INDONESIA
HANDBOOK

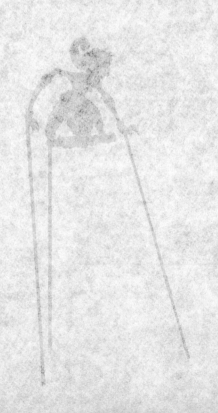

INDONESIA HANDBOOK

SIXTH EDITION

BILL DALTON

MOON
PUBLICATIONS INC.

INDONESIA HANDBOOK
SIXTH EDITION

Published by
Moon Publications, Inc.
P.O. Box 3040
Chico, California 95927-3040, USA

Printed by
Colorcraft Ltd., Hong Kong

ISBN: 1-56691-062-5
ISSN: 1078-5442

Editor: Kevin Jeys
Associate Editors: Taran March, Valerie Sellers,
Gina Wilson Birtcil
Editorial Assistants: Pauli Galin, Charles Mohnike, Jason Ross,
Sheri Wyatt
Copy Editor: Deana Corbitt
Prepress Assistants: Michael Greer, Asha Johnson, Emily Kendrick,
Nicole Revere, Valerie Sellers
Production & Design: Carey Wilson
Cartographers: Bob Race, Brian Bardwell
Index: Nicole Revere

Front cover photo: Hindu carvings at Borobudur, by Lou Corbett
All photos by Bill Dalton unless otherwise noted.

Distributed in the U.S.A. by Publishers Group West
Printed in China

Please send all comments,
corrections, additions,
amendments, and critiques to:

**INDONESIA HANDBOOK
MOON PUBLICATIONS, INC.
P.O. BOX 3040
CHICO, CA 95927-3040, USA
e-mail: travel@moon.com
or bdalton@ttci.net**

Printing History
1st edition — 1977
2nd edition — 1980
3rd edition — 1985
4th edition — 1988
reprinted April 1989
5th edition — November 1991
reprinted April 1992
6th edition — September 1995

CONTENTS

MAPS

MAP SYMBOLS

MAIN ROAD		AIRPORT, AIRSTRIP
SECONDARY ROAD	CATHEDRAL	POINT OF INTEREST
PATH/TRAIL	CHURCH	HOTEL/ACCOMMODATION
BRIDGE	TOWN, VILLAGE	TEMPLE (PURA)
UNPAVED ROAD	CITY	MOSQUE (MESJID)
RAILROAD	MOUNTAIN	WATERFALL
PROVINCE BORDER	WATER	GUESTHOUSE GH
INTERNATIONAL BORDER		SIGHTSEEING ATTRACTION
FERRY		

SPECIAL TOPICS

ABBREVIATIONS

ABBREVIATIONS, MAPS

D.—*Danau* (lake)
G.—*Gunung* (mountain)
Jl.—*Jalan* (street)
Kec.—*Kecamatan* (district)
Kep.—*Kepulauan* (archipelago, islands)
L.—*Laut* (sea)
Ma.—*Muara* (mouth of river, delta)
P.—*Pulau* (island)
S.—*Sungai* (river)
Sel.—*Selat* (strait)
Tel.—*Teluk* (bay)
Tg.—*Tanjung* (cape, point)

ABBREVIATIONS, TEXT

a/c—air-conditioned
C—Celsius
d—double occupancy
pp—per person
Jl.—*Jalan* (street)
s—single occupancy
t—triple occupancy

IS THIS BOOK OUT OF DATE?

Although we do everything in our power to make the information in *Indonesia Handbook* as accurate as possible, the task is sometimes just too much. You can help. If prices have gone up, if services have been discontinued or are now unacceptable, if certain suggestions are misleading, if you can offer shortcuts, warnings, or tips, please write us so we can let other readers know. If you come across a special place we do not mention, fill us in. We value highly letters from resident expatriates, hikers, and outdoor enthusiasts. Letters from Indonesians themselves, with their impressions on *Indonesia Handbook,* are particularly welcome.

If you can improve or add to a map, send it in. Amateur and professional photographers are invited to submit photos for consideration. All photos must be specifically identified if they're to be of any use. Photographers will be acknowledged in the book's photo credits, and receive a free copy of the edition in which their work first appears. By submitting photos, it's understood the photographer is granting Moon Publications the nonexclusive right to publish the photo(s) under the above terms. The publisher cannot, in most cases, undertake to return photographs.

This guide is updated at every reprint and completely revised every 2-3 years, so your contributions will eventually be shared with thousands of other Indonesia travelers. This guide is a sounding board and clearing house, so help keep us in the front ranks of adventurous, independent travel writing. Address letters to:

Indonesia Handbook
c/o Moon Publications Inc.
P.O. Box 3040
Chico, CA 95927 USA

ACKNOWLEDGMENTS

This edition of Indonesia Handbook would not have been possible without fellow travelers Carl Parkes, who updated the Java and Kalimantan chapters, and Bob Nilsen, who did the same for Nusatenggara. Many thanks.

INTRODUCTION

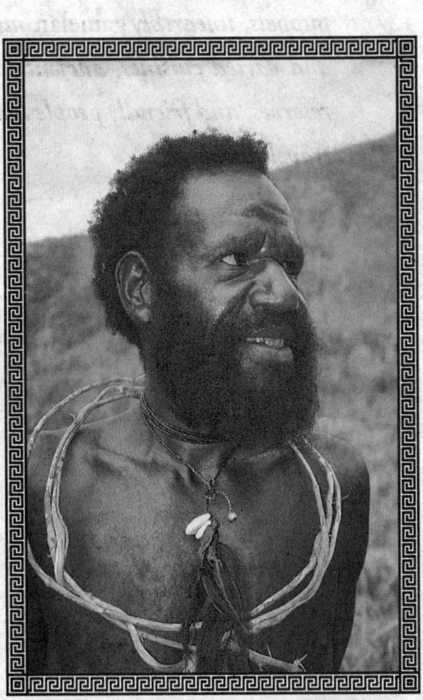

A country of incredible and diverse beauty, Indonesia sprawls across one-eighth of the globe, stretching between Malaysia and Australia. This nation encompasses mind-stupefying extremes: the 5,000-meter-high snow-capped mountains of Irian Jaya, sweltering lowland swamps of eastern Sumatra, open eucalyptus savannahs of Timor, lush rainforests of West Java. Restless volcanos spew lava the whole length. This is the most complex single nation on earth—each of Indonesia's 992 inhabited islands has customs, native dress, architecture, dialects, and geography all its own. Its wayang puppets, unearthly gamelan music, exquisite textiles, matchless and varied cuisines, ancient ruins and historical sites, nature reserves, and friendly people make Indonesia one of Asia's finest travel discoveries.

THE LAND

This 5,200-km stretch of islands embraces a total area of five million square kilometers, about one million square kilometers more than the total land area of the United States. The surrounding sea area is three times larger than the land, and Indonesians are one of the few peoples in the world who include water within the boundaries of their territory, calling their country Tanah Air Kita, literally "Our Land and Water."

Of the country's 17,110 islands, Indonesia claims the better part of three of the world's largest—New Guinea, Borneo, and Sumatra. Only 6,000 are named, and 992 permanently settled. Not all the islands in insular Southeast Asia belong to Indonesia. The massive island of New Guinea consists of Papua New Guinea on the east and Irian Jaya to the west, only the latter an Indonesian territory. The northern one-quarter of the island of Borneo belongs to Eastern Malaysia and Brunei, while the southern three-quarters comprises the Indonesian provinces of Kalimantan.

Volcanos

Inhabiting a portion of the intensely volcanic Ring of Fire, most Indonesians live and die within sight of a volcano. The islands are the site of the earth's two greatest historic volcanic cataclysms, Krakatoa and Tambora, and each year brings an average of 10 major eruptions. This activity not only destroys, but provides great benefits. The Hindu monuments constructed for over 750 years on Java were for the most part built from cooled lava rock, ideal for carving. The chemical-rich ash produced by an eruption covers a wide area of surrounding land; rivers carry ash even farther by way of irrigation canals. Thus Indonesia enjoys some of the most fertile land on the planet. In places it's said you can shove a stick in the ground and it'll sprout leaves.

Indonesia is the place to see volcanic craters seething with bubbling, steaming gray mud, rocks covered in bright yellow sulphur, and vast rivers of black gaseous lava. The trapped heat under the earth is an almost limitless source of alternative energy. It's estimated there are at least 217 geothermal locations in Indonesia with a total potential of 16,035 megawatts.

CLIMATE

Indonesia straddles the equator, and days are all roughly the same length. The sun rises promptly at 0600 and sets just as predictably

INDONESIA

SOUTH CHINA SEA

SULU SEA

THAILAND

PHUKET

HAT YAI

BANDA ACEH   PENANG   KOTA BARU

MALAYSIA

KOTA KINABALU

BRUNEI

TARAKAN

MALAYSIA

MEDAN   KUALA LUMPUR

KO SAMUI

SIBOLGA   SINGAPORE

NIAS ISLAND   PEKANBARU   RIAU ARCHIPELAGO

KUCHING   KALIMANTAN

SAMARINDA

BALIKPAPAN

SUMATRA   PONTIANAK

PADANG

MENTAWAI ISLANDS

BANGKA

PALEMBANG

BANJARMASIN

BENGKULU

INDONESIA

TELUKBETUNG

JAKARTA   CIREBON   SEMARANG   MADURA

INDIAN OCEAN   BOGOR   BANDUNG   SOLO   SURABAYA

YOGYAKARTA   JAVA   MALANG   BALI   LOMBOK

DENPASAR   MATARAM

0   500 km

at 1800. The country has a typical monsoonal equatorial climate with only two seasons: wet (Nov.-April) and hot (May-Oct.). It's always hot and always humid, with the temperature changing very little, so in reality the hot season generally is only slightly hotter and just not quite so wet as the wet season. Sometimes it rains so hard it's like standing under a tepid shower turned on full. With a roar the skies upend, spilling a solid wall of water on the earth below, flattening plants and flowers. The wettest places are in the mountains of all the main islands.

Locales east of Solo in Central Java have sharply defined dry seasons, the duration increasing the closer the area to Australia. The Palu Valley in Central Sulawesi receives less than 50 cm of rain per year. In the far south-eastern islands of Timor and Roti, the dry season can last up to seven months. Sumatra and Kalimantan have no dry season. But don't put off your trip just because of the wet. When it rains the dust on the roads is reduced, flowers bloom, it's fresher and cooler, and everywhere it's green, like bright wet paint. With an extensive and ever-improving surfaced road system throughout the islands, the rains shouldn't slow you down at all.

Indonesians look upon climate differently than people in the West. Warmth is associated with "hard work, pain, terror, bad," while in the West most think "pleasant, cozy, secure, healthy." Indonesians prefer to socialize and promenade in

© MOON PUBLICATIONS, INC.

the cool of the evenings. Because the hard winters of North America and Europe never occur here, there isn't the drive to finish tasks before the season changes. This explains in part the Indonesian *jam karet* (rubber time) mentality.

AGRICULTURE

For Indonesia's rural, agriculturally based population, land is the most important commodity in the country. It's the single greatest source of litigation, poverty, and injustice in Indonesia, particularly where it's scarcest—on overpopulated Java. The government painfully wresting land from peasants has become a fact of life in

the rapid industrialization process of the past 10 years.

The *Desa*

Three of five Indonesians work the soil. The *desa* is the entire productive community of a small village. In a Western sense, the *desa* is an authoritarian, undemocratic system, a sort of oriental kibbutz. Houses are loosely scattered around vegetable plots and fruit trees, with narrow pathways winding in every direction. Sometimes there are also community meeting places, barns, and fishponds. The *desa* is often surrounded by rice fields, hedges, and bamboo groves, with forests beyond. People work hard all day, then return home to pray, sing, dance, smoke, gossip, watch *wayang* or TV, sleep, then rise at 0400 to labor again in the fields.

Controlling every activity in the *desa* is a council of elected villagers. The headman is called the *kepala desa*. An ancient cooperative system, *gotong royong,* in which everyone lends a hand, parcels out land, supervises community seed beds, grows crops, and manages irrigation and rice storage. There are two systems of cultivation used in Indonesia, *ladang* and *sawah.*

Ladang

Ladang means shifting or swidden cultivation, a method characterized by prodigious human labor using uncomplicated, preindustrial implements. It's estimated as many as a third of all Indonesians still work *ladang.* The practice can be very complex; basically, it's an imitation of nature itself. Unirrigated, arable land is prepared by burning the jungle just before the start of the rains; the farmer clears the land and fertilizes and weeds the soil at the same time. Then comes planting of a wide variety of quick-growing, predominantly staple food crops such as rice, corn, yams, taro, or the starchy palm-like sago. Cultivators plant in rows, working usually uphill over fallen trees and rough ground. Men poke holes with sharpened sticks, while women follow behind dropping in unhusked seeds, a few per hole.

Ladang is usually practiced in the nonvolcanic, less fertile soil of the Outer Islands, and the soil soon becomes exhausted. The plot is then abandoned. At least 10 years is needed for the jungle to overgrow the cultivated plot and replenish the soil. The *ladang* farmer can then return and cultivate the plot for another two years, repeating the cycle. If the cycle is abbreviated and the forest denied the time to take root again, tenacious *alang-alang* grass colonizes the cleared forest area and depletes the soil of nourishment, leading to the so-called "Green Deserts" of Indonesia. Farmers can return *alang-alang* fields to cultivation only with much hard work.

The *ladang* system requires roughly 10 times the area needed for wet-rice growing. In most parts of the world this slash-and-burn farming means a nomadic existence, but in Indonesia *ladang* farmers live in permanent villages. *Ladang* usually fosters somewhat archaic clans or genealogical communities, like those found on Flores, Sulawesi, and Timor. Because of the pressure of population and the introduction of improved agricultural methods, *ladang* is giving way all over Indonesia to the more intensive wet-rice cultivation, called *sawah.*

Sawah

Sawah, a type of wet-rice cultivation, is a spectacular form of agriculture which often looks like a soft green stairway climbing into the sky. Although it can be utilized up to 1,600 meters above sea level, *sawah* is commonly found in the monsoon areas of the low-lying plains, where the water supply is more plentiful and regular. Because such complicated irrigation

terraced rice fields

systems and the people to maintain them traditionally required a despot as manager, *sawah* cultivation has encouraged Indonesia's history of strong agrarian communities supporting an aristocratic hierarchy.

Technically very intricate and delicate to manage, this system of complex waterworks is more productive than *ladang,* able to support some of the world's greatest rural population densities. Nowhere has *sawah* succeeded like on Java and Bali, because nowhere is there so little land available to accommodate such high birthrates. Two or even three crops a year are sometimes planted, and *sawah* has the capacity to produce undiminished yields year after year.

During the wet season, the land is planted with rice; during the dry the same fields are often planted with corn and cassava. Backbreaking planting, weeding, plowing, and harvesting are all done by hand, workers elbow- and knee-deep in mud, using iron and wood tools. Plows are pulled by *kerbau* (water buffalo), except on smaller fields close to the edges of terraces. In the southeastern islands, *kerbau* are driven over the fields, turning them into a slushy mire; in effect, the animal acts as the plow. Today gasoline-powered rototillers are appearing on the more prosperous islands of Java and Bali.

Many animist rites persist from the old days, when people were bound by strong religious ties to their communal land. When rice is planted on Java or Bali, a small plaited figure of a fertility goddess is placed under an umbrella and incense burned in her honor to insure good crops the following season. This rice goddess, Dewi Sri, is believed to literally dwell in the rice stalks. At harvest time the stalks must be cut in a certain way so as not to offend her. Using wood-mounted, razor-like handblades concealed in their palms, women deftly cut only three to four stalks at a time so Dewi Sri will not be frightened.

FLORA AND FAUNA

Although covering only one percent of the earth's surface, Indonesia is amazingly rich in animal and plant life. Contained within its land and water territory are 17% of the world's bird species, 16% of the world's amphibians and reptiles, 12% of the world's mammals, and 10% of the world's flora. Not only does this sprawling island nation possess impressive quantity, but also immense variety. Spanning 4,800 kilometers across two biogeographic zones—the Oriental and the Australian—and with landforms ranging from mangrove swamps to glaciers, Indonesia is no doubt the most diverse natural wildlife repository on earth.

To acquaint yourself with Indonesia's incredible biodiversity, visit a Java zoo. The biggest and best zoo in the country is the Ragunan Zoo of Jakarta, with over 4,000 animals and birds, including white tigers, Java rhinos and Komodo dragons. Other zoos include Bandung in Western Java, Yogyakarta in Central Java, and Surabaya in Eastern Java.

Animal Life

Hundreds of different species of mammals are scattered throughout the archipelago. These include the orangutan, with its blazing orange shaggy coat; deep-black wild cattle weighing up to two tons; 35-cm-high miniature deer; clouded leopards; mountain goats; wild warthogs; the Asian sun bear, with a large white circle on its chest; and long-snouted tapirs which gallop like stallions, tossing their heads and whinnying. Two hundred mammal species, of the 500 in the world, are found only in Indonesia.

The fauna of Irian Jaya resembles that of Australia: vividly colored birds of paradise, spiny anteaters, mouse-like flying possums, bandicoots. In northern Sulawesi lives the world's smallest species of monkey, which can easily sit in the palm of the hand. Reptiles include the giant Komodo dragon, the reticulated python, and deep-croaking geckos.

Of approximately 1,500 bird species worldwide, 430 are found in Indonesia and nowhere else. There are peacocks, pheasants, partridges, turkey-sized pigeons, and jungle fowl who incubate their eggs in volcanic steam. Black ibis fly in V-formations, the blue-crowned hanging parrot of the Riaus emits sharp penetrating notes, the glossy black talking mynah of Nias mimics gibbons, and the rhinoceros hornbill of the Kalimantan jungle cackles gleefully with human-like laughter.

Chief among the country's many bird sanctuaries are the small coastal islets of Dua, Rambut, and Bokor, all within easy reach of Jakarta. The island of Sumba in the southeast has 10 endemic species of birds. Bird lovers should check

NATIONAL RESERVES OF INDONESIA

NOT TO SCALE

© MOON PUBLICATIONS, INC.

IRIAN JAYA

CYCLOPS MOUNTAINS RESERVES

PULAU BIAK–SUPERIORI RESERVES

MEMBERAMO PEGUNUNGAN FOJA ROUFFAER RESERVES

PULAU DOLOK RESERVE

RAWA BIRU –WASUR RESERVE

GUNUNG MEJA RESERVE

PEG. WANDIWOI/ WANDAMEN RESERVE and CENDRAWASIH MARINE RESERVE

RAJA AMPAT ISLAND RESERVES

LORENTZ RESERVE

MALUKU

P. BAUN & ARU TENGGARA MARINE RESERVE

MANUSELA RESERVE

PULAU KASA and PULAU POMBO MARINE RESERVES

PANUA and TANJUNG PANJANG RESERVES

TANGKOKO-BATUANGAS and DUA SAUDARA RESERVES

TANJUNG API RESERVE

LORE LINDU RESERVE

DUMOGA - BONE NATIONAL PARK

MOROWALI RESERVE

SULAWESI

BUKIT RAYA RESERVE

HULU-BAHAU –SUNGAI MALINAU RESERVE

NUSATENGGARA

KOMODO NATIONAL PARK

GN. RINJANI RESERVE

PULAU MOYO RESERVE

KALIMANTAN

KUTAI RESERVE

PADANG LUWAI RESERVE

BALI

BALI BARAT NATIONAL PARK AND MARINE RESERVE

HUTAN SAMBAS RESERVE

MANDOR NATURE RESERVE

GUNUNG PALUNG RESERVE

JAVA

PLEIHARI –MARTAPURA RESERVE

TANJUNG PUTING RESERVE

UJUNG KULON RESERVE

SUMATRA

GUNUNG LEUSER NATIONAL PARK

KERINCI SEBLAT RESERVE

SIBERUT RESERVE

WAY KAMBAS RESERVE

out the spectacular native avifauna at Jakarta's Ragunan Zoo, as well as the bird park at Beautiful Indonesia in Miniature.

Insect and arachnid forms number in the hundreds of thousands: aquatic cockroaches, praying mantises like bright green banana leaves, beetles in the shape of violins, submarine-diving grasshoppers, and the world's most extraordinary moth, the Atlas, with a wingspan of 25 cm. There are spiders that catch and devour small birds in giant webs, and scorpions with bites like bee stings. The fabulously colored butterflies are world famous.

In Indonesia's seas are found the world's rarest shell, the Glory of the Seas; crabs who clip down coconuts and open them on the ground; bony-tongued and luminous fish; freshwater dolphins; fish that climb mangrove trees looking for insects; seaweed that reaches lengths of 75 meters; and the world's only poisonous fish.

Plants

Due to its extreme geographic fragmentation, Indonesia is richer in plant species than either the American or African tropics. Its flowering plant species number more than 40,000, representing 10% of all plant species in the world. There are 250 species of bamboo and 150 species of palm. In the more fertile areas flowers are rampant—hibiscus, jasmine, allamanda, frangipani, bougainvillea, lotus lilies one-half meter wide. Java alone has 5,000 plant species; there are twice as many species on Borneo as in all of Africa.

Of the world's 350 species of the commercially important dipterocarp tree, over half are found in Indonesia—155 species in Borneo alone. The tall, hardwood rainforest trees of Irian Jaya rival the giant sequoias of California. This island also possesses alpine moss and heath forests, the equivalent of South America's cloud forests.

Sumatra is home to the insectivorous corpse plant, which smells like putrefying animal flesh to lure insects, and the world's largest bloom, the one-meter-wide rafflesia. The luxurious vegetation of Borneo hosts seductive orchids which glow in the perpetual twilight of the jungle. Here is found the world's only black orchid, *Coelogyne pandurata*. Because of the unbelievable humidity, strong sunlight, and fecund volcanic soil, when you build a fence in Indonesia, six months later it's no longer a fence—it's a living wall of vegetation.

Nature Reserves

The most expedient way to view Indonesia's plant and animal life is to visit one of its 150 state-run reserves. To gain entry, you must obtain permission from Dinas Perlindungan dan Pengawetan Alam (PHPA), the Forest Authority, which maintains offices in all the major towns throughout Indonesia. The PHPA also staffs branch offices inside the reserves, where you may register and pay a nominal fee. Many also provide inexpensive accommodations in basic lodges, as well as the use of kitchens.

An outstanding reserve is Ujung Kulon National Park in far western Java, where you might see wild cattle, *rusa*, leopards, gibbons, and one of the last remaining Javan rhinos. The largest of Indonesia's reserves is the mighty 900,000-hectare Gunung Leuser National Park of northern Sumatra, which still marks extensive tracts of land as "unexplored." One of the least known, least visited, yet most accessible reserves is the remarkable Wasur National Park in southeast Irian Jaya, an excellent place to see a variety of large birds and mammals in the wild.

When looking for animals in the rainforest, be patient and go slow. The forest is packed with animals, most of whom hide or flee when loud, clumsy humans come crashing through. You'll see more animals if you walk slowly, stopping frequently, or sit very quietly. Scan the canopy for subtle branch movements. A tactic used by naturalists involves sitting on a rain poncho beneath a large fruiting forest tree. It's almost certain something will arrive to dine in a relatively short time. Sitting also gives you an opportunity to contact the diverse life on or near the forest floor. Use coconut tobacco juice to fight the leeches.

HISTORY

When you read Indonesian history, you read world history. This country is a subtle blend of every culture that ever landed here—Chinese, Indian, Melanesian, Portuguese, Polynesian, Arabian, English, Dutch, American . . . wave after wave of invaders and migrants who either absorbed earlier arrivals, killed them off, or pushed them into more remote regions. This ongoing and unending process explains Indonesia's astounding ethnic diversity.

PREHISTORY

Java was one of the earliest places where human beings lived. In 1891 the fossil skull of Java Man (*Homo erectus*) was discovered at Trinil in Central Java. This erect near-man lived at a time when Europe was under ice and most of Indonesia was a part of Asia. The species ranged from Africa all the way north to the glacial border of Europe and east to China, thriving some 500,000 years ago at the very beginning of the Pleistocene epoch. Charcoal and charred bones indicate these people used fire. *Homo erectus* was not an ancestor of present-day Indonesians but a vanished race all its own; the species either couldn't adapt or was wiped out by more advanced incoming beings.

Excavations at Sangiran in Central Java uncovered an even more primitive type. Then, in 1931, 11 skullcaps were found at Ngandong, belonging to a more advanced race than *Homo erectus*—the so-called Solo Man. All 11 skullcaps had been deliberately cracked open: it is assumed Solo Man was a brain-eating cannibal. Found with the busted skulls was an astonishingly rich fossil bed of 23,000 mammalian bones, mostly of extinct oxen, elephants, and hippos. Also uncovered were scrapers, borers, choppers, and stone balls for use in slings.

Starting about 40,000 years ago, early Australoids entered New Guinea and the Lesser Sunda Islands. Other groups expanded into the archipelago from southern China about 30,000 years ago. Negritos, a pygmy people who began to radiate through the islands about this time, were some of the first known fully human migrants into Indonesia. There are still genetic traces of these short, woolly-haired, round-headed people in eastern Sumatra, the Lesser Sundas, and the deep interior of Irian Jaya.

More advanced than the Negritos were the two humans whose skulls were found at Wajak in East Java. The true ancestor of present-day Indonesians, the Wajak Man is the earliest known *Homo sapiens* found on Java, living about 10,000-12,000 years ago. These groups seeped and percolated into the archipelago from many directions over the span of centuries, rather than arriving in a series of coherent, monolithic, and coordinated mass migrations.

THE HINDU/BUDDHIST PERIOD

Indian chroniclers wrote of Java as early as 600 B.C., and the ancient Hindu epic the Ramayana also mentions Indonesia. By the 2nd century A.D. Indian traders had arrived in Sulawesi, Sumatra, and Java. At the time of its colonizing efforts, India, then the pinnacle of civilization, was at the apex of its cultural vigor. Bronze Age Indonesians had many similar cultural traits that made the Indian culture easy to absorb. Indonesian feudal rulers most likely invited high-caste and learned Brahmans to migrate and work as a literate bureaucracy. Indian influences, including Hinduism, touched only the ruling classes; there was no significant impact on the rural people, who have always leaned more toward animism. By the 5th century, Indonesians were using southern Indian script to carve Hindu inscriptions.

Sanskrit words found in the Indonesian language today indicate the specific contributions Indians made during their period of influence in the islands, which lasted 1,400 years, from A.D. 200 to 1600: healing practices, astronomy, navigation techniques, the potter's wheel, horses and elephants, textile dyeing, plank boats and wheeled carts, figure sculpture and decorative arts, written literature, monumental architecture, spices. Sanskrit words such as *angsa* (duck) and *gembala* (shepherd) suggest Indians introduced techniques of animal husbandry. Many Hindu legal practices were also carried to Indonesia, as well as numerous titles relating to social rank and regal pomp.

The most far-reaching and significant Indian exports were metaphysics, philosophy, and the Hindu concept of a divine ruler with unchecked powers. Indians practiced a more integrated religious system than the Indonesians, featuring a hierarchy of gods with specific roles to play. By the 5th century, Brahmanist cults worshipping Shiva had sprung up on Java and temples confirmed the authority of Hindu religious beliefs. By the 9th century, syncretism appeared on Java, a belief system regarding both Shiva and Buddha as incarnations of the same being. In the 10th century Indonesian students were sent to the great Buddhist university of Nalanda in northeastern India; Indonesians even went as far as Tibet for learning and philosophy. The Sriwijaya Buddhist kingdom rose in southern Sumatra during the 7th century and exercised a wide sphere of influence over all of Southeast Asia. On Java, early Hindu states rose and fell— Pajajaran, Sailendra, Kediri, Singosari. Most, though very rich and powerful, were mainly coastal empires.

The Arrival Of Buddhism

Indian missionaries took Buddhism to Indonesia at a time when the religion was declining in India itself and as Indonesians were ready to go beyond the confines of their indigenous belief systems. Though adherents of Hinduism and Buddhism were enemies in India, in Indonesia most followers of these two religions lived side by side in peace, blending with and borrowing from one another. On the fertile ground of Southeast Asia, Mahayana Buddhism evolved into a new kind of polytheism. Sumatra remained primarily Buddhist, but Hinduism eventually took over on Java, though the world's largest Buddhist monument, the imposing Borobudur *stupa,* was built in the 9th century by Buddhist Sailendras in Central Java.

The Majapahit Empire

The Indonesian-Indian era reached its apogee in the 14th century East Javanese Majapahit Empire, considered the Golden Age of Indonesia. Though it thrived for barely 100 years (1294-1398), Majapahit was Indonesia's greatest state. Gajah Mada, its famous prime minister, worked so hard in his life to unite all the islands that it took four officials to do his job when he died. During this last mighty Java-Hindu kingdom, Indonesian sculpture and architecture suddenly veered away from Indian prototypes and a revitalized native folk art emerged. When Islamic traders arrived in the 15th and 16th centuries, they found a complex of well-established Indianized kingdoms on Java and Sumatra. Borneo was still only marginally Indianized, Sulawesi barely at all.

Even though Islam ostensibly erased Indian cultural traditions from Java by the 16th century, much is still visible from Buddhist-Hindu times. The *kraton* courts of Solo and Yogyakarta are today hardcore enclaves of Java-Hindu culture. The religion and culture of Bali, the *gamelan* orchestra, and the five-note scale were also inherited from India. *Bopati* was the term used by the old Hindu aristocracy for a governor of a province, and the Indonesian *bupati* holds this power to this day.

Many motifs and styles of the earlier Hindu culture permeate Indonesian art: all over Java you can see Hindu-style gates leading to

mosques and the cemeteries of the Islamic high saints. Indian epic poems have been adapted into living Indonesian theater and Indian mythic heroes dominate the plots. Place-names of Indian derivation are found all over Indonesia, and Indian scripts persisted until Indonesian was latinized in the 20th century.

ISLAM

Arabs started arriving in Indonesia as far back as the 4th century, engaged in trade with the great civilizations of the Mediterranean, India, Southeast Asia, and China. These early traders brought the oil palm and kapok tree from Africa. In the 14th century the Mohammedans consolidated their hold on Gujerat in India and began to expand their trade considerably in Indonesia. This was the beginning of the archipelago's Islamic period.

Islam caught on in far northern Sumatra first, then spread to Java. The capture of Melaka by the Portuguese in 1511 scattered Muslim merchants and their faith all over insular Southeast Asia. Islam took hold most solidly in those areas of Indonesia least affected by the earlier Hindu civilizations: the north-central Java coast, Banten in West Java, and the Aceh and Minangkabau regions of northern Sumatra. Demak was the first important Javanese city to turn Muslim, in 1477, followed by Cirebon in 1480. In 1478, a coalition of Muslim princes attacked what was left of the Hindu Majapahit Empire, and Islam was here to stay.

The Lure Of Islam
Indonesia is one of the few countries where Islam didn't supplant the existing religion purely by military conquest. Its appeal was first and foremost psychological. Comparitively egalitarian and possessing a scientific spirit, Islam arrived in these islands as a forceful revolutionary concept that freed the common people from feudal bondage. Until the appearance of Islam, Indonesia was a land where the king ruled as an absolute monarch and could take away a man's land and even his wife at whim. Islam, on the other hand, taught that in Allah's eyes all men are made of the same clay, that no man shall be set apart as superior. (Women, of course, are another story.) There were no mysterious sacraments or initiation rites, nor was there a priest class. With its direct and personal relationship between individual and God, Islam possessed great simplicity. Everyone could talk to Allah. Though Mohammed was Allah's only prophet, each follower was an equal of Mohammed.

Islam is ideally suited to an island nation; it's a trader's religion stressing the virtues of sound commercial law, prosperity, and hard work. It compelled people to bathe and keep clean, to travel and see the world, or at least Mecca. One could pray anywhere, even on board the deck of a ship. In short, Islam exerted a democratizing, modernizing, civilizing influence over the peoples of the archipelago. Islam also had a great political attraction, serving in the early 16th century as a force against Portuguese colonial domination, and 100 years later against the Dutch.

Java's Hindu princes were probably first converted to Islam by a desire for trade, wealth, valuable alliances, and power; then the people took up the faith of their ruler en masse. Pre-Islamic signal towers became Muslim minarets and the native Indonesian meeting hall was transformed into a mosque. Rulers placed their royal *gamelan* in the mosques and people came to listen, then returned converted to the new religion.

Islam And The Arts
During the 15th and 16th centuries, the arts, especially literature, were deeply affected by Islam. Arabic styles and themes provided models upon which local literature could be based. Stimulated by the coastal Javanese sultans, textile-decorating arts and armory flourished. *Wayang* and *gamelan* went through their most refined development during the fully Islamic 18th century.

Because Islam prohibits the worship of idols and bars portraits of all living creatures, early Islamic art was stiff and formal. This prohibition has been the main source of uniqueness and intrigue in Indonesian art forms; even on today's *batik* you often see the wings of birds or the antlers of deer, but not the animals themselves.

THE PORTUGUESE PERIOD

The Portuguese were the first Europeans to enter Indonesia. Carrying their God before them, these vigorous and bold traders arrived in Indonesia 87 years before the Dutch. The Portuguese period lasted only about 150 years, from about 1512. Portuguese was the lingua franca of the archipelago in the 16th century and initially even Dutch merchants had to learn it. Portuguese involvement was largely commercial and did not involve territorial expansion; the period was of small significance economically and had little effect on the great intra-Asian trade artery stretching from Arabia to Nagasaki.

In 1570, the Portuguese murdered the sultan of Ternate in hopes they'd gain favor with his successor. The inhabitants revolted and threw them off the island, the beginning of Portuguese decline in Indonesia. The sun set permanently on Portuguese possessions in the area when Portugal decolonized East Timor in 1974.

What did the Portuguese leave behind? For their small numbers and the brevity of their tenure, the Portuguese had a deep impact. Much musical influence is evident: *kroncong* music, named for the sound of guitar strumming, is still a popular folk entertainment in Jakarta. Indonesian is sprinkled with hundreds of Portuguese loan words: *mentega* (butter), *pesta* (festival), *sepatu* (shoe), *gereja* (church), and *meja* (table), as well as many geographic locations. Tobacco was introduced by these medieval adventurers. Portuguese shipbuilding techniques and designs are still followed in Sulawesi and Nusatenggara. Old Portuguese helmets and spears are kept as family heirlooms, and scores of Portuguese forts are scattered around Maluku and other eastern islands.

THE ENGLISH PERIOD

Early in the 17th century the English were direct rivals to the Dutch in the exploitation of the East Indies. The two great maritime powers even maintained outposts alongside one another in Banten, Makassar, Jakarta, and on Ambon. Although treaties dictated the two chartered companies would peacefully cooperate, they were far from amicable partners. Underlying enmity erupted at last on Ambon in 1623, when the personnel of an English factory were tortured and executed, accused of conspiring to seize the local Dutch fort. Vivid woodcut illustrations of the Amboyna Massacre printed in the popular press enraged the English public.

Almost 200 years later, during the Napoleonic Wars, Java was occupied by English forces and the sultan's *kraton* in Yogyakarta stormed and subdued. The young and energetic Lord Raffles, founder of Singapore, was appointed governor. He immersed himself enthusiastically in the history, culture, and customs of Indonesia, uncovering the famous Borobudur temple and meticulously recording the cannibalistic habits of the Batak of northern Sumatra.

But because England wanted to prepare Holland against attack by France and Prussia, most of the Indies were handed back to the Dutch in 1816. Raffles tried to perpetuate British interests in the islands—principally in Bengkulu, southwestern Sumatra—but by 1824 the English had shifted their attention to Singapore, and eventually abandoned Indonesia altogether. The most long-lasting result of British rule in Indonesia is left-hand driving.

THE DUTCH ERA

By the time European traders reached the East Indies in the early 16th century, the islands had government, cities, monumental temples, irrigation systems, handicrafts, orchestras, shipping, art, literature, cannon-fire, and astronomy. With the notable exception of maritime prowess, it was Europe that was undeveloped, not Asia. The Dutch started their involvement here as traders, first entering Indonesia at Banten in 1596 with just four ships. When these ships returned safely to Holland with their valuable cargos of spices, the result was wild speculation. Backed by private companies, 12 expeditions totaling over 65 ships were sent to the East Indies between 1598 and 1605. The Vereenigde Oost-Indische Compagnie (VOC) was chartered in 1602, a private stock company empowered to trade, make treaties, build forts, maintain troops, and operate courts of law throughout the East Indies.

The Dutch did everything they could to isolate the islands from all other outside contact. They gained their first foothold in Batavia in the early 17th century and within 10 years were sinking all foreign vessels found in Indonesian waters. The Dutch opened strategic fortified "factories," or trading posts, over the length of the archipelago. Indonesian dynasties, continually feuding amongst themselves, were easy prey for such a strong external force, and by the mid-17th century the Dutch found themselves the new masters of huge amounts of territory. When sultans asked for Dutch arms and assistance to help put down rival sultans or usurpers, the Dutch would always assist—gaining more land in the bargain. Using a combination of arms, treaties, perfidy, and puppets, they became increasingly involved in the internal affairs of Indonesian states.

Dutch Hegemony

Not content with the roles of mere middlemen and carriers, the Dutch began to seek control of the sources of production. New crops were introduced and plantation agriculture established and expanded. When the VOC went bankrupt in 1799 because of corruption and mismanagement, it was gradually replaced by institutionalized imperialism in the form of a huge bureaucracy of colonial civil servants. The commercial enterprise had been transformed into a colonial empire.

An infamous forced cultivation system, the Culture System, was instituted in 1830, and soon coffee, sugar, indigo, pepper, tea, and cotton were raised to supply European demand. Virtually all of Java was turned into a vast state-owned labor camp, run somewhat like the antebellum slave plantations of the United States. Javanese farmers were starved to produce cash crops: in 1849-50 serious rice famines occurred in the great rice-producing area of Cirebon. Java made the Dutch such profits they were able to build railways, pay off the national debt, and fight a war with Belgium. By 1938 the Dutch owned and controlled over 2,400 estates, equally divided between Java and the Outer Islands.

Colonial Rule

The history of Dutch colonial rule was based on a racial caste structure perpetrated by a class of emigrant Dutchmen. Swimming pool signs read No Natives Or Dogs, and the formal position from which to address a Dutch master was from the floor. The Dutch regarded Indonesians as "half-devil, half-child"; they carried their White Man's Burden with pride.

Under Dutch rule no higher education was available until the 1920s. In 1940, about 90% of the people were illiterate, only two million chil-

dren were in school, and just 630 Indonesians had graduated from Dutch tertiary institutions. The Dutch, running an efficient, immense island empire with just 30,000 government officials, lived in big, stolid, one-story houses and plantation homes maintained by numerous servants, washing down huge lunches with vast quantities of beer. The men wore native costume around the house, and second-generation Dutch women freely intermarried with Indonesians. The Netherlanders pointed to Indonesians with pride as a happy people weaned from savagery, reared in prosperity by a system of paternal despotism.

The imperiousness of Dutch administration began to soften in the early 20th century, with the implementation of the Ethical Policy, which indicated a desire to begin a true partnership with the Indonesian people. But the colonialists never really considered handing these regions over to the indigenous peoples.

NATIONALISM

Intellectuals and aristocrats were the earliest nationalists. Diponegoro, the eldest son of a Javanese sultan, was the country's first nationalist leader. In 1825, after the Dutch built a road across his estate and committed various other abuses, Diponegoro embarked on a holy war against them. He was a masterful guerrilla tactician, and both sides waged a costly war of attrition in which 15,000 Dutchmen and 250,000 Indonesians died, mostly from disease. At one point the Dutch even considered pulling out of Java. Diponegoro fought for five years until treacherously lured into negotiations and arrested, living a life of exile until his death in 1855.

Early 20th-Century Nationalism

It was Raden Kartini, the daughter of a nobleman, who first asserted publicly the right of Indonesians to enjoy the same access to Western knowledge and ideas as Europeans. Although often reading like the jottings of a self-pitying pampered princess, her *Letters* (first published in 1911) were also sensitive, visionary, and full of fire. They caused people in both Europe and Asia to wake to the new spirit in the air. Kartini, also celebrated as Indonesia's first women's emancipationist, died in childbirth at age 24.

victims of the Dutch,
interred at Marga

Her memory and ideals are kept alive each 21 April when parades, programs, and social activities are held in her honor all over Indonesia.

Indonesians were intrigued when little Japan defeated mighty Russia in 1905. Indonesia didn't pass completely into Dutch hands until 1911, and that's when these foreigners started to lose it. Guided by the mistaken notion of to-know-us-is-to-love-us, gifted Indonesians from high-bred families were sent to Holland for higher education. Many of these same Western-educated Indonesians later became fiery nationalists; by providing education to Indonesians, the Dutch made themselves redundant. By the time WW I arrived, a number of nationalist organizations had sprung up suddenly and almost simultaneously, revealing the extreme dissatisfaction and impatience the Javanese masses felt for colonial rule. The Javanese were waiting for a Ratu Adil, a Righteous Prince, who would free them from their oppressors.

An organization of middle-class traders started the Sarekat Islam (Muslim Society) in 1912. Originally intended to help Indonesian *batik* and textile businessmen meet growing Chinese competition by sponsoring cooperatives, SI grew at a spectacular rate into Indonesia's first mass political organization; by 1919 it claimed a membership of two million members. The Indonesian National Party (PNI) was founded in 1927. PNI sought complete independence through Gandhi-style noncooperation, and an ex-engineer named Sukarno emerged as its chairman. With his oratorical power and dominating,

charismatic style, Sukarno soon became Indonesia's most forceful political personality.

Grappling with the world depression of 1929, the Dutch were in no mood to bargain, determined to make up for their losses by increasing the exploitation of Indonesia's natural resources. A ruthlessly efficient secret police force imposed order throughout the islands. Increasingly repressive measures were enforced against nationalist leaders—Sukarno and his compatriots Hatta and Sjahrir were rounded up, exiled, released, rearrested. The Dutch broke up political parties and waived petitions. Anti-Dutch feelings grew. In 1940, when the Germans invaded the Low Countries, the capitulation of Holland had a shocking, sobering effect on the Dutch community in Indonesia. To the Indonesians the Dutch suddenly didn't seem so powerful. But instead of seeking to improve relations with Indonesians to form a united front against a possible Japanese invasion, the Dutch continued their repression.

WORLD WAR II

Invasion Of The Indies

With the crippling of the U.S. Pacific Fleet at Pearl Harbor, the subsequent conquest of the Philippines, and the capture of Singapore, the Japanese brought the war to the doorstep of the Dutch East Indies. The loss of the British destroyers *Prince of Wales* and *Repulse* left the islands wide open to attack. The whole of the Indies suddenly became militarized. In January 1942 Japanese troops landed on Sulawesi and Borneo, and by February the Japanese launched a full-scale invasion of Sumatra.

The crucial battle for Java was joined on 27 February when a small force of 14 Allied ships met a superior Japanese invasion fleet in the Sundra Strait and were blown out of the water. On 1 March 1942, Japanese forces landed in Batavia; the Dutch forces surrendered on 9 March.

The Japanese Occupation

The Indonesians were at first gratified that their Asian brothers had freed them from white oppression. The Japanese immediately backed the nationalists and orthodox Muslims, the two groups most opposed to Dutch rule. The new masters even spoke reassuringly of one day granting Indonesia its independence. But the Japanese soon proved themselves more ruthless, fascist, and cruel than the Dutch had ever been. Indonesia suffered terribly at the hands of its conquerors. The invaders forced 500,000 young men to serve as slave laborers in the jungles of Burma and Malaysia; only 70,000 returned. The Japanese also routinely rounded up Indonesian women to serve as sex slaves in army camp brothels.

Indonesia was included in Japan's mythical "Greater Southeast Asia Co-Prosperity Sphere," which in reality meant the country would be exploited of every possible resource. The islands were plundered of all raw materials: oil, rubber, rice, and spices. Cities were stripped clean of gold and jewels, as well as tons of wrought-iron fences and ornaments—shipped to Japan and smelted down to make pig iron for the war machine.

During their occupation, the Japanese also encouraged Indonesian nationalism and allowed political boards to form, but only with the intention of using these for their own war aims. Sukarno, who was retained by the Japanese to help them govern, cleverly used every opportunity to educate the masses, inculcating in them nationalist consciousness and fervor.

At first it was forbidden to speak in public any language but Japanese, and Indonesians were forced to learn it. But when the Japanese realized how difficult it was to implement this policy, they began to promote Bahasa Indone-

sia, which was eventually used to spread their propoganda out to the smallest villages. The language grew to become a gigantic symbol of nationalism and was disseminated on an ever-wider basis, further unifying the islands. The Japanese also created an armed home guard, later to become the core of a revolutionary militia that would fight the Dutch. As the war progressed and the Japanese began losing, greater real power began passing into the hands of Indonesians.

THE REVOLUTION

The British Role

Eleven days after Hiroshima, on 17 August 1945, Sukarno and Hatta declared independence in Jakarta and the Republic of Indonesia was born. Fearing the return of the Dutch, the Indonesians desperately tried to secure as many Japanese weapons as they could. Meanwhile, remnants of a shattered Dutch colonial army, weakened by the war, tried to regain a foothold on their precious islands.

The British, who first arrived in Jakarta in September 1945, were charged with the thankless task of rounding up Japanese troops and maintaining order. Duped into fighting for the Dutch, they got more than they bargained for in bloody street battles with Indonesian fighters, culminating in the furious month long Battle of Surabaya in November 1945. Convinced the republic was supported wholeheartedly by the Indonesian masses, the British informed the Republican government it was responsible for law and order in the interior. This constituted de facto recognition of the new Indonesian government.

Surprise, Surprise

The Dutch were back and they intended to start up just where they'd left off. But they were mistaken; it was not going to be business as usual. Once the Japanese army left their posts, bands of politically passionate young people (laskar) emerged. The total strength of these irregular armed troops surpassed by many times the numbers of the official Republican army. During the internal revolution against the Dutch (1945-49), communications were nonexistent and the provinces were on their own, administratively and militarily.

Internationally, in the early years of the struggle the Indonesians were almost alone in their fight against the Dutch. It was the independent Asian states, the Soviet Union, Poland, and the Arab states who first gave the new republic their support, not the U.S. and other Western powers. The latter tried to push compromises and watered-down solutions; United Nations resolutions were ignored, that world body's role a fiasco.

In January 1946 Sukarno considered Jakarta too vulnerable and moved the Republic's capital to Yogyakarta, where he could depend on the powerful sultan for support. In April negotiations began to decide the question of independence. The Dutch only used the resulting pacts and treaties to buy time. Dutch troops embarked on "pacification" exercises, attacking many key cities on Java and Sumatra in July 1947 and butchering hundreds. In 1948 an ultraconservative government was voted into power in Holland, one that considered further negotiations futile. In December, Yogyakarta was bombed and strafed, then occupied by Dutch paratroopers. Sukarno and most of the members of his revolutionary cabinet were taken into "protective" custody while three divisions of the Republican army evaporated into the countryside.

In spite of Dutch military successes in the cities, the countryside was controlled by Republicans, who launched endless guerrilla attacks. Outraged world opinion eventually rallied behind the new Republic and the UN applied real pressure. It was also pointed out that the amount the Dutch were spending to regain the islands was embarrassingly close to the sum the U.S. had granted Holland for war reconstruction aid under the Marshall Plan. The U.S. Congress rebelled, and in 1948 withdrew its support of the Dutch.

Indonesian Republicans controlled the highways, the food supply, and the villages. What they didn't control, they burned or blew up. *"Merdeka!"* ("Freedom!") was on everybody's lips, the emotive word emblazoned across the railroad cars rumbling through the cities. Finally, the Dutch transfered sovereignty to a free Indonesia on 27 December 1949. On that day, all over Indonesia the Dutch red, white, and blue flag was hauled down and the red and white flag of Indonesia hoisted in its place.

Not turned over to the Indonesians was the territory of West New Guinea, over which the Dutch retained provisional control. Their stated intent was to keep the region from falling into the hands of Javanese "imperialists," to provide a home for dispossessed Indo-Europeans, and to exploit the great mining potential of the region. Since Irian was very much a part of the Dutch East Indies and never separated from it constitutionally, the Indonesians looked upon the territory as their natural legacy. They suspected the Dutch of trying to preserve colonialism in the region. The issue was a festering sore for the next 15 years.

POST-INDEPENDENCE

On 16 December 1949, the Indonesian House and Senate unanimously elected Sukarno president of the new Federal State of Indonesia. Indonesia was quickly recognized by most nations, and the UN admitted it as its 60th member in September 1950. After all the suffering, sacrifice, and fighting, it was now time to rebuild the nation.

"It was not enough to have won the war," Hatta said. "Now we must take care not to lose the peace." It would not be easy. When the Dutch left, the Indonesians had nothing—no teachers, no higher-level civil service class, no national income. The mills and factories were closed or destroyed. There was serious fighting against secessionists, communists, and religious fanatics. Politicians who put the good of their party over the good of the country scrambled after power. The new Republic turned over cabinets every six months, and there was chaotic bickering and dissension among the military, religious, left-wing, and conservative factions in the embryonic government. In 1955, 169 different political parties fought for 257 seats.

To stop the chaos, Sukarno declared in 1956 his policy of "Guided Democracy," involving the creation of a National Council made up of members handpicked by himself. Sukarno declared the age-old Indonesian tradition of *mufakat,* or decision through consensus, would best suit Indonesia as a method of decision-making. Political parties and legislative bodies were abolished.

The Outer Islands continued to prove unruly, claiming rightfully that the central government was neglecting them and that Jakarta was too lenient toward communists. In February 1958, West Sumatra and North Celebes revolted, demanding more Outer Island, Muslim-oriented autonomy. Calling themselves anti-communists, they received aid, equipment, and arms from the United States. Thus commenced full-scale, though lackadaisical, civil war. Seventy army battalions were mobilized to suppress the insurgents. Sukarno ordered the landing of troops on the eastern coast of Sumatra and by 17 April 1958 central government troops took Padang. On 5 May Bukittinggi fell.

The Irian Jaya question came to a head in 1962, when Sukarno ordered amphibious landings and paratroop drops into the Dutch-controlled territory of West New Guinea. These forays stirred the U.S. to put relentless pressure on the Dutch to capitulate. The Netherlands turned the territory over to UN administration in 1962, which in turn handed it to the Indonesians in 1963 under the stipulation that an Act of Free Choice occur within five years. Predictably, an assembly of tribal leaders agreed without a vote to integrate with the Indonesian Republic in 1969.

Pariah Among Nations
By the late 1950s, Sukarno was accumulating ever more power, press censorship had appeared, and the jails were filling with politicians and intellectuals. During the early 1960s Indonesia left the UN and became militantly anti-Western. To prevent Sabah and Sarawak, the British-controlled sections of Borneo, from joining the proposed Malaysian federation, Sukarno initiated an aggressive konfrontasi military campaign. Raiders were sent to attack the Malaysian peninsula and skirmishes broke out in northern Borneo between Indonesian, British, and Australian troops. Sukarno aligned himself with Communist China, parroting its official anti-imperialist line.

For 20 years this visionary and mesmerizing leader welded the islands together by adroitly playing off powerful groups against one another, his government a hectic marriage of widely disparate political ideologies. When he told his people that Marxism, nationalism, and Islam were all reconciled in one political philosophy, "Sukarnoism," they embraced it. Sukarno squandered billions on colossal stadiums, conference halls, and grandiose Soviet-style statuary. The inflation rate was running at 650% per

year; mammoth foreign debts had accumulated; opposed factions of the military, communists, Muslims, and other groups were grappling for control of the government. The political polarization between Army generals on the one side and the Indonesian Communist Party (PKI) on the other was nearing the breaking point.

The 1965 "Coup"
What happened before dawn on 1 October 1965 and all the events that followed have come under increasing scrutiny over the last 20 years. The truth will probably never be known, but the official Suharto version and Western conventional scholarship would have the world believe the PKI attempted a coup early that morning. Accumulating evidence, however, points to the possibility it was Indonesian army leaders and the American CIA who at least partly engineered events.

On the night of 30 September 1965, six top generals and their aides were abducted and brutally murdered. What followed was one of the most massive retaliatory bloodbaths in modern history. An unknown general named Suharto, provided with CIA-supplied death lists, mobilized the army strategic reserve (KOSTRAD) against "communist conspirators." The Indonesian army had never forgiven the communists for an attempted coup in 1948. While the armed forces stood aside, fanatical Muslim youths burned the PKI headquarters in Jakarta to the ground. Over the following months all of Java ran amok, resulting in the mass political murders of as many as half a million people—shot, knifed, strangled, and hacked to death. Tens of thousands were imprisoned without trial. The Communist Party was obliterated and the government bureaucracy purged. The army assumed control of the country, eventually developing a system of authoritarian domination and repression without precedent in Indonesia. A complete ideological and economic reversal occurred which continues to this day. In 1966 Indonesia's militant konfrontasi campaign with Malaysia was called off and the Jakarta-Peking axis abruptly ended. Suharto opened the country to Western investment and the Indonesian congress announced plans to rejoin the UN. Although his role in the plot was never made clear, Sukarno's power was systematically undermined by the new regime until his death in June 1970.

Ascent Of Suharto

A mild-mannered speaker, quiet, pragmatic, and a shrewd professional soldier, Suharto is today Indonesia's head of state. Born of humble parents in 1921 in a village near Yogyakarta in Central Java, the second president's personal style stands in stark contrast to his flamboyant and magnetic predecessor.

Suharto first distinguished himself in 1948 as the leader of an attack against Dutch forces occupying Yogyakarta. His first important military assignment was in 1956, as commander of the army's Diponegoro Division. In 1959 he was cashiered for collecting illegal levies. Two years later, however, he was appointed commander of KOSTRAD, the army's strategic reserve. Suharto was put in charge of the military campaign to wrest control of Irian Jaya from the Dutch, but happened to be in Jakarta at the time of the 1965 coup. In the right place at the right time, Suharto's troops played a decisive role in the turmoil of October. After dismantling Sukarno's Guided Democracy, Suharto installed a neo-monarchial, patrimonial regime which soon became popularly known as the Ordu Baru ("New Order").

Javanese rulers traditionally use their scribes to concoct accounts of their reigns that shower the ruler with glorious achievements. What's different about Suharto's 1989 autobiography *Soeharto: I Did it My Way* is that it was written while he was still president. The book's photos reveal a man who thinks of himself as a respected equal of the greatest leaders of the Western world, a refined Javanese *priyayi* who maintains Javanese customs, dress, and values. The book itself reveals a man with a thin skin and a long memory.

GOVERNMENT

Indonesia is easily the most broken-up country in the world, and its sheer expanse and diversity make it awesomely difficult to govern. On the state crest are the old Sanskrit words Bhinneka Tunggal Ika, "We are many but we are one." This line is played hard by Indonesia's leaders, who try to bring unity to the country by invoking nationalistic ceremonies; claiming a mystical, divine mandate to rule; and pushing a national fitness program of *senam pagi* (morning exercise), practiced every morning in even the most remote hill villages. The Indonesian language is another effective unifying force.

To bring all the diverse people of this sprawling island nation together within the political and geographic entity called Indonesia will always be the greatest single problem facing its leaders. Along with such typical fundamental problems of a developing Third World nation as overpopulation, unemployment, and lack of an industrial base and technical expertise, the widely dispersed group of 17,000 islands suffers from an uneven population and unequal distribution of natural wealth. In addition, it's a massive job trying to usher a feudal agrarian society into the 20th century.

The country's gigantic conservatism, low-key Indonesian temperament, almost feudal deference to established authority, docile resignation of the masses, and omnipresent army keep the government in power. Resignation is in fact a great asset, providing people with the patience to endure a succession of demagogic, inept, and unjust rulers. Indonesians are most concerned that the government satisfies them—food in their bellies, a roof over their heads, clothes to cover them.

Indonesia's most pressing issues are independence movements in Aceh, East Timor, and Irian Jaya; tension between *pribumi* and the Chinese; the role of the armed forces in an increasingly complex society; uneven distribution of wealth; and the political frustrations of the middle class at a time of rising expectations. There's a widespread feeling of resentment over the business activities of Suharto's children, several of whom are the richest people in Indonesia. Their avarice offends not only *pribumi* businessmen, but the World Bank, which is pushing for abolition of the wildly lucrative monopolies hampering vital sections of the economy. The behavior of his own family is Suharto's Achilles' heel.

THE NEW ORDER

The soft-spoken Suharto rose to power in 1965-66 because he controlled a key position in the

Indonesian army during a crisis. During the 30-year period since his ascension, Suharto has excelled in clever political maneuverings, controlling internal army politics, and accumulating and reinforcing his power by gathering around him committed and powerful people. The armed forces under his command have played a central role in the nation's development, and provide Suharto with his pervasive base of power.

Suharto receives high marks for guiding the aggressive political, economic, and social reforms of the 1970s. The basic policies he has instituted have resulted in a remarkably stable political and economic climate. The enormous increase in the power of the state has made the rule of law firmer. For those who lived through the turbulent Sukarno years, this is no insignificant gain.

Since 1967 competing power blocs have unceasingly struggled for greater influence and position in the government. Although Bung Harto maintains a firm grip, the military, cabinet, civilian bureaucracy, parliament, technocrats, academics, businesspeople, foreign investors, ethnic Chinese, Islamic groups, and Christians all jockey for increased power and prestige.

The left is something Suharto doesn't need to worry about. The massacres of 1965-68 wiped out the left; yet Suharto cruelly presides over pathetic purges to this day. A few tired old communist leaders were executed as late as 1985; several oil companies were then required to dismiss more than 1,500 employees said to have been associated with the PKI. In the outskirts of Jakarta, a Communist Party Treachery Museum has opened, and in 1992 superpatriot Try Sutrisno, Indonesia's vice president, warned against a possible resurgence of communism. Those who speak out for human rights and democracy come from the new left, said he, damning them as "fourth generation" communists. BAKIN, the state political security organ, keeps an ever-watchful eye.

The Islamic population is more problematic. Indonesia is the largest Muslim nation in the world, and rising Muslim consciousness poses one of the greatest potential threats to the regime. In September 1984 there were bloody Muslim riots at the port of Jakarta; troops clashed with extremists, leaving hundreds dead. The burning of a few Christian churches in East Java and an attack on a busload of Chinese workers in the 1990s have been the most hostile manifestations of Indonesia's new radical Muslim fundamentalism, although many see this violence as aimed more at the Chinese (most of whom are Christian) than at Christianity. Some fear modernization, the influx of Western culture, economic injustice, and rampant government corruption may push alienated youth in the direction of Muslim extremism.

Succession

All agree Suharto has lingered too long. Yet he's always claimed legitimacy by cloaking himself and his regime in the garments of the constitution, saying he'll step down only if the reins of state are passed in an orderly manner according to the precepts of that document.

Anyone interested in Indonesia's next president should look carefully at the country's new vice president. Try Sutrisno was elected vice president with the support of all factions at the MPR assembly in 1992. He was nominated by the armed forces bloc, the same bloc that so vociferously opposed Suharto's previous choice.

BILL WEIR

Merdeka Gateway art, Lhokseumawe, Banda Aceh province, Sumatra

Born in Surabaya in 1935, Sutrisno entered the army in 1956. He served as Suharto's aide-de-camp in 1974 and became the top military man in 1987. A masterful consensus builder is he, but a diplomat he is not. As commander of the armed forces he defiantly dismissed the army's 1991 massacre of 171 unarmed civilians in Dili as a trifling "incident" and declared all opposition on East Timor should be shot. During the entire crisis Sutrisno unflinchingly supported the army's explanation of events.

In the tradition of Javanese kings who rule by divine right and only part from their rule by death, Suharto will probably remain president—health permitting—through the late 1990s. With four coordinating ministers at his disposal, his job will be less taxing. But a well-prepared and well-managed transition will not be easy. His successor will begin with much less power than Suharto enjoyed during his 30 years as president, and will probably have to share what power he does have with other state bodies.

One never knows what Suharto will do next. He has built and maintained his position of power by outmaneuvering and outguessing his opponents. The preeminent Australian journalist David Jenkins has written that during the past 30 years "Suharto's greatest asset has been an inscrutability so pervasive that at times not even his closest associates have been quite sure what he is thinking."

SYSTEM OF GOVERNMENT

Administratively, Indonesia is divided into 27 provinces, each headed by a governor nominated by a provincial legislature and approved and appointed by the central government. Akin to the U.S. states, each province has its own provincial capital. The provinces are further divided into regencies, subdistricts, and municipalities.

Pancasila

The concept of Pancasila ("Five Principles"), authored by Sukarno during the Japanese occupation, is the basis of civilized rule. The government urges all Indonesians to accept this state ideology as their fundamental political philosophy, crucial to national unity. Displayed on practically every government building, the emblem of the five *sila*, or principles, are: 1) belief in one supreme God; 2) a just and civilized humanity; 3) nationalism, the unity of Indonesia; 4) democracy, guided by the wisdom of unanimity arising from discussion (*musjawarah*) and mutual assistance (*gotong royong*); and 5) social justice, the equality of political rights and the rights of citizenship, as well as social and cultural equality. Each regime tends to interpret these five concepts in a way that will further its social and political goals.

Indonesian political leaders point out that since the majority of Indonesians share strong cultural values—adhering to a sort of a pan-Indonesian superculture—it follows that Indonesians should share the same political culture as well. They argue that the collectivist *adat* of traditional village culture is ideally adapted to consensual politics, with the weight of decision-making falling on the shoulders of a society's elders. The Pancasila state philosophy is often used to justify the military's heavy-handed grip on both civilian and government affairs.

The State Organs

According to the text of the country's 1945 constitution, still in effect, the nation is a republic, with sovereignty residing in the people. Functions of the government include executive, legislative, and judicial, but there is no specific separation of powers, no system of checks and balances. The constitution provides for a strong president who serves a term of five years. Apparently, this highest government executive may be reelected indefinitely; it's up to the president to accept or reject another term. Suharto was overwhelmingly reelected to serve a sixth five-year term in March 1993. Only Cuba's Fidel Castro has served longer as a head of state.

Suharto's cabinet, officially called Development Cabinet VI, is responsible only to him. With a current membership of 41, the new cabinet is the world's largest, after China's. Previous cabinets promulgated policies to improve agriculture, as the president has always had a soft spot for farmers. The present cabinet, however, is intent on turning Indonesia into a modern industrial state. The man most responsbile for the realignment of the president's priorities is Minister of Research and Technology B. J. Habibie. This German-trained aeronautical engineer has turned to politics to advance his vision of a

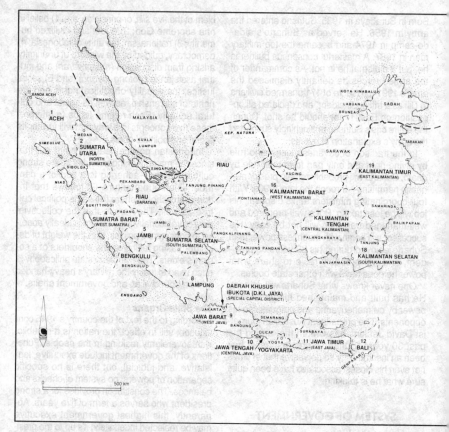

modern Indonesia that can take its place beside the tigers of Southeast Asia—Malaysia, Singapore, and Hong Kong. Habibie is equally committed to developing a qualified, skilled workforce to implement Indonesia's ambitious technological programs.

The president himself is directly responsible only to the Majellis Permusyawaratan Rakyat (MPR), the People's Consultative Assembly. This "super parliament" consists of 1,000 farmers, workers, students, businesspeople, clergy, intellectuals, and military types—a heterogeneous body meant to represent a wide cross-section of society. The MPR meets every five years to select a president and endorse the general policy guidelines for the president's next five-year term.

Just because Indonesia has a parliament doesn't mean it's a democracy. Although empowered by the constitution with the highest authority of state, in reality the MPR is a classic rubber-stamp body that rarely meets and never decides important issues. Members must pass an ideological screening administered by the military, and the president has the final right to approve MPR appointees. At least 60% of the body works for the government party; nearly 200 are admirals, generals, or air marshals.

The 500-member Dewan Perwakilan Rakyat (DPR), or House of Representatives, is a legislative body that sits at least once a year. Only 400 members are elected; the remaining 100 seats are reserved for armed forces personnel. DPR representatives are not known for their

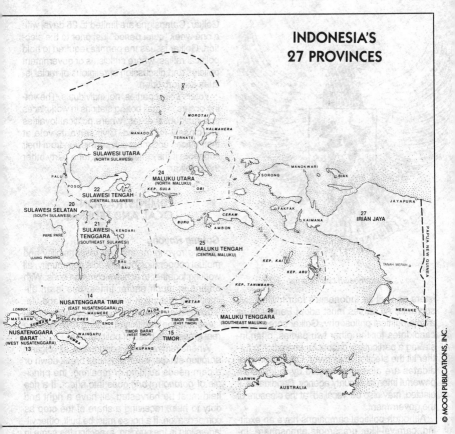

INDONESIA'S 27 PROVINCES

candor and outspokenness. Every statute passed by the DPR requires the approval of the president.

The judiciary cannot impeach, nor can it rule on the constitutionality of decrees or legislation promulgated by the other branches of government. The number of sitting supreme court judges varies from 15 to 20; they preside over 300 subordinate courts scattered across the country's 27 provinces. Adequate qualified staffing is a major problem bedeviling the scope and speed of settlements.

Political Parties And The Electoral Process

The government Golkar party, founded in 1964 as a counterbalance to growing PKI influence,

enjoys the full backing of the army and bureaucracy. This all-powerful government political machine, with almost unlimited resources, dominates all levels of government. Golkar represents the armed forces, the bureaucracy, farmers, women's organizations, students, and many other "functional groups" (*golongan karya*). Golkar always wins.

The Muslim United Development Party (PPP) is plagued by internal friction. The Indonesian Democratic Party (PDI), also weakened by internal bickering, is a coalition of Christians and Sukarnoists. Nine political parties challenged Golkar in 1971; in 1973 the government forced them all into the PDI and PPP. No additional parties are permitted. Golkar has a virtual monopoly on the political loyalty of all cabinet min-

Indonesian coat of arms

isters as well as Indonesia's four million civil servants. All parties must adopt Pancasila as a sole political philosophy. Golkar screens the candidates for the other two parties, often installing a particularly unpopular character to further tilt the election in its favor. Opposition candidates are also investigated by Indonesia's powerful internal security agency. Candidates, if elected, may also be "recalled" at the pleasure of the government.

Although political campaigns have an exciting, carnival-like, grassroots atmosphere, Indonesia's electoral process is actually heavily managed and controlled. Little effort is expended in educating the people to inform their political choices. Indonesians have a vote but not a say. The whole process is designed to demonstrate the government's legitimacy to its people and the world, while avoiding as much as possible any real contest among competing political parties.

Electioneering by opposition forces is not permitted in villages, where four out of five Indonesians live. Since only Golkar can organize on the village level, if you don't vote for Golkar you won't get a new village school or agricultural co-op. Voting is not compulsory, but government officials in provincial districts apply pressure on village heads to get out the vote for

Golkar. Campaigns are limited to 25 days, with a one week "quiet period" just prior to the election. Golkar issues the permits required to hold political rallies, where criticisms of government policies and discussion of religious or racial issues are forbidden.

Voters select parties, not individuals. The voting occurs in small polling stations in workplaces and residential areas, where political loyalties are closely monitored. Civil servants vote at their offices and must ask permission from their superiors if they intend to vote for a party other than Golkar.

ADMINISTRATION— LOCAL AND FEDERAL

Gotong Royong

Gotong royong means joint responsibility and mutual cooperation of the whole community, all working together to achieve common ends. With origins in much earlier times, this is an all-important institution in Indonesian village life. Indonesia consists of tens of thousands of villages and the tradition of *gotong royong* is the real grassroots base of political rule.

Whenever fire, flood, earthquake, or volcanic eruption strikes, when pipelines break down or a dam needs building or repairing, the principle of *gotong royong* goes into effect. If a rice field must be harvested, all have a right and duty to help, receiving a share of the crop as compensation. If a house must be built, other villagers join in the building, expecting the same in return. Men usually work with their own tools and without pay. Sometimes neighboring villagers are expected to help. If a village follows this communal organization, no household will be without land to farm, work to subsist, food to eat. Anyone in trouble will receive help.

The system revolves around thousands of village headmen (*lurah* or *kepala desa*), who coordinate *gotong royong* programs and carry out government policies. *Lurah* rule by assigning friends and assistants to tasks, a sort of administration by relationships. Loyalties to family, village, and friends are more important than self-advancement. The government greatly encourages this village socialism—it makes the government's job much easier, enabling the country to almost run itself.

Musjawarah And Mufakat

The native political process is built on ancient Javanese customs. The Arabic words *musjawarah* (discussion) and *mufakat* (consensus) describe methods of resolving political, policy, and personal differences by prolonged deliberation ending in unanimous decision. These methods are used both in the state's highest legislative body and at the humblest village meetings. Indonesians don't believe in the Western-style system of decision-making by voting, where the majority of 50% plus one gets its way, a method disdained as "dictatorship of the majority." Indonesians believe this system isn't fair; the will of the minority is just as important as that of the majority, so the council just talks itself out until all parties come to an accord, too exhausted or too hoarse to discuss the issue any further. The process proceeds slowly, but all points of view are eventually brought together in one compromise agreement.

The Bureaucracy

You'll have ample opportunity to observe at close range Indonesia's ponderous, octopus-like, highly centralized bureaucracy. In the outer areas, you'll often have to seek information or aid from the local *camat,* or apply for a *surat jalan* from the office of the *bupati* (mayor). If there's any possibility an official may get in trouble for granting you permission, he'll insist upon the decision first clearing Jakarta. Petty officials are everywhere. Indonesia is a land of a million dictators.

The bureaucracy is a privileged class. Positions in local government bring prestige, job security, and steady pay, and openings are hotly contested. Local authorities in Indonesia's 3,500 subdistricts and 62,900 villages function as extensions of the central government, charged with imposing Jakarta's tight political and administrative grip on local affairs. But in spite of its hierarchal appearance, the real glue holding the whole structure together is the phenomenon of *bapakism,* which encourages a collectivist, familial attitude toward society. A father figure, the *bapak,* supervises a circle of loyal underlings in every bureaucratic office.

After three centuries of Dutch rule, the Indonesians achieved independence in 1949 with virtually no skills in administration and government service above junior-management level.

Indonesian officials were allowed to decide inconsequential departmental matters, but for weightier issues the Dutch decided for them. During this period there evolved a tradition of invariably channeling the more important decisions to the top, a time-honored practice that explains the extreme paternalism and painfully slow decison-making process in the Indonesian bureaucracy today.

THE ARMED FORCES

Indonesia's armed forces were founded in 1945 during the revolution against the Dutch. From that time to the present, the army has been the most powerful of all the services. Most of the soldiers and officers in the army were former members of the Dutch colonial army and the Japanese-sponsored militia Pembela Tanah Air (PETA). During the period of Guided Democracy (1959-65), Sukarno promoted the navy, air force, and police as distinct branches in an attempt to curb the power of the army.

Under the direct control of the president and the ministry of defense, the armed forces consists of the army (Angkatan Darat), navy (Angkatan Laut), air force (Angkatan Udara), and police (Polisi Negara). A central command (ABRI) coordinates all four services. Armed forces personnel number 284,000, with another 800,000 in reserve. Duty in hazardous counterinsurgency war zones like East Timor, Irian Jaya, and Aceh does wonders for the career track of a professional soldier. The military's arsenal includes F-16 fighter planes and A-4 Sky Hawks; work is progressing on ballistic missiles.

The military is the nation's only credible political power. The service provides the country with its president, half its ambassadors, two-thirds of its regional governors, and half its ministers. From its inception, retired military men have secured up to 80% of the leadership posts in Golkar, the government party. The army's power and prestige in national affairs is a legacy of its role in the war against the Dutch. Since the armed forces feels it won independence, saved the country from 1948 and 1965 communist uprisings, and came to the rescue on several other occasions when civilian authority was found wanting, it believes it has a god-given right and moral duty to continue to rule over Indonesia's civilian population. In nearly every village of Indonesia you find the inevitable memorial to the brave martyrs of the revolution, as if the government never wants the people to forget to whom they owe their gratitude for freeing them.

The Dutch occupation of western New Guinea and the retaliatory 1957 takeover of Dutch businesses and property greatly expanded the army's role in the economy. Army officers began managing businesses, the income supplementing the meager funds available to them through conventional channels. Today Javanese "financial generals" and retired generals own monopolies, corporations, shipping lines, hotels, import firms, factories, mines, and oil wells.

Dwi Fungsi

The army also considers itself a sociopolitical force, a role enshrined in the doctrine of *dwi fungsi*, or dual function, which calls for its extensive participation in politics and government. Thus, there's an army level of command corresponding to each function of the civil government from the provincial level right down to the village. Starting in 1980 with the *ABRI masuk desa* program, the military began to assist in public works projects in the countryside to improve its public image and help rural development. The military also views its participation in the day-to-day running of the country as a necessary part of the national defense strategy. A typical military officer's career consists of serving alternate stints in both regional and combat commands; he then "retires" into the civil bureaucracy.

The Dili Massacre

In November 1991 Indonesian troops killed 171 peaceful, unarmed East Timorese mourners at a Dili funeral, a blunder that sparked an outcry all over the world. Jakarta claimed the "regrettable tragedy" was an overreaction by low-level soldiers who believed they were defending themselves. But the massacre was the most serious abuse of military power since independence. Canada, Denmark, and Holland immediately cut off aid, there were protests at the Indonesian embassy in Australia, and the massacre was the root of a 1993 foreign-relations crisis with the United States.

The subsequent investigation of what the government insisted on calling an "incident" was

the first independent inquiry into military conduct under the New Order regime. Two top generals in East Timor were fired, and, eight months after the massacre, 10 soldiers were sentenced to one year in prison. Though this was the first time in Indonesian history that soldiers were prosecuted for human rights violations, the sentences were grossly disproportionate to the number of people killed.

CENSORSHIP, PROPAGANDA, AND CIVIL LIBERTIES

Although the Indonesian constitution guarantees freedom of the press and speech, censorship is taken for granted in Indonesia. Accompanying the economic deregulation of 1988 was a tendency towards *keterbukaan,* or openness, in Indonesian society, but by the early '90s the publishing industry was under siege once again. In June 1994 the government banned three weeklies in one day—*Tempo, Petik,* and *Editor.* Their crimes included reports on conflicts between the military and the research and technology minister over refitting 39 German ships, and disclosures that the trial of a Chinese businessman accused of "losing" $430 million in state funds involved associates of Suharto. Information Minister Harmoko damned the publications as purveyors of "alcoholic journalism."

In Indonesian government circles, freedom of the press is regarded as less important than stability and harmony among the people. There is no exchange of opinions, only a one-way monologue from the government down to the people. In the past 10 years, the New Order regime has banned the publication of over 120 books and periodicals. As a result, the country's domestic newspapers often stretch or omit the truth. A law requiring all publications and press corporations to obtain an operating license means not only an offending publication but also the parent company can be closed down. Publishing management staff must receive police clearance and vow never to engage in anti-Pancasila activities.

No formalized, institutionalized censorship guidelines exist. Whim and whimsy determines what will be censored. If Indonesia's attorney general determines a book has the capacity to disturb law and order, it is banned. Ban orders may not be debated openly in public, and the Indonesian Publisher's Association has not once remonstrated against a government ban order. Journalists work under extreme constraints and can be blacklisted. Artists and performers likewise lament that the government's obsession with security is like a black hole swallowing all independent thought and ideas. They fear that 30 years of repression has slowly killed the country's cultural life and that Indonesia will never produce important literature or drama. In 1989 the authorities arrested two Yogyakarta students for circulating the works of Indonesia's greatest living novelist, Pramoedya Ananta Toer, a former PKI sympathizer. After a show trial condemning those who would "disturb the stability and success of national development," the students were sentenced to eight years in jail. If you go to a movie and wonder why the main character suddenly vanishes, that's the long reach of the government. The hero was too antisocial or amoral, or the film too sexually explicit. Films of primitive Indonesian people such as the Asmat of Irian Jaya, or films depicting poverty or environmental pollution, cannot be shown, as the authorities believe they portray the country in a bad light. In July 1993 a student was prosecuted in Central Java for circulating a calendar cataloging incidents of abuse by the military.

Sure-fire ways to guarantee your publication will be yanked from the shelves include negative commentary about the president or his family's multibillion dollar investments, direct criticism of the army, accounts of demonstrations or insurgency movements in East Timor or Irian Jaya, and any news item that offends religious sensibilities. Licenses may be revoked for leaking a proposed economic program. Three journalists for the weekly magazine *Jakarta-Jakarta*, who published interviews with crucial eyewitnesses to the Dili Massacre, subsequently lost their jobs. In mid-1986 a whole planeload of Australian tourists was barred from entry because of a scathing editorial by David Jenkins in the *Sydney Morning Herald* that compared Suharto to Marcos and accused the president, his family, and business associates of "waxing fat on government capital, credit, and concessions, and accumulating $2-3 billion." Pages critical of Indonesia are often blacked out of such imported weeklies as *Far Eastern Economic Review, Time,* and *Newsweek.* Foreign journalists may be denied visas if they're too candid in their reporting. Steven Erlanger of the *New York Times,* who also wrote about the Suharto family's business dealings, was banned in 1990. Pat Walsh, a prominent Australian human rights activist, was refused entry to Indonesia in November 1992. And the book you hold in your hands has, since the mid-'70s, been unavailable for sale in Indonesia.

Civil Liberties

Indonesia's military bureaucratic state can best be described as an open patriarchal dictatorship. Don't think Big Brother is always watching. The Javanese are a softer civilization than the North Koreans or Saudis. There's authoritarianism, but not mind control.

The rule of formal, court-upheld law doesn't exist here. Legal rules are made up day-by-day according to need. Regulations can be stretched much more in Indonesia than in the West; problems can often be worked out before they come to a confrontation. Because *adat* affords so much latitude and reinterpretation, the amount of personal liberty in practice is astonishingly high. Government controls actually felt by the people are extremely limited compared to places like the U.S., where government regulations, laws, and taxes touch every individual every day.

All this social freedom should not hide the fact that legal injustices occur. P. Kooijmans, who visited Java and East Timor at the behest of the United Nation's Commission on Human Rights, reports that torture during detention is particularly apt to occur in politically unstable areas like East Timor, Irian Jaya, and Aceh. A law passed in 1992 bars the return of Indonesian citizens who engage in "anti-Indonesian" activities abroad. Another law requires all "social organizations" to submit to scrutiny by the ministry of the interior. The military also routinely intervenes in industrial disputes.

Dissent

One of the most significant challenges to the Suharto regime was an open petition signed by 50 prominent national figures, including 1945-generation military men, politicians, academics, and students. This document became known as the "Petition of 50 Group." Reacting to an

April 1980 Suharto speech, where he implied he was the embodiment of Pancasila, the group accused the president of virtually usurping the government and heading a corrupt and maladministered regime. The government's reaction was swift and unrelenting. All news coverage of the event was banned, members of the group were prohibited from overseas travel, and firms associated with the dissidents had their government contracts cancelled. The petition's most famous signatory was A.H. Nasution, founder of the Indonesian army and Suharto's former superior.

These tensions led to violence during the parliamentary campaign of May 1982, when opponents of the government attempted to disrupt what they believed were rigged elections. In Benteng Square rioters hurled rocks and burned automobiles; troops were ordered to "shoot on the spot" anyone who attempted to disturb the polling. Admiral Sudomo, head of national security, assured a group of ASEAN journalists, "we will shoot very cautiously, for this is a democracy." Sixty people were killed and 1,334 injured. In 1984 there were more riots and bombings, and show trials were staged in 1986.

These days the president, the military, and various important ministers are attempting a reconciliation. Former adversaries have been photographed smiling and shaking hands with the president; Nasution and Suharto have even met. All this high media drama has led optimists to believe the government is genuinely committed to openness and the right of its citizens to nonviolent dissent. Though there has recently been an unprecedented amount of dissident views expressed in the Indonesian press—unthinkable even several years ago—harsh prison terms are still meted out. East Timorese students who protested the Dili massacre in front of the UN building and other diplomatic missions in Jakarta in 1992 were sentenced to 10 months to 10 years for "hostility toward the government" and "subversion."

JAKARTAN CENTRALISM

The government is centered on Java, and is also intensely Java-centered. Indonesia's is not a truly representative government; the Javanese are in effect the new colonialists of the archipelago. An elite of perhaps 2,000 Javanese men manipulate Indonesian politics. With only a dozen or so exceptions, they all speak English, drive new Japanese cars, live in Jakarta, and are Javanese.

There has always been tension and conflict between the seafaring, mercantile Muslim states of Indonesia's Outer Islands and the bureaucratic, powerful, Hinduized forces of Java. Outer Island ethnic groups have come to resent Java's heavy-handed overlordship. Colonialism, whether by white Dutch Europeans or brown Javanese Asians, is equally unacceptable to Indonesia's Outer Island peoples. Many would prefer a looser federation to ensure a more just distribution of national wealth and power.

The Threat Of Separatism

The threat of secession always looms large in this scattered island nation. Overpopulated Java couldn't possibly survive on its own; when any of the resource-rich Outer Islands gets uppity, Java sends bombers and assault troops to quell secessionist uprisings. There were serious revolts in 1949 in southern Maluku and in 1959 in Sumatra and North Sulawesi because Java took too much of the revenues from these regions for its own enrichment. It's now deliberate government policy to constantly rotate provincial chiefs of police and military district heads throughout Indonesia to prevent power consolidation and keep secessionist challenges to a minimum. In the civilian sector, the central government also appoints provincial as well as *kabupaten* (regency) and *kotmadya* (municipality) heads, even though elected local assemblies are in place.

INTERNATIONAL RELATIONS

Foreign Aid

Since Suharto's takeover in 1967, Indonesia has received hundreds of millions of dollars in diplomatic, economic, and military support from the developed nations. Japan provides the largest share of Indonesia's foreign-development capital. Lesser but still substantial sums come from the U.S., Germany, the Netherlands, France, and Australia. More than humanitarian interest motivates investment in the region. Indonesia sits on Southeast Asia's largest and richest oil reserves, is an influential member of OPEC, possesses an unlimited and untapped labor pool, and controls the strategic Straits of Malacca, through which ships must pass from the Pacific to the Indian Ocean and the Persian Gulf. Maintaining Indonesia's position as the largest country in Southeast Asia, and perhaps the only one with the potential to become a major world power, is of prime importance to the stability of the entire region.

Suharto and his ministers, understandably sensitive over their human rights and environmental records, have reiterated again and again that aid, loans, and trade must not be predicated on Indonesia's internal policies. No amount of Western aid has ever guaranteed Indonesian support of *donar contries*. In March 1992, Jakarta asked the Netherlands to discontinue its aid program following Dutch protests over the 1991 Dili Massacre. It further requested the Dutch-directed IGGI be dissolved.

The U.S. also became increasingly critical of Indonesia's handling of events in East Timor. The Senate Foreign Relations Committee unanimously approved an amendment linking arms sales to Indonesia to human rights in East Timor, the first time arms sales to a U.S. ally were tied to human rights concerns. Indonesian leaders reacted by calling for diversifying their arms sources and reducing ties to the U.S.

The Nonaligned Movement
Indonesia founded the nonaligned movement (NAM) at the historic Asia-Africa Conference in Bandung in 1955; President Suharto assumed the 108-member movement's leadership in 1991. The 10th summit was held in Jakarta in 1992, when 60 heads of government and assorted dignitaries heard Suharto outline future priorities in the wake of the end of the Cold War. Indonesia considers itself a stable role model for other NAM nations. Though Suharto encourages members to place greater emphasis on economic and human concerns, political and ideological issues still dominate the organization. Indonesia's own human rights and environmental records point to a gap between what it says and what it does—there were mass detentions in Dili before and during the NAM conference to quell protests designed to capture the attention of the international press.

During the Sukarno years, Indonesia developed close ties with China and the Soviet Union and was openly hostile to what Sukarno called the Old Established Forces (NEFOS), the developed nations of the West. Although Indonesia today vigorously espouses Asian neutralism and an independent approach to foreign affairs, in reality Suharto has aligned his nation closely with the West. The G-7 industrialized countries were invited to attend the NAM economic cooperation and development meeting on Bali in May 1993.

Regional Relations
The Association of South East Asian Nations (ASEAN) was formed in 1967 along the lines of NATO, the European-based multinational alliance, and consists of Indonesia, Malaysia, the Philippines, Singapore, and Thailand. In the post-cold war world, it was hoped ASEAN would become an important vehicle for Asia/Pacific consultations and dialogue aimed at promoting economic development through regional cooperation. In reality, little has been achieved. Members have consistently disagreed on the level of developed nation participation in their economies. ASEAN's most recent success has been acting as intermediary for the warring parties in Cambodia, with Suharto an active player.

Indonesia also hopes to provide quality products at competitive prices to the Asean Free Trade Area (AFTA). Yet another new interregional body, the 10-member Council for Security in Asia Pacific (CSCAP), coordinates discussions between nongovernmental groups on Pacific security matters.

Suharto himself has launched a number of diplomatic initiatives in the past several years. Indonesia suspended its relations with China after the 1965 coup, but in 1989 Suharto bypassed his foreign minister and minister of trade to normalize relations with China. Suharto also visited Moscow in 1989 to established bilateral trade with Gorbachev's government. Another remarkable foray was Suharto's November 1990 state visit to Vietnam, ending that country's 15-year isolation in Southeast Asia—a gesture Vietnam will never forget.

ECONOMY

Before WW II, Indonesia exported substantial percentages of the world's rubber, tin, petroleum, pepper, cloves, nutmeg, quinine, coffee, tea, palm oil, and copra. But by 1965, President Sukarno's disastrous economic policies had left the economy in chaos, with a foreign debt of $2.5 billion and a population among the poorest in the world.

Following the crises of the 1960s, Suharto's New Order changed a badly managed economy to a liberal market economy backed by foreign investment and state planning. Within three years, the new regime managed to get the nation's debt under control. By balancing the budget and controlling the money supply, Suharto brought down inflation from a staggering 639% in 1966 to under 15% in 1969. Resources were redirected from wasteful prestige projects to producing food and clothing and the building of roads and harbors.

The new administration wholeheartedly adopted Western development strategies and encouraged foreign investment with such major incentives as tax exemptions and assurances of free profit. With billions of dollars in Western aid and food imports pouring into the country, Indonesia became a model of a successful developing nation.

Foreign Investment

This transformation was executed by a handful of U.S.-trained technocrats—popularly known as the Berkeley Mafia—who reorganized virtually the entire economy. In 1967 the government began allowing 100% equity ownership by foreigners. When this law was held partly responsible for anti-Japanese riots in Jakarta in 1974, it was changed to force foreign investors to take on local partners. Increasing competition for capital among ASEAN nations resulted in the 1992 reinstatement of the 1967 regulation.

Today, Japan is by far Indonesia's biggest trading partner, accounting for about 40% of the nation's exports. Japan is also Indonesia's largest supplier. The rapid appreciation of the yen against all other currencies induced many companies from Japan to relocate manufacturing facilities to Indonesia to take advantage of lower labor and material costs. The lure was powerful enough to induce the Taisei Corporation of Japan to build a $206 million industrial estate in Cikampek, West Java, in 1993.

Foreign investment rose by more than 1,000% between 1985 and 1990. Primary areas of investment include chemicals, hospitality, metals, mining, textiles, and food. Indonesia's greatest asset in the regional competition for foreign investment is its gigantic pool of manpower, the country's one inexhaustible resource. For unskilled labor, the minimum wage on Java is only Rp2100 per day; on Bali, Rp3000 per day. While Indonesia's glut of workers will keep wages low for decades, the booming economy has created an acute shortage of middle-level managers.

Deregulation

From the 1950s to the late 1980s, the state retained control or ownership over so many vital industries and installations the health of the economy was primarily determined by the vicissitudes of the state budget. Initially established to protect vital and strategic industries, the monopolies date back to 1957, when the government nationalized Dutch companies as a part of its West Irian campaign. But the state-owned monopolies frequently created inefficiency and high prices, and suffered from low productivity and a cumbersome and excessively bureaucratic decision-making process.

Very slowly at first, the government began deregulating the economy in the late 1980s. A particular goal has been to privatize the 215 state-run monopolies controlling such crucial commodities as oil, cloves, and palm oil. Hotels, banking, travel agencies, and numerous other industries have been privatized as well. For the first time, privately owned megaprojects have emerged in the mining, manufacturing, and agribusiness sectors. One of the largest and fastest growing conglomerates in Indonesia is the privately owned timber company Barito Pacific; its exports alone in 1992 accounted for 13% of the global trade in plywood.

By the end of the century the private sector is expected to play a much stronger role. It is

COSTS OF EVERYDAY GOODS AND SERVICES IN INDONESIA
(US$1 = Rp2100)

average monthly electrical bill for average family: Rp10,000

bread roll: Rp200

can of soda pop: Rp1000

cassette tape of domestic artist: Rp4500

cassette tape of Western artist: Rp7500

child's school uniform: Rp10,000

cooking oil: Rp7000 per liter

film, Fuji 36-shot, 100 ASA: Rp7000

14-inch color TV: Rp600,000

gasoline: Rp700 per liter

Imodium diarrhea medicine: Rp1000 per pill

kerosene: Rp300 per liter

man's haircut: Rp2000

new American movie, a/c, nice seats: Rp4000

new Chinese bicycle: Rp250,000

pack of *kretek* cigarettes: Rp1100

postcard to Europe: Rp1000

Time or *Newsweek*: Rp4000

water: 1 liter Rp1000

hoped deregulation will increase the relocation of manufacturers from industrialized countries to Indonesia, taking advantage of the country's abundant natural resources, cheap energy, strategic market location, rapidly expanding domestic consumer market, suppressed labor movement, and exploited and underemployed labor force of 80 million.

Problems And Gains

Between 1970 and 1990 Indonesia achieved one of the highest annual average reductions in poverty in the Third World. When Suharto took office in 1967, the average per capita income was just over $70 a year; today, it's over $600. Average life expectancy at birth is now 61. The inflation rate was five percent in 1992, the economic growth rate 5.7%.

Evidence is everywhere of Indonesia's newfound wealth. TV antennae and new housing complexes break the skylines of every city, health-care centers have sprung up all over the archipelago, farmers are subsidized with lime and fertilizers, poor students are sent to universities. A modern network of roads, highways, and bridges is in place, with snarling traffic jams in the centers of all the big cities. Available consumer goods have increased fivefold in the past 10 years.

Yet all is not rosy. The country suffers from serious foreign debt and debt service problems. Low-income groups do not benefit from development. There is widening inequality between the urban and rural populations, a shortage of skilled labor, labor unrest, and military intimidation. The country faces an enormous task in educating its 26 million elementary-school-age children, 60% of whom receive little more than perfunctory schooling. The wealthiest 20% of the population derives an income roughly seven times greater than that of the poorest 20%. Twenty-seven million Indonesians live in poverty. Sixty percent of the national wealth is concentrated in Jakarta. The health of the country's banking system was thrown into question when Indonesia's tenth-largest bank, Bank Summa, went bankrupt in 1991.

INDUSTRY

During the pre-WW I colonial period industrial development was not a priority. But after the war the Dutch realized how vulnerable and dependent the colonies were on imported manufactured goods. Employment opportunities were also needed for Java's growing population. The first cautious step toward creating an industrial base was a paper factory built in Bandung in 1923.

Though Suharto opened Indonesia to foreign investment in 1967, until the mid-1980s the economy relied too heavily on oil, timber, rubber, and other highly localized products. Foreign exchange was generated through the sale of these raw natural resources, extracted mostly by Japanese and American multinational corporations. The slump in oil prices in 1982 caused a serious economic downturn and again raised questions of overdependence on oil. The government redoubled its efforts to develop the country's non-oil manufacturing industries. By the early 1990s manufactured goods accounted for 27.7% of total Indonesian exports, overtaking agriculture as the greatest contributor to Indonesia's economic output.

Manufacturing

PT Astra International dominates the domestic vehicle industry; Indomobil Utama is the nation's second-largest automaker. An automotive deregulation package announced in 1993 is expected to attract Japanese, U.S., and European auto firms. General Motors already plans a $110 million assembly plant in Indonesia.

Indonesia has also entered the high-tech aerospace industry. The state-owned Indonesian National Aircraft Industry (IPTN) in Bandung produces passenger aircraft and helicopters for both domestic and overseas markets. Other industries manufacture ships, tankers, electric trains, aerobridges, railway coaches, telecommunications equipment, heavy diesel engines, and jetfoils. Indonesia also plans to build nuclear reactors on earthquake-prone, overpopulated Java; Australia will support and supply uranium for the project.

The country's light manufacturing facilities produce tires, furniture, clothing, footwear, electronics, audiocassettes, drugs, toiletries, and cigarettes. Electrical appliance production has grown at a rate of 80% per year since the late 1980s. Textiles are Indonesia's largest non-oil export commodity, totaling $6 billion in 1992.

Oil And Minerals

The first oil wells in Indonesia were drilled near Surabaya, East Java, in 1889. These were soon eclipsed by oil fields in southern Sumatra and East Kalimantan. A Dutch subsidiary of Standard Oil dominated the East Indies petroleum industry until WW II. It was, in fact, a U.S. oil embargo the Japanese used as a pretext for invading the Indies in 1941.

The process of Indonesianizing the oil fields began after WW II. Indonesia eventually took its place as a major oil producer, joining OPEC in 1962. In 1968 the government entered into production-sharing agreements with foreign oil companies, launching a period when petroleum became the driving force behind the economy. When oil prices quadrupled in 1973, Indonesia's export earnings doubled, with oil providing almost 50% of state revenue in 1974-75. This period of abundance ended with the global recession, political scandal, and the near-bankruptcy of Pertamina, the state-owned oil and gas company.

Today oil continues to play a major role as a source of government revenue and foreign exchange. Crude oil production increased from 508.9 million barrels in 1988 to 572.8 million in 1992, an average of about 3.5% per year. Oil now accounts for 20% of total exports. With only 34 of the country's 60 oil basins explored and only 14 developed, Indonesia's recoverable oil reserves will last well into the 21st century.

Natural gas is playing an important role as an alternative energy source. Indonesian production rose dramatically with the discovery of huge reserves in northern Sumatra and East Kalimantan; today Indonesia is the world's largest exporter of natural gas.

Low-sulphur coal deposits were first tapped during the steamship era, and the first commercial mines opened in 1846 in South Kalimantan, East Kalimantan, and West Sumatra. Indonesia's prewar level of annual production was two million tons. In the mid-1980s, Indonesia intensified exploration, rehabilitation, and expansion of its state-owned mining enterprises, diversifying its coal products in an attempt to break away from oil. With greater opportunities for foreign and domestic investment, production increased from two million tons in 1987 to 22.5 million tons in 1992. With proven reserves of at least 1,730 million tons, production is expected to reach 40 million tons by the year 2000.

Although the legends of Indonesia's huge and diverse mineral riches have been exaggerated, the nation does possess huge deposits of tin, copper, nickel, and gold, and limited deposits of bauxite. Indonesia lies in the world's tin belt, and is the fourth-largest producer on the globe. The tin from Riau's Bangka Islands is generally considered the best in the world. Bauxite is mined entirely on Pulau Bintan by Alcoa; another major reserve has been confirmed in West Kalimantan. At present, 90% of Indonesia's bauxite is exported to Japan. A joint-venture aluminum smelter was completed at the massive Asahan industrial complex in North Sumatra in the mid-'80s.

With reserves of over 40 million tons, Indonesia's nickel production accounts for spectacular revenues. A large nickel mine was opened by Canadian-owned INCO at Soroako in southeast Sulawesi in 1978; today it's the site of the largest nickel-smelting plant in the world. Significant nickel deposits have been mined on Pulau Gebe by the state mining company, Aneka Tambang. Copper has been mined in Java, Sumatra, and Timor since Indonesia's Early Metal Phase (around 1000 B.C.), when it was used in the production of bronze. Indonesia's largest copper mine lies in the high, rugged Ertsberg Mountains of Irian Jaya. Opened by Freeport Minerals Inc. of Lousiana in 1967, it is also the largest gold mine in the world.

AGRICULTURE

Indonesia is still very much an agricultural nation. Agriculture continues to employ more than half the workforce and contributes about 25% of the gross domestic product. The current five-year plan calls for increasing the role of the private sector in agribusiness and shifting priorities from food production schemes to agricultural product processing, also known as agroindustry. The agricultural sector enjoys the full support of President Suharto, son of a Javanese rice farmer, who is seen on television more often talking with *petani* (farmers) than with assembly-line workers or bureaucrats.

Rice is Indonesia's most important crop and is grown virtually everywhere in the country. It is considered the tastiest of all grains and is eaten at least three times a day. Whole dynasties in Indonesia have grown up around the apportionment and control of water for rice growing. As a result of the introduction of high-yield, genetically engineered strains, Indonesia achieved self-sufficiency in rice in 1984. The downside of this "Green Revolution" is that traditional rice varieties are now grown only in mountainous areas, forced out of the plains by hybrid varieties. The cost of the native varieties are twice that of the IR64 hybrid. Another drawback is that production gains have not been achieved without skirting ecological disaster.

Indonesia ranks among the world's top five producers in rubber, coffee, cocoa, and soybeans. Indonesia is currently the third biggest coffee exporter after Brazil and Colombia. Even though cocoa prices have fallen to a 20-year low, Indonesia produced 215,000 tons in 1992, 160,000 for export. Other significant exports include copra, palm oil, sugar, bananas, tea, spices, and orchids. Indonesia accounts for 70% of the world's production of the fabled nutmeg fruit and boasts the best quality, although poor marketing and smuggling cut into earnings.

About 30% of the population smokes *kretek* (clove) cigarettes, making Indonesia the largest producer and importer of cloves in the world. The country's biggest cigarette maker is PT Gudang Garam. The Clove Buffer Agency (BPPC) exercises a nationwide monopoly over the purchase of cloves from farmers and cooperatives.

Fishing

Fishing has always been a major Indonesian industry, employing directly or indirectly about 1.5 million people. Salted fish, a valuable item of trade between coastal and inland peoples since early times, still provides the main source of animal protein in the Indonesian diet. There's a large inland catch in lakes and waterways as

angler's hut

BURNING DOWN THE HOUSE

Environmental consciousness is new to Indonesians. The nation's environmental movement began in 1982, when, after indiscrimate logging ravaged large tracts of forests on the large islands, the government passed the Basic Law of the Environment. Subsequent regulations introduced in 1987 attempted to control pollution. Now there are more than 300 environmental and nature clubs throughout the country confronting Indonesia's gigantic problems with water, forests, and soil.

Industrial Pollution

The chemical, textile, and cement industries contribute greatly to the country's pollution problem. The nation's waterways and canals are becoming toxic dumps of poisonous industrial waste. Most of Indonesia's water supplies are contaminated with human and industrial waste and almost 90% of the population does not have access to safe drinking water. In many of Indonesia's metropolitan areas, the air is befouled by industrial pollution. Rising sea levels caused by global warming may submerge large areas of Indonesia's arable land, its ports and railways by the year 2010, displacing millions of people.

Logging

Indonesia is home to as much as 10% of the world's tropical rainforests, over a third of which have already been destroyed. The country is losing its remaining forests—the most valuable in Asia—at a frightening rate. Logging and slash-and-burn agriculture destroys an estimated 1.3 million hectares a year. Bob Hassan, the head of Indonesia's largest timber company and a spokesperson for the timber industry, swears Indonesia will triple its production by the 1999 fiscal year through the opening of new concessions. There are presently 550 concession holders, most retired military or former government officials. The continuing sharp environmental exchange between Indonesia and the West has been exacerbated by a boycott of tropical timber by a number of developed countries. This pressure has prompted efforts at reforestation, and concessionaires are now required to pay between $5 to $55 per cubic meter of cut log to support government replanting projects. As an additional measure, 121 million hectares of land were set aside as reserves and national parks by 1991.

Nuclear Energy

Another danger is posed by nuclear power plants.

With the vigorous backing of the German-trained Minister for Research and Technology Dr. B. J. Habibie, the government has already approved the construction of a $2 billion plant in central Java. There are plans for five more across the island of Java by the year 2000. Java is one of the most densely populated islands in the world, subject to earthquakes and volcanic eruptions. Fallout from an Indonesian meltdown could affect the neighboring countries of Singapore, Malaysia, Brunei, Papua New Guinea, and Australia.

Crisis Areas

Some areas suffer more serious environmental degradation than others. Because of deforestation, Maluku has great problems preserving its natural environment. The islands of Seram, Buru, and Kei have been serverely deforested. Yamdena in southeast Maluku is imminently threatened by timber concessions owned by Pak Sioe Lim, who is desparately trying to maintain his status as the fifth richest man in the world. Farther east, the Asmat region of Irian Jaya has been hard-hit by loggers. On Java, Indonesia's most populous island, a 1993 government study warned that air pollution will double over the next two decades.

According to satellite data, an astonishing 30% of Sumatra's forests disappeared between 1982 and 1990. Two-thirds of the stunning and unique ecosystem of the island of Siberut off western Sumatra has been destroyed by clearcutting, great and varied forests replaced by oil palms. Farms, plantations, oil fields, *transmigrasi* settlements, mining operations, and clearfells are laying waste to eastern Kalimantan's magnificent rainforests—the second largest expanse in the world—where 50 logging camps chew up to 10,000 logs per month.

Golf Course Fever

There are now over 80 golf courses in Indonesia, 24 in the Jakarta area alone. The construction of golf courses inevitably leads to popular protest and reflects a widening gap between rich and poor. An 18-hole course consumes about 50 hectares of productive agricultural wetlands, often purchased from poor *petani* at below-market prices. The sellers are frequently unaware of their full legal rights.

The president's son Bangbang, under the guise of one of his many companies, systematically purchased all the prime beachfront real estate in the areas around Manado in North Sulawesi. He plans to fill the land with golf links, despite laws protecting waterfront real estate as public property to within 100 meters of the high water mark. Bangbang also bought the delicate dune areas of Kuta in South Lombok, and is reputed to be behind a move to drive all the small *losmen* and *rumah makan* off Gili Trawangan in West Lombok to make way for a huge resort and another dreaded golf course. This despite the fact there is nowhere near enough water on the island to cope with any more accommodations, much less a golf course. Bangbang also owns all the land adjacent to Bali's Tanah Lot, future home of more mausoleum-style hotels. Then there's his planned golf course and casino on Bali's offshore island of Nusa Penida.

Dams, reservoirs, and other redevelopment projects have sparked protests all over Indonesia by people dissatisfied with the low compensation rates for land paid by the government. In 1986, 5,000 families were forcibly moved to make way for the huge Kedung Ombo dam in Central Java, causing an international uproar. These farmers still refuse to accept the low rates offered by the government for their flooded land, crops, trees, and houses. Four persons were killed in Madura, East Java, in September 1993, when hundreds of villagers demonstrated against the building of the Nipah Dam.

Endangered Species

Indonesia has more endangered species than any other country in the world. The Worldwide Fund for Nature has named Indonesia a culprit in the worldwide traffic in protected species, failing to curb exports of thousands of rare plants and animals. The orangutan, a forest-dependent species living only on Sumatra and Borneo, is down to only around 8,000 individuals, its numbers dwindling due to illegal trading and habitat destruction. Even more threatened is the Javan rhinoceros, with only about 57 individuals left in the Ujung Kulon Reserve of West Java.

The country's 150 reserves and national parks are designed to protect endangered species, but many are parks in name only—"paper parks."

Traders deal in a large range of species, particularly in sea turtles, whose shells are openly on sale in shops in Jakarta, Pangandaran, and on Bali. The fabulously colorful Bird of Paradise of Irian Jaya are relentlessly hunted for their skins; as many as 50,000 specimens are destroyed each year. In Europe a skin sells for as high as $30,000.

What Is To Be Done

Founded in 1980, the country's most powerful mainstream conservation organization is Wahana Lingkungan Hidup Indonesia (WAHLI), the Indonesian Forum for the Environment. The Indonesian equivalent of the Sierra Club, WAHLI is highly respected. It advises government ministries, organizes antipollution campaigns, publicizes violations, and files suits against perpetrators of environmental crimes. Thanks to WAHLI's intervention, a shipment of plutonium bound for Japan was prohibited from passing through the congested Strait of Malaka in 1992. WAHLI is presently concerned with promoting environmentally sound development, especially in the Outer Islands. The organization is funded almost entirely by industrialized countries.

WAHLI and other organizations encourage recycling schemes, waste minimalization programs, and energy efficiency. They also promote such clean energy alternatives as the harnessing of geothermal power. Members of parliament are urging the government to popularize the use of domestic natural fertilizers, and the government is beginning to require major industries to be more responsible for the impact of their ventures on the land and quality of life.

Environment impact assessments are now required of industries before they set up operations. The new environmental minister, Sarwono Kusumaatmadja, recently announced that the credit companies receive will now be linked to their environmental record. An ecolabeling program, to assure the production of environmentally safe goods, may be adopted as early as 1995. A well-equipped Environmental Management Center (EMC) has been established in Serpong, West Java, to monitor the quality of Indonesia's environment.

---

well. People all over Indonesia also cultivate fish in ponds and rice paddies.

While Indonesia has twice as many ocean fishermen as Japan and perhaps the greatest potential fish stock of any tropical country, productivity is about one-tenth that of Japan's.

Dominating the industry today are large mechanized commercial fleets owned by Chinese or Indonesians who've entered into joint ventures with the Japanese and Taiwanese. They account for up to a quarter of the catch yet make up only two percent of the total fleet; their trawlers and purse seines are resented by traditional fishermen, who angrily destroy boats, nets, and engines. Trawling was banned off Sumatra and Java in the early 1980s, and everywhere else except far eastern Indonesia in 1983. Illegal fishing is common off Maluku, where the Indonesian coast guard occasionally takes into custody Taiwanese fishing vessels.

Forestry

Indonesia has the largest tropical forest reserves in the world after the Amazon basin, about 122 million hectares. The hardwoods of Indonesia have been in high demand since ancient times. During the Japanese occupation, large tracts of forests were cut down to plant cash crops, and in revolutionary times more forests were cleared during fuel shortages. Because start-up costs were low and logging permits easy to attain, the forestry industry attracted major foreign investment from the very beginning of Suharto's New Order regime. After petroleum, timber became Indonesia's second largest export earner, the industry selling 18 million cubic meters of tropical timber overseas in 1973. Between 1970 and 1980, production grew by almost 10% per year, peaking in 1978 when Indonesian timber exports comprised over half the world's total.

In 1985 the government finally prohibited the export of raw, unprocessed timber. Exports dropped abruptly at first, but a steady increase in plywood production returned Indonesia to the ranks of the world's leading timberfellers. Almost 30% of Indonesia's landmass is presently logged by 550 logging concessions, about 60% joint ventures with foreign companies. A staggering one percent of the country's irreplaceable rainforests is cut annually—faster than any other place in the world. Environmentalists fear that in 20 years the lowland forest areas of Sumatra, Kalimantan, and other large islands will be totally gone. Because of the worldwide clamor over Indonesian clearcutting, the government has in the last several years made reforestation a priority.

TOURISM

The government looks to tourism to increase foreign exchange earnings, provide employment opportunities for the nation's huge labor force, and attract investors. It's hoped profits from resort development will eventually trickle down; this proved to be the case on Bali, where a major village handicraft industry appeared in the wake of the first tourist boom in the early 1980s.

The government began shoring up the industry in the mid-'80s, with visas-on-arrival, inflight immigration formalities, easier customs clearance, facilities for foreign air carriers, and joint services with Garuda by foreign carriers. There were over 2.5 million visitors to Indonesia in 1991, the highest in ASEAN in spite of the Persian Gulf War. Backpackers and surfies, who spearheaded the tourism boom of the 1970s and '80s, are now being replaced by family groups and leisure visitors. *Prestige,* the U.S. magazine of affluent lifestyles, awarded Indonesia eight awards for excellence in 1993. Now $200-per-day cruises, unabashedly tapping upmarket clientele, are common. There are 12,000 five-star hotel rooms in the country. Sheraton plans to open as many as 20 hotels before the end of the century.

Two-thirds of all visitors to Indonesia arrive from the Asia-Pacific region. Of these, the largest number—around 70%—come from Singapore, taking the 30-minute boat ride to Batam and Bintan, two rapidly developing islands between 20 and 30 km south of Singapore. The next largest groups journey from Malaysia, Japan, and Australia. Europe accounts for 21% of all visitors; that percentage is growing.

Tourist Development

Minister of Tourism Joop Ave declared that $295 million was invested in tourism projects in the first seven months of 1993. Road, rail, ferry, and shipping infrastructures have improved spectacularly, more cruise ships and commuter aircraft are coming on line, and modern international airports have opened in Jakarta and Bali. In 1991, the government initiated a Tourism Awareness Program to protect indigenous cultures and help local people adjust to changes caused by tourism.

To fulfill the need for skilled workers in the industry, there are now 66 tourism training schools throughout the country. Presently, the best tourist facilities are found on the western, more densely populated islands of Sumatra, Java, and Bali. The trend, however, indicates foreign tourists are visiting in greater numbers more remote portions of Java, as well as Sumatra, Sulawesi, Maluku, and Lombok. To divert business from overburdened Bali, the government is improving the tourist infrastructure on other islands. At least 10 new megaresorts, modeled after Bali's large-scale, integrated Nusa Dua complex, are under construction in places like Biak, Tasik Ria in northern Sulawesi, Palau Belitung in the Java Sea, Baturaden in Central Java, and Merak Belantung in South Sumatra. All should be operational by the year 2000.

Indonesia has yet to realize 10% of its tourism potential. The eastern islands, with their huge potential for coastal/marine recreation, remain relatively untouched.

CORRUPTION

Corruption (*korupsi*) in Indonesia has been refined into a complex art—the perfection of rottenness. It permeates every level of government, from the lowliest post office clerk to the first family in the land. The government admits at least 50% of the annual GNP disappears through institutionalized and illegal levies, and it's estimated 30% of all development funds are skimmed off by dishonest officials. One can't help but wonder how prosperous Indonesia might be if so much weren't lost through graft. Most Indonesians have come to accept petty graft as a way of life. The right amount to the right person at the right time is like applying oil to a big unwieldly machine.

Before the arrival of white people there was no such thing as corruption on these islands. When the first European trading companies set up shop there were few guidelines governing salaries or benefits, yet employees were still expected to carry out their duties. Often left to fend for themselves, they were forced to impose illicit levies in order to survive. From there the practice grew. It's accepted that widescale corruption crippled and finally brought down the Dutch East Indies Company in 1799.

Corruption became entrenched during the Japanese occupation; the bewildering number of regulations and permits gave officials ample opportunity to demand unofficial levies to supplement worthless wartime scrip. During the revolution, salaries were so erratic and ludicrously low, and resources so limited, that corruption ran rampant in the Indonesian bureaucracy and armed forces.

Corruption stems in part from the traditional Asian attitude of paying deference and presenting gifts to one's superiors. Low salaries are a prime cause as well, with civil servants looking for other sources to buttress their meager wages. A man of standing in the community must maintain an appearance of affluence—good clothes, a car, comfortable home, ritual feast every so often. He also has weighty responsibilities on his Rp120,000-180,000 per month salary: support relatives, send his kids to good schools. He feels he *must* seek and accept bribes. Many officials don't even look at it as corruption but rather as the way things ought to be. Those who have the education, competence, and power to sign papers or make decisions believe bribes are their due. Skimming and off-budget administrative "fees" enable an official to accomplish much—a Hari Raya bonus for his staff, a new village school, a fishpond.

Corruption starts at the top and filters down. A legislator who gets a substantial discount on a car purchase sells the purchasing permit to a car dealer. Many small bureaucratic offices are managed like a family agricultural plot, where only kin, family, and ethnic group can play any real role. A poor peasant must pay the teacher a bribe so his child may graduate from the fifth to sixth grade. Even the judicial system is not immune. Indonesians say the best way to tip the scales of justice is to first tip the judge trying your case. This is true whether you're up for a traffic ticket or murder. In fact, people don't even use the legal system unless they have the money. Bribes of Rp210 million are not uncommon in important cases, and during preliminary negotiations the verdict may go first one way and then the other as rival bids are put in. About Rp100,000 can get a month lopped off a sentence. Poorly trained and underpaid guards running the prisons demand bribes to allow prisoners to obtain a mattress, work in the kitchen, or sleep away from the lavatories.

Graft is practiced with equal elan by foreign investors. For any capital-intensive project, whether financed by private funds or government aid, 10-15% of the investment routinely goes to bribes and kickbacks for officials whose signatures are required to move the paperwork through to completion. In 1991 the chairman of the Association of Construction Companies told the press he regarded it as only natural to pay money to government officials who award contracts. It's a way of thanking them, he said.

Of course every few years a presidential commission announces a big anticorruption drive, headed by some highly vocal and visible general. In the end, a couple of petty offenders are suspended while the big fish go free or accept early retirement. The real objective of these purity drives is mollification of students and the foreign press. Chronic corruption in the 1980s was so acute the government took the extraordinary step of contracting a Swiss firm to carry out customs inspections on its behalf, completely bypassing the notorious Customs and Excise Service.

THE PEOPLE

There has been such an influx of peoples from China, Arabia, Polynesia, Southeast Asia, Indochina, and Europe that Indonesia is an ethnological gold mine, the variety of its human geography—336 ethnic groups—without parallel on earth. Shades of skin vary from yellow to coal black. Welded together by a unifying lingua franca and intermarrying freely, Indonesians represent all the Asian cultures, races, and religions. They worship Allah, Buddha, Shiva, and Jehovah—in some places an amalgam of all four. Living in a collection of local archipelagic nations, many Indonesians identify themselves in local terms: Orang Toraja, Orang Sawu, Orang Mentawai. This sense of local identity with one's tribe and clan has fostered an attitude of tolerance toward other cultures summed up in the Indonesian expression *"lain desa, lain adat"* or "other villages, other customs."

Cultural Differences

Due to the archipelago's size and terrain, many of Indonesia's ethnic pockets have remained extremely isolated. You can find ways of life separated by some 5,000 years—a journey through time. People live in the Neolithic, Bronze, Middle, and Nuclear ages. Some Indonesians wear rings and rat ribs in their noses, others read the *Asian Wall Street Journal* and mimic Western rap.

If the races have mingled at all, it's been near the sea. Many mountain tribes were scattered into the hills by Muslim, Christian, or Hindu-Buddhist conquerors who moved into the richer valleys and prime coastal areas. Sumatra's elusive Kubu and Mamak tribes, the Penan of Kalimantan, the Alfuro of Maluku, and the Dani of Irian Jaya are descendants of the so-called Austronesian groups who drifted into the archipelago between 8000 and 7000 B.C. These tribes are considered "uncivilized" by present-day coastal inhabitants.

A theme in much Indonesian folklore and *wayang* is the constant struggle between the dark-complexioned highlanders and the lighter-complexioned lowlanders, or between the noble

lain desa, lain adat

princes and the black giants of the jungles and mountains. Indonesians can be quite color-conscious; many are outright racists. Village women and little girls smear white powder on their faces to "beautify" themselves; Indonesian women take all possible precautions against exposing their skin to the sun. It's believed that the darker the skin, the more primitive the person, the lower his or her class.

The government takes the position that the "backward" tribal peoples must be brought into the mainstream of modern Indonesian life. In 1990, the term used to describe tribes was changed from *suku terasing* (isolated tribes) to *suku yang sedang dibina* (tribes not yet developed). The government counts around 1.2 million people in this category, 50% of them on Irian Jaya.

POPULATION

Indonesia has the fourth-largest population in the world—some 180 million—which equals the population of all other Southeast Asian nations combined. Better health care, decreasing infant mortality, and longer life expectancy keep more people alive. The population of Java, about the size of New York state and comprising only seven percent of Indonesia's total land area, has tripled this century, reaching 110 million. That's well over a third of the population of the U.S., and 60% of Indonesia's total.

In spite of the government's best efforts, the Asian Institute of Management projects that by the year 2020 the country's population will be 253.7 million, 52% comprising a huge middle class living in urban areas. Over the next 30 years Jakarta will double in size, from 10 million to 20 million people. Indonesia has probably the world's largest collection of cities with populations over 200,000—26 at last count. Around 20% of Indonesia's population now lives in urban areas.

Dua Cukup

When Suharto launched his birth control program in 1974, it was risky business. Though the Muslim clergy were at first against it and the Nationalists condemned it, the president's unflagging commitment to family planning was the key to the program's success. In the early days the program focused on birth spacing; now more

long-term, permanent methods—sterilizations and implants—are preferred. Coercion and deception are often employed on unwilling recruits.

With a mixture of Madison Avenue hoopla, Islamic teaching, and the motto *"dua cukup"* ("two is enough"), Indonesia's family planning campaign is now well entrenched. A whole battery of government, military, and community agencies cooperate in its implementation. A recent survey indicated that 94.5% of Indonesian women from 20 provinces were familiar with birth control. Songs extolling the virtues of a "small, happy, and prosperous family" are played for motorists stopped at traffic lights; if you practice birth control you earn discounts of 5-30% at cinemas, doctors' offices, pharmacists, gas stations, and grocery stores. The largest condom factory in Southeast Asia, producing 130 million untrustworthy condoms a year, is in Banjaran, West Java. Between 1974 and 1991, fertility declined from an average of 5.6 to three births per woman and the number of couples using contraceptives increased from less than 10% to more than 45%. The government hopes that by the year 2005 the birthrate will drop to 2.1, the replacement level at which the population ceases to grow.

Transmigrasi

The country's controversial *transmigrasi* policy has also failed to reduce Indonesia's overcrowded urban populations. The idea of the scheme is to move people from the overcrowded inner islands of Bali, Lombok, and Java (over 800 people per square km) to sparsely populated islands like Sumatra (about 182 per square km), Kalimantan (38 per square km), and Irian Jaya (8.5 per square km). Since 1969 more than two million people have been relocated. Critics charge the scheme amounts to cultural genocide—the biggest colonization program in history. Financed and granted technical support by international development agencies, these migrations are really state-sponsored invasions by surplus populations. Transmigration is expensive (about $9000 per family), and since 1978 the World Bank has poured $300 million into the program.

Living conditions in the transplanted communities are supposed to be better, but in many cases disastrous ecological deterioration has followed the settlers' arrival. Because the sites

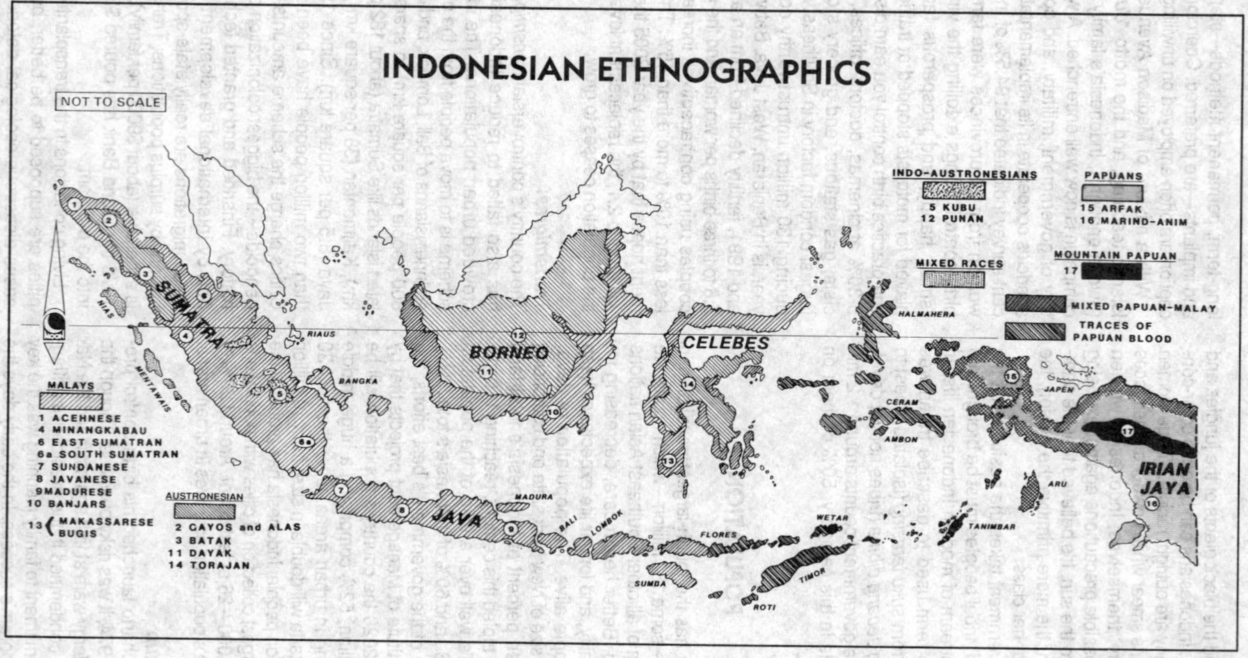

INDONESIAN ETHNOGRAPHICS

PAPUANS
15 ARFAK
16 MARIND-ANIM

MOUNTAIN PAPUAN
17

INDO-AUSTRONESIANS
5 KUBU
12 PUNAN

MIXED RACES
MIXED PAPUAN-MALAY
TRACES OF PAPUAN BLOOD

AUSTRONESIAN
2 GAYOS and ALAS
3 BATAK
11 DAYAK
14 TORAJAN

MALAYS
1 ACEHNESE
4 MINANGKABAU
6 EAST SUMATRAN
6a SOUTH SUMATRAN
7 SUNDANESE
8 MADURESE
9 JAVANESE
10 BANJARS
13 MAKASSARESE
   BUGIS

IRIAN JAYA
JAPEN
ARU
TANIMBAR
CERAM
AMBON
HALMAHERA
WETAR
TIMOR
ROTI
FLORES
SUMBA
SUMBAWA
CELEBES
BORNEO
JAVA
MADURA
BANGKA
RIAUS
SUMATRA
NIAS
MENTAWAIS

NOT TO SCALE

© MOON PUBLICATIONS, INC.

INDONESIAN DEMOGRAPHICS

INHABITANTS PER SQ. KM.
UNDER 10
11-19
20-39
40-79
80 - 299
300-599
600-799
800 +
(JAKARTA RAYA)

0   500 km

© MOON PUBLICATIONS, INC.

are poorly chosen, transmigrants are lucky to get three years of harvests before the land becomes infertile. An estimated 3.5 million hectares of tropical forests have been destroyed to build *transmigrasi* sites.

From the government's point of view all its people belong to one nation, so transmigration is not colonization but national integration. Colonies of transmigrants also serve as deterrents for regional secessionist movements. The government claims locals don't mind transmigrants because they bring with them money, skills, and agricultural techniques, creating thousands of job opportunities and clients for local businesses.

THE INDONESIAN FAMILY

Ever since nomadic Malay hunter-gatherers began cultivating rice in the fertile ashes of burned forests some 4,500 years ago, rice has been at the very center of Indonesian culture. The structure and pressure of this intensive cultivation has given rise to very close-knit, cooperative families, especially on the island that supports the bulk of the population—Java.

The heart and soul of Indonesia is the village. About 80% of the people still live in 60,000 agricultural communities throughout the archipelago.

The village council of elders is the foundation of Indonesian democracy, and village and family loyalties come before all others. Even Jakarta, the capital of Indonesia, has all the habits and manners of a village.

The extended family is a sophisticated structure that makes alliances and friendships, keeps people happy, and offers a superbly supportive environment for children and elders. A family could include grandparents, grandchildren, father's and mother's relatives, nieces, nephews, and cousins, all living under the same roof. An adult child working outside the home turns over wages to the family, submits to opening of personal mail, is expected to help in the cost of sending younger siblings to school, and must contribute to the expenses of supporting mature members of the family. Most Indonesians have never slept in a room where they couldn't hear someone else breathing.

The nation as a whole is looked upon as a family. Both the president and schoolmasters are referred to as *bapak* or *pak* (father). A schoolmistress or *warung* proprietor is addressed as *ibu* (mother). Don't be surprised if an Indonesian friend refers to scores of peers and acquaintances as "brothers" and "sisters." Children must forever honor and respect their parents. Newspapers annually publish photos of

Pak Harto kneeling reverently before his mother-in-law during Lebaran.

ADAT

Meaning indigenous customary law, this is the word Indonesians utter when you ask about a custom with obscure origins. They just say, "it's adat." The closest Western equivalent to adat is common law. This unwritten, unspoken traditional village law governs the actions and behavior of every person in every village and city kampung in Indonesia. Evolving from a distant time when villages were largely collectivist and self-governing, the dictates and taboos of adat dictate what foods are eaten and when, ceremonies for the ill or dead, ownership of land and irrigation systems, architecture of family houses and granaries, criminal and civil law covering theft and inheritance, relations between siblings, marriage, the treatment of guests—everything, the total way of life.

Adat is particularly useful in times of economic or political instability. Adat helps to ensure peace between the various religious communities—all have adat in common. Although rooted in religion, adat is not a religion. Indonesians say, "religion comes in from the sea, but customs come down from the mountains." Islam was in many instances radically modified to fit local adat. Rules and behavior from other imported religions have also become a part of adat.

Most of the more elaborate and cultic manifestations of adat have been forgotten; it now covers only the basic necessities and social obligations of life. Though the original meaning of many acts and gestures may be lost, they are rigorously performed without question. Adat is not in the law books, it's in the genes. Some say adat strangles the people because it encourages superstition instead of reasoning, that it stifles progress because all actions are based on precedent. Change from within Indonesian society is very slow.

THE CHINESE

The Chinese are Indonesia's most important ethnic minority and largest alien group. Chinese Buddhist pilgrims visited Java and Sumatra on their way to and from monasteries in India as early as the 5th century. Chinese traders began arriving in the 10th century, setting up culturally advanced trading communities on Java's north coast. Chinese Muslims from Yunnan played a role in converting Java to Islam in the 15th century. In the 18th century the VOC allowed large numbers of Chinese to immigrate as an intermediary class.

The Chinese eventually worked their way into the bureaucratic and merchant classes, becoming tax collectors, moneylenders, pawnshop owners, farmers, and traders in salt and opium. Though economically powerful and able to enjoy many privileges in Dutch society, they were forbidden to own land and were excluded from the political process—a situation that exists to this day. In the 20th century, nationalist fighters remember with bitterness the indifference or opposition with which most Chinese viewed the revolutionary struggle. This very class of native Indonesians today forms the Old Guard of the civil bureaucracy and officer corps.

The Chinese are also resented for their religion, wealth, and business skills, despite the fact wealthy Chinese businessmen (cukong) work closely with high-placed Indonesians—even the president himself—advising and financing them, giving them a cut of the profits. Although the Chinese comprise only about two percent of the total population, they control about 75% of the country's private domestic capital. They succeed in all fields: as professionals, bankers, tour guides, traders, shopkeepers, plantation overseers, machine shop workers, and mechanics.

Unlike the Philippines or Thailand, where the Chinese have been integrated fully into society, the Chinese in Indonesia are resented and envied. They have traditionally been ostracized from the mainstream of Indonesian society, with periodic purges perpetrated against them. In an uprising in Batavia in 1740 thousands of Chinese were slaughtered. After the 1965-66 coup as many as 200,000 lost their lives. Indonesia repudiated a dual-citizenship treaty between Indonesia and China in 1969, leaving 80,000 Chinese citizens stateless. In 1980, there were widespread anti-Chinese riots in Central Java. Much of the present resentment is due to the rapid growth of Chinese business groups following the financial market liberalizations and corporate scandals of the late 1980s. Anti-Chinese sentiments are exacerbated by Indonesian Chinese investment in China, rather than in Indonesia. Other Indonesians suspect the Chinese are ultimately loyal to Beijing, not Jakarta.

In 1959, the government prevented Chinese from settling in rural areas, resulting in a mass exodus to the cities, where the majority live today. Chinese are not allowed to run their own schools, publish their own newspapers, import Chinese-language publications, or form political parties. Chinese characters are prohibited, by government decree, from all of Indonesia's Chinatowns. The authorities have even outlawed the physical fitness exercise tai chi, which employs a few Mandarin words and soothing music.

If your father is Chinese, you're Chinese until you die; Indonesia and Korea are the only countries in Asia that base nationality entirely on paternal lineage. Enrollment of Chinese in state tertiary institutes is limited to two percent; in private institutions, 30%. Chinese may not hold dual citizenship and in the armed forces may not rise above the rank of colonel. They must also take on Indonesian surnames; often they choose high-class *priyayi* Muslim names, which enrages the Javanese.

Peranakan And Totok

Peranaken refers to people of non-Indonesian ethnic origin who were born in Indonesia, usually Chinese. These Chinese-Indonesians have lived in Indonesia for generations and have become thoroughly Indonesianized. *Peranakan* have intermarried with Indonesians and are usually completely illiterate in Chinese languages. This group has evolved its own customs, *adat,* dialect, *batik,* and cuisine, adapted from local Malay culture. *Peranakan* have lost more of their Chineseness than most of the world's 30 million or so overseas Chinese. They're looser and less inhibited than Singaporean or Taiwanese Chinese, for example.

Totok, on the other hand, is a colonial term refering to Indonesia's unacculturated immigrant Chinese, brought in by the Dutch to work as coolies in the mines of West Kalimantan and on the plantations of North Sumatra. Today, *totok* are concentrated in business districts like Jakarta's Kota, in typical shophouse dwellings like those found in southeast China. *Totok* are the exception in Indonesia.

LANGUAGE

BAHASA INDONESIA

Such is the diversity of tongues in Indonesia (200 indigenous speech forms, each with its own regional dialects) that often the inhabitants of the same island don't speak the same native language. On the tiny island of Alor there are some 70 dialects, on Sulawesi 62 languages have been identified, and Irian Jaya is home to an astounding 10% of the world's languages.

One language, Bahasa Indonesia, is taught in all schools to all students from age five; it's estimated about 70% of the population is literate in Bahasa Indonesia. This language is the only cultural element unifying the entire geographically splintered population. First used as a political tool in 1927 with the cry "One Nation, One Country, One Language!," it's the only language used in radio and TV broadcasting, in official and popular publications, in advertisements and on traffic signs. Films shown in Indonesia are required by law to be dubbed in standardized, modern Indonesian. Most of the country's regional languages change forms and endings to show deference to the person addressed; Bahasa Indonesia does not. Thus, Indonesian has been a force for the democratization and unification of the different races and classes of Indonesia.

Indonesian, or a dialect of it, is the native language in northern and eastern Sumatra (especially the east coast); the coasts of Borneo, Manado, and environs; in scattered locales around the Lesser Sunda Islands and Maluku; and in large urban centers such as Jakarta and Semarang. About 30,000 residents of Hong Kong and 35,000 residents of Australia speak Indonesian.

Characteristics Of Bahasa Indonesia

Although Indonesian derives from Old Malay, the proliferation of acronyms and infusion of foreign words makes Indonesian reading material barely comprehensible to Malaysians. Although known for economy of vocabulary and simple, even childish phrases, Bahasa Indonesia is actually an elaborate, subtle, and ambiguous speech form for expressing complex thought.

Initially, this nontonal language is sublimely easy to learn. It's written in the familiar Roman alphabet, words are pronounced the way they're spelled, the morphology is very simple. Nouns and verbs lack cases, genders, declensions, confusing conjugations—no verb "to be." Perhaps the most difficult aspect of the language is its use of prefixes and affixes to turn roots into nouns and verbs.

Indonesian is a poetic language. *Matahari* means sun, or, literally "eye of the day"; *rumput laut* means "sea hair" or seaweed; *merah muda*, for pink, translates literally as "young red." It's also very picturesque—*bunga uang* means bank interest, from *bunga* for flower and *uang* for money; *seperti cari ketiak ular* (searching for the armpit of a snake) means looking for something nonexistent or impossible to find. Words you may have already run across include *amok* (blind terror), *sarung* (the Malay skirt), and *bambu* (bamboo).

Indonesian has a tremendous amount of dialectical variation and each ethnic group speaks its own accented form. The Javanese speak it very slowly and monotonously, the Sundanese use a sing-song manner, while the Irianese employ an archaic form taught only by missionaries. All dialects are mutually intelligible.

History

Modern Bahasa Indonesia began as a trader's language, used throughout the archipelago. The prototype of present-day Indonesian was spread by the 12th-century Sriwijaya Empire of Sumatra. This archaic language, called Old Melayu ("Malay"), is still spoken in almost pure form in the small Riau and Lingga archipelagos off eastern Sumatra.

During colonial times the Dutch used Malay as the official language of administration. In the early part of the 20th century, Indonesian nationalists realized the need for a national language when they found themselves addressing their revolutionary meetings in Dutch. Because it features no feudalistic levels of speech

and was not used by any major ethnic group, Bahasa Indonesia was adopted as the future national language at the Second Indonesian Youth Congress of 1928. When the Japanese army occupied Indonesia in 1942-45, they banned Dutch but found it impossible to impose their own language. To disseminate propaganda they encouraged the use of Indonesian. When the war ended, the Proclamation of Independence was written and broadcast to the world in Indonesian. When Indonesia achieved nation status in the 1950s, a modern version of the language was quickly developed and expanded to apply to all the higher requirements of a fully modernizing, developing country.

Bahasa Indonesia is perhaps humanity's most highly evolved pidgin language, devouring thousands of words from Indonesia's local languages, as well as Arabic, Chinese, Dutch, Portuguese, Sanskrit, Tamil, French, English, and American. Many words of Western origin found in Bahasa Indonesia have obvious roots: *hotel, doktor, polisi, cigaret, musik, paspor, revolusi, subversif, demokrasi.* Some 7,000 words in Indonesian can be traced to Dutch.

New words generally begin in colloquial usage or among intellectuals and scientists. Many newly adopted words come from sports, economics, military science, or some advanced technological field. Although Javanese and Sundanese, spoken by over 110 million people, have also had a significant impact on the development of the lingua franca of the country, Indonesian has become so important and sophisticated that regional languages have not been able to grow into modern languages serving as vehicles of communication for complex contemporary issues.

LEARNING INDONESIAN

When traveling in a foreign land, it's impossible to really understand the culture without some knowledge of the language. Language teaches culture, not the other way around. Learning the language also helps minimize culture shock, enabling you to settle in more quickly.

Using a phrasebook is alright, as long as you realize you're not really using the language. You're simply holding up verbal signs: "Where is the toilet?" God forbid you get back an answer

BECOMING *BAHASA*-LINGUAL

- First learn the number, time, and calendar systems and how to spell your name in Indonesian; this will spare you much frustration and money. Next, learn how to greet people, as the formality of welcoming people is of paramount importance to Indonesians. Then, master the forms of polite speech, a social skill Indonesians place great weight on. For example, there are at least six ways of saying "please" and 12 ways to say "no."

- Avoid Indonesians who try to speak to you in English; they're your most formidable obstacle to learning the language. The fastest way to learn another language is to never speak your own. If you live with a non-English-speaking family, you'll be semifluent within a month. You'll have to learn—to survive.

- Concentrate at first on just listening and speaking. It takes only a few weeks to learn the sound system properly. You must hear Indonesian spoken and speak it every chance you get. Immerse yourself in it. Listen and constantly repeat words and phrases, impressing them on your memory. Take the word *menandatangani*, meaning "to sign something," a bit of a stumbler. Have Indonesians teach you how to pronounce it. The more times you use it, the quicker you'll learn to pronounce it correctly and the quicker it'll become part of your vocabulary. Only after you've learned pronunciation should you take on the written language.

- Don't worry about grammatical errors or common mistakes; this self-consciousness is a tremendous block to learning. You have to make mistakes to learn. Children are quite willing to be wrong; that's why they can learn a foreign language so quickly. They don't care about being grammatically correct. Speaking "perfect" Indonesian is of little concern to Indonesians, who'll always give you the benefit of the doubt. You always get points for trying.

- Try to use what words you do know skillfully. You'll be flabbergasted at what you can get across with a vocabulary of only 200 words or so. You can cruise for weeks with variations on *makan, tidur, mandi, terlambat, sebentar lagi, sekarang, belum,* and *sudah* (eat, sleep, wash, too late, in a little while, now, not yet, already). Infinite combinations of sentences! In one month of diligent work you'll be speaking *pasar melayu,* or "market talk"—all you need for bargaining, getting around, and meeting and relating to people.

- After a while you'll find you're actually understanding. The plateau to strive for is the ability to ask questions in Indonesian and quickly integrate the answers. The most important phrases toward this end are, *"Apa namanya ini dalam Bahasa Indonesia?"* ("What is this called in Indonesian?") and *"Bagaimana anda menyebutnya?"* ("How do you say this in Indonesian?").

- If you move around and stay with the people, all you really need is a good dictionary. Never go anywhere without it and never stop asking questions. Listen to the radio and TV. Translate songs, labels, posters, signs, newspapers, tickets, handouts.

- If tackling a regional Indonesian language, use Bahasa Indonesia as your learning medium. Always ask for the Indonesian word for the Bahasa Daerah (local language) word.

- Force yourself to say complete sentences. Don't be lazy and speak pidgin Indonesian. Start with a proper opening and always include subject, object, and predicate. Speak whole phrases, not expletives or one or two word sentences.

not in the phrasebook. In truth, the most important sentence in the phrasebook is "I don't speak the language." Then ask your questions. If you don't profess your ignorance, you're likely to receive an outpouring of verbiage impossible to comprehend.

Warung, bus stops, markets, kiosks, and offices are the best language classrooms in the land. Head toward any foodstall and start up a conversation. Educated people will make themselves known; they delight in teaching you.

They're very patient, repeating and writing words for you, teaching aphorisms and idioms, breaking sentences down. Indonesians are very encouraging, crying *"Wah, pintar sekali!"* ("Wow, very smart!") the moment you utter a few intelligible words. These daily, regular Indonesian lessons with the people are easily the equal of a $1200 Berlitz Total Immersion Course.

Many Indonesians in regular contact with tourists obligingly speak an abbreviated, simplified form of Indonesian, a sort of "Tourist Indonesian" involving much gesticulating and use of body language. Listeners sensitive to your very limited vocabulary and struggles to find the right word will begin to use the same words as you, obligingly adopting your method of expression.

Dictionaries

The best dictionary for the truly serious Indonesianist is the brilliantly compiled *An Indonesian-English Dictionary* by John M. Echols and Hassan Shadily. Covering modern Indonesian in its entirety, this dictionary has become the standard work used by English speakers since the first edition was published in 1961. The companion volume is the 660-page *An English-Indonesian Dictionary*. Softcover versions of both dictionaries are available in Indonesia for around Rp20,000.

Selected Indonesian Vocabulary for the Foreign Executive by Helen and Russel Johnson lists the root word in alphabetical order according to prefix. A very good 400-page pocket-size dictionary is *Tuttle's Concise Indonesian Dictionary* by Kramer and Koen. This tome contains all the vocabulary a traveler or new student would need to learn, read, or speak Indonesian. Also beginning to appear in Indonesia are handheld pocket-sized electronic dictionaries; type in an Indonesian word and immediately the English translation of the word is displayed. A Japanese brand name, Wiz, costs around Rp190,000.

Phrasebooks

If staying for a month or less, a good phrasebook will serve you well. Allegedly designed with the traveler in mind (though it doesn't contain "truck"), the handy, bilingual Periplus *Pocket Dictionary* contains 2,000 Indonesian words commonly used in asking directions, bargaining, simple conversation, and other everyday situations. Brief spelling and pronunciation guide included.

Everyday Indonesian: A Basic Introduction to the Indonesian Language and Culture by Thomas Oey contains relatively new written and spoken words and phrases divided into the usual phrasebook categories. It's also a useful guide to Indonesian etiquette and body language.

A good phrasebook available only in the U.S. is *Say It In Indonesian* by John Wolff. Compiled by a professional linguist; very thorough. Widely available in bookstores in English-speaking countries is the pocket-size *Indonesia Phrasebook*. Memorizing this little booklet will serve you well for a stay of thirty days or less.

Books And Magazines

Children's School Readers, available in bookshops all over Indonesia for Rp1200-25,000, are well suited for foreigners. The Indonesian is idiomatic and has everyday applications; they also contain valuable information about Indonesian culture and history. Some you can almost read by following the pictures. Cost Rp1200-25000.

Pelangi (*Rainbow*) is a marvelous educational magazine about the Indonesian language, culture, and geography. With both Indonesian and English printed in parallel text, this attractive quarterly is useful for anyone interested in Indonesia. For subscriptions (A$23 per year in Australia, A$25 overseas), write to Pelangi, USQ Press, University of Southern Queensland, P.O. Box 58, Darling Heights, Toowoomba, 4350 Queensland, Australia, tel. (076) 312-768, fax 355-550.

A cheap, endlessly reprinted, and competent study book available in bookstores and tourist kiosks all over Java and Bali is A.M. Almatsier's *How to Master the Indonesian Language*. Almatsier's *The Easy Way to Master the Indonesian Language* costs Rp8000 and is just as widely available. This book provides a step-by-step method of learning Indonesian, designed especially for the long-term resident. Chapters cover everyday situations frequently encountered by expats—Basic Colloquial Expressions, To the Supermarket, Sports, and the like.

The Indonesian language courses at UC Berkeley use the classic *Beginning Indonesian Through Self Instruction* by John U. Wolff, Dede Oetomo, and Daniel Fietkeiwicz. *Indonesian: A Complete Course for Beginners* by J.B. Kwee is a difficult work, but one that will provide you with a sound working knowledge of formal spoken and written Indonesian. *Bahasa Indonesia: Introduction to Indonesian Language and Culture* by Yohanni Johns is becoming a standard introductory text in universities around the world. This excellent, in-depth two-volume set is completely self-contained, providing clear explanations of basic grammar. Extensive notes on usage and etiquette.

Indonesian Language Tapes

Language/30 Indonesian tapes provide an excellent introductory, self-taught program which will put you in tune with the language in about six hours. This concise course stresses only conversationally useful words and phrases. Two cassettes of guided greetings, introductions, requests, and general conversation for use at hotels, restaurants, businesses, and entertainment venues, using only natives speaking flawless Indonesian.

The standard tapes for audio Indonesian language training in the English-speaking world are *Indonesian Conversations and Beginning Indonesian Through Self-Instruction,* an extensive set of 60-minute study tapes duplicated from professionally recorded masters. This expensive course ($441 for the complete 83-tape set) is accompanied by text supplementing the oral training.

A program offering individual and group instruction in Indonesian is located on Bali at the Centre for Foreign Languages (SUA Bali), Jl. Abimanyu 17 A, Denpasar 80231, tel. (0361) 234-256. Apply to Director Dra. I.A. Agung Mas. The standard fee for a two-week intensive course, including accommodations, is $650. Individual courses can be designed for specific needs. Another well-respected program, sponsored by the Council on International Educational Exchange, is offered at the Institut Keguruan Dan Ilmu Pendidikan (IKIP) in Malang, East Java. Students learn language, history and society, literature, anthropology, and art. Regular field trips are a part of the program. For further information, contact Marcia Tavares Maack at the CIEE Academic Programs Dept., 205 E. 42nd St., New York, NY 10017, tel. (212) 661-1414, ext. 1236.

BODY LANGUAGE

Such aggressive gestures and postures as crossing your arms over your chest or standing with your hands on your hips while talking, particularly in front of older people, are regarded as insulting. These are the traditional postures of defiance and anger in *wayang* theater.

Anger is not shown openly. Loud voices are particularly offensive. In their efforts to make themselves understood, many Westerners speak with exaggerated slowness, raise their voices, or wave their arms about. To Indonesians, all these gestures convey anger.

The feet are considered the lowliest part of the body and, especially on Java, it's offensive to sit with the soles of your feet pointing at people. It's also impolite to use your toes or the tip of your shoe for pointing, as when indicating something displayed on the ground in the *pasar*.

To beckon someone with a crooked index finger is rude. If you need to call to someone—e.g., a passing *becak* driver—extend your right hand and make a motion using the cupped fingers turned downward. Neither should you point with your forefinger; instead use your right thumb for pointing.

Since Asians consider the left hand unclean, never use it to touch someone or to give and receive things. If you should use your left hand, say *"Ma'af"* ("Excuse me"). When giving or receiving something from someone older, or in a high office or elevated status, extend your right arm (but not too far), bring your left arm across the front of your body, then touch your fingers to your right elbow. When passing in front of an elder or high-born person, or person of equal rank whom you don't know, bend your body slightly, particularly if that person is sitting.

RELIGION

All the great religions have come to these islands over the centuries; Indonesia has absorbed them all. The Muslim faith is the most widespread; Indonesia has the world's largest population of Muslims, more than in the entire Arab world.

A source of motivation and visionary power, religion is enormously important in Indonesian life. To obtain your National Identification Card you must state your religious affiliation. National law requires religious instruction in all schools from the elementary level through the first two years of university. Each religious community develops its own curriculum for use in the schools, and each student must pass an examination on the religion of his or her family.

Animism

Animism, the belief that every object has a hidden power, influences huge sections of the population, no matter what their professed religion

RICHARD LONGLEY

may be. Though technically it's illegal to be an animist, all over Indonesia people are strongly moved by the spirits of ancestors, rice, trees, rocks, rivers, mists, and the nature gods controlling the sun, rain, and other natural phenomena. Animists believe the entire universe is mysteriously present in every place and at every instant. Mountains, the source of fertilizing water and soil, are the border between the human world and the world of the dead. Explosive mountains are dangerous, always to be appeased.

In Indonesia the sea unites and the land divides; coastal Muslims have more in common with each other than with the animists inland. Many of Indonesia's highland-, jungle-, or swamp-dwelling people have been cut off from the coastal peoples for centuries, retaining their own superstitions and singular methods of cultivation and hunting and gathering. Semi-animist groups such as the Badui of West Java and the Donggo of Sumbawa retired to the interiors long ago rather than adopt the Muslim faith.

Since animism is against the law, the government has classified the multilayered belief systems of such basically animist groups as the Torajans, Dayaks, and Tenggerese as "Hindu." Although officially labeled "Christian," the highlands of Irian Jaya are crawling with animists. Sumba is another heavy animist enclave absurdly slotted "Christian." The millions of so-called *abangan* Muslims of Java's interior still adhere to many syncretic, pre-Islamic, animist practices, such as acknowledgment of spirits, meditation, and asceticism.

ISLAM IN INDONESIA

Islam reached Indonesia soon after its birth in the Middle East. The religion first took hold in the trading ports of the archipelago—Pasai, Melaka, Aceh, Makassar, and the north coast of Java—from the 14th to 17th centuries. It was carried into the region by peaceful Gujerati merchants from India, and had, in fact, mellowed considerably by the time it arrived, dipping into Persian and Indian philosophies along the way. It arrived a much less austere form than was found

ISLAMIC INDONESIA

PERCENT MUSLIM
0-5%
5-10%
10-25%
25-50%
50-75%
75-90%
OVER 90%

PROVINCE BOUNDARY

0   500 km

MEDAN
P. SIMEULUE
P. SIBERUT
SUMATRA
JAKARTA
BANDUNG
SURABAYA
JAVA
BALI
P. SUMBAWA
P. FLORES
TIMOR
NUSATENGGARA
SULAWESI
MANADO
BANJARMASIN
KALIMANTAN
AMBON
MALUKU

© MAGON PUBLICATIONS, INC.

in the Middle East—the work of a personal, mystical, salvation-conscious sect from Persia called Sufis, who practiced an emotional approach to God and whose mystical leanings blended in nicely with existing Buddhist and Hindu beliefs.

At first, spreading Islam was tough going: Hinduism was entrenched. The areas of Indonesia today which practice the most orthodox forms of Islam—Ternate, the north coast of Java, Banten in West Java, Aceh, and the Minangkabau region of Sumatra—are located far from the regions where the ancient Hindu-Javanese civilizations were strongest.

Today, all aspects of Indonesian life reflect Muslim traditions, and the propagation of Islam enjoys full government support. The government routinely backs national Islamic religious festivals. Muslim greetings and gestures are common, scrupulous attention is given to cleanliness, and many men have more than one wife, though this is becoming increasingly unacceptable.

Although pork is popular and plentiful in Christian areas and on Bali, it is absent in Muslim Indonesia, where it's considered unclean and cannot be sold within municipal meat markets. Nearly every town on Java has an orthodox Islamic quarter, called the *kauman,* usually located near both the main mosque and the central market, and the home of traders, craftsmen, and their families. Roughly one-half of all Javanese are *santri,* orthodox Muslims.

Arabic is taught in Muslim schools so the Koran may be read and studied in its original form. In strongly Islamized village areas of Indonesia one awakens to the hum of small boys and girls chanting from the holy book. Phrases are endlessly repeated for years until committed to memory.

The call to prayer is sounded from minarets, reminding Muslims to pray five times each day. The poorer the neighborhood, the louder and more persistent the prayer calls. Friday, the holy day, is a half working day when long lines of *sarung*-clad men stream to Indonesia's tens of thousands of shiny metal-roofed mosques. Mosques are centers of social, educational, and cultural activities, sponsoring soccer teams and organizing fundraisers. Muslim leaders play an active role in community health programs, promoting appropriate technology, and setting up cooperatives to improve the lives of impoverished Muslims.

Those who wear the white *peci* (headgear), *haji* who have been to Mecca and kissed the black stone in Kaaba seven times, are greatly respected men in the community. Though many younger men nowadays would rather buy a motorcycle or travel to Germany with the money, others diligently save for this pilgrimage. A record 122,885 Indonesians performed the *haj* in 1993.

Islamic Animism
Malay-speaking Muslims live in the periphery of the Islamic world and the majority of communities conform more to animist and Hindu-

Buddhist practices than to the formal precepts of the Koran. Dogma has never been as important to Indonesians as the ritual and social aspects of religion. Each region of Indonesia practices the faith with a peculiar twist of its own. The Minangs of Sumatra are matrilinear, and only portions of the Javanese Islamic population strictly perform all the duties of Islam. Few Indonesians actually understand Arabic. Orthodox Muslims believe abortion under any circumstances is against the faith, yet Indonesia passed a law in 1993 allowing "certain medical procedures" (i.e., abortions) in emergency situations. Unofficial figures estimate as much as 17% of the Indonesian population is preoccupied with mystical matters, their spiritualism eclipsing the basic rationalism of Islam. Even the president believes in a Javanese brand of mysticism heavily concerned with omens. *Kebatinan* (mysticism) is alive and well in central Java, where the sultan of Yogyakarta is looked upon as a god. Army generals helicopter into mystic camps for spiritual consultations.

Selamatan (ritual ceremonies) are attended by neighbors and friends to appease the spirits and restore calm and balance during important transitional events. *Dukun* witch doctors exorcise evil spirits from granaries, temples, cars, hotels, and swimming pools. *Dukun* can transport themselves to a parallel world and communicate with god. Thieves use black magic to rob houses. There are devils, *wewe* (ghosts who steal children), and *pontianak* (spirits who lure young men). On Ambon, *mawang* (white-magic priests) work harmoniously alongside Christian or Muslim religious leaders. The Islamic Makassarese of southwestern Sulawesi worship large stones, flags, swords, umbrellas, and plows, presenting regular offerings of food and betelnut to these sacred objects; on important occasions animals are even sacrificed to them. The Catholics of Yogyakarta use *gamelan* music to celebrate mass, some Christians of Kalimantan pay homage to God by spitting, and the Christians of Torajaland in southern Sulawesi sacrifice bulls to the memory of a dead *raja*.

Orthodox Vs. Secular

There has always been conflict in Indonesia between those who want the country run as a fundamentalist Islamic state enforcing Islamic law, and those more interested in a modern 20th-century nation. In the early days of the New Order, Islam was perceived as a threat to the state ideology of Pancasila. Several of the most serious armed rebellions since independence were incited by Muslims, and on several occasions Darul Islam extremists were nearly successful in attempts to assassinate Sukarno.

In the late '60s, Muslim merchants were marginalized, as foreign investors in Indonesia invariably chose Chinese partners. The indigenous Muslim bourgeoisie, frustrated as their economic power declined, gradually became attracted to a more doctrinaire, dogmatic form of Islam based on a stricter interpretation of the Koran. They united with modernist urban intellectuals interested in establishing Indonesia as an ideal Islamic state. Some became politically radicalized, turning to religion as a way of venting their impotence, circulating fiery literature and enlisting the support of heretofore apathetic young Muslims. In September 1984, 1,500 angry Muslim youths rampaged through the streets of north Jakarta's port district, shouting antigovernment and anti-Chinese slogans, attacking police posts, burning Chinese homes and businesses. Heavily armed soldiers were mobilized to quell the riot and more than 100 demonstrators were killed. The government's overreaction reflected its deep-seated fear and distrust of Islamic fundamentalism.

In the 1990s, the movement has become assertive in a different way. The fundamentalist revival has been joined by young middle- and upper-class Indonesian businessmen, civil servants and students disillusioned with the corrupt, materialistic, Westernized ways of their parents. A return to the true religion is very much in vogue. Glossy magazine articles feature the latest in women's Muslim apparel, fashionable veils (*kerudung*) are appearing in the classroom and the office, *ulama* (Muslim scholars) attend the most chic social gatherings, billboards advertise Swiss Watches "Made Especially for the Muslim Executive." Bumper stickers proclaim Islam Is In My Blood.

All religious organizations must profess loyalty to Pancasila and the Indonesian Constitution. The New Order has always been reluctant to hand over real political power to organized Islam, and in 1973 the government diluted Muslim influence by forcing the merger of four Islamic political parties into the officially sanctioned Development Unity Party (PPP). The government forbids the PPP from using the shrine in Mecca as its symbol, and the forces of Islam can legally propagate Islam only through government-approved social organizations such as the modernist Muhammadijah and the more traditionalist Nahdlatul Ulama.

The president has recently tried to build bridges between the palace and organized Islamic groups in the interests of broadening his political base. In the 1980s Suharto tended to associate Islam with the extreme right, but in the late 1980s and 1990s he is resolutely attempting to cultivate a better public image among Indonesia's giant Muslim majority. The founding of the Muslim Majlis Ulama (Religious Leaders Council) and the Indonesian Muslim Intellectuals Association (ICMI) were seen as an effort to lure Muslim intellectuals with the possibility of political power. In 1991, the government licensed the state's first Islamic bank. Laws were passed in 1992 that give more autonomy to religious schools and more authority to Islamic Law over the daily affairs of Indonesia's Muslims. The Muslims rewarded Suharto by nominating him for his sixth term as president in 1992.

Still, orthodox Muslims want more. They advocate the implementation of God's will in all aspects of human life. They demand the whole population observe religious holidays, the government protect and encourage Islam, the social and legal system be based on Shariah (Islamic law), the government ban the state lottery as gambling, and the interest banks charge be done away with as usurious and contrary to Muslim law.

Islam And Women

Women generally have fewer privileges than men in Muslim societies. But in Indonesia, women are not considered second-class citizens; they're more socially and politically advanced than their Islamic sisters in other Third World countries. Women are active in business and government, are allowed to vote, and sit on the Indonesian Supreme Court. One of the most dynamic Muslim women's movements in the world is the Aisjijah of Muhammadijah. Even in devout *santri* (traditionalist) circles, women are not kept secluded as in the majority of Islamic nations. Except in houses of worship, women

and men are not segregated. Only in a few areas in Indonesia do girls and women wear *purdah* (facial veils), and nowhere is it required. Young Muslim women may wear the less severe, distinctive Islamic headdress (*kerudung*) to school, a practice gaining in popularity, though the majority of Indonesian women walk bare-headed.

The Minangkabau of West Sumatra determine descent and inheritance through female family members, a practice that flies in the face of Islamic social philosphy, where women are looked upon as chattel. Among Indonesia's most significant holidays is Kartini Day, honoring Raden Kartini, the Javanese princess, feminist, and activist whose writings ignited an early 20th-century movement to improve the lot of Indonesian women by asserting their right to education and freedom from polygyny and child marriage.

MINORITY RELIGIONS

Muslims here are tolerant toward religious minorities. In fact, religious tolerance is a tradition in Indonesia. As early as the 5th century the Hindu and Buddhist faiths coexisted peacefully in Indonesia, building temples next to each other and even mixing Buddhist and Hindu iconography and statuary in one structure. Some early mosques in central Java combine Hindu and Islamic architecture, using Hindu *yoni* for pillars.

It's not uncommon to see a Christian community helping Muslim neighbors build a mosque. In Jakarta, the biggest mosque in the country, with a capacity for 100,000 people, stands opposite the oldest Catholic church in Indonesia. In the late '60s, a presidential decree recognized not only Islam and Christianity but also Hinduism, Buddhism, and Confucianism as "official" religions. It was hoped belief in one of these universal religions would immunize citizens against godless communism.

As missionary religions, Islam and Christianity inevitably compete for converts. Protestant and Catholic missionaries have proselytized here for centuries, yet there are only 12.5 million Christians scattered throughout Indonesia, about seven percent of the total population. Muslim groups regularly complain about Christian missionaries who entice converts with food, clothing, medical care, and educational scholarships.

The Chinese of Indonesia are either Christian, Taoist, Confucianist, or Buddhist. Most Indonesian Buddhists live on Java; there are various scattered Buddhist sects in Solo, Cirebon, and Yogyakarta. The Badui of West Java are Buddhists in some of their beliefs. The 3.5 million people of Bali are Hindu, or to be more precise, Bali-Hindu.

CUSTOMS AND CONDUCT

A first-time Indonesian traveler flying into Jakarta from Los Angeles, Munich, or Perth might go into immediate culture shock. Although the airport is modern and efficient, the city itself is crowded, noisy, and humid. It can seem like everyone is after your money and in all the world there are no people as cold and metal-eyed as these. Not trusting the buses, you take overpriced taxis. You're the only overseas guest in your hotel, and there's no one about to help soften the shock of a decidedly strange place. In the middle of the night Muslim loudspeakers start blaring, calling foreign people to alien prayer. You feel totally alone.

It's time to start adjusting and adapting. You need to stay a week in a *kampung* before you can start to understand what it's like to be an Indonesian, but in the beginning consider spending a bit extra to retain a room in a comfortable hotel. Meet other Western travelers, become part of the traveling community—but remember to use your own imagination and daring to avoid following the well-worn paths of others. It also helps to go to Indonesia the first time around with a set purpose—climbing volcanos, studying dance, collecting *batik*, absorbing *gamelan*, visiting classical Hindu monuments.

In Indonesia you must learn to live with the idea of being a freak. Be prepared for treatment considered rude in the West. If your hat flies off or you stumble, people will probably laugh. But don't remake your whole personality and temperament for Indonesians. If you're really the outrageous and flamboyant type, observe the most important social etiquette but go ahead and show people who you are. These cultures aren't at all fragile and delicate; there are at least eight civilizations buried under this soil. The people will love you for providing them with your own brand of street theater.

Besides, there are plenty of *kasar* (rude, loud) people around, great characters who are not really frowned upon. These types are usually described by the gesture of a forefinger held vertically in front of the nose and between the eyes, meaning the character is mad, stupid, or "does not speak his brain." Most Indonesians leave outrageous behavior to village idiots, traveling gypsy theaters, *becak* drivers, and Westerners.

THE INDONESIAN PERSONALITY

Most Indonesians possess split personalities, divided between Western logic and Eastern feeling. The Hindus taught them how to escape, the Muslims how to accept, and the Dutch how to fight.

Indonesians usually hide such negative feelings as jealousy, envy, sadness, and anger. A Westerner quarreling with an Indonesian is generally assertive, direct, and confrontational. Yet the angrier the Westerner becomes, the quieter and softer the Indonesian. Indonesians have been trained to cope with stressful interpersonal situations with yielding, nonassertive smiles. An Indonesian will maintain a calm appearance and ultimately withdraw from a quarrel, usually choosing to deal with the issue later through a third person.

Prolonged eye contact is avoided, as it may be interpreted as a challenge that could anger another. A subordinate always refrains from direct eye contact with a superior. Indonesians rarely show anger, but when they do they run amok and stab someone. Indonesians believe Westerners get angry so quickly because they eat too much meat, take themselves too seriously, and don't know how to laugh at themselves.

When under intolerable stress, the normal Indonesian reaction is to retreat deeply within so that it seems the soul no longer inhabits the body—cut off from the outside world and its unbearable pressure. On Bali after a fatal automobile accident, groups of relatives can be seen sleeping at the accident site. And nothing prepares the Westerner for a Javanese driver's smile as he tells you his child has just died.

In Indonesia the traveler must be willing to be seen as well as see.

Individual Vs. The Group

There is no place in Indonesian society for the individual. Indonesians seek the security and support of others. Each person feels at one with a group, self-identity deriving from group identity. Indonesians believe the man or woman who stands alone is unnatural, even absurd.

Indonesians are accustomed to sharing their beds with other family members and may feel lonely and frightened when sleeping alone. Someone looking over your shoulder while you're writing is unthinkable in the intensely private societies of the West, but is considered normal in Indonesia. Why should anyone want to write personal thoughts that no one else may read?

Indonesians want to know your marital status immediately. If you're over 20 years old and say you have no children, Indonesians pity you. To respond, in fact, with an outright "no" is much too blunt. Say instead *"Say belum beranak"* ("I do not yet have children"). Indonesians commonly use at least four other expressions to denote "no": *"belum"* ("not yet"), *"tidak terima"* ("I cannot accept" or "you're joking!"), *"tidak senang"* ("not happy"), and *"tidak boleh"* ("not allowed to"). These are softer, more refined, and less provocative ways of saying "no." Anything to avoid unpleasantness and confrontation.

Time

Many Indonesians place little importance on time. You will learn here that not only is time not money, but that life is better than money. In Indonesia, you'll discover how to wait, be pa-

tient, observe. The Indonesian attitude toward time is summed up in the phrase *jam karet* or "rubber time." But note that even though Indonesians themselves have a remarkably flexible attitude toward time, punctuality will be expected of you as a Westerner.

According to the Armed Forces newspaper *Angkatan Bersenjata,* only about 20% of all government employees actually get to work on time, and only about 20% really do their jobs. Office workers spend most of their time reading newspapers, playing cards, or talking about the lottery. Slow-moving *wayang* shows, circumcision feasts, *gamelan* music, and lovely *batik* give more pleasure than getting rich.

Sex And Intimacy

Indonesians of the opposite sex may not be openly affectionate with one another, while pairs of Indonesian males or females will frequently touch, link arms, or hold hands. The whole nation seems involved in a conspiracy of intimacy, unaffected and casual, considered a mark of friendship and sociability rather than a manifestation of romance.

This is a country where grown men walk you across the street, holding your hand to make sure you reach the other side safely, but lovers of the opposite sex may never touch each other in public. Such touching would bring shame to those involved. Thus, Western couples should never kiss or hold hands in public.

Also avoid extreme dances in Indonesia. The older generation—partbcularly in rural areas—

considers modern dancing blatant vulgarity. Prolonged eye contact between young unmarried people of the opposite sex is discouraged as it may be interpreted as a sexual invitation.

GETTING ALONG

Hygiene

Indonesians bathe at least twice daily, early in the morning and after school or work. A male who needs to urinate in a populated place can just squat in a ditch with knees spread. Give and receive only with the right hand; the left hand is used in the toilet to wash yourself with and is considered unclean. Giving or receiving something with the left hand is insulting.

After a *beruk besar* (bowel movement) in an Asian-style squat toilet, throw in five or six dippers of water until the water becomes clear. Cleanse yourself with your left hand, not toilet paper. In Indonesia, people don't blow their noses in front of others; sniffing is okay. Indonesians clean the house every day and usually wash their clothes every day as well.

Do you hate cigarette smoke in crowded places? About 60% of Indonesians smoke, puffing away in hotel lobbies, on packed buses, in restaurants, on planes. Get ready for it, because there's little you can do about it. Many Indonesian men believe if a man doesn't smoke he must be gay.

Dealing With Bureaucrats

Rule-breaking tourists make it hard for those who follow, so be law-abiding. However, don't always assume you need permission to do something or go somewhere. It's easier to ask forgiveness than permission. The more questions you ask, the more questions will be asked of you. Just go ahead and do it. (Obviously such advice does not apply to ecologically or militarily sensitive areas.)

Since government offices are so busy, you'll learn to behave aggressively, never letting anyone cut in front of you. Once you reach an official, open with a friendly exchange, then bring up your business. When confronting Immigration, be extra respectful, even ingratiating. Play the game. Dress neat and clean.

If you're trying to move paperwork through an office, or clear something through customs,

be courteous but volunteer as little information as possible. Go through the proper channels even though you know lower-ranked employees can serve you just as quickly and capably. As is true anywhere, a smart and competent subordinate must always defer to a dull-witted and plodding superior. Use the telephone whenever you can; it's cheaper than waiting weeks for the mail. Never get angry, no matter how long and frustrating the wait.

In places unaccustomed to tourists, you'll find the police may harass you. As well as wanting to know who you are and what you're doing in their territory, they'll quickly let you know they run the place, then show off their English and prance their authority in front of the local people. If plunged into a hassle with annoyingly officious cops, customs, or *imigrasi* officials, act stupid, meek, friendly, and innocent. In most cases, they just want you to acknowledge the fact they're real and exercise power over you.

Religion

Religion plays a central role in the lives of Indonesians. Don't tell people you're an atheist; people will react with confusion, disbelief, even scorn, believing you're a godless communist. To an Indonesian, the idea of a person living without religion is like living without a heartbeat.

Ask permission to enter or take photos in a mosque. Remove your shoes before entering, and remain silent and respectful as you would in a church or synagogue. Women should dress modestly with long sleeves, trousers, or skirts; men should wear long pants. Menstruating women should not enter. Smoking is prohibited. Don't touch anyone. While the Islamic holy book, the Koran, is being read, don't drink or smoke; never put a book or anything else on the holy tome.

Chinese temples and religious monuments such as Borobudur are used for religious worship and ceremonies by those practicing Confucianism, Taoism, and Buddhism, and should be granted the same respect as mosques. A sash—usually available at the entrance—should be worn around the waist when entering a Balinese temple.

Never touch anybody's head. Most Indonesians regard the head as the seat of the soul and therefore sacred.

Dress And Grooming

You'll be the object of constant scrutiny. Indonesians are very conservative, so be neat, clean, and fairly careful about what you wear. A *sarung* tied above the breasts is only acceptable on the way to bathe, and wearing shorts, undershirts, and thongs in the streets can be insulting—these are clothes worn only by lower-class people such as fieldworkers and *becak* drivers. Do disheveled shorts-and-undershirts Westerners realize how poor, desperate, and unloved they look to Indonesians?

Long hair is no problem because many Indonesian freedom fighters vowed not to cut their hair until they won independence from the Dutch, and that struggle went on for five years. If you sport a beard you'll be known as *Bapak Jenggot*, "Father Beard." Indonesians will ask how you keep from getting food caught in it, mothers will tell their children you'll eat them up, and others will think you appear angry all the time, like a *raksasa*. Whether bearded or not, children outside of tourist areas—and older people too—will often be afraid of you, though they'll try not to show it. Some children only see white people when they're punching, shooting, or killing each other in the movies. This is why many Indonesians in untouristed areas start screaming and running the moment they see you.

Interactions

Don't get too annoyed about constantly being asked where you're going. Think up some zany answers, or use the standard ones, like exactly where you're going, if you know, or just *"jalan jalan"* which means roughly "out walking" and covers everything from aimless wandering to purposeful trips to the toilet. Or try the Malay response, *"Saya makan angin,"* "I'm eating the wind." This phrase often gets rid of *becak* drivers who won't leave you alone.

If people join you on the path or road, make conversation—usually they're not latching onto you forever. A lot of people ask for your address, which you shouldn't give unless you desire occasional requests for money, photographs, sponsorship, or help.

Knowing Indonesian allows for a greater range of encounters, as Indonesians are less self-conscious speaking to foreigners in their own tongue. Even better is speaking a few words in the local dialect. For example, you can amuse a whole *bemo* full of Torajans by calling lurking figures on the side of the road *bombo*, the Torajan word for ghost.

Youngsters still call Western tourists by the Indonesian word for Dutchman, *Belanda*. So when you hear *"Belanda!"* shouted out behind you, turn around and come back with *"Bukan Belanda! Saya orang Selandia Baru!"* ("I'm not Dutch! I'm a New Zealander!") or some such reply. The fixed look of suspicion turns into a smile of appreciation at words in roughly recognizable Indonesian. News of who you are will then seem to travel far ahead of you.

Begging

Encourage Indonesian pride. If small children offer their services as guides, render payment in ways other than money or candy. Begging creates an endless cycle of dependence, diminishes self-worth, and does more harm than good. Say *"tidak boleh"* ("you may not") to begging children. Offer a look through your binoculars, some pencils, pens, balloons, safety pins, or a small notebook. When in Jakarta or Bali, buy a quantity of the amazing postcards available there, then proffer them as gifts in the Outer Islands.

Don't give medicines unless you know what you're doing and can provide follow-up care. This misuse of antibiotics, especially with children, can be dangerous and is a big problem in developing countries. Encourage the use of local health clinics.

Adult Indonesians who do you a favor may ask for *uang rokok* (literally, "cigarette money"). A small gratuity to a driver or lad to fetch coffee or a newspaper is not a handout.

Hassles

If a pickpocket probes your jeans or shoulder bag for money, remove the strange fingers, point, and announce to everyone, *"pencopet!"* In the countryside, a crowd will sometimes wrestle a thief to the ground, holding the malefactor until a police official arrives with handcuffs.

On occasion in such places as southern Sumatra, Flores, or Sulawesi, you may be taunted by young boys who just want to torment foreigners to see how they react. It's absolutely essential not to get angry—this is what delights them most. Move in quickly among responsible-looking adult Indonesians. In some outlying towns of Indonesia—such as in southern

Sumatra or Sumbawa—a jeering crowd may follow you around, teasing, taunting, and verbally abusing you. In these cases, try to find a public official, schoolteacher, or police officer with whom you can establish a respectful rapport. Or enter an outlying, untouristed area only with an authority figure to evade encounters with rude, unsavory, or hostile individuals. Often you have surprise on your side and you're gone before a crowd can even gather.

Many Indonesians are skilled at coaxing you into doing things you really don't want to do. Get in the habit of saying, *"Bukan adat kami"* ("It's not our custom"). Surrounded by hundreds of dissimilar ethnic groups, Indonesians understand well that different people practice different customs.

In tourist locales, sellers on foot can be unbelievably pushy and will stick to you like glue. Always be polite at first, expressing your disinterest. But if these people persist, following you and aggressively hounding you, turn around, face them, and state firmly and unequivocally you're just not interested. Keep repeating this in Indonesian and in English, looking them straight in the eye, until they back off. Usually this works quite well, but if it doesn't, say vehemently *"silahkan pergi!"* ("please go!"). Another technique effective for use with a nagging vendor is to make an offer so ridiculously low the pest will give you up as a lost cause. Also be wary of predatory touts who offer to show you around different arts and crafts shops, expecting a commission from the owners or in the end charging you for "guide" services.

The ultimate hassle in Indonesia is a bust for selling dope, an offense Indonesians take very seriously. Even your hotel owner or a passerby on the beach can turn you in.

Women Traveling Alone
Women are more likely to be raped in the U.S. or Australia than in Indonesia, but you can expect men and boys here to touch you indecently. Sleazy types tend to hang around train and bus stations, movie theaters, ferry docks, and ports. If obscenely approached, just spit out *"Kau babi!"* ("You pig!"); this will get his and the crowd's attention. Hopefully, the humiliation will prevent him from continuing.

When traveling alone, a woman should choose her clothes with care. Except when going to the

beach, it's not a good idea to wear short skirts or shorts, braless tank tops, or strapless tops. In particularly strong orthodox Muslim areas, such as Aceh, women shouldn't even wear bathing suits or short shorts to the beach. Don't ask a man to accompany you to the beach as protection; this will be interpreted as an invitation to sex. Don't ever hug an Indonesian man; it will be misinterpreted.

On Bali and in other tourist areas, drivers say such filthy things to women most soon prefer to avoid taxis altogether. If you want more comfort than a *bemo* provides, hire a car—but eschew all expressions of intimacy with the driver. Never take one driver overnight or for long-term. Don't eat meals with him. Another way a single woman can avoid trouble is to join a group tour. Either way, you will never receive so many marriage proposals in your life.

Staying With People
Conversations on buses, trains, and boats can often lead to great places to stay. You may never have to stay in a hotel if you're friendly, humble, and patient. But be forewarned: staying with a family means absolutely no privacy. This could get old fast, unless you enjoy forever standing in the spotlight.

As a visitor you must adapt to many roles. Friends and relatives will visit, and anyone in the *kampung* who speaks English will come around to practice. You'll be invited to do things with the family so they can parade you around the village or city street, showing you off to everyone. On occasion you'll be used as a vehicle to boost someone's standing in the community.

Small gifts and souvenirs (*ole-ole*) are a common way of showing gratitude and affection to the family you're staying with. When you go off for the day, bring back a small edible gift; if you visit the mountains, bring back fruit or flowers. If you're invited to dinner, bring a gift of chocolate or a tin of cookies. Gifts are usually not opened when presented, but opened later in private.

When attending an event in someone's home, it's customary to leave your shoes outside, then wait to be seated. Don't initiate action; wait to be told what to do. Don't take photos without permission. Wear clean, decent clothes.

At a wedding, the presence of a Westerner is believed to be a sign of good luck and is much appreciated. Take your place in the formal receiving line and offer best wishes to the couple with *"selamat berbahagia."* If you take pictures, send copies of the photos to the wedding couple. To acknowledge a birth, send a card with the words *"selatmat dating kelahiran putri/putra"* ("best wishes on the birth of your daughter/son"). When attending a Christian baptism or infant *turun tanah* ("touching the earth") ceremony, bring a small gift of clothing or toys. At a circumcision celebration, slip the boy Rp10,000-15,000 in a plain white envelope.

Avoid climbing walls or trees if there are priests or religious officials about as it is disrespectful to occupy space above them.

Conversation

Indonesians usually don't join in conversation unless invited to do so. It's not easy for them to initiate conversations and they're often relieved when spoken to. Indonesians are very proud of their country and will always ask if you like Indonesia, if you plan to come back. Foreigners can ask Indonesians almost anything and get away with it. Do talk politics, but always in private and never with the army or police. Talk about children (yours or theirs), where they come from, places they've traveled to at home and abroad. Don't introduce business into social situations.

High value is placed on deferential or submissive behavior. It is the duty of the individual to obey communal law and defer to group elders. Indeed, one cannot help but get the impression that the entire country of 190 million people is run like one great boarding school.

In the West members of the same family in the same house often greet each other with "hi," "hello," or "how are you?" Indonesians feel this is very formal. People in the same household here launch straightaway into conversation. Also, you don't have to say "please" and "thank you" in Indonesia as much as in the West.

Children will constantly yell "Hello Mister-r-r-r!" or "Hello Mi-s-s-s!" You can simply answer *"pergi ke mana?"* ("where are you going?") or *"dimana jalan kaki?"* ("where is the footpath?"). Watching wide-eyed as you walk by, they'll think the foreigner can greet, so perhaps can also understand. Learn the traditional greetings in the local languages of each region you visit.

Table Manners

Indonesians always offer to share the meals they're eating when visitors arrive at house, office, or park bench. If invited to dinner, arrive 10 minutes late; it's expected. Once seated, watch your Indonesian host; a guest may not start until the host offers the invitation *"silakan makan"* ("please eat") or *"silakan minum"* ("please drink"). All guests are expected to bring a small gift of flowers or cookies.

While at the table, never eat with the left hand. Take a small helping the first time around because your host will be offended if you don't take seconds. It's polite to keep pace with your host. If you empty your plate, it means you want more. If you don't like what's served, it's acceptable to just take a sip or bite. To ask for salt, pepper, soy sauce, or *sambal* is an insult, implying the cook didn't know what spices to add to the dish.

Be careful not to offend your Muslim friends, who are forbidden to eat pork. In their company never ask for or offer dishes prepared with pork or lard. Indonesians are also unaccustomed to eating uncooked food such as salads, cold meats, and dairy products; sometimes Western food can even upset their stomachs. Westerners rarely eat the insides of cattle or sheep, but in Indonesia virtually every part of an animal is consumed. Many traditional families in Indonesia do not talk during meals; conversation starts only after the meal. Cover your mouth with your hand when picking your teeth; only animals show their fangs.

Visiting

Unannounced visits are a tradition in Indonesia. The best time to drop in on people in their homes is between 1600 and 1800—after work, food, and siesta, and, in Islamic areas, before evening prayers. It's less polite to visit or call later in the evening, after 2100. It's common for Indonesians to be on your doorstep at 0630 as everyone gets up early. Visits between 1230 and 1530 are considered impolite.

Visitors are never turned away. Allow enough time with your host, as a rushed guest leaves a bad impression. If you're kept waiting for your host to appear, it's a compliment: s/he's changing into nice clothes to receive you. Conversely, s/he'd be offended if you visited only in a *sarung* or T-shirt. The polite way to turn down a visit to someone's house is *"ya, kapan-kapan, kalau ada waktu"* ("okay, sometime, if there's time").

It's polite to introduce yourself when meeting strangers without waiting for someone else to initiate the ritual. Shake hands when greeting people; men, women, and children will all offer their hands when introduced. Respect is shown by bowing from the waist when passing in front of people, especially older people. Share your

cigarettes, and maintain a supply of biscuits for children.

Travelers should also be prepared to forego an occasional night's sleep. Make of the night the day. Many forms of entertainment, prayers, and religious festivals run all night long. In some places people stay up the whole night of the full moon simply for the coolness and magic of it. There's plenty of magic in Indonesia.

ON THE ROAD

Nothing is easy in Indonesia, especially traveling. The obstacles blocking a smooth, leisurely journey are formidable. Road conditions are often deplorable, seas are rough, flights delayed or canceled, schedules constantly changing. If traveling by sea, your kapal motor will undoubtedly have no radio, lifevests, or compass. Rented cars aren't fitted with seatbelts and motorcycle helmets are flimsy. Public transportation is overburdened and inadequate, the country's bus stations like overfilled car parks. Traveling Indonesia is a neverending battle against banal Westernized food, sugar, MSG, grease, noise pollution, heat, seething throngs of people, overabundant insect life, foul lodgings, and shady arts and crafts dealers. Yet this spellbinding, kaleidoscopic country will return your investment twentyfold in the variety of its landscapes, its endlessly fascinating natural phenomena, and its inhabitants whose friendliness and hospitality are the equivalent of an abduction.

MINISTRY OF TOURISM

ARTS AND CRAFTS

With giddy variety, competitive prices, and unique motifs and themes, Indonesia is one of the world's great shopping adventures. You'll find here a vast array of fashionable clothing, inexpensive leather goods, exquisite textiles, and stunning jewelry. Indonesia offers everything from primitive artifacts to sophisticated art produced by palace artisans, colorful contemporary decorative furnishings to priceless antiques. Unfortunately, there are also untold quantities of mass-produced souvenirs, repetitive carvings, and dreary bric-a-brac.

Superb craftsmanship and long traditions are exemplified in the simplest domestic crafts: the mats, sun hats and bamboo implements of Java; the basketry of Roti; the flute-making of the Torajans; the bamboo *angklung* of Sumba.

Because of the country's tropical climate, stone temples and megaliths are the only remnants of ancient Indonesian art—the work of *rajas,* priests, and royalty. The art of the common people, rendered in cloth, papyrus, palm leaf, and wood, long ago disintegrated. But the motifs and symbols survive: in Indonesia nothing is destroyed, everything is preserved. Designs and techniques of prehistoric painters and sculptors are still widely used in textiles, metalwork, and woodcarvings on houses and ships. The same sort of fish with human faces carved on Prambanan stone reliefs a millennium ago can be seen today in Balinese paintings. Primitive art, such as that practiced by the Asmat and Tanimbar islanders, uses models and themes found in ancestor worship.

TEXTILES

The scattered isles of Indonesia offer probably the world's greatest collection of traditional handmade textiles. You'll find many regional and island specialties, with unique patterns, designs, and colors. The brilliant flaming *ikat* of the Torajans of south-central Sulawesi; the primitive bark cloths of Irian Jaya; the ancient appliqué technique of the Dayaks of Borneo; the sophisticated *ikat* designs of the Lesser Sundas; the color-rich *lurik* of Central Java; the dazzling *songket* scarves and *sarung* of Sumatra, where gold threads seem to float atop the material.

At one time textiles had a religious significance. The Sundanese women of West Java weren't allowed to marry until they'd woven a *samping*; Pekalongan women of the north spent half the night meditating and burning incense before starting work on a *batik.* Organic dyes were sometimes ritually made from the blood

SHOP TALK

- If shopping is your main reason for going to Indonesia, plan an itinerary that will expose you to the crafts that most interest you. If you're trolling for ethnographic artifacts, for example, route your journey through Irian Jaya, Southeast Maluku, Sulawesi, Kalimantan, Nias, and North Sumatra. If *batik* turns you on, travel to Yogyakarta, Solo, Pekalongan, and Cirebon on Java.

- You'll usually find the best buys in the town or island where a particular craft is produced—there's a much wider selection and the artisans are more amenable to bargaining. In remote areas, however, you may be considered a rich foreigner capable of paying ridiculously inflated prices. Peer pressure from other vendors also drives prices up.

- For the cheapest prices, frequent the small back-lane shops, open-air "art" markets, cottage industry home-shops, factory shops, privately owned galleries, and big department stores. For higher quality, try the glitzy shops in the arcades of the best hotels—but be prepared for high prices. If you find something you really like, buy it. You'll probably never see something exactly like it again.

- Many villages or city *kampung* specialize in particular crafts. If you want to know an area or city's specialty, just ask the locals what gifts they send to relatives out of town. With their answers, you'll learn what's cheap, unique, rare.

- You can save money, hassles, and time by shopping in one of Indonesia's big-city, modern, fixed-price, all-in-one department stores. Sarinah in Jakarta and Matahari in Denpasar both have wide selections organized by island. You can browse at your leisure without being pestered by shop owners or vendors.

- Regional crafts may not be available in tourist areas. For example, Torajan crafts from Sulawesi, Timorese crafts from Timor, and Batak crafts from Sumatra are not widely available in Jakarta and Bali. Asmat carvings, however, or at least knock-offs of Asmat carvings, seem to be everywhere.

- The morning price is often the lowest of the day: sellers believe if they make a sale right off, the rest of the day will go well.

- If you let third parties—guides, *becak* drivers, chauffeurs—take you into a shop, count on a commission of 10% to 30% tacked onto the price. Shops working on low overhead don't want anything to do with commissions. To get a better price, ask your driver or guide to stay out of the shop and tell the shopowners they're not obligated to pay a commission.

- Bring Western clothes for trading. T-shirts with cartoons, messages, or emblems are very popular. You can easily sell or swap them. Western jewelry and flashy wristwatches are also popular with Indonesians.

---

of human sacrifices. Today, *sarung* are often wrapped around the bride and bridegroom to symbolize unity, or spread over a seriously ill person to increase the power to fight off illness. The dead are honored with a covering of precious textiles.

Weaving

In Indonesia, fabrics are sometimes woven in three and four directions. Similar to tie-dying, *ikat* textiles are created by tying off already dyed weft or warp threads to retain various designs and colors while the rest of the fabric is dyed. Each completed, hand-woven *ikat* represents a colossal amount of human labor; most of these tribal fabrics survive only in the more remote parts of the archipelago.

Ikat has always been used throughout Nusatenggara for local ceremonies, and for many years was produced because imported printed cloth wasn't readily available. *Ikat* is still very much used for ritual purposes, but increasingly it's made to supply a healthy tourist demand. Most of these striking woven textiles are used as *sarung,* head cloths, *selendang,* banners, or as ceremonial cloths for the wrapping of the dead. They're in high demand in the West as wall hangings, runners, tablecloths, upholstery material, and curtains. *Ikat* dyes are made from local plants and minerals, giving the cloth a rich, rustic appearance.

To bone up on the rather abstruse topic of Indonesian textiles, and to keep from being charged antique prices for new textiles, study *Indonesian Textile Techniques* by Michael Hitchcock, or the more venerable *Splendid Symbols: Textiles and Tradition in Indonesia* by Mattiebelle Gittenger.

Batik

Indonesian artists love animal motifs: buffalo, elephants, crocodiles, snakes, and lizards, as well as dragons, lion-birds, and other mythological creatures. You can see these motifs vividly represented in Indonesia's most renowned textile craft, *batik*. These beautiful handmade works of art on cotton are made by using a "wax-resist" method whereby wax is applied to the cloth to resist the dye. The wax can be applied by hand (*tulis*) or with a metal stamp (*cap*).

Batik means "to dot." In *batik tulis,* hot wax is poured into a small, bamboo instrument called a *canting,* which features a copper reservoir for holding molten wax. With one, two, or even three spouts of varying thicknesses, the *canting* is used like a pencil to apply a wax pattern. The material is dipped in one color and all parts of the cloth not covered in wax take up the dye. Wax is then removed from a section of the cloth and applied to the newly dyed section. The material is dyed in another color, and then another—from the lightest color to black. This labor-intensive waxing and dying process is repeated many times until the desired colors and shades appear on the cloth. One completed cloth can incorporate hundreds of different patterns.

In *batik tulis* the colors on both sides of the cloth are equally vibrant, as the wax is applied to both sides. In *cap batik* the inside colors are duller, as wax is applied to one side only. Some *batik* makers employ a combination of both *batik tulis* and *batik cap. Cap,* or stamped *batik,* where the same motifs are repeated over the entire cloth, is by far the most widely used method.

The majority of *sarung* sold in Indonesia are actually not *batik,* technically speaking, but "*batik* motif," also known as "hand-print *batik*". It takes experience and keen observation to identify *batik* produced with the print/*cap*/*tulis* combination. Sellers can be very unhelpful; sometimes it seems everything is *halus.* Always ask where your *batik* was made.

Although several "wax-writings" inscribed with a *canting* date back to the 16th century, *batik* didn't reach its zenith until the introduction of high-quality white cotton from Europe in the late 19th century. During this period, *batik* of unbelievable detail and quality came from a number of private workshops in Central Java. Today the main *batik*-producing centers are Cirebon, Yogyakarta, Solo, and Pekalongan on Java. *Batik* is also produced as far north as Jambi in South Sumatra. Almost any shop will demonstrate *batik*-making, and a number of schools in Yogyakarta teach the process to Western students.

Tailoring

Bali is unquestionably the fashion capital of Indonesia. Hundreds of Indonesian and foreign designers maintain factories and shops along Jl. Legian in Kuta and Legian. In this shopping district, as well as in the art markets of Yogyakarta and Solo on Java, shopping takes an exorbitant amount of time and energy—there are literally hundreds of shops, the dust and noise are nerve-wracking, the climate sweltering, the bargaining draining, the flood of kitschy, copycat products seemingly endless.

In the tourist areas of Bali and Yogyakarta, you can buy very inexpensive ready-made clothes, but they often fade, wrinkle, and finally fall apart. Cause: cheap material. Colors also tend to be very loud, and successful patterns and designs are mass-produced over and over. Many shops carry defective merchandise. Large and extra-large sizes are in chronic short supply.

It's better to hire a tailor or seamstress to sew your clothes. You can replace all your clothing with cheap, lovely Indonesian-style garments you designed yourself. Indonesians are very skilled at copying an existing piece or a photo from a fashion magazine. Take apparel that fits you very well so the tailor can make a paper pattern. Bring at least a sketch of what you want.

Tailoring costs vary. In Flores you can have a simple shirt copied for Rp3000; the price rises on Bali. In Kuta, it's Rp10,000 for the same shirt; in Ubud only Rp5000. Avoid tourist ghettos. Explain everything, specifying even button selection, pants length, the slant of the pockets. More elaborate designs cost more and require more time. Names and addresses of competent local tailors and seamstresses are available from fabric shops and tourist offices. Or ask your *losmen* or hotel owner.

ANTIQUES

In Indonesia you'll find Ming china, old coins, bottles and inkwells, embroidery, 300-year-old trading beads, chandeliers, brass lamps, delft ware, pewter ware, canopied beds, old chests and carved doors, *wayang* puppets, vintage tools, clocks, walking canes, and Indonesian tribal masks. There's still a lot of traditional art here, despite the onslaught of ruthless collectors who've turned to Indonesia after plundering West Africa.

The best antique flea markets are on Java, particularly in Solo, Jakarta, Cirebon, Semarang, and Surabaya. Don't miss Solo's Pasar Antik, one of the largest and most colorful antique markets in Indonesia, especially for period artifacts from the Dutch years.

Learn as much as you can beforehand so you can separate the gems from the junk. Visit museums, take tours. Attend cultural lectures sponsored by Jakarta's Ganesha Society and run by the American Women's Association. These events are usually publicized well in advance in the special-interest sections of the local press. Jakarta's City Museum and National Museum offer excellent examples of the various antiques and regional styles found in Indonesia.

In a large city like Surabaya or Bandung, antique shops are frequently located close to one another on one or two streets. Java's most famous row of antique shops is along Jakarta's Jl. Surabaya, dominated by shrewd Minang merchants. Other antique haunts include the shops along Jl. Kebon Sirih Timur Dalang, Jl. Majapahit, and Jl. Kamang Bangka. In Yogyakarta, check out the shops in Kota Gede and along Jl. Malioboro and Jl. Taman Garuda. Shops are usually cluttered and disorganized, so you really have to dig. Sometimes you have to travel a bit to find the genuine stuff. Timor and Flores are known for antique ivory, Medan for old Batak tribal artifacts, Maluku and Kalimantan for old china. Banda Aceh, in far northern Sumatra, is famous for its antique gold, old knives and swords, Dutch porcelain, and rare woven textiles.

Warnings: beware of peddlers of old VOC coins. These fakes are extremely convincing, but don't fall for the scam. The price—Rp10,000 for a Dutch silver 12.5 guilder piece—is too low for them to be real. Also be wary of vendors who want antique prices for "very old" textiles that may have come into being two weeks ago. For big-ticket textiles, stick with reputable, established sellers.

CARVING

Indonesia's hundreds of ethnic groups produce some of the world's most sought-after and exciting primitive art. Here are fascinating forms of woodcarving: *si gale gale,* life-sized wooden puppets the Bataks of North Sumatra jerk to life when a child dies; eerie two-meter-high ancestor figures from the Leti Islands in Maluku; the menacing demons, *naga,* and human-like fish of Java; the handsomely grained ebony animal figures and mythical birds of the Balinese; the posts, house gables, and window shutters of the Sumbanese and Alorese; frightening masks, war shields, arrowheads, stone axes, and spears from Irian; attractive shields from the Dayaks of Kalimantan.

Woodcarving

The woodcarving center of Java is Jepara, famous for its ornately carved furniture and panels. Torajaland and Asmat are the carving centers for the eastern islands. On Lake Toba in North Sumatra, the Bataks skillfully carve ancestor figures, masks, magic augury books, and wands. Traditionally, Mas is the woodcarving center of Bali, though the work occurs all over the island. Bare teak or mahogany are favored by some Balinese carvers, but many use bright pastel oils to paint feathers or scales on wooden objects.

Indonesian carving falls into two categories: the ancient Dongson style, found in the Outer Islands, dating from 350 B.C. and derived from Indochina; and the "high" Hinduized style of the Javanese and Balinese court cultures which dominated Java and Bali from the 7th century on. The wood available for both styles is teak, ironwood, sandalwood, "crocodile" wood, mahogany, and young ebony imported from Sumatra and Borneo. On Bali, sweet-scented hibiscus is popular. Rare tropical woods require special care so they don't dry out, split, or rot in temperate climates.

Unique examples of Dongson-style primitive art may include war shields, spears, masks, staffs, storage containers, baby carriers, panels, posts, window shutters, ancestral statues, effigy figures, and musical instruments. Perhaps the most spectacular examples of ethnographic carving are the magnificent phallic ancestor *bisj* poles of the Asmat of southern Irian Jaya. Some artifacts, such as a Dani digit chopper, are hung with dog hair, chicken feathers, and pig scrotums, and would tend to clash with typical Western decor. Other carved pieces, such as a marvelous carved Batak door resplendent with mysterious lizard motifs, would fit into a Western home perfectly.

Many traditional handicrafts would have disappeared long ago if it weren't for tradition-loving tourists. Tourist interest is also why so many items have become so expensive. A good Balinese carved statue or an authentic Batak magic wand now costs up to Rp525,000.

Other Carving Media

The detail on buffalo horn, bone, ivory, or hornbill beak can be so extreme you need a magnifying glass to truly take in the work. For the best and cheapest carved tortoiseshell, seashells, and other sea ornaments, go to Ambon and Ternate in Maluku and Manado in North Sulawesi. In Maluku clove stems are used to create tiny figures of sailors on the decks of miniature sailing ships. For stonework, using smooth lava rock, visit Magelang. Batubulan is Bali's stonecarving center.

Leatherwork is prepared mainly on a crude grade of buff-colored buffalo hide. On Jl. Malioboro in Yogyakarta, Indonesia's leather-carving capital, sidewalk vendors sell luggage, briefcases, lampshades, pendants, belts, purses, and sandals. The workmanship is amateurish and the styles old-fashioned, but the prices are incredibly cheap. Another major leather carving center is Bandung in West Java.

The best-known carvings in hide are the gilded shadow puppets used in the *wayang kulit* of Central and East Java. These flat puppets, representing different characters from the Hindu epics, make excellent decorative wall pieces, particularly if backlit. Rows of wooden puppets-in-the-round (*wayang golek*), also depicting Hindu characters, make striking displays.

METALWORK

Metalworking in bronze, brass, tin, and iron still thrives in areas where Hindu influence was once strongest—the prosperous seaports of Java, Bali, South Sulawesi, coastal Borneo, and West Sumatra. The most praised examples of ancient Dongson-derived artifacts are the remarkable bronze kettle drums (*moko*) of the Pantar and Alor islands of eastern Nusatenggara.

Students of metallurgy can see percussion-type *gamelan* instruments made at Pak Sukarna's foundry in Bogor. Brasswork is the specialty of the Makassarese of southwestern Sulawesi. Probably the most popular metal souvenir is the legendary *kris,* the ceremonial dagger worn by Javanese and Balinese. Antique bejeweled specimens can cost well over Rp21 million, though keepsake varieties with wooden handles are available for less than Rp21,000.

Jewelry

Indonesian artists excel in such precious metal crafts as silversmithing and the setting of semi-precious stones in silver and gold. Gold is quite cheap in Indonesia; try the gold shops along Jl. Hasanuddin in Denpasar on Bali. Silver is also inexpensive, especially the way it's cut in Indonesia. Some workshops cut the stuff by as much as 50%; good quality work is 92.5% pure. No matter what the silversmiths of Bali, Yogyakarta, and Bukittinggi tell you about the excruciating hand-tooled work they poured into pieces, don't pay more than Rp8000 for a ring, brooch, or small pendant. The silver centers of Indonesia are Ujung Pandang in South Sulawesi, Kota Gadang in West Sumatra, Kota Gede in Central Java, and Celuk, Mas, and Denpasar on Bali. It's usually quite easy to see artisans working in the shops and factories of Kota Gede and Celuk.

Banjarmasin in South Kalimantan is a center for rings set with stones as well as for Dayak polished stone beads. Martapura in South Kalimantan has a booming trade in jewelry; Pangkalanbun in Central Kalimantan is the place for lovely black opals and purple amethyst. Contemporary jewelry is plentiful in the resort shops. Jakarta, Yogyakarta, and Kuta on Bali are the best places to shop for antique jewelry.

PLAITING

Indonesia's oldest craft. Woven containers are still made where rural people are unwilling to spend precious cash on tin or plastics. Bamboo, rattan, *sisal,* nipa, and *lontar* palm are ingeniously utilized all over Indonesia, probably most creatively by the Sundanese of West Java, the Dayaks of Kalimantan, the Sasaks of Lombok, and the Balinese. The palm-leaf offerings set outside the houses and temples of Bali are greater works of art than the island's world-famous paintings and carvings.

Since sophisticated "modern" tools like iron hatchets, axes, machetes, small planes, and knives are needed to gather bamboo and to work it, the plaiting crafts are associated with the more advanced cultures of western Indonesia. Split bamboo is made into nets, hats, wickerwork, mats, and umbrella frames. Indonesians turn out ingenious tables, comfortable chairs, chests, standing closets, four-poster beds, and cabinets from wood and vegetable fibers. They're extremely adept at refurbishing antique furniture or creating new antique-looking pieces. The largest collection of furniture shops in the country is the two-km-stretch along Jl. Ciputat Raya in Pondok Labu, a suburb south of Jakarta on the old road to Bogor. Many of the shops will arrange shipping.

CERAMICS

Since plentiful bamboo is so easily made into vessels, ceramic firing techniques have never developed into an advanced craft in these islands. Glazed earthenware is crafted in Kasongan village near Yogyakarta, Plered in West Java, and Kediri on Lombok.

Indonesia was once a trading center for ceramics, and today contains the largest, most comprehensive collection of Chinese ceramics outside China. Well-preserved pieces are found throughout the archipelago: dug from old graves on Sumba, in the Dayak longhouses of Borneo, on the shelves of dusty souvenir shops of Ambon. Though traces of exquisite Han dy-

nasty ceramics have been unearthed, more common is "Kitchen Ming," so-called because they were items of everyday use by the Chinese from A.D. 1400 to 1800. Celadon ware, known for heaviness and subdued decoration, is encountered all over Indonesia.

The farther you travel from the tourist haunts, the cheaper the pottery. Giant Tang vases cost Rp500,000 in Ambon, and whole sets of Kitchen Ming will run as little as Rp250,000 in Samarinda.

Porcelain from Japan, Thailand, Vietnam, and Burma also turns up in Indonesia. Arabian and European earthenware is quite scarce. Jakarta's National Museum on Medan Merdeka and the Adam Malik Museum in Jakarta Pusat feature Indonesia's most stunning collections of antique Chinese ceramics and porcelain.

PAINTING

Not until the late 19th century did an Indonesian painter, the Javanese Raden Saleh, attain fame in the European art world. Most of the Indonesian art of this period merely imitated Western styles and was devoid of originality in concept or design. Just before WW II, artists in associations such as Pelukis Rakyat and Seniman Indonesian Muda began working with genuine Indonesian expression through the adaptation of Western techniques in oil and batik. The impressionist Affandi, the "Picasso of Indonesia," was one of the leaders of that early effort. Direx Gallery, across the road from his old studio on Jl. Solo just west of the Ambarrukmo Palace Hotel in Yogyakarta, sells Affandi's work. Also check out the batik paintings in the shops along Jl. Tirtodipuran.

Concentrations of talented contemporary artists display work in galleries in Jakarta, Yogyakarta, and on Bali.

HOLIDAYS, FESTIVALS, AND EVENTS

Indonesians take their festivals and holidays seriously. Colorful spectacles celebrating religious, patriotic, or tribal holidays are so frequent and elaborate it's a wonder people have time for anything else. On holidays, Indonesians dress in resplendent white clothes or appear in bright new *sarung* and *kebaya,* immaculately groomed. Because of the incessant Indonesian heat, celebrations are usually scheduled early in the morning or late at night.

For events on Java and Bali, consult the free, full-color, and very detailed *Calendar of Events* booklet available at Garuda offices, Indonesian consulates or embassies, and tourist offices in Jakarta or Denpasar. Some regional tourist offices might also provide lists of annual local events.

Because they can explain what's going on and introduce you to the different players involved, it's best to accompany an Indonesian or two when attending local events. Don't be shy: the presence of a Westerner is often considered a good omen at weddings, circumcisions, and *selamatan.*

Family Transitional Events

At an Indonesian wedding you'll experience many attributes of the culture. Check out the lengthy prenuptial ceremonies, ethnic wedding costumes, elaborate dais, endless toasts and speeches, lavish reception with buffet and traditional song and dance, ostentatious exchange of gifts. It's not uncommon to come across a glittering wedding procession complete with band and bride in a *palanquin.* In southern Sumatra following the pepper harvest in October there are weddings everywhere.

Yellow tags tied on trees or poles, or an open-air gathering under an awning, signals a funeral. When a death occurs in a Muslim family, hundreds of relatives, friends, neighbors, and associates converge on the home of the deceased. The dead are usually transported to the cemetery on the shoulders of family members and interred in the ground within 24 hours.

Javanese *selamatan* ceremonies launch new businesses or bless the birth of a new child. Ceremonies for newborns and mothers-to-be are common. Each ethnic group practices its own rites, the pomp and formality dependent upon the social level of the family. There could be a procession, feast, ritual bathing, special foods, prayers, and blessings. Many groups hold "touching the earth" ceremonies (*turun tanah*) for infants.

Visitors may well encounter a young boy, usually between 11 and 12, on his circumcision day (*sunatan*), an important rite of passage for the Muslim male. The youth is paraded about like an elegant prince on an elaborately caparisoned

cremation procession

J. WEISS

horse or decorated *becak*. On Bali, a tooth-filing ritual celebrates the passage from childhood into adulthood.

RELIGIOUS HOLIDAYS

Islamic religious holidays are predominant in Indonesia. The Islamic calendar is based on the lunar year (354 days), so festivals move backward through the solar months, the dates varying from one year to the next. Hindu Bali has its own festivals, reckoned with a calendar of 210 days per year. Indonesia's Christian population uses the Gregorian calendar of the West, but put their own spin on Christian holidays. The Portuguese descendants of Flores, for example, wear grass pompoms, black costumes, and triangular-shaped caps as they carry statues of the Virgin Mary in barefoot Good Friday processions. During May and October, thousands of Roman Catholics in Yogyakarta journey to the Holy Spring of Sendangsono near Muntilan in Central Java, where pilgrims light candles at the feet of a statue of Mary.

Ramadan

A monthlong fast in the ninth month of the Javanese calendar. Islamic fasting is less drastic than the Hindu custom of total abstinence from all food and drink. During Ramadan (*puasa*) Muslims visit family graves and royal cemeteries, reciting prayers and burning incense. Special prayers are chanted at mosques and at home. Brand-new velvet *peci* (caps) are everywhere. Each day begins with the whole family rising at 0300 or 0400 and gorging themselves on as much food as they can force down their gullets. Those who strictly observe *puasa* eat nothing during the daylight hours. The fast is broken each day at sunset, usually in groups. During *puasa*, business slows to a crawl. Workers are less productive, bureaucrats less patient, stealing and "borrowing" rampant, servants more demanding. The fasting month ends when the crescent of the new moon is sighted with the naked eye.

Lebaran

Also called Hari Raya (or, in Arabic, Idul Fitri). The first day of the 10th month of the Arabic calendar, marking the end of the monthlong Muslim fast. A celebratory outburst of banquets releases pent-up tension. Tom-tomming and firecrackers all night long precede 0700 festivities, when everyone turns out for an open-air service and mass prayers in the village square. This is followed by two days of continuous feasting and public holidays. Verses are sung from the Koran; sometimes there are religious processions.

Lebaran is like Christmas, Valentine's Day, and New Year's rolled into one. No matter what the obstacles or cost, millions of Indonesians return to their villages to feast with their families. With this annual gathering, the simplicity of life in the *desa* provides psychological healing. It's a joyous time of mutual forgiveness, with pardon asked and received for the wrongs of the past year. The heads of households buy new clothes for children, servants, and relatives. Big city relatives lavish gifts on their country cousins. There are presentations of specially prepared food, the best each family can afford. Tea is served with helping after helping of sweet doughy cake and bright cookies. Lebaran continues until all visits to relatives are ended. A large extended family can celebrate for as long as a week.

Other Islamic Holidays

Idul Adha, on the 10th day of the 11th month, is the Muslim day of sacrifice, commemorating Abraham's willingness to sacrifice his son Isaac. In Islamic areas goats and cattle are sold on village greens. After the slaughter, mosques distribute the meat to the poor. Devotees attend special ceremonies at the mosque and visit burial grounds; family graves are cleaned and strewn with flowers and holy water. Tahun Baru Hijriah is the Islamic New Year. Maulud Nabi Mohammed, on the 12th day of the new year, commemorates the birth of Mohammed. Mi'raj Nabi Mohammed celebrates the Ascension of the Prophet, when Gabriel led Mohammed through the seven heavens.

Other Religious Holidays

Christmas (Hari Natal) is a national public holiday, ardently celebrated among the Minahasans of North Sulawesi, the Irianese of Irian Jaya, the Batak of North Sumatra, and the Catholics of Flores. Wafat Isa Almasih (Good Friday) is observed in the traditional manner. Easter is known as Kenaikan Isa Al-Masih; businesses usually remain open.

The Balinese celebrate religious festivals almost unceasingly, particularly during the full moons of April and October. Cockfights, social gambling, music, and dance are all part of the festivities. As in India, Bali honors the goddess of learning on Saraswati Day—no reading or writing allowed. Nyepi, the Balinese New Year, is an enthusiastically celebrated holiday. Following a night of noisemaking and merriment, the Lord of Hell, Yama, rids Bali of devils. While Yama is about his work, the whole island closes down—no driving, no music, no smoking, no sex, no talking. Nyepi usually falls during the spring equinox at the end of March or beginning of April.

Waicak Day draws Buddhist visitors the world over to participate in mass prayers and ceremonies at the massive Borobudur monument in Central Java. Art, musical, and theater performances, *wayang kulit,* and other Javanese theater presentations feature the history of this great 9th century Buddhist sanctuary.

Imlek is the Chinese New Year; Indonesian Chinese visit temples and elders, attend family reunions, gamble, eat special foods. Jakarta's Glodok and the Chinese quarters in other urban centers run on overdrive during this period, though pageants and fireworks are banned. While Imlek is not an official state holiday, you'll realize how much Indonesia's economy depends on the Chinese when you see the number of shops and businesses closed for the festivities.

SECULAR HOLIDAYS

The secular Indonesian calendar is packed with celebrations of the founding of cities, the births and deaths of famous people, the accomplishments of cultural and military heroes, and feasts and ceremonies to appease animist spirits. The government also participates in overseas events (the Indonesian float won awards at Pasadena's Tournament of the Roses three years in a row) and honors foreign patriotic holidays. On 25 April, Ambon acknowledges Australia's Anzac Day, which commemorates those Australian soldiers and other Allied troops who lost their lives defending the island during WW II.

Hari Proklamasi Kemerdekaan is Independence Day, marking the anniversary of Indonesia's declaration of independence from Holland on 17 August 1945. The biggest Indonesian national holiday, it's celebrated differently in each of Indonesia's 27 provinces. In Aceh on North Sumatra there are Arab ceremonies; in Wamena, Irian Jaya, you'll find Papuan tribal dancing and athletic events; Manado in North Sulawesi celebrates with parades saluting the growth of industry; Tenggarong in East Kalimantan features Dayak blowpipe competitions. Indonesian flags are sold everywhere, and the day is filled with ceremonies, speeches, and public entertainments. Children and youth organizations march in parades while the older generations look on fondly. Also see village sports and games in the *kampungs.* Related to Indonesia's independence is Pattimura Day, when a flaming torch symbolizing the spirit of a guerrilla fighter is carried by a team of relay runners through the villages of the island of Ambon to Kota Ambon, the capital.

Bersih Desa occurs at the time of the rice harvest. Houses and gardens are cleaned, fences whitewashed, village roads and paths repaired. Once intended to remove evil spirits from the village, Bersih Desa has lost most of its ritualistic significance. In some Indonesian societies, it expresses gratitude to such fertility figures as Dewi Sri, the rice goddess. The memory of Raden Kartini, early nationalist and Indonesia's first women's emancipationist, is celebrated on 21 April. There are parades, lectures, programs, and social activities attended by women, schoolgirls, university teachers, female workers, and members of women's organizations, all wearing gorgeous regional dress. Mothers aren't allowed to work—children and fathers do the cooking, washing, and housecleaning. Busloads of pilgrims pay their respects at Kartini's grave near Rembang in Central Java. New Year's Day is celebrated here as in the West. The new year is greeted with fireworks and village and district fairs. Businesses are closed. In Christian areas, there are church services.

REGIONAL EVENTS

Ethnic festivals occur constantly throughout the islands. The mountain-dwelling Tenggerese of East Java annually toss live bulls and chickens into a molten crater to placate the gods. Each

April at the Pasola in remote Sumba Island, mock battles and jousting tournaments recall an era of internecine warfare. In communities along the coast of Java, fishermen load flowers and bull heads onto decorated sailing *prahu,* then throw them overboard as an offering to the South Sea goddess. These sea festivals are often accompanied by water sports competitions, communal dances, all-night *wayang* shows, and *pencak silat* contests.

On Sumba daylong ceremonies herald the arrival of the *nyale,* sea worms considered sacred for their ability to foretell the fortunes of the people. Near Negara in West Bali, thundering bull races celebrate the harvest. The Balinese and Torajans are famous for their lavish funeral ceremonies—like great medieval country fairs filled with pageantry and color, where animal effigy sarcophagi are burned and buffalo and pigs slaughtered. The Garebeg Besar of Yogyakarta is an age-old ceremony that begins with a parade of palace guards marching through the city carrying a huge mound of food (*gunungan*) symbolizing Mount Meru. The Sekaten of Solo features a procession of sacred *gamelan* instruments from the *kraton* to the Grand Mosque. In Maluku and Nusatenggara, bloody whip fights exorcise demons.

Performing Arts

In addition to the religious, national, and regional holidays and festivals there are also regular performing arts presentations—the graceful dances of Java, the dynamic martial arts of Sumatra, the mesmerizing dance dramas of Bali. In the Batak Cultural Center of Prapat, visitors are enthralled by Batak songs. *Wayang* puppet shows, for both tourists and Indonesians, often accompany holiday celebrations. The dazzling court dances of Java are staged at open-air theaters in Prambanan and Pandaan each May during the dry season. On Lombok, the popular *cupak gerantang* dance is omnipresent. Upscale hotels are likely venues for regional dance performances; ask your hotel or check schedules at tourist offices.

Arts And Crafts Fairs

Usually organized by the government or the community, these fairs promote the arts and crafts of a particular area. Among the regular annual events are the Jakarta Festival in the third week in May; the Bali Arts Festival in June and July; the June Lake Toba Festival in North Sumatra; North Sulawesi's Bunaken Festival, held in July; the Krakatoa Festival in July in West Java; the August Lake Poso Festival in Central Sulawesi; and East Kalimantan's September Erau Festival. These fairs are a time for processions, boat races, songs, dances, and fairs.

HOLIDAY TRAVEL

Religious and secular holidays can seriously inconvenience travelers. Many of Java's resort towns and hill stations are crowded with domestic tourists during major public holidays like Independence Day. Traveling the week before Lebaran can be exhausting—more than 25 million Indonesians flock to their villages for spiritual rejuvenation and to indulge in an orgy of banquets, gift-giving, and familial warmth. From Jakarta alone, three million people hit the road. This mass exodus is utter chaos; impatience and frustration reign supreme.

You certainly won't feel lonely. Make train or bus reservations at least a week in advance; even then it's difficult to find an empty seat. During holidays prices go up; accommodations throughout Indonesia fill to capacity. Although the holy fasting month of Ramadan is a slow travel period, it's not always easy to find something to eat. The only joints open in orthodox Islamic areas are dark, secretive *warung,* hidden away in back alleys.

ACCOMMODATIONS

Choose your lodgings carefully. Take some time to look around so you don't get stuck in an airless, mosquito-infested room filled with the sounds of traffic. Always check the electricity, fan or a/c, lights, toilet, and shower to see if they work. Some rooms are definitely better than others, so state what you want and tour several before deciding. You may be shown the most expensive or avoided rooms first, but you'll be surprised how a cheaper or superior room somehow materializes once you show a lack of interest.

Other travelers are the greatest single source of information on the best places to stay. Second best is tourist offices. *Becak* and taxi drivers often know the most popular tourist accommodations. In smaller villages, ask the *hansip* (district civilian militia) about homes that put up travelers. The same person who tells you a hotel or *losmen* in this book no longer exists will also point you to another good one.

In airport receiving lounges or at taxi desks, you'll often be besieged by clerks and touts pushing hotels with which they enjoy familial or employment connections. Touts in Outer Islands airports like Kupang and Pontianak flash color brochures and offer "special package rates." Sometimes these are good deals, sometimes not. Often the special-rate rooms are somehow full when you arrive. At least these offers include a free ride into the city.

Noise

Indonesian towns, cities, and resorts are invariably noisy, so try to secure a place away from the main roads. One great advantage of putting up the extra money for an a/c room is that the white noise of the air conditioning unit drowns out street clatter and considerably muffles the noise from hallways and other rooms. Avoid cheap accommodations near bus/*bemo* stations; in these neighborhoods, the only culture you'll encounter is noise and hustlers.

Many low-end accommodations are located near mosques, so the loud wails of the Muslim call to prayer booming over static-wracked loudspeakers will function as automatic alarms to awaken you in the early hours before dawn. Roosters crow, babies cry, children scream, music blares—all commencing promptly at dawn. Indonesians get up early. Your proprietor and his family will probably spend evenings sitting like zombies mesmerized by a loudly blatting TV. Radios and TVs are often played at top volume, blaring through paper-thin walls. Bring earplugs.

Of course some travelers enjoy this sort of chaos. One reader writes to recommend a Kupang homestay run by "Abdul, a friendly, guitar-strumming, pot-smoking, betel-chewing, alcoholic lecher and adulterer. If you want to do any of the above, except with his wife, then Abdul's the man. Abdul's wife covets Cleopatra-brand soap and Abdul enjoys Jim Beam. Pay for your room with these. Bob, a long-term Aussie expat on sickness benefits, 56 years old and drunk by 5 a.m. every morning, is a character. Ask for the room next to him. The sound of him urinating over the balcony and chundering onto the 'slanty-eyed bastards' below is an excellent alarm clock and adds authentic Aussie culture to the city."

Holding Down Costs

Room tariffs throughout the islands vary considerably. Rates for accommodations in remote places like Ambon or Wamena can run three to four times higher than on Bali or Java.

If you follow the well-worn travelers trail through Sumatra, Java, and Bali, you'll find Indonesia offers some of Southeast Asia's cheapest lodgings. Probably the best values on lower-end accommodations are found on Samosir Island (North Sumatra), Yogyakarta, and on Bali. Because of the competition and high concentration of tourists, Bali has by far the best accommodations anywhere in Indonesia for the money—as low as Rp5000 per night. In the past few years prices have increased sharply in Indonesia's outlying islands; for an economy room the average is now Rp15,000-20,000. On Java, a Rp25,000 hotel room in a small town like Blitar is a bargain. Accommodations in mountain resorts are expensive. In some, like Sarangan and Kaliurang on Java, the farther down the slope of the mountain, the cheaper the accommodations.

Two people traveling together always cuts expenses. A double room may cost Rp30,000 while a single runs Rp25,000. In many hotels you pay a flat rate for the room no matter how many people occupy it. Classes of rooms, and even individual rooms, are priced according to their particular assets or drawbacks—as perceived by Indonesians. You'll find Indonesians attach importance and value to amenities we may not find necessary or even comfortable. For example, a large, dark, dingy room could cost thousands of *rupiah* more than a small, cramped, clean room. Or a foam mattress might be more expensive than a *kapok* mattress, even though *kapok* is cooler. Or they feel fluorescent lighting is more desirable—and should be more expensive—than single bulb lighting. Indonesians consider a luxury room a stifling windowless box with no a/c. Westerners want an open, spacious room with windows and tile—what some Indonesian hotels consider cheap transit rooms.

Just as you bargain for other services, be sure to bargain hotel rates. A discount is definitely in order if there are a lot of empty rooms or you arrive in the slow season. Always try for a "student discount." Particularly for first-class deluxe hotels, if you book your hotel reservations through a local travel agent you could receive a 10-20% discount. At the front desk, if you ask for the "special business discount" you could knock as much as 20-40% off the price.

Government tax and service tax may be added to your bill. This can total as little as 10% in lower-priced hotels up to a preposterous 21% in swankier joints. Always determine if there's added tax before you check in. Taxes are usually in effect only in the upmarket hotels, starting at about Rp25,000. Also make sure there aren't two *daftar tarip* (hotel room rate cards), one showing taxes, the other not. Read all the small print. Any extra charge should be prominently posted and if it's not, you shouldn't have to pay. Expect to pay for each "extra" you get. A fan is invariably Rp2000 or more extra, a/c runs up to Rp15,000 extra, a private *mandi* costs an additional Rp10,000-15,000.

If you're only going to be in town for an afternoon—waiting for a bus, train, or *bemo*—try to work a deal with a *losmen* or *penginapan* proprietor to rent a room on an hourly or half-day basis. Indonesians are naturally hospitable and should be amenable to this type of short-term arrangement.

Baggage Storage

Travelers may leave their packs at a bus station office (*kantor terminal bis*), tourist office (*kantor pariwisata*), mayor's office (*kantor bupati*), or the home of the village chief (*rumah kepala desa* or *rumah kepala kampung*), depending upon which is friendliest, obligated by *adat,* or most convenient.

It's extremely common for hotels—no matter the class—to offer to store luggage in special storage rooms while you're traveling around. In lower-priced homestays, *losmen,* and *penginapan,* the owner will store your gear in the family quarters with the tacit understanding you'll stay there again upon your return.

Disabled Access

Indonesia is not known for its facilities and services for disabled travelers. If you use a wheelchair, you'll probably have to stay in a large hotel with low ramps, elevators, wide doors, and special facilities. Some restaurants and a few department stores are also equipped to handle disabled travelers. However, it's very easy and not that expensive to arrange for a roomy vehicle or van, and Indonesians are so naturally curious—too curious—and helpful you'll be overwhelmed by their attention, open-mindedness, and patience. Wherever you plan to stay, phone or fax ahead and ask about street access, stairs, railings, doorway measurements, and staff assistance.

Mandi And WC

The verb *mandi* means to bathe or wash; *kamar mandi* is the place where you bathe or wash. A *kamar mandi* could be a bamboo-partitioned enclosure along a riverbank in Sumatra; an open-air, shoulder-high cement bathing enclosure in a Balinese courtyard; an ornate, tiled bathroom with bathtub and jacuzzi in a high-priced hotel. Even low-priced *losmen, penginapan,* and *pasanggrahan* ordinarily possess running water, and a growing number now have showers and Western-style toilets. You may still find some accommodations in the outlying islands where water must be carried in by hand or refilled with a hose attached to a hand pump.

The *kamar mandi* is equipped with a large water tank and moist, lichen-covered walls. Bobbing in the middle of the cement water tank is a plastic or metal scoop with which you throw water over yourself elephant-fashion. Don't climb into the tank and bathe; you'll foul it. Instead, soap yourself down and rinse off while standing on the *mandi* floor. Sometimes fish or even frogs are kept in the water tank to control mosquito larvae.

The water is warm to cool and you'll welcome its refreshing tingle after a day in the humid tropical sun. In mountain resorts or in those *losmen* fed by underground wells, the water could be icy cold. In these cases, wait until the hottest part of the day to bathe. If you ask for hot water, it'll be provided in buckets, and there may be an extra charge of Rp2000-3000. All over this geophysical active island region are hot springs (*air panas*) where you may luxuriate in piped-in water from hot underground springs.

The abbreviation WC stands for "water closet," and is the European designation for toilet. Another Indonesian phrase for toilet is *kamar kecil* (little room). *Pria* means "men," *wanita* "women," though only in airports, train stations, department stores, and big hotels are there separate men's and women's restrooms. Sometimes the WC is located in the *mandi* room itself, but more often it's a separate, darkened enclosure. If you need to urinate, it's socially acceptable to use the floor of the *mandi*; just rinse the floor afterwards.

An Indonesian WC consists of two foot pads and a drainage hole in molded cement. You squat on the pads, take aim, then clean yourself by splashing water from a nearby can or plastic dipper. Fill the dipper (*gayung*) or can from the *mandi* water or a nearby faucet. Increasingly, Asian-style WCs are giving way to Western-style, sit-down toilets, especially in heavily touristed areas like Bali. This is a shame: there's not a more comfortable and anatomically natural position in which to relieve yourself than squatting. Besides, Western-style toilets in Indonesia are so cheap nine out of ten leak and drip all night long. The lack of running water in numerous accommodations still necessitates flushing the toilet with the *gayung* (five dippers for bowel movements, two for urine).

Also, using water instead of paper is a more hygienic method of cleaning. Squat toilets are not designed to flush down paper products. Westerners, who are reluctant to do as the Romans, often clog up WCs with their copious use of toilet paper.

TYPES OF ACCOMMODATIONS

Places to sleep are limited only by your imagination. For example, if you're really stuck in a remote area it's often possible to sleep on a *warung* bench without charge if you agree to eat there. You can sleep in your rented vehicle or on the floor of a restaurant. You probably would be able to stay on the floor of the local school, police station, *hansip* post, or church. All these places will provide mats and mosquito coils.

If you want real contact with the Indonesian people, insulating yourself in neocolonialist splendor in large, glitzy international-class hotels won't do. Generally speaking, the more money you spend on accommodations the more distant you'll find yourself from the people. But don't stay in real dives. Be choosy. Typically, low-cost Indonesian-style accommodations are family-run, spartan, and dismal, with one chair, a cabinet, and a window. They have short beds and low doorways—painfully undersized for large-framed Westerners. The lighting is terrible. Kerosene lamps and even candlelight are found in some remote areas. At least half of Indonesia's inexpensive lodgings turn off the electricity during daylight hours and turn it on again at around 1700 or 1800 until 2300 or 2400. Expect electrical failures at any time.

If there are prostitutes in residence it will probably prove noisier at night; also, keep a closer watch on your gear. In inexpensive accommodations security is lax and the flimsy doors are easy to open even when locked. Take your valuables with you or leave them with the proprietor for safekeeping. It's also common in cheap *losmen* for the boys who work there, or even the manager himself, to work hidden peepholes spying on couples and single women.

The more expensive hotels and *wisma* are well-screened, but few cheap hotels provide mosquito nets. Bring your own or use mosquito coils. Mattresses, sometimes without a top sheet, may be so thin you have to pile one on top of the other to get a good night's rest. Check your mattress for bedbugs. If you find the critters, ask the management for a new mattress or change rooms. Don't leave food out in your room. Pack it away in containers impregnable to ants, cockroaches, and rats.

Cheap Indonesian-style accommodations ordinarily offer only a slimy shared seatless squat

toilet and *mandi*. Sewage systems don't always work well and waves of stench could pass through the coziest *losmen*.

Some *losmen* owners seem unwilling to accommodate Western travelers. They may say they're full when it's obvious there are plenty of unoccupied rooms. They're probably balking at the time and expense of police registration. Or perhaps the police or some local tax official will hit them up for *uang rokok* (cigarette money) or a tax which could reduce the profit on a cheap single room to practically nothing. If you go directly to the police and ask them to help you find accommodations, they may take you right back to the reluctant *losmen*.

Staying With People

In Indonesia, someone is always inviting you home to meet the family. Muslims take care of strangers; it's part of the Islamic tradition of hospitality. Even if your *enemy* comes to your front door, you must shelter, feed, and succor the creature. If you stay with a family in a *kampung* or in a fishing village on an offshore island, it's polite to drop in on the *kepala kampung, kepala desa* (headman) or *penghulu* (village chief) to register. His house is usually the largest one in the village, with a big veranda for meetings. As a foreign visitor, you're often obligated to stay with the *kepala desa* and not in a lesser-ranking household.

If the village is very small and you have no other place to stay, the *kepala desa* will fix you up for free or for a nominal charge of around Rp10,000 per day. Be prepared for anything. When traveling deep inside East Kalimantan or Nias in West Sumatra, longhouse floors may be the only places to sleep. The dogs, fleas, roosters, and crying children will guarantee you'll arise at 0500. People in Outer Island, preindustrial societies now expect payment of about Rp5000 for a meal and a night's lodging.

Don't expect a room to yourself. You'll most likely get just a bed—no privacy, no quiet. It's a nice gesture to give notebook paper, pens, pencils, postcards, coins, or stamps to children, and cigarettes, soap, or perfume to adults. Make it known these gifts are not compensation but just meant as a kindness. Travelers coming after you will benefit from your thoughtfulness.

You may also stay in someone's house or in a rented house as a long-term paying boarder.

For example, private residences renting rooms to foreigners for around Rp150,000 per month are found along the coast on either side of the small seaside spa of Yeh Sanih in Buleleng Regency, northern Bali. And there are literally thousands of foreigners living along the southern coasts of Bali who lease bungalows for months at a time.

Camping
There are hundreds of campgrounds throughout the archipelago, usually designated for youth groups. In rural areas you can "camp" on village *bale* platforms or even in the fields. Because of wild animals, however, this last is not recommended in Sumatra. It's also possible to camp in the isolated agricultural estates of Java if you receive permission from the *kepala perkebunan* (plantation manager).

Permits are necessary to visit almost all reserves and national parks, obtainable either from Dinas Perlindungan dan Pengawetan Alam (PHPA), Jl. Juanda 9, Bogor, West Java; at the PHPA offices in the reserve itself, or in the nearest large town. Facilities for visitors in nature reserves and national parks are usually quite basic. Bring food with you, something to sleep in or on, insect repellent, and a small, portable, one-burner kerosene stove. Don't underestimate either the terrain or the chill, especially if visiting mountain reserves or climbing volcanos. Take rain gear; precipitation is a possibility even in the dry season, particularly at higher altitudes. In backcountry areas you may need to pack in water.

Penginapan
A lodging house with very basic facilities—table, chair, bed, thin walls, and a single, low-powered, unadorned light bulb hanging from a cord. *Penginapan* means simply "place to spend the night." You'll find these trader's accommodations all over Indonesia, down little back lanes, often advertised with a sign reading PENG-X followed by the owner's name. The average rate ranges anywhere from Rp5000 to Rp25,000 per night. Most common in small or coastal towns and deep in the interiors of Indonesia's islands. The differences between *penginapan* and *losmen* are becoming blurred—they're essentially the same sort of accommodation.

Losmen
A cheaply run hotel but still quite livable. Bathrooms are usually shared. Room service depends on the particular *losmen*. Here you find interesting people—itinerant merchants, students, *pegawai,* other budget travelers. Architecturally—with their narrow verandas, row of low bamboo chairs, coffee tables, and louvered double windows—*losmen* are descendants of the *pensions* popular at the turn of the century in the Dutch East Indies. Prices range from Rp5000 to Rp25,000. Usually *losmen* are efficiently run by an *ibu* (your hostess, meaning "mother") or a small staff of boys. In Jakarta and other places on Java, a *losmen* could mean a brothel. You'll seldom find *losmen* in the hill stations of Java, where more expensive *wisma* and guesthouses predominate.

Homestays
The phenomenon of homestays, or licensed private homes in tourist villages, is found mainly on Bali and in other areas of the islands popular with travelers. Often named for the family who owns the accommodation (e.g., Homestay Adiyasa), they share many of the characteristics of *losmen* and *penginapan,* but are usually more homey and familiar. You mix more with the family, and simple meals like *nasi goreng* and *mie kuah* are provided.

Wisma
A *wisma* is an Indonesian lodge or small guesthouse with pretensions. Usually it's one story, efficiently run, family owned. *Wisma*-class hotels are actually some of the best accommodations for the money in Indonesia. Costing Rp30,000-50,000, they're comfortable and homey, with first-rate service. *Wisma* often offer flush toilets, and a simple breakfast is included in the price of a room. The name *wisma* is also used for public buildings or even blocks of offices—a *wisma budaya* is an art gallery. Falling in the same price and comfort category are privately or company-owned *pondok* (private lodges, cottages, or cabins) and tourist guesthouses.

Pastoran
A Catholic priest's residence or parish house. In Outer Island towns you can stay as a guest in the local *pastoran* for a modest payment, which always includes meals. Though the food isn't

the greatest, it's still a tremendous deal: you sit down with the brothers in the evenings and listen to the day's stories. These priests are extremely well-informed about the area and you learn a great deal.

Youth Hostels

Hostels really aren't that widespread or necessary in Indonesia because of the ubiquity of inexpensive hotels. The only legitimate youth hostels in Indonesia are the Bali International Hostel (Jl. Mertasari 19) and Wisma Taruna (Jl. Gedung 17) in Denpasar, the Wisma Delima (Jl. Jaksa 5) in Jakarta, and the Kopo International Youth Hostel (Jl. Raya 502) 70 km south of Jakarta. All offer dorm beds, and, except for Wisma Taruna, a/c rooms.

Modern showcase hostels like those in Jakarta are not really hostels but function essentially as student or youth-group dormitories. They're booked months in advance by Indonesian middle-school students. Protect your valuables in hostels, not only from Indonesians and hostel staff but also from thieving Westerners.

Kost

A family boardinghouse which rents out small cubicles on one floor, usually to female students, *kost* are overseen by an *ibu kost* who is on site at all times. Some *kost* host both male and female students. Found wherever there are secondary or tertiary students. Ask in any *kampung* or at the Dharma Wanita (Women's Center). Best time to find an opening is May or June.

Kost are about the cheapest and safest accommodations in Indonesia. If you share a room, the cost ranges from Rp20,000 to Rp30,000 per month. A private room runs Rp50,000-75,000. Sometimes meals are included, sometimes you pay Rp50,000 per month for two meals per day. Occasionally there's a resident *pembantu* (housekeeper) who does the laundry, washes the floor, and cooks. Laundry runs around Rp10,000 per month.

This environment is ideal for foreign students staying in Indonesia for six months to a year; some *kost putri* accept women for as short a period as one month. Accept that you'll live under certain restraints. First, everybody will

know everything about you. The *ibu*, in particular, will want to know where you are at all times. Her word is law. On weekdays you must be in by 2100, on weekends 2230. Restricted visiting hours. Staying in these student dorms is a crash course in Indonesian culture.

Asrama

Similar to *kost putri*, an *asrama* is a student dormitory, hostel, residence hall, coed dorm, or barracks. You might find spare beds for hire, particularly during school holidays. Or stay there free as a guest of a student.

The designation *asrama* can also mean a detention center. The jail for visa overextenders and narcotics violators on Bali is called Asrama Tahanan Imigrasi.

Pasanggrahan

These are forestry huts, park lodges, or reserve rest houses. *Pasanggrahan* are found primarily in Sumatra, Kalimantan, Sulawesi, and Maluku. There may be several in one locale. Usually quite cheap, sometimes even free. *Pasanggrahan* could also mean a more upscale commercial lodging house, frequently located in remote locales like the mountain resorts of Java.

Hotels

Hotel associations, with government backing, are cracking down on the heretofore loose use of the term, and now prevent anyone from using the "hotel" appellation without meeting certain standards. My litmus test: if the front desk clerk speaks English, you're probably in a hotel.

The tourist industry has devised two official rating systems to grade the services and facilities of Indonesia's hotels. The *melati* jasmine system is applied to standard hotels, while the *bintang* star system rates the more luxurious joints. There are about 50 high-priced international-class *bintang* hotels in Indonesia's big cities, tourist resorts, and provincial capitals. Five-star (*lima bintang*) hotels cost Rp231,000 to Rp357,000 double occupancy. Most feature all the modern conveniences: a/c, coffee shops, continental and Japanese restaurants, swimming pools, tennis courts, shopping complexes. Four- and five-star hotels must maintain a *gamelan* ensemble and a set of *wayang*. An increasing number of hotels offer international di-

LAUNDRY SERVICES

Your hotel will almost always offer laundry service, either in-house or out of house. Always check the per-item price first—it can be really expensive. The hotel could also tack on a service and government tax of 21%, rendering an average load of laundry an astronomical Rp31,500. Even otherwise reasonable hotels overcharge for laundry.

So exit the hotel and find an *ibu* (literally "mother," but figuratively any older woman) who does washing. Ask for the *tukang cuci* (launderer). If you're in the city frequent a Chinese laundry, which will charge according to article. Dry cleaners are found only in Indonesia's metropolitan areas.

Laundry is always ironed after it's washed, no matter how destitute the *kampung* or *losmen*. Allow at least one day of full sunshine to get your clothes back. Since back-lane *ibu* often use cheap soap containing lye and enzymes that can destroy clothes and plastic scrubbing brushes that wear fabric thin, many travelers choose to wash their clothes themselves in the sink, bathtub, or *mandi*. An inexpensive, light nylon clothesline and a few clothespins are smart items to take to Indonesia.

rect dialing (IDD). Hotels like Jakarta's Aryaduta Hyatt, the Jakarta Hilton, and Bali's Kartika Plaza include full-scale gyms, fitness rooms, jacuzzis, and running tracks.

A handful of luxury hotels—like the Amandari and the Four Seasons on Bali—are in a class all their own, off the charts. They feature fully-equipped, self-enclosed compounds, private staffs, sumptuous surroundings, peerless service, and start at Rp525,000 per night. Bali

has the country's swankiest international-class hotels, located mostly within the Sanur/Nusa/Kuta tourist triangle; it even has a Club Med.

For a listing of Indonesia's three-, four-, and five-star deluxe hotels, refer to the "Pacific Hotel Directory" in *Pacific Travel News,* published each June and December, or contact either the Directorate General of Tourism (Jl. Kramat Raya 81, Jakarta) or any Indonesian Tourist Office.

There are also small, efficient, clean, well-managed business hotels all over Indonesia. These offer very good value. Hotels such as the Mutiara (Jl. Malioboro) in Yogyakarta and the even less expensive Nakula Familiar Inn (Jl. Nakula 4) in Denpasar offer better value than the big hotels, with more local flavor and personalized service.

Colonial-Style Hotels
Try to stay in one of the aging Dutch colonial-era hotels while they're still standing. Many retain their distinct glamour and charm, but are slowly turning musty, dank, foul-smelling, and run-down with age.

Refusing to lower their rates and compete with the new generation of hotels, many have gone out of business. Still, the traveler can sometimes find real bargain accommodations in these bygone relics—Rp30,000 for a gigantic suite with anteroom, dressing room, veranda, and huge bath. Indonesians snub these dinosaurs, so a modern annex with a/c rooms and full facilities at exorbitant rates is often found behind or in front of the original hotel.

The best of these splendid art deco era hotels have been completely remodeled and modernized. Historical relics dating from the Sukarno era are the grand old spacious 1960s-style hotels like Jakarta's Hotel Indonesia and the Bali Beach Hotel.

FOOD

Indonesia has one of the world's great cuisines, drawing on influences from around the world. Foreign culinary art is subtly distinguishable in Indonesian cooking, yet each alien ingredient is blended creatively with the islands' own cooking secrets. Indonesia is located at the crossroads of the ancient world, astride the great trade routes between the Middle East and Asia. Wave after wave of traders, adventurers, pirates, and immigrants have been drawn by the riches of these Spice Islands. All brought their native cuisine with them. From India came curries, cucumber, eggplant, and cowpeas. From the Americas, chili, pepper, vanilla, soursop, pawpaw, and pineapple. The Chinese brought the wok and stir-fry, Chinese mustard, and such vegetables as brassica and cabbage. From Arabia arrived Middle Eastern gastronomic techniques and ingredients such as kebab and flavorful goat stews. Peanuts, avocado, pineapple, guava, papaya, tomato, squash, pumpkin, cacao, and soybeans were all introduced by Europeans. Nature and history have conspired to give Indonesia a culinary tradition as varied and seasoned as its thousands of islands and hundreds of ethnic groups.

Yet it's also true that Indonesian food can be mediocre and lacking in variety, even a constant, dreadful carbohydrate overload. After the culinary delights of Thailand, Malaysia, and Vietnam, Indonesia can really bring you down to earth. With the exception of Bali, food does not play a major role in Indonesian culture. In Thailand, as in France, if they're not eating, they're talking about eating; the cuisine is highly refined. It has nothing to do with money—Vietnam is desperately poor, but the food is wonderful. Sumatra's Padang food is excellent, and food on Bali good, but on an island like Flores hunger can eventually force you out. Still, if you know the dishes and spices, you can order good food anywhere.

INGREDIENTS

Travelers should stick to a light diet of rice and fish, which will provide all the protein anyone

needs. A tropical climate calls for a tropical tempo. Lighten up on meat; you don't need to overload on all that fat and protein. Fat keeps you warm; you want the opposite here.

Staples

The basic diet on most of the islands is rice (nasi), lots of it, supplemented with vegetables, a bit of fish, and, once in a while, savory meat and eggs. Anything with the word nasi in front of it means it's prepared or served with rice. All traditional Indonesian food is designed to complement or be complemented by rice. For Indonesians, the whiter the rice, and the more it's been hulled and slipped, the tastier it is. White rice serves as a sharp counterpoint to the spiciness and heat of Indonesian food.

The soybean is the vegetable cow of Asia. A major subsidiary crop in Indonesia, soybeans are grown on wet-rice land after the rice harvest. Because of this wonderful bean, Indonesia's country folk tend to eat more nutritiously than the rich, who gorge themselves on such empty Western status foods as meat, bread, beer, soda pop, and chocolate. Rural people feast on such hearty and organic soybean-based foods as tahu (beancurd), tempe (fermented soybeans), and kecap (soy sauce). They're also fond of coconut candy and cane syrup.

Beef products are consumed mostly by urbanites. Rural consumption of beef is kept in check by the need to maintain buffalo as draught animals and cows as milk producers. Chicken tends to be scrawny and tough in Indonesia, but at least it has flavor. Pork is produced and consumed by the Hindu Balinese, the urban Chinese, and the Torajans. In Islamic Indonesia, pork must be served—if served at all—on a separate table, and never on the same plate with other foods. If you hire a Muslim cook, he won't touch pork or even get near it. Goats, bred all over Indonesia, are the Muslim staff of life. Any dish with the word gulai in it denotes a blend of goat, coconut milk, and spices—the Indonesian curry (kare). Sop kaki kambing is leg of goat soup: other ingredients include goat lung, muscle, intestines, bladder, and chopped penis.

Coconut adds richness to curries and sauces. Indonesians perform wonders with freshly grated coconut, which is first kneaded and sieved, then blended with water. As it cooks, the coconut milk thickens; with the addition of flour or corn starch it becomes a sauce (*santen*). The subtle sweetness of Javanese cooking comes from *santen* (coconut milk), not from sugarcane. The Balinese eschew *santen* except on special occasions.

Spices

Indonesia taught the world the use of exotic spices and herbs. Indonesian cuisine is known for its deliberate combination of contrasting flavors (spicy, sour, sweet, hot) and textures (wet, coarse, spongy, hard). The carefully orchestrated contrast will catch your taste buds by surprise. The most humble, dilapidated *warung* can conjure an array of exquisite foods with flavors, textures, and aromas you never dreamed existed.

Indonesians have developed original gastronomic themes with lemongrass and *laos*, cardamom and chilies, tamarind and turmeric. All find their way into delightful, sometimes scorchingly hot dishes. In complex Javanese dishes, vinegar and tamarind are added to palm sugar to produce a sweet-sour spiciness.

Surprisingly, you seldom come across the spices—nutmeg, pepper, mace, and cloves—that gave the "Spice Islands" their name. Some areas of Indonesia lack spices, like much of Kalimantan and southern Maluku, where food tends to be bland and unappetizing. When traveling through these areas of Indonesia, bring your own dehydrated food, spices, and hot sauce.

Indonesian saffron (*kunyit*) is used to color rice dishes an intense yellow and provide rice with spicy flavoring. *Terasi*, a red-brown fermented shrimp paste with a pungent aroma, is used in small amounts in most sauces. It's considered absolutely essential to a successful *rijstaffel* (smorgasbord).

Salty soy sauce (*kecap asin*) is a necessary adjunct to many Indonesian meals. *Kecap asin* is made by inoculating boiled beans with *Aspergillus oryzae* fungus, then exposing it to sunlight and adding anise, aren, and ginger. There are many kinds of hot chili pastes (*sambal*) invariably made from red chilies, shallots, and tomatoes; the *sambals* from Padang in West Sumatra are some of the hottest in Indonesia. Almost every dish features its own kind of *sambal*. Each Indonesian family makes its differently; the Chinese make theirs differently still.

When in doubt as to whether a dish is spicy-hot, inquire of the waiter *"Pedas atau tidak?"* ("Hot or not?"). Don't get the idea that all Indonesian food is hot. Many dishes are quite mild. Central Java's food is sweet and spicy, while East Java's is salty and hot. Sumatran food is very spicy-hot. If the dish is too hot, squeeze a little lemon with salt over it. A *kretek* cigarette will cool down your throat after a chili burning.

Fish And Seafood

Indonesia offers a staggering amount of fresh seafood: tuna, shrimp, lobster, crab, anchovies, carp, prawns, and sea slugs, all prepared supremely by coastal peoples for Rp3500 to Rp7500 per dish.

Ujung Pandang, the home of the Makassarese and Buginese, has some of the best seafood in Southeast Asia. Try the succulent baked fish (*ikan bakar*), or a huge plate of perfectly prepared prawns in butter and garlic sauce. The mouthwatering freshwater prawns you're served in Samarinda or the Baliem Valley were probably caught that morning; they explode with freshness. *Baronang* is a big fat fish with a great taste and very few bones. Some freshwater fish such as the buttery *belanak* (gray mullet) are bred in compounds; take the bones out, mix with coconut milk and spices, then wrap back in its skin and bake.

The country's rice farmers raise a supplementary fish crop by letting fish loose to spawn in flooded rice fields. Dinner is caught by opening a sluice gate or scooping up fish in a net. *Belut* (eel) are caught at night in the rice fields; buy a good-sized bunch of this crisp delicacy wrapped in newspaper. Sea slugs are another delicacy, a textural, hallucinogenic experience. Cook with chicken or some other kind of meat, and the slugs take on the flavor of the meat. Sea slugs are the magic mushrooms of the ocean.

NATIONAL DISHES

Fried rice (*nasi goreng*) and fried noodles (*mie goreng*) are rice or noodles fried in coconut oil with eggs, meat, tomato, cucumber, shrimp paste, spices, and chilies. Sold at roadside stalls for Rp750-1500, these are among the most popular everyday foods in Indonesia. Each vendor serves up the dish with a special regional or ethnic twist. Both *nasi goreng* and *mie goreng* are common breakfast dishes. If *istimewa* (special) is written after either dish, it means it comes with egg on top.

Probably the world's earliest known barbecue, *sate* consists of bite-sized bits of marinated or basted chicken, beef, mutton, shrimp, or pork skewered on veins of coconut palm, grilled over charcoal, then dipped into a hot sauce made of chilies, spices, and peanuts. The *sate* man comes with his whole kitchen on his shoulders. Listen for the sound of his feet rhythmically hitting the mud. He squats in the gutter and fans the embers of his charcoal brazier until it glows red hot, then turns out sizzling kebab.

Served from pushcarts, *warung, rumah makan,* and restaurants everywhere, *nasi campur* is a filling plate of steamed rice with flavorful beef, chicken, mutton, and/or fish, plus a mixture of eggs and/or vegetables, crisp onions, roasted peanuts, and shredded coconut heaped on top. A thin sauce covers it all. If you're alone, just ask for this classic one-plate version of *nasi padang* cuisine—cheaper than asking for a la carte dishes. Go up to the window and just point at what you want. A good *nasi campur* will set you back a whole Rp1500-4000; it's the best deal in Indonesia.

Soto means thick *santen* has been added to a soup; a breakfast dish. *Sop* is similar to meat and vegetable stew; only water is added. A popular Chinese soup with meatballs is called *bakso*, sold from small pushcarts on the streets and lanes of Indonesia. The liquid could be broth or spiced water, the meatball may consist of meat, fish, shrimp, or pork. *Soto ayam* is a delicious chicken soup flavored with lemongrass and other herbs and spices. Add glass rice noodles, shredded chicken, hard-boiled eggs, chopped shallots, bean sprouts, *emping* (crackers), fresh squeezed lime juice, and *sambal*. *Soto ayam* is often eaten as a main meal with a side plate of *nasi*. A very filling staple in Chinese eateries is *mie kuah*, noodle soup in broth. Vegetarians can order a meatless *mie kuah sayur*.

Rijstaffel (rice table), a sort of Indonesian smorgasbord, is a legacy of the Dutch. In colonial days, a ceremonial *rijstaffel* could include as many as 350 courses. Today, 10-15 courses is the norm. The total meal offers a variety of tastes—some sweet, others spicy, all eaten with steaming hot rice and condiments. Today you can experience a bona fide colonial-style *rijstaffel* at the Oasis (Jl. Raden Saleh 47) in Jakarta as well as in upscale hotels like the Bali Hyatt. Poor man's *rijstaffel* can be sampled in any *nasi padang* restaurant.

The stuffed pancake *martabak,* originally from Arabia, can be hearty enough to qualify as a main course. Also try *apam,* a sweet pancake filled with nuts and brown syrup and sprinkled with sugar. Another widespread nourishing dish is the Chinese *cap cai,* a kind of Indonesian meat and vegetable chop suey. A standard served in "tourist" Chinese joints is *fu yung hai,* a vegetable/meat omelette with sweet and sour sauce.

Krupuk is the Indonesian pretzel, a big, crispy, oversized cracker made from fish flakes, crab claws, shrimp paste, or fruit mixed with rice, dough, or sago flour. *Krupuk* is dried until it looks like thin, hard, colored plastic, then fried in oil. To keep it fresh, the barefoot *krupuk* man carries two huge insulated containers, which look like big milk cans, on a bamboo pole on his shoulders. Indonesians use *krupuk* for bread; some people like to dip it in their tea. *Krupuk* is also used as scoop for curry or *gado-gado.*

Regional Dishes

Indonesians identify very closely with their regional foods and are very pleased if you try them. Food is a tremendous icebreaker, frequently used as a pretense to invite you home. The attitude seems to be: if you like me, you'll like my food. Indonesia's regional specialties are rarely, if ever, found anywhere else. There are foods prepared by isolated tribes and ceremonial foods cooked only on festive occasions. The aboriginal Penan of South Kalimantan eat roast lizard, while a single python can feed a whole village of inland Irianese. The Minangkabau of North Sumatra serve *nasi kunyit* and *singgang ayam* only at weddings or memorial celebrations.

Maize and the root of the cassava plant are staples in the eastern island groups; flour prepared from the pith of the sago palm is the food center in Maluku, Nusatenggara, and West Irian. Cassava, which looks like a long, thin, shriveled

Indonesian
snack wagon

turnip, has a ridiculously low protein count of one percent; a starchy, unappetizing, fibrous mass millions of Indonesians subsist on. Westerners know it in its refined form as tapioca. Sago is sometimes served in highly unusual ways, such as the glue-like *papeda* of Ambon.

Always sample the home cooking in whatever area you find yourself in. In regions such as Minahasa, mice and dog are considered savory delicacies. *Tritis,* a specialty of the Karo of North Sumatra, is partially digested grass taken from a cow's stomach. The Torajans of south-central Sulawesi cook meat or fish in buffalo or pig blood. The Sundanese of West Java specialize in cooked goldfish. The Balinese cook ducks and pigs to perfection, and are very fond of sweet and/or sticky foods made of rice (*lontog* and *ketan*). They also prepare a *sate* from a paste made of chopped turtle meat mixed with coconut milk and spices. Said to be superb but the turtle is an endangered species, so consumption should be discouraged.

EATING VEGETARIAN

An ever popular vegetarian dish is *gado-gado,* which doesn't travel well outside of Jakarta. This is a healthy, warm vegetable salad combining potatoes and other boiled vegetables, a rich peanut sauce, and prawn-and-rice crackers called *krupuk.* Similar to *gado-gado* is tasty *nasi pecel.*

Tofu-based dishes are widespread through the islands. *Tempe,* made by inoculating parboiled soybeans with the *Aspergillus oryzae* fungus, is one of the few plant sources of vitamin B12. Found in the greatest abundance and variety on Java, each small cake is wrapped in shiny pieces of banana leaf. Leaves of bamboo, mangos, papayas, and cassava are often used in cooking main dishes. Coconut, coconut milk, chilies, ginger, and peanuts are popular in Indonesian cooking. To make sure you get your point across, say, *"Saya senang sekali makan sayur-sayuran"* ("I like vegetables very much"); in Padang restaurants point to each dish and ask *"Tanpa daging?"* ("Without meat?").

Bali and Java are the easiest places to secure vegetarian dishes. There are tasty, cheap, and clean vegetarian restaurants in Jakarta (Paradiso 2001, Jl. H. Agus Salim 30) and Medan (Restaurant Vegetarian Indonesia, Jl. Gandhi 63A). On Bali's rural roadsides, you can get freshly steamed vegetables and *lontong* for pennies. The Karos of Brastagi in North Sumatra serve vegetable soups that would earn praise in Seattle's gourmet restaurants. Raw vegetables (*lalap*) are a favorite of the Sundanese of West Java. Anywhere in Indonesia where there are Chinese restaurants—which is everywhere—there are plenty of vegetarian items on the menu. In Outer Island regions like the Baliem Valley of Irian Jaya the sweet potato (*ubi*) is particularly favored.

FRUITS

Discovering the new tastes of inexpensive local fruits, delicately crisp and bursting with flavor, is one of the delights of Indonesian travel. Although you'll find many of the same fruits you encounter in Thailand and Malaysia, there are dozens of varieties available here that are found nowhere else. Fruit stands occupy the busy streets of every Indonesian town and village; local markets offer an even greater variety. Stands selling fruits and/or juice stay open long after most other stalls close down. Price depends on season. To deflect disease, all fresh fruit should be washed and peeled before eating.

There are pineapples (*nanas*), pomelo, melons, and guavas. The delicious mango tastes different on every island; the varieties here are distinct from the rest of Southeast Asia. Jackfruit (*nangka*), an enormous fruit weighing up to 20 kg, is also used in cooking *nasi gudeg*—yellow *nangka* meat cooked in *santen* and served with rice, bits of chicken, and spices. The citrus (*jeruk*) family is also well represented on the islands: tangerines, oranges, grapefruits, lemons, limes. Sweet *jeruk* (oranges) run about Rp1500 per kilo. Lemonade is *air jeruk sitrun*. Also sold everywhere—when in season—are *salak, rambutan*, litchis, breadfruit (*campedak*), papaya, and avocados.

Endemic Fruits

Try splendid local fruit like mangosteen (*manggis*), praised by Queen Victoria and hailed by some as the perfect fruit. The outside is round and purple, the inside like an orange, but creamy and cool. The smelly, infamous *durian*, spiked like a gladiator's weapon, tastes simultaneously like onions and caramel—a fruit much enjoyed by those not put off by its evil aroma. Believed to be an aphrodisiac: an old Malay expression goes, "When the *durians* are down, the *sarung* are up." *Durian* on Java cost as much as Rp5000, but it's often difficult to find a really good one. Sellers seem eager to push rotten *durian* on innocent tourists. Ask your driver or guide to make the selection.

The litchi-like *rambutan* has a prickly rind of a pale rose color. Within this delicacy is a dark green transparent jelly, tasting something like a grape but far more luscious. Don't be alarmed by the *rambutan*'s hairy exterior; this is an easy fruit to love. Gently squeeze open the fruit and enjoy the sweet, translucent flesh. *Salak* is called snake-fruit because of the remarkable pattern of its skin. Carefully peel and enjoy; it's similar in taste to an apple. *Jeruk Bali* is a large pomelo-like grapefruit and *jeruk Garut* are sweet tangerines from the Puncak area south of Jakarta.

The tiny, delicious *blimbing* is another favorite; *gambu* is a cousin of the *blimbing* and equally delectable. The bell-shaped *jambu air*, though tasteless, is an effective thirst-quencher. The *sawo* is shaped like a potato but tastes like a ripe, honey-flavored peach or pear. The unbelievably juicy *zirzak* means "sour sack" in Dutch, and features warty green skin and a lemonish tart taste. Unforgettable. Called soursop or custard apple in the West.

Then there are sweet, gooey, sumptuous fruits like *langsat* and *marquisa*. When you bite into the jelly-like *tuih* fruit, it tastes like sweet, fine coconut milk. You can buy essences of *durian, salak, nangka,* and *zirzak* in the country's supermarkets. They're used in cakes and cookies just like we use vanilla extract.

The Banana Family

Pride of place among all Indonesian fruits must go to the cheap and ubiquitous banana (*pisang*). Indonesia boasts 42 varieties of every shape, flavor, texture, and size, from the tiny fingerlong *pisang tuju* to the half-meter *pisang raja* (king banana), which grows upward instead of down. Some bananas are big and fat and redskinned, some feature edible skins, some are fit only for baby food. There are seedless bananas and bananas with big black seeds, wild bananas, bananas edible only when cooked.

One of the sweetest varieties is the small *pisang mas* (golden banana), with a thin skin and incomparable taste; the leaves are used to wrap rice. *Pisang susu* (milk banana) is not too sweet, just the right size, and tastes wonderful. Bananas are also used frequently to season meats and stews; on Ambon plantains are cut into very small cubes to resemble *nasi goreng* and prepared in the same way. Bananas seldom cost more than Rp500-1000 for a small bunch.

DRINKS

Thirsty foreigners are provided, in most cases, with boiled water at their *losmen,* homestay, or hotel and thus needn't be paranoid about drinking unclean water. Fortunately for visitors and the Indonesian middle class, about 20 brands of commercially produced "mountain spring water" are available in plastic containers. The usual price is Rp1500 for a 1.5 liter bottle and Rp600-800 for 0.5 liters; more expensive if cold. Cheaper on Bali, more expensive on distant Flores. Most Westerners carry bottles of Aqua like security blankets. If you hang onto the empty plastic bottle, you can ask for *air putih* or *teh tawar* at your *losmen* or guesthouse, let the liquid cool a bit, then refill your bottle.

Caffeinated Drinks

About the only drink Indonesians themselves take with meals is China tea (Rp100-500). For sweetened tea, say *"teh gula"*; for unsweetened tea say, *"teh pahit"* or *"teh tawar."* Tea helps stimulate the appetite and digestion and will keep you awake after a heavy lunch. Buy attractive packets of tea on the way to almost any hill station or mountain resort on Java.

Powerful coffee, introduced by the Dutch in 1699, is grown widely on Java, Bali, and Sumatra. Served pitch-black, sweet, thick, and rich, with the grounds floating on top, coffee in most spots costs Rp500-1500 per tall glass. In the markets of Bali, coffee powder (*kopi bubuk*) can go for as little as Rp3000 per kilo. Indonesian *kopi* is sometimes laced with chicory or chocolate. The best Indonesian coffee is cultivated south of Semarang in Central Java.

Native Drinks

Since there are so many mineral- and vitamin-rich natural fruit drinks here, both hot and cold, it makes no sense to drink Fanta or Coca-Cola. Instead, quench your thirst at ice juice stands (*warung es jus*) or carts along the street. These sometimes contain delicious, though overly sweetened, natural drinks like citrus juice (*air jeruk*), *es zirzak,* or the incredible avocado drink *es pokat* (*es avocad* on Bali), made with coffee essence, palm sugar, and condensed milk. Sounds terrible; tastes delicious.

Bajigur is made of coconut milk thickened with rice and sweetened with palm sugar. *Es soda gembira* is like an ice cream soda without the ice cream. Other dessert drinks include glasses of lumpy *es cendol* filled with doughy rice-flour droplets. Anywhere but in Yogyakarta and Solo fresh milk is rare and considered unsafe, so Indonesians use powdered whole milk or cartons of long-life milk. If you order milk for your coffee, it will almost always come as sweet condensed milk or sterilized milk. You can drink coconuts as a form of sterile milk; they contain potassium, are a great source of glucose, and are found everywhere. Almost any boy or man walking by with a *perang* will cut open a coconut for you. He'll then make you a spoon of the same material to scoop out the meat. A young coconut (*kelapa mudah*) is the most refreshing. *Kopyor* is a lighter coconut than the more plentiful *kelapa mudah,* and its subtle, velvety flavor is much in demand.

Alcoholic Drinks

Is it just a happy coincidence that Dutch beer goes so well with Indonesian food? Heineken of Holland taught Indonesians how to brew the country's ubiquitous pilsner-style Bintang lager beer, the best accompaniment to Indonesia's hot, spicy food. Very popular with travelers, it comes in a big 620 cc bottle and costs Rp3000-4000. The Dutch connection continues with Anker, a sweet-tasting beer from Jakarta brewed in cooperation with Holland's Breda Breweries. San Miguel, also brewed in Indonesia, doesn't go down that well, but locally produced Guinness Stout does. Irish whiskey and every brand of hard liquor you can name are served in the bars of Bali's resort areas. Drinks such as whiskey and soda are known here by their English names.

For native brews, mildly alcoholic *tuak* (palm toddy), brewed from various palm sugars a month before consumption, provides you a mellow slow-motion high. In Torajaland, *tuak* is prepared by filling a length of hollow bamboo with palm juice, then burying it for a week to allow fermentation to take place. Very popular in non-Muslim regions of Indonesia. *Brem,* usually home-produced, is rice wine made from glutinous rice and coconut milk. Old *brem* (more than three days old) is sour and contains more alcohol; new *brem* is sweeter and packs less of a kick. Either costs Rp1200-2000 per bottle. A commercial variety, Bali Brem, is also available; Rp3000 per small bottle. *Badek* is another fermented liquor obtained from rice. *Tipple arak* is an insidiously potent distilled rice spirit made from fermented molasses. Tourists like to drink *arak* with Sprite or 7UP.

SNACKS AND DESSERTS

Indonesians love snacks. Smooth and steamy, soft and crunchy leaf-wrapped hors d'oeuvres are sold from carts and markets in every village and town. Varieties of sweets and finger snacks are endless: vivid pink puffed rice; gaily colored rice pastries; luminous green, red, and blue sweets made from cassava; lentil pastes; a vast array of *kue* (cakes); coconut and crunchy peanut cookies; sweet mung-bean soups; sticky banana cakes. *Lemper* is a sweet, glutinous fruit pudding; it's no coincidence the word sounds like *lumpur* (mud). *Kolak* is a sweet coconut broth filled with cassava, banana, and jackfruit. *Kue dadar* are crepes filled with shredded coconut and sweetened with brown sugar. Bananas steamed, deep-fried, or boiled cost about Rp200 each.

Most desserts derive from sticky or glutinous rice. *Ketan* is rice pudding cooked in coconut milk and sugar syrup; *kue lapis* is a layered pudding of rice flour or mungbean flour. *Lontong,* a main ingredient in *gado-gado,* is rice cooked in banana leaves—tastes something like cold Cream of Wheat. *Bubur santen* is rice porridge cooked in palm sugar and coconut milk. After cooking, what sticks to the bottom of the pot is brown, crunchy, and sticky—a paste much coveted by Indonesian children.

Ice cream is available in all the usual flavors, plus *durian,* coconut cream, and litchi. Sweet corn kernel ice cream is another Indonesian treat. Bakeries often specialize in homemade ice cream, or you can stick with locally manufactured brands like Peters and Flippers.

A common *kampung* dessert is *es campur*—the Indonesian equivalent of the banana split. A typical *es campur* consists of sweet syrup water, milk, gelatin, sweet bread cubes, *tape* (tapioca), and various other coagulated pulpy substances in snake-like curls, balls, pellets, or mash, in colors ranging from bright green to chartreuse. *Es campur* costs anywhere from

Rp500 in a small *warung* to Rp1500 from a restaurant concessionaire.

During Hari Raya, pastries, homemade cookies, and sweetmeats are offered to guests. On Asjura, a Muslim holiday, you may be confronted with *bubur asjura,* a rice porridge of peanuts, eggs, and sweet beans. Akin to eating sweet slimy worms.

VENDORS AND VENUES

In Indonesia, food comes to you. Meals and snacks are pushed through the windows of trains and buses, served piping hot on top of volcanos. The streets fill each morning and afternoon with walking restaurants. Beverage vendors push carts full of poisonous-looking concoctions. Ask around for the different *kaki lima* vendors (meaning "five feet"—the vendor plus the three legs of the cart). They deliver chickens, streaky bacon, crab, and frog legs. Traditional food trolleys (*gerobak makanan*) sell hot food virtually everywhere. Housewives, servants, and children who buy from *kaki lima* bring their own dishes to be filled. One of the most nutritious meals around is *bungkusan,* containing rice, side dishes, and condiments, skewered with a short sharp stick or palm leaf rib.

Warung

When hunger strikes, follow your nose to the rows of glowing hissing gas lamps illuminating Indonesia's night markets (*pasar malam*), located on the perimeters of bus, minibus, and train stations. Here you'll discover a collection of smoky ramshackle mobile *warung*. By far the best food for the money is served in these makeshift food-stalls—the poor person's restaurant. *Warung* are especially active at night, though they also do a brisk business at midday, serving the "Businessman's Lunch" of Indonesia. *Warung* dispense pure Indonesian cuisine and usually specialize in *soto, sate, nasi goreng, mie goreng, lontong,* or *cap cai.* Also available are such snacks as *krupuk, pisang goreng* (fried bananas), thinly sliced sweet potatoes, and fried *tempe.*

If sitting in one *warung,* you can still order from others nearby. Choose one with good food and a friendly atmosphere, then walk around to the various neighboring *warung* and order different food items: 10 sticks of *sate* from one tent, *sop sayur* from another, *gado-gado* from a third, all the while pointing back toward your table. If you don't speak Bahasa Indonesia, simply point to anything that looks good. After eating and before paying, ask how much, and make sure it's figured correctly. If you eat Rp6300 worth of roadside food you're an absolute glutton.

Warung that serve only coffee (*kopi*) and biscuits (*kue*) are the exclusive domain of menfolk who sit around and gossip, read the newspaper, or listen to the radio. Men often stop in the local *warung* to exchange news. *Warung* are important sources of information and make excellent language labs for learning Indonesian. These coffee shops also sell domestic supplies such as kerosene, batteries, buttons, medicine, dried fish, and salt. At night a well-lit, convivial *warung* could be the only happening place in the whole village.

Rumah Makan

Meaning "eating house," a *rumah makan* is a full-service Indonesian restaurant with a complete menu offering dishes cooked to order. *Rumah makan* also typically offer a wide selection of precooked foods wrapped to go. Menus can number 12 or more pages, but this doesn't always mean all ingredients are always on hand. It only means the staff can cook the dishes if provided the ingredients, and that such a complete menu is expected of them. Rather than listen to interminable replies of *"Sudah habis"* and *"Ma'af, tidak ada"* ("Sorry, we're out"), just ask outright *"Sedia makanan apa?"* ("What do you have?"), or, even better, *"Apa keistimewaan di rumah makan ini?"* ("What's the specialty of the house?").

Nasi Padang

The Minangkabau region of West Sumatra produces some of the best cooks in Indonesia, and it is in their *nasi padang* restaurants where the visitor will find the tastiest, spiciest Indonesian food. If you're in a hurry, *nasi padang* restaurants offer the quickest service of any eatery; they're also some of the most expensive. A *rumah makan padang* is sure to occupy the main street of any town or village in the country, no matter the size.

You're first brought a cold napkin, a free glass of hot tea, a lit candle to keep the flies away, and your eating utensils, semi-sterilized in a glass of hot water. No menu is needed. All you have to do to start the unending procession of food is utter the simple word *"nasi,"* at the same time pointing to the window filled with great basins and platters piled high with spicy-hot food. Waiters will then descend with up to 10 small dishes balanced precariously on each arm, setting them all on the table before you. You pay only for those dishes you eat, so get the prices right before diving in. Vegetable dishes are always cheapest—meat dishes can really run up the tab. The sauce from each is free so you can just order a lot of rice, eat only a couple of dishes, and use the sauce from the rest; this is what the Indonesians do. Afterwards, you're given a fingerbowl and wet napkin to clean yourself.

Stick with the old standbys—fried fish (*ikan goreng*), curries, fresh vegetables (*sayur-sayuran*). Or try something more exotic—spiced prawns, calf's brains, steamed sweet potato leaves. West Sumatrans are especially fond of curries, eggs with chilies, and a great variety of *kambing* (goat), *ayam* (chicken), and *lembu* (beef) dishes. *Rendang*, a wonderfully flavored beef and sauce dish, requires a long time to cook and is tantalizingly seasoned with ginger, garlic, hot chilies, coconut, lemongrass, and coriander.

Chinese Restaurants

Most major towns, cities, and tourist areas feature Chinese restaurants, often called *restoran*. These are generally more expensive than Indonesian-style eating places but offer more variety and culinary sophistication. A typical Chinese-style restaurant charges about Rp7000-9000 per person minimum for an average meal, including beverage. Indonesian-Chinese food can be similar to classic Indonesian food, and is just as individualized. Each restaurant includes its own family recipes. Although influenced by Indonesia, the food comes from a different culinary tradition. A Chinese restaurant, for example, uses mustard greens (*sawi*) frequently, and is the only place where you can indulge in pork (*babi*), crab (*kepiting*), frog legs (*kodok*), and springrolls (*lumpia*). During Ramadan, Chinese *restoran* are often the only places you can grab a meal in the daylight hours.

Tourist Restaurants

A menu written in English is a menu meant for tourists. Prices are invariably higher than in a *rumah makan.* In tourist restaurants you'll also probably be charged for hot tea (*teh pahit*)— Rp200 for hot scented water. A typical tourist restaurant offers uninspired Western-style dishes, Western music, and ridiculous prices. Don't expect the food to come in the sequence ordered either. Indonesians don't understand the correct order of courses in Western food—soup first, then salad, then the main course, then dessert. The only way to make sure your dishes arrive in the right sequence is to order dishes separately or write them down in the proper order.

As a rule, Indonesians aren't really able to pull off passable Western food. French and Italian dishes, particularly, suffer here. Though the atmosphere may be superb and the music excellent, the majority of tourist restaurants prepare bland, tasteless food. The spicy hotness and "funny-tasting" spices are reduced or eliminated.

Restaurants or *warung* catering exclusively to tourists are not always bad value, however. Take, for example, the amazing fish dinners in Padangbai, East Bali, or the noteworthy vegetarian pizza at Bu Sis and other tourist restaurants in Yogyakarta's Pasar Kembang area. Where there are large concentrations of expatriates—Sentani in Irian Jaya, Balikpapan in East Kalimantan—you'll find numerous restaurants with steaks, hamburgers, and other foreign dishes.

You can usually project the prices in a restaurant by the cost of its *nasi goreng*. If that dish is overpriced, other dishes will be too. Too many Western-style restaurants charge up to Rp3000 for a *nasi goreng* or *mie goreng* without *udang*, *telor*, or *daging*—just fried white rice with microscopic bits of vegetables. For more authentic food stick to the *warung* and *rumah makan* on side streets.

ORDERING AND EATING

Unlike the chopstick users of Japan and China, Indonesians like their rice in a mound, surrounded or heaped with other cooked food. In the country, *warung* meals are often served cold on banana leaves. If you want a dish served hot, say *"Yang masih panas."*

Learn the ingredients that go into various dishes before you order in a restaurant. *Soto babat telor*, for example, is a soup prepared with cow intestines. Quite good if you like that sort of thing, but if you don't, understanding the words *soto* (soup) and *telor* (egg) is obviously not enough. Whenever you order any meat dish, specify whether you want the flesh (*daging*) or the innards (*isi perut* or *babat*).

Indonesians prefer not to eat with a spoon and fork. Since fingers taste better than metal, most prefer to eat with their fingers. Rice is scooped up with the fingers, molded deftly into a neat ball, then placed on the tongue without a grain out of place. Always eat with the right hand; the left hand is used as toilet paper.

HEALTH

Traveling in Indonesia can be medically safe. In fact, you could return in better health than before you left. Don't be preoccupied with sanitation and prevention; it'll spoil your trip. The traveler is more likely to get hurt or killed riding a motorcycle on Bali the first week in Indonesia (snuffs out about three tourists per month) than contract some hideous tropical disease.

Take common-sense precautions, but avoid paranoia ("How were these dishes washed? Was this tea boiled long enough?"). Even in swank hotels hygienic techniques aren't always de rigueur, so if it's your turn to get sick, you're gonna get sick. And know that once you suffer through your first bout with diarrhea or prickly heat, there's seldom a recurrence.

Prevention
If you take care with personal hygiene, use caution in what you eat and drink, and get plenty of rest, you'll avoid most health problems while in Indonesia. Most illnesses among travelers are resistance diseases, a result of poor health, eating badly, overindulgence, or overexposure to heat and sun. Upon arrival, first become acclimated to the tropical environment: maintain adequate fluid and salt levels, avoid fatigue, dress light. Jet lag may change your sleeping patterns and eating habits, so schedule early extra rest.

Information about what and where the risks are and how to avoid them is your best protection. If you hear there's a cholera epidemic in Cirebon, don't go to Cirebon. You don't walk barefoot in the tropics because several different types of infections—such as *cutaneous larva migrans,* which can enter the body through the skin—thrive in the tropics. If you try to swim to another island, understand that it may be farther than it looks and the channel currents very strong.

Have a complete dental checkup before your trip. Travelers who've spent months traveling in the Outer Islands should get a complete medical checkup once home. And don't forget to continue taking your malaria pills for two weeks once you've reached home.

Insurance
Check whether your health insurance entitles you to reimbursement of medical expenses incurred overseas. If not, obtain special health or travel insurance for as little as $3 per day. Read the small print—some policies available in Australia, for example, do not pay damages on motorcycle injuries unless the insured possesses a current Australian motorcycle license. Evidently, insurance companies were taken to the cleaners by people who obtained an easy-to-get Balinese license and then attempted motorbiking for the first time. One of the best travel health insurance outfits is Travel Guard Internationale (1-800-826-1300) with a 24-hour Emergency Claims Service.

IMMUNIZATIONS

First take a look at the latest World Immunization Chart from the International Association for Medical Assistance to Travelers (IAMAT), 417 Centre St., Lewiston, NY 14092, or find out from an official vaccine center which immunizations are currently required for travel to Indonesia. Then double-check with the Indonesian embassy.

Get your immunizations over a couple of months rather than in a single rush shortly before you leave. The whole series doesn't have to be repeated but you should receive boosters for any immunization for which the effective period has elapsed. Tetanus, polio, and yellow-fever vaccines are very effective; others, such as cholera, are not. Most Westerners received polio immunizations as children and need only a booster. You should be protected against tetanus, which is more prevalent in the tropics. A yellow-fever vaccination is only required for those arriving within six days after leaving or transiting a yellow fever locale. Typhoid and paratyphoid vaccinations are optional but advisable.

Consult your doctor concerning immunizations for children, which may include triple antigen (DPT), polio, measles, rubella (German measles), and mumps. You should get a measles shot if you've never had one, or were vaccinated against it before 1969. A gamma-

(CONTINUED ON PAGE 88)

TRAVELER'S MEDICAL KIT

A medical kit takes on extra importance if you're planning trips to remote Outer Islands like Kalimantan and Irian Jaya. The contents of the kit listed herein will prepare you for almost any common problem.

Many of the following supplies can be bought in Indonesia after your arrival, so don't pack too many medicines. You can also obtain prescriptions easier and cheaper in Indonesia than in the West. Generic names are used whenever possible.

When traveling, tablets are always more convenient than liquids. Keep your medicines in small hard-to-break plastic bottles. Label each with a full description of its purpose and dosage. If you suffer from any medical problem—allergies, reactions to medications—bring a letter from your doctor and a written medical history to ensure proper treatment in an emergency.

Analgesics
Bring aspirin to relieve minor pain, lower temperature, and provide symptomatic relief of colds and respiratory infections. Codeine is a more powerful drug used for the relief of pain and cough.

Antibiotics
If in remote areas carry antibiotics (penicillin or tetracycline) for emergencies (skin or urinary-tract infections), though they can cause some complex side effects. Antibiotics break down your resistance, so use only after you've exhausted every other means of treatment. Don't take more than one antibiotic at a time, and don't stop the full course of treatment just because the symptoms seem to have receded. The usual course is at least seven days. Many different varieties exist: tetracycline, penicillin G tablets, penicillin V tablets, ampicillin, amoxicillin, and broad-spectrum cephalexin capsules. If you're allergic to penicillin, don't take amoxicillin or ampicillin.

Antidiarrheals
Highly concentrated tincture of opium or less-concentrated camphorated tincture of opium are superb remedies against diarrhea; paregoric or charcoal tablets are also effective. Brand-name drugs include Stop Trot in Britain and Kaopectate in the United States. The active ingredient in both is powdered psyllium husks; these may be mixed with water, juice, or soda. Papaya seeds are also said to work well. More powerful medications such as Lo-

motil or Imodium (Streptotriad in U.K.) should be used sparingly. Lomotil, a prescription drug, also helps to ease the abdominal cramps, nausea, chills, and low-grade fever that are frequently byproducts of diarrhea. Any antidiarrhea drug is contraindicated if the diarrhea is persistent, associated with high fever, or accompanied by blood in stools, jaundice, or drowsiness. Enterovioform, sold over the counter virtually everywhere in Indonesia, has been found to cause neurological damage.

Antihistamines
Eases and soothes the debilitating symptoms of allergies, hay fever, colds, vomiting, irritating skin conditions, insect bites, and rashes. The cream is also effective for jellyfish stings.

Antiseptics
Handy for minor cuts and scrapes—Indonesian mercurochrome doesn't even sting. Savlon is a great antiseptic cream available in the U.K., called Cetavlon in the rest of the world. Outstanding ointments to use against tropical ulcers include F.G. Ointment, Neosporin, and Polysporin. Antibiotic Cicatran Cream or Betadine work well for cuts and mosquito bites gone septic. Sepsotupf from Germany heals small cuts by morning. Bacitracin is a very good bacterial ointment available in Indonesia.

Clove Oil
For toothaches. Cotton wool soaked in *arak* serves the same function in relieving tooth and gum pain.

First Aid
Assorted bandages are light, take up little room, and make fantastic gifts out in the villages. More practical, however, are the ectoplast strips that can be cut to a variety of sizes and shapes. Bring a roll of sterile cotton gauze and a roll of adhesive surgical tape, elastic bandages for strains and sprains, and moleskin felt padding with adhesive backing for prevention of blisters (adhesive tape can be used as a substitute). Also pack disinfectant, soap, thermometer in hard case, tweezers, scissors, safety pins, needles, a sterile razor blade, and plastic dropper bottles for your tincture of opium. For rinsing out cuts or tooth and gum infections, use sodium bicarbonate, which is like a toothpaste, soap, and deodorant all in one. Rinsing with hydrogen peroxide three times a day is equally effective.

Insect Repellent

Take some preventatives against insects. Roll-ons or sprays are not readily available. Take Off! or Cutter's on expeditions to heavy mosquito areas, such as river trips in South Sumatra and Kalimantan, or backpacking trips to remote or inaccessible areas of the Outer Islands. Otherwise go into any *apotik* and buy Minyak Sereh mosquito repellent. Really works, but doesn't last as long as Off!. Many people swear by Avon's Skin So Soft lotion; mosquitos seem to hate the scent. Use Kwell (not available in Indonesia) or Pyrinate shampoo to combat head lice and scabies.

Laxatives

Metamucil, a mild laxative with natural dietary fiber, aids digestion and combats constipation, but is bulky to carry. A natural fiber laxative in pill form would be better.

Leech Repellent

Dibutyl Phthalate applied to the skin is effective for four hours. If sprayed on your clothes, it's effective for up to two weeks. Skin coated in a mixture of tobacco juice and water repels leeches, as do clothes soaked in a concentrated salt solution. Many insect repellents are also effective. If you put soap on your skin, leeches will slip off. Others believe citrus juice works as well.

Motion Sickness Remedies

For motion sickness and nausea, take one to two antihistamine tablets such as meclizine (Antivert). Nonprescription Dramamine can also help prevent and relieve discomfort, but could cause drowsiness three to four hours later. Paspertin (metoclopramid hydrochloride) relaxes the stomach. Chewing ginger also helps. If you don't have a preferred brand, try chlorpheniramine maleate tablets. In Canada, Gravol is effective; in the U.K., try Sea-Legs. Chew glucose-based tablets; they are also effective if you need energy. Transdermal scopolamine (prescription required in the U.S.) is another medicine that prevents motion sickness.

Odds And Ends

Also take antifungal powder, calamine lotion to soothe itching, and eyedrops for infections (choloromycetin available in North America, Albucid in the U.K., both in liquid or ointment). Include water-purification tablets such as tetraglycine hydroperiodide, iodine in various forms, or Potable-Aqua. Chlorine compounds such as Halazone are ineffective against amoebas. Chloroquine or chloroquine-sub-stitute prevents malaria attacks. Meat tenderizer works outstandingly well for stings of all kinds. If you regularly use them, don't forget skin cleanser, birth control pills, cotton tipped swabs, dandruff medication, foot powder, laxative, rubbing alcohol, sleeping pills, and nasal spray (phenylephrine HCL, one-half percent, or xylomethaciline solution) or nasal decongestant for sinuses and stuffed noses. Women should bring tampons in plastic (not paper); tampons are almost impossible to find in Indonesia. Also bring protein pills (concentrated soybean), particularly if trekking. If taking long treks, take along a cheap bottle of baby powder for rubbing rashes. Bring dry powder to dust infections; wet ointments draw flies.

Pepto-Bismol

In case of stomach trouble, use Pepto-Bismol or antacids. Sodium bicarbonate will also neutralize acidity.

Sunscreens

Expensive in Indonesia, so bring your own. Paba or zinc oxide, an opaque ointment, is widely available. Reapply after heavy sweating or swimming. Hat and sunglasses are critically important items to carry in the tropics. Use a lip salve like Chap Stick or Carmex. Comfrey cream also works well.

Tiger Balm

Relieves itching from insect bites; soothes headaches and muscle pains if massaged vigorously into the skin. The red variety is the strongest.

Tinactin Or Micatin

Available in the U.S. without a prescription. Used to treat prickly heat, jock itch, athlete's foot, and ringworm. Native herbal skin treatments include *bajamaduri* (spiny spinach) for treating burns, and Cap Pagoda Cream for tropical ulcers. Desenex also works well.

Topical Eye Antibiotics

Very useful for treatment of eye irritations and conjunctivitis. Avoid penicillin products, as you're more likely to suffer an allergic reaction to penicillin when it's applied to the skin. Good antibiotic eye creams include those containing bacitracin, neomycin, or polymixin.

Vitamins

Vitamin tablets are fiendishly expensive and of dubious pedigree in Indonesia. The country's fruits and vegetables should instead provide most of the

(CONTINUED ON NEXT PAGE)

TRAVELER'S MEDICAL KIT
(CONTINUED)

vitamins you need. Because of the lack of dairy products, however, take iron and calcium. An iron supplement is especially important for women; if you feel run down or have trouble with menstruation, take one ferrous sulfate tablet (200 mg) per day or eat liver in *nasi padang* restaurants until you feel better. If you eat too much rice, you'll lack Vitamin B. Take Vitamins B12 and B6; they work as catalysts for each other. Beriberi is a severe thiamine (B1) deficiency that often appears in the tropics among people who subsist for the most part on polished white rice.

globulin injection will give you about six months' protection against hepatitis; this shot, however, only protects against infectious hepatitis and not serum hepatitis, which is spread by using unclean hypodermic needles. Rabies vaccinations are unnecessary unless you plan to play with bats, hire on as a zookeeper at a wild rodent park, or work as a temple guard on Bali.

Vaccination Centers

Since no vaccinations or inoculations are at present required except for visitors arriving from infected areas, you won't even be asked for your Buku Kuning ("Yellow Booklet"). This is the International Certificate of Vaccination, which records all immunizations and vaccinations. The booklet is available from designated vaccination centers around the world or direct from your doctor.

In the U.S., many local public-health departments give shots for free, charging only a small fee for the stamp in your vaccination certificate. In Australia, contact the Commonwealth Office Health Centers. In Indonesia itself, cholera vaccinations are dispensed at Jakarta's Sukarno/ Hatta Airport in Cengkareng, though the cheapest place to get immunized in Jakarta is Dinas Kesehatan, Jl. Kesehatan 10. Foreigners can get shots at their embassy health unit, set up for use by embassy staff and contract employees, and staffed by foreign service doctors.

FOOD AND DRINK

Food- and water-borne infections are perhaps the greatest threats to the traveler in the tropics. Bacterial infections (typhoid, paratyphoid, cholera, salmonella, shigella), infectious hepatitis, and such parasitic infections as guineaworm, bilharzia, bacillary dysentery, amoebic dysentery, worms, and giardiasis can all be transmitted by contaminated food, water, or ice.

As dairy products are often made with untreated water and unpasteurized milk, they're outstanding media for the breeding of many pathogenic bacteria. It's therefore advisable not to drink local fresh milk or eat ice cream sold by street vendors. Stick to dairy products labeled as pasteurized. Diamond, Peters, and Campina are quality brand-name ice cream products sold locally. Fresh milk should always be boiled; drink it quickly before germs immediately begin breeding again. Use instead powdered whole milk (Dancow brand), cartons of long-life milk, or sweetened condensed milk (Indomilk). Yogurt, relatively more acidic, is considered safer, and is sometimes used as a remedy for an upset stomach.

All vegetables and fruit eaten raw should be thoroughly washed, rinsed, or peeled before eating. Vegetables used in raw salads may have been fertilized with "night soil" (human excrement), and contaminating organisms may remain on the vegetable surface. Lettuce and cabbage are particularly difficult to clean. Salad dressings—particularly mayonnaise-based products—may be a source of bacterial infection.

All meat and fish should be cooked well if you wish to avoid worms. Eat seafood while fresh; never carry shellfish in the hot sun and always cook thoroughly. Cold meats provide an excellent medium for the multiplication of bacteria, particularly in the heat and humidity of the tropics. If you have to eat meat, stick to well-cooked meals served hot. Stay away from rare meats and avoid cold buffets.

Contaminated Water

One of the biggest culprits in transmitting disease. Diseases transmitted by water include cholera, typhoid fever, bacillary dysentery, and giardiasis. The water in most tropical countries must be considered unsafe to drink because of poor sewage disposal and improperly treated water supplies.

By Indonesian law, water and ice served in restaurants must be boiled first. Of course, not everyone obeys the law. Avoid ice cubes unless they've been made from boiled water. Hot beverages carry fewer disease-causing organisms than cold beverages. Beer or soda water are about the only non-sweet beverages to drink. Though it contains a load of sugar, Fanta is safe for children to drink—it hydrates the body, and contains no caffeine. Plastic bottled water (Agua) and water you have treated yourself are the only waters you should consider safe. Noncarbonated bottled drinks may or may not be safe to drink. Use carbonated, bottled, or boiled water for brushing your teeth. In restaurants unboiled water is often used for washing dishes and cooking certain foods. The freezing of water does not kill organisms, nor does alcohol in a drink.

Several practical methods make water safe to drink. If boiled briskly for 10 minutes, all the major disease organisms will die. Chemical sterilization, such as water-purification tablets like Halazone, is popular, but watch for side effects. Also, be forewarned that chlorine-based sterilization has proven effective against neither amoeba nor protozoan organisms, including giardiasis. Another chlorine-based method involves adding laundry bleach until a slight chlorine odor is detectable in the water. Let stand 30 minutes before drinking. Adding 5-10 drops of tincture of iodine per liter also works well; let stand for 20 minutes.

Salt

When your body sweats you lose salt, so you should add more to your diet. Jet lag and fatigue can be caused by salt deprivation. Loss of body fluids as a result of diarrhea or dysentery also calls for increased salt consumption. Salt tablets are not really necessary, but after heavy physical exercise you might pour a little extra salt on your food. If trekking into remote areas of Indonesia, take along ordinary sea salt. A mixture of salt and water serves as a mild antiseptic. If you have a sore throat gargle with this solution.

EXHAUSTION AND HEAT EXPOSURE

Travelers need to adjust to a climate that is extreme by temperate zone standards, possibly producing fatigue and loss of appetite. Acclimating to the enervating heat and humidity of Indonesia, it must be said, could take weeks. First, slow down the pace. Don't overdo; no one else does. Get plenty of rest. Follow the Indonesian custom of *tidur siang* (napping) sometime between 1200 and 1600, the hottest part of the day. Drink increased amounts of water with fresh lemon and lime juice, and make sure there's salt in your diet. Restrict alcohol and smoking. Avoid rich, fatty foods. Don't eat too much fruit; this can cause stomachaches and diarrhea.

Adapt yourself to the sun gradually. Actually, it's healthy to get out in the sun's torrid heat for a while each day; it has a purifying, acclimating effect. Use sunblock, zinc oxide, or coconut oil as protection. Small children should be especially careful. Wear loose cotton clothing, light in color and weight. Don a floppy hat. If you carry an umbrella, as Indonesians do, you'll walk in the shade all the time.

DIARRHEA

Travelers' diarrhea constitutes 90% of travel health problems, affecting about half of the five million visitors to the tropics each year. Diarrhea often begins within a few days of arrival in a tropical climate, as travelers are exposed to organisms they're unused to. Many stomach troubles like diarrhea are often a result of sudden changes in climate, food, and water, rather than poor hygiene during food preparation. This is equally true for travelers from the tropics visiting the West. Emotional upsets or the stress of travel can also play a role in simple diarrhea.

People frequently refer to acute diarrhea as dysentery but this is a misnomer. Diarrhea is much more common than dysentery. Dysentery is a serious disease characterized by blood, mucous, and/or pus in the stool. If you have severe diarrhea that lasts more than two to three days, accompanied by fever, black-colored stools, or painful stomach cramps, you may have amoebic or bacillary dysentery. Seek medical attention, as this disease can cause severe damage to the intestines.

Diarrhea is generally a self-limiting disease lasting only a few days. If it persists for more than five days, see a doctor. If you're experiencing persistent watery diarrheal illness (eliminating more than a liter an hour) within a week after

(CONTINUED ON PAGE 92)

AILMENTS, IRRITANTS, AND PLAGUES

Aches And Pains
Indonesians think it ludicrous that Westerners take aspirin for a headache when the only sensible thing to do is get a massage. During a massage, Indonesians use exotic body lotions composed of many ingredients—scented wood, hibiscus seeds, eucalyptus oil. The Danis of Irian Jaya tie smoked charmed grasses around the neck; some Indonesians wear little white tapes containing an anesthetic on their temples. There's also a green paste to smear on the forehead to cure headaches. The *krok* treatment consists of rubbing I Ching coins on the muscles in combination with eucalyptus oil to produce a friction rash so the pores can open to let out the pain, heat, and evil. Sweet-tasting *kayumanis* (cinnamon) is chewed for throat ailments. *Kesambi* oil is used to enrich and add body to the hair.

Cuts And Bites
Since bacteria breed so quickly in this climate, the tiniest cut or sore can soon become ugly, a festering tropical ulcer requiring prolonged antibiotic treatment. Most tropical ulcers and sores are due to mosquito bites. At night use mosquito coils, the electric "mosquito mat" device, or netting. Wear long sleeves and trousers at sundown, apply insect repellent after dark, and cover legs and wear protective footgear when walking through tall grass or on coral reefs.

Whenever the skin is broken, it requires more attention than in colder climes. Clean the opening with soap and water, apply antiseptic, and cover well with a bandage. Reclean the cut and change the bandage every day, more often if it gets damp or wet. If it's a large cut or wound, use a nonstick sterile gauze dressing. Use scotch tape if you lack surgical tape. If you can't have the wound sutured, at least try to join the skin edges or use butterfly plastic strips.

As long as you have open wounds, swimming in the sea is also best avoided. If you can't resist the beautiful beaches, wash the wound and apply a new dressing after leaving the ocean. If infection sets in—inflammation, itching, and pain after two days—soak the wound in hot water for 15 minutes, cover with a sterile dressing, then apply or take antibiotics.

Ear Infections
People with ear infections usually contract them from snorkeling and/or swimming. In most cases the infections are severe, keeping you out of the water for weeks. Take penicillin orally every six hours until the infection has been absent for two days. Ingest a systemic decongestant to reduce swelling around the opening of the ear's eustachian tube. A hot water bottle applied to the ear, aspirin, and warm olive oil inserted into the ear will reduce pain.

Food Poisoning
Food poisoning lasts about three days. Little can be done for this awful illness. Prevent it by avoiding raw foods not adequately refrigerated, including shellfish, salads, mayonnaise, and custard-filled pastries served under unsanitary conditions. Treatment consists of lots of bed rest and plenty of clear, slightly sweetened fluids for rehydration.

Fungal Infections
These include athlete's foot and ringworm. Avoid by using only your own towel, wearing flip-flops to bathe, choosing open sandals, and eschewing nylon or other synthetic garments. Ringworm is not really a worm, but a fungal infection that produces a red-ringed patch, usually on the trunk, accompanied by itching, pain, and scaling. When cured it leaves a small red spot. Within a year, new skin appears. Dab on a Chinese medicine called Three-Leg-Brand Ringworm Cure. One application is enough. Go into a Chinese apothecary and point at the fungus—they'll know what you need. Or use a benzoic acid compound. Tinaderm, available in the U.K., is a cream applied at night. In the U.S., try Micatin, a broad spectrum antifungal. Selsun Blue dandruff shampoo can also be used in the treatment of fungal infections. First wet the area, rub shampoo on like soap, leave for 5-10 minutes, then rinse off with water. Treat in this manner two to three times. In Indonesia, buy the wide-spectrum antifungal Mycolog. You need the cream or lotion, or powder in case infected areas get soaked with sweat. With vaginal infections, fungus is caused by a bacterial imbalance. Yogurt is a bacterial culture, so yogurt on a tampon neutralizes the fungus and soothes the itch.

Infections And Skin Ailments
In a tropical climate, you need to be more careful about personal hygiene. Bacteria thrive in hot humid areas, causing an increase in the variety of infections. Bacteria can enter the body through wounds or insect bites, especially those you scratch. Extra care should be taken in drying yourself, particularly

around the ears and crotch area, so rashes won't develop. Corn starch, baby powder, or arrowroot powder help keep skin dry. A highly effective lotion called Caladine can be bought in Indonesia and is highly recommended.

Cutaneous larva migrans is caused most frequently by the larval form of dog and cat hookworms and is picked up by direct skin contact with contaminated soil. These larvae penetrate the skin. They don't grow to maturity but travel a tortuous path just under the skin, leaving a tiny trail behind them, progressing about two to five cm a day. The presence of the larvae often produces severe itching at the site; secondary infection, signaled by scratching, may be a problem.

Leeches

Usually a problem only in the damp, cool rainforests or at higher elevations, leeches wait insidiously at the sides of trails, cling to trees, or hang from leaves overhead along dense tracks used by deer and wild pigs. They smell human perspiration, then wait to fall onto your hair, beard, or neck, push their suckers through boot eyelets, squeeze under your belt, even penetrate the anus. They also attack at night while you're sleeping.

Clothes only offer a catchhold for leeches. You might try walking barefoot and half naked like the Dayaks of Kalimantan, who cover their bodies with mud. Also effective is a skin application of tobacco juice and water. If you're naked you can flick leeches off as you see them. Usually leeches can't be felt until they drop off saturated with blood; sometimes you feel a trickle of blood or a warm sticky spot under your clothes or inside your boot. If they've attached themselves, either hold a lighted match or cigarette to the things or apply salt or iodine. Then stick on a cigarette paper to help stop the flow of blood; leeches inject an anticoagulant.

Plants

Don't be too quick to blame insects when you return from a hike with your hand or leg swollen or tingling with a rash. A great variety of plants harbor toxic chemicals in their leaves or sprout nasty nettles. Merely brushing against them results in nagging skin irritations. Some people are more sensitive than others. Exercise caution with garden and house plants, particularly when children are around; some are poisonous if eaten. Carry an antihistamine cream to soothe severe skin irritations. Rainforest streams can be acidic and laden with plant toxins, especially in the dry season, causing rashes after bathing. If the water is rust-colored, beware—it's probably

loaded with tannins and other goodies leached from the soil and trees.

Prickly Heat

An intensely irritating skin rash quite frequently encountered in the tropics, usually soon after arrival. Red pimples or blisters break out on areas of the body that are always moist from sweating: under a tight-fitting belt, in the armpits or crotch area, behind the knees. You can reduce your chances of contracting prickly heat by wearing loose-fitting cotton clothing and avoiding synthetic materials that don't breathe. To treat, splash cold water on the rash to cool it, dab dry, then apply a dusting powder. Calamine lotion can be used to soothe the skin. In severe cases, when the rash keeps you awake at night, use an antiseptic powder and even an antihistamine. Cut down on your use of soap.

Sea Creature Injuries

Avoid all contact with cone shells in reefs and shallow water, as these inject a dangerous venom. Handle only with forceps. Don't ever put live cone shells in your pocket. While swimming in the ocean, always wear enclosed shoes or flippers covering the whole foot. Never walk in bare feet on coral as stonefish inflict nasty injuries and live coral also hurts the skin, cutting or poisoning. For coral cuts, wash out the coral with fresh water and soap within the first hour of injury. To prevent infection, once the wound is clean keep it covered for five to seven days. Change the dressing daily.

Remove single urchin spikes carefully. Multiple small spikes cannot be removed. To destroy the toxin and relieve the pain, soak the injured area in hot water or vinegar for 10-15 minutes. If stung by a Portuguese man-of-war, wash the area off gently with alcohol or whiskey. Heat is not recommended. Apply meat tenderizer paste for 10-15 minutes. Large areas of hives or difficulty in breathing indicates a serious emergency that requires medical treatment within 15-20 minutes.

Snakebite

Of Indonesia's 450 species of snakes, only five are considered dangerously poisonous. Cobras you should treat with great caution, since they're venomous and can even be found in cities. Other common poisonous snakes include the *krait,* easily recognized by alternate black-and-white bands.

Snakebite treatment consists of convincing the victim to lie down in an attitude of complete rest. Don't wash or suck the bite site. Cutting should be avoided; the snake can often be identified by the

(CONTINUED ON NEXT PAGE)

AILMENTS, IRRITANTS, AND PLAGUES
(CONTINUED)

shape of the wound. Washing and sucking also doesn't prevent the blood from spreading. Instead, immobilize the limb and apply firm pressure over the afflicted area with a roller bandage. Do not apply a tourniquet. If bitten on the foot or ankle, bind one leg to the other for support; if bitten on the hand or wrist, use an improvised splint. If the victim becomes unconscious, turn the person on the side and keep airways clear. Alert the nearest hospital immediately, while keeping the victim as calm and as immobile as possible.

Venereal Disease

Indonesia is very receptive to the AIDS infection because almost all favorable conditions which can facilitate transmission exist—high-risk sexual behavior, poverty, high prevalence of sexually transmitted diseases, a tourist industry, and seaports visited by sailors from AIDS-infected countries. The Indonesian government is finally, slowly fessing up to its AIDS problem, though the number of cases is certainly much larger than it would dare to admit. It's estimated there are now 16,000 people in Indonesia infected with the virus. If the government does not fully implement its AIDS prevention program, now floundering because of lack of funding, Indonesia could suffer an AIDS epidemic similar to the ones in India, Thailand, and Burma.

Everyone should practice precautions (use condoms, avoid dirty or shared hypodermic needles) to avoid this deadly disease, particularly in centers with large prostitute populations. Condoms provide reasonable protection; however, condoms sold in Indonesia are not to be trusted, so travel there with a good supply. Nine out of 15 brands tested in 1992 by a Dutch consumer organization failed to meet minimal standards of effectiveness and durability. One brand had a surprising number of holes.

Gonorrhea has spread to most ports of the archipelago. Syphilis is much less common. If you do get gonorrhea, it's only serious if ignored or unrecognized. Don't try treating it yourself; you need a full lab test in a private clinic or public hospital plus two injections and a course of ampicillin. A private hospital or one run by a church group could charge you around Rp25,000 for this routine and simple treatment.

Worms

Worm (*cacing*) infestations are common in warm countries like Indonesia where rainfall is plentiful. Hookworm eggs are passed into the soil in human or animal feces. Eggs hatch in the soil and the larval form enters the bloodstream when the skin comes in contact with the contaminated soil. Severe itching and burning may occur at the site where the parasite enters the body, often the area between the toes. Roundworm infection may occur when you eat vegetables fertilized with human feces. The eggs hatch in the stomach, then the larvae enters the blood and may migrate to affect other organs of the body. You may display no obvious symptoms, or the worms may cause abdominal discomfort, diarrhea, or sometimes a generalized rash. Pinworm infestations are likewise common. Their eggs are often swallowed, then hatch in the stomach, where they enter the intestines and ultimately to the anus where they lay their sticky, white eggs. Pinworms (also called threadworms), about a half-cm long, are easy to detect in the area around the anus.

Roundworms, hookworms, and pinworms are common infections easily spread, so all members of a traveling group should simultaneously take worm medicine. To prevent worms, wear footwear. One extremely effective nonprescription antiworm medicine available in Indonesia is Combantrin (one two-pill treatment, Rp2500). Stool lab exams are widely available, even in remote areas.

leaving an epidemic area, it could be cholera, and you might require intravenous feeding.

Prevention

Take antibiotics to treat diarrhea, not prevent it. Don't overconsume fruits, especially during December and January. Even the Balinese contract the infamous "Bali belly" during this season. Avoid all obvious sources of contaminated food and drink. Before you consider eating in a *warung* or restaurant, look closely at the faces and hands of the cooks and people serving you. They also eat the food they sell. If their faces reflect ill health, their fingernails are dirty, or their establishment unkempt and unsanitary, walk on by.

Diet

When diarrhea strikes, you lose a considerable amount of fluid and salt. These must be replenished immediately by drinking lots of fluids (but no alcohol or strong coffee). Take in clear fluids such as water, weak tea, juice, clear soup, broth, or soda that has lost its carbonation. The very best liquid is an oral rehydration solution, available in pharmacies everywhere. Experienced travelers in remote areas often carry their own special preparation: a teaspoon of salt, one-half teaspoon baking soda, four teaspoons cream of tartar, and six teaspoons sugar. Add this to a liter of water. You can prepare the dry mixture ahead of time and pack it along in case you need it.

When recovering from diarrhea, gradually add such plain foods as biscuits, boiled rice, bread, and boiled eggs to your diet. Indonesians, if they eat at all, drink *jamu* (an herbal medicinal tea) and eat the young *jambu* fruit and plain rice. Bananas are good because they're bland and contain the binding agent pectin. Pawpaw fruit contains digestive enzymes, and is easily digested. Avoid fatty or spicy foods while under treatment, and add milk products last. Often, after a serious diarrhea attack, your body is dehydrated and you may experience painful muscular contractions in the stomach. Fruit juice or cola with a teaspoon of salt will counteract this.

Medicine

Against mild dysentery or fever, try 10 drops of tincture of opium in a small amount of water, up to five times daily. Or 10 papaya or pumpkin seeds a day. Another native cure involves eating the skin of the papaya or swallowing small brown pills made from papaya skin; no constipation afterwards. Active charcoal tablets are dirt cheap. They absorb the toxins in your bowels so cramps disappear and your body gets a chance to rid itself of the bacteria/virae naturally. This only works, though, if you have the time, and are in proper shape.

An over-the-counter drug sold in Indonesia that clears up diarrhea is Diatabs. If you believe in white man's medicine, and if your immune system can handle it, a well-tried and effective remedy is codeine-phosphate, available only by prescription. One ounce of Pepto-Bismol liquid taken every 30 minutes provides symptomatic relief for most people with diarrhea. Isogel is a natural vegetable material that soothes and regulates the stomach. In the stronger stuff, Lomotil comes in the form of minuscule white

tablets. The A-Bomb of diarrheatic medicines, Lomotil should only be used for a day or two; it can potentially lock in the infection. Lomotil usually completely stops bowel movements for two or more days. Imodium (Arret in Britain) is one of the best non-antibiotic treatments for diarrhea. Milder than Lomotil, it allows you to at least continue to function. Enterovioform and Mexaform are dangerous—can cause eye and nerve damage—and should be avoided. Remember that many of these remedies only relieve the symptoms and do not actually cure the disease. Diarrhea could be a symptom of a wide variety of maladies. Don't use these medicines if you have high fever or chills, or persistent or bloody diarrhea.

MEDICAL TREATMENT IN INDONESIA

Doctors And Dentists

Although doctors in Indonesia charge only Rp5000-10,000 per visit, they can make some big mistakes. They often pretend to know what they don't. To make up for a dearth of diagnostic skills, they tend to prescribe standard recipes of antibiotics, antihistamines, tranquilizers, and vitamins, figuring this should cover just about any affliction. Also, no matter what your malady, an Indonesian doctor is going to stick you with a needle.

Try to find a Chinese doctor in a mid- or fair-sized Indonesian city. The proprietor of any hotel or *losmen* can usually come up with the name of a reliable and reasonably priced sawbones or two. If you feel language will be a problem, get the names of English-, German-, or French-speaking doctors from your respective embassy or consulate. Many foreign physicians serve as house doctors in four- and five-star hotels. Although there are English-speaking doctors, there are no foreign doctors with private practices in Indonesia. The government no longer issues work permits to foreign physicians.

Routine dental care such as cleaning and fillings can be performed in all the main cities. Locate a good *dokter gigi* (dentist) through your embassy or consulate. Complicated root-canal therapy, surgery, or bridge construction and repair is often referred to specialists in Singapore. No certified orthodontists work in Jakarta. Dental floss is hard to find, so bring an ample supply.

SERIOUS DISEASES

Bilharzia (Schistosomiasis)

Although you can catch bilharzia by drinking infected water, you're more likely to be infected swimming in still or slow-moving fresh water. Tiny snails breed in the water and serve as hosts to parasitic worms, or "flukes," which penetrate the skin. If in doubt, rub off the water with a towel right after bathing because evidence indicates the worms burrow into the skin only after the infected water evaporates. Symptoms: blood in urine, diarrhea, blood and mucous in the stools, general feeling of ill health.

Cholera

Among travelers who stay in popular tourist accommodations and avoid potentially contaminated food and water, the risk of cholera is very small. It would be really bad luck if a traveler contracted it—there have been only nine confirmed cases among all U.S. travelers in the last 17 years. The ultimate preventative is to eat only cooked foods which are still hot, and drink only carbonated bottled soft drinks or beer, and boiled or safely treated water. The cholera vaccine is only about 40% effective and can't be relied upon.

Dengue Fever

Although travelers run a low risk of contracting this mosquito-borne, haemorrhagic fever, take precautions against mosquito bites. Symptoms include sudden chills, headaches, muscle and joint aches, swollen lymph nodes, a pale pink facial rash, and a fever as high as 104° F. Treat by staying in bed and drinking rehydration liquids. Take Tylenol for headache and muscle ache. Don't take aspirin.

Hepatitis

Exercise the same precautions in avoiding this disease as in preventing dysentery and diarrhea. Unsanitary eating utensils and unwashed salads and fruits are prime suspects. Hepatitis is a debilitating liver disease which turns the skin and the whites of the eyes yellow, the feces whitish, and the urine deep orange or brown. These symptoms—as well as sleepiness, nausea, depression, and a dramatically diminished appetite—appear around three weeks after infection. See a doctor. Don't drink alcohol, use tobacco, or take antibiotics while under treatment. Though it doesn't prevent the disease, a gammaglobulin shot beforehand ameliorates the symptoms.

Malaria

This disease strikes more than 150 million people worldwide each year and causes more than a million deaths. Malaria is an acute and sometimes chronic infectious disease caused by protozoan parasites within red blood cells. A malarial infection results in various derangements of the digestive and nervous systems. The parasite is transmitted to humans by the bite of the female anopheles mosquito. Symptoms include high fever, headaches and body aches, sweating and shivering, with progressive anemia and splenic enlargement.

A vicious form of cerebral malaria, Falciparum, which attacks the brain, is unfortunately found in Indonesia. The first symptom is a violent headache; the victim can be dead in six hours. Mefloquine is one antidote against this killer strain. In some areas, such as East Kalimantan and Irian Jaya, some malarial strains have developed immunity to chloroquine. Consult your physician to make sure your malaria suppressant is effective against all strains of malaria. One option is to supplement a weekly dose of 300 mg chloroquine with 100 mg of proguanil taken daily.

Call the Centers for Disease Control's (CDC) travelers' health information hotline, tel. (404) 332-4559, before leaving home. The malarial season in Indonesia lasts all year and the whole country is affected below 1,200 meters in altitude, though Jakarta, Surabaya, and surroundings are without risk. Malaria has greatly decreased on Java but is still found on the Outer Islands.

In areas of Indonesia where malaria and other insect-borne diseases are endemic, sleep in a room with screened windows, keep well-covered after dusk, and use insect repellents, mosquito nets, and electric mats or burning coils. For the average tourist entering a malarial zone, the mainstay of protection is Larium, taken once weekly. A prescription of 20 tablets costs a devilish $77, but Larium is state-of-the-art protection. It's essential to take your malarial suppressant two weeks before arrival and for four weeks after leaving. If you take your medicine faithfully, you most likely won't be stricken. Just remember that no antimalarial is 100% effective.

People who contract malaria should get to a doctor or hospital quickly for an injection that will cure if applied in time. Otherwise victims are subject to recurrent bouts of malaria. Pregnant women should consult a doctor before taking any malaria prophylactic.

Jakartan optometrists do satisfactory lens-work, but take an extra pair of glasses or contact lenses, your lens prescription, and contact lens cleaning and storage fluids.

Hospitals

If you're seriously ill, go to Jakarta, Semarang, Bandung, Surabaya, or Medan—major cities with the best-equipped hospitals and 24-hour emergency service. Very possibly the best medical facility in all of Indonesia is S.O.S. Medica (tel. 021-750-6001 for emergencies) in Jakarta. For treatment of the most serious illnesses, medical evacuation to Singapore may be required.

Jakarta has Indonesia's best medical services. Your first choice for emergencies should be St. Carolus Hospital, Jl. Salemba Raya 41, Menteng, tel. 858-0091 or Pertamina, Jl. Kyai Maja 43, Kebayoran Baru, tel. 707-211. Particularly good for cardiac cases is Dr. Cipto Mangunkusumo ICCU, Jl. Diponegoro 69, Menteng, tel. 334-636. Sumber Waras, Jl. Kyai Tapa, Grogol, tel. 596-011 also has a sound reputation, as do Pondok Indah, Jl. Metro Dua, Kava UE, tel. 769-7525, and Setia Mitra, Jl. Fatmawati 80-82, Cilandak, tel. 769-6000.

With the exception of Jakarta, hospital equipment—especially in the provinces—is generally pretty rustic. A doctor may not even be in attendance and the staff may be trained only in first aid. It really helps if you know someone. In a provincial capital, it might be necessary to ask the assistance of the local Department of Health, Dinas Kesehatan Propinsi. In a regency capital, ask for Dinas Kesehatan Kabupaten. In many remote areas, the only treatment available is at small, foreign-supported missionary clinics or crowded, poorly outfitted government health centers, employing medicos who are overworked and underqualified. Bali's general hospital in Sanglah offers really substandard medical services; malpractice is virtually a plague. Balinese doctors stitch you up with what resembles thick string. There's not a single X-ray machine on the entire island. The best hospital on Sumatra, run by missionaries with English-speaking staff, is the Immanuel Hospital on Jl. Sudirman in Bukittinggi, West Sumatra.

Hospitals are reluctant to bill—it's usually cash on the line, or at least half payment in advance. The hospital will not file an insurance claim but will give you all the information necessary for you to do so. Fees may include meals, though by Indonesian custom families supplement these with food from home. Relatives even supply medicine and, in some cases, equipment like wheelchairs and portable potties. Many Indonesian hospitals have no buzzer system for summoning nurses, so relatives sleep beside the bed to provide round-the-clock attention. Hospitals can be very noisy, resembling a crowded hotel more than the recuperative morgues common in the West.

If you've been struck by a *bemo,* a clinic won't take you—only a hospital can accept emergency cases. In some areas, you're hours away from medical treatment. On Samosir Island in the middle of Lake Toba (North Sumatra), the only contact to the mainland—and the nearest hospital—is by radio. Pregnant women should consider delivering in one of Jakarta's maternity hospitals.

Pharmacies

You can buy most medicines in Indonesian pharmacies without a prescription. Most international-standard hotels contain pharmacies, and the state-owned pharmaceutical company Kimia Farma maintains outlets in midsized towns and cities. In smaller nonchain pharmacies, feel free to bargain. Many U.S. medications are available and are only slightly less expensive than in the West. Because brand names may differ, it helps to know a medicine's generic name. If you can't read Indonesian, be sure to ask the pharmacist to explain the proper dosage, which might be different from what you're accustomed to. The pharmaceutical directory *Iso Indonesia* (Rp9000) provides an explanation of the nature and dosage of available drugs; it's also available in English.

If you require a particular medicine over a long period of time—birth control pills, vitamins, blood pressure medication—you'd better bring your own supply. Keep all medicines out of reach of Indonesians; pills are like candy to them.

Jamu

The great Dutch botanist Rumphius (1628-1702) was one of the first Westerners to recognize the curative powers of *jamu* in his remarkable 1741 work *The Ambonese Herbal.* These over-counter herbal medicines are derived from the forests of Indonesia—hidden pharmacies of potent medicines in the form of plants, grasses, minerals, fungi, roots, barks, mammals, birds, and reptiles. They come in the form of pills, capsules, powders, beans, peas, flat seeds, and leaves.

Today you see tricolored *jamu* stalls in the markets, painted like barber poles with row upon row of small packages, jars, and bottles lining the shelves. No doctor's prescription required. Explain your problem to the vendor and he'll know what you'll need. The *jamu* manufacturer Portret Nyonya Meneer publishes a very useful *List of Jamu* which explains uses in English. Follow the dosage directions on the packet or bottle. *Jamu* is cheap, about Rp300-500 per packet; the "super" is served with an egg, two kinds of wine, a cup of sweet tea, and a piece of candy, all for Rp2500-4000.

There are hundreds of different *jamu,* one for every conceivable malady. Women over 40 drink a special *jamu* to keep themselves from getting too thin. Jelok Temu is given to year-old babies for strength. Jantung fortifies the heart. Lular paste, made from rice mixed with pulverized bark and flowers, slows the wrinkling and aging process. Mangir is a yellow powder put on the skin to make it clear, fragrant, and refined. Ginjal treats an inflamed appendix, making an operation unnecessary. Kumis Kucing (cat whiskers) cures urinary tract infections. Beras Kencur peps you up. Other *jamu* treat colds, tightness or dizziness in the head, runny nose, bronchitis, flu, and "starry eyes." There are anticough herbs and herbs for sore bones, backaches, and listlessness. There are men's tonics to increase strength and aphrodisiac *jamu* to increase sex appeal and fertility. Strong. Pa is the trademark for medicinal capsules that increase male potency, extracted from the *pasak bumi* root of central Borneo. There's even a special *jamu* for *becak* drivers and others who perform extreme physical labor, as well as herbs to strengthen and increase the health of hard-working women. If women, especially mothers with many children, take "Magic Formula No. 125," they'll find their husbands more considerate. If you're tired or depressed, take a 40-day course of the antidepressant Colasan, which will really blast you out of whatever's hanging you up.

Dukun

The Indonesian folk doctor. Long-established opponents of Western medicine, these barefoot doctors have used locally made remedies and treatments for thousands of years. Though most *dukun* medicine has never been laboratory tested, many *dukun* remedies have a sound scientific basis in modern medicine—*dukun,* for instance, were the first to use quinine to cure malaria. Whenever one of these old men die, it's akin to the loss of an entire medical library.

Great numbers of Indonesia's (mostly rural) people place their faith in the *dukun.* For the villager he's cheap and on the spot—they'll visit him before a hospital or clinic. In the cities you'll often see *dukun* standing or squatting in parks or street corners, surrounded by a crowd, shouting out the wondrous properties of medicines spread out on blankets before them. *Dukun* often receive no consultation fee but derive income from the sale of herbs and potions only. It's believed some *dukun* are men of supernatural powers, containing the souls of dead people who talk through them, often in tongues or Old Javanese. Some are witch doctors who exorcise evil spirits from houses and heal illnesses by faith. They claim to be able to cure people who've been secretly poisoned or purge them of spells cast by less powerful *dukun.*

These native medicos believe mind rules over matter; for psychosomatic sicknesses they dispense psychosomatic cures. Secret Islamic sayings and prayers are written on pieces of paper, then dunked in a glass of water. After downing the liquid the patient is cured. *Dukun* can also improve a client's sex appeal. A "diamond blown onto the lips" by a *dukun* will give his customer an irresistible smile. A great many *dukun* are also quacks.

COMFORT

The visitor is engaged in an unremitting effort to stay comfortable. In Indonesia, the battle never ends against fried food, sugar, MSG, noxious cigarette smoke, noise, the heat, insecticide spray, over-air-conditioned rooms, pestering kids, and pickpockets.

Do what Indonesians do to maintain comfort. When relaxing they wear cool *sarung* and *kain,* ideal for this climate. Chemical fabrics are too

DEALING WITH MONKEYS AND OTHER VERMIN

If feeding wild monkeys, always look out for the dominant male. He should be given food first to avoid fighting. When you smile at monkeys, never show your teeth—in monkeydom this is considered an aggressive gesture. Because of scorpions, take care collecting wood or coconuts. Look first. In low-priced accommodations, check the underside of mattresses for bedbugs. You won't get any sleep with these beasties about unless you change rooms or change mattresses. If you lay your mattress out in strong sunlight, bedbugs will vacate it. Don't leave food open in your room but seal in plastic containers. Rats can chew through backpack canvas.

hot and sticky, so just wear drip-dry, loose-fitting, light-colored cotton clothes. If caught in a torrential downpour, there's no need to change clothes. The sun and heat from your body will dry out your clothing quickly.

If your room is damp, clammy, and dark, air out your bedding the next morning on a line in the sterilizing sun; Indonesians do. You can get another day from a sweaty shirt or blouse simply by hanging it out all day in the scorching Indonesian sun, making it fragrant and wearable again. When you're too hot, drink water or hot tea. Beards can be quite itchy in the heat, and they scare Indonesian children.

At night Indonesians of all ages love to cuddle a skinny, sausage-shaped bolster, the *bantal guling* (Dutch wife), which looks like a long, soft punching bag. Lying lengthwise on the bed, this pillow absorbs sweat and delightfully fits the contours of arms and legs. If a *bantal guling* isn't available, use a piece of cloth such as a *sarung* for absorbing sweat from delicate areas.

In cheap hotels keep mosquitos at bay by moving your bed under a fan or by using mosquito coils (*obat nyamuk*), which are quite effective, a little nauseating, slightly dangerous (you hear of mattresses burning), and available anywhere for Rp800 for a box of five. Quite repugnant is the practice of spraying insecticide all over your room and under your bed. This problem is easily remedied by simply telling the person armed with the sprayer "*Tak usah, terimah kasih*" ("Thank you, but it's not necessary"). Electrically powered anti-mosquito devices, known as *mosquito mat,* are much better and not as toxic; the whole setup (device, small sealed packages of tabs or mats) costs around Rp12,000.

Few travelers use mosquito nets (*kelambu*) while sleeping, yet you can buy them in both single or family sizes for a song. Nylon nets cost Rp8000 for a single, Rp12,000 for a double; cotton are Rp15,000 and Rp20,000 respectively. Cotton is more comfortable and cooler than nylon but is also heavier. They weigh only 100-200 grams. Take a double net because singles are only about 1.25 by 0.7 meters. If you buy one with long enough strings, you can put it up practically anywhere. Makes sleeping in the tropics a breeze.

Take a *mandi* as frequently as necessary to stay cool and grunge-free. Use a dipper to throw cold water over your red-hot skin. When staying in a hotel with a *bak mandi* outside the room, don't go into the bath fully clothed. Just wrap a towel around you and take in shampoo, soap, scrub-brush, and the like. If you bring in clothes, they may get wet, as water is flung with abandon over walls, floors, and ceilings. The happy sound of splashing *mandi* water is heard throughout the day. It's a great boon to travelers in Indonesia that *bak mandi* are often found in airports, train and bus stations, and restaurants the length of the land.

IMMIGRATION AND CUSTOMS

For many nationalities, tourist visas are no longer required to enter Indonesia. Tourists and those delegates attending conventions and conferences receive a "tourist pass" or "entry stamp" upon arrival, a stamp in your passport that allows you to stay up to two months anywhere in Indonesia. As long as they exit and enter through certain air- and seaports, nationals of 37 countries do not need a visa. Visitors from other countries can obtain a tourist visa from any Indonesian embassy or consulate; two photos are required, together with a small fee. All visitors must possess a passport valid for at least six months after arriving in Indonesia.

A tourist must possess an onward ticket by plane or boat out of Indonesia, or a letter from an air carrier, shipping or cruise company, or travel agency confirming the purchase of those tickets. If you fly into Kupang without a return air ticket to Australia, the Indonesian authorities want to see A$1000 dollars. Of course, sometimes *imigrasi* don't bother to ask, often the case in Biak and Batam.

Don't lose the white arrival/departure card you receive with your entry stamp. If you do lose it, go to the nearest immigration office and obtain a replacement. Don't wait until your departure date to inform immigration officials it's lost. The two-month tourist pass cannot be extended. If you want to stay longer you must leave Indonesia, then reenter.

Restrictions

If you have an entry pass in Indonesia, it's impossible to change the status of your visa unless you do so outside of Indonesia. Apply for other types of visas months (years) in advance in your country of origin. Citizens of Israel and Portugal may not enter Indonesia on their passports. Businesspeople from the former Soviet Union and other countries of eastern Europe are granted a one-month, nonextendable visa that allows them to travel freely within the country. Visitors with a Hong Kong Certificate of Identity may obtain a 30-day group travel visa from the Indonesian consulate in Hong Kong. You must enter and exit Indonesia in Medan, Jakarta, or Denpasar, and all tour details must be arranged through a travel agent.

Immigration officials reserve the right to deny entry to any visitor who, in their opinion, is not properly dressed or groomed, lacks the proper funds, or, in their words, "may endanger the country's security, peace, and stability or the public health and morals." These unfortunate undesirables will receive a transit visa that allows them to stay at the airport until the first available flight out.

VISA TYPES

Tourists entering through designated sea- and airports do not need visas, but if you enter via other points or have a reason to stay in Indonesia longer than two months there are several other stay permits available. A business visa, for example, can be obtained on application; extensions are granted at the discretion of authorities in any of Indonesia's 74 immigration offices. In these offices, the prices for visas are standardized. A fixed price list is usually posted on the walls so you know exactly what you should pay. For God's sake wear a clean shirt, and don't try to bribe an immigration official.

Probably the best place to get visas approved is right in the heart of the beast—Jakarta. To accommodate all the extra stamps required for special visas, when you apply for your passport try to get additional pages. In the U.S., ask for a businessperson's passport.

If you stay over three months in Indonesia on any visa, you must register as an alien, pay Rp1500 plus Rp400 for two forms, and be fingerprinted. After residing in Indonesia six months, any foreign resident wishing to leave the country must obtain an exit permit and pay a foreign fiscal tax of Rp250,000. This tax constitutes an advance payment of income tax. Only the diplomatic corps, members of international aid organizations, airline personnel, and government-sponsored people are exempt.

Visitor's Visa

Unfortunately, this type of visa isn't granted as much as it used to be. You must either have a legitimate reason to travel (relatives in Indonesia? study a martial art? practice meditation?),

SELECTED INDONESIAN CONSULATES ABROAD

Australia

Indonesian Consulate General, Beulah Park S.A., Adelaide 5067, tel. (08) 318-108

Consulate of The Republic of Indonesia, 22, Coronation Drive, Stuart Park, Darwin-NT 0801, tel. (089) 819-352

Consulate of The Republic of Indonesia, third floor, 52 Albert Road, South Melbourne, Victoria 3205, tel. (03) 690-7811

Indonesian Consulate, Judd Street South Perth, Western Australia 6151, tel. (09) 367-1178

Indonesian Consulate General, 236-238 Marcubra Road, Marcubra, New South Wales 2035, tel. (02) 344-9933

Belgium

Indonesian Consulate General, Suikerul 5 Bus No. 9, 2000 Antwerp, tel. (031) 3225-6136

Canada

Indonesian Consulate, 425 University Avenue ninth floor, Toronto Ontario M5G 1T6, tel. (416) 591-6461

Indonesian Consulate, 1455 W. Georgia Street, second floor, Vancouver, B.C. V6G 2T3, tel. (604) 682-8855

France

Consulate D'Indonesie, 25 Boulevard Carmagnole, 13008 Marseille, tel. 9171-3435

Germany

Indonesian Consulate General, Eplanade 7-9, 0-1100 Berlin, tel. (030) 472-2002

Indonesian Consulate General, Berliner Alle 2, Post Fach 9140, Duesseldorf, tel. (0211) 353-081

Indonesian Consulate General, Bebellallee 15, 2000 Hamburg 60, tel. (040) 512-071

Indonesian Consulate, Widermayer Strasse 24d-8000, Muenchen 22, tel. (089) 294-609

Hong Kong

Indonesian Consulate General, 127-129 Leighton Road, 6-8 Koswick St. Entrance, tel. (5) 2890-4421

Malaysia

Indonesian Consulate, 467 Jalan Burma, P.O. Box 502, 10350 Penang, tel. (04) 374-686

Spain

Indonesian Consulate General, Rambia Estudios 119, Apartado 18, Barcelona-2, tel. 317-1900

United States Of America

Indonesian Consulate General, Two Illinois Center, 233 North Michigan Ave. Suite 1422, Chicago, IL 60601, tel. (312) 938-0101

Indonesian Consulate, Pri Tower 733 Bishop Street, P.O. Box 3379 Honolulu, HI 96842, tel. (808) 524-4300

Indonesian Consulate General, 3457 Wilshire Blvd., Los Angeles, CA 90010, tel. (213) 383-5126

Indonesian Consulate General, 5 East 68th Street, New York, NY, 10021, tel. (212) 879-0600

Consulate of The Republic of Indonesia, 1111 Columbus Avenue, San Francisco, CA 94133, tel. (415) 474-9571

---

or be involved in an accredited education and culture study program. You must apply in advance in your country of origin and display a letter of invitation from an influential sponsor or guarantor in Indonesia—a government official, high-ranking military officer, respected non-Chinese business owner, sometimes even another Westerner. Visitor's visas are easier to obtain in remote embassies and consulates like Kota Kinabalu, Seoul, or Vientianne, where they're not used to dealing with many tourists and may just hand one over in less than 24 hours for US$3.

Visitor's visas are normally given for a four- or five-week initial stay but can be extended up to five times for one or more month's duration each time, for a total of six months. Don't stay the full six months or the government will hit you with the dreaded foreign fiscal tax. Extensions are granted at the sole discretion of *kantor imigrasi* personnel, and each could mean a two-day bureaucratic hassle. Each extension costs Rp10,000, but for the first extension you must pay an additional Rp30,000 "landing fee" (some European nationalities excluded). Reserve lots of room in your passport as each extension oc-

SELECTED DIPLOMATIC OFFICES IN INDONESIA

Australia: 15 Jl. M.H. Thamrin, tel. (021) 323-109

Belgium: Wisma BCA, 15th floor, Jl. Jend. Sudirman Kav. 22-23, Jakarta, tel. (021) 578-0510

Denmark: Wisma Metropolitan, 16th floor, 29 Jl. Jend. Sudirman, Jakarta Selatan, tel. (021) 516-565

France: 22 Jl. Lembang, Jakarta, tel. (021) 365-301

Germany: 217 Jl. S. Parman, Medan, tel. (061) 324-073

Great Britain: 75 Jl. M.H. Thamrin, Jakarta, tel. (021) 330-904

Japan: 24 Jl. M.H. Thamrin, Jakarta, tel. (021) 324-308

Malaysia: 6 Jl. Dr. Cipto, Medan, tel. (061) 517-150

Netherlands: Royal Netherlands Embassy, Jl. H.R. Rasuna Said Kav. S-3, Kuningan, tel. (021) 511-515

New Zealand: 41 Jl. Diponegoro, Menteng, Jakarta, P.O. Box 2439 DKT

Singapore: 3 Jl. Tengku Daud, Medan, tel. (061) 513-134

Sweden: 2 Jl. Hang Jebat, Medan, tel. (061) 511-017

Switzerland: Swiss Restaurant, Legian Kelod Kuta, P.O. Box 2035, Kuta 80361, Denpasar, tel. (0361) 51735

United States of America: 5 Jl. Merdeka Selatan, Jakarta, tel. (021) 360-360

had to see that official in the first place. Apply early, because it might take as little as two days or as long as three weeks to obtain an extension for a visitor's visa, and you might have to return four or more times. *Imigrasi* appreciates it if you bring an Indonesian friend, as they hate to speak English. It gets more difficult for stays beyond three months; small offices refuse to handle extensions of this duration. You may need to be fingerprinted and fill out additional forms. Your sponsor may have to write new letters. When you've used up your six-month limit, the words "Final Extension" are stamped in your passport.

It's generally easier for Europeans to obtain visitor's visa extensions than it is for North Americans or Australians. The latter are processed with the most prejudice because the Australian government makes it difficult for Indonesians to enter Australia and remain there for any length of time. Dutch travelers are given a lot of slack because of nostalgic historical/cultural ties between the two countries. Indonesians seem to go out of their way to show the Dutch they hold no grudge. Dutch travelers have an even better chance if the *imigrasi* officer speaks Dutch.

Business Visa

A business visa, available at Indonesian consulates, allows a stay of up to 30 days and can be extended to three months. Single entry costs Rp11,550. Submit forms in duplicate with two photos, plus a letter in duplicate from a business firm or employer stating the purpose of your visit and providing financial guarantees. If you're a writer, journalist, or photographer, don't say so.

Under certain circumstances, this type of visa might be easier to obtain than a visitor's visa. A business manager or firm owner must vouch for the fact that you're carrying out some service for the company in Indonesia. Some foreigners, in order to export handicrafts and textiles, start into business with Indonesians, then have "the company" sponsor them. Patience, a little knowledge of Indonesian, good manners, and a friendly approach go a long way. For a businessperson who intends to remain in Indonesia less than six weeks, it makes more sense to enter Indonesia with a tourist pass.

cupies a full page. To apply, you'll need your sponsor's extension request letter, sponsor's ID card copy, the application for visa extension, and crossed fingers. You also need a good measure of serenity—even a saint would lose patience with the *imigrasi* people. Typical is when they ask you to wait a few minutes to see an official. An hour later, you're told the man will be in his meeting until 1400, the time the office closes. Then comes the oft-heard "come back tomorrow." Finally, it turns out you never

PORTS OF ENTRY AND DEPARTURE

Official air and sea entry points change frequently. If you enter Indonesia at any other point, you're required to obtain a proper visa beforehand and will receive only 28 days upon arrival. If you enter Indonesia overland from Papua New Guinea, or take a boat from the southern Philippines to East Kalimantan, you're entering Indonesia illegally. If caught, Indonesian immigration officials may put you in jail or send you right back.

However, these policies seem to change constantly, subject to bureaucratic caprice. You sometimes get the impression regulations are dreamed up on the spot. For example, every Indonesian embassy and consulate in the world insists you need a permit from Jakarta to travel in the interior of Irian Jaya. This is a myth. At Jayapura's police station, permits (*surat jalan*) for the interior are issued routinely while you wait. Your guide can secure a *surat jalan* for you and your party if you give him money for the fee (Rp2000) and four passport photos per person.

OVERSTAYING AND REENTRY

It's possible to get an extension over your 60-day maximum stay to meet a ship or plane. *Imigrasi* routinely grants a three-day overstay, particularly if you're leaving by ship. For a longer overstay, the only legitimate excuse is you've lost your passport or are in the hospital or can bring a note from a doctor or hospital verifying a medical problem.

If you know you're going to overstay your visa—even for a lousy day—go to the immigration office and obtain an official extension. Don't try to talk your way through the immigration checkpoint at the airport because they're stickier than you might expect and will require you to straighten the matter out at the *imigrasi* office. They can really make you squirm and sweat; you may have to pay a fine—bargain—and may even miss your flight.

If your flight is booked up to a week after your last day, you should be able to obtain an extension from the *imigrasi* office. It will probably require a letter from your travel agency ex-

plaining the situation. Don't even bother showing up without a confirmed ticket out and a reason why you can't make an earlier flight.

Reentry

If you use up your two-month maximum stay but want to spend more time in Indonesia, one oft-used solution is to leave the country, return, and get a new entry stamp or visa. You must obtain a visa if your place of arrival is not an of-

---

IN THE DENPASAR JAIL

Apropos of Indonesian penalties for visa overstays, narcotics violations, and the like, a reader writes:

"The Immigration Detention Centre in Denpasar is called 'quarantine' among the staff there. They do treat you very well, but the quantity of food provided leaves a lot to be desired. Lunch at 10 a.m., dinner at 5 p.m., but no breakfast, so you've got 17 hours to wait between feeds from one day to the next. Of course you can pay to get extra food, cups of coffee, and the like. I spent four days there for one month's overstay while they claimed they were referring the matter to a higher authority—their euphemism for waiting until they were done haggling over the price with my husband. They behaved as if I didn't know what was going on.

"While I was there a Frenchman was transferred in on his way home from the real jail, which I gather was not such a pleasant experience. He'd been detained for five months—two months awaiting trial and three months sentence—for overstay. I don't know how long he'd overstayed, but I think his real problem was language. (How can one stay in Indonesia long enough to overstay without knowing what *"dari mana"* means?) Presumably he threw their system into confusion; as he didn't understand when they were asking for money, they had to process him according to the law.

"There was also a Dutchman on his way home after serving four years for narcotics offenses, and a Chinese man who's been in detention since 1960—something to do with not having any papers and the Chinese didn't want him back. He seems quite well settled there, though. His room is well furnished and he always seemed to have cigarettes and extra food. It baffles me how he still has money after so long."

ficial entry point. Most people in this situation spend Rp420,000 on a roundtrip ticket from Jakarta to Singapore, spend a few days shopping, then fly right back to Bali or Jakarta. Cheaper is to leave Indonesia at certain points as close as possible to neighboring countries from where you can re-enter. Some obvious exit points are not that reliable. For example, Indonesian authorities may not allow you to exit Jayapura for Wewak, and you may not cross the border from Merauke into Papua New Guinea. The following are the most convenient, least expensive routes out:

1. by air from Medan (North Sumatra) to Penang (West Malaysia). You can also take the speedboat from Medan to Penang; leaving twice weekly, Rp65,000 one-way, Rp130,000 roundtrip.
2. by air from Pekanbaru (East Sumatra) to Melaka (West Malaysia), then by taxi to Kuala Lumpur.
3. by air from Jakarta to Singapore; one-way Rp163,800, roundtrip Rp294,000 on Sempati Airlines.
4. by air from Pontianak (West Kalimantan) to Kuching (East Malaysia); Rp104,000 one-way, Rp208,000 roundtrip, leaving once weekly on Friday. Returning you get an entry stamp.
5. by road from Pontianak (West Kalimantan) to Kuching (East Malaysia). There are four daily buses over the land border separating the two countries, costing Rp22,000.
6. by air or boat from Tarakan (East Kalimantan) to Nunukan and Tawau (East Malaysia). The boat connection leaves three times weekly and costs Rp34,000 one-way, Rp68,000 roundtrip. You need a visa before reentering Indonesia.
7. by air from Kupang (Timor) to Darwin (Australia).
8. by ferry from Melaka (Peninsular Malaysia) and Dumai (East Sumatra). The problem with this reentry is you need a visa and have to go to Kuala Lumpur to get one.

From Pekanbaru To Singapore By Boat

The visa run from Pekanbaru to Singapore has vastly improved over the past several years. Gone are the 40 hours of slow-boat hell. Now you can board a fast launch leaving Pekanbaru

at 1700 and arrive in Selatpanjang at 0600 (Rp15,000). Speedboats leave frequently, zipping you to Batam in three hours for Rp30,000, a bone-crunching journey on rough seas. From Batam hop across to Singapore for Rp73,500 roundtrip. If all goes to plan you can be in Singapore for a late lunch. Alternatively, you can fly to Singapore direct from Padang (West Sumatra) or Pekanbaru.

CUSTOMS REGULATIONS

Indonesian Customs

Customs procedures have become even more relaxed with the installation of green and red routes at international airports. Tourists with nothing to declare use the green route with no baggage inspection. Indonesian customs and immigration people are pretty mellow and approachable, but it all depends on the place, time of day, mood of the official, who's watching, the crush of the line, and your nationality. They're mostly concerned with just moving tourists through as quickly as possible.

Duty-free items acceptable for import are: 200 cigarettes or 50 cigars and .9 kg of tobacco; cameras (no limit) and reasonable amounts of film; two liters of liquor; and a reasonable amount of perfume for personal use. All weapons and ammunition, narcotics, anything considered pornographic (read: *Playboy*), books with Chinese characters, and Chinese medicines are forbidden entry into Indonesia, though customs officials may be relaxed about enforcement.

Technically, photographic equipment, computers, radios, typewriters, cassette recorders, TV sets, cordless telephones, and transceivers should be listed on your passport, declared to customs, and displayed upon departure, but officials don't check. All movie films, videocassettes, laser discs, records, and computer software should first be screened by the Film Censor Board. You must clear printed matter using Indonesian languages with the minister of culture.

If you need to carry prescription medication, get a letter from your doctor. The import of pets, plants, and fresh fruit is strictly controlled. Owners must show dogs and cats were inoculated against rabies at most six months before arrival, and a good-health certificate is required from your veterinarian.

Home Country Customs

Importation into other countries of souvenirs bought in Indonesia can be problematic. Be sure any souvenir you buy can legally enter your home country, as some items are confiscated and destroyed. One reader reported *wayang* puppets she attempted to take into Australia were quarantined. Seems the puppets were treated with forma gas, which required a six-day wait. Anything purchased with feathers or furs or made in part with organic matter is also high risk.

MONEY

The Indonesian monetary unit is called the *rupiah*, issued in notes of Rp100, Rp500, Rp1000, Rp5000, Rp10,000, Rp20,000, and Rp50,000. Bills are the same size but different colors. Be careful with the old Rp10,000 notes; they're maddeningly similar to Rp5000 bills.

If heading into the countryside or to remote places like the interior of Irian Jaya, take lots of small denomination notes—it's nearly impossible for people out there to make change for Rp20,000 notes. Bring wads of Rp1000 and Rp5000 bills. Always keep on hand lots of Rp100 notes: taxi drivers and small vendors are invariably "out of change" and you'll need small change for public WCs and snacks.

Coins are valued at Rp25, Rp50, and Rp100. Though it's not frequently seen, a Rp500 coin also exists; useful for some public phones. Study the coins until you're familiar with all of them. You'll sometimes see worthless Rp5 and Rp10 coins. Keep them as souvenirs.

Attitudes

To swagger with your money in Indonesia is against your interests—you're just asking to be taken advantage of. To the man in the street a dollar's worth of *rupiah* has the same emotional impact as $10 to us; $2000 is enough to run a rural Indonesian family of four for a year.

In Indonesia a price is attached to everything "extra"—a better seat on the bus, extra sugar or ice in your drink, to urinate at the market, for the use of a fan, for each and every application form at a government office. There's even a per-letter fee just to pick up poste restante letters. Someone who carries a 7UP halfway up a mountain on his head will sell it for twice the price you can buy it cold in the city.

The marketing concept of the "giant economy size" is unknown in Indonesia. The smallest size is nearly always the best value. Three *martabak* at Rp350 offers twice as much food as

the Rp1000 sizes. Same for laundry soap or packets of peanuts. Neither do Indonesian retailers seem to value the "return customer"; they want your money now, up front, not sometime in the future.

EXPENSES

First rule: don't ask how much Indonesian currency is worth in "real money"; it's just as real as American or Australian currency. Don't make the mistake of always translating Indonesian prices into U.S. or European currency, then feeling relieved and grateful for the cheap price. Instead, think in *rupiah*. It doesn't cost "just" 50 American cents, it costs a thousand damn *rupiah!*

Second rule: it's not even worth going to Indonesia if you're constantly obsessed with getting the cheapest price. Indonesia is cheap by any foreign standard, but instead of paying Rp3500 for a great meal many travelers pay Rp500-1000 at the same restaurant for a simple plate of fried rice. Why travel and save $50 if you only eat rice or stay in fleabag hotels the whole time? A lot of these characters hang out at the Mona Lisa in Bukittinggi, eating the cheapest thing on the menu for breakfast, lunch, and dinner.

Third rule: a common hotel practice is to give prices in U.S. dollars, and they're very glad if you pay in dollars with U.S. traveler's checks. However, the price in *rupiah* is nearly always considerably lower. For example, the Graha Beach Hotel in Senggigi on Lombok asks US$50 per night. At the current exchange rate, you'll shell out about Rp105,000 if you pay in dollars. Yet the price in *rupiah* could be only Rp85,000. Always compute the hotel's dollar price in *rupiah* before deciding which currency to use.

How much money you spend per day depends upon your tastes, comfort level, destination, and mode of travel. If you're on the move, buying tickets on buses, taxis, and trains, count on spending at least Rp31,500-42,000 per day. In places like Jakarta, Irian Jaya, and Maluku, where prices are much higher, expect to spend Rp42,000-52,500 per day. Prices are considerably more stable on Sumatra than on Java and Bali. In provinces like Irian Jaya and Central Maluku, your only choice is to trek for weeks on end or travel on excruciatingly slow boats, so you'll wind up having to fly and your expenses will soar. On Sumatra, Java, Bali, and Nusatenggara overland travel opportunities are plentiful and cheap.

If you're staying put, your daily expenses will be much less. There are tens of thousands of villages where you can live for Rp10,500 per day or less—if you live like the villagers. Due to the intense competition, the cheapest spots are right along the traveler's trail—Lake Toba, Yogyakarta, Bali, etc. Mountain resorts and big cities are the most expensive. Jakarta is significantly more expensive than any other city in Indonesia.

Entrance Fees

Guards (*penjaga*) and attendants (*juru kunci*) frequently make you pay a fee to enter a parking lot, historical site, temple, or museum, plus an additional Rp100-250 for your camera. At numerous high-traffic tourist sites there's a fee for your video camera as well.

Don't pay an entrance or parking fee without obtaining an official receipt—unless only a "donation" is requested, then Rp100-200 is acceptable. Remember that in many cases the attendants make their living from tourists. There will also be beggars at holy places (*tempat kramet*) and graveyards, as it's believed a person has a bigger heart when visiting ancestors.

Tipping

A few annoying Western customs, like tipping, have caught on. Never tip waiters in *warung* or *rumah makan,* bartenders and reception people in small hotels, hairdressers, medical personnel, tailors, or taxi drivers. Don't contribute to this cancer! Tipping in the Western sense is not part of Indonesian culture. When you do tip—to your houseboy or cook—it's always unexpected and thus has more impact. Save tipping for those instances when it's really deserved.

In places where you're supposed to tip for individual services, a 10% service charge plus 10%

government tax is added to your bill. Expect these charges in the big tourist hotels of Lake Toba, Jakarta, Bali, Ujung Pandang, Tanatoraja, and other tourist centers. As in Europe, only high-priced hotels and leading restaurants add these charges. Airport porters generally expect a payment—not a tip—of Rp500-1000 per bag. Hire-car drivers (*sopir*) and guides (*petunjuk*) may be tipped Rp5000-10,000 per day, but only if you're pleased with their performance. Although bribery in the civil bureaucracy exists, it's unlikely travelers or tourists will ever need to resort to it. In most cases you won't even know if you've paid a bribe—such corruption is deftly institutionalized and masked behind some official fee or charge.

MONEYCHANGING

Bank deregulation has brought about a great improvement in the moneychanging situation. The U.S. dollar, accepted all over Indonesia since WW II, is still the most useful foreign currency here; the *rupiah* is based on it. Though the U.S. dollar will probably bring the most favorable exchange rate, it's possible to cash other well-known currencies like Australian dollars, German Deutsche marks, Netherlands florins, and French and Swiss francs. Canadian dollars are more difficult. Gold is freely and legally traded in

APPROXIMATE CURRENCY EQUIVALENTS
(March 1997)

Australia: A$1 = Rp1890
Canada: C$1 = Rp1752
France: Fr1 = Rp415
Germany: DM1 = Rp1404
Hong Kong: HK$1 = Rp310
Japan: 100¥ = Rp1967
Malaysia: M$1 = Rp968
Netherlands: G1 = Rp1244
New Zealand: NZ$1 = Rp1690
Singapore: S$1 = Rp1678
Sweden: Kr1 = Rp312
Switzerland: Fr1 = Rp1622
United Kingdom: UK1 = Rp3847
United States: US$1 = Rp2400

The most widely used "people's money" is the Rp100 bill. The image is that of the revolutionary war hero General Sudirman (1912-1950), a gifted military tactician.

Indonesia and there are gold shops in every good-sized Indonesian city.

Cash

Though you can change traveler's checks in most places, cash is sometimes a different matter. Many smaller banks frown on the good old British pound. Large denomination U.S. notes ($100s as opposed to $20s) fetch a higher rate of exchange. Indonesian banks, even on Bali, refuse to touch foreign banknotes that are soiled, worn, or physically damaged. If you do a good job taping them with transparent tape, you'll probably get away with passing damaged notes. Banks also won't exchange foreign coins.

Indonesian paper currency tends to stay in circulation longer, so Indonesian banknotes start to take on the appearance of filthy scraps of torn cloth. This worn money will not be accepted, so you shouldn't accept it either. The only place you can change it is the bank.

Exchange Rates

Exchange rates for various currencies vary. For example, the rate for the German mark is 10% better in Jakarta than in Sumatra. Medan offers infinitely better rates than anywhere else on Sumatra. Estimate your spending for the whole of Sumatra and change money in Medan—the main drag has more banks than Patpong has brothels. Brastagi is wholly without banks and Bukittinggi offers only the Bank Negara Indonesia (BNI) with bad rates.

Rates can also depend on the bank and even on the branch of the bank. In many cases, the headquarters bank changes money, but city branches do not. Bank Bumi Daya consistently gives good rates. BNI is usually at least as good. Bank Expor Impor always changes foreign checks or cash. All have branches virtually the length and breadth of the country. The best rates tend to be in tourist areas. In the far reaches of Indonesia the exchange rates could be downright criminal, or there could be no banks at all. Venture to such outlying areas—where they might not have ever heard of a Swiss franc—only with stacks of Indonesian cash, with no denomination higher than Rp20,000. Avoid, if you can, exchanging money at hotel front desks, where you'll receive at least five percent below the rate offered by state banks. Airports usually offer very competitive rates.

A stamp duty of Rp500 is often charged for amounts from Rp101,000 to Rp1 million and Rp1000 for amounts more than Rp1 million. If you change less than Rp100,000, no stamp duty is charged. Bank hours are generally Mon.-Fri. 0800-1200, Saturday 0800-1100; get to the bank early to avoid lines. You'll need your passport and tourist entry card for each transaction.

Moneychangers

Moneychangers generally don't charge a fee for their services, so you can change money as often as you want. They also offer quicker service and better exchange rates. They're open both earlier and later than banks.

The main roads of Kuta and Sanur on Bali and Jalan Jaksa in Jakarta are literally choked with moneychangers. In remote places like the Baliem Valley in Irian Jaya, there are no moneychangers, only banks. Changing money is still a problem in Banda, Kei, Aru, and the Alor/Solor group where Chinese shop owners might change U.S. dollars at lousy rates. Bring wads of the filthy stuff to these outlying locales.

Reconversion

When leaving the country, you can exchange up to Rp50,000 for foreign currencies; be sure to keep your exchange receipts. Reconvert *before* you clear airport security; once past the security check you can't go back. Shops and coffee shops beyond the security point sometimes accept dollars at so-so rates. Keep your departure tax (Rp20,000) tucked away for use in exiting Indonesia.

TRAVELER'S CHECKS AND CREDIT CARDS

There's no black market in Indonesia, so for safety's sake bring only a portion of your funds in cash. Though rates are often better for traveler's checks than for cash, always carry some $5, $10, and $20 bills in case you need quick money when banks are closed or refusing traveler's checks. The bulk of your traveling funds should come in the form of a widely accepted brand of traveler's checks such as American Express. Some places like Lombok do not use the Indonesian phrase (*trapel cek*) for traveler's checks. *Cek jalanan turis* is probably a more widely understood term.

American Express (AmEx), Bank of America, First National City Bank, Barclays, and Thomas Cook traveler's checks are accepted all over Indonesia. Wells Fargo Traveler's Checks are difficult to cash in the Outer Islands. AmEx is best, replacing lost checks the fastest. Once authorization is received through Sydney, replacement checks are issued within the hour. All the above companies maintain offices in Jakarta and Bali. Some Australian savings banks and smaller banks without agents in Jakarta will let you starve before they replace your lost TCs.

Bank Bumi Daya, Bank Expor Impor, Bank Rakyat Indonesia, and Bank Negara Indonesia accept most Australian and better-known TCs. Upon presentation of your passport, it usually takes about 20 minutes to cash TCs at a bank. If the clerks won't accept your brand of TCs, ask for the manager. Major hotels, department stores, and many pricey shops will also take TCs, at lousy rates.

Credit Cards

Indonesia is very much a cash-oriented society. Visa, MasterCard, and AmEx credit cards can be utilized only in the major tourist and business centers equipped to process charges—Medan, Lake Toba, Palembang, Jakarta, Yogyakarta, Solo, Bali, and Lombok. Midrange to upscale hotels, tourist-oriented souvenir shops, domestic and international airline offices, and the more expensive restaurants accept them. Different branches of the same store will have different policies; for example, Sarinah's fifth floor won't accept AmEx but the first floor will.

Travel agencies will usually accept credit cards. Not all retail outlets accept the American Express card; Diner's Club is gaining strength. Most Java and Bali merchants can't authorize your limit, so you can only purchase goods equal to a total value of Rp250,000. Also, it's common for Indonesians to add a two to five percent "commission."

Your passport and credit card are needed for all transactions. Be sure to verify the total amount charged. Ask the retailer or service provider to convert the total amount into dollars and cents, then write the amount on the charge slip. That way, in spite of currency fluctuations, you'll know exactly what you owe your credit card company. Maintain a list of your card numbers so you can cancel your cards if you lose them. Leave a duplicate list with a friend back home. Always keep the customer copy because charge slips can be altered and used to defraud. Don't discard slips until charges have been paid. Later, if you discover you've been cheated by a merchant who switched or misrepresented merchandise, write your credit card company to resolve the problem. Always keep your credit cards in sight when making a purchase.

Cash Advances Against Credit Cards

You can also use your Visa, MasterCard, or AmEx (but not Diner's Club) credit card to obtain cash advances (normally up to $500) from moneychangers, though they'll charge a steep six percent commission. On Bali, BNI doesn't charge a fee if you use your credit card to get cash. Other banks may charge three percent.

Bank Duta does not charge a commission on cash advances in Medan, Palembang, Jakarta, Yogyakarta, Solo, Legian, Ubud, Cakranegara, Ambon, or Jayapura. Neither does Bank Central

Asia (BCA), with branches all over Indonesia. In other banks you may give the clerks apoplexy if you hand over your Visa card for cash.

Dutch Postcheques

Dutch tourists or people with a Dutch giro account at the state Postbank can use postcheques to obtain up to Rp200,000 per cheque at most Indonesian post offices. It takes about a month for the money to be deducted and is about five percent more expensive than a cash charge.

Postcheques are also cheaper than traveler's checks. Because there's no such thing as a Dutch guilder TC, the Dutch have to change guilders to dollars, buy TCs, and then cash them. That's three transactions, which comes out to more than a five percent commission. Postcheques are insured against loss, and are also accepted in Malaysia, Thailand, Hong Kong, and Japan. The Dutch may also use Postgiro credit cards to draw cash from main post offices.

Wire Transfers

Also called remittance orders. Take enough money with you—US$2000 for two to five months of budget travel—so you won't need to have money wired, which can cost up to US$15. Travelers who've been caught short may find it requires several weeks for money to be remitted by wire from Australia, North America, or Europe. If you're really stuck, a telex is a much faster way to transfer money.

BARGAINING

In Indonesia, always bargain hard for everything everywhere, including medicine in drugstores, hospitalization, immigration fees, entrance charges to small museums or temple sites—bargain no matter what type of establishment it is, even in "fixed-price" shops. Bargaining is most critical in open markets, with anyone who quotes you a ridiculous price, when taking *becak,* and with vendors of tourist souvenirs the natives themselves seldom buy. Always ask for a lower rate for your hotel room. Bargain for transportation on *bemo* and buses only if you know you're being overcharged. Prices for tailors and hairdressers are standardized and fixed, but bargain with your mechanic and tire-fixer.

The Chinese are seasoned businesspeople and are often the easiest to deal with. Merchants from other ethnic groups can be more irrational, unpredictable, and less motivated. The Bataks and Padang are the pushiest entrepreneurs.

Buying and bargaining in Indonesia can be good-humored or infuriating. It's a social vehicle by which one requests and receives favors, a means to solidify one's status in the local economy. The price is always set in consideration of the merchant's need on that day, an assessment of the potential buyer, how much the merchant likes you, plus the sporting spirit of the exchange. An item has many prices, each reflecting the correct charge for a particular customer from the shopkeeper's point of view. Indonesians also have a tendency to misrepresent goods and services. Every boat you're about to charter has a new engine, every hotel is quiet and safe, every *batik* painted by the seller's father.

Bargaining isn't a one-way process at all. Indonesians enjoy it and will respect you more if you bargain. It's a pleasurable way merchants have to relate to you. It should be leisurely, lighthearted, and friendly. Never get angry. Bargaining is a game won by technique and strategy, not distemper and threats.

Bargaining can be a prolonged exchange lasting days and even weeks. Take your time; if you're impatient, you'll pay more. Often if you wait, you'll receive a substantial discount. Get to know the seller and his family, build a personal relationship, go back again and again, have tea, always keep it civil. The merchant might be in a better mood or need the money more in a few hours, days, or weeks.

It's challenging to try to obtain the same price as the locals. There's a second, higher price for out-of-town Indonesians, and a third and even higher price for Chinese, *orang besar* (big men), Jakartans, Indonesians from other islands, and foreigners like you. The Japanese, thought to be ignorant and richest of all, are overcharged constantly. You pay according to your station in life. If you say you're poor, they laugh. If you're so poor, how come you're here?

Admittedly, being overcharged gets very tiresome after a while. Though it's only a matter of pennies, the practice eventually manages to annoy every Westerner as a matter of principle. The very best bargaining is done with your feet, by going back to the good places. But

BARGAINING TECHNIQUES AND STRATEGIES

- Don't ever assume a price is accurate or believe a (perhaps biased) bystander. Spot-check prices in a hotel shop; if a smaller hotel, ask your hotel proprietor, houseboy, driver, or someone else uninvolved with the shop the correct price of an item. Indonesians themselves are always swapping price information as a means of keeping costs down.

- Don't stop and buy at the very first stall, vendor, or shop you come across. Compare prices first; learn about quality. Do all your heavy buying during your last week in Indonesia, when you're the most knowledgeable.

- Start by asking the seller the price. He'll start too high, but you can bring him down by counteroffering a reasonable price. The remainder of the exchange will then become more realistic. In hopes you'll be over-generous, many Indonesians when you ask "how much?" will reply, "it's up to you." When the seller smiles, it means he knows you know an item's value.

- For luxury goods like carvings, jewelry, textiles, and paintings, start at 50% of the asked price, then inch up. For services like *becak* and laundry, start with 50-75% of the price. Sundries like canned goods, soap, and cigarettes are usually purchased at set prices from small convenience stores or hotel kiosks. In tourist areas, you can't bargain for these; in non-tourist areas bargain for a break of 25% or so.

- When a merchant reaches a final price and won't budge, try for some extras. Throw in an inexpensive item and say you'll accept the offer if this small item is included. Or try to gain acceptance of your credit card without a commission charge. Get the merchant to absorb packing and delivery, or share some of the freight and insurance costs.

- As a last resort, try the walkaway. Feigned disinterest makes for many a good deal. Your posi-

tion is strongest when you seem not to care. This is almost always necessary with *becak* drivers. Just smile, shrug your shoulders, and walk slowly away. Often the driver or seller will call you back, agreeing to your last bid.

- Don't show interest in the item you want. Don't hover around or fondle it; try not to provide clues to your true interest. If you show enthusiasm, the seller will be less flexible. Include the desired item with other articles you wish to purchase, almost as an afterthought. Throw it in at the last minute before clinching your negotiations, innocently asking "oh, how much for this too?"

- Remain flexible. There's a vast difference between opportunistic tourist-oriented stores, markets, and street sellers, and those businesses offering goods and services mostly to Indonesians. You tend to see less overcharging in the country than the city.

- If you buy more than one item, you should qualify for a bulk-purchase discount of at least a portion of the price off each item. On a large bulk purchase or on a multiple luxury purchase, many thousands of *rupiah* should be removed from the retail total.

- Bid for goods early in the day, just as the shop opens for business. Indonesians believe making an early sale will bring good luck the rest of the day, and are often willing to take a lower price.

- An Indonesian friend will probably obtain better prices than you. Expat residents always send their cooks and houseboys to the market to do the shopping.

- It's bad form to continue bargaining after an amount has been agreed upon or a deal struck.

- Ask for a receipt listing the specific items and the prices you paid as proof of purchase for clearing customs. Observe the wrapping process—sometimes merchants substitute an inferior product for the one you actually purchased.

never pass up an item you really want—even if you have to pay an inflated price for it. Chances are you'll not run across the same item again. Some travelers are just too stubborn and aggressive and won't pay that extra Rp200. Here they've traveled halfway around the world to become livid over a lousy dime. When you get

back home, the money you spent will seem a paltry amount indeed.

Shops offering only fixed prices (*harga pas*) are becoming more common, offering a shopping environment Western consumers will feel immediately comfortable in. In these stores, the price is set, with no discounts or reductions. If you see a price posted or attached to an item, it's a fixed-price shop. If no fixed price sign is posted or no prices are attached to merchandise, there's room for haggling. All verbally stated prices are merely starting points from which you should receive anything from a 10% to 50% discount.

MEASUREMENTS AND COMMUNICATIONS

The Indonesian measuring system is based on the European metric system. In other areas, however—such as time, power, and phone and postal services—the Westerner will find things quite different in Indonesia from back home.

POWER

Electrical service is gradually spreading into the most remote corners of the archipelago. In North Sumatra alone, the number of villages with electricity more than doubled in the four years from 1989 to 1993. Still, electricity in the *kampung* and even in some larger towns can be minimal—you'll get used to solitary dim bulbs and oil lamps.

Power is fairly reliable, but brownouts are not uncommon. If you're renting a home it's wise to secure one with its own generator. Street-lighting is haphazard. Since the sidewalks and streets of Indonesia are full of pitfalls and debris, always carry a flashlight. The country's drainage ditches are really treacherous, particularly at night. They're poorly marked and streetlights are mostly nonexistent, even on streets frequented by tourists. Most public entertainment venues lack air-conditioning, so a woven fan is indispensable.

Current

In the past, current has run 110 volts, 50 cycles AC, but most areas are changing over to 220-240 volts, 50 cycles AC. Some districts may feature both 110 and 220. Check to make sure which current is running before plugging in expensive electrical appliances. Transformers are readily available and reasonably priced, as are 220-volt appliances. Bathroom shaver plugs usually feature a transformer switch. If you carry a computer or hair dryer, bring a stabilizer and adapter if your plugs are not of the round, slim, European two-pronged type. Power surges at night mean the current can fluctuate between 180 and 220 volts, so unplug that razor.

Electronic Media

Indonesia became one of the first developing countries to launch a nationwide TV network, linking Indonesia's 17,000 islands with telephone, television, and data communications services. Television, broadcast some six hours a day, is expanding rapidly in Indonesia, with 27 companies serving 2.5 million television sets. Wherever there's an electric generator, there's usually a TV.

Broadcasters are spread throughout the country, competing with each other for viewers. The government-operated TV network, connected with Jakarta via domestic satellite and microwave, is called TVRI. Another big station is RCTI, a quasi-private company in which the Suharto family has controlling interest. TVRI is a tool of the state and programming is dominated by Indonesian-language, paternalistic, nationalistic local and international news, speeches, welcoming addresses, and endless coverage of handshaking ceremonies between Suharto and his ministers or other heads of state. There are also progovernment educational and religious programs, Indonesian music and drama, soccer and badminton matches, Taiwanese kung fu movies, and American programs dubbed in English and subtitled in Indonesian.

Indonesian TV is so boring that in the early 1990s people started buying parabolic antennas to go global rather than watch TVRI or subscribe to RCTI. Cable News Network began broadcasting via Indonesian satellite in 1991 and today its signal is accessible by two-meter dish. News, music, films, and other entertainment emanate from Hong Kong's Asiasat and are now available 24 hours a day throughout Indonesia.

American TV sets aren't compatible with Indonesian signals. American black-and-white sets can easily be converted locally, but for color it's best to buy or rent a set here. Many long-term U.S. expats bring their sets for use with videocassettes and games. Local TV sets are okay in quality but more expensive than sets in most other countries. Rental rates are around Rp50,000 per month. Don't bring stereo equipment from the U.S.; it must be adjusted and is difficult to readjust back to American speed. Just buy your stereo in Indonesia and sell it when you leave.

The government radio network, Radio Republik Indonesia (RRI), with 45 stations, comprises the national system. Radio is still important, keeping most of the population informed and entertained. RRI broadcasts news and commentary in English about an hour each day. In addition, many private radio stations broadcast RRI news and Indonesian and Western music on AM and FM. About 20 foreign radio stations broadcast programs to Indonesia in Indonesian. Shortwave reception takes in English-language programs such as BBC, Voice of America, and American Top 40.

Laser video discs are now the rage, rented in most larger towns for about Rp5000 per movie. In Bali free laser disc movies are offered in restaurants and bars. Satellite dishes are also popping up all over the country; you may find one in even the most remote villages. Dishes receive a variety of foreign channels, including CNN. Four-star hotels also routinely subscribe to international satellite signals.

Software is still copied freely here, though it's now harder to buy illegal copies in stores. Computer viruses are rampant in Indonesia and copying bootlegged software in this country is asking for trouble. Virtually all computers suffer from one or more viruses. Even the very latest antivirus software may not be sufficient protection against Indonesian virus attacks. Antivirus software sold here may itself contain a virus. If you plan to bring a computer into Indonesia, make sure you have a copy of the very latest antivirus software, and arrange for updates to be sent regularly.

TIME

There are three time zones in Indonesia. West Indonesia Standard Time (Sumatra, Java, the western half of Kalimantan, Bali, Lombok) is Greenwich Mean Time plus seven hours; Central Indonesia Standard Time (eastern Kalimantan, Sulawesi, Nusatenggara) is G.M.T. plus eight hours; East Indonesia Standard Time (Maluku, Irian Jaya) is G.M.T. plus nine hours. This means that if it's midnight in London, it's 0700 in Jakarta and Denpasar, 0800 in Sulawesi, and 0900 in Ambon.

For the correct time in Jakarta, dial 103. Most of Indonesia is on or so close to the equator that the days and nights are about the same length. On Bali, about midpoint in the archipelago, the sun rises at 0600 and sets at 1800.

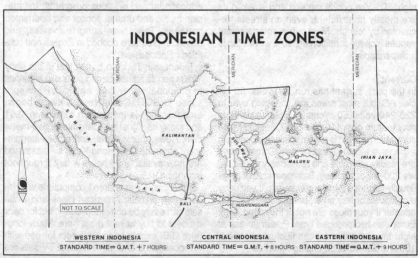

INDONESIAN TIME ZONES

NOT TO SCALE

WESTERN INDONESIA
STANDARD TIME = G.M.T. + 7 HOURS

CENTRAL INDONESIA
STANDARD TIME = G.M.T. + 8 HOURS

EASTERN INDONESIA
STANDARD TIME = G.M.T. + 9 HOURS

© MOON PUBLICATIONS, INC.

Business Hours

Very flexible, depending on numerous variables. Hours vary from one business to another, from city to city, and from season to season. Even more complicated is the convolution of the Indonesian work week due to the mixing and simultaneous use of two religious calendars, the Islamic and Gregorian. Banks, offices, and schools close early on Friday because it's the Sabbath, but in order to fit in with the world at large, Sunday is also observed as a day of rest. Saturday, meanwhile, is a partial work day, so the Indonesian work week consists of four full days and two partial days.

In the small towns, restaurants and *warung* usually close several hours after sunset. Expect businesses to take midday lunch breaks of an hour or more, during which time no one answers the phone. During major religious holidays such as the monthlong Muslim fast (*puasa*), restaurants in Islamic areas are closed during daylight hours.

Generally speaking, government offices open at 0800 Mon.-Sat., closing at 1500 or 1600 Mon.-Thurs., 1130 on Friday, and 1400 on Saturday. Always get an early start for government offices, before the lines get too long and the day too hot. Banks are open 0800 or 0830 to 1200 or 1300 Mon.-Fri., and 0800-1100 on Saturday. Bank branches in hotels often remain open into the afternoon, and moneychangers in the tourist centers stay open at night. Shopping centers, supermarkets and department stores operate from 0900 to 2100 or even later, seven days a week.

POSTAL SERVICE

Sending Letters

You can drop letters, aerograms, and postcards into mailboxes on the street or mail them at hotel reception desks, regardless of whether or not you're a guest. You can purchase stamps at hotel front desks, and sometimes in shops selling postcards. Very useful on Bali are the postal agents of Kuta, Sanur, and Ubud, who sell stamps, postcards, and stationery. These agents also send telegrams and offer poste restante pickup. Less conveniently, you can buy stamps at the post offices found in any midsized Indonesian town. Go to a window with a scale, as your letter must first be weighed and assigned a stamp value. Then proceed to another window for the actual stamps. Elbow through the clump of people and push your letter as far as possible through the barred window, seeking to gain the attention of the postal clerk. He'll often recognize you as a foreigner and cut you some slack. Try to squeeze your money into another gap between the hands. Fear not: these are considered acceptable manners at Indonesian post offices.

After securing your stamps, take them over to the glue stands and apply glue to the back; the glue on Indonesian stamps is weak. If possible, watch the stamps until they're cancelled to assure they're not stolen.

Aerograms are the cheapest and fastest way to send a letter abroad from Indonesia. They cost but Rp20 apiece for five at the post office; then comes the correct postage. Sample rates include Rp400 to ASEAN countries, Rp550 to Japan and Australia, Rp700 to Europe, Rp900 to North America.

Not all of Indonesia's postal branches offer complete postal services. Some don't accept parcels. Post offices in the big cities and tourist centers are fast and efficient, with the latest in digital scales. Philatelists will find commemorative stamps and first day covers at Jakarta's main post office on Jl. Pos Utara. If you want to be 100% sure of delivery, use a reputable courier service like Elteha, Usaha Express, or DHL; which have offices in all major Indonesian cities.

Postcards

Another inexpensive way to send news back home is on postcards costing anywhere from Rp1000 for 10 at Borobudur to Rp1000 apiece in the Baliem Valley of Irian Jaya. Cards of Balinese dancers display some of the most beautiful card art you'll find anywhere. Postage rates run from Rp275 to ASEAN countries to Rp1000 for a large card to North America.

Registered Mail

Register anything of value. The charge for registering a letter is about equal to the charge of postage, but the odds are your missive will actually reach its destination. Letters may be registered at any post office branch. A signed form should be returned to the sender indicating the letter was received.

Express Mail

Two forms of express service are available for domestic mail: blue envelopes marked Kilat ensure Air Mail Service, while yellow envelopes reading Kilat Khusus are the equivalent of Air Mail Special Delivery. These envelopes are available at all post offices. Express service costs an extra Rp65 and usually saves at least one or two days. Kilat letters, like ordinary letters, may be put into any mailbox along the street.

Always use Kilat service for international mail; letters sent to the Americas, Europe, or Australia will arrive in five to seven days. Bring strong envelopes to Indonesia to make sure your exposed film or important papers arrive safely.

Packet Post

It's always best to ship your parcel from the post office yourself; don't rely on anyone else to do it right or even to do it at all.

Professional shippers may wait until they receive the money, often three months later. Parcels mailed to small towns in Indonesia may gallop quickly to the local post office, only to sit there for several months waiting to be processed by customs officers.

Prices are cheapest when sending 10 kg parcels. If you're shipping 17 kg, it's probably cheaper to pack two 10 kg parcels instead of a 10 kg and a 7 kg. Minimum box size is 14 cm by 9 cm, with a maximum length of 100 cm, and a total circumference of 200 cm. Include your name and address on a slip of paper inside the package as well as on the outside. Provincial post offices may lack the proper custom forms for overseas shipping, or they may be out of stamps. To mail packages surface post to foreign destinations, you'll need form CP2, an expedition document, and C2/CP3, a customs declaration form. Since you'll need five copies of C2/CP3, bring spare carbon paper; post offices often fail to stock carbon paper.

A customs officer will check your parcel to confirm you're not mailing antiques. After the inspection, pack and seal the parcel in front of him. Be sure to secure proper documentation for any statue or antiquity to show to customs officials at the airport or docks. A receipt with a certified dealer's registration number should suffice.

To Europe or North America, international seamail can take up to six months, though the average is two to three. If you don't have much to send back, surface post is less expensive than a shipping company, which charges a minimum of $175 for a portion of a container.

Wrapping And Packaging

Shops will usually wrap your purchases in a flimsy layer of newspaper, binding the whole in plastic twine with a convenient carrying handle, an arrangement that will never withstand the rigors of travel. To protect your purchases during overseas shipping, use light packing material. The best padding available in Indonesia is foam carpet backing from carpet stores.

In big city post offices men will wrap your package in a nylon jacket for a fee of Rp3000-5000 or so per package. Chances are, after you buy the paper and string and get together everything you need, you'll have spent that amount yourself. Using this wrapping service also tends to move your parcel along faster through the system. These men are available only in the main cities where the volume makes it worth their while.

Parcel contents must be inspected at the post office before mailing, so don't seal your package ahead of time. If you decide to take purchases back yourself, have the airlines paste a Fragile sign on your package and check it in at the baggage counter. Hand-carry your most precious purchases.

There are specialized air-express companies on Bali, so if you're buying crafts in the Outer Islands wait until you get back to Bali to airfreight them. These companies are expensive, charging about Rp16,800-21,000 per kilo (five-kilo minimum), and taking 7-10 days. PT Golden Bali Express, Jl. Kartini 52, Denpasar, is one of the most competent companies on the island. If you pack it yourself you might get the price down. Also, check on the "unaccompanied baggage" rates on your flight home. At about Rp7350 per kilo, these rates may be cheaper than airfreight.

Receiving Mail

It's best to receive letters at your hotel rather than rely on poste restante. If you must use the latter, have your mail sent to one of Jakarta's two main post offices: Central Post Office (Kan-

tor Pos Pusat), Jl. Pos Utara, open Mon.-Sat. 0800-1600; or Jl. Kapt. Tendean 43, open Mon.-Thurs. 0800-1600, Friday 0800-1100, and Saturday 0800-1230. Bali's main post office is in the administrative district of Denpasar called Renon; you can also have your mail sent to post offices in Kuta, Ubud, or Singaraja.

All mail should include your last name underlined and in caps, with only your first and middle initials, or letters could get missorted under your first name. Follow your name with your address, the town name, the island name, then Republik Indonesia. A fee of Rp50 is charged to retrieve a poste restante letter.

Receiving goods in Indonesia is still risky. Approximately half the items mailed to you in Indonesia will get ripped off, especially medicine, books, and magazines. Don't send anything valuable in letters mailed to Indonesia; 30% of all letters never arrive. Postal workers know a $100 bill could lurk inside any letter; poorly paid as they are, the temptation is just too great. Aerograms and postcards, however, almost always get through.

PHONE SERVICE

Indonesia has largely shed its reputation as a purveyor of one of the most agonizingly frustrating phone systems in all of Asia. Telephone system overloading used to be so severe that it was almost impossible to place a call during normal business hours. Though it still requires a bit of persistence, you can now routinely place both domestic and international calls. The latter are handled by Indosat, a state-owned enterprise utilizing satellites. Both domestic and international calls can be placed from pay phones, hotel rooms, the local telephone office, or in a *wartel,* a privately run retail telephone service shop.

Expect inefficiency. You might wait 45 minutes and suffer excruciating difficulties the entire time. The person in charge might chant over and over, "Do you want to cancel?" Persevere: eventually you'll get through (probably).

Jakarta has the highest ratio of service in the country, with 10.9 telephones per 100,000 people, and the highest successful call ratio (SCR). The SCR for Indonesia as a whole stands at about 35% but is projected to increase to 65%

INTERNATIONAL TELEPHONE COUNTRY CODES

Australia: 61	Malaysia: 60
Austria: 43	Netherlands: 31
Belgium: 32	New Zealand: 64
France: 33	Philippines: 63
Germany: 49	Singapore: 65
Hong Kong: 852	Taiwan: 886
Indonesia: 62	Thailand: 66
Japan: 81	United Kingdom: 44
Korea: 82	United States: 1

by the end of the century. As much as 45% of all unsuccessful calls is attributable to human error. The government has launched a Telephone Etiquette National Campaign to encourage correct, efficient, friendly phone conversation.

About half of Indonesia's 67,000 villages have phone service; the government is installing nearly a million lines per year. Still, phone installation is so expensive and the wait is so long that cellular technology is increasingly filling the gap. While businesses and individuals wait for phones they rely on radio telephones, which behave like real phones and cost about Rp500,000 per month.

Local Calls

You'll find yellow-and-gray public pay phones here and there, but they're usually out of order. Also make local calls from pay phones in hotel lobbies and airport terminals. To continue talking, you must plug in Rp100 coins every two minutes. Oftentimes tourists can use phones at reception counters in hotels and restaurants. Ask. Indonesians, however, will prefer to dial the number for you. Phone books are difficult to come by and don't always list all businesses and residences. On Bali, where the system is computerized, dial 108 for information.

Long-Distance Calls

Place long-distance calls within Indonesia by dialing direct. Dial first the city code number, then the local number. The archipelago is divided into five zones; calls are priced according to zone. The rate from Jakarta ranges from Rp300-500 per minute for Zone V calls (Java, Sumatra, Sulawesi, Nusatenggara, and Kalimantan), to Rp1000 per minute for Zone I calls (Biak, Nabire, and Manokwari). Indonesia's country code is 62. When calling Indonesia internationally, dial 011, then the city code *without the zero,* then the phone number. For example, the city code for Jakarta is 021, but when calling from a foreign country you dial 011-62-21 plus the number. This is true for many European countries as well.

Twenty cities offer International Direct Dialing service. Completely computerized, the system links 127 countries. IDD phones are standard in upscale hotels in all the main tourist areas of Indonesia. Reception is usually quite good. For IDD calls, just dial 00-801 plus the country code, then the local number. Where direct-dialing is unavailable, obtain quick operator assistance by dialing 104 in Jakarta, 108 on Bali, and 101 in the rest of Indonesia. Your time starts as soon as you start talking to the home country operator.

Although it's a wonderful feeling dialing direct to a friend in New York from your hotel room overlooking the Surabaya skyline, hotels levy a preposterously high surcharge on calls. A call from Kuta to Los Angeles could easily cost Rp60,000. Instead, take a *becak* to the nearest *wartel* or city telephone office; in the larger cities, these offices are open 24 hours a day, seven days a week.

Credit card calls are extremely convenient, especially for intercity calls, and much cheaper and faster than *wartel* offices. With Kartu Telpon cards (Rp5000 minimum), you can phone for about one-third the hotel price, with no minimum duration. Use them anywhere in Indonesia with card telephones—and nearly all towns in In-

donesia now have card phones. You purchase different denominations or units: a 140-unit card is Rp11,000, a 500-unit card Rp40,000. A three-minute call to Amsterdam is 140 units.

Dutch travelers may use the Telecom Telecard (P.T.T), which allows callers to phone Holland from Indonesia and other points in Asia, with the charges added to their regular monthly phone bill.

Special Home Country Phones are available at major airports, some *wartel* offices, in big star-studded hotels, and at big shopping centers. These phones enable you to automatically connect with an operator in your home country by simply pushing a button adjacent to the name of the nation you wish to reach. Within 30 seconds you'll reach an operator in that country. The charge is billed to your home phone in your home country. Once you get through to a home-country operator, you can reverse the charges. The charge from the U.S. is cheaper than dialing direct from Indonesia. If there's no answer or the receiving party refuses to accept your call, there's no charge—even if it took five minutes trying to get through. Collect calls are accepted only between Indonesia and Europe, North America, and Australia.

Faxes And Cables

Any *wartel* and many hotels will send faxes for you; Rp10,000 to Rp15,000. You can receive a fax at any *wartel* for Rp1000. For overseas cables, allow 36 hours. A 15-word full-rate cable to the U.S. runs Rp8050, telexes Rp10,000-15,000. Cables sent to points within Indonesia are much cheaper.

INFORMATION

Really valuable and up-to-date travel information you'll receive from other travelers along the way—the cheapest and friendliest *losmen,* where to eat and drink, best beaches, most beautiful walks, unusual things to see and do. The many Indonesians you meet can fill you in on *wayang,* dance, and folk dramas, crafts outlets, sources of medicine, tickets for the best buses. This book should cover the rest.

Tourist Offices

Overseas, the Indonesian government maintains Indonesian Tourist Promotion Offices (ITPO) where brochures, maps, and timetables are available. There are ITPOs, for example, in Los Angeles, San Francisco, Singapore, Tokyo, and Frankfurt. Many have tourist promotion offices attached, as well as a Garuda office.

In Indonesia itself tourist offices usually go by the name Bapparda, Diparda, Kanwil Depparpostel, or Kantor Pariwisata. Or you can simply ask for the *kantor pariwisata.* In large provincial capitals, these offices are usually found in or near the governor's office. Although tourist offices in big tourist centers like Jakarta, Bandung, Yogyakarta, Solo, Bali, and Ambon are quite efficient, providing good information and brochures, others may not be as helpful. Woefully underfunded, the staff could be uninformed, not conversant in English, their files neglected. In the smaller cities, the best hotel or biggest travel agency often takes the place of the *kantor pariwisata.* Many tourist offices are inconveniently located out of town to take advantage of cheap rents.

Tourist Literature

Most printed matter is sent to overseas embassies; what's left is often rationed and undisplayed. Distribution is so haphazard and irregular you might find the most complete collection of brochures about West Sumatra in Lombok. Publications quickly go out of print and are seldom reprinted, so whenever you find anything available, snap it up. There may be only an "office copy"—ask to borrow it for a quick photocopy.

Some regional offices publish excellent booklets and pamphlets. Obtain a calendar of events listing all major religious and public holidays and annual cultural events. One of the best information centers on things Indonesian is the Directorate General of Tourism, Jl. Kramat Raya 81 (P.O. Box 409), Jakarta, which publishes literature and maps on all 27 Indonesian provinces.

GOVERNMENT TOURIST OFFICES

The Directorate General Of Tourism (DGT) is located in Jakarta and administratively is under the Department of Tourism, Post, and Telecommunications, which has offices in all main tourist destination areas. These offices are known as Kanwil Depparpostel, or Regional Office of Tourism, Post, and Telecommunications.

Each of the 27 provinces of Indonesia also has its own tourist office, identified by the designation Diparda, or provincial tourist service. All offices can offer assistance and information.

BALI

Kanwil X Depparpostel Bali, Komplek Niti Mandala, Jl. Raya Puputan, Renon, Denpasar 80235, tel. (0361) 225-649; Diparda Tk.I Bali, Jl. S. Parman, Niti Mandala, Denpasar 80235, tel. (0361) 222-387

IRIAN JAYA

Kanwil XVII Depparpostel Irian Jaya, Jl. Raya Abepura 17, Entop, P.O. Box 999, Jayapura 99224, tel. (0967) 22446; Diparda Tk.I Irian Jaya, Jl. Soa Siu Dok II, P.O. Box 499, Jayapura 99115, tel. (0967) 2138 ext. 263

JAVA

Central Java: Kanwil VII Depparpostel Jawa Tengah, Jl. K.H. Achmad Dahlan 2, Semarang 50241, tel. (024) 318-021; Diparda Tk.I Jawa Tengah, Jl. Imam Bonjol 209, Semarang 50241, tel. (024) 510-924

East Java: Kanwil IX Depparpostel Jawa Timur, Jl. Jend. A. Yani 242-244, Surabaya 60235, tel. (031) 815-312; Diparda Tk.I Jawa Timur, Jl. Darmokali 35, Surabaya 60241, tel. (031) 575-448

Jakarta: Kanwil V Depparpostel DKI Jakarta, Jl. K.H. Abdurrohim 1, Kuningan Barat, Jakarta 12710, tel. (021) 511-742; Diparda DKI Jakarta, Jl. Abdurrohim 2, Kuningan Barat, Jakarta 12710, tel. (021) 510-738

West Java: Kanwil VI Depparpostel Jawa Barat, Jl. K.H. Penghulu Hasan Mustafa 22, Bandung 40263, tel. (022) 72355; Diparda Tk.I Jawa Barat, Jl. Cipaganti 151-153, Bandung 40161, tel. (022) 81490

Yogyakarta: Kanwil VIII Depparpostel D.I. Yogyakarta, Jl. Adisucipto Km 7-8, P.O. Box 003 YKBB 55001, Yogyakarta 55282, tel. (0274) 5150; Diparda D.I. Yogyakarta, Jl. Malioboro 14, Yogyakarta 55213, tel. (0274) 62811 ext. 218/224

KALIMANTAN

East Kalimantan: Kanwil XIII Depparpostel Kaltimur & Kalteng, Jl. Belibis 227, Samarinda 75117, tel. (0541) 32286; Diparda Tk.I Klaimantan Timur, Jl. Ade Irma Nasution I, Samarinda 75117, tel. (0541) 21669

South Kalimantan: Kanwil XII Depparpostel Kalimantan Selatan, Jl. Pangeran Samudera 92, Banjarmasin 70111, tel. (0511) 68707; Diparda Tk.I Kalimantan Selatan, Jl. Mayjen D.I. Panjaitan 23, Banjarmasin 70114, tel. (0511) 2982

West Kalimantan: Kanwil XIX Depparpostel Kalimantan Barat, Jl. Sutan Syahrir 17 Kota Baru, Pontianak 78116, tel. (0561) 39444; Diparda Tk.I Kalimantan Barat, Jl. Achmad Sood 25, Pontianak 78121, tel. (0561) 36712

MALUKU

Kanwil XVI Depparpostel Maluku, Jl. Sultan Hasanuddin Tantui, Ambon 97128, tel. (0911) 43762; Diparda Tk.I Maluku, c/o Kantor Gubernur KDH Tk.I Maluku, Jl. Pattimura, P.O. Box 113, Ambon 97124, tel. (0911) 52471

NUSATENGGARA

East Nusatenggara: Kanwil XI Depparpostel NTT & Timor Timur, Jl. Ir. Soekarno 29, Kupang 85112, tel. (0391) 21160; Diparda Tk.I Nusatenggara Timur, Jl. Jend. Basuki Rachmat 1, Kupang 85117, tel. (0391) 21540

Timor Timur: Diparda Timor Timur, Jl. Dr. Yose Carvalite, Dili, tel. (0390) 21530

West Nusatenggara: Kanwil XX Depparpostel Nusatenggara Barat, Jl. Indrakila 2A, Pajang Timur, Mataram 83121, tel. (0364) 22327; Diparda Tk.I Nusatenggara Barat, Jl. Langko 70, Ampenan 83114, tel. (0364) 21730

SULAWESI

North Sulawesi: Kanwil XV Depparpostel Sulawesi Utara & Tengah, Jl. Diponegoro 111, Manado 95112, tel. (0431) 51723; Diparda Tk.I Sulawesi Utara, Komplek Perkantoran, Jl. 17 Agustus, Manado 95117, tel. (0341) 64299

South Sulawesi: Kanwil XIV Depparpostel Sulselra, Jl. Andi Pangeran Pettarani, Ujung Pandang 90222, tel. (0411) 321142; Diparda Tk.I Sulawesi Selatan, Jl. Sultan Alaudin 105B, Ujung Pandang 90222, tel. (0411) 83897

SUMATRA

Aceh: Kanwil XVIII D.I. Aceh, Jl. Mesjid Raya 6, Banda Aceh 23121, tel. (0651) 22888; Diparda D.I. Aceh, Jl. TGK Chik Kuta Karang 3, Banda Aceh 23121, tel. (0651) 23692

Lampung: Kanwil IV Depparpostel Lampung & Bengkulu, Jl. Kotaraja 12, Tanjungkarang, Bandar Lampung 35111, tel. (0721) 55208; Diparda Tk.I Lampung, Jl. W.R. Supratman 39, Gunung Mas, Bandar Lampung 35111, tel. (0721) 45265

North Sumatra: Kanwil I Depparpostel Sumatra Utara, Jl. Alfalah 22, Kampung Baru, Medan 20146, tel. (061) 322-838; Diparda Tk.I Sumatra Utara, Jl. Jend. A Yani 107, Medan 20151, tel. (061) 511-101

Riau: Kanwil XXI Depparpostel Riau, Jl. Merbau 16, P.O. Box 296, Pekanbaru 28141, tel. (0761) 31452; Diparda Tk.I Riau, Jl. Gajah Mada 200, Pekanbaru 28116, tel. (0761) 25301

South Sumatra: Kanwil III Depparpostel Sumatra Selatan & Jambi, Jl. Lebak Daun, Palembang 30137, tel (0711) 358-948; Diparda Tk.I Sumatra Selatan, Jl. Bay Salim 200, Palembang 30126, tel. (0711) 24981

West Sumatra: Kanwil II Depparpostel Sumatra Barat, Jl. Khatib Sulaeman, Padang Baru, Padang 25137, tel. (0751) 55711; Diparda Tk.I Sumatra Barat, Jl. Jend. Sudirman 43, Padang, tel. (0751) 34231

Also well informed and fluent in English are the people at the Visitor Information Center, Jakarta Theatre Building, Jl. Thamrin 9, which boasts a wide selection of publications and maps. Here's where you can pick up the really useful *Jakarta Bus Routes and Train Services* and *Jakarta General Information*.

Other Sources

The American Women's Association, Jl. Lauser 12, Kebayoran Baru, Jakarta, tel. (021) 722-1947, is very active in welcoming newcomers. The AWA provides a wealth of information about living in Indonesia, including an excellent handbook called *Introducing Indonesia: A Guide to Expatriate Living*. Although this guide is directed more toward meeting the needs of resident expats rather than tourists, there's much information of benefit to both. AWA also operates a lending library (open only to members), a thrift shop where foreigners can purchase used books and clothing, and a servant's registry.

The local Garuda, Merpati, or Bouraq airlines offices, although not strictly in the tourist information business, may employ personnel more knowledgeable than those in official government tourist offices. Garuda staff often dispenses informative, full-color brochures on each Indonesian province. Travel agency personnel can also be extremely helpful. In small towns, the Department of Education and Culture (Kantor Pendidikan dan Kebudayaan, or PDK) is the best place to go for inquiries of a historical or cultural nature. PDK people can sometimes provide the exact locations of old ruins, or distribute maps and literature on sites, art forms, architectural attractions, and dance venues.

PRINT

Newspapers And Magazines

English-language dailies published in Jakarta include the *Indonesian Times* (morning), the *Indonesian Observer* (afternoon), and the *Jakarta Post*. Singapore's *Straits Times* also frequently publishes stories on Indonesia. Other English-language papers include the *Surabaya Post* and the *Bali Post,* newspapers providing limited world coverage. Local newsstands also sell overseas editions of the *Asian Wall Street Journal, London Times, Bangkok Post, International Herald Tribune,* and *The Australian. Time* and *Newsweek* are readily available, though sections critical of the government are sometimes heavily censored.

Reading Indonesian newspapers is a good way to improve your Indonesian. Most of Indonesia's 271 domestic publications are privately owned and most are based in Jakarta. Leading-circulation dailies include the far-sighted and daring Catholic newspaper *Kompas* and the *Jakarta Pos Kota*. Major news magazines focusing on current events include *Editor* and the *Newsweek*-like *Tempo*.

Specialty Publications

Specialized magazines serving the business community include the weeklies *Review Indonesia* and *Asiaweek*. Both magazines are excellent sources of news on Indonesia, with an emphasis on the economy, and both are available from newsstands in the metropolitan and tourist areas of Indonesia. *Inside Indonesia* is a hard-hitting, incisive Australian magazine with brilliant insights on Indonesian politics, new technologies, lifestyles, culture, and the business community. For a subscription, write P.O. Box 190, Northcote, Victoria 3070, Australia, tel. (03) 419-5588. The monthly *Indonesian Journal* publishes information and articles (mostly in Indonesian) pertinent to the Indonesian-American community in the United States. Copies are available free at the Indonesian embassy in Washington D.C., as well as at the Indonesian consulates in Los Angeles, San Francisco, Houston, Chicago, and New York.

The Indonesian Documentation and Information Centre (INDOC) is an independent organization collecting and disseminating information on political and social developments in Indonesia, with a particular emphasis on human rights, labor, and the environment. The American Gamelan Institute, tel./fax (603) 448-8837, produces a journal, as well as videos, cassettes, and CDs featuring Indonesian music. John Mac-Dougall of Indonesia Publications sponsors a number of periodicals. *Indonesia News Service* digests current news stories about Indonesia from leading magazines and newspapers. *East Timor Reports* is a series of topical briefing books updated every three months; MacDougall is also the editor of *Antara Kita*, a bulletin of the Indonesian Studies Committee. This 12-page bulletin, issued four times a year, contains articles and book reviews on scholarly research in Indonesia. Subscriptions are $6 in the U.S., $9 in Europe, $10 in Asia and Africa. Address: 7538 Newberry Lane, Lanham-Seabrook, MD 20706, U.S.A., tel. (301) 552-3251, fax (301) 552-4465; e-mail apakabar@access.digex.net.

Books And Guidebooks

The most active publisher of both reprints and new titles on Indonesia is Oxford University Press, Walton St., Oxford OX2 6DP, London, England, or 16-00 Pollitt Dr., Fair Lawn, NJ 07410, U.S.A., which carries at least 30 titles on Indonesia. Topics range from a discussion of the *prahu* to nostalgic rambles of 19th-century adventurers, from archaic social customs and history to Asia's natural wonders. Of a more scholarly persuasion are the publications of the Cornell Modern Indonesia Project, 102 West Ave., Ithaca, NY 14850, U.S.A. Ask for a complete list of publications. Another estimable press dealing with Asian subjects is University of Hawaii Press, 2840 Kolowalu St., Honolulu, HI 96822, U.S.A. E.J. Brill, Postbus 9000, 2300 PA Leiden, the Netherlands, tel. (071) 312-624 publishes Dutch-, English-, German-, and French-language reprints of old out-of-print Indonesian classics such as F.M. Schnitger's *Forgotten Kingdoms of Sumatra* and A. Hoogerwerf's *Udjung Kulon: The Land of the Last Javan Rhinoceros*. Ask for the South and East Asia catalog. AMS Press, Inc., 56 East 13th St., New York, NY 10003, U.S.A. publishes a fascinating selection of reprints of such arcane classics as Claire Holt's *Dance Quest in Celebes* and *The Community of Erai*. Ask for the Southeast Asia mail-order catalog.

Bookstores

Jakarta and other major cities are the best places to buy foreign-language publications. Prices for imported books and magazines are high but selections large. Books published in Indonesia are cheaper in Jakarta than at tourist sites. In Jakarta, try Gunung Agung (Indonesia's largest bookshop), Jl. Kwitang 6, with a wide selection of English paperbacks as well as books, guides, and maps on Indonesia. Also check out the Gramedia bookshops at Jl. Melawai IV/13, Blok M, and Jl. Gajah Mada 109; the bookshop at Sarinah Department Store; and hotel bookshops and newsstands. In Medan, North Sumatra, try Toko Buku Deli, Jl. A. Yani 48; a Gramedia bookstore is located at Jl. Gajah Mada 23. There are a number of bookshops in Kuta, Ubud, and Sanur on Bali, where you can find ample reading material, including plenty of used books.

In Singapore, Select Books Pte. Ltd., 19 Tanglin Rd. #03-15, Tanglin Shopping Centre, third floor, Singapore 1024, tel. 732-1515, fax 736-0855, has one of the world's largest retail selections of books on Southeast Asia currently in print. For out-of-print books on Indonesia, head for Antiques of the Orient, 19 Tanglin Road #02-40, Tanglin Shopping Centre, Singapore 1024, tel. 733-0830, fax 732-8652. The huge Toppan Bookstore in the Orchard Plaza Shopping Centre on Orchard Road, and MPH Bookstore, 71-

77 Stanford Rd. both have very respectable Indonesia collections. These big Singapore chain stores may have a wider selection of books on Indonesia than many shops in Indonesia itself.

In Holland, Wout Vuyk Antiquariaat, Spuistraat 316, 1012 VX, Amsterdam, tel. (020) 220-461, stocks a very respectable collection of used books and folios on Indonesia. For the rare find, scour Amsterdam's flea markets and other antiquarian bookshops.

FILM

Indonesian Films

The domestic film industry is dying. Only 30 films were produced in 1992, half the output of 1991. One company has a monopoly on film distribution; it alone decides which films are shown—for the most part kung fu and horror thrillers. Films are also subject to censorship. The Indonesian film *Langitku Rumahku (My Sky My Home)* earned high praise at international film festivals in Germany, France, and the U.S., but was yanked off the screen after a single showing in Jakarta.

Films About Indonesia

Check your nearest major library or video rental store for films and videos on Indonesia. See the movies *The Year of Living Dangerously* and *Max Havalaar,* the first Australian and the second Dutch, both before and after you visit Indonesia. Anthropological film archives may have copies of Margaret Mead's *Island of Bali*; the strong, primitive feeling depicted in this 1930s film no longer exists on Bali. *The Sky Above and the Mud Below* is a splendid documentary made by a Dutch-French expedition, the first to cross what was then the Netherlands New Guinea, walking 450 km from the Arafura Sea to the north coast. An exciting whitewater river video is Sobek Adventure's *The River of the Red Ape,* recording the first descent of Sumatra's Alas River through the world's largest orangutan rainforest.

An award-winning Australian documentary TV series, *Riding the Tiger,* examines contemporary Indonesian society and the forces that shaped it. The producers spent two years traveling the archipelago, capturing Indonesians at every level of society, from plantation workers to generals. *Ring of Fire* documents the extraordinary ten-year voyage of two British filmmakers, brothers Lorne and Lawrence Blair. As much a spiritual travelogue as a report of a harrowing physical journey, this avant-garde series consists of four volumes, each an hour long: *Spice Island Saga, Dance of the Warriors, East of Krakatoa,* and *Dream Wanderers of Borneo.* The set is available for $99.50 from Mystic Fire Video, Inc., P.O. Box 1092, Cooper Station, New York, NY 10276, U.S.A., tel. (800) 727-8433.

Mitra Tourism Development Division, Jl. Ciputat Raya 64, Pondok Pinang, Jakarta 12310, tel. (021) 769-6004, produces videos on popular tourist performances and attractions. *Film on Indonesia* is a valuable, informative, and very readable catalog for those interested in Indonesian studies, anthropology, and ethnographic film. Send $5 to Yale Southeast Asia Studies, Yale University, P.O. Box 208206, New Haven, CT 06520-8206.

MAPS

The best folded maps of Indonesia are produced by Nelles Verlag GmbH, Schleibheimer Str. 371 b, D 80935, Munich 45, Germany, tel. (089) 351-5084, fax 354-2544. These beautiful creations feature vivid color printing, topographic features in realistic relief, and major city plans in margin inserts. Widely available in U.S. bookstores for $6.95; cheaper in Indonesia (around Rp5000).

Periplus Editions publishes a three-map series with a focus on Java. Another high-quality folded map is Hildebrand's *Travel Map of Western Indonesia,* which covers Sumatra, Java, and Sulawesi. This up-to-date map clearly presents the country's topography, roads, and towns. Also useful is *Indonesie Reisatlas* (ISBN: 9025721273), available in both Dutch and English, published by Intermap bv, Enschede and J.H. Gottmer/H.J.W. Becht, Haarlem, the Netherlands.

Map Link stocks the Periplus and Nelles Indonesia maps, as well as several series published in Southeast Asia. Contact Map Link at 25 East Mason St., Santa Barbara, CA 93101 U.S.A., tel. (805) 965-4402, fax (800) 627-7768 (U.S.A. only), (805) 962-0884 (everywhere). A valuable resource for the serious traveler.

Domestic Sources

It's hard to get good maps in Indonesia. Maps have military associations, and government officials are very hesitant about giving them away. The Directorat Topografi Angkatan Darat in Jakarta has up-to-date, comprehensive maps, but won't sell them to tourists—topo maps are classified. You may have better luck at Seksi Publikasi (Publications Section), Geological Survey of Indonesia, Geological Museum, Jl. Diponegoro 57, Bandung, W. Java, which has on file the 1962 series (1:50,000) of full-color U.S. Army Mapping Service (AMS) maps, as well as geologic maps. Open 0800-1200.

The *Falk City Map*, available for Rp9500 at any major hotel or bookstore in Jakarta, is the best map to Indonesia's capitol. The PT Starnico maps of Kalimantan, Maluku, and Irian Jaya are a joke; the company seems to have determined village locations by throwing darts. Starnico's maps of Sumatra and Java are better. PT Pembina, Jl. Pajaitan 45, Jakarta, tel. (021) 813-886, publishes regional maps of Sumatra, Java, Bali, and the Outer Islands, complete with distance charts. Both series may be purchased at most bookstores.

Indonesian tourist offices dispense national, regional, and local maps free, but you can't always rely on their accuracy. Try to get hold of the *Indonesia Tourist Map*, a handy, full-color booklet of maps and facts that should last about as long as your two-month pass. Regional tourist offices also give away town plans of the main cities of Sumatra, Java, and Bali. Many airline offices, travel agencies, police stations, and tourist and *camat* offices display big wall maps, some of the best area maps available. Hotels frequently publish their own maps so guests won't get lost and will be able to find their way to the owner's sister's restaurant.

Overseas Sources

The most extensive stocks of maps for sale in Australia are at Angus and Robertsons, 107 Elizabeth St., Melbourne; Sydney's Angus and Robertsons on Pitt St.; Dymock's on George St., Sydney; and the Rex Map Centre in Sydney, 412 Pacific Highway, Artaron, NSW.

Topografische Dienst, Westvest 9, Delft, the Netherlands, has many maps of Indonesia. Very

helpful proprietor. This is the place if you want a copy of a map on, say, Wetar Island or the Talaud Archipelago. Most of the maps are old, but recent maps of the outlying islands are nearly impossible to find. Despite the passing of years, maps based on topographic survey work by the Dutch are still very informative. Most old Dutch maps are usually available as dyeline (*diazo*) copies only.

TPC Maps

Probably the best maps you can buy are *USAF Tactical Pilotage Charts* (TPC). These cost about US$5 each and are available from Distribution Center CH4, National Ocean Survey, Riverdale, MD 20737, U.S.A.; Air Touring Shop, Elstrea Aerodrome, Hertfordshire U.K.; and the Rex Map Centre, 412 Pacific Highway, Artaron, NSW, Australia. Though TPC maps are excellent with coastlines and rivers, the urban areas are out of date. Available in Indonesia and Malaysia; difficult to find in Singapore.

U.S. Army Maps

You can acquire good topo maps of the main Indonesian islands from the U.S. Army Topographic Command, Washington, D.C. Unfortunately, these maps are made from aerial and satellite photos with very little local input—fairly important towns may be shown as little villages and vice versa. Also, roads are not current.

Atlases

The Library of Congress Geography and Map Division has cataloged over 48,000 atlases, the largest such collection in the world. The official prewar atlas of the tropical Netherlands territories, *Atlas van Tropisch Nederland*, was produced in 1938. Many of its social, economic, and political assertions are long outdated, yet for Outer Island Indonesia it's still one of the few complete sources. Another useful resource is the 975-page *Gazeteer of Place Names of Indonesia and Portuguese Timor* (1978), published by the U.S. Army Topographic Command, Washington, D.C. This unbelievably detailed tome provides the exact coordinates and spellings of tens of thousands of Indonesian place-names. Cross-referenced with 32 maps. Write for publication list, prices, and shipping details.

GETTING READY

Documents And Paperwork

You need a passport to cross borders, exchange currency, cash traveler's checks, pick up mail, rent a room, and please police, immigration, and bank officials. If entering Indonesia through an unofficial gateway, you'll also need a visa from an Indonesian consulate or embassy. Write down your passport number, traveler's check numbers, credit card numbers, vital contact addresses, and any other pertinent information. Make two copies. One copy you should carry with your luggage; leave the other with a friend or family member back home. Register all valuables such as cameras and tape recorders in your passport. If these items are insured before you leave your home country and are registered in your passport, that's vital proof if the items are stolen.

It would also be wise to jot down your plane ticket numbers, place and date of issue, and how tickets were paid for (credit card number, cash, personal check); this information is invaluable if the ticket is lost or stolen, and could save you enormous hassles. It's advisable to travel with a copy of your birth certificate in case you lose your passport.

If you wear glasses or contacts, or take medication on a regular basis, make sure you carry a copy of the prescription. Have your doctor make out prescriptions using scientific names that are internationally understood. Unless you are entering Indonesia from an infected area, you won't be asked for your International World Health Certificate. Indonesia only has a few official youth hostels so you really don't need an International Youth Hostel Association (IYHA) card here. Just pay the few dollars extra.

An International Student Identification Card (ISIC) could be useful in obtaining discounts of up to 25% on rail and flight tickets. To apply, write CIEE Student Travel, 205 East 42nd St., New York, NY 10017, U.S.A., tel. (212) 661-1414. Obtain an International Driver's License, valid for a year, from your local automobile association. You never know when you'll want to rent a car or van; an Indonesian license on Bali costs Rp63,000.

Bring at least 10 passport photos, then have 30-40 more printed cheaply from the negative in Singapore, Penang, Hong Kong, or Indonesia. Passport photos are necessary when filling out applications or applying for a *surat jalan,* and they make great mementos—you'll use up dozens on a trip through Asia. Don't leave home without a small electronic or conventional address book or organizer to fill with the names of new friends. Your business card is highly sought and prized by Indonesians. Bring a stack to save the trouble of writing out your address all the time.

Packing

Pack light. A week before leaving, gather up everything you're planning to take, put it all in your pack, and go for a walk. How will it feel maneuvering that much weight through jostling, crowded Indonesian rail and bus stations under a humid tropical sun?

A top-loading duffel bag with a strong shoulder strap is probably the best traveling companion. Choose a sturdy, well-designed bag with heavy-duty zippers and noncorrosive Fastex and Dacron thread. Make sure your backpack includes a hip belt and semirigid frame. It's absurd to see travelers buried beneath big backpacks. People who travel with large cumbersome packs are having an equipment experience, not an Indonesian experience. All that's necessary is a half-empty soft canvas bag about the size of a gym bag. In fact, you don't really need to take anything but money: you can buy everything you need in Indonesia.

Affix an identifying badge or mark on your pack. It's also wise to put an identifying badge inside each piece of your luggage in case the one on the outside is lost. If you're going camping, bring a light tent, inflatable pillow, poncho, and a portable one-burner kerosene stove. All other gear you can buy in Indonesia. Since the country is generally too hot for your standard sleeping bag, run a seam down a folded cotton bed sheet to make a light sleeping bag, or simply use a sleeping bag liner. Standard bags will be useful if you're planning to ascend to high altitudes. In Indonesia, nights and mornings are cool above 300 meters; count on the temperature dropping about 0.6 degrees C for every

SNAPPING SHOTS

With its lush landscapes, colorful markets, architectural and historical sites, and friendly people, Indonesia is an endlessly photogenic country with thousands of potential subjects. But to enhance the photographic experience and ensure the quality of your shots, some advance preparation is necessary.

First of all, pack light. If you're struggling with two bags full of still-camera photographic equipment, all you'll do is worry about your gear—and you should worry. Two SLR camera bodies plus two lenses are the maximum you should carry. Be sure both bodies are in good working order and the meters have fresh batteries.

Equipment And Accessories

Because of the sharp light and shadow contrasts in the tropics, a camera with through-the-lens metering is essential. Beginners should start with a model from a major manufacturer. With the new generation of fully automatic, auto-focusing 35 mm subcompacts, travelers are beginning to discard their clunkier, heavier SLRs. You might also consider an instant Polaroid camera when visiting the country's outlying areas; these cause great delight among the local populace.

It's best to take a spare set of fresh batteries for both camera and flash. A 24-mm wide angle and an 35-110 or 80-200 zoom will probably handle about 80% of the situations you'll face. Zoom lenses aren't very fast so also bring along a basic 50-55 mm lens for available-light photography using fast film. Take the smallest camera bag that will hold your gear. Use a skylight filter (1A or 1B) to reduce the bluish haze of scenes in color, and a yellow, orange, or red filter to add tone and contrast to black-and-white photos. Filters also protect your expensive lenses. A lens hood is highly recommended to keep direct sun off the lens.

Indonesian heat and humidity can easily ruin your film and camera. Heat gives color film a greenish-yellow tone impossible to eradicate in normal processing. Silica gel packets, stored with your equipment, can keep moisture at a minimum; dry tea leaves are also effective. Never leave your camera and film in the sun or any hot place for any length of time. Don't allow film to sit in your camera for more than a week as the emulsion will stick and sweat, resulting in wavy lines in your pictures.

Tropical mildew growth can be a problem for cameras and slides. Storage in cool locations, like the inside of a rucksack, will cut down on this problem; check periodically for mildew build-up and use silica gel. Insist on hand inspection of your carry-on camera bag and film at domestic airport security checkpoints.

Film

One of the finest films in the world for tropical photography is Kodachrome 64. Also take along faster 200 ASA film and even some 400 (or higher) ASA film for use in poor light situations like caves and Chinese temples. Color film is widely available throughout Indonesia. The most popular 35 mm brand is Fuji, sold everywhere in a full range of ASA/DIN ratings and costing about the same as in the West. Fuji 50 ASA Velvia film is probably the best film available in Indonesia, sold in larger metropolitan areas and tourist centers. It can be processed reliably and cheaply in Jakarta, Yogyakarta, and Bali. Although Kodachrome and Fuji slide film are sold in Jakarta and Bali, the processing is unreliable.

Always check the expiration date on the film box, especially in Indonesia's outlying areas.

When To Shoot

Light diffusion on the equator is different than in temperate zones so beware of the intense sunlight and haze from 1000 to 1500—causes color film to flatten and wash out. Sometimes you can increase the vibrancy of your daytime pictures by deliberately underexposing by at least a half f-stop. Polarizing filters also help a great deal. The very best light for rich, warm color photos under the tropical sun usually arrives between 0700 and 1000. Rise with the Indonesians in the early hours for cleaner air and crisper light and colors. The sun is straight overhead by around 1100, which usually causes a bluish cast. Careful underexposure by one f-stop or so will help put wispy clouds back in the sky.

Remember that the lush tropical green of rice fields or jungle usually photographs better when backlit by the sun. Shadows are harsh and strong in the tropics, especially at midday, causing high contrast. Find those films that show more shadow detail, or take careful light readings from the shadows. Or use a flash to fill in the shadows; if you don't have a flash, you'll need at least ASA 200 film for Borobudur. Sidelighting also helps achieve greater depth in most subjects. You'll get the brightest colors from your sunset shots if you take the exposure reading off the eastern sky, then turn and shoot directly into the sunset.

Although the use of a flash is terribly distracting to the audience, a powerful flash is often the only means by which to capture the nighttime dances of Bali. Always be mindful of scale; when you shoot a picture of an immense volcanic crater, without a tree or human figure it will look like a scale model made of sand and mud.

Photographing People

Indonesians are polite and congenial and usually willing to let you record them on film. In fact, a big problem is keeping bystanders and city crazies out of your compositions. The Baliem Valley of Irian Jaya and possibly Torajaland in South Sulawesi will probably be the only places you'll be asked for money (Rp100-200 is enough). Among traditional peoples the belief is common that photography will capture their souls. The Sakai of the Dumai area of South Sumatra are downright hostile when you try to take pictures, Toba Batak women are shy, and in some orthodox Islamic areas such as Aceh religious prohibitions bar photos of people in prayer. It's also impolite to photograph people bathing in streams, rivers, or lakes.

As a courtesy, first ask for permission with the word *permisi,* or use expressive hand gestures, making your intention clear. Please respect refusals. The discreet use of a telephoto lens obviates the need to ask permission. In street photography, hire a canopied *becak* for use as a blind. Be aware of the sacred nature of many of the ceremonies you witness; act accordingly when using a flash or maneuvering for shots. Disrespect for monuments and a pushy demeanor will not only result in unpleasantness for you but trouble for photographers who follow.

Photographing Objects

Always ask first before photographing the interiors of mosques, churches, or temples. It's highly unlikely permission will be refused. If you wish to photograph government buildings, museums, or monuments, a fee of Rp500-3000 is charged for a still camera and Rp3000-5000 for a video camera. This fee may apply to the exterior, interior, and even surrounding grounds.

In some exhibits or museums, the use of a flash will fade the priceless exhibits and is prohibited. All over Indonesia it's forbidden to take pictures of airports, military barracks, bridges, railroad stations, harbors, and port or military installations without the necessary papers—even asking for these may arouse suspicion. If in doubt, ask officials or guards, or your film might be confiscated.

Processing

Color print film is developed and printed locally in just one hour. Slides take two to seven days, depending upon where you are. At only around Rp500 per 35 mm print, color print costs are lower than in most Western countries. Developing black-and-white film in Indonesia could be a real problem, with the film sent to Jakarta for a 10-day wait.

The quality is generally good at the better shops and photo studios, but it can vary widely. No processing facilities for Agfa exist in Indonesia. An alternative is to just store your exposed film, which can keep up to two months before processing, or airmail exposed film to processing centers back home.

Mail-order processing is convenient, low-priced, and guarantees quality results. One of the risks, though, is loss or damage in the mail. Kodak mailers, small prepaid envelopes selling for around Rp23,000 (including film) in drugstores and camera shops, cost less if ordered through the big New York mail-order houses. Using mailers is especially recommended if you work with Kodachrome.

---

100 meters of altitude. Local outfitters may rent sleeping bags or these may be supplied by your guide.

Clothing

Choose patterned or dark-colored fabrics that won't show wear or soil quickly. In a tropical climate, cotton clothes are most comfortable. But since 100% cotton requires ironing, bring along a few half-cotton, half-synthetic, wrinkle-free garments for special occasions and visits to

bureaucratic offices. Indonesia is too hot for Western-style sportcoats, so either buy a light *batik* sportcoat or an attractive *batik* long-sleeved shirt for dress-up—quite acceptable and very fashionable.

Except in the mountains, denim is too hot for Indonesia and it also takes too long to dry; perhaps pack one pair of jeans for high-altitude trekking or cycling. Looser corduroys or light summer trousers are better suited for this climate. Take along a warm light sweater or cardigan for the mountains. A water-resistant jacket packs light and if worn over sweaters keeps you warm. Long-sleeved shirts or light sweatshirts are appropriate for cool evenings and as protection against sunburn or insects. It's generally considered inappropriate for men to wear shorts for anything but the roughest manual work, long-distance cycling, hash runs, or trips to and from the bathroom or beach.

Recommended also is a cloth or khaki fishing hat deep enough to stay on your head in heavy winds and with a brim to protect you from rain and sun. Spray with water repellent. It'll look frumpy, but will do the job. A helmet is a life-saving investment for bicyclists and motorcyclists; buy one with a bubble to protect your face from rain, sleet, and insects.

Women should take long-sleeved blouses and longish skirts. Skimpy clothing, backless dresses, shorts, and even slacks can be offensive in this Muslim country, especially if worn in mosques, temples, churches, or on formal occasions. Your bikini will pass provided it's worn only at the swimming pool or on Kuta or Sanur Beach on Bali. Experienced female travelers replace nightgowns with T-shirts. Bathing suits can double as underwear; they're easy to wash, quick-drying, light, and comfortable. Take one wrinkle-proof dress that's easy to wash. Dresses of double-knit cotton T-shirt material are excellent. Scarves are stylish, lightweight, and compact, and can be used as belts, shawls, or temple sashes.

You need one pair of hiking shoes, one pair of sandals, and one pair of dress shoes. Sandals you can wear anywhere—everyday traveling, hiking, snorkeling, coral walking, dancing, motorcycle riding, even to the immigration office. Perfect for Indonesia. Dress shoes come in handy for meetings with officials. Although flip-flops almost always come with your hotel or *losmen,* they're invariably too small for Westerners.

Don't expect to buy good quality footwear in Indonesia; such shoes are hard to find. The international chain Bata sells inexpensive shoes in leather, canvas, or plastic, but a U.S. size nine is about the largest size they make. It's extremely hard to find size nine shoes for women.

GETTING THERE

The prices and air routes into Indonesia change constantly. As soon as the *Official Airlines Guide* is published, it's out of date. Check the latest and cheapest means of getting to Indonesia in the Sunday travel section of a major metropolitan newspaper. Check also the Yellow Pages and adventure travel media.

The International Air Traffic Association (IATA) is a cartel of air carriers that fixes high fares for all participating carriers—you'll pay the same inflated rate no matter which airline you use. Avoid paying full IATA fares by refusing to patronize the airlines, which must charge full IATA fares. Instead, buy your tickets from travel agencies and consolidators. These discount agencies often offer gray-market tickets at low rates that cannot be advertised. To know what fare, features, and restrictions you're trying to beat, check first with Garuda, the Indonesian national air carrier.

Ask about special promotional fares. Before paying for your ticket, inquire after restrictions, refunds, cancellation fees, and stopovers. Those under 26 should ask if airlines grant discounts to those with student IDs. Infants and children four to 12 could also receive substantial discounts.

A good deal could be an Advance Purchase Excursion (APEX) fare, which must be reserved and paid for two to three weeks before departure. There's a substantial penalty for cancellation, with no stopovers allowed. Since APEX tickets require rigid departure and return dates, purchase one-way tickets only. Rates are lower in the off-season, February to November.

Consider buying a one-way ticket from Europe or the U.S. direct to Bangkok, Hong Kong, or Singapore; from these points it's relatively inexpensive to continue on to Indonesia. From Bangkok you can travel down to Penang; from there it's an easy hop on a boat or plane to Medan, North Sumatra.

To obtain an Indonesian entry stamp you need a ticket out of Indonesia.

Gateways

You can fly into Indonesia from all over the world. The three main international air gateways are Jakarta, Denpasar, and Medan. By far the largest number of flights arrive in Jakarta's international Sukarno/Hatta Airport, 20 km west of Jakarta in Cengkareng.

Unbelievably, except on expensive cruise ships or by private yacht, it's really difficult to reach the largest island nation in the world by water. There are only two regular entry points by ship. Ferries depart Penang in Malaysia for Medan and a daily ferry connects Singapore with Palau Batam in the Riau Archipelago; from there you can board another ferry to Pekanbaru, East Sumatra, or Jakarta. Ocean liners and cruise ships of the Holland American Lines, Garuda's Spice Island Cruises, and Lindblad Travel call at remote Indonesian ports at luxury prices. These upmarket tour companies offer fly/cruise arrangements whereby you're flown to Surabaya, Bali, or Medan to meet your cruise vessels. See your travel agent.

Circle-Pacific And Round-The-World Tickets

Using a combination of airlines out of the U.S.—Air New Zealand, Qantas, MAS, Singapore Airlines—travelers can spend up to a year circling the Pacific and Southeast Asia. For Qantas and Air New Zealand, you're looking at around US$2449 roundtrip, 14-day advance purchase, with four stopovers. Additional stopovers are US$75-200 extra. Some require that you use all your tickets within 12 months, others give only six months. To save money, either ask your travel agent to do business through a consolidator offering flights to Asia, or call a consolidator directly. The cheapest fares feature midweek departures.

Air Brokers International, Inc., 323 Geary St., Ste. 411, San Francisco, CA 94102, U.S.A., tel. (800) 883-3273 or (415) 397-1383, fax (415) 397-4767 sells more round-the-world tickets than any other consolidator on earth. It's also the largest non-Indonesian consolidator of Garuda tickets in the U.S., selling a Los Angeles-Denpasar-Jakarta ticket for the unbelievable price of US$850 roundtrip.

Indonesia may be included as a stopover on many round-the-world tickets. The infinite possible variations in round-the-world itineraries

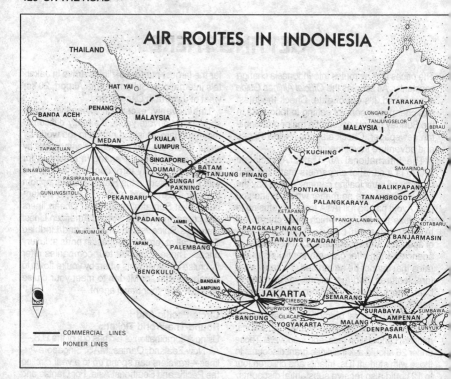

AIR ROUTES IN INDONESIA

COMMERCIAL LINES
PIONEER LINES

depend on the ticketing alternative the traveler selects. The best and most expensive is the full-fare, full-service ticket. You can go where you like on almost any airline and take six months or a year doing it. The main drawback is you have to zig-zag around the world in one direction only, booking individual flights as you go without the privilege of switching carriers. Plus, all your flights may not be available when you want them. You sacrifice some flexibility but save some cash by buying a round-the-world package offered by an individual airline or specific group of airlines. It's cheaper still to string together several discount tickets, acquired in such bargain centers as London, Bangkok, or Hong Kong. There is considerable variation in price, length of validity, and number of stopovers permitted. If your round-the-world ticket doesn't offer a stop in Indonesia, try to land as close as possible—Singapore or Bangkok—then hop down to the archipelago. Singapore Airlines (SIA) sells a US$2570 economy ticket with stops

in at least three cities; six-month validity, 14-day advance purchase. Qantas has a US$3000 ticket with 21-day advance purchase.

FROM MALAYSIA

From Penang

Malaysia is a good place to buy cheap air tickets. Refer to the *Straits Times* for ads. Popular with travelers is the low-priced hop from Penang across the Strait of Malacca to Medan in North Sumatra. The MAS flight leaves Penang daily, takes just 20 minutes, and costs around M$54 one-way, M$108 roundtrip. An excellent high-speed ferry service operates between Penang and Medan every Tuesday and Friday at 0800, then returns from Medan to Penang the same day at 1330. First-class fare is M$100 one-way, M$180 roundtrip; economy class is M$90 one-way, M$160 roundtrip. Children 2-12 fly half price. Free refreshments and snacks and free

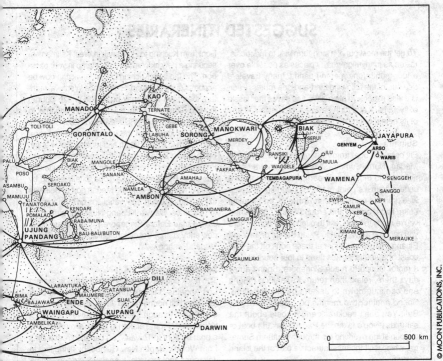

transfer from the port of Belawan to Medan city center are included. Belawan customs doesn't seem to check tickets out. In Penang, buy ferry tickets at the KPLFS office, PPC Shopping Complex, Jl. Pusara King Edward, 10300 Penang, tel. (04) 625-630 or 625-631, fax 625-508. In Medan, call (061) 514-888 or 518-340. Travel agencies and hotels along Chulia Street in Penang sell tickets.

From Kuala Lumpur
Malaysia's capital is a real travel bargain center. It's now just as cheap flying to Indonesia from Kuala Lumpur as from Singapore. The flight to Medan with MAS or Garuda is around M$78 one-way, M$156 roundtrip. MAS now flies from Kuala Lumpur to Surabaya, and twice weekly to Pontianak on West Kalimantan. **Student Travel Australia,** sixth floor, UBN Tower Letter Box 32, 10 Jalan P. Ramlee, 50250 Kuala Lumpur, Malaysia, sells a Kuala Lumpur-Denpasar MAS or Garuda ticket for about half the price of other

agencies. On the same street as STA in Kuala Lumpur are other cheap ticketing agencies.

From Melaka
Two ferry services leave Melaka for Dumai, East Sumatra. The trouble is you need a visa (obtainable in Kuala Lumpur) to enter Indonesia through Dumai, an economically and militarily sensitive oil installation. One operates once weekly for M$80 one-way, M$150 roundtrip, departing Melaka on Saturday at 1000 and arriving in Dumai around 1430. Buy tickets at **Atlas Travel Service,** Jl. Hang Jebat, tel. (06) 220-777, in Melaka. The other ferry, operated by **Tunar Rupat Express,** Jl. Merdeka 17 A, also costs M$80 one-way, M$150 roundtrip, but takes only 2.5 hours.

From East Malaysia
First hop a Straits Steamship Co. ship or fly MAS from Singapore to Kuching on Sarawak for M$242 roundtrip. Then, from Kuching, grab the Merpati flight to Pontianak in West Kali-

SUGGESTED ITINERARIES

To get the most out of a long-term visit to Indonesia, to see as many high-quality places as possible over a four-month (one reentry) period, many travelers use one of the following land-and-sea routes. Each is a less expensive alternative and saves the hassle of flying back and forth between Indonesia and any of its neighboring countries more than once.

Sumatra-Java-Bali

Fly or take a boat from Penang, West Malaysia, to Medan, North Sumatra. Northern Sumatra is the richest and most scenic part of the island from a cultural/tourist's point of view. Spend six to seven weeks in the wilds of Aceh Province, on beautiful Lake Toba, and in and around Bukittinggi. When you're ready to leave, exit through Pekanbaru, where you can ride a riverboat to Palau Batam or Tanjung Pinang, Riau. From either of these ports off the east coast of Sumatra it takes three to four hours aboard a motor launch to reach Singapore. Spend a few days there, relax, then return to Tanjung Pinang and continue down to Jakarta by ship or plane. Spend another two months on colorful Java and Bali. You don't backtrack and it costs about the same as if you'd taken the Padang-Jakarta boat or the punishing overland trip through southern Sumatra, which isn't the most attractive part of the island anyway.

Outer Island Route

Leave Bali for Surabaya, then make your way for two months by boat or plane through Sulawesi and Kalimantan, exiting Indonesia at Tarakan for Tawau. Spend some time journeying across East Malaysia, then return to Kalimantan on the regular Merpati

flight from Kuching to Pontianak in West Kalimantan, securing a new Indonesian entry stamp in your passport. The trip from Kuching to Pontianak can now be accomplished overland. Experience West Kalimantan, then from Pontianak board the cheap Bouraq flight to Singapore or take a ship from Pontianak to Tanjung Pinang in the Riau Islands off East Sumatra.

Next, board one of the launches to Singapore, then return to Palau Batam and receive a new entry. From Palau Batam board an oceangoing ferry to Pekanbaru, East Sumatra. From Pekanbaru take a bus up to Bukittinggi, Lake Toba, finally exiting by cross-channel ferry from the Medan port of Belawan to Penang. You can work variations on this theme—for instance, Darwin-Kupang-Nusatenggara-Bali-Java-Pulau Batam-Singapore-Pulau Batam (with new entry stamp)-Pekanbaru-Bukittinggi-Lake Toba-Medan-Penang.

Easterly Route

The back door approach is to take Garuda's direct Los Angeles-Bali-Jakarta flight, deplane at Biak (an island off northern Irian Jaya), then fly and take boats west through Maluku to Sulawesi and East Kalimantan. From Tarakan in East Kalimantan take a boat or flight to Tawau. You can also reach Biak from Wewak, Papua New Guinea, by flying first to Jayapura, the capital of Irian Jaya. Indonesian officials may not give you an entry stamp when you arrive in Jayapura, so you may need a visa from the Indonesian Embassy in Port Moresby, Papua New Guinea (Sir John Guisa Dr., tel. 253-116). Obtain the very latest info about PNG-Indonesia cross-border restrictions from travelers you meet along the way.

mantan. You can also now travel by road from Kuching to Pontianak. It's possible to fly visa-free from Brunei to Balikpapan, East Kalimantan on a regular Garuda flight. From Tawau in East Malaysia to Tarakan on East Kalimantan board a MAS or Bouraq flight.

FROM SINGAPORE

By Air

Singapore is a popular and convenient departure point for Jakarta, Denpasar, Medan, and

Padang. You can also reach the Riau Archipelago and Kalimantan from Singapore. Remember that 30-day excursion fares are usually cheaper than regular fares. Check travel agencies for the cheapest fares. Many advertise in the *Straits Times*. **Airmaster Travel Center,** 36-B Prinsep St., Room 1, Singapore 0718, tel. 338-3942 or 337-6838, sells a 30-day Singapore-Jakarta excursion fare. Price varies depending on airline and length of stay. Airmaster also sells a Singapore-Jakarta-Denpasar ticket and a Singapore-Denpasar ticket with a stopover in Yogyakarta.

Another reliable agency, one that's been around for at least 15 years, is **MAS Travel Center Ltd.,** 19 Tanglin Road, #06-01 Tanglin Shopping Center, Singapore 1024, tel. 737-8877. Cheapest is Myanma Airlines, which flies Fokker F-28s from Jakarta to Singapore for S$70 one-way. Friendly, with good food. Also cheap: Sempati Airlines, flying to Jakarta daily for as little as S$106 one-way. Sempati also flies from Tanjung Pinang to Jakarta for Rp150,000. Qantas flies three times weekly to Jakarta.

One great route involves flying MAS from Singapore to Medan with stops in Penang and Kuala Lumpur on the way back to Singapore. Good if you want to see a bit of Malaysia—Penang is like paradise compared to noisy, dusty Medan. For a four-week trip you need less than S$500, excluding the flight. Garuda also flies from Singapore to the Sumatran cities of Padang, Palembang, and Pekanbaru. Also consider flying all the way from Singapore to Sydney, Darwin, or Perth, paying only a small extra amount for stopovers in Bali or Yogyakarta.

Student discount tickets (ID card needed) are available from Singapore to Jakarta or to Denpasar with a stopover in Yogyakarta. Check with **Student Travel Australia** (STA) 02-17 Orchar36d Parade Hotel, 1 Tanglin Road, Singapore 1024, tel. 734-5681, fax 737-2591. Garuda also serves Pontianak from Singapore; S$125 one-way, S$250 roundtrip. MAS schedules nonstop daily flights from Singapore to Kuching. From Kuching, Merpati has flights every Friday to Pontianak, or you can take the bus. Singapore Airlines (SIA) and Garuda both offer daily flights from Singapore to Medan. SIA's excursion fare is S$261 roundtrip; you have to stay five days but no more than one month; otherwise, the price is S$374.

Airline Offices: Cathay Pacific, Ocean Bldg., Collyer Quay, tel. 533-1333; Garuda, Gold Hill Sq., 101 Thomson Rd., 13-03, Singapore 1130, tel. 250-5666; KLM, Mandarin Hotel, 333 Orchard Rd., tel. 737-7211; MAS, Singapore Shopping Centre, 190 Clemenceau Ave., tel. 336-6777; Qantas, Mandarin Hotel, 333 Orchard Rd., tel. 737-3744; Singapore International Airlines, SIA Bldg., 77 Robinson Rd. tel. 223-8888. Call around for a different kind of routing that takes in Australia or New Zealand.

By Sea

Travelers can enter the Riau Archipelago, three hours south of Singapore, on their own and visa-free by taking a ferry (S$20, 40 minutes) from Singapore to Palau Batam or Palau Bintan. Launches leave every couple hours from Finger Pier, Prince Edward Rd., Singapore. There's also a speedboat direct from Singapore to Tanjung Pinang for S$45 (2.5 hours). From Tanjung Pinang you can either head for Pekanbaru in East Sumatra or Jakarta. From the Tanjung Pinang dock boats sail up the Siak River 36 hours to Pekanbaru. This journey has been praised by readers for its scenery and adventure—a unique and increasingly popular way to enter Sumatra.

A Pelni ship sails from Tanjung Pinang to Jakarta every other Sunday, the cheapest way of getting to Jakarta from Singapore (only about S$30 total). However, it leaves early in the morning and requires at least one night in Tanjung Pinang. If you plan to arrive in Tanjung Pinang from Singapore on Saturday, you'll encounter another problem. The Pelni office—Ketapang 8, tel. 2151—closes at 1300 Saturday and the direct ferry from Singapore to Tanjung Pinang (S$46) won't get you there in time to buy your Pelni ticket for the following day. Solution: take the smaller, faster boat from Singapore to Palau Batam (45 minutes). Go through customs in Sekupang and catch a taxi across the islands to Kabil. From Kabil, speedboats leave constantly for Tanjung Pinang (crossing time 30 minutes); when you arrive catch a minibus (Rp200) to the Pelni office. This route will leave you with time to spare.

Rooms are booked full before the ship sails. Johnny's Guesthouse in Tanjung Pinang should have space; Johnny can arrange transport to the port of Kijang. You can also buy tickets at the port, providing you can fight your way through the crowd. If you want comfort, upgrade yourself to second class—it's only Rp40,000 more and worth it for the food and *air panas* alone. The fee for upgrading goes straight into the purser's pocket; you don't get a receipt. Arrive refreshed in Jakarta two days later.

Find the Pelni office at 50 Telok Blangah Rd. #02-02, Citiport Centre, Singapore 0409, tel. 272-6811, 271-5159, or 271-8685.

To East Malaysia

Flights to Tawau and Kuching in East Malaysia are usually S$20-40 cheaper out of Johore Bahru, just across the narrow strait separating Singapore from the Malay Peninsula. Also ask about MAS advance-purchase fares and night flights; MAS even provides free transport from its downtown Singapore office to the Johore Bahru airport.

From Tawau, East Malaysia you can enter Indonesia at Tarakan. No direct flight to Tawau from Singapore exists; you have to fly to East Malaysia's Kota Kinabalu first. Bouraq flies from Tawah to Tarakan, East Kalimantan for M$100. Or you can take a speedboat, running three times weekly for Rp34,000 one-way, Rp68,000 roundtrip. In Tawau, obtain a visa first from Wisma Indonesia. Wait: three hours. You'll be offered many cheap spots on many illegal boats heading down to Tarakan. Or take the MAS flight that leaves Monday and Saturday at 1300 for M$63 one-way, M$126 roundtrip. From Kuching you can also reach Pontianak in West Kalimantan by air (Rp104,000) or bus (Rp22,000). At Pontianak Airport obtain a two-month Indonesian entry stamp. MAS flies from Singapore to Kuching.

FROM OTHER ASIAN NATIONS

From The Philippines

You can take the flight from Manila to Kota Kinabalu for $250 on Royal Brunei Airlines, or try the connection between Davao in the Philippines and Manado, North Sulawesi on the white-and-green Bouraq turboprop. The latter flight, which the two cities have waited 20 years for, takes one hour and 40 minutes and costs around $200. Garuda also operates a 2,179-km-flight from Manila to Jakarta on Wednesday and Saturday for $570 roundtrip; minimum stay five days, maximum 180 days. For good tickets check **YSTAPHIL,** 4227 Tomas Claudio St., Manila, Philippines, tel. (02) 832-0680.

From Thailand And Vietnam

A number of travel agents in Bangkok offer cheap tickets that can be paid for in Penang, issued in Kuala Lumpur, and collected in Bangkok. Fares and departure dates fluctuate, and getting a straight answer to a seemingly simple question is like trying to bite the wind.

Near the Malaysia Hotel in Bangkok are travel agencies selling cheap tickets; some also sell fake student ID cards for $6. Walk around and compare prices. There are discounts for off-season and student flights, as well as package deals offering no-frills indirect flights. **K Travel Service,** 21/33 Soi Ngam Dupli, Bangkok 10120, tel. (2) 286-1468 has a good reputation among travelers. Several other agencies are located along Sukhumvit Road. STA in Viengtai Hotel is expensive but honest. Garuda now services Jakarta to Ho Chi Minh City on Friday and Sunday for $353 one-way, $564 roundtrip; minimum three days, maximum 30 days.

From Japan And Korea

Tokyo is a better place to buy air tickets than is generally realized. In addition to the local market, there's a large population of *gaijin* (foreigners) required by Japanese immigration to periodically leave the country and reenter rather than easily extend their visas in Tokyo. This requirement has created a ready market for cheap excursion fares. Many discount travel agencies specializing in overseas flights advertise in English-language media like the *Japan Times* and *Tokyo Journal.* Tokyo's a big place, so it's best to phone around and compare prices.

The following agencies are worth checking: **Council Travel,** Sanno Grand Bldg., Room 102, 14-2 Nagata-cho, 2-chome, Chiyoda-ko, Tokyo 100, tel. (03) 3581-7581; **STA,** seventh floor, Nukariya Bldg., 1-16-20 Minami-Ikebukuro, Toshima-Ku, tel. 5391-2889, fax 5391-2923; **A.B.C. Air Bank Co.,** tel. 233-1177; **Asahi International Travel,** tel. 584-5732; **E.H.L.,** tel. 351-2131; **M.I.C.,** tel. 370-6577; **N.L.C.,** tel. 988-7801. The only nonstop flight from Tokyo to Bali is offered by Garuda on DC-10 widebody jets for US$1021 one-way coach fare; US$1752 one-way first class.

There aren't that many discounters in Korea. The travel agent in the **USO Club** outside the gates of the Yongsan U.S. Army Garrison is worth a try: 104 Kalwol-dong, Yongsan-gu, Seoul, tel. (2) 792-3063 or 792-3028. He sells mostly roundtrip tickets to Asian destinations for GIs and dependents. Also try the **Korean International Student Exchange Society** (KISES), YMCA Bldg., Room 505, Chongno 2-ga, Seoul. Tickets to Jakarta sometimes sell for as little as US$550. Garuda provides service on Monday, Wednesday, and Saturday from Jakarta to Seoul, with a stop in Singapore. The fare is US$844 one-way, US$1412 roundtrip; minimum five days, maximum 30 days.

From Hong Kong

Hong Kong is just as cheap as Bangkok and Penang for air tickets in Southeast Asia, with direct flights to Jakarta and Denpasar. Return flights are even better bargains. Sample fares to Jakarta are HK$9390 one-way, HK$7190 roundtrip; to Denpasar HK$9390 one-way, HK$7190 roundtrip. Many discount travel agencies advertise in English-language morning newspapers like the *Hong Kong Standard, South China Morning Post,* and the monthly magazine *Business Traveler.* Shopping and calling around should prove fruitful. The following agencies are consistently good: **Phoenix Travel Service** at Tjim Tja Soi in Kowloon, tel. 2722-7378, (talk to Rocky); STB, 26 Des Voeux Rd., Central Bldg., 26/F, tel. 2810-7272; **Time Travel,** Chungking Mansions, 16th Fl., A Block, tel. 2366-6222; **Hong Kong Student Travel Bureau,** Room 1021, 10th floor, Star House, Tsimshatsui, tel. 2730-3269. Ask agents about the Cathay Pacific flight for around HK$5000 roundtrip to Denpasar and the direct flights to Kota Kinabalu.

From Taiwan

For discount travel agencies in Taiwan, see the notice board at the Taipei Hostel near the Lai Lai Sheraton Hotel. Travelers tend to gravitate towards **Jenny Su Travel Service,** 27 Chungshan N. Road, 10th floor, section 3, Taipei, tel. (02) 595-1646.

FROM AUSTRALIA, NEW ZEALAND, AND PAPUA NEW GUINEA

From Australia, even economy-class tickets are expensive. Either Qantas or Garuda offers frequent services to Bali and Jakarta from Adelaide, Brisbane, Cairns, Darwin, Melbourne, Perth, Port Hedland, and Sydney. Only Garuda and Merpati offer the Darwin and Port Hedland services, while Qantas and Garuda operate from the other departure points. Flight time from Melbourne is about six hours. Qantas and Garuda offer precisely the same fares and flight restrictions to Jakarta (A$898 one-way, A$1090 roundtrip) and Bali (A$753 one-way, A$915 roundtrip), with seven-day minimum stay, maximum 45 days. During the Dec.-Feb. high season flights from Australia to Indonesia are heavily booked, so reserve your place at least three months ahead. It's usually significantly cheaper buying Garuda tickets for internal Indonesia travel before leaving home. You can get to Bali for A$999 roundtrip from Sydney. It's A$800 roundtrip from Darwin direct to Jakarta. Garuda flies to Indonesia from Auckland for NZ$1000 one-way, NZ$1438 roundtrip. Auckland-Denpasar airfare is NZ$1518 roundtrip with Air New Zealand.

Fly to Jakarta from Perth for A$596 one-way, A$937 roundtrip (peak); A$504 one-way, A$787 roundtrip (low). Flight time is only 3.5 hours. Perth-Denpasar-Jakarta flights leave twice weekly. Cathay Pacific has a four-hour morning flight from Perth to Jakarta. If you have an International Student ID card, check out STA flights from Perth to Jakarta. There are also STA charter flights to Kuala Lumpur with connecting flights to Denpasar.

Very popular with travelers is flying from Darwin to Kupang, then island-hopping to Bali. From Kupang there are regular flights to Denpasar for A$190 one-way. From Darwin, Merpati flies to Kupang twice weekly for A$200 one-way, A$350 roundtrip in the low season. This flight leaves each Saturday morning and takes just two hours; return flights leave Fridays. Upon arrival in Kupang you'll receive a 60-day entry stamp.

Package And Group Tours

There are numerous package deals from Sydney to Bali and Lombok for around A$600. A 7-10 day all-inclusive holiday package to Bali can cost as little as A$1200-1300, including airfare, transfers, accommodations, and continental breakfast in a three-star hotel. Certain conditions, as the ads say, may apply. Departure and return schedules are usually immutable. Find a flexible agent who can arrange for you to use vouchers in a selection of hotels so your movement won't be restricted.

One of the cheapest ways to get to Indonesia from Australia is to join a tour group, which can cost even less than APEX fares. Even though you pay for places and services sight unseen, the prices are unbeatable: Sydney to Bali, A$855 (peak), A$710 (low); Perth to Bali, A$610 (peak), A$520 (low). These tour packages issue hotel vouchers, which you exchange for accommodations; other vouchers you can use in restaurants or even to rent bicycles or motorcycles. Many travelers take advantage of the cheap airfares and ignore the vouchers. Look for deals in the travel sections of Australia's big city newspapers.

From Papua New Guinea

Land approaches from Papua New Guinea to Irian Jaya are illegal. Flying from Vanimo across the international border to Jayapura costs K78 roundtrip, which satisfies Indonesia's onward ticket requirement. Or you can buy them K39 each way. Tickets are sold by Air Niugini; departure tax is K10. Boarding an Air Niugini jet after flying Merpati is like a breath of fresh air—literally. The No Smoking policy results in much cleaner planes and a more pleasant flight. Before arriving, get an Indonesian visa at the Indonesian embassy in Port Moresby; Jayapura is not an official entry point into Indonesia. If you have no plans to visit Port Moresby, convince a tour company like Trans Niugini to send your passport and visa application to the Indonesian embassy in Port Moresby. It'll take about five days and cost K25 plus the visa fee, but it's worth it.

FROM THE U.S. AND CANADA

Airlines serving Indonesia from North America include Garuda Indonesia, Hong Kong Airlines, Japan Airlines, China Air, KLM, and Pan Am. An hour or so spent calling toll-free numbers will provide the most up-to-date info on current airfares, timetables, and connections. Call (800) 555-1212 for airline numbers. If you work through travel agents, have them contact an Asian consolidator for the best fares. If you plan to travel in the high season (June-Sept., December, and the Chinese New Year), you'll need to book months in advance.

Garuda Indonesia

Direct flights travel four times a week between Los Angeles and Bali. Take off at 2140, flying first to Hawaii (six hours), then to Biak (nine hours), then four more hours to Bali. You change to another plane for the final leg to Jakarta. Total air time: 21 hours. The fare from L.A. to Jakarta (good food and liquor, solicitous crew) is US$1350 roundtrip Jan.-May and US$1450 in June, July, August, and December. No discounted tickets. From Los Angeles to Biak is US$1160 in the high season (Jan.-May) and US$1060 in the low (June-Dec.). The US$1350 fare from Los Angeles to Bali is the same as to Jakarta. You get one "free" stopover in Bali or Yogyakarta on the flight from Los Angeles to Jakarta; an additional stopover costs US$50. You get only one stopover each way, with no repeat on your return trip. As one of your stopovers en route to Bali or Jakarta, consider deplaning in Biak for a week or so. Within two flights of Biak is the famed Baliem Valley, perhaps Indonesia's most remarkable and untouched tribal area—superb weather, exhilarating trekking. If you were to fly there from Jakarta, it would cost over US$450 roundtrip; if you stop on the way from L.A. it's free but for the Biak-Jayapura and Jayapura-Wamena roundtrip hops.

Ask about Garuda's Visit Indonesia Pass, which allows you to visit three cities in Indonesia for $300. Each additional city costs US$100, to a maximum of 10 cities. To take advantage of the pass you must stay in Indonesia a minimum of five days and a maximum of 60 days. Also check into Garuda's tour packages, for five, 10, and 15-plus days. The price depends largely on the rating of the hotel you stay in. For information, call (800) 247-8380. North American Garuda offices include GIA, 3457 Wilshire Blvd., Los Angeles, CA 90010, tel. (800) 342-7832 inside California or (800) 826-2829 outside California; GIA, 360 Post St., Ste. 804, San Francisco, CA 94108, tel. (415) 788-2626; GIA, 51 E. 42nd St., Ste. 616, New York, NY 10017, tel. (800) 248-2829 outside New York or (212) 370-0707 inside eastern region; GIA, 1040 W. Georgia St., Vancouver B.C., Canada V6E 4H1, tel. (604) 681-3699; GIA, 1600 Kapiolani Blvd., Ste. 632, Honolulu, HI 96814, tel. (808) 947-9500.

Other U.S. Flights

The travel sections of the *Los Angeles Times* and the *San Francisco Examiner* are full of ads for cheap transpacific flights. Other good sources are *Great Expeditions Magazine*, 242 W. Milbrook, Suite 102-A, Raleigh NC 27609, tel. (800) 743-3639, fax 919-847-0780; and ITN, 520 Calvados Ave., Sacramento, CA 95815. Tickets from the U.S. west coast to Hong Kong, Singapore, or Bangkok average US$1150 one-way or US$1400 roundtrip. From these points board a flight to Jakarta or Bali. If you're planning extended travel in Asia, buy an open ticket valid for one year. There are some incredibly cheap tickets between Los Angeles, San Francisco, Seattle, and Singapore with stops in Hawaii, Japan, Korea, Taiwan, Hong Kong, and Bangkok.

Continental, tel. (800) 231-0856 offers a ticket from San Francisco to Denpasar for US$1450 roundtrip via Honolulu and Guam. The low season fare is US$1350 roundtrip if you depart by 31 May. You're allowed one stopover, for up to six months. If you get a ticket just to Jakarta, you can exit through northern Sumatra, travel up to Bangkok, then back to the U.S. with stops in Hong Kong, Taiwan, Korea, Hawaii, Los Angeles, and San Francisco.

Other possible routings start from New York. Scan the *New York Times, Chicago Tribune, Los Angeles Times* and the *San Francisco Examiner* for cut-rate airfares. KLM, tel. (800) 556-7777, flies to Jakarta via Amsterdam; one-way coach fare is US$1234, first class US$2059 one-way. Icelandic Airways, tel. (800) 223-5500, connects New York with Luxembourg for US$159; then fly to Asia with one of the cut-rate European charters.

Cheap U.S. Ticket Agencies

Overseas Tours, 475 El Camino Real, Ste. 206, Millbrae, CA 94030, tel. (800) 323-8777 in California or (800) 227-5988 outside California, claims to match any advertised ticket price to the Orient. Overseas represents 20 scheduled airlines, 300 tours, and 500 hotels in Asia. Travel agencies owned by Indonesians or with strong connections to Indonesia are well placed to offer bargains, and include **Canatours Inc.,** 427 Bernard St., Los Angeles, CA 90012, tel. (800) 345-2262 outside California or (213) 223-1111 in California, fax (213) 223-1048; and **Royal Express Tours and Travel,** 731 S. Atlantic Blvd., Monterey Park, CA 91754, tel. (818) 289-8520. Also with great prices to Asia are **Adventure Center,** 1311 63rd St., Ste. 200, Emeryville, CA 94608, tel. (503) 654-1879; and **Community Travel Service,** 5237 College

Ave., Oakland, CA 94618, tel. (415) 653-0990. The latter sells Japan Airlines roundtrip tickets for US$952 with stops in Tokyo.

OE Tours, 275 Post St., 4th Floor, San Francisco, CA 94108, boasts low airfares to Asia. **Council Travel Services,** 2511 Channing Way, Berkeley, CA 94701, tel. (415) 848-8604, is a well-known student discounter; nonstudents may also use its services. **Pan Express Travel,** 209 Post St., Ste. 921, San Francisco, CA 94108, tel. (415) 989-8282, sells a US$475 one-way (US$830 roundtrip) ticket for a San Francisco-Honolulu-Biak-Denpasar-Yogyakarta-Jakarta flight. **Student Travel Network** is a budget student ticket agency with offices worldwide. **STA** sells Garuda tickets from anywhere in North America to Indonesia. Prices aren't the cheapest but the service is dependable. Main office: 5900 Wilshire Blvd., Suite 2100, Los Angeles, CA 90036, tel. (213) 937-1150.

From Hawaii

Asia Travel Service tel. (808) 926-0550 Interisland or (800) 884-0550 sells tickets to Bali or Jakarta for US$799. Also check out **Panda Travel** tel. 734-1961, fax 732-4136. A great deal is **Emerson Travel's** seven-day tour of Bali for only US$950; price includes five nights in a hotel, daily breakfast, airfare, transfers, day tours, fruit basket. Optional tour to Yogyakarta. Emerson also sells tickets to Jakarta, Bali, Yogyakarta, Solo, and Surabaya for US$799.

From Canada

With persistence, some good bargains are available. Look for cheap flights and travel agencies specializing in Southeast Asia in the *Toronto Globe and Mail.* In Vancouver, see Susan Maddon of **Bali Orient Holiday Inc.,** 1150 W. Georgia 208; she sells a Vancouver-San Francisco-Los Angeles-Biak-Bali-Singapore ticket for as little as C$1558 (Bali return C$1150). Probably the best bucket shop in Canada is **Adventure Centre,** 17 Hayden St., Toronto, Ontario M4Y 2P2, tel. (800) 661-7265, with offices in Calgary, Edmonton, Toronto, and Vancouver. Also look up **Travel Cuts,** the Canadian student travel bureau, which sells consistently inexpensive fares; C$850 one-way (C$1340 roundtrip) to Jakarta. Travel Cuts main office is located at 187 College St., Toronto, Ontario M5T 1P7, tel. (416) 979-2406.

FROM LONDON

London is famous for its low airfares to the Orient—the best place in Europe to buy air tickets. In fact, you won't be able to find anything *but* budget airfares. This is because of the many discount ticket outlets called "bucket shops." Each shop may or may not have its own advance-purchase requirements and cancellation penalties, and cheap tickets may not be available at peak periods when airlines can fill their planes at higher prices.

Compare prices on Aeroflot, Pakistan, and Air Lanka. Start inquiries at London's **Garuda** office, 35 Duke St., London W1M 5DF, tel. (071) 486-3011. To Jakarta, Garuda offers a fare of £708 one-way or £1159 roundtrip, minimum stay seven days, maximum 180 days. Garuda Indonesia, known for its monopolistic practices and high prices, even takes part in the slashed airfares business in London. It has no choice; the market is so big. The U.K. was the source of 165,844 visitors to Indonesia in 1992.

When buying a ticket through a bucket shop, don't pay more than a deposit before receiving the ticket, as these agencies have a high rate of closure. Make sure they belong to the Association of British Travel Agents (ABTA); its members guarantee a refund in case they go broke.

An appealing option is to fly London-Singapore, for which fares are deeply discounted (around £600 roundtrip). Then—after a trip into Malaysia—buy a roundtrip Hong Kong-Jakarta ticket. Or try for a good fare from London to Australia (around £500) with a stopover in Indonesia. A roundtrip ticket from London to Sydney with a stopover in Singapore and Bali will run around 1000 pounds. Fares from London straight to Bali cost 400 pounds one-way, 700 pounds roundtrip. There are also various low-cost London-Australia and London-New Zealand flights available for about £500-800 roundtrip, with inexpensive stopovers in either Singapore or Bali. The fewer the stopovers, the cheaper the ticket.

A reliable travel agent for cut-rate tickets is **Trailfinders Travel Centre,** 194 Kensington High St., W8, tel. (071) 937-5400; take the tube to High St., Kensington. The largest budget agency is **Student Travel Australia** (STA), 74 Old Brompton Rd., SW7, tel. 937-9962. Also worth a look are **Council Travel,** 28 A Poland St., London W1, tel. 437-7767, and **Campus Travel,** 174 Kensington High St., tel. 938-2188.

The weekly *Time Out,* available at London newsstands, contains ads for many bargain airfares and bucket shops. The *Sunday Times* and the *News and Travel Magazine* may also prove very useful.

FROM OTHER POINTS IN EUROPE

It's not difficult to find low discount fares from Amsterdam, Athens, Basel, Brussels, Frankfurt, Paris, Rome, Vienna, or Zurich. Indeed, Indonesia-bound traffic has become so frantic that European countries now offer unbelievably cheap package deals. Sample roundtrip fares from Frankfurt include Jakarta, DM3869 roundtrip, DM2757 one-way; Denpasar, DM3902 roundtrip, DM2828 one-way excursion fare. Recommended is **SRS Studenten Reise Service,** Marienstrasse 23 (U-Bahn and S-Bahn: Friedrichstrasse) for discounts to students up to age 34. Travel agencies offering cheap tickets advertise in the travel section of such publications as *Zitty.* Also try **Alternativ Tours,** Wilmersdorfer Strasse 94, U-Bahn Adenauerplatz, tel. (069) 881-2089, a well-known and trustworthy consolidator.

The biggest student travel agency in Austria is the **Osterreichisches Komitee fur Internationalen Studentenaustausch** (Okista), with head offices at 9 Garnisongasse 7, Vienna, tel. (0222) 401-480. Open Mon.-Fri. 0900-1730, Saturday 0930-1200. Try other Okista offices at 9 Turkenstrasse 4-6 and at 4 Karlsgasse 3, tel. 505-0128 in Vienna.

In Switzerland, get a recent issue of the best Swiss travelers' publication, *Globetrotter-Magazin,* which lists loads of cheap airlines. The **SSR** offices are also outlets for cheap Indonesia-bound tickets: try first the head office at Rue Vignier, Geneva, tel. (022) 29-97-33; open Mon.-Fri. 0900-1730. Another good ticket agency offering budget fares to Asia is **Globetrotter.**

You can fly from Amsterdam to Singapore at very reasonable prices—sometimes even cheaper than flying from Sydney to Singapore. To find the cheapest flights, check the Saturday editions of Holland's main national newspapers. The best is *Volkakrant.* It's wise to ask if your agent is a member of ANVR, a union of travel agents which requires its members to join a fund that guarantees your ticket in case anything goes wrong. One of the cheapest flights from Holland to Indonesia is with Czechoslovakian Airlines: the 20-hour Amsterdam-Prague-Abu Dhabi-Bombay-Singapore-Jakarta jaunt. KLM and Garuda operate a weekly B747 joint service between Amsterdam and Bali/Jakarta for around G800. Garuda's office is at Singel 540, 1017 AZ Amsterdam, tel. (020) 272-626. The fare to Jakarta is G4039 one-way, G7343 roundtrip; to Denpasar G4075 one-way, G7416 roundtrip. Garuda APEX fares from Amsterdam to Jakarta/Bali: G1593 one-way, G2950 roundtrip (minimum seven days, maximum 180 days, valid only until 31 May). Cheaper is **NBBS,** Rokin 38, tel. 624-0989, or Leidsestraat 53, tel. 638-1736, the official Dutch student travel agency. Another good outfit is **Amber Reisbureau,** Da Costastraat 77, 1053 ZG Amsterdam, tel. (020) 685-1155; 100% reliable. Also worth a try is **ILC Reizen,** NZ Voorburgwal 256, tel. 620-5121.

In Belgium try the student travel agency **Acotra,** Rue de la Madeleine 51, tel. (02) 512-8607, and **Connections Travel Shop,** Rue du Marche-au-Charbon 13, tel. 512-060, both in Brussels. **Nouvelles Frontieres** of Italy and France offers cheap airfares to the Far East; the Rome-Jakarta ticket costs only 950,000 lira roundtrip. In Rome, the student travel center **CTS,** Via Genova 16 (off Via Nazionale), tel. (06) 46-791, has some great fares to Southeast Asia. In Paris, investigate **Selectour Voyages,** 29 Rue de la Huchette, tel. (01) 43-29-64-00, open weekdays 0945-1830; and **Council Travel,** 31 Rue Saint Augustine, tel. 42-66-20-87, open Mon.-Fri. 0930-1830, Saturday 1000-1400.

CRUISES

The trouble with cruises is that passengers are able to stop for only three or four hours at some ports. The luxury and service, however, are undeniable. **Royal Cruise Line's** "Golden Odyssey" departs Bangkok for Semarang, Yogyakarta, and Bali on its way to Hong Kong. The **Pearl Cruises'** "Bangkok, Bali and Beyond" itinerary visits Jakarta, Semarang, and Bali. **Royal Viking's** "Jewels of the Orient" cruise aboard the *Royal Viking Star* departs Singapore and Bangkok for Bali; the *Sea Goddess* calls on several Indonesian ports. Inquire at your travel agency.

Those cruisers who prefer a more localized experience may be interested in the *Island Explorer* operated by **Spice Island Cruises** and marketed in the U.S. by Salen Lindblad. In spring 1972, the *Island Explorer* made its first visit to the eastern archipelago, visiting islands ignored by Westerners since before WW II. On its 14-day cruise, the ship carries 36 passengers and 20 crew, visiting such remote destinations as Flores, Komodo, Ambon, and Nias for US$4260. Facilities onboard include satellite telephones, glass-bottom boat, water skis, and a complete scuba-diving facility. Spice Island Cruises also operates a 22-passenger high-performance dive ship. For cabin costs and complete details on winter and summer voyages, contact **Lindblad Cruising Inc.,** 133 E. 55th St., New York, NY 10022, tel. (800) 223-5688.

TOURS

To reach remote locales like Ujung Kulon and Komodo, some find it easiest to sign on with a tour. Beginning in the 1990s, Indonesia became a major player in the special interest/adventure travel and study tour market. The country offers mind-boggling cultural and natural diversity, volcano trekking, river rafting, scubadiving, snorkeling. You can learn *batik*-making, study colonial architecture, take up the language, canoe through an elephant reserve, search for Javan rhinoceros by swamp boat.

But do your research first. Many tour companies promise the stars but deliver mud. You might see a tour advertised out of New York City or Sydney for "A Borneo Jungle Safari" that costs US$1800 for the airfare plus another US$4000 for the ground arrangements. At this level of touring you have a perfect right to expect the absolute best in hotels when in the big cities. But when you arrive in Jakarta, you're shunted off to the tatty old Hotel Indonesia. Things get worse from there.

Contact the Indonesian embassy or consulate in your country for tour companies specializing in Indonesia. You can reach the **Indonesian Tourist Promotion Office for North America** at (213) 387-2078, fax (213) 380-4876. In Indonesia itself, a visit to any of Indonesia's regional tourist offices can help you select the right tour company.

You can also sign up for package tours in Singapore. **German Asian Travels (Pte) Ltd.,** 9 Battery Rd., #14-03 Straits Trading Building, tel. 533-5466 has a solid reputation. **Swib Tour-Travel Indonesia,** Louis Bourwmeesterplein 17, 5038 TN-Tilburg, the Netherlands, tel./fax. (013) 420-117, is a Dutch outfit run by J.A. Brouwer, a veteran tour guide since 1978. Swib specializes in Kalimantan, Sulawesi, Maluku, and Irian Jaya, leading groups and individual travelers.

Bolder Adventures, tel. (800) 397-5917 for the U.S., fax (303) 443-7078, is an innovative Colorado company run by Southeast Asia specialists. Bolder offers many tours to Indonesia, including the extraordinarily well-designed 17-day "Indonesia Wildlife Adventure," in which participants explore virgin rainforests; observe orangutan at the Camp Leakey Research Station on Borneo; watch giant monitor lizards on Komodo Island in Nusatenggara; and visit the largely animist island of Sumba, known for its mammoth megaliths and savage funerals. Cost: US$3,195 plus air. **Maluku Adventures,** P.O. Box 7331, Menlo Park, CA 94026-7331, tel. (800) 566-2585, fax (415) 321-1387 can arrange anything from treks across the island of Ceram to live-aboard dive tours of the Maluku Sea on an Indonesian Navy oceanographic research vessel. Maluku also offers an air-and-land Bali Program for US$1,300 pp. Package includes airfare San Francisco-Bali-San Francisco, coach class, garden rooms, roundtrip transfers, and full-day volcano tour with Barong Dance. With a two night extension to Yogyakarta, add another US$165 pp. Maluku works with **Festival of Asia,** (800) 533-9953, which also offers creative tours at excellent prices.

Mountain Travel Sobek, tel. (800) 227-2384 or 510-527-8100, fax 510-525-7710, conducts a 10-day foray into the highlands of Irian Jaya, a popular nine-day "Sulawesi Adventure," and an "Islands of Fire: Java, Lombok and Bali" for US$2690. The company limits tours to 12 people, and is well known for its in-depth cultural explorations and high-quality tour leaders. **Wilderness Travel,** tel. (800) 368-2794 for U.S. and Canada, fax (510) 548-0347, a Berkeley, California group, offers "Indonesia: Through the Ring of Fire" which takes in Torajaland, Mt. Bromo, Java, Lombok and Bali. This 17-day tour includes dance performances, shadow plays, and visits to Indonesia's foremost *gamelan* musicians, woodcarvers, and *batik* makers. Also ask about the "Irian Jaya Expedition," a 24-day hiking and cultural expedition led by adventurer Magnus Andersson. Land cost: US$3795, 13-15 members.

California-based **Danu Enterprises,** tel. (408) 476-0543, fax (408) 476-0543 presents some really offbeat study tours such as "The Healing Arts of Bali," which explores forms of traditional healing and massage, and offers daily yoga classes and visits to Balinese *balian* (shaman) practicing both black and white magic. Made Surya, who lives half the year in Indonesia and the other half in the U.S., is a maskmaker, dancer, and bon vivant. He's also a sensitive, garrulous, and informative host who'll give you an Indonesian's perspective on Indonesian culture, conveyed in colorful, forceful, American English.

High-end **Zegrahm Expeditions** presents "Where the Spirits Dwell," a 25-day cultural tour of the Asmat area of Irian Jaya, the Banda Islands of the Maluku Sea, and the Bird's Head Peninsula. A real plus is expedition lecturer Tobias Schneebaum, legendary anthropologist, author of *Where the Spirits Dwell,* and adopted son of an Ocenep tribal village. All-inclusive land and sea cost: US$7,960, not including air. **Ecosummer Expeditions,** tel. (800) 688-8605 in the U.S., (800) 465-8884 in Canada, fax (604) 669-3244, is a hardcore, cutting-edge adventure company offering treks on Irian Jaya. Trips range from moderate to extremely strenuous. Exclusive adventures to the rainforest areas of the Upper Asmat. Also check out **Asian Pacific Adventures** of Los Angeles, specialists in Indonesia's outlying islands. The 22-day "Irian Jaya Exploratory" takes you to Indonesia's least known tribal region, the Yali Valley of the eastern highlands of Irian Jaya. Worth looking into is **Overseas Adventure Travel,** based in Cambridge, Massachusetts. Berkeley, California-based **Backroads Bicycle Tours,** tel. (800) 245-3874 for U.S. and Canada, fax (510) 527-1444, offers bicycle touring, including an 11-day package featuring luxury hotels, guesthouses, and a Balinese bus that ferries cyclists to the top of the island's volcanos. **Close Up Expedi-**

tions, tel. (510) 465-8955, fax (510) 465-1237, sells photographic expeditions to Indonesia.

Indonesia-Based Companies
Established in 1984, experienced and professional **Nusa Dua Bali Tours and Travel,** Jl. Bypass, 300 B, Box 3419, Denpasar 80034, tel. (0361) 51-223, fax 52-779, organizes tours and travel within Indonesia. Working with an impressive network of affiliated tour operators throughout the archipelago, the company offers both packaged programs and first class tours. Competitive rates, excellent service, and a consistently high standard of accommodations and guides. Nusa Dua cut its teeth in the business by catering to demanding and discriminating European clients.

Sea Trek, Jl. Tukad Bilok 15 B, Sanur, tel./fax (0361) 237-507, has run modified Pinisi-style ships in central and eastern Indonesia since 1985, visiting such remote islands as Tanimbar, Kai, Aru, Sula, Halmahera, Bacan, Misool, Waigeo. The ships provide 10 double-cabins, common showers and toilets, lounge, small dining area, and snorkeling gear—comfort, not luxury. Many have tried to copy Sea Trek's formula but most have failed. In Holland, contact managing director Dick Bergsma, Sea Trek, Stationsplein 3 H Rosmalen, tel. (020) 4192-20235, fax 4192-19522. **Garuda Orient Holidays,** (800) 247-8380 for U.S. and Canada, fax (213) 389-1568, is a subsidiary of Garuda Indonesia Airlines. **Natrabu,** with more than 34 years of experience in leading tours, maintains its U.S. headquarters at (800) 628-7228 for U.S. and Canada, fax (415) 362-0531. Award-winning **Vayatours Inc.,** tel. (800) 999-8292 U.S. and Canada, fax (213) 487-0838, one of Indonesia's largest tour companies, staffs a sales office in North America at 6420 Wilshire Blvd., Suite 420, Los Angeles, CA 90048, tel. (213) 655-3851.

GETTING AROUND

There are two ways to travel—the tourist way and the native way. Monied tourists hire cars and minibuses, use taxis and planes, join package tour groups. But for economy, mobility, and firsthand contact with the people, the native way is best. Indonesians make do, and, given enough time, everyone gets where they're going.

The government is straining to keep Indonesia's internal infrastructure moving and improving at the same rapid rate as its economic growth. The strict traffic laws passed in 1992 were an effort to unclog the highways of the big cities. A new container port is under construction at Jakarta's Tanjung Priok, work has begun on a $100 million elevated light rail system for the capital, and the existing telephone system is undergoing overhaul. The government has invited the private sector to invest in energy, communication, highway, and port development.

Presently, traffic in the big cities is horrendous. How do you cross a street in Jakarta? Walk out into the traffic with your arm outstretched and outstare the drivers—there's no turning back. Crowded interisland rail and sea transit systems are inadequate to meet the needs of the people. In the interiors of most of the Outer Islands roads exist only in the dry season; to get from one village to another means riding on top of bags of rice or onions in the rear of a truck.

Best And Worst Times To Travel
The most important thing to understand about travel in Indonesia is the concept of *jam karet,* or "rubber time." Departure times are stretched or contracted depending on the whim of the driver, pilot, or captain and how full or empty the vehicle is. Don't be in a hurry—no one else is. For physical comfort, the best time of the day for travel is from 0600 to about noon, and after the sun goes down.

Because Indonesia's climate is tropical, people travel here year-round. At the end of the rainy season in January and February, bridges, railroad tracks, and airfields could be washed out in the more remote islands of the archipelago. It's also difficult getting across Indonesia in the alloted two months; it's better to split the main islands up into two 60-day segments. In the peak tourist seasons (June-Aug. and Dec.-Jan.) it's sometimes impossible to get a ticket. Everything is full; you might have to wait several days, particularly for extraordinarily busy connections like Ujung Pandang to Denpasar.

like a bridge over troubled waters

Some flights are booked for more than three weeks ahead of time. A lot of people are stranded on Bali during the peak season—confirmations disappear at the drop of a bribe.

The period around the *haj* can be a challenging time to get in and out of Outer Island cities such as Ujung Pandang—Garuda aircraft are busy ferrying pilgrims to Jakarta, where they change planes to the Middle East. Avoid traveling during religious holidays such as Idul Fitri (the end of Ramadan), when millions of Indonesians hit the road to visit relatives. You must compete with them for transport and tourist facilities, and prices skyrocket. This lasts about two weeks, when it seems half of Sumatra and Java goes by bus to visit the other half. Even ships change schedule during this difficult travel period.

On Friday, the Muslim holy day, most offices and many businesses are closed and transportation almost stops at 1100 or so when Muslims go to pray. If you're prevented from getting a seat on a long-distance night bus or train, just start taking local transportation and cover the distance in 100- to 200-km segments. You'll get there paying about the same amount, it'll just take you longer.

Travel Information

Tourists who don't speak Bahasa Indonesia will have difficulty communicating with drivers/operators, but what a wonderful incentive to learn. Tourist offices in the cities dispense info, brochures, and maps, and can also be useful in booking hotels and arranging tours, transport and boat charter, and train tickets. They're plugged into many of the local travel service vendors and many actually function as mini-travel agencies. In remote areas don't hesitate to avail yourself of the army or police when trying to find places to stay and eat. Usually, they're extremely friendly and helpful. Some train and bus stations, airports, and Pelni shipping offices feature special *loket turis* (tourist ticket windows) with English-speaking ticket clerks. Always ask for the *loket turis* if you want to buy tickets or make reservations.

Asking Directions

When you reach a town and want to find the bus, *oplet,* or minibus station appropriate for continuing on to your destination, just ask *"Dimana stasiun . . . ?"* If people give the answer or say yes too quickly it probably means they don't know what they're talking about. It's sometimes difficult to get correct information from Indonesians because of their infuriating habit of telling you only what they think you want to hear. Often the integrity of the relationship is more important than the objective information; if you're lied to, it means the Indonesian wants to please you.

Minimize this problem by asking very specific questions. If you're driving your own car, lean out the window and ask *"Dimana Sukamade?"* ("Where is Sukamade?"). No doubt you'll receive the traditional reply, *"terus"* ("straight on") regardless. Or *"terus, kiri"* or *"terus, kanan"* ("right, left"), which will cover all options. Never ask a leading question such as, "this is the right way, isn't it?" Ask several people, then take a mean average. If it's an obscure place, keep asking as you go along and eventually you'll get there. Single out the man or woman with a khaki, light gray, or deep blue safari uniform with the Indonesian Pancasila emblem pinned to the shirt. These are *pegawai,* one of the nation's three million civil servants. They're often better educated and more helpful in giving directions.

Indonesians also tend to report distances as less than they really are; if it's 500 meters, they'll say 100. If seven km, they'll estimate two. Try asking *"Berapa menit?"* ("How many minutes?"); this inquiry of time rather than distance is more likely to generate an accurate response. Most Indonesians don't have the foggiest conception of linear distances, but they know how long it takes them to walk or ride somewhere.

Names are frequently shortened: Cibadak becoming Badak, Sukabumi Bumi, Cilegon Egon—all cried out to solicit passengers as *bemo* speed down the road. Indonesians could also use an altogether different name than the official public name, such as the old name Badung for Denpasar.

Several different names may be given to a single street. Indonesia has so many heroes to commemorate a single street may change names four or five times in the space of three kilometers. Name changes usually occur at major intersections. In Surabaya, for example, Jl. Gresik starts in the west, then mutates into Jl. Rajawali, Jl. Jepun, Jl. Kapasan, and Jl. Keneran as it proceeds to the sea. Thankfully, street numbering is no longer as confusing as it once was, when houses and buildings were assigned lucky numbers or reflected the number of children in a family.

Don't rely on maps, even those published by the government. Maps may indicate Indonesia has a superb road system, but in truth many of those roads haven't existed since Dutch times; others are planned for the future.

Transport Costs

Intercity bus fares are roughly Rp14 per km on Java, Sumatra, and Bali; Rp19 per km in Nusatenggara and Timor; and Rp19-24 per km on Kalimantan, Sulawesi, Maluku, and Irian Jaya. Regional administrators could fix additional charges to reflect local road conditions

or seasons. You can count on up to two or even three times these rates for end-of-the-line segments in the mountains.

Some Indonesians will try to take advantage of your ignorance by overcharging, so you must constantly exercise your bargaining skills. You eventually develop a sense of what's the correct price to pay, a feeling that a Rp2000 *becak* ride offer is really worth only Rp1000. When riding in any private, native-style transportation, one way to learn the correct charge is to first ask the passengers or bystanders the standard fare (*harga biasa*). Always settle on the price before you get in the vehicle; if necessary, bargain each and every time you travel the same route. Don't get out without receiving your change. When you know you're going to be doing a lot of *bemo* riding take lots of small change; drivers don't always have much.

If traveling with a large backpack on a *bemo* or small bus, you'll be asked to pay another adult fare, as your pack takes up an extra seat. You're expected to understand this. Often there's a day price and a night price (sometimes double). On big national or religious holidays such as Hari Raya, transport companies customarily raise prices.

Ticket Touts And Guides

Though some are downright unsavory, you don't necessarily have to be paranoid about the touts hanging around the bus stations and harbors of Indonesia. These people will claim to have special connections with the ship's captain, stationmaster, harbormaster, or whomever. This might actually be true, and touts could save you a lot of trouble and money. Be open. Touts might help you get a ticket when all other channels fail. The fee, tacked on to the base price, might, if not ridiculously high, be worth it.

The same goes for self-appointed multilingual guides who attach themselves to you at airports, in cities, and at tourist sights. These contacts could lead to exciting experiences. Local guides and their strongly accented English and peculiar sales pitches are a part of the color and personality of a place. Their rates can be quite reasonable, Rp525-1050 per day. Some of these freelance guides check out flight manifests at airports to see who's arriving, or hang around tourist information offices or travelers' hotels. They seem to have friends everywhere.

Guides usually don't have telephones and can only be contacted through friends working in tourist agencies, tourist information offices, or hotels. Official guides are available for tours of museums, temples, and palaces. These certified, specially trained and registered guides may or may not be as knowledgeable and honest as freelancers.

Paperwork And Permits
Always carry your passport; police will often ask to see it. International student ID cards can sometimes secure discounts on flights, ferries, or trains. An International Driver's License is available from your local motorist's association. When hiring a bicycle, you can use your license as a deposit rather than your passport.

Permits are required to visit many of the country's reserves and national parks. They're available for around Rp2000 from the Dinas Perlindungan dan Pengawetan Alam (PHPA) office in the park itself, or at a PHPA office in the town nearest the reserve. You can also apply at an Indonesian consulate before leaving for Indonesia. Stays of five days are permitted. Anyone wishing to stay longer should apply directly to PHPA's main office in Bogor, West Java at Jl. Ir. H. Juanda 9; open 0730-1100. Include date of planned visit, length of stay, number of participants, nationality, and passport information.

A *surat jalan* is a letter travelers may be required to carry while traveling in restricted areas of the Outer Islands. Obtainable only from local/regional police stations, this advance permit is sometimes necessary to secure connecting transportation: requires two to three passport photos, and takes at most an hour to obtain.

TRAVEL BY AIR

For internal destinations, surface transportation is generally cheaper and easier than flights. However, you'll find that often the only alternative to a lengthy land or sea passage—particularly in the Outer Islands—is to fly. Most big towns in Indonesia are connected to Jakarta by air. Flying in Indonesia is a breeze; the skies are empty and the weather usually clear. In-air service is generally good, though the food is often cold.

There are 45 private or semiprivate airlines in Indonesia, a number involved primarily with mineral development. Most fly a zany collection of aircraft. State-run Garuda Indonesia Airways, offering both domestic and international services, is the largest and slickest Indonesian airline. Other airlines, offering mainly domestic flights, include Merpati (swallowed up by Garuda in 1989), Mandala, Bouraq, Sempati, Pelita, and Seulawah. These alternative airlines concentrate on the low-traffic outer-fringe areas not covered by Garuda, and their fares average 15-25% less. Different airlines often cover the same route and there can be quite a difference in fares offered by competing airlines between the same two points. Routes, fares, and airlines change frequently, so it's best to call to find out what's available or to confirm specific flights. It may be cheaper to purchase internal tickets in Australia, Japan, or Bangkok before you leave home.

ASEAN students, and occasionally Western students, might receive a 25-30% reduction in airfares upon presentation of student IDs—if they talk to the right person long and hard enough. You'll need an International Student Identification Card (ISIC), as well as a special letter from your school registrar. For international flights, the age limit for eligible students is 26; there's no age limit for domestic flights.

You can obtain the various nationwide timetables from each airline at the main airline offices or tourist information centers in Indonesia's big cities. These list routes, fares, flight frequencies, and addresses of provincial offices. Charter aircraft cost US$300-800 per hour, depending on the type of aircraft. You can rent helicopters in Irian Jaya for around Rp2.1 million per day.

Try to secure a seat in front of the wings so you can enjoy the spectacular scenery. Smoking is still permitted on Indonesian aircraft, but only in the back of the plane. The pilots and other crew members on Indonesian aircraft can be extremely accommodating and hospitable. If you're a pilot you could get invited into the cockpit; Indonesian pilots often swoop low over volcanos to oblige passenger requests.

Stay loose. Your flight to Ujung Pandang or Medan is likely to be late. Perhaps the plane won't take off at all. Or you could be asked to move to the front of the plane for some inexplicable, slightly foreboding, reason. Garuda is the exception—very reliable service.

You can't trust some travel agencies to make reservations for flights; you can't even rely 100% on confirmation promises made in airline offices. Always confirm flight availability and book a seat as far in advance as possible at the local airline office in your city of departure. This is especially important in the eastern islands, where flights are less frequent; for the most popular routes, Jakarta-Yogyakarta, Surabaya-Denpasar, and the like; and during the peak tourist seasons of July-Aug. and Dec.-Jan., when flights are booked solid two or three weeks at a time. Reconfirm your flight no sooner than three days but no later than a day before departure. Hotels or travel agencies will reconfirm for Rp2000-2500 per ticket. Also get in the habit of reconfirming onward or return flights as soon as you arrive at your destination. You're in the airport already, where the airline has an office, so get it over with.

Finally, don't forget good manners. Don't treat the Indonesians like idiots. One traveler reports she was able to apply the full value of a Denpasar-Ujung ticket she didn't use towards a Ujung Pandang-Manado ticket, achieved in just 30 minutes with persistent and unerring politeness.

Airport Tax And Baggage
Airport tax ranges from Rp4000 to Rp6000 for internal flights and should be included in the price of your ticket. For international flights the tax is Rp20,000. Baggage allowances range from 10 kg on smaller planes such as the 18 seat DHC Twin Otter up to the normal allowance of 20 kg. The 10-kg restriction for the Twin Otter applies even if your ticket states you're entitled to 20 kg; booking agents are unaware of the restriction. You can still use the 20 kg on the ticket to try and get away with more weight. This restriction is especially important to remember in Irian Jaya, where most flights are serviced by Twin Otters.

The excess baggage charge is about Rp7500 per kg for every kilo over the maximum allowance. That's if they even bother to charge you. If you're carrying a lot of gear, you may have to grit your teeth and just pay it. Avoid paying too much by maxing out your carry-on baggage allowance, or try including yourself in a group standing nearby so the total weight will average out under the limit. Or look around for locals traveling light, and ask if you can put your luggage on their ticket. Also claim you got away with more luggage on your last Twin Otter flight yesterday.

Airport Transport
Indonesia's three main air gateways are the Sukarno/Hatta International Airport in Jakarta, the Polonia Airport in Medan, and Ngurah Rai Airport in Bali. A good number of Indonesia's provincial airfields—particularly in the eastern islands—are served only by Skyvans and consist of nothing but a grassy strip. Goats and cows must be chased off before planes can land, and the "terminal" consists of a thatch hut, a chair, a table, and the Indonesian flag flapping in the wind.

In the Outer Islands, airstrips are often far from town. You can usually hitch a ride in with the crew. The airlines or your hotel may provide transport, or you can walk out to the nearest road and hail a passing *bemo,* minibus, or motorcycle *pengojek.*

In the larger cities, taxis into town are available through the terminal taxi desk. Fares are always fixed. In places like Ambon, Torajaland, and Jayapura, high fares—up to Rp25,000—are demanded for relatively short distances. If you spy a private taxi, wait until most of the other passengers have left the terminal; the driver might then come down in price.

From town out to the airport, bargain. Jakartan taxi drivers try to gouge Rp40,000 for the 20-km ride. When drivers demand such absurd and astronomical fares, charter a *bemo* or threaten to charter one.

Garuda Indonesia
Named after Vishnu's legendary mount, Garuda is the largest airline in the Southern Hemisphere. It flies long-distance international routes to major Asian, European, and Australian cities, and provides service to 35 domestic destinations. Whereas most other Indonesian airlines use propeller-driven planes, Garuda utilizes a variety of modern jets. Garuda is subsidized by the government and is therefore more efficient and better equipped than other Indonesian airlines.

Curiously, the lack of competition has not meant poor service; Garuda's staff is courteous, its pilots professional, its aircraft well maintained, its ticketing and seat reservations service fully computerized.

If you want to visit a number of cities inside Indonesia within a set period of time, Garuda offers a bargain Visit Indonesia Decade Pass with domestic flights discounted up to 50%. The condition: you must fly to Indonesia on Garuda and purchase the ticket in your country of origin. You're allowed three stopovers for US$300. Each additional stopover costs US$100, up to a maximum of 10 stopovers. Children pay 67% of the adult fare. You must still pay all relevant taxes and airport departure taxes. The VIDP requires a minimum stay of five days and a maximum stay of 60 days. The pass is a particularly good value if you want to visit the outer reaches of the archipelago, like Irian Jaya—normally a whopping Rp735,300 from Jakarta—or Aceh, usually Rp440,000 from Jakarta.

The fare is applied only to economy class solely on Garuda or Merpati domestic flights. A completely unused pass is fully refundable; portions are not. To learn more, in the U.S. call (800) 3-Garuda.

In Indonesia, Garuda's head office is at Wisma Dharmala Sakti, Jl. Jend. Sudirman 32, Hotel Borobudur Intercontinental, tel. (021) 360-033. At the Jakarta airport, the number is 550-500. The airline maintains offices in 34 other Indonesian cities, from Merauke on Irian Jaya to Banda Aceh in northern Sumatra.

Merpati

Merpati, the second-largest Indonesian carrier, flies turboprop aircraft to 110 destinations within Indonesia, as well as a few border crossing flights to Australia, Brunei, and East Malaysia. The head office is located on Jl. Angkasa 2, Kemayoran, Jakarta, tel. (021) 417-404, 413-608, with branch offices in the major provincial capitals. Owned by Garuda since 1989, Merpati serves the more remote destinations, providing an air bridge to district centers and provincial capitals. Merpati flies to virtually all parts of the country, but is particularly active in eastern Indonesia. Garuda's timetables also list Merpati flights; Merpati publishes its own timetable as well.

Merpati flies a laughable variety of outlandish aircraft. These include Vanguards, 707s, Viscounts, Skyvans, and Twin Otters. It now flies all the old Garuda Fokker F-28s and DC-9s, and will gradually replace its Twin Otters with the new CASA, coproduced by Spain and Indonesia.

Everybody has Merpati horror stories. The most important rule is this: a Merpati ticket doesn't entitle you to anything. All that counts is the presence of your name on the flight manifest in the Merpati office in the city of departure. Best to book well in advance, preferably in person at the city's main Merpati office. Make sure your name actually goes on the manifest. Many people list themselves on several flights, just to be sure. This doesn't cost anything, so feel free. If in trouble, a few *rupiah* will probably slide your name onto the manifest. Most often you can't buy your ticket until the night before the flight; it's only then the company's reasonably sure the flight will actually go.

It's almost impossible to book Merpati in the U.S., especially on short notice. It's even difficult to book Merpati in Indonesia, unless you book from the city of departure. All tickets must be confirmed before purchase. Getting your money back for a cancelled Merpati flight is like squeezing water from a rock. The company is also notorious for making it difficult to replace lost tickets.

Other Airlines

Bouraq Airlines is a private company offering mostly domestic flights linking Jakarta and other points on Java, Nusatenggara, Kalimantan, Sulawesi, and Maluku. Bouraq emphasizes comfort, speed, regularity, and simplicity. Though long wedded to propeller planes, Bouraq recently began switching to Boeing 737s. Many travelers use Bouraq's flight from Tarakan in East Kalimantan to Tawau in Sabah, East Malaysia, to obtain a new Indonesian entry pass. Bouraq staffs 28 offices in Indonesia; the head office is located at Jl. Angkasa 1-3, Kemayoran, Jakarta, tel. (021) 629-5150 or 659-5179. Bali Air is a subsidiary of Bouraq and offers charter flights only.

Sempati, Ground Floor Terminal Bldg., Halim Perdana Kusuma Airport, tel. 809-4407, fax 809-4420, is a passenger/cargo airline that operates throughout Indonesia. It also offers international flights between Jakarta and Singapore, Kuala Lumpur, and Penang. Sempati uses modern Boeing 707s and Fokker F-27s.

Mandala, Jl. Garuda 76, P.O. Box 3706, Jakarta Pusat, tel. (021) 420-6645 operates four-engine prop planes in the far reaches of Sumatra, Kalimantan, Sulawesi, Maluku, and Irian Jaya, with connecting flights to Java. Consistently a little bit cheaper than Merpati, and a lot cheaper than Garuda. With 22 branch offices. Also check out Pelita Air Service, Jl. Abdul Muis 52-54, tel. 375-908. Airfast is a private air company that accommodates paying passengers when there's room. Indoavia flies from Ambon to the isolated Banda Islands in the Maluku. These private companies can fly only where official domestic airlines do not, and sometimes have to renew their permits to fly every week.

Oil Company And Missionary Aircraft

On the Outer Islands you could get lucky and hitch a free ride with a lone charter, but you should expect to pay. You may also have to use the more expensive oil company or missionary fixed-wing aircraft or helicopters. Missionary aircraft companies such as Missionary Aviation Fellowship (MAF) and American Missionary Alliance (AMA) are the only outfits that penetrate deep into the interiors of Kalimantan and Sulawesi; they also provide very important air links in Irian Jaya. You can buy a seat on a space-available basis only. Priority is given to cargo resupplying mission stations.

TRAVEL BY SEA

Sea transportation in one form or another is available to and from all the inhabited islands of Indonesia. Interisland passage on large seagoing ships (*kapal laut*) is still seriously deficient for an archipelagic nation of this size; smaller boats are required to reach the more remote attractions. On these craft you'll meet a fascinating cross-section of locals and travelers.

The most reliable oceangoing shipping company is state-owned Pelni. Other shipping lines, such as Samudra and Trikora Lloyd, also have vessels working the archipelago, but they're principally cargo carriers, carry few passengers, and don't sail according to fixed schedules.

Check with the *syahbandar* (harbormaster) in the tens of thousands of ports of Indonesia about the comings and goings of boats and their prices. A port may be no more than a copra shed on an isolated beach, or a rickety pier along a marshy riverbank, but you'll always find the *syahbandar* office located on the waterfront.

Ask around harbors to find a boat or ship sailing to your destination, then inquire at the shipping company office. Even if you have the captain's permission, it's difficult to leave the country by ship—you must also clear your passage with immigration, the harbormaster, and sometimes naval authorities.

If you pay a bit more and go second or first class, the Indonesian archipelago is a place where you can experience leisurely travel in the stateroom style of Joseph Conrad and Somerset Maugham. Don't fall for an agent's pitch for *asuransi*; by the time you collect insurance you'll be too old to enjoy it. Usually there are no student discounts on vessels, but you can always try, especially in Nusatenggara and Sulawesi.

Pelni

Pelayaran Nasional Indonesia (Pelni) is the national shipping company, with over 70 cargo and passenger ships connecting the country's major and provincial harbors. Some of the ships in the Pelni fleet should have been torpedoed years ago—the dirtiest, stinkingest rustbuckets ever to sail the seven seas. These blemishes on the good name of Pelni are being retired one by one, replaced by more modern vessels with standardized and reasonable fares.

The pride of the fleet, Pelni's 15 German-built passenger vessels, are favorites of travelers because they follow regular schedules and sail in loops around the archipelago, stopping at ports along the way to refuel and take on cargo. In fact, these showpiece ships are so popular—2,862,489 passengers in 1992—there's not enough room for all the people who want to take advantage of the very low tariffs. Fourteen more passenger liners are expected to join the fleet by the year 2000.

Although Pelni gets to just about everywhere at two- to three-week intervals, a roundtrip usually requires 2-2.5 weeks to complete. Pelni's comprehensive timetable is very useful. Pelni ships seem to be the only transport enterprise in Indonesia that keeps to schedules. You can plan your whole trip around the Pelni brochure.

If a truly long, leisurely sea voyage of two weeks is what you desire, book passage on the KM *Kambuna,* embarking Belawan in North Sumatra for Jakarta, Surabaya, Ujung Pandang, Balikpapan, and Bitung in North Sulawesi, then back along the same route. Inquire at any of

PELNI NETWORK

JAYAPURA

SORONG

TERNATE

AMBON

BITUNG

TOLI-TOLI

PANTOLOAN

BAU-BAU

TARAKAN

KUPANG

ENDE

WAINGAPU

BALIKPAPAN

UJUNG PANDANG

BIMA

BANJARMASIN

KOLEMBAR (LOMBOK)

PONTIANAK

PADANGBAI (BALI)

KETAPANG

SURABAYA

SEMARANG

TG. PRIOK (JAKARTA)

MUNTOK

BENGKULU

DUMAI

PADANG

SIBOLGA

BELAWAN (MEDAN)

LHOKSEUMAWE

MALAHAYATI (BANDA ACEH)

-·-·-·- = KERINCI ROUTE
+ + + = KAMBUNA ROUTE
——— = RINJANI ROUTE
————— = UMSINI ROUTE
———— = KELIMUTU ROUTE
— — — = LAWIT ROUTE
·········· = SERIMAU ROUTE
(ACTUAL ROUTES MAY VARY)

500 km

0   500

© MOON PUBLICATIONS, INC.

these ports for details. A shorter voyage on the KM *Kerinci* sails from the port of Padang down the coast of West Sumatra, passing volcano after volcano. Flying from the Irian Jaya capital these days is expensive business—Rp735,000 one-way to Jakarta. To save money, fit your trip to the Baliem around voyages of the KM *Umsini,* Rp151,000 economy, Rp557,000 first class.

Two relatively new Pelni ships, the *Serimau* and the *Tatamailau,* are a great boon to travelers exploring Indonesia's eastern regions. The *Serimau* sails from Ambon to Jayapura, the *Tatamailau* to Banda, Fakfak, Agats, Merauke, Dili, Maumere, Ujung Pandang, and Surabaya on a three-week circuit. Though they've lost money for Pelni, these ships are a lifeline to these far-off haunts.

Rates And Classes

You can obtain a schedule from the Pelni head office at Jl. Angkasa 18, Jakarta, tel. (021) 421-1921, fax 421-1929. The company also staffs a number of provincial offices. You can purchase Pelni tickets through travel agencies or direct through a Pelni office in one of 32 ports. Travel agents widely advertise Pelni tickets. Child fares are usually half the adult rate, and Pelni provides a 25% discount for children under twelve. If you cancel, you lose 25% of the cost of the ticket.

Reservations made in Pelni offices in such inland cities as Rantepao or Bukittinggi are not reliable. Reservations for the upper classes sometimes aren't necessary—on the day tickets are sold you're given first priority as a tourist. Economy class is another matter. Onshore offices sell tickets but allocation of sleeping spaces occurs on board; spaces are sometimes oversold.

Economy class, formerly known as deck class, bunks 50-60 people at a time. You're assigned a numbered two-by-one meter space on long, low, wooden platforms, each with an overhead baggage rack. The economy section is located in the rear of the ship on decks five, four, and three. At night it's hard to sleep, what with the bright flourescent lights, droning calls to prayer, and loud, incessantly violent movies. Six days in Pelni's economy class will send you around the bend ("WHERE YOU GOING?" a thousand times a day!). Hand out photocopies of standard replies to give yourself some peace. Sneak into the higher classes to use the facili-

ties. Food is included in the price; in economy class you get a half cup of rice, a tiny piece of fish, a hard-boiled egg, and some veggies, served on a plastic dish with a spoon and a cup in a cardboard box. Plenty of hot water to fill mugs and tin cups.

First Class fare includes two single beds, a/c, TV, day and night videos, a table, comfortable beds, bathroom with hot showers, and palatable meals on white tablecloths. When booking, they make every effort to keep couples and families together, and you have your choice between male and female quarters. Food is Indonesian. Take books and games because this is not a cruise ship and there are no organized activities.

Pelni Travel Tips

- Avoid the school holidays in June. People pack Pelni boats like sardines; tickets sell out weeks in advance.

- Pelni officials and crew are bribemasters. A few *rupiah* often opens space on a full boat. You soon find *habis* (finished) and *penuh* (full) are fluid concepts in Indonesia.

- Traveling first or second class is definitely worth the extra money. Luxurious cabins and ample food.

- If traveling economy class, arrive at dockside at least three hours before sailing to secure a good bunk on deck five, highest above the waterline and the most stable.

- It's essential to bring survival rations if traveling economy class. The food is slop—disgusting—and the shop prices exorbitant.

- In economy class, there's always a mad scramble for mattresses. People who clamber aboard first snatch up mattresses and hurl them down wherever they wish to sleep; those who arrive later are left without a thing to rest on. And after you grab a mattress, expect an official to come around and demand Rp2000 for it.

- Always take your valuables with you during fire drills.

- Couples seeking to share second class cabins should buy economy class tickets and upgrade on board. Sometimes you can effectively secure first class cabins at second class prices.

Other Shipping Companies

Check with other shipping companies, which may offer small, clean, fast ships with friendly crews, good food, and cheaper fares than Pelni. At least nine other shipping companies run ships regularly throughout the archipelago. Use Pelni's fare structure as a reference; consult with travel agencies. Not all agents will have every ship listed, so check several.

You can take Perintis Lines, for instance, for half the cost of Pelni passage. Perintis ships, however, usually carry only two small lifeboats, so you risk the sort of catastrophe that claimed the *Tampomas II* in 1981. That old Perintis favorite, *Dharma Nusantara,* and her ugly sisters *Daya* and KM *Nusana* still ply their routes, though they're not recommended even for your worst enemy. Mats on deck rent for Rp1000 per person. Don't plan on washing because the *mandi* is a leaky pipe. The eight toilets reek of ammonia—like squatting above an open vial of tear gas. Later in the voyage they give off quite a different odor. From Ambon, the *Dharma* requires 24 hours to reach Banda.

Kapal Motor

On the smaller *kapal motor,* First Class means you're situated under a canopy on the upper deck. Deck Class means you're frying on the uncovered lower deck, scorched by the sun. On smaller boats, try going directly to the captain himself and paying him your fare. If you go through a ticket agent it could work out to 10-15% more. Force the agent to itemize each "extra" charge on your ticket, or you'll end up paying for his lunch. It might be difficult to buy your ticket from an office or agent, so always be prepared to buy it second-hand from sharks who add at least Rp2000-3000 to the original fare.

Still one of the best deals in Indonesia, and an increasingly popular way to see the eastern islands without traveling by road, is a 6-8 day voyage on a *kapal motor* from Bangsal on Lombok to Labuanbajo in West Flores. Cost: Rp250,000 pp. Highlights are the islands of Komodo and Rinca, but you also stop at islets and beaches along the way. The price includes transport, accommodations (sleep on deck), food, and equipment. The return trip is cheaper—Rp100,000 pp—as there aren't as many people heading west as east.

Prahu

Indonesia possesses an astounding variety of indigenous sailing craft known by the generic term *prahu,* craft known for their beauty, speed, and strength. Each region boasts its own design: the *pinisi* of Bugis, *janggolan* of Madura, *lambo* of Bali, *nade* of Sumatra. If the world's oil wells were to dry up tomorrow, goods and people would continue to move around Indonesia, just as they always have.

It's an unforgettable experience riding on these wind-powered Indonesian vessels. A passage on a ship is also an ideal language-learning opportunity, as other passengers and crew seldom speak European languages.

Boarding one of the bigger Buginese cargo boats as a paying passenger from Surabaya or Jakarta to the Outer Islands is more difficult than might be imagined. Indeed, it's something of a privilege, as passengers are in truth nothing but encumbrances. Unless you show up with all your luggage and just sit on the boat, a lot of times they'll sail off without you. They make enough money shipping cargo, and don't really need your piddly Rp20,000. It's easiest sailing amongst the Outer Islands, where captains depend more on passenger fares.

These huge motorless boats, which look like fat, round-bilged sailing hippopotami with enormous and unwieldy lateen sails, can sometimes drift on a windless sea for a week. Or you could run into a tremendous storm at sea—lightning everywhere, driving rain, big waves tossing the small *prahu* like a coconut shell. Get sick; get washed overboard.

But if you have the ability to endure cramped, rolling conditions for three or more days, try a *prahu* just for the sheer medieval thrill of it. Play bottlecap checkers or dominoes with the crew, catch up on your letterwriting, learn the Bugis alphabet, try cooking curried fish and chilies. A bottle of Chinese wine will get you through the night like the north star. Under a full moon you can sometimes see dolphins riding the bow wave above a luminous night sea.

Other Vessels

You'll find all kinds of river, lake, and oceangoing craft in Indonesia, from luxurious love boats to exploratory schooners, from shallow-draft yachts to rusty freighters. Bali offers the most variety of recreational seagoing vessels—vintage sailing ketches, hydrofoils, exotic tall ships, specialized dive boats, underwater boats.

The *longbot* of Kalimantan is a long, narrow, sausage-shaped boat powered by two outboard motors and equipped with bench seats for passengers. Its nose lifts high out of the water when underway. These craft work the water where passengers and goods must be ferried over shallow rivers or reefs. Outrigger canoes are used to hop across narrow straits and channels. Fees are set and the boats are available for charter. Speedboats are rare, used to carry passengers to classy joints like Pulau Seribu in the Bay of Jakarta or Nusa Lembongan off the east coast of Bali. They're considerably more expensive than *longbots* or outriggers, about Rp150,000 per day.

Inexpensive ferries connect Sumatra and Java, Java and Bali, Bali and Lombok, and all the islands of eastern and western Nusatenggara. These ferries can transport motorcycles and bicycles; some are designed to carry cars and trucks. Ferries run once or twice a day or several times a week. Some ferries, like the one that runs from Sumbawa to Komodo and on to Flores, travel both ways, passing each other en route. The rivers of Kalimantan—the island's highways—are served by large, sluggish river ferries chugging up- and downriver carrying people, purchases, and merchandise, stopping frequently in innumerable small port towns for an hour or so. They almost always feature canopied sections where you can stay dry and seek cover from the sun.

To crew on private yachts, try the port of Benoa on Bali from August through October. You could hitch a ride to Indonesia's Outer Islands, Singapore, Australia, Sri Lanka, Capetown, Brazil, or the West Indies. It's rare to find yachties who simply cruise the Indonesian islands; most sailors you meet are circumnavigators who want to clear the area as fast as possible because of government red tape and the threat of piracy. Most are on their way from Australia to the Indian Ocean, the Red Sea, or the Cape of Good Hope.

Government regulations require that all crew members and passengers possess valid passports, visas, and necessary inoculations. Vessels of all types are potential targets for pirates, who strike mostly in gangs of not less than five when the vessels slow in the dark between 2000 and 0400. Most of the 200 attacks in 1992 occured in

the narrow 32 km Phillip Channel, the southern half of the waterway between Singapore and Indonesia, and south of the Strait of Maluku and the Anambas and Karimata Islands of Indonesia.

Boat Hire

To visit such remote places as Krakatoa or the pearl-diving islands of the Arus, it's necessary to hire a boat from a fisherman or charter agency. Hotel or tourist offices can often suggest, if not arrange, a reputable captain and reliable boat. If you can't secure a referral, shop around for the best boat at the cheapest price. Make it clear exactly what you're paying for: does the price include gas and the return trip? Food? Cover everything so there won't be any misunderstandings. Rent for the trip rather than by the hour as the engine could die and the boat drift for miles. Or maybe the thing will lose a rudder. Take some plastic to cover your gear when it rains. Stock plenty of supplemental food and water.

Several companies operate modern schooners from Bali to Timor via the eastern islands of Nusatenggara. Leading companies include Sea Trek, tel. (800) 227-8747 U.S. only, fax (510) 654-4200; Odyssey Cruises, tel. (800) 825-1680 for the U.S. only, fax (213) 935-3156; and Discovery Ecotours, tel. (800) 825-1680 U.S. only, fax (213) 935-3156, an Alice Springs, Australia company that operates a tall-masted square-rigged schooner.

The Ride

When traveling by sea, your schedule must be flexible. In other words, don't have one. Sometimes you wait 30 hours on deck for your *kapal motor* to leave port. If it's a school or religious holiday, you haven't a prayer trying to find a place on a large intraisland ship. Most smaller boats don't carry flares, two-way radios, lifeboat, or spare parts and you might ride anchor four days in the middle of the Makassar Strait with a missing propeller before help comes.

On many of the bigger ships, go onboard early on the night before to secure a good place and to keep from sleeping amongst masses of people and merchandise. For the cheapest passage—deck class—take along a woven rattan mat (*tikar*) or a stack of newspapers to stake out your territory. The *tikar* serves as carpet by day and mattress by night. On a crowded boat try a hammock, hanging it on deck and swaying with the current. Sometimes you can rent a folding bed from the crew. Crew members might also rent out their own cabins for Rp5000-10,000, depending upon length of passage. As a Westerner, you may be able to use the officers' toilet and shower.

Deck class in the upper decks is not only cheapest but often superior to the small, hot, sometimes windowless cabins. Except for the new Pelni ships, even first- and second-class cabins can often be too stuffy to survive in during the day. If it's too crowded below decks, foreigners usually exile themselves aloft where it's cooler, cleaner, and windier, bereft of rats and cockroaches. There's also more privacy, and better security if you take turns watching each other's gear.

During the wet season, deck class passengers on some ships get drenched, so a small tent is a must. Plan on washing in a *mandi* consisting of one leaky pipe; bring a plastic container. To save money on hotels during two- or three-day layovers, ask the captain if you can sleep on board while the ship lies in harbor.

Unless you fancy rice and egg twice a day, or chunky cold white rice and fishheads, bring your own food. Some smaller boats serve fresh-caught fish, but many heave you salted dehydrated fish that smells like wet dog. There's always hot water. Cork up a couple of bottles of drinking water. Bring your own tin cup, plate, and eating utensils, as these are usually in short supply. On bigger ships you can sometimes slip the second-class kitchen or officer's mess some money or a shirt and they'll deliver meals to you even if you're traveling deck class. Sample the first couple of meals to make sure their grub is really superior to deck class slop.

TRAVEL BY TRAIN

Sadly, Indonesia's unique state railway system (PJKA) has been neglected, while stinking, noisy *bemo, oplet,* and minibuses proliferate. Indonesian railways date back to the late 19th century; at one time, the Java State Railway held the world record for the longest nonstop narrow gauge, running between Batavia and Surabaya. In those days all trains ceased running at dusk because of the "hazards of the jungle." During the Japanese occupation, most of the country's motive power and rolling stock was removed to Manchuria.

There are now 7,891 kilometer of track, all on Java, Madura, and parts of Sumatra. Java's rail system, the most extensive, runs the whole length of the island, connecting the east coast with the ferry for Bali and the west coast with the ferry to Sumatra. In Sumatra, trains operate around Padang, Medan, South Sumatra, and Lampung. A train connects the port of Teluk-betung with Palembang and Lubuklinggau in the south, while other tracks connect Padang with inland Lake Singkarak and the port of Belawan to Medan in the north.

For longer distances, trains are slower, less tiring, and more comfortable than buses, minibuses, or *bemo*. Trains are also cheaper. They offer color and scenery without the numbing discomfort and moments of pure terror which typify a long-distance bus or minibus ride. On trains you sit in relative comfort, fresh air blows in, you can read or get up and stretch your legs, vendors walk up and down the aisles selling refreshments, and it's easy to strike up conversations with other passengers. Another big advantage of train travel is the convenience of journeying from city center to city center with no transfer fares to pay, no weather delays, no road obstacles. Big cities such as Surabaya and Jakarta feature several different stations serving west-, south-, and eastbound trains. On Java you can travel day or night from Jakarta to Surabaya by fast, diesel-fueled, air-con express trains. The Bima passes through Yogyakarta and Solo, while the Mutiara takes the northern route through Semarang.

Fares

Anyone used to the fares in other parts of the world—Europe, for example—will find the cost of rail travel in Indonesia astonishingly cheap. Where else, except perhaps India, can you travel in comfort at express speeds for three hours for a fare of around $1.50? Try it, between Jakarta and Bandung, on the Parahyangan trains. Nine departures daily, the first at 0530. Fares: first class Rp29,000, executive A class Rp23,000.

Nowadays both fares and schedules are posted at most train stations. Student discounts are given at the ticket window, reduced by as much as 10-25%. Trains charge different prices at different times of the day, and discounts usually only apply to the cheaper third-class day trains.

Fares vary from train to train, too, as well as by class. There are many different types of trains. Some are decrepit, lumbering, and noisy, with hard wooden seats; others are sleek, fast, comfortable, expensive. Travel in the more expensive but infinitely superior trains—even third class is okay.

The Indonesian names and characteristics for classes of seating are *eksekutif, bisnis,* and *ekonomi. Eksekutif* (first class) features a/c, free meals and videos, and no vendors are allowed in the stations. *Bisnis* (business class) offers fans, meal service (for a price), and no vendors. *Ekonomi* (economy class) . . . well, it's a cultural experience. Fares range from Rp35,700 to Rp105,000 for the Jakarta-Yogyakarta-Semarang-Surabaya journey, depending on the train and class. The Bima and the Mutiara Utara on Java are luxury trains, linking Jakarta and Surabaya. The Bima is the only one with sleepers. An executive class seat on the air-conditioned Mutiara Utara or the Bima train from Jakarta to Surabaya costs Rp51,000-58,000, while a business class seat runs Rp31,000-36,000. The Bima passes through Yogyakarta and Solo, while the Mutiara runs on the northern route through Semarang. The Senja Utama Solo is an express service, with reclining seats but no air-conditioning, from Jakarta to Yogyakarta and Solo. From Jakarta to Solo, the fare is Rp46,000 executive class, Rp24,000 business class. The Senja Utama Semarang runs Rp40,000 executive class and Rp18,000 business class from Jakarta to Semarang. If your ticket costs Rp200-400 more than the fare you see listed, a "station fee" (*bea stasiun*) has been added. The amount of the fee depends on the ticket price.

Reservations/Buying Tickets

Obtaining a train ticket can be an infuriating experience. As trains are heavily booked, it's difficult to buy tickets at the last minute. Seat reservations at some stations and for some trains are available only one day in advance; in other cities you can buy tickets three days before departure; in yet other cities, only one hour before leaving. Double-check schedules. If you board a train without a reserved seat, you'll stand and sway the whole way. You can't book a roundtrip by train; you must make return reservations at the point of departure.

In Jakarta, you can order tickets as long as a week in advance, at least for the express trains. In other cities, tickets are available only on the day of departure. So rise early, get in line, and expect to wait for as much as one or two hours. Observe Weber's Rule: the longer you stand in line, the more likely it's the wrong line. A corollary of this rule is that the supply of tickets could be exhausted before you reach the agent. If this happens, it sometimes helps to make a direct appeal at the *kantor kepala stasiun* (Stationmaster's Office), where they may conjure up an extra ticket or two for *pegawai* and frustrated Westerners (ask for the *loket turis*). To save the hassle of getting to a station and waiting in line, for a small fee you can make reservations one to three days in advance through a travel agency.

The Ride

Regular day trains make more stops than night trains. They also have no air-conditioning, but offer an ever-changing view of rural Java or Sumatra for a cheaper rate. Many travelers opt for cooler nighttime travel, particularly on long- and medium-distance hauls. Most trains don't run to their timetables, though they nearly always leave exactly on time from their starting points. Schedules also change frequently. Arriving later than expected can be a nuisance, though many trains arrive one or two hours early. Stations offer secure luggage service. If you are going to be in the station for just a few hours, the stationmaster will keep your bags for around Rp500 apiece; you can then leave the station and walk around. Ask for the *kantor stasiun,* usually located on the ground floor.

It's wise to bring your own food and water, since the food on trains and platforms is often bland, expensive, and carelessly prepared. Buy *nasi campur* (Rp3000) at a good *warung* prior to boarding; it'll keep the night. Fruit, snacks, and drinks you can purchase from vendors at each station stop. For meeting people, the dining car is best.

Vintage Trains

Just 15 years ago Java was a sanctuary for rare engines, with over 700 active steam locomotives. No steam engines were ever built on Java; those now retired are all of unique European design. Almost all the huge, black, lum-

(CONTINUED ON PAGE 152)

BEATING THIEVES

There are thieves throughout all Indonesia. Snatch thieves, pickpockets, cat burglars, scam artists—on Sumatran buses travelers are even drugged to make them easier to rob.

Since they must carry their money and valuables on or about their persons, travelers are prime targets. Suspicion and wariness are not very agreeable states of mind, but they do prevent thefts. Take all available precautions, because practically anything you have, people want. Wet wash is stolen from the line, shower shoes from in front of your door. Indonesians often borrow things—surfboards, sunglasses, rings, guitars, books—and "forget" to return them. The Indonesians you move among when traveling on the cheap—like the denizens of U.S. Greyhound bus stations—frequently confuse generosity with abundance, taking advantage of your good nature and desire to be friendly. Travelers also rip off other travelers, so exercise just as much caution around Westerners, especially in dormitory-style accommodations.

All over Indonesia theft increases dramatically as holiday seasons approach. Indonesians themselves take extraordinary precautions to avoid being robbed during these times. Theft is so bad that for several weeks prior to Ramadan the Javanese customarily turn their homes into fortresses. This is because poorer Indonesians try to obtain money and goods before the monthlong fast begins, when they must forgo all. Indonesians are also under great pressure to buy gifts for friends and relatives at the end of the fast, a cash outlay as financially devastating as Christmas is to us. There's also a big increase in stealing prior to some of the more important religious festivals on Bali.

Discouraging Theft

The best preventative is to travel through the islands without jewelry, watch, or camera. The less you bring, the less there is to steal and the less your risk of bodily injury. Never carry a lot of cash; only Rp210,000 or so at a time, or enough to see you through the week.

The following precautions should quickly become second nature. Almost all hotel rooms have doors with locks. Use them. Even better, take your own lock and key along to prevent inside jobs by hotel staff. If a door doesn't close tightly or the lock seems flimsy, jam a chair underneath the door handle. If you have the slightest doubts about the security situation in a fleabag losmen or penginapan, stay in a more

expensive hotel with better security. Try never to rent a room without strong bars on the windows. If you do, take all your valuables with you when you go out, or ask if you can store them in the proprietor's residence. Spend that Rp10,000-15,000 extra for a safer hotel with bars on the windows, a penjaga (guard), everpresent staff, and a good high stone wall with barbed wire or broken glass on top. It's essential the general public be prevented from entering the hotel compound. Your room window shouldn't face an alley or sidestreet but open toward the interior of the hotel. Beware of leaving bags on floors; they can be hooked with a line or pole and pulled to the window.

If you're staying with Indonesians, the word that a Westerner (translation: rich) is in town spreads instantly through the whole kampung. Quick and quiet, thieves will enter your room through the window while you sleep and steal the camera from the hook above your head or the backpack from underneath your bed. Don't set anything valuable near an open window or on a curbside table while dining al fresco. Beware of instant friends dressed a little too slickly and speaking English a little too glibly; likely con artists.

When sailing on board a Pelni ship, take all your valuables with you during lifeboat drills. When trains stop at stations, never leave anything valuable unattended on the seats or on the table while windows are open. Don't leave valuables in a vehicle; to show you haven't, leave the glove compartment open.

Muggings are practically unheard of except in the wrong parts of Jakarta and Surabaya at the wrong time of day. If you go into a redlight district, go sober; thieves most often accost drunks. Carry the minimum amount of cash you'll need for the night in your shoe or a hidden pocket. Finally, when hiking, leave your belongings with the local cops in exchange for a half-hour passport inspection and/or English conversation practice.

Pickpockets

When your mind is not on your money, you're vulnerable to pickpockets. Carelessness is a pickpocket's best friend. Like a mosquito, you don't know you've been bit until the itching starts. Heed Awas Copet (Beware of Pickpockets) signs. There's even a school for pickpockets in Cirebon, West Java. Graduates of this school are said to be able to remove your wallet from your back pocket while you're sitting down or extract money from deep inside your front trouser pockets. Be wary of minor accidents—being shoved or bumped, somebody stepping on your foot. These may simply be ploys to distract you while your wallet is lifted. When big interisland ships dock, avoid passenger crushes. If you're pushed around in a crowd, drop your arms and turn to face the person bumping you. The pickpocket will usually turn aside and move away smartly. Don't be taken in by commotions, distractions, or "accidents" of any kind.

If you're traveling with somebody else you're less likely to get ripped off. You can keep an eye on each other and on each other's gear. Be extra wary of the *bemo* of Bali. Travelers are victimized by young pickpockets dressed as schoolkids who work in groups: one or two divert you while another steals. Sit in the traveler's seat in the back of the *bemo* with your side next to the cab. Keep your bag or pack against the cab with your eye on it, pockets facing the wall. On the buses of Jakarta, a gang of young hooligans may surround you and pick your pockets while you're standing there. Though you may even realize what's happening, there's little you can do about it, squashed as you are. With Jakarta's heavy gangsterism, the other passengers will probably be too scared to help.

Wallets, Purses, Shoulder Bags, Backpacks

In Indonesia, the whole concept of the wallet in the hip pocket must be discarded. Pickpockets also know exactly how to get at wallets and purses in shoulderbags. Never put purses in coat pockets or shopping bags or on counters. The less you open your bag in public, the better. The only safe way for a woman to carry her purse is to hug it tightly against her side, away from the street, protected by her arm.

Avoid zipper-type shoulder bags—you don't always close the zipper all the way, leaving enough room for a hand to reach inside. Instead use a latch or snap to fasten the bag, or choose a bag with a small opening you must pry apart to get into. In the Yogyakarta area, thieves specialize in slitting open clothes and packs with razors. Don't put valuables in a camera case; thieves have caught onto this practice. An ice cooler is better. Try not to carry cameras hanging around your neck; thieves are tempted to yank them off. Beware of approaching motorbikes—purses and bags can be snatched from your shoulder by rear-riders, a Surabaya specialty. Some travelers bear scratch marks from thieves who tried to tear off necklaces, backpacks, or watches.

Leave your address book, traveler's check serial numbers, passport number, photographs, heavy money, air tickets, and other hard-to-replace papers in the bowels of your backpack. You're less likely to lose your backpack, and can remove valuables in the privacy of your room as you need them. Your backpack offers the most security because it either remains in your room or rides on your back, making it difficult for a thief to get deep inside without discovery. Keep only those possessions you can do without in side pockets or on the top layer of backpacks.

Moneybelts

Moneybelts are recommended for Indonesia, especially if you're heading on to Southeast Asia and India. If you hang a compact pouch around your neck under your shirt, it can be yanked off in crowds. Better is a tight moneybelt fastened around your waist under your clothing. On long hauls, wrap a cloth around the belt so your skin isn't irritated by the wet canvas.

Select a moneybelt with a buckle in front so it doesn't eat its way into your back when carrying your pack. Wrap your traveler's checks, passport, and other documents in plastic so they don't become soiled and stained with sweat. Make canvas moneybelts slitproof with steel, chicken wire, or leather backing. In cities, some travelers lock the contents of their moneybelt with a tiny padlock.

Insurance Against Loss Or Theft

If your goods are stolen, put word out on the street you'll pay a reward for the return of your gear. Going to the police can be futile and even additionally expensive. Before an investigation the police may ask to talk about it over dinner, which you pay for. Some accounts tell of travelers appealing to the police upon thefts of items like cassette recorders; when the police recover a deck by sheer accident they ask the traveler to donate Rp5000 for "finding" it.

On the other hand, a policeman can end up as your only friend. He might console you, feed you, start up a collection to return you safely to your friends. You can also settle a serious disagreement over money, usually in your favor, by taking the matter to the police. This, a disputant Indonesian rarely wants to do. Even raising the possibility of using the police as mediators often results in negotiations moving along quickly and in your favor.

Your homeowner's insurance policy should cover loss of personal property while traveling abroad. If you don't have coverage or don't want to risk increased premiums on your homeowner's policy, consider separate travel insurance. Cameras, video cameras, tape recorders, and the like insured and registered in your passport, with receipts kept and a police report filled out, all serve as valid proof in the event of loss.

(CONTINUED ON NEXT PAGE)

BEATING THIEVES
(CONTINUED)

Lost Air Tickets/Passports

It's always a good idea to write down your flight ticket number, flight number, issuing agent, date of issue, and method of payment, and keep the accumulated info in a safe place. Detailing all this information will make your ticket easier to refund in case of loss. You still have to pay at least a $10 fee to the airline to replace your lost or stolen ticket. Since the airline wants to be sure tickets haven't been used, they can only be refunded three months or more after the expiration date.

Try not to store your passport and money in the same place. If a victim of thieves, you lose everything at once. Report passport losses immediately to the nearest police station and ask for a letter of reported theft/loss. Without this letter, required Imigrasi stay-extensions can be difficult. You can obtain new passports or letters of travel through consulates and embassies. You'll most likely find your embassy or consulate in Jakarta; many of Indonesia's major trading partners also maintain consulates in Surabaya, Bali, and Medan.

---

bering, coal-burning locomotives have been phased out of passenger operation. A few of the country's steam locomotives—museum pieces in the West—still haul freight and sugar in East Java; two run in Medan. Now India and China are more relevant destinations for rail enthusiasts. Occasionally you see old locos puffing out of the railyards in Madiun, East Java. These yards should be visited sooner rather than later. Behernoths such as Mallets or Hartmanns, their smokestacks belching steam and soot, haul rolling stock up severe gradients in the vicinity of Bandung at Cibatu. A big draw for rail buffs is the open-air museum at Ambarawa in Central Java, where 22 steam locomotives have been put out to pasture. Charter groups can enjoy the thrill of a steam-hauled ride aboard a vintage Swiss-built cogwheel tank locomotive from Ambarawa to Bedono through scenic hilly Central Java terrain.

TRAVEL BY BUS

Buses are cheaper and slower—but with assigned seating, slightly less crowded—than a *bemo* or minibus. The most comfortable seats on the whole bus, as far as riding out the bumps, are in the middle (*di tengah*), but not over the wheels. Local public buses are frequent and very useful for short sightseeing jaunts.

Daytime bus travel on congested roads is slow and exhausting; they move much faster in the cool of the night. Long-distance buses require about an hour to cover 40-45 km. Use this formula to calculate the length of time it takes to get somewhere; if it's 170 km, it'll consume around 4.5 hours. On the run from Lahat to Bukittinggi in West Sumatra, for example, seating is five across and you sweat nonstop for 20 hours. The bus is closed up tight as soon as it gets dark.

Buses still aren't as cheap as third-class rail, and for the longer distances on Java it's generally more relaxing to take trains. On many routes—such as most of Sumatra and Irian Jaya—there are no rail connections. You have no choice but to take buses.

Bus travel can provide its share of comic adventures. A reader reports that on the Liman Express run to Rantepao, the bus suffered a flat tire in the mountains south of Makale. There was a spare but of course no lug wrench. After the driver hitched to Makale for help, his son and a passenger borrowed a wrench from a passing truck and changed the tire in the rain. So the bus took off again, with the passenger driving. They picked up the driver down the road; he just grinned and allowed the passenger to drive all the way to Rantepao.

Bis Malam

Many big cities are connected by *bis malam* (night buses). These custom-built nonstop buses usually leave in the late afternoon or early evening and arrive the next morning or afternoon, with a limited number of stops, about once every two or three hours. The best are luxuriously equipped, with reclining airline seats, onboard toilet, nonstop *Rambo* videos or karaoke, even a *nasi padang* meal, snack, and drinks. *Bis malam* could be sleek, purring, modern buses advertising "Full A/C and Video" or veritable rolling piles of lurching scrap metal. Generally *bis malam* are safer, cooler, faster, and more expensive than regular day buses, the Indonesian equivalent of the U.S. Greyhound system.

Ask other travelers and *losmen* proprietors which bus companies are currently the best. They might also advise you where to book seats. For shorter, heavily trafficked runs like Denpasar-Surabaya, buses leave frequently throughout the day. For longer distances, *bis malam* usually leave early, often by 0630 or 0700. Indonesian hotels are very conscientious about waking you up to catch a bus, train, or plane.

If you're just passing through, book a seat on a bus out as soon as you arrive in town, even if it doesn't leave until a few days later. If you wait until the day you want to depart, get to the bus company office early, as tickets are often sold out by 1300. If you roll into a town during the day and buy your ticket in advance, you can safely store your things in the company office or even at the local bus station office. Choose a seat in the front, where there's not as much bounce. Try to get control of a window, and never sit under a ceiling speaker if you wish to retain your hearing and sanity. Pick a seat from the seating chart in the bus company office. Try not to sit next to young children, 90% of whom will be sick. Inquire if standing passengers are allowed—you don't want them to be. Buy a ticket as far in advance as possible so you can be assured of getting a good seat to accommodate your long Western legs.

On the road, your money and valuables should be kept in your shoulderbag or handbag which you should lean against or sleep on. If your backpack is put on the roof, personally see it's properly tied down. Some travelers even habitually padlock and chain their packs to the roof rack.

Local Buses

Local buses offer slow but frequent service between and around most small towns and cities. Destinations are posted above the front windshield. Big city bus stations usually feature a row of buses, engines running, ready to pull out. If the first bus is full, just climb on the one behind. It will leave within minutes. Once these local buses hit the road, wherever a passenger

awaits is a bus stop. Often there's standing room only. Be extra careful with your money and valuables—lots of pickpockets.

Bis Kota

These inexpensive, crowded, noisy, hot, fast, uncomfortable intracity buses are available only in major cities. In some locales, like Jakarta, these creaking goliaths stop only at designated bus stops. In other cities, like Yogyakarta, you can flag them down on the street. Fares are usually Rp300, Rp200 for students, to anywhere in town. City bus route maps are not available except in Jakarta; walk up to the men in the white shirts in the *kantor setasiun* (bus station office) and ask directions.

Fares

Buses are the cheapest way to get around within Indonesia. You can figure the fare if you know the distance: by government regulation, bus companies in Indonesia can't charge more than Rp16 per km for good roads, Rp19 per km for bad roads. This means road conditions in Kalimantan, Irian Jaya, and Sulawesi may dictate higher fares.

Fares for short distances, especially on Java and Bali, are extraordinarily cheap. Few local 20-km-plus rides ever cost more than Rp2100 and more than Rp20,000 worth of bus travel in one day is unbelievably exhausting. With minibuses you can often haggle the price, but on the big express buses there's usually a standard fare—fixed and inarguably cheap. The price of intraisland ferry crossings is often included in the ticket price. Children ages 4-11 are usually charged half the adult ticket; children under four ride free. Some travelers succeed in obtaining a student discount; it might be worth a try. Excess baggage costs about a fifth of adult fare. For local buses, fares are almost always posted over the ticket window (*loket*) at the bus station.

INTER- AND INTRACITY TRAVEL

Most of the following types of public transport vehicles run regular routes and make regular stops at terminals, street corners, or intersections, but they also frequently pick up passengers anywhere they find them. Particularly if you're willing to tip the driver, they'll also make detours to let you off. If the driver tries to renegotiate the fare halfway to your destination, ask to be let out and insist upon paying the fare only up to that point. Faced with the possibility of losing the whole fare, the driver will return to the original price.

All of the following contraptions bump and lurch on all the islands of the Indonesian archipelago. They carry baby chicks, goats, pigs, coconuts, plows, bicycles, cases of soda pop, sneezing children, and pickpockets. Experience life at the village level while being driven pell-mell to your final destination by kamikaze drivers.

Horse-Drawn Carts

Though slow, a horse-drawn cart or carriage can be a delightful little adventure. They come in a variety of shapes and styles, each a pleasant mode of travel in many small towns and villages. Look for these covered horse buggies standing in rows near train stations, around the grassy *alun-alun*, or on the edge of town waiting for fares. The two-wheeled kind (one horse) are called *dokar* or *sado*, and can carry up to four people. In Yogyakarta, Solo, Malang, and Surabaya, the carriages are large, with four wheels, sometimes drawn by two horses, and able to accommodate six to eight people. These are called *andong* or *bendi*.

When it rains, the driver covers the *dokar* with plastic. Horse manure, sold later for fertilizer, is collected in a bag suspended behind the horse. Small bells are attached to the horse harness. When darkness falls, small oil lamps to the sides of the coach are lit. The lights, together with the bells and the sound of the horse's hooves, are a great pleasure to see and hear.

Dokar are still part of the scene in and around such regional centers as Bandung, Bogor, and Yogyakarta on Java, but in larger cities they're fighting to operate alongside their motorized competitors. You'll be hard-pressed to find a *dokar* in or around Jakarta. They're particularly prevalent in hill stations, and are popular in Lombok and on the other islands of Nusatenggara. On Lombok, they're called *cidomo*. In the hill resort of Gedong Songo in Central Java you can hire sturdy, indefatigable ponies to take you up an ancient pilgrim's path to seven 8th century temples set amongst the hills.

Fares are set by bargaining, the average being Rp1000-1500. The farther the distance and the more passengers, the greater the fare. Drivers of horse-drawn carriages operate on a fixed-fee basis, particularly when offering local sightseeing trips. In Kuta Beach, *dokar* run down to Legian, catering to yuppie tourists at inflated fares.

Becak

The pedal-powered *becak* looks like a big painted rocking chair on wheels. A *becak* (pronounced "BEH-jack") is best described as a man-powered tricycle-taxi, an enjoyable form of transport for up to two passengers. Passengers sit side by side in front of the driver, a canvas or cloth canopy providing some measure of protection from the sun, fumes, and dust. When it rains, a large flap of transparent plastic is brought down over the passengers in front.

Truly one of the great experiences of Asia is riding a *becak*. At the flick of a wrist you can signal a turn to the left or right. In the evenings glide under starlight, trees, streetlamps, with just the sound of rubber tires rolling over the pavement. No other form of conveyance combines all the viewing advantages of walking-pace travel with the comforts of a city taxi. But unlike taxis, *becak* are slowly being legislated out of the larger cities because of the disruption they cause to the flow of traffic. Though still an important means of transport in cities as large as Yogyakarta and Ujung Pandang, they're completely excluded from North Sulawesi and are not spotted on Timor either.

In the gaudily painted, congenial *becak* you'll drink in more sights and become more immersed in the local atmosphere. You can even converse with passersby as you roll along. A *becak* can take you to places completely inaccessible to cars. They're able to negotiate the narrow *kampung* streets where other vehicles cannot go. A parked *becak* also makes a great blind for taking photographs.

Few work harder for their bowl of rice than the *tukang becak*, who usually chooses this hot, heavy work because he has few other choices. Though he speaks rudimentary English, you won't find a better guide. He knows where to change money, the location of the best crafts shops and entertainment districts, where to find the cheapest hotels. He'll walk up hills, pushing you from behind, though if it's too steep, please get out and walk to give the guy a break. His thighs are enormous, his shirt wet with sweat, his lifespan an average of 50 years. Most die of an overworked, enlarged heart.

Becak are usually leased by the drivers. Since up to a third of the fare goes to the owner, *becak* are often more expensive than *bemo*. Costing Rp500-2000 for a one- to five-km ride, *becak* are considered by Indonesians slightly extravagant. Indonesians use them mostly to take their kids to school, to carry home produce from market, or when they're late. If you have many errands or stops to make, you can hire *becak* at about Rp2000 per hour.

Always, always agree on price before climbing in. If you can take the *becak* driver out of earshot of his cronies, he'll be more likely to agree to a *harga biasa* (normal fare). Don't try to bargain with "tourist" *becak* drivers in and around popular tourist sites. Just walk a block away in any direction and look for another one. The walkaway technique works really well with *becak* drivers. There are always 10 more drivers ready to step in if he doesn't accept your offer. Another tactic is to ask a local the correct fare. Try to choose an older *becak* driver; older men know better the true value of money, and will bargain more easily. The younger, more ambitious drivers want up to Rp5000 per hour. On occasion, they refuse to take the money agreed upon; if a driver won't take it, just put it on the seat and walk away. Don't argue.

Taxis

Taxis—licensed and metered, as we know them in the West—are available only in Jakarta, Bandung, Yogyakarta, Solo, Semarang, Surabaya, and on Bali. In the rest of Indonesia you'll find private cars or unmetered taxis, for which you pay an agreed-upon or fixed amount. You can usually find taxis on certain streets in inner areas of the city, in a special taxi stand beside the *alun-alun*, outside the larger hotels, or cruising the streets looking for fares. Taxi drivers speak little English, often know only the names of major streets, drive on both sides of the road, and do not heed speed limits.

With the notable exception of Jakarta, highly trafficked, profitable routes, such as between airports and major cities, are seldom serviced by buses or other modes of transport. In these cases, taxis are the only game in town. To save

in taxi costs from airports into cities—sometimes as far as 25 km and as high as Rp30,000—befriend someone on the plane or wait at the taxi desk for someone to share a taxi with. It's also frequently possible just to walk 500 meters or so outside the airport gate to a main highway and flag down a public *bemo* or minibus. You can even hire one and keep it all to yourself at a cheaper rate than an airport taxi. When heading from cities out to the airport, hire local transport like a *bemo* or minibus, not a taxi.

If you have friends to share the fare with, taxis can be a better value than public transport. Licensed taxis (yellow number plates) equipped with a meter usually charge Rp800 for the first kilometer plus Rp500 for each additional kilometer. It's your responsibility to have the exact fare because the driver will never be able to make change. Most drivers expect a small tip.

You can charter taxis at about Rp6500-8000 per hour, or by the day or week. In Outer Island areas, like Biak on Irian Jaya or Palopo in Central Sulawesi, where vehicles are scarce, taxis won't take you for less than Rp10,000 per hour.

For longer distances, shared taxis can be a comfortable, streamlined way to travel. Get a group of up to five people together, go down to the taxi stand, and bargain for the best hourly rate. Or call a taxi company and line up a vehicle a day in advance.

Helicak

A cheap alternative to taxis, these motorized three-wheeled vehicles consist of a cabin mounted on a motorcycle, sheltered from the sun and rain by a tinted plastic bubble. A *helicak* can fit two passengers, who sit in the bubble in front of the driver. Quite common in Jakarta, they run Rp1000-2000 for short distances.

Bajaj

Making deep inroads into the traditional *becak* (pedicab) market in many cities is the *bajaj*, a two-seat, three-wheeled vehicle that is essentially a motorized version of the *becak*. Built more for Asians than for larger Western frames, the chugging *bajaj* look like a cross between a pickup truck and a golf cart. Over-revved, loud, dirty, and dangerously unstable, *bajaj* can pack six to eight passengers and are quicker than taxis because of their ability to squeeze between trucks and buses. *Bajaj* drivers charge

There are three ways you can die in a bemo—a head-on collision, suffocation, or fright.

a negotiable fare on a trip-by-trip basis and can be hired in almost all large towns. A bit less comfortable but a lot faster than a *becak,* though they often have engine trouble (repaired in about 10 seconds).

Bemo, Oplet, Microlet

Bemo is short for *becak motor.* This is an open-backed canopied pickup truck running on a regular route. Made in several sizes, a *bemo* is outfitted with two rows of low, wooden passenger benches down the sides. Large four-wheeled *bemo* can carry 12-16 people sitting knee-to-knee. There are three ways you can die in a *bemo*—a head-on collision, suffocation, or fright.

An *oplet* generally operates on specific routes and between cities and nearby suburbs. The word comes from the Dutch verb *opletten* (to watch out for) from the days when servants were ordered to *oplet* for a taxi scheduled to pull up in front of the house. In Sumatra, an *oplet* could be a rainbow-colored Chevrolet bus or minibus, reminiscent of the Filipino jeepney, while on Java it's a canopied pickup truck with seats. In bigger cities such as Jakarta, *microlet* are replacing the *oplet.* These light blue vehicles charge the same fares and run the same routes. Actually, all the fine distinctions between different types of small public vehicles are becoming redundant now as old-style vehicles are gradually giving way to Japanese-made minibuses, usually Mitsubishi Colts or Toyota Commandos.

Minibuses

Also called colts (pronounced "koll"). Assembled in Mitsubishi's Surabaya plant and from there spewed out all over Indonesia, minibuses feature 11 seats holding up to 20 people with the conductor hanging out the side. The name colt applies to all minibuses, not just Mitsubishi Colts. A good way to get a feel for the landscape is to climb on top of a minibus, but only if the road leads through the mountains. Otherwise, the thing goes too fast.

These small vans travel the middle-distance runs on most of the major and secondary roads throughout the archipelago, shuttling passengers back and forth between neighboring towns. Operating on the shorter, heavily trafficked routes more frequently than the big public buses, minibuses have in fact replaced buses on many transport routes. Minibuses are generally Rp400-1000 more expensive than buses because they're not controlled by the government, so they can charge almost anything—as long as it's competitive. Though they cost more than buses, minibuses are considerably faster and are a lot more convenient and comfortable. They're also more prone to accidents.

Ask officials at bus and minibus stations for the correct fare. In many cases the fares are also posted, although the actual fares asked by the drivers and their assistants are invariably higher. Before taking off, your minibus driver might circle around the town or city for 20 minutes soliciting passengers to fill all remaining seats, only departing once they're full. Midway through the journey you might be asked to board another minibus to take you the rest of the way; be sure the new driver doesn't charge you again. You can also charter minibuses for your personal use at rates cheaper than taxis. How much to offer? Multiply the number of passengers the bus can hold by the usual individual fare to your destination; that will give you a rough estimate of the fair price.

In Indonesia's cities minibus companies specialize in city-to-city, door-to-door service. For example, if you want to go from Cirebon to Jakarta, phone the 4848 Bus Co. in Cirebon. They'll ask where you are and where you want to go and at what time; buses leave almost every hour to Jakarta for a fare of Rp20,000. One advantage of door-to-door service is that it's much easier to arrive in a new city without having to find local transport. The disadvantage is you drive around for sometimes as long as 45 minutes picking passengers up at one end and at the other you spend just as much time dropping them off.

The Ride

Whatever the vehicle, the custom is to flag it down along the main routes of a city or on main highways between towns. Vehicles are invariably overcrowded as the driver will not leave until he's convinced no one else can possibly be stuffed in. You will learn at very close range the driver's musical preferences as he will play his favorite tapes at full volume for hours on end. Tell him to turn the volume down with, *"Tolong turunkan musiknya."* It won't do any good, but will allow you to practice your Indonesian.

Small public vehicles operate on irregular schedules on fixed routes like buses, and can also be hired. They're always stopping for and dropping off passengers, and will pull over anywhere you want. *Bemo* prices often go up at least Rp50-100 at night, especially in popular tourist areas. On longer routes between cities, bargaining is the rule. Fares vary from region to region, but are usually higher on less frequented routes. For rides within a city, Rp300 or so is the usual fare, no matter how long or short the distance. If the driver insists the fare is Rp400, just give it to him—it's not worth arguing about. Don't climb into an empty *bemo* without making

it clear you do not want to charter it but intend to pay the public fare only (*harga umum*).

PRIVATE AND TRAVEL AGENCY VEHICLES

Older, unlicensed "taxis"—look for black license plates—ferry passengers from village to village in the countryside. Crammed full of people, animals, and goods, they shuttle back and forth over short distances. The rate is approximately Rp5000 per hour or Rp40,000 per day, depending on how well you bargain, how badly they need the fare, the type and age of car, length of hire, and distance. In many cases, a friendly bout of haggling can quickly produce quite acceptable results. Two hours is usually the minimum charter period. Find someone else to go in on the fare.

In the towns of Indonesia, you can rent jeeps and off-road vehicles from the local travel agent. In the cities, rent through an agency or from a car rental firm. The local tourist office can suggest people or businesses who rent vehicles; someone in the office might even have one to rent. Before sealing a deal for a long-term rental, take your driver on a day outing to test his character and personality and determine how well he drives.

The cost of hiring a car varies wildly, depending upon where you are. In the Baliem Valley of Irian Jaya it can cost Rp150,000 per day; in Jakarta, Rp100,000 per day; in Bali as little as Rp40,000 per day. Also expect a lot of parking and entrance fees. Anywhere but Bali, the rental automatically comes with a dependable driver. You're expected to pay for the driver's meals and accommodations in special rooms hotels provide for drivers (around Rp15,000 pp per night).

Cars that would have been diverted to the junkyards 20 years ago in America are on the road in Indonesia. Even in the outskirts of Jakarta, 1950s Austins and Chevrolets are used for city-fringe transportation needs. These old cars, with heavy-gauge steel bodies, seem to run forever. Indonesians are ingenious at fashioning spare parts or rendering outlandish repairs to keep cars running almost indefinitely.

Bemo Hire

It's easier and cheaper to hire an *oplet, bemo,* minibus, or private car than deal with a taxi or official car rental agency. Small *bemo* naturally cost less than the large ones. To hire a *bemo* for a whole day, count on Rp35,000-45,000. If chartering by the hour (Rp5000-6500), make it clear each quarter of an hour beyond the estimated number of hours will be charged at one-fourth the hourly rate—they often expect you to "round it off." Write down the starting time on a piece of paper and put it up on the dashboard. Don't let the driver and helper jam in 16 of their friends. *Bajaj* are the cheapest of all motorized transport to rent, for as little as Rp3000 per hour.

Car Rentals

There are numerous car rental agencies, including **Avis**, Jl. Diponegoro 25, Jakarta 10310, tel. (021) 334-495. Daily rates are around Rp147,000 per day. **National Car Rental** Kartika Plaza Hotel, Jl. Thamrin 10, Jakarta 10320, tel. 333-423, offers competitive rates. Another rental agency is **Bluebird** Jl. HOS. Cokroaminoto 107, Jakarta 10310, tel. 332-064, 333-000, fax 332-175. It's also possible to rent by the hour. Avis in Jakarta and Bali offers chauffeur-driven cars starting at Rp21,000 per hour for a Toyota. There's usually no tax, and gasoline is included. You must be at least 25 years old, 19 for National. An International Driver's License is also necessary. **Nitour**, Jl. Majapahit 2, Jakarta 10160, tel. 346-347, 346-344, 340-955 and **Pacto Ltd.**, Jl. Taman Kemang II/Blok D-2, Jakarta Selatan, tel. 797-5874, 797-5879, are trustworthy, long-established Indonesian-based companies found in all the bigger towns. On Bali, hundreds of hotels, travel agencies, shops, and people on the street can arrange car rentals.

Hiring A Driver

Most newcomers to Indonesia think it wise to use a driver (*sopir*) because he knows the language and is used to the country's crowded and hazardous road conditions. The streets in most Indonesian cities, and also the main roads between cities, are very busy from dawn to dusk, especially on Java and Bali. If you're not confident driving in a sea of thick, fast-moving, noisy traffic—surrounded by everything from buzzing mopeds, trucks, and buses to plodding oxcarts, *becak*, and pedestrians—it's best to leave your first Asian car trip in the hands of a capable local driver. You may not have a choice in the matter, as private vehicles usually aren't rented without an accompanying driver.

An Indonesian driver can probably get you to your destination hours faster and safer than if you drove, and if there's an accident, your driver will be responsible, not you. A *sopir* is also less useful in explaining things to you than in explaining you to the people. A driver/guide frees you from always explaining where you're from and what you're doing. He'll also clean and maintain the car.

MOTORING IN INDONESIA

Driving Your Own Car

A personal car for sightseeing and shopping adds a great deal of convenience and independence. The drawback to driving your own car is that you may not truly experience Indonesia, only drive through it. Only when you step from the metal box will you taste Indonesia firsthand. Unexpected hazards of the road are another drawback. Until very recently the Indonesian government restricted the import of privately owned vehicles to diplomatic passport holders. But now you can bring your own car into Indonesia, as long as you take it out again when your visit is over. Importing a car for personal use is tax-free and, provided international documents are produced, the procedures are simple. You'll need an International Certificate of Insurance; motor vehicle registration book or ownership (*Buku Pemilik Kendaraan Bermotor*), obtainable from the police; and a *carnet de passage*, which is a letter of guarantee the vehicle will be exported after completion of your visit or proof onward passage has been booked.

Alternatively, you can buy a car while there, though cars are very expensive by U.S. or Australian standards. Road taxes can run Rp1 million-1.9 million per year. Insurance, at Rp1 million-1.7 million per year, is a necessity. Insurance companies all staff offices in Jakarta. You can obtain an International Driver's License in your home country upon presentation of a valid license. You can't drive anywhere in Indonesia—even on a motorcycle—without this license.

Traffic Laws

Draconian traffic laws passed in 1992 are meant to encourage greater discipline on the road. These laws call for set fines of Rp5000 to Rp25,000. The most important rule a newcomer needs to remember is to drive on the left-hand side of the road, a lasting legacy of the brief British occupation of Java.

The 1992 law calls for the officer to issue a motorist stopped for a traffic offense a ticket stipulating the fine. The motorist also has the option of requesting the officer issue a ticket stipulating the date of a court hearing, supposedly scheduled within a week of the issuance of the ticket. Don't do this. Normal practice is to settle with the policeman on the spot by handing over Rp5000 as a *hadiah* ("gift"). The actual amount will depend upon the seriousness of the offense. This practice forms a vital portion of the income of lower-grade policemen. If stopped by a cop, talk to him for a few minutes to make sure he's serious. If he is, nip it in the bud and pay him Rp10,000 right away (foreigners are expected to pay more *hadiah* than Indonesians). Don't relinquish your license, registration, or title papers or it'll cost you Rp60,000-70,000 in legal fees to get them back.

Road Conditions

Roads and bridges are undergoing constant improvement and new roads and superhighways are laid at a frenetic pace. Still, of the 85,000 kilometers of roads in Indonesia, only 21,000 are paved. Java's roads are the best. Depending on the season and local road conditions, it's possible to drive from Jakarta to the eastern tip of Java, over 1,200 km, in two or three days. In the Outer Islands few roads are sealed and road conditions are utterly unpredictable. One year a road is well paved and in excellent condition, the next it's a bumpy riverbed. Agricultural estate roads are rarely asphalted, but usually feature a good all-weather gravel surface. On rainforest roads, the rain can get so dense it clatters on your hood like nails, steaming up the interior until you run with sweat. Because of heat, humidity, dust, and traffic fumes, most people prefer air-conditioned cars. Make sure the a/c works before settling on a per diem rate. On long journeys, pack snack foods and drinks in a styrofoam cooler.

When traveling by car, remember that maps mislead as to the size, importance, and conditions of roads. A curio of road travel is the amount of signposting left from Dutch times. Should you follow the wrong road to an unexpected or unfamiliar destination, seek assistance from the local

government office. The *kepala kampung* (village headman), *bupati* (district head), or *lurah* (area head) can help you find the right road or accommodations for the night.

Fuel And Mechanics

Called *bensin* or premium in Indonesia, gas costs around Rp750 per liter. Only the state-owned Pertamina oil company may sell gasoline from *pompa bensin,* or filling stations. Look for the famous seahorse emblem. Watch for attendants who stick the nozzle in your tank and pull it out moments later, telling you they've pumped 10 liters though the pump registers nothing. "Machine broke, mister."

Lower-octane gasolines are sold from unofficial roadside stands where *bensin* is measured out in cans. In small villages, gas is sometimes dispensed in Fanta or Bir Bintang bottles. Some readers report the gas sold in these *warung* is watered down, in which case your engine will sputter.

If you're renting a car or *bemo* with driver, be sure it's understood who'll pay for the gas (usually you). It's not necessary to carry extra gasoline while motoring in Java, but since the distances between stations are sometimes great, fill your tank when you have the chance.

Car repair (labor costs only) averages Rp4000-5000 per hour. When carrying out roadside repairs, the custom is to place a big stone or tire in the middle of the road so oncoming traffic can swerve and avoid hitting you. If you have a flat or slow leak, find a *tambal ban* or *press ban* (tire repair shop).

TRAVEL BY MOTORCYCLE

Motorcycling is a fast and inexpensive way of getting around, and often the only way to negotiate dirt roads in the rainy season. Indonesians call a motorcycle simply *motor,* or *honda*. Petrol is cheap at Rp750 per liter, though it's occasionally in short supply.

Indonesia is not the place to learn to ride a motorcycle. Ride one with great caution as serious motorcycle accidents on Indonesia's madcap roads are all too common. Chickens, dogs, and children dart out unexpectedly into the road, there are giant potholes, big trucks lumber down the road straddling both lanes, and cars travel at night without using their headlights. Boulders, small rivers, and landslides on the road in the rainy season are other hazards.

Bring warm clothes, as it gets cold when it rains, and in the highlands the temperature drops considerably. Also bring an International Driver's License (endorsed for motorcycles), which is required to rent a bike. International Licenses are available at automobile clubs.

Traveling With A Motorcycle

For long term use, you're best off buying a local *honda* for Rp300,000-500,000; you can then resell it for maybe half what you paid for it. If you travel from island to island with your own bike, make sure it's a lightweight machine, as you'll be loading and unloading it frequently. Pay a crew member Rp2000 to help you. Freighting costs aren't that high. It'll cost you around Rp125,000 to transport your motorcycle by ship from Surabaya all the way to Timor, or about Rp735,000 from Jakarta to Australia. If traveling through the islands by ship, obtain a customs clearance for the bike the day before and a pass from the harbormaster to enter the harbor, then just show up with your ticket. When arriving at dockside, to avoid getting bogged down in hours of customs paperwork, try driving off the ship and right through the gate, saying hello to everyone without stopping. You might make it.

Rentals

You can rent motorcycles in Yogyakarta, Solo, and Pangandaran on Java, and Kuta Beach, Candidasa, Sanur, and Denpasar on Bali for around Rp10,000-12,000 per day; rates are cheaper by the week. Most are 90-125 cc bikes, and you won't need anything heavier or more powerful. The longer the rental period the lower the per day rate; the newer and more powerful the bike the higher the rate. Trail bikes are the most expensive. Most are rented by private parties, usually young men hoping to make the bike pay for itself. On Bali it's big business: a family saves money so it can buy a motorbike to rent. Check not only *losmen* but restaurants, travel agents, and shops for rentals. On Bali approach any group of young men you see lounging around their bikes on street corners.

Carefully check the battery, oil, brakes, cables, and clutch before you agree to a rental

fee. Leave your passport or student ID as collateral and take the bike for a test drive. You should possess at least a crude knowledge of motorcycle mechanics if you plan to rent a bike here. It's also advisable to bring a few simple tools—screwdriver, wrench, pliers, and the like.

Ojek Or Taxi-Motorcycle

Another type of motorcycle transport is called *ojek*, or *honda sikap*. Here you pay the motorcycle driver for the privilege of riding on the back of his bike. The *ojek* driver, for both motorcycles and bicycles, is called a *pengojek*. *Ojek* drivers usually cluster at road junctions with infrequent *bemo* service or none at all. Passengers getting off buses on the main road negotiate with *pengojek* to get them and their goods out to their villages, or mount an *ojek* from a city bus terminal to their homes in the *kampung*.

If you're really stuck, try asking for the *honda sikap* arrangement anywhere, or just simply hitch motorcycles at the side of the road. Pushbike riders can be approached for *ojek* rides as well. When riding double, females are expected to sit sidesaddle while holding onto the packrack—a real trick. When dismounting from the back of a motorbike, watch the hot exhaust pipe. Quite a few travelers receive severe wounds caused by inadvertently touching the exhaust, wounds that heal very slowly.

TRAVEL BY BICYCLE

Besides walking, bicycle riding is the cheapest form of transport. Bicycles here serve as pack mule, dating jalopy, family car, and vendor's shop. A pushbike is what people use until they can afford a motorcycle or scooter. For the traveler, few other modes of transport offer such versatility. It can be ridden, carried by almost every other form of transport from outrigger canoes to jets, and can even be lifted on one's shoulders across streams or over lava-strewn volcanos. Cycling offers minimal transport costs, complete freedom from schedules, and, next to walking, unsurpassed closeness to nature. From a bicycle you can hear the birds singing, see clouds float over volcanic peaks, cruise by vignettes of village life, hear little tykes shout "I love you"—really *experience* Indonesia.

Road Conditions

Bicycling in Indonesia is rewarding but demanding. Because they're Indonesia's most densely populated and developed islands, Bali and Java offer the best highway systems—each features good-quality roads reaching to every corner of the island. All but the most minor roads are sealed. By contrast, long stretches of roads in the Outer Islands are unpaved, potholed, or partially washed away. Where roads are nonexistent, ride in motorcycle ruts or along footpaths.

Since it can be dangerous to ride a bicycle in the more heavily trafficked areas, most main roads on Java include cycle/pedestrian paths. Where there are no bike paths, motorists seem to be more aware of cyclists than in the West. In many Javanese cities, such as Yogyakarta in Central Java, cyclists are the majority and motorists the minority. As usual, Jakarta is the exception; it's not possible to ride around Jakarta.

Get used to judging the different speeds of traveling vehicles, adjusting to oxcarts, *becak*, motorcycles, buses, and cars. Cyclists who won't get off the road for anybody should not ride in Asia. Be prepared to pull off the road to let large vehicles pass. Keep to the smaller roads wherever possible. Signposting is generally good.

At first it seems there are no traffic rules except "Yield to those who are bigger and faster than you." But after a while you learn the rules are there, they're just different. For a right-hand turn, for example, you turn onto the right-hand side of the road first, then cycle against the traffic until there's a gap in the traffic before crossing over to your side of the road. If you want to go straight ahead at intersections, put your hand straight out in front of you while keeping eye contact with oncoming drivers. At really busy intersections, dismount and walk your bike across.

The physical shock of riding long distances over the washboard roads of backcountry areas can be a huge strain. If you're not a physical-fitness freak and grow tired of the torment of the highway, load your bicycle on top of a bus or minibus for long hauls or journeys up into the mountains. That way you won't arrive too hot and exhausted to enjoy the local attractions.

Equipment And Repair

If you're an ardent cyclist, consider taking your own bike. For long-distance touring, it's important to use a thoroughly robust machine. Airlines are surprisingly lenient about accepting bicycles as luggage (often free, but check first). For air travelers, the easiest is a bike that disassembles and fits in a bag. Your bike should have low gears and be 100% reliable. Avoid bikes with skinny 2.5-cm tires; three-cm or 3.5-cm tires are stronger and absorb greater shocks. Make sure all parts conform to accepted international specifications so you can easily find replacement wheels, spokes, and gears. Choose the best-quality, strongest back panniers—they'll take a lot of punishment. Bring a small, comprehensive tool kit and a pump.

At the places in Indonesia where it's most pleasant to ride a bicycle—Yogyakarta and Solo on Java, Candidasa and Ubud on Bali, Senggigi Beach on Lombok—rentals are plentiful and cheap, about Rp3000 per day. Elsewhere it takes some searching, and you may never find a bike that really works. Most Indonesian machines will definitely not win you a place in the Tour de France. Rental choices run from one-speed clunkers with terrible seats to one-speed clunkers with terrible seats and no reflectors, bell, lights, or brakes. Most are sturdy black machines that resemble two-wheeled tanks. For rentals, count on a rate of Rp3500-4000 per day or Rp8000-12,000 per week. Mountain bikes rent for Rp10,000-20,000 per day.

An alternative to renting involves buying a used bicycle. *Toko sepeda* (bike shops) in the cities sell cheap 10-speed Taiwanese models, a few Japanese mountain bikes, and low-priced kids' BMXs. If you're going to occupy an area for a month or more, try to work out an arrangement with a bike shop whereby you buy a good used bike for around Rp100,000-150,000 and undertake to repair and upgrade it if the shop agrees to buy it back when you leave for 20-25% less. This arrangement results in a very low daily rental cost.

If you're renting a local bike, a carrier rack over the rear fender is quite adequate for carrying your shoulder bag or knapsack. Fasten with a couple of elastic spider shock cords with hooks. A critical accessory is a horn or very loud bell. Tires and tubes are available in urban areas in all the usual sizes. High-tech parts and tools might prove difficult to obtain.

Since bikes are used so much by the Indonesians themselves, even the smallest villages feature bike shops or someone whose specialty is fixing bikes. The *tukang sepeda* (bicycle repairer) usually sets up shop on a corner. His labor charges are low, mending your puncture while you wait for only Rp500 or so, using only rubber from an old inner tube, a pot of glue, and a homemade hammer.

The Ride

Don't carry a lot of personal gear; you may want to park and explore an area by foot, and you'll tire easily if you have to lug a bunch of stuff with you. Find a headman, friendly resident, or *warung* owner to safeguard your gear.

Bring zinc oxide or a sunhat for protection against the ferocious tropical sun. A good helmet is also essential. A rearview mirror, reflectors, and a dynamo light provide added protection. Be prepared to use a sharp stick or your pump to defend against hostile dogs. Local bikes are equipped with a claw-like key lock, which locks around the wheel, but a heavy-duty hacksaw-proof steel cable lock (*kunci*) offers more security.

At public places—post offices, markets, schools, big stores—leave your bike at the *titipan sepeda* (bicycle parking area), where the attendant guards the bikes and gives you a claim ticket. The service may be free or cost Rp50-100. At night bring your bike inside your room, or ask the proprietor for the safest storage place.

JAVA

When fossil remains of the erect ape Homo erectus were found on Java in 1891, scientists surmised that Java was the original location of the Garden of Eden. The most famed of all of Indonesia's islands, Java is still one of the richest, lushest, most densely populated places on Earth, and ranks among the loveliest regions anywhere. Deep purple fiery volcanos tower majestically over a land of intense green plains, twisting mountain passes, cool hillside resorts, remote crater lakes, extraordinary Hindu temples, wild game parks, botanical gardens, serene beaches, dense rainforests, savannahs, thick bamboo groves, stands of teak, and squalling, teeming cities. Java is both young and old. It was the genesis of Indonesia's powerful maritime and agricultural kingdoms, and contains the best-preserved and largest number of classical monuments, many built centuries before Columbus came to America.

COURTESY OF THE ROYAL TROPICAL INSTITUTE IN AMSTERDAM

INTRODUCTION

Though Java is the smallest of the Greater Sunda Islands, and comprises only seven percent of the country's land area, it contains 60% of Indonesia's population. Here live most of Indonesia's urban population, as well as the majority of its poorest peasantry. Many areas of Java resemble India because of the congestion, the rice paddies, the explosive colors. "I see India everywhere, but I do not recognize it," said the great Bengali poet Tagore when he visited Java in 1927.

The Dutch concentration of resources on Java for several hundred years greatly increased the differences between it and Indonesia's other islands, which the Javanese still consider "Outer Islands." Educationally, it's the most advanced island. Java's universities and technological institutions form the backbone of Indonesia's tertiary education. Java is top-heavy with industry, processing, and modern transport and telecommunication facilities. With 60% of Indonesia's investments concentrated on Java, it's the island of opportunity, the place where young men flock from the rural areas of Indonesia to find jobs. Java also processes raw materials from Indonesia's productive regions: tobacco, foods, bever-

ages, rubber, timber, textiles, machinery. Yet, because of its giant population, Java could never survive if it were left to its own resources; it would be like a head without a body.

THE LAND

Java's total land area is roughly 130,000 square km. The island is 659 km in length and its width varies between 60 and 200 km. A chain of high volcanic mountains extends the whole length of the island; 15 peaks exceed 3,000 meters. There's a vast contrast between the sluggish, muddy, isle-enclosed Java Sea of the north coast and the wild deserted southern shoreline which borders the Indian Ocean. Here, the continental shelf drops off sharply, and tremendous waves crash against steep, dangerous beaches.

Though the island's original lowland and coastal vegetation have virtually disappeared after centuries of intensive land use, there are still areas of mangroves on the coasts, rainforests in the west, and monsoon forests in the east, as well as some casuarina woodlands and savannah lowlands, and pristine montane forest on the slopes of some of its volcanos (especially in the east). Although all these various ecosystems are somewhat represented in the island's 84 conservation areas, the island is in trouble because of the intense population pressure.

Agriculture

Java's level of fertility and agricultural productivity is without parallel in any other equatorial land, and most of its people make their living by farming. Because of Java's miraculously rich volcanic soil—with loam so dark it looks like melted chocolate—farmers often harvest two or even three rice crops a year. Shifting cultivation is almost unknown, while wet-rice cultivation (*sawah*) is extensive, irrigated by water systems up to 3,000 years old. Terraces, often only one meter wide, are etched in steep hillsides with wooden handtools. Everything that grows on Java has its use; nothing is thrown away unless it's made into compost or used to feed chickens or goats. From planting time to harvest, the rice crop is watched with the same love and concern lavished on a child. Rocks and stones are removed by hand,

and stray soil on the roadside is swept up with brooms and returned to the paddy.

Who Owns The Land?

In principle, land is village-owned, and established villagers have a right to work land cultivated by their ancestors. Today, however, there just isn't enough land to go around. Large families are common, and land is split up many times among sons. With each generation, the size of family farms—already small—grows ever smaller as the land is divided among the male heirs. Javanese farmers must support families of five or six children with the same area an average Australian farm family uses to park its cars and tractors. Javanese work an average farm of less than 0.6 hectare (about two acres); a farmer with two hectares is considered a big landowner. Of this 0.6 hectare, half is set aside for rice; the rest is covered with fruit and vegetable gardens, house, and stables. Plots too small to farm are sold (often to the rich), and more and more families become landless. Present surveys show that about 50% of Java's population is landless, another 25%

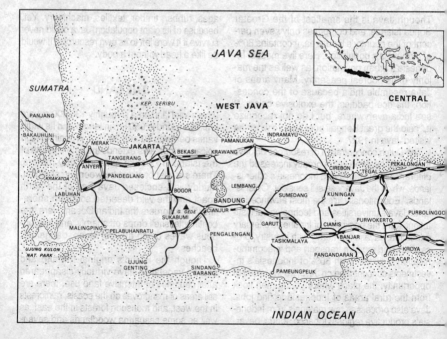

nearly so—tragic figures for a predominantly rural farming society.

In some areas, export crops are even given emphasis over food crops; in East Java the government uses as much as 30% of the land for sugarcane cultivation, a lopsided practice carried over from the Dutch colonial period. Traditional village welfare and harvesting institutions once ensured the poor would at least have enough to eat; because of population pressure, modernization, and socioeconomic inequalities this is no longer always the case.

The Future
Many observers fear Java is careening inexorably toward an ecological disaster. Under the enormous pressure of population, deforestation is progressing at a frightening pace; East Java alone consumes 14 million cubic meters of firewood per annum, equal to two-thirds the peak lumber export of both Sumatra and Kalimantan. No more forests can be cleared for farming or firewood without further silting of the island's reservoir and irrigation systems, some of the most extensive, intricate, and delicate in the

world—the lifeline of the country's rice cultivation.

The island is already involved in a race against time, its precious topsoil sliding into the sea. The cycle of floods and droughts also has exacted a deadly toll on lowland rice fields, causing serious food shortages. Pollution problems have reached critical mass. Because of its expanding population, most of Java's mountain lakes are now cesspools. The canals and rivers winding through Java's cities are a lethal gray color, putrifying with slime and rotting garbage, receptacles for industrial and human waste. Cities like Surabaya, Temanggung, Solo, Magelang, and Bogor have taken action, but elsewhere conditions worsen.

Climate
It's a myth of temperate peoples that the tropics boast perpetual blue skies. Since Java is so mountainous, it helps create a variety of climates, and is often cloudy. There's a distinct dry season at the far eastern end of Java from around April to November. Though the sun doesn't stay hidden for long, bright clear days are rare. From December to March it rains, es-

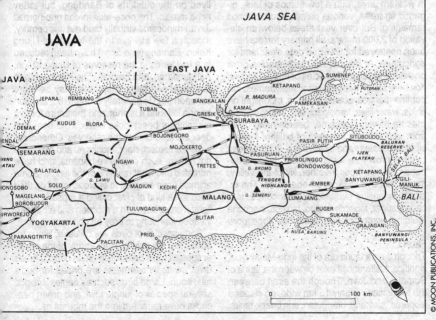

KRAKATOA JAKARTA BANDUNG SLAMET 3428 m MERAPI 2950 m LAWU 3265 m SEMERU 3676 m BROMO 2392 m RAUNG 3332 m

SUMATRA SUNDA STRAIT YOGYAKARTA JAVA SEA

INDIAN OCEAN

PRINCIPAL PEAKS OF JAVA

NOT TO SCALE

© MOON PUBLICATIONS INC

pecially in western Java, which has one of the country's highest levels of precipitation. The heaviest rains come in February. Although violent thunderstorms occur, there are no true hurricanes. The Javan "winter" is June, July, and August, one of the best times to visit.

FLORA AND FAUNA

Flora
Native vegetation forms a dense tropical forest in western Java, with a few stands of teak, gigantic fig trees, various palms, and bamboos remaining. But over vast areas below an elevation of 2,000 meters, all primary forests have been destroyed for firewood or to clear land for agriculture. At least 5,000 plant species grow on Java, including 35 species of fruit—20 found nowhere else. There are giant strawberries, turpentine mangos, scarlet hibiscus, moonlight orchids, water lilies, frangipani, and the lotus (*padmasna*) flower. Gossamer beards hang down from *kapok* trees, showers of brilliant flowers sit atop *cassias* and trees of fire. In high forest regions grow tree ferns, azaleas, wild rhododendrons, yew trees, heather, lily-of-the-valley, myrtle, honeysuckle, even edelweiss. The island's extensive plantations grow coffee, tea, cacao, sugar, tobacco, indigo, tapioca, cinchona (quinine), *kapok*, cloves, and rubber for export.

Fauna
Though Java's fauna are of the Indo-Malay type, significant differences exist between the fauna of Sumatra and Java. Though the strait between the two islands is only 15 km wide, no clouded leopards, *siamang*, orangutan, sun bears, tapirs,

or elephants are found on Java, and no *banteng*, leopards, or *rusa* are native to Sumatra. For millions of years Java was covered with rich tropical jungle and mountains, an animal zoo with *Homo sapiens* the prey. Since man and beast shared the island for eons, it's little wonder Javanese myths and legends are filled with animals and animal-like creatures, their common enemy volcanic eruptions and fire.

As people multiplied and began increasingly cutting into the jungle slopes, the animals started losing out. Even as late as 1940 tigers still lived on the outskirts of Bandung, but today none remain. The once-widespread one-horned Javan rhinoceros virtually died out this century, though a few still live in the forests of Ujung Kulon. *Banteng* (wild oxen) have been reduced to a few herds in the reserves of Ujung Kulon, Pangandaran, and Baluran. The black panther, nocturnal and fairly adaptable, may be more common than is generally thought, but as soon as one is found it is shot, and the future for this magnificent beast looks bleak. Wild boar and deer are restricted to the reserves. Other creatures—anteaters, deer, monkeys, and birds—do not require such extensive habitats, and have retreated into what remains of the jungle. Some animals have adapted to encroachment on their habitats; a kind of civet called a *musang*, a delightful cross between a raccoon and a badger, invades *kampung* to prey on chickens.

Forty species of birds live on Java. Since Indonesians are avid hunters, many of the smaller species have been killed off. In coastal areas dwell swifts whose nests are prized for bird's nest soup. Large birds such as eagles, hawks, several species of jungle fowl, and green peacocks have retreated into the mountains.

MAJOR RESERVES OF JAVA

JAKARTA

C. JAVA

MADURA I.

W. JAVA

YOGYAKARTA

E. JAVA

NOT TO SCALE

© MOON PUBLICATIONS, INC.

1. Pulau Dua and Pulau Rambut bird sanctuaries
2. Ranca Danau Reserve
3. Ujung Kulon National Park
4. Gunung Halimun Reserve
5. Gunung Gede Pangrango National Park
6. Pangandaran Nature Reserve
7. Dieng Plateau Lake Reserves

8. Arjuno-Lalijiwo Reserve
9. Gunung Semeru Reserve
10. Yang Plateau Reserve
11. Baluran National Park
12. Ijen-Merapi Reserves
13. Nusa Barung Reserve
14. Meru Betiri Reserve
15. Banyuwangi Selatan Reserve

There are still 100 varieties of snakes, but crocodiles no longer exist anywhere on Java. The island's frogs sound like birds, and giant iguana, up to two meters long with thick bodies and eerie humanoid hands, are found near Bandung on the Citarum River. Colonies of lizards can be observed on some of the islands of Seribu; they also live on Pulau Krakatau and Pulau Sanglang off West Java, and in the caves of Pelabuhanratu. One does not have to sit for long in the rainforest to see thousands of insects—species you never dreamed existed.

HISTORY

Java is the physical center of all the islands, and has always been the metropolitan trading focus for the archipelago. It's the golden mean in both size and location, long the most favored isle for human habitation and thus the most populous and politically powerful. Java's history is long. Compared to the poor archaeological records of the Outer Islands, Java possesses a fantastic amount of documents and monuments. With the wealth generated from huge surpluses

obtained from wet-rice cultivation, great pre-colonial inland empires rose on this island: Majapahit, Singosari, Kediri, Mataram. Ancient Java was a land of peasants and princes, with the peasants laboring and producing for the princes enthroned in their cities and temples, providing the massive agricultural wealth to fuel the empire's maritime trade.

Written history in Indonesia began with the coming of Hinduism. For centuries Hindu culture overwhelmed Java, and is still very much in evidence today—mystic vocabularies, trains, even noodles are named after the heroes of the Indian epics. Buddhist and Hindu religious symbols remain everywhere you turn.

Starting in the 14th century, another import from India appeared: Islam. The new religion first entrenched itself in Demak and Gresik; these footholds eventually grew into a series of powerful commercial Islamic city-states. With the arrival of Europeans in the 16th and 17th centuries, the political power of these states was sharply curtailed. Yet Java's glamorous past lives on in the royal courts of Yogyakarta and Solo, where Hindu culture remains, a cloistered flower of aristocracy scarcely touched by Islam.

Colonization

The Dutch took possession of the island while Shakespeare was still alive. For a period of 200 years, beginning in about 1723, Java was the key island in the Dutch East Indies empire, paying shareholders in Europe an average dividend of 18% per annum. Under Dutch rule Java became known as the garden of the tropics, one of the best-governed tropical islands in the world. It was a wonder of colonial management, a land of railroads, schools, swank resorts, vast well-run estates. You could telephone any point on the island from your hotel, and travel on some of the best-paved roads in Asia. Batavia, present-day Jakarta, offered steep white-walled mansions, a maze of canals, overhanging roofs of red tiles, signs all in Dutch—like a street in Rotterdam or The Hague. For 40 years during the 19th century, while the peasants starved, all of Java was turned into a huge work farm, subject to a system of enormously profitable forced deliveries of cash crops. The Java War (1835-40) was the last stand of the Javanese aristocracy, the Javanese equivalent of Bali's *puputan*. The Javanese have said the Dutch had good heads but cold hearts, and claim they lost all their lands because it was precisely the reverse with them.

ARCHAEOLOGY

Irrigation farming long ago created an intensely cooperative society in which villages were grouped together under strong district rulers needed to control the flow of water. The ability to support such luxurious pastimes as immortalizing oneself or one's god with the erection of impressive stone monuments, requiring decades of construction involving massive human toil and suffering, indicates gigantic agricultural wealth. For roughly 750 years, starting with the advent of Indian culture, temples were built all the way from the Dieng Plateau in Central Java to the Candi Kedaton, near Bondowoso, in East Java. Ruins are still being unearthed.

The highest concentration and best-preserved Hindu-Buddhist temples lie in Central and East Java, a region comparable to ancient Egypt's "Realm of the Dead." Most of the early Hindu period art has perished and relatively little is known of its development until the 8th century, the beginning of the Hindu-Indonesian period. Because of the tropical climate, only the work of stone sculptors and megalith builders has survived, leaving remains of temples not only on Java but all over Sumatra, Borneo, and Sulawesi.

Visiting Monuments

Pace your visits to monuments lest you find yourself templed out early in your journey. When searching for ancient ruins on Java, signs on the roadway will almost always point the way to important monuments. There's always an attendant or guard (*juru kunci*) at primary temples or monuments, ready for you to sign the guestbook (*buku tamu*) and fork over the nominal admission fee. Don't feel compelled to provide the same amounts registered by the names of those who've preceded you; the *juru kunci* occasionally affixes additional zeroes to the true sums to make it seem past visitors were excessively generous. Also be prepared to run the gauntlet of souvenir stalls and sellers who swarm over tourists and travelers.

Candi

This word is derived from the Sanskrit *chandgrika* (house of the goddess of death) or *candika,* another name for Durga (goddess of death). Regardless of the temple's purpose or its symbolic religious source, the present-day meaning of *candi* is roughly "temple." Many Javanese *candi* were dedicated to the cult of the dead or linked to the idea of an afterlife. Evident on supposedly "Hindu" temples on Java is a combination of Hindu symbols and deities, plus a monument to a god-king, ancient nobleman, ancestor, or teacher whose ashes were buried underneath or in a niche of the *candi.* In some temples, such as at Mendut, the dead king is actually depicted as a Hindu god, his spirit residing in a statue of a god which could be contacted ritually. Thus, *candi* were magic centers radiating power.

The *candi* you see today were once surrounded by flowering trees, high walls, and tall gates opening on inner courtyards. All around these sumptuous temple complexes were shady lanes, rice fields, and the bamboo homes of the people, stretching to the horizon. The long-lasting stone *candi* were rich Brahman structures. The temples of the people were built of wood and bamboo; none have survived.

Seldom do you see any of Java's ruined classical temples venerated today. Indeed, compared to the temples of India, which are crowded and throb with life, Java's temples are archaeological specimens only, maintained to promote tourism. Temple construction had all but stopped by the end of the 15th century, with the Mt. Lawu Group (Sukuh and Ceto) two of the last remnants of the Hindu-Javanese period.

Candi Construction

It's believed most temple plans in Indonesia originated in India, though this has never been proven. No monuments in India are quite like the *candi* of Java. Indonesian artisans and sculptors struck out on their own, coming up with a new way of building, sometimes even surpassing the artistry of the motherland. Hindu-Javanese religion, cosmology, monotheism, and aboriginal cult worship all came together in these monuments. The ground plan of many of these complexes reproduces the human body lying face down on the earth. This is related to the parallelism between the microcosm and macrocosm—in the very small is found the very large.

Many *candi* were built in the shape of the Buddhist sacred mountain, Meru. In their simplest form, these sepulchral monuments consist of three parts: base, temple, and roof, forming a cube-like terraced pyramid usually featuring a platform for walking around to view the carved pictures. A stairway often leads to the terrace. In the more elaborate *candi* are additional platforms, niches, porches, and bases. Hindu-Javanese temples were frequently enlarged long after they were first built, their foundations replaced or annexes added. This happened so often it makes for much confusion among scholars.

One striking characteristic of classical Hindu-Javanese stone architecture is the large amount of hewn stone required for walling in space. Often the enormous masses of stone making up the straight-walled temple body surround just one small inner chamber (*cella*) housing the cult image of the god or ancestor in whose memory the structure was erected (today these images are almost always missing). At the *cella* entrance, space was provided for only a single priest to pray. Javanese techniques of construction make little use of pillars or true arches. Mass is always given more emphasis than space; the structure is often piled high with heavy, overlapping layers of giant stone blocks. Borobudur is a stunning example, a huge ponderous heap of stone covering the top of a hill, with only a small room in the central *dagob* (the highest pinnacle) housing the holy relics.

Reliefs

The characters and themes from Indian epic poems on temple bas-reliefs on Java are often quite uniform; in the 12th century a courtly *kakawin* poem became immensely popular, greatly stimulating the plastic arts of Java. These Indonesian narrative poems carved in relief aren't as sexually explicit as their counterparts in India. Instead the everyday life of ancient tropical Java is clearly depicted, featuring pots, pans, ropes, small lizards, birds robbing grain bins, fruit markets, and parading priests. Archaeologists can derive the date of a monument by "reading" certain animals on a structure. Three frogs, two crabs, three iguanas, and an eel, for instance, somehow add up to A.D. 1455. Highly durable "diamond plaster" provided a base for the application of bright colors, enabling carvers to add extreme detail, and helping preserve the images.

Still, equatorial wind and rain have worn smooth the now-exposed carvings and ornamentation to such an extent that many reliefs have lost much of their vividness and definition even in the 60-odd years since they were first photographed in the 1920s and '30s. The finest bas-reliefs and sculpture from the Central Javanese period are today part of the royal collection in Bangkok, presented by the Dutch colonial government to the visiting king of Thailand in 1896. Other outstanding pieces are found in Leiden and Amsterdam.

THE *KRATON*

When the temple city concept arrived from India, the *kraton* developed as its Indonesian counterpart. The fortified palaces of Javanese rulers became the centers of political power and culture. As in India, these fortresses contained all the surrounding region would need in the way of commerce, art, and religion. Cities within cities, they encompassed banks, baths, shops, temples, massage and meditation chambers, schools, workshops, scribe and concubine quarters—everything royalty had a use for.

Only the *kraton* was open to all the new values and attractions Indian civilization had to offer. The *kraton* adopted and modified first the Hindu caste system, then the philosophical structure of Islam. Only these courts possessed enough wealth for the arts and crafts to flourish. Handcrafted objects were made as ornaments and utensils for the king and court. Though the *kraton* was their origin, crafts eventually spread beyond their walls and into the villages and countryside. Dance also found a home in the *kraton*. The princely courts of Solo and Yogyakarta created their own dance dramas, each style evolving differently. During the colonial period, for the most part a time of peace on Java, artistic expression flowered intensively. The princes, though politically powerless, were still extreme-

ly wealthy. The finest *wayang* puppets, masks, and dance costumes in Indonesia were and are produced in and for the *kraton*.

During the Forced Cultivation Period, the twin *kraton* regents of Yogyakarta and Solo were partners with the Dutch in the ruthless exploitation of the people. Yet the *kraton* have always been regarded by the masses as the center of the world, reservoirs of spiritual power. They were even built in such a way as to reflect a microcosm of the universe. The titles of the hereditary rulers who live in them today testify to their supernatural cosmic function: the *susuhunan* of Solo is called Paku Buwono ("Axis Of The World"), and the sultan of Yogyakarta is known as Hamengku Buwono ("He Who Cradles The World In His Lap").

THE PEOPLE

With their light brown skin, straight black hair, high cheekbones, and small and slender builds, the Javanese originally belonged to the Oceanic branch of the Mongoloid race. But the Javanese "race" is actually a blending of every race that ever established itself on the island. Most of Java's people belong to four major cultural-lingual ethnic groups: the Sundanese of West Java (about 30 million), the Javanese of Central and East Java (about 79 million), the Tenggerese from the area in East Java around Gunung Bromo (300,000), and the Madurese inhabiting Madura Island. Of these, the Javanese are numerically the largest group and the most influential culturally and politically.

Population

In 1805, Java's population was only five million. While Asia as a whole doubled its population between 1800 and 1950, Java's increased sevenfold. With the island's population growing by over two million per year, Java is a precise working model of Malthusian theory: the crude death rate operates to keep the total population always just within the means of subsistence. If population growth and urban immigration levels continue at their current rates, Java will most likely double its present population in 30 years.

Java is one vast village. Though it's home to Indonesia's biggest and most crowded cities, 85% of the island is rural. With over 800 people per square km, Java offers the densest agricultural population in the world. Because the countryside is so economically depressed, the people surge into the cities. But today even the countryside is feeling population pressure, and the incredible absorption capacity of the Javanese village is finally starting to break down. With 60% of Java's land already cultivated and the burgeoning population overflowing onto what is now farmland, gigantic problems lie ahead.

The Suharto government, realizing a runaway population could undo even its most far-reaching development efforts, began to accelerate family-planning programs soon after it took power. The success of these programs is largely attributable to the thousands of village-level family-planning associations throughout Java. Folk traditions also serve to limit family size, with the village *ibu* meeting once monthly to coordinate efforts. Often a Javanese village will hold elections for the "King of the Condom" and "Queen of the IUD." Signs on house-fronts announce the occupants are enrolled in family planning programs, stating the type of contraceptives used, and the proud results achieved.

In the past, the government's solution to the overpopulation and erosion crisis was the magic cure-all *transmigrasi*, instituted by the Dutch as early as 1905. Transmigration involves relocating

the slums of Jakarta

JR & WM KIRWIN

ETHNIC GROUPS OF JAVA

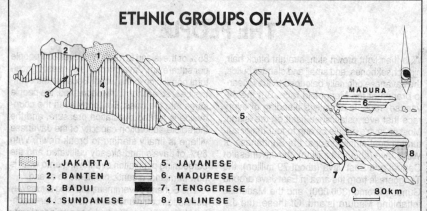

MADURA

1. JAKARTA
2. BANTEN
3. BADUI
4. SUNDANESE
5. JAVANESE
6. MADURESE
7. TENGGERESE
8. BALINESE

0   80km

© MOON PUBLICATIONS, INC.

people from densely populated Java to the more sparsely populated Outer Islands. In general, these underfunded schemes have never really worked; they're rather like transplanting a malignant cancer from the breast onto the leg. Although the *transmigrasi* program continues unabated, it's now generally recognized the main cure for Java's overpopulation must lie with vigorous family planning.

Shared Poverty

Java's overcrowding has led to a phenomenon known as "shared poverty." There are often far too many people for what jobs do exist; this results in many people undertaking a job requiring only a few. Half a dozen people may work on a car, three men milk a goat, *becak* drivers share territories, and stall owners haggle and peddle intensively, then trade goods constantly among themselves to keep business and money circulating at all times. In Solo, many university teachers may teach only four to eight hours each per week. This unique system is able to absorb most everyone in need of work, providing all with at least some means by which to earn their daily bread. Instead of some being *really* poor, everybody is just a *little* poor.

RELIGION

Once again, out of sheer numbers, the religion of Java is beyond doubt Indonesia's most potent political and social force. An estimated 150

religious sects (*aliran kepercayaan*) exist on Java. The indigenous Agama Jawa religion has evolved into an incredible blending of doctrines and practices: in the Javanese story of creation, all the world's major religions are represented.

For centuries Javanese feudalism was the island's true religion, not the law of the Koran. From its early years, Javanese Islam has merged Sufism, Hinduism, and native superstition. Only in the 19th and 20th centuries did Islam penetrate rural Java so deeply as to upset the traditional patterns of authority. Today Islam is the professed religion of 87% of the island's inhabitants. Yet only 5-10% adhere to a relatively purist form of Islam; some 30% conform to a syncretic and Javanized version of Islam, while most of the remaining consider themselves only nominal Muslims. The latter are known as *abangan,* professed adherents of Islam whose practices and thinking are actually closer to the old Javanese mysticism. Vast parts of Java, especially Central Java, are still Hindu-Buddhist.

Mysticism

The current widespread *abangan* cultural awakening arose in part because of the aggressiveness of Java's organized politicized Islam, in which hardline Islamic views and ways of life were pushed upon the majority. The beliefs of the unorthodox *abangan* are attractive to the powerless and powerful alike. Although calling themselves Muslim, members of the Javanese ruling class are preoccupied with mystical religious views and metaphysical philosophy. Traditionally, many of Java's kings became hermits when they grew old, and today a strong *abangan* undercurrent runs through Indonesia's military leadership, including the president himself.

Javanese *pamong* (tutors), black magicians, and *dukun* (healers), famous for their oracular powers, have often influenced powerful politicians. The symbol of Golkar is a banyan tree; its shade is a place of sacred and mystical importance in Javanese villages. Incense is burned before beautiful works of art—a *topeng* mask, *kris,* gong. Worshipped by individual families or by whole villages, these *pusaka* (talismanic heirlooms) often attract legends around themselves. *Pusaka* are said to be able to charm people, ward off sickness and evil, and make the rains come.

CUSTOMS

The Javanese claim the level of a people's civilization is measured by the refinement of its system of etiquette. So strongly do they feel this, the Javanese commonly refer to etiquette as *busananing bangsa,* "the garments of a nation." And by this measure, the Javanese pride themselves on being one of the most refined, polite, and cultivated peoples on earth. This cultivation stems from the *priyayi* tradition. *Priyayi* is the gentry class of Java, the old Hindu-Javanese aristocracy who guard and hold such values and ethics as extreme politeness, deference to the aged, soft-spokenness, proper conduct, sophistication, social arts and graces, and artistic skills (dance, drama, music, and verbal eloquence). As a class they consider manual labor undignified—if you can read and write, you must "have clean hands."

This official class eventually became the civil servant class under the Dutch; today they're the white-collar workers, businesspeople, civil administrators, ruling elite. Indonesia's so-called New Order regime has adopted the paternalistic and feudalistic Javanese *priyayi* political system, and rules the country more or less like a traditional Javanese kingdom with its elaborate system of palace-centered patronage.

Priyayi Etiquette
On this overpopulated island people would be at one another's throats if they were too intimate, too loud, too vulgar, or too blunt. It's a virtue "to talk Javanese," i.e., not to say what you really mean. Granny won't ask outright for her afternoon cup of tea, but will say only, "it's awfully hot and dusty, isn't it?" Even *priyayi* children are extremely well behaved. Mastery of formal etiquette receives so much emphasis that a child who has not yet learned its subtleties is said to be *durung Jawa,* or "not yet Javanese."

Priyayi values still have a strong hold on people of all ages on Java; you often see written on signs or hear Javanese say, "people must have etiquette-feeling." Complicated Javanese etiquette dictates eye direction, the position of the hands, the way one sits, stands, points, greets people, laughs, walks, and dresses. Javanese even flash different smiles for anger, sorrow, suffering, and grief. Most Javanese art forms—dance for example—reflect this discipline and patience.

Of course there are other ways of viewing *priyayi* etiquette. Like the English Oxford or "educated" accent, it's a way of wielding oppressive superiority over others, of denying status and power to those who came from society's lower or *kasar* (rough and ill-bred) classes. Elaborate cultural refinements have always set Java apart from the Outer Islands. But one should also bear in mind that the authority of formal etiquette is not recognized on every island and by every Indonesian. By the same token, most Indonesians practice in varying degrees the same traits as the Javanese. Even scrupulously polite Javanese will sometimes get angry or quarrel. And the same Javanese who are so gracious and considerate in their homes are among the world's most rude and inconsiderate drivers, or grossly *kasar* to Western women at bus stations. Traditional etiquette has been eroded by imported cultural elements and Western technology.

Rules Of Etiquette
Four principal elements make up *priyayi* etiquette:

- The ability to recognize and honor age and rank. In a word, you may not differ with your elders.

- The ability to avoid shocking and offending others. This skill is manifested most superbly in the Javanese art of conversation, characterized by its mild and indirect nature. The cultivated man or woman always tries to put others at ease and ensure no unexpected offense to a listener. Since open dislike or disagreement would create a strained or uneasy atmosphere, which the true *priyayi* prefers to avoid by any means necessary, it's very common for Javanese to express agreement with something they actually do not agree with. Thus, when a Javanese says "yes," interpret *the way* s/he says it to determine what s/he really means.

- The ability to conceal one's real feelings. The Javanese approach possibly delicate subjects in a roundabout fashion and rarely speak bluntly or frankly. No one looks for disturbance; everyone seeks peace.

- The ability to exercise an almost catatonic self-control. Jerkiness and unpredictability are signs of a lack of inner refinement. The less refined people seem to be, the more they fall in the eyes of their peers. Loud voices, flamboyant behavior, bragging, roars of laughter, wails of sorrow are all considered ill-mannered. Passion or anger is expected only of children, wild animals, peasants, the retarded, and foreigners. The Javanese keep it all inside; you only see the placid exterior and the seemingly calm smile.

LANGUAGE

The Javanese language is far more complicated than the archipelago's other languages. As a direct result of the strong influence of the Indian caste system, the Javanese language is the most intricate device ever created to indicate social rank. Many Javanese in fact prefer to speak Bahasa Indonesian so they aren't forced to speak up or down to people.

When Javanese first meet, a sort of extended introduction occurs in which individuals are classified according to ethnic group, rank, and place in society. This ritual must be performed before social interaction can begin. The Javanese spend an inordinate amount of time classifying each other; some conversations never move beyond this stage.

It's impossible to speak Javanese without expressing your view of the social status of the listener. The Javanese lexicon contains a great number of honorific speech forms, which, if used correctly, demand an extreme awareness of the proper respect due age and rank. There are high, middle, and low levels of speaking to inferiors, equals, or superiors. Separate languages include one for the gods and ritual feasts, an ancient poetic language, a classical Old Javanese which is a sort of Javanese Latin, and even special formal vocabularies for the royal court. A sultan always uses the low language and servants the high language when talking to one another. Village schoolteachers address pupils in low *nongko* while pupils answer back in high. Another level is used only in expressing anger.

Their language also shows the Javanese obsession with politeness, that instrument for making others—as well as oneself—feel peaceful within. Thus, you never ask a tailor outright, "how much?" but instead inquire "what will it be in exchange for the thread?" Referring to his wife a husband says, "friend in the back of the house." In addition, different speech tones, *halus* (polite) and *kasar* (crude), are used. One is soft, slow, tender; the other loud, rapid, rough.

CRAFTS AND CULTURE

BATIK

Java produces the world's finest *batik*. A traditional method of decorating cloth, *batik* is an art of great antiquity. The earliest evidence of *batik*-making dates back to the courts of Central Java. *Batik* centers later developed on the north coast, then spread to other parts of Java. Formerly, *batik* fabrics were used mainly to make *sarung*, skirts, scarves, and men's headgear; nowadays *batik* is used in housecoats, dresses, blouses, ties, belts, slippers, hats, umbrellas, sport coats, upholstery—anything that can be made of cloth. Even school uniforms in Indonesia feature subdued *batik* patterns.

Most Javanese women cannot afford to wear traditional dress every day, donning instead cheaper Western clothes. During national holidays, however, all women and girls wear the traditional *sarung-kebaya* outfit, the national woman's dress of Indonesia. A great demand for *batik* has always existed on Java; it isn't just tourists who've guaranteed that *batik* survives and prospers. Still, tourists have undoubtedly accounted for an increase in the making of *halus*, or high-quality, handmade (*batik tulis*) pieces.

Java's principal *batik* centers are Yogyakarta, Solo, Pekalongan, Cirebon, Tasikmalaya, Indramayu, Garut, and Lasem. Each area still produces its own distinctive design and color. Several sizes of *batik* are available. A *kain panjang*, for example, is one meter wide and 2.5 meters long. The *sarung* is one meter wide and two meters long, sewn into a cylindrical shape and worn as a skirt. *Sarung* are usually worn by men, *kain* by women. A *dodot* is used for high-court ceremonies; its length is four times its width. The *selendang* is a breast and shoulder cloth worn by women.

THE *BATIK* OF JAVA

Batik Tulis

The most prized and expensive *batik*, *batik tulis* are usually drawn on fine cotton, linen, or silk. Finely detailed designs are sometimes first drawn freehand with a pencil on the textile. Then hot liquid wax, impervious to dye, is applied with a pen-like instrument called a *canting*, which has one, two, or three spouts and a small bowl on top which is dipped into the hot wax. Areas not slated for coloring are filled in with wax. The cloth is then passed through a vat of dye. The wax is removed with hot water, scraped from the portions of the dried material still to be dyed. Next, other areas are waxed over. This is repeated during each phase of the coloring process, up to four or more times, until the overall pattern and effect are achieved.

Women generally perform the designing and waxing, which require great care and skill. Men normally do the dyeing. A *batik tulis* could require up to 40 days to complete. Really high-grade pieces can consume as much as six months, especially if deep-toned vegetable dyes are used. Until recently there's been a move away from the time-consuming, painstaking *batik tulis* work toward the quicker but usually inferior *batik cap* stamped process. But with increased tourist knowledge of Indonesian artforms, the demand for expensive, hand-drawn *batik* has grown.

If you want older, used *batik sarung*, try the vendors in the markets of Yogyakarta and Solo. Or journey to a village and let it be known you want to buy. Then sit back and see what turns up.

Batik Cap

This is a faster and cheaper method, using the same traditional patterns. Copper stamps (*cap*) are used to impress wax patterns onto the fabric. *Cap* are made from strips of metal and wire meticulously soldered together, and are themselves collector's items and art objects. Some *batik cap* can be superior to *batik tulis*.

Designs

Batik designs are as infinite and variegated as Javanese society itself. You find crazy quilt patterns, circles, ovals, rosette shapes, stars, flowering tendrils, checkered and round patterns, rhombuses, wavy lines, S-like flourishes, swastikas, and bird

(CONTINUED ON NEXT PAGE)

THE *BATIK* OF JAVA
(CONTINUED)

tails. Even partly completed *batik,* such as a cream or white background with some unfinished patterns, is very striking. Sometimes the waxed cloth is crackled by hand to create a shattered effect. Indigenous designs abound, such as the *sawat* pattern forming the wings and tail of *garuda* or the Siliwangi tiger. Some designs are asymmetrical, others are rigid; the freeform variety is endless. Most artisans copy from patterns but the more talented designers can draw intricate floral, geometric, and wildlife patterns from memory—flowing designs filled with stunning colors.

Batik designs offer a fascinating window onto the history and mythology of Java. In traditional *batik,* three types of designs are used: horizontal (called "soft rain"), vertical, and diagonal. Diagonal motifs are considered less harsh than either vertical or horizontal. The designs for the courts of Yogyakarta and Solo were basically indigenous, although some influence from India is seen on the higher-quality cloth.

The introduction of Islam, which forbade depicting lifelike figures, led to stylized patterns without direct representation of human or animal forms. Chinese and European influences are evident in the design and color combinations of Pekalongan and Cirebon *batik,* where bright colors and filigree-like birds, flowers, and trees all form part of the pattern. The motifs of central Java vary greatly from those on the north coast. Other regions prefer Western themes, still others utilize ancient, stylized motifs simple yet mysterious.

Colors

Historically, *batik* has employed natural organic dyes. Indigo is the oldest dye; human blood was once prized. Europeans in the 19th century introduced synthetic dyes, which are now widely used. If chemical dyes are used (usually for really bright colors), *batik* lasts 25-30 years; cloths dyed organically, which fade into rich deep colors, last 45-50 years.

Colors still differentiate certain regions: turkey red for Sumatra, blue-black from Indramayu. Yogyakarta and Solo hold to the official court colors: indigo, dark browns, deep blues, and maroon—colors of dignity. Mauve is considered suitable only for young unmarried girls. West Javanese *batik* is punctuated by golden yellows and light browns with rich, dark, blackish-blue backgrounds. In the northern coastal districts and on Madura, bright reds, yellow, glowing russets, and greens are dominant. Modern *batik* makes use of multicolored combinations: crimson, yellow, and green mixed with blue, yellow, and black.

Cirebon stormy cloud motif

JAVANESE METALCRAFTS

Blacksmiths have always been highly revered members of the Javanese community. According to Javanese mythology, in fact, it is a blacksmith named Panji who is the primal ancestor of the Javanese people. The Javanese were particularly renowned for their skills in metalworking during the Bronze Age (2500-1000 B.C.). These skills included the creation of large bronze kettledrums that may have been used for mystical rainmaking. But by far the crowning achievement of Javanese bronzework is found in the great bronze *gamelan* orchestras of Central Java.

The *Kris*

At one time all Javanese men, from the age of three, were required to wear this magical, wavybladed dagger, and most Javanese are still fond of wearing them. The *kris* is often worn formally by the groom at weddings and by young men to their circumcision ceremonies. Rank is denoted by the method of wearing the *kris,* and it must be worn according to set rules: stuck in the belt in back so that the end of the sheath points to the left, the hilt to the right.

On the best *kris,* hilts incorporate exquisite carvings in ivory or metalwork, decorated with *raksasa* figures (demonic images that drive off evil spirits), little gnome-like men, snakes, or monkeys. The grips of the *kris* of noblemen were often sculpted of gold and set with rubies, diamonds, and sapphires. The ornaments on the blade also provide protection: delicate leaves, *garuda,* or *kala*-figures, and very frequently a *naga* (serpent). *Kris* blades sometimes include up to 31 *lok* (undulations), though more often just seven or nine. An odd number of *lok* insures good luck. These waves are designed to "saw" flesh for a deeper, ripping stab, and also make the wound difficult to heal.

A high mystic value is attached to this instrument of death. Traditionally, old *kris* are part of the family's heirlooms, kept in the back of the house and stored in silk with other objects of the cult of the ancestors. The making of a *kris* was a work of great craftsmanship, created by the *empu* or *pande* (smiths and armorers), members of a secret and holy craft. Though he usually came from a poor and humble family, the *pande* was addressed as if he were an honored lord. The smithy was a hallowed place and the *empu* never failed to complete a very detailed ritual before beginning work on a new *kris.*

In an elaborate rite still practiced in Central Java, once a year the *kris* is taken out and cleaned, a sacrifice shown to it, incense burned, prayers offered, and the blade rubbed with ointments. At one time the exclusive possession of the noble class, the *kris* had to suit the wearer's disposition and character exactly—the ideal alter-ego. The number of times it had drawn blood added to its power. Before a battle or assassination, arsenic was applied to the blade to ensure a fatal wound. The owner would even bathe the blade in the entrails and brains of snakes and scorpions to increase its power.

Some *kris* have a spirit and are capable of sorcery: they can talk, fly, swim, turn into snakes, even father human children. Designs on the blade can ward off demons or render the wearer invulnerable. If pointed at someone or if stabbed into the shadow or footprint of an intended victim, the invisible venom of the *kris* could kill a man. When danger is near, *kris* have been known to rattle in their sheaths.

FOLK THEATER

Each locality of Java boasts its own exciting folk drama. The best place to see this popular theater is in small villages, where the admission price is low and performances are spiced with lots of humor. In the cities people have been conditioned by modern films and fast-paced life and want their entertainment *hebat* (violent, sensational). For villagers who can't read and don't own TVs, these dramatizations of folk tales, proverbs, and poems provide them with new ways of thinking and behaving. Also used as a political vehicle; almost all troupes nowadays are financed by pro-Suharto army officers.

When an entertainment troupe arrives in a small village, it's a big night. Actors barely make a living from their profession, traveling like gypsies with their pots, pans, bedding, and children in tow. Most come from poor families, have little education, and work at unskilled jobs when not touring. As they seldom have time to rehearse, the actors become professional improvisors. The director distributes roles and provides a brief sketch of the story about an hour before each performance.

The gradual but steady appearance of communal TV sets in even the most remote villages is slowly eroding the popular demand for these traveling theater troupes. Folk drama does survive, however, on TV and in People's Amusement Parks in all the big cities of Java, where the following forms are regularly staged.

Ludruk

A modern day, mostly East Javanese transvestite musical theater form. Plays aren't based solely on Javanese mythology and history but are taken as well from everyday life, with many satirical allusions to contemporary events. No fixed repertoire. All roles are improvised by male actors renowned for their flawless ability to imitate women. In the countryside, *ludruk* performances cost as little as Rp250. Get backstage if you can to watch the performers apply makeup and don costumes.

Ketoprak

A folk melodrama originating in Yogyakarta. More traditional that *ludruk, ketoprak* is more movie-like and costly to stage, most often per-

INSTRUMENTS OF THE *GAMELAN* ORCHESTRA

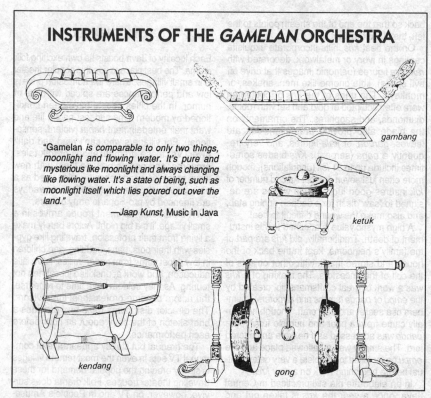

gambang

"Gamelan *is comparable to only two things, moonlight and flowing water. It's pure and mysterious like moonlight and always changing like flowing water. It's a state of being, such as moonlight itself which lies poured out over the land.*"

—Jaap Kunst, Music in Java

ketuk

kendang

gong

formed in Javanese accompanied by *gamelan.* Dancing and singing appear in the beginning and end, but not in the middle. A show usually starts at 2100 and ends at 0100. Serials are frequently divided into seven installments, lasting through the week. This genre takes its stories mostly from East Javanese folklore and history, as well as from Chinese and Arab sources. Traditional moral lessons with contemporary social issues are woven into the plot. *Ketoprak* instructs and entertains simultaneously, passing on new ideas in subtle ways.

In this peformed literature, past, present, and future are all incorporated into the storyline— kings, court scenes, enchanted rings, magic incantations, village doctors, elections, bandits, dwarves, battle scenes on man-powered horses—you could see anything. Even the Christmas story or *Hamlet,* with traditional Javanese dress and mannerisms and all kinds of local

elements mixed in to guarantee box office success. Clowns perform hilarious mimicry of the courtly *serimpi* dancers, including all the simpering expressions. *Ketoprak* is sometimes so popular local authorities close the shows because villages spend too much time and money there, neglecting family responsibilities and local taxes. Truly a theater of the people.

GAMELAN

Gamelan is the broad name for many varieties of xylophonic orchestras with bronze, wooden, or bamboo keys on wooden or bamboo bases or resting on tubular resonators, balanced on pegs, or suspended. This type of percussion ensemble is found in other forms in Thailand, the Philippines, Madagascar, and Cambodia. *Gamelan* orchestras are the most widespread type of orchestra in the archipelago, especially on Java and Bali. The most sophisticated is the native Javanese *gamelan*, usually composed of about a dozen musicians and used as accompaniment in *wayang* and dance performances. In its complete modern form, a *gamelan* orchestra could comprise 70-80 instruments, with solo vocalists (*pasinden*) and up to 15 choir (*gerongan*) members. Native *gamelan* seldom play outside Indonesia because of transportation expenses.

The ethereal sound of the *gamelan* is created when rows of small bronze kettle-shaped discs of varying sizes, with raised nipples, are hit with cudgel-like sticks. These bronze instruments give the *gamelan* its highly distinctive musical range, from thin tinkles to deep booming reverberations. *Gamelan* music can't be compared with the compositions of the West's great polyphonic composers such as Bach, whose music is so mathematically precise. *Gamelan* is much looser, freer, more flighty and unpredictable. Some even feel it is curiously melancholy, even disturbing.

Indispensable to *gamelan* aficionados is a subscription to *Balungan* ($15 for three issues per year), a publication dedicated to *gamelan* in all its forms. Write to: *Balungan*, P.O. Box A36, Hanover, NH 03755, U.S.A.

History

The bronze kettledrum originated from the Dongson culture of Vietnam, reaching the archipelago via China around the third century B.C. Gongs were imported into Java and the rest of the major islands during the Sriwijaya dynasty, whose empire dominated Southeast Asia in the 9th century. In that period *gamelan*, together with drums and blown conch shells, were used for ceremonial occasions; you can find these predecessors of the *gamelan* on 10th century Borobudur bas-reliefs. *Gamelan* as we know it today attained the pinnacle of its refinement in the Central Javanese *kraton* of the 18th and 19th centuries. Although strange to the European ear, the inimitable quality of *gamelan* has attracted Western composers ever since Claude Debussy first "discovered" and praised it at the end of the 19th century.

Tonal Scales

The Javanese *gamelan* owes its origin to the influx of peoples from Southeast Asia, who brought with them the *pelog* scale. A complete *gamelan* consists of two almost identical-looking sets of instruments, with some gongs and drums common to both. One set is tuned to the five-tone *slendro* scale, the other to the seven-tone *pelog* scale. No two orchestras are tuned exactly alike.

Each tone system offers a different feeling. Generally, the *slendro* is more festive and cheerful while the *pelog* sounds more solemn and sad. Scales are divided into unfamiliar intervals and can be constructed to fit any kind of performance. Modulations don't exist, melodies aren't based on a fixed key note, and the tonal material is very flexible. Though *gamelan* is more rigidly structured, as in jazz there's no written score. Neither is there as much soloing as in Western bands; *gamelan* relies more on an integration of sounds. The playing technique is handed down through successive generations, and *gamelan* orchestras hundreds of years old often carry such proper names as "Venerable Dark Cloud," "Flowering Success," and "Drifting in Smiles."

Instruments

The main theme is carried by the *saron*, a set of convex metallic resonating keys beaten with small mallets. These are the most striking instruments; *saron* look like round, bell-shaped pudding dishes with covers. The sound is given more depth and paraphrased by the xylophone-like *gender*, a row of resonant tubes. The *ketuk* offers short, flat, dull accents, while the *kenong* contributes deep resounding notes. The various gong tones and subtle beats are difficult to distinguish at first. The gongs reverberate with shimmering, echoing notes. The *kendang* provides the beat for the melody, accelerating or slowing the tempo as the composition requires. The beat of the *keprak* (wood block) provides the rhythm for the dancers. The sorrowful violin-like two-stringed *rebab* accompanies the chorus, which sings in unison or recites in nasal tones speeches from the plot of a *wayang*. There might also be a zither, and several light, magical reed flutes (*suling*)—the only wind instruments in the *gamelan*, used to paraphrase the nuclear theme in a higher key. Half a dozen drums complete this amazing ensemble.

The *Angklung*

Very popular in West Java, the *angklung* is a portable instrument of bamboo tubes cut to different lengths and freely suspended in a frame. Although restricted to four notes, a strange xy-

DANCE DRAMAS OF JAVA

Bedaya

Javenese perform many different versions of *bedaya*. One of the oldest and most sacred forms is *bedaya ketawang*, performed on the second day of Ruwah on the Javanese calendar—the anniversary of the *susuhunan* of Solo's ascension to the throne. Originating over 400 years ago, this dance is dedicated to the dreaded South Sea goddess Nyai Loro Kidul, who was said to have appeared to the first ruler of the dynasty, Sultan Agung, expressing her love by dancing and singing before him.

The nine dancers, also called *bedaya,* are traditionally selected from families related to the sultan. They belong to the innermost ceremonial circle of the *kraton,* where this dance form has reached its highest development. Performances are kept secret, and no photographs are allowed so as not to anger the South Sea goddess, who is invisible but present. If the dance displeases her, the Javanese fear she might carry one of the dancers off to the bottom of the sea.

The dancers' period of training is long and includes voice training, as dancers must also sing. The dancers (girls aged 15-16 years) are dressed like brides with their hair piled up in buns, wearing beautiful, intricate haircoils of gold, precious stones, and jasmine buds. They fast before the dance to purify mind and body, and none may be in her menses. The dance lasts 90 minutes. First, there are offerings to the gods. While a female choir sings a litany, dancers move languidly, their movements punctuated by chanted, hypnotic bell-like sounds, flicks of long sashes, gentle kicks beneath long swirling trains. Incense permeates the air; petals are showered over the audiece. Dancers are like priestesses in their detachment and solemnity, their gowns undulating like the waves of the sea.

Serimpi

A slow, graceful, disciplined classical dance of Central Java perfected over centuries, *serimpi* features highly controlled movements of arms, hands, fingers, and head. Its sources are the same as those of the *bedaya,* the old Amir Hamzah stories depicting a battle between two rival princesses. Impersonal poise, subtle restraint, and an intense inward meditation are maintained throughout; faces tilted downward, staring fixedly at the floor. The dancers create such uncanny imagery as a fish swimming through the water. They fly across the

lophonic sound is produced when the frame is shaken. The *angklung* was used in ancient times by troops marching into battle. It has now been adapted to Western scales; large *angklung* orchestras can play European as well as Indonesian songs. The *gamelan angklung* orchestra combines these bamboo instruments with gongs and drums.

DANCE

After the split of the Mataram Kingdom into the vassal states of Yogyakarta and Solo in 1775, the art of court dancing evolved differently in the *kraton* of each of these cities. As cultural capitals, they've always been artistic rivals: Solo considers Yogyanese dancers too stiff; Yogyakarta believes Solonese dancers are too slack and casual. The differences in the two schools are still recognizable.

In court dancing, the emphasis is on angular graceful poses and smooth subtle gestures.

This type of dancing is far removed from Western theories of art and reflects the ultra-refinement of the Javanese courts. Conceived during a time of warring states, classical dancing is executed with all the deliberation of a slow march and the precision of a drill maneuver. Sometimes years of arduous muscular training are required to execute certain gestures—such as arching the hand until the fingers touch the forearm, meant to imitate the opening of flower petals. Dancers are incredibly detached, yet their inaction and long periods of immobility are considered just as important as the action. All these pauses, silences, and motions arrested in space, with lowered eyes and meditative poses, make Javanese dance hypnotic to watch.

The tradition of classical dancing was once considered a sacred legacy by the courts. Dancers selected from lower-class families could serve only in supporting roles in the royal plays. It wasn't until 1918, when the Krida Beksa Wirama Dance School was founded in Yogyakarta, that the dance moved outside the

floor on their tiptoes with a dagger in one hand and a fluttering scarf in the other—a sort of stylized combat. Dancers' heads move slowly from side to side while executing "bird movements" or "make-up miming," the hips arching back slightly, the torso leaning forward. Hands usually stay at hip level, elbows slightly bent. *Serimpi* ends in a sitting position with a Hindu blessing.

Reyog

A *wayang topeng* masked dance, *reyog* features a great leering tiger's head or monster's headmask crowned with peacock feathers. Weighing as much as 50 kg and up to 50 cm tall, the mask rests on the nape of the neck and is held in place by the teeth. Though of small build, *reyog* dancers possess incredibly strong neck muscles. It's said to be impossible to strangle these dancers by hand.

The *reyog* story concerns a local king who desires the daughter of a neighboring king. In an effort to discourage the unwanted suitor, the princess assigns him an impossible task: to dig a tunnel from his palace to her father's palace. The average villager sits enthralled and wide-eyed throughout this performance, which can last for up to 12 straight hours.

Kuda Kepang

This is East Java's famous horse-trance dance, in which up to eight performers ride black cutout bamboo-weave hobbyhorses to the rhythm of drums, gongs, and flutes, while a man beats a steel pipe with a hammer. Variations of *kuda kepang* are found in different parts of Java, involving more masked players, monsters, and mysterious rites. In a Chinese-influenced version, there's even a role for a dragon. No stage or enclosure is required for this dance. It can be dangerous, and requires the aid of a *dukun* (medicine man or mystic teacher) who uses mantras to control the dancers.

Often there's a sham battle, then one of the dancers suddenly becomes *jadi* (possessed), believing he's a horse. This state is usually induced by the pain caused by whips, which sometimes draw blood. The entranced dancer then gallops, canters, rears, and prances like a circus pony. There's a bundle of hay in a corner which the "horse" chews. A dancer often loses control—shrieking, twitching, slurping water from a pail, running wild and whinnying, rolling in the grass, charging with stiff body and voided expression. The *dukun* finally calms the performer and brings him out of the trance with incense and incantations.

walls of the *kraton*. Many village groups have since imitated and diluted the courtly style.

Private dance groups perform for anniversaries, wedding receptions, or a *selamatan*. A group can be hired for anywhere between Rp100,000 and Rp600,000; the average cost is Rp250,000. If you hire a troupe to perform, you'll repay the family you're staying with for their kindness, their prestige in the village and *kampung* will rise, and their neighbors will share in the pleasure.

WAYANG

A Javanese word meaning literally "shadow" or "ghost," *wayang* is a theatrical performance of living actors, three-dimensional puppets, or shadow images projected before a backlit screen. The word can also refer to the puppets themselves. In most forms, the dialogue is in Javanese or Sundanese; sometimes Indonesian is used. Most often the chants are in Kawi (Old Javanese), as archaic a language on Java today as Shakespearean English in Great Britain.

All *wayang* drama forms reflect Javanese culture. Characters are judged not by their actions but by their devotion to what is appropriate to their castes, and by their predetermined roles in the drama. Gestures are appreciated more than common sense, style more than content. Courage, loyalty, and refinement always win out in the end, and fate is accepted without question. The *wayang* plays do not just show the direct victory of good over evil. They also display weakness as well as greatness in all the characters and, by implication, in society as a whole.

Besides the abbreviated tourist performances held in Yogyakarta and Solo, *wayang* is staged when some transitional event occurs in a person's life: birthdays, weddings, important religious occasions, or as ritual entertainment during family feasts or *selamatan*. Coming of age (puberty), circumcision, promotion, even the building of a new swimming pool—all could be excuses for a show. While providing entertainment, *wayang* also teaches the meaning, purpose, contradictions, and anomalies of modern life. The policies of the military government are

(CONTINUED ON PAGE 186)

WAYANG THEATER FORMS OF JAVA

WAYANG KULIT

A shadow play using two-dimensional puppets chiseled by hand of buffalo or goat parchment; like paper dolls, but with arms that swivel. This shadow play can be likened to a Punch-and-Judy show. Since a *wayang kulit* puppet is a stylized exaggeration of a human shape, it's really a shadow of a shadow. Of the many different styles of *wayang kulit*, by far the most popular is the form practiced in Central and East Java, where its developed as a spellbinding medium for storytelling.

Other forms, such as *wayang golek* and *wayang orang,* find it difficult to compete with *wayang kulit*. The latter is the cheapest form to present, requiring no costuming or elaborate sets, just puppets and a sheet with a bright electric light behind it. With TV and radio, *wayang* has spread to a much wider audience. These media are not killing *wayang kulit,* as many people maintain; if anything, the mass media increase exposure.

Wayang Making

A complete set of *wayang kulit,* including duplications of a single character to show different ages and moods, could number 350-400 puppets, the smallest only 23 cm high and the tallest over one meter. The *penatah,* or *wayang* making artist, first cuts out contours from buffalo leather or goatskin. Cutting and coloring is executed with the help of a special pattern book that uses 12 different motifs to make the figures more recognizable. Before painting, the hide is rubbed smooth, then given a plain white background. Next, gold or yellow paint is applied to provide a gilded effect. The hide is then stiffened with glue. The best designs, when finished, seem worked in delicate lace filigree.

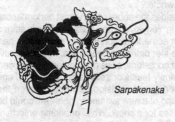

Sarpakenaka

During a performance, each figure is held by a flexible rod of split buffalo horn. The sharp bottom end of the rod, when not in use, is stuck into a banana trunk. Rods are also attached to the puppets' elbows and shoulder joints so the arms may be manipulated. Faces are always in profile, the body turned to the front and both feet pointed in the same direction as the face.

Ramabargawa

Performances are uncannily realistic, with the characters jabbing each other in the chests and waving their arms about to punctuate the action. The puppets can tilt, advance, retreat, fall, pivot, dance, fight, come down from the sky, or fly like a bird. For an otherworldly effect the puppets are moved toward or away from the screen, the shadows becoming sharp black outlines or blurry grays, always fading and wavering. Small boys love to sit in back on the *dalang* side of the screen to watch his deft hands and better appreciate the designs and colors of the puppets.

WAYANG GOLEK

Since *wayang golek* is the imitation by human actors of the movements of the shadow puppets, the three-dimensional *wayang golek* puppets imitate human beings imitating the shadow puppets. The idea for this most recent *wayang* form might have been borrowed from the Chinese communities of Java's northern coastal ports where, in the 15th century, mention is first made of wooden doll puppets. Today, these puppets are more like those in the West, except that rods are used to manipulate them, not strings. The show is performed in the round; no shadow or screen is used. The audience faces the *dalang* and watches realistic people in miniature. Different *gamelan* pitches set the mood. *Wayang golek* plays are closely tied to the history of Islam in Indonesia and were used in propaganda campaigns introducing the new religion.

This *wayang* form is most often performed in the daytime. Traditional *wayang golek* has a less ceremonial, less magical, more worldly atmosphere than *wayang kulit*. To see one of the top new *dalang* in action, with incredible use of characterization and ventriloquism, attend a show at Lingkung Seni Wayang Golek in the village of Giri Harja III. Here, the *dalang* is really jazzed, keeping the audience in a constant uproar. Pyrotechnics are used to compete with the movies: heads pop up from bodies, fake blood spills, characters smoke cigarettes. Modern, highly topical themes and social issues are played out, with actual exchanges between the *golek* puppets and the audience. By contrast, tourist performances of *wayang golek* in Yogyakarta tend to be dispirited and poorly produced, the puppets almost paralytic.

Puppet Making

No room for innovation exists in the sculpting of a modern *golek* puppet; the artisans are strict copyists. Puppets consist of a trunk and head plus arms that rotate at the shoulder and elbow joints, moved from beneath by means of thin rods attached to the palms. The *batik* puppets are enameled and bejeweled, and have surprisingly human features. Since a *dalang* must stand for so long with his arms upraised, the puppet is carved from strong but light *arbasia* wood. The neck is elongated and the head swivels on a central bamboo pole hidden under the flowing *kain* or *sarung*. Puppets are dressed by the local seamstress, often the carver's wife.

The shape and color of the head, face, and headdress follow the same conventions as the leather puppets, though *golek* are less stylized and more individualistic. *Golek* faces are like masks, meticulously painted, showing the full range of expressions: smiles, hideous mean-tempered scowls, dumb stares, haughty composures. See the puppets pant and shake with fright, heads turning in all directions, arms going a mile a minute.

WAYANG TOPENG

This masked theater mimes the stories of the *wayang golek,* employing dancing men acting like puppets. This form probably stems from the ancient Javanese practice of masked dancers performing at primitive death rites. Dance masks are an important part of Indonesian culture, known all over Java and Bali. Sometimes the dancers themselves speak their roles, other times a *dalang* speaks for them. Although classical Kawi is most often used, it's spoken in a less stylized form than in *wayang orang.* Troupes on Java consist of male dancers; female roles are taken by boys from ages 8-14, before their voices change.

Masks are often similar to the heads of *golek* puppets. Older masks from both Java and Bali have pronounced sculptural qualities; masks were held in position by the actor biting a leather strap or wooden prong.

Dasarata

Today the masks are flatter, features painted rather than carved; a strap around the head is used, freeing the mouth for speech. The eyes are mere slits, requiring the dancer to throw back his head to see, which gives his movements a birdlike quality. On stage the shiny, beautiful masks with big mysterious eyes seem suspended in the air. An entire *wayang topeng* troupe consists of perhaps 20-25 people, and a set of *topeng* traditionally contains 40-80 pieces. Some masks are rare and prized, guarded as *pusaka,* and found only in the collections of princes and museums. The acclaimed *reni* masks on display at the Sonobudoyo Museum in Yogyakarta attain this classic standard.

Each region of Java features a different style of *topeng* masks, costuming, and dancing. The most active *topeng* centers are in East Java and on Bali. Javanese masks feature tapered faces, sharp noses, and small mouths, while Balinese masks have full oval faces, broad noses, and heavy lips. The Javanese maintain a few standard comic masks, whereas Balinese comic masks are limited only by the carver's imagination. Many Balinese masks are elaborately decorated, with real hair or hair-like fibers, bright colors, bulging eyes, and hinged jaws. In all *topeng* forms, face, hair, and headdresses are painted in a color appropriate to the character. Faces are generally round, the shape and size depending upon the stature of the character. White masks are usually reserved for the king and queen; features are calm and elongated, with half-open lips displaying the front teeth. A red *topeng* often depicts a powerful rival, with a fuller face and larger features.

WAYANG ORANG

Called *wayang wong* in Javanese, these are abstract, symbolic dance plays, with or without masks, employing actor-dancers who dress up like *golek*

(CONTINUED ON NEXT PAGE)

WAYANG THEATER FORMS OF JAVA
(CONTINUED)

puppets. Masks are usually worn only by actors playing animals. A *dalang* may recite and chant, but the dialogue is most often spoken by live actors and actresses wearing shiny gold-and-black costumes and rich, deep-colored *batik* silks.

Dewi Renuka

As in a good Shakespearean play there's a little something for everyone—clowns, demons, magic, juggling, tricks, bawdy jokes—a mixture of circus, vaudeville, and ballet. Because of its hilarious antics, *wayang orang* is more intelligible and more of a spectacle to Westerners than other *wayang* forms. *Wayang orang* is also by far the most expensive to stage. A boxful of leather or wooden puppets is much cheaper to maintain than a whole troupe of live actors. Consequently, *wayang orang* is quite rare.

Wayang orang is pre-Islamic, perhaps once a cremation celebration, male initiation rite, war dance, or chant recital. The modern form first flowered in the 18th and 19th centuries, and was staged solely for the aristocracy. It reached its peak from 1900 to 1940, when huge performances were presented in the royal courts of Central Java. Presided over by the sultan, Javanese and Dutch dignitaries and splendidly dressed court ladies and gentlemen would sit in long rows enjoying an opulent feast and glittering dance-drama lasting up to three days. Now only the four-day dance festivals at Prambanan and at Pandaan each year from June to October can compare with those bygone extravaganzas.

Dancers

Wayang orang's highly controlled dance style so closely imitates the gestures and movements of the leather cutout marionettes the dancer seems to move on a two-dimensional plane; feet, knees, and thighs held at extreme angles so the body appears flat. Thus the term *wayang orang*, or "human puppets." Many other parallels exist between *wayang orang* and *wayang kulit*. The actors' waiting room is called a *kotak*, the same name given to the chest that contains the *wayang kulit* puppets. The dancers usually show only their profiles to the audience, just like *wayang kulit* puppets. The costumes, makeup, lavish jewelry, and tall headdresses are also similar.

The dialogue is High Javanese, intoned with melodic, almost ecclesiastical monotony except for the high-pitched cackle of mockery, or a sudden roar of anger. As many as fifty different scenes are enacted in a performance that can last from six hours to several days.

even explained in terms of *wayang* theater, not only by the puppetmasters, but also in newspaper editorials and even in government statements. For example, Krishna, the most widely venerated Hindu deity, has been compared with President Suharto.

History

Wayang dates from before the 9th century B.C., preceding Indian influence. In ancient, pre-Hindu times, *wayang* puppets were perhaps corporeal manifestations of deceased ancestors who came down to earth during the performance to visit and communicate with their descendants. *Wayang's* function was to placate and please the gods so as to increase fertility or exorcise or propitiate various ghosts and evil spirits. Since the moving, flickering silhouettes were considered the very souls of the dead, the puppeteer (*dalang*) was probably first a shamanistic priest, a medium between the dead and the living.

With the arrival of Hinduism from India sometime after the 1st century A.D., the dramatic Ramayana and Mahabharata epics were incorporated into existing *wayang* dramas. During the time of intense Hindu influence (8th-15th centuries), Hindu teachers used *wayang* as a vehicle to propagandize and popularize their religion. Indian heroes, gods, demons, and giants eventually began to supplant the ancestor figures, and Indonesian backgrounds were supplied for the Indian epics.

These shows also had a strong influence on Hindu-Javanese sculpture. On 13th-century bas-reliefs you can see figures similar to *wayang* puppets of the time, portraying all the same characters and events found in *wayang* today. When Hinduism started to give way to Islam in the 13th century, Indonesian Muslims simply turned Islamic literary figures into puppet characters. Shadow plays were used by sultans to flatter themselves and their courts, to glorify and perpetuate the feudalistic court rituals of Javanese royalty. *Wayang*, by reinforcing the class system, kept people in their place. Because Muslims banned the reproduction of the human form, both good and evil puppets were made ugly and grotesque so they wouldn't resemble living beings, and the puppets' faces, coloring, hairstyles, clothes, and jewelry are still so strongly stylized they're more symbols than actual human figures. *Wayang* puppets are the only surviving figural representations from the graphic arts of the early Islamic period.

The Audience

You won't be able to follow all the stories, but you can't help but be infected by the atmosphere. The audience is the best show of all. Twenty to a thousand Javanese sit up all night long in an overflowing theater reeking of clove cigarettes. Babies fall asleep on mothers' laps, people tip off chairs in hysterical laughter, kids alternately sleep and come awake, giggling in front of or behind the screen until dawn. The audience already knows all the stories and roles, and though they're constantly moving around eating, sleeping, and talking, they never lose the thread. This 3,000-year-old work of myth still applies today; it's living and dynamic—much more of an electric and kinetic exchange than the movies could ever be. A *wayang* show is like eavesdropping on neighbors, or more accurately, friends and relatives. The audience loses all sense of time as the gods themselves—not merely their shadows—are felt to appear on the screen.

Forms Of *Wayang*

Today there are more than 10,000 individual performers of the *wayang kulit* shadow play on Java and Bali. In addition, there are *wayang orang* dance plays and *wayang topeng* masked dancing. The Sundanese prefer *wayang golek*, carved wooden puppets, to the flat leather figures of the *wayang kulit*. In addition to these

well-known forms, there are a few rare, vestigial forms such as *wayang beber*, a narrated presentation in which drawings are unrolled, and new forms like Jakarta's *wayang karya*, which features a large puppet stage. On Madura, one troupe of *wayang orang madura* wears masks covering only the top part of their faces, so their mouths are exposed to speak freely. The Chinese of Java have their own form of *wayang golek*, performed only in temples. It's believed *wayang golek* is the last development of all the native *wayang* forms.

Lakon

The plot of a *wayang* performance, the *lakon* is usually divided into three primary, escalating phases, each with many scenes. Lasting from four to 10 hours, *wayang* plays are more exciting and spectacular than tragic or funny. Everything is illusion, symbolism, dream, fairy tale, mysticism. The true origins of the plots are almost untraceable. Stories are a combination of sacred old myths, the adventures of nobles, various historical plays, ancient Javanese folk poetry, and the newer Indian epic tales. Or themes could be extremely contemporary, concerning liberated women, problems of marriage, and social issues. Despite the differences, all themes tend to emphasize absolute good against absolute evil. Western and Chinese cinema have exercised a strong influence on *wayang* forms; today there's kung fu fighting in the battle scenes. In spite of the inroads TV has made in the villages, *wayang*'s popularity remains strong.

Some plots are drawn from an old Arab story, the Menak cycle, but have been completely Javanized and "improved" upon; even old Javanese folk tales such as the Panji cycle have been worked over extensively for presentation in *wayang gedog*. There are plays about the shrewd, brave little mouse-deer (*wayang kancil*) who outwits the stronger animals of the jungle. Mystics use *wayang* to propagate their cults. *Wayang josuf* concerns Joseph of the Bible and his brothers.

Plots became more politicized after WW II; during the independence struggle they were used to politically indoctrinate the masses. *Wayang* applauded heroism in guerrilla warfare; the communists had the puppet Arjuna use the hammer and sickle as a weapon. In

*from the Ramayana:
Sinta's trial of purity*

wayang pancasila, the history of the republic is glorified: the five Pandava brothers from the Mahabharata symbolize the five Pancasila principles of government. *Wayang* plays have also been utilized to explain the meaning of five-year economic plans.

Epic Indian Poems

By far the most popular form of *wayang* is that based on the Indian classical poems, the Ramayana and the Mahabharata. Themes are usually variations on the struggle between gods and demons, with people choosing sides, sharing glory with the gods, helping the gods ward off demon attacks, or being destroyed by them. The original epics were brought from India and translated into Kawi over 1,000 years ago, but were only adapted for Javanese theater in the 19th century. For many Indonesians these classic stories, and not the Koran, are the true holy books. In fact, *wayang* mythology has been called "the Bible of Java" because it alludes to a time when the gods were still on earth, a time when they established the great rules and traditions of life.

The *Dalang*

In the *wayang* forms in which puppets are used, the *dalang* is the puppeteer. The *dalang* is the playwright, producer, principal narrator, conductor, and director of the shadow world. He's an expert in languages and highly skilled in the techniques of ventriloquism. Some *dalang* (or their wives) carve their own puppets, maintaining a cast of up to 200 which are kept in a big wooden box. The *dalang* must be familiar with all levels of speech, modulating his voice and employing up to nine tonal and pitch variations to suit each puppet's temperaments. The *dalang* has a highly developed dramatic sense, and, if he has a good voice, his chants are beautiful and captivating to hear. He must also be intimately versed in history, including complex royal genealogies, music, recitation, and eloquence, and must possess a familiarity with metaphysics, spiritual knowledge, and perfection of the soul. Traveling from village to village and city to city, he has as many fans as a film star.

A man of unbelievable physical endurance (some chew betelnut for strength), detachment, and self-control, the *dalang* must be able to work his many characters for hours, keeping as many as six puppets moving and talking at the same time. With movements of arms, hands, fingers, feet, and voice, the *dalang* must maintain different body rhythms all at once. Battle scenes show best of all the degree of the *dalang*'s skills. For *wayang* small children sit in the front rows; sometimes the *dalang* increases the number of battles in the plot in proportion to the number of children.

In ancient times the *dalang* was nothing less than a priest officiating at religious rituals. On Java the *dalang* retains to this day vestiges of his priestly role, particularly in the *ruwatan* performance, a ritual used to ward off evil from a vulnerable child.

Once passed down from father to son, the puppeteer's art is now taught only in special schools in Central Java. The working *dalang's* fees depend on his reputation and popularity. It's common for *dalang* of the first rank, such as Nartosado of Yogyakarta, and Amarnsoroto, Durmoko, and Supraman of Solo, to demand two million *rupiah* for one night's work. Special appearances can incur additional costs. When a first-class *dalang* performs, only the very best orchestra can be hired; if the *gamelan* is second- or third-rate it will not do the *dalang* justice.

Characters

The easiest way to pick out the speaker is to watch the arms of the puppets or actors. If they stretch out, they're speaking. Javanese can tell the good and evil characters as easily as an American can discern the good and bad guys in any cowboy film. Audiences look for such indications as the placement and shape of eyes, nose, mouth, body hair or chin whiskers, the pose of the head, the coiffure, the headgear, clothing, jewelry—each of these immediately identifies the character. Soft or raging voices also assist in picking out specific character types.

Six facial and body colors indicate individual character, temperament, and mood. Vishnu's face is black, Shiva's face gold; Krishna's enemy brother Baladewa has a red face. White depicts noble descent, youth, beauty; a blue or green face means cowardice. Black stands for inner maturity, adulthood, virtue, and calmness; gold indicates beauty or royalty or glory. Red shows uncontrolled passions and desires. A dozen mouth shapes express emotion, and about 25 varieties of stylized coiffures and headgear denote priests, princes, warriors, queens, or gods. Arjuna and his twin brothers Makula and Sadewa wear their hair in an upward curl, like a scorpion's tail or lobster's claw, indicative of their royalty. Gods wear long cloaks, shawls, and footwear; kings wear pleated *kain*. A warrior often wears a belt for his *kris*. The eyes of priests and high nobility are almost closed.

The size of the puppets depends on whether they're demons, giants, gods, or ordinary people. Puppets representing the highest deities are smaller than the noble heroes, who in turn are smaller than their opponents. The bulky demons are the largest puppets of all. Large figures like Bima and Kumbakarna are an indi-

cation of physical power but not necessarily of greatness, passion, or violence. Generally, the large villain figures belong to the negative "left" side of the screen or stage, while the smaller good guys belong to the positive "right" side, though exceptions abound.

Warriors and rough characters stand with legs apart; females are shown with legs close together. Different shapes of eyes and noses denote nobility, patience, crudeness, steadfastness, power, loyalty, clownishness, wisdom. Basically, almond eyes and pointed noses mean benevolent puppets, while bulging round eyes and bulbous noses denote crude figures. Arjuna epitomizes aristocracy and refinement with his almond-shaped eyes, finely turned long-pointed nose veering in a straight line from the tip to forehead, slightly bowed head showing humility, no moustache, and absolutely no jewelry or finery. Finally, witches, animals, and demons—exempt from the ceremonial behavior of noble humans—have license to adopt hilarious styles of their own, and often provide an element of raucous comedy.

The *wayang* repertoire also serves as a character chart by which to judge people. Javanese sometimes use proper names from the Indian epic poems to refer to people they meet. "He's a Suyudana" (the ambitious and deceitful leader of the 99 Korawa brothers) or "he's just like Gatutkaca" (brave). A person's face and body can also typecast him: "he walks like a Raksasa!" (threatening and lumbering). *Wayang* characters also provide types to be emulated, giving the young a clear audiovisual message on which qualities and virtues to strive for and which to avoid.

Panakawan

The deformed *panakawan* (clowns) Semar, Gareng, and Petruk are the trusted and loving servants of the heroes. But they're also much more. With their short legs, ugly shapes, fat stomachs, sagging breasts, jutting jaws, forever limping, trickstering, or fighting, they're the *wayang*'s most laughable and lovable characters. They find joy in spreading strife.

Genealogically speaking, Semar is the father of all clowns. Many in the audience look upon him as a deity, the chief of all the gods, and actually worship him as such. When he meets with the gods they always use honorific language when addressing him; he in turn speaks *down* to them. Every once in a while Semar loses his temper, soars up to heaven, and starts knocking heads about. He's even been known to throw the great god Brahma down a well. The gods apologize and defer to him, because Semar is there to lead as well as serve. This is the crux in understanding what the Javanese view of god is. God should be the strongest force there is, yet he's available—like a servant—to anyone who needs him. Semar represents the common people—the source of his awesome power—and he can do no wrong in their eyes.

Semar is as well a comic, a symbol of wisdom and humor. He's a figure of great and abiding

mystery. When he comes on stage, the chorus sings a song of praise. "Who is Semar? *What* is Semar? He has the genitals of a man, yet the dress of a woman. He is a midget, and yet he is very big. He is very old, yet he wears his hair like a child." This clown even goes around as a sort of spy, eavesdropping and ferreting out information. He could be in disguise, for example, as a sleight-of-hand magician—but using *real* magic. In many of the stories the princes try to prevent him from having his way, but if the tide goes against him he merely changes into another one of his infinite godlike aspects, such as that of a bold young knight. Even though his role, appearance, and voice change, the audience knows very well it's still Semar.

JAKARTA

Also known as Ibu Kota, the "Mother City," this sprawling urban center of 10 million people is Indonesia's capital, its brain and nerve center. The world's ideas, technology, and fashions first touch Indonesia here. Jakarta is the nation's literary center and headquarters for its mass media; 21 newspapers are printed here. The city has a film industry, modern theater academy, and prestigious university. Jakarta is where the big contracts are signed, the strings pulled, the rakeoffs diverted. Base for 12,500 companies, 80% of all foreign investments come through here, and most of the money stays here.

The chief drama of this city is in its contrasts, a fascinating collision of East and West. Air-conditioned diesels hurtle by peddlers and sleek office towers throw shadows across cardboard hovels. Jakarta contains Indonesia's most expensive buildings and its murkiest slums—great rivers of steel, glass, and granite winding through endless expanses of ramshackle one-story *kampung.* Here live the most and least educated people of Indonesia. Jakarta is Indonesia's most dynamic, problem-ridden city.

Since its founding in 1619, Jakarta has possessed a reputation as run-down and hectic, a city of suffocating heat, stinking canals, endless shantytowns, blaring horns, traffic-tangled grimy streets—Asia's most overcrowded, underplanned, and least-visited capital. However, the serious Indonesianist cannot afford to bypass this megalopolis. Jakarta's National Museum contains one of the finest collections of Orientalia in the world, and virtually all government departments locate their head offices in the city. Travelers' expenses will run two to three times higher here than anywhere else in Indonesia. A thin slice of pineapple could put you back Rp200, a second-rate Western movie Rp5000, while cheap *losmen* are now in the Rp10,000-15,000 range. Another hard reality is the audacious pickpocketing on Jakarta's buses, and the gangs of youths who relieve travelers of their possessions at knifepoint.

Climate

Jakarta is hot. The flat coast of Java can be unbelievably oppressive—humidity as high as 95%, for days on end, with few breezes. The temperature drops dramatically within 20 minutes on the drive to Bogor or the hills of Bandung. On the weekends everyone tries to escape to these climes; the traffic backs up for miles. November to May is often drenchingly wet. Because of the city's outmoded sewage and drainage systems, expect flooding.

People

Jakarta is a city of a thousand villages, each with its own shops, schools, police, and customs. The city epitomizes the Indonesian national motto, "Unity in Diversity"; it's a melting pot of Javanese, Chinese, Balinese, Batak, Minangkabaus, Maluku Islanders, and Europeans. The population is so mixed it almost constitutes a separate race—the Dutch called them Batavians. Jakartans even speak their own vivid dialect, Jakartanese. Despite a 1971 edict declaring Jakarta a "closed city," over 200,000 migrants enter the city each year from Java's economically depressed countryside and Indonesia's outlying islands. Four-fifths of these newcomers make their living as laborers, *becak* drivers, one-man manufacturers, hawkers, servants, *warung* cooks—all contributing to the substratum world of the underground economy.

One-fourth of Jakarta's people are squatters. The thousands who sleep in the streets are known as *orang gelandangan,* "people on the move." Apart from garbage collection, peddling and sidewalk trading are the first occupations open to new migrants. Even though urban development is elite-oriented, 70% of the city's workforce is employed in the informal sector.

HISTORY

Jakarta has the longest continuous history of any modern Indonesian city. The Tarumanegara inscription, found near Tantung Priok,

JAKARTA BAY

OLD SHIPS

MARINA
(BOATS TO PULAU SERIBU)

HORIZON HOTEL

ANCOL AMUSEMENT PARK

JL. MARTINADATA

TO TANJUNG PRIOK HARBOR AREA (1 km)

PASAR IKAN

MARITIME MUSEUM

JL. PULIT SELATAN

TO AIRPORT (8 km)

DRAWBRIDGE

JL. KOPI

MUSEUM WAYANG

MUSEUM OF FINE ARTS

JAKARTA CITY MUSEUM

OLD BATAVIA (KOTA)

KOTA TRAIN STATION

PORTUGUESE CHURCH

JAKARTA TOWER HOTEL

CHINATOWN (GLODOK)

JL. GAJAH MADA

JAKARTA

CHINESE TEMPLE

NIGHT WARUNGS

NIGHT WARUNGS

NATIONAL ARCHIVES BLDG.

TO KALIDERES BUS TERMINAL

JL. HASYIM ASHARI

JL. JUANDA

GPO

BHARATA THEATER

GROGOL BUS TERMINAL

JL. MERDEKA UTARA

ISTIQLAL MOSQUE

PASAR SENEN TRAIN STATION

JL. SUPRAPTO

JL. CARINGIN

LAPANGAN MERDEKA (FREEDOM SQUARE)

GAMBIR TRAIN STATION

SENEN BUS TERMINAL

TO PULO GADUNG BUS TERMINAL

JL. PARMAN

INSCRIPTION PARK

NATIONAL MUSEUM

JL. MERDEKA SELATAN

HYATT ARYUDATA

JL. KRAMAT RAYA

ORCHID PALACE HOTEL

JL. KEBON SIRIH

INDONESIA TOURIST OFFICE

Since

TOURIST INFORMATION

JL. JAKSA

BUDGET HOTELS

JL. MENTENG RAYA

TANAH ABANG TRAIN STATION

JL. HASYIM

SARINAH DEPT. STORE

JL. SUMATRA

TAMAN ISMAIL MARZUKI (TIM)

TEXTILE MUSEUM

TANAH ABANG BUS TERMINAL

GRAND HYATT

HOTEL INDONESIA

MANDARIN ORIENTAL HOTEL

JL. BONJOL

PASAR SURABAYA ANTIQUES

JL. DIPONEGORO

PASAR BLORA

KARTIKA PLAZA HOTEL

PROCLAMATION MEMORIAL

JL. SUBROTO

PARLIAMENT

REGENT HOTEL

JL. RASUNA SAID

TO TAMAN MINI INDONESIA PARK

SAHID JAYA HOTEL

TAMAN RIA REMAJA

MERIDIEN HOTEL

TO KEBAYORAN BARU AND BLOK M

JL. THAMRIN

TO RAMBUTAN BUS TERMINAL (8 km)

TO ZOO

STADIUM

JAKARTA HILTON

0   1 km

© MOON PUBLICATIONS, INC.

dates from A.D. 500. For centuries merchants met near the mouth of the Ciliwung River, a site destined to be conquered later by empire-mad Dutch, opportunistic English, and Japanese expansionists. When the Portuguese made the first European contact with a Javanese kingdom in 1522, Jakarta was called Sundakelapa. The Hindu *raja*'s control of Sundakelapa was broken by Islamic troops on 22 June 1527, a date still celebrated as the city's birthday. The conquering Muslim prince, Fatahillah, then renamed the small Javanese coastal settlement Jayakarta—"City of Victory."

In the early 1600s, Dutch traders established a fortified trading post in Jayakarta. In 1619, they overcame the Bantenese rulers and burned the village to the ground. The Dutch then built a small garrison that withstood twin assaults in 1628 and 1629 by a mighty army of 80,000. Repelling subsequent attacks, the Dutch grew more entrenched. Renaming the site Batavia, for a medieval Germanic tribe, the Dutch built a completely new city of intersecting canals, small gabled houses with tiny windows, and red-tiled roofs—a Little Holland in the tropics. Batavia soon became the trade center for the Dutch East India Co.; from here, Dutch governors sent voyagers out to open new trading routes. Batavia became known as Koningin van het Oosten ("Queen of the East"). Massive agricultural wealth flowed through its seaport, which Captain Cook called "the best marine yard in the world."

These same European ships also carried malaria to the once healthy seaport, turning it into one of the world's worst pestholes. Known for 100 years as "the Graveyard of Dutchmen," its silted-up canals became perfect breeding grounds for diseases. By the mid-18th century, many families had moved to the new suburb of Weltevreden (meaning "well-contented") in

the city's healthier southern reaches. Batavia's outskirts were dotted with spacious country estates occupied by the Dutch elite. From 1811-1816 Batavia was the base for Sir Stamford Raffles, Java's English administrator while the British occupied the Indies during the Napoleonic Wars.

Many of Jakarta's modern (post-1700s) relics and architecture have survived. Thus in Jakarta, more than anywhere else in Indonesia, you can see and feel the effects of the Dutch and English presence.

The Twentieth Century

With the proclamation of Indonesian independence in 1945, the name Jakarta—an abbreviation of the native name Jayakarta—was adopted. Most historical buildings remained standing at the end of WW II, though many had been looted by the Japanese. During the Sukarno era, Jakarta was a collection of villages barely held together by the slogans of bombastic nationalism. In the subsequent Suharto years the main avenues were widened and buildings shot up in all directions. The better-known sections of Jakarta are relatively new. Menteng is largely the product of the early 20th century; Kebayoran Baru was laid out by the Dutch after WW II.

Over the last 15 years, the government has begun to revitalize Jakarta's rich collection of historical attractions: colonial fortifications, country estates, cemeteries, mosques, Chinese temples. The old Dutch section of Kota has undergone restoration, along with a number of Jakarta's classical buildings and monuments, reopened as museums and memorial halls. In addition, the establishment of greenbelts, parks, offshore resorts, and an ultramodern international airport has begun to draw tourist revenue away from more popular Asian destinations such as Bangkok and Hong Kong.

mansion of the Javanese painter Raden Saleh

SIGHTS

Jakarta lies on a north-south axis. Fronting the city's main drag, Jl. Thamrin, are many of the city's largest office buildings, major hotels, theaters, and banks. At Jl. Thamrin's southern end is the new suburb of Kebayoran Baru; at the northern end lies Lapangan Merdeka ("Freedom Square") with the towering National Monument. To the north are Kota and Sunda Kelapa, sites of the city's Dutch beginnings and oldest remains. Posh Menteng, Gondangdia, and Cikini (where the diplomats now live) were the most exclusive Dutch residential areas; you still see white villas with tiled roofs and floors and shaded porches. See also the millionaires' row of Kemang. Tour the city on Sundays, when the streets have 30-40% less traffic.

KOTA (OLD BATAVIA)

With its Old World atmosphere, Kota is the oldest part of the city. This relatively small northern area was the waterfront swamp where the Dutch first settled, remaining for 330 years. Surrounded by a moat and thick wall, Old Batavia stretched from Pasar Ikan south to Jl. Jembatan Batu/Jl. Asemba. The Dutch stored their spices in warehouses along the harbor; from majestic buildings surrounding a cobblestone-paved square they administered a vast mercantile empire. The heart of

Old Batavia lies where the Jakarta City Museum is today. From Jl. Thamrin, take bus no. 70 (Rp400) or Patas bus no. 16 (Rp600) to Terminal Bis Kota, also called *stanplats*.

Most Kota sights are within walking distance of the *stanplats*. You can visit all the museums in one morning. Near the *stanplats* on Jl. Nelayan Timur see the one remaining 17th-century drawbridge, **Chicken Market Bridge,** which marked the southwest corner of the old Dutch fort. From **Museum Wayang** on Jl. Pintu Besar Utara cross the drawbridge over the Kali Besar to view the only 17th-century building left, the shop owned by PT Satya Niaga. Through the 18th century, ships could sail under the drawbridge and continue up the Ciliwung River.

Glodok

Go wandering in the daytime around Glodok, Jakarta's Chinatown, in the immediate area around Jl. Pintu Besar Utara. After the 1770 massacre of Chinese, survivors were forcibly relocated here outside the city walls. Glodok is now a thriving banking, trade, and entertainment center. Hunt for temples along the narrow back streets, lined with Chinese food vendors and shops. Take Jl. Pancoran beside the five-story Glodok Plaza. The Dutch architecture contrasts strikingly with the Chinese buildings with their slanting red-tiled roofs and balconies.

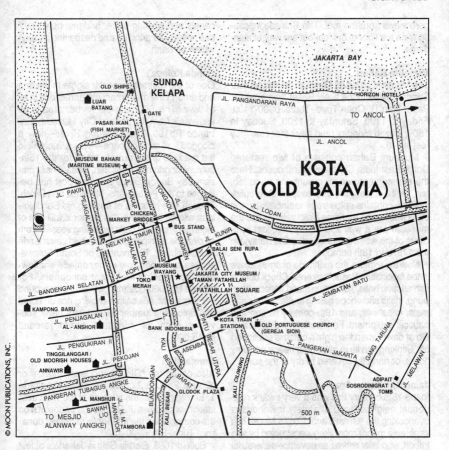

At Jl. Gajah Mada 188 is the **Candra Naya,** the former home of the Chinese "captain" hired by the Dutch to help them administer Batavia's Chinese community. At Jl. Gajah Mada 111 is the **National Archives,** built in 1760 and formerly the home of Governor-General Reinier de Klerk.

Near the Petak Sembilan fish market is the famous, very large **Dharma Jaya Temple,** dating from 1650. Beside Museum Bahari are *bajaj* which will take you back to Terminal Bis Kota for Rp300; get back into the city from here for another Rp200.

Gedung Syahbandar
This tower-like building overlooking Pasar Ikan in northernmost Kota is a good point to begin your

tour. Early in the 17th century, the Javanese erected a military post on this spot to control the mouth of the Ciliwung River and keep an eye on the Dutch who, in 1610, were granted permission to build houses and a *godown* (warehouse). Within months of signing the contract, the unruly Dutch violated it, changing the building material to stone. By 1618, through a series of similarly deceitful moves, the Dutch were firmly entrenched in Jayakarta, their cannons trained on their host's *kraton.* This watchtower, built in 1839 by the Dutch, is one of the few remains of Kasteel Batavia. Gedung Syahbandar or Menara Syahbandar ("Harbormaster's Building") was once a lighthouse and meteorological station equipped with all the high-tech instruments of the day. Superb views from the roof. The Chinese inscriptions on the floor of the lookout are weight standards.

Museum Bahari

The Maritime or Naval Museum is located near Sunda Kelapa in the lively Pasar Ikan area (Jl. Pasar Ikan 1). Open Tues.-Thurs. 0900-1400, Friday to 1100, Saturday to 1300, Sunday to 1500, closed Monday (and any other time they feel like it).

Museum Bahari consists of two restored Dutch East India Company warehouses. Here the company stored its mountains of coffee, tea, cloth, spices, tin, and copper. One building now contains spice trade memorabilia; the other addresses maritime history. In front of the museum are a wall and sentry box, last remnants of the wall that surrounded Old Batavia in the 17th and 18th centuries.

Nearby, explore the multitude of small alleys in the fascinating Pasar Ikan area. Check out the fish auction halls, fishermen's and sailor's *kampung,* stalls and shops selling stuffed exotic animals, seashells, and 19th-century fishing and nautical equipment. Few tourists and no hotels. Go at dawn when the night's catch is auctioned off. Stinking fish lie in glistening heaps on slimy floors, or hang fly-covered to dry in the sun.

Jalan Kali Besar Area

In the 18th century this was a very swank residential neighborhood of stately townhouses overlooking the "Great Canal." **Toko Merah** is a venerable manor most likely constructed by van Imhoff, who later served as governor-general. Its name, meaning Red Shop, derives from the building's unusual red brick exterior and the red-painted woodwork and furniture. Inside are fanlights, a fine wooden staircase, carved doors, and inner courts and hallways, all in rich, dark mahogany. Toko Merah was the first nautical academy in the Orient, known as Academi de Marine (1743-55). In the 1940s, Toko Merah was restored and taken over by the Bank voor Indie; it's now occupied by the Dharma Niaga Company.

Journey east of Kali Besar to see the slums of Jakarta. Indonesians are ingenious in hiding their slums behind tall buildings, so tourists don't usually see them. But they're everywhere. Head east of the Jakarta Museum, sticking to the canals and walking under bridges; here you'll see poverty as grinding and despairing as anywhere on earth.

Sunda Kelapa

One of the most spectacular sights in Jakarta and among the great maritime attractions in all of Java. This 500-year-old harbor area is an easy walk from the Jakarta City Museum. Entrance Rp100. The Ciliwung River—now a clogged and stinking canal—was a vital link to the markets of the outside world for the 15th-century kingdom of Pajajaran, located near present-day Bogor. Since then the port has belonged to the Portuguese, Muslims, and Dutch. Though little remains of bustling old Sundakelapa except the name, the harbor is still one of the most important calls for sailing vessels from all over the archipelago—you could catch a ride to Palembang, Kalimantan, or South Sulawesi. See row upon row of handmade shallow-draft oceangoing Makassar schooners. For around Rp3000 boatmen will take you around the waterfront; see sailors cooking rice on board and unloading lumber as peddlers hawk souvenirs such as miniature *prahu* (around Rp15,000).

Gereja Sion

Also called the "Old Portuguese Church" or "Gereja Portugis," on Jl. Pangeran Jayakarta 1. Emerging from the left side of the Kota train station, walk down Jl. Batu to the bridge; it's on the corner. View the interior (guestbook, donation) Tues.-Sat. 0900-1500.

Built in 1693, Gereja Sion is Jakarta's oldest standing house of worship. The Portuguese themselves never built a church in Jakarta, but they imported Portuguese-speaking Indian slaves. Their descendants—freed when they converted to Christianity—eventually became a prominent social class known as Mardjikers or "Black Portuguese," though they had only a drop of Portuguese blood.

Gereja Sion was restored in 1920, and again in 1978. The interior contains fine 17th-century carved wood pillars, a baroque pulpit, lavish ebony pews, and big copper chandeliers. Wooden shields lining the walls commemorate former governor-generals and military men. Many prominent people of Old Batavia are interred in the church graveyard. The most beautiful tomb is that of Governor-General Zwaardecroon; he asked to be buried here so he might "sleep amongst the common folk."

Taman Fatahillah

In front of the Jakarta City Museum is stone-paved Taman Fatahillah, once Batavia's main square. The fountain in the middle—faithfully reconstructed from a 1788 sketch—sits on the foundation of the original. Here the early inhabitants fetched—and later died from—their drinking water. In this square criminals were flogged or beheaded; merry festivals and public markets occupied the site on other days.

North of the fountain is a 16th-century Portuguese cannon with the honorific title Si Jagur ("Mr. Sturdy"). Because of its phallic shape and clenched fist with thumb protruding between the fingers (a symbol for sexual intercourse on Java), women believed the cannon could cure infertility. Barren women used to offer the cannon flowers, then sit on top of it; the Dutch attempted to end this practice by removing it to a museum. Its Latin inscription, *"Ex me ipsa renata sum"* ("I am reborn from myself") alludes to the fact the cannon was recast from an older weapon. In front of Si Jagur 0600-1400 every day except Sunday is a bustling flea market.

Balai Seni Rupa

This Museum of Fine Arts (tel. 021-271-062) is located on the east side of Taman Fatahillah in a large building with a classical facade. It was built in 1870, and once housed the Department of Justice. Open Tues.-Thurs. 0900-1400, Friday to 1100, Saturday to 1300, Sunday to 1500; entrance fee Rp200, children Rp100.

Balai Seni Rupa houses a permanent exhibition of Indonesian paintings from the Raden Saleh era up to contemporary times, including a number of carved tree trunks. A ceramics museum, Museum Keramik, shares the same building. Open daily 0900-1400 except Monday and Friday; tel. 177-424.

Old Batavia Museum

Also known as Museum Kota, or "Fatahillah." Located on the south side of Fatahillah Square right behind Kota station. Entrance Rp200, plus a Rp500 camera charge. Open Tues.-Thurs. 0900-1400, Friday to 1100, Saturday to 1300, Sunday to 1500.

Once the City Hall of Batavia (Stadhuis), this magnificent 1710 two-story building is a fine example of Dutch colonial architecture. The whole edifice was converted in 1974 into a museum charting Jakarta's long and dramatic history. The interior is almost devoid of decoration, the floor plan pragmatically designed to serve the needs of bureaucrats and a populace that for 250 years flocked here to obtain marriage licenses, hear sermons, pay taxes, and legalize contracts.

After torture-exacted confessions, criminals were executed or severely flogged in the square while solemn judges looked down from the balcony. The basements in the wings contained the infamous "water prisons" where up to 300 unfortunates were chained in cells flooded with filthy water for weeks on end; see the strong double bars on the basement windows along Jl. Pintu Besar.

Most exhibits are annotated in Indonesian; no numbering system, catalog, or explanations in English. The building contains an amazingly rich collection of massive antique furniture, domestic items, and VOC memorabilia. See the rogue's gallery of old oil portraits of past Dutch governor-generals; their hard-set, heavy faces reflect the stern mentality of the times. The museum also exhibits maps dating from 1619, a fine numismatic collection, archaeological exhibits, historical sketches, and blunderbusses of every variety. In the back courtyard, see the stone "in loathsome memory of" Pieter Erbervelt, a Eurasian who planned an indigenous uprising to overthrow Dutch rule. He was executed in 1722.

Museum Wayang

A puppet museum on Jl. Pintu Besar Utara 27 (tel. 021-279-560). Open Tuesday, Wednesday, Thursday, and Sunday 0900-1400, Friday to 1100, Saturday to 1300. Entrance Rp200. This long, narrow building (1912) and the structure behind it (1939) were built to serve as "the Museum of Old Batavia." In 1975 the collections were moved to the Jakarta City Museum and this building was turned into the Museum Wayang. Construction workers excavated gravestones dated as far back as 1650, when this site was the principal church graveyard for high officials—the Westminster Abbey of colonial times. This two-story building has nine rooms, each containing priceless collections of puppets from all over the world. Because seawater seeps into the ground floor, only the second floor is used for exhibits, sealed off and air-conditioned to combat salty air, humidity, and dust. This makes the museum a welcome refuge from sticky Jakarta. Go on an off day such as a Tuesday morning, when you'll find the museum almost empty.

This is a museum for lovers of *wayang,* dolls, and dollmaking—all highly developed art forms in Indonesia. Along with Indonesian *wayang* forms, it contains puppets from India, Thailand, China, Cambodia, even a Punch and Judy troupe presented by the English ambassador. The museum includes a 1,500-volume library (Dutch, English, and German books) on *wayang.* In back of the museum is a stage surrounded by *wayang beber* scrolls from Solo. At 1000 or 1100 every alternating Sunday *wayang kulit* and *wayang golek* are performed, accompanied by *gamelan.*

CENTRAL JAKARTA

Lapangan Merdeka

One-square-kilometer Lapangan Merdeka ("Freedom Square") is one of the world's largest city squares. Once a muddy grazing field, in 1809 Governor-General Daendels turned it into a military parade ground. After the British occupation in 1818, the vast field was renamed King's Square, or Koningsplein, and the state bureaucratic headquarters were built around it. Medan Merdeka is surrounded by government buildings, banks, hotels, and businesses. The modern Parliament building resembles the Sydney Opera House. The Ministry of Finance, northeast of Lapangan Banteng, is a copy of Amsterdam's Sutick Palace. In the north part of the square is the Presidential Palace complex containing the Istana Merdeka and the Istana Negara. To the east is a military police compound.

National Museum

Also called the Museum Pusat (Central Museum), at Jl. Merdeka Barat 12 on the west side of Medan Merdeka, a 10-minute walk from the Jl. Jaksa area. The building was erected between 1862 and 1868 by the Batavian Society for the

Ganesha, Jakarta National Museum

Arts and Sciences—the oldest scientific institution in Southeast Asia. Converted into a museum in 1947, it contains the world's richest collection of Indonesiana. Although poorly lit and not dusted since the Dutch left, you could spend a whole day in the prehistory and ethnographic sections, and the Hindu-Javanese antiquities exhibit rivals Leyden Museum in Holland. The museum also houses one of the largest, rarest collections of Oriental ceramics outside China—it's particularly strong on Han period pieces, 300 B.C. to A.D. 220. Scale models of traditional dwellings, villages, and *prahu* show the astounding variety of building styles throughout the islands. The Gold Room, with its statuettes, crowns, and medallions, protected by guards and steel gates, is open only on Sunday.

The museum is open Tues.-Thurs. 0830-1400, Friday to 1100, Saturday to 1300, Sunday to 1500; closed Mondays. Admission Rp200. On intermittent Sundays at 0930 *gamelan* performances are open to the public. Informative guided tours are offered Mon.-Wed. 0930-1030 (free).

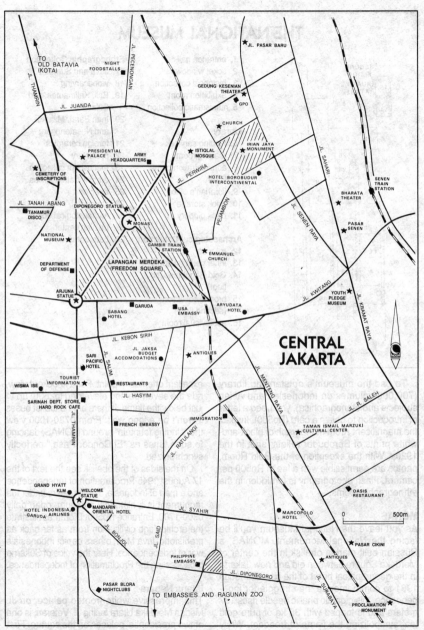

CENTRAL JAKARTA

TO OLD BATAVIA (KOTA)

JL. THAMRIN

JL. PECENONGAN

NIGHT FOODSTALLS

JL. PASAR BARU

JL. JUANDA

GEDUNG KESENIAN THEATER

GPO

CHURCH

PRESIDENTIAL PALACE

ARMY HEADQUARTERS

ISTIQLAL MOSQUE

IRIAN JAYA MONUMENT

JL. PERWIRA

HOTEL BOROBUDUR INTERCONTINENTAL

CEMETERY OF INSCRIPTIONS

JL. TANAH ABANG

DIPONEGORO STATUE

TANAMUR DISCO

PEJAMBON

JL. SAHARI

SENEN TRAIN STATION

BHARATA THEATER

MONAS

NATIONAL MUSEUM

GAMBIR TRAIN STATION

EMMANUEL CHURCH

JL. SENEN RAYA

PASAR SENEN

DEPARTMENT OF DEFENSE

LAPANGAN MERDEKA (FREEDOM SQUARE)

ARJUNA STATUE

GARUDA

SABANG HOTEL

USA EMBASSY

ARYUDATA HOTEL

JL. KWITANG

YOUTH PLEDGE MUSEUM

JL. KRAMAT RAYA

JL. KEBON SIRIH

SARI PACIFIC HOTEL

JL. SALIM

JL. JAKSA BUDGET ACCOMODATIONS

ANTIQUES

JL. MENTENG RAYA

JL. R. SALEH

TOURIST INFORMATION

RESTAURANTS

WISMA ISE

JL. HASYIM

SARINAH DEPT. STORE, HARD ROCK CAFE

FRENCH EMBASSY

IMMIGRATION

TAMAN ISMAIL MARZUKI CULTURAL CENTER

JL. THAMRIN

JL. RATULANGI

GRAND HYATT

KLM

WELCOME STATUE

MANDARIN ORIENTAL HOTEL

JL. SYAHIR

MARCOPOLO HOTEL

OASIS RESTAURANT

HOTEL INDONESIA

GARUDA AIRLINES

JL. BONJOL

JL. SAID

PHILIPPINE EMBASSY

PASAR CIKINI

ANTIQUES

JL. DIPONEGORO

JL. SUMBAYA

PROCLAMATION MONUMENT

PASAR BLORA NIGHTCLUBS

TO EMBASSIES AND RAGUNAN ZOO

0   500m

© MOON PUBLICATIONS, INC.

THE NATIONAL MUSEUM

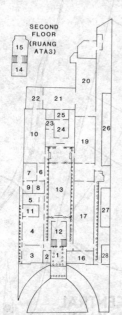

SECOND FLOOR (RUANG ATAS)

1. entrance hall
2. ticket windows
3. historical collection
4. exhibition room
5. numismatic collection

Library
6. lending service
7. reading room
8. administration of the library
9. librarian's office
10. book storage
11. book bindery

Archaeological Collection
12. rotunda
13. inner court (statuary)
14. Gold Room (second floor)
15. bronze collection (second floor)
16. audiovisual room

Ethnographic Collection
17. Java and Sumatra
18. woodcarving
19. Bali, Kalimantan, and Sulawesi
20. Irian Barat, Maluku, and Nusatenggara
21. foreign ceramics
22. prehistory
23. manuscript collection
24. administrative offices
25. director
26. storage of archaeological objects
27. training center
28. bathrooms

© MOON PUBLICATIONS, INC.

To use the museum's outstanding library (700,000 volumes on Indonesian and Asian subjects and ethnographica), you need a letter of introduction to obtain a card (Rp500). Inspect the magnificent Krom monograph of black-and-white prints of Borobudur reliefs, shot in the 1920s. With the exception of the Gold Room, photos are permissible with a fee of Rp500 per camera. Flash photography is forbidden in the ethnographic rooms.

MONAS

As you leave the National Museum you'll be facing the National Monument, MONAS, a Russian-built marble obelisk in the center of Merdeka Square between old and new Jakarta in the geographical heart of the city. Started in 1961 to commemorate the struggle for independence, this gigantic phallic needle rises 137 meters and is topped with 35 kg of pure gold leaf symbolizing the flame of freedom. Wryly called "Sukarno's last erection," it provides an excellent orientation point. For a knockout view, ride the seven-person elevator (Rp2500) up to just below the flame. If there are no tourist buses it won't be a long wait. From 0730-1000 view the "singing fountain" around MONAS, dancing to such tunes as "El Condor Pasa," perfectly synchronized.

On the sides of the obelisk see the text of the 17 August 1945 Proclamation of Independence and a map of Indonesia. Three meters under the monument is a historical museum, open daily 0800-1700. Entrance Rp500. Dioramas illustrate the archipelago civilization from as far back as prehistoric Java Man; others depict Indonesia's war of independence. Hear the voice of Sukarno broadcasting the Proclamation of Independence.

Istana Negara

This impressive white-fronted palace, on Jl. Medan Merdeka Utara facing Jl. Veteran, is one of two presidential palaces on the square. First a country house built by a wealthy Dutchman in the late 1700s, it once served as the governor-general's residence. View the front from Jl. Veteran. The lavishly appointed interior boasts Dutch colonial furniture, a neoclassic dining hall, and ceiling decorations resembling Ambonese lace. For a tour, first get permission from the Chief of the Presidential Household, Istana Negara, Jakarta; give it two weeks. Dress or shirt and tie obligatory.

Istana Merdeka

Built by the Dutch nearly 100 years after Istana Negara to replace that aging palace, this stately edifice was called Koningsplein Paleis. It's been occupied by 15 Dutch governor-generals, three Japanese military commanders, and two presidents of Republik Indonesia. In an emotion-filled ceremony, the Dutch flag was hauled down forever on 27 December 1949. Eyewitnesses state that when the Indonesian bicolor red and white Dwiwarna was raised above the building 100,000 people roared *"Merdeka! Merdeka!"* ("Freedom! Freedom!"), ending three centuries of Dutch colonial rule. The palace was renamed Istana Merdeka, or "Freedom Palace."

The building is more a formal reception hall than a residence. The portico's marble steps lead up to enormous Corinthian pillars. From the terrace one first enters the so-called Credential Hall, where foreign dignitaries were received by the head of state; you can still see the bullet hole in a hall mirror, a reminder of a MiG-17 strafing run during an unsuccessful 1960 assassination attempt on Sukarno. Official rooms lead off the Credential Hall; the president's private quarters were in the wings. In the back, a terrace looks out upon a tranquil garden.

Emmanuel Church

At Jl. Merdeka Timur 10 on the east side of the square opposite Gambir train station, this unique classicist Dutch Protestant church was erected between 1834 and 1839. The architect, J.H. Horst, incorporated elements from Greek temples, Renaissance theaters, and the Roman arena in the circular construction. The congregation surrounds the pulpit while the sun bathes the entire interior. Some precious articles in the Emmanuel Church were preserved after several Kota churches were demolished: silver and gilt dishes, boxes, chalices, an elaborate baptismal font, a baroque organ built in Holland in 1843 (only two others like it in the world). On Sunday services are delivered in Dutch at 1000, Korean at 1115, and English at 1700.

Istiqlal Mosque

In the northeast corner of Lapangan Merdeka is the massive six-level Istiqlal Mosque. With its minarets and grandiose lines, this is Jakarta's most central and grandest place of Muslim worship. Its size is more impressive than its beauty: the huge white dome can be seen for 15 km and is easily identified from aircraft far out over the Java Sea. On Friday the mosque is crowded with thousands of worshippers; after Ramadan up to 200,000 people crowd around. Reputed to be the largest mosque in Southeast Asia and the second largest in the world, this was one of Sukarno's pet projects. Seventeen years in the making, it was finely crafted from the best materials. English-speaking tours are offered for Rp1000; photos allowed.

Lapangan Banteng

As you stare out the lush lobby of the Hotel Borobudur Intercontinental onto Lapangan Banteng it's difficult to believe that in the mid-17th century this whole area was a primitive swamp, inhabited by crocodiles, tigers, and rhinoceros. During the 18th century, it became a vast military area with barracks, administrative buildings, and parade grounds. By the 19th century, this small square was the lively, genteel hub of Dutch social life.

Only two buildings remain from that era: the neoclassical **Supreme Court** and the empire-style **Department of Finance.** Built between 1809 and 1828, the Department of Finance was formerly the monumental palace Witte Huis ("White House"), Weltevreden's capital during the 19th century—the nerve center for the whole VOC commercial network.

On Jl. Budi Utomo is a pharmacy now called Kimia Farma; this typical building was the 19th-century Masonic lodge, **De Ster in het Osten,** "The Star in the East," which the local people called Gedung Setan ("Devil's House") because of the unremitting secretiveness of its members.

About 100 meters farther, on the corner of Jl. Pos and Jl. Gedung Kesesian, is the **Jakarta City Theatre** or Gedung Kesenian. Built in 1821, this was formerly the Schouwburg Theatre. Lastly, the Roman Catholic cathedral, Jl.

Kathedral 7 on the northwest corner of Lapangan Banteng, was built in 1901—a uniquely grotesque Gothic structure with three black spires.

A symbol of Sukarno's megalomaniacal sense of nationalism is the statue of a man breaking the chains of bondage. This 1963 piece commemorates the "liberation" of West Irian from the Dutch—crude but unforgettable.

National Awakening Museum

On Jl. Abdurrakhman Saleh, open 0900-1400. On 20 May 1908 (now known as National Awakening Day), students of the Stovia Medical School founded here Budi Utomo, the first modern national independence movement. A fine example of tropical Jakartan architecture, the building now houses a small historical museum and library.

Youth Pledge Museum

At Jl. Kramat Raya 106. Also called Gedung Sumpah Pemuda. On 28 October 1928, students first pledged "One Country, One People, One Language" here. This famous oath ignited the desire for freedom in Java's populace and became an underground battle cry.

Proclamation Monument

On Jl. Proklamasi 56 in Menteng, open daily 0800-1600. The Proclamation of Independence was first read on this site on 17 August 1945 by President Sukarno, urged on by students who'd kidnapped him at gunpoint. The original building, now destroyed, was Sukarno's home during the Japanese occupation. A stone (Batu Peringatan Proklamasi) and statues of Sukarno and Hatta now commemorate this seminal nation-building event.

Gedung Pancasila

From in front of Hotel Borobudur, follow Lapangan Banteng Selatan and walk down Jl. Taman Pejambon until you reach a "palace" with Ionic columns and pilasters in front of the new Department of Foreign Affairs (Departmen Luar Negeri). Erected in the 1830s, it originally housed Dutch army commanders. After 1918, the big hall—as wide and long as the entire building— served as the meeting place for the Volksraad, the advisory People's Council, which represented minorities in the segregated Dutch colonial system. In 1945, at the end of the Japanese occupation, a committee convened here to prepare for handing the Dutch East Indies to the Indonesian people. In this hall—with its typically overdone Dutch interior of dark wood walls, stained-glass ceilings, and marble floors— Sukarno delivered his benchmark speech "The Birth of Pancasila," which laid the constitutional foundation for the modern Indonesian state, and gave the building its name. In the Treaty Hall of the building, now a national monument, is the text of the Preamble of the 1945 Constitution.

Textile Museum

A permanent exhibition of cloths and weavings from all over Indonesia, located in the Tanah Abang area in the southwest section of the city (Jl. Satsuit Tuban 4, tel. 021-593-909). You'll see two giant, stylized *canting* and an Indonesian flag in front of an ornate 19th-century house. Open Tues.-Thurs. 0900-1400, Friday 0900-1100, Saturday 0900-1300, Sunday 0900-1400; entrance fee Rp200.

The museum contains 600 pieces representing 327 different styles and processes. If you're planning to spend serious money on fabrics, do some research here: peruse the books in the museum's library and study the pieces on display. Exhibits include old weaving contraptions, all nine processes of *batik* making, the different types of *canting* and *cap* used, plus all the various dyes. Almost every *batik* center on Java is represented; also view the gorgeous and rare woven arts of the Outer Islands. Several of the ticket takers will give you a tour of the museum, conducted in Indonesian only.

Cemetery Of Inscriptions

Northwest of the National Museum on Jl. Tanah Abang. The large Tanah Abang cemetery, which received Jakarta's dead for hundreds of years, was leveled in 1976 to make way for urban growth. Luckily, a small section was spared; tombstones have also been gathered from other demolished churchyards in Kota and reflect the diverse ethnic, racial, and social backgrounds of 17th- and 18th-century Batavian citizens. Olivia Raffles, wife of Sir Stamford, is buried here. The tombstones are romantic, gothic, baroque, and sinister, with touching and mysterious inscriptions. Open Mon.-Thurs. 0800-1500, Friday to 1100, Saturday to 1800.

Abri Satriamandala Army Museum

This museum, on Jl. Gatot Subroto, contains a huge display of weapons and dioramas commemorating the 1945-49 war for independence. Open 0900-1600; closed Mondays.

VICINITY OF JAKARTA

Taman Mini Indonesia

This 120-hectare open-air cultural/amusement park is a window into the cultural and environmental complexity of Indonesia. Traditional-style pavilions exhibit artifacts and crafts of the peoples of each of Indonesia's 27 provinces.

It would take a week to see everything. In fact, Indonesians will proudly tell you there's no need to see the rest of Indonesia if you visit this park, which they compare to Disneyland. Apparently, Madame Suharto visited Disneyland in 1971 and became so enraptured with the place that when she returned she immediately applied her almost embarrassing talent for fundraising, buying out surrounding farmlands and eventually gracing Taman Mini with the usual tourist schlock of cement *anoa*, artificial waterfall, and miniature Borobudur. The complex was formally opened in 1975.

The result is an impressive, sprawling complex; an instant albeit superficial introduction to Indonesia. Dozens of souvenir stalls and restaurants dot the grounds; there's also a friendly *warung* complex. On Sunday between 1000 and 1400 are outstanding free traditional dance performances, films, and cultural shows at the various pavilions. Get a Taman Mini monthly program in any Garuda office, VIC office, or hotel. Open daily 0800-1700, but most pavilion hours are 0900-1600. They close the gates at around 2000. Entrance fee Rp1000.

Attractions: The cultural exhibits and the genuine Indonesian architecture are the most valuable aspects of this park. Many structures were dismantled in outlying provinces, then reconstructed here: replicas of houses, temples, mosques, and churches. Every important ethnic group of Indonesia is represented. The bigger structures are showrooms for arts and crafts, historical artifacts, clothing, and dioramas of heroic events. At the **Asmat Museum** is an excellent collection of war shields, original statuary, and *bisj* poles. The **Dayak Pavilion** features mockups of Dani huts.

Near the park entrance, the **Indonesia Museum** is billed as the country's best collection of artifacts and handicrafts—one of the highlights of Taman Mini. Inside is a stunning exhibit of 35 mannequin couples dressed in distinctive local wedding costumes. The second floor features "Man and his Environment," with model houses and exhibits of tools and cooking utensils. The 30-minute "Indonesia Indah II" show in the **Keong Mas Theatre** tries to cover the vast cultural tapestry that is Indonesia.

A wildlife and natural history museum is featured inside the **Komodo Dragon Museum**,

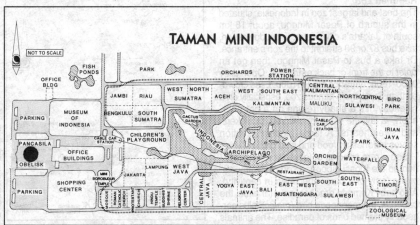

TAMAN MINI INDONESIA

which towers 25 meters above the ground. The six-hectare **bird park** contains 650 bird species native to Indonesia—a great spot to relax. The latest addition is a museum displaying the superb private art collection of the Suharto family.

Getting There: Located 12 km southeast of the city, the long bus trip through Jakarta's neighborhoods gives a good overview of the size and diversity of this Asian megalopolis. From Jl. Thamrin in front of the Sarinah Department Store, take bus P16 to Rambutan bus terminal, then bus T01 or T02 to the park.

Lubang Buaya

Means "Crocodile Hole." This massive monument commemorates seven Indonesian officers tortured and killed on 30 September 1965 during the alleged communist coup d'etat, their bodies ignominiously stuffed down a well. The official name is Pancasila Cakti. Replicas of the six murdered generals and one army officer stand on top of a wall. Ironically, a brother of one of the six senior officers was a high-ranking communist ideologue. The monument is built upon a *pendopo*; take your shoes off as if you were entering a mosque. In front is a parade field where military ceremonies take place.

Lubang Buaya is located in a rural setting 16 km southeast of Jakarta in Pondok Gede, three km east of Taman Mini Indonesia. Board a minibus from the highway in front of Taman Mini to the entrance.

Ragunan Zoo

The best and largest zoo in Indonesia, situated in the suburb of Pasar Minggu, about 16 km south of Jakarta's city center. From downtown, take bus 87 or 90 straight to the zoo's entrance. Or take a bus to Pasar Minggu, then get an *oplet* to the front or back entrances. Open daily 0900-1800; entrance fee Rp1000. Less crowded than Surabaya's famous zoo, especially on a weekday, it's a shady refuge on a hot afternoon—a favorite place for children, picnickers, and sweethearts. A large foodstall section serves Indonesian food and iced drinks.

See a rare species of lesser ape here, misnamed the Klossi gibbon, a sort of pygmy *siamang* (only one other specimen in captivity). Also baby Komodo dragons, several *anoa*, the *babirusa,* the megapode bird (*maleo*), plus gorgeously plumed birds of paradise. The animals

are kept in humane enclosures, not cages, maintained in conditions as near to their natural habitats as possible. Signs in English and Indonesian point the way to each of the animal groups' environs. The zoo plays a direct role in conservation—several species of threatened fauna are bred here. Also view the oceanarium and the botanical gardens (one of Indonesia's best) with a wide variety of indigenous plants labeled in Latin.

Pulau Seribu

Pulau Seribu means Thousand Islands and refers to 114 or so small islands situated in the shallow waters off Jakarta's coast. These tiny tropical islands, the Key West of Java, can best be seen just after takeoff from Jakarta's Airport. Only seven islands are populated, with most of the people living in the northern group; the rest are covered with coconut palms, wildlife, and beautiful virgin beaches of white sand—it's difficult to believe Jakarta is so close. Unfortu-

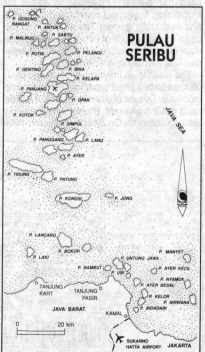

nately, their location in the Bay of Jakarta means the muck of the city washes directly around the islands, making the water indescribably filthy. The farther out the better; try to visit those islands located as far into the north Java Sea as possible.

Of the seven islands developed as holiday havens, the more accessible are just 10-15 km from Jakarta. Small hidden coves, emerald water, and totally isolated beaches—better than Bali. Coral gardens are found off Pulau Putri, Pulau Papa Theo, Pulau Genting (Besar and Kecil), and Pulau Opak Besar, all promoted as dive sites. Superior diving is found on the more outlying islands—some of them privately owned—such as Burung, Pabelokan, Sibaru Kecil, and Sibaru Besar, with their talcum powder beaches and coconut plantations. On Pulau Untung Jawa, site of a Sunday market, are picnic facilities and a campground. Camping is also possible on Pulau Perak and Pulau Khayangan. About 100 km north of Jakarta is a marine nature reserve.

Marine Recreation: Exploring its coral shores is one of the great attractions of visiting Pulau Seribu; unfortunately, raw sewage from Jakarta is affecting the environment, particularly the coral reefs. Pulau Papa Theo offers a dive camp that can accommodate groups of up to 15 people; contact Pulau Seribu Paradise in Hotel Borobudur (tel. 380-8426), or at its offices in the Setia Budi Building, Block C1, Jl. H.R. Rasuna Said, Jakarta (tel. 515-884). You can either take snorkeling gear or rent while there. Count on about Rp42,000 per dive or around Rp73,500 per day, including equipment and instructor.

Accommodations: The most developed islands have native-style bungalows, restaurants, even "discos" (bluegrass music in the middle of the Java Sea). Bungalows and/or cottages on Pulau Putri, Pulau Panjang, Pulau Pelangi, Pulau Kotok, Pulau Pantara, Pulau Hantu Barat, Pulau Hantu Timor. Accommodations are cheaper than the international-class hotels of Jakarta; weekday rates are even less, though still not cheap. On weekends and during holiday periods a surcharge of 25% is common. Add to this boat fare, local taxes, food costs, and a service tax of 21%.

Getting There: Pulau Panjang, 64 km and 25 minutes by Skyvan from Jakarta, is the only island with a landing strip. Airfare includes the 25-minute boat transfer from Pulau Panjang's airstrip to Pulau Putri. From Pulau Panjang take boats to other islands in the Kelapa Group. Jakartan travel agents should be able to give you details and prices; for example, a three-day, two-night full board package costs around Rp304,500, which isn't a bad deal. Don't believe them if they imply you can't visit the island of your choice without renting a bungalow first.

The main islands can be reached by boat from Marina Jaya Ancol between 0800 and 1000, or from Muara Kamal north of the airport on the way to Tangerang. From Ancol ferries leave around 1030 for touristy Pulau Bidadari; from there you can embark to the outlying islands. You can reach Pulau Panjang in four hours by chartered boat from Sunda Kelapa; if you want to go for the day, it costs around Rp9000 roundtrip (one hour each way) to Pulau Bidadari. Boats return in the afternoon. Both Pulau Onrust and Pulau Air Besar are accessible on day-trips by boat from Tanjung Priok. Travel among the outlying islands by private or hired boat for about Rp10,000 per hour—you'll feel like a temporary castaway.

Pulau Bidadari: Only 15 km from the mainland, Pulau Bidadari is pleasant enough, especially if there aren't many other visitors. On the island's highest point are the remains of a mighty round fort, today held intact by the tentacle-like roots of trees and shrubbery. See the second-floor entrance and the big gunpowder magazine. A leper hospital was built here in 1679; another name for the island was Pulau Sakit, "Island of the Sick." All the gravestones were removed to Pulau Kelor when Bidadari was developed into a "paradise." The shallow sea is safe but somewhat overdeveloped and polluted now.

Prices are probably too steep for the budget traveler: Rp20,000 roundtrip boat ride from Ancol, Rp25,000 d for the cheapest bungalows. Along the path are bungalows that include bath and toilet; other bungalows (*pondok*) are built on stilts over the sea and reached via a small pier. Lying in bed, look out over the water to see fish gliding over coral beds. Food in the open-air restaurants is so-so. Boat trips can be made to nearby islands like Pulau Khayangan, Pulau Untung Jawa, Pulau Kelor, and Pulau Onrust (Pulau Kapal), which features the ruined foundations of a fort and wharf. Captain Cook's ship, the *Endeavor,* put in here for repairs here in 1770. In his journal Cook praised the carpenters on Onrust as "the ablest in the East."

Pulau Putri: The most developed island, only 20 minutes by air or 40 minutes by speedboat from Ancol. Although high-priced, this resort island is marvelous in every way. Accommodations range from cottages to family bungalows. Furnishings are spartan, but all units have electricity at night, and come equipped with a/c, western plumbing (hot and cold water), outside showers, kitchenettes, and ocean views. The bar and restaurant offer 24-hour room service.

Book in advance through a travel agent or through Pulau Putri Seribu Paradise, Setia Budi Building, Block C1, Jl. H.R. Rasuna Said, Jakarta, tel. (021) 515-884. The island's dive shop rents equipment for scuba diving and snorkeling; sailboats and sailboards are also available.

ACCOMMODATIONS AND FOOD

ACCOMMODATIONS

The area for inexpensive accommodations in expensive Jakarta is the Jl. Jaksa/Kebon Sirih district, within walking distance of the tourist office, sightseeing attractions, and Gambir Station (Rp1500 by *bajaj*). Accommodations run Rp8000-25,000; a few offer higher-end annexes with air-conditioning. All fill up fast, so book early in the morning. The area is a bit noisy because of its mosques and in the rainy season the *gang* are a muck of mud and car oil. The majority of accommodations here are double rooms with shared bathrooms; most charge the same price for single or double. Tea and/or drinking water are usually included in the price, but other extras must be paid for.

The Visitor Information Center at the airport can book you into moderate hotels like the Sabang and the Marcopolo cheaper than if you book yourself by phone. Your travel agent at home, or in Indonesia, can also usually get better rates.

Arriving/Departing Jakarta
Cengkareng Transit Hotel, tel. (021) 611-964 or 614-194, is only 15 minutes from Sukarno/Hatta Airport. Tries to be fancier than it is, but offers a/c and free minibus to and from the airport every half-hour. A good place to spend one's first or last night in Indonesia, free of anxiety and perspiration. Rates: Rp84,000-136,500.

If you arrived in Ancol too late to catch the boat to Pulau Seribu, spend a night (or longer) at the **Youth Hostel,** Graha Wisata Remaja Ancol, about 30 minutes' walk from the marina at Ancol. It looks like a high-class hotel; there are a/c rooms with *mandi* for Rp20,000 as well as fan rooms and dorms. Simple all-you-can-eat meals are available at specified hours (Rp2000 pp). Staff members don't speak much English but are quite helpful. The hostel is empty during the week but booked solid on weekends.

Budget On Jalan Jaksa
Best known is **Wisma Delima** on Jl. Jaksa 5, tel. (021) 337-026, which has been sabotaged by its own success. Hasn't changed a bit in 10 years —bad lighting, slimy *mandi,* stuffy, noisy, cramped dormitory beds for Rp6000. Rooms upstairs are nicer. All right for a few days. The receptionist, Ricky, is a nice guy. Be aware you'll have to come home at midnight (0100 on Saturday), when the gate is locked.

For more comfort but also more hassle, head for **Hostel Noordwijk,** Jl. Jaksa 14, tel. 330-392, where you get a telephone, extraordinary security, outdoor lounge, multilingual managers, free tea, laundry and food service, and 20-cm-thick mattresses. Norbek charges Rp16,000-35,000 and could stand to be friendlier—instead of saying hello when you enter, staff says *"Silahkan bayar"* ("Please pay for your room"). Be prepared for a rude staff and an unbelievable number of house rules—bad vibes all around.

Borneo Hostel, Jl. Kebon Sirih Barat Dalam 35, tel. 320-095, on a side street off Jl. Jaksa, has rooms from Rp15,000-25,000. **Borneo Hostel 2** (tel. 337-873) is cleaner than the original spot next door. **Hostel Bintang Kejora,** Jl. Kebon Sirih Barat Dalam 52, tel. 323-878, 100 meters from the Borneo Youth Hostel, costs Rp15,000-22,000 and is quite friendly in this not-so-friendly neighborhood. On the same street is **Family Homestay,** Jl. Kebon Sirih

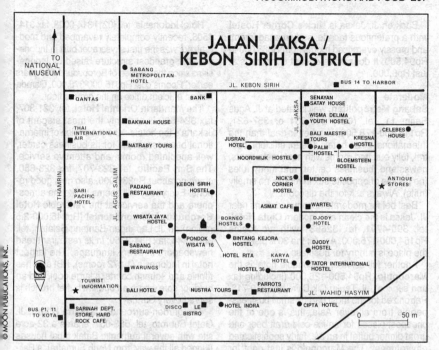

JALAN JAKSA /
KEBON SIRIH DISTRICT

Barat Dalam 1, tel. 335-917, a spacious family home with about six extra rooms upstairs for guests. Clean and friendly—Vilhelm speaks Dutch and English.

On the same street are other small *losmen* with rooms cheaper than Jl. Jaksa—**Pondok Wisata 16** (tel. 326-747) with dorm beds for Rp6000 and rooms at Rp12,000, and **Pondok Wisata Jaya** (tel. 314-4126) with rooms Rp12,000-20,000. Also recommended is the friendly **Jusran Hotel** (tel. 314-0373) with low-priced rooms Rp8000-14,000. Well situated at the end of a quiet alley. Good spot.

Djody Hotel, Jl. Jaksa 35, tel. 315-1404, asks Rp15,000-35,000, which is grossly expensive because the rooms are not ventilated, the bathrooms stink, and no breakfast is offered. Down the street, at no. 27, is a branch called **Djody Hostel** (tel. 314-1732), with beds for Rp18,000-25,000; also overpriced. **Bloemsteen,** Jl. Kebon Sirih Timur 173, is a small, tight, really hot, cheap place just off Jl. Jaksa; Rp8000-10,000 downstairs rooms, Rp10,000-15,000 upstairs. Nice garden. If full, check out the **Kresna** next door.

Hotel Karya, Jl. Jaksa 32-34, tel. 314-0484, fax 314-2781, is also worth mentioning, with a variety of a/c rooms for Rp52,500-72,500; overpriced.

A new place on Jl. Jaksa is the **Tator International Hostel** (tel. 325124) with fan rooms Rp14,000-24,000 and a/c rooms from Rp35,000. It's very well run by a Torajan man: good security, exceptionally clean, nice dining area, good restaurant with Indian/Indonesian/Western food, laundry service with ironing, and other nice little touches like use of the phone in the office. Good value.

Call from the airport to reserve a room at popular **Wisma Ise,** Jl. Wahid Hasyim 168, third floor, tel. 333-463, reached by walking from Jl. Jaksa along Jl. Wahid Hasyim, then crossing Jl. Thamrin and walking on the right side. Wisma Ise offers 20 newly remodeled rooms for Rp12,000-24,000—a nice, quiet, spotless place with magnificent large patio and good breakfasts. The family will wake you for your 0500 flight and even drive you to the airport. Only a five-minute walk east from Sarinah Department Store.

Back on Jl. Jaksa is **Nick's Corner Hostel** with a pretentious facade, surly management, and grossly overpriced rooms from Rp63,000 to Rp94,500. It does have decent dorm beds at just Rp8,000.

Moderate

Sabang Metropolitan, well located at Jl. Agus Salim 11, tel. (021) 345-031 or 357-621, Rp115,500-178,500, is a better deal than the international-class hotels. Clean, efficient, central, fully outfitted rooms with pool, restaurants, newsstand, business center, and funny rules (no people of opposite sex in rooms, no smelly fruits). Always ask for the discount.

Best bet for moderate accommodations near Jl. Jaksa is the clean and modern **Cipta Hotel,** tel. 390-4701, fax 326531 with a/c rooms Rp154,000-175,000. Ask for the 30% discount; the place is hungry for business.

Another full-service, reasonable hotel is the **Marcopolo,** Rp94,500-126,000 (including tax and service), Jl. Teuku Cik Ditiro, tel. 310-713. Patronized for the most part by small business-people from all over Asia, this is one of the cheapest places for an ice-cold draft beer and great dinner buffet in an a/c, fairly sophisticated environment. The Marcopolo is just right for cleaning up and resting after some hard traveling.

All the rooms at **Guesthouse Yanie International,** Jl. Raden Saleh Raya 35, tel. 320-012, are a/c with bath and toilet; Rp73,500-94,500 with breakfast of *nasi goreng.* Service is friendly. The manager, Mr. Anang, speaks good English. Situated in a shopping area and opposite a hospital.

Luxury

Most all the top hotels are found in central Jakarta, either on or around Jl. Thamrin. In this class you'll find essentially the same high standards as in any European or Asian capital. Rates start at about Rp252,000. Though you must add 10% tax and 11% service charge to room rates, business discounts of 10-20% are sometimes granted. Jakarta recently experienced a mini-hotel boom, adding a Meridien, Regent, and second Hyatt. Most of the city's eight five-star hotels feature nightclubs with floor shows hosting local and imported talent; all have Olympic-size swimming pools, restaurants, bars, shopping bazaars, health and business centers.

Hotel Indonesia, tel. (021) 314-0008, fax 314-1508, recently completely revamped and modernized, was the first skyscraper built in Indonesia—the grandest structure raised by Indonesians since the erection of Borobudur 1,000 years earlier. Rooms cost Rp315,000-378,000. Garuda has an efficient office on the ground floor.

The **Mandarin Oriental Hotel,** tel. 321-307, fax 324-669 is certainly the most elegant of Jakarta's top hotels—the top choice of international businesspeople for its business center, well-appointed rooms, and attentive service. The **Sari Pacific,** tel. 323-707, fax 323-650, charging about Rp336,000, also gets good reports. Everybody still seems to like the atmosphere and the service at the venerable **Hotel Borobudur Intercontinental** (Rp945,000-2.5 million) on Jl. Lapangan Banteng Selatan, tel. 380-4444, fax 384-2150; in its restaurant read newspapers in every language. The largest hotel in Indonesia (1,172 rooms), HBI also has tennis and squash courts, a large pool, and an outdoor cafe where an opulent buffet brunch is served every Sunday.

The garden-surrounded **Jakarta Hilton,** Jl. Gatot Subroto, tel. 583-051, shares a 32-acre site with several authentic Batak tribal houses (lugged all the way from North Sumatra), a Balinese temple, and even a jogging path; this whole complex is a luxurious enclave (Rp420,000-630,000) well insulated from the downtown bustle, with swimming pool, health club, tennis courts, bowling alley, shopping arcade, nursery, and an American restaurant that serves authentic hamburgers, fancy drinks, sundaes, and pizza. Get in on its famous buffet-style *rijstaffel* on Friday nights.

The new **Grand Hyatt,** tel. 390-1234, fax 310-7300, is a luxurious 455-room hotel in the heart of the business district with a huge pool and several high-class restaurants—another favorite among those who can afford it (Rp630,000-1 million). The downstairs shopping complex has several bookstores, inexpensive cafes, a *wartel* office for cheap phone and fax services, and a KLM center.

FOOD

The food in Jakarta is really magnificent. Expats who work here say it's the immense variety of

Jakartan food that makes it all bearable. There are not only Thai, Korean, Vietnamese, Chinese, and Japanese places but also fine European restaurants, Mexican food, pizzas, American fast-food franchises, nouvelle cuisine, and even a Sicilian restaurant and Mongolian barbecue.

Food Markets

Akin to Singapore's food markets, the *pujasera* is an assembly of inexpensive *warung* representing the entire spectrum of Indonesian cooking, where one is likely to find BMWs alongside *bajaj* and beat-up taxis. Behind the National Museum are some excellent and friendly lunch *warung*. Along Jl. Mangga Besar, in northern Jakarta off Jl. Hayamwuruk, foodstalls sell *nasi padang*; Chinese and Indian stalls as well (Indian food is curiously under-represented in Jakarta).

The Jl. Cikini Raya area blossoms in the early evening: follow your nose. These *warung* along Jl. Kendal serve the famous goat's foot soup (*sop kaki kambing*), Makassarese broiled fish, and typical Batawi cooking. Bring coins for strolling minstrels.

At Blok M, a major shopping center in Kebayoran Baru, is a staggering array of stalls near the bus terminal, open 0600-0100. The emphasis here is on Central and East Javanese cuisine, as well as tasty snacks like coconut cakes and *es pokat*.

Jalan Jaksa

Many of the Westernized restaurants on this street serve banal food with dishes in the Rp2000-3500 range. Best is **Asmat Cafe** and **Memories Cafe**, though you'll find better food on nearby Jl. Agus Salim.

Jalan Agus Salim

West of Jl. Jaksa, this is a tatty, frenetic street filled with cassette tape stores, haberdashers, *sate* carts, fast-food restaurants, a Japanese bakery, and numerous Chinese and Padang-style restaurants. The **Natrabu,** Jl. Agus Salim 9A, is a good, though pricey, Indonesian restaurant. For vegetarian food, the **Paradiso 2001,** Jl. H. Agus Salim 30, is tasty, cheap, and clean. Down the small alley next to the A&W, Dozens of smoky streetside *sate* vendors set up their carts at the south end of the street at night. The spotless new **Sizzler** offers great buffets and a well-stocked salad bar.

To observe how the Colonel goes over in Indonesia, look in at the palatial **Kentucky Fried Chicken** on Jl. Agus Salim near Jl. Jaksa. In deference to local tastes, the chicken is served with rice and *sambal.* **McDonald's** at Sarinah Department Store doesn't push *gado-gado,* but is otherwise a real novelty in Indonesia—a non-smoking restaurant.

Jalan Pecenongan

This street, filled with car dealers by day and foodstalls by night, has been around for as long as anyone can remember. Directly north of the giant MONAS statue near the big mosque, the Jl. Pecenongan food mart runs north to south between Jl. Batutulis and Jl. Juanda. It specializes in Jakarta-Chinese, as well as such Central and East Javanese food as *tahu pong* (fried beancake slices with egg and ketchup), the crispy *babi kluyuk* (sweet-sour pork), and *lumpia semarang.*

Indonesian Restaurants

Nowhere in Indonesia is there such a variety of regional Indonesian cuisines as in Jakarta (an exception is a Balinese eatery; not one exists in all of Jakarta). *Rumah makan nasi padang* can be expensive. Reliably good is the **Salero Bagindo** chain with restaurants at Jl. Panglima Polim Raya 107, Jl. Wolter Monginsidi 67, and Jl. Kebon Sirih 79.

From the shortage of Javanese restaurants one would think the Javanese were outnumbered in their own capital. For the finest Javanese and Sundanese food, try **Indah Kuring,** Jl. Wahid Hasyim 131A near Wisma Ise. For a refreshing break while museum visiting, **Restaurant Fatahillah** is a great spot—an old building full of dusty curios for sale. On Fatahillah Square opposite the City Museum. For East Javanese cooking, **Handayani,** Jl. Abdul Muis 36E, serves such typical dishes as *sop buntut* (oxtail soup).

For *sate,* go to the good, inexpensive, a/c **Senayan Satay House,** Jl. Kebon Sirih 31-A, Kebayoran (on the corner of Jl. Jaksa); the place also serves a fantastic *gado-gado batawi.* Featuring an overabundance of waiters; meals range Rp3000-6000. The best known Javanese-style fried chicken restaurants are **Ayam Bulungan,** Jl. Bulungan 64, and **Ayam Goreng Mbok Berek,** Jl. P. Polim Raya 93.

Chinese Restaurants

Bakmi Gajah Mada, Jl. Gajah Mada 92 and Jl. Melawai IV/25 in Blok M, specializes in all kinds of delicious noodle dishes. The **Cahaya Kota,** Jl. Wahid Hasyim 9, tel. (021) 353-3015, is one of Jakarta's finest Chinese-Indonesian restaurants, where the capital's rich and powerful go. Matchless Chinese food and superb frog legs.

The **Shantung,** Jl. Antara 37, also receives high praise. The **Moon Palace,** Jl. Melawai VIII/15A, Kebayoran, has excellent Chinese food. In Kota, the **Blue Ocean,** Jl. Hayam Wuruk 5, open daily 0700-1200, serves up high quality dim sum.

Other Asian Restaurants

Omar Khayam, Jl. Antara 5-7 across from the main post office, open 1200-1500 and 1830-2400, offers an extensive menu of Indian specialties. Buffet lunch every weekday (Rp9000).

Jakarta's numerous Japanese restaurants are expensive, less so than in the West but more so than in Yogyakarta. You can get a nice meal for Rp40,000 (sushi and tempura for two) at the **Tokyo** right at the corner of Jl. Jaksa and Jl. K.H. Wahid Hasyim. Frequented by Japanese businesspeople, it's costly, but you really get what you pay for. Less expensive but still good is the **Taichan Rarman** Japanese restaurant on Jl. Gondangelia Dalam. The finest and priciest Japanese restaurants are found in the multistar hotels.

For Korean food try the **Korean Tower,** Bank Bumi Daya Plaza (30th floor), Jl. Imam Bonjol, though only the set lunch is affordable. The **Korea Garden,** Jl. Teluk Betung 33, is also recommended.

Seafood Restaurants

In Glodok, the **Jun Nyan** on Jl. Batuceper 69 off Jl. Hayamwuruk, closed Monday until 1800, is very possibly the best seafood restaurant in Indonesia. Frequented by American Embassy types, its popular specialties include cracked crab with fantastic sauce, fried whole fish, boiled shrimp, squid and frog legs in black sauce, and chicken feet in soy sauce. Be sure to make a reservation; tel. (021) 364-063 or 364-434.

If the Jun Nyan is full—and it often is—head to the **Tak Seng** in Tanjung Priok, a highly atmospheric restaurant that triples as a pharmacy, boutique, and hawker's hangout. **Ratu Bahari,** Jl. Melawai VII/4 in the Blok M shopping center in Kebayoran, has sizzling Chinese seafood.

European Restaurants

The best Western cuisine is found in the top-rated hotels. For unbelievable spreads, many of the hotels serve all-you-can-eat breakfast and lunch buffets—a real pig-out. Both the Hotel Borobudur and the Hilton offer buffet lunches every day, worth the price if you're hungry, and especially if you like desserts. The **Marcopolo** on Jl. Teuku Cik Ditiro offers a dinner buffet for under Rp10,000. The **Nirwana Restaurant** in Hotel Indonesia puts on a smorgasbord lunch every Friday.

The **Bavaria** is a German restaurant in the Prince Centre Bldg. 3-4, Jl. Jen. Sudirman. For inimitable Dutch colonial *rijstaffel,* check out the **Club Noordwijk,** Jl. Ir. H. Juanda 54; **Art and Curio,** Jl. Kebon Binatang III/8A (near TIM), Cikini; and the lavish **Oasis Restaurant,** Jl. Raden Saleh 47, Kebayoran (closed Sunday), decked out in true Casablanca style.

George and Dragon is an English pub a short walk from the Sheraton at Jl. Teluk Betung 32. Sip a Guinness while dining on cheese with pickles or farmhouse liver pâté. The place also serves Indian cuisine. The *Far Eastern Economic Review* recently reported that "clandestine information gathering activities" (translation: spying) occur in this establishment, owned by an Australian military officer.

In Kebayoran, **Le Bistro,** Jl. Wahid Hasyim 75, serves excellent, expensive French food; live music. Enjoy Italian dishes at the **Rugantino,** Jl. Melawai Raya 28. Troll for pizza at the several American **Pizza Huts**; one is located in the Jakarta Theatre Bldg., Jl. Thamrin 9.

ENTERTAINMENT AND EVENTS

Jakarta has a full range of expensive and free, seductive and sedate, instructive and zany entertainments. Only in Jakarta can one attend a Batak tribal concert, a shadow puppet play, and an Irian Jaya dance performance all in the same week. Indonesian cultural events as well as Western entertainments (except gambling) are well represented. Jakarta has at least five bowling alleys (more than in Amsterdam!) and over 25 movie theaters.

NIGHTLIFE

There are a surprising number of bars, nightclubs, discos, and massage parlors in Jakarta. Most of the city's nightlife revolves around the luxury hotels. For example, the **Hyatt** happy hour runs from 1900 to 2100, with half-price

drinks and free snacks; **Hotel Indonesia** offers the same 1800-2000.

Bars And Nightclubs

A fairly active scene has grown up on Jl. Wahid Hasyim near Jalan Jaksa. Prices are high but early-bird discounts are often available before 2200. Some of the best discos, where flashy young Indonesians flock on weekends, include **Faces,** a videotheque that also presents live performances; Rp10,000 entrance fee but free before 1030. Sunday nights are "White Nights," when Caucasians are admitted free. Down the same street (Jl. Wahid Hasyim) is **The Parrots,** a four-story restaurant and discotheque that caters to all ages (Rp5500 for first drink). Jakarta's oldest but still most popular disco is the infamous **Tanamur** within walking distance of Jl. Jaksa.

TAMAN ISMAIL MARZUKI

JL. CIKINI RAYA

ENTRANCE

1. College of Fine Arts
2. mosque
3. food kiosks
4. outdoor theatre
5. food kiosks
6. Sanggar Tari Huriah Adam (dance studio)
7. Theatre-in-the-Round
8. exhibition hall
9. indoor theatre
10. open air theatre
11. Star Theatre, art gallery, office space
12. new construction
13. Sanggar Baru (miscellaneous studios)
14. planetarium
15. fire house

The venerable old **Jaya Pub,** behind the Jaya Building roughly across from the Sarinah Department Store on Jl. Thamrin, is a nice piano bar featuring music and a relaxed atmosphere (usually no cover) where artists, writers, musicians, and filmmakers congregate.

The latest addition to the bar scene is the fairly tame but comfortably familiar **Hard Rock Cafe** fronting the Sarinah shopping center.

Red Lights

While prostitution is illegal, it's officially underestimated that Jakarta has five unauthorized redlight areas, 21 illegal brothels, and 5,000 prostitutes working the streets. Jakarta's largest and only authorized redlight district is **Kramat Tunggak** in north Jakarta, home to 1,700 prostitutes and procurers. The city government has limited to three years the working life of prostitutes, procurers, and brothel owners; then they must enter some other line of work. Beware of Buaya Kemayoran ("Kemayoran Crocodiles"), the riffraff operating in the Kemayoran District.

Jakarta's "sister boys," beautiful female impersonators and transsexuals, deck themselves out in sleek dresses and hang out at Tamang Lawang near Kartika Plaza.

ANCOL AMUSEMENT PARK

A mammoth 551-hectare family recreation park for round-the-clock entertainment. Probably Southeast Asia's largest amusement complex, this shoreline resort lies 10 km from downtown on the bay between Jakarta and Tanjung Priok. If you're already in Kota, you could easily visit Ancol at the same time; from the *stanplats* near Jembatan Dua, get an *oplet* for Rp300 to Ancol. Avoid the park on weekends if you don't like crowds. Prices are high, particularly for some of the Euro-style attractions. In fact, Ancol is all very Western. Jakarta's only waterfront hotel, the expensive Horizon, is here, as well as the Jakarta sports hall where at 1900 each evening you can see jai alai matches.

A concert at Ancol's Pasar Seni, open 0900-2000 daily, is a nice way to spend an evening. From the marina at Ancol's beach, take boats out to Pulau Seribu in the bay. Beyond Ancol by the sea is a haunting graveyard, Ereveld ("Field

of Honor"), for 2,018 military and civilian victims of the Japanese occupation.

PERFORMING ARTS

The tourist office brochure titled *Jakarta Permanent Exhibitions and Regular Performances* includes a useful guide to theater and dance venues; current listings are available in the monthly "Guide to Jakarta." Also watch the English-language newspapers for announcements of performances at the various hotels. The best listing of events is found in the monthly guide, aptly called *What's On*.

Taman Ismail Marzuki

The Jakarta Arts Center, Jl. Cikini Raya 73, tel. (021) 322-606, is open daily 0900-2400; low admission. This is Jakarta's Lincoln Center—a large complex of exhibition halls, outdoor cafes, planetarium, and theaters with performances almost every night of the year. Get TIM's monthly bilingual program from the box office, shops, travel agencies, the Jakarta Visitor's Center, or most big hotels or embassies. Events are also listed in the English-language *Jakarta Post.*

The cultural showcase of the nation, TIM sponsors an incredible variety of Indonesian and international cultural events, from avant-garde ballet to Australian rock bands, harp concerts to Ibsen plays. The cultural performances are really worth seeing; unfortunately, they're generally scheduled more or less simultaneously, starting between 0900 and 1100 Sunday mornings. Several art galleries in the complex exhibit modern Indonesian art; open Mon.-Sat. 0900 to 1300 and 1700 to 2100. Take a Manggarai bus from Lapangan Banteng, or catch this same bus from the Jl. Jaksa area as it heads down Jl. Merdeka Timur.

Museum Wayang

Gamelan performances are held at this puppet museum on Jl. Pintu Besar in Kota on alternate Sundays at 1000 for Rp500.

School Of Folk Art

At the Faculty of Fine Arts, National University of Indonesia, see teachers and students playing Cirebon-style *gamelan,* Sundanese traditional dancing, *suling* orchestras, and *wayang* puppet theater. Located at Bakti Budaya, Jl. Bunga 5, Jatinegara near Jl. Matraman Raya.

Taman Mini Indonesia

Open 0900-1700 each day, this park is in Pondok Gede in east Jakarta near Halim Airport. Take a bus from downtown to Rambutan, then a *bemo* to Taman Mini. Dances and cultural performances are held on Sunday 1000-1200 in the pavilions for West Java, Yogyakarta (*wayang kulit*), East Java, and West Sumatra. The park is choked with people but worth visiting for the shows alone.

National Museum

Excellent Javanese *wayang kulit, wayang golek*, and *gamelan* concerts are staged every few Sunday mornings at 0930 for only Rp300. A must stop for anyone passing through Jakarta on a Sunday.

Bharata Theatre

On Jl. Kalilio 15, near Pasar Senen. Authentic *wayang orang* dramas are presented nightly at 2000 except Monday and Thursday, when there are *ketoprak* performances. This is one of Java's few remaining theaters sponsoring classical drama. Tickets cost Rp3000-4000. Packed with Javanese—abundant local color.

Cultural Centers

The **Ganesha Society** puts on weekly talks and films about Indonesian culture at the **Erasmus Huis,** the Dutch cultural center on Jl. Rasuna Said, tel. (021) 772-325, next to the Dutch Embassy. Get the schedule at the National Museum at Jl. Merdeka Barat. Also check out the **Indonesian-American Cultural Center,** Jl. Pramuka Kav 30, tel. 881-241, which offers Indonesia-related films, lectures, and exhibits. The **Gedung Kesenian,** a whitewashed Romanesque theater near the main post office, sponsors traditional *wayang orang* performances several times monthly.

SHOPPING AND SERVICES

SHOPPING

Although Yogyakarta's sidewalk vendors and shops are cheaper places to shop, Jakarta's outlets contain crafts from all over the archipelago—often at prices five times their cost at the place of origin. Because of the heat, shops close in the afternoon and reopen in the evening.

Sarinah Department Store

Near the Jl. Jaksa area on the corner of Jl. Thamrin and Jl. Wahid Hasyim, open daily 0900-1800. Like an Indonesian Macy's, Sarinah has everything from Borneo *perang* and coral jewelry to *batik* slippers and Batak woodcarvings. A visit to this well-organized department store is sure to satisfy your shopping appetite. Sarinah is a good place for newcomers to acquaint themselves with what's available, though at rather high, fixed prices. Hunt for bargains. Most clerks speak some English. Don't miss the Batik Center on the third floor, with its special salesroom for *batik tulis* (very complete and fairly priced); reasonably priced handicrafts are found on the fourth floor and a well-stocked bookstore occupies the fifth.

Handicraft Markets

Notable are the 30-40 a/c boutiques of the Jakarta Hilton's **Indonesian Bazaar,** and the 200 kiosks of Ancol's Arts Market, **Pasar Seni,** a delightful outdoor art fair open 24 hours a day. This market is a permanent setting for working artists and craftspeople from all over Indonesia. As at art markets everywhere, you'll find some high-quality items but a lot of junk as well. Good prices. Excellent seafood restaurants abound; stick around for the evening live music concert.

Shopping Centers

See Indonesian yuppies in action. Jakarta's big department stores have really gone upscale: escalators carry hordes of shoppers between floors, the video arcades are filled with teenagers, chic coffee shops sell cappuccino, women push shopping carts down crowded supermarket aisles. A welcome refuge from the heat, these a/c shopping complexes have fixed prices, some great bargains, and a wide variety of goods under one roof. The various municipal *pasar* and their *toko* usually go by their city section name: Senen, Pasar Baru, Glodok, Blok M.

Blok M in the elite suburb Kebayoran Baru offers myriad shops selling everything under the tropical sun. Also visit the three-story a/c **Ald-**

iron Plaza shopping center on Jl. Melawai inside Blok M. The **Pasar Raya Shopping Center,** Jl. Iskandarsyah, has a much better selection of traditional goods than Sarinah. **Pasar Senen** is a well-planned shopping complex near central Jakarta specializing in housewares and daily needs, open since 1733. Although the prices are generally quite reasonable, you still must haggle.

Antiques

Jakarta's densely packed flea market stretches for several blocks along Jl. Surabaya in Menteng. These shops offer a bit of everything. Unearth treasures among the fakery and hopeless discards. Many items are of dubious antiquity, having been made the week before in local crafts shops. Arrive in the late afternoon when vendors want to make last sales and go home. To get there, walk or take a bus for Manggarai and get off at Jl. Mohammed Yamin.

Pricier concentrations of antique shops also found at: Jl. Palatehan I in Kebayoran, an easy walk from Sarinah Department Store; Jl. Agus Salim; Jl. Kebon Sirih Timur Dalam, Menteng; Jl. Majapahit, Kota (antique porcelain); and Jl. Gajah Mada, Kota.

Clothes

When buying ready-to-wear garments, style and quality vary sharply and sizes seldom conform to Western standards. **Tanah Abang,** Jl. H. Fakhrudin, is the heart of Jakarta's textile operations. **Pasar Baru,** near the post office, is one of Jakarta's oldest and most popular markets, selling just about everything, but best for fabrics. *Batik* cloth and garments are available in all the city's *pasar,* particularly in Blok M, Senen, and Glodok. The price depends on your bargaining skills. The *batik* in the **Batik Keris** shop in Sarinah is generally high quality—one of the largest selections in Indonesia. Textiles from Nusatenggara sell for fair prices at **Cakrawala,** Melawai Raya 28, Blok M, tel. (021) 717-226; the Smithsonian buys textiles here. Visit the boutique of **Iwan Tirta,** Jl. Panarukan 25, considered Indonesia's foremost *batik* designer.

Birds And Flowers

Bird markets (*pasar burung*) are on Jl. Pramuka in the Matraman District. See birds and other small pets from all over Indonesia. Sellers usu-

ally speak only Indonesian. Open 0800-1800. The **Orchid Nursery** in Cipete displays hundreds of different kinds of orchids; in the laboratory see botanists cross-fertilize specimens. Open daily 0800-1800. **Taman Anggrek Ragunan** orchid garden is near the zoo.

Bookstores And Print Media

In Kebayoran, **Gramedia,** Jl. Gajah Mada 109, tel. (021) 274-397, has Jakarta's best collection of English books and magazines. **Gunung Agung** is Indonesia's largest bookstore chain; check out the branch at Jl. Kwitang 24-25. The huge **Ayumas** bookstore, Jl. Kwitang 6 near Pasar Senen, sells a multitude of English books, magazines, and maps. The whole fourth floor of Pasar Senen, one kilometer east of MONAS, consists of bookshops. Some of the best bookstores, including a Gramedia, are in Blok M shopping center in Kebayoran Baru.

Foreign publications are quite dear and newspapers arrive days late. Purchase them at most of the international-class hotels. The shop at the National Museum has a small selection of books in English on Indonesia. Jakarta has three English-language newspapers, the *Indonesian Times*, *Jakarta Post*, and *Indonesian Observer*. The *Post* is a surprisingly candid and freewheeling paper that will help you quickly understand many of the important political and social controversies raging across Indonesia.

The best map of Jakarta is the *Falk City Map*.

SERVICES

Tourist Information
The **Visitor Information Center** (VIC) at Sukarno/Hatta Airport is open daily 0800-2000, closed Sunday. The city's big **VIC** is in the Jakarta Theatre Building, opposite Sarinah Department Store on Jl. Wahid Hasyim, tel. (021) 315-4094. Open Mon.-Thurs. 0830-1600, Friday to 1700, Saturday until 1300. Specializing in the Jakarta area, staff here hand out free theme-oriented maps, train schedules, and brochures, but you have to ask specifically for what you want.

The **Directorate General of Tourism**, way out on Jl. Kramet Raya 81, tel. 310-3117, carries very little useful information and is not worth visiting.

Health
Jakarta offers the best medical services in Indonesia. The best hospitals are: in Menteng, **St. Carolus Hospital**, Jl. Salemba Raya 41, tel. (021) 858-0091; in Cikini, **Cikini Hospital**, Jl. Raden Saleh 40, tel. 374-909; in Grogol, **Sumber Waras**, Jl. Raya Kyai Tapa, tel. 596-011. For **24-hour emergency** service, go to **Fatmawati**, Jl. Fatmawati, Cilandak, tel. 760-124; or the **Pertamina Hospital**, Jl. Kyai Maja 43, tel. 707-211.

For **inoculations,** the Dinas Kesehatan (Health Department), Jl. Kesehatan 10 in Grogol, offers cholera vaccinations for only Rp5000. Open Mon.-Thurs. 0800-1400, Friday 0800-1100, Saturday 0800-1300. The Health Port near the airport's international terminal also provides inoculations.

Post Offices
The Jakarta general post office (*kantor pos pusat*) is on Jl. Lampangan Banteng, northeast of MONAS, a six-minute walk from the Chainbreaker statue or Rp2500 by *bajaj* from Jl. Jaksa. Windows are open for stamp sales Mon.-Fri. 0600-2400, Saturday to 1300. The poste

restante service is a bit disorganized; open Mon.-Fri. 0800-1600, Saturday to 1300; each letter costs Rp100.

A special annex on Jl. Pos, called Pos Paket (open Mon.-Thurs. 0800-1300, Friday 0800-1100, Saturday 0800-1300) is for mailing parcels; it's just around the corner from the post office. Pay a modest fee for packaging and fill out your forms; allow about 30 minutes. Ten kilos to the U.S. will cost around Rp90,000.

A small branch post office is in the Sarinah Department Store, open Mon.-Thurs. 0900-1430, Friday 0900-1200, Saturday 0900-1230.

Telephone And Fax
Although the system is improving, it's still frustrating and time-consuming to make local calls. A long-distance telephone office (*kantor telekommunikasi*), open around the clock, is on the ground floor of the high-rise Jakarta Theatre Building (opposite the Sarinah Department Store) on the corner of Jl. Wahid Hasyim and Jl. Thamrin. Other offices are on Jl. Merdeka Selatan 21 (open 24 hours) and in the Jayakarta Tower Hotel, Jl. Hayamwuruk 126. *Wartel* offices are located all over Jakarta, including a useful branch in the shopping complex below the Grand Hyatt Hotel. To call the U.S., three minutes is around Rp14,000; slightly less for Europe.

The Jakarta area code is 021.

Banks And Moneychangers
No problem changing traveler's checks or cash in any currency in Jakarta. Go in the morning. **American Express** is on Jl. Rasunah Said; open Mon.-Fri. 0815-1400, Saturday until 1100. If holding an Amex card, the company will give cash against a personal check. **Bank Dagang Negara** (BDN) is on Jl. Kebon Sirih and usually offers very good rates. Many other big banks are located along Jl. Thamrin; most are open Mon.-Fri. 0800-1200, Saturday 0800-1100.

Moneychangers also offer a wide variety of services, but you trade the convenience of longer hours for poorer rates. The tourist infrastructure around Jl. Jaksa is quite unimpressive compared to Bali, Yogyakarta, or even Bukittinggi. Of the few moneychangers in the area, one is in a travel agency on Jl. Wahid Hasyim. **PT Ayumas Gunung Agung**, Jl. Kwitang 24-25, tel. (021) 349-490 (near Jl. Jaksa), consistently gives good rates. Also check the moneychanger on the first floor of the Sarinah Department Store.

Immigration

The **Directorate General of Immigration,** Jl. Teuku Umar 1, Menteng, tel. (021) 349-811 or 349-812, is the head office for all of Indonesia—where the buck stops. Ironically, it's often easier to get a break here than in most *imigrasi* offices—here you can at least see the right person. Open Mon.-Thurs. 0800-1500, Friday to 1200, Saturday to 1400.

For relatively quick processing, get there when the doors open. For visa extensions, go to the office at Jl. Cikini Raya 93. Don't bother showing up without a confirmed ticket out and a reason you can't get an earlier one; they're stickier than expected when giving out one-day extensions.

TRANSPORTATION

As Indonesia's principal gateway, Jakarta is served by 14 carriers directly from Europe, Southeast Asia, India, the South Pacific, and Los Angeles. Jakarta is only an hour by air from Singapore and four hours from Hong Kong. For a thorough discussion on how to get to Jakarta, see the "Getting There" section of the On The Road chapter. Jakarta is also a principal hub of domestic travel: most bus, rail, air, and sea connections either start or eventually end in Jakarta. The newspaper *Jayakarta* prints a list of timetables for trains, planes, and boats leaving Jakarta—a very useful resource.

GETTING THERE

By Air

Jakarta's superdeluxe Sukarno/Hatta Airport is built in the international style. Squads of yellow-shirted porters will want to carry your bags, but you can grab a free baggage cart. A toll road connects the airport, 20 km west of the city, to downtown. If you want to avoid Jakarta altogether, take the bus to Gambir and catch the first train departing to Bogor, Bandung, or Yogyakarta. Or go to Rambutan station, where you can board a bus to Bandung or Yogyakarta and leave Jakarta behind in about one hour flat.

Public Buses: Although taxi drivers will approach you right away for a fare, blue-striped Damri buses with a/c and reclining seats leave regularly from right in front of the terminals for only Rp3000, taking 45 minutes. Running every 30 minutes from 0300 to 2200, these fast and comfortable buses take passengers direct to Gambir train station.

Taxis: Metered taxis wait on the other side of the train station, at the main entrance. Bluebird taxis are the cheapest—*never* take an unmetered taxi. From Sukarno/Hatta, taxi drivers want Rp30,000 (30 minutes), limousines ask Rp40,000, and private hotel shuttles (when available) Rp5000.

By Sea

Pelni ships dock at Tanjung Priok's Dock no. 1, 20 km east of the city. From the harbor, take bus P14 to Jl. Kembong Sirih, near the budget hotels on Jl. Jaksa. Or share a metered taxi with several people, about Rp15,000.

Perhaps even better is the bus that meets most boat arrivals. Take this bus all the way to Rambutan, from where buses depart to Bandung or Yogyakarta. This way, within about an hour after getting off the boat you'll find yourself amid beautiful countryside rather than wilting in muggy Jakarta.

By Train

Five major train stations are scattered around Jakarta. Most passengers arrive at the centrally located Gambir station, within walking distance or short taxi ride of the budget hotels on Jl. Jaksa. A taxi costs only Rp2500. If arriving at Senen station, walk up to the corner of Jl. Kramat Raya and Jl. Kwitang and take bus 913 or 40 to the hotel area of Jl. Jaksa. Or, if over-burdened, hire a *bajaj* (Rp1500-2500) from the train station to your hotel.

By Bus

Bus stations are out in the boondocks but are served by local buses into the city center. From Rambutan bus terminal (arriving from Yogyakarta and Bandung), take Patas express bus P2, P3, P11, or P17 to the Sarinah Department Store on Jl. Thamrin, then walk a few blocks to Jl. Jaksa. From Pulo Gadung bus terminal, take Pata bus P7 or P7A to Jl. Thamrin, then any bus south to Sarinah. Metered Bluebird taxis are amazingly cheap and will help avoid serious schlepping.

GETTING AROUND

Indonesia's ultimate city—sprawling, bustling, congested—is a bitch to get around in. It's 25 km north to south (nearly 600 square km), hot and muggy, and hardly any non-Indonesian ever walks. Even if you hire a taxi, the traffic is horrendous, and you end up crawling to your destination. Streets maddeningly change names every two or three blocks and major thoroughfares are freeways without pedestrian overpasses. Lie low from 1200 to 1600 or collapse from heat exhaustion.

It seems like every third person you meet has been ripped off while getting around Jakarta—cameras pinched, hit by snatch thieves on motorcycles, robbed on the buses. Carrying your rucksack, you're viewed as easy meat. Single women are particularly vulnerable. Beware of pickpockets, especially at train stations like Gambir. There aren't enough cops to go around, and few citizens will help you as they fear getting harmed themselves.

To avoid rip-offs, don't leave your hotel with a lot of money or valuables. Walk the streets wearing only a cheap watch; carry a Rp10,000 note to buy off robbers. On the buses enter through the front door only. Stand clear of groups of young men; sit or stand up front. Stick with your Indonesian friends; they know the safest areas of the city. Always try to travel with at least one other person. Do your eating and drinking in the relatively safe Jl. Jaksa area.

Finally, remember that Jakarta is much safer than most American cities—it's highly unlikely you'll encounter any problems.

By City Bus
The city has at least 20 private bus companies. Craft in all sizes and colors charge a Rp300 flat fare. All over Jakarta there are metropolitan bus stations—Pintu Air (near the post office in Pasar Baru), Grogol, Tangung Priok, Kota, Blok M—from where you can take buses in every direction. Buses post signboards announcing their ultimate destinations, but it still helps to know the city. Patas buses, marked with a P, offer better service and security than other bus lines.

The most popular bus for visitors is Patas P1, P11, or P01 (a/c) from Jl. Thamrin to Old Batavia and the sailing ships moored at Sunda Kelapa. Or try the fun doubledecker; sit upstairs for great views.

By Taxi
Bluebird, tel. (021) 333-000 or 325-607, is the most efficient taxi company, with pale blue cabs and completely honest meters. Rates are extremely low for a major city. For example, from Gambir train station to Jl. Jaksa is only Rp2500, while direct service to most international hotels is just Rp3000-6000. At these prices, you might want to skip the buses.

Rental Cars
The agent for **Avis** rental cars is PT Multi Sri Service Corp., Jl. Diponegoro 25, tel. (021) 341-964 or 349-206. **Car Rental** is on the ground floor of Hotel Kartika Plaza, Jl. Thamrin 10, tel. 332-006 or 322-849. You can rent a chauffeur-driven Toyota Corona from any of these companies for around Rp147,000-189,000 per day. Rates will definitely be cheaper once you leave Jakarta.

GETTING AWAY

By Air
Jakarta offers some good discounts on airline tickets; check the bulletin boards in the Jl. Jaksa hotels. Domestic departure tax is usually included in the price of your ticket. International departure tax is Rp17,000. At the airport, you can store luggage for Rp1000 per piece; inquire at the information counter.

To reach the airport, take a Damri bus from the west side of Gambir station (Rp4000, every 30 minutes). Taxis cost about Rp20,000; take a metered taxi, not a "special charter." Beware of the rip-off airport transport services advertised on the bulletin boards around Jl. Jaksa.

Garuda, Singapore, and other airlines offer standard rates to Singapore of about Rp294,000 one-way. Discounts are often available from smaller, hungrier airlines like Sempati and Myanmar Air. Another option is to fly Merpati or Garuda to Batam Island, then board the one-hour ferry to Singapore. Price wars, however, now make it almost as cheap to fly direct.

One of the cheapest ways to get to the U.S. is with Korean Airlines via Bangkok; six North Pacific stops for only US$800. Also check out the UTA flights every Monday night to the U.S., stopping in Sydney and Papeete en route to Los Angeles or San Francisco. The travel agent Indosangrila offers discounted student fares to Bangkok, Manila, Hong Kong, and Europe.

By Sea
All ships depart from Tanjung Priok, about 20 km northeast of the city center. Take Patas no. 14 express from Jl. Kebon Sirih, then a minibus to the harbor. Or take city bus no. 70 from Jl. Thamrin to Kota, then bus no. 64 or minibus 14 to the Tanjung Priok bus station, then a *bajaj* to Dock One. Taxis to the docks cost under Rp10,000 from Jl. Jaksa.

Pelni ships ply all corners of the archipelago. For the unbelievable price of Rp30,000-50,000 per day you can stay in very comfortable first-class cabins with private baths and private dining room. Pelni's head office at Jl. Angkasa 18, tel. (021) 421-1921, fax 421-1929, is open Mon.-Fri. 0830-1200 and 1300-1400, Saturday to noon. Another office is at Jl. Pintu Air 1, behind the National Mosque. Buy tickets in advance or just show up at the harbor and grab the first available deck space. Cabins should be reserved well in advance.

Hardcore adventurers might inquire about sailings at the harbormaster's office (*kantor Syahbandar*) in the small harbor at Sunda Kelapa. With some luck, it's possible to sail on fantastic Makassar schooners to Sulawesi and Kalimantan. Just be prepared for third-world hardships.

Pelni sails every Thursday at 1500 for Tanjung Pinang, the small island just south of Singapore. Local boats continue across to Singapore. The KM *Lawit* sails weekly from Jakarta to Dumai, Riau Daratan, from where you can go overland to Bukittinggi via Pekanbaru. Pelni sails to Medan every Saturday at 1300. Continue down to Lake Toba, or take the cargo boat across to Penang in West Malaysia. Avoid the Medan-bound Pelni ship when it's packed with Bataks going home for Christmas.

Pelni departs for Padang twice monthly on Tuesdays at 1900. The KM *Kerinci* makes this run in about 36 hours for Rp76,000 first class or Rp35,000 economy class. This large, clean, and comfortable ship sails nonstop and seems almost to fly over the water. Get ready for the cooler weather of Sumatra's west coast.

By Train
Jakarta's five major stations offer trains departing for all points on Java and southern Sumatra. Most trains leave from Gambir station, centrally located on Jl. Merdeka Timur and within walking distance of Jl. Jaksa. Others leave from Pasar Senen station, east of Gambir station. Trains heading west leave from Tanah Abang station, west of Jl. Thamrin. Another important station is Kota in Old Batavia; the Bima and the Mutiara Utara leave for Surabaya from Kota.

Train departure times change frequently and should be checked at the Visitor Information Center just opposite Sarinah. Tickets are sold several hours before departure from the station's *loket*; expect a crush. Always go to the proper station and allow plenty of time to get there, especially during rush hour. If trains are full or lines too long, don't give up—see the stationmaster. At Gambir, you can buy tickets several days in advance.

The travel agency **Carnation,** Jl. Menteng Raya 24, tel. (021) 344-027 or 356-728, open Mon.-Fri. 0800-1500, Saturday to 1400, Sunday 0900-1300, handles reservations for such trains as the Bima, Mutiara, and Parahiyangan. The modest service charge is well worth it.

Trains to Palembang and southern Sumatra depart at 0830 from Kota and at 0600 and 0905 from Tanah Abang; the trip takes about four hours. Morning trains are better. Take the train to Merak, then board the ferry to cross the Sunda Strait. The ferry in Merak waits for the train to arrive. From Srengsem a train continues north 400 km to Palembang. Most people now prefer to take faster buses from Jakarta's Kalideres station, leaving for Padang and Medan practically around the clock.

Trains to Cirebon depart Gambir at 1014 and 1640. For Bogor, trains leave Gambir every 30 minutes until 2000; Rp1000. For Bandung, trains depart Gambir six times daily, the first at 0539. The Parahiyangan ("Abode of the Gods") train is more convenient than the bus and gets you there in about 3.5 hours. This well-maintained train features a good restaurant; coaches are

On the outskirts of Jakarta, before dawn on 1 October 1965, the corpses of six kidnapped and killed Indonesian generals were tossed in Podok Gede, the "crocodile hole," igniting a year of bloodshed that resulted in the deaths of over 500,000 Indonesians.

well ventilated with large fans. On weekends, even standing-room tickets may be sold out. On the day of departure, get in line early. Tickets for the 0933 go on sale at 0830. On weekends and holidays, it's best to pick up your ticket a day in advance.

Trains depart Gambir seven times daily starting at 0620 and reach Yogyakarta in about 10 hours. Most travelers take the Senja Utama, which departs Gambir at 1920, arriving Yogyakarta 0528. Buy meals on the train, or bring your own. You also have the option of taking more luxurious trains. The cheapest train is the very full Senja Ekonomi, which Indonesians appropriately call Kereta Ayam, or "Chicken Train."

There are at least seven trains a day for Surabaya (859 km, 14-17 hours), with prices starting as low as Rp9800 for third class on the Senja Ekonomi and rising up to Rp65,000 on the Mutiara Utara with a/c and reclining seats. Most comfortable and expensive are the Bima and Mutiara Utara a/c night expresses; they have the advantages of speed, a better clientele, clean washrooms, and decent dinners. The Bima departs Kota station at 1600 and travels the southern route through Cirebon, Purwokerto, Yogyakarta, Madiun, Kertosono, and Surabaya. Travel time from Jakarta to Yogyakarta is 12 hours, from Yogyakarta to Surabaya six hours. The Mutiara Utara departs Kota station at 1630 and takes the northern route from Kota station via Cirebon, Tegal, Pekalongan, and Semarang; 15 hours. Jakarta to Semarang requires nine hours, Surabaya to Semarang about six. You get a comfortable reclining seat and footrest; no berths. The Mutiara Utara continues east to Banyuwangi and Denpasar, with bus connection.

By Bus
Jakarta has three major bus stations. Buses heading east depart from the **Pulo Gadung bus terminal.** Buses heading south leave from the new **Rambutan bus terminal,** a helluva long distance from central Jakarta. Take Patas bus P3, P7, P11, or P17 from Sarinah Department Store to Rambutan.

Kalideres bus terminal, three km northwest of Lapangan Merdeka, has buses heading west and to Sumatra. Get to Kalideres by taking bus no. 913 from in front of Gambir train station. From the MONAS side of Gambir station, a/c Damri buses leave for Sukarno/Hatta Airport (Rp3000, one hour) every 30 minutes. Fast, dependable, and cheap.

The Jakarta-Bogor run costs Rp1,000 (45 minutes), departing Rambutan station about every 15 minutes. However, the most convenient way to reach Bogor is by train from Gambir station; hourly departures. Buses leave Rambutan for Bandung every 20 minutes around the clock; the journey takes three hours. Trains are better since buses are crowded and weekend services don't go over the Puncak Pass but travel via Sukabumi—a long, long trip.

From Pulo Gadung station, there are frequent departures for Cirebon (five hours), Pekalongan (six hours), Tasikmalaya (eight hours), Banjar (nine hours), Yogyakarta (12 hours), Solo (13 hours), Malang (18 hours), and Surabaya

(20 hours). The best bus companies for Yogyakarta are **Raya** (via Salatiga-Magelang), Jl. Alydrus 13, tel. (021) 372-246, and **Dewi Jaya**, Jl. Sawah Besar, tel. 649-4916. It's best to reserve your seat in advance. You can usually get a seat if you just show up at any of the terminals and wait for the next bus out, but expect the bus to be badly overcrowded. Prices depend on the company; the age of the bus; whether the bus is equipped with a/c, reclining aircraft seats, videos, and toilets, and the route. Most buses are direct, with one or two stops for food and a break. Travel time by *bis malam* and train is about the same. For advice on the latest and best bus companies, inquire at the Jakarta Visitor Information Center or ask other travelers.

To Denpasar, it costs about Rp45,000 (32 hours) for an a/c night bus. Buy your ticket at **Continental Ekspres**, Jl. Antara, Pasar Baru (five-minute walk from the post office), or **Lorena** on Jl. Hasim Ashari. The best company is the **Bali Indah**. The trip involves about 28 hours of hard driving. Passengers receive a *nasi padang* and drink along the way. Buses leave at about 1630 from the Pulo Gadung bus station. Get there early to book a good front seat.

Buses to Serang, Merak and Banten, Carita Beach, and Labuhan leave from the Kalideres Station about every 15 minutes. Buses (a/c with reclining seats) to Padang and Bukittinggi cost Rp35,000-45,000 (36 hours), but it's better to break your trip at Carita Beach and in southern Sumatra. Best company for Sumatra: **Bintang Kejora**, Jl. K.H. Mas Mansyur 59 (behind Hotel Indonesia in the Tanah Abang area), tel. 336-672 or 375-662. Several other companies with buses to Sumatra also have their offices on this street; some will even send someone to pick you up at your hotel.

WEST JAVA

Extending from Krakatoa to Central Java, this 44,118-square-km province is a diverse, historic, and culturally rich region of beautiful mountains, deep-green tea plantations, rugged wildlife reserves, lush botanical gardens, fertile rice paddies, isolated communities, musty royal courts, holiday resorts, and unspoilt beaches with magnificent coral formations. But population and industry is fast taking over: only about five percent of the area's original forest remains.

The province's historical name, Sunda, meaning "white," refers to the white ash that covers the land after volcanic eruptions, rendering the soil rich and fecund. West Java volcanos are exceedingly active: in 1982 Galunggung erupted, killing 20 people and causing an estimated $25 million in damage, covering villages in the area with mud and thick dust. More recently, a 1993 explosion of Krakatoa killed two American tourists.

The giant metropolitan capital enclave of Jakarta is located within the province, though the capital and cultural center of West Java is the cool mountain city of Bandung located on a plateau 180 km to the southeast. The main attractions for visitors are the wildlife reserves of Ujung Kulon and Krakatoa, Bogor's world-renowned botanical gardens, and the fine beach resort of Pangandaran.

Aside from traces of Hindu-Buddhism and scattered relics, West Java is not the place for ancient remains. But the region is well endowed with dilapidated old colonial estates dotting the countryside on the outskirts of Batavia, formerly peaceful havens for the Dutch landed gentry.

The Sundanese

Several racial groups are indigenous to this part of Java. The interior plateau of West Java is the Priangan, heartland of the Sundanese, who make up the majority of the province population of 28 million. Of all the peoples of Java, the Sundanese are nearest to the Malay, and they have their own distinct, non-Javanese culture. Acclaimed for the beauty of their women, dreamy melancholy music, and evocative poetic imagery, the soft-spoken Sundanese tend to be earthier and more lighthearted than the refined, hierarchal, and aloof Javanese; they're also more strongly Islamized.

The Sundanese language has its own literature, writing, and levels of formal address, a legacy of the Hindu kingdoms dominant from the 8th to the 16th centuries. *Wayang golek* is associated with this region; the Sundanese also have a rich tradition of performing arts and orchestras with the *angklung* (bamboo percussion instrument) and the mournful *kecapi suling* (lute and flute music).

The mysterious and isolated Badui people live in the remote mountainous region south of Rangkasbitung. Some scholars believe the ancestors of this tribe were the original inhabitants of the region; they fled to the mountains in the 16th century to escape the Islamization of Java.

THE FAR WEST

SERANG

The small town of Serang, 95 km west of Jakarta, serves as the crossroads turnoff to Banten, 10 km north, and the beaches near Carita. You can also set out from this densely populated town to visit regional attractions like Bird Island. The best of the town's lackluster hotels are the **Serang** on Jl. Jen. A. Yani and the **Abadi**, Jl. Jen. Sudirman 36, tel. (0254) 81641. Friendly **Peng-** **inapan Bugis** is Serang's best budget hotel. Regular buses run from Jakarta's Kalideres station to Serang (Rp2100, two hours, 95 km).

BANTEN

Banten is renowned for its short-legged bantam hen, *ayam katik,* and its valuable historical remains signifying the advent of Islam in Java. Banten was one of Java's two dominant states

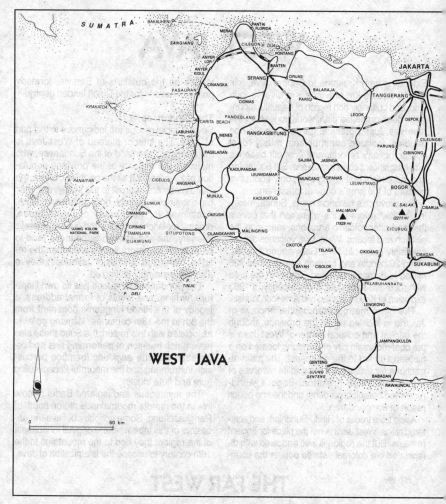

WEST JAVA

in the 17th century. You can view the ruins of the once great Bantenese Islamic kingdom; some portions of a palace have been restored, and a museum houses 200-year-old archaeological objects.

History

Once a powerful and wealthy 16th-century center for the pepper trade between the Spice Islands and India, Banten figures largely in West Java history. By 1545 the Portuguese had es-

tablished a trading station here. The Dutch first set foot on Java at Banten in 1596, part of an expedition that founded the first Dutch settlement on Java. Their rivals, the British, set up a factory at Banten in 1603 but were expelled in 1683. In 1684 the Dutch vanquished the sultan of Banten's forces and consolidated their power. By the 19th century the Banten harbor had silted up, becoming a sleepy backwater fishing village. Today the harbor is one of the main spots in Java where Bugis *prahu* stop.

© MOON PUBLICATIONS, INC.

Banten was so continuously rebellious toward Dutch rule it became known as "The Aceh of Java." The Bantenese are still a proud and culturally distinct people. They practice an orthodox form of Islam; at the Islamic school nearby you'll see scores of veiled schoolgirls in white. The area is also known for *debus* "dancing" by religious ascetics known as *nayaga,* men who can control fear and pain. Accompanied by traditional drums and recitation, men are pounded with iron stakes, burned or buried alive, cut and slashed, and emerge unscathed. They also show their invulnerability by eating glass fragments, cutting their tongues, and rolling over barbed wire.

Sights In Town
If you're here for just the day, leave your pack at the police post so you can view unimpeded the many well-preserved historical sites.

Towering over the village is the majestic **Mesjid Agung,** built in Hindu-Islamic style by the son of Sultan Hasanuddin in 1559. It contains a small historical museum of weapons, kitchen utensils, and terra-cotta wares; closed Sunday afternoon. Visitors may also climb the steep spiral staircase of the nearby white *menara* for a fine view over the coast. Graves of the royal family lie in a neighboring building.

Northwest of the mosque is **Speelwijck Fortress,** constructed in 1682 and defended until the early 1800s. Though now in ruins, it's still a pleasant spot to wander. A lichen-covered ancient graveyard with some European tombstones lies behind the fort's eastern gate. Climb the single remaining watchtower for another marvelous view.

Klenteng is a newly renovated 200-year-old Chinese temple with a small museum. Located opposite the fort entrance, it was a gift of the sultan to Banten's large Chinese community, given out of gratitude after the Chinese supplied medicine to curb a malaria epidemic. Here dozens of deities are enthroned.

Surosawan Palace was a heavily fortified compound with archways, main gate, and massive four-meter-high walls built around what is now a completely pastoral setting. Originally constructed by a Dutch Muslim, Henrik Lucas Cardil, it's reminiscent of European bastions. See the ruins of Chinese temples and an old minaret inside the grounds. As a result of Dutch intrigue and manipulative politics, this *kraton* was destroyed by the son of the sultan, driven by the Dutch against his own father. The palace was burned down again by Dutch Governor-General Daendels in 1832. Inside the old walls excavations are still taking place and underground you can see evidence of a fire. A great many iron and bronze pieces have been unearthed from workshops where armaments, ammunition, swords, and musical instruments were made.

Pulau Dua Bird Sanctuary
Near Banten, off the northwest coast of Java, is the sea-level island of Pulau Dua, within easy reach of Banten's Karanghantu Harbor. With Peru's guano islands and the Norwegian Bird Cliffs, Pulau Dua is one of the world's foremost bird islands. During the breeding season (March-July) its eight hectares are a favorite breeding ground for 40,000-50,000 migratory birds, including species of ice birds.

Species from as far away as India and China touch down on Pulau Dua: ibis, egrets, snake birds, doves, teals, pelicans, cormorants, black-crowned night herons, coastal seabirds, parakeets, parrots, Indonesian *beos, burung buntul, bangau,* and *jepelins.* Even after the end of the breeding season in September, you can still see the white-bellied eagle, herons, and thousands of wading birds from the north.

There's a *losmen* that charges a "tourist price" of Rp5000. Most visitors base themselves in Serang, Merak, or Cilegon, where there are ample accommodations, and make Banten a day-trip. Board a bus from Jakarta's Kalideres station to Serang (Rp2100, two hours). From Serang's Pasar Lama minibus station it's only 10 km and Rp500 by minibus to Banten. Take a short boat ride from the Karanghantu harbor in Banten, or simply walk across the mudflats at low tide.

MERAK

A dirty port town on the northwestern tip of Java; here you board ferries to Sumatra. The big petroleum base in Merak is run by Pertamina; on the north side of Merak foreign oil workers live in fenced housing estates with their own golf courses, schools, community centers, and stores. Most travelers head straight through Merak on the first available ferry to Sumatra.

Vicinity Of Merak
Cilegon, a steel industry center, lies 15 km southeast of Merak. The giant **Krakatoa Steelworks** was a Soviet project, abandoned and left to rust after the 1965 coup, then taken over by Pertamina with the help of Western foreign aid. This is the country's biggest steel mill and, with an estimated investment of US$250 million, one of the largest industrial projects ever undertaken in Indonesia. Because of corruption, including a million-dollar home and personal helicoptor for the director, the project cost three times the price of a similar steelworks in Taiwan. It took 20 years to design and bring on line the massive complex.

Florida Beach, on the northwest tip of Java and five km from Merak, offers several well-patronized stretches of white-sand beaches. During weekdays the village, on a tiny protected bay, is quiet, but on Sundays it's swamped. Though it lacks the charm of Carita Beach, there's lots of activity, with freighters, banana boats, outriggers, and fishing platforms out in the bay, and old men walking up and down the beach netfishing. Restaurants and *warung* sell snacks and greasy *mie goreng*.

Accommodations

Losmen Robinson, Rp10,000-15,000, is spacious and each room has a fan. Next door is **Hotel Anda,** Jl. Florida 4 (pronounced "PLOR-i-da"); same prices as the Robinson for a room with a fan. A bit noisy but comfortable enough. Both are opposite the bus station.

More expensive is the **Merak Beach Hotel,** Jl. Raya Merak, three km east of Merak; Rp48,000-65,000 for individual a/c units facing a sandy beach. Restaurant, bar, water sport facilities. It's very quiet during the week but packed with Jakarta high-rollers on the weekend.

Getting There And Away

Buses from Jakarta's Kalideres station via the new toll road run 0500-2400 and take only 2.5 hours (Rp3000, 125 km). Trains depart at 0600 and 1700 and take about four hours from Jakarta's Tanah Abang station. All trains connect with the ferry to Srengsem. To Jakarta, trains leave Merak at 0630 and 1630. Ferries from Merak to Srengsem on the southern tip of Sumatra leave at 1100 and 2300 every day from the dock near the Merak train station; Rp1250-3750. Ferries also embark hourly from the dock near the Merak bus station for the much closer ferry terminal of Bakauheni; Rp700-1700, 1.5 hours. Buses waiting in Bakauheni leave continuously for Bandar Lampung (two hours) and Palembang (12 hours) in Sumatra.

ANYER

In this coastal town, halfway between Labuhan and Merak, is an old and very photogenic iron lighthouse built by the Dutch in 1885 at the behest of Queen Wilhelmina. Anyer was the largest Dutch port on this coast before it was wiped out by tsunamis from the 1883 Krakatoa eruption. Anyer was also the start of the old Java Highway (Postweg) begun during the rule of Daendels (1762-1818). You can still recog-

nize fragments of this highway by the gnarly old tamarind trees by the side of the road. Great views from here over the Sunda Strait.

Sangiang Island

Anyer Kidul, just south of Anyer, is the jumping-off point for Sangiang Island, off the coast to the northwest, about Rp35,000 roundtrip and 1.5 hours by *kapal motor*. This uninhabited island is covered in 700 hectares of jungle, completely surrounded by spectacular coral reefs. Take food, water, sunscreen, salt tablets, and mosquito repellent. The lagoon on the northwest coast offers incredible diving and snorkeling—even octopus and a sunken wreck. Brown monkeys, delectable fruits, shells, coral, and lonely beaches abound. To menace shipping traffic through the channel, the Japanese built fortified shore batteries on a clifftop on the south peninsula facing the Sunda Strait; a road leads from the barracks to the top, where huge guns poke through creepers. The best camping spots are on the southeast part of the island on coral beaches under shady trees.

Accommodations

A modern, expensive, Pertamina-owned resort complex, the **Anyer Beach Motel,** has a/c beachfront cottages with hot water, swimming pool, bar, restaurants, and bowling alley for around Rp147,000-200,000 including tax and service. Nearby upscale resorts with rooms from Rp126,000-252,000 include the new **Mambruk Beach Resort, Marina Village** with attached marina, and the Balinese-style bungalows at **Puri Retro Resort.**

CARITA BEACH

The whole way down the west coast, from Merak to just south of Labuhan, are some of the most idyllic beaches on Java—shady, sandy—and a warm sea perfect for swimming, snorkeling, fishing, water-skiing, and sailing.

Only three hours by car from Jakarta, this is a beautiful, two-km-long, immaculate white-sand shoreline within the protective enclosure of a U-shaped bay. The swimming beach, without rocks or undertow, has innocuous surf one to two meters high. The steady breeze assures a fresh climate and a paucity of mosquitos. The distant silhouette of Krakatoa can be seen from the beach, and the Carita serves as a convenient base for outings to Krakatoa or Ujung Pandang. Masks, flippers, and snorkels can be rented from the hotels.

Vicinity Of Carita

The twinkling lights you see at night out at sea all along this coast are from platforms built on stakes. Beneath the platforms (*bagan-bagan*), rectangular flat nets are drawn up when a large number of fish, attracted by the bright kerosene lamps, have gathered over them.

From Carita, enjoy walks in the surrounding countryside. **Curug Gendang waterfall** is six km over a few hills. The nearby village of **Sindanglaut** marks the furthest reach of the tsunamis from the 1883 Krakatoa eruption.

Karangbolang is a recreation spot facing the Sunda Strait, six km south of Anyer Kidul. Legend has it the huge perforated boulder here landed during the Krakatoa eruption. A very nice beach meanders in and out of inlets lined with coconut trees. With a long, narrow slope, the surf is safe for children (though Dec.-Jan. it could get choppy). Admission Rp200. Every Sunday there's a crowded market, but on weekdays the beach is nearly deserted.

Accommodations

Over 20 hotels and bungalow resorts now line the beach between the Anyer lighthouse and Labuhan.

A former German aid worker, Dr. Axel Ridder, arrived in Indonesia in 1970 and fell in love with the area around Carita. Ridder eventually built a row of wooden bungalows along the beach. **Carita Krakatau Beach Hotel,** tel. (0254) 201-043, Jakarta (021) 314-0252, has since become a popular destination for Jakartans on weekends. Simple bamboo bungalows, with water and electricity, line the beach to the right. Rates Mon.-Thurs. are around Rp52,500 pp, Rp94,000 on the weekend. More expensive concrete beachfront deluxe units are to the left. Check out the display boards in the hotel lobby: a wealth of information on Krakatoa and, to a lesser extent, Ujung Kulon and the Baduis.

Hostel Rakata, 50 meters back from the beach, has 20 simple rooms for Rp8000-12,000. Other accommodations include the newer **Wisma Wira Carita,** with spacious clean rooms

for Rp35,000 during the week and Rp55,000 on the weekends, and **Desiana Cottages** along the beach, which offers tidy bungalows with kitchens at about the same prices as the Carita Krakatau.

The most popular place to eat is the Carita Krakatau Beach Hotel open-air restaurant, where European food (even lobster) is available—really delicious but expensive meals for Rp20,000 and up. Or just eat *nasi goreng* and tasty noodle dishes in the *warung* down on the main road to Labuhan.

Getting There

Buses leave every hour from Jakarta's Kalideres station for Rp3500 (158 km, three to four hours); look for the sign Jakarta-Labuhan. Do not take the bus to Merak or Anyer. From the Labuhan bus halt, walk up the road and flag down a colt minivan to the town of Carita; from there colts continue north to Carita Krakatau Beach Hotel (Rp600).

LABUHAN

A fishing village and junction town Rp3500 by a/c bus and 160 km southwest of Jakarta. Two km north on the road to Carita is the PHPA office where you get permits for Ujung Kulon and Krakatoa. Go in the morning.

Accommodations

Stay at adequate **Hotel Citra** for Rp8,000-12,000; bargain down if business is slow. Another option is the **Hotel Caringin;** Rp9000 for rooms with *mandi*. Most travelers choose to stay at more scenic and comfortable accommodations at Carita Beach to the north.

KRAKATOA VOLCANO

In the early misty hours of 27 August 1883, Krakatoa disintegrated in the most violent explosion in recorded history. When the central mountain erupted, it heaved out 20 cubic kilometers of rock, causing the island to collapse and allowing sea water to rush into the fiery crater. The resulting explosion was catastrophic. Countless tons of rocks, dust, and pumice were hurled 20 km into the sky. Volcanic de-

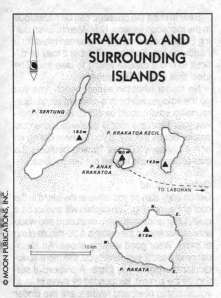

KRAKATOA AND
SURROUNDING
ISLANDS

P. SERTUNG

182m

P. KRAKATOA KECIL

P. ANAK
KRAKATOA

60m

143m

TO LABUHAN →

813m

P. RAKATA

0   10 km

© MOON PUBLICATIONS, INC.

bris landed on Madagascar on the other side of the Indian Ocean. The boom was heard in Brisbane over 4,000 km away, atmospheric waves circled the globe seven times, and for three years volcanic dust and clouds from the explosion circled the earth, creating sensational multihued sunsets.

The destruction was terrific—not from volcanic debris but from the seismic sea waves (tsunamis) which followed. These "tidal" waves reached 30 meters high, wiping out 163 villages along the coasts of western Java and southern Sumatra and rocking vessels as far away as the English Channel. A chain of explosions all but destroyed Rakata Besar, leveling its original peak and digging a submarine cavity 400 meters below sea level.

All remained calm in the middle of the demolished crater until 1927 when a thick plume of steam roared from the seabed, and before long rocks and ash rose far enough to form a small cone. Ominously named Anak Krakatoa ("Son of Krakatoa"), the new mountain rumbles occasionally, and has since risen 150 meters above the sea. Renewed seismic activity was detected in 1979.

On 15 June 1993, Krakatoa suddenly erupted and engulfed a group of five tourists from Eng-

land and America, killing two Americans in the firestorm. The Indonesian government now forbids visits closer than three km, a safety precaution that precludes landings on the highly volatile Anak Krakatoa. However, local boat operators still make the landing against regulations; proceed with caution.

Flora And Fauna

Just 17 years after the island was blown to bits, Krakatoa was again astonishingly covered in plantlife, carried by wind, birds, or sea. Although this awesome volcanic disaster killed an estimated 36,000 people, the eruption of Krakatoa became immensely instructive ecologically, a boon for biologists and geophysicists who study these islands' renascence for clues to the earth's evolution. After the eruption, the Netherlands East Indies government, at the time entirely geared to maximizing agricultural returns, studied Krakatoa intensely. Thus, it was here that tropical soil science originated. The ecological principle of "primary succession" unfolded dramatically on Krakatoa as the biological slate was wiped clean and the small group of islands slowly became colonized once again from surrounding land by increasing numbers of species. Now dense vegetation covers all the surrounding islands, along with insects, amphibians, snakes, land snails, lizards, spiders, rats, bats, and birds. Pine trees, bush, alang-alang, casuarina, and spinifex are all in evidence, having gained a foothold on the far corner of Anak Krakatoa. The remnants of the outer rim of the original mammoth crater are now covered in trees.

Supplies And Equipment

Bring water bottles, lunch, canned food, rice, or order takeout meals through a rumah makan to see you through the day. Camp on an island about 30 minutes away by boat from Anak Rakata, where anglers sometimes spend the night. And don't forget that 24-mm wide-angle lens to fit it all in.

Getting There

Krakatoa is about 44 km west of Carita Beach and Labuhan. Day-trips to Krakatoa can be arranged in Labuhan, Carita, or Pasauran. Though Pasauran is geographically the closest to Krakatoa, it's easier to arrange boat transport from Labuhan, 4.5 hours by boat, if the weather cooperates. Krakatoa is in most cases a one-day roundtrip. The earlier you leave (at least by 0600), the more time you'll have. Stay the night before in Carita or Labuhan. For boat rentals, the PHPA staff in Labuhan can help you or any villager can lead you to the homes of fishermen who will take you. Once the word gets out you're after a boat, a number of middlemen will offer you vessels of varying condition, age, and size at varying prices.

Rent a good boat; don't take any chances. Get one at least 12 meters long with a reliable engine that can stay afloat in rough seas. Take the advice of the PHPA people. The least expensive rental is with local fishermen for Rp110,000-120,000, with a four- to five-man crew. Boats from hotels on Carita Beach cost Rp210,000 roundtrip (eight hours in the boat, two hours hiking), or Rp420,000 roundtrip on a speedboat (four-hour journey, two-hour trek). Refunds are never given, even if your boat is forced to turn back, so withhold a portion of the payment until your safe return.

As you approach Krakatoa, instruct the captain to make a slow tour around half the island (takes about 1.5 hours); upon exiting cover the other half of the island. There's a shack built by Dutch environmental scientists where you can rest from the long, hot boat journey, though the ants may drive you mad.

Organized tours can be arranged in Jakarta through **Krakatau Ujung Kulon Tours** (tel. 021-314-0252, fax 330-846) in the Hotel Wisata International on Jl. Thamrin, behind Hotel Indonesia

Bear in mind the passage can be hazardous in the monsoon season, Nov.-March. Even during September winds and waves can make for a harrowing trip. Starting in October it may be difficult to find a captain willing to take you. The ideal time is April-September.

No matter what the season, each time you go the volcano will be in a different mood. Surrounding waters could be 60° C. Hot ash blackens your face, the roar is deafening, charcoal smoke clouds the sky. If you're there during an active phase, you'll see flaming boulders the size of basketballs tossed out like pebbles.

Getting Around

Get an early start so you arrive at the island in the cool of the morning. The captain will anchor off a quiet, lunar landscape; jump overboard and wade ashore. Ascending the crater is a 30-minute climb at most. Wear good walking shoes. An abundance of beauty surrounds you, the more spectacular the higher you climb. A primordial setting. At the summit, surrounded by rivers of lava, volcanic slag piles, and ravines, are two cinder cones and a long ridgeline you can follow over the top. The soles of your shoes will grow hot. The gaseous areas should be avoided as they can cause breathing difficulties, or worse. On the other side of the island is a long curving beach with bizarre driftwood and jettisoned rubber sandals; the swimming is not tempting. Back on the boat the crew will be cooking dinner, caught on the journey out; dine on delicious curried fish only two hours old served with hot tea.

on the boat to Krakatoa

© MOON PUBLICATIONS, INC.

UJUNG KULON NATIONAL PARK

This completely untamed wilderness lies on the far western tip of Java, connected to the rest of the island by a narrow boggy isthmus. Two national parks here total more than 420 square km—one located on the Ujung Kulon peninsula, the other on the main island of Panaitan across a narrow strait.

Opened by the Dutch in 1921 as a refuge for the threatened Javan rhinoceros, the establishment of this last large area of lowland forest on Java has since been credited with saving a number of rare life forms from extinction. Observation towers have been erected at Cigenter, and grazing fields where wildlife can be observed are found at Cijungkulon on Pulau Peucang. On the western tip is a lighthouse, standing near the ruins of an older lighthouse built by the Dutch. Unspoiled beaches with coral formations off the south and west sides of Pulau Peucang and Pulau Panaitan make for spectacular diving, snorkeling, and swimming. No scuba facilities, so bring your own equipment. Best time to visit is April-Aug., when the sea is calmer and the ground not as marshy.

Flora And Fauna

The reserve features broad open meadows, reedy swamps, estuarine shallows with crocodiles, steam rising from *alang-alang* grass, flocks of peacocks, rooting wild pigs, hornbills, gibbons, river otters, miniature deer, and *rusa*. There are also wild buffalos, around 250 blue panthers, and over 200 bird species. Fifty protected rhinos remain. Similar to its Indian relative found now only in small pockets in Assam and Nepal, the armor on this one-horned rhino's back is divided into four sections. The beast's small pig eyes don't see well; he'll attack blind anyway. These rare behemoths sometimes seek refuge on the sandy beach of Nigur, or on the peninsula's neck to the southwest. Look for fresh three-toed hoofmarks, and make sure a tree is always nearby.

Permits And Supplies

Permits are available from the friendly Forestry Office (PHPA) two km north of Labuhan on the road to Carita. The permit is free, and staff will help with everything, including boat transport and lodging reservations. Pay Rp2000 for a man to go to the market to stock up on provisions. The PHPA office is open Mon.-Thurs. 0700-1400, Friday to 1100, Saturday to 1200.

The PHPA camps at Pulau Handeleum and Pulau Peucang offer cooking facilities, water, and cooks, but be sure to bring food and beverages. The last place to shop for supplies is Labuhan, Carita, and (the most expensive) Tamanjaya.

Accommodations

Before taking the trip into the park, you may want to spend the night at Carita or in Labuhan. Book through Labuhan's PHPA office to stay either on Pulau Handeleum or Pulau Peucang. Both islands are posts for the park where guards and their families live.

Pulau Handeleum, one hour by boat from park headquarters at Tamanjaya, has a PHPA guesthouse that sleeps eight and offers reasonably central access to the eastern park. About 20 km farther west on the other side of the peninsula, only 10 minutes and Rp5000 by boat from Cidaun, is **Pulau Peucang,** a nice island with a small rainforest. Accommodations here are older bungalows (Rp10,000-15,000) and two new a/c lodges with hot water and full service restaurant.

Visitors can also camp out or stay the night in PHPA shelters built at intervals along the trail; found, for example, at Citadahan and at the post at Karangranjang.

Getting There

Get an entry permit first from the PHPA office in Labuhan, about midway down the west coast and the usual jumping-off point for the park. In Labuhan hire the PHPA guard boat for around Rp250,000 roundtrip, or charter a less expensive motorized fishing *prahu* (plenty of offers, but bargain determinedly).

It's important to find a reliable boat; in 1988 eight surfers and four Indonesian crew spent 12 days drifting between Java and Sumatra. The 90-km passage from Labuhan to Pulau Peucang off Ujung Kulon normally takes 6-10 hours, depending on the weather. Gasoline is not plentiful within the park so make sure there's enough for daily trips from Pulau Peucang to the mainland.

Jakartan travel agents offer tours of Ujung Kulon and Krakatoa for Rp265,000-735,000, including all transportation, accommodations in a guesthouse on Pulau Peucang, photo safari with guide, meals, and two nights at relaxing Carita Beach Hotel. Tours are often advertised in the *Jakarta Post.*

Entry is cheaper by land. From Labuhan take a minibus (Rp3000, three hours) to Sumur via Cigeulis; *kapal motor* also depart Labuhan almost every day for Sumur (Rp3500). From Sumur reach Tamanjaya (park headquarters) via motorcycle-taxi (Rp5000 pp). Show your permit at the PHPA office in Tamanjaya, then hire a guide to take you into the peninsula, a six-hour walk to Pos Karangranjang. Buy food for both of you, plus some *kretek* for him. Motorcycle drivers are always hanging out, waiting to take you into the park via Cijawung and Karangranjang. Passage on a local *prahu* from Tamanjaya to Pulau Peucang costs around Rp75,000 one-way.

Getting Around

A guide can show you the other side of Pulau Peucang for Rp5000. On the peninsula portion of Ujung Kulon, be prepared with supplies and equipment to camp overnight, hire a guide, plus pay mandatory insurance (Rp1500). Take along a medical kit, water, and, if you've hired a boat, lifevests and an ice chest full of cold drinks. Pay Rp5000 per day for food for you and your guide; the guide will cook. Stick to the walking tracks. The walk from Cidaun along the whole southern coast via Karangranjang to the park headquarters at Tamanjaya is a total of 45 km and will take about three days.

BOGOR

Located sixty km south of Jakarta, Bogor sprawls among hills between the Ciliwung and Cisadane rivers. Its population is 250,000, the majority *pegawai* and their families.

The name Bogor is taken from the extinct *bagor* palm. Founded over 500 years ago, the city is built around a huge, verdant botanical garden, one of the most magnificent in the world and one of Indonesia's major tourist attractions. Bogor is one of the most important scientific centers in Indonesia, and at least 17 affiliated institutes are scattered all over the city, most of them progeny of the gardens. A lovely town of pretty villas, magnificent trees, and banana, mimosa, and wild almond plants.

Climate
Set in the more exposed uplands (200-300 meters), Bogor maintains a cooler and more refreshing climate than Jakarta. And with the amount of rainfall the city receives, it's no wonder Indonesia's largest botanical garden is located here. Bogor probably leads the world in thunderstorms, which arrive precisely at 1600 two out of three days year-round. It's said that if the peak of Gunung Salak to the southwest of the city is clouded, then it will rain that day.

ISTANA BOGOR

The road from Jakarta runs smack into the lawn of this gleaming white former Dutch governor's mansion, a magnificent site complete with spotted deer herd roaming over undulating lawns under big shady trees. The palace has not served as a residence since Sukarno's time; the main building is used for official occasions, installations, and ceremonies. The palace interior covers an area of about 14,000 square meters; the grounds cover 24 hectares. Inside the mansion are sumptuously appointed rooms, lavish reception chambers, and a fabulous international collection of fine art.

History
This was the official residence of the Dutch governor-generals from 1870 to 1942. While on a duty tour of the upper interior territories, Baron Gustaf Willem van Imhoff, governor-general for the Dutch East Indies Company, became fascinated with the peaceful village of Bogor. In 1745 he built a small resthouse here, naming it Buitenzorg ("Without a Care"). Used as a retreat from the busy social life and government responsibilities in Batavia, over time pleasant Bogor village developed into the noisy city of today, and the humble country estate evolved into a splendid colonial palace. Huge glamorous parties were held here, the Dutch elite coming up from Batavia for riding, hunting, and dancing on the immaculately kept grounds. Deer were fattened by the Dutch to provide venison for their banquets. In 1950, the palace was taken over by the Indonesian government. Suharto doesn't ever stay here because the ghost of Sukarno is said to haunt the corridors at night. Certainly his presence is almost palpable.

The Collections
The Japanese in WW II looted the Dutch treasures, so what you see now is what Sukarno collected during his political career. Sukarno fancied himself quite the art connoisseur: there are incredible paintings by some of Indonesia's most renowned painters, a few it's said he "improved" to suit his tastes. Among the 219 paintings and 136 sculptures are many voluptuous nudes from every race. Sukarno's private collection of erotic paintings and sculptures is locked in a special room. In the left wing is a famous painting by Le Maire of his wife Ni Polok in 12 different aspects. See Sukarno's bedroom, the half-ton chandeliers from Czechoslovakia, the wonderful statuary in the palace garden.

Tours
The palace, not normally open to the public, can be visited by prior arrangement through tour agencies like Safairiyah Tours on Jl. Sudirman and Mulia Rahaya Travel in Muria Plaza. You can also arrange tours through most *losmen* and hotels. The Tourist Office, Jl. Juanda 38A, tel. (0251) 21350, can sometimes fit you into a group on a last-minute basis, though you may have to wait a week. A group must consist of a

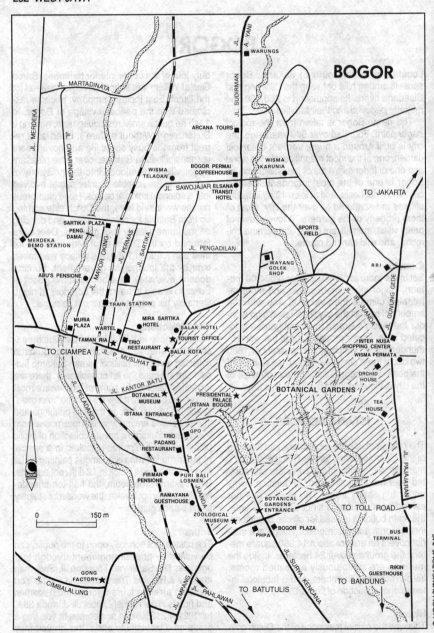

BOGOR

JL. MARTADINATA
JL. MERDEKA
JL. CIWARINGIN
JL. SUDIRMAN
JL. A. YANI

WARUNGS
ARCANA TOURS
BOGOR PERMAI COFFEEHOUSE
WISMA KARUNIA
WISMA TELADAN
JL. SAWOJAJAR ELSANA TRANSIT HOTEL
TO JAKARTA

SARTIKA PLAZA
PENG. DAMAI
JL. PERMAS
JL. SARTIKA
JL. PENGADILAN
SPORTS FIELD
MERDEKA BEMO STATION
ABU'S PENSIONE
JL. MAYOR OKING
WAYANG GOLEK SHOP
RRI

TRAIN STATION
MIRA SARTIKA HOTEL
SALAK HOTEL
MURIA PLAZA
TAMAN RIA
WARTEL
TRIO RESTAURANT
TOURIST OFFICE
BALAI KOTA
INTER NUSA SHOPPING CENTER
WISMA PERMATA
JL. IR. JUANDA
JL. GUNUNG GEDE

TO CIAMPEA
JL. P. MUSLIHAT
ORCHID HOUSE
JL. KANTOR BATU
BOTANICAL MUSEUM
JL. PELADANG
ISTANA ENTRANCE
PRESIDENTIAL PALACE (ISTANA BOGOR)
BOTANICAL GARDENS
TEA HOUSE

GPO
TRIO PADANG RESTAURANT
JL. JUANDA
JL. PAJAJARAN

FIRMAN PENSIONE
PURI BALI LOSMEN
RAMAYANA GUESTHOUSE
ZOOLOGICAL MUSEUM
BOTANICAL GARDENS ENTRANCE
TO TOLL ROAD

0   150 m

PHPA
BOGOR PLAZA
BUS TERMINAL

GONG FACTORY
JL. CIMBALALUNG
JL. EMPANG
JL. PAHLAWAN
JL. SURYA KENCANA
RIKIN GUESTHOUSE
TO BANDUNG
TO BATUTULIS

minimum of 10 people. While admission to the Istana is free, travel agencies charge Rp5000-8000 for their reservation services.

If you don't want to go through a tour agency, make a request by letter, including the name of each visitor, the date, and exact time you hope to view the palace. Send to: Head of Protocol, Istana Negara, Jl. Veteran, Jakarta.

KEBUN RAYA

The Bogor Botanical Gardens, right behind the presidential palace, occupy an incredible 87-hectare estate; this is one of the world's leading botanical institutions as well as an important scientific research center. The gardens have been here for over 170 years; Bogor rose around them.

The gardens are essentially a cultivated park of paths, pools, lawns, cactus gardens, great twisting foot-thick overhead vines, and enormous water lilies, with a river bubbling through it all. The collection includes 12,695 specimens of native plants from all over the Malay Archipelago and many other tropical regions.

Kebun Raya is also a favorite trysting place for lovers. Because of the great number of married couples who met here for the first time, another name for the gardens is Kebun Jodoh, or "Garden of Betrothal."

History
These world-famous gardens were conceived by the Dutch governor-general van der Capellan, who expanded a garden established in 1811 by avid British botanist Sir Stamford Raffles. During the Forced Cultivation Period early Dutch researchers used these gardens to develop cash crops to provide profits for the mother country. Today, the gardens are still used to collect and maintain living plants, with special emphasis on varieties with profit potential.

The very first specimen of oil palm introduced into Indonesia in 1848 still grows in the gardens. It's the ancestor of the high-grade oil palms now cultivated throughout Indonesia and Malaysia; the crop remains one of Indonesia's main exports.

Practicalities
Kebun Raya is open 0800-1700. Admission is Rp1600, Rp1300 on Sunday and holidays,

when it's particularly crowded. To miss the crowds, visit Kebun Raya on a weekday; to avoid the rain, visit in the morning. Guides, some quite knowledgeable and entertaining, are available; negotiate a fee in advance (about Rp6000 per hour).

Museum Zoologicum Bogoriense
This depository of 300,000 specimens of birds, mammals, reptiles, amphibians, fish, insects, mollusks, and other invertebrates is right next to the botanical gardens entrance on Jl. Ir. H. Juanda. It was founded in 1894 to study the fauna of the Indonesian archipelago.

Open daily 0800-1600, Friday until 1100; admission Rp1600. The majority of the stuffed specimens are in pretty sad shape, but don't miss the giant Japanese crabs, the blue whale skeleton, and the last, stuffed rhino from Tasikmalaya. A scientific library, **Bibliotheca Bogoriensis,** containing several thousand scarce books and hundreds of magazines, is also on Jl. Ir. H. Juanda.

SIGHTS NEAR BOGOR

Batutulis
Despite the fact Bogor was the capital of the immensely powerful Hindu kingdom of Pajajaran from the 12th to the 16th century, there are few reminders of this period. One of the few remaining physical traces the all-conquering tropical climate has not claimed is Batutulis (meaning "Writing Stone"), an ancient nine-line inscription in Sundanese Sanskrit etched on a conical stone. The inscription attests to the king's supernatural powers, and served to protect the realm from enemies. King Surawisesa decreed in 1533 that the message be written in stone.

The stone is housed in a small building nearly opposite the gate to Sukarno's former home, three km southeast of Bogor's Ramayana Cinema. Open from 0700 until late at night, the *juru kunci* accepts a small donation to let you in, shoeless. The inscription is still sacred to many, and despite the *bemo* whining by outside, the spot still possesses the feel of a place of meditation and devotion. Inside, a ritual of some sort could be going on, people genuflecting on mats, incense burning. One set of footprints, which look like someone stepped onto wet cement, is said to have been imprinted into the stone by the

THE BADUI

This tribe of 2,000-4,000 Sunda-speaking people—the mysterious "Amish of West Java"—live in 27 villages in a 50-square-km forest territory around Gunung Kendang, southeast of Rangkasbitung. A visit to this area is not easy and usually appeals only to dedicated students of isolated cultures.

For 400 years the White Badui have maintained almost complete isolation from the outside world, preserving intact an ancient way of life. Despite anthropological study, little is known of the Badui. They're reputed to possess strong mystic and clairvoyant powers; it is said the Badui predicted both world wars. Today their isolation is receding, as the growing population on the plains north of Gunung Kendang increasingly encroaches on Badui lands. New schools and low-cost housing are also drawing the Badui away from their traditional territory.

The origins of the Badui are uncertain. One theory maintains they're the remnants of the aristocracy of the Sunda kingdom of Pajajaran, who lived near Batutulis in the hills around Bogor; Badui domestic dwellings most closely resemble traditional Sundanese architecture. To escape invading Muslims in the 16th century, Badui ancestors are believed to have fled into the mountains. Badui still pay their respects to Siliwangi, the last of the Hindu kings.

Badui villages are divided into Badui Dalam (the inner three villages of Cibeo, Cikartawana, and Cikeusik) and the Badui Luar (outer 24 villages).

Badui Dalam

The inner, or White Badui, consist of 40 families. This inner clan dresses only in coarse white cloth, and follows rigorous rules of conduct first laid down by an ancestral divinity called Batatunggal. They have no police, no schools, and recognize no government. They're forbidden to get drunk, eat food at night, take any form of conveyance, wear flowers or perfumes, touch money, or cut their hair. Other taboos are meant to render Badui lands unattractive to invaders: they may not cultivate *sawah,* utilize fertilizers or modern tools, raise cash crops, or keep large domestic animals. The Badui Dalam live in *tanah larangan* (forbidden territory), where no stranger may spend the night.

Badui Luar

Outside the sacred inner circle live the Outer Badui, or Badui Luar. This outer clan wears bluish-black turbans and all-black *sarung,* lives less strictly, may sell crops and trade, and generally serves as a go-between for the White Badui and the rest of the world. This group oversees both the entry of strangers into Badui lands and the exit of Badui people. In the past no one was allowed to leave this jungle fastness, but now you sometimes see Badui men in the streets of Jakarta, or as far away as Bandung. Two things are certain: they've come on foot, and have a good reason for being there.

---

sheer magical strength and power of King Surawisesa. The monarch's knee marks are further evidence of his divinity.

Batutulis Ciampea

Another mysterious inscribed stone is located in Ciampea northwest of Bogor. Take a minibus from the stand near the Bogor train station about 18 km to Warungborang village; on the corner a track leads off to the right for 2.5 km over *sawah* to the small farming *kampung* of Ciampea. From here it's easy to find your way without a guide. After an hour's pleasant walk you come to an enormous gorge. A large polished black boulder has been moved out of the river, where it was embedded and half-submerged for many years, and placed in an enclosure on the top of the bank, complete with guards and donation book. This 1,500-year-old stone, one of the first written

records on Java, also bears the footprints of the Hindu King Purnawarman; those of his elephant imprint another stone nearby. The stone dates from the kingdom of Taruna, one of the earliest (6th-7th century) Indian-influenced kingdoms on Java. The inscription, in Old Palava script, is so immaculate and precise it seems as if it were carved only yesterday. Very friendly area. Not many visitors make it to this ancient relic.

Southwest Of Bogor

One of the most popular outings from Bogor is southwest to a waterfall, hot springs, and river, plus visits to a gong factory, traditional cracker makers, and a look at ageless agricultural techniques. You'll find tour guides at all *losmen;* full-day tours with lunch cost Rp25,000. Two-day tours include an overnight in a small village

Getting There

The rigid taboo system prevents tourists from visiting the inner territory, but you may enter the outer villages of Leuwidamar, Lebak, and Kadukatug. Although the Outer Badui resist contact with large numbers of people, they're known to be friendly to small groups who journey into their midst. At Rangkasbitung, obtain written permission from the local government office, (*kantor kabupaten*), by showing your passport, signing the application, and surrendering Rp3000 and one photograph of yourself.

This trip is suitable only for those who are physically fit, have planned and packed wisely, and can adjust to local living. Bring gifts and enough money to reciprocate a stay in village homes; also take food to supplement village meals. Adopt quiet, attentive behavior during your stay with the Badui.

The journey is probably best accomplished in groups no larger than eight people. Ideal would be locating a Badui Luar guide in Rangkas going home to one of the outer villages. It takes about three days to walk over the hills to Kadukatug. The trek starts from Leuwidamar village, at the end of a fairly good road, about 20 km south of Rangkas by minibus. Stay in the residence of the *kepala polisi* (police chief) in Leuwidamar. This kind man doesn't ask for money, but offer a donation for food, snacks, and tea. From Cisimeut you cross the river and travel 30 km by foot or motorcycle over about 12 hills to the Muslim village of Muncang. Some travelers spend the night in Muncang before continuing on the next day at dawn—another 20 km to the outer Badui village of Kadukatug.

(Lokspurna) and a four-hour trek to the summit of Genung Salak.

ACCOMMODATIONS

Budget

An excellent choice is the small and cozy **Puri Bali Losmen,** tel. (0251) 317-498, at Jl. Paledang 30. It's clean, spacious, and centrally located, only 400 meters from the entrance to Kebun Raya; Rp15,000-25,000. The 80-year-old Balinese proprietor, I Made Taman, former head of Indonesia's national parks, is a delightfully knowledgeable, helpful, garrulous man who speaks good English, German, and Dutch and plays the guitar and violin. He and his two sons make gracious and lively hosts.

Next door is the friendly, family-run **Firman Pensione** at Jl. Paledang 28, tel. 323-246, with rooms Rp10,000-30,000, dorms for just Rp4000. Firman has evolved into the primary backpackers lodge because of its low prices and friendly managers. Clean with Balinese touches is the **Ramayana Guesthouse,** tel. 320-364 just opposite the gardens with rooms from Rp20,000 to Rp45,000. Great location and plenty of services—guides, taxis to Bandung, trekking tips.

Moderate

Because of its superb location, the best mid-priced place is **Abu's Pensione,** Jl. Mayor Oking 15, tel. (0251) 322-893, just behind the railway station. Abu Bakar rents clean dorm beds for Rp6300, rooms overlooking the river for Rp16,800 with outside bath or Rp21,000 with inside bath, and Rp63,000-94,000 for deluxe rooms. Abu's provides great meals on a garden patio next to the local ravine, and also offers a number of tourist and travel services.

North of the gardens are several moderately priced guesthouses in quiet neighborhoods. Comfortable **Wisma Karunia,** Jl. Sempur 35-37, tel. 323-411, is close to the gardens and charges only Rp21,000-35,000 for large, clean rooms. Nearby **Wisma Teladan,** Jl. Sawojajar 3 A, tel. 323-327, is an equally good value.

On the north side of town is guesthouse-style **Elsana Transit Hotel,** Jl. Sawojajar 36, tel. 322-522; there are three classes of rooms, the cheapest running about Rp29,500 for second-class rooms with pavilion, up to Rp45,000 for bigger rooms. There's also a plush lobby, small kiosk, and quiet courtyard. Not very central, Elsana is just off Jl. Jen. Sudirman, one of the main approach roads into Bogor from the north.

A recommended guesthouse is family-run **Rikin's,** Jl. Cibural Indah, tel. 314-070, which offers lodging for Rp30,000 with all meals included. Rikin speaks Dutch and a little English. For moderate costs, he will drive you around to remote rubber plantations, tapioca factories, and *desa.*

Luxury

Bogor's newest is the **Mirah Sartika Hotel**, tel. (0251) 312-343, fax 315-188 in a small alley. Central location plus spotless a/c rooms for Rp63,000-126,000. Another *tempo doeloe* relic is the very nice **Wisma Permata**, at Jl. Raya Pajajaran 35, tel. 318-007, fax 311-082), rooms Rp70,000-95,000, with hot water, huge rooms and bathrooms, big beds, breakfast, and adjacent steakhouse restaurant.

The venerable Dutch-era **Salak Hotel** is currently undergoing renovation and expansion and, if additional investors can be found, will someday open as Bogor's largest and most exclusive hotel. In the meantime, the half-finished hotel rots in the tropical heat.

FOOD

Sundanese food is a little drier and less spicy-hot than *nasi padang*; it also tends to be cheaper. One of the most popular Sundanese dishes is *asinan,* a mixture of fruit, vegetables, and peanuts in a hot peanut sauce. The best places to sample *asinan* are **Asinan Bogor,** Jl. Kapt. Muslihat, and **Asinan Segar,** Jl. Veteran, next to the barber shops. Also try the local *bandrek* and *bajigur* drinks.

Wagons and carts clog the streets; eat well for Rp1000. The liveliest food scenes are the stalls and *warung* on Jl. Veteran just across the river. Popular *warung* are found at the intersection of Jl. Sudirman and Jl. Yani. Bogor is a famous fruit and vegetable center and all along Jl. Oto Iskandardinata and around the main gate of Kebun Raya—especially on Sunday—an immense variety of fruits and vegetables (even blackberries) is on sale.

Try spacious, modern **Bogor Permai Coffee House,** Jl. Jen. Sudirman 23A (near Jl. Sawojajar), tel. (0251) 2115, for Chinese/Indo food upstairs and Western food downstairs, with bakery and supermarket. For *nasi padang,* go to **Hidangan Puti Bungsu** and **Hidangan Trio Masakan Padang** on Jl. Kapitan Muslihat. Many restaurants are located along the main Bogor/Jakarta road; the number of cars parked in front is indicative of their popularity. Some offer such Sundanese delicacies as golden carp and fresh vegetable salad.

SHOPPING

Dase Spartacus is a partially blind carver of high-quality *wayang* puppets. Get to his workshop by walking east from the entrance gate of Istana Bogor; turn left and descend the steps into the small neighborhood of Lebak Kantin. Ask someone to direct you to his residence. Return to the palace gate and walk north up Jl. Sudirman, exploring the red-tiled old Dutch neighborhoods down in the valley on the right.

One of the two remaining gongsmiths on Java is **Pak Sukarna's,** Jl. Pancasan 17, one-half kilometer from Istana Bogor down Jl. Empang near Bogor's town center. When buying a gong, listen for clear undulations in tone. The means of creating these undulations remains a secret. The pitch of the gong depends upon its size and the thickness of the metal. In the showroom workers take special orders for gongs, other *gamelan* instruments, and professional-quality *wayang golek*. If the *wayang* maker is there, he'll sign his products.

SERVICES

The tourist office for the regency of Bogor is located at Jl. Veteran 2. The **Bogor Tourist Office,** Jl. Ir. H. Juanda 10, tel. (0251) 321-350, will provide maps and information on events and places of interest in and around Bogor. Open Mon.-Thurs. 0800-1400, Friday 0800-1100, and Saturday until 1300.

On the same street (no. 9, tel. 21014) is the headquarters for the **Dinas Perlindungan dan Pengawetan Alam (PHPA),** the official body for the administration of Indonesia's wildlife reserves. This is the place to get information on reserves, though entry permits to national parks and reserves can usually be acquired directly from branch PHPA offices in or near the reserves.

The Red Cross Hospital, **Umum P.M.I.** (pronounced "pay em ee"), Jl. Raya Pajajaran, tel. 24080, near the Kebun Raya, has physicians on duty weekdays 0800-1400.

Bogor's telephone city code is 0251.

TRANSPORTATION

Getting There

The most convenient way to reach Bogor from Jakarta is by train from Gambir station; hourly departures.

To Bogor by bus from Jakarta's Rambutan bus terminal takes two hours (Rp1000). More direct buses ride the smooth new expressway, which cuts at least half an hour off the trip. From Bandung to Bogor by bus consumes three hours. The Bogor bus station is only about a 10-minute walk from Kebun Raya and two km from most of the town's budget accommodations. Take minibus 03 from the bus terminal to reach Abu's Pensione. Ask to be dropped at the PLN.

Getting Around

Because of the massive gardens in its center, Bogor is very spread out. *Angkutan kota* (*angkots*) rides around town cost Rp200-500. Pasar Bogor and the *bemo* terminal on Jl. P. Muslihat near the train station are the central stands. You'll also find *delman* (horse drawn passenger carts) stands at Pasar Bogor and near the railroad station at Jl. Mayor Oking. There's a taxi stand in front of Pasar Bogor next to PHPA; bargain, as the cabs are unmetered.

Getting Away

The *terminal bis* is on Jl. Pajajaran southeast of town. Reach Merak by bus for Rp2500 (four hours). From the bus station minibuses head south to the beach resort of Pelabuhanratu; change buses in Cibadak, roughly the halfway point.

To Puncak, take a bus (Rp2000) up to the pass. Get off the bus at the turnoff to Cibodas, where most of the better guesthouses are located.

There are no direct trains from Bogor to Bandung, but you can board three trains a day southeast to Sukabumi, departing 0630, 1130, and 1630. To Bandung by bus costs Rp3750, four hours via the Puncak. Buses stop at Kebun Kelapa bus terminal, from where minibuses head to the hotel district. Otherwise, stay on the bus to Cicaheum terminal for onward buses to Garut, Pangandaran, and Yogyakarta.

Tours

Folks at Abu's Pensione can arrange transport to and from the airport, confirm flights and purchase air tickets even when the plane is full, lead eight-hour city tours and one-day tours of Bogor's environs, plus lead all kinds of walking tours up in the mountains. You can also make arrangements through Firman Pensione, Ramayana Guesthouse, and Rikin Guesthouse. A reliable travel agent is **Arcana Tours and Travel,** Jl. Jen. Sudirman 23A, tel. (0251) 28629, run by Mr. Safariyyah.

THE PUNCAK

Stretching under monsoon clouds from Bogor all the way to Cianjur, the Puncak ("summit") is an invigorating mountain district and favorite West Java domestic tourist area. On weekends, bumper-to-bumper traffic stretches all the way from Bandung to Jakarta. Foggy 1,200-meter-high Puncak Pass is very scenic when not covered in clouds, rain, or traffic. Nights can be surprisingly cool—average 22° C—so bring warm clothing. Enjoy fairy tale walks out of Cisarua, Cibodas, and Cipanas.

Tea Cultivation

The best tea thrives on these high, cool mountain slopes—the cooler air slows growth and increases flavor. Constant pruning keeps plants short and bushy. Harvesters, mostly young women earning Rp2000 per day, take only the young leaves and buds; each can pick up to 25 kilos daily, enough for five kilos of dried tea. Black tea is fermented; green tea is not. Tea bush roots are made into carvings which are sold alongside the road.

About six km on the Puncak side of Cianjur is the entrance to the Gunung Gedeh Tea Estate, which leads to many picnic places and beautiful views of the mountains. Another eight km southeast is the entrance to the Malabar Tea Estate, open to visitors.

Accommodations

The entire stretch of highway across the Puncak is lined with expensive hotels and bungalows where, on weekends, it's difficult to find a room for under Rp30,000. Midweek prices frequently start at half of weekend prices.

The best place to stay for trekkers and budget travelers is in the small town of Cibodas, just below the entrance to Cibodas Botanical Gardens. Highlights include superb views of tea plantations, countless hikes, the gardens, and daylong treks to the summits of Genung Gede and Genung Pangrango. Upscale visitors should stay in one of the resorts in the towns of Puncak or Cipanas.

Transportation

The Puncak area is about one hour and 34 km southeast of Bogor by bus; 110 km from Bandung. If you intend to stay in one of the small guesthouses near the botanical gardens, take a bus from Bogor for Rp2000 all the way to the

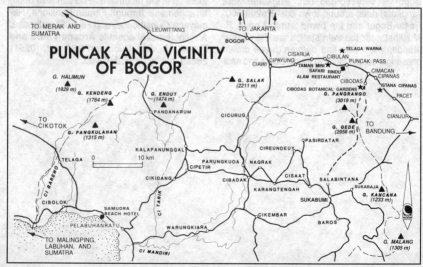

PUNCAK AND VICINITY OF BOGOR

TO MERAK AND SUMATRA

LEUWITTANG

TO JAKARTA

BOGOR

CISARUA CIBULAN TELAGA WARNA

CIPAYUNG PUNCAK PASS

CIAWI TAMAN MINI RINDU

SAFARI

ALAM RESTAURANT CIBODAS

CIMACAN

CIBODAS BOTANICAL GARDENS

ISTANA CIPANAS

G. PANGRANGO (3019 m)

PACET

G. HALIMUN (1929 m)

G. KENDENG (1764 m)

G. ENDUT (1474 m)

G. SALAK (2211 m)

CIPANAS

TO CIKOTOK

G. PANGKULAHAN (1315 m)

PANDANARUM

CICURUG

G. GEDE (2958 m)

TO BANDUNG

CIANJUR

TELAGA

KALAPANUNGGAL

CIREUNDEUY

OPASIRDATAR

0   10 km

CIKIDANG

CIPETIR

PARUNGKUOA

NAGRAK

CISAAT

SALABINTANA

CIBADAK

CIBODAS

KARANGTENGAH

SUKARAJA

G. KANCANA (1233 m)

SAMUDRA BEACH HOTEL

WARUNGKIARA

CIKEMBAR

SUKABUMI

BAROS

PELABUHANRATU

TO MALINGPING, LABUHAN, AND SUMATRA

CI MANDIRI

G. MALANG (1305 m)

© MOON PUBLICATIONS, INC.

town of Cimacan, then another bus up to Cibodas. Or you can hop off the bus at one of the highway villages described below.

CISARUA

Cisarua is the first big town you encounter enroute to the Puncak; nothing special but the only budget alternative to Cibodas. The town lies at the bottom of the mountain and offers little aside from cheap rooms at the Kopo Hostel and a swimming pool ideal for escaping the lowland heat.

Just before Cisarua you'll find the turnoff for **Taman Mini Safari,** which bills itself as a miniature Kenya. One traveler reports, "My guess is that if Kenya looked like this, it wouldn't be so popular. But it's rather a nice place to spend a day." Includes a big amusement park.

Seventy km from Jakarta and ten km from Bogor, the **Kopo International Youth Hostel,** Jl. Raya Cisuara 537, tel. (0251) 4296, offers Cisarua's cheapest rooms (Rp15,000), with dorm beds for Rp5000. Very clean, no mosquitos, cool fresh air; restaurants, supermarkets, and swimming pool nearby. Request directions to nearby sights. From Bogor, ask to be dropped at the Cisarua Pertamina gas station; the hostel is adjacent.

CIBULAN

Cibulan, a few km beyond Cisarua, is a busy lowlands town with little charm or character. Still, it's a useful base for visiting the nearby tea plantations.

Cisarua Indah is a nice, good-value place to stay. In Jakarta ask at the Hostel Norbek (Jl. Jaksa 14) for a letter of introduction, which will save you Rp5000 per night. Rates are higher on weekends and holidays. The restaurant closes at 1700; another restaurant stays open across the road.

Hotel Cibulan is an old Dutch hotel in creaky condition with rooms from Rp12,000 weekdays and Rp18,000 weekends.

PUNCAK

Puncak is the name of the entire region, the pass itself, and a small town situated right at the top of the pass. Best views from here, nearly to Jakarta.

Ask the bus driver to drop you at the superbly located **Rindu Alam Restaurant,** where the food is decent and the views some of the best in all of West Java. From the restaurant, hike down the hill to tour the enormous **Gunung Mas Tea Estate,** which welcomes visitors in its processing rooms.

From Rindu Alam, hike up the road about ten minutes to the turnoff to **Telaga Warna,** a small lake often packed with Indonesian tourists. Nothing special, but a nice hike.

Puncak Pass Hotel, tel. (0255) 2503, is an old colonial hotel with rooms from Rp52,500 to Rp126,000. The hotel is situated just over the pass, facing the rolling valley stretching from Puncak to Cianjur.

CIPANAS

This area of recreational hot springs is a good place to break the journey between Bogor and Bandung. Visit the picturesque market that sells cut flowers, plants, vegetables, and fruit. The hot sulphur baths here (Cipanas means "Hot River") are famous for their remedial powers; the water originates from natural springs on Gunung Guntur. The mountain's top is still bare from an 1889 eruption.

Sights

Cipanas can be a bit hectic and unpretty at times, a traffic-snarled noisy town surrounding a single peaceful oasis—the president's holiday home. This elegant country house (built in 1750), called **Istana Cipanas,** lies in a park with gardens, triple-canopy jungle, and hot springs. On the grounds is a bungalow where Sukarno composed some of his most famous speeches. Suharto seldom uses the six presidential retreats dotted all over Java, preferring to tend cattle on his gentleman's farm on the slopes of Gunung Gede. A Catholic church near the palace is presided over by an old Dutch priest, Father Vanderland.

On the left after the turnoff to Cibodas Botanical Garden and several km before the town of Cipanas, see the small sign pointing up a dirt track to the right to **Santa Yusup Convent.** This nunnery is a simple and quiet retreat where it's possible to rent rooms if you book in advance.

Of the three Buddhist *vihara* in Cipanas, the one in town with all the electric lights is hilarious to look at, while the retreat in the hills is quite nice. Ask for Gereja Buddhist; the entrance is near the Simpang Raya II Restaurant in the town of Pacet. All the *vihara* are under the same *bhikku*, one of Indonesia's leading Buddhist religious leaders, who lives in Pacet. You're given a booklet which explains his philosophy, though it's also okay if you want to practice your own form of meditation here. The people are very nice.

The monastery is set in a really beautiful spot, and serves outstanding vegetarian food. What you pay for room and board is up to you; no one asks for money, but you should contribute a daily donation of at least Rp5000. Bring a good sleeping bag for the many two-blanket nights. During the day it's sunny and you can look down the valley with mountain streams in the distance, a lovely and peaceful view.

Visitors may also stay at the **Biara Catholic Camp,** next to Padang Sati restaurant, Rp8000 pp.

Accommodations

Lots of places to stay and eat in different classes and tastes, although all are comparatively expensive. Cipanas is crowded on weekends with visitors from Bandung, Bogor, and Jakarta.

The top-end choice is **Summit Panghegar,** tel. (0255) 511-335, fax 512-785, with conference center, tennis courts, spacious restaurant, and comfortable rooms for Rp136,500-189,000. Or try **Villa Cipanas Indah,** run by a nice Indonesian woman; 100 meters from the main street near the market. A more expensive place to stay is the **Bukit Raya,** with large swimming pool. The **Lembur Kuring,** south of Cipanas, has Sundanese-style bungalows; clean and sparsely furnished, with hot water from the springs. Bring your own towel, top sheet, and soap. Eat at the Padang-style restaurants **Roda** or **Padang Sati.**

CIBODAS

The town of Cibodas is the best destination in Puncak for great scenery, mountain treks, botanical gardens, and a good selection of budget guesthouses.

Cibodas Botanical Gardens

A cool, high-elevation extension of the Bogor gardens. Indonesia's first botanic reserve, Cibodas was established in 1862, primarily to protect the region's unusually rich mountain flora. Today the scene of important botanical research, beautiful Cibodas Park covers about 125 hectares and attracts 80,000 visitors a year. Admission Rp1000; open daily 0800-1600, but avoid Sundays unless you love crowds. A rough map is posted at the park entrance.

During the last century the Dutch planted mountain trees collected from Australia, the Canary Islands, South Africa, and many other temperate areas. Alongside the original plantings stand the thick tropical jungle covering the slopes of Gunung Gede. Good paths run through the jungle, some stone-paved; names, both Latin and popular, are displayed on the trees. See 15-meter-high tree ferns (*alsophila*), beds of roses, begonias in full bloom, and an elfin forest where moss-strewn ground and lichen-draped trees impart a fairyland look. Also check out the eucalyptus and lily collections, and the superb view of Gunung Gegerbentang, covered in dense rainforest.

Attached to the garden is a forest reserve of more than 1,200 hectares extending up to the summit of Gunung Pangrango and the crater of Gunung Gede.

Transportation

Cibodas is about 10 km beyond Puncak Pass and five km uphill from the town of Cimacan. The turnoff has been improved but you still need to look carefully for the small sign Kebun Raya, or the enormous billboard Cibodas Golf Course. Ask the bus driver to drop you at the turnoff, then wait for a minibus heading up the hill to the gardens. No need for a special charter.

Accommodations

Several small homestays are located just down the road from the entrance to the botanical gardens. Young touts pitching hotels often meet you at the bus stop.

Probably the most popular choice is the small but clean **Freddy's Homestay** on the right side of the road tucked away in a small lane. Rooms here cost Rp5000-10,000; good views over the adjacent tea plantations. Another possibility is the nearby **Wisma Jamur** ("Mushroom House") run by Miss Nina, who asks Rp12,000-25,000 for rooms with private bath. The mushrooms, I may add, are in no way magic.

Pondok Pemuda Cibodas, the local youth hostel, is located near the parking lot and minibus terminus and has dorm beds for Rp6000 and rooms from Rp12,000-18,000. Nothing special but easy to find. A final choice is the **Cibodas Botanical Gardens Guesthouse,** wonderfully situated directly inside the boundaries of the park. Here, class A rooms run Rp12,000-30,000 depending on meal plan, while class B rooms (three beds per room) cost just Rp5000. Rooms can be reserved at the Bogor Botanical Gardens.

GUNUNG GEDE NATIONAL PARK

An easily accessible park with excellent trails, waterfalls, and spectacular scenery. Pick up your hiking permit, park brochure, and trail map at the Forestry Office (PHPA) near the Cibodas Gardens parking lot; open daily until 1600.

Wear warm clothing and good footwear. Local guesthouses and Kopo Youth Hostel can help you prepare and find tents, sleeping bags, and the like. The best time for the hike is May to October; the park is closed from January to March. The 10-km hike to the rim of Gunung Gede (2,958 meters) takes four to six hours on a well-maintained path. You can easily reach the summit in a single day with an early start; clouds often roll in around noon. Approaching the perfect cone of Gunung Pangrango (3,019 meters) takes seven to eight hours.

Follow the trail up from the Cibodas gardens parking lot. On the way up, you pass a turnoff down to the waterfall (the sign says Cibeureum), then go over the (hot) waterfall to a ruined cottage. To reach the waterfalls requires only 90 minutes and provides a compromise hike for visitors short on time. Ignore the left fork 30 meters before the ruins. Directly after the ruins, the trail forks again; take the right fork to the summit or the left fork to the crater.

You'll get the most out of this experience by camping overnight near one of the hot springs, reaching the top at sunrise. To camp overnight, follow the blue-painted stones along the crater lip and down into the valley. Or start at around 2000, making the walk at night during the full moon, timing your arrival at the top for sunrise.

PELABUHANRATU

This isolated fishing village 90 km southeast of Bogor is the site of the large Samudra Beach Hotel, a popular weekend destination for Jakarta and Bandung residents. The beaches are splendid along this coastline, but don't venture too far out. Though the water appears serene, it's best to heed the posted warning signs; the Bulgarian ambassador drowned here.

The swimming "accidents" and other strange happenings around Pelabuhanratu are invariably attributed to Nyai Loro Kidul, goddess of the South Seas. In fact, the name Pelabuhanratu means "Queen's Harbor." Homage is paid to her every June with a garish thanksgiving festival, Pesta Nelayan, celebrated all along the coast. Featured are lines of colorfully decorated fishing boats, *pencak silat* martial arts contests, *ketuk tilu* dances, and various sporting competitions such as rowing and swimming. Flowers are scattered on the water and a buffalo head is sacrificed to the sea.

Accommodations

This busy seaside holiday resort has high prices and sometimes substandard service. A number of seaside bungalows and motel-type accommodations lie along the four-km stretch between the village market and the Samudra Beach Hotel.

The cheapest *losmen* are near the bus terminal on Jl. Siliwangi—**Karang Naya, Wisma Putra,** and **Penginapan Laut Kidul.** The renovated **Karang Sari,** 200 meters beyond Pondok Dewata on the right on a hill overlooking the sea, has about 15 neat rooms, apartments, and bungalows, Rp31,000-105,000, all situated around a garden.

Pondok Dewata, just beyond the gas station, is probably the best place for families—safe beach and reasonably priced. Dewata's set of Balinese-style a/c bungalows go for Rp52,000-126,000. Pool, small restaurant, and shady gardens. Just beyond the Karangsari is a steep hill turning left to **Bayu Amirta,** more commonly known as the Fish Restaurant or Hoffmann's. Hangs right on the edge of a cliff; superb sunsets. Rp21,000-63,000.

Samudra Beach Hotel, tel. (021) 340-601, is four km past Pelabuhanratu village, Rp350 from the market by minibus down a picturesque wooded shore road. Standing in astounding contrast to disheveled Pelabuhanratu, this modern high-rise sits alone in a truly beautiful location. Built by Sukarno in the 1960s, he always promoted it mightily: suites, swimming pool, mini-golf and tennis, expensive dining rooms, *gamelan* playing in the lobby. The management charges Rp105,000-315,000 for rooms that saw better days in the Sukarno era. You can swim right in front of the hotel but heed the sign *Hati-Hati!* (Dangerous!). A room at the hotel is always kept unoccupied for Nyai Loro Kidul.

Food

The colorful *pasar ikan* in town does a roaring trade in the early mornings. In-season tuna and other seafoods are incredibly cheap. Don't pay any more than Rp500 for coconuts. A *nasi padang* restaurant is right by the pier in town, and an excellent seafood restaurant, the **Bayu Amirta,** cooks fish to perfection. It's crowded on weekends so reserve ahead and bring your own wine.

Getting There

Pelabuhanratu is 2.5 hours from Bogor. Buses, minibuses, and *bemo* regularly head down here on a good road from Bogor via Cicurug and Cibadak. It's about one hour by bus or minibus from Bogor to Cibadak, then another 1.5 hours to Pelabuhanratu. A direct bus to Pelabuhanratu also leaves Sukabumi; this ride takes you through rice fields and rubber and tea plantations. You can also take a train from Bogor to Cibadak, then change there to a minibus.

BANDUNG

Roughly 180 km southeast of Jakarta, Bandung is Indonesia's fourth-largest city, with 1.7 million people. Lying in a high valley surrounded by mountains covered in tea plantations, the city is a bustling center of Sundanese culture. It's the site of some 50 universities and colleges, many small academies, and such prestigious institutions as the Nuclear Research Center, the Volcanologists Monitoring Center (VSI), and Indonesia's aircraft industry (IPTN). Indonesia's elite army divison, Siliwangi, is headquartered in Bandung, occupying the former command center of the Netherlands Indies Army. Splendid colonial architecture is another Bandung attraction.

Bandung is also a center for the textile and food processing industries. In the fine arts, musicians, dancers, and artists are lured here from all over Indonesia to study. Once referred to as the "Paris of the East," the Dutch loved Bandung and their long occupation is reflected in the architectural gems as well as the somber middle-class architecture recalling early 20th-century Western European cities—an overabundance of ferroconcrete buildings.

Downtown Bandung has unfortunately lost much of its charm and glamour; nowadays it's choked with exhaust fumes and dust. The real charm of Bandung lies in the northern neighborhoods constructed by the Dutch, an historic district of tree-lined boulevards, handsome old houses, and art deco municipal buildings. If you only experience the messy downtown district, you've missed the real highlight of Dutch-era Bandung.

History
Bandung sits on an ancient lakebed; the rich alluvial soil nourished a successful farming community for hundreds of years. The area was first mentioned in writing in 1488 in connection with the Hindu kingdom of Pajajaran, which at the time reigned over all of West Java. This thinly populated feudal kingdom deep in the Preanger Mountains enjoyed a peaceful existence until the arrival of the Dutch in the late 18th century, attracted to the region for its coffee-growing potential.

In 1810, the residence of the Bandung regent was moved from Dayeuhkolot to where the newly built Great Post Road (present-day Jl. Asia-Afrika) crossed the River Cikapundung, and the city of Bandung was born. It quickly became one of the principal operating bases for the Dutch colonial government; in 1856 Bandung became the residency capital, in 1884 the railway arrived.

Tired of the heat and malaria of Jakarta, the Dutch intended to move the capital to Bandung in the 1930s. Although never completed, this plan left Bandung with Indonesia's richest collection of art deco architecture and one of the finest city layouts on the island.

During WW II Bandung was the main defense position of the Dutch government; Allied headquarters here was captured by the Japanese on 7 March 1942. During the struggle for independence, Sukarno first emerged as a nationalist leader at the Bandung Institute of Technology (ITB), the "MIT of Indonesia." In 1955, Bandung was the site of the famous Asian-African Conference that launched the nonaligned movement—one of the greatest triumphs of Indonesian foreign-policy efforts. In the post-WW II period Bandung was a hotbed of fanatical fundamentalist Islamic movements such as the murderous Darul Islam group.

The People
Bandung is a cosmopolitan city with the usual Indonesian mix. The city is split by the railroad tracks: to the north are the richer neighborhoods, to the south the poorer. Because of the numerous universities and colleges housing some of Indonesia's brightest students, this is a youthful city, a haven for academics and intellectuals. Bandung's ITB student leaders pride themselves on being the most radical in all of Indonesia, the catalyst for nationwide student protests and strikes.

Youth groups are constantly agitating for social and political change, regularly disseminating propaganda in vituperative underground print and broadcast media. In 1978, ITB students published the famous *White Book of the 1978 Students Struggle,* railing against corruption

BANDUNG

JL. CEMARA
LINGGA PUB
TO TANGKUBAN PRAHU
JL. SUKAJADI
JL. CIPAGANTI
ADVENT HOSPITAL
STUDIO EAST DISCO
TAMAN SARI
ZOO
TAMAN OKEWAH
BANDUNG INSTITUTE OF TECHNOLOGY
JL. SILIWANGI
TIZI'S RESTAURANT
JL. I.R.H. JUANDA
SHERATON INN
PATRA JASA HOTEL
GANECA
JL. DIPATIUKUR
JL. HASBANUDIN
JL. PROF. EYC*
PONYO RESTAURANT
JL. CIPAGANTI
JL. CHAMPELAS
TAMAN GANECA
JL. TAMANSARI
JL. SURAPATI
PURI GARDENIA HOTEL
TO PAK UJO'S ANGKLUNG STUDIO
LAGA PUB
JL. PASTEUR
JEANS PARADISE
JL. SULJANA
JL. PASIRKALIKI
JL. CIPAGANTI
S. CIKAPUNDUNG
FLOWER MARKET
JL. H. JUANDA
LAPANGAN GASHIBU
JL. DIPONEGORO
GEOLOGICAL MUSEUM
GEDUNG SATE BUILDING
JL. SAGUNG
JL. DR. CIPTO
BOURAQ
JL. WASTUKANCANA
JL. LAKSMANA
ANGGREK HOTEL
OLD DUTCH HOMES
TO AIRPORT
JL. PAJAJARAN
YOUTH CENTER
QUININE FACTORY
HOTEL SANTIKA
JL. SUMBAWA
TAMAN MALUKU
JL. ACEH
SEE "CENTRAL BANDUNG" MAP
JL. PASIRKALIKI
JL. WASTUKANCANA
JL. MERDEKA
BIP PLAZA
JL. ACEH
CITY
TAMAN LALU LINTAS
SILIWANGI STADIUM
GOVERNOR'S HOUSE
JL. SUMATRA
JL. KEBON KAWUNG
JL. GAREJA
HOTEL GUNTUR
HOTEL SAHARA
TRAIN STATION
BANK OF INDONESIA
JL. BRAGA
JL. JAWA
JL. GUDANG SELATAN
SAKADARNA LOSMEN
MINIBUS STATION
JL. KEBON JATI
HOTEL MELATI
PANGHEGAR HOTEL
JL. LEMBONG BUNGSU
HOTEL SURABAYA
JL. SUNDA
RUMENTANG SIANG CULTURAL HALL
PASAR BARU
WAYANG THEATER (YPKI)
ISTANA HOTEL
JL. NARIPAN
TO JAKARTA
POST OFFICE
LOSMEN INTERNATIONAL
JL. JEN. A. YANI
TO CICAHEUM BUS TERMINAL
JL. JEN. SUDIRMAN
TOURIST OFFICE
MERDEKA BLDG.
GRAND PREANGER HOTEL
JL. NARIPAN
JL. CIBADAK
JL. ASIA-AFRIKA
JL. PAJAGALAN
SAVOY HOMANN HOTEL
ALUN-ALUN
JL. LENGKONG KECIL
JL. JEN. GATOT SUBROTO
HOTEL PAPANDAYAN
JL. ASTANA ANYAR
JL. ISKANDARDINATA
JL. DEWI SARTIKA
LOSMEN MAWAR
WAYANG MAKER
JL. TAMBONG
JL. PANGARANG
PACIFIC HOTEL
PA AMING PUPPETS
JL. KARAPITAN
JL. PASIRKOJA
HOTEL BRAJAWIJAYA
KEBUN KELAPA BUS TERMINAL
JL. PUNGKUR

0   200 m

© MOON PUBLICATIONS, INC.

and cronyism in high places. The first Indonesian rock festival took place in Bandung in 1975.

SIGHTS

A highly recommended tour starts at the *alun-alun* (visit the tourist office), passes the Merdeka building and continues to Hotel Savoy Homann. Walk up Jl. Braga, then north to the historic Bank of Indonesia, City Hall, and east along Jl. Aceh past Taman Maluku to the impressive Gedung Sate building. Continue north to the ITB campus and Bandung Zoo before returning by bus to city center. Allow a full day.

Early Architecture

Few of the city's buildings predate the 20th century. What exists today is a curious mixture of neglected dignified colonial structures, old homes and decrepit emporiums near the Central Market, and restored Dutch municipal buildings such as Gedung Sate in the northern section of town. Pre-1900 remnants include **Gedung Merdeka** ("Freedom Building"), on Jl. Asia-Afrika, **Gedung Pakuan**, on Jl. Oto Iskandardinata (official house of the governor of West Java), and **Gedung Papak**, on Jl. Wastukancana, constructed in 1819 by order of Governor-General van der Capellan. One of the city's oldest buildings (1850), the **Pendopo Kabupaten** on the south side of the *alun-alun*, was entirely reconstucted in 1993. The huge tree planted to commemorate the birth of Queen Wilhelmina in 1880 still stands.

Downtown Attractions

The 1920-40 period was Bandung's Golden Age of art deco/nouveau architecture, a time when concrete was used with flair and grace. The area north of the railway was designed and built by famous Dutch architects of the art deco period.

Start your walking tour at the tourist office in Bandung's *alun-alun,* created at the same time (1850) as Gedung Pakuan and the Great Mosque. Surrounded by shopping centers, offices, and cinemas.

The **Savoy Homann Hotel** is probably this vigorous period's most superb specimen. One of Asia's grand hotels, all its rooms are mini-suites, with quarters for drivers and servants. Even the furniture and fittings bespeak the art nouveau look. The dining room is a spectacular replica of a food station aboard a 1930s trans-Atlantic oceanliner.

Jalan Braga, though it retains only a shadow of its former splendor, still boasts beautiful stained glass. More glimpses of this era can be seen along Jl. Braga, around Jl. Pasar Baru and Jl. Banceuy. Also check out the **IKIP Building** on Jl. Setiabudi, and several private homes in the Dago area, particularly the one on the corner of Jl. Sultan Agung.

The **Army Museum** (Museum Mandala Wangsit Siliwangi), on Jl. Lembong near the Istana Hotel, contains a collection of weapons used in the freedom struggle against the Dutch in the 1940s. Also see graphic photos of the work of the Darul Islam movement. Open Mon.-Thurs. 0900-1300; free.

Gedung Merdeka

Also known as the Asia-Afrika Building, Gedung Merdeka is right in the center of the city on Jl. Asia-Afrika 65 on the corner of Jl. Braga, near the city's *alun-alun*. Built in 1895, it was renovated to its present form by Van Gallenlast and Wolf Shoemaker in 1926. Open 0800-1300 daily, Friday to 1100, Saturday to 1200.

In 1955, President Sukarno invited leaders of 29 developing nonaligned nations to a solidarity conference in this building. Bandung hit the headlines that year and nothing of like magnitude has happened since. Such figures as Nehru, Nasser, Ho Chi Minh, and Chou En Lai attended, with Sukarno acting as the Grand Dalang. It was said he employed dozens of professional, specially trained prostitutes to spy on the delegates.

In this building the first openly anticolonialist conference took place, laying the groundwork for today's nonaligned movement. All nations attending had recently achieved independence and, with the exception of Japan, all were underdeveloped; all announced themselves independent according to "Ten Principles of Nonalignment for Peaceful Co-existence." In the building's museum is a fine, well-annotated exhibit commemorating the conference.

Gedung Sate

Perhaps the finest piece of Dutch art deco architecture in Indonesia. Nicknamed after the

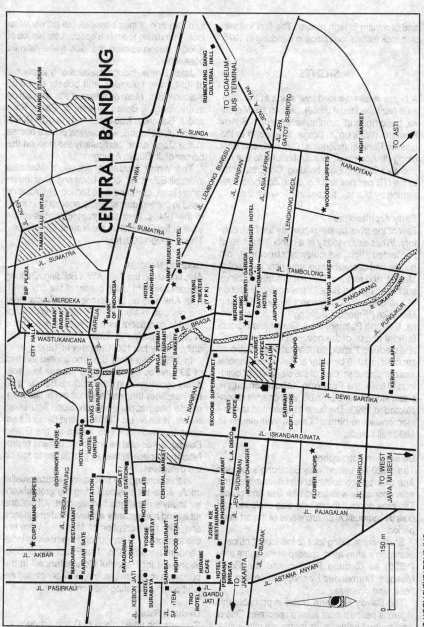

CENTRAL BANDUNG

SILIWANGI STADIUM

TO CICAHEUM BUS TERMINAL

RUMENTANG SIANG CULTURAL HALL

JL. ACEH

JL. TAMAN LALU LINTAS

JL. SUMATRA

JL. SUNDA

JL. JAWA

JL. LEMBONG BUNGSU

JL. JEN. A. YANI

JL. NARIPAN

JL. JEN. GATOT SUBROTO

NIGHT MARKET

TO ASTI

WOODEN PUPPETS

KARAPITAN

JL. ASIA - AFRIKA

JL. LENGKONG KECIL

JL. SUMATRA

ISTANA HOTEL

ARMY MUSEUM

HOTEL PANGHEGAR

WAYANG THEATER (Y P K)

GRAND PREANGER HOTEL

JL. TAMBOLONG

WAYANG MAKER

JL. PANGARANG

BIP PLAZA

JL. MERDEKA

BANK OF INDONESIA

GAREJA

TAMAN BADAK PUTIH

MERDEKA BUILDING

MERPATI / GARUDA

SAVOY HOMANN HOTEL

JAIPONGAN

S. CIKAPUNDUNG

JL. PUNGKUR

CITY HALL

WASTUKANCANA

JL. BRAGA

BRAGA PERMAI RESTAURANT

FRENCH BAKERY

TOURIST OFFICE

ALUN-ALUN

PENDOPO

WARTEL

KEBUN KELAPA

GANG KEBUN KARET (WARUNGS)

GOVERNOR'S HOUSE

HOTEL SAHARA

HOTEL GUNTUR

JL. NARIPAN

EKONOMI SUPERMARKET

JL. DEWI SARTIKA

SARINAH DEPT. STORE

POST OFFICE

JL. KEBUN KAWUNG

TRAIN STATION

OPLET / MINIBUS STATION

CENTRAL MARKET

L.A. DISCO

JL. SUDIRMAN

JL. ISKANDAR DINATA

MONEYCHANGER

FLOWER SHOPS

JL. PASIRKOJA

TO WEST JAVA MUSEUM

CUPU MANIK PUPPETS

MANDARIN RESTAURANT

KARDJAN SATE

SAKADARNA LOSMEN

YOSSIE HOMESTAY

HOTEL MELATI

SAHABAT RESTAURANT

NIGHT FOOD STALLS

TJOEN KIE RESTAURANT

PHOENIX RESTAURANT

JL. JEN. SUDIRMAN

JL. PAJAGALAN

JL. AKBAR

JL. KEBON JATI

HOTEL SURABAYA

JL. SA ITEM

TRIO HOTEL

JL. GARDU JATI

HURAME CAFE

HOTEL PERDANA WISATA

JL. CIBADAK

JAKARTA

JL. ASTANA ANYAR

JL. PASIRKALI

150 m

© MOON PUBLICATIONS, INC.

curious roof spire, which resembles a *sate* stick, this superbly restored gem was once intended as the new capital of the Dutch East Indies empire. Several other worthwhile sights are nearby.

The **Museum Post and Philateli,** in the left wing of Gedung Sate, Jl. Cilaki 73, contains an extensive stamp collection and a graphic history of Indonesia's postal services. Open daily 0900-1300. For contemporary architecture, visit the **Government Office Building** on the football pitch next to Gedung Sate on Jl. Diponegoro. The tallest building in Bandung, with fantastic views, it looks like a water tower in disguise—a four-story office block supported on 14-story slender concrete columns sweeping stylishly upward.

Don't miss the **Geological Museum,** near Gedung Sate, with its huge floor space of fossils, minerals, models of volcanos, photos of eruptions, and relief maps. Open Mon.-Thurs. 0900-1400, Friday 0900-1100, and Saturday 0900-1300.

Bandung Institute Of Technology

Premier among Bandung's many colleges and universities is the Bandung Institute of Technology, or ITB, on the north side of the city; take a Dago-bound Honda and get off at Jl. Ganeca. This is the oldest, largest, and one of Indonesia's most prestigious technical universities.

ITB was established in 1920 by a group of enterprising Dutch planters, merchants, and industrialists led by the Malabar planter H.A.R. Bosscha. The curriculum, based on the famous Technical High School in Delft, was designed to provide training for native engineers and architects. Yearly, around 30,000 students attend 17 higher educational institutions on campus. ITB has produced many of Indonesia's foremost engineers and political personalities, including Sukarno.

Initially criticized for its remoteness from the central area of Bandung, the ITB campus is high, cool, dry, drained, and able to expand. Graceful, soundly built, and functionally brilliant, ITB's original complex is one of the most architecturally important 20th-century buildings in Indonesia.

Taman Lalu Lintas

Also known as the "Traffic Garden," Taman Lalu Lintas, on Jl. Belitung, was established to give small children their first lessons in traffic regulations. It's dedicated to the memory of General Naustation's daughter, killed in the 1965 coup by bullets meant for him. There's a library, minitheater, small cars and trains, and miniature roads with traffic signs.

Bandung Zoo

At the zoo (Kebun Binatang), discover a wide variety of unusual bird species from all over Indonesia and Southeast Asia, the usual Komodo dragons, and other protected species. Crowded on holidays and Sundays. Admission Rp600.

ACCOMMODATIONS

Budget

In the budget area, the newest and cleanest choice is **Yossie Homestay,** Jl. Kebon Jati 53, tel. (022) 420-5453, fax 420-9758, owned by Josep and his American wife. Rooms in immaculate condition cost Rp9000-12,000; dorm beds just Rp4000. Yosep also runs tours to nearby volcanos, hot springs, and silk weaving villages, and sends direct minibuses to Pangandaran. Live folk music in the evenings.

Sakadarna, Jl. Kebon Jati 50/7B, now has a second branch: **Sakadarna International Travelers Homestay,** tel. 420-2811, Jl. Kebon Jati 34, which includes a restaurant. Clean; dorm Rp4000 and rooms from Rp10,000-12,000. The friendly owners offer tours of the surrounding area (Lembang, Tangkuban, Ciater, Dago), can arrange direct minibuses to Pangandaran, and dispense free brochures with maps and useful information.

A favorite of Javanese and Western couples is **Hotel Melati II,** Jl. Kebon Jati 27, tel. 420-6409, Rp25,000-40,000. All rooms include private bath and complimentary breakfast. Good value. **Hotel Sahara,** Jl. Oto Iskandardinata 3, tel. 420-1684, is located across from the governor's residence, only a five-minute walk from the railroad station. Go over the pedestrian overpass, then walk straight along the street perpendicular to the tracks; it's at the end of the street on your right. Comfortable rooms with verandas start at Rp25,000.

A final choice near the train station is the old Dutch art-deco **Hotel Surabaya,** tel. 436-791 with economy rooms Rp10,000-18,000, standards Rp12,000-20,000, and elaborately furnished (period beds, antiques) rooms in the rear from Rp45,000. An old world experience.

Moderate

Hotel Melati is probably the best of the moderate hotels near the train station. **Hotel Guntur,** tel. (022) 50763, is less conveniently located, but rooms are clean and reasonably priced at Rp37,000-45,000.

Trio Hotel, tel. 615-055, may be situated near the redlight district, but it's a spotless place with rooms for Rp70,000-105,000. Actually a great location: lively at all hours plus dozens of nearby *warung, durian* stalls, nightclubs, and excellent Chinese restaurants.

The final moderate choice, **Hotel Braga,** tel. 420-4685, is an old Dutch hotel with large but dirty rooms at Rp35,000-60,000. A new coat of paint and new furnishings would make this a great place in a good location. The owners don't have a clue what a gold mine this hotel could be with some work.

Luxury

Plentiful, pleasant, with all the modern conveniences, **Hotel Perdana Wisata,** tel. (022) 438-238, fax 432-818, is a brand new deluxe hotel which claims to be managed by the Holiday Inn group. Strange location on a busy street, but rooms are superb at Rp147,000-210,000. Pool and Japanese restaurant.

On Jl. Asia-Afrika is the venerable art deco classic **Savoy Homann Hotel,** tel. 432-244, fax 436-187, with large rooms off a lovely inner garden; rooms cost Rp210,000-357,000. Though the hotel is a recognized architectural masterpiece and retains a distinct bygone charm, the place seems disorganized and rooms badly need upgrading. The Garuda/Merpati office is right across the street.

Hotel Panghegar, Jl. Merdeka 2, tel. 432-286, fax 431-583, is an older three-star hotel with executive rooms for Rp130,000-210,000. Despite the general decline of this once luxurious hotel, it remains popular with budget tour groups and Indonesian business travelers. From the hotel's revolving restaurant—Indonesia's first—you can watch beautiful equatorial sunsets over the city.

Bandung's best five-star hotel is the superbly managed **Grand Preanger Hotel,** tel. 431-631, fax 430-034, with a renovated art deco wing and 150 rooms in the new tower, plus pool and nightclub with rockin' Filipino bands. Rooms cost Rp315,000-462,000, or try the Garuda Suite for Rp4.2 million. One of the best hotels on Java.

FOOD

Do you salivate over luscious avocados and corn on the cob? Do you crave strawberries, blackberries, and other temperate treats? Well, due to the higher elevation, nearly every kind of fruit and vegetable is not only grown in Bandung but available in abundance. What's more, they're very flavorful and cost next to nothing.

Street Food

Many *warung* and night markets downtown serve a Bandung specialty, tasty *soto ayam.* Clusters of *warung* are found all over the city, specializing in their own dishes. Many are set up at night on Jl. Gardu Jati, in Bandung's old Chinatown, and inside Ekonomi Supermarket. Low-priced food, as always, can also be found around the railroad station.

Some of the best coffee in Bandung is served just opposite the tourist office in a *warung* called **Bejo.** Downstairs in the same building is **PA Edeng**'s modest *warung,* serving high-quality, cheap Sundanese meals.

Opposite Hotel Guntur, Jl. Oto Iskandardinata, right around the corner from Penginapan Malabar, is a whole alleyway (Gang Kebun Karet) full of small, cheap *warung.* For noodle dishes, the *gang* next to the Dian Cinema is the place. Fantastic *bakso tahu* (tofu and fishball soup, an Asian standby) is available at several *warung* on Jl. Dalem Kaum just west of the *alun-alun.*

The **PLN Complex** sells delicious *martabak* and side dishes; for around Rp2000 you can eat your fill. A final recommendation is **Kardjan Sate** across the railroad tracks—the best *sate* in Bandung.

Restaurants

Bakmie Raos, Jl. Kepjaksaan 19, is a good *bakmie* noodle place; Rp850 for a bowl. Noodles, *nasi goreng,* and *pangsit* dishes are served, all with a Chinese accent. Always crowded, with a convivial *kampung* atmosphere.

Jaya Bailu, Jl. Alkateri 2 across from the Asia-Afrika Plaza Building, has good cheap food—

Rp1250 for a full meal. The curbside carry-out restaurant **San Francisco** makes the best sweet *martabak*; people line up out to the parking lot. **Koja Sate House**, Jl. Pasir Koja 1, and **Pakarjan**, Jl. Pasirkali, are both outstanding.

Sate Ponorogo, Jl. Jen. Gatot Subroto, specializes in *sate* served in an open-air garden atmosphere. Tasty *sate* in the restaurants in front of the *stasiun kereta api* (train station); try **Hudori.**

Pak M. Uju, Jl. Dewi Sartika 7A (near the *alun-alun*), and the marvelous **Ponyo**, Jl. Profesor Eyckman, are traditional Sundanese restaurants with sound reputations. At the Ponyo, you sit on cushions on the floor and are served fish plucked from a pool. **Rumah Gudeg Tera**, at Jl. Tera 4, near the railroad tracks, is a small Javanese restaurant. Stick to the *gudeg* and *pecel* dishes; eat really well here for under Rp1000. The best Javanese restaurant is **Handayani**, Jl. Sukajadi.

At the snake restaurant **Naya**, Jl. Pasteur, dine on cobra, or python fried in butter, steamed, or in soup (Rp5000), also fresh snake blood.

Chinese

The best Chinese restaurants and open *warung* are found along Jl. Gard Jati. The **Sahabat** and **Phoenix Restaurant**, around the corner, are the best in the neighborhood.

The Rose Flower, Jl. Jen. A. Yani 32, is only 150 meters from Jl. Asia-Afrika. Outstanding food—sample the asparagus and cream soup. **Queen**, Jl. Dalam Kaum 53-A, is crowded on Saturday nights; moderate prices. **Tjoen Kie**, Jl. Jen. Sudirman 46, is a well-known Cantonese restaurant in a colorful section of town. **Mandarin Restaurant** on Jl. Pasankali is a new spot recommended by locals.

Western Food

Because of its great popularity with Europeans, Bandung developed a number of first-class bakeries, some in business for decades.

Jalan Braga, the main shopping street, is the place for sidewalk cafes, French pastries, marzipan, and ice cream. Try the popular **French Bakery** (no. 18): good coffee. Another dessert place, popular with Westerners, is the **Braga Permai**, Jl. Braga (open 0900-2400), for fresh strawberries, strawberry pancakes with whipped cream, or ice cream.

Take a Dago-bound minibus to **Tizi's**, Jl. Dago, for such Western delights as T-bone steaks (fantastic), delicious breads, cookies, and pastries.

At **Rasa's**, Jl. Tamblong 15, enjoy all kinds of expensive baked goods—waffles, eclairs, chocolate cake, superb ice cream, 30 different kinds of cookies, plus everything from a fruit pancake to an American hot dog and Indonesian-style meals. The **Steak Rasa**, Jl. Tamblong 36, is a small shop famous for its desserts, especially puddings; good steaks

Local Delicacies

These include *sate, rujak, lotek, bajigur* (coconut juice, the best on Jl. Supratman near RRI), and *bandrek* (ginger drink). *Oncom* is fried beancake, peanuts, and yeast; Rp300 for a small. *Peuyeum* is made of cassava with yeast added (a little sour); buy it at any market for Rp500 per kilo—more than enough for two. Another Sundanese favorite is *lalap-lalapan*, a mixture of veggies with a gooey soy sauce on top known only in Bandung. Also try *roti bakar*, a sort of Indonesian submarine sandwich filled with whatever's available. In the markets Bogor papayas sell for around Rp1000. Order luscious *comro* sweets; they'll laugh when you ask for them because *comro's* usually for kids.

The best yogurt place is **Yoghurt Cisangkuy**, Jl. Cisangkuy (eight-minute walk from *kantor gubernur*), serving Lychee Special Yogurt Juice (Rp900), fresh fruit, and yogurt desserts. This outdoor cafe is also a good place to meet students.

ENTERTAINMENT

By virtue of its many schools, rich artistic traditions, and pride of place as the capital of Sundanese culture, Bandung since the 1920s has been considered a cultural hub—"the Yogyakarta of the Sundanese." There's also plenty of sleaze.

Discos

Bandung's large student population keeps a half dozen discos filled to capacity on most nights.

Studio East Disco, Jl. Cipaganti, is the old favorite and considered one of the largest discos in Southeast Asia. **L.A. Disco** on Jl. Asia-Afrika is well located in a musty old shopping complex. Wednesday is gay night.

Maraba Disco on Jl. Suniaraja is a low-class joint favored by assorted forms of Sundanese night creatures. The official redlight district is just off Jl. Saritem, south of the Hotel Surabaya in the old Chinatown. Great cafes and restaurants, but the small brothels hidden in the alleyways are rather sad.

Pubs

Local expats hang out at the **Laga Pub** on Jl. Terusan Pasteur; clean, comfortable, with live music most nights. You'll think you're in England. **O'Hara Tavern** in the Hotel Perdana Wisata is also popular with local Westerners. Another possibility is the **Lingga Pub** in northern Bandung; reggae music on Saturday nights. Although quite a distance from downtown Bandung, it's worth the hassle.

Jaipongan Dance

Jaipongan is a local dance tradition which some consider a traditional art form; others call it an excuse for prostitution in a *sarung*. Basically, it's rent-a-dance with traditionally dressed hostesses. An inexpensive way to enjoy an evening and learn something about contempoary Indonesian lifestyles. Clubs are scattered around town and tend to open and close with the seasons. The tourist office can make recommendations.

One spot is **Purwa Setra**, Jl. Oto Iskandardinata 541A, where the hostesses dance in Sundanese-Jaiping-style and the audience is asked to join in. Open 2100-2400 every night; entrance fee Rp2000 plus Rp1000 per dance. Also check the hall called **Fajar Parahiyangan** on Jl. Dalem Kaum beside the river and department store.

Hostesses will sit and chat for Rp10,000 per hour or dance for Rp1000. Low class; several beers will help.

Banci

Along Jl. Sumatra, you can view female impersonators called *banci*. These ultra-glamorous "females," inhabiting the bodies of males, will sometimes approach male travelers on the street and ask if they'd like to "play." Many speak Dutch and English.

Bandung has an international reputation in gay circles. Gay hustlers sometimes approach people in the downtown area, basically cruising for money.

Ram Fighting

These exciting spectacles are local, low-level competitions which lead to championship matches held annually on the first Sunday after 17 August (Independence Day), when hundreds of rams are brought to the Bandung area to battle for "the cup." The sport is closely tied in with breeders' efforts to upgrade the quality of their rams. Champion rams, which can weigh up to 60 kg and are adorned with names like "Bima" and "Si Kilat" ("Sir Lightning"), are quick to attack and cunning in evasion. A contest usually consists of around 50 ferocious head-on collisions. The Sundanese are orthodox Muslims and forbidden to gamble. Thus no money changes hands at these matches; they're staged purely for the pleasure of handlers and breeders.

Ram fights are held far less frequently than in the past. Fights are occasionally scheduled at Aki Bohon's house in Cilimus on Jl. Cibuntu, or in the town of Cisuara en route to Lembang. Check with the tourist office or the budget guesthouses near the train station.

Sir Lightning, a veteran combatant in the ram fighting amidst the Bandung hills

DIANA LASICH HARPER

THE PERFORMING ARTS

SMKI And ASTI

The Bandung **Music Conservatory** (Konservatori Karawitan), Jl. Buah Batu 212, consists of two parts: ASTI (academic, professional level), and SMKI (for high school students). Ask at the Tourist Information Office, tel. (022) 420-6644, on the *alun-alun* about performances. Take a *bemo* from the Kebun Kelapa bus station or a bus from Perapatan Lima, east of the *alun-alun* on Jl. Asia-Afrika.

ASTI, the Institute of Fine Arts, often stages performances by its students. Visit any time to see students practice and to ask the lecturers any specific questions.

Rumentang Siang

This theater hall, also called **Gedung Kesenian,** is on Jl. Baranang Siang 1 (Pasar Kosambi area); take a city bus toward Cicaheum. Theater, music, or dances are held every Friday night and sometimes on other nights—*calung* dance-dramas, special film presentations, *wayang orang,* Western theater productions, ballet, drama, *reyog,* even Sundanese country music (*musik keroncang*). Entrance Rp1500.

West Java is the home of *wayang golek,* which the Sundanese prefer over shadow play. Since no curtain separates the puppets from the spectators, you can enjoy the puppets as both characters in a story and as sculptural creations. The shows are attended mostly by the Sundanese themselves and last all night (1830-0400). Other performance art takes place 2000-2300. Check with the tourist office.

Yayasan Pusat Kebudayaan (YPK)

Now called **Restaurant Sindang Reret** (Jl. Naripan 7), with shorter performances geared to tourists and local Sundanese. Free admission but you'll need to purchase a modest dinner. *Wayang golek* performances take place here every Saturday. Other entertainment, most often on weeknights, might include *wayang orang* or *gamelan.*

Other Venues

Sundanese cultural performances are staged every Wednesday night at 1900 at the **Pasundan Restaurant** in Hotel Panghegar. Rp2100 buys a great buffet plus traditional music and dance, *wayang golek, debus* magicians, and *angklung.* Sit on the floor for the best view.

Also call **Pak Ujo's,** Jl. Padasuka 118 (tel. 71714), in the middle of a genuine Javanese *kampung* on the outer fringe of Bandung on Cicaheum, for tourist performances of Saung Angklung Padasuka. First ask at the tourist office. Pay Rp8000, or go down a small *gang* and watch over the fence with the neighborhood kids for free. Very popular with the Dutch; it's really a sight: high-spirited Dutch women kicking up their heels with whirling Indonesian children dressed in traditional Javanese attire.

SHOPPING AND CRAFTS

Bandung shops are filled with the products of this far-flung archipelago as well as imported goods—souvenirs abound. West Java accounts for 60% of Indonesia's commercial textile production, mostly concentrated in Bandung. For back street exploring, cruise Pasar Baru and the streets around Jl. ABC (electronics), Jl. Oto Iskandardinata (gold shops), and Kosambi Blok (everything). Pasar Jatayu, a flea market on Jl. Arjuna behind the motorbike parts shop, is a great place to find antiques and secondhand junk.

Shops And Workshops

Shops in the *pasar* are normally open until 2100; others are open 0830-1400 and 1700-2030. Except for those in the markets, shops are closed on Sundays and public holidays. The nearest Bandung gets to Paris is Jl. Braga, the city's Champs-Elysées. Many shops are also found on Jl. Asia-Afrika.

Recommended shops: **Aneka Lukisan,** Jl. Cihampelas 96, for paintings, textiles, and *batik*; **Batik Semar Solo,** Jl. Dalam Kaum 40, for *suling* and ceramics; **Gang Umar 2,** for *suling*, puppetry, and ceramics; **Lumayan,** Jl. Cicendo 5, for paintings, lacework, and basketry; **Mayang Sari,** Gang Madurasa 275, for *gamelan* instruments.

Cupu Manik on Gang Haji Umar (off Jl. Kebon Kawung), only 500 meters from the Sakadarna Losmen, is a small *wayang golek* factory. **Pak Ruhiyat,** on Jl. Pangarang (behind no. 22), is another fine *wayang golek* craftsman working out of his home. **Sarinah,** Jl. Braga 10, tel. (022) 52798, sells new *wayang golek* at very good prices (Rp2200-6875).

Try **Pritico,** Jl. Braga 72, for *batik* and paintings; **Saung Angklung,** Jl. Padasuka 118, for *wayang* and *angklung*; **Sin Sin,** Jl. Braga, for antiques. **The Leather Palace,** Jl. Braga 67, sells well-made, inexpensive shoes and other leather goods. For snakeskin articles, visit **Banowati,** Jl. Geger Kalong Hilir.

Ceramics

The government-sponsored **Ceramics Research Institute** (Balai Penelitian Keramik), Jl. Jen. A. Yani 392 near Pasar Cicadas, is concerned with each facet of the operation of turning clay into practical, beautiful objects. The institute turns out everything from small, coarsely finished eggcup-size plant pots and miniature ornamental horses to exquisite copies of classic Chinese vases.

The **Bandung Institute of Technology** is also known for its ceramic products, notably convincing copies of Chinese porcelain, ornamental pots, and figurines. On Jl. Sukapura in Kiara Condong, one km from Balai Penelitian Keramik, is a Kasongan-type ceramics center selling lampshades, wall decorations, and the like; located in an alleyway. Farther afield, **Plered** is an active traditional ceramics center southwest of Purwakarta (70 km northeast of Bandung), and the site of an experimental station of the Bandung Ceramics Research Institute.

Textiles, Plaiting, Bamboo

Both modern and traditional *batik* designs in cotton, silk, and synthetic fabrics are widely available in Bandung. At the **Textile Research Institute,** Jl. Jen. A. Yani, watch *kapok* processing and weaving. Free tours are offered, particularly interesting for children. Cane, bamboo, and rattan handicrafts and furniture from West Java are reputedly some of Indonesia's best. Traditional woven crafts are available in the excellent **Craftworks Shop** on Jl. Tirtaywasa, about a three-km walk from the main *alun-alun*—very fine quality and reasonable prices.

One of the renowned products of the province is the bamboo *angklung*. Each one, cut from different lengths of bamboo, produces a different tone when shaken. Mini "souvenir" sizes of this

instrument are available in almost every souvenir shop or from vendors on the street. You can buy other works of bamboo art, such as sailing ships and home furnishings, from **Gallery 16,** Jl. Raya Cibeureum 16.

Painting And Sculpture

Bandung is home to many commercial landscape painters; now and then the city hosts art fairs. Local painters use every conceivable media, which gives the art fancier a wide choice—from world-class works of recognized masters to *batik*-painting and mass-produced schlock. A number of shops and art galleries deal exclusively in painting, styles mostly leaning toward the Western genres. For high quality, visit **Decenta,** Jl. Dipatjukur 99 (expensive, ITB's best artists); **Tatarah's,** Jl. Braga 51C; and **Naini's Fine Arts,** Jl. Tamblong 26. Check both streets for paintings, graphic arts, reliefs, and sculptures. Vendors will also set up paintings and sculptures on the sidewalks and near the *kantor pos.*

SERVICES AND INFORMATION

Shop around for the best exchange rate; hit first **Bank Negara Indonesia 1946** and **Bank Dagang Negara** on Jl. Asia-Afrika.

The main **Immigration Office** is located on Jl. Suci. The **Dutch Consulate** is in the Panin Bank building, third floor, Jl. Asia-Afrika 166-170, tel. (022) 439-482.

There are 12 hospitals in Bandung. An outstanding one is the **Seventh-Day Adventists Hospital,** Jl. Cihampelas 135, tel. 82091, with English-speaking missionary staff. Bandung's **Boromius Hospital,** Jl. Ir. H. Juanda 80, tel. 81011, has a very fine outpatient clinic.

The Bandung telephone city code is 022.

Tourist Information

The **Bandung Tourist Information Office** is located in the northeast corner of the *alun-alun*; open daily 0900-1700. Staffed for the most part by well-informed volunteers who hand out basic city maps and provide sound verbal information on cultural happenings. They also dispense advice on other points of interest on Java and Bali and make hotel and train reservations.

TRANSPORTATION

Getting There

Although the airport lies only four km from town in the northwest of the city, taxi drivers want Rp8000 to take you into town. Instead, just walk out the gate, turn right, and walk down to the main road and take a *microlet* for Rp300.

Buses from Jakarta and Bogor usually stop at Bandung's Kebun Kelapa Bus Station. Take one of the yellow minibuses marked Karang Setra to Jl. Kebon Jati, where you'll find the budget hotels near the train station. Too far to walk with a heavy pack. Buses arriving from the east end up at Cicaheum bus station, way off in far, far east Bandung. To reach the *losmen* near the train station, take Damri bus 1 past the *alun-alun* and get off at Jl. Dulatip. Express buses often blaze right past Bandung, with only a brief pause at Cicaheum. Ask to be dropped on the main highway where *angkutan kota* head north to the town square.

From Bogor the bus costs Rp2000 and takes four hours (129 km). The bus often drops you off outside town on the main highway; some buses go to the Kebun Kelapa bus terminal. You can also take a minibus from Bogor to Bandung for around Rp1500. By Patas bus from Rambutan bus terminal it costs Rp4500 and takes five hours.

Bandung is also served by air (Garuda, Merpati, and Bouraq) from Jakarta on a 30-minute flight; planes land at Husen Sastranegara Airport. Garuda and Sempati also connect Bandung and Yogyakarta by air; one flight daily.

From Jakarta the Parahiyangan (first class) runs Rp25,000, 3.5 hours, but some *ekonomi* trains cost as little as Rp6000 third class, four hours. After arrival at the train station, walk to the right (south) to reach the *losmen* across the tracks. Three trains serve Yogyakarta and Bandung daily and take about six hours. Air conditioned *bis malam* costs Rp10,000 (12 hours, 486 km).

A shared taxi from Jakarta, costs Rp7500, takes only four hours, and goes straight to your hotel. Sari Harum Travel and Luta Travel in Pangandaran run daily minibuses direct to the hotel of your choice. Or take a regular bus from Pangandaran to Banjar, then transfer to another bus headed for Bandung.

Getting Around

Public transport is complicated, so always ask around first. The only major east-west connecting street (Jl. Asia-Afrika) is at the southern end of the city.

Angkutan kota carry passengers within the city and to Lembang and Dago, the fare dependent on distance. Use the term *angkutan kota* rather than *bemo*. There are no *bemo* in Bandung, or Java for that matter. Inquiring after *bemo* will often bring but quizzical stares.

Bandung **taxis** are metered and quite cheap.

Tour Guides

Local tours can be arranged through the large Indonesian operators, but more personalized service is available from local guesthouses such as **Yossie's** and **Sakadarna.** Several possible one-day tours: north to Tangkuban Crater and surrounding areas, southeast to Gunung Papandayan and Garut, or southwest to Cibuni Hot Springs and the 8th century Hindu temple in Kawah Putih. Tours cost Rp20,000-40,000 depending on the number of participants.

Other local guides include **Soehardhie Yogantara** (Yoga for short) or **Mamun Rustina** at the tourist office. Very flexible, willing to make arrangements to suit individual needs. Yoga, who speaks excellent English, takes tourists on overnight trips to rustic villages, staying in traditional houses to view Sundanese circumcision ceremonies, weddings, and the like.

Getting Away

Garuda and Merpati fly daily to Jakarta, Yogyakarta, Surabaya, and Denpasar. Airline offices include: **Bouraq,** Grand Preanger Hotel, Jl. Asia-Afrika 81, tel. (022) 431-631 or 437-896; **Merpati,** Jl. Veteran 46, tel. 437-893 or 439-742; **Garuda,** Jl. Asia-Afrika 73, tel. 51497 or 56986.

At least seven daily express trains run to Jakarta. Trains depart hourly and take three or four hours to reach Jakarta. Take the train to Yogyakarta rather than endure 18 miserable hours on the bus. Three trains depart daily. The most convenient are the 0730 Pajajaran, which arrives in Yogyakarta at 1515, and the 1730 Mutiara, which arrives in the early morning. Make reservations the day before. The train passes through a number of stations, such as Kutoardjo, where you can hop off for a quick bite.

Bandung has two bus terminals: Cicaheum for buses going east and Kebun Kelapa for buses heading west. Kebun Kelapa station is quite central, but Cicaheum station is 45 minutes (Rp350) by *ankut* out of town. Take Damri bus 1 direct to Cicaheum from in front of Yossie's Homestay or the Panghegar Hotel.

Bis malam companies offer the best long-distance services; to get good seats, book the day before. The best companies for Yogyakarta are **Bandung Express,** Jl. Dr. Cipto 5; **Muncul,** Jl. Cendana; **Yogya Express,** Jl. Sunda 54, tel. 52507, not far from the intersection with Jl. Asia-Afrika; **Apollo Express,** Jl. Lengkong Besar; and **Maju Makmur,** Jl. Martadinata, tel. 58854.

Most *bis malam* leave at around 1900, arriving in Yogyakarta at around 0600. The charge is about Rp16,000, with a/c and snacks.

To Jakarta buses leave all day from the bus offices, arriving at Jakarta's Rambutan station. Buses take 3.5 hours (129 km) to reach Bogor; just going over the beautiful Puncak Pass makes this trip worthwhile, though buses take a different, less crowded route on weekends. Bandung's Terminal Bis Cicaheum runs buses every hour to Banjar, four to five hours. Continue by bus or minibus down to Pangandaran. Most travelers take the daily direct minibus from Sari Haruna Travel. Tickets are sold at Yossie's and Sakadarna.

VICINITY OF BANDUNG

JUANDA PARK

The northern third of Bandung lies on the slopes of a series of hills rising to the volcano Tangkuban Prahu. Flag down a northbound *oplet* on Jl. Merdeka or simply hop on a minibus from the railroad station, telling the driver you want to get off at the park. The park (Rp400 entrance) is built on a grassy bluff surrounded by lawns, pathways, and wooden benches. You can view the whole city from here—great sunsets, and at night a marvelous festival of lights.

It's a fantastic five-km walk from Juanda Park to Maribaya on a well-beaten road—incredibly busy on Sundays with students, a large part of its charm. Just before reaching the thunderous 25-meter-high falls on the Cikapundung River near Maribaya you'll be hit up for another Rp400. At the bottom are tunnels carved out by the Japanese during WW II for ammunition storage; one goes right through the hill. Fun to hear kids hollering and singing in the caves. A very pretty area.

MARIBAYA

A small, overcrowded park with dirty pools and hot springs in a steep walled valley five km east of Lembang. Bathe in colored volcanic water said to contain natural healing agents. Although Maribaya itself is too commercialized to be in-

spiring, there are some magnificent waterfalls and tall evergreens in the area. A restaurant serves European, Chinese, and Indonesian meals. Small refreshment *warung* sell snacks.

To get to Maribaya, take a minibus from Lembang or Tangkuban Prahu; from Juanda Park it's a two-hour (five-km) walk with lovely views and friendly locals. Another way to walk to Maribaya is from a parking area almost four km from the Tangkuban Prahu crossroads, just before the road descends steeply into the valley. Start on the track near the small restaurant. The right-hand trail follows the ridge to Lembang; the left-hand trail rises to the hilltop above Maribaya. At the point where the road takes a sharp right turn, walk directly into the pine trees towering 300 meters above a gorge with jagged cliffs—one of the best sights around Bandung.

LEMBANG

A cool upland (elevation 1,400 meters) village 16 km north of Bandung, nestled in the wooded lower slopes of Tangkuban Prahu volcano. An agricultural community, Lembang has been a favorite tourist destination since the time of the Dutch. The houses and villas are built in the style of a different era, with masses of flowers and neatly tended gardens strangely at odds with the tropical landscape. The surrounding mist-shrouded peaks, lush pastureland, and rolling lower hills heavy with fruit and vegetables make sections of this mountain town a place of peace and beauty. Reach Lembang from Ledeng by boarding a minibus from in front of Bandung's train station; Rp450, 45 minutes.

Accommodations And Food
The Grand Hotel, Jl. Raya 228, tel. (022) 82393, exudes old colonial charm, despite heavyhanded restoration in the early 1990s. Opened for business in 1926, a number of different classes of rooms are spread out inside a giant shaded yard. Popular with Dutch tour groups. In the evenings, full-course *rijstaffel* is available for Rp7500. With bar, restaurant, pool, and tennis courts.

The newest hotel is the **Yehezkiel,** tel. 286-199, fax 286-677, with clean rooms for Rp30,000-45,000. Cheaper *losmen* and *penginapan* lie down the mountain between Lembang and Ledeng.

Shopping
The fruit market is on Jl. Raya Lembang in the town center, where vendors sell a wondrous variety of produce seven days a week. Try mouth-watering corn on the cob (*jagung bakar*), refreshing *bajigur,* and the best avocados. Sometimes at night a small circus with dancing dogs entertains the market. Another outlet for vegetables is the nunnery, down a small track

VICINITY OF BANDUNG

TO JAKARTA AND PURWAKARTA

TANGKUBAN PRAHU (2076 m)

TO SUBANG

CIATER ESTATE

DOMAS CRATER

CIATER HOTSPRINGS

GATE

4 km.

8 km.

5 km.

LEMBANG   JAYAGIRI   MARIBAYA

TO CIREBON

WATERFALL

QUININE ESTATE

WATERFALL
1 km.

JAPANESE CAVE

JUANDA PARK

DAGO

SUMEDANG

TO JAKARTA AND BOGOR

4 km.

CIMAHI

BANDUNG

CITARUM

CATARACTS

TO TASIKMALAYA

CICALENGKA

NAGREK

SOREANG

MAJALAYA

LAKE CANGKUANG

LELES

BANJARAN

PASEH

NOT TO SCALE

KAMOJANG

TAROGONG

BLACKSMITH VILLAGE

PACFT

G. GUNTUR (2244 m)

CIPANAS

GARUT   G. GALUNGGUNG (2241 m)

CIWEDY

KAMPUNG NAGA

RANCABALI

KAWAH PUTIH HOT SPRINGS

G. PAPANDAYAN (2622 m)

CISURUPAN (G. CIKURAI)

SITU PATENGGANG

PANGALENGAN

MALABAR SANTOSA

G. CIKURAI (2841 m) TASIKMALAYA

TO

CIBUNI HOT SPRINGS

TO PAMEUNGPEUK

© MOON PUBLICATIONS, INC.

almost opposite the entrance to the Grand Hotel; walk in at the Karmel Gereja Katolik sign. For crafts, the Lembang Art Shop (Jl. Raya 264) sells long flutes, small *wayang golek,* and handmade baskets. At the *kampung* north of Lembang ask directions to the statue of Dr. Junghun, who introduced the cinchona tree, the bark of which is used to make quinine.

TANGKUBAN PRAHU

This smoldering 2,081-meter-high volcano, distinguished by its low, flat top, lies 13 km north of Lembang. Tangkuban Prahu's crater—actually 10 craters—is the remnant of a gigantic collapsed volcano which also formed the huge depression between it and the jagged peak of Gunung Burangrang to the west. Tangkuban Prahu last erupted in 1969, filling the area with black clouds, ash, and mudflows.

The name Tangkuban Prahu stems from a Sundanese legend. Queen Dayang quarreled with her son, Prince Sangkuriang, and he left the palace. Years passed, and the prince prospered. One day he met and fell in love with a beautiful woman—Queen Dayang, of course—who'd lost none of her youth and beauty. Discovering in horror that her lover was her son, she promised to marry him if, between sunrise and sunset, he could dam the Citarum River so the Bandung Plateau would become a lake. Sangkuriang, with the assistance of the gods, managed the herculean task, flooding the whole plateau. But his mother caused the waters to quickly subside, overturning her son's canoe and drowning him. She then took her own life. To this day the volcano, in the shape of an overturned boat (Tangkuban Prahu), bears this name to commemorate this agonizing oedipal tragedy.

The lake is now the city of Bandung.

The Craters
Go early in the morning before the clouds roll in. Entrance Rp250. This highly commercialized volcano is visited by tourists from all over the world—it's one of the few live volcanos in Indonesia you can reach by car. As soon as you arrive the vendors begin to descend. The weather is cold until you go down into the steaming craters.

The main and most accessible crater, Kawah Ratu ("Queen's Crater") is not so active now: it looks like a big muddy gray pancake. Other areas farther down are still going strong. You have to walk for about 20 minutes around the edge of the first crater before the others come into view. Descend into the depths and walk amidst sulphur fumes, thick yellow crust, and bubbling mud. Don't try to go to the very bottom of the craters: several years ago three young boys died doing so.

Plan on a three- to four-hour rugged hike for thorough exploration. Wear sturdy shoes and take a sweater. Guides want Rp5000 to accompany you down into the craters, but you can do it yourself quite easily; it's not very dangerous if you watch your step.

Getting There
Take a Subang-bound minibus from the Lembang market, Rp600 (nine km) to the volcano turnoff. From the entrance gate, it's four km uphill through an exotic wood to the top; walk or hitch another minibus. On weekends minibuses from the Lembang market run straight up to the crater. After hiking around the crater rim, follow the rocky trail downhill past smoking calderas to the main road, where you can flag down a minibus back to Bandung.

CIATER TEA ESTATE

From the gate at the base of the Tangkuban Prahu, take a minibus (Rp400) to the former British tea factory; ask for *pabrik teh.* Travel along a road through rice fields, which gradually give way to forested terrain. As you climb higher, take in glorious views of distant peaks and densely forested valleys. Then, at about 1,000 meters, everything suddenly turns dark green. Across hills rolling in all directions, like an enormous petrified ocean, undulate tens of thousands of healthy tea bushes in closely packed rows. The total planted area of the estate is 757 hectares; another 1,633 hectares is used for other purposes and set aside as reserve land. Most of the plantation lies on a single massive lava flow from Tangkuban Prahu, generating some of the highest yields of tea on Java. The pickers—smiling Sundanese girls in bright dresses and wide sunhats—gingerly hoist loaded wicker baskets and sacks.

Proceed to the factory and take in the magnificent vista from the lookout tower, with clouds scudding below the enormous plantation; then walk through the blackened gateposts and request a tour. Visitors may taste samples and purchase packets of No. 1 Export Blend.

SUMEDANG

A pleasant highland town 45 km northeast of Bandung as yet unspoiled by commercialization. At 450 meters above sea level, the temperature is pleasant year-round. Opportunities abound for hiking and camping, and the mostly ethnic Sundanese are known for their friendliness; people will invite you to their homes to get to know you.

History
The kingdom of Sumedang was founded in 1578 and became a Dutch regency in the early 1700s. Dutch Governor-General Daendels ordered the local people to construct a road, which can still be seen between Bandung and Sumedang near Cadas Pangeran. Many people died from hunger and disease, breaking up rocks for this road. Taking pity on his people, the regent, Pangeran Kornel, informed Daendels he didn't wish to sacrifice any more of his subjects, telling Daendels to use his own army to build the road. Daendels agreed, and to this day Pangeran Kornel is revered as a symbol of courage for standing up for his people against the Dutch.

Sights
Sumedang Museum contains many artifacts of Sundanese culture: crowns, *kris,* musical intruments. Western visitors are admitted daily except Friday 0800-1200. Northwest of town lie the remains of a fort and bunker built by the Dutch, the cannons aimed at the regent's mansion.

A cemetery, **Gunung Puyuh,** south of the *alun-alun,* contains the remains of Sumedang nobles, as well as the grave of Indonesian hero Cut Nyak Dhien, an Acehnese guerrilla banished here. Three ancient graves lie to the east of town; locals visit them during the month of Mualud to make offerings and ask for blessings. This area is also popular with young people, especially on moonlit nights. Each Octo-

ber, a *kuda renggong* (horse-dance festival) is held. Check at the tourism office (Jl. Pangeran Suriaatmadja 6) for dates.

Recreation
The hilly area around Sumedang is good for hiking and camping. To make advance plans, contact **Dadi Kjukardi,** Mountain and Jungle Rover Association, Jl. Kebon Kol 11, Sumedang 45311, West Java. You can visit two tea plantations by car or on foot. Sumedang has two swimming pools: one six km from town on the main Bandung-Sumedang road, the other at the foot of Gunung Tampomas. Also near Gunung Tampomas are two hot springs.

Practicalities
There are *losmen* in the Rp5000-20,000 range along Jl. Pangeran Geusan Ulun and Jl. Mayor Abdurahman. **Penginapan Kencana,** on Jl. Pangeran Kornel near the *alun-alun,* charges Rp16,000-25,000 d.

Sumedang is also known as Kota Tahu ("Tofu Town"). Try tofu with *lontong* and chili sauce; tofu vendors abound. Along the main road are restaurants specializing in Sundanese and Chinese food. For good *bakso* try **MM** or **Mirasa,** both on Jl. Mayor Abdurahman, or **Ahaw** in the market block; Rp1000-1500 per bowl.

Sumedang is a 1.5-hour, Rp700 bus ride from Bandung, or take a minibus for Rp1000. From Cirebon the bus is Rp1300, three hours.

PATENGGANG LAKE AND KAWAH PUTIH HOT SPRINGS

South of Ciwedy is this high (1,600 meter) circular mountain lake surrounded by forests and tea plantations and shrouded in swirling mists. With its nearby steam craters and hot springs, the area is quiet, blessed with cool gentle breezes and attractive landscapes. Visitors can fish, rent boats, and swim, though the water is cold. Hire a rowboat out to the island in the middle; see the old Buddha statue beneath the cliff. The lake tends to get crowded on Sundays with domestic tourists, but it's easy to get away on the many trails in the vicinity. Keep a lookout for the Monster of Patenggang Lake, which resembles a giant black fish with golden fins. Sighted intermittently since Dutch colonial times, this mysterious creature only appears at dusk when it's quiet. Fishermen make offerings to it before going out on the lake each day.

There's one **penginapan,** only Rp6000 s with cheap meals. A **guesthouse** overlooks the lake near the parking lot. Visitors may stay here as guests of the tea estate; contact the estate manager for reservations.

Organized tours from Yossie's Homestay and Sakadarna also include **Kawah Putih Hot Springs,** Patenggang Lake, a traditional blacksmith village north of Ciwedy, and the newly opened **Cibuni Hot Springs.** A very relaxing tour.

MALABAR TEA ESTATE

A government-controlled tea plantation at the base of Gunung Malabar in the hills around Pangalengan, south of Bandung. With wide vistas over the valleys below, immaculate buildings, splendid roads, and cultivated fields, this vast estate is an unending delight to the eye. In 1896 K.A.R. Bosscha pioneered its development, and it quickly became famous for its beauty, efficiency, and top-quality tea. Bosscha's name is attached to the Bosscha Observatory, just outside Lembang, north of Bandung. The Bosscha memorial, together with the beautiful house where he once lived, is fastidiously maintained.

Guesthouse Malabar is located high on the slopes of Gunung Malabar (2,321 meters) in the middle of the Malabar Tea Plantation. Very quiet, relaxing, and very cold at night. Reservations recommended.

KAWAH PAPANDAYAN

A mighty 2,622-meter-high crater and nature reserve 65 km southeast of Bandung, towering 1,950 meters above the Garut Plateau. Papandayan forms the southernmost cone in one long row of volcanos. Originally, a large mountain here consisted of more than a cubic mile of rock, which exploded sideways across the Garut Plateau on the night of 11 August 1772. This catastrophe killed 2,957 people and completely devastated 40 villages. It left a gaping notch in the side of the crater that is still visible today. During the 1920s there was so much volcanic activity here the crater was virtually unapproachable.

Visiting this fiery crater is a more primeval experience than the over-touristed Tangkuban Prahu, and is even more otherwordly than Bromo. Accompanied by a guide, you can walk into the crater's seething heart. Numerous geysers, which spout 10 meters high and roar like jet engines, are found in the active crater. An astonishing sight.

Sights

Four big craters make up the complex; Kawah Alun-Alun alone possesses the classic volcanic shape. Kawah Papandayan is the youngest, with active fumaroles and visible indications of last century's eruptions. Kawah Mas, or Golden Crater, is so named because its most active area is a gigantic dome of sulphur. Yellowstone this isn't, but under high pressure steam hisses from its many fissures.

Wonderfully fragile crystals form around the jet holes, mud boils, streams flow with milky blue water, and pillars of mud and rocks of fantastic colors are scattered in piles. Early in the morning, before the crater is covered with mist or clouds, enjoy the view over the city of Garut; from the summit you might see the Indian Ocean.

Kawah Mas can be a very dangerous place. You could scald your feet in boiling mud, or be poisoned by gases. Mummified animals are occasionally found in gas-filled valleys, where they were overcome by sulfurous fumes—trapped in valleys of death. Take precautions. No one will stop you from entering the active area, but if you want to get really close be sure to hire a guide. Camping can be unbelievably cold; bring warm clothing, sleeping bag, and tent.

Getting There

Most visitors arrive on organized tours from guesthouses like Sakadarna or Yossie's. These tours include the summit, the 8th-century Hindu temple Candi Cangkuang, the town of Garut, local *batik* factories, and a *krupuk* producer. Tours cost about Rp30,000 and receive excellent reviews from most travelers.

Another highly recommended, often-skipped sight is **Kampung Naga,** a traditional Sundanese village near Garut; figure on an additional Rp10,000. Recent visitors report a homestay now welcomes Westerners in one of the last old-style villages in West Java. Could be something special.

GARUT

Garut, a typical Sundanese highland town, is an area of mountain lakes, volcanos, hot springs, ancient ruins, and excellent hikes, as well as a center for tobacco and citrus. Garut is literally ringed by volcanos; it was very heavily struck in 1982 by eruptions of nearby Gunung Galung-gung. The north part of the *kabupaten* consists of a plateau area of *sawah,* while the slopes to the south are crossed by 12 rivers, in a region of big tea, rubber, citrus, and apple plantations, with forests in relatively sound ecological condition.

Garut, at 717 meters above sea level, was once known all over the Far East as the "Switzerland of Java." One of Indonesia's oldest tourist regions, wealthy English and Dutch tourists vacationed here in splendid, fashionable hotels. Today, travelers usually pass right through or use Garut as a refreshment stop.

Accommodations

Stay in one of the many *penginapan* in town; there are also plenty of budding English speakers anxious to put you up. **Penginapan Gelora Intan,** Jl. Karacak 4, Rp7000 d, is very comfortable, with friendly staff; coffee and tea are served, and sometimes bananas. Other places to try include: **Hotel Nasional,** Jl. Kenanga 19; **Pribumi,** Jl. Raya 105; and **Biasa,** Jl. Cigong 57.

Cipanas

A superior option to overnighting in Garut is the mountain town of Cipanas, about six km southwest. Less traffic, better atmosphere. Accommodations include the rudimentary **Penginapan Nasional** for Rp6000, **Wisma PKPN** from Rp10,000, and the clean, popular **Tirta Merta** with rooms for Rp10,000-20,000. Or try upscale choices **Kota Indah Guesthouse** and the top-end **Tirtagangga,** with pool, tennis courts, and rooms priced from Rp21,000 to Rp84,000.

Other Towns Near Garut

Tarogong, five km north, has a hot springs and pool containing health-giving minerals. Find a wide range of accommodations and restaurants here. **Cititis,** six km north, is a waterfall with a beautiful panorama and a recreation area for hiking and camping. Also in this area is **Gunung Guntur** (2,244 meters), approachable from Leles. Guntur is a veritable witch's cauldron of magnificent scalding-hot steam geysers shooting 30 meters into the air. In 1843, an eruption poured out a massive flow of lava in the shape of a boot. The toe of the boot lies just above the hot springs resort of Cipanas. Visit the Oven, a steamy pool of gurgling gray mud, actually used for cooking. The old *penjaga* will demonstrate some tricks guaranteed to invoke disbelief.

GUNUNG GALUNGGUNG

Another looming volcano. **Kawah Talagabodas** is a large geothermal area 2,000 meters above sea level on the slopes of Gunung Galunggung, 27 km east of Garut. The turnoff to the crater is about 13 km from Garut in Wanaraja village; though the track is bad, it's accessible by automobile and definitely worth it.

This steamy sulphur lake, about 215 meters in diameter, is a pale greenish-white. Its color comes from the sulphur and alum at the bottom; the surface is disturbed only by the constant noisy bubbling of escaping gases.

Recently, villages around Galunggung have been damaged or destroyed by volcanic rocks, which go right through clay-tile roofs. Ashfalls and lava flows have afflicted the populace as well. Once-lush paddies, forests, and gardens have been pelted by rocks blown out of the crater; the whole place is buried under heavy gray ashfall. Permission might be needed to visit some areas—check with police.

The easiest way to climb the mountain is to ascend by minibus from Tasikmalaya, then hire a motorcycle taxi to the village of Sinagar. From here it's a two-hour hike to the summit. Inquire at the English school just opposite the Crown Hotel in Tasik; students will provide free guide services in exchange for informal English conversation.

SITU CANGKUANG

About 17 km north of Garut, this is one of Indonesia's oldest temples and the largest temple in West Java. According to archaeological evidence, this 9th-century *candi* predates Prambanan and Borobudur. In comparison, however, the structure is no larger than a shrine. About 40% of the building is original, the remainder carved over the course of a very successful reconstruction completed in 1976. Candi Cangkuang is the only ancient building of its type in West Java.

In 1893, a Dutch archaeologist, Vorderman, noted that Desa Cangkuang contained the ancient tomb of Arif Muhamad and a deformed stone statue. On the basis of that information, an Indonesian archaeologist in 1965 led an expedition that discovered not only the tomb and statue but also the remains of a classical Hindu temple, Candi Cangkuang. Further explorations and excavations have established that this location in the Leles Valley was for several centuries the center of a number of Neolithic, megalithic, Hindu, and Muslim cultures. The more animist aspects of Java-Hinduism still linger today: near the *candi* is a watchman's hut complete with a site for religious ceremonies.

From Leles, 15 km north of Garut, follow the small road to Desa Cangkuang. At the large grass *alun-alun* next to the *mesjid* in the center of town turn left down a good rock road and continue for about three km. Near the village of Cangkuang the hills form a peninsula jutting out into the lake; you'll see the temple among a group of trees. Cross the lake to the island on small boats or on unusual bamboo rafts with seats, or walk around on a small road for two km to reach the temple.

TASIKMALAYA

A rattan-weaving center 57 km east of Garut and 116 km southeast of Bandung on the road to Yogyakarta; Rp25,000 by bus or take a train from either city. A volcanic area, Tasikmalaya is surrounded by curative hot springs, yet there's not a tourist in sight.

Crafts

Tasikmalaya is a center for woven rattan and pandanus articles such as baskets, sandals, hats, handbags, and floormats. High-quality wares from Tasikmalaya are seen all over Java and exported around the world. Beautiful handpainted canvas and wooden umbrellas are sold cheap, but it can be very difficult finding the best-quality goods; factories export and don't bother stocking the local shops.

Though shops usually carry a variety of goods, specialties are noted: **Agung,** Jl. Paseh, Gg. Ciparaga I/9 (wooden thongs); **Aquarius,** Jl. Raya Rajapolah 118; **Alas,** Jl. Galuh 11/4 (caps, garments); **Enjo Karo,** Jl. H.Z. Mustofa 262 blk (embroideries); **Panyombo,** Jl. Pasar Wetan 65 (knittings); **KUD Mukti,** Jl. Rajapolah 2 (bamboo and pandanus pieces); **Motekar,** Jl. Cicariang (embroideries). The **Kusumah Art Shop,** on Jl. R.E. Martadinata 216, is known particularly for its baskets.

Batik

A special high-quality cloth found only in the Tasikmalaya area, this style uses local motifs (mostly detailed floral patterns) and colors (mostly red backgrounds). At any of the shops listed below, ask someone to take you to see *batik tulis*-making; different processes take place in different home workshops. Embroidered *batik* is also available.

For generally cheaper prices and a more unusual selection try Rajapolah village 12 km north, where the weavers actually work. The rattan furniture and pandanus weaving industries are also centered in and around this village. In Tasikmalaya itself, shop for *batik* articles at **Batik Bordir Kota Resik,** Jl. Seladarma 96, tel. (0265) 41385; **Batik Kartika,** Jl. R.E. Martadinata 127; **Kabinangkitan,** Jl. Sutisna Senjaya 20, tel. 41548; **Mitara Batik,** Jl. R.E. Martadinata 81, tel. 21253 or 21322; and the *batik* cooperative **Kopinka Ciamis** on Jl. Raya Timur.

Accommodations And Food

In the center of town near the big mosque is the decrepit but cheap **Kencana Hotel,** tel. (0265) 332-621, with rough rooms for Rp7000-10,000. The upscale **Yudanegara Hotel,** tel. 331-922, offers a/c rooms from Rp45,000. **Widuri Hotel,** tel. 334-342, is a clean old Dutch art-deco hotel with fan rooms for Rp10,000-20,000 and a/c rooms from Rp30,000 to Rp40,000. Nearby **Crown Hotel,** tel. 330-269, fax 333-967, is the top-end choice, with a conference center, "Music Cafe," and small a/c rooms for Rp60,000-75,000. The lobby has photos of nearby sights, such as Kampung Naga and the south coast beaches.

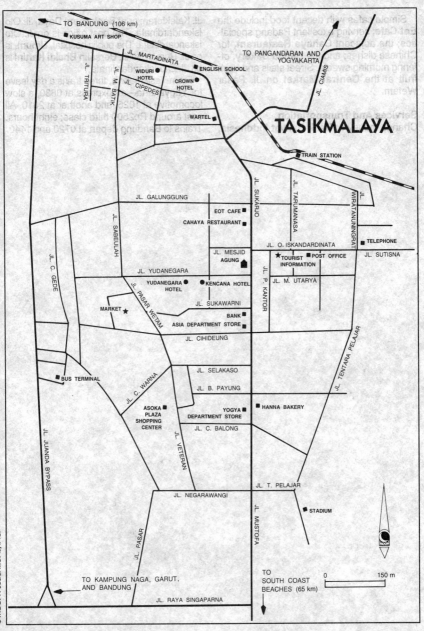

TASIKMALAYA

TO BANDUNG (106 km)

KUSUMA ART SHOP

JL. MARTADINATA

JL. TRITURA

JL. M. BATIK

JL. CIPEDES

WIDURI HOTEL

CROWN HOTEL

ENGLISH SCHOOL

TO PANGANDARAN AND YOGYAKARTA

JL. CIAMIS

WARTEL

TRAIN STATION

JL. GALUNGGUNG

JL. SABEULAH

JL. SUKARJO

JL. TARUMANASA

JL. WIRATANUNINGRAT

EOT CAFE

CAHAYA RESTAURANT

TELEPHONE

JL. O. ISKANDARDINATA

JL. MESJID AGUNG

TOURIST INFORMATION

POST OFFICE

JL. SUTISNA

JL. C. GEDE

JL. YUDANEGARA

JL. P. KANTOR

JL. M. UTARYA

JL. PASAR WETAM

YUDANEGARA HOTEL

KENCANA HOTEL

MARKET

JL. SUKAWARNI

BANK

ASIA DEPARTMENT STORE

JL. CIHIDEUNG

JL. TENTARA PELAJAR

BUS TERMINAL

JL. C. WARNA

JL. SELAKASO

JL. B. PAYUNG

ASOKA PLAZA SHOPPING CENTER

YOGYA DEPARTMENT STORE

HANNA BAKERY

JL. C. BALONG

JL. VETERAN

JL. T. PELAJAR

JL. NEGARAWANGI

JL. MUSTOFA

STADIUM

JL. JUANDA BYPASS

JL. PASAR

TO KAMPUNG NAGA, GARUT, AND BANDUNG

TO SOUTH COAST BEACHES (65 km)

0   150 m

JL. RAYA SINGAPARNA

© MOON PUBLICATIONS, INC.

Simple cafes with decent food include the **Eot Cafe,** serving excellent Padang specialties; the adjacent **Cahaya Restaurant,** for Chinese dishes; and the **Hanna Bakery,** offering morning sweets. Street stalls and fresh fruit at the **Central Market** on Jl. Pasar Wetam.

Services And Transportation
Change money at **Bank Rakyat Indonesia,** Jl. Kalektoran; or at **Bank Bumi Daya,** Jl. Oto Iskandardinata. The post office is on Jl. Oto Iskandardinata. The public hospital, **Umum,** is on Jl. Rumah Sakit; **Bersalin Bhakti Kartini** is on Jl. Oto Iskandardinata.

From Tasikmalaya, three trains a day leave for Yogyakarta—an express at 0830, a slow locomotive at 1026, and another at 2010. All cost around Rp2500 third class; eight hours. Trains to Bandung depart at 0720 and 1440.

PANGANDARAN

A favorite beauty spot 88 km southeast of Ciamis and 223 km southeast of Bandung on the south coast near the border of Central Java. This once-small fishing village at the entrance of a small peninsula is almost completely surrounded by the Indian Ocean. The whole peninsula, Cagar Alam Pananjung, is now a wildlife reserve. Hike along the long white-sand beaches, swim in the gentle surf, dive on coral reefs.

Pangandaran offers accommodations, restaurants, souvenir shops, a cinema, recreational facilities, and a bank—a good place to unwind. Domestic tourists swamp the place during weekends and holidays, and it's quickly developing a scruffiness typical of many beach resorts. The travelers' cafes serve the standard fare and young guides overcharge for unnecessary tours.

Pangandaran is booming. Once a backpackers spot known for the potency of its mushrooms, it's now chiefly patronized by tourists from Germany and Australia. Big hotels are sprouting like weeds and trendy cafes occupy every corner. Fishermen are politely asked to move elsewhere as beach roads are pushed through traditional fishing villages.

What's going on? Quite simply, Pangandaran was recently included in the government's official list of "upcoming tourist destinations." Tons of cash have been poured into new roads, sewage systems, and the like. Pangandaran has a good beach—an asset in surprisingly short supply on Java—and can be reached easily from Yogyakarta and Bali. An airport opened in 1995. Dozens of kilometers of pristine beach wait undisturbed for investors.

SIGHTS

Pangandaran Beaches

Watch the sun set on the west beach and the moon rise on the east beach. The eastern beach has rough, dangerous surf. On the west side, the beach near the park entrance is safer, but toward the north, currents make swimming dangerous. Because the western beach is so broad, sharks don't enter these waters. Snorkeling is good off Pasir Putih, an excellent coral beach for sun-

bathing on the west side of the peninsula. Visit the beach south of Pasir Putih and watch turtles and monitor lizards bask in the sun. A nice half-hour walk from the park entrance; wear good shoes, as the path passes over sharp rocks. It costs Rp5000 to reach the reefs by sailboat; beware of boatmen who agree to take you out to see the *kebon laut* for a certain amount, then demand twice as much once you're out to sea.

Superior beaches are found a few kilometers west of Pangandaran on the coastline stretching toward Pelabuhanratu. Nothing out here but a few lonely hikers, ambitious real estate developers, and a handful of *losmen* owners wondering about the future.

Pangandaran Nature Reserve

This 530-hectare *cagar alam* (nature reserve) is south of the village and takes up a whole three-km peninsula. Entrance fee Rp1000. The PHPA office stocks maps identifying wildlife habitats and tracing the different paths through the park. An intriguing place. Some segments of the beach are right out of *Robinson Crusoe*; you can really get away from it all. Some portions of the reserve are difficult to reach, which helps preserve the animals. Study the map carefully to find a path to take you into the heart, tag along with a walking tour group, or hitch on a jeep. The beach path is a 10-km walk around the entire peninsula at low tide. By motorboat you can travel the same circuit in 1.5 hours for Rp25,000, 15 to a boat. Around Rp4000-5000 per hour for a motorless *prahu*.

Within its relatively confined area, the park seems to have everything: caves, teak forests, shady banyan trees, grazing fields, scrub areas, mytho-historical remains, seashores, WW II Japanese pillboxes. The abundant wildlife includes black monkeys, tapir, tame deer, porcupine, peafowl, lumbering hornbills, green snakes draped from trees. Watch enormous wild *banteng* emerge to graze on the grassy clearings in the late afternoon; climb the observation towers to get a better look. A *taman laut* (coral garden) lies on the south tip of the preserve.

Most of the peninsula is limestone; be sure to visit the spectacular caves. Ask at the entrance

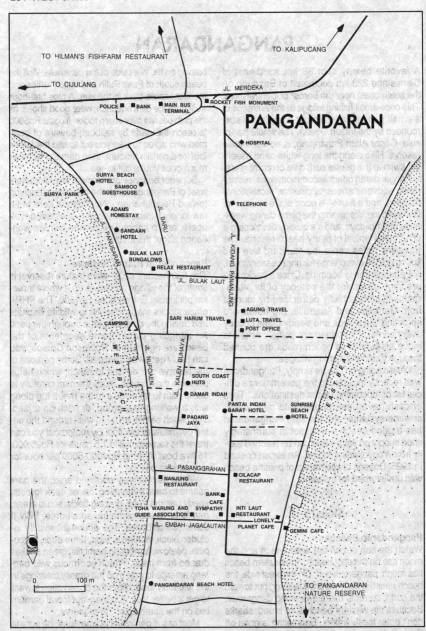

PANGANDARAN

TO HILMAN'S FISHFARM RESTAURANT

TO KALIPUCANG

TO CIJULANG

JL. MERDEKA

POLICE   BANK   MAIN BUS TERMINAL   ROCKET FISH MONUMENT

HOSPITAL

SURYA BEACH HOTEL
BAMBOO GUESTHOUSE
SURYA PARK
ADAMS HOMESTAY
SANDAAN HOTEL
BULAK LAUT BUNGALOWS
RELAX RESTAURANT

TELEPHONE

JL. BARU

JL. KIDANG PANANJUNG

JL. PANUSARAN

JL. BULAK LAUT

CAMPING

AGUNG TRAVEL
LUTA TRAVEL
POST OFFICE

SARI HARUM TRAVEL

WEST BEACH

JL. NUADAEN

JL. KALEN BUHAYA

SOUTH COAST HUTS
DAMAR INDAH

PANTAI INDAH BARAT HOTEL

SUNRISE BEACH HOTEL

PADANG JAYA

EAST BEACH

JL. PASANGGRAHAN

CILACAP RESTAURANT

NANJUNG RESTAURANT

BANK
CAFE
SYMPATHY

TOHA WARUNG AND GUIDE ASSOCIATION

INTI LAUT RESTAURANT
LONELY PLANET CAFE

JL. EMBAH JAGALAUTAN

GEMINI CAFE

MOON

0   100 m

PANGANDARAN BEACH HOTEL

TO PANGANDARAN NATURE RESERVE

for the short path leading to the *gua,* or use one of the local guides. The charming Mr. Toha, who can be contacted through his *warung,* just west of the Cafe Sympathy, is an older, more experienced guide who has great respect for the reserve. His tour fee is Rp5000.

Near Pangandaran

Rent a motorcycle and you'll escape the mercenary guides who seem to hover around every hotel and guesthouse in Pangandaran.

The popular spots are a narrow river gorge called **Green Canyon** and a few rather disappointing beaches such as **Batu Hiu** and **Batu Karas.** Without a bike or car, you'll need to take a *becak* up to the main bus terminal in the town of Pangandaran. Take any bus heading west to the beach. Several cheap hotels here.

Batu Hiu Beach

A picturesque rocky area 12 km west of Pangandaran where a dramatic cliff drops right down into a sea of huge violent waves. Get tips on local handicraft villages, remote caves, and waterfalls from the folks at Delta Gecko Homestay.

This part of the West Java coast is visited often, especially during holidays. Duplicate the famous photograph shot from the cliff with a single palm tree in the foreground. The name Batu Hiu ("Shark Rock") is derived from the shark-shaped boulder. During the colonial era a beautiful park was laid out here; some old buildings remain. Hire a bike in Pangandaran and ride to Batu Hiu. Good exercise, level the whole way. Pay the admission fee at the gate, then ride down the dirt road and through a palm grove until you reach a grassy plateau. The cliff lies just beyond. Also accessible by car.

Batu Karas Beach

Take a bus from Pangandaran to Cijulang (Rp400), then a motorcycle (Rp500) to the beach; about an hour. Or set off on a nice one-hour walk from Cijulang. A remote spot with nice scenery, good surfing, and deep-sea spearfishing. The beach is brownish, but the consistent waves attract a steady stream of surfers. On the road from Cijulang, look for the old bamboo bridge spanning the palm-fringed river.

Several hotels face the arching bay. **Batu Karas Beach Cottages,** where the road meets the sea, is acceptable, but most travelers head

500 meters west to a private cove where **Alana's Bungalows** (note the cool surfboard sign), upscale **Teratai Cottages** (with swimming pool), and **Hotel Pusaka Indah** have rooms for Rp10,000-45,000. Bargain hard if the places look deserted.

Green Canyon

A narrow, jungle-shrouded river some 20 km west of Pangandaran, just beyond the village of Cijulang. Boat tours take three hours and cost about Rp3000 per person. Bill Jones and Slim at so-called "Harbor 5" have been recommended.

The scenery will remind you of the jungle in *Apocalypse Now.* The magical enclosed swimming pool is clear only during the dry season. Avoid the expensive "guided tours" from Pangandaran (Rp30,000). Instead, take any bus west 30 minutes to the large signs marking the boat launches. Walk around and haggle with a few of the young guys; a half-day trip from Pangandaran.

ACCOMMODATIONS

Standards and cleanliness of the 60 or so *losmen,* hotels, and bungalows are improving all the time. Prices are rising as well. In five years, Pangandaran has gone from a backpacker's heaven of cheap smoke and powerful mushrooms to a midmarket yuppie resort. Bare-bones *losmen* under Rp10,000 are still available in the back streets, but most places now charge Rp12,000-20,000 (with fan) or Rp25,000-50,000 (with a/c).

Budget

Try for a cheaper rate if you stay longer than three days. Be prepared for no vacancies in the *wisma*-class accommodations—many of the hotels cater to big groups coming down from Bandung. During the crowded Lebaran holidays rates can quadruple.

Budget places priced around Rp10,000 include the old and decrepit **Laut Bira** and the equally sad **Losmen Mini.** Better budget spots are located in the small streets between the east and west beaches, and include **Jaya, Budi, Damar Indah, Surya Indah,** and the clean **South Coast Huts.** Inspect a few, then negotiate a discount for longer stays.

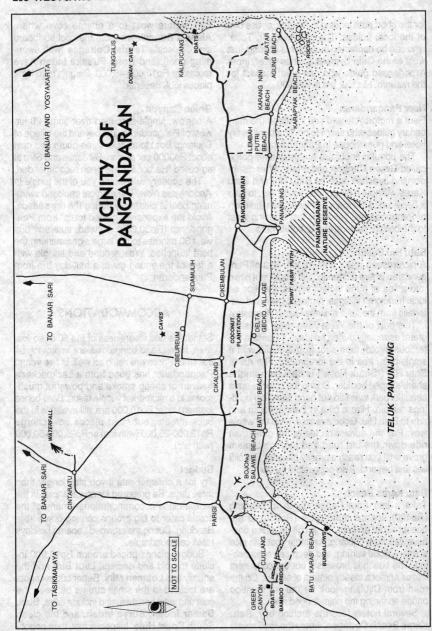

VICINITY OF PANGANDARAN

TO BANJAR AND YOGYAKARTA

TUNGGILIS

DONAN CAVE

KALIPUCANG

BOATS

PALATAR AGUNG BEACH

ROCKS

KARANG NINI BEACH

KARAPYAK BEACH

LEMBAH PUTRI BEACH

PANGANDARAN

PANANJUNG

PANGANDARAN NATURE RESERVE

POINT PASIR PUTIH

TO BANJAR SARI

SIDAMULIH

CIKEMBULAN

CIBEUREUM

CAVES

COCONUT PLANTATION

DELTA GECKO VILLAGE

TELUK PANUNJUNG

CIKALONG

WATERFALL

BATU HIU BEACH

CINTARATU

BOJONG SALAWE BEACH

TO BANJAR SARI

TO TASIKMALAYA

NOT TO SCALE

PARIGI

CIJULANG

GREEN CANYON

BOATS

BAMBOO BRIDGE

BATU KARAS BEACH

BUNGALOWS

Another good choice for backpackers is the ultra-quiet and very friendly **Bamboo Guesthouse** on Jl. Baru, tel. (0265) 379-419, one block back from the beach. Cozy rooms in a funky environment for Rp8000-10,000. The simple but wonderful **Delta Gecko Village Homestay** is located five km west of Pangandaran in a coconut grove near the village of Cikembulan. Vegetarian restaurant, lamps at dinnertime, free coconuts, psychedelic bicycles, small library, deserted beach—all run by resident artist Delta Agus and his garrulous German-Australian wife, Kristina. Rooms cost Rp10,000-20,000, dorms Rp6000. Take a bus west from the main bus terminal in Pangandaran, then a motorcycle taxi through the coconut groves. A great place for quiet contemplation.

Moderate

Most of the decent mid-level spots priced around Rp20,000-30,000 are located in the northwest section of Pangandaran, a 10-minute walk from the center of town. A good strategy is to check into one hotel and examine other options the following day.

Bulak Laut features pseudo-Bukittinggi cottages with fan-cooled rooms for Rp20,000-25,000—a nice change from the dismal, totally uncreative architecture plaguing most of Pangandaran. Good, central location. **Adam's Homestay**, tel. (0265) 379-164, is owned by a German woman and her colorful world-traveling Indonesian husband. Small pub, authentic cappuccino, and attractive rooms from Rp20,000 to Rp40,000. Excellent library, too.

Another outstanding choice is the **Sandaan Hotel**, tel. 379-165, with inexpensive fan-cooled rooms and better a/c rooms in the rear (Rp40,000-50,000) facing a small but attractive pool. **Pangandaran Beach Hotel**, tel. 773-667, at the southern end of the beach is older but has acceptable rooms in the Rp20,000-40,000 range.

Luxury

Best in town is the newish **Surya Beach Hotel**, tel. (0265) 379-428, fax 379-289, with a lovely pool, two restaurants, and friendly staff. Small fan-cooled rooms with common bath cost just Rp20,000, but most visitors stay in the standard a/c rooms with TV and refrigerator for Rp84,000-110,000. Or try the best in the center of town, the **Pantai Indah Barat Resort Hotel,**

tel. 379-004, fax 379-327, with swimming pool, tennis courts, and a/c rooms for Rp75,000-125,000. **Sunrise Beach Hotel,** tel. 379-220, fax 379-425, also has a pool and a/c rooms in the same price range. Avoid the older and poorly managed **Bumi Pananjung** and the crumbling **Hotel Bumi Nusantara.**

FOOD

At the southern end of Jl. Kidang Pananjung leading through town is a whole nest of greasy-spoon *warung*—a wonderful place to sit and watch village life while sipping *orang tua* with ice. **Cafe Sympathy,** on the main street near the *warung* on the right, is very popular: a good value, and cheap. **Inti Laut** in front of the Cafe Sympathy serves some of the better seafood in town. **Cilacap Restaurant** also serves delectable food but the 1994 death of the owner may end the restaurant's long and triumphant run as master of the local cafes. Other *rumah makan* can be found all along Jl. Pantai Pananjung. For dessert, mouthwatering mangosteens go for Rp200 apiece.

Local experts suggest the following cafes and restaurants: **Lonely Planet Cafe** (great seafood), **Gemini** (seafood pizza), **Warung Jambu** (Sundanese), **Padang Jaya** (Sumatran food at Pasar Seni Market), **Nanjung** (Chinese), **Sunrise Hotel** (international), **Relax Cafe** (homebaked breads, ice cream, and a very friendly European manager), **Adam's** (cappuccino), and **Hilman's Fishfarm Restaurant** (fresh seafood), this last in a memorable location completely surrounded by fishponds.

TRANSPORTATION

Getting There

The typical visitor books a minibus direct from a hotel in Bandung or Yogyakarta to a guesthouse or hotel in Pangandaran. You'll pay premium, but the convenience is often worth the extra cost.

Of course, you can do the journey independently, thereby saving some money. From Bandung, take a bus to the town of Banjar and a second bus down to Pangandaran (six hours total), then a *becak* (Rp1000) to the guesthouse or hotel of your choice.

From Yogyakarta, take a very early bus to Cilacap (five hours) to catch the 1300 boat to Kalipucang, a town near Pangandaran. An early start is necessary to avoid having to overnight in Cilacap. It's a fabulously relaxing five-hour boat journey between Cilacap to Kalipucang—a great change from a steady diet of trains and buses. River experiences are rare in Java and guarantee a fine diversion from the drudgery of overland travel.

Getting Away
You can book an express minibus to Bandung or Yogyakarta from **Luta Travel** or **Agung Travel** in the center of Pangandaran. Both agencies also rent motorcycles—a great way to tour the surrounding countryside. Some say the best minibus to Bandung is from **Sari Harum Travel,** just opposite the post office.

You can also take a bus from the bus station in Pangandaran to the town of Banjar, then continue by bus or train to Yogyakarta or Bandung. Or take a *bemo* from the Pangandaran bus terminal to Kalipucang, then the ferry at 0700, 0800, or 1100 to Cilacap (over the border into Central Java). It's four hours to Cilacap—via Segara Anakan, Klaces, Mutean, and Candi—along a densely vegetated waterway that passes stilt houses, men fishing from dugouts, and many species of birds. You'll hear the constant calls of the marabou storks in these swampy wilds. Excellent photo opportunities.

From Cilacap's wharf it's a few kilometers to the bus station on the other side of town. From the Cilacap bus terminal, take a bus to Yogyakarta. This entire picturesque route takes about 12 hours; a beautiful journey.

CROSSING INTO CENTRAL JAVA

CILACAP

In an area known for its cliffs and wild seas, Cilacap sits on the coast of what Indonesians call the Indonesian Sea. Most travelers only visit Cilacap to catch the boat to Kalipucang and Pangandaran. There's a big industrial estate under development here; Royal Dutch Shell built a $1.5 billion petrochemical complex, and it's hoped the complex will allow Indonesia to attain near self-sufficiency in oil-derived chemicals. Cilacap's natural harbor, open to large seagoing ships, is protected by the long penitentiary isle, Nusa Kambangan. Seashell crafts are sold in souvenir stalls; billiard halls for sailors; and a children's park.

Enjoy views of Teluk Penyu (Turtle Bay) Beach and the mysterious ruins of **Benteng Pendem** ("Buried Fortress"), a massive 19th-century edifice buried under sand and earth. This scenic fort, built by the 17th-century Sultan Agung of Mataram, has undergone numerous restorations, most recently by private investors seeking to develop it as a tourist site. Prior to WW II the fort was restored by the Dutch to guard Cilacap, Java's only south-coast port accessible to oceangoing vessels.

Accommodations And Food
Losmen Bahagia and **Losmen Akhmad** are both on Jl. Jen. Sudirman, near the Sleko boat jetty. Each is spartan but okay for one night. Visitors arriving by bus from Yogyakarta can stay at the nearby **Losmen Anggrek** or **Losmen Genung Hamita,** just across the street from the bus terminal. Both have rooms for Rp8000-15,000. Eat at nearby **Cafe Lestari**; the elderly owners speak Dutch. Also check out friendly **Losmen Tiga** downtown at Jl. Mayor Sutoyo 61; Rp8000-10,000 with clean *mandi.*

Cilacap's luxury hotel is **Wijaya Kusuma** on Jl. Jen. A. Yani 12/A, tel. (0282) 22871, also in the city center; rooms with hot water, a/c, and color TV go for Rp90,000. Other high-priced hotels include the **Cilacap Inn,** Jl. Jen. Sudirman 1, tel. 22428, and the **Grand,** Jl. Dr. Wahidin 5-15, tel. 21332. Charges are in the Rp40,000-80,000 range.

Most travelers eat in the area around **Losmen Tiga**; the **Perapatan Restaurant,** just around the corner, specializes in seafood. The **Grand,** Jl. Dr. Wahidin 5, is a more expensive but excellent restaurant serving Indonesian, European, and Chinese dishes. Cheaper fare in the *warung* along Jl. Mayor Sutoyo.

VICINITY OF CILACAP

TO BANDUNG

CENTRAL JAVA

TO PURWOKERTO AND GUNUNG SLAMET
TO KROYA

KESUGIHAN

KALIPUCANG

KR. ANYAR
MAJUNGKLAK SEGARA
ANAKAN MUTEAN CILACAP

PANGANDARAN KLACES CANDI

NUSA KAMBANGAN

0   10 km

INDIAN OCEAN

© MOON PUBLICATIONS, INC.

Getting There

From Yogyakarta, take the 0700 train to Kroya for Rp3200 (five hours), then the minibus (one hour) to Cilacap. Or take a bus from Yogyakarta to Cilacap via Purworejo (Rp2500, five hours, 216 km). A number of travel agencies on Jl. Sosrowijayan in Yogyakarta sell minibus tickets direct to Cilacap's jetty, getting you there by noon before the ferry leaves for Kalipucang.

Or take a bus (six hours) from Wonosobo, 150 km to the northeast. If you get the very first bus out of Wonosobo, you'll be able to make the last ferry to Kalipucang at 1300. Another popular way to reach Cilacap is by bus from Pangandaran to Kalipucang, then by ferry (four to five hours), which docks at Cilacap's Sleko dock area. Minibuses wait at the jetty to take you all the way to Yogyakarta.

Getting Away

If heading east, many travelers prefer to visit Dieng Plateau before arriving in Yogyakarta. Minibuses leave Cilacap to Wonosobo, from where minibuses depart all day for Dieng (Rp1000, 1.5 hours). Get an early start. If head-

ing west, take the four- to five-hour ferry through endless mudflats and twisted mangroves to Kalipucang, then bus down to Pangandaran.

NUSA KAMBANGAN

The convict isle, near Cilacap, is the Indonesian Elba. For many years hundreds of detainees who participated in the abortive 1965 coup were imprisoned here. There's even a verb in Indonesian, *menusakambangankan,* meaning "to send into political exile."

In spite of the island's spectacular natural beauty, fine beaches, and the remains of an old Dutch fort, it remained closed to tourists until 1992, when hotels in Pangandaran initiated escorted tours to the once forbidden island.

GUNUNG SLAMET

The climb up the 3,428-meter-high Gunung Slamet volcano, 15 km north of Purwokerto in Central Java, winds through vegetable gardens, steep riverbanks, dense jungle, and treacherous ravines. Wild forest pigs frequent this region. **Baturaden** is a mountain retreat on the slopes of Gunung Slamet with a beautiful camping reserve and nice panoramas. The climate is cool, the trees tall, the earth fertile. Get there first by *angkutan kota* from Purwokerto's terminal to a certain point in town from where minibuses climb to Baturaden (Rp500).

You'll see lots of accommodations along the last half km before Baturaden's terminal, but a good one is **Losmen Indra Prasta,** five minutes' walk uphill from the terminal, Rp10,000-20,000. The 1.5-hectare park (entrance fee Rp450) is well laid out with a swimming pool, hot springs (Rp250), mountain stream, and a green carpet of grass and trees.

THE NORTH COAST

CIREBON

The north-coast town of Cirebon is not on the popular Javanese tourist routes. It boasts no golden sandy beaches or trendy restaurants or hotels, but it's a clean, pleasant town, well worth a diversion—especially for its rich variety of arts and crafts and historical attractions. Lying between the sea and the mountains, Cirebon's hot temperatures are often buffered by cool mountain breezes.

An ancient precolonial port town near the border of West and Central Java, Cirebon is the meeting point of the Sundanese and Javanese cultures, and the local dialect is a blending of the two. The city's name, in fact, derives from the Javanese word *caruban*, or "mixture." The sultanate here was split into two main houses, Kanoman and Kasepuhan. Both palaces are open to visitors, occasionally hosting court dances and *gamelan* recitals.

Also, it must be said the citizens of Cirebon are among the friendliest in all of Java—perhaps due to the scarcity of visitors and the small-town atmosphere. Spend some time chatting with the schoolkids, *becak* drivers, and anyone else who approaches you during your walks. The people you meet will provide you with your fondest memories.

History

Wedged between the warring kingdoms of Banten to the west and Mataram in the interior, caught between the Javanese and Sundanese, Cirebon has experienced a turbulent history. One of the *wali sanga*, the saints credited with bringing Islam to Java, set up Cirebon as a religious and artistic center around 1552. He took the title Sunan Gunung Jati ("Sultan of Teak Mountain"). His gravesite, six km north of Cirebon on the road to Indramayu, is still a highly revered spot, drawing pilgrims from all over Java. The sultanate came under the domination of the Dutch East Indies Co. in the 17th century, and by the early 18th century the administration of native affairs was the joint responsibility of three courts.

Through Cirebon's fine harbor vast quantities of rice, sugar, pepper, and wood were exported.

KRATON

Seven *kraton* were built in Cirebon; four are extant. The remaining three are either in ruins or absorbed by surrounding *kampung*.

The largest, Kraton Kasepuhan and Kraton Kanoman, were built around 1697 when the sultanate split. The court for the older prince, Kasepuhan, was erected on the site of the 15th-century *kraton* of Cirebon's earlier Hindu-Javanese regents. Kanoman was raised for the younger prince; it's smaller and less elaborate.

These native courts, quite distinct from the reserved and stately courts of Central Java, reflect the many cultural influences that have passed through this busy port city over the centuries. Elaborate Chinese phoenixes, cranes, and peonies coexist with Dutch inlaid decorative tiles. The Muslims made their mark in such architectural details as dark brown woodcarving, while the terra-cotta stepped walls evoke Hindu influence. Kraton Kasepuhan even features as its crest the white tiger that once guarded Siliwangi, a venerated Hindu ruler, linking the new Islamic court with its Hindu ancestors. Since Indonesian independence, the royal status of the different *kraton* have gradually evaporated.

Kraton Kacirebonan

An offshoot of Kraton Kanoman, Kraton Kacirebonan lies close to Jl. Pulosaren west of Kraton Kasepuhan. This *kraton* is less touched by Dutch and Western influences than Cirebon's more famous palaces. The house is still occupied by members of the royal family, but visitors can gaze in over the gate.

Kraton Kasepuhan

The town of Cirebon had long been ruled by Demak Muslims when Sunan Gunung Jati

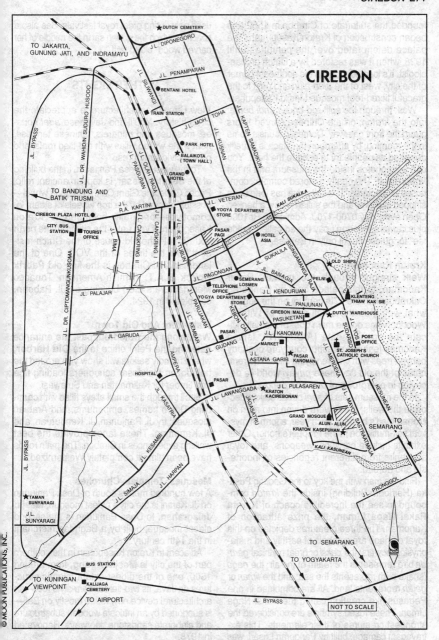

CIREBON

TO JAKARTA,
GUNUNG GATI, AND INDRAMAYU

★ DUTCH CEMETERY

J.L. DIPONEGORO

J.L. PENAMPARAN

■ BENTANI HOTEL

J.L. SILIWANGI

■ TRAIN STATION

J.L. MOH. TOHA

J.L. KAPTEN SAMADIKUN

J.L. KUSNAN

● Park Hotel

■ BALAIKOTA
(TOWN HALL)

● GRAND
HOTEL

J.L. OLAH RAGA

J.L. PASGURAN

J.L. WAHIDIN SUDIRO HUSODO

J.L. BYPASS

TO BANDUNG AND
BATIK TRUSMI

J.L. R.A. KARTINI

J.L. VETERAN

▲ YOGYA DEPARTMENT
STORE

KALI SUKALILA

■ CIREBON PLAZA HOTEL

CITY BUS
STATION

■ TOURIST
OFFICE

J.L. BIMA

J.L. CANGKRING II

J.L. CANGKRING I

J.L. K.S. TUBUN

PASAR
PAGI

● HOTEL
ASIA

J.L. SUKALILA

J.L. SISINGMANGA RAJA

■ OLD SHIPS

J.L. DR. CIPTOMANGUNKUSOMA

J.L. PALAJAR

J.L. PAGONGAN

J.L. BANAGIA

● PELNI

J.L. SEMERANG
LOSMEN

■ TELEPHONE
OFFICE

▲ YOGYA DEPARTMENT
STORE

J.L. KENDURUAN

★ KLENTENG
THIAW KAK SIE

J.L. PARJUAKAN

J.L. PANJUNAN

★ DUTCH WAREHOUSE

J.L. GARUDA

J.L. KEMBAR

KEBON CAI

J.L. PASUKETAN

■ CIREBON MALL

J.L. YOS SUDARSO

POST
OFFICE

PASAR
■ GUDANG

J.L. KANOMAN

J.L. MERDEKA

■ MARKET

J.L. ASTANA GARIE

PASAR
KANOMAN

■ ST. JOSEPH'S
CATHOLIC CHURCH

■ HOSPITAL

J.L. AMPERA

PASAR
■

J.L. KASATRIA

J.L. PULASAREN

J.L. KESINEAN

TO
SEMARANG

J.L. LAWANGGADA

★ KRATON
KACIREBONAN

J.L. JAGASATRU

J.L. MAYOR SASTRAATMAJA

GRAND MOSQUE ■

ALUN - ALUN

KRATON KASEPUHAN

KALI KASUNEAN

J.L. KESAMBI

J.L. BYPASS

J.L. HARPAN

J.L. SIMAJA

TO SEMARANG

TO YOGYAKARTA

J.L. PRONGGOL

★ TAMAN
SUNYARAGI

J.L.
SUNYARAGI

■ BUS STATION

TO KUNINGAN
VIEWPOINT

■ KALIJAGA
CEMETERY

TO AIRPORT

J.L. BYPASS

NOT TO SCALE

© MOON PUBLICATIONS, INC.

founded the sultanate of Cirebon in 1552 and began construction of Kraton Kasepuhan. The palace deteriorated over the centuries until 1928, when it was restored by a Dutch archaeologist. It's located today in the southeast corner of the city, west of the *alun-alun* and next to the graceful tiered-roof mosque Mesjid Kasepuhan.

Walk through the split red-brick *candi bentar* into the *kraton*; ornate Chinese carved tigers guard the front gateway. Domestic tourists come in the morning; by afternoon the place is usually deserted as people try to escape the heat. You can take photos inside the museum and in the *kraton* itself. The neatly restored complex comprises 25 hectares. The sultanate has long been stripped of power and the sultan is now a banker. Open every day 0700-1700. Admission Rp1000 plus camera fee; don't pay the so-called "guide fee" for guides fluent only in Bahasa.

Kraton Kanoman

Walk straight through the market, Pasar Kanoman, to this palace built by Pangeran Cakrabuana in the 17th century on the edge of what was then the small village of Witana. Woodcarvings on the main door of the hall indicate the opening date (A.D. 1670). Istana Kanoman features a restful courtyard of shady banyan trees with children flying kites. The remnants of the old Javanese *priyayi* world lie decaying in overgrown plazas and *pendopo*.

In the museum sets of *seni debus* stakes decorate the walls; these were driven into men on Mohammed's birthday each year, a form of mystical self-mutilation in the Prophet's honor. Other exhibits include carvings, weapons, and royal souvenirs from different regencies of Indonesia and abroad.

Find the man with the key to the Gedung Pusaka (Heirloom Building) inside the *kraton* compound to see the incredible coach of **Kareta Paksi Naga Liman,** the prize attraction of Kanoman. The three creatures depicted on this royal carriage are symbols of earthly and metaphysical powers: the *paksi* or great mythical *garuda* bird represents the realm of the air; the *naga* (snake bird) represents the sea; and the *liman* or *gajah* represents land. All are combined in one Pegasus-like creation called the Paksi Naga Liman. These fused symbols are considered the strongest creatures of their elements. This extravagant carriage, built by Pangeran Losari, was used only during great royal festivals. See also a coach on which the queen sat in the middle of her carved wood "cloud puff."

OTHER SIGHTS

View Cirebon's architecture to appreciate the city's history. You'll find Javanese *adat* houses, mosques and minarets, Chinese temples, neat white-walled villas with red-tiled roofs, and ornate civic structures.

To the west of Desa Panjunan, in the building of the **Sekolah Dasar,** is kept an ancient relic, Pedati Gede, the Giant Cart. This huge wheel—possibly inspired by the iron wheels of steam locomotives—originally belonged to Kraton Kasepuhan. If you enter the city from the north you run into the old house of the Dutch resident from the times of the VOC. One of the landmarks of Cirebon is the fine old **Pabrik Rokok B.A.T.** (British-American Tobacco Manufacturers Ltd.) building on Jl. Pabean, completed in 1924.

Waterfront And Old Town

Walk along the waterfront past the entrance gate and the Pelni office to the **Old Harbor,** where friendly sailors will show you around the half-dozen Makassar schooners loading rice and timber for Kalimantan and Sulawesi.

Stroll through the small alleys filled with crumbling Dutch homes, emporiums, and Arabian mosques; try Jl. Panjunan, Jl. Kenduruan, and Jl. Kanoman. These lanes provide the best walking experiences in Cirebon. The main roads have been almost completely Westernized.

Mosques, Temples, Churches

A few hundred meters south of Desa Panjunan on Jl. Kartini is the city's oldest mosque, **Mesjid Jalagrahan.** In Desa Panjunan is the second oldest mosque, built by a Baghdad merchant in the 14th century.

Adjacent to Kraton Kasepuhan in the southern part of the city is **Mesjid Agung,** from around 1500, one of the oldest extant Islamic structures on Java. Its two-tiered *meru*-style roof—an architectural device now found mostly on Bali—is supported by an intricate wooden substructure and elaborate sandstone doorways. Renovated in 1978.

Near the harbor on Jl. Kantor to the left of Bank Dagang Negara is one of the most beautiful Chinese temples on Java, **Klenteng Thiaw Kak Sie**; built in 1658, it's also Indonesia's oldest. A number of well-preserved wall frescoes are inside. **Klenteng Dewi Welas Asih** lies a few hundred meters to the south of Jl. Benteng. **Saint Joseph's Catholic Church** was built in 1878 by Theodores Gauntsoltez; it's located on Jl. Yos Sudarso.

Town Hall

A magnificent example of an architectural style that flowered between the two world wars. This is a town hall like no other you'll ever come across—eligible for a Ripley's entry. Over the door of the mayor's room is a stained-glass window with a pink curled-up shrimp in its center. High on top of the building eight giant stone shrimps seem to cling to the two square towers flanking the entrance. Once painted contrasting colors, one could not mistake, even from afar, the town hall of Kota Udang—a monument to Cirebon's status as an important processing center for this popular shellfish.

Taman Sunyaragi

A grotesque three-story red brick and concrete grotto, 4.5 km southwest of town on Jl. Sunyaragi. Take minibus BS on Jl. Sisingamanga Raja.

Taman Sunyaragi has passed through several transformations since its initial construction as a resthouse for 15th-century royalty. Sunan Gunung Jati used it as a country palace for his Chinese bride, Ong Tien, who died just three years after arriving on Java. It is, in fact, still referred to locally as "the Pleasure Gardens of the Chinese Princess." At that time the building was adorned with cascading waterfalls and the area was landscaped with small lakes and gardens.

The name Gua Sunyaragi actually means "Place of Isolation." In Hindu-Javanese history, remote sites were traditionally used by royalty to seek inner knowledge and strength, or as testing places where adherents practiced a form of spiritual discipline. In these secret chambers practitioners were taught such pursuits as meditation and military science.

Sunyaragi later became the site of a weapons workshop and armory. Legend has it the partisans fighting the Dutch operated out of Sunyaragi during and after the Java War (1825-30), when the whole structure was turned into a guerrilla post. Before the Dutch could attack, all the weapons were spirited away to the countryside and the building abandoned. In their fury, Dutch troops destroyed the decorations and statues.

In 1853, Sunyaragi was restored and redesigned by a Chinese architect in a curious Chinese architectural style. Restoration continues. Wander through secret chambers, narrow gates, caves, miniature doors, and corridors and staircases leading to nowhere.

Gunung Jati Tomb

Take minibus GG on Jl. Sisingamanga Raja at the Cirebon Harbor to this tomb of Sunan Gunung Jati, a 16th century missionary who brought Islam to Java. This spiritual conquistador ruined the Hindu Pajajaran Kingdom in overcoming Jakarta; after subjugating the kingdom of Cirebon, he died. His tomb is one of the holiest places on Java. A series of courtyards are filled with gravestones, all surrounding the tomb. This site is visited by both Indonesian and Chinese pilgrims. Take off your shoes before entering. The inner sanctum of Sunan Gunung Jati's grave is closed to the public. If you're going to give money, give only to the *juru kunci.* Empty bottles are sold for Rp100 so pilgrims may take holy water away. Across the road, walk up the small hilltop covered in graves for a nice view of the sea. The best time to visit the complex is on Jumat Kliwon (Holy Fridays) on the Javanese calendar, when the complex is filled with worshippers burning incense.

ACCOMMODATIONS

Budget

For those on a real budget a whole row of inexpensive hotels (Rp5000-8000) is located in front of the train station—**Kejaksan, Budi Aslih,** and **Palapa** on the north; **Leksana, Indonesia,** and **Famili Hotel** on the south.

Hotel Asia, tel. (0231) 202-183, is a Chinese-run hotel and the best-value *losmen*-style accommodation in Cirebon. Located in an old Dutch home, the whole building is itself an antique. Quite centrally located down a quiet street facing a canal at Jl. Kalibaru Selatan 15; rates range from Rp12,000 to 20,000. *Nasi gudeg* vendors come around the courtyard in the mornings. A masseuse works the premises (Rp2500). The English-speaking manager can answer any specific questions and offers a useful information package with local transportation tips.

Two simple hotels compete with the popular Hotel Asia. **Semerang Losmen** on the main street is an old Dutch place with rudimentary but cheap rooms from Rp7000, while **Hotel Baru** on Jl. Siliwangi seems popular with *becak* drivers, perhaps because of kickbacks.

Moderate
Cirebon Plaza Hotel, Jl. Kartini 54, tel. (0231) 2061 or 2062, is a clean, modern hotel on the road from Bandung; Rp30,000 s or d for a/c rooms with *mandi*; coffee shop and restaurant. **Grand Hotel,** tel. 208-623, has all the amenities, plus great service and style. This old colonial hotel at Jl. Siliwangi 98 offers a multitude of large rooms in every price range: Rp35,000-60,000 for a/c rooms in a central location.

A step up is the **Sidodadi Hotel,** tel. 202-305, fax 204-821 with 54 a/c rooms for Rp63,000-84,000.

Luxury
The top range is occupied by two new hotels. **Bentani Hotel,** tel. (0231) 203-246, fax 207-527, has a pool, three restaurants, and decent a/c rooms for Rp105,000-160,000. Upscale **Park Hotel,** tel. 205-411, fax 205-407, features a deluxe lobby, pool, and 91 rooms priced at Rp126,000-210,000. A favorite of expats working the Pertamina oil refineries to the west of Cirebon. This hotel also operates the **Sangkan Hurip Park Resort** in the mountain town of Kuningan just outside Cirebon.

FOOD

Specialties
Nasi lengko is made of rice, *tempe, tahu, sambal,* lemon, cucumber, sprouts, fried crispy onions, and meat. *Nasi jamblang* consists of sour fish, beef jerky, dried cow's lung, vegetables, and *tahu goreng,* served with a specially prepared rice. Try some at Hotel Asia around

0900 when the vendors arrive. You can also buy it at the harbor and bus station.

Another place to try local dishes is **Pasar Pagi,** open until 2100. **Warung Nasi Lengko,** near the Golden Cinema, and **Nasi Jamblang** on Jl. Gunung Sari feature good Cirebon-style *nasi campur* and *nasi goreng* with lots of vegetables. **Pasar Kanoman** is another colorful, noisy market selling fruit, *tahu,* and crab. For all kinds of baked goods and crackly *krupuk,* head for **Toko Famili,** Jl. Siliwangi 96.

Restaurants
A number of inexpensive restaurants serve Chinese and Indonesian food in the center of town on Jl. Karanggetas. For excellent Padang-style food, delicious ice juices, and stereo music, hit **Sinar Budi,** Jl. Karanggetas 22. Right across the street at no. 9 is **Restaurant Kopyor**; *es kopyor* for Rp1100.

Other good restaurants on this street include: **Kecil,** no. 14, and the **Jatibarang,** no. 1. For Sundanese cuisine, try **Kencana,** Jl. Karang Kencana, or the **Lembur Kuring** farther out of town on Jl. Bypass. Most high-priced hotels have restaurant/coffee shops and bars too.

Seafood
Cirebon's specialty is shellfish, although environmental problems and overfishing have dramatically reduced the catch in recent years.

The best seafood restaurant in Cirebon is **Maxim's,** Jl. Bahagia 45-47. There are over 50 items on the menu; the best deals are the freshly caught crab and shrimp dishes. The old black-and-white photographs in the front lobby, snapped by the grandfather of the present owner, illustrate the history of Cirebon's *kraton.*

Other high-quality seafood restaurants include the **Jumbo Restaurant** on Jl. Siliwangi and the **Citra Restaurant** on Jl. Sisingamanga Raja. At the south end of Jl. Bahagia, a Chinese *pasar malam* sets up each evening at around 1800; prices are lower than in the restaurants.

ARTS AND CRAFTS

Since the 15th century, Cirebon's well-established Chinese community has influenced the city's unique arts, both in motifs (*megamendung,* or "rock and clouds") and lacquer techniques. Stylized rocks and clouds decorate monochromatic carved door panels, and wooden *wayang* puppets are carved specifically as wall decorations.

Much of the wood comes from the *sawo* fruit tree. A Jepara woodcarving (*ukiran jepara*) shop is on Jl. Bahagia 53. Also look up Kardita, a *pelukis becak* (*becak* painter). Cirebon is a very active bamboo furniture center, turning out many different styles of chairs, stools, and tables. West of town, near Weru, stalls sell economical rattan furniture. In Sura Nanggala Lor, 12 km from Cirebon, see a *wayang topeng* carver at work; specimens for sale cheaper than in Bandung.

Batik

The stylistic nuances and bright accents of Cirebon *batik* are found nowhere else on Java. Traditionally, the motifs most associated with Cirebon *batik* are Chinese in origin: dragons, tigers, lions, and elephants, and, of course, "rock and clouds." Sealife, so vital to the economic wellbeing of the city, is also frequently portrayed.

Since the artists' guilds decreed only men could work in *batik,* Cirebon became one of the few places on Java where females did not draw and paint the cloth. Thus the *batik* of this area features bold, masculine designs; large, dramatic portions of free space; and a minimum of busy detail. Quite distinct from other north coastal or central Javanese areas. View the zenith of this art form in Cirebon's *kraton* museums, though the finest pieces have been sold and only small collections are left.

Batik cap sarung cost Rp12,000-20,000. *Batik kain* in the shops start at Rp20,000. The more expensive *batik tulis* goes for Rp40,000; don't expect lively bargaining as most shops stick to a *harga pesti* (fixed price). Too expensive for the local market (Rp40,000-90,000), most of the traditional rock and clouds *batik* is sent to Jakarta, marked up fivefold.

Around Pasar Pagi on Jl. Karanggetas are numerous *batik* shops, though much of the work is from Solo, Pekalongan, and other cities. You'll also find many examples of the Indramayu *batik* style, with more involved red and blue patterns. *Batik cap* sells for Rp20,000-25,000, still quite pricey but unique.

Also, try **Pasar Balong** until 1600. **Toko Batik Permana,** Jl. Karanggetas 18, and **Toko Batik**

Saudara, Jl. Karanggetas 46, are also worth a visit. Finally, check out the **GKBI** (Batik Cooperative) at Jl. Pekarungan 33, which sells a wider selection of Cirebon *batik* than any other outlet. Walk easily to GKBI from Hotel Asia, or take a *becak.* Open Mon.-Fri. 0800-1200, Saturday 0800-1230.

Trusmi

Some of Cirebon's finest *batik* is made in Trusmi northwest of Cirebon. Take minibus GP from Cirebon Harbor.

Although the *batik* is actually made here, it's not necessarily cheaper—there's just a wider selection. Visit **H. Mohammed Masina**'s workshop in the long one-story white building opposite a grass clearing. Masina and his wife Ibu have rejuvenated some of the old Cirebon court designs, using mostly traditional creams and browns against tan backgrounds, with superb Chinese reds and blues depicting birds and oversized lions. Family workshops such as these proliferated during the 1920s and '30s; the Masinas' extraordinary hand-drawn technique is a throwback to that golden age. Many of the best pieces are destined for the GKBI Institute in Jakarta, so prices depend on how low the stock is.

Another workshop, one of the largest in Trusmi, is **Budhi Tesna**'s, noted for *batik* printing. Numerous other workshops are located both here and in the neighboring village of Kalitengah.

SERVICES AND TRANSPORTATION

Change money at the banks along Jl. Yos Sudarso. **Bank Dagang Negara** on Jl. Kantor offers the best rates. The **main post office** is on Jl. Yos Sudarso near the harbor. The **telephone office** is on Jl. Pagongan. The **tourist office** (Dinas Pariwisata), featuring local maps and a staff speaking fragmentary English, is located outside town near the city bus terminal. For books and stationery supplies, try **P.D. Equator,** Jl. Bahagia 41, or the bookstore in the modern **Cirebon Mall.** The Cirebon telephone city code is 0231.

Getting There

The quickest way to cover the 266 km from Jakarta is by the daily train, which leaves Jakarta's Kota station at 0700, 1350, and 1644. Trains depart several times daily from Yogyakarta and Semarang.

If driving your own vehicle from Jakarta, the north coast road via Bekasi, Cikampek, and Jatibarang is rather flat and boring but much faster (five to six hours) than the scenic route via the Puncak and Bandung. From Bandung, Cirebon is 2.5 hours by car. Or take the bus from Bandung; Rp2500, four hours.

Getting Around

You can reach any place of interest in this small city by minibus, bemo, or becak. Stasiun Taxi Kota on Jl. Gunungsari has taxi kota traveling in all directions. Try to negotiate a full hour for around Rp3000. Taxis are metered and very cheap.

Getting Away

Pelabuhan Udar Penggung Airport is five km from the city toward Kuningan. Garuda/Merpati offers twice daily flights to Jakarta; another Garuda flight leaves for Ujung Pandang, Balikpapan, Pekanbaru, and Palembang.

To Jakarta the train takes only three to four hours. Gunung Jati trains depart for Jakarta three times daily early in the morning. Sometimes you can buy a ticket the day before your trip. There are also trains east along the north coast to Semarang (tracks could be flooded in the monsoon season) and to Yogyakarta. Train schedules are posted at the station and at Hotel Asia.

Take minibus G8 to the stasiun bis, five km southwest of town on the road to Kuningan. The reputable **4848 Bus Co.** at Jl. Karanggetas 7 offers buses to Semarang, Yogyakarta, and Bandung.

VICINITY OF CIREBON

Indramayu

Fifty-four km northwest of Cirebon, this area has developed its own style of batik, character-ized by subdued mengkuku red (terra-cotta or Turkish red) and various shades of traditional indigo. The dramatic and continued use of blue and red in the Indramayu area is thought to be a result of the long Chinese presence here: blue symbolizes mourning and melancholy, while red is symbolic of happiness, fertility, and good fortune. For the best batik, visit the nearby village of Pamuan. Batik tulis pieces average Rp50,000-75,000.

Linggarjati

This 300-meter-high resort, 13 km north of Kuningan and 22 km southwest of Cirebon, is a clean, cool village with beautiful panoramas. Perched on Gunung Ciremay, with hills and green sawah all around, this is where the people of Cirebon go to relax. The resort includes bungalows, hotels, good walks, and gardens. Take a minibus from Kuningan or drive from Bandung via Majalengka.

Linggarjati is famous as the site of 1946 negotiations between the Dutch and the Republican government of Indonesia. The building where the conference was held has been fully restored and turned into a museum. Nearby are relics from prehistoric diggings around Cigugur and other excavations at Cipari village in the Kuningan District. People have lived at the foot of Gunung Ciremay (3,078 meters) for thousands of years; remains and stone tools span the New Stone Age to the Megalithic Age (2500-1500 B.C.).

There are no losmen; hotels cost anywhere from Rp6000 to Rp35,000. **Hotel Linggarjati,** Rp12,000-25,000, features swimming pool, tennis courts, and full resort amenities. **Linggarjati Cilimus** occupies a nice setting, with dining room, tennis courts, swimming pool, and some bungalows. Only two km to the hot-water mineral baths.

PEKALONGAN

Pronounced "Pek-ALLO-ang." Known as Kota Batik ("Batik City"), Pekalongan (pop. 125,000) is an important textile center famed for colorful hand-waxed and stamp-printed *batik* using distinct motifs. This is Indonesia's third leading *batik*-production center after Yogyakarta and Solo; Pekalongan even has a Batik Museum on Jl. Majapahit, open 0900-1330, closed Sundays.

SIGHTS

Dutch Architecture
This town has always been a fortress and trade city. The old Dutch Quarter just north of the **Loji Bridge** is comprised of several stately buildings surrounding a grassy park: the old **Resident's Mansion**, imposing **post office**, **Dutch Reformed Church** (1852), **Kota Madya** (former Dutch city hall), **Societeit Corcle** (Dutch clubhouse), and the remains of a **VOC fort** built in 1753, and later turned into a prison by the Dutch.

On 7 October 1945 the Pekalongan residency became the first in Indonesia to free itself from Japanese rule, touching off a violent social revolution which became known in this part of Java as the Tiga Daerah Movement.

Pekalongan *Batik*
Pekalongan has always played a leading role in the development of modern *batik* designs and techniques. Instead of the traditional muted motifs of central Java, here you'll see bright, bold, exuberant colors and naturalistic figures. Recognizable by red and blue birds and flowers on white or pink backgrounds, Pekalongan *batik* is some of the most *halus* on the island; you could easily pay Rp250,000 for a fine piece. The town includes numerous *batik* factories and shops; as in Yogyakarta, peddlers with bundles of *batik* approach you on the street, interrupt your meals in restaurants, gesture from doorways, hang around hotel lobbies. Coming directly from the *kampung* where the *batik* is made, these pieces are generally cheaper than in shops. The whole town is involved in *batik*.

Batik Shops
Shop at **Nirwana** on Jl. Dr. Wahidin and **Kencana** off Jl. Mansyur (Gang Podosugih 1/3). **B.L. Pekalongan,** Jl. K.H. Mânsyur 87, tel. (0285) 1358 or 589, is one of the largest *batik* shops; open 0800-1700. **Nulaba Batik** at Jl. Iman Bonjol 47 offers a large selection of designs from all over the northern coast.

For lower prices, buy directly from the factories: **PT Rimbung Djaya,** Jl. Jen. Oerip Sumoharjo 20, is opposite *kantor perdangan,* two km from the city; open 0800-1600. **Pandawa Graha,** run by Suryanto Tri, is at Jl. Jawa 24, tel. 1499. For really superb work, visit the Leonardo of *batik,* **Pak Oey Tjoen,** at Jl. Raya 104 in Kedungwuni, nine km from Pekalongan. Unbelievably intricate designs, with eight or nine colors on one piece. Other factories include **Batik Susilo** in the nearby village of Wiradesa and **Umar Hadi Batik** in Buaran village in south Pekalongan. See the *batik* process at these factories any day of the week except Friday.

Prices vary considerably. *Batik cap sarung* costs Rp10,000-15,000 while handmade *batik tulis* runs Rp25,000-100,000 and up.

ACCOMMODATIONS AND FOOD

Pekalongan has a number of good *losmen,* some more expensive hotels include breakfast. Several have swimming pools.

Three convenient cheap accommodations lie opposite the train station on Jl. Gajah Mada, all in the Rp10,000 range: **Hotel Gajah Mada** (no. 11A, tel. 0285-222-185) is more cheery and personable than the others; **Losmen Ramayana** (no. 9) has a billiard hall. **Losmen Asia,** Jl. Wahid Hasyim 49, tel. 22125, is also popular.

Hotel Hayam Wuruk, Jl. Hayam Wuruk 152-158, tel. 22823, has a wide selection of rooms. Rates are Rp18,000-24,000 with fan and Rp28,000-45,000 with a/c. **Hotel Istana,** Jl. Gajah Mada 23-25, tel. 23581, fax 21252, just down the street from the train station, asks Rp24,000-30,000 with fan and Rp42,000-60,000 with a/c. A really nice hotel; well-priced.

The **Nirwana,** Jl. Dr. Wahidin 11, tel. 22446, fax 23841, has 63 rooms and is considered the town's

PEKALONGAN

JL. SUPRATMAN

TO PORT
SEE INSET

JL. K. BANGSA

JL. INDRAGIRI

JL. PROGO

JL. DIPONEGORO

JL. BLIMBING

JL. PATIUNUS

JL. PERENTIS

JL. VETERAN

PASAR BANJAR SARI

JL. SURABAYA

★ ARAB QUARTERS

JL. TERATAI

JL. CEMPAKA

JL. SALAK

NULABA BATIK

JL. BONJOL

JL. S. AGUNG

JL. BANDUNG

JL. AGUS SALIM

JL. SERUNI

HOTEL GAJAH MADA
HOTEL ISTANA
HOTEL MELATI

CINEMA

JL. MERDEKA

★ MONUMENT 4

HAYAM WURUK HOTEL

REMAJA RESTAURANT

ES TELER CAFE ★

JL. GAJAH MADA

TRAIN STATION

LOCAL BUSES

A KARIM RESTAURANT

WARTEL

PASAR ANYAR

BANK

JL. CIPTO

TO CIREBON AND JAKARTA

JL. SLAMET

AL JAMI ▪

ALUN ALUN

JL. KINTAMANI

JL. MANSYUR

JL. JAWA

JL. IRIAN

PEKALONGAN RIVER

JL. MANINJAU

★ BATIK MUSEUM

JL. SUMATRA

JL. WAHID HASYIM

JL. WAHIDIN

JL. MAJAPAHIT

BUS STATION

JL. SUDIRMAN

JL. SUTOMO

TO SEMARANG →

PEKALONGAN

TO KEDUNGWUNI

0   100 m

© MOON PUBLICATIONS, INC.

INSET

POST OFFICE ★

★ CITY HALL

DUTCH RESIDENTS MANSION ★

★ VOC FORT
TOURIST INFORMATION

DIPONEGORO

PO AN THIAN

JL. PATIUNUS

★ CHINESE HOMES

JL. S. AGUNG

BLIMBING

PASAR BANJAR SARI

top-drawer hotel. Rooms cost Rp50,000-80,000.

Sample such typical delicacies as Pekalongan-style *sayur asam* and *sambal tempe* at the foodstalls that spring up around Pasar Ratu at night. The **Remaja**, Jl. Dr. Cipto 20, serves good-value Chinese meals. **Buana Restaurant,** Jl. Mansyur 5, specializes in Chinese-style seafood. **A Karim** is unpretentious, with excellent *sate* and *gulai kambing*. Afterwards indulge yourself with an iced fruit drink at the popular **Es Teler 77.**

TRANSPORTATION

By bus from Cirebon to Pekalongan is Rp1800 (136 km, four hours); from Semarang it's Rp1250 (two hours). Pekalongan's **bus station** is 1.5 km east of the town center, Rp500 by *becak* or Rp200 by minibus; if arriving from the west, ask to be let off in the town center.

Pekalongan is also on the main Jakarta-Semarang-Surabaya rail line; by train to and from Semarang or Cirebon costs Rp4100-7000 depending on class.

The local minibus station is behind the Pertamina station on Jl. Hayam Wuruk. From here take minibuses to the *batik* villages around Pekalongan.

An a/c bus to Jakarta costs Rp5600 (402 km); to Bandung it's Rp2500. Early in the morning buses to Cirebon and Semarang pick up passengers in front of Hotel Gajah Mada.

SEMARANG

The administrative capital of Central Java, Semarang is a busy harbor city; a government, trading, and industrial center; and a major fishing port. The population is 1.2 million, of which 40% are Chinese.

Semarang is divided into two sections. The mainly residential Candi section is up in the cooler hills, where many of the luxury hotels are located; the markets, restaurants, government offices, harbor, and transportation terminals lie in the lower section. The oldest and most picturesque part of town is around Pasar Johar; in this area are the taxi, train, and minibus stations and the post and telephone offices.

Semarang is in many ways a more orderly city than Java's other important ports, Jakarta and Surabaya. It offers lively nightlife, with many clubs and massage parlors. In fact there's so much business traffic hotels are often over-booked. Although more a commercial center than a city for tourists, Semarang is a good starting point for many holiday resorts in the mountains to the south. It's the only port open to large ships on this stretch of coast, and cruise ships often call here. From Semarang you can easily visit Ambawara, Kudus, and the temples on Gunung Songo.

History

Great wealth has always passed through this city: agricultural produce going out, industrial raw materials and processed goods coming in.

Semarang served a huge population of Dutch traders and officials during colonial times, and the city is still crowded with old Dutch churches, warehouses, and administrative buildings. Long known as "The Red City," a center of socialist activity in the archipelago, the Communist Party of Indonesia was born here in 1920, and eventually grew into the world's largest outside of communist-controlled countries. At the end of WW II, Indonesian irregulars tried to wrest weapons from crack Japanese troops garrisoned in Semarang to oppose the landing of Allied Forces intent upon retaking Java. These guerrilla bands fought a pitched battle in the city 14-19 October 1945 and lost 2,000 men.

SIGHTS

Dutch Architecture
See the remnants of an old **Dutch Fort** on Jl. Imam Bonjol behind Poncol train station; around Tawang station are a number of big dilapidated former **Dutch warehouses.** Distinctive colonial architecture is on display all over the old town north of Pasar Johar; go on foot. The old Dutch section along Jl. Suprapto is wonderfully photogenic.

The **Catholic church** on Jl. Karanganyar recites its liturgy to *gamelan* music on Sunday. **Gereja Blenduk**, Jl. Jen. Suprapto south of Tawang station, was built in 1753; *blendoek*

SEMARANG

means "to swell," and refers to the building's unique copper dome roof. See the baroque facade of the organ inside. **Gereja Bangkon,** Jl. Mataram 908, about the same age as Gereja Blenduk, has been beautifully restored.

The amazing **Lawang Sewu,** which used to house the Dutch Railway Authority, is easily discernible amongst all the buildings surrounding the Tugu Muda roundabout. Now occupied by the army, it's a hassle to photograph this remarkable structure; you must get permission from the military commander at Bintaldam IV Dina Sejarah, on the other side of the traffic circle.

Chinatown
The city's oldest Chinese temple (1772), the colorful Klenteng Gang Lombok, sits right in the heart of Chinatown; to the Chinese this temple is better known as **Tay Kak Sie.** This is a well-maintained, living temple, used by Buddhists, Confucianists, and Taoists. Also wander along the canal roads and view crumbling homes reflecting ancient Chinese styles.

Museums, Memorials, And Shrines
Because of its large Chinese community, Semarang has been a center of herbal medicine

(*jamu*) production for centuries: you can visit the factories of both **Cap Jago,** Jl. Setia Budi, tel. (024) 285-533, and **Nonya Meneer,** Jl. Raya Kaligawe Km 4, tel. 285-732, by appointment. **Museum Jamu Nyouya Meneer** is Indonesia's first facility dedicated to traditional herbal medicine: old photographs, tools, and ingredients. Take a Kudus-bound bus (45 minutes); open Mon.-Fri. 1000-1530.

Museum Jawa Tengah, on Jl. Abdul Rahman one km from Semarang's Ahmad Yani Airport, features fossils, Hindu-Javanese reliefs and statues, and *wayang.* Free entrance. A military museum, **Museum Perjuangan Mandala Bhakti,** lies south of the Tugu Muda Monument. Members of the Dutch military who fell during the Japanese invasion are buried in two immaculate cemeteries, **Ereveld Kalibanteng** and **Ereveld Candi** in Candi.

In the center of the city, the candle-shaped **Tugu Muda Monument** commemorates the five-day battle by ragtag Indonesian partisans against elite Japanese soldiers at the end of WW II. Murals on the base show the sufferings of the people under both Dutch and Japanese domination, painted communally by one of the oldest artists' organizations in Indonesia.

The modern **Mesjid Baiturahman,** northwest of Simpang Lima, is Central Java's largest and most elegant mosque.

Sam Poo Kong Temple

Also known as Gedung Batu ("Stone Building"), this great cave temple lies on the main road to Kendal about five km west of the city. Take a Daihatsu to Karang Ayu, then another to the temple.

One of the largest and most honored Chinese temple complexes in Indonesia, Gedung Batu houses the spirit of a Ming dynasty Chinese admiral, Cheng Ho, a legendary Muslim eunuch who landed on Java in 1406 with a fleet of 62 vessels and 27,000 sailors. Twice a month, on Jum'at Kliwon (Friday) and Selasa Kliwon (Tuesday) of the Javanese calendar, multitudes of pilgrims arrive. The main hall, with its tall red columns and beautiful curved roof, is constructed around an inner chamber flanked by two huge dragons. Pilgrims vigorously shake incense and containers of bamboo sticks before these beasts, seeking their fortunes.

Since Cheng Ho (or Sam Poo Kong, his saintly name) helped carry Islam to Java, Gedung

Batu is a rare "double sanctuary," sacred to Buddhists and Muslims alike. Seeing Indonesians wearing *peci* in the temple's interior, carrying incense sticks, praying in a Chinese-style temple to a Chinese admiral, gives one hope that these two races will one day live in harmony.

In the back room is an old iron anchor, the object of worship for scores of pilgrims each week. The Chinese believe the anchor once belonged to a sailing ship from China. According to the official Javanese history of West Java, however, the anchor belonged to a VOC ship, the *Leiden,* which burned and sank in Cirebon's harbor in 1835.

Gombel

A cool, quiet recreation area in the hills south of Semarang. At 270 meters above sea level, the park provides views of all of Semarang, including ships anchored offshore. Lots of restaurants.

ACCOMMODATIONS

Budget

A number of the smaller accommodations don't accept foreign guests—a way of avoiding police paperwork.

Several dozen small, inexpensive (Rp6000-10,000) *losmen* are concentrated along busy, noisy Jl. Imam Bonjol, a 15-minute walk from Tawang train station. Try **Hotel Singapore,** tel. (024) 543-757, a clean and quiet hotel with friendly managers. Rooms here cost Rp9000-12,000, probably the best cheapie in Semarang. Basic, clean rooms are also available at **Losmen Rahayu,** no. 35-37, tel. 542-532, up to Rp25,000 with a/c. Centrally located is drab **Losmen Poncol,** no. 60 near the Poncol train station; bring mosquito coils.

The old Dutch colonial **Hotel Oewa-Asia** is on Jl. Imam Bonjol right in the noisy center of the city. Rooms in a quieter back part of the hotel run Rp8000 with wall fan and two beds. In the front building rooms run Rp15,000 with *mandi,* toilet, and plenty of noise. The ice water is a nice touch. Another choice is big, breezy **Hotel Jaya,** at Jl. M.T. Haryono 87, tel. 23604; Rp10,000 for large, fairly clean rooms with inside *mandi.* Secure; gate closes at night. Isolated location but one of the better cheap hotels in town.

CENTRAL SEMARANG

TO OLD SHIPS
TO HARBOR
JL. MPU. TANTULAR
PARK
CHURCH
TO TERBOYO BUS TERMINAL (2 km)
JL. R. PATAH
JL. RONGOWARSITO

DUTCH WAREHOUSES
PELNI
JL. KAKAP
JL. SUPRAPTO
JL. KEPODANG
PERTAMINA PETROL

JL. TAHIR
JL. SUGIYONO
MINI BUS STATION
PLAZA
JL. HARYONO

JL. PETEK
TELEPHONE
POST OFFICE
PASAR
SHOPPING CENTER

BANK INDONESIA
JOHOR PLAZA
SEMERANY PLAZA
TAY KAK SIE TEMPLE

METRO DEPARTMENT STORE
JL. AGUS SALIM
JL. PETALONGAN

HOTEL SINGAPORE
METRO HOTEL
PASAR JOHAR
JL. PEDANARAN
JL. PEKOJAN

LOSMEN RAHAYU

JL. GENDINGAN
HOLIDAY RESTAURANT
TOKO OEN RESTAURANT
JL. KAUMAN

JL. IMAM BONJOL
JL. PEMUDA
GARUDA/MERPATI
CHINATOWN

TO TUGU MUBU
JL. W. HASYIM

PERTAMINA PETROL
JL. TANJUNG
BANK
BANK
JL. DEROK

JL. TENDEAN
JL. GAJAH MADA
JL. PRINGGER

CINEMA
JL. M.H. THAMRIN

TO TUGU MUDA
TO SIMPANG LIMA AND CANDI

0   250 m

© MOON PUBLICATIONS, INC.

Moderate

A good deal on higher-priced rooms is the well-run **Blambangan Hotel,** Jl. Permuda 23, tel. (024) 21649, with dorm beds from Rp6000 and rooms for Rp15,000-25,000. Popular and often filled with Indonesian tourists. Another good midpriced hotel is the **Surya,** Jl. Bonjol 28, tel. 540-355, fax 544-250, with economy rooms from Rp22,000 and a/c rooms Rp25,000-30,000. Rates include tax, service, and breakfast.

Luxury

These hotel rates include government and service tax, plus breakfast and afternoon tea. Most accept credit cards.

The **Metro,** Jl. H.A. Salim 2-4, tel. (024) 547-371, fax 510-863, is centrally located but showing its age. Rooms are overpriced at Rp105,000-160,000. **Queen Hotel,** Jl. Gajah Mada 44-52, tel. 27603, charges Rp25,000-47,500 for clean rooms really not worth the price. Colonial-style, centrally located **Hotel Dibya Puri,** Jl. Pemuda 11, tel. 27821 or 24934, charges Rp63,000-105,000 for dirty, smelly rooms; one of the saddest hotels in Indonesia.

The **Telomoyo,** Jl. Gajah Mada 138, tel. 20926 or 25436, is central, with 67 a/c rooms and large open courtyard. Nice lobby with a homey feel. Popular with Dutch package tourists and Japanese business travelers. Higher-priced rooms are a better value; European food is served in the restaurant. **Hotel Santika,** Jl. A. Yani 189, tel. 314-491, offers Rp26,000-31,500 rooms with a/c; telephone, in-house video, restaurant. This flashy hotel is located opposite Es Teler, one of the best *bakso* restaurants on Java.

Luxury In The Hills

If you've got the money and want knockout views, head for one of the plush hotels in the hills of Candi Baru. **Siranda Hotel,** Jl. Diponegoro 1, tel. (024) 313-272, offers beautiful views at night. Air-conditioned rooms start at Rp60,000 for the first floor, and descend in price as you ascend in height. There's no elevator, so you'll get a lot of exercise. Built in 1974 for Indonesia's first PATA conference, today the Siranda is a little frayed at the edges, but still a good value.

For something less pretentious, check out the comfortable **Green Guest House,** Jl. Kesambi 7, tel. 312-787; neat a/c rooms for Rp25,000-45,000. The **Patra Jasa,** Jl. Sisingamangaraja, tel. 314-441, fax 314-448, sits lordly above the city with beautiful rooms complete with a/c, refrigerator, and TV for Rp210,000-525,000. Restaurant, coffee shop, bowling alley, tennis courts, swimming pool, billiards, travel bureau, drugstore, bank—the best tourist hotel in Semarang.

FOOD

Foodstalls

Scores of eating tents serve food and drink at all hours on Jl. Depok, Jl. Pringgading, and along Jl. M.T. Haryono. These tents offer some of the best eating in Semarang. An amazing concentration of foodstalls is found nightly in the Simpang Tiga area near the flashy shopping centers and big mosque.

A great cheap place to eat is **Pasar Yaik** (open 1700-2000) near Pasar Johar for Semarang specialties such as *sate kerang* (oyster sate), *bolong baling* (a big puff donut), and *lumpia* (spring rolls).

Because of its demographics, this city's culinary strength is its wide selection of Chinese eateries. Along Gang Lombok, off Jl. Pekojan near Tay Kak Sie Temple in Chinatown, is a string of oustanding Chinese *warung* and seafood restaurants at moderate prices; open 0800-1300. Probably the city's best seafood is found in the a/c **Kit Wan Kie,** Jl. Pinggir 23-25, tel. 20973.

There are also excellent Chinese restaurants adjacent to Sam Poo Kong Temple in the western part of the city. Of the many Chinese restaurants along Jl. Gajah Mada, the **Gajah Mada** (no. 43) is best known for its seafood—a bit dear, but worth it. Don't miss the Sunday morning dim sums.

Experience the oldest and quaintest eating establishment in Semarang, **Toko Oen,** Jl. Pemuda 52 (open 0900-2130). The pricey Chinese and European dishes aren't such a good deal, but the atmosphere is pure *tempoe doeloe.* The very good **Istana,** Jl. M.T. Haryono 836 near Gereja Bangkon, tel. 21754, serves Indonesian, Chinese, and European food in the Rp5000-7000 range. Drink with the expats at the **Ritzeky Pub,** Jl. Sinabung Buntu; open Tues.-Sat. 2000-1200.

on the streets of
Semarang

For Indonesian food, try **Nglaras Roso,** Jl. Haryono 701, tel. (024) 314-555. **Timlo Longtong Solo,** Jl. A. Yani 182, is renowned for its Javanese *lontong.* **Es Teler,** Jl. Jen. A. Yani 178, is always crowded; the *bakso* is only Rp750. Take a *bis kota* on Jl. Pemuda to Jatingaleh and ask to get off at the **Gombel Indah** for nice views of the city while dining. **Mickey Mouse** is an Indonesian restaurant in Ungaran, south of the city. Worth an evening excursion.

ENTERTAINMENT

Ngesti Pandowo, Jl. Pemuda 116, puts on rather pallid performances of Solonese-style *wayang orang* in a theater with wall-to-wall mosquitos and a primitive bathroom. Of higher quality are the performances broadcast at least once monthly on RRI (Radio Republik Indonesia) on Jl. A. Yani. There's also no shortage of nightclubs, massage parlors, and discos.

Semarang's 400-hectare **Tegalwareng Zoo** on Jl. Sriwijaya has comical chimpanzees and *wayang* and *ketropak* dramas, as well as rock bands and exhibits of traditional arts. The **Semarang Fair** takes place near the zoo during the month of August, featuring *warung* and regional entertainments. **Dugderan** is a traditional bazaar and carnival held yearly in front of Mesjid Agung in the Pasar Johar area for three consecutive days starting the first day of the fasting month, Bulan Puasa. Dugderan is essentially a huge night market drawing vendors

from both the countryside and other cities. Sample numerous regional specialties.

Besides the New Year, the Chinese of Semarang hold a traditional religious festival called **Jaran Sam Poo** in honor of Sam Poo Kong's historic arrival in the 15th century. The highlight of this event is the Pek Kong procession, which leaves the Tay Kak Sie Temple on Gang Lombok in Chinatown with a statue of Sam Poo Kong, a Chinese dragon, and Chinese of all ages in colorful costume. The procession proceeds to the Sam Poo Kong Temple. A ghastly, bloody, nervewracking sight—one of the most incredible in Indonesia.

SHOPPING AND SERVICES

Shopping

Semarang features about 20 markets and shopping centers filled with everything from rice cookers to diamonds. For textiles, earthenware, and leatherwork head for lively **Pasar Johar** near the Metro Hotel just off Jl. Pemuda. A good public market, especially for foodstuffs, is **Gang Baru** (also called Pasar Cina), where you can buy almost anything at the best prices; open only 0600-1200. Try **Batik Danar Hadi,** Jl. Gajah Mada 186, and **Batik Keris** in the Gajah Mada Plaza, for *batik*. **Jalan Kranggan Timur** features numerous shops selling jewelry, gold, and precious stones. Go to **Jl. Pemuda** for antique shops. Silver items, leather puppets, ceramics, and other Javanese crafts are available at **Panjang,** Jl. Widohargo 31A. A bird market, **Pasar Burung** on Jl. Kartini, is open all day.

Services
The **Semerang Tourist Office** is on Jl. Sriwijaya 29, tel. (024) 311-220 ; open Mon.-Thurs. 0800-1400, Friday to 1100, Saturday to 1330. Worth a visit only if you're in the neigborhood. The **Central Java Tourist Office** (Kanwil Depparpostal VII Jawa Tengah) at Jl. K.H.A. Dahlan 2, tel. 515-720, dispenses brochures, maps, and regional calendars of events; hours are Mon.-Thurs. 0800-1400, Friday to 1100, Saturday to 1330.

Change traveler's checks at **Bank Rakyat Indonesia,** Jl. Pattimura 2; **Bank Bumi Daya, Jl. Kepodang 32-34;** BDN, Jl. Kepodang 6-8; or **BNI,** Jl. Haryono 16. The **kantor imigrasi** is on Jl. Siliwangi in Krapyak. The **post office** is near Pasar Johar, right beside the telephone office. The best hospital, with English-speaking doctors, is **St. Elizabeth** in Candi at Jl. Kawi 1, tel. 315-345.

TRANSPORTATION

Getting There
From Jakarta flights take 45-60 minutes; Garuda's shuttle costs Rp126,000. A taxi from the A. Yani Airport (eight km west of the city) into Semarang costs Rp6000. Alternatively, it's a 15-minute walk to a *bemo* that will take you into town.

Semarang has deep-water berthing facilities for large seagoing vessels. The harbor is often used as a port of call for excursion ships with passengers embarking for Borobudur and other areas of Central Java. A taxi from the harbor into town costs Rp5000.

Trains depart Jakarta at 0800, 1630, 1753, 1950, and 2100; the most comfortable is the Mutiara Utara, which departs at around 1630, arriving at 0013. From Surabaya's Pasarturi station, trains depart at 1630 (arriving 2145) and 1730 (arriving 2252). All trains pull into Semarang's central and historic Tawang train station, though Poncol station is closer to the budget *losmen*.

The large **Terminal Terboyo** is on Jl. Kaligawe, six km east of downtown Semarang on the road to Kudus. Frequent city buses depart this station for the city for only Rp250. Exit the

bus terminal and walk out to the main road; buses heading west will reach city center in about 15 minutes.

Getting Around
Becak cluster around the municipal bus and Daihatsu stations, but are banned on Jl. Gajah Mada and Jl. Pemuda.

Bright orange Daihatsus (small Japanese *microlets*) run like ants all over town and charge Rp200-500 according to distance covered. Flag one going in your direction, or go to Terminal Baru, centrally located on Jl. H. A. Salim behind Pasar Johar. From this station, Daihatsus and city buses spew forth in all directions.

To get to Candi, take a bus on Jl. Pemuda marked Perumnas or Jatinealeh. There are taxi stands at the Metro and Dibya Puri hotels. Taxis are metered and very cheap.

Getting Away
Catch a taxi to the airport at the Metro Hotel or the Hotel Dibya Puri , or call the Indra Kelana Taxi Service, tel. (024) 312-515. The fare is around Rp6000. Or flag down an orange Daihatsu and try to bargain a ride for around Rp4000.

Garuda, Jl. Gajah Mada 11, tel. 20910 or 20178, offers a handy shuttle service seven times daily to Jakarta (Rp126,000) and twice daily to Surabaya. Buy your ticket at the cash window or at the office, open Mon.-Fri. 0800-1600, Saturday to 1300. **Merpati,** Jl. Gajah Mada 58/D, tel. 23027 or 23028, is open Mon.-Thurs. 0900-1400, Friday to 1100, Saturday to 1400. **Bouraq,** Jl. Gajah Mada 61/D, tel. 23779, and **Mandala,** Jl. Pemuda 40, tel. 285-319, also fly to Jakarta. Most airlines provide free transport to the airport.

Inquire about Pelni services at Jl. Mpu Tantular 25, tel. 20488, near Tawang train station; open Mon.-Fri. 0800-1600, Saturday to 1300. Pelni's KM *Kelimutu* calls at Semarang twice weekly, picking up passengers for Banjarmasin, Surabaya, Padangbai, Lembar, Ujung Pandang, Bima, Waingapu, Ende, and Kupang.

Semarang's Tawang station is along the main Surabaya-Pekalongan-Jakarta northern rail line; Semarang is very accessible by rail from these cities. From Semarang the Mutiara Utara and SBM Utara depart at 2145 and 2252, arriving in Jakarta about eight hours later. The most civilized way to get to Jakarta is on this train—the night bus dumps you in at some horrendous hour in a location far from the city. Trains take three hours to Pekalongan and five hours to Cirebon. The Cepat leaves Semarang at 0013, arriving in Surabaya at 0545.

The majority of *bis malam* and express bus offices are at the Terboyo bus station. Sample fares: Jakarta (500 km, nine hours), Rp5200-11,000; Bandung (368 km), Rp3900-8100; Yogyakarta (118 km), Rp1300-2600; Surabaya (379 km via Solo), Rp4000-8300; Surabaya (316 km), Rp3300-7500.

Buses leave early in the morning for Wonosobo for around Rp3000 (four hours). Express minibuses travel to Cirebon for Rp8000 (five hours) and Jakarta for Rp13,000 (eight hours).

VICINITY OF SEMARANG

AMBARAWA

In this small mountain town a pivotal clash took place between the Dutch and Republican irregulars in 1949; a huge ugly statue commemorates the famous action. There was also a notorious massacre of Dutch women and children by revolutionaries here in 1945.

Sights
The **Railway Museum** (Museum Kereta Api) exhibits locomotives built from 1891 to 1927 in Germany, Holland, and elsewhere. Free admission; two km from the bus terminal.

Ride the only cog railway still running on Java on a special chartered tour from Ambarawa to the village of Bedono, 17 km uphill. The steam line running Semarang to Ambarawa to Magelang was fully operational until 1977, when it was driven out of business by faster and cheaper private road transport. They still fire up a 1903 steam cogwheel, however, its beautiful engine with all original working parts in excellent shape. The engineer starts burning wood and coal in the steam locomotive around 0400 and by 0900 the engine is ready to roll. Ride in antique coaches, remodeled according to the original designs. A highlight is the 4.5-km section of track southwest of Jambu with a notched center rail gripped by a cogwheel. In the middle of the climb the train stops to let passengers hop down and take pictures.

The roundtrip journey consumes a day. A group of up to 80 people may sign up for this special tourist attraction, but a week's notice is required. It's possible to join a group of domestic tourists. Inquire at Exploitasi Jawa Tengah, Kantor PJKA, Jl. Thamrin 3, Semarang, tel. (024) 24500, or at the main PJKA office in Yogyakarta.

Accommodations And Transportation
Both **Losmen Sederhana** and **Losmen Aman** on Jl. Permuda rent rooms for Rp9000-12,000. **Losmen Tentaram** is somewhat better, priced from Rp15,000.

The bus from Semarang to Ambarawa (40 km) takes one hour. Yogyakarta to Ambarawa (90 km) via Magelang requires about three hours. Ambarawa is a good embarkation point for Wonosobo and the Dieng Plateau. Six to eight buses a day connect Ambarawa-Wonosobo-Purwokerto, or you can take a bus heading for Yogyakarta until Secang (Rp300), then transfer to a bus to Wonosobo (Rp700). In all, the Ambarawa-Wonosobo route takes about two hours.

BANDUNGAN

Bandungan is a popular 981-meter-high hill resort and a good base for exploring the Gedung Songo temple group. First take a minibus to Ambarawa, then from Ambarawa's Pasar Projo take another bus northwest off the main road for about seven km (Rp350, 30 minutes) to Bandungan.

Bandungan produces abundant vegetables, fruits, and decorative flowers. The locals hire out horses to explore the surrounding mountain roads.

Accommodations And Food
Numerous hotels and *penginapan* rent rooms for Rp4000-60,000. Check out **Penginapan Sri Rejeki** and the nearby **Riani I,** charging Rp5000-12,000 with small *mandi*. **Wisma Kereta Api,** run by the Railway Authority, is a classical 1930s art deco structure; picturesque bungalows rent for Rp8000-20,000. The *wisma* overlooks a public swimming pool and the plains of Central Java. Avoid the restaurant, which serves terrible food. The **Madya Hill View** is

modern and better kept; Rp8000 for rooms with bath, beverage included.

The 40-room **Hotel Wina** (Rp12,000-35,000), higher up the mountain, offers sweeping views. **Pondok Sarimaryn Indah,** with 32 rooms from Rp6000-12,000, provides hot and cold water and egg and coffee for breakfast. About one km out of town is Bandungan's top hotel, the **Rawa Pening,** with rooms and cottages for Rp25,000-38,000 in a complex of gardens and terraces. Restaurant with exquisite views.

Lots of *warung* in town. Shop for fruit in the *pasar* near the intersection to Gedung Songo. Flower sellers gather here in the early morning starting at 0700.

THE GEDUNG SONGO GROUP

This archaeological park is seven km uphill from Bandungan on the slopes of a small valley on the southern side of Gunung Ungaran. The name means "Nine Temples," though there are actually seven, built A.D. 730-780.

At 900 meters elevation, this is perhaps the most breathtaking temple location on Java. The site was chosen with great care for its magnificent views, encompassing Gunung Ungaran, Lake Rawapening, Gunung Merbabu, and even hazy Gunung Merapi. Although most of the main *candi* in each group were dedicated to Shiva, one shrine was set aside for Vishnu, a Hindu god rarely worshipped on Java. See Temple II with its well-preserved *kala-makara* relief on the portal.

Though vehicles can drive to the first temple up an incredibly steep road, it's far better to walk the six kilometers to Gedung Songo from Bandungan through a beautiful region of vegetable patches, roses, and pine trees. There's a 2,427-meter-long walking path which connects all five complexes. Entrance fee Rp350; camping Rp550. It takes about 20 minutes to walk from the parking lot to temple Gedong V.

The horseback riding here (Rp5000 for 1.5-2 hours) is one of the best deals in Java. You can either ride or be led. These noncomplaining, small, sturdy beasts are on automatic pilot—they know all the trails and seem indefatigable. Ride through gorgeous gardens of papaya, bananas, potatoes, tobacco, cabbages, beans, grapes, tomatoes, and corn, with cloud-scudding temples above and volcanos looming in the distance.

DEMAK

Twenty-five km northeast of Semarang on the road to Surabaya, Demak was once the capital of Java's first Islamic kingdom. Although a prosperous seaport until the 16th century, due to the heavy silting of its harbor Demak is now three km inland.

In 1479, the Islamic ruler Raden Patah built Demak's wooden mosque, **Mesjid Agung.** This is the oldest mosque on Java, considered so holy that seven pilgrimages to it are the equivalent of one pilgrimage to Mecca.

The structure is a prime example of the joint architectural influences of the Java-Hindu and Islamic cultures. Legend has it the great mosque was built in a single night. The mosque's eight great pillars are the only remaining original features; the rest was completely rebuilt in 1845. Symbolism abounds. The three tiers of the roof, for example, are said to symbolize the three main levels of religious consciousness, while the five doorways represent the five fundamentals of Islamic teaching. Newly refurbished and renovated, President Suharto himself officiated at the rededication ceremonies in April 1987. Inside are many relics.

Behind the mosque, visit the venerated grave of the founder of the Demak kingdom, Raden Patah. **Sunan Kalijaga's Mausoleum** is found at Kadilangu, two km south of Demak. On Besar

DIANA LASICH HARPER

Mesjid Agung

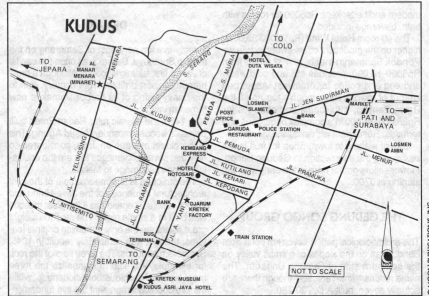

KUDUS

© MOON PUBLICATIONS, INC.

10 of the Javanese calendar, tens of thousands gather here to celebrate Idhul Adha Day.

KUDUS

Kudus, 54 km northeast of Semarang, originated with the founding of a mosque here in 1546 by Sunan Kudus, a Javan *wali* (holy man). Though a staunch Islamic town—censuring looks if you wear shorts—some old Hindu customs prevail: cows may not be slaughtered within the city limits and schoolboys still spend a night at the shrine of Sunan Muria to improve their chances in exams.

Kudus is famed as a center for the clove cigarette industry, producing nearly 25% of Indonesia's annual output. The *kiajis* of Old Town Kudus have a reputation as healers. It's easy getting around town, either walking or by *becak*, which are really cheap here.

Sights
Wander the narrow streets of the staunchly Islamic *kauman*; ask directions to the ruins of the Hindu-period **Mesjid Bubar.** One kilometer beyond the *alun-alun* is ancient **Al Manar Mosque,**

containing a famous minaret. Built by Sunan Kudus in 1549, this mosque has undergone numerous improvements and modifications. The 20-meter-high, red-brick minaret in front, built around 1685, closely resembles the temple-building style of East Java. Combining both Hindu and Islamic architecture, it actually looks like a Javanese Hindu temple. This *menara* is radically different from minarets in Saudi Arabia or Egypt; it's really just a modified *kulkul* (watchtower) added to fortified temples during Hindu times to warn rice farmers of danger. Now used to announce daily prayers; you can climb the wooden ladder inside for a view of the city.

Malam Dandang takes place annually during Ramadan; this traditional ceremony is connected with the opening of the Al Manar Mosque. In the rear of the complex is the elaborate mausoleum of Sunan Kudus.

Kretek Factories
Clove cigarettes were invented in the 1890s by an entrepreneur who claimed the smoke ameliorated his asthma. Indonesians now smoke over 36,000 tons of cloves a year, outstripping domestic supplies and even importing cloves from Madagascar and Zanzibar.

Take free tours of the factories of Djarum, Noryorono, Seokun, and Jambu Boh. Chinese-owned Djarum's 17 factory buildings each produces a million handrolled *kretek* cigarettes per day. Five hundred people work in the rolling shed; some roll up to 5,000 a day. In the packaging building 2,000 women work like ants, dressed in dainty *kebaya* and jewelry. Visit Djarum's modern offices on Jl. Jen. A. Yani and take a free tour.

Accommodations And Food

About 10 *penginapan* and hotels range from Rp10,000 to Rp25,000. **Losmen Amin,** Jl. Manur 448, is cheap and adequate. On Jl. Jen. Sudirman (no. 63) is **Losmen Slamet**; Rp10,000-15,000. You'll find the **Flamingo Cafe** at the same address. The menu is in Indonesian; the real thing.

Hotel Duta Wisata, Jl. Sunan Muria-Barongan 194, tel. (0291) 22694, is a poor person's plush hotel. From Rp15,000, not including 10% service charge and 10% tax. A quiet place on a back street. Moving up in price, the town's premier hotel is **Notosari,** Jl. Kepodang 17, tel. 21245. Within walking distance of the bus station, rooms start at around Rp18,000 with breakfast and go up to Rp31,500 with a/c. Friendly people; clean, quiet, good service. Best in town is the **Kudus Asri Jaya Hotel,** tel. 22449, with pool and a/c rooms from Rp68,000.

A *pasar malam* springs up around the *alun-alun* each evening. Kudus is known for a few specialty dishes, among them *soto ayam, soto kudus* (chicken soup), and *jenang kudus* (made of glutinous rice, brown sugar, and coconut); sample at the bus terminal *warung* or at **Simpang Tujuh** in front of the *kantor kabupaten.* The people of Kudus are for the most part prohibited from eating beef, but buffalo meat, chicken, goat, and fish are all available. **Garuda Restaurant,** Jl. Jen. Sudirman 1, offers Javanese, European, and Chinese dishes in the Rp2500-3500 range.

Getting Away

The minibus station is right behind the bus station. Sample fares: Demak, Rp500; Semarang, Rp650; Surabaya, Rp6000; Jakarta, Rp7500; Jepara, Rp500; Rembang, Rp600; Mayong, Rp500; Solo, Rp2000.

Kembang Express, Jl. Jen. A. Yani 90, tel. 282, runs night and morning buses to Yogyakarta, Rp2000.

VICINITY OF KUDUS

Colo

Colo, 18 km north of Kudus at the foot of Gunung Muria, is a recreational spot with cool, healthy, cloudy weather. Catch a minibus from Simpang Lima and ride up the mountain; stay at the *penginapan.* About 1.5 km north of Colo are **Montel Falls.** West of the resort, climb the thousand steps to the grave of Sunan Muria. You can buy Colo's specialties, *nasi pecel pakis* and *ayam panggang,* at many of the *warung.*

Mayong

The birthplace of Raden Kartini is in Mayong, 12 km northwest of Kudus or 25 km south of Jepara. The house is 50 meters from the highway.

The daughter of a Javanese civil servant in the Dutch colonial government, Raden Ajeng Kartini wrote the most important Indonesian literary work of this century. Titled originally *Through Darkness to Light* in 1911, the work was reissued by the University Press of America in 1985 under the title *Letters of a Javanese Princess.* It provides a fascinating picture of the life and spirit of the times. Although she died in childbirth in her 20s, posthumously Kartini became a spokesperson for the liberation and education of women and an advocate of Indonesian independence. Pilgrimages are still made to her grave near Rembang every 21 April on Kartini Day. In Rembang's *kantor kabupaten* is the **Kartini Museum.**

JEPARA

A small, scruffy, country town 90 km northeast of Semarang on the north coast. Jepara was a main port for the "Second Mataram" of the 17th century, playing an important role in rice export until the harbor silted up.

Today Jepara is noteworthy as home to some of the best traditional carvers on Java. Jepara's other name is Kota Ukir, "Carving Town." Except for the hinges, no nails, screws, or metal joinery are used. The wood comes from Blora and Cepu (East Java)—teak mostly, but also mahogany, *kayu meranti,* and *sono.* Coming into town you'll see shops overflowing with tables, chairs, and cabinets piled high inside and out.

Paid by the meter, men come in from the surrounding villages to carve. To see them in action, visit the nearby villages of Tahunan, Mantingan, and Blakanggunung. Many shops are concentrated along Jl. Pemuda. Want to learn carving? S.T.N. (Bagian Ukir) offers a three-year course in both modern and traditional styles.

Accommodations And Food

Right next to the noisy bus station on Jl. Kol. Sugiono is **Hotel Terminal**; a/c rooms with European toilet cost Rp25,000 d. Rooms for Rp8500 have just a sink inside; no fan, good lighting. Many rooms face a garden; restaurant attached.

Losmen Asia, Jl. Kartini 36, and **Losmen Jakarta**, Jl. Pemuda 16, are in the Rp6000-9500 range; women travelers report hassles at both places. The Ritz of Jepara is **Menno Jaya Inn**, Jl. Diponegoro 40/B, Rp9000-18,000; friendly owners, excellent value. Another good value is the inexpensive outdoor restaurant **Pondok Rasa,** Jl. Pahlawan 2—excellent atmosphere. At the *terminal bis,* eat at **Rahayu.**

Vicinity Of Jepara

Kartini Beach is two km from town. Rent a *prahu* and visit nearby Pulau Mandalika; nice swimming. Seven km east of Jepara is Pantai Bandengan, one of the few beaches in all of Central Java that's clean with clear water. Also a camping area here. A Portuguese fortress lies on the steep coast in Desa Kelet east of Jepara; take a *bemo* first to Keling, then on to Kelet for Rp550, then by foot to the fort.

At **Mantingan,** locally known as Makam Sunan, eight km from Jepara or 20 km south of Rembang, are remains of a 1559 mosque and cemetery. Get there by minibus for Rp3000, or by *andong* down a lovely country lane for Rp1500. Examine the Hindu-style medallions on the tomb of Ratu Kalinjamat, a Jeparan warrior-queen who attacked the Portuguese fortress in Melaka twice in the 1500s. Though they appear as leaf decorations, when viewed from a distance you can make out the figures of monkeys. Although Islamic religious laws forbade representing living creatures, the desire to depict people and animals was so strong the sculptors composed them of leaves and flowers.

CENTRAL JAVA

Central Java is the island's cultural, geographic, and historic heartland. Lofty mountains march across the entire central portion of the province; the cool slopes contain numerous hill resorts. This range roughly divides the trading and administrative center in the north from the cultural and emotional center in the south.

Central Java was the site of the first Islamic kingdom on the island, the sultanate of Demak, founded in 1511. From this beachhead the new creed quickly spread, destroying the already weakened Hindu kingdoms to the south. Southern Central Java is extremely rich in archaeological sites, from Hindu to Portuguese, all easily accessible.

The island's most crowded and most feudal province, Central Java has 28.5 million people, but only about 10% live in cities. The rest dwell in villages. The population density is about 690 people per square km over a total area of 34,205 square km. Large industry occupies Cilegon (cement), Solo (handmade *kretek* cigarettes), and Tegal (boatbuilding). Moderate industries include *jamu,* food and soft-drink production, and *batik*. The rainy season runs from October through April; the rest of the year is dry.

Because of its low cost, easygoing pace, physical beauty, rich culture, and superlative shopping, Central Java is the most popular region on Java for foreign travelers. The towns most noted for their handicrafts are Solo and Banyumas for *batik*; Sukoharjo for carvings; and Solo, Salatiga, and Secang for textiles. A few pottery villages, like Kasongan outside of Yogyakarta, produce whimsical, fragile animals and decorative objects from red clay.

YOGYAKARTA

One of the largest villages in the world, Yogyakarta is Java's cultural capital and an important center for higher learning—Java's Kyoto. The name means Prosperity Without War and is often shortened to Yogya—pronounced "JOAG-jah." For centuries a royal city and major trade center, the Yogyakarta *kraton* is the highest-ranking court in Indonesia and "Special Region Yogyakarta" (pop. three million) is responsible directly to Jakarta and not to the provincial head of Central Java. From 1946 to 1950, Yogyakarta was the grassroots capital of Indonesia and the headquarters of the revolutionary forces. Today, with its rich culture, economy hotels, and restaurants, it's a city streamlined for travelers.

Well known as the "main door to traditional Javanese culture," the city draws thousands of talented people from around the world. There are numerous music and dance schools, brilliant choreographers, drama and poetry workshops, folk theater and *wayang* troupes, artists excelling in the plastic arts. It's also one of the best places to shop in Southeast Asia. Yogyakarta is a major *batik*-producing center, and, due to increased tourist awareness, this art is developing ever higher standards. The painters and sculptors here are Indonesia's elite, strongly individualistic but increasingly commercialized.

History
Yogyakarta lies in the center of Java's Realm of the Dead. It's a city surrounded by ancient ruins. Only an hour away are the great temples of Borobudur and Prambanan. The Mataram Empire of Central Java fell apart and formed the states of Surakarta (Solo) and Yogyakarta in 1755. Yogyakarta is still governed by an ancient line of sultans and is the only remaining functioning sultanate in Indonesia. The layout of the city still reflects the traditional formal relationship between the sultan, marketplace, and mosque.

For the Javanese, Yogyakarta has always symbolized nationalistic passion and resistance to alien rule. A stubborn center of the guerrilla struggle against the Dutch, during Indonesia's war of independence it was the first capital of the infant Republic. During the Dutch occupation, the sultan locked himself in his *kraton,* and

CENTRAL JAVA

120 km

COURTESY OF THE ROYAL TROPICAL INSTITUTE IN AMSTERDAM

when he finally consented to negotiate with the invader it was from the top of his palace wall, looking down on them, with all his people watching. A three-nation committee tried to bring the Dutch and Indonesians together here, but they agreed only on minor points. Finally, in 1948, the Dutch launched an all-out attack on the city, dropping 900 paratroopers and heavy bombs while U.S.- and British-built planes strafed the streets. With the Republican leaders captured and their ministries closed down, the rebel forces retired from Yogyakarta to the countryside, carrying out a people's war.

The U.S. Senate, noting its Marshall Plan money flowing to support Holland's fight against the Indonesians, threatened to cut the Dutch off. Finally, in December 1949, Holland formally recognized the new Republic. With the Javanese now in command, Solo's sultanate—which had sided with the Dutch—was summarily dissolved, while Yogyakarta's was rewarded with status as a Special Region. The territory was allowed to govern itself and its sultan was appointed as its first governor—a lifetime position—as well as Indonesia's first vice president.

SIGHTS

Taman Sari

A pleasure park built in feudal splendor between 1758 and 1765 for the sultan and his family. Taman Sari once featured lighted underwater corridors, cool subterranean mosques, meditation platforms in the middle of lily ponds, *gamelan* towers, and galleries for dancing—all in mock Spanish architecture. Princesses bathed in flower-strewn pools, streams flowed above covered passageways, boats drifted in artificial lakes. Tour on foot 0800-1700; Rp500 admission. Students will offer to guide you to secret places.

See the men's and women's bathing pools, and the underground mosque. Though sections of the ruins are under renovation, the ornate swimming pools and crumbling walls rebuilt, and many of the gates replastered, the gardens on the whole exist in a charming state of disrepair.

The "living ruins" are equally interesting. The area of narrow dusty lanes and small houses behind the Water Palace is a center of the *batik* industry, where many painters work in bamboo studios. Also visit the Batik School.

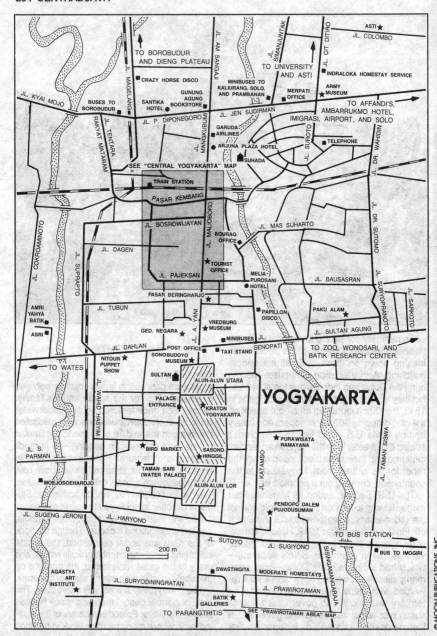

Bird Market

Pasar Ngasem, the grotty, cacophonous bird market north of Taman Sari, features parrots, orioles, roosters, singing turtle doves, and even eagles. Also see such animals as squirrels, rabbits, guinea pigs, and monkeys. A popular tourist attraction; hang out in the back and watch children training pigeons for competitions.

The *Kraton*

Built in 1757, this is the palace compound of Yogyakarta's sultans—classical Javanese palace-court architecture at its finest. It costs Rp1000 to get into the front portion of the *kraton,* called Pagelaran, and Rp1400 to enter the Di Dalam, the inner sanctum. Open Mon.-Thurs. 0830-1400, Friday 0800-1130, Saturday 0830-1300, Sunday 0830-1400. Dress conservatively; men should wear long trousers.

The *kraton* features *batik* and silver workshops, mosques, schools, markets, offices, and two museums, all enclosed by three-meter-thick white walls imitating European fortifications. The interiors are especially reminiscent of prewar Dutch bourgeois mansions. During the war of independence, guerrilla commander Suharto dressed as a barefoot peasant and peddled vegetables at the rear of the *kraton* to confer with the sultan on tactics to use against the Dutch.

See the ornate and heavily gilded Bangsal Kencono ("Golden Pavilion"), with its carved teak pillars. The Glass Pavilion combines Hindu motifs, Buddhist lotus flowers, stylized opening words from the Koran, marble floors, and vortex ceilings. The sultan's collection includes *wayang* puppets, royal carriages, Raden Saleh portraits, and life-sized costumed figures. A museum displays trappings of the sultanate—a saddle of gold and silver thread, huge 600-year-old brass gongs, a *gamelan* inaugurated during the Majapahit Empire.

At the souvenir concession, buy copies of old photographic prints for Rp300 apiece—a good selection. The *batik* factory in the *kraton* is run by one of the sultan's sons, and is well worth a visit. The process is completely unmechanized, his prices are pretty reasonable, and he carries the full range of traditional court designs. To visit all portions of the palace, apply at the Kraton Office. Permission is required from the Kraton Office to videotape; Rp12,500.

Kraton Performances

The inner court, with male and female steps to the entrance, includes two small museums and a pavilion where you can see classical dance rehearsals each Sunday 1030-1200. On Monday and Wednesday 1030-1200 traditional *gamelan* rehearsals are staged. Both performances are included in the price of admission.

The performance standards here are the highest in the country. The Yogyakarta dance style, created by Sultan Hamengku Buwono I (1755-72) in time of war, requires an almost military discipline of mind and body. Dancers are distant and withdrawn, consumed by pauses and meditative poses. Even the jangle of bells is considered coarse; anklets are used only by men for monkey and animal roles.

The Pakualaman

On Jl. Sultan Agung, this is the other *kraton* of Yogyakarta, a princedom founded within the sultanate of Yogyakarta by Paku Alam I in 1813. After considerable intermarriage, the Pakualam royalty has many connections with the *kraton* family in Solo. This court also receives visitors. *Gamelan* concerts are staged about once every fifth Sunday. Open 0800-1300; donation requested.

Yet another fine example of Javanese *kraton* architecture is the Ambarrukmo Palace, built by Hamengku Buwono VII in the 1890s.

Museums

Musium Biologi, Jl. Sultan Agung 22, displays a collection of plants and stuffed animals from throughout the archipelago; Rp500 entrance fee, open Mon.-Thurs. 0800-1300, Friday until 1100, Saturday and Sunday until 1200.

The **Army Museum** (Dharma Wiratama), Jl. Jen. Sudirman 70, is open Mon.-Thurs. 0800-1300, Saturday and Sunday 0800-1200. This museum records the Indonesian revolution, displaying documents, photos, historical articles, homemade weapons, uniforms, and equipment from the 1945-49 struggle.

Located on Alun-alun Utara, the square north of the *kraton,* is the **Sonobudoyo Museum,** a building constructed in the classical Javanese *kraton* style. Open Tues.-Thurs. 0830-1330, Friday 0800-1115, Saturday 0800-1200, and Sunday 0830-1300; closed holidays. A first-rate collection of Javanese, Madurese, and Balinese

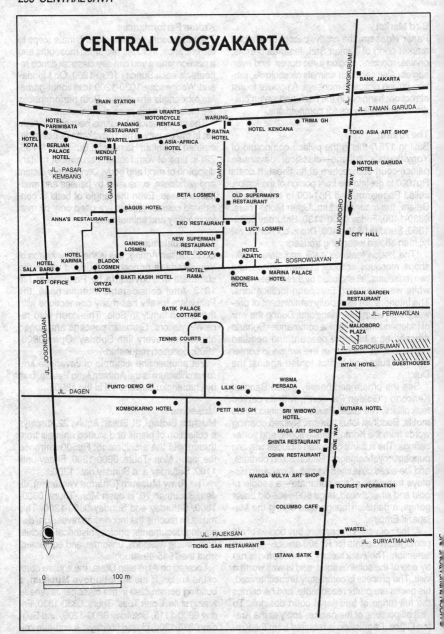

CENTRAL YOGYAKARTA

BANK JAKARTA

JL. MANGKUBUMI

JL. TAMAN GARUDA

TRAIN STATION

URANTS
MOTORCYCLE
RENTALS

WARUNG

TRIMA GH

TOKO ASIA ART SHOP

HOTEL
PARIWISATA

PADANG
RESTAURANT

WARTEL

RATNA
HOTEL

HOTEL KENCANA

HOTEL
KOTA

BERLIAN
PALACE
HOTEL

MENDUT
HOTEL

ASIA-AFRICA
HOTEL

NATOUR GARUDA
HOTEL

JL. PASAR
KEMBANG

GANG II

GANG I

JL. MALIOBORO

ONE WAY

BETA LOSMEN

OLD SUPERMAN'S
RESTAURANT

CITY HALL

BAGUS HOTEL

ANNA'S RESTAURANT

EKO RESTAURANT

LUCY LOSMEN

GANDHI
LOSMEN

NEW SUPERMAN
RESTAURANT

HOTEL JOGYA

HOTEL
AZIATIC

HOTEL
KARINIA

HOTEL
SALA BARU

BLADOK
LOSMEN

JL. SOSROWIJAYAN

POST OFFICE

ORYZA
HOTEL

BAKTI KASIH HOTEL

HOTEL
RAMA

INDONESIA
HOTEL

MARINA PALACE
HOTEL

LEGIAN GARDEN
RESTAURANT

JL. PERWAKILAN

BATIK PALACE
COTTAGE

MALIOBORO
PLAZA

JL. SOSROKUSUMAN

TENNIS COURTS

INTAN HOTEL

GUESTHOUSES

JL. JOGONEGARAN

WISMA
PERSADA

JL. DAGEN

PUNTO DEWO GH

LILIK GH

KOMBOKARNO HOTEL

PETIT MAS GH

SRI WIBOWO
HOTEL

MUTIARA HOTEL

MAGA ART SHOP

SHINTA RESTAURANT

ONE WAY

OSHIN RESTAURANT

WARGA MULYA ART SHOP

TOURIST INFORMATION

COLUMBO CAFE

WARTEL

JL. PAJEKSAN

TIONG SAN RESTAURANT

JL. SURYATMAJAN

ISTANA BATIK

0   100 m

arts and crafts, excellent *batik* exhibits, musical instruments (a complete seven-ton iron and copper *pelog gamelan*), palace furnishings, 18-carat gold Buddha, *wayang golek* puppets, woodcarvings, and weapons. Contribute Rp500 as you enter.

About 60 meters from the *kraton's* main gate is the **Kareta Museum,** with old royal coaches and carriages.

Monumen Diponegoro

A reconstruction of Diponegoro's residence, destroyed by the Dutch in 1825, is located four km west of Yogyakarta at Tegalrejo. A 15-minute bicycle ride from town, Rp1000 by *becak,* or take bus no. 1 from Jl. H.O.S. Cokroaminoto.

This museum is dedicated to Prince Diponegoro (1785-1855), who led partisans during the Java War (1825-30). His *kris* are hung with flowers in glass cases; see also photos of his other sacred possessions and the large commemorative *pendopo.* Visit the hole through which he and his followers escaped to reach Gua Selarong near Parangtritis. After five years of bloody war this nobleman was tricked into negotiations at Magelang, arrested, and exiled to Sulawesi for the remaining 25 years of his life.

Gajah Mada University

With 17,000 students, this is Indonesia's largest tertiary-level institute. It opened in December 1949 with a total student body of 483, many part-time guerrilla fighters among them. Since there was no campus or any other facilities, from 1949 to 1973 the northern courtyards of the Yogyakarta *kraton* were utilized as lecture halls; its first medical faculty worked out of the *pendopo* of the crown prince's palace, and the *gamelan* store became the university dispensary. Informal places to meet students include the main building (Gedung Induk) in the middle of the campus and the Balai Budaya, the art and cultural exhibits building.

Mosques And Churches

Best to visit mosques between sunrise and noon. Dress straight. Two-hundred-year-old **Mesjid Agung** is on the western side of Alun-alun Lor. This is where the *kraton's* royal *gamelan* are kept during Sekaten week and where the famous *gunungan* procession terminates.

Mesjid Soko Tunggal, opposite the main gate (Pintu Gerbang) of Taman Sari, was built in the *kraton* pavilion style; stories from the Koran are carved on its pillars. Ethereal Batak hymn-singing vibrates from the **Huria Kristen Batak Protestant Church,** Jl. Nyoman Oka 22, Kota Baru, early Sunday mornings. Attend the Indonesian-style Catholic mass in Yogyakarta's oldest church, **St. Francis Xavier,** Jl. P. Senopati (near the post office); masses are held Saturday at 1730 and Sunday at 0530 and 0700.

ACCOMMODATIONS

Although inflation has affected Yogyakarta's reputation as Indonesia's *losmen* mecca, the city still offers remarkably good value. During the Ramayana ballet (four days only, each May, June, July, and August), Yogyakarta hotels are packed. The following is a small sampling of the accommodations available.

Pasar Kembang Area

The area between the two parallel streets Jl. Pasar Kembang and Jl. Sosrowijayan is the cheapest, but it's too close to the train station; you hear noisy locomotives running all night. Most *losmen* here charge Rp5000-10,000.

On the small lane Gang I are a number of small *losmen.* Most don't allow you to come in later than 2330 or 2400. Take care with the super bargains on this lane; make sure your room is secure or you may find yourself minus your backpack or camera. **Beta Losmen,** with its own *kampung,* is one of the largest; clean, friendly, secure; usually full in July and August. **Hotel Jogya** is relaxing, clean, and central—a pretty good value.

The other small gang, Gang II, offers comparable values. **Bagus Hotel** charges Rp5000-8000 with fans, tea only. More *bagus* than Bagus is the **Gandhi Losmen,** one of the cheapest and best accommodations around. The family is very friendly and helpful, and there's free tea as well as laundry service—a secure place with a beautiful garden. **Gandhi II** nearby is very basic, damp, and dirty. **Losmen Prastha Jaya** has fans and an outside *mandi.* Clean, but no breakfast.

Jalan Pasar Kembang

The slightly decrepit **Ratna Hotel**, no. 17A, is set back from the road and quiet; Rp10,000-15,000 d, including private *mandi* and toilet. Across Gang I from the Ratna is **Hotel Kencana**, with doubles (king-size beds) and private *mandi* for Rp15,000. At no. 41 is **Hotel Mataram**; Rp8000-10,000 with private *mandi* and toilet. The **Rachmat** and the **Shinta** offer rooms in the Rp8000-10,000 range.

At the end of Jl. Pasar Kembang is **Hotel Kota**; Rp12,000-20,000. Beautiful, spacious rooms, nicely laid out, secure, clean, showers in some rooms, leafy gardens, tea. Drawbacks: the front rooms are noisy, it's run like a boarding school, Rp20,000 pp deposit required. No guests admitted between 2330 and 0530.

Asia-Africa Hotel, no. 25, tel. (0274) 66219, fax 4489, rents economy rooms for Rp13,000-30,000 and a/c rooms with private patio for Rp28,000-45,000.

Newer hotels on Jl. Pasar Kembang include the **Mendut Hotel**, tel. 63435, fax 64753, with a small pool and a/c rooms for Rp32,000-85,000, and the **Berlian Palace Hotel**, tel. 60312, fax 3181, with overpriced a/c rooms at Rp63,000-90,000.

Jalan Sosrowijayan

Just around the corner from Gang I is the Arab-owned **Hotel Aziatic**, Jl. Sosrowijayan 6. The Aziatic (Rp12,000) is clean and comfortable, with large beds in big rooms. Super security; no fans. **Indonesia Hotel**, tel. (0274) 87659, across the road at no. 9, features rooms from Rp6000 with common bath, Rp9000 with private bath, and Rp14,000 with fan and bath. Garden courtyard, pleasant environment, good laundry facilities. Down the street is the new but claustrophobic **Marina Palace Hotel**, tel. 88490, with overpriced rooms at Rp84,000-105,000; the **Bakti Kasih Hotel**, tel. 4890, with desultory a/c rooms for Rp47,000-84,000; and the completely disorganized **Bladok Losmen**, tel. 60452, rooms priced at Rp31,000-42,000 with fan and private bath.

Jalan Sosrokusuman

The **Puri** gets the most tourists; Rp8000-12,000. If traveling with children, rent the large room with TV, fan, refrigerator, and two extra beds—less expensive than two regular rooms. Com-

fortable **Prambanan Guesthouse**, no. 18-20, tel. (0274) 3303, charges Rp8000-12,000 with bath. The **Intan Hotel**, no. 1/16, offers rooms for Rp7000-12,000. Extremely central and clean. Mostly Indonesians stay here. **WHW Hotel** has rooms for Rp5000 s or d with fan and outside *mandi*. **Hotel Zamrud** has extremely clean rooms for Rp10,000 s, Rp15,000 d, all with inside *mandi* and fan.

Jalan Dagen

A quieter street with better value hotels, though not as well-priced as those on Jl. Prawirotaman.

By far the best of a half-dozen choices is the clean, quiet, and nicely decorated **Peti Mas Guesthouse**, tel. (0274) 61938, fax 71175, with attractive pool and garden restaurant; fan rooms for Rp20,000-45,000, a/c rooms at Rp46,000-82,000.

Jalan Prawirotaman

A European yuppie enclave in a peaceful neighborhood just 10 minutes by *becak* south of the *kraton* area. *Becak* from city center cost a fixed Rp1500.

Small guesthouses and private homes on this street rent out the majority of their rooms to European package tourists. These guesthouses are a much better value than accommodations near the train station. All are about the same price, some of the best deals in Yogyakarta. Usually included in room rates are breakfast, tea, juice, and snacks. Often built around attractive gardens, these guesthouses are very comfortable, with Western toilets, and offer postal, laundry, taxi, and ticketing services. Nearly all take credit cards. During the high season, July-Aug., call or fax first to inquire after vacancies. Sending a fax is the most reliable way to make a reservation.

Sartika Homestay, no. 44A, tel. (0274) 72669, receives rave reviews from travelers. Afi, the friendly English-speaking manager, is always ready to answer questions and provide any services for a pleasant stay. Many travelers think this the best accommodation in the neighborhood, and wish they could stay much longer. Room rates are Rp15,000-20,000 including breakfast, tasty snacks, and drinks. **Sumaryo Guesthouse**, tel. 77552, fax 73507, is also recommended; swimming pool, nice rooms, quiet, good breakfast, cold beer, can get your washing done.

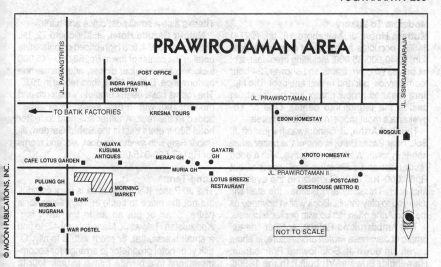

© MOON PUBLICATIONS, INC.

PRAWIROTAMAN AREA

JL. PARANGTRITIS

JL. SISINGAMANGARAJA

POST OFFICE

INDRA PRASTNA
HOMESTAY

JL. PRAWIROTAMAN I

← TO BATIK FACTORIES

KRESNA TOURS

EBONI HOMESTAY

MOSQUE

WIJAYA
KUSUMA
ANTIQUES

GAYATRI
GH

CAFE LOTUS GARDEN

MERAPI GH

KROTO HOMESTAY

MURIA GH

PULUNG GH

MORNING
MARKET

LOTUS BREEZE
RESTAURANT

JL. PRAWIROTAMAN II

POSTCARD
GUESTHOUSE (METRO II)

WISMA
NUGRAHA

BANK

WAR POSTEL

NOT TO SCALE

Another nice place is **Perwita Sari,** no. 31, tel. 77592, Rp10,000-25,000 including breakfast; large clean rooms, friendly staff, swimming pool. **Wisma Indah Guesthouse,** no. 12, tel. and fax 76021, is a family-run Indonesian-style hotel with private bath, shower, fan, complimentary snacks and tea; very clean and friendly. Rates are Rp15,000-25,000 economy, Rp20,000-30,000 standard with fan, Rp35,000-45,000 a/c, and Rp40,000-50,000 deluxe. See Anton, who knows all about Yogyakarta, especially its archaeological sites.

Duta Guesthouse, no. 20, tel. and fax 72064, is very relaxing, with showers and Western-style toilets, electric fan, a lovely courtyard, and refreshing swimming pool. Clean and friendly; Rp10,000-15,000 with common bath, Rp20,000-25,000 private bath, Rp30,000-35,000 with a/c.

Right next door is the **Rose Guesthouse,** tel. 77991, very friendly, great pool, and a full range of services including laundry and tours. Economy rooms are Rp12,000-20,000, better rooms go for Rp20,000-50,000 including tax and breakfast. Another outstanding value is **Metro Guesthouse,** no. 7/71, with free tea, swimming pool, clean, friendly service, and a fair-priced restaurant. Rates are Rp9000-12,000 in the nearby Postcard Guesthouse annex, Rp14,000-17,000 economy, Rp20,000-35,000 standard with fan, and Rp40,000-50,000 with a/c.

Cheaper places are often subsidiaries of larger guesthouses, such as **Delta Homestay,** owned by Duta, on Jl. Prawirotaman II. Economy rooms run Rp10,000-15,000 and a/c rooms are Rp24,000-28,000. The clean, new, small pool has a bright red water slide. **Agung Guesthouse,** tel. 75512 on the same street is another popular spot with rooms in the same price range. **Makuta Guesthouse,** tel. 71004, lacks a pool but has an attractive small garden and decent rooms for Rp8000-20,000. Dutch and German tour groups often stay at the modern five-story **Airlangga Hotel,** at Jl. Prawirotaman 6, tel. 63344, fax 71427. Lacks character.

The neighborhood's cheapest option is the simple but friendly **Vagabond Youth Hostel,** tel. 71207, with decent rooms, helpful travel tips, and unusual tours to Creme Cave and Krakal Beach, and Kaliurang trekking. Dorms are Rp5000, rooms Rp10,000-15,000.

To stay with a Dutch- or English-speaking family and enjoy home-cooked meals in a family atmosphere, use **Indraloka Homestay Service,** Jl. Cik Ditiro 14, tel. 3614 or 0274. See Mrs. Moerdiyono. Expect to pay around Rp22,000 d, plus 21% service and tax. She caters to intellectuals and won't take just anybody. She also arranges excursions to tourist sites near Yogyakarta, and is plugged into a network of homestays in other Javanese cities.

Moderate To Luxury

Mutiara Hotel, Jl. Malioboro 18, tel. (0274) 64531, occupies an excellent downtown location; Rp40,000-85,000, including breakfast, a/c, all taxes, Western baths and shower, 24-hour room service, bar and restaurant, pool. The Mutiara features a new annex just up the street beside the tourist info center. One of Yogyakarta's most modern downtown hotels.

The **Puri Artha,** Jl. Cendrawasih 9 just off Jl. Solo near Pasar Baru, is one of the better small hotels in town. Well-run, attractive, with a good restaurant and swimming pool, costs about Rp63,000-105,000. *Gamelan* in the evening, and each Thursday and Sunday the staff will take you to play tennis. Book well in advance as the Puri Artha often fills up with package tourists.

The **Ambarrukmo Palace,** another fine example of Javanese *kraton* architecture, is about seven km down Jl. Solo toward Prambanan. Hamengku Buwono VII built it in the 1890s. Rates are Rp178,500 for the cheapest single room, Rp745,000 for the presidential suite. The shops in the arcade charge ridiculous prices.

There's also a small post office and bank.

Natour Garuda Hotel, Jl. Malioboro 72, tel. 66353, fax 63074, is a high-priced colonial-style hotel in the center of town; Rp252,000-745,000 including tax, service, dinner, and Ramayana performance. Built in 1911, then rebuilt in 1938. The rooms have been completely restored and modernized, with a new seven-story annex added in the rear. Another splendid four-star hotel 500 meters east is the **Sahid Garden,** Jl. Babar Sari, with swimming pool, a/c, and rooms for Rp157,500-315,000.

Long-Term

The Jl. Pasar Kembang area is very colorful, but not the place to settle in Yogyakarta for a while. Scan or put an ad in the town rag, *Kedaulatan Rakyat,* Jl. Mangkubumi 42, to find a small house, flat, or room with a family. Or ask your hotel proprietor to arrange for accommodations in a private home, usually four to five km from the city center, for Rp20,000-30,000 per month room only.

FOOD

Specialties

Yogyakarta is god-sent for vegetarians: bean cakes, *rempeyek* (peanut cookies), and vegetable soups galore. The *makanan asli* (native foods) of Yogyakarta, *gudeg*, is jackfruit cooked in coconut milk with a mixture of eggs, tofu, chicken, and spicy sauce. Served in Indonesian-style restaurants all over town. One of the best *warung* deals in town is *nasi rames*—a very healthy, tasty meal with four or five different vegetables.

Also try tasty Javanese *opor ayam,* slices of chicken simmered in coconut milk; and sumptuous *mbok berek,* one whole fried chicken for Rp4000. The best *mbok berek* restaurant is the famous **Suharti Mbok Berek** on Jl. Solo seven km east of Yogyakarta.

Street Food

Jalan Malioboro is particularly popular as "restaurant row," but the Chinese restaurants are inconsistent, overpriced, and not recommended. Eat instead at *warung,* where the people eat.

A cheap and lively market exists on Jl. Malioboro, selling *nasi gudeng* and Jakartan food. At the end of the lane where Gang I joins Jl.

chicken becak, *Yogyakarta*

H.S. PARISER

Pasar Kembang is perhaps the best *nasi sayur* in all of Indonesia for Rp500. **Warung Makan** on Gang I serves excellent food; very cheap and friendly. After 2100 on Jl. Malioboro vendors sell delicious chicken, rice and veggie dishes, and even deep-fried dove (*burung dara goreng*); tasty meals for Rp800-1000. Eat from banana-leaf fronds on mats spread on the sidewalk and watch the street life. Few beggars. Stands on Jl. Alun Utara sell Arabian pancakes (*martabak*) for around Rp1500; open till midnight.

Nasi Padang

Some simple *nasi padang* places lie just south of the train station on Jl. Pasar Kembang. **Mama's** has been a favorite for almost two decades. On the right-hand side are *sate* and soup tents serving *sate, kambing,* and *sop kaki sapi* (buffalo-feet soup).

Travelers' Eateries

In many of these popular hangouts, enlivened by resident Indonesian hipsters, Westerners sit sardined with other Westerners, playing Western music, eating Kuta Beach-style food. The current hot place is **New Superman's,** Gang I, which serves up a huge variety of inexpensive meals, desserts, and drinks. Though the quality is often questionable, it's a convenient place to meet other travelers. A buoyant social center in the evenings, opening promptly at 0700, closing at 2100. **Lima French Grill** just opposite New Superman's serves tasty steaks with varied sauces.

On Gang II, **Anna's** serves good tourist fare—try the *tempe* club sandwich with fries. Around the corner is **Restoran Bu Dhari**; Rp5500 for specials like chateaubriand or sukiyaki. Best pseudo-Western food for the price is **N&N** on Gang I. **Pesta Perak,** Jl. Tentara Rakyat Mataram 8, has buffets for Rp9500—excellent food, fantastic variety, and great service. A hardcore tourist hangout is **Helen's.** At Jl. Malioboro 57, the **Shinta** has a full menu and delicious drinks, including *es kopyor* (fermented coconut) for Rp1000.

Restaurants

On Jl. Prawirotaman, down the street from the Metro Guesthouse, is **Cafe Lotus Garden,** which specializes in authentic Indonesian food. Reasonable prices for generous portions, consistently good, many vegetarian dishes. The owner, Mas Untung, possesses a wealth of information about Yogyakarta—a good place to exchange notes with other travelers. Cafe Lotus Garden features Indonesian dance and *wayang kulit* three times weekly; Rp2500 cover charge.

A good new restaurant, **Slomoth,** is found at Jl. Parangtritis 75D. The food, a combination of Western, Chinese, and Indonesian, is fresh and reasonably priced. The menu includes English descriptions, and the friendly waiters speak English. Located in a pleasant garden, the Slomoth features good prices for beer and soft drinks, live concerts, and music videos and sports events on a large-screen TV.

A good Japanese restaurant is **Yuriko,** Jl. Parangtritis near the mosque. Excellent Japanese food (Rp3500), plus Indonesian (Rp1500), Chinese, and European. Friendly owners. **Hanoman's Garden Restaurant** on Jl. Prawirotaman 9B, has so-so food, but you can enjoy a different performance every night at 1930—*wayang kulit, golek,* or dance—for Rp2500. Cheap and good is the **Legian Garden Restaurant,** one block from the Natour Garuda Hotel on the corner of Jl. Perwakilan and Jl. Malioboro, serving European, Javanese, and Chinese food.

On a small *gang* off Gang I between Superman's and Bu Sis is **Eko Restaurant.** The young manager really pays attention to the quality of the food—pepper steak cooked to perfection with an incredible sauce for Rp2750. Near the tourist info building is the **Hari Restaurant**; reasonably priced; mostly Indonesian clientele.

Fruits, Desserts, And Drinks

A plethora of fruits are available on Jl. Malioboro. Inside **Beringharjo** market is a feast for the senses: women in colorful *batik sarung,* a delightful mélange of earthy aromas, great crimson mounds of fresh chilies, grains, and beans bulging in handwoven baskets.

Tip Top Ice Cream Parlor, Jl. Mangkubumi 28, tel. (0274) 3682, sells excellent ice cream in many flavors, including *durian,* mocha, and tutti frutti; open 0900-1330 and 1700-2100. For more pastries and ice cream, try **Chitty Chitty Bang Bang** and the **Holland Bakery.** Next to the President Movie Theater.

Yogyakarta's wide variety of street stalls serve many special Javanese beverages: *es strop* with *kelapa* on top, delicious *tapi, coklat* with *cingkong* and *kelapa* (this one has a mocha-vanilla-butterscotch flavor—delicious). For black rice pudding (the perfect breakfast, Rp700), vendors pad down Gang I and II in the Pasar Kembang area between 0730 and 0900.

THE PERFORMING ARTS

Wayang and dance dramas are performed for both tourists and Javanese. Tourist performances are usually shortened, with just the epic highlights presented. Plays held at **Sasono Hinggil** south of the *alun-alun* are true marathons that start at 2100 and last for nine hours without a break. Tourist performances are not necessarily inferior to the genuine article; often they're better-funded and include more lavish props and costumes than an authentic *kampung* production. You won't be able to understand the words but the magical scenes will fascinate nonetheless. Go to the tourist office, Jl. Malioboro 16, for information on the latest venues and a schedule of performances. The following is only a partial list.

Wayang Kulit And Golek
The **Agastya Art Institute,** Gedongkiwo MD III/237, is a training school for *dalang*. Shadow plays are staged here 1500-1700 except Saturday. Entrance Rp3000. *Wayang golek dalang* is also taught; every Saturday 1500-1700 you can see one in action for Rp1750.

Nitour, Jl. Dahlan 71, stages almost paralytic, poor-quality *wayang golek* performances every day 1100-1300 except Sunday; Rp1750 admission.

Also see *wayang kulit* at **Ambar Budaya** in the Yogyakarta Crafts Center, opposite the Ambarrukmo on Jl. Adisucipto, every day 2000-2230; Rp3000. **Habiranda Dalang School,** on the northeast side of the *alun-alun* in the Pracimasono pavilion, puts on free rehearsals each evening 1900-2000 except Sunday and Thursday. At **Sentolo,** 20 km west of Yogyakarta (Rp250 by bus), famous *dalang* can be hired out for *wayang* performances; fee negotiable.

Dance And Drama
Ask at the tourist office about exact performance times and the addresses of the city's many dance companies.

At the **Yogyakarta Kraton** see classical dance rehearsals 1000-1200 on Sunday. Tickets are sold at the door of the palace. *Gamelan* rehearsals Monday and Wednesday 1030-1200; Rp1000. At the **Purawisata** on Jl. Brig. Jen. Katamso, *wayang orang* performances are held nightly with the Ramayana plot; Rp10,000. The biggest venue in town—worth the steep admission fee.

Grhadika Yogyakarta Pariwisata (GYP) is an institution that arranges performances of *wayang orang* at Pendopo Dalem Pujodusuman, Jl. Brig. Jen. Katamso 45, on Monday, Wednesday, and Friday 2000-2200; Rp8500 admission. This is the finest and most authentic Ramayana venue in Yogyakarta; highly recommended for lovers of serious dance.

Krido Beksa Wirama in Dalem Tejokusuman on Jl. K.H. Wahid Hasyim has packed classes—watch Old Java come alive in the story of *Ken Angrok,* episodes from the Ramayana, and ancient mask plays. Rehearsals 2000-2100 on Sunday on the Tejakusuman *pendopo.* Classical Javanese dancing was the exclusive prerogative of the courts until this school opened in 1918. **ASTI,** a dance academy on Jl. Colombo, attracts some of the most talented young contemporary dancers in Central Java.

Each Saturday at 0900 the **kuda kepang** (horse trance dance) is performed near Candi Sewu in Prambanan village. Nightly shows start at 1800 in the *alun-alun,* and in front of the tourist office at 2000.

A superb dancer and choreographer, Bagong Kussudiardjo, whose studio is on Jl. Singosaren 9 off Jl. Wates, teaches his own interpretation of modern jazz ballet. Rehearsals 1600-2000 except Friday. Vishnu Wardhana, Jl. Suryodiningratan 13, teaches a whole range of dance styles, from traditional Indonesian to modern improvisational.

Hotel Performances
In the lobby of the **Ambarrukmo** a small *gamelan* performs each day 1030-1230 and 1600-1800; free. There are also nightly cultural shows at this hotel. A worthwhile Ramayana performance at the **Natour Garuda Hotel** costs just Rp12,600, though you'll need to buy a drink.

Avoid the performances at the **Arjuna Plaza Hotel**; the *wayang orang* is pathetic and the *gamelan* consists of old women and children struggling to play from sheet music. **Hanoman's Garden Restaurant,** Jl. Prawirotaman 9B, stages nightly modern and classical Javanese dance, as well as *wayang kulit* and *golek* puppet shows; Rp2500. There could even be an Italian or Australian rock group, or jazz or pop singing.

Ramayana Ballet

These de Mille-like spectacles take place on the enormous stone stage of the Lorojonggrang open-air theater near the Prambanan temple complex on four successive full-moon nights each month from May to August. Cancelled if it rains. This four-episode contemporary *sendratari*-style ballet is based on the traditional *wayang orang* dancing of the classical Javanese theater. The plot is a modernized, dramatized version of the Indian epic poem the Ramayana. The Prambanan temple panels are, in effect, reenacted live.

See and hear an entire *gamelan* orchestra, scores of beautifully and grotesquely costumed dancers, singers and musicians, monkey armies, acrobatic miracles, giant kings on stilts. The performance lasts 1900-2100. Bring cushions or a sleeping bag to soften stone seats. If taking a camera, don't use the flash. After the show, a whole herd of minibuses will take you right back to Terminal Terban in Yogyakarta.

The tourist info center, major hotels, and almost any travel agency can sell you roundtrip tickets; Rp8000-30,000, depending on the seating. The Rp15,000 seats are the best value. It's of course cheaper just to go early and take the local bus to Prambanan village, sightsee some of the temples, have a rest and a cold drink, and be ready when the ticket office opens.

The Ramayana is also perfomed in the covered theater in Prambanan, just opposite the new open-air theater, every Tuesday, Wednesday, and Thursday throughout the year 1930-2200; Rp7000-15,000.

Discos

Yogyakarta has several discos. At the **Rainbow** in the Mutiara Hotel on Jl. Malioboro, the cover charge is Rp5000, but on "ladies nights" women get in free. A better disco is **Crazy Horse** on Jl. Magelang in the Borobudur Plaza. The Rp5000 cover includes a beer; hobnob with hip young Indonesians. The newest hot spot is **Papillon Disco** on Jl. Surtotomo.

Other Entertainment

For events such as traditional dances, pop concerts, and musical performances, watch for information banners stretching across streets and buildings. Current Western movies might be running too—check the paper. The **French Institute,** Lembaga Indonesia Perancis, Jl. Sagan 1/1 behind Cinema Rahayu, offers French classes and frequent cultural presentations. The Germans (Jl. Jen Sudirman 18, in front of Hotel Merdeka) and Dutch also operate cultural institutes where they too present cultural shows. **Karta Pustaka,** the Dutch club at Jl. Jen Sudirman 46, has a big theater which regularly hosts lectures, concerts, and films.

FESTIVALS AND EVENTS

Most Yogyakarta festivals center on the *kraton*. In the past their purpose was to reinforce the prestige of the reigning sultan and his court. Even today the sultan's bathwater is considered holy and his fingernail clippings kept for their latent power. Since the current sultan is democratic, Yogyakarta's festivals aren't nearly as grandiose as they once were; more like folk festivals now.

The Garebeg procession, held three times within the Islamic year, was at one time a pre-Muslim charity feast carried over and grafted onto the Islamic feast days of Maulud and Idul Fitri. In fact, there is such a mixture of animism, Hinduism, and Islam in the rites of Yogyakarta's festivals that no one really knows the origins of many of the symbols or what they mean. All is buried under centuries of custom.

The following are the more important events; refer to an Islamic calendar for dates.

Sekaten

Also called Garebeg Maulud, and commemorating the birth of the Prophet Mohammed, this great festival centers on the *kraton* and the Royal Mosque, Mesjid Agung. A big fair is held on the square north of the *kraton* with continuous prayer in the mosque compound. The ceremony begins at midnight with a procession of the palace guards; two sets of sacred *gamelan* are brought from the palace to the mosque. The climax is the great procession carrying the beehive-shaped *gunungan* (rice mountains) on bamboo frames from the *kraton* to Mesjid Agung, escorted by 800 palace guards (*prajurit*) all dressed in zany uniforms with zebra-striped shirts, slipper shoes, and Napoleonic and top hats. Armed with bows, arrows, spears, swords, and rifles, they parade in 100 platoons while firing blanks into the air. Accompanying the *gamelan*, bulky female *kraton* guards march with *kris* in their sashes; dignified *kraton* officials in white turbans and flowing white robes sit on thick cushions. Vendors sell sweets and balloons; the fair includes night markets and folk theater presentations.

Garebeg Besar

In this religious festival, mass prayers are held in mosques and public squares. Then goats, sheep, lambs, cows, and buffalos are ceremonially slaughtered to commemorate Abraham's willingness to sacrifice his son to God. The meat is distributed to the poor. The sultan, with a retinue of nobility, court dignitaries, and large floats of *gunungan*, takes part in a procession from the *kraton* to Mesjid Agung. A big bamboo theater is set up in the northern *alun-alun*.

Labuhan

Means "Offering." Held yearly the day after the sultan's birthday. At 0800 offerings are taken from the *kraton* to Punden Krendowahono on the Indian Ocean. Here the sultan's old clothes are dedicated to the queen of the South Seas, Nyai Loro Kidul, and put out to sea on a raft. Other offerings, such as nail clippings and hair trimmings, are buried in the sand. Each Jumat Kliwon, every 35 days, Chinese women come and offer sacrifices. Once every eight years, similar offerings are sent to the volcanos Merapi and Lawu and to the village of Dlepih near Wonogiri.

Sendangsono Pilgrimage

During May a religious ceremony is observed by Catholic devotees at Sendangsono, 32 km northwest of Yogyakarta, where a statue of the Virgin Mary stands in a cave on the slopes of the Menoreh mountain range. Sendangsono is the Javanese Lourdes; the well water here is considered holy. On the way you pass through Boro, a Catholic village populated by people with names like Josuf, Petrus, and Maria.

Waicak

A solemn festival commemorating the birth, enlightenment, death, and final ascension of the Buddha, Waicak occurs at the 1,100-year-old Borobudur and Mendut temples, 41 km northwest of Yogyakarta.

CRAFTS AND SHOPPING

Spend several days in Yogyakarta before buying so you can discover the right prices at the right places. Be prepared to bargain, with grace. To get acquainted with the full range of crafts offered, visit first the government-sponsored **Yogyakarta Crafts Center,** Jl. Adisucipto across from the Ambarrukmo Hotel. Check out the **Handicrafts by the Handicapped** shop in the Crafts Center. Open daily 0900-1000, this shop sells handicrafts made by disabled people, offers reasonable prices, and provides daily demonstrations.

Also visit **Pasar Beringharjo,** a giant market on Jl. Jen. A Yani, an extension of Jl. Malioboro. Swarming with brazen rats, this one-km maze of market stalls features everything from macrame to mutton to mangos. The people selling textiles and old *batik* here lie like snakes; the unprepared will be robbed blind. Leather goods and an endless assortment of food, baskets, dry goods, and everyday craft items are sold at reasonable prices in front of and around the market.

Yogyakarta's newest and largest shopping complex is the enormous **Malioboro Plaza** with McDonald's, Matahari Department Store, and Texas Fried Chicken. **Sinar Mas Department Store,** Jl. Malioboro 38, tel. (0274) 4490 or 2613, is a nice department store right downtown. **The Art Shop,** opposite the Hotel Garuda, sells high-quality arts and crafts.

Wayang

For the most part, Yogyakarta's *wayang kulit* puppets are made from goat skin, not buffalo hide; the best cost at least Rp20,000. You'll find *wayang* puppets all over town, but the best place is probably **Pak Ledjar** on Jl. Mataram DN I/370. From Helen's on Jl. Malioboro walk east down the alley to Jl. Mataram, then turn left. Another good place is **Toko Jawa,** Jl.

Malioboro opposite the Mutiara Hotel, which also sells musical instruments and Ramayana costumes. *Wayang golek* puppets are made at master **Pak Warno's** on Jl. Bantul, eight km south of Yogyakarta. High-quality *wayang kulit* puppets are created at **Moejosoehardjo's,** Jl. S. Parman Taman Sari 37B, tel. (0274) 2873, west of the Winingo River; he specializes in large *gunungan* screens.

The *wayang kulit* schools are also good-value places to shop for puppets. **Swasthigita Studio and Workshop,** Jl. Ngadinegaran MD 7/50, tel. 4346, is located in a small alley to the left at the beginning of Jl. Panjaitan south of the *kraton*. See the hundred-year-old set of *wayang kulit* animals and demons in the back; watch the craftsmen carve puppets. The *wayang kulit* with the light transparent rods are more desirable than those with black rods. **Delly Art Shop and Antiques,** Jl. Tirtodipuran 22B, sells several types of puppets; the owner is helpful and honest.

Antiques

Toko Asia, Jl. Malioboro opposite the Hotel Garuda, sells an outstanding collection of old *kris*. Several other small shops are close by. **Madiyono,** Jl. Tirtodipuran 36 (open 0900-2100), has a full range of art antiques. Also worth checking is the group of antique shops in the vicinity of the Ambarrukmo, and the four shops on Jl. Prawirotaman.

Saptohudaya, Jl. Solo km 9 Meguwo, tel. (0274) 62443, sells museum-quality textiles, carvings, Irianese artifacts, and antiques; the best of the best and prices to match. Most *batik* factories also sell antiques. Jalan Taman Garuda is good hunting ground: try **Seni Jaya** (no. 11), and **Pusaka** (no. 22). Probably the most soulful antiques in all Yogyakarta, all at exorbitant prices, are found at **Ardianto,** Jl. Magelang.

Leather

Leather prices have gone up; now you pay Rp30,000 for a large briefcase, up to Rp70,000 for a large suitcase. Make sure the leather is thick and treated. Sometimes the handtooling is lousy, or a layer of cardboard is glued between two thin layers of leather. Note carefully how the buckles are fastened; they tend to break off first.

In Indonesia you can still sit down with a craftsman and decide together on design, hide, reinforced stitching—a creative process involv-ing you and the artisan. You can have a pair of high boots made to order for about Rp50,000 that would cost you US$250 in Italy. Leather sandals on Jl. Malioboro go for as low as Rp7000, though shops along Jl. Pasar Kembang tend to be cheaper. A few of the many leather outlets include **Aries Handicraft,** Jl. Kauman 14; **B.S. Store,** Jl. Ngasem 10; **Kusuma,** Jl. Kauman 50; **Budi Murni,** Jl. Muju Muju; **Balai Penelitian Kulit,** Jl. Sokonandi 3; **Amie,** Jl. Kemasan, in Kota Gede.

Silver

Kota Gede, five km southeast of Yogyakarta, is the hub of Yogyakarta's silver industry. You needn't confine yourself to only those items you see on display. Though it may take as long as a week, almost any workshop will produce special-order pieces. Make a sketch, supply a photograph or a specimen, and they'll skillfully produce a facsimile, priced usually by the weight and grade of the silver used. Outlets in town include **Tan Jam An,** Jl. Mas Sangaji (go several streets past Tugu Monument and it's on the right-hand side); **Tjokrosuharto,** Jl. Panembahan 58; and **Sri Moeljo's,** Jl. Mentri Supeno UH XII/1, tel. (0274) 88042. A new, dynamic shop, **Borobudur Silver and Art Shop,** Jl. Menteri Supeno 41, sells nifty stuff at reasonable prices, and is a pleasant place to relax and watch the *batik* process. Sally Sagita, the friendly owner, speaks fluent English.

Miscellaneous

At **Tjokrosuharto,** Jl. Panembahan 58, buy *angklung* for Rp5000 and medium-quality *wayang kulit* puppets for Rp3000-4000. Chinese *kebaya* are sold at **Busana Dewi,** Jl. Dr. Sutomo 9/B, but come cheaper from the sidewalk sellers and in the shops along Jl. Malioboro; Rp8000-10,000 for the better ones. **Tan Jam An,** Jl. Mas Sangaji, carries, in addition to silverware, a fine collection of old Chinese *sarung*. Hire fine embroidery on pants and shirts at clothing shops for Rp3000-4000. Genuine Javanese *petani* hats on Jl. Malioboro cost Rp750. Custom-made rubber stamps run Rp2000 with handcarved personal logo, weird emblems, family crest, address, or whatever—a real steal.

The best shops for cassette tapes are **Podomoro** and **Atlantic** on Jl. Malioboro, and the shops on Jl. Solo. On Jl. Taman Garuda on the left-hand side coming from Jl. Pasar Kembang, basketware and mats are for sale; large baskets go for Rp1500-Rp2000. At **Agastya Art Institute,** Jl. Gedongkiwo MDIII/237, you'll find paintings on canvas.

Crafts Out Of Town

For woodcarvings, visit Moyudan village northwest of Yogyakarta. Ceramics enthusiasts should travel to Kasongan. *Kuda kepang* (flat hobbyhorses made from plaited bamboo) are created near Candi Sewu in the Prambanan temple complex. **Supowiyono,** son of the late Empu Supowinangun, has reestablished the once-vanished art of *kris*-making at his residence in Jitar/Moyudan, about an hour by *bemo* west of Yogyakarta.

Direx Gallery

On Jl. Adisucipto, at the large bridge before the river. Indonesia's best-known contemporary artist, Affandi, was born in 1908 in Cirebon and died here in 1990. When the Japanese asked him to paint a poster to help recruit more Javanese labor for Burma, he submitted a canvas showing starving men slaving in a hellhole jungle. See some amazing self-portraits from the '30s and '40s. It's best to view his paintings from a distance; he was farsighted. Affandi finished his paintings on the spot, most of them within an hour. The starting price is Rp1.5 million. Also exhibited are the works of promising young artists.

Amri Yahya

For modern *batik* paintings, visit this dynamic, internationally known Sumatran artist. A permanent oil and *batik* painting exhibition is on display at his large gallery at Jl. Gampingan 67, next to ASRI. Be prepared: these slick, top-of-the-line paintings sell for as much as Rp2 million. See artists at work on the premises.

ASRI

The School of Fine Arts on Jl. Gampingan. With 78 faculty and 2,000 students, this is one of Indonesia's top art academies. Sculpture, graphics, commercial and industrial arts, and primitive, symbolic, and decorative painting taught here. People at ASRI are rediscovering the lost Javanese art of stone sculpture, and the school maintains a huge interior-design department with excellent facilities. Their big art carnival is held in the second half of January each year, and there's a permanent exhibition of paintings always on sale. ASRI students journey to Bali for artistic inspiration.

BATIK

Most of Yogyakarta's hundreds of *batik* outlets open in the mornings, close 1300-1630, then open again at 2100. Look around the galleries before you buy. High-quality *batik* paintings, cheaper than oils, run Rp210,000-525,000 average, but it's worth paying a bit more if it helps improve the art. When shopping, avoid being led into the galleries; it's better to deal directly with the outlets.

Batik Painting

You could search the factories and shops for a full day and find nothing original. Many a young "artist" will approach tourists to invite them to see an exhibition, which it's said will be in town only another day before moving on to Jakarta or Singapore. Don't buy this line, or the one about a portion of the cost of the paintings going to the Ministry of Culture and Education. Pay only as much as you would to any other artist.

Factories And Shops

You can tour most of the 25 *batik* factories on Jl. Tirtodipuran and Jl. Parangtritis. The majority produce soulless junk. Lots of classy salerooms, but generally they're not the place to buy *tulis* work as most of the pieces are created with the *cap* method.

On Jl. Tirtodipuran, see the Chinese-style *batik* at **Plentong,** no. 28; **Batik Srimpi,** no. 22, offers Solo-style work. **Winotosastro,** no. 34, has an excellent selection, including some fine *tulis* pieces and ready-made clothing. **Rara Jonggrang,** no. 6A, displays paintings by at least 15 artists. Another large factory is **Suryakencana,** Jl. Ngadinegaran, with a wide selection in its showroom. **Terang Bulan,** Yogyakarta's *batik* supermarket at Jl. Jen. A. Yani 76, is especially rewarding if you don't know anything about *batik*. All kinds of material at fixed, honest prices to give you an idea what you should pay elsewhere; browse and learn. Another *batik* store with fixed prices, **Juwita,** is on the same side of the street toward the *pasar*.

BATIK STUDY

Batik is a lot more technical than you might imagine. Batik courses range from Rp4000 to Rp60,000 per week, including materials and sometimes meals and accommodations. Most tourists who study *batik* in Yogyakarta are quite satisfied with some of the mediocre courses offered because they're actually able to produce something—a moon rising over rice fields, peasant's hut, cane stalks, soaring *garuda* . . . other such tourist drivel.

The one-week courses offered in the Water Palace area generally aren't good value because the teachers are too young and inexperienced, most just learning the trade themselves. Also beware of courses taught by "world masters"; students are supposed to get a charge out of studying under prestigious names, but most learn little. The teacher doesn't teach but employs assistants—who sometimes don't speak English—to instruct you.

Batik Research Center

The most thorough course with the best facilities is Balai Penelitian Batik Kerjaninan (Batik Research Center), Jl. Kusumanegara 2, tel. 3753, about three km east of the town center. Open Sun.-Thurs. 0800-1330, Friday until 1130, Saturday until 1230. The institute carries out research and provides assistance on technical problems faced by artisans. The center offers three-month courses, six days a week, 0900-1200, three people per class. Call for fee information. The emphasis here is on the industrial approach.

The research center isn't the usual tourist circus but a real bit of Javanese culture. Buy *batik* here with the wax still smelling hot; the selection isn't huge, but it's representative. Visitors may tour the center's workshops and take photographs. For the free tour by an English-speaking guide, check in at the front desk.

Studios And Galleries

F. Agus Mudjono, Merangsang Kidul, Mg. III/102, creates traditional *batik* paintings selling for Rp10,000-350,000. Agus has exhibited his work all over the world. **Tjokrosuharto,** Jl. Panembahan 58, is a large fixed-price shop with a variety of crafts including *batik*. **Siti Astana Bilai-Batik,** Jl. K.H. Dahlan 29, features *batik tulis*; workshop nearby. **Gallery Yo-** **gyakarta,** Jl. Gampingan 42 (behind ASRI), is an excellent source for *lurik*, the Javanese homespun. If the color you'd like is not in stock, order it; view the weaving process in the rear.

Ardiyanto Batik, Jl. Taman Garuda, adopts traditional designs for fabric in cotton and silk for dresses, blouses, pillows, and pictures. Limited selection of good-quality *batik* at fixed prices. **Saptohudoyo Gallery,** Jl. Adisucipto near the airport, exhibits works of a variety of artists. **Lod Gallery,** in Taman Sari, sells highly original work by younger artists. The Water Palace area has the best bargains for *batik* paintings—as low as Rp6000—but much of it is amateurish. Also check for possible bargains by top-of-the-line artists at **Amri Gallery,** Jl. Gampingan 67, tel. (0274) 5135, and **Bagong Kussudiardjo,** Jl. Singosaren 9.

Avoid **Professor Purnomo's Batik School and Art Gallery,** which preys on foreigners with mendacious hard-sell tactics and prices three to ten times the going rate.

SERVICES

Tourist Information Center

Stop here first, at Jl. Malioboro 16, tel. (0274) 66000. From Jl. Pasar Kembang the office is located halfway down Jl. Malioboro toward the main post office; open Mon.-Sat. 0800-1930. An extremely helpful staff, with a town plan, regional maps, and calendar of events. Complete train and bus schedules posted. Beware of strangers who try to pass themselves off as officials from the tourist office.

Public Services

The **main post office** occupies a historic building on the corner of Jl. Senopati and Jl. Jen. A. Yani. Small philatelic department. The *pos paket* in a side room will wrap your parcel securely in nylon for only Rp750.

The **immigration office** is open Mon.-Thurs. 0730-1330, Friday 0730-1100, Saturday 0900-1230. Located eight km out of town on Jl. Adisucipto on the road to Solo. *Bemo* drivers will let you off right in front.

A *wartel* is attached to the Batik Palace Hotel, offering international telephoning, fax, and telegrams. Fax machines are also found at the better hotels and most guesthouses in Yogyakarta. The Yogyakarta telephone city code is 0274.

Changing Money

Better rates of exchange than Bali or Jakarta. Shop around for the best rate. **Bank Niaga** (Jl. Sudirman) usually provides a good rate; open 0800-1400, Saturday until 1300. Compare the rate with **Bank Bumi Daya,** on Jl. Sudirman beside the Merpati office. **Bank BNI,** adjacent to the main post office, is also worth a try; enter through the foreign exchange door. Other authorized moneychangers located on Jl. Pasar Kembang and Jl. Parangtritis. The moneychanger on Jl. Pasar Kembang near the *wartel* is open daily until 2130.

Medical

Yogyakarta on the whole offers good medical treatment; Gajah Mada University is an important center for medical studies. **Bethesda,** Jl. Jen. Sudirman 70, tel. (0274) 2281, is the local hospital, open 0900-1400; usually a mob of incompetent interns descends on you. Instead, try a private doctor, 90% of whom speak English. Recommended are **Dr. Gandha,** Jl. Pringgokusuman 1, and **Dr. Sukadis,** Jl. Dagen.

Books, Film, And Massage

The largest bookshop in Yogyakarta is **Gunung Agung,** corner of Jl. Mangkubumi and Jl. Diponegoro; open Mon.-Sat. 0900-2000. Also try **Gramedia** on Jl. Sudirman and **Sari Ilmu** on Jl. Malioboro. A real library, **Perpustakaan Negara,** is on Jl. Malioboro opposite the Garuda's new wings.

Old women up to age 95 give massages for Rp3500 per hour on the lane off Jl. Sosrowijayan. One of the most competent practitioners is **Panti Pijat,** a blind man living at Jl. Gowongan Kidul 6 beside Pramitha Hotel; ask for Tuna Netra. Another *pijat* works in the back of Losmen Jaya, Gang II off Jl. Sosrowijayan.

PT Modern Photo Film Co., Jl. Malioboro 159 very close to Jl. Sosrowijayan, charges only Rp195 per glossy print and takes only 25 minutes if there's no line; open 0800-2100.

GETTING THERE

Flights between Jakarta's Sukarno/Hatta Airport and Yogyakarta are heavily booked; confirm reservations and get to the airport at least an hour early for check-in. Rp135,000 on Garuda.

At Yogyakarta's Adisucipto Airport, catch a minibus into town on the highway in front of the terminal. It costs Rp300 to Terminal Terban; from there take a *becak* to the Jl. Pasar Kembang area for Rp500. Taxis to or from the airport charge Rp6000.

From Gambir station in Jakarta, trains leave nine times daily; 7.5-12 hours, Rp7500-57,000 depending on the train. The Bima has first-class Rp44,000-58,000 tickets. By train from Surabaya requires seven hours; six trains run daily. Three trains run daily from Bandung, Rp6800 third class on the Cepat; Rp21,500-33,000 second class (eight hours) on the Mutiara.

Once at the Yogyakarta train station, walk out the back entrance onto Jl. Pasar Kembang, closer to hotel row. There's no need to walk down the main street to Jl. Malioboro. Hotel Asia-Afrika and Hotel Mendut, very near the train station, are always open, even very early in the morning.

Night buses between Jakarta and Yogyakarta cost around Rp14,000 (Rp20,000-25,000 with a/c); 14 hours, 585 km. The night bus from Bandung is Rp8500 (Rp10,000 with a/c); six to seven hours. From Surabaya the night bus costs Rp8500 (Rp10,000 with a/c), 8.5 hours. From Semarang, Rp1350, three hours; Rp2700 by minibus, 2.5 hours. The bus from Solo costs Rp750 and takes 2.5 hours; the minibus is Rp1250 and takes two hours.

When you arrive at the station, ignore the bullying *becak* drivers who want Rp3000 to Jl. Malioboro; instead go through the archway to the right of the main entrance and catch a local bus.

GETTING AROUND

The best way to see the city is to walk or ride a bicycle, like everyone else. The streets are filled with friendly hellos and the jangle of bicycle bells. Getting around town is easy: Jl. Malioboro is the main drag, with the railroad station at the north end and the *kraton* at the south; all the inexpensive places to stay are just off this street. The main bus station, Terminal Umbulharjo, is in the southeast of town, Rp250 by minibus.

Bikes And Motorcycles

At about Rp1500-2000 per day, bikes are cheaper than *becak*. For the best rate, rent one for a week for around Rp5000-7000. Hotel Bagus on Gang II, Hotel Aziatic (Jl. Sosrowijayan 6), and Hotel Kartika all rent bikes. Get there early before 0900-1000, when all the good bikes are gone. Check your bike carefully, and read the fine print. Always lock your bike, and keep an eye on it. At the main market, post office, and cinemas, watchmen guard your vehicle for Rp100.

You can rent motorcycles at Yogyakarta Rental, Ana Rental, Java Rental, and Indonesia Rental, all on Jl. Pasar Kembang, for Rp10,000-12,000 per day. Negotiate cheaper weekly rates. Buy a bicycle or motorcycle at Pasar Sepeda on Jl. Haryono, where there are hundreds of them, row on row. Good used 100-cc motorbikes run about Rp450,000, bicycles Rp6000-15,000. New bicycles cost Rp60,000.

Becak, Andong, Bis

Becak here are extremely reasonable, charging only around Rp4000 an hour. There's no shortage of the things, so if you don't get this rate or near it, just walk away and take your business elsewhere. Many *becak* drivers approach you proposing Rp300-500 per hour, but their intention is to take you on a shopping tour. If you're interested, this is an excellent way to shop around, though you have to pay the cost of commissions from the shopowners if you buy anything. Hire a *becak* to tour the back streets in the cool of the evening—a wonderful experience.

Horsedrawn *andong* (capacity three people) are a delightful way to get out to places like Kota Gede or Kasongan. *Andong* hang around Jl. Senopati to the east of the post office, behind Pasar Beringharjo (Jl. Suryotomo), and down the small streets on the edge of town.

Orange *bis kota,* which run only 0600-1900, cost Rp250, as do the much smaller minibuses that circulate constantly on set routes around the city. The tourist office has a book of 17 minibus routes around town; No. 4 and 11 run down Jl. Malioboro. No. 4 heads south to Kota Gede and the main bus terminal. No. 11 reaches the same places on a longer, more circuitous route.

Catch minibuses to Prambanan (Rp400) from Terminal Terban, Jl Simanjuntak. Kota Gede and Imogiri are accessible by bus. Local *kobutri* minibuses depart from the terminal beside the Jl. Senopati shopping center for all points in the city.

Taxis, Rented Cars

Hire taxis from Jl. Senopati beside the main post office or from in front of big hotels like Garuda and Mutiara. Taxi fare to the airport is Rp6000. Within the city, the fare is Rp4500 per hour (minimum two hours). To charter taxis or minibuses, go through your hotel; try the taxi stand beside the post office, or catch an a/c taxi. Dial (0274) 5819 for Indra Kelana Taxi or 2548 for Centris Taxi.

Out-of-town taxi trips feature fixed rates: Prambanan, Rp27,000, 32 km roundtrip; Borobudur, Rp50,000, 84 km roundtrip; Solo, Rp70,000, 130 km roundtrip. You can charter taxis (up to four people) and minibuses (eight to nine) for approximately Rp120,000 per day within the city, Rp150,000 per day outside.

If you get together with five or six people you can rent a Suzuki van and driver to Dieng and Borobudur for about the same Rp20,000 price as a package tour.

GETTING AWAY

By Air

Fly **Garuda**, Jl. Mangkubumi 56, tel. (0274) 5784, closes at 1600; **Merpati,** Jl. Sudirman 63, tel. 4272, closes at 1500; or **Bouraq,** Jl. Mataram 60, tel. 86664, closes at 1700. Garuda sample fares: Jakarta, four flights daily, Rp135,000; Denpasar, three flights daily, Rp130,000; Surabaya, Rp75,000. Also check out Bouraq; one flight to Tarakan (East Kalimantan) daily.

For the airport, take a minibus from the minibus terminal on Jl. Simanjuntak in north Yogyakarta toward Solo and get off in front of the terminal.

By Train

The railroad station is right in the middle of town just off Jl. Mangkubumi. Trains to West Java are generally uncomfortable and more expensive than buses, but the trains to East Java are cleaner, faster, and less expensive. For the Bima, buy a ticket on your day of departure at the stationmaster's office (room 4) 0800-1200. For the Fajar Utama, buy your ticket one day before, and for the Senja Utama Yogyakarta on your day of departure. Alternatively, for the Fajar Utama and the Senja Utama Yogyakarta, make ticket reservations one or two days before at the Pusaka Nusantara Ticket Agency, Jl. Brig. Jen.

Katamso 49, tel. (0274) 88375, open 0800-1400. Buy snacks for the train from the *warung* and shops along Jl. Pasar Kembang.

To Jakarta: Ten trains daily, 9-12 hours, Rp8500 third class to Rp58,000 VIP on the Bima. The most popular trains to Jakarta are the Fajar Utama I at 0700 (arrive 1600, Rp18,000-40,000), the Senja Ekonomi at 1700 (arrive 0400, Rp8000 third class), the Fajar Utama II at 0900 (arrive 1800, Rp18,000-40,000), and the Senja Utama Soli at 1915 (arrive 0500, Rp18,000-33,000).

To Bandung: Three trains per day; Rp5000 third class, Rp15,000 second class, Rp36,000 first class. Best choice to Bandung is the Senja Mataram at 2130 (arrive 0530, Rp16,000).

To Mt. Bromo: A train leaves at 0735 (third class only) and arrives in Probolinggo at around 1700, which leaves plenty of time to get to Ngadisari by nightfall to rest up for the Bromo climb the next morning.

To Surabaya: Six trains daily, from Rp8000 on the Argopuro to Rp51,000 first class on the Bima.

To Bali: Take a Surabaya train, with further connections to Banyuwangi, then ferry and bus to Denpasar. If you catch the Ekspres Siang at 1420 from Yogyakarta, it puts you in Surabaya at 2030, time enough to catch the Mutiara Timur leaving Surabaya at 2200 for Banyuwangi.

Local Buses And Minibuses
The main bus station, Umbulharjo, is in the southeast corner of the city near Kota Gede, on Jl. Veteran and Jl. Menteri Supeno. Buses leave every 10-15 minutes 0330-1900 for all the towns in the immediate area: Kaliurang (Rp1000), Imogiri (Rp600), Parangtritis (Rp1200).

Buses north to Magelang and Borobudur depart from Terminal Umbulharjo and Terminal Pingit (Jl. Magelang), a 10-minute walk north of the Jl. Pasar Kembang area. The bus from Yogyakarta to Muntilan is Rp700, then change buses at Muntilan for Borobudur, Rp500. Be very careful of pickpockets on local buses out to Borobudur. They're particularly deft at cutting shoulder bags with razors and extracting valuables without alerting the victim.

Long-Distance Buses/Minibuses
Many bus offices are on the Jl. Mangkubumi/Jl. Malioboro extension, just up the street from the train station, while ticket agencies conveniently line Jl. Sosrowijayan, where express buses also pick you up. Learn from other travelers or the tourist office about the latest, best buses and fares. Long-distance buses usually leave between 1500 and 1930 and travel straight through the cool night. Get there at least 30 minutes before departure.

To Bali: Buses leave for Denpasar 1600-1800, and pull in at 0630-0830. Rates are Rp22,000-35,000 including ferry trip and tasteless meals; no standing passengers allowed. Companies with good night buses to Bali include **Cakrawala** (Jl. Surapati 124), **Panorama Indah, Javatu,** and **Puspasari.** All drive like madmen. The **Safari Dharma Raya** gets high marks from travelers: plenty of leg room, a/c set to nonarctic temperatures, easy on the music videos. Avoid the **Bali Indah** bus company; drivers pick up extra people and overload the bus. The buses are always late and serve terrible food.

Buy tickets at **Terminal Umbulharjo** or at Jl. Sosrowijayan where there are dozens of agents. It's cheaper to do it step by step: train to Surabaya, another train to Banyuwangi, minibus to ferry at Ketapang, ferry to Gilimanuk.

Tours
If you're short on time or would like a quick introduction to a specific site, dozens of small tour companies and hotels offer four- to eight-hour tours around the city and to surrounding areas. Examples: "Borobudur Sunrise Tour," "Merapi Volcano Close-up Tour," and tours to the Dieng Plateau. The "City Arts and Craft Tour" (three hours) takes you around to silversmiths, *wayang* plays, a *batik* factory, and an art gallery. If you want to spend longer at certain sites, take a tour to Dieng (with visits to Borobudur en route), then stay overnight at Dieng and catch the same tour company going back the next day.

Ask the tourist office, Jl. Malioboro 16, about other, higher-priced special-interest tours. **Intan Pelangi,** Jl. Malioboro 18, tel. (0274) 3644, offers daily cultural tours of Yogyakarta by bus. For organized tours to Imogiri (Rp31,500) or Borobudur (Rp37,800), inquire at **Pacto,** Jl. Mangkubumi, tel. 2740, and **Nitour Inc.,** Jl. K.H.A. Dahlan 71, tel. 3165 or 2114, ext. 4.

VICINITY OF YOGYAKARTA

Kasongan

This potters' village 45 minutes (Rp400) by minibus from Yogyakarta is well known for its animal-shaped, brightly painted children's money-boxes; Rp1000-4000. Large pots, vases, and bowls for sale. See the potters bisquing pieces in big blazing straw fires. In front of each shop is a display showcase. Customers haggle over prices, which are half what the pieces go for in Yogyakarta's Pasar Ngasem. Can also special-order; allow 10 days.

Bapak Suwarno in Nidiro village near Kasongan is renowned for his *wayang orang* masks; Rp25,000-50,000.

Sentolo

See the entire *wayang golek*-making process, and buy expensive but very nice puppets in this village, about 17 km from Yogyakarta. Take a bus from Jl. Sutoyo/Jl. Sugiyono to Wates, and ask to get out at Sentolo.

KOTA GEDE

Six km southeast of Yogyakarta's city center, Kota Gede, founded in 1579, was once the capital of the old Mataram Kingdom and is older than Yogyakarta itself. Silver workshops sprang up to serve the king; nowadays Suharto orders gifts for state guests from here.

Senopati Grave

The grave of Prince Senopati, Mataram's founder, is only one-half km from the *pasar*. Coming from Tom's Silver, take the first left after the market and enter the mossy burial ground (donation): Shady courtyards and an ancient mosque. Dress conservatively. Only go to the graveyard on Monday 0930-1200 and Friday 1330-1600 when there's activity; otherwise there's nothing to see but sacred turtles in a dirty pool. Many other royal personalities, under ornamental parasols, are entombed in Makam Senopati, less than one km beyond. Visit the village country market, which sells all kinds of fruits, clothes, and implements. Not many tourists; no accommodations here.

Silverworking

The many busy, clanging silverware shops here consume some 50 tons of silver annually. You're free to wander through big workshops full of men and boys using the simplest of handtools, hammering on anvils, filing, polishing, heating, and soldering strips of bright silver. There are two grades of silver: 92.5% sterling, and 80%. Display rooms sell a huge variety of pieces, from Rp3000 for a ring set with a semiprecious stone up to several million *rupiah* for a complete silver dinner service for 12. Most of the silver shops inventory the same items, seldom deviating from the sure sellers, but all will make anything to order.

Visit **Tom's Silver,** Jl. Ngeksigondo 60, tel. (0274) 2818, the largest and most established workshop, with a large showroom. The workmanship is better, but the prices are also higher. Credit cards accepted, bargain only if you buy wholesale or very expensive items. At **MD Silver** down the street on Jl. Keboan, jewelry sells for less; here you can see *wayang kulit* made from *kerbau* hide. The showroom is open 0800-2000, until 1700 on Sunday; workshop open 0800-1700. Numerous other shops line the streets of Kota Gede, many selling not only silver but tortoiseshell and horn handicrafts, curios, and fake antiques as well.

Getting There

Pedal the back way down Jl. Gembira Loka through the countryside. Travel first straight down the road past the zoo until you come to a bend to the left, then head straight until you reach a paved road. Turn right at the sign Kota Gede 3 Km. Costs around Rp6000 for a chartered *andong* or Rp3000 for a *becak* for two from Yogyakarta. Or take the *bis kota* for Rp250.

IMOGIRI

A cemetery for the royal houses of Yogyakarta and Solo since the early kings of Mataram, Imogiri lies 20 km southeast of Yogyakarta, a 30-minute (Rp450) minibus ride. Climb barefoot up the 345 warm stone steps to the sacred burial ground at the top. The mighty Sultan Agung was the first Ja-

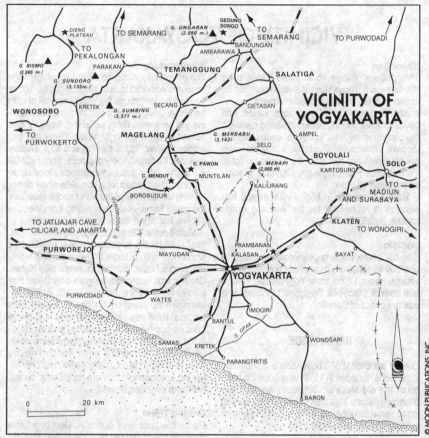

VICINITY OF
YOGYAKARTA

© MOON PUBLICATIONS, INC.

vanese king interred here, his tomb built in the mid-17th century on a small rocky promontory. Since then, nearly every king has found his final resting place on this highly venerated hill.

This is not a place where crowds of tourists come on buses; you have to make an effort to get here, but it's worth it. You may be the only Westerner present; it could be one of the highlights of your visit to Yogyakarta. Hardly anyone speaks English.

Pay the entrance fee (Rp800) and sign the visitors book. An important pilgrimage site of ancestor worship, you must wear formal Javanese dress to enter. On the premises men may rent a *sarung* and women a *kain* and *kebaya* for a modest fee. Three major courtyards are laid out

at the top of the stairway: to the left are buried the *susuhunan* of Solo, to the right the sultans of Yogyakarta, in the center the Mataram kings. Some graves are over 400 years old.

The Royal Tombs are only open Monday 0900-1300 and Friday 1330-1600; the tomb of Sultan Agung is open around 1430 on Friday, the best day to visit. The graves are closed during Ramadan and no photography is permitted in the graveyards.

PARANGTRITIS AND VICINITY

The place to go if you want to take a break from Yogyakarta, Parangtritis is 27 km south on the

Indian Ocean. This is the most popular and accessible of the beaches south of Yogyakarta—a simple seaside resort with wild seas, horse rides on the beach, friendly people, and a handful of foreigners. Take books, *sarung,* and a musical instrument. Accommodations are reasonable, food cheap and plentiful. During the week, life can be simple here and quiet; on holidays and weekends the place swarms with thousands of local tourists.

Sights

Visit the excellent freshwater swimming pool and *mandi.* The surrounding area is dramatic, with many jagged cliffs and beaches of meadow-like gray sand dunes and eerie moonscapes stretching for kilometers. Also, walk up the paved road for superb views from the lookout, and do a lunchtime splurge at the stunning Queen of the South Resort.

One km before the village is the hot spring **Parang Wedang,** entrance Rp200. Nice walks up into the hills in this weirdly beautiful area. Watch men gather the ingredients for Chinese bird's-nest soup on elastic-like bamboo scaffolding over steep cliffs. The soup isn't actually made from the whole nest but from the saliva the birds use to glue their nests together.

During the war for independence, caves in the vicinity were used as hideouts by General Sudirman and his band of guerrillas. Follow the marked route of the guerrillas toward the top, then turn right where a rock points to **Gua Langse.** The trek to this cave travels through undergrowth; rough getting there but upon your arrival there may be a pot of tea waiting. Ceremonies often held here—strange Javanese witchcraft. Swim in the pools (Rp350) fed by spring water flowing through bamboo pipes. Another path eventually leads to cliffs with superb views down the coast and out to sea.

Nyai Loro Kidul

Parangtritis is the domain of Nyai Loro Kidul, the legendary goddess of the South Seas. Like Neptune, her hair is green and full of shells and seaweed; she holds court over sea nymphs and creatures of the deep. Venerated and feared by the Javanese, Loro Kidul is summoned by a gong on the evening of the Muslim day of rest (Thursday), when a bamboo tray of rice, bananas, jasmine flowers, cosmetics, and coconuts is offered to the eternally youthful goddess. Don't wear green; that's *her* color, and she's been known to yank people into the sea for the transgression.

Parangkusumo, one km down the beach, is where Sultan Senopati lived for some months with Nyai Loro Kidul in the 17th century. The sacred spot of their rendezvous, enclosed by a fence, contains a symbolic tree, a lamp, and remains of flowers and incense offerings from Javanese (including the mayor of Jakarta) who come to ask direction and aid from Nyai Loro Kidul. Visitors may enter this enclosure; the *juru kunci* will offer your questions to the goddess for Rp200, plus take your offerings.

Accommodations And Food

About 15 *losmen* line the main road down to the beach. Facilities are similar, a bit limited and unhygienic but passable. Rooms rent for Rp6000-10,000 but could be cheaper off-season or during the week.

Right at the entrance is **Suharjo's,** the cheapest *warung* and the place to socialize. One of the best and coolest *losmen,* with good food, is **Widodo's**; Rp5000-8000. **Penginapan Parang Endong** is a little beyond the village. Another good choice is **Yenny Homestay,** operated by the affable Mr. Supripto—a gold mine of information on local sights. He often hangs out at Superman's in Yogyakarta. Rooms at Yenny's cost Rp7500-10,000 with breakfast. Wild mushroom omelettes are a speciality in Parangtritis.

The top-end choice is the new **Queen of the South Resort,** tel. (0274) 67196, fax 67197, at the east end of the beach, about four km from the main beach area. Swimming pool, billiards, and a/c rooms for Rp147,000-294,000. One of the most stunning boutique resorts in all of Indonesia; the *pendopo* restaurant is worth the visit alone.

Getting There

Catch a big bus on the corner of Jl. Kol Sugiyono and Jl. Parangtritis in Yogyakarta all the way to Parangtritis for Rp1000 (includes beach area admission); some go via Imogiri, others more directly via Kretek. Alternatively, rent a bicycle in Yogyakarta and cycle all the way. The last bus returns to Yogyakarta around 1700.

Other Beaches

Samas Beach is Rp1000 by minibus from Yogyakarta via Bantul: violent surf, hot black sand, lagoons, eerie landscapes, steel-colored dunes, several *warung*.

Baron Beach is 55 km southeast of Yogyakarta. First take a minibus to Wonosari (one hour), then catch another to Baron (one hour). Relatively isolated, a long narrow beach. A sign forbids swimming, but go to the mouth of the underground river where the locals bathe; beware of strong currents. Stay at **Losmen Bintang Baru**; Rp5000. Get good cheap food at

Titi Sari; the other half dozen *rumah makan* are only open weekends and holidays. On weekends there could be busloads of Muslims who frown on Western-style sunbathing.

Kukup Beach is yet another white-sand beach east of Baron, with several caves and limestone shallows. The Kukup turnoff is one km before Baron; take the road all the way. Though safer than Parangtritis, be careful of currents while swimming.

THE PRAMBANAN PLAIN

It took staggering agricultural productivity to enable pompous feudal monarchs to erect these temples to their own glory. On the rich Prambanan Plain, 17 km northeast of Yogyakarta, are the most extensive Hindu temple ruins in all Indonesia. There's no telling how many more are still under the earth. Lying today among villages and green rice fields with the sharp peak of Gunung Merapi in the background, most of these temple complexes were built from the 8th to 10th centuries. They were abandoned when the Hindu kings moved to eastern Java in the 10th century. Around 1600, all extant temples were toppled by an earthquake. In the 19th century, their blocks were carried off to pave roads and build sugar mills, bridges, and railroads. The Dutch started restoration in the late 1930s.

PRAMBANAN TEMPLE COMPLEX

Java's largest temple complex. Prambanan's central courtyard contains three large structures: a main temple dedicated to Shiva, flanked by one each to Brahma (to the south) and Vishnu (to the north). The complex originally contained 244 minor temples (*candi perwara*), all arranged in four rows. Only a couple have been restored. The two small *candi* at the side of the main terrace were probably the treasuries where jewels and gold were kept.

Rp4000 admission to the main complex. Open 0600-1800; go early. Vendors line the walkways, plus there's a food and souvenir stall area. See the Ramayana ballet performed here during full moon nights from May to August. Performances nightly in the new, indoor pavilion.

Shiva Temple (Candi Lorojonggrang)
This large central temple was dedicated to Shiva the Destroyer. Built to contain the remains of the Mataram King Balitung, who reigned in the middle of the 9th century and claimed to be a reincarnation of Shiva. Much of the structure had collapsed by the last century and not until 1937 did reconstruction begin. Now a wonder of restoration, this tall, elegant temple is a synthesis of both north and south Indian architectural styles. Almost 50 meters high, for 1,000 years it was the tallest building on Java. Its lavish decorations, statues, and other details all show an outstanding sense of composition. The whole structure is perfectly balanced; while walking around its 20 sides, it never seems to change. See it late in the day when the crowds thin out and the sun turns it gold.

Reliefs
Candi Prambanan's relief sculptures, realistic and humorous at the same time, are among the finest in all of Indonesian art. With the renovation of the Brahma temple, the panels are now complete. Four stairways lead to the walk-around gallery that takes you entirely around the temple. The body of the terrace is decorated with the unique Prambanan motifs. On the outer walls are 62 panels of dynamic dancing figures and celestial musicians taken from the ancient *Manual of the Indian Art of Dancing*; see the beautiful, haunting, cosmic dance of Shiva.

To follow the story, go up the east stairway first, down to the left after the gallery, then slowly around the temple proper. On the inner-wall gallery are Ramayana scenes. Rama stories, of an unknown version, were first depicted in Indonesia on this temple in the 9th century.

THE PRAMBANAN PLAIN

(map showing: CANDI SEWU, CANDI PLAOSAN, CANDI BUBRAH, CANDI LUMBUNG, PRAMBANAN COMPLEX, PRAMBANAN VILLAGE, TO SOLO, CANDI SARI, GATA, CANDI SAJIWAN, LAWU, CANDI SAMBISARI, KALASAN VILLAGE, CANDI KALASAN, S. OPAK, KRATON RATU BOKO, CANDI BANYUNIBO, S. SOROGEDUNG, S. KONGKLANGAN, SAMBISARI VILLAGE, TO YOGYAKARTA, 0 — 2 km)

© MOON PUBLICATIONS, INC.

Sprinkled throughout are trees of heaven surrounded by animals, pots of money, creatures half-women and half-birds. Trees, rocks, and water are more stylized, earthy, and responsive than those in Borobudur, with monkeys frolicking in fruit trees and busy kitchen scenes. Here and there you can even see traces of Buddhism—many stupa. In the office at Candi Prambanan, ask to see the erotic bas-relief.

Sculpture
A three-meter-high statue of the four-armed god Shiva is enshrined in the main eastern chamber; there are minor rooms for the Divine Teacher, Ganesha. In the northern cell the goddess Durga kills a demon-bull. The Prambanan temple is often called Candi Lorojonggrang after the statue of the "slender cursed virgin" in the north room, her nose missing, her breasts worn shiny smooth by the rubbing of adoring hands. Legend has it this cursed virgin was turned to stone when she refused to wed a *raksasa*. In the courtyard in the small shrine opposite Shiva's great temple is a statue of Shiva's bull, Nandi, the only freestanding stone statue of an animal

in ancient Indonesian art. Sculpted in a simple, powerful, yet natural style.

Getting There
Only Rp700 by minibus from Jl. Sumanjuntak or a flat, easy bike ride from Yogyakarta on a special bicycle lane to Prambanan village. From Solo take a minibus (Rp1000) from the station near Cilingin terminal to Prambanan village.

OUTLYING TEMPLES

Numerous other temple complexes are found along the road between Yogyakarta and Solo. Watch for the small signs posted by the Archaeological Service. Temples Sambisari, Kalasan, and Sari lie between the airport and Prambanan village. Lumbung, Bubrah, Sewu, and Plaosan temples all lie more or less north along the same side of the road from the Prambanan complex. To start, follow road signs pointing toward Candi Lumbung. To visit these outlying temples, hire *andong* near Prambanan's minibus terminal for about Rp1000 per hour.

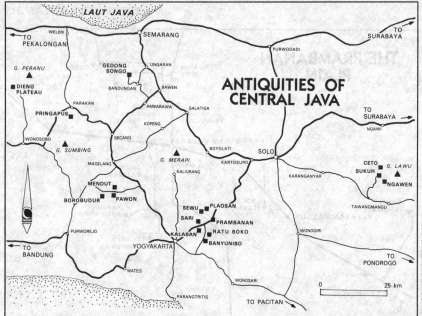

ANTIQUITIES OF CENTRAL JAVA

© MOON PUBLICATIONS, INC.

Kalasan, a Buddhist temple of 8th-9th century vintage, was founded in 778. Its present structure, is the product of a partial restoration in 1927-28; patches of the original white plaster covering Kalasan's exterior have been preserved.

The **Dieng Plateau** contains the oldest temples in Java. The earliest inscription is A.D. 809; several are older. Eight of these 7th-century Shivaistic temples are still standing.

Borobudur is the world's largest stupa, built with more than two million cubic feet of stone. This Buddhist monument was consecrated in the early 9th century (A.D. 824-850). **Mendut** is a temple of worship and **Pawon** a porch temple; both lie within this complex.

Banyunibo: this 9th-century *candi,* was originally part of a larger Buddhist site; it has now been completely restored. Known for its very fine double-*makara* motif.

Sewu is a large complex of 250 temples. The symmetrical configuration of this 9th-century Buddhist site is intended to generate harmony in the kingdom, creating a miniature replica of the world.

Plaosan, a 9th-century temple complex, incorporates a mixture of Buddhist and Hindu elements.

Pringapus holds the remains of a small Shivaistic complex of the 9th century.

Ratu Boko is a former *kraton* with hermitages, dance platforms, gateways, and pillars. These fortified palace-monastery remains show traces of both Shivaite and Buddhist elements.

Prambanan, a large 9th-century temple complex, houses one of the most beautiful Shiva temples on Java. Realistic and humorous relief sculptures.

Sari is a two-story, rectangular Buddhist *candi* of the 9th century. See the beautiful, sensuous dancer reliefs.

Ngawen originally consisted of four sanctuaries; a 9th-10th century Buddhist *candi.*

Sukuh was built late in the Hinduized 1400s, but includes many Javanese aboriginal elements that would appear to predate the arrival of Hinduism. This high-altitude temple is of the Bima cult.

Ceto is similar to Sukuh in age and origin, but lies at an even higher altitude and contains many more terraces. One interesting remain here is an intricate design of stones laid flat on the ground.

Gedong Songo is Shivaistic-Hindu in origin, built in the 8th-9th centuries. Most of this group is elaborately built and in excellent condition.

It's more enjoyable walking in the cool of the morning on the network of trails. Or take a bicycle. Only Kalasan and Prambanan ask for money (Rp200 each); none but the Shiva temple charge for photography (Rp200).

Candi Sewu

The "Thousand Temples," one km north of Prambanan; take the road behind Candi Lorojonggrang. Built in the first half of the 9th century, today Sewu is largely in ruins. It consisted once of a large central temple and 250 minor temples and shrines with two rows of side chapels. To assist pilgrims in meditation, the whole complex was built in the shape of a mandala. Many niches and dark passageways; two-meter-tall *dwarapala* demons armed with swords and clubs guard the entrances. The main temple has been completely dismantled and removed for restoration with only a slab remaining to mark its position.

Candi Plaosan

About one km east of Candi Sewu, this Buddhist complex consists of three groups of principal

H.S. PARISER

Shiva's bull

temples set in a row. Attributed to a 9th-century Sailendra princess, Plaosan combines the function of both temple and monastery. Statues and well-preserved reliefs show devout pilgrims in procession with downcast eyes. An image of a *raksasa dwarapala* was carved from a single block of stone. Although the outside is still rough, the *kala*-heads over the windows inside are in mint condition. Both Hindu and Buddhist religious symbols and ornamentation exist here side by side, indicative of peaceful coexistence of the two religions on Java.

Candi Lumbung

Five hundred meters northeast of Candi Lorojonggrang, this Buddhist- style temple consists of one main temple surrounded by 16 smaller ones.

Candi Sari

Near Kalasan village, 200 meters north of the 14 Km signpost from Yogyakarta, set in the middle of coconut and banana groves. Its design is woven together superbly, like a basket. The second floor served as a priests' dormitory. The famous decorations on the panels between the windows, with 36 large semi-divine beings dancing and playing instruments, are similar in style to Candi Kalasan's reliefs.

Candi Kalasan

Just 50 meters from the Yogyakarta-Solo highway at the 14 Km signpost, Candi Kalasan is one of the easiest of the outlying group to visit. Kalasan is the oldest Mahayana Buddhist temple in Indonesia to which a date can be fixed: A.D. 778. The present exterior was created much later. In fact, there are actually three Candi Kalasans: the present one, still standing, turned out to be the third, erected on top of and around the second, within which are the remains of the first. This Buddhist royal mausoleum is set in a lush garden landscape. Once completely covered in multicolored shining stucco. Unique niche decorations and Central Java's most beautiful *kala*-heads are surrounded by heavenly musicians. Beautiful craftsmanship. The exquisite lichen-covered interior is bathed in light.

Candi Sajiwan

Two km southeast of the Prambanan complex near the village of Sajiwan. Turn south at the sign on the eastern outskirts of Prambanan village and walk about two km. At the foot of this Buddhist temple are reliefs depicting the Tantric tales, with the main theme education. The base and staircase are decorated with animal fables, the *Jatakas*.

Ratu Boko

Also called King Boko's Temple, located a few kilometers south of Prambanan village on the road to Piyungan. Coming from Yogyakarta, turn right at the large triangular intersection in Prambanan village, then walk 2.5 km down the road. It's a steep, rocky 15-minute ascent from the 18 Km signpost. Look for the Dinas Purbakala-Ratu Boko sign. Once the site of a huge fortified 9th-century *kraton*, Ratu Boko overlooks luxuriant rolling green fields, bamboo groves, and the feathery palms of Prambanan Plain. With its beautiful views, it's well worth an early morning walk. The entire plateau is full of ruins; a few bathing pools, still used by villagers, waterspouts, and gateways are in good shape. Some sites have yet to be completely excavated. Don't pay "admission" to the guys working on restoration.

Candi Banyunibo

After Ratu Boko, turn left (southeast) and walk one km. This temple is near a small village on the other side of a gully. See the beautifully carved double-*makara* motif above the niche framing a seated female deity. With its strong facial and bodily form, the goddess statue points to Java's ancient links with Ceylon. A duplicate goddess occupies a niche above the entrance of the House of Pilgrims behind the Temple of the Tooth in Kandy, Sri Lanka. You can reach the other scanty temple remains of Ijo, Mtring, and Tinjong by crossing the river beyond Banyunibo and climbing the hill.

Candi Sambisari

Two km from the village of Sambisari, at the end of a country lane (see the giant sign). If driving, turn in at the 10.2-km signpost and drive for about two km. This 8th- to 9th-century Shiva temple was discovered in 1966 when a farmer broke the blade of his plow against a stone. Unearthed from five meters of volcanic ash, Sambisari could be part of a larger complex. See stone images of Durga and Ganesha, a lovely tree-of-heaven motif, and the *makara*-ornamented doorway. Sambisari is perfectly preserved, unmarred by plunderers or the elements. The lintels are roughly cut but *kala*-heads have hardly changed from the day they were chiseled. About 90% of the restoration is new stone.

GUNUNG MERAPI

The name means "Fire Mountain." More or less in a constant state of eruption, this 2,950-meter-high mountain 25 km north of Yogyakarta is one of the world's most destructive volcanos. There are six volcanologist posts high on its slopes to keep an eye on it, plus a crew of up to 1,000 men on call. When Gunung Merapi erupted in 1006, it covered Borobudur 48 km away and so devastated the land around the monument it remained uninhabitable for generations.

The mountain erupts about once every 5.5 years and has killed nearly 1,600 people in 26 eruptions since 1930. The last major eruption was in November 1994, when a 220° C burst of gas, steam, and ash killed more than 80 people. More than 1.3 million cubic yards of lava poured down the mountainside in a few short hours during the '94 blast. Today more than 40 check-dams and dikes attempt to protect the populace, and large areas beneath the volcano are "forbidden zones."

Merapi can be climbed easiest from Selo; from Kaliurang it's much more challenging. First get to Selo, a small village near Boyolali. Two routes to Selo are possible from Yogyakarta. Most people journey to Kartosuro, then bus to Boyolali and finally Selo. The western approach is by bus to Magelang, then minibus to Selo.

If arriving from the north, take the bus to Wonosobo, Magelang, then Selo (Rp2250). Once in Selo, register at the police station. Stay overnight in the dormitory at the **Agung Merapi Hotel,** or perhaps at your guide's house.

When the minibus stops, a guide should present himself. Look around for a good guide so you don't walk to your death; your guide *must* have experience with the mountain. Police recommendation helps. The guide will charge depending on the size of the group, usually about Rp5000 pp.

Bring a sleeping bag, waterproof clothing, food, water, and good boots. Time your climb for the dry season; during the rainy season the whole area is covered in clouds. The very steep route first takes you through a countryside of lantana flowers and misty ridges, then up through raspberry country to the barren peak. The view before sunrise is unbelievable—the whole Milky Way. It's possible to descend into the crater until the sulphur burns your throat. Four to five hours to ascend the 2,950-meter peak; only two hours to scrabble back down. Little lava stones, like ball bearings underfoot, help your descent immeasurably.

If you want to view the gates of hell, go up at night while Merapi is erupting; see huge red globs of molten rock glowing in the darkness. This night climb is extremely dangerous without a guide who knows the mountain intimately. It's about a 10-minute walk from the summit to the gas jets, which at night glare red hot, with rivulets of orange-red molten lava and sparks spilling over the rim, black acrid smoke, and enormous clouds of steam. During this hot lava

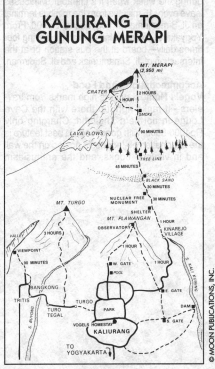

KALIURANG TO GUNUNG MERAPI

© MOON PUBLICATIONS, INC.

stage, Yogyakarta's normally tranquil river is turned into a cocoa-colored torrent.

Organized Tours

Travel agencies and hotels along Jl. Sosrowijayan in Yogyakarta also organize climbs up Gunung Merapi, charging anywhere from Rp20,000 to Rp60,000 pp with transport, breakfast, snacks, and drinks.

KALIURANG

A 900-meter-high mountain resort on Merapi's southern slope, with guesthouses, restaurants, tennis courts, swimming pool, waterfalls, and fantastic hiking. Merapi is usually visible around 0600-0700 but is cloud-covered the rest of the day. If you want to while away some time, head up here. Kaliurang is the closest resort to Yogyakarta, and is only busy on weekends. Go up during the week when it's cheaper. Minibuses leave every 15 minutes from the minibus terminal on Jl. Simanjuntak in Yogyakarta, Rp900. From Yogyakarta you can also take a bus leaving four times daily—board at the bus station or at the intersection of Jl. Simantunjak and Jl. Sudirman.

Accommodations And Food

Vogels Homestay gets high marks from travelers—it ranks right up there with the Cave Lodge in northern Thailand. Charging only Rp4000-8000, with good food, its best feature is the information on Indonesia posted on the wall and in visitors' books, and the enthusiasm

shown visitors by the Christian host. You'll see Vogels as soon as you get off the bus.

Comfortable old **Hotel Kaliurang** lies on the right just before you reach the top of the hill. Good location and nice garden; Rp6000-9000, but you can bargain below that, particularly on weekdays. During the weekend most hotels charge steeper rates. Many cheap *warung* in the vicinity of the market and the parking lot.

To Gunung Plawangan

Two gates (Rp200 each), the West and the East, and two trails lead to the seismological station on Gunung Plawangan (1,260 meters), but from there neither trail continues to the summit. It takes less than 1.5 hours to climb to this observatory, where you can observe activity on Gunung Merapi. Friendly guys here—their only instruments seismographs and binoculars. See photos of the big 1954 eruption. The *warung* near the observatory sells drinks, fruits, and biscuits; if there are too many tourists, prices will be high. You can't see the crater from here.

To Gunung Merapi

The beginning of one path up the mountain, the South Gate, lies at the end of the road where the bus stops. Follow an easy, well-trod footpath with log steps to the northeast; you can't really lose your way. Walk about an hour from Kaliurang to the small village of Kinarejo on the northeast side of Gunung Plawangan, and from there make your ascent to Merapi's peak. A long way. A very strenuous but rewarding six- to seven-hour climb from Kaliurang.

BOROBUDUR

This colossal, cosmic mountain is one of humanity's most imposing creations—nothing else like it exists. Erected 200 years before Notre Dame and Chartres cathedrals, it predates the Buddhist temple of Angkor Wat in Cambodia by three centuries. Built with more than two million cubic feet of stone, Borobudur is the world's largest stupa and the biggest ancient monument in the Southern Hemisphere. See it on a rainy day when water spews from the mouths of its gargoyles. To prep yourself, read Jacques Dumarcay's books *Borobudur* and *The Temples of Java*.

Go very early in the cool of the morning to avoid the large crowds. Admission Rp4000; Indonesians pay Rp1000. Walk to the top of the hill (four hours, bring water) behind Borobudur for a splendid view. You can reach other antiquities in the immediate area—Mendut, Pawon, Banon—with local minibuses.

Inside the privately managed park you'll find a small archaeological museum, tours on a simulated train, and an audiovisual show on the historical background of Borobudur.

History

Its name is probably derived from the Sanskrit Bhumian Bhara Bhudara, "Mountain of the Ac-

cumulation of Merits of the [Ten] States [of the Bodhisattva]." Artisans and specialists from India undoubtedly visited the site. Although the structure features many characteristics of the Central Javanese style (A.D. 700-950), it has little else in common with other Buddhist temples in Southeast Asia. Persian, Babylonian, and Greek influences are present in Borobudur's art and architecture. Planned by people with a profound knowledge of Buddhist philosophy; on Borobudur, Buddha and Shiva are spiritually the same being.

Used for veneration, worship, and meditation, this giant monument was an achievement of the Vajrayana sect of the Tantric School of Buddhism, which found acceptance in Indonesia around A.D. 700. The feudal Sailendra princes—highly advanced technicians—erected it with peasant labor between 778 and 850.

No one really knows how this great structure was built, in a time when modern engineering techniques, it is believed, had not yet been developed. No nation or group of humans could possibly build it today. Thousands of laborers, slaves, carvers, and supervisors worked for decades rolling logs and working ropes, levers, hammers, mallets, and chisels, using only hands and arms. Records indicate the population of the countryside of Central Java was drastically

Borobudur, circa 1920

LEGENDS AND LEGACIES

Borobudur was built on the confluence of two rivers, always considered a holy spot in India. It's a magic place, one of the most magical in Indonesia. When you stand on top it feels like you're floating over the mountains—greenery, volcanos, fantastic landscapes.

According to tradition, the architect who designed the monument was Gunadharma, whose face you can see to the right of the largest pinnacle in the Menorah Mountains, just behind the monument.

Kenari trees were planted around Borobudur in 1840. At the foot of the east stairway once stood a sacred fig tree, said to descend from the original *bodhi* tree under which the Buddha attained enlightenment. This particular tree had been brought to Borobudur in 1928, a shoot of the holy tree in Ceylon which was itself a shoot of the original tree brought from India in the 3rd century B.C. It was chopped down to get the crane in for restoration work.

Later, in the early 1980s, hundreds of families were evicted—with meager compensation or none at all—to make way for the archaeological park.

reduced after the 9th century completion of Borobudur; it exhausted five generations.

In 856, the Sailendras were overthrown by Hindus and Borobudur was abandoned soon after its completion. It might have begun collapsing just when the sculptors were applying their finishing touches; there's evidence of work initiated to reinforce the base, and some panels have trace marks on them. The monument was buried under a thousand years of volcanic eruptions and tropical growth until discovered by an English colonel in 1814. In 1855 Borobudur was cleared, and the long process of restoration begun.

Shape

Borobudur's famous layout, in the form of a giant mandala, can only be appreciated from the air. The structure was constructed to look like the holy Mt. Meru of India, a mythological model of the universe. You can't enter the stupa because it consists only of terraces built over the top of a hill. Greek columns and the Gothic cathedrals of Europe feature a vertical structure, but in Asia the pattern is horizontal. Temples are laid out in square or rectangular enclosures and rise to a gently culminating pyramid. This massive, perfectly symmetrical stupa is one of 84,000 all over Asia, many said to contain the remains or essence of Buddha.

But Borobudur is a stupa with a difference. A historical hodgepodge, it was built in five different stages. The first was the work of Hindus. This unique building combines symbols of the circle (heaven), the square (earth), and the stupa into one coherent whole. Many projections make 36 corners in all. The foot is 122 meters square and the temple goes up tier by tier.

Turn left upon entering to pay tribute to the gods; those who turn right pay tribute to devils. There are 10 terraces from the base to the main topmost stupa, each representing the individual stages toward perfection. The pilgrim's walk takes you around the temple nine times before reaching the top. The east side's third gallery has the best preserved and most beautiful gateway. Visitors are swallowed up symbolically by the *kala*-monster upon entering, then granted new spiritual life.

Reliefs

One of the largest and most complete ensembles of Buddhist reliefs in existence, Borobudur amounts to a virtual textbook of Mahayana Buddhist doctrine in stone. There are 1,500 pictorial relief panels of Buddha's teachings, plus 1,212 purely ornamental panels. Once glistening with bright purple, crimson, green, blue, and yellow paint, over 8,235 square meters of stone surface are carved in high relief, telling scholars much about the material culture of 8th- to 9th-century Java. There are lessons on history, religion, art, morality, literature, clothing styles, family life, architecture, agriculture, shipping, fighting arts, and dancing—the whole Buddhist cosmos. Sculptors trained in the best tradition of Indian classical temple building poured their abundant talents into delicate, intricate detail.

The walk through the labyrinth of narrow corridors to the summit is over five km. To read all the reliefs from the beginning of the story, go through the door on the east side. Because of so many right-angle corners, you're able to see only a few steps ahead. This was designed to force you to take in each phase of the story a frame at a time—like 9th-century TV.

Terraces

The five-storied pyramid is subdivided vertically into three spheres of Buddhism, symbolizing religious microcosms: the base, *kamadhatu,* means "world of passion," with reliefs illustrating worldly life and toil; *rupadhatu,* above the base, consists of four terraces with beautiful reliefs depicting Buddha's life; and *arupadhatu,* the three circular terraces, represents the "world of formlessness." Lower, richly adorned square terraces signify the senses, the round top terraces the soul.

The base-terrace, or "hidden foot," wasn't discovered until 1885. It contains a series of reliefs showing the human form shackled to greed in a world dominated by desire, lust, and death. The lower terraces are full of scenes of karma and earthly existence, woe and desire, good and evil deeds, rewards and punishments—all the *samsara* of the world. As one climbs to the higher levels, reliefs become more heavenly. By the time you emerge on the square terraces near the top, you've eliminated desire, though you're still tied to the world of the senses. You finally attain perfection and are released from all earthly bonds when you reach the round terraces.

Each sphere shows striking differences, from the richly decorated squares to the round terraces devoid of all decoration. The top is spacious and simple: the topmost central stupa (15-meter diameter) is the symbol of heaven, where all suffering ends. This pinnacle was once 10 meters higher than it is now, visible from kilometers away to guide the pilgrim.

Buddha Stupas

On the upper round terraces are over 72 stupa that look like inverted lotus blossoms, each formerly containing a sitting statue of an athletic young Buddha. Through the apertures the Buddha could be seen half in sunlight, half in shadow, each statue only partly visible—calculated to bring home to the visitor both the formless and absolute reality, the two faces of god. Buddha's hands are held in different positions to represent various *mudras,* or symbols, for different actions: teaching, blessing, preaching. Reaching in through the lattices and touching Buddha's hands brings good luck. Most of the heads are missing, knocked off or destroyed by Muslim vandals. You can find some of them today in museums in Bangkok, Holland, Paris, London, and Boston. In the niches above the galleries are statues of reincarnated Buddhas, each pointing to a different compass direction.

Restoration

Over the last 12 centuries, Borobudur held on through the ravages of moss and lichen, heavy tropical downpours, and devastating stone cancers. It took almost 100 years (1814-1911) to uncover the monument and bring it fully back to life. Theodor van Erp launched a major four-year restoration project in 1907, but over the following decades the monument continued to deteriorate rapidly. By the 1960s the foundation was so badly weakened the whole structure was in danger of collapse.

Finally, in 1973, restoration began in earnest, financed by funds from the Indonesian government, private organizations, and member states of UNESCO. No other archaeological rescue of such magnitude had been attempted since the raising of the Egyptian temple of Abu Simbel in 1966 to protect it from the floodwaters of the Aswan Dam. A technique used at Angkor Wat was employed; the ruin taken apart stone by stone, the stones and blocks numbered, the pieces cleaned and chemically treated, then assembled again. The lower galleries were completely dismantled and rebuilt on a reinforced foundation with adequate drainage.

For years the whole project fell prey to bureaucratic ineptitude, corruption, and financial mismanagement, but the work was at last completed in 1983 at a cost of some US$25 million. In January 1985 nine bombs destroyed parts of the stupa; the government blamed either Muslim extremists or local people evicted from their homes to make way for the archaeological park. The massive stupa is still in an almost continual state of reconstruction.

Waicak Day

An annual Buddhist ceremony commemorating Buddha's birth, death, and the day he received enlightenment under the *bodhi* tree. This event usually falls during the full moon on the most auspicious day in May. Since 1959 Waicak has occurred at Borobudur, attended each year by Indonesian Buddhists and by a great many Buddhists from abroad, particularly Theravada Buddhists from Sri Lanka.

The festival begins at Candi Mendut with the bearing of holy water to Borobudur. The climax comes at 0400 when all worshippers converge on the monument. Thousands of men in saffron robes and women in white *saris* carry lighted candles, moving barefoot in a slow, solemn procession up the stairs of Borobudur, chanting and praying. They circle the temple clockwise toward the main stupa at the top, where they wait for the moon to appear on the horizon—the legendary time of Buddha's birth. The highlight of the ceremony is the call of the Buddha, welcoming the audience with the song "Maha Manggala Suta."

Accommodations

To really understand Borobudur, spend a few days at the comfortable and friendly **Lotus Guesthouse**, tel. (0293) 8281, about 500 meters up the road on the east side of the monument.

Decent rooms with breakfast cost Rp7500-10,000. Very quiet, oil lamps, no electricity.

A fallback choice is the **Ramayana Losmen** near the park entrance. Same prices but less atmosphere.

Getting There

Borobudur lies 42 km northwest of Yogyakarta and 17 km southwest of Magelang. From Yogyakarta, buses north to Muntilan and Borobudur depart from terminal Umbulharjo and Terminal Pingit on Jl. Magelang. The whole trip takes 1.5 hours one-way. Beware of pickpockets on these buses.

Hotels in Yogyakarta, as well as many tour agencies, conduct early morning minibus or taxi tours out to Borobudur. Or you can charter a taxi. Driving your own vehicle from Yogyakarta takes one hour.

VICINITY OF BOROBUDUR

MENDUT

Make the beautiful walk to Candi Pawon (two km), then on to Mendut (three km east of Borobudur). After the left-hand turn to the southwest beyond Muntilan, the first temple is Mendut, which stands quietly alone in the middle of a grassy garden. Mendut is a genuine 9th-century temple of worship, not a *candi* to the dead. It faces Saranath, where Buddha spoke his first words of deliverance. Originally over 27 meters tall, Mendut was a mound of rubble, home to grazing cows, until it was cleared in 1836. Complete Dutch restoration occurred between 1897 and 1904. The temple dates from A.D. 850, about the same time as Borobudur, and features extensive galleries, terraces, a pyramid-shaped roof, and stupa on top. Erection required very sophisticated knowledge of Buddhist and Shivaistic texts, Indian inconography, symbolism, and monumental architecture. The builders no doubt visited the Indian holy land. Admission Rp100.

Relief Panels

Mendut's 30 relief panels are among the finest and largest compositions in Hindu-Javanese art. The stories are drawn from the *Jataka* tales,

old Buddhist folk myths involving Buddha's previous incarnations. The stone images in the temple interior are very well preserved, including a 2.5-meter-high Buddha between two bodhisattvas. These colossal statues weren't stolen, simply because of their great weight. Buddha's feet rest upon a stylized lotus blossom; his hand is held in the aspect of a preacher. Architects placed a shaft to one side of the chamber to let in rays from sun and moon to illuminate the Buddha. What was holy to the ancestors of the Javanese is still holy; often there are fresh offerings of flowers and food in the laps of the statues, with incense burning at Buddha's feet. A profound air of tranquility.

Vicinity Of Mendut

The temples belonging to the Borobudur complex—Mendut, Borobudur, and Pawon—fall along a straight east-west axis connecting them to Deer Park in Saranath in India. Pilgrims had to pass each temple to reach Borobudur. **Candi Pawon** lies about two km east of Borobudur and about 800 meters from the road; see the turnoff and sign. Pawon probably served as a porch temple dedicated to Kuvera, god of riches. A little jewel of a temple with tiny windows and dwarves pouring riches from bags above the door. Exquisite body decoration.

Near the village of Muntilan is **Candi Ngawen.** The corners of the base are decorated with lions. Candi Ngawen is actually a collection of four temples in a row, each about three meters apart; only one has been restored. On a plateau just south of Muntilan (ask directions), the temple remains of **Gunung Wukir** could date from as early as the 8th century, making it the oldest identified Shiva sanctuary on Java. Only foundation stones remain.

MAGELANG

The cool city of Magelang (pop. 115,000) is a crossroads town connecting Yogyakarta, Semarang, and Purworejo. On the way from Yogyakarta to Magelang you pass the turnoff to Borobudur to the west.

Magelang is a town of heroes. During the Java War (1825-30), the guerrilla leader Prince Diponegoro was tricked into negotiating with the Dutch and captured here. Visit the room where he was taken prisoner. Later, the town's residents fought bravely in the revolution (1945-49); on the town's crest two bamboo spears symbolize the struggle against the Dutch.

In keeping with its bellicose traditions, Magelang is today the location of the national military academy, AKABRI. **Musium Akabri,** one km from the city's center on the AKABRI campus, features historical artifacts and displays explaining the training of academy cadets. Also see **Musium Soedirman,** Jl. Badaan, Blok C-F.

Out of town is **Ambarawa,** a remarkable Dutch colonial rectangular stone security fortress surrounded by blockhouses.

WONOSOBO

The district's largest town, busy Wonosobo is a favorite stop en route to Dieng. In this mountainous area (elev. 772 meters), rain falls about half the days of the year; the average temperature is 20-25° C. The district produces an abundance of vegetables, tobacco, *klembak, cayuputi, pyrethum,* and *kecang babi.*

For details about Wonosobo and environs, try the **Tourist Information Center** in the Gedung Sasana Bhakti 45, Jl. Pemuda 1, tel. 194, on the south side of the *alun-alun.* Two banks, **BNI** and **BRI,** are on Jl. A. Yani.

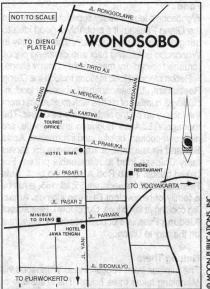

The best source of information about the Wonosobo District is Mr. Agus at the Dieng Restaurant on Jl. Kawadenan. This Jerry Garcia lookalike and his attorney wife can help with maps, photos, trekking tips, and hired transport.

Accommodations

Right opposite the train station is **Hotel Selamet,** Jl. Siliwangi 93, tel. 32961; Rp16,000 and up, very friendly and helpful staff. **Losmen Jawa Tengah,** Jl. Jen. A. Yani 59, tel. 202, offers rooms for Rp6000-14,000; best value in town. **Hotel Nirwana,** Jl. Tanggung 18, is comfortable, though more expensive at Rp25,000. If it's not full of tour groups, try to bargain the staff down to Rp15,000. You might secure a room usually reserved for tour drivers for as low as Rp6000.

Avoid very run-down **Hotel Merdeka. Hotel Bima,** Jl. Jen. A. Yani 5, has clean, Western-style *mandi* with hot water; Rp27,500 d including breakfast. Basic rooms for Rp11,000. Friendly **Family Losmen** occupies a renovated Dutch hospital on Jl. Parman; superb clean rooms for Rp8250. Free tea all day; in the morning women come by to sell snacks.

Food

Wonosobo's food is vastly superior to the fare on the Dieng Plateau; it's probably a good idea to bring snacks up the mountain. The specialty in Wonosobo is *kacang babi* and *dendeng gepuk* (crushed spiced dry meat), sold in many shops.

Recommended food stations include the **Dieng Restaurant,** Jl. Kawedanan 23. Excellent food, including a number of dishes with mushrooms from the factory up on the plateau. Ice-cold beer. The managers, L. Agus Tjugianto and his wife, are nice, soft-spoken, helpful, and informative. **Anda Bar and Restaurant,** Jl. Kawedanan 25, serves tasty Chinese food at reasonable prices. For baked goods, **Toko Roti ABC** is the best. **Asia Restaurant,** Jl. Kawedanan 35, tel. 165, is run by a family of benevolent Chinese albinos. Amazing cooking at fair prices. Out of town, **Restaurant Kledung Pass** is a popular roadside restaurant on the way to Dieng.

Getting There

The minibus from Yogyakarta to Wonosobo via Magelang takes three hours. The first stage of the journey to Magelang is about Rp1000; there may be a slight wait in Magelang for a minibus to Wonosobo (Rp1500). If you want to take in Borobudur on the way to Wonosobo, start *really*

early. Since the Wonosobo bus terminal is about one km from town, tell the driver you'd like to get off on Jl. A. Yani, the location of several good hotels. Or you can just go straight to the minibus terminal in the center of town and head right for Dieng. If driving your own vehicle, Wonosobo is a full-day's hard drive from Jakarta.

Getting Away

The last minibus to Dieng departs around 1800. The 85-km road linking Wonosobo and Banyumas runs beside a foaming, rocky river called Kali Serayu; enjoy green valleys to both sides of the river. To Cilacap, buses leave Wonosobo early morning and midmorning; Rp3000, six hours.

If you intend to take the ferry from Cilacap to Pangandaran, take the Purwokerto bus at 0530 (three hours). To Semarang, buses depart early in the morning and travel via Secang and Ambarawa; Rp3000 (four hours). For Jakarta, Remaja Travel (Jl. A. Yani 83) runs *bis malam* at 1600; Rp10,000, 14 hours.

Vicinity Of Wonosobo

Kalianget is a hot spring three km north of Wonosobo on the road to Dieng. The sulphurous water is said to cure skin disease, stiff

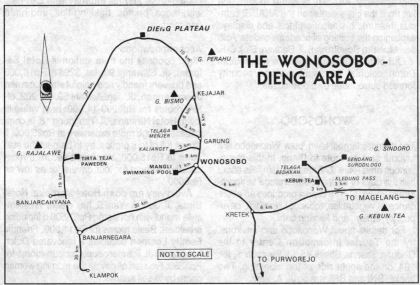

THE WONOSOBO - DIENG AREA

DIENG PLATEAU

G. PERAHU 10 km

KEJAJAR

G. BISMO 6 km

TELAGA MENJER 3 km

KALIANGET 3 km

GARUNG

8 km

G. RAJALAWE

TIRTA TEJA PAWEDEN

MANGLI SWIMMING POOL 1 km

WONOSOBO

TELAGA BEDAKAH

KEBUN TEA

G. SINDORO

SENDANG SURODILOGO

KLEDUNG PASS 3 km

TO MAGELANG

G. KEBUN TEA

BANJARCAHYANA

30 km

8 km

KRETEK 6 km

BANJARNEGARA

30 km

NOT TO SCALE

TO PURWOREJO

KLAMPOK

aching muscles, and the weariness brought on by long, tiring journeys. **Telaga Menjer,** a 1,200-meter-high cool mountain lake, lies 12 km north of Wonosobo; you can reach it in 30 minutes by minibus for Rp700.

Kebun Tea plantation is 17 km east of Wonosobo. **Telaga Bedakah** is three km north of Kebun; the springs at **Sendang Surodilogo** are four km farther east. **Tirta Teja Paweden** is a swimming pool and playground 19 km north of Banjarnegara and 50 km west of Wonosobo. **Klampok** is a ceramics center 30 km south of Banjarnegara.

DIENG PLATEAU

The oldest temples in Java lie at 2,093 meters on this pear-shaped plateau, 26 km northwest of Wonosobo. Sacred since early times, this enchanting highland area offers lovely mountain scenery, a cool climate, fascinating volcanic fissures, and ancient Hindu temples named for *wayang* heroes. The name Dieng comes from Di Hyang, which means "Abode of the Gods." Dieng was once a huge volcano; after a great eruption, the resulting caldera, after thousands of years of weathering, became the present soggy plateau.

That the Sailendras built the Dieng monuments is only surmise; some say the Sanjaya did. In any event, the small Indian-style temples were built at the end of the 7th century. Archaeologists first believed present-day remains indicated Dieng was a ruined city, but realized later the site was a flourishing complex of hermitages for housing priests, attendants, servants, and visiting pilgrims. At that time Dieng was reached by two huge stairways, one reputed to contain 4,000 steps. An elaborate system of irrigation ditches kept the ground dry and level, but after 1,000 years of neglect Dieng has reverted to swamp.

Dieng is still an extremely active geothermal area and you can walk right up to the rims of boiling, smoking, odorous cauldrons. In June 1979, poisonous gases rose from underground passages and several lakes, killing 150 villagers.

You can spend days just hiking around; sturdy footwear recommended. The energetic can walk to many sites within minutes, including Sembungan, the highest (2,160 meters) village

on Java. Try to visit Dieng in the dry season; in the wet there's often a cold wind, and it might be dry for less than an hour each day. In the dry, night temperatures could drop to freezing; dress accordingly. Arrive in the morning; by early afternoon a thick silvery mist creeps down the wooded slopes and wraps the whole plateau in a chilly white blanket. The mists are an excellent environment for the rich green grasses and dozens of species of flowers—dahlias and marigolds, lupines and roses—that enhance the strange beauty of the plateau. Bring paints, charcoal, or crayons; this eerie plateau has always been a favorite subject of artists. At the entrance road to Dieng, pay Rp300 at the tollgate where a man sells Dieng Plateau maps for Rp100.

Kawah Sileri And Kawah Sikidang
Among the many natural wonders here are Kawah Sikidang and Kawah Sileri, as well as a number of other crater lakes, each sparkling with strange shimmering colors, boiling with sulphur mud, whitish smoke hovering over the surface. To the sides of the craters crystals of bright yellow sulphur outcroppings glitter in the sunlight. Kawah Sileri ("Hot Lake") looks very hot indeed, with smoke and vapors rising from it, accompanied by a strong sulphur smell. A magical area. Walking can be dangerous: if you step on a weak spot in the caked mud you'll boil your feet.

Gua Semar
Several small caves are situated on a peninsula between the lakes Warna and Pengilon. Gua Semar is popularly believed to be the dwelling place of the clown-god Semar. Many Indonesians meditate in this famous cove; when things begin to pile up, Suharto has been known to spend the night. The fate of Portuguese Timor may have been decided in this cave when Suharto and then-Australian Prime Minister Gough Whitlam conferred within its dank walls in 1974.

There's a whole ritual involved in visiting the cave. Bathe first at Bimolukar to attain "a pliable heart" and "swift mind," then walk into the cave, where flowers lie and incense burns. The cave is said to be the exact physical center of Java. There's nice camping along Telaga Warna but stay away from the sulphur fumes rising from portions of the lake.

DIENG PLATEAU

Dieng Village to:
Bimolukar	50 m
Hindu temples	1 km
Kawah Sileri	4 km
Gua Jimat	6 km
Candradimuka Crater	8 km
Samur Jakatunda	8.5 km
Telaga Siwiwi	3 km
Telaga Merdeka	3.5 km
Candi Gatotkaca	1.5 km
Kawah Sikidang	2 km
Candi Bima	1.5 km
Suaka Alam Reserve	1 km
Telaga Wama	1 km
Telaga Pengilon	1 km
Gua Semar	1 km
Tangga Buddha	2 km
Sembungan village	3 km

Temples

Only eight of perhaps 200 temples have been restored over a 10-square-km area; for most, only the foundations remain. In the swampy center of the plateau see a group of five Hindu-Buddhist temples. All monuments are dedicated to Shiva. They were built as places of worship, not to glorify kings.

The *candi* are very compactly built, none over 15 meters high, with sparse ornamentation. Most have the same basic shape: a square, squat base with a vestibule in front and projections for niches on the other three sides. Strong vertical and horizontal lines bring strength and character to the structures, most of which are two-storied. Often a *kala*-head is

placed over the entrance; also peculiar to the Dieng site are sinister animal mounts. Many of the temples share uncanny resemblance with temple architecture in southern India, in particular a group of 7th-century temples at Mamallapuram.

All extant temples on Dieng were named after members of the Pandava clan from the Mahabharata, the names chosen by the local population over 100 years ago. Candi Bima, to the south 1.5 km from Dieng Village, is unique in all of Indonesia: faces in the roof appear as spectators looking out windows. Its elegant lines, pyramidal roof, and lovely sculpture are reminiscent of its more sophisticated descendants Prambanan and Mendut.

Other Sights

Gua Jimat, a volcanic vent, pours out so much carbon dioxide animals cannot live here; a world-famous ecological site. You can see traces of a palace in the center of the plain east of Gua Semar and Arjuna Temple. Stone staircases once led to this site, and you can still see remains of the complicated underground tunnel system that once drained the crater floor. Along a rocky woodland path two km south of the lakes is a pool of hot bubbling mud where geysers shoot skyward and sulphur fumes from the earth. About 10 km east of Dieng Village is a Trappist monastery. A guesthouse is set aside for visitors; women cannot enter the monastery itself.

Accommodations And Food

Consider sleeping in a tent under the brilliant stars, but bring a good sleeping bag or shiver. Or stay in Wonosobo and make Dieng a day-trip. **Bu Jono's,** the small *losmen* as you come into Dieng, is the worst of the lot. Spare menu; better fare (European and Indonesian food) at **Restaurant Gunung Mas.**

A little bit past Bu Jono's is **Losmen Gunung Mas,** Jl. Raya Dieng 42, Dieng's largest, most comfortable hotel; Rp5000 with outside bath to Rp35,000 for a room with hot water, private bath, tea and coffee. Also try **Losmen Asri,** a couple of hundred meters down the road from Bu Jono's. Probably the most popular *losmen* at Dieng.

One of the great pleasures of Dieng is eating cornbread, beans, and potatoes—what the locals eat, since rice doesn't grow here.

Getting There

From Yogyakarta, take a minibus to Magelang, then another minibus or *bemo* to Wonosobo (Rp1200). From Wonosobo take a minibus or *bemo* up to Dieng (Rp1000), passing tobacco plantations, rugged steep landscapes, bamboo aqueducts, pale eucalyptus, and sleeping volcanos. From Yogyakarta the total direct trip to Wonosobo takes almost four hours and costs Rp4000-6000. Or join one of Yogyakarta's myriad tour groups; each does Dieng for roughly Rp12,000-18,000. Inquire at your hotel desk.

If coming from Bandung, consider stopping at Dieng before arriving in Yogyakarta. Take the 0510 train to Kroya, then a minibus to Wonosobo.

Getting Away

Buses and *bemo* leave Dieng every five minutes or so for Wonosobo. A unique exit from the Dieng Plateau is the 13-km walk north to Bawang, leaving the plateau by Gunung Sipandau. This walk requires good shoes with traction as the stepped path is often slippery. Pass through villages that seldom see foreigners.

You could also hike south to Garung, where you can catch a taxi to Wonosobo. Start early and don't plan to camp along the way; you might get hassled. It takes one to two hours to walk from Dieng to Sembungan and another five to six hours to reach Garung. Hiking is beautiful in this area—obtain a map from the Dieng tourist information center or from the Dieng Restaurant in Wonosobo.

misty dawn on the Dieng Plateau

SOLO

The cultural linchpin of Java. Sometimes called Surakarta, often spelled Sala, but always pronounced Solo. The population of 500,000 is larger than Yogyakarta's, its sister city. Java's oldest cultural center, considered the island's most Javanese city, Solo is a *priyayi* stronghold. It's the only Javanese city where you see the Javanese written language widely used on buildings and signs. In the hearts of its people, Solo is the traditional capital of the Javanese kingdom—not Yogyakarta.

Solo offers everything found in Yogyakarta but the tourists. There are art galleries, theaters, mystical fraternities, dance and music academies, extensive markets, traditional crafts, Chinese temples, inexpensive *losmen,* good restaurants, and a frivolous nightlife, where the women of Solo "walk like hungry tigers." The city never sleeps; people roam the streets 24 hours a day. There are two *kraton,* one even larger and more venerable than Yogyakarta's. Religion is soft and flowing here, unlike the more orthodox form of Islam practiced on the north coast and in West Java.

But change is overtaking this ancient capital. Traffic lights are found on all the major intersections; the slick Purwosari shopping center introduced consumer mentality; then, in 1987, the huge new Singosaren Plaza shopping center replaced the venerable old downtown household market Pasar Singosaren.

History

Once just a village in the middle of a forest, founded by the legendary Kyai Sala, Solo became the seat of the Mataram Kingdom when the previous capital at Kartosuro was reduced to rubble during a war with the Dutch. An auspicious site near the Solo River was chosen by the sultan and the palace completed in 1745. In one magnificent procession, the entire *kraton* moved from Kartosuro to the new palace, called Kraton Surakarta Hadiningrat. This dynasty lasted only 10 years, until the realm was partitioned in 1755 after the death of Sultan Paku Buwono II. The *susuhunan's* uncle, claiming Yogyakarta as his territory, became the first sultan of that royal city.

The reigning *susuhunan* of Solo, in spite of his diminished authority, was permitted by the Dutch to continue receiving income from his holdings. This vast revenue went toward the promotion of music, dance, and *wayang,* which flowered under royal patronage. During the Java War of 1825-30, most of Yogyakarta's *priyayi* families supported Diponegoro, while those in Solo remained loyal to the Dutch. When the Dutch occupied Solo, the *susuhunan* held a reception for them in his *kraton.* This was remembered 116 years later in 1946 when Indonesia became a republic, and the *susuhunan* of Solo was stripped of all authority.

In the 1960s Solo was a center of Communist Party activity; the PKI enjoyed here some of its most fervent support.

KRATON HADININGRAT

Also called Istana Kasuhunan, or the Susuhunan's Palace, located southeast of the city center. *Susuhunan* means "royal foot placed on the head of vassals paying homage," a title dating from the 1600s.

Before 1985, gaudy vulgarity was the dominant theme. The gold vessels, gilded furniture, mirrors, and flamboyant hangings seemed like stage props in the home of a colossal profiteer. Rumors about the *raja's* womanizing and extravagances were rampant and neverending. Living in Jakarta, he neglected upkeep of the palace and failed to propitiate hidden powers. Finally, in January 1985, catastrophe struck. The main core of the *kraton,* the Dalem Gede—with all its priceless wood architecture and furniture—caught fire. What followed was a comic tragedy. Fire engines which could easily have doused the fire responded quickly but couldn't fit through the main gate. Since the gate was sacred, a powerful symbol of authority, the firefighters refused to smash it down. Consequently, some 60% of the palace burned to the ground. The official cause of the fire was a faulty electrical circuit, but it's local belief the prodigal king no longer deserved the protection of the palace spirits, who, as the Javanese say, "went back home."

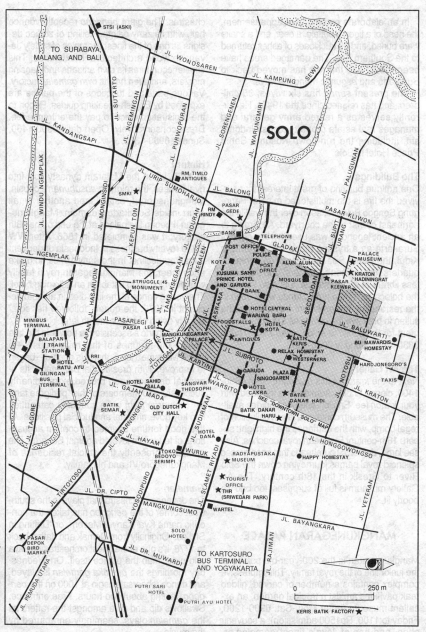

TO SURABAYA,
MALANG, AND BALI

SOLO

STSI (ASKI)

JL. WONOSAREN

JL. KAMPUNG
SEWU

JL. SUTARTO

JL. SORENGENEN

JL. WARUNGMIRI

JL. NGEMINGAN
JL. NGEMINGSIDI
JL. PURWOPURAN

JL. KANDANGSAPI

JL. WINDU NGEMPLAK

JL. BALONG

JL. PALIGUNAN

JL. URIP SUMOHARJO

RM. TIMLO
ANTIQUES

SMKI

PASAR
GEDE

JL. MONGINSIDI

JL. KEPUN TON

JL. WIDURAN

RM
RINDY

PASAR KLIWON

JL. SUPIT
URANG

JL. HASANUDIN

JL. NGEMPLAK

BANK

TELEPHONE
GLADAK

POST OFFICE
POLICE

PALACE
MUSEUM

STRUGGLE 45
MONUMENT

KOTA

POST
OFFICE

ALUN ALUN

KRATON
HADININGRAT

JL. KEBALEN

JL. TAMBAKSEGARAN

KUSUMA SAHID
PRINCE HOTEL
AND GARUDA

MOSQUE

PASAR
KLEWER

JL. SEGOYUDAN

BANK

MINIBUS
TERMINAL

JL. PASARLEGI
PASAR LEGI

HOTEL CENTRAL

WARUNG BARU

HOTEL
KOTA

JL. BALUWARTI

JL. ASRAMA

FOODSTALLS

BU MAWARDIS
HOMESTAY

BALAPAN
TRAIN
STATION

MANGKUNEGARAN
PALACE

ANTIQUES

BATIK
KERIS

HOTEL
RATU AYU

JL. TOTOGAN

JL. SUBROTO

RELAX HOMESTAY

JL. NOTOSU

HARDJONEGORO'S

WESTERNERS

RRI

JL. KARTINI

GARUDA

PLAZA
SINGOSAREN

TAXIS

GILINGAN
BUS
TERMINAL

JL. WARSITO

HOTEL
CAKRA

JL. KRATON

JL. GAJAH MADA

HOTEL SAHID
SALA

SANGYAR
THEOSOPHI

BATIK
DANAR HADI

SEE "DOWNTOWN SOLO" MAP

JL. TAGORE

BATIK
SEMAR

OLD DUTCH
CITY HALL

BATIK DANAR
HARU

JL. PASARNONGKO

JL. SUDIRMAN

JL. HONGGOWONGSO

JL. HAYAM

HOTEL
DANA

TOKO
BEDOYO
SERIMPI

WURUK

RADYAPUSTAKA
MUSEUM

HAPPY HOMESTAY

JL. TIRTOYOSO

JL. YOSODIPURO

JL. SLAMET RIYADI

TOURIST
OFFICE

JL. DR. CIPTO

THR
(SRIWEDARI PARK)

JL. VETERAN

MANGKUNGSUMO

WARTEL

JL. BAYANGKARA

JL. PEMUDA UTARA

PASAR
DEPOK
BIRD MARKET

JL. RAJIMAN

SOLO
HOTEL

JL. DR. MUWARDI

TO KARTOSURO
BUS TERMINAL
AND YOGYAKARTA

0   250 m

PUTRI SARI
HOTEL

PUTRI AYU HOTEL

KERIS BATIK FACTORY

© MOON PUBLICATIONS, INC.

In an elaborate ceremony of appeasement, the head of a tiger, a buffalo, a deer, and a snake were buried, and 30 truckloads of ashes returned to the Southern Sea. The damaged areas have been rebuilt and the *raja* has moved back to Surakarta and begun to mend his ways.

The present *sunan* has six wives, 35 children, and has reigned since the 1940s. He currently serves as a retired army general and manages real estate property across Indonesia, including the run-down Kusuma Sahid Prince Hotel in Solo.

The Buildings

One antique building of great interest that survived the fire is the multistoried minaret Panggung Songgo Buwono, seen over the wall in the northeast corner of the courtyard. According to an ancient legend, it was used by the *rajas* of Surakarta as a trysting place with Nyai Loro Kidul, the South Sea goddess. The servants' quarters, the women's quarters, and the priceless library of *lontar* manuscripts also survived the holocaust. Since public funds were used in the restoration, the president has charged the sultan to preserve the palace as a cultural monument for the public to enjoy; open Mon.-Thurs. 0830-1400, Sunday 0830-1500.

The Art Gallery

Next to the *kraton* is this museum, open 0830-1400, closed Friday. Admission is included with your *kraton* fee. English-speaking guides available. The museum contains a lavish collection of regal pomp, with the carriages the highlight: superb 18th-century European royal coaches. Also see large, demonic figureheads that once graced splendid royal barges journeying down the Solo River to Gresik in the 18th century. The Art Gallery museum is full of surprises; too bad it's poorly lit.

MANGKUNEGARAN PALACE

Mangkunegaran is the 200-year-old palace of the junior line of the royal family. This impressive complex contains a number of carved, gilded teak pavilions amidst a tropical garden, an excellent museum (open Mon.-Sat. 0900-1200, Friday to 1100, Rp1500 admission), a souvenir shop, and one of Java's finest *gamelan* orchestras. The giant *pendopo* reception/dance hall, with its zany painted ceiling of zodiac designs, is one of the finest examples of stately Javanese wood architecture in existence. This smaller court hires its own artisans and dancing masters, and even has its own *gamelan* factory. Various parts and functions of the palace are explained by English-speaking guides. Report to the registration office to pay the entrance fee. Dress conservatively. Open daily 0900-1400, Sunday 0900-1300.

History

In 1755, when the Mataram dynasty split into rival houses, the reigning *susuhunan's* cousin, Mangkunegoro I, established another small court inside Surakarta's domain. Mangkunegaran II began the palace at the end of the 18th century; it was completed in 1866. After WW II, the royalty business in Indonesia underwent a marked decline. In the early 1970s, to make ends meet, the Mangkunegaran royal family was even forced to establish an adjoining hotel. The young prince of the line died in an auto accident in 1979; the queen "followed her son," literally dying of grief a month later.

After Suharto's ascension to power in the late 1960s, the fortunes of this royal house—to which Madame Tien Suharto is related—began to improve. With presidential patronage, its financial dealings soon proved extraordinarily successful and members of this "pedigree family" (*keluarga trah*) were suddenly catapulted into key governmental and judicial positions. All this good fortune seemed to confirm accusations of feudalism leveled against Suharto. The palace is presently the official residence of Mangkunegoro VII and his family.

Gamelan

The Javanese orchestra that plays in the southwest corner of the *pendopo* has taken the honorific name Kyai Kanyut Mesem, or "Drifting in Smiles." Originally from Demak and dating back to 1778, it's one of the finest orchestras on Java and older than the palace itself. On Wednesday mornings the *pustaka gamelan* is played, and dance rehearsals begin at 1000 on the *pendopo*, lasting about two hours. Free entrance. Swallows dip and dive amongst the rafters as the *gamelan* plays, seemingly enraptured by the music.

OTHER SIGHTS

Neighborhoods

Solo's real flavor can only be experienced by exploring the small alleyways in the central part of town near the two *kraton*. Whitewashed walls and fences, balconies, families hanging out on the doorsteps. Stroll the two fine alleys: Jl. Kusuma and Jl. Hasyim Asyari just west of the *alun-alun*.

The Buddhist community occupies Prawit in the northern fringe of town. A Confucian group in Chinatown gathers each Sunday at the main temple, Lithang, on Jl. Jagalan. The Catholic church at Purbayan is built in the old cathedral style. A small Hindu *pura* is at Kentingan (Komplex UNS); a new Protestant church lies on the eastern end of the city's main street, Jl. Slamet Riyadi. You'll find the Arab quarter around Pasar Kliwon. The imposing homes of merchants dominate the Lawiyan neighborhood, their holdings often protected by high walls from the dusty roads crowded with oxcarts, laden donkeys, and bicycle cabs. A small museum of *kris* and other artifacts is at Jl. Kratonan 101, west of the palace. See **Mesjid Besar** (The Great Mosque), west of the *alun-alun*, with its *pendopo* and minaret, a combination of Javanese and Muslim styles.

THR Sriwedari

Located on the western end of Jl. Slamet Riyadi, this amusement park is open daily to the public. Admittance charge only during special events. It offers an uncrowded, park-like atmosphere, with children's playground and a zoo containing the widest selection of animals in Central Java. Buy souvenirs in the art shops around and inside the park and treat yourself to a Bintang beer at one of the good cheap *warung*. Or try the interior *warung*, which serves *cobra sate*. Watch the skinning. On Monday evenings, or when it's raining, you may find the park deserted.

SOLO MEDITATION

Sanggar Theosophi Sala

Solo is a center for spiritual groups. The **Theosophical Society** is located at Jl. Gajah Mada 102. The sign reads simply Theosophic. Theosophy is the science of metaphysics, the study of the cosmos as it applies to humans and earth. There is no worship, but every Sunday members discuss theory, read texts, and lecture.

Sumarah

A mystical white magic fraternity founded by a bank clerk in 1937, its name is an acronym for Sujud Marang Allah, which means "Devotion, Dedication, and Surrender to God." With 10,000 followers worldwide, the organization accepts aspirants from all creeds. Sumarah is founded on the concept that every religion, at least in its original form, believed all paths lead to one god, that all spiritual development was for the good of everyone. Every religion merges, and Sumarah does not hesitate to take wisdom from other sources. Students try to maintain contact with the world and remain aware of what exists outside their perception. As in the Zen concept of the "such-ness" of things, one must realize his or her essence and individuality.

Each *pamong* (teacher) uses a different technique; for example, Pak Hardjanto is a follower of a mixture of Hinduism, Javaism, and Bali Hindu religions. None practice levitation or other spectacular public demonstrations of their faith, believing any outward manifestation of God's favor is irrelevant. The idea is to maintain the spirit of humility and self-surrender and to constantly worship God, while at the same time live at peace within society.

Studying Sumarah

Many resident Europeans study under the tutelage of a *pamong*. Meditation sessions usually last two to three hours. If you're interested, first visit the Joyokusuman Guesthouse at Gajahan RT 9/I no. 16 between 0900 and 1000 and ask for Laura. The introductory booklet costs Rp500. To further familiarize yourself with metaphysical thought, Pak Sujono (Jl. Bonggowarsito 60) maintains an outstanding library which you can peruse. There's no registration fee, and admission into a meditation group is by invitation only. Go along to a meeting or two to see how you like it. Comfortable rooms for rent, from Rp60,000 per month, for long-term meditation students at Joyokusuman Guesthouse, Gajahan. To make ends meet, most of the meditators teach English.

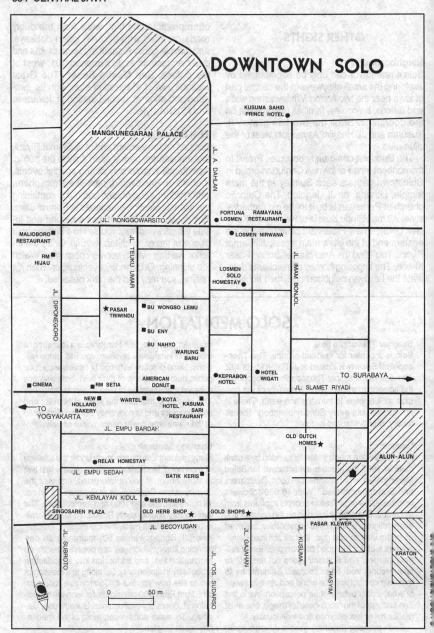

DOWNTOWN SOLO

MANGKUNEGARAN PALACE

KUSUMA SAHID
PRINCE HOTEL ●

JL. A. DAHLAN

JL. RONGGOWARSITO

FORTUNA   RAMAYANA
● LOSMEN RESTAURANT ■

MALIOBORO
RESTAURANT ■

● LOSMEN NIRWANA

RM ■
HIJAU

JL. TEUKU UMAR

JL. IMAM BONJOL

LOSMEN
SOLO
HOMESTAY ●

JL. DIPONEGORO

★ PASAR
TRIWINDU

■ BU WONGSO LEMU

■ BU ENY

BU NAHYO
WARUNG ■
BARU

■ CINEMA   ■ RM SETIA

● KEPRABON
HOTEL

● HOTEL
WIGATI

TO SURABAYA ➡

AMERICAN ■
DONUT

JL. SLAMET RIYADI

NEW ■
HOLLAND   WARTEL ■
BAKERY

■ KOTA
HOTEL KASUMA
SARI ■
RESTAURANT

⬅ TO
TO YOGYAKARTA

JL. EMPU BARDAH

OLD DUTCH
HOMES ★

ALUN-ALUN

● RELAX HOMESTAY

JL. EMPU SEDAH

BATIK KERIS ■

JL. KEMLAYAN KIDUL ● WESTERNERS

SINGOSAREN PLAZA   OLD HERB SHOP ★ GOLD SHOPS ★

JL. SECOYUDAN

PASAR KLEWER

JL. SUBROTO

JL. GAJAHAN

JL. YOS. SUDARSO

JL. KUSUMA

JL. HASYIM

KRATON

0   50 m

At night, take in one of the musical extravaganzas: rock groups, female vocalists, string quartets. From 2000 to 2400 (Sunday 0900-1200) view a variety of Javanese dramas. The Sriwedari *wayang orang* troupe is considered Indonesia's finest; Sukarno used to fly the whole troupe to Jakarta for the evening. During Ramadan a giant night market, **Maleman Sriwedari,** sets up in this people's park.

Radyapustaka Museum

Founded in 1890 by the Dutch, the Institute of Javanese Culture is the oldest such organization in Indonesia. The institute's first task was to build a museum, create a library, and publish a monthly magazine. The institute developed rapidly, well known in the world of scholarship, with many foreign cultural historians and Oriental culture experts contributing to its archives over the years. The present aims of the institute include standardizing the Javanese alphabet and offering courses in Kawi (Old Javanese), painting, sculpture, *kris-* and *batik-*making, and puppetry.

Located right next to the Sriwedari Amusement Park, the museum contains a fascinating collection of royal paraphernalia, exquisite *kris,* and Javanese crafts. Open daily (except Monday) 0800-1200, Friday until 1100; Rp100. The **City Library** right next door is open 0900-1300, Friday until 1100.

ACCOMMODATIONS

Budget

On or around Jl. Ahmad Dahlan is a neighborhood of old Dutch buildings, narrow alleyways, trendy cafes, and almost a dozen decent *losmen* in the Rp5000-10,000 price range.

Probably the most popular is **Losmen Solo Homestay** in the narrow lane to the north; spacious courtyard, friendly help, and acceptable rooms (sometimes noisy) for Rp5000-8000. **Keprabon Hotel,** at Jl. Dahlan 12, tel. (0271) 32811, is a real rarity—an old Dutch hotel with art deco touches in the period windows and furniture. Simple but clean rooms face a quiet inner courtyard.

Two other options are located on Jl. Ronggowarsito near the palace. **Fortuna Losmen,** tel. 48791, has dirty but quiet rooms facing an

inner courtyard, while **Losmen Nirwana** is an older, rambling building with rooms from Rp6000. **Hotel Central,** no. 32, tel. 42814, is another older Dutch hotel but rooms with common bath are overpriced at Rp10,000. **Losmen Timur** has dark closed rooms with no windows; bathrooms are ill-lit and decrepit, but it's cheap.

Hotel Wigati, Keprabon Wetan IV/4, tel. 37341, right down the lane from Penginapan Timur, is an old and dark 37-room hotel. A new wing is planned; it's worth a look. In the mornings vendors sell *nasi liwet* out front.

Homestays

A favorite of travelers is **Westerners,** on Kemlayan Kidul 11, tel. (0271) 33106, well known to *becak* drivers. Except for the screeching birds in the morning and the almost compulsive sweeping, let nothing untoward be said about this delightful family-style accommodation; Rp5500-7000 for small but adequate rooms, plus two VIP rooms for Rp8500-9500. There's a kitchen (with utensils), telephone, laundry area, bicycles for rent, breakfast, and a good notice board. Relax in open-air sitting areas with flowering plants—an island of peace in the center of the city, where, as the name implies, only Westerners can stay.

An excellent nearby alternative is the popular **Relax Homestay** on Jl. Empu Sedah, with six fabulous rooms in the main building for Rp7000-10,000 and 10 smaller cubicles for Rp6000.

A new homestay recommended by travelers is **Sinar Mulaya Homestay,** Jl. Dr. Rajiman 576, tel. 37903. Prices (Rp6000-20,000) include fan, breakfast, tea and coffee all day, use of mountain bikes, and laundry; staff will pick you up from your arrival point and guide you around town for free. The friendly owners also own three *batik* factories they'll be proud to show you; they don't push you to buy.

Visitors studying Indonesian mysticism and other spiritual arts often stay at the **Joyokusuman,** just off Jl. Gajahan, south of the *kraton.* Lovely grounds, pleasant atmosphere, and rooms from Rp8000 make for a pleasant stay in this old mansion of a former Solonese prince. Discounts for monthly stays.

Train Station Vicinity

Handily located near Balapan train station, though a bit far from town center, is clean, well-organized **Hotel Gajah Mada,** Jl. Gajah Mada 54;

Rp8000-12,000. Rent a room surrounding the large inner courtyard and fountain, as the rooms facing Jl. Gajah Mada are too noisy and expensive. Quiet **Hotel Wismantara**, Jl. R.M. Said 53, runs Rp10,000 with *kamar mandi*. Right down the street toward the city is friendly *losmen*-style **Hotel Kondang Asri**, Jl. R.M. Said; Rp7000.

Moderate
One of the best deals in the Rp15,000-24,000 price range is the **Hotel Dana**, Jl. Slamet Riyadi 286 across from the tourist office. Spacious doubles come with fan, *mandi*, and veranda; nice courtyard, quiet for downtown. More conveniently located right in the center of town is the old but tidy **Hotel Kota**, at Jl. Slamet Riyadi 123, tel. (0271) 32481, with budget rooms and common bath for Rp7000-9000 and a/c rooms with color TV Rp25,000-35,000.

Also try homestyle **Ramayana Guest House**, Jl. Dr. Wahidin 15, tel. 2841; large a/c rooms, including breakfast (0700-2100), tea, and evening snack. Nearby check out the **Putri Ayu Hotel,** Jl. Slamet Riyadi 293, tel. 6154, for commodious, quiet, extremely clean rooms. Though about 2.5 km out of town on the road to Yogyakarta, a *bis kota* passes by right out front (Rp150)—or take a *becak* for Rp500. Closer is the **Indah Jaya,** only a few minutes from the train station, with large a/c rooms and adjoining Indonesian-style *mandi*. Clean and comfortable. Chinese-owned **Hotel Trio,** opposite Pasar Gede, is a good value; ask for the rooms in the back.

Luxury
The 50-room **Kusuma Sahid Prince**, Jl. Sugiyopranoto 22, tel. (0271) 46356, fax 44788, was once considered the top hotel in town. On estates formerly owned by members of the royal family, this aging relic charges from Rp178,500 up to Rp2.1 million for a luxurious suite. If you feel heatstroke coming on, pay Rp3500 to plunge into the Olympic-size pool. The Kusuma, however, sorely needs restoration and a new a/c system that works.

Small **Hotel Cakra**, Jl. Slamet Riyadi 171, tel. 45847, fax 48334, in the Rp84,000-126,000 price range, has a restaurant, good central location, and efficient managment.

Top choice in town is the plush **Hotel Sahid Sala,** Jl. Gajah Mada 82, tel. 45889, fax 44133, where rooms cost Rp105,000-210,000. A major 1994 addition now provides the cleanest and most modern rooms in Solo. Swim at the Kusuma, but stay at the Sahid.

FOOD

Street Food And Cafes
A venerable old custom in Solo involves snacking (*jajan*) at all hours of the day or night: cassava cakes, sticky rice (*jada*), *mie bakso,* hot tea. The *warung* with cheap and lousy food look the same as the *warung* with cheap and superb food—you have to know your *warung.*

One of the jolliest spots in Solo is the small but popular **Warung Baru** on Jl. Dahlan in the center of town. Great music, reliable travel information, and wonderful food, from mountainous fruit salads to local specialties. The whole affair is presided over by a beautiful, vivacious woman appropriately named Sunny; her bicycle tours of Solo receive rave reports.

A Solo specialty is delicious *nasi liwet,* rice served with chicken and vegetables in coconut cream sauce. Another great dish is *nasi gudeg*—rice served with stewed jackfruit, coconut cream, and your choice of chicken, fermented eggs, or tasty tofu. Excellent. Try it on Jl. Teuku Umar: Rp750-900 including meat, vegetables, sauce, and boiled egg. A specialized *nasi gudeg* place is the friendly Bu Mari near Relax Homestay and Westerners.

At **Restaurant Wijaya's** try the Solonese dish *gampol plered,* made from rice flour, coconut milk, and spices; even the mayor of Solo eats here. The best *gampol plered* is sold by vendors who travel around the different *kampung.* Cheap eating places also cluster around the train station; you'll find another row of *warung* on Jl. Diponegoro near the entrance to Pasar Triwindu. For Solonese chicken rice soup (*nasi timlo*), go to **Timlo Solo,** Jl. Jen. Urip Sumoharjo/Mesen 106. **Pak Dul's,** on the corner of Jl. Imam Bonjol and Jl. Ronggowarsito, is an eating tent serving tasty "100% *halal*" rice dishes; order cold beer from the Ramayana Restaurant across the street.

Jalan Teuku Umar
Here, on tents with Nasi Gudeg blazoned across them, sample Solo's filling specialty consisting of egg, beans, *nasi,* coconut sauce, and vegeta-

bles—a deal at Rp1000. Other Indonesian cuisines available: *wedang ronde* (soup), *telur puyum* (quail eggs), and *sosis* (meat dish). On this same street hot milk tents open at night, cozy meeting places where *becak* drivers, businesspeople, Chinese laborers, schoolchildren, and travelers all eat together. Rp300 for milk with honey, Rp600 for Susu ltb, a male virility tonic promising new strength.

Many of the legendary stalls moved several years ago over to Sriwedari and have since gone bankrupt, but a few survivors have returned to Jl. Teuku Umar. Try **Bu Wongso Lemu** for *nasi liwet* served on banana leaves, *nasi gudeg* at **Bu Yatis,** and other dishes at **Bu Eny** and **Bu Nahyo.**

Sate

Several *sate ayam* places lie about five minutes from Hotel Central. **Sate Ayam Madura** offers *nasi soto* and *nasi rames*; **Sate Ayam Pak Dul,** Jl. Nonongan 73, is better known. A good *sate kambing* place occupies the corner of Jl. Nonongan and Jl. Slamet Riyadi.

Restaurants

Escape the heat in the conveniently located a/c **Kusuma Sari Restaurant** in the heart of Solo. The food is average, but check the photo menu—curious shots of hamburgers decorated with miniature corn, and a grinning Pinokio Sundae.

Restaurant Sari, Jl. Slamet Riyadi 351, about 2.5 km from the tourist office, features such specials as sausages and smoked ham, as well as the best restaurant versions of Solonese dishes. **Populair,** Jl. Achmad Dahlan 70, serves very good Chinese-style meals. The *cap cai* (Rp1500) is hard to beat; enough for two. Another Chinese restaurant is the excellent **Centrum,** serving seafood dishes in the Rp3000-4000 range near the Westerners.

The **Ramayana Restaurant,** on the intersection of Jl. Imam Bonjol and Jl. Ronggowarsito, is a cozy little place with well-prepared Chinese cuisine, *sate,* and cold beer. **The Orient,** Jl. Slamet Riyadi 337A near the Sari, is Solo's top Chinese restaurant; dishes cost Rp3000-4000. The **Diamond,** down the street toward town, serves the same quality food at higher prices—which explains why it's usually empty. Probably the best *nasi padang* restaurant in town is **Pasar Pon,** Jl. Slamet Riyadi near

Bioskop Dhady. For something cheaper, **Bakso Taman Sari,** Jl. Gatot Subroto 42C, offers tasty dishes and competent ice drinks; about Rp1500 for a meal.

Madukoro Restaurant, six km west of Solo on the road to Yogyakarta in the little town of Kartosuro, serves the best *burung dara* and *seger ayam* around; sample the special *"madukoro* drink." **Kantin Bahagia,** Jl. Gatot Subroto 97, across from the Matahari shopping center, is a nice place to relax after shopping; good cheap food in a pleasant atmosphere; you can also rent bikes and receive travel info here.

Desserts

At night try the local sweet, *serabi*—rice custard on a crispy pancake. Available in the Pasar Pon area. Best served hot with sprinkled chocolate shavings, pineapple, or *pisang* slices on top. Also try *jenang gulo,* sweet, sticky rice cakes. At Jl. Slamet Riyadi 76 is the **New Holland Modern Bakery,** which peddles delights like cheese danish (Rp500), hamburgers with the works (Rp2000), chocolate jimmies, *kelapa muda* pastry, all kinds of cakes, confections, and very good ice cream.

Nearby, also on Jl. Slamet Riyadi, flashy **American Donut** offers the best selection of baked goods. **Orion,** Jl. Urip Sumoharjo, is another outstanding bakery. Ice cream carts are everywhere; taste coconut ice cream—an overwhelming bowl for Rp300. Superlative ice juices mixed at **Tentrem Ice Cream,** Jl. Urip Sumoharjo. In **Pasar Gede** and **Pasar Sinjosaren** select from a mouthwatering cornucopia of local and imported fruits.

ENTERTAINMENT

Dance And Music

Although the Sasono Mulyo, the Kraton Hadiningrat's royal dance pavilion, survived the 1985 fire, the *kraton's* troupe of dancers moved to the ASKI building—an academic, sterile environment out of town. The pavilion now stands hauntingly empty. In its day this court was the origin of many lyrical dances, such as *golek* and *bondan* ("mother tending her baby"), a fusion of professional (*taledek*) and classical Solo dance styles.

The body movements of Solonese dancers are more liquid than the rigid discipline in Yogyakarta. The zenith of the refined court dance form is practiced at the *kraton* dance school; here you can see the emphasis the Javanese place on composure and perfection.

The *bedaya* and *serimpi* are the last vestiges of the old ceremonial *kraton* dances. At **Mangkunegaran Kraton** every Wednesday at 1000 you can see these traditional dances practiced for two hours free. In Kraton Hadiningrat, only one very old woman still teaches the traditional *serimpi*. An American university has videotaped her instruction method so her great art and skill will not be forever lost.

Solo has also always occupied a prominent place in *wayang* development. *Wayang* themes are everywhere in this city—in inlaid work, carvings, paintings, court dances. It's said there are 1,000 *wayang kulit dalang* working in the Solo area. Performances of *wayang kulit* and *wayang orang* are performed here for the populace, not just for tourists.

Clubs, Concerts, And Films

Pop concerts in Solo occur at least once a month; most groups seem to try to emulate the Talking Heads. Pubs and discos are presently the rage: **Nuansa Pub** and **Dinasti** on Jl. Honggowongso, **Sasmaya** on Jl. Dr. Rajimani, **Legend Disco** on Jl. Honggowangso, **Nirwana Disco** on Jl. Urip near Pasar Gede, and the **Dew Drop Inn** behind the stadium. These are the places to go if you get tired of *nasi gudeg*, want some Western food, and enjoy listening to small bands play new Indonesian pop music. Dancing, Rp3000-5000 cover; open at 1200. Some also serve as informal venues for local prostitutes, often college students moonlighting on weekends.

Melodramatic Indian films and violent kung fu movies play at the **Trisakti Theatre,** Jl. Kratonan, and the **Solo Theater** in Sriwedari Park. Try to see a traditional Solonese wedding in Bulan Besar: the groom crushes an egg with his foot and the bride then washes his foot in flowery water.

Before *puasa,* Solonese make pilgrimages to graves and visit bathing places at Cokrotulung and Pengging to take ceremonial baths. Occasionally, horse races take place at the Manahan Sportsfield, with visitors pouring in from surrounding cities.

STSI (ASKI)

In recent years, ASKI has become STSI. Under any acronym, it's still Solo's music conservatory, next door to the Law Department at Pagelaran Alun Utara. Over 60 years ago this prestigious academy devised a system of ciphers to mark traditional Javanese *gamelan* notes so that songs and music could be preserved. Before, musicians learned songs and meters by heart. Some royal *gamelan* musicians and dancers rehearse and teach here every morning—except Sundays—from around 0900 until 1400. Also a museum. Here you may see *wayang kulit* free of charge, Malaysian or Balinese dances, and art exhibits.

Sriwedari Theater

The Sriwedari Amusement Park, in the middle of town on Jl. Slamet Riyadi, is home base for the celebrated Wayang Orang Sriwedari. Because performances are put on every night except Sunday, this park is one of the easiest places to see versions of not only the Hindu epics but also more popularized productions such as *ketoprak* and *wayang orang.* Tickets cost Rp400, or stand for free at the side of the building and look through the wire mesh with the kids. Starts at 2000, ends by 2300. Realistically painted stage props—palace hall, dense wild forest, rice fields, mountains. The dance style is sometimes learned second- and third-hand from the court masters down the street in the *kraton* dance schools. The Saturday night shows are the most popular, so buy those tickets in advance. While waiting, wander around the park and snack at the small restaurants.

Also see *dangdut* on Saturday nights—Indonesian/Arab pop music fronted by provocatively dressed female singers.

Radio Republik Indonesia

Wayang shows are held at the RRI Bldg. near the railroad station, which is Rp500 by *becak* from city center. Broadcast live all over Central Java, *wayang orang* performances (Rp400-750) are staged approximately twice a month every other Wednesday, *wayang kulit* (Rp500-1000) every third Saturday of each month. Keep your eyes and ears open and always check with the tourist office; don't believe anybody else. At the RRI entrance the month's upcoming events are generally posted. Performances at the RRI are at least as good as those put on in Sriwedari Park, with better acoustics and generally younger dancers.

SHOPPING AND CRAFTS

Jalan Secoyudan is Solo's shopping street, known for dozens of goldsmith shops. For one of the largest collections of ancient *kris* in Indonesia, visit **Hardjonegoro**, Jl. Kratonan 101. Some of the *kris* are quite famous; expect to pay anywhere from Rp100,000 to five million *rupiah*. To see an *empu*, or *kris* smithy, in action, go to **Pauzan**, Jl. Yosoroto 28/82. A craftsman of *kris* scabbards is **R. Ng. Prodjotjendono**, Jl. Nirbitan RT 16, no. 3. For the princely sum of Rp2500, select from a vast variety of cassette tapes at dozens of audio shops around town. A bird market, **Pasar Depok**, lies at the northwest end of Jl. Tirtoyoso near Balemkambang Sports Center. Solo's newest addition to the consumer economy is the **Purwosari Plaza**, a good place for Western items. Many boutiques, gold and shoe shops, fabrics, and a big supermarket.

Pasar Triwindu

Off Jl. Diponegoro, just north of Jl. Slamet, an easy walk from Kraton Mangkunegaran. In this flea market you'll find bric-a-brac of every description, often at prices cheaper than in Yogyakarta or Jakarta. Some prize items but a lot of worthless junk as well. Ask to see more refined items often kept under or inside the stalls. Bargain hot and heavy for everything.

Antique Shops

The best include **Eka Hartono**, Jl. Dawung Tengah 11/38; **Toko Parto Art**, Jl. Slamet Riyadi 103; and **Toko Singowidoyo**, Jl. Urip Sumoharjo (heaven for the lapidarist). On display in these dusty shops is a fascinating assortment of relics and curios of the era of Dutch colonialism—delftware, silverware, bronzes.

Other shops along Jl. Slamet Riyadi sell extremely convincing reproductions of 17th- and 18th-century Javanese furniture: herb chests, cabinets, and chairs that look so antique you'd better obtain written verification they're not to avoid problems with customs. Noteworthy also for very fine reproductions is **Mirah Delima**, Jl. Kemasan RT XI.

Wayang

For good-quality *wayang kulit*, expect to pay about Rp15,000 for small ones and Rp20,000 for those larger. Visit the workshop of **Usaha Pelajar**, Jl. Nayu Kidul north of the bus station. The hub of *wayang kulit*-making in the Solo area is **Desa Manyaran**, 35 km southwest; take a bus from Solo's *terminal bis*. Ask for the *kepala desa*, who'll take you around to view the different craftsmen. **Subandono**, Jl. Sawu 8/162, Perumnas Palur, still works in the virtually extinct form of *wayang beber*. In this, the most ancient *wayang* form, the *dalang* unrolls long illustrated scrolls while narrating the pictured tales. His office address is SMKI Konservatori, Jl. Kepathihan, tel. (0271) 2225. He asks Rp10,000-15,000 for a two-meter scroll painted on cloth; 12 scrolls form the complete *Panji* tales.

Toko Bedoyo Serimpi

For theatrical supplies and dancing costumes, visit this small shop at Temenggungan 116 on the corner of Jl. Hayam Wuruk and Jl. Ronggowarsito. A diverse collection of *wayang* accoutrements: gilt slippers for both males and females; all kinds of armlets, headbands, and bangles; different kinds of hats; splendid belts; glittery vests. A classy *batik* shop, Batik Serimpi, lies across the street.

Gamelan Workshop

In **Bekonang** village (10 km from Solo), *gamelan* instruments are made and sold: *kencong* (five in one complete set); *rebab* (two-stringed zithers), Rp40,000; big brass gongs with dragon-stands; whole sets of iron gongs (iron doesn't resonate nearly as well as brass). Browse around the workyard; play the instruments or have them played for you. Another supplier of *gamelan* instruments to the court is **Pak Sarwanto**; his family workshop is at Jl. Ngepung RT 2/RK I in Semanggi, two km southeast of town.

Others

For clicking, clacking, handmade toys, some cut from scrap metal, visit the toy shops in Sriwedari Park. Also find 19th-century dollhouse furniture, small painted tea sets, orange clay dolls, cardboard *wayang kulit* puppets, and miniature *gamelan* sets with silver xylophone keys and painted wooden frames, perfectly tuned to the *slendro* scale. Ceramics are not so common on Java, as bamboo receptacles obviate the need for pots; **Slametho W.S. Kara-gan 291,** Panularan, sells extremely ornate pottery at reasonable prices. The *batik* pots are Rp3000; those made in the shape of geese are Rp4000. The biggest pots, about one meter high, sell for Rp5000-6000. **Glasscutter Hosanna,** Jl. Kerinci 10, Manahan, makes elaborate mirrors that look like cut crystal; Rp100,000 to over one million.

BATIK AND TEXTILES

Solo is a *batik*-producing center of long standing. The art form generates both revenue and local pride. Solo-style *batik* designs and the somber classical colors of indigo, brown, and cream are noticeably more traditional than Yogyakarta's. Solo is a better place to buy *batik* than Yogyakarta.

Look for *Solo malam,* a peculiar local style featuring bright colors against a black backdrop. You can take a *batik*-making course in Solo, usually offered privately in someone's house, or at Warung Baru or Relax Homestay. For traditional *batik* painting, visit **Lawiyan.** Twenty km south of Solo, the well-known weaving village of **Pedan** uses ancient motifs, producing fabric from cotton yarn and silk interwoven with golden and silver thread.

Shops

Three major producers of *batik*—Danar Hadi, Batik Semar, and Batik Keris—are based here, well-known brand names that enjoy worldwide sales. These large shops are reliable places to buy; you at least get what you pay for. You pay 10-20% more than when shopping in the villages, but at these shops there's a full range of quality—from a Rp5000 shirt to an exquisite Rp222,000 *batik tulis sarung.* You can visit the workshops in back; the shops accept credit cards. Traditional **Batik Semar,** Jl. R.M. Said 132, is best, with friendly and helpful people; watch the *batik* process. The more modern **Batik Keris,** Jl. Yos Sudarso 37, sells fabric and nice *ikat* work.

Centrally located **Danar Hadi Batik Shop,** Jl. Dr. Rajiman 8, is another fixed-price outlet; see the *batik* process here. Open 0800-1600,

closed Sunday. Danar Hadi runs another, smaller shop on Jl. Slamet Riyadi, open 0900-1500 and 1700-2100 and on Sundays. There are over 70 other *batik* shops in Solo, many concentrated on Jl. Dr. Rajiman. On Jl. Honggowongso, find several fashion shops where you can buy T-shirts and jeans much cheaper than in Europe or the United States.

Markets

The largest *batik* and textile market in Indonesia is **Pasar Klewer** ("Hanging Market") on Jl. Secoyudan near the Susuhunan's Palace; open 0800-1600. A mad bustle of stalls offers bright *batik,* Western, and ready-made Indonesian clothes, including stunning *lurik* shirts. Unless you're trained, it's difficult to tell the difference between the extensive variety of mass-produced and fine-quality pieces. The second floor offers better *batik,* but less bargaining. Pasar Klewar doesn't have as much rubbish as Yogyakarta's big Pasar Beringhardjo.

While at Klewer buy some striking *lurik* material, one of the few natural cotton fabrics on Java. With striped, colorful patterns, *lurik* is rough to the touch, like Indian cotton, but it softens with age. Rather than buying poorly sewn ready-made clothes, employ one of Solo's thousands of tailors to sew a dress (Rp3000), shirt (Rp2000), or skirt (Rp2000).

Textile Factories

Solo contains at least 300 *batik* factories of various sizes. Most are scattered around the southern part of the city, many others are out along Jl. Adisucipto, and several more are located on Jl. Gremet. The spot to visit is the **Keris Batik Factory** on Jl. Cemani, southwest of the tourist office. Here, in an almost preindustrial atmosphere, 100 men and women produce elaborate *batik.* A great learning experience. This fascinating factory is included with bicycle tours from Warung Baru, or take a *becak* from the tourist office for Rp1000. No direct bus service.

In the factories you can see the *batik* and *ikat*-making processes, but you can't buy material or *sarung* for a *rupiah* less than in the shops. For outstanding, elegant, and expensive *batik tulis,* visit the studio of Ibu Hartini, located behind Pasar Klewer, one of Java's most famous *batik* designers.

SERVICES

Do your official business early in Solo as most offices close between 1400 and 1700. The **Surakarta Municipality Tourist Office** is at Jl. Slamet Riyadi 275, tel. (0271) 41435; open Mon.-Sat. 0800-1700. Free maps and leaflets, as well as information on events and sites and tour arrangements. Find the **central post office** on Jl. Sudirman 8, tel. 4642. The best bookstore in town is **Sekawan,** with two branches: Jl. Slamet Riyadi and Jl. Kartini.

Banks lie within walking distance of the inexpensive hotels in the Jl. A. Dahlan area. Try **Bank Bumi Daya,** Jl. Slamet Riyadi 16, tel. 5028; **Bank Negara Indonesia 1946,** Jl. Jen. Sudirman 19, tel. 2668, with probably the best rate; and **Bank Niaga,** Jl. Slamet Riyadi 8, tel. 7977. The **telephone office** is located downtown on Jl. May. Kusmanto 1, tel. 108, open 24 hours. The most convenient place for overseas calls and faxes is the *wartel* office on Jl. Slamet Riyadi in central Solo. Another *wartel* office is adjacent to the tourist office. The Solo telephone city code is 0271.

Imigrasi is located on Jl. Adisucipto, 10 km out of the city on the way to the airport. Take a *bis kota* from Jl. Ronggowarsito.

Health

Consider **Dr. Benny Tahapari,** an Ambonese who speaks Dutch and English, on Jl. Ir. Sutami in Jebres, three km west of the center. Or approach English-speaking **Dr. Amien Romas** in Kauman Sememen. The government health service, **Dinas Kesehatan,** is on Jl. Kampung Baru opposite Warung Sate Pak Jaman; see Dr. Johan Vandenberg.

Solo has a wide reputation for traditional, natural healing. The city is a center for *jamu* processing, with the large *jamu* manufacturer Air Mancur based here. Visit the small factory on Jl. Riyadi in the western outskirts of Solo, or the main factory outside town in Palur enroute to Surabaya. A traditional medicine store on Jl. Socoyudan, **Jamu Akar Sari,** is within an easy walk of the Westerners; here they concoct made-to-order *jamu* for consumption on the spot. Chinese medicine is also a developed science here. At **Toko Sin She,** behind Pasar Gudeg on Jl. Ketan Dan, mime your illness and the staff will prescribe a medicine, herb, or elixir for you. Acupuncturists here charge Rp2000 per session; ask at Toko Sin She. Some of the best tai chi teachers around are in Solo.

Massage is just the ticket after returning with aching bones from the Gunung Merapi climb, performed by *tukang pijet,* many of them old women. Your hotel will order for you; Rp5000-10,000 per session. Other, less common masseuses (called *tukang urut*) specialize in therapeutic massage, and put you right back together. For yoga, see Mr. Anda Suyono, Jl. Ronggowarsito.

TRANSPORTATION

Getting There

The airport is nine km west of town. Garuda schedules two flights daily from Jakarta, Surabaya, and Denpasar via Surabaya. Merpati and Sempati also serve Solo.

Trains from Yogyakarta run as cheap as Rp1000. From Jakarta, the overnight first-class Bima travels via Yogyakarta for about Rp35,000; there are also slower, much less expensive second- and third-class non-a/c trains. Arriving at Solo's train station on Jl. Balapan in the north side of town, it's Rp1000 by *becak* or Rp7000 by taxi to the hotel area off Jl. Slamet Riyadi.

Minibuses leave constantly from 0700 to 1700 for Rp3000 from Yogyakarta's Terminal Terban. Or climb on a bus or minibus anywhere on Yogyakarta's Jl. Sudirman/Solo. Or take a shared taxi (Rp3500 pp) from Yogyakarta's post office. From Semarang, Solo is Rp2500 by bus or Rp3500 by minibus. From Surabaya it's Rp5000 by bus; six hours. In front of Solo's Gilingan bus station, just north of the train station on Jl. A. Yani, stand by the roundabout to catch a *bemo* three km into town (Rp250) or take a *becak* (Rp1000-1500).

Getting Around

Solo is a city for walking. Pedicabs are ubiquitous, Rp500-1500. Short *becak* rides should cost Rp500, longer journeys Rp1000-1500. You can rent bikes at Westerners and other guesthouses. The minibus station is by Kraton Hadiningrat, or flag one down along the main streets. Longer distances cost Rp400 from the minibus station. Double-decker *bis kota* run continually from west to east down Solo's main street, Jl. Slamet Riyadi, then circle round and head west up Jl. Secoyudan; Rp200 fixed fare.

Outstanding bicycle tours for Solo and the surrounding countryside leave daily at 0930 from Warung Baru. You'll cross the Solo River south of town, look at *batik* selections and a *gamelan* workshop, sample fruits and fried snake, visit the Arab quarter and a weaving village, then return to Warung Baru by sunset. Recommended by many travelers as a Solo highlight. Find, however, a good bike—many are trashed.

Getting Away

The Garuda office is located in the forecourt of the Kusuma Sahid Prince Hotel, Jl. Sugiopranoto, open Mon.-Fri. 0700-1600, Saturday 0700-1300, Sunday and holidays 0900-1200. Solo's airport is nine km, 25 minutes and Rp9000 by taxi from the city; taxis are available at the private stand on Jl. Gatot Subroto. Garuda fares: Jakarta, Rp147,000; Surabaya, Rp74,000; Ujung Pandang, Rp252,000. For Denpasar, change planes in Surabaya.

Five trains per day connect Yogyakarta to Jakarta. To Semarang, two trains depart daily at 0500 and 1300. For longer hauls, book at least a day in advance. To Surabaya, trains depart six times daily; the 1440 is the most popular with travelers, arriving in Surabaya at 1955. For Mt. Bromo, the train to Probolinggo leaves at 0920, third class only. The train to Malang leaves at 0145.

The big Gilingan bus terminal is three km north of central Solo on Jl. Tagore, Rp1000-

1500 by *becak*. Many long-distance bus companies here. Day buses make this 298-km, nine-hour run to Malang via Surabaya, but the best route involves changing buses in Jombang and continuing to Malang on the beautiful mountain road through Batu. No need to first go to Surabaya. A night bus runs directly from Solo to Malang, six hours.

Damri, Agung Ekspres, and Mira all maintain offices at Terminal Gilingan, charging Rp15,000-22,000 and taking about 12 hours to Denpasar on Bali. To reach Pacitan, take a direct bus from the Giligan bus terminal, three hours. For Sukah and Ceto, climb aboard the doubledecker bus on Jl. Riyadi to Palur (10 km), then take a regular bus to Karangpadan, and finally a minibus north to Kemuning. Then hike 20 minutes to Candi Sukuh, or take a minibus from Kemuning to Candi Ceto and hike two hours down to Candi Sukuh. Then continue down the trail to Tawamanggu. A full day of adventure.

Because buses are so crowded, you may prefer to use a faster van that holds only 8-10 people and leaves every half-hour or so, heading straight to your address in Yogyakarta (Rp2500-4000) or Semarang (Rp3500-5000). Catch these at Jl. Honggowongso 90, tel. (0271) 32375, or make reservations through your guesthouse or hotel.

On the *alun-alun,* in front of the Great Mosque, board tiny minivans west to Kartosuro, east to Karanganyar, and south to Sukoharjo. From the taxi stand on Jl. Gatot Subroto, catch taxis (private cars) to Semarang, Yogyakarta, or anywhere else.

VICINITY OF SOLO

SANGIRAN

This region is known mainly in scientific circles for its extraordinary finds in the fields of paleontology, anthropology, and geology. Since 1891, when a Dutch professor found the skull of Java Man (*Pithecanthropus erectus,* now called *Homo erectus*), this area 15 km north of Solo has been the center of intense research. Many prehistoric fossils—human and animal—have been unearthed here. Most of the fossilized remains were buried under layers of fallow earth, laden with lime which helped preserve them. After heavy rains, especially, the fossils turn up in landslides. All the early hominid finds laid the foundations for theories of the earliest human life on Java 250,000 years ago.

Plestosen Sangiran Museum
This small, unique, and well-organized museum exhibits extinct elephant tusks; teeth and horns from extinct giant deer, antelope, and other small animals; fossilized mollusks; remnants of stegodon, oxen, rhinoceros, crocodiles, pigs, and apes; and models of *Homo erectus* craniums. Entrance Rp100. Tags identify the items in Latin and Bahasa Indonesia. Although the ape people in the diorama have Indonesian faces, in reality the humans of that time were of a completely different race. Books in the small library

may be read on the premises; of special interest is the *Quaternery Geology of the Hominid Bearing Formation in Java.* It's illegal to collect or remove fossils, especially of humans; besides, the locals are much better at it. Visitors can overnight in rooms on the grounds of the old museum up the road; Rp7000. Nice setting.

Getting There
Located in Krikilan village 15 km north of Solo on the highway toward Purwodadi via Kalioso. From Solo, take a Purwodadi-bound bus from the main bus terminal to Kalijambi (one km beyond Kalioso); it's then an easy 3.5-km, half-hour walk from the intersection to the museum. Or flag down a motorcycle and ride on the back. Returning, try to hitch a ride to the turnoff, or perhaps all the way back to Solo.

CANDI SUKUH

This Hindu temple on the slopes of Gunung Lawu was built in the 15th century, late in the Hindu period and just as Islam was penetrating coastal Java. The temple was approached in ancient times by a long flight of steps. The terraced pyramids at Sukuh and nearby Ceto have been compared with the ruins of ancient Mexico and Egypt. Both are dedicated to Bima, the giant warrior god of the Mahabharata.

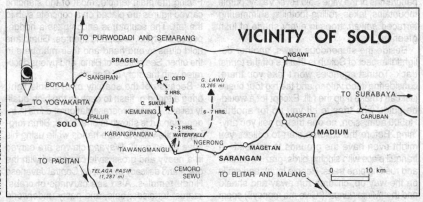

VICINITY OF SOLO

TO PURWODADI AND SEMARANG

SRAGEN
NGAWI
BOYOLA — SANGIRAN
C. CETO
G. LAWU (3,265 m)
2 HRS.
TO SURABAYA
C. SUKUH
KEMUNING
6 - 7 HRS.
TO YOGYAKARTA
SOLO — PALUR
MAOSPATI
CARUBAN
2 - 3 HRS.
KARANGPANDAN
WATERFALL
MADIUN
NGERONG
TAWANGMANGU
MAGETAN
TO PACITAN
SARANGAN
TELAGA PASIR (1,287 m)
CEMORO SEWU
TO BLITAR AND MALANG
0   10 km

© MOON PUBLICATIONS, INC.

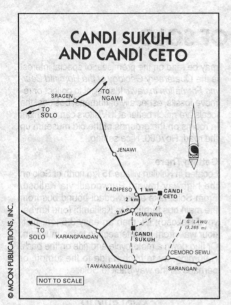

CANDI SUKUH AND CANDI CETO

SRAGEN
TO NGAWI
TO SOLO
JENAWI
KADIPESO — 1 km — CANDI CETO
2 km
2 km — KEMUNING
G. LAWU (3,265 m)
TO SOLO — KARANGPANDAN — CANDI SUKUH
CEMORO SEWU
TAWANGMANGU — SARANGAN

NOT TO SCALE

© MOON PUBLICATIONS, INC.

Often referred to as Java's only erotic temple, Sukuh is highly distinctive, with elements not found in other temples in Indonesia. Scholars have conjectured Sukuh was the temple of worship for a family or clan cult, and might have been used for sex education. At 910 meters above sea level, the sites were chosen with great care: these temples overlook the whole Central Javanese plain, a superb location. From the upper terraces you're treated to sweeping panoramas of the wide Solo River Valley: purple mountains, lakes, rolling foothills, shimmering terraced *sawah,* trees in every shade of lush greenery.

Beside the stupendous views, another delightful aspect of Sukuh is that it's off the tourist track. Tourist agencies won't take you there, considering it too vulgar, and the big tour buses just can't make it up the hill. Except for a would-be guide who tries to hit you up for another Rp500 admission, no one tries to sell you anything. Before the children start to collect, you might even have the grounds to yourself—a tranquil place with singing birds, grazing horses, and rustling pine trees. People laugh and smile on the way up, children run away and shriek, and the *"Minta uangs"* ("Give me money!") seem halfhearted, even frivolous. Offerings are placed on this site by the sultan of Yogyakarta each year, and the temple receives regular visits by Javanese pilgrims.

The Complex

The architecture alone sets Sukuh apart. The shape of Candi Sukuh, with its steps leading to the upper part of the temple, is strikingly similar to the Mayan temples of Yucatán and Guatemala, under contruction at the same time. Walk up three grassy pyramids, passing through three gateways, each atop a flight of stairs, until you come to the main structure, a large stepped pyramid of rough-hewn stone. The temple gate is next to the *kantor,* where you register and flash the tickets you've bought in Nglorok. After, walk down to the bottom of the temple so you can climb up through the gateways. Stay in the *pondok* to the right as you're facing the temple; Rp2500 s plus food. A *kampung* nearby offers excellent goat milk; the watchman will take you there. Trails behind the *pondok* lead to the misty heights of Gunung Lawu.

Sculpture

Though tame in comparison to India's Konarak or Khajuraho, Sukuh is one of the only explicitly erotic temples in all of Java. On the stone floor at the top of a steep stone tunnel leading into the complex, large realistic sexual organs are lovingly carved in relief. Devotees still leave flower petals here. Other symbols of love and procreation are found in and around this temple, all executed in an exuberant and unabashed style. Facing the main temple, most of the standing carved figures are placed on a concrete slab to the left. The sculptures encompass a hodgepodge of styles, eras, and themes. Guardians hold clubs in one hand and their members in the other. See statues of Bima, and pylons decorated with the story of Garuda.

Because of the scarcity of available light, bring a tripod or flash to capture the high-quality reliefs. The first representation of a *kris* in Indonesian art is shown in one panel: Bima forging a knife with his bare hands while using his knee as an anvil. *Wayang* clowns are carved in a heavy and gross style compared with the grace and delicacy evident on Central Javanese Hindu temples. Also see carvings of crabs, lizards, tortoises, bats, and nasty underworld creatures. Yoni and phalluses are found in reliefs that depict sexual acts and fetal growth in the womb.

Getting There

Sukuh is just an hour's drive from Solo. From Solo take the road to Tawangmangu; get off at Karangpandan, 29 km east (Rp800 and one hour by bus) of Solo. You'll see a sign at an intersection pointing to Candi Sukuh.

From Karangpandan, take a bus five km to Kemuning, the beginning of the road leading to the *candi*. This is where you buy your ticket; don't throw it away as you'll need it to see the temple.

It's an hour of hard, steep slogging on a surfaced road to get to the top. On the 20-minute trip back down, children will sing you songs as they carry 25-kilo baskets of pine cones to sell at the market. You can also approach easily from Madiun via Sarangan and Tawangmangu.

From Candi Sukuh, take the path that leads to Tawangmangu through villages with incredible and varied scenery and friendly people. The path comes out at the Grojogan Sewu Waterfalls just below Tawangmangu's Kebon Hortikultura. Ask people along the way for directions or pick up a rough map at Warung Baru in Solo.

Makam Suharto

Near Kapending, on the way to Candi Ceto, Makan Suharto is a nice place to spend an afternoon. Like the pharaohs of Egypt, President Suharto built an enormous *pendopo* with huge gilded columns for the remains of his parents and to serve as a final resting place for himself and the rest of his family. One would think Suharto was trying to rival the memorial to Sukarno—a man whose shadow he's always labored under—but Suharto's mausoleum was finished long before the government ever considered a memorial to Sukarno.

Construction of this lavish memorial upon a hill reserved for royal graves was completed in 1977 and immediately became the center of controversy; it even sparked a student riot in Jakarta. One student leader reportedly said, "While the people starve, the boss builds his grave." To further exacerbate the situation, a Suharto business associate inadroitly answered charges the mausoleum had cost US$10 million by saying the true costs were "only" US$1 million.

It's strictly forbidden to enter the *pendopo* or take photos of it, but since it's so big, it's not at all difficult to see from a distance.

CANDI CETO

Built around the same time as Candi Sukuh, this impressive terraced temple lies 28 km from Karanganyar near the small village of Kadipeso. At 1,500 meters, Ceto is 600 meters higher and more northerly than Sukuh, one of the most spectacular temple locations on Java. In addition, it's been fantastically restored. Though smaller than Sukuh, the fascinating, lavishly decorated Ceto ruins contain terraces, statues, guardian figures, linga, reliefs, and a wooden *pendopo*, plus stupendous views. Almost no foreign visitors.

Two main narrow terraces make up the complex. At least some portions were built in the 15th century, at the very end of the Majapahit era. Animal themes and figures play an important role, particularly on the higher terraces. As at Sukuh, the Hindu religion was given only nominal obeisance, and it's supposed this temple too was used for fertility rituals.

Getting There

Candi Ceto is a one-hour hike north of Candi Sukuh. A complete tour would start with a minibus from Kemuning direct to Candi Ceto, then a hike down to Sukuh for a three-hour trek down the weathered cobblestone path to Tawangmangu and the nearby waterfall. Buses and *bemo* from Tawangmangu head west to Solo and east to Sarangan.

TAWANGMANGU

Tawangmangu lies near the provincial border, on the slopes of Gunung Lawu 42 km from Solo. This pretty 1,050-meter-high hill resort can be enjoyed for its natural beauty, fresh breezes, clear streams, refreshing weather, and hilly woodland walks to historical remains and pilgrimage spots. Delicious drinking water and a variety of accommodations, including campgrounds, make it a nice place to get away to. Crowded with vacationers on holidays.

Kebun Hortikultura is an herbal laboratory and horticultural experimental garden which also produces ingredients used in traditional *jamu* folk medicine. Located on the left about 1.5 km up the hill from the bus station; turn in at two white posts. Two km from the *stasiun bis* toward Sarangan is a bathing place; Rp400 entrance fee. As an alternative to walking around town, take the occasional *bemo* that labors up and down the main street, or rent a horse from the villagers (Rp2000-3500 per hour).

Accommodations And Food

Most hotels and guesthouses are in the Rp8000-15,000 range, though it's possible to find a few for as low as Rp5000. **Pak Amat's** is the most convenient hotel and restaurant, only about 50 km from *stasiun bis*; all individual units with verandas are separated from the main building by a nice garden. Expect to pay around Rp8000-12,000 after bargaining.

Losmen Pondok Garuda, on Jl. Lawu, one-half km up the hill from the bus station, has quite attractive rooms and superb views over the valley. **Wisma Yanti** on Jl. Lawu offers good facilities and nice grounds; very quiet. No meals, just coffee and tea. The rooms at **Pasanggrahan Mali'jawan,** about 1.5 km toward Sarangan, aren't in the best shape, but the place has a huge *rumah makan* open 0700-2300. Across the street is **Pondok Indah** at a firm Rp24,000. **Camping Tawangmangu Baru,** four km from *stasiun bis*, comes complete with tents, camping equipment, electricity, cafeteria, sports field, swimming pool, and tennis courts. Campsites including tent cost Rp6000; rooms range Rp8400-32,500.

A specialty of Tawangmangu is *sate kelinci* (rabbit shish kebab). Buy vegetables and fruit at roadside stands along Jl. Lawu and make your own picnic salad. Many eating stalls around the *stasiun bis*.

From Pasanggrahan Mali'jawan, turn left and go back 200 meters toward Tawangmangu bus station; see the Ayam Goreng sign. This *rumah makan*, called **Sapto Argo,** offers *nasi gudek, nasi opor,* and *nasi rames*. Try the *es soda gembira* (a blend of soda, syrup, and milk), a delicious drink. Other good restaurants along Jl. Balai Kambang include the **Bangun Trisno** and **Puas Siti Sari.** Also try **Lesehan Pondok Indah,** 300 meters past Sapto Argo, where Indonesian specialties are served on bamboo platforms overlooking the rice fields. Quite refreshing.

Getting Away

It's 14 km to Sarangan, 10 km to Cemoro Sewu, and 42 km to Solo. Take very crowded minibuses over the top to Sarangan, Rp800. Or make the cool, five-hour walk on a precipitous road that climbs over 1,800 meters, one of the highest roads on Java. Quite an unspoiled area. Climb the trail up to Gunung Lawu from Blumbang village. On top is the tomb of Sunan Lawu, a much visited pilgrimage spot. Because of its isolation and height (3,265 meters), you can see Gunung Lawu from as far away as Solo and Madiun. For Candi Sukuh, take the bus out of Tawangmangu west to Karangpandan; it's only 11 km and Rp300 farther by *bemo*. Or try the easy, scenic path to the temple leading from Tawangmangu's Grojogan Sewu Falls; three to five hours.

Vicinity Of Tawangmangu

Reach **Grojogan Sewu** waterfall on a small road from Kebon Hortikultura, or take the path nearly opposite Pasanggrahan Mali'jawan. Grojogan Sewu, a 100-meter waterfall, lies in the middle of pine forest with lovely natural panoramas. Unfortunately, there's also trash everywhere. Descend to the bottom of the falls to the swimming pool; Rp150 entrance. In the forests around Tawangmangu live many wild monkeys. A Hindu temple, **Reca Menggung,** lies in Desa Kelurahan Nglurah, a 30-minute, 1.5-km walk from the Tawangmangu bus station. Hot spring **Sumber Air Panas** is five km from Tawangmangu. At Pablengan, 17 km from Tawangmangu, you'll find carbon dioxide and natural gas holes, oxygen vents, saltwater holes, and hot springs.

SARANGAN

This picturesque hill station (elev. 1,287 meters) between Solo and Madiun is a restful and enjoyable overnight stop. Situated on the slope of Gunung Lawu, the shape of the mammoth volcano looms large above the town. A small, placid crater lake sits right in the middle of Sarangan, with *losmen,* guesthouses, and hotels dotting the banks. A beautiful area, ideal for boating, swimming, fishing, tennis, horseback riding, and mountain climbing. Cabbages grow up and down the hills, right outside your hotel.

Friendly mountain people live here; very little stealing as it's bad for tourism. Not many budget-minded travelers visit Sarangan, but in the tourist season—July, August, and September—a great many elderly Dutch tourists arrive, and every Sunday Indonesian day-trippers from Madiun and surrounding areas descend in droves. Sarangan is also popular with wealthy Chinese and during holiday seasons, when all prices double.

Accommodations And Food

Most hotels have dining rooms and offer meals included in the room rate, plus free tea and coffee. The most expensive place is **Grand View Cottages**, with breathtaking views and two-bedroom cottages from Rp105,000. On the other end, there's **Losmen Baru** at Rp6000-8000 with a small sitting room and no view of the lake. Turn right at the intersection just before town where the road from Madiun to Tawangmangu turns into Sarangan.

Wisma Cemara, cheapest on the hill, charges Rp8000 with *mandi*, Rp12,000 with fireplaces. The **Nusa Indah** is quite reasonable at Rp6500 s, Rp8500 d; it also offers a modern small apartment for Rp10,000 with breakfast, Rp15,000 full board. The proprietor, Sugimani, is very knowledgeable about the Gunung Lawu climb. **Losmen Kartika,** 30 meters up the hill from Nusa Indah, features 12 rooms around a courtyard; Rp8000-18,000. **Losmen Lestair, Penginapan Tentrem,** and **Penginapan Purnama Jaya,** all a five-minute walk from the lake, charge in the Rp8000-12,000 range. **Hotel Lawu,** the last going up the hill, wants Rp5000 for a room with annex. **Hotel Sarangan** is spacious with a terrific view, garage, parking area, children's playground, and restaurant. English and Dutch spoken. Rooms (Rp42,000-58,000) feature porches high over the lake, bedroom and sitting room, fireplace, inside hot-water *mandi*, and room service.

On the lanes and streets you'll find *bakso mie* vendors, and women who sell boiled eggs, still hot, five for Rp500. **Sari Rasa,** right up the street from Nusa Indah, is popular with the Chinese. **Asia Restaurant** and **Shinta** both sell low-cost Indonesian food. Near the *bemo* terminal are 10 depots serving Indonesian cuisine. **Warung Sederhana** is the best and one of the cheapest; try the *nasi goreng*—fantastic at Rp800. Everyone eats with their fingers and they're tickled if you join in.

Getting There And Away

From Solo it costs Rp800 to Tawangmangu, then board a *bemo* (Rp1200) over the mountain to Sarangan. From Sarangan, it's another Rp800 to Madiun. With the influx of visitors, many more minibuses shuttle between Tawangmangu and Sarangan on Sundays.

From the bus terminal, *bemo* or minibuses don't start for Tawangmangu until around 0800, so if you're in a hurry wait at the intersection of the road into town and try to hitchhike a passing truck. Or charter a minibus from Sarangan to Tawangmangu for Rp20,000—but expect at least three "helpers," frequent stops for "cousins," and a chockfull "chartered" minibus by the time it reaches Tawangmangu. The twisting mountain road to the summit is so steep that many cars can't make it over the top and your vehicle might have to let half the passengers off at every other bend. A dramatic, spooky climb.

GUNUNG LAWU

Heavily forested Gunung Lawu (3,265 meters) is an ancient, eroded volcano that has retained its symmetrical shape. The trail to the top is used by local people who make pilgrimages to the Hindu-Buddhist temple near the summit to offer food and baskets of flowers. On the way up are remnants of old temples, terracing, and Majapahit graves. Stay overnight for giddy views and incredible photos of the sunrise.

Hire a guide at Blumbang village near the top, halfway between Tawangmangu and Sarangan. The trail, however, is well marked, and guides are unnecessary, unless you intend to overnight and need proper equipment.

The Climb

From Sarangan to the peak of Gunung Lawu (Puncak Lawu) takes six hours; to the crater (Kawah Lawu) only 3.5 hours. The climb begins 300 meters northwest of Cemoro Sewu (five km from Sarangan and seven km from Tawangmangu) where you'll see several radio/TV towers. Just beyond the bridge, near Pos 1, is the start of the well-maintained and heavily used trail. Water is available at several points as the trail winds up the mountain; the final ascent is actually from the northeast. There are several huts plus emergency shelters on the way: at 2,400 meters, 2,850 meters, and 3,100 meters.

During the full moon, it's possible to climb up and back in one day and night. Leave Sarangan at 0400, reach the peak at 0900, spend two hours at the top, then take two hours to descend to Sarangan. If you spend the night on the summit, expect frigid temperatures. Ample firewood. The rainiest season is Nov.-May, but the hike is possible all year.

EAST JAVA

A heavily populated area of 30 million people, East Java is packed with bursting cities, towns, and *kampung* along roads running ceaselessly through carefully nurtured rice and cane fields. Mountain slopes are home to fruit, coffee, and tea plantations. This rural region was the site of the last powerful Javanese Hindu kingdom, the Majapahit.

The island's least touristed province, East Java is more traditional and religious than Central Java; it features few plush tourist amenities, accommodations are relatively more expensive, and it's more difficult and time-consuming to travel here. But for those with the time and transportation, the area's far-flung attractions offer some unusual sidetrips through magnificent countryside. East Java is to Central Java as Mississippi is to Virginia: deep, deep Java, considerably more rural and less touched by the West.

THE SOUTHWEST

MADIUN

Madiun is a pretty town 118 km east of Solo—abundant vegetation, but very dry, hazy, and dusty in summer. A respected *pesantren*, **Pondok Gontor**, a religious boarding school for Muslims, is located in Madiun. An abortive revolt in Madiun in September 1948 was the first serious attempt by Indonesian communists to seize power by force; it was crushed in surprisingly short time by loyal troops. The Indonesian Communist Party (PKI) was routed at Madiun and its leader forced into exile. The political openness of the 1950s allowed the PKI to rebuild its influence through mass organization, until its ultimate obliteration in the mass purges of 1965-67.

Accommodations And Food
Cheap hotels are clustered around the east end of town. **Hotel Madiun** charges Rp3000 d; cheaper is **Hotel 7777**. The best is central **Hotel Merdeka** on the main street, Jl. Pahlawan 42, tel. (0351) 2547, Rp10,000. A giant complex, bright and organized, with nice gardens. Across the street is **Ramayana** with standard prices. Also check out large Dutch-style **Losmen Pussat**, Jl. Dr. Sutomo 66; Rp9000. Comfortable, breezy, with nice front porch. **Hotel Tedjo**, Jl. Dr. Sutomo 55, opposite Losmen Pussat, is a clean family-run place; Rp8000. Try the local specialty, *babat,* a little cake filled with *kelapa muda.*

Getting Away
From Terminal Sleko to Surabaya is Rp6000. To Solo or Yogyakarta from Madiun, the train is the most direct; on the way to Yogyakarta you'll pass the Prambanan temple complex.

PACITAN

A fair-sized but easygoing village, 100 km southeast of Solo on the southern coast. Splendid beaches stretch along a huge bay to either side. Bring good books, snacks, and a lover—the place is all your own. The road south from Solo leads to Wonogiri, then passes through Girimoyo on the provincial border. Next comes the really bizarre section: a landscape of rows and rows of cone-shaped barren limestone hills containing dozens of caves, many open for exploration.

The road then winds gently down through teak forests until the wide expanse of Pacitan Bay comes into view. Fishing *prahu* sway gen-

EAST JAVA

© MOON PUBLICATIONS, INC.

PACITAN

JL. A. YANI

PASAR

HOTEL BALI QUEEN LOSMEN REMAJA WISMA WIJAYA

BUS STOP LOSMEN SIDOMULYO

HAPPY BAY BEACH BUNGALOWS

DESA TEMPERAN

TELUK PACITAN

TO SOLO

MOON

NOT TO SCALE

© MOON PUBLICATIONS, INC.

tly on the sheltered waters; behind the pier and storehouse is the marketplace for the day's catch. A small park with swimming pool is an ideal place to sit back and drink in the view—all the way to the craggy summits of the distant Kidul Mountains.

The beach is seven km from town on the large bay. Visit **Desa Temperan,** a little cove five km down the coast that offers some of the area's best swimming. A *warung* in the nearby *desa* serves rice, fish, and vegetables. The *dokar* ride out to Desa Temperan and back (Rp2000) is a joy. On the way you pass a classical Greek mortuary temple.

On the road to Solo, nine km from Pacitan, is a monument to Sudirman and Slamet Riyadi and an overlook of the coast; nice spot for a picnic. Two other beaches in the area: Watu Karung (22 km) and Latiroco Lorok (41 km).

Accommodations And Food

The **Bali Queen** is the town's big hotel; Rp15,000-25,000. The cheapest places in town are **Losmen Remaja,** Rp6000; and the really basic **Losmen Sidomulyo,** Jl. A. Yani, Rp5500. Next door is **Wisma Wijaya. Happy Bay Beach Bungalows,** tel. (0357) 81474, is right on the beach. Spacious individual bungalows facing the bay cost Rp12,000-25,000; a second-floor veranda restaurant offers sweeping views of Pacitan Bay.

Back in town and on the other side of the minibus station, **Restaurant Adem Ayem** dish-

es out *nasi campur, nasi rames, gule,* and *sate.* Behind Losmen Sidomulyo, *sate* is sold at night.

Getting Away

Numerous buses depart for both Ponorogo and Solo. To Solo via Wonogiri (Rp2500, 100 km, four hours) buses depart 0400-1400. To Ponorogo, the road climbs up through a scenic valley and gorge to a pass, then winds down onto plains (Rp1500, four hours).

GUA TABUHAN

Four km beyond Punung village is **Gua Tabuhan,** or "Musical Cave." This giant limestone cavern was reportedly a hideaway for Prince Diponegoro; the guerrilla leader General Sudirman also made his headquarters here during the struggle against the Dutch. Follow the signposts down a dirt track to the cave; for Rp1000 boys will guide you through slippery 50-meter-high caverns. In the main chamber an old man and his assistants present an amazing reproduction of a *gamelan* orchestra. Played by striking rocks against stalactites, each in perfect pitch, the three-toned melody vibrates and

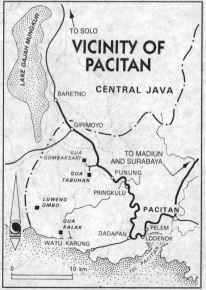

LAKE GAJAH MUNGKUR

TO SOLO

VICINITY OF PACITAN

BARETNO CENTRAL JAVA

GIRIMOYO

GUA GOMBAKSARI

GUA TABUHAN

LUWENG OMBO

GUA KALAK

WATU KARUNG

TO MADIUN AND SURABAYA

PUNUNG

PRINGKULU

PACITAN

PELEM LODENOK

DADAPAN

TEL. PACITAN

MOON

0   10 km

© MOON PUBLICATIONS, INC.

echoes with each blow. Offer Rp2000 for the performance. Cut and polished agate stones and rings sell for Rp850-15,000; have jewelers on Bali set raw stones for you.

Cave enthusiasts can also detour to **Gua Gombaksari** to see some beautiful white calcite formations; no admission fee. In nearby Danaraja village lives one of the last *dalang wayang beber* on Java, Pak Sarnen, who performs and reads using 16th-century scrolls. **Kalak Caves,** which some say are the finest caves on Java, lie 12 km south of Punung, near the south coast, accessible only on foot. **Baksoka River Valley,** four km from Punung toward Pacitan, features petrified wood; many Neolithic stone tools have been found here.

BRANTAS RIVER VALLEY

PARE

Twenty-four km and Rp600 by minibus northeast of Kediri, and just over 100 km from Madiun, Pare is best known as a base for visitors to the nearby temples of Surawana and Tingawangi. The town has cooler, nicer weather than Kediri, and the people are friendly and helpful. It was in Pare where anthropologist Clifford Geertz studied social change in Java in the 1950s. Geertz's classic work, *The Religion of Java,* is still a highly readable, fascinating account of the crosscurrents of beliefs and customs on Java.

Accommodations And Food
Of Pare's two good *losmen,* the cheaper is **Sederhana,** with electricity, bathrooms in the back, coffee and tea; Rp5000-8000. **Hotel Selamet,** Jl. Kandangan 1, is a poorman's five-star hotel—quiet and secure. The proprietor can tell you about the surrounding area and arrange transportation. In a nearby forest see *kalong* (flying foxes) at night when they come to eat fruit. From Hotel Selamet it's a short walk up an alley to the town's main street, containing all the shops and other conveniences. Additional accommodations include **Losmen Centrum** and **Losmen Surakarta,** both Rp5000 for smaller rooms.

Several food stations on Jl. Kandangan serve some of Pare's best Javanese/Indonesian food. Always crowded.

Getting Away
Minibuses from Pare to Jombong cost Rp1000; from Jombong board another minibus to the Trowulan ruins or Mojokerto. For Malang, take the rough 75-km-long road heading east through a kaleidoscope of landscapes: *sawah,* forested wilds, mountainous passes, apple orchards, wobbly bridges.

Pemanang
Also called Memang, this site 15 km from Pare was the supposed capital of the 13th-century Kediri Kingdom of the Oracle King, Jayabaya, whose prophecies, without exception, have all been fulfilled. There's a small commemorative stone here as well as Jayabaya's restored *pendopo.* Many pilgrims arrive here to pray.

Candi Surawana
Located in Desa Canggu, about six km from Pare. In front of Hotel Selamet on Jl. Kandangan, negotiate for a 30-minute *becak* ride out to the temple; Rp3000 roundtrip. If you have the time, though, it's better to walk. When you arrive at Canggu, find the *juru kunci* to get into the compound.

Candi Surawana sits under a banyan tree in the midst of a beautiful tropical garden. All that's left of this *candi,* built around A.D. 1390, is its gigantic unfinished base; on the grounds are scattered thousands of carved blocks, at least as intriguing as the temple itself. Architecturally, Surawana belongs to the *wayang* style, its reliefs resembling modern Balinese puppets. The depiction of nature in these reliefs is some of the most exciting in East Javanese temple art. Panels illustrate humorous animal stories and erotic situations; dwarves decorate the corners. By Indonesian standards, these ruins have been maintained superbly.

A bathing place near the *candi* dates from the same era; ask the villagers for directions. A half km beyond the temple is the opening to an underground river; once a tunnel connecting Teguwangi and Surawana.

ANTIQUITIES OF EAST JAVA

LOSEM

TUBAN

MADURA

S. SOLO

GRESIK

SURABAYA

S. MAS

MOJOKERTO   PORONG

REMBANG

TROWULAN   KEMANGGUNGAN   BANGIL

MADIUN   NGANJUK   JALATUNDA   BELAHAN

PASURUAN

TIGUWANGI   SURAWANA   MALANG   JAWI

PROBOLINGGO

S. MADIUN   SELAMANGELENG   PARE   ANJASMO   ARD   PENANGGUNGAN

KEDIRI   JAGO

BONDOWOSO

PONOROGO   WILIS   KELUT   KAWI   SINGOSARI   BROMO   LAMONGAN   ARGOPURO

TULUNGAGUNG   BLITAR   PANATARAN   MALANG   JAGO   TAMPANG   SEMERU   KEDATON   S. JATIROTO

SELAMANGELENG   BARA   S. BRANTAS   KIDAL   LUMJANG

SUMBERJATI

0   50 km

© MOON PUBLICATIONS, INC.

Candi Teguwangi

Travel by minibus to Teguwangi village (seven km, Rp400), or hire a *sepeda motor* from Pare. You may also meet someone at Surawana Temple and get a ride over on a motorbike. Travel about two km along the road to Kediri to a Y; the left fork goes to Kediri, the right to Desa Teguwangi. It's only about four km from the fork to a small school and a dirt-road turnoff to the right. Go up this road for about one km and you'll come to the fenced-off temple.

An unfinished Shivaistic complex built in the latter half of the 14th century, Teguwangi is not as intact as Surawana. The temple's north face has not been carved, and part of one of the corners has caved in. The carvings are not quite as accomplished. There are scenes of people delivered from dangers and spells, comical stories from the Sundamala, and exquisite landscapes. Scenes flow around the corners without a break.

TULUNGAGUNG

Thirty km south of Kediri, known as Kota Banjar, or "Flood City," because the Brantas River overflows in April or October every year, partially inundating the city. About 30 Hindu-Buddhist statues occupy the Halaman Kabupaten on Jl. Kartini. For recreation, walk around the *alun-alun* in the cool of the early evening; there's often a soccer game going on. Antiques are sold in Pasar Wage and on Jl. Wakhid Hasyim. For unique *batik tulungagung* check out Kalangbret, six km by minibus from Pasar Wage on Jl. Kapt. Kasinhin. Tiban is a whip-fight festival popular in the area.

Attractions

A clove plantation at Trenggalek is owned by local people. Two beaches lie south of Tulun-

EAST JAVA ANTIQUITIES

Trowulan, a 14th-15th-century Hindu site, was once the captial of the Majapahit Empire; today just relics and ruins of the all-brick temples remain.

Surawana sits under a banyan tree in a fantastic tropical garden. This 14th-century Shivaite temple displays intriguing carved reliefs. All that remains of this *candi,* originally dedicated to a prince of Wengkur, is its giant unfinished base.

Tiguwangi is an unfinished Shivaistic complex built late in the 14th century. Its carvings are not as well-preserved as Surawana's. The temple was dedicated to Prince Matahun.

Selamangeleng are cave hermitages used by ancient Javanese rulers and mystics as retreats. These 10th-11th-century Buddhist caves are filled with bas-relief.

Sumberjati, a Shivaite *candi* of the 14th century, is dedicated to King Martarajasa, the first king of Majaphit.

Bara is a 13th-century Shivaite *candi* featuring a giant image of Ganesha.

Jalatunda, a Shivaite bathing place, was built in the 10th century. Exquisite carvings were added to the stone pool in the 14th century; many are now on display at the National Museum in Jakarta.

Panataran consists of ruins from seven major buildings and many more building foundations. This 10th-century Shivaite sanctuary was one of the most important sites of the Majapahit kingdom, visited several times by the Gajah Mada.

Belahan is a bathing place east of Jalatunda; a Vishnuite site of 11th-century vintage. The ashes of King Airlangga of Java were interred in this brick pool in 1049.

Jawi and **Singosari** are Shivaite-Buddhist temples of the 13th-14th century. Both are dedicated to King Kartenagara, the last king of Singosari.

Kidal, a 13th-century Shivaite *candi,* is dedicated to King Anushapati, the second king of Singosari. Three sides of the base are adorned with *garuda* statues.

Jago, built in the 13th century, is a funerary monument dedicated to Tantric Buddhism and a memorial to King Vishnuvardhana of Singosari. The temple's best statues now reside in the National Museum, though many remain in the monument's courtyard.

Kedaton is a small 14th-century Shivaite *candi* that features relief panels illustrating Garuda's search for the elixir of immortality.

gagung: **Pantai Popoh,** 20 km away, has comfortable hotels and bungalows. Visit 900-meter-long **Trowongan Air,** not far from Popoh, and the marble factory **Pabrik Marmar Tulungagung.** Twenty-five km south of Tulungagung at Parigi is a 10-km-long beach consisting of hills and thousands of chattering coconut trees; Rp1200 by minibus to either beach from the Tulungagung Tamanan station.

Accommodations And Food

Losmen Centrum, Jl. Yani Barat 37, is the best. A cheerful little place where you can enjoy hot ginger drinks and Arabian-style coffee; very cheap *nasi pecel* in the morning. **Losmen Indonesia** lies on a little lane off Jl. Kapt. Kasinhin in Kampung Plandaan; Rp4000-6000. No meals, but you can eat at **Depot Arumdalu** nearby; good *nasi* dishes. **Losmen Rahayu** (Rp4000-6000) is near the train station; eat at **Warung Sederhana** close by. Six km out of town is the more expensive **Pasanggrahan**

Argo Wilis, Rp8000 a night. Newer hotels include the **Gajah Mada Losmen,** Jl. Kartini 10, tel. (0355) 81996; **Nasional Losmen,** Jl. Pahlawan 3, tel. 81642; and the **Panorama Losmen,** Jl. Supratman 12, tel. 81857.

The best restaurant in town is the **Sumber Rasa,** Jl. Teuku Umar 58, filled with stuffed teddy bears. There's a *sate gule* place at Jl. Diponegoro 57. Try the *sate kambing* and *nasi gule* at Jl. Diponegoro 45. Frequent also **Depot Apollo,** Jl. Wahid Hasyim 7. Visit **Es Djus Segar,** Jl. Teuku Umar, for iced juices.

Getting Away

It's Rp400 from Losmen Centrum by *becak* to Tamanan, the minibus and bus terminal near the Pertamina gas station. To Kediri, Rp800 by bus; Trenggalek (32 km), Rp400. For Pacitan, go first to Trenggalek by minibus, then ride through the hills to Ponorogo, then to Pacitan. To Blitar, 35 km east of Tulungagung, it's Rp700 by bus or Rp900 by minibus.

TULUNGAGUNG AND BLITAR AREAS

Gua Selamangeleng

Cave hermitages, which ancient Javanese rulers and mystics used as retreats, are a curious feature of East Java not found elsewhere on the island. Sanggrahan village, southeast of Tulungagung, features rare examples of 10th-century bas-reliefs carved on the walls of a cave gouged out of solid rock. Four rooms present scenes of mountains, mysterious clouds, and burials. One of the first known versions of the Mahabharata epic was carved here. The story of Arjuna is also carved in an earthy style—voluptuous heavenly nymphs astride clouds descend and attempt to seduce the meditating god.

From the intersection on the southeast side of Tulungagung, head south about five km to Sanggrahan. Locals will direct you to a house where you sign a guestbook, then children will take you on a one-km trail through rice fields and across a small river. Signs show the way. This cave lies in a populated area at the foot of the Wajak Mountains; use the great pinnacle of rock as a landmark. Candi Cunkup, the foundation of a recently excavated small temple, lies on the northeast side of Sanggrahan. Nice view.

Gua Pasir

Gua Pasir, four km beyond the first cave, also has scenes of Arjuna resisting temptation, though they're not as well executed. These scenes show the love life of the comic dwarves, the *panakawan*. Tragically, Gua Pasir's carvings are now nearly invisible beneath graffiti. The walk out to Gua Pasir through rural East Java is as rich an experience as the cave itself. The area around Boyolinggo village is a black-

and white-magic center. In Balairejo, call in on the most renowned magician (*orang sakti*) of them all, Gipowikromo.

BLITAR AND VICINITY

A typical middle-sized Javanese community 50 km southeast of Kediri, 80 km east of Malang. Blitar is the birthplace of Sukarno, Indonesia's first president. Blitar is also known as Kota Lahar. *Lahar* is a river of lava, water, and ash that gushes out of a volcano—in this case, Gunung Kelud. This small town, with just one main street, Jl. Merdeka, is a useful base for touring the sights and temples in the surrounding countryside.

Attractions
Pasar Legi, two blocks west of Hotel Sri Lestari, is a superbly organized market worth a morning visit. **Museum Blitar,** just west of the city park, is a small open-air museum with an impressive central image of an eight-armed deity.

A **cattle market** is held at Sananwetan, about two km from Blitar's center. **Pantai Tambak Beach** lies 20 km southeast of Blitar; get there by minibus from Pasarpon. For more seascapes and shining beaches, try **Pantai Serang** 60 km south of Blitar; take a minibus to Lodoyo, another to Bangunrejo, then one more to Serang—a three-hour ride in all. **Krisik** is a quiet retreat 15 km northeast of Blitar, Rp600 by minibus. The Blitar area is known for its export-quality coffee; at least seven coffee plantations lie within 30 km of town.

Accommodations And Food
Central and comfortable is **Hotel Sri Lestari,** tel. (0342) 81766, on the main street at Jl. Merdeka 173. Rooms in the main building go for Rp8000-12,000; also some a/c rooms with hot and cold water in the Rp40,000-55,000 range. The owners can help with transportation to Sukarno's Tomb and the temple complex at Panantaran. The newish **Blitar Indah Hotel,** tel. 81779, on Jl. Ahmad Yani, east of city center, costs Rp6000-15,000, but the Sri Lestari is a better choice in a more convenient location. The moderately priced **Mandala Plaza,** Jl. Slamet Riyadi 37, tel. 81810, near Sukarno's Tomb, has rooms with private baths and refrigerators but no a/c.

Blitar is known for its *sambal pecel,* exported to Holland. **Hotel Sri Lestari** serves up outstanding Javanese country home cooking; in the courtyard of the same hotel is a *warung* serving Indonesian food and a few European dishes. Try the excellent baked fish served in stone bowls. The big **Ramayana Restaurant,** Jl. Merdeka 45-47, is like a Chinese delicatessen. At the bus terminal are a number of *warung* serving delicious chicken dishes. Jalan Anggrek is the best place to buy fruit and veggies.

Getting Away
Make an offer to the minibus drivers at the terminal to tour all the temple complexes in the area—Panataran, Sewentar, Gadusari, Wlingi, Gado. Start at Rp25,000—it'll take a full day. See if the owner of Hotel Sri Lestari will rent you a motorscooter or motorcycle.

Several trains travel to Malang. Trains to Solo leave at 0400 and 1725. The bus station is just a 10-minute walk west of the Sri Lestari Hotel. By bus to Surabaya requires four hours. Buses to Solo leave early in the morning and take six hours. Damri Bus Co., Jl. Mayang 92, runs buses to Jakarta via Kediri and Solo. If you want to go to Yogyakarta, get off in Solo and take a minibus. Buses also leave for Banyuwangi via Malang at around 1800, arriving 0600. Purchase your ticket the night before.

Sukarno's Tomb
On the way out to the Panataran complex is Sentul, the site of Sukarno's elaborate grave. Open daily 0800-1700; no entrance fee. The site is also called Makam Proklamator, or "The Grave of the Declarer of Indonesia's Independence." For eight years after his death in 1970, Sukarno's body lay in a plain unmarked grave beside that of his Balinese mother in Blitar's small cemetery for war veterans, as he explicitly requested in his will. But to counter the growing power of the Muslims and to recapture the loyalty of young intellectuals, Suharto in 1978 revived Sukarnoism. To this end, Sukarno's grave was lavishly refurbished and the marble monument is now a big tourist attraction. There are restaurants and souvenir stands nearby; vendors even hawk T-shirts and poster portraits of the country's first president.

Holy Gong Of Lodoyo
An artifact of the Mataram Kingdom, found in Lodayo, 12 km southeast and Rp800 from Blitar. The proper name of the gong is Kiai Prada. The

BLITAR

TO MALANG

JL. PAHLAWAN

JL. DIPONEGORO

JL. A. YANI

JL. BALI

TO LODOYO AND SERANG BEACH

TO PANATARAN AND SUKARNO'S GRAVE

JL. SUNGKONO

JL. WAHIDIN

WARTEL

Bank

OLD CINEMA

RAMAYANA RESTAURANT

Bank

STADIUM

JL. KELUT

CITY PARK

JL. MERAPI

JL. KENONGO

JL. ANJASMO

Bank

POLICE

POST OFFICE

JL. MERBABU

Bank

JL. SEMERU

JL. MELATI

JL. MERDEKA

JL. LAWU

JL. MASTRIP

TRAIN STATION

JL. KACAPIRI

HOTEL SRI LESTARI

ONYX SHOP

LAWAR RIVER

JL. ANGGREK

TO TULUNGAGUNG

JL. MAWAR

JL. KERANTIL

PASAR LEGI

JL. TANUNG

BUS TERMINAL

TO KEDIRI

© MOON PUBLICATIONS, INC.

100 m

0

structure containing the gong is located right next to the Pembantu Bupati Building on the *alun-alun,* opposite Pasar Lodayo. The gong is removed and rung only twice a year, on Hari Raya and Mohammed's birthday.

As is the case when visiting many sacred objects on Java, it's the traveling that's most memorable. The whole trip is a study in the mélange of Javanese traditional behavior: village hospitality, customs, bureaucracy, hierarchal social systems, and religious syncretic beliefs. You might have to deal with as many as three officials to get in to Kiai Prada. After a moment of silence, you sign the guestbook; then they uncover the gong. It's swathed in a saffron cloth and surrounded by white textiles to keep it warm and holy. The whole atmosphere is filled with quiet, loving, expectant reverence.

PANATARAN

Ten km north of Blitar and 80 km southwest of Malang is East Java's largest and most imposing complex of ruins.

The Panataran temple group took 250 years to build, starting in the 12th century; most probably the work of the Majapahit. Three gradually rising walled courtyards are laid out on a long field; see dance-play platforms, terraces, shrines, and the same *gapura* gateways found in almost every village in East Java. Temple reliefs show the transition from three-dimensional to two-dimensional representations. The whole complex is very well maintained. Get here really early to have the place all to yourself.

The Dated Temple
So called because of the date 1291 (A.D. 1369) over the entrance. A fine example of East Javanese *candi* architecture, this temple is richly decorated with exuberant detail. Carvings show a contrast between a vegetarian and a corpulent meat-eater, the left and right paths of a yogi, the corpulent Bubukshah and the thin Gagang Aking. The bands in the roof are filled with carved animals.

Naga Temple
One of the most striking structures is the Naga Temple, on the second terrace. Once used to store sacred objects, all around it are colossal carvings of protective coiled serpents carried by priests—a sight to make any medieval thief shudder. On the base are reliefs of animal tales.

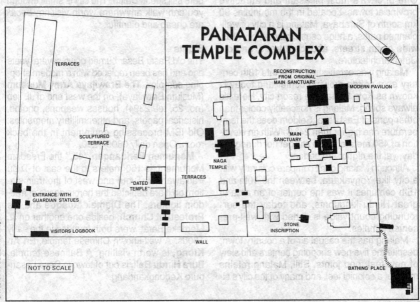

PANATARAN TEMPLE COMPLEX

TERRACES

RECONSTRUCTION FROM ORIGINAL MAIN SANCTUARY

MODERN PAVILION

SCULPTURED TERRACE

NAGA TEMPLE

MAIN SANCTUARY

"DATED TEMPLE"

TERRACES

ENTRANCE WITH GUARDIAN STATUES

STONE INSCRIPTION

VISITORS LOGBOOK

WALL

BATHING PLACE

NOT TO SCALE

The Main Temple

Just the substructure remains of what was once the main sanctuary. On its bas-reliefs the monkey general Hanuman leads his army through the air past the flying wounded, clouds of fighting monsters, battles, and monkeys building a dam across the sea. On the first terrace scenes from the Ramayana are carved in *wayang* style. These figures are permeated with supernaturalism—animals or spooky beings camouflaged in intricate motifs—so the atmosphere seems charged with life. Along the second terrace, in a much more naturalistic style, view fables from the Krishnayana—the adventures of Krishna as he abducts the princess Rukmini just before she's betrothed to another suitor. Winged monsters gaze menacingly from the third terrace.

Bathing Places

Southeast of the main temple. Panataran was constructed more for the commoner than the Brahman. This bathing place built in 1415 shows

flying tortoises, the bull and the crocodile fable, winged snakes, and a lion plowing a field. Reliefs also depict Indian Tantric tales, the Eastern equivalent of *Aesop's Fables*.

You'll find another bathing place on the road between Ngelok and Panataran. Go through the village toward the complex; around the corner on the left by a river, just before the bridge, is a bathing temple with live spouts. Villagers still use this 16th-century structure for washing clothes and bathing.

Getting There

From Blitar, take a *bemo* or minibus past Jiwut and Ngelok villages to Desa Panataran. The temple complex is down a little road surrounded by rice fields. Open 0600-1700. If you walk back you can visit the bathing place en route. It's also possible to visit Panataran on a day visit from Malang if you hire a motorcycle from Duta Transport in Malang. The Sri Lestari Hotel in Blitar charges Rp21,000 for a jeep up to the temple, including a stop at Sukarno's Tomb.

MALANG

One of Java's most pleasant and attractive provincial towns. Located in the mountains 90 km south of Surabaya, Malang is a city of well-planned parks, a huge central market, big villas, wide clean streets, abundant trees, and old Dutch architecture.

Malang was established in the late 18th century as a coffee-growing center and today is known as Kota Pesiar, the resort city. Here it's always spring: Malang is noticeably cooler than other parts of East Java. Seldom does the temperature rise higher than 24° C. With an elevation of 450 meters, it can still get hot during the day, yet the nights are perfect.

Although Malang can't compare culturally with a city like Yogyakarta, between the 10th and 15th centuries it was the center of an area of great Hindu kingdoms, and today the surrounding countryside is dotted with well-preserved temples.

Malang has the casual air of a country town, despite the five new shopping centers and slew of new fast food joints. Still, Malang retains much of a colonial feel, and many of the city's el-

ders still speak Dutch. The city is small enough you can walk anywhere worth visiting; *becak* are cheap and plentiful.

Sights

The old Pasar Besar burned down several years ago and has been replaced with a modern shopping complex. The **Brawijaya Army Museum** (Musium Brawijaya), on the west end of Jl. Ijen (no. 25, tel. 2394), houses weapons, photos, historical papers, and other military mementos. Old IBM processing equipment in the back room. Open daily 0800-1200.

Monumen Perjoangan "45," the Freedom Monument, is 150 meters to the east of Tugu Pahlawan (Jl. Tugu) and west of the train station; on it are depicted the heroic deeds of freedom fighters. The **Djamek Mosque** and the **Protestant Church,** beside one another on Jl. Merdeka Barat, were both founded in the early 1800s. A well-known Chinese temple, **En An Kiong,** is worth visiting. A Balinese temple, **Pura Hindu Bali,** is out of town in Desa Lesanpuro Kedungkandang.

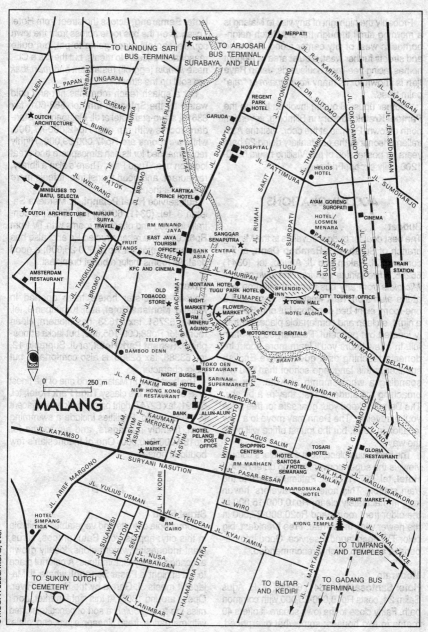

MALANG

Probably the highlight of any visit to Malang is a morning stroll through the old Dutch neighborhoods west of city center along Jl. Bromo and streets further west, a quiet area of elegant homes facing tree-lined boulevards. **Jalan Raya Ijen** is known for its many *koningpalm* or "raja" palm trees.

Another unusual outing involves touring the **Pantoel Kretek Factory** in Blimbing, seven km north of town. Permits at the door. Visit the Australian prisoner at the penitentiary doing 20 hard years for possession of pot. Visiting hours 0800-1200 daily except Friday.

ACCOMMODATIONS

Budget
The best deal for budget travelers is the Malang branch of Surabaya's **Bamboo Denn,** at the corner of Jl. Hakim and Jl. Arjuno, tel. (0341) 66256, a five-minute walk from the town square. *Microlets* from any bus terminal will drop you at the *alun-alun;* walk west from there. Just a one-room, eight-bed dormitory but only Rp4000 a night, a clean and comfortable place, centrally located but peaceful. Popular, so it's often full. In a few hours you'll learn more about Indonesia teaching as a guest native English speaker in this language school than you will spending a whole month at Kuta. Try approaching the students first; they're a bit shy. The Denn will keep your gear safe for free while you're traveling. The Denn may move to a new location in 1995, but the tourist office will point the way.

The best-value place, from a traveler's point of view, is the super-convenient and quiet **Helios Hotel,** tel. 62741, on Jl. Pattimura close to the train station. This hotel is a travelers' haven kept immaculately clean; Rp10,000-15,000 in the older front rooms and Rp20,000-27,000 in the newer wing in the rear. Free breakfast, big color TV, good laundry service. Good info dispensed here too. Highly recommended.

Moderate
Hotel Santosa, tel. (0341) 66889, Jl. H. Agus Salim 24, costs Rp18,000-25,000 with common bath. Fairly close to the town square, it offers 40 rooms in two houses; somewhat overpriced.

Hotel Semarang, across the street from Hotel Tosari, is on the bus route across from the town square—an old place going to pot, but quite reasonable prices. No meals, but there's a Chinese *lumpia* (eggroll) restaurant and *martabak* are sold up the street.

For a splash (each room has hot and cold water) try the **Splendid Inn,** tel. 668-601, fax 63618, a two-star hotel at Jl. Majapahit 4. Standard rooms with fan cost Rp42,000-47,000, while a/c rooms are Rp47,000-99,000. Highly recommended for its rich atmosphere and great location near Tugu Park. There's also a library, restaurant, and good tourist info; it feels more like a guesthouse.

Full-service **Hotel Pelangi,** Jl. Merdeka Selatan 3, tel. (0341) 65156, fax 65466, is centrally located and offers a/c rooms with TV from Rp65,000. The reconstructed Pelangi also has economy rooms for Rp15,000-25,000; a good deal. All rooms include buffet breakfast.

Luxury
Several three-star hotels have opened in Malang. **Montana Hotel,** at Jl. Kahuripan 9, tel. (0341) 62751, fax 61633, has modern, clean rooms for Rp68,000-105,000, but lacks atmosphere. **Regent Park Hotel,** at Jl. Suprapto 12, tel. 63388, fax 62966, is also comfortable but lacks character.

The best hotel in Malang, and one of the finest in all of Java, is the classy **Tugu Park Hotel,** tel. 63891, fax 62747, right on the park and adjacent to the Splendid. Facilities include a swimming pool, friendly managers, and a/c rooms for Rp168,000-210,000. One of Indonesian's few boutique hotels.

FOOD

Street Food
A cornucopia of fruits and vegetables available in this city: apples from Batu, grapes, citrus, giant Indonesian watermelons, locally grown avocados, papayas, tomatoes. A colorful place to eat at night is **Pasar Senggol,** where Jl. Majapahit meets Jl. Gareja by the Brantas River. Opens around 1800. At this night market, don't miss the *terang bulan,* a sort of pancake stuffed with margarine, fresh pineapple jam, chocolate,

and sweet milk. The flower market nearby is also a must. The night market on Jl. Branwijaya has faded and you'll find a greater selection of foodstalls on Jl. Suryani Nasution and around the train station.

Restaurants

The **Minang Jaya**, Jl. Basuki Rachmat 111, tel. (0341) 5707, specializes in West Sumatran cuisine. Open 24 hours a day, the restaurant will provide 20 different combinations of food—a real adventure in eating. Taste some *gulai kilkil* (buffalo feet curry). Since it's better than the food you'll find out in the villages, order a packaged lunch if you're going out to the temples on a day-trip.

Minang Agung also serves Padang specialties in a lovely old Dutch cafe filled with antiques and comfortable wooden furniture. A better choice than the Minang Jaya, which has modernized and lost most of its old-world atmosphere. **Restaurant Cinta**, Jl. Sukarjo, is usually crowded with diners—a good sign. **Miramar Restaurant**, Jl. Pasar Besar 117, is pretty classy, with a neon sign. **Ayam Goreng Suropati** on Jl. Trungjoyo near the train station is a fried-chicken place only a five-minute walk from the Helios Hotel.

The **New Hong Kong**, Jl. A.R. Hakim near the *alun-alun*, is Malang's best Chinese restaurant. For something different, the Arabian restaurant **Cairo**, Jl. Jagalna 1, specializes in Indonesian food with a Middle-Eastern accent; reputedly the best *sate kambing* in town. **RM Marhaen**, Jl. S. Wiryo Branoto, is the place to sample Javanese and Arabian food combined.

Or try moderately priced Chinese food at **Gloria Restaurant** near the Pelangi Hotel, and the **Amsterdam Restaurant** on Jl. Kawi; a favorite of expats who recommend the Western dishes.

Just off the square near Hotel Pelangi, **Toko Oen** serves high-quality Western, Chinese, and Indonesian food, as well as iced drinks and great ice cream. Like an old-fashioned Dutch coffee shop, this is a real oasis with an authentic colonial atmosphere. The place even serves such anachronistic standbys as *uitsmijter* (Dutch sandwiches), *kaasstengels* (cheese sticks), *droptoffee* (licorice toffee), *kroket* (meat snacks), and *haagsehopjes* (Dutch mocha candies). Clean, spacious, good service. Open daily 0900-2030. Next door is a well-stocked bakery.

ENTERTAINMENT, SHOPPING, SERVICES

Performances

Watch dancers rehearse on Sundays at 0900 at Sanggar Senaputra on Jl. Rumah Sakit. At night stroll by the **Katolik Sasono Budoyo** (Catholic church, built in 1934) on Jl. Gareja to hear *gamelan* music and see medieval Javanese dances during services.

Malang has long been a center of *topeng* culture and is host to a number of troupes. *Wayang topeng* is practiced all over the Malang area to celebrate marriages, circumcisions, and village events; it's not difficult to see one of these masked dances, especially in the Pakisaji in the Kepanjen area southeast of the city or in the clove-growing Senggreng area, seven km southeast of Kepanjen. To learn *wayang topeng,* see Pak Karimun in Pakisaji, south of town en route to Blitar.

Shopping

Visit the many *pasar* of Malang, liveliest 0600-0630. Though not much of a place for crafts, some unique pottery is for sale on Jl. Slamet Riyadi northwest of city center.

A wonderful selection of flower stalls and shops are found on Jl. Majapahit. **Pasar Burung**, the bird market, is on Jl. Brawijaya. The best bookshop in town is **Gramedia** in front of Sarinah Supermarket on Jl. Basuki Rachmat; **Toko Buku Siswa** is on Jl. Agus Salim in the shopping center opposite Gereja Katolik. Wisma Batik (Danar Hadi) is on Jl. Basuki Rachmat.

Mitra Shopping Center, Jl. Agus Salim 10-16 on the same block as the post office, has Westernized food, coffee, and cheese—a deli-type environment. **Gajah Mada Plaza** and **Malang Plaza** are also on Jl. Agus Salim. The all-alit **Sarinah Supermarket** is not cheap.

Services

The **Malang City Tourist Office** (Baparda) is located beside the Balai Kota on Jl. Tugu; open 0700-1400, Friday and Saturday until 1100. See Mr. Tontowi; moderately informative. The **East Java Tourism Office** on Jl. Semeru is hopelessly disorganized and not worth visiting unless you're conducting a study of Indonesian work habits.

The **main post office,** on the south side of the *alun-alun,* is open 0800-1400. **Bank Bumi Daya** accepts only U.S. and Australian dollars. The **Eksim Bank** accepts only U.S. dollars and Lloyd's of London traveler's checks. Bank Bumi Daya is faster. After the banks close at 1500, you can change money at the very efficient and marvelously friendly **Murjur Surya Travel** on Jl. Bromo.

Kantor imigrasi is on Jl. R. Panji Surosoy, tel. (0341) 41039, north of town near the Arjosari bus terminal. A big **public library** on Jl. Ijen sits in front of Musium Brawijaya. At least 10 **medical specialists** practice at Jl. Kawi 13. Consultation hours: 1700-1900. Swim at Tugu Park Hotel (Rp2500).

The Malay telephone city code is 0341.

GETTING THERE

Trains run between Surabaya and Malang at least seven times daily. From Surabaya's Kota station, a train leaves at 0715, while another leaves Gubeng station at 0723—both cost Rp2000 and take 2.5 hours. Two trains depart daily from Blitar.

Buses leave for Malang from Surabaya constantly, Rp1500, 1.5 hours. Unusual approaches to Malang include the route via Lumajang (120 km) south of Probolinggo; this road passes by monstrous Gunung Semeru. The route from Solo via Jombang and Pare, then minibus to Kandangan and Batu, gets you into Malang by the back door.

Travelers coming to Malang from Yogyakarta or Solo need not visit Surabaya. Get off the bus in Jombang and catch the small bus from the rear of the Jombang bus terminal to Malang via Batu. Great scenery over the mountain pass.

You can rent motorcycles for Rp10,000 per day, and bicycles for Rp1000, from **Duta Transport,** at Jl. Majapahit 40, tel. (0341) 62568. Reserve your vehicle one day in advance. A motorcycle is a good way to quickly tour the coun-

tryside, see the isolated temples, and appreciate the natural beauty of East Java.

GETTING AWAY

The Malang Airport reopened in 1995. Garuda, tel. (0341) 69494, is at Jl. J. Suprapto 41. Sempati has an office in the Regent Park Hotel.

Several trains leave daily for Solo and Yogyakarta, but the best is the 1515 express, which has both third and second class seats. Trains also reach Surabaya and Probolinggo and continue east to Bali. Departures are listed at the train station.

Malang has three bus terminals, all situated about five km from the center of town. Take a minibus to the proper terminal, then board the first available bus to your destination. Local *microlet* around town are easy to understand: A means the minibus is heading to Arjosari Terminal, G goes to Gadang, L reaches Landung Sari. Most minibuses pass the *alun-alun.*

For long distance destinations, take a night bus from the office adjacent to the Toko Oen Restaurant. This office represents almost a dozen different companies serving every conceivable destination in Java, Bali, and Sumatra. Sample prices: Cirebon Rp25,000, Semarang Rp13,000, Bali Rp15,000-21,000, Yogyakarta Rp10,000-15,000, Bandung Rp32,000, Jakarta Rp35,000-43,000.

For Surabaya, Bromo, and Bali, go to **Arjosari bus terminal** for destinations to the north and east. To reach Arjosari, take any local minibus marked A. Buses to Blitar and Telungagung depart from the **Gadang bus terminal,** five km south of city center. It's easier to take the train (70 km, three hours) on a refreshing, variegated route through the mountains. The **Landang Sari terminal** serves destinations to the west (Kediri, Batu, Selecta, Mojokerto). To reach Solo or Yogyakarta, take a *bemo* to Landung Sari, then a bus to Jombang, then another bus west to your destination.

VICINITY OF MALANG

Gunung Kawi

A pilgrimage place 40 km southwest of Malang on the southern slopes of Gunung Kawi. A revered spiritual leader, Mbah Yugo, is buried here. The actual site is called Pesarean Mbah Sujono, which means "The Grave of Grandfather Sujono," another Muslim pioneer who is also interred here. Crowds, sometimes numbering in the thousands, continuously worship at the graves. All faiths, including non-Muslim Chinese, visit Gunung Kawi from all over Indonesia seeking healing, fertility, a blessing for the mother of the paddy fields, success in exams, or just good luck. Stalls open all night sell everything from stuffed alligators to hair-growth stimulant. People are friendly to the point of being tiresome.

Mats are provided for the thousands of devotees staying the night. If you sleep in the public dorm, you'll be stared at like you just fell from the moon, your every gesture followed by at least 20 pairs of eyes. Alternatively, there are some *losmen*.

The site is accessible by minibus from Malang's Gadang bus terminal via Kepanjen. Thursday evenings minibuses frequently leave for Gunung Kawi, returning Friday morning after the passengers have spent the night worshipping and watching puppet shows.

Pantai Ngliyep

A magnificent rocky beach, 60 km south of Malang, with dense coastal forests, beautiful seascapes, and giant waves. Take a minibus (Rp1500) or bus (Rp1000) toward Blitar and transfer at Kepanjen, 18 km south of Malang. Crowded on holidays. Stay in **Penginapan Ngliyep,** with outside *mandi.* A campground near the beach is usually crammed with young

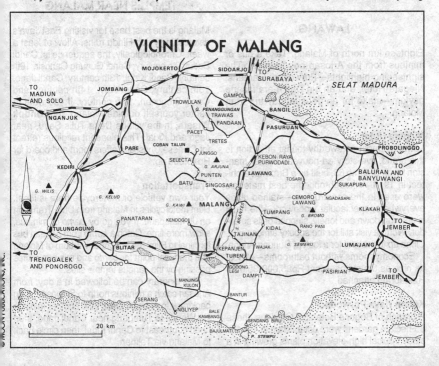

VICINITY OF MALANG

campers. The beaches are cleaner northwest of Ngliyep. You can reach Bale Kambang Beach on foot from Sujono village, six km away; this white-sand beach features a coral reef stretching 250 meters out to sea.

Since 1913, Ngliyep has celebrated Labuhan with a procession to Gunung Kembang, where an offering of a goat's head is thrown into the sea. For five days preceding the ceremony there are *wayang kulit* shows dedicated to Nyai Loro Kidul.

Bale Kambang Beach

Considered the best beach near Malang, Pantai Bale Kambang features three offshore islands graced with Balinese-style temples, all accessible by bridges. Take care when swimming—bad rips.

A solitary *losmen* is located here, but most visitors make this beach a day-trip from Malang. To reach Bale Kambang, take a *bemo* from Gadang terminal to Godong Legi, another to Bantur, and a final *bemo* to the beach.

LAWANG

Eighteen km north of Malang. Take a bus or minibus from the Arjosari bus terminal. The sightseeing highlights—Purwodadi Gardens, Niagara Hotel, and an old Dutch-era insane asylum—make for an unusual day-trip from Malang.

Niagara Hotel

Lawang's most noteworthy tourist attraction is this grand, five-story art-nouveau former mansion on Jl. Sutomo 63, built by a Brazilian architect in 1918. Although only the best materials were used in the construction—stained glass everywhere, spectacular woodwork—the hotel is now run-down and lonely, stripped of its splendor. Worth a visit still for the spooky atmosphere. Climb up to the roof for a look at Gunung Arjuna.

Economy rooms without bathrooms—almost as nice as the suites—cost Rp25,000-35,000. Restaurant attached.

Kebon Raya Purwodadi

A branch of Bogor's Botanical Gardens, these 85-hectare gardens were established in 1914 to study tropical high-elevation plants growing in a dry climate. More remote and less well-known, this attractive botanic park is less crowded than the Bogor Gardens, particularly on weekdays. The staff are helpful and friendly. The park is especially invigorating in the early morning when everything is hosed down and smells fresh. Don't miss the tropical cacti, dozens of rare palms, the small, well-organized orchid house, and the waterfall. Open daily 0700-1000; entrance Rp100. From Purwodadi you can also take one of the back ways up Gunung Arjuna.

Sumber Borong

This classic Dutch-era mental institution is located one km east of Lawang in a peaceful, rural setting. Visitors are welcome to watch the music show put on by inmates every Wednesday and Saturday at 0900—a mad cross between Metallica and Perry Como with Javanese gong orchestras. Ask for the amiable Pak Wayan or director Dr. Rusman.

TEMPLES NEAR MALANG

Malang is the best base for visiting East Java's astonishingly rich Hindu ruins. Allow at least a week. Chronologically, the sequence is: Candi Badut, 9th century; Candi Gunung Gangsir, 10th century; Candi Kidal, 13th century; Candi Jago, 13th century; Candi Jawi, 14th century; and Candi Singosari, 14th century. If you want to center yourself outside Malang, try **Pondok Wisata,** in the village Desa Tulis Sayu, near Jago and Kidal. This pleasant religious retreat for Chinese Christians offers room and board for Rp15,000 pp.

Transportation

Your own vehicle or motorcycle here is ideal. Rent motorcycles in Malang from Duta Transport on Jl. Majapahit. If you go by *bemo* or minibus, allow more time. Catch a *bemo* from Arjosari bus terminal to Blimbing, a northern suburb of Malang and the focal point for *bemo* and minibus routes passing by the various temple sites.

This itinerary can be followed in a day: from Arjosari catch a minibus north to Singosari, then backtrack to Arjosari. Next, take another minibus via Wendit to Tumpang near Candi Jago, then head southeast to Candi Kidal, then circle back to Malang via Tajinan.

A separate outing must be made to Candi Badut from Malang; take a *bemo* to Landung Sari bus terminal five km northwest of Malang, then a *becak* out to the village of Sumbersawi near Dinoyo. From Sumbersawi, walk about 30 minutes to the temple remains. Nearby is an old graveyard.

Candi Singosari

Ten km north of Malang is the town of Singosari; the local name is Candi Linggo. Dating from the 13th century, this Shiva shrine is the most imposing monument remaining of the murderous Singosari dynasty. It was built to honor King Kartanegara and his priests, killed in a palace revolt. This monarch and his cohorts were the same folks who mortified Kublai Khan's emissaries by cutting off their noses and tattooing "NO!" across their foreheads, an act that precipitated the launching of 1,000 Mongol troop ships against Java in 1293.

Candi Singosari's unique feature is its base, serving also as the central *cella* or inner sanctum of the temple. Thus it's called a "cellar-temple" or "tower-temple" by archaeologists. Only the top of Singosari is ornamented; because of

Candi Singosari

COURTESY OF THE ROYAL TROPICAL INSTITUTE IN AMSTERDAM

time, finances, or civil catastrophe, ornamentation was never completed. Carving always began at the top of a *candi*, working downward so as not to damage lower, finished sculptures with falling pieces. Most of the statues originally at Singosari now form the backbone of the world-famous Hindu-Javanese collection at Leiden Musuem in Holland.

From Arjosari, it's Rp400 by minibus to Singosari village. At the intersection in the northern fringe of town, near where the *bemo* stops, turn west down Jl. Kartenegara next to Bioskop Garuda; the temple is about 600 meters down the road on the right. Ask directions.

Candi Sumberawan

From Candi Singosari, go toward the guardian statues, then turn right down a country road and head northwest for six km until you reach Sumberawan village. Turn right, head up the dirt road about 300 meters, and turn right on a narrow track. You'll probably need a guide, as the narrow trail is unmarked and almost impossible to find. Ask for the gate key if you want to go right up to the stupa, which is about 300 meters further on a trail through rice paddies and across the dam. Spectacular scenery.

Candi Jago

Eighteen km east of Malang, Candi Jago is a memorial to the Singosari king Vishnuvardhana. Although the roof and body have caved in, it's still one of the most attractive and remarkable temples of the period. Candi Jago dates from the late 13th century, yet has distinct connections with the prehistoric monuments and terraced sanctuaries in Java's mountains.

The monument incorporates Buddhist sculptures, Krishna reliefs, Arjuna's fretful night in his hermitage, earthy scenes from everyday life, and some early and grotesque *panakawan* carvings. See clearly the shift towards two-dimensional figures during this tumultuous dynasty. *Wayang*-like "moving picture" sculptures are placed right next to one another, like figures in stiff parade; the action unfolds counterclockwise. Temple reliefs are bolder, more vigorous than any earlier style—change was definitely taking place. Jago's gatekeeper will provide a handout about the reliefs with explanations in English. The Sumberwringin watering place is nearby.

At Arjosari catch a minibus or *bemo* to Tumpang. About 100 meters before Tumpang's *pasar*, 150 meters down a side road to the left, is Candi Jago. Look for the signpost.

Candi Kidal

This small but lovely sanctuary is an architectural jewel, a nearly perfect example of Singosari temple art. Next to a papaya grove is the richly carved 13th century *candi*—a 12.5-meter-tall burial temple honoring a Singosari king. The recently renovated structure appears quite slender since the base towers up so high, the temple tapering at the top to form a pyramid. To the left of the steps are well-crafted episodes of Garuda carrying the nectar of immortality. Kidal also offers elaborate carvings of medallions and *kala*-heads on the main body, with statues of Garuda guarding the base. There used to be a tunnel beneath the temple leading all the way to Candi Singosari.

Kidal village is five km southwest of Tumpang. At Tumpang market catch a minibus straight to Desa Kidal. On the far side of Desa Kidal, you'll see the sign for the temple. Continue on the road clockwise back to Malang; fabulous scenery.

BATU

Seventeen km northwest of Malang, this 1,200-meter-high hill station is an upscale, concrete resort town with broad boulevards, modern shopping centers, and plenty of traffic. The vegetable-growing area of Batu also offers hot springs, a variety of sports, and rest and relaxation. Because of its high, bracing climate on the slopes of Gunung Arjuna, Batu has since Dutch times been a tuberculosis center and recuperative resort. Many of the hotels feature curative *air panas* and swimming pools. Take a minibus from Malang's Landung Sari terminal.

Accommodations And Food

Batu is somewhat expensive; most hotels cost Rp42,000-89,000.

Losmen Kawi, Jl. Panglima Sudirman 19, tel. 228-8139, is a cheerful place and quite central, with 17 large rooms for Rp9000-14,000. Eat in the *rumah makan* next door to save money. Also check out the **Mustika**, Jl. Budiono 2; **Hotel Perdanan Wisma**, Jl. Trunojoyo 102;

and **Hotel Batu**—all clean and reasonable. Other hotels have dining rooms and some include meals in their room rates.

Hotel Asida, Jl. Panglima Sudirman 99, offers a swimming pool and tennis court. Better values are the **Palem Hotel,** Jl. Trunojoyo 26, tel. 228-8177, with 22 family rooms with bath; the **Arumdalu,** tel. 228-8266, with full resort facilities; the **Batu Hotel and Village,** Jl. Hasanuddin 4, tel. 2340, with rooms and villas; and **Hotel Selecta,** Jl. Tulungrejo, Box 30, tel. 228-825, with rooms and bungalows with private *mandi*.

Batu is well known for its delicious fruits and vegetables, especially apples, citrus, onions, potatoes, and cabbage. Near the *alun-alun* is a lively *pasar malam*. For excellent Chinese food at low prices, try **Restaurant Kenangan** beside the market.

Coban Rondo Falls

Nine km from Batu. For Rp200, take a minibus to Sebalo village, a little *desa* about six km from Batu. Turn down the signposted trail by the memorial to the cows and walk five km to this 65-meter-high waterfall at the foot of Gunung Panderman (3,037 meters).

Back out on the main road, continue through mountainous countryside to Pare and Kediri. On the way at Pujon, nine km from Batu, is a bathing pool called **Dewi Sri**; an experimental agricultural project is underway here.

If heading back down from Batu to Malang, stop in Junrejo and visit the **Buddhist Dharma Putra Asramam Temple**; you'll see the stupa.

Songgoriti Hot Springs

From Batu walk four km or catch a motorbike or minibus to these hot springs. Songgoriti is a popular recreation area with a large swimming pool, surrounded by restaurants, gardens, casuarina trees, and rice fields. Of the two classes of hot springs offered, the better bargain is the public bath—the only one in East Java.

SELECTA

Only 6.5 km northwest of Batu, nestled on the side of Gunung Arjuna, Selecta is a fine resort surrounded by gorgeous mountain scenery, landscaped flower gardens, vegetable patches, and apple orchards. Enjoy the rock garden and swimming pool with its clear, fresh water, and several fine restaurants and souvenir stands.

Accommodations
Hotel Santosa II on Jl. Selecta-Tulungrejo charges only Rp12,000 including food. **Hotel Selecta** has 33 rooms and three bungalows; Rp18,000-35,000. Good service and food, but the restaurant is quite pricey. Request hot water for baths, and plenty of blankets. It costs Rp800 to enter and use the pool.

Also try the **Purnama Hotel,** Jl. Raya Selecta, Box 18, tel. 228-8195, an excellent hotel in the Rp84,000-110,000 range, with very friendly waitresses as well as tennis courts. **Kartika Wijaya** has full facilities, fitness center, billiards, swimming pool, pub, good views, and rooms for Rp80,000-120,000.

Vicinity Of Selecta
North of Selecta, visit the little mountain town of Sumber Brantas, the source of the Brantas River. Selecta is also a good place to strike off from for the tropical volcanos to the north. From Junggo, hike three to four hours to the top of Gunung Anjasmoro (2,277 meters), Gunung Welirang (3,156 meters), or Gunung Arjuna (3,340 meters). These mountains are in a clump; hit all three by hiking along the connecting ridges.

Take a minibus from Batu or Selecta, then wait for an onward bus to continue up the mountain past several large tea plantations. Ask to be dropped at the trailhead to Gunung Arjuna.

PANDAAN

A cool and refreshing town 45 km south of Surabaya on the road to Malang. Known for its nearby temples and Ramayana performances.

Ramayana Ballet
At the **Taman Candrawilwatikta** amphitheater here (capacity 2,000), on the first and third Saturdays of the month from May to November, East Javanese classical dances, dramas, and temple rituals dating back to the 8th and 9th centuries are staged against the flawless cone of Gunung Penanggungan. There's no dialogue, so concentrate on the music and dancing as costumed players mime shortened versions of the Ramayana ballet in the *sendratari* school style.

Candi Jawi
Two and a half km from Pandaan bus station on the road up to Tretes. An early 14th-century masonry gem, built on a terrace of river rocks and surrounded by a dry moat, this Shivaite *candi* was dedicated to the murdered King Kartanegara. After the great earthquake of 1331, a Buddhist stupa was added to the base of red bricks. The structure is still quite beautiful, thanks to a superb restoration project several years ago. Unidentified reliefs are carved all around the temple in a mixture of Shivaite and Buddhist elements. In a barred concrete structure in back of Candi Jawi you'll find a statue of Shiva amidst other artifacts.

TRETES

An 850-meter-high mountain resort, Tretes lies nine km off the Surabaya-Malang road near Pandaan, easily reached by *bemo,* taxi, or bus. A very popular Dutch retreat before WW II, Tretes is still the place to go to escape the steamy heat and humidity of Surayaba. Tretes offers good swimming pools, souvenir shops, restaurants, hotels, spectacular views, and trails crisscrossing the mountainsides.

Accommodations
Motel-style hotels, with private entrances and balconies or terraces, offer meals, hot water, private *mandi*, and blankets for the cool nights. Dozens of cottages, bungalows, and rooms are available, ranging from Rp15,000 to Rp40,000. Bargain for less on weekdays.

The **Tanjung Plaza,** Jl. Wilis 7, tel. (0343) 81102, full of slot machines, is noisy on weekends, though clean and comfortable; attached restaurant. **Pemandian Tretes** offers excellent views, restaurant, and swimming pool; non-a/c rates include meals. Frequently full. The **Natour Bath Hotel Tretes,** Jl. Pasanggrahan 2, tel. 81776, fax 81161, features extravagantly expensive rooms and bungalows with TV; stroll in to sample the superb swimming pool and panoramas. Rooms here cost Rp126,000-273,000.

Tretes Raya, Jl. Malabar 166, tel. 81902, is very comfortable and, with its full resort facilities, including bungalows around a swimming pool, is almost worth the price. **Dirgahayu Indah,** Jl.

Ijen 5, tel. 81932, is a small hotel with family-style rooms. Cheaper than Tretes are the hotels in the *kampung* on the lower slopes of Gunung Welirang, where rooms go for as little as Rp6500. Try **Hotel Semeru** in Prigen.

Vicinity Of Tretes
Ibu Jaya's in Prigen is a big collection of bizarre antiques and artifacts from the days of the Dutch and even before; lots of kitsch junk too. Take a *bemo* from Tretes. Open every day in the mornings. Visit the nearby waterfalls **Kakek Budo** and **Putuk Truno,** and the **Air Pasanggrahan** complex.

You can climb **Gunung Welirang** in five to six hours from Tretes. No problem finding a guide who speaks Bahasa Indonesia. Welirang means "sulphur" in Javanese; just follow people looking for the sulphur baths.

You can reach the old temples of **Belahan** and **Jalatunda** on the slopes of Gunung Penanggungan from Tretes on foot or on horseback. Pacet, a small high-elevation village to the west, offers stunning views and cool, crisp air.

MOJOKERTO

Forty-two km southwest of Surabaya. Sukarno attended Dutch primary school here; at that time in the 1920s, it was a very small town. Visit the important **Museum Purbakala;** from the south side of the *alun-alun,* head east along Jl. A. Yani to the museum (no. 14), next to *kantor kabupaten.* Open 0700-1400, Friday till 1300, Sunday closed. Leave a donation.

A magnificent sculptural group of Vishnu carried on the back of Garuda is the centerpiece of

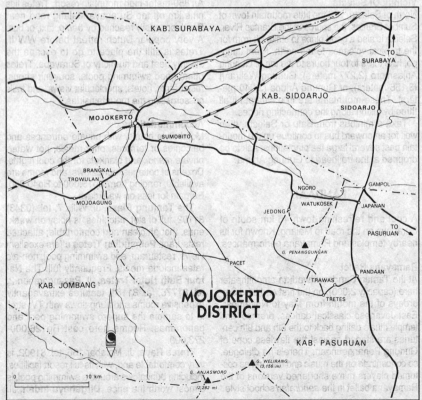

a fascinating series of reliefs around the main room. Also known as the Airlangga Statue, one theory holds that the Vishnu figure is a representation of King Airlangga. Taken from the Belahan Bathing Place near Trawas, this piece was probably carved as early as the 11th century. The museum is filled with many other lifelike statues, relics, carved stoned reliefs of daily scenes, and umpteen plaques covered with ancient writing. Afterwards, wander through the original quarter of town with its fine old Dutch houses.

Accommodations And Food

Penginapan Barat, Jl. Kartini II/93 down a quiet path along a canal, is Mojokerto's nicest *losmen* for the money—clean and well kept. **Penginapan Mutiara,** Jl. Setia Mulio, is behind Pasar Kriwon. This cheerful worker's place is the cheapest in town, and often full. Another good place to stay is **Losmen Nagamas,** Jl. Pahlawan 23, on the southeast side of Mojokerto; Rp5000 s, Rp7000 d including breakfast. **Wisma Tenera,** Jl. H.O.S. Cokroaminoto toward the *terminal bis,* wants Rp6000 s, Rp9000-14,000 d. Travelers also seek out **Losmen Merdeka,** Jl. Pamuji 73; Rp7000 s or d including light breakfast. The most expensive hotel in town is the **Sriwijaya** on Jl. Desa Pacot.

Getting Away

Two bus stations here, one on Jl. Majapahit, the other on Jl. Pahlawan. From the Jl. Pahlawan station, buses depart for Madiun and Surabaya, Rp2000. There are no buses at night from the Jl. Majapahit station, so you have to rely on minibuses. If you're going to Trowulan, right after Pasar Kliwon take a left on Jl. Achmad Dahlan and catch a *bemo* or minibus for Rp600. For Malang, take a minibus to Jombang, then ride another through the hills southeast to Malang.

TROWULAN

This small agricultural community was once the capital of the mighty Majapahit Empire which, under the ruthless Gajah Mada, controlled most of the archipelago in the 14th century. This ancient capital and major trade center was once completely surrounded by a high brick wall en-

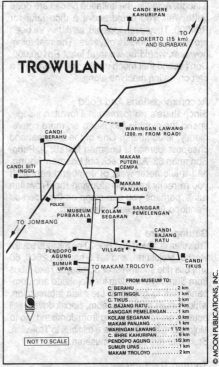

CANDI BHRE KAHURIPAN

TO MOJOKERTO (15 km) AND SURABAYA

TROWULAN

WARINGAN LAWANG (200 m FROM ROAD)

CANDI BERAHU

MAKAM PUTERI CEMPA

CANDI SITI INGGIL

MAKAM PANJANG

POLICE

MUSEUM PURBAKALA KOLAM SEGARAN

SANGGAR PEMELENGAN

TO JOMBANG

CANDI BAJANG RATU

PENDOPO AGUNG   VILLAGE

SUMUR UPAS   TO MAKAM TROLOYO

CANDI TIKUS

NOT TO SCALE

FROM MUSEUM TO:	
C. BERAHU	2 km
C. SITI INGGIL	1 km
C. TIKUS	3 km
C. BAJANG RATU	2 km
SANGGAR PEMELENGAN	1 km
KOLAM SEGARAN	0 km
MAKAM PANJANG	1 km
WARINGAN LAWANG	1 1/2 km
C. BHRE KAHURIPAN	6 km
PENDOPO AGUNG	1/2 km
SUMUR UPAS	1 km
MAKAM TROLOYO	2 km

© MOON PUBLICATIONS, INC.

closing pools, palaces, playing fields, plazas, and temples. Today, remains lie scattered over a 15-square-km area. Impressively, all the temples were made from brick, with no stonework, granite, or sandstone. All have lost their centerpieces, either to thieves or museums.

Museum Purbakala

This large, new, well-lit museum is renowned for its remarkable collection of terra-cotta figurines, toys, clay masks, bronze statues, and priestly accoutrements. A superb collection of statues and photographs of ancient sites in East Java is located just behind the museum; don't miss it. The interior collection is a museum of fragments; use your imagination. Open Tues.-Thurs. 0700-1400, Saturday until 1200, Sunday until 1400, Friday until 1100, Monday closed.

Kids will hustle you here to buy "authentic" 600-year-old Majapahit relics and terra-cotta figurines. Ask them if the piece is *"imitasi"*—for a laugh. Actually, the imitation pieces are done quite well; you could score a nice fake for Rp4000. They even *look* old, as if they've been around for hundreds of years. The real thing, however, would be worth at least Rp100,000. Don't spend that much unless you've brought a carbon-dating machine along.

Accommodations And Food
Since there's no *losmen* in Trowulan village, spend the night in Mojokerto or, more conveniently, in Jombang. One of the cleanest and cheapest *losmen* is **Losmen Melati,** Jl. Pang. Sudirman 63. Also check out **Losmen Agung,** half a kilometer west of Jombang center. If you're really keen on studying the Trowulan ruins, perhaps you can sleep on the open-air Pendopo Agung near the museum.

Getting There
Trowulan is 12 km and Rp600 by minibus southwest of Mojokerto, and a 1.5-hour (Rp2000, 60 km) bus ride southwest of Surabaya. Take a bus from Surabaya heading for Mojokerto and Jombang. Ask to get off at the main intersection, which heads to the museum. *Becak* drivers will pounce on you. If coming from Jombang, go to Mojoagung first, then take a minibus to Trowulan. Start your tour from the museum.

Touring The Temples
You need only good footwear and an adventurous spirit. Allow one day. Leave your pack in the souvenir shop at the museum. Follow the museum's tabletop map for directions. It's more fun to walk than to take a *becak* though you'll end the day dog tired.

Spending 15-20 minutes at each site, looking and resting, it'll take six hours walking or two to three hours by *becak*. When hiring a *becak,* try for the *tur komplet* for Rp8000-10,000, a better deal than visiting a site at a time. The walk or ride to each temple, down lanes filled with laughing children and past people working *padi,* is at least as satisfying as the temples themselves.

Pendopo Agung is a restful midpoint between the museum and Candi Bajang Ratu, built by the Indonesian army during a wave of tourist development as an exact reproduction of the 14th-century pavilions traditionally built in front of Majapahit nobles' residences.

Only the base of ancient **Siti Inggil** remains; a new temple with shrines has been built atop it. The devout still practice sleepless, waterless three-day fasting meditation here. The *juru kunci* of Jalatunda lives just down the road from the locked compound. **Candi Berahu** is thought to have stored the cremated remains of Majapahit royalty. This fine building has been recently restored.

Waringan Lawang, three km from the museum, east of the highway, is a split gateway which once led toward the palace of Gajah Mada. Not much is left except the two sides, which can be seen in many famous photos and sketches of the area. A reconstruction project now underway will make this a worthwhile spot by the late 1990s.

At **Kolam Segaran** Majapahit received royal guests. Once a great wide pool of water; in the middle floated a pavilion (*bale kambang*). The brick monolith of **Bajang Ratu** hardly looks like a temple; it's well maintained and appears quite new even after almost six centuries. The ride out is really nice. Though the best preserved of all the temples, all that's left of the Bajang Ratu compound is a doorway and a bit of the outer walls. Glowering *kala*-heads on all four sides add veracity to the curse thought to linger over the ancient doorway: it's said that anyone who walks through it will never marry.

Five hundred meters southeast of Bajang Ratu is **Candi Tikus,** wistfully named the Mouse Temple by present-day farmers wishing to rid themselves of field mice. Candi Tikus was once a splendid bathing place with terraces, turrets, and spouts along the walls of the now-dry basin.

Two km south of the museum is the cemetery of **Makam Troloyo,** containing possibly the oldest Muslim grave on Java, dating from 1376. Though members of the royal family buried here had already become Muslims, some of their graves are decorated with the six-point Sun of Majapahit. Another grave contains a Champa princess from Cambodia, who died in 1448.

Getting Away
To get back to Surabaya or Mojokerto, just flag down a returning bus or hitchhike. To Malang, take the road via Jombang and Batu, a nicer route than via Mojokerto and Surabaya. Another beautiful sylvan road leads from Trowulan to Pacet, then through to Tretes.

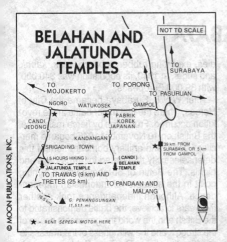

BELAHAN AND JALATUNDA TEMPLES

NOT TO SCALE

TO SURABAYA

TO MOJOKERTO

TO PORONG

TO PASURUAN

NGORO   WATUKOSEK   GAMPOL

CANDI JEDONG

PABRIK KOREK JAPANAN

KANDANGAN

SRIGADING TOWN

(5 HOURS HIKING)

(CANDI) BELAHAN TEMPLE

39 km FROM SURABAYA, OR 5 km FROM GAMPOL

JALATUNDA TEMPLE

TO TRAWAS (9 km) AND TRETES (25 km)

TO PANDAAN AND MALANG

(9.5 km)   G. PENANGGUNGAN (1,511 m)

★ = RENT *SEPEDA MOTOR* HERE

© MOON PUBLICATIONS, INC.

GUNUNG PENANGGUNGAN

A revered nine-peaked mountain 35 km southeast of Mojokerto, Penanggungan is shaped like India's mythical Mt. Meru. In 1935, 81 monuments, sacred bathing places, meditation grottos, and ruined sanctuaries were discovered under dense jungle grass and rainforests covering Gunung Penanggungan's northern and western slopes. These ruins, dating from A.D. 977-1511, encompass many different and peculiar East Javanese styles. Most are still in excellent condition; the *juru kunci* at Jalatunda will guide you to some of the more accessible sites.

Getting There
The closest place to stay is in Pandaan. Alternately, stay at Mojokerto and do the whole outing in a day. The easiest way to the two most important temples from Watukosek or Ngoro is by rented motorcycle.

Jalatunda is easily reached on a paved road (watch for small signs), but Belahan is almost completely inaccessible without a jeep. The road is horrendously steep and rocky—only for the completely crazy temple nut. Obviously, these temples get very few tourists.

Belahan
This bathing place, dating from A.D. 1049 and still in use, lies in a quiet clearing in the jungle on the west side of Gunung Penanggungan. This could be King Airlangga's burial monument. There are two four-armed spout figures of the goddesses Lakshmi and Shri, Vishnu's wives. The locals consider the water trickling from their nipples to be nectar of the gods.

Jalatunda
Four km higher than Belahan on a paved steep road. Built at the end of the 10th century, Jalatunda might be East Java's oldest *candi*. Relief panels depict simple tales with evocative, thin-limbed females and dancing males. Sleep under the *pendopo* with Javanese-Hindu pilgrims who've come to meditate and light incense. It's 14 km from Ngoro to Jalatunda via the village of Jedong. Alternatively, Jalatunda is a nine-km walk from Trawas. The site was restored in 1994.

Other Sights
On the northern slopes of Gunung Penanggungan is the gateway of **Candi Jedong,** dating from 1385, which resembles the facade of a temple. **Candi Gunung Gangsir,** or Candi Bankal, is nine km west of Gampol, then a 1.5-km walk north off the highway through villages and sugarcane fields; see the small sign on the highway between Gampol and Bangil. Built entirely of bricks in the Hindu style during the Singosari dynasty, the walls of the *candi* contain superlative reliefs from the Ramayana of monkeys, messengers, and birds. Bring a flashlight to make out reliefs on the ceiling.

SURABAYA

The melodious name belies the city's true nature—hot, dirty, and noisy, an industrial hub on Java's swampy northeast coast. This is East Java's biggest metropolis as well as its provincial capital. Extending over 300 square km and supporting a population of 3.6 million, Surabaya is the country's second-largest city, a modern center for manufacturing, agriculture, and trade, its bustle and din in sharp contrast to the serene agrarian countryside around it.

Travelers use Surabaya as a stopover between Bali and Yogyakarta or Jakarta, or as a place to hang around while waiting for a ship or a plane. The pace here is less frantic than in Jakarta and it's generally cheaper. The city has broad, busy streets, red-tiled houses with neat little gardens, a six-lane boulevard, horrendous traffic jams, quiet cul-de-sacs, technical universities and religious schools, thriving nightclubs, 40 cinemas, bowling and billiards centers, four railway stations, a splendid zoo, and multistory shopping complexes with speed lifts and freezing air-conditioning.

The city is the main base for the Indonesian navy; for hundreds of years it's been one of Indonesia's most important ports, its facilities second only to Jakarta's. This is also an active center for theater and East Javanese dance forms such as the mesmerizing horse trance dance, *kuda kepang*. Surabaya is also the last Indonesian city to display its historical lineage in great fashion—vast neighborhoods of Dutch colonial architecture, weedy graveyards, Islamic enclaves, messy Chinatowns. Despite its rough reputation, Surabaya deserves a second look.

History

Allegedly founded at the site of a legendary battle between a shark (*sura*) and a crocodile (*buaya*), Surabaya has served as East Java's commercial center and chief harbor since the fall of the Majapahit Kingdom. Formerly, it consisted of islands and swamps; King Wijaya battled Kublai Khan here in 1293. In the 16th century, the inhabitants converted to Islam and fought long and bitterly against the onslaught of the Mataram armies. Surabaya became the largest and most important seaport in the Dutch East Indies, exporting rubber, tobacco, teak, *kapok*, and sugar. In 1940, its population was 340,000, with 39,000 Europeans.

After WW II, Surabaya became the City of Heroes, where the first major battle in the revolution occurred. Frustrated by fierce resistance, the British on 10 November 1945 began a merciless aerial and artillery bombardment of this defenseless city that lasted for three days and nights. The Battle of Surabaya was a turning point in the struggle for Indonesian independence. Although independence took another five years to achieve, the battle demonstrated to the British and the world the grassroots nature of the struggle and the willingness of the masses to sacrifice their lives. The Tugu Pahlawan monument in the main city square commemorates the intense resistance against the Dutch and their allies.

During the political upheavals of 1965-66 there were numerous street executions. Bodies clogged the water under bridges, and Surabaya's canals ran red for months. Outside the city near the airport thousands of "communists" were massacred by villagers cranked on *jihad*. The captives were led to believe they were being driven to the airport for deportation and were murdered along the way.

SIGHTS

Historical Sights

In the heart of the hotel district is the Buddhist stone statue, **Joko Dolog** ("Fat Boy"), a remnant of the Singosari dynasty. Joko Dolog depicts the great King Kartanegara seated on a pedestal, inscribed 1289. The statue was transferred to this spot from its site near Malang by the Dutch about 300 years ago. This magic place lies in Taman Apsari, behind Suryo Monument. Bring flowers and a few *rupiah*. On Jl. Pahlawan Surabaya is the towering **Heroes' Monument** (Tugu Pahlawan), which commemorates the victims of the terrible bombing of November 1945.

The **Rakhmat** and **Sunan Bungkul** mosques, built in 1836, are Surabaya's oldest and contain

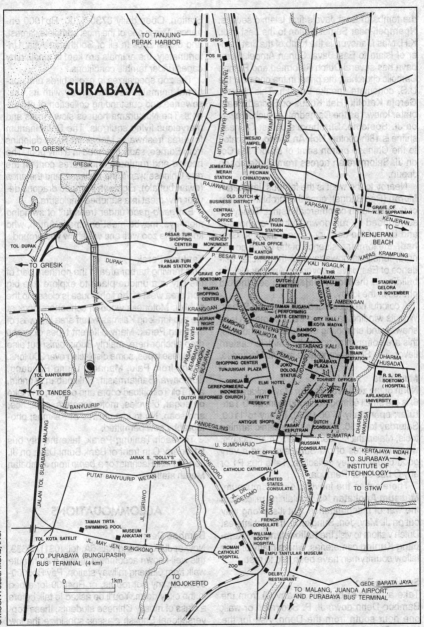

SURABAYA

TO TANJUNG PERAK HARBOR — BUGIS SHIPS
POS III

TANJUNG PERAK BARAT — TIMUR

TO GRESIK →

GRESIK

NYAMPLUNGAN

PEGIRIAN

MESJID AMPEL

KAMPUNG PECINAN (CHINATOWN)

JEMBATAN MERAH STATION

RAJAWALI

INDERAPURA

OLD DUTCH BUSINESS DISTRICT ★

KOTA TRAIN STATION

KAPASAN

KAPASARI

GRAVE OF W. R. SUPRATMAN

CENTRAL POST OFFICE

TOL DUPAK

PASAR TURI SHOPPING CENTER

HEROES' MONUMENT

P. BESAR W.

PELNI OFFICE

KANTOR GUBERNUR

KENJERAN
TO KENJERAN BEACH

← TO GRESIK

DUPAK

PASAR TURI TRAIN STATION

KAPAS KRAMPUNG

KALI NGAGLIK

SEE "DOWNTOWN CENTRAL SURABAYA" MAP

GRAVE OF DR. SOETOMO

KRANGGAN

WIJAYA SHOPPING CENTER

DUTCH CEMETERY

THR SURABAYA MALL

KUSUMA BANGSA

STADIUM GELORA 10 NOVEMBER

TAMAN BUDAYA (PERFORMING ARTS CENTER)

GARUDA

EMBONG MALANG

GENTENG WALIKOTA

CITY HALL / KOTA MADYA

AMBENGAN

BLAURAN NIGHT MARKET

ARJUNA RAYA

KEMBANG KEDUNGDORO

BLAURAN

BAMBOO DENN

KETABANG KALI

GUBENG TRAIN STATION

DHARMA HUSADA

TOL BANYUURIP

TUNJUNGAN SHOPPING CENTER
TUNJUNGAN PLAZA

PEMUDA

JOKO DOLOG STATUE

SURABAYA PLAZA

TOURIST OFFICES

R. S. DR. SOETOMO (HOSPITAL)

← TO TANDES

BANYUURIP

JL. BANYUURIP

GEREJA GEREFORMEERD INDONESIA (DUTCH REFORMED CHURCH)

ELMI HOTEL

HYATT REGENCY

JL. PANGLIMA SUDIRMAN

JL. RAYA GUBENG

FLOWER MARKET

DHARMA WANGSA

AIRLANGGA UNIVERSITY

ANTIQUE SHOPS

PASAR KEPUTRAN

DUTCH CONSULATE

JL. SUMATRA

PANDEGILING

U. SUMOHARJO

POST OFFICE

RUSSIAN CONSULATE

JL. KERTAJAYA INDAH
TO SURABAYA INSTITUTE OF TECHNOLOGY

JARAK S. "DOLLY'S" DISTRICTS

DIPONEGORO

CATHOLIC CATHEDRAL

KALIMAS RIVER

TO STKW

PUTAT BANYUURIP WETAN

JALAN TOL SURABAYA - MALANG

JL. GIRIAYO

UNITED STATES CONSULATE

JL. DR. SOETOMO

FRENCH CONSULATE

RAYA DARMO

TOL KOTA SATELIT

TAMAN TIRTA SWIMMING POOL

MUSEUM ANKATAN '45

JL. MAY. JEN. SUNGKONO

WILLIAM BOOTH HOSPITAL

TO PURABAYA (BUNGURASIH) BUS TERMINAL (4 km)

ROMAN CATHOLIC HOSPITAL

EMPU TANTULAR MUSEUM

ZOO

DELBY RESTAURANT

0   1km

GEDE BARATA JAYA

TO MOJOKERTO

TO MALANG, JUANDA AIRPORT, AND PURABAYA BUS TERMINAL

© MOON PUBLICATIONS, INC.

MOON

the tombs of East Java's first Islamic settlers. **Ngampel,** near Semut station to the east of Jl. K.H. Mas Mansyur, is the tomb of the first carrier of Islam to East Java, Sunan Ampel. Surabaya has several Dutch Reformed and Roman Catholic churches; the priest in the one near the U.S. consulate speaks English. This church, **Gereja Katolik** (Hati Kudus or Sacred Heart, better known as the Cathedral), is tucked away on Jl. Soetomo. Surabaya's oldest Chinese shrine is 18th-century **Hok An Kiong,** dedicated to the Chinese patron saint of sailors Ma Co, on Jl. Selompretan across from Jl. Kembang Jepun.

Nearby to the west is the famous **Jembatan Merah** (Red Bridge), once the throbbing center of the old Dutch commercial district. Today it's surrounded by run-down Dutch warehouses and turn-of-the-century office buildings. **Grahadi,** the former residence of the Dutch governors, functions nowadays as the official residence of East Java's governor. Another historic building is the **Hotel Majapahit**; see the old photos in the lobby.

A colorful neighborhood is **Kampung Sasak.** With its winding narrow streets, women in lace shawls, and crumbling old Dutch warehouses, this area offers a good dash of Middle Eastern flavor. The Simolawang area is 75% Madurese.

Museums

North of the zoo, at Jl. Taman Mayangkara Mpu 6, is the small ethnographic museum **MPU Tantular;** open daily 0700-0200, Friday to 1100, Saturday to 1230. It houses mesolithic farming tools, Majapahit statuary, Koranic manuscripts, *wayang,* photos of old Surabaya, and a very good paper money collection. Take bus P1 or any C bus on Jl. Pemuda.

There's also the inevitable army museum, **Museum Angkatan '45,** containing relics from the war of independence, but it's a long way out on Jl. May. Jen. Sungkono. It might interest Dutch visitors to visit the **Kalibanteng** and **Kembang Kuning** cemeteries, where many of their fellow countrymen have been laid to rest.

Surabaya Zoo

Take a *bemo* or bus (P1 or any C) from the Bamboo Denn down Jl. P. Sudirman or walk one hour south from the Denn. Ask for the Kebun Binatang; it's just north of Joyoboyo Bus Station. Open daily 0730-1700; Rp1000 entrance. This is one of the most complete, largest, and oldest zoos in all of Southeast Asia. Unfortunately, the animals are kept in small, dirty cages under terrible conditions.

The zoo specializes in exotic birds and nocturnal animals. See the aviary with its cassowaries and outstanding collection of pheasants. The Nocturama houses slow lorries and marvelous flying squirrels. The Dolphinarium features freshwater Mahakam River dolphins from Borneo, sadly cramped in a tiny pool. The hoofed and ruminant enclosures contain the rare Chinese *wapiti,* the *babirusa,* and the *anoa* (dwarf buffalo). Eighteen Komodo dragons devour raw meat in a sandbed enclosure.

Eat *gado-gado* under trees full of swinging monkeys; maybe meet enigmatic Anton, who knows the zoo well and will show you around.

Tanjung Perak

This thriving harbor area in the northern part of the city is a unique place to explore (the big port area west of the lighthouse is closed to the public). Motorless wooden schooners dock at the two-km-long Kalimas wharf area just west of Tanjung Perak. Many different types of *prahu* drop anchor here, mainly Bugis *pinisi* but also Madurese types, some displacing over 200 tons. *Prahu* from Palu, Manado, Ujung Pandang, Sumbawa, Banjarmasin, Balikpapan, Kendiri, and Toli Toli offload copra and pepper, and take on sugar, bicycles, motorscooters, cars, rice, and soap. No tourist crowds at Kalimas; photography now permitted.

To reach Tanjung Perak, take the city bus P1 or any C in front of Bank Bumi Daya on Jl. Jen. Basuki Rachmat or a *bemo* from Jembatan Merah station.

ACCOMMODATIONS

Bamboo Denn

Now at Jl. Ketabang Kali 6A, tel. (031) 40333, this well-known accommodation is a 20-minute walk from Gubeng railway station. Pay Rp5000-9000 for tiny hot rooms, or Rp4000 for a bed in the okay dorm. You'll be asked to talk before a class of mostly Chinese students; these conversational English classes subsidize the low cost of the rooms. Perhaps a convenient place to stay for those overnighting in Surabaya on their way to Yogyakarta, Jakarta, or Bali. Dismal, but definitely cheap. Public transport, travel agent, and public telephone nearby. The Bamboo Denn also runs a very similar and very useful language school/dormitory setup in Malang, 60 km south.

Gubeng Station Area
If the Bamboo Denn is full (unlikely), try **Hotel Gubeng**, Jl. Sumatra 18; Rp18,000. Nothing special and a positively hostile owner. Come out of the station and turn left, then walk down the road about 300 meters; look for the white sign. **Hotel Kayoon**, Jl. Kayoon 5, tel. (031) 63522, wants Rp8000 for very basic rooms; an old and scuzzy hotel.

About an eight-minute *becak* ride from Gubeng station is Jl. Embong Kenongo, with a wide variety of accommodations from Rp15,000-36,000. It's quiet and the good value, restful open-air nighttime eatery **Pasar Kayoon** is just down the street. **Hotel Santosa**, no. 40, tel. 43306, rents rooms for Rp10,000-15,000. The front row of rooms, facing a small garden, is best—tolerably clean, and not a bad deal for a major city. Communal *mandi*. Family-run **Bina Dirga Angkasa**, no. 52, tel. 42687, charges Rp12,000 for the cheapest rooms; it's very secure and has a travel agent in front. The **Pavilyun**, an old centrally located Dutch-style hotel at Jl. Genteng Besar 98, asks Rp14,000—the best budget alternative to the Bamboo Denn.

The **Remaja Hotel**, Jl. Embong Kenongo 12, tel. 41359, fax 510-009, is in the Rp55,000-65,000 range plus 21% tax and service—a small, efficient businessperson's hotel, with a/c and mice. Another midmarket choice is the **Wisma Mawarani**, tel. 44839, fax 45435, with high-ceilinged rooms with a/c for Rp55,000-75,000—a good alternative to the Remaja.

If you want to be right in the middle of it, the **Olympic Hotel**, Jl. Urip Sumoharjo 65, tel. 43216, is the place—Rp12,000-26,000. Located on a busy extension of Jl. P. Sudirman, this old hotel couldn't be more central. *Bemo* stop just 50 meters south, Nitour and Garuda offices are close by, and you can eat at nearby Wiena Restaurant.

Hotel Stasiun, Jl. Stasiun Kota 1, is right down the street from Stasiun Semut. This inexpensive, secure hotel is located in a lively neighborhood with good bus connections. The **Merdeka I**, Jl. Bongkaran 6 (near Kota station), has rooms for Rp8500-12,000.

Kampung Sasak
A number of cheap hotels lie along Jl. K.H.M. Mansyur in the middle of the orthodox Arab Quarter (Kampung Sasak), a busy warehouse and market neighborhood. Try **Hotel Indah** (no. 86), but avoid the rather decrepit Hotel Islam. Although Hotel Kemajuan is very cheap, it's a fleabag. The best deal in Kampung Sasak is on the other side of the Kalimas canal: **Hotel Kalimantan**, Jl. Pegirian 202-A, charges Rp9000 non a/c, Rp13,000 a/c. It's secure and has a garden, travel agency, and restaurant in front that gives room service. Next door, at Jl. Pegirian 202, tel. (031) 311-846, is **Penginapan Gajah Mada**; Rp4000-5000 rooms but no a/c. Both these hotels are within walking distance of Jembatan Merah, the historic Mesjid Sunan Ampel; the Kalimas wharf area is only two km away.

Luxury
Most are in the business/entertainment district, and charge Rp69,000-140,000. The **Majapahit**, Jl. Tunjungan 65, tel. (031) 69501, with a/c, balcony, refrigerator, bar, and restaurant, is a fully equipped and historic hotel. It was here in 1945 that the Dutch flag was ripped down and the Indonesian flag raised in its place, an incident that helped precipitate the Battle of Surabaya.

Mirama Hotel, Jl. Raya Darmo 68-72, tel. 69501, offers a/c rooms with TV and refrigerator, restaurant, and bar. **Garden Hotel**, centrally located at Jl. Pemuda 21, tel. 47000, has a/c, a swimming pool, a good Chinese restaurant, and a bar—one of the best values in this price range.

Try the plush **Ramayana**, Jl. Jen. Basuki Rakhmat 67-69, tel. 46321. Also in this category is the **New Grand Park**, Jl. Samudra 3-7, tel. 270-004, with a/c rooms in a downtown location. Eat at the excellent Kit Wan Kie seafood restaurant across the street. The **Elmi Hotel**, Jl. P. Sudirman 42-44, tel. 47157, and the **Simpang Hotel**, Jl. Pemuda 1-3, tel. 42219 or 42220-5, offer rooms in the Rp168,000-210,000 range.

The elegant four-star **Hyatt Regency**, Jl. Basuki Rakhmat 124-128, tel. 511-234, fax 521-508, with its beautiful decor and service, is one of Indonesia's best high-class hotels: Rp420,000-

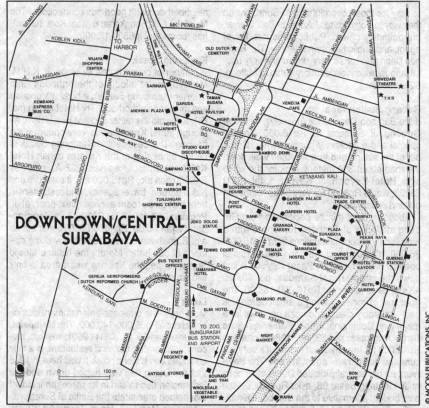

DOWNTOWN/CENTRAL SURABAYA

630,000. Features video movies, health club, business center, and nightclub. The **Garden Palace Hotel,** the city's newest international-class hotel on Jl. Yos Sudarso 11, tel. 479251, has spacious a/c rooms with video, bar, TV, pub, ballroom, 24-hour coffee shop and restaurant.

FOOD

Night Markets And *Warung*

Pasar Kayoon, right along the banks of the scenic Kalimas on Jl. Kayoon, is a superb night market with scores of open-air foodstalls. Open 0900-2300, it's a very cheap, picturesque, and convenient place to eat. Nearby, in front of Gubeng station, stalls also offer inexpensive night meals.

On the side streets near the THR, vendors sell tasty snacks such as *terang bulan* (full moon)—hot pancakes with chocolate, peanuts, and sweetened milk. At night exit the THR and turn left, walk about 500 meters, and locate the *martabak* stands. On Jl. Tegalsari, about 100 meters up on the righthand side, is a pretty good *soto madura asli, soto ayam* open-air restaurant, Chinese wok place, and coffee and drink vendors. For *soto madura,* head for the *warung* at Stasiun Gubeng and the THR Complex.

An excellent night market is located just five minutes from the Bamboo Denn on Jl. W. Kota Mustajab.

Indonesian

Restoran Aquarius at the zoo is surprisingly good. Also check out **Wiena** on Jl. Urip Sumoharjo, and the **Beringin Jaya** on Jl. Darmo. Excellent Indonesian food is served at the **Tirta Indah Garden**, Jl. Mayjen Sungkono 47-A. For Padang food try **Sari Bundo** on Jl. Walikota, or **Antika**, Jl. Raya Darmo 1.

Sample East Javanese regional specialties such as *kilkil* (a hearty soup made from the hooves of goats and cows) in **Kombes Duryat** behind Bioskop Ria and at **Pasar Blauran Baru** near Wijaya Shopping Center.

East Java is also famous for its *krupuk*; buy kilos wholesale in the Sidoarjo District, the number one *krupuk* center in Java. In Pasar Genteng, or on Jl. P. Sudirman near Hotel Tanjung, myriad kinds of *krupuk* are offered for sale. Indonesians who pass through Surabaya always stock up on *krupuk* and *bandeng* (a smoked river fish).

At **Soto Ambengan** on Jl. Ambengan try *soto madura* (Madura-style soup); *bakwan* (soup with pork balls and wonton); *semanggi* (small boiled leaves eaten with peanut sauce); and *bumbu rujak* (chicken in chili sauce).

Downtown

Near the intersection of Jl. Pemuda and Jl. P. Sudirman are some good eating places. Take a left on Jl. P. Sudirman toward the city. The air-conditioned **Chez Rose**, at Jl. Raya Gubeng, has European, Japanese, and Chinese food as well as imported beef, great pastries, and homemade bread; get a good meal with drinks for two for Rp21,000. Next door is cheaper **Depot Banyuwangi** for *nasi pecel* and *nasi tumpeng*. Air-conditioned **Panglima Sudirman**, serving good big portions of Chinese food for reasonable prices, is still crowded most evenings.

The **Taman Sari Indah**, Jl. Taman Apsari 5, is next to the main post office. The **Bamboo Denn** offers seafood and Chinese food. For dessert, **Cafeteria Michiko**, Jl. P. Sudirman 10 nearly opposite the Surabaya Post Bldg., sells delicious yogurt/fruit/ice drinks—quite thick, the real thing. The food is good too.

Chinese

Kit Wan Kie, Jl. Kembang Jepun 51, offers superb Cantonese cuisine. **Agung**, Jl. Baliwerti 1, is famous for its fried pigeon and other delicacies. The **Oriental**, Jl. A.I.S. Nasution 37, has great but expensive seafood; the lobster is especially tasty. **Bima Garden**, Jl. Pahwalan 8 next to the Surabaya Movie Theater, is noticeably cheaper than the Kit Wan Kie and nearly as good.

Other Chinese restaurants along Jl. Pasar Besar are even more reasonably priced. **Elmi Restaurant**, Jl. Samudra 37, tel. (031) 333-004, has excellent food at moderate prices, with live music most evenings. For a cheap Chinese meal, try Jl. Kembang Jepun, sampling the food at small stalls along the side streets (open only in the evening). Also check out the restaurants in Tanjung Plaza.

Miscellaneous

Tired of *nasi*? The Hyatt Regency's **Hugo's Restaurant** charges Rp15,000 for a European meal. At **Yakiniki** in the Surabaya Delta Plaza (Jl. Pemuda) serve yourself all the Japanese barbecue you can eat for Rp7500. High marks—and high prices—for steaks and Japanese food at the **Gandy Steak House and Bakery**, Jl. Sumatra 51. Other steakhouses include: **Bon Cafe Steak House**, Jl. Raya Gubeng 44; **Venecia Cafe**, Jl. Ambengan 16; and **Max's Pub**, Jl. Nasution 27. For fried chicken try **Ayam Goreng Pemuda**, Jl. Pemuda, near Jl. P. Sudirman.

Sweets And Drinks

The best ice cream and other goodies in Surabaya are at **Hoenkwe's**, Jl. Tunjungan 98, laid out in full Dutch colonial splendor. **Zangrandi Ice Cream Parlor** on Jl. Yos Sudarso near Jl. Pemuda serves high-quality Italian ice cream. Another good spot is **Puri Ice Cream**, Jl. Embong Trengguli, one street over from Jl. Pemuda. The **Granada Modern Bakery** sells Danish pastry, donuts, small cakes, and pies. Surabaya also offers fantastic deep-fried treats like puffy *cemblem* (jam donuts) as well as biscuits.

The oldest *jamu* shop in East Java is on Jl. Kedung Doro; hand-beaten fresh drinks served in coconut cups. Lemon drinks like *es limon* and *es juruk* are a real luxury item in drier East Java, fetching prices as high as Rp1000.

Shopping Centers

Overheated visitors can cool off inside the city's major shopping centers. **Surabaya Plaza** features a discount food bazaar on the fourth floor, a **McDonald's** on the ground floor (see the bizarre Balinese entrance on the east side), **Kentucky Fried Chicken**, and a **Dunkin Donuts**. Similiar fast food selections in the **Tunjungan Plaza** on Jl. Basuki Rakhmat.

ENTERTAINMENT

THR (Surabaya Mall)

On Jl. Kusuma Bangsa, north of Gubeng train station. For purely mindless entertainment, this is one of the best Taman Hiburan Rakyat parks in Indonesia. Open daily 1800-2400, and not all that crowded.

There are actually two parks here: the one on the left as you're facing the main entrance is the THR park, while the one to your right is the children's amusement park, Taman Remaja. Both are open throughout the year. THR features souvenir stands, clothes boutiques, cassette stores, movie theaters, band amphitheater, small train, and Ferris wheels and other carnival rides. Directly to your right inside the entrance are various *warung*; deeper in are ice cream shops, small, fine restaurants, and numerous foodstalls. THR is also a venue for folk performances: *sri mulat* (Javanese comic drama), *ludruk,* and regular performances of *wayang wong* and other open-stage dramas, sometimes featuring live *kroncong* pop bands. Local dancing on Thursday 2000-2300, live rock music on Saturday (same times), and *srimulat* twice monthly.

Taman Remaja is a sort of Indonesian Disneyland; Space cars floating amongst trees, spooks in the ghost house, merry-go-rounds, popcorn, American fried chicken stands. Notice in the bumper car arena that polite Javanese children seldom intentionally collide with one another as do kids in the West.

Taman Budaya

In the mornings you can watch students at this Performing Arts Center rehearsing dances like *negremo* and *gandrung*. Located at Jl. Gedengkali 85, it's only Rp500 by *becak* from the Jl. Pemuda tourist office. Also bamboo *kolintang* music rehearsals, *ketoprak,* classes in Javanese singing accompanied by *gamelan,* as well as *janur* (young coconut leaf arrangement), Chinese historical dramas, and old Javanese legends like *Aryopenangsang* and *Angreni Larung*. Tickets run Rp1000-Rp2500. Shows last until 2400. Lots of snack carts outside.

Surabaya's leading institute for the study of traditional dance and music is the **Sekolah Tinggi Karawitan** (STKW) in southeastern Surabaya.

Discos

Discos are a good place to meet young Indonesians. Most venues have a cover charge that may include a drink. Try **Studio East,** Jl. Simpang Dukuh; **Top Ten,** Tanjungan Plaza; **Juliana's Club,** Hyatt Regency, Jl. Basuki Rakhmat; **Atum,** Pasar Atum Shopping Center; and **Blue Sixteen,** Jl. Pemuda. Most discos charge a Rp10,000 cover and Rp6000 per beer.

Red Lights

The Jarak and Bangunrejo red-light districts are world renowned. Take a taxi (Rp5000), *becak* (Rp3000), or W bemo from Jl. Pemuda. Jarak presents row upon row of gaudy little dollhouse shanties, where 15,000 women work and live. Lanterns are strung out in the night; muddy streets are clogged with *becak*; lines of gas-lit carts sell antibiotics; groups of men, hustlers, beggars, minstrel groups, and *ronggeng* (street dancers who sing and dance for small change) rove the streets.

Tandes is another entertainment district; take a *becak* all the way from the Bamboo Denn to Tandes to avoid the aggravation from the Jembatan Merah *becak* drivers. A fascinating ride through market and canal areas that never sleep.

Transvestites (*waria*) haunt Jl. Irian Barat on the other side of the river. Said to be the only government-approved pickup spot in the country.

Other

Pemandian Taman Tirta, an olympic-sized, crowded (except at noontime) public swimming pool, lies on Jl. May. Jen. Sungkono next to the TV tower. Another swimming pool is behind the mammoth Surabaya Plaza (Rp3000). Also check out the movie theaters: **Mitro,** Jl. Pemuda; **Delta,** in the Surabaya Delta Plaza; **Studio,** in Tunjungan Plaza; and **Golden** at the THR/Surabaya Mall. Some of the Chinese restaurants, such as the Bima Garden, feature bands.

The **Chez Rose,** Jl. P. Sudirman 12, is a traditional place to meet foreigners. Expats also hang out at the **Hyatt Regency.** For tennis or squash go down to the **Tennis Club** behind the Ramayana Hotel and play for Rp2000 per game (nonmembers fee). Tennis courts are heavily booked. Take in some **karaoke** at the Diamond Ace on Jl. P. Sudirman.

Events
The anniversary of the city's founding is celebrated in May. The birthday of Mohammad, Maulud Nabi, is commemorated in weeklong traditional ceremonies, carnivals, and mask festivals in the streets of Surabaya. The final nights of Ramadan are wonderful in Surabaya, with huge crowds in the street and much excitement in the air. Ask the tourist office for exact dates for all events. The Chinese temple, **Hong Tik Hian,** just south of the holy tomb of Ngampel at Jl. Dukuh II/2, is the site of daily *potehi* performances.

During the dry season (May-Oct.), a dance festival is held on the first and second Saturdays of each month at **Candrawilwatikta,** a large, open-air theater an hour (40 km) south of Surabaya.

SHOPPING

Textiles
Surabaya is not known as a source for original *batik*; Gresik, Sidoarjo, Madura, and other coastal towns have always produced *batik* for the Surabaya market. The city *is* known, however, for its Chinese and Javanese tailors, who'll cut you a pair of made-to-measure trousers in an hour or so for only Rp15,000. Visit the "Street of a Thousand Tailors," Jl. Embong Malang; *becak* drivers know the location.

You'll find **Batik Semar** at Jl. Raya Gubeng 41 at Toko Metro; **Batik Keris** in Toko Sarinah at Jl. Tunjungan 7; and **Rumah Batik Danar Hadi** at Jl. Pemuda 1 near the Simpang Hotel. Besides these big chains, Indonesian fabrics and *batik*, as well as fine jewelry and Javanese artifacts, are displayed at **PT Santi Art Shop,** Jl. Sumatera 52, and **Mirota,** Jl. Sulawesi 24. **Pasar Tunjungan Surya** on Jl. Tunjungan is the place to go for East Javanese handicrafts. The government runs a showroom, **Dinas Perindustrian Jatim,** at Jl. Kedungdoro 86-90; reasonable prices. There are crafts exhibits at least once a month at the **Balai Pemuda** near Mitro Cinema; stalls represent nearly every district of East Java. The **GKBI** *batik* cooperative at Jl. Kranggan 102

is also worth a visit. Some outstanding Indian textile shops lie along Jl. Panggung and Jl. Sasak in the Arab Quarter around Mesjid Ampel.

Antiques
A whole row of small antique and curio shops lies near the Hyatt on Jl. Basuki Rakhmat and along Jl. Urip Sumoharjo. On Jl. Raya Darmo you'll find **Rokhim** (no. 27) and **Whisnu** (no. 68-74). If you know what you're looking for and know how to bargain, you'll find some good buys. Good hunting also along Jl. Tunjungan; try **Sarinah** (no. 7) for paintings, silver, and brasswork; and **Kundandas** (no. 97, tel. 43927), for statues, embroidery, and shell handicrafts. The **Bali Art Shop,** Jl. Basuki Rakhmat 143, tel. 45933, opposite the Hyatt, offers a large selection of Chinese porcelain and uncut agate. **Rais Art Shop,** at no. 16 on the same street, near the Hyatt Regency, features other unique antiques.

Shopping Centers
Tunjungan Plaza, the city's premier shopping center, is Surabaya's Ginza. Walk down the main street, Jl. Tunjungan, an extension of Jl. Basuki Rakhmat, and follow the bright lights. This pretty, colorful area that doesn't shut down until around 2100. An area especially strong on consumer goods such as cameras, sound systems, cassette recorders, and other electronic gadgets.

Also in the Tunjungan district, check out the **Wijaya, Siola, Romano,** and **Aurora** shopping centers and the big art shop **Sarinah.** Surabaya's newest shopping center is the mammoth **Surabaya Plaza,** as extravagant as anything you'll find in Dallas or Singapore. Giant, ice-cold a/c blowers, escalators, marble floors, shops selling gold jewelry for Rp600,000. Strategically located right in front of the Jl. Pemuda tourist office.

Goldsmiths
Dozens of goldsmiths are located on Jl. Baluran; take the street between Jl. Tunjungan and Bank Bumi Daya. Jewelry sellers are found on the first floor of the Wijaya Shopping Center, on Jl. Kapasan, and in *kampung* Gipo and Nyamplungan.

Markets
A black market behind the zoo sells shoes, jeans, T-shirts, and other cheap goods. **Pasar Keputran,** Surabaya's main night market, livens

up around 1900 and is positively chaotic by 2300. The walk to Pasar Keputran is very enjoyable: proceed to the main junction of Jl. Pemuda and Jl. Kayoon and walk one km south. Another big market is **Pasar Pabean,** a dirty, sprawling spot in Chinatown. Worth a visit for the color and clamor and bustle.

Kayoon Flower Market, along Jl. Kayoon on the banks of Kalimas River, is a park for strollers and lovers. The market sprouted spontaneously after flower hawkers were thrown off public roads in 1960. Here you'll find a variety of tropical shrubs and trees, as well as fresh- and saltwater fish for home aquariums. South of the flower stalls is an active open-air food market. Another flower and bird market is located near Terminal Bratang on Jl. Barat Jaya.

SERVICES

The **central post office,** Jl. Kebon Rojo next to Tugu Pahlawan, is open weekdays 0800-1600, Saturday 0800-1230; several telex booths for rent. A more convenient branch is located on Jl. Pemuda, just before the Joko Dolok statue. All packages must be inspected, so leave the contents visible.

The **telephone office** (*kantor telpon*) in Tunjungan Plaza offers direct dialing to key cities in Indonesia and the world. *Kantor imigrasi,* Jl. Achmad Yani (seven km south of downtown), is open Mon.-Thurs. 0800-1400, Friday 0830-1030, Saturday 0800-1200.

The Surabaya telephone city code is 031.

Information
The **East Java Regional Tourist Information Office** (Kantor Penerangan Pariwisata), Jl. Pemuda 118, tel. (031) 472-503, is very helpful; get maps and brochures, and ask for the booklet *Events of East Java.* Inquire after the Madura bull races. Check out the huge *reyog* mask from Ponorogo in this office, open daily 0800-1600, Friday until 1100, closed Sunday.

Read books, magazines, and newspapers at **Perhimpunan Persahabatan Indonesia-Amerika,** a small lending library at Jl. Dr. Sutomo 110. Lectures and films sometimes occur here. Open Mon.-Fri. 0800-1300 and 1600-2000, Saturday 0800-1200.

The **U.S. consulate** is at Jl. Sutomo 33, tel. 67545 or 68037. The **U.K. consulate** is at Jl. Sutomo 46, tel. 66773, near Marmoyo petrol station. You'll find the **Dutch consulate** at Jl. Sumatra 79, tel. 45202. **Goethe Institute,** the German Cultural Center, faces the Bambu Runcing Monument. **Public libraries** are located at Jl. W. Kota Mustajab 68, tel. 42707, Jl. Pemuda 15, and Airlangga University. Major booksellers include **Toko Buku Sari Agung,** Jl. Tunjungan 5; and **Gramedia,** Jl. Basuki Rakhmat 95.

Health
At least six *jamu* shops occupy Jl. Kedungdoro; the old Chinese lady at no. 239 really knows her stuff. For shots or a new International Health Certificate, go to **Dr. Sutomo** (Karangmenjangan), Jl. Dharmahusada 6-9, or **Dinas Kesehatan Pelabuhan** (Health Department), Jl. Perak Timur 514-516.

William Booth Hospital is one of Indonesia's best, a reasonably priced outpatient clinic on Jl. Diponegoro, employing Western doctors and nurses. No emergency service, however.

GETTING THERE

Flying into the city, Gunung Semeru glows red as the brown Kalimas River snakes below. Tourist information booth and authorized moneychanger at Juanda airport. From Jakarta, Garuda flies a shuttle every two hours to Surabaya, Rp210,000 (one hour), no reservations required. It's almost as easy to fly to Surabaya from Sulawesi, Kalimantan, or Maluku, as Surabaya is a major air link for the eastern islands.

Surabaya's Juanda Airport is 15 km south of town and taxi drivers demand Rp10,000 to take you into the city. Alternatively, take a special bus marked Alloha-Juanda (Rp2500), then bus J to city center (Rp400). Or go directly to the Purabaya bus terminal and head east to Bromo and Bali.

The Gubeng train station is closest to the best hotels; the new station lies just across the tracks. The Bima and Mutiara a/c express trains leave Jakarta daily in the late afternoon for the 18-hour (Rp32,000-65,000 depending on class) trip to Surabaya. Make reservations at least two days in advance through **Carnation Tours,** Jl.

Menteng Raya 24, Jakarta, tel. (021) 344-027. From Yogyakarta, take the Ekspres Siang (Rp3800-5000, 6.5 hours), the Mutiara Selatan (Rp9000-13,500, six hours), or the Bima (Rp17,000 first class).

The 15-hour trip from Jakarta by a/c night bus costs Rp35,000; from Bali (10 hours) it costs Rp15,000; from Yogyakarta (eight hours) the fare is Rp12,000. These deluxe buses include reclining seats, cold drinks, and complimentary meals.

Surabaya is a one-day (800 km, 12 hours) drive from Jakarta; follow any of the well-marked routes via Yogyakarta or Semarang.

GETTING AROUND

Very good city transport system. The main street of Surabaya is Jl. Jen. Basuki Rakhmat/Jl. Tunjungan, which runs roughly north to south, changing its name every kilometer or so in order to honor as many of Indonesia's heroes as possible. Grisly car wrecks, along with warning signs, are on permanent display at major intersections.

Good *bemo* system with routes all over the city; Rp200 within city limits. The tourist office stocks a complete list of *bemo* itineraries. Learn which letters—A, B, K, M, V—will take you where. The two biggest *bemo* stations in Surabaya are at Wonokromo (near Joyoboyo) and at Jembatan Merah, both accessible by V *bemo* from Jl. Pemuda and M *bemo* from Jl. Kayoon.

Also cheap are the city buses that travel three main routes: north to Tanjung Perak, from Jl. Demak to Kutisari, and from Wonokromo to the Jembatan Merah station. Flat rate of Rp400.

Becak are about Rp400 per km. The blue ones (*becak siang*) are for daytime use; the white (*becak malam*) serve the night. Ask the drivers to wend their way around the back streets, often the most fascinating way to go. Indonesian life is seldom seen so close and so anonymously.

Metered taxis, charging about Rp400 per km, are available at stands, hotels, and the airport. There's also a taxi stand in front of the Weta Hotel and Andhika Plaza. Sample fares: Pelni office (Rp3000), Perak Harbor (Rp4000), Gubeng (Rp2000), Purabaya bus terminal (Rp8000), Juanda Airport (Rp10,000).

GETTING AWAY

By Air
Surabaya's airport is an important domestic air link to the whole eastern half of Indonesia and one of the country's busiest international airports and cargo terminals; it was expanded to welcome foreign visitors for "Visit Indonesia Year 1991." The airport lies 15 km south of the city, Rp10,500 by taxi; call **Taxi Cab Surya**, Jl. Kranggan 100, tel. (031) 471-340, or go to Gubeng station and hire a private car. The latter option is cheaper.

By Sea
Surabaya is a major port and at least 15 ships a day take passengers to virtually all Outer Island and international ports. Tramp the docks and check around the dozens of shipping offices in Surabaya; see what's going out. Inquire at the ticket agent **C.V. Usaha Bersama,** Jl. Pahlawan 7. **Dwidjaya,** Jl. Slompretan 31, sends ships to Balikpapan and Samarinda, Kalimantan. Also check the shipping news sections in the daily *Surabaya Post* and *Jawa Post*. Departure times are always changing. You might actually have better luck taking a smaller ship to Ujung Pandang or Kalimantan from Kaliangat on the eastern tip of Madura.

With Pelni's new line of ships, it's hardly worth shopping around the other companies for interisland travel. The office is at Jl. Pahlawan 20, tel. (031) 21042; from Jl. Pemuda take *bemo* M and get off by Tugu Pahlawan. Open Mon.-Fri. 0800-1200 and 1300-1600, Saturday 0800-1300. When the line is long, walk upstairs and ask for Mr. Riffai, the very helpful manager. In most cases you can go directly to the harbor and buy your ticket on the ship or at the nearby information counter.

Pelni runs modern, comfortable ships constantly circling the archipelago: Kalimantan every three days; Sulawesi every two days; Irian Jaya and Maluku every eight days. For Nusatenggara, use the Pelni ship KM *Kelimutu,* which departs Surabaya every other Tuesday at 1800 for Semarang (Rp28,400) and Banjarmasin (Rp23,000). Returning to Surabaya, it then leaves for Padangbai, East Bali (Rp16,700); Ujung Pandang (Rp21,000); Bima on Sumbawa (Rp24,000); Waingapu (Rp42,500); Ende (Rp47,800); and Kupang (Rp53,200).

Kalimas, just behind the Port Authority Building in Tanjung Perak, is the harbor for *kapal*

AIRLINE OFFICES IN SURABAYA

Garuda; Jl. Tunjungan 29; tel. 44082

Merpati; Jl. Urip Sumoharjo 68; tel. 40773, 470-568, or 45870

Mandala; Jl. Raya Diponegoro 49; tel. 66473

Bouraq; Jl. P. Sudirman 70-72; tel. 46428/42383

British Airways; Jl. P. Sudirman 70-72; tel. 470621, or 42383

Cathay Pacific Airways; Hotel Hyatt Bumi, Jl. Basuki Rakhmat; tel. 45052

Japan Airlines; Simpang Hotel, Jl. Pemuda 1; tel. 42151

KLM; Jl. Yos Sudarso 11; tel. 479-251

SAS; Hotel Bumi Hyatt, Jl. Basuki Rakhmat; tel. 40861

Thai Airways International; Jl. P. Sudirman 72; tel. 40861

---

layar and *kapal motor.* Although technically illegal, some managers of these Makassar schooners will take you to Kalimantan, Sulawesi, or the Malukus for reasonable fares. One of Indonesian's great adventures.

By Train

Surabaya has three train stations: Pasar Turi serves trains that run along Java's north coast, while Gubeng trains head south and southwest, and Semut trains go east. Gubeng is the most convenient station; purchase tickets two hours in advance. Schedules are posted in the lobby.

To Banyuwangi, trains depart at 0815 and 2200, arriving at 1720 and 0530, Rp2800-3500. The Mutiara Selatan departs for Bandung at 1730, the Ekspres Siang at 0515. To Jakarta, the Baybaru economy train departs at 1215, the Jayabaya business train at 1500, the Bima at 1600, and the Mutiara at 1630. The Katumapel departs Gubeng station for Malang six times daily; the GBM Utara departs for Semarang at 1745, arrives 2333. Seven daily runs to Yogyakarta; best are the Jayabaya at 1500, the Bima at 1600, and the Mutiara at 1745. Economy trains depart at 0540, 0830, 1215, and 1400.

To Denpasar the Mutiara Timor departs at 0815 and 2215 from Gubeng Station. It's a 370-km, 16-hour run to the Bali ferry terminal at Ke-

tapang. Train fares include ferry crossing and onward bus to Denpasar. The train is more comfortable than the grueling bus ride and is very possibly the only train in Indonesia that actually runs on time.

By Bus

Surabaya has two main bus terminals. All buses from Bali, East Java, and Central Java arrive at the new **Purabaya bus terminal,** 10 km south of city center. On arrival, walk past the shops for the local bus marked Perak to reach the downtown hotels. The other major bus terminal, called **Jembatan Merah,** is located in the old Dutch business district. Come here for buses to north coast cities.

Take bus P1 or C on Jl. Basuki Rakhmat to the Madura ferry terminal at Ujung Baru in the Tanjung Perak area, then the ferry over to Kamal on Madura. For Mt. Bromo it's Rp600 from Surabaya's Purabaya terminal to Pasuruan, then on to Tosari. A more popular approach is to take an early morning bus from Purabaya to the Bayuangga bus terminal, two km before the Bromo turnoff. You can also ask to be dropped directly at the Bromo turnoff, five km west of Probolinggo, then take the first *bemo* up the mountain. You don't need to go to Probolinggo, a truly hellish town.

Tours

Discover East Java with one of Surabaya's 38 official tour companies; contact the head office of the **East Java Department of Tourism** (Dinas Pariwisata), Jl. Darmokali 35, tel. (031) 65448 or 65449, for recommendations. **PT Aneka Kartika,** Jl. Stasiun Kota Pusat Perniagaan Semut Indah, Blok D-28, tel. 20981, offers a three-hour "Surabaya City Tour" for two for Rp24,000 pp, a 10-hour "Malang and Nearby Temples Tour" for two for Rp147,000 pp, and a five-hour "Madura Bull Races Tour" for two for Rp178,500 pp. **Vaya Tours,** Jl. P. Sudirman 11, is another possibility. Or try **Pacto Tours,** tel. 45776, in the Hyatt Regency Hotel.

For something really different, take a cruise on a customized traditional Bugis sailing vessel (*pinisi*) to Flores, Lombok, Kalimantan, or Maluku. **PT Wisata Bahari Indah,** Jl. Tanjung Priok 6, tel. 291-633 or 293-313, offers 16- to 35-day luxury *pinisi* cruises for Rp630,000-1.5 million.

VICINITY OF SURABAYA

On the city's hilly northern outskirts, huge factories loom everywhere. Over five million people live in the 30 square km area along the Brantas River. Besides Madura, there are other islands off Surabaya; tiny Bawean, north of Surabaya, is the only home of the very rare Bawean deer, a subspecies of the Indonesian *rusa*.

Beaches
Visit the beaches east of town, which are actually beach parks with small entrance fees. Packed with people; *prahu* pull right up on the beach to take you for rides. **Pantai Kenjeran,** an eight-km *bemo* ride from Jembatan Merah, is one such recreational beach. You can hire *alis-alis,* especially on Sundays. Not as scenic, white, or distant as **Pasir Putih,** but you can enjoy yourself. Or take the ferry over to Madura for closer beaches, such as **Camplong.** Reach

SURABAYA DISTRICT

Puger Beach on the south coast by minibus via Gumukmas for Rp2300.

Sidoarjo
This whole area 23 km south of Surabaya is known for its wide fishponds, mainly containing *bandeng* (milkfish). Sidoarjo is also known for its *batik kenongo* and fish and shrimp *krupuk petis* (congealed fish paste) processing. Every year in Sidoarjo's *alun-alun,* during birthday celebrations for the Prophet Mohammed, a *bandeng* as big as a baby goes on the block at public auction. One fish sometimes fetches as much as six million *rupiah.*

GRESIK

This old seaport, 25 km from Surabaya on the road to Semarang, was where the first Islamic traders from India landed, eventually overthrowing Java's native Hindu religion and setting up the island's first Islamic outpost. Quite a few minibuses (Rp800) leave Surabaya from Terminal Jembatan Merah until 2000. It takes a long time to get from the outskirts of Gresik to the center.

Muslim heroes are buried in an ancient cemetery two km south of Gresik; reverently interred here is one of Java's nine early Islamic missionaries. This was also the first Java town visited by a European: the Portuguese discoverer of Maluku, Antonio d'Abreu, stopped here in 1511 and found a thriving seaport housing many foreign merchants. With its strong Islamic traditions, Gresik survived as a sacred, tax-exempt enclave until finally subjugated by the VOC in 1680.

In recent times, Gresik has become an important industrial estate. The biggest woodworking complex in Southeast Asia is here, processing the razed forests of Kalimantan, 80% of the factory's products for export.

Sights
Wander the old narrow streets of the **Arab Quarter** where women glide by in white shawls and veils. In Desa Candipuro, visit **Makam Maulana Malik Ibrahim,** the grave of a pioneer

of Islam. His tomb and those of his wife and children are dated 1419. Until the discovery of some Majapahit graves at Trowulan, these were long thought to be Java's oldest Muslim graves. Also see the very old school (*pesantren*) where Islamic texts are studied. In the port area, hire a boat to tour the harbor; you'll see amazing and unusually shaped sailing and cargo vessels such as the tubby-hulled *leti-leti*. **Pasar Bandeng,** a traditional fish market, sets up along Jl. Basuki Rakhmat and Jl. Raden Satri every year on the day before Idul Fitri.

Accommodations

There are few hotels in Gresik. Try a day outing from Surabaya—have lunch, wander around, and get back to Surabaya by dark. If you do decide to stay a few days, the best Gresik *losmen* is the **Putra Bengawan,** Jl. Ny. Ageng Penati 166; Rp6000 s or d. Other accommodations include **Bahagia,** Jl. H.O.S. Cokroaminoto; **Cempaka Putih,** Jl. Jaksa Agung Suprapto 11; and the large **Sekar Kedator** (16 rooms), Jl. K.H. Zubaer 52.

Crafts

Hidden away in Gresik's back streets are many small textile cottage industries making *songket* from gold or silver thread with simple backgrounds and colorful designs of floating leaves. Outstanding quality. Just wander through and you'll be invited to view a selection; *sarung kembang* and raw silk also for sale. Check out Pasar Gresik along Jl. Basuki Rakhmat. Gresik is also

known as a center for copper implements, woven mats, and Muslim caps (*kopiah* and *songkok*).

Giri

Just two km south of town in Giri is **Makam Sunan Giri,** the grave of one of Java's most famous *wali*. Take a minibus from Terminal Gresik (Rp200) to Giri, then walk. This revered hill, drawing pilgrims from all over Java, is guarded by two mythological Hindu creatures. Many steps lead to the bathing place of the *wali,* a man who, it is said, could fly and work miracles. The mystic saint's shrine is appointed with fine lace, Persian tapestries, and Chinese carvings. A yearly religious festival, Khol Sunan Giri, commemorates the death of Sunan Giri; at this time the "flying jacket" is brought out, and if you wear it, you can fly. Makam Panjang, another holy Islamic gravesite in Manyar, eight km northwest of Gresik, is known for its unusual mix of Buddhist and Islamic elements.

Vicinity Of Gresik

For centuries Gresik has been noteworthy for its salt production; in the hot season see the salt pans being worked along the road southy to Surabaya. Among the most impoverished groups in Indonesia are the fishermen who eke out an existence along the fished-out shores of northern Java, where fish are contaminated by Gresik's petrochemical industry. Java's longest and biggest river, the Bengawan Solo, disembogues in the district around this town. In other words, this area is one of Java's main sewerpipes.

MADURA

An undiscovered gem, this beautiful rugged island is one of the poorest parts of the province. Yet it's blessed with numerous fine white-sand beaches, unpeopled countryside, inexpensive and uncrowded *losmen,* and unique cuisine. Although only 30 minutes from Surabaya by ferry, Madura is almost totally free of tourists. The island is worth more than just a day-trip. Madura is famous for three things: women, salt, and bull races. Some of the best stockbreeders in Indonesia live here. Crowded farmers' festivals, held frequently in special arenas all over the island, attract visitors from around the world. The best day to visit Madura is Sunday, market day.

The Land

Madura belongs geologically to East Java; the strait between the two islands flooded over only during the last ice age. Madura is a generally flat, dry island measuring 160 km long by 30 km wide. Much of the island consists of treeless, infertile, rocky limestone slopes. The northern coast around Ambunten features high dunes and strong waves; the island's lovely southern beaches are more suitable for small children. There are rambling fruit gardens and endless tobacco estates. Bougainvillea bushes overhang the roads and brighten lanes, fishing villages stretch along the whole southern coastline, and the island's cemeteries with their mossy gravestones and craggy trees are the best haunted graveyards in Indonesia.

The People

Glimpse a bygone rural life, extinct in other areas of Java. The younger Madurese wear the *peci* but the older people cling to the *destar* (headcovering). Even though tens of thousands of Madurese have moved to Java, they still retain their own language.

The Madurese relish their reputation for tenacity; they're a people of independent spirit. They're also well known for their energy, thrift, and hot-temperedness. The men are black-mustachioed with high cheekbones and narrow faces; the mere sight of one strikes fear in the hearts of effete Surabayans. They are all thought to carry knives and practice a mystic form of *pencak silat* with no sporting application, used only to kill.

The women of the island are small and dark with very fine features. They walk with a sensual grace, carrying most everything on their heads in enamel wash basins or trays. Madurese women are renowned all over Indonesia for a special style of movement and massage during lovemaking called *goyang madura.*

Food

Corn, introduced by the Portuguese in 1625, is the staple grain in Madurese cuisine. Don't miss the island's *perkedel jagung,* corn-and-shrimp fritters. The best *salak* grow here, and 20 *jambu* cost only Rp200 in season. Try the regional beverage, the nutritious *la'ang. Blaken,* a fish paste used in *nasi goreng, sambal,* and sauce

MADURA ISLAND

for *gado-gado*, costs Rp1500; it comes in old handmade jars of rough glass. Madura's chicken and other kinds of *sate*, as well as *soto madura* (a rich, spicy soup), are famous and prepared all over Indonesia. For sweets, yam taffy is made from pulverized tubers.

Crafts
Madurese craftsmen were inspired by Chinese and European imports, and the island is perhaps best known for its fine beds, screens, chests, and cupboards. Also look for *tempet kue*, three-legged bamboo containers used to store cakes; buy one in the morning *pasar* for Rp1200. Unusual, pre-Malayan pottery comes from **Sodar** in the mountains northwest of Sumenep. Basketry is the specialty in **Satubaru** near the north coast.

Madura *batik* uses rich, bold *mengkudu* red, red-brown, or indigo coloring, incorporating vigorous winged *naga*, sharks, airborne horses with fish tails, and other strange aquatic animal representations. Visit the *batik*-making center, **Tanjung Bumi**, about five km from Bangkalan. In **Telaga Biru**, a ship-building village 15 km west of Ketapang, women draw *batik* designs on cotton cloth loomed at home. Fantastically gnarled, lucky seaweed (black coral) bracelets are also fashioned on Madura. Worn to ward off sickness, these amulets are believed to cure rheumatism.

TRANSPORTATION

Getting There
From Surabaya it's only 30 minutes by ferry (passenger Rp450, car Rp3500) to Kamal. The ferry leaves every half-hour 0630-2000. Several land and sea transport craft make continuous but unscheduled trips from a nearby dock; ask directions. On the ferry you might meet a minibus driver who'll invite you to climb aboard for the ride from Kamal to Pamekasan (100 km, two hours, Rp1400) or Sumenep (160 km). From the Bamboo Denn, take bus P1 to Perak Harbor (Rp400), the ferry across to Kamal (Rp400), then a bus from Kamal to Bangkalan (Rp600), Sepulu (Rp1500), or Pamekasan (Rp2800).

An alternative approach starts in Panarukan, west of Situboudo; ferries leave daily at 1300 (Rp2000, four hours) for Kalianget, returning at

0700 the next day. *Bemo* leave Kalianget for Sumenep (11 km); from there you can take buses to all over the island. Flights are also possible from Surabaya airport to the Trunojoyo Airstrip near Sumenep. There is serious talk of building a three-km bridge from Surabaya to Madura, but don't plan on using it soon.

If you're heading to Madura during bull race season in your own vehicle, be sure to make car ferry reservations the day before and be at the ferry no less than 30 minutes before departure time.

Getting Around
Minibuses travel to practically everywhere on the island worth reaching, and there's even a train that departs Kamal each day for Pamekasan on a slow six-hour journey. Careening *oplet* or *bemo* crammed with people run frequently along the main highway that encircles the island. The roads have very few cars, so hitchhiking can be slow. Since Madura is such a poor island, with bargaining *becak* rides are quite cheap. It's possible to catch freighters from Kalianget back to Bangkalan or Sampang or even to Kalimantan and Sulawesi. Obtain *syahbandar* clearance.

PAMEKASAN

Madura's capital, Pamekasan, is a slow-moving city, very easygoing, quiet, and undeveloped. The town center is lined with casuarina trees. The *kerapan sapi* are held in a field about one km from city center.

Accommodations And Food
Hotel Garuda, on Jl. Mesigit 1, tel. (0324) 81589, is a large complex opposite the town park—about the best for your money, very central, near the shopping district, theaters, and eating places. Huge rooms for Rp9000 d up to Rp15,000 with *mandi*. **Losmen Bahagia**, Jl. Trunojoyo 47, is Chinese-run with stuffy rooms, poor security, and dirty bathrooms. Worst but cheapest in town. A Chinese restaurant, **Depot Bahagia**, is attached.

Hotel Trunojoyo, tel. 81181, is located on a small *gang* off Jl. Trunojoyo; from Rp8000 (including breakfast) to Rp18,000 for a/c rooms with *mandi*. The **Government Guest House**

lies on the south coast between Sampang and Pamekasan, set on a nice shallow beach. Eat in the numerous **rumah makan** surrounding the *alun-alun*.

Crafts

Textiles are quite reasonable here: a 2.5-meter piece of Madurese fabric bought in Pamekasan for Rp15,000 sells for up to Rp100,000 in Jakarta. For special Madurese-style *batik,* Keluarga Muhammed offers a wide selection, from *sarung* (Rp25,000 for two) and *kain* (Rp25,000) to the more expensive *prisma*. For rocking chairs (*kursi goyang*), go to Jl. Segara 10. Jewelry shops line the main street. The village of Kardulak is a center for Madurese arts and crafts.

Getting Away

It's Rp2000 by minibus over the mountains up the island's center to Temberu, then another Rp2000 by minibus from Temberu to Arasbaya. Another route leads to Sotabar, intersecting the north coast road. The people in the central region are quite distinct from the coastal people, with more of a Mongoloid appearance: slanting eyes, high cheekbones, slender frames, knotty hands—mountain folk.

On the Pakong side of the central mountains forests are more numerous than on the Pamekasan side. On the road north from Pamekasan to Sotabar stop at Puncak, the island's highest point, where tobacco fields seem to stretch to the horizon. At night see clearly the thousands of lights of Pamekasan and the fishermen's lamps off the coast.

Vicinity Of Pamekasan

A natural gas field where fire spouts out of the earth, the **"Eternal Fire"** (Api Abadi) lies on the road to Kamal. Legend has it the flames come from the mouth of a giant, interred by the gods. Turn in at the sign Tak Kunjung Padam, meaning "It will never go out." The site lies 800 meters from the highway, surrounded by a metal fence. Try to see it on a moonlit night. Rain or dirt can sometimes extinguish the flames but it's relit again immediately. You can even cook *sate* over it.

The **Tomb of Pangeran Jimat** and other old graves are in a cemetery near Kalpajung Laur, north of Pamekasan. On the way east to Sumenep, stop at **Prenduan**'s lively country market.

Sampang And Vicinity

On the way from Kamal to Pamekasan you pass through this coastal town where you can catch a *bemo* north to Ketapang. In Sampang, stay at **Losmen Setia,** Jl. Imam Bonjol 63, or **Puri Trunojoyo,** Jl. K.H. Wakhid Hasyim. Both hotels may be full.

Gua Lebar is an extensive cave complex with stalagmites and stalactites located on top of a mountain near Sampang. Pleasant swimming and sunbathing at **Camplong,** with a long row of casuarinas and views of East Java's volcanos across the Madura Strait. Rent an outrigger or *sampan* from fishermen (Rp3000-4000 per hour) to see the reef.

SUMENEP

Remote Sumenep, 53 km northeast of Pamekasan, is sleepy, rural, almost a village, but definitely more interesting than dull Pamekasan. More history and more tradition. In the 13th century, Sumenep was an established regency of the Singosari kingdom; the first governor was crowned by King Kartanegara himself. This makes Sumenep one of the oldest *kabupaten* in Indonesia. Bulls race at Sumenep's Giling Stadium; catch a local meet 0900-1300 each Saturday.

Sights

The *alun-alun* is in the center of town, surrounded by the *kraton,* main mosque, government buildings, and markets. The 18th-century mosque, **Mesjid Jamik,** is the religious center for the people of Sumenep, who are nearly 100% Islamic. The mosque has a Javanese Hindu-style gate and a three-tiered Balinese-style *meru* roof. Very cool inside. The *juru kunci* isn't pushy about asking for donations. Excellent morning market nearby. See the old columned houses that look like Roman funerary temples, and visit the great *pasar pagi* near the mosque.

A remnant of Majapahit-style architecture, **Kraton Sumenep** is surrounded by a high white masonry wall. The *pendopo,* with carved pillars, dates back to 1763. The structure is filled with ancient *pusaka* and a fortune in 19th-century Dutch brass lamps, converted now to electricity. Ask to visit the mysterious Islamic praying room, the Kamar Tempat Ibadah, inside the *kraton. Gambu*

Sumenep
street market

and *wayang topeng* dances are occasionally held on the palace porch. A pool and well-kept flower garden are off to the side. Inside the complex is a good museum; donation Rp300.

The **Royal Carriage House**, formerly a garage for the *raja's kereta*, is opposite the *kraton*. It houses a magnificent 300-year-old Chinese marriage bed and the throne of Queen Tirtonegoro.

Accommodations And Food

Chinese-run **Hotel Wijaya I**, Jl. Trunojoyo 45-47, tel. 233, is near the *stasiun bis* on the south side of the highway. All the conveniences, kitchens, and clean bathrooms for Rp6000-10,000. Rent motorcycles here. A little kiosk sells cookies, snacks, *krupuk*, and cigarettes; the restaurant serves good cheap food. **Hotel Wijaya II** is nearby and charges about the same. **Losmen Damai**, Jl. Jen. Sudirman 39, is an old Dutch-style hotel on one of the main streets with rooms for reasonable prices. **Losmen Matahari**, just down the street at Jl. Jen. Sudirman 42, is another possibility, though these two hotels may be closed to Westerners.

17 Augustus on Jl. Diponegoro (five-minute walk from the *alun-alun*) serves delicious *ayam* dishes, tasty *nasi goreng, nasi campur,* and good drinks—a popular place at night. Other food stations include **Mojo** (also on Jl. Diponegoro), **Sederhana, Candra Restaurant, Osaka Restaurant,** and the **Wijaya Restaurant** in Hotel Wijaya. The best Chinese food is probably served at the **Mawar**, Jl. Diponegoro 47A. Eating stalls

open in the evening north of the *alun-alun* sell *soto madura* and *sate.* The **Nasi Burung,** on Jl. Trunojoyo next to Station PIKNJ in front of Jiwita, is a breakfast place which locals rate highly.

Crafts

Mustika Kempang, Jl. Trunojoyo 78, specializes in Madurese-style *batik.* Delftware, old Chinese pottery, furniture, *kris,* and all manner of antique jewelry are on display at the **A. Ba'bud Shop,** Jl. A. Yani, run by an Arab who specializes in *batik.* Eddy, the proprietor of **17 Augustus,** sells old Madurese *batik* and *wayang topeng* masks.

Getting Away

The *terminal bis* for westbound buses is in the south edge of town. Minibuses for easterly destinations depart from the terminal near the Giling Stadium. The fare to Ambunten by *bemo* is Rp500. From Sumenep's *terminal bis,* it's Rp3500 by bus to Surabaya, or Rp1500 by minibus to Pamekasan. Or take a minibus from Sumenep to Surabaya through **Travel and Pikat Kilat,** Jl. Jen. Sudirman 43; Rp3000, departing at 0400. Allow plenty of time to reach Arasbaya as the stretch of road in the northwest is really rough. To Panarukan, East Java, ferries depart Kalianget at 0700 each day (four-hour passage).

Vicinity Of Sumenep

The royal graves, **Asta Tinggi,** are two km west of Sumenep. Once a resthouse for Sumenep royalty, the main building was constructed in the 17th century. The sultan and his ancestors are interred here. Sumenep's export harbor, **Kalianget,** 10 km southeast, has silted up over the centuries—ships must anchor 11 km from the landing, and people are ferried in by launch. There's also a salt factory here.

At **Batang Batang,** on a highway rising into the mountains, is a superb view over the Sumenep area; the road is difficult to negotiate by taxi, car, or *bemo,* so drive the 25-30 km on a motorcycle. On the north coast are the glistening white sands of **Dasuk** between the seacoast towns of Ambunten and Sergong. **Lombang,** on the island's far northeast coast, boasts one of Madura's most scenic and isolated beaches; take a minibus from the Sumenep terminal (Rp600).

Offshore Islands
Catch a *kapal motor* from Kalianget to Palau Sapudi off the east coast. This pretty island is well known for its superior cattle. Visit the picturesque fishing village of **Tlaga** on the north coast, 18 km from Gayam. **Pulau Kangean,** east of Sumenep, is known for a bird species, *ayam bekisar,* and for its beautiful panoramas. Coral reefs encircle the whole island; visit the **Mamburit** sea gardens and natural aquarium. Reach Palau Kangean by ship once weekly from Kalianget; Rp5000-6000, 12 hours.

THE NORTH COAST

In the north, agriculture, not fishing, is the principal source of income. The earth is redder than on the south coast; here you start seeing banyan trees, cactus, rubbly volcanic rock, dense coconut groves, rolling dunes, sandy yellow beaches, more vegetation and varied crops. The trees lining the road (*pohon asam*) bear sour berries used in cooking *galok, rojak,* and other sour-tasting dishes. Around **Arasbaya** you'll find cornfields and haystacks.

The north coast is more isolated than the south; the people here have retained more of their traditional customs and benefited less from the government: one out of every 10 kids seems to have a bad eye. You'll see more oxcarts and *dokar,* and few hotels. The women wear colorful traditional *sarung kebaya* and turbans. It's like another century up here, difficult to grasp that

the area is only a few short hours from Surabaya. **Pasongsongan** and **Pasean** are small fishing villages with rows of *prahu* and dazzling beaches.

Lombang And Slopeng
Lombang and Slopeng are considered the two most attractive beaches on the island. No formal accommodations but you can camp or stay with villagers.

At Slopeng, 20 km north of Sumenep near Ambunten, are giant dunes, Gunung Pasir ("Mountains of Sand"), that stretch for three km. Along this coastline grow graceful fan palm trees. The reefs go out much farther than those on the southern coasts; ask a fisherman to take you out in a uniquely carved *prahu.* No hotels in Slopeng, only a decrepit little whorehouse on the west part of the beach called the "special place" (*tempat istimewa*). Travel by *bemo* from Slopeng to Ambunten for Rp400.

Pasongsongan
Stay at Bapak Taufik Rahman (Rp5000-7000), run by Mr. Taufik. He'll take you fishing or to the bull races. Take the *bemo* from Kamal, just over the hill from Pamekasan.

Ambunten
In this large, traditional village the people are extremely friendly—too friendly. It's another Pied Piper scene, with hundreds of children trailing around after you. An important fishing center, boats are packed together here in a sheltered bay, with the fishermen working on their craft and mending sails. Get *prahu* rides to all over—Kalianget for only Rp2500. Unique salt factory. Watch the occasional thunderous bull race. Although there are no *penginapan,* some travelers have reported sleeping on the beach down the coast a bit. One of the island's most beautiful sights is the rolling yellow dunes here.

Ketapang
Just before crossing the bridge into town on the left-hand side is a rocky graveyard. The cemeteries of Madura, with their small Islamic tombstones blackened with age and rain, seem always to be located between a tobacco field and a house. Legions of dead inhabit this island. Just after the bridge a road leads three km to a

THE RUNNING OF THE BULLS

Like a scene out of *Ben Hur,* these thrilling, high-speed spectacles take place two Sundays each month at Bangkalan's stadium. The idea of racing bulls caught on from racing plowing teams; the word *kerapan* stems from an old Madurese word meaning "to work the soil." The island's small, sturdy breed of cattle is descended from the wild *banteng* that once roamed freely over western Indonesia. Only the strongest, handsomest bulls are chosen for competition. For details on upcoming races, contact one of the East Java tourist offices in Surabaya.

Kerapan Besar

After a series of regional competitions, beginning in April, comes this grand finale, the all-Madura championship race held in October in the stadium at Pamekasan. The championship cup is sometimes awarded by President Suharto himself. During the week prior to Kerapan Besar, traditional games, ceremonies, parades, *gamelan,* and night bazaars spring up all over town.

Each day the bulls are given herbs, raw eggs, honey, and beer. The night before the big race, cattle raisers sing their best bulls to sleep. The next morning they're bathed, brushed, and tenderly massaged. At race time the bulls are decorated with gilt and tinsel leather bibs, flower-tasseled horn sheaths, silver-studded head harnesses, and jangling bells.

The Race

The competition is held on a grassy straightaway 120 meters long. Twenty-four pairs of racing bulls are matched up, their ornaments removed, and the beasts teamed with their brightly dressed jockeys. Each is given a generous tote of *arak* from a bamboo tube, then *gamelan* music is played to excite the bulls. The three-man judging panel takes its place. Dead silence reigns.

The bulls look heavy and awkward, but they're actually sleek racing animals. The starter drops the flag and the teams lunge forward, the riders straddling skids slung between the yoked bulls. Jockeys prod and flog the animals mercilessly with thorns and spiked rods. With much snorting and flying mud, the bulls can cover 100 meters in nine seconds, faster than the world's human track record. The winner's front legs, not nose or head, must cross the finish line first. The triumphant teams are raced again in tournament fashion, and the losers also race, so in the end there will be two winners—the winner of the winners and the winner of the losers. The winning teams then parade around the stadium.

That night, the bulls are rubbed down and soothed with quiet *gamelan.* The owners of the fastest bulls are held in high esteem in their villages, the respect of the community considered more a reward than the material prizes. The fastest bulls are used as studs.

---

waterfall. At the Ketapang minibus station is a little *warung* serving fruit and drinks. A *pasanggrahan* here charges Rp4000 d.

Air Mata

Madura's oldest and most beautiful cemetery sits on a hill near Arasbaya. Its name means "Water of the Eye," or tears. Coming from Ketapang, right after the bridge when you first enter Arasbaya, take a left-hand turn. The minibus driver will drop you off here, or perhaps turn in. About two km down the road is an intersection where you can board another minibus to take you to a little *desa* called Tampegan. If you arrive in Tampegan in the morning, you'll find *dokar* for people going to the market; to Air Mata it's Rp300.

Walking is recommended. About one-half km from Tampegan see the sign Air Mata and a

long staircase leading to another walkway. Within the actual burial compound, you'll be stunned by the vast complex of very old graves. There's one group of family and relatives of the Cakraningrat royal line. Ask the *juru kunci* to show you the involved genealogical chart depicting the connection between the Mataram rulers buried at Imogiri and those royal personages resting in Air Mata. You'll find all of Sultan Agung's crowd on the chart. You can easily spend an hour at Air Mata, worth the entrance fee for the tranquility alone. Leave a donation.

The pièce de résistance of this complex, the grave in the back of the cemetery on the highest terrace, contains Ratu Ibu (1546-69), a descendant of Sunan Giri, the great East Javanese saint. Knockout view over a cultivated river valley; you can see why this spot was selected as a holy burial place. The 16th-century gravesite was consecrated at a time when the doctrines of Islam were just gaining strength and influence. Though prohibited by Islam to depict the human figure or even animals, carvers couldn't resist the temptation to embellish, so living forms are represented within very stylistic flower motifs.

Bangkalan

Bangkalan surrounds the usual *alun-alun* of stately old jacaranda trees. At one end of the *alun-alun becak* drivers gather; opposite Pasar Bangkalan is the minibus station and a line of shops. The bull-racing arena is one km from downtown; a tall white wall surrounds the stadium and *sawah* grows to all sides.

From Bangkalan, it's 18 km and Rp450 by minibus to Kamal. It costs Rp2000 by *bemo* to Sumenep, and Rp1500 to Pamekasan.

Accommodations And Food

Most tourists only come over to Bangkalan on package tours for racing day, so there's a scarcity of accommodations. *Losmen* choices include the **Hotel Ningrat,** on Jl. Cholil, tel. 388, with fan-cooled rooms for Rp12,000-16,000 and a/c rooms from Rp22,000, and the **Wisma Pemuda** on Jl. Veteran with rooms for Rp8000-14,000.

In front of Losmen Purnama is a small *warung* serving *nasi goreng.* Down the street are small, cheap Madurese *warung* offering all kinds of *nasi* dishes. Opposite the *pasar* building in the minibus and *bemo* station is **Manalagi,** Jl. A. Yani 5, specializing in *soto madura* and *nasi krengsengan,* a *kambing* dish in rich sauce. You'll find many other *warung* near Pasar Bangkalan, such as **Warung Amboina** at the end of the minibus terminal beyond the roundabout; reasonable prices and giant *krupuk.*

MOUNT BROMO

The most popular of all of East Java's travel destinations, this active 2,392-meter-high volcano lies 112 km southeast of Surabaya. The caldera is like a vast, arid amphitheater enclosed by perpendicular walls 350 meters high. This awesome, 2,200-meter-high "sand sea" contains three mountains: Widodaren ("Bride"), Batok ("Cup"), and Bromo ("Fire"), all within one huge crater, the Bromo-Semeru Massif. There are three small crater lakes inside the larger crater, with waterfowl and excellent hiking.

The ideal time to visit is in the dry season (April-Nov.) when you have a better chance of seeing a blood-red sunrise. In the wet, you may as well sleep late and stroll across the sand sea during the warmer part of the day, after the heavy fog has blown away. The temperature on top of Bromo is around 5° C; in July it can drop to zero, so dress warmly. Three times a year the site is overrun by tourists: when an annual festival takes place, over Christmas, and during July and August.

From Bromo's peak are stunning views of active Gunung Semeru, Java's highest mountain. Although Bromo can still vent steam and ash, smoke profusely, and occasionally boom from the central crater, it has not spewed lava in historical times.

Gunung Batok

The extinct volcano Gunung Batok sits behind Bromo, ridged from top to base like a giant lemon squeezer. This is the mountain everyone first thinks is Bromo. You can walk around Gunung Batok also, and if you feel really energetic you can climb it. Just as rewarding a climb as Bromo. From the top see Gunung Semeru shooting up clouds of gas every 15 minutes. Difficult to find the path.

The Legends

The whole crater, it is said, was dug out by an ogre using half a coconut shell. He performed this Herculean task in a single night, to win the hand of a princess. When the king feared the ogre would succeed, he ordered his servants to pound rice, at which time the cocks started crowing, thinking dawn had come. The ogre couldn't finish the job, and died of grief and exhaustion.

Inside Widodaren in the Bromo crater complex are buried the legendary ancestors of the Tengger, wife Roro Ateng and husband Joko Seger. They were childless and prayed for offspring, vowing to sacrifice one of their children to the gods if their prayers were granted. The couple went on to produce 25 children, but never lived up to their promise. Joko Seger was

Gunung Bromo comes alive

finally reminded of his debt when pestilence and death swept through the village. Finally, the sacred couple took their youngest child, Kusuma, into the sand sea to appease the gods. Immediately, a volcano erupted, and Gunung Bromo was born. Roro Ateng and Joko Seger still live in a cave on Widodaren called Gua Adam, where the Tenggerese go to pray and make wishes. The name "Tengger" is derived from the last syllables of the founding couple's names.

Kasada Festival

Also called the "Karo Feast," this Tenggerese festival is held in the Bromo crater once a year, at midnight, on the 14th day of Kasada—the Surabaya tourist office will know the exact date. This annual ceremony to commemorate deceased ancestors and relatives goes back to Majapahit times. Offerings are carried by thousands of worshippers who hold oil torches and climb to the top of Gunung Bromo on foot and horseback. Hundreds of people at a time perch along the razor-thin edge over roaring jets of steam boiling 200 meters below. Those who wish to ask special favors of Bromo bow their heads in front of the village priest and make their wishes known to him. The priest then utters a prayer, and the people throw offerings of fruits, flowers, goats, and chickens into the crater. A fantastic air of unreality, like a Black

Mass, until the sun comes up, dispelling the magic and fear.

Be prepared for massive crowds, foreign TV crews, thousands of unruly teenagers toting boomboxes, admission gates, clicking cameras, and the greatest gathering of thieves and pickpockets in the entire archipelago.

Getting There

From Surabaya's Purabaya bus terminal ride a bus 2.5-3 hours (Rp2000, 93 km) to the turnoff to Bromo. Unless you're arriving late at night, there's no reason to stop in Probolinggo. Leave Surabaya early so you can make it to Ngadisari, below Bromo, the same day.

The same rule applies from Bali. Continue by bus straight through the messy town of Probolinggo and ask the driver to drop you at the Bromo turnoff. Only overnight in Probolinggo if you arrive after 2000.

From the Bromo turnoff to Ngadisari it's two hours and Rp2000-2500 by minibus, leaving every hour or so until 1800. You might have to change buses at Sukapura. The turnoff to Bromo is five km west of Probolinggo on the main highway between Surabaya and Banyuwangi.

From Ngadisari to Cemoro Lawang, walk, catch a truck, or take a horse to the rim. There's a bus stop under construction in Cemoro Lawang; regular service might be available by the time you arrive.

THE TENGGER

Some 60,000 mountain people with almost Tibetan features live in some 40 villages ranging from 1,500 to 2,745 meters elevation around Gunung Bromo. Speaking an archaic dialect of Javanese, the Tengger are esteemed by other Javanese as intelligent, placid, hard-working people with high moral values and a history of opposition to foreign influences.

Guests are invited deep inside Tengger houses and placed next to the brick hearths, because tradition holds that visitors must be kept warm. Tengger hearth-fires burn perpetually, warming kitchens and drying vegetables hanging from the rafters. Onions, leeks, potatoes, carrots, maize, cabbage, and cauliflower are grown in expertly cultivated gardens on the steep mountain slopes surrounding these highland villages. Rivaling even the Baguio rice field builders of the Philippines, these climbing terraces are amazing feats of engineering.

Religion

When armed conflict broke out in the 1400s between the Islamized coastal districts and the Majapahit Empire of East Java, Hindu nobles, priests, and artisans fled to Bali, while the ordinary people withdrew to the Tengger Highlands. Today, the Tengger are the only people in East Java who practice the Hindu religion openly. The Tengger call their religion Buddha Mahayana, though their belief system incorporates only traces of Buddhism. The Tengger don't believe in reincarnation, but their caste system and calendar are similar to those of the Balinese. They have their own priests, but no temples; an altar is maintained in each home. A place of worship, usually located on a hill overlooking the village, consists of a smooth, flat rock or a neatly fenced area of one or two overhanging trees, sometimes strewn with flowers and crowded with people uttering prayers and performing religious duties. Since Majapahit times the Bromo crater has also been a Tengger center of worship.

PROBOLINGGO

Famous for its mangos (*arun manis*) and grapes, Probolinggo offers few other charms. Beware of thieving *becak* drivers at the railway station, robbers masquerading as hotel owners, ripoff tour operators, and the completely phony "tourist of-fice." Persistent crowds of gawkers, hecklers, and harassers will attack faster than flies on feces the moment you step off the bus. The sane should avoid Probolinggo and proceed directly to Bromo.

Accommodations

If you're stuck in this hellhole, try one of the hotels on the main road. **Hotel Victoria,** at the crossroads of Jl. Pang. Sudirman and Jl. Suroyo 1-3, is the nicest hotel for the money (Rp8500-17,000). **Hotel Kemayoran,** Jl. Pang. Sudirman 75, above the restaurant of the same name, is very convenient. Also recommended, at Jl. Pang. Sudirman 94, is **Hotel Ratna**; quiet, central, comfortable beds, real furniture, TV, shower, flush toilet, big breakfast, and good service. **Hotel Bromo Permai II** is opposite the bus station—an excellent source of info on Bromo and the principal stop for backpackers.

SUKAPURA

This big Tengger town is a scenic place with a few *losmen* and homestays. Few people pause here, however, as it's quite a distance to Bromo and the town suffers from truck traffic.

Stay in the only **guesthouse** in Sukapura—a grand and spacious establishment for such a little town. The big lounge/dining room is a nice place to sit, read, and relax. Rooms are Rp9000-

PROBOLINGGO

NOT TO SCALE

HOSPITAL
POST & TELEGRAPH OFFICE
BANK
GAS STATION
HOTEL VICTORIA
RM MALANG
R.R. STATION
HOTEL KEMAYORAN
PASAR
BANK
BUS STATION
MINIBUS STATION
TO BROMO TURNOFF   TO BANYUWANGI AND BALI AND SURABAYA

© MOON PUBLICATIONS, INC.

15,000 with two large double beds. Across the road is a small **rumah makan** with reasonable, tasty meals.

A new upmarket addition just up the hill from Sukapura is the **Grand Bromo Hotel**, tel. (0335) 23103, fax 23142, with fan-cooled rooms priced from Rp105,000 to Rp159,000. Popular with tour groups but otherwise extremely isolated and not worth the price.

NGADISARI

A friendly mountain village of shiny tin roofs, fishponds, and misty mornings, just three km down from the crater rim.

Visitors must pay an entrance fee of Rp1500 on arrival; this is legitimate, not a ripoff. Stay away from the local tourist office, which has a terrible reputation for cheating Western visitors.

If you get into Ngadisari early enough (two hours before darkness), continue the final steep three-km (one-hour) ascent to Cemoro Lawang on the crater's rim, where you can secure accommodations.

Yoschi's, tel. (0335) 23387, two km below Ngadisari in Wonokerto, has rooms for Rp6000-24,000. The friendly German/Madurese owners offer a sunrise tour to Bromo. The restaurant serves Indonesian and European food. Superb potato dishes. Yoschi's also offers money-changing, book exchange, games, travel information, and chartered minibuses to Yogyakarta and Denpasar. Ask for the day tours hiking map. Tell the driver you want to be let out at Yoschi's, since the drivers have a secret deal with the adjacent *losmen.*

Adjacent **Bromo Homestay** handles the overflow from Yoschi's. A clean and comfortable place, if somewhat sterile. Another option is **Hotel Tengger Permai;** double rooms for Rp15,600 with breakfast and private bathroom. The hot spiced wine is ideal for the cool weather.

You could also stay with villagers or in one of the nameless *losmen,* which offer really bad rooms for Rp3000-7500—like sleeping in a cupboard under a 10-watt lightbulb. Bargain vigorously. Several *warung* serve coffee and *nasi goreng*—reasonable food but not wonderful.

CEMORO LAWANG

Three km higher than Ngadisari and right on the rim. Hire a jeep from Ngadisari for Rp1000; it's too far and steep to walk. Public bus service may now be in operation. From Cemoro Lawang it's a 20-minute descent into the crater.

Several guesthouses and small hotels are situated right at the crater's rim. **Motel Bromo Permai,** just 30 meters from the crater's edge, is similar to a youth hostel, but for all classes and ages. Cozy gatherings at night in the restaurant. Room choices include a 20-bed dorm for Rp3500, very basic double rooms with common bath from Rp10,000, and first-class rooms with hot showers and breakfast for Rp32,000-46,000. All the rooms need work but the rim location is superb and the managers a friendly lot. Make reservations from the office in Probolinggo, tel. (0335) 21626.

Smaller, friendlier, with better food and cleaner rooms is the new **Losmen Lava,** tel. 23458, located about 30 meters below the hotel entrance. Rooms are Rp5000-8000 including breakfast, and the cafe is a perfect spot to meet other travelers. Highly recommended. A third possibility is the newish **Cemara Indah Hotel** up the road to the right and directly on the crater rim. Great cafe. Decent rooms from Rp10,000.

You can also pitch a tent in a designated zone and sleep outside in a warm sleeping bag. Local *warung* reasonably priced, serving excellent food—fresh, delicious *pisang goreng* for only Rp100 each.

THE CLIMB

From Cemoro Lawang

No matter how much you've heard about it, you won't be prepared for this ethereal, unforgettable spectacle. The ascent to the Bromo crater from Cemoro Lawang takes about two hours by foot or 1.5 hours by horseback. For the sunrise, walk down the wall of the big crater so as to arrive on Bromo's narrow rim by daybreak. Take a flashlight. Your motel will wake you up at 0300; you'll hear all the commotion, with horses whinnying outside.

Although guides can be arranged in Ngadisari, it's really easy to walk to Bromo without one—just fall in behind the tourists. About Rp5000 to hire a horse.

Under clear skies sparkling with stars, the wind whistling, follow the guides and the sure-footed packhorses across the crater floor up through the corridor of white-painted rocks. Stay behind the person with the torch.

By the time you've crossed the lava plain and started up Gunung Bromo, it'll be getting light. At the top of a rise you'll see a steep 256-step concrete staircase up to the rim. It's possible to walk all the way around the rim, but it's precarious in places and very dusty. You can climb right down inside Bromo's crater, but if you fall into its maw, that's it.

After sunrise, you might walk over to the newly constructed Balinese-style temple and then continue around Gunung Batok. A jeep trail heads to the caldera wall, where a paved road zigzags at impossible inclines up to a viewpoint. Superb panoramas. The road splits at the viewpoint, down to the town of Tosari or up to the summit of Gunung Penanjakan.

The ascent to the viewpoint is extremely difficult for hikers but those with rented jeeps or motorcycles shouldn't miss this outstanding excursion.

Sunrise From Gunung Penanjakan

Most visitors do the standard trek to the rim of Mt. Bromo for sunrise. However, the most spectacular views and sunrises are experienced at the summit of Gunung Penanjakan, a one-hour hike from Cemoro Lawang. Local guesthouses can provide maps to the trailhead. The views from Gunung Penanjakan are otherworldly—across the entire volcanic caldera to smoking Gunung Semeru. Stay two days and experience both sunrises.

From Tosari

Take a bus from Pasuruan to Tosari, 19 km from Bromo. The Pasuruan minibus stop is a *becak* ride across town from the bus stop. Minibuses leave to Tosari when they fill up, about every hour. Once above the flatlands, the road is very steep, curvy, and narrow. The main part of town by the market is a really nice area with terraces, pretty homes, and vegetable gardens.

The walk from Tosari to the rim of the crater takes about two hours on a paved road; not at all steep. Trek it in the early morning, before the sun's high enough to hit you in the face. If you start from Tosari at around 0300 or 0400, you can catch the sunrise over Bromo. You could also hire a horse or catch a ride.

Tosari is becoming the leading alternative to Cemoro Lawang. Hotel choices include the expensive (Rp63,000-84,000) **Bromo Cottages,** and the budget **Pendopo Agung** (Rp2400-3000) and **Pondok Wisata** (Rp1050-1800) in the nearby town of Wonokitri.

From Malang/Ngadas

Attempt this trip only in the dry season; in the wet, dangerous mudslides block roads and could sweep you away. If up early enough, hire a minibus or *bemo* from Malang to Tumpang, then take another to Gubuklakah (12 km). From Gubuklakah a steep 16-km-long road leads to Ngadas; one hell of a hill. The Tengger village of Ngadas, built upon a great slope, receives few Western visitors. Incredible views of Gunung Semeru and the valley. Stay with a villager; the *kepala desa* can arrange accommodations.

From Ngadas it's about three km (30 minutes) uphill to the lip of the crater. The track then branches south to Gunung Semeru, then over to Ngadisari, about a 3.5-hour (15 km) steady walk. Three hours in all to walk from Ngadas to Gunung Bromo; something of an ordeal, but worth it. Rows of stones mark the shortest path across the sands at the east end. For maximum dramatic effect, cross the crater east to west. Vegetation gradually disappears as you enter the great sand sea.

Getting Away

Take a *bemo* (Rp2000) down the mountain to the Bromo turnoff. If heading to Bali, flag down the first bus heading east and continue to Banyuwangi. You might need to change buses in Probolinggo.

If you're going to Surabaya, catch a *bemo* at the Bromo turnoff and continue two km north to the new Bayuangga bus terminal. From here a/c buses leave frequently for the Purabaya Bus Terminal in Surabaya. Most *bemo* coming down from Bromo continue to this terminal; ask the driver whether his destination is Bayuangga or Probolinggo.

GUNUNG SEMERU

Also called Mahameru, or "Great Mountain," Semeru is one of the world's most beautiful peaks, and at 3,676 meters is Java's highest mountain. It sits above a sparsely populated region of volcanic highlands, wooded hills, and picturesque crater lakes which offer excellent camping and trekking opportunities.

Gunung Semeru, which means "One Mountain," is named after the Indian World Mountain Meru. According to legend, all the other mountains of Java fell away from Gunung Semeru on its mythical journey from the Himalayas. Semeru is still quite active, on occasion spewing out hot ash and solidified chunks of lava, though usually contenting itself with a huge belch of smoke every 15 minutes. In 1911 an eruption destroyed 200

houses, and in 1946 six people were killed and 81 houses destroyed. In 1994, a violent explosion killed a half-dozen Javanese peasants and temporarily closed the mountain to trekkers. Inquire in Malang or at Bromo on current conditions.

At night hot red twinkling lava and dancing red showers cascade down the steep sides of the volcano, disappearing in the dark forests below. Inside the crater you'll walk in white sand up to your knees; you might be chased from the summit by thundering explosions of gases and globs of red ash. The sunrise is spectacular over the crater's eastern rim, with all the mountains of East Java visible when the weather is clear. Ideally, you should allow about three days for the climb.

South of the immense Tengger crater are the lakes **Rano Pani** and **Rano Regulo,** situated on a 2,200-meter-high plateau rising gently toward

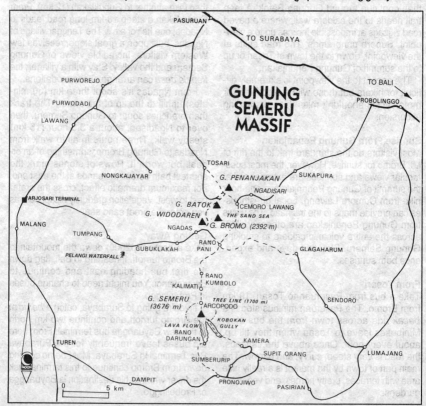

the peak. Set in open pasture and *cemara* woodlands, these lakes are attractive camping spots and a favorite starting point for the climb. This rolling, beautiful countryside is kept clear by annual fires set by the Tenggerese to promote new grass growth. Rano Pani village, on the lake of the same name, has a small four-bed resthouse—no bedding, no food, no charge—mostly used by youth groups.

Travelers with extra time or hired transport might stop at Pelangi Waterfall between Tumpang and Gubuklakah—reputedly the most impressive falls in the entire Malang district. Tour groups often stay in the nearby upscale hotel.

Flora And Fauna

An abundance of wild animals is found in the area, including *rusa, muncak,* wild pigs, snakes, and leopards. Flying squirrels are common in the forests, and ducks are often seen on the lakes. Finches and thrushes frequent even the highest screes, where they feed on the purple berries of the *vaccinium.* A number of rare or endemic plants are established here: the dwarf shrub *Styphelia javanica* grows in cushions and has sharp-tipped narrow leaves and fragrant white flowers, found only in the mountains of East Java. Outside the sand sea are casuarinas, Sunda Island oaks, and large-leaved *homolanthus* trees.

Climate

Climb Semeru only in the dry season. All of East Java has a marked dry season May-Oct., but the high mountains collect moisture during the southeast monsoon and thus there are pockets of fine wet forests on Semeru's southern slopes. It's warm in the villages in the Kobokan Gully, but at night and early mornings temperatures near the peak can be freezing. And it's always cloudy in the afternoon.

The Climb

Though all the approaches to Gunung Semeru are strenuous, the mountain is a far easier climb

than Merapi. If you're spending a night on the summit, bring a friend, a tent, flashlights, sleeping bags, warm clothing (especially windbreakers), campstove, food, and at least one liter of water per day per person.

Semeru's sand can be troublesome; you climb up two steps and fall back one. At the top there are explosions every 15 minutes, and you may also see stones thrown up by the other peak. You need oxygen for that one. The two peaks are only about 300 meters apart. Actually, you'll climb to the peak of Gunung Mahameru, as Semeru is too dangerous due to volcanic fumes and gases. Get off the summit no later than 1200—the wind sometimes shifts from south to north and carries with it poisonous sulphur. By that time visibility is nil.

Getting There From Malang

From Malang it costs Rp1500 for minibus or *bemo* to Gubuklakah. It's best to wait here for the next available vegetable truck rather than hiking. Take the minibus or truck from Gubuklakah all the way to Rano Pani village. Stay in the uninhabited climbers' house in Rano Pani or in the solitary guesthouse. Register and pay a fee at the ranger's office. You can also hire a guide (not really necessary) and rent camping equipment in Rano Pani (necessary).

From Rano Pani, it's a four-hour hike to Ranu Kumbulo and another three hours to the base camp at Kalimati. It will turn very cold, with freezing rains, and ash and sand will fall after each eruption, extinguishing your fire. At midnight, climb four hours to reach the top.

Time your arrival at the summit between 0800 and 1000 to avoid the release of deadly volcanic gases. The air might become thick with ash, but this isn't a problem if you breathe through a handkerchief. Electronic cameras may fail. Sliding back down the mountain is an exhilarating 30 minutes.

It's fairly easy to return to Malang in a single day. Total time for the Semeru sojourn is three days and two nights.

NORTHERN COAST

PASIR PUTIH

The principal resort on East Java's north coast, 175 km east of Surabaya. Minibuses and *bemo* run from Probolinggo (Rp1000), or take a bus direct from Surabaya or Banyuwangi. Pasir Putih offers a narrow, unimpressive beach with surf, graceful painted outriggers lined up on shore, a few coconut palms, and easily accessible coral sea gardens. Admission Rp500.

Although the name means "white beach," the sand is really dark gray, though clean. This is a favorite beach resort for Indonesian families, offering shallow, calm swimming. Visit during the week to avoid the crowds; on weekends it's elbow to elbow, packed with tourists from Surabaya and Malang. When you're ready to head for Bali, just hit the road to Banyuwangi and flag down a minibus.

A dozen hotels and guesthouses lie between the highway and the sea. Could be a lot of noise from the road (overnight buses) and from hotel generators.

Accommodations charge Rp10,000-45,000, though you may find a few as low as Rp6000. One of the cheapest is the **Sidho Muncul,** Panarukan, tel. 2273, on the east end. Also check out the **Wisma Bhayangkara**; tight double rooms face the highway, more expensive rooms face the beach. **Pasir Putih Inn** is the large complex near the restaurant on the west end. Attached to the Pasir Putih Inn is a Westernized restaurant serving average-priced meals, the menu written in English and Indonesian. Some hotels feature charcoal-broiled fish, but the best seafood is available in the several beach *warung.* Well-stocked fruit stands.

THE BONDOWOSO AREA

Bondowoso

Coffee plantations dot the valley floor surrounding Bondowoso, 196 km southeast of Surabaya.

Bondowoso and nearby Situboudo are both renowned for their bullfighting contests, bull against bull. **Aduan Sapi,** the runoff for the winning bulls, is a popular annual event. For months, sets of bulls are pitted against one another in separate heats, fighting their way up to regional *kecamatan* level, *kabupaten* level, then to "residency" level championships. Upcoming fights are listed in the tourist magazine *Panorama,* available at most tourist offices in East Java.

Also visit the big livestock market at **Wonosari,** where people haggle over cattle, sheep, and goats; in the *pasar* a wide range of traditional farming implements are available for sale.

In Bondowoso, stay at the **Palm Hotel,** Jl. A. Yani 32, tel. (0332) 21505 or 21201, with rooms ranging from Rp15,000 (outside *mandi*) to Rp50,000 (a/c, hot water, TV, and video). All prices include breakfast and a free pass to the swimming pool. Also try the very clean **Anugerah Hotel** on Jl. Mayjen Sutoyo with rooms from Rp8000, or the slightly cheaper **Kinanti Hotel** on Jl. Santawi.

Situboudo

On the main street is **Hotel Asia,** Rp3500 d. **Losmen Baru,** on the Pasir Putih side of town, charges only Rp2500; across the road is **Losmen Mustika.** Also try **Losmen Sarworini** near the *stasiun kereta api.*

Prajikan, 12 km south of Situboudo or 24 km north of Bondowoso, is a pilgrimage spot containing the grave of Kiai Emas Atmari. Kayumanis is an apple and coffee area 29 km from Situboudo; before Asembagus, turn right and travel 14 km.

Nusa Barung

An uninhabited island 12 km off Puger on the south coast of Java, designated as a nature reserve. The collection of edible swiftlet nests in cliffs on the wind-hammered southern shore, and of green turtle eggs on the island's beaches, are concessions granted by the local government. The structure of this 6,000-hectare island is limestone, which forms handsome undercut sea cliffs; crevices in the rocks are full of crabs, limpets, and snails. Along this same coast, egrets and blue and white reef herons are commonly seen. Small, deep bays at the northwest end make good anchorages where local fishermen from Puger often shelter overnight. Hitch a ride with them, though their fishing schedules are erratic. Camp on the sandy beaches, but watch the sandflies. Allow at least two days to explore the island.

THE EASTERN END

BANYUWANGI

Banyuwangi means "fragrant water" in Javanese. Known as "Kota Jajah" ("City From Which to Explore and Then Colonize"), this is the embarkation point for Bali. Banyuwangi was the capital of Blambangan, the final Hindu empire on Java, ultimately destroyed by the Dutch in the 18th century.

Sights
See Banyuwangi's elegant mosque, **Mesjid Baiturrachman,** and visit the small but informative **Museum Blambangan,** just behind City Hall. For exotic textiles, visit the fabric shops on Jl. Suit Ubun—like an Indian bazaar. The **THR** amusement park is the most cacophonous you've ever experienced. Not very good for relaxation or food either.

Accommodations And Food
Banyuwangi has over 20 *losmen* and hotels. Very popular with travelers, **Hotel Baru,** Jl. Pattimura 82-84, tel. (0333) 21369, has 42 spacious, airy rooms for Rp6000-9000. Another cheap place, usually quiet but often full, is **Wisma Blambangan,** Jl. Dr. Wahidin 3, tel. 21598, opposite one corner of the public square; Rp10,000-18,000. Next door **Hotel Banyuwangi,** Jl. Dr. Wahidin 10, tel. 41178, offers expensive a/c rooms with private baths.

Hotel Manyar, just one km south of Ketapang ferry terminal (Jl. Situbondo, tel. 41741), is plush but pricey; conveniently located if you're traveling to Bali the next morning. The **Pinang Sari Hotel,** Jl. Basuki Rachmat 116, tel. 61266, has spacious rooms with fans for Rp12,000-15,000 and a/c rooms at Rp30,000-48,000. **Hotel Ishtiar Surya,** Jl. Gajah Mada 9, tel. 21063, is similarly priced.

Eat nights at the *pasar malam* on Jl. Pattimura: *sate gule, kaldu, soto madura,* and *kambing* dishes. Packed with Indonesians at dinner time. A *soto madura* place is next door. Opposite Hotel Baru, **Warung Baru** serves good cheap food. Near Hotel Selamat are **Depot Aida** and **Selamat,** the latter a *bakso* joint.

Services
Visit the **tourist office,** Jl. Diponegoro 2, tel. (0333) 41761, for information, maps, and leaflets. The office is useful for booking any hotel in the area, and for arranging tours and chartered vehicles. A very convenient tourist information center is located at the Ketapang ferry terminal. The manager, Isman, arranges four-man jeeps to Gunung Ijen for Rp75,000. To get information on Baluran Park, the surfing area of Blambangan, or any other government reserve area in East Java, try Banyuwangi's **PHPA Office,** Jl. A. Yani 108, tel. 41119. Open Mon.-Thurs. 0700-1400, Friday until 1200, Saturday until 1300.

Getting There
The only consistently dependable road follows the north coast from Surabaya, but during the dry season, experience rural East Java by cutting south at Probolinggo and traveling on small country roads via Jember or Besuki. This is a longer (375 km vs. 300 km) and slower yet more attractive route. The train from Surabaya, the Mutiara Timor, arrives at 0545. Another fast train arrives from Yogyakarta at 1910. The train station is near the boat terminal in Ketapang.

Getting Away
Trains to Probolinggo and Surabaya depart three times daily.

If you're heading for **Bali,** catch ferries from Ketapang, eight km north and Rp500 by minibus from town. The first ferry terminal you come to from Banyuwangi is the cheaper one; Rp300. The other main terminal is farther down the road. Ferries cross to the Balinese port of Gilimanuk 12 times a day; Rp700, 30 minutes, then

BANYUWANGI DISTRICT

KAB. PANARUKAN

BAJUI MATI

BALURAN GAME PARK

KAB. BONDOWOSO

TO WONOSARI

BATANGAN

PANDEYAN

KAYUMAS

WONOREJO

SUKASAN

JEDING

BLAWAN

SEMPOL

ALASBULUH

TO
BONDOWOSO

SUMBERWRINGEN

PONDOK
MOTOR

JAMPIT

KAWAH IJEN
CRATER
(2,400 m)

TURAH

G. RAUNG
(3,332 m)

MACAN

G. MERAPI
(2,800 m)

KALIKLATAK

UNGKUP
UNGKUP

KAB.
JEMBER

SODUNG

LICIN

KETAPANG

TO JEMBER

BANYUWANGI

KALIBARU

KALISETAIL

ROGOJAMPI

GLENMORE

GENTENG

CELURING

MUNCAR

BENCULUK

TEL. PANGGANG

SUMBER SARI

KEBONDALEM

PURWOHARJO

TEGALDHIMO

SUKAMADE
BARU ESTATE

SUNGAILIMBU

PASANGGRAHAN

REJEGWESI

SARONGAN

SUKAMADE
BEACH

GRAJAGAN

MERENGAN

GUA
PADEPOKAN

GUA PUTRI

TEL. BANYUBIRU

TG. KUNCUR

TEL. GRAJAGAN

PANCUR

LAKE

BLAMBANGAN

BOAT

SENDANG
SURYA

PENINSULA

GUA
HAJI

PLENGKUNG

GUA
(CAVE)

LOGI

TG. PURWA

SUMUR
TONG

0   10 km

© MOON PUBLICATIONS, INC.

three more hours by bus to Denpasar. Car and passenger ferries cross frequently until 2100.

The city has three bus stations. **Terminal Brawijaya,** in the southern outskirts, runs buses to points south. From **Terminal Banjarsari,** take minibuses (Rp400) up to Licin on the slopes of the Ijen Plateau. From **Terminal Blambangan,** north of town on the road to Ketapang, take minibuses to Ketapang (Rp400), Kaliklatak (Rp850), Baluran (Rp750, 30 minutes), Pasir Putih (Rp1000, two hours), Probolinggo (Rp2500, four hours), and Surabaya (Rp3000, eight hours). Catch *bis malam* from this station to Surabaya (Rp5000) or Malang (Rp8500, eight hours). Reliable nightbus companies include **Pemudi,** Jl. Kapten Ilyas 6, and **Jawah Indah,** Jl. Dr. Sutomo 86.

KALIKLATAK

This government agricultural co-op in high-elevation Kaliklatak, 20 km northwest of Banyuwangi, grows such crops as coffee, cacao, rubber, citrus, cloves, and *marakisah* on the slopes of Merapi. The co-op is accessible by *bemo* or bus from the Banyuwangi *terminal bis.*

Accommodations

Stay as a paying guest of the plantation in nice bungalows. **Wisata Irdjen,** tel. 24061', no a/c, has a restaurant; Rp42,000-63,000. Quite popular with Dutch tour groups. Make reservations at least 30 days in advance. Wisata arranges tours of the nearby rubber and coffee processing plants.

BALURAN

The entrance to this 250-square-km reserve in the northeast corner of Java is Batangan, just north of Wonorejo, 37 km north of Banyuwangi. The park headquarters at Bekol is 12 km from the main Surabaya-Banyuwangi coastal road. A reserve since Dutch times, a national park only in 1980, Baluran is one of Indonesia's most accessible game parks. Little-known Baluran encompasses a mountainous area which gives way to open forests, scrubland, and white-sand beaches washed by the Bali Straits. Baluran features coastal marshes, open rolling savan-

nah, swampy groves, crab-eating monkeys, and grasslands with huge wild oxen. This is Java's one bit of Africa.

The Land

The whole park is dominated by the towering volcanic cone of Gunung Baluran (1,247 meters). Park lands completely surround the cone and the open-sided crater, and are bound on three sides by the sea. Java's northeast corner is exceptionally dry, with little rain between April and October. Thus the north side of Baluran features extensive savannah grasslands threaded by seasonal stone-bedded streams. South and west of Gunung Baluran the monsoon forest is largely secondary, splendid for birdwatchers. Nearly all species typical of dry monsoon forests are found here; peafowl are particularly common. The park's western boundary is encroached upon by teak and *turi* plantations.

Preparations

Wear good shoes and bring food, binoculars, and a flashlight. The best time to see wildlife is at dawn or dusk during the drier months (April-Oct.), when the herds move to the waterholes. Just sit in the watchtower and observe; let the game come to you. When there's plenty of water

BALURAN

© MOON PUBLICATIONS, INC.

(in the beginnning of July, for example), you have to go out and search for the animals. In the wet season bring a mosquito net; in the dry season the bloodthirsty creatures aren't quite as bad. You can pick up your permits at the park.

Sights

Baluran is the best place on Java to see a wide variety of wild animals. With its high grasses, flat-topped acacias, dried-out water courses, and herds of animals grazing peacefully, this reserve is strikingly similar to East Africa's famous game parks. Climb up through the mahogany and teakwood forests or tramp across the open grasslands bordering the Madura Strait. You can approach as close as 50 meters to herds of wild buffaloes.

There are also wild dogs, deer (groups of 30 or more are common), leopards, civet cats, squirrels, fruit bats, macaques, leaf monkeys in the upland forests, and monitor lizards. See wild pigs thunder across savannahs of acacia trees, and a plethora of such birds as green jungle fowl (*ayam hutan*), prancing peacocks (*burung merak*), drongos, and kingfishers. It's not wise to venture out of the jeep or off well-trodden tracks.

The guesthouse sits on a little raised area; behind is a hill with a 500-meter path up to an old game observation tower with a telescope for viewing the animals. To the right is Gunung Baluran, with swamp forests and open savannah all around, cleared to create a grazing area for the *banteng* (wild oxen). A real joy to watch the sun rise and set from this tower.

From Bekol take the 2.5-km-long path through the savannah to the beach at Bama. If driving, it's accessible only by 4WD and only in the dry season. Though not a very pleasant beach and unsuitable for swimming, the marine environment boasts crab-eating macaques

and a shore nursery of milkfish. At low tide the beach turns to mudflats which stretch for 400-500 meters out to sea.

This shoreline is generally broken and rocky, interspersed with small coves and mangroves where fishermen construct pond traps. The milkfish spawning grounds lie between Baluran and Madura and in season the shallow waters are thick with them. Whales and dolphins are sometimes seen out in the Madura Strait.

Accommodations And Food

There's a campground near the entrance to the park. At the foot of the hill in Bekol, 12 km from the park entrance at Batangan, is a comfortable, modest *pasanggrahan* belonging to the PHPA (Forest Service); capacity 14 people. Rooms cost Rp4000-10,000. No electricity, just lamps and candles. Friendly staff. There's a guard at all times, so your gear is safe. In the early morning you'll be awakened by the strident calls of peafowl and jungle fowl. Plenty of water and cooking facilities, but no meals available. Some *warung* near the park entrance sell *nasi campur* in banana leaves, but it's best to bring your own food.

Getting There

Five hours (Rp2500) and 264 km by bus from Surabaya, about 18 km north of Ketapang (Rp600 by *bemo*), the entrance to Baluran is quite easy to reach. You can also take a bus from the Joyoboyo station in Surabaya to Situboudo (four to five hours), then a minibus to Batangan, the park entrance. Report to the guardpost, open 0700-1700. Mr. Sukri might lead you into the park; be sure to tip him. It's possible to stash your heavy luggage safely at the guardpost for one to three days. You don't need a guide; just head down the all-weather dirt road leading from the south into the reserve.

THE IJEN PLATEAU

Containing six volcanic peaks 1,200-3,050 meters high, the whole eastern end of Java is dominated by the high and seldom-visited Ijen Plateau. The volcanic cones of Gunung Ijen and its neighbor Gunung Merapi loom over the landscape. This plateau offers savannah landscapes, ruggedly beautiful panoramas, cool weather, grand hiking, and a placid, bright yellow crater lake. The peaks are surrounded by villages, home to 7,500 people working the coffee plantations and sulphur mines high on the slopes. Still quite primitive.

Sights
From the crater rim of Ijen, its barren screes colonized by low, tenacious *Vaccinium* bushes with long trailing roots, long ridges lead down toward Baluran. The northeast slope, called **Maelang,** is wild rolling country with lots of deer—a former hunting reserve. Tracks lead from **Bajulmati** through old coffee and teak plantations on the lower slopes and up into the hills. To the west is the Ijen Plateau, its dry grassy plains frequently burned to encourage young growth.

This is high country, easy to walk in, but the only water comes from the Banyupahit ("Bitter River"), flowing from Kawah Ijen's acid yellow-green crater lake. Sumatran pines and coffee plantations occupy the west end of the plateau. Just beyond Blawan is the small **Jeding Nature Reserve,** where the Banyupahit River plunges 30 meters through deep limestone gorges. Because of settlement, disturbance, and fire, Ijen is not an outstanding wildlife area. *Rusa*, leopards, pigs, peafowl, and jungle fowl are found in Maelang; civet cats, muncak, pigs, and tame silverleaf monkeys inhabit the moist forests.

Preparations
Officially you're supposed to apply to Banyuwangi's Forestry Service (PHPA) for a permit, though most travelers are never questioned. You

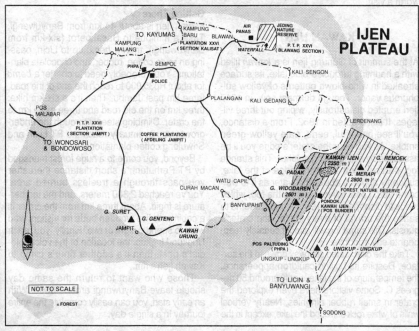

may need to show it to obtain accommodations, however. Up on the plateau, State Forestry Corporation (Perum Perhutani) officers can offer assistance and advice. **Jampit,** which you can reach by bus, jeep, or small truck, features shops to replenish your supplies. It's best to buy food beforehand in Situboudo or Bondowoso. Bring warm clothes; the higher the elevation, the wetter and colder the weather. The rainy season is Nov.-March, the dry April-October.

Accommodations And Food

Pondok Kawah Ijen, a former Dutch resthouse near Ijen's crater, is in bad shape—only two rooms left, windows broken, no toilet. The **Jampit, Ungkup-Ungkup,** and **Blawan** guest-houses are controlled by the local forestry officers; you need permission to stay. The big old *pasanggrahan* at Sempol has four beds for Rp5000 without breakfast. In Sempol, however, you may stay at the **Asrama Polisi** (Police Mess) or the **PHPA House** if you're with a group of four. At Sumberwringin, or Fig Tree Spring, a very pleasant old *pasanggrahan* provides food and accommodations in the old Dutch style; worth a visit.

KAWAH IJEN

At the summit of Gunung Ijen is a *kawah* filled with a haunting turquoise-blue lake, its surface streaked in wind-blown patterns of yellow sulphurous vapor. Though dormant now, in 1817 Ijen erupted distastrously, wiping out three villages. It last erupted in 1952. From a distance, you'll see beautiful, eerie, pale yellow-green smoke. As you near the crater's edge you'll be assaulted by evil-smelling sulphur. This strange fog, particularly thick at the edge of the lake, suddenly appears above the water as if to welcome you. Local folklore claims the fog, which tends to disappear in a few seconds, seems to sense the arrival of every visitor, the crater's guests. This same fog will almost certainly reappear to say goodbye.

Take the dilapidated stairway down to the surface. Despite its boiling-cauldron appearance, the temperature of the lake is only around 50 degrees C. Some visitors have even explored the crater in small rubber dinghies. Nearly vertical walls of white rock surround the lake, except in the northwest where the wall has collapsed. A dam regulates the flow of water into the Banyupahit River; the lake has been known to boil over when volcanic activity increases. From a tunnel dug through the crater rim on the south side, the lake can be watched for any unseemly activity, and the volcanology post at Ungkup-Ungkup (one km from the nearby mining cabin) is manned year-round. Don't shout, or you'll disturb the sensitive seismographic monitor at this station.

Sulphur Mining

A continuous upwelling of sulphur from fumaroles at the level of the lake is the basis of a thriving enterprise. Pure hot red sulphur, oozing out of hissing fissures, turns bright yellow as it dries. It's then broken up into big chunks with hammers and loaded, 50-60 kg at a time, into baskets carried by men and horses down the trail to a factory at Jambu. Nine to 12 tons of sulphur are delivered each day. A natural source of sulphuric acid, the sulphur is used by oil refineries and in the production of fertilizers. These sturdy carriers also work as guides and can be hired to show you the area (Rp4000-5000 for half a day).

Getting There

Kawah Ijen is about 44 km from Banyuwangi. Take a minibus to Sasakperot (six km from Banyuwangi), then a *bemo* up to Licin, passing en route coffee, rubber, and chocolate plantations. You'll probably need to charter a *bemo* for about Rp35,000 to reach the end of the road, three km past Jambu. Then it's a six-km hike; three km on the old road and three more km to the crater. Climbing steeply through the undergrowth you eventually reach the PT Lijen and Sriwulong coffee plantations.

Beyond, you come to a huge forest managed by PT Perhutani; a short distance thereafter you pass through a treeless burned area. You've reached 2,300 meters, and the temperature is frigid. About three km from the crater is a cabin with five wooden beds for visitors who want to spend a night or two. Finally, you reach Ungkup-Ungkup, the location of the volcanologist's post, then it's another hour's climb to Kawah Ijen's rim.

Those who want to return the same day should leave Banyuwangi around 0600. With an early start, you can easily complete the entire journey in a single day.

Other Approaches

Climbing Kawah Ijen is less strenuous from the Bondowoso side. First get to Wonosari or Bondowoso; arrive the night before so you'll be ready for an early start. The bumpy road from Wonosari, which begins two km north of town, leads all the way to Sempol (48 km, three hours, Rp3000 by *bemo*).

You could also catch a ride on a PTP truck; wait in front of Toko Hijau on Jl. R.E. Martadinata in Bondowoso. If you come from Wonosari, you have to stop at Pos Malabar to sign the guestbook.

In Sempol, a village in the middle of a coffee estate, stay in the *pasanggrahan*. The police also put up travelers at the Police Mess, 200 meters beyond the gateway to the estate. At Sempol, hire a guide (the police or the estate officers will suggest someone) for Rp5000 and take the footpath to Jampit-Turah-Macan, walking four hours over plank bridges and jagged ravines. From Macan to the volcanologist's post at Ungkup-Ungkup takes another two hours, then it's only one km and one hour to Kawah Ijen. You can rent a guesthouse run by the estate in Jampit.

THE SOUTHERN COAST

BLAMBANGAN PENINSULA AND GRAJAGAN SURFING CAMP

This remote region was the last stronghold of institutionalized Hinduism on Java, the legendary 17th-century kingdom of Menak Jinggo. Battles for control of Blambangan were waged back and forth until Sultan Agung marched to the coast in 1639, eventually conquering western Bali. Balinese troops rallied and drove the Muslim Mataram troops into the sea and the peninsula remained under the control of Balinese kingdoms until 1768.

Today Blambangan is the relatively unexplored **Banyuwangi Selatan Reserve**. The whole of **Teluk Grajagan** is a very popular swimming, boating, and recreation area, particularly for surfing, which is fantastic, though expensive. Foreign surfers claim **Plengkung** has the best surf in Indonesia: waves up to four meters high and three km long. If there are no waves elsewhere on Java and Bali, there will always be waves at Plengkung.

The Land

In general, the peninsula is dry and thickety, with the driest months April-October. Teak plantations have encroached on the landward side of the peninsula; its dry climate is ideal. Elsewhere, mixed monsoon forests still exist. Blambangan is outstanding for its turtle-nesting beaches, and as perhaps the last area in Indonesia where the *ajak*—the handsome, rufous, bushy-tailed wild dog—still thrives. Only on Blambangan are *ajak*

safe from ruthless persecution. Packs of *ajak*, once common all over Java, have always been blamed for livestock losses, but on Blambangan their natural prey is deer, pig, and *muncak*. Jungle fowl, macaques, leaf monkeys, *banteng*, *muncak*, *rusa*, and leopards also inhabit Hutan Purwo, Blambangan's forest reserve.

Sights

Muncar, 41 km south of Banyuwangi, is East Java's largest fishing *kampung*. Watch the fishermen work along the beach; visit the fish market. **Sitihinggil** is a historical site near Muncar. At **Pancur**, 80 km south of Banyuwangi, stone pedestals are the only remnants of the kingdom of Menak Jinggo. Attractions include a good swimming beach, as well as a clean freshwater spring. Nearby, at **Desa Kedungrejo**, 90 km south of Banyuwangi, you'll find scattered large stone blocks which once formed the foundation of the palace Umpak Songo. Other ancient archaeological sites are accessible on foot: at **Logi** find the remains of a building erected by the Dutch in 1811; at **Sumur Tong** there's an old well; at **Gua Haji** a statue honors a famous *haj*.

Accommodations

The surfing season is May to July. It costs around Rp15,000 per day to stay at the surfers' camp at Plengkung in bamboo bungalows. Only *warung* food is available so stock up beforehand and take along a cooking stove. It might be possible to stay on the boat you arrived on, or pitch a tent on the sand.

Surfing Tours

Surfing expeditions from Kuta Beach cost about Rp840,000 per week, including transportation, accommodations, and meals. A cheaper alternative is to take a *bemo* from Banyuwangi south to the town of Tegaldhimo. The PHPA office in Tegaldhimo arranges surfing tours to Plengkung at Rp25,000 per day; significant savings but something of a hassle. You can also arrange budget tours at PT Plengkung Indah in the Banyuwangi Hotel on Jl. Wahidin in Banyuwangi.

Getting There

From Banyuwangi's Terminal Brawijaya, take a minibus all the way to Benculuk, then a *bemo* or minibus on a rough road to Grajagan. The road ends at this fishing village; from here you embark by local fishing boat (Rp5000-6000) to Plengkung on the westerly corner of the Blambangan Peninsula. The passage to the surfing locale is easy but coming back you have to go against the wind.

Other approaches: walk two days along the bay from Grajagan to Plengkung; charter a boat from Benoa Bali; use the surfing camp's expensive diesel cruiser direct from Bali. Plengkung can also be reached by minibus from Banyuwangi to Trianggulasi (76 km), then from Trianggulasi to Plengkung along the shore's edge for 12 km. Before setting out for Blambangan, obtain a permit from the PHPA office in Banyuwangi.

THE MERU BETIRI RESERVE

One of the most important reserves on Java. Established in 1972, this 50,000-hectare game park lies on the rugged southeast coast where thickly wooded hills rise steeply to over 1,000 meters. The World Wildlife Fund assisted Indonesia's Forestry Service in drawing up a management plan for the relatively new reserve. To explore, you must be accompanied by a PHPA officer or local guide. A newly built observation tower rises from a cleared savannah.

Though best known as the last refuge of the now-extinct Javan tiger, Meru Betiri is also of considerable botanical importance as one of Java's few remaining areas of relatively undisturbed primal montane forest. It's the only known habitat of two of the island's endemic plant species, the *Rafflesia zollingeriana* and *Balanphora fungosa.*

The reserve's two highest peaks, Gunung Betiri and Gunung Tajem, create a sort of rain pocket; this makes the reserve wetter than surrounding areas and accounts for the unbelievably thick jungles. There are even enclaves of true natural rainforests—almost the last on Java—ranging in elevation from sea level to the peak of Betiri.

Fauna

The steep, densely wooded hills of Meru Betiri provided the final stronghold for the indigenous Javan tiger (*harimau macan jawa*), which once inhabited the hilly eastern boundary of the estate. A 1978 study revealed that five or six still survived, but the tigers are now believed extinct. Human interference was the major reason; plantations took over the tigers' traditional valley habitat.

Sleek long-bodied panthers (*macan tutul*), pigs, *muncak,* rabbits, squirrels, civets, leopards, black and silverleaf monkeys, and the long-tailed macaque also inhabit the reserve. Sea and shore birds are common. Two species of hornbills (wreathed and the smaller pied hornbill) and egrets and terns are seen most often.

Most of the government's conservation efforts are concentrated on the sea-turtle nesting beaches where, in the right season, five species of turtle (green, loggerhead, hawksbill, Pacific ridley, and the leatherback) arrive to lay their leathery, golfball-sized eggs.

Accommodations

A comfortable PHPA resthouse, **Taman Rekreasi,** provides food and lodging at Rajegwesi, a small fishing village on a bay within the reserve, about two hours by road from the Sukamade Baru Estate. You can order meals in advance. Another resthouse, closer to the turtle nesting beach, is **Wisma Sukamade** in the Sukamade Baru Estate.

SUKAMADE BARU ESTATE

Founded by Dutch planters in 1927, this bustling plantation comprises 1,200 hectares in rubber, coffee, and coconut palms, surrounded by dense jungles and a breathless expanse of coastline.

Accommodations
The estate's *pasanggrahan* is extremely comfortable, with giant home-style meals; five rooms hold up to 25 people; Rp20,000 pp. Sometimes you can rent the plantation jeep.

Sukamade Beach
Also called Turtle Bay or Pantai Penyu, this famous three-km-long beach lies at the reserve's east end, about 90 km southeast of Jember. Dark forested hills descend to the shoreline, pounded by the deep green surf of the Indian Ocean. This long blinding beach, usually empty, is one of the few locales on Java where you can still observe huge sea turtles laying their eggs in the sand. From Sukamade Baru Estate it's a one-hour walk to this protected, penned-in area. You can't camp or swim on the beach, but villagers might be willing to put you up. The best time for catching sight of the laying turtles is 2100-0200 every night Nov.-March; take a flashlight and watch for notched tracks in the sand. Observing these magnificent reptiles emerging from the surf on a moonlit night to dig their deep nesting pits is a rare experience.

Vicinity Of Sukamade
A small cove called **Teluk Hijau** ("Green Bay") has deep green surf; the 20-minute walk from the narrow track down to the beach leads through some fine primary jungle. The smaller sandy beaches of **Nanggalen, Sekar, Permisan,** and **Pisang** to the west are worth visiting. Only one truck daily, at around 0600, leaves the estate and travels to **Rajegwesi,** a fishing village close to the southern sea. A spectacular environment of seascapes and steep-sloped mountains, *sawah,* and sailing *prahu.*

Getting There
The streams, rivers, and rough mountain trails make the trip a real adventure. Sukamade Baru Estate lies about 100 km southwest of Banyuwangi. Take a *bemo* from Banyuwangi to Pasanggrahan then a pickup to Sarongan. A truck to Sukamade departs daily at noon; otherwise charter a vehicle. The truck returns from Sukamade daily at 0600. Total travel time about five hours.

BALI

This tiny island of nearly three million Hindus, surrounded by a sea of 160 million Muslims, lies just two km from the far eastern tip of Java. When the first Dutch war yacht pulled into Bali on 22 February 1597, those aboard found a heaven on earth. In the 1930s several popular documentaries featured this island paradise; then the world knew, and Bali has been degenerating ever since. It's a tourist colony now, an Isle of Capri in the western Pacific. Earnings from tourism have risen spectacularly each year since 1970, and the industry is now aiming at one million tourists a year—one visitor for every three Balinese.

COURTESY OF THE ROYAL TROPICAL INSTITUTE IN AMSTERDAM

INTRODUCTION

Once known as "Anthropology's Shakespeare," Bali's unbelievably complex and durable social and religious fabric is now breaking down under the foreign onslaught. Today you see signs like "Cremation! Rp5000! Book here!" and revered Hindu priests in graffiti-art T-shirts. When groups of men go to pray, they wear hibiscus in their ears, clean bright *sarung,* and crisply pressed, soulfully faded Levi jackets.

Big-business tourism is foisted upon the Balinese by the international consortiums that build hotels and megaresorts—most recently at Tanah Lot—without the consent or consultation of local residents. Most of the money earned by these swank hotels is siphoned back to Java or overseas. Tourism has brought corruption, crime, and disease. You used to be able to leave your bag in the open anywhere on the island for three days and nothing would move it but the wind. Not anymore. Thefts of

tourists' belongings occur regularly; prices are higher; vendors in tourist ghettos like Sanur, Kuta, and Lovina hassle you; the sound of motorbikes is constant; quality of painting and carving is declining—you've heard it all before.

Fortunately, the law prohibiting building any structure higher than a palm tree has saved the island, otherwise developers would have taken over completely. Although Bali is only 135 km long by 90 km at its widest, you can still get as lost as you want. There are hundreds of villages that haven't changed in 50 years. You don't need directions; just head for the hills. The best things are still free: orange and gold tropical sunsets, an astoundingly rich culture, the smiles of the children, the sound of the palms, the talcum-powder beaches and coral dive sites. You can still get into temple dances and tourist sites free, and live well for about Rp31,500 a day or less.

BALI

G. PENULISAN (1,745 m)
G. BATUR (1,717 m)
LAKE BATUR
G. ABANG (2,152 m)
G. AGUNG (3,014 m)
G. BATUKAU (2,276 m)

TO LOMBOK

NUSA PENIDA

SAMPALAN
TOYAPAKEH
NUSA LEMBONGAN

UJUNG
BUGBUG
PADANGBAI
KUSAMBA
AMLAPURA
TENGENAN
TIRTAGANGGA
CULIK
KUBU
TIANYAR
TEMBOK
TEJAKULA
KUBUTAMBAHAN
SANGSIT
SINGARAJA
SUKASADA
GITGIT
LOVINA
SERIRIT
LAKE BUYAN
BUBUNAN
MAYONG
PUPUAN
MUNDUK
BEDUGUL
LAKE BRATAN
PACUNG
PENELOKAN
PENULISAN
KINTAMANI
BATUR
TRUNYAN
BESAKIH
RENDANG
BANGLI
KLUNGKUNG
GIANYAR
GUNUNG KAWI
TAMPAKSIRING
PEJENG
UBUD
PELIATAN
MAS
SAKAH
CELUK
BATUAN
BATUBULAN
KESIMAN
SANUR
P. SERANGAN
TANJUNG BENOA
NUSA DUA
KUTA
DENPASAR
KAPAL
MENGWI
KEDIRI
TABANAN
MARGA
SANGEH
TANAH LOT
ANTOSARI
JIMBARAN
PECATU
ULUWATU

PULAKI
NEGARA
MENDOYO
PULUKAN
CANDIKESUMA
MELAYA
BELIMBINGSARI
P. MENJANGAN
TERIMA
GILIMANUK

JAVA
BANYUWANGI

BALI

30 km

© MOON PUBLICATIONS, INC.

THE LAND

Bali is one big sculpture. Every earthen step is manicured and polished, every field and niche carved by hand. Once a geographic extension of Java, Bali still resembles it, mountains and all, sharing much the same climate, flora, and fauna as the mother island. There are few flat areas; hills and mountains are everywhere. The surface of the island is marked by deep ravines, fast-flowing rivers, and, in northern Bali, a west-to-east volcanic chain 1,500-3,000 meters high, an extension of Java's central range. On the plains of southern Bali you see rice fields exquisitely carved out of hills and valleys, sparkling with water or vividly green. All seasons are one: in fields side by side there is rice that's just been planted, rice that's still growing, rice that's ripened. Balinese terracing and irrigation practices are even more sophisticated than on Java, employing a remarkable system of aqueducts, small dams, underground canals, and tunnels through rock hillsides. A village organization, the *subak,* controls the distribution of water from a reservoir or main pipeline.

In southern Bali, besides rice, crops of tea, cacao, groundnuts, and tropical fruits flourish.

As you head north, the lands........... from tiers of rice fields to gardens of onions, cabbages, and papayas. Thatched palm huts give way to sturdy cottages made of wood, tile, stone, and volcanic rock. In the higher altitudes you find mountain streams, prehistoric ferns, wildflowers, creepers, orchids, leeches, butterflies, birds, and screaming monkeys. Bali's western tip, Pulaki, is the island's unspoiled, uninhabited wilderness. Legend has it Bali's first inhabitants originated here in a lost, invisible city.

Climate

Bali lies only eight degrees south of the equator and has an eternal summer, warm sea breezes, and high humidity. Tropical showers can quickly give way to blinding sunshine. Rainfall, which usually is not heavy and continuous, arrives mainly in the late afternoon and night. From November to April the rains really come; the wettest days are in December and January. The dry season is May to October. From June to the end of September, Bali is very pleasant.

HISTORY

Bali is a living museum of the old Indo-Javanese civilization that flourished on East Java over 400 years ago. Prior to 1815 Bali had a greater population density than Java, suggesting its Bali-Hindu civilization was even more successful than Java's. Majapahit refugees were not the first to bring Hinduism to Bali; Indian culture was present in parts of the island as early as the 9th century, and Balinese writing is derived from the Palava script of southern India. Bali today provides scholars with clues about India's past religious history in old sacred texts that have vanished in India itself.

When Gajah Mada of Java's Majapahit Empire conquered Bali in the mid-14th century, East Javanese influences spread from the purely religious and cultural spheres into fine art, dancing, sculpture, and architecture. When that empire fell in the 16th century under pressure from Islamic military and economic invasion,

there was a mass migration of Java's Majapahit scholars, dancers, and rulers to Bali. Priests took their sacred books and mythical records, and on Bali they developed unique Bali-Hindu customs and institutions. But Hinduism is only the veneer; the Hindu practices of the new masters were merely superimposed on the deeply rooted aboriginal animism of the Balinese natives, who cling to beliefs dating back to the Bronze Age.

In the early 19th century, Bali's sole export was its highly prized slaves; its imports were gold, rubies, and opium. The island remained obscure for so long because of its lack of spices, precious metals, or aromatic woods, and because of its steep cliffs rising from the sea, deep straits with treacherous tidal currents, and encircling reefs. Surprisingly, the fertile, lava-rich lowlands of Bali were among the last areas occupied by the Dutch and only came

their colonial rule following prolonged resistance. When a wrecked cargo ship off the south coast was looted by the Balinese at the turn of this century (a traditional practice of island peoples), the Dutch used the incident as a pretext to control the island. One sunny morning in 1906 in Puputan Square, Denpasar, Hindu princes and their families, wearing splendid ceremonial costumes and waving priceless *kris,* charged deliberately into Dutch rifles. This mass suicide (*puputan*), and another two years later in Klungkung, resulted in the annihilation of Bali's most powerful and highest ranking royal families.

THE PEOPLE

The Balinese are small, handsome people with round, delicate features, long sweeping eyelashes, and heart-shaped lips. Their cults, customs, and worship of god and nature are animist, their music warm-blooded, their art as extravagant as their nature. Culturally, the Javanese lean more toward refinement and modesty, keeping themselves in check in life and art, while the Balinese prefer the headier, flashier sensations—laughs, terror, spicier and sweeter foods. They're more lavish and baroque in their colors and decorations; they like explosive music and fast, jerky dancing.

Today there's still a distinction between the *majapahit,* descendants of 16th-century migrants of East Java's fallen Majapahit Empire, and the Bali Aga, the original inhabitants of the island who retreated into the mountains where they're found to this day, indifferent to outsiders. Among the Hinduized Balinese, the three classical Hindu castes are indicated by surnames: the Brahmans with the title Ida Bagus; the Satria with the titles Anak Agung and Cokorda; and the Vaishyas with the title Gusti. Nearly every village has a *puri,* the elaborate residence of a Satria, and a *geria,* the residence of a Brahman. The Bali Aga are Sudra, or casteless, though no Balinese is considered untouchable.

Ninety percent of Bali's population practice Bali-Hinduism. There's also a sprinkling of Muslims in the coastal towns, Buddhists in the mountains, and Christians everywhere. Several thousand Arabs and Indians, many hoteliers and textile dealers, live in Denpasar. Some 25,000 Chinese live in the main trading centers of Denpasar, Singaraja, and Amlapura, running the majority of the small retail businesses and restaurants.

Women And Family Life

Women often have independent incomes and are in charge of raising pigs and cultivating the fields. They also prepare for all the milestones in family life considered important or magical: birth, the first cutting of a child's nails and hair, filing of teeth, piercing of earlobes, marriage, and death. Women carry loads weighing up to 30 kg and standing 1.5 meters tall on their heads, while men take up the rear cradling just their *parang.* A young Balinese girl can train herself to carry up to 40 coconuts, stacks of fruit, or great water jars on her head while riding a bicycle down a bumpy country road. Women delouse each other and their children as a social pastime and an affirmation of familial love. Balinese women wear bras like Western women wear bikini tops. Unmarried girls often sport a loose lock of hair hanging down the back over one shoulder with a *gonjer* (flower) dangling in it.

As in many Indonesian societies, menstruating women are sent out of their homes to board in a special house or compound. A Balinese man believes if menstrual blood ever touches his scalp he will be impotent for the rest of his life and follow his wife around like a dog. The birth of boy and girl twins is a calamity, an evil omen. It's thought the twins have committed incest in the womb, and rigorous purification ceremonies are required. If such twins are born in a house, the house must be destroyed; a woman who knows she's carrying twins gives birth in a hospital or outdoors to save her house.

The Balinese believe each part of the house corresponds to a part of the human anatomy: the arms are the bedrooms and the parlor, the navel is the courtyard, the sexual organs are the gates, the anus is the backyard garbage pit, the legs and feet are the kitchen and granary, and the head is the family shrine.

The *Banjar*

Each Balinese village is like a little republic, self-contained and independently run by the *banjar,* a sort of town council. More than any other factor, this village organization kept intact the Balinese way of life after the decline of the local *adat* princes and chieftains. Each family pays a subscription fee and when a man marries, membership is compulsory; otherwise he's looked upon as morally and spiritually dead. Attendance of all heads of household is required at regular meetings; absentees are fined.

The *banjar* runs its own communal bank from which villagers may borrow to buy farm equipment, cattle, or other necessities. The *banjar* supports and maintains village temples, roads, and ditches; owns a *gamelan*; handles taxation, cockfighting, divorces, and duck herding; and helps to arrange and finance weddings, family celebrations, temple festivals, cremations, and community feasts. The *banjar* advises villagers on matters of religion, marriage, and morals, all regulated carefully by its elected members. Each *banjar* has its own meeting house where members gather in the evenings to sip *tuak,* talk, and gamble. The leader of the *banjar* is elected by its members and approved by the gods through a medium. No other political system has yet broken through the patriarchal shield of the *banjar,* though increasingly its cohesiveness is weakened by consumerism, modern lifestyles, and the travel industry. Many members now send a monetary contribution in lieu of their presence.

RELIGION

Outside of India, Bali is the largest Hindu outpost in the world. Put in another way, it's the furthest reaches of the Hindu empire. On Bali Hinduism has developed along lines all its own. In fact, the way in which the Balinese practice their frontier Hinduism is still their greatest art.

Hinduism is at least 3,000 years old and dates from the creation of the Vedas, compilations of prayers, hymns, and other religious writings. Hinduism doesn't have a single founder or prophet. There is only one god, though its many different manifestations are named and classified in great detail.

The Balinese call their religion Agama Tirta ("Science of the Holy Water"), an interpretation of religious ideas from China, India, and Java. Agama Tirta is much closer to the earth and more animist than Hinduism proper; the two sects are as different from each other as Ethiopian Christianity from Episcopalian Christianity. If a strict Hindu Brahman from Varanasi ever visited Bali, he'd think them savages. Although the Hindu epics are well known and form the basis of favorite Balinese dances, the deities worshipped in India are here considered too aloof and aristocratic. Often the Balinese don't even know their names. The Balinese have their own trinity of supreme gods, the Shrine of the Three Forces. Because of the caste system, 200 million people are shunned in India. On Bali only the older people still believe in the caste system; the young ignore it. In India a Hindu must be cremated at once in order to enter into heaven; because of the expense, on Bali sometimes a whole village will temporarily bury its dead and later stage a mass cremation. In India widows must not remarry but on Bali they can—here, even high priests marry. In India, worship at home is all-important but on Bali group worship is preferred.

Balinese Animism

The Balinese are scared witless of ghosts, goblins, and the like, which disguise themselves as black cats, naked women, and crows. Spirits dominate everything the Balinese do, and they are constantly offering fruit and flowers to appease angry deities. If put in our society, a Balinese would show all the classic symptoms of paranoia and neurotic disorders, but on Bali these traits are ritualized and institutionalized. There are sun gods, totemic gods, deer gods, secretaries to the gods, mythical turtles, market deities. Clay figures of the fire god are put over kitchen hearths, bank clerks place pandanus-leaf offering trays on their desks. *Ngedjot* are placed in the courtyards of every house; these offerings consist of little squares of banana leaves holding a few grains of rice, a flower, salt, and a pinch of chili pepper. No one eats until *ngedjot* are placed at the cardinal points in the family courtyard and in front of each house. Though mangy dogs eat the offerings as soon as they touch the ground, their essence has already been consumed by the spirits.

Gods and goddesses, who protect or threaten every act performed by a person during his or her lifetime, inhabit stone thrones and statues or simply hover in the air. Gods are often invited down to visit earth and are gorged with offerings and entertained with music and dance, but eventually they must go back home because they're too expensive to maintain. The Balinese always try to stay on the good side of all the forces. If the spirits are kept happy, the people can relax and even grow lighthearted. Children carry flowers to shrines and learn to dance at an early age to please the gods and the *raja*.

Feasts mark special periods in an infant's first year: three days after birth, 42 days after the first bath, 105 days after birth, and 210 days after birth—the first birthday celebration. At each stage of the agricultural cycle ceremonies are held, offerings made, and holy texts chanted. Even cockfighting was originally a temple ritual—blood spilled for the gods. During the 1965 political bloodletting in which 50,000 Balinese were killed, victims dressed in spotless white ceremonial attire before being led away to execution. Devils were believed to live in the communists or their sympathizers, and their deaths were necessary to cleanse the island of evil. Heaven? The Balinese believe heaven will be exactly like Bali.

Dualism

The Balinese religion divides most concepts into polarities: heaven and earth, sun and moon, day and night, gods and demons, man and woman, clean and unclean, strong and weak, hot and cold. The interaction of these contrasting pairs runs the world, creates harmony, and determines one's fate. Thus the Balinese witch, Rangda, who symbolizes evil, plays a useful role in guarding the temples. In Balinese folk medicine, headaches are cured by spraying the head with a mixture of crushed ginger and mashed bedbugs—a heated or irritated condition cured with a cooling medicine.

Spatial Orientation

The Balinese are one of the few island peoples who don't look towards the sea but upward towards the mountains. They believe everything high is good, powerful magic, healthy. The ocean below is sinister, filled with poisonous fish, sea snakes, and sharks. The highest of the island's mountains, Gunung Agung, is known as the "Navel of the World." The sacred mountains are "north," the sea "south"; these are the cardinal points and their villages, houses, and even their beds are aligned in these directions.

Festivals

There's an unending chain of festivals, over 60 religious holidays a year. The basic tenet of the Balinese religion is the belief the island is owned by the supreme god Sanghyang Widhi, and has been handed down to the people in sacred trust. Thus the Balinese seem to devote most of their waking hours to an endless series of physically and financially exhausting offerings, purifications, temple festivities, processions, dances, and cremations. Festivals are dedicated to woodcarving, the birth of a goddess, and percussion instruments; there are temple festivals, fasting and retreat ceremonies, parades to the sea, celebrations of wealth and learning.

Get a Balinese calendar; besides offering faithful pictorial representations of simple, realistic folk scenes, they show the most propitious days for religious activities. Try to catch one of the full moon ceremonies, a traditional affair that can last for some days. Lots of praying, singing, and dancing—a wonderful opportunity to interact with the people in their own environment on a special occasion. Your hotel owner will tell you what to wear or perhaps even dress you in traditional attire. Incidentally, ceremonies concerning people take place in homes rather than temples. The temples are only used for ceremonies to gods.

Cremation

On this extravagant occasion you'll see most of Bali's popular art and all the more important religious symbols. Cremation liberates the soul of the dead, allowing it to journey to heaven to rejoin the Hindu cycle of reincarnation. Bodies are buried twice on Bali: once at death, and again after being exhumed and cremated. These funerals are a time of tipsy hilarity, gossip, offerings, and dances, all brightened by continuous *gamelan* music. First the deceased is "re-awakened," the grave opened, and the remains placed on a decorated wood and bamboo tower, a fantastic creation of tinsel, paper, flowers, mirrors, silk, and white cloth. Because of pervasive power lines all over the island, the really tall towers of the past are seldom used today.

The corpse is then carried in a noisy procession to the cremation grounds. On the way it's spun around on top of men's shoulders to confuse the soul and prevent it from finding its way back to its house, where it might make mischief for the living. While tourists trip over themselves taking pictures, the splendid tower, offerings, and coffin are then set ablaze. As matches are considered unclean, blowtorches ignite the pyre, blasting both the cranium and feet, enabling cremations to take place even when it rains. Up until 1903, widows were burned in the great fires of the dead. After the blaze subsides, the eldest son rakes the ashes to make sure all the flesh is burned. To free the soul, the ashes are carried out to sea and scattered.

The Balinese don't sell tickets to their cremations, but they sell transport to the ceremonies. In tourist resorts you'll see signs announcing the event, as well as the address and telephone number of the transport agency. The local tourist office also knows when and where cremations take place. Some don't need advertising: the 1993 funeral for the last *raja* of Gianyar drew 50,000 people, almost two percent of the total Balinese population.

Temples

At least 20,000 temples grace Bali. If you see *pura* in front of a word, it means temple: *puri*, on the other hand, means palace. All temple complexes and historical sites now charge Rp550

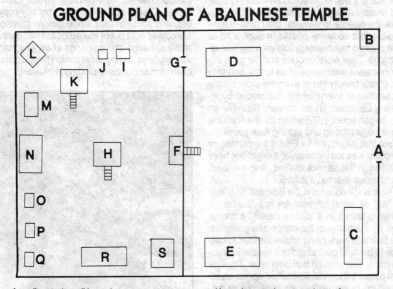

GROUND PLAN OF A BALINESE TEMPLE

A. split gate (*candi bentar*)
B. *kulkul* tower
C. kitchen (*paou*)
D. *bale gong* (*gamelan* orchestra)
E. *bale* (pavilion)
F. ceremonial gate (*padu raksa*)
G. side gate
H. *parungan* (seats of the gods)
I. *ngurah alit* (secretaries of the gods)
J. *ngurah gede* (secretaries of the gods)

K. *gedong pesimpangan* (seat of ancestor-founder)
L. *padmasana* (throne of sun god, Surya)
M. Gunung Agung (three-roofed *meru*)
N. 11-roofed *meru*
O. Gunung Batur (one-roofed *meru*)
P. Maospait (dedicated to Majapahit settlers)
Q. *taksu* (seat of interpreter of the deities)
R. *bale* (shed for offerings)
S. *bale* (shed for offerings)

admission, and you must be appropriately dressed. Not all sites require a sash, but all require at least a *sarung*. It's also common to sign a guest book. At some of the more obscure sites beware of guest books in which zeros have been added to all the preceding figures, making it appear donations have been substantial. Menstruating women are barred. Notice the exuberant ornamentation; carvings on temples are like the flowers and the trees. Bring binoculars to observe the extreme detail.

There are temples everywhere—in houses, courtyards, marketplaces, cemeteries, and rice paddies; on beaches, barren rocks offshore, deserted hilltops, and mountain heights; deep inside caves; within the tangled roots of banyan trees. At most intersections and other dangerous places temples are erected to prevent mishaps. Even in the middle of jungle crossroads, incense burns at little shrines. Four sites in particular stand out: **Gunung Kawi, Ulun Dau Batur, Ulun Danu Bratan,** and **Besakih.** The last is the Mother Temple of Bali, the state temple. It lies on the slopes of Gunung Agung, the "Navel of the World," the holiest mountain on Bali, where all the gods and goddesses live.

THE ARTS

The island's well-organized cultivation system and its astounding fertility have given the Balinese the leisure to develop their arts. It's incredible that so many people in such a small area pour so much energy into creating beautiful things. Their worship of life and the gods encompasses a wide range of art forms, and they can create beauty out of even the most simple necessities of everyday life. Influenced by incoming European artists, modern Balinese art only began about 1927, when for the first time artists began dating and signing their paintings. Before that, all art was for God. If the painting or sculpture was too innovative, it might not have qualified in the service of God, and the work would be considered a failure.

There is still no word in the Balinese language for "art" or "artist." A sculptor is a "carver," a painter is known as a "picture maker," a dancer goes by the name of the dance she performs. The Balinese have never allowed artistic knowledge to become centralized in a special intellectual class. Everyone on Bali is an artist. The simplest peasant and most slow-witted worker create something, or are aesthetically conscious as critical spectators. A field laborer will chide a clumsy instrument maker for a job poorly done. Even *dagang,* young girls who run small foodstalls, are skillful practitioners of Bali's classical dances.

But Bali's art is living on borrowed time. Communities are increasingly unwilling to subsidize the sumptuous ceremonies, music and dance troupes, and new costumes and masks, preferring the comforts of the modern lifestyle. The Balinese are very susceptible to fads: fashions, theater themes, new painting styles, dance crazes. They're unabashed and uncanny copyists, and some of their stone temple carvings are copied right out of magazines. Their earthy stone carvings and paintings show pregnant women, boys playing, beer drinking, seductions, even atomic bombs exploding in heaven.

VILLAGE HANDICRAFT SPECIALTIES

Babat: Sandstone carvings; silver- and gold-work.

Bangli and **Tampaksiring:** Coconut, cattle-bone, and buckhorn carvings.

Batuan: Woven goods. Known for traditional woven cloth and carved and decorated painted wooden panels. Also some painting.

Batubulan: Stone sculpture center. Lining the roadsides are fantastic stone figures and statues of divinities and demons sold as protective figures for family shrines, crossroads, or temples. Also known for stone bas-relief of mythological heroes. Watch the stonecarvers and their apprentices at work. Packing and shipping agents here as well.

Blaju and **Gianyar:** Weaving. Where most of the good *sarung* come from. Excellent places to shop for textiles.

Bona: A center of the plaiting industry. Baskets, hats, sandals, bags, and fans. They also build bamboo chairs, tables, birds, and flowers.

Bratan and **Celuk:** Weaving, gold- and silver-work. In Celuk the tourist buses disgorge the hordes on the main road shops, but the back lanes are where it's happening. Celuk has over 25 silver shops.

Goa Gajah: Baskets, shell carvings, and other curios. Cheaper than Denpasar.

Klungkung: Wood and horn handicrafts, bone carvings, fine woven silk. Several antique shops sell Chinese porcelain, ornamental gold and silver jewelry, and some old Gelgel dynasty relics.

Mas, Peliatan, and **Ubud:** Carving and painting centers. Some of the best-known Balinese carvers live in Mas.

Puaya: Puppets made from old Chinese coins. Leather puppets are also made here.

Perishable Art

The purest and oldest example of Balinese art is the ancient mosaic-like *lamak,* which last only a day. Woven by women for Balinese feasts, *lamak* are made from strips of palm leaf, bamboo, and yellow blades of sugar or coconut palm pinned or folded together to form fancy borders, rosettes, and diminutive tree designs. There are hundreds of different designs. After hanging a day on an altar or rice granary, they wilt by night. Other perishable arts include five-layered stacks of organic temple offerings, outrageous adornment on cremation towers, cones of edible fruits and cakes, and long rectangular panels of sculptural tapestry hung on temples and shrines. Hourglass-shaped palm-leaf fertility figures (*cili*) with round breasts and long thin arms appear when rice seeds first sprout.

Wayang

The Balinese form of *wayang kulit* has the same repertory as on Java, but puppets are smaller and more realistic than the Javanese variety. On Bali, *wayang* shows are performed in the open air, and men aren't separated from women, as on Java. In addition, Balinese theater forms aren't as strongly influenced by the two-dimensional shadow play. On Java the art of *wayang topeng* is dying, but on Bali it's still going strong. More expressive and typical of the characters than the *topeng* masks of Java, these pantomimes act out deeds of local kings and warriors in Balinese history, with usually two or three players impersonating the heroes. The preeminent maskmakers on the island are I Wayang Tangguh, Cokorda Raka Tisnu, and I Wayan Tedun of Singapadu; and Ida Bagus Oka, I Wayan Muka, and Ida Bagus Anom of Mas.

CARVING

The Balinese sculpt with natural media: wood, stone, bone, horn, even deadwood or gnarled tree roots. For the most part, souvenir-caliber woodcarving is turned out now, and successful creations are mass produced. There are only about a dozen places in Singakerta, Pengosekan, Kemenuh, and Mas, the main wood-carving centers, that sell high-quality carvings—and they want as much as Rp420,000 for one. You can negotiate a better price for a far superior product by taking note of the artist's name and visiting him in his home workshop. Bring cash. If you want something made to order it'll usually take about two weeks. Bring a photo or picture of what you'd like copied.

If you're looking for quality woodcarvings, go to Tegallalang, Pujung, and Sebatu, all north of Ubud. This is a great area to meet woodcarvers. Using very simple tools, top-class carvers earn only Rp5000 a day. Prices are cheap, and you'll see items unavailable in the expensive galleries of Mas. The wood used is ebony, jackfruit, teak, tamarind, hibiscus, or frangipani. Statues are usually finished with neutral or black shoe polish.

Balinese woodcarving is grotesque, almost psychotic, expressing vividly the people's fear of the supernatural. Features are distorted to emphasize a subject's special character—a frog's bulbous eyes, the sleek movement of fish, the graceful legs of deer. Figurine carving is unique, with faces rendered in painstaking detail. Still often seen are examples of the slender fluid form of figure sculpture with elongated arms and faces, inspired by a style born in the '30s when artist I Tegelan of Belaluan refused to cut a beautiful piece of wood in two.

Such mythological images as Hanuman wrestling with a serpent, or a dancing Sita, are common motifs. Painted woodcarvings of a heavenly nymph or mythical bird cost Rp20,000-35,000. Called The Bird of Life, the creature is used in cremation ceremonies to bear the deceased's soul to heaven. Chess sets of carved teakwood or bone pieces are quite distinctive; Vishnu riding on the shoulders of Garuda is the King. In Kuta the starting price is around Rp100,000, but sellers will come down to half that or less. For carved chopsticks, foot peddlers want as much as Rp8000 a pair, although you can get them as cheap as Rp3000-4000. Each stick is beautifully carved with owl or Garuda heads, abstract designs, etc. Boxed sets (12 pairs) go for only Rp15,000.

Bali is an ideal place for Western artists to study their crafts. Students of maskcarving, for example, can learn under the tutelage of masters like Muka or Anom in Mas. These teachers charge about Rp5000 per lesson. If you attend lessons every day you can learn to carve your own mask in about three weeks.

Stonecarving
Stonecarving is related to the craft of woodworking; since soft volcanic rock (paras) is used, the technique is much the same. Because Balinese believe constant maintenance of their stone temples is a moral obligation, stone sculpture is also a religious function. Stonecarving is relatively unaffected by tourist consumerism because most pieces are too expensive to ship. Stonecarving skill is most vividly seen in the distinctive split gates (candi bentar), swirling stone friezes, and absurd and menacing mythological statuary. The centers for stonecarving are Kapal and Batubulan; shops selling statues depicting characters from Balinese scriptures line both sides of the road. For something nontraditional, Wayan Cemul, just up the lane from Han Snel in Ubud, makes wild and wonderful paras sculptures.

PAINTING

Painting virtually died out on Java when the Majapahit Empire migrated to Bali during the 16th century. On Bali it's been practiced continuously for the last 400 years. For centuries Java was the Mother Country, and this is reflected in the subject matter of traditional Balinese art. Now most Balinese artists work solely for money, reasoning it's senseless to go to the trouble of making a good painting when a bad painting will sell for just as much, just as fast.

Try to visit artists at home (which you can find after persistent inquiry), and save yourself a percentage of the price which otherwise goes to the guide, driver, agent, or shop. The same paintings that sell for Rp5 million in the galleries on Ubud's main road sell for Rp420,000 just down the path in the kampung. High-quality paintings, if you can find them, cost roughly Rp420,000-840,000 per square meter. You'll often find that when you get back to Australia, the U.S., or Europe, the frame will cost more than the painting. Be sure to buy your frame in Bali, too.

Traditional Painting
Religious narrative paintings derive from the 14th and 15th centuries when the Hindu population of East Java relocated to Bali. They're characterized by a flat, stiff, formal style, painted according to a very strict traditional formula devoid of emotion. Figures of Hindu gods, demons, and princesses in lime watercolors are placed row on row in high state in the realm of the gods. Each god is distinguished by details of dress which set him or her apart. Shading to indicate perspective is traditionally not used. These paintings are read like a comic strip, the characters and events represented in separate

frames, the scenes all taking place in a divine world. Cloud and wind patterns, and flame and mountain motifs, separate the scenes.

Sometimes up to 15 meters long and four meters wide, these paintings are hung along temple eaves as festive decoration. Modern examples of these cloth paintings are still turned out, especially in Kamasan village. Although influenced by Western art, Balinese painters have retained many artistic traditions from their Javanese cultural ancestors. Balinese painting is still limited in subject matter, treatment, symbolism, and particularly in the colors used: blue, yellow, black, white, and Chinese red, with dull browns and greens mixed from the pigments.

Modern Painting

The period between the world wars brought heavy changes. Balinese artists stopped painting according to rules and started to re-create their own visual experience. During the years 1933-39, the European artists Walter Spies and Rudolph Bonnet, among others, demonstrated to Balinese artists that painters can be free of set formulas or a single stylistic convention, encouraging them to unfold individually. These Europeans taught them the concept of the third dimension. You can see Rousseau's style, which greatly influenced Spies, evident in Balinese painting. Tourist demand for paintings "suitable for framing" again changed the technique and content of the painting style.

Balinese painters are filled with stories and myths from childhood and never lack for an inspirational theme. Dozens of stories are depicted simultaneously in many of their paintings. In jungle scenes there's elaborate, riotous decoration of leaves, flowers, and animals, with every leaf carefully outlined. Reminiscent of Persian miniatures or the work of the English artist Beardsley, tiny blades of grass and insects are found in the farthest corners of the paintings. Artists are now working mostly for a European market. Birds and banana-leaf panels have lately become the rage—more decoration than art.

Art Galleries And Museums

To familiarize yourself with high-quality historical works, visit the collection of paintings at Ubud's Puri Lukisan Museum. Many of Bali's finest painters live in and around this village. To understand contemporary Balinese painting, see the Neka Gallery in Ubud, the Neka Museum north of Campuan, and the superb Agung Rai Gallery in Peliatan. Also visit the Art Center on Jl. Nusa Indah in Abiankapas, Denpasar, and its permanent exhibition of Balinese painting (open 0800-1700, tel. 0361-222-776), only a 15-minute walk east of Kereneng station. Called the Taman Werdi Budaya, the center also features Balinese and Indonesian maskmakers and woodcarvers. A car park, museum, and small, fixed-price handicraft shops with reasonable prices are also found in the complex.

You must ferret out the talented artists as it's difficult to find anything of quality—usually the same tropical scenes of birds and frogs, and copies at that. Prices vary wildly. The government store Sanggraha Kriya Asta in Tohpati (Badung) used to be a good place to determine fair bargaining prices, but in 1994 its silver, woodcarvings, and clothing were more than double what you'd pay at most shops in Ubud. Mobiles are still inexpensive, though.

SHOPPING

Due to the extravagant sums package tourists pay for Balinese artifacts, prices have become ludicrously high. Clothing, woodcarvings, bone work, and batik are usually cheaper in India and other Asian countries, and often of equal or better quality. Although Bali's silversmiths are more inventive, silverwork is just as cheap in Yogyakarta. The serious shopper needs to obtain the latest edition of Shopping and Traveling in Exotic Indonesia (Impact Publications, 9104-N Manassas Dr., Manassas Park, VA 22111, U.S.A., tel. 703-361-7300).

French tourists start raining down in July and August, and Australians and domestic tourists overrun the island at Christmas and New Years. From March through June crafts are about one-fourth to one-half the high-season prices. Bargains are unusual—at any season—particularly in silverware, watches, and clothing. Watches are cheaper in Kuta than anywhere else in Indonesia. They make excellent trading material in Lombok and the other Outer Islands. Use your bargaining skills and know the prices. Great places to shop for clothes are the giant supermarkets of Denpasar. Be careful when selecting loud and radical clothing—consider whether you'll wear the stuff back home.

On Bali, the asking price in a local market or from a peddler is not necessarily lower than that of an exclusive shop—they both start out at escalated prices. Vendors approach you constantly. If you don't like it or can't afford it, say vehemently, *"Sing ngeleh pipis!"* (Balinese for "I'm dead broke!"). You'll have plenty of chances to see a wide selection of items again and again at prices "only for you." If you let a guide take you into a crafts shop, he expects a commission of 10-20% or more.

Generally speaking, air-conditioned stores with glass doors and/or windows, price tags, and American Express signs are fixed-price shops. Also beware of art shops with huge gravel parking lots to accommodate tour buses: prices will be ridiculous. Sometimes it's smart to buy in fixed-price shops—if you find an honest, reasonably priced shop, at least you won't get cheated. A non-rip-off *harga pasti* shop will also give you a good idea of what you should pay for arts, crafts, and clothes.

If you've bought a lot of stuff and want to ship it back home, there are plenty of reputable shipping agents who'll do it for you. As a guide, it costs about Rp73,500 for 10 kg or Rp126,000 for 20 kg to Australia, including packing and insurance. Delivery requires six to eight weeks. Anything under 20 kg is usually delivered to your door.

Jewelry

Balinese silver is 92.5% pure and 7.5% other metals. When buying jewelry, the price depends on the weight, the design, the stone, or all three. Sample prices: silver bracelets start at about Rp252,000 with gold, Rp126,000 without gold; silver necklaces, Rp47,000; rings set with semiprecious stones, Rp105,000. Sellers will often come down 10-20%. Many jewelry shops also sell paintings, woodcarvings, and other souvenirs. Go in the back to watch them make silver articles.

Gold used in jewelry is three grams of gold to one gram copper. Almost any Balinese town features a gold shop, selling mostly traditional jewelry like earplugs and the large gold rings Balinese men like to wear. Dozens of Europeans sell their own personalized jewelry around Kuta and Legian. Denpasar's Jl. Sulawesi has a number of gold shops where you can buy attractive gold articles at a fair, fixed price. This is not the case in the art shops of Celuk, where you have to bargain like mad for a decent price. An option is to buy gold cheaply in other places in Southeast Asia and have it reworked into rings, brooches, and necklaces on Bali. Or trade silver or high-content silver coins for handmade jewelry. Artisans usually want a little cash in hand as well. Also bring stones for setting with striking backgrounds, or buy Indonesian stones like lapis lazuli, garnet, amethyst, onyx, and turquoise and have them set.

Want to learn silversmithing? Some *losmen* owners silversmith on the side. Or ask around for a *kampung* craftsman and work with him directly. A good place to start is the backroads of Celuk and Singapadu. Dozens of metallurgists and jewelers live and work in Banjar Sangging in the vicinity of Kamasan, producing by ancient methods delicately ornamented large silver and gold bowls. Ask for Banjar Pande Mas, where the gold- and silversmiths work.

Textiles

Take advantage of the inexpensive pants, shirts, and blouses available in shops and from beach peddlers—Kuta, Legian, and Sanur are the designer clothes capitals of Asia. In Ubud it costs only Rp5000 and three or four days to secure a perfect fit made to order in a tailor shop, so you shouldn't ever pay a peddler more than that amount plus the cost of material (Rp2000-5000). The most striking and distinctive cloth native to Bali is *ikat*, known on the island as *endek*, Bali's most visible craft. With its luscious colors, soft diffused look, and primitive patterns, *endek* is worn all over the island for all occasions. The most famous *endek* comes from the village of Tengenan in eastern Bali—double-*ikat*, or *gringsing*. Some villagers on Nusa Penida weave a red, brown, or yellow-patterned *ikat* that may be purchased in a few shops in Sampalan, Toyapakeh, and Klungkung.

Javanese *batik* garments are plentiful. Also keep a lookout for *kain prada* fabrics woven of silk or cotton and decorated with silver or gold threads or gold leaf. These very colorful kerchiefs are worn by temple girls during festivals. A ceremonial two-meter-long cloth could take from three weeks to a month to weave, depending on the intricacy of the design. Not washable; clean by dusting, then let it air in the sun. In the Klungkung area you might still find traditional gold-embroidered *songket* and amazingly elaborate *silk ikat*.

Shells And Trinkets
Two-hundred-year-old perforated Chinese coins (*kepeng*) with Chinese characters on one side and Pali script on the other are used in casting the I Ching. Puka shells are small, round, and white, sometimes dotted with brown. They're found only in Hawaii, the Philippines, and Bali. Buy small necklaces with uniform-sized shells. You'll pay premium prices in Kuta, but out at the *warung* around the surf hangouts of Bukit you can find really long chains for much cheaper. Turtle Island (Serangan) has the most gorgeous seashells.

Miscellaneous
If you want to buy decent leather products here, you're out of luck. Reasonable prices and average quality at Goa Gajah. You pay a bit more for marginally better quality in Denpasar, but the goods don't match Yogyakarta's standards. The village of Belaga near Blahbatu specializes in bamboo tables, chairs, and other furniture made of attractive spotted bamboo. Conical-shaped straw hats (around Rp3500) used by fieldworkers cut out the sun's rays exactly below the eyes and also make good umbrellas.

Bali is fast becoming an international center for primitive art. The highest concentrations of antique shops are in Kuta, Legian, and Sanur. Pejatan and Kapal are the ceramic centers of Bali. A ceramics cooperative in Pejatan makes neat little clay animals with dull matte finish and celedon glazes. Brent Heslin's shop next to Sanur's Batu Jimbar Restaurant exhibits high-fired functional ceramics. Many of the major hotels carry his stuff. For something different, *lontar* palm-leaf books are masterpieces of art and calligraphy; buy them in Tengenan. There's a shop in Denpasar's Pasar Kumbasari that specializes in kites.

THE PERFORMING ARTS

Music
Enormously loved by the people. The sound of echoing xylophones, drums, and clashing cym-

CLARA PRYOR

bals is heard all hours of the day and night. Bathers sing in the rivers, rattles clack in the fields, looms tingle with bells, kites vibrate in the wind, little boys walk along lanes imitating the sound of gongs, and flocks of pigeons circle overhead with whistles attached to their feet.

Some of the finest *gamelan* are made on Bali and cost up to Rp42 million. Every village has its own orchestra, given such names as Sea of Honey or Snapping Crocodiles. All musicians are unpaid amateurs. Anyone may play—a musician might hand over his *gendang* to a spectator during a performance. The Balinese *gamelan* is played more vigorously and passionately than the slower, more haunting Javanese variety. The Balinese like their music electrifying and very loud, with sharp changes in tempo and volume. Similar instruments are tuned slightly out of pitch with each other to make the sound shimmer. It's a perfect music for spells and animist rites. Old men play flutes in the background, dogs prance across the dance floor, infants suckle, children play—the musicians oblivious to it all. Many village orchestras practice in the evenings, when entry is free.

Listen for *genggong*, the Balinese mouth harp, a short thin strip from the rib of the sugar palm leaf with a grooved tongue. Tugging a string causes the instrument to vibrate; you "breathe" the tune. There's a whole repertoire of *genggong* pieces played by orchestras of up to 24 players. Two examples are "Crow Steals Eggs" and "Frog Song"; the latter sounds like the blissful rhythms of a frog's breeding chorus. These instruments can bleat, trill, croak, laugh, or lull you to sleep. Another unique Balinese instrument is the *rejog*: two deep gongs fastened to hang vertically at each end of a stick.

Dancing

Balinese dance will probably be the most impressive sight you'll see. With over 1,000 troupes, dance is at the very center of Balinese life. On Java dance is the prerogative of the courts, but on Bali it's most prevalent in the villages. The Balinese consider Javanese dancing boring, while the Javanese think Balinese dancing noisy and vulgar. Dancers on Bali perform for the pleasure of the gods, prestige, and the entertainment of friends and family.

In 1992, Bali's governor decreed that 11 sacred dances may not be performed in hotels. However, a great number of performances are staged especially for tourists; programs are written in Italian, Spanish, French, Dutch, German, Japanese, Korean, Chinese, and English. Many dance forms have been shortened to please the easily bored foreigner, but just because dances are put on for tourists doesn't mean they're of inferior quality. Restaurants and most hotels are not really sympathetic environments for Balinese dance, so try to choose an amphitheater or open-stage venue. If you don't like people in front of you popping up to use their flash cameras, get there on time so you can sit in one of the front rows. Please leave your cameras at home; flashes are very disrupting. Performances last an hour. Audio tapes are available at the entrance for Rp6000.

Try to see dancing in conjunction with a temple festival or other local ritual event. These are free and more spontaneous than tourist performances. On any night of the week you could see a number of different dance-dramas and ballets, honoring a local temple god, dedicating a new temple, exorcizing evil, or celebrating a wedding, tooth filing, or cremation. The stage could be an open dusty courtyard in front of a temple gate or a crossroads beneath the starry sky and towering palms. The dance area will be encircled by hundreds of squatting, sitting, standing people of all ages. The mood is electric.

Dance Choreography

Balinese dance is generally easy to understand; all you need is the thread of the story. In Balinese classical dance all movements and limbs speak—the joints, facial features, fingers, wrists, neck, eyes, hips, knees, feet, ankles. There are over 200 different kinds of dances, many religious, each a composite of not only dance, but also drama, music, spoken poetry, and ballet. Balinese dance styles stem from everyday work; dancers simply work gracefully and wear beautiful clothes when they perform. Men climb coconut trees with prehensile toes, which you also see utilized in some dance steps. *Pikulan*-carrying is excellent training for male dancers, the work giving them rhythm and good breathing technique, allowing them to effortlessly rise and fall in dance.

Women carry burdens on their heads, flicking their eyes in dance to greet each other and to watch where they step. Their fingers, trained from childhood to make small things, flutter with agility in dance, expressing feelings. Virtually everybody cracks their finger joints, enabling them to flutter their fingers in an exaggerated way. A good Balinese *legong* dancer can be judged solely by the suppleness of her little finger. Women's dance is pure form. Only in the men's dancing is the content open to interpretation. The Balinese don't dance upward and away from the earth, but move along its surface in slow, zigzagging circles. Female postures are characterized by an outcurved spine, buttocks pushed back, with the shoulders off center. With breasts and buttocks protruding, many poses are blatantly erotic. In both female and male dancing the limbs form angles. Elbows point upwards and the head sinks down so that the neck almost disappears.

Sudden changes of direction and precise jerky steps are marked features of Balinese choreography. They dance with a mesmerizing intensity; the only exceptions are the comic or grotesque characters who show shocked surprise or fear. Violence is shown on stage during a dance where it's not permitted in real life. You must have fire to dance, and it must come from the eyes. The complete lack of emotional expression of the other

BALINESE DANCES

Gambuh
The oldest dance practiced on Bali, over 1,000 years old, from which all other dances descend. Its mysterious music and slow, stylized form are unique.

Pendet
The welcoming or offering dance, performed by young girls before all dance performances. The basic female dance.

Kecak
This dramatic pre-Hindu dance is said to derive from the choral element of the trance dance, *sanghyang dedari*. Also called the "Monkey Dance" because of the savage ape sounds made by the performers; 100 or more seated men all shake, clap, and shout as one being. *Kecak* takes place in a big shadow-filled area at night with only burning torches set around the all-male choir. No *gamelan* accompaniment, just the massed voices chattering in perfect unison. Fierce eerie hissing and moaning, bellows, and other weird primeval sounds pierce the night. All bodies appear as black, throwing their arms out at once and shaking their fingers wildly. *Kecak* has borrowed some typical movements from Kuntao, a secret fighting art imported from China. The plot is taken from the Ramayana.

Barong
Also called the *kris* dance. A dance pantomime of a fantastic dragon-like holy animal, the *barong*, pitched in battle against the witch Rangda. This most violent of Balinese dances is often used in exorcism. The open-air *barong* dance is usually held in the middle of the road. Rangda is queen of the witches, a ruthless child-eater and black magician who brings sickness and death. Some scholars say her origin is Shiva's wife Durga in her evil aspect. *Barong*, a hairy, eerie, mythical lion, sides with human beings against Rangda to thwart her evil plans. *Barong*, manipulated by two men who take him through comic, yet complex, dance movements, has a beard of human hair, and hair, feathers, and bells all over his body.

Legong
Considered the most dazzling of all Balinese dances. Swathed in cocoons of gold-plaited fabrics, dancers perform interpretations of literary classics. A pair of young girls is chosen for good looks and supple physiques. If they look alike, so much the better. They're chosen before they begin menstruation—only then are they considered pure and limber enough to perform the necessary movements. Training begins at age four or five; they retire at about age 13. Extraordinary muscular control and great physical endurance are required in this dance.

Baris
A stately, un-Javanized native war dance performed for festivals and ritual feasts, *baris* is very typical of the most masculine aspects of Balinese life. Featuring heroic poses, expressive faces, sham battles, duels, and violent music, the *baris* is a male dance which passes through all the emotions: passion, pleasure, rage, tenderness, love.

Tari Tenum
A typical example of contemporary dance, portraying a woman making a *sarung*.

Sanghyang Dedari
Held only in time of trouble to alleviate sickness or misfortune, this celebrated shamanistic dance is a means of contacting the gods. This dance is often closed to tourists; tourist versions are laughable shams. Two autohypnotized little girls become possessed by the spirit of a god and dance on men's shoulders. They never open their eyes, yet their performances coincide perfectly. The girls have never had formal dance lessons, and after being revived by the priests they don't remember any of the performance.

Kebyar
An interpretive dance of many moods, *kebyar* is performed while squatting; the audience's attention is forced to focus on movements of the torso, arms, hands, and face.

Janger
A modern dance performed in a large square, with two rows of young men and women moving opposite one another. The story tells of a prince's search for a magic arrow. Led by a man, those at the side accompany the dance with rhythmical movements, tinkling music, and singing.

Joget
A popular Balinese dance. Each girl who performs chooses a partner from the audience, tapping him on the shoulder with her fan. Partners change every five minutes. Especially hysterical when a French clerk or Australian crayfisherman is tapped, with all his mates egging him on.

facial features can be likened only to a trance state. It's said experts can tell a dancer's teacher by the style in which she dances.

Dance Study

Watch or study *gamelan* and dance at SMKI, the High School of Performing Arts in Batubulan. There's also Sekolah Tinggi Seni Indonesia (STSI) on Jl. Nusa Indah in Denpasar. Though at this dance college you may sit in on classes, to seriously study Balinese classical dance you need a permit from Jakarta identifying you as a guest student. You can't really get involved with dance within the time allotted on an ordinary tourist pass—an average course lasts one to two years. For short term, it's more rewarding to go up to Ubud or out to a village to study dance

informally. One way to find a teacher is to first find a style you like by watching performances, then approach the artist directly for lessons. Stay for several weeks; they're glad to have you. Many of Bali's dance teachers are elderly women, who know the complete repertoire of the dances. It's a great pleasure to watch these masters teach their young students in the villages. The interpersonal dynamics between teacher and pupil are captivating to watch.

The biggest problem is language. Another problem is money. The teacher usually leaves it up to students to decide how much they should pay. A teacher may ask Rp5000 per lesson, but it's highly negotiable. Alternatively, the student may make a substantial donation to the *gamelan* orchestra.

ACCOMMODATIONS

Half the hotels in Indonesia are on Bali. The more than 4,000 accommodations fit every budget, from the refined sensual indulgences of the five-star Aman resorts for Rp630,000 per night to remote places like Toyabunkah on the shores of Lake Batur for Rp63,000 per night. There are Japanese hotels, Aussie hotels, hippie hotels, family inns, and *losmen* dives.

If you prefer top-end accommodations, complete hotel information and reservation services are available at the airport upon arrival. In the high-priced places a 15.5% government tax and service charge is added to your bill. There's usually no extra charge for children under 12 occupying the same room as their parents if no extra bed is required. If you want a cultural experience, family-run guesthouses, homestays, and *losmen* are preferable to hotels. You live right inside the family compound and participate in daily life. You learn how to make *lamak* from the grandmother, flutes from the father, kites from the small ones, *bebek tutu* (smoked duck) from the mother. The grandfather will take you to the next cockfight, the daughter will show you the shortest way to the market or how to sew a *sarung* into a skirt. The owner can find you the best dance, painting, or *wayang kulit* teachers, take you to a wedding or special ceremony, give transport advice.

The nicest, best-value places are often located down lanes on the wings of such resorts as Legian, Candidasa, Lovina, and Ubud; these accommodations tend to be lower-priced and more relaxing. Most are built in the Balinese style with cool *atap* roofs, quiet courtyards, and plain, sparsely furnished but comfortable rooms with electricity, shower, and private bath. The tariff is around Rp8000 s, Rp15,000 d. Your gear is usually quite safe in the family compound. The houseboys are good-natured, unsophisticated boys from nearby villages. They're overworked and underpaid and give the rooms occasional perfunctory cleanings that are friendly but mostly symbolic.

The low season is Feb.-May, when even Bali's expensive hotels will offer as much as 50% off standard rates. But during the high season (July, August, December, and January), accommodations are booked solid all over the island. Then it's essential to book in advance. If a small hotel has a swimming pool, it will charge Rp73,500 and up, but other comparable accommodations can be just as comfortable and cost only Rp42,000. No matter what the price, breakfast (coffee or tea, toast, fresh fruit salad, egg) is almost always thrown in for free. Accommodations in a given class can be so dissimilar in price, furnishings, location, atmosphere, and extras that it pays to search around for the place that best suits you.

For longer stays, Westerners gravitate to Penestanan (rice paddies, views, country life) and Peliatan (its music and dance appeal to the cultural tourist). Some Westerners even take out a 10-year lease at around Rp231,000 per month, make improvements on the property, then hand it over to the Balinese family at the end of the lease. Others negotiate a special per-day rate at a hotel or rent "under contract" a room or section of a *pondok wisata* (bungalow for rent) for several months while studying dance, music, painting, or puppetry. Since the 1930s Bali has been considered the perfect working environment for artists. Look for Rumah Disewakan (House For Rent) signs at the start of lanes.

Quite often when arriving in a resort you'll be approached by locals offering rooms. These rooms could be excellent, newly opened, the owners eager to please. Touts also work Kereneng station but most frequent Batubulan station in Denpasar. Many homestay owners, like Pande in Peliatan, meet tourists arriving in Bali at Kereneng and take them back to their homestays. Be open, listen carefully, and ask about services and discounts. Owners of newly opened accommodations tend to bend over backwards to find and keep guests.

Homestays of the highest rank are found all over the island—in the villages of Kuta, Legian, Ubud, Peliatan, Penestanan, and Candidasa; in the vicinity of Amlapura; in Lovina near Singaraja; and even in Denpasar itself. For extended vacations, there are beautiful isolated hotels on the south coast at Petitinget, Canggu, and Berawa Beach, far from nerve-racking, sybaritic Kuta. Some believe the posh hotels, immaculate boutiques, and well-groomed lawns of Nusa Dua to be the ultimate vacation get-away. Others consider them tourist ghettoes. But you can't dispute the luxury of these extravagant and elegant resort properties.

FOOD

Balinese food, when prepared and eaten by the Balinese, is very spicy and peppery (*pedas*). Often it's served cold. Frying is done in coconut oil. Grated coconut meat (*nyuh*) is an essential ingredient. Thick, rich coconut cream (*santan*), made by squeezing grated coconut, is used in many native dishes. Since the Balinese have a repugnance for dairy products, *santan* is substituted for cream. It doesn't keep, so it must be used the same day. By far their favorite food is *lawar,* a mixture of fresh pig's blood, raw flesh, and grated coconut in an obligatory spicy sauce. The men are generally better cooks than the women. At about 0400 on the morning before a ceremony, the old men of the *banjar* will gather for a few hours to make this delicacy. Each man returns home soon after dawn carrying his portion, which is immediately devoured with relish by the whole family.

Balinese also eat worms, frogs, dogs, flying foxes, snakes, porcupines, anteaters, lizards, wild boars, centipedes, grubs, birds, and ricefield eels. A child will take you out dragonfly-hunting, using a long thin pole with a sticky end. Take the wings off, fry the bodies in coconut oil until crisp, and eat with spices and vegetables. If you want to experience authentic Balinese royal banquet food, attend Pura Krambitan's **Puri Night** in Krambitan outside Tabanan town. Contact Mr. Ajus Erawan, tel. and fax (0361) 233-774.

Markets in most villages open every three days; here you'll find a cornucopia of grains, beans, greens, and fruit. Tropical fruits include *zirzak, salak* (best from Rendang), *nangka, jeruk* (pink are better), *durian, blimbing* (star fruit), breadfruit, mangosteens, passion fruit (from Kintamani), and white mangos (they'll melt in your mouth). You'll also come across such exotic vegetables as acacia leaves (*twi*), greens (*kankung*), edible ferns (*paku*), and tapioca leaves (*ketela pohon*), all ingredients in many of the roadside *warung* dishes. Sweet potatoes (*ubi*) with coconut, fresh groundnuts, rice porridge, and *sambal* or spicy peanut sauces also constitute the staples of nearly every *warung.* In these simple bamboo eateries you can sample some of the best food on the island for less than Rp1000.

Babi Guling

Although most Indonesians are Muslim and don't eat meat, on Bali pigs are bred and cooked magnificently. Don't miss the island's famous delicacy, *babi guling,* suckling pig roasted on a spit and stuffed with red chilies, garlic, turmeric, ginger, aromatic leaves, and peppercorn. The flesh is juicy and tender, the skin crisp and covered with a golden-brown glaze. Serves four or five. Roast duck (*bebek tutu*), an equally famous Balinese delicacy cooked in banana leaves, serves two or three; the best is prepared in Peliatan. Order these specialty items at least 24 hours in advance. Or you can try the very best *babi guling* in several *warung* in Pasar Gianyar, where they roast more than a dozen animals a day and the food is always fresh and delicious. Allow Rp10,000 for two people.

Western And Indonesian Dining

As for Western food, dishes like lobster, home-style steak, and pizza are found in all the tourist resorts of Bali, though the dishes lose something in the translation, perhaps because of the use of local ingredients. For example, tacos are usually stir-fried vegetables on a big cracker, bearing no relation to a real taco. Pancakes are made without leavening, and Balinese curry bears about as much resemblance to Indian curry as Westminster Abbey to the Taj Mahal.

The island's best Japanese restaurants are in the Galleria in Nusa Dua and the Shima Restaurant in Sanur. Thai food has recently become the rage; try the beautifully appointed Swasdee Restaurant on Jl. Pura Bagus Taruna in Legian and the elegant, open-sided Kokokan Club on Jl. Pengosekan in Peliatan, both featuring dishes spiced with lemongrass, lime, and mint.

Such Indonesian national dishes as *mie goreng, sate,* and *gado-gado* are served in restaurants everywhere. Lombok-style eateries offering scrumptious *ayam taliwang* are found on Jl. Teuku Umar on the way from Denpasar to Kuta. Look for a nontourist restaurant with plenty of Indonesian patrons. They are very fastidious eaters and you can bet the food will be good. A tip: if you don't write your order down precisely, half the time they'll get it wrong. Very popular in the big hotels of Sanur, Kuta, and Nusa Dua is Balinese-style *rijstaffel* (Rp9000 to Rp19,000), made of well-spiced regional fish, vegetable, and meat dishes, often accompanied by a haunting *tingklik* orchestra. The Saturday night *rijstaffel* in Sanur's Tanjung Sari Restaurant is spectacular.

There's even a growing health food consciousness evident in restaurants, particularly in Ubud, with vegetarian items regularly appearing on menus. Whole-wheat bread (called "brown bread") is becoming widely available in Ubud, Sanur, Lovina, Kuta, and Legian.

Liquid Refreshment

Sample some mellow homemade native brews: *arak* (distilled rice brandy), *tuak* (sweet palm beer), and *brem* (rice wine). *Brem* is available either by the bottle (Rp3000) or glass (Rp1500). *Brem tua* (old *brem*) is more expensive than *brem manis* (sweet *brem*). You won't find a decent bottle of grape wine on Bali, but high-quality mixed drinks and cocktails are served in most tourist restaurants for Rp5000-Rp12,000. Big plastic containers (1500 milligrams) of water can be bought at grocery and convenience stores for around Rp1000, in the corner *warung* for Rp1500. Because of the heavy influx of European tourists, in the sophisticated cafes of Kuta, Sanur, Ubud, and Lovina you can sample not only Balinese but Colombian and Brazilian coffees and frothy, piping hot cappuccinos and espressos. Balinese sweets (*lak-lak, gilinggiling, culek, batun cluki*) are traditionally served with grated coconut and palm sugar on top.

SPORTS AND RECREATION

Water Sports

Bali is a popular scuba and snorkeling destination, famous among divers for its marinelife, superb visibility, and sensational drop-offs. It was on Bali that drift diving became popular, following the development of techniques to accommodate the deep ocean currents surrounding the island. The spectacular **Menjangan Wall** in the northwest part of the island is commensurate with northern Sulawesi's Bunaken.

A great number of dive operators offer gear, tanks, wetsuits, lunch, transport, experienced dive masters, excellent Balinese-style accommodations, and porters to and from the beach for about Rp126,000-147,000 per dive. A PADI Advanced Course takes two days and costs Rp504,000. **Baruna Diving,** the largest dive operator on Bali (offices in Kuta, Sanur and Nusa Dua) is a good place to start.

The surf breaks for which Bali is famous are at Uluwatu and Padang, best when the southeast winds blow onshore during the dry season. During the wet (Jan.-March) surfers nip over to the other side of Bukit Peninsula to Nusa Dua, Sri Lanka, and Sanur where the wind will be offshore. Surfing is the big attraction of the offshore island of Nusa Lembongan; three of Indonesia's most outstanding surf breaks are here.

One of Bali's nicest and least known beaches—with good swimming and warm water—is located next to the airport in Tuban and Jimbaran. Off Kuta Beach the waves can be very deceptive; seven or eight people drown each year, caught in the vicious undertows. For your own safety, swim only between the clearly marked red and yellow flags, and don't swim deeper than your body length. Lifesavers constantly patrol the beach during daylight. Never swim after sunset.

You can enjoy dolphin-watching in the early morning in Candidasa and Lovina. Catering to Japanese demand, fleets of game fishing boats are based in Benoa, Bali's main port. One of the favorite sportfishing spots for wahoo, Spanish mackerel, and tuna is under the awesome 100-meter-high cliffs of Nusa Penida. For more information on sportfishing, contact **PT Tour Devco Benoa,** tel. (0361) 231-591.

A wonderful diversion is **Sobek Rafting Tours,** tel. 287-059 or 289-448, down the 11-km-long Ayung River; you'll find brochures on hotel reception desks all over Bali. With four, five, or six persons per raft, the Class III trip runs about two hours through Bali's last original rainforest—a botanist's delight. The Rp119,700 price includes a big, delicious catered buffet. Just dangerous enough to be scary but definitely not life-threatening. **Bali Adventure Rafting,** tel. 751-292 is another, Australian-trained professional rafting outfit.

Cockfighting

Fights have been declared illegal by Muslim Indonesians but still take place on the sly in almost every village, usually in the mornings. Ask around to find them. They may coincide with *upacara* temple ceremonies and festivals. You see only men at the cockfights, though tourist women may attend tourist fights.

Fighting cocks are given the greatest loving care, massaged, bathed, and trained every day. Their feathers, combs, and wattles are trimmed so they won't provide a beakhold for opposing birds. The owner concentrates on the bird's diet and strives to develop a lean and tireless fighter. Pet, mascot, child, dream, income, the owner always carries the bird around the courtyard and to the *warung* or clubhouse. Their bell-shaped wicker cages are placed at roadsides so the cocks may be amused by passersby.

Two cocks eager to fight are decided upon, then bets are placed. A village will put as much as a million *rupiah* on its favorite cock. Then the fight is blessed. Evil spirits receive offerings that will hopefully satisfy them and ensure a good harvest. The birds are teased by their handlers—tails pulled, feathers ruffled, palm wine spit down their throats, all intended to arouse the fighting spirit. The trainers then tie a sharp scissor blade to each cock's stronger leg. The birds are riled up some more, then let go. Predominantly a male-bonding event, the crowd is fused in a single gesticulating, shouting, hysterical body. The fight is often finished in 15-20 seconds. The cocks display amazing ferocity even when crippled. If both refuse to continue they're put inside an upside-down basket, where one almost always kills the other. Often a badly wounded cock can be revived by artificial res-

piration or special massages. Then it will fight again, and win.

Bull Races

Outside Negara in western Bali, thrilling regional water buffalo races (*mekepung*) are held on the Sunday before Indonesia's Independence Day, and again every other Sunday each September and October. Only the island's handsomest, sleekest bulls—which are not used for plowing or as beasts of burden—are chosen to compete. After extensive training, the huge beasts are dressed up in silk banners with painted horns and big wooden bells. Each team is judged for speed, strength, color, and style. Like Roman charioteers they come thundering down to the finish line, whipping and shouting, mud flying. Jockeys twist the tails of the bulls to gain speed. Much gambling. This festival is staged to please the harvest god. The winning bulls are used for stud and fetch up to twice the market value when sold.

Golf

One of the world's top 50 golf courses is on the grounds of the **Bali Handara Kosaido Country Club** in Pancasari near Lake Bratan. Judged fifth in the world for technical design and service, this 18-hole championship course features tall trees and flowers in riotous colors separating the fairways. Other fine golf courses are at the **Bali Beach Hotel** in Sanur and at Nusa Dua.

Running

Begger's Bush, tel. (0361) 975-009, on the right in Campuan just after the bridge when coming from Ubud, is the headquarters of the Bali chapter of the Asia-wide **Hash House Harriers,** a running club. Your host, Victor Mason, who runs barefoot with his two dogs, steps larger than life out of a Somerset Maugham short story. Victor also escorts amateur ornithologists through the fertile countryside surrounding Ubud on his very entertaining and informative "Bali Bird Walks." The price of Rp58,800 includes guide, Balinese-style lunch, drinks, and use of binoculars.

GETTING THERE AND AWAY

By Air

For details on international flights into Indonesia, see "Getting There" in the On the Road chapter. The Denpasar airport is large, well-organized, and modern. Bali now has a beautiful, air-conditioned, two-level international terminal with color TVs, gift shops, spacious departure halls, lounges, and comfortable seating. For international flights, get there at least two hours before departure. International departure airport tax is Rp13,000; domestic departure airport tax is Rp6000. Airport storage is Rp3000 per item per day.

To keep the stress low upon arrival, it's nice to get a place to stay without running around. After you emerge from customs inside the terminal you'll see a well-staffed visitor's desk. This helpful service offers a great choice of accommodations in all price classes, and you can learn of "specials" or discover new places to stay not in any of the brochures. Staff will also call a hotel to make sure there's a vacancy before you get there, reconfirm a room, and arrange for pick-up. Outside the terminal are moneychanging offices. You might as well change money here as these offices give just as good a rate as anywhere on the island.

Outside the terminal lurk touts and hotel proprietors. If you don't have a place to stay, these could be viable and good-value—they may be new and eager to please. Listen, peruse photos and brochures, ask about location, services, and rates, and try to get a discount. Some try to push expensive rooms with the argument that the lateness of the hour makes it difficult to find a room (not true). If it doesn't work out, at least you get a free ride into town. The higher-priced hotels have vans waiting outside to give guests who book ahead free rides. Boys hold up signs announcing the names of the hotels.

If you just want a reliably clean, comfortable, friendly, moderately priced, nearby overnight accommodation, take a taxi to the **Mastapa Garden Cottages,** tel. (0361) 751-660, in Kuta or the quieter **Orchid Garden Cottages,** tel. 751-802 or 752-852, in Legian, a village just north of Kuta. Call and they might pick you up. If you want to shift down from the tourist mecca

into a laid-back beach resort, take a taxi (Rp40,000, three hours) direct to Balina Beach in eastern Bali. To discover the attractions of rural Bali, beautiful upland alternatives are Tirtagangga or Sideman, also in east Bali.

If you already know of a good place to stay, right outside the main hall there's a taxi counter where you can purchase regulated and fixed-priced transportation to anywhere on the island. Pay in advance. If you're going to Ubud and you want to save money, get a taxi to Denpasar's Batubulan station (Rp10,000), then a minibus to Ubud (Rp1000). Or take a taxi straight to Ubud for Rp35,000 (one hour). Alternatively, to avoid taking a taxi from the airport, walk about 500 meters to the road outside the airport where cheaper transport runs until 2200. Just hop on any *bemo* heading north. One can more easily bargain for a cheaper taxi charter-rate *bemo* outside the airport. Ask around to share a vehicle.

By Road

Be very aware that theft is rampant on the night buses from Java to Bali. Carry anything of value (like a camera) with you at all times. Even if your luggage is locked, thieves can get in. Be extra cautious where the bus loads onto the ferry at Ketapang on the tip of East Java. If you're late for the ferry, go down the beach to the ferry depot. The passage across the Bali Strait takes 45 minutes. From the ferry depot on the Bali side in Gilimanuk, take a *dokar* to the terminal and board a bus or a minibus for Denpasar (Rp3000). Alternatively, Lovina Beach is 87 km distant; this coastal resort strip, which begins about 10 km west of Singaraja, is more tranquil and less expensive than the over-touristed south.

Getting Away

If heading for Java, take a taxi or *bemo* to Denpasar's Ubung station, which has many bus company offices. There are pages of bus company listings in the yellow pages of the Bali phone book. The last bus to Yogyakarta leaves at 1730, but there are plenty of buses to Surabaya with free meals, cold water, a/c, and video (violent Chinese kung fu movies). If you're catching a flight out of Jakarta, allow three days to get there no matter what they say in the bus company office.

If you intend to leave the island by air, you can order a ticket anywhere on Bali. It takes 48 hours for your money to be sent to Denpasar and the ticket returned via shuttle or other courier service. To reconfirm reservations costs Rp4000-6000 if done through a travel agency, or you can phone Denpasar air offices yourself for less. Continental, Qantas, and many other international airlines staff offices at the Bali Beach Hotel.

GETTING AROUND

By Foot

The best way to see Bali is to walk in the countryside. Take half-hidden narrow pathways at roadsides and follow them inland, sometimes as far as 15 km. You'll reach places about as outlandish as you want to be, with no cold drinks, police, shops, electricity, or transport connections. Children pop up and yell out a singsong "hello!"; infants may start screaming at the sight of you.

By Bicycle

If you ride a bicycle around Bali, you'll have much more contact with the villagers and enjoy more scenery than if you're on a speeding, smelly, noisy, dangerous motorcycle. Bicycles rent for only Rp5000 per day (Rp8000 for mountain bikes), and are cheaper by the week or month. Consider buying a bike from a *toko sepeda* in Denpasar, then arrange to have the place buy it back after you use it for several weeks or months. Because the seats are hard and uncomfortable, buy a cushioned saddle and a seat post for long-distance riding. Repair costs are very reasonable.

To get to the Bali highlands, load your bike on the back of a *bemo* or minibus; when you get ready to come back it's two days coasting downhill. It'll usually cost you an extra passenger's fare to put your bike on a *bemo*. Bring your bike inside your accommodations at night to prevent ripoffs.

By Motorcycle

Renting motorbikes may at first appear the best option, but they often prove more trouble and expense than they're worth. Intrusiveness in quiet villages, pollution, breakdowns, and injuries all argue against them. Even experienced bikers are victims of shattered nerves after just a week of riding on Bali, where trucks drive right down the center of the road, and chickens, dogs, and children dart out everywhere. Driving at night is especially hazardous; insects batter you, piles of sand litter the road, visibility is nil. You also have to worry about gas (Rp750 a liter) and oil money, as well as parking fees at nearly every tourist site. Basic rules for driving a motorcycle on Bali: always wear a helmet and goggles or glasses; don't drive too fast; never stop on sand or loose gravel; slow down on curves; always toot your horn when approaching people or animals; carry a windbreaker at higher elevations; and stop driving before sundown when the insects come out.

Off-season rental rates for an ordinary 100-125 cc motorbike are Rp12,000-15,000 per day, Rp75,000 per week. More difficult to find but easier to drive are motorbikes with automatic starting and shifting; just insist on it and one will show up sooner or later. The more powerful and newer the machine, the higher the daily rate; the longer the rental period, the lower the rate. Rental costs rise when the Europeans or Australians arrive in August, December, and January. You'll be approached constantly by guys offering to rent you bikes. A good place to start your inquiries is in your hotel or homestay. Be wary of overcharging for faulty equipment. In most cases, a helmet comes with the bike.

By Ojek

Look upon any vehicle as a potential taxi. To *naik ojek* is to ride with the driver on the back of a motorcycle for a fee. You can spot *ojek* drivers because they carry two helmets. Also called *honda sikap*, *ojek* drivers collect passengers at the start of country roads and take them to remote temples, villages, and tourist sites. Journeying by *ojek* is also the cheapest, quickest, and most convenient way to travel short distances on Bali. Flag them down anywhere.

By Taxi

For short distances metered radio taxis are extremely handy. These air-conditioned Japanese cars are blue and yellow with a taxi sign on the roof; a/c, and quite comfortable for up to three adults. Most drivers are friendly but usually speak little English. Always insist the driver switch on the meter and don't agree to pay a fixed price for a trip. The asking price is always much higher. When they say "it's up to you," it means the trip is going to be really expensive; sometimes there are nasty misunderstandings. Minimum fare at flag-fall is Rp800, and most trips within the Kuta/Legian area are around Rp2000-4000. The fare from Kuta to Sanur is around Rp6000. If you go from Kuta to Sanur and then Ubud, letting the car wait and using it for four or six hours altogether, the fare should be about Rp8000-10,000 per hour by the meter.

By Bus, *Bemo,* And Minibus

Bali's cheapest and fastest motorized transport are 30-passenger Izusu minibuses and *bemo,* excellent for observing Balinese native life. The island's transport system is now so extensive you can go virtually anywhere on day-trips from Denpasar, Ubud, or Singaraja. If there's no direct express service, travel in stages. *Bemo* run along the roadways at a steady rate and, when approaching the cities, in a constant stream. It's just a matter of making the connections. The driver or his assistant will know where to drop you to connect with your next *bemo.* Batubulan, 10 km northeast of Denpasar, is the *bemo* hub for central, northern, and eastern Bali. When traveling by *bemo,* always allow plenty of time for your return trip. If you need to return to Ubud after visiting Amlapura, make sure you get the last minibus leaving Amlapura around 1700.

Being charged the proper fare without a lot of bargaining and hassle is the exception rather than the rule. Usually *bemo* drivers start by asking 50-100% above the appropriate fare and must be bargained down. Watch what the Balinese are paying; pay what they pay. Also ask your *losmen* or homestay owner for the normal fare. *Bemo* within cities, like Denpasar and Singaraja, cost only Rp400-500 for an average ride. *Bemo* prices in the country, for the same distances, are cheaper. You can charter a *bemo* for about Rp40,000 per day between five or six people, but watch these street robbers, as they normally charge at least double the price of the metered taxis. Always have the correct change; driver's assistants never have the correct change. Pay at the end of the journey. Many *bemo* have internal buzzers that you use when you near your destination. Otherwise tap lightly on the window or shout *"stop!"* Be prepared to step over sacks of rice, trussed chickens, bundles of copra, etc.

Thefts of travelers' belongings on *bemo* are not as frequent as in the past, but they still occur. Once confined only to Denpasar, special robber *bemo* now cruise the roads looking for unwary travelers. Once on board, the traveler is pickpocketed and/or manhandled out of his or her money by a group of young men who crowd around to intimidate and confuse. As a rule, don't get into "rogue" *bemo* occupied only by young men. Bona fide, registered *bemo* have yellow-black license plates.

By Shuttle Bus

A godsend for travelers, travel agencies and hotels all over Bali offer regular shuttle-bus service to points all over the island. Shuttles save you the trouble of renting or chartering vehicles, yet are quick, inexpensive, and safe. They're also a good alternative to public transport. The Kuta-to-Ubud shuttle departs five or six times per day, takes an hour, and costs Rp7000. Public transport from Kuta to Ubud takes several hours and costs Rp3000. Shuttles also operate from Ubud to Bedugul and Lovina twice daily, and even to Gili Trawangan on Lombok. All of them also run vice versa. You can usually order tickets through your hotel. Fares range from Rp7000 from Kuta to Ubud to Rp25,000 from Kuta to Gili Trawangan.

The most efficient shuttle outfit is **Perama Landsea Adventure,** with offices in tourist areas throughout Bali. The drivers are always on time, fast, and well-organized. Most shuttle services offer a bonus: no extra charge for stopovers en route; just pick up another shuttle the next day.

By Rental Vehicle

There are hundreds of hotels, restaurants, and travel agencies where you can rent four-wheeled vehicles, priced according to type, age, and condition of the vehicle. The price should always include insurance and unlimited mileage. Kuta, Tanjung, and Sanur have the largest concentration of car rental agencies. Jimmys rent for Rp35,000-40,000 per day. Toyota *kijang* cost up to Rp60,000 per day for one to three days, and Japanese compacts like Mazda sedans or Suzuki four-wheel drives are also widely available for around Rp45,000 per day. Air-conditioned cars are more expensive. If you rent a vehicle for a month, you could get it for as little as Rp30,000 per day. If you want to cover long distances, a four-wheel drive or gutsy Katana is the way to go. Landcruisers cost Rp75,000 per day and up.

You can save yourself hassles if you rent a car with driver, which costs only a bit more than a car without driver and you don't have to buy insurance. Before committing yourself, make sure the car's emergency brake and odometer work. Check the oil; the vehicle is often empty of oil when turned over to you. Examine the tread, as Bali roads are rocky. Cars don't come with seatbelts, which is really scary since you need them here perhaps more than anywhere else in the world.

Traffic conditions worsen by the day. It's now very stressful to drive a car, let alone a motorcycle, in the Tabanan-Denpasar-Gianyar-Klungkung area. In the high season the drive to Ubud is sometimes bumper-to-bumper trucks, vans, cars, motorbikes. If you're going to tackle Bali's mountains, do so in the daylight so you can take in the scenery; it's also safer. Honk your horn when you see people on the road ahead and before dangerous turns to let other drivers know you're coming. It's better to be an obnoxious asshole than to kill or be killed.

Driver's License And Insurance

An International Driver's License is all that's needed to legally drive; get one for a small fee through your local automobile club. If your IDL is not valid for motorbikes, then you need a Balinese Driver's License. If you don't have a valid license, you might be assessed a hefty fine at police roadblocks set up occasionally. The police station is on Jl. Seruni, about a 15-minute walk from Stasiun Kereneng. A license costs Rp30,000 or Rp40,000, depending on the mood of the officer. Answers to the license test are: BCCACACCCCCCACBCABABAA. If you don't know an answer, just ask the attendant what

the question means and she'll swiftly provide the solution.

Gas

Pertamina stations, found on all the main roads, charge around Rp750 per liter. Roadside vendors, recognizable by the sign *solar* (diesel) and premium (gas), charge only Rp650 per liter, but they water down the gas, which can cause your engine to sputter. Gas can be scarce, and they may refuse to sell it to you. Have the person you hire the car from fill the tank. Always check prices when you stop for gas because attendants may try to rip you off by as much as Rp10,000.

By Boat Or Yacht

Sailfish-shaped *prahu* look like a sort of elephant fish with a long double trunk and big bloodshot eyes. Sail close to shore; a *prahu* takes two people to handle. Larger, longer, native-style public boats take passengers from Kusamba, Padangbai, and Sanur to the offshore islands of Nusa Lembongan and Nusa Penida for Rp15,000 pp. One-way charters from Sanur or Kusamba to the islands cost Rp60,000-75,000. The whole-day charter rate is Rp250,000 depending on size and speed of boat.

Benoa is Bali's main port where foreign yachts call; take a canoe out and ask around for a ride. High-end **Rasa Yachts,** tel. (0361) 288-756, operates luxury yachts on day-trips or extended cruises. Other yacht charter outfits to check out are **Bali Yacht Charter,** tel. 887-739, and **Golden Hawk Cruises,** tel. 887-431. For Rp147,000 per person, the **NL Reef Club,** tel. 231-591, embarks on exciting day-trips aboard the *Wakalouka,* a prestigious 23-meter-long catamaran. For the eastern islands, ferries leave the Balinese port of Padangbai for Lembar on Lombok.

Tours

Numerous travel/tour operators are listed in the Bali phone book under "Travel Bureaus." Most operators are reliable, and the tours can be an excellent value. Most only run if there are at least four people, so if one place can't run the tour you want when you want it, check out the next place. On all tours you're picked up at your hotel. Most also take in sites along the way, and the tour could last all day. Don't let them stop in too many silverware and woodcarving shops; the drivers and guides get commissions, so shop prices will be inflated.

Tour participants may modify the tour by pitching in and paying extra. For example, from Penelokan down to the crater floor costs an extra Rp5000 on the **"Kintamani Volcano Tour,"** which takes in Goa Gajah, Pejeng, Tampaksiring, Penelokan, Bangli, and Gianyar for Rp20,000. Most budget hotel owners also offer personalized tours. Ask your hotel proprietor about the **"Pony Day Tour"** (Rp115,000 per person, 0830-1400) or call (0361) 751-672 or 751-746 for reservations. These retired, spirited racing ponies from Java take you down narrow paths between rice fields. The tour ends with a gallop on the beach. Another unique adventure is the **whitewater rafting** tour down the Ayung River (Class III); arrange booking (Rp119,700 per person) from almost any hotel or by calling 287-059 or 289-448. **Iskander Wawo-Runtu,** tel. 288-441, explores the untouched side of Bali (Rp126,000 per person) on high-tech mountain bikes from his farm in Pupuan down to the sea. You'll see beautiful rice fields, forests, rivers, steep ravines, and remote villages.

DENPASAR REGENCY

Once part of Bandung Regency, in 1992 the Denpasar area split off and became Bali's ninth *kabupaten.* In addition to the island's capital, Denpasar Regency encompasses Sanur, Benoa Port, and Serangan Island, leaving Bandung more pencil-shaped than ever.

DENPASAR

Denpasar is the largest and busiest city on the island. An old trading center, its name means "east of the market." It's the headquarters for the government, the media, the island's principal banks, airline offices, and hospitals. Bali's two universities, Udayana and Warmadewa, are also based here. The city's local name is Badung, its old name, and you'll hear "Badung" sung out by *bemo* drivers all over Bali. Though it's been the capital of Bali since 1958, it's no longer the administrative center of Badung Regency. In 1992, Greater Denpasar and Sanur split off from Badung and formed their own administrative entity—Denpasar.

A hot, dusty, cacophonous, former Brahman-class city, Denpasar has grown fifteen-fold over the past 10 years, and is now home to 367,000 people. Its citizenry consists of Badung's landed gentry, the priest class, and the new Balinese techno and bureaucratic elites, as well as Indonesians drawn from other islands to this economic magnet. Denpasar is one of Indonesia's most fully integrated and tolerant cities, with separate *kampung* of Bugis, Arabs, Indians, Chinese, Madurese, and Javanese. Without doubt it's the richest, most important city in eastern Indonesia.

Unless you've got business here, the city has few charms, other than those quiet back alleyways where people are quite friendly. The most important government offices are located in a tree-shaded administrative complex of handsome reddish brick and gray stone. Industry is low-tech and non-polluting. Denpasar is actually best at night, when it's not so hot and the individual *kampung* resume their normal rhythms. It seems the whole population is either directly or indirectly involved in the tourist industry and you can easily engage people in conversation.

Denpasar's main one-way east-to-west shopping street, Jl. Gajah Mada, is crammed with chauffeured cars, noisome put-putting *bemo,* roaring motorcycles, and smelly spewing buses. The city's limited attractions include a spacious *alun-alun,* tourist information offices, the island's main bus stations and best-stocked markets, some good Chinese restaurants, a spirited night market, dance and drama academies, a major art center, first-class museum, and five big cinemas heralding the coming of the next kung fu epic.

DENPASAR REGENCY

NOT TO SCALE

© MOON PUBLICATIONS, INC.

SIGHTS

A great place for families to hang out in the evenings is the huge well-kept park in the middle of town, **Puputan Square,** named for the bloody 1906 extermination of the island's ruling class by the Dutch. An heroic-style monument facing Jl. Surapati commemorates this tragic event. Note the woman with the *kris* in one hand and jewels in the other. Eyewitnesses of the time reported that female members of the court tauntingly flung their jewelry at the Dutch troops before being mowed down by rifle fire.

On every side of Taman Puputan are the traditional symbols of the power elite. North of the square is the **Governor's Residence,** built in Javanese *pendopo* style. Facing the Bali Museum is the stolid, modern military headquarters complex. Just south of the square in the middle of the city's busiest intersection is a five-meter-high, four-faced, eight-armed statue—Mukha, representing Batara Guru, "God of the Four Directions," who is even-handedly blessing all the cardinal points simultaneously.

The Bali Museum
The largest collection of Baliana in the world is located on the east side of Taman Puputan on Jl. Mayor Wishnu just south of the tourist office. The Bali Museum was established in 1910 by the conquering Dutch, who sought to collect and preserve artifacts they felt were disappearing overseas or succumbing to the elements. In 1917, an eruption of Gunung Batur and subsequent earthquakes destroyed hundreds of Denpasar's buildings, including the museum. Rebuilt in 1925, it was used as a storehouse for artifacts and temporary exhibits until 1932, when it was established as an ethnographic museum. The German painter Walter Spies helped assemble many of its original treasures from private collections and donations.

The grand, well-kept complex consists of a series of attractive, grassy courtyards containing all the archetypes of Balinese architecture—*bale agung, candi bentar, kulkul.* The main structure, with its many pillars, is built in the manner of Puri Kanginan in the eastern regency of Karangasem. Standing next to it is a reproduction of Singaraja Palace on the north coast. With rich ornamentation both inside and out,

the museum's architecture combines the two principal edifices of Bali, the temple (*pura*) and the palace (*puri*).

The museum's four buildings contain a splendid collection of Balinese art—Neolithic stone implements, a hoard of Buddhist clay seals excavated near Pejeng, Balinese folk crafts, carved and painted woodwork, cricket-fighting cages, dance costumes, textiles, masks, weaving looms and fabrics, agricultural tools, musical instruments, furniture, scale models of ceremonial events, ethnographic exhibits. The first pavilion is a two-story building containing high-quality, early traditional, Kamasan-style paintings; classical Balinese calendars; modern Batuan and Ubud-style paintings; and work of the Academic and Young Artists (or Naive) schools. Another pavilion displays carved media—wood, stone, clay, and bone—including sculpted windows, doors, pillars, ceiling beams, friezes, old guardian figures, demons, and specimens of Bali's extraordinarily earthy and vigorous folk art. The building, dedicated to prehistoric artifacts, displays Bronze Age implements, including the famous Gilimanuk bronze spearhead, the largest ever discovered in Southeast Asia. Also see ritual objects, priestly accoutrements, and a veranda lined with old stone statues. One building is devoted entirely to masks, weapons, and costumes of the performing arts, including rare *barong* pig masks and primitive dance masks from remote villages. There's also an incredible display of *topeng*.

A good part of the displays are annotated with English explanations, and clear maps in the central building show all the important prehistoric and historical sites of Bali. The museum also has a library and a shop selling postcards and books in English. However, there's no ground plan of the museum nor is a guide available to show visitors around. Open Tuesday, Wednesday, and Thursday 0800-1700, Friday 0800-1530, closed Monday. Admission Rp500. Wear long pants.

Temples
Just east of the big *alun-alun* on Jl. Mayor Wishnu, next to the museum, is a Hindu temple, **Pura Jagatnatha,** built in 1953. In the afternoon, people from the surrounding *kampung* come here to pray; the temple's especially busy during the full moon. On a towered throne of

DENPASAR

UBUNG
BUS STATION

TO BLAHKIU

TO TABANAN

JL. MARUTI

JL. HOS COKROAMINOTO

KOKAR
ACADEMY
OF ART

JL. RATNA

JL. SERUNI

JL. KARTINI

JL. YUDISTIRA

JL. PATIMURA

JL. VETERAN

JL. NANGKA

BELIMBING

POLICE
HEADQUARTERS

JL. SUPRATMAN

TO GIANYAR
AND UBUD

BARATA
BOOK
SHOP

JL. SETIABUDI

HOTEL
ADI YASA

JL. N. A. KEDODONG

JL. TERATAI

GARUDA
AIRLINES

MERPATI
OFFICE

WISMA
TARUNA INN

JL. G. K. SAHADEWA

JL. RAMBUTAN

JL. KEPUNDUNG

ANGSOKA

JL. D. PATJAR

JL. PALAWA

TO LEGIAN

JL.
DR. WAHIDIN

ATOOM
BARU

JL. ARJUNA

JL. MELATI

JL. KAMBOJA

NATOUR
BALI
HOTEL

LOSMEN ELIM

KERENENG
BUS STATION

BANK
NEGARA
INDONESIA

BADUNG REGENCY
TOURIST OFFICE

JL. RIDJASA

ART CENTER
(TAMAN WERDI BUDAYA)

HONG KONG RESTAURANT

G. SEMERU

KUMBASARI
SHOPPING
COMPLEX

GAJAH MADA
BANK DAGANG
NEGARA

JL. UDAJANA

PUPUTAN SQUARE

JL. KALIASEM

G. MERPATI

G. BATUR

JL. THAMRIN

JL. KAWI

JL. TERNATE

PASAR
BADUNG

JL. BELITON

BALI MUSEUM

JL. LET REGUL

JL. HAYAM WURUK

TO SANUR

PEMECUTAN
PALACE HOTEL

JL. HASANNUDIN

SUCI TERMINAL

JL. DEBES

JL. SUTJI

JL. MADJ. JEND.
SUTOJO

JL. PUTRA

JL. KADJENG

TERMINAL
TEGAL

TWO BROTHERS INN

JL. G. WILIS

JL. BUKTUNGGAL

KERTA WIJAYA
SHOPPING CENTER

AYAM BAKAR
TALIWANG

JL. LIMA BESAR

JL. PITJA

JL. IMAM BONJOL

HOTEL
DENPASAR

JL. DIPONEGORO

JL. M. T.
HARYONO

JL. SUDIRMAN

TO AIRPORT AND
KUTA BEACH

JL. YOS SUDARSO

PJKA (TRAIN TICKET OFFICE)

MATAHARI
SHOPPING CENTER

GOVERNOR'S OFFICE

BALI GOVERNMENT
TOURIST OFFICE

POST
OFFICE

IMMIGRATION
OFFICE

JL. NITI MANDALA

BOURAQ
AIRLINES

BALI BARU WISATA
RENTAL CAR

JL. NIAS

TO BENOA

0   250m

© MOON PUBLICATIONS, INC.

white coral sits a bright, gold statue of Ida Batara Sanghyang Widhi in his typical pose. This is the supreme god of Balinese Hinduism. The *padmasana* rests on the back of the sacred turtle, clasped by two *naga* on plinths carved with scenes from the Mahabharata and Ramayana. The central courtyard is surrounded by a moat containing gigantic carp.

Also visit **Puri Pemecutan** near Tegal bus station on the corner of Jl. Thamrin and Jl. Hasannudin, built in 1907 to replace the original palace of the *raja* destroyed by Dutch artillery. Pemecutan, which shares the complex with Pemecutan Palace Hotel, houses old weapons and a renowned *gamelan mas* which survived from the original *puri*. Don't miss the handsome, four-tiered *kulkul* diagonally opposite the palace with its eight small *raksasa* statues. Chinese porcelain plates decorate the topmost tier.

Another unique and archaeologically important temple is **Pura Masopahit,** located in a small alley in the middle of the city off Jl. Sutomo. Enter through a door in the alley. This temple, one of the oldest on Bali, has its origins in the great 14th- and 15th-century Javanese Majapahit Empire when Hinduism was first introduced to Bali. The massive statues of Batara Bayu and Garuda guard the split gateway. On the imposing facade is a pantheon of carved demons and deities, including Yama and Indra. Heavily damaged in the 1917 quake, the earliest, now-restored buildings are in the back. Look for the terra-cotta statues.

Pura Melanting, in the midst of Pasar Badung, is a market temple where vendors make offerings on their way to their stalls. Northeast of Denpasar on Jl. Ratna (near the Sekolah Menengah Musik), off to the left and just before the signpost to Kesiman, is old **Dalem Pura Tastasan** with a monolithic altar and *batu hitam.*

ACCOMMODATIONS

Unless they have business in the city, most tourists and travelers prefer the cheaper accommodations and more agreeable surroundings in the nearby beach resort areas of Kuta, Legian, or Sanur. Most of those who use Denpasar's 100 or so hotels are Indonesian businessmen, tour groups, and domestic tourists. Book ahead during high seasons.

Budget

For the budget traveler, **Wisma Taruna Inn,** Jl. Gadung 31, tel. (0361) 226-913, lies on a quiet back street, two km from the city center (Rp200 by *bemo* or a 20-minute walk). From downtown Denpasar, walk up Jl. Hayam Wuruk and turn left at the Arya Hotel, approximately 100 meters down on the right. Rates Rp5000 s, Rp10,000 d (without breakfast); in the off season even lower. Rent motorcycles and bicycles here. Other amenities include laundry service, beverages, and food. Friendly houseboys. This hostel is only a 10-minute walk from the Kereneng bus terminal, which provides transport to all of eastern Bali.

Catering exclusively to travelers is **Two Brothers Inn** on the main road (Jl. Imam Bonjol) to Kuta Beach. It's only a five-minute walk from the Tegal *bemo* terminal and a 10-minute fast walk from downtown. Go down the lane (Gang VII/5) to the right of Banjar Tegal Gede. One of the cheapest *losmen* in Denpasar (Rp10,000 to 15,000 d without *mandi*), the Two Brothers is clean and safe, with electricity, sitting toilets, showers, fragrant flowers, free tea and coffee. It's also quiet, except for the dog chorus at night. Excellent value; please don't try to bargain. Try local meals in nearby *warung* and a small restaurant 200 meters away; ask proprietor Ibu Anom for the best eateries. From Two Brothers you can easily walk or take a *bemo* into town (Rp350), or just stroll down the lane in your swim gear with your towel over your shoulder and thumb a *bemo* (Rp800) to Kuta Beach.

If Two Brothers is full, try the noisier 31-room **Hotel Tamansari,** Jl. Iman Bonjol 45, tel. 226-724, for Rp10,000-Rp15,500. Some rooms have Indonesian-style *kamar mandi*; some have a fan. The pool is a surprising addition to a budget hotel. Also with a pool, and near the Two Brothers toward the city, is **Hotel Dharma Wisata,** Jl. Imam Bonjol 83, tel. 222-186; Rp15,000 d for rooms with their own *mandi*. Cool, clean, efficient, pool.

Quite central and cheap is **Hotel Adi Yasa,** Jl. Nakula 23 (tel. 22679), asking Rp8500 s, Rp15,000 d with bathroom and breakfast. The 22 rooms, which may be hot and muggy and badly need refurbishing, all face a pleasant, central garden. Request a fan. When getting off the long-distance bus at around 0500, this is a convenient transit place to stay as it's only

1.5 km from Ubung station. Another reasonable place is the family-run **Penginapan Tambora,** Jl. Gunung Tambora 6, tel. 226-352: Rp15,000 d, Rp10,000 s, plus Rp1500 extra for a fan. **Penginapan Mertapura,** Jl. Belimbing 22, tel. 225-036, charges Rp15,000 s or d. Can be noisy, as it faces the street.

Two centrally located *losmen* catering primarily to Indonesian businessmen are **Losmen Intan Sari,** Jl. Thamrin 1-3, tel. 224-521, Rp9000 s or with wall fan Rp12,000, and nearby **Losmen Rakta Usadi,** also on Jl. Thamrin, tel. 224-421, with 13 rooms for Rp10,000 s. Basic **Hotel Ratu,** Jl. Yos Sudarso 4, tel. 226-922, is a small businessman's hotel with a central location, yet cushioned somehow from city noise. Rooms cost Rp15,000 s and Rp20,000 d including tax, are clean, with showers but no hot water. Breakfast not included.

Moderate

The **Sari Inn,** Jl. Mayjen Sutoyo, tel. (0361) 222-437, has 15 large, comfortable rooms with *mandi,* fan, and tea—very reasonable for Rp15,500 s, Rp20,000 d. An inexpensive *rumah makan* is 200 meters away. Call the inn from the airport and the owner will pick you up for Rp10,000. Seventeen-room **Losmen Elim,** Puri Oka, Jl. Kaliasem 3, tel. 224-631, charges Rp15,000 s, Rp25,000 d; Rp50,000 for a/c front rooms. Breakfast extra, no hot water, all the hot tea you can drink. **Hotel Denpasar,** Jl. Diponegoro 103 (P.O. Box 111, Denpasar), tel. 28336, features Bali-style cottages for Rp30,000 s, Rp45,000 d with a/c, private *mandi,* and hot water. Hotel Denpasar also offers a number of spartan, lower-priced fan-cooled rooms. Restaurant. Located in the south of the city on the road to Suwung. In the heart of Denpasar, **Hotel Puri Alit,** Jl. Sutomo 26 (P.O. Box 102, Denpasar), tel. 228-831, fax 288-766, has 22 rooms. With fan Rp16,000 s, Rp20,000 d; with a/c Rp30,000 s, Rp35,000 d. Private bath, tub, shower. For reservations, call the head office at Jl. Hang Tuah 41, Sanur, tel. 288-560, fax 288-766. Part of the Alit chain; if you like it here check out **Alit's Beach Bungalows** in Sanur and **Alit Kuta Bungalows** in Kuta.

Luxury

Recently renovated **Pemecutan Palace Hotel,** Jl. Thamrin 2 (P.O. Box 489), tel. (0361) 223-491, has 45 rather ordinary rooms ranging from Rp30,000 s to Rp45,000 d, most with a/c and phones; no hot water. The restaurant serves Chinese, Indonesian, and Western food. Amenities include laundry and a car rental service. Quiet, despite its central location. The hotel is housed in a rebuilt palace—the royal occupants were annihilated in the 1906 *puputan.* Today, you may observe the day-by-day activities and rituals that still take place in the extensive courtyards of the *puri.* The singing birds add a nice touch. Ask to see the old *meriam* (cannon), an 1840 gift to the *raja* by the Dutch.

For more spacious surroundings, away from the hustle and bustle, stay in nearby Tohpati at **Hotel Tohpati Bali,** Jl. Bypass Ngurah Rai 15, tel. 236-273, fax 232-404, northeast of Denpasar. Luxury facilities—cottages surrounded by tropical trees and flowers, pool and sunken bar, piano bar, restaurants, shops, fitness center, putting green, tennis courts, and a contracted beach in Sanur with "every water sport available."

Centrally located at Jl. Veteran 3, just a short walk from Jl. Gajah Mada and the Bali Museum, is the closest thing to first-class accommodations in Denpasar—the venerable three-star, 73-room **Natour Bali Hotel** on Jl. Veteran 3 (P.O. Box 3, Denpasar), tel. 225-681. Built by a Dutch shipping company in 1927, this was Bali's first tourist hotel, and though it's becoming rather frayed, it still retains vestiges of its charming past with a palm-shaded lobby, antique black fans, art-deco lamps, dark wood finishings, and shady walkways. Here stayed the early Western anthropologists and writers who arrived to study Bali. The hotel charges Rp92,400 for rooms with a/c, ceiling fans, private bathrooms, hot water, TV, video, and a sound system. Suites are Rp150,150. Other amenities include gift shop, bar, and the Puri Agung Restaurant.

FOOD

With its sizable population of bureaucrats, businessmen, laborers, and service personnel, Denpasar offers an abundance of well-established *warung, rumah makan,* and restaurants serving Indonesian specialties at very reasonable prices. The city's densest concentration of Indonesian-style eating establishments is on Jl. Teuku Umar, which eventually joins Jl. Imam Bonjol, the road to Kuta.

Food Markets

For an instant introduction to Indonesian cuisine, visit the colorful open-air *pasar malam* in the parking lot 150 meters behind the multistoried **Kumbasari Shopping Complex** just off Jl. Gajah Mada by the river. Open 1800-2000. Dozens of stalls under plastic covers serve Chinese noodle soups, fried rice, *sate,* excellent *martabak, babi guling, nasi campur, pangsit mie,* chocolate donuts, and hot drinks. Try steaming *kue putu* smothered in coconut shavings. At night, the *pasar malam* is a splendid place to visit, with hundreds of milling people of all ages, races, and islands. Other *pasar malam* include the Kereneng bus station (the Asoka Night Market), serving *babi guling* and other native dishes; and opposite Tegal station. Both are good, cheap, and entertaining.

Virtually all of Denpasar's six big shopping centers feature good quality, cheap, and genuine bakeries and cafeteria-style food marts with a wide range of Indonesian, Chinese, Muslim, and Western meals for Rp2000-Rp5000. The huge **Tiara Dewata Food Centre** on Jl. Mayjen Sutoyo serves 150 different kinds of foods, with meals starting at Rp1000.

Nasi Campur

Near Hotel Adi Yasa, on Jl. Judistira at Tapakgangsul, clean and simple **Rumah Makan Wardani,** tel. (0361) 224-398, serves a delicious Balinese-style *nasi campur* for only Rp3000. Open only from early morning until 1300. After 1500, nearby **Warung Satriya** (Jl. Kedongong 13, off Jl. Veteran) opens, serving Denpasar's best *nasi campur.* The **Tiara Dewata** food mart serves superb *nasi campur* for only Rp2000-3000.

Specialty Foodstalls And Restaurants

A simple *warung* on Jl. Kartini opposite the cinema serves fantastic crab soup (Rp2000) with green vegetables and egg plus a plate of rice. It also specializes in excellent shelled fried crab. A bottle of Sari Temulawak (ginger drink) caps the meal (Rp500 with ice).

The **Puri Agung Restaurant** in the Natour Bali Hotel features a memorable *rijstaffel* (Rp15,000) as well as fixed-price meals. For inexpensive but first-class and not too spicy Indonesian/Javanese food in a clean environment, eat at **Restaurant Betty** at Jl. Sumatra 56—a popular hangout for expats. For East Javanese specialties, try the excellent **Kikel Sapi** on Jl. Sumatra downtown. Tasty *gado-gado, gule, and rawon.* So popular at night you may have to share a table. Open 0800-1600. **Ayam Bakar Taliwang** on Jl. Tengku Umar, open 1000-2000, serves complete dinners of extra fat and juicy Sasak-style Taliwang chicken, with rice, *sambal,* vegetables, and delicious *es kelapa muda* (Rp1000). Outstanding fish *sate* with hot sauce. Particularly popular with high-placed government people. Another above-average chicken place is **Ayam Goreng Prambanan,** Jl. Hayam Wuruk 69.

Chinese Restaurants

Denpasar has some of the best Chinese restaurants on the island. The chicken dishes at **Restoran Gajah Mada,** close to the traffic lights on Jl. Gajah Mada, are beautifully prepared. The unpretentious but excellent and central **Atoom Baru,** Jl. Gajah Mada 106-108, tel. (0361) 234-772, offers tasty *nasi goreng, cap cai,* fishball soup, and fish and vegetables with tomato sauce. A local favorite. Also try the popular, fancier, and air-conditioned **Hong Kong Restaurant,** Jl. Gajah Mada 85, tel. 234-845, fax 235-777, across the road from the Atoom Baru and right in front of Kumbasari Shopping Complex. Prices start at Rp6000-7000; each dish can be ordered in small, medium, or large portions. Specialties include stewed seafood and bean curd, Sichuan hot and sour soup, and fried fresh carp. Nice atmosphere; good for groups.

Baked Goods And Desserts

There are dozens of bakeries in Denpasar providing fast food for people on their way to work. The biggest is **Amsterdam Bakery,** Jl. Diponegoro 122, tel. (0361) 235-035—also a steak house, ice cream parlor, and restaurant. On Jl. Sumatra (no. 34A) is **Toko Roti Matahari,** tel. 234-447, with bread, cheese and raisin rolls, donuts, and muffins. Ice cream too. The city's new shopping centers also feature bakeries; **Tiara Dewata** on Jl. Mayjen and **Sutoyo** are especially good.

EVENTS AND EXHIBITS

Dances and musical performances take place throughout the year. Keep your eyes and ears open. There are many tourist dance venues in southern Bali within easy reach of Denpasar, especially at Sanur's pricier hotels and restaurants. For cheaper, longer, and more traditional dances, see the celebrations and festivities in the villages.

The best way to follow religious ceremonies and festivals is to obtain a calendar of events at one of Denpasar's tourist offices. In Denpasar itself, full moon ceremonies occur at Pura Jagatnatha (next to the Bali Museum) with its white coral lotus-throne shrine to Sanghyang Widi. You can watch if you wear the traditional Balinese costume, *sarung* or sash.

Sanggraha Kriya Asta Handicrafts Center

Located in Tohpati (P.O. Box 254, Denpasar, tel. 0361-222-942) in the northeast suburbs, seven km east of Denpasar, is an art cooperative supervised by the Department of Industry. Displayed here are samples of nearly all the crafts produced on Bali today: woodcarvings, paintings, *batik*, dresses, shirts, and silverwork. There are five spacious buildings, each devoted to a major craft. Open daily 0900-1730, Saturday 0900-1700, Sunday closed. Call for free transportation in the Denpasar, Kuta, and Sanur areas.

The Art Center

Also called Taman Werdi Budaya. Located on Jl. Nusa Indah in Abiankapas, a Denpasar suburb in the direction of Sanur, a 15-minute walk east of Kereneng station. Set in a restful garden with lotus ponds amid richly carved baroque Balinese buildings, The Taman Werdi Budaya houses exhibits of modern painting, woodcarvings, shadow puppets, and giant *barong landung* puppets. This is one of Bali's finest art exhibits. Open Tues.-Sun. 0800-1700, tel. (0361) 222-776. A car park, museum, and small, fixed-price handicraft shops are also located in the center.

Visitors can view dance and music rehearsals in two open-air amphitheaters with modern lighting. Dances are also regularly staged for the public, including works incorporating modern Balinese choreography. In the *kecak* performance, staged each night 1830-1930 (Rp5000), traditional flickering oil lamps are still used. Eerie and powerful.

The Art Center also hosts a summer art festival each year from mid-June to mid-July, with competitions for costumes, dance, drama, *sendratari* performances, music, woodcarving,

metalworking, and food. Every year is different, with each of Bali's regencies sending its best teams. Also see art events, crafts exhibits, and an extravagant production of the Ramayana Ballet. If it's the high season, be sure to book your hotel in advance. These entertaining and exciting cultural shows draw tens of thousands of visitors from around the world.

The Balinese Art Development Center Program, Jl. Bayusuta (in the Art Center), is open 0800-1700 daily except Monday. This tertiary-level institute offers work on the undergraduate through master's degree levels. Besides staging dances, plays, and pop concerts, it houses permanent exhibits offering handicrafts, paintings, carvings, and silver. Student discounts available.

STSI And SMKI

More advanced students attend Sekolah Tinggi Seni Indonesia (formerly ASTI), the Institute of Arts and Dance on Jl. Nusa Indah near the Art Center in Abiankapas, tel. (0361) 272-361. Classes are 0700-1300 daily except Sunday. STSI director Made Bandem is responsible for a virtual renaissance in the Balinese arts. Tourism revenue is recycled into larger and grander ceremonies for the gods that, inevitably, include Balinese theater, music, song, and dance, and thus contribute to the development and preservation of Balinese art.

SMKI is the Conservatory of Instrumental Arts and Dance (tel. 975-180, fax 975-162), for high school students in Batubulan. Opened in 1960; all Balinese dances are studied here. Visitors are welcome in the mornings to watch teachers train their pupils.

Hotel And Commercial Performances

In Sanur (nine km southeast of Denpasar), the Ramayana, *joged,* and *legong* are frequently staged at such big hotels as the Bali Hyatt just about every night of the week starting about 1900. Performances last 45 minutes to an hour, and are often accompanied by buffet dinner. Cost: Rp25,000-30,000. *Wayang kulit* is performed every Monday, Wednesday, and Saturday 1900-2000 for Rp6000 in the Laghawa Beach Inn.

A high-quality, dynamic *barong* is put on especially for tourists at Batubulan, a suburb northeast of Denpasar, on one of three open-air stages every morning, 0900-1000. Jammed with hundreds of Europeans, and suffocating with peddlers, admission is Rp5000. In the afternoon, 1630-1730, is a *kecak* fire dance. At Tanjung Bungkah, between Denpasar and Sanur, a *kecak* and fire dance has been staged 1930-2030 regularly since 1972, admission Rp5000. While here, see the small but colorful Pura Dalem temple.

SHOPPING

Denpasar is where the Balinese shop for staples and necessities. Small shops and businesses are generally open 0830-1400, close for several hours, then reopen in the evening around 1700, then close again around 2100. On Sunday, everyone goes home at 1200 or 1300. The best way to shop in Denpasar is on foot. Denpasar's shopping street and business center is Jl. Gajah Mada, where anything—cassette tapes, textiles, medicine, stationery, tacky souvenirs, electronics, shoes—is available. The chance of being overcharged here is just as great as in Kuta or Sanur. Downtown is not the only place to shop. Other shopping streets include Jl. Thamrin for textiles, tailors, souvenirs, and leather ware, and Jl. Diponegoro for clothes and books. The big, bustling shopping centers, a few km from the downtown, are open from 0900 or 1000 until 2000. The tourist corridor between Kuta and Ubud is choked with art shops carrying every conceivable native craft.

Downtown Markets

One of Denpasar's main attractions is the massive, multistoried, visually fascinating central market, **Pasar Badung** on Jl. Gajah Mada alongside the river. With droves of people and amazing colors, this market is especially strong in plaited ware and inexpensive trinkets. Good cheap eateries. As you enter the market, kids will offer to carry your merchandise for Rp1000. Lines of *dokar* wait to take shoppers and their goods home.

Different goods are sold in different sections. The cool, dark, basement level houses a huge, bustling fruit and vegetable market, as well as meat and fish markets. The first floor is devoted to hardware, flower offerings, and spices. The top floor features textiles, *songket, sarung* from

Java, dance and ceremonial accoutrements, kitchen utensils, hardware, tinware, brassware, bags, inexpensive clothes, basketry, a giddy variety of things made from palm leaves, and a great view over the city.

West of Pasar Badung, just across the river, is the giant **Kumbasari Shopping Complex,** a rabbit's warren of small wholesale and retail shops selling clothes, bedcovers, *batik,* paintings, Mas-style carvings, Celuk silver, and scads of junk. Cinemas cap the complex. This is the closest Denpasar gets to an art market. Opens at 0800.

Shopping Centers

To satiate the increasingly urbane appetites of Bali's growing middle class, there's been an alarming proliferation of huge, air-conditioned, well-scrubbed, Western-style shopping centers. At last count the city had seven. Each contains a comprehensive supermarket, bookstore, department store, food center, and playground, as well as beauty salons, music stores, cosmetic counters, and sports, houseware, and hardware departments. Kitchen utensils like stainless steel pots, glassware, and wooden spoons are a real bargain, cheaper than in the *pasar*. The guitars are better quality than those sold in Bandung. If buying foreign-brand items like high-pressure kerosene lamps (Rp40,000) or staplers, remember spare parts. Also buy conventional, Western-style, ready-to-wear clothing, children's clothes, and all types of consumer articles: electronics, office and art supplies, housewares, crafts, and jewelry. All offer free parking with security guards and luggage counters (*tempat titipan*) where you can check in your valuables.

Other Markets

A morning market, **Pasar Kereneng,** is also a major terminal for buses to central and east Bali. Fruits and vegetables are sold here, as well as a limited selection of woodcarvings, paintings, and crockery. Denpasar's *pasar malam,* just south of the Kumbasari complex, is clogged with vendors selling cheap clothes, jewelry, shoes, and *batik.*

Pasar Satriya

Located by the temple Pura Satriya, on the corner of Jl. Veteran and Jl. Nakula, this small art dealer's wholesale market sells woodcarvings, paintings, and other crafts, plus produce and good Bali-style takeout food. Look in on the only bird market on Bali—the **Satriya Bird (Pasar Burung) Market** at Jl. Veteran 64, where 40 shops sell parrots, cockatoos, partridges, and parakeets, as well as tropical fish and aquariums.

Craft Shops

C.V. Nuratni, Jl. Gianyar 15, is a large and well-known art shop on the road from Denpasar to Tohpati. Painted 2.5-meter-high Tegalalang *garudas* go for Rp3 million; small ones are Rp31,500. Carved wooden ducks, Rp735,000; a realistic banana tree for Rp630,000. Nuratni is an exporter and also accepts credit cards, traveler's checks, and personal checks. Prices not marked. **Ellis Koleksi,** Jl. Imam Bonjol 337, tel. (0361) 226-110, and the **Garuda Art Shop,** Jl. Setiabudi 36, tel. 226-736, are worth checking into. Or try **Emi Handicraft,** Jl. Hasannudin 53, tel. 236-215, for *batik,* books, silver, and crafts—plenty crammed into a small space.

Peep in at **Mega Art Shop,** Jl. Gajah Mada 36 (open 0730-1700, tel. 224-592), for its wide range of Balinese arts—jewelry, leather, puppets, paintings, ceramics, and fine textiles, including reasonably-priced framed weavings from Timor for Rp210,000-262,500 and Sumbu *ikat* for Rp105,000-262,500. Ten percent cash discount. See the incredibly delicate, museum-quality antique gold artifacts from Flores. An even larger Mega (tel. 228-855) is located at Jl. Gianyar Km 5.7 on the outskirts of Denpasar. Ask to see the owner's private collection of *kris* and *ikat.*

Fabrics And Textiles

Jalan Sulawesi is the fabrics street, especially for Indian or Muslim-style fabrics. Several well-stocked shops, including **Dua Lima** and **Toko Murah,** carry everything from gingham to velvet, nylon net to the finest cotton. Fair prices. At Jl. Sulawesi 58, tel. (0361) 225-421, **Meubal Yani** carries *bantal guling* (Dutch wife) for only Rp6000.

Indonesians themselves shop for clothes at **Galuh Tenun and Batik Bali** (tel. 98304) in Batubulan on the main road out of Denpasar on the right. Here you can buy a *sarung* for as little as Rp4000. Enough of the staff speak English so you can make yourself understood. For high quality *batik sarung* and *batik,* try **Wino-tosastro** on Jl. Hayam Wuruk 102 on the road

to Sanur. Silk is the specialty of the **Duta Silk House** in Duta Plaza, Denpasar. **Panca Mulia Textiles,** Jl. Gajah Mada 78, is a great place to buy *sarung* and three-meter-long *kain,* mostly traditional designs, Rp10,000-15,000.

Ikat

Toko Pelangi at Jl. Gajah Mada 54 specializes in fine *ikat* from Bali, Sumba, and Savu. **Sekana House,** Jl. Diponegoro VII/4, tel. (0361) 235-776, offers traditional antique *ikat.* **Surya Jaya,** Jl. Gajah Mada 62, sells convincing copies of *ikat* for curtains, bedspreads, and the like.

Antiques

Antique lovers should try the well-established **Arts of Asia,** Jl. Thamrin 27-37, Blok C5, behind the Lokitasari Shopping Centre, which sells jewelry, paintings, carvings, Chinese porcelain, old *wayang* puppets, and high-standard *ikat.* Said to be among the best antique shops in Indonesia. **Alit's,** on the east end of Jl. Thamrin, and the **Meteor Shop,** Jl. Kartini 32, are known for their antiques as well as carved chess sets and sandalwood fans. Antique shops on Jl. Gajah Mada include **Yudistira Art Shop** (no. 52), tel. (0361) 222-712, and **Pelangi Art Shop** (no. 54), tel. 224-570. **Mario Antiques** in Batubulan has a lot of junk but also some gems. The nicest pieces of furniture come from wealthy families, and they won't part with them cheaply. The shop is a half km past the market on the left.

Gold And Silver

A number of silver shops sell 22-24 carat pieces on Jl. Sulawesi beside the household market. Some offer wholesale prices competitive with Hong Kong and Singapore. As is the case throughout Indonesia, you buy gold jewelry by the weight; the actual workmanship is free. Worth investigating is **Merlin Jewelry** on Jl. Gajah Mada, tel. (0361) 222-417.

A very specific place for gold is the row of gold shops on Jl. Hasannudin. At any of them you may also have gold articles made. The **Kenanga Gold Shop** at no. 43A, tel. 225-725, has a fine selection. If you change your mind after your purchase, you may return the item and they'll refund your money, less 10%. Peep in at **Melati** (no. 41 F, tel. 237-854) and the **99 Gold Shop** (no. 31 D, tel. 237-169) while you're in the neighborhood.

Bookstores

The biggest bookstore on Bali is **Barata Book Shop,** Jl. Kartini 156-160, tel. (0361) 226-716. The second largest is Gramedia in the **Matahari Shopping Center** on Jl. Dewi Sartika. Other bookstores include **C.V. Garuda Wisnu,** Jl. Teuku Umar 90 X, tel. 238-010, and **PT Gunung Agung,** Jl. Teuku Umar 110, tel. 223-999. **Kios Corsica,** Jl. Sumatra 46, has 20 titles on Bali (in English), but specializes in magazines and newspapers. **Boko Buku Muda,** Jl. Gajah Mada 18, sells books as well as office and art supplies, sports equipment, and typewriters.

SERVICES

Tourist Services

The **Denpasar Regency Tourist Office,** Jl. Surapati 7, tel. (0361) 223-399 or 23602, is a five-minute walk from the Bali Museum. Pick up a map of Denpasar and a calendar of events. Open 0700-1400, Friday until 1100, Saturday until 1230. This is the best, friendliest, and most convenient source of information on both the regency and all of Bali. You can temporarily store your backpack here during office hours.

The tourism headquarters for the entire island is the **Bali Government Tourist Office** on Jl. S. Parman, tel. 222-387, a 10-minute walk behind the post office in Denpasar's government complex. Present yourself at the reception desk and fill in the request form. More of an administrative office than one geared for tourists. Open Mon.-Thurs. 0700-1400, Friday until 1100, Saturday until 1230. The area code for Denpasar is 0361.

The **immigration office** is on Jl. Panjaitan, off Jl. Puputan Raya, tel. 227-828. If staying in or near Kuta, *kantor imigrasi* at the airport on Jl. Ngurah Rai (near the post office) is more convenient. Open 0700-1400, Friday until 1100, Saturday 0700-1230, Sunday closed.

Consulates include Australian, Jl. Moh. Yamin Kav 51, Renon, tel. 235-092; Danish and Norwegian, Jl. Jayagiri VIII/10; Dutch, Jl. Imam Bonjol 599, tel. 751-904 or 751-497, fax 752-777; French, Jl. Raya Sesetan 46 D, Banjar Pesanggaran, tel. 233-555; German, Jl. Pantai Karang, tel. 288-826; Japanese, Jl. Moh. Yamin 9, Renon, tel. 231-308 or 234-808.

Medical And Legal Services

The most modern hospital is **Sanglah,** Jl. Nias, tel. (0361) 227-911, ext. 11. Another hospital, **Wangaya,** is located on Jl. Kartini, tel. 222-141. **Surya Husada Clinic,** Jl. Pulau Serangan 1-3 in Sanglah, tel. 225-249, is the best private hospital. Though it's double the price of public hospitals, the service is better, and the staff better trained and more proficient in English. Open around the clock.

For private treatment, see **Dr. Ketut Swastika,** Jl. Kamboja 55, tel. 224-468. Another physician with experience treating tourists is **Dr. Tjokorda Gde Subamia,** Rapco Station, tel. 226-531. **Dr. Gst Putu Panteri** runs a psychiatric clinic on Jl. Raya Denpasar, tel. 225-744. **Sin She Bobby Lok,** Jl. Diponegoro 216 A, is a popular Chinese acupuncturist.

The city's largest pharmacy is **Kimia Farma,** Jl. Diponegoro 125, tel. 227-812, just up from the Matahari Shopping Center. It's also the busiest and has the longest wait; get there early in the morning. Open 24 hours. Another Kimia Farma pharmacy is located in front of Sanglah hospital. At smaller pharmacies you get faster service. A handy apothecary is **Toko Obat Jaya Abadi,** Jl. Gajah Mada 71-73, tel. 232-077 or 235-236, which specializes in Indonesian and Chinese medicines. Also try **Apotik Sehat,** Jl. Diponegoro 205, tel. 752-284, and **Apotik Kresna Farma** on Jl. Thamrin, tel. 222-133. A small, inviting *jamu* opposite Pasar Badung on Jl. Sulawesi has an outstanding selection. There are many others. **Toko Jaya Abadi** on Jl. Gajah Mada sells *jamu* and traditional Chinese medicines. A wonderful traditional Chinese apothecary, **Toko Sentosa,** on Jl. Gajah Mada, carries everything from ginseng root to Ho Shou Wu.

Dentists working in Denpasar hold to a surprisingly high standard. Emergency treatment is administered by **Dr. Indra Guizot,** Jl. Patimura 19, tel. 222-445 or 226-445, appointments 1000-2100. Or contact **Dr. Gede Winasa Kesama,** Jl. Diponegoro 115A; call for an appointment 0900-1400 and 1700-2000, tel. 233-907, emergency tel. 224-030.

For traffic problems, contact the **police headquarters** on Jl. Supratman near the stadium. Open Mon.-Sat. 0800-1200. Police stations are located at Jl. Diponegro 10, tel. 234-928, and on Jl. A. Yani, tel. 225-456.

Going by the name *notaris,* there are many lawyers in the Denpasar area. Start with **Amir Sjarifudin,** Jl. Veteran 11 A, tel. 226-288, or **Francisca Teresa,** Jl. Patimura 7, tel. 227-110.

Photo Shops, Postal Service, And Banks

Folks at Denpasar's leading photographic supplies store print photos (21 minutes) and slides (one day), enlarge, repair cameras, and take passport photos in both black and white and color— **Tati Photo,** Jl. Sumatra 10-14, tel. (0361) 226-912, on the corner of Jl. Sumatra and Jl. Thamrin. Photo services also available from **Prima Photo,** Jl. Thamrin 41, tel. 222-471, and **Diamond Photo Studio,** Jl. Thamrin 5, tel. 226-903.

The **central post office** is on Jl. Raya Puputan in Renon, tel. 223-565, and is difficult to get to. Hire an *ojek* from Kereneng station for around Rp2000. Open Mon.-Thurs. 0800-1400, Friday 0800-1100, Saturday 0800-1100. They won't forward mail, although they say they will. Although it has poste restante service, it's more secure to get your mail sent to a poste restante counter at a post office in Ubud, Sanur, or Kuta. Even better is to have mail sent directly to your hotel. Other major post offices are near Kereneng station and at Sanglah near the Udayana University on Jl. Diponegoro.

To send parcels, go to the *paket pos* building at Jl. Diponegoro 146, tel. 227-727. Open Mon.-Fri. 0800-2000, Friday and Saturday until 1100. From Ubung terminal, take a *bemo* to the corner of Jl. Sudirman and Jl. Niti Mandala Renon, then walk 500 meters to the west. This is a good place to have parcels sent, as the clerks charge only Rp4000 to wrap and bind your box, with a plastic cover sewn on tightly and securely. **DHL Courier Service,** Jl. Tanjung Bungkak 92, will send an envelope to Europe, Australia, or the U.S. in 24 hours for Rp31,500.

For packaging and forwarding bulk shipments overseas, use **Air International Cargo,** Jl. Ngurah Rai Bypass, Tohpati, tel. 234-699; **Bali International Cargo,** Jl. Hang Tuah 2, Renon, tel. 288-563 or 287-041; **PT Pacific Express,** Jl. Arjuna 21, tel. 237-842; or **PT Sucofindo,** Jl. Teuku Umar 5, tel. 236-403. There are scores of other cargo shipping companies in Sanur and the Kuta area. Allow about three days to send a container.

There are several banks to choose from. Many lie at the eastern end of Jl. Gajah Mada near the intersection with Jl. Arjuna. You'll get quick and continuous service (no break for lunch) at **Bank Negara Indonesia** at Jl. Gajah Mada 20. One of the best banks for telegraphic transfers is **Bank Bumi Daya,** Jl. Veteran 2, which will also cash most traveler's checks. **Bank Ekspor-Impor,** Jl. Udayana 11 (tel. 23981), cashes Thomas Cook traveler's checks and is reliable for wire transfers. A 24-hour moneychanger is at the airport.

GETTING AROUND

Denpasar is the travel hub of Bali. Here you can catch *bemo,* minibuses, and long-distance buses to every part of the island. Denpasar drivers are reckless and inconsiderate, with one foot on the accelerator at all times. Pedestrians take their lives in their hands crossing Denpasar's streets. There are more vehicles here per capita than even Jakarta, and if the sheer volume and cacophony of the traffic don't get you, the oppressive heat and humidity will.

If you try to drive on your own, use a map. Tourists have spent hours circling the city's confusing pinwheel of one-way streets, trying to escape. You can obtain a local license for motorbiking or driving at the Denpasar police station on Jl. Supratman. It's far better, however, to get an International License before you reach Bali.

Bemo, Taxis, Dokar

The minimum *bemo* or minibus fare to anywhere in Denpasar is Rp300 for the inner city, Rp500 maximum for the rest of the place. Three-wheeled contraptions known as "baby *bemo*" run up and down Jl. Gajah Mada and from there circulate endlessly all over the city. You'll be wedged among nine or even ten people in a space designed for six.

Denpasar now has new metered taxis—yellow, with a sign reading Taxi. Still, the **Praja Taxi** (tel. 289-090 or 289-191) drivers may claim the meter is broken, or may choose a longer route than necessary, so it's best to settle on a fare before climbing in. With the recent rise in gasoline prices, flagfall is now around Rp1000. From the Matahari Shopping Center to the Denpasar Tourist Office the fare should run around Rp3000. Taxis from Denpasar to the airport cost about Rp12,000; to Kuta, Rp10,000; to Sanur, Rp8000. Don't tip.

The most expedient and least expensive way to get somewhere in Denpasar quickly is to charter a three-wheeled *bemo* for around Rp2500 for an average run. Or just flag down anything going in your direction—private cars, trucks, or motorcycles. Many drivers cruise for paying riders, charging Rp1000-1500 for a two-to-five-km ride.

You'll find pony-drawn *dokar* outside Kereneng station or just off Jl. Sulawesi beside the household market. They aren't allowed on main streets such as Jl. Gajah Mada. *Dokar* charge tourists at least Rp1500 for a short ride. Capacity three Australians or four Indonesians.

Car And Motorcycle Rentals

Jeeps with drivers can be rented through **Utama Motors,** tel. (0361) 222-073, or **Bali Wisata,** tel. 224-479, both on Jl. Imam Bonjol, or ask your hotel desk clerk or homestay owner. **Taman Sari Hotel,** Jl. Danau Buyan 31, tel. 288-187, also rents cars. Rent a motorcycle from **Koperasi Jasa Bakor Motor,** Kompleks Pertokoan and Terminal Tegal Sari 33 B, Jl. Imam Bonjol, tel. 226-576.

You'll have to pay for parking almost everywhere in Denpasar; as soon as you start to turn the key, attendants appear out of nowhere to collect Rp200 per car, Rp100 per motorcycle.

GETTING AWAY

By Air

From Terminal Tegal, take a *bemo* to the airport, Rp800. The number for the Ngurah Rai Airport international terminal is 751-011. Store your baggage at the airport for Rp2000 per day. Domestic airport tax depends on destination. The international airport tax is Rp11,000 for all flights. Garuda, Merpati, Sempati, and Bouraq all charge about the same for the Denpasar-Jakarta flight. During December and January flights out of Denpasar can be booked solid.

Garuda, Jl. Melati 61, tel. (0361) 222-028 or 227-825, is near Kereneng bus station. **Merpati** is at Jl. Melati 59, tel. 222-864. Both are opposite the stadium, near each other, and maintain similar business hours: Mon.-Fri. 0700-1600, Saturday until 1300, Sunday 0900-1300. Use **Bouraq,** Jl. Sudirman, tel. 223-564 or 222-252, in front of Udayana University, for flights at competitive prices to Nusatenggara, Sulawesi, and Kalimantan. Many foreign airlines—**Thai, Qantas, Cathay Pacific**—staff offices in the Bali Beach Hotel in Sanur. Check literature for addresses. **UTA** is at Jl. Bypass Ngurah Rai, tel. 233-341.

By Boat

Pelni's **KM Awu** leaves Bali once every four weeks for Ujung Pandang, Flores, Kupang, and other destinations. Contact Pelni agents at the Pelni office on Jl. Diponegoro or in the small port of Benoa (in the Sanur area). Try the **Bali Hai** catamaran service to Nusa Lembongan for Rp142,800 or the sunset dinner cruise for Rp71,400. Children under 15 half-fare. Leaves in the afternoon. Book through a travel agent or call (0361) 234-331. Inquire around Benoa Harbor for a lift on a private yacht. Benoa is also the place to find a variety of small *prahu,* including some carrying turtles to Bali.

Take a minibus from Batubulan to Padangbai (Rp2000) on the east coast of Bali. From Padangbai, the ferry departs for Lembar every two hours, except at midnight. The standard fare is Rp4000; 3.5 hours. Another way to Lombok is by jetfoil from Benoa for Rp50,000 (two hours) with **Mabua Express,** tel. 72370. For info on hydrofoil service to Lombok, call 31327 or 88901. Heading east from Bali, you can island hop all the way to Timor. Or charter a boat roundtrip to Komodo for Rp560,000 with your own cook and guide.

By Bus

Long-distance buses from Bali now travel all the way to Sumbawa Besar on Sumbawa and Medan in northern Sumatra. It's easy to shop for the best deal because most bus companies are on just two streets: Jl. Hasannudin (near Jl. Sumatra) and Jl. Diponegoro. Start with **Java Indah Express,** Jl. Diponegoro 14, tel. (0361) 227-329; **Simpatik,** Jl. Diponegoro 31 A, tel. 226-907 or 238-204; and **Lorena,** Jl. Hasannudin 3, tel. 234-941. A number of other companies also at Ubung station (Jl. Cokroaminoto) offer similar quality and service. In the busy season, it's best to buy your ticket the day before and choose the best seat. In the slow season, just show up at the time of departure and you'll probably get on. There are dozens of ticket agents in Kuta, Legian, Ubud, Candidasa, Lovina, and Sanur.

For Surabaya, *bis malam* leave Ubung at 1900, 2000, and 2100, arriving in the early morning. At least 10 buses per day. If leaving in the cool of the evening (last bus at 2100) you'll miss the scenery. The fare, Rp21,000, includes a meal halfway through the 11-hour trip. The Jawa Indah air-conditioned bus with toilet leaves at 0600 and 1800. To Malang (East Java), the 10-hour trip costs around Rp25,000. If there's a long delay and you're in a desperate hurry, just climb on a public *bemo* and leave Ubung as early as possible for Gilimanuk. In Ketapang in East Java, on the other side of the Bali Strait, climb on a bus for Surabaya.

To Yogyakarta, long-distance air-conditioned buses cost Rp38,500. They leave Ubung at 1530 or 1600 and arrive at around 0700. Two meals (*nasi campur* and drinks) are included in the fare. Look for a bus with comfortable reclining airline seats, pillows, and an inside toilet. For Jakarta, take a bus from Ubung at 0630 or 0700, arriving at Jakarta's Pulau Gadung Station by 0930 the next day (Rp58,000).

By *Bemo*

Four-wheeled *bemo* emanate from Denpasar's five *bemo* stations on the perimeter of the city to points all over the island. Go to the station closest to your destination. If you find yourself in the wrong station, there are three-wheeled *bemo* constantly going around in circles, zipping passengers back and forth between stations.

Denpasar is so big that in most cases you must pass through it on your way to someplace else. For example, if heading from Kuta to Sanur you must first get a *bemo* from Kuta to Tegal station (Rp800), then transfer to Kereneng where you board another *bemo* to Sanur (Rp500).

From Tegal, in western Denpasar, *bemo* depart for Kuta, Legian, the airport, and Nusa Dua; from Ubung station on Jl. Cokroaminoto in the north of town, *bemo* head west and north to Gilimanuk (Rp3000), Bedugul (Rp2500), Singaraja (Rp3000), and points east on Java. From Kereneng, on the east edge of town off Jl. Kamboja, *bemo* serve Denpasar and the suburbs of Batubulan and Sanur. From the big Batubulan station east of town, just before the village of Batubulan, big vans and minivans leave for every major tourist destination. From Suci, take *bemo* to Benoa Port and Sanggaran. From Wangaya, *bemo* depart for the Sangeh Monkey Forest, Plaga, and Petang. *Bemo* arrive and leave Denpasar's stations in all directions until around 2000. If you plan on returning to Denpasar the same day, plan ahead because after nightfall the *bemo* of Kuta, Legian, Sanur, Ubud, and Singaraja are the only ones still running (at jacked-up prices) on the island.

Organized thieves sometimes work *bemo* out of Denpasar. Beware of pairs of young men: one will get on carrying large parcels, used to cloak his attempts to pick your pocket, moneybelt, or backpack while his cohort distracts you with friendly conversation in quite intelligible English.

SANUR

A prosperous and historic beach resort area, Sanur is Indonesia's answer to Waikiki. It's nine km southeast of Denpasar and crowded with high-priced luxury hotels and clusters of serene bungalows in leafy compounds along the shoreline of a gentle, reef-sheltered lagoon. Bali's oldest tourist resort; guesthouses began appearing here as early as the 1940s. Large hotel enclaves, shady lanes, trees, and coral walls give the village a park-like setting. The sunrise over Nusa Penida Island each morning is magnificent. At sunset, sailboats dot Sanur's horizon.

Sanur is smaller, quieter, prettier, safer, and more sheltered than Kuta or Legian. It's also more expensive, though less expensive than Nusa Dua. The big luxury hotels which made Sanur famous are on such side streets as Jl. Danau Tamblingan, Jl. Tanjung, and Sari.

Despite throngs of tourists, the village still retains its Balinese character, especially early in the morning when only locals fill the streets. In fact, Sanur is one of Bali's largest traditional villages. It feels more established than Kuta or Lovina; the trees are mature, the streets in good repair, there's less construction. Sanur is the preferred long-term residence for those Bali expats who prefer the ocean and the city.

History
In 1904 the Chinese steamer *Sri Koemala* ran aground off Sanur and was pillaged by local fishermen. Badung's king refused the subsequent Dutch request for compensation; the Dutch used this as a pretext to invade southern Bali. Netherlands East Indies troops came ashore on 15 September 1906. The Dutch marched on the king's *puri* in Denpasar, annihilating the entire royal family.

The first commercial bungalows were built in the 1950s. The era of mass tourism didn't begin, however, until the building of the ugly, eight-story Bali Beach Hotel at Sanur during the early '60s. Today, it's still Bali's tallest structure, visible from 20 km away. When it was finished in 1965, the Sanur *banjar* decided it was disrespectful to the gods to build any more structures higher than a coconut palm. The palm height limit was then adopted all over the island.

Tourism
With its elegant resorts and quiet cottages, Sanur is particularly popular with older European package tourists who luxuriate on the beach, attend glamorous poolside parties, look out at the lovely view while eating veal parmigiana, and join evening cruises on the *Bali Hai* over to Nusa Lembongan. At night people get dressed up and walk along the road parallel to the beach on their way to favorite restaurants. Sanur tourists tend not to occupy the village during the day; long convoys of buses move out of Sanur every morning at 1000, returning late in the afternoon. Tourists are found on the beach only in the high season; at other times long stretches of beach seem nearly deserted.

Although it has three discos, a bowling alley, cocktail lounges, and a wide variety of restaurants with international cuisine, Sanur's nightlife doesn't compare with Kuta's. Nor does Sanur have Kuta's noise, pollution, crime, or mosquitos. The sellers are not as numerous—though they can be just as intolerable. Overall, Sanur has a more quaint, mellow, and cosmopolitan feel than Kuta.

The Balinese of Sanur are full of pride and their behavior is more mannered than that of the people of Kuta, who've become sour and short as a result of the constant influx of poking, prying, demanding tourists. In Sanur, the village atmosphere still survives. People go earnestly about their business oblivious of the tourists.

SIGHTS

Museum Le Mayeur
Also called the Ni Polok Museum. Formerly the home of the late Adrien Jean Le Mayeur, the Belgian impressionist painter who moved to Sanur in 1932. Just 100 meters north of the Bali Beach Hotel (take the lane to the right), smothered by buildings on all sides, the house is wedged between the Diwangkara Beach Hotel and the Bali Beach Hotel. You can also reach the museum from the beach. Open at 0800 every day except Monday and Sunday; closing

SANUR

TO GIANYAR

TO DENPASAR

JL. SANUR

WATERING HOLE HOMESTAY

ALIT'S BEACH BUNGALOWS

DIWANGKARA HOTEL

★ MUSEUM LE MAYEUR

GOLF COURSE

BALI BEACH HOTEL

HOTEL TAMAN SARI

HOTEL SANUR INDAH

HOTEL RANI

POLICE

JL. SEGARA

POST OFFICE

U.S. CONSULATE

SEGARA VILLAGE HOTEL

BORNEO BAR AND RESTAURANT

SPLASH BAKERY

BERINGIN 59

SINDHU BEACH HOTEL

BALI MOON RESTAURANT

CAFE LOTUS POND

LA TAVERNA

GAZEBO COTTAGES BEACH HOTEL

IRAMA

TANJUNG SARI

KALPATHARU BAR AND RESTAURANT

SANTRIAN BALI BEACH BUNGALOWS

LAGHAWA GRILL

SETIA TOURS

KITA

LAGHAWA BEACH INN

PACTO TOURS

THE SWAZTIKA II

LAGHAWA TERRACOTTA GARDEN RESTAURANT

HOTEL RAMAYANA

PENJOR RESTAURANT

TAMAN AGUNG BEACH INN

CAFE BATU JIMBAR

NEW SEOUL

KUL KUL RESTAURANT

MELANIE RESTAURANT

TELAGA NAGA RESTAURANT

PENEEDA VIEW

BALI HYATT

OKA'S

JL. BAJA LETKOL NGURAH RAI

TANJUNG SARI

0   0.5 km

TO KUTA, AIRPORT

TRATTORIA DA MARCO

SURYA BEACH HOTEL

HOTEL SANUR BEACH

© MOON PUBLICATIONS, INC.

time varies from 1100 to 1400. Entrance fee Rp100-200. Ni Polok's daughter is the guide; she owns the adjacent Polok Art Shop.

Set in a tropical garden of hibiscus and bougainvillea and adorned with statues, the gallery contains 92 paintings captioned in English and Indonesian, local artifacts, and some superb specimens of traditional Balinese carvings. Later works dramatically capture the people and scenes of Bali; earlier paintings, which depict Le Mayeur's extensive travels around Europe, tend to be in poor condition. Some paintings were rendered on rough canvas made of woven palm leaves which Le Mayeur was forced to use during the Japanese occupation. The dark interior makes it difficult to view the works.

Le Mayeur first settled in the village of Klandis, east of Denpasar, where he met Ni Polok, a star *legong* dancer and famed beauty. She agreed to model for Le Mayeur and became the subject of a number of his paintings, bringing him great success in Singapore. In 1935, Ni Polok and Le Mayeur married. The couple lived in a lovely beach home on Sanur until his death in 1958. Ni Polok died in 1985. Today the Indonesian government manages the house and collection.

Pura Belanjong

Southwest of Hotel Sanur Beach is one of Bali's most significant archaeological sites, an inscribed stone victory pillar erected by the Buddhist king Sri Kesari Varma in A.D. 914. Only partially deciphered, the inscription—in both Old Balinese and Sanskrit—refers to a military expedition against eastern Indonesia, where the Balinese once obtained their slaves. It's believed Kesari, a king of the Warmadewa dynasty, founded the Besakih sanctuary on the slopes of Gunung Agung. The pillar lies behind Pura Belangjong, about a kilometer past the entrance to the Hotel Sanur Beach.

SPORTS

Boating And Sailing

There are generally more complete marine sports facilities in Sanur than in Kuta. Surfing, windsurfing (Rp10,000 per hour), snorkeling, skin diving, water-skiing (Rp60,000 per hour), Jet-Skiing (Rp120,000 per hour), parasailing (Rp20,000), paddleboats (Rp8,000 per hour), Balinese outriggers, speedboats (Rp63,000 per hour), and fishing excursions are offered by water sports offices right on the beach in front of the big hotels.

A good place to start is **Baruna,** which maintains offices in the Bali Hyatt (tel. 0361-288-271), Bali Beach Hotel (tel. 288-511), and Hotel Sanur Beach (tel. 288-011). The Bali Hyatt's leisure activities desk (tel. 287-777) sells luxury cruises, deep-sea fishing, and snorkeling adventures on two fully equipped, diesel-powered speedboats for Rp630,000-840,000 full day (eight hours) or Rp420,000-630,000 half-day (four hours).

Prahu jukung are more economical; they rent at a fixed rate of Rp10,000-15,000 per hour. One of the most exciting Sanur experiences is to rent one of the brightly painted motorized outriggers for either a sail around the lagoon, beyond the reef to the port of Benoa, or to offshore islands such as Serangan (Rp105,000 roundtrip), Nusa Lembongan, or Nusa Penida (both Rp10,000 one-way, Rp30,000 roundtrip). Boats to Nusa Lembongan depart from the end of J. Hang Tuah. The passage takes about an hour.

Charter the *Wyeema,* a sturdy, 24-ton, 14-meter-long steel-hulled sailing yacht for safe and comfortable sailing adventures. Marvel at the unpeopled islands, deserted beaches, and spectacular reef diving. The crew prepares delicious food. Their specialty is a seven-day, six-night package to Komodo Island (Bali, Komodo, Sape, Bima, then return by air to Bali). This package may be extended to 12 days and 11 nights. Bookings: **Wyeema Adventure Sailing, Surf N' Dive,** Jl. Pemamoran 12, Taman Sari, Sanur, tel. 287-593, fax 231-592.

Diving

An efficient and well-managed dive outfit is **Oceania Dive Center,** Jl. Bypass Ngurah Rai 78, tel. (0361) 288-652 or 288-892, fax 288-652, which sells dive packages (two-person minimum) to Sanur and Nusa Dua (Rp94,500), Padangbai (Rp73,500), Tepekong (Rp136,500), Menjangan Island (Rp178,500), and Nusa Lembongan (Rp178,500). It also offers full-day introductory dive courses, two-day open-water courses, and four-day advanced open-water courses. Prices (Rp210,000-735,000) include tanks, weight belt, lunch, transport, and dive guide.

Also check out **Bali Diving Adventure,** Jl. Duyung 10 just south of the Bali Hyatt, Semawang, tel. 288-871, for affordable dive tours and water sport activities. Other dive outfits include **Bali Dive Sports Club,** Jl. Srikesari 38, tel. 288-582, fax 88743, and **Jeladi Wilis,** Jl. Segara, Beach Market, tel. 287-096 or 288-574.

Swimming And Surfing

Although Sanur's beach remains white and sandy, in front of La Taverna the shallow and weedy shore has been eaten away by lime removal; Semawang's beach, south of the main Sanur Beach, is nicer. At low tide, swimming is impossible; this is when the Balinese fish. At high tide the beach is completely nonexistent.

Although the waves within the lagoon are tame, there's occasionally more dramatic surf at the north beach off Alit's. In front of the Bali Beach Hotel is a right reef break; in front of the Beach Market a fast left-hander. The only consistently good surf is two or three km out in the channel in front of the Bali Hyatt; at high tide hire a parasailing boat to take you out and back for around Rp42,000. At low tide, either wade out into the reef for almost a kilometer or rent a *jukung* to take you out farther. These reefs are inhabited by colorful fish as well as hundreds of sea urchins (wear shoes). The ideal time to snorkel is a little past low tide when clear water flows into the lagoon and the waves are not so high nor the current as strong.

Penyu Dewata, P.O. Box 666, Sanur, tel. (0361) 289-211 or 289-212, is a new nine-hectare water park in Padang Galak in the delta of the Agyung River near Sanur, the largest of its kind in eastern Indonesia. Here children can learn to swim with qualified and experienced instructors. Facilities include three olympic-sized pools, certified lifeguards, cafeteria, lockers, and changing rooms.

Other Sports

The Bali Beach Hotel features a nine-hole seaside golf course that's all right for an easygoing round. Open to nonresidents, the green fee is Rp52,500, club hire Rp23,100. Bali Beach Hotel guests receive a 25% discount. Ten-pin bowling in the same hotel is Rp3500 pp per game.

Kite flying is a distinctive event in Sanur. Sponsored by the local *banjar* in the windy, low-lying *sawah* behind the village, competitions take place from July through September. Teams dressed like samurai in white bandanas charge through the rice paddies to keep the monstrous paper kites aloft. It takes two men to carry the heavy spool of nylon cord and up to six to get the 10-meter-long kites airborne. Once a kite is flying, the cord is tied to a tree. Buy your own kites from local craft shops.

ACCOMMODATIONS

The beachfront is crowded with a whole string of expensive (Rp231,000-420,000) luxury hotels, some sprawling over vast areas. Smaller, family-run, bungalow-style hotels (Rp105,000-210,000) offer greater personal attention and a more intimate atmosphere. Cheaper still (Rp15,000-20,000) are the homestays (no view of the sea) on the lanes running back from the main road. Accommodations differ tremendously in environs and services. Bookings are necessary in the high season, July-Aug. and Dec.-Jan.; during this period the larger hotels will frequently add an Rp21,000-31,500 surcharge to your hotel bill.

Budget

There are now a growing number of homestays away from the beach and off the main road. You're seldom more than a five-minute walk to a pool, such as the one at Santrian Bali Beach Bungalows, open to nonguests for Rp3000 or so.

A sweet and helpful family runs **Prima Cottages** at Jl. Bumi Ayu 15 behind the Arena Restaurant, tel. (0361) 289-153, fax 288-548. It has an intimate atmosphere, is completely walled-in so you can't hear traffic, yet is only two blocks from the beach. Many places in this price range are like jail cells, but Prima's rooms are clean with private, Western-style bathrooms and mosquito nets. Fans or a/c; pool. The popular **Yulia Homestay,** tel. 288-089, behind Yulia Art Shop and kitty-corner to the LG Club, has eight cheap, clean rooms in a family compound for Rp15,000 s, Rp20,000 d. Coffee and tea included in the price. Only eight rooms; popular with travelers.

To the south on the main road of Jl. Tanjung Sari is the **Taman Agung Beach Inn,** tel. 288-549 or 288-006. Twenty rooms with bath (no hot water) cost Rp21,000 with fan, Rp42,000 for a/c; the restaurant is good but overpriced. Farther up and only five minutes from the beach is **Hotel Ramayana,** tel. 288-429, telex 235-307; Rp26,000 for fan rooms, Rp40,000 for a/c rooms, and Rp54,000 for private bungalows. Down the street from the post office on busy Jl. D. Buyan are three *losmen*-style guesthouses, **Hotel Rani, Hotel Taman Sari,** and **Hotel Sanur Indah.** All offer more or less the same prices and services, with plain but adequate rooms in the Rp15,000-20,000 range; a/c rooms with hot water cost Rp35,000-40,000. The least together, tidy, and friendly of the three is Hotel Taman Sari, no. 31, tel. 288-187. My personal favorite is Hotel Rani, no. 33, tel. 288-578; good service, clean, and the "economic room" is only Rp14,500 s or d (plus 15% tax, no breakfast).

The well-run **Watering Hole Homestay,** Agung and Sue's, tel. 288-289, has 13 rooms for Rp30,000 s or d (fan, fridge), surrounded by an interior garden. Four rooms are a/c; Rp40,000 s or d. Relatively cool and quiet for downtown Sanur. The restaurant in front serves good Indo/Chinese food and nightly seafood specials—delectable frog's legs. The homestay features a bar, hosts a buffet with *legong* every Thursday night for Rp10,000, and is close to the landing place for boats to Pulay Lembongan. Mostly Dutch stay here.

The **Kalpatharu Bar and Restaurant,** Jl. D. Tamblingan, tel. 288-457, is a small family hotel (only eight rooms) across the street from the Gazebo and Irama. Prices have been consistent for the past few years: Rp30,000 s, Rp35,000 d for rooms with fan, hot water, shower *mandi,* continental breakfast; Rp45,000 d for a/c rooms. Pool. Friendly people. The restaurant serves pretty good Italian, Indonesian, Chinese, and seafood.

Moderate

Ibu Beach Bungalows, P.O. Box 223, Denpasar, tel. (0361) 288-046, next door to Respati's, costs only Rp63,000 d for a bungalow facing the beach; includes breakfast, afternoon tea, and cookies. Simple rooms in Balinese style with no a/c or hot water, but excellent views, sea breezes, and the beach is just meters away.

Highly recommended is the Bali-style **Laghawa Beach Inn,** Jl. D. Tamblingan, Batu Jimbar, P.O. Box 357, Denpasar, tel. 288-494 or 287-919, fax 289-353, on the ocean side of the

strip. Only 100 meters to the beach. Rooms with a modern bathroom and hot water for Rp52,500 s, simple fan-cooled rooms for Rp63,000 d, a/c rooms for Rp73,500 s, Rp84,000 d. Pool, excellent food. Credit cards accepted.

Gazebo Cottages Beach Hotel, Jl. D. Tamblingan 35, P.O. Box 134, Denpasar, tel. 288-212 or 289-256, fax 288-300, charges Rp73,500 s, Rp84,000 d for standard rooms; Rp88,200 s, Rp98,700 d for bungalows; Rp98,700 s, Rp115,500 d for studios. All rates subject to 15.5% service and tax. High-season surcharge is Rp31,500. Credit cards honored. Great location, excellent service, pool, and private beach area with restaurant and bar. Gazebo bought out **Irama** and **Peneeda View,** tel. 288-999, with comparably priced rooms. **Santrian Bali Beach Bungalows,** Jl. Tanjung Sari, P.O. Box 55, Denpasar, tel. 288-181 or 288-184, fax 288-185, offers a/c in rice barn-style bungalows or rooms and a wide variety of dining and entertainment options. Good sized pool. Rates: Rp105,000 s, Rp115,000 d.

Less expensive, though showing its age, is **Alit's Beach Bungalows,** Jl. Hang Tuah 41, P.O. Box 102, Denpasar, tel. 288-560 or 288-567, fax 288-766, at a great location at Sanur's north end next to the beach. Alit's has 100 a/c Balinese-type bungalows with hot water and shower; Rp78,000 s, Rp84,000 d standard, Rp86,000 s, Rp94,000 d for superior. Don't bother with higher-priced, newer units. Amenities include restaurant, pool, squash and tennis courts, billiards, mini-golf, open stage, dance floor, TV lounge, barber and beauty shops, drugstore, and conference hall.

Luxury

There are scores of first-class hotels, with luxurious four-star properties as well as more intimate bungalow compounds at two-thirds to one-half the price. Be sure to book ahead in the peak tourist seasons.

Well-designed **Sativa Cottages,** Jl. Tamblingan, P.O. Box 163, tel. (0361) 287-881, is a good deal for the price—only Rp126,000 s, Rp163,800 d. Full-on comfort in attractive thatched roof bungalows. Nice pool too. About 10 minutes south of the Bali Beach Hotel is the older and popular **Segara Village Hotel,** P.O. Box 91, Denpasar, tel. 288-407 or 288-408, with rustic, beachfront a/c bungalows, recreation room, gym, sauna, pool, sunken bar, and international restaurants. Standard rooms cost Rp84,000-105,000 pp, bungalows and suites run up to Rp231,000. Just south of Segara Village is the **Sindhu Beach Hotel**, Jl. Danau Tondano 14, P.O. Box 181, tel. 288-351, which has 189 bungalow-style rooms (Rp105,000 s, Rp136,500 d) overlooking a quiet part of the lagoon.

At the south end of Sanur beach is top-grade, 200-room **Surya Beach Hotel**, Jl. Mertasari, P.O. Box 476, Denpasar, tel. 288-833, fax 287-303. Thatched-roofed, cottage-style rooms start at Rp157,500. Solar-heated water, conference facilities, tastefully decorated—just the right balance of luxury and simplicity. Watch "Balinese Cultural Night" on the moonlit open-air stage. European-trained chef, sports facilities, pool. **La Taverna Hotel**, Jl. Tanjung Sari, P.O. Box 40, Denpasar 80228, tel. 288-497, fax 287-126, consists of 44 quiet, a/c, thatched-roof and stucco bungalows. Rates: Rp189,000 d garden standard, Rp231,000 d garden superior, Rp399,000 d duplex suite, Rp366,000 family unit. High season supplement: Rp31,500. All rates subject to 15.5% tax and service charges. Pizzeria, bar, pool, private beach. Excellent Indonesian cuisine served in a beachside restaurant.

The 346-room **Hotel Sanur Beach**, P.O. Box 279, Denpasar, tel. 288-011, IDD 71793, fax 287-566 or 287-749, is a four-star international-class hotel owned by Garuda. Located on a small, quiet side street, rooms are Rp220,500 s, Rp241,500 d standard; Rp283,500 s, Rp304,500 d deluxe; Rp315,000 s, Rp420,000 d studios. Bungalow suites with marbled bathrooms and private pools go for Rp735,000-Rp1.7 million. All rates subject to 15.5% service tax. Good buffet breakfast. Disco, volleyball, tennis, badminton, putting green, moneychanger, carving and painting gallery concessions, and pools. Visit the Perahu Lounge, Tirta Poolside Bar Restaurant and Pizzeria, East West Restaurant, or Warung Seahorse on the beach. The smaller, family-owned **Tanjung Sari**, P.O. Box 275, Denpasar, tel. 288-511, fax 287-917, south of the Irama, has 29 native-style bungalows with outside pavilions and sitting rooms, all impeccably furnished. Most cost Rp210,000 s, Rp231,000 d; seafront sites are Rp250,000 s, Rp315,000 d. The restaurant, pool, and beach bar—a popular

rendezvous spot—overlook the bay, with Gunung Agung in the background. A beautiful outdoor dining room is noted for its lavish *rijstaffel*, exquisite dancing, and haunting *gamelan* music.

The **Bali Beach Hotel**, P.O. Box 275, Denpasar, tel. 288-511, fax 287-917, on the north end of the beach, is the only skyscraper on the island. It's been rebuilt since the fire of November 1992 destroyed it. (How did the fire start? Four rumors abound: 1) divine punishment for the height; 2) torched for insurance purposes; 3) since it was built in 1966 with Japanese war reparations money the place was cursed from the beginning; and 4) the Qantas Airlines people started it when they were laying a new carpet, heating the glue with open fires. Once it started to burn, flames leapt all the way up to the 11th floor; the fire department had equipment useful only for battling fires in one-story structures.) Today there are 605 a/c rooms in a tower block, plus a low-rise garden wing and cottages. Staff of 1,000, three pools, massage, four restaurants, nightclub, open-air stage with *topeng* performances, shopping arcade, barber and beauty salon, indoor games room, post office, banks, conference halls, tour offices, airport transfers, its own fleet of buses. Bali's American Express, Garuda, and Qantas offices are here. Recreation includes fishing, bicycling, bowling, billiards, tennis, and golf. Units run Rp210,000 s, Rp231,000 d for standard rooms; Rp220,500 s, Rp252,000 d for superior; Rp231,000 s, Rp273,000 d for deluxe. Nonsmoking rooms available.

Get an elegant sniff of the retro-Bali theme at Sanur's most beautiful luxury hotel, the big, flamboyant, 390-room **Bali Hyatt**, P.O. Box 392, Denpasar, tel. 288-271, fax 287-693. For 17 years this hotel was the only show in town, the trendsetter for everyplace else. Today it must compete with the luxury resort hotels of Nusa Dua, not to mention another Hyatt. Sanur's Bali Hyatt, in contrast to the Grand Hyatt of Nusa Dua, has a mellow, aged feel to it. The 36-acre complex, the biggest hotel property in Sanur, is made up of rooms (Rp262,500), low-rise bungalows (Rp315,000), and suites (Rp525,000-840,000). Fresh fruit bowl everyday. Activities include tennis, sailing, windsurfing, snorkeling, and palm tree climbing demonstrations. Private beach. Child-care facilities.

FOOD

Sanur's restaurants offer a wide choice of high-quality food. The restaurants along Jl. Tamblingan and Jl. Tanjung Sari are competitively priced, about equal to what comparative meals cost in Kuta or Ubud. Nearly all the better restaurants offer free transport in the Sanur area.

Observe where the *bemo* drivers, waiters, and hotel workers eat; *warung* sustain Sanur's vast service staffs. Sample inexpensive fresh fish and banana-leaf packets of *nasi campur*. Plenty of cheap eating and drinking *warung* face the beach at the end of Jl. Pantai Sindhu.

Visit **Sanur Food Market** on Jl. Tanjung Sari for snacks, baked goods, and Indonesian and Western meals. **Galael Dewata Supermarket** on Jl. Ngurah Rai, next to the Kentucky Fried Chicken, has great imported food and wine. Excellent ice cream parlor.

The **Bali Moon Restaurant**, Jl. Tamblingan 19, tel. (0361) 288-486, near the New Subec nightclub, serves Italian and European food in a garden setting on a high, thatched, open-air *bale*. Good food and attractive surroundings. The circular bar serves a full spectrum of exotic drinks. All prices subject to 15.5% tax and service. **Oka's,** tel. 288-942 or 288-630, recently underwent a facelift. Unique menu and lots of variety; open kitchens, live entertainment, ice machines with a guarantee of 100% safe ice. Free roundtrip transport in the Sanur area to any of the family's four restaurants (Oka's, Istana Garden, JJ, Bella).

The **Swaztika II** sits adjacent to the Swaztika Bungalows and the Hotel Ramayana. The name derives from *su* (goodness) and *asti* (to be); delicious seafood, especially the grilled prawns and fresh tuna. **Made's Bar and Restaurant,** Jl. Tanjung Sari 51, is a popular tourist hangout opposite the Kalpataru Hotel. Much like a sidewalk tavern, in the off season it's very low-key and casual but in the high season it's packed. Very good seafood, Indonesian, and Italian. If you have a hankering for Western food, you can get huge, delicious hamburgers at the **Borneo Bar and Restaurant** on Jl. Pantai Sindhu. The joint advertises "the coldest beer in town," a Wyoming cowboy breakfast (Rp5000), and nightly specials like grilled teriyaki chicken (Rp5000).

A good breakfast place is **La Lagune** at Jl. Tamblingan 103, tel. 288-893, open 0800-2300. For an inexpensive lunch of *sate*, fresh fried fish, grilled lobster, *nasi goreng,* or other Indonesian dishes, try the **Sanur Beach Market,** a village cooperative on the beach end of Jl. Segara. Set menu (Rp25,000) on Wednesday and Saturday nights during dance performances.

The **Cafe Batu Jimbar** on Jl. Tamblingan, tel. 287-374, is the bright spot nowadays, the "health food" restaurant of Sanur, serving reliably tasty, wholesome, imaginative dishes and lavish desserts (chocolate fudge cheese cake, baklava), wonderful salads (average Rp6000-8000), and real eggplant parmesan (Rp4800). Other exotic dishes include spicy Thai chicken soup (Rp7600), french fries (Rp2500), and gazpacho. A meal for two costs about Rp20,000.

The **Cafe Lotus Pond,** tel. 289-398, is excellent. As in all good restaurants, the staff here makes their own bread, pasta, and cakes. Although the a la carte menu leans toward Mediterranean, the Balinese *bebek tutu* (Rp9500) is brought all the way down from Ubud. Best smoked duck on the island. The all-you-can-eat Balinese-style *rijstaffel* (Rp14,000) is justly praised. Pizza, too. And don't miss the desserts.

A good *padang*-style restaurant, **Beringin 59,** Jl. Tamblingan 5, tel. 288-602, is a favorite of drivers and hotel personnel. **Jawa Barat,** Jl. Kesumasari, Banjar Semawang, tel. 288-252, is popular in south Sanur. Here affordable Indonesian, European, and Chinese cuisines are served up: grilled fish, chips, and vegetables Rp4500; *nasi goreng* Rp2000; *mie kuah* Rp1500; *kare ayam* Rp1500. One of the best places for authentic Indonesian dishes. *Selamat menikmati!* For traditional Balinese festival dishes, as well as Western and Chinese cuisine, go to the **Kul Kul Restaurant** near the Hyatt just south of Hotel Taman Agung; pick a night when the frog dance is staged. Free transport.

Shima Japanese Restaurant is considered one of the best on the island. The manager is Japanese, and so is the cook. Independently owned, not attached to any hotel. Though expensive, try **Kita** at Jl. Tamblingan 104 for Japanese dishes such as tempura, yakitori, and sukiyaki. The **New Seoul** in Batu Jimbar serves Korean specialties; the **Swiss Restaurant** on Jl. Segara just south of the Bali Beach Hotel offers fondue.

Trattoria Da Marco in south Sanur serves excellent but pricey Italian food—a must is the spaghetti Viennese. Open at 1800; listen to live Italian and Spanish songs. Also in south Sanur on the beach is the small **Terrazza Martini**; very good garlic spaghetti (Rp6500). Nearly as good for pasta, as well as Indonesian buffet, is **La Taverna,** tel. 288-497, a pleasant beachside bar and restaurant with superb seafood and Italian brick-oven pizzas.

For fresh food at reasonable prices, try the **Laghawa Terracotta Garden Restaurant** at Jl. Tamblingan 51, tel. 287-919. The **Laghawa Grill** is just up the street to the north. **Telaga Naga Restaurant,** tel. 88271, belonging to and across from the Bali Hyatt, offers high-quality Sichuan-style food, and overlooks a carp-filled lotus pond. Open 2030-2300; super service. **Kalpatharu Bar and Restaurant** is a good breakfast place, open 0700-2300; breakfast buffet Rp3900, American breakfast Rp3850, continental breakfast Rp2950.

The Hyatt, Sanur Beach, and Bali Beach contain a variety of premier restaurants with expensive Indonesian, Chinese, Italian, and Japanese menus; extravagant buffets; 24-hour coffee shops; and beachside cafes. The place for desserts is the Bali Hyatt; enjoy all the cakes you can eat for Rp5000.

The Tanjung Sari Hotel on Jl. Tanjung Sari, tel. 288-441, is known for its genuine Indonesian and continental food prepared by a French chef. The dining area is on an elevated terrace by the beach. The *ikan pepes* is first class. On Saturday evening there's a splendid, colonial-style *rijstaffel* for Rp50,000, accompanied by *gamelan* music and *pendet, topeng,* and *baris* dancing. Nice seaside bar.

Opposite the Batu Jimbar *bale* is **Choice Bakery and Cafe,** selling fresh bread and croissants daily, specializing in European food at prices half those charged at Batu Jimbar Cafe next door. **Splash Bakery,** tel. 288-186, on the corner of Jl. Bypass and Jl. D. Buyan opposite the Biro Reklame Plastic Centre, is a perfect place for a quick breakfast. Very good prices: whole wheat bread for Rp2000 (or Rp1500 if day-old), whole carrot cake Rp4000, fruit scones Rp500, all-meat pies and sausage rolls Rp2500. Australian-trained baker. Another bakery with a wide range of items is the **La Lagune Restaurant and Cafe,** Jl. Tamblingan 103, tel. 288-893.

ENTERTAINMENT AND EVENTS

Sanur's big hotels are some of the best places to see regular commercial cultural shows performed by professionals. Keep your ears open and look for banners and fliers. Often you have to pay for dinner (about Rp42,000), which will get you a great seat. Or you can just stroll in, stand behind a chair, and watch. Dress well.

Independent restaurants put on buffet dinners and dances for around Rp31,500 pp. The Penjor Restaurant, tel. 288-226, near the Bali Hyatt, for example, has a "Bali Night" with *legong* on Tuesday, Thursday, and Sunday 1930-2100; the frog dance every Monday at 2015; *joged* every Wednesday at 2015; and *janger* every Friday at 2000. Other restaurants with dinner/dances include Kul Kul, tel. 288-038, Paon, tel. 288-263, and Swastika, tel. 88373. A *kecak* dance is performed on an open-air stage under a giant *waringin* tree at Tanjung Bungkak from 1830 for Rp4500; get there on a Denpasar-bound *bemo* (Rp500, four km).

Nightlife

Sanur is much tamer than Kuta and the nightlife starts and ends earlier. It's a 35-and-up tourist resort, not really the haunt of Australian/Euro all-night ragers. Pleasant company, good food, a watchable TV, and an ample collection of books to borrow at the **Borneo Bar and Restaurant** on Jl. Panti Sindhu. The crowd is an interesting collection of expats, visitors, and locals.

LG Club Sehatku at Jl. Tamblingan 23, tel. 287-880, fax 253-635, is a sauna, steam, shiatsu, and traditional massage spa south of the Bali Moon Restaurant. Get a voucher from the guard before opening (1100-2300) for the special Rp10,000 rate. The standard price is Rp35,700, VIP room Rp113,400. All prices subject to 15.5% tax and service.

The huge, flashy **New Subek Disco** is next door to the Sehatku where, for Rp10,000, you can enjoy its elaborate sound and light system from comfortable chairs placed amphitheater-fashion around a dance floor. The disc jockey churns out a remorselessly loud wall of house music with lyrics flashed in red letters on an electronic sign.

The dancing in **Matahari Disco** in the Bali Hyatt starts at 2000; sometimes there's a cover of Rp3000. Mostly tourists here. The **Number One** in Batu Jimbar, tel. 288-097, farther south, is also fun—lots of singles. Dress casually, but no beachwear. Open 2000-0130. A happy hour every night 2100-2200 features half-priced drinks (beer Rp1500, mixed drinks Rp3000). Ask about complimentary transportation for guests staying in Sanur.

Events

The village has eight full *gamelan* (you can often hear the sound of gongs drifting over the *kampung*), an infamous Black Barong, and the island's only female *kris* dance. Sanur's temple festivals are famous for their color and grandeur. Public performances of authentic Balinese dances occur when a local business, *banjar*, or family celebrates an opening, temple anniversary, or tooth filing.

An unsual *odalan* is staged at the Pura Dalem nearly opposite the main gate of the Bali Beach Hotel. A long procession of girls carrying high offerings arrives in the late afternoon, followed by the cleansing of the temple's *pratima* and a performance by regimented and entranced *baris gede* dancers with long spears.

SHOPPING

Scores of shops, fashion boutiques, and convenience stores line Sanur's main drag. **Sari Bumi-Earth and Fire,** next to Cafe Batu Jimbar, sells fine Indonesian handmade ceramic lamps, dinner and tea sets, bowls, and vases. Open Mon.-Sat. 0800-2000, Sunday 1000-1800. Visit the exclusive showroom of **Linda Garland Designs** on Jl. Tanjung Sari for high-quality, high-priced Indonesian crafts, *batik* quilts, cushions, bedcovers, and bamboo furniture.

Yulia Art Shop, Jl. Tamblingan 38, tel. 288-089, sells traditional *batik* items, woodcarvings, antiques, and reasonably-priced silver. At the end of Jl. Pantai Sindhu, take a right to the **Sanur Beach Market** for beach garments, textiles, woodcarvings, leather goods, jewelry, seashells, *ikat* bags, and distinctive folk crafts.

Pisces, Jl. Tamblingan 105, tel. 289-373, fax 288-040 in Semawang, is just down the street from the Bali Hyatt near the La Lagune restaurant. This shops deals in well-sewn, double reinforced black-and-white garments in unique

designer cuts; prices from Rp16,000. These original and continentally designed clothes are the creation of Kim and Made Patra. For elegant apparel and stunning handwoven *ikat* fabrics, try **Nogo** at Jl. Tanjung Sari 173.

Asmat Arts, Jl. Tamblingan 200, deals in "primitive arts made by 20th-century Stone Age people." Several antique shops are on the north end of Jl. Tanjung Sari; hunt for unique textiles, baskets, tribal artifacts from the eastern islands, and reproductions of antique furniture. Try **Tjek Lai** on Jl. Bypass near the Bali Beach Hotel for old wooden boxes and Chinese wedding beds. Bargain hard; Kuta is better for antiques. Also check for antiques in the shopping arcades of the big hotels, especially that of the Bali Hyatt.

SERVICES

The majority of Sanur's tourist services are found along Jl. Tamblingan. Besides moneychangers, travel agencies, rental agencies, beauty salons, tailors, photo processing shops, mini-markets, kiosks, major airlines offices, and telephone, fax, and telex services, Sanur has loads of packing and shipping companies to send home all your souvenirs.

For communications needs, go to the *wartel* (open 0800-2200) on the southeast corner of Jl. Segara Ayu and Jl. Ngurah Rai. The Beach Market Bar and Restaurant on Jl. Segara Ayu has a card pay telephone in front. A great many of the hotels have IDD telephones. Sanur's telephone code is 0361.

Postal agents are found all over town. One is just a few doors south of Cafe Batu Jimbar, next to Golden Bali Bar and Restaurant. Most hotels offer postal services.

A good, central place to shop for toiletries and liquor is the Kartika Jaya (Rai's Drugstore), Jl. Tanjung Sari 15, tel. 288-209. For just about everything, shop in the popular but expensive Gelael Dewata Supermarket on Jl. Bypass.

For photo processing, try the Sanur Foto Center III, kitty-corner from the New Seoul Restaurant, or the Mercy Photo Studio, Jl. Tamblingan 58, tel. 288-603. The latter is a good place to order passport photos; one-day service Rp900 for three, Rp2700 for 10.

For a wide selection of Indonesia books, English novels, and varied international periodicals, try the Kika Book Shop (tel. 287-374) in the Batu Jimbar Cafe.

Learn Indonesian from Australian Anita Goldman, tel. 751-557 or fax 753-693. She charges Rp25,000 for a 1.5-hour lesson and is available any time, your place or hers (Jl. Bethngandang 16 X, Sanur).

A Pentecostal church is on Jl. Bypass Ngurah Rai, tel. 287-334 or 89346, with an Indonesian service 0800-1000, Korean service 1030-1200, and English service 1830-1930.

For a "Health Massage," see Pertuni and Iwapi at Refleks Pijat, near the Bayu Restaurant, tel. 8037. For medical needs, see English-speaking Dr. Kt. Rina on Jl. Bypass, or the house doctor at the Bali Hyatt, tel. 288-271.

TRANSPORTATION

Charter *bemo* for short trips around Sanur for about Rp3000-5000, or simply walk anywhere within 10-15 minutes. Motorbikes rent for reasonable rates at Yulia Art Shop and Homestay, Jl. Tamblingan 38, tel. (0361) 288-089, diagonally opposite the LG Club. Many rental offices, travel agents, hotels, and shops on Jl. Tanjung Sari rent Suzuki Katanas, minibuses, Kijangs, and sedans for Rp73,500-115,000 per day; try first to strike up a good rental deal with your hotel manager.

Getting There
From Kuta to Sanur, take a *bemo* first to Terminal Tegal (Rp500) in Denpasar, then a green *bemo* all the way to Sanur (Rp500). A four-lane highway runs six km from the edge of Denpasar to Sanur. The official taxi fare for the 20-minute drive from the airport to Sanur is Rp12,000. If you have prior booking, look for the name of your hotel on signs or vehicles at the airport for a free, air-conditioned ride to Sanur. Another way to get to Sanur is to walk along the beach from Lebih, south of Gianyar, to Sanur. This involves crossing the mouths of several rather large rivers—exercise caution.

Getting Away
On Jl. Tanjung Sari, flag down a green public *bemo* heading northwest to Denpasar (Rp600), or a blue one heading south to Tegal station (also Rp600). From here take another *bemo* to Kuta for Rp600. Take yellow, metered Praja taxis for Rp10,000 to the Matahari Shopping Center in Denpasar; additional *rupiah* if going farther. Private cars or minibuses into Denpasar cost Rp20,000 first price.

If you have your own vehicle, drive the beautiful new superhighway via Batubulan in the direction of Ubud. This highway makes Sanur a good base from which to explore the regencies of Bangli, Gianyar, and Klungkung.

Tour Companies
The biggest and busiest ticket agent in Sanur is **Tunas Indonesia Tours and Travel,** Jl. Tamblingan 107, tel. (0361) 288-581 or 288-450, fax 288-727. Daily air-conditioned coach tours are offered by **Santa Bali Tours and Travel,** Hotel Bali Beach Arcade, Sanur, tel. 287-628 or 288-057, ext. 799, fax 236-508, to Bali's Art Villages (Rp30,000), Singaraja and Lake Bratan (Rp40,000), and Karangasem East Coast (Rp38,000). **Satriavi Tours and Travel,** Jl. Cemara 27 in Semawang (Sanur), tel. 287-074, fax 71921, offers tours to Kintamani, Tanah Lot, and other tourist sites.

Meru Bicycle Day-Trips
Iskander Wawo-Runtu (or simply Alexander), of the same family that owns Cafe Batu Jimbar, guides adventure tours on mountain bikes from his upland farm in Pupuan down to the sea. The hotel pickup time in Sanur is 0800, and the tour starts from Batungsel at 1000; drop-off at your hotel is around 1800. Cost: Rp126,000 pp, five person minimum. Contact Alexander at the Tanjung Sari, Private Bungalows, Jl. Tamblingan 41, Sanur, tel. (0361) 288-441, fax 287-930, or at Cafe Batu Jimbar on Jl. Tamblingan, tel. 287-374.

BENOA PORT AND SERANGAN ISLAND

BENOA PORT

For hundreds of years, reef-sheltered Labuhan Benoa was the entry point from the sea for all of south Bali. The accumulation of alluvium has long since rendered much of this natural harbor unnavigable, but a long causeway was built by the Dutch after their 1906 invasion. At the end are fuel tanks, a big wharf, warehouses, a lighthouse, fisheries, charter-vessels offices, and a Pelni office.

Reach Benoa from Denpasar's Tegal Station by *bemo* for around Rp1000. A chartered *bemo* from Kuta will run about Rp9000-12,000. If traveling by car, 10 km from Denpasar turn right and travel down a two-km-long jetty (Jl. Pelabuhan), which stretches toward the northeast corner of the Bukit Peninsula.

Large cargo ships, fishing boats, oil tankers, cruise ships, private yachts, and intraisland *kapal layar* moor in this wide and shallow bay. The port is also the location of the Bali International Yacht Club, tel. (0361) 288-391. If you'd like to crew on one of the visiting overseas yachts, hire a *jukung* to take you around to the different vessels; ask if there are any openings. Visiting ocean-going yachts usually arrive at this anchorage in the high season.

Catch the high-speed hydrofoil to Lombok. With its twin hulls and high-tech design, this vessel will get you to Lembar in West Lombok quickly, comfortably, safely, and reliably. Enjoy stunning views while you luxuriate in a spacious air-conditioned lounge with TV, video, and refreshments. Departs Benoa at 0830, arrives 1030; departs Lembar 1300, arrives back in Benoa 1500. Book through your travel agent, or call the offices directly, tel./fax 72370. The fare from Bali to Lombok is around Rp40,000; return about Rp35,000.

SERANGAN ISLAND

Also known as Turtle Island or Pulau Sakenan, this dry, low-lying, 73-hectare, three-km-long island is formed on the sandbar at the entrance to Labuhan Benoa, only one kilometer off the southeast coast of Bali. The island's lovely palm-lined southern beach is visible from the village of Benoa. At the northern end of Serangan are two villages, Pojok and Dukuh, connected by a bridge over an inlet.

Unfortunately, Serangan has become a tourist trap. The island's main attraction seems to be a muddy pool inhabited by greenback turtles (*kura-kura*). Shops selling seashell and turtle-shell artifacts and cold drinks surround the pond, but there are no accommodations. You'll likely be hounded by vendors.

Green sea turtles (*Chelonia mydas*) are caught in the surrounding shallow coastal waters, or simply turned on their backs when they come ashore at night to lay eggs. First kept alive in bamboo pens, then fattened on seagrass or leaves, they're eventually slaughtered at Pegok on the outskirts of Denpasar. The meat is then sold to restaurants for turtle steaks and *sate,* or used as a vital ingredient in Balinese ceremonial *lawar*. There used to be a balance between supply and demand on Bali, but now hundreds of these magnificent animals must be imported from the eastern islands and Maluku. If you're fortunate, on a moonlit night you can watch them lay eggs on Serangan's beach. Eggs are imported from West Java and buried in the sand so tourists can see them hatch here. There's also a turtle egg hatchery on the island.

Serangan's slender **Pura Sakenan** is a two-part sea temple sacred to all south Bali. A feature of this *pura* is its peculiar, graceful *bersayap*-style winged *candi bentar*. Inside is an obelisk to the rice goddess, Dewi Sri. Legend has it Pura Sakenan was founded by the 10th century wanderer-priest Mpu Kuturan. The more squarish **Pura Susunan Wadonan** nearby contain *prasada,* but without the *cella*. This combination of *candi* and prehistoric pre-Hindu stepped pyramid is seldom seen in Balinese temple architecture.

Events
It's best to visit the island at festival times. Once every 210 days, a **Turtle Festival** (Manis Kuningan) is held at the Pura Sakenan sea temple in

the north of the island. For the two-day *odalan* anniversary festival, droves of people cross over the sandbars bearing offerings to the sea gods. At the same time, towering giant puppets for the *barong landung* dance are carried by canoe in a water procession. A big colorful fair takes place outside the temple, with throngs of people in all their finery streaming in and out.

Getting There

The most common method is by boat from Desa Suwungan, about a kilometer south of Sanur; you'll see the sign pointing to Serangan Island. Take a right turn off Jl. Bypass, then drive past shrimp farms to the channel through the man-

groves. The price is Rp15,000 (15 minutes); bargain the fare while waiting for other passengers to fill up the boat. Once on the island, get to Pura Sakenan from the north by walking south over the bridge to the *banjar* of Dukuh-Sekenan.

From Tanjung Benoa, plan on about 20 minutes each way to cross the bay by *prahu motor*, and at least a half-day on the island. The fishermen ask as much as Rp30,000 first price, but will come down to Rp20,000. From Tanjung's tip, it's possible to walk across the mud to Pulau Serangan when the tide is low. Also, inquire at the water sport centers about day snorkeling excursions to coral formations off Serangan's east coast.

BADUNG REGENCY

Bali is divided into nine *kabupaten* (administrative districts, or regencies), based on the old post-Majapahit kingdoms; of these, Badung contains the neon-lit tourist swath of Legian, Kuta, and Nusa Dua. Badung also extends inland to the overtouristed monkey forest of Sangeh and on to the slopes of Gunung Catur (2,096 meters), high in the central mountains.

Badung has the island's highest prices and the poshest, most sophisticated hotels. Yet central and northern Badung are regions of fertile rice fields carved exquisitely out of hills and valleys, with small, densely settled villages surrounded by groves of coconut palms. Wealthy southern Bali's temple festivals, ceremonies, and dance performances are lavish and unending.

The drier, sparsely populated club-foot shaped peninsula known as Bukit ("The Hill") is attached to the southernmost body of the island by a narrow isthmus. Here, high cliffs fall steeply into the Indian Ocean and surf pounds stretches of isolated coast; this is among the earth's top surfing spots. Although the soil is thin, water scarce, and the climate arid, Bukit is fast becoming an overflow residential area for the mushrooming population of Nusa Dua, Jimbaran, and Tanjung. Between Bukit and southern Bali's fertile plains is Ngurah Rai International Airport, which receives hordes of tourists from all over the world. The bulk of Bali's tourists visit the concentrated international beach enclaves of the south, taking day-trips to sites all over the island.

History

Since it's the most accessible seaport in the southern part of the island, the Badung region has always been an important point of contact with the outside world. The Javanese Majapahit army came ashore at Kuta in 1343 to conquer Bali. The first Dutchmen landed on Bali at Kuta in 1597. In the 1830s an ambitious Danish trader, Mads Lange, established a thriving trading post at the same site.

Once ruled by the *raja* of Mengwi, Badung split from Tabanan in 1885. This historical event explains the regency's odd vertical shape—like an exclamation point—and accounts for Meng-wi being included within its territory. The Pemecutan clan of Denpasar defeated Mengwi in 1891, but held sway only briefly, until the incursion of a new and increasingly powerful player, the Dutch. Though the Dutch subdued the northern part of the island in 1849, the fertile, lava-rich lowlands of the south came under colonial rule only after prolonged resistance. Badung was pounded into submission in 1906, setting the stage for the conquest of all of southern Bali.

Since the establishment of the Ngurah Rai International Airport in Tuban in 1969, the provincial government of Bali has attempted to confine tourist development to the south. A whole generation of local residents have built *losmen* and restaurants in the south's tourist enclaves of Kuta and Sanur, and entrepreneurs from all over Indonesia flock here for money-making opportunities. Thousands of laborers from Java are also attracted to work on the new roads and hotels of the constantly expanding economic infrastructure. Thus Badung Regency is where Balinese culture has undergone the most radical and deepest changes.

NORTH OF DENPASAR

Near **Sempidi**, north of Denpasar on the road to Kapal, are beautifully decorated *pura desa* and *pura dalem*. Sempidi's **Pura Puseh** is known for its very colorful *odalan*. Also visit the cut-rock cave **Goa Krebing Langit** on the east bank of the river between Sempidi and Lukluk. Lukluk's *pura dalem* is worth a visit; its decoratively painted bas-reliefs portray mischievous village scenes as well as mythological themes.

Mengwi

Sixteen km northwest of Denpasar, Mengwi is Rp600 by minibus from Denpasar's Ubung station. If driving, take the main road to Tabanan through Kapal to the Mengwi turnoff, then proceed north. This quiet town is important as the former seat of a long dynasty of kings; its large temple belongs to the group of Bali state or "national" temples. Since its beginnings in 1634

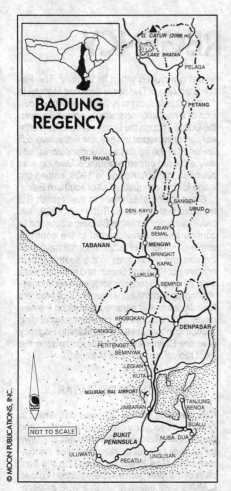

BADUNG REGENCY

NOT TO SCALE

© MOON PUBLICATIONS, INC.

under Raja I Gusti Agung Anom until its demise in 1891, Mengwi was a separate kingdom that extended its political power as far as Blambangan, East Java. The dynasty was ultimately defeated by the neighboring Balinese kingdoms of Badung and Tabanan.

The elegant **Pura Taman Ayun** is the second largest temple complex on Bali, and one of the island's most beautiful shrines. This trim, impressive garden complex lies only one-half km east of the main highway (turn in at the market), accessible by a long entrance walkway.

The original structure dates from around 1740 when ruler Cokorda Munggu built what was to be his state temple on high ground. It's partly surrounded by a wide moat with lotuses, which gives the impression the temple is floating. Consisting of 50 separate structures, this clan temple evokes a palpable sense of calm and beauty. Constructed in four spacious, rising levels, the *pura* symbolizes the Hindu divine cosmos. Carved demons stand silhouetted against the sky; ancient gray stone contrasts against the brick-red plaster. Restored and enlarged in 1937, today Pura Taman Ayun is looked after by descendants of the royal family. It's clean, with toilet facilities, trim gardens, and an orchid nursery. Donation Rp500-2000.

Notice the tall, beautifully crafted split gate with wooden doors and a half *kala*-face to each side. Inside the older, second courtyard is a long row of 29 shrines where visiting deities can relax and enjoy themselves. The stone altar facing east is dedicated to Ibu Paibon, the royal ancestor. A great number of shrines are replicas of Bali's sacred volcanos or major temples built by Mengwi's rulers. They sit on moss-covered stone foundations, topped by slender, tiered black-thatched roofs, their small wooden doors masterfully carved. The replicas are located in the temple so the people of Mengwi can worship and derive benefit from them without the expense and trouble of traveling to the originals. Climb the small tower in the lower left-hand corner for the best view of the temple and surroundings.

There's a lot going on in and around this complex. Hire a little boat and tour the sanctuary from the moat. Pavilions display paintings for sale as well as postcards, textiles, terra-cotta figurines, and fashions. Before the entrance is a huge *wantilan* where cockfights, *barong* dances, and other cultural events are staged. Farther on is a big collection of orchids; on the banks of the moat grow fruit trees and perfumed flowering *cempaka* and frangipani. Visit Pura Taman Ayun when the three-day *odalan* occurs; watch hundreds of women file over the bridge into the courtyard carrying high, multicolored offerings. The temple filled with people, music, dance, and processions is a magnificent sight.

The Mandala Wisata ("Museum of Cremation"), near the Taman Ayun temple, contains palm-woven offerings. Climb on the small raft pulled by ropes for a ride across the moat to the rather high-priced and touristy Royal Garden Restaurant. Visit only if tour buses aren't parked out front. The Indo/Chinese food is delicious and the view over the moat and the tall *meru* towers superb. Or eat more cheaply and authentically in the market or at the *bemo*/bus station. A very nice homestay, the only one in town, lies south of the temple in Banjar Alang Kajeng. The owner, I Ketut Arya, is informative and helpful; six double rooms at Rp8000, breakfast included. Other meals for around Rp1000.

Sangeh

Travel fifteen km beyond Mengwi on the road to Gunung Catur, Rp1000 by *bemo* from Wangaya station in Denpasar to Sangeh's parking lot, filled with Super-Kijangs and Suzuki Katanas and surrounded by a big souvenir shop scene. Here, under towering 30-meter-tall trees, is the holy Monkey Forest, with three clans of sacred, very aggressive monkeys crawling over lichen-covered Bukit Sari ("Nectar of the Mountains") Temple. Built by the royal family of Mengwi in the 17th century, the temple is dedicated to the god Vishnu and was initially used as a place of meditation. Restored in 1973, today it functions primarily as a *subak* temple where offerings to agricultural deities are made. Notice the old statue of Vishnu's mount Garuda, and the relief of a Japanese shooting at an airplane.

Legend says the monkey general Hanuman seized the giant cosmic mountain Mahameru in order to deal the evil demon Rawana a death blow. A piece of mountain with monkeys still clinging to it fell on Sangeh and there they live to this day. There are 10 hectares of *pala* (nutmeg) trees here, a species not native to Bali; their presence has never been explained, thus contributing to the mystery of the place. Another puzzle is that no monkey bodies or skeletons are ever found.

Buy a bag of peanuts and watch for the King of the Monkeys; also watch out for monkey claws and teeth (carry a stick). Don't get too close to their young, hang on to your glasses, cameras, and hats, and for God's sake don't go with money sticking out of your pockets. These descendants of Hanuman's warriors will grab at any protrusion and won't return a thing unless you divert them with a stick, peanuts, or a banana. Pestering peddlers and begging children are even worse.

Between the tour buses, absorb some of the quiet and serenity of Sangeh's magnificent forest. Walk down the pathway by the river gorge in back. From Sangeh, take a rocky side road that crosses over to Mengwi. From Sangeh an unpaved path leads through the rice fields to Ubud. A poor road leads from Sangeh to Ubud.

North of Sangeh is the rugged Petang district, with lots of fresh air, coffee, cloves, vanilla, and chocolate. Beyond, climb up to Pelaga through rice fields, vegetable gardens, bamboo stands, and more plantations.

LEGIAN

This once dusty, poor seaside village is now just an extension of Kuta, though with slightly more chic energy. Legian offers good music, outstanding food, both luxury and budget hotels, sophisticated fashion boutiques, banks, souvenir markets, and *arja, barong, kecak,* and Ramayana performances at least every other day. From Denpasar, Legian is Rp600 by *bemo,* or a two-km walk from Kuta Beach on a congested sidewalk beside a busy road running south. It's more pleasant to walk via the beach, though this trek is only safe in the daytime.

ACCOMMODATIONS

No lack of accommodations in and around Legian. The northern section features unique, relaxed places surrounded by spacious gardens and coconut palms, with only the sound of birds, insects, and geckos. Nowhere, however, will you escape the 15.5% tax and service charge.

Budget

The inexpensive **Janji Inn,** Banjar Legian Kelod, tel. (0361) 753-328, in a quiet coconut grove off Gang Uluwatu, offers eight large, well-appointed rooms with *mandi* for Rp10,000 s, Rp15,000 d. Good security, free breakfast, tea all day, nice people. A welcome oasis not far from the madding crowd. **Wisata Beach Inn,** a short walk from the beach behind Glory's Restaurant, has very nice, quiet, two-room bungalows in a garden setting for only Rp10,000 s, just Rp9000 per day if you stay a week. Cheap, comfortable **Surya Dewata Beach Cottages** is a small complex of little bungalows with 24-hour security down a small alleyway off Jl. Padma Utara; the path is very dark at night. A kitchen is available for preparing meals. For something closer to the beach, try the 10-room **Sri Beach Inn,** Rp8000 s and Rp12,000 d, light breakfast included. Set in the middle of a beautiful and well-maintained orchid garden. The place is run by Wayang Tampa, who speaks better than average English and employs tireless houseboys.

On Jl. Padma, central little seven-room **Three Sisters** is a bargain at Rp12,000 s or d with outside *mandi,* Rp15,000 s or d with inside *mandi.* One of Legian's first *losmen*; still popular. Family-run **Korti's Beach Inn** is down a small lane off Jl. Padma. Korti's feels like a Balinese *kampung* despite heavy traffic outside. Rates are Rp10,000 s, Rp12,000 d. Very hidden. Also check out the **Dawan Beach Inn,** tel. 224-493, next door. Another old Legian favorite and just as quiet, with private bathroom, garden, hot water, and fan.

Oka Melati Hotel, tel. 751-085 or 751-306, has patio and upstairs rooms with balconies, each with wrought iron table and chairs. Rooms are simply but pleasantly furnished and include *mandi.* Features include an attractive courtyard with palms, a well-staffed front desk with fax, birdcages, and lovely roof garden. Staff will keep your passport and valuables in a locked compartment. Price depends on length of stay and your negotiating abilities. Directly across the street is another hotel with a pool you can use. Next door is the relaxing and attractive **Orchid Garden Cottages** Jl. Pura Bagus Taruna 525, P.O. Box 379, Legian Kaja Kuta, tel. and fax 752-852, with 23 rooms on 900 square meters. The restaurant entrance is covered in bougainvillea. A store, film processing, laundry, and tour service also on the premises. Other restaurants and lots of services within easy reach. Rates are Rp20,000 for fan room, Rp32,000 for a/c room with hot water, attached bathrooms, and breakfast. Clean rooms and beautiful garden. **Bali Indra Resort** (behind Depot Viva) has air-conditioned rooms for Rp38,500 and a great swimming pool.

Moderate

An old Legian fixture is **Three Brothers Bungalows,** tel. (0361) 751-566, now with a small but nice swimming pool. Still a comfortable place to stay in spite of the sometimes lackadaisical service. Prices run Rp25,000 d, meals not included, for bungalows with tiled floors, ornate wooden furniture, and double louvered doors opening onto tiled verandas. The garden *mandi* is big, modern, roofless, completely tiled, and

JL. DHYANA PURA

JL. LEGIAN

KUTA
PALACE
HOTEL

OKA MELATI
HOTEL

RUM JUNGLE

ORCHID
GARDEN
COTTAGES

JL. PURA BAGUS TARUNA

POCO LOCO

BENNY'S CAFE

BALI
COCONUT
HOTEL

GLORY BAR AND RESTAURANT

POSTAL AGENT AND CARGO CENTER

BHUWANA
BEACH
COTTAGES

THREE BROTHERS
BUNGALOWS

SURYA DEWATA
BEACH COTTAGES

WARUNG KOPI
JL. KUTA PALACE

BALISANI HOTEL

LEGIAN

SERENDIPITY
COTTAGES

WARUNG KOPI

JL. PADMA UTARA

GARDEN VIEW
COTTAGES

BALI SEA

LEGIAN
SNACKS

LEGIAN VILLAGE
HOTEL

BALI MANDIRA
COTTAGES

JL. PADMA

RAMA GARDEN
COTTAGES AND
RESTAURANT

THREE
SISTERS

LEGIAN BEACH HOTEL

JANJI INN

GOSHA
RESTAURANT

BALI INTAN
COTTAGES

JL. MELASTI

BAIK BAIK

KULKUL BEACH
RESORT

BRUNA BEACH
HOTEL

JL. PANTAI (BEACH RD.)

JL. LEGIAN

RAMA GARDEN COTTAGES

KUTA JAYA

SERENDIPITY FINE ANTIQUES

THE BOUNTY

DEPOT VIVA

ZA'S BAKERY AND RESTAURANT

MAMA'S

KRISHNA
BOOKSHOP

SOUVENIR
SHOPS

PROTESTANT CHURCH

EL DORADO RESTAURANT

GANG BENA SARI

MASTAPA
GARDEN COTTAGES

GANG MENUH

TO KUTA

0   300 m

© MOON PUBLICATIONS, INC.

filled with plants. More expensive rooms are quite luxurious, with garden baths and beautifully carved wooden furniture; some on upper floors open to the outdoors. These last cost an incredibly cheap Rp40,000-50,000. Peaceful, well-kept grounds. The restaurant on the premises is a tranquil hangout and gathering spot. **Puri Wisata Bungalows,** on Jl. Legian Kaja three blocks south of Jl. Melasti, tel. 751-637, fax 753-185, has 22 rooms for Rp30,000 economy class with fans or Rp50,000 d for a/c rooms with fridge. Rooms are clean and furnished with rattan furniture. The small restaurant is inexpensive and serves free tea or coffee; free airport transfers if you stay three or more nights. Cars and minivans available for tours and transport. Manager speaks English very well.

Just a few minutes walk from the beach, **Garden View Cottages,** Jl. Padma Utara 4, tel. 751-559, offers bungalows for Rp60,000 s and Rp75,000 d. Well-kept grounds, quiet location. **Bhuwana Beach Cottage,** tel. 752-234, offers nice cottages including furniture, fridge, and fan. Rp25,000 for the larger units. Friendly people. Also near the beach is the **Bruna Beach Hotel,** tel. 751-565, fax 753-201, with ordinary, clean rooms for as low as Rp60,000 s, Rp70,000 d. Prices vary depending on fan or a/c, hot or cold water. Deluxe family rooms run Rp157,500. Rates don't include breakfast (Rp6000) or the 15.5% tax and service charge. Amenities include pool, beachside restaurant and bar, volleyball games on the beach, TV room. Bruna staff sell bus tickets; reconfirm air tickets; rent cars, jeeps, motorbikes, and surfboards; and offer deep-sea fishing and island cruises. Popular with Germans.

Rama Garden Cottages, on Jl. Padma, P.O. Box 334, Denpasar, tel. 751-972 or 751-971, fax 751-866, 200 meters from the beach, has clean, comfortable rooms with fridges and all modcons in Bali-style two-story modern bungalows. Pool, restaurant, bar. Right in the middle of Legian, close to the action. Also on Jl. Padma is the 90-room **Legian Village Hotel,** only a couple of blocks from the beach, with nicely appointed a/c rooms, hot water, pool, restaurant, and laundry service for Rp63,000 s, Rp74,500 d.

Mastapa Garden Cottages, Jl. Legian, P.O. Box 13, Denpasar, tel. 751-660, fax 751-099, opened in 1973 in the midst of jungle. In a decade, Kuta and Legian eventually enveloped it, and Mastapa is now ideally located between the two towns. Remarkably quiet and safe despite its eye-of-the-storm location, Mastapa's is perfect for a few days' rest at reasonable rates (Rp37,800-84,000 s, Rp42,000-94,500 d). Its a/c rooms and bungalows, set in from the street, surround a small, clean pool and gardens. Enjoy an American (Rp5500) or continental (Rp2500) breakfast in the upstairs restaurant, painting exhibitions, occasional Balinese dances in the inner courtyard, and special buffets. Mastapa's arranges island tours in its own vehicle. Particularly suited for families. Business travelers may avail themselves of fax, IDD, secretarial services, and a small conference facility. Laundry and luggage storage. This family-style guesthouse is run by extremely gracious manager Kade and her father Wayan Mastra, a renowned Christian theologian. Almost opposite Mastapa's is a lane that takes you right to the beach.

Luxury

Hotels in this feel-no-pain class are near to or on the beach, and feature a/c, fridge, mini-bar, telephone, color TV, in-house video, bed control panel, private baths, hot water, pool, safety deposit boxes, laundry and dry cleaning, travel service, spacious lobbies, and restaurants serving European, Chinese, and Indonesian food. Credit cards accepted. Taxi service, car or motorbike rental, and free transport from the airport.

The elegant **Legian Beach Hotel,** P.O. Box 308, Denpasar, tel. (0361) 751-711, fax 751-715, lies at the end of Jl. Melasti near the center of Legian. The 140 rooms spread out over enormous grounds amid luxuriant facilities: bar, restaurant, Olympic-size pool, free airport transfers. Wide choice of rooms. Those with fans in three-storied blocks go for Rp70,000 s, Rp80,000 d; a/c beachside bungalows are Rp150,000 s, Rp160,000 d. The 96-room **Bali Mandira Cottages,** P.O. Box 1003, Denpasar, tel. 751-381, rent for Rp168,000 s, Rp189,000 d (plus 15.5% tax and service) with a/c, hot water, IDD, sound system, lush courtyard gardens, pool, tennis and squash courts, bar, restaurant, and nice view of the ocean. Friendly service. **Kuta Palace Hotel,** at the end of Jl. Pura Bagus Taruna, P.O. Box 244, Denpasar, tel. 751-433, has 135 rooms for Rp110,000-300,000. Open-air theater, lots of sports and entertainment. Located in northern Legian right on the beach.

The **Balisani Hotel,** Jl. Padma Utara, tel. 752-314 or 754-058, fax 752-313, is a small, beautifully designed hotel that re-creates a traditional Balinese village in luxurious style. Well-trained staff. Standard rooms cost Rp100,000 s, Rp110,000 d; cottages with king-size beds Rp140,000; two-story villas Rp160,000. High season surcharge Rp25,000; rates include tax and service charge. The Meru Restaurant overlooks the pool. Water sports are easily arranged. The modern **Bali Coconut Hotel,** Jl. Padma Utara, tel. 754-122, fax 754-121, is built in a tropical style but offers all the conveniences with snappy service. Restaurant and karaoke bar, coffee shop. Rates Rp90,000 s, Rp100,000 d, with high season supplement of Rp20,000. Walk down a short private alley to the beach.

On Jl. Pantai Kuta is the small but special **Kulkul Beach Resort,** tel. 752-920, telex 235-505, with 40 thatch-roof bungalows comprising 76 rooms, some with open-air baths. Staff and management eager to please. The quaint, rustic feel appeals to a younger clientele. On the premises is the popular Blue Cactus Mexican restaurant, a karaoke bar, traditional beauty salon, and tour and travel desk. Drawback: the resort is located next to the Baruna Night Club, which pulsates with raucous music until 2300. The **Kuta Jaya** on Jl. Raya Pantai Kuta, tel. 752-308 or 752-378, fax 752-309, is completely self-contained, with its own shopping arcade, photo center, doctor, drugstore, bank, travel agency, postal and dry-cleaning services, and an open-air performance stage. Some 150 rooms (Rp147,000-315,000 per room), nice garden, clean interiors, peaceful atmosphere. Just north of the Kuta Jaya is the large **Bali Intan Cottages,** Jl. Melasti 1, P.O. Box 1002, Denpasar, tel. 751-770, fax 751-891, with 146 rooms in two-storied blocks for Rp136,500 s, Rp178,500 d, plus family suites for Rp294,000. Seafood restaurant, coffee shops, bar, room service, table tennis, tennis and squash courts, seaside pool. Closest upmarket hotel to Kuta.

Long-Term
The **Serendipity Cottages,** Jl. Padma Utara, tel. (0361) 751-331, consist of 12 fully equipped, comfortable bungalows well-suited for long-term

rental: complete kitchen, private garden, hot water, cassette stereo, maid and laundry service, good security. One bungalow sleeps four or more people. Costing Rp63,000 per day not including tax; not a bad deal for a family. Bargain for an even better monthly rate.

FOOD

An outstanding place to eat Indonesian food at reasonable prices is **Warung Loji,** the restaurant attached to Loji II supermarket. Excellent *nasi campur* for Rp2000; great fried chicken. For home-cooked meals try **Warung Murah,** one-half km from Legian toward Seminyak. Sells classic Bali-style *nasi campur* with meat, egg, veggies, and *sambal* for around Rp2000. Closes around midnight.

If heading toward Legian from Kuta, the first good place to eat is the small **El Dorado Restaurant,** on Gang Bena Sari off Jl. Legian, an excellent traveler's eatery serving a variety of international dishes—a good restaurant for the money. Especially popular for breakfast and with Hollanders; Chinese owner Tjipto Wiyono speaks Dutch. Wonderful fruit *lasi* (Rp1000-1200) and ice juices. Open 0800-2000. About midway between Kuta and Legian.

Depot Viva, on Jl. Legian, serves tasty Indonesian and Chinese food at quite good prices; also lots of mosquitos. **Benny's Cafe,** Jl. Pura Bagus Taruna, is an above average breakfast place serving oatmeal bread, homemade cakes, and Aussie and Italian food. Useful bulletin board. The **Lido Restaurant and Pub,** Jl. Melasti, specializes in Chinese and European food. Medium-sized, upmarket **Gosha Restaurant,** also on Jl. Melasti, is one of the best restaurants in the area for seafood and European dishes. Always crowded; friendly staff. Giddy variety of food offered. Just as classy, in its own way, is **Bruna Beach Hotel,** tel. (0361) 751-565, on the beach road parallel with Jl. Legian overlooking the beach. Bruna serves delicious Indonesian and Western dishes. The **Bali Rock Cafe,** also on Jl. Melasti, tel. 754-466, boasts international cuisine in a friendly atmosphere. Nice garden setting, ice cold beer, low-priced performances, children's meals, buffet, party nights, open-air dance floor, clean kitchen. Opens at 1600. Every Monday and Thursday evening is "Big Bopper Burger Night"; eat as many hamburgers as you like for Rp6000. The **Balisani Suites** on Jl. Batubelig, tel. 754-050, puts on an occasional Asian buffet dinner with *legong* dance at poolside for Rp30,000 pp. For times and reservations, call 754-050, ext. 222.

The small garden courtyard in the back of **Warung Kopi**, Jl. Legian 427, tel. 53602, is a great place to relax and enjoy very good food: Greek salad with real feta and olives (Rp3000), curries (Rp5000) and other vegetarian Indian dishes, Lebanese green beans, yogurt and tahini salad (Rp4000), black rice pudding (Rp2000), superb cappuccino (Rp1500). The special breakfast of fruit salad, juice, two eggs, whole-wheat toast, jam, and Balinese coffee (Rp3000) is particularly popular. Extensive variety of desserts, cakes, and chocolate mousse. Reasonable prices, nice atmosphere. Close to central Legian. Also on Jl. Legian is award-winning **Za's Bakery and Restaurant,** tel. 752-973, known for its breakfast, brunch, and seafood. Try the flavorful fish soup with spicy tomato base and thick slice of multigrain bread (Rp3500). Great juices, fruit, and divine yogurt, homemade jams, toasted muesli, whole-wheat bagels, croissants, raisin bread, and cheesecakes. Cheapest margaritas on Bali (Rp5500). Fast, friendly service.

Goa 2001 Restaurant, just beyond Legian toward Seminyak, is a popular eatery with Indian dishes and a sit-down sushi bar. Also Indonesian, Italian, and German food. Limited menu, but what's there is adequate to good. Tasty pumpkin soup. Meals with drink average Rp10,000-12,000. A warm-up place before the discos open; most of the Beautiful People lounge around listening to great music while downing exotic drinks ordered from a three-page-long drink menu. The magnificent building has a vaulted ceiling of ribbed bamboo and interlocking thatch. The **Swiss Pub and Restaurant,** behind the Kuta Palace Hotel on Jl. Pura Bagus Taruna, tel. 751-735, is a Swiss oasis in the middle of Indonesia. Run by a Balinese woman and her Swiss husband, Jon Zurcher; they import wine from France, steak from New Zealand, and bratwurst sausages and cheese from Switzerland. Asia buffets every Saturday, plus daily *rijstaffel.* Try the

smoked fish (Rp5000), banana flambé (Rp2200), and superb omelettes. Jon, who also serves as the official Swiss Consul, can be recognized by his pipe and bare feet. He eschews shoes even when climbing volcanos, and will personally lead treks to places you'd never go alone. Ask to see his photo albums.

A traditional English self-service buffet brunch (Rp7000) is served every day between 1100-1300 at **The Bounty** on Jl. Legian. On the Bounty's upper deck English dishes like steak and kidney pie are served; drink in the Captain's Bar. Nearby is **Mama's,** Jl. Legian 354, specializing in German food—*schweine braten mit rotkohl, fassbier, gulaschsuppe, hahnchen mit pommes frittes.*

At the **Kurumaya,** Jl. Padma 1, tel. 752-111, in central Legian, you can savor teppanyaki, tempura, shabu-shabu, and other traditional Japanese cuisine. Open 1800-2300. Enjoy Mexican food at the Kulkul's **Blue Cactus Restaurant,** tel. 752-520. The biggest margaritas in Bali, using José Cuervo tequila, are served up at Kulkul Resort's rooftop **Blue Cactus Mexican Restaurant and Bar** (tel. 52520) on Jl. Pantai Kuta. Open 1700-2400 nightly, with a live mariachi singer from 1930 to 2100 and the Cactus Combo laying down a Latin beat from 2130 to 2400. Also well-prepared guacamole, nachos, seafood tacos, and tortilla soup. The Indonesian food in the Kulkul's **Kamboja Restaurant** isn't modified to suit Western tastes. At 2000 the place is transformed into a karaoke bar, patronized mostly by Indonesians.

For international buffets, as well as Outback (Rp6950), American (Rp5500), Indonesian (Rp4500), or continental (Rp3500) breakfasts, head for the **Glory Bar and Restaurant** on Jl. Legian, tel. 751-091, fax 753-219. On Saturday night Glory serves an excellent Balinese feast for Rp8000; buffets are Wednesday night. Open 0800-2400. Try the Happy Harvey Hour, when popular cocktails are served by the jug. Plastic accepted. Call Glory Ride Transport for a free ride in the Kuta area only. Good, inexpensive Aussie delicacies like Toad in the Hole and baked beans on toast are available at **Legian Snacks** on Jl. Padma Utara. High-quality meals, cold drinks, low prices, always packed. The specialty is Aussie food, with some Indonesian and Chinese dishes. Especially good for breakfast.

ENTERTAINMENT

The **Poco Loco** is a well-known, high-quality Mexican restaurant. Tequila shots from a portable minibar. One of the cheapest places to drink beer and watch the street crowds is **Loji II,** an open-air cafe and market; Rp3000 for a large, cold *bir bintang*.

Movies are shown every night at the **Swiss Pub** on Jl. Legian; also see the latest world news, sports, music, and Bali travel videos. For details, call (0361) 51735. Movies are shown free every night at **The Bounty** at 2100, 2300, and 0100. A large beer costs only Rp4000 during happy hour. **The Legend** on Jl. Melasti advertises Balinese dishes, movies every evening, and free dance performances Friday nights. Free transport for those staying in Kuta or Legian. Each night the fully a/c **Jaya Pub,** Jl. Seminyak 2, tel. 752-973, features live jazz, rock, oldies, and country with the Jaya Pub Band, Hendrix and Lia, and the Surf Trio. International menu. Happy hour is 1900-2000. Opposite the Jaya Pub is **Cafe Luna**—a row of big motorbikes out front, humming clusters of people, perhaps the hottest late night hangout in south Bali. Especially popular with expat Kuta entrepreneurs and garment industry exporters.

Double Six and the **Gado Gado** alternate disco nights. Dine in the beachside pavilions at sunset or later—much later; closing time is 0400. The **Strand Bar** on Jl. Double Six is a night spot featuring continuing exhibitions of local and Western artists. Displays change on a monthly basis. On Sunday, Wednesday, and Friday there's a fish barbecue and hard rock at the **Rum Jungle** on Jl. Pura Bagus Taruna off Jl. Legian. A secluded and unique nightspot with a jungle hideout atmosphere. Locals and tourists party hearty on a raised dance floor. **Dracula's Cabaret Restaurant,** two km north of *bemo* corner at Jl. Legian 494, tel. 751-790, bills itself as the world's most outrageously funny cabaret restaurant. Complete with chains, rabbit traps, Igor the three-foot house hangman, chamber of horrors, animated corpses, and over 200 sculptures ranging from tiny spiders to a giant Frankenstein. Feast on a sumptuous four-course meal, guzzle cocktails, scream at the mad antics of the grotesque staff. Suitable for all ages. Doors open at 1900; turns into a disco after midnight. Bookings essential.

SHOPPING

The shops along Jl. Legian in north Legian feature creative, unusual clothes and cheaper prices than Kuta. Run-of-the-mill clothes easy to find. At **Baik Baik,** tel. (0361) 751-622, opposite the start of Jl. Melasti, buy print shirts in bold colors, trendy men's pleated pants, long-sleeved floral *batik* evening blouses of original and zany design. Check out **Mr. Bali,** tel. 751-232, for designer men's shirts, pleated Europants, and safari shorts. Find these ambitious designs at three locations: Jl. Bunisari near *bemo* corner, on Jl. Pantai Kuta, and down Jl. Legian on the left. **The Kidz Shop,** Banjar Legian Klod, specializes in made-to-order clothes for children.

Purchase ceramics and other tasteful, classy material at okay prices at **Nacha,** tel. 753-991, at Legian Kaja 456/490. Good quality, 100% leather articles are sold in the **Matahari.** Painted leather belts a specialty; Rp12,000 to Rp27,000. Very creative and well-made merchandise. Two addresses: on Gang Three Brothers behind Studio Lala in Central Legian, and at Legian Kaja 459. Mick Jagger shops for leather at **Composition,** Jl. Legian 453 B, tel. 752-376. Really wild stuff.

Toward Kuta is a row of shops selling antiques and artifacts from Nusatenggara; on Gang Menuh near Mastapa Garden Cottages. Worth checking out; prices are lower than in the shops on Jl. Legian. **Alia Jewelry,** Jl. Legian Raya 360, deals in elegant Indonesian black and chameleon opal, available only in this country, as well as Indonesian cultured pearls, blue sapphires, rubies, emeralds, topaz, and aquamarines.

Zaz is a specialist retailer of sunglasses, hats, beads, shell buttons, hairpins, brooches, earrings, bracelets, necklaces, seashells, and name plates. Two locations on Jl. Pura Bagus Taruna, at 9 and 506. Also handmade jewelry made to order. Leonard Karwelo's **Soerya Prima Art Shop** on Jl. Pura Bagus Taruna deals in traditional *ikat* and antiques from Sumba, Flores, Timor, and Kalimantan. **Serendipity Fine Antiques,** at the start of Jl. Tunjung Mekar in Legian Kelod, tel. 238-535, 753-333, is strong on cupboards, boxes, and sets of drawers. **Kaliuda II,** Jl. Legian 452, features sculpture from Nusatenggara.

SERVICES

Each of Legian's side streets is an entire community unto itself. The **Loji II supermarket** on Jl. Padma Utara is extremely well-stocked: stamps, Guinness, cosmetics, Special K cereal, Western canned goods—a little bit of everything. A branch office of **Bank Negara Indonesia,** with safety deposit boxes, is located on Jl. Legian about 75 meters before the Swiss Pub. **Krishna,** an outstanding bookshop with unenthusiastic clerks, lies diagonally across from the Mastapa. Attend Sunday church service with Rev. Ketut Suyaga Ayub, manager of Orchid Garden Cottages, tel. (0361) 752-852. The **Legian Church,** on Gang Menuh off Jl. Legian, holds services at 1700. There's a **Protestant Church** (GKPB) down the lane opposite Gang Benasari with 1000 Sunday services by Preacher Sudira (tel. 224-862) in English. The **Synod of Bali** offers a tour; contact Wayan Sudira (tel. 24862).

The **Kuta Fitness Center and Barbell Club,** on Jl. Tunjung Mekar, charges Rp7500 for a one-time workout, up to Rp150,000 for one month. Full member dues are Rp100,000. Open every day 0800-0900 except holidays. Aerobics offered three days a week. The traditional Balinese beauty salon of the **Kulkul Beach Resort,** tel. 752-520 or 752-921, offers facials and baths using *jamu,* and three different types of massages. Another traditional salon, specializing in acne, hair care, and body massage, is the **Ratu Ayu,** tel. 751-660, in the Mastapa.

NORTH OF LEGIAN

Seminyak

Voyeur tourists from Java, who come to gawk at the topless women, no longer target Kuta but travel beyond Legian to Seminyak. Seminyak and points north are where you go if you seek relative tranquility. Just keep your children away from the ocean in this area—the ferocious dropoff is absolutely lethal.

Seminyak is home to most of the Europeans and North Americans who work in Bali's clothes/jewelry/handicrafts export businesses. Many live in rented bungalows far from the road, or lease property from Balinese families and build thatched structures among the trees along the beach. For information on the sale and lease of available private residences, holiday homes, and commercial properties, contact PT Bali Intouch, Jl. Raya Seminyak 22, tel. and fax (0361) 751-683. For postal services, try **Ida's Postal Agent,** at the start of the road to Seminyak.

Accommodations: Dhyana Pura on Jl. Dhyana Pura (P.O. Box 1010, Interport Ngurah Rai), tel. 751-047, fax 730-683, e-mail: intouch@denpasar.wasanteranet.id, is a clean, comfortable place with nicely furnished bungalows on well-kept grounds. Beautiful beach, seaside pool, free shuttles to town. Rooms (a/c, bathtubs, hot water) cost Rp50,000-Rp60,000; rooms with fans are Rp30,000. Prices include continental breakfast in an attractive 24-hour restaurant and bar on a raised, open pavilion. Operated by a branch of the Bali Protestant Church, the Dhyana Pura is also a training center for young Balinese Christians. Very nice people. The **Raja Gardens** (P.O. Box 41, Kuta), tel. 751-494, fax 751-556, next door to the Dhyana Pura, is also very friendly. It's cheaper than the Dhyana Pura but there's no a/c or hot water and it's not on the beach.

Bunga Seminyak, tel. 751-239, fax 752-905, offers seven private guesthouses on a beautiful beach between the Nusa di Nusa and the Dhyana Pura. The best unit is Bungalow no. 3 (Rp50,000), at the end of the garden beyond the main house—a/c, hot water, small kitchen with fridge, nice veranda within the sound of the surf. All rates include tax and service. Bicycles, motorbikes, and jeeps for rent. Go down Jl. Camplung Tanduk 800 meters toward the sea and turn left at the sign.

Nusa di Nusa, P.O. Box 191, Denpasar, tel. 751-414, means "Island in the Island," perfectly describing this serene, secluded row of ricebarn shaped bungalows surrounded by tropical gardens. Rp60,000 s, Rp75,000 d for a/c; Rp50,000 s, Rp60,000 d for fans. Amenities include a restaurant, pool, sunken bar, Italian pizzeria, and snack bar on the beach. Ask about houses available for monthly lease.

For a little luxury, the **Bali Agung Village** in the rice fields near Bunga Seminyak is phenomenal. The rooms have all the perks: TV, a/c, hot showers, room service. If you stay a few days, bargain down to Rp60,000 per night. The whole complex is beautifully designed, small and cozy, peaceful, extremely tasteful.

Good restaurant. Nice pool with swim-up bar. Walk 500 meters to the beach and the Gado Gado nightclub. **Legian Garden Cottage,** tel. 751-876, three minutes from the beach at the end of Jl. Double Six, is very nice with a big yard. Rates for small cottages are Rp100,000 s, Rp120,000 d. Next to Double Six Disco, so it can get noisy at night. The **Blue Ocean** on Jl. Double Six, tel. 751-580, charges Rp100,000 s for a/c rooms with hot water. The beach in this area is clean and refreshing and the restaurant serves an excellent set breakfast (Rp3000).

South of the Bali Oberoi on Jl. Dhyana Pura is the **Bali Imperial,** P.O. Box 384, Denpasar, tel. and fax 751-545, which looks like a gigantic ultramodern Zen temple with lush gardens, tranquil ponds, and the last word in kitsch sculpture (a *kecak* dance in stone!). The first hotel on Bali operated by a Japanese chain, it features 17 independent villas (Rp315,000 and up) and exclusive maisonette suites (Rp840,000 and up) catering to wealthy Japanese. Each bungalow has its own pool, jacuzzi, and bath. Embarrassingly devoted staff of 350. Restaurants serve Japanese, Balinese, and European cuisine. Other amenities include business services, shopping arcade, full recreational facilities, and private beach. In Jakarta, reserve with Bali Imperial, Medco Building, Jl. Ampera Raya 20, Cilandak, Jakarta 12560, P.O. Box 757 JKS, tel. (021) 780-4766, ext. 505, fax 780-4666. Designed to resemble a Balinese village, the spacious Indian-owned **Bali Oberoi** on Jl. Kayu Aya, Box 351, Denpasar, tel. 751-061, fax 752-791, features private thatched-roof cottages on 35 acres of immaculate tree-filled grounds enclosed by a weathered stone wall. Each villa has its own split-gate entrance, each room its own sumptuous garden bathroom with sunken bath partially open to the sky. The aesthetically pleasing bungalows start at Rp441,000 and move up to the Rp1.2 million presidential villas with their own private pools and isolated beach fronts. The open-air poolside Kura Kura is a first-class restaurant.

Food: The *warung* in Seminyak are more reasonably-priced than those in Kuta. The **Taman Sari** at the north end of Jl. Legian specializes in authentic German dishes as well as creative vegetarian dishes like spaghetti with tofu. The formidable breakfast (Rp7000) comes with whole-wheat bread, smoked ham, cheese, eggs, toast and jam, fruit, tea or coffee. If you want food in a pleasant, quiet atmosphere, this is it. Near the entrance to the private road to the Oberoi is the **Arisky Ay** (Jl. Oberoi Basangkasa) serving *cap cai* for Rp3000, crab soup for Rp2000, and fried rice for Rp3000. **Shanti** is a restaurant and bar owned by Goa 2001. Just after Ida's Postal Agent, at the start of Jl. Oberoi, is the **Sweet Corner** for Chinese seafood.

Warisan Resto is located in the middle of the rice fields; the candlelit atmosphere is quite romantic. Elegant nouveau cuisine—avocado vinaigrette with blue cheese and walnuts, veal scaloppini with prosciutto, sautéed baby lobsters, leg of lamb, tournedos, artichoke hearts. Dishes are beautifully presented with fine wines from California and France. Count on about Rp50,000 pp for a full dinner. Opens every day at 1600. the **Aura** is a nice bar downstairs. Turn right after the Oberoi turnoff and travel one km in the direction of Krobrokan; it's on the left-hand side, about two km north of Legian. Sophisticated crowd, so dress accordingly.

Crafts: Citra Batu Alam, Jl. Tanjung Mekar 27 A (Banjar Pelasa), tel. and fax 752-065, specializes in gemstones, coral, fossils, rocks, minerals, beads, eggs, spheres, old coins, jewelry, and lapidary work. On the bottom floor of Warisan Resto is a very chic antique shop called the **Gallery,** which displays antiques, textiles, and curios. Buy something to use and remember at **Dalung Village,** 3.5 km past Krobokan. The Dalung makes and sells ceramic products—delightful ashtrays, tissue and toothpick holders, condiment sets. Design your own, specify the color, and pick it up a month later. Prices run Rp2,000-Rp12,000.

Petitingit

A few km beyond the private road to the Oberoi is the three-star **Pesona Bali Beach Hotel and Cottages,** Jl. Kayu Ayu (P.O. Box 1085, Denpasar), tel. (0361) 753-914 or 753-733, fax 753-915. Popular with European tour operators, it has 69 rooms (Rp147,000-210,000), seven bungalows (Rp231,000-378,000), big beautiful pool, coffee shop, game room, and a lobby in the shape of a huge *bale banjar*. The restaurant serves continental breakfast for Rp12,500, American breakfast for Rp16,000. Lunch is Rp25,000, dinner Rp30,000, and a mind-boggling once-weekly *rijstaffel* goes for Rp25,000. All prices subject to 15.5% tax and service. The strength of the Pesona is its isolation. There are only a few *warung* and practically no shops nearby; the hotel operates a handy roundtrip shuttle service to Legian and Kuta six times daily. The Petitingit temple is a 10-minute walk on the road north.

Safely cushioned from the Legian/Kuta scene is five-star, villa-style **Puri Ratih,** Jl. Puri Ratih, Petitinget, Krobokan, P.O. Box 1114, Tuban, tel. 751-546, fax 571-549, winner of the RCI Design Award. Huge bungalows resemble private homes, incorporating every modern convenience. Prices fluctuate with the seasons. Units incorporate Bali-style bath, original paintings, color TV, and electronic safes. Facilities include an ocean-view restaurant, a library, squash court, and pools with water spouting from Balinese statues. Also in Petitinget is **Intan Beach Bungalows,** tel. 752-191, which recently added deluxe facilities and a 200-room complex on four levels. Prices start at Rp136,500 and top out at Rp2 million for the presidential suite.

Berawa Beach
The best thing about the **Bolare Beach Bungalows,** P.O. Box 256, Denpasar 80001, tel. and fax 235-464, is its location on a pretty white beach, surrounded by coconut palms and rice fields—sixteen km from Kuta, 11 km from Denpasar, 20 km from the airport. Bali-style bungalows equipped with a/c, private bath, hot water, shower, spacious patio, and your own garden run Rp100,000 s, Rp110,000 d plus 15.5% tax and service. Suites are Rp130,000. Great sunsets from the beach bar by the pool. Services include a hotel shop, travel agency, car rental service, library, launderette, doctor on call. Drugstore, safe deposit box, and restaurant (breakfast Rp10,000, lunch Rp20,000, dinner Rp30,000). If you can afford it, it doesn't get much better than this. Removed from the frenetic pace of Kuta, yet with your own vehicle it's within easy striking distance.

Canggu
A surfing break about three km north of Petitingit, which dissolves if there's no swell. At low tide, reach Canggu by motorbike or bicycle. Or take a *bemo* down Jl. Legian toward Krobokan, then turn west toward the beach.

Krobokan
About 22 km beyond Seminyak. This can be a dangerous strip of road, especially at night, when thugs may accost you, even in your car. Krobokan's *puri* contains over 75 temples. From Krobokan, take the back road via Gaji north to Sempidi—rural Bali at its best. For a complete loop, turn east from Krobokan to Denpasar, then motor back to Kuta.

KUTA

The tree in the middle of *bemo* corner, that struggled for years against pollution and the onslaught of tourists, is dead. In late 1992, this solitary outpost of nature was finally cut down and replaced with a guardian statue. This event was part of a continuum that began in the 16th century, leading to today's rollicking honky-tonk tourist encrustation 10 km south of Denpasar on Bali's southwest coast. Kuta was just a sleepy fishing village on the way in from the airport when it was discovered by seasoned travelers in the late 1960s. Since then, tens of thousands of travelers, surfies, and package tourists have turned Kuta into a gigantic First World yuppie resort. If Sanur is Indonesia's Riviera, then Kuta is its Tijuana.

Kuta is essentially five kilometers of close-packed pubs, chic boutiques, tacky restaurants, juice bars, bookstores, supermarkets, surf shops, tie-dye T-shirt outlets, travel agencies, moneychangers, beauty parlors, and blaring cassette shops. You can't walk 10 meters without encountering someone demanding you buy something. At night when the sun sets, Kuta Beach Road (Jl. Pantai Kuta) is an evil-smelling maze of bicycles, motorbikes, pedestrians, honking *bemo,* and cars plying their way through a smoggy layer of dust and thousands of milling people.

At least five of 10 visitors here are free-spending Australians—they're particularly in evidence during the Australian school vacation period of December and January. When you have restaurants serving Vegemite sandwiches and Toad in a Hole (hot dog in a bun), and a pub called Koala Blu, you know Australia isn't far away. Most never leave the Kuta area the whole time they're

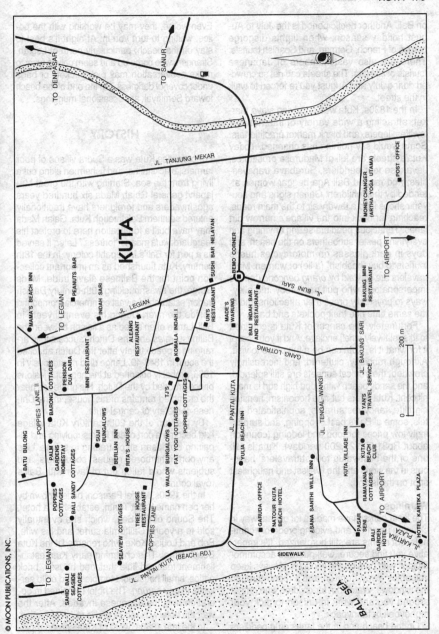

KUTA

© MOON PUBLICATIONS, INC.

TO DENPASAR

TO SANUR

JL. TANJUNG MEKAR

POST OFFICE

MONEYCHANGER
(ARTHA YOGA UTAMA)

TO AIRPORT

BEMO CORNER

MAMA'S BEACH INN

PEANUTS BAR

TO LEGIAN

INDAH SARI

SUSHI BAR NELAYAN

JL. BUNI SARI

JL. LEGIAN

BAKUNG MINI
RESTAURANT

MADE'S
WARUNG

UN'S RESTAURANT

ALEANG
RESTAURANT

BALI INDAH BAR
AND RESTAURANT

MINI RESTAURANT

KOMALA INDAH I

PENSION
DUA DARA

GANG LOTRING

BARONG COTTAGES

BATU BULONG

TJ'S

JL. BAKUNG SARI

POPPIES LANE II

JL. PANTAI KUTA

FAT YOGI COTTAGES

POPPIES COTTAGES

YANS
TRAVEL SERVICE

SUJI
BUNGALOWS

BERLIAN INN

TO LEGIAN

PALM
GARDENS
HOMESTAY

RITA'S HOUSE

LA WALON BUNGALOWS

YULIA BEACH INN

JL. TENGAL WANGI

KUTA VILLAGE INN

BALI SANDY COTTAGES

POPPIES
COTTAGES

TREE HOUSE
RESTAURANT

POPPIES LANE

KUTA
BEACH
CLUB

SEAVIEW COTTAGES

GARUDA OFFICE

RAMAYANA
COTTAGES

ASANA SANTHI WILLY INN

NATOUR KUTA
BEACH HOTEL

SAHID BALI
SEASIDE
COTTAGES

JL. PANTAI KUTA (BEACH RD.)

PASAR
SENI

TO AIRPORT

BALI
GARDEN
HOTEL

SIDEWALK

JL. KARTIKA

HOTEL KARTIKA PLAZA

BALI SEA

200 m

0

on Bali. Another hectic period is the July to August holiday season, when flights disgorge hordes of French, German, and Spanish tourists. There are also vast numbers of Japanese tourists of all ages. The streets can get so crowded during July and August you're forced to walk in the street.

In the 1830s, Kuta was a thriving slave market, attracting a wide variety of international lowlifes, lepers, and black market practitioners. Some would say nothing has changed. Today Kuta's streets are full of Madurese prostitutes, Javanese foot peddlers, Surabaya transvestites, and ragged Bali Aga beggar women attended by their children. Garish signs and souvenir shops lend a tawdry air to the main roads, reaching far back into the village's narrow dirt lanes. Tenacious peddlers selling anything and everything pester sunbathers on the beach, and boys in dark glasses on motorcycles hustle tourists to buy "hashish" (a lie) or women. Male travelers are waylaid by *orang bencong* (female impersonators) who pull passersby into alleyways to physically press their affections and at the same time rifle their pockets and bags.

Fortunately, the cancer of Kuta is confined to this relatively small enclave. And if you accept it for what it is, Kuta can be a fun place to visit. Although rubbishy, cluttered, and increasingly crowded, the tropical sunsets are still splendid, and the sandy beach with good high surf is magnificent. Kuta offers cut-rate hedonism, nonstop nightlife, fancy restaurants, sophisticated hotels, some of Bali's best shopping, and surprisingly low prices for food and lodging (count on about Rp21,000-25,200 per day). Kuta is still one of the best-value tourist/travelers' hangouts in the world and the liveliest and naughtiest spot on the island.

Warnings

The local *banjar* have made a lot of headway in cleaning up crime and evicting predatory criminals, but rooms are still burglarized. It's imperative you find secure, well-guarded accommodations with bars on the windows. Always keep valuables away from an arm's reach through the windows. Watch out for children who gather around you and work in unison to pick your moneybelt or fannypack.

On the beach and in the lanes drug peddlers may seem friendly, but four of five will cheat you.

Even worse, they may be working with the police, waiting to turn you in. At night it's best to stay off the beach, particularly north of Legian. Strangers who come up and seem only to want to make conversation may pick pockets or bags under cover of darkness. On the end of the beach toward Seminyak are occasional muggings.

HISTORY

For centuries Kuta was a Sudra village of poor farmers, blacksmiths, and fishermen eking out a living from the sea. Starting with the great Majapahit general Gajah Mada six hundred years ago, invaders and foreigners have traditionally entered southern Bali through Kuta. Gajah Mada may have built a fortification here to protect his rearguard; *kuta* means "fortress." Later, it served as a port for Bali's Majapahit colony. In the 18th century, Kuta flourished as an important collection point for the Balinese slave trade. Mads Lange, the swashbuckling 19th-century Danish trader, established a vast commercial compound beside the river. During his eventful years in Bali, Lange often acted as a liaison between the Balinese *rajas* and the Dutch, successfully arranging a peace treaty after the Dutch attacked the south in 1848-49. Lange died mysteriously in 1856, probably poisoned at the hand of a jealous prince prodded by the Dutch. His grave lies near the crumbled remains of his house, in the Chinese cemetery of central Kuta.

By the turn of the 20th century Kuta village had become a port of call for resupplying and repairing European ships trading in spices. Like any port, it harbored rogues, scoundrels, and subjects who'd fallen out of favor with Bali's royal courts.

In the 1930s, Muriel Pearson, better known by her pen name Ketut Tantri, established a hotel, The Sound of the Sea, which she eventually sold to a young California surfer and his wife, Bob and Louise Koke, who renamed it the Kuta Beach Hotel. This charming early Kuta establishment featured little thatched houses, brick patios, small household temples, and child servants in gay *sarung*. The hotel remained in operation until the Japanese invaded. After the war, the hotel was rebuilt and is still in operation.

In the late 1960s, word of Kuta spread rapidly along the travelers' trail and a constant stream of wanderers was drawn to its sunny wide beach, cheap bamboo *losmen,* and relaxed beach life. At first travelers stayed in Denpasar and ventured to Kuta on day trips, but soon the villagers began renting out thatch huts to visitors, also opening makeshift restaurants serving *lassi* and Western dishes. In 1975, the first large luxury hotels were built, catering to the needs of tourists. The cows and buffalo that used to graze in the fields between the *losmen,* with their big tick-tocking wooden bells, have long disappeared, and the farmers and fishermen lugging their plows or nets down the dusty back lanes were long ago replaced by tipsy revelers and sputtering motorcycles.

The massive tourist influx has transformed this whole coastal strip from Bali's poorest district to one of the most prosperous in all of Indonesia. Kuta and Legian have grown spontaneously and exponentially, without a plan. While the big, swank hotels of Sanur were built by businesses from other islands, the budget hotels and restaurants on Kuta are for the most part the work of local entrepreneurs. In spite of the dozen upmarket hotels, to this day Kuta and Legian retain their reputation as resorts catering to budget-conscious travelers.

SPORTS AND RECREATION

The Beach

Kuta's six-km-long crescent-shaped surfing beach, protected by a coral reef at its southern end, and long and wide enough for Frisbee contests and soccer games, is famous for its beautiful tropical sunsets and broad swath of gray sand. Too bad it's so polluted. You can't swim without catching plastic trash in your mouth, hands, and feet.

You'll see everything here—Western kids doing wheelies with BMXs, topless Italian women, Euromen in G-strings, beach-tennis players, California joggers, patrolling Indonesian soldiers, clusters of carts selling steamed corn and bags of peanuts, hefty Dutch matrons, packs of mangy dogs, hordes of Javanese tourists, cyclists, horseback riders, hippies, masseurs, and whole Australian families with Whoopi Goldberg hairdos. Huge crowds gather at sunset, setting up tripods, reading novels, strumming guitars, swigging cold beer, tripping on magic mushrooms.

Vendors, who may not venture beyond an official demarcation line, offer massages, drinks, souvenirs, and bikinis. Large sun umbrellas are for rent. Nude swimming and sunbathing, as well as motorcycle and surf buggy riding, are frowned upon by the local police. The beach is extremely crowded in August and December. For any semblance of seclusion you have to walk north for at least a kilometer past Legian.

Although Kuta's beach is inviting, watch the treacherous undertow and strong currents. Since 1958, over 100 tourists have drowned here. Always swim within the flag markers on the beach, keep near the crowds and lifeguards, and remain within the reef.

Surfing

Kuta became a hippie haven and surf paradise in the early '70s. The best waves are the left-handers out on Kuta Reef; the best surfing is from March to July. Kuta Reef is accessible by motorized outrigger from Jimbaran for about Rp30,000-40,000. Young Kuta cowboys tend to be real possessive about their waves, so make friends with them first. For surfing equipment, head for the dozen or so surf shops on Jl. Bakung Sari and Jl. Legian. Run by veteran surfers, these shops rent and sell surfboards, boogie boards, and such accessories as watersport wear and tide charts. These guys can also give you current information on the state of the surf. Surfboards can also be rented on the beach.

Scuba Diving

Wally Siagian, who gained world fame after the publication of Periplus Edition's best-selling *Underwater Indonesia* (1991), takes small groups on tours to his favorite dive sites. Wally specializes in night dives, spear fishing, and marine photography. Contact **Baruna Water Sports,** Jl. Bypass Ngurah Rai 300 B, Kuta, tel. (0361) 753-809, fax 752-779, the longest-established and best scuba dive operator on Bali. Another well respected operator is **Bali Dolphin** at the Bali Garden Hotel, Jl. Kartika, tel. 752-725, ext. 139; these people can also arrange parasailing, fishing, Jet-Skiing, and water-skiing activities.

North Of Kuta

At low tide, bicycle rides or walks along the firm, moist sand are refreshing. Heading north of

Kuta, you can ride for about seven km. At this point either retrace your tracks or turn inland at the thatched roofs of Seminyak's Bali Oberoi and return to Kuta via Jl. Legian. Although the new tourist accommodations springing up north of Legian in Canggu and Pererean are bringing more people to previously isolated beaches, the crowds thin the farther north you get. If you're walking or riding northwest to Tanah Lot, you have to cross several rivers and stretches of deep black lava sand where the coast is rocky and unsuitable for swimming.

Along the beach to the northwest of Kuta, on the estuary of a lazy river, is the unusual temple of Pura Petitenget. Built entirely of white coral, this traditional temple was founded by one of the first Hindu-Javanese priests, Sanghyang Nirantha, on his journey along the beach to Uluwatu. After defeating a local *bhuta,* this Balinese-Hindu saint invited the people of the village of Krobokan to build a temple here to commemorate the place where the sacred books of India, the Vedas, were first brought to Bali. Pura Petitenget shares a common forecourt with the *subak* temple of Pura Ulun Tanjung. This was also the spot where the first Dutchman, Captain Cornelis de Houtman, set foot on Bali in 1596.

ACCOMMODATIONS

There are hundreds of *losmen,* beach inns, bungalows, cottages, and hotels here. Since the main roads Jl. Pantai Kuta and Jl. Legian are all built out, new accommodations appear down the lanes to either side of these roads. Each lane is actually a little neighborhood unto itself, with its own *warung,* shops, hotels, and strip of beach where the neighborhood gathers at sunset.

There are about 15 international-class (Rp210,000 and up) accommodations, 75 medium-priced (Rp73,500-157,500) accommodations, and about 350 budget joints with the cheapest class of rooms in the Rp40,000-80,000 range. In the low season (Mar.-June), you can bargain prices down by as much as 20%. Don't get stuck paying Rp50,000 (plus tax) for a mosquito-ridden hole just because it's near the beach when a really together place like Dua Dara (Rp12,000 d) off Poppies Lane II is a much better value.

At the airport or along the road Balinese owners, houseboys, and touts pitch *losmen* in person; some of these leads are worthwhile. Signs erected at the start of many lanes point the way to hidden accommodations. Avoid places along or near noisy, smelly, and polluted Jl. Panti Kuta and Jl. Legian; opt instead for accommodations in the back lanes nearer the beach or in the outskirts of Kuta. The villages north of Legian along the coast—Seminyak, Petitenget, Canggu—tend to be quieter and more easygoing, with lower prices and fewer peddlers. There are also many private, fan-cooled bungalows for rent in these villages; expect to pay about Rp20,000-30,000 per day. The drawbacks to staying here are lack of public transport to goods and services and the possibility of break-ins.

In the high season (July-Sept., December, January), hotels are booked solid so make reservations far in advance. There are so many places now and such intense competition that proprietors are often inclined to give a discount for stays of three or more days, so the inevitable first question is "how many nights?" Bargain. Following is a sample of the many accommodations available.

Budget

Kuta villagers created Indonesia's first budget seaside accommodations, which exist to this day—rows of concrete cells hastily erected in the family compound, with a basic *mandi* in back of each cubicle and a long, narrow veranda in front. Cheap bamboo furniture and spartan breakfast.

Relatively nice, with a secure inner courtyard, is **Puspa Beach Inn,** tel. (0361) 751-988, on a lane off Jl. Bakung Sari. Rooms have fans, private bathrooms, and showers—a good deal in the heart of Kuta. A bit higher priced but still reasonable is **La Walon Bungalows** with pool; Rp40,000 d in high season, Rp37,800 d low season. The **Kuta Suci** (tel. 52617), off Poppies Lane II, charges Rp30,000 s, Rp40,000 d per room. Basic but quiet and clean; two higher-priced cottages. Two minutes from the beach is **Yulia Beach Inn** on Jl. Pantai Kuta 43, tel. 751-862, fax 751-055. The 48 rooms start at Rp20,000 s, Rp25,000 d for fans and shared bath and rise to Rp45,000 s, Rp50,000 d for bungalows with fridge, a/c, private bath, and hot water. Also available are safety deposit boxes; postal and laundry service; car, motorbike, bicycle, and minibus hire; and daily tours starting at about Rp15,000 pp. The sixteen-room **Mama's Beach Inn**, tel. 751-994 or 751-512, is close to restaurants and clubs. From Jl. Legian, enter the lane beside Panin Bank. It's best suited for indestructible Aussie surfers who don't need a lot of sleep and like to stick with their own kind. Rates are Rp15,000 s, Rp20,000 d with cold shower, fan, no breakfast. Very conveniently located—maybe too much so, as street sounds intrude.

Treat yourself well at **Yasi Sudi's**, a couple doors down from Seaview Cottages. The staff is great, especially the manager; Rp79,800 d, plus a beautiful swimming pool and hot baths. Good value **Berlian Inn**, tel. 751-501, is quiet and close to the beach. Rooms with private bath, shower, hot water, fans, and bamboo decor go for Rp31,500 s, Rp42,000 d. With a/c Rp46,200 s, Rp56,700 d. If heading for the beach, turn right into the lane just before the Tree House Restaurant. **Rita's House**, tel. 751-760, in an alley between Poppies Lane I and Poppies Lane II, is close to the beach and costs only Rp15,000 s, Rp20,000 d. Quiet and away from the intense hustle. Rita's sets up tours, has parking spaces, and can recommend *batik,* music, and painting teachers.

Many Rp15,000-plus places on Poppies Lane II are on the grungy side, both inside and out. An exception is the amazingly clean and tidy **Pension Dua Dara** on Segara Batu Bolong Lane, just off Poppies Lane II. Each room (Rp8,000 s and Rp10,000 d for a small, Rp12,000 d for a large) has bath, fan, and terrace. An incredible deal if you don't mind such inconveniences as no bathroom mirrors or towel racks. Safety deposit boxes, free breakfast including coffee, toast, and jaffle, plus tea all day. The drinks are cheaper than in restaurants. Phone available. Caters mostly to young Australian surfers. **Palm Gardens Homestay**, tel. 752-198, consists of clean brick cottages (Rp20,000-25,000 d) with showers, nice private gardens, moneychanger, and tour service. Towels changed everyday, floor mopped, bathrooms cleaned. Several good restaurants nearby. Very private, little noise. Clean, safe, reasonably priced **Suji Bungalows**, tel. 752-483, asks Rp20,000 s, Rp30,000 d for double bungalow with fan. Pool, nice staff. Price includes breakfast. Recommended. **Bali Sandy Cottages** is

close to the beach yet set off the road away from the motorcycle traffic. Clean rooms and lovely balconies overlook a courtyard. Awesome breakfast—jaffles, fruit salad, big pot of tea. All for the surprisingly low tariff of Rp20,000.

The little lane of Gang Bena Sari comes closest to what Kuta was like in the old days. Halfway to Legian on the left-hand side, running between Jl. Legian and the ocean, **Gang Bena Sari** is diagonally across from the Mastapa Cottages. It has relatively sparse traffic, a great traveler's eatery (El Dorado), about five quiet *losmen*/homestays, and a *warung*. One of the quietest, prettiest *losmen* on Kuta is the **Lusa Inn** with spacious yard/garden, good security, and big rooms for only Rp15,000 s, Rp20,000 d. Also noteworthy is **Komala Indah II**, which has rooms with Asian toilets for Rp8,000 s, Rp12,000 d; newer rooms with Western flush toilets are Rp12,000 s, Rp15,000 d. Here you can live in a Balinese compound in a bungalow with shower, bath, sink, fan, mosquito nets, good beds, tile floors, and private garden. The place is clean, safe, quiet, private, and only a five-minute walk to either Jl. Legian or the beach. Free tea, jaffle breakfast. Nice boys run it.

Moderate

Medium-priced hotels have a/c, hot water, and pools, and many offer IDD telephones in the rooms. They do not, however, have the range of sports facilities and cultural activities of the luxury class hotels, though they do provide vehicles for rent and can take small groups of guests on personalized tours.

Pride of place goes to **Poppies Cottages**, P.O. Box 378, Denpasar, tel. (0361) 751-059, fax 752-364, which offers luxury, charm, privacy, and security in the heart of Kuta for Rp121,800 s, Rp132,300 d in 20 delightful Bali-style bungalows. Poppies is peacefully enclosed in its own complex on Poppies Lane, a maze of stone paths meandering through lush gardens and lily ponds. Each unit has a/c, ceiling fans, fridges, hot water, baby cots; some have kitchens. Efficiently managed, Poppies provides complete room service, babysitters, pool, free airport transfers, even parking. Book early—steady and loyal clientele. Poppies runs another set of bungalows on Poppies Lane II without pool for Rp48,300 s, Rp121,800 d.

The **Pendawa Inn**, tel. 52387, in south Kuta lies down a lane across from the Hotel Kartika Plaza. Beautiful, well-kept garden, clean rooms with showers and Western toilets, friendly people. Tranquil and a bit away from the rush, this is a little oasis in the midst of bustling Kuta. It's about a five-minute walk to the beach, near a good and inexpensive restaurant, the Puspa Ayu. Rates: Rp14,700-29,400 s, Rp33,600 d (three classes). Discounts for stays of a week or more. Jimmys with a/c can be hired for about Rp42,000 per day. Near Legian is **Wina Cottage**, tel. 751-867, fax 751-569, with 129 Bali-style rooms around a tropical garden with Western-style interiors. Prices vary; fan-cooled rooms run Rp63,000 s, Rp73,500 d; a/c studios are Rp94,500 s, Rp115,500 d; and a/c deluxe units Rp126,000 s, Rp157,500 d. Amenities include private bath, hot water, wall-to-wall carpet, sound system, refrigerators, TV, tropical gardens, pool, videos, drugstore, bar, safety deposit boxes, bicycles and motorbikes for rent, complimentary fruit basket, tea, ice water, and free transport to and from the airport. Great value. The 45-room **Ramayana Cottages** on Jl. Bakung Sari, P.O. Box 334, Denpasar, tel. 751-865, fax 751-866, has rooms for Rp67,200 s, Rp84,000 d, depending on whether you have fan or a/c. Tennis courts. Only 200 meters from the beach and across the road from active nightlife. Between the Kuta Beach Club and Yan's Travel Service on Jl. Bakung Sari is reasonable **Kuta Village Inn**, with different classes of rooms and a very quiet, beautiful backyard with pool. For three people you pay Rp67,200 for a simple room with shower and ventilator fan.

A good deal for Rp63,000-94,500 is **Asana Santhi Willy Inn**, in the middle of Kuta at Jl. Tengal Wangi 18, tel. 751-281. Willy's 26 rooms feature antique furniture, tasteful art, verandas, and private open-air garden bathrooms under big mango trees—cheap, quaint, cool, quiet, beautiful, and full of character. Small pool, IDD telephones. Go down the lane before Lita Beach Club and turn right. Popular **Barong Cottages** on Poppies Lane II, tel. 751-488, fax 751-804, has rooms with two double beds, a/c, shower, and hot water for a bargain Rp57,000. Price includes breakfast of toast, juice, coffee, and sliced fruit. Facilities include a pool, gardens, restaurant, bar, and nice views from the terrace. Beachfront **Sandi Phala Beach Resort**,

Jl. Kartika Plaza, tel. 753-042, fax 753-333, has spacious, well-designed two-story bungalows (Rp73,500 s, Rp84,000 d). From the private terrace is a great view of the pool, the beach, the sea, and the sunset. High season surcharge is Rp21,000; tax and service 15.5% extra. Sunken bar. Great sandwiches and cocktails in the beachside Warung Sunset Restaurant. Rent *jukung* or Jet-Skis out front for Rp50,000. Modestly priced and quite comfortable **Fat Yogi Cottages**, Poppies Lane I, tel. 751-665, has rooms with fans, showers, bathtubs, and hot water for Rp25,200-35,700 s, Rp31,500-42,000 d including breakfast. Facilities include pool, restaurant, bar, laundry, and taxi service. Plastic accepted. **Bali Anggrek Inn**, P.O. Box 435, Denpasar, tel. 751-265, fax 751-766, has 151 rather ordinary rooms in four classes, with all the usual amenities. The large pool offers nice views over the beach.

Luxury

Kuta boasts world-class, high-end resort hotels featuring every convenience, including open-air dining rooms, luxurious gardens, Olympic-size pools, volleyball and squash courts, kids' playgrounds, mini-golf courses, jogging tracks, and fitness centers. Rooms usually have color TVs, a/c, refrigerators, minibars, IDD telephone, hot water, and private balconies. Many of these more expensive places deal only in dollars and may even find it difficult to figure out *rupiah* amounts.

The 32-room **Natour Kuta Beach Hotel**, Jl. Pantai Kuta, P.O. Box 393, Denpasar, tel. (0361) 751-361, has quiet bungalows, lush gardens, and overlooks the beach. The oldest (1936) of Kuta's hotels, it was built on the site of Ketut Tantri's hotel. Rooms, built in the native style first introduced by Bob and Louise Kokes, are priced at Rp150-235,000, while suites run Rp346,300. There's a Garuda agent in the hotel. To the south along the beach, the **Bali Garden Hotel**, P.O. Box 1101, tel. 752-725, under joint Japanese-Balinese ownership, has international-standard rates of Rp226,800 d in the low season. Amenities include regular cultural performances, a Japanese restaurant, tour desk, and disco. Five-star **Hotel Kartika Plaza**, P.O. Box 84, Denpasar, tel. 751-067, fax 752-475, has 304 elegant rooms and suites, plus 81 Balinese-style bungalows set in a huge 12-hectare garden. Clearly in the splurge category, it boasts an Olympic-size pool and an impressive full-size and well-equipped fitness center, including three clay tennis courts with instructors, massage rooms, weight room, and two jacuzzis. Rooms in the four-story wings, which wrap around the giant pool and gardens, cost Rp210,000 for garden view or Rp231,000 for ocean view. Standard bungalows (Rp220,500 s, Rp241,500 d) are cozy with their own pool.

Nearby and towards Kuta is another first-class resort, **Bintang Bali Hotel,** Jl. Kartika Plaza, P.O. Box 1068, Kuta, tel. 753-292, fax 752-015, with 401 rooms and suites forming two wings surrounded by a six-hectare garden. Though a blockish-looking property, it boasts sophisticated restaurants with sumptuous buffets, bars, piano lounge, disco with "unrivaled lighting system," karaoke supper club, swimming pool with waterfall, jacuzzi and cold dip, tennis court, gym, sauna, billiards, game room, massage, shopping arcade, and conference facilities. Prices start at Rp199,500 s, 220,500 d and climb to around Rp1.9 million for the presidential suite.

Dead center to all the action, 200 meters from the beach but peacefully set back 300 meters from Jl. Bakung Sari, is the **Kuta Beach Club,** P.O. Box 226, Kuta, tel. 751-261, fax 71-896. Its 120 plushly furnished bungalows cost Rp94,500 s, Rp115,500 d. Pool, sundecks, tennis, mini-tennis. Right across from the beach, with landscaped gardens and the biggest pool on Kuta, the big, upmarket **Sahid Bali Seaside Cottages** on Jl. Pantai Kuta, P.O. Box 1102, tel. 753-855, part of the Singapore-based Sahid chain, charges an average of Rp126,000 s, Rp147,000 d. In a class by itself, sprawling over 10 hectares, is handsome **Pertamina Cottages,** Jl. Pantai Kuta, P.O. Box 121, Denpasar, tel. 751-161, with 255 modern, two-room, four-square, redbrick, beautifully appointed cottages from Rp189,000 to around Rp1.7 million per day. Though comparable accommodations can be found for less, the isolation is splendid with closed-circuit TV, fresh flowers daily, shopping arcade, open-air stage, two restaurants, bars, convention facilities, tennis courts, pool, badminton, and three-hole golf course. A minibus conveys meals and guests through the grounds. A favorite with package tourists and Indonesian businessmen. Only a five-minute drive from the airport, the southernmost hotel in Kuta.

FOOD

Kuta's streets are lined with literally hundreds of restaurants serving a truly international, mind-boggling range of cuisine. They come in every size, price range, and degree of sophistication, serving Chinese, pseudo-Western, and Indonesian food, and all play the latest hit songs or videos. Don't leave without trying the seafood Kuta is famous for: succulent lobster, barbecued bluefish and mackerel, crab dishes, tuna steaks. Compared to Ubud or Candidasa, Kuta's food is not cheap. Lobsters here cost as much as Rp90,000. Ridiculously expensive jumbo shrimp are another favorite of free-spending tourists. An average meal is about Rp6000-7000, not including drinks. But its restaurants are as cheap as Singapore's, three times cheaper than New York's, and five times cheaper than Tokyo's. Look for fliers offering discounts of up to 50% at various restaurants. Some of Kuta's cheapest food is in the *pasar senggol* behind the post office.

On hotel row along Jl. Kartika Plaza is a whole series of restaurants that target hotel guests who balk at the Rp20,000 required for extravagant buffet breakfasts and dinners or hanker after a different dining experience than those offered in the monster hotels. One such opportunistic restaurant is **Bali Sunrise,** opposite the Kartika Plaza, where American and continental breakfasts are Rp6000 and Rp3500 respectively. Ask other travelers for the latest, best places to eat. Back-lane eateries are naturally quieter and less dusty and noisy than those in downtown Kuta and along Jl. Legian. Most of Kuta's restaurants close at around 2000.

Soups, Javanese *rujak tahu, nasi* and *mie goreng, pisang goreng,* wok stir-fries, steamed corn, steamed peanuts, and sweets are sold from carts that trundle down the main streets and back lanes of Kuta—heaps of food for under Rp2000.

Indonesian/Balinese

A multitude of *warung* are found scattered along Kuta's alleyways and side streets, most catering to Indonesians who work in Kuta, but many also patronized by budget travelers. Disappointing is the fact that not one restaurant in Kuta exclusively serves up genuine Balinese food. Lots of *gado-gado* and *soto ayam* from Java, *gulai* from Madura, and Chinese *cap cai,* but no *lawar.* In the labyrinth of alleys a few Balinese *warung* survive. One standout is on Jl. Tengal Wangi, where a fantastic *nasi campur* is served for about Rp1000; walk down from Willy's and it's on the left just before Jl. Buni Sari. Catering as it does to locals, it could close early; the *ibu* might run out of food, or go to a festival. The **Bakung Mini Restaurant,** Jl. Bakung Sari 7, serves up a *nasi campur* special consisting of spring rolls, mixed *sate,* fried chicken, steamed rice, eggs, *cap cai,* and shrimp crackers for only Rp7000. Fast, tasty, affordable, and hot *nasi padang* fare is the specialty of **Rumah Makan Ny.**

Another style of Indonesian cuisine—authentic, spicy Lombok food—is sold at **Rumah Makan Taliwang Bersaudera** on Jl. Imam Bonjol on the right-hand side about one km up from Kentucky Fried Chicken, near the outlet where Lombok clay pots are sold. Decidedly superior cuisine to 90% of Kuta's restaurants. A chicken dinner with vegetables and a drink at the Taliwang will set you back about Rp7000.

For good eating in a truly Indonesian environment at very good prices, head for the night market at the north end of Kuta. See the sign across the start of Jl. Bakung Sari. Although most popular with locals, tourists have also discovered the Indonesian, Chinese, and Balinese eateries here. Available are tasty and traditional dishes such as Yogyanese-style *kalasan* chicken, fresh fish in all sizes, steamed crab, sizzling *sate kambing,* and unmodified *nasi padang.* A wonderful place to eat and drink if you don't mind a few flies.

Chinese

With high customer turnover and international menus, the steaming, busy, open-fronted Chinese restaurants of Kuta specialize in seafood and barbecue dishes. After picking out your size or quantity of fish from ice trays in front, order the dish prepared either spicy or bland. The freshness of the food compensates for the lack of intimacy and personal attention. Reservations not necessary.

At big, lively, smoky, open, central, and crowded **Mini Restaurant,** opposite the disco on Jl. Legian, pay about Rp15,000 for a big fish that feeds two to three. Try such seafood dishes as the incomparable sweet and sour shrimp with rice, delicious crabs, or lobster. Mini is packed at night, so go early. Another Chinese seafood restaurant, **Bali Indah Bar and Restaurant** on Jl. Buni Sari, tel. 751-937 or 752-433, prepares sumptuous food in an authentic Chinese style. Across the street from the Mini is the slightly higher-priced **Indah Sari,** where you can see seafood grilled on an open fire, then dine in a pleasing atmosphere of natural bamboo and old-fashioned Casablanca fans.

Ethnic Foods

If you get misty for home, many places offer milkshakes, steaks, ham and eggs, toast and Vegemite, and peanut butter and honey sandwiches. For example, the menu at the **Jaya Pub Garden Restaurant** in Legian lists not only *sate* from Madura, but lasagna from Napoli, steak *au poivre comme à Paris,* Texas T-bone, and *hutspot op z'n Hollands,* all prepared by a team of chefs experienced in Jakartan restaurants. Some of Kuta's restaurants claim to serve such authentic Australian specialties as "vegetable pie," but somehow the dish gets lost in the translation—it could end up as just a rolled pancake with spiced veggies inside. Hotel restaurants generally offer better Western food than Kuta's street restaurants.

With the coming of the Japanese, sushi bars are on the ascendant. The small **Sushi Bar Nelayan,** where Poppies Lane I meets Jl. Legian, is a top buy. You get a good choice, 10-15 pieces for Rp7000-11,000. For more elaborate fare, the **Yashi Japanese Restaurant** in Pertamina Cottages in south Kuta near the airport is very good. Japanese beer too. For Korean barbecue, seafood, *bulgogi, sam gae tang, doe jee sam kyub sal,* lobster with *yaki* sauce, and *gyaza musi,* the **Agung Korean House,** tel. (0361) 752-899 or 752-238, on the first floor of the multistoried Kuta Supermarket on Jl. Bakung Sari, is the place.

The latest craze are pizzerias selling medium pizzas for Rp8000-12,000. **Cappuccino,** Jl. Wana Segara Road, tel. 753-797, is part of the well-run Cafe Lotus group. It specializes in pizzas, pastas, black pepper steak, and fresh seafood. Free pick-up service. **Fat Yogi's,** on Poppies Lane I, has delicious Italian food as well. Two of the best Italian restaurants, with surprisingly well-stocked wine cellars, are the remarkable and beautiful **Warisan** in Seminyak, and

Cafe Latino on Jl. Ngurah Rai on the way to the airport. For dedicated carnivores, there are now two Mama's German Restaurants, tel. 751-805, on Jl. Legian specializing in steaks, famous homemade sausages, and "big soups from Mama's kettle." Under German management.

The Griya Delta on Jl. Legian (behind Panin Bank) serves wonderful *tandoori* dishes. For Swedish food, try Restaurant Lilla Sverige Mamma's Kottbullar on Poppies Lane II—*kottbullar* (Rp3900), *jausous frestelse* (Rp3900), *lok sas med flask och kokt potatis* (also Rp3900).

In A Class Of Their Own

The in place is still age-old Made's Warung, right on Jl. Pantai Kuta, with great food and an inimitable atmosphere. Made's serves the very best jaffles, smoked salmon on rye with cream cheese (Rp12,000), chili, cappuccino, fresh-squeezed carrot juice, and an absolutely top-class *nasi campur*. Dinner specialties include *gado-gado,* Tuna Fish Dinner with spicy Bali sauce (a winner at Rp6500), sushi deluxe (Rp10,000), and *rijstaffel* (served on Saturday at 1700 only; get there early). European breakfast (fresh-squeezed juice, fruit yogurt, muesli cereal, eggs, bacon, whole-wheat toast) for Rp7500. A lively, crowded place and a peerless venue for people-watching—front row seats face the madness. Though every dish is good, the place isn't cheap; it's difficult to eat well here for less than Rp12,000-15,000.

The best Mexican food on Bali is served at TJ's, tel. (0361) 751-093, down Poppies Lane toward the beach. Particularly prized are Jean's tacos, chips, and salsa, but the varied, tantalizingly worded menu also includes Seafood Bahian (Rp6500), famous chocolate diablo cake (Rp2000), and chocolate mousse (Rp2200). The fajitas are made with high-quality flank steak; the flour tortillas ground by hand, then rolled with a beer bottle. A wait to eat. Great wide wooden bar with long drink menu, free snacks, and racy Latin music in the background. Here you could meet anybody. The Kopi Pot, Jl. Legian tel. 752-614, is a good place for vegetarian dishes, salads, soups, continental cooking, seafood, and the better known Indonesian dishes. Well known for its steaks. Open daily until 2300. Relaxing, terraced garden setting; also an upstairs area away from the noise. Of-

froad parking. Look for fliers offering a 15% discount for meals over Rp20,000.

The Bali Bagia Bar and Restaurant on Jl. Bakung Sari serves some of the best steaks in Kuta. Monday night is Barbecue Party Night; choice of steaks, spareribs, or fish fillet plus smorgasbord (Rp10,500). Wednesday is Seafood Party Night (Rp22,500), Thursday is Roast Dinner Night (Rp12,500). The BB offers free transport (tel. 751-357, 752-757); bookings necessary. Dinners start at 1900.

A dazzling evening can be spent at the Hotel's Kartika Plaza's Legong and Rijstaffel Night. For Rp46,200, dine on an authentic *rijstaffel,* including many of Indonesia's most delicious dishes: *bihun goreng, oseng oseng sayuran, pepes ikan, rendang, sate campur, gado-gado, perkedel kentang.* The excellent buffet is accompanied for 45 minutes by sequences from Bali's most famous dances—*legong, kebyar, baris.* Absolutely first class.

Poppies Lane I And II

Some of Kuta's best restaurants are located on Poppies Lane I. Poppies Restaurant is in a delightful and romantic setting, featuring above average Western and Indonesian food, local Balinese specialties, seafood salad, and excellent Mexican dishes. To get a table, reserve ahead by calling 51149, or arrive early in the evening—it fills up fast. Un's Restaurant, in a small lane off Poppies Lane I, has an Indo/Chinese/Euro menu—excellent steaks, schnitzels, and fish, though the service isn't the best. Nice atmosphere, listenable music, comfortable chairs, big portions, good food. Expensive, but worth it.

There are dozens of small restaurants on Poppies Lane II, some quite good. An old standby is Batu Bulong with average quality but reasonable prices. A great place to watch all the errant activity is from the second floor of the Twice Bar and Bakery. Decent breakfast is served starting at 0800. The croissants are in high demand.

Desserts And Drinks

An ancient Kuta fixture, Aleang's still has superb yogurt; the place looks brighter and cleaner nowadays. The Kopi Pot, Jl. Legian, tel. (0361) 752-614, is known for its mouthwatering homemade desserts, cakes, and pies, and a wide variety of shakes, juices, coffees, and imported teas. Also praiseworthy is **Made's Warung** on Jl. Pantai Kuta: homemade ice cream, chocolate cake, and top-notch black rice pudding. At the beach end of the same street is **Made's Juice Shop,** also a long-standing favorite.

Magic Mushrooms

Perhaps half a dozen restaurants in Kuta and Legian prepare soups, omelettes, and pizzas spiked with magic mushrooms, which contain hallucinogenic psilocybin, similar to mescaline. Though not openly advertised, mushrooms in a dish can be recognized by the words "magic" or "special" written on the menu.

ENTERTAINMENT AND NIGHTLIFE

Like any city, Kuta has it all. You have your choice of enclosed, air-conditioned places where you don't even feel like you're in Bali, huge dance halls with strobe lights, or open-air clubs facing the beach.

For at least two months (December and January) each year, Kuta is Asia's approximation of the United State's Palm Springs at Easter break. Get ready for a real scene, in which the tourists provide the richest source of entertainment for other tourists. Alcohol is served in copious quantities in scores of drinking establishments designed to entice the Australian collegian. You'll see pubs packed with beer-swilling Australians dressed in singlets, shorts, and rubber thongs guzzling cans of Foster's Lager and eating meat pies while watching live broadcasts of Australian football matches on big screen monitors. Should the motto "rage with us!" appeal to you, you can join one of Kuta's organized "Pub Crawls," in which large groups of Australian revelers are transported by bus from pub to pub where they drink, ingest godawful food, and become more and more inebriated, until finally they're deposited semiconscious at the doors of their hotels in the middle of the morning. The promoter's advice: "Avoid Hangovers—Stay Drunk!"

The local rice beer, *tuak,* is served in bamboo mugs. Anytime after 2100 or 2200, you have to run the gauntlet of pimps, whores, and hashish sellers on Jl. Legian. Kuta really doesn't sleep until 0500 or even later, and even then you'll find a few Italians wandering around looking for cappuccino.

Gay men cruise the beach at night. There's no gay bar to speak of—every place is mixed now—but some bars are more gay than others. The gay scene is a lot healthier than it used to be as a tremendous effort has been put into AIDS prevention and education. You'll see anti-AIDS posters all over the island.

Movies

Taking in a movie at one of Kuta's cinemas costs Rp3000-4000. Indonesian subtitles provided at the bottom of the screen, smoking and drinking allowed. The Multiplex three-screen cinema (exceptionally comfortable seats) on the top floor of the big shopping center on Jl. Legian shows popular American films starting at 2100. New videos are shown on huge screens in bars and restaurants, drawing big, loyal crowds of tourists every night. **Bonten Video Movie Bar and Restaurant** in the heart of Kuta at the Gelael Top Plaza shows free films daily; meals served and a happy hour (1600-2100) with cocktails and large Bintangs for only Rp3000. **Un's,** in a small lane between Poppies Lane I and Made's Warung, also shows videos every night.

Dances And Events

Kuta is an artificial tourist bubble and most dances staged here are not the real thing. Major tourist hotels like Pertamina Cottages and the Oberoi present dances, usually accompanied by dinner for Rp42,000 and up. In Kuta, tickets are sold for performances in other southern villages (Bona, Batubulan). If you have your own transport, tickets are cheaper at the venues themselves.

At the **Sari Wisata Budaya** on Jl. Bypass Ngurah Rai near Gelael Supermarket, a *janger* dance is staged (Rp5000) from 2000 to 2100, and a *barong* from 0900 to 1000. Visit a Western shopping center, **Plaza Bali** on Jl. Ngurah Rai in Tuban, tel. (0361) 753-301, to see a woodcarver or silver craftsman demonstrate his skill. Traditional dance and music are performed nightly at the Balinese Theatre; dancers and musicians from all over the archipelago participate. Open 1000-2300 every day.

Pubs, Clubs, And Discos

No less than 15 clubs operate in Kuta, Legian, and Seminyak. Most open late, have no dress code, charge Rp4000-5000 entrance fee, and close at around 0200 (officially, 2400). Stay tuned for weekly events advertised on fliers distributed on Jl. Legian.

The **Gado Gado** (open only on Tuesday, Thursday, and Saturday nights), a relaxing al fresco beachfront disco, attracts a good mixture of older Indonesians, Westerners, and expats. **Peanuts** is preferred by Australians. The convivial **Koala Blu** caters to Australians as well. Others like to hang out at **Goa's** in Legian, which has a sophisticated sushi bar, exotic and reasonably priced drinks, and outstanding vegetable curry. Goa's is a good place to get in the mood before the discos start, and the volume and quality of the music allows you to talk.

At **Shanti**, near the Oberoi Hotel in Seminyak, there are jazz and reggae nights each week starting at 2100. The accompanying *rijstaffel* costs Rp7000. For live music, the **Jaya Pub Bali**, Jl. Legian Kaja, tel. (0361) 752-973, employs the same musicians as the Jaya Pub Jakarta. **Double Six** is packed with exotic people. The restaurant has very good salads, pastas, Italian dishes, and buffets, and becomes a disco Monday and Friday. Balinese rastas dance to live reggae music at **Baruna's,** a long-time favorite of hardcore Australian party animals. The **Strand Bar** features art exhibits and a colonial plantation bar with superb drinks. No dancing, geared to conversation, the crowd nearly 100% Western expatriates. **Cafe Luna** in Seminyak, right across from the Goa, is very small, a place where everybody knows everybody.

On Poppies Lane II behind the Sahid Bali Hotel is **Tubes,** "The Surfer's Bar and Restaurant." Here you'll find good vibes, pizza, fruit smoothies, a swimming pool, and MTV and movies (at 1500 and 2000). During happy hour (1700-1900) and nightly dancing (starting at 2000), watch spunky Japanese women press their attentions on Kuta cowboys, who by now speak very passable Japanese. Another hangout for the beautiful people is the **Blue Ocean,** where the waves are first class and the sunsets at times enthralling. Happy hour at **Eagle One,** Jl. Buni Sari 3, tel. 753-418 or 751-743, is from 1700 to 2000; drinks are 20% off. Free transport to and from your hotel. **Kuta Seaview Restaurant** on Jl. Pantai Kuta has a full bar, great food, and live music every night, with no admission, tax, or service charge. Open 0700 to 0200. Free pickup (tel. 751-961 or 753-524).

SHOPPING

Kuta's best buys are clothes. Sun hats, visor hats, and straw hats are also excellent value, as are colorful cloth beach bags and rattan bags. Another great bargain is sunglasses, in every style imaginable, for Rp6000-10,000; sunglasses are the only product for sale at **Mr. Sunny** on Jl. Legian. Pick up the latest tapes at numerous cassette shops for Rp6000-9000. Imitation watches are cheaper in Kuta than anywhere else in Indonesia. Use your bargaining skills and know the prices (as little as Rp6000). Watches make good trading material in Lombok and on other Outer Islands, and they sell for big money in India. Gucci perfume is not a good buy, though the packaging is brilliant.

For general goods, **Gelael Dewata Supermarket,** on the right just before you enter Kuta from Denpasar, sells a full range of cosmetics, toiletries, disposable diapers, imported foodstuffs, baked goods, drinks, stationery, and clothing. **Loji I** and **Loji II** supermarkets in Legian are smaller but well-stocked. The 15,000-square-meter **Plaza Bali** on Jl. Ngurah Rai in Tuban, tel. (0361) 753-301, offers a vast array of shops—an international duty-free store, souvenir shops, boutiques, galleries, restaurants, cocktail bar, cultural exhibits, drugstore, postal and international telephone service, car rental service, overseas packing and shipping office. Open 1000-2300 every day. Plaza Bali is just a five-minute drive from the airport.

Vendors

The hustling on the beach can be horrific—a wild and open free market. If you decide to come to Kuta, you better get used to it. Your only defense is to joke around and try to have a good time. Roving vendors aggressively hawk giant polished sea turtle shells, hen-feather dusters, Sumba blankets, postcards, silver jewelry, cold beer, and wind chimes. Every craft and fakery from every workshop on Bali seems to eventually find its way to Kuta. Ninety-five percent of the items are mass-produced for tourist consumption. The silver articles may be silver-plated copper or brass, glass is sold as semiprecious stone, and horn and bone articles are passed off as ivory. Peddlers ask up to Rp20,000 for unbelievably bad paintings—

acrylic on cloth—but they'll come down to Rp3000. It's all pure junk.

Women come up carrying baskets full of fabrics and garments; check carefully because the seams and zippers on clothing sold on the beach often give way in two or three days. Everything is bargainable. First prices are astronomical but soon the seller will offer a special price "only for you." After a few days, the sellers get to know you and you become friends. Don't buy anything for the first few days; talk to people and learn the prices.

Kids on the street trying to sell you stuff can be as pesky as flies. They also invade your space by touching you, getting in your way, and even picking your pocket. Kids will even pester you while you're getting a massage.

Shops
Some shops specialize in leather and silk, others in *batik* and designer fashions. **Madona** shops sell Lycra hats, belts, headbands, footwear, and dazzling sequined garments. Fixed-price places will give you a good idea of

persistent street vendor

what you should be paying. Shop the side lanes for the best bargains—these shops are hungrier. Prices in Legian are generally lower than in Kuta, and the clerks are friendlier. Kuta shopkeepers sometimes get mad if you don't make an offer on something you've looked at. Good shops are hard to find in both ends of town. Because of the vast number of shops and the uneven quality and prices, shopping takes great patience—hours of it. Shop in the evening when it's cooler.

Clothes
Kuta and Legian, along with Thailand, are the fashion capitals of Southeast Asia. Indonesian, Italian, French, Japanese, and American designers use native tie-dyeing and *ikat* techniques to turn out brilliantly original garments exported worldwide. The best buys produced in Kuta's backlane sweatshops are beachwear—bikinis, bathing suits, boxer and Bermuda shorts, T-shirts, singlets—in lightweight cotton and rayon. A decidedly Australian bias in the bold colors and zany designs. If you bargain vigorously, you can buy merchandise in the shops cheaper than from the vendors on the beach. Stick to your offered price. It's also cheaper to patronize shops off Jl. Legian, the main drag.

A number of classy designer boutiques take American Express and have high, fixed prices, which vary according to the material used and originality of design. Stunning shirts are available for Rp25,000-30,000; *batik* sundresses Rp30,000; *batik* shirts made from old *sarung* Rp8000-12,000; jackets Rp45,000-75,000; dress trousers Rp50,000 and up; dresses Rp40,000-75,000; T-shirts Rp8000-15,000; *ikat* purses Rp2000-10,000; *sarung* Rp8000-15,000. All very eye-catching and continental, but watch the quality. Examine goods carefully.

Carmen Dixon Collections, Jl. Pura Puseh 22, Legian Kelod, tel. (0361) 751-717, carries contemporary designer fashions, resort wear, and cocktail dresses. Really good buys. **Sundance** on Poppies Lane I sells unique T-shirts and shorts. **Noa'noa,** Jl. Pantai Kuta 44 G, second shop on Jl. Legian Kelod, carries bikinis and beach clothing. Children's clothing is another Kuta specialty. **Kuta Kidz,** between *bemo* corner and Made's Warung, is filled with children's clothes. **Hop On Pop,** Jl. Pantai Kuta 45 C, also specializes in children's wear.

A great concentration of shops filled with ethnic-exotic beach garb, most with reasonable prices, is located at **Pasar Seni,** the crowded Kuta Art Market at the beach end of Jl. Bakung Sari. More than a hundred shops on both sides of the road comprise this market. Competition is intense and the consumer is lord. These micro-retailers deal for the most part in cheap clothing and leisure wear, but carvings, *batik,* paintings, masks, textiles, mobiles, and other bric-a-brac are also available.

Jewelry And Antiques

Kuta offers a wide choice of jewelry, in both antique and contemporary designs. Whole shops are devoted to seashell jewelry or painted wooden earrings with dangling parrots, fish, cats, or stars. Silver is imported and ingeniously and meticulously worked into bracelets, pendants, and rings in local workshops.

Genuine antiques and tribal artifacts are ridiculously expensive, the starting prices so high you don't even feel like bargaining: Sumba blankets Rp450,000; Dayak baby carriers with handmade brass bells and colored beads Rp250,000-350,000. Kuta's fake antiques are products of inspired genius. If a woodcarving is claimed to be 50 years old but costs only Rp150,000, it isn't 50 years old. It may have been artificially aged by burial in the earth or exposure to the elements.

Nogo Bali Ikat Centre, tel. (0361) 754-335, across from the Kopi Pot on Jl. Legian, specializes in textiles, carvings, and paintings. This chain of shops is best known for *endek.* Designer Lily Coskuner shied away from the wildly mixed colors favored by the Balinese, limiting combinations to varying shades of one or two colors in a single pattern. Nogo sells jackets (Rp150,000), slacks (Rp75,000), dresses (Rp120,000), and sashes, as well as lengths of *endek* for Rp15,000 per meter. Also check the mother-of-pearl and seashell buttons at Rp1000-4000 apiece and beautiful ties for Rp20,000. A Nogo shop dealing in Asmat art is located at Jl. Tanjung Mekar 55 in Legian. The owner, Iwan Sumichan, claims to have the largest collection of Asmat artifacts on Bali.

Leather

Leather is really popular and there are scores of shops. Leather jackets go for as little as Rp200,000—if you bargain. Some are interwoven with rattan designs. Very unusual chic leather belts, multicolored and studded, cost Rp30,000-Rp100,000. Again, for the best prices, work the back lanes and make sure the sewing and stitching is first rate. Large leather bags go for around Rp80,000-150,000, small ones for Rp40,000-75,000.

Bookstores

Along Jl. Pantai Kuta and Jl. Legian are at least six secondhand bookstores selling used paperbacks in all languages; most will buy back books you've bought from them. Don't throw away any books or magazines, as they can always be sold or exchanged. English, German, and French daily newspapers are available in shops such as **Kerta Bookshop** off Jl. Legian, and **Kiosk Widyasari** on Jl. Bakung Sari, which sells the *Herald Tribune, USA Today,* and The *Australian.* **Krishna Bookshop,** also on Jl. Legian, has a good selection of new English-language books and periodicals on or about Indonesia.

SERVICES

With banks, moneychangers, physicians, pharmacies, postal agencies, police station (tel. 751-998), fire station (tel. 225-113), market, cinemas, photo-processing shops, and ticket agencies, Kuta is almost completely self-contained. There's even an Alcoholics Anonymous (tel. 751-442 or 751-443) chapter holding morning meetings in the coffee shop at the Dhyana Pura Hotel on Jl. Dhyana Pura in Seminyak.

Post And Shipping

The postal agent on Jl. Legian sells stamps and aerograms at the official price. Other services include registered post and do-it-yourself poste restante service, with dictionaries, phrase-books, stationery supplies, and picture post-cards for sale. There are other poste restante services at postal agents on Jl. Padma and Jl. Melasti in Legian. Parcel rates at these postal agencies are the same as official government rates but they charge high fees for packaging: Rp5000 for parcels weighing one to three kg, Rp7000 for three to five kg, Rp10,000 for five to 10 kg. Denpasar's *kantor paket pos,* on the corner of Jl. Teuku Umar and Jl. Diponegoro, tel. 223-568, employs packagers who charge a bit less. For larger shipments, Kuta's international freight forwarding companies pack, arrange transport, and insure goods to Europe, the U.S., and Australia. Expect to pay a minimum of Rp367,500.

Kuta's small *kantor pos*, central post office Kuta, Bali 80361, Indonesia) is down a small lane off Jl. Kaya Kuta, near the cinema. Open Mon.-Thurs. 0800-1400, Friday 0800-1100, Saturday 0800-1230. You may also have poste restante letters sent here; Rp60 per letter pick-up fee. This post office and the postal agent on Jl. Legian across from the Sari Club are more convenient places to pick up mail than Denpasar's main post office in Renon.

Telephone

On Jl. Pantai Kuta, facing the beach, is a *wartel* where you can place international telephone calls, Rp20,350 for three minutes. Open Mon.-Fri. 0800-1800, Saturday 0800-1100. Faxes cost around Rp13,000 per page; a great deal if you have lots to say. Also Rp1000 to receive a fax. Rp6050 for each minute of an international telex. Another telephone office, with IDD capability, is located at the airport to the west of Hotel Regent. The area code for Kuta is 0361.

Moneychangers

There's a moneychanger in every other doorway from around 0800. They generally give better service and more competitive rates than Kuta's banks. Moneychangers are open as late as 2200 and can change money in five minutes with presentation of a passport and the completion of a short form. You'll find several cordial, efficient changers near the crossroads of Jl. Legian and Jl. Pantai Kuta. Or try **Artha Yoga Utama,** situated where Jl. Bakung Sari meets the road to the airport.

Photography

Instant photo processing and printing are streamlined, cheap, and convenient all over Kuta. Most places offer half-day service. Fresh film too. Kodak products sold and processed at **PT Inter-Delta,** Jl. Legian 52, tel. 751-857, in Legian. **Bali Fotografie Centrum** on Jl. Kaya Kuta offers photo supplies and fast slide processing and framing.

Churches

Kuta has several churches. Try Catholic **St. Francis Xavier** on Jl. Kartika Plaza (Sunday mass begins at 0800); Pentecostal **Gareja Pantekosta** (tel. 0361-751-504, services 0800 and 1800) on Jl. Kaya Kuta near Supermarket Nova; or ecclesiastical, **Jl. Raya Tuban** (tel. 553-674, services Sunday at 0900 and 1800). There's a small mosque near the Pentecostal church.

Massage

Platoons of masseuses in conical hats and yellow T-shirts cruise the beach seeking customers. The majority give competent and thorough rubdowns. Go in the morning for the best price; don't pay more than Rp10,000 for a 40-minute massage. Sometimes halfway through the massage they demand more money. Special prices are offered if you get a massage from the same masseuse every day. Older women are usually better than the young ones; old blind women are the best, giving traditional massages using *lulur paste* from Java. You can also get massages at many hotels—Mastapa has an excellent masseuse—or at traditional Indonesian salons such as Selamat Datang at the Kulkul Beach Resort on Jl. Pantai Kuta, tel. (0361) 752-520, which also offers hair and skin care and steambaths.

Beauty Salon

Eyeliner and eyebrow tattoos, eyelash curling and implants, hair and body treatments, computerized facials, perms and tints, leg waxing, cream baths, hair treatments, cutting and blowing, styling, and manicures and pedicures are available at **Bravo International Hair and Beauty Parlour,** Jl. Kaya Kuta 105, Block 4-5, tel. (0361) 754-096 or 754-097, just 500 meters north of the Gelael Supermarket.

Health And Fitness

Doctors are on call at **Kuta Clinic,** Jl. Kaya Kuta 100 X, tel. (0361) 753-268. Or make an appointment with **Dr. Tjok Gde Subamia,** who has an office on Jl. Raya Bypass Kuta, tel. 751-315 or 753-008. The closest clinic outside of Kuta is the excellent **Nusa Dua Clinic,** Jl. Pratama 81 A-B, tel. 71324, with 24-hour service, doctors on call, and an ambulance.

If you crave a real workout, the equipment and professional assistance at the **Fitness and**

Relaxation Centre, tel. 751-067, at the Kartika Plaza Hotel is topnotch. Open Mon.-Sun. 0600-2000, with an entrance fee of Rp10,000 pp per day. Fee includes use of gymnasium, pools, squash courts, lockers, showers, whirlpool baths, steam sauna, dry sauna, lounge, game room, aerobic classes, and mini-golf. A great deal for five bucks.

TRANSPORTATION

Getting There And Around
If arriving by air, take a taxi from the airport (Rp6000). Or walk out the airport gate and hire a *bemo* for Rp500 to the start of Jl. Pantai Kuta. Get to Kuta from Denpasar by boarding a *bemo* from Stasiun Tegal in southern Denpasar (Rp600). *Bemo* from Denpasar travel only one direction—Denpasar to Kuta, then to Legian via one-way Jl. Pantai Kuta, then back through Kuta down Jl. Legian before returning to Denpasar. Stay on the *bemo* until you're closest to your destination.

Professional motorcycle taxis will give you a ride anytime to anywhere, but most commonly from Legian to Kuta and vice versa if you're willing to pay around Rp2000. Depends on if it's the busy season and/or how much they need the money. You can find them anywhere; they sleep on their bikes at night. Late at night, *dokar* are available for, say, Rp5000 from Peanuts to the Bintang Bali Hotel. *Bemo* leave as soon as they fill up, and once you pay your fare you can get off anywhere you want. Bear in mind that public *bemo* prices soar between 1900-2100, and ratchet up again around 2200 when you'll probably have to private charter.

Rentals
Sturdy bicycles rent for about Rp2500-3000 per day; you must pay in advance and sign a contract. Motorcycles rent for Rp10,000-12,000 per day. Rental cars are available from scores of agencies in Kuta, though you could get a better deal per diem if you go through your hotel proprietor. Expect to pay at least Rp40,000 per day (three-day minimum). If you plan to use Kuta as a base, know that the traffic, confusing one-way streets, and paucity of parking make using a car here very trying.

Travel Agencies And Tours
Kuta agents offer airline tickets to just about anywhere at good prices, but for long-haul airfares you can do much better in Singapore or Bangkok. Agencies also rent cars, bicycles, and motorbikes; offer tours; sell long-distance bus, train, and ferry tickets to the islands east and west of Bali; confirm flights (Rp2500 fee); change money; dispense postage stamps; and sell books. Get an idea of what's available from **Perama Tourist Service,** tel. (0361) 751-551, on Jl. Legian; this excellent agent also runs a handy shuttle service to Ubud at 0830, 1100, and 1500 for Rp12,000. For flight reservations and confirmations, Garuda (tel. 224-664) has an office in the Kuta Beach Hotel, open Mon.-Fri. 0730-1600, Saturday and Sunday 0900-1300.

Tours include two to five day trips with overnight accommodations to Java, Lombok, Komodo, Sulawesi, and even Irian Jaya. One takes you on a climb up Gunung Bromo's crater for around Rp250,000, a bargain as the roundtrip is over 700 km and you get a wonderful look at East Java. You even see surfing trips advertised to Grajagan on the Blambangan Peninsula (East Java) at around Rp63,000 per day, or one-day snorkeling trips in south Bali for around Rp30,000.

Getting Away
A thick and endless stream of motorcycles, *bemo,* cars, vans, and buses travel to Legian via the beachfront road, Jl. Pantai Kuta. *Bemo* from Denpasar's Tegal station (Rp600) stop very briefly at *bemo* corner to let out passengers, then travel down traffic-snarled Jl. Pantai Kuta and the beachfront road to Legian. *Bemo* from Kuta to Legian are Rp500 before 1800; then drivers begin asking as much as Rp5000. After 2200, *bemo* become scarce and those that are available charge exorbitant fares. It costs at least Rp2000 to ride on the back of a motorcycle from Kuta to Legian, or around Rp3500 by taxi.

To Denpasar, get a *bemo* by walking down from *bemo* corner in the direction of Denpasar to Jl. Kaya Kuta, just where it turns in front of Kuta Market. From there head to Tegal station (eight km, 12-15 minutes) in southern Denpasar, then walk to downtown Denpasar in about 10 minutes, or hop on a three-wheeled *bajai* for Rp300. *Bemo* into Denpasar start getting scarce around

1900, after which you may be assessed a "surcharge." To get to Sanur you must travel via Tegal, transfer to Kereneng, then get on a *bemo* to Sanur. To Candidasa, take a *bemo* to Tegal, then Kereneng, then Batubulan, then a minibus to Amlapura, alighting at Candidasa en route. Sometimes the minibus only goes as far as Klungkung, at which point you have to change to another for Amlapura. To get to Ubud, go first to Tegal, transfer to Kereneng, then transfer again to Batubulan, then board a final *bemo* to Ubud. To Singaraja and Lovina, take a *bemo* first to Tegal, then to Kereneng, then to Ubung station, then to the north coast.

The heat, congestion, and time-consuming changes required to get to Ubud, Candidasa, or Sanur by public transport convince many people to charter a *bemo* direct. Don't worry about finding charters; they'll find you. You'll pass motorcycle, minibus, and *bemo* drivers soliciting fares by shouting *"transpor!"* and *"charter!"* every ten paces. To take you and all your stuff from Kuta to the airport in Tuban, they'll first ask Rp10,000. Just laugh at them—the going charter rate is Rp4000-5000. Unlicensed *bemo* can't enter the airport and must drop you off at the gate, where you have to walk 300 meters to the domestic terminal, or 600 meters to the international terminal. Taxis to Denpasar cost around Rp8000. Shuttles to the airport and Sanur leave at 0930, 1100, 1430, and 1730 for Rp4500; shuttles for Padangbai and Candidasa run at 0930 for Rp15,000; Ubud at 0930 for Rp15,000; Lovina at 0930 for Rp17,500. You'll see shuttles advertised on sandwich boards in the doorways of almost any kind of Kuta business.

THE BUKIT PENINSULA

Bukit ("Hill"), a lemon-shaped peninsula at the southernmost extremity of the island, is a dry, rocky land. Oval-shaped and about eight km from north to south, 17 km from east to west, with a maximum elevation of 200 meters, Bukit offers limestone caves, temples perched on the edge of dizzying cliffs, stretches of immaculate isolated beaches, and a dramatic coastline pounded by Bali's most challenging surf. This 100-square-km tableland of stunted bush and prickly pear cactus once lay at the bottom of the sea but now sits 100-200 meters above sea level, its sides in the south rising 100 meters straight up. For years the Dutch called this curious windswept geographic feature Tafelhoek, the "Tableland." Bukit might once have been a separate island, one which eventually attached itself to the mainland. It shares climate, topography, and geology with Nusa Penida, a small island off Bali's southeast coast. Standing out in stark contrast to the lush, alluvial plains of southern Bali, the barren, underpopulated Bukit plateau has no streams and the land cannot be artificially irrigated. On the clifftops of the undeveloped west and south coasts are remains of ancient sea temples. Inland, stone blocks are mined from karst quarries.

There's a drastic difference between the dry season (May-Sept.) and the rainy season (Oct.-April). During the dry, few crops grow, there's almost no surface water, the area is denuded of vegetation, and the concrete water cisterns are empty. In the wet season (average 65 rainy days per year), rice, manioc, sorghum, corn, soybeans, peanuts, beans, coconuts, bananas, oranges, and flowering trees grow out of the thin layer of topsoil. Extensive erosion has created caves and deep cracks in the rocky earth. When the Nusa Dua complex was started, 14 deep bore holes had to be drilled and a water treatment plant built to provide the resort with a source of potable water.

With the building of the spectacular Bali Cliff Hotel, the peninsula made the transition from copra and lime to tourists and surfers. Today Bukit's flat, far eastern corner is the ritzy beach resort of Nusa Dua with its dozen or so four- and five-star hotels strung out along an idyllic, five-km-long stretch of palm-lined, white-sand beach.

History

Bukit has played an important role in Balinese mythology. Legend tells how the gods created Bali by taking a piece of land from Java, then shaping the island to make it hospitable to human beings. They created the high mountains of Batukau in the west, Agung in the east, and Bukit in the south.

In ancient times, Bukit was considered a dangerous area where great herds of wild *banteng* and water buffalo roamed, driven south by population pressure. Bukit served as hunting grounds for pheasant, wild boar, and deer for the *rajas* of Denpasar and Mengwi; cattle still graze there. So inhospitable is this land that criminals, political enemies, and debtors were once banished here.

JIMBARAN AND VICINITY

On the west side of Bukit's narrow isthmus is one of Bali's finest and cleanest white-sand beaches, curving for five km from just south of the airport to the jutting cliffs of eastern Bukit. The warm water is suitable for swimming and bodysurfing, but not for surfing. The east side of the isthmus is an ugly, smelly, mangrove swamp, now being converted to fishponds. In the middle of the isthmus is Jimbaran, the principal town of Bukit. This fishing village is making the jarring metamorphosis into an upscale tourist resort. Some of the hotels here have planted Balinese rice fields *inside* the hotel complex. From Jimbaran, it's only 10 minutes to the airport, 20 minutes to the Galleria in Nusa Dua, and 40 minutes to Denpasar.

To enter the heart of Bukit, head south on the old road from the airport. On the way, see beautiful yet simple Pura Ulunsiwi with its multi-roofed *meru, kori* entrance, and *candi bentar*. West of town early in the morning fishing boats pull up on shore and women with buckets balanced on their heads line up to unload fish, then

THE BUKIT PENINSULA

TANJUNG BENOA

NUSA DUA

SEE "TANJUNG - NUSA DUA" MAP

BUALU

BENOA HARBOR

SUWUNG MANGROVE SWAMPS

BEMO TERMINAL

BALI EDELWEISS (AUSTRIAN RESTAURANT)

JL. DARMANANGSA

SEA-WEED FARM

PURA GEGER

PURA KARANG BONG

SAWANGAN

KAMPIAL

TV TOWER

KUTUH

PURA TEGEH SARI

TV TOWER (163 m)

UNGUSAN

SATELLITE DISH

PURA BATU PAGEH

TELUK JIMBARAN

JIMBARAN

PURA MUAYA

YOUTH HOSTEL

PURA SARIN BUANA

PURA GUAGONG

TV TOWER

PUNCAK PESONA RESTAURANT

SALAKAN

BONGOL

BAKUNG

PURA MASUKA

BALI CLIFF HOTEL

GUA PETENG

G. INGAS (203 m)

BALANGAN

CENGILING

TELUK SAIT

PAK RODAS WARUNG

PAK LOTENG'S MASSAGE

CEPLUK SILVER

MICROWAVE STATION

PECATU

(184 m)

PURA BALANGAN

BINGIN

BANGKET

PADANG PADANG

(125 m)

BUKIT PENINSULA

SULUBAN

PURA ULUWATU

© MOON PUBLICATIONS, INC.

2 km

0

walk to the cooperative to weigh, sort, and sell. By midmorning the catch is in and the work done.

Accommodations

Across the road and south of the Keraton Bali Cottages is **Puri Indra Prasta**, Jl. Ulu Watu 28A, with clean, comfortable rooms, restaurant, bar, and swimming pool. At Rp35,000-45,000, including breakfast, this is Jimbaran's least expensive hotel. Small **Hotel Puri Bali**, tel. (0361) 752-227, near the beach, offers 41 modern a/c rooms and good service for Rp273,000 s or d including tax, breakfast, and dinner. Many types of food—Italian, European, etc. Free shuttle to Kuta three times a day. The 99-room (Rp115,000) **Keraton Bali Cottages**, Jl. Mrajapati, P.O. Box 32023, Kuta, tel. 753-991, fax 753-881, features fine Balinese architecture and landscaping. Every Wednesday night there's either a Ramayana, *kecak* fire dance, *joget*, or *legong* on the grounds from 1930 to 2030 (Rp42,000). Built in 1990; superior large new rooms are Rp231,000. Looks like a village of condos in a palm-shaded tropical garden decorated with mythical stone statues; very self-contained with snappy service. Amenities include two restaurants, open-air stage, and tennis courts. The **Four Seasons**, tel. 701-010, with 125 rooms, is perhaps the most traditional resort on Bali— the Amandari idea taken to its ultimate conclusion. The grounds were designed by famed landscape architect Michael White of Sanur, who designed David Bowie's home in the Caribbean. Rates start at Rp780,000 for a one-bedroom villa and increase to Rp3.6 million for the two-bedroom Royal Villa. Rates are higher over the Christmas holidays.

Food

Eat at Jimbaran's main street *warung* or at the market on market days. Stroll along the beach where open-air hotel restaurants provide meals and drinks under umbrellas for Rp21,000 and up. **Cafe Latino**, Jl. Airport, Nusa Dua, tel. (0361) 754-580, is only a five-minute drive from the Keraton Bali Cottages. It specializes in high-quality Italian food—seafood, salads, appetizers, imported meats, Italian wines. Balinese-style entertainment and disco parties every Tuesday and Friday. Free transport from your hotel. Very popular with expats.

SURFING BUKIT

Since the early 1970s, Bukit has been a popular destination for surfers, beachcombers, seekers of solitude, and budget travelers. It boasts some of southeast Asia's best surfing beaches, and is considered among the top ten surfing spots in the world. Be prepared for huge breakers, which can dwarf those of Kuta and Sanur. A bonus is the dramatic backdrop of sheer cliffs which start at the northwest corner of Bukit and extend all the way around to just south of Nusa Dua.

Go early in the morning to catch the best waves. The best time to surf is the dry season from April through October. Strong winds during the wet season make surfing impossible. There are no official accommodations, and only one *losmen* at Bingin. But if the surf is really good, surfers customarily crash on the beach or at one of the full-service beachside *warung*. Bukit *warung* rent surfboards (Rp5000) and sell Indonesian *nasi campur* and simple Western meals, iced drinks, and a bed for the night. The best *nasi campur* is at **Warung Widari** in Pecatu; only Rp1000.

It costs little or nothing to surf. At most spots, the surfer need only pay a "board carrier" Rp10,000 or so. This work provides employment to local youths; there's even an official Board Carrier Association. Motorbike drivers will transport surfers and boards to the beach for Rp10,000-15,000. Drop in at the **Surf Information Warung** in Bongol and ask for Hank; he runs a *warung* at Balangan and provides guide services to all of Bukit's surfing spots.

Balangan

This long, beautiful, white-sand surfing (left-hander) beach, accessible by four-wheel drive or motorbike, lies six km northwest of Bongol. From Balangan's parking lot, it's a 10-minute walk to the beach—hard to find, as there's no sign. Six *warung* here. A cave temple sits on the beach. Walk up to Lookout Point for a grand panorama over Bukit and the airport.

Bingin

A great place for surfing (hollow left-hander) and relaxing. From the main highway in Pecatu, take the dirt road to Bingin; this is the same pretty, shady country road you take to Padang

Padang. On the way, refresh yourself with a cold drink or *nasi campur* at **Pak Roda's Warung** at the turnoff to Bingin; from this *warung* to the homestay the road is seriously rutted. **Homestay Wayan,** just below the parking lot at Bingin, has three rooms (Rp15,000 s, Rp20,000 d), a living room for guests, small restaurant, veranda, and a nice garden. There's a river below the homestay, and you can take fresh showers thanks to the homestay's water tank. From the homestay it's a 10-minute walk to the beach.

Padang Padang

From the parking lot, it's a short walk to the caves where you start surfing; really nice beach here too. There are at least 10 *warung* at Padang Padang selling jaffles, noodle soup, cold drinks, and the like. Ketut Sugi's *warung* has the best selection. Kelly's Bar is also okay. On the road to Padang Padang there are two places of note. **Pak Loteng** gives massages and administers traditional herbs. The other is **Cepluk Silver,** which produces made-to-order Gianyar-style silver.

Suluban

Called Ulu by surfers, this is the most famous—and crowded—surfing spot on the island. Waves sometimes reach eight meters in height with straight-line swells. Purportedly one of the best left-handers in the world, for daredevils and goofy-footers only. A footpath, which starts 200 meters before Pura Uluwatu's parking lot, leads down to the beach; look for the sign Suluban Beach 2 km. Boys will offer to carry your surfboard and equipment for the 45-minute trip. Motorbikes will take you most of the way down, but this is a narrow, dangerous path so drive cautiously if you're on your own. From the covered motorcycle parking area at the end of the trail, climb down to the large sea cave at the bottom of the cliff, which opens to the ocean.

There are some other isolated and lovely beaches for surfing, sunbathing, and swimming to the southeast and east of Uluwatu. One such beach, with outstanding surf, is Nyang Nyang; the turn is about 2.5 km inland.

Bali Cliff Resort

The first major hotel built on Bukit is set high above the crashing surf of the Indian Ocean just south of Ungusan, 25 minutes from Ngurah Rai Airport. It's said President Suharto himself invested in this new, five-star hotel. The only hotel on Bali offering views of both the sunrise and sunset, its 200 beautifully appointed rooms range from superior (Rp359,000) to executive (Rp924,000) to various classes of luxurious suites (Rp945,000-Rp4 million). Special features include an elaborate laser/video entertainment program, in-house doctor, bank, Japanese restaurant, pizzeria, outdoor stage, and art market. The Olympic-size pool comes right up to the edge of a 75-meter-high cliff, water cascading down its face. A "travelator" (outdoor elevator) lowers guests to the beach; decent surfing nearby. A walkway from the hotel leads to the cave temple of Pura Batu Pageh. Call (0361) 771-992 for reservations.

PURA ULUWATU

On the south coast of Bali is a whole series of sea temples—Tanah Lot, Pura Sekenan, Pura Rambut Siwi, Pura Petitenget, and Pura Uluwatu. All pay homage to the guardian spirits of the sea, but none is more spectacular than Uluwatu.

This well-maintained temple, one of the *sadkahyangan* group of the holiest temples of Bali, is the least overwhelmed by tourism and commercialism because of its remote location on the southwestern tip of Bukit. For years entrance was forbidden to anyone but the prince of Badung. He visited right up until his death at the hands of the Dutch in the *puputan* of 1906. Administered now by a royal family in Denpasar, Uluwatu actually belongs to the Balinese people, but is particularly sacred to fishermen, who come here to pray to the sea goddess Dewi Laut. The full name of the temple is Pura Luhur Uluwatu, which roughly translates as "The Temple Above the Stone," an accurate description as this temple perches on a cliff overhanging the Indian Ocean 90 meters below.

At the end of a beautiful country road, Uluwatu may be reached by public *bemo* from Kuta or Tegal station in Denpasar. From Kuta, it'll cost Rp12,000-15,000 (20 km) to charter a vehicle, though it's faster if you take a motorbike. From the parking lot, walk 300 meters down a path to the temple (open 0700-1900). Get there early in

Pura Uluwatu

Java 50 km away. As white breakers crash against the rocks below, watch sea turtles swim in a hundred shades of churning blue-green sea water; wide-winged white frigate birds soar against the sky, moving to and from nests in the cliffs. Beware of mischievous resident monkeys who snatch unguarded items.

When the temple is bathed in gold at sunset, streams of jeeps, cars, and buses head to Uluwatu for the spectacular view. Since the temple is so small, it can get very crowded. While here, refresh yourself with an *es kelapa muda* (Rp1500), sold at stands on a shady slope off the parking lot. Served with a straw and a spoon to scoop the soft gooey meat from the coconut; one of Asia's greatest pleasures.

the morning for a quiet hour before the tourists start arriving. Contribute a donation for temple upkeep and take a sash, or *sarung* if you're wearing shorts. For some obscure reason, visitors are prohibited from wearing black-and-white checkered cloths or red hibiscus.

Layout And Construction
Walk up the 71 steps through a strikingly simple limestone entrance to the rectangular outer courtyard. All three courtyards—representing the spiritual, earthly, and demonic realms—are surrounded by hard weathered coral which has enabled the temple to survive for centuries and gives it a brilliant white appearance. Towering over the middle courtyard is an enormous arched *kala* gate flanked by Ganesha guardians, reminiscent of East Javanese temple architecture.

From the center of the northwest wall is a beautiful view of the sheer cliffs and ocean below. Descend down into the outermost courtyard—from there you can see the tip of East

BUALU

About 3.5 km beyond Kampial is Bualu, once a sleepy dusty fishing village, but transformed since the start of the Nusa Dua resort project into a scruffy, bustling service and bedroom community. Not really attractive—an untidy hodgepodge of makeshift shops, car rental shops, tour agencies, beauty salons, tailors, and small restaurants sprawling in all directions. Bualu stands in vivid contrast to the immaculate lawns, gardens, and grand hotel properties of the exclusive resort next door. Bualu is where Nusa Dua guests can step out and experience "the real Indonesia."

In the southern part of the village is another exit out of Nusa Dua, Jl. Pantai Mengiat—a useful street with many services. This garish, Kutaish street, which starts on the other side of the roundabout opposite the entrance to Nusa Dua's Hilton, is more pleasant to walk along than Jl. Pramata, which heads north up the Tanjung Peninsula.

Food
The best place to eat for the money is the **Amanda Food Center,** just a six-minute walk west of the Tragia Supermarket. A Singapore-style food park with class, Amanda caters to the tastes of the vast and multiethnic Indonesian service community. Especially good for lunch. Go around to any of the 31 reasonably priced individual stalls serving Padang and Solonese food—many of the traditional foods of Indonesia,

as well as European dishes. After you've made your choices, the food is brought over to your table. Great smells, squeaky clean, roofed, like a cafeteria with an upbeat atmosphere. Three times the value of Kuta. Live music seven days a week, starting at 1900.

Along this strip are a number of half-empty restaurants. **Rumah Makan Beringin** has a giddy assortment of *nasi padang* dishes, even late in the day. The newer, flashier **Nusa Dua Grill** is across the street from a big car and motorbike rental place near the Bank Rakyat Indonesia.

Just behind the row of souvenir stalls on Jl. Ngurah Rai Bypass is the **Novi Restaurant,** serving Westernized dishes at inflated prices. **Terminal Bualu** with lots of *warung* is a good place to eat. Check out the old market next to the Sentral Theatre. Later, this area turns into a night market selling *nasi kuning, soto,* and *ayam bakar.* In front of the Tragia Supermarket is **Papa Bob's Donuts,** with pizza by the slice (Rp2000). Inside the Tragia is a very good bakery (delicious danish) and lots of snacks. On Jl. Pantai Mengiat you'll find a whole row of seafood restaurants—the **Koki Bali, Maschere, Galliano** (Italian and Chinese food), and **Ming Garden. Ulam Restaurant** serves traditional Balinese seafood; lobster Rp29,000, Indonesian dishes Rp8000. Across the street is another lobster house, **Ulam II.**

Shopping

Bualu is a more pleasant shopping experience than Kuta. You can take your time, and the vendors are more polite. Though the crafts and souvenirs are identical to those found in all of Bali's tourist centers, the selection isn't as large. In the art market visit the *batik* painter Surarta. A few classier, pricier boutiques are found on Jl. Pantai Mengiat in south Bualu. Just west of the post office is refreshingly air-conditioned **Tragia Supermarket,** tel. 71271, open 0830-2000, the pride of Bualu, offering useful, convenient shopping for those staying in Nusa Dua or Tanjung. The big building in the center houses the supermarket (first floor), department store (second floor), and arts and crafts (third floor).

Services

Not only food and accommodations, but laundry, taxis, and other services tend to be more expensive in Bualu, Tanjung, and Nusa Dua than in other tourist areas. The *kantor pos* is just east of Tragia Supermarket. The moneychanger, **PT Batuan Indah,** is located on the Nusa Dua side of the Tragia complex, while **Panih Bank** is on the other side.

Transportation

It's a pleasant one-kilometer walk from Nusa Dua's big hotels to downtown Bualu. The Nusa Dua shuttle bus runs to the Tragia Supermarket regularly. Up the street from the Tragia is Terminal Bualu, where you can catch blue Isuzu to Denpasar (Rp1000) or Kuta (Rp750). You can also hop on a green *bemo* for Tanjung Benoa; it passes all the hotels and restaurants of the east coast strip.

Diagonally across from the Amanda Food Center is a *wartel* which accepts faxes and sells long-distance bus tickets to Denpasar, Yogyakarta, Semarang, Bandung, and Jakarta. Taxis to the airport are now Rp15,000. From Bualu's main intersection, a road leads south to Sawangan, another travels north to Tanjung Benoa, and yet another heads east to Nusa Dua.

NUSA DUA

The most luxurious hotels on Bali are located in this beach enclave on the east end of Bukit, 27 km south of Denpasar. Named after two raised headlands connected to the east coast by sandspits (Nusa Dua means "Two Islands"), this full-scale, totally self-contained tourist resort has its own parks, roads, golf course, deep-water wells, sewer system, fire station, police, telephone exchange, banks, emergency clinic, mall, travel and tour agencies, and airline offices. The resort may be divided into south Nusa Dua, where the big international hotels are concentrated, and north Nusa Dua (Tanjung), which includes Club Med, the Bali Tropic Palace, Mirage, and Puri Joma.

Kuta, Sanur, and Ubud—Bali's oldest tourist areas—grew spontaneously, and limits have since been placed on their expansion. In 1971, it was decided that only at Nusa Dua would further luxury hotel development be permitted. The area was chosen because of its breathtaking location, its proximity to the airport, and the fact that its relative isolation from Bali's population

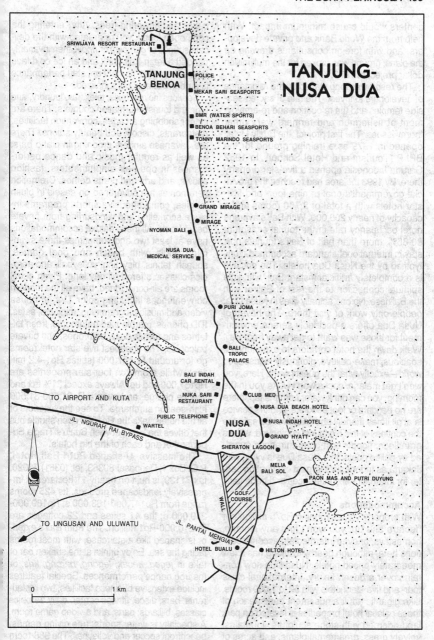

SRIWIJAYA RESORT RESTAURANT

TANJUNG
BENOA

POLICE

TANJUNG-
NUSA DUA

MEKAR SARI SEASPORTS

BMR (WATER SPORTS)
BENOA BEHARI SEASPORTS
TONNY MARINDO SEASPORTS

GRAND MIRAGE
MIRAGE

NYOMAN BALI

NUSA DUA
MEDICAL SERVICE

PURI JOMA

BALI
TROPIC
PALACE

BALI INDAH
CAR RENTAL

TO AIRPORT AND KUTA

NUKA SARI
RESTAURANT   CLUB MED

PUBLIC TELEPHONE   NUSA DUA BEACH HOTEL

JL. NGURAH RAI BYPASS   WARTEL   NUSA INDAH HOTEL

NUSA
DUA   GRAND HYATT

SHERATON LAGOON

MELIA
BALI SOL

PAON MAS AND PUTRI DUYUNG

GOLF
COURSE

TO UNGUSAN AND ULUWATU

WALL

JL. PANTAI MENGIAT

HOTEL BUALU   HILTON HOTEL

0   1 km

centers would cause minimum impact. With help from the World Bank and private developers, and with foreign consultants drawing up the plans, ground was broken for the multimillion dollar project in 1973.

The resort was long stalled by the reluctance of developers to invest. The fate of sacred seaside temples and the relocation and re-employment of fishermen and farmers were other thorny issues. The first project, the Bualu Hotel, opened in 1979 as a training ground for the BPLP (Tourism and Hotel School). In 1982 Garuda Indonesia opened a five-star property there. By 1993 the area had reached the provincial government's goal of nine four- and five-star hotels with a total of 2,700 rooms and a capacity of nearly 200,000. With Bali's average hotel occupancy rate in the tourist season at 80-85%, more than half of Bali's tourists now stay in international-standard accommodations typified by the Nusa Dua hotels. The enclave is a completely artificial instant Bali, with little spiritual connection to the rest of Bali or with the Balinese. No one actually *lives* in Nusa Dua; people only work or visit there. The haven of Nusa Dua offers a decidedly serene environment for those who want to get away from Bali. Walk down the hotel corridors to experience a spacious, make-believe, gloriously landscaped world—exactly what the guests want. Here, you won't get malaria, cocks won't wake you in the morning, you can drink water from the tap, there are no beggars or foot peddlers, and the service is at all times friendly and attentive. So safe are the confines of this big tourist compound, with its grandiose, floodlit split-gate entrances guarded by police posts, that Nusa Dua is vying with Jakarta as Indonesia's largest convention center for international conferences and trade fairs.

Accommodations

With property values running Rp75 million per hectare and up, you won't find any *losmen,* homestays, or even intermediate accommodations here, although nearby Tanjung has a few moderately-priced hotels. Nusa Dua now contains over a dozen luxury, international-class four- and five-star hotels with 50 to 1,000 rooms. Like gigantic adult amusement parks, each of these palatial hotel properties is located on park land adorned with stone sculpture, fountains, velvety grass, ornamental plants, and acres of palms and flowering trees. After entering the cool, open lobby, you're greeted with the delicate sounds of *gamelan* or *rindik,* then invariably handed a fresh-fruit drink and an ice cold face towel. From that moment on, staff performance is embarrassingly personalized.

Services include taxis, telex, fax, laundry, and tour and tourist information counters. There are indoor shopping arcades, convention facilities, restaurants, discos, and beauty salons. There are Javanese singers crooning in piano bars, as well as regular music and dance performances in open-air amphitheaters, fashion shows, and arts and crafts demos. Cremation ceremonies are advertised on easels in plush lobbies; comprehensive sports programs include snorkeling and windsurfing from private beachfronts. All these deluxe accommodations have at least two and sometimes three swimming pools, with beach and pool games, squash, tennis, bicycling, volleyball, and aerobics classes offered all day long. Plush guest rooms are air-conditioned, have all the modern conveniences including color TVs, in-house video and music programming, minibars, safes, IDD phones, marble-tiled bathrooms, fresh toiletries and towels daily, bathrobes, and private balconies. The cheapest five-star hotel rooms go for around Rp157,000 (suites Rp1-4.2 million), while rooms on four-star properties are Rp157,000 and up. Always expect 21% tax and service charge, and even a Rp21,000-31,500 high-season surcharge. To see the exteriors of all the hotels, take the Rp1000 open shuttle bus that drives the loop between Bualu's Tragia Supermarket and each of the big hotels.

The massive, U-shaped **Putri Bali Hotel,** P.O. Box 1, Denpasar 80363, tel. (0361) 71020, fax 71139, is built on nearly 11 hectares of impressively landscaped grounds. Its 425 rooms range from Rp147,000-168,000 s, Rp189,000-210,000 d; the 41 suites and 22 cottages are Rp210,000-Rp1 million. The Putri Bali's exterior is shaped like a staircase, with most rooms facing the sea. Enjoy drinks at the sunken bar or take in *jegog, kecak, legong, barong, kris,* or the frog dance performances. Special features include extensive business facilities, two restaurants, bars, disco, fitness center, daily aerobics classes, billiards, darts, and a video game room. A specialty is water sports: free diving demos, beachfront soccer and volleyball. The 388-room

Melia Bali Sol, P.O. Box 1048, Tuban, tel. 71410, fax 71360, is owned by Spain's leading hotel chain and caters to package tours from Europe as well as conferences. Rooms are Rp189,000-199,500 s, Rp315,000-Rp1.2 million d. Meeting rooms with complete audiovisual equipment accommodate 40 to 500. This graceful, attractive hotel is noted for its fine cuisine, particularly the Asian dishes at the Lotus Restaurant. Enjoy entertainment at any of several piano bars. Discos, shops, health center, kid's playground, library, three tennis courts, jogging track, beautiful open-air theatre. See the 1,200-square-meter lagoon-style swimming pool with three islets.

The 450-room **Nusa Dua Beach Hotel,** P.O. Box 1028, tel. 71210, fax 71229, is run by Aerowisata, a subsidiary of Garuda Indonesia. Beyond the magnificent *candi bentar* and within the four-story hotel are four restaurants, two bars, a coffee shop, and a disco. All the principal styles of Balinese village architecture are represented: *puri, bale banjar,* and *kulkul.* Almost three-quarters of the guests are domestic tourists, incentive travelers, or conference attendees—impressive business services. Rooms are Rp189,000-252,000 s, Rp210,000-315,000 d. The jogging track, tennis and squash courts, and a huge swimming pool are surrounded by 8.5 hectares of lush park land under hundreds of graceful palms. With its long beachfront, marine sports abound. Guests may receive instruction and use equipment for scuba, snorkeling, boating, and water-skiing, then take a sauna or massage at the hotel's fully equipped gym. **Club Med,** P.O. Box 7, Nusa Dua, tel. 71521, accommodates 700 in three- and four-story Balinese-style bungalows geared toward packaged stays for families and couples. A highly organized nonstop sports program is part of the Rp210,000 pp daily tariff: sailing, windsurfing, snorkeling, tennis, aerobics, yoga, volleyball, badminton, and archery. Emphasis is given to arts and crafts like *batik* and kite-making. Entertainment includes regular performances of Balinese theater, periodic talent contests, arts festivals. The environment can be raucous—announcements blare over squawk boxes, noisy crowds leave the small pool dirty—but the food is very good and the sports facilities first class. The rooms, though spartan, are comfortable. The majority of guests are Japanese and Aus-

tralian. Extraordinary security; nonguests are not allowed to walk along the beach.

The breathtaking US$170 million **Grand Hyatt,** P.O. Box 53, Nusa Dua, tel. 71234, fax 72038, is one of Asia's classiest hotels. Inspired by the design of the Tirtagangga water palace, its four "villages" are linked by simulated ponds, gardens, and pools. Its environs and rooms (11 categories Rp315,000-Rp12 million) are decorated with millions of dollars worth of original art. The staff of over 500 responds to your needs instantaneously. Fine restaurants; breakfast buffet is Rp310,500. The swimming pool is a continuous inland "lagoon" that flows beneath footbridges, by sparkling waterfalls and water slides. The Grand Hyatt is recreation oriented: snorkeling (Rp65,100 per hour), windsurfing (Rp16,800 per hour), and kayak flotation (Rp10,500 per hour). Or take the "Archaeological Tour" (Rp65,100). Forty percent of the clientele is European. Use your Hyatt Gold Passport in the Bali Hyatt in Sanur. For reservations, call (800) 233-1234 in the United States. The U-shaped, 400-room **Nusa Indah,** P.O. Box 36, tel. 71565, fax 71908, overlooks the beach. Nice gardens, four restaurants, and extensive convention facilities—in fact, the largest in Indonesia, with 2,000-person capacity and simultaneous translation service.

The 276-room **Sheraton Lagoon,** P.O. Box 2044, Kuta 80361, tel. 71327, fax 71326, consists of four-story room blocks with attractive terra-cotta roofs on one side of the complex, with food and beverage facilities, the lobby, and other public areas on the other side. Ultra-personalized services include special check-in, complimentary coffee, tea, and American breakfast, round-the-clock butler service in the suites, and "daily surprise." Rates are about the same as the Grand Hyatt's—Rp346,500-378,000 s, Rp409,500-430,500 d, suites Rp463,000-3.7 million. The Sheraton boasts the largest free-form pool on Bali; on the beach are pedal boats. Great views of the sea from the open-air Cascade Bar, while the Cafe Lagoon Coffeeshop overlooks the "lagoon" meandering through seven hectares of landscaped grounds. A spacious outdoor amphitheater hosts cultural performances. The opulent **Amanusa Resort,** P.O. Box 33, Nusa Dua, tel. 71267, fax 71266, sits on a grassy knoll overlooking the Bali Golf and Country Club, commanding spectacular views of the ocean and Gunung Agung. Thirty-five free-standing luxury suites (Rp630,000-1.4 million) are linked to the public facilities by pathways. Special features: sunken baths, queen-size four-poster beds, walled private courtyard, suites with private pools, two restaurants, a library, cruise boats, floodlit tennis courts, massage and beauty salons, free airport transfers. The last word in luxury vacation living.

Food

The **Tragia Convenience Store** in the Galleria sells a limited selection of drinks, snacks, fruit, and dairy products; it also has a bakery/coffee shop where a loaf of whole-wheat bread costs Rp4000.

The gourmet high-priced, high-quality restaurants in the hotels serve international, European, Chinese, Balinese, and Indonesian cuisine. The Grand Hyatt's **Salsa Verde** restaurant is said to be one of the best Italian restaurants on the island—complete with a traditional Old World pizza oven. Superb seven-course French dinners at the **Pavilion Restaurant** in the Melia Bali Sol. Outside the hotels, the Galleria offers a few outstanding—but pricey—restaurants. Every Monday night at 2000, the **Paon Mas** features a *rijstaffel* buffet for Rp25,000; call (0361) 71981 for reservations. Next door is the **Putri Duyung,** tel. 72051, with a wide choice of fresh fish and seafood; open for lunch and dinner 1100-2300. Galleria's **Chikara Tei,** tel. 72267, is a Japanese restaurant highly praised by the Japanese themselves.

Beyond the Nusa Dua barricades altogether, though not far to walk, is Jl. Pantai Mengiat in the southern part of Bualu, the supply base for Nusa Dua. On this street are the popular seafood restaurants **Koki Bali, Maschere, Galliano, Ming Garden,** and **Ulam.** Lobster is the big item here. Call the Ming (tel. 71545) or the Ulam (tel. 71590) for free transport from your hotel. The long-established Ulam is frequently recommended by hotel managers.

Water Sports

Nusa Dua's beach hotels front a three-km-long beautiful white sand beach with gentle waves and not a rock in sight. However, barriers constructed to create a protected swimming environment have moved the surf quite a distance from shore. There's an excellent lagoon, and

in the rocky outcroppings to the south are spectacular blowholes, natural waterspouts created when waves blow up through fissures in the coral.

For surfers, the right-hander in front of Club Med is a lark; park in the lot south of Club Med. Another right-hander, at high tide only, is found between the two headlands south of the Nusa Dua Beach Hotel. Also, rights and lefts up to two meters high peel off Nusa Dua channel, but watch the strong riptide. Take a *prahu* (Rp5000) about one km offshore to ride swells in three different directions. Beware of strong winds.

Shopping

Nusa Dua's newest shopping center is **Galleria**—the largest on Bali and, at 3.5 hectares, one of the biggest in Indonesia. Opened in 1993, it's laid out like a Western mall. Here, tourists are made to feel comfortable browsing in air-conditioned shops among familiar surroundings while paying familiar prices. As long as you have money, Galleria offers something for everyone. Even though prices are supposed to be fixed, some stores will negotiate.

The **Tantra Gallery** exhibits exceptional Ubud artists including Yan Tino (oils), Made Nusa (oils on canvas), and Wayang Pundah (watercolors). The **Keris Gallery,** tel. (0361) 71303, is Bali's largest department store—like a huge Nordstrom or Filene's—carrying silks, handicrafts, traditional *batik,* Sumatran pearls, and Euro-style clothing from the collections of Yves Saint Laurent, Ettiene Aigner, Kenzo, and Paloma Picasso. Like most shops in the Galleria, Keris offers super Gucci. Open 0900-2000. **Country Interior** features a stunning selection of folk art and home furnishings from Java and Lombok. Probably the nicest shop in the Galleria for tasteful decorator items is **Stiff Gallery.** Displayed attractively on its sand floor are beautifully glazed teapots, basketry from Java, and many other folk items. A showroom for both shops is located at Jl. Gatot Subroto 128A, tel. 234-029, Denpasar. **Folk Art Antiques** carries eye-catching items, such as an ornate blowgun from Kalimantan (Rp157,500) and other Outer Island tribal artifacts. The **Duty Free Shop** carries leading world labels from Hermes to Harley Davidson with prices to match, as well as exclusive lines of locally manufactured products.

Services

A clinic, **Nusa Dua Medical Service**, tel. 72118, is across from the Galleria; there are several others in Tanjung. An interdenominational church service is held each Sunday at 1730 in the Nusa Dua Beach Hotel. Most hotel rooms have IDD telephone service and card-operated telephones are common.

Transportation

A smart new highway whisks arrivals the 10 kilometers from the airport to Nusa Dua in about 20 minutes. Public *bemo* leave Kuta for Nusa Dua (Rp1000) from the intersection of Jl. Pantai Kuta and the road to the airport. From Tegal station in Denpasar, take a *bemo* (Rp1000).

The resort offers easy access to Denpasar (25 minutes). There's a Garuda Airlines counter in Building A2 in the Galleria, tel. (0361) 71444 or 71342, where tickets can be reconfirmed, luggage checked in, and boarding passes obtained. Open Mon.-Fri. 0800-1900, Sunday and holidays 0900-1900. Extremely convenient. Taxis from Nusa Dua to the airport charge a fixed Rp15,000. Shuttle buses leave each hotel every hour or so for Bualu, the shopping center just outside the gates of Nusa Dua. Or just walk. It's agreeable sauntering around this park-like ghetto. The manicured scenery and luxuriant tropical vegetation is a delight and you don't have the traffic, noise, fumes, dirt, and street vendors typical of other tourist areas of Bali. There are even sidewalks.

Taxi drivers in Nusa Dua are ruthless; there aren't that many of them and they have you captive on the big hotel properties. The only way to get cheaper fares is to walk from your hotel out to the main road, where you still might be quoted the same rip-off fares. Coming back from Kuta it's cheaper. Alternatively, charter a vehicle from an agent in Bualu for around Rp50,000-55,000 per day. Avis Rental Car has offices at Club Med (tel. 71521) and the Nusa Dua Beach Hotel (tel. 71220).

Vicinity Of Nusa Dua

Visit the Kuburan Katolik (Catholic Cemetery) of Bualu. Northeast of Bualu are the extensive mudflats of Suwung, which extend for about seven km to Jimbaran; bridges cross over swampier sections. A commercial seaweed farm is located two km south of Nusa Dua. A road leads south to the small farming community of Sawangan; large banyan-like *bunut* trees grow in the town's center. Pura Geger, a temple dedicated to agricultural deities, is a short distance east of town on a rocky promontory. A track leads for two km south to remote Pura Karang Bona, which looks out over the sea.

TANJUNG

Three km north of Nusa Dua, the five-km-long peninsula of Tanjung Benoa points toward Benoa Harbor like a long finger. This once sleepy expanse of coconut palms and shallow beach has been transformed into a growing resort area with luxury hotels, dive agents, restaurants, and open-air cafes. Tanjung doesn't have the same feeling of sterile isolation as neighboring Nusa Dua. It's Nusa Dua's wild side. The rhythm of the peninsula is more like Costa Brava in the late '70s than the frantic pace of a modern Balinese resort. New hotels, shops, and restaurants are constantly being built, affording tourists plenty of options and all the conveniences, but there's not nearly the level of traffic, congestion, crime, and vice that plagues Kuta.

A nice place for evening strolls is the relatively quiet village of Benoa on the peninsula's tip. For hundreds of years this was an embarkation point for ferries crossing over to Suwungan; the overland journey to the main part of Bali via Jimbaran was too arduous and time-consuming. Offshore are foreigner's yachts along with smaller Indonesian vessels, Navy boats, and traditional Bugis *prahu*. Sit and drink a cold beer while watching the village life at the Sriwijaya Resort Restaurant. More romantic is to walk along the beach southeast of Benoa, past rows of *jakung* pulled up on shore. In Benoa village is a Bugis *kampung* with its small *mesjid*. Don't miss the large, garish Chinese Buddhist *klenteng* picturesquely sited looking out to Benoa Harbor. The annex of this local temple contains bronze icons salvaged from the shipwreck of a Chinese vessel in the 15th century. Recently renovated, the Ratu Cina shrine in the local *pura dalem* shows the long history of Chinese contact. Occasional *gong* or *legong* dances are held at the temple.

Accommodations

It all begins a half km north of the entrance to northern Nusa Dua's Club Med. If you're staying for a while, look for the many *rumah disewakan* (house for rent) signs on village lanes. The up-market hotels on this strip have all the usual tourist features: a/c, private terraces or balconies, minibars, fridges, IDD telephones, sound systems, color TVs, 24-hour room service.

The **Bali Tropic Palace**, Jl. Pratama 34 A, P.O. Box 41, Nusa Dua 80361, tel. (0361) 72130 or 72107, fax 72131, is a small version of a Nusa Dua hotel. It has 108 lavishly appointed cottages. With garden view Rp241,500, with sea view Rp273,000, junior suite Rp525,000, deluxe suite Rp735,000. Amenities include two restaurants, pizzeria, two bars, butterfly-shaped swimming pool, and beautiful private beach. American buffet breakfast Rp18,900, set lunch Rp31,500, dinner Rp44,100. Serene atmosphere. Small but high-class **Puri Joma**, Jl. Pratama, Terora, Nusa Dua 80361, tel. and fax 71526, offers 10 Bali-style bungalows decorated with stone carvings and traditional golden painted doors. Idyllic, safe, relaxing garden. Nice quiet rooms have a/c, IDD telephones, fridge, and no TVs. Enjoy the breezy, scenic beachfront seafood restaurant, swim in the modern pool. Only Rp107,100 s, Rp130,200 d. Lower prices during the off-season. Discounts for stays of more than seven days.

The cheapest accommodation on Tanjung—and very central—is Hasan Homestay, with a *losmen*-style row of rooms with baths, fans, and Kuta-type breakfast for Rp17,000 s or d. Only full during the high season, when the price goes up to Rp20,000. Big, cold beers Rp4000.

Food

A number of seafood specialty restaurants have opened up on both sides of Jl. Pratama just south of Benoa village. All have a weary sameness, and are 50-90% empty except in July, August, and December. Those on the beach offer good views of the Nusa Penida cliffs. Most have full bars, and offer fare at prices about 10% higher than Kuta. Menus are generally too Western.

Just across from the Mirage Hotel is the **Nyoman Bali**. Packed every night, it drains plenty of business from the higher-priced restaurant in the Mirage. The clean and reasonably priced **Nusa Sari Restaurant** has excellent Balinese food and the portions are generous. Though European food is also served, it's best to stick with the native stuff. There's a great *nasi campur* place, **Puri Panca Setia**, opposite the Grand Mirage Hotel. **Warung Jakarta**, also on the strip past Puri Joma heading north has great *nasi campur* (Rp1200) and Betawi-style *gado-gado* (Rp800) with mixed corn kernels. Unbeatable prices for genuine Javanese cuisine. **Bali Gonsaga** is a tourist restaurant specializing in Italian food. Heading north on Jl. Pramata, it's just before the turnoff to Club Med and the Nusa Indah Hotel. Also at the start of Jl. Pramata are a number of small *warung makan* and street vendors selling less expensive, genuine food.

Recreation

Tanjung is popular with marine sports enthusiasts. Tourists enjoy parasailing, water scooters, scuba, snorkeling, water-skiing, glass bottom boats, reef fishing, trawling, power boating, and banana boat rides. The intensive training for parasailing takes all of 12 seconds. It costs Rp25,000 for only two to three minutes in the air—a blast. There are dozens of water sport clubs and shops. Most employ divemasters who offer five-day scuba certification courses for Rp420,000. The reef lies about 200 meters off the northeastern end of the peninsula—easy to reach, with a gentle current and a surprising variety of fish and scattered outcrops of coral. The dives are perfect for beginners. When the tide's in, board the dive agent's *prahu motor* for the five-minute trip. Visibility's about 10-15 meters along a gradual downslope.

Services

There are well-stocked shops and *warung* up and down the Tanjung strip. A public telephone (accepts cards) is at the lower, Bualu-end of Jl. Pratama; see the blue sign between Warung Karina and the bank. A small shop opposite the Grand Mirage offers laundry service.

Getting There

If you're coming from Bualu, the start of Jl. Pratama leading to Benoa village (no sign) looks like the entrance to a crowded, noisy, dusty, Javanese *kampung*. Green minibuses run up and down narrow Tanjung until sunset; Rp300 for foreigners. If you're still in Bualu after dark and want to get back to your hotel, find a taxi (Rp4000-5000).

Per day rental car prices are relatively stable: Rp42,000 or so for a Jimney, about Rp52,500 for a *kijang*. **Bali Indah**, Jl. Pramata 51 B, tel. (0361) 71701, rents Suzuki Katanas for Rp35,000 (plus insurance). Also an authorized money-changer with reasonable rates. **CV Puri Sarana,** which rents cars, is just before the Mirage Hotel. All the water sport agencies handle car rentals.

Because of speeding traffic, the narrow road, and the absence of sidewalks, walking Jl. Pra-mata is unnerving and potentially dangerous. From Nusa Dua you can walk 1.5 hours on the beach north to Tanjung Benoa. Another approach is by boat; boats shuttle back and forth all day long if the tide is right (Rp5000 pp). From the beach in Benoa village, boatmen will take you across to Pulau Serangan for Rp30,000. It's cheaper to take one of the many small *prahu* from Desa Suwungan; take a right off Jl. By-pass on the way from Kuta to Sanur.

GIANYAR REGENCY

The roundtrip from Denpasar to Kintamani through Gianyar makes an excellent introduction to the art and culture of Bali. Indeed, Gianyar is Bali's richest and oldest cultural region, where much of today's religious life was forged in ancient times. The town of Gianyar is the regency's administrative capital, while Ubud is its cultural capital and most populous town. No part of Gianyar Regency is farther than an hour's ride from Denpasar.

Consisting of 244 *desa,* 504 *banjar,* 2,732 temples, and a population of about 350,000, this geographically and economically diverse region features both undeveloped coastline and cool, fresh hills and mountains. The northern border lies only three km away from the active crater of Gunung Batur. Rivers run from this crater lake through the valleys, hills, and terraced fields of the regency.

History
Around the area of Bedulu and Pejeng lies Bali's most ancient capital, a 10-km-long strip of land known as the Land Between the Rivers. Many of the island's archaeological wonders are found here, hidden away in secret valleys—the Elephant Cave hermitage at Bedulu, the ghostly, monumental royal tombs at Gunung Kawi, and the crude and energetic carvings on a rock face at Yeh Pulu—as well as the mysterious 2,000-year-old Moon of Pejeng bronze drum. All of Bali regards these sites as holy.

Legendary rivers Petanu and Pakrisan course through this region, their sources in the slopes of Gunung Batur. The Pakrisan is particularly rich in historic remains, the river having cut its way through rock cliffs and giant boulders. All along its banks are rock-cut *candi,* monasteries, meditation cells, sacred watering places, shrine compounds, and famous temples. These remnants, as well as Bronze Age statuettes, rock inscriptions, and bronze plates, all point to the existence of a powerful and cultured kingdom that experienced an extraordinary flowering of religion, architecture, technology, and art 400-600 years ago.

The irrigation tunnels in the mountainous regions north of Gianyar, the terracing of the slopes, and the intricate planning of the rice-field system are all products of this period. Many of the Balinese have no knowledge of this ancient pre-Hindu kingdom, believing the master-pieces in rock were carved with the thumbnails of a mythical giant, Kebo Iwo. Great mythological battles between the gods and the evil King Mayadanawa of Bedulu are said to have taken place in this holy land. Details of these ancient conflicts have been passed down orally in folk tales and recorded in Bali's epic poem, the *Usana Bali,* composed in the mid-16th century during the golden age of Middle Javanese literature. These stories depict the coming of Hinduism to Bali and the end to the old customs. Historians have surmised the evil king may have been a rebel leader who opposed Hindu influence on Bali.

The sacred bathing place, Tirta Empul, was created by the gods to revive the dead warriors of this mythic conflict. Blood ran from the bodies of the dead into a river, the Petanu ("Cursed One"), and until 1928 its waters were not used for drinking, bathing, or irrigation. Because of this curse, no ancient monuments are found along the banks of the Petanu (the Goa Gajah

GIANYAR REGENCY

PUAKAN

PENYABANGAN

PUPUAN

TARO

PUJUNG — SEBATU
MANUKAYA · TIRTA EMPUL

BAYAD
· PRESIDENTIAL PALACE

KEDISAN

TAMPAKSIRING

PAYANGAN

· GUNUNG KAWI

TEGALLALANG

CELUK

KELIKI

KENDERAN

BUNUTIN

SEBALI

KEDEWATAN

GENTONG

PETULU

SAYAN

CAMPUAN

UBUD

TATIAPI

PENESTANAN

PELIATAN

PEJENG

BEDULU · GEDONG ARCA

TEGALINGGAH

GITGIT

TEGES · GOA GAJAH

BITRA

BENG

PENGOSEKAN

KUTRI

SIDAN

MAS

BURUAN

GIANYAR

BONA

TULIKUP

KENGETAN

BEKUL

SAKAH

BLAHBATUH

BELAGA

MEDAHAN

SIYUT

KEMENUH

KRAMAS

LEBIH

BELANGSINGA

NEGARA

BATUAN

GUTRI

SUKAWATI

BANDA

MASCETI

TUGU

SINGAPADU

CELUK

PINDA

TEGALTAMU

GUANG

SABA

BATUBULAN

KETEWEL

PABEAN

PETANU RIVER

PAKRISAN RIVER

0   5 km

© MOON PUBLICATIONS, INC.

complex is located on one of the tributaries of the Petanu). This victory of the gods over the forces of evil is celebrated annually in the Galungan festival.

Prior to the 18th century, the region now called Gianyar had been divided among the kingdoms of Klungkung, Bangli, Mengwi, and Badung. By the late 18th century the *raja* of Klungkung had lost much of his power after suffering defeat at the hands of the armies of Karangasem. This allowed the ambitious and ruthless *punggawa* of the village of Gianyar to emerge as the ruler of the new rajadom and extend his control over a vast area, including neighboring states. He took the name Dewa Manggis ("Sweet God") after the village in Klungkung where he was born.

During the remainder of the 19th century, there was a confused series of wars between the kingdoms of southern Bali, which accelerated Dutch involvement in the area. The sons of Dewa Manggis were pitted against the allied states of Badung, Bangli, and Klungkung, and they sought help from the Dutch. In 1900, the colonial army was sent to protect Gianyar, which meant automatic annexation and Regentschaap status.

Tourism began in the regency in the 1930s when Tjokorda Agung Sukawati, of the old Sukawati line, set about establishing Ubud as the center of a renaissance in Balinese arts. In 1935 he sponsored the painter's cooperative Pita Maha and invited foreign artists, musicians, anthropologists, and writers to stay at his palace.

In the 1950s the region began to open up to international tourism—dances and music recitals were staged, art shops opened, hotels built, antiquities excavated, museums established. Although taking up only seven percent of the island's total land area, Gianyar today is Bali's most important region for tourism.

Economy

More than half the population of this primarily rural region works in the tourism industry; the rest grow rice, sweet potatoes, and soybeans. The plantation districts of Payangan and Tegallalang also grow coconuts, litchi nuts, cloves, and vanilla, the Sukawati District grows tobacco, and Bali's best-quality coffee is harvested during August and September around the upland village of Taro. The villagers of Kramas and Ketewel on the south coast fish for a living, and the regency's freshwater ponds produce about 130 tons of fish each year.

Gianyar is the center of Bali crafts production, where the weaving, plaiting, and wood- and stonecarving industries are major employers. The Technical High School in Guang provides vocational training in sculpture and carving. Celuk is an important center for silversmiths and goldsmiths, Batubulan for stonecarving, and Mas, Ubud, and Batuan for painting and woodcarving. Sukawati is known for its puppet sculptors, Pujung and Sebatu for expressive wooden statues and wooden jewelry, and Tampaksiring for tusk and bone carving. Bona is the center for bamboo furniture and is a thriving tourist-oriented performance venue.

The Arts

The agricultural wealth of these densely populated plains—sometimes referred to as the Balinese Valley of Culture—has always provided nobility with the means to develop the arts. The villages of Blahbatuh, Batuan, Sukawati, Bona, and Ubud are preeminent centers for music, dance, drama, woodcarving, and other arts. With its flourishing culture, impressive handicrafts, warm climate, and monumental antiquities built as long ago as 200 B.C., Gianyar Regency is the heart of Bali, the focus of tourist interest on the island.

GIANYAR TOWN

The small, bustling administrative center of Gianyar Regency, 23 km from Denpasar's Terminal Kereneng (Rp700 by *bemo*). Gianyar's importance from a tourist point of view is its use as a *bemo* stop for those heading north to Kintamani or east to Klungkung, and its attraction as a center for native Balinese *ikat* weaving, called *endek*. It also has several jeweler's shops selling traditional gold jewelry, a large cockfighting arena (*wantilan*), and its *babi guling* stands and *joged* group are famous all over the island.

The poorly staffed tourist office for Gianyar District (Dinas Pariwisata Gianyar) is at Jl. Ngurah Rai 21, opposite the telephone office. Their only function is to direct you, in rudimentary English, to the various weaving factories. It's easier to get info in Ubud. Change money at Bank Rakyat Indonesia 200 meters down the road by the palace; turn in at the sign to Lebih.

The *Puri*

The old palace, visible through a gate, is in the middle of town facing the *alun-alun*. First built in 1771 on the site of a priest's house, it barely survived a number of 19th-century wars, then was destroyed by a 1917 earthquake. Rebuilt in the 1920s, the *puri* is a traditional and well-preserved Balinese palace, one of the only ones still lived in by a royal family. Its spacious courtyards are decorated with beautiful examples of stonework and carved wood pillars. You may tour the courtyard on the western side with its two impressive gates and gilded *bale*; visiting the palace requires permission. In the *alun-alun* stands a *waringin* tree, a symbol of Balinese and Javanese royal courts.

During the wars of the 1880s, pressed in on all sides by belligerent neighbors, Gianyar's *raja* Dewa Manggis agreed to pay liege homage to the Dewa Agung of Klungkung. Ultimately, the *raja* and his whole family were imprisoned. In 1889, two sons escaped from Klungkung and reestablished their kingdom in this royal palace. Placing themelves under the protection of the Dutch, the kingdom was spared when the Dutch conquered the other principalities of south Bali. In the 20th century, the Gianyar royal line became leaders in the colonial government of Bali.

Accommodations And Food

Most travelers are not dedicated enough to stay overnight here; Ubud, only 10 km away, has an infinitely larger selection of accommodations and restaurants. Gianyar has two places to stay. **Sari Gadung Homestay,** Jl. Dalem Rai, tel. (0361) 93104, on the *alun-alun,* offers seven rooms (Rp7000 s or d) with a front sitting room. No breakfast, but free tea and coffee. Very plain, drab, tolerably clean, cool, central. Another *losmen,* **Pondok Wisata,** Jl. Anom Sandat 10 X, tel. 93239, is down a little street off the *alun-alun.* Owned by the family that runs the weaving factory Cap Putri Bali, nine rooms cost Rp20,000 s, Rp35,000 d each (no a/c or fans), simple breakfast included. Without breakfast, rooms are Rp15,000.

The big culinary attraction of Gianyar is the **Pasar Senggol,** which takes place out in the main street near the market every night beginning at 1700 and lasts until 2000 or 2100. All the best traditional dishes are found here: grilled chicken (*ayam kampung*), rice mixed with sweet potatoes (*tepeng*), and all the Balinese *kampung* sweets. People from Denpasar drive all the way here because the night market offers such a concentration of authentic Balinese village food in a nontouristy atmosphere.

Shopping

The shops along the main street are not cheap; prices are driven up by tour buses. There's a thriving art market where you can bargain for just about any form of art or craft product made on the island, and a few that aren't. Prices are higher than in the villages but still not bad, if you know how to spot the genuine article.

A woodcarving training center is located in Abianbase only a few blocks from Gianyar's police station. Visit before 1200. Called Sasana Hasta Karya, the program was set up in 1983 by the Denpasar Catholic church to help unemployed youth. The carving follows Balinese traditional style with some thematic inspiration from the Borobudur and Prambanan temples in Central Java. The executive manager, Father Maurice Le Coutour, escaped from Cambodia in 1975.

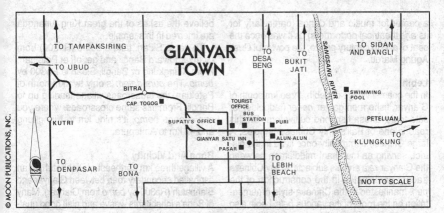

Shop for handwoven and hand-dyed textiles and *sarung* here. Just outside town are several textile shops and factories with showrooms selling *sarung,* colorful T-shirts, shirts (Rp30,000 and up), and stunning *ikat* (Rp10,000-15,000 per meter). Prices are high and items are generally not that good a value, but the designs and colors are utterly unique. Best to shop in the off-season. You could even pay more than in Denpasar or Kuta—a *sarung* costing Rp7500 in Legian runs Rp15,000 here. The Gianyar market sells *kain ikat* cheaper, but the lighting is so dim it's difficult to make out the colors and quality. When shopping, the clerks can only come down about 10-15% at most; the boss has to authorize bigger discounts. Always ask for a quantity wholesale price if you buy more than three of anything. Wander back to the sweatshops in the rear to view and photograph the tying, dyeing, and weaving processes, which use such antiquated machinery as bicycle wheels to separate the cotton thread from the loom.

There are at least 50 hand-weaving factories in Gianyar. The textile factories pay the young girls and boys Rp60,000 to Rp70,000 per month to work 0800-1600 every day but holidays; it takes about six hours to complete a *sarung.* The workers are too poor to wear any of the *sarung* they make—they wear cheap dresses instead.

At Jl. Astina Utara 11, tel. (0361) 93046 or 93443, fax 93442, **Cap Togog** is the largest and oldest weaving factory in Gianyar. Open 0800-1630 every day. No women's clothes, but *endek* fabric at Rp17,000 per meter, men's shirts starting at Rp30,000, silk *sarung* for Rp80,000. All fabrics made by 300 people working looms in the back. Colors won't run, as there is good quality control. For discounts, see manager Pande Nyoman Gede Maruta.

One of Gianyar's best known mills is **Cap Cili**, at the start of town next to the *puri,* Ciung Wanara 7, Gianyar 80511, tel. 93023, fax 93724. Owned by Pande Wayan Sira, this *ikat* hand-weaving factory is also well-established. Lengths of *endek* cloth (Rp10,000-12,500 per meter), hand-painted *batik,* short-sleeved shirts (Rp17,500), long-sleeved shirts (Rp25,000), purses (Rp5000), *sarung* (Rp10,000), and swim trunks (Rp6000). Big display room, helpful clerks, fixed prices; open 0800-1800 every day. Also check out the Bakti and Cap Putri Bali weaving centers.

Getting There And Away
Bemo pass often through Gianyar, a main crossroads and urban center. Distances and prices: Denpasar, 23 km, Rp700; Kutri, 10 km, Rp400; Bedulu, five km, Rp300; Sidan, three km, Rp300; Pejeng, 10 km, Rp400.

VICINITY OF GIANYAR TOWN

Bitra
In the village of Bitra, two km to the northwest, is a famous death temple (*pura dalem*) under a big banyan tree beside a river. A state *pura* dedicated to the descendents of the throne of Dewa Manggis is found at Beng, three km northeast of Gianyar. Kramas, four km to the south, is

a center for music and dance (particularly for its *arja* theatrical performers) as it was once the seat of a 17th century prince, the powerful Gusti Agung Maruti.

Lebih

In the coastal village of Lebih, three km south of Gianyar, fishermen gather *nener* (tadpoles) for sale to Javanese fishpond cultivators. On this road is one of Bali's only Chinese temples. A large Chinese community once lived in the district, serving as merchant middlemen between the Gianyar *raja* and his subjects. Many Chinese traders participated in the construction of the *puri,* manifested in the Chinese-style ornamentation on the roofs of the various *bale.* Lebih also features a Pura Segara (sea temple) with a view of Nusa Penida. Balinese from all over the district bring the ashes of their dead to this temple for final liberation of the soul in a ceremony known as *melasti.* The prettiest beach in the area is at Siyut, 10 km south (via Tulikup and Bekul) of the main Gianyar-Klungkung road. Because of the undertow, swimming here is dangerous.

Saba And Masceti Beaches

Seven km south of Gianyar, west of Lebih and near the mouth of the Pakrisan River, are the restful black- and gray-sand beaches of Saba and Masceti. A motorcylist will take you down to Saba Beach for around Rp2000. Watch the fishermen repair their boats and nets. Surfers will find a good right break over a sand and rock bottom. People from all over Gianyar stage a huge appeasement rite here annually to placate the forces that bring disease and calamity to people and crops.

Sidan

There are many exceptionally beautiful temples in the Gianyar area. A small but exquisitely carved temple is in Sidan, a village three km east of Gianyar town on the road to Bangli. Located right on a curve in the road near the village, this is a particularly fine example of a *pura dalem.* The *kulkul* tower is covered with extraordinary stone reliefs showing devil giants punishing tormented evildoers. Gates are flanked by deities of death, the main motif of the entire temple. Notice semi-divine Boma and Durga in the form of the terrifying widow-witch Rangda. The *pura* is dedicated to Merajapati, the caretaker of the dead. Some believe the ashes of the great King Airlangga are interred in this temple.

To get to Sidan, take a *bemo* (Rp300) from Gianyar toward Bangli and get off at Peteluan. From Klungkung or Bangli, Sidan is Rp300 by *bemo.* The *pura dalem* is only two km north of Peteluan, the crossroads village leading up to Bangli. From this same crossroads, where you can change *bemo,* it's nine km to Klungkung and 47 km to Amlapura.

Bona And Vicinity

A village three km northeast of Blahbatuh on an asphalted secondary road between Gianyar and Blahbatuh (Rp300 by *bemo* from Gianyar). Many of Bona's inhabitants weave and plait good quality baskets, hats, sandals, wallets, handbags, fans, dolls, birds, flowers, and enormous Christmas trees made of dried *lontar* palm leaves. You can order plain and spotted bamboo chairs, beds and tables, or wooden furniture here. Bona is also the venue of an extraordinary version of the modern *kecak,* the fire dance, first performed here in the 1930s. It happens at least six days weekly from 1800 to 2000. Entrance is Rp5000, including transport from Ubud at 1700; you can buy tickets at the door.

Visit the readymade *batik* and *ikat* outlet **Anoman Handicrafts Shop** up the road from Bona toward Gianyar. To see the *ikat* process, visit the weaving factory in Beng or one of at least 50 weaving factories and dozens of showrooms in and around the town of Gianyar, three km to the northeast. At Masceti, 10 km south of Bona via Medahan, is a much venerated sea temple, one of nine believed to protect the south coast of Bali from the forces of the sea. From Medahan, follow the signs to the sea through rice terraces and you'll come to the impressive rough coral *candi bentar* that marks the entrance to the temple. An attractive lily pond lies to the east, but the black-sand shore is marred by a hideously ornamented swimming pool and stage.

BLAHBATUH

Located four km east of the Sakah turnoff to Ubud on the main Denpasar-Gianyar highway, or seven km west of Gianyar. Blahbatuh District is known for the number of reservoirs where freshwater fish are raised. Bamboo furniture is made in Belaga near Blahbatuh and Bona. While in town, visit the orchid nurseries and the remarkable Pura Gaduh at the top of a steep stairway shaded by overhanging trees. Though it dates from the 14th century, the temple's statuary doesn't resemble Hindu-Javanese iconography of the time; it might be a native Balinese creation. There are numerous fanciful carvings inside the gate on the main stairway.

Blahbatuh is a minor kingdom founded by Gusti Ngurah Jelantik, prime minister of Gelgel, who led a famous military expedition against Java in the early 17th century. During the conflict, booty was brought back to Bali, including 21 extraordinary portrait masks of important Majapahit personages. Said to be the prototypes of all Balinese dance-drama masks, these *topeng* have been kept for over 600 years in rather dilapidated Pura Penataran Topeng near Blahbatuh's *puri*. These mysterious and powerful totems can only be viewed during the temple's *odalan* festival.

VICINITY OF BLAHBATUH

Blahbatuh is an important junction town from where you can head up to historic Gunung Kawi via Kutri, proceed to Bangli and the spectacular Batur region, or head for Klungkung, Rendang, and Besakih. About one km to the west of the town's crossroads is a small road to the south to **Belangsinga** village, the location of a waterfall on the Petanu River known as **Srog Srogan** or Air Terjun Tegenungan; it's reputedly a place of healing. Don't go on Sunday, but do go on the night of the full moon when *pedanda* come to pray at the nearby Pura Merta Jiwa ("Water of Immortality"). In the village of **Belaga,** one km to the east between Blahbatuh and Bona, look for the celebrated bamboo artisans who craft and sell implements and furniture of "black" and natural bamboo.

Kutri

Opposite Blahbatuh's *pura* is the road leading straight to Kutri (five km). About 400 meters south of the village is Pura Pedarman. This temple was built in honor of King Airlangga's mother Gunapriadarmapatni, a Javanese princess who married King Udayana, a prince from the Warmadewa dynasty, at the end of the 10th

century. She ruled Bali until her death in A.D. 1006. This royal widow-sorceress cursed and plagued her son's kingdom. Scholars speculate she is the historical origin of the witch-queen Rangda. The queen was cremated on this hill, her ashes then taken to Gunung Kawi where her tomb was carved out of the riverbank.

In the inner sanctum of the temple are several statues of eight-armed death goddess Durga in the small, white shrine on the right. From the lower temple, climb the steep stone steps up to the summit of Bukit Dharma through a forest of banyan trees gripping huge volcanic boulders. At the top is a sanctuary with an 11th-century stone frieze of Durga standing on a *nandi* (bull), possessed by a demon as she delivers the deathblow to the animal. Though well worn, her face is still arresting. In her hands are the trappings of supernatural power: javelin, shield, bow and arrow, winged conch shell, flaming sharp-edged disk (chakra), and flask containing *amerta* (holy nectar). With its fine classic Indian lines, this relief is considered one of the most finely wrought sculptures from the early Pejeng Kingdom.

Vicinity of Kutri: Bedulu lies three km north of Kutri, between Denpasar and Gunung Batur. The Archaeological Museum (Gedong Arca), two km north of Bedulu, houses historical objects and Song, Yuan, and Ming dynasty ceramics from the 13th to 19th centuries, a period dominated by Chinese and European merchants and navigators. The second courtyard contains 15 stone *sarcophagi* set around a small pool. Their design usually represents animals; others are shaped like modern coffins. The museum's architecture is a typical and well-preserved example of the local style. Visit nearby Goa Gajah, 1.5 km to the east, while you're in the area.

South of Kutri is the small village of Buruan, the home of well-known sculptors and dancers. In the *banjar* of Bangun Liman to the west, the *pura desa, pura puseh,* and *pura dalem* have been built all in a row; usually on Bali these temples are in different locations throughout the village. Down on the riverbanks, to the west of Bangun Liman, troupes of wild monkeys live in a natural habitat.

Gongmaker

About 500 meters north of Blahbatuh's main crossroads in Blahbatuh Kaja is a small road to the east (turn in at the *bale banjar*) which leads to Banjar Babakan, about 150 meters down on the left; ask for Kerajinan Gong Sidha Karya. This is the home and workplace of Bali's only surviving gongmaker, I Made Gabeleran, a world authority on bronze casting and Balinese instrument-making. Gongsmiths are held in high esteem on Bali, in a caste of their own. The Blahbatuh gong factory is the largest on Bali, a must-see for lovers of *gamelan*. This *pabrik gong* is bigger and deeper than it looks; at least five rooms are given over to the production of musical instruments. Go in the morning when the barefoot workers are the most active and it's not so hot. They start work at 0730 and finish at 1630. All kinds of Balinese musical instruments—*gangsa, trompong, kendang* drum, tiny bells—are forged here. In the rear of the factory, scenes from the Ramayana are ornately carved and then painted in red and gold on stands, frames, and cases made of jackfruit wood. These carvers are amazingly fast; two working from either end are able to carve a whole *gangsa* in a day.

This workshop's capacity is about five or six *gamelan* sets per year. Since there is no standard concert pitch, each *gamelan* is tuned slightly differently so the ensemble's unique character can emerge when played. You're allowed to sound the gongs here. A complete gong *kebyar*

sells for around 25 million *rupiah*. In the big display room in the middle of the complex, large gongs cost 1.5 million *rupiah,* small gongs go for Rp300,000, bell sets are Rp150,000, *kempur* run Rp800,000, *rebab* sell for Rp200,000, *cengceng* are Rp150,000, and xylophone-like *gangsa* range from Rp550,000 to Rp800,000.

Kemenuh

A major carving center about nine km southwest of Gianyar, Kemenuh is more active and considerably cheaper than Mas, especially for huge *garuda* statues and other mythic figures up to three meters high. The "driftwood carvings" of Kemenuh, if you can find them, are unique. Most of the carvings are created inside family compounds; the only advertisements are small signs on the compound gates. Three spacious, well-laid-out shops to visit here: Bali Budaya, Ida Bagus Marka, and Ida Bagus Komang Menaka. A wide range of woodcarvings, from fine art to functional pieces, can be seen at Gallery Marka in Banjar Sumampan, P.O. Box 277, Denpasar 80001, tel. (0361) 235775, fax 287-073. Over the years I.B. Marka has acquired the best work from the best artists—at high prices. Also see the *pura dalem* of Kemenuh for its intricate and beautiful carvings.

NORTHERN GIANYAR REGENCY

TARO

Between Pujungklod and Pujungkaja, take the road northwest for six km to the small village of Taro. Set on a hillside and hidden behind a palm forest, Taro seems removed from the world. The village marks the exact center of Bali. This area is known for its litchis, picturesque buff sandstone quarries, and unique architecture. These highlanders own the largest coffee plantation in the regency, a remnant of the big Chinese-owned estates of the last century. Taro domesticates the only hybrid breed of white cattle on the island. Since the locals believe this albino stock is holy, they are not used for work, may not be sold or eaten, and are strictly quarantined to keep the breed pure.

In Taro is the longest and one of the largest and most beautiful *bale agung* on Bali. This great pavilion, located in the village's *pura desa,* is the heart of the political and religious life of the community. Note the little bridge placed over a hole in front of the temple gate over which only the pure—gods and virgins—can pass.

SEBATU

Two km east of Pujung, take the road opposite the road to Taro. On the way, stop and see the Duckman, the first Balinese sculptor to carve ducks on a commercial scale—he's quite famous now. The Sebatu area is the best place on Bali to buy small wooden crafts. There's a cluster of shops in the countryside selling painted wooden suns, moons, stars, flying goddesses, and animals for only Rp1000-4000 apiece.

See the huge elephants at the shop **Sedana Yogya.** In Telepud, Wayan Astika carves fanciful suns and moons in natural browns and black stains, as well as stools in the shape of striped cats (Rp6000-10,000). He and other carvers create made-to-order work as well. When the road goes down, turn right toward Sebatu. In a small valley before the village is the **Pura Gunung Kawi,** a bathing place with stone stautes of maidens spouting water, carved stone *naga,* sacred golden carp, and lichen-covered ancient walls. The temple is in an exceptionally pretty spot against a backdrop of rich green foilage. At dusk small bats fill the air.

Sebatu is a village of woodcarvers and musicians. In front of the temple are a few shops displaying a mass of wooden crafts. Look for sensual figures and exquisitely carved *garuda* statuary. Note the difference between the masks of Mas and those of Sebatu; the lines and colors of masks from Mas are pure, while those of Sebatu are more exuberant. Mas makes god's masks, Sebatu devil's masks. Bargain as much as possible; the sellers are receptive. Every three days the village *pasar* takes place in the area in front of the temple.

From the temple, the road continues to the peaceful village itself, which few tourists ever visit. It consists mainly of one street of houses decorated with plants and flowers. The village is very active in dance and music, renowned as much as Peliatan. It's home to a noted dance troupe that once toured the world. Ask to see the photos of Balinese in fur coats in London. Incredibly, this small village possesses three orchestras. Rehearsals take place at 2000 every night, except during harvest. This is an opportunity to see people performing without enduring the clicking of cameras and flashes. Travelers without their own transportation should be aware that *bemo* back to Ubud stop running around 1600 or 1700. From Sebatu, a small road before the temple leads to Tampaksiring and on to Gunung Batur.

PUJUNG

A woodcarving village in the mountains five km north of Tegallalang. Between Tegallalang and Pujung are exquisite rice fields to the right side of the road. Coming from the south, 500 meters before turning right toward Sebatu, is a small shop selling handmade chess games starting at Rp30,000—a bit expensive, but beautiful work.

An even more spectacular road is from Gentong to Bayad. Heading east out of Ubud, turn left at the T-junction and travel northward towards Petulu. At Gentong turn right towards Kenderan. This road takes you through untraveled rice terrace landscapes all the way to Bayad; from here you can turn left to Pujung or right to Tampaksiring. Pujung village is divided into two *banjar,* Pujungklod and Pujungkaja. Visit the workshops of Anantaloga, Kresna Asih, Nyoman Pugra, Sri Sedana, Wayan Gede Artha, Wayang Nyungkal, and Wayang Tata, all specializing in different styles and sizes of *garuda* carvings, painted wooden banana trees, jewelry, and colored spirit boxes. Generally, the prices are better than in Mas or Kemenuh. The selection is immense, including some old woodcarvings, so take your time. Copies of old woodcarvings are a good deal. Always check for cracks; this can be a problem with cheap wood.

Leaving Pujung, travel another 20 km on the back road to Lake Batur. Just when you've had enough of this dirt road, Gunung Batur pops up. From Pujung, several roads head east to Tampaksiring; take the smaller one which bears left off the main road as it turns down to the *pasar.*

TAMPAKSIRING

The source of the Pakrisan River and one of the earliest centers of Hinduism on Bali, Tampaksiring lies on the road to Bangli and Kintamani, just 14 km northeast of Ubud. The town is south of the sacred bathing place of Tirta Empul near the source of the Pakrisan River and upstream from monumental Gunung Kawi. Get there by taking a *bemo* first to Gianyar, then another to Tampaksiring (Rp600). The weather here is cool and it often rains lightly in the evenings.

Accommodations And Food

The only place to stay in the area is **Gusty Homestay,** just 100 meters from the main road, but it's a grotty dive (Rp5000 pp, no breakfast). If coming from the south it's on the left, behind the market in the middle of town. Gusty does serve meals. Chinese-style **Tampaksiring Restaurant,** on the left as you come into Tampaksiring from the south, is good but pricey. The *warung* in front of Tirta Empul are okay for snacks and light refreshments. At the top of the stairs at Gunung Kawi enjoy *bubur sayur bayan* (porridge and vegetables) for only Rp200.

Tirta Empul

Situated in a valley in the northeast corner of Tampaksiring under a spectacular banyan tree, 37 km northeast of Denpasar at the end of a well-signposted road, the Tirta Empul temple and its 20 small sugar-palm thatched shrines are beautifully decorated and maintained. Savor the serene atmosphere of the complex, which is set against a backdrop of surviving forest. Even the souvenir shop outside the temple is neat and orderly. Tirta Empul is on nearly every tour group's central Bali itinerary. Fleets of tour buses visit the site. From the parking lot, visitors have to run the usual gauntlet of souvenir stands to the temple compound, which you may enter after renting a sash. Seeking protective bless-

ings and deliverance from illness, people journey from all over Bali to bathe in this sacred cleansing spring where terrifying *garuda* scowl down on naked bathers floating among the lily pads. Seeing it on a rainy day adds even more mystery to the site.

There's a large square altar dedicated to Batara Indra and elaborate carvings adorn the lichen-covered walls surrounding the pools. Built under the rule of Sri Candrabhaya Singha Warmadewa in the 10th century, the complex was completely restored and given a new paint job in 1969. Tirta Empul conforms to the structure of most Balinese temples. It's divided into three main courtyards: the front, the middle, and the inner sanctum. Backing the outer courtyard are two rectangular bathing pools, one each for men and women. According to tradition, each of the pool's 15 fountains has a specific function: spiritual purification, cleansing from evil, antidote to poison. The natural freshwater spring at a higher level is the source of the water that bubbles up under the pools. The water is so clear plants growing at the bottom of the pool are clearly visible, as are a number of fish and a rather large eel. Because it's believed that from this spring bubbles the elixir of immortality, it's surrounded by a wall to prevent it from being profaned.

The Balinese use holy water as an essential part of almost every ritual. Their religion is in fact called Agama Tirta, or "The Religion of the Holy Water." Tirta Empul's water is looked upon as the holiest on Bali, widely thought to possess magical curative powers. The spring is believed to have been created by the god Indra, who pierced the earth to tap *amerta,* the restoring waters that brought back to life his army, which was poisoned by the demon-king Mayadanava.

Events

Regular ceremonies are held at this sanctuary, particularly during Galungan when dance clubs from the surrounding area bring their sacred *barong* masks to be purified by the spring's water.

An inscription in Old Balinese found in the village of Manukaya states that two ponds were formed here in A.D. 962. When the badly worn inscription was finally deciphered by Sutterheim in 1969, it described in detail the ritual cleansing of a holy stone during the full moon of the fourth month in the Balinese calendar. For more than 1,000 years, villagers from Manukaya carried a stone to the spring for purification rites on the precise day each year of Tirta Empul's founding, never knowing the origin or the reason, only that it was *adat*. Since none of the villagers then knew what the old inscription read, the date of the temple's founding must have been handed down orally through 33 generations of invasions, dynastic changes, and natural disasters.

Crafts

In the parking lot are 400 meters of stalls selling everything from bone and ivory carvings to coconut shell ornaments and chess sets. The best deals are the painted wooden jewelry and carved cow bone ornaments. The bone- and ivory-carving industry is centered around Manukaya to the north of Tirta Empul.

This is also the area for Bali quilts, handpainted fabrics quilted by machine, as well as colorful and cleverly designed bedcovers. Two or three km beyond Tampaksiring you'll see quilts flapping in the wind, draped on lines outside at least 12 shops specializing in color-rich—bordering on garish—quilts in a variety of sizes. Prices run Rp75,000-250,000. You can usually bargain down from there. Dacron-filled quilts are nearly twice as expensive as those filled with foam. Hand-painted cotton shirts and kimonos also for sale. **Gardana Shop,** beyond Tampaksiring in Kayuambua, offers a good selection.

Vicinity Of Tampaksiring

Pura Gumang is a 30-minute walk northeast of Munukaya. Surrounded by large mossy trees, this early Shivaite temple has a large gateway, a huge linga and trident, carvings of mythical Hindu-Javanese sea monsters, and a worn statue of Shiva's bull Nandi. **Pura Mengening,** a little west of Tirta Empul, is a sacred and picturesque spring under a large tree. The freestanding *candi* here, containing some ancient statues, is similar to those at Gunung Kawi. Atop a nearby hill is a venerable old *pura* which may have been dedicated to King Udayana. The connection between the three holy sites of Tirta Mancingan, Tirta Empul, and Gunung Kawi is obvious.

ISTANA TAMPAKSIRING

Two km north of Tampaksiring, the road branches to the right for Tirta Empul, while the left road climbs to a hilltop retreat built by Sukarno in 1954. Park for Rp500 and pay an entrance fee of Rp500. With its large, well-kept lawns, this is a lovely place to walk. Since you can't enter any of the buildings, content yourself with looking in the windows.

This splendid presidential palace, its two main buildings connected by a footbridge, is a classic example of the first truly Indonesian national architectural style. The sprawling, one-story buildings, built along the lines of a Javanese *pendopo,* feature grooved plaster columns and the geometrically hardlined look of the art deco era. Sukarno is said to have designed the whole complex, a sort of ranch-house/social realism combo, an architectural amalgam he picked up during his engineering training at ITB in Bandung. Sukarno was half Balinese and he visited the island frequently, usually staying in this resthouse. The *istana* purposefully and incongruously overlooks the Balinese Fountain of Eternal Youth, as if it were the dictator's intention to prolong his "President-for-Life" status indefinitely. When Suharto visits, he always stays in Wisma Negara rather than Wisma Merdeka, where Sukarno's ghost is said to roam.

On the palace grounds are four complexes: Wisma Merdeka, the personal residence of the president; Wisma Negara, guesthouse for friends or guests of state; Wisma Yudistira, for use by the press corps; and Wisma Bima, for presidential bodyguards. There's also a beautiful *pendopo* for dance performances and a small aviary with hornbills, eagles, and peacocks. Completely restored in 1957 and well-maintained ever since, all buildings are in mint condition with some of the original furnishings intact.

Hordes of Japanese, fascinated with Sukarno memorabilia, visit the *istana.* The palace provides an excellent view of the whole Tirta Empul sanctuary; the story goes that the dictator could look down through a telescope upon naked women bathing below, sending for those who pleased him and eventually siring a few children upon them. You may meet Sukarno's daughter, now in her thirties, working in Warung Bitar in the parking lot/souvenir market.

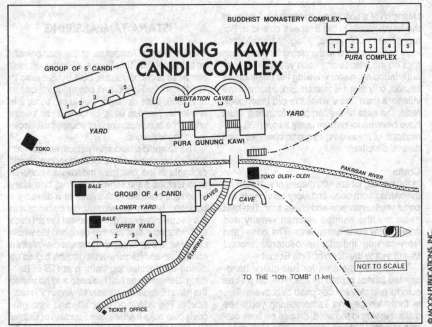

GUNUNG KAWI CANDI COMPLEX

BUDDHIST MONASTERY COMPLEX

1 2 3 4 5
PURA COMPLEX

GROUP OF 5 CANDI
1 2 3 4 5

MEDITATION CAVES

YARD

YARD

TOKO

PURA GUNUNG KAWI

PAKRISAN RIVER

TOKO OLEH - OLEH

BALE

GROUP OF 4 CANDI
LOWER YARD

CAVES

CAVE

BALE

UPPER YARD
1 2 3 4

STAIRWAY

NOT TO SCALE

TO THE "10th TOMB" (1 km)

TICKET OFFICE

© MOON PUBLICATIONS, INC.

GUNUNG KAWI

Two km south of Tampaksiring, on the banks of the upper course of the sacred Pakrisan River, Gunung Kawi ("Mountain of Poetry") lies in the heart of the archaeologically rich Pejeng area, a region where Hinduism first took hold on Bali. This is one of the more impressive historical sites on Bali: a blinding green watery canyon where two rows of ancient blackened tombs have been hewn out of natural rock hillsides as royal memorials.

The whole complex is well-swept and well-maintained and should be visited in the cool mornings or late afternoons when few tourists are about. At the lookout on top of the long, steep stairway, look down upon overwhelming scenery: sunlit waterfalls and palm-studded rice terraces plunging to a deep ravine with a rushing river flowing through it all. The holy water of the river was meant to sanctify the site. Carved into niches on two facing cliffs, the somber and un-embellished temples contain no interior chambers, only facades. Built in the late 11th century,

the temples are remarkably well-preserved. There are 10 temples in all. Across the gorge is an abandoned hermitage for the keepers of the tombs. All around flows holy water and steep-sided rock walls covered with dripping moss, all of which gives the site an elevated and venerated atmosphere.

History

Goa Gajah and these temples are the earliest known monuments of Balinese art. The Balinese knew of the Gunung Kawi *candi* long before they were "discovered" by H.T. Damte in 1920. Local lore says the legendary Kebo Iwo carved the ancient structures in one night with his fingernails—he's credited with carving nearly all the ancient monuments between the Pakrisan and Petanu rivers.

Heavily weathered inscriptions etched over the sham doors of the *candi* date construction to the 11th century. The highly decorative script used here was in vogue during the East Javanese Kediri period. The Balinese usually prefer ornamentation to bulk, but not at Gunung Kawi, where the monolithic-style architecture obviously originates from Java. Urs Ramseyer observed that the tombs resemble Indian temples.

Stone monuments are rare on Bali, a fact which only adds to the mystery surrounding the purpose of the structures. The structural difference between these and Javanese *candi* is that the impressively-scaled Gunung Kawi monuments are not freestanding but are hewn in relief out of a solid rock hillside. There's little doubt each temple served as a memorial to deified royalty, as they're shaped like the burial towers found all over Central and East Java. The exact identity of the royal personages honored here is unknown. One very credible theory suggests the five *candi* in the main group were built for King Udayana, his Javanese queen Gunapriya, his concubine, his illustrious eldest son Erlangga who ruled over East Java, and his youngest son Anak Wungsu. Reigning over Bali from A.D. 1050 to 1077, Anak Wungsu is believed to have given up his kingdom to become a religious hermit.

The *candi* on the far left in the row of five, placed higher than the rest, may be that of King Udayana. The four *candi* on the other side of the river were built for the chief concubines of Anak Wungsu. Another theory suggests this whole mausoleum complex enshrines the memory of only Anak Wungsu and his royal wives and favorite concubines, who most likely immolated themelves to follow their sovereign into the afterlife.

Attractions

The "Tenth Tomb," discovered only a few years after Gunung Kawi's discovery by W.O.J. Nieuwenkamp, is either a memorial to a high priest or a high-caste state official, possibly Anak Wungsu's prime minister, Rakryan, who died after his master. A boy from the *toko oleh-oleh* (souvenir shop) near the bridge will take you along a path through *sawah* to this odd *candi* removed from the main complex. The one-km-long walk takes you by a small gateway hewn from rock. To the left of the Tenth Tomb are more niches.

To the right of the main ensemble of temples is a Buddhist monks' cloister (*patapan*) with five cells carved out of rock. In the confluence of the Oos River in Campuan, near Ubud, several other ascetic cells were also discovered, indi-

cating the monastic tradition was entrenched in 11th-century Bali. Gunung Kawi's cloister inmates most likely were caretakers of the *candi*. There's a second hermitage near the main cloister, consisting of niches around a central courtyard, which might have served as sleeping quarters for visiting pilgrims.

Getting There And Away

From Tampaksiring, Gunung Kawi is a two-km walk south on the road to Pejeng, or take a *bemo* for Rp300. The small road to the tombs is on the left in Desa Panaka. From the main road, walk 600 meters to the ticket office—Rp550 entrance, Rp300 parking—then walk through a fortress-like gateway and descend 315 stone steps that wind down into the gorge, at one point through a stretch of solid rock, emerging onto the bank of the river.

Souvenir and drink stands line the walkway down to the ravine but their presence is not cloying. During the descent, pause along the way to catch the views. At one point you can make out the tip of Pura Mengening. There are actually two Gunung Kawis, so don't be confused. In Sebatu village five km to the north is the bathing spot of Pura Gunung Kawi.

TEGALLALANG

From Keliki, there's a good road to this village north of Ubud, about five km before Sebatu. Or take the path on the right between Ubud and Campuan, go down to the river, and at the bottom of the ravine take the right fork up to Tegallalang—you'll be transported back to the Bali of the 1950s. For the Gunung Kawi monuments and Tirta Empul temple in Tampaksiring, take the road from Tegallalang via Pujung, or enjoy the very scenic drive from Tegallalang to the Bali Aga mountain village of Taro.

The Tegallalang area is the place to buy woodcarvings—flowers, animals, birds—at better prices than in Ubud. Particularly known for superb *garuda* statues. Look in at the Bunga Mekar Art Shop, run by Ketut Tunas; it's cheaper and has more creative suns and moons than the shop next door. Few tourists ever visit these shops so you'll be received enthusiastically.

UBUD

Ubud lies only 36 km from the resorts on the southern coast. The name for this royal village is derived from the Balinese word *ubad* (medicine), the moniker of an herb with healing properties which grows along the nearby Oos River. If you aren't interested in tourist hype but want comfortable accommodations at good prices, a central location, and all the facilities in a less hurried rural environment than the south, the Ubud area is for you. Even with the bumper-to-bumper traffic and thousands of tourists during Bali's peak tourist seasons, when it's difficult to find a parking space, Ubud still shows glimpses of its basically rural character.

However, this may not be your first impression. When you first arrive, you might get the feeling there are more visitors here than Balinese. With its hundreds of art galleries, studios, and souvenir shops, and the flurry and congestion around the two-story market on the main road, Ubud looks like a big commercial scene—totally disenchanting. A monster, Sarinah-style department store, with crafts from all over Indonesia, has gone up on Monkey Forest Road. Development is so frenetic now that shops, homestays, hotels, and restaurants ring the soccer field. The Menara has been taken down—the end of an era—and a Kuta-style glitzy restaurant put up in its place.

The village now seems to be moving toward Padangtegal, with new businesses always opening. The newest area to develop is Jl. Sukma. Some years ago it was just a sleepy dirt road with homes and a few *losmen* and shops, but now it's paved all the way from the main road to the junction with the highway to Gianyar, cluttered with scores of accommodations, shops, and new restaurants.

The town and its surrounding collection of villages offers the best value accommodations on Bali, and certainly the best food. In the immediate outskirts, as little as 100 meters from the main road, traditional culture and the demands of the tourist industry coexist to some degree. Culture goes on in spite of the influx of tourists and their dollars, and most of the town is touristy without being tacky. It's classier than Kuta, with upper middle-class tourists and young travelers in the majority. Although new tourist services are added constantly, part of the Ubud area's charm is that these villages have a very spotty power supply, with electricity always at a premium. A flashlight is definitely needed to wend your way safely at night along rutted, muddy back lanes. Also make sure your room is secure; thievery is worst on Monkey Forest Road.

The air here is pungent—it smells of earth, river, and rainforest. Ubud is higher and cooler than the south, with delightful fresh air and fewer flies and mosquitos. The stars over Ubud almost crowd out the sky they're so bright, and during the day the heavens are crowned with fluffy cumulus and wispy cirrus clouds. Wandering around in the crisp night air is pleasant and safe.

Culturally speaking, Ubud is to Bali what Yogyakarta is to Java. Ever since the German painter Walter Spies made his home here in the 1930s, Ubud has been a haven for both native and European artists. In an area of 10 square km in and around this village live Bali's most accomplished dancers, musicians, painters, and carvers. Temple festivals, celebrations, and performing arts are offered somewhere in the area every day of the week. Ubud is also the expat capital of Bali. A permanent Western community is here because cultural and natural attributes make it the ideal place for those who wish to stay for any length of time in Bali. Long-term accommodations are plentiful, low-cost, and comfortable. From your *losmen* or homestay family you can learn how to make a bamboo mouth harp, study painting, maskmaking, and *gamelan,* or learn the art of the *dalang.*

History

The royal village of Ubud grew to prosperity in the fertile land between rivers in the 19th century, ruled by feudal lords who paid allegiance to the *raja* of Gianyar. Foremost among them were the greatly respected Sukawatis, who at one time controlled most of the surrounding districts. The Sukawatis learned to work within the Dutch colonial system through their membership in the Volksraad, the People's Council based in Batavia, and they became politically powerful on Bali by

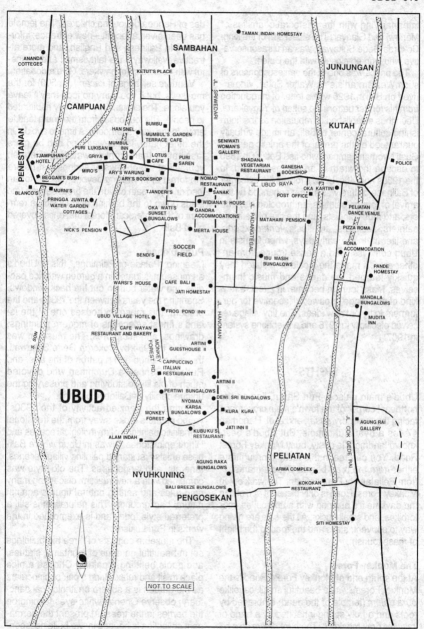

TAMAN INDAH HOMESTAY

SAMBAHAN

JUNJUNGAN

ANANDA COTTEGES

KETUT'S PLACE

KUTAH

CAMPUAN

BUMBU

HAN SNEL

MUMBUL'S GARDEN TERRACE CAFE

SENIWATI WOMAN'S GALLERY

SHADANA VEGETARIAN RESTAURANT

GANESHA BOOKSHOP

POLICE

PENESTANAN

PURI LUKISAN

MUMBUL INN

GRIYA

LOTUS CAFE

PURI SAREN

TJAMPUHAN HOTEL

MIRO'S

ARY'S WARUNG
ARY'S BOOKSHOP

NOMAD RESTAURANT

OKA KARTINI

BEGGAR'S BUSH

SANAK

JL UBUD RAYA

POST OFFICE

BLANCO'S

MURNI'S

TJANDERI'S

WIDIANA'S HOUSE

PELIATAN DANCE VENUE

PRINGGA JUWITA WATER GARDEN COTTAGES

OKA WATI'S SUNSET BUNGALOWS

GANDRA ACCOMMODATIONS

MATAHARI PENSION

PIZZA ROMA

NICK'S PENSION

MERTA HOUSE

JL PADANGTEGAL

RONA ACCOMMODATION

SOCCER FIELD

PANDE HOMESTAY

BENDI'S

IBU MASIH BUNGALOWS

WARSI'S HOUSE

CAFE BALI

MANDALA BUNGALOWS

JATI HOMESTAY

MUDITA INN

FROG POND INN

JL HANOMAN

UBUD VILLAGE HOTEL

CAFE WAYAN RESTAURANT AND BAKERY

ARTINI GUESTHOUSE II

UBUD

MONKEY FOREST RD.

CAPPUCCINO ITALIAN RESTAURANT

ARTINI II

PERTIWI BUNGALOWS

DEWI SRI BUNGALOWS

JL COK GEDE RAI

AGUNG RAI GALLERY

NYOMAN KARSA BUNGALOWS

KURA KURA

MONKEY FOREST

JATI INN II

ALAM INDAH

KUBUKU'S RESTAURANT

PELIATAN

AGUNG RAKA BUNGALOWS

ARMA COMPLEX

NYUHKUNING

BALI BREEZE BUNGALOWS

KOKOKAN RESTAURANT

PENGOSEKAN

SITI HOMESTAY

S SON

NOT TO SCALE

© MOON PUBLICATIONS, INC.

intermarrying with the aristocratic families of Mengwi and Gianyar. The eldest son of the king, Cokorda Gede Sukawati, was an ultraconservative who worked closely with the Dutch.

The prince was one of the earliest sponsors of such Western artists as Walter Spies, who arrived on Bali in 1925 with a letter of introduction from his former patron, the sultan of Yogyakarta. Ubud thus established its reputation as the flourishing cultural center of Bali, an image virtually guaranteed by the arrival of the artistic genius I Gusti Nyoman Lempad, who fled Bedulu in 1890 to escape the wrath of an oppressive lord. In the 1930s and '40s, Ubud's role as the epicenter of Balinese culture was further enhanced by the arrival of foreign painters, anthropologists, writers, and musicologists, and the rise of Balinese painters, sculptors, architects, *lontar* experts, and literati. In the early days, when tourists in Ubud commissioned a dance troupe from another area, it made the locals so agitated they quickly learned the dance and music themselves. Mass tourism became, in effect, a new kind of patronage, a powerful incentive for performers to try out new ideas. The tiny village received electricity in 1976 and a telephone system in 1987.

SIGHTS

Ubud's main palace, Puri Saren, lies on the northeast corner of the town's main crossroads facing the two-story *pasar,* and at Jl. Hanoman 47 lies a beautiful temple. But Ubud's best-known landmark is dusty, busy Monkey Forest Road. You can reach this tacky thoroughfare either from the road beside Ubud's market or from Peliatan via Pengosekan. The walk down Monkey Forest Road is only pleasant at night; in the daytime it's buzzing with automobiles, motorbikes, and small trucks. All the *bale* are giving way to souvenir stalls and the road to the blight of mass tourism.

The Monkey Forest

At the south end of Monkey Forest Road is the Monkey Forest, with a beautiful small, cavelike *pura dalem* (temple of the dead) embraced by roots and a holy spring inhabited by a band of irascible gray monkeys. The *pura dalem* on a hill around the corner contains well-executed statues of Rangda devouring children. The temple has been given a facelift—new entrance, information in Balinese and English, and more attractive walkways. It's fairly small and peaceful with no persistent hawkers. Give a donation.

Vendors sell bags of *kacang* (Rp500) for the monkeys, but if you carry no food they'll leave you alone. The simians are definitely habituated to people. The tour buses from the south tend to arrive in the early afternoons, a time to avoid. On the other hand, tourist-watching can be more fascinating than monkey-watching. Refresh yourself at the cold-water springs just before the forest or in *warung* beyond (Rp500 for an iced drink). A path beside the great banyan tree leads down to the bathing place inside a remnant of the dipterocarp forest that once covered all of Bali.

Puri Lukisan

Meaning "Palace of Paintings," this is Ubud's art museum, situated in a garden with rice paddies and water buffalo out the back windows. Spanning the years between the 1930s and the present, this museum houses one of the island's finest selections of modern paintings, drawings, and sculptures. The museum was founded in 1954 by Cokorda Gede Sukawati, the *raja* of Ubud and a patron of the arts, and Rudolph Bonnet, a Dutchman who devoted much of his life to studying and preserving the unique quality of Balinese painting.

During the frenzied activity of the 1930s, young painters broke away from the traditional formalistic paintings of mythological scenes and Hindu epic stories. It was in Ubud where Balinese artists first started painting village scenes, funerals, and landscapes. The old style was combined with a new realism, discarding many rigid rules and setting natural figures against natural backgrounds. This naturalism is still a preferred style today and is exemplified in the works in Puri Lukisan.

The museum consists of three big buildings set in beautiful gardens of fountains, statues, and pools befitting a palace. Choose a nice place to sit and relax. Bring a pair of binoculars as the garden is a superb ornithological sanctuary; observe Oriental white-eyes feeding on the berries in the trees. At present the permanent collection is housed in two buildings, containing hundreds of sculptures and paintings displayed in chronological order, covering the whole evolution into modern idiom with paintings of dances, temples, feasts, rice harvests, *wayang* stories, and Balinese folklore. The third building is operated by a local painters' cooperative. Here you'll get an overview of all the different stylistic trends in Balinese art. The works in the cooperative are for sale and prices are negotiable; if you see an artist you like, note his name and village and visit his private gallery. Use the works in this museum as standards of excellence by which to judge the paintings in Ubud's galleries and studios.

Tragically, the works in Puri Lukisan's permanent exhibits have fallen into serious disrepair. Because of the lack of air-conditioning in this humid, tropical climate, the paintings are steadily deteriorating—green fungus under the glass eats away at the canvases. Open daily 0800-1600; entrance Rp500. The spacious garden alone is worth the price of admission.

ACCOMMODATIONS

The Ubud area offers the largest selection of inland accommodations on Bali, suiting everyone's tastes and budget. Even the upscale places are a bargain. There are over 300 homestays and *losmen*, most inside family compounds, so you have plenty of choice and plenty of bargaining power. The majority are "illegal," meaning they don't pay taxes and operate without a license. These inexpensive inns open and close practically overnight.

The Ubud area now has six international-standard accommodations: Puri Komandalu, Amandari, Kupu Kupu Barong, Ulun Ubud, Villa Cahaya Dewata, and Ubud Village. There are 80-odd places on the Monkey Forest Road alone. Jalans Hanoman, Kajeng, and Banjartegal are also full of ritzy homestays. And the frenzied building goes on everywhere.

Walk along the back lanes of Ubud's various *kampung* off the main road to discover Ubud's cheapest, cleanest, quietest, and most picturesque *losmen* and homestays. You've got to look around; many places charge Rp52,000 for terrible rooms. Despite the multitude of tourists, it's still easy to find the perfect guesthouse—a lovely bungalow with gilded doors, shower, and porch facing a quiet, storybook garden. Far from the night cries of those dreaded Ubud dogs, only Rp8000-15,000. Because of the intense competition, in the off season every accommodation gives a discount of at least 10% if you stay a week or more. Be sure to negotiate. Although you can find every class of accommodations all over the Ubud area, in July and August the village is flooded with French and German tourists and lodging is expensive and difficult to find.

Except for the higher priced hotels (Rp63,000 and up), breakfast is always included in the price, and staff will bring you tea all day long. In upscale hotels, Western breakfasts cost at least Rp10,000. Most Rp8,000 to Rp15,000 places really knock themselves out serving you an extraordinary breakfast of fruit salad, banana pancakes, eggs, jaffles, tea or coffee—the best value in all of Bali. Only in the higher priced categories do Ubud accommodations offer hot water and air-conditioning, but you really don't need them. This class of hotel will invariably be able to arrange such recreational activities as transport to *gamelan* and cultural performances, whitewater rafting, pony-riding tours, birdwalks, trekking, volcano climbing, and mountain bike riding. The following is only a sampling of Ubud's 300-plus accommodations.

Budget
The average price for a small, tidy room in a family lodging is around Rp8000 s, Rp15,000 d. You share clean, Balinese-style bathrooms with the family or with other travelers. These low-end places don't normally have telephones, but you may store your baggage and souvenirs for free. An excellent example is **Alinda**, Jl. Hanoman 64 (opposite Dewi Sri Bungalows), with very clean new rooms with toilet, cold shower, and *mandi* for Rp12,000 d in the off season, Rp15,000 d in the high season, including above average breakfast.

An unusual homestay is **Arimurti and Sukadana Homestay**, Jl. Jembawan in Banjar Padantegal Kaja, Lorong Rinjani 4. Take the road beside the post office south, then turn left and follow a long, bamboo-shaded lane to this quiet and secluded cottage-like accommodation—like a treehouse in the jungle. The owner is a primary school teacher and *wayang* puppeteer who teaches tourists the Balinese and Indonesian languages on the side. Doesn't get many guests because it's too far a walk from Ubud's *bemo* stop. Only Rp15,000 d with attached shower, toilet, and breakfast of *pisang goreng,* omelette, black rice pudding, hardboiled egg, tea or coffee all day.

At **Arja Inn,** Jl. Kajeng 9, you have your own *mandi,* mosquito net, and comfy bed. Lovely family, very private—all for only Rp15,000 d. The friendly **Artini I** asks Rp7000-8000 s, Rp12,000-15,000 d for rooms with their own *mandi,* sizable veranda, magnificent garden, and award-winning breakfast. Quiet. Artini Restaurant is opposite. **Frog Pond Inn** gets consistently wonderful reviews. The owner is friendly and the rooms have billowy beds, clean white sheets, private *mandi* and toilet, and bottled water; surrounded by a tropical garden.

Gandra Accommodations, Jl. Karna 88, Ubud Kelod, 100 meters from Yuni's, charges only Rp8000-10,000 s, Rp10,000-13,000 d. Beautiful gardens, clean rooms, great breakfast of fresh fruit and jaffles, free storage service, helpful family, nice garden. Dip into some of the old novels. One of the best accommodations for the price in Indonesia, yet only five minutes from Ubud's center. Walk down Monkey Forest Road 100 meters and turn left at the sign. A small shop sells blankets, clothes, and film at reasonable prices. Go out the back entrance and take a right to **Warung Seroni**—a great place to eat. **Matahari Pension** (Rp12,000 s) is far from places to eat and there may be no other guests there at the time, but so what? **Merta House,** Jl. Karna 96 (parallel with Monkey Forest Road), charges Rp8000 to Rp12,000 (all rooms the same). The smiling woman who runs this place is a real character; bargain with her. **Mimpi's Bungalows,** Jl. Hanoman 60, Padangtegal (see the sign Friendly Place to Stay), is owned by an elegant man, Made Suarta, a dancer and painter of miniatures. The front looks really rustic but in the back are several spotless bungalows (Rp15,000 d).

Mumbul Inn on Jl. Raya near Lotus Cafe has Rp25,000 d rooms upstairs. Really airy, with swarms of fireflies and an amazing frog chorus each night. Rooms downstairs have fans. Nice people. The restaurant serves whole wheat bread and inventive, nutritious meals. Pay just Rp2500 per day to swim in the pool next door. **Nick's Pension,** tel. (0361) 975-636, 15 meters from Oka Wati's down a ravine, is only Rp12,000 d and quite comfortable, offering a beautiful view over rice fields on Monkey Forest Road. Rates are Rp18,000 s or d or Rp25,000 with hot water. Good service, and considering its proximity to the town's center, it doesn't get much better than this. Clean, quiet, **Nyoman Warta Accommodations** (Banjar Tebesaya 25) offers some of the finest bungalows in the Ubud area for only Rp10,000 s, Rp12,000 d. You get coffee and tea all day long, as well as a nice breakfast of fruit salad, pancakes, and coffee. This is a family business run by very kind people. It lies about 200 meters from the center of Ubud down a small road near the cemetery.

Oka Homestay is tucked behind Puri Saren at Jl. Bingung 18. It's quiet, secure, small—just four rooms, each with *mandi,* shower, toilet. First and foremost a traditional family home. Oka speaks excellent English and will patiently and cheerfully encourage your *bahasa.* You feel like you're staying with friends—they always make time to chat, answer your questions, loan and help you dress in *adat* clothing, and include you in family and community life and ceremonies. Breakfasts are sensational and often extra treats appear. **Pande Permai** is recommended highly. Built in 1990, it has clean rooms with hot showers overlooking a gorge. Quiet and peaceful, with very nice people. The owner is principal of a high school. A disadvantage is that the delicious breakfasts are served late. It's also on top of the hill on Monkey Forest Road so it's a bit of a walk to downtown Ubud. In the low season bargain easily to Rp15,000 s. **Rona's Accommodations and Book Exchange,** Jl. Tebesaya 23, tel. and fax 975-120, is the ideal place to acclimate. Rona's is hardly ever empty, but when it is call for a free pickup in the Ubud area. The rooms, though basic, are excellent—comfortable, cleaned daily, and cheap (Rp10,000 s, Rp12,000 d). Price includes mosquito net, fan, towels, soap, toilet paper, wardrobe, private bath. Rona's also has Rp20,000 bungalows with showers (no hot water) and deluxe rooms for Rp30,000 with double bed, wardrobe, shower, flush toilet, and sink. The Indonesian food served in the restaurant is high quality and cheap, with a large and varied two-course breakfast and free tea or coffee all day. Luggage storage, security box, and use of multilingual library are free. Also available: laundry service, moneychanger, dance and shuttle bus tickets, tour service.

Sudana Homestay, Jl. Goutama 11, run by one of the friendliest families in Ubud, is in a traditional Ubud neighborhood not far from the town's center, just down from the Nomad office on a small street between Jl. Hanoman and Monkey Forest Road. The homestay is basic (Rp8000 s, Rp12,000 d) with only two rooms carved out of an old banana garden. Very clean, inside *mandi,* no fans, but an airy shared porch; fruit salad and jaffle breakfast, endless tea and coffee. A good place to learn and practice Indonesian and gain insight into local festivals. Relaxing **Taman Indah Homestay,** off the main road on Jl. Sandat, has a beautiful view of rice fields. Walk down Jl. Sandat onto a dirt path and you'll come to a clearing in the middle of *sawah;* turn left. Rooms are equipped with two beds, *batik* bedsheets, toilet, shower, mosquito net, fan, cool tile floor, furnished patio—all this and breakfast for only Rp20,000 d. At the start of Monkey Forest Road, on the left, is **Tjanderi's,** tel. 975-054, a central, lively, long-established *losmen* with five rooms with bath and toilet (Rp10,000 s or d), or high bungalow rooms in the back for Rp12,000 s or d with inside *mandi.* Banana sweets in the morning. You can arrange for motorbike rental here. Ask about the two beautiful, secluded bungalows up in the rice paddies (for Rp25,000) with electricity, plumbing, and a nice breeze, surrounded by a goldfish pond and accessible by motorbike.

Warsi's House, on Monkey Forest Road, has upstairs rooms for Rp35,000 overlooking the family compound and beautiful gardens. Rooms have fans, two double beds, Western toilet, shower with ventilator, inside tub with hot water, towels, and good security. Upstairs rooms have possibly the best view of the Monkey Forest. The room rate includes a large breakfast of banana pancakes, fresh fruit salad, tea or coffee; toast and eggs also available. Warsi is a sharp businessperson and also owns a boutique. She likes to dress her guests up in traditional attire and take them to temple festivals. Or try **Widiana's House** (Jl. Karna 87), down a small alley behind Ubud's market, with large airy clean bungalows with inside *mandi* nestled in a dense, shady, cool array of trees—very private yet extremely centrally located; Rp8000 s with breakfast. Recommended.

Moderate

Artini II Guesthouse, on Jl. Hanoman in Padangtegal Kelod, tel. (0361) 975-348, is in a beautiful, peaceful walled compound with 18 rooms and bungalows (Rp25,000-35,000) lined with bamboo matting. It features inside baths, hot/cold water, fans, bamboo frame beds, and a porch facing a nice garden. **Dewi Sri Bungalows,** Jl. Hanoman in Padangtegal, P.O. Box 23, Ubud 80571, tel. 975-300, is a haven in the rice fields with three different classes of self-contained bungalows: standard Rp63,000, second story Rp84,000, or suite Rp105,000; American or continental breakfast included. The duplexes are really nice, with a private bedroom upstairs, relaxing open-air living area below, and walled open-air bath. Hot water, pool, attentive staff, coffee shop. A ten-minute walk from Jl. Raya, its main draw is the antique exterior and interior. **Kubu Ku's Guesthouse** is a magical environment where guests lounge on couches, watching the sun set over rice paddies while listening to a whole collection of elegant windchimes. The artist who runs it speaks English well. He serves vegetarian and Indian food prepared by a French meditation teacher. Get one of the two beautiful airy rooms right on the rice paddies, complete with Western bathrooms, hot water, and large beds for only Rp38,000 d. A favorite spot.

Among the quietest places is **Ibu Masih Bungalows,** tel. 975-062, on Monkey Forest Rd. with bed, breakfast, fan, private bathroom and shower for Rp20,000-50,000. A new place with the same proprietor is **Masih Accommodations,** about 20 meters beyond the football pitch off Monkey Forest Road. Prices for the six bungalows range from Rp15,000 s to Rp25,000 d; enormous upstairs rooms have pyramidal ceilings and magnificent bathrooms and verandas. Ibu Masih is a marvelous lady who'll teach you dancing, talk to you about art, and make a royal tour of her guests each morning. Masih's personable homestay is just a 10-minute walk from Ubud's "downtown." **Oka Kartini,** tel. 975-193, fax 975-759, is on Jl. Raya in Padangtegal on the left about 150 meters before the post office, as you're entering Ubud from Peliatan. Out of the busy center of Ubud with all its traffic and sellers, Oka's restful, Balinese-style bungalows with intricately carved reliefs and palm thatch, surrounded by pool and gardens, are in the Rp63,000-84,000 range with hot showers; other rooms go for as little as Rp21,000. Oka worked for six years as a guide in the Puri Lukisan and is well informed about painting. She'll store your luggage while you travel around, find you a dance teacher, and hand out free treats. Public transport is close at hand, or ask for airport transfer by private car (Rp42,000 for two).

Near the start of Monkey Forest Road is **Oka Wati's Sunset Bungalows**, P.O. Box 158 Ubud, tel. 96386, fax 975-063), a superbly run family operation. Three classes of accommodations: standard for Rp52,500 s, Rp63,000 d; a suite Rp94,500 s, Rp115,000 d; family Rp126,000 (plus 10% service charge). Peaceful surroundings. Balinese-style rooms upstairs over beautiful *sawah* and lily ponds with ceiling fans, big oval bathrooms, nice furnishings, bedside lights, balcony, pool, and a restaurant only 30 meters away. All units have hot water. You can arrange adventure rafting and tours here, or rent bikes for Rp3500 per day. In June or July, make reservations one month in advance. **Pertiwi Bungalows**, Monkey Forest Rd., tel. 975-236, fax 975-559, has eight standard rooms for Rp63,000 s, Rp73,500 d; 22 superior rooms for Rp73,500 s, Rp84,000 d; and eight deluxe rooms for Rp126,000 s, Rp147,000 d. Meals are extra: Rp6300 for continental breakfast, Rp7400 for American breakfast, Rp11,600 for lunch, Rp14,700 for dinner. All rates subject to 15.5% service and tax. Visa and MasterCard accepted. Rooms are very large in typical Balinese decor with peaked thatched roofs, bamboo wall matting, ceiling fans, and private baths with hot and cold water. Facilities include a fantastic pool, poolside bar, open-air pavilion restaurant, and parking lot. Staff is very helpful. If you want to be in the middle of the action, this is one of the best hotels on Monkey Forest Road.

The classy **Pringga Juwita Water Garden Cottages**, Jl. Bisma Ubud 80571, tel. and fax 975-734, has 25 rooms in two different classes: standard Rp78,000 s, Rp84,000 d and deluxe Rp105,000 s, Rp115,500 d (plus 15.5% tax and service). You get the service, decor, and comfort of any of Ubud's six international-standard hotels at half the price. All rooms have hot water, private verandas, fans, Balinese-style furniture, and woodwork finishing. The generous, high-quality breakfast (0700-1000) comes with whole-grain bread and homemade jam. The bungalows for Rp115,500 are the best deal, with lux-

uriant gardens, jungle-enveloped swimming pool, restaurant on leafy pavilion, plus lots of conveniences. Only about an eight-minute walk from Ubud's center, yet very quiet with only the sound of birds in the mornings. Ideal for groups. Well-run by a charming and conscientious manager. The **Puri Saren Agung Hotel,** the town's oldest hotel, was the former palace of Cokorda Gede Sukawati, the late *raja* of Ubud. When this *puri* burnt down in the 1950s, the *raja* had small guesthouses constructed with Balinese antiques and Western conveniences—one of Bali's first accommodations to combine traditional and Western features. At one time the best paintings in Ubud could be seen in this *puri,* and it was the custom for painters to bring their works to Cokorda for approval before selling them. Peek in to see the fantastic carved wood panels, but stay elsewhere. The bungalows leave much to be desired.

Han Snel's Siti Bungalows, Jl. Kajeng 3, tel. 975-699, fax 975-643, 150 meters up the lane next to the Lotus Cafe, consists of five bungalows (Rp84,000-105,000, plus 15% tax and service) with all the modern conveniences in the garden of the artist's home. One of Ubud's best-kept secrets, Snel offers one of the best rooms around for the price—solar-heated showers, away from traffic noise, nice garden, and privacy. Just four rooms, so you'll be lucky to find one empty. Elegant restaurant.

Long-Term Stays

If it's real peace you require, consider staying in one of the villages around Ubud—Campuan, Penestanan, Kedewetan, Sayan, Peliatan, or Pengosekan—where you're almost assured of finding a secluded place out in the rice fields or over a jungle-filled ravine, as quiet as a convent, with the smell of fresh *sawah*. Work out a special per-day rate for a long-term stay in a hotel or with a family.

FOOD

Half the fun of Ubud is finding new places to eat. Most of the best *warung* and restaurants are concentrated along Monkey Forest Road or the various other tracks and roads running adjacent to it. The best *babi guling* is served in a *warung* opposite the entrance to Puri Saren. On request, almost any family-style homestay or *losmen* will cook up a wonderful Balinese dinner of smoked duck, fish cooked in leaves, steamed jackfruit with special sauce, and vegetable side dishes for around Rp20,000. In the morning you can buy huge portions of *nasi campur* (Rp1000) and black rice pudding (Rp500) to the side of Ubud's market. In the late afternoons and evenings, treat yourself to *pisang goreng* from market vendors.

Restaurants

Ubud's restaurants are clean and decent, but even in the best restaurants the food quality can be erratic. One nice service provided by many restaurants in Ubud is transport. Pick your restaurant by its specialty. For Mexican food, go to **Kura Kura,** though the prices have gone up dramatically and the portions have shrunk. For barbecue try **Griya**; for Japanese food, **Mumbul's.** Balinese village food aficionados should go to **Bendi's,** Indian food-lovers to **Bumbu.** For the best sandwiches go to the **Coffee Shop,** with prices varying from Rp2600 to Rp3500 for a club sandwich with the works. For vegetarian food, **Shadana's** on Jl. Raya is one of the best.

The best restaurants offer a good balance of food from east and west. Catering, as they do, to French and Italian tourists, restaurants have featured more international fare of late—Thai, vegetarian, pasta. The **Cappuccino Italian Restaurant** on Monkey Forest Road serves up pizza and homemade fettuccine. The best pizza in Ubud, prepared in a real pizza oven, is made by **Cafe Roma** on Jl. Sukma, about 300 meters from Jl. Raya—good spaghetti, too. Ubud is so far from the sea that seafood is not the town's forte. **Murni's** (by the bridge) and **Lotus Cafe** have fresh grilled seafood specials two or three times weekly, but you never know when or for how long.

There are also more families traveling to Ubud now. At the **Gayatri Restaurant** a children's play area is provided upstairs so parents can enjoy a meal in peace. **Oka Wati's** boasts perhaps one of Ubud's most romantic dinner settings. A great number of restaurants advertise daily specials on big sandwich boards outside.

Jalan Raya

After the style of Made's Warung in Kuta, **Ary's Warung** has tables set up over the street. Incredible wine list, liqueurs, and cocktails at fair prices, plus snacks and sandwiches such as

Ubud market

hummus, BLTs, and granola. Quite tasty food. Check out the old black-and-white photos of old Bali and Java on the wall. **Garden Roof Restaurant,** next to I Made Sadia Homestay and more or less opposite Griya, offers a wide variety of Indonesian and Western dishes. It's not cheap, but the food and service are good. Try the roasted chicken with fried potatoes and salad (Rp4500).

Some readers swear by it, others consider it overrated, but eating at **Lotus Cafe** on Jl. Raya near the tourist office is unquestionably an elegant experience. Recline on pillows and sip coffee in a gazebo on the edge of a beautiful lotus pond with jazz music in the background. The homemade baked goods are excellent; other winners are fresh carrot juice, rich cheesecakes, chocolate brownies, and the Greek salad with feta cheese. Count on about Rp17,000 for dinner for two. For a place to hang out, Cafe Lotus is clean and friendly, with good service. Closes at 2100 and doesn't open Monday.

Casa Luna is a big three-story restaurant with a wonderful selection of food. Really inventive dishes: black rice pudding with nutmeg ice cream (Rp3000), magnificent salads (around Rp3000), herb fettuccine in fresh tomato-basil sauce (Rp4000), Moroccan chicken (Rp7500). Casa Luna is situated in an elevated *wantilan* with colonial-style antique furniture—pure *tempoe doeloe*. Live music on Saturday night. The **Honeymoon Bakery** in the foyer of the restaurant sells croissants, brown bread, and multigrain muffins. **Mumbul's Garden Terrace Cafe**, tel. (0361) 975-364, just up from the Lotus Cafe on the same side of street, features high-quality food at excellent prices. Definitely one of the most varied menus in town—an oasis in the desert of repetitive fare. Beautiful table settings, comfy chairs, very good service, with an airy view over a deep gulley. The menu has evolved from what people crave, resulting in an international array including Japanese and Thai dishes. Try the pork fillet in mustard sauce—delicious! Smoked duck available every Saturday night.

Toward Padangtegal on the right, **Nomad Restaurant** stays open until 2300 and offers very good, expensive food like spicy guacamole with *krupuk* (Rp2000), seafood salad, and mango juice *lassi*. A *gamelan* plays in the background; food is served by waiters and waitresses in traditional dress. Chic atmosphere, and the bar has the largest selection of beer, wine, and cocktails in Ubud—a great place for a nightcap. A real sleeper is **Shadana Vegetarian Restaurant** featuring superb homecooked vegetarian dishes like *tahu* burgers (Rp2500); vegetarian *sate kebab* (Rp2500); cheese, egg, and avocado jaffles (Rp2000); artful *nasi campur*; and brown rice with *tempe* and fresh vegetables with a subtle sauce. Ask for the *sambal bali* hot sauce. Most people miss this small restaurant just opposite Jl. Hanoman east of Ubud's town center. And, unfortunately, it's shrinking, the tables gradually giving way to more lucrative clothes and souvenirs.

Monkey Forest Road

Opposite the soccer field on the Monkey Forest Road is open-air **Bendi's**. Never a disappointment, the staff prepares simple and delicious Balinese village food such as ferns and grated coconut, chicken, vegetarian dishes, or an admirable *nasi campur* for only Rp2000. Count on dinner for two costing around Rp15,000. **Yogyakarta** is a new place to eat near the soccer field; try the

chicken cooked similar to the way it's grilled in the West—delicious. Half a chicken, french fries, and salad costs Rp4000. **Cafe Bali,** across from Warsi's on the far side of the football pitch, is a small up-and-coming restaurant with a variety of food at decent prices. Watch the fireflies at night. The management is gentle, friendly, and kind, the premises clean and charming, and the Indonesian food and pizzas good. Try the corn *pacora*, veggie lasagna, or special duck. Two entrees and sodas will set you back Rp6500. **Tjanderi's** lays out delicious, cheap, and generous meals—pizzas, scones, yogurt, coconut pie, and *gecok*. The cheese and vegetable tacos and banana-coconut tacos are acclaimed, and the vegetable soups just as hearty as they were 20 years ago. Expect gregarious gatherings in the evenings, as it's right on the main drag.

Elsewhere

Bumbu Restaurant, within the walls of the former *puri* near the town center, specializes in Balinese, Indian, and vegetarian dishes. This remarkable gastronomic phenomenon is run by the owners of Mumbul's. The Indian Thali plate comes with either chicken or fish curry (Rp8000); also try *tandoori* (Rp4000), *dhal* (Rp1500), and *moghlai saag*. Authentic Balinese foods include traditional village-style *sate lilit, lawar, telor pindang,* and curried *tempe*. If you can't make up your mind, Bumbu's will serve you a sample platter with a generous combination of house specialities. Drinks include frappes (Rp3500), cocktails, nonalcoholic "mocktails," liqueur coffees, and long drinks. Desserts are equally weird and wonderful.

Mira's, under new management, has a very nice ambience, beautiful garden, waterfall, and an imaginative menu. Tuna fish curry (Rp6500) is a sure bet. Outrageous desserts. **Sanak,** Jl. Hanoman 7, has Padang-style food, one of the few *nasi padang* restaurants in Ubud. **Griya Barbecue and Restaurant,** opposite the lane next to the school, specializes in barbecued chicken, pork, and beef. Check out the daily specials. A classy place to dine is **Han Snel's Garden Restaurant** with its Oriental-Indonesian menu. Everyone raves about the dazzling mini-*rijstaffel* (Rp10,500 pp for seven dishes). The specialty of the house is steamed *bebek tutu* cooked to perfection and served in sumptuous garden surroundings.

Oka Wati's, a little out of the town center off Monkey Forest Rd., is a full-fledged restaurant in the emerald paddies. The establishment offers a winning combination of friendliness, reasonable prices, and excellent Western food. Tuna sandwiches (Rp2500), scrambled eggs (Rp3000), and vegetarian items are always available; Balinese ceremonial banquet dishes like *bebek tutu* (Rp25,000) or a whole suckling pig (Rp50,000) must be ordered 24 hours in advance. Oka still makes excellent yogurt and banana sweets in the mornings. **Wayan Cafe and Bakery** is the swank place to eat—it's easy to drop Rp30,000 for two. Tables set at different levels in a leafy garden create a nice atmosphere. Wayan herself is hospitable and generous. Popular homemade baked goods (whole-wheat bread) and *ayam sate* (Rp2500) with superb peanut sauce. There are wonderful salads, pizza, "prawns *a la ketut*" (lots of garlic), and the chicken curry is without peer. Great carrot juice and desserts. It's always crowded; in the peak season, make reservations for the evening.

Desserts And Baked Goods
Wayan Cafe and Bakery and **Casa Luna** are superb. Casa Luna is the only place in town with frozen yogurt. **Cafe Lotus** is said to have the best chocolate cake on Bali. Cafe Wayan's Death by Chocolate cake is renowned; Wayan also serves an inimitable coconut pie. Nomad's serves perfect apple strudel plus *gulek,* a Balinese dessert of boiled bananas and pineapples. At Mumbul's, don't pass up the thick passion fruit shake with jackfruit ice cream and other delicious desserts.

In the market early in the morning, get an ample serving of black rice pudding sprinkled with coconut and brown sugar syrup for Rp500—a healthy, filling breakfast. Not many restaurants are open for breakfast because most accommodations serve breakfast as part of the price of a room, but street vendors do business long before the restaurants open at 0800.

Many of Ubud's eating establishments now offer whole-wheat bread (known as "brown bread"), Danish, and French bread. The **Honeymoon Bakery** in Casa Luna offers very good brown bread. **Tino Drug Store,** tel. (0361) 975-020, sells all kinds of baked goods at good prices (brown bread Rp1500, apple cake Rp1000). The ticket for a breakfast on the run, it's open 0800-2000.

SHOPPING

Ubud is a pleasant, enjoyable place to shop. Shopkeepers are easier to deal with than those in southern Bali. The prices are cheaper than in the south. Ubud used to be known just for its galleries but now you can come here and buy clothes, souvenirs, and crafts as well. Ubud's main street and lanes are lined with a great variety of shops and kiosks, filled to bursting with woodcarvings, basketry, toy *gamelan* sets, dangling earrings, antiques, clothes, *batik,* bamboo windmills, and paintings. Because of recurring waves of free-spending visitors, the sellers can be a bit pushy at times, and first prices are high—you're expected to bargain. The best time to shop is in the cool evenings. The majority of shops are open from 0900 to 2030 or 2100. A tip: for basic necessities, go to Gianyar to shop. It's closer than Denpasar and has a bigger market than Ubud.

Ubud lies in the middle of the surrounding villages of Campuan, Penestanan, Peliatan, and Pengosekan, which have all more or less grown together. In these thriving craft villages live hundreds of painters, carvers, and weavers who create a surprising percentage of the wares sold in the island's galleries, art shops, and boutiques.

Pasar Ubud
Pasar Ubud on Jl. Raya in the middle of town and its surrounding area houses several hundred shops and stalls. This central market offers low-end clothes in booths upstairs as well as tawdry handicrafts, fans, bags, baskets, and jewelry. Look in on I Nymoan Latin's shop behind the market, with excellent *batik,* fabrics, machine-woven *ikat,* and scarves at great prices. A quarter of these booths target the Balinese themselves with sandals, cheap belts, jackets, and white shirts—some nice things at reasonable prices. Produce is available on the grounds and in the back. Vanilla pods make nice gifts (Rp2500 for 20 sticks). A big lively crowded market takes place every three days, spilling over into the street as women come in to sell and buy goods.

Bookshops

The largest selection of guidebooks, new books, and expensive large format picture and culture books on Indonesia, as well as current issues of European, Asian, Australian, and American magazines and newspapers can be found at the **Ubud Bookshop** opposite Puri Sakenan on Jl. Raya. A few minutes away, at Monkey Forest Rd. 68, tel. (0361) 975-359, is **Dewa House Book Shop.** Open 0800-2130, Dewa sells a fair selection of new and used books at the usual high prices. Books are bought back at half price. In Campuan, check out the small and tasteful selection of Oxford in Asia paperbacks in Murni's; the *Herald Tribune* (Rp3500) is also for sale.

Ganesha Bookshop, also on the main road (opposite the post office), is more user-friendly than Ubud Bookshop. Here you can buy a used book for Rp10,000, then sell it back for Rp5000. Open 0700-1700 seven days a week. The closest thing to a metaphysical bookshop on Bali is the **Meditation Shop** on Monkey Forest Rd., which sells multilingual spiritual and self-help literature and tapes.

Clothes

Have a tailor make a shirt that you design, or a seamstress create a *kebaya* to fit; Rp15,000 for the material, Rp5000 for the labor. A seamstress works upstairs in the Ubud market on big market days. There are many stores on the main drag that sell unexceptional, touristy clothing and trinkets, but **Made Lastri's** produces clothing of good quality and design in unusual *batik* fabric. Lastri will make clothing to order if provided with a sample or pattern to work from. She needs only one day to create a simple skirt, a week for a jacket or full-length kimono robe. Buy fabric from the market and have a beautiful, lined robe made for about Rp31,500.

Another very good shop, though relatively expensive, is **Bali Rosa,** fax (0361) 975-162, Jl. Raya Ubud (opposite the start of the road up to Pringga Juwita), with a fine collection of Western fashion clothing designed by Nadine Thompson. Hand-painted silk and rayon print outfits with shoes to match are sold at fixed prices. Painted wooden jewelry and beadwork is also available. On Monkey Forest Rd. is a women's clothing shop, **Balinka,** that makes high-quality, colorful clothes in cotton and rayon. The styles are simple, elegant, and very different from what's sold nearby. Some of the most original and fashionable clothes are found at **Neo Primitive** on Monkey Forest Rd. (left side, coming from town, right after Dian's Restaurant).

PJ Collection, Banjar Tegallangtang, fax 975-120, has a nice line of *batik* and contemporary hand-painted designs and cuts on cotton knit material. This retail, wholesale, and export business has fixed but reasonable prices: sleeveless tops for Rp5000 and lined pants for Rp25,000. **Puspa Shop** at the corner of the soccer field will make something for you, or do alterations on the spot. Good prices. Excellent selection of men's shirts and pants and women's dresses, blouses, and shorts for Rp12,000-40,000 first price. For an attractive made-to-order T-shirt collection, go to **Sama Sama Shop III** on Jl. Hanoman, tel. 975-072, Padangtegal. Original hand-painted designs. Buy a nice quality *batik*-lined jacket at **Warsi's** for Rp35,000. Handsome cotton *batik sarung* cost around Rp12,000-15,000. Elsewhere, expect to pay Rp6000 for a machine-printed *batik sarung* and Rp15,000 for a *batik* outfit.

Miscellaneous

An excellent music shop, **Ubud Music and Photo Color Service Centre,** tel. (0361) 975-362, is opposite Cafe Lotus on Jl. Raya Ubud, offering the most extensive collection in Ubud, including a very decent Indo-Javanese pop and classical music section. There's also a good choice of guidebooks, ice cream, perfume, toiletries, and film processing. Open 0900-2000. **Baliku** has an above-average selection of all types of music at reasonable prices, plus photo services. Located about halfway down Monkey Forest Rd. on the eastern side opposite Ubud Village Hotel. You'll pay about Rp12,000 for processing and printing a 36-exposure roll of film, and about Rp6000 for a prerecorded tape of fair quality.

Near the Monkey Forest is **Kubu Ku Windchimes** for unusual and elegant tinkling, clapping, whirling noisemakers. Odds and ends like kitchen stools and clay figurines also available. **Ganesha Bookshop,** Jl. Raya, sells musical instruments, beads, jewelry, and other collectibles. Visit the village of Nyuhkuning southwest of Ubud, a woodcarving center since the 1930s. Other woodcarving villages north of Ubud are Pujung, Sebatu, Taro, and Jati.

ARTS AND CRAFTS

Antiques And Primitive Art

Upscale **Murni's** in Campuan is one of the most fashionable antique shops in the Ubud area. **Art Gecko,** beside Rona's Accommodations at Jl. Tebesaya 23, carries a fascinating selection of reasonably priced imported primitive art; while little is from Bali, many artifacts come from the Outer Islands. The proprietors go really far afield to find items. If something carried here starts to catch on in the rest of Bali, they drop it. This very tasteful retail/export shop is the only one of its type in Ubud, with pieces costing up to Rp150,000.

Jewelry

Mirah Silver on Jl. Raya has some beautifully designed rings, earrings, pendants, and necklaces, or try **Putra Silver** on Monkey Forest Rd., which sells all kinds of quality silver jewelry at good prices (no bargaining). Putra's wholesale office is in the Puri Agung in Peliatan. Also recommended is **Purpa Silver Gallery** on Monkey Forest Rd., tel. (0361) 975-068 or 975-234, fax 975-016. More than just a silver shop, Purpa has a very fine selection of contemporary and abstract art.

Paintings

The Ubud area is noted for its painters. Signs point the way to studios all over town and there's also a massive array of galleries. It's more satisfying to buy directly from the painter and you may get a better price. Fame has not diminished the open nature, friendly demeanor, and hospitality of Ubud's painters, but you have to be dogged to find those working in a distinct style. The vast majority of paintings have a monotonous sameness to them—the same village and jungle scenes ad nauseam. Be prepared to look for days and not find anything original except for the colors and frame.

A commission is tacked onto the price if a painter puts his work in a gallery. Count on a good 50 cm-by-70 cm painting costing around Rp420,000 minimum. Additionally, if you allow yourself to be led around to the art shops by locals, your driver will get 10% and your guide up to 15% of the price of a painting, so you could actually pay 25% more than you would if

you negotiated directly with the painter. Don't forget the back lane galleries. The same painting that would cost you Rp10 million in a high-class gallery may go for only Rp2 million in a lesser-known gallery.

Sanggar Seniwati

In Bali, women are not encouraged to be artists, as art is considered men's work. With all their religious and family obligations, it's remarkable that Balinese women are able to produce art at all. To help publicize and support the efforts of women artists, the Sanggar Seniwati (Art Association) has been established. If a woman wants to study art, she may enroll in one of the association's study programs. Exhibition space for one-woman shows, studios for visiting artists, and a large open area for workshop/practice sessions are available on the premises. No studio fee is charged.

One artist the association actively promotes is Putu Suriati. Stricken by polio early in life, Suriati overcame unbelievable odds to become a painter. She paints in painstaking detail using a dazzling range of colors. Other women artists who belong to the *sanggar* are Tjok Istri Mas Astiti, Dewa Biang Raka, and Ni Made Suciarmi. Over 40 artists have exhibited their work in the association's Seniwati Gallery nearby.

To learn more about the nascent women's art movement in Bali, contact assistant director Mary Northmore, herself a noted artist. The association's office and studios are just off Jl. Raya in Ubud at Jl. Sriwedari 2 B, Banjar Taman, Ubud, Gianyar, tel. (0361) 975-485, residence 975-568. The gallery is open 1000-1700; closed Monday. The association publishes attractive full-color calendars picturing the works of women painters; Sanggar Seniwati recently sponsored exhibitions in London and Washington.

Noted Balinese Artists

I Bagus Made Poleng, in Tebasaya near Padanggtegal, doesn't paint for the money. This eccentric Brahman only sells paintings when his village needs money for a religious festival. He deliberately starts with a high price—Rp6 million—so his paintings won't sell, then gets angry when they do.

I Nyoman Meja is one of Bali's most successful artists. You'll see only a few of his works in Ubud's local galleries. His studio is in Taman near the Nomad Restaurant. He asks Rp4.2 million for an average painting and recently sold one of his works to a Japanese museum for the unheard-of price of Rp23 million. Murjawan, in Kuto village near Ubud, is an experienced artist who paints in extreme detail.

Noted European Artists

Ubud hosts a small European and Australian artist's colony: Australian Donald Friend, Dutch-born Han Snel, and the Catalan artist Antonio Blanco, whose specialty is erotic art and illustrated poetry. The paintings of these expat artists, who've devoted most of their professional lives to depicting Balinese life and culture, can be seen in the Neka or Agung Rai galleries, or in their home studios. One km through the rice fields beyond Campuan is Penestanan village, where the Young Artists School developed under the influence of the Balinese artist Cakra and Arie Smit, another Dutch-born artist who came to live in Ubud in 1956. These compelling paintings, rendered in a naive, exuberant style and using strong primary chemical colors, often depict scenes from daily village life.

Galleries

In most of Ubud's art galleries at least five different contemporary styles are represented, with works by old veterans as well as brash young artists. Also on exhibit are modern forms such as Japanese-influenced screens. In many of the galleries—even the big ones like Agung Rai in Peliatan and Neka Gallery in Ubud—you get a personal tour guide. Sometimes there are special exhibits or collections on loan from museums. Always ask to see the dealer's private collections, usually hidden away behind a locked door. Most galleries charge Rp500 to enter the showrooms; in some you may watch artists at work in the back.

At **I Gusti Nyoman Lempad's house** on Jl. Raya, on the north side of the road in the center of Ubud, his grandchildren carry on the painter's tradition, turning out some excellent work. Lempad, who died in 1978 at the extraordinary age of 121, originally painted in the traditional *wayang* style, evolving eventually toward an expressionistic, exaggerated stylization of the *wayang* figures. Toward the end of his life he developed a very distinctive sketching style using only black Chinese ink on paper. A few of these

remarkable sketches are on display in the gallery, which feels more like a private home than a public gallery. A visit gives you an insight into the traditional home of an upper-caste Balinese family.

Han Snel's Gallery is back from the road, very quiet. A former Dutch solider who deserted the colonial army after the war for independence, Snel eventually married a Balinese woman and lives here today with his family. His style is abstract, with a stunning use of color. Han is now more a hobbyist painter; his most productive, provocative years are over. These days he turns out only three or four paintings a year. His gallery is well laid-out, well-lighted, and contains fine decorative works.

A must is the **Neka Gallery,** established in 1966 in Peliatan. Whereas Puri Lukisan represents only Balinese artists, the Neka Gallery exhibits painters from all over Indonesia, as well as foreign artists who've lived and worked on Bali. The Neka Gallery in eastern Ubud in Padangtegal consists of five different buildings. Paintings cost Rp31,500-21 million; you can get a discount of 10-25%. Suteja Neka no longer pays commissions to agents for taking tourists around to his gallery—he's so famous he doesn't have to. In 1982, the Neka Museum north of Campuan (about 2.5 km from Ubud) formally opened. Affandi, Sujono, Sobrat, Kebot, Ida Bagus Made, Lempad, and other famous artists are exhibited here. The art students of Bali's Udayana University must study the works in the Neka Museum to graduate. The Neka Museum exhibits and sells some of the highest-quality contemporary paintings found anywhere in Bali. Paintings range from impressionism to abstract expressionism. Open daily 0830-1700.

Also visit the equally important **Agung Rai Gallery** in Peliatan and the **Agung Raka Gallery** just before Mas. These big commercial galleries, which feature Balinese, European, and Indonesian paintings, deal with international art connoisseurs and do a high-end, high-turnover trade in overseas markets. Agung Rai even buys paintings in Europe and sells them here to Europeans. The **Rudana Gallery,** south of Teges on the right side, is a marvelous private collection put together over 14 years, comprising a great variety of painting styles—contemporary works by local artists as well as masterpieces by famous painters. The artwork of Blanco, Bonnet, and

Spies enhances the collection. In the traditional art room hang works by Made, Djudjul, Kasta, and Kobot. Modern work includes pieces by Wianta, Nidjara, and Soeporno.

ENTERTAINMENT AND WORKSHOPS

From the early 1920s, the royal family ensured that the most talented teachers of dance, music, and drama were brought to Ubud, both to entertain the king and to impart their knowledge to local performers. The brilliant ethnomusicologist Colin McPhee based himself here, assiduously conducting groundbreaking research and writing his classic *A House in Bali* (1944) about his prewar experiences in Ubud. Even earlier, the Dutch musicologist Jaap Kunst published *Music of Bali* (1925), in which he lauded the *gamelan* of Peliatan. Ubud and its neighboring villages are still major dance centers where every night of the week a performance, music recital, or dance class is happening somewhere. Get info about dances and events from the tourist office on Ubud's main street, or wait for one of the touts selling tickets around the town's main crossroads.

Dance

The *kecak* and *barong* are the most spectacular and interesting Balinese dances. People sell tickets in the streets—their commission is already included in the price, so helping them earn a living isn't costing you extra. Tickets are also available at the door. At only Rp5000, which sometimes includes transportation, the performances are a great value. These dance dramas are actually short demonstrations of up to six separate dances in one. Most start at 1930 and last about 90 minutes. It's first-come, first-served, so get there early.

Because of its temple surroundings, the dances put on almost every night at Puri Saren are outstanding. The *legong kraton* is staged each Monday and the *barong* every Wednesday night. Package tour operators drive clients here from Denpasar. The dancers are extremely talented, but the frequent camera flashes and street noise can be distracting.

See children practice dance at the *puri* on Sunday and Tuesday afternoons at 1500. It's free, fun, and fascinating to watch. Foreign kids can join in. At the Padangtegal stage every Thursday at 1900, a Ramayana ballet is staged by the Sekar Alit children's troupe. Performed on the same stage every Tuesday at 1930 are *legong* dances; every Saturday at 1930 see *legong* and *barong* dances. The huge Gunung Sari dance and music pavilion, in the *pura dalem* between Padangtegal and Peliatan, stages *legong* every Thursday and Saturday nights at 1930-2045. The performances of the Ciwa Ratri Dance and Classical Gamelan Gebyug at 1930 at the dance venue on Jl. Tebesaya are very popular. Audiences marvel at the dancers wearing big cowbells.

The Gamelan Semara Ratih ensemble in Banjar Kutuh, northeast of the post office, performs the best tourist *gamelan* every Tuesday night at 1930. Better than the Ubud Palace show, this *gamelan* is healthy, young, vibrant, and has a varied program. It is made up of dancers and musicians from all over, including many students, graduates and teachers from STSI, the Bali Arts Academy in Denpasar. The group is new and still building a reputation with the show *The Spirit of Bali*. Gamelan Semara Ratih also performs recent works by Nyoman Windha, a leading composer from the music and dance academy STSI, as well as other modern compositions and some classical dance pieces.

A *wayang* theater performance, *The Sacrifice of Bima*, takes place on Wednesday and Sunday from 2000 to 2100 (Rp5000) at Oka Kartini's on Jl. Raya in Padangtegal. This is an authentic shadow puppet show with a torch behind the screen, preceded by a short explanation. Upward of a third of the audience watches the skill of the *dalang* from behind the screen.

Workshops

Choose your family accommodations according to your interest, be it *wayang* theater, instrument-making, jewelry, or carving. The sign Painter and Homestay, for example, means the *losmen* is owned or managed by a painter. If you stay with a dancer, you'll be able to watch private *gabor*, *oleg*, and *tari tenun* dance lessons in the flowered courtyard. Guests are sometimes treated to special demonstrations.

I Nyoman Warsa at Pondok Bamboo (opposite Kubu Ku Windchimes) teaches the bamboo *tinglik* instrument for Rp5000 per hour. Nyoman is very patient. His son teaches music too. You'll find it's difficult to follow the rhythm

DANCE PERFORMANCES IN AND AROUND UBUD

DAY	DANCE	TIME	PLACE
Sunday	kecak dance	1900-2000	Padangtegal, Ubud
	fire dance	1900-2030	Bona, Gianyar
	legong dance	1900-2000	Puri Agung, Peliatan
Monday	legong dance	1930-2030	Puri Saren, Ubud
	fire dance	1900-2030	Bona, Gianyar
Tuesday	Mahabharata epic	1900-2030	Br. Teges, Peliatan
	rajapala dance	2000-2130	Bale Banjar Ubud Klod
Wednesday	fire dance	1900-2030	Bona, Gianyar
	barong dance	1900-2030	Bale Banjar Ubud Klod
	wayang kulit	1900-2030	Oka Kartini, Peliatan
Thursday	mask dance	1930-2100	Pengosekan, Ubud
	gabor dance	1930-2100	Bale Banjar Ubud Klod
Friday	fire dance	1900-2030	Bona, Gianyar
	legong dance	1930-2100	Peliatan stage, Peliatan
	calon arang	1900-2030	Puri Saren, Ubud
Saturday	legong dance	1930-2100	Pura Dalem Puri, Peliata

and count time, but don't despair. In the *ikat* shop next to Dian's Restaurant, take lessons on the happy, galloping *klintik* for Rp5000 per hour. I Wayang Karta runs a Balinese dance and music school and guesthouse at Jl. Sugriwa 20 in Padangtegal. Learn one of Bali's traditional dances from this very patient man.

At the Ganesha Bookshop on Ubud's main street opposite the post office, sign up for an informal introductory workshop in Balinese music. No previous musical knowledge is necessary. Participants are given a brief history of the *gamelan* and are then invited to choose an instrument on which to learn some basic music. Instruments are provided and the tutors all speak English. The workshop costs Rp15,000 and runs every Tuesday evening 1800-1930. Alternate times and group bookings available on request.

The Meditation Shop on Monkey Forest Rd., is the venue for silent meditation ("spiritual sharing") each day at 1700. Practice group meditation 1800-1900. Five-night courses also offered. The shop sells metaphysical literature and tapes

in English, French, German, Dutch, Cantonese, Japanese, and Indonesian. The Fibra Inn on Monkey Forest Rd., tel. (0361) 975-451, offers meditation, dancing, *gamelan,* painting, and woodcarving courses.

At the **Crackpot** on Monkey Forest Rd. you can learn *batik*-making. Make your own *batik* T-shirt, painting, *sarung,* or postcard with help and instruction from *batik*-makers. Create your own designs or use the ready-made design templates. You can get into as much detail as you want and come and go as you please, no time limits. Adult T-shirt costs Rp20,000, child T-shirt Rp15,000, cushions Rp20,000-25,000, paintings Rp15,000-25,000. Organic dyes that change with the light are used. The Crackpot also has a book exchange service and a coffee shop where you can relax, read magazines and newspapers, play games, and enjoy the best sandwiches in town in a friendly atmosphere.

Learn Balinese cooking at **Casa Luna** on Wednesdays. The course covers cooking techniques, alternative ingredients, and menu planning. Each session costs Rp15,000, runs 2.5 hours (1100-1330), and includes lunch and tea or coffee. Booking is essential as there's a five-person minimum. Classes can be arranged for other days as well if minimum booking requirements are met.

SERVICES

On Ubud's main street and all the way down Monkey Forest Road are moneychangers, international freight forwarders, postal agents, film processing outlets, and travel agencies. A unique, locally managed, nongovernmental tourist information center, established by contributions from 12 *banjar* and the Indonesian Hotel and Restaurant Association, is on Ubud's main street across from the dance hall/cinema. Staffed by at least three English-speaking Indonesians, this is a great place to find out what's going on. Staff post dance schedules, shuttle bus costs and times, and notices of ceremonies; hand out a good map of Bali; sell tickets to dance performances; and provide a convenient message board for travelers.

Public bulletin/notice boards are all around town, posting information about events happening around the island, details of transport costs, and other points of interest to tourists. It pays to check them each day. A useful one is at the Crackpot on Monkey Forest Rd. Behind Ubud's News Stand by Ary's and diagonally across from Lotus Cafe, a printer will make you 100 single-color business cards for Rp12,000.

Tino Drug Store, tel. (0361) 975-020, on Jl. Raya next to Casa Luna, is Ubud's best-stocked supermarket; open 0800-2000. Want to get married on Bali? I Nyoman and Warti Sujana can help make the arrangements. Make inquiries at Tebesari Homestay and Dressmaker, Banjar Tebesaya 29, in Peliatan.

There's now a Kodak photo processing shop called **Era Drug Store and Photo Color Service Centre**, tel. 975-341 or 975-362, at the start of Monkey Forest Rd.; a branch is down the road toward the monkey forest. **Segara**, near Nomad Restaurant, does photocopying and laminating, sells stationary, and offers binding service—the best services of its kind in Ubud. A laundry service is advertised beside the sign to the Frog Pond Inn on Monkey Forest Road.

Ubud's Children Club, Jl. Pengosekan 9, tel. 975-320, is run by an Australian woman; open 0800-1200, 1300-1600. AA meetings are hosted by the Mumbul Inn on Jl. Raya each week.

If your hotel doesn't have a swimming pool, for a small fee (Rp2000-3000) you can swim as a guest in a number of hotel pools—Puri Suraswati, Villa Rasa Sayang, Dewi Sri Bungalows, Fibra Inn, Grand Ubud, Oka Kartini's, Oka Wati's, and Pertiwi's. The entrance to the pool at the Ubud Village Inn is Rp3000 but includes a drink, towel, and nice relaxing music.

Tourist Services

It's a harbinger of Ubud's maturity as a tourist center that agencies like **CV Three Brothers Wisata** on Monkey Forest Road have arrived. These people do everything: car, motorbike, and pushbike rentals; insurance; packing and shipping; postal service, stamps, and parcel delivery; coach tours; shuttle bus tickets; moneychanging; cash for credit cards; bus tickets for Java; international and domestic air ticketing; importing/exporting; document clearance; hotel reservations; and laundry. Another full-service agency is Surya International on Jl. Raya, tel. (0361) 975-133, fax 975-120; staff will make hotel reservations for you for a fee.

Banks And Moneychangers

The Ubud branch of **Bank Duta**—Indonesia's best bank—offers the most services. It's located near the major intersection in north Peliatan just before Ubud. You can get a cash advance on your credit cards and change traveler's checks here. Another good bank is **BCI** beside Nyoman Communication Service. You don't have to look far for a moneychanger—virtually every shop in Ubud will change money. Look for the best rate.

Postal Services

There are postal agents all over Ubud where you can buy postcards and stamps or mail letters and parcels. **Rona's**, Jl. Tebesaya 23, sells stamps and posts letters. The poste restante service at Ubud's post office in Padangtegal is free, though not too reliable; it's better to have letters sent to a hotel. The post office also offers *paket pos* service; first have your parcel inspected, then wrapped by a *tukang bungkus* in a shop outside for Rp400-10,000, depending upon the size and material (Rp10,000 for a wooden box filled with protective foam). The post office is open Mon.-Thurs. 0800-1400, Friday 0800-1100, Saturday 0800-1400. The postal code is 80571.

Book Exchanges And Lending Libraries

Rona's Accommodations and Book Exchange, Jl. Tebesaya 23, tel. (0361) 975-120, has a library of over 2,000 books in English, German, French, Italian, Swedish, Norwegian, Danish, and Dutch. There's a lending library behind the Menara Cafe where you can borrow books for Rp1000 each with a Rp5000 deposit. All the books have been shelved but are not yet cataloged. Because of lack of air-conditioning, these valuable volumes are in pretty bad shape. Most books are in English, including all the classics about Bali; some books are available in Dutch and German.

Telephone

From Ubud's center walk east to the T-intersection in north Peliatan, make a left, and walk 200 meters north. On your left, just in front of the police station, you'll find the fully-computerized, efficient government telephone office. Here you can dial your home country direct by entering a booth and pressing the button marked with the country you want to call (choice of 20 countries). Pay with Visa or an Indonesian telephone charge card, or call collect. The telephone code for Ubud is 0361.

Another good, convenient place to make international (IDD) calls via satellite is **Nomad's Telecommunications Center,** which takes up the whole top floor of Bank Central Asia on Ubud's main street. Most other telcom businesses charge you for a minimum of three minutes but at Nomad's you pay only for the actual time you're on the phone. Collect calls must go through Denpasar and it could take anywhere from 30 to 90 minutes; open 24 hours. East of Nomad's is a *wartel* telephone service where it's also cheap to make short calls abroad. Open 0800-2300.

Ary's Wisata Travel Service, next to the Ubud Bookshop and beside the restaurant of the same name, offers a fast, efficient fax service (Rp10,000 to the U.S.), reconfirms tickets, offers a poste restante service, and allows you to leave messages for people. Very handy and central for people who don't have telephones. Open 0900-2100.

Freight Forwarding And Shipping

Dozens of reliable international air and sea freight forwarding companies are based in Ubud. These companies also offer container service, packing, custom clearance, guaranteed parcel delivery with insurance, and handicraft and garment exporting. Check out **PT Sakura Citra Cargo,** Jl. Suweta 9, Ubud 80571 Gianyar, tel. (0361) 975-070 or 975-634, fax 975-581, and **Ary's Wisata Travel Service,** Jl. Raya, tel. and fax 975-162 or 975-523. **PT Purnama Cargo,** Jl. Jembawan 1 X (near Ubud's post office), P.O. Box 119, tel. 975-033, will ship one container to Europe for about Rp556,000, less to the west coast of the United States. Will wrap and prepare an average size box for sea shipment for Rp5000, not including postage. See manager I Wayan Rarem.

Beauty And Health

An indulgent treat for both men and women can be found at **Nur's Beauty Salon** at Jl. Hanoman 28. A friendly and professionally run operation. The herbal bath is not to be missed—an hour and a half of pure relaxation for Rp38,000. You can spend the better part of the day at Nur's receiving a manicure, pedicure, facial, massage, herbal bath, shampoo, trim, and style—for Rp86,000. Nur also offers two-hour body massages for both men and women. Another good beauty salon is **Marie's,** which does manicures for Rp7500, wash and cut for Rp15,000, plus facials, baths, and massages. Very friendly. **Salon Traditional Massage** on Jl. Hanoman offers face masks, cream baths, waxing, braids, beard cutting, and *jamu* treatments.

TRANSPORTATION

Ubud's central location is ideal for tourists who visit Bali for only a week or so, as the town can be used as a handy base for trips around the island. You can reach almost any tourist site, get back the same day, and go to the theater that night. It's even possible in Ubud to arrange a seat on a bus from Denpasar to Yogyakarta. Book two days in advance; the bus usually departs from the travel agency's office in Ubud.

The *bemo* stand is in the middle of town by the market. It's easy to board public transport out from 0500 right up until evening. Sample fares: Mas Rp600, Blahbatuh Rp600, Gianyar Rp800, Klungkung Rp800, Denpasar Rp1000. The *bemo* to Denpasar goes straight to the big Batubulan station, from where you can catch another *bemo* to Denpasar's Kereneng station near the city center within walking distance of the market and Merpati and Garuda offices. When returning to Ubud from Denpasar, remember the last *bemo* for Ubud leaves Terminal Blahbatuh around 1800. Going from Ubud to Kuta and Sanur is a bit complicated, taking four *bemo* and about two hours. First take one of the large brown vans from near Ubud's market to Batubulan (Rp800, 27 stops), then a *microlet* to Kereneng station (Rp500), then another *bemo* to Tegal, then another to Kuta. It's easier to take the shuttle bus, which drops you off at your door.

The Sakah Connection

For many destinations, you first have to go to the crossroads village of Sakah, seven km south down the road. *Bemo* leave all the time for Sakah (Rp500). From Sakah connect with other *bemo* heading for Singaraja, 102 km; Gianyar, 10 km via Bedulu; Tampaksiring, 19 km; and Amlapura, 60 km via Gianyar with a stop in Candidasa. Sakah to Candidasa is normally Rp2000 but *bemo* drivers try to charge tourists Rp3000. Remember, if you want to head east or north from Sakah, there's no need to go all the way into Denpasar and get another *bemo* out. Just take a *bemo* to Gianyar, the junction town for the eastern half of the island. To the villages bordering Ubud, like Peliatan and Campuan, *bemo* cost only Rp300-400 from Ubud's center.

Shuttle Buses From Ubud

Take advantage of the express services in vans from Ubud to Kuta/Sanur/Airport for Rp7000, departure times 0800, 1000, 1300, and 1730; Candidasa/Padangbai Rp8000, departure times 0630 and 1100; Kintamani for Rp7000, departure time 1100; Lovina Rp12,000, departure time 1100. Shuttle buses also depart for Lombok from Mataram for Rp16,500, departure times 0630 and 1100; Senggigi Rp17,000, departure times are 0630 and 1100; Gili Trawangan Rp22,500, departure time 0630. Book the day before for shuttle service.

The shuttle bus south usually drops people off at Sanur first, then drives on to the airport,

then to Kuta. If you have something to do in Sanur, you may stop over there and take another shuttle bus later in the day on the same ticket. There are two shuttle buses a day (40-50 minutes) to Denpasar's Terminal Ubung, one in the morning that connects with the bus to Jakarta and one in the afternoon that connects with the bus to Yogyakarta.

Travel Agencies

There are dozens of good travel agencies all over Ubud. A good one is **PT Cahaya Sakti Utama,** Jl. Raya 33, tel. (0361) 975-520, 975-721, or 975-131, fax 975-115. **PT Sapta Nugraha Kencana,** Jl. Hanoman 17, also gives great service and the staff is knowledgeable. Sells plane and shuttle bus tickets, reconfirms tickets, and has been known to change flight departure times on tickets, charging you only Rp5000 and saving you a trip to Denpasar.

Surya International on Jl. Raya, tel. 975-133, fax 975-120, opposite Puri Lukisan, confirms tickets on Garuda, Qantas, JAL, and MAS flights for Rp2500. Bus and shuttle bus tickets are available; also offers daily sightseeing tours to Bali, Lombok, and Java. Very handy location in Ubud's center. **Perama Travel Agency,** which sells shuttle tickets and tours, has an office (tel. 975-513) in Pengosekan. **Rona's,** Jl. Tebesaya 23, tel. 975-120, is an agent for Perama and sells shuttle bus tickets.

Long-Distance Buses To Java

Although ultimately departing from Denpasar, in Ubud you can choose your seat and confirm your ticket. The bus to Surabaya leaves 1900, arrives 0700 the next day, Rp21,000; to Yogyakarta leaves 1530, arrives 0800, Rp24,000 non-a/c, Rp38,000 a/c; to Semarang leaves 1530, arrives 0800, Rp37,000; to Bandung leaves 0630, arrives 0800, Rp50,000; to Jakarta leaves 0630, arrives 0700 the next day, Rp56,500. Book two days in advance at any of Ubud's dozens of travel agencies, but cancel 24 hours in advance. Departure is from Denpasar's Ubung station. Get yourself there by *bemo* for Rp1500 via Batubulan or take a shuttle bus direct to Ubung for Rp12,000.

Vehicle Rental

If there are three or four of you, consider hiring a *bemo* for a day or two of leisurely sightseeing.

Your hotel or *losmen* can usually arrange car or motorcycle rentals. A decent four-wheel drive vehicle rents for about Rp50,000 per day including driver and insurance; a self-drive Suzuki jeep is Rp40,000 per day including insurance.

On Monkey Forest Road, **I Nyoman Hertia Car Rental,** tel. (0361) 975-360, has a large fleet of cars to choose from. It costs Rp25,000 to hire a taxi to the airport at 0430 or 0500 in the morning, which is a bargain when you consider a taxi straight from the airport to Ubud is Rp30,000.

Pushbike And Motorcycle Rental

Pushbikes are one of the best ways to explore the Ubud area—you're able to cover more territory than if you walked. There are a number of bike rental places with big one-speed models that fit Western frames for around Rp3000 per day, or newer, fat-tired mountain bikes for Rp8000-10,000 per day. If you rent long-term (over a week), a bike costs only Rp2500-3000 per day. **Alit's** on Monkey Forest Rd., a little down from Tjanderi's on the right, has bicycles for Rp3000 per day; many mountain bikes to choose from. Near the Monkey Forest, **I Kt. Sudarsana Shop** rents new bikes with baskets for Rp3500 per day or Rp3000 per day for six to seven days.

It's very easy to cycle around Ubud, though it's difficult to stay on the right track, even with a Pathfinder map. It's also difficult not to end up on one of the crowded main roads. One warm-up ride is through Campuan to Keliki, then west to the main road and back to Ubud. This tour will take a leisurely three to four hours for nonathletic types and offer some great views. Another outing is to cycle to Tampaksiring and Goa Gajah.

A good day tour is the ride from Ubud down the back roads via Kengetan to Denpasar, coasting almost the whole way. Watch those big lumbering tour buses. From Denpasar, put your bike on top of a *bemo* for the return trip to Ubud. Motorcycle rental costs about Rp15,000 per day including insurance. Might as well go for a vehicle, which offers better protection and costs only Rp20,000-30,000 more. The nearest place to gas up is in Peliatan.

Tours

Many storefront travel agencies offer a comprehensive, well-priced range of coach tours all over the island for Rp15,000-Rp80,000, depending upon distance, carrier, and destination. Sample tours: the "Kintamani Volcano Tour" (Rp15,000), which includes Goa Gajah, Pejeng, Tampaksiring, Penelokan, Bangli, and Gianyar, runs 0900-1700. The full-day "Besakih Mother Temple Tour" (Rp30,000) takes in Celuk, Bukit Jambul, Kusamba, Gianyar, and Taman Gili. The "Bedugul Tour" (Rp20,000) includes Mengwi, Alas Kedaton, and the Lake Bratan area.

PT Cahaya Sakti Utama Tours and Travel (Nomad's), tel. (0361) 975-520 or 975-131, sells a snorkeling day-trip to Turtle Island for Rp20,000, including transport and equipment. Book one day ahead. A very popular tour is Sobek's whitewater rafting trip down the Ayung River gorge near Ubud. The price of Rp120,000 includes transport to and from your hotel, world class guides, hot and cold showers, changing rooms, and an excellent meal. Also ask about Sobek's Class IV whitewater rafting trip for Rp147,000 and the kayaking tour for Rp105,000.

The Pony Day Tour includes a/c transport from your hotel to the stables in picturesque Tabanan Regency, instruction in the basics of riding, catered lunch, and a guided circular tour on ponies of rice terraces, woodlands, river courses, and the beach—a nine-hour ride for Rp115,000 pp. Book at many hotels in the Ubud area or call the Campuhan Tourist Service, tel. 975-298, located on Jl. Raya at the bottom of the hill. From Ubud you can also arrange for accommodation and tours to other areas of Indonesia. Ask Perama Tourist Service in Pengosekan, tel. 975-513, about the "Land-Sea Adventure to Komodo Island" (Rp525,000), "Lombok Countryside Tour" (Rp200,000), and "Trekking Mt. Rinjani" (Rp300,000). The per person price includes transport and ferry ticket with no extra charge for stopovers.

Back Roads From Ubud

Ubud is a more convenient base than the south for exploring inland Bali. With your own *bemo* you can take the shortcut to Gianyar via Bedulu or travel north from Ubud via Campuan, Sayan, and Kengetan to Sangeh—an infrequently traveled route with few public *bemo*. If heading south, take the quiet back road out of Ubud instead of the really busy main road via Mas. This country road, which starts at Banjar Tegal in Ubud, passes by art shops and through working agricultural villages, and emerges in Batuan. These narrow, paved back roads are ideal for mountain bikes. By the early 1990s, tour buses had begun to discover them and, although they're still a lot less traveled than main roads, it's not as virgin an experience as it used to be.

A variation on this route is via Campuan to Kedewetan, Payangan, and Punggang to Batur's crater rim. This back road from Ubud is now paved for all but six or seven km, but features potholes and ruts the whole way, making it an easier trip by motorcycle than by car. The road intersects the main north-south road at Kalanganyar, the village between Kintamani and Penelokan. An even more adventurous route for a private vehicle is the one via Peliatan to Pujung and Jasan. The surfaced mountain road that passes through Pujung emerges onto the road along the crater rim northwest of Penelokan. Check out the woodcarving centers and artshops of Tegallalang, Pujung, Jati, and Sebatu on the way. Jati, where the great carver I Tjokot lived, is just off the road beyond Tegallalang. The Peliatan/Tegallalang/Pujung/Batur road is much nicer than the one passing through Pejeng and Tampaksiring.

Walks From Ubud

Go to Ubud to get close to the real Bali. All around this sprawling village are scenic rice fields, forested gullies, deep river gorges, lush vegetation, half-overgrown shrines and grottos, beautiful and diversified landscapes, Tarzan pools, moss-covered temples carved from rock hillsides, even a Monkey Forest. Wake with the sun and set off on foot or bicycle down any of the village's many lanes. Indispensable companions to bring along are Victor Mason's *Bali Birdwalks*, the Pathfinder trail map *Ubud and Environs,* and bottled water.

Any track leading off Ubud's main road, Jl. Raya, will do. The path will lead to pristine native *kampung* with a contingent of yapping dogs. You'll get an inside look at the enormously durable community life of the Balinese. A walk from Ubud to Kubuh, Tunjungun, Yeh Tengah, Keliki, Campuan, and back to Ubud will take only a day. Rest during the noonday heat, then set off again in the late afternoon. Or just walk straight to Keliki; the trail starts from beside the Pura Campuan Batu Lebah in front of Murni's in Campuan. This very nice two-hour walk up through a river

valley takes you by rice paddies and jungle with no vehicles or shops and few people.

For total and instant immersion into Balinese rice culture—really beautiful and only minutes away—walk up through Ubud's *pura dalem* on the east side of town, or pay to get in to the Puri Lukisan. After taking in the exhibits, go around the back of the last building and start walking north along the gradually rising path between irrigation canals. This is as real as Bali can get, and you'll probably be completely alone. You'll see pond herons, rare Malay facewings, Javan Mooniers, white-bellied swiftlets, Troides Helena butterflies, and Lucinea spiders.

To walk to Kintamani, leave Campuan at 0500 and walk steadily uphill through Sebali and Keliki—you'll reach Kintamani around 1700 or 1800 the same day. Most of the mountains of central Bali can be seen on this beautiful walk. If it starts to get dark, stay on one of the village platforms. It's a big event in the village when a car or motorcycle drives by or a person arrives on foot.

On the walk to Pejeng, you'll take in surpassing views of rice fields. This is also a great cycling and jogging road. East of Ubud at the T-junction, go straight ahead instead of turning south to Peliatan. This bitumen road (Jl. Laplapan) heads straight east to Tatiani (30 minutes). Cross a river and ask the local boys in Tatiani to take you to the waterfall. Farther on, in Pejeng Timor east of the *kepala desa's* office, is a temple with two amazing reliefs with very deep dimensions and almost animated carvings. In Pejeng, see the Moon of Pejeng, then walk south via Bedulu to visit the Archaeological Museum in Bedulu.

Victor Mason's Bali Birdwalks

This three-hour guided tour is not just for those who love birds but for anyone who appreciates natural productions—butterflies, trees, brilliant scenery. Meet at 0900 in Victor's Bali-style restaurant and pub, Begger's Bush, by the bridge in Campuan. After a drink, the group sets out, getting back at around 1300 for lunch. The cost is Rp59,000 (10% goes to the Bali Bird Club), which includes the birdwalk, binocular use, lunch, bottled water, coffee, and tea.

The biggest draw is the inimitable humor, panache, and wit of Victor, your host, who has lived on Bali since 1970. Victor really plays the part of the eccentric British ornithologist. He started his vastly entertaining nature rambles in 1990; as the years go by, it's getting harder and harder to find good paths into the countryside, but Victor seems to know them all. He'll lead you into the exquisite gardens of Puri Lukisan, demonstrate how to paste a *cingke* leaf on your forehead to cool you down, teach you how to suck sweet nectar from a Cardinal's Hat or whistle birds up. Of the 100 bird species found around Ubud, you're bound to see 30 or so, as well as some quite abrupt alterations of habitat. The best way to go is barefoot. Sharp-eyed Sumadi is his able assistant. Call (0361) 975-009 to make a reservation.

VICINITY OF UBUD

Nyuhkuning

This village lies beyond the Monkey Forest, far from the hubbub of Ubud. See the woodcarving museum in the middle of the paddies. Exhibited are 30 or so carvings dating from the 1950s. Each piece is displayed with a plate providing the sculptor's biographical information. This is the first real effort to show the wide variety in Ba-

linese carving. Stay in isolated, peaceful River Garden Homestay, with five rooms and two bungalows. Managed by an American, River Garden is to be developed as a health spa.

Singakerta

From Nyuhkuning, it's an hour's walk (crossing en route a dizzying girder bridge over the Oos River) to Singakerta's *purah puseh,* with elaborate gargoyles on the gate and *kulkul* tower. From this temple walk about 50 meters west to Pura Gado, a strange temple which combines both stupa-like Buddhist and primitive Polynesian features. In Singakerta, some of Bali's best woodcarvers make their living. South of the village on a well-trod path is the extravagant Pura Penataran Agung next to a big *wantilan* tree. Refresh yourself in the picturesque bath behind the temple. Beyond, in the rice fields, is Goa Raksasa, a perfect meditation spot in a cove of hibiscus and poinciana bushes framing a Javanese-style *candi.*

Tegenungan

Relax and enjoy Balinese village surroundings twenty minutes south of Ubud by taxi. Walk 300

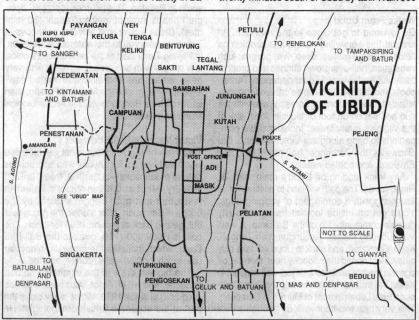

meters from the main road through rice paddies and invigorate yourself at the **Waterfall Restaurant,** which affords outrageous 360-degree views of lush tropical paradise. Stand under the waterfall and receive the ultimate cold, clean water massage.

Sanginggan

There are many places to stay north of town, like in **Wisata Cottages** in the small village of Sanginggan a little past Campuan. The Wisata has Rp40,000 bungalows, which include a nice breakfast. Rooms are right on the edge of a dropoff to a ravine with the river below. The problem with this locale is that it's too dangerous to walk along the narrow road down to Campuan and back. There are deep ditches on both sides, into which you'll surely be forced to escape the roaring trucks. This road desperately needs a sidewalk.

CENTRAL GIANYAR REGENCY

PETULU

A scenic area and bird sanctuary about an hour's walk up a gradual uphill road running north of Peliatan. Another approach is via the road by Coconut's in Ubud. As you approach Petulu, it feels like olde Bali—the people aren't burned out on tourists yet. The population is 4,500 farmers and 15,000 herons.

Famous dancers, teachers, musicians, and wood- and stonecarvers live here, including dance master I Ketut Tutor, who teaches *baris*; I Ketut Tutur, a renowned *topeng* performer and teacher of dance; and I Wayan Gandra, a *gamelan* musician of international acclaim. On the road, especially near where the road to Petulu turns west off the main highway to Tampaksiring, are a number of shops selling woodcarvings in huge display rooms. The woodcarving village of Pujung lies 11 km north of Petulu.

From the roundabout in north Peliatan just before the entrance to Ubud, flag down a *bemo* (Rp300) toward Tampaksiring and get off at the start of the road west up to Petulu village, then walk 2.25 km to the heron-viewing site Petulu Gunung. In the northern part of the village are souvenir shops, a traditional bathing place, and a carved temple with water pouring from the mouths of stone animals.

The Heronry

Start this pleasant afternoon excursion so you arrive no later than 1700 to see the great flocks of thousands of large white herons (known collectively as *kokokan*) wheeling, drifting, sailing, landing in a number of tall palms and *bunut* trees to roost for the night. The next morning they fly north to the cool climes of Gunung Batur, where they feed for the day. It's an impressive sight, seeing flocks of herons shift whole trees. Considered sacred, plumed egrets, cattle egrets, and Javan pond herons may not be disturbed while they roost. Only if they fall to earth or become caught in a tree may they be captured and turned into a delectable sort of pâté wrapped in plantain leaf.

The birds began roosting here for the first time in 1966, just one month after an elaborate sacrificial ceremony petitioning for protection and blessings after the political butchering of thousands of "communists." Many Balinese believe the herons embody the souls of the dead, come to reunify the people of Petulu. Twice a year on Saniscara Kliwon Landep the people of Petulu hold a special ceremony for these birds.

Accommodations And Food

The **Mudita Inn** has four rooms with showers and flush toilets for Rp25,000 d (a bargain during the slow season). The **Puri Asri,** P.O. Box 37, Ubud 80571, fax (0361) 975-120, a peaceful village house, lies just at the start of the smaller road up to Petulu from the main Peliatan-Tampaksiring road. Room rate is Rp40,000 d for any of five bungalows, hot water and breakfast included. Free jeep transport into Ubud for dinner. Quiet in spite of the location between two highways.

Five-star **Hotel Puri Kamandalu,** owned by Suharto's daughter, rents bungalows starting at Rp210,000 per day. Food is expensive if you eat in the restaurant with formal dinner settings: Rp21,000 for breakfast, Rp42,000 for dinner.

THE PEJENG AREA

With over 40 old temples in the region between the rivers Pakrisan ("Kris River") and Petanu ("Cursed One"), the Pejeng area contains Bali's richest collection of antiquities—from the earliest known kettledrum and clay stupa to relatively modern Shivaite sculptures and rockcut Buddhist sanctuaries and bathing places. Most antiquities are in the form of worn statues kept in important area temples. Because Balinese Prince Udayana married a Javanese princess, East Javanese cultural influences started to appear in Bali in the beginning of the 11th century and the language used in inscriptions changed from Old Balinese to Old Javanese.

The town of Pejeng, 48 km northeast of Denpasar, is named after an illustrious kingdom concentrated in the Bedulu-Pejeng area from the 9th century to the 14th century, when it fell to Majapahit invaders. Today it has a powerless but high-status *puri* (Pemahyun) and is full of Brahmans. Most visitors drive from Denpasar right through Bedulu and Pejeng on their way to Tampaksiring and Penelokan, sometimes stopping at the Gedong Arca archaeological offices in Bedulu en route. No accommodations or restaurants in Pejeng, but some good markets. From Pejeng, take the wonderful walk to Manggis—lots of small villages, emerald green rice fields, and dense green forests.

The Moon Of Pejeng

If heading north, Pura Panataran Sasih (*sasih* means "drum") is on the right side of the road after Gedong Arca, recognizable by its stone sculptures of wild boars and *naga*. The chief shrine of the 10th century Pejeng kingdom, this *pura* is linked to the Bali Aga mountain sanctuary of Penulisan north of Kintamani. Heading north from Bedulu, the temple is on the main road on your right just as you enter Pejeng.

Hanging in a high pavilion to the left, surrounded by a wooden fence, is a superb example of Bronze Age art, the sacred monumental bronze gong known as the Moon of Pejeng. Considered a masterpiece of bronze-casting, this 186.5-cm-tall hourglass-shaped gong is thought to be the largest in the world cast in a single piece and the oldest surviving archaeological artifact on Bali.

Legend has it that in the beginning of time, one of the earth's 13 moons fell from heaven and landed in a tree. This moon was so bright it stopped the shameful work of a thief. This so annoyed the criminal he climbed the tree and urinated on the heavenly object. With a loud boom the moon exploded, killing the thief and falling to earth as a gong. The fall damaged it—a crack can still be seen on its base—and the urine explains the green coloration. To this day no one dares touch the gong and daily offerings are made to it.

Other legends hold the gong is the wheel of the chariot of the moon or the earplug of the mythical giant Kebo Iwo or moon-goddess Ratih. A highly revered object, the richly ornamented gong is believed by most Balinese to possess magic power. Its sounding surface measures 160 cm in diameter. The piece is thought to date from around 300 B.C., the beginning of the Indonesian Bronze Age.

No one knows whether the gong originated in Bali or northern Vietnam. With its horizontal bands, diagonal and vertical lines, triangles, spirals and double spirals, it has definite connections with the Dongson culture (300 B.C. to A.D. 100) of Vietnam. The gong could have been carried to insular Southeast Asia by royal personages fleeing the Chinese. Some scholars speculate it precedes the Mings, and may have been a gift from Kublai Khan to a *raja* of Bali.

The Pejeng gong has been on continuous display in the Pura Panataran Sasih since the Old Balinese period. It's believed to be about 1,000 years older than the Pejeng dynasty. When the great naturalist Rumphius visited Bali over 300 years ago, the kettle gong was already ancient. The treasure is so high up in a tower-like shrine you can't make out the detail—bring binoculars. Donation requested.

A row of large shapeless rocks to the right of the courtyard are said to be shooting stars dislodged by the moon when it fell to earth. Also kept here are ancient commemorative statues of former kings and a well-weathered statue of Ganesha recovered from the Pakrisan River valley. Open pavilions in the complex contain an odd assortment of 10th- to 12th-century sculptures: commemorative statues of old rulers and a group of standing gods joined in prayer.

Getting Away

There are many archaeological odds and ends in this "Valley of the Kings" in the middle of Bali's rice belt; follow the directory on Pejeng's main street. A strange 120-cm-high linga, surrounded by eight upper-body statues of Shiva, is found in the open *bale* of Pura Ratu Pegening east of Pura Panataran Sasih. It's a nice walk to the 14th-century cut-rock *candi* at Kalebutan near Tatiapi, one km west of Pejeng Timor. To reach this group, which looks like a scaled down version of Gunung Kawi, start on the path from the second crossroads after the *puri* leading to Pejeng's graveyard. A landslide uncovered the existence of this *candi* in 1928; vegetation covered it again after the war and yet again in the 1950s. The 3.5-meter-high temple has been carved in relief from a two-meter-wide niche cut into solid rock. In 1951 a cloister with cut-rock niches and a courtyard were discovered on the other side of the ravine.

IMPORTANT TEMPLES OF THE PEJENG AREA

Pura Kebo Edan

South of Pejeng is Pura Kebo Edan ("Mad Buffalo Temple"). As you head north from Bedulu, you first pass the archaeological museum on the right; a bit farther on your left is Pura Kebo Edan. Small but historically significant, this temple features a huge statue under a wooden shelter. The figure goes by the local name of Bima. There is considerable conjecture about whether this horned and fanged giant, which probably dates from the 13th or 14th century, represents a demon or a god. Urs Ramseyer, in *The Art and Culture of Bali,* claims Pura Kebo Edan is probably a Balinese version of the East Javanese Singosari magic temples built on Java during the 12th century.

The 3.6-meter-high male dancing figure towers over the courtyard. Snakes curl around his ankles and wrists and he's endowed with a magnificent penis. On his head is an ornate mask and headdress. He stands on the bodies of a copulating couple. Legend says Bima wanted sex with this woman but his penis was too large for her. When he found her with a mortal, he crushed the man beneath his feet. The giant is flanked by a pair of lesser *raksasa* in

threatening postures and decorated with skulls. In front are two reclining buffalo, one male and one female. The statue was restored in 1952.

Pura Puser Ing Jagat

A large, very old temple dating from A.D. 1329 with unique reliefs, thought to be the center of the old Pejeng kingdom. A major pilgrimage site, during the full moon this *pura* draws couples desiring children and people hoping to increase their healing powers. The temple is part of a legend about Bali's last indigenous king, Bedaulu, and his escape from the Majapahit army in 1343 through an underground tunnel to the bandit isle of Nusa Penida. In the *pura* is a stone that no one may ever move—it's believed to be the secret entrance to the tunnel.

See the four dancing mustachioed demons in Gedong Puser Tasik on the temple's east side—sneering expressions, bulging eyes, swinging penises, clubs in their right hands, conch shells in their left. This type of statuary, with figures on all four sides, is called *catuhkaya.*

Housed in a shrine behind the temple is the Pejeng Vessel, or Mandala Giri, a cylindrical stone vase entwined with serpents and portraying the churning of the sea of milk. The carvings on the bowl relate the story of nine gods, each corresponding to a different quarter of the compass. A chronogram dates the vessel at around A.D. 1329.

Pura Pengukur Ukaran And Goa Garba

This walk to the Pakrisan River Valley, near the village of Sawangunung, is a total immersion into rural Bali in an area untrafficked by tourists. Start your walk by turning east at the intersection by the *pasar* just north of Pura Panataran Sasih. The small road bears to the right, then to the left. Walk for one km to the T-junction, turn left, then walk past the school to Pura Pengukur Ukuran. Below is Goa Garba.

Pura Pungukur Ukuran means "The Temple from which All Things are Measured." Built by King Jayaprangus on the edge of a ravine at the end of the 12th century, the temple's inner courtyard contains numerous *bale,* pre-Hindu megaliths, carved stones, and an ornate shrine with linga. Out a side gateway take the flight of huge stone steps descending to Goa Garba ("The Womb") on the western bank of the Pakrisan River. A gouge on a boulder step is said to be the footprint of the giant Kebo Iwa himself.

In this small valley is a carved stone gateway, ancient disused bathing places (the king's on the left, the queen's on the right), and three meditation niches hewn out of the rockface, with slanting roofs and carvings decorating the wall above. Inscriptions in Kediri script above the hermitage cells are still legible; inside are a few pieces of ancient sculpture and pedestals.

KEDEWATAN

A small village in the foothills two km north of Sayan on the road to Kintamani via Payangan. At the T-junction the road to the east leads after about six km to Ubud, passing Neka Museum on the left and Ananda Cottages on the right. Take a swim or sunbathe on the black rocks along the river below by walking 25 meters south of the shrine, which is south of Kupu Kupu Barong Cottages. Then follow a winding path through terraces carved out of the hillside down to the river. Take a shower under one of the many chilly, naturally fed springs. Another path starts north of Kupu Kupu Barong down a dramatic cliff face of switchbacks through rice fields and palms right to the edge of the foaming river. See the bat cave at the bottom of the gorge.

North of the T-junction is a *warung babi guling,* said to be the best in the area. This and several other Kedewatan *warung* are the last genuine *warung* in the whole Ubud area. The reasonably priced **Ubud Indah Garden** in Banjar Lungsiakan/Kedewatan serves good Indonesian and European food, has clean washrooms, and serves ice made from boiled water. It also prepares Italian, Chinese, Japanese, Indian, Balinese, and seafood dishes. Friendly service. Open for breakfast, lunch, and dinner. The restaurant offers free transport to and from accommodations in the Ubud area. In Sayan Kutuh, visit the gallery of painter I Nyoman Weda, a particularly pleasant person.

Accommodations

Because of the unique and coveted location lining a precipice over a deep and fertile river valley, Kedewatan's accommodations tend to be very intimate, very exclusive, and very expensive. If you have to think about money, you prob-

ably can't afford it. These fine resorts typically offer delicious seclusion, spa bathrooms, gym facilities, flexible check-in/check-out, airport transfers, valet and tour services, courtesy shuttle buses into Ubud, even golf driving ranges. At least stop in these cool hillside hotels for a cup of tea or a glass of wine and enjoy the view of the rushing Ayung River 75-100 meters below.

One of Bali's most exquisite hotel properties is the **Amandari,** tel. (0361) 975-333, fax 975-335, part of the Hong Kong-based Aman Resort group. This ultradeluxe two-million dollar hotel achieved world prominence in November 1990 when Mick Jagger and Jerry Hall were married on the premises. Designed by Peter Muller, who also designed the Oberoi, the Amandari simulates a Balinese village with 27 walled garden suites—virtual house complexes. The cheapest bungalow rents for Rp525,000 per night, the most expensive is Rp1.5 million (plus 15.5% tax and service). Each fully tiled bungalow, with teak beams, rattan furniture, sliding floor-to-ceiling glass walls, and sunken marble outdoor tubs, is connected by walkways leading to the resort facilities. On the grounds are lily ponds, a large (29-by-19 meters) hillside pool in the shape of a rice terrace, and a tennis court. Both simplicity and elegance are the rule—no signs, no noise, no plastic, no unnatural materials, no radios, no music, no telephones ringing. Free transport to and from the airport. Bikes and guides are available free of charge. Extraordinary security; sentinels in white tunics guard the grounds.

One of the area's premier accommodations is the **Kupu Kupu Barong,** P.O. Box 7, Ubud, Bali, tel. 975-478, fax 975-079, in Kedewatan, perched on the edge of a cliff above the impossibly green Ayung River. Out nearly every window of its 19 luxurious a/c bungalows are breathtaking views, in some ways superior to the Amandari's because you're closer to the river. Structures are built in traditional *lumbung* style, with thatch roofs, bath and shower, fridge, ceiling fans, separate entrances, and private balcony and terrace. Each unit is set at a different level amidst organic, leafy, extravagant gardens and pathways overgrown with bougainvillea and sprays of orchids. The property boasts three pools, a resort shop, and Balinese massage and whirlpool. Part of the complex is an excellent and spectacularly situated restaurant.

Rajapala and Mahabharata dances are put on each evening. Rates (subject to 15.5% tax and service) begin at Rp640,000 and go up to Rp3.1 million for the Barong Suite with private pool. Tranquil Balinese exoticism.

Completely self-contained **Puri Kamandalu** consists of 20 rooms combining classical Chinese and Indonesian motifs. Located right by a rafting river, you can take paths and walkways all the way down to the river. Great meditation place. Lowest priced bungalows with two-meter-long baths cost Rp368,000, 75-square-meter suites are Rp473,000. **Putra Ubara Homestay** has four big, comfortable, cool, well-furnished rooms for Rp35,000 apiece, including breakfast and houseboy attendance. Off the road at the southern end of the Sayan chasm, the view over terraced *sawah* is less spectacular but also 30 times cheaper than the Amandari.

Vicinity Of Kedewatan

Seven km beyond Kedewatan and about 13 km north of Ubud is Payangan, from where the road continues to climb toward the eastern mountains. You can also get to Payangan from Keliki. Walk west via Keliki Kawan, noting its gargantuan banyan tree. After Klusa, cross over a river and end up in Payangan's marketplace. This is a nice, cool village with a busy fruit and vegetable *pasar* every three days, less commercialized than Ubud's market. The only place on Bali where litchi (*longan*) are cultivated; also in this region are vanilla, *durian,* pineapple, and coconut plantations.

CAMPUAN

A crossroads village one km west of Ubud. Walk down a road between huge green embankments, then cross the bridge over a deep river gully. The bridge 25 meters above the river is a vital link between Ubud and the villages of Campuan, Penestanan, Sangginan, and Kedewatan to the west. The walk to and from Ubud has become quite hair-raising because of the traffic but staying in a slower-paced village is incentive enough to brave it. Below the Campuan bridge flows the River Oos, which serves as a laundromat and bathing site. Down on the right side two branches of the river meet, a spirit-

ual spot for Hindus. The word *campuan* actually means where two rivers meet, a corruption of *campuran* (as in *nasi campur*). On the spur in between is moss-covered 12th-century Pura Gunung Labuh, an agricultural and fertility temple. Bathe under pure mountain spring water pouring out of a bamboo spout.

History

Legend has it that a wandering Hindu priest named Rsi Markendya founded the temple of Pura Gunung Lebah in the 8th century at the confluence of Campuan's two rivers. Near this spot in 1906, Nieuwenkamp discovered a nine-by-one-by-two-meter hewn-rock cave supported by two columns. Characters were written on the roof, which had caved in during the 1917 earthquake. Ever since the German artist Walter Spies took up residence in the 1930s on the grounds of the present-day Hotel Tjampuan, the lush, tranquil beauty of the village has attracted famous painters, scholars, and celebrities from all over the globe. While here, Spies and Rudolph Bonnet made important contributions to modern Balinese art by coaching Balinese artists and providing them with paints and canvases. These Europeans inspired the Balinese to forsake the rigid conventions of the traditional style and adopt some European painting techniques.

Pura Gunung Lebah

This beautiful, tranquil, and impeccably maintained temple lies beside the river just north of the Campuan bridge, easily accessible from the Tjetjak Inn. The celebrated *batik* painter Nyoman Suradnya considers it the most important temple in the Ubud area. It was the site of the Penyegjeg Bhumi, the "Great Ceremony to Straighten the World" of October 1991, a ceremony held only once a century. An exciting discovery, the temple doesn't seem to be in anyone's maps or guides, so it has no sash-hawkers or other sellers lying in wait outside the front gate. Sit in the temple and listen to the river. You'll probably be the only person in the place.

Neka Museum

This nicely laid-out museum, one km north of Campuan, sits in a traditionally designed compound of four galleries containing the works of the greats of Balinese art. The museum portion, where works are not for sale, makes up only one small corner of the complex; the rest of the art is for sale. In the first gallery are exhibited the works of well-known traditional Balinese painters. In the second gallery are the works of modern Indonesian artists with formal academic training who've worked on Bali. In the third gallery are the works of three European artists— Walter Spies, Rudolph Bonnet, and Arie Smit— who greatly encouraged and influenced the direction of Balinese art. The art of other foreign painters who lived for extensive periods on Bali is displayed in the fourth gallery.

Besides these permanent exhibits, you can view paintings from an adjoining, continuously changing exhibit. In the small bookshop you can buy postcards of some of the gallery's best known works and copies of the book *Perceptions of Paradise*. Although a good variety of modern and traditional paintings are for sale, unfortunately there are no labels, no price list, and no information about the paintings. The Neka Museum was founded by Suteja Neka, who's collected works for this exhibit since 1966. Admission Rp500.

Galleries

It's easy to strike up a rambling, enjoyable conversation with Antonio Blanco, an eccentric Catalonian artist who welcomes visitors to his home/gallery. He's an intriguing character, which is great for business. Blanco calls his style renaissance; many of his paintings are bawdy and erotic, yet possess grace and rhythm, attractive colors, and lots of hidden meanings. Blanco paints in a pit below floor level so he can view his subjects at eye level. The steep driveway to Blanco's home is on the left immediately after the bridge on the way into Campuan from Ubud. Definitely worth a visit.

Accommodations

Family-operated **Ananda Cottages**, P.O. Box 205, Denpasar 80001, tel. (0361) 975-376, fax 975-375, has three classes of rooms: standard downstairs Rp63,000 s, Rp73,000 d; superior upstairs Rp73,000 s, Rp94,000 d; and family units Rp160,000. Add 15.5% tax and service. All rooms have private facilities, hot and cold running water, 24-hour room service, and veranda or terrace. Intercoms connect the rooms to the front desk. An open-air restaurant serves Euro-

pean or Indonesian food. Nice surroundings and hospitable and friendly staff. Relax at the bar and take a swim or sunbathe in the natural spring-fed pool. Recreational activities include badminton and a jogging track nearby. The cottages are between the Campuan bridge and the Neka Museum, facing beautiful rice fields. **Tjetjak Inn,** on the right as you're approaching Campuan, charges Rp31,500 s, Rp42,000 d (includes tax) for small, sparsely furnished bungalows overlooking the river. Breakfast is included, served either on your veranda or in the open-air restaurant. No phones in rooms. Close to the main Ubud-Campuan road, with a sweeping view, good vibrations, a nearby natural springs, and superb walking tracks in the vicinity. Call 975-238 or fax 975-052 for reservations, especially in July and August. **Made's and Uli Pering's Cottages,** a 20-minute walk uphill from the Tjetjak Inn, rent for Rp35,000 and look out over a magnificent ravine. For people who like to walk or meditate. Quiet, except for the sound of the rivers below. Negotiable seasonal rates.

Long a favorite of Jakarta-based expats, **Murni's Houses,** tel. 975-165, lies below the restaurant of the same name; Rp94,500 per day for an apartment and Rp158,000 per day for a private house (capacity eight people). Pool, maid service, and helpful staff. Each accommodation is whimsically decorated with Balinese paintings and hanging winged gods. From your veranda contemplate some of the area's most impressive examples of agricultural engineering. **Puri Sekar Ayu Bungalows,** Jl. Raya Campuan, tel. 975-671, on the right on the road down to Campuan, offers five bungalows on a hill. Rates are Rp46,000-63,000, with delicious breakfast included. Nice patio restaurant, peaceful surroundings.

On the slope of a green hill overlooking a deep gorge, the luxury-class 26-room **Hotel Tjampuan,** P.O. Box 15, Denpasar 80001, Bali, tel. 975-368 or 975-369, fax 975-137, is on the right, about 200 meters up after the bridge. The embodiment of the rustic charm architectural movement of the 1950s, with a decided air of neglect, the property is much bigger than it looks. The rates are Rp94,500 s, Rp109,000 d for standard Agung rooms; Rp137,000 s, Rp168,000 d for Raja rooms; all are subject to 15.5% tax and service. Each large bungalow has its own bathroom with hot and cold water, jacuzzi-style bath, shower, ceiling fan, and veranda, but no in-room telephone. Spies and Bonnet both lived here during the 1930s; in fact, you may sleep in Spies's old house. Facilities include a 1930s-style pool and tennis court (reportedly built for Woolworth heiress Barbara Hutton), badminton courts, bar, restaurant, and lots of exquisite privacy. Take a stroll through the scenic, rambling, and well-kept grounds. **Ulun Ubud Cottages,** P.O. Box 3, Ubud, tel. 975-024 or 975-762, fax 975-524, is actually in the outskirts of Campuan beyond the Neka Museum in Sanggingan, 2.5 km north. This top-class hotel boasts some truly distinct features: dramatic location with stunning views, fine performance and study spaces, good restaurant, bar, pool, and a variety of spacious traditional-style rooms with hot water, bath, shower, and antiques. Priced at Rp94,500 s, Rp116,000 d for standard rooms; Rp105,000 s, Rp137,000 d for studio bungalows; Rp231,000 twin, Rp189,000 triple for family units; Rp137,000 s, Rp189,000 d for suite rooms. All rates include breakfast, tax, and service. Clean, quiet, beautifully designed and decorated.

HILLTOP CAMPUAN

If you'll be staying in Ubud for three days, stay in one of the area's homestays. If you're staying for a month, rent one of the bungalows above the main road on the Penestanan side of Campuan. Pure country. The more picturesque and peaceful places—surrounded by rice paddies and overlooking gardens—are often under contract for months on end. On the higher levels of the village on a clear day you can see Gunung Agung towering in the distance. You're out of earshot of the main road and far away from Ubud's hustle, bustle, noise, and pollution.

Reach this peaceful area by taking the steep road to the left after the Campuan bridge. With its *warung,* restaurants, clusters of bungalows, lanes, swimming holes, and shops, it's an entirely self-contained community from which you never need venture. As it's uncertain where Campuan ends and Penestanan begins, just call it "Hilltop Campuan." Dotting the ridge are a dozen idyllic family-run homestays overlooking some of Bali's most beautiful *sawah,* only a few

minutes walk from the road. These private compounds consist of two to five bungalows that rent long-term. There's almost always a waiting list, but in September it really slows down. Typically, on the bottom floor is a bathroom, a kitchen with cooking facilities, and an open-air living room. On the second floor you'll find a large bedroom and porch with great views of cascading terraces and forests. Outside are beautiful gardens and sometimes even a lotus pond. There's usually a delightfully cool breeze from the south blowing through, keeping both the heat and the bugs down. Instead of paying Rp400,000 per day at Nusa Dua for make-believe Bali, see the real Bali in one of the many accommodations in this area for a fraction of the cost.

Accommodations

A wonderful place to stay is **Made Arta's**—three comfortable houses in the middle of paddies. Each costs Rp30,000 per day and can hold up to four people. Made comes every morning to prepare a delicious breakfast. He speaks English well, and is a valuable source of local information, customs, and conversation. Climb the Penestanan steps and follow the path to the right. About 230 meters past Kori Agung, turn left down the path and find Made Arta's on the right. To reserve a bungalow, write Arta Bungalows, Campuan, Ubud 80571, Bali, Indonesia.

For Rp30,000 you can occupy a whole house at isolated **I Nyoman Gelis Bungalows.** Up to four people may share a big quiet bungalow with hot water. Nyoman gives great massages for Rp20,000 per hour. His place is about a 10-minute walk from Warung Ibud Putu. Bathing place down the path below the homestay. **Garebig Bungalows** in Penestanan Kelod offers a full range of accommodations at different prices. The two-story bungalows for Rp30,000 are the best; others go for Rp15,000. All rooms overlook rice paddies. Price includes a nice breakfast, plus bananas and tea in the afternoon. The room service is a real advantage to staying here, as is the daily maid service.

Melati Cottages, P.O. Box 15, Ubud, tel. (0361) 975-166, nearby, offers sumptuous quarters. Turn left after Blanco's and at the top of the hill take the little path near Hotel Penestanan and wander around the rice paddies. Nyoman Rata, the proprietor, knows what Westerners like. His 12 bungalows, Rp21,000-52,500 d, offer hot water, floor-to-ceiling glass walls, 360-degree views over *sawah*, wide wooden plank floors, life-size woodcarvings, a pool in the middle of rice paddies, and a library. Very quiet, good service, and well-protected in an enclosed area. Nyoman will pick you up at the airport and take you to Ubud. **Pugur Bungalow,** P.O. Box 10, Ubud, on the edge of the rice fields, is a beatific spot of peace and quiet still close to restaurants and other conveniences. After Warung Ibu Put, take a left and walk two minutes; it's on the right. All bungalows feature well-equipped private kitchens so you can cook for yourself, or you can hire a Balinese cook for Rp100,000 per month. Very private with beautiful views of both Gunung Agung and Gunung Batukau. The owner, Pugur, who studied with Arie Smit in 1963, may invite you to his house for *kuningan*.

Food

A tiny place with only three tables, **Warung Dewi,** on the right at the bend of road as you come down the hill from Ubud, serves black rice pudding topped by an enormous fruit salad (Rp1500), as well as excellent vegetarian *nasi campur* (Rp2000). Dewi takes special orders of *bebek tutu* for four (Rp25,000).

Siddharta's is an open-sided restaurant with accommodations in the rice paddies near the Penestanan steps. Service is friendly, food inexpensive and well-prepared, the premises clean and attractive, the views nourishing. Recommended is the Buddha's Delight, a vegetarian dish of steamed fresh vegetables (Rp2000), or *nasi campur* with fried *tempe* chicken (Rp2500). Down the path from Siddharta's, near the stairway, is **Warung Ibu Putu**—shady, quiet, inexpensive, and friendly. Excellent soup, guacamole, first class *gado-gado*—everything on the menu Rp2000 or less.

On the Campuan side of the bridge, **Beggar's Bush Bar and Restaurant,** tel. (0361) 975-009, continues to enjoy a solid reputation for excellent Western and Indonesian food and nice atmosphere. The best steak, spareribs, and baked potato in town, plus real Balinese food like *ayam takir* (steamed running chicken) and *pecel paku* (ferns). Owner Victor Mason, founder of the Bali Bird Club, author of *Bali Bird Walks*, and enthusiastic ornithologist, is an af-

fable, highly literate, and charming English gentleman. In Victor's office is a 19th-century English polyphone, one of the first mechanical gramophone-type musical instruments.

Set in the midst of rice fields is an excellent restaurant called **Kori Agung.** A lovely couple runs this establishment, offering eight tables with a beautiful view. Everything on the menu is fresh and well-prepared at moderate prices—a dinner for two includes appetizers, main dishes, desserts, and coffee for about Rp42,000. The black rice pudding is some of the island's best.

Entertainment

Laser disc videos are screened at **Coconut's,** but movies are not thoughtfully chosen—usually violent. Not only is this the clearest screen around but there's also a crystal-clear stereo system and pleasant dining area. Another place that shows big-screen movies is the **Bridge Cafe** near Campuan's suspension bridge. The person who picks the films has good taste. The food is good but expensive.

The Beggar's Bush, on the right just after the bridge, captures the feeling of an English pub. Victor Mason's bar is named after a notorious 19th century tavern outside London. Truly cold draft beer is served at sensible prices (half pint Rp3000, full pint Rp5500); also try Beggar's Grog, a spiced *arak* from Karangasem brewed from a guarded family recipe. The Bush possesses a killer 1940s jazz and blues record collection. Balinese cowboys, regular irregulars, locals, police, and Brits love this sacred temple of low debauchery. The kitchen doesn't close until midnight to serve hungry late night revelers, many of whom are thankful for the free transport back to their hotels.

Shopping

Kunang-Kunang I in Campuan, tel. (0361) 975-714, fax 975-282, is an importer of stylish, collector-quality art objects, silver jewelry, textiles, pottery, musical instruments, furniture, and antiques from Lombok, Sumatra, Timor and all the outlying islands—you name it, they've got it. Not a souvenir shop, this place displays expensive stuff in locked glass cases: contemporary jewelry, silver, precious stones, and some *ikat* pieces. The staff speaks good English. A branch, Kunang-Kunang II, tel. 975-716, is on Jl. Raya in Ubud.

Daigo Yasugi sells Balinese art on T-shirts for Rp10,000-50,000. All are original works by Balinese painters living in Ubud—so original the other T-shirt makers copy his designs within a few days after they come out. His shirts are colorfast and fixed priced. Daigo can also make T-shirts to order. See his creations at the **Bali Art Co-op** on Jl. Raya, tel. and fax 975-087.

Services

Campuhan Tourist Service, P.O. Box 10, Ubud, tel. and fax (0361) 975-298, is the only travel agent in Campuan, handling faxes (Rp10,000 to the U.S.), airline ticketing and confirmations, hotel reservations, car rentals, moneychanging, and various tours.

Sekolah Seni Rupa Indonesia (SSRI) is opposite the Tjampuan Hotel. Several Westerners attend this inexpensive government art school. Telephone services are available at **Kori Agung Bungalows and Cafe,** which obviates visiting any of Ubud's telecommunications offices.

Walks From Campuan

The surrounding area is quite beautiful and setting out for a walk is a good way to kill half a day. Generally speaking, the north is cleaner and less polluted than the south. To the west is the painter's village of Penestanan, an easy walk from Campuan. From here turn north and walk to Sayan where the rice terraces and views from the hills are magnificent. Get a reasonably early start for the best views and photo opportunities, as the mist and light provide tremendous ambience.

Penestanan

Five km from Campuan via Kedewatan. However, there's a nice shortcut through rice fields to this village that lies only about two km from the Campuan-Kedewatan road. After crossing the bridge in Campuan, bear right and after 200 meters turn left at the homestay signs and ascend a steep flight of stone stairs. Continue on this path for one km to the main village of Penestanan. Just before the village, cross a deep river gully. On the left, down a path, is a refreshing bathing, washing, and drinking spot with ancient stone statues. Note the mixture of architecture along the way. There are several airy and extravagant private residences in the area occupied by jetsetting expats and foreign-service personnel. The best beadwork in the area is produced in the studio of Wayan Candra.

Accommodations: Reasonably priced Penestanan Bungalows, tel. (0361) 975-803, is situated in magnificent rice fields. Negotiate a price of Rp31,500 per day for nice-sized rooms high up on the second floor with privacy, fantastic views, and hot water. Life here is altogether pleasant and extremely quiet. The place is just half-full even in the high season because you can't drive there.

SAYAN

Head west out of Penestanan until you hit a bigger road. This is the start of the village of Sayan, about seven km from Ubud. In the 1930s the Canadian-born composer and ethnographer Colin McPhee built a house here, hired a lazy houseboy and a querulous Madurese cook, and wrote his classic *A House in Bali.* Parallel with the road, but not visible from it, is one of the most spectacular views in all Bali—a deep, lush river valley formed by the fast-flowing Ayung River. A famous photographic subject, this scene is portrayed on many postcards.

Take any of a number of paths to the west that lead through the trees and you'll come to the lip of the gorge. A number of private bungalows are available in the area—excellent value for those planning to spend three to four weeks. **Sayan Terraces,** P.O. Box 6, Ubud 80771, tel. (0361) 975-384, offers idyllic, quiet cottages for Rp35,000 s or d with free breakfast, hot water, and lovely porches overlooking the magnificent river valley. The owner/manager, I Wayan Ruma, is a kind and gentle man who'll pick you up at the airport if you write or call ahead. Nearby, on the northern side of Sayan Terraces, **Aman Bebek** offers two small houses for rent. The *warung* opposite Sayan Terraces serves the best *nasi campur* in Sayan; the one next to it offers excellent chicken *sate.*

Bongkasa

The largest blooming banyan tree in the Malay Archipelago—100 meters across—is in Bongkasa, near Sayan. To get there from the Bale Banjar Kutuh in Sayan, walk 80 meters south and take a right on the footpath to Bongkasa.

The trail leads past a temple, across bridges over an irrigation canal, then to the Ayung River. Continue north to the Pura Puseh of Bongkasa, an ornate temple built of brick surrounded by a spacious lawn. Walk on to stone steps that lead to the Tanggayuda *banjar* and on to Pura Desa Tenggayuda, where you'll see the tree. It's so large that from a distance it looks like a whole forest. The central bole has been entirely engulfed by a huge tangle of aerial roots and a mass of epiphytes. The tree is the habitat of a sizable population of birds, squirrels, and lizards. Proceed north to the sand-collecting gorge where laborers scoop sand from the bottom of the river using hand-operated pulleys, then haul the sand in buckets on their heads up the slope to the main road. From there it's collected by middlemen and sold for Rp4500 per cubic meter.

Getting Away

The ambitious may continue on to Sangeh, a beautiful walk through rice fields, shadowy lanes, and palm plantations, crossing little canyons over split-bamboo bridges. If you take it easy, it requires about four hours. Just keep asking for Sangeh; everybody knows the way. From Sangeh, take a *bemo* down to Denpasar (Rp800), then another *bemo* back up to Ubud again (Rp800)—a satisfying day-trip.

PELIATAN

Just 1.5 km southeast of Ubud, Peliatan spreads out along a very busy kilometer-long throughfare from Ubud to the bend in the road at Teges. The Peliatan *puri* actually predates Ubud's but because of a 17th century argument between two princes, two separate courts were created—Puri Saren in Ubud and Puri Kaleran in Peliatan. The Ubud aristocracy still pays respects to their higher-ranking royal cousins in Puri Kaleren.

The village of Peliatan and its neighboring hamlets are known among the Balinese for their internationally famous *legong* troupes and fine *semar pegulingan* orchestra. In 1931, under the leadership of Anak Agung Gede Mandera, a Peliatan ensemble was the first to leave Bali and perform abroad, creating an international sensation in Paris. The same troupe of dancers

and musicians took New York, London, and Las Vegas by storm in 1952 in a lavish tour organized by the British entreprenuer John Coast. Since the 1950s, Peliatan's *gong kebyar* group has dominated Bali's musical scene. In Ubud there are so many dance groups now it's difficult for individual groups to succeed financially, but in Peliatan there's ample opportunity to see both live dances and frequent rehearsals. With no less than 15 *gamelan* orchestras, Peliatan is a popular place for Westerners to study the performing arts.

Except—and this is a big exception—for the amount of traffic speeding down its long main street, Peliatan hasn't experienced the phenomenal growth that has afflicted Ubud. Because its relative isolation is conducive to studying, Peliatan makes an ideal language lab for learning Bahasa Indonesia or Balinese. For walkers, Peliatan is close to such historical attractions as Gajah Mada and Pejeng. Take off in any direction and you'll find something of interest. The lesser-known places can only be reached by foot or bicycle.

Accommodations

With about 15 pleasant, low-budget homestays and hotels in and around Peliatan, this village serves as an alternative to Ubud, especially when places in Ubud are too expensive or full in the peak season. Several accommodations are located just off the very busy and noisy main street, Jl. Cok Gede Rai, which runs right through town, but most lie down paths and lanes running into the surrounding countryside. Many rooms and bungalows are occupied semipermanently by Westerners studying dance and *gamelan*.

The **Andong Inn** is on the road from Peliatan to Petulu. In all, 11 rooms face a beautiful garden. The five Rp15,000 rooms without hot showers are the best deal; others with hot showers and bathtubs go for Rp35,000 s, Rp40,000 d including breakfast. Genuine Balinese food is served in the cafe. Very relaxing except for the humming of a nearby telephone tower. The **Gunung Merta Bungalow** is in Andong in north Peliatan by the police station, tel. (0361) 975-463, fax 975-120, a collection of eight comfortable rooms (Rp34,000-60,000 s or d) fashioned in traditional Balinese red and gray stone and set in a lovely tropical garden. Each room features a writing table, bamboo chairs, paintings, separate bathroom with tub, hot/cold shower, sink, flush toilet, and private patio. Rates include Indonesian, continental, or American breakfast. Amenities include a pool, IDD, fax, postal, transport and tour services, packing and shipping, and bicycle rental. Mr. Lilem, the owner, epitomizes Balinese hospitality, and possesses a broad knowledge of Bali and its people. The hotel's small size allows personalized attention.

Ibu Arsa Homestay, tel. 295-817, in a walled-in compound under the banyan tree on the main road, offers three classes of rooms: a bungalow facing the family temple for Rp25,000, two small bungalows for Rp10,000 each, and two standard rooms for Rp5000 each. Price includes breakfast of your choice. All rooms are spotless with attractive bamboo furniture and Balinese-style squat toilets and *mandi*. There's no private sitting area, but guests can linger in the courtyard on bamboo couches and chairs or in the restaurant out front. **Madra Homestay,** Banjar Kalah, tel. 975-749, is a quiet place in the rice fields in a beautiful garden, only 150 meters from the main road. Graded by size, location, and type of bathroom, three classes of bamboo and thatch-roofed *pondok* are available: Rp10,000 and Rp15,000 for older rooms (popular with long-term residents), and Rp20,000 s, Rp25,000 d for rooms with shower, good breakfast included. All prices subject to 10% tax. An ideal location for study, relaxation, peace, and quiet, Madra's is strongly recommended for both the budget traveler and the student of Balinese culture. The staff works hard to keep the place tidy and the atmosphere friendly. There's no restaurant, but you can arrange to have meals prepared. Excellent security, storage service, parking. Make reservations at least one month in advance for June, July, and August by sending a fax care of Ary's Wisata Travel Service in Ubud, fax 975-162.

Central Mandala Bungalows, tel. 975-028, in the middle of town, is actually the site of the Puri Kaleran palace of the former *raja* of Peliatan. Clean rooms with fan, cupboards, big inside bathrooms, showers, and hot water for Rp25,000 s, Rp30,000 d. The grounds of the *puri* are large—a very private, enclosed environment. Mandala's has been taking in guests since 1962, when Helen and Frank Schreider wrote of their stay here in *The Drums of Tonkin*. Students are always living in the compound. Ask to see the

photo album. The Mandera Cafe (reasonable prices) is only open in the high season.

The newly remodeled **Puri Agung Homestay** offers Balinese-style bungalows in five different classes, ranging from Rp6000-8000 s to Rp12,000-15,000 d. The more expensive feature living rooms, wardrobes, and small libraries. Bright, clean, spacious, peaceful. Cockatoos and parrots cackle in the attractive courtyard with its variety of trees and flowering plants. Since this has been the home of the old ruling clan of Peliatan for 12 generations, 16 different families live in 16 individual *kampung* within this large complex. Anom, the hostess, will regale you with tales of her dance troupe's tour of the world in the 1950s. Travelers have written glowingly of **Siti Homestay,** Banjar Kalah, tel. 975-599, which has six comfortable double rooms with attached *mandi* for only Rp8000 s, Rp10,000 d (larger rooms), and one deluxe room for Rp15,000. Price includes a big, delicious breakfast. The proprietors, Wayan and Siti, are both schoolteachers, and Wayan is articulate, well-informed, and speaks excellent English. Absolutely the top of the list for family homestays. Authentic Balinese atmosphere, quiet, pretty garden. The grounds are beautiful. Small bistro and cafe serving praiseworthy food. It's easy to get *bemo* on Jl. Peliatan one minute away, and Wayan can advise you about entertainment, best places to eat, celebrations, local transport, and good walks.

Food
Ageless **Ibu Arsa Restaurant,** tel. (0361) 975-817, under the banyan tree on the main road, was Peliatan's first restaurant, offering excellent and inexpensive Balinese food since 1968. Noteworthy are *sayur bayam* (stewed spinach) for Rp1000, *gado-gado* for Rp1000, and *mie kuah* for Rp1500, plus European food including oatmeal, omelettes, and ham steak with pineapple. Desserts include lemon pancake (Rp800) and black rice pudding with fruit (Rp1500). Ibu Arsa also serves special orders if you ask a day in advance: stewed chicken in sauce, smoked duck or fried chicken for Rp20,000. *Bubur* and *lawar* stalls located nearby.

Pande Homestay on Jl. Cok Gede Rai presents a smoked duck dinner for two served with rice and vegetables for only Rp18,000; order a day in advance. Next door is a very cheap *warung* serving *nasi goreng, sayur, ijo, ikan goreng, cap cai, and funghung hai.* You'll also find a bunch of excellent *warung* (try the Balinese-style *nasi campur*) near the T-junction east of Ubud where the road north leads to Petulu and the road south heads for Peliatan.

Mudita Inn, popular with travelers, cooks up huge *gado-gado,* freshly made from scratch for only Rp1500. Cheese omelettes with tomato are Rp1400, large cold Bintangs cost Rp3000, soft drinks Rp700. Mudita also offers soups, Balinese food, or lunch and dinner with two hours' notice. Open 0900-2200. Mudita is a guide and speaks good English. The kitchen staff of **Sita Homestay** in Banjar Kalah, tel. 975-599, makes superb homemade yogurt that took two years to perfect. Their smoked duck dinner, prepared by the grandfather (who is nearing 100), is the absolute nectar of the gods.

Performances

The big draw is the only all-woman *gamelan* on Bali, the famous *gamelan pegulingan* Mekar Sari, which performs at the Tirtasari Dance Stage under Mrs. Anak Agung Raka Mas. Members range from little girls and teens to regal-looking white-haired matrons. The music accompanies a children's *legong* group performing fairy tales. Very professional, very good lighting, brilliant costuming. In addition, there's a stylized staff fighting dance (*baris tombok*) performed by four boys. This unique, spirited presentation takes place on Sunday night 1930-2100.

Legong and *kecak* tickets for performances in the Peliatan/Ubud area can be conveniently purchased at the centrally located Mudita Inn on the main street (Jl. Cok Gede Rai), tel. (0361) 975-179. A sample of area performances: the tiny *legong* dancers, as well as the Mahabharata, every Tuesday 1930-2100 at Teges Kanginan; the *legong* with *barong* every Wednesday (same time) one km south of Pande Homestay at Banjar Teruna; and the *kecak* at Puri Kaleran in Mandala Bungalows at 1930-2030 every Thursday (over 200 performers, but it lasts but an hour). The **Kokokan Club** on Jl. Pengosekan, tel. 975-742, in the nearby hamlet of Pengosekan presents a traditional Balinese buffet with live entertainment like *joged gudegan, barong buntut,* the frog dance, or even Western-style experimental theater, such as the black comedy *Shamlet* (a takeoff on *Hamlet*) by the Frequent Flyers. Dinner and show Rp35,000, show only Rp10,000; every Thursday at 2000.

Dance Instruction

Peliatan is one of the few places on Bali where dancers are still trained in the traditional manner. The instructor glides through the dance movements, mimicked by a brace of little girls, all synchronized perfectly to the beat of the *kenong.* Some instructors invite European pupils to join in. Watch young Balinese students practice *gamelan* and dancing each day at around 1400 in the village *puri,* Puri Kaleran, otherwise known as Mandala Bungalows, tel. (0361) 975-028, on Jl. Cok Gede Rai, the palace of the former *raja.* Anak Agung Raka, a daughter of Anak Agung Mandera, runs a dance school next to Puri Agung Homestay. She has many Japanese students and starts a new class every six months or so. The dance master Sang Ayu Ketut Muklin teaches dance to young trainees at Teges Kanginan.

Shopping

With art galleries lining its main street and the din of workshops in its back alleys, Peliatan is a major center for carving and painting. Some Peliatan specialties are the carved wooden fruit, flowers, ducks, fish, frogs, tiny birds in frames, and mobiles produced by young carvers. Carved horses, deer, and tigers are produced in Teges, a village to the south of Peliatan. Gifted carvers worth visiting are Nyoman Togog and I Wayan Pasti. The neighboring villages of Mas and Nyuhkuning have been centers for woodcarving since the 1930s.

Djujul, whose studio is down the street from the Dok Putu Putera Homestay, is a well-known painter who works only when he's inspired. Djujul usually has a work in progress so you're able to see a real master paint. It's cheaper to buy directly from him than from a gallery—expect about 25% off the gallery price of Rp2.1 million for a small painting. **Dewa Windia Handicraft** showroom and workshop in Peliatan (west of the banyan tree) sells napkin holders, mirror frames, miniature ducks, giant Garuda statues, and tropical fruit sculptures. A selection of attractive *sarung* sell for Rp10,000-12,000 at the bistro in Siti Homestay in Banjar Kalah, tel. (0361) 975-599; also look for dresses and drawstring pants hand-tailored by Siti. Well-stocked groceries, dry goods, and appliance stores lie on the Teges end of town.

Banjar Kalah

This small hamlet is noted for its woodworking shops producing giant flowers, banana trees, small creatures, and fruits—an ideal place for those interested in wood handicrafts. Several *warung* and small restaurants here are popular with budget travelers. Drop in on toymaker I Made Greriya, tel. (0361) 975-241, who turns out educational toys, wooden animals, clever mobiles, puzzles, trees, flowers, and ducks. On the road west toward Pengosekan, which turns at the bend in the road to the east, is the workshop of Dewa Nyoman Batuan, who produces decorative boxes, handcarved mirror frames, and small cabinets.

Art Galleries

The painter, poet, writer, director, actor, musician, dancer, and choreographer Madi Kertonegoro, born in Ambarawa on Java, is a child of the Indonesian New Art Movement (Gerakan Seni Rupa Baru) and is reputed to be Indonesia's only antinuclear artist. His **Future Peace Art Gallery** is at Jl. Andong 1, tel. (0361) 975-467, only 450 meters north of the T-junction at the northern end of Peliatan. You can't miss it; there's a big sign. Works on permanent display include landscapes, still lifes, portraiture, and experimental art. Examine some of the books Madi has written in the **Pustaka Bayu** bookshop next to his studio; also check out the 1991 video about him and the cassette tape of his band Wild Roots.

The **Agung Rai Gallery** lies beyond Peliatan but before Negara, one km south of Pande Homestay. One of the finest galleries on Bali, a mammoth art complex of thatch-roofed, traditional-style *bale,* each building houses a different school of Balinese art. Schoolboys, some only six years of age, are regularly invited to the gallery to practice line drawing and to make copies of paintings under the guidance of a senior artist. Works from this well-known gallery have been exhibited in Singapore, Holland, Germany, and Guam. Agung Rai established the gallery in 1978; he got his start in the art business by peddling his paintings to tourists on the hot sands of Kuta Beach in the early 1970s. At least as much an educational experience as

Ubud's Puri Lukisan, these co-op showrooms give you a clear view of the scope and development of modern Balinese painting. See the marble-floored room filled with works costing up to Rp31.5 million. In the private collection in back are the haunting works of noted prewar Dutch, German, and Austrian artists who lived and worked on Bali, exerting a major influence on local painting styles.

Services

Change money at **Bakti Art Shop, Diana Express, Mudita Inn, Bank Duta, Bank Utama, and Bank BRI. Wayan Sidhakarya** (Puri Saren Kangin 31, Peliatan) is a professional Bahasa Indonesia language instructor who works for the Experiment in International Living. He can be contacted through the Mudita Inn, tel. (0361) 975-179. **I Wayan Paksa** of Siti Homestay, tel. 975-599, in Banjar Kalah, is also an effective teacher of Indonesian, insisting upon good grammar and correct usage.

Rent bicycles from **Mudita Inn** on Jl. Cok Gede Rai, for an average daily rate of Rp2000 for one-gear bikes and Rp3000 for mountain bikes; 10% discount if you rent by the week. Bikes are also available (Rp3500 per day) from the Andong Inn.

Getting Away

A *bemo* to Ubud center, Petulu, or Mas costs Rp300, to Denpasar Rp700 (baggage extra). If traveling farther afield, catch a *bemo* (Rp300) down to the Sakah intersection on the main road between Denpasar and Amlapura. From Sakah, you can travel to most of the attractions to the north, west, and east. For Gunung Batur, go straight up via Pujung if you have your own vehicle. You can make it in a *bemo,* but since they're so rare it's faster to first get a *bemo* to the Sakah turnoff, then another *bemo* to Tampaksiring, then head on to Batur. Get an early start; head back from Penelokan no later than 1700. For Besakih, take a *bemo* to Sakah, then another one to Klungkung. Leave by 0800 so you can see Klungkung's Kerta Gosa en route.

North of Peliatan, an asphalt road with nice scenery leads into the mountains to the quiet, rural woodcarving villages of Jati, Pujung, and Sebatu. The famous woodcarver I Nyoman Tjokot came from the village of Jati, 15 km north of Ubud. His sons, Ketut Nongos Cokot and

Made Dini, have carried on the family tradition, carving huge statues of Garuda and other mythological figures. Nongos's shop is in Teges at the crossroads of the roads east to Bedulu and west to Peliatan; Dini's shop is just west of the bridge before Goa Gajah, if coming from Teges.

TEGES

Just south of Peliatan, Teges is divided into two communities. Teges Kanginan, east of the main road, is renowned for its musicians, dancers, *wayang kulit* puppeteers, and teachers of the *kecak, kebyar,* and *legong,* as well as an accomplished children's gong orchestra and a beautiful, sweet *gamelan* of the *semar pegulingan* type. The people of Teges Kawan, west of the main road, are mainly sculptors who specialize in unusual giant woodcarvings like a whole eggplant tree with leaves, fruits, flowers, and branches.

Nyoman Sumertha Fine Arts Gallery, Banjar Teges, tel. (0361) 975-267, fax 975-655, displays every style of Balinese painting: stylized puppets, pastoral scenes, young artists. A special section showcases the distinctive individualism of modern Indonesian painters. Talented artists demonstrate their skills on the spacious grounds.

PENGOSEKAN

This artists' village of 70 painters lies about four km south of Ubud and one km west of Teges. A haven for painters since the 1930s, Pengosekan gained world notice in 1974 when Queen Elizabeth II visited Gina, an artist she admired. In those days it was a poor, isolated, dusty village cut off from Peliatan by a river which could be forded precariously only in the dry season. The Community of Artists, Bali's first artist's cooperative, was established here in 1979 under the direction of teacher turned artist Dewa Nyoman Batuan. Internal bickering broke up the co-op in 1985.

Pengosekan is peaceful yet within easy reach of restaurants and entertainment. Since it's about a 25-minute walk into Ubud, a bicycle or motorbike is handy if you're staying for any length of time. The village is only a 10-minute walk west from the main road at the corner in Banjar Kalah,

where you can easily catch public transport in the direction of Ubud or Denpasar.

Desak Putu Warti Stretton, tel. (0361) 975-647, is a Balinese master dancer-musician who provides individual and group instruction in English. She also arranges performances and leads private tours.

Accommodations

Bali Breeze Bungalows, P.O. Box 67, Ubud, 80671, tel. (0361) 975-410, fax to Ary's 975-546 or 976-162, lies on the edge of the village with nice views of rice terraces: five two-story bungalows for Rp21,000-31,500 (one or two people), three family units for Rp52,500 (four people), breakfast included. Facilities include beautiful gardens, open lawns, table tennis, and badminton court. This very secure place features bars on the windows and night guards roaming the grounds. An informal, unpretentious, and comfortable place with lots of personalized service.

Puri Indah Exclusive Villas, also on Jl. Pengosekan, tel. 975-742, fax 975-332, is a small hotel set amidst beautifully landscaped gardens overlooking a small river, palm forest, and rice terraces. Each individually decorated *pondok* features overhead fans, mini-bar, large modern bathroom with hot and cold water, and private terrace. Room rates: superior Rp126,000 s, Rp147,000 d; deluxe Rp252,000 s, Rp273,000 d; VIP deluxe Rp483,000 s or d. Family houses cost Rp252,000-420,000. All rates subject to 17.5% tax and service. Facilities include safe deposit boxes, beautiful pool, poolside bar open till midnight, restaurant, and complimentary transport to and from Ubud's main restaurants. Credit cards accepted. **Jati Homestay,** Jl. Hanoman, offers beautiful rooms right on the rice paddies; Rp8000 s, Rp12,000 d, also one upstairs for Rp15,000 s or d. Can't beat the location. Run by the painter Mahardika, who is also a masterful *kebyar* player. Dinner fare includes delicious fish steamed in banana leaves with spices, great fried crispy noodles, and well-made rice wine.

Food And Entertainment

The elegant, open-sided **Kokokan Club** on Jl. Pengosekan, tel. (0361) 975-742 or 96495, is rapidly becoming the place to be seen in Ubud. Located in front of Agung Rai's small hotel, Puri

Indah, and adjacent to his large new museum, this is the first authentic Thai restaurant in the Ubud area, featuring dishes fragrantly spiced with lemongrass, lime, and mint. Order succulent seafood, innovative vegetarian dishes, mouthwatering cocktails, mixed drinks, fruit juices, wines and coffee, espresso and cappuccino, all at reasonable prices (by Ubud standards). Open 1100-1400 for lunch, 1800-2000 for dinner. Every Saturday at 1930 is a special traditional Balinese buffet with smoked duck, prawns, seafood, chicken curry, vegetable, and salads—12 courses for Rp35,000 adult, Rp15,000 child under 15 years. Book a day ahead. Dinner is accompanied by live dance and drama; on alternate Saturdays hear live acoustic music and vocals. Free transportation in the Ubud area.

Painting

Even during the 1930s, when Rudolph Bonnet was exerting a profound influence over Ubud area painters, the *wayang* style persisted in Pengosekan, most notably in the magnificent works of I Gusti Ketut Kobot. He painted classical puppet-like figures, but in a softer, more humanized, and naturalized style. Kobot was an active member of the Pita Maha Painter's Cooperative created by the cosmopolitan Ubud Prince Cokorda Gede Sukawati, Rudolf Bonnet, and Walter Spies in 1935. The group dissolved by the end of WW II. A post-Pita Maha painters' cooperative was established here in 1969 by brothers Dewa Nyoman Batuan and Dewa Mokoh. Known as the Community of Artists, these brothers and their colleagues rediscovered the hidden beauty of nature with delicate and graceful depictions of leaves, insects, birds, and legendary creatures. This phase became known eventually as the Pengosekan Style. They laboriously painted large canvases symbolic of Bali's myths. Each canvas looked like a detail of a larger painting or a colored photograph shot with a macro lens. The colors used were refined and muted, yet pleasingly matched, conveying a sweet and cheerful feeling.

Inspired by the Bali International Style of Irish designer Linda Garland, the commune's production in the 1980s concentrated on the more lucrative decorative arts, turning out partitions, screens, big parasols, tissue boxes, wooden fruit, toilet seats, children's furniture, floral mirror frames, small watercolor paintings, and other useful products—rendered with the same carving and fine drawing found in their less commercialized art. Strife and jealousy put an end to the cooperative by the mid-'80s. Now the thirty-some artists of the village produce work independently.

The brothers Barat and Kobot on the road to Padangtegal are the elders of the Pengosekan Style, still painting religious subjects. Just south is Sena, another advocate of the style. Under the banyan tree is Sana, known for his temple scenes and depictions of Hindu deities. Mangku Liyer, whose studio is behind Oka's Homestay, paints dark and mysterious phantasmagoria. In Batuan's studio, located just east of the bridge near Peliatan, you can see a large selection of carved furniture and flowers, paintings, and decorative parasols. Older brother Mokoh's paintings reflect his naughty sense of humor. Putralaya paints meticulous submarine landscapes. Gatra, at the southern end of the village, paints unearthly, moody scenes of nymphs and demons.

Plaiting And Carving

This village is also known for its basketry, a thriving cottage industry. The beautifully pleated *lontar*-palm basketry of Pengosekan and neighboring Nyuhkuning combines harmonious colors with utility: baskets that fit inside one another or ones shaped like a mangosteen or an egg. Opposite Pondok Impian Bungalows is a shop specializing in baskets of all shapes, sizes, and patterns. Wayan Ludra, whose workshop is in Pengosekan, produces attractive picture frames, boxes, trunks, chairs, and medicine cabinets. This family of woodcarvers owns an art studio on Monkey Forest Road, tel. (0361) 975-271.

GOA GAJAH

This mysterious complex, two km east of the statue of the dancer in the Teges intersection, is probably the oldest excavated relic of ancient Balinese art. Epigraphs found at this site date Goa Gajah ("Elephant Cave") with certainty back to the 11th century, about the time of King Airlangga's reign in East Java. Until 1923 the site was known only to local people, and only in was an elaborate and extensive bathing place discovered nearby. Today it's a major tourist site.

The easily accessible artificial cave lies below the road between Peliatan and Bedulu, on the side of a steep ravine. It can be a restful place, especially when there aren't mobs of tour buses disgorging passengers into the mammoth parking lot. It's best to visit Goa Gajah either in early morning or late afternoon to avoid the buses arriving from the southern resorts. Soft *rindik* and lyrical flute music wafts from two expensive tourist restaurants, Puri Suling above the cave and Sari Gading at the other end of the parking lot.

To get there, take a *bemo* from Ubud to Teges (Rp400, four km), then continue by *bemo* or walk two km in the direction of Bedulu. The road from Teges passes over the Petanu River just before reaching the cave. Once over this bridge you've entered the old kingdom of Pejeng, a long tongue of land between the Petanu

GOA GAJAH

NOT TO SCALE

© MOON PUBLICATIONS, INC.

and Pakrisan rivers strewn with Bali's most famous and treasured monuments and relics. If coming from the other direction, it's two km from Bedulu.

You'll know you've arrived when you see the rows of tacky curio stands selling *batik*, leather goods, garments, carvings, and baskets, plus fruit, snacks, and drinks. Parking fee is Rp300; entrance fee to the whole complex Rp550 (Rp300 children), plus Rp500 for sash/*sarung* rental if your legs are uncovered. A long flight of steps leads down to the site. It's possible to go on foot to Yeh Pulu from Goa Gajah, but the way along *sawah* dikes is a little tricky. Ask a local boy to guide you.

History
Goa Gajah is a curious name. Elephants have never inhabited Bali and the many elephant motifs seen in Balinese art likely have artistic origins in India or Java. The old Javanese *lontar*-leaf chronicle, the *Nagarakertagama* (written in A.D. 1365), mentions that a high Buddhist official kept a hermitage at Lwa Gajah ("Elephant River"). This probably refers to the Petanu River which runs near the cave through a deep gorge; the name Elephant Cave perhaps originated from early visitors who named the cave after the river. Other theories say the cave got its name from the statue inside of the elephant-god Ganesha, or the monster's head above the cave was mistakenly identified as an elephant's head. Legend has it the great hollowed-out boulder was the supernatural work of Kebo Iwo, the builder of Gunung Kawi and Yeh Pulu—some have even suggested the monster head is in Kebo Iwo's image.

The decorations and interior plan of the cave are very similar to the hermit cells of East Java. Other hermitages with rock reliefs are found near Ubud (Goa Raksasa), on the River Oos (Jakut Paku), and in caves near Kapal. Archaeologists estimate Goa Gajah was built around A.D. 1022. Whether Goa Gajah was a hermitage for Buddhist or Hindu monks is uncertain. Both Buddhist and Hindu sculptures are found inside and nearby. It's quite possible, given the intermingling between the two religions, that recluses of both sects sought peace and solitude at the site; a Shiva-Buddha belief system is found to this day among a small group of Brahman priests in eastern Bali. In any event, the 1954 excavation of a large bathing place in front of the cave proved the whole complex held an important place in the religious life of ancient Bali.

In modern times, Goa Gajah was first mentioned in 1923 in an Archaeological Service report filed in Singaraja by a young Dutch civil servant who visited the site after hearing villagers speak of "a monster's head with elephant ears." The indefatigable Dutch artist Nieuwenkamp, during his fourth visit to Bali in 1925, also heard rumors of "a cave overshadowed by an enormous elephant's mouth" and reached the cave by automobile—the first tourist ever to do so. In subsequent visits he proved the head above the cave was that of a demon and not an elephant. Still, the name stuck.

The Facade

The cave was cut into a protruding rock wall, flat on top, with a flight of steps carved into the right side. It's been postulated the flat top was used by ascetics for meditation. The wall to either side of the entrance, curving slightly outward, is riotously decorated with stylized mountain scenery, forests, entangled leaves, rocks, ocean waves, animals, monsters, and phantom human shapes running in panic from the gaping mouth which forms the cave's entrance.

Directly over the entrance is the head of an enormous bulging-eyed demon that has mysti-

Goa Gajah

fied scholars and tourists alike. With its arched hairy eyebrows, long menacing fingernails, floppy ears, and long tusk-like fangs, it appears to be splitting and pushing the rock apart with its pudgy bare hands. Seeming to swallow everyone entering, the baroque facade seems a thing apart from the earthly civilized world of humans. The function of this carved goblin is to safeguard the heavenly character of the sanctuary. Balinese are quite comfortable with menacing, ugly faces on temples; they make the people feel safe from dangerous forces. Eerie monsters guarding hermit's caves, in the form of *kala*-heads, are also found in East Java. The figure may also represent Rangda, the widow-witch (its large earplugs are a woman's).

Another interpretation maintains the impressive head may represent Shiva Pasupati, who divided the cosmic mountain Mahameru into two parts, creating the rival mountains Agung and Batur as well as the *candi bentar*. Yet another theory holds the head may represent Bima, son of Vishnu and Pertiwi, goddess of the soil. If this were the case, this would be the earliest representation extant of Bima, today a common sight guarding many of Bali's temples.

The Interior

The entrance of this hewn-rock cave, which opens to the south, is two meters high and one meter wide. The dark, musty interior is T-shaped. If you haven't brought a flashlight, a boy holding a candle, cigarette lighter, or oil lamp will take you inside. The grotto contains 15 niches cut out of its walls; these may have served as either meditation chambers or sleeping berths for ascetics. The niches prove the cave was not a temple.

In the cave's westernmost wing is a 100-cm-high four-armed statue of the elephant-god Ganesha holding an axe and broken tusk, symbols of his warlike nature, and a drinking vessel and beads, symbols of his wisdom. On the easternmost wing of the crossway are three 46.6-cm-tall stone phalluses arising from a common base—distinctive features of a Shivaite sanctuary. Bits of statues, bases, and fragmented *raksasa* heads fill other niches. Notice the ancient graffiti on the wall to the right, written in Old Javanese and probably dating back to the second half of the 11th century.

The Bathing Place

In 1954, figurative torsos with waterspouts on their stomachs were found on either side of the entrance to the cave; it was surmised a bathing place had to lie nearby. In that same year a sunken, rock-bottomed courtyard of dressed stone was struck in front of the cave, and farther down the hill to the south a threefold flight of steps leading to the remnants of a former bathing place were unearthed. These were the most significant archaeological discoveries in post-WW II Bali.

Found were two distinct bathing partitions, one for men and one for women. Only the bases remained of six standing nymphs, but the upper portions of the statues previously found in front of the cave entrance fit perfectly. Today, the bathing place is fed by a pond east of the cave, water spouting from large, round urns held by the six Greek-looking statues. The elaborate carving and style of these divine female figures display Buddhist as well as Hindu religious symbols. The connection with Java is unmistakable: almost identical water nymphs grace the bathing places of Belahan on Gunung Penanggungan in East Java.

Goa Gajah's discoverer, Krijgsman, took his daily bath there. The Balinese cheerfully joined in until leaders decided the ancient bathing pool was too holy a spot for such an earthly use.

Surrounding Antiquities

Other antiquities at the site cover a large time span. On a pavilion to the left of the cave are three ancient stone statues. One is an image of the Buddhist goddess Hariti, which may date from the Old Balinese period (circa A.D. 1000). Originally a child-eating ogress worshipped in India, she was converted to Buddhism and metamorphosed into a fertility goddess and child-protector. Hariti is always seen with a large number of lively children. On Bali, she, or any poor woman with many children, is known as Men Brayut.

Other Buddhist figures are found by taking the stairway south of the bathing place down into a gorge which falls away to the Petanu River. Most tourists miss this well-kept, park-like hillside environment which, because of its serenity and beauty, is reminiscent of a Babylonian garden.

In the remains of a small *candi* are two curious, five-meter-wide stones in the shape of a stupa with lotus flower motifs that once sup-

ported Buddha images. The arrangement of the stupa represents the superimposed heavens of the Buddhist religion. The Buddhist stupa, as well as the bas-relief fragments, date most likely from the reign of Kesari, a Buddhist king who ruled Bali during the Central Javanese period (10th century).

YEH PULU

This rarely visited carved cliff face is about one km from Goa Gajah. Water is all-important to the Balinese culture and economy, and *yeh*, the Balinese word for "water" or "spring," occurs frequently in Balinese place-names.

To get there, start from the Bedulu crossroads. Heading west on the road to Ubud is Goa Gajah; the road east leads to Pura Samuan Tiga; the road south to Gianyar. On this road (Jl. Yeh Pulu) you'll see a sign after one km; take a right, then a left, then a right again. This small road leads almost all the way to Yeh Pulu. Park in front of the small open *bale*. It's a nice cool 300-meter walk on a well-built walkway by an irrigation channel and bathing place to the site. Village boys will volunteer to accompany you, although you don't really need a guide. Pay an entrance fee of Rp550, Rp300 for children. The old woman caretaker (*pemangku*) cleans and maintains the reliefs and a statue of Ganesha. For a donation, she'll tell you who's depicted on the reliefs, show you some worn-out carvings on the northern side, and dispense holy water from a clear spring feeding a sacred pool filled with fish. Very calm surroundings, rarely any disturbances.

Lying between the Petanu and Pakrisan rivers, the ruins of this unique late 14th-century high rock relief on a two-meter-high tuff wall lay buried for centuries under volcanic eruptions and vegetation, but its figures remained intact. Once unearthed, the wall revealed perhaps the most important and mysterious sculpture of the Middle Balinese period. The 25-meter-long, life-sized frieze deviates radically from other carvings on Java or Bali. The carvings are enigmatic and naturalistically done, depicting not religious scenes but short vignettes from everyday village life. Stylized decorative leaves frame the work and the chiseling is crude, earthy, almost homely, but with a primitive vigor and realism. When the site was finally excavated in

1925, water seepage from the rice fields above the rock wall soon damaged the exposed figures. Measures have since been taken to prevent further decay.

Bernet Kempers has pointed out in his book *Monumental Bali* that the relief represents stories from the life of Lord Krishna, one of Vishnu's incarnations. A hunting scene, for example, corresponds to the Hindu legend of Krishna defeating the bear Jambavat. The only deity directly represented is two-armed Ganesha, the elephant-headed son of Shiva, carved into his own niche to the far right.

Accommodations And Food

There's a whole little scene here, a cluster of drink and snack *warung* at the top of the pathway, with an art gallery and Made's Cafe looking out over rice fields. For accommodations at **Ketut Lantur,** pay Rp10,000 pp for an old set of rooms with Indonesian-style *mandi,* or Rp15,000 pp for a newer set of rooms facing the street. Lantur prepares meals and you can also buy traditional earthenware pottery in his ceramics shop. This is a quiet, laid-back place to stay. A *nasi bubur* (Rp100) stand just up from Lantur's opens in the afternoon.

Getting Away

Walk up to the main road to catch *bemo* to Ubud. Ketut, who lives 50 meters behind the *warung,* or any other boy from the nearby *kampung,* will give you a fascinating tour of the surrounding countryside, including a rice temple he claims is the only one of its kind on Bali. See also a waterfall, beautiful rice terraces, and a nice place to view the sunset. On the way there's a good swimming spot in a big river. Have your guide take you to the small bathing place 200 meters north of Yeh Pulu, with stylistic reliefs cut into the rock behind the two basins. These sites aren't easy to find without a guide. Depending on the length and quality of the tour, pay your guide Rp5000-Rp10,000.

BEDULU

A farming village south of Pejeng, at the start of the road to Yeh Pulu, approximately 26 km north of Denpasar. Bedulu was once the seat of the Old Balinese kingdom of Pejeng and the last indigenous dynasty to hold out against the mighty Majapahit Empire, which invaded Bali in 1343. After the invasion the Hinduization of Bali accelerated, culminating in the massive cultural migration to Bali of the Majapahit court in 1515.

Legend has it Bedulu's pre-Majapahit ruler, Sri Aji Asura Bumibanten, possessed supernatural strength and powers. He proved this by having his head cut off and put back on, experiencing no injury or pain. He got such a thrill out of this he had his servants decapitate him often. One day, however, during this neat parlor trick the gods made his head roll into a river, where it washed away. His servants panicked and in desperation chopped the head off the first available animal, that of a wild boar happening by, and placed it on the neck stump of their master. Understandably, this caused the ruler some embarrassment, so he hid in a high tower out of sight of his subjects, forbidding anyone to look at him. A child eventually discovered the secret and the bestial king became known as Dalem Bedulu ("He Who Changes Heads"). A less theatrical explanation is that Bedulu comes from Bedaulu, which simply means "upstream."

Pura Samuan Tiga

Down a stony path about 100 meters east of the Bedulu crossroads is Pura Samuan Tiga ("Temple of the Meeting of Three Parties"), probably built by the great sage Mpu Kuturan. During the reign of King Udayana and Queen Dharmapatni (988-1011), religious sects were rife on Bali, each with its own tenets and peculiar practices. Because this situation brought about instability and confusion, six holy men met at this temple to promote the Principle of the Hindu Trinity, unite all the different sects, and establish island-wide customary law (*desa adat*), bringing about religious conformity on Bali.

Gedong Arca

An archaeological museum two km north of Bedulu on the road to Gunung Kawi. One of only five museums on Bali, it contains a scant and unlabeled collection of pre-Hindu artifacts: megaliths, bone ornaments, pottery, earthenware, stone axe heads, adzes, weapons, copper plate inscriptions from A.D. 885 and 903, utensils, bronze jewelry, Chinese ceramics, and Hindu statues and relics. Note the impressively decorated egg-shaped sarcophagus, hewn from a single block of stone, with a turtle and human features carved in high relief on the cover. These coffins, which contained bodies in the fetal position, were used long before cremation was practiced on Bali. Small library. Open Mon.-Thurs. 0800-1400, Fri.-Sat. until 1300, closed Sunday.

MAS

An affluent center for the arts 20 km northeast of Denpasar and five km south of Ubud. Historically, the Brahmanic village of Mas ("Gold") is thought to be the place where the wandering high priest Nirantha finally settled. Nirantha emigrated from East Java in the 15th century and founded temples all over the island. The majority of Bali's Brahmans today claim descent from this venerated Hindu sage.

Beautiful Pura Taman Pule, on the east side of town behind the soccer field, only 100 meters from the road, is believed to have been built on the original site of Nirantha's hermitage (*griya*). A statue of the wandering holy man is near the temple and the *tangi* tree he planted is located behind an altar in the middle courtyard. Note the temple's ornately carved wooden doors overlaid with gold leaf. Twenty-two sacred *topeng* are stored in the *pura*.

Regular performances of the *kecak* dance are staged in Mas, and during the three-day Kuningan festival the ancient *wayang wong* drama is staged in Pura Taman Pule's umbrella-studded courtyard. In the early morning one of the largest and most frenetic cockfights in Bali is held in a nearby arena.

Accommodations And Food

Stay in the enormously pleasant **Taman Harum Cottages,** (P.O. Box 216, Denpasar 80001), owned by the famous woodcarver Ida Bagus Tantra. The only restaurant here is **Puri Rasa,** down the street from the Puri Rasa Gallery, serving Indonesian/Chinese dishes, or you can eat noodle soup with meatballs (Rp1000) and *rujak* (Rp500) at any of the *pedagang kaki lima*. The *warung* sell snacks for Rp100.

Woodcarving

Modern Balinese woodcarving had its origins in Mas. Formerly, carvings were made only by priests for religious purposes and exclusively featured characters from the Mahabharata and Ramayana. During the 1930s, the themes became more realistic and commercialized, depicting such subjects as animals, farmers, and villages. Several old masters who created Balinese woodcarvings famous throughout the world in the 1930s are still alive and working today in Mas. Their families carry out their work in traditional compounds with impeccably decorated and maintained carved doors and pillars, themselves fine examples of gorgeous Old Bali art and architecture.

For the best prices, comb the workshops in the back lanes of Mas. Just follow the ubiquitous tap-tap-tapping of mallets and the sound of gentle sanding. The typical master carver is, in fact, a designer, making an original model or motif which is then copied by a young team of apprentices who work under his supervision. Pieces do not leave the studio without his approval or before the wood is properly dried.

In Mas they carve everything—weeping Buddhas, fishermen, mass-produced Vishnu and *garuda* figures, rice goddesses, yogi, roosters, herons, deer, prancing horses, key rings, chess pieces, carved and painted fruit trees (*pulusan*). Typically, Mas carvings are smooth, unpainted, and made of high-quality wood, but carvers also shape pieces of gnarled driftwood and tree roots into lizards, turtles, abstract faces, and fishheads.

To find quality, you have to tour a lot of shops. If you can't find what you're looking for, ask to see the inventory in back. Craft shops line both sides of the road. The largest and most expensive lie on the edges of Mas, on land large enough to build big turnaround driveways able to accommodate tour buses carrying hundreds of tourists; commissions are paid to drivers and tour leaders. In these huge display rooms prices are quoted in U.S. dollars. Tell the clerks you want to buy goods for export to America or Europe; this will give them a good excuse to drop prices. Depending on the size and the type of wood used, statues three inches high made of polished ebony cost Rp5000, while taller and higher quality pieces are Rp6000-8000. In more expensive shops, yogi statues cost Rp25,000. Look for detail: fingernails, toenails, fingers, muscle delineation, even hair. An artist signs and dates his important pieces.

The Master Carvers

Ever since he was chosen to represent Indonesia at the 1964 World's Fair in New York, Ida Bagus Tilem's work has been sought by collectors worldwide. The internationally acclaimed artist seems to have inherited considerable talent from his father, Ida Bagus Njana, a great innovator of carving styles—some dub him the inventor of modern Balinese carving. The work of both Tilem and his father is exhibited in a fashionable and spacious multilevel, multiroom gallery in Mas; open 0930-1730. To view this high-priced collection is to take in at one glance all aspects of traditional life on Bali—a lifetime of carving. In the back room is a very rare collection of old ivory, mostly from Sumatra, and wonderful old Balinese *topeng* (not for sale). In the downstairs courtyard is Tilem's collection of old Balinese religious carvings and statues. About 75 apprentices work for Tilem, who is now very ill.

Wiryati's Art and Handicraft Collection, tel. (0361) 975-542, is a wholesale shop selling attractive painted statues of cats and other animals. Individual pieces cost Rp3000-5000, sets of three are Rp7500-15,000. Other art shops to visit are Ketut Roja's **Siadja and Son** and **Adil Artshop,** featuring the works of Ida Bagus Taman.

Maskmaking

Some of Bali's most famous maskmakers work at home, down the back lanes of Mas; you'll see their signs hanging from many compound gates. Most produce what actually function as wall hangings, not true masks. The Balinese seldom buy them for use in performances. Many of the more established craftsmen teach maskmaking for around Rp5000 per lesson. Wander from workshop to workshop. Each specializes in different kinds of masks—traditional, birds, monkeys, lions, characters from the Ramayana. Take your time and bargain. Prices range from Rp30,000 to Rp150,000, depending on the mask's size, color, and complexity; better prices later in the day. I.B. Sutarja retails his masterpieces for Rp2.1 million; the masks of his 12 children are much cheaper.

A nephew of Tilem's, nontraditional maskmaker Ida Bagus Oka, began carving masks at age six. Oka has recently gone into business with Canadian artist and designer David Trevelyan. Their carved faces and figures draw inspiration and motifs from indigenous African, Oceania, Northwest American Indian, and Tlingit-style carvings. The phantasmagoric, traditional masks of Ida Bagus Anom are in high demand by *topeng* players and pantomines all over Bali. An accomplished dancer, Anom is a more original maskmaker than Tilem. His yawning masks are copied by dozens of carvers. Anom offers a three week east-west *topeng* dance mask workshop and gives lectures to groups on the maskmaking process. Sadana, Anom's brother, carves surrealistic statuary and fantastical masks.

I Wayan Muka, the head of the *banjar* of Batan Ancak, is another highly original and skilled maskmaker with a sound reputation as a teacher. He instructs up to 15 students at a time (more than any other maskmaker), with 25 additional employees. Muka is very good at miming the emotion of the character depicted in his masks. In his studio are two enormous masks, wide as tree trunks, commissioned by President Suharto. These 1.5-meter-high masks required 18 months to complete. He still creates a lot of traditional painted *topeng* (Rp125,000); his plain masks usually run Rp75,000-90,000. Visa and MasterCard accepted. Open 0800-1700.

Vicinity Of Mas

From Mas, take the back lanes to Ubud via Lod Tunduh, Pengosekan, and Padangtegal. About two km south of Mas is Sakah. Ida Bagus Oka of Mas first visualized the gigantic baby statue in the middle of the crossroads at Sakah. Made from 45,000 kg of sandstone, it represents the beginning of life. The baby statue also marks the "beginning of art," as beyond it lie the art villages of Mas, Peliatan, and Ubud. From Sakah's T-junction, the road to the east leads to Gianyar; the road to the south takes you to Sukawati.

SOUTHERN GIANYAR REGENCY

BATUAN

An old Buddhist-Brahman village 13 km southwest of Gianyar and 18 km northeast of Denpasar. The name Batuan ("Stone") probably refers to a circle of plinths erected as a ceremonial meeting place for ancestor worship in ancient times.

Batuan's golden age ranged from the early 1600s to the early 1700s, when the royal family of Gusti Ngurah Batulepang controlled most of southern Bali. Their power was eclipsed when a splinter court of the Klungkung royal family established itself in nearby Sukawati in the early 1800s. All that remains of the Batulepang kingdom is a small temple honoring Gusti Batulepang. In the early part of the century royal patronage by Anak Agung Gede Oka (1860-1947) made Batuan a very active center for woodcarving and the fine arts.

Gamelan Gambuh

Batuan is celebrated for its dancers. Students from around the world visit this village to learn baris and topeng in the homes of several topeng dance masters, namely I Made Jimat and I Ketut Kantor. Kantor is the son of the late dance master I Nyoman Kakul, who excelled at the gambuh repertoire, arja operettas, and the masked wayang topeng. In Banjar Dentiis, a troupe of wayang wong dancers performing Ramayana stories is favored by a number of Bali's premier hotels.

During Batuan's elaborate, colorful odalan celebrations, exquisitely poised old women perform the offering dance and episodes from old Javanese stories in the courtyard of the village's main temple, accompanied by a superb gamelan ensemble, Bali's oldest extant orchestra. This stately gamelan, which exists only in a dozen or so villages, consists of just a rebab, drums, and one-meter-long, deep-voiced, ghostly sounding bamboo flutes.

Painting

Like the painters of Kamasan near Klungkung, Batuan artists enjoyed a long tradition of painting in the wayang style until the 1930s, when some artists came under the tutelage of Spies, Bonnet, and other influential Pita Maha members. Two brothers, I Patera and I Ngendon of Batuan, were the first to adopt Bonnet's principles of human anatomy and introduce themes of daily life into their early black ink drawings. Dewa Ketut Baru was another accomplished practitioner of distinctive China-ink drawings.

Short, dynamic figures dotted the landscapes of Batuan painters. Reds, browns, and blacks were the dominant colors used by these early painters. By contrast, Ubud's painters rendered tall and glamorous figures. The best paintings of other masters of the Batuan school of the 1930s can be seen in the Puri Lukisan museum of Ubud. That same attention to detail and magical atmosphere is retained in contemporary painting. The most important exponents of the Batuan style today are Ida Bagus Putu Gede, Made Tubuh, and Wayan Rajin. The painter I Made Budi is noted for his colorful and ribald depictions of tourists. Budi's home is near the schoolhouse.

The painter Dewa Ketut Rai, Banjar Tengah, practices a wide variety of styles. Dozens of young apprentices outline paintings in the courtyard. Their forte is miniatures, very original and fine work, not the same old schlock of rice paddies and bare-breasted women. A valuable insight into Balinese painting as a business.

Galleries And Art Shops

Batuan is a good place to shop for patung (statuary) and carved wooden panels, doors, furniture, screens, and reliefs. Also check out the masks of Dewa Cita, son of the celebrated maskmaker Dewa Putu Bebes, and Dewa Mandra of Batuan and Made Regug of Negara. Owned by the family of I Patera and I Ngendon, **Dewata Art,** tel. (0361) 298-426, displays a large selection of handwoven textiles, paintings, and woodcarvings. Fantastic erotic carving on coffee table tops sells for Rp8.4 million. Boys demonstrate the carving technique out front. Reasonable prices.

Gelombang Gold and Silversmith, on the main road between Celuk and Gianyar, employs 20 experienced gold and silversmiths, who make uniquely designed export-quality jewelry at competitive prices, ranging from plain gold rings to intricate gold brooches set with precious stones. Traditional Balinese-style cutlery sets are also available. Special orders accepted.

SINGAPADU

Only 1.5 km to the northwest of Celuk is Singapadu ("Two Lions"). In the center of the village sits a huge banyan tree and a *pura desa*. Next to the temple is the main *puri*, home of an old ally of the ruler of Sukawati, who defeated the Kingdom of Mengwi in the 19th century.

Singapadu today is known primarily for its consummate maskmakers, notably I Wayan Tangguh, Cokorda Raka Tisnu, I Wayan Teguh, Nyoman Juala, and I Wayan Tedun. Expect to spend from Rp75,000 to Rp150,000 for a mask at any of these workshops, the price depending on the style and type of wood used. Tedun's son, Made Hartawan, and Ketut Muja and Wayan Pugeg also do high-caliber work. They sell *topeng* at good prices, perfect for souvenirs. Teguh's workshop houses a collection of the principal characters in Balinese *topeng* theater, some of the finest specimens on the island. *Barong* masks are still crafted in Singapadu's palace.

Singapadu is also renowned for its *gong saron,* an archaic and somber seven-tone *gamelan* played only at funerals in the *banjar* of Seseh and Apuan. Singapadu's sacred ensemble *gamelan luang* is a rare mixture of bronze and bamboo instruments. The town is also noteworthy for its accomplished *barong* performers, as well as *arja* singers and dancers.

SUKAWATI

A large crafts village northeast from Celuk, 14 km southwest of Gianyar, and 15 km northeast of Denpasar on the road to Ubud. Many Chinese have settled here, so Sukawati is a flourishing market town, now nearly indistinguishable from neighboring Batuan. A produce market opens every morning in the town center; park in the Art Market lot right on the highway (Jl. Raya Sukawati) for Rp300.

An excellent little place to eat is **Depot Selecta Sukawati,** a Chinese-run *warung* beside the art market. All the main Indonesian dishes: Chinese omelettes, *mie kuah* (Rp2000), chicken *nasi campur* (Rp2500), iced drinks. Good food, inexpensive, popular with the Balinese. During the village *odalan,* there are up to three processions per day (one for each *banjar*) for four days in a row, with girls in long trailing dresses walking from Sukawati's striking temples to a nearby holy spring.

History

Sukawati was an old center of power and a hotbed of the arts during the Dalem Dynasty in the early part of the 18th-century. I Dewa Agung Anom set about establishing a kingdom along the lines of the grandiose Majapahit of East Java, bringing with him from Klungkung a whole company of high-bred dancers and musicians who entertained the *raja* on the lavish grounds and gardens of his palace. So sweet and intoxicating were the sounds of the *gamelan* wafting from the great gilded *bale* that the populace gave the palace the name Sukahatine, which means "my heart's delight." This eventually evolved into Sukawati.

I Dewa Agung Anom's reign was long, but because of quarreling and greed among his sons, the choice of succession was thrown into turmoil. Tormented by the fact his sons were ill-suited to rule, Anom declared that when he died whichever son would dare take his corpse's tongue into his mouth would inherit the kingdom. Upon his death, the *raja*'s body became so decomposed that none of his sons were willing to perform the repulsive task. When a close relative, the *raja* of Gianyar, stepped forward and took the hideous tongue into his mouth, the corpse shrank to normal size and began to exude a pleasant aroma. Soon after, the disgraced heirs of the kingdom were defeated in war by the armies of Gianyar, and the palace was abandoned.

The village still sponsors preeminent dance and *topeng* troupes, and is the home of famous *tukang prada* (makers of gold-painted umbrellas and costumes) and *tukang wadah* (builders of cremation towers). Sukawati is also credited with inventing, in the early part of this century, the choreography for the modern form of *legong,* an enchanting dance featuring two prepubescent girls.

Temples

Sukawati's complex of temples is rivaled in its status and stateliness only by Besakih. Pura

Penataran Agung in the center of Sukawati is sacred to members of the royal houses of all the surrounding areas—Ubud, Tegallalang, Peliatan, Batuan, Negara, Mas, and Singapadu. Destroyed in a 1917 earthquake, the temple was rebuilt on a smaller scale. Next door, in Pura Kawitan Dalem Sukawati, check out the panel carvings of Tantri fables. In the northeast part of town is Pura Desa, with its huge *candi bentar*.

Dalang And Wayang Kulit

Sukawati's 25 or so *dalang* and their troupes hire themselves out to perform all over Bali. They regularly win the island's Grand Puppeteer title, it is said, because of the potency of the *taksu* shrine in Sukawati's *pura dalem,* before which the shadow puppeteers appeal for power before a *wayang*. On Bali, the status of *dalang* is almost equal to that of priests. The most renowned of the town's *dalang* are I Wayang Nartha, I Wayan Wija, Ganjreng, and the brilliant *gender wayang* performer I Wayang Loceng, who is an expert on all aspects of shadow puppetry—music, mythology, and language.

Shops all over Bali sell souvenir-quality *wayang kulit,* but it's in Sukawati that you can buy the real thing. Wija, the popular *dalang* who lives in Babakan just behind the *pasar,* has developed a theater based on the Tantri fables using an utterly original set of leather animal puppets. In the puppeteer workshops of this neighborhood, prices range from Rp15,000 to Rp45,000 depending on the size, quality, and complexity of the carved, punched, and brightly painted *wayang kulit.*

Handicrafts

The *ibu* at Kios Adi Putra, Jl. Raya Sukawati on the north side of Pasar Sukawesi, offers a wide selection of extraordinarily durable *ata* baskets. *Copot* baskets from Lombok start at Rp9000. Large, attractive, patterned *lontar*-palm baskets dyed natural brown, black, and white are sold for Rp5000-15,000. Sukawati also produces woven bamboo baskets, bamboo birdcages, colorfully painted woodcarvings, miniature *jukung* (Rp3000), and ornate long-handled temple umbrellas. In addition, Sukawati is the windchime-making capital of Bali. These musical pinwheels, *pindakan,* can also be seen at Kubu Ku Windchimes outside Ubud.

For first-class, fairly priced, custom-made gold- and silversmithing, visit I Nyoman Sadia at Jl. Sarsan Wayan Pugig 5 just off the main road in Banjar Babakan at the north end of town. Nyoman takes one or two weeks for delivery. At the *bale banjar* on the left side of the road, turn right down a steep hill, then turn east after 200 meters down an unpaved road; his workshop is on the left.

Opposite the *pasar* is the two-story **Art Market,** a crowded warren's nest of stalls selling woodcarvings, textiles, clothes, curios, paintings, stone statues, dance costumes, and temple accessories. Flimsy junk and cheap souvenirs abound, so keep your sense of humor when bargaining. The prices are already very good. Art shop owners and hawkers from all over Bali come here to buy articles in their original state, then finish the items themelves to save money.

Vicinity Of Sukawati

North of the market after the police station is a side road to the left that leads to Puaya (about one km from the main road), a center for the production of *wayang kulit* made from hide, *topeng* masks, traditionally painted dance costumes and theater ornaments, and dolls made of old Chinese coins. Take the dirt road east to Banjar Delod Pangkung, a traditional village of walled compounds and small thatched shrines. From here continue east to the village of Banjar Babakan, famous for its puppetmasters. Heading east past the *banjar,* the path leads through a cold, dark bamboo forest. Carry on over the bamboo bridge spanning the Tukad Palak River, then past another bamboo bridge, then beyond bathing places, fields of *alang-alang,* peaceful *subak* temples, and a rice hulling station, until you reach the amazing 20-meter-high Tegenungan Waterfall. After the hike, bathe in the public bath of Pura Musen, the river temple of the *desa* of Belangsinga. The path ends in Belangsinga, where you can pick up the asphalt road to Blahbatuh.

CELUK

This gold- and silverworking center just beyond Batubulan is noted for its delicately detailed work and fine filigree-style silver pieces produced with the simplest of hand tools. Stay in

Dharma Samadhi Accommodations and Silversmith, only 200 meters from the main road.

In the classier showrooms on the south side of town prices are usually given in U.S. dollars and credit cards are accepted. Tourists on buses usually pull into these shops between 1000 and 1130—after the *kris* dance in Batubulan—to inundate a shop owned by the brother-in-law of the driver. Avoid visiting the shops during these hours; the crush inflates prices. The display rooms claim fixed prices, but bargaining is usually acceptable—nay, *necessary.* Sample starting prices for original designs: earrings with red coral inset, Rp15,000-20,000; beaten silver necklaces, Rp30,000-40,000; large embossed silver tray, Rp150,000; dragon bracelets, Rp60,000-125,000. The smaller silver workshops in the back of the village are cheaper. If heading toward Sukawati, turn down either of the small lanes on the left; just follow the tap-tapping from small family compounds down the lanes off the main road. These workshops will always fulfill special orders, and can design modern jewelry, particularly if you provide a prototype. They also offer contemporary silver and gold designs of their own creation, suited to European and American tastes. Wayan Kardana and Wayan Kawi have earned solid reputations as skilled artisans, but don't stop there—at least 1,700 silver and goldsmiths live and work in the cottage industries of Celuk.

Bali Souvenir Artshop sells some original articles—amber beads and bracelets—different from the usual tourist pap in the other shops. Another unusual *toko* is **Suardana Gold and Silver Jewelry,** tel. (0361) 298-011, run by I Ketut Suardana. The prices in these shops are better than those in Kuta or Denpasar.

Vicinity Of Celuk

Don't plan to eat in Celuk; move on to Sukawati where the food is better and cheaper—there's a large marketplace. Four km west of Celuk is Tegaltamu, where artisans of all ages fashion stone images of gods and demons. Leaving Celuk head east, but before reaching the concrete bridge alongside the old suspension bridge, take the smaller road to the right, which runs through the villages of Guang and Ketewel. Guang is well known for its *garuda* statues made of black ebony or brown *sabo* wood. A technical high school in this village trains students in sculpting and carving.

BATUBULAN AND VICINITY

Batubulan

Heading northeast out of Denpasar up the tourist corridor, Batubulan ("Moon Stone") is 17 km before Gianyar. Batubulan and the neighboring villages of Celuk and Singapadu are heavily involved in handicrafts, music, dance, and other arts.

In Batubulan are the headquarters of SESRI (High School of Indonesian Fine Arts) and SMKI (High School of Indonesian Performing Arts), where tourists can watch morning dance classes. The director of SMKI is I Nyoman Sumandhi, an accomplished dancer, *dalang,* and musician, who trained at Wesleyan University, KOKAR, and UCLA. After graduation, SESRI and SMKI students are expected to return to their villages to teach the arts. A great number continue their studies at STSI in Denpasar.

Arts And Crafts

Renowned for its decorative and fanciful stonecarving, Batubulan features sculptures and bas-reliefs in temples, houses, yards, public buildings, hotels, restaurants, and adorning bridges and crossroads all over the island. Visit the many shaded outdoor workshops along both sides of the main road, where child artisans chip away at stone blocks to liberate the heroes, gods, demons, and Buddhas of Bali's rich syncretic mythology.

Though a surprisingly soft carving medium, soapstone is costly and cumbersome to ship. Thus, stone sculpture is seldom bought by tourists and remains a nearly intact art form. Most of Batubulan's customers are Balinese who use statues as guardian figures for family shrines, courtyards, and doors. Semireligious statuary also serves a civic function as guardians for government buildings.

Don't miss the workshops of I Made Sura and I Made Leceg on the main road. Shops also carry a wide variety of other crafts, antiques, and furniture—chests, trunks, carved door frames, bamboo sofas with big pillows. For old *topeng,* wooden friezes, and mirror frames, try Kadek's Antique Store. For woven textiles and *batik,* Galuh Artshop on the main road is the place. For quality arts and crafts from Bali and beyond, visit Satya in Banjar Tegeha, tel. (0361)

298-032, also featuring *barong* and *kris* dances at 0930 every morning.

Pura Puseh

The talent of the local stone sculptors is on display on the gate of Batubulan's *pura puseh,* only 175 meters east of the main road, where statues of Hindu deities and mammoth elephants coexist with meditating bodhisattvas with Balinese facial features. Those familiar with Indo-Javanese art will recall the well-known statue of Vishnu from Belahan (East Java), King Airlangga's portrait statue. The sculptures aren't old, but are copies of statues in library books borrowed from the Archaeological Service. This temple is dedicated to the village founder, who is worshipped along with the gods who own the ground. A particularly strong *barong* mask lives here; people say they can hear it now and then shuffling around in its guarded storage shrine.

Performances

Except for the war years and during Nyepi each year, dances have been held in this village almost continually since 1936. Batubulan's first dance troupe, Denjalan Barong, was established in 1970 and has performed the *barong* drama every morning without a break since then. The Puri Agung and Tegaltamu groups were formed in the 1980s. Altered and abbreviated for tourist consumption, these are basically recreational, commercialized performances imbued with a certain languor born of playing year in, year out. Nevertheless, they're vastly entertaining. The clowns, monsters, monkeys, and pantomine are first-rate.

Batubulan is the home of the enthralling *kecak* monkey dance, created in 1928 by the painter Walter Spies for the German film director Baron von Plessen, then producing the first feature film on Bali, *The Isle of Demons.* The story goes that while the two were watching a performance of *sanghyang dedari,* one dancer spontaneously leapt onto the stage and assumed the *baris* posture. This gave Spies the idea of combining the chorus of the trance dance with the gestures of the formalized war dance. Spies even rescored an original *gamelan* composition for that stunning film, experiencing great disappointment when it was never used.

Today, a total of four dance venues with rising rows of bamboo seats are busy with almost continuous weekday performances. One airy theater is located out in the rice fields—a really inspiring setting. *Barong* and *kris* dances are performed at 0930 before busloads of domestic and foreign tourists; Rp5000 fee. When the 90-minute show is over, the spectators emerge into a swarm of peddlers. In a few minutes the buses drive off in a cloud of exhaust fumes and dust, leaving the village to take up its daily rhythm again. On another stage every Saturday night the *tari kecak* and *sanghyang* are performed. This is actually a medley of popular dances featuring a *kuda kepang* firewalker in deep trance and two tiny *sanghyang dedari* dancers under very shallow trances.

KETEWEL

South of Sukawati and 18 km southeast of Gianyar is one of Bali's largest fully cooperative villages, consisting of 14 *banjar* and around 1,500 heads of household. As in many of these Olde Bali villages on the slopes of Gunung Batur, the headman is the spiritual leader, decides legal matters, and heads the village temple (*pura puseh*). The village possesses a remarkable set of female masks used in an archaic form of the *legong* dance. The *legong bededari* was first conceptualized in the late 19th century by a priest of Ketewel who'd seen two angels in a dream.

The houses, temples, and public structures of Ketewel are classic examples of the spare but beautiful south Gianyar style of architecture. Sights include the handsome *wantilan,* and the grand Pura Peyogaan Agung, its scale and craftsmanship equal to any of the island's state temples. Check out the inner courtyard of this temple during the biannual *odalan,* when the ghostlike *ratu dedari* mask dance is staged. Also see Ketewel's Pura Beji holy water temple, fed by a mountain spring, and the communal baths. From Ketewel's T-junction, the road east leads to the beach at Pabean, where purification ceremonies occur at sacred Pura Segara sea temple. On this same road, in the southern part of the village, is a cemetery and death temple with a view of the sea. From the same T-junction, the road to the south leads to the village of Gumicik; nice beach.

KLUNGKUNG REGENCY

Klungkung is the smallest regency on Bali, roughly divided between the fertile terraced slopes of the uplands, the coconut and banana groves of the narrow coastal strip, and the poor, arid, and sparsely populated islands of Nusa Penida, Nusa Lembongan, and Nusa Ceningan. Only Lembongan, the Kerta Gosa courthouse, and Goa Lawah are regularly visited by tourists.

History

From the 16th century until the beginning of this century, Klungkung was the royal capital of Bali. The Gelgel dynasty, governed from Gelgel, four km south of present-day Klungkung, played a major role in government and diplomacy, exerting a pervading influence over the whole island. This was the Golden Age of Bali, when dance, drama, music, and painting flourished.

The last Majapahit king fled Islamic Java to set up court in Gelgel around 1515. The Brahmans and Satrias of the court commenced to divide Bali into a number of kingdoms, administered by relatives and generals. The Javanese-Hindu cultural influence emanating from here laid the foundation for Bali's unique religion and society.

The greatest of the Gelgel dynasty kings was Batu Renggong, who called himself Dalem. After assuming the throne in 1550, he launched a military, political, and cultural renaissance, conquering Bali and sending roving bands of Balinese troops into large areas of East Java and the islands of Lombok and Sumbawa. Indonesia's first contact with Europeans occured under Dalem's reign, when three Dutch ships put in near Kuta in 1597. Also dating from this critical era are the magnificent old courthouse, floating pavilion, and gardens of Klungkung. During Dalem's reign the Brahman priest Nirantha arrived on the island, assuming the position of the court high priest and exerting a considerable influence on arts and literature. Besakih became Bali's state temple and the abode of royal ancestors.

In the 17th century the brilliance of the Gelgel court began to flicker. Under the reign of Dalem di Made the dynasty steadily lost land, power, and status. An ambitious general, Gusti Agung Maruti, launched an attack on Gelgel in 1686 and proclaimed himself *raja*. The kings of Badung and Buleleng, refusing to accept Maruti's sovereignty, helped the rightful Majapahit descendant regain his throne in 1705. Five years later, for superstitious reasons, a new capital was built in Klungkung a few kilometers to the north. Klungkung's first king, Jambe, was the first to use the title Dewa Agung ("Great King"). The first major dynastic genealogy was compiled by this court in 1819. The Klungkung court also created new art forms, such as *arja* and the *geguritan* poetic form, and held elaborate state rituals to assert its status as Bali's spiritual capital.

The Dutch military campaign against Klungkung began in 1849. Troops landed at Padangbai and marched as far as Kusamba. Hearing the enemy's ranks were stricken by dysentery, the virgin queen Dewa Agung Istri Kanya launched a deadly night attack, inflicting heavy casualties on the Dutch and fatally wounding the Dutch commander. A peace settlement was negotiated by the wily Danish trader Mads Lange, and the next day the Dutch troops were ordered back to their ships.

Thus the conquest of south Bali was postponed for another 60 years. A full scale Dutch invasion of the south was mounted in 1906, obliterating the royal houses of Denpasar and Tabanan. In April 1908 Dutch warships arrived from Batavia and both Klungkung and Gelgel were bombarded into submission. Dewa Agung Jambe and 300 of his relatives and followers chose collective suicide (*puputan*) over the colonial yoke. Clad in white and armed only with *kris,* the royal retinue marched straight into Dutch rifles. Dewa Agung was shot down and six of his wives stabbed themselves to death, falling over his body. When the smoke cleared, 108 Balinese had died without the loss of a single Dutch soldier. Today, across the road from the Kerta Gosa, a monument commemorates this ghastly event.

Economy

Once one of the most prosperous and fertile districts in all of Bali, 20% of Klungkung's arable land was destroyed in the 1963 eruption of Gunung Agung, which took 1,600 lives and drove

KLUNGKLUNG REGENCY

SIDEMEN

TENGANAN

MANGGIS

BUGBUG

PANTI

SELISIHAN

TABOR

BUKIT JAMBUL

AAN

KLUNGKUNG

PAKSABALI

TIHINGIN

DAWAN

PADANGBAI

GIANYAR

TAKMUNG

SAMPALAN

BANJAR ANGKAN

SALAKAN

TENGAH

KAMASAN

GELGEL

KUSAMBA

TANGKAS

GOA LAWAH

SELAT BADUNG

NUSA LEMBONGAN

JUNGUT BATU

KUTAMPI

SAMPALAN

TOYAPAKEH

SENTAL

KANJIN

DESA LEMBONGAN

SELAT LOMBOK

NUSA CENINGAN

PENIDA

NUSA PENIDA

BATUKANDIK

TANGLAD

DEBULUH

PELILIT

TANJUNG MALING

0   20 km

INDIAN OCEAN

87,000 from their homes. Bali was unable to absorb the homeless, and many were resettled in *transmigrasi* areas of the Outer Islands. Survivors eke out a subsistence living growing chilies, scraggly corn, and onions on gravelly land long since denuded of heartier vegetation.

The People

The people of Klungkung still claim a cultural and social superiority over other Balinese. One of every three Satria priests hails from Klungkung. The area is home to the island's most strict and traditional caste rules. Klungkung nobles may use the formal Balinese language to speak down to everyone else. The regency's rigid class structure is obvious in such societal extremes as the Resi Bhujangga sect of Takmung, a priestly class of Vishnu worshippers, and the *desa* of Anjingan, inhabited by dogeaters, scavengers, beggars, and corpse-robbers.

KLUNGKUNG

A historically important town 40 km from Denpasar (Rp1500 by minibus) and 13 km east of Gianyar (Rp500 by *bemo*), Klungkung was the seat of the Gelgel dynasty from 1710 until 1908. Most Balinese nobles are descended from Klungkung's *raja,* his family, or retinue. Until his death in 1965, the last Klungkung *raja* was regarded as the most exalted prince in Balinese aristocracy. Throughout his life Ida Dewa Agung Geg bore the scars of the 1908 *puputan,* when he was stabbed in the side and shot in the knee. He was exiled to Lombok until 1929, then returned to Bali to occupy the old palace with his 40 wives and 100 children.

THE TAMAN GILI PALACE COMPOUND

Meaning literally "island garden," the Taman Gili complex consists of the Bale Kambang and the Kerta Gosa, set within an extensive garden enclosure and framed by a tall gateway to the west called the Pemedal Agung. These are all that remain of the Semara Pura Royal Palace after it was pounded by Dutch artillery.

In 1710 the Dewa Agung himself, Gusti Sideman, took a personal hand in the design of his new *puri.* A great lover of the arts, he employed the realm's best carvers, carpenters, masons, and sculptors, working with only the very finest materials. The result was Bali's first and most opulent example of Hindu-Balinese court architecture. Indigenous forms blended with Majapahit motifs and techniques resulted in a unique complex, 150 meters on each side, built in the shape of a mandala—a microcosmic representation of the universe. Semara Pura ("The Palace of the God of Love") contained courtyards, gardens, and moats surrounding elegant pavilions, each serving a different function. In the northwest corner is a *kulkul* tower; on a side street to the west is the great stone gateway the Pemedal Agung, riddled with bullet holes during the *puputan.* Its main door, side doors, and arch are extensively carved; note the ridiculous-looking Dutchmen in top hats.

Pay the entrance fee of Rp550 at the *loket* in the parking lot opposite the complex. Since the ceiling of the Kerta Gosa is high, it's a good idea to bring binoculars for more detailed study. Hire one of the wordy, vacuous, and virtually incomprehensible guides

Museum Semarajaya

To the west of the Kerta Gosa is this small but functional museum you can visit on your ticket (Rp550 adults, Rp300 children) for Taman Gili. No English labels. The museum contains a number of old Dutch newspapers recounting the *puputan*—fascinating examples of the hyperbole of the day. Exhibits include the royal litter bearing the *raja* when the Dutch opened fire. Black-and-white photos of the *raja* and his family, miniature cannon, ancient pounding stones, water jars.

Bale Kambang

One of the most important structures, built in the most sacred area of the compound, is open-air Bale Kambang, the Floating Pavilion. Surrounded by an artificial pond once covered in water lilies, this rectangular structure served as a reception pavilion for the *raja's* important visitors and a place of relaxation for Brahmanic judges.

The Bale Kambang was restored and enlarged by the Dutch in the early part of this century; note the whimsical statues of Dutchmen on both sides of the entrance. The date of the paintings on the ceiling is not known, but the last original work was completed, most likely, by the celebrated Kamasan artist Wayan Kayun in 1945. The paintings were last restored in 1983. Eight rows of paintings are decorated with symbols from Balinese astrology and scenes from the tale of Pan Brayut, concerning a poor couple with 18 children. Other paintings depict the legend of Sang Sutasoma, the wise old man of Balinese folk literature.

Kerta Gosa

The royal Court of Justice of the Gelgel dynasty lies at the beginning of the town center on the right, on the south side of Klungkung's main intersection. Located in the northeast corner of the Taman Gili complex, it's an elaborate open-sided pavilion reached by climbing a steep, short flight of brick steps with *naga* as balustrades.

In precolonial times the pavilion was a meeting place for the Dewa Agung and the princes and lords of the district, who assembled to discuss matters of state. It later became a courthouse where the king and his high priests sat in judgement. The *raja,* with his Brahman judges and ministers, would hear cases of murder, political conspiracy, sacrilege, and breaches of caste rules. Summary justice was traditionally administered on the accused. Because of the severity of the sentences—mutilation was the most favored form of punishment—most cases were settled at the village level before a council of elders. Only the most important cases, beyond the jurisdiction of clan or village leaders, would climb to the level of this high court.

Although the 1908 fire destroyed most of the palace compound, the Kerta Gosa was officially reopened in 1909, designated as a court for cases involving *adat* law, as opposed to colonial law. It functioned as a court of justice until Indonesian independence in 1949.

The Dutch sponsored a renovation of the Kerta Gosa in 1920, remaining faithful to its original design. In 1930 a group of master painters under the direction of Pan Seken completely replaced earlier, deteriorated paintings drawn on cloth. The only visual record of this group's work, applied directly on the wood of the ceiling, is a photograph taken by Walter Spies. The complex was again restored in 1960, when the Kerta Gosa's famous murals were repainted. The entire ceiling was replaced; new paintings by Pan Semaris (son of Pan Seken) depicting the story of Bima Swarga were rendered on asbestos sheeting. The last paintings, executed in 1989 to replace faded panels, are woefully inferior acrylic works. Carbon monoxide fumes, Bali's hot and humid climate, and the moisture of monsoon rains have exacted an irreversible toll on the superb 1960s work, in which no artificial dyes were used.

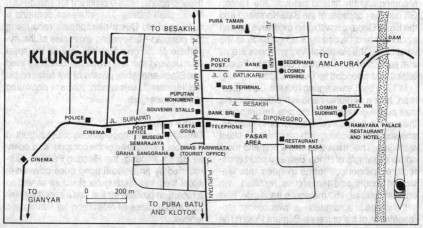

Every square centimeter of the walls and ceilings is covered in concentric murals painted in the traditional *wayang* style popular at the time the *puri* was constructed. The large, vaulted roof rests on carved columns, and the paintings ascend the pyramidal ceiling to a central gilded wood lotus surrounded by four fluttering doves. The various levels of heaven and hell are described through the story of Bima, the hero who journeys to the underworld to save the souls of his parents. Bima has a darker complexion than the other princes and is bereft of their wing-like epaulets—he's relied upon for his strength, ferocity, and courage and has no need for such finery.

The scenes picture terrifying episodes defendants would meet after their deaths, before rebirth as dogs, snakes, or poisonous mushrooms. Thieves are boiled in oil in large copper kettles; souls are castrated, beaten, burned, and torn; birds peck out eyes; decapitated whores walk planks over seas of flames; unfortunates are sawn in half for disrespecting their parents; liars get clawed by tigers; women who underwent abortions have their breasts gnawed away by rats; miscreants are crushed by the elephant-king Gajahraja. All these lurid punishments are executed by fierce little demonic spirits called *buta* who work in the Kingdom of the Dead. They place wrongdoers under sword-trees which they then shake; they remove the intestines through the anuses of those who farted in public. Old maids are chased by boars and poked with tusks; childless, promiscuous women are forced to suckle a huge caterpillar.

Lawbreakers were obliged to attend their own trials. While relatives waited in the adjoining Bale Kambang, the accused would kneel before the all-powerful tribunal, their eyes taking in the horrendous punishments portrayed on the ceiling above. But if the wrongdoers lifted their eyes from the horrors of hell, they could perhaps find some comfort. Above hell's gruesome miseries and agonies shine the delights and beauty of heaven. The highest panels show pious souls attended by councils of the divine—the just rewards for those who lead good and honest lives.

PURA TAMAN SARI

You can reach Pura Taman Sari ("Flower Garden") by taking the road north to Besakih. After the police station, make a right at the small intersection and walk 300 meters until you see the sign announcing the temple. Built in the 17th century, this *pura* of *meru* towers, quiet ponds, and gardens is a welcome refuge from the noisy and polluted town.

PRACTICALITIES

Accommodations

Klungkung is not blessed with good places to stay—it's better to base yourself in Padangbai (15 km) with its much better selection of hotels and eateries, and do Klungkung on a day-trip. **Graha Sanggraha** is located behind the tourist office near the mosque; Rp7000 pp, no meals. **Losmen Wishnu,** Jl. Gunung Rinjani 4, is a three-minute walk from the *terminal bis*; Rp6000 s or Rp8000 d. Rooms upstairs are better, with a balcony over the street. Central, but the place is noisy and bare-bones. Of late the odor of gasoline seems to permeate the place.

Losmen Sudihati, Jl. Diponegoro 125, is a ten-minute walk from the minibus station in the direction of Amlapura; Rp6000 s, Rp8000 d. Grubby and dark—okay in an emergency. Just around the corner, and in the same price range, is the **Bell Inn.** Down the road on the right on the edge of town, also toward Amlapura, is Klungkung's finest accommodation, **Ketut Oka Odean's Ramayana Palace Restaurant and Hotel** (Jl. Diponeogoro 152); Rp20,000 s, Rp35,000 d for any of three large, clean, well-furnished rooms. Five smaller rooms in back without *mandi* go for Rp8000 s, Rp10,000 d. Nice sitting areas on open pavilions in a flowery garden.

Food

The restaurant at the **Ramayana Hotel** serves Indo-Chinese food (*ayam goreng* Rp7000, omelette Rp2000), or eat at the **Sumber Rasa** on Jl. Nakula across from the old *stanplatz*. Just a couple doors down is the Chinese-run **Bali Indah** on Jl. Nakula—fairly clean, quite inexpensive, and only several minutes from the Kerta Gosa.

Sederhana, Jl. G. Rinjani 13, tel. (0366) 21524, is a Muslim restaurant next to Losmen Wishnu. Friendly service and cheap, local prices for delicious *sate kambing* (Rp2500), *gulai kambing* (Rp1500), and *sup ayam* (Rp1000). At dusk the bus terminal offers many *warung* serving delicious and inexpensive Balinese and Indonesian food—the best place to eat for the least money in town. The *sate* stalls are particularly good.

Shopping And Crafts

Klungkung is right on the interisland trade route and derives most of its wealth from commerce. Down some steps behind a row of shops to the east of the Kerta Gosa, right in the center of town, is Klungkung's huge, covered, old-style Asian marketplace—the largest on Bali. This excellent *pasar* is divided into different sections—to the left is bamboo, in the back are *warung,* to the front clothes. You'll also find spices, vegetables, fruits, flowers, sweet cakes, traditional implements, basketry, handmade housewares, *songket, ikat,* and jewelry. A real people's market. Prices are good; very crowded. Ponies, with tassles and bells on their foreheads, pull carts to and from the busy *pasar.*

Hard-sell vendors in the parking lot in front of the Kerta Gosa push souvenir-quality necklaces, fake coins, wooden sculpture, and cloth reproductions of the Court of Justice paintings (Rp25,000, first price). Along Klungkung's main street (Jl. Diponegoro) is a row of souvenir shops selling inexpensive woven *lontar* articles, gold and silver jewelry, traditional *endek, songket, batik,* temple parasols, *wayang*-style paintings, carvings, and antiques. Find here also ceramics, old *selendang,* and clever reproductions sometimes not available in other parts of Bali.

Services

Klungkung features a row of general goods stores, a Bank Rakyat Indonesia, and a *perumtel* office with pay phone. Klungkung's telephone code is 0366. The tourist office is in front of Museum Semarajaya on the grounds of Taman Gil. There's also a gas station, an *apotik,* and good doctors. Working in the town's hospital (RSU) on Jl. Flamboyan (tel. 0366-21172) is Dr. Julius Tanasale, who studied in Thailand and specializes in tropical diseases.

Getting There And Away

From Denpasar's Terminal Kereneng, board a *bemo* to Klungkung for Rp1500. From Ubud, take a *bemo* to the Sakah intersection, then change to one for Klungkung (Rp1500 total). If coming from Candidasa (25 km) or Amlapura, make sure the *bemo* is heading straight to Klungkung; some stop and wait for ferry passengers in Padangbai. Klungkung's *bemo* station is a transport hub for *bemo* and minibuses heading for Besakih (Rp1000), Penelokan (Rp1200), Padangbai (Rp700), Amlapura (Rp1000), and Candidasa (Rp600). To Batubulan station in Denpasar it costs Rp2500 by minibus, Rp1250 by big bus. Transport out of Klungkung to Batubulan starts to wind down at around 1900. After that, if you want to get back to Denpasar you have to charter (Rp20,000 and up). It can also be problematic to reach Besakih by public transport after 1500.

VICINITY OF KLUNGKUNG

WEST OF KLUNGKUNG

Takmung

The highly revered temple of Pura Kentel Bumi ("The Temple of the Creation of the Earth") lies on the bend in the main road west, separated from Klungkung by a wild, deep ravine. Takmung is the base for the priestly Resi Bhujangga sect who worship Lord Vishnu. North of Takmung is Aan, the home of high priest Pedanda Aan, who must be consulted each time it's necessary to determine the auspicious day to begin an important undertaking.

Tihingan

A *gong kembar* instrument-making factory near the village of Aan, Tihingan is an obligatory stop for lovers of *gamelan.* On the main road from Denpasar to Klungkung, take the turnoff at Salakan north to Tihingan (five km). You can also reach Tihingan from a road north of Sankanbuana, two km west of Klungkung (if coming from Klungkung, just keep straight ahead). The foundaries are on the right in the rice paddies; there's a sign out front.

There are a number of gongmakers in this village, employing over 100 people. The best known is the small factory run by I Ketut Lunga

Yasa, whose father is a master player and instrument maker. This is a very warm and approachable family. Here they make smaller instruments—*gangsa, tawa-tawa, cengceng*. Gongs are forged on Sundays by men stripped to the waist wielding hammers against anvils set around a roaring pit in the ground. The pieces are then filed and polished the rest of the week. A *gender* goes for around Rp200,000, large gongs cost Rp600,000, *cengceng* around Rp50,000. These are not tourist souvenirs but actual musical instruments used in orchestras.

While in Tihingan drop by the Puri Penetaran Pande in the village center, consecrated by the local *pande* gong. There's a magnificent *kulkul* tower supported by *rangda* columns. In front of the temple is a stone statue of Twalen, the lovable clown of the Mahabharata. Under the *waringin* tree is a statue of the goddess of winds, who supplies the air for the bellows of foundaries.

Brickmaking is another cottage industry in the area. Wander through the countryside and brickmakers will show you how bricks are formed in rectangular wooden molds, stacked to dry for seven days, then fit into a kiln and fired for a week using rice husks as fuel. Since the clay is dug out of the nearby topsoil, the brickmaker's factory looks like a house with a moat around it.

Banda Village

Near Tihingin, the internationally acclaimed modern Balinese artist Nyoman Gunarsa has built a three-story concrete museum devoted to 16th-19th century Balinese traditional paintings. Gunarsa has collected these rare classical paintings, many drawn on bark paper, for about 12 years. The museum is also a center for dance, music, and the other fine arts of Bali. Gunarsa's studio is filled with old furniture, antique woodcarvings, impressionistic paintings, and traditional dance costumes. Born in 1944, Gunarsa has twice been named the best painter in Indonesia by the Jakarta Arts Council and has put on one-man shows all over the world. His oil paintings now fetch up to Rp20 million apiece.

GELGEL AND VICINITY

This was once the seat of the old court of Gelgel, the capital of the kingdom of the same name. Founded by Javanese lords and priests,

Gelgel was Bali's first unitary kingdom. It reached its apogee during the reign of Batu Renggong in the late 16th century. In 1710 I Gusti Sideman moved his capital to the more strategic site of Klungkung, which controlled the road from Gianyar to Amlapura as well as the approach to Besakih, Bali's holiest temple.

Today, Gelgel is known for its pottery and beautiful hand-woven ceremonial *songket.* Get here by simply turning south at the main crossroads by the Kerta Gosa in Klungkung and traveling three km, then taking a left one km to Gelgel. Except for the royal state temple of Pura Dasar and a few ruined gateways, nothing remains today of the noblest of all the Balinese rajadoms. Pura Dasar is entered through a huge outer courtyard. When the descendants of Gelgel's far-flung aristocracy arrive, this temple plays host to elaborate ceremonies on its large *bale* and *wantilan.* Try to make it here for the impressive *odalan.* Don't miss the mysterious ancestral stones placed on a stone throne, and weathered Pura Nataran.

Not far away, to the east of Pura Dasar, is Gelgel Mosque, the most ancient mosque on Bali, established by Muslim immigrants who served the Dewa Agung during Bali's Golden Age. The story goes that when Muslim missionaries tried to convert the Dewa Agung, he balked at the circumcision requirement, and thus Bali remains Hindu to this day. Visitors are discouraged from entering the *mesjid,* which is smack in the center of the Muslim quarter.

The most significant temple in the neighborhood is Pura Jero Agung ("Great Palace Temple") built on the grounds of the former Gelgel *puri* to the west of Pura Dasar. Unusual and mysterious Pura Kuri Batu, in Jelantik village northeast of Gelgel, features beautiful carved doors of solid stone. Who carved the doors and when no one knows. The villagers just say "the doors have always been here."

East of Gelgel is a large complex of *kuburan* and temples connected to the many noble families of Bali. North of the graveyards is Pura Dalem Gandamayu, thought to have once been the residence of the wandering Hindu priest Nirantha. One of the shrines in the temple is dedicated to the blacksmith clan; the other is kept by the descendants of Nirantha.

The nearby village of Tangkas, south near the coast, is known for its sacred *gamelan luang,* a rare and archaic ensemble combining both bamboo and bronze instruments. One km to the west of Tangkas is Jumpai, noted for its powerful *balian* and sacred *barong*. Visit the nearby beach of Klotok, frequent destination of pilgrims. To get there from Klungkung, take the road directly south past Gelgel until you hit the ocean.

KAMASAN

Descendants of the Hindu-Javanese Majapahit court artisans still work in the villages surrounding Klungkung, practicing the same professions as their ancestors of 25 generations ago. The coppersmith guild settled in Banjar Budaya, the ironsmiths in Klungkung and Kusamba, while the artists and silver- and goldsmiths established themselves around the villages of Kamasan and Desa Tojan.

Originally a village of gold- and silversmiths who produced the crowns, body ornaments, and jewelry for the *raja* and his family, Kamasan later became known as a center for painters. Their art was devotional work (*ngayah*) for god or a leige lord, sent all over Bali to decorate *puri*.

When the Dutch arrived, Kamasan artists lost their royal patronage and the art of *wayang*-style painting nearly died. Kamasan underwent a resurgence when the Dutch commissioned the restoration of the Kerta Gosa paintings in the 1920s and 1930s. In the 1960s tourists and art and souvenir shops became an important source of revenue. High-ranking officials now commission works for their homes and offices.

Kamasan lies four km south of Klungkung. From Klungkung's main intersection, take a *bemo* (Rp300) down the hilly road in the direction of Klotok and ask to be dropped off at Kamasan. You know you've arrived when people start to invite you into the compound to buy directly from the artist. Since tourists only occasionally visit the village, it has only one showroom. Its proprietor, I Made Sondra, is quite knowledgeable. He sells painted wooden eggs and other collectibles like bamboo boxes, wallets, and basketry.

Painting

The traditional *wayang*-style paintings produced here were the only form of painting on Bali from the 14th century until the early 1920s, and it's the oldest school of painting still practiced here. The 140-plus painters in the *banjar* around Kamasan belong to a specialized guild working as a collective enterprise in home workshops and studios. Many of the best-known painters trace their lineage to I Gede Modara, a classical painter of the 18th century who enjoyed the patronage of the Dewa Agung.

As in the Kerta Gosa frescoes, the highly conservative, formalized Kamasan style imitates the two-dimensional shadow puppets, with faces drawn in three-quarters profile. The heroes and demons depicted are taken from the Ramayana, *Suthasoma, Pan Brayat,* and other Javanese and Bali-Hindu mythologies and literary classics. The village was once a lively center court for *dalang,* dancers, and musicians, all serving as inspiration for local painters.

It used to be paintings that depicted themes or characters that did not correspond to the accepted, cherished age-old values of the community risked severe criticism, but Kamasan's new patrons want painters to produce work with lighter themes. Kamasan painters also specialize in pictorial Balinese calendars costing Rp20,000 or less.

Kamasan paintings are actually colored drawings. Traditionally, rocks, leaves, soot, crushed limestone, bone, and other vegetable and mineral dyes produced yellow, blue, red, green, orange, caramel, dark ochre, and dark brown colors. Now poster paints are beginning to replace hand-pounded natural dyes. Cotton cloth is stretched, a layer of white rice flour starch applied, scenarios sketched from memory with charcoal, outlines drawn in with China ink, and the pigments filled in with a homemade, very fine bamboo paintbrush. Figures are usually colored orange. In the best pieces, look for figures set off by fluid and distinct black outlines. Colors are dabbed on the canvases before the black outlines, which are usually drawn by the master artist when finishing the piece. Colors should remain clear and separate without being muddied by overlapping. It takes about a month to finish a one-half-square-meter painting, including preparing the canvas and paints.

Because Kamasan lies outside the usual tourist routes, and because of the system of guide commissions that controls tourist marketing in Bali, these artists are unable to sell many paintings at a reasonable profit. The best of the Kamasan paintings are seriously undervalued and masterpieces can be purchased practically for the price of day labor and materials. The cheapest place to buy paintings is Banjar Sangging. The cloth paintings aren't usually framed and range in price from Rp100,000 to Rp750,000. Be generous; these fine traditional craftsmen are an endangered species.

Painters

The most famous and sought-after painter is I Nyoman Mandra, whose works are a favorite of international collectors and hang in European museums and galleries. Mandra is a delightful person and speaks fairly good English. His students do amazing work as well, which you can observe in a government-sponsored school. Here, village children are trained to carry on this 500-year-old-tradition by imitating the master. Another well-known painter is Mangku Mure in Banjar Siku (the closest *kampung* to Klungkung), who sells his really big paintings for as high as 2.5 million *rupiah*. With Pan Semaris, Pak Mure directed the restoration of the Kerta Gosa paintings in 1960. Nyoman Serengkog, a rare female practictioner in what used to be a male-dominated profession, is the wife of Pan Semaris and works in the adjoining *kampung*. Ketut Rabeg in Banjar Sangging is also considered a gifted artist.

PAKSABALI AND POINTS EAST

About a 10-minute drive east of Klungkung is the village of Paksabali, well known for the making of ceremonial parasols and flags. Don't miss the Dewa Mapalu ("Clashing of the Gods") festival celebrated at Pura Timbrah during Kuningan. Get to the temple by crossing the bridge, then taking the first asphalted road to the north; the temple's on the right side of the road. *Pratima* are carried on litters down a steep ravine for ritual bathing in the Unda River. When the bearers return, the *pratima* "refuse to go back" to the temple, so a wild free-for-all (or god fight) ensues in which participants often fall into trance.

In Sampalan Tengah, the next village (one km) east of Paksabali, visit the *ikat* factory, which weaves designs on cotton (Rp12,500 per meter) or silk (Rp30,000 per meter). This village is also the home of Mangku Putu Cedet, Bali's preeminent traditional *undagi* (architect), his status equal to that of the island's highest ranking *dalang* or *pedanda.* Sadly, temples, ceremonial *bale,* and the occasional small Balinese-style hotel are the only opportunities left for the diversified talents of the *undagi,* his job having been largely taken over by modern-day building contractors and developers.

Three km after Sampalan Tengah, take the small paved road to the left and travel two km to the small *desa* of Dawan at the foot of Bukit Gunaksa. Dawan is the home of Pedanda Gede Keniten, a direct descendant of the court priest of the Gelgel dynasty and a man believed to possess supernatural powers. The village lies in the middle of a *sawo*-growing area and is also renowned for its *tuak* and high-quality brown palm sugar. In the adjoining village of Besang, visit the *pura* with the ancient *kawi* inscription under a soaring pagoda.

EASTERN KLUNGKUNG

KUSAMBA

Take a *bemo* from Klungkung (Rp500) in the direction of Amlapura. On the descent, you'll come across gigantic lava beds, effluvia from Gunung Agung's 1963 eruption. Where the main road meets the sea, and where your nostrils meet the aroma of drying fish, is the working fishing village of Kusamba. On its sparkling, black-sand beach you can see many *jukung* in daily use. Turn south at the Y-junction in the center of town and drive about one km.

Upon Kuta's decline in the mid-1800s, Kusamba became southern Bali's busiest and most important entry port for agricultural products and slaves. It was also the center for a specialist clan of blacksmiths skilled at weapons-making. In 1849, Kusamba was the site of a pivotal fight between the Dutch and Queen Istri Kanya; the Balinese emerged victorious and Istri Kanya has been a national heroine ever since.

Saltmaking

The mixed and rather dour Hindu and Muslim population also mines seasalt, the other major area industry. Driving the coastal road east of Klungkung, you'll see small, brown, thatched, peculiarly shaped beach huts—salt-making factories. Across the road from Goa Lawah, three km east of Kusamba, they'll ask for money just to peer into one of the briny troughs; go farther up or down the coast to observe this centuries-old technique for free.

Wet salt-rich black sand is first carried by yoked buckets from the sea and spread out on flat terraces along the beach. After drying, the sand is dumped in a large palmwood vat inside a hut. Next, seawater is leached through the sand, producing a clear, salty water which is then poured in hollowed-out coconut-log troughs set in low platforms in rows beside the huts. Under the sun's blazing heat most of the water evaporates, leaving a salt slush which is further processed into salt crystals. Weather permitting, the whole process takes two days. The salt panner can make three to five kilos of salt per day in the dry season. The coarse white seasalt, used in salting fish and not as table salt, is sold to distributors who in turn sell it in the markets of Klungkung, Amlapura, and Nusa Penida.

Getting Away

From Kusamba, *bemo* to Padangbai run Rp500; Denpasar Rp1000. Kusamba is also a port of embarkation for Nusa Penida. For the old harbor, drive east through town past the market and take a right at the sign Dermaga Penyebarangan Kusamba; to Banjarbias Harbor it's about 500 meters from the main Klungkung-Amlapura road. Motorized *prahu* require 45 minutes to 1.5 hours to reach the island of Nusa Lembongan or the landing stage at Toyapekeh on Nusa Penida. The fare for tourists for either of these destinations is Rp15,000 pp. The first boat, carrying seasalt, peanuts, fruit, and rice, leaves at around 0600. With enough passengers, a second boat departs in the afternoon. There are seldom any boats after 1600. The number of departures per day depends on weather, demand, cargo, and destination. These sprightly boats can carry up to 1.5 tons of cargo. They're available for hire if you want to go snorkeling on the stunning coral reefs of Nusa Lembongan. The older harbor, on the beach in the village of Kusamba itself, also features boats to Toyapekeh, but they run less frequently.

GOA LAWAH

The famous Bat Cave lies just three km northeast of Kusamba on the left side of a dramatic road paralleling the sea. The holy cave begins at the foot of a rocky cliff and is said to extend all the way to the base of Gunung Agung. The ceiling is alive with thousands of fluttering, squeaking, vibrating, long-nosed fruit bats—an awesome sight. The wheeling, squealing bats are drawn again and again into the deep and dusky cavern; the noise is deafening.

A thick layer of slippery, sickly sweet bat droppings carpets the cave floor, through which bat-gorged pythons ooze in a state of surfeit. Bat excrement also covers the small shrines of a

Shivaite temple guarding the cave's entrance. It's believed Pura Goa Lawah was founded in 1007 by the peripatetic holy man Empu Kuturan. The cave and temple, one of the great *sadkahyangan* state temples of Bali, are both associated with religious rites surrounding death. The locals believe the cave harbors an enormous snake, Naga Basuki, the mythical sacred serpent of Gunung Agung and the caretaker of the earth's equilibrium. Homage is paid to this deity in the *pura.*

In 1904 the princes of Bali held a historic conference in this cave to plan action against the encroaching Dutch. Oral tradition says the cave leads by way of an underground river to Pura Goa ("Cave Temple") within the Besakih complex some 25 km away. A tale is told of how a prince of Mengwi actually entered the cave and emerged at Besakih, but his feat was never duplicated—entering the cave is now forbidden.

Today Goa Lawah is a real tourist trap. After alighting from the minibus, sellers of postcards and necklaces descend upon you; the parking lot is choked with *warung makanan* and souvenir stands. Watch for cheeky young girls who drape a shell necklace around your neck as a "welcome gift," then demand payment. Entrance fee Rp550. If traveling by public transport, don't arrive at Goa Lawah later than 1700; after that *bemo* to Klungkung or Denpasar (55 km) are scarce.

NUSA LEMBONGAN

A low, protected island about 11 km southeast of mainland Bali, measuring only four by 2.5 km and ringed with palms and white sandy beaches. Inland the terrain is scrubby and very dry, with volcanic stone walls and processional avenues crisscrossing the small cactus-covered hills. Crops are meager, and the only fruit available is melon. All other food must be imported from the market in Denpasar or from the neighboring island of Nusa Penida.

The island is small enough to explore on foot, offering beautiful beaches and coves, majestic views of Gunung Agung, unique Balinese architecture, and friendly country folk. With a lack of arable land and a severe shortage of tourist attractions, the island's economy is limited to its underwater wealth—seaweed.

There are just two villages on Nusa Lembongan—the large, spread-out administrative center of Desa Lembongan, and the village of Jungut Batu. Surfers and backpackers hang out in the latter—about 150 per month, for an average stay of three to five days. The only other visitors are European, Japanese, and Australian day-trippers on excursion boats. Jungut Batu offers the island's best accommodations and water sport opportunities. There's motorcycle traffic between the two villages and it's easy to get a lift.

Both villages are heavily involved in the cultivation of seaweed. Before government-supported commercial seafood production in 1980, the people of the island lived on maize, *singkong, ubi,* beans, and peanuts. Today most everyone is involved in one way or another with cultivation of the weed, and the air is permeated with its smell.

Visit the seaweed gardens at low tide; they look like gigantic underwater botanical gardens. Two kinds are grown, the small red *pinusan* and the large green *kotoni.* Almost the entire crop is exported to Hong Kong for use in the cosmetics and food processing industries. After harvesting, gatherers leave a floating offering of rice and flowers that gently drifts away on the outgoing tide.

Life on Nusa Lembongan is very relaxing, with cool breezes, little traffic, no big hotels, no pollution, no stress, no photocopy machines, and hardly any telephones. Best of all, there are almost no *pedagang acung* (pushy vendors) and few thieves. Jungut Batu's charming "tree house" bungalow-style accommodations—with outdoor open-air *mandi,* rickety wooden furniture, sand-floor restaurants and offices—are reminiscent of Kuta Beach 20 years ago.

Water Sports

Since the seaweed gardens must be protected from petrol-based pollutants, motorized boats are restricted in these waters. Nusa Lembongan and the adjacent island of Nusa Ceningan are therefore known for superb snorkeling, diving, and surfing. You can rent surfboards, masks, and flippers in Jungut Batu, or they may be supplied "free" by the captain whose services and boat you hire.

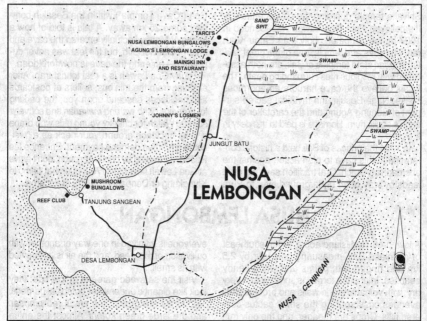

It's not possible to arrange for scuba diving on Nusa Lembongan. You must either bring all your gear and your own dive-equipped boat or accompany a dive excursion with one of the specilized sea sport companies on the mainland. When the tide is low, it's possible to wade out to see reef animals and colorful fish in amazingly clear water. Because of the seaweed farms, it's difficult to wade out that far; most people take a motorized *jukung* to the reef, about 150 meters offshore.

If you're part of a small group, bargain with one of the captains to take you out snorkeling or trawling for tuna. Try not to pay more than Rp30,000 or at the most Rp40,000 for three people for two hours. The price includes snorkels, fins and masks, lines and bait, the boat, and petrol. Not many fish but the snorkeling is great. The captains know the best places.

Getting There

Public boats run from Kusamba and Padangbai, but the most popular point of embarkation is from Sanur, where *prahu motor* depart from in front of the Ananda Hotel. Ask for *stasiun bot.*

Buy your ticket in the small ticket office on the left at the end of Jl. Hangtua. It's Rp15,000 one-way for tourists and Rp3000 for locals. Boats usually leave only in the morning; in the afternoon the waves are too rough.

It's quite a trick to board. You run out to the boat between the waves while carrying your stuff on your head to keep it out of the waist-deep water, trying to climb aboard before the next big wave crashes over you. Sometimes help is required to push the boat over the sand and out to sea. The 11 km crossing requires 1.5 hours, depending on the currents. The strait separating Bali from these offshore islands can be fickle and even treacherous. Lives have been lost. You never know what the weather or sea will bring, so hire something substantial.

Sit in the back near the motors—you won't get as wet and you'll be first off the boat. You'll alight at either the Reef Club at Tanjung Sangean or at Jungut Batu. If the ferry deposits you at Jungut Batu, the *losmen* are right there in front of you on the beach. If you arrive at the Reef Club, it's a one km walk into Desa

Lembongan. From the main road in Jungut Batu, it's about a 500-meter walk to the beach.

Smaller morotized *jukung,* which carry about 15 people, sail from Kusamba to Nusa Lembongan. Turn right down Jl. Pasir Putih and ask for the *dermaga* in Banjarbias. A few captains will try to charge you Rp25,000, but the proper overcharged Westerner rate is Rp15,000. Sometimes the morning boat from Kusamba sails only to Toyapekeh on Nusa Penida; in this case, just hop on the first *jukung motor* (Rp3000, 45 minutes) leaving Toyapekeh for Jungut Batu on Nusa Lembongan.

One-way charters from Sanur or Kusamba cost around Rp60,000-75,000 to Nusa Lembongan or Nusa Penida. Per day the charter rate is Rp250,000, depending on the size and speed of the boat. If four or five people contribute to a charter, you can visit not only Nusa Lembongan but also Nusa Ceningan and Nusa Penida. The boatmen always want their money in advance, "to buy petrol."

Returning To Bali

The boats to Sanur leave Jungut Batu at 0400 or 0500. After 0600 it can prove expensive—Rp60,000 and up for a charter. Be prepared to get pretty wet even in a calm sea. Alternatively, you can grab a boat from Jungut Batu to Toyapekeh at around 0500; from there take the local boat to the mainland. Or climb aboard the speedy *Bali Hai* back to Sanur for Rp100,000; a small canoe will take you from Jungut Batu's beach out to the hydrofoil by 1400. The *Bali Hai* sails back to Sanur at around 1500. From Jungut Batu to Banjarbias in Kusamba, there's only one regular boat in the very early morning. The fare is a flat Rp15,000 pp—no bargaining. You could possibly find a seawood farmer in Jungut Batu who will take you across cheaper. Again, you may have to get yourself over to Toyapekeh on Nusa Penida to catch a boat.

Cruises To Nusa Lembongan

At least a dozen companies offer marine recreational tours to Nusa Lembongan. Craft range from slick high-tech specialized vessels to romantic tall ships. All pick up passengers early in the morning at Bali hotels, take them to Nusa Lembongan for two or three hours, feed them a lavish hot buffet lunch, then sail back to Bali into a tropical sunset.

A very elegant experience is the sleek catamaran *Wakalouka* (Rp142,000), boasting pool, oceanarium, glass-bottom boat, and barbecue seafood lunch. If it's swashbuckling you desire, take the gaff-rigged ketch the *Golden Hawk* (Rp157,000), older than the Statue of Liberty and looking like something that sailed out of *Seven Years Before the Mast.* For a relaxing day excursion, and an extraordinary banquet, try the hydrofoil *Bali Hai* (Rp139,000), which thunders and bounces in a straight line to Nusa Lembongan. The *Bali Hai* also offers an Hawaiian-style "Sunset Dinner Cruise" for Rp69,000, departing at 1800 and returning at 2030. Bali Yacht Charters runs day cruises to Nusa Lembongan on the 47-foot sloop *Ocean Lady II.* The Rp142,000 pp price—good value—includes all food and drinks, coral viewing, and island exploring. Call Dewi, Atik, or Captain Patrick (tel. 287-739).

DESA LEMBONGAN

With a population of around 4,000, Desa Lembongan is the largest village on the island. Its inhabitants also cultivate seaweed. Besides the temple high on a hill up a long flight of steps, about the only other *obyek wisata* in Desa Lembongan is the Underground House. Not really a house but a damp, cool, earthen cave with many passages, dips, tunnels, and exits. Watch your step and don't get lost in this rather forbidding labyrinth. The candle provided isn't really enough; you'll also need a flashlight. Built by the puppeteer Jero Mangku from 1961 until he died; they say the old man believed in black magic and wanted to hide. An eerie place. From Desa Lembongan, it's a three km walk north to Jungut Batu.

JUNGUT BATU

The island's only tourist-oriented beach inns, homestays, and restaurants are concentrated in this small seaside village on the northwest coast. With just the sound of the waves, distant radios, crowing roosters, and an occasional motorbike, this is Bali at its best. The beer is cold and cheap and the clothing super casual—*sarung,* surf shorts. There's not much to do except surf, snorkel, read, sleep, eat, drink, hang out. You go mad if you stay longer than two weeks.

Come in January in the off season—no one's here and the waves are good. Jungut Batu is also one of the best places to take children on Bali. Nothing to do but play with the local children; there's a karate club for young ones, and during each full moon a festival and cockfights. There's always lots of activity on the long beach or in the water—children flying kites, boats loading and unloading goods and passengers, seaweed gatherers walking and weaving between their gardens. The sun sets right over Sanur's Bali Beach Hotel and at night lights twinkle all along the southeast coast of Bali.

Lining the beach are five eco-friendly bamboo surfer-style restaurants, several with TVs and videocassette players. Bring your CD player—lots of CDs, as well as books. If you bring your own tapes, they'll play them in the restaurants, though the blaring TVs and stereos seem out of place and drown the sound of wind and waves. Also bring lots of cash, because there's no place here to change money.

From Jungut Batu walk to observe the island's birdlife. It's a hot but level three km walk (30 minutes) to the main village of Desa Lembongan on the southern coast of the island. Take the stairs at the south end of the beach up into the hills; from there you get a fine view over Nusa Lembongan and the island of Nusa Penida. Tanjung Sangean is a 4.5 km walk. Also explore the sandspit extending off the northwest coast.

Water Sports

Three of the best surf breaks in the world are off the Jungut Batu beach: Playground, Shipwrecks, and Lacerations. Why the foreboding names? Because you're surfing over deadly coral formations. If you slip and fall into these mushrooms of multicolored, razor-sharp coral, it's like jumping into a rubbish bin of broken glass. And there's only one doctor (in Desa Lembongan) on the whole island.

Lacerations is a tubey righthander with a name that speaks for itself. The tunnel waves are so big you can drive a bus through them. One of the best righthanders in the world, it's perfectly round with a perfectly calm channel in the middle. The tunnels occur only during high tide with the right sort of moon. A perfect right breaking over a coral reef grown over an old shipwreck is appropriately called Shipwrecks. From the beach you can see the prow of the ship sticking out of the ocean.

This righthander, the most consistent wave on the island, ranges from a small mellow hot dog wave to a hairy stand-up tube. You can surf this break at any tide, but it usually fades at low tide. Watch the strong riptide. It's a long crawl—10-15 minutes—to Shipwrecks, but a *jukung* will take you out for Rp1500. Playgrounds is a lefthander, less consistent than Shipwrecks. It's a good fun wave that can get pretty scary at low tide, as the reef is sharp and the water shallow.

JUNGUT BATU WAVES

PLAYGROUNDS

LACERATIONS

'NO MANS' (UNRIDEABLE)

RIDEABLE WAVE

SHIPWRECKS

BEACH

BEACH

NOT TO SCALE

© MOON PUBLICATIONS, INC.

Accommodations

All accommodations face the beach—there's nothing between you, the crashing waves, and the setting sun. All water here tastes salty. Almost all accommodations feature generators turned on only from 1830 to around 2300. Places with two-story treehouse-style bungalows like the Nusa Lembongan Bungalows offer the best ventilation. Choose a bungalow with mosquito nets and screens on the windows. Few places have bars on the windows, just flimsy door locks, but thievery is kept to a minimum since everybody knows everybody. Ask for a lower per day price for extended stays. The tariff is less in the low season (Nov.-Feb.). The farther south you go, the cheaper the accommodations. There's a place between the police station and No. 7 that costs Rp3000 s, but it offers only grass huts with holes in the walls. Breezy atmosphere, no electricity. Most remote is Mushroom Beach Bungalows, two coves and ridges south of Jungut Batu. It's almost too remote because you have to take a boat to Jungut Batu for a decent meal, unless you want to pay Rp20,000 for the smorgy at the nearby Reef Club.

As soon as you get off the boat **Bobby's and No. 7** is on the right. This *losmen* is at the south end of the beach, farthest from the sunken ship. Nice people and nice rooms (Rp7000 s in the off season, Rp15,000 s in July and August), breakfast included; good food. Staff will even help argue the price of the boat back to the mainland. **Johnny's,** south of Agung's and 50 meters from the beach, charges Rp7000 s. Indonesian-style *mandi*. A favorite of budget-surfers.

Agung's Lembongan Lodge and Restaurant offers four two-level bungalows big enough for a family, with electricity, WC, *mandi*, and porch for Rp15,000-Rp30,000. Clean and pleasant, the clientele is mostly surfers. Agung's also has *losmen*-style rooms with two beds, bathrooms, and electricity for Rp8000-10,000 d. Good food. **Tarci Bungalows and Restaurant,** north of Agung's, has bungalows for Rp25,000. Each can hold up to four people. The four bungalows in front are split into upper (Rp15,000) and lower (Rp10,000) units. A single bungalow called **Eka Dharma** must rank as one of the best places to stay on the island. A very agreeable young man, a family member, oversees the bungalow. His name is I Nyoman Yudana; his seaweed storage barn and boat are next door. Nyoman will

take you out snorkeling on his boat (Rp10,000). Facing Agung's with the water to your back, it's down the beach to the right about 150 meters.

Nusa Lembongan Bungalows lies in the middle of a coconut grove. Eight bungalows rent for Rp20,000 s, Rp25,000 d; the bungalows in the back are cheapest. Each two-story treehouse-style bungalow features a bath and sitting room, bamboo furniture, a skylight roof for cool breezes, a large double bed with clean sheets and mosquito net, and tea whenever you want it. The owner and his family treat you real good, on occasion even dishing out young coconuts, *nasi campur,* or a fish dinner. Good security. **Mainski Inn** has nine spacious double-story bungalows featuring nice upstairs rooms with thatched roofs, bamboo walls, and balconies open to the sea. Cost: Rp10,000 to Rp20,000, plus seven percent tax and service; rates go up in the busy season. Breakfast sometimes included. The most solid, well-built bungalows on the island, with big rooms, easy access to the path to the main road, and an outstanding second-story restaurant. There's a good sound system—mostly loud disco and rap music—so bring tapes if you want your own music. The walls are covered with surfing decals.

Mushroom Beach Bungalows is a quiet, modest, isolated place charging Rp20,000 including breakfast of tea, coffee, and toast. Four rooms in two buildings; electricity from 1700 until 0700. Simple meals are served; remember, houseboys are not known for their culinary skills. If there's fish, it's served. Great view over a private cove.

Food

North of the main part of the village are a number of quite stylish beachfront tourist restaurants with luxurious oversized furniture. Menus include Aussie jaffles, vegetable soups, Euro-breakfasts, delicious ice drinks, *gado-gado,* salads, and yogurt. Many items are unavailable, but the food is surprisingly good for such a remote area. The fresh fish, including lobster, are the best deals. If you go fishing or spearfishing and catch a reef fish or a lobster, the restaurants will cook it up for you. Suckling pig may be ordered in advance. Several *warung* in the village serve *nasi campur.*

With its tile floor and color TV, **Agung's** is one of the more popular places to eat. Certainly it's the most Westernized. The best place to view the sunset is Mainski Inn's upper-level restaurant. **Mainski's** has an unusual menu with lots of variety, and it changes every day. Try the killer vegetable pie (Rp3000)—great with an order of guacamole on top. Ask for the grilled tuna, the best dish. If you walk straight back from Mainski Inn to the main road, turn right to the pool hall and stroll 50 meters past; on the left is a *warung* with the coldest beer on the island. The restaurant in front of Tarci's has a full menu with good chili pizza. Small beers Rp1700, big ones Rp3500.

Shopping

Original woven articles are sold in the **Mermaid Shop** in the village. From 1100 to 1500 take a boat (Rp1500) out to the *Bali Hai* and shop in the big kiosk on the upper deck. Purchase film, batteries, shaving cream, razors, souvenirs, T-shirts, and coolers. This boat plugs you into the world; use your American Express card.

Services And Getting Around

A small post office is open 0800-1400; there's a larger post office in Sampalan on Nusa Penida. One doctor practices in Desa Lembongan. A dozen motorcycles are for rent at Rp10,000-15,000 per day. *Jukung motor* rent for around Rp10,000 per hour or Rp150,000 per day. A few bicycles rent for Rp5000 per day but they're so primitive you have to push them up hills. Get one with springs in the seats.

From Jungut Batu To Nusa Penida

A motorized ferry leaves at high tide at 0500 or 0530 and costs only Rp3000 pp. It's filled with people who shop for chicken, vegetables, and fruit in the market in Sampalan. Leaving Jungut Batu, you get a very picturesque tour of the bay: the adjacent ridges, beaches, and coves, the moored *Bali Hai,* the shipwreck, workers gathering seaweed from their farms. The channel

separating Nusa Lembongan and Nusa Penida is unexpectedly deep, in some places over 120 meters. This early morning trip is beautiful, but it's possible to charter a trip later in the day for Rp15,000-20,000. It's about a 10-minute walk from Jungut Batu's beach inns to where the *jukung motor* picks up passengers for Nusa Penida.

NUSA CENINGAN

The small, neighboring isle of Nusa Ceningan can be reached by boat (Rp5000) from Desa Lembongan or by simply walking out to it across the narrow, shallow channel at low tide. The sea between the two islands is filled with seaweed gardens. The four-by-one-km island, with a limestone and chalky landscape and a 100-meter-high hill in the center, only has one village and no places to stay. It does offer great surfing, sandy beaches, and lazuli and cobalt-blue coral pools filled with starfish.

Great snorkeling and scuba diving, with superior visibility and infinite small sealife, is possible in the calm, warm, crystal-clear channel between the two islands. Off the temple is a surf break which can jump in size quickly, as the waves come straight in from deep water onto a shallow ledge. The best way to get out to the breaks and around the indefinite channel between the two islands is to hire an outrigger: Rp10,000 for two to three hours.

The Balinese spearfish here, using homemade wooden spears. They even spear two-inch fish. Watch the sharks in this area. A Balinese was killed off Nusa Ceningan in 1988. He'd speared a sea turtle and was dragging it bleeding through the water when he was attacked. His headless corpse was found two days later. A dangerous sport, spearfishing.

NUSA PENIDA

Rarely visited by tourists, the towering southern seacliffs of the mysterious and foreboding island of Nusa Penida are clearly visible from Sanur Beach. The district capital is Sampalan, the island's principal town. There's only one other town of any size—Toyapekeh—and about 15 villages scattered along the coasts and in the highland interior of the island.

Because of its mountains, Nusa Penida gets more rain, produces more crops, and is therefore better off economically than Nusa Lembongan or Nusa Ceningan. Nusa Penida and its satellite islands offer fine swimming, surfing, snorkeling, scuba diving, and sunbathing, with delightful,

friendly villages. Not an island rich in elaborate temples, dance and drama performances, or the plastic arts, Nusa Penida is like a Balinese outpost transplanted to some alien shore. It's off the radio map, metaphorically speaking.

Radio communication between Klungkung and Sampalan wasn't established until 1985. The island has one hospital and one post and telegraph office. Generator-supplied electricity—and TV reception—exist only in the Sampalan area. The highlands feel like the interior of Sumbawa. The roads are generally good, though there's very little traffic. People are easy to meet and talk to. The island is cooler than

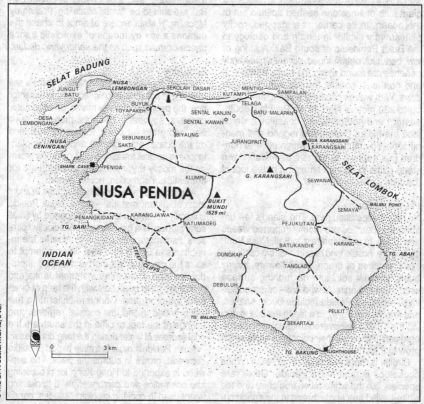

the mainland, there's less pollution, and the air seems to circulate more freely. Sampalan and Toyapekeh have the only official accommodations. Rice, fish, and vegetables are the main staples in the island's *warung*. Most visitors stay in Jungut Batu on Nusa Lembongan and come over to Nusa Penida island on day-trips.

Land And Climate

The body of water separating the three islands from Bali roughly marks the division between Asia and Oceania. As the Balinese say, "Here the tigers end."

The trench in the Lombok Strait between Nusa Penida and Lombok is even deeper, with the sea plunging to depths of over 300 meters just four km off Nusa Penida's east coast. The main island, nearly rectangular—22 by 16 km—with a total area of 203 square km, is basically a giant slab of limestone seabed uplifted out of the ocean. In its center is a stepped, rocky plateau very similar in terrain and geology to the Bukit Peninsula of south Bali. A string of low, beautiful, palm-fringed, silvery white sandy beaches are found along the north, northwest, and northeast coasts, fringed with coral gardens. With waves crashing against sheer cliffs up to 230 meters high, Nusa Penida's southeastern and southwestern coastlines, which face the Indian Ocean, are rugged and magnificent. You can drive to within several hundred meters, hike to the top, then walk down steep paths to springs emerging at the foot of the cliffs just above the sea.

Flora And Fauna

No native vegetation here. The island's few uncultivated patches are mostly imported weeds and grass. In stark contrast to Bali, Nusa Penida is a dry, hostile land of arid hills, big cacti, low trees, patches of green, small flowers, thorny bush, shallow soil, and no running surface water. The few animals who live—or rather, survive—on Nusa Penida include birds, snakes, and *kra*. Walter Spies, in a trip to the island during the 1930s, discovered unusual copper-colored bats that derive their color from algae which grow in their hollow hair.

Birdlife is more Australian than Asian. White cockatoos inhabit Nusa Penida. Other rare species, like the white-tailed tropicbird and the white-bellied sea eagle, breed in the spectacular cliffs of the southeast coast. The island is also the home of the exceedingly rare Rothchild's mynah and a breed of cock much prized as an offering in exorcistic rituals.

History

Once known as the Siberia of Bali, Nusa Penida was formerly a penitentiary island of banishment for criminals, undesirables, and political agitators fleeing the harsh and unyielding reign of the Gelgel dynasty. The inhabitants were overwhelmingly of the *sudra* caste, with few *ksatria* and *brahmana* among them. In Balinese mythology, the island is the home of the fanged giant Jero Gede Macaling, who periodically sends his invisible henchmen to southeastern Bali via the beach at Lebih, spreading plagues, famines, droughts, and rats. The word *caling* means "fang" and those dying of cholera on Bali are said to be *"ambil Macaling"* ("taken by Macaling"). Mainlanders attempt to chase the demons away by means of exorcistic trance dance-dramas such as the *sanghyang dedari*.

Economy

The level of chalk content in Nusa Penida's soil makes it impenetrable to water; lacking water for rice, the people grow only maize, sweet potato, cassava, soybeans, peanuts, mangos, *sawo bali*, and grass for cows. Except for seaweed off the coasts and coconut and cashew plantations in coastal areas, agricultural crops grown on the mostly dry, mountainous terrain are for domestic consumption, not for export.

All garden terraces are faced with the island's most abundant material—stone. Nusa Penida is literally covered in terraces supported by small coral stones. The government periodically sponsors *transmigrasi* programs to resettle the inhabitants in South Sulawesi. In an attempt to stem the devastating runoff and irrigate unproductive land, lined rain-catchment tanks and reservoirs have been built with the help of overseas aid programs. Concrete cisterns, a few wells drilled in the low coastal regions, and springs at the foot of cliffs in the south are the only sources of water during the long dry season.

Nusa Penida's most lucrative export is edible seaweed, grown in submarine pens. The seaweed is exported to Hong Kong for processing into cosmetics and carrageenan, a thickening agent used in cooking crackers, sauces, condiments, and other food products. There's a big difference between the traditional, poor, cassava dependent, rural hill villagers of the arid interior and the more prosperous seaweed-farming villagers of the coast, which have become market dependent and can at least fish for their protein.

A small-scale fishing industry catches mostly sardines and Bali's largest and most succulent lobsters. On the south coast fishermen descend paths down to the sea, where they fish from platforms protruding from the sheer cliff walls.

The People

The island's lack of infrastructure, meager resources, and harsh living conditions account for Nusa Penida's relatively small population of 47,000. The bulk of the population is Hindu. Toyapekeh is the only part-Islamic village, consisting of a mixture of Sasak, Bugis, Malay, and Javanese settlers whose ancestors migrated hundreds of years ago.

Nusa Peniders are commonly thought to possess knowledge of black magic and are avoided by other Balinese. Most speak or understand a little Indonesian, but use their own peculiar vernacular of Old Balinese sprinkled with many words borrowed from Lombok. They have their own *adat,* dances, puppetry, weaving arts, and architecture. The people of the central plateau live in austere one-room huts built of jagged limestone blocks, surrounded by rustic stables, storage sheds, the family shrine (*sanggah*), and terraced dry fields.

Most festivals and religious events are devoted to appeasing, deceiving, or exorcising the black-faced demon-king Jero Gede Mencaling and his white-skinned wife Jero Luh. Personified in giant puppets (*barong landung*), these terrifying deities dance and strut through village streets at festival times. Another popular exorcistic dance is *sanghyang jaran,* held during times of catastrophe in the Sakti area of west Nusa Penida.

Water Sports

As a dive and snorkeling locale, Nusa Penida is at least as spectacular as Bunaken in North Sulawesi. But it's a long and expensive ride, and, once there, strong, unpredictable swells and currents make conditions challenging and even hazardous. Not the place for beginners. A well-organized dive outfit, a knowledgeable guide with plenty of experience in the area, a reliable

craft, skilled boatmen, and a good engine are all necessities. The best dive sites, in the channel between Nusa Penida and Nusa Ceningan, are close together and you can move to alternate locations as conditions dictate.

Two of the most convenient sites lie off the *dermaga* east of Toyapekeh. Fish life is common; manta rays collect on the southwest end of the island. The variety of coral along the dropoffs and steep slopes is incredibly rich, but because of deep upwellings the water can be uncomfortably cold, dropping to below 19° C during the Balinese winter. Visibility, up to 15 meters, is quite good.

Getting There

Turn in at Jl. Pasir Putih about 1.5 km east of the town of Kusamba and walk 500 meters to Banjarbias, where you'll see small, bullish outboard-powered outriggers taking on cargo. Boats usually leave twice daily, but only when there are enough passengers. Another departure point, preferred by Nusa Penida residents, is from Kampung Kusamba about 100 meters from the *pasar.* These motorized outriggers carry passengers to, among other places, Toyapekeh on Nusa Penida. Make sure you're on the right boat. The charge for Westerners is Rp15,000 one way and the 10-km passage takes 45 minutes to one hour, depending on the wind and the choppiness of the water. When you arrive in Toyapekeh, there are frequent *bemo* to Sampalan (Rp500, nine km). To charter a boat from Kusamba to any point on Nusa Penida's north coast costs Rp100,000-150,000 roundtrip. Boats must return to Kusamba by 1400.

From Padangbai the charge is the same. Buy your ticket in the *loket* to the north of the main Lombok ferry ticket office. The first express ferry departs at around 0630, but you have to wait for it to fill up. And you might wait awhile, what with its 45-passenger capacity. The crossing takes just 30 minutes, docking at Buyuk just east of Toyapekeh. From there you can hop a *bemo* east into Sampalan (Rp500, five km). From Jungut Batu on the northwest coast of the neighboring island of Nusa Lembongan, small *jukung motor* shoot over to Nusa Penida for Rp3000 pp.

Prahu sail from Sanur to Toyapekeh (25 km, 1.25 hours, Rp15,000) very early in the morning. Check out the day cruises offered by Bali International Yacht Club, tel. (0361) 288-391, in

Sanur; Bali Intai Tours and Travel, tel. 752-005 or 752-985 in Tuban; and many other outfits which visit the south coast of Nusa Penida. These cruises charge around Rp150,000 pp, that includes free transport to the boat, drinks, packed lunch or Indonesian buffet, and fishing and snorkeling equipment.

Getting Around

Roads cover the island; good roads run from Toyapekeh to Sampalan and on to Karangsari, and from Toyapekeh to Klumpu. The roads from Klumpu to Batumadeg, Tanglad, and Pejukutan are winding and bumpy but asphalted and traversable. Because of the island's rocky, undulating topography, only motorcycles, trucks, or tough canopied *bemo* can manage the bumpy, dusty roads of the outlying areas.

Bemo run irregularly between the main villages, connecting north coast towns and inland settlements. From Sampalan, *bemo* begin carrying passengers out to the villages early in the morning, but by the afternoon the terminal is all but empty.

The best way to get around quickly is by motorcycle. As soon as you get off the boat at Buyuk or wander into the Sampalan terminal you'll be approached by motorcycle owners or drivers. You can either drive or be driven. It's cheaper to drive yourself, though the drivers know all the best places, can introduce you to people, and speak better Indonesian. It's Rp20,000 for a motorcycle and driver for just a few hours; for that price don't accept anything less than six hours. Expect a per diem price reduction if you take the motorbike for more than a day. Or wait a few days to meet someone, and convince a newfound local friend to drive you around for free. Make sure your rental agreement makes it clear who pays for gas and oil. Try to get a free dropoff at your embarkation point back to Bali or Nusa Lembongan.

You can charter a whole *bemo* for Rp50,000-75,000 per day; inquire at Toko Elektronik. You may also opt for an hourly rate, though drivers will demand at least Rp15,000 per hour. At Mentigi harbor, it's Rp75,000 for a small, two-engine boat; Rp100,000 for a larger one.

Getting Away

Take boats to Padangbai (30 minutes) and Sanur (1.25 hours) from Buyuk, eight km west of Sampalan. Get there by 0700 to buy your ticket (Rp15,000) at the Departemen Perhubungan office near the pier. Each boat holds about 30 people. If there are enough passengers, a boat sometimes leaves for Padangbai in the afternoon. From Mentigi Harbor, one km west of Sampalan, hire boats to Banjarbias, then a *bemo* into Kusamba where other *bemo* pass by to Amlapura or Klungkung. The cost is Rp15,000.

SAMPALAN

The largest settlement and Nusa Penida's administrative center, Sampalan is a long town around one narrow, tree-lined street crammed with shops selling food, necessities, agricultural tools, and cheap clothing. Don't miss the *pasar* north of the *bemo* terminal—traditional, classic, an example of a Bali gone by. Sampalan is a study of a growing "outer island Bali" urban culture, a delightful little town with just enough places to sleep, eat, snack, and drink. Sampalan is your best base on the island, with beautiful views across the Badung Strait to Bali; at night, try to guess which town belongs to which set of lights.

Accommodations And Food

Bungalow Pemda, the government resthouse, is in the east part of town, a 10-minute walk to Pasar Sampalan and the *bemo* terminal. The bungalows, opposite a soccer field and only 50 meters from the police post, face a beach lined with *junkung*. Very convenient location. Five units, each containing two rooms with bathroom, cost Rp5000 s, Rp8000 d. The beds are too small and narrow, the place could be cleaner, and the mosquitos are bad, but what do you want for two bucks?

You can try to stay in cleaner rooms with local families. Ask the *bemo* drivers to drop you off at Made Latoni's house (Banjar Sental Kawan, Desa Ped, Nusa Penida); he can arrange accommodations in one of several private homes for Rp10,000-15,000 per night. For Rp20,000 per day, Made offers motorcycle guide service.

On the road are small *warung* which serve *nasi campur, nasi goreng* (Rp1500), and cold drinks. **Warung Ceper** (Jl. Nusa Indah 54) offers local foods like *lawar, urab, ayam kampung,* and veggies. A knockout *kampung*-style *nasi campur* with all the fixings is only Rp1500, though the food is generally gone by 1800. Great value, though there's no compromise with the fiery spice. **Kios Dewi** is neat, clean, and well-lit but lacks the character of Warung Ceper. **Toko Anda** on Jl. Nusa Indah offers groceries, as well as stationery, snacks, ice cream, cosmetics, and color film.

Getting Away
It's easy to find *bemo* or a minibus east to Toyapekeh (Rp500, nine km). When full, *bemo* leave for Sewana to the southeast, usually starting at around 0900 (Rp500, eight km). The *bemo* fare to Klumpu is Rp1500, Tanglad Rp3000.

TOYAPEKEH

A small, attractive Hindu coastal village nine km east of Sampalan, with the island's only mosque, inhabited by fishermen and seaweed farmers. This is the main market town of northwest Nusa Penida. When the boat from Nusa Lembongan pulls in on the beach, *bemo* are waiting to take passengers to Sampalan (Rp500).

Stay at **Losmen Tenang,** right on the beach. Price: Rp6000 s, Rp10,000 d. Order meals there or from a few simple *warung* on the main road. East of town is a nice beach. Motorized *jukung* from Toyapekeh to Jungut Batu on Nusa Lembongan cost Rp3000, and leave only in the mornings because of the tides.

Pura Dalem Penataran Ped
From the Toyapakeh minibus stand, ride or walk four km northeast down a tree-lined road along the sea to this temple in Desa Ped. The temple is 50 meters from the beach, north of the main road. Built almost entirely of limestone blocks and patchwork cement, with rough *paras* carvings, guardian statues, and the leering face of Bhoma looming over the gate, it's architecturally very homely and sinister-looking. One of Bali's holy *sad-kahyangan* temples, this rather crude and poorly maintained *pura* is considered magically powerful. It's the destination of devout pilgrims from all over Bali who seek to ward off evil and sickness by praying to the sorcerer and destroyer of evil Ratu Gede Macaling, a spirit who occupies a high place in the Hindu-Buddhist pantheon. Beyond the outer west wall of the temple is a shrine dedicated to this terrifying protective deity.

ROUND THE ISLAND

Circumvent the whole island by starting from Sampalan and heading first to Toyapekeh, then Penida, Batumadeg, Tanglad, Sewana, Karangsari, and back to Sampalan. Traveling by rented motorcycle or *bemo* you can make it in four days: one day in the Sampalan-Toyapekeh region; another spent exploring the southwest coast; the third day touring Batumadeg, Debuluh, and Tanglad; the fourth wandering Sewana and Karangsari.

The seacoast village of Penida is nestled at the bottom of a valley filled with coconut palms, surrounded by a peaceful woods. This pretty village offers a short beach and nice scenery but has only one *warung* and no place to stay. Rent a *junkung* and visit Shark Cave offshore. The road east from Sebunibus leads to Klumpu, about 15 km southeast of Sakti. One-half km east of Klumpu, a paved road takes you north to the coastal road between Toyapekeh and Sampalan. The Klumpu area features the island's best indigenous architecture.

From Klumpu, the road heads south and then southwest to Batumadeg, passing Bukit Mundi, Nusa Penida's highest point and the dwelling place of Dewi Rohini, the female spouse of Shiva. Climb Bukit Mundi from Batumadeg up through grassy ridges; there's a temple in a small patch of forest on the western slope. On the way down pass through the small village of Ratug.

The first tourist didn't reach Batumadeg until 1977. Today there are some *warung,* a few shops, and *bemo* connections. From Sebuluh Waterfall near Batumadeg take the steep path two km down to the sea. The road southwest from Batumadeg ends in Debuluh; from here a path leads down to yellowish sea cliffs. All along the coastline you can stand on spectacular promontories and watch the dazzling green sea 200 meters below. Offshore, rock pinnacles eroded from the cliffs shoot straight up, completely surrounded by water.

Another road from Batumadeg takes you across a plateau for seven km to Batukandik, which possesses "male" and "female" shrines.

This unique temple also has a prehistoric stone altar: a woman with enormous breasts supports a stone throne on her head, two roosters standing on her shoulders. The Holy Forest of Sahab hides a temple, said to be the exit of a mythical tunnel connecting Bali with Nusa Penida; the hole apparently starts in Pejeng.

Tanglad

This stark, rolling country feels a million miles from Bali. From Batukandik a bumpy road takes you along a gently rising and falling ridge four kilometers to the village of Tanglad; from Klumpu turn right and climb the hill 10 km. You can catch a *bemo* to Tanglad (Rp3000, 25 km) from Sampalan at 0800 or 0900, after the market. The same *bemo* leave Tanglad for Sampalan at 0500.

Tanglad is a very traditional, preindustrial, rocky mountain village of steep-roofed stone houses, inhabited by bare-breasted, betel-chewing, middle-aged women. Of a population of 2,000, sixty are weavers. *Capuk* cloth costs Rp6000-10,000 per meter here. You'll be shown "antique" pieces for Rp50,000, woven with hand-spun cotton 15-20 years ago. The rough designs and crude techniques are light years away from the sophisticated *ikat* and designs of Sumba and Flores.

Small *warung* serve noodle soup and very strong coffee. The only entertainment is two billiard tables in the town *bale*. In the temple, see the throne of the sun-god Surya in a sculptural style reminiscent of East Java's Candi Sukuh. From Tanglad, head north to Pejukutan. Take the road south to Sekartaji, or visit the traditional houses of Pelilit on the south coast.

The East Coast

The nicest part of the island. This undiscovered coastal strip lacks the laid-back quality of Nusa Lembongan's Jungut Batu but offers full Bali culture. If you can spend only a short time on Nusa Penida, just start walking south from Batu Malapan. *Bemo* leave Sampalan for Batu Malapan when full; Rp500 is the correct fare.

This stretch of coast is even more scenic than the east coast of Karangasem. Sewana and Karangsari village are lovely, as are the adjacent offshore sea gardens. Here, industrious women use inflated inner tubes to move heavy baskets of seaweed. Long lines of bright *jukung* pull up on shore. At the side of the road are mats covered in drying seaweed.

From Tanglad, it's nine km northeast to the small fishing/seaweed village of Sewana. From Pejukutan, the road north leads down to the sea. The high cliffs of the southern part of the island give way to open beach and seaweed gardens. The village starts as soon as you come down the mountain, as the road levels out. Walk this beautiful coastal road; if you've rented a motorcycle, have the driver wait for you three km up the road at Gua Karangsari.

To the south of Sewana are several pagoda-like temples. Malibu Point, with visibility up to 20 meters, is a favorite scuba-diving spot with an excellent variety of fish, including pelagic, tuna, and manta ray, as well as hawksbill turtles. With a current of up to four knots conditions can be fierce, and the water is cold.

Gua Karangsari

Northwest 3.5 km from Sewana and about five km southeast of Sampalan, within sound of the ocean, is an immense limestone cave known by the locals as Gua Giri Putri. Hindus worship at the holy spring inside. The entrance lies 150 meters up a steep stairway. Climb down through a small opening, crouch under a low ceiling, then descend down into tremendously deep, vaulted grottos—still and silent except for the squeaking of bats, which grows louder the deeper you go. Tradition has it the cave leads eventually to Pura Puser Ing Jagat in Pejeng.

Some of the branch tunnels lead to openings; at the far end of the cave is a fantastic view of fertile rolling hills and green mango farms. The main shaft rises to a small lake. The villagers will provide you with a big lamp for Rp2000. Without their assistance, entrance should be free. For safety's sake, bring a friend. Besides the bats and some birds, there's a certain species of crab found in this cave. During Galungan, a torchlit procession of women bearing offerings visits the underground lake.

BANGLI REGENCY

Stretching north to south in central-eastern Bali is the only landlocked regency on the island. Only tiny Klungkung has fewer people than Bangli's population of 180,000, divided into 187 community groups in 73 villages.

With its rugged, overgrown hillocks, wooded ravines, and steeply tiered gardens leading up to immense volcanic craters, the regency encompasses some of the most superb natural scenery on the island. The roads north from Bangli or Tampaksiring climb gradually, the air becomes cooler, and upland crops such as peanuts begin to replace rice. North of Bangli, the road meanders through eerie forests of giant bamboo, finally emerging on one of Bali's most dramatic vistas: the huge 10-km-wide basin of Lake Batur, with the smoldering black cone of Gunung Batur rising behind it.

The region offers mineral hot springs, volcano-climbing, boat tours of beautiful Lake Batur, unique archaeological sites, venerated temples, the mountain towns of Penelokan and Kintamani, and the Bali Aga village of Trunyan. Isolated corners of the mountainous Bangli region are home to a number of aboriginal, pre-Majapahit communities, ethnically and culturally distinct from the Balinese mainstream. These mountain folk don't believe in priests, holy water, or cremation. They speak archaic dialects, expose their dead to the elements, uphold a fine stone-carving tradition, and practice an archaic, non-Javanized form of Hinduism.

Tourism is not well-developed in Bangli, with the exception of the Penelokan/Kintamani area. Most independent travelers visit the regency on a fast roundtrip from the south, climbing the Batur volcano on their way to Lovina, then head back down via Bedugul and Lake Bratan in the western range.

The region's higher altitudes are quite cold at night, so bring warm clothes and shoes. Make certain your accommodations provide dry blankets and firewood. Visit the mountains in the morning because by the afternoon the volcano and lake are shrouded in clouds and fog. Thievery is just as much a problem here as in the madcap alleys of Kuta, so watch your gear.

HISTORY

This regency was born of cruelty, incest, betrayal, and murder. In Bali, where legend and history are so intertwined, the history of Bangli reads like a story from one of the *Panji* tales. In the 18th century, the ruthless King Dewa Rai of Taman married his cousin, Dewa Ayu from the Bangli Denbancingah family. Dewa Rai then adopted Dewa Gede Tangkeban, the son of the ruler of Nyalian, but the son fell in love and had an affair with his adoptive father's wife, the queen. She persuaded her lover to turn Dewa Rai's dissatisfied subjects against their despised king. After Dewa Rai was murdered in the courtyard of the Puri Agung of Bangli, Dewa Gede Tangkeban married his stepmother and became king of Bangli. Since this marriage was not sanctioned by the religious *adat* of the time, seven generations of rulers were cursed with bad luck.

In the 18th and 19th centuries, a time when maritime trade was paramount, only those kingdoms with ports were economically and politically powerful. To trade, Bangli was forced to transport its goods through other territories, paying heavy tribute to their sovereigns. Bangli's luck changed in 1849, when its king Dewa Gede Tangkeban II was appointed by the Dutch to rule the northern regency of Buleleng. This vast area came under Dutch control after Buleleng's King Gusti Ketut Jilantik committed *puputan*. This confederation was of great advantage to Bangli; it was then able to gain access to the sea. Buleleng could irrigate its rice fields with Bangli water. But the union was short-lived. In 1854, Buleleng rebelled against Bangli; in 1882, all of northern Bali came under direct Dutch colonial administration.

Bangli first became known to the Western world when a German doctor, Gregor Krause, was appointed to the Dutch hospital here from

BANGLI REGENCY

TO SINGARAJA

KEDERAN

LUPAK

LOTENG

DUSA

BANTANG

PURA TEGEH KURIPAN

PENULISAN

LAMPU

CATUR

BELANTIH

YEH MAMPEH

KINTAMANI

G. BATUR
(1717 m)
TOYA BUNGKAH

SONGAN

VIEWPOINT

LAKE BATUR

BATUR

PRAJURTI

PELAGA

PENELOKAN

KEDISAN

BUAHAN

TRUNYAN

ABANG

G. ABANG (2153 m)

KATUNG

BANUA

WOS RIVER

SUTER

TARO

BANGKLET

PEMPATAN

PENGLIPURAN

0   5 km

KAJUBII

BESAKIH

TAMPAKSIRING

KUBU

MENANGA

RENDANG

DEMULIH

BANGLI

SELAT

ISEH

APUAN

BUKIT JAMBUL

PEJENG

BUNUTIN

PALAK

GIANYAR

PETELUAN

KLUNGKUNG

© MOON PUBLICATIONS, INC.

1912 to 1914. An avid photographer and amateur ethnologist, Krause took over 4,000 photos
during his tenure. Four hundred of them, together with his reports on Balinese cultural life,
were published in Germany in 1922 and distributed worldwide. The book's effect on Europe, having just emerged from four years of
war and still struggling with poverty, was electric. The majority of photos were shot in Bangli
and constitute an invaluable historic record of
the time—the *puri,* aristocratic life, *raja* and
princesses in ceremonial attire, royal *topeng*
dancers.

Scottish-born Muriel Pearson, under the pen
name Ketut Tantri, wrote *Revolt in Paradise,* a
fascinating tale of life in Bali and Java from 1932
to 1947. Inspired by the early Hollywood film
The Last Paradise, she came to Bali, settling
first in Denpasar. Soon growing restless, she
drove inland in search of the real Bali. Her car
ran out of gas in front of the Puri Denpasar in
Bangli. The *raja* of the time invited her into the
palace and eventually she became his quasi-
adopted daughter. He gave her the name Ketut
Tantri, *ketut* meaning fourth-born child. She
wore traditional clothes and at the *raja's* sug-
gestion dyed her red hair black—only *leyak* (evil
spirits) have red hair on Bali.

EVENTS

Bangli's temple festivals are known for their
stunning offerings. Ceremonies often last all
night, and the dances are more traditional than
in the south. Here, the dancers fall into a real
trance; this is usually the only district where you
can see a genuine *sanghyang dedari* (exorcistic
dance).

The highlight of your stay here may be stum-
bling upon a *gamelan* competition. Only in the
Bangli area can you still find the powerful, deep,
and reverberating *gong gde,* a huge ensemble
of *calung, jegogan, trompang,* gong, big drums,
half a dozen *saron*-style *gangsa* and large *cengceng.* In feudal times, the *gong gde* was perhaps the most important symbol of a court's op-
ulence. Rare, streamlined versions of this archaic orchestra can be found outside Bangli
town in Demulih and Sulahan, and in Kintamani's Pura Batur.

The *balian* of Bangli are renowned for their supernatural powers, for their practice of the science of black magic (*pengiwa*), and for their
ability to heal psychically through the medium of
trance. Those patients the *balian* are unable to
treat are sent to Bangli's lunatic asylum.

BANGLI AND VICINITY

A friendly, scenic town in the cool, sloping, rich
farmlands of central Bali, Bangli is an hour's
drive (40 km) northeast of Denpasar. Bangli
dates back to A.D. 1204. An offshoot of the
early dynasty, the ancient kingdom of Bangli
became Bali's most powerful upland court in
the second half of the 19th century, largely as a
reaction to the Dutch presence in Buleleng.
Bangli's prominence, however, never eclipsed
the grandeur of the lowland courts, and its influence was not deeply felt in island politics.

Bangli today is perhaps the quietest and most
easygoing of all the regency capitals. Dominated by one-story buildings, the town is spread
out for some distance along the highway. Neat
and trim concrete administration buildings and
houses are surrounded by gardens and near-
empty streets; no souvenir shops, tourist restaurants, or nightlife. You have the whole town to
yourself.

Travelers use Bangli as a transit stop halfway
between Denpasar and Penelokan. Lying on
the slopes of Gunung Batur, Bangli has one of
the most temperate climates on Bali. When
skies are clear, the town offers superb views of
the still-active volcano.

SIGHTS

Eight royal *puri* were once situated around the
main crossroads of town, but now only Puri Denpasar is open to the public. Note the sculptures of
lions and bodhisattvas inspired by early photographs of Borobudur, and the remarkable painted mural and frieze in the *bale loji* depicting Chinese life in Bangli during the last century. The
mural is in bad shape but you can still make out
detail. Also worth seeing is the 100-year-old *bale
kulkul,* about a five-minute walk from the Artha

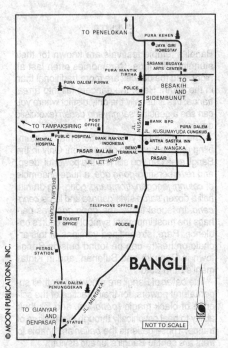

Sastra Inn. This well-preserved three-story pagoda-like structure with coconut tree columns once functioned as an alarm/signal tower to warn or call for an assembly. From the top tower hang two *kulkul,* one male and one female.

Pura Kehen

Thousands visit this lovely old terraced temple in the northeast corner of town—the largest and most sacred temple in the regency. To get there, follow the road to Penelokan, then turn right at the T-junction and walk 300 meters. Approaching it through surrounding woodland and coconut groves, Pura Kehen has the appearance of a full-scale *wayang* performance in the middle of a breathtaking rice paddy. Brave the usual crush of vendors, some very aggressive. Children accost tourists with flowers, asking for money.

One of the finest temples of its kind, Pura Kehen was founded in the early 11th century by Sri Brahma Kemuti Ketu as a state temple. Kehen is derived from the word *kuren,* meaning "household" or "hearth"; the temple is under the protection of Brahma, the Lord of Fire. Below the

first long flight of steps is Pura Penyimpenan ("Temple of Safekeeping"), an old temple containing a collection of historical *lontar* and inscribed *prastasis.* Here, a 9th-century bronze plate alludes in Sanskrit to a dedication ceremony in honor of Hyang Api (Brahma).

Pura Kehen's layout, as well as the temple's high platforms and megalithic stone construction, betrays a link with the animistic terraced mountain sanctuaries dating from the earliest periods of Balinese history. Like Besakih, Pura Kehen was built on eight terraces on the southern slope of the hill. Each of the three main terraces is connected to the one above by a flight of stairs. The first five terraces make up the outer courtyards (*jabaan*), the sixth and seventh are middle courtyards (*aba tengah*), while the eighth is the sacred inner courtyard (*jeroan*). Steep stairs lead to Pura Kehen's splendid gateway, the *pamedal agung,* known as "the great exit." Above it are the splayed hands and hideous face of a *kala-makara* demon who prevents malevolent spirits from entering the sacred grounds. *Wayang kulit*-like stone statues on pedestals depicting characters from the Ramayana line both sides of the 38 steps leading up the main entrance. The forecourt and middle courtyard are shaded by a venerable old *waringin* tree with a *kulkul* in its branches. The courtyard's walls are inlaid with chipped Chinese porcelain plates, the balustrades of the steps decorated with ornamental carvings.

The inner sanctuary features a shrine of 11 tapering *meru* roofs, resting places for the visiting mountain gods. The 11-tier *meru* is the highest honor that can be offered. In the northeastern corner of this courtyard is the *padmasana,* the three-throned shrine of the holy Hindu triad. Go around the back and check out the superb carvings. Ornamentation on the highest temple is so overdone and uncontrolled it's rare even for Bali—a stirring testament to the virtuosity of Bangli's stonecarvers.

EVENTS

During the *odalan* temple festival, beginning in the afternoon, high offerings are carried up the long stairway to Bangli's Pura Kehen. At night, this temple anniversary is celebrated with sacred *rejang* dance. Even bigger than the state temple's *odalan* is Bangli's *ngusaba* ceremony. Unusual dance forms practiced in the Bangli area include various archaic types of *baris* typical of Bali's mountain regions: *baris presi* (eight men with leather shields), *baris dadap* (men with shields made of *dadap* wood), and *baris jojor* (eight men in line with spears).

Besides temple festival days, Bangli's main event is market day, when you'll see products like sweet potatoes, peanuts, and spices not found in the south. The *pasar* is south of the Artha Sastra Inn. Dances and *wayang kulit* are sometimes staged in the town's *bale banjar* every *hari raya,* but not with the lavishness or regularity of Gianyar. A resident *dalang,* Dewa Made Rai Mesi, lives just 700 meters from the Artha Sastra Inn.

The **Sasana Budaya Arts Center,** one of the largest cultural complexes on Bali, is about 2.5 km northwest of the town center, just around the corner from Pura Kehen. Here you can see *gamelan* and theater performances, *baris* dances, and art exhibits. Obtain a schedule of events from the local tourist office. Tourist dances—the fire dance, *kecak,* and ballet—are

PURA KEHEN

PADMASANA
MERU TOWER

JEROAN
(INNER SANCTUARY)

CANDI BENTAR

ABA TENGAH
(MIDDLE COURTYARD)

CANDI BENTAR

BANYAN TREE

JABAAN
(FORECOURT)

MAIN GATE

TERRACES   TERRACES

0   10 m

© MOON PUBLICATIONS, INC.

performed nearly every day in Bona, 13 km southwest of Bangli (Rp5000). Buy tickets 15 minutes before show time at 1900.

ACCOMMODATIONS AND FOOD

The **Artha Sastra Inn,** Jl. Merdeka 5, tel. (0366) 91179, an original *raja's* palace, has seen better days. Still, the potted plants and palace court architecture give this place a unique feel. You can sleep in the bed of the last king of Bangli and participate in the ritual life of a *triwangsa* family. The inn is ideally located in the center of Bangli near the bus station. Coming into town from Denpasar, the palace complex is on the right. The inn is managed by an obviously overworked adolescent boy. Funky, decaying rooms outside with *kamar mandi* are Rp6000 s, Rp9000 d. Slightly less run-down are the five larger rooms in the interior of the *puri*; with inside *mandi,* costing Rp10,000 s, Rp15,000 d. These are adapted from traditional Balinese *bale* and feature ancient carved doors and antique furniture. Prices include breakfast of banana or pineapple pancakes. Inexpensive menu, but the food is not that great.

The *pasar malam* to the east of the bus station serves cheap, delicious meals; *ayam goreng* with vegetables for Rp3000. Or dine at several *warung makanan kecil* around the bus station; get there early as they stay open no later than 2100.

SERVICES AND TRANSPORTATION

Services
You'll find many shops in the local market south of the Artha Sastra Inn where you can buy the necessities of life. Though it takes up a whole block, it's not much of a market. The tourist office is on Jl. Brigjen Ngurah Rai, but is of minimal use—just a pamphlet or two. Change money at BPD on Jl. Nusantara (open 0730-1400) or use a bank in Gianyar, 13 km and Rp500 by *bemo* to the southwest. There's a pay telephone in front of the Artha Sastra Inn.

Getting There
Bemo from Denpasar's Terminal Kereneng cost Rp800 (40 km). From the town of Gianyar *bemo* cost Rp500 (13 km); from Kintamani Rp700. If

coming from Klungkung (19 km, Rp500), you may have to change *bemo* in Peteluan or simply board a Singaraja-bound *bemo* and get off in Bangli. Magnificent views on the way up.

From the new *bemo*/bus station opposite the Artha Sastra Inn in Bangli, get rides to Gianyar (13 km, Rp500), Penelokan (26 km north, Rp600), Kintamani (33 km, Rp700), Tampaksiring (22 km), and Denpasar's Batubulan station (40 km, Rp1000).

Bangli lies on the border between central and eastern Bali and it's easy to reach Besakih (21 km) from here on a lovely meandering surfaced road which runs by impressive rice terraces and along fast, clear, cold rivers at the bottom of deep ravines. The road emerges at Bangbang on the main Klungkung-Besakih road; from Bangbang turn south two km to enjoy the majestic vantage point from 300-seat Bukit Jambul Garden Restaurant. From Bukit Jambul, head north to Besakih via Rendang (12 km). *Bemo* run from Bangli direct to Rendang for Rp500, or take a *bemo* to Bangbang for Rp400 and walk a little. From Rendang, you can head east to Selat, then turn south on the postcard-scenic road to Klungkung via Iseh and Sidemen. About an eight-hour trip via motorbike; too many changes if you take public transport.

VICINITY OF BANGLI

For starters, try a nice walk through *sawah* to the east, bringing you to Pura Dalem Cungkub. Dewa at the Artha Sastra Inn takes guests to this temple. An even bigger temple lies to the west.

South Of Bangli

One-half km south of Bangli toward Gianyar is **Pura Dalem Penunggekan,** a temple of the dead. Detailed panels show scene after vivid scene of unimaginable and grotesque horrors heaped upon evildoers—impaled by arrows, boiled alive, devoured by demons, strung up from trees, roasted over flames. Bukit Jati occupies a scenic hill south of Bangli; take a *bemo* first to Guliang, then walk 500 meters to the top, the site of many temples. Not generally known to tourists, **Pura Tirta Harum** ("Temple of the Fragrant Spring") is a royal temple six km south of Bangli, about an hour's walk up a long uphill path. It's believed the ancestor of

the present-day dynasty of Bangli was born in a small thatched-roof building here. Enter through the *candi bentar.* Pura Tirta Harum derived its name from a nearby holy spring. An important *odalan* takes place here, attended by all castes.

In Bunutin, seven km south of Bangli, turn east. Overlooking a lake, Pura Langgar is designed along Islamic lines with four central pillars and four gateways in the direction of the four winds. The legend goes that, during the 17th century, a local Hindu prince fell gravely ill. Seeking a cure, a *dukun* was consulted; he advised the family to build a temple in honor of an Islamic ancestor of the prince, I Dewa Mas Wili, who joined the Gelgel court after immigrating from East Java's Blambangan peninsula. In accordance with the *dukun*'s wishes, a beautiful mosque-like temple was built on the shore of the lake. Today both Muslims and Hindus worship at Pura Langgar.

West Of Bangli

Turn west at the main crossroads toward Tampaksiring. After about one km, on the south side of the road, is the lake-fed spring of Tirta Empul, located at the bottom of a big ravine. Take the long flight of steps down to the springs. About two km farther west you'll see the signpost and the road south to Bukit Demulih ("Hill of No Return"). If you continue straight, you'll reach Penelokan. Perched on top of Bukit Demulih is the small temple of Penataran Kentel Gumi. From the hilltop, you can see the Balinese Pyrenees, a range of nine mountains named after the nipple-like *trompang* percussion plates in the *gamelan* orchestra.

Also visible is Pura Kehen, under a giant banyan tree north of Bangli; the whole Bukit Peninsula to the south; and the ugly box of the Bali Beach Hotel along the east coast at Sanur. There's a sacred waterfall on the way to Demulih Hill. Apuan is a five-km walk south of Bukit Demulih, or take a *bemo* (Rp500) from Bangli. The house of the *kepala desa* here, with its gold-leaf decoration, is as beautiful as a king's palace.

Sulahan village, six km west, is known for its basketry and wonderful old *gong gde.* This venerable orchestra, which most likely dates from the 18th century and today is known as Gong Gde Sekar Sandat, once belonged to the kingdom of Klungkung. It was cast in an amalgam of gold and bronze, which made it very durable. Before the advent of the *gong kebyar,* this powerful class of *gamelan,* with its deep melancholy tolling and unusual melody, was once widespread on Bali. It is rarely heard today.

North Of Bangli

The largest bamboo forest on Bali is in Kubu, four km north of Bangli. The sound of the wind blowing through the bamboo strikes some as eerie, but can be quite relaxing when you grow used to it. The locals believe the bamboo took root from bamboo sticks used in the making of camp shelters and *pikulan* abandoned by the army of Panji Sakti in the early 17th century. The most famous aboriginal village in the regency is Trunyan on the northeast shore of Lake Batur; few people know about Kajubii, eight km north of Bangli. Like most archaic Bali Aga villages, Kajubii is surrounded by a protective wall. Here the children are considered

more important than the old people, looked upon as servants of God.

Eleven km north of Bangli, In Kubu District, is Penglipuran, a much-ballyhooed "undiscovered" village of 164 families which looks like a well-groomed stage set from pre-Javano-Hindu Bali—neat as a pin and set against a backdrop of great natural beauty. Though it's not really "undiscovered" (note the parking lot for tour buses), a visit nevertheless provides a valuable glimpse into Bali's past. Every highland village in Bali once had this unique street plan. The original outer walls of each compound form two unbroken walls on either side of the long street, sloping gradually north to south. A *pura penataran* and a *pura dalem* lie at the north end. Each compound has retained the old-style domestic gateway. If you're invited into a household, give the oldest woman at least Rp500. Sit in the town *warung* and chat with the people, the best thing about visiting Penglipuran.

NORTHERN BANGLI REGENCY

PENELOKAN

Its name means "Place to Look." From Denpasar's Terminal Kereneng it's 56 km and Rp3000 by *bemo.* This cool, 1,450-meter-high village perches on the rim of a caldera looking out over the sacred, blackened, smoking volcano of Gunung Batur and Lake Batur, an all-important water catchment for south-central Bali's agricultural wealth. Sometimes the lake's colors change from glassy blue to platinum, a perfect mirror of the sky and mountains.

Get here by 0800 or 0900, before the clouds move in. Better yet, wake up early to catch the sunrise. In August and September the sunrise is too high, coming up over the middle of the peak, but in June and July it rises to the left of the peak in a golden yellow. At night see the moon sail over the volcano.

Though not a particularly attractive village—the roads untidy, the corrugated tin-roofed buildings decrepit, the vegetation sparse—views here are magnificent. In the mornings you can see not only all the surrounding mountains, but also Gunung Agung to the east, and sometimes even the sea and beyond. Penelokan has a high, fresh

climate and reasonable *losmen.* There are some great walks across the mountains, and along the road the views of Lake Batur, 300 meters below Penelokan, are unequaled. On the debit side, its vendors and street hustlers are rude and unscrupulous. There's also an admission charge for entering Penelokan, payable at checkpoints as you enter from the south or north. Keep the ticket so you don't have to pay again. To get down to the lake, public *bemo* drivers charge Rp1000 one-way for rides up or down the hilly road. If driving yourself, make sure you have good brakes before descending this extremely steep, hairpin road.

Warnings

The Penelokan/Kintamani area has one of the worst reputations in all of Indonesia for horrid, money-hungry, aggressive people. The many food peddlers hound tourists mercilessly. Beware of road sellers who pull the big switch—substituting a low-quality item for the high-quality piece you agreed to buy. Try not to show even the slightest interest in the wares pushed by the clutch of vendors on the street. If you stop and start bargaining a crowd of pushy, grabbing people will surround you, sticking items in your face. They really come out in numbers when the tourist buses start rolling into Penelokan from the southern resorts around 1030 or 1100. Don't stop when people on the road try to flag you down to sell you tours or boat rides across the lake. They may reach for the ignition key, or say your oil is leaking or they smell gas or you need air in your tires—all lies. One reader reports this happened to him five times within three kilometers. Don't leave your motorbike unattended. Bystanders may steal a part, then offer their help—for an inflated price—when you can't start it.

Bemo drivers mercilessly hassle women travelers, and have been known to threaten physical violence during price disputes. By the mid-'80s the situation had become so grim the government stepped in and implemented fixed prices on local transport. Now the situation has improved somewhat, though freelancers offering transport deals are still a big problem. One scam perpetrated by *bemo* drivers involves offering to haul you down the hill to accommodations in Kedisan. Even though the driver will insist the service is included in the price of the hotel, he'll ultimately charge you Rp2000 pp. Segara Bungalows has been known to employ this trickery. Motorcycle drivers offering to take you down to the lake won't accept anything less than Rp5000. Some *bemo* drivers want Rp8000 for a charter down to the lake. Just laugh and start walking. Someone will come along and offer to take you for the standard fare of Rp1000.

Accommodations
From Penelokan's *losmen* you'll discover one of the town's most pleasant activities is just sitting and gazing at the mountain and lake. You'll pay a lot for the view, though, if you stay in the generally overpriced, damp, run-down, and very basic *losmen* here. Penelokan does not have many comfortable and reasonable accommodations. Power outages are a fact of life. Be prepared for cold evenings and nights when bracing fog creeps over the crater's edge. Except for the most bare-bones places, blankets are provided with your room. You'll need them.

As Penelokan accommodations go, **Lakeview Restaurant and Homestay**, tel. (0362) 223-464, is above average, though it doesn't really have the right to call itself a homestay. Its tiny

Rp15,000 rooms, Rp40,000 bungalows, and Rp55,000 "superior" rooms with private baths are damp and smelly. Twenty rooms in all. The free breakfast is okay. Facilities include showers, hot water on request, safety deposit box, laundry service, and bar. But even with the 20% discount for guests (ask for the yellow menu, not the black one), the restaurant is overpriced—Rp8500 for *nasi goreng*, Rp4700 for a large beer, Rp2500 for a pot of coffee. Nonetheless, it's a fine place to admire the 11 km expanse of the crater. The management can arrange for a guide to take you up Gunung Batur. Make reservations at (0361) 232-023 in Denpasar.

Below and behind Lakeview, check out the **Caldera Batur Bungalows** with a good restaurant and clean rooms with private baths and bamboo beds (Rp15,000). For the money it's one of the best budget places in Penelokan. Sitting on its own promontory, **Losmen Gunawan** lies to the north 250 meters past the road down to Kedisan on the right. The most expensive rooms with baths, which can hold a family of three, sit directly over the volcano and cost an outrageous Rp25,000 d (no bargaining). A word of advice—check your room first. The blankets could smell of urine, the water barely trickle, the shower and toilet leak, with dirt in the corners and no towels, soap, toilet paper, or hot water. Demand a nice room. Tiny rooms with one bed are Rp15,000 s or d; no views. These smaller box-like rooms, however, are warmer, desirable during Penelokan's chilly nights. Large, uncarpeted rooms with big bathrooms cost Rp20,000. The tariff includes a decent breakfast (banana pancake, tea, and fruit salad). You must pay before you take the room.

Another option is to stay up the road in Kintamani, a 10-minute (Rp300) *bemo* ride north. Mellower, but not as close to the lake, and without the views. Yet another possibility—perhaps the most desirable for the budget traveler—is to stay right down on the lakeshore in either Toya Bungkah or Kedisan. These villages are more relaxed, with inexpensive eateries. The locals are a couple notches friendlier, and it should cost only Rp1000 to go up and down the hill by *bemo*.

Food
A major drawback to staying anywhere in the Batur area is the poor food. There's a critical

shortage of good *warung,* though the fruit stands opposite the road to Kedisan sell *jeruk,* passion fruit, and other exotic fruit. For less costly fare, try the *nasi campur* at a few local fly-blown *warung* for as little as Rp1500-2000, though they tend to be bland. Request *for be jahir,* a small, lipsmacking variety of lake fish. Toyah Bungkah has the area's best budget restaurants.

Then there are the big, sprawling tourist establishments. A string of expensive restaurants—the **Puri Selera,** Kintamani Restaurant, Danau Batur, **The Caldera,** and the 400-seat **Batur Garden**—are found along the road north to Kintamani, with meals in the Rp12,000-17,500 range. These restaurants, which serve Indonesian/Chinese food and Western bar drinks, cater mostly to tour groups. Open for lunch, the **Kintamani Restaurant**'s excellent buffet costs about Rp12,000. Meals at **Danau Batur,** one km up the road, are also delicious.

Between Penelokan and Kintamani are several cheaper restaurants—**Puncak, Gong Dewata, Gunungsari** and the **Mutiara Cafe**—with views just as nice as those offered by the tourist traps. **Gunawan's** has an assorted menu including fresh fish dishes such as *ikan goreng a la Batur,* or "Bali Island Noodle," with secret ingredients. Some items wildly expensive (cheese sandwich Rp7000!). They kick you out of the toilets and the restaurant at 2130 after you're finished eating—no reading or writing allowed. **Lakeview Restaurant and Homestay,** tel. (0362) 223-464, open for dinner, specializes in lake fish.

Shopping And Services
The shops along the road include some bargain buys. Chess sets sold in Kuta for Rp30,000 go for Rp20,000 here (no bargaining). Bone shell bracelets cost Rp500. The shop owners are friendlier than the foot vendors. A post office located between Peneloken and Kintamani handles parcels. Open 0800-1600. A postal agent is located next to the police post, about a five-minute walk north of the market.

Getting There
The most popular way to reach this mountain area is on the highway out of Denpasar by *bemo* from Batubulan station (Rp3000). *Bemo* pick up more passengers in Bangli, then head straight up to Penelokan. Or take a *bemo* from Batubulan first to Bangli (Rp1500), then on to Penelokan (Rp600). The road north to Bangli and Penelokan begins at the crossroads town of Peteluan, just east of Gianyar. There you can always find public transport during the day for a ride up to Penelokan.

From Singaraja in the north, a minibus costs Rp2000. The majority of tour groups stop at Goa Gajah, Gunung Kawi, and Tampaksiring's Tirta Empul before arriving in Penelokan in the late morning. These tours on air-conditioned buses are advertised all over Bali; a lunch at one of Penelokan's swank restaurants is usually thrown in. If traveling on public transport, from Ubud you must first go to Gianyar (Rp800), then to Penelokan. Or from Ubud take a *bemo* first to Sakah (Rp500), then flag down a minibus heading for Singaraja; get off at Penelokan.

There are also some great back-road approaches to Penelokan from Ubud. Try the narrow, potholed road through Tegallalang, Sebatu, and Pujung. This road offers nicer landscapes than the one through Tampaksiring. Even wilder is the road from Ubud via Payangan; drive a 100 cc (or more) motorcycle through the deep upland interior of Bali. On the way you'll experience variegated scenery, bamboo forests, and remote, hilly, pre-Hindu walled villages. To walk from Ubud via Payangan takes about 12 hours. The higher you ascend the more changes you'll encounter. The aboriginal natives of the Gunung Batur region even look different from the people of the coasts—darker, shorter, more wiry. In few other places is there a folk as stony-eyed as these.

Getting Away
Even getting out of this place is a hassle: men come out of nowhere to claim you promised you'd go in their car. To get to Lovina, you may end up paying Rp25,000 for a private taxi. Too much maybe, but it's a quick way out. Neither is it easy finding direct transport to Ubud. The closest place one can easily reach is Bangli; then you have to get another *bemo* to Gianyar, another to Sakah, and another to Ubud. Regular *bemo* travel between Kintamani and Batubulan (Rp3000); they may stop in Ubud en route. The *bemo* drivers of Penelokan have established a monopoly on transport down to the shore of Lake Batur.

VICINITY OF PENELOKAN

An exciting, fun ride is to take a bicycle up to Penelokan on top of a *bemo,* then freewheel it all the way back down to the southern coast. From Penelokan, you can hike around the crater rim to the rainforest on top of Gunung Abang (2,153 meters) in about five hours, eating raspberries along the way to quench your thirst.

From Penelokan to Besakih, travel southeast over a fascinating road running high above the lake across the foothills of Gunung Agung. Move through remote villages; not many tourists take this route and the Balinese are surprised to see you. A little before Rendang (14 km south of Penelokan) at Menanga is the turnoff to Besakih. Southwest of and downhill from Penelokan is Taro, near Jati on the road to Ubud. In these mountainous Bali Aga villages, the *bale agung* (council house) is the heart of the political and religious life of the community. The longest council house on Bali is in Taro. In the highland jungle, among the slippery ravines and steep hills between Gunung Batur and Gunung Catur, are the Bali Aga villages of Selulung, Batukaang, and Catur. See remains of primitive pre-Hindu monuments, lichen-covered stone statues, small Polynesian-style megalithic pyramids.

Climbing Gunung Abang

This old 2,153-meter-high volcano ("Red Mountain"), on the eastern side of the crater southeast of Penelokan, is the highest point on Batur's outer crater. Climbing it is demanding but easier than climbing Gunung Batur. The trailhead lies about six km southeast of Penelokan. Drive or walk down the Penelokan-Suter-Rendang road for five km. Go one km past the turn south to Suter until you see several *warung.* Continue on this trail to a temple, then head down a steep incline for another one km. Walk straight along the rim of the caldera up through a slippery and muddy scrub forest. You'll pass another temple, then after an hour you'll reach the windy, misty summit. The view is sensational. The climb up and back from the trailhead takes about four or five hours, depending on the season.

BATUR

A mountain village, Batur is north of Penelokan on the western rim of the crater, with no distinguishable border separating it from Kintamani. The newcomer on the ridge, Batur until 1926 was a prosperous village located at the foot of Gunung Batur. In 1917, the volcano erupted and buried most of the village in lava. This cataclysm took the lives of 1,000 people, destroying 65,000 homes and 2,500 temples. Miraculously, the molten lava stopped at the gateway of Batur's village temple. The survivors looked upon this good fortune as an auspicious sign from the gods, and thus rebuilt their village in the same location.

Nine years later the volcano erupted again. This time the village as well as the temple were completely buried under 30 meters of lava, but only one life was lost—an old woman who died of fright. Only a high shrine to the goddess of the sea was spared destruction. Finally getting the message, the community relocated high on the crater rim. With help from Dutch engineers, the villagers dismantled the surviving shrine and transported it piece by piece up the flank of the crater on the backs of horses and laborers. Once reassembled, the ancient dark stone shrine was incorporated in a new brick-and-stone temple, Pura Ulun Danu ("Head of the Lake"), with obvious Indian influences.

This is one of the most significant religious complexes on Bali. Lake Batur is the source of dozens of underground springs which help regulate the flow of water for the farmlands and sacred pools throughout the whole south-central region. Farmers from all over the island pay homage here to Ida Batari Dewi Ulun Danu, the life-sustaining and highly venerated goddess of the lake, who supplies the rivers, tributaries, dams, and irrigation canals between here and the sea with water. The temple's high priest is an important advisor on agricultural and water-use issues. In times of drought or crop failure, elaborate rituals are performed to secure help and blessing from the goddess of the lake. In the temple is housed a grand old *gong gde,* which accompanies the sacred dances of *baris gede* and the ceremonial *rejang* dance for women, a major 11-day *odalan* that usually takes place in March.

The nine-temple complex, with its impressive tall gateway, contains a maze of 285 shrines and pavilions dedicated to the deities of water, agriculture, holy springs, and arts and crafts. The largest temple, Pura Penataran Agung Batur, consists of five spacious well-swept black-gravel courtyards filled with rows of thatched-roof *meru* towers. In the northwest corner the Chinese-style shrine honors the patron saint of commerce, Ida Ayu Subandar. See the solid gold bell in the *bale gedung,* the storage place for valuable temple artifacts.

KINTAMANI

A windblown market town strung out along the highway, 68 km from Denpasar, Kintamani is a cool, fresh retreat; bring warm clothes, as it's cold at night. The fog comes rolling into Kintamani early, transforming it into a ghost town of howling *anjing,* so you'd best settle in before nightfall. The coldest months are July and August; lots of rain from October to March. Get up early to watch a superb sunrise.

Most travelers prefer to stay here instead of Penelokan. With its weather-beaten wooden buildings, the place has the feel of a frontier town. There are fewer annoying locals and you're treated with slightly more respect. Still, Kintamani has more barking dogs per square meter than any other place on Bali. The town boasts the world's finest specimens of the famous Bali Dog, now registered with the AKC. A particularly endearing characteristic of this breed is its habit of following you for upwards of a kilometer, barking in fits and starts the whole way, triggering mass barking frenzies in dozens of other dogs which linger on long after you're gone.

There's a busy market every third morning along the highway in the north part of town, right in front of Losmen Miranda. Mountain people come into Kintamani from the surrounding villages to trade. Traditional and turbaned, these rustics are seldom without their *parang.* This damp climate encourages a variety of fruits and vegetables unknown elsewhere on the island: peanuts, cabbages, passion fruit, citrus, flowers, coffee beans, and Bali's best *kritik* (cassava chips). This spectacle of local color and produce is over by 1100.

The temples of the area look out over the crater. People come from all over the island to pray here, especially during *odalan.* A grand old *gong gde,* one of only three on Bali, plays for the ceremony. Its heavy somber tolling hearkens back to a Bali now forever part of the past. Hear it on a moonlit night.

Accommodations

Most *losmen* are located on the main street, Jl. Pasar Kintamani, each offering cold, cubicle-like, damp-smelling rooms. This condition is somewhat alleviated by a crackling log fire at night—order the wood earlier in the day. Though in July and August there are many visitors, Kintamani's accommodations are generally not full. Bargain if business is slow.

Kintamani's best budget hotel is small, friendly, family-run **Losmen Miranda** in the upper end of town. Six rooms: Rp6000 s and Rp10,000 d with *mandi,* Rp8000 d without *mandi.* Services include free baggage storage, hot water at no charge, and a log fire. This clean, well-kept hotel and its good food are excellent value. Nothing glamorous but no bugs in the bed and bars on the windows. The owner, Made Senter, works as a guide. Between Puri Astina and the market, **Losmen Sasaka** has four rooms with hot water, bath, and showers for Rp25,000 d, including breakfast. Meals available at reasonable prices. The market is just south of this *losmen.* In the south end of town, **Supermen Inn** offers small unpretentious rooms with breakfast and *mandi* for Rp5000 s, Rp8000 d. Run by Kintamani's hippest, youngest hotelier, I Made Rubin, this *losmen* is the best place in Kintamani to eat cheap.

The most northerly accommodation, about 800 meters in from the road past a little village, is **Puri Astina,** tel. (0362) 95254, the classiest and quietest place in town at Rp30,000 d (no bargaining) for six front rooms with views; four bargain rooms go for Rp15,000 d. A clean, friendly place with a big sitting room, private baths with hot water, showers, Western toilets, and an expensive and rather cheerless restaurant with tourist menu (Rp2500 for soup, Rp8000 for Johnny Walker). Beautiful floor-to-ceiling views of three volcanos and the lake—worth rising at 0500 for. Postal service. Ask the owner Agus Sartono to arrange horseback riding and experienced guides for trekking or climbs up Gunung Batur (the path starts here). To get to Puri Astina, watch for the big sign just north of Kintamani's market before the radio tower. Don't confuse Puri Astina with **Astina I,** which has minimal bath, no view, and costs Rp12,000-20,000.

Food

Try **Warung Makanan** up from Puri Astina in the market. Losmen Miranda has a pretty good fully Westernized 28-item breakfast and dinner menu, including fried noodles (Rp1700), veggie omelettes (Rp1500), black rice pudding (Rp1500), and vegetables, eggs, and sauce (Rp2500). Miranda claims to have the best pancakes (Rp1800) on Bali—banana inside, coconut on top.

A number of food stations are located on the left-hand side of the road if heading toward Penelokan. Some big fancy tourist restaurants on the right overlook lovely gardens to Lake Batur. Tour buses dump hundreds of Taiwanese and Korean passengers at the 400-seat **Batur Garden,** which serves only lunch—Chinese and Indonesian dishes plus Western bar drinks.

Buy export quality Robusta powdered coffee at **P.T. Perkebunan** in north Kintamani for Rp1600 (250 grams). This plantation office, at the 6 km Penelokan marker, is a branch of the head office in Jember, East Java.

Getting Away

From Kintamani to Penelokan by *bemo* is Rp400, to Singaraja by bus is Rp2500 (1.5 hours), to Denpasar by bus is Rp2500 (1.5 hours). The Denpasar-Singaraja bus passes in front of Losmen Miranda. Ask Made Senter, the helpful owner, about his coffee and coconut plantation tours. For Gunung Batur, it's possible to start your climb from Kintamani at 0600 and return by 1200. Expert local guides, available through the hotels, will lead you down the old bridle path that drops steeply from the lip of the outer crater, then climbs up and over the rim of the inner crater before descending into the innermost crater. It's only about a 45-minute hike to the rim of the inner crater, then another 1.5 hours to the top of Gunung Batur. All the guidebooks recommend **Gede's Trekking,** on Kintamani's main street near the market, for tours in almost any direction. **Made Senter** also offers guide services up Batur. Guides will ask

Rp20,000 for one or two people, Rp40,000 for groups of more than two, but may accept as little as Rp25,000 for as many as six people. Depends on the demand. Or ask for detailed directions (Losmen Miranda has a map). Be prepared for hard going on Gunung Batur's ascent and the descent to Toya Bungkah. Catch a *bemo* back from Toya Bungkah, but leave by 1300 or you may have to charter (Rp6000 and up to Penelokan).

There are lots of other good walks in the area—to Gunung Abang, Gunung Agung, and the sea. The more people, the cheaper the guide rate. The track down to Ubud begins just south of Kintamani in Kubupenelokan, next to the Batur Garden Restaurant. It can be negotiated by motorcycle or by bicycle. Travel past walled-in villages and wild mountain scenery, bouncing into Ubud about three hours later.

PENULISAN

Peninsulan means "Place of Writing." You'll find this site eight km north of Kintamani at a left bend on one of Bali's prettiest roads. Take the soaring, 333 high-stepped stairs covered in slippery green mold up to lonely Pura Tegeh Kuripan, almost invariably covered in mist.

Spectacularly situated on the outer edge of the Batur crater, this remote temple is the highest and perhaps oldest on the island. On Bali, high places are considered sacred—where the gods dwell. Archaeological evidence indicates the existence of a sanctuary here as early as 1500 B.C., 2,000 years before the arrival of Hinduism. This royal *pura* was the highest structure on Bali until the Perumtel station was built on the opposite knoll. Now it shares that distinction with a TV tower.

Dedicated to the god of the mountains, Sanghyang Grinatha, a manifestation of Shiva, Penulisan is believed to have been the mountain sanctuary of the kings of the Pejeng dynasty. Today, people in the surrounding villages worship here; it's also visited by pilgrims from all over Bali. In the highest courtyard under a number of austere open *bale* are a whole row of linga and yoni, fragments of sculptures, finely wrought stone statues, and pagan phallic symbols and prehistoric divinities dating from the 9th century and before. The highest point of the temple, the tall Panerajon shrine, is a representation of the Hindu mythic mountain Mahameru. The pyramidal form of the complex, the site's eleven rising terraces, and its large megalithic stones are all typical of the arrangement of archaic Indonesian mountain sanctuaries.

Scholars conjecture the standing portrait statues of a king and queen with the inscription Batari Mandul and Anak Wungsu, dated Saka year 999 (A.D. 1077), may represent King Udayana and his consort Gunapriya. Another theory is that the royal personage is the Chinese Buddhist princess Subandar. Since *mandul* means "childless," it's been surmised the princess became infertile as a result of a curse hurled by a Shivaite priest.

For years outsiders were forcibly prevented from entering this temple by armed natives. It wasn't until 1948 that the ruler of Bangli allowed the Netherlands Indies Archaeological Service to carry out some technical renovations. Since then, the site has been in an almost continual state of restoration. Because of the high, mist-laden elevation, the statuary and reliefs are in a pretty decrepit state.

Very early in the morning is the quietest and most pleasant time to visit. Surrounded by mountains, caressed with a cooling breeze, on the rare clear day you can see half the island from the highest terrace—all the way to the Indian Ocean in the south and Singaraja and the gleaming Java Sea to the north. Sometimes you can even see the deep purple volcanos of East Java. Just below the temple is the village of Sukawana, the highest village on Bali.

Vicinity Of Penulisan

From the village of Sukawana, take the high road that follows the northern rim of the outer crater. The road plunges to Pinggan on the crater's north side, then curves southeast to Songan. Through pine forests and coffee, clove, and citrus plantations the road north of Penulisan winds its way down to the ocean at Kubutambahan, 47 km away. From there you can either head west to Singaraja and Lovina or east to Tirtagangga and Amlapura. Down the road from Penulisan, toward Kubutambahan, is *desa adat* Loteng, where local *banjar* keep a traditional trinity temple.

Between Penulisan and Bantang, turn on the rough mountain road west through isolated Old Bali villages on the slopes of Gunung Catur. Belantih consists of two long, broad, east-west avenues that serve as communal living rooms. These flat avenues, sectioned off by gradual shifts in levels, reflect ancient class groupings. Lined with family dwellings, the houses contain just a kitchen, sleeping rooms, and a *sanggah* house temple. Houses are constructed of wood with bamboo tile roofs, effective at keeping the occupants warm through the cold nights. A *pemakssan* ancestor temple lies just north of the village and another temple in south Bali style sits at the western end of the main avenue. Belantih's rustic, rough-hewn dwellings and its unusual layout make it a must for anthropologists. The road, which runs along the watershed between the north and the south of the island, takes you through Lampu and Catur, eventually leading to Pelaga in Badung Regency.

LAKE BATUR REGION

The crescent-shaped crater lake of Batur is 7.5 km long, with a maximum width of 2.5 km, and a depth of between 65 and 70 meters. The western side is barren lava rock while the eastern side is lined with trees. Eight villages huddle along its shores: the ancient Bali Aga settlements of Seked, Prajurti, Kedisan, Buahan, Abang, Trunyan, Songan, and the newer village of Toya Bungkah. These small fishing settlements are characterized by their archaic layout and unusual houses—steep bamboo shingle roofs and walls of clay, mud, woven bamboo, or wooden planks. Fish provide most of the protein for these lake dwellers.

After your three-km corkscrew descent from Penelokan down to the lake (Rp1000 by *bemo,* or walk it in 45 minutes), turn left and journey two km on the northwest side of the lake through a strange moonlike landscape. Rivers of black lava, a layer of gravely volcanic ash, sparse scrub, a few onion fields, and scattered houses now occupy an area where villages stood before the 1926 and 1963 eruptions. After seven km, this switchback road arrives in Toya Bungkah.

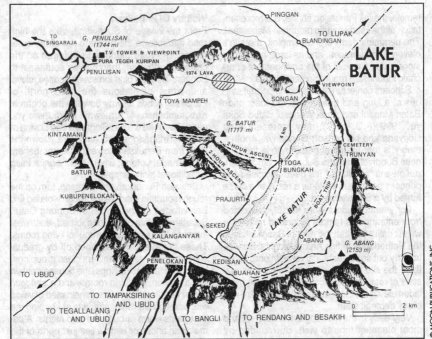

KEDISAN

The fishing and farming village of Kedisan, the community almost directly beneath Penelokan, offers foodstalls, *pasar* area, extensive gardens (oranges, corn, peanuts), souvenir shops, *bemo* terminal, ticket office, and boat landing. A number of accommodations, several in attractive settings, are only minutes from the water.

The big drawback of these *losmen* is the swarms of peddlers demanding you buy *sarung*, shorts, and paintings. They will flash you large, sad eyes, and show you guest books filled with signatures of tourists who've bought from them before. Don't fall for it unless you want to buy mass-produced and tacky merchandise and encourage obnoxious behavior in doing so. Kedisan is also full of people trying to get you to pay them to guide you up the mountain. Again, don't do it; you don't need a guide.

Accommodations

Cheapest is **Segara Homestay** near the ferry terminal and close to the road, next to the bar/restaurant and shops. Turn right after descending from Penelokan. Five basic rooms with *mandi* cost Rp8000 s, Rp10,000 d. The restaurant offers the standard menu, though it would be nice if someone taught them the basics of cooking; it's a shame a chicken has to die to be covered in such a vile sauce. North along the western side of the lake toward Seked village is **Segara Bungalows,** separated from the lake by peanut and cabbage fields. Accommodations start at Rp10,000 s for bargain rooms with *mandi* and go up to Rp65,000 for larger rooms with hot water, fan, shower, and bathtub. Rooms in the middle cost Rp15,000 to Rp35,000. The restaurant serves Indonesian and Balinese food, margaritas, and other mixed drinks. A few meters farther, **Surya Homestay** offers private baths, hot water, shower, laundry service, good views of the lake, and 18 clean rooms for Rp7000 and Rp8000 s, Rp15,000 d—all with breakfast (pancake, toast, egg, choice of coffee or tea). There are also Rp10,000 d rooms. It's a two-minute walk to the lake; good food in the restaurant. A bit noisy—dogs at night, cocks in the morning. Park your vehicle in the car park where it'll be safe.

Getting Away

For the lake trip, buy your tickets at the fixed-price ticket office in Kedisan. There are 82 boats in all. Standard price is Rp35,000 (maximum seven people) for a two-hour tour of Trunyan, the hot springs, and back to Kedisan. It's slightly cheaper if you just go to Trunyan and back (20-minute passage each way). This ferry is only 500 meters from the Segara Homestay. If you like crowds, Sunday is the best day. Beware of scalpers and independents who try to con you into paying several times the official price. Lying through their teeth, they'll tell you anything—that they're cheaper, that the government boats no longer operate. They're also inclined to renegotiating the price halfway across the lake or once they have you captive in Trunyan.

A self-propelled dugout canoe is probably not a cheaper alternative at Rp10,000, unless you're prepared to paddle a hell of a long way. Don't try to paddle across unless you're very strong and race kayaks for a living. No matter what kind of boat you take or no matter when you leave, take jeans and a jumper or freeze your ass off.

Yet another alternative involves no boat across to Trunyan—walk it. Take a *bemo* (Rp500) or ride your motorbike from Penelokan to Buahan; from there it's about a one-hour (seven-km) hike along the well-maintained lakeshore path to Trunyan. A longer hike runs from Kedisan north to Toya Mampeh, looping around southeast to Songan, then back to Kedisan via Toya Bungkah.

Vicinity Of Kedisan

In Buahan, four km from Kedisan, stay at **Far From The Madding Crowd**, Rp8000 s including breakfast. Nice, clean, friendly. A good trail from Buahan takes you around the shore of the lake to the village of Abang, about four km from Penelokan and two km before Trunyan. To walk from Kedisan to Abang and back takes about 3.5 to four hours at a moderate pace.

The village of Abang, relocated more than once due to shifts of the mountain slope, lies four km before Trunyan. Abang's main attraction is its small, primitive marketplace. Every morning lines of village women from the other side of the mountain climb down the steep slope carrying sweet potatoes and vegetables to exchange for a few fish from the lake. After your visit to Trunyan, return to Abang and negotiate for a canoe or motorboat back to Kedisan or across to Toya Bungkah. From Toya Bungkah, it's about seven km along hair-raising terrain back to Kedisan.

TRUNYAN

Bali's best-known Bali Aga village (pop. 600) nestles under a precipitous crater wall on the eastern shore of Lake Batur. You can walk to Trunyan from Buahan. Take a motorized boat or canoe from Kedisan, or travel by boat across the lake from Toya Bungkah. A path from Trunyan zigzags up the inside face of the crater wall on the southeast slope of Gunung Abang.

The Bali Aga are the island's oldest inhabitants, aboriginals who lived here long before the Majapahit invasion. The first direct evidence of Indic influence on Bali dates from an early copper plate, inscribed A.D. 882-914, referring to the founding of a temple to Batara Da Tonta in Trunyan. His title, Batara, indicates that the Bali Aga's most important ancestor figure was incorporated into the Hindu religion.

Trunyan is a real tourist trap and you may not get to experience much more than villagers clamoring for money. Still, the setting is spectacular—green mountain backdrop and deep blue lake, mist-shrouded Gunung Batur rising up from the water.

Culturally and ethnically outside the mainstream, Trunyan provides evidence of how Bali's earliest people lived. The inbred inhabitants are mostly fishermen, their harsh expressions mirroring a harsh life. Women wearing warm red *kain* pound *padi* in giant stone mortars. Although they plant cabbage and corn in plots near the lakeshore, the Bali Aga have no rice fields. Since ancient times they've relied on begging to supplement their meager diet. Much of the village—houses, walls, alleyways—has been cut crudely out of volcanic rock. Without trees and gardens, their homes present a bleak impression, unlike any other village on Bali. Modern Indonesia is now making heavy inroads, with the construction of new brick, concrete, and zinc-roofed buildings. The few traditional architectural oddities include special boys' and girls' clubhouses (*bale truna* and *bale daha*), a pavilion where married women meet (*bale loh*), and a great wooden ferris wheel put in motion during ceremonial occasions. The giant contraption is revolved by foot power. Trunyan's *bale agung,* where married men sit in council, is one of the largest traditional buildings on Bali.

Visitors to Trunyan are not made to feel welcome. Except for the temple, which seems to take up half the village, you don't really see the ancient ways of the Bali Aga, and there are a lot of hustlers around. A guide will attach himself to you and expect a fee of at least Rp5000. Most visitors just get out of the boat, pay Rp5000 for stepping ashore, go up to a temple (also Rp5000) which Westerners may not be allowed to enter, then march right back down to the boat again for a trip to the cemetery (another Rp5000) in Kuburan.

Pura Pancering Jagat

Trunyan's old temple, Pura Pancering Jagat ("Temple of the Navel of the World") stands under a massive banyan tree. Unusual architecture abounds in this austere *pura*—a fossilized relic of aboriginal Balinese society. The Bali Aga never came fully under Javano-Balinese domination, and the Polynesian features found in their temples are not seen elsewhere on Bali. One must cross over a symbolic little bridge (*titi gonggang*) before entering. Hidden away in a seven-tiered tower inside is Bali's largest statue, the megalithic-style Ratu Gede Pancering Jagat, the powerful patron guardian of the village. Known locally as Da Tonta, this unique 3.5-meter-high stone and clay statue, adorned with ornaments, is considered very ancient and many magic powers are attributed to it. Every three years virgin boys ceremoniously clean and paint the surface of the colossus with a mixture of water, chalk, and honey. You won't be able to see this great statue, as it's jealously guarded by the villagers. Only they, and only during rituals, may gaze upon it.

The Kuburan

The Bali Aga prefer exposing their dead in the open air rather than cremating them. Valuable land cannot be given over to the burial of the dead. After complicated rituals, the naked body is first wrapped in white cloth, then placed in a shallow pit, protected from scavengers by a triangular bamboo fence. Those who have committed suicide or who have died of horrible disfiguring diseases are buried.

The eerie cemetery, full of skulls and bones and bush, might have a fresh rotting body in it. Those selling boat-trip tickets might accost you in Kedisan screaming "A new body at Trunyan!" Bizarre. Curiously, there is no stench of decomposing flesh—because, it is said, the bodies are placed near a *taru menyan* tree, which smells of incense.

TOYA BUNGKAH

Lying on the western shore of Lake Batur, along the roller-coaster road from Kedisan to Songan, the resort village of Toya Bungkah features an invigorating hot springs, massive cinemascopic views, and a black-sand beach. Many travelers choose to stay in Toya Bungkah rather than Kedisan. Watch your gear in both places—lotta thieves.

Toya Bungkah gets busy only during July and August, otherwise there's little traffic or motorboat noise. Just roosters crowing and flies buzzing. There are worse places to stay for a few days. Free of city lights, at night the stars are brilliant and the air fresh, filled with the sound of generators supplying power to the restaurants and color TVs.

Just before the village is a tollbooth where you're hit with another irritating entrance fee: Rp1500 for two adults and a vehicle. Keep your entrance ticket so you can reenter each day. Popular tourist activities include bathing in the lake, fishing (Rp1000 for bamboo poles and worms), touring the lake via motorized boat (Rp40,000 per hour with boatman), visiting Trunyan and/or the cemetery on the other side of the lake, walking along the scenic shore, getting up at 0400 to climb Gunung Batur, or simply hanging out and enjoying the view and the cool air. At least five small open-air pool halls liven up the evening and somewhat occupy the many shiftless young men of the village. Although Toya Bungkah presents fewer hassles than other Batur communities, the males can be pretty aggressive to single women.

Hot Springs

This sulfurous hot springs is known to soothe muscle aches and pains, as well as cure rheumatism and skin diseases. The volcanically heated water bubbles up from under the lake in several places among the lava rocks. The water is not really that hot, though it becomes warmer as the day progresses. A private hot springs lies north of Amertha's. Admission fee of Rp300 just to look, Rp1000 for hot-tub style baths. Facilities include changing room and toilet. Bring your own towel. Signs ask patrons not to wash clothes, shampoo, or wear shoes in the bathing area.

The public *air panas* is on the other side of Amertha's and free. However, since villagers wash their clothes and cows in these shallow pools, and there's lots of litter around, you don't always feel like bathing here. After a long, relaxing dunk, swim Finnish-style from the mineral pools straight into the chilly lake. Very therapeutic, especially fresh from a hike up Gunung Batur.

The Art Center

Also called the **Balai Seni Toya Bungkah.** Above the *air panas* is a retreat for the study of the arts, including a dance academy and amphitheater. Rooms and bungalows spread out among nice peaceful gardens. If you stay here, you can watch the dances and an occasional *wayang kulit* for free. Good selection of books available to guests, with the emphasis on painting, from Dyer to the Fauvists. If no visiting study group is in town, the center seems virtually deserted; no one can provide any information on anything other than the rooms and restaurant.

Accommodations

Toya Bungkah contains about fifteen *losmen,* most surrounded by neatly landscaped gardens. Look around before you settle on one. Except for the Art Center, all offer quite plain rooms for Rp8000 s, Rp10,000 or Rp12,000 d, which includes toilet, shower, and front veranda. Unlike other budget accommodations on Bali, breakfast is sometimes not included in the price. Most *losmen* are located in the west end of the village. If the room doesn't offer a view of the lake, you could probably bargain down to Rp6000 s, Rp8000 d. Whatever the price, insist upon clean bed linen and a towel or threaten to move to another *losmen.* Try to avoid places close to the road, as hikers set out at 0400 accompanied by a chorus of dogs; sputtering motorcycles and *bemo* start up in earnest at around 0500.

Darma Putra Homestay and Restaurant has only four rooms, with comfortable beds, bathroom, and shower for Rp10,000 s, Rp15,000 d (breakfast included). Behind Marini's Bar and Restaurant are three fairly quiet, nice bungalows run by I Nyoman Mertha; Rp12,000 s, Rp20,000 d (includes breakfast) with nice views and clean tile floors. The very reasonable **Awangga** is just past the Art Center, about 75 meters from the Toya Bungkah-Songan road. Small rooms without showers overlook the lower baths of the hot springs; Rp8000 s, Rp15,000 d with hot water. Four bungalows with hot showers cost Rp25,000 d. Quiet, enclosed courtyard. Jero Wijaya provides great information as well as maps of the crater area.

Another good place is **Arlina's,** past the Art Center on the bend of the road, which charges Rp10,000-15,000 for rooms with one bed, Rp15,000-20,000 two beds. Also included: breakfast, *mandi,* shower, and the clearest and most unobstructed views of the lake. The nice woman manager also runs the restaurant where you can get inexpensive meals. Join the card-playing guides in front of the *losmen* and banter with them over their "fee" for taking you up Gunung Batur. **Tirta Yatra,** right on the lake, wants Rp8000 s or Rp12,000 d for very basic rooms—virtual cells separated by bamboo mats. Outhouse in the back. This is like camping, so bring your own soap, drinking water, and sleeping bag. Rooms have a squat toilet, no shower, oil lamp lighting. A fine cheap restaurant overlooks the lake. Despite the noise from children, roosters, dogs, and the nearby road, **Nyoman Pangus Homestay and Warung** is often full because it's the best known. Located right in the village center, Nyoman asks Rp10,000, Rp12,000, and Rp15,000 s or d for rooms (no breakfast) in the back with bath, shower, and a place where you can do laundry. A friendly, gentle man eager to please; an okay place to stay.

Behind Nyoman Pangus Homestay is **Mawa Bungalows.** The service-oriented owner charges Rp6000 s and Rp8000 d for rooms in front, Rp10,000 s and Rp15,000 d for rooms in back. Laundry service. **Asri Inn,** tel. (0361) 753-645, fax 754-784 in Denpasar, charges Rp15,000 d with *mandi*. Separate bungalow for Rp20,000 d. Nice location, though perhaps too central. **Amertha's Accommodations** is right on the lake, overlooking the hot springs. Bungalows for Rp20,000 and Rp25,000 s or d face the lake with private garden bath, walls of volcanic rock, and open verandas. Other, smaller rooms go for Rp12,000 and Rp15,000 s or d. All four classes of rooms have private *mandi*. Since it's very close to the hot springs, hot water is pumped up for showers. Wide parking lot and good restaurant. More secluded than Toya Bungkah's other *losmen* and homestay, the **Art Center** has the most expensive rooms, each with *mandi* and European toilet. Standard rooms with hot water cost Rp17,500. The suites in front go for Rp25,000—very nice, they look out over landscaped gardens, near the lake, with attached *mandi*. Family rooms (capacity four or five) are Rp40,000. The Art Center is often booked by groups. Performances take place when hotel guests charter a dance troupe.

Food

There's an abundance of small restaurants and shabby small *warung* offering the usual tourist fare at cheap prices. Many specialize in grilled lake fish, small and bony but tasty.

The **Marini Bar and Restaurant**, attached to Amertha's Accommodations and almost hanging over the hot springs, is the best place to eat. The resort's best grilled fish, but some dishes—like the vegetables—tend to be greasy. The **Art Center Restaurant** asks higher prices than any other eatery (fruit salad Rp2000), but the food is well prepared. **Under the Volcano** is also a good place to eat, and even stocks cold beer. Daily specials include wonderful fish and chicken dishes—only Rp2500 for three lake fish, grilled to perfection. The owner buys fish twice daily; the chickens run around out back until you order them.

Getting There

From Penelokan, there's a good paved road via Seked and Prajurti. Since Toya Bungkah gets little traffic, *bemo* drivers first want Rp1500; when you get in the price suddenly skyrockets to Rp15,000, eventually falling to Rp8000. Just wait until a public *bemo* comes along and pay Rp1000. Alternatively, you can hitch a ride down to the crater from a tourist or a truck, then walk

to Toya Bungkah from Kedisan in an hour. Or take a boat from Kedisan.

Getting Away

Hop on a *bemo* up to Penelokan (Rp1000); they leave from 0400 to 1300. After 1300, the *bemo* are more infrequent; you may have to charter (Rp6000 and up) or accept an outrageous price. Have your *losmen* or hotel owner make return transportation arrangements for you (bring this up before you take a room). Or hitch a ride with a construction truck for around Rp2000 to Penelokan. With a five-person minimum, you can arrange shuttle service to Ubud, Rp6000 pp; Kuta, Rp8500 pp; Lovina, Rp8000 pp. Ask Nyoman Pangus at Under the Volcano, who can also arrange treks.

At Toya Bungkah's tiny harbor and concrete pier, boatmen ask Rp10,000 up front for a row-boat across the lake to Trunyan's Bali Aga cemetery; you row. You'll die if you row by yourself, then they'll go through your pockets for the Rp20,000 to see the cemetery. Motorized boats to the boneyard cost Rp40,000 for up to seven people. Not worth it unless you're a serious maggot aficionado.

Vicinity Of Toya Bungkah

Walk north to Tirta, where there's only one *losmen*. The proprietors are desperate for guests. Take the path from Awangga to the north, crossing over black lava rocks; newer lava flows along the way. Many travelers arrive in Toya Bungkah in the afternoon, stay the night, rise early to climb Gunung Batur, then descend from the mountain and reach Kedisan via Prajurti and Seked by midday. Houseboys and "professional guides" everywhere in Toya Bungkah available for the climb. They'll quote Rp15,000-Rp25,000, but the final price depends on the age and experience of the guide, the size of the group, your bargaining power, and supply and demand.

SONGAN

From Toya Bungkah, walk one hour to Songan on the northeast corner of the outer crater. Songan is also accessible by boat from Kedisan and Toya Bungkah. This is the largest village on the lake, with a population of around 5,000. The people make their living from fishing and cultivating the flatland beyond the village. The remote hamlet has only one *losmen,* **Restu Inn Homestay and Restaurant,** with rooms for Rp12,000. There are no *bemo* but you can get rides on gravel trucks; the drivers ask for lots of *rupiah* but are happy with Rp2000; some travelers wrangle free rides. Many sulfur wells and natural springs in the area. If you need to go back up to Penelokan in your own vehicle, gas up here.

Turn right at Songan and travel to the end of the road to reach a beautifully situated temple. Since the headwaters of Lake Batur are considered holy throughout the whole eastern half of Bali, a ritual drowning of live animals occurs here every 10 years in honor of Dewi Danu, the goddess of the lake. In 1984 two buffalo, a pig, a goat, a goose, and a chicken, adorned with gold, *kepeng,* and other decoration, were taken out into the middle of the lake and drowned with solemn grandeur. The floor of this lake is no doubt littered with incalculable wealth from the millennia of ceremonial sacrifices.

From the temple, climb 15 minutes up to the remote viewpoint on the crater rim; you can see Bali's east coast. It's a 12 km walk on an old trade road to Lupak on the highway running northeast along the east coast. Walking over streams and through little villages and beautiful forests, it's about a five or six hour hike. Take water, as the more you descend, the hotter and more barren it becomes. The path ends in the middle of Lupak's small local market. Turn left on the highway and catch a blue *bemo* to Lovina for around Rp3500.

GUNUNG BATUR

After Agung, Batur is the most sacred mountain on Bali. Most often the mountain's only sign of life is an occasional wisp of smoke that drifts across its lava-blackened slopes. But when this 1,717-meter volcano erupts, it glows red, bellows, and throws out rocks and showers of volcanic debris. If you arrive in Penelokan at night, you'll awaken to an unforgettable sight. The next morning, the mist will lift from the shining lake and roll across the crater like a mammoth white and gray curtain. When the weather is clear there are also spectacular views of Gunung Batur's smoking cone.

The crescent-shaped lake takes up about one-third of the basin's total area. Measuring 13.8 km by 11 km, this is one of the largest and most beautiful calderas in the world. The crater's outer walls, about 30,000 years old, range from 1,267 meters to 2,153 meters above sea level. There are actually two calderas; the floor of one lies 120-300 meters lower than the other. Plan on a full day to explore them both.

History

Like Krakatoa, Batur was initially formed in the shape of a sharply pointed cone. A terrific explosion blew the point off the cone, atomized a large portion of the volcano, and collapsed the bulk of the mountain into the magma chamber emptied by the initial cataclysm.

Before the present caldera was born,

abode of the gods

Penelokan and Kintamani lay on the western slope of the "first" Gunung Batur. Now Penelokan and Kintamani are spread out along the top of the caldera's outer crater rim. The present younger, smaller volcano—of the effusive rather than explosive type—gradually grew out of the crater floor over a period of hundreds of thousands of years.

Batur erupted in 1917, destroying 65,000 homes, 2,500 temples, and 1,372 people. Its last major eruption was in 1926, when the village below was covered in lava. In 1959 a crack in the lakebed emitted poisonous gases, coloring the water green and killing all the fish. There was further activity in 1963 during the Gunung Agung catastrophe, when lava spilled down Batur's southeastern flank. The lava flows from those eruptions can still be seen beside the lake.

Guides

Guides will approach you everywhere, offering their services for a starting price of Rp30,000. They'll eventually settle on Rp15,000 for two or three people. For six people, most guides won't accept anything less than Rp25,000 or Rp30,000. You can easily find a guide if you arrive at the trailhead at 0330. They'll come out of the dark and offer to lead you for as little as Rp10,000.

Although you don't really need a guide, the fellow can help you find your way out of the clouds that can envelop the slopes of Gunung Batur without warning. If you decide to hire a guide, choose a younger man or boy; it's an arduous ascent. It's unnerving to hike up the mountain sweating and gasping for breath while your nimble guide scrambles up playing the flute, puffing away on cigarettes.

The guides in Toya Bungkah offer three different climbs. The short one, up and back for the sunrise, is Rp25,000-30,000 (four hours). The medium one involves a walk around Batur's three craters, a visit to the bat cave, and a breakfast of eggs boiled by volcanic steam for Rp30,000-40,000 (five hours). The third option is the more interesting tour. Here you get the volcanically boiled eggs with banana and bread, the sunrise, a hike down to the other side of Gunung Batur plus a trip to the "lucky temple" of Toya Mampeh, where lava stopped just meters before the gateway. For this tour they ask Rp60,000-70,000 (all day). All these prices apply to a group (maximum four people) and reflect first offers only.

At least six guides work in Toya Bungkah. Consider I Nyoman Toto ("Charlie"), whom you'll meet sooner or later if you hang around Amertha's. Nyoman Mertha works in Marini's in the village center opposite Under the Volcano; he's very bright, has studied history and geography at the university, and speaks good English. Ketut Lanus, a pleasant and honest man, also leads tours. Jero Wijaya (Toya Bungkah, P.O. Box 01, Kintamani, Bali 80652) is very knowledgeable about the volcanic history of the area.

Approaches

You can attempt the climb from many different directions. As a rule, always take the widest, most obvious and worn path, not necessarily the most direct.

The easiest approach is from the northwest, beginning at Toya Mampeh. This climb, by way of the volcano's back door, can also begin from the west at Kintamani. Guides here ask Rp25,000 for one to two people plus around Rp5000 for each additional person. If you start on the path from Puri Astina at 0630, you can climb the volcano, rest in the hot springs, and grab a *bemo* back to Kintamani by 1200 or 1300. It's also possible to ascend the volcano directly from Kedisan, though this is an unrelentingly steep climb. Simply walk 20 minutes out of town in the direction of the mountain and follow signs on the left directing you to the trail. Don't be alarmed when the trail branches off; they all lead to the same place. Just keep walking uphill. You can also start from the northeast, from Songan. Drive or walk on the good road west to Toya Mampeh; on the way climb up through the lava fields on the volcano's northern side, a product of a 1974 eruption.

One of two "tourist" approaches starts from Prajurti. In this lakeside village, about three km southwest of Toya Bungkah, a big sign marks the start of the trail. Two hours up and 1.5 hours down. Or go up from Prajurti but descend via Toya Bungkah, passing through a beautiful pine forest. As a reward, soak in the *air panas* in Toya Bungkah. The hike from Toya Bungkah is the most popular. If you start at 0400, you'll make it to the peak of Gunung Batur in time for the sunrise. The climbs from Toya Bungkah and from Prajurti end in exactly the same spot, so ascend one way and descend the other. From Penelokan take a *bemo* to Toya Bungkah (Rp1000) or the boat from Kedisan. From Toya Bungkah, walk the gully with the rocky entrance behind the WC on the other side of the Under the Volcano parking lot. The path veers to the left; just keep going up. A group of locals—men with sodas in a bucket and would-be boy guides—will follow any tourist who takes this path. Sometimes they block the trail with plywood barriers, hoping to confuse you or force you to hire them. Ignore this behavior. Take the same trail down.

Climbing It
Though a strenuous ascent, Gunung Batur is the easiest Bali volcano to climb—you can drive to the base and you don't have to struggle through vegetation. Regardless of your approach, tackle the mountain only in good weather. Make sure you have sturdy shoes; it's slippery near the top. Wear long pants and a warm sweater, windbreaker, or sweatshirt. Start up the scoria- and pumice-strewn slope by at least 0600. Take sunscreen and water to prevent burning and heatstroke.

As you start your ascent locals try to sell you drinks. When you say you don't need any, they'll accompany you anyway. As you get higher and higher you grow more and more thirsty. When you finally reach the top you realize you've bought all their drinks without really intending to. So bring your own food and water (two liters) or be prepared to pay for the most expensive drinks on Bali—Rp3000 for a soda and Rp2500 for a plastic bottle of water. It always amazes

people when they find three *warung* on top of Batur's north crater, serving pancakes or jaffles (Rp2000) and reasonable tea and coffee (Rp500-700).

As you climb, the towering mountain is frequently hidden by dense fog and mist, revealing the summit momentarily, then surrounding it again. The way is well-trodden, well-marked, and well-maintained, but if you get lost don't expect anyone to show you the way without exacting payment.

The Summit
There could be 100 people on the summit, but this is likely to occur only in the tourist season. Most tourists are guided to the sandy top of the middle crater. The topmost crater to the north is another hour's climb, along a narrow rim only one meter wide, and the view isn't as fine. At the top is a small shrine to Vishnu. See the sun slowly lighting the whole lake, catch glimpses of Gunung Rinjani on Lombok to the east. Peer into the volcano's steaming core and sit awhile on warm rocks. Take in the sweeping panorama across the shimmering waters of the lake, spot the rivers of lava diverted by huge boulders. Look for relatively recent, all-black lava flows. From the rim take the trail down inside the crater to the bat cave. If you intend to stay in the Batur region for just a day, get down to Toya Bungkah by 1300 or you may have to spend a lot of money chartering a *bemo* up to Penelokan. Allow time to bathe in the cool lake or in Toya Bungkah's hot springs below—just what you need.

KARANGASEM REGENCY

With mighty Gunung Agung dominating the landscape, this regency's scenery is some of the most spectacular on the island. Karangasem is Bali's most traditional region, with rustic villages, hospitable people, and unique festivals. The 861-square-km regency is one of the

most untouristed on Bali, removed from the frenzy of development. This is the only area of Bali where a number of archaic dance and musical forms are still regularly practiced and where the High Balinese language is still in common use.

GUNUNG AGUNG

This sacred mountain is to the Balinese what Olympus was to the ancient Greeks—the Cosmic Mountain. The Balinese, who consider this vol-

cano "the Navel of the World," always sleep with their heads toward Agung. The mystical Balinese believe the mountain was raised by the

KARANGASEM REGENCY

gods as a vantage point to view the unceasing pageant of life below. To them, it's a central, heavenly point of reference, the geographical and religious center of the world. With an elevation of 3,014 meters (3,142 meters before the 1963 eruption), the foot of the mountain stretches northeast right to the sea. To the southeast its slope is blocked by a line of small extinct volcanos; to the northwest Agung is separated from Gunung Batur by a narrow valley.

When you fly into Bali, you'll see the shad-

owy outline of the giant blue-black mountain dominating the landscape. Early in the morning its peak can be seen poking through the clouds from almost any part of Bali. Whether in the bright sunshine or moonlight, a stream of clouds on the crest always trails off in the wind. From the summit, you can see Pura Besakih, Gunung Rinjani on Lombok to the east, Singaraja, and the whole north coast. The lower portions of the mountain are heavily forested, and farmed up to about 1,000 meters.

Climbing The Mountain

Between July and October the fit and adventuresome can attempt the ascent of Gunung Agung. It's exhausting, and can be downright dangerous. Climbers have become lost, never to be found. Don't climb alone, and bring a flashlight, water, warm clothes, an umbrella (a necessity), and trail food. Because of sharp grass, long pants are also a good idea. Good hiking shoes with nonslip soles are a must for the final steep scramble over loose scree to the summit. Since there are innumerable trails leading skyward, you should have a guide, particularly in the early part of the climb. The cost depends upon how many climbers make up your group and what services, if any, are provided.

The most popular route begins on the trail to the right of Pura Besakih, still a difficult six-km climb to Agung's usually cloudy peak. Leave no later than 0630 if you don't want clouds to obscure the view from the top. After climbing about 1.5 km past some houses, you come upon a *meru* temple at about 1,200 meters, where it's possible to sleep. From this point on, your trek will vary from thick vegetation to rubbly volcanic debris to an icy summit ridge.

Another well-worn route starts above the small 900-meter-high village of Sebudi on the southern slopes of Agung, about 2,100 meters below the summit. Take a car or *bemo* (Rp500) from Rendang to the small agricultural village of Selat. Let the police in Selat know your route;

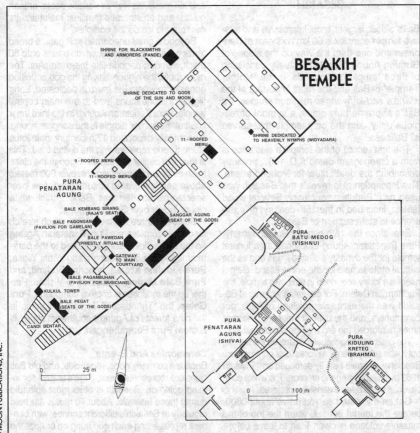

check in with them again when you get back. At the start of the village is **Puri Agung Cottage** with nine rooms (Rp20,000-40,000).

From Selat, allow several hours for the five-km drive north on a rocky lava road to Sebudi. The road ends about four km beyond Sebudi; it's possible to spend the night here. This is your last chance to hire a guide for the rest of the way up the mountain—well worth the price since trails are so poorly marked. Fit climbers can complete the whole ascent in a single day. Head back down by 1430 so you can arrive in Sorga, the uppermost hamlet of the slope, by 1730 for the drive back to Selat.

BESAKIH

Bali's oldest, largest, most impressive and austere temple complex is 60 km northeast of Denpasar and one-third the way up the slopes of Gunung Agung. Besakih, actually consisting of three temple compounds, is the "Mother Temple" of Bali and the most important of the island's *sad-kahyangan* religious shrines. It's Bali's supreme holy place, a symbol of religious unity, and the only temple that serves all Balinese.

The first record of the temple's existence is from a chronogram dated A.D. 1007, possibly describing the death ritual for Mahendradatta. This inscription also reveals that Besakih was used as a Buddhist sanctuary. Several wood tablets, inscribed in the 15th century, give reference to state support of Besakih.

Ever since the 16th century Gelgel dynasty, Pura Penataran Agung functioned as a funeral temple for the dynasty's deified kings and as the central state temple for the entire island. Gelgel rulers are today enshrined in their own temple, the Padharman Dalem. For centuries worship at Besakih was the exclusive privilege of *rajas*, not commoners, and the difficult trek here in former times reinforced the ardor of the devotional act.

The great 1917 earthquake destroyed the temple, but it was subsequently restored to its original form. Besakih was again heavily damaged on 17 March 1963 by a Gunung Agung eruption. The whole complex has since been extensively restored.

Get an early start so you arrive about 0800, before the tourist hordes, when the top of the massive volcano is clear. Plan to leave before early afternoon rains. From Besakih, head down the hill to Pesaban, south of Rendang to the west, to the Bukit Jambul Restaurant for its delicious afternoon Indo/Chinese buffet (Rp10,000). Look out over rice terraces all the way to the sea. Outside the restaurant, tour buses clog the highway.

Layout And Design

Besakih is a very complex architectural structure venerating the holy Hindu trinity. Via a series of long stairways, the temple group ascends parallel ridges toward Gunung Agung, the honored birthplace of Bali's deities, tantamount to heaven. The temple is continually enlarged as municipalities, regencies, and wealthy honored Brahman families add more shrines. Each caste and kin group, as well as various sects, artisan guilds, and artistocratic families, maintains its own temple inside the complex.

Beyond a great unadorned split gate, a broad terrace leads to a *gapura*, which opens onto 50 black, slender, pagoda-like *meru* temples. The more roofs, the higher-ranking the god or deified ancestor to whom the *meru* is dedicated. Long flights of stone steps lead to the main central temple, Pura Penataran Agung. In the third inner court of the central temple is the *sanggar agung*, a beautifully decorated 17th-century triple lotus stone throne representing the divine triad. This is the ritual center of Besakih. Through the clear, fresh air of the topmost terrace, over 900 meters above sea level, is an unsurpassed view over spectacular rice terraces. Behind, thick white clouds hover over Gunung Agung.

Besakih's three main temples, which stretch for over a kilometer, are **Pura Penataran Agung** (in the symbolic center), dedicated to the paramount god Shiva, or Sanghyang Widhi Wasa; **Pura Kiduling Kreteg,** honoring Brahma; and **Pura Batu Medog,** dedicated to Vishnu. Farther up the mountain is another compound, **Pura Gelap,** the "Thunderbolt Temple." Highest, in the pine forests of Agung's southwest slope, is austere **Pura Pengabengan.**

Ceremonies And Events

Because so many gods, regencies, and old Bali clans are represented here, there's always something going on. Besakih is at its most splendid during these festivals. About 70 rituals are held regularly at Besakih's different shrines, with banners representing each god hung on or near the temple and long lines of women walking up the terraces, their heads piled high with offerings.

Each of Besakih's temples has its own *odalan,* and on the full moon of the 10th lunar month vast crowds pack the entire compound to celebrate the visit of the gods; this rite also commemorates Besakih's founding. During Galungan, enormous throngs of pilgrims turn Besakih into a hive of activity. An important island-wide Water Opening ceremony also occurs here.

The most majestic event is held only once every 100 years, the spectacular **Eka Desa Rudra,** a purification ceremony in which harmony and balance in people and nature are restored in all 11 directions. This rite last occured in March 1963, some 16 years before the proper date, apparently because Sukarno wished to impress a convention of travel agents. Midway through the opulent ceremony, Gunung Agung began to shower the whole area with ash and smoke, finally exploding in its most violent eruption in 600 years. Earthquakes toppled temples, hot ash ignited thatched roofs, volcanic debris rained upon the earth. As the molten lava moved toward them, Hindu priests prayed frantically, hoping to appease the angry gods, assuring worshippers they had nothing to fear. In the end, 1,600 Balinese were killed and 86,000 left homeless. The catastrophe was attributed to the wrath of the god Shiva in his most evil aspect as Rudra. It ultimately became a damning judgment on the entire Sukarno era. Miraculously, the flaming lava flowed around Besakih, sparing most of the temple, though shrouding it with black ash for months.

The ceremony was held again in 1979, this time on a Saka year and with all the proper officiations. The sacrifice of an elephant, a tiger, an eagle, and 77 other animals seemed to do the trick—Eka Desa Rudra was completed without incident, and Besakih reestablished its place as the principal Hindu sanctuary in all Indonesia.

Getting There

Besakih is about a two-hour (61 km) drive northeast of Denpasar, or one hour northeast of Klungkung. On holidays take a *bemo* or minibus directly from Klungkung (Rp1000). Otherwise take one first from Klungkung via Rendang to Menanga (Rp750), then another up the steep six-km climb (Rp500) to the Besakih parking lot. Or get a *bemo* to Rendang (Rp600), then travel another nine km up the road to Besakih.

If you're coming from the north, take it slow over the potholed road from Penelokan, which begins along the route to Abang. From the Besakih parking lot, walk 600 meters past souvenir stalls, drink stands, and pay toilets to the start of the stairway up to the main sanctuary. The walk is a steady, gradual grade.

Unless you're Hindu, you may not enter any of the terraces, though you may walk around the entire complex. Well-informed and friendly students will volunteer themselves as guides. About Rp2000 is adequate. After 1400, it may be difficult to find a public *bemo* back down to Klungkung.

THE EAST COAST

PADANGBAI

A tiny, charmingly scruffy port of transit for the neighboring island of Lombok and beyond, Padangbai lies 29 km northeast of Gianyar. One of the most relaxed beach places on Bali, the port faces out on the Bali Strait to Nusa Penida. Benoa and Padangbai are the main shipping ports of south Bali. From Denpasar, take a bus from Batubulan (Rp1100) or Amlapura (Rp700) or a *bemo* from Klungkung (Rp400). Or just hop on any bus out of Batubulan heading for Amlapura, get off at the turnoff to Padangbai, and hitch a ride down to the port.

As many as 80 travelers may be staying in this small port village at any given time. About half are either leaving for or arriving from Lombok; the other half are just hanging out. Listen to travelers' tales; play soccer with the local kids; sometimes there's dancing on the beach at night. The big craft item in Padangbai is miniature *jukung* (Rp1500 small, Rp2500 large), though they aren't even made here—Padangbai merchants buy them from the Sukawati Art Market.

The waterfront is lined with *warung* and restaurants serving cheap, fresh seafood din-

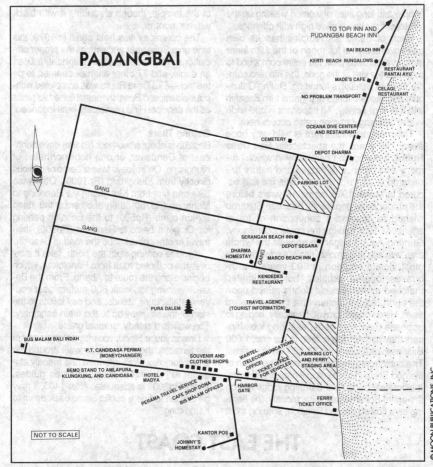

PADANGBAI

TO TOPI INN AND
PUDANGBAI BEACH INN

RAI BEACH INN

KERTI BEACH BUNGALOWS

RESTAURANT
PANTAI AYU

MADE'S CAFE

CELAGI
RESTAURANT

NO PROBLEM TRANSPORT

OCEANA DIVE CENTER
AND RESTAURANT

CEMETERY

DEPOT DHARMA

PARKING LOT

GANG

GANG

SERANGAN BEACH INN

DEPOT SEGARA

DHARMA
HOMESTAY

GANG

MARCO BEACH INN

KENDEDES
RESTAURANT

TRAVEL AGENCY
(TOURIST INFORMATION)

PURA DALEM

BUS MALAM BALI INDAH

P.T. CANDIDASA PERMAI
(MONEYCHANGER)

SOUVENIR AND
CLOTHES SHOPS

WARTEL
(TELECOMMUNICATIONS
OFFICE)

TICKET OFFICE
FOR VEHICLES

PARKING LOT
AND FERRY
STAGING AREA

BEMO STAND TO AMLAPURA,
KLUNGKUNG, AND CANDIDASA

HOTEL
MADYA

PERAMA TRAVEL SERVICE

CAFE SHOP DONA

BIS MALAM OFFICES

HARBOR
GATE

FERRY
TICKET OFFICE

NOT TO SCALE

KANTOR POS

JOHNNY'S
HOMESTAY

© MOON PUBLICATIONS, INC.

ners. On the beach along this sheltered bay are dozens of painted outriggers. Accommodations are inexpensive and there's a good variety. Prices rise during August and December by at least 25%.

You can sunbathe on the beach stretching north of the Pantai Ayu Restaurant, though the water is too polluted for swimming. A 15-minute walk over a grassy hill will bring you to quiet, sandy, beautiful Pantai Kecil, lined with palm trees. Nude bathing is frowned upon: this is a Muslim area. To the southwest are more gray-sand beaches. The idyllic beach to the north,

on Blue Lagoon Bay, is a longer walk, but has better snorkeling because of shallower water and some hard coral outcrops on the sandy bottom.

At least three dive spots are found off Padangbai, all a 10-15 minute *jukung* ride out into Amuk Bay. The water is cold; use a wetsuit. Pura Jepun, only 50 meters from shore, is a mixed reef with a flat, sandy bottom and a visibility of 10-12 meters. On the way, you'll pass the entrance to Blue Lagoon Bay. South of the harbor is Tanjung Bungsil, where the sloping bottom flattens out at between 9-10 meters.

A ferry arrives from and departs to Lombok about every two hours. Private sailing yachts from Singapore and Australia moor in the landing stage, and cruise ships stop about once a week.

Accommodations

Part of Padangbai's charm is its inns and restaurants run by humble anglers turned entrepreneurs. Though the land is potentially very valuable, there are no international chains or fancy beach inns here. The accommodations opposite the beach have a quiet rhythm, and you get some of the best "included" breakfasts in Indonesia.

Perhaps the best value is the three-story **Pantai Ayu Homestay,** characterized by brightly painted doors built into the side of a hill. Rooms vary from Rp10,000 s to Rp20,000 d. All have *mandi* and fresh-water showers. The top floor contains a restaurant; great homemade ice cream. In the center on Jl. Pelabuhan (tel. 35393) near the harbor gate is the town's original **Hotel Madya,** not luxurious but okay. Rooms without *mandi* run Rp6000 d, rooms with *mandi* Rp10,000 d. Safety deposit box. **Johnny's Homestay** lies behind the post office. Rooms are secure but overpriced, with *mandi* and small fans. Eat elsewhere.

Topi Inn and Restaurant (Jl. Silayukti) at the north end of the beach is a large chalet-like building with five rooms running Rp7000 s, Rp10,000 d with breakfast. The dormitory, which sleeps 20-29, just might be the cheapest accommodation on Bali (Rp2500 pp). Fresh-water showers. One of the best places for the money is **Kerti Beach Bungalows**; each bungalow is situated under a palm tree with a nice sea view. Rp12,000 s, Rp15,000 d, Rp20,000 t with breakfast. Farther down the beach is comparably priced **Rai Beach Inn,** near the beach and opposite the Pantai Ayu Restaurant. Mediocre service, two- or three-bed rooms Rp15,000 s, 25 bungalows Rp20,000—all with fans.

Food

Padangbai is known for unbelievably cheap food—whole platters of seafood for around Rp4000. The best value eating is in the many *warung* and cafes along the waterfront and the beach. The three restaurants in one continuous building up from Ibu Komang are all outstanding.

One of the top restaurants in town is Ibu Komang's **Pantai Ayu** ("Tropical Seafood") on Jl. Silayukti on the beach next to colorful *jukung*. Enjoy great curries, salads, hot chips, and hamburgers, all in the Rp1000-3000 range. Open 0700-2000. Souvenirs, library, snorkeling equipment, car rental, post. **Topi Inn and Restaurant** on the north edge of town serves lunch and has perhaps the closest thing to a health food menu in Padangbai. Besides the *warung,* several restaurants offer similar fare at similar prices. Restaurants like the Segara have popped up along the waterfront. **Cafe Shop Dona** serves good *nasi campur* (Rp2000).

Services

At least three **moneychangers** here; rates slightly lower than in Kuta. At *kantor telepon* make calls to anywhere in the world; three minutes to Denpasar costs about Rp3000. A small *kantor pos* is just around the corner from Warung Jawa.

Getting Away

Arriving from Lombok, a line of *bemo* waits to take passengers to all the major points on Bali. For Klungkung (Rp700), Candidasa (Rp500), and Amlapura (Rp800), walk 100 meters from the harbor gate to catch *bemo*—blue for Klungkung, orange for Amlapura and Candidasa. For Batubulan direct it's Rp1200, or go first to Klungkung, then another Rp700 into Batubulan. After 1800, it's difficult to find a *bemo,* unless you walk out to the main road and flag one down. Bus tickets to Probolinggo (East Java) run Rp20,000; Surabaya, Rp25,000; Malang, Rp20,000; Yogyakarta, Rp35,000. Tours and shuttle bus service to Ubud, Rp7500; Lovina, Rp15,000; Sanur/Kuta/Airport, Rp10,000; Kintamani, Rp15,000; and Mataram and Bangsal in western Lombok, Rp15,000-Rp20,000. An ultrafast catamaran to Bangsal, roundtrip, is Rp20,000. The shuttle bus to Senggigi is worth the extra Rp2000. Speedboats to Nusa Penida depart from near the large parking area next to the pier (Rp3000).

The ferry ticket office is near the pier, under the Cepebri sign. A ferry departs every two hours from 0200 to 2000. For the popular and crowded 0800 ferry, buy your ticket at 0700. Economy Rp4800, first class (a/c) Rp9000. Lembar, 22 km south, costs Rp1000 by *bemo* from Ampenan. The ticket office for passenger

CANDIDASA-BALINA
BEACH AREA

© MOON PUBLICATIONS, INC.

cars (Rp59,200), motorcycles (Rp30,800), and pushbikes (Rp800) is just after the harbor gate heading toward the concrete *dermaga*. On board the ferry, keep a sharp eye on your stuff.

BALINA BEACH

About five km beyond the turnoff to Padangbai is a small steel bridge. About 500 meters beyond, turn right down a small lane to Buitan village. This is the heart of Balina, a lovely beach strip with scant sellers, few tourists, a nice wide black sandy beach, tame waves, no treacherous currents, and seldom the sputter of a motorbike. You'll find a real beach here. All the amenities of Candidasa are accessible by *bemo* four km to the northeast, while the urban center of Amlapura lies 18 km to the northeast.

Balina is known for its diving excursions in a marine reserve offshore. If you reach the beach by late afternoon, you can go night fishing with local fishermen. The Balina Diving Centre has an

impressive team of five instructors supervised by a PADI Open Water divemaster; can arrange fishing and outrigger sailing trips. Dive trips, instruction, and snorkeling are offered every day starting at 0900. Minimum two people, except for the three-person minimum to Nusa Penida and Menjangan. Sample pp rates: Rp14,700 snorkeling/Rp84,000 diving, Blue Lagoon; Rp42,000 snorkeling/Rp147,000 diving, Nusa Penida; Rp52,500 snorkeling/Rp178,500 diving, Pulau Menjangan. Discounts for 15 or more.

Accommodations And Food

The best upmarket place to stay is 34-room **Puri Buitan,** east of the Balina Beach Bungalows on one of east Bali's most beautiful, safe beaches. Definitely worth the price if you're looking for easy living near the beach—nicely furnished rooms with hot water, swimming pool, great snorkeling, and shuttle service to Ubud. Puri Buitan's motel-style units are clean and tidy: Rp63,000 s, Rp73,500 d for fan-cooled rooms; Rp84,000 s, Rp94,500 d for a/c rooms; Rp136,500 s, Rp157,500 d for deluxe a/c seaview rooms. Restaurant on premises. Book through I Made Patera, P.O. Box 444, Denpasar 80001, tel. and fax (0361) 287-182. **The Nelayan Villages** (or Balina Beach Bungalows, P.O. Box 301, Denpasar, fax 0361-87948) next door offers accommodations with private verandas and baths. Forty-one Balinese-style bungalows range from two-bed units for Rp33,600 s, Rp42,000 d, up to Rp136,000 for family units. Prices include continental breakfast; credit cards are honored, and there's a moneychanger. The restaurant is terrible; at the nearby Java Restaurant, the food is somewhat better. Fishing families will offer you drab rooms in the *kampung* for Rp10,000 s or d (first price).

To the west is the isolated **Ampel Bungalows** in Manggis village—beautiful seascapes, nice gardens, restaurant. When you pass Manggis and the turnoff to Amankila, the road winds down to the coastal flats heading for Candidasa. The turn to Ampel is 300 meters before the bridge, about one km before Balina Beach. All *bemo* drivers know the place. For Rp15,000 you get a simple, clean room (no hot water or electricity) and an exceptional view. Verandas are lit with oil lamps provided for the evenings.

Getting Away

The man at **Kios Melati,** just up from the Puri Buitan, rents vehicles for Rp50,000 per day. You may also charter vehicles for the airport, Kuta, or Nusa Dua (Rp40,000). In the high season, a shuttle service may be in operation with shared rides to Ubud, Sanur, Kuta, and the airport for Rp10,000. For much cheaper public transport, go up to the main road and flag down a *bemo*. Kios Melati also develops film in one day.

CANDIDASA

Candidasa, meaning "Ten Temples," is named after a shrine in the eastern part of the village. It's a tidy, well-kept, three-km-long European tourist retreat on Bali's southeast coast where the local people are unobtrusive and the hotel folks eager to please. Attracting refugees from the frenetic southern honeypots, Candidasa is the type of place where you think you'll stay two days but end up staying a week. Best in the off-season. The smallest resort area on Bali; the rhythm is noticeably more laid-back than Kuta,

Lovina, or Sanur. Tenganan, a traditional village nearby, exerts its influence—many Candidasa businesses are owned by Tenganan people. An Italian influence is also heavy.

Candidasa also makes an excellent base for trips to Tirtagangga, Kusamba, Goa Lawah, Klungkung, Bangli, and eastern mountain towns like Putung and Iseh. For a scenic land tour, rent bicycles. Visit nearby Tenganan to shop, and for a fascinating look at the ancient rituals of a traditional society.

Sights And Recreation

At high tide predatory waves pound the seawall, chasing beachcombers to higher ground. At low tide, the beach west of the lagoon is only eight meters wide and you can walk as far as 50 meters on the shelf (wear sneakers) and observe rock pools and reef life (great for children). During all but the rainy season, the water is crystal clear—this is also the village bath. Cement walkways and sitting pavilions surround the inland lagoon at the east end of town. The community's fresh water is handpumped from wells.

The sea currents here are unpredictable; swimming is not advisable. If there's no pool where you're staying, you can use a pool in any of the ritzier hotels for around Rp6000.

Take in views of the rocky Batu Manggar islet offshore, the lighthouse off Padangbai's headland, the looming island of Nusa Penida, and neighboring Lombok. Sunbathing is best on the seawall several meters above. Watch the wind and rain chase fishing craft across the sea. At street level is a statue of the giantess Hariti, surrounded by her many children. Childless couples often come to the temple seeking help from this goddess.

Accommodations

Until a few years ago this small village had only a few thatched huts and one private homestay. Today it boasts over 60 *losmen,* with more sprouting monthly. Tourist accommodations are everywhere. Largely a budget resort, big, expensive hotels just wouldn't make it here—it's just too far from Denpasar. Prices and services are comparable to Kuta's moderately priced hotels. Accommodations across the road tend to be cheaper than those close to or facing the sea. Prices, which normally average Rp8000 s, Rp12,000-15,000 d for a basic bungalow, go up at least 25% in August. Top-of-the-line beachfront bungalows, with private *mandi* and luxurious bamboo verandas, go for Rp40,000-80,000, while new first-class hotels run Rp105,000-190,000.

Clean, quiet **Dutha Seaside Cottages** is a nice, family place on the north end of the village—run like a large commune. Dutha has its own beachfront, with good swimming. Rooms run Rp8000 s to Rp20,000. Tariff includes breakfast, or just go in the kitchen and make your own tea or coffee. Frequent parties and Balinese feasts. A real traveler's place.

Kelapa Mas has rooms ranging from Rp10,000 to Rp30,000; very popular and almost always full. Simply and minimally maintained, with a lovely seaside location in a banana and coconut grove. Cottages facing the sea are the best. **Agung Bungalows** is a great place to stay, starting at Rp10,000 with fan, private bathrooms, and breakfast. Contact Mr. Supadnya, manager, at (0361) 355-535 (Denpasar). Near the sea, the **Dewa Berata,** east of Agung's, has comfortable bungalows and a pool. For three people the charge is Rp40,000. The quiet and friendly **Nani Beach Inn,** near the Ramayana, has bungalows with *mandi* for Rp15,000 d, which includes a good breakfast. Very close to the beach. **Losmen Geringsing** is one of the more comfortable low-priced *losmen,* with rates varying from Rp8000 s to Rp15,000 d.

Candidasa's first-class hotels tend to be on the wings of the central downtown strip. Located on oceanfront property amid palms, most of these accommodations feature European toilets and showers, hot water, a/c, pools, refrigerators and minibars, gift shops, restaurants, sea sports, airport transfers, and big dish TVs. All take credit cards. **Nirwana Cottages,** Sengkidu, Amlapura 80871, tel. 236-136, fax 235-543, has a superb location, nice rooms, and wholesome homecooked food. Ten traditional one-story cottages go for Rp73,500-Rp105,000. Close to the water, Nirwana is clean, private, and low-key. Centrally located **Candidasa Beach Bungalows II,** tel. 751-205, is a big two-story hotel with an open-air bar and a pool. Despite the packed-in feeling, rooms are spacious, and breakfast—especially the banana pancakes—is excellent. All rooms have fans, a/c, hot water, Western-style bath, fridge, and TV. Cost: Rp58,800 s, Rp69,300-84,000 d.

The elegant **Watergarden,** tel. and fax 235-540, has 12 luxurious Balinese-style cottages. All bungalows (Rp126,000 s, Rp136,500 d) have a/c, ceiling fans, and large wooden-decked verandas. Amenities include pool with waterfall, room service, restaurant, IDD, laundry and ironing, safety deposit, library, flight reconfirmation, mountain bikes, and tour and transport services.

Relaxing, clean, and comfortable **Puri Bagus Villa** is tucked away amid the palms in Sumuh fishing village past the lagoon: 50 well-designed, spacious bungalows rent for Rp126,000 s, Rp136,500 d. Nine units (Rp31,500 surcharge) and two suites (Rp367,500) face the ocean. Terrace verandas, but beware of slippery tiles after it rains. Good 24-hour security, an unobtrusive, friendly staff. Pool, restaurant. Coral reef out front. Reservations: Jl. Bypass I Gusti Ngurah Rai 300 B, P.O. Box 419, Denpasar 80001, tel. 751-223, fax 752-779, or direct to the hotel at 235-238 or 235-291, fax 235-666.

Out Of Town

To get away from the crowds, head 10 minutes west of Candidasa to Sengkidu. **Anom Beach Bungalows** asks Rp25,000 for one of eight bungalows with fan, shower, and breakfast. Excellent restaurant on the premises. Snorkeling equipment for rent. Also check out **Homestay Dwi Utama** (Rp7000 s, Rp10,000 d) with four rooms facing the ocean. High-class **Candi Beach Cottages,** on the white sands of Mendire Beach in Sengkidu, charges Rp126,000-189,000 for luxurious rooms. Amenities include two bars, two restaurants, water sports, pool, tennis courts, a fitness room, spa, occasional *barong* dances, tour service, and free shuttle into town. One of the best accommodations a bit away from Candidasa is the **Bayu Peeneda Bungalows**; Rp30,000 includes breakfast. Uncrowded, six-room **Homestay Ida** is in the eastern part of town just before the lagoon. Ida's charges Rp30,000-40,000 for traditional bungalows in a coconut grove. No hot water.

Food

Dinner is the big social event around here. Candidasa's imposing eateries, many set back from the road in big pavilions among the palms, offer the usual Kuta/Legian menus—but with a Mediterranean twist (pasta or German dishes always included on menus). There are even several authentic Italian restaurants. The fish dinners are the best buy.

Family-run **Arie's Restaurant,** on the western edge of town, is one of the best for budget Western, Balinese, and Chinese food. The fish dinners are good value; also try the *gado-gado* and the fish curry with vegetables. **Chez Lily** is Candidasa's premier gourmet restaurant. Excellent and unusual food, reasonable prices, slow service. Open 0800-2000.

The first and still one of the best restaurants in Candidasa is the candle-lit **Pandan Restaurant** on the beach—fantastic grilled fish with vegetable salad. The buffet dinner (Rp9000, with free beer) is highly recommended. Fancooled and well-posted **Raja's Restaurant and Bar** boasts international cuisine. Nightly videos at 1930.

Probably the best place for Western food is **TJs,** tel. and fax (0361) 35540, by the Water Garden Cottages. Homemade bread, stuffed baked potatoes, lots of salads, delectable grilled fish, and a clean, lovely and authentic Balinese-style *nasi campur* with *urab* and not much oil. Also a popular place for cakes and expresso. East of the village on the left is the **Mandara Giri Pizzeria,** the best Italian restaurant in Candidasa with extremely good, inexpensive food—crab with cognac, pizza with seafood, outstanding spaghetti and lasagna.

Entertainment

Barong and *legong* dances are put on at *Pandan Harum* twice weekly (Tuesday and Friday), starting at 0900-1000 (Rp4500). During the tourist season, performances are also staged at the Candidasa Beach Hotel and other upscale hotels. If you like a lot of noise, Tina Turner on a big screen, and high priced-drinks, go to the **Legend.** The only place open late at night, this is where all the gigolos hang out. Jam with the local musicians. The **Tirta Nadi** also has live music. You can also stay up late drinking and listening to high-volume music at the **Sanjaya Beer Garden.**

For recent movies, **Raja's** has a huge monitor for videos, or see them on laser disc at **Molly's Garden Restaurant** (around 1930). Molly's also serves California-style cuisine with international influences. Try to focus on your meal while the screams from horror videos split the evening air.

Services

Kubu Bali Rental, tel. (0361) 235-532, Rp3000 per day for mountain bikes, Rp2000 for ordinary bikes, is reliable. If by the week, it's Rp500 per day cheaper. Motorbikes also for rent. You can rent motorcycles unofficially from the locals. Car rental runs Rp25,000 for 12 hours or Rp22,500 per day for three-day minimums. The nearest **gas stations** are on the right side coming from Denpasar just before the Tirtagangga turnoff, right after the turnoff to Padangbai (heading for Klungkung), and in Amlapura (13 km). At least 15 **tour operators** have offices in Candidasa, and all the hotels have tour desks. You can arrange English-, Japanese-, or German-speaking guides through your hotel. The fancy hotels charge astronomical prices for **fax** service; Ayodya Homestay is cheaper. There are two *wartel;* the best known is at the Kubu Bali. There's a postal agent at Asri Market (open 0800 to 2000). At a small shack southwest of town about one km is a **laundry service,** Monalisa—about one-third cheaper than the hotels. Another *tukang cuci* (Wayang Resiyani) works near the temple; ask for her in one of the nearby *warung.* She charges Rp300-500 per piece, including ironing and washing.

Shopping

Baskets and offering trays from *ata* vines made from Candidasa's hillsides are an important home industry of this area. They're sturdy enough to last 100 years; better ones start at Rp30,000.

Across the street from the Candidasa Beach Bungalows II is Chinese-run **Asri,** a combination film developing/grocery/crafts retail store with fixed prices and computerized checkout. Some readers report engaging in 90% of their Bali souvenir/gift shopping here. No pressure and reasonable prices.

Eddy's Market, near the *wartel,* has photo service, moneychanging, groceries, and souvenirs. **Tanteri's Ceramic** is a showroom for remarkable Pejaten pottery, a unique variety of glazed stoneware produced exclusively in Pejaten village.

Getting There And Around

From Klungkung or Padangbai, take a *bemo* headed for Amlapura. If traveling from Denpasar, first take a minibus to Batubulan station (a foreigner with luggage pays Rp1000), then catch another minibus to Candidasa (another Rp1500—many stops along the way). Regular shuttles run from Kuta for around Rp10,000. Minibus and *bemo* travel up and down the coastal road between Amlapura and Klungkung from 0500 to 1900. Sample fares: Padangbai, Rp700; Amlapura, Rp700; Goa Lawah, Rp700; Klungkung, Rp1000; Denpasar, Rp1500; Singaraja, Rp3000.

Shuttle buses to Ubud leave five times daily for Rp10,000; to Sanur, Kuta, and the airport, 0930 and 1000 for Rp10,000; to Kintamani, only at 0800 for Rp15,000; and for Lovina, 0800 and 1200 for Rp18,000.

Candidasa is about 2.5 hours from Bali's airport. Virtually all the better hotels in Candidasa offer private transfers to and from the airport, Kuta, Nusa Dua, Tanjung Benoa, or Ubud for around Rp30,000 one-way (minimum two people).

MG International Ticketing, midtown, sells air and shuttle bus tickets, rents bikes and cars, and changes money. Buy long-distance bus tickets to Java here, too. MG is useful as an agent for such international airlines as SIA, MAS, UTA, KLM, Pan Am, JAL, Thai, and Qantas. **Perama Tours** near Arie's Restaurant has very good prices for tickets and offers tours to Lombok, car rentals, and other tourist services.

On the western corner of the lagoon, across the road, is **No Problem Transport,** tel. (0361) 29110, for changing money, postal service, tours, shuttles, and international bookings. The only problem with No Problem is you must call Denpasar (Rp6000) to confirm your international ticket purchases.

TENGANAN

This is an original pre-Hindu Balinese settlement, long a stronghold of native traditions, located about halfway between Padangbai and Amlapura. At the end of an asphalt country road up a narrow valley, Tenganan is far removed from the Javano-Balinese regions of Bali. Like Trunyan to the northwest, this small village is inhabited by the Bali Aga, aboriginal Balinese who settled the island long before the influx of immigrants from the decaying 16th-century Majapahit Empire. It might appear to be a stage-managed tourist site, but is actually a living, breathing village—the home of farmers, artists, and craftspeople.

The people have completely adapted to the tourist economy; nowadays tables selling palm leaf books are set up at intervals the whole length of the main street. Tenganan is a great place to just hang out; the walled village's quiet pace and somnolent air is all the more accentuated by the complete lack of vehicular traffic, except for the occasional motorcycle. There are no accommodations for tourists; the nearest hotels are in Candidasa.

The lowland people of Tenganan have preserved their culture and way of life through the conviction they're descended from gods. They practice a religion based on tenets dating from the kingdom of Bedulu, established before the Hindus arrived.

Except for such visual blights as the row of green power poles down the center of the village's unique pebbled avenues, Tenganan is a living museum in which people live and work frozen in a 17th-century lifestyle, practicing their own architecture, kinship system, religion, dance, and music. Signs of the 20th century are the TV antennas on bamboo poles piercing the thatch rooftops, the motorcycles parked outside the compounds, and the occasional tinny sound of a cassette recorder or radio.

About 106 families with a total of 49 children live in Tenganan—a significant drop from the estimated 700 at the turn of the century. A council of married people decides the legal, economic, and ritual affairs of the village. The village *adat* prohibits divorce or polygamy, and until recently only those who married within the village were allowed to remain within its walls; others were banished to a section east of the village called Banjar Pande.

By the 1980s, this custom resulted in Tenganan achieving less than zero population growth, a result of inbreeding. Mandates from the gods were recently reinterpreted, allowing villagers who marry outside the clan to stay, provided the spouse undergoes a mock cremation ritual from which he or she is brought back as a Tenganian.

Layout

The most striking feature of this 700-year-old walled village is its layout, totally different from any other community on Bali. Rectangular in shape (500 meters by 250 meters), Tenganan shares many characteristics with other primitive villages on Nias and Sumba.

Broad stone-paved streets, which serve as village commons, rise uphill in tiers so the rain flows down, providing drainage. Each level is connected by steep cobbled ramps. There are also three streets running east to west. The only entrance to this fortress-like village is through four tall gates placed at each of the cardinal points. The main entrance in the south is called *lawangan kelod.*

Events

Most rituals take place early in the morning. Around 18 June each year begins the three-day Udaba Sambah. At this time one of the area's five primitive ferris wheels is erected. The unmarried girls of the village sit on chairs and the giant contraption is revolved by foot power for hours on end. For the past several years, however, the ceremony has not been held because of a shortage of young marriageable girls. The high point of Udaba Sambah is the killing of a black water buffalo, followed by a ritual trance fight (*makara-kare*) between young men who attack each other with prickly pandanus leaf whips. This duel, similar to the *peresean* whip fights of Lombok, is staged to the intense martial sounds of *kare* music. During the festival the streets of Tenganan are thronged with people from all over Bali. Wayan Suwirta at the Nuri Arts Shop has a photo album of the ceremony.

Kawin pandan is also practiced here once yearly: a young man throws a flower over a wall and must marry whomever catches it. *Rejang* is a formal and sedate ritual offering dance, originally performed by virgin boys and girls. In this quiet, hypnotic dance, girls in three rows wear magnificent costumes and colorful sashes, their hair adorned with blossoms of hammered gold. It's accompanied by the slow, haunting *gamelan* music found only in Bali Aga villages.

Flaming Cloth

Tenganan is the only place in Indonesia where double-*ikat* textiles are made. Rather loosely woven, these so-called "flaming cloths" (*kamben gringsing*) are used only in rites of passage or for ceremonial purposes: weddings, tooth filings, covering the dead, or during a child's first haircut. It's thought the *sarung*-length cloths can immunize the wearer against illness; small pieces for wrapping around the wrist are sold for this purpose. Only about six families still know all the

double-*ikat* processes (coloring, tying, dyeing), and only about 15 people still weave *gringsing* on small makeshift breastlooms. Within the cloth, reddish or dark brown backgrounds, once dyed in human blood, are used to highlight intricate whitish and yellow designs of *wayang* puppet figures, rosettes, lines, and checks. Great care is taken to ensure that even tension is applied throughout so the patterns will match exactly. It can take up to seven years to complete a fine piece of *gringsing,* and they're generally sold only upon the death of the owner. The really precious *gringsing,* prized by serious textile collectors for their rarity, cost US$3500-5000.

Lontar Books

Lontar are palm leaves on which intricate drawings have been etched, usually depicting scenes from Hindu epics. I Wayang Muditadnana makes about one five-page *lontar* book per month, which he sells mostly to tourists for Rp100,000 and up. On holy days or upon request he can be heard reading passages from his books. I Made Pasek is another *lontar* carver in the village. He, too, spends about a month inscribing one palm-leaf book with miniature Ramayana scenes and stories. A third artist, I Nyoman Widiana, asks Rp100,000 for his seven-page wordbooks. He also sells lesser quality *lontar* made by his students. Most cheap (Rp10,000) versions sold on the street are of low quality. The finer, antique works fetch Rp500,000.

Ata Baskets

Ata baskets are a good buy, so sturdy they're said to last 100 years. They're made from a vine collected from the hills behind Tenganan. Basketry has been developed into a fine art on Lombok too, but baskets there are made from rattan. *Ata,* in fact, is much stronger than rattan because it's water, heat, and insect resistent. *Ata* baskets come in all shapes and sizes, and cost from Rp5000 to Rp250,000. An average-size basket takes two to three weeks to make.

Shops

Tenganan is a fantastic place to shop—both for local and Gianyar crafts, as well as fine textiles from the eastern islands. Many vendors have a good eye, ask reasonable prices, and don't hassle you to buy. The craft shops on the outside of Tenganan's southern entrance carry handsome tasseled shawls, *ata* baskets, offering trays (*du-longs*), wickerwork, woven reeds, betelnut containers, and a good variety of woven eastern isle (Sumba, Flores) textiles. Watch for imitation Sumba blankets, carving from Gianyar, and other crafts which may be bought cheaper in Denpasar's Pasar Badung or in the villages of origin. You'll get a better price for crafts in the off season (February to May), and in the morning before the tour buses start arriving and prices skyrocket.

Gagaron, located through the entrance gate from the parking lot in the lower part of the village, is a good place to start. The owner sells smallish *gringsing* for Rp350,000 to Rp400,000, as well as an extensive collection of *kain ikat.* Art shop **Dewi Sri** is on the right on the top parking lot. It carries a large selection of new bronze pieces, single and double *ikat,* and *ata* baskets. At **House of Music and Gamelan Centre,** toward the top of the village (fifth terrace), I Nyoman Gunawan makes distinctive nine-piece Tenganan-style *gong selonding.* He also sells gongs (Rp300,000), *rebab* (Rp150,000), carved *rindik* (Rp150,000), and tapes (Rp6000). This is a better place to buy more elaborate musical instruments than Gagaron's in the lower part of the village.

Getting There And Away

Tenganan is three km off the main road between Klungkung and Amlapura, just before Candidasa, and 17 km southwest of Amlapura. Catch a *bemo* from Klungkung or Padangbai to the Tenganan turnoff, then mount the back of one of the 15 or so waiting motorcycles (Rp1000, after negotiations) and travel up through a tunnel of banana trees and bamboo. You can also stay in Candidasa (there's no lodging in Tenganan), then early in the morning walk from the main road up to Tenganan. Or hitch a minibus, *oplet,* truck, or anything that's going along the way. Another option is to rent a bicycle in Candidasa; it's a nice, though uphill, one-kilometer ride. The road ends at the southern entrance gate to Tenganan, where you'll be asked for a donation. Foodstalls, inside and out, sell cold drinks and snacks.

THE NORTHEAST COAST

This coastal strip offers some of Bali's best snorkeling, the island's most splendidly located self-contained dive *losmen,* and Bali's largest concentration of traditional *jukung.* On a beautiful bay is the solitary village of Amed; visit the fish market in the morning when the tuna come in (both Rp2000 and Rp3000 sizes). The road south from Amed is paved but very narrow, with Hindu fishing settlements hugging the shore all the way to Ujung. A poor, very dry part of Bali.

European snorkelers and divers have discovered the coastline southeast of the village with black-sand beaches, unpolluted waters, and perhaps the best variety of fish on Bali. Snorkeling begins east of town where the currents are calm year-round, visibility is 10-20 meters, and the hard coastal reefs are superb. Dive along the reef wall to see schools of cardinal fish, triggerfish, black snappers, pyramid butterflies, bannerfish, and damselfish among the sand slopes, table corals, big fan gorgonians, and magnificent staghorn *Acropora* and *Dendronephthya* trees—all within just 20 meters of shore.

Getting There

Take a *bemo* from Tirtagangga to the turnoff at Culik (Rp400), then hire an *ojek* to take you the three km to Amed (Rp300), or all the way to accommodations at Hidden Paradise (Rp1500), Vienna (Rp1500), or Good Karma (Rp2000). From Amed, hitch a ride or catch an infrequent *bemo* two km to the small fishing community of Cemeluk.

Accommodations

The three places to stay on this coast are real escapes, perhaps fulfilling most people's popular paradisical visions of Bali. Six km southeast of Amed is isolated Lipah village, with a very good coral reef starting about 15-20 meters offshore. **Kuchit and Gillian's Hidden Paradise Cottages,** tel. (0361) 231-273, fax 751-749, offers rooms with fan for Rp63,000 d, Rp84,000 with a/c, and spacious, beautiful suites for Rp110,000 d. Breakfast for two included; pool, laundry service, safety deposit box, mountain bike rentals, and a whole wall of snorkeling gear (Rp4000 for 12 hours) available. The restaurant out front serves good seafood dinners (under Rp5000). Farther south in grape-growing Bunutan is I Wayan Utama's pristine 10-bungalow **Pondok Vienna Beach Bungalows** (Rp20,000 s or d), in a very nice location in a garden at the end of a small fishing village. Good service, generator for 24-hour electricity, fresh well-water showers, and laundry. Reservations: Box 112, Amlapura 80801. The restaurant serves straightforward food—the kitchen may be out of menu items like *tahu,* as staff must drive to Amlapura each day to shop and may not get back by mealtime. Local *warung* sell snacks but no rice; you'll have to eat at the *losmen.* Get a massage with coconut oil for Rp5000, or take a ride out to the reef in a *jukung* for Rp10,000-Rp12,000.

The most southerly accommodations are at **Good Karma Homestay** in Selang, Bunutan township. Simple, clean bungalows (five in all) go for Rp7000 s, Rp15,000 d (includes breakfast). Extremely quiet, just the sound of the waves. Only basic services: no telephone, cold showers, generator power, laundry, cold beer, nice beach—all you need. Snorkeling starts just 5-10 meters from the homestay, or you can hire a *jukung* for Rp5000-6000 per hour to travel farther from shore. Guides are available for trips into the hills.

TULAMBEN

Bali's parched northeast coastal road is one of the few areas where rural life is largely unaffected by tourism. The only intrusion of Western culture is the pool table, set in makeshift bamboo pool halls frequented by young men of the village. On the drive to Singaraja, you'll pass villages of waving people, temple festivals, banana and coconut plantations, and subsistence farmers eking out a living gathering seasalt and coral. Beautiful tiered rice fields give way to dry country ravaged by volcanic rubble from Agung's 1963 eruption.

The small fishing village of Tulamben lies along this hot, dry coast, 23 km from Tirtagangga. Due to its proximity to some of the island's best diving, it has attracted snorkelers and scuba divers from all over the world and is the area's main attraction. Tulamben Beach is peppered with black rocks that scald your feet in the noonday sun. There's not much to do here but dive, eat, read, sleep, and stroll down the village street in the cool of the evening.

All the *losmen* here cater mostly to divers, so don't expect fancy services or facilities. As yet, none have swimming pools, and generator-powered electricity is only on from 1800 to 2300. Bargain if the accommodation is not full. If you stay at least three nights, most hotels will give you a 10% discount in the low season. There's a country doc-

tor in Kubu, as well as a post office and small *warung* selling simple food, snacks, and fruit. Dining rooms at each of the four accommodations.

Diving And Snorkeling

The best months for diving are July and August, but even in the rainy season the diving can be very satisfying. The numerous dive operators in Kuta, Bali, and Lovina bring large groups of enthusiasts here. Hardcore divers end up staying for days. A large variety of big fish is accessible right out in front of most accommodations; some fish are so tame, they'll eat bananas right out of your hand.

Snorkeling gear can be rented from any of the accommodations in the village for Rp3000; if you're not a hotel guest, it's Rp4000. **Paradise Palm Beach Bungalows** offers 40-minute dives for Rp63,000, including gear and an excellent guide, and gives a 10% discount on dive equipment for guests. A government forestry official will ask a Rp500 fee pp (per day) from anyone snorkeling or diving off the coast.

A sunken American Liberty ship, torpedoed by the Japanese in 1942, is the big diving attraction. This eerie ghost lies about a kilometer to the west of the main hotels, only 30 meters from the beach. Swim straight out from the toilet block on the beach; it doesn't take much strength to reach it. The ship stretches for over 100 meters along a steep sandy slope, its hull parallel to shore. The top is only three meters below the surface, the bottom is about 30 meters down. Visibility is 12-15 meters. Large encrusted holes in the hull and deck allow exploration of the interior of the wreck. Plenty of soft corals, sponges, hydrozoans, and gorgonians. It's estimated 400 species of reef fish inhabit the wreck, as well as 100 species of surface organisms.

Avoid diving from December to January when waves are high. During the dive season, as many as 60 people may swarm over this popular site. If you overnight in Tulamben and go out early in the morning or late in the afternoon, you can avoid the crowds. Kal Muller, the author of *Underwater Indonesia,* writes that a full moon dive on the wreck "is among the most memorable dives you'll ever make."

Accommodations And Food

Dewa Nyoman Chandra's **Paradise Palm Beach Bungalows** is the oldest and most pleasant budget accommodation in the area. Make reservations at Friendship Shop, tel. (0361) 229-052, in Candidasa, or write P.O. Box 111, Amlapura 80811, Bali. Seventeen rooms: Rp17,000 s, Rp20,000 d; also a Rp15,000 s or d set of rooms. If you stay for three or more nights, ask for a discount. The most expensive rooms are the four facing the beach. Very nice, surrounded by a lush garden. The restaurant is good: fish curry (Rp3500), *tahu campur* with vegetables (Rp2000), jaffles (Rp1500 to Rp1800), *ikan laut* (about Rp2000, depending on size), and drink. A small kiosk sells snacks, cookies, toiletries, and clothing; the dive shop has batteries, film, snorkeling equipment, and books. Laundry service costs Rp500 for a T-shirt, Rp1000 for long pants.

East of the Paradise is the neglected-looking **Bali Timur Bungalows** with six rather forbidding cinderblock bungalows for Rp10,000 s, Rp12,000 d. Price includes breakfast (pancake, fruit salad, or omelette). The **Ganda Mayu Bungalows and Restaurant** has two big rooms (Rp12,000 s, Rp17,000 d) and two small rooms (Rp8000 s, Rp12,000 d) facing the beach. Good parking. Very impressive menu.

At the top end is the **Saya Resort** east of town. Make reservations through Bali Marine Sport on Jl. Ngurah Rai, Blanjong, Sanur (see manager). Four rooms go for Rp84,000 s, Rp147,000 d or t, including breakfast and dinner.

Getting There

From Candidasa, reach Tulamben by *bemo* via Amlapura (Rp1400). Or from Singaraja it's Rp2000 by van. Paradise Palm Beach Bungalows offers transport to the airport (up to four people) as well as a tour service. If you call from Candidasa, the Paradise will send a vehicle to pick you up (Rp30,000 pp, up to four people). Motorbikes and *jukung* (Rp5000 per hour) also for rent.

AMLAPURA

At one time Amlapura was the seat of one of the richest kingdoms of Bali, which traced its origins back to a 16th century Balinese prime minister known as Batan Jeruk. During the waning days of the Gelgel dynasty, this rajadom rose to the pinnacle of its power. In the 19th century, the kingdom owed its wealth mainly to the fact that its *raja* cooperated with the Dutch invaders, thus saving his title and autonomy. Lying at the foot of the holy mountain Gunung Agung, Amlapura is today the capital of Karangasem Regency.

During Gunung Agung's monthlong eruption in 1963, massive lava streams devastated almost all of eastern Bali. Although the lava did not reach the town itself, the accompanying whirlwinds and earthquakes destroyed many of the buildings. The town was cut off for three years after the eruption, isolating this formerly prosperous trading community from the rest of Bali. To the visitor, Amlapura still has a sleepy air about it, although the city is the commercial and administrative center of East Bali.

Amlapura is the smallest of Bali's *ibukota* (regency capitals), with only about 30,000 people. Shops shut down for the afternoon and open again at 1700; restaurants close early at night. Every three days there's a good open market. Change money—but not traveler's checks—at Amlapura's Bank Rakyat Indonesia, or more easily in Candidasa. Telephone calls can be made at Amlapura's 24-hour, seven-days-a-week telephone office; *bemo* pass it on the way into the *pasar*/terminal (see the tall signal tower). The post office is near the two hotels. If you drive in Amlapura, watch for a lot of unmarked one-way streets. The nearest gas station is in Subugan, just west of town.

Puri Kanginan

Of Amlapura's four palaces, each facing the cardinal points, the most famous is that of the last *raja,* Anak Agung Anglurah Ketut. Puri Kanginan (also known as Puri Agung) is a big complex, surrounded by a thick redbrick wall. Enter the complex through an elaborate three-tiered gate. Inside, an air of slow decay prevails. The fountains have stopped spouting and dragons and serpents sit stonily with wide-open mouths, yet it's a functioning *puri* with connecting walkways over pools and compounds set aside for the royal family.

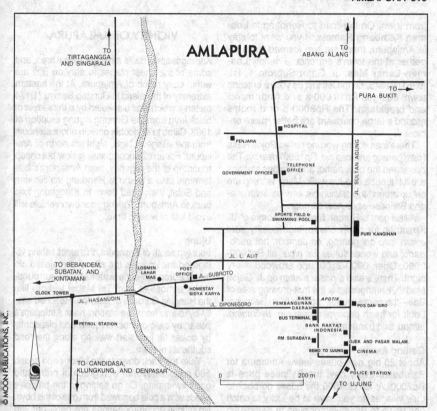

AMLAPURA

TO
TIRTAGANGGA
AND SINGARAJA

TO
ABANG ALANG

TO →
PURA BUKIT

HOSPITAL

PENJARA

GOVERNMENT OFFICES

TELEPHONE
OFFICE

JL. SULTAN AGUNG

SPORTS FIELD &
SWIMMING POOL

PURI KANGINAN

JL. L. ALIT

TO BEBANDEM,
SUBATAN, AND
KINTAMANI

LOSMEN
LAHAR
MAS

POST
OFFICE
JL. SUBROTO

CLOCK TOWER

JL. HASANUDIN

HOMESTAY
SIDYA KARYA

JL. DIPONEGORO

BANK
PEMBANGUNAN
DAERAH

APOTIK

POS DAN GIRO

BUS TERMINAL

PETROL STATION

BANK RAKYAT
INDONESIA

RM SURABAYA

OJEK AND PASAR MALAM

BEMO TO UJUNG

CINEMA

TO CANDIDASA,
KLUNGKUNG, AND DENPASAR

0   200 m

POLICE STATION

TO UJUNG

© MOON PUBLICATIONS, INC.

A combination of European, Chinese, and Balinese architecture and interior design were used in this *puri's* construction. Some of the deteriorating furniture in the palace's Maskerdam reception building was donated by Queen Wilhelmina of Holland. The largest and most striking pavilion is Bale London, with flourishing Edwardian decorations and a long veranda. It was given this curious name because its furniture is decorated with what the *raja* thought to be the British royal crest. Over the *bale* entrance is a widely reproduced 1939 photo of the mustachioed *raja,* shot at a time when the district was granted limited self-rule by the Dutch. The king's own pavilion has all his clothes and belongings preserved under lock and key.

As the *raja* had 35 wives, many families—as many as 150 people—still live inside the palace. Among the residents is the *raja's* grandson,

painter Anak Agung Ardana, who produces brightly colored cubist-style paintings. Several women occupants still weave gold-brocaded *songket.* Princess Mirah and her American husband "Gipper" also occupy the palace; they run Bali Fabrications, tel. (0361) 21496, which features neomodern ethnic *batik* designs. See some of their creations at C.V. Indu Kirana, Jl. Bypass Sanur, tel. (0361) 289-018; their showroom in the U.S. is at 47 Paul Dr., Ste. 1, San Rafael, CA 94903, tel. (415) 472-4410. The *puri* is open to tourists for Rp200 admission plus another Rp200 for a single-page sheet explaining the pictures on the main building. Overnight guests sometimes accepted.

Accommodations And Food
Most travelers prefer to stay at the idyllic **Tirtagangga** or **Abian Soan,** both about five km

from town. On the road to Rendang is **Losmen Kembang Ramaja.** If you want to stay in Amlapura, there are two *losmen* close together at the town's entrance. Friendly **Losmen Lahar Mas,** Jl. Gatot Subroto 1, tel. (0361) 21345, on the left just as you're entering town, charges Rp10,000 s or d (with *mandi* and breakfast). The Rp8000 s or d rooms around a large courtyard are better, more enclosed.

There's an eating *warung* called Pojok Rasa (*nasi goreng* and *cap cai,* Rp1500) nearby. The *pasar* and the bus, *bemo,* and minibus stations are all about a one-km walk. Many *warung* are set up around the *stasiun bis,* serving Javanese- and Balinese-style *nasi campur.*

A little gem is **Rumah Makan Surabaya** on Jl. Kesatrian for really cheap, high-quality *soto ayam, cap cai goreng, es campur,* hot *gado-gado,* and wonderful *es jus nipis,* all Rp1000-2000. Open 0900-2100, and crowded every night. There's also a *pasar malam* on Jl. Gajah Madah. Karangasem is the fruit-growing area of Bali—the name means "sour fruit" in Balinese. Look for fresh papaya, pineapple, *belimbing, jambu,* and bananas.

Getting Away
About 20 big new buses leave Amlapura for Batubulan every day; the Balinese price is Rp2000. At about 1600 the buses go back to their villages so you have to be lucky to catch one going to Batubulan or even to Klungkung after around 1700. At this time, it's best to hire an *ojek,* usually found near the bus/*bemo* terminal. Minibuses or *bemo* to Tirtagangga cost Rp500 (six km); Klungkung, Rp1000 (38 km); Denpasar, Rp2000 (2.5 hours, 78 km); Singaraja (Rp2500, 3.5 hours).

Bemo also travel all the way to Singaraja along the northeast coast via Culik and Tianyar over a paved road with unusual scenery. Starting at 0400, they run up until around 1600. Sit on the left for a better view of the rugged, brooding northern side of Gunung Agung. A good road and new bridges now cross over volcanic washouts and black lava flows along the way. Bicyclists without low gears may want to throw their bikes on top of a minibus up the big hill between Tirtagangga and Culik. Sweeping views of terraced rice fields greet you as you come down into Culik.

VICINITY OF AMLAPURA

Karangasem is Bali's most traditional area, and some of the finest places to stay on Bali are within easy reach of Amlapura. At the eastern extremity of the island is Gunung Seraya (1,174 meters), which was blanketed by a thick layer of black lava from the Gunung Agung eruption of 1963. Climb to its double peak in about six hours from the village of Ngis, eight km north of Amlapura. For an all-encompassing slow but cheap roundtrip of the regency, from Amlapura's bus terminal take a *bemo* to Rendang via Sibetan and Selat, then head down to Klungkung and back to Amlapura. Taking your own vehicle will avoid lots of waiting time.

Ujung
Four km south of Amlapura, this small fishing village on the coast is the site of a majestic old mock European-style water palace surrounded by a moat—a mini Taj Mahal laid out like the Hanging Gardens of Babylon. Reached easily by *bemo* from the station near Amlapura's *pasar,* by *ojek,* or most uniquely and pleasantly by *dokar.* Or just start walking along the road southeast of town.

Take the track down to the black-sand beach 500 meters beyond, with graceful *prahu* and good swimming. Or go fishing in the palace's ponds with a pole borrowed from one of the boys. No official accommodations are here, but you could possibly stay with fishing families up the hill. Bukit Kangin, up a side road to the left just before Ujung, is a Grecian-style temple built to honor the dynasty's royal founder. Nice view. Several villages hold a festival here during the full moon of the fifth month of the Balinese calendar.

The Road To Amed
Only opened since 1990, this incredible 30-km-long road is one of the wildest and most unvisited on Bali—no traffic, no telephone wires. It follows a tortuous route through arid hills high above the coast. Buy fresh *ikan awan* in Seraya village at the start. See cattle being washed in streams, great panoramas of the Bali Strait, isolated farmlets, grape arbors, and villages of Hindu fishermen with long unbroken lines of *jukung* with multicolored sails pulled up on the beach after the night's catch.

It's second and third gear nearly all the way, but the steeply undulating road is fairly well-maintained. It crawls through one of the poorest districts of Bali, where the inhabitants raise goats and grow small ears of corn, peanuts, and sweet potatoes. The road finally drops down to the fishing and salt-making village of Amed. From Amed, either return to Amlapura via Culik and Tirtagangga or head north along the coastal road to Singaraja via Tulamben.

Abian Soan

In the rice paddies just off the road on the northern edge of the village of Abian Soan, five km west of Amlapura on the road to Bebandem, is **Homestay Lila.** It can be difficult to find; there's only a small sign on a post showing the way. Located on the edge of a small ravine, these small, quaint, nonair-conditioned, no-fan little cottages cost only Rp7500 s, Rp12,000 d with sinks, bathrooms, verandas, and continental breakfast. The best deal for a family is the whole-house compound, Rp15,000 per day. All the buildings have electricity. Meals are available or you can shop in Bebandem or Amlapura and cook at the homestay yourself.

Bebandem

Every three days there's a big cattle market (*pasar hewan*) here where you can mingle with the *petani* amidst the market smells of dirt, dung, coffee, cloves, and cattle. Arrive early (by 0800) to see the action, shop, and enjoy Balinese drinks. The market reaches its peak of activity at 0800 or 0900, depending on the season.

Unless it's a long distance, farmers walk their cattle to the Bebandem market; you'll see them strung out along the Subagan-Rendang road before the dawn. With their long necks, soulful eyes, and fine rusty brown coats, Balinese cattle resemble overgrown deer. Bali's special breed (*bos benteng*) is found only on this island and no crossbreeding is allowed. Cattle are raised for many purposes: as beasts of burden, for export, for ceremonial purposes, and for meat. The Balinese farmer will only reluctantly sell his cow if he needs money for a ceremony.

To entice farmers and their families, all of downtown Bebandem is crowded with stalls selling hand-forged knives, cockfighting spurs, farm tools, impressive daggers, irresistible snacks, *cendol* stands, tonics to increase virility, trinkets, rings and baubles, sunglasses, pop posters, *kain,* cassette tapes, and bright, eye-catching clothing. This is a lovely area; go the back way via Asak to the main Klungkung-Amlapura highway. From Bebandem, it's Rp500 by *bemo* (nine km) to Amlapura, Rp800 to Rendang.

Putung

Located 11 km west of Bebandem, 20 km from Amlapura, and 68 from Denpasar, this mini-tourist resort is famous for *salak* grown on vast plantations. At 700 meters above sea level, enjoy the cool fresh air; it doesn't warm up until noon. An ideal place for meditation. The grandiose surroundings will nourish your soul.

From Amlapura, take a *bemo* to Bebandem (Rp400), then another *bemo* (Rp400) to the turnoff in Duda village, then walk or hitch 2.5 km to the **Putung Country Club Accommodations Bar and Restaurant.** Here there are five rooms for Rp15,000-20,000 s, and others for Rp20,000-25,000 d. Although plain and basic, what you're paying for is the stunning view. The bungalows sit on the edge of a high cliff over a deep chasm—no *padi,* just jungle falling sharply away to the sea. This area, it is said, is a favorite haunt of *leyak* who hover over the nearby hills and cliffs. The restaurant serves Balinese/Indonesian meals for Rp2000-10,000. In the off season you'll have the whole place to yourself.

There are also several nice walks in the area. From Putung, take the five-km-long path through gardens and forests down to the coast to Manggis. Or head west along the road to Rendang; the terraced rice fields follow the land's dramatic contours. If you turn south at Selat, you can reach Klungkung via Sidemen.

Sidemen

A Swiss charitable foundation has established a special school here devoted to strengthening and propagating traditional Balinese culture. With 120 students, the school's curriculum includes the study of *adat,* crafts, music, dance, painting, water divination, calendrical traditions, the Balinese language, traditional penmanship, literature, and the Bali-Hindu religion. Visit also the weaving factory Pertenunan Pelangi. There are several outlets where you can purchase expensive silk *kain songket* interwoven with designs of gold and silver thread, as well as distinctive Sidemen-style *endek* garments. Get to

Sidemen by traveling west on the scenic road from Amlapura through Bebandem, Putung, and Iseh, or by waiting for a *bemo* at the turn at Satria (or Sampalan Tenah) northeast of Klungkung, then traveling 12 km through the hills. Stand in front of Sidemen's market for a lift out of town in either direction.

Sidemen Homestay is one of the nicest homestays on Bali: 14 comfortable bungalows with fans, fine food (four-course dinners), good service, and superb views. Enjoy a drink from the bar, with Gunung Agung rearing up behind you. In the vast expanse of *sawah* in front is a wonderful collection of ragged, multicolored scarecrows.

Still, the Rp84,000-105,000 (full board) Ibu Putu charges is inflated, though guests seem willing to pay it. No a/c, *kelambu,* or hot water, nor does she accept Visa, but the rooms are nicely furnished, the beds decent, and the village-like ambience peaceful.

Two km away in Desa Tebola is **Homestay Patal,** a better deal: six spacious, quiet, and well-kept bungalows (Rp105,000 per night) set in a well-tended garden high on a hillside, half a km from the road, with gorgeous landscapes on every side.

TIRTAGANGGA

Fifteen km northwest of Amlapura (Rp500 by *bemo*); the turnoff is just one-half km beyond the bridge after leaving Amlapura. One of the prettiest places in all of Bali, Tirtagangga ("Water of the Ganges") is a pool complex built by Raja Anak Agung Anglurah Ketut in 1947 with corvée labor on the site of a sacred spring that emerges from under a banyan tree, the site of a small water temple. This was only one of the old *raja's* weekend retreats; his other water palaces are at Ujung and Jungutan.

With its shallow pools, pleasant cool weather, few mosquitos, great beauty, quiet star-filled nights, and birds chirping over the constant sound of splashing water, Tirtagangga is perfect for relaxation. Sitting on the slopes of Gunung Agung, the open-air palace's fabled water basins, fountains, bizarre statues, and figures have been repeatedly damaged by earthquakes. Locals and the government are involved in a seemingly ceaseless restoration project.

It's a sublime experience to swim laps in those big flower-strewn pools filled from mountain streams. Pools are drained mornings, but completely fill again by afternoon. It costs Rp700 adults, Rp200 children to use a 45-meter-long pool; you can come and go all day. The water is spine-tingling cold, so wait until noon to plunge in. After 1800 swimming is free of charge, but the water is too cold. The local moneychanger has good rates; for other services, go to Amlapura. Tirtagangga makes the best base for exploring the splendid northeast coast.

Accommodations

During the busy tourist season (July-Aug., Dec.-Jan.), Tirtagangga's seven hotels fill up quickly. The first *losmen,* **Dhangin Taman Inn,** is set in a nice courtyard and garden. Its 13 basic rooms vary in price from Rp10,000 to Rp15,000 s, depending on size, view, and baths. **Tirta Ayu Homestay** offers four bungalows right inside the water palace. Cost is Rp20,000 d, including pool admission and breakfast; laundry service is extra. New two-story bungalows on the homestay grounds are priced higher.

Outside the palace complex is the **Hotel Taman Sari** (Rp7000 s, Rp8000 d), offering 25 rustic rooms with bathrooms, showers, and a view of the sea. The two front rooms are quietest. Electricity is only on 1700 to 0700, and there are far too many ants and mosquitos, but the price is right.

Next door to the Taman Sari is the simple but immaculate **Homestay Rijasu** (Rp7000 s, Rp10,000 d), with complimentary breakfast and tea. Same price as the Taman Sari but the rooms are cleaner and nicer, with 24-hour electricity. Laundry, but no telephone. Excellent food just next door.

East of the water palace, up 99 steep steps, is quiet **Kusuma Jaya Inn.** Its 18 hillside bungalows are Rp15,000 s, Rp20,000 d for the basics or Rp40,000 for a larger unit with huge beds, fan, and big open-air bathrooms. Rates can be bargained down. Superb views (especially at sunrise and sunset) take in the glittering sea and Gunung Agung. Service is excellent, food well-prepared and reasonable. Around the bend from

Kusama Jaya is **Prima Cottages.** Though its five rooms are small, they're very comfortable. Nice atmosphere; less expensive than the Kusuma Jaya.

Food

Tirtagangga's ground-level accommodations all have restaurants that feature fresh fish (Rp2000 with tangy peanut sauce) taken right from the pools. **Tirta Ayu** has the best food of the lot. At sunset, climb the "stairway to heaven" to **Kusuma Jaya** or **Prima** for spectacular views and very good Indonesian menus.

Stalls at the head of the road are cheaper with surprisingly good *nasi campur* (Rp1500); also cold drinks, fried peanuts, fruits, and *bubur*. **Cafe Sawah** is down the hill from the Kusuma Jaya. Nice salads. For great music and a convivial atmosphere, try **Good Karma,** operated by a former clove and vanilla farmer who calls himself Baba ("The King"). Come For Talking And Joking With Baba For Good Karma states a sign. Ask Baba about his five rental cottages up the coast in Lipah—great location.

Getting Away

It's easy to get *bemo* into Amlapura (Rp500); they run until 1700. For Singaraja, buses call on Tirtagangga starting at around 0900 (Rp2000). Red *bemo* also pass from 0400 to 1600 (Rp2500, three to four hours). If you want to visit Kintamani from here, take the *bemo* to Kubutambahan (Rp1500, three hours), then go south one hour to Kintamani (Rp1000). For Candidasa, it's Rp750 by *bemo.*

VICINITY OF TIRTAGANGGA

This area has fantastic scenery. It's a nice walk following the water source of the pools; take a dip in one when you return. Climb the hill 1.5 km up to the village, where locals secretly host the occasional cockfight. Return via the winding road through the valley. You'll see coconut palms, brilliant rice fields, and the distant sea, with Bali's biggest and most sacred mountain towering above.

Another superlative walk is the path leading uphill to Tanahlingis and Ababi. Tanahlingis is known for a choral group peculiar only to Karangasem that imitates the rhythm of *gamelan* instruments; Ababi features a big washing place with walls of brick in a dry riverbed. From the *warung* look down at the men, women, and children as they wash, chat, and fetch water. A major agriculture ceremony is held at the end of the dry season each year. Also worth seeing is the Chinese cemetery, one km beyond Tirtagangga on the right.

Tanaharon

Take the hike up mini-Gunung Agung, Tanah Aron. Make a left at Abang about three km after Tirtagangga and follow the road to Tanaharon for 10 km. It's 45 minutes to the top from where the asphalt ends beyond Pidpid; the roundtrip walk takes five hours. Nice lookout points over steep ravines.

Budahkling

In this colony on the slopes of Gunung Agung live two castes of Mahayana Buddhists who've retained pre-Hindu feasting traditions. Also living here are descendants of a gold- and silversmiths guild that served the princely Karangasem court before WW II. Villagers here make *kain songket* and sell small *selendang* for Rp15,000, *sarung* for Rp50,000, large *kain* for up to Rp150,000.

Bukit Lempuyang

To get to Bali's easternmost hill and the site of an important temple, take an *ojek* from Bajo (Rp2000) to the parking lot about halfway up, then walk to Pura Lempuyang (1,058 meters). About 2.5 km from the main highway is a tollgate (Rp50I0 pp); from where the road ends, it's about a one km walk to the first small temple, Pura Telagamas. From there it's 4,000 steps to the top. Start early before it gets too hot. If you go in the afternoon, the mountain is covered in clouds, but on clearer mornings, you'll spot the islands of Nusa Penida and Nusa Lembongan.

BULELENG REGENCY

This sprawling, 1,370-square-km regency offers mountain hikes, rustic villages, waterfalls, hot springs, untouched marine and forest reserves, silversmiths, beach resorts, a secluded coastline bordering a placid sea, and distinctive temples. The south end stretches across the foothills of Bali's central volcanos while the north's coastal plain faces the Java Sea. Because of Buleleng's geographic isolation from the densely populated south, it has developed distinct cultural differences in architecture, dance, and art. The regency's capital, Singaraja, has a cosmopolitan air with many ethnic and religious minorities existing in harmony. Tour buses from southern Bali seldom venture over the mountain passes; consequently, there are fewer beggars, touts, and hassles in the tourist enclaves of the region. In the early 1990s, the religious leader of Buleleng, the Pedanda Brahmana of Singaraja's Hindu University, attempted to strengthen the beliefs of the region's Hindus, decreeing that Buleleng's faithful must pay obeisance to God three times daily. Tourists complain about being awakened so early, but it's now custom.

HISTORY

During the 14th century, northern Bali came under the rule of Javanese nobles of east Bali's Gelgel dynasty. In 1584, the legendary Panji Sakti built a palace called Puri Sukasada where Singaraja is today, extending his rule all the way to East Java. The Dutch were next on the scene. In 1846, they sent ashore a military expedition to capture Buleleng; the attack ended in a stalemate and a shaky treaty was signed with the ruling princes.

In 1855 Buleleng was separated from Jembrana and became the first of Bali's regencies

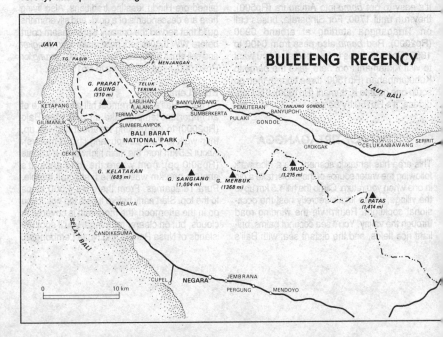

BULELENG REGENCY

to fall under direct political control of the empire-building Dutch. By 1882, Singaraja was the district's Dutch capital, a major shipping point for Nusatenggara during colonial times. The descendants of the local regent became bureaucratic officials working for the Dutch. Feudal rule came to an end here a full 60 years prior to colonization of the more bucolic south.

Today northern Bali has an anachronistic European air, the class system isn't strictly adhered to, and the social order centers more on the family than in the communalized agricultural *banjar* of the south. Since castes don't play a major role in social intercourse, northerners seldom use the High Balinese language.

ECONOMY

The regency is an important cattle export center and a major coffee, vanilla, nutmeg, cocoa, and clove-growing district. Since Buleleng's climate is drier than that of the south, Indian corn, copra, and fruits such as mangos, mangosteen, bananas, passion fruit, and avocados can be grown here. The latest cash crop is red grapes, the sweetest in all Bali, cultivated on bamboo frames in the hills overlooking the coast. The island's best and stinkiest *durian* come from Bestala near Munduk village. Four shrimp cultivation farms lie west of Lovina.

Singaraja, Buleleng's capital, has been an important educational and cultural center since the Dutch were here; the education faculty of Denpasar's Udayana University is based here. Tourism is a nascent but burgeoning industry. Though it's not as culturally rich as the southern half of the island, tourists are attracted to Buleleng's cheaper prices and stretch of relatively quiet beaches, dotted with inexpensive accommodations and restaurants. Shallow reefs offshore offer some of the island's most accessible snorkeling and dolphin-watching opportunities.

TEMPLE ART

The temple architecture of northern Bali differs considerably from the classical lines carved in the gray sandstone of south Bali. The soft pink

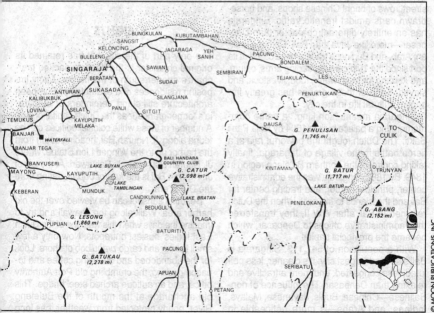

paras quarried near Singaraja allow northern sculptors more exuberance in their work. Because the stone ages so quickly, carving is an art form that must constantly be kept alive. In the north, stones are chosen for their color, white or brown, and often remain unpainted.

Though interior layout is basically the same as in south Bali's temples, northern architecture replaces small shrines with large pedestals—houses for the deities—built with elaborately carved stone. Steep flights of narrow steps lead to airy thrones and shrines, scale is exaggerated, and the tall *candi bentar* are covered with spiky, flame-like shapes; arabesques; and spirals studded with *leyak,* supernatural beings, and sea creatures. On the cartoon-like bas-reliefs of Buleleng, you'll see baroque gone wild—images of plump Dutchmen cramped into a motorcar, men drinking beer and cranking up cars, people copulating in the bushes, men riding bicycles made of leaves and flowers.

GETTING THERE

Reach Buleleng by crossing Bali's central mountain range on one of the island's two main roads, both offering spectacular scenery. If you have your own transport, take the fastest route to Singaraja from Denpasar via Bedugul, then return to Denpasar via Kintamani, a roundtrip covering most of Bali's mountainous backbone. Buleleng can also be reached from Gilimanuk along the northwest coast and from Amlapura along the scantily populated northeast coast. A third northbound road from Denpasar crosses the mountains through the coffee-growing district of Pupuan, offering impressive views.

SINGARAJA

Singaraja is a small seaport and the capital of Buleleng District, featuring tree-lined avenues, quiet residential perimeters, a wide market street, rows of bright Chinese shops, and horse-drawn carts amidst frenetic traffic. Singaraja has an entirely different character than Denpasar—more like Java than Bali. Chinese, Indian, Arab, and Buginese traders have called at its port since the 10th century, trading arms, opium, and *kepang* for fresh water, food, livestock, and slaves. Each of these groups has greatly impacted cultural life in the city.

Singaraja means "lion king," a name commemorating a palace built in 1604 by Raja Panji Sakti. The Dutch fought the powerful *raja* at a fierce battle in the village of Jagaraga, finally taking control of the northern Buleleng region in 1849. By 1882, Singaraja was the administrative center, principal harbor, and trading center for Bali and the islands to the east. When the Dutch returned to Bali after WW II, they transferred their administrative offices to Denpasar, which became the provincial capital.

With a population of 541,113, Singaraja is Bali's second-largest city. It's cleaner, less polluted, less congested, and more attractive and relaxing than Denpasar. The influence of non-Balinese—Chinese, Bugis, Javanese, Malays, Indians, and Arabs—is more noticeable in Singaraja than in other parts of Bali, as this city has been a marketplace for the Java sea trade for over a thousand years.

SIGHTS

The only part of the city that has retained its original character is the densely packed merchant's quarter south of the harbor. Many imposing residences and examples of European architecture still stand, reminders of Singaraja's former grandeur as the Dutch capital of Bali. A number of these white colonial edifices can be found along Jl. Ngurah Rai, heading south from the harbor up to the Winged Lion Statue, where Jl. Ngurah Rai meets Jl. Pahlawan. At the top of Jl. Ngurah Rai is the *kantor bupati,* dating from the Dutch era.

Beautiful sunsets can be viewed over the old harbor area. Walk along the seawall and try to imagine the days when this was one of the Dutch East Indies' busiest entrepôts. Now only a few small fishing and cargo *prahu* bob offshore. Look for the abandoned and decaying coffee and tobacco *gudang,* the crumbling old Port Authority office, and an antique arched steel bridge. This old anchorage at the mouth of the Buleleng River, poorly protected from weather, has long

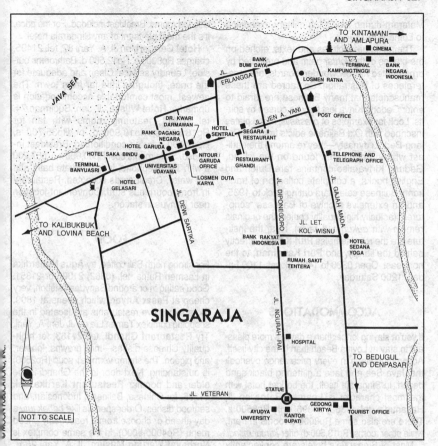

SINGARAJA

TO KINTAMANI AND AMLAPURA

CINEMA

BANK BUMI DAYA

TERMINAL KAMPUNGTINGGI

BANK NEGARA INDONESIA

JL. ERLANGGA

LOSMEN RATNA

JAVA SEA

DR. KWARI DARMAWAN

JL. JEN A. YANI

POST OFFICE

BANK DAGANG NEGARA

HOTEL GARUDA

HOTEL SENTRAL

SEGARA II RESTAURANT

HOTEL SAKA BINDU

NITOUR / GARUDA OFFICE

RESTAURANT GHANDI

TELEPHONE AND TELEGRAPH OFFICE

TERMINAL BANYUASRI

UNIVERSITAS UDAYANA

LOSMEN DUTA KARYA

HOTEL GELASARI

JL. DEWI SARTIKA

JL. DIPONEGORO

JL. GAJAH MADA

TO KALIBUKBUK AND LOVINA BEACH

JL. LET. KOL. WISNU

BANK RAKYAT INDONESIA

HOTEL SEDANA YOGA

RUMAH SAKIT TENTERA

JL. NGURAH RAI

HOSPITAL

TO BEDUGUL AND DENPASAR

JL. VETERAN

STATUE

GEDONG KIRTYA

TOURIST OFFICE

AYUDYA UNIVERSITY

KANTOR BUPATI

NOT TO SCALE

since silted up. Celukanbawang, 40 km west of Singaraja, now serves as Buleleng's principal export harbor.

Near the waterfront, the haunting statue of freedom fighter I Lontong points seaward. After WW II, in the chaotic period between the Japanese surrender and the Dutch return, the crew from a Dutch patrol boat hoisted the Dutch flag in Buleleng Harbor; I Lontong climbed up and replaced it with the red-and-white Indonesian banner. He was machine-gunned from the Dutch boat the minute he stepped away from the pole.

A huge Hindu temple **Pura Jagatnatha** is on Jl. Pramuka. A large Chinese *klenteng* in the eastern part of the city houses priceless vases

and tapestries. On the sea in the west part of town is a Chinese cemetery, Bukit Suci, with unusually marked and decorated graves; turn north just east of Terminal Banyuasri and travel down Jl. Pantai Lingga. There's a fishing village and a swimming beach nearby.

Gedong Kirtya

Holy objects are ordinarily stored out of sight in high places, but in Singaraja you can view sacred *lontar* books at Gedong Kirtya at the east end of Jl. Veteran. The 3,000-odd *lontar* in this library record the literature, mythology, magic formulas, medical science, folklore, religion, and history of Bali and Lombok. Many of the *lontar* were looted from the palace in

Mataram during the Dutch military expedition to Lombok in 1894.

The miniature pictures and texts, etched on the blades of the *lontar* palm and protected by ornamented narrow wooden boards, are masterpieces of illustration. So sacred are these manuscripts that many Balinese are afraid to enter Gedong Kirtya lest they be cursed by spirits. Look for examples of *prasastis,* metal plates inscribed with Old Balinese edicts from the Pejeng-Bedulu dynasty—they're among the earliest written documents found on the island. Gedung Kirtya also contains rare Dutch and English books, a complete collection of traditional Balinese calendars dating back to 1935, and an extensive archive of Balinese "scriptures" (actually high quality copies; the originals remain with *dukun* and *rajas*). Near the institute are the royal temples **Puri Kawan,** directly behind the library, and **Puri Kanginan,** to the northeast. Open 0800 to 1400, closes 1100 Friday, 1200 Saturday.

ACCOMMODATIONS

If you're staying longer than a day, it's more pleasant to stay at Lovina Beach than in the city itself. Accommodations in every price range overlook the Java Sea and face a glittering black sand beach. In Singaraja itself, the budget hotel with the most character is **Losmen Ratna** on Jl. Hasanudin, tel. (0362) 21396, only Rp6500 s. There are also some Rp8000 d rooms in front, while other rooms (Rp13,500 d) offer *kamar mandi.*

Most of Singaraja's hotels are conveniently located on Jl. Jen. A. Yani. **Hotel Garuda,** at no. 76, tel. 22191, charges Rp8000 s, Rp10,500 d with breakfast. The rooms at **Losmen Duta Karya,** tel. 21467, have fans, intercoms, and sinks for Rp10,000 s, Rp12,500 d with bath; five air-conditioned rooms go for twice as much. Breakfast includes toast with egg and coffee. Nice courtyard. A cafeteria serving Chinese seafood and Muslim dishes is only 100 meters away. More central **Hotel Sentral,** at no. 48, tel. 21896, is Rp7000 s, Rp10,000 d with fan, inside *mandi,* and breakfast; air-conditioned rooms run Rp22,500 s, Rp30,000 d. Clean, well-run **Hotel Sedana Yoga,** Jl. Gajah Mada 136, tel. 21715, asks Rp10,500 s, Rp15,000 d for rooms with fans, Rp25,000 s, Rp35,500 d for air-con-

ditioned rooms. Breakfast included. For the price, it's the most pleasant of any Singaraja hotel.

Hotel Gelasari, on Jl. A. Yani 87, tel. 21495, charges Rp8000 s, Rp12,500 d. Bathrooms outside. Laundry service. Clean and adequate for the price, though a little far from town. The newest, most comfortable accommodation is upmarket **Hotel Wijaya,** Jl. Jen. Sudirman 74, tel. 61471, featuring rooms with fan for Rp16,800 s, Rp18,900 d; or Rp35,700 s, Rp42,000 d for air-conditioning. Breakfast included. Suite rooms cost Rp60,900 s, Rp67,200 d with TV, telephone, fridge, private bath, and hot water. Credit cards accepted. Restaurant in front, courteous staff. Convenient location near Banyuasri station.

FOOD

For strong north Bali coffee, try **Agus Mahardika** in Losmen Ratna, tel. (0362) 21396 or 21851. Good eating in or around Banyuasri station, very cheap at **Pasar Anyar,** which opens at 1800. More expensive restaurants are located in the shopping complex Taman Lila on Jl. Jen. A. Yani. Try **Restaurant Ghandi,** tel. 21163, for high-quality Chinese dishes—*mie,* prawns, lobster, and pigeon. The shrimp vermicelli soup (Rp2500) is outstanding. Next door to the Ghandi is the older and popular **Restaurant Kartika,** tel. 41296, for Chinese, Balinese, Indonesian, and seafood dishes. Order specials like *bebek tutu* a day ahead or choose from a reasonably priced menu (Rp4000-5000). In the same complex is **Nurhayat Warung Muslim,** Jl. A. Yani 25 B. Near Taman Lila is **Restaurant Lumayan,** known for good *sate kambing*.

A great Chinese eatery is **Restaurant Segar I** on Jl. Erlangga near the harbor. Though very plain, it serves a great *nasi campur* with lots of shrimp for Rp3000; Indonesian food too. **Restaurant Segar II** is on Jl. Jen. A. Yani; the two Segars, owned by the same family, are widely considered the best restaurants in the city.

SHOPPING

People are friendlier, laugh easier, and are more willing to bargain in this relatively untouristed city, but the craftsmanship doesn't begin to compare with the variety and ingenuity of southern work. Take cash when you shop, as few places accept credit cards or traveler's checks. The souvenir shop **Tresna,** Jl. Gajah Mada 95, tel. (0362) 21816, sells antiques, *kain tenun,* and carvings. The city's retail shops, concentrated along Jl. Jen. A. Yani, are getting bigger and cleaner, with better selections. Self-service shops have arrived too, and in most you don't have to bargain. Visit **Buleleng Market** just south of Jl. Semeru. Each night until 2100 or so—depending on reliability of electricity—this market transforms into a dimly lit, lively *pasar malam.* One km east of Singaraja is the small village of Banyuning, whose people turn out urns, vases, roof tiles, and other pottery.

A major weaving factory is **Berdikari** at Jl. Dewi Sartika 42, tel. 22217. It specializes in reproducing ancient, finely detailed Buleleng silk *ikat,* sold for sky-high prices. **Perusahan Puri Nadiputra,** on Jl. Veteran behind the Gedong Kirtya, sells distinctive hand-woven *sarung* or *kain.* There are looms in practically every home in the *kampung.* To buy *endek, ikat,* colorfast *sarung,* and gold-threaded *songket,* visit the cottage industry **Poh Bergong,** 10 km south of Singaraja. It's where retailers come to buy at wholesale prices.

SERVICES

Most government offices are located near the junction of Jl. Veteran, Jl. Ngurah Rai, and Jl. Pahlawan. Road distances in north Bali are measured from this point, where the Winged Lion statue stands.

The **tourist information office,** Jl. Veteran 23, tel. (0362) 25141, is near the Gedong Kirtya; look for the sign from Jl. Veteran. The friendly staff can supply you with a few pamphlets and maps of Buleleng and Singaraja. Open Mon.-Thurs. 0700-1400, Friday until 1100, and Saturday until 1230. Nyoman Suwela speaks excellent English. The *kantor polisi* (tel. 110) is on Jl. Pramuka, and the post office is on Jl. Gajah Mada where it intersects with Jl. Jen. A. Yani. The official telephone office, where you can also receive and send faxes, is next to the post office at Jl. Gajah Mada 154. Singaraja's telephone code is 0362. Change money at Bank Dagang Negara (BDN), Jl. A. Yani, tel. 41344; Bank Bumi

Daya (BBD), Jl. Erlangga 14, tel. 41245; or Bank Rakyat Indonesia (BRI), Jl. Ngurah Rai 14.

Nitour Tour and Travel, Jl. Jen. A. Yani 57, tel. 22691, is Singaraja's main agent for Garuda, Merpati, and Bouraq. Open Mon.-Fri. 0800-1400, Saturday 0800-1200. Note that Nitour cannot reliably confirm bookings on flights out of Bali: call the main Garuda Airlines office in Denpasar.

Doctor Kwari Darmawan, tel. 21721, is reputable; open 0630-1900, 1600-1900. **Rumah Sakit Kirtha Usada,** on Jl. Jen. A. Yani, tel. 22396, offers the best-equipped medical facilities on the island. A well-stocked pharmacy is **Sumber Waras.**

TRANSPORTATION

Board a minibus from Kintamani (Rp1800) or from Denpasar (Rp2500) to Singaraja. Another route is via Kintamani in the mountains, then through Kubutambahan on the north coast. If you're traveling to Lovina from Karangasem, you'll arrive first at Penarukan terminal, then take a *bemo* to Banyuasri terminal, then another to Lovina. To get around town, take *dokar* (Rp500-1000) from Pasar Anyar, the night market. *Bemo* (Rp500) run a circuit through Terminal Banyuasri, Pasar Anyar, and Terminal Penarukan.

Singaraja's **Terminal Banyuasri** serves destinations west such as Lovina (Rp500) or Gilimanuk (Rp2000). To get to Labuhan Lalang or Negara, catch an *oplet* to Gilimanuk, then take the main highway to Denpasar. Minibuses also leave Banyuasri for Denpasar every 30 minutes from early morning to around 1800; a two-hour trip. Denpasar-bound minibuses can even be found after 1800, but they'll charge Rp3500 instead of the usual Rp3000. The main terminal **Penarukan,** tel. (0362) 61334, is on Jl. Supratman three km east of Singaraja, serving destinations to the east including Amlapura (Rp2500), Kintamani (Rp1800), Tejakula (Rp600), Padangbai (Rp4000), Klungkung (Rp3000), and Batubulan (Rp3000).

By motorcycle or car, it takes 2.5 to three hours to reach Amlapura. Direct buses travel to Surabaya (Rp20,000) from either Singaraja or Lovina; if you're in a hurry to get to Java, you can hop the first thing going to Gilimanuk, where you can connect with long-distance buses for destinations including Yogyakarta or Jakarta.

Check out the long-distance night bus companies **Cakrawala,** Jl. Surapati 124, tel. 41791 or 21925, and **Puspasari,** tel. 41698. Ticket offices are found around the Taman Lila complex on Jl. Jen. A. Yani. You can also catch shuttle buses to Denpasar, Kintamani, Ubud, and Kuta (Rp12,500), which leave from the **Perama Tourist Service,** tel. 21161.

SOUTH OF SINGARAJA

Beratan And Vicinity
Take a *bemo* from Banyuasri station (Rp500) to the *kampung* of Beratan, where silver- and goldsmiths fashion temple accoutrements; brooches in the shape of frogs, geckos, and seagulls (Rp9000-12,000); ID bracelets (Rp35,000); and rings ready for setting. Nearby, in **Jinang Dalem,** Balinese buy *ikat* and gold- and silver-inlaid *songket* cloth used in ceremonial dress (Rp150,000). **Nagasepaha** village is known for unique *wayang kaca,* used as coverings for offerings.

At Panji the **Bhuwana Kerta Monument** honors heroes of the Indonesian struggle against the Dutch. In the 16th century, Raja Panji Sakti, founder of the kingdom of Buleleng, was born in this village. Nearby is a cave believed to have been inhabited by a *raksasa.*

Gitgit
South of Singaraja, off the road to Bedugul, is Bali's most spectacular waterfall, easily accessible at the end of a 600-meter walk through rice fields. Small donation to enter. Restaurant, *warung makan,* souvenir shops, changing rooms, and toilets. Cool off with a swim in the lagoon-like pool at the foot of the 15-meter-high falls.

You could do a lot worse than the **Giggit Hotel and Restaurant** opposite the *air terjun;* clean rooms cost Rp25,000 s, Rp35,000 d, deluxe rooms Rp45,000 s, Rp55,000 d. Tariff includes breakfast (Indonesian, European, or continental). Notice the sweeping panorama over the north coast and the Bali Sea. Meals are also available in Mini Restaurant across the street.

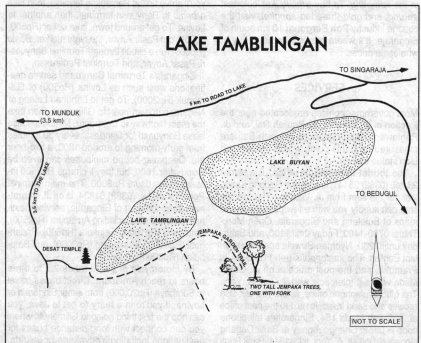

LAKE TAMBLINGAN

TO SINGARAJA

5 km TO ROAD TO LAKE

TO MUNDUK
(3.5 km)

3.5 km TO THE LAKE

LAKE BUYAN

TO BEDUGUL

LAKE TAMBLINGAN

JEMPAKA GARDEN TRAIL

DESAT TEMPLE

TWO TALL JEMPAKA TREES,
ONE WITH FORK

NOT TO SCALE

© MOON PUBLICATIONS, INC.

Danau Tamblingan

A trip to Danau Buyan and smaller Danau Tamblingan has the feel of a mini-archaeological expedition. Both are contained within one vast caldera, lying between 500 and 1,500 meters above sea level. Because of the scarcity of public transport, the trip is best accomplished with a chartered vehicle or motorcycle.

There are two approaches. West of Singaraja, turn south at Banjar and follow the asphalt road to Munduk which then runs east along the tranquil northern shores of Danau Tamblingan and Danau Buyan. For an easier approach, head south on the main highway out of Singaraja. About eight km before Bedugul, bear right and follow the ridge five km through the village of Palu'an. Just before entering Munduk, turn left and bump along a dirt road for 3.5 km down to Lake Tamblingan. Ask for directions frequently, and pause to smell the fields of hydrangeas and coffee plants and hear the sounds of an almost primeval upland rainforest.

When you reach the lake, you'll see a house; ask for Komang, a boy who'll lead you to the site. This road is drivable, but at its end you'll have to park and walk 500 meters to the archaeological site. Look for the old lichen-covered grindstones under a forked *jempaka* tree. The stones themselves are not such a big deal, but the trip there is an adventure, featuring a serene lake surrounded by beautiful peaks. No ticket-takers or tourists.

Munduk

This hilly town in Bali's central mountains has a delightfully fresh climate and is surrounded by the great natural beauty of coffee, cacao, clove, vanilla, and tobacco gardens. Munduk is the largest of a series of mountain villages including Gobleng, Gesing, and Oemegero. To reach Munduk from isolated Danau Tamblingan, go back to the main road and take a left, then travel 3.5 km.

Munduk is blessed with a number of safe, comfortable accommodations in a unique setting. **Puri Lumbung Cottage** has five traditional raised cottages made of thatch, matting, and wood, and is immaculate and nicely furnished. Set on the side of a mountain, the cottages afford magnificent views of rice terraces and *cengke* plantations. Each bungalow sleeps two and has its own water, electricity, and *mandi*. The hotel is part of a Balinese project to involve tourists in the everyday lives of the locals.

The hotel's restaurant, **Warung Kopi,** specializes in traditional homecooked meals—ask the kitchen to cook only Indonesian/Balinese food. The *ares ayam* (Balinese soup with boiled banana stem and chicken) for Rp2250 gets high marks, but the *cap cai* is rather bland. The Balinese desserts are very intriguing. After the meal, relax on the high pavilion with a cup of freshly brewed local coffee and a magnificent view. Peak season rates (15 Dec.-15 Jan.) are Rp74,000 s, Rp84,000 d; off season rates are Rp63,000 s, Rp73,000 d. Stay four nights and a fifth is offered free. The management of Puri Lumbung can also arrange for accommodations in simple, less expensive, but attractive homestays in the area—Meme Surung, Mekel Ragi, and Guru Ratna.

EASTERN BULELENG

Buleleng Timor is known for its rustic farming villages and elaborate temples in which every square inch is covered in curves, arabesques, spirals, flames, and floral ornamentation hewn from volcanic rock. The Balinese have a fondness for caricature, beautifully represented in the bas reliefs of Buleleng's temples. Scenes include corpulent Europeans, Dutch steamers being attacked by sea monsters, and aircraft falling from the sky. Demon hands and heads emerge from the carving, as if three-dimensional figures were imprisoned in stone.

SANGSIT

Eight km east of Singaraja (Rp500 by *bemo* from Penarukan station) lies Sangsit's main attraction, the brilliant **Pura Beji,** dedicated to the goddess of wet rice and fertility, Dewi Sri. It's located about 500 meters down a cactus-lined road to the sea; look for the small sign on the left side of the road. This extraordinarily lavish *subak* temple, one of the oldest in north Bali, was built in the 15th century on the site of a well. Though a bit commercialized, it presents a perfect example of the northern rococo style of temple carving, featuring a strange off-angle symmetry.

Made of easily carved pink sandstone, Pura Beji swarms with carved demons and stone "vegetation." The temple's spellbinding gateway is covered with images of *naga,* imaginary beasts, devils, and *leyak* sentries guarding tiny doors. In the temple's spacious inner courtyard you'll see gnarly old frangipani trees, wooden statues, and a throne of the sun god. Admission by donation. Near Pura Beji is Sangsit's *pura dalem,* containing relief panels showing stories and erotic scenes meant to scare off malevolent spirits.

JAGARAGA

Heading east from Singaraja, turn right at the end of Sangsit village on the road to Sawan. The villages on the steep inland slopes of Buleleng claim ancient origins. Inscriptions dating from the 10th century tell of pirate raids, earthquakes, and volcanic eruptions.

Jagaraga's architecturally extravagant *pura dalem* is dedicated to Durga. It features carved comic-strip panels of cyclists, Balinese flying kites, dog-fighting airplanes, fishermen hooking a whale, a Dutch steamer, some long-nosed Dutchmen in a Model-T Ford being held up by a bandit with a horse pistol, and mammoth fish swallowing a canoe. The detail of the vintage cars is wonderful, with mudguards, lamps, carburetors, and doors intact. Stone owls, roosters, bats, tigers, and crabs cling to the walls. Admission by donation, Rp1000.

A number of temples are found on this road, all featuring effusive, cunning, and mischievous carvings; ask the locals. Get there by *bemo* (Rp750) from Singaraja's Stasiun Penarukan.

BUNGKULAN

Two km east of Sangsit and 12 km east of Singaraja is Bungkulan, with 10,000 inhabitants and 13 *banjar* with three temples each. Though unaffected by tourism, there's always an event worth seeing, with 13 *odalan* and one or more annual celebrations at each temple. Bungkalan's very

old, worn **Pura Sari Pemerajan Agung** is perched on the highest hill overlooking the village. Inside are hand-carved statuary and a fine old *kulkul* with a carved human head on top. The temple's age is uncertain, but there are records of a renovation in 1778.

The village is active, with a market held every day. Take an early morning swim in the local river and watch children doing washing, men and boys taking the family cow to water, and women diving for sand they carry up the bank on their heads.

Bungkalan has one of the best village homestays on Bali, a relaxing and very reasonably priced family accommodation called **Sarah and Dewa's Guesthouse,** P.O. Box 189, Singaraja, Bali. It's set in a beautiful, tranquil garden, ensuring privacy. Nice rooms in the main house are Rp10,000 s or d while two separate bungalows with private bath and overhead fan cost Rp12,500 s or d. Breakfast not included. The owner knows the area well—both she and her husband are extremely helpful and always willing to pass on useful information about Balinese customs. Try Sarah and Dewa's wonderful homecooked meals like Bubble and Squeak (potato pancake), tofu or *tempe,* Spanish omelette, chicken-fried rice, and cold drinks. Staff will arrange for a masseuse (Rp5000), a tailor to copy a blouse or a skirt (Rp3500), bicycle rental (Rp2500 for an 18-speed mountain bike), men's haircuts, or one-day laundry service.

KUBUTAMBAHAN

Reach this important crossroads town by *bemo* (Rp1000) from Singaraja's Penarukan station. Find Kubatambahan where the north coast road intersects the road to the main highway.

The unusual **Pura Maduwe Karang,** the "Temple of the Owner of the Land," is about one km beyond the Kintamani turnoff. This important district temple is dedicated to Mother Earth, who is worshipped to ensure successful fertilization of crops grown on dry, unirrigated land. One of northern Bali's largest temples, its terraced entrance recalls some of Europe's stately baroque gardens. Steps lead past 34 stone figures from the Ramayana to a big, peaceful, nearly empty courtyard. More steps lead to an inner section containing a huge stone pyramid-like base flanked by two *bale* reserved for offerings.

The temple's carvings show ghouls, noblemen, home scenes, soft porn, and a riot of leaves and tendrils, all atop a stupa-like structure. One pedestal shows a horrifying rendition of Durga, another a large figure resembling Christ at the Last Supper. The centerpiece depicts a battle scene from the Ramayana. On the northern wall of the innermost shrine is a famous one-meter-high relief of a Dutch official riding a floral bicycle, a reproduction of a 1904 carving destroyed by an earthquake. The cyclist is W.O.J. Nieuwenkamp, a famous Dutch landscape and portrait artist who rode his bicycle around Bali in the early 1900s, painting as he went. Ask for the key and leave a donation in the shop. Next to Pura Maduwe Karang is a small *warung* that sells black rice pudding (Rp500), possibly the best on Bali, and fantastic coffee.

YEH SANIH

Idyllic beaches and seaside temples are found along the northern coast of Bali. To reach the beach resort Yeh Sanih, catch a minibus (Rp1000) from Singaraja's Penarukan station. This shady seaside spot offers a black-sand beach—a bit rocky, but the swimming is good. Enjoy wooden *bale* for sunning and a beautiful, botanical garden featuring pink frangipani.

Yeh Sanih's main attraction is an enclosed natural swimming pool of clear, fresh water from an underground spring. Known by the locals as a recreation site since the early '30s, the pool wasn't restored until 1971. Cool sea breezes, trees, and a nice panorama over the Bali Strait make for a serene setting. Entrance fee Rp500.

On holidays this retreat could be stampeded by screeching schoolchildren, and it's also subject to tourists at any time. But on weekdays the place may be virtually empty. It's not a scene like Lovina; there are fewer sellers and hustlers. Many tourists pass through, but few stay.

In the mornings, take a swim in the ocean—more like a lake than a sea. Unlike Lovina, there's not a soul to bother you here. Quite passable snorkeling 500 meters out; another good snorkeling spot one km away. Visit the *pura* on the hill, **Pura Taman Manik Mas.** The nearest **Agen Pos and Telephone** is in Kubu-

tambahan five km west. If you want nightlife try Lovina, but remember the last *bemo* back to Yeh Sanih from Singaraja's Penarukan terminal departs at around 1900. There's a small bus station, **Tempak Parkir Roda Empat Air Sanih,** with drink stands and toilet.

Accommodations And Food

Within Yeh Sanih's gorgeous pool complex is two-story **Puri Sanih Bungalows I**; Rp15,000-20,000 for units with fans, mosquito nets, fresh flowers, and breakfast. The manager assumes that the louder you yell, the better you manage. Tennis courts available to the public. The restaurant, with a European and Indonesian menu, is expensive and the food barely edible. To the east, with the freshwater pool in between, is nicer **Puri Sanih Bungalows II,** tel. (0362) 22990, overlooking lily ponds and extensive gardens. Comfortable, spotlessly clean bungalows with sliding doors and private baths face the ocean. Rates: Rp20,000 s, Rp35,000 d in low season, Rp40,200 d, Rp25,000 s in high season. The row of rooms farthest from the ocean are Rp20,000 (Rp15,000 per day if you pay one month up front). Nice breakfast pavilion; eat lunch and dinner at one of the *warung*. Nothing disturbs this park-like setting, just the chirping birds. **Tara Beach Bungalows** charges Rp10,000 s, Rp15,000 d. The manager can arrange for snorkeling, diving, fishing, and sailing excursions or rent pushbikes, motorcycles, boats, canoes, and floats. Enjoy hot and cold drinks in the Tara Pub.

Above the pool, up 33 steep steps, is pleasant **Puri Rena Bar and Restaurant.** Open 0700-2300, serving Indonesian, Chinese, and Balinese cuisine. You pay for the view, though—*gado-gado* is Rp2500, while a vendor down the road charges Rp500. Puri Rena has four small budget rooms available for around Rp10,000 s (after bargaining). This hotel organizes excursions to local festivities, provides travel information, and is planning a center to give guests an inside look at Balinese culture. Eat inexpensively at *warung* across the road from the pool. **Warung Seger** has good Bali *asli nasi campur* (Rp1000), *nasi goreng* (Rp1500), and one of the best *sop ayam* (Rp1500) around.

There are several options for longer stays. When you sit down at any *warung,* you'll be approached by people asking if you'd like to rent a room—anything from a bamboo fisherman's hut on the beach to a room in a private home above the village. Also look for Rooms For Rent signs on the highway. Ask around; expect to pay about Rp150,000 per month.

Vicinity Of Yeh Sanih

Walk south up the mountain halfway to Kintamani. A good paved road along the northeast coast, guarded by gnarled trees, leads to Amlapura. The road hangs over cliff tops, passing sandy coves that shelter fishing *jukung*—one of Bali's most picturesque journeys, with unspoiled views of the island's highest peak. East of Yeh Sanih 1.5 km toward Amlapura is **Antara Bungalows and Refreshment**; Rp9000 for room and simple breakfast. Not in good condition; Pura Sanih Inn is better.

For elegant dining—real silverware, gracious service, table linen—head two km east of Yeh Sanih to the superlative **Apilan Restaurant** in Desa Bukti for wonderful French cuisine including homemade breads and cakes. Lunch is only Rp10,000; a three-course candlelight dinner is Rp15,000. Apilan rents a cottage for Rp25,000 per night s or d. If you're a guest, meals are available any time, otherwise the place is open Fri.-Sun. for lunch and dinner, or by special request. No tax or service charge. Note that the whole building is made of coconut palm byproducts—floor, roof, and walls. One km from Desa Bukti and three km east of Yeh Sanih is **Air Sanih Seaside Cottage**; Rp5000 s for any of four bungalows. Nice place, very quiet, close to the beach. Price doesn't include breakfast but coffee and tea are available. Perfect if you want to be alone.

SEMBIRAN

One of Bali's oldest traditional villages, Sembiran lies 30 km east of Singaraja. Like many of Bali's *asli* villages, it's located high in the hills, off the main coastal road. From Terminal Penarukan take a *bemo* to Desa Pacung (Rp500), then catch a ride on a motorcycle the rest of the way (Rp500). The winding four-km-long asphalt road up to Sembiran is surfaced but extremely steep. This lovely country road passes beautiful hills, valleys, *sonekeling* trees, and forests. As you approach the village, there's a giant *kemit* tree, the base of which is said to have been a place where corpses were laid out in ancient times.

With a population of 6,000, this is one of only a half dozen Bali Aga villages, but one where traditions are not easily forgotten. People speak a dialect of Old Balinese, and the caste system is not followed in Sembiran. Many of the typical Balinese time-marker ceremonies are not observed here. The Sembiranese have two Days of Silence (Nyepi) per year instead of the single day observed by the rest of the island. Marriage is by proposal, not elopement, nor are partners arranged by parents. There are 20 *pura* in Sembiran, 17 containing artifacts and carved stones.

This uniquely laid out village of corrugated iron roofs gets about five or six tourists per week. In the *warung* near the market, enjoy tea and snacks with the friendly villagers, a number of whom speak Indonesian. There are no commercial accommodations, but you can stay in homes. No telephones, but plenty of televisions.

To leave, take the new road out to Tajun, on the main north-south road. This is a windy, rocky, only partially paved route through rolling hills, hidden valleys, and poor *desa*—about as wild as Bali gets.

TEJAKULA

The fishing and farming village of Tejakula is on the way to Amlapura (Rp1500 by *bemo* from Terminal Penarukan), three km east of the turnoff to Sembiran village. Tejakula's well-maintained bathing place is an elaborate, fort-like structure, with water gushing into separate pools for *pria* and *wanita*. It was originally built to wash down horses and cattle but is now reserved solely for the human animal.

Tejakula boasts one of the finest *kulkul* towers on Bali. Typical of the style found in north Bali villages, it's brilliantly carved with *Panji* cycle legends and *wayang* characters. Also in the village is a unique *gamelan* called Gong Tejakula, a *kampung* of gold- and silversmiths called Banjar Pande, and the ancient temple Pura Ponjok Batu ("Pile of Stones") perched on a small rock face and surrounded by hills, valleys, and twisted frangipani trees. It's said the wandering priest Nirantha sat on one of the temple's stones and composed poetry. Nearby on the beach at low tide is a freshwater springs frequented by locals; the water bubbles up from the sand and runs into the sea.

The highest waterfall on Bali is in Desa Les, five km east of Tejakula. There's no road to the falls, just a path through rice fields. Ask directions from the villagers in Desa Les; it's about a half-hour walk. There's just one cascade, and the water can be quite frigid. One of the few unisex communal *mandi* on the island is found in Les.

LOVINA BEACH AND VICINITY

LOVINA BEACH

This area has a lot to offer, not the least of which is its distance from the southern honeypots. The beach is better than Candidasa's and the uphill areas inland are some of the prettiest on Bali. To get there, flag down a *bemo* (Rp500) from Singaraja anywhere on Jl. Jen. A. Yani. Lovina Beach was the first seaside resort to appear in the mid-'70s, taking its name from a restaurant that operated from 1953 to 1960 where Permata Cottages is today. Anak Agung Panji Tisna, the ruler of northern Bali, named this stretch of coast after the English word "love" in 1953. In 1976, the few *losmen* that existed were demolished by an earthquake.

The resort returned to form during the 1980s, when *losmen* and beach inns started popping up all over the area. Lovina has since become the generic term for a whole line of small villages and beaches that it has, touristically speaking, devoured. From east to west, these are: Pemaron, Tukadmungga, Anturan, Kalibukbuk (or Banyualit), Kaliasem (or Lovina), and Temukus. Kalibukbuk has the most activity, while the fishing villages of Anturan (or Happy Beach) and Temukus are the quietest, with less densely packed restaurants and accommodations.

Generally, the restaurants, stores, and services are on the south side of the road, accommodations on the north. Most are only a short walk from the beach or main road. Services include myriad moneychangers, convenience stores, used bookshops, a bank, a postal agent where you can send parcels, a Perumtel office (in Kalibukbuk), and vehicle rentals. The moneychangers here offer rates about 10-15 *rupiah* lower than those in Denpasar or Kuta.

Though not as scenic as the southern coastline, Lovina attracts refugee tourists from fast-paced Kuta. It's about as far away (100 km) and as completely opposite to Kuta and Sanur as you'll find—no flash menus, no surfies, few motorbikes, little music, few dogs—and comparatively cheap. A few years ago, you could easily live on about Rp12,600 a day. Today, the tourist economy makes accommodations and food less than the super-bargains they once were. Lovina keeps growing and changing, with prices rising and falling as demand changes.

In Lovina, enjoying beautiful sunsets involves simply walking out on your veranda. You can dive in glass-clear water, find good trekking paths, temples, and hot sulphur pools in the hills, and use centrally located Lovina as a base for daytrips to Tulamben, Bali Barat National Park, Pulau Menjangan, the Buddhist monastery, Yeh Sanih, and the lakes and volcanos of the central mountain range.

Vendor Overkill

Granted, the Lovina Beach strip is still not as overrun with tourists as the southern beaches. But, like Kuta, its spirit no longer belongs to Bali. In recent years, local entrepreneurs competing for tourist money have appeared en masse. Vendors run from all directions the minute you alight from a *bemo* or park your car, asking if you'd like to rent a room, attend a buffet, see the dolphins, or go snorkeling. On the beach, pushy hawkers offer dance tickets, massages, fruit, *sarung*, cigarettes, or magic mushrooms. Lovina sellers are more familiar and more likely to joke than Kuta's all-business vendors, but they're just as persistent, and will hassle you even when you're lying on the beach with your eyes closed.

What to do? Deal with a limited number of the pests. Buy a few *batik* from X, go snorkeling with Y, buy a pineapple from Z—when someone else approaches, say you already have your own suppliers. Other vendors usually accept this and will leave you alone.

Accommodations

From the road, it appears Lovina hasn't changed much over the years. A great number of new accommodations, however, have crept in on lanes out of sight of the roadside hotels. In the low season, expect to pay Rp10,000 per person for basic beachfront accommodations and Rp73,500 for four-star luxury. There are two types of resort accommodations: the upstart, splash "beach inns" or resort hotels, which have sprouted up along eastern beaches, and the venerable resorts of Kalibukbuk and Kaliasem that've been around for some time. Well-established places like the **Rambutan** and the **Banyualit** are more picturesque, offer more shade, and have more character than the newer hotels. Since these hotels are small, with 10-15 rooms, they can give personal and friendly service. A basic breakfast of toast, butter, jam, fruit salad, and coffee or tea is almost always included in the room rate.

The small street leading to Banyualit is lined with seafood restaurants, garment and convenience shops, and different classes of hotels. It's less congested than most of Lovina, yet all you really need can be found on this street. If you stay in a hotel too near the main highway, mornings and nights could be noisy. Midrange accommodations—upscale but not four-star international—offer the most value for the dollar. For Rp42,000-Rp84,000, they offer security, beautiful bungalows, nice gardens, full services (laundry, postal, safe-deposit boxes, free storage), phones and faxes, rooms cleaned daily, attractive restaurants, free breakfast, stone and tile pools, cheap marine tours and rental of snorkeling gear—and they all take plastic.

Reservations for the most popular accommodations are critical during the high season (July and August) and over the Christmas holidays, when rates rise Rp5000-10,000. Ask for a

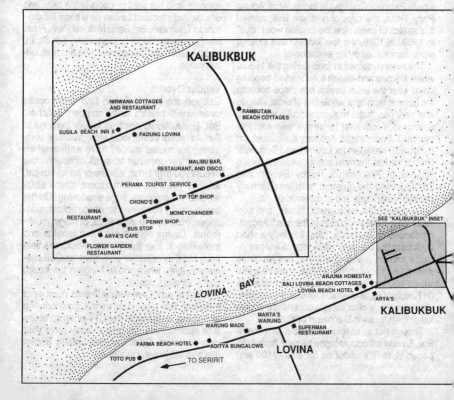

discount in the offseason, or if you'll be staying more than three days.

Susila Beach Inn has opened a branch on the beach next to the Angsoka called—you guessed it—**Susila Beach Inn II,** offering cozy bungalows with verandas, showers, toilets, and a fruit salad breakfast. Rates: Rp9000 s, Rp10,000 d. Lovina's largest and oldest accommodation, **Nirwana Cottages,** tel. (0362) 22288, fax 21090, is 500 meters down the road on the beach. The brick, bamboo, and thatch structures feature flush toilets, showers, and enclosed outdoor patios—but they aren't very well cared for. Five classes of rooms range from Rp10,000 to Rp50,000. Good restaurants are within walking distance. Family-run no-frills **Arjuna Homestay** is a little known, good budget hotel (Rp8000 d) tucked away only 50 meters from the beach.

Thirty-room **Bali Lovina Beach Cottages,** tel. and fax 41385, between Arjuna and Per-

mata, is pure luxury living: immaculate cottages with bath, shower, and hot water cost Rp94,500 s, Rp105,000 d for superior rooms; Rp84,000 s, Rp94,500 d for standard rooms; Rp63,000 s, Rp73,500 d for rooms with fan. Credit cards accepted. Restaurant, beautiful pool, poolside bar, beach access, very few beach hawkers. Water sports offered include sailing, snorkeling, fishing, canoeing, windsurfing, and dolphin-watching tours. Lovina's swankest, largest, and most expensive hotel on the strip is **Palma Beach Hotel,** Jl. Raya Lovina, tel. 62362, 61775, or 61658, fax 61659, a quiet, luxury marine resort that caters to package tourists. Nineteen standard rooms go for Rp126,000 d; superior class rooms are more spacious, with open-air bathrooms, fridge, TV, and garden for Rp157,500 d. Live karaoke weekly, a coffee shop and restaurant, tennis court, large pool facing the beach, and open-air fitness center. Make reservations at the Denpasar office, Jl. Raya Puputan

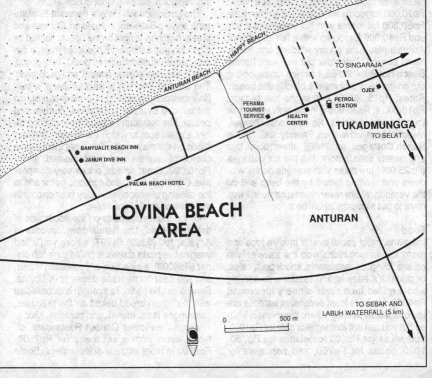

LOVINA BEACH AREA

17 X, tel. 25256, fax 25231. Watch for Palma's business cards offering a 20% discount.

Quiet, family-run **Lovina Beach Hotel,** tel. 23473, was built in 1953 on the site of Lovina's original hotel founded by the late *raja,* Anak Agung Panji Tisna, a direct descendant of the Buleleng kings. The current owner, Agung Sentanu, is the *raja*'s grandson. In a good location on the beach side of the road, the Lovina Beach offers convenience, friendly 24-hour service, good security, laundry and mailing service, and safe-deposit boxes. Rates for the three classes of rooms are Rp52,500 for spacious, air-conditioned beachfront cottages; Rp31,500 for beachfront cottages with ceiling fan; and Rp21,000 for rooms with garden view, shower, and fan. Three air-conditioned beachfront bungalows with inside *mandi* go for Rp35,000 each. An excellent place for children.

Friendly 52-room **Aditya Bungalows,** P.O. Box 134, Singaraja 81101, tel. 41059, charges Rp90,000 for deluxe rooms with a/c, hot water, private terrace, TV, fridge, and sea view; Rp70,000 for rooms with a/c and a garden view; Rp50,000 for rooms with hot water and a fan; and Rp40,000 for rooms with a fan and *mandi.* Aditya's also runs a very efficient and handy travel service. The older but well-kept **Parma Beach Hotel,** tel. 23955, has nice rooms looking out on gardens that meet a black-sand beach. Rates: Rp15,000-25,000 in the low season; Rp18,000 s, Rp30,000 d in the high season for four classes of rooms. No additional charges; reasonably priced kitchen. Friendly staff. **Billibo Beach Cottages,** tel. 61498, offers rooms that are merely satisfactory, but the six cottages (Rp25,000) are clean with screens on the windows and reading lamps by the beds and on the veranda. Make reservations; some will wait days to get a cottage at Billibo's.

Food

In Lovina, most social events involve food and many accommodations woo the traveler with on-site, low-price restaurants, snack bars, cafes, or pubs. It's easy to find restaurants serving whole grilled tuna steak dinners for around Rp4000. Lovina's least expensive eateries are the beachside *warung* where the menu is limited but you can eat *lontong* with *sate* for Rp1000, fruit juices for Rp600, omelettes for Rp750-1000, sodas for Rp700, and pancakes for

Rp750-1000. In the high season, you'll want to start out for dinner early, as the best restaurants are swamped and orders can take a while. At the **B.I.U. Warung** near Chono's, the meals are excellent and the prices the cheapest in Lovina. The small bakery at the **Malibu Bar, Restaurant and Disco** sells loaves of brown bread for only Rp1000.

Competing restaurants try to outdo each other by hosting huge buffets on alternating evenings. Tables sag with curries, grilled meats, salads, noodle dishes, and fruit. After dinner, most eateries sweeten the deal with a free *regog* or *legong* dance performance. These buffets can be good deals, but pay attention to the menus—soy sauce and *krupuk* do not constitute an entree. Both the food and the performance cost Rp5000-Rp9000—one of the best bargains in Asia. The open-air **Rambutan Restaurant** in Kalibukbuk presents a *legong* and Balinese Banquet at 1930 every Sunday and Wednesday night featuring professional dancers performing traditional dances. Cost is Rp6000.

The Lovina Beach Hotel's **Permata Restaurant,** serving Balinese, Indonesian, Chinese and Western dishes, is right on the beach, flanked by a garden and fishpond. Specialties include *betutu bebek* (stuffed steamed duck), *babi guling, sate ayam, nasi goreng spesial,* and *gado-gado.* The pride of Permata is *nasi tumpeng,* a truly Balinese dish consisting of a mountain of rice surrounded by *sate,* vegetables, curries, and *betutu.* The restaurant's beachfront gazebo offers a great spot to watch the sunset. **Warung Made** on the main road offers a set menu with a choice of courses and great dessert, all for Rp10,000. Great salads; prices very competitive. Classical music and acoustic guitar add to the relaxing atmosphere. Happy hour discounts on food and drink. Nice *brem.*

Of the four restaurants on the south side of the main road, the hands-down favorite is **Arya's,** tel. (0362) 61797, where you'll find imaginative pasta dishes, a grilled tuna fish dinner (Rp4000), a selection of vegetarian meals, and the best homemade desserts in Lovina. Service can be so-so; its strength is its breakfast with multigrain bread baked on the premises, homemade jams, muesli, and porridge. Next to Arya's is the **Flower Garden Restaurant,** offering items from a set menu for Rp7500-Rp9500 in more intimate surroundings. Some of the dishes are good, but portions are sometimes skimpy. If Made herself is cooking, count on a superb meal—dishes like guacamole and potato skins, cream of prawn soup, or tuna wrapped in bamboo leaf. Sample Made's Bali wine at your peril. Balinese dancing starts around 2000.

Three nights a week, **Chono's** hosts an extravagant *rijstaffel* buffet at 1930. The meal—15 tasty dishes including rice wine, chocolate milk, peanuts, and fried *tempe*—is followed by Balinese dancing for Rp6000. Chono's also serves fresh seafood at very reasonable prices: fried calamari with garlic butter (Rp3000), grilled tuna (Rp3000), or snapper with choice of sauce (Rp3500).

Entertainment

Kuta-like nightlife spots on the north coast include the **Malibu Bar, Restaurant and Disco** in Kalibukbuk next to the New Srikandi, a meeting place for singles and travelers. It offers dinner and a big-screen movie (starts at 1910), followed by live singers or Balinese reggae music. The disco serves every drink imaginable, and the menu includes Western tourist dishes. Malibu will pick you up if you call (tel. 0362-23671); open into the early hours. The other "downtown" nightclub, the open-air **Wina Restaurant** on the northwest corner of Jl. Seririt and the road to Nirwana, also features big-screen movies and live music until midnight, but has expensive, lousy Chinese food. **Warung Made** is a favorite gathering spot with an interesting but slightly expensive menu. Another popular hangout, the **Toto Pub** in Lovina, is so close to the water it's in danger of being swallowed by the sea.

Recreation

At night fishing fleets head out in their *jukung*, luring fish for netting with kerosene pressure lanterns swaying and glowing yellow along the waterfront. For around Rp5000 you can join them for a two- or three-hour late afternoon trip. The bay is great for swimming: Lovina's warm sea laps lazily at the gray-sand shore during the dry season, quite tame compared to the volatile southern coasts. The wide expanses of sand are great for sunning (especially at Kalibukbuk), and beach masseurs are available for Rp5000.

For a reef so close to the beach, the snorkeling, diving, and boat fishing are above av-

erage in Lovina. The docile sea and the shallow lagoon make this coast ideal for beginners and young divers to safely explore the intertidal zone.

You don't need to venture far for good snorkeling. There are fine spots two to three km from shore where the water is shallow. But the best dive sites lie closer to Singaraja, where the reef juts gradually farther out from the beach. Rent a motorless outrigger (Rp5000 low season, Rp8000 high season) to take you out; you'll see fascinating reef life right from the boat just by sticking your head underwater.

When snorkeling you'll feel as if you're swimming in an aquarium with moray eels, tropical fish, and pastel coral. If the water's over your head, use the boat as your island. Wear sneakers, and watch out for the sharp coral, sea urchins, and catfish-like fish with poisonous spines. Start early before the water gets cloudy: the sand is so dark it can be difficult to see the bottom. In February or March, no snorkeling or dolphin trips are offered due to heavy rain and dirty water.

Boatmen wait on the beach for customers; many provide snorkeling gear. You can rent *prahu* from the hotels, or simply swim out to the reef. Snorkeling gear rents for Rp5000 for two or three hours.

To spend breakfast with dolphins, buy a ticket the day before from boys on the beach. Average price is Rp10,000 per person and the length of the tour may vary from 2.5 to three hours, depending on the season, the boat, and the captain. Determine in advance how many hours you're going to spend snorkeling versus hours looking for dolphins. If you don't, you may end up having to bargain on the boat and pay Rp5000 to see dolphins. When you buy your ticket, give the vendor your room number and someone will wake you with a knock on your door 15 minutes before the predawn departure. It's a 30- to 60-minute trip to dolphin territory.

Most of the motorized boats can fit four to six people; big wooden outriggers can carry up to seven people and are less likely to pitch and roll than smaller craft. If you're lucky (about 75% of the time), for a few miraculous moments your boat will be surrounded by hundreds of leaping, flipping, and blowing dolphins. Watch for the different species, particularly the large, slow swimmers that can weigh up to a ton. In any event, you'll get a boat ride, tea, and *pisang goreng* breakfast, and snorkeling on the return trip. Don't let the boatmen go in before the agreed-upon time.

A good place to obtain diving information and arrange trips is **Spice Dive,** which has an office inside Arya's. Staff is honest and properly qualified. Check out their photo albums of various dive locations (Lovina reef, Tulamben, Menjangan). Scuba certification courses are also offered. **Baruna** rents snorkeling gear by the hour (Rp1500) and books cruises to see dolphins (Rp8000 per person), snorkeling trips (Rp5000), and Sunset Cruises (Rp4000). Make reservations at your hotel. **Perama Tourist Service,** tel. (0362) 21161, in Anturan, also organizes marine excursions. **Permai Dive Sports,** tel. 61471, in Tukadmungga offers a dive trip to Menjangan Island, one of the best dive and snorkeling spots in Indonesia. In the off season, prices may drop to Rp105,000, including one night's free accommodations. Permai's beginner course includes two dives, all equipment, guide, transport, and food for Rp147,000.

Khi Khi's, tel. 21548, offers expensive, quality half-day snorkeling and dolphin-viewing tours for Rp30,000 per person. Its big *jukung* with both outboard motors and sails set out at 0530 from Banjar rather than Lovina, which is often crowded with boats and tourists. Around 0800 or 0900 you'll likely be spotting dolphins, by noon the day's fishing catch will be grilling on the beach, and after a native-style nap under a tree, you'll return to Lovina at 1300. The Cadillac of dolphin-watching outings. Khi Khi's also offers deep sea fishing tours (Rp40,000) and tuna fishing tours (Rp100,000).

Shopping And Services
Women with stacks of *sarung* and blankets on their heads will sell their wares cheaper than in Lovina's shops, but you'll have to bargain.

A little east of Arya's, across the road, is the **Tip Top Shop**, selling bus and shuttle tickets, snack foods, drinks, sundries, English newspapers, guidebooks, maps, medicine, film processing, waterproof cameras, cheap water, and clothes. Best prices in Lovina; it also has a telephone and a postal service (stamps, postcards) and is open until 2300. **Penny Shop,** opposite the street to Angsoka cottages, carries an extensive used book library, film (Rp11,000 per

roll), and offers one-day film processing. Also a cheap laundry service that includes ironing.

Lovina has its share of postal agents where you can send letters and parcels for the same prices charged by the post office. It also offers a bank, moneychangers, and fax services. Lovina's clinic can be found south of the Lovina Beach Hotel in Kaliasem.

Getting There
On arriving from Kuta, the shuttle bus lets passengers off at **Perama Tourist Service** in Anturan, where the passengers are relayed to their hotels free of charge. The Perama shuttle leaves Kuta for Lovina at 0830 and at 1600 (Rp12,5000, 2.5 hours). If you're traveling from Denpasar, take a public *bemo* to Banyuasri station on the western edge of the city. From dawn to dusk, *bemo* travel regularly from the station to Lovina (Rp500) on a road lined with huge trees and emerald-green rice paddies; tell the driver where you'll be staying and he'll drop you off as close as possible. If you're arriving from Surabaya on a long-distance bus, save backtracking by asking the driver to let you off along the highway at either Lovina or Kalibubuk. From Amlapura, the bus arrives at Terminal Penarukan just west of Singaraja, where you can catch a *bemo* to Banyuasri station.

Rentals And Shuttles
Shuttles run to Ubud, Denpasar's Ubung station, Sanur, Kuta or the airport for Rp12,500. Shuttles leave for Kuta (a 2.5-hour trip) at 0700 and 1300. For four or five passengers, drivers will offer service to Candidasa or Padangbai via the east coast for Rp20,000 per person. Or catch the shuttle to Kuta where you find another heading to Candidasa (Rp20,000 per person). Kuta is also the transfer point for shuttles to Senggigi and Mataram. Most hotels and homestays can arrange tickets and provide pick-up service. Ask about Perama's "Stopover Service," offering southbound travelers up to two nights in scenic Bedugul at no charge.

Most Lovina hotels organize minibus tours of Gianyar Regency; some rent cars. Jeeps rent for Rp35,000-40,000 per day (not including insurance); motorcycles cost Rp12,000-15,000 per day, though good machines are hard to find. Scooters with automatic clutch cost around Rp10,000 per day, bicycles about Rp2500-3500 per day, and mountain bikes Rp5000 and up per day. Rent from virtually any homestay, hotel, or travel/tour agency.

For a great day-trip, rent a motorbike or a jeep and travel from Seririt to Mayong, then east toward Kayuputih, Gobleg, and Munduk. The narrow asphalt road to the lakes passes a few small villages as it climbs into the mountains. When you reach Kayuputih, walk back to Banjar or continue on to Munduk, where you'll find superb views of Tamblingan, Buyan, and Bratan lakes. The road joins the Singaraja-Denpasar road at a point approximately 20 km south of Singaraja and 10 km north of Lake Bratan.

Getting Away

Buses to Singaraja (Rp500) stop in front of Arya's. To Gilimanuk or Bedugul, take a *bemo*; there's no shuttle service. If you're heading to western Bali or East Java, you don't have to go into Singaraja to catch a bus—buy tickets at Arya's or wherever buses to Surabaya stop to pick up passengers. Three travel services can be found in Anturan. Perama, tel. (0362) 21161, sells bus tickets to Jakarta for Rp48,000. It's a hellish ride: the bus leaves at 0630, arriving 28 hours and three meal stops later at 1000. Order airline tickets from Perama too; they'll be delivered within 48 hours.

VICINITY OF LOVINA BEACH

Pemaron

Heading west out of Singaraja, the first village you reach is Pemaron. For sheer comfort and relaxation, the **Baruna Beach Cottages,** P.O. Box 149, Lovina Beach, Pemaron, tel. (0362) 21795 or 21746, fax 22252, set amidst landscaped gardens, can't be beat. Rooms or bungalows (the latter feature Western toilets) run from Rp35,700 to Rp109,200. Make reservations at least two weeks in advance.

To get to Baruna, take a *bemo* (Rp500) from Singaraja. Baruna is a totally self-contained resort right on the beach, offering a poolside bar, boutique, cultural shows, sauna and massage services, sailing, windsurfing (Rp12,000 per hour), snorkeling and dolphin trips (Rp3000 and up), and motorbike and bicycle rentals (Rp10,000 per day). American, Indonesian, or continental breakfasts cost Rp8400-18,900, lunch or dinner Rp8400-Rp21,000. Another nice

Pemaron hotel is **Aldian Palace Hotel and Restaurant,** tel. 61549.

Tukadmungga

Accommodations offered in Tukadmungga are resortish, quiet, and attract fewer vendors than the more congested beaches farther west. Though rooms may be spare, they're set back from the noisy road and are often surrounded by beautiful rice paddies. Upon entering Tukadmungga, head toward the sea and you'll reach **Permai Beach Cottages** on Happy Beach, tel. (0362) 61471, catering to water sport enthusiasts. Rooms are Rp15,000 s, Rp35,000 d with a/c, fan, hot water, good ventilation, and shower. Some of Permai's dive trips to Lovina, Pulau Menjangan, and Tulamben include one night's free accommodations.

There are three restaurants and four accommodations at the end of the road to Happy Beach. **Happy Beach Inn** is reasonably priced at Rp8000 s, Rp10,000 d for rooms with fans; cheaper rooms are Rp5000. The two bamboo rooms in the back of Happy's are the best, only Rp10,000. The food is inexpensive and great—try the fish wrapped in banana leaves, black rice pudding with ginger, or the dinners, when staff cooks a big suckling pig and serves *nasi campur* with calamari (Rp2000). This small cluster of accommodations makes a good base for snorkeling tours, and there's an amazing reef just off shore. Close by is the **Suci Jati Reef Hotel,** tel. 21952, with large four-room cottages among the rice paddies on the beach, smaller rooms in a two-story building, and a basic restaurant. Room prices are average, around Rp15,000. Facilities include private baths, safety deposit boxes, fans, laundry service, bar, motorbikes and bicycles for rent, and airport transfers.

Yuda rents 12 small, clean, raised cottages with no hot water, no breakfast, a hole-in-the-floor toilet, and bamboo walls for Rp31,500-42,000. Rooms are grouped around a restaurant pavilion with the waves only five meters away. Private *mandi* cost extra. Farther west and close to the highway is **Bali Taman Beach Hotel,** offering double rooms with a/c, ceiling fan, bath in private garden, shower, TV, fridge, and pool for Rp105,000-126,000. A nice restaurant looks out on the sea; good food. Between Suci Jati and Yuda, down a narrow lane through rice fields, is basic 14-room **Sri Homestay.** Reservations are advised in July and August. Rates:

Rp12,600 for standard rooms, Rp18,900 for bungalows, breakfast included. Sri Homestay offers tours and vehicle, motorbike, or bicycle rentals. **Perama Tourist Service, Accommodations, and Agen Pos,** tel. (0362) 21161, sells bus tickets and stamps.

Anturan

In Anturan is **Homestay Agung,** a popular place among travelers. With bamboo-decorated rooms for only Rp8000 s, Rp15,000 d, Agung's is nearly always booked. Alone on the water is **Lila Cita Beach Inn** with plain second-floor rooms for Rp15,000 s, Rp20,000 d. Rooms with private outdoor *mandi* and flush toilets run Rp20,000 s, Rp25,000 d. The helpful staff creates a friendly atmosphere, and there's superb snorkeling out front. On the same road is quiet, good value **Celuk Agung,** P.O. Box 191, Singaraja 81101, tel. (0362) 23039, fax 23379. Most of the sixteen comfortable bungalows in three classes have private baths, showers, hot water, satellite TV, and fridges. Prices range from Rp42,000 s, Rp52,500 d for standard (no a/c) to Rp105,000 s, Rp115,500 for the suites. Most of the hotel's grounds are devoted to gardens; facilities include a bar, a reasonably priced restaurant, pool, tennis and badminton courts, laundry, safe-deposit boxes, and transport service. Nice views of rice fields and the sea.

Kalibukbuk

The highest density of hotels and restaurants is found down Kalibukbuk's main road to the sea, where the beach is widest. Check around before deciding on a place. One of the cheapest (Rp8000 s, Rp10,000 d with breakfast) is the **Indra Pura Inn,** tel. (0362) 61560, near the Banyualit Beach Inn. On the main road, only a five-minute walk from the beach, is the remarkable **Chono's,** tel. 23569, which rents clean, spacious rooms with good beds and large baths. Cost: Rp15,000-20,000 for rooms with a fan, shower, and private toilet; simple breakfast included. Transport, car rental, sightseeing and snorkeling tours, and laundry and baggage storage service. On its second story, Chono's has a nice restaurant that hosts buffets and dances regularly.

The quiet **Banyualit Beach Inn,** P.O. Box 116, Singaraja 81101, tel. 25889, fax 23563, gets high marks for its concrete and traditional bungalows with clean and tidy rooms, *mandi* with plants,

Western toilets, and bedside phones. Room rates are Rp15,000-45,000 in three different classes. Some units have verandas nearly touching the water, and it's only a 10-minute walk to the main road. Nice surroundings, nice restaurant, good security, and an accommodating staff. Staff can organize tours; transport; snorkeling, scuba, fishing, and sailing outings; and dolphin-watching trips. Credit cards accepted. Down the lane is the family-oriented **Rambutan Beach Cottages,** P.O. Box 195, Kalibukbuk, tel. 23388; Rp25,000 for budget rooms, Rp35,000 for rooms with ceiling fan, Rp40,000 for upstairs rooms, and Rp50,000 for rooms with hot water. Upstairs rooms are spacious, cool, and soundproof, with a veranda, balcony, and electric mosquito coils; all rooms have private bath. Near several restaurants and the beach and surrounded by a garden of *rambutan,* coconut, and banana trees, this is an excellent place to stay.

Spiffy and relaxing **Angsoka Cottages,** tel. 22841, fax 23023, only two minutes from the beach, has cozy rice-barn units for Rp15,000 (outside *mandi*) and detached bungalows with a/c, inside *mandi,* hot water, and a nice veranda for Rp60,000. Amenities include restaurant and bar, helpful staff, laundry service, IDD telephones, pleasant gardens. It's located in the heart of Kalibukbuk, with moneychangers, restaurants, art shops, and ticket agents close at hand. Angsoka boasts an attractive pool with a sunken bar surrounded by bamboo and *angsoka* flowers. Book at the front desk for shuttle service, marine excursions, or dolphin watching. Luxury accommodations at a budget price. Just south of Angsoka Cottages is **Padang Lovina Seaside Cottages** on Jl. Binaria, only a two-minute walk from the beach. Thirteen clean double rooms for Rp20,000 s, Rp30,000 d, all with tile floors, private baths, showers, ceiling fans, and breakfast. One air-conditioned suite costs Rp25,000 s, Rp35,000 d. Also recommended is secure, quiet **Rini Hotel and Restaurant,** tel. 23386, in the center of Kalibukbuk, with friendly service, good food, and a large garden. Rates: Rp20,000-25,000 for economy rooms, Rp30,000 for standard, and Rp50,000 for superior. Bungalows are fully equipped with big beds, fans, mosquito nets, showers, and verandas. It's a one minute walk from the beach, three minutes to the main road, with shops, moneychanger, postal agents, and restaurants nearby.

An established place, nine km west of Singaraja, **Ayodya Accommodations** is enclosed in a serene flower-filled compound and costs Rp8000 s, Rp10,000 d for traditional, clean nipa and bamboo huts. Each room is cool and spacious with a private reading-cum-dining area, efficient food service, and laundry facilities. Good security. North of Ayodya is **Astina's**, P.O. Box 42, Singaraja 81151. Though rooms are a bit dark, rates are only Rp7000 s, Rp8000 d with outside *mandi*, or pay Rp11,000 s, Rp12,000 d for larger Bali-style bungalows with inside *mandi*, sink, shower, carved furniture, fan, and breakfast; cheaper in the off season. This quiet location with nice gardens is away from everything but a short walk to anything. Good value.

Surya Bar and Restaurant is cozy and attractive, with inexpensive, delicious food, particularly the fresh charcoal-grilled fish and chicken *sate*. The **Grace Restaurant**, across from Arya's, has excellent Javanese-Indonesian style food, and the view of the sunset from the open upstairs attracts many. Fresh seafood is the specialty. **Khi Khi's**, tel. 21548, between Ayodya and Nirwana, serves fresh lobster or crab with a choice of seven sauces, grilled fish steak (Rp7500), sweet-and-sour snapper (Rp4000), and a special Thai soup (Rp4000). Main dishes are around Rp6000; free 30-minute dance performance in the evenings. A few rooms in the back rent for Rp12,500-15,000. Open-air **Banyualit Restaurant** specializes in seafood, Indonesian dishes with a Chinese accent, and curries. It's one of the best restaurants in Lovina; even the *bupati* eat here. Complete menu, Western prices (around Rp15,000 per person). For excellent Balinese fish, try **Spunky's Cafe** in Banyualit.

Temukus

Temukus offers a convenient home base if you're touring the Banjar area. **Pondok Wisata Ayu Bar and Restaurant**, tel. (0362) 21338, has five rooms for Rp15,000 s or d plus 10% tax and service. There's not much shade, so it can get quite hot. A better option is **Agus Homestay** across the road, renting nice rooms with fans for Rp10,000 s, Rp15,000 d. Ten-room **Samudra Beach Cottages and Restaurant** is set out of the way one-half km west of Aditya on the road to Gilimanuk. Rates are Rp25,000-Rp30,000 for air-conditioned rooms with hot water. A little dreary. Best of the lot is **Krisna Beach Inn** on Jl. Seririt about 13 km west of Singaraja, with eight clean rooms (Rp10,000 s, Rp18,000 d) in a U-shaped compound facing the ocean. Krisna's has an open-air restaurant pavilion (open 0700-2200) serving fresh seafood. Special features include laundry service, swimming out front on a nice private beach, and a splendid coral reef just off shore.

From Lovina, take a *bemo* (Rp500, one km) to Temukus or walk it in about 30 minutes from the bridge in Kaliasem. At the 14.5 km mark, turn up the dirt road and you'll see a sign for **Air Terjun Singsing** ("Daybreak Waterfalls"). It's about a 500 meter walk, with good eating stalls along the way. Ask for directions to the 12-meter-high falls, where you can swim in the pool below while cool, fresh water cascades over you. In the dry season, you might find that farmers have blocked the falls to divert the water. There's a bigger, more isolated waterfall (Singsing Dua) up the path leading east; a third falls lies off the road from Singaraja to Anturan. Look for the *ojek* drivers waiting at the head of a steep road—for Rp1000, they'll take you up to the falls.

BANJAR AND VICINITY

Banjar is the starting point for sightseeing in the area. It consists of two villages, one a Muslim community, the other an authentic fishing village. Head north at the intersection of Jl. Seririt and the road to Banjar. Banjar-on-the-sea is an authentic fishing village (pop. 50) with no tourists, no hotels, no sellers. Ask to share some fishermen's food with the villagers. Along this coast there are no plastic bottles in the water, which makes for superior snorkeling.

Buddhist Monastery
Go first to Banjar village, about 18 km west of Singaraja on the highway to Seririt. From the highway where the *bemo* lets you off, walk two km; then, at the intersection just before Banjar Tega's market, turn left up the paved road. Climb another two km to the hilltop monastery. Or take a *honda ojek* (Rp2000) all the way up the steep hill from the Banjar turnoff. Wear long pants or a *sarung* as you must arrive respectfully dressed. *Sarung* rent for Rp500. Entering the *vihara,* sign the guestbook, and give a donation.

This storybook monastery, also known as Brahma Vihara Asrama, has a gleaming orange roof, Sukothai-style gold leaf Buddha images,

raksasa door guardians, stupa with Buddha eyes, and exuberant woodcarvings—a dazzling mix of Balinese Hindu and Buddhist components. Opened in 1970, it's the only Buddhist monastery on Bali. Tibet's Dalai Lama paid a visit in 1982, and Bali's Chinese make regular pilgrimages to this peaceful ashram. Severely damaged in the July 1976 earthquake, it has since been completely restored.

The Theravadic *vipashana* breathing technique is practiced here, the aim being to produce clear comprehension and mindfulness. The resident *bhikku* (Buddhist teacher) will guide you on your way to equanimity. The *bhikku* is only here May-June, Aug.-Sept., and Dec.-January. Instruction in English is available only in September and April. All are welcome, but anyone wanting to visit overnight should write first. Quite comfortable, with plenty of good vegetarian food.

Note the panels depicting Buddha fables, a temple bell from Thailand, and a specimen of the *bo* tree of enlightenment. A number of books on Buddhism are for sale. The hall at the bottom is for prayer, the top building is meant for meditation. Unsurpassed views over the north coast.

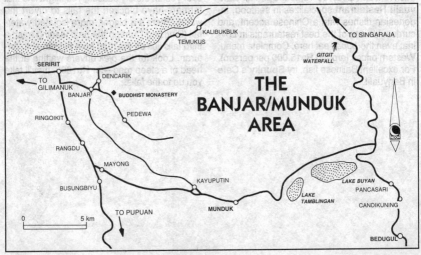

THE BANJAR/MUNDUK AREA

© MOON PUBLICATIONS, INC.

The road continues past the monastery and up the mountain to the village of Pedawa. Walk from the monastery to the *air panas* on a small path in just 10 minutes.

Air Panas
A hot spring lies only 10 minutes away from the monastery (if you take the shortcut). Or drive six km east of Lovina on Jl. Seririt, take a left and travel two km to Banjar Tega's market, then it's a two km farther uphill. Motorcycle *ojek* drivers or *dokar* wait at this turnoff to Banjar to give you a lift and take you back to the main road, Rp1500 each way. Fifty meters on the left after the market, look for the Air Panas 1 Km sign and follow the forested road to the end. After cycling up the hill, the hot water will be a great relief. Arriving, it costs Rp200 to park and Rp450 entrance (Rp200 child), but you can swim all day.

Surrounded by jungle and luxurious gardens, this is the perfect setting for a day's loafing. Lay back in one big lovingly warm pool or another smaller pool of green-yellow sulphur water, which pours out of pipes from the hill above. When you get too hot, take a dip in the river. Neat and clean toilets, showers, and changing rooms available.

Overlooking the pool is a fairly reasonably priced restaurant with a full Indonesian/West-ern menu (*sop ayam* Rp2000, beef *sate* Rp4000, *gado-gado* Rp1500), a cool and re-laxing place to sit, read, or write. Two *warung makan* serving up *nasi campur* (Rp500), snacks, fruit, cakes, and *es campur*, as well as about 10 souvenir shops with very aggressive, hungry sellers peddling Kuta-style garments, are up on the road.

Open 0700-1900, the whole complex is tidy and well-maintained. No nude bathing but you may use shampoo and soap. The pools could be peaceful or they could be crowded with a busload of Japanese tourists. Nevertheless, this beautiful spot makes a worthwhile morning or af-ternoon outing. One hundred meters upstream is another, smaller *air panas*.

Pedawa
From the Buddhist monastery in Banjar Tega, it's a seven-km hike north to Pedawa. Pedawa is a quiet, friendly town. Strike up a conversation with one of the shop owners. At Pedawa's T-junction, turn west, go past the public *mandi*, and stay on this sealed road for four km to Banyuseri through a country of peanuts, corn, and fruit gardens. From Banyuseri walk down to Banjar on the coast. In all, it's 13 km from Pedawa to Banjar on this route. If heading east from Pedawa, the good road ends here.

WESTERN BULELENG

From Lovina, travel the road west toward Gili-manuk through a relatively arid landscape of coconut groves and grape orchards. The ad-ministrative center of Buleleng Barat is the small market town of Seririt, 22 km west of Singaraja. At Seririt, turn inland for the road to Denpasar via Pupuan.

The Pupuan Area
Down the western side of the mountains just north of Pupuan are a few coffee growing vil-lages. Not many visitors arrive here; the chil-dren will shy away from you at first. The very generous and warm people will show you around the plantation and processing plant and offer you *kopi Bali*. Farther down the mountain are some of the island's most spectacular rice terraces. These works of art make incredible viewing around sunset.

Seririt
Twelve km west of Kalibukbuk. Stay at **Hotel Singasari** on Jl. Gajah Mada, tel. (0362) 111, past the bridge in the west end of town. Rates are Rp5000 s to Rp20,000 for a/c double. Check out shops and food stations just north of the *bemo* stop. A good starting point is **Sederhana** on Jl. Surapati near the mosque. From Seririt, take a *bemo* toward Pupuan but get off at May-ong, about 10 km southeast. From Mayong, head east toward Kayuputih; from there you can walk back to Banjar or continue on to Munduk. In Munduk, Pan Wicarna creates *gong besar* and complete *gamelan* sets in a simple foundry next to his house.

From Munduk a track skirts the crater rim with superb views over Tamblingan and Buyan lakes. This small but asphalted road finally joins the Singaraja-Denpasar road north of the Bali Handara Country Club, approximately 20 km south of Singaraja and 10 km north of Lake Bratan. In the rainy season the road from Munduk to the main north-south road may be impassable.

Celukanbawang

Just off the main coastal road 40 km west of Singaraja, this port receives timber and cement from Kalimantan and Java; here you could get lucky and catch Bugis schooners trading between Bali and Kalimantan. The port is also used by the oil company ARBN as a supply base for its offshore drilling explorations. In Celukanbawang, stay, eat, drink, and watch movies at **Drupadi Indah Hotel and Restaurant.** Lodging costs Rp10,000 d, or Rp13,000 d for larger rooms with bigger beds. *Mandi* inside both classes of rooms. Another okay place to eat is **Depot Muslim Abdullah** in the village.

Tanjung Gondol

About 35 km east of Gilimanuk just before the poor fishing village of Gondol. With rows of *jukung* and surrounded by a coconut plantation, this part of the coast is idyllic and peaceful, with no tourists and no facilities but plenty of good swimming and snorkeling. The best post for viewing the extremely rare Bali mynah (or Bali starling) is at Teluk Kelor near Grokgak.

Pulaki

Pura Agung Pulaki, a large, dramatic temple only 25 meters from the sea, is situated 48 km west of Singaraja and 30 km west of Seririt near the grape-growing village of Banyupoh. Cliffs tower behind the temple, surrounded by jungle and overrun by hordes of aggressive simians. Considered sacred, the monkeys are well-fed by locals but always eager for tourist handouts.

This important temple commemorates the arrival of the Javanese saint-priest Nirantha to Bali in the 16th century. It was completely restored with black stone gates and terraces in 1983 in a ceremony presided over by the governor of Bali and the *bupati* of Buleleng. *Pedanda* fanned out all over Java and Lombok to obtain holy water for use in the ceremony.

Legend has it a great village exists here, invisible but for its temple. It is said that when Nirantha lived in Gelgel he was forced to hide his daughter lest she be abducted by the king. He eventually brought her to this remote place, rendering it invisible to keep her safe. To this day, the people who occupy the invisible village are known as *gamang* and are said to wander the countryside.

Time your arrival for the sunset at beautiful Pantai Gondol, which offers clean white sand, coral reefs, and above-average snorkeling. There's another smaller, monkey-infested temple one-half km west of Pura Pulaki where a tunnel has been cut through large rocks hanging over the road.

One km past Pulaki and 500 meters off the road is an *air panas*. A more famous hot springs, known for the medicinal qualities of its mineral waters, is at Banyuwedang (entrance Rp450 adults, Rp250 children) farther west of Pulaki. It's 900 meters off the highway just before the entrance to the Bali Barat National Park.

In a beautiful setting against a mountain, only two km from Banyupoh at the end of a pretty country road, is Pura Melanting. Dedicated to the god of prosperity, this temple with its huge and ornately carved *candi bentar* is set impressively against a mountain. Zero tourists visit this site.

Pemuteran

One of the most idyllic hotels on Bali is **Pondok Sari** in Pemuteran two km west of Pulaki. This charming accommodation charges Rp30,000 s or d for eight very nice clean rooms with electricity. The small restaurant with little outdoor tables has good food; try one of the nightly specials for Rp5000. Ten percent service and tax charged for both rooms and meals. The hotel is located on a scenic cove, and a tidy and quite scenic beach is only 150 meters away, offering some of the island's best snorkeling. An Australian divemaster lives nearby; several nights a week he screens a video of the superlative dive spots on Bali. Fifteen minutes are dedicated to the reefs in front of Pondok Sari. Rent a snorkeling mask and fins for Rp15,000 for five hours.

Pemuteran is 15 km east of Labuhan Lalang and about 50 km west of Lovina. Pondok Sari is 500 meters from the main road; see the sign. There's a homestay next door with similar prices. Visit one of the *warung makan* selling snacks, fruit, and drinks.

Beware of the Muslim mosque about 800 meters distant which blasts early morning prayers. Bring earplugs.

Jayaprana's Gravesite

Near Labuhan Lalang is the sacred grave of the folk hero Jayaprana, the foster son of the treacherous king Anak Agung Gde Murka. In the 17th century, the king sent Jayaprana to Teluk Terima under the pretext of investigating wrecked ships plundered by pirates. His real motive was to steal Jayaprana's wife Layon Sari. During this royal mission, Jayaprana was ambushed and killed by the king's minister. Hearing the news, Layon Sari stabbed herself to death. The king then went insane, ran amok, and was killed by his subjects.

Jayaprana was finally given a proper cremation in 1949, an event accompanied by many strange, unexplained apparitions. The folk hero's grave (Rp400 admission), with figures of the betrayed Brahman and his bride behind glass, is a steep 10-minute climb from the south side of the road nearly opposite Labuhan Lalang. About halfway up the stone stairway are splendid views of the old volcanos of eastern Java, Gilimanuk Bay, and Pulau Menjangan.

BALI BARAT NATIONAL PARK

The Land

The 76,312-hectare Taman Nasional Bali Barat, with its complex of habitats including forests and coral-fringed islands, is the real wild side of Bali. Since Bali is such a densely populated, intensively cultivated island, very little of Bali's forests are left. To preserve a portion of the island as a wilderness zone and resource for forest products, Bali Barat National Park was named as one of Indonesia's ten national parks in 1984. The park today encompasses an amazing 10% of Bali's total land area.

The park is managed by the Indonesian Forestry Service (PHPA), which limits and controls public access. Bali Barat National Park was initially established by the Dutch in 1941 to protect the endemic white starling of Bali (*Loucospar rothschildi*), and the last of the island's wild *banteng*. The Balinese subspecies of the Asian tiger may also have roamed the area, but by 1941 its existence was doubtful. Despite rumors to the contrary, the last animal was probably shot in the 1930s.

Though not nearly as rugged as the areas surrounding the higher mountains of eastern Bali, primary monsoon forests are found along the watershed on the southern slopes of the mountains Sangiang, Merbuk, Musi, and Patas.

The park's southern sector is watered by clear streams and traversed by footpaths that offer steep but relatively easy walking through forested hills. The park's northern sector is much drier than the south.

On the way to the park from the east, immediately before the park entrance on the right, is Banyuwedang hot springs, believed to possess curative powers. Entrance Rp450, children Rp250, insurance Rp50. From the highway walk or drive 900 meters to the gate, pay, then walk 100 meters to the springs.

Fauna

The park offers *rusa* deer, *kancil*, barking deer, long-tailed macaques, civets, monkeys, wild boars, and perhaps 30 or so *banteng*—living ancestors of today's deer-like Balinese cattle. The park's profuse and beautiful birdlife includes the endangered Bali starling (popularly known as *jalak bali*) and sea and shore birds, the most conspicuous being brown boobies and lesser frigate birds. Two species of terns nest in large numbers on a sandy cay at the entrance of Teluk Lumpur ("Mud Bay"), while the boobies and frigates roost on Pulau Burung farther east.

An extremely rare species, the Bali starling averages 23 cm long and has black wingtips and brilliant blue rings around its eyes. The Bali starling lives in groups of two or three in the acacia scrub on the north coast of Cape Prapat Agung. To see live specimens, visit the Bali Starling Recovery Project. Get a *bemo* (Rp500 each way) from Labuhan Lalang to Sumberlampok, then turn right and walk two km to the Recovery Project at Tegal Bunder. Take off your shoes and socks, walk down a hall, and look through the tiny windows of the aviary. The birds live in the trees and are fed from big buckets of bugs. There are only nine birds here and perhaps 100 more in the jungle. Entrance fee is Rp2000.

More like a forest than a jungle, the park offers exceptional walking and first-class panoramas. Day-trips can be arranged by the PHPA office in Labuhan Lalang. Part of the walk is crosscountry with no trails. At times you have to crawl through undergrowth and use paths frequented by wild ox and deer. Birds are everywhere—incredible surround sound.

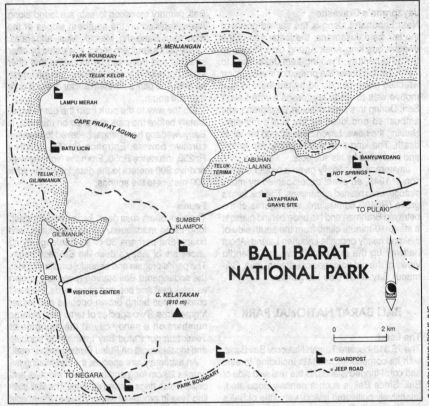

An interesting walk is the 25-km-long track along the coast of Cape Prapat Agung. This cape is cut off from the rest of the reserve by the main Singaraja-Gilimanuk road, as well as by settlements and coconut, teak, and eucalyptus plantations. Into this wilderness bring lots of water, as it can get extremely hot.

Information And Permits
The best info on hiking and guides comes from the Park Headquarters in Cekik, just three km south of Gilimanuk at the junction of the road from Singaraja with the road from Denpasar. Open Mon.-Thurs. 0800-1400, Friday 0800-1100, and Saturday 0800-1200. The PHPA maintains a branch office at Labuhan Lalang with a useful relief map of the park.

You must have a permit and be accompanied by a guide (Rp15,000 per day) to enter the reserve. Permits and guides are available free at the park headquarters in Cekik and the ranger station at Labuhan Lalang, as well as at the Department of Forestry (PHPH) office in Denpasar (Jl. Suwung 40, P.O. Box 320). You don't need a permit to drive through the park from Singaraja to Gilimanuk.

A typical walk lasts from 1000 to 1500. Dress like your guide: jeans and long sleeves for protections from thorns and snags. Take a lunch and sit quietly in the forest to hear the symphony.

Accommodations And Food
Undoubtedly the best place to stay is Pondok Sari just before Pulaki to the east, or in Gilimanuk.

There are no accommodations in the park itself. You can camp in designated campgrounds east of Cekik. Be sure to let the rangers know you plan to stay overnight. For overnights, bring a sleeping bag, mosquito net, and all food and beverages. You can rent camping equipment from the park forestry office at Labuhan Lalang.

In the middle of the complex at Labuhan Lalang, between the Taman Nasional Bali Barat offices and the sea, are two open-air restaurants catering to tourists. Very rustic, with lots of mosquitos and humidity. Cold beer served out of ice chests.

The Marine Reserve

The 6,600-hectare marine reserve includes the shores of the mountainous outcrop of land between Teluk Terima and Gilimanuk, and several sanctuary islands in the bay near Gilimanuk, but is centered primarily on Pulau Menjangan and the excellent coral reefs surrounding it. Because it's a national park, both the number of boats and number of passengers visiting the island are controlled. A PHPA officer accompanies you on the boat; request one who speaks English.

Coral reefs are also found off the mainland. Since these waters are protected, the snorkeling is superb. Go early in the morning when the water is clearest. Just drift along the coral wall; unbelievable. This dive site is particularly suited for beginning and intermediate divers.

It costs Rp42,000 for a four-hour snorkeling trip to Pulau Menjangan (maximum 10 people). Prices are fixed, and one person costs the same as ten. From the jetty at Labuhan Lalang take one of the good-sized boats waiting for passengers. The passage takes about 30 minutes. You can rent snorkeling equipment from the PHPA office in Labuhan Lalang (Rp6000 per set), or hire in Lovina or Kuta before you go.

The sanctuary island of Pulau Menjangan, off the northwest coast at the western entrance to Teluk Terima received its name ("Deer Island") from the wild Java deer that graze upon its open savannahs. One of Bali's premier scuba diving locales, these reefs are frequented by species of fish of every size, shape, and color.

There's a great variety of underwater terrain, for the most part about two meters below the surface extending 100-150 meters offshore, with no dangerous currents or wind-generated waves to contend with. The soft coral walls around the island are almost vertical and extend to a depth of 35-60 meters. The unusually rugged surface of the reef is pockmarked with caves, grottoes, fissures, and hollows, and covered with giant gorgonians and barrel sponges. At 25-50 meters the visibility is crystal clear.

The spectacular 120-meter dropoffs and caves off Pulau Menjangan's south side are only surpassed by the particularly fine species of coral off its northern shores. Menjangan's northwestern end is the site of an old shipwreck near a small pier and PHPA guardpost about 75 meters from shore. The 25-meter-long wreck lies on a sandy slope from seven meters to 45 meters underwater.

There's a break in the wall on the east side; this is where all the boats come in. You'll find the fish are quite cheeky, as the guides feed them regularly with leftover rice. Boats usually visit the same sites day after day; permanent mooring buoys are in place to prevent anchor damage to the coral. Guides allow sightseers to disembark so they can walk the short nature trail on the island and view the plantlife and wild deer. An onshore shelter for divers is located on Pulau Menjangan's western end, but spending the night on the island isn't allowed. Sections of the island are fringed with mangroves.

Everyone in these waters should beware of tiny stinging jellyfish. You could end up with welts all over your torso.

JEMBRANA REGENCY

The Balinese call this rugged, thinly populated region Pulaki, former site of a lost invisible city that one day sank beneath the sea. Except for a strip of coast, most of the district's 841,800-square-km are mountainous, with impenetrable highlands said to harbor strange wild animals. The wilderness area of Bali Barat National Park—with its jungle fowl, boar, wild deer, Javan buffalo, and monkeys—falls almost wholly within Jembrana Regency. So rugged are the lonely mountain forests of Jembrana that the villages are spread far apart. West of Pulukan no roads head north across the island.

Jembrana is the most heavily Javanized regency of Bali. Settlements with typical Javanese names like Palarejo are common in the area; in some instances the people have adopted Balinese *subak*-style irrigation practices. In a subtle area around Negara you can see where Java really starts. You begin to notice more mosques, *peci, nasi padang* restaurants, Javanese-style wooden *cikar* carts pulled by plodding water buffalo. The Balinese culture recedes to the east, almost as if the Balinese had relin-

quished this swath of island to the Javanese. Jembrana is also home to Bali's strongest and most populous Christian communities.

Jembrana is the least populated regency of Bali. The population today is around 215,000, scattered throughout 51 villages, mostly situated along the main Denpasar-Gilimanuk coastal artery. Four of five inhabitants earn income from farming or fishing. Drier and not as agriculturally rich as the rest of the island, revenues derive for the most part from rice fields, coconut plantations along the coastal strip, coffee plantations in the highlands near the border of Tabanan, and vanilla, cocoa, and cloves. One of the main fishing ports of Bali is Pengambengan, 10 km southwest of Negara.

Jembrana is also the least visited part of Bali. Its isolation only came to an end with the Gilimanuk-Ketapang ferry service begun by two enterprising Germans in the 1930s. Today, most tourists speed through the region on buses, racing along the 134-km-long road from Denpasar to Gilimanuk. All Jembrana's traveler's hotels are located in Negara, Medewe, or the ferry ter-

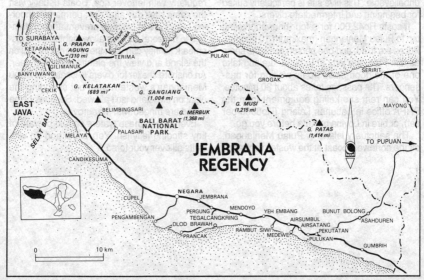

minal of Gilimanuk. Not even rudimentary English is widely spoken. Ample *bemo* and minibuses service the district; *dokar* and *ojek* are available in the smaller towns and villages.

Other than exciting bull races held in the vicinity of Negara, there's a dearth of historic sights and cultural performances. The regency does offer utterly unique dance and *gamelan* forms, isolated sea temples, and a 71-km-long stretch of highway paralleling a coast lined with rocky, sandy beaches pounded by high surf.

HISTORY

The present channel between eastern Java and Bali's northwestern tip was exposed as dry land during the Pleistocene epoch about 20,000 years ago. This enabled settlement by early human beings; Jembrana, in fact, was the first place people lived on Bali. During WW II, pottery fragments, basalt pebble-tools, and Neolithic adzes were found at Cekik, south of Gilimanuk. The remains of a burial site were also discovered.

A Balinese chronicle records that the region came under the jurisdiction of the Gelgel dynasty in the 15th century. Two princes were sent by the king to civilize the wild western wilderness, establishing separate courts near present-day Gilimanuk and Negara. The princes vied with each other over who could develop the most prosperous kingdom, their rivalry eventually erupting into a full civil war which destroyed both courts. Jembrana then slipped again into anonymity until 1803, when another court developed in present-day Negara. When the Dutch subjugated Buleleng Regency to the north in 1849, they assumed control of Jembrana.

Neither wealthy nor powerful, Jembrana never played an important role in Balinese politics. Because of its close proximity to Java, Jembrana was visited early by Chinese, Javanese, and Buginese traders who leased land from the local lords for planting cash crops. The Dutch and other Europeans established huge plantations of cotton, cacao, coconuts, and tobacco in the regency as early as 1860. Coffee land grants were still awarded to Chinese merchant princes in the late 19th century. Sparsely populated Jembrana has also been settled by transmigrants from Java and other parts of Bali, particularly after the devastating eruption of Gunung Agung in 1963.

ARTS AND CRAFTS

The most famous painter in the regency is I Gusti Putu Windya Anaya, who can be found in his home-studio in the village of Yeh Embang. Jembrana's traditional handloom weaving centers are Sangkaragung and Dauh Waru, producing *songket* and *endek* for formal occasions. The best woodcarvers and sculptors work in Pendem village near Negara. Look for silverware and gold jewelry in Dauh Waru. Bamboo artifacts such as lamp covers, bags, and baskets are the specialty of Pulukan near Melaya in western Jembrana, while *lontar* palm leaf handicrafts are produced in Gilimanuk. To see a traditional blacksmith at work, visit the village of Batu Agung.

DANCE AND MUSIC

The intriguing and sonorous *gamelan jegog* ensemble of Jembrana, created by Kiyang Gelinduh in 1912, consists of 14 instruments made of giant bamboo tubes that play a reverberating, low-pitch melody. Likened to the sound of deep, roaring thunder, these instruments formerly functioned as a means of calling people for cooperative village work. So large are these natural resonating tubes, the musicians must sit on top, striking the swaying bamboo beneath them with heavy mallets. The *gamelan jegog* accompanies Jembrana's traditional dances.

It's best to hear the orchestra during a village celebration, or you can commission a performance for around Rp175,000 by contacting Ida Bagus Raka Negara in Tegalcangkring, a village that traditionally produces the finest *jegog* players and instrument makers. Also check at the Office of Education and Culture in Negara for further information.

The largest version of *jegog* is the *jegog mebarung,* in which two *gamelan* compete with one another, accompanied by *kendang, rebana, kecak* and *tawa tawa.* Sets of *jegog* instruments are displayed both at the Institute of Arts and Dance (tel. 72361) on Jl. Nusa Indah in Abiankapas near Denpasar, and at Sangkar Agung, a private museum three km east of Negara near the village of Pangintukadaya. The Grand Hyatt Hotel of Nusa Dua also features *gamelan jegog.*

Balinese trance dance

S. MOONEY

Other musical forms in Jembrana show distinct folk influences from Java and Madura. Examples include the daring *cabang* (knife dance), the *jegog* dance, and *pencak silat*. *Sewa gati* is a "seated opera," found in the village of Berangbang five km north of Negara. The *leko* from Pendem village features two female dancers dressed in classical *legong* garments. *Kendang mebarung* is a duel between two one-meter-wide drums (*kendang*) accompanied by a set of *angklung*. *Genggong*, from Penyaringin village, emulates the sound of frogs. The resonant *bumbung gebyog* employs lengths of bamboo in varying pitches, playing harmonious interlocking rhythms. It accompanies such dance-dramas as Goak Ngajang Sebun ("Crow Building its Nest"). Derived from the pounding of newly harvested *padi*, it's perhaps the only music on Bali created by women.

BULL RACES

Negara is famous for its thrilling water buffalo races (*mekepung*), introduced by Madurese migrants. The races take place on erratic four-km-long tracks outside Negara, beginning about 0600 before the heat makes the big bulls sluggish. Mostly locals attend this festive event—there's lots of rooting and cheering, and the betting is frantic. It's possible to attend rehearsals, trials, and competitions, and even to commission a bull race.

Only the island's handsomest, sleekest water buffalos are chosen to compete. Teams are di-

vided into two clubs, the Eastern Division (east of the Ijo Gading River) and the Western Division (west of the river). Organized by the regional government, trials are usually held the second and third Sundays in September and October to celebrate the end of the rice harvest. Biannual championship races—The Bupati's Cup and The Governor's Cup—take place on the Sunday before Indonesia's Independence Day on 17 August, and again every other Sunday each September and October. Dates and places are different each year, so obtain current info from Negara's Department of Tourism on Jl. Surapati behind *kantor bupati*.

After teams parade before the crowd of spectators, their ornaments are stripped off and the beasts teamed with their brightly clad jockeys. Each pair of bulls pulls a small two-wheeled cart manned by a precariously balanced jockey. To gain speed, the jockeys twist the bulls' tails and lash their backs with whips. Entrants are judged not only for speed, but are also awarded points for strength, color, and style. These heavy, awkward-looking, normally docile animals can reach speeds of up to 80 kph. The winning bulls are used for stud.

A variation of the *mekepung* is the *megembeng*, in which a pair of bulls is harnessed together and decorated with elaborate ornaments. Huge wooden bells are hung around their necks, making a distinctive sound as the bulls race across the field dragging the colorfully dressed jockeys behind.

THE MELAYA AREA

Belimbingsari And Palasari

For many years after conquering southern Bali in 1908, officials of the Netherlands East Indies attempted to bar Christian missionary activity on Bali. The Dutch wanted no interference in the well-integrated religious life of the Balinese, who oftentimes opposed—sometimes violently—Christian proselytizing. But in the 1930s the government relaxed its hands-off policy.

With the tacit consent of the Dutch Resident, a Chinese missionary named Tsang was sent to Bali in 1929 by the American Christian and Missionary Alliance to work among the Balinese Chinese. Tsang soon began to win converts, first among the Balinese wives of the Chinese, then among Balinese of the lower castes. He promised the Balinese freedom from taxes and corvée work gangs if they converted. By the mid-1930s, several hundred converts had been exiled from their own villages. The swelling numbers of new Christians soon caused unemployment and housing problems in Denpasar.

Meanwhile back in Holland, missionary groups protested that an American fundamentalist church had been allowed to establish itself on Balinese soil. Under pressure, the Resident expelled Tsang and allowed Netherlands-based Protestant and Catholic churches access to Bali. The 1930s were a period of worldwide economic recession and a time of unrest on Bali. The number of converts steadily increased throughout the thirties. In 1939, to relieve the tensions between Christians and Hindu Balinese, Christian agricultural communities were constructed in a part of Bali nobody wanted—the sparsely populated, malarial swamps of western Bali, 25 km northwest of Negara.

Belimbingsari (pop. 1,900), a big Protestant community, was hacked out of the jungle in the form of a cross in 1939. The Belimbingsari church features a high, sweeping roof with three distinct tiers representing the island's mountains. Christian congregations from all over Bali consider this striking church with its graceful Balinese lines their "Navel Church." Belimbingsari is one of the best kept villages on Bali, the rice production one of the highest in Indonesia. The Catholic community of Palasari (pop. 1,700), three km to the

southeast, has the largest Catholic church in eastern Indonesia, with a parish of over 700.

The Palasari Dam

Located in a mountainous area in the village of Palarejo near Ekasari, 26 km northwest of Negara, this dam was built to prevent floods, provide a source of water for irrigation, and as a fish breeding pond and place of recreation. The high elevation assures breezes and cool temperatures. *Prahu* for fishing and paddling about for rent.

GILIMANUK

This ferry port at Bali's westernmost tip links Bali with East Java across a narrow strait, Selat Bali. Much of Bali's imports and exports, and most of its domestic tourists, pass through this point. Except as an around-the-clock ferry terminus, Gilimanuk has little to offer tourists, who usually alight the ferry or landing barges from Java and shoot straight through to Denpasar or Lovina. But with its basic no-frills services and amenities, Gilimanuk is a friendly little town for stopovers, for resting up.

History

The strait that separates Java and Bali, less than three km wide and only 60 meters in depth, is said to have been formed by some mythical king who, hoping to excommunicate his son, gouged a line with his finger along the ground. The earth parted and the waters of the Indian Ocean and the Java Sea rushed in, separating Bali from Java.

It was an easy matter for Neolithic humans hunting in the primeval wilderness of East Java to cross this narrow strait. During WW II, stone adzes and pottery fragments were discovered just two km south of Gilimanuk at Cekik. Over time, about 100 burial places were excavated; Bali's earliest human settlement discovered to date. See these Neolithic artifacts in the Bali Museum in Denpasar.

Both Gilimanuk and Negara, the main towns in the regency, show a greater influence from Islamic Java than other parts of Bali. In fact, it was from Java that Balinese revolutionaries derived their material and ideological sustenance in their fight to oust the Dutch. In Cekik is a war memorial commemorating landing operations by the Indonesian army, navy, and police on Bali from April to July 1946. Boarding a large number of outrigger canoes under cover of darkness, Indonesian troops set off from Banyuwangi on East Java and landed at three points—Melaya, Candikesuma, and Cupel—along Bali's southwest coast. The republic's first sea conflict took place during these operations, and fierce land battles erupted as the Indonesians came ashore. Many lost their lives. The survivors fled to the hills, where they joined units from earlier landings and engaged in guerrilla warfare.

Accommodations
There are plenty of places to stay. Cheapest are the **Kartika Candra** and **Homestay Gili Sari** (Rp8000 pp, no breakfast), both on the main street in the east side of town across from a mosque loudspeaker. Coming from Singaraja, just before town near the National Park Headquarters in Cekik, is **Mangarana's Accommodation** for Rp15,000 s or d. The plumbing may not work. Gilimanuk's best hotel, only 500 meters from the ferry, is the **Nusantara Dua,** which faces a quiet beach with a lovely view of the mountains of Taman Nasional Bali Barat across an inlet. Attractive grounds with rooms go for Rp10,000 s to Rp20,000, depending on the size of the room and the bed. There's also a row of dark, depressing rooms with squat toilets for a budget price of Rp8000 (no breakfast). Bungalows farther down the beach run Rp25,000 s or d. No breakfast. More central but noisier **Penginapan Putra Sesana,** on the road toward Denpasar, has 11 small, tight rooms for Rp10,000 s, Rp15,000 d. No fan, small Indo-style toilets. The restaurant serves especially good *ayam kecap* (Rp2500).

Food
There's a long row of *warung* and *rumah makan* by the ferry terminal where you can also buy fresh seasonal fruit. Several *nasi padang* restaurants are right across from the terminal; a good

one is **Meriah.** The **Bakungan** on Jl. Gilimanuk, a half km down from the Putra Sesana, is the town's best restaurant. Order from the English menu if you can't read Indonesian. Particularly good is the *ayam kecap* (Rp2500).

Transportation
Take *dokar* or one of the Hondas clustering around the terminal to anywhere in town for Rp500-Rp1000, or rent a motorcycle for Rp4000 per hour. From Gilimanuk's *bemo* station, *bemo* head out regularly to Denpasar until 2200 (Rp3000, two hours, 134 km). *Bemo* also travel to Singaraja via Lovina until around 1800 (Rp2500). Less crowded minibuses travel to Singaraja/Lovina for Rp3000 or to Denpasar's Ubung for Rp3500.

Crossing from Gilimanuk over the Bali Strait to Ketapang on the Java side takes only 30 minutes and costs Rp600 adult, Rp400 children. Ferries depart every 15-20 minutes during the day and about every 30 minutes at night. Watch for pickpockets. Buses to Surabaya (Rp2500, five hours) wait for passengers on the Java side. If there's room, you can also board one on the Gilimanuk side. Or hitch (politely) from the lorry drivers or domestic tourists driving their own cars. Another ferry terminal is 2.5 km before the main ferry terminal if you're coming into town from the Denpasar side; motorcyclists will take you to the bus station (Rp500).

The Northern Route
Head up Bali's north coast road, visiting some of the island's most serene beach accommodations. The road between Gilimanuk and Singaraja is also very scenic bicycling country, mostly flat with only a couple of hills. Not as much traffic as on the Gilimanuk-Denpasar road.

The lagoons and extensive mangrove swamps north of Gilimanuk feature an unusual variety of wildlife. Pulau Menjangan, off Bali's northwest coast, is famous for its snorkeling and scuba diving. This marine reserve is part of the Bali Barat National Park, the last wilderness area on Bali. Access to the park is easiest from Labuhan Lalang, about 25 km northeast of Gilimanuk. Three km south of Gilimanuk in Cekik is the park headquarters.

NEGARA

Since 1803 Negara has been the capital and main town of Jembrana Regency, 33 km southeast of Gilimanuk. During the revolution, Negara's *raja-puri* was a center of fierce republicanism. Lately, Negara has been spiffed up with a new civic center, a big Honda dealership, and new monuments as centerpieces to new roundabouts. Yet, Negara hasn't lost its market town charm. It's perhaps best known for the *mekepung* between July and October, a sport introduced by Madurese agricultural migrants.

Take a *bemo* from Tabanan (Rp1200) or Denpasar's Ubung station (Rp1500) to travel on one of Bali's busiest roads, through rolling paddy fields with mountains on the right and the sea on the left. If you want the journey to go faster, take a night bus. The downtown consists of two main parallel one-way streets. Along the four-lane bypass road Jl. Surapati in the north are the government buildings and the telephone office. The southern street, Jl. Ngurah Rai, is home to a gas station, bus station, post office, market, and shophouses. Negara is cheap. While a coffee in Kuta costs Rp1500, here it's only Rp300.

Accommodations

Decrepit-looking **Hotel Ana** is a Javanese-style business hotel with 23 budget rooms for Rp4000 s, Rp6000 d, or Rp6000-8000 s with *mandi*. It's set in from the main street at Jl. Ngurah Rai 75, tel. (0365) 41063. No restaurant, and no fan (could be muggy), but very central. Mix with the Indonesians. Cute, garish **Hotel Tis** lies downtown on Jl. Srikandi, tel. 41034, by the river. Nine rooms go for Rp10,000 d, Rp15,000 t; Rp25,000 for rooms on top. Attached is a restaurant serving Javanese-style food like *ayam goreng*. **Losmen Intaran**, Jl. Ngurah Rai 73, tel. 41073, is another inexpensive downtown hotel. At Jl. Ngurah Rai 107, tel. 41161, is Negara's best accommodation, **Hotel Wira Pada,** behind the restaurant of the same name. The tariff is Rp12,500 for quiet back rooms with *mandi*, up to Rp20,000 for front rooms with showers (breakfast included). The hotel's ten spacious rooms with a/c and porch are a pretty good deal. Plenty of parking, moneychanger, secure, above average restaurant, minibus for rent at Rp100,000 per day.

Accommodations Out of Town: The new Bali-style **Penginapan Segara Mandala,** Jl. Sudirman 34, tel. 41839, is opposite the *kantor bupati*. It has three units with two rooms each, equipped with bath and fan. Tariff is Rp7500 s or d. Kind of a lonely, sterile place. About 1.5 km from Negara down the main highway towards Denpasar is a sign pointing to the **Cahaya Matahari Bungalows** in Desa Batuagung. The homestay lies about one km up this country road. Ask one of the guys hanging out on the corner to give you a lift on the back of his motorcycle for Rp600-800, or wait for an infrequent *bemo*. To get back down to the main road, manager I Dewa Ketut Indra will take you on the back of his motorcycle, or you can wait for a *bemo*. Nice view up here 100 meters above sea level. Surrounded by *sawah*, each bungalow has twin beds, Asian toilet, shower, art on the walls, clock, electricity, and porch. The tariff of Rp15,000 s, Rp20,000 d includes breakfast and free tea and coffee served all day. You can order a day's meals for two for Rp30,000; single meal is Rp15,000 for two. Also several small local *warung*. Except for the loud radio, this is a pleasant place run by a nice family. A seven-km walk leads to a waterfall in the hills behind the homestay.

Food

The food served in the *warung* is very Java-oriented. Try one of the many pan-Indonesian *warung* in the bus station. The clean **Wira Pada Restaurant** in Negara, Jl. Ngurah Rai 107, tel. (0365) 161, serves cheap Chinese-style *nasi campur* (Rp1500) and fantastic *cap cai* (Rp2500, but specify if you don't want chicken liver). The *udang goreng* (Rp6000) is among the best on Bali. Try the good grilled fish or chicken (Rp3000-5000), fried prawns (Rp6000), or *es stroop* (Rp500).

A half-km down Jl. Ngurah Rai toward Denpasar is the "100% halal" **Rumah Makan Puas** where you can enjoy classic Javanese entrees such as *nasi plecing, nasi lele, Rawon Jawa, gado-gado,* and *pepes ikan*. Choose from an array of Javanese desserts like *soda gembira* or *es buah*. Standard prices. A smaller Javanese eatery, **Rumah Makan Caterina,** Jl. Pahlawan 17, tel. 41325, specializes in homemade *sambal* and Javanese dishes like *soto ayam* and *nasi rawon*; the *es caterina* is not so great. The foodstalls of the *pasar malam* open up at night around the *bemo* station.

The Padang-style restaurant **Papin** is five km east of town. On the other side of town on the road to Gilimanuk is **Rumah Makan Miranda,** Jl. Gatot Kaca 39, tel. 41195, a real gem with delicious Balinese food. A great *nasi campur* with tea costs only Rp1500.

Services

The tourist office is located within the Pecangakan Civic Centre, Jl. Setia Budhi 1, tel. (0365) 41060. A competent guide who works in this office is Ketut Lanus Sumatra, Jl. Abimanui 15, tel. 41441. The only bank with an authorized moneychanger is **Bank Pembangunan Daerah Bali,** Jl. Srikandi, tel. 41066. For medical attention, go to the **RSU,** Jl. Abimanui 6, tel. 41006; **Poliklinik Kerta Yasa,** Jl. Ngurah Rai 143, tel. 41248; or **Poliklinik Darma Sentana,** Jl. Ngurah Rai 151, tel. 41656. **Apotik Karya Farma** is a big new pharmacy at Jl. Rama 16.

Transportation

By *bemo* it's Rp2000 from Negara to Tabanan, Rp750 to Gilimanuk, Rp2500 to Denpasar. Next door to Penginapan Indra Loka is an office selling bus tickets to Malang, Jakarta, Bandung, and Bogor, as well as Pelni ship tickets on the *Kerinci, Kambuna,* and *Umsini.*

Vicinity Of Negara

Negara's population has a noticeably strong Javanese, Madurese, and Sulawesi element. Muslim Buginese settlers from southern Sulawesi founded the town of Loloan Timur in 1653. Here, Bugis culture is most obvious in the oblong two-level dwellings built on high piles. This architecture is found in no other village on Bali.

Visit the busy fishing port of Pengambengan, 10 km southwest of Negara; sardine canning facilities, prawn-breeding ponds. The secluded beach at Candikesuma, 12 km west of Negara, offers excellent bathing and swimming. Legend says a holy well here, marked by a triangular-shaped monument, was the bathing place of Nirantha's wife. Another beach, Pantai Rening, 10 km west of Negara, features black sand, sea cliffs, and a dramatic view of the mountains of East Java. Swim and windsurf at the beach in the village of Dlod Brawah about four km south of Mendoyo, 11 km east of Negara. The sand is said to be of great benefit to those suffering from rheumatism. A good road to the beach brings you to a parking area, toilet, and *mekepung* arena. Crowded on Sundays and holidays. Up the side of a mountain, 20 km inland from Negara, is a large clove plantation at Asahduren.

MEDEWE AND VICINITY

MEDEWE

Seventy-two km west of Denpasar is the small, peaceful seaside resort of Medewe, offering an excellent sand-and-rock-bottom surfing beach. Formerly this area was a thick forest of thorny trees; the Balinese name for the thorny forest was *alas meduwi.* The forest was cleared and settled in 1912. Today, Medewe gets about 700 visitors a month. Pura Rambut Siwi, six km farther west, is the main tourist site.

Coming from Negara, as you're heading downhill in the eastern edge of the village of Pulukan, turn right just before the bridge and drive or walk down the asphalt road to the turn-around area just before the sea. This headland offers constant, cool sea breezes, a public toilet, fishing *jakung* in the mornings, soft sunsets, and the twinkling lights of Banyuwangi in East Java far in the distance. Brown-sand Pantai Medewe is very quiet with no dogs and few roosters, only the sound of the waves. Up on the main road, catch *bemo* to Negara (Rp1000) or Tabanan (Rp1500).

Surfing

The very rocky, flat shoreline along this coast provides little sand to lie on. The surfing in front of Medewe's beach is known for the length of the ride. Paddle out from Medewe Beach Cottage and try the high, rolling, uninterrupted, left-point break, its peak finishing in the river's mouth. It's easier to get out there in low tide with booties. Or reach the surf via the river to the west—a long paddle. During the full moon, the waves are best at midtide. Lately, Medewe has been popular with Japanese surfers. Another little-known surfing beach is Selabih to the east.

Accommodations

Three accommodations sit at the end of a tarred road. The cheaper one is newly renovated **Nirwana Beach Hotel.** Run by friendly houseboys, everything works—electricity, plumbing, showers, fans. The six upgraded rooms with good mattresses, clean bed linen, and porches cost Rp20,000 s, Rp25,000 d. Pay Rp5000 extra for a fan. Beside the Nirwana is a small *warung* run by I Gede Suyasa where you can order tea, coffee, snacks, *nasi campur,* and drinks. Behind his *warung,* in **Homestay Gede,** Suyasa rents two rooms in raised bamboo bungalows for Rp15,000 s, Rp20,000 d; less in the low season.

Just across the road from the Nirwana is firstclass **Medewe Beach Cottages,** P.O. Box 26, Negara 82217, Bali, tel. (0365) 40029 or 40030, fax 41555; Rp31,500 s, Rp42,000 d for standard units, or Rp115,500 s, Rp126,000 d for ocean view suites with a/c, satellite TV, refrigerator, terrace, private bath, and hot water. Rooms with garden views are Rp84,000 s, Rp95,000 d. Amenities include a pool, welldesigned grounds and gardens, ample parking, bar, and restaurant with fairly high prices—Rp8400 for Indonesian or American breakfasts, Rp21,000 for lunch or dinner (*pisang goreng* Rp2000). All rates subject to 15.5% government tax and service. Major credit cards accepted. Good folks work here. A romantic spot for honeymooners. Every Sunday night there's a *joged bumbung* folk dance in the garden of the Medewe Beach Cottages starting at 2000. Free for guests of all three of Medewe's hotels; just buy drinks and food. Bamboo *gamelan* accompanies this dance.

Food

One can eat cheaply. Boys come around selling lobsters for Rp25,000-Rp30,000 per kilo (two to five lobsters per kilogram, depending on size). Gede will cook them for you in his *warung.* Check out the *warung* on the main road. A Javanese *warung* is on the highway west of the Rambut Siwi sea temple, just up the road from Medewe. The best eating for the money is at Chinese-style **BMC Hotel and Restaurant,** a 10-minute walk along the highway from Medewe Beach. Go toward Denpasar on the main road. It's a little ways up on the left after you cross the bridge. Try the superb *mie kuah ayam* (Rp2500) and *sate.* The BMC Hotel also rents rooms; most are substandard; the few good ones go for Rp25,000 d.

VICINITY OF MEDEWE

Rambut Siwi Temple

On the south side of a deserted stretch of the Gilimanuk-Denpasar highway between the villages of Yeh Embang and Yeh Sumbul is a shrine and several *warung* selling fruit and flowers. Here is the start of the one-km narrow asphalt road to Rambut Siwi Temple. A *pemangku* blesses truck drivers who don't have time to pray at the main temple. At the end of the road is a parking area, garden, toilet, pavilion, and *warung* selling fresh local fruit. At the carved gateway travelers are blessed before proceeding into the red brick and stone temple complex over the beach.

Its name means "Worship of the Hair" in reference to the 16th-century Hindu priest Sanghyang Nirantha. The priest stopped in the village of Yeh Embang in 1546, leaving the symbolic gift of his hair as a gesture of esteem for the devout villagers. View the panorama of rice fields from the pavilion to the north of the complex, walk through the temple, then descend to the long narrow black-sand beach below. East down the beach, take the stairway back up to the small road which leads again out to the main highway.

Special because of its simplicity and natural location, this beautiful clifftop sea temple is shaded by frangipani and *cempaka* trees and hugged on two sides by *sawah.* Except during festivals, it's very peaceful here. The temple anniversary occurs every six months, when worshippers arrive from all over the island to ask blessings for safety and prosperity. Like all temples, Rambut Siwi consists of three principal enclosures. The entrance is guarded by beautifully carved wild boars and *naga*; the structures are of aged red brick and stone. Inside are shrines to Saraswati (symbolized by a goose) and the rice goddess. To the side of the gate to the second courtyard, note the *pedanda* being swallowed by a snake. An impressive *candi bentar* on the southern wall opens onto the cliff with the surf lapping below. Since 1988 the Bali government has been shoring up the more precariously perched buildings threatened by the sea.

Flanking the main temple is **Pura Penataran,** set to the east on the rocks up a winding stone stairway. This is the original temple, believed to be the site where Nirantha first prayed. See small Pura Melanting at the top of another stairway to the west. Dedicated to the goddess of prosperity, Dewi Melanting; merchants often pray at this shrine. Under an overhanging rock is the sacred five-chambered cave Goa Harimau ("Cave of the Tiger God") and the holy spring Goa Tirta ("Holy Water Cave"), where priests obtain holy water, salt-free in spite of its close proximity to the ocean.

Pura Prancak

If you continue west you come to the sea temple **Pura Prancak,** which commemorates Nirantha's landing on Bali. Carved of white stone,

the *pura* overlooks the slow-moving Prancak River about 150 meters to the south. Nice beach, too. To reach the temple, turn left off the highway at the village of Tegalcangkring seven km west of Rambut Siwi. After 1.5 km, turn right and travel nine km down a narrow back road to the sea. The temple lies on the right just before the road turns south.

The Pekutatan-Pupuan Road

About 20 km east of Negara, Pekutatan is where you climb steeply up from the coast to the upland village of Pupuan, then head northwest. This is the only road north other than the one at Cekik, three km southeast of Gilimanuk. If entering Jembrana from Siririt, enjoy sweeping views of Java and the Bali Strait to the west. On the narrow twisting Pekutatan-Pupuan road you'll ride through the gnarly tendrils of a wild *bunut* tree at Bunut Bolong. Farther on is a clove plantation. You'll pass fragrant spices laid out on mats by the roadside. Visit the historic Hindu temple of Bujangga Sakti, then wind down through fantastic rice terrace and coffee-growing country to Pupuan. Another popular scenic route north via Pupuan is from Antosari, also on the Denpasar-Gilimanuk road, Rp1500 by *bemo* from Denpasar.

TABANAN REGENCY

Tabanan is one of Indonesia's richest rice-growing districts, with paddies stretching from the coast to as high as 700 meters on the lower slopes of Gunung Batukaru, the second highest mountain on Bali. Every temple in Tabanan contains a shrine venerating this mountain's spirit, Mahadewa. Tabanan's other major summits are Sangiyang and Pohon.

Three labor-intensive crops of new high-yield rice are grown each year, with soybeans planted in between to rejuvenate the soil. The *subak* of Tabanan average 12-15 tons of rice per hectare, making the inhabitants some of the most productive rice farmers in all Indonesia. Besides rice, there are crops of tea, cacao, groundnuts, and tropical fruits. The regency's higher climes are alpine, with mountain streams, moss, prehistoric tree ferns, wildflowers, creepers, orchids, leeches, butterflies, birds, and screaming monkeys. Lake Bratan in the middle of the regency's central highlands was formed by the volcano Gunung Catur, now inactive. The area is green, opulent, and peaceful, and the people friendly. As you leave Tabanan's southern plains and drive north to Bedugul on Lake Bratan, the landscape changes from tiers of gentle rice fields to gardens of onions, cabbages, and papaya. Thatched palm huts give way to sturdy cottages made of wood, tile, and stone. In the southern villages, the kitchen is separated from the other buildings of the family compound, but in these cold mountain villages, people cook in the same building where they sleep and live.

For the traveler, Tabanan offers remote mountain villages with fresh, crisp air; picturesque hill resorts; overflowing fruit, vegetable, and flower markets; austere lakeside temples; premier montane hiking; one of the world's finest golf courses; a 30-km-long strip of unspoilt black-sand beaches; and the regency's most famous and most photographed temple, the island sanctuary of Tanah Lot.

Tabanan is targeted as the next big tourist area. Why? The region is far from the bustle of city life, hawkers, and everyday hassles. Its attractions are accessible on day-trips from Denpasar or Kuta, or tourists can stay within the regency—new accommodations are built as soon as electricity and water become available. There are big plans for the regency's isolated coastline and a new road is under construction between Kuta, Seminyak, and Tanah Lot.

HISTORY

The regency has a lively history. Records indicate it came under the suzerainty of King Airlangga in 1037. When Majapahit invaded Bali in A.D. 1343, the territory was allotted to one of Gajah Mada's field generals, Arya Kenceng. Tabanan's classical period was in the 17th century, and included the founding of the main *puri* by Raja Singasana. Tabanan, Mengwi, and Penebel were almost constantly at war until 1891 when Mengwi was defeated by the princes of Tabanan and Badung. Through a series of court intrigues, assassinations, truces, and marriages, the principal houses of the district—Kaleren and Krambitan—were formed in the 19th century. When the Dutch conquered Bali in the early 20th century, they captured the king and crown prince (who committed suicide while in captivity), sacked the Tabanan palace, and exiled most of the surviving royalty to Lombok. The Dutch controller's office was established right in front of Puri Kaleren, but it was the outcaste marriage of a ranking princess that finished the kingdom for good. Since the rajadom had not entered into an agreement with the Dutch, the heirs lost their titles and lands, which were parceled out to the regency's *banjar*. Some historians believe this early redistribution of land to the peasants accounts for Tabanan's prosperous rice economy today. In 1929, the Dutch reorganized Bali's kingdoms into eight regencies, restoring the *raja*'s titles and authority, a status that lasted until 1950, when Sukarno abolished Indonesia's royalty with the stroke of a pen.

TABANAN REGENCY

TO SERIRIT
MAYONG
BUSUNGBIU
MUNDUK
GITGIT
LAKE BUYAN
PANCASARI
G. CATUR
(2,096 m)
LAKE TAMBLINGAN
LAKE BRATAN
CANDIKUNING
TO CATUR
G. LESONG
(1,860 m)
G. POHON
(2,069 m)
BEDUGUL
PLAGA
PAPUAN
PUJUNGAN
BATURITI
G. BATUKARU
(2,275 m)
PACUNG
BATUNGSEI
PURA LUHUR
JATULUWIH
APUAN
PETANG
BLIMBING
WANGAYAGEDE
PENEBEL
PEREAN
YEH PANAS
LALANG LINGGAH
MARGA
ANTOSARI
BLAYU
BAJERA
SOKA
ABIAN SEMAL
TABANAN
MENGWI
KRAMBITAN
BERABAN
BANJARANYAR
KLATING
KLATINGDUKUH
KEDIRI
KAPAL
PEJATAN
SEMPIDI
YEH GANGGA
TANAH LOT
DENPASAR

0   10 km

© MOON PUBLICATIONS, INC.

THE ARTS

Though the *rajas* of Tabanan's royal houses lost political power in the early 1900s, they continued to support the arts. Their palaces have long been famous for *gamelan,* dance, and drama groups. The regency's most famous native son was Mario (I Ketut Mario), the consummate dancer and choreographer who dominated Bali's performing arts during the 1920s and 1930s. The solo *kebyar* dance, which he created, is still widely performed. In the seated version, the dancer not only exhibits his skill as a graceful contortionist but also his mastery of the music, parodying every nuance and mood of the *gamelan* rhythm. Tabanan's large concert hall, Gedung Mario, built in 1973, is named after this genius. Commemorative performances are held there each year in his honor.

The Chinese-Balinese painter and *batik* artist Kay It was one of Bali's most promising and unique painters until his sudden death in 1977. Born to a family of shopkeepers in Tabanan, It's brilliant, modern, impressionist painting style was full of life and movement. He was also a master in clay and ceramics, which he learned from the villagers of Pejatan near Tabanan. Today you can see It's ceramics and tall totem poles on the grounds of the Bali Hyatt Hotel in Sanur. It's continuing influence can also be seen in the designs of ceramics for sale in the markets of Bali. View his paintings at the Art Center in Abiankapas in Denpasar and at the Neka Gallery in Ubud.

EVENTS

A genuine Balinese feast is put on for tourists about three times monthly in Puri Anyar. Every year a purification ceremony occurs several days before Nyepi, and every five years a much grander exorcism is held in which thousands of youngsters march from Gunung Batukaru to the sea. Don't miss the splendid *odalan* every 210 days at Tanah Lot, when dances are performed on the beach below Beraben village opposite the offshore temple.

BEACHES

It seems that every side road in Tabanan ends in a deserted, steep, beautiful black-sand beach. Enjoy stunning views of the sea with the mountains and rice terraces behind—no dogs, no tourists, not even a fisherman. Drawbacks, if you're not a surfer, are the three-meter waves and lethal undertows. French and Italian joint venture companies plan to develop the best of these beaches; hotels have already gone up at Yeh Gangga, Beraban, Klating, and Soka. Big waves crash over black sand at Kedungu Beach, west of Tanah Lot and 12 southwest of Tabanan. Nice views, beautiful rice terraces, and a Japanese golf course nearby. Thirteen km from Tabanan is long, wide Kelating Beach, with big rolling waves and beautiful panoramas.

Pasut Beach, near Sungai Ho and Pura Segara, is a quiet beach lying 14 km southwest of Tabanan. The Ho River is navigable by small sampan. Northwest of Pasut and 24 km from Tabanan is Beraban Beach, which offers excellent accommodations. Even more isolated, with great views, is Kelecung Beach west of Beraban. The most westerly of Tabanan's beaches is Soka Beach. See the rocks said to be the pot and old kitchen of Kebo Iwa, the legendary figure who carved Gunung Kawi.

TABANAN TOWN AND THE SOUTH

TABANAN

The regency's capital as well as the commercial and arts center. Lying in the heart of Bali's thriving rice belt, Tabanan's town center is bustling with small industries and many Chinese-owned shops. East- and westbound traffic streams in and out of town on several one-way streets. Prior to 1989 Tabanan was a dirty shophouse town, but when the new *bupati* was elected in that year new buildings and a new market were built. There's now a supermarket, gardens and sidewalks beautify the roadways, and an efficient waste disposal system is in place. The town has even won prizes for cleanliness; some say it's the best-organized town on Bali.

Though seldom visited by tourists and not known as an art center, Tabanan is actually rich in dance and art traditions. There are classical poetry (*kakawin*) clubs, it's been a woodcarving center since the 19th century, and the town is home to a famous *gamelan* and the much acclaimed dance troupe Rama Dewa. Five km east of Tabanan in the village of Abiantuwung, the dance masters at the Sanggar Tari Wrhatnala (School of Dance) train Balinese and foreign dancers. If coming from Denpasar, the school is on the right. See the sign by a big

TABANAN

TO G. BATUKARU AND JATULUWIH
TO GILIMANUK
TERMINAL PESIAPAN
TO MARGA
GAS STATION
PURI TABANAN
POST OFFICE
HOSPITAL
POLICE
BEMO STATION
PASAR
MONUMENT
TO DENPASAR
TO TANAH LOT
NOT TO SCALE

© MOON PUBLICATIONS, INC.

pura and *waringan* tree. Contact director I Gusti Ngurah Supartha, a well-known choreographer and musician.

Gedung Marya

Named after I Ketut Mario, Bali's preeminent choreographer and dance master of the 1920s and '30s, this building is located in front of the Puri Gede Royal Palace of Tabanan. Dances are staged here only in June during the art fair and for Independence Day celebrations on 17 August. During the fair you may see the *kebyar, arja, wayang kulit,* and *lomba-lomba* festival.

Accommodations

There are few hotels in Tabanan. Since the selection is limited and substandard, it's best to push through and stay outside the city in more agreeable seaside accommodations at Yeh Gangga, Tibubiyu, or Balian Beach. If you have to stay, on the east side of town is **Hotel Sederhana** (Jl. Saha Dewa), right across from the police station; Rp5000 s, Rp10,000 d. Clean and quiet. Opposite the *bupati* office is the trader's hotel **Taruna Jaya,** about the same price as the Sederhana. If coming from Denpasar, turn left at the Rumah Sakit, east of the *bupati* office.

Food

Eat bargain meals in the *pasar senggol* (open 1700-2400) east of Gedung Marya. Terminal Pesiapan, Tabanan's bus/*bemo* station, also has good, simple places to eat. One of the best *nasi padang* restaurants around is the **Murah Meriah** in the bus station. People from all over Bali associate Tabanan with a spinach-like vegetable called *gendo* (or *sayur pelecing*); try a dish in the *pasar malam*. Tabanan is also a good place to buy *brem*. In the *nasi padang* restaurant **Pura Bulia,** Jl. Gajah Mada 45, a quite good *nasi campur* is served. Reflecting Javanese influence, there's another Muslim restaurant as well. **Rumah Makan Taliwang** on Jl. Gatot Subroto specializes in *ayam goreng* and *ayam pangang.* **Toko Makanan Sedia,** on the main street Jl. Gajah Mada, is a small Chinese restaurant with tasty food.

Shopping

Tabanan is one of the best places on Bali to shop for everyday articles. The big market for the whole regency is in the middle of Tabanan, which sells exotic items like avocados. This busy *pasar* is neater and cleaner than most markets, and the sellers don't hassle you. Shop here for clothes, shoes, *krupuk,* and household and electronic goods. Also for sale are *sarung,* ceremonial clothes, and temple umbrellas. **Toko Swardana,** Jl. Gajah Mada 41, tel. (0361) 91249, has a beautiful collection of reasonably priced clocks, watches, alarm clocks, perfume, and sunglasses. Check out the supermarket **Nanushka Utama Pusat Perbelanjaan,** about three km before Tabanan on the way from Kediri. About 1.5 km from Tabanan on the road to Kediri is **Miranda Fashion Clothing.**

Services

The Diparda (tourist information office) is on Jl. Gunung Agung on the east side of Gedung Marya, tel. (0361) 91602; see Pak Ketut Suaba. Change money at the BPD Bank, which accepts traveler's checks at fair rates, on the main street Jl. Gajah Mada. For calls to Australia, Europe, and the U.S., try the telephone and telegraph office substation (Perumtel Telekommunikasi) at Jl. Gelantik 4, only a five-minute walk from Gedung Marya. Tabanan has a big hospital on the main road coming into town from Denpasar.

Getting Away

The Tabanan bus station (Terminal Pesiapan) is on the west side of town. From this terminal big Isuzu vans head for Mengwi, Rp500; Denpasar, Rp800; Bedugul, Rp2000; Negara, Rp1750; and Gilimanuk, Rp2500. All *bis malam* leave from Terminal Pesiapan; arrive one hour before departure. A bus ticket office is in Warung Ani, Jl. Gajah Mada 128. Long-distance bus ticket fares are Jakarta, Rp56,500 (departs 0700, 24 hours); Bandung, Rp50,000 (0700); Bogor (0700); Surabaya, Rp21,000 (1900); Malang, Rp21,000 (1800); Yogyakarta, Rp38,000 (1530). Another *bis malam* is east of Bank Rakyat Indonesia.

VICINITY OF TABANAN

Explore the paddies and villages around town. Almost any side road out of Tabanan to the south eventually ends up at the sea, with a wide sandy sloping beach and good surf. The Tabanan coast offers isolated coves and rocky outcrops which provide shade and spectacular ocean views. The black sand is known for its curative, therapeutic properties, and is said to be particularly helpful for arthritis.

The Subak Museum in Sanggulan village houses exhibits on the history and development of Bali's unique *subak* irrigation committees. This is the only museum on Bali to focus on agriculture, displaying tools, farming implements, kitchen utensils used for cooking rice, a scale model of a farming *kampung,* and old-style structures. Open daily 0800-1400, closed Sunday. Donation. Located 19 km northwest of Denpasar.

Yeh Panas

The holy spring of Yeh Panas is in Penetahan, about 12 km north of Tabanan. Japanese soldiers stationed in Tabanan used to visit this spring during the war to refresh themselves in its hot, pungent, sulphurous mineral waters. They widened the track to the spring, and built small bathing sheds. In the 1960s luxury tourist villas were constructed at the best vantage points around the spring, but the project lacked financing and the buildings were abandoned. The shells were soon occupied by invisible spirits (*memedi*); the voices of women were heard whimpering in the night. To discourage these new occupants from settling in permanently, the remaining structures were used to shelter pigs and cattle.

Today, the delightful and relaxing Yeh Panas Hotspring and Spa on the sylvan winding road (Jl. Batukaru) to Gunung Batukaru is Bali's only hot springs specifically designed as a spa. There's a Rp500 admittance charge (plus Rp250 for parking), which pays for just looking (no bathing). You can partake of these facilities for around Rp60,000, plus 17.5% tax and service. No expense was spared in the construction of these nine separate and private outdoor spa enclosures. Each spa has jets and blowers; for "room service" you hit a *kulkul.* The swimming pool is fed by fresh water and has a sunken bar and waterfall. There's a playground for the kids. The naturally hot water from the springs (probably Bali's hottest) contains sulphur, potassium, sodium, and small percentages of minerals, with no additives except an occasional dose of chlorine. The water, it is said, will heal itching and skin diseases.

The comfortable restaurant, overlooking the rushing river, serves expensive drinks (Rp5000 for a large Bintang), and Western, Indonesian, and Chinese food, pizza, and pasta. For more information and reservations, contact Varianusa, Jl. Raya Kuta 15 X, Denpasar, tel. (0361) 52411 or 54881, fax 52411, which maintains radio contact with the spa.

Marga

The Margarana monument in Marga is located 15 km northeast of Tabanan. This memorial park honors a regiment of guerrilla fighters killed here by the Dutch shortly after WW II. The Dutch far outnumbered the Balinese, many of whom were armed only with sharpened bamboo poles. The engagement was a devastating blow to the Balinese resistance movement, killing many of its original leaders. So many high caste cadre lost their lives that the battle marked the beginning of much heavier participation of lower caste guerrillas.

The Margarana ("Battle of Marga") monument was built in 1954. In the middle is a 17-meter-tall, eight-roofed monument shaped like a Javanese *candi,* designed to symbolize the unity of the fallen revolutionaries in their fight for freedom.

A strange, eerie feeling permeates this place. The memorial stones of 1,372 men and women, Muslims, Hindus, and Christians, who died on Bali fighting Dutch forces lie in a cemetery here, including 11 Japanese soldiers who defected to the Indonesians. Christian tombstones bear the cross, Muslims the half moon, Balinese the swastika. The monument is inscribed with the text of a famous letter the Balinese commander Lieutenant Ngurah Rai wrote to a Dutch officer, pledging to give his life for the revolution.

Marga is not a regular tourist stop, so there will probably be few people there. Worth a visit. Every 20 November, Balinese Memorial Day, a Hero's Day Ceremony is held here with a reenactment of the "Long March." Attended by *pemuda,* scouts, and soldiers, this eight-hour march to Denpasar lasts from evening to the early morning. Visit the small museum on the grounds (open 0800-1200) with exhibits of uniforms, weapons, documents, photos, battle plans, and battle remnants.

KEDIRI AND VICINITY

Kediri

Five km south of Tabanan in Kediri is the site of one of Bali's largest cattle markets. Amid a din of human and animal sounds and pungent smells, game cocks, potbellied swine, lumbering oxen, squealing geese, squawking ducks, and soft golden-brown cattle are sold and traded. Other equally animated and exciting cattle markets are held in Biringkit and Bebandem.

In Kediri's *puri* is a particularly honored historical relic, the magic *kris* of the Javanese priest Nirantha. Known as Jaramenara, this holy object was left with the village headman as a token of Nirantha's gratitude just before the saint went off to Ulu Watu and his final transcendence. Every Kuningan festival, the *kris* is removed and washed in a special ceremony.

Pejatan

Just four km southwest of Kediri is this small and friendly pottery village of one-story thatch compounds squeezed between two rivers. Untouched by the modern world, Pejatan has long been known as a center for hand-decorated, wheel-thrown pottery and ceramic roof tiles. The red clay was traditionally mined on village land until it began to run out in the early '80s. In 1985 the villagers started experimenting with high temperature porcelain, and within a few years Pejatan was turning out not only washbasins and pots but porcelain dinner sets, elegant bowls, delicate animal figurines, and open lattice-work filigree vases. High-fired porcelain is much less fragile than traditional terra-cotta. Before long, the ceramic pieces were in high demand at Bali hotels, restaurants, and shops.

Roof tile-making, however, remains the primary economic activity of about 90% of the town's inhabitants. Widely used by the island's building trade, these dull red terra-cotta tiles featuring figures of gods, goddesses, and *wayang* heroes are patterned after a style first introduced by the painter Kay It. Check out the fanciful ornaments, called *jambangan,* popularly used to decorate the apex of thatched roofed houses. Pejatan's humorous, grotesque standing clay figures—inspired by the stories of the Ramayana and Mahabharata—decorate gardens and walls all over Bali. A big jolly clownish terra-cotta fat man goes for Rp50,000, weighs about 15 kg, and is quite fragile since the sculpture isn't high-fired. You'll also see huge 80-cm unglazed earthen water jars for about the same price. Clay is imported from the Malang area of East Java.

Smoke from dozens of coconut husk-fueled brick kilns billows from the yards of the village *kampung.* Any ceramic worker will lead you to one of dozens of workshops. There are only two retail display rooms (open daily 0800-1800), about one-half km from one another—**Tanteri Ceramic,** Dusun Banjar Simpangan, tel. (0361) 91897, and **Pejatan Keramic.** The best pieces are the glazed Chinese-style ceramics with beautiful ornamentation. Look for unique animal shapes—fish, lizards, frogs, turtles, monkeys—which climb out of sugar bowls, lidded bowls, teapots, perfume jars, soap dishes, ashtrays, cups, covered clay glasses, and napkin holders. Colors are flat, gray-green celadon, light blue, or ivory. Order a whole dinner set for 6-12 people, made specifically to your design. As you browse in the showrooms, you'll realize that prices aren't that cheap: Rp10,000-15,000 for simple pieces, Rp45,000 for more involved work. And don't expect startling artistic merit—craftspeople in Europe, Australia, and the States are just as original and charge about the same price. These are more curios than art pieces. On hand are factory-produced sure sellers which are duplicated over and over again. Search out the unusual.

Located seven km north of Tanah Lot, Pejetan is easily reached on a narrow, beautiful country road west of the main west-to-east road. Just follow the signs. An even more scenic approach is the nine-km back-country road from Krambitan. Head east, cross over the bridge in the dip, then turn right at the intersection to Pejetan via Serongga (a popular fishing spot), Curah, Sudirmara, Bedha (a large agricultural temple), then Pejetan. Be ready to stop for festivals and ceremonies on the way. After Pejatan, go to Tanah Lot for the sunset.

Alas Kedaton

Four km north of Kediri in Kukuh village is a temple surrounded by a lovely, state-owned sacred forest with cool, peaceful walking paths. In and around the temple cavort more than 700 friendly monkeys, while *kalong* hang from the treetops. This monkey forest is smaller than Sangeh's, and the monkeys seem better behaved. At least three families live completely separated from one another in the forest.

On the way to the temple from the parking lot, you'll pass through an art market. The custom now is for a young girl to escort you (tip her Rp500) and help you feed the monkeys. These girls will tell you they'll get in trouble with the boss if you don't stop by their shop and buy something on the way out. Just laugh and do it. Near Alas Kedaton in the vicinity of Sangeh is Carangsari village, a miniature Ubud with *losmen,* restaurants, and *warung.* Beautiful rice fields.

YEH GANGGA

Yeh Gangga Beach Bungalows, near Desa Ayagangga, has six four-room bungalows. Each room is well furnished, with two beds, fridge, and fan. Tariff is Rp60,000 d, breakfast included. The owners are conscientious, knowledgeable hosts with exemplary attitudes on local culture. The hotel caters mostly to a European clientele. Javanese-style food at reasonable prices is served in the hotel's small dining room (order dinner in the morning), or try the delicious *nasi bubur* (Rp500) in one of the *warung* up in the village. A spring on the property provides fresh water for the hotel. Watch CNN World News in the restaurant each evening at 1930, or browse in the library. Free pickup from the airport. For bookings, write P.O. Box 32, Tabanan 82151, fax (0361) 92744.

The best thing about Yeh Gangga is the location. The bungalows overlook rice fields, picturesque rocks, and empty Yeh Gangga Beach, where religious processions frequently end. Borrow the hotel's dinghy and explore along the coast. You can't swim in the ocean here; the riptide is too dangerous. The hotel has a nice, unchlorinated pool and bathhouse. You can arrange a car from the village.

To Tanah Lot

It's a six-km walk (one hour, 20 minutes) southeast along the shore to Tanah Lot. Leave early in the morning so you can cross the river at low tide, then walk along the beach to a cliff where there's a small temple complex. Descend to the beach again, totally deserted for about one km.

On the next cliff, after a few small stores, veer left and follow the stone path to the end of the street, then turn left, then right, and follow the path parallel to the ocean. Cross a creek, climb a hill, cross a river, and you arrive in Tanah Lot—missing the parking lot, stores, restaurants, entrance fee, and donation. For more walks in the area, refer to Yeh Gangga Beach Bungalows' photo album and information booklet.

TANAH LOT

Like a delicate Chinese painting, this small, pagoda-like temple 13 km southwest of Tabanan sits on a huge eroded outcropping of rock offshore. Tanah Lot is only one of a whole series of splendid sea temples on the south coast of Bali, all paying homage to the guardian spirits of the sea. So that these spirits may be constantly propitiated, each temple is visible from the next along the entire southern coastline. On crystal-clear days from Tanah Lot you can just make out Pura Uluwatu.

Legend has it the temple was built by one of the last Brahman priests to arrive in Bali from Java, Sanghyang Nirantha, a man remembered for his successful efforts in strengthening the religious beliefs of the populace and for founding several of Bali's most dramatic 16th century *sad-sanghyang* temples. At that time, the area's holy leader, Bendesa Beraben, jealous when his followers joined the newcomer, ordered the Hindu saint to leave. Using his magical powers, Nirantha left by simply moving the rock upon which Tanah Lot is built from the land into the sea, changing his scarf into the sacred snakes that still guard the temple. Later, Bendesa Beraben converted wholeheartedly to Nirantha's teachings.

Incomparably situated off a black volcanic sand shore, Tanah Lot is one of the most photographed and sketched temples in Asia. Watch the dramatic sunset from the lovely park opposite the temple and its oddly shaped rock silhouetted against a blood-red sky. Tanah Lot is actually only one reason to come here; this relaxing nearby park is another. Follow the paths to the other temples in the vicinity—Pura Batu Bolong, Pura Batu Mejan, Beji Taman Sari, Pura Enjung Galuh. There are many vantage points from which to view Tanah Lot, the best from Pura Enjung Galuh on a bluff just west of Tanah Lot.

The whole site is well-maintained; commercial activities are in keeping with its peaceful isolation, charm, and holiness. The tacky souvenir stands are outside the park. A favorite of the multitude of domestic tourists who visit Tanah Lot are the scores of poisonous black snakes (*ular suci*) sleeping in sandy holes just above the waterline along the beach. When the tide is out, they slither into the temple. The locals believe these snakes guard the sanctuary from intruders, and great care must be taken by all who visit the temple not to disturb or anger them. The snakes are the property of the temple's guardian spirit.

Big crowds come to pray here even though the structures which make up the Tanah Lot temple complex are actually quite unremarkable, consisting of just two *meru* shrines of seven- (dedicated to Sanghyang Widhi Wasa) and three- (dedicated to Nirantha) tiered black-thatched roofs, plus two pavilions. Women bear towers of votive offerings on their heads, waiting until low tide to safely walk over a concrete-reinforced walkway and up rockcut steps to the solitary temple. At high tide, when the walkway is submerged, the incoming waves can get pretty ferocious.

Fees are required to park your vehicle, hire a sash, and enter the temple grounds (Rp550). Time your arrival for low tide, which is around noon at times of the full moon.

Accommodations And Food
Tanah Lot has enough amenities—postal agent, minimarket, moneychanger, restaurants, accommodations—to make for a very comfortable sojourn. During the day, escape from the tourist throngs clambering over the temple by sightseeing in Tabanan Regency, returning at night to have the place to yourself and mingle with the small service population of friendly Balinese who are delighted you came to the temple to stay a few days.

The closest accommodations to the temple is **Mutiara Tanah Lot**, tel. (0361) 25465, fax 22672, with eight bungalows facing the ocean. Half with a/c (Rp84,000 s or d), the other half have fans (Rp73,300 s or d). Price includes breakfast, tax, and service. The restaurant offers a pricey tourist menu. A breezy, quiet, and meditative place to stay. A big complex near the art market is **Dewi Sinta Hotel and Restaurant**, P.O. Box 8, Tabanan 82171, tel. 35445, which charges Rp50,000 for deluxe a/c family rooms. The non-a/c standard rooms for Rp32,000 are a better deal. Plain but undeniably quiet. Most rooms have private baths, hot water, and shady veranda overlooking *sawah.* Amenities include safe-deposit boxes, nice grounds, a *wantilan*-style convention hall, and sometimes *kecak* performances at night. See the assistant manager, I Ketut Sudiartana. A *losmen* without a name is located on the other side of the market; Rp20,000 s or d for five pedestrian rooms with Indonesian-style floor-level toilets, no shower, facing the ocean. No meals available, but free tea or coffee. Ask the manager for a discount. There are plenty of cheap, semi-tourist places to eat like **Warung Made.** Cheapest of all are the *warung* in the *bemo* station/parking lot.

Getting There And Away

The most scenic way is to walk at low tide six hours (14 km one-way) up and back from Kuta. Wear a bathing suit, as the rivermouths along the way can be forded. Time your arrival for Tanah Lot's spectacular sunset. You can also reach the temple by driving from Denpasar toward Tabanan and Negara, then taking a left (southwest) at Kediri's stoplight down a side road that leads after 10 km to Tanah Lot's parking lot. About an hour's drive from Denpasar.

Most of the travel agents in Bali's major resorts include Tanah Lot as an almost de rigueur stop. Minibuses and *bemo* depart Denpasar's Ubung station for Kediri (Rp600), from there you get *bemo* onward to Tanah Lot (Rp300, nine km). When you're ready to return to Denpasar or Kuta, don't wait too long after 1600 to get a *bemo* back to Kediri so you can connect with another *bemo* to Denpasar. Otherwise you might have to charter a ride on the back of a motorbike or walk.

Vicinity Of Tanah Lot

Within walking distance is a serene beach called Pantai Nyanyi with black sand, big waves, and beautiful views, especially during the full moon. About 13 km from Tabanan. Kedungu and Yeh Gangga are nice beaches northwest of Tanah Lot toward Negara.

KRAMBITAN DISTRICT

Six km west of Tabanan is Krambitan, a small district located in a prosperous agricultural re-

gion. The main village is Krambitan, about eight km southwest of Tabanan (Rp500 by *bemo*). Though it lacks an inexpensive *losmen,* this village makes an excellent base from which to visit Tanah Lot, Mengwi, Pejatan, Alas Kedaton, Gunung Batukaru, and Bedugul. Five km to the south of Krambitan village are the black sand beaches of Pasut and Klating. Located on either side of the mouths of two rivers, these beaches are clean and graced with native *jukung.*

Krambitan Village

Not by accident is the name Krambitan derived from the Sanskrit *karawitan,* which means "art, music, and dance." This small, attractive village is renowned for its classical literature, *legong* dancing, *wayang*-style painting, stone- and woodcarving, and a *tektekan* orchestra believed to have magical powers. The paintings belong to a school started by the great painters Gusti Wayang Kopang and I Macong in the 1930s. The style is similar to that of Kamasan except that the teeth and costumes are depicted differently. Ask the friendly villagers the way to the unique Ulun Suwi temple dating from the Neolithic period.

The village contains old-style residences as well as two treasure-filled 18th-century gilded palaces, Puri Gede and Puri Anyar, lovingly restored by the family of the *puri.* During the revolution, the Krambitan *puri* sided with the Republicans. Cultural programs and dinners have been presented here since 1967. Identical twin grandsons—Pak Oka and Pak Roi—of the late king preside over the palaces, keeping the traditional dancing and arts very much alive. The *puri* also arranges special tourist events such as traditional-style dinner parties accompanied by *legong, tektekan,* and *joged* performances. Overnight guests are welcome in Puri Anyar Wisata, *gamelan* lessons can be arranged, and you're invited to join the village's *lontar*-reading or kite-flying clubs.

Puri Anyar

Inside the royal compound are peaceful gardens, pavilions with unusual gold-plated carvings, and many charming traditional buildings filled with well-preserved antiques and art objects. In perfect harmony with this setting, Pak Oka maintains an unmistakable royal bearing. Ask him to show you his "celebrity" corner in the family living quarters; on the wall are framed memorablia of the distinguished guests who've visited the palace.

The *bale gong* (concert hall) in front of the *puri* houses art work, the royal orchestra, and an impressive collection of musical instruments, *kris,* and sacred masks. On the right as you enter the *puri* is a courtyard containing the family shrines, embedded with Chinese and Dutch porcelain and tiles. One rare blue Delft piece dates from the Napoleonic period; Bonaparte can be seen on horseback.

Tektekan

Not actually a dance but a procession of men carrying bamboo split drums and giant cowbells, this classical, very old orchestra is played to exorcize malignant spirits when an epidemic, serious drought, or pestilence befalls the village. The ceremony accompanies the Calon Arang, a legend dating from the 10th century in Java. Puri Anyar's *tektekan* is made of bamboo, whereas the typical Balinese *kebyar gong* is made of bronze. This unique ensemble marches through the village only on the day before the Balinese New Year, whenever an exorcism is required, on certain auspicious days, or by special order of the *raja* when a tourist bus arrives. The drama must be accompanied by blood sacrifices (a small chicken or duck) at both the beginning and end.

Puri Night

Your inestimable host Pak Oka puts on monster banquets for as many as 300 Dutch cruise passengers, or big groups of Italians, French, or Germans who really lap it up. This magical evening begins with *tektekan* dancers carrying enormous tick-tocking cowbells and lighted torches greeting tour buses full of astonished European tourists. Behind the men are lines of maidens performing a welcoming dance.

The guests are then invited into the second open-air courtyard to seat themselves around the central *cempaka* tree at candlelit tables with banana-leaf settings. Delicious Indo-Chinese food is brought in by a procession of servers. This buffet dinner (pay extra for beer) is the ultimate dining experience for those who like Balinese food served in the traditional manner. After dinner, the guests are invited to dance the *joged.* What follows is one of the most mesmerizing *kris* dances on the island, a version of the Calon Arang performed to the beat of hypnotically tuned bamboo tubes. To drive away the demons, some of the players become entranced, arm themselves with *kris,* and attack Rangda. The last part of the dance can be so dangerous no one is allowed to use a flash for fear of snapping the dancers out of their deep trance. Half the village is there looking on.

Taking place about three times a month, this special event is usually reserved for private parties only. With permission, individuals may attend a large, already-booked Puri Night paying separately, or commission a private performance with dinner. Call first. For more information, contact Ajus Erawan, Jl. Anyelir 23, Denpasar, tel. and fax (0361) 33774.

Accommodations

Treat yourself to an amazing stay in one of 12 rooms (including four princely rooms) in the maze of **Puri Anyar,** a fully functioning Balinese palace. The full-board tariff is Rp157,000 for a whole bungalow, or Rp42,000 for one room in a bungalow with hot water, fan, and a big bed. One ornate, gold-leaf decorated bungalow is called the royal pavilion and features a bathroom with a cascading waterfall. Breakfast is included, lunch is Rp16,000, dinner Rp25,000. Pak Rai may take you kite-flying on the beach, or you can jog in the countryside north and west of Krambitan. For bookings, contact Raja Anak Agung Giri Gunadhi (Pak Rai) at his office at Jl. Surapati 7, tel. (0361) 23602 or 92668. **Puri Gede** next door also has a few rooms available. Book in advance with a tour agent or through the tourist office in Denpasar. If full, you can still attend a Palace Night.

Vicinity Of Krambitan

One km to the west of Krambitan is Tista, a village renowned for its unique version of the *legong—legong leko,* which is only danced around Tabanan. In this social dance, two tiny *leko* dancers wearing *legong* dress and headdresses are accompanied by the melodies of the *janger.*

Two km south of Krambitan is Panarukan, a village known for its many fine wood and stone sculptors and a smaller version of *tektekan.* Visit the studio of Panarukan's most famous native son, the modern painter Ajin Ida Putu

Cegeg. Only two km beyond Panarukan is the wide and empty black sand beach of Klating-dukuh, offering fine views of the coast. Follow the road about nine km southwest of Krambitan to wide, quiet, black-sand Pasut Beach with waves up to three meters high. At the beach, turn southeast and walk 20 km to Tanah Lot.

Tibubiyu

The ceremonies in the tidy traditional village of Tibubiyu are almost unceasing. As in days of old, performances take place right on the street. *Tek-tekan* dances can be arranged. Tibubiyu consists of 300 families who grow rice and vegetables. This village doesn't even have an eating *warung*, only one small stall that sells cigarettes, salt, coffee, drinks, and batteries; no newspapers or telephones. The market opens daily at 0500.

BeeBees Restaurant and Bungalows, just four km beyond Krambitan in Tibubiyu, is undoubtedly one of the best traveler's hotels on Bali. Run by Australian artist Barbara Miller, these six rustic yet comfortable *lumbung*-style thatched bungalows with garden bathrooms are set in a lovely compound. The tariff is Rp32,000 s, Rp40,000 d, including a breakfast of coffee, fruit, toast, and fruit juice. Book through Drs. Dewa Made Suamba Negara, Tibubiyu, Krambitan 82161, Denpasar, fax (0361) 236-021.

BeeBees open-air restaurant looks out over a broad expanse of rice fields stretching to the sea. The menu offers most Indonesian standard meals plus Western breakfasts. Its strength, though, is the delicious Balinese entrees like *tum* and *gundo*. Try the Village Combination (Rp2000), a vegetarian *nasi campur*. The drink list includes small bottles of Balinese *brem* (Rp2000), ginger tea (Rp800), and brandy coffee (Rp1000). Check the blackboard for three-course daily specials (Rp8000), usually pork or chicken. Not a place for pub-crawlers; this is the gentle side of Bali. Groups of painters attend painting workshops here. There's always a cooling breeze, and in the evenings you often need a jacket. A bucket of hot water is offered to guests at shower time. Airport transfers arranged on request; Rp40,000 for a chartered *bemo*, 46 km, 1.5 hours. Ask the Queen Bee to fetch Pak Guru Rasin for superb traditional massages (Rp5000). Laundry service.

Take local *bemo* on the main street of the village to Ubung station in Denpasar (Rp2000) or to Tabanan (Rp1000). From BeeBees, follow the path through rice fields (10-minute walk) to the well-formed beach—fine, glistening, diamond dust black sand, with not a structure or vendor in sight, and really high surf.

LALANG LINGGAH

Beautiful, unspoilt **Balian Beach Bungalows** lies near the village of Lalang Linggah, 50 km west of Denpasar on Bali's main south coast highway. Situated in a six-acre coconut plantation beside the Balian River and within 300 meters of the Indian Ocean, this tranquil area offers excellent river swimming, surfing, miles of uninhabited coastline, fishing villages, and friendly, unaffected locals. The complex has 24-hour electricity, a small bar and restaurant, superb gardens overlooking Bali's biggest river, and a helpful staff. One of the most peaceful *losmen* on Bali.

Owned by Australian surfing enthusiast Bob Monkhouse and his Balinese manager-partner A.S.B. Hermawan, the Balian offers a range of accommodations from dormitory-style bunkbeds to bungalows supported on piles at varying elevations. The tariff includes simple breakfast; 10% government tax added to the bill. In the *losmen* block (Rp12,000 s, Rp15,000 d), each room has its own *mandi* and WC; each pair of rooms—one overlooking the river, the other the valley behind—shares a balcony. Another, stilted bungalow (Rp15,000 s, Rp17,000 d) overlooks the river. Both Visa and MasterCard accepted. The Balai Gede (nicknamed Honeymoon Suite) is a traditional building with a huge platform bed. It affords the best view across the river and down to the sea (Rp30,000 s or d). Other higher-priced units, similar to the Balai Gede, face the sea. One is suitable for a large family (easily sleeps six) and costs Rp40,000. Enjoy Western/Indo-nesian fare at the Balian's restaurant. Or try **Made's Warung** one km west; reach it from the road at the small *desa* of Surabrata—great place to hang out while enjoying jaffles, noodles, and cold soda.

The Balian is not for ragers or low-low budget travelers either. Some comments in the guestbook: "Big Waves, No Babes!" and "Watch out for bats in your room!" Most of the guests appreciate the quiet, the lack of even one seller on one of the best beaches on Bali, and the simple beauty of the surroundings. The locale is noticeably cooler as it gets sea breezes all day, which helps keep the mosquitos down. The Balian River turns into a blue lagoon in the dry season and offers refreshing swimming.

Visit the small village on the coast at the mouth of the river; the inhabitants make salt and collect rocks. Also visit the fishing village at one end of the bay. If you venture around the point, you'll find a multitude of caves, tunnels, and small bays. Explore the area on foot or rent a motorbike or Suzuki jeep at the Balian.

From Kuta, catch a *bemo* (Rp300) to Terminal Tegal, then hop a three-wheeler (Rp300) to Ubung. The next step is by bus or *bemo* (Rp2000, 1.5 hours) to Lalang Linggah on the way to Negara and Gilimanuk.

All buses from Java to Denpasar pass the front gate; ask the driver to stop at Lalang Linggah just over the bridge on the Balian River. From Lovina, catch a *bemo* to Seririt and on to Pupuan, then continue south to Antosari or Pulukan, both on the main Denpasar-Gilimanuk highway. Lalang Linggah is 10 km west of Antosari and 30 km east of Pulukan. Take the Balian's transport service, or a public *bemo* into Tabanan (Rp1000), Negara (Rp1500), or Gilimanuk (Rp3000).

NORTHERN TABANAN REGENCY

The western uplands of Gunung Batukaru are famous for their magnificent landscapes. From Wangaya Gede, take the narrow mountain road leading east to 700-meter-high Jatuluwih with a peculiar temple embellished with gargoyle-like creatures—mindful of Chinese temples. Fine views from Jatuluwih, Apuan, Pacung, and the slopes of Gunung Batukau. The temples Pura Natar Sari in Apuan and the Pura Bukit Kembar in Pacung are known for their *barong* dances during the temple *odalan*; check with one of the tourist offices about times.

From these heights you can take in the whole of southern Bali to the coast. Get to Jatuluwih early, otherwise you'll be above the clouds; it also tends to rain in the afternoons. If the scenic but rough road through steeply terraced rice fields hasn't been rendered impassable by heavy rains, reach Jatuluwih directly from Pura Luhur.

Perean
On the road north from Mengwi to Bedugul take the turnoff west to the village of Perean, about 30 km from Denpasar. Balinese *meru* are almost always made entirely of wood but in the compound of the grand old temple here, Pura Yeh Gangga, the body and foundation consist of stone. On three sides of the *pura* are niches, on the fourth is a mock door with a stone carving in the shape of a lock. Porcelain plates are embedded in the sides of the temple; steps from the *meru*'s east side lead up to a narrow terrace. Pura Yeh Gangga is crowned with a seven-tiered thatch roof. The simple temple compound is surrounded by a wall broken by a *candi bentar*. Inscribed stones discovered in the vicinity bear the dates A.D. 1339 and 1429. On the opposite side of the river are several hewn-rock caves, and to the east are the hot springs, Yeh Gangga ("Water of the Ganges"), that gave Perean's temple its name.

Pupuan
Beautiful Bangsing Waterfall is in Pujungan village near Pupuan. If coming from Denpasar, the way to the falls starts down a small alley in Pupuan. Drive 10 minutes to the teahouse 500 meters before the *air terjun*, then walk in and swim in the pool beneath the falls, which is quite deep in the middle.

The coffee-growing region of Pupuan is on the spectacularly panoramic road north from Antosari to Seririt, the island's most westerly north-south road. On the way, stop in at Pura Makori in Blimbing village, which consists of a number of stones hidden in the forest. An ideal site for meditation.

GUNUNG BATUKARU

Except for Bali Barat National Park, the pristine rainforest covering 2,275-meter-high Gunung Batukaru is the only wilderness region left on this densely populated island. Known locally as Coconut Shell Mountain, this dormant volcano is the most westerly of Bali's three highest summits and completely dominates the regency of

Tabanan. On Batukaru's slopes is Pura Luhur, one of the island's national *sad-kahyangan* temples, seldom visited by tourists because of its remote location.

To climb Gunung Batukaru, hire a guide for Rp30,000 in Wangaya Gede village south of Pura Luhur. From the outer courtyard of the temple, walk 200 meters to a small river, then cross the bridge and turn north up the steep trail through a thick, damp, slippery forest to the top. Only the trail is visible during the five to six hours of the climb. The view from Gunung Batukaru's overgrown summit is blocked by trees. A small temple of roofless stone shrines is on the top. Don't attempt this climb in the rainy season, and don't even try to reach Pura Luhur by road if you don't have a sturdy vehicle with a cooling system in good working order. If you're on a motorbike, you're going to get wet.

Pura Luhur Batukaru

A unique, sacred mountain sanctuary and royal temple near the peak of Gunung Batukaru, 23 km from Tabanan, built to venerate deities of mountains and lakes. All the regencies of Bali maintain temples at the temple of Besakih except for the Tabanan princes, who have their ancestral temples here. Pura Luhur served as the state temple for all of western Bali when Tabanan was an independent kingdom, and even today every temple in western Bali has a shrine dedicated to it. When the archaeologist Hooykaas visited the site in the 1920s, he discovered a number of large upright linga, so it's presumed this place has served as a sanctuary since prehistoric times. Legend says the temple was founded by the Hindu sage Kuturan, who proselytized on Bali in the 11th century. This date was corroborated in 1925 when Goris discovered statues in a nearby bathing place similar to those found at 11th century Goa Gajah. In 1604, the temple was attacked and partially destroyed by the *raja* of Buleleng, but his troops were beaten back by millions of bees unleashed by the protective spirits of the temple. Pura Luhur was not rebuilt until 1959, even though pilgrims continued to worship in the rubble.

The temple lies in a solitary clearing 1,300 meters above sea level, with a gigantic, uninhabited, humid tropical forest all around it. The site is often cool and has the highest annual rainfall on Bali. Not a very large complex, it consists of a main enclosure to the north, plus two smaller temples tucked away in the forest. Within the complex are a number of symbolically distinct shrines, each representing a different Tabanan dynasty. Many of the shrines have been newly renovated, so the place has lost a bit of its charm. One of the few temples of its type on Bali, Pura Luhur is known as a *pura taman,* which means it has a bathing place and is maintained by a king. Note Pura Luhur's seven-tiered *meru,* similar in shape to a Thai stupa, dedicated to the god Mahadewa who presides over Gunung Batukaru. The shrine also exalts Di Made, a ruler of Gelgel A.D. 1164-1686.

A few meters east of the temple are steps leading past lichen-covered statues and demons down to a square artificial pool with a tiny island in the middle, a symbolic microcosm of the Hindu Mount Meru. On the isle are two *bale,* one dedicated to Gunung Batukaru, the other to the deity of the three lakes—Tamblingan, Buyan, and Bratan—which stand within its catchment area. Nearby is a small temple and sacred *air panas* bubbling up from a riverbank. Several paths lead off into the forest.

Getting There And Away

First turn right a bit west of Tabanan and travel north on a steep narrow road up the southern slopes through lovely rice terraces and untouristed villages. Three km before Penebel a turnoff west takes you to the hot springs of Yeh Panas, then on to Wangaya Gede, the village just south of Pura Luhur, and finally to the *desa* of Batukaru where Pura Luhur Batukaru is located. Pura Luhur can also be reached from the main Mengwi-Bedugul road by taking the road east to Marga. These cool, jungled uplands have sublime landscapes, with green moss everywhere.

BEDUGUL AND THE LAKE BRATAN AREA

A small, friendly lakeside resort in the middle of the central highlands southwest of Gunung Catur, an hour's drive (48 km) from Denpasar on the main road north to Singaraja (30 km away). Bedugul is the name given to a number of villages strung out along the lake's western shore. With its comfortable accommodations, wonder-

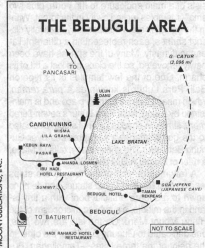

THE BEDUGUL AREA

TO PANCASARI

G. CATUR (2,096 m)

ULUN DANU

CANDIKUNING
WISMA LILA GRAHA

KEBUN RAYA

PASAR

LAKE BRATAN

IBU HADI
ANANDA LOSMEN
HOTEL / RESTAURANT

SUMMIT

GUA JEPENG
(JAPANESE CAVE)

BEDUGUL HOTEL
TAMAN REKREASI

TO BATURITI

BEDUGUL

HADI RAHARJO HOTEL
RESTAURANT

NOT TO SCALE

© MOON PUBLICATIONS, INC.

ful fresh fruit and vegetables, lakeside views, blankets of fog, and an average temperture of 16-20° C, Bedugul has been a popular weekend retreat since Dutch times. It's a welcome change from Bali's tropical scenery and humidity. Few tourists ever stop here.

Serene Lake Bratan fills the ancient crater of long-inactive volcano Gunung Catur (2,096 meters), which towers over the lake. Over 1,200 meters above sea level, Bedugul is nearly as cool as the Gunung Batur region. The cool ride up to this valley through terraced mountain vegetable gardens of cabbage, onion, and papaya is even more scenic than the ride to Kintamani. And Bedugul is more relaxing and quieter—especially in the hot season—than Kintamani, where there are too many grabby sellers. Since Bedugul is a strangely expensive place, it's cheaper to stay in Lovina and charter a car for the day.

The first entrance on the right as you near the top of the mountain is 100% commercial. In fact, there are so many domestic tourists swarming around touristy Hotel Bedugul that sitting quietly on the shore of the lake is impossible. Guides are available at the hotel, but their English needs a lot of work. Across the lake are some 25-meter-deep caves (Gua Jepeng) dug out by Indonesian slave laborers for the Japanese during the war. The caves are accessible

from the rim trail up to Gunung Catur. You can walk there from Taman Rekreasi in about 45 minutes. Don't pass up the beautiful hikes to shrines along the lakeshore and through the steep, jungle-covered hills and pine forests. Bedugul and the mountains that surround it start to cloud over in the afternoon. Overcast skies or rain cause the area to become severely cold (down to 11° C at night), so bring a sweater. A lovely *desa* called Kembangmerta, on the other side of the lake from Hotel Bedugul, is two km from the main road or just one km from Ulun Danu Temple. Dotting the whole hillside are holiday homes of rich Balinese.

Water Sports

It's really crowded on holidays and weekends and during the vacation season, 20 December to 5 January. At other times, the lake is a quiet refuge nearly devoid of tourists both domestic and foreign. Along the pier in front of Hotel Bedugul are moored boats of every size and description. Powerboats stand ready to pull water-skiers and parasailors around the lake, or you may hire a small *prahu* (Rp5000 per hour) and paddle around the placid waters under shady trees, gliding through reflections of steep mountain slopes and fleecy clouds. Lake swimming is chilly, but early in the day when the sun's out the water-skiing on the lake's glassy surface is primo enough to attract international competitions.

In front of Hotel Bedugul is the **Taman Rekreasi Bedugul** (Bedugul Leisure Park) complex (admission Rp500, plus parking fee) where you can go parasailing (Rp20,000 for 15 minutes) and rent water-skiing (Rp25,000 for training, tows, and use of jumping ramp) equipment. Motorboats rent for Rp20,000 (30 minutes, capacity four people), covered boats Rp20,500 per tour of the lake (capacity eight people), Jet-Skis Rp20,000 for 15 minutes. Paddleboats (Rp1000) and wooden *prahu* are also available for paddling across to the temple. Join the children fishing for minnows from the shore; fishing poles and bait cost Rp500 per day.

Accommodations

Don't settle for the limited selection and high prices in Bedugul. Check out accommodations in each of the different communities of the area—Pancasari, Candikuning, Bedugul, Baturiti, Pacung. Three km south of Candikuning in Bedugul village at the junction of the road to the lake is basic, 10-room **Hadi Raharjo Hotel and Restaurant,** tel. (0362) 23467; Rp15,000 for 15 rooms with private *mandi*, cold water, breakfast included. Good value. **Hotel Bedugul,** tel. 29593, on the lake's southern shore, seems to have absorbed all the adjacent, less expensive hotels. This enables the place to get away with charging Rp73,000-94,500 for rather decrepit motel-style lakeside rooms. Also, 36 bungalows face the lake (Rp63,000-Rp105,000) with private *mandi* and hot water plus breakfast. All prices subject to 15.5% tax and service. Patronized by rich Chinese, Jakartans, and Japanese who seem to be the only ones able to afford the waterside restaurant (lunch buffet Rp9325) where the quality of the expensive Chinese-Indonesian food is not that high. A wide range of water sports is offered. A scene for people who like people.

Between Candikuning and Bedugul is the **Mini-Bali,** appropriately named for its six tiny Rp15,000 rooms, small beds, and the truly mini portions served in its restaurant. One room (Rp20,000) has a private *mandi*. Spartan yet clean.

Food

Owing to the temperate climate and heavy rainfall in these mountains, Bedugul offers a giddy selection of European and Asian produce grown on the area's fertile mountain slopes. Bedugul supplies the southern population centers and hotel resorts with most of its vegetables and succulent fruits. The *warung* near the trailhead up to Gunung Catur serve delicious *gado-gado,* fried vegetables, and *nasi goreng.* Bargain. Bedugul also features several grocery stores and lots of fruit vendors.

Getting There And Away

A good road runs from Singaraja's western bus station to Bedugul, Rp1700 by *bemo* or minibus. If heading north to Singaraja, take a *bemo* (Rp2000) from Denpasar's Ubung station to Bedugul—a faster route to the north coast than via Kintamani. Bands of dark, heavy-coated monkeys are often seen along this road. If you're heading back to Denpasar, start early in the afternoon because *bemo* (Rp2000) tend to fill up fast above Bedugul; by the time they reach you there's no more seating room. At the Denpasar

40 km sign at Baturiti, a dirt road drops down to the cultivated plains, emerging just before Mengwi. So full of boulders it'll shake the guts out of anyone on a motorcycle. A nicer experience is to walk the 25-km-long track from Bedugul to Kintamani. You're also within striking distance of the mountain area around Munduk; just head north by road to Giggit and then turn east. Stop in at pristine Danau Tamblingan en route.

Pura Puncak Mangu

This remote temple is located on the rim of the caldera above Lake Bratan. What the temple on top of Gunung Abang is to the people of the Gunung Batur region, this temple is to the people of Bedugul. Though it's one of the sacred *sad-kahyangan* temples of Bali, it's little known. If you're in reasonably good shape, the six-km hike to the top of Gunung Catur takes about two hours. Reach the trailhead by turning right off the main road at the Y before Bedugul; the well-marked path to the top of Gunung Catur starts at the end of this road. The first segment winds through bean and cabbage patches, then climbs through a dank *lantana* and pandanus forest. For the last several kilometers, you must pull yourself by roots and trees up a slippery, muddy, steep slope. On the way, you'll pass an abandoned, dilapidated Dutch country house hidden in the bush. At the top is a large flat area inhabited by monkeys; a dense forest blocks the view. Ancient Pura Puncak Mangu, built by Mengwi's first *raja,* is a simple, peaceful temple with a *padmasana,* shrines, a linga, some nice reliefs, and two *meru.* Camping is possible under the temple's several *bale.* Takes only an hour to get back down. Bring water.

Baturiti

A village five km south of Bedugul, with breathtaking views and wonderful fresh air. Market every three days. Both accommodations and food are less expensive here than in Bedugul.

Accommodations: The **Pacung Hotel and Restaurant,** tel. (0362) 26531, ext. 131, overlooks the valley near Baturiti. With a lovely setting, good service, and small pool, it's expensive at Rp126,000 per bungalow with private baths, hot water, fridge, TV, in-house video. Suite bungalows cost Rp147,000. The restaurant offers well-prepared Indonesian and Chinese dishes (Rp4000-5000), freshwater fish, and a Westernized buffet (Rp12,000) 1200-1500. Add 15.5% to all prices. About one km south of Candikuning market in Baturiti is the **Bukit Mungsu Indah Hotel,** tel. 23662 or 23663, with 13 cottages on a hill looking south toward the lowlands. Standard rooms range Rp40,000-55,000, superior rooms Rp55,000-60,000 with TV, fireplace, and basic breakfast included. The best rooms face the Kebun Raya botanical gardens. Cheaper rooms are smaller and have no TV. In the mornings you can see the surrounding mountains.

The **Green Valley Homestay and Restaurant,** about two km south of Candikuning market, has fantastic views, taking in Gunung Agung and rice fields to the sea. In addition to the lunchtime buffet for Rp11,000, food is available a la carte (drivers eat free). More of a small hotel than a homestay, the rooms are Rp20,000-40,000 with TV and hot showers. The new owner, Ida Bagus Wiryana, also owns restaurants in Lovina and Candidasa. He is studying for the priesthood and is definitely a good Samaritan. **Pacung Cottages and Restaurant,** tel. (0361) 25824, fax 37638, just south of Baturiti and nine km south of Lake Bratan in Pacung village, is a pleasant rest stop. Rates are Rp115,000-136,500 s, Rp126,000-147,000 d, suites Rp294,000 (subject to 15.5% tax and service). Rooms are carpeted, with private baths, hot water, and balconies. The bar and restaurant serves international cuisine (too Westernized). Amenities include 24-hour room service, heated pool, con-ference room, gift shop, dry-cleaning, and ample parking.

Candikuning

Two km north of Bedugul, extending along the road on the west side of Lake Bratan, are the Muslim lakeside villages of Candikuning I and Candikuning II, settled by Javanese, Madurese, and Islamic Sasaks from Lombok. A *wartel* is opposite the market. This is a popular fishing spot.

Be sure to visit the colorful fruit/vegetable/flower market, Pasar Candikuning, north of the turn to Hotel Bedugul; in front is a statue of an ear of corn standing on a fat cabbage. Buy luscious passion fruit, jackfruit, wild strawberries, mangos, pomegranates, and such temperate and tropical vegetables as carrots, potatoes, corn on the cob, and year-round asparagus. The starting prices are high: Rp3000 for a kilo of apples, Rp5000 for a bunch of vanilla pod. Don't believe them when they say they're selling saffron—this is the name for *nasi kuning* coloring and flavoring, for which they want Rp1000. Be prepared to bargain vigorously. In the back is the fresh flower market, with tier upon tier of potted ferns, hydrangeas, begonias, champak, lilies, and beautiful wild mountain orchids. You'll find the widest selection of ornamental plants August to September.

The Ulun Danu Temple Complex

On a small promontory jutting out from the western shore of the lake is this peaceful half-Hindu,

Ulun Danu Bratan temples

DAVE LINDFIELWOOD

half-Buddhist temple complex built by the *raja* of Mengwi in 1633. Lake Bratan is looked upon as the source of irrigation water for the southern districts and the *subuk* shrine here is the focus of island-wide ceremonies meant to ensure a steady and continued supply of water. Periodically the temple is flooded by the rising lake, reclaimed again and again.

Turn in from the main north-south highway and into the parking lot, which faces the usual row of gaudy souvenir shops. Walk under the canopy of a huge banyan tree past a satiny lawn and gorgeous gardens with trumpet-flower trees and gladiolas—a scene of beauty. To the left is a Buddhist stupa with intricate carvings, then enter the main temple Pura Teratai Bang, dominated by a seven-tiered *meru* tower. The goddess of food and drink is revered at the smaller Pura Dalem Purwa. Farther on is Pura Ulun Danu Bratan floating out on the lake with its elegant 11-roofed *meru* dedicated to Vishnu, its seven-roofed *meru* dedicated to Brahma, and its three-roofed *meru* housing a linga dedicated to Shiva. There are also two smaller shrines. This is Bali's most important irrigation temple, the destination of pilgrims from all over the island who come to worship Dewi Danu, the water goddess. Few pushy sellers, lots of native Balinese, occasional busloads of tourists.

You can also approach Pura Ulun Danu from the lake. Any number of boatmen around Hotel Bedugul will take you there for Rp200 adults, Rp100 childen. From the temple, walk around the shore of the lake. If you lose interest halfway around the lake, you can always hire a canoe to take you across to Pura Ulun Danu or Bedugul.

Kebun Raya

The start of the 2.5-km-long road up to Bali's sprawling botanical gardens, arboretum, and mountain orchid collection lies just 200 meters south of the Candikuning market. Founded in 1959, the park is dedicated to the study of the mountain flora of eastern Indonesia. Specimens are labeled in Latin, signs are in Indonesian. Open daily 0800-1630. Entrance Rp300; free for Balinese. Benches and toilets are available inside the park. A superb place for a picnic or a shady stroll. If you're looking for peace and solitude, stay away on the weekends.

A branch of the Bogor Botanical Gardens, this extensive 130-hectare garden features a collection of 500 varieties of orchids and 668 species of local and imported trees. An excellent eight-km-long footpath at the north end of the gardens leads through the foothills of Gunung Tapak at the north end of the valley. The path comes out on the main road in Pancasari.

Accommodations and Food: Two inexpensive places are on the road to the botanical gardens. At Rp15,000, the **Mawar Indah** is highway robbery. Nicer and cleaner is the Islamic hotel **Ibu Hadi**, Jl. Kebun Raya, tel. 23497, a convenient and central place for travelers. Light and airy rooms cost Rp10,000-20,000. Most Ibu Hadi rooms overlook cabbage and onion patches. The scenic front veranda overlooks the town. When not raining, you can see the lake. Ask to see the "special room" (Rp25,000) at the top of the stairs. Downstairs is a restaurant serving very cheap Central Javanese fare, with nothing over Rp3000. Pay extra for the staff to boil up a tub of hot water. Prices include tea and banana pancakes; no tax or service charge. **Ananda,** a small *losmen* just across from the Candikuning market on the main road, is new and clean. At Rp20,000 with breakfast, this is a best buy.

Not a bad deal is the **Lila Graha,** high on a hill looking out over Ulun Danu Temple and the lake, though the barbed wire installed for security reasons makes the backyard look like a concentration camp. An old Dutch villa built in 1935, bungalows were added in 1970. Bungalow rooms cost Rp25,000-30,000 with suites for Rp60,000. Rates include breakfast. The bungalows on the side of the hill are more private, nicer but noisier. Restaurant. Book through the office in Denpasar, Jl. Kamboja 10, tel. (0361) 237-245, fax 36201, or call the hotel directly, tel. 25750. Around the lakeside north of Bedugul, opposite the road to the Lila Graha, is **Hotel Ashram**, tel. (0368) 21101 or (0362) 22439, which caters primarily to groups. Bungalows spread out over a whole hillside with gardens and stepping-stone paths. Tariff is Rp30,000-70,000 for rooms with hot water, bathtub, spring beds, and terrace. The smaller Rp30,000 rooms come with cold water, no shower, no bathtub. The Ashram has two restaurants, one a delightful open-air pavilion looking out over the lake, the other in the middle of the attractive hillside garden.

In Candikuning market, eat cheaply at **Warung Nasi Era** and **Warung Nasi Sari Sedana**, which sell *nasi campur* for Rp2000. Or in the market buy the steamed corn on the cob and sweet rice wrapped in coconut leaves. Try fresh lake fish and Indonesian food across the road at **Ananda**. Next door is **Ayam Goreng Jogya**, specializing in *ayam goreng*. Several doors away is Ananda II for Chinese food. A nice venue for tea and dessert is the open-air patio of the **Perama Tea House** on the lake on the south side of the Ulun Danu temple complex.

PANCASARI

A vegetable-growing and service community north of Bedugul. The Lake Buyan Recreation Area is on the left as you enter Pancasari from the south. There's a very scenic walk around the south side of the lake, up over the saddle, then on to Lake Tamblingan to the road around the northern side of the lakes back to Pancasari. An inexpensive hotel overlooking Lake Buyan is Lake Buyan Cottage, tel. (0362) 21351, close to the post office, just down from the market, 200 meters from the main road.

SUMATRA

COURTESY OF THE ROYAL TROPICAL INSTITUTE IN AMSTERDAM

The "Africa of Southeast Asia," this gigantic island—sixth largest in the world—is 1,760 km long and up to 400 km wide. It accounts for a full 25% of the total Indonesian land area. In just about every way—economically, politically, and strategically—Sumatra is Indonesia's most important island. With its grass huts, lake tribes, wildlife reserves, steamy jungles, swampy lowlands, swift clear rivers, spectacular waterfalls, crater lakes, and immense forests of 30-meter-high tropical trees, Sumatra has become the third most popular tourist destination in Indonesia. Called the "Isle of Hope" or the "Isle of Gold," this island's natural wealth is fabulous.

INTRODUCTION

You'll feel a vast difference between Sumatra and neighboring Java. Sumatra is far wilder, more rugged, more ethnically diverse, and more difficult to get around in. Islam entered some coastal regions of Sumatra more than 300 years before it touched Java. With the exception of northern Sumatrans, the people are generally less educated and poorer than the Javanese, and their culture is not as refined. People are shorter, darker, more wiry—a jungle people. You're apt to find more *kasar* individuals on Sumatra, which—after Java—is sometimes refreshing. Compared to Java, this island has a grand beauty, and the distances and space are enormous.

THE LAND

Sumatra took its name from the early Muslim port of Samudra (from the Sanskrit for "sea"), near modern Lhokseumawe in Aceh Province. About the same size and population as California, almost one-third of the island is continuous lowland and saltwater swamp with nipa palms and mangrove trees extending some 1,370 km down the whole east coast. The rivers are shallow and winding as drainage is poor and flooding common. Fine white sand beaches, but with rugged surf, are found on the west coast and its offshore islands.

An unbroken mountain wall ranging from 1,575 to 3,805 meters marches down the entire western aspect of the island. Called Bukit Barisan ("Parade of Mountains"), this range includes 93 volcanic peaks, 15 of them still active. On its western side the mountains plunge steeply into the sea, while on its eastern side they slope gently down to the plains and swamps.

Based on analysis of French and U.S. satellite data, an astonishing 30% of Sumatra's forests disappeared in the eight years between 1982 and 1990. All major ecosystems are represented in reserves throughout the island, with the exception of lowland rainforests, always the first to come under the axe. The northwest and southwest regions are still quite inaccessible and wild. There's a chain of islands off the west coast—Simeulue, Nias, the Mentawais, and Enggano—with rocky, reef-enclosed coasts.

Climate

The equator cuts this huge island in equal halves. Heaviest rains north of the equator occur Oct.-April, while the dry season is May-Sep-

SUMATRA

0   100 km

© MOON PUBLICATIONS, INC.

tember. South of the equator, the rainy season is Dec.-Feb., sometimes making the roads nearly impassable. Because clouds coming in from the ocean are blocked by the Bukit Barisan range, the climate west of the range is often rainy and hot. The ideal time to travel through Sumatra is Sept.-Oct., when the rains have started, but they're not so torrential that the roads wash out and, unlike in the dry season, dust isn't constantly in the air.

FLORA

The mangrove forests of Sumatra are the largest and most biologically diverse in the world. In the rainforests trees such as the *keta-pang* soar over 60 meters high, supported by six-meter-high buttress roots. In northern Sumatra is the indigenous pine *Pinus merkusii*, extensively used in reforestation schemes on Java. Vines called "wait-a-minute" are tipped with spines that often snare people on jungle tracks. Strangler figs send long tendril roots to the ground from branches of tall trees, gradually suffocating the host tree. The corpse plant, a huge, foul plant that smells like putrefying animal flesh, consists of a central spike over two meters high which rises from a bowl of giant leaves. Its stench attracts beetles and other insects to help it pollinate.

The extraordinary rafflesia grows up to one meter in diameter—the largest bloom in the world. Found on the island's west coast, this fascinating plant rises from the leaf-littered forest floor. A bud develops and grows to the size of a large cabbage, brown in color. Nine months later the flower opens, spreading out brilliant white-spotted orange petals. Finally it rots to a spongy mess on the mossy, damp ground, the plant's large sticky seeds carried to new soil by animals that eat or brush against it.

FAUNA

Sumatra has always been famous for its animals. It has a greater variety of wildlife than any other island in Indonesia: 176 different mammals, 194 reptiles, 62 amphibians, 520 birds. The jungle is near at hand and the island's wild creatures have always played a great part in

its myth and folklore. Observe the many thousands of tigers, mythical birds, and other beasts painted on *becak* and signboards all over Sumatra. Since the island's flora and fauna are largely shared with Malaysia, Kalimantan, and Java, few species are endemic. Elephants, Sumatran rhinoceros, and large free-ranging populations of Sumatran orangutans are the island's best-known fauna. Orangutans, rhinos, and wild pigs are only found in the north, while the tapir and certain species of monkeys are found only in the south.

A cousin to the Javanese tiger, Sumatran tigers occasionally venture into more remote villages to take a pig or calf. It's customary to call a tiger "grandfather" (and when crossing rivers, be sure to address a crocodile as "grandmother"). Tigers' claws are a powerful good-luck charm, and their whiskers grated in alcohol will make one man strong as ten. Other predatory species include the elusive Sumatran clouded leopard, the civet, and a small, striped forest cat called the *macan akar*. Use a flashlight to spot the *macan akar* hunting in the trees at night.

Tapirs, wild dogs, bearded pigs, sun bears, flying foxes, squirrels, wild oxen, the Sumatran hare, and barking and mouse deer also live here. Other unique mammals include the slow loris, the subalpine gray shrew, and the rare goat antelope, which lives above 1,500 meters. Honey bears have footprints similar to people's and can walk upright on their hind legs—characteristics that generated many stories and even search parties in the early 1900s. There are also numerous species of monkeys, such as the pigtailed macaque and the fox-nosed monkey. The flying lemur and the proboscis monkey are found in the island's mangrove swamps.

One species of orangutan lives on Sumatra, a rare primate found only in the most remote parts of the island. Don't be deceived by lookalikes such as red-leaf monkeys, which are orange, hairy, and swing and crash through treetops. To be certain, just look for a tail, as great apes such as orangutans are tailless; also, orangutans do not hoot, as do red-leaf monkeys. Orangutans may be observed in a semiwild state in the Bukit Lawang Rehabilitation Center at Bohorok in northern Sumatra. Another huge reserve, where many of Sumatra's species are found, is the Gunung Leuser National Park of Aceh and North Sumatra.

Sumatra is also the home of Indonesia's grandest animal, the Indian elephant. Moving in herds of 20-30, an estimated 2,000 survive. The Sumatran species has small ears and isn't as hairy or as large as the African variety—it stands only three meters high, a pygmy pachyderm. The Sumatran two-horned rhinoceros is the world's smallest rhino, averaging only 1.37 meters in height and weighing on average 900 kilos. Its body is covered with bristly hair. Only a handful survive in deep rainforests, where they browse on the leaves of small trees.

Sumatra's wide variety of birdlife includes dazzling parrots and cockatoos, hornbills, the great argus pheasant, the crested partridge, the rose-crested bee-eater, woodpeckers, and nearly all the pigeons of Indonesia. Sumatra is also famed for its endemic species of insects, including a submarine diving grasshopper and a very rare olive-and-black moth that has a wingspan of over 10 cm. There's even a cave-dwelling cricket with antennae 20 cm long.

HISTORY

In mythical times, Sinbad the Sailor is said to have landed on an "extremely fertile island of abundance" off Sumatra where he met the "Old Man of the Sea." In the 1st century, a Chinese emperor dispatched an expedition to Sumatra to procure a rhinoceros for the imperial zoo. By the 7th century, Sumatra was the most important island in the archipelago and the cultural heart of Southeast Asia. Two seagoing, piratical, mercantile empires were based near present-day Palembang and at Jambi. The Sriwijaya Kingdom was a 7th-century offshoot of the Buddhist Sailendra cult of *devaraj* (god kings).

Sriwijaya had no agricultural lands to speak of but, guarding one of the main waterways of the ancient world (the Strait of Malacca), this trading empire at its height controlled an area which included Sumatra, the western end of Java, and the east coast of Malaysia. Its commercial and political influence extended as far as ancient Formosa and Hainan. A Sriwijayan prince even became ruler of Cambodia. In the 13th century, the empire finally broke up into city-states, mainly on coasts and rivermouths.

Sumatra has a long history of foreign contact. Accounts of Indonesia's first Islamic community, Perlak (present-day Aceh), were brought back to Europe by Marco Polo, who visited the northern tip of Sumatra in the 13th century. He also recorded that Sumatra was "Java the Less," though the island is three times larger than Java.

Portuguese influence on Sumatra is apparent in some of the island names. The island of Enggano (meaning "Mistake" in Portuguese) off the west coast was probably named after a Portuguese navigational error. In 1602 the Dutch became a major controlling power in Sumatra—and the archipelago—with the establishment of the privately held Dutch East India Company. In 1699 the company went bankrupt, and the Dutch government took over all its holdings. In 1685, the English established fortified factories on the west coast, trading in pepper and other spices, but abandoned this effort by treaty with the Dutch in 1824. The Japanese launched the invasion of Sumatra up the Musi River in February 1942, capturing the oil fields around Palembang, one of the richest prizes of the Pacific War.

ECONOMY

Because of its mineral wealth and cash crops, the Dutch used to refer to Sumatra as the "Isle of the Future." World War II, however, abruptly and permanently interrupted their development plans. Now the Javanese are the chief exploiters of the island's wealth; Sumatra today is the mainstay of the Indonesian economy. The island supplies about 50% of Indonesia's gross import earnings—more than half its oil, three-quarters of its rubber and palm oil, a major portion of its coffee, and the total output of the country's tin, as well as substantial quantities of coal, bauxite, aluminum, and gold. Thirty percent of all Indonesian exports—oil, natural gas, rubber, palm oil, tea, *sisal*, and tobacco—originate from northern Sumatra alone. Sumatra has only nine percent of Indonesia's industry, although the factories of northern Sumatra are among the worst polluters in the country. Only 18% of the island's people live in the towns. Shipping, trading, and fishing in coastal areas traditionally form the backbone of the island's local subsistence economy.

Oil is Sumatra's big money-earner, accounting for nearly 40% of Indonesia's petroleum revenues. Oil was valued in ancient times by the Chinese as a medicine for skin diseases, rheumatism, and other ailments. During Sriwijayan times, jars of the curious substance were brought from southern Sumatra to Peking for the emperor of China. In the 1500s, naval warriors of northern Sumatra poured oil on the waters of bays to keep intruding ships out of their ports. In 1866, American Alvin S. Bickmore was given a bottle of crude oil by a local *raja* on a trip to Palembang, where the first oil in South Sumatra was drilled by the West in 1896—a herald of the great Talang Akar oil fields 48 km north of Palembang. In addition to crude oil, Sumatra produces many refined petrochemical products—kerosene, gasoline, urea, and plastics. Until the oil price slump of 1986, this created an economic boom in the large coastal cities of Pekanbaru, Jambi, Medan, and Palembang.

THE PEOPLE

With its great diversity of tribes (*puak*), and numerous megalithic, aboriginal, and matriarchal societies, Sumatra is one of Southeast Asia's richest cultural areas. During the mesolithic era, while Java and Bali were still connected to mainland Southeast Asia, groups of pre-Malay peoples drifted south from China and Burma. Since that migration, wave after wave of Chinese, Indians, Arabians, and Javanese have also made Sumatra their home. Although Sumatra has the highest birthrate in the nation, the island is today underpopulated, with only 30,750,000 people, a mere 15% of Indonesia's total. While Sumatra has about 33 persons per square km, Java has nearly 900.

Ethnic Groups

Numerous ethnic groups are found in Sumatra, among them some of the most ancient cultures of Indonesia. Besides the main groups (Acehnese, Batak, Minangkabau, Lampungese) are isolated aborigines such as the Sakai in Riau Daratan, the Kubu of southern Sumatra, and the Sakkudai of the Mentawais—all descendants of the archipelago's original inhabitants and bypassed by the mainstreams of the 20th century.

Coastal Malays are another long-settled group, living in Sumatra's southern and eastern parts; they've probably populated the island as hardy seafarers for several millennia. The majority of Sumatra's population does not, however, live along the coasts. In the mountain regions of North Sumatra live the Christian Batak, and the high uplands of West Sumatra around Bukittinggi are the home of the matriarchal Minangkabau. Both groups live as traders and successful agriculturalists. Peripheral groups such as the "Sea Gypsies" (or Orang Laut) still fish and trade in small, unsturdy boats along the swampy shores of eastern Sumatra and in the hundreds of islands of the Riau Archipelago. In northernmost Aceh Province live the staunchest Muslims who, from the late 16th century, ruled the coasts of Sumatra from river-based trading kingdoms.

ARTS AND CRAFTS

Music

Sumatra's pervasive Islamic influence is reflected in its musical instruments. A primitive type of oboe (*serunai*) is almost identical to the *surnai*, originally from Persia. A tambourine-like drum (*rebana*), bamboo flute, and various forms of lutes and string instruments found throughout the island are also common in other Islamic areas of the world. The gong and drum of southern Sumatra show a strong Javanese influence. The various musical structures and differently tuned instruments also indicate Chinese, Indian, Arabic, and Portuguese infusions.

Dance

It's said there's a different dance for every one of Sumatra's 100 districts, and that the island has as many dancers as single girls. Married women seldom dance. Sumatran dancers, known for their *gaya* (grace), are masters of smooth, soft, willowy movements. Candle dances (*tari lilin* or *tari piring*), in one form or the other, are performed all over the island. In the handkerchief dance, men and women each hold one end of a large white square cloth. They perform a kind of maypole dance, winding in and out and turning around, tying the handkerchiefs in a series of knots. At the conclusion, they untangle the cloth immediately and faultlessly.

Textiles

Sumatra produces three types of cloth: *batik* in Palembang and Jambi, dye-resist *ikat* on a backstrap loom, and *songket,* a discontinuous supplementary-weft technique which often incorporates metallic threads of silver or gold into the weave. The dye-resist and supplementary-weft *ikat* techniques are associated with areas—such as Batakland or Lampung—where ancient peoples first migrated to Sumatra. The Neolithic and Dongson-style patterns reflect the limited contact of these with later cultural influences such as Islam. The *songket,* on the other hand, is found in locales such as the Minang Highlands, which has experienced a considerable amount of outside cultural and mercantile influence. Today, the *songket* is produced on a self-standing frame loom employing chemical dyes and gold-foil-covered thread. Used mainly for wedding ceremonies, *songket* clothing is extremely elaborate. The finest examples are found in the Palembang area, where until very recently pure gold and silver thread were used.

Architecture
The traditional architecture, especially of northern and western Sumatra, is magnificent. Large rectangular buildings on wooden pilings are built one to two meters off the ground, with swooping saddle-shaped roofs and high gables at both ends that rise to a point. Structures are often adorned with geometric designs and buffalo horns, and carvings grace the gable-ends. So impressive are these structures that they've served as models for "national" architectural styles. By contrast, houses along the rivers, swamps, and jungles of eastern and southern Sumatra are simple pole cottages with ladders (tigers can't climb ladders).

As for classical monuments, since Sumatra's great Sriwijaya were more concerned with international trade and control over the Strait of Malacca than in governing the interior, no great monument complexes were produced. The few temples and stupas that do exist (such as at Padanglawas, Muaro Takus, and Kota Cina) are in such a state of ruin they don't grab you like Java's finely crafted and preserved monuments.

GETTING THERE

Most travelers opt for the 20-minute flight from Penang, Malaysia, to Medan, or take the hydrofoil from Penang to the port of Belawan 27 km from Medan. From Medan, they then travel down the island in a more or less southerly direction,

exiting via Pekanbaru to Singapore or via Bandar Lampung to Java. You can also approach from the south by taking a boat from Singapore to Tanjung Pinang (four hours) or Pulau Batam (30 minutes) in the Riau Islands, and sailing up the Siak River to Pekanbaru in eastern Sumatra (27 hours). There are also regular flights from Tanjung Pinang and Pulau Batam to Palembang, Pekanbaru, and Medan, and from Singapore or Kuala Lumpur, Malaysia's capital, to Medan.

From Merak, West Java
From Jakarta's Kalideres bus station, take a bus (3.5 hours) to Merak; one leaves every quarter hour. Or take the fast morning train from Tanah Abang train station, which connects with the ferry. The ferry terminal is within walking distance of Merak's train station. The ferry takes five to six hours, passing within 20 km of Krakatoa in the Sunda Strait. First class is Rp4300; third class Rp1695. The railway ferry's RoRo-coaches roll off at the Serengsem terminal five km east of Panjang, while the regular passenger ferries dock at Panjang. Scores of local and long-distance buses at Panjang and Serengsem are ready to depart for such distant destinations as Bukittinggi and Medan.

From Merak, car ferries also sail for Bakauheni east of Panjang at least eight times daily. They take only 1.5 hours and cost Rp2200 first class and Rp1275 third class. The price of the ferry is included in your ticket. From Bakauheni, take a bus (two hours) to Bandar Lampung's Terminal Rajabasa, from where you can catch buses to Palembang and points north. From Bandar Lampung, you can take a train to Palembang and on to Lubuklinggau; from there buses continue to Padang and Bengkulu. You can also purchase a one-way bus ticket from Jakarta to any point on Sumatra.

From Jakarta
Non-a/c buses from Jakarta head for Padang (Rp35,000, two days), Palembang (Rp19,000, 20 hours), and Jambi (Rp25,000). To avoid this experience of your life, fly Garuda to Padang (Rp187,000, three times daily), Pekanbaru (Rp189,000, twice daily), Jambi (Rp133,000, twice daily), Bengkulu (Rp115,500, twice daily), Medan (Rp259,000, daily), or Banda Aceh (Rp398,700, daily). Trains also travel from

Jakarta to Merak, cross the strait to Serengsem, then head north to Palembang and then as far as Lubuklinggau.

If you have more time, take the Pelni ship to Medan. The passage takes 36 hours, arriving in Medan on Monday morning. Jakarta to Padang (and vice versa) on the weekly Pelni ship KM *Kerinci* is popular with those who want to avoid the grueling bus trip or the expensive flight. This modern deluxe a/c ship departs Jakarta's port of Tanjung Priok every other Friday at 1300, arriving in Padang around 1600 the following day, for Rp132,000 first class, Rp40,200 economy. Pelni's Jakarta office is at Jl. Angkasa 18, tel. (021) 421-1921, fax 421-1929.

From Penang, West Malaysia

The shortest, quickest way into Sumatra—and Indonesia—is to take the daily flight from Penang to Medan with MAS. Buy this ticket cheaper in Malaysia than in the U.S. or Australia. The inexpensive Penang-Medan/Medan-Penang hops are the ones most often chosen to fulfill Indonesia's onward-ticket requirement. The MAS flight leaves Penang's airport daily and takes just 20 minutes to Medan (M$125 one-way). In Medan, the MAS office is in the Danau Toba International Hotel, Jl. Imam Bonjol 17, tel. (061) 519-333.

A fast, regular hydrofoil sails from Penang to Medan's port of Belawan. Buy tickets at Penang's Tourist Association Office on Jl. Syed Barakhbah, at the shipping company itself (Kuala Perlis-Langkawi Ferry Service Sdn. Bhd., PPC Shopping Complex, next to PTA office, Jl. Pusara King Edward, 10300 Pengang, tel. 04-625-630), or at a number of travel agencies and hotels along Chulia Street. Tickets cost M$100 one-way. The ferry departs Tuesday and Friday at 0800 from near Penang's Port Commission and the crossing takes five hours. Before you get your boarding pass, pay a compulsory M$6 seaport tax. On board the boat bus tickets from Belawan to Medan's bus station (27 km) sell for Rp4000.

From The Riau Islands

Boats depart for both Pulau Batam and Tanjung Pinang in the Riaus, a small archipelago off Sumatra's southeast coast, from Singapore's Finger Pier 0800-2030. In the Riaus, which serve as stepping stones to Sumatra and Java, go through customs and get an entry stamp in your passport. For Pulau Batam, boats take only 30 minutes and cost S$20 one-way. Fast boats (2.5 hours) cost S$65 one-way; slower boats (four hours) run S$45 to Tanjung Pinang. Pelni has a ship that sails to Medan in North Sumatra from Tanjung Pinang every other Friday. Get a schedule from the Indonesia Tourist Promotion Office, 10 Collyer Quay #15-07, Ocean Building, Singapore, tel. 534-2837, or in Tanjung Pinang at the Pelni office five km out of town on Jl. A. Yani.

Also leaving Tanjung Pinang daily at around noon is a boat up the Siak River to Pekanbaru; Rp7500 deck, Rp12,500 for berths. You arrive in Pekanbaru at around 0700 the next day. Bukittinggi is only Rp5000 and five hours from Pekanbaru. From Tanjung Pinang there are also regular Garuda flights for Palembang (four days weekly), Padang (three days weekly), and Pekanbaru (daily). From Pulau Batam's Hang Nadim Airport, 30 km and Rp10,000 by taxi from Sekupang, there are daily flights to Pekanbaru, Palembang (Rp116,000), Medan, and Padang (Rp117,000) with Sempati, Merpati, or SMAC. From Tanjung Pinang, flights to Pekanbaru cost Rp98,400 and to Palembang Rp117,000.

From Melaka, West Malaysia

A ferry leaves twice a week from Melaka on Malaysia's west coast to the oil port of Dumai in eastern Sumatra (north of Pekanbaru), costing M$80 and taking two hours. From Dumai take a bus to Pekanbaru (158 km), then another bus to Bukittinggi (Rp5000, five hours). Since Dumai is not an official entry point into Indonesia, you won't receive an entry pass upon arrival so you need to obtain an Indonesian visa before departing Melaka. Or you can just taxi up to Kuala Lumpur and catch the twice weekly flight to Medan, or taxi down to Singapore from where you can catch daily Garuda flights to Medan and Pekanbaru (S$87), or fly to Padang (three flights weekly).

GETTING AROUND

Since the weather has such an effect on the condition of Sumatra's roads, it's important to plan your itinerary to avoid road and bridge washouts and swollen river crossings. Also be aware that the exchange rate is infinitely better in Medan than elsewhere in Sumatra so estimate your spending for the whole of Sumatra and change your money in Medan.

By Air
Sumatra has a fairly extensive air network. Using planes will definitely save you time and hassles. Check SMAC, Mandala, Sempati, and Merpati fares, as they sometimes fly identical routes at cheaper prices than Garuda. SMAC is an extremely useful airline plying the northern part of the island.

By Boat
An alternative way to head south from Medan is to take the daily train to Tanjungbalai (archetypal Indonesian port town) where there's a boat going down to Bagansiapiapi about every week. Once there, you're in Riau, where there are many boats to Dumai, Bengkalis, or upriver on the Rokan to Pekanbaru. While there, see what Caltex is doing to the rainforest.

By Train
The island's rail system is concentrated in the south. These trains generally carry a tough clientele; be on your guard for theft. A line starts in Bandar Lampung and heads north to Prabumulih, east to Palembang, and west to Lubuklinggau, the end of the line. Don't reserve seats on a train that hasn't arrived yet because the seats will already be full and people won't move. Only reserve seats on a train that originates from the station you're buying your ticket in. If you want to stretch out, buy tickets for two seats. Vendors working the aisles sell all kinds of fruit, drinks, and rice combos. The dining car is always a relaxing place to hang out—more breathing space and the windows are bigger.

By Bus
The chief interest in Sumatra is the journey through it. If you want to experience the true art of riding a Sumatran bus, take the bus trip north from Bandar Lampung to Medan. The lengthwise journey through Sumatra is one of the last true adventures on earth. Don't be put off by the tales you hear of this journey; the country in between more than makes up for the hardship. Because of the lack of vehicles on this huge island, Sumatran local buses are generally more crowded than on Java and Bali. You could travel on a bus with gunny-sacked pigs, casks of coconut wine, goats pissing on your foot, and occupied coffins resting on the shoulders of relatives.

Whereas delays of an hour or so are normal on Java and Bali, delays in Sumatra can vary by days. Here you'll have a guaranteed breakdown at least once, and a comic repair show. You'll get bogged down in mud, driven over log-strewn cow paddocks, with your head beating against the ceiling and your buttocks resting on spikes. You'll spend more time airborne than on the seat, like being inside a cement mixer. Bus sickness is rampant and companies thoughtfully dispense plastic bags, which Indonesian passengers take frequent advantage of. Endless whining, piercing, nasal Indonesian or Chinese music is played right above your head at full distorted volume. Often on the longer journeys, VCR movies will be shown without pause. Kung fu may be played in English, followed by a tearjerker in Indonesian.

A stoker usually accompanies the driver to do running repairs, perform errands, and collect fares. The driver eats five times a day at Padang-style restaurants along the way, with untold stops for drinks and snacks. On some northern Sumatran runs, the drivers even race each other, the passengers unwilling spectators. Up on the roof is a crawl space provided for the crew, located between the goods covered by a tarpaulin. Try to wrangle a place up here— it's like riding a wild bronco, but the air is much better and there's more to look at.

The Machines: Sumatra's old boxy buses of the '80s are being replaced with a new generation of sleek long-distance Mercedes buses with a/c, reclining seats, and toilet. Mitsubishi minivans, built for nine people but squeezing in 19, handle the short routes. The private "chicken-catcher" local buses must be inspired by the same muse that created the jeepneys in Manila. They're vividly colored, sometimes with a high gloss, and the painting has to be competitive. Given such macho names as Guntur ("Thunderbolt") and Kilat ("Lightning"), some of these beauties also have the most incredible horn systems you can imagine, complete with a full set of keys capable of playing such tunes as "We Are The World." The driver will come down full throttle on an intersection or have a car turn in front of him, and instead of honking will render these great soaring crescendos.

The Roads: During Dutch times they used to hold car rallies that would take ten days from the south all the way up to Aceh. It took a leisurely week to travel by motorcar from Panjang to Medan, overnighting in comfortable motor lodges along the way. Today the magnificent 2,500-km Trans-Sumatra Highway runs right up through the center of Sumatra from Bandar Lampung to Banda Aceh. Though it's been vastly improved, it will never really be finished because it's constantly washed away or blocked by landslides, particularly in the wetter south.

Elsewhere road conditions are extremely variable, with some horrible stretches. About 60% of all roads are single lane. The road from Bukittinggi to Padang is in fair shape, and the roads south of Padang are generally worse than the roads in the north. The only consistently sealed segment is from Sungaidareh to Bukittinggi. Surolangun and the section between Muara Amin and Baturaja in the south may be trouble spots. It's possible to travel by bus all the way from Lubuklinggau to Bukittinggi in two days, a beautiful but hard-slogging section. You can do the whole length of the island in the dry season in three to four days if you meet all your connections. If you don't want to rupture your spleen, however, consider breaking up your journey with rest stops.

One can never really predict what conditions will be like. In April, toward the end of the rainy season, whole stretches of road may have washed out or disappeared under devastating landslides. At night you could come upon a gigantic hole in the ground; pray that the driver sees it. The crew will sometimes lay lumber on the mud and drive through it, or attach a winch to a tree. Some buses without winches could be hung up in the mud in one place for as long as a week, passengers camping in and around the bus and on the roof. Whole caravans could get trapped, stranded in the mud for days.

In the wet season rivers might be swollen too high for vehicles to board the unwieldy rope-bound wooden rafts used as ferries. These rafts are hauled across the river along a steel hawser slung betwen the two banks. If bridges are out in southern Sumatra you can often catch a barge downriver (a bona fide adventure) to town where you can wait more comfortably for another bus.

The Companies: Before boarding, check out your bus. There are now so many bus companies on Sumatra vehicles can range from acceptable to downright dangerous. Non-a/c buses are better and as much as 30% cheaper. Fares are deregulated, an entrepreneureal free-for-all. Scalpers (*calo*) sell tickets in Sumatra's bus stations for exorbitant prices. Ask the local people or other travelers for the correct fare before buying your ticket.

If it's raining, the bus should have a winch. ALS and ANS bus companies both cover wide-ranging networks throughout the island and are usually reliable, though the seats may be painfully narrow for big Western frames. Habeko buses tend to be small, old, and cramped. No matter what the bus, for less wear and tear on your body book ahead as far as possible for a seat in the first two rows or a perch in front of the back axle. Your luggage is safer from theft up front, where the whole bus can keep an eye on it. Make sure your window closes completely. Buy a pillow or foam for cushioning, or use your sleeping bag. Bring a towel and soap along for *mandi* during stops. Watch for pickpockets.

At most meal stops, the food is expensive, so it's better to buy a packaged lunch before starting your journey. Sometimes you can walk a ways down the road from the meal stop and find ordinary *warung*. Bottled water is readily available, even in small villages. To avoid the annoying bus terminal scene, walk or get a *bemo* to some place along the highway and wait for a bus to come along. It pays to find out when buses pass through town; otherwise you could stand at the side of the road for hours assuming your bus is right around the corner. Small, local buses and *oplet* will pick up people even if the bus is already full, whereas express buses won't pick up many extra passengers.

LAMPUNG PROVINCE

A wild, forested district known for its pepper, stunning *tapi* fabrics, and ambitious *transmigrasi* projects. Sumatra's southernmost province has a long coastline with innumerable bays, a rugged mountain interior with game reserves and sea-level swamplands, and some densely populated rural areas that appear to be lifted straight out of Java. It also shares beautiful Lake Ranau with South Sumatra Province. Dormant volcanos of the region range from 2,231-meters-high Gu-

nung Pesagi to 1,645-meters-high Gunung Raya. Pepper, cloves, coffee, and copra are all grown extensively along the rich southern coast, which benefitted enormously from the 1883 Krakatoa catastrophe. Rice, coffee, maize, cassava, and rubber are cultivated inland. Bakauheni, on the southeast tip of Lampung, is the main maritime gateway to Sumatra for overland travelers from Java. Outside of Tanjungkarang and Kalianda there aren't many nice places to stay.

HISTORY

According to folklore, the first people to settle this area came from Batakland. Prior to Islam the Lampungese practiced a syncretic Buddhist-Hindu ancestor cult; *menhirs* and other archaeological remains of this heritage are found on stone inscriptions scattered around the province. To cultivate the valuable pepper spice for sale to European and Asian traders, the sultans of Banten centuries ago sent the first transmigrants to Lampung to carve villages and farms out of the jungle and spread Islam.

From the end of the 16th century until 1808, the sultanate of Benten controlled Lampung and its pepper without interfering in local customs. In the 19th century Lampung became a refuge for Banten rebels protesting Dutch rule. In 1855, after defeating the Lampungese hero Raden Intan II, the Dutch monopolized all trade. Today, Raden's grave, built on an earth mound in his Kalianda fortress, is a popular pilgrimage site. In WW II the Japanese drove out the Dutch and established a base in Kalianda to guard the vital Sunda Strait.

THE PEOPLE

The population of the province is divided into two main groups, the native Lampungese and Javanese transmigrants. Traditional native Lampungese villages can be recognized by their well-constructed brown wooden houses raised two meters above ground on pillars, many with a balcony. Often these "balcony houses" feature decorative latticework under the eaves or around the outside edges. The Javanese began settling the area in 1905 when Lampung was chosen as Indonesia's first transmigration site, selected to serve as a receptacle for Java's surplus population and to supply laborers for European plantations.

The Javanese soon made up 80% of the population. Javanese colonies, with their own traditions, *desa* heads, and social structures, became enclaves in the midst of Lampung, attacking the surrounding rich jungles like swarms of locusts. In 1987, Lampung was Indonesia's second most densely populated province outside Java. In the 1980s, 700,000 hectares of protected forest reserves were illegally cut down for shifting cultivation.

By 1983 overcrowding and habitat degradation had become so critical the government began a massive retransmigration program. In 1988, government-hired thugs on trail motorbikes destroyed or burned 1,000 homes in the Gunung Balak area of central Lampung to drive out the settlers. More involuntary evictions, home burnings, seizures of coffee and clove crops, and violent clashes followed in 1989—over 100 people were killed. The government blamed "fundamentalist Muslim subversives."

SOUTHERN LAMPUNG

KALIANDA AND VICINITY

From Bakauheni, take a bus to the junction three km outside town, then walk or take local transportation to the small port town of Kalianda. Area attractions include hot springs, pretty coastal scenery, 1,284-meter-high Gunung Rajabasa, nice beaches, and trips to offshore islands. Kalianda has had its share of misfortune. It experienced bitter struggles against the Dutch in the late 1800s; Krakatoa's 1883 eruption caused a giant tsunami, destroying the town. WW II brought fierce fighting between Japanese and Australian forces.

Today, Kalianda is small, quiet, and easy.

Most of the town's population is Muslim, while a small Chinese community maintains a temple. Visit the fish market near the harbor to see catches of fish, sharks, and rays auctioned off. The grave and fort of Raden Intan II, a local nationalist hero, is near town; ask for directions. For the Kalianda to Bakauheni run, the *bemo* will stop right in front of Penginapan Beringin if you ask the owner to arrange it for you. Goes via Sukarata and takes about an hour on a bumpy road. From Bakauheni to Merak the boat costs Rp1700 a/c second class.

Penginapan Beringin (Rp9000 s, Rp13,000 d), Jl. Kesuma Bangsa 55 (near the cinemas), is a little paradise. Clean and very spacious room with *mandi* and *nasi goreng* for breakfast. One

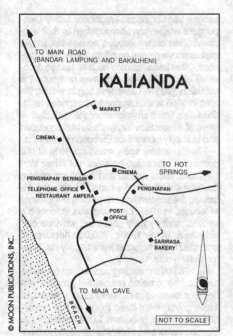

KALIANDA

TO MAIN ROAD
(BANDAR LAMPUNG AND BAKAUHENI)

MARKET

CINEMA

CINEMA

TO HOT
SPRINGS

PENGINAPAN BERINGIN

TELEPHONE OFFICE
RESTAURANT AMPERA

PENGINAPAN

POST
OFFICE

SARIRASA
BAKERY

TO MAJA CAVE

BEACH

NOT TO SCALE

© MOON PUBLICATIONS, INC.

other *penginapan* in town. Eat at very good **Javanese Ampera Restaurant** close to Beringin, or sample the many *warung*. Don't miss the very good **Sarirasa Bakery**; you'll see the beige/blue handcars all over town.

Sights

Weary travelers may revitalize in the beautiful and relaxing sulphurous hot spring baths, **Way Belerang,** only a two-km walk (30 minutes) from town. Take the street beside Penginapan Beringin uphill toward Gunung Rajabasa. Constructed by the Dutch, three pools each have different mineral content; Rp300 admission, refreshments available. Above, **Gunung Rajabasa,** an inactive volcano, is most easily climbed from its south side; take a minibus first to Cugung, then ascend several hours to the summit. Start early. *Cengkeh* (clove) trees are a profitable source of income for the district; the highly fertile lower slopes of Rajabasa are covered with them. Cloves, drying on mats by the roadside, give local villages a sweet spicy scent.

Fishing is the traditional occupation of the resident Lampung Pemanggir people. Boats can be hired for around Rp20,000 per day from Canti (southeast of Kalianda) to visit one of Kalianda's many offshore islands. Bargain hard. The owner of Penginapan Beringin will lend you snorkel and mask. Have the captain dump you on a small island for the day. Crazy people go to Tahiti, when there are islands like these. From Canti, you can also charter boats to visit Krakatoa.

TELUKBETUNG

Telukbetung, Bandar Lampung, and Panjang, all located on the north end of Lampung Bay, are virtually different sections of one city now. Telukbetung, only a 30-minute flight from Jakarta, is a port town and capital of Lampung Province. A 100-year-old ship's buoy lies opposite the Brimob police station in Telukbetung, on a hill under a *pohon ambon* tree. It overlooks the same bay from which it was originally catapulted on a giant Krakatoa tidal wave. At the tourist office, Jl. Selat Gaspar 39, Yaman Aziz (who runs a homestay) is knowledgeable on Lampung's attractions and can help arrange guided trips. While the **Sahid Krakatoa Seaside Hotel,** Jl. Yos Sudarso 294, tel. (0721) 64244 or 62167, is fairly revolting to look at, the views are stupendous. You may receive a 25% discount on the Rp63,000 s, Rp70,000 d standard rooms, or Rp80,000 s, Rp84,000 d superior rooms. Prices don't include 21% service and tax charges.

Getting There And Around

The Panjang ferry terminal lies nine km southeast of Telukbetung. Other ferries from West Java come in at the terminal at **Bakauheni,** 87 km (two hours) by bus from Telukbetung on a good but hilly road. By air, Garuda has five daily 30-minute flights from Jakarta to Branti Airport. Merpati flies from Palembang every day. The airport is 30 km north of Bandar Lampung in Branti; take either a local bus from Bandar Lampung, then walk in from the main road, or take a taxi from Bandar Lampung (Rp15,000). A **Garuda** office is in the Sahid Krakatoa Seaside Hotel. Daily trains arrive in Bandar Lampung from Lubuklinggau and Palembang. Most Sumatran cities have at least daily bus service to Bandar Lampung. Minibuses travel the main streets and to Bandar Lampung and *becak* are plentiful in the downtown areas.

KALIANDA AREA

BANDAR LAMPUNG

Formerly called Tanjungkarang, this modern town lies five km north of Telukbetung, a starting point for the journey north. If it's been a while since you've entered one, visit the department store. Catch *oplet* on the main street or use *kijang* or metered sedan taxis (call Taxi 4848 or 333). With the bus and train terminals situated in town, Bandar Lampung has a wider range of places to stay—and is more convenient—than Telukbetung. **Bank Negara Indonesia (BNI)**, Jl. Kartini 51, changes American Express traveler's checks. Visit the ethnographic and archaeological **Museum of Lampung** on Jl. Teuku Umar.

Accommodations And Food
Penginapan Renny, Jl. Kota Raja 7, has small rooms for Rp3000, "large" rooms for Rp6000: okay, friendly and quiet, but only one *mandi* in the whole place. **Hotel Andalas**, Jl. Raden Intan 89, tel. (0721) 63432, is very clean, friendly, and rip-off free (doesn't even charge for room service). At Rp27,500 for a/c double, Rp24,000 for fan room, it's very good value. Eat at the nearby Padang restaurant. **Kurnia City Hotel**, Jl. Raden Intan 114, tel. 62030, has a/c rooms, TV, hot and cold

water, private baths, and laundry service for Rp40,5000 deluxe, Rp32,000 standard, and Rp19,500 economy. The **Sheraton Inn Lampung**, Jl. Wolter Monginsidi 175, tel. 62721 or 63691, is quite luxurious—huge swimming pool, tennis courts, fitness center, bake shop; Rp98,000 weekend rate for s or d. This includes massive Euro-style or American breakfast and 21% tax and service. Downtown Bandar Lampung is busy at night, with numerous foodstalls.

Vicinity Of Bandar Lampung
Outside Bandar Lampung are popular beaches, islands, and mountains. Six km southwest of Telukbetung, on the west side of Lampung Bay, is **Nusa Indah Permai Beach.** From Lampasing take the two-hour boat out to Pulau Tegal. Past Lampasing to the southwest are more beaches and coastal scenery. On the east side of this bay are several beaches at **Pasir Putih,** 11 km southeast of Telukbetung. Offshore are the small islands Dewi, Cendong, and Tengah, reached by *spetbot.* Twenty km southeast of Bandar Lampung are beautiful land- and seascapes at **Tarahan.** A two-hour drive from Bandar Lampung is the 130,000-hectare **Way Kambas Reserve** with an elephant training center. Hire a motorboat at Way Kanan to tour the **Way Wako River.** The **Pugung Archaeological Site** in Pugung Raharjo village (40 km to the northeast) has megaliths and Hindu and prehistoric relics. At **Padangcermin,** 65 km southwest of Bandar Lampung, are nice landscapes and a beach resort.

Panjang, a port town southeast of Telukbetung, has frequent minibuses to and from Bandar Lampung. The train also departs here for Palembang, usually in the morning and evening. If arriving on the ferry, travelers usually go up to Bandar Lampung, then take trains or buses north. If you have to overnight in Panjang, stay at **Losmen Kastari.**

Getting Away
Most minibuses and buses originate from terminals on the north side of town. Just ask where the terminal is for your destination. Large buses leave from Terminal Rajabasa, where bus companies such as Damri, ANS, and ALS have their offices. City buses to Terminal Rajabasa leave from the bus station near the railway station. From Rajabasa there are plenty of express buses (1.5 hours, Rp1000) to Bakauheni that

stop at the entrance to Kalianda on the main road. From there you can catch a ride into Kalianda as it's a bit far to walk.

Long-distance bus destinations include Lahat, 11 hours; Jambi, 30 hours; Padang, 36 hours; Bukittinggi, 38 hours; Sibolga, 48 hours. The direct bus service to Medan takes three days and two nights and is reserved only for masochists and fugitives. For this long haul north, the first 390 km feature a reasonable dirt road (only about 50 km are really bad), then 290 km on the Trans-Sumatra Highway. Sometimes the bridge is out at Lubuklinggau, where you might have to change buses. **Bengkulu,** on Sumatra's southwest coast, is also connected to Banjar Lampung by daily buses.

The *ekspres siang* train departs for Palembang with connections to Lubuklinggau. Only economy class is available (Rp3500)—wooden bench seats for 10 hours but not bad if you've just come from a bus ride through hell on Java. There's also a night train that departs around 2030 and arrives in Palembang in 4.5 hours; first class only. Trains commonly run an hour or so late; day trains are less crowded.

From Bandar Lampung northward on a trans-Sumatra journey, you have several strategies. One is to train up to Palembang and Lubuklinggau, where you take a bus to Bukittinggi. If you don't want to stop in Palembang, pay only to Prabumulih (an hour short of Palembang) and wait three hours or so for the train, which comes back from Palembang at around 2000 that night, arriving in Lubuklinggau at 0500. Don't get stuck in Prabumulih; it's a real hole. After arriving in Lubuklinggau, if you're still not totally whacked, there could be a place on a bus leaving for Bukittinggi at around 0700, or on to Padang. Or travel by bus from Lubuklinggau west to Bengkulu (four hours, one change), then from Bengkulu take another bus north to Padang. This is a more time-consuming way to get up to Padang, but Bengkulu is worth a stop.

CENTRAL AND EAST LAMPUNG

Metro
The capital of Lampung Tengah (Central Lampung), 50 km northeast of Bandar Lampung. The number of Javanese transmigrants settled in this area make Metro nothing less than a transplanted Javanese country town. Surrounding the *kampung* are irrigation canals and extensive *sawah* fields. But it's not pure Javanese— there's more space and more discretionary income here than in a typically crowded Javanese town. Native Lampungese villages in the area can be distinguished by their solid wood houses on pillars, often with a front porch. Balinese villages are fewer in number but feature the unmistakable Hindu temples (visit the Balinese *transmigrasi* colony at Ramanutara). In Metro, stay at **Losmen Nuban,** Jl. Sukarso, tel. 21784.

Pugung And Vicinity
In the village of Pugung Raharjo is a small museum housed in a funny-looking wooden building; people in an office next door will open it for you. Inside is an unusual one-meter-high stone statue of a man, rendered in what is described as a "Polynesian" art style. Another statue, quite different, is a Majapahit bodhisattva excavated near Pugung. Pottery fragments, diagrams, photos, and maps are also on exhibit. A small library contains books and papers on archaeological studies carried out in the area. No *losmen.*

The direct route from Bandar Lampung lies along the highway west of Panjang. The road climbs up from the coast to a gently rolling plateau of vast rubber and oil palm plantations. Twenty km before Sribawono, turn left at the crossroads, then travel two km north to Pugung. Few commercial vehicles travel this route; it might be easier to approach via Metro using public transportation. From Metro, the road passes through the many villages, gardens, and *sawah* of the Lampungese, Javanese, and Balinese.

Gedung Wani is a Lampungese village 10 km north of Pugung with a 200-year-old wooden gate covered with intricate carvings—a gift from the Banten Kingdom of West Java. Look for a small building near the road. Peer through the windows or ask the man in the house behind to open the building for a better look.

Taman Purbakala
In the beautifully landscaped setting of this antiquities park one km east of Pugung is a ring of

dolmen (stone tables) and menhir (vertical stone slabs). In the center of the ring is an erect two-meter-high stone phallus. Nearby is a giant *punden,* an earth and rock mound; smaller *punden* are in the vicinity. Picnic shelters and a spring-fed swimming hole have been built for visitors (crowded on Sunday only). Stone pathways connect all the sites so it's easy to find your way around this 25-hectare park.

The Road To Jepara

Jepara is a country town probably named after the village of the same name in Central Java. The scenic road from Telukbetung to Jepara via Sukadana passes by date palms; coconut, pepper, and rubber plantations; and flowers in profusion. In **Natar,** toy windmills are sold, some pumped by little mechanical men, all fashioned from wood and decoratively painted. After Natar the road crosses a bridge built by the Dutch in 1932 over the Sekumpung River. For some kilometers the road then follows a canal built with slave labor by the Japanese during the war. The antlers mounted on the houses in the **Gunungnghadji** area indicate the number of stags inhabiting the forests of this region.

Sukadana is an old native Lampungese town of about 100 *asli* families, surrounded by mostly Javanese *transmigrasi* settlements. Here you can see genuine *rumah adat,* the original Lampung-style traditional dwellings. After Sukadana are many cassava gardens; see mounds of cassava in baskets on the back of bicycles along the highway. Refresh yourself at roadside stalls where whole bunches of bananas sell for Rp500.

SOUTH SUMATRA PROVINCE

The Bukit Barisan range, on the western border of the province, is the source of large, sluggish rivers that flow through highland plateaus and rift valleys before dropping onto lowland plains and a belt of brackish coastal marshes along the island's whole southeast coast. These wetlands regions of South Sumatra are up to 250 km wide, some of the largest in the world, supporting at least 50,000 fishermen. Much of the rest of the province, both in the mountains and lowlands, is covered by dark green jungle. Volcanic Gunung Dempo (3,159 meters), on the border with Bengkulu Province, is the highest volcano in the region, followed by Gunung Seminung (1,881 meters). An almost unavoidable stop for visitors to South Sumatra is the important provincial capital of Palembang, the island's second largest city after Medan.

The giant Musi River is joined in its lower reaches by other big rivers: the Lematang, Ogan, and Komering. Ships up to 10,000 tons can travel the Musi upstream as far as Palembang. Smaller *kapal motor* sputter for hundreds of kilometers upstream into the interior. For travelers, the cool highlands hold the greatest attractions: vast primary forests, the breathtaking panoramas of Lake Ranau, the mountain town of Pagaralam surrounded by megalithic sites, an 80-meter-high waterfall in Sugiwaras, the hot springs near Tanjung Sakti. On the islands of Bangka and Belitung, off the province's east coast, are found some of the most beautiful beaches in Asia.

Only about 15 years ago, this province changed from a trading province to one with a strong industrial base: the Pertamina oil refinery, the Pusri fertilizer plant, a tire factory near Palembang, and the coal mines of Tanjung Enim testify to this transformation. The tin mines of Pulau Bangka and Pulau Belitung are another big export earner. Some of Indonesia's largest oil fields are located in the eastern part of the province, while the valleys of the Bukit Barisan range to the west are rich agricultural regions growing coffee, tea, tobacco, cloves, rice, and vegetables. Timber, rattan, resins, fruits, wild latex, and *nibung* and nipa palm are harvested from the jungle.

The population is about five million, a blending of Javanese, Malay, and Minangkabau cultures. Around 700,000 people live in the Palembang area. In the eastern part of the province, not

SOUTH SUMATRA PROVINCE

© MOON PUBLICATIONS, INC.

much is traditional or unusual in the folk lifestyles except for the province's 17,000 or so isolated tribespeople who have yet to be "assimilated" by the government. Eventually they'll be put in settlement centers where they can be better controlled and indoctrinated.

Houses along rivers and in the jungles of the east are pole cottages with ladders on hilltops surrounded by hens, skinny dogs, banana trees, children, and mud. Not much to eat in these hinterlands except *pisang goreng.* Nearer the cities and in the *transmigrasi* projects are row upon row of tract-like houses on stilts with zinc roofs. Houses in old neighborhoods along the Musi are either built on stilts or rafts, and the wealthy live in *limas* houses, which resemble traditional Javanese *rumah adat.*

LAKE RANAU

A giant (40-by-29-km) mountain lake in the southwestern part of the province 330 km from Palembang. Part of the lake lies in Lampung Province. Indonesians go here to enjoy the cool climate, nice scenery, sulphur hot springs, and water sports. This pristine environment—like an untouched Lake Toba—features Gunung Seminung (1,881 meters) soaring up from the southern shore behind the lake. Here, as in much of the Bukit Barisan range, coffee is the most important cash crop; cloves, tobacco, vegetables, and rice are also grown. Culture and language are similar to coastal Lampung to the south.

Sights

Bandingagung, the area's largest town, offers several places to stay. All the buses for Ranau Danau terminate here. The town is 12 km west of the main highway; turn in at Simpangsender village. Quieter and more restful is a small resort, **Wisma Putri,** on the lake's eastern shore. Turn in at the sign, eight km south of Simpangsender, or seven km north of Kotabatu. Double rooms cost Rp25,000 but the manager may let you camp outside or sleep on a folding bed in the recreation room. The restaurant serves generous portions at reasonable prices; freshwater fish is the specialty. A 20-minute walk away on the edge of the jungle, with a view over rice paddies, is a waterfall. An elephant training center is in the area.

Kotabatu is the first town on the lake if approaching from the south, and it has a *penginapan.* Kotabatu makes a good base for hiking up Gunung Seminung. Sulphurous hot water can be enjoyed at **Gemuhak Springs,** three km from Kotabatu on the volcano's lower slopes. Just offshore is a small island, **Pulau Mariza.** Beaches are found on the north shore at Bandingagung, Surabaya, and Senangkalang. You can charter boats to tour the lake from Bandingagung and Kotabatu. Boating is best in the morning, as afternoon winds really whip up the waves. Rent a boat and cross the lake to the hot springs.

Getting There

From Palembang and other points north, this picturesque lake is an eight-hour bus ride over dozens of bridges. The last leg from Muaradura is 90 minutes of dust; you might want to spend the night in Muaradura next to the river at **Wisma Tanjung Raya,** Jl. Pasar Tengah (a waterfall is three km out of Muaradura). From Bandar Lampung and other points south, take a bus on a sometimes bumpy paved road via Bukitkemuning and Liwa (eight hours, 299 km). This southern approach is hillier and more scenic than coming from the north, and you pass through more traditional villages en route.

BATURAJA

A large transit town on the Ogan River, 272 km northwest of Bandar Lampung. An easygoing and relaxing place for a day's rest, with nice people and friendly children, Baturaja isn't beautiful or interesting but the people are talkative (but only in Bahasa Indonesia). Nearby is **Air Terjun Gua Putri,** an impressive cave and waterfall (the Harrison Hotel can organize an outing). If you get into Baturaja late in the afternoon, all the hotels on the main road could be full. **Hotel Kencana I and II** charge Rp3500 s, Rp7000 d. **Hotel Mandala** is dark, gloomy, and dirty (Rp6000-8000 d), and **Losmen Indonesia** is simple and not so clean (Rp5500 d). **Hotel Harrison** is probably the best—good service, large room with TV, *mandi,* and simple breakfast for Rp10,000-15,000 d, Rp21,000 a/c. Chinese **Restaurant Megaria** is reasonably priced and good.

Express buses, which stop on the main road near Losmen Indonesia, head southwest to

BATURAJA

NOT TO SCALE

© MOON PUBLICATIONS, INC.

Danau Ranau, southeast to Bandar Lampung, north to Palembang, and northwest to Lahat. Trains head north to Prabumulih, Palembang, and Lubuklinggau. The train southeast to Bandar Lampung costs Rp2300 third class and takes seven hours. Though it's extremely hot, the trip is great, with friendly people, vendors selling everything, and enough space for sitting, walking, and visiting.

THE PASEMAH HIGHLANDS

In the Pasemah Highlands between Lahat and Pagaralam are 26 sites with stonecarvings, tombs, and terraced sanctuaries. These remains, which may date as far back as A.D. 100, are said to be the most concentrated collection of monumental symbolic culture in Indonesia. Huge queerly shaped stones are carved into fantastic figures: warriors mounted on elephants, men wrestling a huge snake, animals copulating, frogs, a footprint, waterwheel, even ocean waves. A great number of these extraordinary carvings, menhirs, dolmens, stone cist graves, and terraced sanctuaries were erected at a time when metals were already known in the area. Figures carry swords; wear helmets, rings, and anklets; hold giant bronze kettledrums—artifacts and implements all belonging to the Bronze Age. Many of the figures appear at first to be three-dimensional but are in fact bas-reliefs, the illusion created by the skillful use of the curved surface of the boulders. The modern-day Pasemahans

still use some statuary as vow-redemption shrines, calling upon their ancestors to bestow blessings and stave off ill-fortune.

Most sites are found in the subdistricts of Kecamatan Pulau Pinang, Kotaagung, and Pagaralam. The minibus from Bengkulu to Pagaralam takes five hours (175 km, Rp3500). The road via Kepahiang and Tebingtinggi is good. Most sites are easily visited but many are well off the main road. Serious seekers need their own vehicle; Rp60,000-70,000 per day to charter a sedan taxi. It would be difficult to see these sites without a guide unless you speak Bahasa Indonesia; if you don't, consider hiring a guide from your hotel. Allow a full day, between asking directions and arranging transportation, to see the sites just around Pagaralam.

Pagaralam And Vicinity
An interesting place, but the local kids don't leave you alone for one second. Day and night they want to practice their English. Stay in noisy **Hotel Telaga Biru**; very plain rooms, quite small with double bed and small *mandi* for Rp5500. Near Pagaralam is the **Mirasa Restaurant** with excellent food and a pleasant, quiet *losmen* attached. Ask for directions to all the megalithic sites at this restaurant; the Mirasa also has photos.

In **Tegurwangi** village (by *bemo* from Pagaralam, Rp250) are several carved human figures and the ruins of a tomb; pillars are decorated with men riding elephants—very beautiful megalithic stones among amazing scenery. Pay a fee of Rp2000, then a man shows you the sites, crawling into the tombs and rubbing his hands all over the paintings (they won't be visible much longer). It's a pleasant walk to the stone elephant at **Belunai.** You have to charter a vehicle to get to the third site—several tombs, mostly ruined, but one still has good paintings. Children show you the way. If the kids haven't worn you out completely by this time, take a *bemo* to **Tanjungsakti** (Rp1000), 34 km from Pagaralam, where there's a hot springs at nearby Pungar Bunga village.

LAHAT

This large town on the Lematang River southwest of Palembang is a rest stop on the long trip through Sumatra and a jumping-off point for visiting the many megalithic sites between Lahat and Pagaralam. Lahat seems to have a large collection of students and teachers who think your whole purpose in life is to help them practice their English. Even if you escape to your hotel room, several will lurk outside, waiting to pounce when you emerge.

Stay in the very clean **Nusantara Hotel,** Rp16,500 d, *mandi,* fan on request. Try some good Padang food at the clean **Hotel Permata.** The **R.M. Lege** restaurant in the town center opposite the local bus station (Jl. Mayor Ruslan 2) is also quite good. To stock up on long hauls, the town's grocery stores are well stocked with drinks, biscuits, and imported canned food.

A minibus to Lahat from Pagaralam costs Rp1500 (1.5 hours); a bus from Palembang runs Rp6000 (five hours, 226 km). The express bus station is quite far out of town. To leave, take a *becak* to **Singgalang,** a *rumah makan* in the station.

From Lahat's bus station, it may take some time to get on an express bus. You may end up in the aisle, which is okay for the 3.5 hours (Rp400) to Baturaja. For Bukittinggi, it costs Rp20,000 *ekonomi* or Rp30,000 a/c (20 hours). You may also choose to travel to Bandar Lampung (11 hours), or all the way to Jakarta (18 hours) on the Lahat Ratu Agung express buses. The non-a/c ride starts at 1700 and costs Rp17,000 for Jakarta, while the a/c bus leaving at 2300 is Rp25,000.

PALEMBANG AND VICINITY

Most travelers don't bother visiting Palembang because it's off the Trans-Sumatra Highway; they just take the boat direct from Jakarta to Padang or bypass it on the bus. But if you do make the side trip to Palembang, coming in by train, you'll notice the many rubber and coffee plantations and factories. This area is also known for its oil wells and forest products. The main market and oil-export center of South Sumatra Province, located on both sides of the Musi River 80 km upstream from the sea, Palembang, with 700,000 people, is Sumatra's second most populous city. For over 1,300 years, the basis of Palembang's economy has been river and ocean commerce. Nearly one-third of total Indonesian government revenue comes from this oil province alone. Pertamina has donated to the city a large sports stadium, TV station, town clock, and a handsome minaret for its mosque.

As is typical of an outlying provincial capital, this staunchly Islamic city has its own dances, songs, customs, and cuisines. Much of the city

is built on piles over tidal mudflats; the weather could get very sticky and hot. The Musi River divides the city into two sections: the southern half, Ulu, where the majority of the population lives, and the northern half, Ilir, which houses most of the hotels, shops, government offices, and well-to-do residential areas. The symbol of Palembang is the Ampera Bridge, built in the 1960s; you see paintings of it everywhere.

An excursion up- or downriver by speedboat or ferry is mandatory before the city's ammonia factories destroy the Musi. Rent one of the many watergoing contraptions from in front of the *benteng* for Rp8000-15,000 per hour. Be cautious with the piratical boatmen down on the Musi; you hear stories of people being taken out in the middle of the river and pressured for more money. Always go with a friend. A sampan ride across the river costs Rp1000.

History
By tradition an ancient Oriental trading center, from the 9th until the 13th century Palembang

was one of the world's principal ports. The city was born on pepper, raised on tin, and grew rich on oil. Palembang was once the capital of the Sriwijaya Empire, which scholars have called "Phoenicia of the East." The first tangible signs in the whole archipelago of the arrival of Mahayana Buddhism appeared in Kedukan Bukit near Palembang in the early 600s. A full 100 years later traces of this religion showed up in inscriptions of Candi Kalasan in Central Java.

On his way to India in 671, a Chinese Buddhist pilgrim, I Tsing, arrived at the university in Palembang and stayed four years, writing his memoirs and handing down a valuable account of the city. He described a huge marketplace where Tamil, Persian, Arabic, Cambodian, Siamese, Chinese,

and Burmese were all spoken. A thousand ships lay at anchor, and Sriwijaya sent its mercenaries as far away as Mesopotamia to do battle. Thousands of monks learned Buddhist teachings and translated Sanskrit texts here.

The city reached its zenith in the beginning of the 11th century. Then in A.D. 1025 it was brutally attacked by a jealous Chola king from South India; the place never recovered. By the end of the 14th century, Sriwijaya had splintered into eight smaller princedoms, the largest of which, Melayu, was centered at Jambi and became a strong maritime power. Finally, with the rise of Melaka in the 15th century, Sriwijaya became a remote backwater. On 17 June 1983, Palembang celebrated its 1,300th birthday.

© MOON PUBLICATIONS, INC.

Sriwijaya's origins have lately been disputed. Some researchers claim the empire originated near Chaiya, Thailand, and not in the Palembang area. One reason for this theory is that, except for the artifacts in the city's museums, little physical evidence remains of Palembang's past splendor. People in the region around Palembang, however, still weave fine fabrics and perform unique Hindu-influenced dances. South Sumatran dancers wear elaborate tree-like headdresses with glittering pendants and festoons or crowns, and carry gold-gilt fans. Wedding costumes are still patterned after the royal courts of the old medieval empire, with a flap on the groom's headdress preventing him from looking at the bride.

SIGHTS

The **Mesjid Raya** (Grand Mosque) near the bridge greets you as you come into the city; it was built by Sultan Mahmud Badaruddin in the 18th century. Go for a ride along the road heading upstream beside the Musi River—whole residential areas are built out over the water, featuring some superb examples of traditional architecture. During the rainy season this broad river becomes a lake; the residences built on rafts rise and fall with the water. Palembang's old *benteng* (fort), with its tall whitewashed walls, is on Jl. Benteng just back from the river in the center of the city. It was built in 1780 during the reign of Sultan Ahmad Najamudin II. The *benteng* is now occupied by the army, so permission to enter must be acquired from the fort commander.

The area in front of the *benteng* and to the sides of the Ampera Bridge is one of Palembang's unique attractions. Here ships of 10,000 tons lie amidst small, bobbing rowboats and sailboats, as motorized *prahu* dart back and forth across the river. Houseboats are moored along the riverbank, functioning not only as dwellings but as floating *warung*. It was this river life that gave Palembang its prewar nickname, "The Venice of the Far East." Today the scene is reminiscent of Hong Kong, but with a more third world flavor.

Palembang's famous "floating markets" are in the Pasar Ilir 16 area, two km downstream from the bridge. This crowded quarter consists of two km of the scariest, dirtiest markets anywhere, selling anything and everything. Immaculately dressed women shop in the disgusting meat and fish area—the smell is unbearable, there are flies everywhere, sellers wash their cutting boards in the sewer. Just like the *klongs* of Bangkok, boats going to market must travel down these canals. Locals will tell you to be careful walking in this area, which is frequented by "gangsters."

Museum Negeri Sum-Sel

This museum is located about five km from downtown, about 300 meters off the road to Jambi and the airport on Jl. Sriwijaya—take a Km 5 *oplet*. See this traditional Palembang house (Rumah Bari), a solid wooden building made of *kayu tembesu*. The Dutch moved it from the countryside piece by piece in 1931. Megalithic sculpture is displayed as well. Open 0800-1400 Tues.-Thurs., 0800-1100 Friday, 0800-1200 Saturday, 0900-1500 Sunday. Closed Monday.

Chinese Temples

Klenteng Kwa Sam Yo, between the river and Jl. Sungai Lapangan Hatal, is remarkable for its hundreds of fascinating murals and wall paintings depicting the story of the great Kublai Khan and other Mongolian heroes. Ask to see the vicious-looking self-torture chair, a means for attaining spiritual knowledge through pain and suffering. Another pain-inflicting activity was the immersion of the penitent's hands in boiling oil; ask to see the color photos of the old Chinese whose unscarred hands were so honored.

Another old Chinese temple is on Pulau Kemarau downriver at the junction of the Musi, Komering, and Ogan rivers. Hire a motorized *sampan* in front of the Benteng for the 15-minute ride. This temple is also a *kramat* (holy place) to Muslims. Sites like this sacred to both religions are known as "double sanctuaries"; the only others in Indonesia are Klenteng Ancol in Jakarta and Gedung Batu in Semarang.

CULTURE

Entertainment

Palembang has three swimming pools, one bowling alley (at Sungai Gerong), and dozens of billiard halls. The city's 20 cinemas (most with a/c) are a godsend for those who like Shaw Brothers extravaganzas, Italian spaghetti westerns, kung fu movies, and bad old American films. Go to Chinatown and enjoy the pace of life there. Ask the *becak* drivers to take you to one of the city's safe nightclubs.

Events

Palembang's traditional wedding ritual dates back to the Sriwijaya era. Weddings and receptions are usually held on Sunday mornings. The busiest wedding season is the time of the *haj,* when many Sumatrans embark on a pilgrimage to Mecca. Tradition dictates that the bride must propose to the husband and pay him a dowry commensurate with his social and economic stature in the community. This arrangement gives her added clout in the marriage as she figuratively "pays for him." On Java, weddings often take place in the mosque but here the custom is that engagement parties and weddings are held at the bride's home. In the wedding egg-breaking ceremony, the groom crushes an egg beneath his bare foot, which the bride then cleanses; this is supposed to symbolize fertility. Finally, with all the pomp of a sultan's court, the bride and groom sit in state on a white-satin couch blanketed in flowers, fanned by young handmaidens.

The anniversary of the founding of Palembang is commemorated every 17 June. The occasion is celebrated with sports events, community projects, and performances of music and dance on an open-air stage. *Jalur* (canoe) races are held at noon a day or two after the Independence Day celebrations on 17 August. The *jalur,* in the shape of an animal, are manned by up to 40 rowers. This event is very popular among Palembang's citizens.

Arts And Crafts

Influenced by centuries of foreign trade, the weavers of South Sumatra have been deeply affected by diverse cultures. Palembang's traditional *kain songket,* symbols of a family's wealth, are usually made of silk, then given an overlaid design of gold or silver; buy one in Pasar Ilir 16. Also, the tourist office can suggest a few weaving centers to visit. Go in the mornings; weavers tend to take the afternoons off. In Rumah Bari, see the small diorama of weavers, traditional textiles, some spinning

wheels, and an exhibit of the whole nine-phase process.

Palembang's *plangi* cloth is unbelievably involved and colorful. *Plangi* comes from the word *pelangi,* meaning "rainbow." Traditional Palembang *plangi* is rarely made now; even old pieces are quite difficult to find. These cloths are now only seen at weddings, draped around the bride's shoulders after the cleansing ceremony. Ask a family to retrieve some of their old *plangi* and take them out into the sunlight.

A good selection of traditional black and red South Sumatran lacquerware is available from **Mekar Jaya,** Jl. Selamet Riyadi 45A. The factory is right behind the shop and tours are provided upon request.

PRACTICALITIES

Accommodations

Near Pasar Ilir 16 are several dirty *losmen* (Rp6000 s, Rp8000 d), but they're noisy and mostly "full." Other bargain places include the spartan **Hotel Asiana,** Jl. Sudirman 45E (near the Jl. Diponegoro intersection); Rp6000 s, Rp9000 d. Check out also **Penginapan Riau,** Jl. Dempo 409 C (opposite King's Hotel); Rp7500 s. **Losmen Jakarta,** at Jl. Sayangan 769 near the river, is only Rp5000 s, but you get what you pay for.

Stepping up, the **Hotel Sintera,** Jl. Jen. Sudirman 30-38, tel. (0711) 24618 or 24801, P.O. Box 146, charges Rp12,000 s, Rp15,000 d with *mandi*; Rp16,500 s, Rp20,000 d with fan and TV (English movies on the Malaysian channel); Rp27,500 to 33,000 t. Standard rooms are Rp22,000, superior Rp27,500, executive Rp35,750, suites Rp44,000. The people are friendly and helpful. Since it's so central, you get a lot of noise from the street, so be sure to ask for a room in the back. **Hotel Bandung,** Jl. Sayangan 669, tel. 26874, has rooms from Rp7000 to Rp18,000 a/c, but the rooms aren't clean and the staff is lazy. A very good choice is quiet **Hotel Surabaya,** tel. 26874, with rooms for Rp17,500 without *mandi* but including TV, or a/c rooms for Rp35,000.

Palembang's best hotel is **Hotel Swarna Dwipa,** Jl. Tasik 2, tel. 313-322, P.O. Box 198, telex 27203, fax 28999, recently renovated and one of Sumatra's finest. The colonial-era old building has large rooms for Rp20,000, but is rather run-down and stuffy. The cheerier newer building offers modern motel-like rooms overlooking a neighborhood of red-tiled roofs and quiet streets. Everything—telephone, lights, bells, buzzers, and the central a/c—seems to work. Taxi and *becak* service in front. Swarna Dwipa's best feature is that it's located in a quiet neighborhood, across the street from a park. Prices: standard Rp50,000 s, Rp61,000 d, Rp78,500; superior Rp61,000 s, Rp72,000 d, Rp89,500 t; deluxe Rp85,000 s, Rp96,000 d, Rp113,500 t. Credit cards accepted. Outsiders can use the swimming pool if ordering a couple of cokes for the no-nonsense price of Rp3750 per.

Food
Parallel with Jl. Jen. Sudirman, the city's main street, is Jl. Sajangan, which turns into an open-air market at night with foodstalls, fruit stands, and *sate* and snack vendors. The restaurant streets of Palembang are Jl. Jen. Sudirman and Jl. Veteran. The higher-priced hotels also have excellent restaurants. Right around the corner from Hotel Sintera is a small alleyway with many noodle and Padang-style restaurants. A notable Padang restaurant is the **Sari Bundo** on the corner of Jl. Kapt. A. Rivai and Jl. Jen. Sudirman. Another outstanding restaurant is **Mahkota Indah,** 24 Ilir Jl. Letkol. **Iskandar 243,** tel. 312-236, upstairs, serves *Palembang asli* dishes. Menu changes daily. Central location. For a real treat, visit the **French Bakery** at Jl. Kol. Atmo 481 B, opposite the King's Hotel, or the **Warna Warni** ice cream store.

Services
The **post office** is near the Grand Mosque close to the river. The **city tourist office,** tel. (0711) 28450, is in the Museum Sultan Machmud Badaruddin II. The **regional tourist office,** tel. 24981, for South Sumatra is located at Jl. Bay Salim 200. Change money at the **Bank Ekspor Impor on** Jl. Rustam Effendy or at **Bank Bumi Daya** on Jl. Jen. Sudirman. Cash advances (normally up to US$500) are provided by **Bank Central Asia,** Jl. Kapt. A. Rivai 22; or try **Danamon Bank,** Jl. Mesjid Lama 170 (Rp500,000 maximum). A competent travel agent is Suwarso Diyanto of **P.T. Sri Varia Wisata Tour and Travel,** Jl. Letkol Iskandar 16 A, tel. 25669 or 313064.

TRANSPORTATION

Getting There
All roads, rivers, and railways in South Sumatra end up eventually in Palembang; even 10,000-ton ships can voyage this far upriver from the Bangka Straits. Palembang's train station, called Kertapi, is in the Ulu section of the city; taxi drivers will take you the eight km into Palembang for Rp10,000, or take a *bemo* or *oplet* for Rp400. Alternatively, take the bus to Palembang from Padang (48 hours) or Medan (72 hours). There are also one-hour daily flights from Jakarta, as well as from Medan and Singapore. Talang Betutu Airport is 12 km north of Palembang; Rp10,000 for two into town, or just hop on an *oplet,* which runs into town for Rp500. The road to Palembang runs right in front of the airport terminal; board an *oplet* into the city for only Rp400.

Getting Around
Palembang's distinctive vehicle, the *kijang,* looks like a small armored personnel carrier; the standard fare is Rp150. Also rampant is a jeep-like *oplet* with a square back, painted in rainbow colors. The big *oplet/kijang* station, Stasiun Ampera, is at the northern end of the bridge. All the Ilir (neighborhoods) are preceded by their numbers: if you want to go to Hotel Swarna Dwipa, look for drivers and their assistants at Stasiun Ampera holding up four fingers, meaning "Ilir 4."

Charter an *oplet* or a *kijang* for half the price of hiring private cars. Buses, *becak, oplet,* and taxis go all over, except for some restricted areas. From the city's main bus station it costs Rp5000 by taxi to, for example, the Hotel Sintera. To the Talang Betutu Airport take *bis kota* to Km 12 (*kilo dua belas*) and get out at the Jambi-airport junction from where it's only a three km walk, or hitch an *oplet*. Taxis to the airport cost Rp10,000.

Getting Away
Buy air tickets at the **Garuda** office, Jl. Kapt. A. Rivai 20, tel. (0711) 21604. **Merpati** is nearby in the Sanjaya Hotel, also a bit down the road on Jl. Kapt. A Rivai. At least five Garuda flights per day connect Jakarta. Merpati flights depart for Pangkalpinang (Pulau Bangka), Surabaya, Dumai, Tanjung Pinang in Riau, and

Telukbetung. On the Padang flight, the plane climbs steeply from the flat lowlands to clear the 3,000-meter-high mountain peaks, a dramatic experience.

A regular boat departs Palembang for Muntok on Pulau Bangka every day (Rp20,000, 2.5 hours).

Departing by train, first take a *bemo* (Rp400) to the Kertapi train station (eight km from city center); watch for pickpockets. One option, instead of the grueling Padang bus ride, is the 10-hour train trip from Palembang to Lubuklinggau, then a bus the next day to Padang. On the train going north from Palembang keep an eye on your luggage. For Jakarta, three trains leave daily. The night train is much cooler and not as crowded as day trains.

Most of the bus companies are on Jl. Letkol Iskandar and Jl. Diponegoro. **ANS**, Jl. Iskandar 903C (just off Jl. Sudirman), is a reliable bus company. From Palembang's northern Terminal Bis Tujuluh, public buses head out to Jambi, Padang, Medan, and other points north, and to Bakauheni, the terminal on the south coast of Sumatra with ferries to Java. It's about six hours (380 km) to Lubuklinggau. To Bukittinggi takes 20 hours, with one stop in Prabumulih and various other dinner stops. To Lahat it costs Rp6000 (five hours), to Jambi it's Rp6000 (36 hours). To Padang (24-36 hours—depends on the season) it's Rp20,000 a/c, departures at around 1300. To Jakarta is Rp30,500 a/c (20 hours).

VICINITY OF PALEMBANG

One of Asia's largest oil refineries is Rp600 by *kijang* from Palembang. The monstrous **Sungai Gerong Refinery** has a daily capacity of 75,000 barrels. Adjacent is the US$200 million petrochemical complex of Plaju. See it at night when it's all lit up like Cape Canaveral. A virtual city within a city, there are office buildings, clubs, a bowling alley, swimming pool, hospital, and row upon row of housing areas for employees. In contrast, note the squatter villages outside the gates. On the other side of Sungai Gerong is the loading harbor, where you can see the big ships lined up to take on oil. The huge **Pusri** urea complex, also downriver from Palembang, produces 1.6 million tons of fertilizer annually. Go at night

when the mosque is backdropped by the glowing lights of the superstructure, an eerie sight.

River Trips
Rent speedboats (*spetbot*) for Rp20,000-30,000 per hour from the busy waterfront in front of the *benteng* and Stasiun Ampera near the bridge. A *spetbot* is a narrow eight-meter-long boat which rises out of the river at full speed, spraying water over the passengers on the choppier sections near the city. Boats can fit up to eight people, though that's a bit crowded. Traditional stilt houses start up right away after leaving Palembang, as you enter a more industrialized area. Farther downstream, the riverbanks become less populated and the water calmer. The boatman adroitly swerves to avoid wakes of other boats, as well as clumps of palm and stumps, stopping every kilometer or so to clean the propeller of debris. Then you come upon stilt villages that contain few articles of the Western world. Women wash clothes on the shores, villagers fish with bamboo poles. Later, when it turns dark, the trees along the bank glow and sparkle with fireflies, like candle-lit Christmas trees. The boatmen use their lights to navigate down the black river. The spluttering motor drowns out the piercing calls of birds. Riverine Sumatra.

A unique way to reach Jambi to the north is on a ferry for the small town of Bayunglincir, 60 km south of Jambi. The ferry leaves Palembang at around 1400 on Monday, Wednesday, and Saturday. The boat first enters the delta area, then heads up a smaller tributary of the Musi to Bayunglincir. The water is yellow and heavy with mud; navigation is cautious. You pass through dense riverine jungles with fireflies, flying foxes, lemurs, basking crocodiles, exotic birds, plenty of chattering monkeys—an Amazon-like, untraveled region. The piloting takes place mostly at night; you arrive at Bayunglincir early the next morning. Awaiting *bemo* take you into Jambi for Rp3000 (three to four hours).

Transmigrasi Settlements
The adventurous can visit transmigration settlements. Among the most interesting are those on the Delta Upang of the Musi, about two hours downriver from Palembang, accessible only by speedboat. Local guides are available on set-

tlement sites, which are mainly supported by tidal irrigation. For this trip, boats may be chartered at the Ampera Bridge in Palembang for Rp60,000 roundtrip, which covers fuel, boat, and operator. Carry water. The cost of a single fare on a public boat is only Rp4000.

Farther to the southwest, about six hours by road from Palembang, is the older settlement area of Belitang, which received settlers under the Dutch program of *colonisazi* as early as

1937. The base for exploration is **Gumawang,** a center of about 100 shophouses with an active market trading in chilies, peanuts, rice, goats, and vegetables. Again, local guides may be obtained. A good place to stay is **Penginapan Santai,** which offers simple rooms for Rp2000 s. Good local food is available at several *rumah makan* across the street for as little as Rp1000 per meal. The one-way express bus fare from Palembang is Rp3000.

BENGKULU PROVINCE

Few travelers visit this wild, sparsely populated, historic province, which extends for almost 350 km down the spine of the Bukit Barisan range. Bengkulu has been overlooked by tourists because of the decrepit condition of its roads and the consequent difficulty of access, but recently both its road and air transport systems have improved, and undiscovered Bengkulu can now easily be included in a trip through Sumatra. It is, however, still off the beaten track, and you'll see only a bare handful of white faces when traveling here.

The Bukit Barisan range bisects Bengkulu with its rich reserve of natural forests, particularly in the north where rainforests come right down to deserted shorelines and cliffs up to 100 meters high.

In the east rise majestic Gunung Dempo (3,159 meters), Sumatra's third largest volcano, and jungle-covered Gunung Ulupalik, source of the giant Musi River. The province's southern portion is highly fertile thanks to the Krakatoa explosion of the last century. In the south is located a large part of the Kerinci National Park, named after 3,800-meter-high Gunung Kerinci.

Much of Bengkulu is covered in extensive forests. The giant *Rafflesia arnoldy,* the world's largest flower, is found in Bengkulu's mountainous terrain. Wild orchids are rampant. Monkeys, elephants, crocodiles, bears, buffalo, and tigers inhabit the rainforests. Wild pigs are considered pests because they eat farmers' crops; they're hunted not for food but to keep their numbers down. All other animals are protected by the government, and hunting them without a permit is forbidden. Bengkulu is Sumatra's "Hunting Province," and the tourist office can help with guides and permits for game-watching and hunting. It takes just a day's travel to get to almost any area of the province by rented jeep or Land Rover.

Of Bengkulu's 767,980 people, 98% are Muslim. Large numbers of transmigrants have settled in the province, in the last decade at the yearly rate of around 12,000. Many recent settlers were forcibly evicted from the controversial Kedung Ombo project of West Java and settled in the Muko Muko area and in northern Bengkulu. Most are farmers who grow coffee, cloves, pepper, tobacco, coconut, fruit, rice, and vegetables. Three major ethnic groups and numerous minor ones, each speaking a different dialect, are native to the province.

BENGKULU

Formerly known as Bencoolen, this old coastal town of 70,000 is the capital of Bengkulu Province. A famous 18th- and 19th-century British trading settlement, Bengkulu is rich in history. In 1973 it had only 10 cars, one restaurant, and several small *warung*; the first traffic light was installed in 1979. Today development is accelerat-

ing, with paved roads, regular flights, a new port for larger ships, and a dramatic population increase. But Bengkulu is still a small, peaceful town and a pleasure to visit, where long sandy, paradise-like beaches line the coast not far from town. There isn't much to do at night except take in a movie at one of the four cinemas, or go to the town's only disco. Moderate-priced hotels are generally well run and clean, there are good restaurants, and the local people are friendly and easygoing. Bengkulu is blessed with rain almost every day, usually starting after 1200.

History

The British, driven from their last stronghold in West Java at Banten, built several fortresses in Bengkulu. The British East India Company chose Bengkulu as a factory site because Banten was a major importer of Bengkulu pepper, at the time a fabulous cash earner. Their intention was to grab a larger share of the pepper trade, which up until then was controlled almost

solely by the Dutch. After striking a deal with the local *raja* for the exclusive rights to purchase the pepper crop, the first English factory, York, was built in Bengkulu in 1685 about three km north of present Fort Marlborough. Malaria and other diseases soon killed off so many British it was said "two monsoons were the life of a man." At one point in the 17th century, slaves were brought in from Madagascar to man the fort. Due to the lack of European women, it was common for the British to take native women; by 1800 Eurasians rose to high posts in the service of the British East Indies Company. The original fort was finally abandoned, and another built where Fort Marlborough is today.

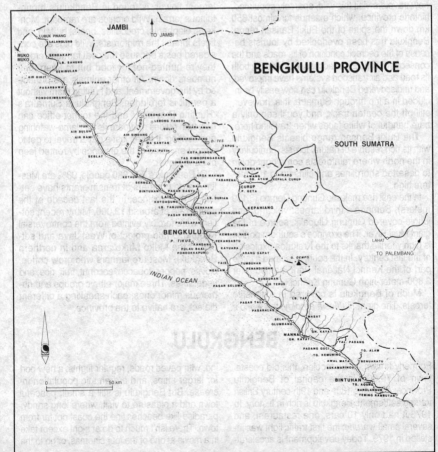

Unwilling or unable to pay the natives enough for their pepper, the British had to resort to coercive and repressive measures to maintain production. By March 1719 relations had deteriorated so badly that the Bengkulunese stormed and burned the fort, forcing the British to flee for Batavia and later India. The British did not return until 1724, when they reoccupied the fort. In the early 19th century, the British administrator was murdered, and bitter reprisals followed.

Sir Stamford Raffles, the founder of Singapore, arrived in Bengkulu in 1818 to revive British fortunes and the failing pepper trade. Raffles preferred Java over Sumatra: "I would not give one Java for a thousand such islands," he said. But this brilliant and ambitious 30-year-old ex-lieutenant-governor of the Indies was charged with edging out the Dutch and building a prosperous new colony for Britain by taking over Sumatra's west coast. Over the next several years he freed the slaves and pacified the pepper chiefs, healing the old wounds.

After Raffles was recalled to Britain in 1823, British rule in West Sumatra was doomed. The Dutch undercut the productivity of Bengkulu's yields, glutting the market and underselling in Europe. This finally culminated in the British handing over the west coast plantations in 1824 to the Dutch, in return for control over Malacca and its straits, a waterway critical to the English company's lucrative China trade.

The greatest sea disaster in history took place in 1942 off the coast of Bengkulu, when a Japanese ship containing 7,000 POWs was sunk by British submarines, with a loss of over 5,000 lives.

SIGHTS

The tourist office at Jl. Pembangunan 3, Padang Harapan (south of the town center), has little printed info but can help arrange guided jungle excursions to view wildlife or the rafflesia. **Kampung Cina** (Chinatown), with its row of buildings with red-tiled roofs, is the old part of town. **Bengkulu Musium Negeri** is on Jl. Pembangunan, Padang Harapan; open 0800-1400 except Monday. The **Parr Monument** is a memorial to the courageous but headstrong governor of Bengkulu who preceded Raffles. Im-

mensely unpopular, Parr forced the natives to cultivate coffee; worse, he attempted to disband the Bugis officer corps at Fort Marlborough. On the night of 27 September 1807 he was stabbed to death and decapitated, most likely by the Bugis officers whose economic interests he threatened. The monument, said to have been built by Raffles, overlooks Kampung Cina. A simple obelisk to yet another English martyr, Hamilton, is located 1.5 km south of Kampung Cina at the intersection of Jl. Sentoso and Jl. Hasan. A cement monument to the monstrous rafflesia flower is in Jembatan Kecil in the middle of the road to the airport north of town.

Sukarno's House

Sukarno, who distinguished himself early in his political career by his vocal opposition to colonial rule, was arrested by the Dutch on Java in 1933, brought to Bengkulu, and put under house arrest for nine years. Later, when the Japanese occupied Sumatra, he was captured again. The first Indonesian president's former house is quite small; it's off Jl. Sukarno-Hatta, and is the one with the flag in front of it. Open weekdays 0800-1400, Friday until 1100, Saturday until 1200; closed Monday. Sukarno was an engineer by trade, trained at the famous Bandung Institute of Technology in the 1920s; he designed **Mesjid Jamik** during his exile here. The mosque is at the intersection of Jl. Jen. Sudirman and Jl. Suprapio.

Fort Marlborough

Built 1709-1719 by the British East India Co., Fort Marlborough is the most formidable fort ever built by the British in the Orient; it is occupied now, as is usually the case with old forts, by the Indonesian army. The whole structure is presently being refinished in cement, which really lessens its historical impact. The well-preserved castle-like parapets around the courtyard contain the original cannon tracks. From its high walls are excellent views of the sleepy harbor, the *pasar,* Kampung Cina, oxcarts, and whirling kites. The back of the fort has been left in its original state; take a walk along the high and windy battlements that overlook the ruins of a rear drawbridge. The old prison with its original bars is now used as a bicycle room for army personnel; inside the compound stand old English gravestones with inscriptions. Admission Rp100.

BENGKULU

NOT TO SCALE

© MOON PUBLICATIONS, INC.

PRACTICALITIES

Accommodations

For real cheap grubbies, go to Kampung Cina. **Losmen Aman,** Jl. Pendakian, is dirty, smelly, hot, and noisy (Rp6000 s). Nearby **Losmen Samudera** on Jl. Benteng (across from the fort) is Rp4000 s, Rp7000 d. If you don't hate yourself, look for something else. The **Ragil Kunung Restaurant and Guesthouse,** Jl. Kenanga, is in a quiet, peaceful spot just outside the center of Bengkulu, easy to reach by minibus or taxi. Very clean and almost without

mosquitos, the five clean and comfortable rooms are built inside a tropical garden. All the food served is excellent and the staff friendly. Tariff Rp5000, with breakfast included.

Friendly **Wisma Rafflesia,** Jl. Jen. A. Yani 925, is very good value at Rp6500 s, including fan and *mandi*. Could get a lot of street noise, so ask for a quiet room. Guesthouse-style **Wisma Kenanga,** Jl. Sentosa 1007, tel. (0736) 390, is a little pricier (Rp9000 d with fan). The people are very nice and can speak rudimentary English. The owner is a teacher of Dutch at Bengkulu University and speaks Dutch fluently. **Wisma Malabero,** Jl. Dr. Hazairin, charges Rp12,500 (bargain down to Rp10,000) for a waterless room with fan. Noisy disco nearby.

The **Samudera Dwinka Hotel,** Jl. Jen. Sudirman 246, tel. 31604, offers 21 large rooms: Rp15,000 for economy class with *mandi*, TV, double bed; Rp35,000 for VIP rooms with color TV, *mandi*, a/c, and hot and cold water. All prices include breakfast and a noon "coffee break." For reservations, contact Harlon Nuzirwan, Jl. Jen. Suprapto 10, Complek Cempaka Putih Permai Blok D/7, Jakarta Pusat 10510, tel. 420-3588. **Wisma Pemda,** Jl. Veteran 1, costs Rp16,000 for big double rooms with *mandi*. Nice place, breakfast included. Right across the street (no. 25) is **Garden Inn,** a fancy place at Rp48,000 d. At Jl. Jen. A. Yani, **Hotel Asia**'s so-so double rooms cost Rp22,000 with hot water.

Offering surf and sand at your doorstep, the most luxurious place in town is **Pantai Nala Samudera International Hotel,** just 20 minutes from the airport and a five-minute drive from downtown at Jl. Pantai Nala 142, tel. 31722, fax 32072, P.O. Box 44. Charge: Rp50,000-59,500 s, Rp62,000-190,000 d (plus 21% tax and service), with 40 a/c rooms with private bath and shower, a/c, color TV, telephone, and airport transfers. There's also a restaurant and showroom for traditional handicrafts and a fitness center. Next door is **Nala Seaside Cottages**; Rp22,000 s, Rp27,500 d for nice bungalows.

Food

Street *warung* are set up at night in many places, such as across the street from the fort. Buy groceries and drinks in one of the numerous Chinese shops along Jl. Panjaitan in Kampung Cina. **Pasar Minggu** is Bengkulu's biggest market and the place to buy fruit—a delight to wander around in and easy to reach. The **Ragil Kuning Restaurant,** Jl. Kenanga, has excellent food at reasonable prices; rooms are also available here. Simple but expensive Chinese restaurants along Jl. A. Yani.

Events

The **Tabot Carnival** is Bengkulu's Mardi Gras. It commemorates the heroism of Hassan and Hussein, grandsons of the Prophet Mohammed. In the festival about 50 colorful towers (*tabot*) made of bamboo and decorated with colored paper, each built in the shape of a minaret, are carried in procession around town, then heaved into the ocean. It's said that Gurkhas from Nepal started this tradition; since some of them were Muslims themselves, they married Bengkulu women. The *tabot* may be carried only by descendants of the Gurkha and Bengkulunese marriages. Huge prayer-drums (*beduk*), made from the slats of coconut and breadfruit trees and covered with goat or cowskin, are beaten continuously throughout the ceremonies.

The festival lasts 10 days, from the first to the 10th of Muharram of the Muslim calendar each year. The climax is on the 10th day with the closing Ceremony of Exile, practiced only in Bengkulu and Pariaman (West Sumatra). Bengkulu overflows with visitors from all over Sumatra who come to participate in this authentic and much-loved folk event. While you're at it, try to get invited to a Bengkulunese wedding, either in the provincial capital or out in the *desa*. A local band is hired and they call people up from the audience to sing, a great way to make friends quickly. If you can sing in Bahasa Bengkulu, the crowd will go wild.

Services

Change money at **Bank Bumi Daya** around the corner from the post office at rates slightly less than in Jakarta. The town's banks won't accept cash against credit cards. The **post and telegraph offices** are across from the domed Parr Monument. **Swadaya Tours and Travel,** Jl. Jen. Suprapto 67, tel. (0736) 31331, and **M.Y. Assik PT,** Jl. Jen. A. Yani 922, tel. 31119, can help with travel arrangements. The telephone city code for Bengkulu is 0736.

TRANSPORTATION

Getting There

Garuda, Jl. A. Yani 922B, tel. (0736) 21416, has direct daily flights from Jakarta and Palembang. Merpati flies from Padang, Jakarta, Palembang, Bandar Lampung, and Muko Muko.

The port at Pulau Baai, 14 km south, handles cargo boats sailing from Padang and Jakarta to Bengkulu; sometimes the regular Pelni Jakarta-Padang-Jakarta ship stops here. Check with Pelni and at the harbormaster's office next to the fort for sailing schedules and prices.

Several bus companies run direct daily bus services to Bengkulu from other Sumatran cities. From the north, Damri and Habeko offer daily buses on the rough coastal road from Padang (560 km, about 20 hours).

Habeko has better, faster buses; Damri's buses are almost falling apart. But it's easier on your body to do it in segments by resting one day in Muko Muko before continuing on to Bengkulu. Access from the south is more difficult, but improving. A rough 60-km road connects Tanjungsakti, just across the border in South Sumatra Province, with Manna in the Bengkulu district. From Palembang, an economy-class train leaves every evening, arriving the next morning at Lubuklinggau; from Lubuklinggau take the Curup bus, from Curup take another bus to Bengkulu (Rp1500).

Getting Around
Minibuses are plentiful and *bemo* travel the main streets from the terminal in Pasar Minggu. It costs only Rp150 to get from Pasar Minggu to the long-distance bus terminal. Or negotiate a ride in a horse cart. To the airport or Pulai Baai (both 14 km from town) a taxi costs Rp8000.

Getting Away
Direct Merpati flights to Jakarta (50 minutes) and Palembang (30 minutes) leave once daily. It's almost impossible to pay for your Merpati tickets with a credit card. Be prepared, because you may want to fly out of Bengkulu after experiencing the Muko Muko-Bengkulu road.

The Pelni ship KM *Kerinci* stops here once or twice a month on its way to Padang from Jakarta. Bengkulu is also an embarkation point for *kapal motor* to Pulau Enggano. Small trucks and buses serve provincial towns from Terminal Panorama, two km south of town. Private buses to other provinces also leave from here. Damri and Habeko are the only companies tackling the rugged coast road north to Padang. If you want to go south, take a minibus to Km 8, then catch one of the big buses farther down the coast to Manna and beyond.

Buses head for Lubuklinggau on the junction of the Trans-Sumatra Highway, 110 km from Bengkulu (Rp4000). Other fares: Curup, Rp1500; Padang, Rp12,000; Palembang, Rp8500.

VICINITY OF BENGKULU CITY

Pantai Panjang
The small boat harbor, with its defecation-littered beach, is right in front of a crumbling English residence; just walk down the little lane to the left of the *warung* which leads to the ocean. Food and drink are available from *warung* in a grove of beautiful native casuarina trees at the south end of Jl. Putri Gading Cempaka, three km south of Kampung Cina. **Pantai Panjang** ("Long Beach"), also known as Pantai Cempaka, is a seven-km stretch of sand, with gently crashing surf, just 1.5 km south of Kampung Cina. Watch fishing *prahu* go out at dusk. Not suitable for swimming because of sharp hidden rocks under the water.

Danau Dendam Tak Sudah
A small beautiful lake, eight km southeast of town, famous for a water orchid (*Vanda hookeriana*) that grows along its shores—the only place in the world where this species grows wild. The orchid is protected and may not be picked. When it blossoms in June, July, and October, the lake is completely surrounded in brilliant pink. The English started to dam the lake during their occupation in the first half of the 19th century, but never finished; the name means "Dam Not Finished." No tourist facilities except makeshift *warung* set up in the busy seasons when the orchids bloom. Near the lake are cabanas where visitors may enjoy the gorgeous view. Two routes lead to the lake. The easiest is by chartered taxi or a public taxi from the village of Dusun Besar. Take the main highway seven km toward Kepahiang, turn left on Jl. Dusun Besar, then walk 1.5 km. Or take the main highway five km toward Manna and turn left on Jl. Danau and walk 2.5 km.

NORTHERN BENGKULU PROVINCE

CURUP AND VICINITY

The district's main town and capital is 85 km northeast of Bengkulu (Rp1500 by bus, three hours) on a spectacular paved road which climbs up through virgin primary forest to a high pass in the mighty Bukit Barisan range. Some points along the way afford glimpses of Bengkulu and the Indian Ocean. One of the best views is from Tabah Penanjung restaurant, about 37 km from Bengkulu. The road descends from the pass to Kepahiang, then follows the Musi River valley upstream to Curup. Stay at clean and quiet **Wisma Bukit Kaba** on Jl. Sukowati for Rp15,000 d for a good-sized room with fan, basic breakfast included. Eat in the hotel's dining room (*nasi goreng* or *cap cai*, Rp1000).

Nineteen km from Curup, **Bukit Kaba** is an extensive sulphuric volcanic crater that has had at least 10 deadly eruptions since the mid-1800s. It makes for a relatively easy day-trip; depart from Curup and head for Kampung Bukit Kaba. There's a very clear, good path up to the crater, and a rather skimpy warm pool on the way up. Climbing to the top takes about four hours. At the summit, climb down into the volcano's three big craters. A thermal hot springs and a 75-meter-high waterfall are both within 30 km of Curup. The high mountain lake, **Danau Tes**, is 50 km from Curup by public bus.

COASTAL ROAD TO PADANG

To see some of northern Bengkulu's deserted beaches and vast jungles, try this adventurous trip. It's about 300 km from Bengkulu to the province's northern border, then another 250 km to Padang. Allow anywhere from 14 to 48 hours. Damri is the only regular bus company to travel the entire run, but local buses, jeeps, and trucks also carry paying passengers. The rainy season (Oct.-Feb.) could cause delays or close sections of the road; ask the bus drivers about conditions. Once you reach Muko Muko, frequent buses head north to Tapan and Padang.

Traveling north from Bengkulu, you can see the culture gradually change from Bengkulunese to Minangkabau. No *losmen* are on this route, but restaurants often put travelers up or you can stay in the Mess Pemda (accommodations normally reserved for visiting government officials) in Lais, Ketaun, Ipuh, and Muko Muko. Most of the road is within the sound of the surf but usually the ocean is separated by a grove of casuarina trees. Beautiful lonesome beaches stretch to the horizon, low cliffs drop straight into the surf.

Ketaun

Seven km after Lais the asphalt runs out; from here on villages are often separated by long stretches of jungle. You'll still find Padang-style restaurants about every 40 km. **Pasar Desa I Ketaun** (80 km) is a Javanese village and market. In the logging town of **Ketaun** (85 km), at the mouth of the large Ketaun River, live the Pekal-Ketaun people. Javanese transmigrants are hacking at the jungle to build new farms and villages in the area.

Two river trips can be made from Ketaun. Take a motorized canoe four hours up Air Langi, a tributary of the lower Ketaun River, to Tanjung Dalam village. **Lubuk Ismael** falls is five km farther. **Napal Putih** is two to three hours up the Ketaun River itself. From there a small train leaves about 0900 each day for **Lebong Tandai**, a gold-mining area. The Aussies may let you take their train, a two-hour trip. From Lebong Tandai it's possible to walk to **Muara Aman** and continue by road to **Lake Tes** and **Curup**. You'll probably need a guide.

Ketaun To Muko Muko

Continuing on the coastal road, **Seblat** (124 km) is a large village on the Seblat River. **Air Rami** (148 km) has a long sweeping beach and a restaurant south of the village. **Ipuh** (161 km) is a small administrative town in two parts: Pasar Ipuh near the coast and Medan Jaya on the main road. Still heading north, the road turns inland, rejoining the coast about 20 km south of Muko Muko.

Muko Muko

Coming from either direction (Padang or Bengkulu), it's a good idea to rest in Muko Muko, a small

MUKO MUKO

TO TAPAN

HOTEL BENTENG

POST OFFICE

PASAR

OLD ENGLISH FORT

KOTA JAYA VILLAGE

PADANG RESTAURANT

TO BENGKULU

NOT TO SCALE

© MOON PUBLICATIONS, INC.

town with an airstrip, before continuing. There's only one *losmen* in Muko Muko, very good and quiet **Hotel Benteng,** offering nice big rooms with *mandi* for Rp7500 (but easily brought down to Rp5000). Have staff fix you a *nasi goreng* in the *losmen* (Rp700) or eat in the good Padang restaurant across the bridge. Take the nice footpath/dirt road to the beach and the small fishing village of Kota Jaya. On the way, you pass the remains of an English fort.

From Muko Muko, Damri runs buses to Bengkulu for Rp5500 (10 hours), and to Padang (also 10 hours).

To West Sumatra Province
Upriver on the Selagan River from Muko Muko are small riverine villages. **Lubuk Pinang** (307 km) is a small market village on the Menyut River and the last village before crossing into West Sumatra Province. **Tapan** is 40 km beyond Lubuk Pinang. It's sad to see so much deforestation along the road; as they say in these parts, *"hutan sudah buka semua"*—"all the forests have been opened."

ENGGANO ISLAND

Largest of a group of six islands in the Indian Ocean 114 km off Sumatra's southwest coast, a subdistrict of North Bengkulu District. Enggano is 29 km long by 18 km wide, and the island's total area, including nearby islets, is 680 square km. Enggano is for the most part flat and covered in secondary rainforest; the coasts are swampy. Swim along the pristine coastline, which harbors numerous coral sea gardens. Buffalo, *banteng,* wild pigs, and many species of birds are found in the wild. The western monsoon lasts from January to June, the southern monsoon from July to December.

Since 1961, Enggano has been a rehabilitation center for Javanese juvenile delinquents. The island's chief commodity is Chinese-owned copra, with about 20 tons exported to Bandar Lampung each month. Coffee, pepper, and cloves are also cultivated.

History
Enggano means "disappointment" or "mistake" in Portuguese, probably referring to some ancient blunder in navigation. The island's Eng-

ganese name is Soloppo, or simply "The Land," and its indigenous inhabitants call themselves *etaka,* or "human beings." For centuries completely cut off from the outside world, the origins of the Engganese are obscure; what little is known has been pieced together from passing accounts of visitors from the 16th century onward. When the Dutch first landed in 1596, the Engganese lacked metal-working, weaving, and rice fields. Skilled workers in wood, they carved elaborate women's headdresses surmounted by crouching human and animal figures. Stone implements were still used here as late as the 19th century. The Engganese language was affiliated with the Austronesian family of languages, deviating radically from the rest of Sumatra.

People
Engganese are thought to be a mixture of the Veddoid race of South India and proto-Malays from mainland Sumatra. Some think they descended from aboriginal Sumatrans who fled when Malaysian peoples began to arrive on the

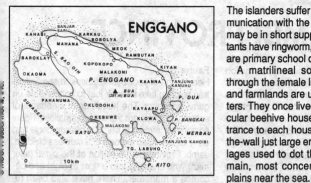

mainland; this helps explain the traces of Hindu influence in their culture. They also bear a striking physical resemblance to the Nicobarese of the Nicobar Islands in the Bay of Bengal. Due to introduced diseases the Engganese have tottered on the edge of extinction since the mid-19th century; in 1928, they numbered but 162. Preventative medicine saved them; by 1961, their numbers had grown to 400.

Presently, the approximately 1,200 surviving Engganese live on fishing, coconuts, and the sale of copra. Most are of mixed blood. The Javanese, Chinese, and other Sumatrans on Enggano far outnumber the native Engganese.

The islanders suffer greatly from a lack of communication with the mainland; food and goods may be in short supply and many of the inhabitants have ringworm, malaria, and anemia. Most are primary school dropouts.

A matrilineal society, descent is traced through the female line; all immovable property and farmlands are usually inherited by daughters. They once lived in fortified hamlets of circular beehive houses raised on piles. The entrance to each house was an elliptical hole-in-the-wall just large enough to crawl through. Villages used to dot the coast. Now only 15 remain, most concentrated along the narrow plains near the sea.

Getting There

Catch a vessel from Bengkulu or Bintuhan to Malakoni, Enggano's largest town and harbor. Boats are not that frequent and you could end up waiting a week. The 500-ton *Bragasena* sails once monthly from Bengkulu; unfortunately, it returns the very next day. Of course, another option is to stay a month until the next time the ship calls, giving you a chance to really experience the local *adat*. There's no *losmen*, so stay with the police or the locals. There are few vehicles—walking is the only means of getting around. Arrive with plenty of *jam karet*.

JAMBI PROVINCE

This east coast province, home to 1.3 million people, faces the Strait of Malacca. Jambi's highest peak, Gunung Kerinci, is the source of Sumatra's longest river, the Batanghari. Because of the river and Jambi's vast patchwork of *transmigrasi* schemes, many racial groups occupy the region. The majority of the transmigrants are forest gatherers and shifting cultivators. In the western part of the province are large oil camps; mineral exploration and production, plus rubber and timber, bring in most of the revenue. With its 70 timber processing plants, this province contributes about 6% of Indonesia's processed timber exports.

Fauna

Here is one of your best chances to see Sumatran wildlife; take a week just to concentrate on game-watching. The hundreds of elephants of eastern Sumatra are the world's smallest. Tigers sometimes wander in from the nearby jungle and carry off domestic animals and careless children. Jambi Province is the region of the *cigau* (tiger man) who changes into a tiger at night and becomes a maneater. There have also been reported sightings in the western regions of the mysterious *orang pendek,* a hairy, very strong 1.5-meter hominid, and strange *kuda liar* or wild horses, both of which terrify the populace.

JAMBI

The capital city of the province, Jambi is a thriving river port on the Batanghari River, about 200 km north of Palembang and 150 km from the sea. Its population (165,000) is ethnically very mixed: Minangkabau, Chinese, Sundanese, Javanese, Batak, Arab, Indian, Pakistani, Japanese, Malaysian, Kubu. Most of the city's traffic is connected to oil or timber activities. Jambi is a connecting point for ships and motorized *prahu,* usually carrying timber, traveling down the Batanghari to Jakarta and the Outer Islands. This small city has a very high rate of rainfall.

Jambi features an unusual mosque with stained-glass windows. There's also a university and library, **Universitas Negeri Jambi,** on Jl. Diponegoro. Walk along the waterfront; take a narrow sampan across the river to visit the orthodox Muslim village, **Olak Kemang,** on the other side. A trip on the Batanghari in a motorized dugout canoe or any other weird rivercraft is a fascinating experience.

Accommodations And Food

Jambi is not a bargain-oriented town. **Hotel Mustika,** Jl. Sultan Agung 31, tel. (0741) 24672, is overpriced and not very pleasant. It's two km from the bus terminal on Jambi's west side. More reasonable is **Hotel Makmur,** Jl. Cut Nyak

Dien 14, tel. 22324, a big two-story place with a very nice lounge room with TV; Rp20,000 d for good rooms, some with a/c, some with fan. Makmur serves only coffee for breakfast.

There are no eating facilities at the Makmur, but it's only a five-minute walk to the downtown area where there are plenty of restaurants—*nasi padang* and a couple of Chinese coffee shops. The **Minang Jaya** gets good reports; also try the **Terkenal,** Jl. Assaat 124. The **Renggali** has tennis courts, patios, a beautiful lobby, and mammoth bathrooms. **Restaurant Sinar Minang** features good food costing only Rp4000-5000 for two; *nasi goreng* is a good deal (Rp1500). Padang food can be enjoyed at **Kejora,** Jl. Laut Tawar.

Getting There And Around

Garuda and Merpati craft fly here from Jakarta in one hour; Jambi is also accessible by air from Palembang and Medan. The Garuda office is located at Jl. Dr. Wahidin 95, tel. (0741) 22401 or 22303; Merpati occupies Jl. Damar 55, tel. 22184. You can also get here by a long bus ride from Palembang, and even on riverboats. For getting around town, taxis are expensive, but there are two kinds of buses—regular minibus at Rp150-200 per ride and so-called "Chevies" (heavy-duty Chevrolet hy-

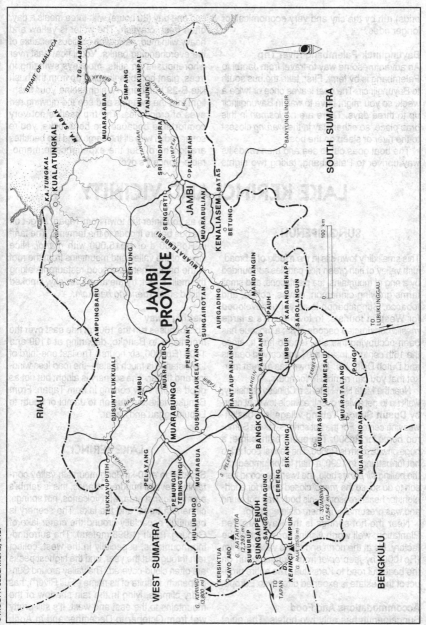

brids) run by the city and very economical for longer rides.

Bayunglincir-Palembang River Trip
An adventuresome way to travel from Jambi to Palembang is by ferry. First, take the bus south to Bayunglincir. The boat leaves once or twice a week, so you might have to wait in Bayunglincir up to three days. There are no *losmen* in this drab place, so either stay in the *warung* closest to the river or sleep on the boat.

The boat goes out to sea and then winds its way upriver to Palembang, taking two nights and one day (30 hours) with three meals a day, often fresh crayfish. The water is yellow and heavy with mud, navigation cautious because of the everchanging banks. You'll float past river whorehouses on stilts, monkeys swinging in trees, giant hornbills flapping up from the bush like B-29 bombers. At night shine your flashlight into the swamps and see the glowing red eyes of crocodiles. The trip itself is not very comfortable because the boat rocks, you're squeezed in with all the cargo, and the benches are too hard. But the experience is memorable—once it's over.

LAKE KERINCI AND VICINITY

SUNGAIPENUH

This small dirty town sits in the middle of a broad, lush valley of rich green rice paddies surrounded by a ring of mountains, tea plantations, and small farms growing cinnamon, cloves, coffee, and tobacco. Sungaipenuh is as yet undeveloped for Western tourists. In town there's a large *mesjid* constructed pagoda-style; a mosque has been occupying this site, legend has it, since the 16th century. Inside are large carved beams and Dutch Delft tiles. The town has a great market that you can ramble in for hours.

Near the Mata Hari Hotel is a Chinese cemetery; walk up to get a view over the whole town. At nearby **Dusun Sungai Tetung** village is a basket-weaving center. For the hot springs, take a Sumurup *bemo* for Rp500. The public bath is free; a huge private room is Rp500. The central pool is too hot for bathing. In 1990, a man fell or jumped into the boiling *air panas* hole, the twenty-second person to do so, so the *mandi* closed down for a fortnight for health reasons—his body was not found and was presumably in there disintegrating.

Near the hot springs is the Kayo Aro Tea Plantation, well worth visiting for a tour of the factory. It's at the north end of the valley, 42 km (Rp1000) by jeep/*oplet* from Sungaipenuh on the beautiful road to Kersiktua. The entire product of this estate is exported directly to Europe.

Accommodations And Food
Sungaipenuh has only two hotels. The quiet **Mata Hari** is the best; it's the first one you come to as you enter the town from Tapan, so get off the bus before it goes to the terminal. The tariff is Rp8000 d or Rp15,000 with *mandi*. Nice views of the valley and mountains from the roof in the back. There are good restaurants along the main street; try the area specialty, smoked grilled steak (*dending batokok*).

Getting Away
Lots of buses run the 160 km ride east over the mountains to Bangko, departing at 1100 and 1400 (Rp3500, six hours). The last one-third of the distance is much faster—the road less winding and flatter. The scenery is alright but not as good as the view coming in from Tapan. From Bangko, take the bus on to Jambi or south to Lubuklinggau and Lahat.

LAKE KERINCI

Situated in a 70-km-long mountain valley containing several hundred villages, this is Jambi's premier tourist area, with volcanos, hot springs, cinnamon trees, and the lake. The scenery is beautiful, especially around the crater lake of Gunung Tujuh (1,996 meters). The surrounding mountains, especially in the west, collect rain throughout the year, and the highest peaks are often cloud-covered. The valley around Sungaipenuh, in spite of its name ("Full River"), has a dry climate, lying in the rain shadow of the mountains to the east and west. It's still pretty wet from October to December and in April, when road travel can be difficult. There are no accommodations at the lake or anywhere outside Sungaipenuh.

Getting There

Lake Kerinci can be reached faster from Padang than from Jambi; the Kerinci District goes by the name Sungaipenuh on bus signs. Sungaipenuh lies about 60 km up in the mountains from Tapan, halfway between Padang and Bengkulu. ALS does the trip, but Habeko is recommended—real buses (Mercedes) with glass windows rarely stop en route. From Padang to Sungaipenuh is 12-14 hours, a scenic drive on a good road along the coast. From Jambi, direct buses depart several times daily for Bangko, traveling part of the way on the constantly improving Trans-Sumatra Highway. Stay the night in Bangko, then take the *bis malam* to Sungaipenuh, a chilly six-hour journey over the mountains. From Bengkulu, it's a 36-hour bus ride (Rp4000, 250 km) to Sungaipenuh.

GUNUNG KERINCI

At 3,800 meters, this volcano is Sumatra's highest, the source of innumerable rivers. It lies inside the northern end of the big Kerinci-Seblat Reserve, which covers a 345-km strip of Sumatra's mountainous spine, straddling four Sumatran provinces. To the north and south are heavily populated farmlands. The volcano's cone is young and bare, while the main crater lies northeast of the remnants of the Berapi/Elok crater system. Kerinci's crater, which erupted in 1934, is filled with yellowish-green water. The mountain is squeezed in between even older mountain complexes to the west and east.

The Climb

Though Kerinci is a very nice mountain to climb, you need to be in good condition. Obtain a permit (Rp1000 per person) in Sungaipenuh to enter the national park. Climbers usually start from Kayo Aro (1,500 meters), a small village south of the peak. Guides will take you to the top, charging Rp15,000-25,000. Ask for Paiman—he's trustworthy, and you can stay in his house for Rp5000 d (only fried potatoes to eat). Paiman speaks only Indonesian but provides accurate information. You can't lose your way on the ascent; there's only one path through the jungle. In the first ascent in 1878, it took van Hasselt a solid week to hack his way to the top and back again.

The first leg is four hours to a covered shelter; from there the climb is steep and hard. In some sections you'll crawl on all fours through tunnels of trees and under roots. You need to rest every 10-15 minutes, the way is so narrow and steep. From Paiman's house, it takes seven-and-a-half hours to reach 3,000 meters—here's a ruined house where you can put up a tent. Fresh water available. Next morning get up early and climb three hours to the peak. There you can see the crater, with huge billowy sulphur clouds. Two hours to descend to the 3,000 meter point, where you can pick up your things and be down off the mountain in just five hours.

WEST SUMATRA PROVINCE

Densely populated and home to the Minangkabau people, West Sumatra has some of the most exciting scenery you'll ever see: peaks looming over deep canyons and splendid sheltered valleys, villages perched atop deep ravines, great high plateaus with natural air-conditioning, giant mountain lakes, steep rocky coastlines, isolated beaches, terraced rice fields, and unique traditional *kampung*. The province's deep crater lakes—Maninjau, Singkarak, Diatas, and Dibawah—were formed by massive volcanic faulting.

Straddling the equator, two-thirds of West Sumatra is still covered in dense forests and thick jungle, with only about 20% under cultivation. Its most important exports are crumb rubber, sawn timber, plywood, cassava vera, vegetable kernels, black pepper, cement, and fresh fish. West Sumatra produces its own rice, and exports a great deal to the U.S.; the rest goes to Bangladesh, Malaysia, Japan, Belgium and Singapore.

Most of the larger Sumatran mammals still inhabit West Sumatra's tropical mountain forests. The giant rafflesia flower is found in the Batang Palupuh reserve north of Bukittinggi and in the forest reserve of Taman Hutan Raya Dr. Mohammed Hatta, north of Padang. On the off-shore Mentawai Islands live such indigenous wildlife as the Mentawai monkey and dwarf gibbons, as well as unusual orchids.

People

This is Sumatra's most densely populated province, with people concentrated for the most part in fertile, rice-producing upland plains. The daily, long, hard labor in the fields has yielded a magnificent countryside. Of the province's 3.7 million people, 95% are Minangkabau. Though West Sumatra is the Minang homeland, their cultural sphere actually extends way beyond the provincial boundaries, as far as Malaysia's west coast. The Mentawai Islands, inhabited by an entirely different society, also fall under the province's administrative yoke.

It can't be overstressed how important dress is in West Sumatra. Because of their unkempt appearance, the Minangkabau feel many travelers lack *baso basi* (good manners). Men should dress just as modestly as women. Dress is important in Padang, but even more important when you head upcountry into the villages. Women should not show their shoulders, knees, or silhouettes of nipples. Men should not wear short shorts or muscle shirts. It's also very offensive for couples to be seen holding hands or kissing in public.

THE MINANGKABAU

Adjacent to Batak territory in West Sumatra is the land of the Minangkabau people, remarkable for their unique matrilineal society. The Minangkabau have a level of political and social equality unique in Southeast Asia. Although sometimes called Orang Padang, they're an interior, not a coastal people. West Sumatra is almost entirely ethnic Minangkabau, who comprise about a quarter of Sumatra's total population and are Indonesia's fourth largest ethnic group.

Most Minang are farmers who live in small independent villages. The rest are skilled traders who live in or near the towns. Due to the rich soil of the rice fields, their villages are prosperous.

They are easygoing, peaceful, self-confident, hardworking, and shrewd commercially—the only ethnic group that can compete successfully with the Chinese in Jakarta. Fervent Muslims, they are one of the best-educated and most vigorous peoples in the whole country; many of the nation's intellectuals, leaders, and authors are Minangkabau.

SOCIETY

Adat

This ethnic group is famous for its matrilineal and matrilocal social system. Minangkabau

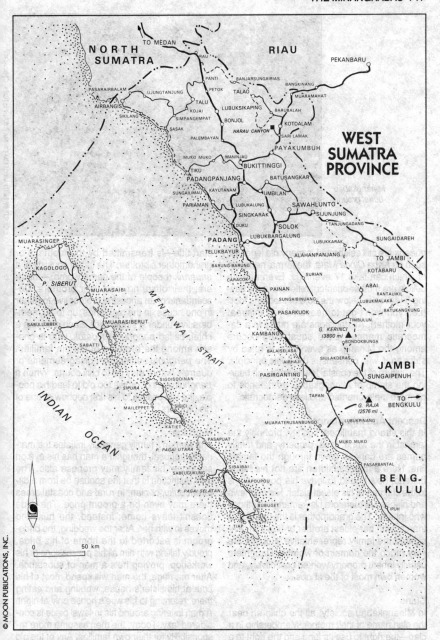

Minangkabau
burial ground

COURTESY FIELD MUSEUM OF NATURAL HISTORY, CHICAGO

queens are still celebrated in many old legends, such as *Kaba Cinda Mata,* the formal narration of which can take 17 evenings. Even afterlife beliefs are mother-oriented, reflected in the saying "Heaven is below the sole of mother's foot" (i.e., you won't get to heaven if you mistreat your mother). All decisions are made in a democratic manner. Little squabbling occurs among the Minang, as everything is ruled by strict *adat,* with consensus the basic principle. The culture of the coastal towns, although bearing the stamp of Minangkabau *adat,* tends to be more male-oriented and less democratic.

Descent And Inheritance

In this strong matrilineal society, probably the largest in the world, titles, property, and family names are handed down through the female line. Here a man's children are not his heirs. Instead, he's bound to leave his possessions to the children of his eldest sister. His nephews and nieces are therefore his *kamanakan,* "those who inherit." The grandmother is the grand matriarch, with her eldest brother or first son considered the family representative. Houses are very much the domain of women. Daughters usually inherit property worked collectively, and women own most of the shops.

Clans

In Minangkabau society, all the children bear the clan name of their mother. Membership in a clan—the right to use its land and the right to a clan title—is transmitted by the mother's or grandmother's brother. The family consists of a *saparuik* (people of the same womb)—mothers, their offspring, and their brothers. Descendants of an ancestral mother live together in one house; in the highlands, up to 30 members live under a single roof. Each clan has a chief, called *penghulu* or *datuk,* who is chosen among the brothers of certain families. The *penghulu* settles clan disagreements or quarrels before they go to civil courts. When a *penghulu* dies or grows too old to lead his people, the title passes to his first nephew or one of his brothers.

Marriage

The woman's family generally initiates the marriage proposal, though if a man has his eye on someone, his family may propose also. The only restriction is that the spouse be from a different *suku,* or clan. In rural and coastal areas there may even be a groom price. The bride doesn't leave home; instead, the husband moves in with her. After the wedding, the bridegroom is escorted to the home of his bride, proudly taking with him all his possessions or his workshop, proving he's a man of substance. After marriage, the man will spend most of his time at his sister's house, working and eating there, returning to his wife's house only at night. A man loitering around his in-laws' place is considered lazy. Today, the men assume more responsibility for their own families. Any of the old ways are changing; in the big towns, married couples spend a symbolic few nights at the mother's house and then go live on their own.

Uncles

Once, it would seem, men were used mainly for procreation, ceremony, and labor. In the past, when a boy was about 10 years old, he would move out of his mother's house and into a *surau* (prayer house) to live and study cooking, martial arts, and the Koran. A child is considered a member of the mother's family group; the father's group regards the child as purely a blood relative without any rights of inheritance. This doesn't mean male privileges are nonexistent or that a man is free from his responsibilities toward his own family; his guidance and wisdom is very much sought. A Minang proverb sums it up: *"Anak dipangku, kemanakan dibimbing."* ("Put your own children on your lap, but give guidance to your nephews and nieces.")

The mother's brothers are referred to as *ninik mamak,* and the eldest among them is called *tungganai.* The *ninik mamak* are responsible for the harmony and welfare of the brothers and sisters, nephews and nieces, as well as for the safety of family property. The real father stays out of family affairs, the *mamak* replacing him and giving advice on business deals and marrying off the children. The *mamak* is also responsible for the education of his sister's children, while his wife's brother is responsible for the education of his own children.

Merantau

The central area of the Minangkabau culture, a group of fertile valleys surrounding three imposing volcanos (Gunung Merapi, Gunung Sago, and Gunung Singgalang), is known as the *darek.* Because of rapid population growth, this central homeland area has expanded along the west coast around Padang and into much of the swampy lowlands extending toward the east coast. Areas outside the *darek* are called *rantau,* originally meaning "outer reaches" or "frontier" but now referring to any area where one goes out in the world to seek his fortune. Thus the word *merantau* today means "to go abroad"—a vital part of Minangkabau custom. From time immemorial Minangkabau men have had to leave the *darek* to do business, for scholastic study, or to seek more land or opportunities.

There's really not that much to keep a man down on the farm except to wait politely until a girl or her family asks for his hand in marriage. Then, all he looks forward to is a life of working on his mother-in-law's farm under the scrutiny of his brother-in-law. With so little industrial development, and population pressure constantly increasing, half the Minangkabau males are driven from the *darek* to Java.

In the past, men would leave the village for 3-12 months, returning to their families with money, goods, and worldly tales of adventure. But since the 1950s more and more are settling permanently elsewhere, and today men often take their families with them. The Minang population of Jakarta today is greater than that of Padang. Though Minangkabaus are found in pockets throughout this island nation, as well as in Malaysia and Singapore, most still retain their *adat.*

Spirits And Magic

Although strong believers in Allah, Minangkabau also believe in many spirits: *urang jadi-jadian* can become tigers; *cindaku* are human-appearing monsters like Dracula who suck people's blood and eat naughty children; *cindai* are beautiful women with long flowing hair who laugh eerily and lure unwary men; *palasik* make children sickly and weak. Visit Bukittinggi's market (Wednesday and Saturday), which has probably the weirdest collection of magicians, charlatans, electrotherapists, acupuncturists, drug-sellers, chanting Muslim holy men, and snake-oil merchants in the whole of Indonesia.

HISTORY

The Legends

The Minang attribute their origin to Adam's youngest son, who married a nymph from paradise and begat Iskander Zulkarnain, purported in some versions to be Alexander the Great. His third son, Maharaj Diraja, sailed to Gunung Merapi when the rest of Sumatra was still submerged in water. There he started the first matrilineal clan. As the water receded, the people spread out into what is now the interior of West Sumatra. Some say the word Minangkabau derives simply from *pinang kabhu,* meaning "original home"—their earliest homeland.

Another legend has it that the name means "Victorious Buffalo" (*minang* and *kerbau*), alluding to a legendary fight with the Javanese. The chiefs of the Javanese and Minang decided to settle an issue with a fight between two *kerbau*. The Minang cunningly starved a calf for 10 days, bound a sharp iron spike to its head, and set it free to run enthusiastically for the belly of the Javanese buffalo, whom it thought was its mother. The starving calf, frantically trying to suckle, gored its adversary to death. To this day, roofs of houses and some women's headdresses are shaped like buffalo horns.

Hinduism

The Hindu-Malay kingdom of Minangkabau rose in the 12th-14th centuries after the decay of the Sriwijaya Empire to the east, when Indian influences began to spread into the highlands. The imprint of this Brahmanic Indian civilization is still evident: a multitude of Hindi loan words, certain agricultural skills, methods of political organization, even remains of Hindu-Buddhist monuments. The Minang once had an Indian-type alphabet, but only the Arabic is used today.

The royal court sat at Pagarruyung; the first royal village was Pariangan. These kings had no strong authority except to settle disputes; they were more symbolic unifiers of the Alam Minangkabau ("Minangkabau World"). They also organized extensive trade and commerce with the outside world. Prior to the 19th century, the most important exports were gold and aromatic forest products. The Minangkabau have a long history of brassworking and forging iron weapons and farm tools. They used cannons and bored matchlocks long before Europeans arrived.

Advent Of Islam

Eventually, small Muslim states ruled by sultans became powerful in West Sumatra, gradually forcing the Minang Kingdom into the central regions, where it hung onto its independence. From 1820 to 1837 a violent struggle in Minangkabau regions raged, with the Dutch and the traditional *adat* chiefs and the Minangkabau royal family on one side, and the Padris on the other. The Padris were ultra orthodox religious extremists who tried to enforce Islamic regulations on a non-Islamic population and to eliminate such widespread pre-Islamic customs as gambling and drinking. In this prolonged and bloody rebellion, the Padris annihilated virtually the entire royal bloodline. This resulted in Dutch resolve to rid Minang territory of the Padris. A religious and political leader, Tuanku Imam Bonjol, along with his Padri defenders, held out until the last fortress fell at Bonjol and the power of the Padris was at last broken. Songs, poems, and books have been written about this folk hero.

Today, the Minang ardently embrace both Islam and their female-oriented *adat,* systems which would at first appear in direct opposition to one another. It's rare that a Minangkabau husband will have more than one wife even though Islam allows him up to four. And even though women have a strong voice they still remain modestly dressed. Being Islamic and matrilineal may seem contradictory, but it is this blend that makes the culture so intriguing.

ARCHITECTURE

Minangkabau architecture is some of the most magnificent and influential in all of Indonesia,

Minangkabau palace

EMILY KROMMENHOEK

even seen in new government offices and public buildings on Java. The peaked, swooping roofs of many Minang buildings are reminiscent of the curved horns of the revered water buffalo and of the women's ceremonial headdress. Traditional houses are disappearing now, replaced with brick and iron-roofed structures; aside from hotels and government buildings, few of the expensive thatch-roof *rumah adat* are being built nowadays.

Rumah Gadang

Means "big house," the traditional Minang dwelling. Each cluster of houses in a village is often the locale of one matrilineage, with a communal *surau* nearby where the men and boys hang out. Bedrooms are set aside for daughters of the household and their husbands, and there's a long common room for living and dining. The back half of the house is divided into small rooms where the married and marriageable women sleep. The maternal uncle, responsible for adding on to a house or building a new one, makes sure each marriageable woman has a room of her own. An annex may be added for each daughter who comes of age, and that structure is home for her lifetime. You can often tell how many husbands and children a family's daughters have by the number of "horn" extensions on the *rumah gadang*, each curving skyward and adorned with swinging ridgepoles.

In front of the *rumah gadang* is a long veranda used for dining and meetings, and as a sleeping area for children, elders, and guests. Raised up to three-and-a-half meters off the ground on wooden pillars with small livestock kept underneath, one must climb up and down *rumah gadang* on a single piece of notched timber that's pulled up quickly to thwart enemies, tigers, or snakes. The traditional house is thatched with thick layers of blackened palm. Exterior wooden walls are often carved painstakingly with scrolls and flowers, each geometric pattern colored in lavender, orange, and other pastels.

ARTS AND CRAFTS

Pencak Silat

A technique of self-defense originating in West Sumatra. Although found in different forms throughout the country, the Minang regional version is feared and admired all over Indonesia.

In fact, the art is accorded the ultimate honor: it's taught in the national military. A male is not considered ready to enter manhood until he's mastered the martial arts.

Pencak silat must be executed with elegance; Minang dance styles, such as the *randai*, are patterned after it, and many basic movements are rich with ornamental gestures. In the Painan area the deadliest form of *pencak silat* has been inspired by a tiger's stalking and killing methods. When performed, most of the wide variety of styles are accompanied by drums and flutes. Women also study this dramatic art form. The fighting style *mudo* is performed by two men. This very technical and potentially deadly mock combat dance, with dramatic pauses after each stance, is called off just before it becomes violent. And well it should: Minangkabau men can kill fish in the water with lightning blows of their feet.

Literature

The Minang have one of Indonesia's highest literacy levels, partially due to strong family support. Their traditional literature is oral, first written down only in the 16th century when Arabic script was introduced. The Minangkabau are very fond of oratory. Whenever any customary ceremony takes place, such as at a wedding party, the maternal uncle opens with an obligatory and formal speech of welcome and gratitude called *panitahan,* which can last up to four hours. Minangkabau men love to argue at length in their mosques and coffeehouses.

The Minangkabau, who are perhaps Indonesia's most precocious, individualistic ethnic group, also excel in modern literature. There are more Minangkabau among 20th-century Indonesian writers than any other ethnic group. They are, after all, practically writing in their native tongue; the Indonesian language was derived in part from West Sumatra. In the 50 years of modern Indonesian literature, such important prewar writers as Rusli, Muis (*Salah Asuhan*), Pustaka, Iskandar, Pane, Anwar, Idrus, and the first noteworthy female novelist, Selasih (*If Fortune Does Not Favor*), all have come out of this region.

These novels in their time were controversial, and some were shattering. One can even go as far as to state that the modern Indonesian novel is virtually a product of the collision between matriarchal Minang *adat,* patriarchal Islam, and the temptations and pressures of modern Western culture—Rusli's *Sitti Nurabaya* and Iskandar's *Salah Pilih* in particular.

The first important modern Indonesian poet, who employed Western poetic devices and concepts in his craft, was Muhammed Yamin. One of the earliest and best known of his poems is "Tanah Air" ("My Fatherland"), published in 1920. In it, Yamin stands on the hills of his native Minangkabau country, singing of its unsurpassed beauty. His efforts revealed the potential of verse written in the Indonesian language. Rustam Effendi is another outstanding poet of West Sumatra.

Dance

In the graceful *tari piring,* or "dish dance," entranced dancers hold plates alit with candles, deftly twisting and turning without extinguishing the flame. Your only chance of seeing a performance is to charter one for two hours for around Rp150,000. *Tari payung,* the "umbrella dance," portrays a young man's loving protection of his girlfriend.

A combination of literature, sport, song, and drama, *randai* is derived from *pencak silat.* Most often held outdoors at night, 9-20 young men in a circle are accompanied only by sharp cries from the audience. The dress is colorful and the dialogue captivating. The dance consists of a succession of slow then rapid steps, depicting the story of a wicked woman driven from her village. Annual *randai* competitions are held at both the *kabupaten* and provincial levels, and this dance form is so popular that over 300 *randai* troupes are now found in the highlands. *Randai* is performed best in the Paguruyung area, the traditional seat of Minangkabau royalty.

Minangkabau also perform one dance demonstrating how a *beruk* monkey climbs a coconut tree and picks choice coconuts for its owner. While under a religiously induced trance, men in the *dabuih* ceremony stick themselves with steel awls, a Hindu-style show of faith.

The Minang *gamelan*-style folk orchestra consists of the *rebab* (a stringed instrument), *talempong* (like a xylophone), *puput* (a straw flute), *gandang* (tambourine), drums, and many different kinds of bamboo flutes (*salung*), some of which are said to put love spells on women.

Handicrafts

Each Minangkabau village is known for its specialty: woven sugarcane and reed purses (Payakumbuh), gold jewelry (Bukittinggi), silver filigree (Kota Gadang), weaving (Pandai Sikat and Silungkang), embroidery (Pariangan), pottery (Sungai Janiah), and metallurgy (Sungaipuar). Artisans in other villages turn out bamboo carving, landscape paintings, wooden models of Minangkabau traditional houses. Antiques galore can be bought in Padang and Bukittinggi.

A very active cottage industry is the handlooming of silk *kain songket,* woven with a supplementary weft of foil thread, which creates a gleaming metallic design. Formerly, these cloths were woven with pure gold and silver threads (very expensive), but now synthetic yarns are most often used. As old *kain songket* decay, the valuable threads are picked out and recycled.

The women's traditional headdress is a turban with sharp conical points called *tanduk,* which resemble the horns of water buffalo or cows. Minang bridal gowns, perhaps inspired by 17th-century European suits, are magnificent pieces of embroidery.

Very light necklaces, pendants, bracelets, and hair ornaments are crafted here, small pieces attached to a string of light metal and then dipped in gold or silver. Intended only for ceremonial use, this jewelry is quite fragile. It's important to ascertain the quality of the gold or silver. Remember, the Minangkabau are shrewd traders; the true carat may not actually be what's stamped on the back of the piece.

EVENTS

Transitional Events

If you're lucky you'll see a Minang procession on the road. These could celebrate, for example, that a man has just become an uncle—an even more significant transition here than when a man becomes a father. Another traditional ceremony, Batagak Panghulu, is held to replace a village headman. This two-day event is enlivened with a debating session. Dress nicely on a Sunday and you may find a wedding to go to; wedding processions could very well take place down any one of Padang's, Solok's, or Bukittinggi's streets. Usually Minang weddings start at 0700 and last all day and night, especially on the last

Sunday before Ramadan begins. Weddings display a curious blend of old and new customs. The bride might wear the traditional Minangkabau wedding attire with a magnificent gaudy golden headdress, while her ladies-in-waiting cover their heads discreetly in Muslim scarves.

Racing
When it's time to prepare the rice fields for planting, many villages hold a *pacu sapi,* or bull race. Cattle compete by racing down a muddy field pulling rice plows behind them. Duck racing (*pacu itik*) is held only in the tiny village of Limbukan near Payakumbuh. Ask about the riotous bareback horse races (*pacu kuda*) held at least once every three months in each of the following towns: Padang, Solok, Padangpanjang, Bukittinggi, Batusangkar, Pariaman, Payakumbuh. They're a major, well-organized event, with vividly dressed jockeys. The Minangkabau also race dogs.

Bullfights
Also called *lagu minang,* this exciting event pits bull against bull. Bullfights are usually held twice a week in the vicinity of Kotobaru, 10 km south of Bukittinggi; fights are also held in Pasarrebo, Kotolawas, and Pincuran Tujuh. Ask *bemo* drivers for times and locales. These events are the province of village men; few women attend. Quite popular; there could be as many as 1,000 spectators.

There are two types: *adu kerbau* (a pair of water buffalo) and *adu sapi* or *adu lembu* (a pair of cattle bulls). They don't actually fight to the death; the contest is more a test of stamina and strength than ferocity. Most of the fun is watching the animated locals make their bets (up to Rp200,000 on a single wager). Buyers from the livestock markets look over the potential stud bulls: a good fighter is a good breeder. The owner, beaming proudly, might get a very good price for the victorious bull.

A bullfight could last for a minute or an hour. Sometimes the bulls are knocked unconscious in their first impact as blood flows from their nostrils and dirt flies and horns lock, grinding and butting. Sometimes the two bulls chase each other around and the onlookers scatter in every direction, having the time of their lives. Magic is also invoked to make the bulls win. The trainers stand by each of their beasts and blow into a length of frayed rope. Called *main angin,* this is said to breathe strength into their animals.

Pig-Hunting
The quintessential male activity in the Minangkabau Highlands. Males of all ages, titles, and classes take part in this violent and exciting sport. There are hunt associations with elected chairmen in nearly every village; from bus windows you often see men with their hunting dogs along the roadside. Locations and times of the hunt are often posted in the town *lepau* (coffee shop), snack house, or *toko*.

Armed with hatchets, knives, spears, and a few old rifles, as many as 50-100 men participate. The hunters pile into a chartered bus early Sunday morning and head for the wilderness. The dogs, snapping and barking, strain at their leashes. Once a pig is flushed out or a fresh trail discovered, the hunt leader (*muncak rajo*) gives the word to release the dogs. When the pig has been run down, the dogs start tearing at its carcass.

Not only is it a traditional sport, but pig-hunting also helps to protect crops. It's believed that embodied in the pig—a religiously taboo animal—is the soul of an evil human sorcerer or magician who is being punished by Allah. The activity is also a sanctioned release from the rigid constraints and formalities of Minang society and its customary laws. It's a time when ordinarily refined and correct members of the community become—for one day—rowdy, roughly dressed, noisy marauders.

PADANG

The main gateway and largest seaport ot the west coast, a center of commerce, the thriving capital of West Sumatra Province, and Sumatra's third largest city. Over 90% of Padang's half-million people are ethnically Minangkabau. Padang has one of the heaviest rainfalls in the world (310 cm per annum) and can be dreadfully hot, even at 0800 in the morning. Most travelers consider the Minangkabau countryside a better—and cooler—experience than Padang, which has undergone fairly steep inflation recently, so most just do their business, go for a walk along the seawall, see the rusting Dutch ships in the harbor, and move on.

On the flight from Java to Padang, the stark differences between Sumatrans and Javanese become immediately clear. Twice declared "Indonesia's Cleanest City," Padang's orderliness is unlike Java, and its economy is unusual for Indonesia: it's a city of native, not Chinese, merchants. It's also a strict Muslim town and a woman can be stopped on the street for not wearing a bra, or an unmarried couple denied a hotel room. Conservative dress is *very* important. A measure of Padang's orthodoxy is the fervor with which they adhere to the Islamic fasting month, Ramadan, when all of Padang's sidewalks are rolled up, its streets empty, its shops shuttered. People are either home or at the mosque. You'll never see an Indonesian city so dead as Padang during this time. The Minangkabau language is close to Indonesian; you'll make progress in your *bahasa* here. An obstacle is that everyone wants to practice their English on you.

Sights

See the lovely old homes set back from wide, tree-lined streets in **Padang Baru,** and old Dutch homes along Jl. Sudirman and Jl. Proklamasi. Chinese temples are in **Kampung Cina** (Chinatown). **Adityawarman Museum,** housed in a huge traditional-style *rumah gadang* with two rice barns in front, lies on the corner of Jl. Diponegoro and Jl. Gereja; open 0800-1800, Friday until 1100, closed Monday. Though poorly displayed, inside are antiques and other objects of historical and cultural interest from all parts of Sumatra, plus a special textile room.

The cultural center, **Taman Budaya,** just across from the museum, stages regular music, dancing, and *pencak silat* performances; open 0900-1400. Also check out the happenings at the **Institute of Minangkabau Studies** (SSMR) in Cengke. Padang's university, **Universitas Andalas,** is in Air Tawar. Don't land in jail here. Padang's prison, built in 1819, has appalling conditions even for Indonesia.

Accommodations

Find cheap *losmen* in Chinatown for about Rp4000 s. Across the street from the bus station are two convenient, inexpensive hotels that attract many travelers. **Hotel Tiga Tiga,** Jl. Pemuda 31, tel. (0751) 22633, offers economy rooms for Rp6000 s, Rp10,000 d; standard with fan for Rp15,000 s, Rp20,000 d; and VIP a/c rooms for Rp18,000 s, Rp25,000 d. Cozy and friendly. A *penjaga* waits outside if you arrive early in the morning on the bus. Right next door is the **Candrawasih Hotel,** Jl. Pemuda 27, tel. 22894; economy rooms Rp5000 s, Rp8000 d; first class Rp7500 s, Rp10,000 d (inside bathroom). Tax, tea or coffee included. Even in the back of these hotels it can get pretty noisy because of the traffic on Jl. Pemuda and the buses across the street.

Better is **Hotel Hang Tuah,** Jl. Pemuda 1, tel. 26556; economy for Rp11,000 s, Rp15,000 d with *mandi* and fan; VIP B for Rp16,000 s, Rp20,000 d with a/c and *mandi*; VIP A for Rp19,500 s, Rp23,500 d with *mandi,* a/c, and TV. Prices include breakfast; an additional five percent tax. Economy rooms have two fans, which you'll need due to heavy rains. Convenient (nearly opposite the bus terminal), the rooms are clean, spacious, well-lit, and the people are friendly and helpful. The restaurant downstairs serves continental breakfast, included in the room price. **Hotel Aldilla,** Jl. Damar 1, has rooms like concrete boxes with no windows; the bar and restaurants are always closed. The seawall for promenading is just down the street.

The staff at the old colonial-style **Hotel Machudum,** Jl. Hiligoo 45, tel. 22333, 22123, or 22010, is not so friendly; Rp12,500 d, Rp15,500 t for very basic "transit" rooms with *mandi* and fan, as well as larger, dirty, bug-filled

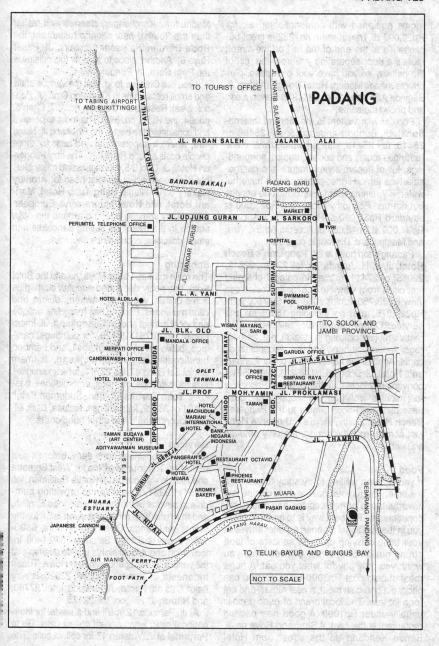

PADANG

TO TOURIST OFFICE

TO TABING AIRPORT
AND BUKITTINGGI

JL. KHATIB SULAIMAN

JL. PAHLAWAN

JL. JUANDA

JL. RADAN SALEH   JALAN   ALAI

BANDAR BAKALI

PADANG BARU
NEIGHBORHOOD

PERUMTEL TELEPHONE OFFICE

JL. UDJUNG GURAN   JL. M. SARKORO

MARKET

JL. BANDAR PURUS

TVRI

HOSPITAL

HOTEL ALDILLA

JL. A. YANI

JALAN JATI

JL. JEN. SUDIRMAN

SWIMMING
POOL

HOSPITAL

JL. BLK. OLO

WISMA MAYANG,
SARI

TO SOLOK AND
JAMBI PROVINCE

MANDALA OFFICE

MERPATI OFFICE
CANDRAWASIH HOTEL

JL. PEMUDA

JL. PASAR RAYA

GARUDA OFFICE

JL. H.A. SALIM

OPLET
TERMINAL

POST
OFFICE

JL. AZIZCHAN

SIMPANG RAYA
RESTAURANT

HOTEL HANG TUAH

JL. PROF.   MOH. YAMIN   JL. PROKLAMASI

JL. BGD.

JL. DIPONEGORO

JL. HILIGO

HOTEL
MACHUDUM
MARIANI
INTERNATIONAL
HOTEL

TAMAN

BANK
NEGARA
INDONESIA

JL. THAMBIN

TAMAN BUDAYA
(ART CENTER)

ADITYAWARMAN MUSEUM

JL. GEREJA

PANGERAN'S
HOTEL

RESTAURANT OCTAVIO

SEAWALL

JL. GURUN

HOTEL
MUARA

JL. NIAGA

PHOENIX
RESTAURANT

SEBARANG PANDANG

AROMEY
BAKERY

JL. MUARA

MUARA
ESTUARY

JL. NIPAH

PASAR GADAUG

JAPANESE CANNON

BATANG HARAU

TO TELUK BAYUR AND BUNGUS BAY

AIR MANIS   FERRY

FOOT PATH

NOT TO SCALE

rooms equipped with nonfunctioning a/c for Rp20,000 d. Transit room no. 222 is great because it's at the end of the hall off the street; there's a door separating you from the rest of the hallway so you have your own patio, plus private *mandi*. Modern **Hotel Bougainvillea,** Jl. Baginda Aziz Khan 2, tel. 22149, is newer, nicer, and priced the same.

Popular with visitors is the **Mariani International,** Jl. Bundo Kandung 35, tel. 25466 or 25410, fax 25410, with a helpful travel office (arranges tours) and secure, tropical surroundings, full of Jepara-style furniture and garage-sale type junk. Higher-priced rooms have hot water, TV, sitting room. Rates include service but not tax. Economy rooms are Rp25,000 s; standard Rp30,000 s, Rp35,000 d; first class Rp36,000 s, Rp42,000 d. Accepts AmEx, Visa, and MasterCard. Discounts possible.

Padang's top hotel is the **Pangeran's Beach Hotel,** Jl. Ir. H. Juanda 79, tel. 22584, 22512, 22085, or 27411, a "marble palace" charging first class front view Rp79,875, first class sea view Rp88,750, junior suite Rp159,750, suite Rp221,875, rates not including 15.5% tax and service. Offers central a/c, telephone, TV, restaurant (specializing in steaks), bar, 24-hour room service, laundry, and taxi. Accepts credit cards. Another top hotel is the two-star **Pangeran's Hotel,** Jl. Dobi 3-5, tel. 26233, telex 55213, conveniently located in the center of Padang, a few minutes' walk from the shopping and business districts. Prices similar to the Pangeran Beach Hotel. Lastly, there's a **Dymen's Hotel** just across from the airport, the only hotel so situated.

Food

If you've been waiting to try spicy food, now's the time. The famous *nasi padang* cuisine is a flavorful blend of fresh spices and, often, coconut cream. The best way is to let them serve you in the traditional manner: a waiter arrives at your table carrying up to 30 saucers of food strung out on both arms. Choose what you want; you only pay for what you eat. A huge meal should cost Rp3000-6000. Or you can choose a one-dish meal, a *nasi ramas,* and eat for a lot less. The local brand of *gado-gado* is usually under Rp1000. A good *nasi padang* restaurant is the central **Simpang Raya** on Jl. Bundo Kendang up the street from Hotel

Machudum; it's cheaper, cleaner, and tastier than the "tourist" *nasi padang* restaurant, the **Roda Baru** in the *pasar* (upstairs, Jl. Pasar Raya 6). Another place to sample this cuisine is the **Pagi Sore,** Jl. Pondok 143.

If you like Chinese food, visit the various stalls and small restaurants in Kampung Cina (Jl. Pondok area): **Restaurant Octavio,** no. 137; **Chan's,** no. 94; the **Ri Ri,** no. 86A. The most expensive and considered the best is the **Phoenix,** Jl. Niaga 138, where a superb meal and beer for three people costs around Rp30,000. The ritzy **Pangeran Hotel,** Jl. Dobi 3-5, has steaks and milkshakes but is expensive. For sweets, head for **Aromey Bakery** on Jl. Niaga. **Hang Tuah Hotel, Mariani Hotel,** and **Hotel Muara** serve European food. Many *warung* open up around the *oplet* station in the mornings selling pancakes and small, delicious, coconut-rice flapjacks.

Shopping

The main market, **Pasar Raya,** next to the Balai Kota, has richly decorated *songket* cloth, plus acres of fruit, vegetable hawkers, *dukun,* and blind musicians. Padang has many fine antique and local artifact shops: **Silungkang,** Jl. Imam Bonjol, tel. (0751) 26426, for paintings, carvings, *batik,* silver, coconut shell, and bamboo handicrafts; **Songket Silungkang,** Jl. Imam Bonjol Sei Bong 47, tel. 23711, for *kain songket,* textiles, paintings, carvings, embroideries, baskets; **Toko Sartika,** Jl. Jen. Sudirman 5, tel. 22101 or 28622, for paintings, statues, *batik,* silver, coconut shell, and other handicrafts.

Services

Get all your business done early, before it gets really hot. The **tourist office** for West Sumatra and Riau is way out on Jl. Khatib Sulaiman, tel. (0751) 28231. In addition to providing pamphlets, several of the staff speak good English, and they can help arrange a *surat jalan* for the Mentawai Islands. Open Mon.-Thurs. 0800-1400, Friday until 1100, Saturday 0800-1400. Information about local sights is also available at the various tourist agencies around town. **Tunas Indonesia,** Jl. Pondok 86C, tel. 22920, is very helpful, as are **Pacto,** Jl. Pemuda 1, tel. 27780, and **Nitour,** Jl. Hiligoo, tel. 22175.

At Jl. Pemuda 12 you'll find a *wartel* for international calls; won't accept collect calls. Go to **Perumtel** at Jl. Veteran 47 for collect calls. The telephone area code is 0751. The **post office** is at Jl. Brig. Azizchan 7, near the junction with Jl. Moh. Yamin. The city's biggest bookstore is **Budi Daya,** Jl. Prof. M. Yamin, Blok D II/4, but it doesn't carry dictionaries (try the shops in the market).

Change money at the moneychanger, **P.T. Enzet Grindo Perkasa,** Jl. Pemuda 17, opposite the bus terminal. At **Bank Negara Indonesia 46,** Jl. Dobi 1, you may also change money. Or try **Bank Pembangunan Daerah,** a state bank next door to Hotel Cendrawasih, which will even give cash against credit cards. Rates are better than Bukittinggi's, but lower than Java's. On the same street, just around the corner on Jl. Prof. M. Yamin, are places where you can get photos developed in "25 menit," i.e., one and a half hours.

Getting There
One of the main gateways on Sumatra's west coast is through Tabing Airport, seven km from the city center. Garuda, Mandala, and Merpati offer frequent flights from Jakarta (Garuda charges Rp186,000, Mandala Rp146,000); Padang is also accessible by air from Singapore, Medan, Dumai, Palembang, and Pekanbaru. Taxis into Padang from the airport cost Rp6000, but a *bis kota* is only Rp300. Or walk 100 meters out to the main road and catch an *oplet* into town for Rp300. A tourist information booth and a taxi stand (take note of the fixed-price taxi fares) are in the airport terminal.

Pelni's KM *Kerinci* departs Jakarta (Tanjung Priok) every other week and takes 28 hours. With its comfortable beds and hot showers, this boat is far less exhausting than the bus ride from Jakarta. Interisland ships dock at Teluk Bayur, seven km south of Padang, from where one can take an *oplet* into town (Rp500).

Padang is connected by bus to all major Sumatran cities. From Jakarta, it's two days by bus with pretty good roads all the way, even in the wet season.

Getting Around
Take an *oplet* or *microlet* anywhere in town for Rp200-300; the terminal is off Jl. Prof. Yamin, between the bus station and the market. Or drive around town in one of Padang's delightful carts (*bendi* or *dos*), drawn by scrawny ponies with gaily colored pompoms. Unfortunately, it's almost impossible for a tourist to hire one for a reasonable price; try to bargain down to Rp1500 for a two-km ride. Taxis hang out on Jl. M. Yamin by the market.

Getting Away
Tabing Airport is seven km from the city's center. Take an orange *bis kota* or an *oplet* out to the airport from Padang, or order a taxi through your hotel. Both Garuda and Merpati offer frequent flights from Padang. The last flight to Jakarta in the afternoon is sometimes cancelled because of rain; try to get a morning flight. Merpati flies to Siberut Island once weekly. Also available is a direct Garuda flight from Padang to Singapore. Airline offices: **Garuda,** Jl. Jen. Sudirman 2, tel. (0751) 23823 or 23224, opens at 0700; **Merpati,** Jl. Pemuda 45A, tel. 21303 or 25367; **Mandala,** Jl. Pemuda 29A, tel. 22350 or 21979.

Check with the **Pelni** office at Padang's port of Teluk Bayur south of the city at Jl. Tanjung Priok 32, tel. 22109 or 21408. For the 28-hour passage to Jakarta, the KM *Kerinci* leaves every second Sunday night at 2300, ariving on Tuesday at 0700. First class (two berths) is Rp100,600, second class (four berths) Rp78,100, third class (six people) Rp58,600, fourth class (eight people) Rp46,600, *kelas ekonomi* Rp34,100. Tickets are also available in Bukittinggi for these prices, which include the agent's Rp5000 fee.

Pay Rp25 (keeps the riffraff out) to get into Padang's central *terminal bis.* Long-distance buses include Jakarta, 32 hours, Rp35,000 a/c; Medan, 24 hours; Palembang, 20 hours, Rp20,000 a/c; Pekanbaru, eight hours, Rp7500; Dumai, 10 hours; Bandar Lampung, 25 hours. Stock up on an incredible variety of snacks at Padang's bus station.

Damri and Habeko, in the *terminal bis,* run buses down the beautiful coastal road all the way to Bengkulu (12 hours). Habeko, the only one to make both the day and night trips, is the best; it leaves at 0900 and arrives in Bengkulu via Tapan at 1800 for Rp4000. Night buses, with a/c or without, leave at 1600. The Bengkulu Indah departs at 1300 and arrives in Bengkulu at 0500 for Rp13,500. This bus goes via Solok and not the coast; get out at Lubuklinggau around midnight for Rp11,500 (a/c).

Or you can do it in stages from Padang. The first day travel to the sleepy fishing village of **Painan,** from where you can try to get a bus farther to Muko Muko. If you're lucky you can flag down a bus or minibus in the early morning or evening to **Tapan**. In Tapan, the locals will tell you every bus to Muko Muko is full but in reality they just want you to take a private car for Rp50,000. Pay no heed; just walk a bit out of town and stop the bus (Rp2000, 2.5 hours). Good road, except for the last 15 km.

For Sungaipenuh (Lake Kerinci), the Habeko bus leaves Padang at 0900 and arrives at 1830 (Rp7500, nine hours). This wouldn't make a good trip at night: the buses are cramped, and the road windy and often bumpy, which makes it hard to sleep. During the day at least you've got the distraction of the scenery and can read if it's not too shaky.

To experience the magnificence of the Minang Highlands, from Padang take an *oplet* or bus up to Bukittinggi (92 km, two hours), the heartland of the Minangkabau. This direct route north passes through the scenic Anai Valley to the market town of Padangpanjang, then over the pass between Gunung Singgalang (2,877 meters) and Gunung Merapi (2,891 meters).

A longer but more scenic route (137 km) heads northeast past the dusty factory town of Indarung, then up into the mountains on a twisting road with spectacular views looking back to Padang and the coast. Lubuk Selasih (37 km from Padang) is the turnoff for the mountain lakes Danau Diatas and Danau Dibawah. Or continue straight for Bukittinggi. On the descent to Solok, stop in Cupak village for a look at intricately carved and painted traditional houses. Solok has little to offer the traveler; continue north to pretty Lake Singkarak. For 10 km the road runs along the lake. Past the lake and 45 km north of Solok is the turnoff for Batusangkar (good views and traditional villages on the way), or head straight to Padangpanjang and over the pass to Bukittinggi.

PADANG VICINITY

SOUTH OF PADANG

Air Manis

The hike along the coast to Air Manis, a fishing village south of Padang with a nice beach, huge waves, and friendly people, is spectacular. First take a *bemo* to Muara, the estuary just south of the city. A *prahu* will ferry you across the river. See the huge Japanese cannon in its concrete bunker near the rivermouth. Follow the wide path over hills covered in clove trees. Walk the three km in about 45 minutes. All over the slopes of this mountain, called Gunung Monyet ("Monkey Hill"), are Chinese graves and monkeys. Here also is the grave of Sitti Nurabaya. A novel of the same name by Murah Rusli relates the Minangkabau counterpart of the Romeo and Juliet legend.

The beach at Air Manis is not so good for swimming, but there's a great view. Stay the night with one of the villagers. At **Papa Cili Cili's Homestay** you get a big bed with a curtain around it and not much privacy. Villagers will probably only be able to speak a smattering of English. Food is basic: fish, rice, vegetables, coconut. Go out night fishing; the fishermen return with fish you'll eat that night. Walk on the path (30 minutes) over the next hill south for a panorama over Teluk Bayur Harbor. During low tide in the mornings wade out to Pulau Pisang Ketek ("Small Banana Island"), but be sure to return before high tide. Pulau Pisang Gadang, farther offshore, can be reached by *prahu*. The beach is rocky.

Bungus Bay

The coastline is very rugged and scenic for the first 100 km south of Padang, with pulse-stopping views from the highway as it twists over rocky ridges and curves along sandy coves. Mountains drop straight into the ocean, forming numerous bays and peaceful beaches. If you're waiting for the Pelni ship or plane, an excellent alternative to killing time in Padang is to stay on one of these beaches. A good place is **Titin's Losmen** on Pasir Putih south of Padang; there's no sign but the *bemo* drivers know where to drop you off.

Bungus is a natural bay, 23 km south of Padang, with great sunsets, a crescent-shaped beach fringed with coconut palms, and white-sand beaches on islands offshore. Get a *bemo* from Padang's *bemo* terminal about 300 meters from the bus terminal. It's only a half hour (Rp450) ride to Bungus. The last *oplet* back to Padang leaves around dusk.

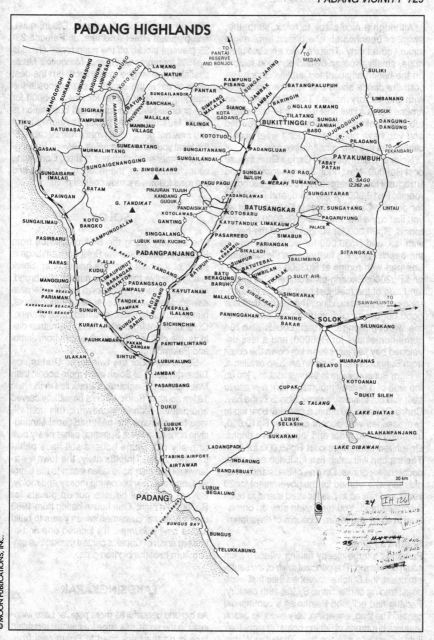

PADANG HIGHLANDS

Although a nice place to relax, sunbathe, swim, or beachcomb, the beach here might strike you as dirty. There's also an absolutely huge, smelly, Korean-owned plywood factory on the beach adjacent to Carolina Beach Resort; the dance stage and speakers compete with the factory noise. The shallow ocean around Bungus is almost too warm—like a bathtub. On weekends the shore is very crowded and you have no privacy. Don't wear scanty clothing as this is a conservative area.

Noisy and dirty rooms at **Carlos Guesthouse** cost Rp6000. Next door, the rather overpriced **Bungus Hotel** charges Rp7000 for economy rooms, Rp16,000 for standard, and Rp27,000 for deluxe. **Carolina Beach Resort,** right as you first come into town, asks Rp6000 for dorm rooms, Rp20,000 for bungalows off the beach with fan, and Rp30,000 for a/c bungalows on the beach. Two km farther south is **Carolina Losmen** with rooms at Rp3000 s, Rp6000 d, and Rp2000; Padang-style dinners. It's on the land side of the road just past a large Minang-style government building. The food at Carlos is good but overpriced; you can eat cheaper in the *warung* along the road. Locals also run some homestays for Rp6000, and a less-developed bay lies just seven km down the coast from Bungus, where *losmen* are also available.

From Bungus, swim in the waterfall two km up the side of a nearby mountain. Hire a *prahu* to take you out to small, nearby islands in the bay. Carlos Guesthouse offers a one-day boat trip to two beaches with decent coral for Rp10,000, including basic meal and inexpensive drinks. Or a hired boat might cost Rp45,000 for four. The captain will catch fish for lunch and crack coconuts for drinks. On one of the islands is an old man who worked for the government for 20 years and retired to this isolated island to open a coffee stand. You may even stay on one island in a hut and return a couple of days later.

South To Painan

Painan is a large sleepy fishing village 77 km south of Padang. The principal town of the southern coast, the Dutch established their first west-coast trading center here. By the 18th century, Padang had eclipsed Painan as a commercial center. The long, sweeping, very beautiful beach features hundreds of fishing boats; at night their lights sparkle out in the bay. Timbulan Water-

falls is nearby. Friendly people. Clean, quiet, and pleasant **Hotel Andhika,** Jl. Pemuda 23-25 (several blocks off the main road), charges Rp7500 for rooms with *mandi*. Mosquitos! Meals available if arranged in advance, but the best place to eat is the *rumah makan* opposite the mosque; very good food for Rp4000-5000 for two people. Near the *pasar* and bus station is **Hotel Mustika** (same prices as Andhika), but you may not get a good night's rest because of the local youths and the noise. Several Padang-style restaurants in the bus station. Continuing south from Painan, the mountains recede and the road follows a sandy coastal plain.

SOLOK

The scenery along the 64-km bus ride from Padang to Solok over the Bukit Barisan range is some of the best Sumatra has to offer. Solok is an attractive town in the middle of a broad, rich plain. The area is known for its extensive *sawah*, tasty white rice, wealthy landowners, numerous *rumah adat*, and traditional clothing. Quite different from other West Sumatran districts, the clothing shows influences from Jambi and Palembang.

Some consider the twin lakes **Diatas** and **Dibawah** south of Solok even more scenic than Maninjau and Singkarak. **Cupak** lies in the hills 19 km south of Solok. With its beautifully carved and painted exterior woodwork, this *adat* village has perhaps the best traditional Minang-style houses in West Sumatra, either newly built or really old. Some houses still have palm-thatched roofs. Unfortunately, the town's waterwheel rice mills have fallen victim to the petrol age, and are now becoming mossy and moldy. Several beautiful houses put up guests for Rp3000 s a night. One house dating from 1983 took traditional craftsmen seven years to build and is now a *losmen*. It's located one-and-a-half km north of Cupak's central market/bus station; turn in at the big iron gate.

LAKE SINGKARAK

As big and beautiful as more popular Lake Maninjau to the north, this large freshwater mountain lake is on the back road to Bukittinggi from

Padang. Make sure you're dropped off at the town of Singkarak if you want to eat. From Singkarak, hitchhike three km up to the accommodations. The highway and railway from Solok to Padangpanjang run 18 km along the shore of the lake; the wide-open view is superb. The shore is gently sloping and clean, with the water warm enough for swimming, boating, fishing, and water-skiing. Women should wear *sarung* to swim in the lake.

There's no regular entertainment, but the area is dotted with recreational facilities, restaurants, and hotels, some as close as five meters to the lake. There's a post office and tourist office here. Hire a *prahu* in Umbilan for a tour of the lake or ask about motorized touring boats. A ferry from Singkarak cruises across the lake to Batu Beragung. **PT Parindo**, Jl. A. Yani 99, Bukittinggi, offers a tour to Malalo, opposite Umbilan, where on occasion traditional dances are staged in the evenings. From Singkarak to Solok by minibus is 45 minutes (Rp300); from Solok to Padang two hours (Rp1000).

Sights

Umbilan is the lake's largest town, where the rushing Umbilan River begins. Take a bus from Umbilan and follow the river to Batusangkar.

Sulit Air is a nice village on a rough road which climbs into the hills, 14 km northeast from Singkarak. Since this village is located on top of a hill, water is rare; its name means "Difficult Water." Sulit Air has some of the most beautiful Minangkabau houses in these highlands, including 70-meter-long houses with 20 families all living in one huge room. No regular place to stay. The best time to go is on market day, when rides are more plentiful. Sulit Air is easy to reach from Padang with the Sulit Air Bus Co., which makes a daily roundtrip. The last bus back to the main road leaves at 1500. Be on it or you'll have to walk the 14 km or stay overnight.

Accommodations And Food

Singkarak village has the only inexpensive place to stay. **Villa Merpati** (no sign) is right on the lake beside a small park. Simple, pleasant rooms cost Rp7500 s; you can probably bargain the price down to Rp3000 s since the place averages only one tourist per week. Three km north of Umbilan right on the lake is **Hotel Jayakarta**; Rp10,000 with *mandi*. The location

next to the highway and railroad tracks does tend to spoil the tranquility, however. There's a *rumah makan* right next door. The **Minang Hotel** in Batutebal, four km northwest of Umbilan, is also located on the lake but away from the road—a beautiful and peaceful spot. Walk a half km north of Hotel Jayakarta and turn left through the gateway. Doubles begin at Rp20,000; also cottages. Food at the Minang is good but expensive; breakfast is served in silver pots, tea mugs—real decadence. The beach here is pebbly and littered. You can rent speedboats and water-skis.

In Umbilan are several quite good *nasi padang* restaurants; another is in Singkarak village. Many other restaurants are found along the lake. The **Lintas Sumatra** has a patio right on the lake and offers *nasi padang.*

PADANGPANJANG

A busy, rainy market town known for its *sate* and cool climate, Padangpanjang lies right on the main Padang-Bukittinggi road 72 km northeast of Padang. Hop on any of the frequent buses or *bemo* heading for Padang from Bukittinggi (30 minutes). The market is worth a saunter to try local foods and take in the array of produce. Thursday is the biggest market day. View Lake Singkarak from the Rantai Lookout point.

Accommodations And Food

It's better to stay in Bukittinggi and make Padangpajang a day-trip. Two basic places to stay are near the market on the main street, Jl. H.A. Dahlan: **Hotel Minang,** no. 18, and the really scuzzy **Hotel Makmur** at no. 34. Both charge around Rp5000 s; noisy, with creepy men. The Minang is marginally cleaner and a little less seedy. On the main road from Bukittinggi, coming down to the market, is **Wisma Singgara Indah,** which bills itself as an "international hotel" though it looks more like a middle-class house. *Rumah makan* and countless *warung sate* nearby.

ASKI

Just north of town is the busy, vital Conservatory of Minangkabau Dance and Music, an organization dedicated to preserving traditional instruments, music, and dance. Dance rehearsals are held most weekday mornings and afternoons until 1400. Possibly see the oldest dance of West Sumatra, the *randai*, derived from *pencak silat*, or maybe some new choreography. Also very fine displays of Minang and Javanese *gamelan* instruments. Listen to the Hindu-style *gamelan* and Minangkabau flutes until your ears ring. Only a little English is spoken here, but just smile. Dress properly. See the director to charter a dance show (expensive).

The Anai Valley

The scenic Anai Valley, 10 km southwest of Padangpanjang on the main highway to Padang, has waterfalls and rivers that twist and wind through gaps in the dense green jungle. A 221-hectare nature reserve has been established here, home to tapir, monkeys, numerous bird species, and the giant *Amorphallus titanum*. With a 40-meter-high waterfall cascading into a pool beside the road, the surroundings are magnificent. Above the clear water of the Anai River a railway bridge was built by the Dutch, considered in its day a tremendous engineering feat.

BATUSANGKAR

A small town and traditional center of the Tanah Datar Plain, Batusangkar lies 30 km northeast of Padangpanjang, or Rp1500 and three hours from Bukittinggi by bus. Once the capital of a Minangkabau Kingdom. Legends tell of a queen named Bundo Kandung who ruled this region in the 14th century. The Dutch established a fort here in the 19th century, their first major garrison in interior Minang country; it later became a strategic stronghold in the struggle against the Padris. You can still see the *benteng*, Fort van der Capelen, a smaller version of Bukittinggi's Fort de Kock. Batusangkar is a pleasant place, smaller and quieter than Bukittinggi or Payakumbuh, with a busy market on Thursday. Walk to the back of town for a nice lookout over both sides of the valley.

Cheap, central, but very dirty is **Penginapan Sri Bunda**, Jl. A. Yani 3. Better to stay at **Hotel Pagaruyung**, Jl. Parak Juar 4, just one street farther than the *penginapan* and only a bit more expensive (Rp8000 instead of Rp6000). The town has several restaurants, *warung*, and night stalls.

VICINITY OF BATUSANGKAR

The surrounding area is quite traditional, with nice views of the countryside and *rumah gadang* with palm-fiber roofs. Most of these villages have maintained their most important social institutions and hierarchies. One such village is **Balimbing,** en route to Umbilan, where travelers may stay in a big *adat* house. Get *oplet* here from Batusangkar three times daily.

Limakaum

Five km southwest of Batusangkar. An old mosque here was constructed with five stories, symbolizing the five villages of the district. Also see a large, very old *rumah adat* with original mountain *atap* roofing. In a small park on the side of the highway near Limakaum are the "stabbed stones" (*batu batikam*), symbolizing a vow of unity between Datuk Perpatih, founder of the Pilang clan, and Datuk Katumanggugan, founder of the Bodi Caniago clan; also here is the unexplained "written stone." This set of ancient inscribed stones is near the only hotel in the area, **Mess Kiambang.**

Pariangan

For a trip into the past, take a stroll through this ancient royal village on the slopes of Gunung Merapi, a living Minangkabau museum where *adat* houses and waterwheel-run gristmills abound, with people relaxing on front steps as the volcano fumes above. See the community house (*balai*), mosque, and *padi* storage sheds. According to Minangkabau folk history, ancestors of present-day Minangs first settled in the vicinity of this *desa*.

Pagaruyung

From Batusangkar, either walk 1.5 hours, or take a *bendi* or *oplet* (Rp200) to Pagaruyung, the former site of the *raja*'s court, heart of the old Minangkabau Kingdom. Here you can see the insides of two palaces (Rp300 each). One of the finest human-made objects in Indonesia is the "big house" (*rumah gadang*), called **Istano Pagaruyung,** located in the middle of nowhere beyond Pagaruyung. The magnificent building (note the 10-point roof) was built on the original location of another structure which burned down in 1976. It's now a beautiful museum—a must-see. Tour buses bring hordes of day-trippers to the site. There are several more palaces in the back of the village.

Tabat Patah And Vicinity

A sweeping view from the ridge of Tabat Patah takes in the entire plain of Lima Puluh Kota to the north: rice terraces, the Payakumbuh area, the Harau Canyon, and distant mountains. The viewpoint is at the pass north of Batusangkar, one km off the main road. If traveling by bus, ask to be dropped at the entrance. Tours often include a stop here. The village itself, and neighboring Rao Rao, are both picturesque *adat* villages. Be prepared for an onslaught of local kids.

Rao Rao, between Batusangkar and Tabat Patah, is noted for its unusual mosque, built in a three-story pagoda style with a smaller version of Bukittinggi's clock tower in front. Like many of the area's mosques, a pond beside it is used as a bathing place by men and a swimming pool for children.

BUKITTINGGI

The administrative, cultural, and educational center for the Minangkabau people, Bukittinggi is one of the loveliest, friendliest, most relaxed towns in all Sumatra—a real oasis after bouncing your buttocks raw on the buses getting there. Cool and sunny, nestled in mountains (its name means "High Hill") just south of the equator, this small university town has the country's oldest teachers' college and features many other schools. There are musical taxis, horsecarts, streetsweepers, veiled schoolgirls, regal women walking sedately under parasols, banks of flowers, good restaurants, and a wide selection of reasonable accommodations.

The town is very compact, with many tourist services and bus pickups concentrated along Jl. A. Yani. Providing you're dressed properly, the women are friendly and the men not cheeky. During Ramadan people are more uptight. Most of the businesses are owned by women and run by men. You don't have to bargain so vehemently here, as the Minangkabau usually start with a realistic first price. The area is worth at least a week and Bukittinggi makes an ideal base.

SIGHTS

In the center of town and overlooking the market is a venerable clocktower constructed by the Dutch in 1827. The "Big Ben" of Bukittinggi, this clock embodies a Dutch idea and Minangkabau design. Nearby is the botanical gardens, where locals may ask to take your picture. The zoo is the highest point in town; just behind the museum, lying within the confines of Taman Bundo Kanduang (Minang for "Kind-hearted Mother") Park. A fantastic place for people-watching; on Sunday the women parade around in their best Minang apparel. It's a must to see the people; the animals are secondary. The zoo (Rp500 entrance) specializes in Sumatran wildlife, and is especially strong on birds, with at least 150 species. For a look inside the belly of the big fish (the aquarium) pay an additional Rp200. See the goldfish swim happily around pathetic plastic shells which every now and then open to reveal plastic mermaids. The animals are not always kept under the best conditions but the hilltop setting is pleasant.

In the center of the park is a beautifully reconstructed traditional-style Minangkabau *rumah adat* (1844) flanked by two rice barns with fine woodcarving. This is the oldest museum (1945) in West Sumatra (entrance Rp200), specializing in local history and culture. Inside are resplendent traditional wedding costumes, headdresses, musical instruments, architectural models, and old firearms. A billboard lists biweekly shows at the museum amphitheater, where you could see eight-year-old boys engaged in traditional knife fights.

Ngarai Canyon

On the southeast edge of town lies Panorama Park (Rp100), which looks out over a four-km-long chasm with sheer rocky walls plunging 100-120 meters down to the riverbed below. The sides of the valleys in the Minangkabau Highlands are so steep the buffalo that feed on the grasslands often venture too close to the edge and are killed in the fall. Thus the Dutch nickname for Ngarai Canyon: "Buffalo Hole." This canyon, which borders Bukittinggi in the south and west and sepa-

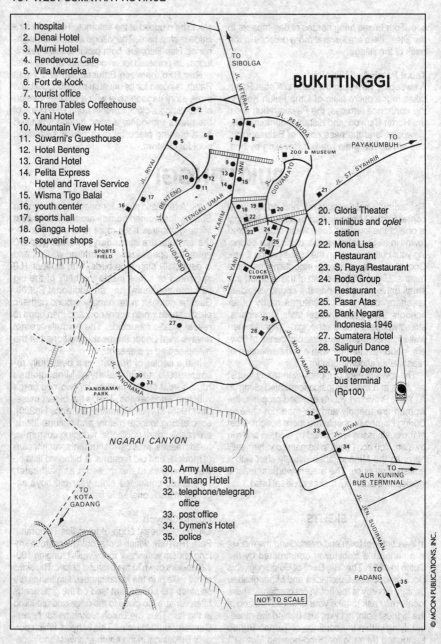

BUKITTINGGI

1. hospital
2. Denai Hotel
3. Murni Hotel
4. Rendevouz Cafe
5. Villa Merdeka
6. Fort de Kock
7. tourist office
8. Three Tables Coffeehouse
9. Yani Hotel
10. Mountain View Hotel
11. Suwarni's Guesthouse
12. Hotel Benteng
13. Grand Hotel
14. Pelita Express
    Hotel and Travel Service
15. Wisma Tigo Balai
16. youth center
17. sports hall
18. Gangga Hotel
19. souvenir shops

20. Gloria Theater
21. minibus and *oplet*
    station
22. Mona Lisa
    Restaurant
23. S. Raya Restaurant
24. Roda Group
    Restaurant
25. Pasar Atas
26. Bank Negara
    Indonesia 1946
27. Sumatera Hotel
28. Saliguri Dance
    Troupe
29. yellow *bemo* to
    bus terminal
    (Rp100)

30. Army Museum
31. Minang Hotel
32. telephone/telegraph
    office
33. post office
34. Dymen's Hotel
35. police

TO SIBOLGA

TO PAYAKUMBUH

ZOO & MUSEUM

JL. VETERAN

JL. PEMUDA

JL. ST. SYAHRIR

JL. RIVAI

JL. BENTENG

JL. TENGKU UMAR

JL. A. KARIM

JL. YOS SUDARSO

JL. A. YANI

JL. CIDUAMATO

JL. YANI

SPORTS FIELD

CLOCK TOWER

JL. PANORAMA

PANORAMA PARK

NGARAI CANYON

TO KOTA GADANG

JL. MHD YAMIN

JL. RIVAI

TO AUR KUNING BUS TERMINAL

JL. JEN SUDIRMAN

TO PADANG

NOT TO SCALE

© MOON PUBLICATIONS, INC.

rates it from the foothills of Gunung Singgalang, is the pride of West Sumatra. Ngarai is sometimes even billed as "The Grand Canyon of Indonesia," though Harau Canyon better deserves this accolade. Viewed from Panorama Park, it's quite a sight, particularly in the mornings when a veil of mist hangs over the canyon. Don't miss the sunset. Gunung Singgalang (2,877 meters) rises in the background.

Underneath Panorama Park are Japanese tunnels (Gua Jepong) built in WW II. With the help of a guide one can penetrate these bare rock caves for hundreds of meters. From the park, a two-km trail leads down through the layers of faulted volcanic ash, across the river on a small bridge, then up the other side of the canyon to the rim and on to Kota Gadang, a crafts village on the other side of the canyon.

Army Museum

A WW II vintage plane stands in front; inside are weapons dating back to the Padri Wars of the 1830s, radios and other military equipment, paintings of battle scenes and national heroes, and photos of the kangaroo courts of the late '60s that "tried" "communists." Admission Rp250. Open seven days a week.

Fort De Kock

The Dutch built a fort on this promontory in 1825 during the Padri Wars. Dutch forts like this eventually became towns. Now the site is a small park and scenic viewpoint. Arrive at dusk when giant fruit bats come out, looking like birds without tails. The bats nest in trees in the canyon below Kota Gadang.

ACCOMMODATIONS

Jalan A. Yani

The tourist belt of Bukittinggi and the center for lodging. Be forewarned, however, that you're awakened each morning by the sounds of motorcycles, cars, and buses—the noise level can be ferocious. Get one of the back rooms. At night it quiets down, with only the sounds of horses' hooves. Walking down Jl. A. Yani from the clocktower, the **Pelita Express,** Jl. A. Yani 17, tel. (0752) 22883, offers both lodging and a tour and travel service. The manager, St. Armen, charges Rp4000 for a basic room and Rp10,000 for a

room with private bathroom. The **Gangga Hotel,** at no. 70, is central with nice sitting areas and a ticketing and taxi service—a big rambling building with rooms for Rp9000 with *mandi.*

Grand Hotel, no. 99, charges only Rp5000 d for cheapie rooms that usually don't have enough water for the shared *mandi* and toilets. The upstairs rooms (Rp10,000 d) have *mandi* and running water. Try **Yani Hotel,** no. 101, with *mandi,* hot water, and breakfast for Rp20,000 d (also Rp6000 rooms). One reader describes the Yani as "filthy, the toilet disgusting, and the breakfast bad," but it's undeniably central and convenient.

Jalan Benteng

To beat the noise and for a generally nicer neighborhood, go up the path on the right just off the bottom of Jl. Tengku Umar (road to the canyon); it comes out near **Hotel Benteng,** tel. (0752) 22596 or 21115, which is highly recommended with reliably clean economy rooms (Rp10,000) with shared *mandi* and views. Higher-priced rooms offer hot water and balconies. The Benteng has a spacious lobby with bar; the restaurant serves expensive European, Chinese, and Indonesian food. Good security. Staff also organizes tours of the area aimed at the highlights of Minang culture.

Suwarni's Guesthouse, Jl. Benteng 2, is a quiet and safe homestay-style place. Dorm is Rp3000, very nice small rooms Rp6000-10,000, big rooms Rp12,000. The landlady cooks really great food, but a few readers have noted the owners tend to be too moneyminded, offering to sell postcards, book flights, or arrange tours around the clock. The food is twice as expensive as elsewhere. Use the laundrette next door, as Suwarni's laundry service is too dear. If Mr. Suwarni organizes a tour, offers to accompany you on a day-trip, or even gives you a ride on the back of his motorcycle, make certain you agree on a price beforehand. Across the street is beautifully located **Mountain View Hotel,** Jl. Yos. Sudarso 3, tel. 21621, with a panorama of the lower town and canyon. Claustrophobic rooms cost Rp12,000 (no windows). Cool and friendly. Good laundry service.

Others

New and pleasant enough, though the rooms are small, is **Wisma Kartini** on Jl. Tengku Umar; Rp10,000 d including good breakfast.

Sumatera Hotel, Jl. Dr. Setia Budhi 16, tel. (0752) 21309, charges from Rp5000 s to Rp17,500 s for three classes of rooms; prices include breakfast, coffee/tea, tax. The affable owner, Eddy Sastri, claims his rates are flexible "depending on our guest's budget." Eddy can help with travel arrangements, tickets, and tours. Clean, friendly, quiet, central, with spectacular views of the surrounding hills; very good value.

Another new place, **Tropic Hotel,** is off Jl. Pemuda, but the staff can be rude and unhelpful, and allow tour guides to hassle you for business. **Villa Merdeka** (also called Homestay Merdeka), is located at Jl. R. Rivai 20 on the corner of Jl. Rivai and the road leading up to Fort de Kock; dorm rooms Rp3500, double rooms Rp12,500 d. A nice old house out of range of the nearest mosque. The manager, Halim, speaks some English and spent many years living in Jambi and Sumatera Selatan as a volunteer worker in villages; he can provide useful information about places to visit.

Guesthouses
A reasonable guesthouse is **Wisma Sitawa Sidingin,** about five minutes from downtown near the public swimming pool on Jl. R. Rivai, just down from the RSAM Hospital. From Bukittinggi's bus station, take a minibus to Murni's on Jl. A. Yani, then walk. Clean, quiet, with a nice family atmosphere. Courtyard garden; free tea, coffee, and toast for breakfast. The **Minang Hotel,** at Jl. Panorama 20, tel. (0752) 21120, is set in a beautiful garden overlooking Ngarai Canyon; Rp35,000 plus tax for the cheapest, smallest rooms, Rp45,000-53,000 for rooms with bathtubs and hot water. Only a kilometer from the *terminal bis,* this well-run guesthouse may be full so make reservations.

Top Hotels
The **Denai Hotel,** below the fort at Jl. Rivai 26, tel. (0752) 21466, is Bukittinggi's top place to stay. The older section starts at Rp25,000 d, while rooms in the new section are Rp40,000 s or d. Detached cottages sleep two luxuriously. The Denai has a nice lobby, TV, and friendly staff. **Dymen's Hotel** is in a quiet area on the south edge and some distance from town on Jl. Nawawi, tel. 21015. Tour groups often stay in this first-class hotel, where the cheapest rooms start at Rp50,000. The meals, though tasty, are

expensive. Two or three times per month in the tourist season (June-Aug.) Minang dance performances, music, and films are staged.

FOOD

Munchie Heaven
The market (Pasar Atas) is piled high with regional snacks. At night, street vendors set up all over town, dispensing *sayak* (a fruit and vegetable dish with sharp sauce), *apam,* and roasted peanuts. *Sate* is famous here. Night stalls sell grilled corn-on-the-cob, *sate ayam, gulai* soup, and noodle dishes. A must is a lunch in one of the *nasi kapan* stalls halfway between the upper and lower markets. Open 0900-1800. Sit down and one of the ladies will give you a plate of rice heaped with about six different Padang-style veggies and whatever other side dishes you point out. Thankfully, no tourist menus—a great experience and very reasonable.

Indonesian Restaurants
Bukittinggi's restaurants, of course, serve Padang food: fantastic curries, *rendang,* smoked eels right out of the *sawah,* and some of the tastiest *soto ayam* in Indonesia. The restaurants aren't that good with vegetables in terms of range and price, but vegetarians can order *martabak sayur* (vegetable *martabak*) at most of the Padang-style restaurants. **Roda Group Restaurant** in Pasar Atas, Blok C-155, has excellent *martabak, dadih campur,* fruit salad, and juices, Padang food, sweet-and-sour vegetables—the menu even comes with a map. Get a table by the window and look out on the market. Even better is **S. Raya** across from the Gloria Theatre, not to be confused with the S. Raya on the clocktower square where the food is poor and served in tiny portions at exorbitant prices by unfriendly waiters. Also avoid the **Famili** on Jl. Benteng next to Hotel Benteng, which serves extremely bad, expensive Padang-style food.

Other Restaurants
The **Mona Lisa,** Jl. A. Yani 58, offers above-average Chinese dishes—good value with efficient service. Classic menu misprint: Greenpeace Soup—perhaps it should be served with Rainbow Warrior trout. Jalan A. Yani has the usual tourist restaurants with Western menus, serving

everything from guacamole to pepper steak, with blaring rock music and local would-be cool guys hanging out in bamboo chairs. The restaurant **Mexico**, Jl. A. Yani 134, has very good food.

The little **Coffeeshop Queen** at Jl. Yos. Sudarso offers dependably good food for a reasonable price. The owner is a friendly Chinese man; besides the Chinese food he also serves delicious European and Indonesian food. The **Three Tables Coffeehouse** across from the Murni Hotel (Jl. A. Yani 142) is another gathering spot for tourists. Fresh milk served hot, new wave music, but skip the day-tour—poor value. The **Rendevouz Cafe** next to the Three Tables has tortoise-like service. Good meals available at the Canyon Coffeeshop on Jl. Tengku Umar; on the walls are posted traveler's tales and suggestions.

Desserts And Drinks
The **Roda Group Restaurant** in Pasar Atas is popular with sweet-toothed travelers. A vast variety of fresh fruit juices is available. The market is the place to buy abundant fruit: passion fruit, *sawo*, *rambutan*, and apples. In the market some people sell *susu kerbau* for about Rp400 for a small bamboo container. One dessert definitely worth trying is *sarikaya* (custard rice pudding) and hearty *dadih campur* (oats, coconut, banana, avocado, molasses, and buffalo yogurt); the best is served in the *rumah makan* in the market. The only good bakery in town is opposite the Yani Hotel.

CRAFTS AND SHOPPING

As a tourist center, Bukittinggi boasts a multitude of craft, souvenir, jewelry, and antique shops. Many are found along Jl. Minangkabau, especially near Gloria Theater. Most shops have fixed prices but you may still bargain a little. You really have to shop around, especially in the antique shops. Some are really overpriced, others are reasonable. **Aishachalik**, Jl. Cindur Mato 94 (an extension of Jl. Minangkabau past the Gloria Theater walking from the market), has good variety and good (fixed) prices. Also try the **Aladdin Art and Antique Shop**, Jl. A. Yani 14, which sells outstanding handwoven articles.

Jewelry
The Bukittinggi area is a center for skilled gold and silver artisans. Both the jewelry itself and the interior of the jewelry shops, done in intricately inlaid wood, are fine examples of Minangkabau expertise. Stones from all over the world are imported and set by craftsmen in their mothers' shops. Also see stones dug from various local mountains, set in brass and hawked in the market, along with colored uncut gems the size of golf balls, and delicate earrings and bracelets hammered out in nearby villages.

Market
A market takes place every day, but Wednesday and Saturday host the biggest, when Bukittinggi is flooded with thousands of Minangkabau who come in from every corner of the highlands. The sprawling market, which literally covers a whole hill, lasts from about 0700 to 1700 and contains everything from antiques and local crafts to produce and spices—a profusion of overpowering smells, colors, and sounds. Get up to it by either climbing the 300-step stairway or use the twisting cart lanes. A sweeping view over the town from the top.

The huge market area is divided into sections: a row of barbers, a row of cigarette-lighter repairmen, rows of crunchy-munchy snacks and sweets stalls, fish market, meat market, countless rows of produce, and perhaps the strangest assemblage of snake oil merchants in all of Indonesia. The market's two levels, Upper Market (Pasar Atas) and Lower Market (Pasar Bawah) are connected by a number of stairways.

Craft Villages
Many craft villages lie within an hour's *oplet* ride from Bukittinggi. **Desa Sunga**, on the slopes of Gunung Merapi near Kotobaru, is a center for brasswork, especially dishes and *sirih* cases. **Kotobaru** produces handwoven gold-threaded weaving. **Ampek Angkek**, on the edge of Bukittinggi, is known for its *kain sulaman*, embroidery, and crochet work. **Sungaipuar** is best known for blacksmithing (from candelabra to plows), **Kota Gadang** for spiderweb-like silversmithing, and **Guguk Tabek-Saroj** for goldsmithing.

Pandaisikat, 13 km from Bukittinggi on the road to Padangpanjang, has woodcarving, fine furniture, embroidery work, and loom weaving. Because of the number of package tourists, many of Pandaisikat's shops have become fixed-priced shops. The **Pusako Weaving House** offers the best quality *songket*. Visit

Silungkang village for woodcarving, bright handwoven gold-threaded *sarung*, scarves, and headwear. When buying *songket*, the quality is determined by the number of metal weft threads used to make the pattern. The best are "two thread," the cheapest "four thread." The two thread is very intricate in detail.

ENTERTAINMENT AND SERVICES

Entertainment
Performances of Minangkabau dance (Rp5000) by the Saliguri Dance Troupe take place almost daily at Jl. Lenggogeni 1 below the clock tower. Sometimes the performances are good, sometimes the dancers lack enthusiasm. Buy tickets at the tourist office. There's a good 50-meter-long swimming pool (Rp500) just off Jl. Rivai. As you come from Jl. A. Yani, go past the *rumah sakit*; it's on the left a few hundred meters along. Open daily 0830-1700. Behind the market is the **Gloria Cinema** with the usual low quality (in content and print) Indo and American films (Rp1500).

For something different, try the bullfights held each Saturday afternoon at 1600, usually near Kotobaru, south of Bukittinggi. It's not necessary to buy a ticket in advance. At Parindo Tourist Service in Yani Hotel they say the ticket guarantees you transport to the site as well as entrance to the bullfight, but it turns out you only pay for transport (Rp3000) and must still cough up the Rp500 admission fee. It's cheaper to take a public bus.

Services
The **tourist office**, in Pasar Atas, tel. (0752) 22403, across from the clocktower, is helpful, offering a few maps and brochures. Open 0800-1400 Mon.-Thurs., until 1100 on Friday, and 0800-1230 on Saturday.

Free maps of the area are also dispensed from various hotels and restaurants. **Uman Pusat** hospital, Jl. Sudirman, has English-speaking doctors. Bukittinggi's **banks**—such as the BNI in Pasar Atas—are renowned for terrible exchange rates; change in Padang before coming up to the highlands. **Parindo Tourist Service** in the Yani Hotel changes money. The **post office** is on Jl. Rivai near the Aur Kuning bus terminal; a 24-hour **telephone service** is offered at the Grand Hotel. Bukittinggi's telephone city code is 0752.

Dhany Laundry Service, next to Suwarni's Guesthouse on Jl. Kesuma Bakti, tel. 21792, is not really cheap but offers very good service. Bring your dirty clothes in before 1100 and get them back by 1700.

GETTING THERE AND AROUND

The two-hour drive from Padang to Bukittinggi is spectacular. The Aur Kuning bus station is three km from town; from here you can easily reach Jl. A. Yani, Bukittinggi's accommodation strip, by *oplet*. Rail service from Padang is only for freight. When arriving in Bukittinggi at 0300 after the 15-hour bus ride from Prapat, ask to be let off at Jl. A. Yani.

Bukittinggi's sights are easily expored on foot. The main *oplet*, *bemo*, and *bendi* station is in the middle of town. Take *oplet* anywhere around town for an Rp200 flat rate. Horsecarts provide a leisurely alternative, Rp1500 for the average one- to two-km ride. These horse-drawn carts (*bendi*), decked out with huge white plumes, scarlet frills, and bells, are always available but it's difficult to bargain with the drivers, who consistently overcharge tourists. There are some *becak*, but the hills are so steep they can only be used on the straightaways. Taxis can be hired from travel agencies and at the major hotels. You can sometimes rent motorcycles through your hotel. Rent mountain bikes next to Wisma Tigo Balai on Jl. A. Yani.

GETTING AWAY

At **Parindo Tourist Service,** Jl. A. Yani, tel. (0752) 21133, students can receive a 25% discount on Mandala Airline tickets. The boat from Padang to Jakarta, Pelni's *Kerinci*, leaves every second Sunday evening at 2300, arriving Tuesday morning at 0700. Tickets are available in Bukittinggi that include the agent's Rp5000 fee. Economy class costs Rp34,100.

Villages and most scenic areas outside town can be reached from the big Aur Kuning station, where buses, minibuses, trucks, and old Chevrolet station wagons provide cheap, uncomfortable, out-of-town service. Buses to Padang (two hours) cruise Jl. A. Yani for passengers from 0500-0600; after that (up to 1900) you have to go to the Aur Kuning station. Most of the major companies staff offices at the *terminal bis*. ANS has an office at the terminal (tel. 21679) and another on Jl. Pemuda (tel. 22626). **Parindo Tourist Service** in the Yani Hotel sells bus tickets.

Watch out when buying tickets from mendacious scalpers who haunt travelers' hangouts, and be careful buying tickets for a/c buses—they seldom are. Always ask to check the bus you'll be riding. There's a special tourist bus to Prapat (Rp20,000!) offered by Rada Tours (inquire at the coffee shop near Yani Hotel), but it's not guaranteed to get you there any quicker than the regular bus (15 hours, Rp12,000, arrival in Prapat 0500). Rada Tours also promises to stop at the equator at Bonjol and a hot springs en route to Prapat, plus provide a snack, but sometimes these promises aren't kept. ANS *ekonomi* is usually a good compromise for long trips. Four-across seating and the buses are not so crowded, with no one in the aisles. ALS *ekonomi* is even cheaper: Rp8500 to Prapat.

If you're heading for Bengkulu, the Bengkulu Indah leaves at 1300 and arrives at 0500; Rp13,500 or a/c for Rp16,000 (1400-0500). This bus goes via Solok and not the coast and you can get out at Lubuklinggau around midnight for Rp11,500 (a/c). Other fares: Batusangkar, three hours, Rp700 (leaves every hour); Sibolga, 15 hours, Rp6500; Medan, 24 hours, Rp18,000 (a/c); Pekanbaru, six hours, Rp5000; Jakarta, 36 hours, Rp50,000 (a/c).

Bukittinggi's tour guides and travel agents are very friendly as long as there's any chance of getting your money. Otherwise they completely ignore you. And it seems as if everyone—hotels, travel agencies, even restaurants—is trying to sell you six- to eight-hour tours to Lake Maninjau, Lake Singkarak, Harau Canyon, and so forth. Most cost about Rp12,000. These small tour outfits will also organize special-interest outings to see butterflies or study biology, archaeology, and architecture. Avoid **P.T. Travina Inti Tour**, which promises and charges a lot but doesn't deliver.

The big thing to do in Bukittinggi now is a 10-day jungle tour to Pulau Siberut in the Mentawai Islands off Sumatra's west coast. Every restaurant seems to have its own guides offering to take you there, regardless of their qualifications, knowledge, or interest in this unique island. Apart from a guy named Lala, who tends to hang around the Three Tables Coffeehouse and is a real con artist, all seem basically honest. They all swear to be the only ones who speak Mentawai, and all have photo-comment books filled with remarks from satisfied customers. To these erstwhile guides Siberut is only a newly discovered tourist gold mine. The charge is Rp210,000 per person (includes meals, boat fare, permit, guide) with a minimum of five people. However, some of the tours take three days to travel back and forth from Bukittinggi, so you only really get seven days on Siberut. If you go for a trip try and get into a small group (under eight people) because the Mentawaians dislike large groups and will not want to have anything to do with you except bum cigarettes.

VICINITY OF BUKITTINGGI

KOTA GADANG

Well known for its fine hand-embroidered shawls, weaving, and silver filigree work, this one tiny village also produced a steady stream of competent colonial bureaucrats in the early 1900s. Since independence it's been the birthplace of a remarkable number of Indonesian professors, government ministers, and diplomats. Lately it's turned into something of a tourist trap, with signs in Dutch advertising coffee all over the village. Kota Gadang can be seen from Panorama Park in Bukittinggi.

Crafts

Prices vary a lot; several places won't allow bargaining, a sure sign of too many package tourists. If you hunt around, you can buy wonderful silver pieces at low prices, such as an exquisite bracelet for Rp30,000 and matching earrings for Rp6000. Also available are brooches, rings (without precious stones), *kris*, and miniature silver Minang houses, all allegedly 90% silver. The **Kerajinan Amai Setia** souvenir center has the widest selection and best prices; signs show the way. Housed in a traditional structure built in 1915, it's open daily 0900-1700, except Friday when it closes for the afternoon. The collection of lacework, handkerchiefs, *sarung,* embroidered *kebaya* (the Minang version differs from the shorter Javanese version), and Minangkabau bridal headdresses is especially good, though difficult to bargain down.

Getting There

Kota Gadang is a one-hour walk up the other side of the gorge from Bukittinggi. To reach the start of the footpath, walk or catch a *bendi* down the twisting road, which begins below Panorama Park, then enter the path on the left after the little *warung.* The path ends at the start of 100 giant steps leading up to Kota Gadang. Or take an *oplet* or bus by paved road five km from Bukittinggi. To get back, you can either take the minibus or walk seven km to Sianok village, where you descend steep dirt steps into the canyon.

On the canyon walk to Kota Gadang, hire a guide (Af or Edison) for Rp1500 to take you to see the flying foxes, giant bats with wingspans of three feet. Your guide will lead you across rice paddies and through the jungle, heavy with swarms of dragonflies. Wear sandals as the rocky path takes you through lots of water. Decide ahead of time on the fee, as you may be taken to a place where you might not easily find your way back; then he'll charge you Rp10,000.

WEST SUMATRA HIGHLANDS

Bukittinggi is the usual choice as a base for exploring the highlands, but the towns of Payakumbuh and Batusangkar also have acceptable accommodations and transport. Your own vehicle would be ideal for touring the beautiful countryside and traditional villages, but *oplet* go almost everywhere. There's superb mountain and valley scenery on the road into North Sumatra Province, where you'll notice a change in the architecture of village houses and will start hearing the familiar *"Horas!"* greeting from the Mandailing Batak people.

Rafflesia Arnoldi

The giant *Rafflesia arnoldi* grows in a reserve 12 km north of Bukittinggi (Rp300 by *bemo,* 30 minutes) near the village of Batangpalupuh. Follow the sign down a path which leads to the edge of a forest to a gate; get the key in the village.

HUNTING THE RAFFLESIA

Sir Stamford Raffles, Bengkulu's British lieutenant-governor from 1818 to 1823, worked tirelessly as the first president of the London Zoological Society; he and the naturalist Arnold were the first to discover and describe the *Rafflesia arnoldi.* The plant's main claim to fame is its huge size—nearly a meter in diameter. This "flower" has no root system, no stem, no leaves, and smells like a 10-day-old dead rat. Its putrid odor is designed to attract carrion insects such as bees and unwary flies; these pests fly inside, and the plant then "eats" and digests them. The attractive flower takes one week to bloom.

It's nearly impossible to grow the rafflesia in a garden, and extremely rare to ever set your eyes on this botanical classic in the wild. But it's worth hunting, for even if you don't catch sight of this wonder you'll still have a fine time exploring the rainforest. Note the plant generally prefers to grow below banyan trees.

The rafflesia has been seen in the areas of Pagar Gunung, Lubuk Tapi, Tabah Penanjung, Bukittinggi, and on Mt. Kinabalu in East Malaysia. It's also found around Tebing Binjai, 15 km southwest of Kepahiang, deep in spectacular rainforest only two km up the mountain from the Tabah Penanjung restaurant. Travel down into a high-canopied primary rainforest of *meranti* trees with splayed trunks, strangler tendrils, wait-a-minute vines, giant ferns, and termite mounds like giant cow droppings. Stop and sniff the air: you should be able to detect the thing at 25 meters.

Tabah Penanjung is the country's official rafflesia reserve, where the plant is protected by the government. A plaque here, found off the road, directs the hiker to the rafflesia. A guide might be needed to lead the way up and down hills through sections of *alang-alang* and prickly grass, with birds crying and wild pigs bolting away. Wear boots and long pants.

Guides to this botanic classic ask Rp2000, or find kids to lead you for less. Some say the rafflesia blooms in January, others say June—no one really knows. It's rare as a tiger print.

Bonjol

About 56 km north of Bukittinggi and 20 km north of Nglau Kamang on the Trans-Sumatra Highway to Medan. Formerly the headquarters of the religious and military leader Imam Bonjol. Old Dutch cannons and Bonjol's prayer house are still found in this village, once the center of intense guerrilla resistance. Bonjol is right on the equator; a line on the road and a small concrete globe to the side of the road mark the spot. Consider taking the tourist bus from Bukittinggi to Bonjol. If you take the public bus and jump off at Bonjol, you'll be stuck there for about 1.5 hours. The tourist bus from Bukittinggi to Prapat runs Rp20,000 with stops at Bonjol and Panti hot springs.

PAYAKUMBUH

Payakumbuh is a market town and government center for the Lima Puluh Kota District as well as a transfer point to the Harau Canyon, only Rp500 by *bemo* from Bukittinggi's Aur Kuning terminal. In the center of a large rice plain, Payakumbuh has a different character from Bukittinggi. The *adat* traditions of the rice plain emphasize chiefly prerogatives with a strict social hierarchy, while the social structure around Bukittinggi is characterized by merchant and artisan family traditions. Payakumbuh is a good base for visiting surrounding villages, there are plenty of places to stay and eat, and it has a large market (best day is Sunday).

Accommodations And Food
Koli Vera, Jl. Pendidikan 54, is the best place to stay (Rp9000 s or d), located outside of town on the road to Air Tabit. **Wisma Flamboyant,** Jl. Ade Irma Suryani 73 on the Pekanbaru side of town, isn't really flamboyant but it's okay value for the money. Rooms are large and clean, in a quiet location. **Wisma Sari,** Jl. Jen. Sudirman KB47 (the main road), is clean but has no inside bathrooms. Scattered around the market are several basic, noisy accommodations, costing around Rp5000. Night stalls and *nasi padang* restaurants line Jl. Sudirman, the main street; **Sari Bunda** is a good one. For *martabak,* fried chicken, and ice juices go to **Minangasli,** Jl. Sudirman. Try the local *kalamai* cakes, like *dodal.*

Crafts
Payakumbuh is a well-known crafts center specializing in pandanus and rattan basketware, cotton mattresses, and birdcages. At **Widjaya,** Jl. A. Yani 83, the embroidery arts are practiced by dozens of young girls. Payakumbuh weaving is characterized by no designs, just plain rattan interwoven intricately in a sort of herringbone pattern. More embroidery and *kain songket* with imitation gold thread can be seen in Payakumbuh's market. Bamboo crafts are another strong point. Visit the handicraft village of **Andaleh,** 11 km from town, where woven-rattan wares such as schoolbags and all manner of basketry are made and sold at **Jolita.** Beyond Andaleh is the beautiful **Taram Valley** and **Taram** village with *rumah adat.*

THE HARAU CANYON

A green fertile valley surrounded by sheer granite canyon walls 100-150 meters high with waterfalls—an astonishing sight. In the Harau Valley is a 315-hectare nature and game reserve, Cagar Alam Harau, with birds, butterflies, monkeys, tigers, steamy rainforests, meadows, wa-

Payakumbuh women in traditional dress

terfalls, a small natural history museum, ranger tours, and an excellent observation point. Pamphlets and map available. The cliffs get steeper as you drive deeper into the park. Only about 20 people a day visit this remote reserve, though on weekends a "study group" as big as 250 could suddenly roll in on three buses. Most Indonesians visit to picnic or to buy exotic orchids at the nursery, which has some very unusual species.

This is an excellent recreation area for mountain climbing and nature hiking. The tigers of the area are protected but the bears are not because of the damage they cause to the fields. Once a week hunters from the surrounding districts gather here to hunt them, assisted by a special breed of hunting dog. These valuable dogs can be seen in Payakumbuh's marketplace, waiting for someone to hire them out to hunt bear. There's no place to stay at the ranger station but you can camp nearby. Bring food. The ranger may be able to arrange for you to stay overnight in one of the nearby hamlets, or in Harau village about three km beyond the ranger station.

Getting There

Harau Canyon is 37 km north of Bukittinggi. The best way to get here from Bukittinggi is to take a Bukittinggi-Pekanbaru bus and ask to be let off just east of Payakumbuh at the turnoff to Lembah Harau. If you take a bus to Payakumbuh, it pulls into the terminal in the western side of town from where you can get a *bemo* (Rp150) to Payakumbuh's market; then take another *bemo* (Rp250) 11 km toward Pekanbaru to the village of Sari Lamak. Get off here at the beginning of the road leading into the park. Unless you hire a *bendi,* minibus, or hitch (fairly easy on weekends), you'll probably have to walk the five km on a narrow paved road to the actual entrance of the park. Admission Rp300.

SOUTH OF BUKITTINGGI

The Singgalang Walk

This loop, one of the highlights of the area, starts at Padanglawas and ends 12 km later at Singgalang. The walk, which skirts along the base of Gunung Singgalang, goes through a countryside of abundance and beauty; you'll see traditional agricultural implements similar to those used in the West over 100 years ago. From Padanglawas, walk across beautiful rice fields to Kototinggi, the next village. Trudge in to Luhung, a high village on the slopes of Gunung Singgalang, then down to Tanjung. Notice that almost every other house has a loom in it. Weavers ask around Rp40,000 for a traditional *sarung tenun pandai sikat.* On the paved road up from **Tanjung** village is a mill where blindfolded *kerbau* on a turnwheel compress sugarcane to pulp—a unique traditional factory. Inside the boiling room observe the cane juice boil down to a syrup which is then made into round cakes; ask to try some, still warm. Walk over the hill from Tanjung to Pagu Pagu, then over to **Pinjuran Tujuh.** Just before this village is an *asli* rice mill by a small waterfall. Keep hiking to Kandang Guguk, Ganting, and then to Singgalang. From Singgalang to Padangpanjang is about four km. About three km after Singgalang is **Lubuk Mata Kucing,** an artesian swimming pool (Rp250 entrance) with cold healthy water. The road finally comes out at Padangpanjang, from where you can board a bus back to Bukittinggi. Allow five to six hours.

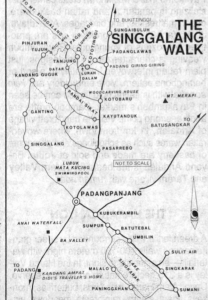

Kotobaru

A dirty, nondescript town at the pass between Gunung Singgalang and Gunung Merapi. Combine a trip here with a visit to the weaving village of Pandaisikat. If you'd like a short walk in this area, take a bus to Pasarrebo, then walk about 15-20 minutes on a beautiful footpath to **Kotolawas.** Check out Kotobaru's market with embroidered scarves and *sarung songket*. On Saturday afternoon (be there by 1600), bullfights are held in one of the nearby villages. Fall in behind other people heading along a picturesque path through the rice paddies. Bulls create pandemonium as they run through the crowded spectators surrounding the unfenced ring—Indonesia's own Pamplona.

Gunung Merapi

Bright green slopes rise up this 2,891-meter-high volcano, the top often obscured by clouds. It erupted last in 1988 and is still considered dangerous enough that climbers are not allowed, though a few guides do take tourists up unofficially at night. Kotobaru is the starting point for the Gunung Merapi climb. In its 1979 eruption, three villages were buried under rivers of rock, lahar, and volcanic debris. Remnants of the upheaval remain and the volcano still spews ash. On its west side is the highest and oldest caldera, Bancah (1,400 meters wide), from where you can see a whole row of smaller craters.

Kandang Ampat

A nice experience is to stay at **Uncle Didi's Traveler's Home** in Kandang Ampat, 1.5 km south of the stunning Anai Valley, 30 km south of Bukittinggi. Pay Rp5000 per person for a place to sleep and two wonderful Indonesian or Western meals a day. The surrounding area has rivers, springs, waterfalls, forests, and *adat* villages. A train passes nearby; if you ask the stationmaster, the train will take you for free to Padangpanjang. Stand in the engine car for beautiful views.

LAKE MANINJAU

Known for its culture, remote location, and beauty, this huge crater lake 38 km west of Bukittinggi is a retreat for famous poets and philosophers. Many visitors consider Maninjau more scenic, cleaner, and friendlier than Lake Toba. The lake is 470 meters above sea level; the 610-meter drop down from the crater's rim is a spectacular drive or walk. The crater holding the lake is one of the largest in the world—a wonder in itself. The lake's deep blue, clear water is always calm. There are facilities for water-skiing, swimming, fishing, and boating (both motorboats and canoes), but no beaches. Lake Maninjau abounds with fish, which are served up in the many restaurants along its shores.

The ride out to Lake Maninjau on the bus or *oplet* is incredibly scenic. From Bukittinggi's Aur Kuning terminal buses run regularly and take only 1.5 hours (Rp700). The last bus back from Maninjau village leaves at around 1600 (but check!) and tends to be very crowded. On market day, buses return to Bukittinngi as late as 1700. If you miss the bus, and don't want to stay over, you'll have to charter a *bemo*.

Embun Pagi ("Morning Cloud") is a small *desa* and lookout (1,097 meters) 30 km from Bukittinggi, just before the descent down to the lake. Children will approach you selling wonderful straw purses and pandanus palm bags in an infinite variety of shapes, sizes, colors, uses, and prices. Stalls sell refreshments. From Embun Pagi, it's a two-hour walk with 44 sharp switchbacks to the bottom of the crater. Cinnamon plantations slope down to the lake, the green reflecting in the shiny blue water, like the picture of a fantasy world in a child's storybook.

A worthwhile trip is the scenic 16-km road following the north shore of the lake from Maninjau to Muko Muko. This good road continues

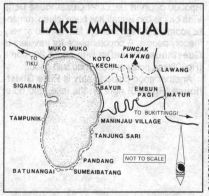

LAKE MANINJAU

NOT TO SCALE

© MOON PUBLICATIONS, INC.

for 139 km all the way to Padang via Tiku and Pariaman. From Maninjau, first take a bus to Lubukbasang (Rp700), then board waiting buses which take you straight to Padang. The trip around the south shore to Muko Muko is more difficult but even more scenic. Small ferryboats leave from the docks beside Hotel Maninjau to various lakeside *kampung*. Or just rent a canoe from someone and go fishing.

The Lawang Top

Take this alternate route to Lake Maninjau and enjoy the beauty of the area. The Lawang Top (Puncak Lawang) is 1,400 meters above sea level and about 1,000 meters above Lake Maninjau. From Bukittinggi, take the bus all the way to Lawang, then walk one hour or take a *bemo* five km past Lawang to the lookout. Friday is best because it's market day. Then walk for two hours (17 km) down a steep, beautiful trail to the lake past houses and cultivated fields. Lots of monkeys. From Bayur walk two km to Maninjau Village, passing some warm springs on the way. Or you can go right from Matur straight on the roadway down to the lake via Embun Pagi.

Maninjau Village

A lakeside village at the bottom of the descent from Embun Pagi. Visit the warm springs, 500 meters down the road from the bus stop and a short walk in. Many places rent bikes for Rp4000 per day. There are 11 guesthouses now, and two hotel/restaurants. **Guesthouse Amai Cheap GH**, Jl. H. Udin Rahmani 54, is in an old Dutch house—the most beautiful in Maninjau. Nice rooms with old fashioned beds are Rp4000 s, Rp5000 d. Often full. Quiet **Guesthouse Della Villa** on the Izin Bupati has huge, clean, romantic rooms with high ceilings for Rp4000 s; very friendly people. A popular place for travelers is **Guesthouse Palantha** with about 20 rooms (Rp6000 s); noisy and the food isn't good.

Another good place to stay is **Pillie Guesthouse** (Rp5000) right on the lake, and quiet

Beach Guesthouse (Rp4000) on the Bayur side of Maninjau village. **Guesthouse Srikandi** has small, hot rooms (Rp4000 s) but the food is the best in Maninjau and reasonably priced; very good breakfast. Another good place to eat is **Goemala Restaurant.** From the porch of one of **Hotel Maninjau**'s 30 rooms, you can literally jump in the lake. The hotel restaurant specializes in fresh lake fish. Rent speedboats for sightseeing or water-skiing. On the north side of town is the quieter **Pasir Panjang Permai Hotel,** Rp30,000-60,000 rooms with hot water and breakfast.

Bayur is two km north of Maninjau, a little *desa* from where you can take a footpath through the jungle up to Puncak Lawang. From here a road leads to Matur and on to Bukittinggi. *Buprestidae* butterflies are as thick as confetti in this area. Bayur is the setting for Frederick K. Errington's brilliantly written and illustrated book on the Minangkabau, *Manners and Meaning in West Sumatra,* the first analysis in English of how the Minang interpret their own customs and etiquette.

Muko Muko

Steep jungle-covered crater walls tower above this village on the west shore of Lake Maninjau, 17 km from Maninjau village, where a river cuts through the crater wall at its weakest and thinnest point, draining the lake. A major hydroelectric project is based here. **Alamada hot springs** are nearby. Speedboats available. Walk to the river an hour before dusk to watch birds and monkeys coming down for a drink.

Stay in the villa on the small island offshore (ask at the PLTA office). Many people from Bukittinggi arrive in Muko Muko on the weekends to dine out. Sample *ikan kecap* in the local *warung*; in *durian* season whole truckloads are exported to other parts of the province. A lakeside *rumah makan,* one km before Muko Muko, is popular for Minang-style fresh lake fish; closes at 1800.

THE MENTAWAIS

The Mentawais consist of four main islands about 100 km off Sumatra's west coast. These islands are actually the tops of a long continuous ridge which became separated from the mainland by a deep submarine trench perhaps 500,000 years ago. This isolation accounts for the islands' separate biologic and geologic evolution. Throughout the Mentawais dwell many endemic animals and plants of Indo-Malay origin.

The islands—Siberut, Sipora, North Pagai, and South Pagai—are generally hilly, especially on the west side, with a few mangrove swamps and gray sandy beaches. Dense tropical vegetation covers 65% of the interiors. Siberut is the largest of the Mentawais, an 86-km-long island with its own subculture quite different from that of the Batu Island to the north and Pulau Sipora and Pulau Enggano to the south. Ringed by untouched coral reefs, Siberut's main town is **Muarasiberut**, inhabited for the most part by Minangkabau, Javanese *pegawai*, Bataks, and Chinese shopkeepers. The principal livelihood of the towns is the export of timber and rattan. The heaviest rainfall is in April and October; February and June are relatively dry. Take your malaria pills two weeks before going.

THE PEOPLE

The Mentawai people (population around 30,000) actually consist of three different ethnic groups: the inhabitants of the Pagai Islands, Pulau Sipora, and Pulau Siberut. All are of Mongoloid blood, with some Veddoid characteristics, and are closely related to the Dayaks of Borneo and the Torajas of South Sulawesi. Long locked in their own time and space, isolated from the rest of the archipelago, this society lacked weaving, rice, pottery, and stonework until the early 1900s. The German ethnologist Maass published in 1902 a landmark travelogue, *Among the Gentle Savages,* a sympathetic portrait of the Mentawai people. Large-scale conversion to Christianity occurred in the 1950s. Today, German Christian missionaries claim the allegiance of perhaps half the inhabitants, while the other half are animists with a thin veneer of Christianity. All schools on the islands are run by missionaries, and there are now about 80 Protestant churches throughout the Mentawais.

These shy, disarming people, formerly a proud, self-assured democratic community practicing hunting and gathering, can be distinguished right away from the coastal townspeople. You can still see a few traces today of their rich traditional culture. Sometimes their black hair is twisted into topknots, and traditional tattoos of blue lines can be seen on faces or peeking out from under the clothes of the older people. The Mentawaians also exhibit a certain alertness and agility missing in the coastal townsfolk.

Traditional Villages

Most Mentawai islanders have traditionally settled inland along riverbanks. In the past, when headhunting raids were an ever-present threat, villages attempted to remain as inconspicuous as possible, separated from the rivers by a wall of seemingly impenetrable tropical forests.

citizens of the Mentawais, circa 1890s

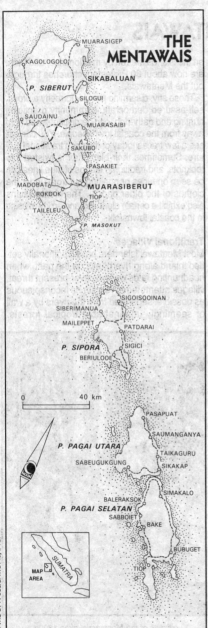

THE
MENTAWAIS

Today, one need travel only a short distance inland before the forest canopy opens on extensive, sunlit gardens. In the center is the village, a vast clearing dominated by thatch-roofed houses. These compact villages may accommodate several hundred people, organized in patrilineal clans made up of five to 10 families each occupying varying sections of the village. Each has its own *uma*, or clan house, a beautifully constructed, massive structure, the focus of Mentawaian social and ceremonial life.

PRACTICALITIES

Tours to the Mentawais have become big business in Bukittinggi. Numerous so-called guides organize 10-day tours for Rp210,000 per person (five or more people); it's also possible to arrange a seven-day tour. Price includes most food, all transportation and accommodations, permit, and guide. You actually only spend seven days on the island; the rest of the time involves traveling to and fro. The boat departs twice weekly overnight from Padang to Muarasiberut, the main town on Pulau Siberut, then it's a fast longboat ride (four to six hours upriver) to Rokdok and Madobat. From there you hike into the interior and stay with families, sleeping on the verandas of huts with the pigs.

Even if you hate organized tours, it's advisable to take a tour to Pulau Siberut unless you have a lot of time and money to spend, or have good contacts on the island. The main problem is language. If you don't speak Bahasa Indonesia or Mentawai you'll be severely handicapped. Finding a longboat might also be a headache. Mr. Moneybags of Muarasiberut owns almost all the boats, plus the only *losmen* and restaurant in town. When he sees tourists, dollar signs light up in his eyes. Hopefully someone will be brave enough to challenge his monopoly, but for now if anything on the island is worth owning, he owns it.

Having said that, you can, of course, do it on your own. The guides will tell you it's dangerous, but then they're hoping to rake in megabucks off you. The guides are an unseemly bunch—when times are tough, they hassle you nonstop, like a pack of hyenas. Guides also snag tourists in the Bukittinggi bus stations. Mostly young and inexperienced, they don't give a damn about the Mentawai, just the dollars in their sticky paws. They steal each other's clients and stab each other and tourists in the back. Don't kid yourself you'll discover a lot about Mentawai culture. The Mentawais may be "primitive" but they're certainly not stupid. They basically view tourists as walking cigarette-vending machines.

Tour Guidelines
1) Put your own group together and choose your guide yourself. Don't let him choose you. Many people go on a tour with people they cannot abide and furious arguments ensue.
2) Six people is the absolute maximum. More is crazy. The Mentawai villages are small and groups of 13 swamp the place. The guides will try and sneak more people in; especially beware of Lala in Bukittinggi. I strongly recommend four people. You'll pay a bit more, but it's worth it.
3) If you can, go and buy supplies with the guide. This ensures you get what you want and not the cheapest junk going. Don't forget you've paid a good price. Bring plenty of smokes. *"Ada rokok?"* is a traditional Mentawai greeting, and they go fast. Buy the cheapest; they won't love you more for Dunhill Internationals.
4) Take as few clothes as possible. You'll get wet and filthy anyway. Plastic bags are handy to wrap dirty clothes and protect what's left of the dry stuff. Good shoes are a must. Indonesian sneakers have no grip and tend to self-destruct. Bring a set of warm dry clothes for the evening; it can get quite cold. Antiseptic ointment is useful and popular with the locals.
5) If you hate mud, pig shit, and leeches, stay away. Siberut has all these commodities in abundance. Leeches just love dark, dank places, so be prepared for a shock.

THE SAKKUDAI

The 5,000 or so native inhabitants of interior Siberut, the Sakkudai, have evolved a unique and fascinating belief system. Their belief in magic is still prevalent and they still practice ritual taboos, sometimes for months on end.

However, their way of life is now being threatened by the intrusion of missionaries, government, and timber concessions. Japanese trawlers, working off Pulau Siberut, have spawned a business in prostitution, which has added even more to the cultural pollution of the island's traditional life.

Religion
The old religion, though forbidden by the government, still persists. The Sakkudai brand of animism is based on the belief that everything, everywhere, is alive and possesses a soul, including states of nature such as floods, rainbows, phases of the moon, and even "nonliving" objects. No object is ever thrown away while it's still functioning for its soul would be greatly offended. Souls and the bodies they inhabit are interdependent, so that what happens to the soul happens equally to the body, and vice versa. Too much soul stress is the primary explanation for illness and death among the Sakkudai, as well as for accidents, long periods of fruitless hunting, and even the withering of plants. It's an insult to ask someone to hurry— *"moile moile"* ("slowly, slowly") is one of their most common calls.

The Taboo System
Taboos (*punen*) exist because the Sakkudai believe that every human enterprise interferes with the environment. When misfortune strikes, the Sakkudai attribute it to something they have done to upset their extraordinary harmony with the supernatural or with each other. They search for the fault within themselves. Harmony is restored by deliberately changing behavior; prohibiting certain foods, for example, or closing the village to all outsiders. Taboos could be in anticipation of violating harmony: building a new house or boat, clearing a field, felling a coconut tree. If the violation is really big, the people's lives could come to a complete standstill. In the same spirit, they beg forgiveness of the animals they slaughter. Fish are killed with poisoned arrows which paralyze them, causing less pain. Under missionary and government pressure, the enforcement of *punen* periods has almost disappeared, so that today they're often observed only on Sunday.

RIAU PROVINCE

A portion of this province, Riau Daratan (Mainland Riau), is located on Sumatra, while the other part consists of thousands of islands, large and small, called Kepulauan Riau or Insular Riau. Both "Riaus" share the same capital: Pekanbaru on mainland Sumatra, gateway to some of the largest oil fields in Asia. Riau Province is an area rich in natural phenomena, historical sites, architecture, and crafts, as well as a popular pilgrimage destination for its old mosques, reconstructed palaces, and tombs containing venerated saints. Twelve generations of sultans have ruled in the area. Today, because of Riau's strategic location on the vital Strait of Malacca, only an ABRI (military) governor is acceptable to Jakarta.

INSULAR RIAU

Insular Riau comprises 94,561 square km of land while its sea territory is 1,176,530 square km—a vast expanse bordered on the north by Singapore, on the west by mainland Sumatra, and on the east by Borneo. Of its 3,214 large and small islands, about 1,000 are occupied, and only 743 named. Politically and economically, two islands take center stage: Pulau Bintan, home to Insular Riau's largest city, Tanjung Pinang; and Pulau Batam, a brash, newly developed, burgeoning industrial estate.

The Riau Islands 300 years ago were the heart of Malay civilization. Little evidence of this remains today, as the small archipeligo is quiet and peaceful, an ideal territory for exploration. You can easily get lost in the South China Sea,

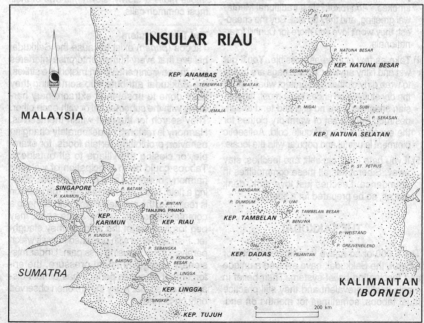

INSULAR RIAU

© MOON PUBLICATIONS, INC.

go diving off the wild coasts of Pulau Mantang or Pulau Abang, or simply search for the ultimate beach—which you'll probably find. If you happen to have a cabin cruiser, this is a safe and tranquil paradise to roam around in. The Riau Islands are also a rich ethnographic area inhabited by many varied cultures. The best primeval forest and wilderness hiking is found on Pulau Lingga.

Climate

The islands have an equatorial climate with a maximum temperature of 31° C and an average minimum temperature of 20° C. The rainy season is October to February; humidity hovers around 80-90%. Rainfall averages 25 cm per month Oct.-Feb., and 15 cm per month March-September. It can be quite cool during December and January, even though most of the islands lie near the equator. If you're planning to visit the eastern islands—such as the Natunas—don't travel during the winter monsoon season of November through March. The South China Sea is notorious for typhoons and hurricanes.

Flora And Fauna

Food crops consist of rice, corn, cassava, chilies, soybeans, peanuts, vegetables, and fruit. Trading crops are rubber (especially on Lingga), cloves, coconuts, coffee, *gambir*, sago, and oil palm. The islands' primary forests yield various timbers, benzoin, palm leaves, resin, rubber, beeswax, and honey. You see remarkable flowers everywhere, including the *nusa indah*, which yields a hallucinogenic drug; and the big red blooms of the *bayam* plant, a species of amaranthus with edible leaves.

The fauna is not very different from mainland Sumatra's: domesticated livestock like cows, buffalo, and goats, and in the jungle wild boar, monkeys, deer, and birds in abundance. The primary fauna reserves are the 200-hectare Pulau Burung, set aside for the protection of turtles and seabirds, and the far northeast island of Pulau Laut. The seas around Riau are generally shallow; *keelong* are built out over the water for catching fish. In these seas are stingrays, hammerhead sharks, marlin, coral fish, and poisonous seasnakes—take care while diving.

History

The earliest known residents of these islands were early Austronesian tribes, thought to have migrated from southern India in the years 2500-1500 B.C. Around A.D. 1000 Bintan and several other island-states rose to prominence. After 1500, Riau's fate was tied to the fortunes of the great seaport of Melaka. The Portuguese seized power in Bintan in 1526, but lost the city by 1539. Their departure marked the beginning of Riau's Golden Age: from about 1530 to nearly the end of the 18th century, the Riau Islands became the nucleus of a high Malay civilization. Its main centers of power were Pulau Penyenget and Pulau Lingga; the capital was moved several times to avoid pirate attacks.

In 1685, Sultan Mahmud Syah II was forced to sign a cooperative agreement with the increasingly powerful Dutch. Over the next century the *raja*'s authority was greatly eroded. From 1784 on, the Dutch exercised absolute control, though the *rajas* had residual authority in the sphere of *adat* law.

Opposition to the Dutch went underground, surfacing in the early 1900s with the establishment of the Rusydiah Club by Sultan Abdurrachman Muazan Syah, the last sultan of Riau-Lingga. While active in the cultural and economic spheres, the Rusydiah Club secretly organized as a paramilitary group. It later joined forces with the famous nationalist organization Sarikat Islam, and its members assisted in the struggle for Indonesian independence.

Economy

Considerable mineral wealth is found on some islands: oil on Batam, granite on Karimun, tin on Bangka, Singkep, and Kundur. Indonesia is today the world's fourth-largest producer of tin, which is second only to petroleum as the country's greatest foreign currency-earning mineral. Thanks to all this mineral wealth, Insular Riau is one of the richest regions of Indonesia. Shipyards, oil depots, and oil-related industries are being built in the Karimun and Natuna islands, and in Tanjung Pinang buildings are sprouting up everywhere. Roads in most towns are neatly lined with parks and gardens, and even the poorest houses have TV antennas. Of course it doesn't hurt to lie so close to commodity-rich Singapore; Riau has always had close economic ties with that island republic and even used Singapore currency until Sukarno's militant 1964-65 *konfrontasi* campaign. There are plans to turn Pulau Bintan's pristine northern coastline into a sort of Indonesian Waikiki, a playground for wealthy Singaporean Chinese.

The People

The main population group of the Riau Islands is of pure Malay stock. Several indigenous population groupings include the Orang Laut (sea gypsies) from the Natuna Islands and the *akit* tribes of the Bengkalis District. Comprised of Malays, ethnic Chinese, Bataks, Minangkabaus, and others, Pulau Bintan is the most populous island. It's said the modern-day Indonesian language originated in the Riau and Lingga archipelagos. On Penyenget, Singkep, and Lingga, a pure, almost classical Bahasa Melayu is still spoken.

The population of these islands is 90% Islam. The remainder are Christian and Buddhist. Riau people are strongly religious. You see new mosques everywhere, Buddhist shrines with incense burning on interisland boats, and no fewer than five Christian denominations in Dabo town (Pulau Singkep).

Arts And Crafts

The islands have a rich cultural inheritance, derived both from the Malay Peninsula and mainland Sumatra. Among the distinctive art forms are stylized woodcarvings and fine "basketweave" cloth woven in the eastern Riaus, Pulau Rengat, and Pulau Pelalawan. The region's most popular dances are the *joget* (a convivial Malay dance), *zapin*, and *dabus*. The latter two have particular religious significance. The *nerdu* and other dance forms are being revived on Pulau Natuna. The traditional theater of Pulau Mantang is known throughout Indonesia. The two main forms are known as *makyong* and *mendu*. On Singkep, traditional Malay theater is still very much alive.

Practicalities

Oriki Money Changer, Jl. Merdeka, Tanjung Pinang, gives a good rate for U.S. dollars. For Australian dollars and other currencies, you'll receive good rates at **Bank Dagang Negara**. Reports of theft can be exaggerated: paranoia breeds paranoia. However, exercise reasonable care and heed Awas Copet (Beware of Pickpockets) signs. No visa is required for a stay up to two months for most nationals; if traveling from Singapore, get your passport stamped in

Pulau Batam. Mosquitos are bad in these islands; antimalarial tablets are advisable.

Island-hop throughout Insular Riau by time-consuming boat. It's quite easy to arrange boat-hire, but use your head. For example, chartered boats demand Rp15,000-20,000 from Tanjung Pinang to Pulau Penyenget. Much cheaper, more expedient, and picturesque is to simply go down to the wharf and hire a public *prahu* for only Rp1000—a delightful passage. On land, the Anglo measurement system is sometimes used to denote road markers, such as Batu V, meaning Five-Mile Marker.

TANJUNG PINANG

Tanjung Pinang is a scurrying, fast-growing, visa-free Malay-Chinese trading center and the principal town of Insular Riau, located on Pulau Bintan 80 km south and just two hours by speedboat from Singapore. This dirty town with a dirty harbor and many obnoxious men is a good place to watch people come and go from all over western Indonesia. Although the wharves in the old harbor area of Pelantan II, with wooden houses lining wooden plank streets and alleys, give the town a unique, timeless feel, most travelers spend only as much time here as it takes to meet a boat or plane.

Tanjung Pinang serves as an important commercial shopping center for such cities as Medan, Jambi, Jakarta, Palembang, and even Padang, so lots of goods are available. Due to the fact that UN employees and oil workers use it as a stopping off point on their way to work, prices have soared and everyone is trying to rip you off. Your first few days here can easily cost you as much as your next few weeks in Indonesia. The main shopping street is Jl. Merdeka, leading to the markets.

Tanjung Pinang lies on the southcentral coast of Bintan, the largest island in the Riau Archipelago (1,075 square km). It's generally flat except for several "mountains": Gunung Bintan Besar (334 meters) and Gunung Kijang. Besides its bauxite mines, Bintan's most notable assets are its nearly deserted, lovely, white-sand beaches. Unfortunately, the water in the area is no longer good for diving, due to Singapore's nearby oil refinery and increased area oil exploration. Better diving possibilities are the hulls of ships sunk during WW II off Tanjung Brakit, Pulau Mapor (east of Pulau Bintan), Pulau Mantang, Pulau Pompong, and Pulau Abang.

History

Situated on important commercial sea lanes, Bintan has always been the trading and working center for the far-flung Riau Islands. The sultan of Tanjung Pinang, Hussein, once held power over Johore, the southern islands of Kepulauan Lingga, and even as far as Tembilahan on Sumatra. He learned the use of gunpowder, and reigned by virtue of a powerful sea fleet. It was from Hussein that Raffles obtained his license to establish a trading post on Singapore Island. The sultan of Tanjung Pinang actually chose to set up his kingdom on Penyenget, a small island opposite Tanjung Pinang. A royal residence was built there in 1803.

Sights

Check out **Embong Fatima,** a smart souvenir shop by the pier. Don't miss Chinatown and its old Chinese temple; there's another Chinese temple in Senggarang across the harbor, accessible by *prahu,* as well as a 150-year-old Chinese *klenteng* complex up the Snake River (Sungai Ular) through mangrove swamps. Climb the hill behind Tanjung Pinang for a fantastic view. Walk down to the fascinating harbor at sunset—it's filled with every imaginable type of wooden craft, from tiny sampan to sleek catamaran. Out of town a bit, have a look at the **Houses of Parliament** at Batu V, a complex of buildings in the traditional Riau architectural style.

Riau Kandil Museum is on Jl. Katamso two km out of town. If you can squeeze through the door, see most of the surviving *pusaka* of the old Riau kingdoms: old *kris,* guns, ceramic plates, manuscripts, charts, and antique brassware. Raja Razak, an enthused and dedicated curator, has moved his family into most of the museum so the artifacts are all crammed in one room. Dusty and without explanations, but worth a visit all the same.

Accommodations

Tanjung Pinang is a busy transit town with people passing through from all over, most seeking cheap rooms. For budget accommodations, stay with families in a number of homestays. Be careful of which house you choose: thefts of foreign-

ers' gear are reported consistently. Ask Indonesians in the street and touts on the quay; they know who takes in tourists. Dorms in private homes run Rp2500-3000, while rooms go for Rp4000-5000 per person. Currently popular with travelers is **Lobo Guest House,** Jl. Diponegoro 8; Rp3000 s including coffee, tea, and light snack for breakfast. To get there, walk down Jl. Samudra from the harbor, up the hill to the right where the road bends, then straight ahead on a dirt path to the guesthouse (no signs). Travelers also recommend **Bong's Homestay,** in operation since 1973, at Lorong Bintan II/20, only a five minute walk from the harbor. Friendly, clean, and cheap; Rp4500 per night including an excellent breakfast. Ask to see Mr. Bong's statistics book.

There are about five hotels with prices from about Rp12,000. **Hotel Sampurna** (Rp8250 s) also has a good *nasi padang* restaurant. **Hotel Tanjung Pinang,** Jl. Pasar Ikan, has a view over the night market and dirty main street. It rents good economy-class rooms for Rp6500 and Rp18,000 with *mandi.* Get your bearings on a large relief map of Riau upstairs. **Wisma Riau** charges Rp63,000 for non-a/c rooms with bath. A hotel on stilts, **Riau Holidays,** tel. 21812, near a long pier with a long wooden veranda over the water, asks Rp52,000-75,000 for carpeted rooms with TV and *mandi.*

Food

There are two vibrant night markets, on Jl. Ketapang and Jl. Teuku Umar. Connoisseurs say Tanjung Pinang has some of the best coffee on earth; try it for only Rp250 at the **Kedai Kopi** at the corner of Jl. Teuku Umar and Jl. Merdeka. Pushcart vendors sell wonderful peanut-filled pancakes (Rp200) in the morning and early afternoon on the street by the *pasar pagi.* But the best eats by far is the **Jalan Ketapang** complex of open-air foodstalls. The whole town converges here at night, a great people-watching place. The seafood stands offer the best value: *kong kong* (conical seashells with oyster-like meat, worth the struggle), prawns, squid, and *kepitang goreng* (crab claws) fried in light crispy batter for only Rp3500.

Services

The **post office** is near the harbor on the town's main drag, Jl. Merdeka. To change money, go to the **moneychanger** on Jl. Merdeka or to **Bank Dagang Negara** on Jl. Teuku Umar. The nearest tourist office is in Pekanbaru on the mainland: Baparda, Kantor Gubernor Riau, TK I, Pekanbaru, Riau.

Getting There And Around

From Singapore, boats depart for Tanjung Pinang from Finger Pier. Jaya Baru Shipping and Trading Co. has boats that leave every day and go straight to Tanjung Pinang for S$65 one-way—a pleasant trip with lunch on board. There's also a slower boat (four hours) for S$40 without food or padded seats. Auto Shipping Pte. Ltd. has boats three times daily to Tanjung Pinang via Batam. If you take the 1230 boat from Singapore, you'll reach Tanjung Pinang around 1830. Don't be alarmed by all the men who jump aboard ship just before you dock in Tanjung Pinang—they're smugglers picking up their haul before the boat arrives at customs.

In Tanjung Pinang, take very cheap and ubiquitous *ojek*; look for motorcyclists wearing white hats. Women shouldn't straddle motorbikes here. The fare should be Rp300 to anywhere in the inner city, Rp500 to anywhere in the suburbs. Taxis, found at the town-clock end of Jl. Merdeka, are only too eager to take you to the seafood restaurants and discos. A taxi to the airport costs Rp8000 (17 km), or take an *ojek* (Rp2500).

Getting Away

The Merpati and Garuda offices are in the same building on Jl. Bintan; Sempati is at Jl. Bintan 9, tel. 21042; SMAC at Jl. Jusuf Kahar 19. Merpati offers service to Jakarta and Pekanbaru; Sempati also flies to Jakarta at least once daily, Pekanbaru twice daily, Palembang three times weekly. Current air fares are Rp169,000-171,000 to Jakarta and Rp103,000 to Palembang.

Pelni boats generally leave from Tanjung Pinang for Jakarta every other Tuesday, although sometimes a boat sails just one Tuesday a month. The cost is Rp30,500 economy. Likewise, the same ship travels to Medan in Sumatra from Tanjung Pinang every other Friday, sometimes stopping in Dumai. This ship is the most inexpensive way of getting to Jakarta from Singapore. You can obtain a schedule from the Indonesia Tourist Promotion Office, 10 Collyer Quay #15-07, Ocean Building, Singapore, tel. 534-2837. Your total transportation cost from Singapore to Jakarta will be S$15 plus Rp37,050. The Pelni office in Singapore is 50 Telok Blangah Road #02-02, Citiport Centre, Singapore 0409, tel. 272-6811.

From Tanjung Pinang to Medan, the Pelni boat *Lawit* leaves every second Friday at 0700 (economy Rp29,000). It's a German boat, quite comfortable, all a/c, but the food isn't that great. The Pelni office is now five km out of town on Jl. A. Yani; open Mon.-Fri. 0800-1400, Saturday 0800-1130. On departure day the office is closed. If necessary, ask in the harbor for a ticket but be prepared to pay double. Everyone in Tanjung Pinang seems to work for a travel agency and is keen on selling you tickets. From Tanjung Pinang's Jl. Merdeka, a share taxi to the harbor in Kijang is Rp2500, or you can take the local bus for Rp1000 (45 minutes).

Leaving Tanjung Pinang almost daily at around noon is a boat up the Siak River to Pekanbaru, East Sumatra; Rp7500 deck, Rp12,500 for berths. Berths 1-17 are the best—the higher numbers are near the engine; they look great until the engine starts, then they become ovens. The trip takes at least 27 hours plus a five-hour stopover at Selat Panjang, an interesting town in the middle of nowhere occupied by many Batak and Chinese. Take a stroll around town and a *mandi* in a room at the dock (Rp200). Some food is served on the boat but bring extra, as well as drinks. The river travel is all done at night so there's no chance to see Istana Siak except on the return trip. Arrival in Pekanbaru is around 0700, then it's three more hours by bus to Bukittinggi.

From Tanjung Pinang there are ferries three times weekly to Dabo on Pulau Singkep; Rp12,500, 10-12 hours. Stopping off at Pulau Galang en route, the ferry pulls in at Sunggai Buluh from where you can board a bus to Dabo (Rp3000), Pulau Singkep's main town on the other side of the island.

For Kijang on Pulau Bintan, take a bus for Rp1000 or shared taxi for Rp2500. The cheapest way to get from Kijang Harbor to Singapore is to take a bus to Tanjung Uban (two hours, Rp3500), then a boat to Kabil on Pulau Batam (30 minutes, Rp2000). From Kabil you can only use a shared taxi to the harbor of Sekupang on the other side of Pulau Batam (Rp10,000, five people). From Sekupang it's a 20-minute, 20-km hop to Singapore by speedboat (every one or two hours, Rp20,000). Return fare is Rp35,000.

Alternatively, from Kijang Harbor take a bus (Rp1000) or share taxi (Rp2500) to Tanjung

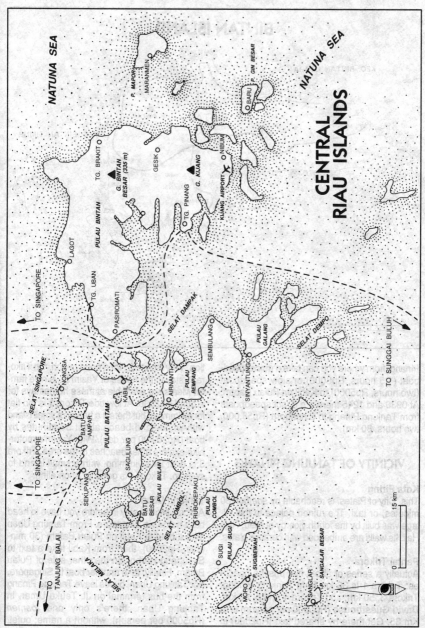

NATUNA SEA

NATUNA SEA

CENTRAL RIAU ISLANDS

P. MAPOR

MARANMEN

BARU P. GIN BESAR

TG. BRAKIT

G. BINTAN BESAR (335 m)

GESIK

NIBUM

PULAU BINTAN

TG. PINANG

G. KIJANG

KIJANG AIRPORT

LAGOT

TG. UBAN

PASIROMATI

SELAT DAMPAK

TO SINGAPORE

TO SUNGGAI BULUH

SELAT SINGAPORE

SEMBULANG

PULAU GALANG

SELAT DEMPO

NONGSA

AIRNANTI

PULAU REMPANG

SINYANTUNGO

KABIL

PULAU BATAM

BATU AMPAR

SAGULUNG

PULAU BULAN

RUBOKEPAKU

PULAU COMBOL

TO SINGAPORE

SEKUPANG

BATU BESAR

SELAT COMBOL

SUGI

PULAU SUGI

SUGIBEWAH

TO TANJUNG BALAI

SELAT MELAKA

MORO

P. SANGALAR BESAR

SANGLAR

15 km

© MOON PUBLICATIONS, INC.

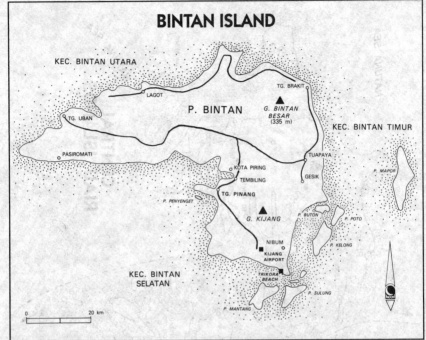

BINTAN ISLAND

Pinang, from where you can take a quick speed-boat (1.5 hours, Rp8000) or slow speedboat (two hours, Rp5000) to Kabil on Pulau Batam. At 0930 and 1245 there are direct speedboats from Tanjung Pinang to Singapore (Rp58,000, two hours, 80 km).

VICINITY OF TANJUNG PINANG

Kota Piring
This "City of Plates" is reachable by *spetbot* (30 minutes) or taxi. The ruined palace in this village was built by the fourth viceroy of Riau, Raja Haji. Its walls are embedded with ceramic plates.

Pantai Trikora
Actually a series of about five pristine beaches: Trikora 1 is 36 km from Tanjung Pinang; Trikora 3, 50 km; and Trikora 4 and 5, 60 km. **David Guesthouse** (Rp5000 per person) is at Km 35. Get there by shared taxi (Rp2500) in the mornings from the Tanjung Pinang bus sta-

tion. Very isolated. Not a good beach. On Trikora 1, stay in the house of Yasim B., a nice family. Meals are available at these homestays for around Rp2000. At low tide Trikora 1 is too flat for swimming, but there's a beautiful small island with white-sand beach about 30 minutes by boat (Rp20,000 per day). With Yasim's motorbike explore other beaches in the area. Trikora 3 is best for swimming, with a small island to swim to. Trikora 4 is good for snorkeling.

Tanjung Uban
A nice village to stay in before you have to head back home via Singapore. From Tanjung Uban take a boat to Kabil on Pulau Batam (30 minutes, Rp2000), then from Kabil take a taxi to Sekupang Harbor on the other side of Pulau Batam. Finally, take another boat to Singapore. For Tanjung Uban, buses leave Tanjung Pinang from the bus terminal on Jl. Teuku Umar. In Tanjung Uban, there's only one *losmen* (Rp5000 per person), without a name; quiet, friendly, lots of mosquitos.

Pulau Penyenget

A tiny island (2.5 square km) off Tanjung Pinang, today inhabited by 2,000 Malay fishermen, once the capital of the *rajas* of Insular Riau who were descended from the Bugis. Chartered boats want Rp15,000-20,000 per person to Pulau Penyenget, but just take a public sampan across for Rp1000 (15 minutes). Go early, when it's cool. This island, which you can walk completely around in several hours, boasts a history and hosts a level of tourism way out of proportion to its size. Everywhere you go along wide, quiet paths under groves of trees are extensive ruins, royal bathing places, ornate watchtowers, Dutch forts, recently renovated burial pavilions, old graveyards. Numerous Muslim pilgrims arrive to pay homage to notables interred in royal graves.

Once on Pulau Penyenget, turn right and walk along the walkway (no motorized vehicles on the island). The principal points of interest are in the island's northwest. Don't miss the magnificent, acoustically perfect, yellow mosque built in 1818 by Yang Dipertuan VII. With its pillars, minarets, and domes, this unusual structure is like something out of Disneyland. Inside is a famous library with hundreds of books on history, religion, culture, law, and languages, as well as five ancient hand-scripted copies of the Koran. Nearby is the graveyard of Raja Jaafar and Raja Ali, and the ruins of the former palace of Raja Ali. All significant sites are marked with small plaques and inscriptions. A new cultural center stages performances of Malay music and dance.

BATAM ISLAND

A 466-square-km island of 100,000 people directly west of Pulau Bintan. Only 20 km south of Singapore, its north shore borders the Singapore Strait. Thirty years ago an almost uninhabited island except for a few fishing villages, its fortunes took a sharp turn in 1969 when it

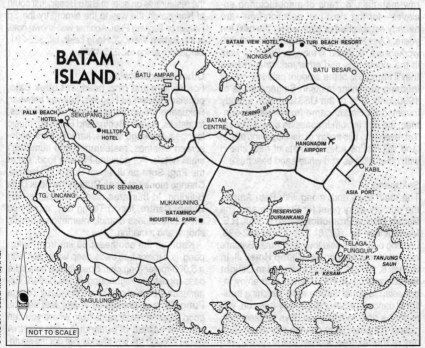

became a support base for the Pertamina oil company and its offshore oil explorations. In 1971 a presidential decree designated Batam as an industrial area, and in the past decade it's also become a major tourist resort, with swank hotels along the northeast coast offering international-standard accommodations and extensive marine sporting activities.

Because of its proximity to Singapore, Batam is an expensive island to visit relative to the rest of Indonesia. The island plays willing host to hundreds of Singaporeans who hop over for a day or weekend visit. Many wealthy Indonesians and Singaporeans own or lease houses on Batam. A big attraction is the fresh seafood restaurants; late night ferries operating out of Batu Ampar even allow diners to eat at a Batam restaurant and return to Singapore that same evening. Cigarettes, alcohol, perfumes, chocolates, and designer bags are the major goodies in the island's numerous duty-free shops.

Attracted by the low labor cost and abundant raw materials, dozens of manufacturing enclaves—for the most part pollution-free—are already established or planned for the next ten years. Over this period, an estimated 750,000 workers are expected to move to Batam to work in the electronics and other industries, where they'll earn 25% of the amount paid to workers laboring at similar tasks in Singapore. As of 1990, only 27% of the US$1.6 billion already invested on Batam came from foreign countries; the rest is from Indonesian businessmen. Yet, even with this frenzy of development, the island still retains a few pockets of rural charm with quiet villages and white-sand beaches.

Sekupang

The main town and, along with Batu Ampar, the primary entry point for Pulau Batam. The **Batam Tourist Promotion Board** is on Jl. R.E. Martadinata, tel. (0778) 322-053 or 322-599. Looking over the whole town and Pulau Batam's hilly interior is the popular **Hilltop Hotel,** Jl. Ir. Sutami 8, tel. 322-482. At **Indonesian Delight Restaurant** on Jl. R.E. Martadinata enjoy Indonesian regional cuisine while watching traditional dances. In Sekupang's duty-free port, you might be able to find good buys on electronic goods. It's possible to change money on Sunday at the tax-free counter in the harbor, but the rates are bad. The moneychanger at the

port does not take traveler's checks and the bank outside the port offers an unfavorable rate. It's best to change just a small amount here.

Nongsa

A coastal area on the north end of the island, one hour's drive (40 km) from Sekupang, with three first-class hotel resorts plus a golf course and country club facing a gorgeous blue ocean. At night you can see the Singapore skyline. In a quiet cove is **Turi Beach Resort,** Teluk Mata Ikan, tel. 321-543 or 322-375, Singapore office tel. 732-2577, with 120 thatch-roof cottages on stilts up the side of a cliff—wonderful views. These bungalows, with balconies and all mod cons, surround a magnificent 43-meter pool. Ideal for sports enthusiasts—surfboards, snorkeling gear, canoes for upriver trips, plus tennis courts (with instructors) and volleyball.

A nice, small beach hotel is the **Nongsa Beach Cottages** on Pantai Bahagia, tel. 321-018, Singapore tel. 221-8433 or 532-2366. Eat in one of the restaurants on stilts at **Batu Besar,** just south of Nongsa on the way to the airport; try the Sri Rezeki or Tanjung Putri. Another well-known hotel is the **Batam View,** Jl. Hang Lekir, tel. 322-281, Singapore office tel. 235-4366.

Other Island Locales

For nightlife and glitz, head for **Lubuk Baja,** popularly known as Nagoya, halfway between Sekupang (15 km) and Nongsa. It has shops, foodstalls, discos (Regina and Rio Rita), music lounges, massage salons, karaoke bars, widescreen cinemas, restaurants, and numerous small hotels. For genuine Padang food, eat at the **Pagi Sore** on Jl. Imam Bonjol in Nagoya. Change money at **Bank Duta** in the Bank Duta Building. In this area also is the huge new **Batam Centre,** facing Tering Bay, a planned city with business district, international hotels, shops, and a marina.

Kabil, in the southeast 30 km from Sekupang, is a major free trade deep water port with a 5,000-meter-long pier. Speedboats here take passengers to neighboring Pulau Bintan. Experience a slice of old Batam in nearby **Telaga Punggur,** a quaint fishing village with several good seafood restaurants from where you can watch a parade of outlandish watercraft. A cruise through the tiny islands that dot the southern side of Pulau Batam is pure bliss. From

Telaga Punggar catch small boats to Pulau Ngenang where, on the eastern side, there are fine deserted beaches.

Getting There And Getting Around
Air-conditioned launches from Singapore (PT Bintan Baruna Sakti, tel. 322-639) leave every day at 0815, 0900, 1000, 1230, 1400, 1500, 1630, and 2030 for Sekupang (S$20 one-way, S$30 roundtrip) and 0900 and 1500 for Tanjung Pinang via Sekupang. The trip takes only 30 minutes. You can save four Singapore dollars on the one-way trip by bypassing all the ticket counters at Finger Pier and going up one more flight and buying the ticket where you hand in passports.

The island has excellent roads. Around Sekupang, taxi drivers tend to charge Rp5000 to take you anywhere in town (or Rp10,000 per hour). The taxi drivers at the pier are total assholes and won't take a Westerner anywhere for less than S$10. A speedboat from Sekupang direct to Tanjung Pinang costs Rp25,000, but you can get there cheaper if you cross the island to Kabil and take a boat from there. The locals pay Rp2500 for a shared taxi from Sekupang's port to Kabil but you might have to pay Rp12,000, or take a taxi to Nagoya (Rp5000) then a bus to Kabil. Or you can take a bus to Nagoya (Rp300), then a shared taxi to Kabil (around Rp2000). The boat from Kabil to Tanjung Uban (west coast of Pulau Bintan) is Rp2000 and the minibus from there to Tanjung Pinang is Rp2250. There's also a boat from Kabil direct to Tanjung Pinang (Rp10,000, 40 minutes).

Getting Away
Pulau Batam is an international gateway into Indonesia both by air and sea. The large **Hang Nadim Airport,** 30 km from Sekupang, provides connections to Jakarta, Pekanbaru, Bandung, Medan, and Padang. Pulau Batam is also served by Sempati, Merpati, SMAC, Deraya, and Airfast. It no longer pays to come to Batam (or Tanjung Pinang) to fly to Jakarta because it's about the same price to fly from Singapore—roughly Rp210,000. The one exception is if you're able to get a 25% student discount from Garuda, available to those under 26. From Sekupang's port, take a taxi to Batam's airport for about Rp10,000.

RIAU DARATAN

Riau Daratan is the mainland portion of Riau Province. An equatorial area (9.5 million hectares) of huge forests with high rainfall, east central Sumatra is a region of swampy lowlands crossed by large meandering rivers. These rivers—extremely important to the communications, transportation, and economy of Riau—are the Siak, Indragiri, Kampar, and Rokan; all drain into the Strait of Malacca. The shallow, coastal estuarine mudflats created by the rivers cover an astonishing 155,000 square km, more than one-third of the island's entire land area. So shallow that even small fishing vessels must keep hundreds of meters offshore, these endless marshlands stink of hydrogen sulphide, the putrid rotten-egg smell of decay.

Flora And Fauna
Most of eastern Sumatra's swamps are densely overgrown with plantlife, especially mangrove, while the open tidal flats literally bubble and seethe with crawling things. Inland, the soil is not really suitable to agriculture and even rice is difficult to grow. Most vegetables and fruit must be imported. Although much of Riau Daratan's land area is Caltex oil country, this region is still one of the least contaminated Indonesian wildernesses.

Even as late as the 1960s, if you took the bus from Pekanbaru to Dumai you could see tigers running across the road. Though this happens very rarely now, the jungle still isn't that far away. Tigers occasionally ravage villages in the deep interior, carrying off cattle, dogs, and people. Small hairy rhinos are found in the Buatan area, a swamp near Pelalawan, and in the Kampar River region. These sullen-faced behemoths love to take mud baths; *durian* is their favorite dessert. To make up for its poor eyesight, the rhino's sense of smell and hearing are keen, so keep alert. Herds of 40 or more elephants move around eastern Sumatra's timber areas.

Hear the black *beo* bird's crazy laughter, croaking 30-cm-high frogs, honking hornbills. In Riau

© MOON PUBLICATIONS, INC.

Daratan are deer, wild boar, monkeys, tapir, bears, explosively colored butterflies, brilliant tropical birds. All kinds of snakes are commonly seen: king and spitting cobras are among the lethal varieties. Unless you're an Orang Sakai (aboriginal Sumatran), don't just go walking off into the jungle.

History
In the lowlands of eastern Sumatra, Indian acculturation can be traced back to at least the 5th century; the Buddhist ruins at Muara Takus near Bangkinang testify to a developed Buddhist culture in the 9th and 10th centuries. But the area's history goes back even further. Today you can still see three-meter-high piles of shells left by Middle Stone Age people. These hunter-gatherers, who migrated with their dogs from Indochina around 2000-600 B.C., sometimes used these shell piles to bury their dead.

Since the shortest sailing route between India and China is through the Strait of Malacca, farsighted rulers have always tried to establish their authority on land to both sides of the strait. Consequently, the east coast of Sumatra has undergone a turbulent history and many kingdoms and powers—Indians, Arabs, Portuguese, Dutch, and British—have come and gone. The strait took on even more economic and strategic importance in 1869 with the opening of the Suez Canal, and since 1950 it has been the main lifeline for tankers transporting crude oil from the Middle East to Japan.

Economy

While tin and timber comprise the riches of Insular Riau, the economy of Riau Daratan is concentrated mainly in oil. Caltex Pacific Indonesia's (CPI) administrative base is at Duri. Indonesia produces about 1.5 million barrels of oil per day in its approximately 50 fields, half of which belong to Caltex. After oil, logging is the largest industry. Loggers usually wait until the oil companies build roads, then go in. Caltex has built and maintains all the roads in the region. Dumai is the export harbor and freight terminal for timber and petroleum. Fishing is another mainstay of the economy—nearly one-quarter of Indonesia's motorized vessels work out of Pekanbaru and Bagansiapiapi. During the '70s and '80s 315,000 transmigrants were brought into Riau Daratan. These were mostly wet-rice farmers working agricultural fields more appropriate for rubber and oil palm, and thus the settlements were for the most part economic disasters.

The People

Islam is Riau's predominant religion (70% of the 2,688,944 people). This province is a very rich ethnographic area. From Pekanbaru all the way down the east coast to Palembang are descendants of the original Malay inhabitants, referred to as Orang Melayu. As authentic a race as the Batak, Minangkabau, and other Sumatran peoples, the Melayu on both sides of the strait between Sumatra and West Malaysia share the same ethnicity, though it's not known for sure who arrived first. Mainland Riau Province is also under much cultural influence from the Minangkabau of West Sumatra. Inhabiting remote regions of the province are numerous proto-Malay and even pre-Malay tribes.

One of the most visible of these preindustrial groups is a nomadic aboriginal people, the Orang Sakai, who trade forest products—rattan, camphor, and wild rubber—for salt and tobacco at nearby villages. These animists also earn money posing for tourists on the Rumbai-Duri road. The government and oil companies have tried to settle the Sakai in communities with schools and clinics near the oilfields to assure a steady supply of labor, but very few have taken root. In some East Sumatran coastal districts beach nomads, Orang Laut, use two-meter-long, half-meter-wide mudboards, curved in front like a surfboard. They cross over swamps by pushing swiftly with hands and feet for hours on end.

Getting There And Around

In western Sumatra rivers are only navigable for short distances, but the large rivers of the east—their waters darkened to a deep brown by tannic acid oozing from millions of swamp trees—are an important means of transport. The muddy Siak is the main river in the province, a busy throughfare of oceangoing ships, barges, fishing boats, and hand- and motor-powered sampans.

Riau Daratan doesn't offer that many all-weather roads; roadbuilding was cut back here once helicoptors began transporting equipment. Now the road system on mainland Riau connects only Dumai, Pekanbaru, Bukittinggi, and Padang; another good road leads from Pekanbaru to Rengat, eventually joining the Trans-Sumatra Highway. To travel by air north or south from eastern Sumatra, fly from Pekanbaru's Simpang Tiga Airport. There's also an airstrip on Pulau Batam, and commercial flights connect Jakarta with Tanjung Pinang, Pulau Batam, Dumai, and Pekanbaru.

PEKANBARU

Capital of Riau Province and the main city of oil-rich Riau Daratan, Pekanbaru is a modern, well laid-out town on the Siak River. It's the gateway to Southeast Asia's largest and richest oil fields, an important and rapidly developing area of Sumatra. A crazy montage of races—about 50% Minangkabau, another chunk Melayu, with a sprinkling of Batak and Javanese—have converged on this busy, hot, lowland city. Pekanbaru is not what you'd imagine of an oil city—

PEKANBARU

© MOON PUBLICATIONS, INC.

it's unexpectedly friendly. The oil companies have made significant contributions to the city's health, communications, agriculture, recreation, education, and transportation projects.

From a tourist's point of view, however, it's singularly unappealing. Oil wealth has driven up prices and Pekanbaru can be expensive. Most travelers who visit this river port do so for one reason: to take the ferry down the river to Tanjung Pinang and on to Singapore. Pekanbaru is also a useful transit point between Insular Riau and the Bukittinggi area of West Sumatra.

Jalan Jen. Sudirman, the main street, runs north to south. The Siak River forms the northern boundary; shops, hotels, banks, and the port lie in the north half of the city, while impressive government offices, military headquarters, and the main bus station lie in the southern part of town. Flat and surrounded by swamps and rainforest, Pekanbaru suffers from an oppressively hot and humid climate.

History

Pekanbaru, which means "New Market," was founded in 1784 at a point as far upstream on the Siak River as big ships could conveniently navigate. In the early years of this century, Hang Tuah was a legendary guerrilla in the war of independence who raided Dutch outposts on the Siak and in the Strait of Malacca. This saboteur fought from a swift little sailboat, which always eluded the Dutch; streets and many shops are now named in his honor.

Prior to the development of the oil industry in the 1930s, Pekanbaru served as the main port for exporting rubber, cloves, indigo, gold, and tin from inland central Sumatra and for importing cloth, machinery, foodstuffs, and other articles. In 1944-45, the Japanese forced Allied POWs and Javanese *romusha* to build a rail link between Pekanbaru and Muara in an attempt to bring coal from West Sumatra to the east coast. Fifteen thousand men died in the process; the first train ran just days before the end of WW II.

Sights

See the **Grand Mosque** on Jl. Sheikh Burhanudin, with its bright onion dome. This mosque and Pekanbaru's church face each other. The old mosque in town features Rajah Siak's grave.

A new *musium* is on the highway to Payakumbuh five km down Jl. Sudirman; open daily until 1400. Stroll around the fish and fruit markets (open daily) where the *durian* are cheap and the men obnoxious. Visit the sleazy harbor area. In front of the DPRD building is a monument to revolutionary heroes. Find furniture makers and other **cottage industries** along Jl. H.O.S. Cokroaminoto heading toward Terminal Kodim. For *rumah adat,* go to Jl. Diponegoro in front of the Riau Hotel, or to Jl. Setiabudi near PT Agung Concern. **Bookstores** and **gold shops** stretch all along Jl. Jen. Sudirman.

Accommodations

Rates tend to be higher than in Java. Get a fan or a/c if you can afford it. Always ask whether all taxes are included in the price. *Losmen* crowd the vicinity of the bus terminal on Jl. Nangka. **Tommy's** is a cheap bed for the night; Tommy also sells tickets for the boat. Another good place is the **Wydia Hotel,** Jl. Kampar 349, tel. (0761) 21180; Rp6500 s. Near the harbor on Jl. M. Yamim are several divey hotels such as the **Nirmala,** Jl. Pasar Bawah, tel. 21314, a handy place to stay if you're taking a boat out. Cheap (Rp8500).

Quite ordinary **Hotel Dharma Utama,** Jl. Sisingamangaraja 10, tel. 21171, is centrally located just off Jl. Sudirman. **Hotel Anom** is a block north of Hotel Dharma Utama on Jl. Gatot Subroto 3, tel. 22636; Rp20,000-50,000 a/c for small but clean rooms around a nice garden courtyard. One of Pekanbaru's best Chinese restaurants, Restoran Anom, is just off the lobby. Rather plain hotels in the Rp45,000-75,000 range include the **Badarussamsi Hotel,** Jl. Sisingamangaraja 71, tel. 22475, and the **Hotel Riau,** Jl. Diponegoro 34, tel. 22986. Of a higher standard is the **Sri Indrayani,** Jl. Bangka 2, tel. 21878 or 23461.

Food

A multitude of restaurants and *kedai kopi* serve up Indonesian, Padang, and Chinese dishes. Fish is plentiful and cheap. A specialty is smoked fish (*ikan salai*); sample it in the downtown market, Pasar Pusat, where the *warung* tend to give you double portions so they can charge twice as much. The best restaurant for *nasi padang* is the **Buana Baru,** Jl. H.O.S. Cokroaminoto 16 near Pasar Pusat. In Pasar Pusat's Chinese section are several excellent restaurants: **Restoran Medan,** Jl. Juanda 28, and **Restoran Glas Mas,** at the corner of Jl. Juanda and Jl. Dago. Not far away from the Buana Baru, on Jl. Jen. Sudirman, is the very good **RM Roda.** Also try the **Badarussamsi,** Jl. Sisingamangaraja 71.

Services

The **tourist office** (Baparda) is at Jl. Gajah Mada 200, tel. (0761) 511-101, Pekanbaru 28116. Change money at **BNI 1946,** Jl. Jen. Sudirman 119. Many other banks (Bank Bumi Daya, BCA, BRI, BPD, etc.) are also found along Jl. Jen. Sudirman, as is the main **post office** (near the corner of Jl. Kartini), telegram and telex offices, police station, and *kantor imigrasi*. The main hospital, **Umum Pekanbaru,** is at Jl. Diponegoro 2. The telephone city code is 0761.

Getting There And Around

Small, slow *kapal motor* as well as fast speedboats make the run between Tanjung Pinang (on Pulau Bintan in Insular Riau) or Pulau Batam and Pekanbaru. By bus from Bukittinggi costs Rp5000. The Garuda flight from Singapore to Pekanbaru departs every day. **Simpang Tiga Airport** is 10 km from Pekanbaru, Rp10,000 by taxi. *Microlets* (small vans) travel constantly up and down Jl. Sudirman and back and forth between Kodim and Loket stations, Rp200 for an average ride. The easiest way to get around town quickly is to charter one of the numerous orange ladybug-like *bajaj*, Rp2000 for an average ride.

Getting Away

The airport is 10 km south, past the bus station, off Jl. Nangka on the way to Bukittinggi, then one km in from the highway. Taxis overcharge; instead take blue *oplet angkutan kota* to Dupa Cinema, then a Simpang Tiga *bemo* to the crossroads (left) to the airport, then walk the last kilometer. Garuda has daily morning and afternoon flights to Jakarta and daily flights to Pulau Batam, Medan, and Singapore, as well as flights to Palembang, Padang, and Singapore. Merpati and Sempati both fly to Tanjung Pinang and Jakarta. SMAC also has regularly scheduled flights to Tanjung Pinang, Jambi, Singkep, Rengat, Medan, Batam. **Merpati** is at Jl. H.O.S. Cokroaminoto 18, tel. (0761) 23558; **Garuda,** Jl. Jen. Sudirman 343, tel. 23906 or 25026; **SMAC,** Jl. Jen. Sudirman 25, tel. 21421. **Sempati** flights can be booked at Jl. Sisingamangaraja 2, or at a travel agency.

To Insular Riau and Singapore by boat, make sure you get what you pay for. Ticket dealers offer a "Batam Express" but they might just put you on a slow boat that takes 32-40 hours. Buy boat tickets (Rp7500 deck, Rp12,500 for berths) at the office just before the gate to the harbor. *Bemo* to the harbor, which is at the end of Jl. Saleh Abbas, cost Rp500. On the slower boats to Pulau Batam (Sekupang), deck class can be so crammed with people and vegetables it's wise to arrive at the docks a couple hours before departure to stake out a good spot. Be prepared for anything: leaving at dusk, getting stuck on a coral reef, stopping off for two hours at Selatpanjang, a Chinese village that builds boats and has a shipyard of sailboats and motorboats.

Fortunately, you now have an alternative to this agonizingly slow passage. Now there's a fast launch, KM *Jelatik Express,* to Selatpanjang, leaving Pekanbaru at least every other day at 1700. It arrives in Selatpanjang at 0600 and costs Rp12,000. From Selatpanjang, fast speedboats leave frequently, zipping you to Pulau Batam in three hours (Rp30,000)—a bone-crunching journey on rough seas. From Pulau Batam hop across to Singapore for S$30 roundtrip. If all goes according to plan you'll be in Singapore for a late lunch.

The city bus terminal (*terminal bis*) is on Jl. Nangka, near most of the bus company offices (ANS, Kurnia, Merah Sari, etc.). Frequent buses travel to Bukittinggi (Rp5000, five hours). Padang is a seven to eight hour ride. Pay extra for reclining seats, extra again for a/c buses. Some taxi companies offer service all the way to Padang or Medan; see **Indah Taxi,** Jl. Karet, tel. 22341. For Medan, either head west first through Bukittinggi or go from Pekanbaru directly north to Medan via Rantauprapat; this takes 24-36 hours depending upon season and the condition of the road.

VICINITY OF PEKANBARU

Dumai
At 18 meters deep, the Siak River is the deepest of all eastern Sumatran rivers, though it still isn't wide enough for the really big oceangoing ships and oil tankers which dock at Dumai, 189 km north of Pekanbaru. Although Dumai is not an official point of departure and arrival, there's an international connection here and departure from Dumai is legal as long as you have a visa or tourist entry stamp in your passport. A hydrofoil to Melaka (West Malaysia) departs three times weekly (Saturday, Tuesday, and Thursday) at 1000, arriving at 0530, for around Rp45,000.

Bangkinang
If you don't want to stay in Pekanbaru and don't want to make the trip to Bukittinggi in one day, stay in **Wisma Samudra** on Jl. A. Yamin in Bangkinang, 64 km to the southwest. Rp10,000 rooms are clean and big, and include your own *mandi* and fan. People are friendly but the village is dull. An alternative is **Wisma Langgini,** Jl. Prof. M. Yamin SH, tel. 28. Eat at **Restoran Cahaya Buana.**

Candi Muara Takus
There's a topless *candi* (actually a brick stupa) among a number of other ruins at a remote Buddhist complex about 130 km west of Pekanbaru.

This site, possibly related to the Padanglawas ruins 100 km north, lies in the foothills of the upper Kampar River near the provincial border between western Riau Daratan and West Sumatra, 26 km from Muaramahat. This place of worship for followers of a Mahayana Buddhist sect is thought to have been built by the Sriwijaya Empire around A.D. 900-1000.

The major feature is a large stupa-form temple called **Candi Maligai,** one of the few stupas ever recovered in Indonesia. Built of red bricks and sand, the outer walls of this structure surround an earlier building impossible to date. The only known parallel to this style of stupa is in Villagaam in Sri Lanka. An inscribed gold plate found in one of the ruins dates from the 12th century; it's believed the complex was used only for a short period. There's a legend of a Batak attack on the site. The whole complex is in a state of partial excavation and renovation.

The *pasanggrahan* outside Muaramahat is called **Arga Sonya,** or you can ask a family in Desa Pongkai (two km from the temple site) to put you up. At Muaramahat, 97 km southeast of Pekanbaru (125 km from Bukittinggi), change to a minibus and proceed on a gravel road for 26 km (one ferry crossing) to Desa Pongkai. Local vehicles travel to Desa Pongkai irregularly, so don't count on a minibus waiting for you when you step from the bus. Get an early start as the road is bad, particularly in the rainy season.

Siak Sri Indrapura
In this small town 120 km downstream of Pekanbaru on the Siak River is impressive Moorish-style **Istana Asserayah Hasyimiah.** It was built in 1889 by Sultan Assaidi Syarif Hasim Abdul Jalil Saifuddin, the 11th Siak sultan, who controlled the region from Langkat nearly all the way to Jambi. His son, Sultan Syarief Kasim II, educated in Amsterdam, lost power in 1946 when the sultanate was taken over by the republican government. Unlike many sultans he openly sided with the republicans and was much admired for his courage.

The Istana was abandoned after the revolution and soon began to fall into disrepair. Caltex has contributed substantially to its reconstruction and renovation; now the local government pays for its upkeep. Some members of the royal family are still alive; Syarifah Fadlon, the widow of the last sultan, occasionally visits Istana

Praduan, the house behind the palace, and is very talkative and friendly.

A small museum inside the palace contains many of the old sultan's possessions and royal paraphernalia: vintage furniture, china and other ceramic pieces, odd historical objects, a still-working 19th-century gramophone (crank it up and listen to old records), and the sultan's gold-plated throne. On the grounds are a mosque, a burial complex for the Siak royal family, and the

High Court Building, in which criminal cases and other lawsuits were tried. Old people can tell you stories of the kingdom.

Get there by bus (Rp1000, three hours) from Pekanbaru or take a regular river ferry (eight hours). The slow boat from Pekanbaru to Pulau Batam often stops here for an hour or two. Not far from the palace, near the pier, is **Penginapan Sraiwangi.** Eat in the restaurant in the *pasar,* 300 meters away.

NORTH SUMATRA PROVINCE

North Sumatra, covering an area of 70,687 square km, is a land of volcanos, high plateaus, waterfalls, lakes, and plantations. Lake Toba, the gigantic crater lake in the center of the province, is so large it's been referred to as an inland sea. Isolated from the outside world until recent times, these upland plateaus of the Bukit Barisan Range are homeland to the Batak people, divided into six tribes. Coastal Malays along the Strait of Malacca and Nias islanders are also included in the population of nine million.

North Sumatra offers some unique experiences for the visitor. Samosir Island in Lake Toba has become one of Indonesia's major travel destinations, so relaxing that many travelers spend weeks here. From Brastagi you can visit traditional villages and climb two active volcanos. Semi-feral orangutan can be seen in a rehabilitation center at Bukit Lawang. Hindu ruins lie in the south, near Padangsidempuan. Nias Island off the west coast is famous for its monumental megalithic sculpture, traditional villages, stone-jumpers, and world-class surfing.

History

Thanks to the silt deposits of rivers, a long strip of land near the eastern coast contains soil of extraordinary fertility. Plantations growing tobacco and other cash crops were established here by the Dutch over 100 years ago. The Dutch government summarily grabbed all unused arable land, transforming the small slash-and-burn farmers of the area into subsistence laborers. The Dutch invited the sultan of Deli to lease land to plantation overseers, and in time both parties became immensely wealthy. The sultan was able to build the fabulous rococo Maimoon Palace in Medan, and commodity-trading houses sprang up all over the city. Chinese, Batak, Indian, and Javanese workers were brought in to work the plantations, many dying of diseases and maltreatment under appalling conditions. Those workers who ran off were pursued by Bengali watchmen, caught, and executed.

By 1930 the plantations of North Sumatra, constituting one of the most intense and successful foreign agricultural enterprises in the third world, were generating 200 million guilders annually. After independence from the Dutch, most of the estates were divided among small holders or nationalized. In 1965 foreign investors were again allowed to invest in cash-crop enterprises.

Economy

Though the region is rugged, it is definitely not undeveloped. North Sumatra is one of Indonesia's richest provinces, accounting for the largest share of the country's agricultural production and more than one-quarter of its agricultural exports, most of which leave via the port of Belawan, 26 km from Medan. The area is completely self-sufficient in food. The visitor will see kilometer after kilometer of rubber estates; extensive palm oil plantations; vast tobacco, clove, cacao, and tea estates; terraced rice fields; many

NORTH SUMATRA PROVINCE

PK. SUSU
BESITANG
TG. PURA
TG. SELATAT
SAWIT SEBRANG
KP. HINAI
SICANGGANG
NAMU UNGGAS
HAMPARAN
STABAT
PERAK
BELAWAN
CINTARAJA
RT. PANJANG
MEDAN
LANGKAT
BINJEI
L. PAKAM
PANTAI CERMIN
TIMBANG LAWANG
KUALA
P. BATU
TG. MOROWA
PERBAUNGAN
TG. BERINGIN
BD. KHALIPAH
KUTACANE
BOHOROK
TG. LANGKAT
TUNTUNGAN
DELITUA
PETUMBUKAN
RAMPAH
SEMBAHE
SIBOLANGIT
BANGUNPURBA
TEBINGTINGGI
LAUPAKAM
BANDARBARU
PENEN
INDRAPURA
BRASTAGI
LAU DUBUK 2
DELI SERDANG
TG. TIRAM
LAKE KAWAR
TG. BARUS
DOLOKMERAWAN
LABUHAN RUKU
LAU BALENG
KOTABULUH
G.G. MERIAH
PERDAGANGAN
LIMAPULUH
T. BINANGA
LINGGA
BARUSJAHE
KABANJAHE
BAGAN ASAHAN
LAU GUNUNG
KARO
HIGHLANDS
PEM. RAYA
KERASAAN
KISARAN
TG. BALAI
MEREK
SERIBUDOLOK
P. SIANTAR
SP. KAWAT
DAIRI
TINGALINGGA
TONGGING P. PURBA
SIDAMANIK
TANAH JAWA
P. MANDI
SIDIKALANG
HARANGGAOL
SIMALUNGUN
JAWATONGAH
ACEH
SILALAHI
TIGARAS
TINGADOLOK
ASAHAN
SIMANINDO
PRAPAT
SEIBEROMBANG
AMBARITA
BOHIT
TOMOK
LUMBAN JULU
L. BILIK
TELE
PANGURURAN
LABUHAN BATU
SIMBOLON
PORSEA
BANDARDURIAN
SUNGKEAN
NEGERILAMA
SELIMBAT
PANGKATAN
MUARA
BALIGE
PORSOBURAN
DL. SANGGUL
BAKARA
WING FOOT
HUTAGINJANG
SIBORONGBORONG
ONANGANJANG
PAKKAT
PARMONANGAN
SIPOHOLON
RANTAUPRAPAT
BARUS
NORTH TAPANULI
TARUTUNG
PANGARIBUAN
KOTAPINANG
AIRNAMULBAS
SORKAM KANAN
PASAR SORKAM
SARRULA
BONANDOLOK
LONGGAPAYUNG
SIBOLGA
CENTRAL
TAPANULI
SIPIROK
PINANGSORI
TAMOSUBAYANGAN
BT. TORU
PAAL XI
GUNUNGTUA
AEKGODANG
PORTIBI
PADANGSIDEMPUAN
BINANGA
AEKNABARA
PIJORKOLING
SOUTH TAPANULI
MUARATAIS
SIHEPPENG
TO
RANTAU
BERANGING
SIMANGAMBAT
SIBUHUAN
UJUNGBATU
SINONDAN
PANYABUNGAN
MUARASOMA
J. MERAH
RIAU
SIKARA-KARA
MUARASIPONGI
RANJAU BATU
NATAL
SP. GAMBIR
KOTANOPAN
TAPUS
SUMUR

LANGKAT
KARO
HIGHLANDS
LAKE TOBA
S. ASAHAN
S. BARUMAN
SELAT MELAKA

0   50 km

© MOON PUBLICATIONS, INC.

vegetable and flower gardens. The province's two basic problems are the poor condition of its roads and the chronic shortage of electricity.

The first priority of the provincial economy has always been farming, with industrialization and tourism second and third. Multinational corporations such as Goodyear, Uniroyal, and Harrison and Crossfield all have substantial investments and facilities here. With the establishment of processing, canning, and vegetable oil plants, even the province's industrial base is farm-oriented. There are also proven deposits of iron, coal, gold, copper, bauxite, quartz, and kaolin, as well as timber. Development has not come without severe environmental degredation. In the Simalungun District, the Porsea Pulp Mill, just two km downstream from the Asahan Dam—made famous by its depiction on Indonesia's 100 *rupiah* note—has destroyed nearby forests and severely polluted the Asahan River.

THE SOUTHERN REGION

THE PADANGLAWAS RUINS

An archaeologist's dream is located near the little village of Portibi, 23 km southeast of Gunungtua. This is a haunting area, even for nonarchaeologists. Because of the area's isolation in the middle of the Sumatran jungle, this collection of ruined 11th- and 12th-century Hindu monuments remained virtually unknown until quite recently. It wasn't until about 1970 that the government attempted to enclose the shattered ruins, enlisting Portibi's *kepala kampung* to double as caretaker and guide. And only since 1976 have the artifacts here received any professional treatment to preserve them.

History

Two large east-flowing rivers, the Baruman and the Panai, spring from sources in the plain. Despite its favorable location on transport routes, the Padanglawas Plain is unlikely to have supported a large sedentary population. Scorching winds from the west coast sweep down through the pass with blistering intensity, creating an extremely dry and inhospitable landscape. The forbidding and gloomy aspect of the site is completely in keeping with the nature of the rituals once performed in the numerous temples on the plain. The sculptures and inscriptions from some monuments show they were funerary sites and sanctuaries reserved for devotees of a form of Tantric Buddhism. The Padanglawas complexes were probably established as a special region reserved for ceremonial activity.

The earliest dated object from Padanglawas is a bronze statue from 1024. The area most likely lay along communication routes during the classical period (13th century), accounting for the variety of Javanese and Indian-derived characteristics on some of the temples. This region lies on a dry plain on the eastern fringe of the Barisan range, precisely at the starting point to the easiest pass over the range; through here the ancients could reach the west coast. The statuary and stoneware are thought to have come from India, transported on barges all the way from the east coast of Sumatra. The Baruman River passes by here and empties into the Strait of Malacca—it's used to this day by river barges trading between Sungai Tapanuli and the east coast town of Labuhanbilik.

The Site

About 1,500 square km of the plain contain at least 26 ruined brick temples, with numerous associated remains. Five broken-down Hindu temples still stand. The best-preserved and least visited are the two temples south of the river across the plain, all accessible by road. You'll find friendly Muslim villagers at Kampung Bahal. The main vaults of the temples remain—the walls are decorated with dancing *raksasa* swinging swords and clubs, lions, many warriors and guardians. The other temple sites are but mounds of bricks. Untold numbers of scattered and broken Buddhist and Hindu statues, carvings, and ancient artifacts lying around have only recently been enumerated and cared for.

The 13-meter-tall temple of Bahal I is in the best shape, and features the strangest iconography—demonic scenes of tyrannical anger and revenge, bursting with thunderbolts and skulls. Some traits, including the asymmetrical floor plan, are reminiscent of the architecture of East Java, though these ancient Batak

*grass atap,
Padanglawas*

peoples actually practiced a distinct form of Buddhism—they were a Tibetan-like Tantric cult full of weird magic. The statuary includes one of the handful of known images of the Tantric deity Heruka, plus a linga on a lotus cushion associated with bodhisattvas in the ruins of Si Joreng Belangah. This linga is characteristic of the blending of various external influences with local Batak culture, producing a unique system of mystical symbols.

Getting There
Since there are no direct buses to Portibi village, you must first take a bus from Padangsidempuan to Gunungtua, 70 km east. Padangsidempuan is 250 km from Medan and 230 km from Bukittinggi. From Gunungtua it's easy to take an *oplet* to the turnoff for the ruins just past the little bridge after Portibi village. Allow a full day, as the ruins are spread out and the weather could be incredibly hot (bring water); leave Padangsidempuan by 0730 at the latest. Once in Portibi, the caretaker, Raja Usin Harahap, will show you around the site. Be sure to tip him for his trouble. Catch a bus back to Padangsidempuan from Gunungtua before dusk.

Padangsidempuan
This town and its surroundings have a lot to offer the visitor. First contact enthusiastic local guide Awaluddin Pulungan, who can arrange jungle trips and a river voyage. In Padangsidempuan is a billiard hall, a *tuak* shop, and Graha Nusantara University, the latter occupy-

ing the top of the mountain and offering great views of the town. Stay at **Samudera Hotel,** Jl. T. Umar 60-A, tel. 476, with VIP rooms for Rp31,000 including breakfast. Economy rooms are Rp8250 (no breakfast). There are several other hotels and *losmen* to choose from. Visit the *salak* garden five km from town and the waterfall near town. On the river voyage to Rianiate Lake, note the 10 kinds of banana trees along the banks. Bring food for the extraordinarily tame sacred fish. You can swim amid beautiful landscapes at Simarsabut and Tao lakes. There's a hot springs at **Sibanggor; Sopogodang** offers ancient *rumah adat.*

SIBOLGA

The approach coming into this port town is dramatic: the highlands abruptly end and the road plunges into a steep-walled valley, then drops to the coast. Beautiful sunsets. It's one of life's little ironies that a town with such a beautiful setting should be so uninspiring. Though Sibolga has little to attract the traveler, it does offer good Chinese food and reasonable accommodations. The port's main claim to fame is as an embarkation point for Nias Island. Sibolga also serves as an overnight stop on the hard bus ride from Bukittinggi to Prapat; the road turns inland at this point. "Hello Mister" calls abound and you'll meet the odd sleazy type characteristic of port towns. Change money at **Bank Dagang Negara** on Jl. A. Yani.

Accommodations

Check out the half dozen or so *losmen* on Jl. Horas near the port, handy for those leaving for Nias. In town, **Hotel Sudimampir,** Jl. Mesjid 98, is cheap. Next door is the **Roda Minang.** The **Hidup Baru,** Jl. Letjen. R. Suprapto 123, tel. 21957, is surprisingly clean and cheap; Rp8500 s, Rp12,500 with *mandi.* Centrally located **Indah Sari,** Jl. A. Yani 27-29, is even more upscale; a/c rooms with private baths cost Rp25,000. Well-heeled and into Maugham-esque colonial nostalgia? Check out quiet **Hotel Taman Nauli,** north of town, with balconied rooms including a/c and bath.

Food

Decent restaurants and an unusually good ice cream cafe are located on the corner across from the big cinema. **Bing Selamat** serves a delicious hot-rice specialty. Chinese restaurant **Telok Indah,** Jl. Jen. A. Yani 63-65, has excellent *funjung hai.* The other Chinese restaurants on the corner closer to the Indah Sari are as good and cheaper; foodstalls outside. **Slamet,** clean and expensive, on Jl. Katamso 30, has quite good food.

Getting Away

Most *ekspres* bus companies maintain offices in the main bus terminal on Jl. Singamangaraja. Another, smaller terminal has local buses to Padangsidempuan, Balige, and Barus, located 1.5 km from Pelabuhan Kecil (Rp500 by *becak*). Bukittinggi requires a trip of 12-18 uncomfortable hours, with buses leaving once daily. Padang is 18 hours away, Medan eight.

Pelni's KM *Kerinci* sails for Padang, Tanjung Priok, Surabaya and points east every two weeks; the office is at Jl. Pelabuhan 48. On both sides of the road leading to the harbor are shipping company offices. Ferries for Nias leave Monday, Wednesday, and Friday from the Pelabuhan Kecil, three km (Rp1000 by *becak*) from the bus terminal. The boat costs Rp7500 and takes 10-14 hours, charging Rp5000 per person extra for a bunk in a four-bed cabin. Departure time is around 2100 or 2200, arriving in Telukdalam at 0900 the next morning. Buy your ticket before 2000, otherwise you'll pay more on the boat. On Tuesday, Thursday, and Saturday a cargo boat also departs for Nias; expect the same conditions. It's better to get a boat to the southern port of Telukdalam rather than the northern port of Gunungsitoli. Try to pick a big, fast boat rather than a small, crowded one. In the event of rain, undercover accommodation on the smaller boats is cramped and unpleasant. Take along a *tikar* (mat), foodstuffs, fruit, and snacks.

NIAS

With its famous megalithic stone altars and furniture, spectacular traditional architecture, and complex religious rites, this fascinating island, 125 km southwest of Sibolga, offers a journey into the past. Isolated for thousands of years, the human populations of Nias and the other islands off Sumatra's west coast have evolved extraordinary cultures. This ancient island, just north of the equator, has rolling mountainous terrain, gorges, ravines, and rivers, and is subject to earthquakes. The northern half of Nias is sparsely populated and features large swampy areas.

A subdistrict of West Sumatra Province, the island's major city and capital is Gunungsitoli in the north, with the main port Telukdalam in the south. Not far from Telukdalam is the surfing hangout of Jamborai village, which boasts fine beaches and some of the best right-handers in Indonesia. Farther inland are traditional hilltop villages with world-class megalithic sculpture and huge wooden handhewn dwellings on tree-trunk pylons. You can easily reach Nias by regular ferry from Sibolga, by air from Medan, or on a cruise ship with 400 other tourists. Exchange rates are poor, so change your traveler's checks in Medan and/or Sibolga before visiting the island, particularly if staying a month or so.

History

A magnificent megalithic heroic culture flourished on Nias well into the 20th century; headhunting and human sacrifices were still practiced as late as 1935. In the south part of the island during the 1800s Acehnese slave raiders regularly went on the rampage. Chiefs would carry off captives from neighboring villages and sell them for gold to slave runners. Today this

ISLE OF NIAS

© MOON PUBLICATIONS, INC.

same gold is used for bride-prices at weddings and adorns the headdresses of Niah dancers.

In the past, northern Nias was vastly different from the south. Poor communications contributed to their mutual isolation, and the inhabitants of each region still speak their own dialect. The north was conquered in the 17th century by the Dutch, but tribes of the south resisted to the bitter end, ensconced in fortified hillside villages. In contrast to the south's megalithic culture and rigid class structure, the people of north Nias became a modern Indonesian/quasi-European culture with few class distinctions.

Missionaries arrived in 1865. After repeated military expeditions, the Dutch finally gained control over south Nias in 1914. A German

Protestant mission was established in 1912 and the Catholics began work in 1937. The Protestants are still in the majority, the professed faith of about 80% of the population.

The Economy

Traditionally, the Niah economy was based on agriculture and pig-raising. To supplement their diet, the people also fished and hunted. Today, most of the 500,000 people of Nias and Batu islands are rice-growers; other main food crops include taro, maize, and sweet potatoes. In swampy areas, wet rice is grown, and in south Nias dry-field rice cultivation is practiced. But due to population pressure, available cultivatable land is shrinking. The island exports copra, pigs, rubber, and *nilam* (patchouli oil).

Pigs are not only an important ritual food but also a source of wealth and prestige. Pig-raising is a profitable and secure business, requiring capital few can acquire. Pork is expensive, usually eaten only once a week. Market day is pig-slaughtering day, when pork is often served for both lunch and dinner.

Since the early 1970s, when travelers first started arriving, tourism has become an increasingly important source of revenues. At Hiliotaluwa in the southwest they're dredging a deep-water harbor for cruise liners and building an airport suitable for widebodied jets, while the Japanese are planning to erect a five-star hotel. Tourism is seen as the way to enter the mainstream economy, a dubious achievement attained by such mainland tourist areas as Lake Toba and Bukittinggi. The industry is supported by the local chiefs, who seek to raise cash to send their children off to technical schools and universities in Medan and Jakarta. Educated offspring are the new symbol of prestige.

THE PEOPLE

The native name for the island is Tano Niha, "Land of the People." Ethnically, the Niah, who call themselves the Ono Niah, are a mixed population of proto-Malays who've had contact with the Asian Mongoloid world. Their exact origin is misty. Many features of their culture and practices are all their own. Niasers speak a language related to Malagasy, yet their sculpture shows uncanny similarities to the woodcarvings made by the Nagas of Assam in the high Himalayas. Because of the similarities of physical type, language, and customs between the two peoples, the Niah may have derived from the Bataks. It's believed their ancestors migrated to the island between 5000 and 3000 B.C. They were strongly influenced by the Bronze Age Dongson culture of North Vietnam, as well as by contacts with Chinese, Hindu, Portuguese, and Muslim traders.

Traditional Culture

When Europeans arrived in the late 17th century, they found the island divided into 50 territorial-genealogical federations. Each village and district traced its descent from a number of original clans which first settled the island. All local authority was vested in the village chief (*siulu*). Above him was a paramount district chief. Elders sat in council to prescribe punishment for taboo breakers and decide questions of boundaries, *adat,* and civil disputes.

The population in the south was sharply divided into three classes: aristocrats (*siulu*), commoners (*si'ila*), and slaves (*sawuyu*). The separation was rigidly enforced. The relationship between the first two was roughly one between creditors and debtors. Slaves were acquired through war or indebtedness; they spent their whole lives toiling in the fields or in the homes of the chiefs. Slaves were symbols of rank and prestige.

Wars were used to exact revenge, capture slaves, or acquire heads to plant under the posts of new *rumah adat*. To acquire full rank and title, "feasts of merit" were staged, with human sacrifices and the erection of stone memorials. Most chiefly ceremonies—birth, naming, cir-

Nias warriors dancing in the village square

cumcision—included mock battles, ritual chanting, animal sacrifice, trance-dancing, and offerings to funerary figures.

In the south, a young man had to perform bride service in the house of his future bride. Marriage involved a complex exchange of feasts and gifts which included a heavy bride-price (*bowo*, usually pigs and gold), the amount set according to the rank of the bride. Today, the bride-price is up to three million *rupiah*. Real estate is still passed down through the sons.

Religion

After 100 years of proselytizing by German Lutheran missionaries, about 95% of the island's population has converted to nominal Christianity, the people now gentle and obedient to authority. Islam (5% of the population) progresses best in the port towns, especially Gunungsitoli. Instead of hunting heads, Niasers now sing hymns; instead of waging war and keeping slaves, they barter copra and pigs for bicycles and boomboxes, and stage melodramatic war dances for tourists. Children attend government elementary and missionary schools.

The old religion is all but dead, the new religion followed with a fundamentalist fervor. The few beliefs that have survived are infused with Christian symbols and practices—Christianity now carries more prestige than animistic beliefs. Strict Sabbath prohibitions are practiced—no work on Sunday, not even picking a coconut. Yet vestiges of the old culture are still evident: village architecture, staged dances, performances of masculine strength, inherited social offices, funerary practices. The dead are sometimes laid out for ceremonies on massive rectangular stones, then placed in a boat-shaped coffin and transported to the cemetery, where they're placed above ground on posts and left to the elements. A short walk behind the chief's house in Bawomataluo is the beautifully restored grave of the last *raja*.

THE ARTS

Crafts

Genuine Niah antiquities can still be found in the north, but they may have to be hammered out of roof beams and are not cheap. A pair of wooden house guardians, for example, could cost Rp300,000. Most antiques were ripped off long ago. When the first missionaries arrived in the 1800s, the statues, effigies, and ancestor figures (*adu*) that weren't destroyed were hustled off to Europe en masse. The best Niah artifacts and sculptures, including whole huts and entire wardrobes, are today in Germany, at the famous Rautenstrauch-Joest Museum of Cologne and in other private collections. In the villages, the people will show you a whole array of traditional gear, such as *kalabubu* (necklaces), *sialu* (earrings), *gare* (swords), *oroba* (crocodile-skin armor), and old photos, but rarely are these heirlooms for sale.

Dance

Warlike southern Niah dances are the only dances in Indonesia featuring high acrobatic jumps. The warrior's dance (*maluaya*) is an eerie dance-song with a hypnotizing sound of rattling shields and men shouting rhythmically, leaping frog-like high into the air. They also perform mock fights and armed combat dances, the "battlefield" dissolving in utter confusion, just like after a real battle. With their horned helmets, flaring shoulder plates, face masks with long protruding boar tusks, and double-edged swords and spears barbed like harpoons, the dancers' battle dress understandably struck terror in the hearts of an enemy. With the cruise ships bringing waves of 400 camera-clicking tourists twice a month, Hollywood has invaded and Niah dances have become jazzier.

Stone Jumping

Vestiges of the earlier Niah culture also survive in the spectacle of *fahombe* (stone jumping). This frightening sport requires great acrobatic skill, particularly when executed with sword in hand. A solid stone column over two meters high and one-half meter broad stands on the great runway of the village between rows of dwellings. In front of the column is a smaller stone, about one-half meter high. A young man runs from a distance of about 20 meters for the smaller stone, and from it launches himself feet-first high into the air over the column. Much like jumping the high horse in gymnastics, jumpers gyrate around in midair to alight on their feet on rough heavy paving stones facing the column.

In olden times stones were covered with sharp spikes and pointed bamboo sticks. *Fahombe* was used to train young loinclothed warriors to clear the walls of enemy villages at night with a torch in one hand and a sword in the other. *Fahombe* also proved a young man's fitness to take a wife. Stone jumping takes place in all south Niah villages—Bawomataluo, Hilisimaetano, Orahili, Botohili—and costs Rp150,000 for a private showing. Another traditional Niah sport is a football game in which players work to keep a rattan ball suspended in the air to "keep the sun from setting."

Sculpture

There were two phases in the history of Niah classical sculpture—the stonework of the ancient proto-Malayans and the woodcrafts of the 1400s. Though it would be difficult to find a single stonecutter on Nias today, much remains of their megalithic culture, which was of a standard found nowhere else in Southeast Asia. Missionaries who first penetrated the island's interior in the 1930s came across abandoned villages in the mountains with entire inventories of stone sculptures still intact.

These islanders once utilized stone as the most important material of civilization. Stone was used for tools, utensils, pillows, even money. Whole villages are paved with great flat stone tiles; at some sites long stone staircases lead to hilltop settlements. Master masons constructed throne-like chairs twisting with serpents, ornamental tables, bathing places, stelae, and obelisks. Horizontal slabs were erected as memorials to the dead.

Stone slabs carved here are similar in shape to those found everywhere in the early history of the planet, from Stonehenge to Easter Island. Hauled from distant riverbed quarries, Niah carvings were executed in light grayish stone with imagination and superb precision. The villagers themselves are ignorant of where the megaliths originated, who carved them or when. They've also long forgotten the meaning of the magical symbols and rosettes adorning stone pyramids and terraces in front of chiefs' houses and in ceremonial places in south Niah villages, at one time the center of sacrifices.

The old religion is portrayed vividly in Easter Island-like armless statues of ancestral beings distinguished by tall Niah-style headgear, elaborate earrings, sharp features, elongated torsos, large male genitalia, heads with small stuck-on beards, right ears with distended lobes. Note the bold, aggressive stance of the Niah *adu*. At the funerals of chiefs, this wooden image was required so the ghost of the deceased could transfer into it. Statues were also used to propitiate spirits in case of family illness. Well-executed wooden statues start at Rp200,000, but the seller may come down as low as Rp45,000. Smaller ones go for Rp10,000-15,000.

Architecture

Southern villages, constructed during the time of internecine warfare, are deceptive fortresses. Bars guarded windows, and trapdoors opened out to roofs. Structures were erected so close together that internal connecting doors made it possible for residents to walk the whole length of the village, sometimes over 300 meters, without ever touching the ground. Many structures featured just a trapdoor in the floor, with no other exits or entrances.

Houses of commoners average four-by-twelve meters; more imposing houses belong to the aristocracy. On these, steeply pitched roofs sometimes soar over eight meters above the height of the walls, with overhanging gables creating a hooded appearance. Rectangular and narrow in shape, these chiefly structures rest on a substructure of stone and massive wooden beams, resisting the tremors that often shake the island. Older houses are made of handhewn polished timbers, ingeniously joined without pegs or nails, with panels and moldings decoratively carved and the roof resting on complicated beamwork.

In remote areas the oldest *adat* houses are still untouched; in the more Westernized villages the people prefer standard Indonesian construction. Nowadays, on more and more *rumah adat,* thatch is replaced with corrugated steel roofs; within a few years old construction techniques will have vanished and the whole silhouette of the typical Niah village will be forever altered. To help preserve what is left, a chief's *adat* house was completely dismantled piece by piece by a Danish professor and shipped back to Europe. In northern Nias, traditional houses are less spectacular, rougher, and more varied.

PRACTICALITIES

Health

Get a cholera shot before arriving—there are still seasonal outbreaks here. Five different strains of malaria are found on Nias, although all villagers assert that in their village there is no malaria (losmen owner Aman Dolyn even sells "antimalarial" T-shirts). Take your malaria pills two weeks before arrival and during your stay. The strains that have evolved here are resistant to chloroquine-based preventatives, so a pyrimethamine-sulfadoxine alternative, such as Fansidar, is suggested. Also bring mosquito repellent and a mosquito net.

Conduct

A number of people on Nias involved with tourism come on strong and pushy, routinely misinforming tourists about prices, routes, losmen, and the like. There are many cheats and thieves. Watch out especially for Andreas—he'll have the shirt off your back while you're not looking. Don't believe people who say their village is safe—never leave your luggage unattended. Be on guard for stone-throwing children. Sometimes kids, such as those in Hilisimaetano, can be downright vicious. Children will inevitably yell "Hello Miste-r-r-r-r!!" and "Hello Miss!!" to which you should simply reply "Ya-ho'wu!" (the traditional Niah greeting, meaning "Strength!"). This usually stops them cold. They watch wide-eyed as you pass by, figuring that if you can greet them you might also possibly understand them. In nontouristed areas, people are usually very helpful and kind. In remote areas, you could suddenly come across menacing-looking hunters with spears and dogs. In these instances, you have surprise on your side, and they're struck so dumb you're long gone before they have time to react.

Your behavior can go a long way towards minimizing negative experiences. Always visit the headman's house first to pay your respects. If the headman is in the sawah, go through a subordinate or a lesser chief. Ask permission to photograph or enter someone's house; there's usually no charge. Most important of all: dress modestly. On Lagundi Beach and at nearby Jamborai, the atmosphere is casual: shorts, swimsuits, no shirts (for males) are the rule. But upon leaving the beach area, women should wear long pants or a long skirt, a short-sleeved blouse, and a bra. Women should never wear just a sarung tied under their arms; that is what Indonesians wear to bathe, not to visit or saunter. Men should wear shirts. To dress otherwise will offend the morals of the local people. Travelers who dress in shorts or undershirts or doff their bras often have stones thrown at them by children. Such children should be reported to the local kepala desa, and not yelled at.

TRANSPORTATION

Getting There

The quickest way in is to fly from Medan to Gunungsitoli. SMAC offers several flights weekly (Rp87,000 one-way, Rp92,000 return). The airport is small: only seven-seat Cessna Islanders can land here. SMAC's office is at Jl. Imam Bonjol 59, tel. (061) 515-934 or 516-617, Medan. SMAC also offers a Wednesday flight from Padang. Gunungsitoli's Binaka Airport is 19 km from town; a bemo costs Rp3000. If flying out, don't forget to reconfirm your return flight. At the airport, prices for minibus hire to the south start at Rp210,000, but you can bargain down to Rp50,000. The public bus from Gunungsitoli to Telukdalam is Rp6000 (six hours, 120 km). You can also get a boat to Nias, to either Gunungsitoli or Telukdalam, departing Sibolga on the west coast of Sumatra at around 2000 two or three times weekly (Rp7500, 9-12 hours).

Getting Around

Since independence many Nias roads have been swallowed by the jungle, and torrential tropical downpours keep most of the remainder in deplorable condition. Buses, trucks, bemo, and jeeps run tortuously along existing main roads. In remote areas walking is your only option; all over the island are forest tracks leading from village to village. In the south many of these paths are paved with stones. Locals will offer to give you a lift on the back of motorcycles. In the tourist villages of the south you can rent bicycles. The influx of tourists has made some bemo and truck drivers greedy; they'll try to convince you to charter and are not inclined to barter. Be home before 1600, when their prices rise 1,000%.

GUNUNGSITOLI

The capital of Nias, where the district's local government and much of the island's commerce is concentrated. This small city features a high school and a good hospital. After exiting the dock, try the tourist office on the right—information on sights in both the north and south, plus a good map. The post office is on Jl. Gomo. Cash traveler's checks at Hotel Gomo or at BNI on Jl. Pattimura at a terrible rate.

It's worth staying in Gunungsitoli at least a day as there are nice walks around the area, which is known for several oval-shaped, free-standing, northern-style *rumah adat* on pylons. See some up the hill from Hilimbawedesolo, 13 km (Rp1000) by bus from Gunungsitoli. More are found four km south of Gunungsitoli.

Dance enthusiasts who speak Indonesian or Dutch should visit Amarojama, the historian. Though his book *Fondroko Ono Niha* isn't much liked in the south (they say it's full of incorrect information), he nevertheless is a wellspring of knowledge on the nitty-gritty details of Niah culture. Ask Mr. Ganda at Wisma Soliga for directions. If you've got Rp75,000, Amarojama will take you to his village to see a dance performance by young men trained in the old dances.

Accommodations And Food

Recommended is **Wisma Soliga**, on the main road two km from town. Though expensive (Rp18,000 for the cheapest double), the hotel's restaurant serves the only good food on Nias (Chinese-style), and Pak Ganda's sons will take you to the *rumah adat* in the hills nearby. (Caveat: Pak Ganda's "genuine" carvings look pretty fishy, and are pricey.) The next best is the **Wisata** in town, which asks Rp12,000 d for rooms with private bath; bargain. Could be noisy. A bit overpriced but quite adequate is **Hotel Gomo**, Jl. Gomo 148, tel. 21926; Rp12,000 d, Rp25,000 d for a/c rooms. Cheaper (Rp5000) is **Hotel Beringin** on Jl. Beringin.

Getting Away

Boats sometimes sail from Gunungsitoli to Telukdalam but the schedule depends very much on the weather. It's better to take the bus departing the terminal on Jl. Diponegoro once daily (Rp6000); the six-hour journey can require as long as 30 hours in heavy rain. The north-south road down the center of the island is potholed and occasionally washed out, the bridges down. The old coastal road is in even worse shape.

TELUKDALAM

Second-largest town on Nias, on the far southeast tip, the main port of entry for southern Nias. You pull into a small palm-fringed bay with the town extending into the surrounding hills. A red church is one of Telukdalam's landmarks. Change money at bad rates in the small shops. Several *losmen* are located on the waterfront, including **Sabar Menanti** and the concrete **Wisma Jamborai,** both Rp8000 s. The Sabar Menanti occupies a large two-story building with big dirty rooms. This combination hotel and restaurant might also have bicycles for hire. Though a filthy dump, it possesses a truly amazing fridge, which cools beer to a temperature fit for Australian consumption in 3.5 minutes flat. A few good restaurants in town serve Padang food and noodle dishes.

Getting Away

The boat from Telukdalam to Sibolga runs twice weekly (Rp7500); you must wait until 2100 for the boat, which arrives in Sibolga the next morning. Boats (about twice monthly, but don't count on it) also sail for Padang (48 hours), saving you the 12-hour bus ride from Sibolga up to Padang. The bus north to Gunungsitoli takes about six hours (120 km), arriving at 1400; the road north becomes wretched after only a few kilometers. Buses also run to Lagundi, Botohili, Hilisimaetano, and Bawomataluo. From Telukdalam's harbor to Lagundi is about 12 km. Transport on motorbikes costs Rp2000 unless a *losmen* owner takes you (Rp1000). For the return trip to Telukdalam, travelers often organize a truck for an evening trip so they can stay at Lagundi Beach until dark. But very often the truck people don't stick to their agreement and triple the prices.

LAGUNDI BAY

Twelve km from Telukdalam lie two villages on this horseshoe-shaped bay: Muslim Lagundi and

SOUTH NIAS

S. GOMO

TUNDRAMBANO
UILIANAA
LAHUSAIDANOTAE
BORONADU
GOMO
ORAHILI
SITAOROASI
S. SUSUA
TETEGEWO
BARAWANU
LAOWI
TUMORI
FANEDANU
HILIDOHONA
TAMIO
SISOBAHILI
RAMBA
S. SUSUA
SITALAGOSUSUA
HILIMBAHO
LAHUSA
TETEZOU
YOBAWAGOLI
HELIZALULU
HILISIMAETANO
BALAEKHA
S. MASIO
SILIMAEWA
TUHEGEWO
HILIAMAZULA
HILIABOLATO
HILIMBOWO
HILIBADALU
BAWOFARONO
S. ARAMO
HILIADULO
S. MEZAYA
ORAHILI
HILIMBULAWA
BALE
HILINDASONIHA
HILINITAEO
GEWA
LAWINDA
HILIMAERA
HILITOTAO
HILIZOROILAWO
HILIZALOOTANO
HILIHORO
SIFAOROASI
HILINAWALO
MAZINO
HILIALAWA
HILIFALAWU
BAWOLANUSA
BAWOGOSALI
HILINAWALO
S. MAZINO
HILIMAGARI
ONOHONDO
SIWALAWA
BAWOGANOWO
LAHUSA
HILINAMOZAUA
HILINAMONIHA
HILISIMAETANO
HILIMONDEGERAYA
S. GEWA
BAWOMATALUO
HILIFALAGO
ORAHILI
HILISAOTO
HILIFARONO
HILISATARO
HILIMAENAMOLO
HILIAMAETALUO
HILISONDEKHA
HILIGANOWO
BAWODABARA
HILILAMETA
HILIZIHONO
BAWOZAUA
LAGUNDI
BAWONOHONO
HILIGEHO
BAWONIFAOSO
BOTOHILI
HILIANAA
TELUK DALAM
LAGUNDI BAY
FAHIL BAY
BALUHO BEACH
HILITOBARA

0 10 km

© MOON PUBLICATIONS, INC.

Christian Jamborai, discovered by Australian surfers in the mid-'70s. If you like to swim and sunbathe it's best to stay in Lagundi, as Jamborai on the point is only good for surfing. Lagundi Bay was the main port of South Nias until the Krakatoa eruption of 1883 wiped it out; the port was then moved to Telukdalam. Join the local soccer games on Sunday afternoon. Take enough money because you get a lousy exchange rate here; to live reasonably comfortably you'll need Rp7000-12,000 per day. Bring lots of reading material. Watch your stuff; theft has become a problem, and a lot of the villagers beg or are always trying to sell you something.

Surfing
The beautiful beach at Jamborai is a 20-minute walk down the shore from Lagundi village toward the west opening of the bay. The waves on the point, where all the right-handers peel off, are much better for surfing than at Kuta. The surf here can reach over three meters high and travels sometimes 200 meters, with wild sea turtles in the water. Out in the wide bay is a coral reef, then white sand, then another reef over 50 meters wide—an unreal world, like a dream. When the surf is up, it's terrific, but when there's no surf you can go crazy because of the remoteness of the place. Sometimes there are up to 35 surfies out in the water, for the most part Australians, but also lots of Europeans—mostly French and Italians—and even a few Brazilians. You can rent surfboards on the beach for Rp2000 per day. Because of the size of the waves and the coral, this surf is not for beginners.

Accommodations
The 30-odd wooden and bamboo *losmen* in Lagundi and Jamborai blend in with the marine surroundings and typically cost only Rp1000-2000 per person. If you stay 10 days or longer you can lodge for free—they make most of their money from the Kuta-style food they serve. Check places out *personally* to make the best choice. Consider good security; bars on the windows, *penjaga* (guards). Most places have mosquito nets and lie only 40 meters through coconut trees to the beach, within sound of the surf. One of the best accommodations is **Yanti's** across the river. The manager has many evenings' worth of information on Niah magic, culture, arts, and language. A real find.

Aman Dolyn, the manager of **Aman Losmen,** is the *kepala desa* of Lagundi. Known also as the Anti-Malaria Guesthouse, his *losmen* is the first on the beach when you arrive by motorbike from Lagundi junction. Some bungalows cost Rp4000 d and simple rooms go for Rp1000-2000. No electricity, but that's the same for all the guesthouses except Yanti's. Watch the peepholes. At **Ama Soni** they really look after you, but rooms will probably be occupied.

Food
Most of the *losmen* provide evening meals at around Rp1000 extra. Meals are okay and normally priced but tend to be monotonous—the same ol' *mie goreng, nasi goreng, gado-gado,* omelettes, etc. Take extra vittles to liven up the fare; peanut butter is like gold. A few *warung* snack bars have opened. **Ama Yanti's** has the best food; **Manuel's** and **Losmen Aman** are also good. The best deal is the tuna and lobster you can buy from the fishermen on the beach in front of your *losmen.* Coconuts cost around Rp200. Make roast fish and lobster dinners on the beach.

Transportation
The Lagundi turnoff lies six km west of Telukdalam, a dirt road that leads six km farther down to Lagundi village. You can reach Lagundi Bay by irregular *oplet* or bus, or you can hitch a ride on the back of a motorbike right to Jamborai village. Truck-buses run only on Saturday from Lagundi to and from Telukdalam for market. Leaving Lagundi for the mainland, allow several days as something might go wrong. Sometimes if you arrive on the afternoon bus in Telukdalam, you can go straight to the harbor and climb on a boat to Sibolga. Beware of David and Martin's shady boat-ticket deals; they tend to hang around the *losmen.* Don't pay in advance.

Botohili
Several southern villages are within easy walk of Lagundi. Botohili is just three km west, the end of the road for vehicles. Two rows of houses are separated by a courtyard of big stone squares. All the *rumah adat* have doors between them that occupants of each house are forbidden to shut; this would mean they have something to hide. If you stay in one of the *adat* houses, you'll sleep in one big room with 30 family members. When you want to be left alone

at night, just say *"Bolehkah saya tidur?"* ("May I sleep now please?"). Young men of the village might play the guitar and talk until midnight. At 0300 sharp the head fisherman starts walking up and down the courtyard calling out the names of his crew. At 0500 the cocks start crowing, and by 0600 the entire family is running through the house. The *mandi* is in the jungle at the end of muddy stepping stones. Don't miss this humble experience. And don't miss going to church on Sunday with the family to hear the exuberant male choir singing hymns in Niah and Indonesian.

BAWOMATALUO

Established in 1878, Bawomataluo (meaning "Sunhill") is the best kept extant traditional village in southern Nias, with superb carvings and high-roofed architecture. It's reached by minibus from Telukdalam (Rp1000, 14 km). Or take the bus to Orahili, then walk a km up the 480 steep stone steps leading to the hilltop village. Bawomataluo is Nias's most accessible, popular, touristy *adat* village. Suharto and Jakarta's police chief have even visited here. Entrance fee Rp5000, camera Rp1000 extra, video camera Rp2500 extra.

Every two weeks a cruise ship brings 400 people, so it's no surprise prices are quoted in U.S. dollars. The inhabitants will try to flog contemporary wood sculpture and "precious family" *pusaka,* kids pester you for money, villagers offer to pose for photos for a fee. Annoying, but not nearly as bad as Torajaland or Penelokan—this is too important a village, culturally speaking, to pass up. People play chess, sculpt, weave, and slaughter pigs as you walk down the long street laid with big stone slabs. Also visit the other villages of the area. Few roads here; most of the time you have to walk on narrow paths through banana orchards and rice fields.

Stay in the *kepala desa*'s house, if not occupied, and give a contribution to his wife: Rp4000 d per night should do, including lunch. As a bonus, you could sit on the sidelines during a village *rapat* (meeting) in the evening. The headman appears to be a sensitive, intelligent, and perceptive man. He speaks some English, but of course Indonesian speakers will get a lot more

out of the exchange. Watch your money and gear, even at the chief's house, as there are reports of thefts. Don't stay in the house opposite the chief's.

Traditional dances are staged, such as the *maluaya,* in which a horde of warriors storms down the wide courtyard, wildly brandishing spears, stamping and rattling their shields, their heads decorated with feathers. Hiring a dance costs a minimum of Rp150,000, which includes the full troupe of 46 people. Stone jumping is extra.

Chief's Palace

By far the most fantastic piece of architecture in the whole village, and the finest and largest of its kind in all of Nias, is the imposing chief's palace, called Omo Sebua. It's built on wooden pillars nearly one meter thick, with a stepped floor of heavy wooden planks. Visitors sit on the level befitting their rank, the highest level accorded only to the chief. Built by skilled artisans and slaves in 1878, the building encloses a great inner chamber 12 meters long and 10.5 meters wide, with carved decorative motifs on one wall in high relief; on the opposite wall is a wonderful carving in low relief of a two-masted European sailing ship, complete with sailors, cannon, and sea creatures lurking in the depths below. All carvings are in great need of restoration. The spikes of the roof soar 20 meters above the ground, and the building's walls are joined with all the consummate skill of a cabinetmaker. The one eyesore is the ugly sheet-metal roof.

Sculpture

In the village courtyard sits an arrangement of 18-ton stone chairs, where the dead were once left to decay. Also see *menhirs,* obelisks, stone ceremonial benches decorated with simple floral motifs, and a stone disk a foot thick resting on four columns. In all there are 287 stone sculptures, both large and small. Check out the stone slab in front of the chief's house: anchor chain, sharks, whales, young boys swimming, all portrayed in a realistic European style atypical of an ancient megalithic culture. The *kepala desa* explains that these anachronistic carvings date from the islanders' first contact with Europeans, who arrived on their sailing ships with iron chains.

OTHER TRADITIONAL VILLAGES

Hilisimaetano

Sixteen km inland from Telukdalam and 20 km north of Lagundi on a good asphalt road. There are 140 *adat* houses here. Stay in **Losmen Mawan**; Rp5000 per person, capacity four people. Stone-jumping by young unmarried men is usually staged on Saturday. A few German missionaries work on agricultural projects; children leave the primary grades and take up training at the project to learn how to build modern houses, irrigation works, and other skills needed for daily life.

Megaliths line both sides of Hilisimaetano's broad stone-paved courtyard, between the rows of traditional houses. There are flat-topped obelisks, benches and dolmens of smooth gray slabs of stone, treasure chests with designs of keys and pistols on the sides. Most of these pieces have been smoothly finished and decorated with spiral designs, triangles, squares, lotus blossoms, hornbills, monkeys, and lizards.

The Orahili-Hilisimaetano Walk

An outstanding one-day walk—as little as four hours, if reasonably fit—via a back northerly path that passes through a number of traditional villages with stone seats, memorial benches, and stairs of honor. People are very friendly, especially once you get past Bawomataluo. Orahili, downhill from Bawomataluo, has by now seen its share of tourists—it's the villages farther along the road that are relatively untourished. Bawomataluo is the best for tribal houses. Siwalawa is rather run-down. Onohondo is a decent, friendly place with a *losmen* (Jirman Hondra, Rp4000), chief's house, swimming pool, and beautiful waterfall one-half km east. Hilinawalo is the most traditional village, over 100 years old. It has a chief's house and a superbly laid central stone walk with stone benches and a pair of thrones. Bawogosali is a pleasant, picturesque village. Hilisimaetano is the worst for rascally kids.

On this moderate 15-km walk, all you have to do is follow the stone path connecting all the villages. No guide required. On rainy days the stones can be very slippery, so wear good shoes. Take mosquito repellent. Stay overnight in the houses of the *kepala desa*; your hosts will probably serve soup or tea or chop up a coconut for you. Ask directions in each village. It's a half-day trip from Bawomataluo northeast to Siwalawa, a difficult segment. From Hilisimaetano at the end of the loop, ride back to Telukdalam by bus or *oplet*. Or have the motorcycle drop you off at Orahili by 0800 and pick you up again at Hilisimaetano at 1600 (Rp2000) at the end of the walk.

GOMO

This village near the Gomo River, roughly halfway between Telukdalam and Gunungsitoli, has been called the cradle of Niah culture. It's believed the ancestors of the present-day Niah orginiated from this area, and it is thus regarded as sacred. From the town center, it's one km to the Gomo police station, where you must show your passport and enter your name in the tourist register. Not many tourists visit the place, which explains why the people are still friendly.

Sights

Gomo is an important site for stone seats, *menhirs,* and phallic stones, representing symbols of authority. Replicas of these megaliths now stand in the yard of the *kantor bupati* in Gunungsitoli, the district capital. There are only six *rumah adat* here; the others burned down years ago. In the old chief's house notice the single- and double-tailed lizard motifs, a larger-than-life monkeyhead carving descending from the forward rafters, and the arm emerging from the wall in a dance gesture. Out front sits a series of round stone tables and a couple of *naga* chairs, one high atop a monolith.

Getting There

From Telukdalam, boats leave for the market town of Helizalulu fairly regularly (three hours, Rp5000). The boat anchors in a small bay; you're dropped on the beach after a five-minute Rp600 *prahu* ride. If the boat arrives late, sleep on the boat, at the *stasiun polisi,* or in one of the *warung* around the marketplace (market day is Wednesday). The hike to Gomo from Helizalulu, over difficult but fascinating terrain, takes about two days. The track passes through a gorge, then follows a river for some distance, passing small villages with occasional *adat* houses. At a point where the road meets the river, a stone stairway rises to a village on the left and a muddy track adjacent to a wide strong river straight ahead. Cross the river here. The water level varies with the rain and could be knee-deep on the trip in but waist-deep on the return; the current can run strong enough to sweep you off your feet.

From the other side of the river, the track is all stone except for some very muddy sections that will ruin any pair of shoes. After about three hours and the crossing of another, shallow river, a stone path on the right leads from the main road, rising through a village with some stone tables and *naga*-head chairs. If you pass through a gap between two not very high, thickly vegetated rises, you've gone too far. People walk along this road with bundles of firewood and sacks of rice on their heads; if in doubt, inquire, though they will not, most likely, speak English. From the village on the hill the road leads down to a wide river, which must be crossed, then passes alongside some rice paddies. There are two more small creeks before a stone stairway leads up through the trees on the right to the village of Gomo.

Another way to reach Gomo is by motorbike,

but it will cost around Rp25,000 as the driver must carry the bike across rivers.

Vicinity Of Gomo
From the police station go down to the river crossing, then walk over one hill through rice paddies along a wide but sometimes unpaved and muddy road out of the forest to a hillside cultivated in sweet potatoes and taro. Here a path leads up past several huts on stilts to a village of three *adat* houses with carved lizard motifs. Another path leads to yet another village, with an enormous conventional wooden house. A path then takes you up through the bushes past some plots of dry rice; another rough path scrambles through some thick grass to a locked iron gate with spikes on top and barbed wire on both sides. Indonesians can squeeze through the bars, but Westerners must carry their large frames over the top without *sate*ing themselves. Inside the fence are dozens of stone tables at various heights around a stone courtyard. Stone chairs with as many as three *naga* heads sit among them, and two large monoliths stand at either end. Ferns grow up between the tables, and vines crawl around the moss-covered stonework. An enchanting, haunted place.

THE BATAK

Some scholars believe the word *batak* was originally a derogatory Old Malay term for "robber"; others translate it as "pig-eater." Another theory insists the word originates from Bataha, the name of a Karen village in the Burma/Siam area, the ancient home of the Batak people.

The sturdy rice-growing Batak live in fertile mountainous valleys extending up to 200 km north and 300 km south of Lake Toba. The Batak are shorter and heavier than the Minangkabau; they've kept their racial stock pure by living inland, and developed an early reputation for ferocity and cannibalism.

Because of mass migrations of Bataks seeking a better life in the lowland regions and Jakarta, modernization in the Batak homeland is slow. Their society is stubbornly traditional, the majority living in small, independent, self-sufficient, tightly knit villages. Many of the Batak's traditional agriculture and land-tenure practices, and thus their way of life, remain almost unchanged.

Well known for their warlike traditions, the Batak have provided modern-day Indonesia with a number of highly regarded military officers. These people also highly value tertiary education, the community sharing the expense of sending the brightest boys in the village to school in Medan or Jakarta. Many Batak are thus well placed in government, academia, and business circles. Batak are very gifted musicians and chorus singers, members of nationally popular bands. They're also some of the best chess players in the East; every village has its master. A barefoot peasant stalemated the Dutch World Champion in the Grand Hotel in Medan in 1939, a major event in Batak history.

The Batak are divided into a number of related ethnolinguistic groups. Though many of their customs are different, they all share the same cultural patterns. The Toba Batak is the only clan that strongly identifies with the name Batak. The word definitely has an unsavory stigma amongst other Indonesians, to whom it's almost a synonym for barbarism, since the Batak once practiced cannibalism and still eat dog cooked in its own blood, a practice repugnant to 90% of Indonesians.

HISTORY

Racially, the Batak are cousins to such "First Wave" tribes as the Igorots of the Philippines, the Dayaks of Kalimantan, and the Torajans of South Sulawesi. The Batak settled in Sumatra after fleeing Mongol warriors who invaded their highland homes in northern Thailand. Numerous cultural, linguistic, and physical indications of early Hindu contact include the Batak style of rice irrigation; their distinctive style of dwellings; the spinning wheel and cotton; chess; Hindu vocabulary, religious ideas, and script; and the use of water buffalo as plows. Several Karo tribes feature darker skin, evidence of South Indian blood.

The Batak tribes retained their own way of life right up to the middle of the 19th century, when Dutch and German missionaries discovered and began to convert them. Although some Batak groups were united under one *raja*, by the time the Dutch arrived they were beginning to evolve into a number of petty states. Their last king, Sisingamangaraja, died in battle against the Dutch in 1907. Today the Batak are still very conservative by nature; foreign elements are accepted only when they can be worked into the people's original cosmic views. Samosir Island was the last bastion of the Toba Batak, conquered by tourists in the early '70s.

Cannibalism

The only human flesh eaters on the island, the Batak were the infamous "headhunters of Sumatra" in tales of yore. Cannibalism was most prevalent among the Pakpak, although usually only token bits of flesh were eaten for ceremonial occasions, to obtain the attributes, luck, or courage of the victim. Herodotus, the Greek historian, first recorded the practice; Marco Polo in 1292 claimed the Batak ate their parents when they grew too old to work. Marsden, in 1783, wrote the first accurate account of cannibalism; when it was published it shocked the so-called civilized world.

Those judged guilty of incest, murder, thievery, or adultery were condemned to be eaten by

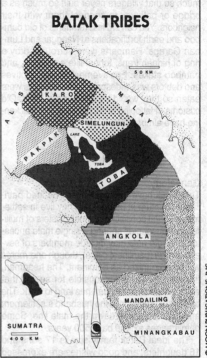

BATAK TRIBES

KARO

ALAS

SIMELUNGUN

PAKPAK

LAKE

TOBA

TOBA

ANGKOLA

MANDAILING

MINANGKABAU

SUMATRA
400 KM

MALAY

50 KM

© MOON PUBLICATIONS, INC.

their fellow villagers, the most degrading of all punishments. An old Batak curse went, "I pick the flesh of your relatives from between my teeth!" In these punitive feasts the victims were not passionately or vengefully killed, but devoured according to fixed ethical rules. Raffles reported in the 19th century, "for certain crimes, a criminal would be eaten alive. The flesh was sometimes eaten raw, or grilled and eaten with lime, salt, pepper, and a little rice. Human blood was drunk out of bamboo containers. Palms of the hands and soles of the feet were delicacies of the epicures." Though this practice largely ceased when the Batak converted to Islam and Christianity, some Batak have indulged in cannibalism in quite recent times.

Traditional Culture

Traditional Batak society was divided into three classes: nobles, peasants, and slaves. Villages were once extremely hostile to one another—so much so that villagers never built so much as a bridge or pathway to connect them with their neighbors. You can still find remnants of old bamboo and earth fortifications at Nanggar and Lumban Garaga. Ramparts were surrounded by a ring of hidden traps, tunnel-like entrances, and bamboo stakes. Enslavement of war captives and debtors was widespread, and enemies were eaten so they would be utterly obliterated. Old customs of tattooing and tooth filing and blackening have almost completely died out.

MODERN CULTURE

Genealogy

The Batak have the most clearly defined patrilineal structure in Indonesia. They live in settlements (*huta*) consisting of small clusters of multifamily households sharing a single male ancestor. A single *huta* may include members of several *marga* (patrilineal clans), though one *marga* will be recognized as dominant. The headman, the *marga-raja*, is responsible for seeing that each individual in the clan has land to work. The bride must move into the husband's settlement and land is passed down the male line. Some patrilineages extend back 500 years.

The ideal Batak family size is 17 sons and 16 daughters, and good wishes are expressed with the gesture of *hagabeon,* which means "have as many offspring as possible." Genealogies are followed intensely. When Batak meet, they rigorously *ertutur,* or cross-examine each other as to lineages and clan. All clan members must marry outside the clan; infant weddings were once commonplace. One *marga* is the bride-providing group and the other is the bride-receiving group. As in other Southeast Asian hilltribes, such as the Karen, the Batak feel the wife-giving group is superior to the wife-receiving group, and that a son ideally should marry his mother's brother's daughter. The tightness of the web of kinship is unbelievably strong amongst the Batak, frequently bringing more than 1,000 people together for weddings and funerals. To be absent could be dangerous to one's health, welfare, and social status.

Batak Women

Batak women are strong-spirited and robust, not as coy as many of their Indonesian sisters. See them smoking foot-long stogies in the rice fields of South Tapanuli, dressing their husbands up like dolls in the market towns of Lake Toba, and breaking out in vibrant hymns on the buses. Premarital purity is not nearly as important among the Batak as among the more puritan Muslims of Java. An old Batak proverb goes, "there is no dainty cake on which a fly fails to sit." Women are unbelievably forward. Actually, the Batak's open, honest directness is refreshing after the masked and refined feelings of the Javanese.

Religion

The Batak are animists with a veneer of Christianity or Islam covering complex and sophisticated beliefs. Little touched by the fervid Islam of the neighboring Minangkabau and Acehnese, two-thirds of the approximately 1.5 million Batak are Catholic or Protestant. Muslim Batak, mostly the Mandailing group, live in southern Batak territory.

The Batak were first converted by a fearless German missionary, Nommensen, who arrived in 1861 with only a Bible and a violin. Many of the older people to this day bear such German names as Luther, Bismarck, and Wilhelm, since nearly all the missionaries in those early days were German. Nommensen decreed the death sentence on the old religion when he persuaded the Dutch government to prohibit collective sacrificial celebrations (*bius*) and the playing of Batak musical instruments, wiping out in one blow their whole "pagan" world. This founder of the church is now buried in Balige, 30 km from Prapat, where there's a memorial marker. You'll often see his portrait on the walls of Batak churches.

Regardless of their nominal faith, half the population still believes in spirits of dead ancestors; sacred trees, stones, and places; and a Hindu-like pantheon of higher deities (*begu*). All Batak trace their descent from one Si Radja Batak, an ancestor-hero of supernatural origin born on a holy mountain near Lake Toba. This god-man gave the Batak their sacred laws; his offspring founded the first *marga.*

The Batak recognize an Upper, Middle, and Lower world, the seats of the gods, men, and dragons respectively. Mula Jati is the creator and Lord of the Universe, linking the three worlds. This lord has a dual nature, manifesting both good and evil and male and female aspects. Decisions must be inspired and sanctioned by ancestors, so elders sit on ancestral stone chairs for communal meetings, channeling the wisdom of the ages. Male priests and wizards (*datu*), skilled in sorcery and the use of natural potions, are also specialists in occult knowledge and divination, using Hindu zodiac and magical tables.

Tondi (soul stuff) determines contentment, temporal wealth, and power; at death it departs to dwell in another organism. Spirits of the dead are contacted ritually through female mediums (*sibaso*). Only in the 1920s could the Dutch compel the Batak to bury their dead. They once kept corpses for days under their houses until, at final rites, they drained the decaying body with bamboo runners. The remnants were then placed in large stone sarcophagi, which you can still see close to the villages.

THE ARTS

Architecture
Older settlements feature a distinctive type of house found nowhere else in Indonesia. Raised on piles soaked for years in mud, these houses are so sturdy they often last 100 years. With not a single nail used, just rope and wooden pegs, the gable ends of these dynamic structures are richly ornamented with mosaics and woodcarvings of serpents, double spirals, lizards, life-giving female breasts, and elon-

gated dark-colored monsters' heads (*singa*) with bulging eyes. The walls are made from heavy planks and the roof rises high, often sloping inward toward the center. Some of these steep, saddle-shaped roofs are made of palm thatch (*atap*), others of bright new galvanized iron. The traditional building stays cool indoors even during the hottest part of the day.

In each house live up to 12 families, each in an apartment (*bilik*) along the two outer sides. The space between is used as a public corridor where children play, men work, women cook, and people visit. A village communal hall (*sopo* or *bale*) serves as council hall, trophy room, and sleeping place for boys and unmarried men.

Language And Literature
All Batak dialects are intelligible to one another, though esoteric idioms are sometimes used by priests or female mourners. When ordering tea in Batak country, call it *tes*, as *teh* means "feces" in Batak. Most homeland Batak speak an almost remedial form of Bahasa Indonesia.

Although there is a native writing system, Surat Batak, no chronicles have been written in that script. Transmitted down through the generations, it's used only as part of the decorative motif on handicrafts, and has little application in everyday life. *Pustaha,* the only "books" which exist, deal mostly with spells and divination, and are rendered on bark, bamboo, and, nowadays, paper. These form the most important part of Batak written literature.

Batak palace

Music And Dance

Village men make their own music. A *gondang* band consists of cloth-covered metal gongs of different sizes, clarinet-type instruments, and two-stringed lutes made of palm fibers. The Toba Batak play a whole row of drums tuned to different pitches. Beaten with sticks, they make a zany sound to Western ears. The Batak are renowned for their powerfully expressive, ethereal hymn singing.

Batak women's traditional dancing is ritualistic and slow. Toba Batak wear turbans and long shawls across one shoulder, bobbing up and down; it's very confined dancing, repetitious, almost solemn. The only truly traditional folk dance left is trance dancing, similar to Balinese trance dances—the big difference is that on Bali they're still part of the people's religion. Dance festivals occur on certain dates fixed each year by the priest-doctors. In one, a pony is tied to a stake in the middle of the road; male dancers form a circle around it, trance dancing to gongs and drums. This ritual dates from the time a sacred breed of horse was regularly sacrificed. Today there are offerings of *selendang* (dance scarves).

Si Gale Gale

The protagonist in this dance-drama is an almost life-sized human puppet called *si gale gale*. This dance is restricted to the island of Samosir and villages on the south shore of Lake Toba. When a child dies, in order that he or she may enter the realm of the dead and not haunt the living, musicians play for the *si gale gale*, which is jerked to life. With its movable palm-wood head, eyeballs, and hands, the marionette moves through grotesque sudden movements while dancing with the villagers. Tears are produced from sponges set behind the eyes.

Each movement of the puppet is controlled by hidden strings which lead into a box mounted below the puppet. A man sits at the other end of the box, his hands concealed, manipulating the strings. The puppet's face is carved in the image of the deceased. The *si gale gale* is wheeled from villager to villager, embracing friends and relatives in its hard wooden arms as tears roll down its cheeks. Unforgettable.

It's difficult to find a genuine *si gale gale* performance on Samosir or even view a puppet in a museum, though an excellent specimen is on display in Jakarta's Wayang Museum. Tourist performances are staged at Tomok and Simanindo once weekly; ask at the tourist office and hotels for details.

Crafts

The art of the Batak is an expression of their religious ideas, and is deeply concerned with magic. The Batak are sophisticated in the arts of metalworking, tie-dying, woodcarving, boatmaking, and bone, shell, and bark fabrication. All show a mixture of Dongson and Indian influences. In the area around Lake Toba, black and white straw is utilized for a profusion of craft items. Tourists pay up to Rp150,000 for a Batak sword, but you also hear starting prices of Rp40,000 for genuine metal antiques. Buy carefully—new artifacts of dubious quality are turned out for tourist consumption.

Prices and quality of Batak textiles are disappointing after all the beautiful *ikat sarungs* of eastern Nusatenggara. Batak *ikat* comes in traditional blue, black, or maroon cloth called *ulos*. This cloth, still important in marriage, birth, and funeral ceremonies, has a central dark panel where the *ikat* is dyed; two white smaller sections top and bottom feature woven patterns of darker thread.

Batak woodcarving incorporates magic signs and fertility symbols. Figureheads of carved hornbills adorn boats, and sorcerors' wooden staffs feature weird figures climbing up the whole length, like grotesque miniature totem-poles. Old *pustaha,* magic augury books of bark or bamboo, cost up to Rp200,000 in the tourist shops of Medan and Prapat.

LAKE TOBA

Lake Toba is the largest lake in Southeast Asia (1,707 square km) and one of the deepest (450 meters) in the world—the Lake Geneva of Southeast Asia. The mythical homeland of the Batak people, it was formed as a result of a mammoth volcanic explosion, believed to be the greatest in the history of the planet. So mighty was this titanic eruption, a veil of incandescent ash wrapped around the earth, plunging it into the darkness of the last ice age about 75,000 years ago. Today surrounded on all sides by pine-covered beaches, steep mountain slopes and cliffs, with Samosir Island sitting right in the middle, Lake Toba is a spellbinding sight. Besides its beauty, this area is also celebrated for its traditional villages, *adat* houses, and rich Batak culture. It's relaxing, relatively inexpensive, cool and pleasant for walking and bike riding, and a nice place to recover from marathon bus rides from Java.

Toba Batak

The best-known Batak subgroup. One million strong, they are considered the most aggressive, direct, and flamboyant of all Batak groups, and proud of it. The original tribe, the Toba Batak have the purest lineages and speak the most uncorrupted dialect. They can trace their family lines back 10 generations, to a time when any stranger who stared upon them was killed and eaten. This fate probably befell the first missionaries in the area; the last recorded instance of cannibalism took place in 1906.

Most Toba Batak live around Lake Toba. Eighty percent are Christian, but their religion is mixed strongly with ancestor worship. Many isolated Toba Batak tribes living on the lake's west side still haven't had much contact with the outside. Entrance gates of some fortress-like Toba Batak villages are still locked at night against hostile intruders.

Getting There

Coming from the south, your first view of Lake Toba will be from the hills above Balige, off the southeast shore of the lake 114 km north of Sibolga; Prapat is another 60 km on a good road. From Medan the direct route through Tebingtinggi and Siantar to Prapat takes five hours (Rp3000, 176 km). A longer but more interesting route (about 260 km) goes via Brastagi, Sipisopiso Waterfall, Pematang Purba (location of a *raja*'s palace), and the Simarjarunjung Lookout. Arriving at Toba, travelers usually head straight for Tuk Tuk village on Samosir Island in the middle of the lake, where accommodations are widely available at good prices and the atmosphere is relaxed.

Transportation

Many lakeside villages have market days; by using market ferries you can hop from village to village. Some of the *losmen* on Samosir Island charter excursion boats and offer roundtrip tours of lakeside villages for around Rp6000 per person, usually leaving Ambarita for Tomok (to pick up more people), then out to the hot springs near Pangururan, and finally back to Ambarita via Tomok.

misty morning, near Lake Toba

J. WEISS

PRAPAT

A busy, congested lakeside resort mostly spoiled by tourism. It has a cool, dry climate, pine-covered beaches, and spectacular views. Evenings are pleasant, whether sitting on a balcony or walking back from the cinema. Prapat is difficult to avoid as it's the main town on Lake Toba and the principal embarkation point for ferries to Samosir.

Most of the upscale tourists are Indonesians and Chinese from Medan and Singapore, while the international travelers come from the post-hippie budget set. Thus Prapat is a place where affluent brown-skinned nationals stay in the higher-priced hotels lining the lakefront while the Caucasians collect in the cheapies along the main highway.

Upon entering Prapat, you must pay Rp200 even if you only want to go to Samosir. A tourist office is located near the arched entrance. Drop in at the Batak Cultural Center, Jl. Josep Sinaga 19, to see what's brewing; dances and musical performances are usually staged on Saturday night (Rp1250). Enthusiastic Batak singing and other forms of entertainment are staged on occasion at Hotel Prapat.

Accommodations

Prapat accommodations are handy if you arrive late or are leaving early on the 0600 bus for Bukittinggi; otherwise just head straight for Samosir, where accommodations are cheaper, quieter, and more idyllic. Most hotels in Prapat cater to wealthy holiday tourists from Medan, Singapore, and Malaysia who like to stay as close to the lakeshore as possible. Many feature bars, restaurants, room service, private baths, nice furnishings, private beach access, and hot water. Bargain if it's off-season or a weekday.

Rather spartan hotels line the main Trans-Sumatra Highway (Jl. Sisingamangaraja); those above restaurants and/or travel agencies are the cheapest (around Rp5000). Buses and trucks roll by all night long honking their horns, so avoid noisy front rooms over the street. Try to find a place off the road—any road. From the gateway, it's about a 30-minute (1.5-km) walk to the main ferry landing over the hill, or take a *bemo* (Rp200).

At the Medan end of town is the **Sudi Mampir,** Jl. Sisingamangaraja 84, nearly opposite the street down to the lake. The rooms at **PT Andilo Nancy** are dusty, grubby, and noisy. Purchase bus tickets here. Walk through the

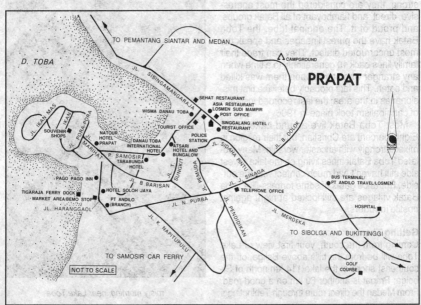

building to the water's edge where ferries leave for Samosir. At the Balige end of town are **Hotel Singgalang** (with a good restaurant) and **Hotel Saudara,** both Rp6000 s, Rp10,000 d.

The old travelers' standby is **Pago Pago Inn,** Jl. Haranggaol 50, between Hotel Prapat and the Tigaraja ferry terminal. The nearby **Soloh Jaya** offers terrific views high over the lake; Rp12,000-25,000 for rooms with bath—a big hotel with spacious verandas.

Higher-priced accommodations (Rp25,000-35,000) include breakfast and full bath, sometimes with hot water. Look around. On Jalan Pulau Samosir, try **Wisma Danau Toba,** nos. 3-6, tel. (0622) 41302 or 41303; and **Atsari Hotel and Bungalow** at no. 9, tel. 41219 or 41725. The **Budi Mulia,** Jl. P. Samosir 9, tel. 41564 or 41465, is a comfortable, moderately priced hotel. Another is the **Tarabunga Hotel,** Jl. Sibigo 2, tel. 41665, 41666, or 41700, with quite basic rooms for the price asked.

Of the several first-class, three-star hotels, **Danau Toba International Hotel** is the best value. On Jl. P. Samosir 9, tel. 41216 or 41485, it features beautiful a/c bungalows for Rp53,000 d right on top of a hill with fantastic lake views, especially from the outside bar. **Natour Hotel Prapat,** Jl. Marihat 1, tel. 41012 or 41019, is a gracious old Dutch hotel with a *tempo doeloe*-style lobby and big lovely rooms overlooking the lake. It's clean, comfortable, with hot water, private baths, and a good, reasonably priced restaurant with Indonesian/Chinese food. Double rooms cost Rp69,000.

Food

Cheapest are the Chinese and Indonesian restaurants along the main highway (Jl. Sisingamangaraja) where you can eat for Rp3500-5000—**Brastagi, Asia, Hong Kong, Paten, Sehat.** At the Asia, one dish will almost feed two. The Chinese-style **Bali Restaurant,** next to the Hong Kong, offers superior food at the same prices as the others, though it sounds like a blowtorch every time they start up the wok. The **Singgalang Hotel** serves a nice ham omelette for Rp4000. Also good food at **B Karo** on Jl. Haranggaol; try the *nasi padang* places along this street too. The market by Tigaraja dock, and other stalls up along the main road (Jl. Sisingamangaraja), sell a wide selection of fruit.

Shopping And Services

Saturday is the big market day, when Pasar Tigaraja by the ferry dock swarms with Batak from outlying villages. Not to be missed. Woodcarvings, leather goods, curios, and the usual tourist fare are on sale at relatively high prices. Souvenir shops also line the highway selling a great variety of overpriced handicrafts: clothing, *batik,* striking *kain ulor* (usually presented as a wedding gift or spread over someone who's ill), woodcarving, and other Batak crafts.

On Jl. Sisingamangaraja is the post office. The telephone office is located on Jl. Josep Sinaga in back of town. Bring sufficient cash, as moneychangers and banks consistently offer poor rates. The nearest bank is 44 km away in Pulau Siantar. Travel agencies (PT Andilo) and a few hotels in Prapat and in Tuk Tuk will change money.

Butar Sinaga (a.k.a. Mr. Jungle) conducts trekking tours of the area, specializing in orchid treks. Contact him through the Post Restaurant.

Getting There

Merpati schedules a Saturday flight from Medan to the Sibisa Airstrip, 16 km south of Prapat.

From Brastagi, take a bus first to Kabanjahe (Rp150), then a Simas/Sepadan bus to the Pulau Siantar terminal (Rp1000), then a bus to Prapat (Rp500). If you arrive too late, the last ferry may have departed for Samosir. The bus pulls into Prapat on the main highway south. Don't believe anyone who tells you the last ferry has already departed in their desperate efforts to install you in a hotel. Continue into the village and check the main ferry terminal at Tigaraja; the last ferry departs around 1800 or 1900.

From Medan, frequent buses drive the four hours (Rp3000) to Prapat via Tebingtinggi; board a PMH bus at Medan's Sisingamangaraja station. The bus from Medan usually stops in front of PT Andilo's on the main road. Many travelers anxious to reach Bukittinggi just rent a room (Rp5000) for the night above or in back of one of the many travel agents on this main road and head out of town the next morning. In Medan hire-taxis to Prapat are available at the airport, Polonia Hotel, train station, and taxi stands. The cost is about Rp50,000 one-way. From Sibolga, frequent buses make the five or six hour trip up to Prapat. From Bukittinggi, take an ANS bus (Rp10,000), which completes the trip in an amazing 15 hours.

Getting Around

A *bemo* anywhere in town costs Rp200. Parking along Jl. Sisingamangaraja—the heart of the town—is now banned to smooth the flow of traffic. Paddleboats run Rp2000 per hour, scooters (mini-speedboats) Rp20,000 per hour. You can often arrange boating and water-skiing through your hotel. Chartered speedboats are expensive—Rp20,000 to Tuk Tuk, first price. Always bargain. Or hire a whole ferry for 50 people for Rp25,000 per hour. Loaded down with bananas, women in bright scarves, children, and merchandise, the public ferries have more character than charters.

Getting Away

The Tigaraja dock in the market area is only a 30-minute walk from the archway into town. About five boats per day go to Samosir Island (Rp800, 30 minutes). The other ferry terminal at Ajibata, over the hill, runs regular ferries at 0830, 1130, 1430, 1730, and 2030. Most travel to Tuk Tuk, then on to Ambarita or Tomok. Passengers are frequently dropped off at the dock of their *losmen*; be sure you get on the right boat. If you take the last ferry to Samosir, someone on the boat may tell you the place of your choice is full, then offer to take you somewhere else. Don't you believe them.

Less frequent ferries depart for other lakeside villages around the island: Simanindo, Nainggolan, Onan Runggu, Pangururan. On Saturday, market day, the dock is wall-to-wall with ferries, with continuous departures until 1300. Nearer the entrance gate to Prapat, behind PT Andilo, is a dock used by tourist boats (Rp800) with more irregular departures; they usually head for Tomok, Ambarita, and Simanindo.

Though the blue-green waters of the lake are normally calm, winds can whip up waves like a stormy ocean. Morning is the best time for lake travel as waves often appear in the afternoon. Rough waters are most likely from June to September.

Those considering a long-distance bus out of Prapat will hear a lot of nightmare stories about promises of an a/c bus, free snack, two bus drivers, sightseeing stops, free entrances to a museum . . . then the reality of a tiny non-a/c bus with no leg space, no free snack, no stop at a museum, and one bus driver who roars along the road like a madman and only stops for petrol. To prevent these horrors, visit the Prapat station and check out the bus before you travel. There are now numerous long-distance bus companies and their vehicles vary from okay to downright dangerous. You could pay Rp12,000 for a rattletrap when Rp9000 would have purchased a safer bus. Night buses can be cold, so take a sweater, sleeping bag, and warm socks.

Obtaining a good seat is your number one priority; don't get relegated to the back seat, which is bumpy at best. Next, listen to the sound of the engine and check the color of the exhaust. Once satisfied, buy your ticket. Try to book at least three days ahead. Among the travel agents on the main highway the most reliable, especially for domestic air travel in Indonesia, is **Adi Sinaga,** Jl. Sisingamangaraja 87, tel. (0622) 41246.

Long-distance buses leave at least every hour up until the early afternoon. If you take the night bus for Sibolga and Bukittinggi, you'll miss the beautiful jungle and mountain scenery along the road.

An alternative is local buses. *Losmen* are available in all the larger towns—Tarutung, Padangsidempuan, Lubuksikaping—on the highway south. If you take local buses, expect delays to load sacks of rice, meal breaks, and stops to repair flat tires or tie wire around broken water pumps. To reach Brastagi you have to transfer at Siantar and Kabanjahe. For the distant villages off the main roads, be ready for spine-jarring, gut-twisting, teeth-chattering, bone-knocking, eye-popping, pot-holed mountain roads. Try this experience on the "back way" to Medan via Tele. Sit in the front seats adjacent to the driver, even if you have to wait 30 minutes for the next bus. It's worth it.

To Bukittinggi, two companies (PT Andilo and Goraharaja, tel. 41246) operate a/c "tourist buses" on Monday, Wednesday, Friday, and Saturday for Rp20,000 including a/c and snack. Rp13,000 for the non-a/c non-"tourist" bus. Buses should start at 0600 or 0700, stop at a few points such as Panti Hot springs and Bonjol on the equator, and arrive around 1830. The bulletin board at Wisma Sibayak in Brastagi is full of warnings about PT Andilo; Goraharaja's service doesn't get many rave reviews either. Just because it's a special "tourist bus" doesn't guarantee you'll get there any quicker. Seldom does the a/c actually work and one traveler reported staggering into Bukittinggi 30 hours, two breakdowns, and a landslide later.

VICINITY OF PRAPAT

Balige
An attractive market town on Toba's southeast shore, 60 km south of Prapat. The buildings in the market feature high, sweeping, traditional-style roofs. Balige is also known for its Batak cloth, available in the market; Friday is market day. Traditional Batak and Chinese food is available in restaurants on the main street. The Batak king **Raja Si Singamangaraja**, who died in battle opposing the Dutch and became a national hero, is buried just outside of town—a tomb of great veneration. To get there, go 2.5 km toward Sibolga, then one-half km down a lane. This *raja*'s former palace is in Bakara to the southwest of Balige, and is now being restored.

Waterfalls
Northeast of the southern shore of Lake Toba, upriver from Balige and 30 km from Porsea, is the impressive Siguragura Falls on the Asahan River—the only one of several rivers in these highlands with its source in Lake Toba. At 200 meters, Siguragura is one of the highest natural falls in Southeast Asia. You have to obtain a *surat ijin* from Inalum Co., Jl. Palang Merah (fourth floor), Medan, to see it.

Sipisopiso Waterfall lies at the northern end of Lake Toba. From the 120-meter-high lookout point above this beautiful falls is a 360-degree panorama of the waterfall, the precipitous valley below, Tongging, Lake Toba, and mountains—an unforgettable sight. From Brastagi take a *bemo* to Kabanjahe, then ask for the bus to Situnggaling (30 minutes). From there it's a one-hour walk to the falls.

Haranggaol
Get a stupendous view above this picturesque market town just before the road from Kabanjahe begins its twists and turns down to the shore of the lake. Haranggaol is a delightful place, one not to be missed. Its strategic location prompts one of the largest bulk markets in the area (Monday): Batak tribes come in from the surrounding areas, and shoppers arrive from as far away as Pulau Siantar. *Ulos* fabrics here cost half what they do in Tomok: starting price Rp75,000 for an old *ulos* (called *sadum sipirok*); for the newer ones the price starts at Rp40,000. Watch for slit thieves.

Haranggaol includes several *losmen* (average Rp5000 d) but there's not much to write home about, though a smart new hotel occupies the main square. Several good Padang restaurants here, but eat early as food becomes scarce after dark. *Besok ada* is not much comfort when you're starving. Buses arrive daily from Medan (140 km), Pulau Siantar (68 km), and Kabanjahe (51 km). The turnoff for Haranggaol is five km south of Seribudolok, then it's 10 km down to the lake.

From Haranggoal, there are many buses to Prapat. Market ferries from Haranggaol leave on Monday at about 1200 to 1330 for Ambarita, Pangururan, Tigaras, Simanindo, and other lakeside villages. The fare is around Rp1500. Other ferries leave Monday and Thursday at 1600. Since ferries very much run on *jam karet,* the fastest way to get to Samosir might be to take the ferry first to Prapat, then board another ferry to the island (at least five per day).

Purba
Fifteen km northeast of Haranggoal. The king of Purba's palace is one of the best preserved in Batakland. Your guide is one of the 80 grandsons of the penultimate king, and judging from his behavior is equally lecherous. He speaks good English and is quite informative. After seeing this fine palace, you can give Simanindo a miss. Few visitors.

SAMOSIR ISLAND

The original home of the Toba Batak, Samosir Island offers a cool, sunny climate, superb hiking and swimming, royal tombs, dramatic Batak architecture, stonecarvings, and very reasonable accommodations and food. Most Toba Batak live either on Samosir Island or south of Lake Toba. This is a musically gifted tribe; a feast of continuous music greets you either from the cassettes of the young or old Batak playing flutes, guitars, xylophones, and drums.

Samosir is a more relaxing and inexpensive place to stay than Prapat—quieter, with cleaner water. No a/c, but you don't need it. If you plan to stay a while, bring good books. Also bring cash; exchange rates on the island are bad. Watch your gear and close your windows at night, as there is theft from rooms all over Tuk Tuk and Ambarita. Though in July 1989 a Dutchman was killed during a robbery, violent crime is almost unknown on Samosir. During the rainy season the mosquitos are vicious. No matter what your religion, attend church on Samosir; the ardor with which the people worship and sing in praise of Christ is something to see.

The Land

Wherever you stand on the shore of Lake Toba, you see this 630-square-km island in the middle. The island is technically a peninsula, connected in the west by a narrow isthmus at the foot of Gunung Belirang. In 1906, the Dutch dug a canal so boats could circle the island. Since then, this channel has silted up and today only the smallest boats can make it through. Samosir was once a piece of a plateau at the same elevation as the cliffs surrounding the lake, but a cataclysmic volcanic eruption blew open a 30- by 90-km depression, collapsing the piece of crust that is now the island. It didn't come straight down, however; the surface slopes gently into the waters on the west side while the east edge forms 500-meter-high cliffs. Some volcanologists believe the ash generated by this terrible eruption may have blotted out the sun and helped plunge the planet into the last great ice age.

Stonework

The Toba Batak interred their dead in stone urns and three-meter-long stone sarcophagi carved in the shape of squatting gargoyles, the faces astoundingly similar to Easter Island statues. Elaborately carved stone heads (*singa*) with three horns and huge round devil eyes are also seen; there's an especially fine one at Tomok. These skull-caskets (*parholian*) contain the skulls of high-ranking Batak dead. In former times, honored heads were first buried for a year, then dug up, dyed red, and ceremoniously placed in coffins. From time to time they were removed so villagers could dance with them and press food to their mouths in festive memorial services conducted by the light of the moon.

More recent are Batak tribal mausoleums, solid mudbrick mounds containing polished bones and topped with rough-cut wooden crosses. Contemporary tombs are sometimes found in the form of a brightly colored Batak house or a lifelike statue of the deceased—see the Soldier's Grave between Tuk Tuk and Ambarita.

The island is also dotted with architecturally magnificent walls fashioned from the colossal cliffs and boulders on the eastern shore. The ruins of these walls circle villages, houses, courtyards, and granaries, keeping them solitary and protected. Carved stone slabs were arranged in a circle to seat the *rajas* and *gurus* (priests) who cast spells and meted out life and death. Basrelief carving and massive statuary were positioned exactly to ward off enemies and evil spirits. Sometimes potions brewed from the remains of visitors were placed nearby to amplify the powers of these statues.

Rumah Adat

Samosir has many of these traditional houses; some can be rented by visitors. The houses are mounted on posts to catch breezes and provide space underneath for firewood and livestock. The swinging curves, sloping sides, and sweeping upturned roofs are reminiscent of sailing ships. The swayback roof sheds water quickly, though now nearly all are made of corrugated metal instead of the traditional thatch. Decorations in the roof gables represent faces of residents looking down in respect on all visitors; conversely, doors are low, forcing guests to bow in respect as they enter. Half a dozen families may

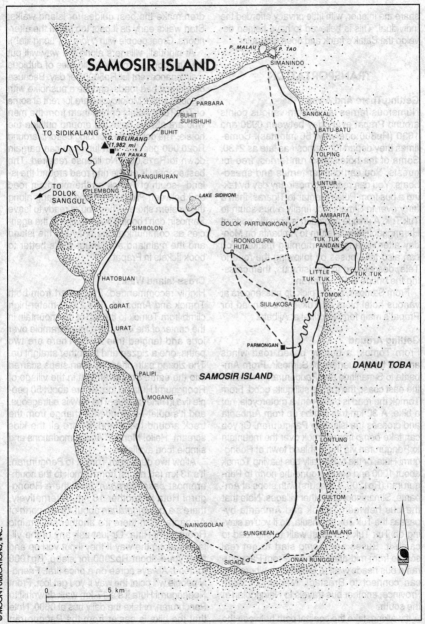

SAMOSIR ISLAND

TO SIDIKALANG

TO DOLOK SANGGUL

G. BELIRANG
(1,982 m)
AIR PANAS

P. MALAU
P. TAO
SIMANINDO

PARBARA
BUHIT SUHISHUHI
BUHIT

PANGURURAN

LEMBONG
SIMBOLON

LAKE SIDIHONI

SANGKAL
BATU-BATU
TOLPING
UNTUR

DOLOK PARTUNGKOAN
ROONGGURNI HUTA

AMBARITA
TUK TUK PANDAN

HATOBUAN
GORAT
URAT

LITTLE TUK TUK
TUK TUK

SIULAKOSA

TOMOK

PALIPI
MOGANG

SAMOSIR ISLAND

DANAU TOBA

PARMONGAN

LONTUNG

NAINGGOLAN

GULTOM

SUNGKEAN
SITAMLANG

SIGAOL
ONAN RUNGGU

0   5 km

© MOON PUBLICATIONS, INC.

share the interior, with little privacy afforded the individual. This is believed to have helped develop the Batak's frank and open character.

TRANSPORTATION

Getting There And Away

Numerous ferries leave from various points around Prapat every day between 0930 and 1830 (Rp800 one-way, 50 minutes). Sometimes they depart for Samosir as late as 2130. Some of the hotels also run ferries, free for guests. You can charter ferries and speedboats. You can reach Samosir any day by taking a bus from Pulau Siantar to Tigaras, then a ferry over to Simanindo, finally a bus south to Tuk Tuk. A unique approach is from the north at Haranggaol; ferries return to Ambarita on Monday after Haranggaol's morning market. You can also take buses by following the road to Tele, descending to the isthmus, then crossing the bridge to Pangururan.

From Samosir, ferries pick up passengers at various hotel piers on Tuk Tuk and head for Prapat's main ferry terminal at Ajibata.

Getting Around

From Tomok, a bumpy paved road winds around three-quarters of Samosir. From Ambarita to Simanindo and Pangururan, and along the east coast, the road is still quite good. From Tomok the road is bad—rent a motorcycle, not a bike. A 30-km trail climbs up from Ambarita and crosses the island to Pangururan. Or you can take *bemo* from Tomok over the mountain to Pangururan via the highland town of Roonggurni Huta, or the twice-daily bus leaving Tomok about 1000 and going around the north to Pangururan (Rp1200, 1.5 hours) with stops at Ambarita, Simanindo, and other villages. Note that the bus between Tomok and Ambarita bypasses the Tuk Tuk peninsula, so if you're staying on Tuk Tuk you must walk to this road to catch it. Buses and *bemo* start to get real scarce from mid-afternoon on. From Pangururan a bus heads west to Sidikalang, where you can connect to Brastagi, Medan, or Aceh Province; another bus travels to Nainggolan in the south.

If walking, take the coastal path between the towns, more picturesque than the road. Children make the best guides for island walks. Start walks early as it gets too hot in the afternoons. Greet people with *"Horas!"* ("Long life!").

At nightfall, villagers along the way will put you up (donate Rp4000). Bicycles of dubious maintenance rent for Rp5000 per day. Because of decrepit bad roads, choose a pushbike with a good saddle. Motorcycles are for rent at some of Tuk Tuk's hotels or hire them from the men who are always hovering around outside the hotels. The going rate including petrol is around Rp20,000 per day; with luck you can bargain down to Rp15,000. No license required. The best scenery is on the ring road around the island—south of Tomok on the mountain road and between Pangururan and Mogang along the western shore. When you're ready to leave Samosir, don't book a ticket at one of the agencies as communications between the island and the mainland are tenuous. It's better to book tickets in Prapat.

Cross-Island Walk

Highly recommended. Paths start from both Tomok and Ambarita. The 1,600-meter-high climb from Tomok to the top of the mountain in the center of the island is a mudscramble over logs and tangled tree roots. There are two paths, one a zigzag and the other straight up. The zigzag path offers wooden steps scarred into the earth. Stay overnight in the village of Roonggurni Huta on top, where about 50 people live in nine houses. The view is outrageous, and it's quiet—a wonderful change from the track around the island, where all the kids scream "Hello! Money!" Accommodations and simple food available.

Allow two days from Tomok to Pangururan. It's 13 km (six hours) from Tomok to the southernmost *pasanggrahan*; from there Roonggurni Huta is another 16 km. Alternatively, there's a *pasanggrahan* about 16 km north of Ambarita; from there it's another six km into Roonggurni Huta. Or just ask any of the villagers along the way if they'll put you up and feed you—about Rp2000 for sleep, Rp1000 for food. Always agree on a price first. Friendly people will point the way if you get lost. From Roonggurni Huta it's a 17-km walk downhill to Pangururan, or take the daily bus at 0600. Note that the hike is easier from the Pangururan side because the climb is not as steep.

Lake Cruises

On Sunday and Wednesday sightseeing cruises depart Tuk Tuk for the hot springs across from Pangururan on the other side of the island, with stops at Ambarita and Simanindo. The enjoyable all-day trip, which includes non-stop music and a floating restaurant, costs Rp10,000. Because the canal is silted up, the boat can't cruise completely around Samosir, so it just does the north side. Guys come around the different *losmen* to ask if anyone wants to go. You can also rent, from a few *losmen,* a mahogany dugout to tour the island.

TOMOK

A traditional village noted for its old stone coffins, Tomok is nine km and 45 minutes across the lake from Prapat. At the intersection of the main and dock roads, climb the steps to the top of a small hill. A huge *hariam* tree houses the spirit of Raja Sidabutar, pre-Christian head of an early tribe. The tree was planted close to his carved tomb 180 years ago on the anniversary of his death. The carved statue of a woman with a coconut shell on her head represents Sidabutar's queen. Mysteriously, the third tomb also bears a woman's face. It is said she was Sidabutar's lover, whom the king said should be killed on the day he died, so they could enter the afterlife together. His orders were followed, and she was allowed her own tomb in the royal cemetery. Her tomb was smeared with her blood; the crimson splotches can still be seen. Nearby are statues and stone chairs. Inland past dozens of souvenir stands is the Museum of King Soributu Sidabutar in a traditional house. Farther inland is another graveyard with stone coffins and old trees.

Accommodations And Food

Just south of Tomok's boat dock is **Silalahi Accommodation and Restaurant. Toba Beach Hotel** is expensive but offers good Indonesian food; it's more cocooned from the island's life, whereas at Silalahi you live right with the family. **Roy's Accommodation,** only 50 meters south of the ferry, has eight double rooms for Rp5000 d. Lots of *kampung* atmosphere, friendly service. Food in the adjacent restaurant is clean, with a variety of European and Indonesian

meals. Hang out and drink *tuak* with local musicians across the road; evenings are filled with music and laughter. Roy also has a phone.

Tomok offers a few *warung* and a weekly market.

Crafts

Over 200 stands sell artifacts, textiles, clothing, Batak calendars, magic medicine staffs, *pustaha* augury books (Rp10,000), whole carved doors (Rp150,000), two-stringed mandolins, and "antiques" made while you wait. Prices go up when the tourist boats disgorge their cargo, so bargain intensely. Young girls and old grannies weave *ulos* cloths in their booths; better quality blankets cost Rp25,000 (Rp40,000 starting price). The older colorfast ones are Rp350,000-500,000. Better prices for textiles on the other side of the island in Pangururan.

TUK TUK

Tuk Tuk is located on a small peninsula five km and a one-hour stroll from Tomok. Here you'll find the island's best selection of low-priced lodgings and restaurants. Although it's getting touristy, with building everywhere, Tuk Tuk is still quieter and more private than Tomok, and offers frequent ferry connections. You can still find a Batak house for Rp2000 with *mandi*. If you go to bed early, you'll miss some of the best music of your life, especially on Saturday nights—buy a bottle of *arak bangkilo* and join the outdoor groups. Climb up on the grassy plateau between Tuk Tuk and the mountain: sweeping view, perfect meditation venue, weird trees.

Accommodations And Food

The cheaper places are the best deal, and the food is good all over Tuk Tuk. The best way to choose a *losmen* is just look around—there's a very wide choice. **Sibayak,** on the Ambarita side, has good food and the people are friendly. **Karidin's** offers comfortable rooms in traditional Batak houses (Rp4000 d), delicious meals, plus a beach nearby—a really nice place to stay. **Losmen Romplan** is gifted with a good reputation, so it's crowded even in the slow season. Bungalows with balcony on the lake with *mandi* and shower cost Rp6000; the small restaurant has fine food. The owner and his German wife speak good English. Rent a motorbike for Rp15,000 per day including petrol; free canoes available.

The **Matahari** receives mixed reviews: some say the bungalows with *mandi* (Rp7000 d, or Rp5000 after bargaining) are okay, others report stories like the manager threatening several guests with a crowbar if they didn't pay a demanded Rp75,000 for a broken door lock. **Bernard's** offers the same price and quality as the Matahari, with rooms overlooking one of the nicest beaches on the island. The **Silintong Hotel** is one of the best on the island and costs only Rp26,000 d (includes breakfast). The restaurant, though, has expensive and awful food. **Pepy's**, between Carolina's and Ferenhi, has very good food; get in on the *rijstaffel* (Rp4000 per person). The excellent "smorgasbord" at **Marfis** costs Rp15,000 for two, Rp24,000 for four. Order the day before.

In a class of its own is **Carolina's** with 30 rooms and Batak-style bungalows on the slope of a small hill overlooking the lake. Truly luxurious motel-style units with hot water are Rp45,000; cheap and simple rooms are Rp7500 with outside *mandi* or Rp12,5000 d with inside *mandi*. The food is reasonable and imaginative—don't miss the breakfast with freshly baked bread—and the service is good. Carolina's has its own pier and a private swimming cove. July and August are very busy so make reservations by phone (tel. 41520) or letter. Rooms at **Uross**, in back of Carolina's, go for Rp3000 with *mandi* and shower, although water is available only on request.

Judita, a short walk from the Toledo, has quiet Batak houses and extra rooms, a charming family, free canoe, and complete menu serving delicious food. Plain rooms with sparse furniture cost Rp2500 d. The **Toledo Hotel** (Rp45,000), which takes package tourists from Singapore and Medan, features hot water, a nice beach, and paddleboats for rent. The barbed wire is an eyesore, but the comfort level is top class. Free ferry service to Ambarita in the morning. The capable proprietress, Mrs. Tobing, is the niece of the Batak national hero, Sisingamangaraja. A good, cheap restaurant is **Antonius**. Try the "Pineapple a la Thorel," a big hollowed out pineapple filled with pieces of different kinds of fruit (avocado, banana, papaya, pineapple), topped with ground nuts and coconut, only Rp750. Rent sportsbikes, mountain bikes, and normal bikes for Rp5000 per day.

VICINITY OF TUK TUK

Little Tuk Tuk
This village on a small cove is a 15-minute walk west of Tuk Tuk. Stay at **Lesley's** (Rp2500 d). John at **Horas Accommodation** has a bookstore where guests may borrow books. Very tranquil location and a good cheap restaurant specializing in German goulash. John also runs a sporadically reliable travel service.

Tuk Tuk Timbul
A 10-minute walk from Ambarita or 45 minutes from Tuk Tuk; ferries stop here also. A Dutch woman married to an Indonesian runs 12 bungalows for Rp3000-6000. Food is cheap but after a few days the pancakes, omelettes, and chapatis all taste the same. No fish or chicken. After swimming and lying in the sun there's not a lot to do. Superb location, very quiet. **Mr. Mas,** near Tuk Tuk Timbul, features a sandy beach.

Tuk Tuk Pandan
This small enclave is a 30-minute walk toward Ambarita. At least five accommodations hang over the lake with spectacular surroundings and convenient ferry connections to Prapat. **Tony's, Abadi's, Nelson's, Caribbean,** and **Murni's** are all popular, all within walking distance of the beach. Other small lakeside hamlets farther down the coast toward Ambarita also offer accommodations. From Tuk Tuk Pandan, it's a 1.5-km walk to **Tuk Tuk Lumban Manurung,** where you can sample Endy's excellent food. **Lekjon** is quiet, with good cheap food. **Poppy's** has two Batak huts right on the beach. **Riston** is friendly and has a nice beach.

AMBARITA

A lovely village with flowered coves, old Batak houses, and few tourists. Samosir's largest settlement, with a post office, small hospital, BRI bank, several ferries a day from Prapat, and a market on Tuesday near the boat dock. Why aren't there any fat dogs on Samosir? Because dog meat is sold in the Ambarita market.

Hang out with the locals in the dozen or so *warung*. Souvenirs are for sale, although there's less choice here than in Tomok. Some of the best mountain trails begin here. In the southern fringes of the village courtyard is a cannibal king's "dinner table," together with stone benches, chairs, and an upright butcher block where captives, enemies, or criminals were beheaded, then chopped up for a ritual repast. The chairs are about 275 years old, once used by prominent people for conferences or court. An enthusiastic guide recounts how the heads of criminals were mounted on poles and stuck out in the lake as a warning.

Accommodations And Food

Gordon's is a lakeside *losmen* on the edge of the village, Rp5000 for rooms, Rp2000 for the dorm. Although quiet, it's located two km toward Tuk Tuk from Ambarita's dock—no joke with a heavy rucksack. Run by a brother and sister; some readers report it's clean and comfortable, others say it's dirty and unfriendly. Whatever the case, be prepared for disco music until 0200 and men hanging around trying to sell you items and services you don't need. The food is well prepared, especially the vegetable and fruit tacos, though a bit overpriced. Cheaper eateries in the village. Average beach.

A better place to stay is Le Shangri-la in Martahan, six km north of Ambarita between the villages of Tolping and Batu-Batu. The Indian/Indonesian owner, Pami, speaks very good English and reasonable French. It's marvelously quiet here, the vegetarian food is high quality, the people are friendly, and big rooms cost Rp5000 per person in eight Batak-style bungalows with showers and thick mattresses. Dorm beds are available for Rp2000. The beach is okay and you can use the canoes. Rohandy's, right on its own peninsula, has good food but has been overrun by tourists and sabotaged by its own success. The best place to eat is Charles Restaurant next to the police station— excellent *nasi goreng* (Rp1000), exotic fruit salad (Rp600), great pancakes (Rp700), and heavenly coconut cookies.

Getting Away

It's a 30-minute walk from Ambarita to Tuk Tuk if you take the shortcut, or 45 minutes on the coastal path. From Ambarita to Simanindo is a seven-hour walk or Rp500 by bus. On Saturday morning boats stop at Rohandy's on their way to the Prapat market. On Sunday, Wednesday, and Friday a boat goes around to the hot springs near Pangururan for Rp2000 one-way. On Monday a boat leaves Ambarita at 0600 or 0700 for Haranggaol's market on the northeast shore of Lake Toba, arriving around 1000 (Rp2000).

SIMANINDO

A traditional village on the north tip of Samosir, 16 km by road. Market on Saturday afternoon in town. Down the road from the museum is a small family homestay, Boloboloni's. Accommodation is basic (Rp4000) and the food revolting. Tao Island just offshore has bungalows from Rp35,000 to Rp45,000—perfect for privacy and relaxation.

The oldest part of the village, Huta Bolon Simanindo, is now a museum. Surrounding the living compound is a two-meter-high earthen wall planted with bamboo. The only entrance is through a stone tunnel just wide enough for the horns of a large water buffalo and just high enough for a woman with a basket on her head. Outside the gate is a long canoe and some tombs. The Rp3000 admission includes a guidebook in English and rather touristy 30-minute dances, including a *si gale gale,* staged three times daily (1130, 1230, 1500) during the tourist season. See it free from the outside. Inside are *adat* houses and rice barns.

All over the island are superb examples of beautiful Batak houses, but the former king's house in Simanindo is the most outstanding. This large earthquake-proof structure has elaborate carvings on the front. The 10 sets of buffalo horns on the outside represent the 10 generations of the dynasty. Inside is a collection of household utensils: large Dutch and Chinese platters, spears and other weapons, carvings, witch doctor charms, and *huda-huda* (imitation horses), formerly used in dances before going off to battle. After the Japanese occupation, armed youths ran riot throughout Batakland, killing aristocrats and ransacking their palaces because they had collaborated with the Dutch. Simalungun, the last *raja,* was assassinated in March 1946.

Getting There And Away

Simanindo can be reached on foot in half a day from Tomok, and by bicycle, bus, or on the roundtrip lake cruises from Tuk Tuk and Ambarita. Buses leave for Ambarita quite frequently but stop early in the day; you might charter one to save yourself from another disgusting *mie goreng* at Boloboloni's. The Ambarita-Haranggaol ferry stops here on Monday. About four ferries a day cross from Simanindo to Tigaras, where you can catch buses to Pulau Siantar.

OVER THE MOUNTAIN

In Ambarita, inquire at Veronica Restaurant about the best way to the top of the mountain. It's a beautiful walk and a guide isn't necessary. Bring water. If you have a tent, there are many nice places to camp. From the main road opposite the bank, take the small road west toward the mountain. Follow the track to the right of the graveyard. Follow the red arrows and begin your ascent. On top of the mountain you'll see the sign for **Jenny Guesthouse**; cross the road, then continue until you reach the village and guesthouse (1,650 meters) a half-hour walk past a forest. Rp2500 for a room with blankets in a comfortable hut with a nice view. Food available. The best sunsets are between June and August.

From Jenny Guesthouse, hike to Tomok (15 km via Siulakosa), Tuk Tuk (about 13 km), Parmongan (20 km), or Roonggurni Huta and then Pangururan via Lake Sidihoni. Another option is to rent a motorcycle or bicycle in Tuk Tuk and ride to Tomok; from there you can reach Parmongan. About two km after Parmongan, take a right, then continue until you reach Jenny Guesthouse—from there you can reach Pangururan. You can also take a public *bemo* from Tomok to Roonggurni Huta, then another one down to Pangururan.

To cross the island from Pangururan to Tomok, first take a bus to Lake Sidihoni (Rp700, eight km) in the middle of Samosir, then walk or ride a *bemo* eight km more to Roongurni Huta. Get another *bemo* or hitchhike down to Tomok (about 25 km). In this part of Samosir they seem to be cutting down all the big trees and replacing them with eucalyptus. Very depressing.

Roonggurni Huta

You'll have no trouble finding a place to stay in this village—the locals will invite you to spend the night in their place. Don't take the first offer; expect to pay Tuk Tuk prices. **Mr. Max** wants Rp7000 for bed, blankets, supper, and breakfast. At the *penginapan* no one speaks English and room and board costs Rp2500. **Love Happy Accommodation and Restaurant** offers inexpensive and appetizing cooking with large portions—a secure and relaxing place. Tariffs start at Rp2500, meals Rp750-1500. Proprietor T.R. Sinaga can guide travelers to the more remote villages such as Jagar-Jagar (a bamboo-fortified jungle village) and Jinlakkosa. His English is good.

From Love Happy, it's 300 meters for magnificent views, 600 meters to a clean swimming pool, one km to a waterfall. Also check out the government plantation nearby. One km out of town on the right just before a stream, up above the track beside a white tomb surrounded by a brick wall, is a giant pre-Christian burial urn with a lid carved of solid rock.

PANGURURAN AND VICINITY

A big village on the west coast of Samosir near the isthmus, 16 km beyond Simanindo. A stone bridge here connects the island to the mainland. Visit the weekly market on Wednesday. In this village you could see dogs roasted whole upon fires, ungutted, with their tongues hanging out. **Barat Losmen,** near the bus stop and wharf, has rooms (Rp2500 s) above a shop with a great balcony. Proprietor Richard Barat speaks English, knows the area, draws maps, cashes traveler's checks, and makes delicious *mie goreng* and *nasi goreng* dinners. Newer and more comfortable is **Hotel Wisata Samosir,** Jl. Kejaksaan 42; Rp15,000, or dorm beds for Rp5000.

Gunung Belirang volcano to the west—the area's major attraction—has hot springs on its lower slopes and great views from its 1,982-meter-high summit. Cross Pangururan's bridge to the mainland, take a right, then walk one hour (3.5 km) on a horrible road to a point 1,000 meters above the lake's surface. Hot water comes from two small valleys amidst sulphur deposits and steam. Bathe lower down where the cascading water has cooled enough. Unfortunately, the hot springs are sadly neglected, with deserted restaurants and dirt-covered dressing rooms—like a ghost town.

Transportation

A bus runs at 0600 from the highland town of Roonggurni Huta down to Pangururan. You can also reach Pangururan by bus from Brastagi; daily buses also leave from Tomok (41 km, 1.5 hours). From Simanindo, it takes 45 minutes by bus or is a seven-hour walk to Pangururan. The road is so bad many prefer the boat to Pangururan from Tuk Tuk or Prapat. From Tuk Tuk the excursion boat costs Rp6000 roundtrip with a stop at the hot springs on the way.

From Pangururan, buses depart daily for Medan, Brastagi, and Sibolga, as well as destinations on Samosir and around Lake Toba.

From Pangururan to Sidikalang is Rp2300 by minibus, then another Rp1500 to Kabanjahe, from where you can ride another minibus to Kutacane. No direct connection between Sidikalang and Kutacane; the Batak people are afraid of the Acehnese, perhaps because of their religious differences. In Sidikalang a lot of dirty *losmen* (Rp3000-4000) are mostly "full" due to police registration. One Western-style hotel offers Rp20,000-30,000 rooms including breakfast. Bargain.

THE KARO

A strong patrilineal society living between Medan and Lake Toba, the Karo are the youngest Batak tribe, remarkable because so much of their close-knit traditional life is still intact. While the lowlands are more influenced by the more worldly Malay culture, *adat* is very strong in these highlands. The Karo dress like the Karen of Thailand, in heavy broad turbans and tightly wrapped dark clothing. Many of the women wear traditional wide-brimmed tasseled headdresses (*tudung*).

The Karo are legendary for their warm natures and speak a very *halus* (soft) dialect, which sounds almost as musical as Italian. Theft is an appalling offense in Karoland—the police take it *personally*. The Karo are the most preoccupied of Sumatrans with witchcraft and spells. Their literature consists mostly of books dealing with magic, medicine, and divination. Chess is widely played by the Karo; the standard is quite phenomenal, a sort of attacking chess of which Kasparov would be proud. In a recent Asian chess tournament, three members of the five-man Indonesian team were Karonese.

Some Karo greetings: *"Majuwajuah"* means the same as *"Horas!"* around Lake Toba, roughly translating as "Good luck!" "Thank you" is *"bujour,"* and *"Kai-berita"* is "How do you do?" The answer is *"Majuwajuah."*

Karoland

The five Karo Batak clans and 83 subclans inhabit a high plateau of mountain slopes, rich volcanic valleys, and deep ravines north and west of Lake Toba. Tanah Karo is approximately 5,000 square km, divided into two main areas, the highlands (700-1,400 meters) and the lowlands (40-200 meters). Roughly speaking, the first half of the year in the highlands is dry and the second half is wet. Most of the 274 villages in the district are named after a geographical feature, flower, or some other local natural wonder. Kuala preceding a name means the village is near a river estuary or the meeting of two rivers. Eleven villages in subdistricts Juhar and Kutabuluh are still so isolated they can't be reached by motor vehicle. It's an easy matter to find villagers to take you around Karoland on motorcycles.

Economy

The high elevation and cool climate make this a highly cultivated area. The Karo run a prosperous cash-crop economy of dry rice and *sawah,* rolling cornfields, and extensive vegetable patches. The Dutch began experimental gardens here in 1911; European vegetables grown in these highlands are in great demand in Medan, which has contributed greatly to the area's economic development.

CULTURE

Kinship

Islam never made deep inroads here. Dutch missionaries started work among the lowland Karo in 1890 and among the upland Karo in 1904. During the political upheavals and slaughter of 1965-66, there were mass conversions to Christianity to avoid accusations of communist atheism. Now 60% of the population is either Islamic or Christian. Though unofficial, the strongest and most widely practiced Karonese

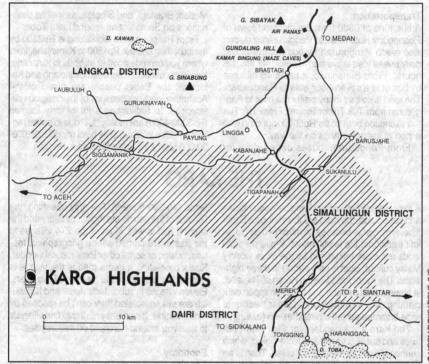

KARO HIGHLANDS

© MOON PUBLICATIONS, INC.

religion is actually kinship. All faiths are bound by clan and *adat* obligations, and if the lineage has been offended, it's believed that illness, drought, and crop failures can result.

An unmarried man without sons is grievously pitied and called *bangkaren* (old bamboo); his social obligations and mission in life were never fulfilled. Couples sometimes have three to five children before they're ceremonially married, at which time the groom's family fulfills its obligation to the bridegroom's family. Karo women obey orders and work for their fathers or brothers in an almost formal relationship; joking or affection is seldom shown.

Architecture
There is a rough-hewn primitive energy in the structure of a Karo village. Karo houses are raised off the ground on heavy posts. Their wide front verandas are used for working, bathing, playing, cooking, and socializing. Nowadays, as with the Toba Batak, the Karo are moving out of

these eight- to 10-family *rumah adat* into single-family houses. They're cheaper, and few big trees are left for use in the imposing traditional structures. Even boys as young as 15 move into their own houses, sharing the rent with others.

Crafts
Karo crafts indicate a strong connection with the Balkans. The spiral heart ornaments found in Croatia are almost identical to the huge ear pendants worn by Karo. Ear pendants (*padung*) are made of silver rods coiled in a flat double spiral. Weighing almost one kilo, some specimens are the size of a baseball. You still see stretched earlobes on the older women from years of wearing these heavy ornaments.

EVENTS

The Karo attend about 60 ceremonial occasions a year. If you're really interested, they're proud to take you around to the different functions for free. Pelawi, the proprietor of Wisma Sibayak in Brastagi, will accompany you to a Karo wedding if one is scheduled in the area. For these formal ceremonial occasions, the attire is *pakan adat* (customary). Men wear a black velvet cap (*songkok*) and coat. Besides a *sarung* and *kebaya,* and long clothes covering their *sarung,* women wear stoles (*uis*) draped over the shoulder and sometimes a folded, heavy, colorful cloth headdress (*tudung* or *uis nipes*), gold bracelets, and necklaces (*sertali*).

The Karonese New Year, Kerja Tahun, is the only time you can see all the *adat* at play and eat special Karonese cake, *cimpa, teritis,* and *cipera.* Ritualized offerings are often made to dead ancestors.

Nurun-nurun is a ritual in which the bones of ancestors are washed and reburied. **Erpangir** is a group hair-washing ceremony which even Christian Karo attend. The **Ngerires Festival** petitions God for a good harvest. It's held at the village of Batukarang near Brastagi at the beginning of the year. In July, **Mejuah-juah** gives thanks for a good harvest. It features the reading of Karo scripts, communal pounding of rice to music, violin playing, and dancing.

Funerals
There's dancing to the music of the *gendang* (traditional Karo orchestra), accompanied by minor-keyed singing. Betel leaves, cigarettes, and money are often placed in the coffin. When a child dies, s/he's laid out in the center of the house and symbolically "married"; with a dead boy the *dukun* enfolds warm bamboo around his penis, a girl has a banana inserted into the vagina. This is perfomed before the burial so the spirit (*begu*) of the frustrated deceased child will not return to disturb the living kinsmen of the village.

KABANJAHE AND VICINITY

Kabanjahe
Kabanjahe is a sizable, modern town, the capital city of the Karo Highlands, 11 km south by bus from Brastagi and surrounded by rich plantation country. Through buses from Prapat and Sidakalang also stop here, or you can grab a northbound bus from Haranggaol. Kabanjahe's big market day is Monday—a sea of Karonese headdresses. The Tugu Abdi Dharma Monument is dedicated to the courageous Karonese of the revolution. The National Building frequently serves as the venue for folk ceremonies, funerals, weddings, the Karonese New Year, harvest festivals, and other traditional performances.

Hotel Penlingdung (Rp6000 d) has clean rooms. Or check out the **Segar** or **Pinjowan.** From the market, take a minibus to any one of them for Rp200. Lots of street *warung* in Kabanjahe. Change money at fairly decent rates at Bank 1946 on Jl. Kapt. Pula Bangun, one km from the bus station.

Lingga
Lingga bills itself as a "typical" Karo village. North of Kabanjahe 4.5 km on the road to Lake Kawar or 16 km south of Brastagi, it's easier to reach than Barusjahe, the other big tourist village. Take a bus first from Brastagi to Kabanjahe, then a *bemo* to the turnoff, then another *bemo* to Lingga (Rp500 in all). Lingga is a complete Karonese village of 32 large, painted, decorated communal Batak longhouses where people work and live practically in the dark. The village architecture is fascinating, with most structures hundreds of years old, but children pester you and adults demand you buy a souvenir costing at least Rp10,000 and pay a Rp300 entrance fee.

Barusjahe
Barusjahe, a very old, uniquely laid-out village with *adat* houses, is about 15 km from Kabanjahe, 10 km from Tongkoh village, or 72 km from Medan. Here lives a cross-section of Karo peoples. A few of the rice barns and monumental buildings (*geritan*), in which skulls and bones of dead Karonese nobility were stored, are more than 250 years old. Not a single nail was used in their construction, only rope and wooden pegs, and they're starting to show their age. The village schoolkids might prove bothersome. Friendlier than both of the above villages is **Batukarang**; take a bus to Kabanjahe (Rp300), then another bus to Batukarang (Rp500).

BRASTAGI

A popular resort town in a mountain forest region 70 km from Medan and almost 1,400 meters above sea level. With its cool healthy climate, beautiful scenery, and fine green plantations, this Karo market center is one of the highlights of the journey through Sumatra. At the turn of the century, the Dutch built roads, bungalows, administration buildings, and clinics in Brastagi, and Dutch merchants used to retire here after prosperous careers in Medan. This is still a rich area for European vegetables (including beets, red cabbage, and lima beans), fragrant flowers, and fruits, which are exported to Penang and Singapore. Carrots are so plentiful they're fed to horses. Flies are numerous—make sure your room has a screen. Brastagi makes an excellent base from which to visit live volcanos and Karo villages.

The post office is on Jl. Veteran. The nearest bank is in the BNI on Jl. Sakti in Kabanjahe, 11 km away, but money can be changed in Brastagi at the Rudang Hotel, Bukit Kubu Hotel, and Wisma Sibayak (up to US$100). Don't bother with the tourist office—it's private, and they only want your business. **Tugu Perjuangan** is a monument to the Karo people who took part in the '45 revolution against the Dutch. The Kolam Renang (swimming pool), with its picture-postcard lawn, costs Rp200 on Sunday when it's crowded; otherwise free. Or soothe those aching muscles in the pool (Rp3000 entrance) at the **Sibayak International Hotel,** tel. (0628) 323-200. Brastagi has one of the most colorful fruit and vegetable markets in Indonesia on Tuesday and Friday. There are also at least five souvenir shops on the main street, Jl. Veteran. Telephone area code is 0628.

ACCOMMODATIONS

Losmen Merpati, Jl. Trimurti 4, is off the main street and very quiet. One of the cheapest (Rp4000 s, Rp7500 d) places in town, it's clean and has good rooms with shower and *mandi* and a small restaurant with good food. **Tolong Inn,** near the monument at Jl. Veteran 128, rents rooms in the Rp5000-8000 range.

The family-run guesthouse **Wisma Sibayak,** on the Kabanjahe side of town, has become a victim of its own success. If you like sleeping in a rabbit hutch with no windows and creaky beds, and enjoy sitting around discussing what you have done and what you're going to do with fellow travelers, then Sibayak is for you. Doubles are Rp5000-7000 in more spacious rooms, or Rp3000 in the dorm. The food isn't that great—cold toast with a minimum of margarine, jam, or cheese—though the fruit salads are okay. The owner is an interesting personality who speaks good English and is a local expert on Karo culture and history, but the place tends to be terribly noisy at night (rats on the triplex roof) and isn't very clean. Don't get Wisma Sibayak mixed up with the very noisy *losmen* by the same name on the main street .

Hotel Ginsata, Jl. Veteran 79 near the monument, is a popular hotel with travelers that charges only Rp3000 s with *mandi*; very clean. The new **Hotel Anda** has good, clean rooms with *mandi* for Rp5000. It's off the main street, adjacent to the Ginsata and less dingy. **Guesthouse Ikut** is on the road that leads up between the gas station and the fruit market, an old colonial building with a splendid view of the Sibayak and more distant volcanos. Tariff is Rp9000 d, not including breakfast—don't order the thing unless you want black burnt toast, undercooked eggs, and a glass of warm water. Also check out a number of medium-priced bungalows (Rp15,000-35,000) on Jl. Jaranguda on a hill 1.5-2 km from town.

You'll feel like a Dutch colonialist at the gracious **Bukit Kubu Hotel,** Jl. Sempurna 2 (one km before town, tel. 20832); Rp90,000 for a suite (no breakfast), Rp25,000 for the cheapest room. Built in 1939, this is one of Indonesia's most faithfully preserved Indies-style hotels, with complete and original Dutch furnishings, restaurant, and a fire at night in the lounge. Nice bar where you can drink Bukit Kubu Slings prepared with real *marquisha* juice. The vast and immaculate lawn surrounding the hotel is a golf course.

Tour groups usually stay at **Rudang Hotel,** Jl. Sempurna, tel. (0628) 43; Rp30,000-80,000, with bar, restaurant, and souvenir shop. At either

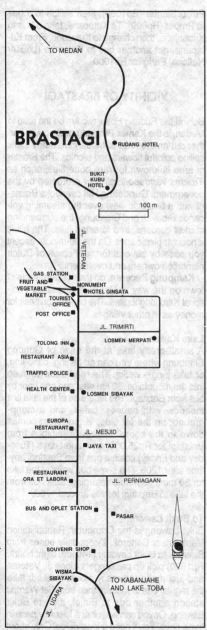

BRASTAGI

RUDANG HOTEL

BUKIT KUBU HOTEL

0   100 m

TO MEDAN

JL. VETERAN

GAS STATION
FRUIT AND VEGETABLE MARKET
MONUMENT
HOTEL GINSATA
TOURIST OFFICE
POST OFFICE

JL. TRIMIRTI

TOLONG INN
LOSMEN MERPATI
RESTAURANT ASIA
TRAFFIC POLICE
HEALTH CENTER
LOSMEN SIBAYAK

EUROPA RESTAURANT
JL. MESJID
JAYA TAXI

RESTAURANT ORA ET LABORA
JL. PERNIAGAAN

BUS AND OPLET STATION
PASAR

SOUVENIR SHOP

WISMA SIBAYAK
TO KABANJAHE AND LAKE TOBA

JL. UDARA

© MOON PUBLICATIONS, INC.

of these expensive hotels one can hire horses. Good views and excellent value at the **Danau Toba International**, Jl. Gundailing, tel. 20946 or 20947, which is quiet, has an accommodating staff, amenities such as hot water, a fine restaurant, and a pool.

FOOD

If you're willing to shoo a few flies away, sample some wonderfully fresh vegetable dishes and soups in small places with rough tables and bare concrete floors along the main street. Local dishes include buffalo-milk yogurt (*minyak susu*) and *tritis*, a ceremonial food made with partially digested grass from a cow's first stomach. *Babi panggang* is a traditional Karonese meal of roast pork, rice, and blood sauce; sample it in the market *warung* and in several places on Jl. Veteran. Another specialty of some Brastagi restaurants is stewed dog meat.

One of the best street restaurants in Southeast Asia is the **Europa** at Jl. Veteran 48 near the billiard hall. Large portions at cheap prices—you could feed an army on the omelettes. The **Tolong Inn** near the monument has great *masakan padang,* the tastiest chicken in all Sumatra. A large Chinese/Indonesian menu and great food can be found in **Restaurant Asia,** Jl. Veteran 9. **Bukit Kubu Restaurant** offers striking scenery from the dining room and quite good, high-priced Indonesian food. It's a shame the amber nectar is so exorbitant, but they take plastic if you feel a thirst coming on.

Abundant fruit is available from the open-air market off Jl. Veteran. A specialty is the vitamin-rich *marquisa* fruit, grown only here and on Sulawesi. Makes a delicious drink; the sour black ones are best. Also try an exotic Brastagi Apple, a cross between a persimmon and a peach. Enjoy hot spiced ginger milk (*bandrek*) at night at Warung Buyun on Jl. Veteran near the hospital. For coffee nuts, northern Sumatra is known for really high-quality coffee. Many of the local *kedai kopi* (cafes) around town also serve *tuak* and *bandrek.* By day meeting places for the men where they sip coffee, smoke *kretek*, and gossip, by night they ring with guitar music, lusty singing, and heated debate—a convivial place to practice your *bahasa* and pit your wits against the local chess champion.

Tuak, made from glutinous rice and visually reminiscent of milk, is served in a water glass (Rp150). Some believe the first sip is dubious, the second revolting, the third stomach-churning, and the rest best spewed into the flower bed. If you do happen to like it, be careful. The stuff's potent. If you abhor *tuak,* try Anggur Vigour (40% alcohol). *Anggur* means "grape" and is marketed as a health builder, an ol'-time patent Karo medicine. It looks like Coca-Cola, comes in a Coke-sized bottle, costs Rp300, and tastes like nothing on earth. Sample at the **Ora et Labora** on the main street.

TRANSPORTATION

Getting There And Away
The bus and *oplet* terminal is on Jl. Veteran. From Haranggaol to Brastagi via Seribudolok is Rp1500 by minibus. Buses also leave Panguru-ran for Brastagi via Sidikalang and Kabanjahe. From Medan, cramped minibuses (Rp1500, 2.5 hours) leave frequently from Stasiun Sei Wampu. From Bukit Lawang, very full buses leave direct to Brastagi at 0530 on a seven-hour ride, of which half is to Binjei.

Kabanjahe is Rp300 by collective minibus. To Barusjahe, go to Kabanjahe first, then take a minibus. To Lingga is Rp500 total (change at Kabanjahe). Board any number of gaudily painted small buses (*sudaku*), pulsating with Indonesian songs, for such local destinations as the Lau Debuk-Debuk turnoff from where you can walk down to the hot springs or farther to the village of Semangat Gunung, then start the climb up Gunung Sibayak. For the impressive Sipisopiso Waterfalls to the south, first take a bus to the center of Kabanjahe, then ask for the bus to Situnggaling (30 minutes). From there walk one hour to the waterfall.

Some minibus companies will take you right to the door of your destination in Medan. Or take a **Jaya** or **Hiba** taxi; both companies will drop you off anywhere in the city, but reserve the day before. To Pulau Siantar by bus is Rp850. A unique and breathtaking way to reach Samosir Island from Brastagi is to take a very early bus on Monday to Haranggaol, then board a ferry and cross the lake. A taxi to Haranggaol costs about Rp50,000. To Prapat, first take a minibus to Kabanjahe's terminal (Rp300), another to

Pulau Siantar (Rp1000), then switch to a bus to Prapat (Rp800). To Kutacane, take a bus to Kabanjahe, then change to Kutacane. From Kutacane, get another bus to Ketembe (Leuser National Park) for Rp1000.

VICINITY OF BRASTAGI

Behind the Rudang Hotel, two km on the road to Medan, is the **Kamar Bingung** maze cave. Farther out on the road to Medan are many stalls selling colorful flowers and orchids. The Brastagi area is known for rare butterflies, such as *Troides vandepolli,* all now protected by the government. **Gundaling Hill** overlooks Brastagi with a fantastic view over the steaming volcanos Sibayak and Sinabung, the surrounding market gardens, and forested hills. The hill is a popular picnic spot. On the 30-minute ascent you pass by several former homes of Dutch plantation owners and overseers.

Kampung Peceren, on the northern edge of town on the way to Medan, features six traditional Karo longhouses. The people don't ask for money as in other villages.

Lake Kawar
A small pretty lake at the base of Gunung Sinabung where you can go fishing, canoeing, or take jungle walks. The road burrows deep into the mountains, 30 km east and one hour by bus from Brastagi. The near side of the lake is a meadow with houses, cafes, and a camp-ground; on the far side, virgin forest comes down to the shore. Charter a minibus from Brastagi for Rp25,000; on market days (Tuesday and Friday) catch a bus from Brastagi anytime after 1200. The same bus waits at the lake for 30 minutes before returning. Last bus from the lake to Brastagi leaves around 1700.

To Bukit Lawang
Bukit Lawang is the Orangutan Rehabilitation Center near Bohorok. Direct daily buses from Brastagi to Bukit Lawang (140 km, eight hours, Rp1900) pick up passengers along Jl. Veteran and just make too many stops. Instead, take the regular bus to Medan, then from Sei Wampu station another bus to Binjei, then to Bukit Lawang. Or you can walk it at a leisurely pace in three days. You'll need a local guide. Only about

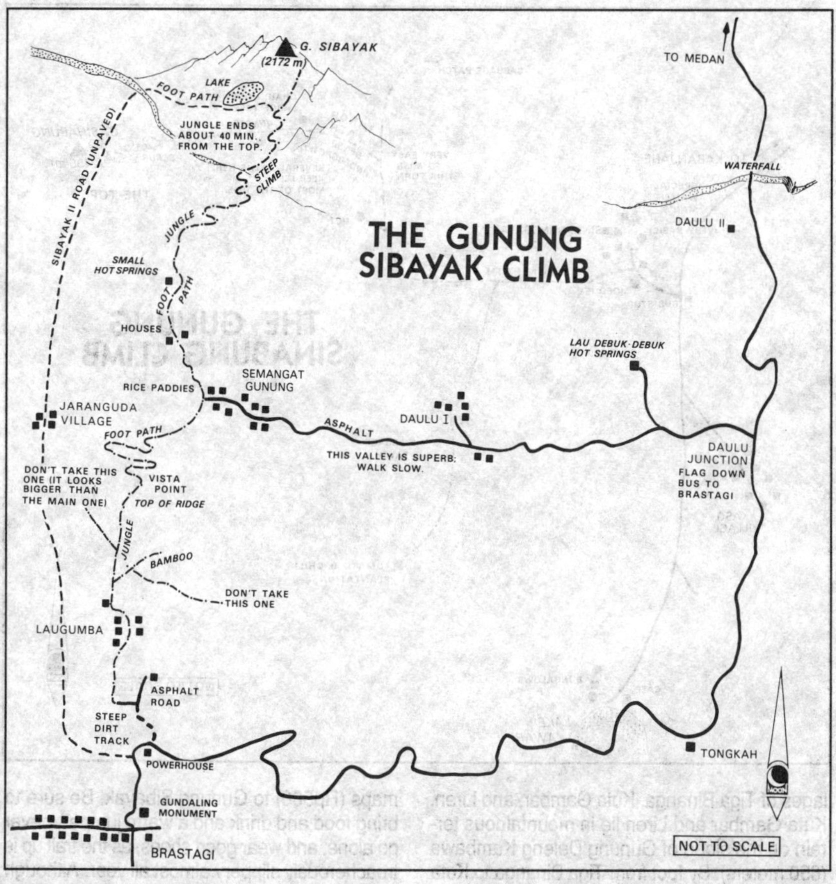

THE GUNUNG SIBAYAK CLIMB

(Map labels, reading across)
G. SIBAYAK (2172 m)
LAKE
FOOT PATH
JUNGLE ENDS ABOUT 40 MIN. FROM THE TOP.
STEEP CLIMB
TO MEDAN
WATERFALL
DAULU II
SIBAYAK II ROAD (UNPAVED)
JUNGLE
FOOT PATH
SMALL HOT SPRINGS
HOUSES
RICE PADDIES
SEMANGAT GUNUNG
LAU DEBUK-DEBUK HOT SPRINGS
JARANGUDA VILLAGE
FOOT PATH
ASPHALT
DAULU I
DON'T TAKE THIS ONE (IT LOOKS BIGGER THAN THE MAIN ONE!)
VISTA POINT
TOP OF RIDGE
THIS VALLEY IS SUPERB: WALK SLOW.
DAULU JUNCTION FLAG DOWN BUS TO BRASTAGI
JUNGLE
BAMBOO
DON'T TAKE THIS ONE
LAUGUMBA
ASPHALT ROAD
STEEP DIRT TRACK
POWERHOUSE
GUNDALING MONUMENT
TONGKAH
BRASTAGI
NOT TO SCALE

© MOON PUBLICATIONS, INC.

25% of the journey passes through primary forest—home to monkeys, snakes, and leeches—the rest winds through burned-up areas and plantations.

The first overnight is in the village of Pamah Sumelir about eight hours down the trail. A guide from Brastagi charges about Rp200,000 for four people, including food, transport, accommodations, and permit to enter Gunung Leuser Park. Ask Mr. Pelawi at Wisma Sibayak in Brastagi for details and arrangements. Without a guide, only ex-jungle soldiers should make this walk alone.

Traditional Villages

Walk to traditional villages of the region where you may stay at the courtesy of the *pengulu.*

These old houses are huge, with lots of children. Moss grows on the thatch, and great swarms of flies blacken the wood. In Wisma Sibayak and Hotel Ginsata there are maps, hiking info, and notices. Also check out hotel guestbooks, particularly Wisma Sibayak's, for some fascinating stories of the adventures and misadventures of previous travelers.

You may stay the night in Pelawi's own family house in **Ajijahe,** 10 km from Brastagi; contact him at Wisma Sibayak. But to see real untouched Karo villages, befriend a native in Brastagi and go home with him—otherwise it's like walking into someone's living room uninvited. Still strict in their adherence to Karo customs and still practicing shifting cultivation are the vil-

THE GUNUNG
SINABUNG CLIMB

CABBAGE PATCH

CHAIR UNDER
LARGE TREE

MINOR
PATH

VERY EASY
TO MISS
THIS TURN

DENSE
UNDERGROWTH

JUNGLE

G. SINABUNG

SCRUB

(2450 m)

THE TOP

SEVERAL PATHS HERE.
KEEP LEFT
MOST OF THE TIME.

TO KABANJAHE

SPECIAL
WHITE
MAN'S
HUT
(VERY BASIC)

SINGARANGGALANG

HUT

MOSQUE

MAIN PATH

BUS STOP

CABBAGE
PATCH

KASO
VILLAGE

TOMATO & CHILI
PLANTATION

NOT TO SCALE

MOON

CAFE

BUNGALOWS

LAKE
KAWAR

© MOON PUBLICATIONS, INC.

lages of Tiga Binanga, Kuta Gambar, and Liren. Kuta Gambar and Liren lie in mountainous terrain on the slope of Gunung Deleng Kambawa (650 meters). By foot from Tiga Binanga to Kuta Gambar is 12 km, three hours; from Kotabuluh to Kuta Gambar is eight km, two hours. More than two-thirds of the people live in *adat* houses and believe strongly in the traditional religion. In this area you can still find spirit mediums (*guru si baso*) and medicine men (*guru*).

GUNUNG SIBAYAK AND VICINITY

The 2,172-meter summit of this volcano dominates Brastagi's skyline north of town. From Semangat Gunung at the base, it's a 1.5- to two-hour climb to the top. Allow six hours up and back. Start early (by 0700) before it clouds over. Wisma Sibayak and Hotel Ginsata sell

maps (Rp500) to Gunung Sibayak. Be sure to bring food and drink and a warm jumper, never go alone, and wear good shoes, as the trail up is treacherously slippery almost all year. Although not a Bromo or a Kelimutu, the heady view from the summit is worth the effort, and the lovely countryside around the mountain is a bird-watcher's paradise.

Get a bus to Daulu junction, nine km down the road toward Medan. Buses leave Brastagi for Medan every 15 minutes starting at 0530. From the junction, walk three km to Semangat Gunung, pay the small entrance fee, and give homage to Nini, the mountain's spirit. You don't need a guide as the trail is easy to follow. The garbage-littered trail is in good shape and even has steps, though it does become quite steep. Be warned that on weekends and school holidays (May-June) a thousand climbers may scamper up Sibayak. After your climb, soak your aching feet and thighs in **Lau Debuk-Debuk** medicinal sulphur springs (Rp500). While in the area see **Sikulikap Waterfall,** only a two-km walk from the hot springs. A new road will someday lead right up to the crater.

Sights
The broken crater, still belching sulphurous fumes, is fascinating. There's a turquoise-colored lake at the bottom, boiling in spots; hundreds of fumeroles deposit gleaming yellow sulphur crystals; and several peaks to climb. Be cautious around the fumeroles; they can be very hot and gases could be poisonous. Don't venture to the bottom of the crater on windless days.

Nini Kertah Ernala ("Grandmother of the Gleaming Sulphur") is the mountain's spirit. Be polite to her (excuse yourself if you have to urinate), or suffer the consequences. Locals perform an incense-burning and betelnut-chewing ritual before the climb; the trappings for the ceremony cost around Rp200. On the trail you'll often see cigarette butts stuck on forked sticks—if the cigarette burned evenly and regularly, the climber proceeded; if not, s/he descended and waited for another, more propitious day.

Perekteken is a sacred place near Gunung Sibayak, about one km northwest of Daulu I. Farmers will point the way across the fields. Strangely shaped twisted trees and sulphurous

gases add an eerie feeling to the site. There are two pools here, thought to contain the spirits of two daughters—one bubbling but cold, the other still hot.

Sikulikap Waterfall is near the highway to Medan. It's a two-km walk from Lau Debuk-Debuk Hot Springs. Don't miss the beautiful panorama—you can see the jungle and lowlands as far as Medan.

GUNUNG SINABUNG

Although the view from 2,450-meter-high Gunung Sinabung isn't as sweeping as the one from the summit of Gunung Sibayak, this active cone-shaped volcano is well worth the climb. Most climbers spend the night in Sigaranggalang village at the base of the mountain. Bring your own food. Stay in the house of your guide, or sleep in the government's office. Guides (Rp10,000-12,000) are advised as there are many crucial right and left turns in the first 30 minutes of the climb; in other places the track disappears into dense jungle. The climb to the top takes three hours, the descent two to three hours. Start the climb early, around 0530; this is the coolest time, and the summit will not yet be obscured by clouds. The track—once you find it—is unremittingly steep. It's unlikely there will be other climbers.

MEDAN

Huge, flat, dusty, sprawling Medan is Sumatra's largest city and Indonesia's third largest, a dominant port and the capital of North Sumatra Province. Medan is notorious for being noisy, dirty, crowded—yet it's a necessary travelers' departure point for Malaysia or points inland like Prapat and Brastagi. With its congested rubbish-strewn treeless streets and choking carbon-monoxide fumes, Medan really has little to recommend it. The city is hit with frequent blackouts and unemployed youths form gangs who sing and shout late into the night. It's one of the worst introductions to Indonesia, so first-time visitors may want to immediately head out to Lake Toba.

But if you get beyond the crazy and ugly parts of the city, there's a fantastic confluence of cultures concentrated here—even more of a pluralistic so-

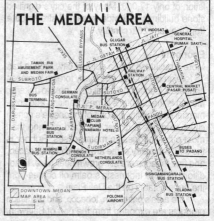

ciety than the average Indonesian metropolis. Medan is big enough to be cosmopolitan with all the conveniences, yet small enough so you can recognize your friends on the street. Medan's expatriate community is composed of diplomats and businesspeople, with their own International School. The huge Toyota dealership on the road west out of town testifies to the city's strong Japanese presence. Medan is also the site of the University of North Sumatra (Universitas Sumatera Utara) in the southwest corner of the city.

Only 25 meters above sea level and just north of the equator, Medan's climate is generally hot and humid. The heaviest rains are in late September, October, and early November. By 1100 the whole city is one blue smoggy haze, as bad as Athens.

History
This area used to be a regular battle site in wars between the sultans of Deli and Aceh; *medan* means "level, open field." The city was founded in the 17th century by Sultan Mahmud Perdasa Alam, who lived in his palace at Labuhan Deli, 10 km away. It grew out of a tiny group of *kampung* in a marshy lowland. Because of the hot climate and immense fertility of this narrow swamp-belt, by 1860 the northeast Deli coastal area had become a highly productive plantation district. The Dutch colonial government decided to make it the residency Oost-Kust van Sumatra (East Coast of Sumatra) in 1887. With the success of Deli Tobacco as a premium cigar wrapper, the city kept growing; it was finally incorporated as a municipality in 1909 with a population of only 17,000. Many of the city's dignified stone buildings and wide tree-lined streets date from the early 20th century.

Economy
More a business than a cultural city, Medan has 15 foreign consulates and many foreign business houses. A leading industrial city—next to Jakarta, Medan is the country's largest banking and commercial community. It's one of Indonesia's richest cities, and has a higher standard of living than most other Indonesian metropolises. Rubber is the staple industry of the area, and coffee, cacao, and fine tobacco are still grown near here. In addition, most of Indonesia's palm oil comes from the huge estates on the Deli Plain.

All the area's petroleum, tobacco, and plantation products are exported from the port of Belawan,

26 km north. About 31% of big businesses, 55% of middle-sized businesses, and 67% of small businesses are owned by Chinese entrepreneurs, although this ethnic group comprises only eight percent of Medan's total population.

The People
Because of its location and the frenetic level of its commerce, all the region's races have converged on Medan. The Javanese originally came to work on the thriving plantations. There are also communities of Sikhs, Acehnese, Riau Islanders, and Arabians, as well as very strong Chinese, Indian, Minangkabau, Melayu, Islamic, and Christian Batak populations who flocked here because the city is the economic center of Sumatra. Ethnically, the city is the hub of the Batak people. Because of its relatively large Batak Christian and Chinese populations, 40% of the city's population is non-Muslim.

SIGHTS

Medan is a well-laid-out city with big parks and wide streets. Though the traffic is Asian, many downtown buildings are Western. Visit the stately residential area of **Polonia,** Medan's old quarter near the airport with elegant government buildings, parks, and large peaked tile-roof houses built by the colonials. Now most are occupied by the government and commercial elite and foreign residents. Most of the city's population, however, lives in a multitude of teeming *kampung* where housing and other facilities have not kept pace with the masses of unemployed rural youths who come in search of a place in the city's economy.

Chinatown is a busy, crowded section of town with a number of *klenteng* and row upon row of shophouses, many with glazed tiles on the roofs. All the Chinese characters above the storefronts were removed in the 1960s by government decree.

Mosques, Temples, Churches
The largest mosque in Sumatra, handsome **Mesjid Raya** (Great Mosque), was built in prewar Moroccan style in 1906. Though seemingly neglected today, this edifice is beautifully and richly decorated, set off by bright stained-glass

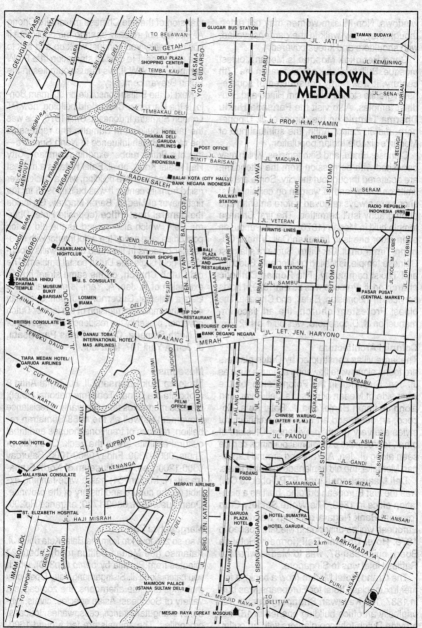

DOWNTOWN MEDAN

windows. Non-Muslim women may not enter, though they may walk in the gardens, veiled, with shoulders and knees covered.

Gang Bengkok Mosque is Medan's oldest mosque. Built by Datuk of Kesawan in the 17th century, it was partly constructed of square-hewn granite stones taken from Hindu and Buddhist temples. Also visit the **Parisada Hindu Dharma Temple** on the corner of Jl. Diponegoro and Jl. Zainul Arifin, the spiritual hub of Medan's sizable Indian population.

Chinese, Hindu, and Sikh temples, which may be visited with permission from the attendant, are scattered throughout the city. Some are off-limits on Friday and to women on certain days; shoes are always removed before entering and photography isn't permitted. The first Chinese temple built in Medan (1870) is on Jl. Pandu; an even older one is in Labuhan Deli. **Vihara Gunung Timur** on Jl. Cik Ditiro, Sumatra's largest Chinese temple, is visited by Medan's Buddhist and Taoist community. The **Roman Catholic church** on Jl. Pemuda was built in 1929; it holds services in Indonesian, Batak, and Chinese. The oldest **Protestant church,** the art deco Immanuel on Jl. Diponegoro, was built in 1921.

Colonial Architecture

The large villas constructed by Dutch planters are found along wide flowering avenues such as Jl. Jen. Sudirman in the Polonia area, on the west side of Medan across the Deli River, and along Jl. Imam Bonjol and Jl. Balai Kota. Rococo, art deco, and art nouveau architectural styles are very much in evidence. Clusters of other, fortress-like old colonial buildings can be seen along Jl. Jen. A. Yani and around Lapangan Merdeka, the old esplanade in Dutch times.

Deli Maatschappij (now PTP Tobacco Co.) was the first European building, built as a plantation office in 1869. The **White Society Club** (present Bank Negara building) was the first European whites-only club in Medan, opened in 1879. **Hotel Dharma Deli** (formerly Hotel de Boer), built 1880-87, was to Medan what the Raffles Hotel was to Singapore.

The **Grand Hotel Medan** (now a bank), a former luxury-class hotel for Europeans, was built in 1887. The **Kesawan Shopping Center** was originally an office building opened in 1874 to provide Dutch tobacco planters with an outlet. On Jl. Jen. A. Yani is the beautifully decorated

mansion of the late Chinese millionaire Chong A. Fie; it's not actually open to the public but if you're cheeky you can just walk up and ask to see the place. Fie died of starvation in a POW camp during WW II; his mausoleum lies in the Pulau Brayan cemetery.

Next to the British consulate on Jl. Imam Bonjol is the **Harrison-Crossfield** building, now PT London Sumatra Indonesia. Until 1970, this was the tallest building in Sumatra and represents the oldest British influence in North Sumatra—that of a British rubber-exporting company. **City Hall** (Balai Kota), on Jl. Balai Kota, is a modest yet lovely square little building, with a clock tower rising from its center; it was built in 1908 for the first mayor of Medan, Baron Mackay. Go inside the **general post office** (opposite Hotel Dharma Deli), which also served as the old Dutch post office, and notice the artful interior with messenger pigeons in tile inlaid on the walls alongside a gold bugle, the Dutch postal emblem. The old **Dutch Church,** on the same street but an extension of Jl. Jen. A. Yani, is now called the Gereja Katedral. **Gubernoran,** Jl. Jen. Sudirman 41, is the imposing mansion of the former Dutch governor, presently the residence of the governor of North Sumatra. Contact **Dinas Pariwisata,** Jl. Jen. A Yani 107, for a tour.

Museums

Museum Bukit Barisan, Jl. H. Zainal Arifin 8 (opposite the Danau Toba International Hotel), features mementos from the wartime resistance movement as well as the 1958 Sumatran rebellion; replicas of traditional houses and tribal cultural exhibits are in the back. Open Mon.-Thurs. 0800-1300, Friday 0800-1000, Saturday 0800-1200; free. The **Museum of North Sumatra,** Jl. H. M. Joni 51, has a wide-ranging exhibit on the culture and history of the province. Open Tues.-Sun. 0800-1700; entrance Rp200.

Margasatwa Zoo

A so-so zoo four km from the Balai Kota down Jl. Katamso (the Medan-Delitua road), about 20 minutes from Polonia by *bemo* (Rp300), which you catch along Jl. Sisingamangaraja. Open only mornings and late afternoons, the zoo cages a variety of Southeast Asian species: civets, gibbons, orangutan, *kancil,* cassowaries, toucans, crocodiles. The animals are fed around 1600. Also visit the crocodile farm near Pam Sunggal six km from Medan, where 1,500 Sumatran specimens—considered the world's most dangerous—are bred for their skins. The reptiles are fed at 1630; open 0900-1700, Rp300 entrance. Take a minibus from Sambu station.

Istana Sultan Deli

The historic palace of the sultan of Deli at Jl. Katamso 66, also called the Maimoon Palace, is an ornate building open all day to the public. For a private visit, apply to the sultan's aide, tel. 22123. Tours can also be arranged. The building and grounds are sadly neglected; a small donation toward the ongoing and underfunded restoration project is requested.

Designed by an Italian architect and built in 1888, the highest technology of the day was used in its construction, incorporating an astounding mixture of Oriental, Middle Eastern, and Western architectural styles. Some elements derive from the Weimar Palace in Vienna, yet all the elaborate pillars, porches, arches, and colonnades reflect Arabic art. The sultanate, in existence since the 16th century, was terminated by the central government after independence. Though the sultan has been pensioned off by the government, he and his family still live in the palace.

ACCOMMODATIONS

Budget

In the lower-priced category (Rp3000-9000, Rp2000-3000 dorm), there's not much choice and many are often full. Better value and more pleasant than any of Medan's hotels are the dozens of losmen in Bukit Lawang. Or stay in **Cafe de Malioboro** in Binjei, 22 km west of Medan; from Binjei, both Medan and Bukit Lawang are very accessible.

In Medan, **Krishen's Yoghurt House** (formerly Jacky's Traveler's Centre), Jl. Kediri 96, is still popular with travelers. Dorm beds are Rp3500, rooms Rp7500 d. The restaurant's walls are plastered with insider's travel info, photos, and notes proclaiming what a wonderful man Jacky is. This copious collage of information ranges from the basic to the most obscure, from the markets of Medan to the rainforests of Aceh. There's even a signed photograph of Joe Cummings on the wall. The restaurant

serves decent fruit juice, homemade yogurt, and tasty Indian food. Jacky is undoubtedly helpful and speaks impeccable English. He maintains a book exchange so you can top up on reading material here, in any language.

Tapian Nabaru, Jl. Hang Tuah 6, tel. (061) 512-155, is in an old Dutch home by a river and tree-filled park. It's only a 10-minute walk from Kampung Keling (the "Ginza strip" of Medan), and five minutes by mesin becak from the airport. Not the cleanest or friendliest of places but it's cheap and quiet. Big or small rooms cost Rp5500 per person; dorms Rp2500. Breakfast (Rp1000) consists of bread, jam, egg, and coffee or tea, or eat in Kampung Keling.

Sarah's Guesthouse, Jl. Pertama 10 (behind Astra Toyota on Jl. Sisingamangaraja) has Rp6000-7500 rooms, or Rp10,000 with mandi. Dark and spartan, but quiet, clean, and safe. Buy bus, ferry, and airline tickets here—transport is available to the airport.

Losmen Irama, in a little alley off Jl. Palang Merah 1125, is centrally located only 50 meters from the intersection of Jl. Imam Bonjol and quite close to Danau Toba International Hotel. Though its rooms could be small, hot, and stuffy, it's cleaner than many. Some rooms have been upgraded with bunkbeds, so you now have to pay for three, even if you're only two. Rooms with mandi cost Rp7500, dorm beds Rp2500.

Clean rooms with fans are available for Rp7500 s (including breakfast) at **Wisma Yuli**, Jl. S. M. Raja Pagaruyung 79B, tel. 323104. The street is off Jl. Sisingamangaraja, opposite Mesjid Raya.

Moderate

At Jl. Sisingamangaraja 21, tel. (061) 24973, is **Hotel Sumatra**, with sweatboxes for Rp25,000 s; Rp35,000 d with fan and mandi. Clean and central near Mesjid Raya, the **Kenanga Hotel**, Jl. Sisingamangaraja 82, tel. 712-426, has nice rooms from Rp5000 to 30,000 with tourist information desk, moneychanger, and small bar. Good value. The restaurant serves either a continental, American, or Indonesian breakfast for under Rp4000. Avoid the **Garuda**, Jl. Sisingamangaraja 27; Rp35,000 s for a dirty room, little insects, dirty sheets, and dirty towels. Not to be confused with the Garuda Plaza at Jl. Sisingamangaraja 18.

Expensive

At Medan's expensive class of hotels, if you book through a travel agent or make an appeal at the reception desk itself, you can often receive a 10% discount. **Hotel Dharma Deli,** Jl. Balai Kota 2, tel. (061) 327-011, is an old colonial-style hotel, the former Dutch Hotel de Boer. The hotel's famous gardens have now been turned into private suites (Rp350,000 and up). The cheapest rooms cost Rp100,000, with an extra bed. Amenities include hot water, a/c, a great lobby, bar, and shops. Right across the street is the historic old post office.

Tiara Medan, Jl. Cut Mutiah Medan 20152, tel. 516-000, is Medan's leading hotel, with full facilities and outstanding service. Its elegant, lavishly appointed rooms are expensive. Try booking at Natrabu Travel to the left of the hotel; Morris will sell you a voucher for Rp90,000 d. The Tiara features two international restaurants, bars, a coffee shop, taxi service, pool, and health club. Ideal for businesspeople as the commerical district is nearby.

Danau Toba International Hotel, Jl. Imam Bonjol 17, Box 490, tel. 327-000, is a large, well-established, high-priced hotel with bar, restaurant, pool, and bowling alley. This modern hotel has a/c rooms (Rp90,000-150,000) with high balcony views looking out over the city, swimming pool, and tennis court. Avoid the hotel's restaurants: the food is either fiendishly expensive or demonically dreadful.

Polonia Hotel, Jl. Jen. Sudirman 14-18, Box 303, tel. 325-300, asks Rp90,000 per room or Rp150,000 for a suite. The Polonia is centrally located with very good service and in-room video, swimming pool, health center, and reputable Chinese restaurant. **Pardede International Hotel,** Jl. Ir. H. Juanda 14, Box 490, tel. 323-866, near the airport, offers 120 clean a/c rooms (Rp90,500 s, Rp120,000 d) with bath, fridge, TV, garden views, pool, tennis court, restaurant, bar, and nightclub. Service is good. A busy pickup joint for Medan's goodtime girls.

FOOD

The **Tip Top Restaurant,** on the shopping street Jl. Jen. A. Yani 92, tel. (061) 24442, specializes in Western food and *nasi padang*. Quite good fish and meat dishes, delicious ice cream and cakes. This attractive sidewalk cafe is a nice place to sit day or night and take in the street life while sipping a cold beer. **Lyn's Cafe and Restaurant** next door is an expat watering hole with probably the city's best Western meat dishes, including chateaubriand steak and spaghetti Bolognese.

For Indonesian cuisine, **Garuda,** Jl. Pemuda 20C-D, tel. 327-692, has very good Padang food (a *nasi campur* costs about Rp1500). The fruit juices are a knockout. A good place for Minang food is **Family** on JL. Brig. Jen Katamso. **Surya Sea Food,** Jl. Imam Bonjol 8, tel. 323-433, and **Columbia,** Jl. Putri Hijau 8J-K, tel. 526-374, serve some of Medan's best seafood. The third floor of the **Deli Plaza Shopping Centre** on the corner of Jl. Getah and Jl. Balai Kota houses dozens of fast-food vendors specializing in cheap and delicious Chinese, Indonesian, and European food.

For Chinese food at night, visit **Jalan Semarang,** between Jl. Bandung and Jl. Pundu, about a five-minute walk from Jl. Jen. A. Yani. Delicious food and beer at good prices, and plenty of atmosphere. Many open-air foodstalls, which serve such delights as snake, frog, and goat testicles, are open from around 1800 until 0100. **Kampung Keling** on Jl. Zainul Arifin is another *warung* area, with Chinese, Indonesian, and Indian food. All the *becak* drivers know where these places are.

Chinese

For Chinese banquet-style cuisine at its best, go to the **Bali Plaza Restaurant,** Jl. Kumango 1A, tel. (061) 514-852—remarkable cooking and very fast service. Only the best ingredients are used, very fresh veggies. You're treated like royalty: hostesses light your cigarettes, continually fill your glass with beer, ladle soup for you. Try the shrimp hot plate, fried chicken, soups, and desserts. Outrageous Shanghai Pancake—three people have trouble finishing it. Upstairs is a restaurant where hostesses rent themselves out as dancing partners.

The **Polonia Restaurant,** Polonia Hotel, Jl. Sudirman 14, tel. 325-300, is an outstanding dining experience where meals are served up to 2300. Stick to the Chinese menu; prices are moderate to expensive. Other good Chinese restaurants include the **Asean,** Jl. Glugar Bypass; the **Cafe De Marati,** Jl. Gatot Subroto, tel. 321-751; and the **Batik Cafe,** Jl. Pemuda 14-C, tel. 24132.

Ethnic And Vegetarian

Heartily recommended is the hospitable and moderately priced **Koh-I-Noor Indian Restaurant,** Jl. Mesjid 21, tel. (061) 513-953, Kesawan District near the post office (Jl. Mesjid runs parallel with Jl. A. Yani). Sample North Indian curries and tandoori chicken. The owners are kind and hospitable and fluent in English. For Japanese food, check out the rather expensive **Yoshiko Yokohama,** tel. 327-000, in the Danau Toba International Hotel on Jl. Imam Bonjol. Medan is blessed with an uncommonly good vegetarian restaurant, **Restaurant Vegetarian Indonesia,** at Jl. Gandhi 63A beside Bioskop Benteng, tel. 526-812. It's run by people from the Buddhist temple next door. They speak no English and have no English menu but provide lots of photographs of their varied and delicious fare.

Baked Goods And Desserts

Royal Holland Bakery, Jl. Taruma next to Hotel Dharma Deli, has outstanding baked goods, inexpensive good Indonesian food, and ice cream delights. Another great ice cream place is **Batik Cafe,** Jl. Pemuda 14C. For baked goods, check out the very good **Medan Bakery,** Jl. Zainal Arifin 148; the **Tip Top Bakery,** Jl. Jen. A. Yani 92/A; and the **President Bakery** on the ground floor of the Deli Plaza Shopping Centre at the corner of Jl. Getah and Jl. Balai Kota.

ENTERTAINMENT AND EVENTS

Most of Medan's dozens of air-conditioned movie theaters are located in the city's new multi-storied shopping plazas. The **Deli Plaza Cinemas** on Jl. Perdana specialize in Western films dubbed in Indonesian. These are the nicest cinemas in town; easy parking, crowded on weekends. When Medan's heat, dust, and fumes get you down, take a dip in one of the hotel swimming pools (Rp2000-3000)—Hotel Dharma Deli, Danau Toba International, or Tiara Medan Hotel.

Taman Ria Amusement Park, on Jl. Binjei, houses permanent cultural, agricultural, and industrial exhibits. The park is the site of the Medan Fair from May to June, with sports contests, *adat* dwellings, and extensive trade exhibitions.

The city has many nightclubs and discotheques, such as **Casablanca** in the Dirgasurya Hotel and **Bali Plaza** at Jl. Kumango 1A. An expat hang-out filled with fortyish Australians, Americans, and Europeans is **Lyn's Bar and Restaurant** on Jl. Jen. A. Yani near the Tip Top—the only *real* bar in Medan. Good draft beer. The private **Medan Club,** Jl. Kartini, is another focal point for expat social life—tennis, squash, golf, badminton, bowling, swimming, and horseback riding.

Cultural performances occur twice weekly at the **Taman Budaya,** Jl. Perintis Kemerdekaan (near PT Indosat); free admission. Also check out the **RRI** (Radio Republik Indonesia) auditorium, Jl. Lt. Kol. Martinus Lubis near the central market, where public concerts, lectures, and cultural shows take place. No a/c, but usually comfortable.

Events

Medan takes its religious and dance festivals seriously, and due to its polyglot, multiracial nature there are many. First find out what's going on at the North Sumatra Tourist Office, Jl. Jen. A. Yani 107. One of the most exciting is the Indian community's **Tabut Kaling,** highlighted by a colorful nighttime *tabut* procession around the city.

Lebaran is also lavishly celebrated here. On the Islamic holy day of **Idul Fitri,** hundreds of devotees and well-wishers converge on the Maimoon Palace in traditional dress. Malay women wear the *baju panjang* and a gold woven *songket,* while men dress in the long-sleeved *teluk belang* and *tengkuluk* headdress. This is the best time to visit the palace. Medan's founding anniversary takes place on 1 July, celebrated with sports events and cultural entertainment.

SHOPPING AND SERVICES

Shopping

The **Central Market** (Pasar Pusat), off Jl. Sutomo near downtown, is one of Southeast Asia's largest. It was *the* largest until half of it was destroyed by fire in 1971. Very old, colorful, and crowded; opens at dawn. Rows of huge two-story warehouses. Hang on to your belongings and wear thongs, as it's muddy. In this area there are actually a number of markets: Pasar Ramas, Pasar Kampung Keling, and Pasar Hong Kong, plus one of Sumatra's most modern shopping complexes, the **Olympia Plaza.** You can buy almost anything in these markets.

For both souvenirs and antiques, Jl. Jen. A. Yani is Medan's main shopping street, offering stores like **Toko Bali Arts** (no. 68), **Toko Rufino** (no. 64), and **Toko Asli** (no. 62). Beware: genuine Batak antiques are very rare and reproductions are quite convincing. Ersatz buffalo "powder horns" swirling with Neolithic carvings go for Rp45,000. Toba Batak calendars are also reproduced en masse. Bamboo weaving, woven blankets (*ulos*), and woodcarvings are probably the best values, but bargain intensely. Buy an old, good quality *ulos* blanket for around Rp120,000.

Services

For maps and information on Medan and North Sumatra Province, visit the **North Sumatran Tourist Office** (Dinas Pariwisata), Jl. Jen. A. Yani 107, tel. (061) 511-101 or 512-300. Open Mon.-Thurs. 0800-1500, Friday 0800-1200, Saturday 0800-1400. There's also an "information booth" at Polonia Airport that seems more interested in changing your money than in dispensing a few meager handouts. Another tourist office is **Kantor Wilayah I Sumatera Utara-Aceh**, Jl. Alpalah 22, tel. 322-838. The best bookshop in Medan is **Toko Buku Deli**, Jl. Jen. A. Yani 48. The **Gramedia**, Jl. Gajah Mada 23, is also well stocked.

You can also obtain good information from such travel agencies as **Nitour Inc.**, Jl. Prof. H. M. Yamin 21-E, Box 248, tel. 23191 or 513-074; see Sales and Operations Manager Suyanto Sastra Negara. Another recommended travel agent is **Natrabu Travel**, tel. 516-000, on Jl. Cut Mutiah; Morris can arrange a driver and accommodations to Brastagi, Prapat, and Samosir Island—very good prices despite a location near the expensive Tiara Medan Hotel.

Be sure to change your money in Medan if you're venturing inland, where banks are few and far between and offer lousy rates. **Bank Negara Indonesia**, Jl. Pemuda 12, tel. 22333, gives the best rates. Also try the **Bali Bank**, Jl. Balai Kota, and the several moneychangers around town. The worst rates are at the airport and at Krishen's. Dutch citizens must go to the general post office on the main *alun-alun* to acquire cash with Dutch *giro* cards.

At **PT Indosat** at the corner of Jl. Thamrin and Jl. Ngalengko you can make direct dial international telephone calls. The telephone city code is 061. Medan's **general post office** is a historic structure on Jl. Bukit Barisan, tel. 23612 or 25945, on Merdeka Square (the *alun-alun*). This full-service office will take parcels as well as ordinary mail. There's another post office at Polonia Airport, but it won't accept parcels. Immigration is at Jl. Jen. A. Yani 74. The Dutch consulate is at Jl. A. Rivai 22, tel. 519-025. Medan's **Rumah Sakit** (general hospital) is located on the corner of Jl. Prof. M. Yamin and Jl. Thamrin, tel. 23332.

TRANSPORTATION

Getting There

Medan is the western air gateway to Indonesia, only a 35-minute flight across the narrow Strait of Malacca from Penang, Malaysia. Garuda flies from Jakarta three times daily (2.5 hours). From Singapore to Medan flights run about S$275 (one hour). Medan's Polonia Airport has no luggage storage. No problems changing money in a small office. Emerging from customs, a mob of porters in yellow jumpsuits will descend upon you, intent on carrying your gear. Metered taxis into the city cost Rp2000-4000; cheaper are sputtering *mesin becak* to anywhere in Medan for Rp3000-4000. *Becak* are not allowed in the airport area, but walk 300 meters to the outside gate and hire one for Rp2000-2500. Alternatively, *bemo* cost Rp2000 into town. If you're not burdened down, walk into the city (two km).

A fast, efficient twin-hulled hydrofoil now makes the Penang-Medan crossing. Tickets cost M$100 one-way, M$180 roundtrip. Not cheap, but a good service. No need to buy a return ticket as nobody is ever asked by immigration (if necessary, you may buy one in Belawan). Arriving by hydrofoil in Belawan from Penang, buses are there waiting for you. Buy tickets on the boat (Rp4000) for the Belawan-Medan bus, or bargain hard with the unscrupulous *bemo* drivers for a ride into Medan. You should be able to get to a bank and a *losmen* for around Rp2000.

The ferry departs Tuesday and Friday at 0800 from near Penang's Port Commission, docking in Belawan (26 km north of Medan) five hours later. From Jakarta, the Pelni ship KM *Rinjani* sails every week and docks in Belawan. This nice cruise on a beautiful new boat takes two days. First class is absolutely luxurious.

By bus from Prapat is Rp3000, a five-hour trip; buses leave every hour. Buses from Padang take 26 hours. Buses from Banda Aceh arrive at the station on Jl. K.W. Hasyim in the northern part of the city. From Bukittinggi, buses require 22-24 hours to reach Medan.

Getting Around

Medan's traffic is noisy and congested, with swarms of fume-spewing motorized *becak*, motorcycles, new Japanese cars, buses, trucks, bicycles, *becak*, and jaywalking pedestrians. City roads are in chaos, with small parking spaces, endemic road repair, few intersections with lights, and no direction signs. A one-way street system has helped unsnarl monumental traffic jams, but street names change maddeningly every kilometer or so, making the city a navigational puzzle for the newcomer. The acrid fumes can be worse than Bangkok's.

Four-wheeled *oplet*, filled to overflowing, whiz down streets at incredible speeds, along established routes in town and out to the suburbs. Watch for pickpockets. *Mesin becak*, powered by motorbike engines, cruise the streets; charter rate Rp2000-3000 for one to two km.

If you're in a small group, Medan's plentiful metered taxis are a cheap (Rp700 flagfall, then Rp300 per km), fast, and convenient way to get around. Long-distance share taxis pick you up at your hotel—Rp10,000 to Prapat, Rp27,500 to Pekanbaru, Rp10,000 to Kutacane (six hours instead of nine hours by bus). The best of these private taxi companies are **Indah Taxi** Jl. Katamso 60, tel. (061) 516-615; **Sumatera,** tel. 29137; and **Cantik,** tel. 327-532, on Jl. Semarang.

Getting Away

Medan's Polonia Airport is two km from downtown. If you take a *becak*, get off outside the gate and walk 300 meters to the terminal. If in a hurry or burdened down, charter a minibus for Rp1500-2000. The price of a one-way Medan-Jakarta ticket is Rp170,250 with student discount, Rp202,000 without discount. Merpati flies to Gunungsitoli, as well as to Padang, Aceh, and Palembang.

International flights are available to Penang, Kuala Lumpur, and Singapore. Make sure to get confirmed booking through your airline of-

fice, as you hear many stories of reserved seats failing to materialize. This situation worsens when Malaysians and Indonesians swap sides on weekends. If you miss a booking, get out to the airport and onto the waiting list; seats are almost always available at the last minute. Airport departure tax is Rp10,000.

Garuda has two offices, in the Tiara Hotel Convention Centre on Jl. Cut Mutiah, tel. (061) 25702 or 515277, and in the Hotel Dharma Deli, Jl. Balaikota 2, tel. 516-400. Other offices: **Mandala,** Jl. Brig. Jen. Katamso 37 37-E, tel. 513-309 or 516-379; **Merpati,** Jl. Brig. Jen. Katamso 41, tel. 514-102 or 514-057; **MAS,** the Danau Toba International Hotel, Jl. Imam Bonjol 17, tel. 519-333; Singapore Airlines (SIA), Jl. Imam Bonjol 16; **SMAC,** Jl. Imam Bonjol 59 and at the airport.

From Belawan, 26 km north, high-speed hydrofoils depart Tuesday and Friday at 1330 for Penang, West Malaysia. Buy tickets (Rp90,000 deck, Rp125,000 cabin) at any number of Medan's hotels, *losmen,* or travel agencies. Get to Belawan by taking tourist buses (Rp5000, one hour) arranged by your hotel, or a Damri bus (Rp500) from Medan Plaza, then walk to the harbor area (1.5 km). A metered taxi to the harbor costs around Rp17,000. The **Pelni** office, Jl. Sugiono 5-7, tel. 518-980 or 518-533, is an easy walk from the Garuda and tourist office, one block back from Jl. Pemuda.

All trains from Medan to other destinations run pretty much on time, but on the return trip they're sometimes far behind schedule, especially the 1505 train from Pulau Siantar. Nowhere in northern Sumatra does a train ride cost more than Rp3000. Only second and third class available. Taking the morning train from Medan is a splendid way to travel to Lake Toba. A train leaves for Rantauprapat at 0930, traveling through beautiful plantations and arriving at 1050. A train also departs for Tanjungbalai, with a stopover in Kisaran, at 0730; arrives 1132.

Big **Amplas bus station** in south Medan (Jl. Pertahanan off Jl. Sisingamangaraja) runs buses in every direction; get there from downtown Medan for Rp250. The largest bus companies are ALS, ANS, and Medan Raya, all operating Mercedes buses on scheduled routes. Many bus company offices are found along Jl. Sisingamangaraja and its side streets. Long-distance buses to Banda Aceh cost Rp20,000; Bukittinggi or Padang, Rp12,000-15,000, depending upon the condition of the bus. Reserve two days in advance if you want the more comfortable front seats.

For those short on time, **Krishen's** offers a seven-day tour of northern Sumatra for four people for Rp24,000 per day. Shop around for the best prices on transport. For example, a shared taxi to Kutacane costs around Rp6000 while Jacky asks Rp20,000. Jacky provides a share minibus to Bukit Lawang for Rp3000-4000 per person, but all you have to do is walk down the street and grab the public bus for Rp2000.

From Amplas Station it's Rp3000 (four hours) to Prapat on good Mercedes PMH buses, which roll from 0600 until around 1700. Buses for Prapat and Brastagi also cruise along Medan's main streets (Jl. Sisingamangaraja and Jl. Iskandar Muda) looking for fares. Alternatively, you can take a bus first to Pematang Siantar, then to Prapat. The longer drive via Brastagi (Rp1000, 71 km from Medan) to Prapat is the most scenic; reach Haranggaol on Lake Toba via Kabanjahe.

The ALS and ANS buses drop their loads of backpackers at **PT Andilo**'s who pays the drivers Rp200 per person for delivering them to his place on the Trans-Sumatra Highway. There he sells them terrible banana pancakes, fruit salads, and corn-made "coffee," and rents them grubby rooms. Medan Raya is a cooperative with drivers who sometimes try to drop backpackers at another place in Prapat, claiming the bus stops there. Don't believe them—insist on going to Tigaraja, where the last ferry leaves around 1800.

VICINITY OF MEDAN

PEMATANG SIANTAR

Located 128 km southeast of Medan, in one of Sumatra's richest tea- and tobacco-growing districts, Pematang Siantar is North Sumatra's second-largest city, a smaller, cooler version of Medan but just as noisy. This city is the capital and largest town of the Simalungun Batak tribe, though there are many non-Simalungun people here, including Chinese, Indians, Karo, and Toba Batak. Also the site of Universitas Simalungan, north of town. Pasar Horas, Siantar Plaza, and Pantoan are the town's new, glitzy shopping centers.

The Simalungun Batak

Their tribal name means "He that is lonely, quiet, or sad." The Simalungun branch of the Batak are a gentle, soft-mannered people with many sad, nostalgic songs, who speak with a slow, lilting intonation. These people were evolving from sedentary *ladang* cultivators into a feudal society when the Dutch arrived; they weren't conquered until 1910. Half the Simalungun are animist, the other half Islamic or Christian, though all attend animist ceremonies such as the group hair-washing ritual (*erpangir*). A number of traditional Simalungun events are held in early December at the royal village of Pematang Purba, west of Pulau Siantar. To really understand the Simalungun culture, visit this village.

Sights

The **Museum Simalungun** on Jl. Sudirman houses a special exhibit of the Simalungun Batak clan. Open Mon.-Sat. 0800-1200 and 1400-1700. Donation. Check out the sculpture in the front yard dating from Portuguese times—a purely animist, powerfully carved seated woman cradling children. The lizard on the door that looks like a crocodile is really a *cicak*; this small lizard lives in the home and offers protection against thieves. Inside are manuscripts in Batak script, spears, gongs, masks, artwork, textiles, and bygone children's games. All labels are in Indonesian. Also visit the town's flower gardens, the **Bah Sorma Swimming Pool** (with restaurants), and the **Senang Umum** clove cigarette factory.

Accommodations

A small clump of hotels in the middle of town are a 10-minute walk from the bus station. The best deals include **Hotel Segar** (Rp5000 s), Jl. Merdeka 234—a bit noisy, but the rooftop overlooks a *pasar* neighborhood. Also try **Losmen Pahala** (Rp6000 s) at Jl. Sokro 133. **Hotel Garuda**, Jl. Merdeka 33, asks Rp15,000-25,000, but you can sometimes bargain them down. Rooms aren't particularly clean and there are no inside *mandi*; the ones in back have no windows. **Hotel Bali**

(Rp8500 pp) is near Hotel Garuda at Jl. Merdeka 52. **Hotel Delima,** Jl. Thamrin 131, is on the other end of town; Rp4000 per person (bargained down from Rp5000).

Siantar Hotel, Jl. W.R. Supratman, is the only high-standard accommodation. For Rp40,000 s, Rp50,000 d, you get private bath, hot water, breakfast, and the privilege of paying government tax. The Siantar also offers a small but select library, nice garden, souvenir shop, billiards, and a restaurant with Euro and Indonesian food—a nicely maintained colonial-style hotel with excellent service.

Food

Numerous Chinese shops sell fresh-baked goods along the town's main street. Good *mie* places as well. **Miramar Restaurant** has tasty Indonesian food. For *nasi padang,* try **Asmara Murni** on Jl. Sutomo; Rp3000 for a nice meal. Also check out **Warung Sederhana** at Jl. Diponegoro 2H.

Crafts

Batak and Karo tribal artifacts are sold in Pasar Besar. Though each tribe uses different colors and patterns, *ulos* fabrics generally feature vertical stripes with horizontal ends and blue backgrounds in red and white designs. *Ulos* are still regularly produced—when a Simalungun Batak male marries, he must present these blankets to his in-laws. The best now cost up to Rp200,000. Check out old specimens in the Simalungun Museum. *Ragidup* cloths are sold in Pasar Besar.

Transportation

Pematang Siantar is a major transport hub for the whole Simalungan area. The train to Medan (Rp1300) is slow but nice. The two bus stations are Stasiun Sentral on the Medan end of town and Stasiun Parlusan two km from town. Stasiun Sentral is just another creepy bus station, but the only way to avoid it is to take a through bus. From Parlusan, catch buses to Haranggaol, Brastagi, Kabanjahe, Prapat (Rp1000, four hours), Sibolga (on this eight-hour ride you pass Balige with its riotously colorful fruit market), and Bukittinggi.

PEMATANG PURBA

A 200-year-old village of Simalungun tribal chiefs, 140 km south of Medan. Pulau Purba used to be the site of an old "execution tree," under which men were judged and then ritually eaten by villagers. The tree was cut down by Dutch soldiers, to help put an end to cannibalism. The village's former entrance tunnel and some earthworks can still be seen.

Within the complex are the ancient courthouse, carved pillars, rice barns, and *raja*'s palace (Rumah Bolon). This beautiful 150-year-old longhouse was inhabited by Batak royalty until 1945. Inside are fireplaces for the many wives (the last *raja* had 12) and attendants. The king signaled his desire to sleep with a certain wife by instructing his eunuch to present her with a betelnut offering. Today, busloads of tourists pass through in the mornings. A guide hits you up for a donation and tries to sell you souvenirs. It's sad to see descendants of kings beg. A living village, like in the Tiga Gambar hinterlands of Karoland, would be more interesting.

This museum village is 200 meters south of the highway, about midway between Pematang Siantar and Kabanjahe, and Rp1500 by bus from Haranggaol. From Pematang Purba, a scenic, bumpy road eventually leads to Kabanjahe. Also, there's an ancient path from Pematang Purba all the way down to Lake Toba.

BUKIT LAWANG

In complete contrast to filthy, smelly, noisy Medan, Bukit Lawang is a relaxing village of several hundred people 90 km west of Medan and 15 km west of Bohorok on the edge of 900,000-hectare Gunung Leuser National Park, deep in North Sumatra's backcountry.

Most travelers venture here to view our distant cousins the orangutan in a right environment, but then discover Bukit Lawang is a delightful place to relax as well. People are very friendly and some speak quite good English. A high-quality Swedish-made video is shown twice weekly and your questions answered at the **Bohorok River Visitor's Center.** From the government's *pasanggrahan,* it's an easy 20-minute walk to the free canoe crossing and entrance to the reserve. Obtain three-day permits (Rp3000) at the PHPA office in Bukit Lawang or from the office in Medan (Jl. Sisingmangaraja Km 55). Try to arrive on weekday mornings to avoid hordes of domestic tourists.

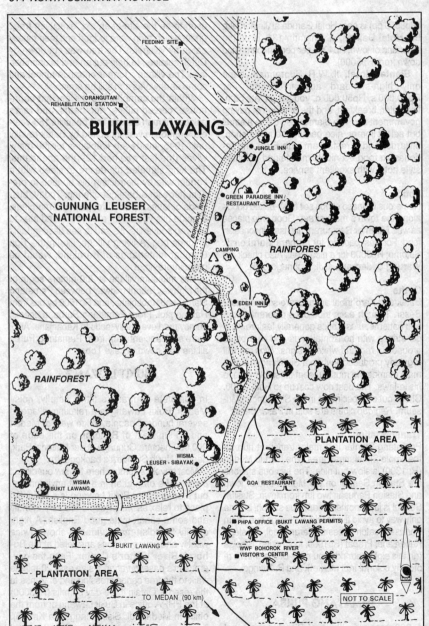

FEEDING SITE

ORANGUTAN
REHABILITATION STATION

BUKIT LAWANG

JUNGLE INN

**GUNUNG LEUSER
NATIONAL FOREST**

BOHOROK RIVER

GREEN PARADISE INN /
RESTAURANT

CAMPING

RAINFOREST

EDEN INN

RAINFOREST

PLANTATION AREA

WISMA
LEUSER - SIBAYAK

WISMA
BUKIT LAWANG

GOA RESTAURANT

PHPA OFFICE (BUKIT LAWANG PERMITS)

BUKIT LAWANG

WWF BOHOROK RIVER
VISITOR'S CENTER

PLANTATION AREA

TO MEDAN (90 km)

NOT TO SCALE

At night visit the house where the singers and musicians play; really nice voices. In the nearby village visit the rubber-processing factory; the manager will show you around. Swim in the Bohorok River. You can also rent a rubber inner tube from **Wisma Leuser Guesthouse** or other places (Rp1000) and shoot the rapids downriver for 2.5 hours. It's great fun but can be literally an ass-ripping experience if you have the misfortune to clip a submerged rock at high speed. Wear shoes because of the river's rocky bottom and bring some money in a plastic bag for the bus back.

Accommodations
In the slow season, prices for accommodations fall Rp1000-2000. The spartan **PHPA Guesthouse** asks Rp3500 pp plus Rp1000 for a very plain dinner. This government-run guesthouse, which sleeps eight, is the last house beyond the village, directly across from the river. There's also a two-hectare camping area with a shelter and toilets halfway between the village and the Rehabilitation Center.

Wisma Leuser Sibayak has bungalows along the river for only Rp7000, other huts Rp5000, dorm beds Rp2000. Good value, friendly people, good food. Mr. Burhan charges Rp6000 with mosquito net (Rp5000 without), Rp3000 for the dorm, Rp1500 for the floor. This gentleman can help arrange the jungle trek to Brastagi or a raft trip down the Bohorok—great fun. **Wisma Bukit Lawang** is better than Wisma Leuser Sibayak, with even tastier food, great views, and similar prices.

Besides the places in the village itself, which charge Rp4000-5000 for rooms, there are other places to stay upstream—the **Eden Inn, Jungle Inn,** and **Green Paradise.** The best is Green Paradise, a 15-minute walk upriver toward the orangutan center. Small and friendly—in fact, one of the best places to stay on Sumatra. Plain, clean, and okay bungalows with a nice veranda overlooking the river cost Rp1500 s or Rp3000 d; the dorm is Rp1000. The food is quite disappointing, though. The owner is a bearded character named Ewan. He spends his days swinging on a hammock, ogling passing women, and preening his beard for his next conquest.

Food
Not a strong point, though the barbecue chicken and amazing fruit salad at **Wisma Sibayak** is highly recommended. But if you hate cats, don't eat there—the place is crawling with them. Good food for very cheap prices at **Goa Restaurant,** where an excellent *gado-gado* is only Rp750. Restaurants have limited menus and serve Euro-style Indonesian food, french fries, fruit salads, etc. Some have balconies which extend right over the river.

Pusat Rehabilitasi Mawas
Since the orangutan (*mawas*) is now headed for extinction (only about 1,000 are left in Sumatran jungles), this center and others like it elsewhere in Sumatra and in Kalimantan preserve wild *mawas* from slaughter or capture, and rehabilitate confiscated specimens. At Pusat Rehabilitasi Mawas you can observe orangutan undergoing training for a return to their original habitat—a rare opportunity. Up to 500 tourists visit the center each week, most from Medan. The center is well-maintained—regulations are followed and the animals receive the care they need. Another rehabilitation center in Tanjung Puting in Central Kalimantan serves the quite distinct Bornean subspecies of this endangered ape. Both centers are a joint project of the World Wildlife Fund and the Indonesian Nature Conservation Agency.

The center is a 45-minute walk from Bukit Lawang at the end of a river trail. A canoe on a cable is provided for crossing the river, where visitors are met by a ranger who accompanies them to the station to sign in. Don't forget your permit. The rangers will ask for a donation of Rp1000. From the station it's a strenuous 15-minute hike up a steep hill to watch the feeding of the semiwild orangutan. Feeding times are at 0800 and 1500. During the rainy season (October, November, and December), fewer orangutan show up for feeding, as they get enough food in the forest. On your way back, cool off in the river.

Getting There And Away
A memorable part of a visit here is the ride out to the reserve through tropical rainforests and rubber plantations. Direct buses from Medan depart each day in the morning and between 1300 and 1500 from Stasiun Sei Wampu; three hours (Rp1500 one-way) on a fairly good road. Buses also depart Medan for Binjei (22 km west of Medan, one hour) all morning long. From Binjei, the last bus leaves at about 1400 and you roll into Bukit Lawang about three hours later. Or you can take a collective minibus from Binjei

ORANGUTAN REHABILITATION CENTER

With orangutans (*mawas*) headed for extinction, this center and others like it aim to preserve the species and rehabilitate confiscated individuals. At Pusat Rehabilitasi Mawas, you can observe orangutans undergoing training to return to their original habitat—a rare opportunity. Like a rehabilitation center located in Central Kalimantan, Pusat Rehabilitasi Mawas is administered by the World Wildlife Fund and the Indonesian Nature Conservation Service, financed largely by the Frankfurt Zoological Society and private donations.

The center is a 45-minute walk from Bukit Lawang at the end of a river trail on top of a steep hill. A canoe on a cable allows crossing of the river; there, visitors are met by a ranger who heads up a strenuous hike to watch the feeding of the semiwild orangutans. The ranger asks a Rp1000 donation.

Officially, only 50 tourists are allowed into the center each day, but in reality up to 500 visit it each week—the government really pushes the place as a tourist attraction. The rehabilitation station has great propaganda value. "Animals belong in their natural habitat and not in cages" is the message, and that message is worth transmitting. If you have a great love of nature, are capable of silence, and will only stay half an hour or so, you'll be welcome at the center.

The Orangutan

One of the great apes, the usually vegetarian, tailless *mawas* is the Asian equivalent of the African gorilla and chimpanzee. The orangutan is the most arboreal of all the great apes. Their name, in Indonesian, means "man of the forest." Orangutans cause trees to sway to reach other trees, and sometimes use forked tree branches as tools to get at fruit. The simian has few natural enemies, though clouded leopards occasionally seize youngsters. Orangutans are most often loners, and don't travel in large families. Their wiry hair offers protection from the rain; sometimes they use large leaves to cover themselves.

The *mawas* at this center were captured illegally and kept as pets in Indonesian homes. The orangutans at the center have either been voluntarily donated by former owners, confiscated by the PHPA, or captured from poachers. Even "responsible" senior government officials in Medan still domesticate them, a legacy from Dutch times when owning a gentle, shaggy orangutan was the prerogative of a colonial gentleman. As *mawas* grow older, however, they move from cute bundles of wispy orange fur to large, powerful 90-kg adults who bite, defecate in-

discriminately, and are most often eventually confined in cages.

The Weaning Process

It is the task of the rehab station to retrain about 20 animals at a time to live again in the wild. The tame and semitame orangutans are also studied here, and much is learned about orangutan behavior in a setting more natural than any zoo.

At first the orphans are fed bananas and milk, but gradually their food supply is decreased, forcing them to forage for themselves. It's a very good sign if one shows up late for a feeding session. They must also learn how to climb and build nests in the trees and how to camouflage themselves with leaves for protection against tigers and panthers. Most difficult, however, is learning to become wary of human beings. Although magnificently strong, the vulnerable orangutan is an utter pacifist and never attacks. Its most aggressive gesture is hurling branches down at woodcutters below.

When their dependence on human care has lessened to the point where they seem able to fend for themselves, they're flown by helicoptor to a distant part of the reserve and released. Like a child's first day at preschool, orangutans are sometimes reluctant to leave their cages and venture into the unknown.

In modern nature conservation practice, much emphasis is placed on the conservation of entire ecosystems. It's impossible to preserve orangutan populations in the wild without giving just as much attention to the preservation of the rainforest which provides the orangutans' lines of communication, sources of food, and safe resting places. Yet in the so-called Gunung Leuser "Reserve," logging operations occur with the tacit approval of the Indonesian authorities; more than 4,000 hectares have already been logged. In the long run this poses the greatest danger of all to the survival of the released *mawas*.

subadult orangutan

(Rp1750, two hours), which leaves when full; ask the driver on the bus from Medan to drop you off at Binjei's taxi stop. You can board buses for Bukit Lawang starting at 0630 (Rp2000) along Jl. Veteran in Brastagi.

Direct, crowded buses for Brastagi depart at 0530 and take seven hours, half to Binjei. Direct buses for Medan leave every hour from 0530 to 1630, but for the afternoon buses you must change in Binjei to reach Medan. In Binjei there's a marvelous, friendly place to stay, the **Cafe de Malioboro,** which has terrific rooms for only Rp5000 s or d, including breakfast. The rooms are very large, and clean, and look out on a beautiful, quiet garden.

Rainforest Trekking
The going rate (all inclusive) for a trek is Rp15,000 pp per day, or Rp20,000 for overnight trips. For day-trips, have a restaurant pack you a lunch in banana leaves. The trek all the way to Brastagi takes two to three days. Price includes food (plain rice, dried fish, *sambal*), tent, guidance, and, if you're lucky, some good information. The guide Mudjeni Ario has the best reputation. He works full time so can only take you on weekends. Meet him at the Visitor's Center.

The walk is beautiful, but only about 25% or less is through primary forest and you won't see a lot of animals. You'll cross swollen rivers, slide over muddy sections while gripping liana vines, and sleep in a different village each night. Take *mandi* in the rivers to refresh yourself. Bring warm clothes because it's cold at night. Check your guide's tent for leaks, as it could rain every day around noon. Use ASA 400 film, as the vegetation cover makes it dark.

ACEH PROVINCE

Sumatra's northernmost province and the westernmost province of Indonesia, Aceh seems a nation apart from the rest of the island and the country, and it could indeed support itself very well from its natural-gas revenues alone. Few travelers make it up this far because of Aceh's mostly unfounded reputation for religious extremism.

If you don't wear shorts or go braless, and you speak some Indonesian, you may find this the friendliest, most civilized province in Indonesia. Its hospitable people, historic architecture and remains, rugged mountains, superlative beaches, and picturesque rural areas will make your trip quite memorable. Two points to keep in mind: beer is largely forbidden to Aceh residents, though foreigners can buy it in hotels and restaurants. And do not carry or smoke marijuana, though locals may offer it to you. The police search likely looking foreigners and throw them behind bars for a few (or many) months if anything is found.

THE LAND

Sumatra's second-highest peak, still-active Gunung Leuser (3,381 meters), is located in southern Aceh Province, in one of Indonesia's largest and least-explored wildlife reserves. Gunung Bandahara (3,012 meters) is another of the province's formidable peaks. Aceh's lowland rainforests are immensely tall, with hundreds of different species of trees, some up to 60 meters high. The pristine coastlines offer clear water and unpolluted beaches; the west coast is generally more scenic than the east coast. Two to three hours from Banda Aceh down the Indian Ocean side is some of the best scenery northern Sumatra has to offer. The central region is mostly sparsely populated mountain wasteland, except for a few fertile districts such as the Takengon area, where the Gayo people cultivate coffee.

Fauna
When Marco Polo landed in Aceh Province in 1292, he claimed he saw a unicorn; it was most likely the one-horned hairy Sumatran rhinoceros, restricted now to the Gunung Leuser National Park and pockets along southeast Sumatra. Tigers and elephants (about 600) are concentrated in the province's more remote central and western regions. In 1985, 55 elephants went on a rampage, smashing homes, chasing villagers, and trampling crops in an attempt to

reach the sea to obtain badly needed salt. With the aid of a helicopter and 350 beaters, they were driven back into Gunung Leuser National Park, but by mid-1986 they were trickling back to the sea.

HISTORY

Lying almost 1,700 km northwest of Jakarta, Aceh is historically and culturally quite distinct from the rest of Indonesia. Contrary to its image as an isolated Indonesian province, Aceh has been trading with Malaya, China, India, Sri Lanka, and the Middle East for well over 1,000 years. During most of its history this state, which possessed an advanced culture and excelled in statecraft, has been an independent kingdom. Because of its critical location at the head of the Strait of Malacca, its territories were always fought over by colonial powers.

Early Islamic Sultanates

The 5th-century *Liang* annals of China mention a Buddhist state in the Aceh region. In the 7th and 8th centuries Indian traders introduced Hinduism, and by the 9th century Islam made its first inroads into Indonesia at present-day Lhokseumawe. When Marco Polo visited Aceh on his return journey from China in 1292, he wrote an account of the first well-established Islamic sultanate in Southeast Asia. The small sultanates in regions such as Perlak, Bonua, Lingga, and Pidie were all gradually consolidated under one sultanate, with its capital in Great Aceh, where Banda Aceh is today. In 1507 began a long line of sultanates which lasted until the final sultan, Tuanku Muhamat Dawot, capitulated to the Dutch in 1903.

The kingdom fought the Portuguese almost continually after the latter conquered Melaka in 1511. Fatahillah, the prince who founded Jakarta, is believed to have come from Pasai in Aceh Province, and local legend claims even Jakarta was first settled from Pasai. Sunan Gunung Jati, the sultan of Cirebon and one of the nine *wali*, is also thought to have come from Aceh.

Golden Age

During the 16th and 17th centuries the capital, Banda Aceh, was a major international trading center that attracted settlements of Indians, Chinese, Arabs, Persians, and Turks. In the 17th century, under the great ruler Sultan Iskandar Muda, Aceh reached the height of its political and economic power. During this Golden Age (1607-36) the Acehnese had a representative in Istanbul, and even engaged in diplomacy with London through the English sea captain James Lancaster. Its navy once held sway over virtually all of the Strait of Malacca as well as large tracts of the Malay Peninsula and the Riau Archipelago, including Singapore. The tolls levied on shipping brought untold wealth into the state's coffers.

Colonial Resistance

Aceh was fiercely rebellious during Dutch colonial times. The maritime power of the Dutch East Indies Co. broke Aceh's economic control of the pepper trade, but when a Dutch expedition was sent to pacify Aceh in 1873, it was driven into the sea. The Dutch declared war on Aceh that April, and a bitter "holy war" (*perang sabil*) broke out, which pitted the Acehnese against approximately 10,000 colonial army troops and the ablest field commanders the Dutch could muster. When the *kraton* of Aceh fell at last in 1878, the struggle had cost 107,000 lives.

Decades of guerrilla warfare and skirmishing ensued; smuggled British arms were purchased in large part by the fruits of trade in the rebel-controlled inland areas. Many heroes rose to fame during this period. In one of the many rebellions against the Dutch (1896), a guerrilla band under the fearless Teuku Umar "defected" to the Dutch side, then escaped with a whole company of men, rifles, and ammunition. For over 40 years this rabid holy war dragged on, costing hundreds of thousands of lives. It was the longest war in Indonesia's history.

In desperation the Dutch employed counterinsurgency measures, arming their Ambonese troops with modern firearms and deadly *klewang* sabers. This tactic soon brought partial success, and the Dutch were able to build a railroad along the coast from Medan all the way up to Banda Aceh. But the colonial army was virtually barricaded in the coastal towns of Bireuen, Sigli, and Langsa. This epic struggle has been commemorated in perhaps the finest film ever produced in this country, *Tjoet Nya' Dhien* (1988).

The turning point came when a famous Islamic scholar, Snouck Hurgronje, advised the Dutch on how to neutralize the *ulama's* authority over the people, and break the bond between the *ulama* and the traditional chieftains, the *uleebalang*. By the early 1900s this new policy enabled the Dutch to maintain an uneasy peace in the province. But the Acehnese were never conquered, just held in check. Dutch troops had to be stationed in Banda Aceh right up to the eve of the Japanese invasion in 1942.

Under their new oppressors, the Japanese, the Acehnese were forced every morning to face to the east toward Tokyo, exactly the opposite of praying to the west toward Mecca. This made the Japanese even more hated than the Dutch. After the Japanese surrender, most of the hereditary chiefs and their families, who had served as administrative officials under the Dutch and Japanese, were wiped out. During the struggle for independence only Aceh remained republican territory while the rest of the archipelago fell again to the Dutch.

In the early years of the new republic the Darul Islam movement, based in West Java, attempted to establish a theocratic state in Indonesia. The Acehnese joined the rebellion and it took from 1953 to 1961 for them to reach a compromise with the central government. Although Jakarta has wisely declared Aceh a "Special Autonomous Territory" (Daerah Istimewa) where Islamic law applies, today it is still a very tender area politically. The governor is a native son; Jakarta wouldn't dare install a Javanese governor here. Aceh was the only province to defeat the army-backed Golkar Party in the 1987 parliamentary elections.

POLITICS

The Javanese have never really understood the Acehnese, and there is little historic, political, cultural, or geographic connection between them. In spite of this, during the war of independence the resource-rich Acehnese always remained loyal to the revolutionary government. They contributed the first airplane to the revolutionary cause in 1945, and financed fighting against the Dutch in Medan. In the 1953 civil war in North Sumatra, Kalimantan, and North Sulawesi, Aceh, although it remained independent, never raised its sword against the central government. During the North Sumatra uprisings in 1965, Aceh again sided with Jakarta.

From the start of Suharto's new order in 1967, however, the Acehnese became increasingly restive, resentful of the fact the Javanese centrists were taking more from the province than they put back in. In the late '70s the long-standing bitterness finally broke into open rebellion with the creation of a shadowy independence movement led by a group calling themselves Aceh Merdeka ("Freedom for Aceh"). Military forays were mounted, but in the face of sustained counterattacks by Indonesian troops, Aceh Merdeka's back was broken by the early 1980s with the death of five of the movement's 10 "cabinet ministers." The fiercely independent Acehnese today revere these dead militants as martyrs.

In 1990 about 80 people were killed in the region, mostly soldiers and Javanese settlers. Nongovernment sources attribute the violence to a revival of Aceh's nationalist movement, though the government blames common criminals involved in the area's thriving marijuana production. But the problem is more complex and deepseated than the government claims. The Acehnese have always resented outsiders; it exacerbates the situation when thousands of Javanese transmigrants are given acres of good land and other benefits while the native Acehnese are barely able to eke out a living.

ECONOMY

Aceh Province is one of the nation's most productive and prosperous regions. The East and North Aceh districts are industrial areas where 75% of the province's economic life is concentrated, while West, South, Southeast, and Central Aceh are the province's agricultural zones. The per capita income of Aceh—not including wealth from oil or natural gas—is above the national average. The *batik* the people wear isn't as faded as in other parts of Indonesia, and Aceh now has 17 television stations, the second largest number of any province in Indonesia.

Aceh has a surplus of meat, 400,000 tons of rice are exported each year, and large quantities of fish are caught off its coasts and in the high plateau region of the Gayo. The main export commodities are wood, rubber, palm oil, pepper, cloves, timber, and coffee. About 70% of the province consists of forests. Timber theft and uncontrolled logging is a serious problem in West, South, and Southeast Aceh, causing floods and landslides.

The province's mineral wealth is substantial and provides badly needed export dollars for the central government. The US$400 million natural gas project at Arun—the biggest of its kind in all of Asia—is expected to net Jakarta US$10 billion over the next 20 years. The Acehnese cannot sell their commodities directly to the export markets—all goods must go through Jakarta. Although the consensus among the Acehnese is to remain with Indonesia, they've always demanded more consultation and compensation for the wealth Jakarta gouges from the region. If there isn't a more equitable distribution of Aceh's wealth, the Javanese face growing bitterness among the native population.

THE PEOPLE

The 3.2 million native inhabitants of northernmost Sumatra are divided into earlier pre-Malayan hill peoples, the Gayo and the Alas, and the more recent lowland coastal people who are a product of centuries of inbreeding with the Batak, Dravidians, North Indians, Javanese, Arabs, Chinese, and Minangkabau. The heterogeneous coastal Acehnese are taller, stouter, and darker than most other Sumatrans, an indication of their Arabian, Indian, and Portuguese descent. But the Malay- and Chinese-looking types are just as Acehnese as everyone else. As the Acehnese say, the word A-C-E-H stands for Arabic, Chinese, European, and Hindu.

The older Gayo do not incorporate as much of the Indian and Arab admixtures, and they're not fighters like other Acehnese. There are even traces of forest pygmies, called Orang Mante, deep in the Gunung Leuser National Park, survivors of an aboriginal race. The Chinese minority handle most of the retail business and do most of the construction work. The Chinese of Aceh are gradually converting to Islam and intermarrying. At one time the Acehnese in remote areas were not friendly to foreigners, especially the Dutch. But their reputation for religious fervor, Islamic fundamentalism, and savage militancy is overwrought. In truth, the Acehnese will treat you with the utmost warmth.

Language

The five dialects of Acehnese are related to Bahasa Indonesia and the other languages of western Indonesia. Acehnese includes Arabic loan words and bears some similarities to the Cham languages of Indochina. People's names, such as Cut Nyak Dhien, have obvious Indochinese origins. Acehnese is written in Latin script. Children speak Acehnese until they are three, then they start learning Bahasa Indonesia. Formerly, most Acehnese could read and write Arabic; the marriage law and statute books are written in that language. The Acehnese often pray in Arabic and are still more likely to understand Arabic than other of the country's ethnic groups. The Gayonese language of the highlands is closer to Karonese than Acehnese.

Village Life

The Acehnese are very attached to their villages and invitations to someone's home occur frequently. Village dwellings, which are well cared for, neat, and clean, are built of bamboo with thatched roofs. These multifamily structures feature separate quarters for males and females, marrieds and unmarrieds. The *kepala desa* and other village men meet at centrally located *meunasah* communal halls (open-air, pile-raised platforms), structures not often seen in other areas of Sumatra. Members of a council of elders in a village are consulted on questions of inheritance and marriage laws. *Meunasah* are also used as schools, sleeping places for young men, guest quarters, prayer sites, and for public ceremonies. It is not uncommon for relatives and loved ones to be buried in the front yard of the family house right under the deceaseds' favorite trees.

Marriage

Marriage is a contract between the father of the bride and the bridegroom. In return for the bride-price, the bride's parents support their daughter and her children; this sometimes includes the purchase of a house. Characteristic of Acehnese weddings are elaborate costumes—the bride is dressed in all the finery of a Balinese *legong* dancer. In rural areas for a certain period after the wedding the bride and bridegroom are not allowed to remain alone in a room with the door locked, and are forbidden to have sex. To ensure this, their hands and nails are painted red and the bride's body is examined each morning by the mother to make sure she has not been touched—all of which only encourages very subtle and contortionist acrobatics. After the wedding, the bride and groom won't usually move in together until they can throw a big party.

Family Life

Strangely, in this male-dominated society, the family is matriarchal, although this is a relatively recent development. The woman and her sisters, particularly in Pidie District, often own the home and inherit the land. The term for wife is *nyang po rumoh,* or "the one who owns the house." In northern Aceh, the bride often receives a house as a dowry from her parents, or the couples may take up residence in the home of the bride's parents, although today many young couples set up their own households soon after marriage.

Husbands are nearly powerless in the home, playing a minor role in raising children and maintaining the house. The Acehnese are primarily farmers, fishermen, laborers, and businessmen. As is often the case throughout Sumatra, men leave the village for long periods to take care of business, coming back during Ramadan. The wife manages the fields and household with the help of the cash provided by the husband—or her parents, if the bride-price was high enough.

Religion

The Acehnese are socially conservative but religiously radical. Along with Yogyakarta and Jakarta, Aceh is designated a "Special Autonomous Territory" where Islamic law is enforced. A thief's arm may be broken for stealing an old banged-up tape recorder. Cruel and unusual punishment? Perhaps, but stealing in this province is seldom heard of and there is no juvenile delinquency problem. Zealotry is relative, and if you compare Aceh with Iran or Saudi Arabia—where the arm would surely be severed—the Acehnese could be considered flaming liberals.

Islam is incorporated into the Acehnese constitution, and has served as inspiration for Aceh's literature. Aceh was the first part of the archipelago to be converted, and today it's a bedrock of Islam, where the faith is practiced with unusual intensity and severity. When the Acehnese are agitated over some religious matter, they are *really* agitated. Mention religion, and these people are ready to die.

Along with the village headman, the local religious leader (*ulama*) is very influential in village life. Knowledgeable in the Islamic religious code (*teungku meunasah*), he conducts public prayer meetings and supervises the religious boarding school (*pesantren*), the administration of which is not a village function.

Yet with all their strict adherence to the precepts of Islam, the Acehnese still give great credence to heretical, almost pantheistic practices. The Islamic judicial system (*hukom*) is the law of the land as long as it does not interfere with *adat*, which remains very strong. Ritual offerings are still employed when planting and harvesting, there is implicit belief in the paranormal such as "invincible" stones, and the interpretation of dreams and omens is widespread. Like so many other places in Indonesia, religion has been adapted to fit local needs.

Christianity has been furiously resisted by the Acehnese. The Bible may not be translated into the phonetic, Latin-script Acehnese language, nor may cassette tapes of the Bible be sold here. Still, churches are found in Banda Aceh, and there's even a Catholic church with a resident Italian priest on Pulau Weh off the coast.

Conduct

Considering its religious orthodoxy, Aceh's moral climate is not that restrictive as long as you respect their culture, their religion, and their women. Here, more than anywhere else in Indonesia, you should dress respectfully—no shorts or see-through blouses please. *Sarung* are not that popular; most girls wear short skirts. Women always show their faces and you'll never see full veils in the towns; it's more common in the *kampung*. A woman need not worry at night; she can wander anywhere safely.

However, the Acehnese are very quick to take offense if you don't respect their customs. If you get fresh with their women, you better hope the police arrive in time to protect you. If you tell the local people their society is too strict, they may ask how many women are hurt or killed in rape or robbery attempts where you come from.

Foreigners and local girls date, but are strictly chaperoned. Though in Banda Aceh young couples are often seen together, it's not a good idea to hold hands with the opposite sex on the street, even if you're married. The rule is that if you want sex, you get married. Be careful about photographing women; ask permission first. Dancing isn't acceptable, and women wade in the ocean clad in dresses. Drinking is not really sanctioned behavior: when you go to a restaurant with your Acehnese friend, you may have a beer, but s/he'll have a Coke.

Movies are censored in Aceh *after* censorship by the Indonesian government. If you go to a two-hour movie and it runs only 45 minutes, you'll know why. During the month-long Ramadan no one may smoke on the street during the day; if you do, citizens will ask you not to. All restaurants and *warung* will be closed during the day.

Arts And Crafts

Traditional technology still survives in the interior, but sewing, metalwork, filigree, weapons, and fine unglazed earthenware pottery are all slowly disappearing with the importation of synthetic goods. The lack of tourism hastens their disappearance. Acehnese metalworking is superlative—lamps ornamented with large bird figures, copper bowls intricately engraved, elaborate brocades. The finely crafted weaponry, an art developed over decades of holy war, includes shields with Moorish designs and swords with mystic Arabic markings. Very attractive and unique, if you can still find them.

Gold and silver are worked extensively. The Acehnese identified very early with New England traders arriving here in the early 1800s: if you go into the goldshops today you can still find imitations of early American gold coinage. Gold jewelry here is sold by weight and you pay nothing for the exquisite work. Gold is occasionally treated with acid to give it a reddish tint, considered more appealing than its true yellow color.

Acehnese cotton and silk fabrics, embroidered clothes, tapestries, cushions, fans, and gold-threaded *songket* are imaginative and of high quality. Embroidery centers are Banda Aceh, Sigli, and Meulaboh. Pieces take several months to complete. The traditional Acehnese loom is made of bamboo with one end tied around the weaver's waist and the other around a post. Silk weaving is undertaken especially for weddings in the area around Banda Aceh. Embroidered pillow coverings (Rp10,000-12,500) are popular all over the province as wedding gifts.

Traditional dancing is undergoing a revival. The *seudati* folk dance, popular in Banda Aceh, North Aceh, and Pidi areas, is staged during important village and family rituals, public holidays, and harvest times. It's performed by 10 men wearing white trousers, long white shirts, red folded hats (*tengkuluk*), and Acehnese daggers (*rencong*). The dance is led by a *syech,* the stage director and choreographer. The dancers stand in two rows facing each other. The *syech* then leads the group in a chorus of narrative songs, rhymes, and spells, the dancers moving rhythmically with varying tempos, occasionally beating their chests and snapping their fingers. The stories revolve around local historical events, but can also convey criticism of members of the community or describe the consequences of neglecting religious studies. The government uses the *seudati* to instruct the people on birth control or health matters. To hire a group of *seudati* dancers might cost Rp350,000-500,000. In some of the more orthodox villages the dance is not allowed because it's considered too worldly and lasts too long into the night.

The *laweut,* performed in the Tangse area, is an Acehnese war dance featuring dancers in brocaded costumes accompanied by a sweet, solemn song, characterized by graceful dips and swirls. Special instruments played in Aceh are the three-stringed bamboo zither, a vase-shaped drum with a single drumhead, types of tambourines (*geudrang*), and the flute (*seurne kale*). Acehnese games, such as the fertility rite *geudeu-geudeu* (team wrestling), have a religious function.

TRANSPORTATION

Getting There

Garuda flies out of Jakarta daily to Banda Aceh, with stops in Medan en route; also from Pulau Batam south of Singapore. From Medan, SMAC flies to Banda Aceh in less than an hour. The Blang Bintang Airport is 14 km east of Banda Aceh. Access by fast modern buses (Rp20,000, 12-14 hours) is easy from Medan via the 608-km fully paved east coast highway. More adventurous is the bus up the mountainous west coast road via Sidikalang, Tapaktuan, and Meulaboh, which takes twice as long. Most adventurous of all is the road through the rugged center from Karoland via Kutacane and Blangkejeren to Takengon. From Kabanjahe to Kutacane is Rp2500 by bus. There's no telling how long this trip may take—you might even have to walk part of the way.

Getting Around

The roads in Aceh's backcountry are ill-maintained. When the Dutch fought to occupy the territory, they established their military camps in the coastal areas and built roads all along the coasts, but neglected roadbuilding in the inland areas. Minibuses, *bemo,* public buses, taxis, and open-bed pickup trucks run all over the province; in the towns small buses and minibuses are used. The three main ports of Aceh are

Sumatran ferry

J. WEISS

Langsa, Lhokseumawe, and Kreung Raya. Smaller ports are Uleelheue and Malahayati in north Aceh (from where ferries to Sabang Island depart), and Tapaktuan and Meulaboh on the west coast. Aceh's regional airports in Tapaktuan, Sinabang, Meulaboh, and Sabang are serviced by small aircraft.

LHOKSEUMAWE AND VICINITY

This unspellable, unpronounceable town on the Strait of Malacca about halfway between Medan and Banda Aceh is located near one of the world's largest reservoirs of natural gas. The opening of this gas field by Mobil Oil Indonesia in 1971 began the disruption of the traditional life-patterns of the farmers and fishermen of northern Aceh. The main entrance to the **PT Arun Natural Gas Field** is at Blang Lancang, 8.5 km northwest of Lhokseumawe, though it's not possible to tour because of "security." A 32-km-long pipeline carries natural gas and condensate from the Arun field to the gas liquefaction plant in Lhokseumawe.

The town center is a few km off the main highway. Eat at **Tiara** (Indonesian/Acehnese) on Jl. Cut Meutia, **Jurzia** (Acehnese) on Jl. Suka Ramai, or at **Golden** (Chinese) on Jl. Perdangangan. From Lhokseumawe to Bireuen, the turnoff for Takengon in the mountains, costs Rp800 (60 km, 45 minutes). **Pase** is a small village nearby where several of the queens of the sultans are buried.

Bireuen

A market and junction town on the province's north coast, 60 km west of Lhokseumawe. A bustling produce market here sells tobacco, coffee, cloves, and cinnamon; it's especially lively during the tobacco season (June-August). Most tobacco is grown by the Gayo in the Takengon area. Stay at **Losmen Fajar,** Jl. Bioskop Gajah 5, tel. 21379; although near the bus station, it's not that noisy. Rooms are clean and prices reasonable—Rp6000 economy, Rp8000 for *mandi* and fan, Rp10,000 for *mandi* and a/c.

Clean and pleasant **Norma Restaurant,** 1.6 km down the road to Takengoan, has a great variety of excellent, cheap food: turtle eggs, very good chicken, Acehnese sauces, giant crabs. Two can eat well for Rp6000-8000, which includes fruit salads. At Bireuen is the turnoff for Takengon on Lake Tawar, a Rp2000 bus ride on a paved road (101 km, three hours). Bus transportation from Bireuen to Banda Aceh is Rp4000 (216 km).

SIGLI

A little over 100 km west of Bireuen, at the mouths of the Krueng Tuka and Krueng Baru rivers, three hours by bus from Banda Aceh. Sigli is where the bloody and protracted Padri War (1804-37) broke out. The Padris were puritanical Muslim religious reformers who attempted to violently introduce their orthodox teachings into the strong *adat* society of the Minangkabau. See the remains of the Padris *kraton* a bit out of town on the main road. Sigli, which used to be called Padri, was once a principal embarkation point for Muslims leaving for Mecca on the *haj*. It was also a major railhead and the old decaying wooden station is a nostalgic colonial edifice. Tour the railyard to see rusting locomotives.

Basic *losmen* are located around the bus station. If you prefer a quieter place, stay at the **Riza** (Rp35,000 for an a/c room) outside of town. If your bus, heading for Medan or Banda Aceh, stops here, be sure to eat at **Stasion Atra Family** on Jl. Perdanganan, tel. 21254, in front of the bus station. Excellent food; don't miss the *sop sapi ayam* and other chicken dishes. For about Rp5000-7000, eat a great Sumatran meal. Sigli is also known for its curries.

In a coconut grove on the other side of the Krueng Baru River is a cemetery with sections for Europeans, Chinese, and Muslims. In the Islamic cemetery, the tomb of Aceh's first Islamic sultan, Sultan Maarif Syah (died 1511), continues to be venerated. Gold embroidered articles may be found in **Garot,** eight km from Sigli; ceramics are made in **Klibeit.**

THE GAYO HIGHLANDS

The Gayo and Alas are the dominant ethnic groups of the isolated lake plains and high river valleys of Central and Southeast Aceh districts, around and to the southeast of Danau Tawar. Isolated from contact with Westerners until the early 20th century, they live in a mountainous range with some peaks over 3,000 meters, bounded on the west, east, and north by the Acehnese and to the south by Batak highlanders. These proto-Malay agriculturalists, closely related to the Batak, don't consider themselves Acehnese but are proud of being Indonesian. They practice wet-rice and swidden cultivation of tobacco, *ganja*, maize, and tuber crops. Most of the people in the mountain towns speak only Gayo.

The Gayo and Alas have borrowed heavily from their neighbors; consequently, their customs are almost the same as those of the Acehnese, except for some groups deep in the mountains (Orang Lingga) who still practice a syncretic 19th-century Islamic/animist religion, believing strongly in local spirits, transmigration of souls, and omens. Having converted to Islam at a later date than the coastal Acehnese, the Gayo and Alas have their own patrilineal culture, language, and traditional arts. In 1904 the ruthless Dutch General van Daalen penetrated these uplands and subdued both tribes, wiping out whole villages as he went.

TAKENGON

The "capital" of the Gayo and the principal town of Central Aceh, deep in the hinterlands 331 km from Banda Aceh. This sizable mountain resort town, 1,120 meters above sea level, is located on beautiful and placid Lake Tawar, surrounded by mountains and coffee plantations. Some of the best coffee in Indonesia grows in this fertile region. The town gets just over 100 visitors a year—a quiet backwater with no souvenir stands or Western menus. You'll be continually mobbed by a sea of chirpy schoolchildren in brown and tan uniforms.

Takengon is renowned for its *didong* choral circle groups, staged to raise funds for community projects; seek out Pak Armas. Traditional Gayo/Alas clothes, pillows, and tapestries are made in this area. Your hotel staff can put you in touch with the right people. Explore the market for sets of ornately engraved pottery (*keunire*). Swim in the lake. Some of the most potent marijuana in Southeast Asia is grown in the Aceh Tengah and Aceh Tenggara regions, though its cultivation is gradually being eradicated. The government attributes the violence of 1990, in which a hundred people were killed, to *ganja* syndicates. Don't buy marijuana or even smoke it here. Police may even search travelers on their way back down into North Sumatra Province through Kutacane via Blangkejeran.

Accommodations And Food
It's a shame there's no *losmen* near the lake. Highly recommended is homestay-style **Losmen Batang Ruang** on Jl. Mahkamah 5, tel. 104, with very clean rooms (Rp5000 d with *mandi*) and friendly people. The manager speaks good English and is very helpful. Nice

views overlook the village from the balconies. **Motel Triarga,** Jl. Pasar Inpres near the main bus terminal, is good and clean; Rp12,000 t but you can bargain down to Rp6000 if there aren't many guests. **Losmen Danau Laut Tawar,** Jl. Lebe Kader 39, has a friendly and competent staff; Rp20,000-30,000 per room. The best deal for the money is the two-star **Hotel Renggali,** Jl. Bintang, on the edge of the water with fantastic views over the quiet, unspoiled lake; Rp50,000 and up. The Renggali offers tennis courts, patios, a beautiful lobby, and mammoth bathrooms. **Restaurant Sinar Minang** serves good food for only Rp4000-5000 for two; *nasi goreng* is a good deal (Rp1500). Enjoy Padang food at **Kejora,** Jl. Laut Tawar.

Getting There And Away

Takengon is about 100 km off the main coastal highway. From Bireuen south to Takengon is a three-hour ride (Rp2000), sitting sardine fashion in a minibus. This curving road features breathtaking scenery, and coming into town—with Takengon's crater lake and the surrounding cultivated fields, mountains, and forests—is a glorious sight. Another approach is by bus from Banda Aceh (Rp5500, 10 hours), or from Blangkejeran northwest of Kutacane. There are also *ekspres* buses to Takengon from Medan, 10 hours on a good road.

Minibuses run daily south to Blangkejeren (156 km). Takengon to Isak is 34 km (Rp2000, one hour), Isak to Uwak 40 km, Uwak to Ise Ise 21 km, and Ise Ise to Blangkejeren is 61 km. You can make this trip in one day, or you can sleep in **Kalampoo** (seven km after Uwak) or in other villages. In Kalampoo, look for the blue-and-white building where you can eat and sleep for Rp5000; it's the only one with two stories. The stretches from Takengon to Isak, Kalampoo to Lumut, and Ise Ise to Blangkejeren, are beautiful. The rest isn't that attractive—once there was a rainforest, but not anymore. This road is now being surfaced so the adventure of riding through Aceh's mountainous center past Gayo villages with their long, low, seldom-visited communal houses will soon be a thing of the past.

Lake Tawar

A big, peaceful, untouristed 25-km-long crater lake, smooth as glass and surrounded by forests and plantations, Lake Tawar is a half-km walk from Takengon's center. Because of local superstitions and abundant seaweed and algae, the locals refuse to swim in its cool water. A famous protein-rich fish called *depik* is harvested from this lake, and is one of the area's best-known delicacies. Rent a vehicle and tour the road around the lake, or hire a *perahu motor* to cruise the lake. Bathe in the natural hot springs at **Simpang Balik,** about 20 km from Takengon. Take the local boat across the lake to **Bintang** village.

Blangkejeren

At Jl. Besar 15 is **Hotel Losmen Mardhatillah,** one of the best places to stay in all of northern Sumatra. Since it's next to the mosque, take a room (only Rp6000 s or d) on the left side of the building. The hotel is very clean and the people friendly. If you want to star in the local peep show, stay in **Losmen Juli,** Jl. Kong Buri 12, with a *mandi* featuring a meter-"high" wall that seems to attract a curious number of passersby. **Losmen Nusantara** costs about the same (Rp3000-4000), depending on your bargaining ability. The market is worth seeing, particularly for color-rich Gayo fabrics. SDA grade school teacher Mr. Hardensah is more than willing to act as your guide; he speaks quite good English. From Blangkejeran, buses leave for Kutacane everyday (four to five hours). Kabanjahe in the Karo Highlands is another four hours by bus from Kutacane.

From Blangkejeren To Takengon

This road is time-consuming, and the satisfaction limited. Trees are down everywhere; only about five km feels like real jungle. Coming from Blangkejeren, the public bus takes you to **Rikit Gaib** (Rp1000); from there to Godang is another Rp1000 by bus. In **Godang** stay with a family or in a *warung kopi* for Rp500 per person, plus Rp500 for a meal (rice, veggies, one egg). Next day, walk 10 km to **Ise Ise.** The vehicles that come by tend to be full; offer to ride on top. Ise Ise is a mere three houses, but has a lovely *wisma;* stay with Pak Warsito and his family. Payment up to you. It should cost around Rp1500 per person from Ise Ise to **Lumut,** a nice village with many rice fields and buffalo, though some drivers want Rp10,000 per person. From Ise Ise it's a 2.5-hour walk to Lumut. In Lumut, sleep in a *warung* for Rp500 per person; meals Rp800. From here, a bus departs at 0800 for Takengon (Rp4000), or try to hitch on private vehicles. You can overnight in Kalampoo, seven km from Uwak. From Takengon, take a bus to Bireuen, right on the Banda Aceh-Medan highway (218 km from Banda Aceh).

GUNUNG LEUSER NATIONAL PARK

The largest national park in Southeast Asia and the most important in Indonesia, the massive Gunung Leuser National Park (9,000 square km) northwest of Medan remains largely unexplored. Formerly a group of reserves surrounding the well-populated Alas Valley of northern Sumatra, Gunung Leuser became a national park in 1980. The World Wildlife Fund, whose representatives are in Bogor and Kutacane, assist with the park's management. Increasing population pressures in the valley continue to be the biggest management problem, particularly since Gayo, Alas, and Batak immigrants are hardly fazed by the rules and regulations emanating from Jakarta. By tradition, these tribes practice shifting cultivation, which is now illegal. The construction of a new highway along the steep Alas Valley has succeeded in cutting the park in two. November is the coolest and rainiest time of year.

The Land

The park lies for the most part in Aceh Province, though a finger projects into North Sumatra Province almost as far as Brastagi. This wild and beautiful area consists of full and submontane primary rainforest, lowland and swamp forest, and a moss forest above 1,600 meters. Plant species include orchids, dipterocarps, and 50-meter-high hardwood trees. Most of the reserve is rough and mountainous, part of the Bukit Barisan range, with Gunung Leuser the highest point at 3,381 meters. The only lowland areas are the Alas Valley and the lower Kluet River Valley, which slopes down to the west coast of Sumatra at Kandang. Natural salt licks are found in several places; they attract herbivores from elephants to mouse deer, and probably orangutans and some carnivores as well. The park is also a world-class study area for primatologists, with orangutans, gibbons, leaf monkeys, and macaques. Its colorful tropical birds include hornbills, Argus pheasant, and many other species common to Southeast Asia.

Practicalities

Obtain a park permit (Rp1000) at Wisma Rindu Alam in Kutacane. Since most buses arrive in Kutacane from Medan in the late afternoon when it's too late to try to get a permit, it's better to spend the night in this *wisma* the day you arrive. Pak Maringgan, who runs the *wisma*, is on the staff of the national park and can help you obtain a permit first thing the next morning. Then you can head for the park. Permits are also available directly from the PHPA office in **Tanah Merah,** two km north of Kutacane, open Sun.-Thurs. 0730-1430, Friday 0730-1200, Saturday 0730-1400. Cost is Rp1000 plus three passport photos.

Kutacane

An unappealing Muslim market town, with a strong Batak Christian minority, Kutacane is right in the middle of Gunung Leuser National Park, surrounded by steep mountains, a full five-hour bus ride from Brastagi. In contrast to the slash-and-burn agriculture practiced by the Batak and Gayo in the park, wet-rice cultivation is common around Kutacane. To get away from the crowds while waiting for a bus, take refuge in the stationmaster's office. From Kutacane straight to Blangkejeren is Rp3000 by shared taxi. If you have to stay the night in this town, which has a reputation for being rough (especially on women), the best place to stay is **Hotel Mamasta,** about one km south of the bus station; a good room here will cost you about Rp10,000.

Wisma Rindu Alam, right on the main street of Jl. A. Yani, is where foreigners usually stay. Dorm beds go for Rp2500, other rooms with fans are Rp5000, Rp7500, and Rp10,000 depending on the size and whether it has a single or double bed. There's a nice garden, and a little store selling soap, toothpaste, sandals, rain ponchos, and books and pamphlets with information on the animals and plants in the park. Drawbacks are that the rooms and *mandi* may not be so clean and you're subjected to massive amounts of street noise. The *wisma* is an easy walk from the bus station; just mention the name and anyone can point it out to you. The small restaurant offers simple dishes like fried rice.

The worst *losmen* in Kutacane is **Wisma Rangali**; Rp2500 s, Rp5000 d, Rp7500 for "deluxe." Avoid this place. **Lau Pakam** is about 32 km south of Kutacane and if you've had enough of the frustrated boys of Kutacane stay here at **Penginapan Kasih Sayang** (Rp4000 s). Buses in the direction of Brastagi leave at about 1000 opposite the *penginapan*.

Ketembe

A research station on the Alas River about 30 km north of Kutacane. There are usually three or four long-term scientific research projects in tropical plant and animal biology in progress at all times at this station. Entry to the research station, however, is strictly forbidden to tourists. To ensure productive research, only those associated with research are allowed within the borders of the study area between the Ketembe and Alas rivers. Field research is so easily disrupted that even visits by authorized guests must be carefully organized and conducted. There are designated tourist areas near Ketembe such as **Pulau Latong, Lawe Gurah,** and the **Bohorok** area in the eastern part of the park. For soft adventurers, **Wisma Cinta Alam** (Rp2000 per person) on the main road a half km south of the Ketembe Research Station, is nicer, cleaner, and friendlier than the accommodations offered at Pulau Latong and Lawe Gurah.

Pulau Latong And Lawe Gurah

Not villages but areas set up by Gunung Leuser National Park specifically for tourists. Pulau Latong is just across the rushing Alas River from Ketembe. Of the two, **Pulau Latong** has better facilities, including three relatively new houses built in a regional traditional style, each with two to three "bedrooms." There's one guesthouse at **Lawe Gurah,** but it isn't in very good condition. There may or may not be beds in the houses, nor electricity (take candles), nor running water, though river water is drinkable after boiling. The houses do have *mandi*. Eat in Pak Ali's *warung*, a few minute's walk from the Pulau Latong facility, which is the only source of simple cooked food and beverages (including excellent homegrown coffee) or staples. Travelers can also take public transportation along the road to eat in one of the larger villages downriver, but this is generally not worth the trouble. The Pulau Latong and Lawe Gurah areas are essentially campgrounds with modest accommodations providing primarily shelter.

You can make trips into the forest from both campgrounds. Guides cost about Rp10,000 per day and offer two- or three-day treks. Pak Maringgan and his staff at Wisma Rindu Alam in Kutacane can arrange for guides, take guests to the market for shopping, arrange motorcycle rental, and find innertubes for river recreation. Lawe Gurah is within a few hours walk of a pleasant hot springs; you can also reach the area from Pulau Latong, though it takes a little longer. When walking alone in the rainforest on trails, you must be patient and slow-moving in order to observe animals. Don't forget binoculars.

The Mamas Valley

Most of the park, except for the area set aside for research at Ketembe, is officially open to tourists. One place that has traditionally been good for backpackers is along the **Mamas River.** The Mamas Valley, however, has fallen victim to logging—it's now necessary to hike several hours through more deforested areas before penetrating the forest proper. Get an early start from **Jongar** and spend the morning walking through various coffee and *kemiri* plantations on the west side of the Alas River. Reaching the best parts of the Mamas Forest requires crossing the Mamas River, which involves clambering across a wire bridge. Local guides will carry backpacks for less coordinated travelers. In November and December the river is a torrent.

Other Options

Another area adventurous backpackers may enjoy is the walk to and climbing of one of the local mountains—**Gunung Loser, Gunung Leuser,** and **Gunung Kemiri.** The trek to Gunung Leuser takes about 7-10 days roundtrip and is not that difficult. There are rafting trips down the **Alas River** organized by Sobek (contact Pacto Ltd., Jl. Brig. Jen. Katamso 35-D, Medan, tel. (061) 510-081. They start not far upriver from Ketembe and then follow the Alas for a few days. Very comfortable with excellent food. You'll see less wildlife, though, than if you actually enter the forest for long periods. Besides the fun of rafting, the main attraction of these trips is freedom from worry about food, lodging, guides, discomfort, and the like.

BANDA ACEH

Located on the northern tip of Sumatra, this city faces two oceans: the Strait of Malacca and the Indian Ocean. The Sungai Aceh River flows through this busy, noisy, shophouse town, while a big mountain rears up behind it. The center of town is dominated by a massive five-domed mosque. In front is Simpang Lima, the busiest intersection of the city and its transport hub. Universitas Darusalam, in the direction of Krueng Raya (Rp300 by *bemo*), has 15,000 students and 575 lecturers. Also on campus is an Institute of Islamic Studies (I.A.I.N.).

The main city of one of Indonesia's staunchest Islamic regions, Banda Aceh's religious orthodoxy and its harsh treatment of criminals ensures that it is very safe. Everyone prays in Aceh, if only to keep up appearances. Nightlife and entertainment will take all of 10 minutes to experience. Yet the atmosphere is not severe. You don't see that many *peci* and there aren't as many veils as in other parts of Indonesia. You even see women walking around the grounds of the city's holiest mosque in blue jeans. One's first impression is its neatness and orderliness; it's noticeably more prosperous than other Sumatran cities, and the people seem better dressed, friendlier, and more respectful to outsiders.

History

In the Middle Ages, this city was a huge multiethnic metropolis with international markets and compounds of Indians, Arabs, Turks, Chinese, Abyssinians, and Persians. At that time Banda Aceh was known as the "Doorway to Mecca," a stopping-off place for pilgrims journeying by ship to the Holy City. Great teachers, poets, and philosophers taught here; schools were everywhere. During the 17th century, under Sultan Iskandar Muda, Aceh reached its height of political power and wealth. In Aceh's struggle to gain total supremacy over the northwest archipelago, it engaged in great sea battles with the Portuguese (1629) and almost succeeded in capturing Melaka, though its fleet was destroyed in the process.

Banda Aceh was one of the centers of fierce resistance during the 19th and 20th centuries, when the Acehnese launched a 40-year guerrilla war against the Dutch, whom they fought almost singlehandedly. Descendants of the wealthy aristocrats (*uleebalang*) ousted by the Dutch in 1873 and subjected to persecution and execution during the revolution in 1945 today form the elite ruling class in the Acehnese community.

SIGHTS

Kherkop

Cared for meticulously, almost affectionately, this Dutch cemetery on Jl. Iskandar Muda contains an estimated 2,200 graves of Dutch soldiers who died during the Acehnese resistance movement. Nicknamed by the Acehnese "the former Dutch neighborhood," this is one of Aceh's main tourist attractions. Its name means "churchyard" in Dutch. Open 0800-1200 and 1400-1700; visitors should first report to the office. Like a 19th-century Dutch equivalent of the U.S. Vietnam Memorial, the names of the thousands interred have been engraved on the commemorative wall of the wrought-iron art nouveau entranceway. The lanes of this good-sized cemetery are named after Dutch officers.

The first grave you come to when you walk in is that of General Kohler, the first major officer killed while storming the mosque in the very first expedition against Aceh in 1873. Walk through stubbly grass between row upon row of ornate Christian stone markers and tombstones; there's even a section in the rear for Banda Aceh's Jewish community. The Dutch provide money for upkeep and still send out an official once a year to see that the grounds are properly cared for.

The caretaker will proudly point out to you all the more interesting inscriptions. On the gravestones you'll see the names of not only Dutch who were killed but also names of German and Indonesian mercenaries (mostly Ambonese) who fought for the Dutch. Some local Acehnese, considered traitors, were buried here in great disgrace amongst the enemy.

Aceh State Museum

This large three-story museum, **Musium Negeri Aceh,** on Jl. S.A. Mahmudsyah 12, displays local artifacts, weapons, a great range of handicrafts, and ceremonial clothing. Free admission. Open Tues.-Sun. 0830-1800. In the same museum complex is **Rumah Aceh,** a model of an Acehnese aristocrat's home built in 1914 in Semarang. Open Tues.-Sun. 0800-1800. A giant cast-iron Chinese bell, **Cakra Donya,** sits in front of the building; it's said to have been presented by China in the 15th century. Nearby are some old cannons and the gracious old *pendopo gubernor* where the Dutch governors once lived, now the residence of the governor of Aceh. On both sides of the governor's house are the former billets for the Dutch military. All these sites were once inside a palace compound destroyed and rebuilt by the Dutch; now only remnants of a wall are left.

About 100 meters to the south of the museum on Jl. S.A. Mahmudsyah are **Islamic graves** of Acehnese rulers, including that of Sultan Iskandar Muda. Another group of royal tombs, dating from the 15th and 16th centuries, is on Jl. Kraton. On Jl. Panglima Merah (Komplek Neusu) rows of former Dutch military barracks have survived, occupied now by military families.

Mesjid Baturrachman

This unusual mosque with its marble interior is a beehive of religious activity. Built in 1879 by the Dutch as a peace offering to the Acehnese, it failed in its purpose—all through the 1880s and 1890s Dutchmen were still dying. The structure replaced a grand mosque which the Dutch destroyed, together with the sultan's

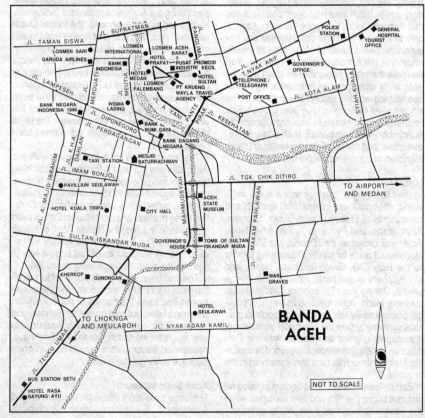

BANDA ACEH

NOT TO SCALE

© MOON PUBLICATIONS, INC.

palace and fortress. The elaborate multi-arched facade is a mixture of styles from Arabia, India, and Malaysia. Behind the mosque are two minarets; you can climb one for views over the city. In front is an expanse of gardens and pathways. The *mesjid* may be visited by non-Muslims during non-praying times (0700-1100, 1330-1600). Rules: veiled dress, take off shoes, get the guard's permission (at north gate), no women in menses.

Gunongan

The baths and pleasure gardens of the former sultan's ladies, on the banks of the river on Jl. Teuku Umar near the clock tower. As you come through the front gate of the yard, ask for the key in the building facing you. The story goes that this "Walking Palace" was built for a Malay princess who married one of the sultans of Aceh, enabling her to take an evening walk, not permitted to women at that time. Some also speculate that this stark white structure served as an astronomical observatory, reminiscent of one in Jaipur, India built in the mid-17th century. From the top of Gunongan you can see a small white structure, the sultan's bathing place, on the other side of the road close to the river. It's also locked, so get the key first.

ACCOMMODATIONS

Banda Aceh tends to be expensive, with a scarcity of rooms. A 10% tax is often added to rooms and to restaurant bills, even in quite modest establishments. On Jl. A. Yani in Penayong (Chinatown) you'll find all sorts of places, from cheap to expensive (Rp5000 up to Rp80,000). The *pasar malam* is nearby—great eating at night.

Budget

Opposite **Losmen International**, no. 19 (Rp5000), is **Losmen Pacific**, nos. 22-24, with clean rooms and *mandi*. The Chinese proprietors are quite friendly. **Hotel Prapat**, no. 17, tel. (0651) 22159, is Chinese-run, with clean rooms, verandas, and a lively courtyard. Next door is **Hotel Medan**, no. 15, tel. 21501, one of Banda Aceh's best deals: clean but simple rooms with *mandi* and Western-style toilets for only Rp25,000; a/c rooms for Rp35,000. **Wisma Prapat**, at Jl. A. Yani 11, is in the same price range.

Not far from Jl. A. Yani is Jl. Ch. Anwar, where **Losmen Aceh Barat** and **Losmen Palembang** (no. 51) are located—both have rooms for Rp8000 to Rp15,000. Closer to town, **Wisma Lading**, Jl. Cut Meutia 9 on the left past the police station when coming from the mosque, is an old colonial building set back from the street. Rooms range from Rp8000 to Rp25,000 (with a/c), but it's rather run-down. Less expensive is **Losmen Sari**, Jl. Merduati 12, tel. 22919.

Losmen Aceh, Jl. Mohd. Jam 1, tel. 21345, is right on the main square to one side of Mesjid Baturrachman. An old colonial hotel built in ornate, gingerbread style and in need of a little paint, the Aceh Hotel was 40 years ago *the* prestigious first-class hotel of Banda Aceh. With its stained ceilings, peeling walls, and dripping faucets, it even *smells* old. But it's central and cheap (Rp4500 s or d) by this city's standards.

Moderate To Expensive

Higher-priced (Rp25,000-40,000) hotels include one-star **Hotel Seulawah**, Jl. Nyak Adam Kamil IV 1, tel. (0651) 21749, with a/c rooms, hot water, and fridge. Nice people. Located right opposite a sports field, it's quiet, with well-kept gardens. Another one-star hotel is **Pavillium Seulawah**, Jl. A. Majid Ibrahim II, tel. 22788. Near Simpang Lima is two-star **Hotel Sultan**, Jl. T.P. Polim 127, tel. 22581, with 40 clean a/c rooms, good service, and a restaurant; Visa and AmEx cards accepted. **Hotel Rasa Sayang Ayu**, Jl. Teuku Umar 439, tel. 21983, is another upmarket hotel. The city's premier accommodation is three-star **Kuala Tripa**, Jl. Mesjid Raya 24, tel. 21879—deluxe spacious rooms, full facilities, opposite a park, and only a seven-minute walk from Mesjid Raya.

FOOD

Acehnese food is as hot or hotter than *nasi padang*. Curried mutton (*gule kambing*) and *ayam goreng* are regional specialties, and the dried beef jerky (*dendeng aceh*) is pretty good too. The best *gule kambing* is found at **Samahani**, Km 17 on the main road to Sigli—the locals love it. Other common dishes are *ikan panggang* (fish), *sayur bayam* (spinach and eggs), and black "twice-cooked" rice dessert (*pulot hitam dua masak*).

The *warung* opposite the Gadjah Theatre are open until late at night. Also at night in the lanes and streets off **Jl. A. Yani** are *warung* serving *nasi goreng, nasi padang,* ice juices, *martabak, sate,* and *kerang* (clams)—a pleasant, lively, and inexpensive place to relax, enjoy delectable Indonesian dishes, and take in the local crowd.

Restaurants

The restaurant district is Jl. A. Yani in Chinatown. You can't go wrong in such eateries as **Happy, Gambira,** and the **Dian.** At Jl. A. Yani 92, **Restoran Tropicana** serves delicious Chinese food, including fresh seafood. The crabmeat is worth raving about, and the shark's fin soup is as good as anywhere in the world. The best Padang restaurant is the **Minang Surya** on Jl. Safiatuddin on the other side of the river opposite Hotel Medan. Also sample **Aroma Restaurant,** Jl. Cut Nyak Dhien, for well-prepared Chinese and Indonesian dishes. For some of the best eating, go out the airport gate and turn right at the Welcome To Aceh sign. Two stalls feature superb curried chicken and *kambing* made from genuine Acehnese medium-hot curry, very filling and rich. An excellent way to kill time if your plane is late.

Desserts And Drinks

Fruit markets are scattered around town. An outstanding bakery is the **Satya Modern** on Jl. Ch. Anwar 3. Coffee (on the bitter side) is widely available for Rp500 per small glass; ask for *kopi tok* (always without sugar).

Out Of Town

Braden, tel. (0651) 22056, nine km from the city on the road to Lhoknga and surrounded by rice fields, specializes in Acehnese cooking like *ikan lele* (swamp fish), *ikan gabus,* and *sia reuboh.* On the road to Kreung Raya in the fishing village of Ujung Batee, 16 km south of Banda Aceh, is the **Ujong Batee Restaurant,** specializing in seafood—one of the best restaurants on Sumatra. It's open only 1130-1400. Fabulous fresh crab, squid, giant tiger prawns, and whole fish.

CRAFTS AND SHOPPING

Special crafts to look for in Banda Aceh include *rencong* (traditional Acehnese daggers), deli-

cate gold filigree jewelry, and embroidered cloths and clothing. The best place to shop for *rencong* is at **H. Keuchik Leumik,** Jl. Perdagangan 115, tel. (0651) 23313; ivory ones cost Rp60,000-150,000. Souvenir models go for Rp4000-10,000. Also for sale are Acehnese, Chinese, and Dutch antiques—perhaps the largest collection in Banda Aceh. High-quality cotton and silk embroideries, wedding accessories, *opo adat, kain adat,* and rattan and pandanus purses and handbags are sold at the excellent government-run **Pusat Promosi Industri Kecil,** Jl. S.R. Safiatuddin 54.

Another important souvenir shop is **Usaha Souvenir Aceh Nyak Ni** on Jl. Singgahmatga SK I/7 A, no. 2, tel. 22091. Several gold and jewelry shops are on Jl. Perdagangan; here you may observe craftsmen designing and hammering out pieces. Look for the distinctive *pinto aceh* design. Buy good *batik* (real wax) in big Pasar Aceh near the mosque for Rp9000; ask for Batik Ibu. Men's sarungs from India are good and cheap (Rp7000); Indonesian men's *sarung* are Rp4500-5000.

SERVICES

Change money at **Bank Dagang Negara** on Jl. Diponegoro (tel. 22010), **Bank Bumi Daya** on Jl. Cut Meutia, tel. (0651) 22081; **Bank Impor-Ekspor** on Jl. Nyak Arief, tel. 22131; or **Bank Negara Indonesia 1946** on Jl. K.H.A. Dahlan, (tel. 22551). Open Mon.-Thurs. 0800-1130, Friday and Saturday 0800-1030—decent rates for a place so far away from Jakarta. The **post office** is on Jl. T. Angkasah. Along Jl. Nyak Arief are all the most important government offices—telephone and telegraph, immigration, police, hospital, *kantor bupati.* The telephone city code is 0651.

The **Aceh Province Tourist Office** (Kantor Dinas Pariwisata Prop. Aceh), at Jl. Teuku Nyak Arief 92, tel. 22697 or 23692, hands out well-researched brochures and maps. This is one of the best-organized tourist offices in Indonesia. Your hotel reception desk will also be very helpful with advice on Banda Aceh's local sights and events. Hop on a *bemo* from Simpang Lima (Rp300), or just take one of the numerous blue Darusalam buses from in front of the big mosque, Rp150.

TRANSPORTATION

Getting There

From Takengon to Banda Aceh is 10 hours by bus (Rp5500). The bus from Bireuen, south of Banda Aceh on the coast, is Rp4000. Banda Aceh is also linked by air and road from Medan, but there's been no rail connection since 1968. Well-built, modern, and comfortable a/c buses with reclining seats, videos, and fans do the Medan-Banda Aceh run frequently in 12-14 hours for about Rp20,000 one-way. Buy bus tickets in Medan at **Melati,** Jl. Gajah Mada, tel. (0651) 521-216; **ARS,** Jl. Asia 218, tel. 515-734; **ATS,** Jl. K. Wahid Hasyim 118; or **Kurnia,** Jl. Gajah Mada, tel. 520-093. Most a/c buses depart around 1600. Non-a/c buses could depart anytime from Medan's big **Amplas bus station** (Jl. Pertahanan off Jl. Sisingamangaraja). Book a day or two in advance to get a good window seat. Several Medan-based minibus taxi companies take passengers: **Widuri,** Jl. Asia Simpang Bakaran Batu 218, tel. 515-734; and **Inda Taxi,** Jl. Brig. Jen. Katamso 60, tel. 516-615. For the return trip to Medan, these companies also maintain offices in Banda Aceh's main *terminal bis.*

Garuda, Hotel Rasa Sayang Ayu, Jl. Teuku Umar 439, Banda Aceh, tel. 21983, schedules two one-hour flights a day from Medan. SMAC, Jl. Cut Nyak Dien 93, Banda Aceh, tel. 21626, also services Banda Aceh. Flights could differ in their routes, but you eventually arrive in Banda Aceh. There are also flights from Jakarta via Medan, and from Pekanbaru. Blang Bintang Airport is 17 km from the city, Rp8000-10,000 by taxi. No moneychanger works at the airport and the info booth is usually closed. Touts hang out in the terminal offering free rides to hotels.

Getting Around

City roads are narrow, with uneven pavement, undisciplined drivers, and congested traffic, all motorized. Use *labi labi* (means "turtle"), small passenger vans holding 12 people, costing Rp300, and running everywhere in town. *Mesin becak* are also available. Taxi, bicycle, and motorcycle rentals are available though the hotels.

Getting Away

Quite useful is SMAC, Jl. Cut Nyak Dien 93, tel. (0651) 21626, a specialized, efficient north Sumatra airline with twice-weekly service to the west coast towns of Meulaboh, Tapaktuan, and Sinabang, plus daily flights to Medan and weekly flights to interior Aceh. Instead of riding 14 hours on a bus to Meulaboh, fly with SMAC in 50 minutes in a nine-seater Islander. A travel agency, **PT Krueng Wayla, Ltd.,** Jl. S.R. Safiatuddin 3, tel. 22066, is very helpful. Another agent for ticketing is **PT Sastra** on Jl. Supratman, tel. 22207.

A ferry sails for Pulau Weh's main port of Balohan every morning at 0800 from Malahayati Harbor in Kreung Raya 35 km east; get this bus (Rp1500, 45 minutes) from Jl. Diponegoro before 1300 or you'll miss the ferry. Ferry tickets cost Rp2900 economy, Rp3500 a/c. A Pelni boat, KM *Lawit,* sails from Banda Aceh every two weeks for Medan's port of Belawan, Dumai, Tanjung Priok, in Jakarta and beyond. Inquire at the offices at Jl. Cut Meutia 51, tel. 23976.

Terminal Jl. Teuku Umar, in front of Rasa Sayang Ayu Hotel in the southwestern part of the city, is the long-distance bus station with buses to Sigli, Takengon, Bireuen, Lhokseumawe, Idi, Kuala Simpang, Medan, Langsa, Meulaboh, and Tapaktuan. Most long-distance buses start at 0600-0700, but there are departures throughout the day as well. Short-distance buses depart from near the big mosque in the center of town. From Jl. Diponegoro near the mosque, board a bus four km to the old harbor area of Uleelheue (Rp800), Lhoknga (Rp1000), and Krueng Raya (Rp1500).

VICINITY OF BANDA ACEH

Lhoknga, 15 km southwest of Banda Aceh, is the city's nearest beach and the most scenic spot on the northwest Aceh coast. From Jl. Diponegoro in Banda Aceh, catch a *bemo* (Rp600). Don't pay the beach "fee" without receiving a ticket in return. On Sunday it's overrun with citified Acehnese strolling around and picnicking beneath the row of palms near the village. Several *warung* serve meals, snacks, and coffee. Foreigners may swim wearing modest bathing attire, but be warned that the undertow off this coast can be lethal.

The most popular part of the beach lies two km beyond Lhoknga village opposite a coconut grove echoing with the reverberations of a giant cement factory, Semen Andalas Indonesia. Stay at **Homestay Darlian/Yusnidar** on Jl. Maimun Saleh in front of the entrance to the Seulawah Golf Club. The homestay (five rooms, Rp2000 per person) has a nice atmosphere, friendly people, and a good beach only 300 meters away. Charter a *prahu* for skin diving and snor-

keling or to explore the area's coastline. To an island offshore it might cost Rp15,000.

Lam Puuk Beach, 17 km from Banda Aceh, is further down the west coast on the road to Meulaboh, a gorgeous white-sand beach with breathtaking sunsets. Stay in the small fishing *kampung* here. **Ujong Batee Beach** is 17 km east of Banda Aceh on the road to Kreung Raya.

WEH ISLAND

A delightful discovery, this small 154-square-km island is near the westernmost tip of the world's largest archipelago; only uninhabited Pulau Rondo is more westerly. The population of 26,196 is mixed, with Acehnese, Javanese, Batak, Minangkabau, and Chinese, plus about five Western expats. Islam is the main religion but there's also a Christian church and Chinese temple. Many Chinese shops. Great food, especially fresh fish. Rent a house for Rp530,000 a year. If you're up as far as Banda Aceh, it would be a shame not to take the ferry (1.5 hours) over.

Sabang is a slow-paced port town which comes to life only in the evenings. Visitors enjoy the island's white-sand beaches, as well as snorkeling, swimming, fishing, and hiking. Narrow twisting roads weave through spice groves and coconut plantations past scenic coves and small villages. Its good hotels and restaurants are cheaper than Banda Aceh's. Though Sabang is administered as a part of Aceh Province, the atmosphere is more akin to a Caribbean or Indian Ocean port. It is, in fact, a sort of escape valve from Acehnese social and religious orthodoxy.

History
Sabang has a glamorous history. Though now only one ship arrives per week, before WW II the port was bigger than Singapore's. Most of the facilities are still here, decaying. Sabang is strategically located at the northern entrance to the Strait of Malacca, one of the world's busiest waterways, right on the main trade artery between Singapore, Melaka, Penang, and Calcutta.

In 1900 it was a tiny fishing village. A coal depot was soon established by the Dutch, the harbor deepened, land reclaimed, wharves built capable of storing 25,000 tons of coal. Foreign steamships used to stop here regularly to collect

coal and put on water from Sabang's huge freshwater lake, Anak Laut. There was a drydock for repairing ships, and a large oil-storage depot. It's said the Russian fleet took refuge here during the Russo-Japanese War, and the Germans used the island as a base during WW I.

In its heyday Sabang boasted elegant nightclubs, fine restaurants, and private clubs. Sabang's harbor before the Great War berthed up to 16 major-sized steamers. The port area was a hive of activity, with hundreds of passengers wearing pith helmets and white shorts filling the streets. It appeared as if that era would never end. But after Singapore gained ascendency and diesel ships came into wide use, Sabang's importance as a port diminished. In the 1960s, during *konfrontasi* between Malaysia and Indonesia, Pulau Weh was turned into a fortress. Today there's an overgrown, bygone air to the island.

Economy
In 1970, to improve the island's economy, the port was made a duty-free zone. In 1978, in an attempt to attract more tourist dollars, there was discussion about opening parts of Sabang for gambling, drinking, and nightclubs, like a little Monaco. Everybody agreed it would bring in a lot of money—everybody also agreed it would be better not to have the money. Instead, it was decided to develop Sabang in other ways, opening the island to industry, providing shipping facilties, generally creating an attractive investment climate. Luckily, none of these plans have been implemented, and even the island's duty-free status was eliminated in 1986. Sabang slumbers on, of little economic importance. Three-quarters of the population is engaged in agriculture. Copra and cloves are the main products of the island; there's also a fish- and shrimp-processing factory here.

SIGHTS

Pulau Weh's great attraction is its natural beauty, rocky coves, Lake Anak Laut, hillside lookouts, harbor views, beaches, and unpolluted marine environments. Though most of the coral is dead, the water around the offshore islands of Pulau Weh is so clear the seabed is visible up to 15 meters. To rent snorkeling equipment in Sabang costs Rp5000—expensive when you consider you can rent a whole motorbike on Bali for Rp7000 per day. On the north coast between March and September and on the south coast between November and May the island's beaches are safe from monsoonal waves.

At **Losmen Pulau Jaya,** Jl. Perdagangan Balakang, tel. 21344, contact Dodent, who runs tours around Pulau Weh and to offshore islands.

Other, self-appointed guides will also approach you; hire one for about Rp10,000 per day. A nine-hole **Golf Club** is near the airstrip. Refrain from photographing military and coastal installations or the airport as the police might confiscate your film. Change money at better rates in Aceh before arriving.

Sabang

See the northernmost Chinese temple in Indonesia, **Tua Peh Kong Bio.** Sabang has three tennis courts where guest players are welcome. At the town cinema, opposite the Pulau Jaya Hotel, the sound system is very bad and the censored films quite short. The post office, tel. 21217, and immigration office, tel. 21343, are both on Jl. Seulawah. The police station, tel. 21306, is on Jl. Perdagangan, and *kantor bupati,* tel. 21018, is on Jl. Diponegoro.

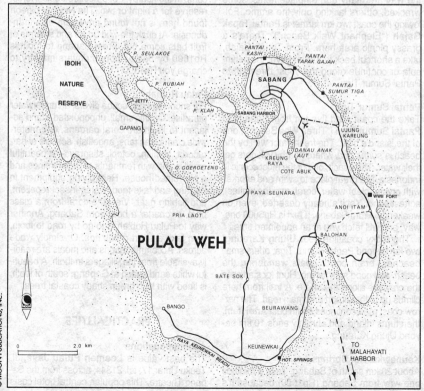

The old port is the place to view beautiful sunsets. Tour this area with its scores of abandoned buildings, factories, and warehouses. All the piers are now in a shambles. The cannons are still there from the various militarizations of the island, covered with canvas, well-greased as if ready for action. Houses have been built over many of the old Japanese fortifications.

Vicinity Of Sabang

About two km from Sabang, go past the old, disused swimming pool and continue a bit farther to the large, picturesque freshwater lake, **Danau Anak Laut** ("Child of the Sea"), which lies in a crater. Beyond it the road climbs to a nice vantage point over Sabang's harbor, the bay, and offshore islands. The nearest beach to Sabang is **Pantai Kasih** ("Love Beach"), a two-km stroll under palm trees along a peninsula. On the way are many gun emplacements, some wrecked, others lacking only the ammo. Following the coast two km farther is **Pantai Tapak Gajah** ("Elephant Walk Beach"). There's a grassy picnic area here. From Tapak Gajah, take a shortcut back to Sabang over the peninsula or continue along the coast three km to Pantai Sumur Tiga.

Pantai Sumur Tiga

Take the coast road five km from Sabang to **Pantai Sumur Tiga** ("Three Well Beach"), one of the island's best. The freshwater well by the beach is *sumur tiga,* where nearby villagers get their water. The beach, one of the most scenic in Indonesia, is a great place to swim and snorkel, with crystal-clear water, coral, and the whitest, softest sand. Yet it's nearly deserted, even on weekends. From Sabang, a taxi is Rp5000 one-way, and will fetch you at an appointed time.

The rocky coastline near **Ujung Kareung,** two km beyond Pantai Sumur Tiga, offers small beaches, brain coral, goats wandering the beach, and good rock fishing. Hunt for starfish in the crevices along the shore. A trail from here climbs up to the airport and main road. The narrow coast road continues south past **Anoi Itam,** then turns inland and abruptly ends 10 km beyond Ujung Kareung.

Keunewkai Hot Springs

About 20 km south of Sabang. Take a minibus one-way from Sabang (Rp1000) because it's

easy to hitch back. The people of this village have built small bathing pools near the shore. Two paved roads lead to Keunewkai from Sabang and together make a scenic loop around the island.

Iboih

In the vicinity of this village 23 km from Sabang are the best snorkeling sites and beaches on the island. Stay with the villagers for as little as Rp2000 pp for a space on the floor; meals cost Rp1500 (rice, vegetable, fish). Other families charge Rp7500 per night plus Rp7500 per meal. In the evening the tourists meet in a coffee shop that serves sweets, noodle soup, and snacks. A nearby beach is good for snorkeling, and you can swim to Rubiah Island if there's no current. There's a steamy volcano and an impressive cave in the area and it's possible to hike and camp in the nearby 1,300-hectare tropical forest reserve for a night or two. The Nicobar pigeon found here is not found anywhere else in Indonesia. At dusk the wild boars and swarms of fruit bats come out. From Sabang to Iboih is Rp1000 by *bemo,* though drivers may try to charge you Rp1500.

Pulau Rubiah

For snorkelers and scuba divers, an underwater paradise. On this small, unpopulated island adjacent to Iboih are coral gardens, one-meter-wide clams, sea fans, angelfish, schools of barracuda, lionfish, octopi, stingrays—a beautiful small island with remnants of British mines and a big ruined house. Rent diving equipment in Sabang and take food, water, insect repellent, and fishing gear. View the coral from a glass boat, or charter a boat from Sabang. Another way to Pulau Rubiah is to go by road to Iboih, then take a short *prahu* ride. Or simply wade across. Accommodations and meals are readily available from the villagers in Iboih. A beautiful white sand beach at **Gapang,** south of Iboih, is lined with lush green shady coastal trees.

PRACTICALITIES

Accommodations

The best value is **Losmen Pulau Jaya,** Jl. Teuku Umar 17, tel. 21344, across from the Sabang Theatre. This popular, central hotel costs

Rp2350, including tax for single rooms with fan—but thin walls and only a screen partition at top. Doubles are Rp4500 including fan. The management is friendly; ask for the map of Sabang. Bathrooms are outside the rooms; no meals; good lighting; clean, free drinking water. Sit out on a nice balcony over the street and watch the people.

Nearby **Losmen Irma,** Jl. Teuku Umar 3, tel. 21235, charges Rp8000-12,000 with fan in rooms upstairs. Downstairs is a good restaurant serving Indonesian food. The **Losmen Sabang Merauke,** also on Jl. Teuku Umar near Irma Losmen and the cinema, asks Rp8000 s or d.

Food

On the streets at night buy delicious *gado-gado, sate,* and *martabak.* Cross the street from the Pulau Jaya Hotel, walk 50 meters, and eat good Indonesian food with the always smiling woman; Rp1500 for two including tea and bananas. A reasonably priced restaurant for Indonesian food is the **Rilzky** on Jl. Teuku Umar. For Chinese food, **Ten Sun's Restaurant** is down a little lane off the main street (Jl. Perdagangan).

Ask to see the old photos and rare wide-angle postcards of turn-of-the-century Sabang.

TRANSPORTATION

Getting There And Around

At 1500 everyday a twin-hulled, comfortable ferry leaves Malahayati Harbor in Krueng Raya, 35 km east of Banda Aceh, Rp1500 (45 minutes) by minibus from the *bemo* station near the big mosque on Jl. Diponegoro. Buy tickets at the port an hour before departure. In fine weather the two-hour trip is enjoyable. The ferry comes in at Balohan Harbor, 11 km south of Sabang. To get to Sabang from Balohan, take a bus or share-taxi (Rp1000, 12 km). The ferry returns from Balohan to Banda Aceh the next day at 0900 (Rp2900 economy, Rp3500 a/c). In Sabang motorcycles rent for Rp15,000, minibuses or taxis cost Rp50,000 per day, and fishing boats about Rp60,000 per day. Ask in **Pasiran,** only a short walk from Losmen Pulau Jaya. A one-day boat trip around the island costs Rp75,000 per person (minimum five people).

THE WEST COAST

Between Lhoknga and the old Dutch lookout is one of the prettiest coast roads in the world. The really nice scenery begins just one hour west of Aceh and continues all the way to Meulaboh. Say good morning to the monkeys. In this untouched area tigers still come down from the mountains to steal livestock.

Calang

About halfway between Banda Aceh and Meulaboh, Calang is a really nice village with good, cheap restaurants (vegetables, bananas, and curry are free) and friendly people who don't cheat. Stay at **Penginapan Sari Jaya** (Rp3500 per room). Since Canadians built the road following the coast, people often ask if you're from Canada. Other sights include a beautiful fine yellow-sand beach, two nice bays, an Australian holiday camp, and a deserted graveyard.

Lhok Geulumpang

Fifteen km north of Calang. Stay at **Dieter's Farm** for Rp10,000 per person, including three

meals and free tea. Though the beach is like paradise the sea is dangerous. Dieter's is a basic *losmen,* the rooms built among the trees. Unfortunately, the owner is a German ex-hippie who thinks that travelers will eat anything, so the food is terrible. It actually looks like dog food. Better to get a room in one of Calang's *losmen* and take a minibus up to Lhok Geulumpang (Rp400). There are no shops in Lhok Geulumpang so bring snacks and water. After a day of swimming, eat a nice meal in Calang.

Meulaboh

Eight hours and 246 km by bus from Banda Aceh. The contrast of ocean, jungle, and rocky shore offers nature at its wildest. Like Big Sur with monkeys. Or take an SMAC flight from Banda Aceh to the airport, 16 km south of Meulaboh.

In Meulaboh, stay at homestay-style **Losmen Mustika,** Jl. Nasional 76, with friendly people and clean rooms. Meulaboh has a number of other *losmen* and hotels. Swimming is safe at

Lhok Bubon, 16 km north on the road to Banda Aceh; other beaches could be dangerous. **Tutut,** 60 km north of Meulaboh, is the site of an abandoned Australian gold mine which ceased operations in 1945.

Tapaktuan

The road between Meulaboh and Tapaktuan is very good; the four-hour bus ride is Rp3500. With the road passing over mountains as spectacular as Java's, the scenery is some of the nicest the province has to offer. You can also

reach Tapaktuan from Medan. Tapaktuan is friendly and has nine *losmen;* the best value is **Wisma Sinabang** (good food, stay for Rp2000). **Hotel Panorama** is the best in town; rooms with fan and no *mandi,* Rp10,000; rooms with fan, *mandi,* and sea view, Rp15,000; rooms with a/c, *mandi,* and sea view, Rp20,000. Prices include towels and soap. Stroll along the main road in the evening. Be sure to see the town's wonderful seven-tier waterfall. In this area the beaches are not as lovely as in the north.

NUSATENGGARA

Afascinating experience for the hardy traveler, Nusatenggara ("Southeastern Islands") is home to hundreds of ethnic groups speaking scores of different languages and practicing widespread animistic beliefs. Flores and Sumba produce some of Indonesia's most exquisite handwoven ikat. Adat architecture is pervasive: the Balinese-style temples of Lombok; the shaggy, elliptical thatch houses of Timor; Sumbanese native houses resembling gigantic straw hats. On Sumbawa megaliths are carved in cryptic reliefs and on Sumba massive stone-slab tombs occupy people's front yards. The region's astounding natural wonders include Komodo's three-meter-long monitor lizards, the colored volcanic lakes of Keli Mutu, superlative snorkeling on Flores, seashell collecting on Gili Trawangan, the virgin game reserve of Pulau Moyo, and the huge rocks of Amanuban in West Timor, which look like the ruins of ancient castles. The area is also rich in dances, fighting arts, animist ceremonies, and unique religious holidays.

INTRODUCTION

Stretching 1,500 km east from Java, the Lesser Sundas include the six major islands of Bali, Lombok, Sumbawa, Sumba, Flores, and Timor, as well as hundreds of smaller islands and islets. The northern string of islands is a continuation of the volcanic belt that runs through Sumatra and Java as far east as Banda, while Sumba, Savu, Roti, and Timor, forming the "Outer Arc" of the Lesser Sundas, are nonvolcanic. The entire region is known as Nusatenggara, meaning "Southeastern Islands." Administratively, the islands are further divided into Nusatenggara Barat (NTB), including Lombok and Sumbawa; Nusatenggara Timur (NTT), comprising Sumba, Flores, West Timor, and the Solor and Alor archipelagos; and Timor Timur, the eastern half of Timor island. The provincial capitals are Mataram (Lombok), Kupang (West Timor), and Dili (East Timor).

Nusatenggara includes some of the country's poorest, least productive, and least developed areas. Though the government has greatly improved communications, transportation, education, and tourism facilities, Nusatenggara's infrastructure is still in its developing stages. Travel there can be inexpensive; a realistic average for two months is US$750 for all food, accommodations, and transport.

THE LAND

Nusatenggara comprises less than four percent of Indonesia's total land area. Unlike Bali and Java, these islands are typically steep and mountainous, with narrow coastal plains and little arable land, surrounded by deep seas and fierce currents. Forests are not as widespread here as elsewhere in Indonesia; instead, most of the land is covered with dry savannah, scrub and open grassland, eucalyptus groves, and monsoon forest.

The region is characterized by prolonged dry seasons interrupted by often heavy rains. Dry months are May to October, though droughts sometimes last months and even years—especially on Sumba and Timor, raked by hot winds blowing north from the Australian deserts. The wet season is November to April, when the arid landscapes turn a lush green, dry riverbeds roar with floodwaters, and dirt roads become impassable quagmires. Timor and the nearby islands are the only regions in Indonesia hit by tropical cyclones, at a rate of three to five per year.

FLORA AND FAUNA

About 120 million years ago, melting ice caps cleaved Bali and Lombok, creating the 48-km-wide, 600-meter-deep Lombok Strait, the archipelago's deepest. The strait marks the so-called "Wallace Line," named after the great naturalist Sir Alfred Wallace. Sir Alfred observed that all the islands west of Lombok feature tropical vegetation, monkeys, elephants, tigers, wild cattle, and straight-haired Asiatics, while the islands east of Bali are home to thorny arid plants, cockatoos, parrots, giant lizards, marsupials, and frizzy-haired Papuans, typical of Australia. The more advanced placental animals and flora beginning to evolve at that time in Asia proper could not cross the turbulent strait between the two islands. Thus, zoological Model-T Fords such as kangaroos and echidnas were allowed to proliferate on the islands

east of Bali because of the absence of predatory mammals.

On the easternmost islands of the chain reside spectacular New Guinea parrots, plus a few Australian species like the cockatoos and honeyeaters who braved the 480-km hop across the Timor Sea. Other than these, Nusatenggara is remarkable for the scarcity of its bird species. Whereas Java and Bali have nearly 200 breeding species of Asiatic birds, just across the strait on Lombok there are 68 fewer.

HISTORY

For over 800 years, Chinese and Arab traders have called at the remote ports of Nusatenggara. The 14th-century Majapahit Empire claimed the whole of Nusatenggara as part of its domain, though theirs was more a mercantile relationship than direct rule; there is little evidence today of Hinduization. Via Ternate and later Makassar, Islam began making inroads in the 15th and 16th centuries. During this period,

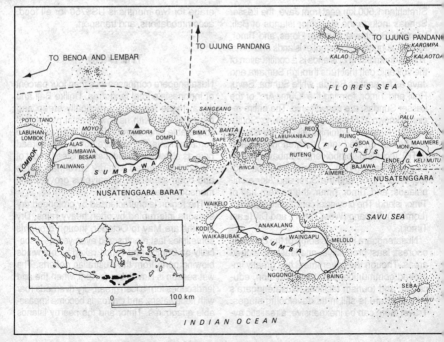

slaves and ponies were major export items. The Portuguese explorer Antonio de Abreu reconnoitered the coast of Flores in 1512, giving the island its present name. From that time on, Portuguese ships stopped frequently along the island chain to replenish their supplies of fresh water and food, and to trade for sandalwood. A Portuguese priest was converting souls on Timor and Solor as early as 1522. With alms from Macao, a fortress was constructed on Pulau Solor and a seminary erected in Larantuka (East Flores) in 1566.

Except for the sandalwood-producing islands of Flores and Timor, there were few resources in Nusatenggara to interest the Dutch, and the VOC did not become active in the area until the 17th century. In 1613, the Dutch, allied with Muslim groups, overran the fort on Solor, and the Portuguese fled to Flores. The Dutch took Kupang in 1653, but for over 100 years competed with the Portuguese for control of the sandalwood trade on Timor. A Portuguese-speaking Christian mestizo group, the "black Portuguese," attacked Kupang in 1749 but were soundly de-

feated. This ended the stalemate, and the Portuguese retreated to East Timor. In 1859, Portugal signed a treaty with Holland renouncing all its rights in eastern Flores.

Savu was forced open in 1860, and within nine years 50% of the population died from a European-borne smallpox epidemic. In 1843, the Balinese lords of West Lombok succumbed to Dutch sovereignty, but it wasn't until 1891, when a Sasak rebellion in East Lombok broke out, that the Dutch found a pretext to intervene and rule the island directly. A Dutch regiment invaded in 1894 but was nearly massacred by a Balinese counterattack.

With the sudden and horrific end of Balinese independence in the ritual suicides of 1906, the Dutch began to consolidate their hold on the islands to the east. Using slave-trading and native looting of shipwrecks as justifications, expeditions were launched against Flores in 1838 and 1846, but that island and the remainder of Nusatenggara were not brought under effective control until the first decade of the 20th century. Ruling through tribal chieftains (*rajas*), the

NUSATENGGARA

© MOON PUBLICATIONS, INC.

Dutch governed Nusatenggara until the Japanese invasion of 1942 rudely shook the region out of its lethargy and political isolation.

Economy

Nusatenggara has virtually no modern industry. Most goods must be imported from Java and paid for with cattle and horses, coffee, beans, copra, and fish. Besides limited deposits of sulphur, oil in East Timor, and salt from the flood pans near Bima, the region has few mineral resources. The great majority of Nusatenggarans eke a livelihood from fishing or subsistence agriculture. In the interior of Sumba and Timor, primitive *ladang* is still used in cultivating taro and yams. The staple crops are corn and sago. Generally, little rice can be grown in such dry weather and generally poor land; there is limited rice cultivation in lowland valleys, irrigated areas, and the extensive paddy fields on the southern slope of Gunung Rinjani on Lombok.

On the small islands of Lembata and Solor, whaling with harpoons is still practiced by the last two whaling communities in Indonesia. On Roti and Savu, the economy is based on exploitation of the sap from the *lontar* palm. Horses have been raised for export in Sumba since the 1840s, and Balinese cattle bred for export on Timor since 1910. Tourism is in its infancy.

THE PEOPLE

The population is estimated at close to 10 million, a highly diverse and fragmented cultural conglomeration with hundreds of ethnic and linguistic distinctions. Many of these peoples still exhibit the rudiments of ancient cultures, with beliefs in spirits, ancestor cults, and magic.

For the most part, the people are friendly. But you should know you'll cause a great stir when you venture into the interior of the islands, where Westerners are a rarity. In some outlying villages, a hundred people may crowd around a white traveler, wanting to touch the hair on white skin. Though this is amusing at first, it can grow annoying in a hurry. In certain areas, such as parts of Flores, isolated villagers may be quite hostile to outsiders. To some groups, travelers represent a cultural threat. And in predominantly Muslim territory like East Lombok and Sumbawa, it's important to respect the conservative codes of dress and

behavior lest you incur local disfavor, which can include fruit and rock throwing. Women should wear bras, long pants or skirts, and full shirts or blouses. Women who travel alone through the heavily Islamized islands can expect to be hassled.

Religion

Having been converted over the last four centuries by Portuguese and Dutch missionaries, most of the population today is at least nominally Christian. Muslims are the majority on Lombok and Sumbawa, but Lombok also has a sizable faction of Hindu Balinese. On Timor, it's about half and half, while the neighboring island of Roti is almost entirely Christian. Despite the veneer of Christianity or Islam, animism is still pervasive, kept alive by numerous ethnic groups scattered throughout the region. Some religious prayers and services, such as the Portuguese-influenced Good Friday Procession in Larantuka on East Flores, have been observed unchanged since the 16th century.

Crafts

Weaving and plaiting are practiced throughout Nusatenggara. Though strictly a cottage industry, weaving—particularly *ikat* —has reached its most sublime expressions on these backwater islands, especially on Sumba, Lembata, Flores, and Timor. The colors and motifs are as yet undiluted by the tourist trade, and goods sell at a fraction of the price you'd pay on Java or Bali. Plenty of fine porcelain is found on Sumba. Visit Flores for fine old ivory and silverwork. The tiny island of Ndau, west of Timor, is noted for its silversmiths.

GETTING THERE

Nusatenggara need no longer be an out-and-back trip from Bali. Bali is still the logical and least expensive jumping-off point; from Padangbai in East Bali there are numerous daily ferries (four to five hours) to Lombok, and regular Merpati flights from Denpasar to Lombok, Sumbawa, Flores, Timor, and Sumba. Merpati flights also depart Darwin in northern Australia for Kupang and Denpasar each Wednesday and Saturday at 1530. This marvelous connection costs only A$198 one-way (1.5 hours to Kupang). Merpati flies from Jakarta to Kupang and from Denpasar to Kupang. Sempati has flights from Denpasar to Mataram, Dili, and Kupang, and from Surabaya to Mataram. Bouraq also flies to Mataram from Denpasar and Surabaya, and from Denpasar to Kupang, Maumere, and Waingapu.

The sleek Pelni ship KM *Kelimutu* sails every two weeks from Banjarmasin to Surabaya, Benoa, Lembar, Bima, Waingapu, Ende, Kupang, Dili, Kalabahi, Maumere, and Makassar, then back to Surabaya. The new KM *Dobonsolo* connects Kupang and Dili to cities along the north coast of Irian Jaya on a two-week circuit. Twice a month, Dili, Larantuka, and Labuhanbajo are connected by the ship KM *Tatamailau* east to points in Maluku and west to Java and Kalimantan. The KM *Awu* links Bima to many ports in Sulawesi and West Kalimantan. If you've got the time, Perintis ships sail between Java, Bali, Lombok, Sumbawa, Sumba, Savu, Roti, Timor, Flores, Lembata, and Alor on less regimented time and route schedules.

GETTING AROUND

Merpati has fairly reliable flights connecting all the major cities and many smaller towns within this island chain. Using mostly small prop planes, new routes are added all the time. Flights are so frequent now that booking for flights between major cities often isn't necessary. For flights that run only once or twice a week, however, reserving a seat is a good idea. Booking can be a hassle, as there is no computerized reservation/flight information connection outside of Denpasar and Kupang. Flight requests must be radioed to the appropriate town and you must wait for a reply by radio, sometimes a day or more. Agents receive a commission on tickets sold so they're helpful if you reserve and purchase through them; they may not be so eager if you only want to make a reservation, buying your ticket at the point of departure.

By Air

Flights depart Bali to anywhere in Nusatenggara; flights leaving from Lombok travel only to Sumbawa, Sumba, and Timor. From Sumbawa, it depends where you are: from Bima you can fly almost anywhere, but from Sumbawa Besar you can go only to Lombok, Bali, and Java. From Sumba, flights are scheduled only to

Bima, Denpasar, and Kupang. From Flores, it again depends where you are: Labuhanbajo now has an airport, making Komodo a bit more accessible for the jet set; from here there are direct flights to Bima, Denpasar, Ende, Kupang, Mataram, and Ruteng. From Ruteng or Ende, you can fly to almost anywhere. Maumere has flights only to Bali (and on to Java), Kupang, and Bima. From Larantuka you can fly to Kupang and Lewoleba. From Lewoleba, flights only go to Kupang via Larantuka, and from Alor there's a connection only to Kupang. Savu and Roti are connected to Kupang only.

By Sea

Motorized and sailing vessels ply the coasts and travel between islands; in the Solor and Alor archipelagos east of Flores, boats are the principal interisland option. Take plenty of books to read during layovers in sleepy port towns. Also, good passenger ferry services link Bali, Lombok, Sumbawa, Komodo, Flores, Sumba, and Timor. These frequent ferries are run by Angkutan Sungei Danau dan Penyeberangan (ASDP), which tends to be even more reliable than Pelni. Frequent non-ASDP ferries also link Larantuka to Adonara and Lembata, and less frequently to Alor.

In Ende, it's fairly easy to get on a cargo boat for Kupang; the trip consumes 35 hours, so choose a big one. If you hang around Maumere or Bima long enough, you'll find boats going to Singaraja and Surabaya. Better fly if you can't wait forever, or don't have the time for the island-to-island overland/ferry trip. For the right price, you can charter small boats, motorized outriggers, or canoes from any port to visit outlying islands and reefs.

By Land

The larger islands offer buses, canopied trucks with benches, bemo, dokar, and minibuses, and you can often hitch a ride (for a fee) with a passing transport truck or motorcycle. With asphalt roads all over Lombok and straight across Sumbawa, it's easy to get around. Move on to Flores and good roads are scarce. There is currently much road work in progress due to earthquake damage on Flores and long stretches are still in fairly poor—yet passable—condition. On Adonara, Lembata, and Alor, land travel is a bone-cracking ordeal in the dry season; in the wet, it could take days to slog 100 km through the mud. On Timor, a well-surfaced road goes from Kupang to Dili. And on Sumba a paved road runs between Waingapu to Waikabubak, with good extensions farther on to the east and west.

The best rule in Nusatenggara is not to plan your schedule too tightly; otherwise you'll just wind up frustrated and angry. One way to get around the transport problem is to bring a motorcycle, which you can take aboard for as little as Rp3500 on all the ferries connecting the islands. Bicycles are another alternative, though it's best to bring your own. Additional ferry charge Rp1000 and up.

Tours

A number of specialized tourist agencies have sprung up in Nusatenggara in the last several years. Most offer various day-trips around Lombok and longer journeys to other islands in the chain. Several also run land/sea tours from Lombok to Komodo. Of the land/sea tour companies try **Perama Tour and Travel,** with offices in Mataram, Senggigi, Kuta Beach, Bangsal, and the three Gili islands; Bima and Sumbawa Besar on Sumbawa; and Labuhanbajo on Flores. **Island Adventures** packages similar weeklong trips. **Swastika Tours and Travel** offers a dozen different options for tours of Lombok and the other major islands in Nusatenggara. In Bima, look for **Parewa Tour and Travel,** tel. (0324) 2525, for special tours to various locales on Sumbawa, Flores, Sumba,

and Komodo. Also in Bima is **Grand Komodo Tours and Travel.**

Floressa Tours, tel. (0361) 289-253, in Sanur arranges dive trips to Maumere on Flores for some of the best skin-diving opportunities in Indonesia. In Kupang, the popular Darwin-Kupang air connection has spawned a number of tour services. **PT Pitoby Travel Service** offers tours to Komodo, Kelimutu, and Sumba, one-day local tours of Kupang, and trips to Roti, West Timor, and Flores dive sites. Offering similar service is **Natrabu,** with offices in Dili and Mataram.

Miscellaneous Tips

In interior areas, you might be expected to register with the police or other local officials; they're not so much keeping tabs on you as just keen on meeting and talking with you. Plan on using Bahasa Indonesia almost exclusively in Nusatenggara. Locals who speak English or European languages in this relatively remote area are plenty rare, so it's wise to be able to handle at least Bahasa Pasar ("Market Indonesian").

Each of the region's major cities features at least one bank that will change U.S. traveler's checks. When you get into the backcountry, be sure to carry your *rupiah* in small denominations. There are small missionary hospitals in Mataram, Ende, Maumere, and Kupang; elsewhere you must rely on missionaries for medical assistance.

LOMBOK

This lush, noncommercialized island, fringed by untouched white sand beaches, is currently in the throes of development. The island isn't as clean as Bali, there are fewer road signs, and the people overcharge too much, especially in East Lombok. It's a poor island, subject to famines. One of the biggest annoyances on Lombok is that travelers are considered curiosities—people stop and stare at you wherever you go. Sometimes whole villages of children will trail after you.

There's a surprising lack of reliable information about Lombok. The Balinese say you'll find only rice and bananas to eat, no roads, no places to stay, and people easily provoked and

quite skilled at knife-fighting—all untrue. The Balinese just want to keep the tourist business all to themselves. Slightly smaller, and drier, than Bali, there's an intact Balinese culture in the western part of the island, with serene temples and palaces. Accommodations in the three main towns—Ampenan, Mataram, and Cakranegara—offer outstandingly good value; the best are owned and run by Balinese.

THE LAND

Lombok is in the same time zone as Bali and the rest of Nusatenggara. Like Bali, Lombok has volcanic mountains in the northern half. The island's landmass, some 4,595 square km in area, is dominated by Gunung Rinjani, rising 3,726 meters above the ocean. Lake Segara Anak fills most of Rinjani's crater. Lombok has similar climate and soil to Bali, favorable for growing coffee, tobacco, market vegetables, rice, and other crops.

Lombok's driest areas lie in an arc that swings from the coastal north around the east and into a broad belt across the south coast. The island's south-central area, a place of scrubby barren hills, is chronically dry; the government calls it "the critical area," with crops frequently wiped out by mice, insects, too much rain, or too little rain. In 1966, 50,000 people starved to death during a famine on the island. It's a very hard life, which is why the government steadily transmigrates the inhabitants of central Lombok to Indonesia's Outer Islands. The midmountain central and western slopes are well watered and green. Here are fertile alluvial plains with picturesque, finely crafted rice terraces.

Fauna

Rusa, buffalo, barking deer, wild pig, long-tailed macaques, civets, and other wildlife proliferate in the southwest and northwest. Lombok is noteworthy as the westernmost island inhabited by the sulphur-crested cockatoo; there are also honeyeaters, bee eaters (an Australian species, *Merops ornatus*), and a mound-builder (*Megapodius reinwardti*). Ducks frequent Lake Segara Anak on Gunung Rinjani. Whales are often spotted off the south coast, where there's also turtle fishing, especially at Kuta Beach.

HISTORY

In the 14th century, Lombok was settled by Hindu-Javanese under the auspices of the powerful Majapahit Empire. Islam was brought to Lombok between 1506 and 1545 by Sunan. In the 17th century, the island was divided into a number of petty princedoms. In return for Balinese support in their struggle against the *raja* of Sumbawa in the early 18th century, the native Sasaks allowed the Balinese to settle in western Lombok. The Balinese king of Karangasem, exploiting the disunity of the feuding princes, conquered Lombok in the mid-17th century, enslaving the Islamic Sasaks in the western part of the island. At the same time, Islamic Makassarese traders from Sumbawa colonized Lombok's eastern half, converting the Sasak to Islam. Though the Makassarese were expelled by a joint Balinese/Sasak force in 1677, the Sasaks soon found themselves oppressed by the newcomers from Bali. Over the next several hundred years, they became second-class citizens on their own island.

The Dutch colonialists used the conflict between the two groups to their advantage. In the late 19th century, the Sasaks sought assistance from the Dutch, who'd occupied northern Bali in 1882. In 1894, the Dutch mounted an elaborate military expedition to Lombok and demanded a war indemnity of one million guilders from the old *raja.* The *raja* accepted but the princes rose up and attacked the main Dutch encampment in Cakranegara. After three days of fierce fighting, the Dutch retreated toward the sea, leaving nearly 300 wounded and 100 dead.

Large reinforcements of men and heavy artillery were mustered and sent from Java. After a bitter monthlong campaign of destruction, with the Dutch razing Balinese villages and the Sasaks looting them, the Balinese stronghold at Cakranegara finally fell. The crown prince, Anak Agung Ketut, a bitter enemy of the Dutch, was murdered; the old *raja* was captured and sent into exile. Soon after, Lombok formally became a part of the Dutch East Indies. Strained feelings still exist between the Sasaks and the Balinese.

THE PEOPLE

Lombok's 1.7 million people are a mixture of Islamic Sasak and Hindu Balinese. The poorer Sasaks live in the eastern part of the island, while the Balinese live mainly in the towns and villages of the western central plain. If you want a Bali without the intense culture, religion, and arts, go to Lombok. Here are found Balinese food, customs—even such Balinese festivals as Galungan are celebrated at full throttle. Most of Lombok's Chinese were killed off in the 1965-66 purges; together with Arabs they now comprise only five percent of the population. The aboriginals of Lombok, called the Bodhas, live in the isolated southeast corner—what's left of them.

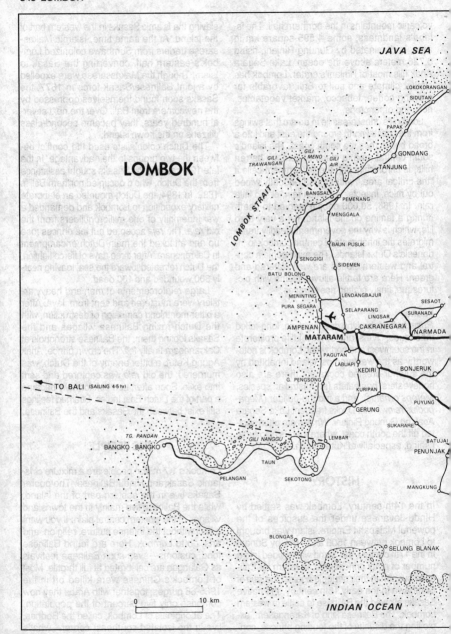

LOMBOK

JAVA SEA

LOKOKORANGAN
SIDUTAN
PAPAK
GONDANG
GILI MENO
GILI TRAWANGAN GILI AIR
TANJUNG
BANGSAL
PEMENANG
MENGGALA
BAUN PUSUK
SENGGIGI
SIDEMEN
BATU BOLONG
MENINTING LENDANGBAJUR
PURA SEGARA SELAPARANG
SESAOT
LINGSAR
SURANADI
AMPENAN CAKRANEGARA
NARMADA
MATARAM
PAGUTAN
LABUAPI KEDIRI
BONJERUK
TO BALI (SAILING 4-5 hr) G. PENGSONG
KURIPAN
PUYUNG
GERUNG
SUKARARE
TG. PANDAN GILI NANGGU LEMBAR
BATUJAI
BANGKO - BANGKO
PENUNJAK
TAUN
PELANGAN SEKOTONG
MANGKUNG

BLONGAS SELUNG BLANAK

0   10 km

INDIAN OCEAN

LOMBOK STRAIT

AMOR AMOR
ANYAR
BAYAN
BATU KOK
SENARU
BANGSALKAMPAR
OBEL OBEL
SAJANG
LEPELAANG
GILI LAWANG
BLANTING
GILI SULAT
SUGIAN
PLAWANGAN
SEGARA ANAK
PADEBELONG
G. RINJANI
(3726 m)
SEMBALUNLAWANG
SEMBALUNBUMBUNG
SEMBELIE
LABUHAN PANDAN
GILI LAMPU
SAPIT
GILI LEBUR
TO SUMBAWA
SWELA
KETANGGA
TIMBANUH
LABUHAN LOMBOK
TETEBATU
AIKBUKA
AIKMEL
PRINGGABAYA
KOTARAJA
ANJONI
APIT AIK
SURALAGA
AIRDAREK
LILIN
MANTANG
PAOHMOTONG
MASBAGIK
KARLEKO
KOPANG
SURADADI
SELONG
TANJUNG
PRAYA
SAKRA
LABUHAN HAJI
LANGKO
BATUNYALA
PEJANGGIK
MUJUR
MARONG
KERUAK
KAWO
SENGKOL
RAMBITAN
SADE
EKAS
TANJUNG RINGGIT
KUTA
AWANG
TG. CINA
TANJUNG AAN
GILI SAYA

ALAS STRAIT

© MOON PUBLICATIONS, INC.

The Sasaks

An Islamic hill tribe with dark skin, long heads, wavy hair, and Caucasian facial features, the Sasaks are thought to have come overland from northwest India or Burma to Java, then migrated across the Lombok Strait to Lombok. The Sasaks are divided into two groups, the secular **Waktu Telu** ("Three Prayer Islam") and the more orthodox **Waktu Lima** ("Five Prayer Islam"). The Waktu Telu, comprising about 30% of the Sasaks, celebrate only three religious occasions: the Prophet's birthday, the holy day of Friday, and Lebaran. Instead of praying five times a day like conservative Muslims, they pray only three times daily. Reminiscent of the worship of linga by the Hindu Balinese, the Waktu Telu also revere monoliths set in the ground. Only a few still eat pork and drink alcohol. The Waktu Telu live mostly in the south-central region in villages with traditional round thatched huts.

Customs

One way to tell the difference between Sasaks and Balinese is that the latter don't mind being photographed. Both the Waktu Telu and Waktu Lima show their Hindu roots by the adoption of a watered-down caste system and the linguistic codes used in addressing commoners and noblemen. Though Muslim, Sasak boys are carried in a Hindu-style circumcision ceremony borrowed from the Balinese. The boy rides on a lion with a tail of palm fronds. No anesthetic is used: the boy is expected to suffer pain for Allah. Much pageantry also comes into play in Sasak courting rituals. Traditionally, if a girl accepts a gift from an admirer, she must marry him.

Native Sasak dances can be chartered. Lombok's shadow play, *wayang kulit sasak,* is one of the few *wayang* forms in Indonesia in which the stories are not based on the Ramayana or Mahabharata legends. Instead, Islamic stories from *Wong Agung Menak* are used. **Sada Loteng,** 20 km from Praya in Central Lombok, is the home of Lombok's only *wayang orang* troupe. Dancers dress like and imitate puppets. Wearing costumes of old cracked leather, they dance with startled, jerky, puppet-like motions. Accompanied by traditional *gamelan,* each dancer recites his own part. The tourist office in Ampenan can arrange shows.

Arts And Crafts

Gorgeous fabrics are woven on this island. Men wear a *batik kain* with an attached *ikat* (*sapuk*) border. The women, who aren't allowed to wear gold ornaments, don the traditional black *baju lambung* with a black *kain* and red shawl (*beberut*). With its several commercial weaving mills, Cakranegara is the best town in which to buy native fabrics and textiles, usually with splashy colors, plus glittery tinsel types of *kain.*

Sukarare is the main rural weaving center, but the villages of **Sengkol, Puyung, Punjuruk** (near Puyung), and **Ketap** also produce fabrics using such traditional technology as backstrap looms, spinning wheels, and bobbin winders. Threads are dyed and woven by hand. Surprisingly, pieces are more expensive in the actual weaving villages than in Cakranegara. Go out on Thursday when people are wearing their traditional black blouses; you'll hear the clack-clack-clack sound of women weaving. Prices range from Rp20,000 to Rp200,000 for a *songket,* depending upon the thread and material used.

Basket weaving in traditional colors of black, yellow, and red is found everywhere on Lombok, but particularly around **Kotaraja** and **Suradadi**; also see samples at **Sweta's** market. The famous **Beleka** baskets are made in the village of the same name outside Mujur. Made from rattan from Taliwang on Sumbawa, these baskets have traditional oval shapes with tight-fitting lids; women and girls take one to four weeks to make one. Big baskets cost Rp20,000-30,000, tiny ones Rp1500. If it weren't for tourism, plastic would have killed off Lombok's plaiting arts; they wouldn't be able to compete.

Giant vases and water pots, which you see carried down country roads, are made at **Banyumulek** in West Lombok, and around the **Kediri** area. See the whole process of building and firing the pots. Pieces are grass-fired at 480° C and thus can be quite brittle. Clay is dug right out of the ground, then chemicals, sand, and ash are added.

Lombok is also a treasure trove of third world toys—all kinds of pushing, turning, wheeling contraptions that clatter, wobble, whirl, and spin. There are little cars with propellers, cars on sticks, and cars made of wood, cans, tin, cardboard boxes, and bamboo, which whole groups of boys gleefully play with and race for hours on end.

Guna Guna

It's a legend on the other islands that Lombok people use a sort of *guna guna*, or black magic, to steal things while you sleep or walk down the street. You may be asleep in your hotel, only to wake up suddenly the moment the thieves leave, having put a spell on you.

TRANSPORTATION

Getting There

Merpati, Bouraq, and Sempati all fly from various cities around Indonesia into Mataram's Selaparang Airport. With Merpati, it's only Rp43,000 and 30 minutes from Denpasar, or slightly more from Sumbawa Besar. Sempati and Bouraq fly into Mataram from Denpasar and Surabaya. Arriving at Selaparang Airport you'll find a taxi booth (price list is posted, all fares fixed), tourist information booth, and a few upper-scale hotel booths.

Ferries every two hours from early morning to midafternoon depart Padangbai on East Bali for the port of Lembar, 26 km south of Ampenan; Rp4800. Add Rp1000 for a bicycle and Rp3500 for a motorcycle. Most travelers bus to Padangbai in the morning, though some choose to stay the night at Padangbai to get an early start and enjoy a smoother crossing. The crossing generally requires 3.5-5 hours; snacks are sold on board. Watch your gear on this route—there have been reports of pickpockets and thefts. Don't trust anyone to look after your things.

Arriving at Lembar, you'll find mobs of minibuses waiting to take you the 25-30 km to your address in Mataram, Cakranegara, or Ampenan. They'll want Rp1500-2000. Transport may be scarce or higher priced if you arrive after dark. When departing, minibuses drop you off right in front of the ticket office in Lembar. Lots of trucks travel the ferries so it's easy to hitch a ride into Denpasar. Several ferries also depart Poto Tano on West Sumbawa for Labuhan Lombok daily; Rp2000, one hour.

Leaving from Padangbai are daily catamaran ferries to Lombok. Departing at 1130, the ship makes a two-hour crossing to Senggigi, then continues to Lembar, arriving at 1615. Rp20,000 for either destination. A second boat departs Padangbai at 1300 for a two-hour crossing to Bangsal; Rp20,000. From Lembar, this ferry leaves at 0830 and goes via Senggigi to reach Padangbai at 1230. From Bangsal the departure time is 0930; arrive in Padangbai at 1130. Contact PT Saranadwipa Citrakarya in Mataram, tel. (0364) 27295; Senggigi, tel. (0364) 93045; or Padangbai, tel. (0366) 34428.

An alternate way between Lombok and Bali is aboard the smooth-sailing *Mabua Express*. Sleek, comfortable, and spacious, this air-conditioned catamaran shuttle runs from Benoa Harbor, located between Kuta and Sanur on Bali, to Lembar Harbor on Lombok. It leaves Benoa twice a day at 0830 and 1430 for a two-hour crossing. At 1130 and 1700 it departs Lembar for the return to Bali. The upper deck fare is Rp48,000 one-way. This includes a snack, drink, and transfer to your destination in the Mataram and Senggigi areas. The lower deck, still comfortable but not so posh, costs Rp33,500 and includes a drink. For reservation and tickets contact a travel agent, hotel tour desk, or the PT Mabua Intan Express offices at Benoa harbor, tel. (0361) 72370, or Lembar harbor, tel. (0364) 25895.

Getting Around

Transport is improving all the time and the roads are not that congested. Quite cheap horse-drawn *cidomo* (*dokar*) are the main means of transport in the towns. Charter one for around Rp10,000 per day, a slow and earthy way to explore the towns and countryside. *Bemo* run between Ampenan, Mataram, Cakranegara, and farther east to Sweta terminal; Rp200-250 for any distance along this route. Some acceptable roads run around Lombok, but the best one stretches between Ampenan and Labuhan Lombok. Along this central highway are a number of crossroad towns—Narmada, Mantang, Paohmotong, Masbagik—from where you can take *bemo* or *dokar* to the island's main tourist attractions. Clusters of waiting *dokar, bemo*, a little marketplace, children playing, and one-story buildings mark each of these highway towns. Lombok isn't a large island; the long, narrow, fertile corridor between the east and west coasts can be traversed in only two hours by bus.

Lying right on the main cross-island road, Cakranegara's Sweta terminal is the focal point for transportation to all of Lombok. A good many of the temples, palaces, traditional villages, and historical sites worth seeing lie within 20 km of Cakranegara. You can view an awful lot of sights in West Lombok by rented taxi and save yourself a lot of time and hassle. Or charter a *bemo* or old car for about Rp50,000 per day with driver.

Motorcycles rent for Rp10,000 per day from people who hang out on the street near Losmen Srikandi in Cakranegara. Cheaper rates for longer rental periods. Some *losmen* owners will also arrange motorbike rentals. Most motorbike owners require you leave your passport as security, either with them or your *losmen*. Bring your bicycle over from Bali because there's some really superb riding country here—one loop winds from Mataram through Suranadi, Lingsar, and then back to Cakranegara. Put your bike on top of a *bemo* if you get tired. In Ampenan, it's possible to rent a bicycle for Rp4000 a day.

WEST LOMBOK

AMPENAN

Formerly Lombok's main seaport but now a crumbling shadow of its former self. Of the three large towns—Ampenan, Mataram, and Cakranegara—Ampenan is the most colorful, with a concentration of inexpensive accommodations and restaurants. The town has a market, shopping area, movie theater, and a few decent restaurants. *Dokar* cost Rp500 to anywhere in town. The west coast beaches are readily accessible from Ampenan.

The **West Nusatenggara Museum** is on Jl. Ponji Tiler Negara, south of Jl. Majapahit. Open Tues.-Thurs. 0800-1400, Friday 0800-1100, Saturday and Sunday 0800-1400; closed Monday and holidays. A small collection, with only a few explanations in English. Best are the displays of cloth and *kris*. The **West Nusatenggara Government Tourist Office**, at Jl. Langko 70, tel. (0364) 21866 or 21730, employs a very helpful staff and offers some useful literature, maps, and brochures. Open Mon.-Sat. 0700-1600; closed Sunday and holidays. Across the street is the **post office**; open 0700-1600 Mon.-Sat., and Sunday 0800-1200. For poste restante, go to Mataram's new central post office. Next door to the post office is the *wartel*; open 24 hours for telephone, telex, and fax services. Several travel agencies are located on Jl. Langko. Change money at any of the several authorized moneychangers near the cinema. While in Ampenan, visit the copra factory near Losmen Pabean, toward the harbor.

Accommodations

The cheaper hotels run about Rp4500-12,000. If you like a city scene, try the Chinese-owned and well-run **Losmen Pabean,** Jl. Yos Sudarso 146; Rp 4500 s, Rp6600 d. A popular *losmen* with travelers, Pabean features laundry facilities and a simple breakfast. *Rumah makan* and Chinese restaurants are down the street.

Several other hotels and *losmen* lie along Jl. Koperasi, also called Jl. Adi Sucipto. At no. 9 is **Zahir Hotel,** tel. (0364) 34248, run by nice people, with a breezy garden, for Rp6500-10,000. At no. 65, **Losmen Horas,** Rp5000-9000, is a bit cramped and too close to a mosque.

Wisma Triguna, tel. (0364) 31705, farther up at Jl. Koperasi 78 toward the airport, is more comfy and a very good value at Rp7500-16,000. Here you get in-room baths, wide verandas, a flower-filled yard, and travel information and services. Each spacious room has a private bathroom. Eddy Barubara, the proprietor, will take you on tours of the island, arrange motorcycle rentals, help you climb and camp on Gunung Rinjani, provide information on Gili Air and Komodo, and let you call home collect from the *wisma*.

The best accommodation in Ampenan is the **Nitour Hotel** at Jl. Yos Sudarso 4, tel. 23780. Pleasant a/c rooms sit separately in a garden, with TV, hot and cold water, and private bath. Rooms run Rp35,000-60,000, including breakfast. Rates decrease during the low season. There's a fine restaurant on the premises serving Indonesian, Chinese, and Western food. A car rental service is available, and a Merpati agent is located in an attached building. A delightful place.

Food

At night the street stalls open up, as well as rolling *apam* and *kolak* wagons. *Kolak* is made from *ubi* with steamed bananas mixed with red sugar—a third-world treat. Two very good Chinese restaurants side by side on Jl. Yos Su-

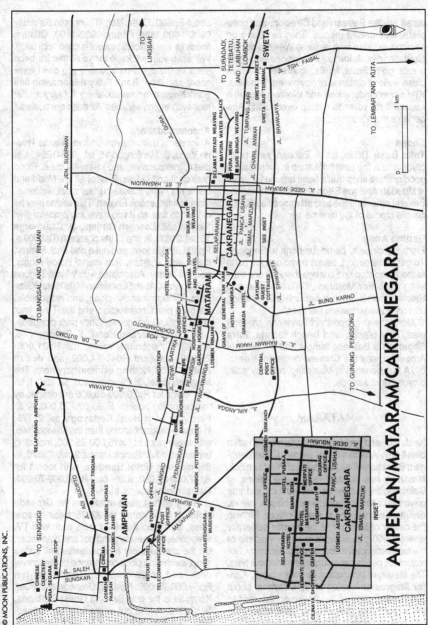

AMPENAN/MATARAM/CAKRANEGARA

TO LINGSAR

TO SURADADI, TETEBATU, AND LABUHAN LOMBOK

SWETA

JL. TGH. FAISAL

Sweta Market

Sweta Bus Terminal

JL. CHARIL ANWAR

JL. BRAWIJAYA

TO LEMBAR AND KUTA

1 km

Selamat Riyadi Weaving
Mayura Water Palace
Pura Meru
Sari Bunga Weaving

JL. TUMPANG SARI

JL. GEDE NGURAH

JL. JEN. SUDIRMAN

JL. ST. HASANUDIN

JL. GOYA

CAKRANEGARA

JL. PANCA USAHA

Suka Hati Weaving

Selaparang

JL. ISMAIL MARZUKI

SEE INSET

Saying Guest Cottages

JL. SRIWIJAYA

Hotel Kertayoga

Perama Tour and Travel

Hotel Handika

Granada Hotel

MATARAM

JL. BUNG KARNO

Grave of General Van Ham

Losmen Rinjani

Garden House

Hospital

Governor's Office

Pejanggik

JL. A. RAHMAN HAKIM

Central Post Office

JL. COKROAMINOTO

JL. DR. SUTOMO

JL. HOS. COKROAMINOTO

TO BANGSAL AND G. RINJANI

Immigration

JL. DEWI SARTIKA

BRI

BNI

Bank Indonesia

JL. PANCAWARGA

JL. PENDIDIKAN

Lombok Pottery Center

JL. UDAYANA

JL. AIRLANGGA

TO GUNUNG PENGSONG

Selaparang Airport

JL. ADI SUCIPTO

Losmen Triguna

Losmen Horas

Losmen Zahir

JL. LANGKO

JL. SUPRAPTO

JL. MAJAPAHIT

Tourist Office

Post Office

West Nusatenggara Museum

AMPENAN

TO SENGGIGI

Chinese Cemetery

Bemo Stop

Pura Segara

JL. SALEH

Cinema

Losmen Pabean

Sungkar

Nitour Hotel

Telecommunications Office

© MOON PUBLICATIONS, INC.

INSET

JL. GEDE NGURAH

Losmen Srikandi

Post Office

Hotel Pusaka

Bank BRI

Merpati Office

Bouraq Office

JL. PANCA USAHA

Selaparang Hotel

Sempati Office

Cilinaya Shopping Center

Hotel Mataram

Losmen Ayu

JL. ASTITI

Losmen Astiti

JL. ISMAIL MARZUKI

CAKRANEGARA

darso are the **Pabean** and **Cirebon,** with complete, well-priced menus. They're strong on seafood, but also feature some Western dishes. Next door is **Jakarta.** For Indonesian-style meals, go to **Setia, Mulia,** or **Arafat,** all within close walking distance of downtown Ampenan. **Kiki** serves Indonesian and Western food in a second-floor veranda setting overlooking Ampenan's main intersection.

Shops
Toko Buku Titian, on Jl. Pabean, sells postcards and is the best bookshop in Ampenan. A good antique shop that's been around for years is **Musdah Antique Shop** on Jl. Saleh Sungkar. Several other antique and art shops lie within a couple blocks of the cinema.

Getting Away
From the cinema, *bemo* run north to Senggigi. To get to the airport, take a *bemo* one km north to the *bemo* stop and change there for one traveling east. For Mataram, Cakranegara, and Sweta terminal catch a *bemo* (Rp 250) along Jl. Yos Sudarso toward the river.

Along the coast north of Ampenan are temples, holy places, and beach resorts. **Pura Segara** is a Balinese temple one km north of Ampenan; see the Chinese cemeteries nearby. A fine beach is at Meninting, an easy walk, bicycle, or *dokar* ride.

MATARAM

Neat, tidy, and well-tended, Mataram is a rather bland city. Administrative center of Nusatenggara Barat as well as the capital of West Lombok, Mataram has spread out to the towns of Cakranegara and Ampenan. Now it's just one continuous strip of government offices, banks, cinemas, homes, and business offices. Right in the center of Mataram is the *kantor gubernor* where 1,000 people work, a prime example of the featherbedded Indonesian bureaucracy. Bureaucratic needs can usually be sorted out here. The **Mataram Hospital** is down the block. *Kantor imigrasi* is located on Jl. Udayana, about 500 meters north of Jl. Langko on the road to the airport. The new **central post office,** the only one on Lombok with poste restante service, lies south of town on Jl. Sriwijaya; hire a *dokar* for

about Rp500. Open Mon.-Thurs. and Saturday 0800-1400, and Friday 0800-1100. Custom check for international parcels is open from 0900. Will wrap your package for you (after it's been seen by the customs agent) if you don't have paper and tape. **Bank Rakyat Indonesia** and **Bank Negara Indonesia,** along Jl. Langko, offer moneychanging services. All rates are posted.

Accommodations
A wonderful Balinese-run *losmen,* **Wisma Tresna Yana,** Jl. Menjangan 15, tel. (0364) 22454, is clean, inexpensive, and relatively quiet. Good breakfast and dinner. Best of all are Made and his family, who make you feel most welcome. Most of them speak English. This *wisma* may be difficult to find, so if you have any problem give them a call. **Losmen Rinjani,** Jl. Caturwarga 18, tel. 21633, is one of the cheapest (Rp5500 s, Rp10,500 t) in town and not a bad deal. Breezy, clean, and spartan, with *mandi* inside rooms; free tea all day. Associated with Wisma Triguna of Ampenan. At Jl. Supratman 10 is **Hotel Kamboja.** Though friendly, clean, and reasonable, it's on a main intersection and the TV is kept on all night. *Dokar* conveniently park alongside.

At the **Selaparang Hotel,** Jl. Pejanggik 40, tel. 32670, economy rooms run Rp21,000-25,000, standard Rp40-44,000, and deluxe Rp42-47,000. Nothing extraordinary here. The **Mataram Hotel,** Jl. Pejanggik 105, tel. 23411, offers rooms for Rp20,000-50,000 or cottages by the swimming pool for Rp65,000-75,000. At Jl. Pejanggik 64 is **Hotel Kertayoga,** tel. 21775, in a more pleasant setting than the previous two, with lower rates at Rp15,000-25,000, including breakfast. At Jl. Panca Usaha 3, tel. 33578, is the pleasing **Hotel Handika,** with rooms for Rp17,000-30,000; suites cost Rp60,000-70,000. Restaurant, gardens, travel desk.

The grandest place in town is the **Granada Hotel,** Jl. Bung Karno, tel. 22275, featuring spacious, well-appointed a/c rooms each with TV, telephone, refrigerator, and hot and cold water. On the premises are a huge restaurant, coffee shop, swimming pool, conference center, travel desk, and broad gardens. Room rates run Rp59,000-79,000. Past the Granada at Jl Bung Karno 31 is the new **Sayung Guest Cottages,** tel. 25378. A little out of the way, but refined. Built in Lombok rice barn-style, each has a spacious room with loft and covered outdoor bamboo veranda. The restaurant serves Indonesian, Chinese, European, and Italian foods. Rooms go for Rp48,000-58,000 including breakfast.

Food

Don't miss the *ayam pelicing* (hot curried chicken) at **Taliwang** on Jl. Pejanggik. The **Garden House**, across from the Toko Buku Rinjani, specializes in Chinese, European, and Indonesian cuisine, but is a bit more expensive. Near the gas station at Jl. Pelikan 6 is the upscale **Denny Bersaudara Restaurant** for Indonesian food. Across Jl. Pejanggik is **Vanini Steak House Restaurant**. On Jl. Cilinaya, to the side of Cilinaya Shopping Plaza, are two great mid-priced restaurants, **Asano** and **Dirga Haya Restaurant**. Can't go wrong at either place.

CAKRANEGARA

Lombok's shopping and market center, Cakranegara—familiarly known as Cakra—is a relatively wealthy city, home to many Chinese, Balinese, and Arabs. In contrast to Ampenan and Mataram, Cakranegara has a modern air, full of concrete and steel, and a rather expressionless main street. The back streets are frumpy and somewhat run-down. While possessing little charm, Cakranegara offers some pearls of pleasure in its palace, temples, and craft factories. You can sometimes see Balinese women wearing beautiful *sarung* and *kebaya* on their way to the temple with offerings on their heads, just like on Bali. Cakranegara is also a bustling crafts center, well known for weaving and basketware. The basketware is bought by the Balinese and sold to tourists on Bali at ridiculous prices. Visit the public market to see silver- and goldsmiths at work; here you may also find clay animal figurines and elegant ceramics.

In the center of town all you'll need lies within walking distance. Bank Exim is on Jl. Pejanggik, the main street. The branch post office is located on Jl. Kebudayaan. The telecommunications office is on Jl. Gede Ngurah; across the street is the Bouraq airline office office. Opposite Bank Exim is the Merpati office, while the Sempati office is located in the Cilinaya shopping center. Other shopping complexes and markets are on or just off the main drag, as are the town's several cinemas.

Sights

See the grave of General Van Ham, second in command of the Dutch expeditionary force during the Lombok War of 1894, in **Karang Jangkong** between Cakranegara and Mataram near the petrol station.

The well-kept **Mayura Water Palace,** Jl. Selaparang, is a huge ceremonial pond built in 1744 during the Balinese occupation. In the 18th century, Cakranegara was the center of the Balinese royal court; the floating pavilion (Bale Kambang), surrounded by a moat, served as a meeting hall and court of justice for the island's Hindu overlords. A small hall is filled with old photographs and Dutch colonial memorabilia. See cockfights nearby. The surrounding park contains fountains and shrines—a pleasant place to stroll around, though you may be wading through children. Wear a sash or the ticket-taker will put one on you; Rp500 fee.

Across the street is **Pura Meru,** one of Lombok's main Hindu temples and the largest Balinese temple on Lombok. Built in 1720 by the Balinese Prince Anak Agung Made Karang, it was meant to symbolize the unity of all the small kingdoms on Lombok. The *pura* is constructed with the usual three separate courtyards with 34 *meru*-roofed shrines. Pura Meru is often locked up and you get the usual runaround with the key.

Accommodations

Losmen Srikandi, Jl. Kebudayaan 2, tel. (0364) 35591, is in the heart of Cakranegara, across from a mosque. Rooms are Rp11,000-35,000 (including breakfast) with tiled bathrooms, fans, and showers. Close to the post office, night market, and motorcycle rental shops. Take a *bemo* right out front for Terminal Sweta. Also central at Jl. Hasanuddin 23, **Hotel Pusaka,** tel. 23119, costs Rp12,500-60,000 for nice cool rooms, some with private *mandi* and fan. Opposite Bank Bumi Daya, this is a central hotel with peaceful courtyard and a good breakfast. **Hotel Ratih,** Jl. Pejanggik 127, tel. 31096, is a pleasant place that charges Rp14,500-23,5000 for an economy room, Rp38,000-43,500 for standard, and up to Rp57,000 for a superior room.

Cheaper places are also available. Clean, convenient, and friendly **Losmen Ayu,** Jl. Nursiwan 20, tel. 21761, features large rooms with fans, cool courtyard, laundry service, and simple breakfast. Rooms cost Rp8000-15,000; higher-priced rooms have inside *mandi*. The owners recently constructed a new building across the street with larger and fancier a/c rooms that go for Rp25,000. At no. 9 on the same street is **Adi-guna Homestay,** tel. 25946, with the same basic setup and amenities for the same price; almost as clean. One block to the west on Jl. Subak III is the Balinese-run **Astiti II,** tel. 27988, with rooms for Rp 7000-12,000. Nice garden but a little cramped. Can be noisy if full of Lombok beach boys. All three offer helpful staff and useful information about the island; and can help arrange motorcycle rentals. Around the corner of Jl. Panca Usaha is **Hotel Astiti,** a rather typical, middle-class Indonesian hotel.

Food

Plenty of *warung* around Cakranegara serve such real *asli* eating as spicy-hot beef curry. For *sate kambing,* try **Warung Istimewa** on Jl. Selaparang. **Depot Dua Em** is across the street from Hotel Ratih. For Indonesian food, Jl. Hasanuddin offers **Madya.** On the same street try **Andala** or **Akbar** for very tasty Padang-style food. For local food, go to **Taliwang,** Jl. Rajawali; fried chicken is the specialty. Sample mouthwatering Arabic *kambing* dishes like *sate* and *gule,* West Lombok's specialty, in open-air **Pasar Gili** near the *bioskop*. **Sekawan Restaurant** on Jl. Pejanggik is the place for Chinese food. A number of hotels have very good restaurants.

Shopping

Unique fabrics and striking *sarung* and *selendang* woven with gold thread are available in Cakranegara; try the weaving factories where they're actually made—**Selamet Riady** at Jl. Ukir Kawi 10 and **Giri Kusuma** on Jl. Selaparang. Two others known for fine craftsmanship are **Sari Bunga** at Jl. Umar Madi 1, and **Suka Hati** at Jl. Majeluk Gang II/7. The shops inside the factories display high-quality authentic weaving, tie-dye pieces, and color-rich embroidered wall hangings. Pieces are usually cheaper in Cakranegara than in the outlying villages.

For antiques, **Wayan Wika Antique Shop,** Jl. Bangau 12 in the western part of Cakranegara, is second only to Sudirman's in Senggigi. Nice porcelain collection at excellent prices. On Jl. Selaparang is **Made's Antique Shop.** Small but friendly. If he doesn't have what you're looking for, Made will try to locate it for you. **Sindu** village near Cakranegara makes all the walking sticks you see on Bali.

Motorbike Rental

Other than your hotel, the best place to rent motorbikes on Lombok is on Jl. Kabudayaan, about a one-minute walk from Losmen Srikandi. Don't take just any machine; stick to it until you get a bike that's in reasonably good shape. One will show up eventually. Motorbikes rent for Rp10,000 a day. You'll be asked to leave your passport as security.

Lombok market

Sweta Market

Sweta is the biggest market complex on the island—a real bazaar. A covered warren of shops, *warung,* and stands selling food, crafts, clothes, cloth, and a multitude of household items. It's good entertainment for a couple of hours, even if you're not buying. Open everyday. See the bird market with good cockfights and bicycles bearing up to 60 chickens.

Terminal Sweta

Next to the Sweta Market is **Terminal Sweta,** the island's central transportation hub with buses and *bemo* to nearly anywhere on the island, buses to major cities on neighboring islands, and *dokar* (Rp 500) to Cakranegara. From here, city *bemo* (Rp 250) run on proscribed routes through Cakranegara and Mataram to Ampenan.

Check the posted prices in the terminal building before you board your bus and pay for your seat. Station attendants can help you find your bus and determine the correct fare. Sample local fares are Narmada (Rp 200), Mantang (Rp600), Labuhan Lombok (Rp2000), Selong (Rp1400), Praya (Rp700), Mujur (Rp110), Kuta (Rp1500), Pemenang (Rp700), Tanjung (Rp900), Bayun (Rp1800), Lembar (Rp700), and Senggigi (Rp500). Sample long-distance fares, including ferry fees, are Sape (Rp26,000), Bima (Rp24,000), Dompu (Rp21,000), Sumbawa Besar (Rp10,000), Yogyakarta (Rp37,000), and Jakarta (Rp70,000).

Some long-distance buses are a/c, some are not; many travel through the night. Some run once a day, others have several daily departures. Check the schedule for exact times and departures, and type of bus. Local buses leave throughout the day and follow a semi-regular schedule of sorts. To distant points, you may need to change buses at midpoint during certain times of the day.

OTHER SIGHTS IN WEST LOMBOK

Gunung Pengsong

About five km south of Mataram, a small group of shrines has been built on a rocky promontory. Climb the long flight of steps and scramble over the rocks at the top for a magnificent view. Gunung Pengsong is Lombok's equivalent of Bali's Gunung Agung. Many visitors on Sunday. Go early in the morning for a clear view over the Lombok Strait toward Gunung Agung, and the surrounding agricultural land and tri-cities to Gunung Rinjani. Take a *bemo* first to Pagesangan (Rp300), then get a *dokar* (Rp1000) the rest of the way.

Pagutan Village

About five km southeast of Ampenan. One of Lombok's most historic temples, this was where the ancient *Nagarakertagama* manuscript was kept. Written in about 1365 by Prapanca, it's one of Java's Kawi (high literature) classics. Only after the 1894 Dutch invasion and occupation of the *raja's* palace in Cakranegara did this precious *lontar* chronicle become known to the West. Now stored in the National Museum in Jakarta, the *Nagarakertagama* is one of the main sources of information on the ancient Majapahit Empire.

Labuapi

A few km south of Cakranegara is the rural town of Labuapi. It's known for its woodcrafts—furniture, wood turning, and woodcarving. Several shops and factories display and sell these wares. The furniture is simple and functional, the turnings utilitarian, the seated human figures and oblong masks of simple design and style and not particularly refined.

Banyumulek

Four km southwest of Labuapi is Banyumulek, a village where nearly everyone is involved in the pottery trade. Literally dozens of shops sell what the village produces. Traditional are the water pots and urns without woven rattan mesh coverings. Pieces with mesh coverings—which adds additional cost and production time—are created principally for tourists.

Pots are constructed either on a wheel or with coils of clay that are then beaten into shape with a flat wooden paddle. These are left to dry in the sun. The outside is scraped to a rough finish and burnished by stone or metal until shiny. Pieces are then fired in an open fire. No glaze is added.

Supported by a New Zealand government grant, this industry has helped to improve the quality of life in the village. Pieces are distributed and sold both in Indonesia and overseas. Stop in at the Lombok Craft Project office to obtain a full explanation of the pottery-making process. The villages of Penunjak in the south and Masbagik in the east are also pottery-making villages involved in the project and worth a visit. When in Mataram visit the **Lombok Pottery Centre** at Jl. Majapahit 7, tel. (0364) 23804.

Southwest Lombok

Lembar harbor is the point of departure for ferries to Bali. Take a *bemo* from Terminal Sweta to the harbor and buy a ticket there for the ferry, or arrange a bus (with ferry included) to Denpasar from Terminal Sweta. Two km up from the harbor is the simple *losmen* **Pondok Serumbung Indah**; rooms for Rp12,000. Ask about ferries from Lembar to **Gili Nanggu**, where there's good swimming and plenty of peace and quiet. The one place to stay charges about Rp25,000. The end of the road at **Bangko-Bangko** is a favorite spot for surfers. Good waves roll in off the headland. Few *bemo* run out this far. No *losmen*; stay with the *kepala desa*.

Narmada

Ten km east of Cakranegara, seven km from Sweta by *bemo* (Rp250). From Narmada's *bemo* stop, cross the road and walk down a side street to the entrance (Rp200) of Taman Narmandi (Narmandi Park). In 1801, a *raja's* summer palace was built here upon an artificial plateau. From a hidden place above the three-tiered pools, the old *raja* used to make his selection of the village lovelies. The top pool is formal and ornamental, with a fountain; the middle is a Western-style swimming pool; and the bottom pool, the largest, is a free-form mini-lake where many people come to fish and boat.

Built by the king of Karangasem, the large complex encompasses a mixture of Balinese, Islamic, and Sasak architecture. The complex slopes down in tiers to the river valley below. The overall design is typically Balinese, the series of compounds laid out as a miniature replica of the summit of Gunung Rinjani and its crater lake, Segara Anak. Since the king in his old age could no longer make the ascent up the volcano to lay his offerings, he had this palace constructed to fulfill his spiritual obligations. Worth an hour's walk or swim (Rp300). Several *warung* are inside the complex, with plenty more in town. Crowded on weekends.

Behind the *bemo* stop, see village handicrafts, clothing, and food in the Narmada market, one of Lombok's largest.

Suranadi And Sesaot

Suranadi is a small temple and gardens, one of Lombok's oldest, four km north of Narmada and 15 km from Mataram in the hills. See the rebuilt baths of kings carved in the Balinese style with icy clean water bubbling up from natural springs; the pool is said to have been built in exactly the same shape as Lake Segara Anak. At the **Temple of the Holy Eels,** eels swim out of conduits if you drop an egg in the water. Donation requested—Rp500 is enough.

For a little self-indulgence, stay at the formerly colonial **Hotel Suranadi,** tel. (0364) 23686. Reputed to be the finest upland hotel on Lombok, rooms and cottages rent for Rp48,000-96,000; amenities include swimming pool, restaurant, and tennis courts. Service and rooms are not a bad value and the location is fantastic. Perhaps the most unusual thing here is the swimming pool, which consists of sand, round rocks, and ice cold spring water. Meals are rather expensive; up the road is **Wisata** for an alternate Indonesian meal.

Take a *bemo* up the river five km through farming villages to Sesaot, with *bemo* station, market, and forest nearby. The deeper you go, the more proud and *asli* the people become. See people carrying 40-kilo loads of firewood on their heads, trudging in from the rainforest to sell their loads in the market.

Lingsar

At Lingsar is another sacred eel pool and a large, Balinese temple complex—oldest and holiest on the island—which combines Hindu and Islamic motifs. This worn and faded temple and its pretty courtyard, believed to have been built in 1714, feel more like an Indian *pura* than anything on Bali. The Waktu Telu Muslims and Balinese Hindus worship together here, using different levels of the temple. The Hindu *pura* in the northern part of the complex has four shrines, each dedicated to the gods and god-kings of Bali and Lombok. The Waktu Telu temple, in the southern part of the complex, contains an eel pond dedicated to Vishnu. On all-night festivals during the full moon, sleep in the temple on mats. Lingsar is a highlight of Lombok, an extremely enjoyable experience. Donation Rp500. Buy eggs in the *warung* for the slug-like holy eels. A second, smaller temple is located in the village 200 meters behind.

In the countryside between Suranadi and Lingsar is **Tragtag,** a pure Balinese village on a small hill, as well as many other traditional Balinese villages. Take a *bemo* from close to Cakranegara's *bioskop* direct to Lingsar. You can also take a *bemo* from Terminal Sweta to Narmada, then board another for Lingsar. From Lingsar's *bemo* stop, it's only a five-minute walk to the temple complex.

West Coast Beaches

The whole of northwest Lombok is popular with sunbathers, skin divers, and snorkelers. Aside from popular Senggigi, try the quieter and more scenic beaches **Meninting, Batu Bolong, Mangsit, Malimbu,** and **Sira,** as well as the three islands off **Bangsal.** Farther up the coast, the beaches turn whiter. See a regatta of colorful sailing vessels float by in the mornings; view Bali's Gunung Agung in the distance through the clouds. Don't stroll naked on the beach here; save that for the offshore islands. To get to each beach except Sira, catch a *bemo* near the cinema in Ampenan.

Batu Bolong, north of Meninting, is worth a visit for the scenic views of Bali from the cliff that juts out over a quiet beach. The Hollow Stone temple underneath was built by the Balinese. About Rp500 by public *bemo* from Ampenan. Go at sunset. Donation requested.

Senggigi Beach

No longer just another pretty beach along Lombok's west coast, Senggigi, about eight km north of Ampenan, is now in the throes of serious development aimed at mid- to upper-end travelers and tourists. Hotels, bungalows, and *losmen* are going up along the 2.5 km stretch between Batu Bolong and Senggigi, with more planned here and farther north along the coast road to Bangsal. Heralding this surge in development are the high corrugated metal fences that dot the road, advertising new and forthcoming construction projects. Here too are new shopping complexes, large restaurants and bars, bookshops, tour and travel centers, post office, telecommunications office, dive center, motorbike rental shops, car rental agents, and art shops. Even the well-known Sudirman's Antiques has moved here from Ampenan. On a prominent spot on the beach is Lombok's swankiest hotel, the Sheraton Senggigi Beach Resort.

Still, the swimming is good, the snorkeling and scuba diving fair, and the colorful armada of fishing boats in the Lombok Strait every morning provide a pleasant local feel. A few small shops front the beach (catch the evening market as well) selling fruits, snacks, and clothes, while strolling vendors try to interest you in the usual array of T-shirts, wood carvings, and the like—all available at Sweta Market at a fraction of the cost charged here.

Here you can rent diving gear to explore the coral offshore or charter a boat (Rp40,000-50,000) to one of the Gili islands for a day of swimming, snorkeling, and salty air. Lots of good walks in the area pass through coconut groves and unfrequented villages. *Bemo* from Ampenan will let you off wherever you want along this stretch. Some *bemo* continue on to Bangsal.

Reminiscent of a fine Hawaiian beach hotel, the 156-room, four-star **Sheraton Senggigi Beach Hotel,** tel. (0721) 486-666, is the premier hotel on Lombok. Plush accommodations, several fine restaurants, luxurious beachside swimming pool, tennis courts, fitness center, and shops will make your stay more than comfortable. Rooms start at Rp230,000. Also at the upper end is **Puri Bunga Beach Cottages,** tel. (0364) 91013, up the hillside across the road from the Sheraton. Great views over the bay, with its own restaurant and bar, swimming pool, and fitness center. Air-conditioned and fan rooms starting from Rp115,000; up to 50% discount in the low season. The **Senggigi Beach Hotel,** tel. 93210, is the original high-class hotel in Senggigi and offers the best location. Full complement of services includes restaurant and bar, swimming pool, and tennis court. Tariffs for the thatched-roof bungalows run from Rp115,000 standard to Rp306,000 for the deluxe; the Grand Bungalow goes for an astonishing Rp1 million a night. The **Lombok Intan Laguna,** tel. 93090, features aesthetically pleasing architecture with rooms from Rp160,000. All have a full range of services, facilities, and offerings.

Plenty of midrange accommodations are available as well. The **Graha Beach Senggigi,** tel. 93101, has garden-view rooms from Rp84,000 and ocean-view rooms from Rp94,000. **Mascot Berugaq Elen Cottages,** tel. 93365, offers a/c bungalows for Rp60,000-68,000. Rates are Rp20,000-70,000 for a room at **Melati Dua Cottages,** tel. 93288. At **Lina Cottages,** tel. 93237, rooms cost Rp25,000-35,000. **Batu Bolong Cottages,** tel. 93065, which is located about 1.5 km south of central Senggigi, rents rooms for Rp30,000-40,000. Each of these has its own restaurant and a selection of services.

Those on a budget should try **Pondok Senggigi,** tel. 93273. With a multitude of rooms from Rp10,000 to Rp76,000, this is perhaps the best deal in town. Large, well-maintained, and pleasant, the buildings constructed of native materials. Ask for a room in the back, as the restaurant hosts a loud live band several evenings a week.

OFFSHORE ISLANDS

The three tiny islands of Gili Air, Gili Meno, and Gili Trawangan off Lombok's northwest coast are magnificent. All once depended on the copra trade, but now money comes from tourism. Coconut trees still cover the interior of all three islands, and there is limited cattle grazing and goat herding on Gili Trawangan. The lack of freshwater springs and limited land size has traditionally kept the population small, but water catchment schemes and water transportation from the mainland has changed that. As everything must be brought from Lombok, prices are slightly inflated. While electricity is generated during the evening hours at some establishments, most still use lanterns. Though there are no banks, moneychangers occupy all three islands; a *wartel* office is located on each isle for local and international telephone calls. And while small—you can walk around each isle in a leisurely two or three hours—there is *dokar* transport on all three islands charging Rp500-1000 for a ride along the limited beachfront paths. These drivers meet passengers at the boat landing to vie energetically for business. A few shops even rent bicycles for Rp2500 an hour. Many of the accommodations are built up off the ground, have outside *mandi,* thatched roofs, woven bamboo walls, covered verandas, a few chairs and tables, and mosquito nets. Bring mosquito coils, however, as malaria is entrenched here during the rainy season. Cases of cholera, dengue fever, and intestinal disease have been reported during the dry season.

No longer unpopulated or unspoiled, these islands are now definitely on the tourist circuit, rapidly becoming very popular. So popular, in fact, that at the height of the late summer tourist rush all rooms are rented and some people must sleep on the beach. Other small islands off Lombok—particularly south and west of Lembar—now receive travelers looking for more tranquil climes.

On the Gias you can still find peace and quiet, lots of sun, reasonably good white-sand beaches, seashells, fine swimming, and some very good underwater scenery. Many accommodations rent snorkel masks and fins for Rp3000 per day while shops usually ask slightly more; look around for the best deal. There are frequent boat connections from Bangsal to and between all three islands.

Gili Trawangan

With its active nightlife, Gili Trawangan enjoys the reputation of a "party" island, and is therefore the preferred destination of many foreign travelers. The most distant from Lombok, it offers the best snorkeling and skin diving. While the center of the island is full of coconut trees, the periphery is more sparsely vegetated, so the island seems hotter than the other two. There's a lighthouse on the west side. Lodgings and restaurants line the eastern shore fronting the best beach area. A few shops and the *wartel* office are located near where the shuttle boats land. There are rumors the government may build a first-class hotel and golf course here, but that seems unlikely until the water problem is addressed in a permanent manner.

Gili Trawangan is the only one of the three islands offering any height. Located at the south end, the hill is an easy walk. From here you have the best view of sunrise over Gunung Rinjani on Lombok and sunset over Gunung Agung on Bali. At the far south end of the hill are remnants of WW II Japanese gun emplacements. There's not much to see there today except for the crumbling cement carcasses of the bunker fronts—the hand-dug tunnels that once honeycombed the hillside have been blocked up.

There are two dozen bungalow complexes catering to travelers along the island's eastern shore, stretching about one km both ways from the boat landing site. Up from the landing are several shops, businesses, and private residences. The interior of this 340-hectare island is one large coconut plantation with a handful of private houses scattered about. Each accommodation offers a simple breakfast with the price of a room; some offer three meals a day for an extra charge. Generally speaking, room prices range from Rp6000-8000 s and Rp10,000-12,000 d, with some higher-priced triples and bungalows. Most have attached toilet and shower/*mandi*. The cluster of establishments toward the south end are larger, packed relatively close together, and built in strips of facing bungalows that back away from the water rather than run along the shore. Somewhat more modern and upscale in appearance, most have restaurants attached. Along the northern portion, the accommodations are smaller, simpler, quieter, and farther apart. Perhaps the quietest are those at the extreme ends of the island—**Marva II** at the south end under the hill and **Nusa Tiga** on the northern tip. Several recommended places are **Pak Majid Losmen, Paradise Bungalows,** and **Rainbow Losmen** on the south end, and **Sudi Nampir Cottages** and **Good Heart Bungalow** on the north end. If one of these doesn't suit you, another is only a few steps away.

In August 1992, the government unexpectedly sent in a special squad of army troops to destroy several bungalow complexes, claiming the owners lacked title to the land. Many suspect government officials and/or wealthy businessmen with government connections covet this land for future hotel development. The majority of the places destroyed have not been replaced, and many still look like they were razed in a war. Then, in October 1993, a devastating fire burned about 50 closely-set bungalows to the ground. Dozens of foreign travelers lost everything—passport, money, clothes—and received almost no compensation from the Indonesian government.

Most restaurants are located along the southern portion of this community; several take turns hosting parties on various nights of the week. Remember: if you prefer undisturbed sleep, look for a bungalow away from these restaurant/bars. Larger *losmen* have their own restaurants and serve seafood, Indonesian, and European fare. The few local *warung* have abbreviated Indonesian menus with food about half the price of the fancier restaurants. Each will post a signboard out front giving the menu and specials for the day. A select few recommended places are the **Excellent Pub and Restaurant,** next to Sudi Nampir cottages; **Borobudur Restaurant,** which also serves Chinese food; **Mountain View Restaurant,** near the *wartel* office; and the **Rainbow Seafood Restaurant,** at the south end.

Gili Trawangan features four competent dive shops, each renting snorkeling and scuba equipment and dispensing information. They are **Albatross Diving,** with perhaps the best reputation, **Blue Marlin Dive Shop, Dive Rinjani,** and **Dive Lombok.** Shop around for the best prices and most personable, experienced staff. Sample rates are in the vicinity of Rp40,000 for a single dive off the beach to Rp150,000 for two dives off the west coast by boat.

Gili Meno

The middle island is the smallest, most tranquil, and least visited. There is good beach all around Gili Meno, the best lying on the southeast corner by the oldest accommodations. Lots of coral and seashells wash up all along the beach. Off the northwest corner of the island is some very good snorkeling and diving, some say the best on the three islands. Water is brackish here; a couple of places desalinate their water while others bring it in from Lombok. Gili Meno is the only one of the three islands with standing water—a salt pond on the west side, from which islanders get a minimal quantity of salt every year. This is the most laid-back of the islands, with two or three shops, less than half a dozen *dokar,* and almost no hype or hawkers.

There are less than a dozen places to stay on Gili Meno. All have restaurants on the premises. There's a concentration on the southeast shore in front of the best beach area. Accommodations run Rp10,000 s and Rp15,000 d for those on the beach; smaller, simpler rooms up the path from the boat landing are somewhat less at Rp5000-8000. Three upper-end establishments cater to those who seek a bit more luxury and refinement. Popular are **Kontiki Bungalows** at the extreme south end, **Mallia's Child Bungalows** on the best part of the beach, and **Janur Indah Bungalows** at the boat landing. **Blue Coral** is located out on the far north end for those who want to really get away. Cheaper and away from the beach are **Rawa Indah Cottages, Fantastic Cottages, Mata Hari Bungalows,** and **Pondok Wisata.**

At the high end is the **Gazebo Resort Cottages,** tel. (0364) 31276, the original top-end accommodation on the island. Neat and pleasing buildings in pleasant surroundings; the constant muffled background noise is the generator used in the desalination process. Here you'll also find the *wartel* office. Rooms for Rp76,000 s and Rp86,000 d, breakfast extra. Vying for the top-end trade are the newer **Casa Blanca Cottages,** tel. 33847, with rooms for Rp48,000-67,000, and the finer **Zoraya Pavilion,** Rp19,000-63,000 including breakfast.

Mata Hari's Restaurant specializes in seafood. **Kontiki, Brenda's,** and the **Blue Lagoon** all have good reputations.

Ask your manager about renting snorkels and fins or try one of the shops. **Zoraya Pavilion** has a wide variety of water-sport equipment for rent, including fins and masks, motorboats, sailboards, and diving gear. Some accommodations also own boats and can arrange day-trips on the water.

Gili Air

The "tourist" island, the one nearest to the mainland. The coral reef near the boat landing is dying or dead; there's a pearl-harvesting operation there now. The best beach area lies on the southeast corner of the island. With about 1,000 residents, Gili Air has the largest permanent local population. Homes are scattered throughout the island's coconut groves. The population is large enough to support a mosque, elementary school, clinic, and a handful of shops. Some accommodations generate their own electricity here. For diving try either the **Blue Marlin Dive Shop** or **Barongang Dive Shop**; masks and fins Rp10,000, one dive off the beach Rp63,000. Both **Perama** and **P.T. Wammen** maintain tour and travel offices here.

The premier accommodation on Gili Air is the **Gili Indah.** On the south coast to the left of the boat landing, its bungalows blend nicely with the well-tended grounds, and the restaurant is one of the best on the island. Rooms for Rp14,000-60,000. Here also are a small sundries shop, boat rental, foreign exchange, *wartel,* and the Perama travel office. Farther to the west, a short walk past Gili Indah, are the more spartan **Lucky's, Anjani's,** and **Salabose** cottages. At the boat landing find **Bamboo Cottages** and **Bupati's Place.** Fronting the best section of beach are **Gili Air, Gili Beach, Fantastic,** and **Nusa Tiga** bungalows. An up-and-coming place at the north end of this stretch is the **Bulan Madu Beach Cottages.** With slight pretensions of grandeur, it's stuck behind a wall and entered through a fine gate. Rooms for Rp40,000-65,000; pleasing gardens. At the north end of the island are **Han's Cottages and Restaurant** with rooms from Rp15,000 to Rp20,000, and on the western point are **Hink** and **Grenica** cottages. Except for exceptions listed above, the prices of most rooms on Gili Air run Rp8000-15,000; prices fall during the slow season. Each accommodation has its own restaurant.

Getting There

Take a bus from Terminal Sweta to Pemenang (Rp700, 45 minutes), or catch a *bemo* in Ampenan traveling to Senggigi and on along the beautiful coastal road to Pemenang. On the bus from Sweta you first pass **Gunungsari,** known for bambooware, then **Sidemen,** where palm sugar is made. From Sidemen, the road climbs through forests inhabited by monkeys, often seen playing along the roadway. Nice views of the north coast as you descend from the pass. From here the road continues five km through Baun Pusuk to Pemenang. Once in Pemenang, catch a *dokar* (Rp300) or *bemo* (Rp200), or walk the one km to the harbor village of **Bangsal.** Bangsal is a small port with a few restaurants and shops, moneychangers, ticket offices, and lots of hawkers selling T-shirts, blankets, hats, cloth, and other souvenirs. A few long-distance buses to various points on Bali and Sumbawa leave from here. Bangsal also offers a few basic bungalows—cheaper than those on the Gilis—where you can perhaps park your motorbike for a small fee while you visit the islands. From here you can walk the few kilometers to Sira Beach, which you'll have nearly all to yourself. Rumor has it a big hotel is planned for this wonderful spot.

Tickets for the boats are sold at a small kiosk at the end of the street, just before the beach. On each island, a ticket booth opens for a short time before the boats are scheduled to arrive. There is no dock at Bangsal or on any of the three islands. You must wade to the boats on departure and arrival so be prepared to get your feet wet. Anytime the wind is up—it's usually stronger in the afternoon—you can count on getting wet, even soaked to the skin. Be sure all your belongings are sealed in plastic. The boats are piloted by men who know the waters well and who choose their routes according to the winds and waves. Small and fairly stable, these boats are often loaded with more passengers than are really safe. They've been known to capsize as they're maneuvered onto the beach, spilling everyone and everything into the water.

Three classes of boats make the connection from Bangsal to the Gili islands: public, charter, and shuttle. Although the service is different, the actual boats used are the same. Be sure to confirm departure times and fares in advance at the ticket booths. The public boat leaves when there are 20 passengers on the list—sometimes up to 30 people actually crowd on. As there's no fixed schedule, the wait for these boats varies according to the season; fewer people in the slow season means longer waits. On the return, boats leave the islands around 0800. Fares and times from Bangsal are Rp900 and 20 minutes for Gili Air, Rp1100 and 40 minutes for Gili Meno, and Rp1200 and one hour for Gili Trawangan. Leaving when anyone wants to charter a whole boat of up to 10 people, the charter boat fares are Rp15,000 for Gili Air, Rp18,000 for Gili Meno, and Rp21,000 for Gili Trawangan. The shuttle boat has a fixed schedule, leaving pretty much on time twice a day at 0930 and 1500. Fares are Gili Air, Rp3000; Gili Meno, Rp3500; and Gili Trawangan, Rp4000.

The three islands are also connected to each other by an interisland shuttle, called the island-hopping boat. This shuttle leaves from each island twice a day around 0900 and 1500. The fare is Rp3000 between Gili Meno and the other two, and Rp4000 between Gili Air and Gili Trawangan.

Aside from these passenger boats to the Gili islands, there is one passenger ferry and two adventure boats that stop here. Tickets for these ships are sold at separate ticket booths—look for signs at the restaurants in Bangsal. The catamaran ferry MV *Putri Anjani* or its sister ship MV *Putri Senggigi* leave daily for Padangbai, Bali (Rp20,000) at 0930, and arrive from Padangbai every day at 1500.

Islands Adventures runs an all-inclusive seven-day program that takes you by coaster from Bangsal to Gili Sulat, Moyo, Bima, Komodo, and Labuhanbajo on Flores for Rp280,000. All you have to do is enjoy the scenery, swim, fish, and eat. The *Heldwati IV* also makes a run along the north coasts of Lombok and Sumbawa. **Perama Land Sea Adventure** offers a less extensive coastal service. Perama transports you from Bangsal to Labuhan Lombok with a day of sightseeing at craft centers on the island. From there you go by boat to the Perama Resort on Moyo, ending at Komodo. Leaving every Thursday and Sunday, this three-day program costs Rp100,000.

NORTH LOMBOK

GUNUNG RINJANI

Famed for its great beauty and eerie isolation, Gunung Rinjani (elev. 3,726 meters) is the fourth-highest mountain in Indonesia, towering over every corner of Lombok. Shrouded in clouds throughout the afternoon, the best time to catch an unimpeded view of Gunung Rinjani is in the calm early morning hours.

The enormous crater of this semi-active volcano is about four km across at its widest, nearly filled with the bright emerald-green water of Lake Segara Anak. The lake lies nearly one km below the crater rim. Virtually this whole mountain complex, its steep slopes covered in dense forests, has been declared a national reserve.

The mountain is sacred to both the Balinese and the Muslim Sasaks on Lombok. Balinese make a twice-yearly pilgrimage to the top to throw ritual rice and goldfish into the lake, a Hindu offering to the goddess of the mountain. The Sasaks may tramp up the mountain several times a year, especially during the full moon when the caldera is sometimes invaded by groups of noisy *pemuda*. Others come just to soak in the regenerative hot springs below the crater rim.

The Caldera
Puncak Rinjani is the highest and steepest point on the edge of the caldera, while the crescent-shaped **Lake Segara Anak** within the caldera lies at a height of just over 2000 meters. About 3 km at its widest, its depth is 230 meters. Plentiful fish inhabit its waters, and waterfowl can be seen. Part of the year, water flows out at a point on the northeast shore called **Kokok**

Putih. Just below this water exit, in a section of pools and cascading falls, are hot springs reputed to ease skin ailments. Water in the top pools is near boiling; each pool down the cascade seems to get cooler. You can pick the most comfortable temperature and try a delightful soak to ease your tired muscles.

The volcanic peak inside the caldera is considered quite young. **Gunung Barujari** (2,375 meters), which sits at the edge of the lake, rose only during the last century or two. Barujari still smokes occasionally but its last known eruptions were in 1884 and 1901, when it expelled showers of ash. It's been estimated the force necessary to create Gunung Barujari and form the lake was equal to about 300 Hiroshima-type atomic bombs.

Climate

Definitely a place to visit in the dry season; it's too dangerous in the wet. In October the weather starts to become questionable and rain will fall for short spurts during the day or night. The steep paths are much safer and the views clearer in the dry; in the wet season the trails become oozy mudslides, the temperature plummets, the wind picks up, and lightning is a potential killer. Follow the advice of locals, who know the mountain well. Gunung Rinjani is cloudcapped most of the year, except for early mornings during the dry season. Pay attention to the elevation. The crater rim, very exposed in any season, can be quite cool. In the mornings the heavy mists gather on your tent like rain.

Climbing

You'll need a tent, cooking gear, matches, flashlight, sleeping bag, warm clothes, stout shoes with good traction, and enough food and water for at least three days. Buy food in Ampenan, or you'll be forced to get it all from a shop at the trailheads for steeper prices. Buy enough food for your guide, too, and he'll do the cooking. The guide sometimes provides a pot and water jug. All camping and cooking equipment can be rented in Senaru or Batu Kok. Ideally, three people should make the climb: one can care for the sick or injured while the other goes for help. Eddy Batubara at Ampenan's Wisma Triguna can arrange the climb for you, as well as rent you complete camping equipment for around Rp25,000. Other hotels and travel services ren-

GUNUNG RINJANI APPROACHES

der similar service. You can also rent needed equipment from a shop or homestay at the northern trailhead. As of yet, no equipment is available for rent at Pesugulan or Sembalun Lawang.

This is one of Indonesia's unique experiences. Unless you're a serious hiker, your destination is not actually Gunung Rinjani, but the beautiful lake inside the caldera. It's a steep, arduous climb, so be in shape, be cautious, and be careful. Though the favorite approaches are from Senaru in the north or Pesugulan to the east, several less frequented routes also lead to the crater rim. You can hire guides and porters from the Senaru, Pesugulan, and Sembalun Lawang departure points. Guides run Rp25,000 a day, porters Rp10,000-15,000. Porters and guides are not really necessary, as the trails are obvious except for a few spots where they split like the channel of a river delta only to come together again farther on. But with at least a porter you'll have a more relaxing time—someone will lead the way for you, lighten your pack, provide companionship, and set up camp and cook for you.

The trails are well used. A few decent shelters are located along the trails and good camping spots are found on the shore of the lake. Inside the crater it's seldom deserted, but you're still rewarded with solitude and overwhelming beauty. At night at this elevation the moon is bright and the stars brilliant and countless.

From Senaru

This is the shortest and easiest way to climb Gunung Rinjani, making maximum use of motorized transport. First board the 0900 bus (Rp1800, 70 km, two hours) from Terminal Sweta to Anyar near the north coast, or Bayan, an isolated, traditional Muslim village where Hindu-style dances are still practiced. Anthropologists have for years been fascinated by the customs of the complex societies living in sparsely populated northern Lombok, the source of the Waktu Telu religion.

From Anyar or Bayan, catch a *bemo* (Rp1000) to the village of **Batu Kok,** or one km farther up to the village of Senaru, the end of the road. The park headquarters is at Batu Kok, where you're asked to check in, register, and pay a Rp1500 entrance fee and Rp500 insurance fee if you intend to climb the mountain. See the spectacular **Sindanggila Waterfall** from Pondok Senaru in Batu Kok. A slender ribbon of lace, it's only a 15-minute walk (Rp100 fee) down a good path into the valley to the pool at the bottom. A second, smaller, less-visited waterfall is a 30-minute walk up the river; the trail starts from the cement steps at the valley bottom and follows the water flume much of the way.

The traditional Sasak village of Senaru features two rows of 20 thatched wooden huts; to the side lie newer shops and *losmen*. When hiking from Senaru, start early. Head up the hill through slash and burn agricultural fields and into the forest. A walk of four to five hours will bring you past the first shelter to the second shelter, where you can spend the night. Water is found at a spring a short distance from the second shelter—look for the sign. An additional two to three hours will bring you out of the forest, across a rocky slope, and up to the cool and breezy crater rim (2,900 meters) at a point called Plawangan I. Only from here and from Plawangan II on the east edge of the rim can you descend into the crater. Inside the crater, stands of pine dot the steep rocky slopes, the otherworldly

green expanse of Segara Anak spreads before you, and Gunung Barujari pokes its small volcanic head up from the crater floor. Views here are reminiscent of those at Crater Lake in Oregon in the United States. If it's clear, you may be able see as far as Bali's Gunung Agung, the whole north coast, and the peaks on Sumbawa to the east.

A good three-hour walk will bring you down the precipitous inner wall of the caldera to the lake. This trek is not for the weak of heart—there are narrow stretches and sections of loose gravel where you must definitely watch your step, struggling to maintain balance. Every year people die when they slip and fall off this trail.

The bottom of the trail comes out at a series of fine lakeshore campsites, from where the path continues around the edge of the lake to a shelter at the lake's outlet. The trail to Gunung Rinjani peak starts from behind this lakeside shelter. If you intend to hike to the summit, plan a day just for this trip. Start at midnight for the six-hour climb and arrive in time for the spectacular sunrise views. A second trail leads through the outlet at Kokok Putih and down the outside of the crater rim to the hot spring pools of the multi-stepped waterfalls.

The hike out from the lake to Senaru takes six to eight hours. In and out, the hike can consume two long days. It's preferable, however, to use three or four days to climb to the summit, rest at the lake, read a book, fish, sit in the hot pools, or swing in a hammock under the trees along the shore.

After your climb down, stay the night at Senaru or catch a *bemo* to Bayan, from where you can get another *bemo* back to Terminal Sweta or travel east along the north coast to Labuhan Lombok. The last *bemo* from Senaru leaves about 1600, and from Bayan to Sweta about 1700; less frequent *bemo* run to Labuhan Lombok.

Accommodations In Senaru/Batu Kok

There are half a dozen accommodations at this trailhead; at least one more is under construction. All charge Rp8000 s and 12,000 d (Rp5000 and Rp10,000 in the low season), including simple breakfast and tea. Near the park headquarters in Batu Kok are **Losmen Segara Anak** and **Losmen Rinjani. Pondok Gurubakti** and **Pondok Senaru** both include views of Sendanggila Waterfall. The owner of Gurubakti was the schoolteacher who once welcomed foreign travelers to this trailhead village long before any accommodations were available. One km up the road at Senaru you'll find **Bale Bayan Senaru** directly across from the traditional Sasak village, and **Gunung Baru Homestay** about 200 meters up the trail toward the mountain, where you can see Gunung Agung on Bali on a clear day. Each place has a restaurant. All will store your luggage while you're on the mountain—ascertain first if there's a storage fee. A couple of places rent camping and cooking equipment, all for the same prices. Try Bale Bayan Senaru. Tents run about Rp5000, a full package roughly Rp20,000.

From Pesugulan

More difficult than the northern approach from Bayan. First take a bus from Sweta to Pringgabaya, then catch a *bemo* (Rp500) north to Pesugulan. On the way you'll pass the town of Swela, once the starting point on this approach. With transportation to and accommodation in Pesugulan you can now give Swela a miss. But if you want to have a look around the Swela area, see the natural spring-fed swimming pool of Lemor (half-hour walk, Rp200 entrance fee), monkey forest, Sunday market, and the graves of the Selaparang kings. Also at Swela is a neglected colonial-style guesthouse with ice-cold *mandi* only 100 meters from the road on top of a hill, surrounded by a huge garden; three rooms at Rp5000 with big iron beds and Dutch embroidered bedsheets. Swela is 100% Muslim: the minaret's loudspeaker blares from early morning to late evening.

The start of the trail is now at Pesugulan, about six km farther along the road past Swela. In Pesugulan you'll find the new **Hati Suci Homestay,** with a commanding view over the paddy fields to the east coast of Lombok and western Sumbawa. Here you can pick up much information about what to do and see in the immediate area (waterfalls, monkey forest, and the village of Sapit one km farther up the road) as well as tips for climbing the mountain. Friendly staff, tasty food, and spacious comfortable rooms with verandas that go for Rp8000-9000 s or Rp10,000-12,000 d, breakfast and blankets included. Porters can be arranged here or in the village for Rp10,000-15,000 per day. You must arrive with your own gear because there's no place to rent it here, though you can purchase basic food supplies in the shops of Pesugulan.

The trail heads north from Pesugulan to **Sembalun Bumbung;** a road now under construction will eventually connect these two villages. It's about a five to six hour walk over hills and through the forest to this cool picturesque valley. Seven km north of Pesugulan and several hundred meters down a secondary trail to the right is a hot spring. Some people camp here on their way up the mountain. From Sembalun Bumbung, another two km will get you to the friendly and simple Sasak village of **Sembalun Lawang,** where you'll find a homestay with rooms for Rp6000 s and Rp8000 d; the food is slightly expensive. The local farmers in this onion and garlic growing region sometimes hire out as guides and porters.

From here turn west toward the mountain. The walk is gentle but hot, traversing mainly open country. It's a full day's hike to the campsite just below the ridge. In the morning, hike up to the rim at **Plawangan II,** and then down to the lake at Kokok Putih. If you want to make it all the way to the summit for sunrise, start this portion of the climb about midnight. Allow three to five days for the roundtrip from Pesugulan. You will almost certainly need a porter from this side, even if only to carry the water you'll need to cover the distance. Alternately, you could go up this side and down the north face.

From Sembalun Lawang *bemo* run periodically throughout the day to Labuhan Lombok, and even as far as Masbagik. If you're going to Bayan, change *bemo* at Kali Putih, though not too late in the afternoon.

SOUTH LOMBOK

The trip to the south coast of the island is a journey through time. All of Lombok was once like Lombok Selatan. You'll pass by whole villages of thatched houses built on hilltops to defend against human predators. Surrounding these Sasak villages are cultivated fields of *ubi kayu* and *ubi jalar*, types of sweet potato, as well as other subsistence crops. March is rice-harvesting time, when you'll see women in the fields cutting and men carrying. Hilltop graveyards of tiny upright stones, like gnarly black toothpicks, remind one of Torajaland, though these are Muslim graves and not animist/Christian. Life is hard in this isolated, sparsely populated, dry, and scrubby region, a land of water buffalo, women in black clothing, and men tilling fields by hand hoe.

Praya And Vicinity

Praya lies 40 km southeast of Mataram. Refresh yourself at **Ria**, Jl. Gajah Mada. From Praya's *bemo* terminal, the road leads south to **Sengkol,** a poor agricultural village with one of Lombok's first mosques. Sengkol's market day is Thursday. Transport south to Kuta is not frequent, except on Sunday. The morning, of course, offers the best chance, so you must leave Sweta for Praya quite early. If you have your own transport, right before Praya is a road that leads south to Penunjak, a village that produces traditional pottery.

Sukarare

An Islamic weaving center 25 km southeast of Mataram and about one km from Puyung. From Sweta, proceed to Puyung by minibus, then hire a *dokar* or walk to Sukarare. Nearly everyone in the village is involved in making intricate traditional fabrics such as *songket* and *lambung* (black blouses), as well as *sarung* and *selendang* (shawls).

Bobbin winders sell for Rp5000 apiece, though you have to bargain half the afternoon to get the price down to a realistic level. Other wares include tablecloths, blankets, Sasak woven belts, poor-quality *kris* (Rp25,000 first price), and some pottery. Tourists have had a negative impact on this place, as reflected in the prices, but people are still friendly and accommodating. You can watch the women weave in front of the several shops in this village.

Pejanggik

Another village known for its weaving is Pejanggik, located about eight km southeast of Praya. Here the motifs and designs are different than at Sukarare. No shops are set up to cater to the tourist. In fact, you may find little evidence of weaving until you hear the clack of the looms as you walk the village street. In this village, some men also weave. Near here lies the burial place of the kings of the ancient Pejanggik Kingdom.

Kuta Beach

Kuta is an oasis in the midst of barren hills. A rather extensive village, it starts about two km inland and heads right down to the sea. Coconut trees fill the valley. Kuta is a strongly Muslim area, so conduct yourself accordingly. Fishermen mend nets on the beach, and on Thursday a busy market offers lots of produce, *dokar*, dogs, and people. Kuta has a post office and *wartel,* several shops, a couple of restaurants, and lots of fresh air and open space. Every year the traditional festival **Bau Nyale** is performed here at Seger Beach in Kuta, as well as at Kaliantan Beach on the eastern side of Awang Bay.

An increasing number of people are finding their way to Kuta, which is rapidly developing as a mini-resort area for the budget traveler. The long, white beach that gently dips into the water is good for sunbathing, though the bottom is too rocky for good swimming. Much better is **Tanjung Aan Beach,** four km to the east. This perfect crescent beach is gentle and beautiful, remote enough to keep most visitors away. Between Kuta and Tanjung Aan is a gigantic rock; climb to enjoy fantastic seascapes. You can also take any path into the hills above Kuta for superb views of the ocean, beaches, and mountains. Waves roll in off the headlands along the coast here, making the points of Seger and Grupuk especially popular with surfers. There are no accommodations in Tanjung Aan, so walk the four km from Kuta, or take an infrequent *bemo* (Rp 400) or *dokar* (Rp700). A few *bemo* run all the way to Awang.

There's a large government tourism development office on Tanjung Aan and this can only mean large hotels, fancy restaurants, organized leisure activities, and the like—probably for an upscale crowd. Rumor has it the land surrounding Tanjung Aan has been purchased for development. In fact, one private entrepreneur recently nearly completed a big hotel here only to be denied permission to finish the project (inadequate government connections, perhaps?). Another rumor claims the current inexpensive accommodations in Kuta will be torn down, replaced by larger, more expensive hotels, or by nothing at all.

Currently Kuta offers about a dozen accommodations, all but one stretching along the beach road to the east of the village center. Most have rooms in the Rp6000-10,000 s, Rp8000-15,000 d range, a couple are cheaper—all discount rates in the slow season. Each has a restaurant and serves a simple breakfast with the price of a room. The larger provide music in the evening. In the cheaper range are **Rambitan Cottages** and **Mascot Cottages**. At the upper end are **Anda Bungalows, Florida Hotel,** and **Rinjani Agung Beach Bungalows.** Other accommodations include **Segara Anak Bungalows,** tel. (0364) 54834, which also has a small shop, bookshop, postal agency, and the Perama travel office; **Wisma Sekar Kuning,** tel. 54856; and **Cockatoo Hotel.** In town near the main intersection is the **Mata Hari Inn.**

Ekas

A more remote spot for surfing lies across the Awang Bay south of **Ekas,** a small fishing village. **Laut Sorga Cottages** near here go for Rp25,000 per room. Surfers try the waves farther down the road at the end of the peninsula.

Selong Blanak

West of Kuta is the more remote Selong Blanak beach. Though these two beach areas are now connected by a road, no public transportation exists as yet. Virtually deserted, except for a few fishing huts, this long beach is great for swimming and sunbathing. Walk down to the far end and you'll virtually have it to yourself; you can probably hang out au naturel without bothering anyone. Before swimmers began to enjoy this beach, surfers found the points off this bay a wonderful spot to ride the waves. Several times a day a *bemo* run between Praya and Selong Blanak (Rp800), but there's only one accommodation. The **Selong Blanak Cottages,** tel. (0364) 54643, is located about two km inland. With six comfortable and traditionally designed rooms, it's small but well-appointed. Rooms run Rp20,000 s and Rp25,000 d, and the restaurant prepares fine filling meals. Offsetting the surrounding barren hillsides are the garden and coconut trees.

Sasak Villages

The whole of south and southeast Lombok is dotted with Sasak villages, some with traditional architecture. The most picturesque are a tight warren of beehive thatched houses and rice barns capping hills, formerly for protection against raiding villages. The once genuine village of **Sade** is now heavily promoting itself; it seems like every second house has a shop out front selling cloth and handicrafts. The village looks more authentic from a distance than from within. Young boys latch onto you as soon as you enter the village, some speaking surprisingly good English, and vie to guide you around for a fee. You must look beyond the commercial surface to find anything of traditional value. Focus on the village layout, building style and technique, household and craft implements, costume and dress.

Nearby is a second, only slightly more traditional village that attracts tourists with a large Welcome To Our Village sign along the road. Many tour companies include these villages on their routes and often busloads of tourists will spill into their narrow lanes all at the same time. Farther to the east, the village of **Batu Rintang** has been affected in a similar manner. Here and there throughout the countryside you'll see clusters of houses in the traditional style. To see the real thing you must spend some time traveling down country roads; follow footpaths through fields to reach these settlements.

EAST LOMBOK

On the road east across Lombok, catch intermittent views of Gunung Rinjani looming above. The lower slopes are terraced in rice paddies, and broad acreage is cultivated in corn and vegetables. Weaving, plaiting, pottery, and wood-carving home industries are still vibrant in this area. The greenery of the lower mountain region changes abruptly to the east of Pringgabaya, turning to brown parched land similar to southern Lombok. Mostly mountainous, there's only a strip of narrow land along the east coast. It seems here you're closest to Gunung Rinjani, it looms so mightily directly above. This far eastern region is strongly Muslim. It's an area where farmers grow lots of onions and garlic, which can be seen drying on roadside racks before the rainy season.

The dry eastern half of Lombok has much less contact with tourists than the western half. Instead of asking for money when photographed, the people *thank you.* Like the Javanese, the women wear the typical *sarung kebaya.* The fieldworkers wear large conical straw hats and live in straw and bamboo huts. An older race, their faces are longer, with higher cheekbones and more Mongolian features. Chinese are noticeably absent from East Lombok; the people will tell you they fled long ago and their houses were burned to the ground.

TETEBATU AND VICINITY

Tetebatu

Located 50 km east of Mataram and four km north of Kotaraja on the cool slopes of Gunung Rinjani, Tetebatu ("Stone Bridge") is a place to relax and rest. An up-country setting, with rice paddies terraced down the mountainside and deep valleys cut into the earth. All is lush and green, thick with foliage. Here you can rest in peace and quiet, literally next to the rice fields, listening to the frogs croak in the evening. The agricultural scenery here is superb—one of those places on Lombok that conjures up images of the best of the Balinese countryside. Three km above the village is a thick forest full of butterflies, dragonflies, and screaming black monkeys swinging in the trees. Spectacular forest views. The surrounding area is thick with a

maze of fields and paths so you may need a guide (many will offer) if you venture far. Start early in the morning for a glimpse of the monkeys, or simply spend the day wandering the fields and forest, or visiting the two nearby waterfalls. **Joben Waterfall** (Otak Koko) is about five km to the northwest. Start from Tetebatu village; there's a small sign at the turnoff. A taller waterfall is **Jukut Waterfall,** about 10 km up on the side of Gunung Rinjani. Each has a pool for swimming. Don't be surprised, however, if, even in a place as remote as this, you're asked to buy an entrance ticket. The other drawback to the place is that everyone must greet you and every second person wants to guide you to the forest or falls for a fee, usually Rp4000-5000 for a half day.

Two other relaxing and tranquil spots on the slopes of Gunung Rinjani are at **Timbanuh,** a Dutch colonial hill resort, and **Loang Gali.** For Timbanuh, go by bus/bemo via Pringgasela. For Loang Gali, as yet little affected by tourism and in a very rural setting, take a bus to Masbajik, from there a *bemo* (Rp250) to Lenek, and then a motorbike (Rp500) to **Loang Gali Cottages.**

Unless you have private transportation, Tetebatu, Timbanuh, or Loang Gali are not the best places from which to explore the craft villages

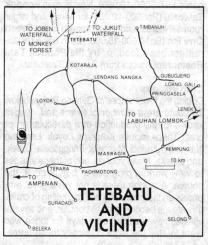

farther down the mountainside. More central to these villages are Loyok or Lendang Nangka.

Take a bus from Terminal Sweta to Paohmotong (Rp1000). From there, catch a *bemo* (Rp250) to Kotaraja where you can change *bemo* (Rp250) or take a horsecart (Rp500) for Tetebatu. Some *bemo* from Paohmotong travel all the way to Tetebatu. Also in Paohmotong, motorbikes will offer you a ride to Tetebatu (Rp1000) or other destinations nearby. This is an accepted means of transportation in this hill area. Check to see that the motorbike is in good working order and that it seems sturdy enough to carry you and your travel bag.

Accommodations: Set in a garden and surrounded by fruit orchards, **Soejono Hotel** is an old colonial house, with a chilly spring-fed swimming pool. Formerly owned by a rich country doctor from Java, it's actually located two km beyond the village of Tetebatu at the end of the road. The *wisma's* neat and clean modern- and Sasak-style bungalows are set in the garden, each equipped with Western-style toilets and TV. Rooms cost Rp15,000-35,000 per night. The proprietress fixes excellent suppers (Dutch, Indonesian, or Javanese) and makes delicious bread, though meals are not included in the room price. The hotel can arrange a rental car or motorbike, or you can hire a local guide (Rp15,000 per day) for a walk around the area.

Additional places to stay include **Wisma Dewi Enjeni,** which has small rooms but a pleasant garden (Rp5000-10,000). Next door is **Pondok Tetebatu** (Rp8000-12,000) for newer and larger rooms. Newest and most modern is the **Green Orry Inn** (Rp10,000-15,000). Each has a restaurant for basic food, or try the **Pondok Tani Restaurant** across from Pondok Tetebatu.

Craft Villages

Dotting the lower slopes of Gunung Rinjani below Tetebatu are a number of towns and villages known for the production of a particular art or craft. These include Kotaraja, Loyok, Lendang Nangka, Suradadi, Masbajik, Pringgasela, Lenek, and Beleka. Make your rounds of these villages to view work in progress or buy items at the source. Although there is not yet a great emphasis on the promotion and marketing of crafts, this area is becoming quite popular, and several villages now include homestays for those who want to stay the night. Typically these homestays rent rooms for Rp10,000 s and Rp15,000 d, including one or two meals. Other food is available at local *warung.* Each place has information about the village crafts and the surrounding area. Although it's possible to go from village to village by *dokar* or *bemo,* it's most convenient to rent a motorbike for Rp12,000 a day.

Four km before Tetebatu is the unimpressive, strongly Muslim village of **Kotaraja.** This village is known for blacksmithing, primarily farm tools and implements. It's also a center for the weaving of bamboo and other natural fibers. In the market here you can find all sorts of local craft items. Bargain hard; they're used to visitors here.

Four km south of Kotaraja is **Loyok,** a village known for bamboo and rattan plaiting. Traditional are various sizes and shapes of baskets, bags, and rice containers; some items, like lampshades, are made solely for visiting tourists. Balinese take woven goods back to Bali and sell them as Balinese goods at Balinese prices. A handful of shops in this village sell local wares, along with woodcrafts from nearby villages. You must venture into the back alleys to see people at work. On the south side of town is the **Jati Ayu Homestay.**

Six km east of Kotaraja is **Lendang Nangka,** a Sasak village of iron smithies, silver jewelers, and decorative woodcarvers. The surrounding area is full of great scenery—terraced rice fields, waterfalls, natural springs, country roads. Traditional Sasak-style houses in the village of **Kesik** are only two km away; closer is the pottery-making village of **Rungkang.** It's here you'll find the much-admired English-speaking schoolteacher Mr. Radiah of **Radiah's Homestay.** Rooms run Rp10,000 s, Rp15,000 d including three meals. This is a known traveler's stop, often crowded during the busy season. Most unusual is the traditional Sasak food served here, an experience you won't find elsewhere. To accommodate the growing number of visitors, **Pondok Wira** recently went up at the west end of town.

On the cross-island highway, **Masbagik** is a large town and transportation center, with post office, *wartel,* and Monday cattle market. Two km east of town in the village of **Penaka** is a pottery center, part of the Lombok Crafts Projects. Here you'll find large water jugs and medium-size pots decorated with traditional geometric designs and some animal-shaped figures. Here too you'll encounter pieces produced just for the tourist, with no traditional foundation. Several shops along the main road display the finished products, so you must ask to be taken to homes down the back alleys to actually see throwing and firing.

Up the road toward the old colonial retreat of Timbanuh is the weaving center of **Pringgasela.** Small-scale production of woven cloth is the specialty here. There's almost no effort to widely distribute here; the intent is to keep all marketing local. Distinctive stripped designs on cloth require up to one week for a single yard. Two or three small shops display a few cloth items. For more variety of cloth and a peek at the weaving, ask for a tour around the village. If staying, find a room at **Rainbow Cottages** close to the center of town. While the name is more impressive than the place, it fits the distinctive color combinations in the locally produced cloth.

Other villages in this region also have their own specialties. **Beleka** is known for woodcarvings and plaited rattan handicrafts, while in **Suradadi** you'll find baskets and mats of other natural fibers. Villagers in **Lenek** and **Kembang Sari** still perform traditional music and dance.

THE EAST COAST

Labuhan Lombok
A poor Muslim town on the northeast coast. From Sweta by bus the trip costs Rp2000 and occupies three to four hours. Located on a beautiful bay with fine views of Gunung Rinjani, but kind of run-down, with scraggly dogs in the street and strictly Islamic people. Not much to entertain yourself with, though some of Lombok's finest blankets are produced in the area.

There are two places to stay here, none too clean and none too quiet; both charge Rp5000. **Losmen Manawar** is on the road toward the new harbor, while **Dian Dutaku** is located at the main intersection in town. *Warung* and several *rumah makan* cluster around the *bemo* station/market selling basic but edible meals and beverages. Try the popular vegetable soup called *bayam*.

Leaving Labuhan Lombok
Labuhan Lombok features a new port located about two km from the town center. From here ferries leave for Poto Tano, Sumbawa. Buy

your ticket (Rp2000) at the harbor office; Rp3200 extra for a motorbike. At this port are a few small kiosks, shops, and *warung* for last-minute food and snacks. There are six ferries a day to Sumbawa, 0700-1700; the crossing takes about two hours. As this schedule seems to change periodically, check departure times at the tourist office in Ampenan or query travelers who've just come from Sumbawa. At the Labuhan Lombok harbor bus drivers will try to sell you tickets for seats on long-distance buses to Sumbawa Besar, Dompu, and Bima at slightly more than the regular fare. Wait and catch a bus at Poto Tano. You can also catch a bus from the harbor to Terminal Sweta or any point along the cross-island highway.

Some people going to Sumbawa find it easiest to rise early in Ampenan or Cakra and take a morning bus to Labuhan Lombok to catch the morning ferry. Alternately, stay in Tetebatu, Lendang Nangka, or even Pesugulan, *bemo* to the highway, and catch any of the frequent buses to Labuhan Lombok. If you want to catch the earliest ferries stay in Labuhan Lombok.

Bemo from Labuhan Lombok run north infrequently to Labuhan Pandan, Bayan, and Sembalun Lawang. *Bemo* run periodically to Pesugulan and south down the coast to Labuhan Haji. You can start the eastern approach to Gunung Rinjani from either Sembalun Lawang or Pesugulan.

Other East Coast Towns
Something to do in East Lombok? Climb **Gunung Kayangan** on the path that starts near the old harbor; takes only 30 minutes. Good view of Selat Alas from the top, with *prahu* slicing through the strait to Sumbawa. Heading four km north toward Labuhan Pandan is **Kampung Nelayan,** a fishermen's *kampung* easily seen from Gunung Kayangan. Ten km north of Labuhan Lombok (Rp500 by *bemo*) is the tiny fishing harbor of **Labuhan Pandan,** featuring a small *penginapan* with cottages (Rp12,500 s, Rp17,500 d including meals). The village is quiet and you can find solitude. It's possible to charter a boat to the three nearby offshore islands for about Rp20,000 a day. Good swimming and snorkeling on these islands off the northeast coast. Currently there are no accommodations or ferry service so you must charter a boat and camp if you want to stay.

About five km south of Labuhan Lombok is **Pringgabaya,** where a side road goes up the mountain to Pesugulan. Four km up a secondary road is **Makan Selaparang,** containing the graves of the kings of the Selaparang Kingdom.

Labuhan Haji, 30 km south of Labuhan Lombok, is an old port that once served as an embarkation point for pilgrims sailing to Mecca. From the small beach beyond the market, boats sometimes go to Labuhan Lalar on Sumbawa. There's a small *losmen* in Labuhan Haji, **Pondok Meliwis,** which charges a hefty Rp25,000 for a bungalow without breakfast. For swim-

ming it's not the best; lots of fishing boats pulled up on the beach.

Some five km inland from Labuhan Haji is **Selong,** which hosts a Monday cattle market. The **Wisma Erina** has rooms for Rp6000-10,000 including breakfast, but you also get an earful of morning prayers starting at 0400.

At **Tanjung Ringgit,** 110 km south of Labuhan Lombok, are large caves where, it's said, a legendary *raksasa* lives. First take a *bemo* south to the canoe-building center of Keruak, then hire another *bemo* to the fishing village of Tanjung Ringgit.

SUMBAWA

Sumbawa (15,600 square km) is made up of rolling uplands, eroded foothills, volcanic ridges, and ancient crater walls. Wildlife here is abundant, and although flora and fauna are predominantly Asian in origin, Australian climatic influence is also obvious: spiny bush, acacia, thorn, cactus, and extensive savannah. Sumbawa's south coast is lined with dormant volcanic peaks that plunge straight into the Indian Ocean. For the most part, the north coast consists of plains and river basins, except for the jagged, towering peak of **Gunung Tambora** on Teluk Saleh. Fertile valleys with bright green rice fields surrounding the towns occur mainly along the rivers on the northern coast and in river valleys in the central uplands. As you travel east on the island's single paved highway, much of the land is covered with a park-like landscape of large, open tracts of countryside alleviated only by small clusters of trees and shrubs, brown hills, and a mountainous coast with picturesque bays and harbors. Eastern Sumbawa is a rocky, dusty, parched country of stubbly growth and bamboo villages on stilts. The island's rainy season is usually November to April, with little daily variation in temperature.

HISTORY

Certain areas, particularly in the east, are known for their megaliths and sarcophagi which date from Sumbawa's Neolithic period over 2,000 years ago. The Javanese epic *Nagarakertagama,* written on *lontar* leaf in 1365, mentions four principalities on Sumbawa as dependencies of the Majapahit Empire; the names of these early princes indicate Hindu influence. The earliest known indigenous kingdoms in western Nusatenggara were the comparatively small states of the Sasaks in Lombok, the Sumbawans in western Sumbawa, and the Bimans and Dompuese in eastern Sumbawa.

For several centuries the Makassarese of southwestern Sulawesi indulged in pillage and slaving raids along Sumbawa's north coast, using the concept of holy war to justify conquest. It was they who first brought Islam to Sumbawa. The Kingdom of Goa in southern Sulawesi subjugated Bima in 1616 and established many small sultanates. Even today, the political system, the descent of the royal sultanate families of the north coast, and the world view derive from that Makassarese kingdom. The palaces of the old sultans still exist; Bima's palace is now a museum and the stilted, barn-like palace of Sumbawa Besar was also restored in the mid-1980s.

The Dutch first landed in 1605, but since the island had little commercial value, they stationed only representatives there and did not rule effectively until the start of this century.

The most violent event in Sumbawa's history was the awesome 1815 eruption of Gunung Tambora; its suffocating rain of ash either directly killed or eventually starved to death 90,000 people, most of this and the neighboring islands' population at the time. The explosion reduced Tambora from nearly 4,000 meters to 2,821 meters.

ECONOMY

As early as the 14th century, Sumbawa had become very wealthy through its timber and horses. Along with Timor, this island was the source of the fragrant woods sapan and sandalwood, valuable commodities which Asian and later European trading powers exported for over 300 years. The island's exports today are almost completely agricultural: rice, coconuts, corn, tobacco, cotton, peanuts, and beans. Cattle and some of the country's best-bred horses are also exported; the Sumbawa horse is in high demand all over Indonesia as a draft animal for pulling *dokar* and *andong*.

Many of the island's forests are virgin, and raw timber has recently become a major export commodity, the result of a joint venture with Filipino companies. The denuding of Sumbawa's forests is causing the usual ecological devastation.

About 90% of the Sumbawanese farm for a living, growing mainly rice, and those inland even hunt for their protein. During the dry season, but just before the rains, much of the farming populace migrates from their permanent villages to flimsy makeshift huts in their fields in the mountains, guarding the fields against animals and pests until the harvest is in. Sumbawa is well known for its honey, which is believed to increase sexual potency.

THE PEOPLE

This island, as big as Lombok and Bali together, has about 800,000 inhabitants. Lying at a transitional point between the Indianized "high" cultures of western Indonesia and the traditional pagan cultures of eastern Indonesia, Sumbawa is a fas-

cinating ethnographic area. From prehistoric times, Sumbawa has been inhabited by two linguistic groups who for centuries couldn't understand each other: the Sumbawa-speaking states to the west and the Bima-speaking clans of the east. The western Sumbawans and Lombok's Sasaks share similar customs and language. The Bimans, on the other hand, are shorter, darker-complexioned, more fiery-tempered, and earthier than the Sumbawans, and speak a language resembling that of Sumba and Flores. Today, Bahasa Indonesia bridges the linguistic gap.

Except for a few villages in the Donggo-Mbawa area, there has never been any Christian missionary activity on the island and both groups are today strict Muslims; there is, how-

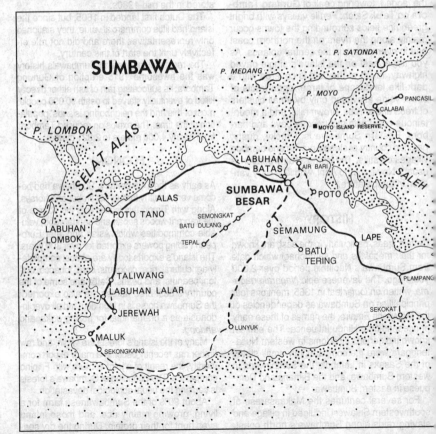

ever, a powerful undercurrent of animist beliefs and adherence to *adat*. The Biman-speaking Dou Donggo people, living in the mountains of the Donggo area west of Bima Bay, are the descendants of the island's aboriginals and number around 20,000. Yet another small, linguistically separate group, the Dou Tarlawi, inhabit the mountains east of Bima Bay.

Sumbawa is heavily Islamic: many of the women still cover their heads, and the eastern districts send proportionally more *haji* to Mecca than any other region of Indonesia. The western part is a mixture of cultures and customs. Mountaineer rustics live in the interior villages of the western peninsula's foothills; see them come down to the more prosperous urban lowlands to

trade their horseloads of woven mats and baskets. These upland Sumbawans often carry large *berang* (machetes) ornamented with carved dragons. The Dompu area is well known for its cloth worked with silver thread.

Events

Especially during Ramadan, the loudspeakers from the mosques can keep you up into the wee hours. But people in the eastern end, at least in Bima, are not that fanatical and food is available all day during this religious holiday. Mock battles, with men wearing Arabic rolled turbans, can be seen on this island. On holidays, at festivals, and during harvest times, you might see traditional Sumbawan boxing matches. The combat-

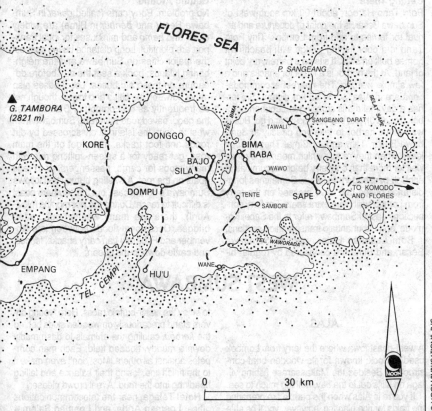

ants bind their hands with sharp rice stalks, which can inflict ugly cuts; this nearly bare-fisted boxing, called *berempah,* usually ends in a draw.

Sumbawan men are skilled archers and still hold contests occasionally, firing their arrows into targets moving along a high wire. Water-buffalo races take place at festival times and also nearly every Sunday in some district or another. A few indigenous dances survive; one is the *barapan kebo,* which depicts the *kerbau* race. Sumbawan orchestras, made up of drums and flutes, sound like bagpipes. *Kulkus* (long hollow drums) are still used for sending messages, and fine violins are crafted by hand on this island.

TRANSPORTATION

Getting There

Poto Tano Harbor, about 90 km southwest of Sumbawa Besar, is the point of departure and arrival for ferries to and from Lombok. Tiny Poto Tano is a poor fishing village with beachfront homes built on stilts. It sits on a barren, dry point of land. At the harbor is a kiosk for snacks and a few simple *warung.* The nearest accommodations are in Alas, some 25 km distant. Six ferries a day make this crossing to Labuhan Lombok (Rp2000); just buy your ticket and go. Buses wait at the harbor to take you directly to Sumbawa Besar, Taliwang, or Bima. These buses leave when they're full, which means they may wait for more than one ferry before accumulating enough passengers to leave. Sometimes long-distance buses that have crossed on the ferry from Lombok will have extra seats. For ferry connections east of Sumbawa refer to the Sape, Komodo, and Labuhanbajo transportation sections.

Both Labuhan Batas, outside Sumbawa Besar, and Bima are connected by regular bi-

monthly Pelni service. Refer to each city's transportation section.

On Sumbawa, Merpati services the cities of Sumbawa Besar and Bima. From Sumbawa Besar flights are routed through Mataram (Rp50,000) to Denpasar (Rp81,000), with connections to Surabaya, Semarang, and Yogyakarta. Flights from Bima to Denpasar, direct or through Mataram, cost Rp125,000, with onward connections to Surabaya, Jogyajarta, Semarang, Solo, Bandung, and Jakarta. Merpati also offers a number of connections from Bima to other towns in Nusatenggara: Labuhanbajo (Rp52,000), Ruteng (Rp85,000), Ende (Rp85,000), Kupang (Rp196,000), Waingapu (Rp77,000), Maumere (Rp104,000), and Bajawa (Rp85,000).

Getting Around

No problem. Pony carts (called *dokar* in Sumbawa Besar and *benhur* in Bima) are widely used, and *bemo* and minibuses for local transport are plentiful. Long distance buses connect the major cities on Sumbawa and the neighboring islands; book a seat the day before departure on these a/c buses. Local buses also move between the cities and towns, though not as frequently as on Lombok or Bali. Besides the good, paved road traversing Sumbawa from west to east, the island is crisscrossed by dirt roads and foot tracks. If you get off the main road, get ready for a spleen-splitting ride with many stops for cargo, passengers, or to retie goats on the roof. A twisting bumpy trail follows Sumbawa's north coast, but the southern coast is difficult to reach. During the wet months (Nov.-April), there are many washed-out, rotted bridges. Occasional floods between late November and February can carry shacks, fences, and cattle down to the ocean.

WEST SUMBAWA

ALAS

A west-coast town where the ferry from Lombok used to dock; known for its wooden boat construction. Besides the Makassarese fishing village on stilts out in the bay, nothing much to see.

If you're in Alas when the people are preparing the fields for rice planting, however, you'll be able

to enjoy the water-buffalo races. Here, young drivers stand precariously on wooden skids behind the *kerbau,* cajoling the animals to dash madly down a muddy, flooded field. Each man competes against all others. Most don't even make it to the finish line, losing their balance and falling headlong into the mud. A real crowd pleaser.

Hotel Telaga, near the telecommunications office, **Losmen Anda,** and **Losmen Salemat**

are all located on the main highway. As Alas holds little attraction and as the ferry doesn't stop here any more, many people find it most convenient to bus straight through to Sumbawa Besar, or start from Sumbawa Besar in the morning to catch a ferry for Lombok.

TALIWANG

In spite of a long, indented coastline and deep bays, Sumbawa's population is not oriented to the sea and most villages, like Taliwang, lie five km or more from the coast. Just before Taliwang is beautiful **Lebok Lebo,** a lake choked with water lilies and men fishing from dugout canoes; visited by waterfowl, hawks, and wild iguanas; and nestled against a fishing village. Dirty, dusty Taliwang attracts few tourists but has a neat atmosphere at night with people strolling down the main street. Sumbawan hospitality is incredible—you might receive six invitations to stay the very first afternoon you arrive. **Tamuren Waterfall** is only a short walk away through the rice fields.

Accommodations And Food
Losmen Tubalong is the best, although that doesn't say much. The restaurant serves only *nasi campur.* Taliwang has several *rumah makan,* and a daily *pasar* sells cool melons and green bananas deep fried in fresh coconut oil.

Vicinity Of Taliwang
Taliwang is Rp1000 from Poto Tano (sometimes possible to hitch trucks), Rp3000 and 115 km by bus from Sumbawa Besar. Visit the coastal resort of Potobatu, 15 km from Taliwang. Eight km and Rp300 by *bemo* south of Taliwang is the fishing village of **Labuhan Lalar,** a natural harbor surrounded by beautiful scenery and a nearby tranquil beach. Nicer than Taliwang, it's a pity there are no *losmen* here. Get to Labuhan Lalar and back to Taliwang early because available *bemo* drop off in the afternoon and you might end up walking, or possibly finding a *dokar.* From Labuhan Lalar there's an occasional boat to Labuhan Haji, Lombok. Beyond Labuhan Lalar, the road continues past Jereweh to Berete and Sekongkang. At **Maluk** there's a fine beach

and waves to surf. The waves here are of three kinds; they include the well-known "scar reef." Sea turtles lay eggs at the beach below Sekongkang and on those farther to the east. Extremely isolated.

SUMBAWA BESAR

The lowland *ibu kota* of Sumbawa Barat (West Sumbawa) and, after Bima, the island's second-biggest town. The main street consists of shops, *rumah makan,* and government offices, with *benhur* raising dust. Stilted houses climb up the hills behind the town. Sumbawa Besar is small enough so you can walk to anywhere, except perhaps the new post office and Labuhan Batas harbor. In the middle of town, at the intersection of Jl. Urip Sumoharso and Jl. Setiabudi, is the *bemo* and *dokar* stand. *Dokar* charge Rp200 for an average ride; *bemo* around town charge a flat rate of Rp250.

The rebuilt wooden *istana* is of passing architectural interest. It's opposite the mosque and only a 15-minute walk from the bus station. This former sultan's palace, with its rusty cannon and creaking carved doors, is called the **Dalam Loka.** It's a solid-wood structure raised high off the ground on hardwood logs. This two-story wooden structure was built in 1885 on the site of three former palaces, and rebuilt from 1979-1985 with government aid. It's divided into rooms for various purposes: reception, living quarters, kitchen, household activities. Until her death in 1990, Sultan Jalaluddin III's fourth and only surviving wife lived in the building. The daughter of the last sultan lives in the new palace a short way away. There were 17 sultans of West Sumbawa from the 1600s to 1958. The last sultan is buried behind the mosque across the road, and seven former sultans are buried on the hill above town.

There are plans for opening a portion of this rebuilt palace as a museum containing *pusaka* and historical objects. Every Sunday morning around 0900 dances are performed here. You can look around inside the palace and grounds; someone will be in attendance to give you an explanation in rudimentary English. Donations accepted. Also visit the **Pura Agung Girinatha** Bali-style Hindu temple, next to the midtown post office.

SUMBAWA BESAR

TO BIMA

TO SEMONGKAT

TO AIRPORT, POST OFFICE, and POTO TANO

NOT TO SCALE

LOSMEN SURABAYA

MARKET

BEMO STATION

DALAM LOKA

JL. PUNCAK

JL. SUDIRMAN

LOSMEN ASIA

JL. KAHARUDIN

TERMINAL BERANG BARU

STADIUM

JL. GURAMI

JL. SETIABUDI

URIP SUMOHARSO

LOSMEN BARU

JL. WAHIDIN

MUCHSIN TALIWANG

NEW PALACE

MERDEKA

BNI

KARTINI

JL. HASANUDDIN

PURI AGUNG GIRINATHA

POST OFFICE

NIGHT FOOD STALLS

LOSMEN INDRA TELECOMMUNICATIONS OFFICE

BUS TERMINAL

ANEKA RASA

JAYA RESTAURANT

PUSPA WARNA

JL. YOS SUDARSO

SURABAYA

LOSMEN TAQDEER

KAMBOJA

JL. MAWAR

HOTEL DEWI

LOSMEN MEKARSARI

PERAMA TOUR AND TRAVEL

RUKUN JAYA

JL. DIPONEGORO

LOSMEN SAUDARA

HOTEL SUCI

LOSMEN TUNAS

CIREBON

HOSPITAL

MERPATI OFFICE

HOTEL TAMBORA

JL. CENDRAWASIH

GARUDA

Accommodations And Food

Many good and clean mid-range *losmen* are within easy walking distance of the bus station, on or near Jl. Hasanuddin. **Hotel Suci,** tel. (0371) 21589, has a nice courtyard and garden. Rooms range from Rp7500 to Rp35,000, but most are in the Rp11,000-15,000 range; *mandi* in all rooms, fan in some. The restaurant serves basic Indonesian food and cold drinks. The management can arrange bus tickets. Across the street is the clean and friendly **Losmen Saudara,** tel. 21528. Rooms Rp5500 s and Rp8500 d share a *mandi*; rooms with *mandi* and fan are more expensive. A small restaurant with limited selection is attached.

Perhaps the best deal for the money is the immaculate and cheery **Losmen Mekarsari,** down an alley off Jl. Hasanuddin. Rooms with *mandi* are Rp7500 s and Rp10,000 d. **Losmen Dewi** is a multistoried hotel with well-furnished a/c rooms. Rates start about Rp20,000, but may drop lower to attract business.

On the cheap end is the basic **Losmen Tunas,** down the street from Hotel Suci, with rooms from Rp6000 s with *mandi*. The double front rooms are larger and nicer but the place overall is a tad claustrophobic and dark. Perhaps a bit better is **Losmen Taqdeer,** closer to the bus station on an alley off Jl. Kamboja. Here you must share a *mandi*; rooms are small but only Rp4400 s and Rp8800 d. If you're really pinching pennies try **Losmen Indra,** at the bus station, or **Losmen Baru** and **Losmen Asia** near the sultan's palace. Don't expect anything clean, tidy, or quiet; not recommended.

Sumbawa's top hotel is the **Tambora Hotel,** tel. 21555, a Rp200 ride from the bus station or a 15-minute walk. This 60-room hotel has fine gardens and a decent restaurant; the Merpati office is next door. Rooms range from Rp8250 s and Rp11,000 d in the economy class to Rp93,500 for a suite. These rooms shouldn't be overlooked as they give you the best surroundings with good value. Here too are rooms for three and four people for Rp16,500-22,000.

Sumbawa Besar has two excellent Chinese and seafood restaurants. The cook at the **Aneka Rase Jaya** is said to be the premier Chinese chief on the island. **Puspa Warna** was started by one of his former apprentices and also offers wonderful dishes. **Surabaya** is okay for a quick bite. The Hotel Tambora has a mediocre restaurant; down the street is **Cirebon.** Close to Hotel Suci try **Rukun Jaya,** small, simple, and wholesome. Across the street from the new palace is the **Muchsin Taliwang.**

Services

The new and not-so-central central **post office** is located way out past the airport about two km west of town, offering poste restante and international parcel service. Take one of the *bemo* that cruise Jl. Hasanuddin. Change money only at **Bank Negara Indonesia,** Jl. Kartini 10, tel. (0371) 21936. Open Monday through Saturday. It's easy to change the better-known traveler's checks and major currencies, but the bank will balk at anything weird, like Spanish *pesos.* The new *wartel* is located across the street from the in-town postal branch office; open 24 hours a day for International telephone, telex, and fax services.

At the intersection of Jl. Cendrawasih and Jl. Garuda, near Hotel Tambora, is the hospital. Also at this intersection are the **PHPA office** and the **Kantor Departmen Perindustrian Kabupaten Sumbawa** on Jl. Garuda, where some native handicrafts are on display. For reservations and flight information, check with the Merpati office next door to Hotel Tambora, open Mon.-Fri. 0730-1600, and 0800-1400 on Saturday and Sunday. A Perama travel office lies next door to Losmen Saudara. It's run by a Mr. Iyat, a one-man fount of travel and tourist information for all of Nusatenggara. He's traveled the length and breadth of these islands and offers useful, exact information. He can also arrange almost any kind of adventure. Pay him a visit.

Getting Away

The airport in Sumbawa Besar is right on the edge of town, 500 meters past Hotel Tambora. Merpati flies to Ampenan and Denpasar three times a week at 1115.

The bus station for points west is in the center of town on Jl. Diponegoro. All fares are posted. Some afternoon buses traveling to Dompu (Rp5000), Bima (Rp6000), and Sape (Rp6800) also leave from this station—through buses from Poto Tano, or buses connecting with those through long-distance buses. Direct, reserved-seat a/c buses to Mataram on Lombok (Rp10,000) leave the station at 0600; non-a/c buses run later in the day.

*traditional
Sumbawa granaries*

If going east, catch a bus at Terminal Berang Baru near the river. Reserved seat, a/c buses to Dompu and Bima leave the Terminal Berang Baru at 0900. Other fares include Poto Tano, Rp2500; Taliwang, Rp3000; and Batu Dulang, Rp1000. Buses to the weaving village of Poto (Rp750), the harbor Air Bari (Rp1500), and Lunyuk (Rp4500) leave from near the market.

For boats to Lombok and beyond, check with the *syahbandar* in Sumbawa Besar's port of **Labuhan Batas**, accessible by public *bemo* for around Rp500. The only Pelni ship that calls at this port is the KM *Tatamailau*. It stops twice a month on its run to and from Surabaya and other points west on Java and Kalimantan, and Flores, Timor, and Maluku to the east. If going to Labuhan Lombok, start early by bus to catch a ferry at Poto Tano; you'll have daylight to travel through Lombok.

Vicinity Of Sumbawa Besar
Saliperate is a sandy beach with coconut trees five km west of the city. It's near here that you'll find the **Tirtasari Resort,** with Chinese food, a swimming pool, and lots of locals on the weekend. Eleven km west at another beach is the **Kencana Beach Inn,** with rooms in the traditional Sumbawan style (Rp1000-84,000) and a restaurant. Here you can fish, snorkel, swim, or take a boat ride. The weaving village of **Poto** makes a fine part-day trip. Nearly everyone here is involved in this cottage industry; it's the only village on Sumbawa with such a reputation for producing cloth. At **Semongkat** you'll find a

swimming pool; 17 km from Sumbawa Besar in the cool mountains. In **Berang Rea** is an interesting geological phenomenon: if you put a stick in a pool called Aik Kawat, the water supposedly solidifies around it.

In the foothills southeast of Sumbawa Besar are a number of megaliths dating from Neolithic times. A particularly rich archaeological area is around the village of **Batu Tering,** near Semamung. One km from Batu Tering, the **Liang Petang Cave** contains breast-shaped stones (supposedly with magical powers), stalagmited and stalactited. Bring a flashlight or hire a lamp and guide for Rp5000. Seven km beyond Batu Tering is a megalithic sarcophagus with human and animal figures carved in high relief. Scholars believe these were the tombs of tribal chieftains who lived here over 2,000 years ago. These burial containers show similarities to the existing burial culture on Sumba. From Batu Tering, it's about a three-hour walk roundtrip; hire a guide for Rp5000. To reach Batu Tering, take a bus from Terminal Berang Baru in Sumbawa Besar; start early in the morning. Another archaeological site is at **Punik,** 35 km from Sumbawa Besar, featuring a cryptic stone pillar.

Crossing the island over the twisting, bumpy mountain road will take you to **Lunyuk.** Beyond Lunyuk at the sea are long strands of white beach where three varieties of sea turtles swim ashore to lay eggs. These huge turtles breed year-round so chances are good you'll see some. There are no accommodations or food at the beach so bring all you'll need. You may have to hire a vehicle from Lunyuk to the beach. The permit to visit is Rp1000, Rp5000 for a guide. Turtles can also be seen at **Sekokat**, about 70 km southeast of Sumbawa Besar. This remote spot is also gaining a reputation for good swimming and surfing. Bus to Plampang and then *bemo* to the new *transmigrasi* village of Labangka II.

The most traditonal of west Sumbawan villages is **Tepal**, situated high in the mountains southwest of Sumbawa Besar. Very few people visit here so it's still relatively untouched. Unlike the lowlands, this area is green and forested, with lots of flowers. Bus to Batu Dulang, from where it's a pleasant nine-hour walk up to the village along a track used by the locals going to and from market. Stay with the *kepala desa*. Make it a couple-day trip. People here speak a different language than those of the lowlands. Bring staple items to give as a donation for your stay (no coffee, as it's grown in this area) or pay Rp3000 a night. If you have time and are interested in the Sumbawan culture, this is the place to go.

Pulau Moyo

Of this island three km off the north coast of Sumbawa, two-thirds is a virgin game reserve. Moyo's central plateau, with its grassy savannahs and intermittent monsoonal forest, is ideal country for *rusa* and feral cattle. Wildlife is easy to see; even as you're approaching on the boat you'll see deer running wild. Hunting requires a permit from the police, then you can bag a deer in five minutes. There are also wild boar and abundant birds: orioles, drongos, koels, coucals, and sunbirds. There are good beaches with fine coral sand and a splendid coral reef at the south end of the island, great for swimming and snorkeling. From Pulau Moyo there are magnificent views of Gunung Tambora to the east.

All the human settlements are concentrated at the north end of the island; the main town is **Sebaru**. To get to Pulau Moyo, take a *bemo* from the market in Sumbawa Besar to Air Bari (Rp1500) on the coast. There hire a fishing boat (Rp15,000 roundtrip) to take you to Air Manis on the southwest coast of Moyo Island. At Tanjung Air Manis it's possible to rent a tent for Rp10,000 a day. Bring all your food and cooking supplies. A little farther up the coast is Amanwana, a posh hunting resort frequented by kings, celebrities, and the very rich. Some guests arrive by helicopter. Some way around

the south coast is an Indo-Australian-operated resort that arranges hunting and diving tours in the range of Rp250,00-400,000 a night. Contact P.T. Moyo Safari Abadi, Jl. Garuda 84, Sumbawa Besar, tel. (0371) 21838.

The PHPA office in Sumbawa Besar is of little assistance for information in English about Moyo Island, but its motorboat occasionally visits Moyo from Air Bari. Plan your trip for the dry season, and if you're camping bring supplies, food, and water—there are no shops on the island.

GUNUNG TAMBORA

The Eruption

The massive 1815 eruption of Gunung Tambora was one of the most destructive and powerful in world history. For several years prior to the blast, dark, thick smoke poured from the cone as the rumblings and thundering grew increasingly powerful. Finally, on 5 April, the volcano exploded; in Batavia, 1,250 km from the blast, the sounds of the eruption resembled distant cannon fire and prompted the English governor-general, Sir Stamford Raffles, to march troops into the city to defend it against rebel attack.

The volcanic paroxysm reached its greatest magnitude during 10-12 April, when the whole mountain turned into a body of liquid fire, blowing 100 cubic km of debris into the sky. The thunder could be heard 1,775 km away at Bengkulu on Sumatra. Tremors were felt in Surabaya, and stones as large as two fists were catapulted 40 km from the demolished peak.

The Aftermath

The fine ejecta that circled the globe caused the planet's temperatures to drop almost one degree Celsius below normal for a whole year, resulting in the famous "year without summer" of 1816 and creating spectacular orange sunsets around the world—which some art historians theorize inspired the moody lighting in paintings by the great British artist J.M.W. Turner.

A thick blanket of ash settled over an area of 2.5 million square km, darkening the whole region for three days, while the sea around Sumbawa was clogged with thousands of uprooted trees and huge islands of floating pumice. Earthquakes, whirlwinds, and tsunami caused by the collapse of the peak killed 12,000 people outright, while another 78,000 died of cholera, exposure, and starvation during the ensuing drought and crop failure throughout the whole of Nusatenggara—the word *tambora* in the Dompu language means "to loose." All the arable land on Sumbawa was rendered infertile, its surface covered in a half meter of ash and mud, making it impossible to plant rice for several years.

Tambora Today

Tambora formerly consisted of two soaring peaks, each over 4,000 meters high, its majestic cone visible from 30 km away at sea. The gigantic eruptions of 1815 reduced the volcano to a jagged 2,821-meter-high crater, Doro Afi Toi, which is today made up of four cones: Tahe (877 meters), Molo (602 meters), Kadiendinae, and Kubah (1,648 meters). From the top of Gunung Tambora are spectacular views over Teluk Saleh; the volcanic peaks of Gunung Agung (Bali), Gunung Rinjani (Lombok), and Gunung Sangeang (Sumbawa) can be seen from here. Beautiful forests cover its western slopes, for the most part *Duabanga molluccana* trees up to 60 meters high. In the crater is a lake. It's possible to hike to the crater rim and down to the lake where you can camp. Make at least a three-day hike of it. To get to the trailhead, start by taking a truck or bus from the Dompu bus station to Calabai (Rp5000, 10 hours). In Calabai, catch a truck or *dokar* to Kandidi village, from where you can get a truck to Pancasila village (Rp3500). In Pancasila, hire a porter/guide for Rp15,000 a day. Bring food and supplies from Dompu; they're limited in Calabai and Kandidi.

Pulau Satonda

Just off Gunung Tambora's northwest coast and surrounded by a fine coral reef, Pulau Satonda is itself an old volcanic cone, its crater now submerged. Try to stop at Satonda's coral reefs on the way to Labuhan Kenanga.

EAST SUMBAWA

Greater racial and cultural diversity is found among the darker-skinned Biman-speaking people of East Sumbawa than among the West Sumbawans. In the east live lowland people, descendants of 18th-century sultanates, as well as the hill-dwelling Dou Donggo, and descendants of earlier Makassarese, Kalimantan, and Javanese immigrants. The Biman language is related to the Savunese and Manggarai of Flores.

History

Local folklore claims the realm grew from a line of 52 princes, the tenth of whom founded the independent kingdoms of Bima and Dompu, which eventually ruled over Sumba and parts of Flores to Timor. The Goa Kingdom of southern Sulawesi subjugated Bima in 1616, and the 38th sultan of Bima was converted to Islam in 1640. When the Dutch conquered Makassar in 1667, Bima was liberated from Goa but strong cultural influence from the north continued even under VOC rule.

The Bima area has mellowed since its days as a notoriously fanatic Islamic stronghold. Darul Islam, a group that wanted Indonesia to become a theocratic state, conducted a terrorist guerrilla campaign in West Java from 1949 to '62 which amounted to open rebellion. In 1957, three fanatics from Bima who tried to assassinate President Sukarno at Cikini School in Jakarta managed instead to kill 13 schoolgirls.

DOMPU

One hundred and twenty-nine km east of Sumbawa Besar, Dompu is a good place to break up the long cross-island bus ride. You may need to stay if you're going to Gunung Tambora, or if you arrived after the last bus has left for Hu'u. Dating back to the Hindu-Javanese period, Dompu was once the center of a sultanate probably founded by a Makassarese nobleman (*datu*) in the early 17th century. Ask around to see the town's *pusaka*: fine handwoven silver-brocaded cloth, helmets, chain mail armor, and rusted swords bequeathed by the Dutch to the old sultan generations ago. The archaeological site of **Doro Batu** is believed to be the burial place of royalty.

Practicalities

If you must stay the night try **Wisma Manaru Kupang,** Jl. Kartini no. 1, tel. (0371) 21032. It has its own restaurant. One block farther into town, near the *bemo* stop, are **Losmen Anda,** with rooms for Rp2500, and **Wisma Praja,** where the rate is Rp7500. Both are dark, cramped, and of dubious cleanliness. Nearby are the restaurants **Pondok Bamboo, Jawa Timor,** and **Bina Baru.** *Bemo* fare from town to the bus station is Rp250. Dompu has both a post office and *wartel.*

Lots of buses, starting at about 0630 and running late into the night, travel to Bima (Rp1500, two hours). Buses from Dompu also run to Sumbawa Besar (Rp5000), Hu'u (Rp1000), and Calabai. On the way to Dompu from Sumbawa Besar, you pass Pulau Rak on your left, an island rich in wildlife; charter a motorized *prahu* (Rp25,000) from Jamu on the north coast.

HU'U

Thirty-nine km south of Dompu over sealed road, on the eastern shore of Campi Bay, are the tiny village of **Hu'u** and **Lakey Beach.** Since about 1990, when surfers discovered this area, it's been known as the best surfing spot on Sumbawa. This coastal region is green and thicker with vegetation than that around Dompu. Lakey Beach is a long, wide strand fronted by reef. Much of the bottom is rocky but three km farther up the beach it's sandy and good for swimming. Waves break in at least four separate spots, including the famous "periscopes." From March-Aug. (best in June and July) surfers, mostly Australian and American, come and ride the waves. During the surf season it's a busy place, often so crowded that some people have to sleep on the beach or at the none-too-comfortable beachside raised platforms. There are far fewer guests Oct.-Dec. as the waves are not as good. It's a place where you can join in a soccer game on the beach with local boys in the afternoon, watch the villagers fish in the tidepools at low tide, or try spearfishing when the tide comes in. During clear weather, you'll be blessed with fine sunsets across the bay.

There are currently eight places to stay. The best is the 32-room **Mona Lisa Cottages.** The well-maintained breezy bungalows are made of solid wood and woven bamboo, and have tables, chairs, storage shelves, and a veranda. The restaurant here has a variety of Indonesian and European food. Billiard tables are for rent and the management maintains safe-deposit boxes for valuables. Electricity is generated in the evening. Taxi service is available to Dompu (Rp20,000), Bima airport (Rp54,000), and Bima (Rp64,000). Rooms (with *mandi*) are Rp10,000 for those facing the beach, and Rp5000 for the ones in the back with shared facilities; breakfast included. Also in this little cluster of accommodations is the **Intan Lestari Cottages.** Rooms here (Rp4000-5000) are in rows facing each other across a walk that runs up from the beach. It's a nice, friendly place where the restaurant has a good reputation. There are a number of surf camps, **Camp Lakey** and **Camp Unicorn** among them, for very basic rooms in the Rp4000-5000 range; 30 minutes down the beach is the surf camp **Periscopes.** During low season, some of these surf camps close. All accommodations except for camp Periscopes lie about three km past Hu'u village; Periscopes is one km beyond. Be sure to let the bus driver know at which place you want to stay, as he'll drop you off in front.

Buses (Rp1000) make the hourlong run several times a day from Dompu bus terminal to Hu'u, starting at about 0600. The morning buses run out to the end to the road; the afternoon buses often just stop in Hu'u village so you'll have to take a horsecart from there. Beware of the *bemo* drivers who wait at the bus station and hound you to charter a vehicle at a rate of Rp20,000 for the trip to Hu'u. The price is steep, but the trip is quick, you're dropped off at the door, and you don't have to wait for the next bus at the station.

BIMA

Sumbawa's main port is a strongly Muslim town; take care with your dress and demeanor. Bima is a handy pit stop on your trip across the island to Komodo, but has little else to recommend it. Many travelers go straight on to Sape. Experience the town first by *benhur.* The only tourist sight is the restored former sultan's palace, now a museum. There are some articles on display that are historically and culturally of interest, but none of the royal family's priceless personal articles are visible. You can view duplicates of *pusaka* such as *kris,* crowns, and belts. Open Mon.-Thurs. and Saturday 0830-1330 and 1530-1730, Friday and Sunday 0830-1100 and 1530-1730. A donation is requested

POST OFFICE

TO KOMBE BUS TERMINAL AND SAPE

NOT TO SCALE

TELECOMMUNICATIONS OFFICE

TO JATI BARU BUS TERMINAL AND WERA

JL. DIPONEGORO

HOTEL PAREWA

MERPATI OFFICE

SULTAN'S GRAVE

BIMA

JL. HASANUDDIN

LOSMEN KOMODO

SULTAN'S PALACE

GRAND KOMODO TOUR OFFICE

TOLOLALAI

JL. SULTAN IBRAHIM

BRI

JL. SUMBAWA

LOSMEN LILA GRAHA

JL. POMPA

HOTEL SANGHYANG

BNI

JL. PUTERASARI

BIM...

JL. MONGONSIDI

JL. KOTO LAMA

MUTMAINAH SHOP

MARKET

JL. SULAWESI

SIMPANG TICO

LOSMEN PELANGI

LOSMEN VIVI

ANDA

BUS TERMINAL

LOSMEN KARTINI

RM SAYONARA

BERINGIN INDAH

JL. KAHARNUDDIN

PERAMA TOUR AND TRAVEL

RM PADANG

JL. KARANTINA

JL. TERMINAL BARU

TO AIRPORT AND SUMBAWA BESAR

TO PORT (2 km)

© MOON PUBLICATIONS, INC.

for the upkeep—perhaps Rp1000, with an additional Rp1000-2000 if you take a volunteer guide. The first sultan's grave is on the hillside south of town; the last sultan's grave is just north of the city center.

Stroll around the *pasar malam,* especially the area set up for *warung* where the food is inviting. The post office is on Jl. Gajah Mada, out beyond the palace; open Mon.-Thurs. and Saturday 0800-1400, Friday 0800-1100. It has poste restante and international parcel service. The *wartel* is in Rabo just beyond the Bima city limits; open 24 hours.

Change major currencies at Bank Negara Indonesia, near Hotel Sanghyang. The rate is better than Bank Rakyat Indonesia, which is just around the corner.

Accommodations
Lots of places of varying standards are concentrated in the town's center near the market. You may try several, only to be told they're full and you should "try the Lila Graha." **Losmen Lila Graha,** Jl. Lombok 20, tel. (0371) 2740, is run by a cheerful, mustachioed Balinese sergeant-major and his guitar-strumming nephew; Rp7000 and up. It's clean, very safe, central (only 10 minutes from the bus station), and offers breakfast. Next door is **Losmen Pelangi,** new and clean but with small rooms; singles start at Rp7500.

Government-run **Losmen Komodo,** next to the *istana,* charges Rp7500 with shared *mandi* and Rp10,000 with *mandi* in room. The manager can be overbearing if you don't speak Indonesian, laying on stories about his sexual exploits with Western women, which the townspeople just lap up.

Opposite the Komodo is **Hotel Sanghyang,** supposedly the town's swankiest. All rooms have a/c and hot and cold water, and the more expensive offer TV; Rp30,000-35,000 s, Rp40,000-45,000 d. Also in this upper end is the **Hotel Parewa.** Nothing great here but the rooms are big, with a/c, hot and cold water, and TV; Rp20,000 standard, Rp35,000 VIP. **Losmen Vivi** is a dirty rathole; not recommended. Across the street is the slightly better **Losmen Puterasari,** with rooms from Rp5000. Both are right next to a mosque. On the cheap end, **Losmen Kartini** is recommended. Ask for a room on the second floor; rates start at Rp5500. Out of town along the bay are two additional hotels. One kilometer beyond the bus station is **Sonco Tengge Beach Hotel** and restaurant, with rooms from Rp17,500. It's fairly quiet for a place on the highway. A few kilometers farther on, set on a rocky point, is the **Lewata Beach Hotel.** This is a spot where the sultan and his wife used to come to relax on the bay. Full amenities, restaurant, and swimming pool; rooms run from Rp39,000 standard single to Rp100,000 for the presidential suite.

Food
Stroll in the market at night for *sate, nasi goreng,* desserts, etc. There are also a number of good *warung* around town. **Anda** has good value Chinese-Indonesian food. Try also **Sayonara.** A Padang-style restaurant, predictably named **Padang,** is quite good but slightly expensive. Also for *padang* try **Beringin** or **Simpang Tico.** Ice-cold beer and bottled water are available at **Losmen Lila Graha,** along with a good selection of Indonesian food. The better *losmen* each feature a restaurant.

Getting Away
The Merpati office is located next to Hotel Parewa. The Bima Airport is about 18 km south of town, next to the salt plains at the bottom of Bima Bay. To get there, try a local bus heading south (Rp4000, 20 minutes) or call the special airport taxi service (tel. (0371) 2455), which will pick you up at your hotel. From Bima, Merpati schedules flights to 15 cities of Java, Bali, Lombok, Sumbawa, Flores, Sumba, and Timor.

It's fairly easy to get a boat from Bima's harbor to Labuhanbajo or Reo, Flores, but most don't stop at Komodo. Bargain with the captain; a fair price to Labuhanbajo is Rp15,000. There are also boats from Bima to Lombok's port of Lembar, but they could take up to eight days. At least three cargo ships per week sail from Bima to Surabaya, sometimes carrying passengers. Motorized *prahu* regularly run from Bima to Ujung Pandang, a 36-hour trip (try CV Suasana Baru, Jl. Pelabuhan); and to Banjarmasin. Two Pelni ships call at Bima. The KM *Kelimutu* sails from Bima twice a month going east and north to Waingapu, Ende, Kupang, Dili, Kalabai, Maumere, and Makassar—a one week trip. Sailing back the same route it continues on to Lembar and Surabaya (two days). The KM *Awu* also connects Bima with major coastal cities on Kalimantan, Sulawesi, and northern Maluku on a twice a month run. Fares on the *Awu* are Rp40,000 to Makassar and Rp19,200 to Surabaya. To buy your ticket and find out what's next in port, go to the Pelni office, Jl. Pelabuhan 27, tel. (0371) 224, in Bima's port.

A regular ferry service offers many departures a day across the Bima Bay from Bima's port to Bajo, from where you can catch a bus to Donggo. The long-distance bus station is a 10-minute walk from town, Rp200 by *benhur*. Bemo will drop you at your *losmen* door or anywhere in town for Rp250. For Denpasar the departure is daily at 0730 and takes about 24 hours. There are also bus trips as far as Surabaya. Several long distance bus companies have offices along the road to the terminal.

For Sape, first get a *bemo* (Rp300) from Jl. Hasanuddin in Bima to Raba's **Kumbe station**, three km inland, then take a bus for Rp1100 to Sape; allow one to two hours. Buses leave Raba for Sape approximately every half hour 0700-1630. Chartering a *bemo* from Bima to Sape will cost around Rp50,000 after bargaining. Buses to Wawo and Maria are Rp550. If going north to Tawali or Sangeang Darat, first take a *bemo* to the **Jati Baru** bus station, then get a bus from there.

VICINITY OF BIMA

Several Muslim pilgrimage spots are near Bima. The most important is the grave of Bima's last sultan to embrace Islam, located in the village of **Tololalai. Raba,** the administrative capital of eastern Sumbawa, was the Dutch administrative center for the island. A few buildings with Dutch influence can be seen here. Raba has less character than Bima, yet is home to several hand-woven cloth cottage industries. This cloth has a predominance of orange, green, and blue (mostly in stripes) with some geometric designs in gold or silver thread. **Mawar** is on the main road; the **Dahlia** is down an alley farther to the east. Samples of this cloth, other crafts, T-shirts, and the like can be seen in Bima at the **Mutmainah Shop** near the market. Other similar craft shops are nearby.

For swimming and relaxing, **Pantai Lawata** is four km and Rp600 by pony cart or Rp250 by *bemo*. Nothing special but popular on the weekends. Another sandy beach is at **Lewa Mori,** 35

km away; take a bus first to Sila, then a *bemo*. In the hills at **Wawo** is a swimming pool built by the Dutch over 65 years ago. Also near Wawo, traditional Biman granaries standing outside the village on stilts can be seen from the highway.

South of Bima past the airport is a huge area of **salt flats.** At certain times of the year, water from the bay is let into these enclosures and left to evaporate. The remaining crystalline salt is then scraped up into piles, bagged, and shipped off for processing.

A back road cuts over the shoulder of the mountain, leading down to the north shore of this northeast peninsula. This road goes to the **Wera** district. Take a bus from the Jati Baru bus station past traditional villages to Wera, then another to the fishing village of **Sangeang Darat.** From here you can sometimes get a boat across the strait to the volcanic island of Sangeang. Gunung Sangeang last erupted in 1986, when all the farmers were moved off the island. Some still maintain their old fields there, and travel daily to and from the island. It's said you can climb to the volcanic crater and back in a half day.

High in the hills above Tente, to the south of Bima, is the small village of **Sambori.** Many of the houses in this village are built in the traditional, tall-peak, A-frame style. Put together with posts, beams, and wooden pegs, they are set on stilts. The bottom level is open and used for family and friends to gather. In the thatched upper portion, usually with just one or two tiny windows, is the living and kitchen area, reached by ladder from below. Above the living room, at the peak of the structure, is the granary.

This is a poor agricultural region where rice, corn, and beans are grown. Young and old can be seen pounding rice in carved-out logs to loosen the husk from the kernel. The village is Muslim. There is no public transportation to this village but trucks make a run at least once a week.

The Donggo Area

A traditional mountain area west of Teluk Bima, the home of 20,000 swidden farmers called the **Dou Donggo** ("Mountain People"). Speaking an archaic form of Bimanese, they live in patrilineal clans in a dozen villages. Though the Dou Donggo share many cultural traits with Biman lowlanders, they preserve a unique ethnic and religious identity, wear distinctive black clothing, observe their own hierarchical order, and build traditional houses called *uma neuhi*. These rectangular, high-gabled *adat* dwellings, raised on piles and located next to steep cliffs high on mountain ridges, represent probably the original East Sumbawanese house form, once prevalent all over the region.

The darker-skinned Dou Donggo, believed to be descendants of the island's indigenous peoples, practiced until recently an animist religion. They adopted Christianity or Islam only in the last 20 years and practice those faiths with varying degrees of orthodoxy. This mountain tribe also weaves outstanding cloth on breastlooms. Ask to see the sacred places (*ntsala*), marked by linga, where the gods gather to copulate.

To the Donggo area, about 40 km from Bima, first catch a ferry (Rp2000) from Bima harbor to the port of Bajo, then take the bus from Sila to Donggo. Walk to **Kali** and **Moawa**. Near Donggo, see the stone inscription and the graves of two folk heroes. **Mbawa** is the only village where the black clothing and *uma neuhi* can be seen in everyday use. Alternately take a bus from Bima to Sila; then change buses there. If you get an early start, it's possible to reach Donggo and return to Bima in the same day.

SAPE

A harbor town on Sumbawa's east coast, the departure point for Komodo Island and Flores, Sape is peopled by boat-making immigrants from Sulawesi. Take a bus from Raba's Kumbe station to Sape (Rp1100, two hours); the earliest buses leave around 0700 and run until 1630. If you arrive late on the bus, Sape looks like a ghost town. You'll find very friendly people in Sape—a million "Hello Misters," even from the police.

The **PHPA office** is located in the green house just past the *kantor polisi* on the north side of Jl. Pelabuha. These gentlemen can also handle inquiries about transport and chartering. If heading directly to Komodo, Sape is your last chance to pick up a few supplies. *Benhur* charge Rp1000 from the bus station to the harbor.

Accommodations
Losmen Give offers tiny rooms with thin walls; the back garden is nice. Have the bus driver drop you off at the door or take a *benhur* from the bus station. Nearby are **Losmen Anda**

and **Losmen Friendship.** Several *rumah makan* are near the cinema. It's better to eat in the *losmen* at night; the *mie telur goreng* is laudable, and sometimes fish and chicken are available. Directly outside the harbor gate is the newer and nicer **Losmen Mutiara Beach** (Rp5000 s, Rp8000 d). Clean and set on stilts over the water (mudflats at low tide), the view is good but the mosquitos and smell may not be so pleasing. Across the road are two very basic eateries, **Sulawesi** and the slightly better **Selara Anda.** Both feature limited menus, but the food is acceptable and the service friendly. Good places to meet other travelers going to Komodo.

Getting Away
The ferry to Komodo and Flores leaves from Sape harbor, called simply *pelabuhan,* about four km (Rp1000) by *benhur* from Sape. The regular Sape-Komodo-Labuhanbajo ferry costs Rp9000 pp (bicycles, motorcycles, and cars extra) to Komodo or Labuhanbajo, and an additional Rp4000 from Komodo to Labuhanbajo if breaking your journey in Komodo. The harbor tax is Rp100. On Komodo there's an additional Rp1500 fare (each way) for the transfer *prahu* from the ferry to the national park pier.

The ferry leaves from Sape to Komodo (and on to Flores) at 0800 everyday except Friday; allow five hours to Komodo and seven to Labuhanbajo. During the wet season, the Sape Strait is notorious for dangerous whirlpools, high waves, powerful currents, and riptides, thus the crossing to Komodo may then take extra time. When the ferry service is down you'll have to take one of the many Bugis boats making the direct crossing to Flores. Avoid chartering a boat to Komodo from Sape as it's substantially cheaper in Labuhanbajo. Reasonably priced private tour boats from Labuhanbajo also run to Komodo and other islands in this crowded strait. Motorized outriggers from Sape are only Rp50,000, but not so seaworthy. At least two large sailboats are available for hire from here.

Vicinity Of Sape
If you're bored, wander west of town to admire the picturesque irrigation system; the surrounding countryside is quite photogenic. The Bugis harbor consists of a row of houses on

stilts and a shipyard where you can watch the building of all types of handmade ships.

Check out the catamaran (*bagan*) fleet that fishes at night using bright paraffin pressure lamps to attract fish. Once the fish have collected above a lowered net, the net is raised and they're hauled aboard. More a fixed fishing contraption than a boat, the square, twin-sailed *bagan* are equipped with a platform up to 18 meters long on which sits a small hut where the crew rests during the day.

North of Sape 25 km is the fishing village of **Toronaru,** with white-sand beaches, coconut

palms, and good coral reefs just outside town. **Gili Banta** is a small islet off Sape, where giant turtles swim in a jade lagoon. Gili Banta has a secluded cove protected on three sides, very calm, with a fine sandy beach and tall stone cliffs—a pirate's hideout. This is the kind of utter solitude that makes you wish you had your own boat. At the foot of the cliffs are incredibly craggy perforated rocks. From the clifftops you can just make out Komodo. Reach Gili Banta by chartered *prahu* from Sape (about Rp20,000 a day); giant turtles will splash away as you glide into the cove. Bring plenty of water and food.

KOMODO ISLAND

One of the world's great wildlife regions, this small archipelago nestled between Sumbawa and Flores is home to the Komodo dragon, the sole survivor of carnivorous dinosaurs that thrived in tropical Asia 130 million years ago. The giant monitor lizards—the largest on earth—were only a myth until the turn of this century when a few pearl fishermen were forced to land here one night in a storm. Today, isolated by the strong, unpredictable currents in the straits that separate them, these dry and barren islands draw thousands of travelers from all over the world to view the lizards in their natural habitat. Komodo, as well as the neighboring islands of Padar, Rinca, Motong, and two small areas on Flores south of Labuhanbajo, were made a national park in 1980.

THE LAND

Thirty-six km long by 16 km at its widest, and 500 km east of Bali, Pulau Komodo lies in one of Indonesia's driest regions. The highly permeable soil is shallow and poor. Above 500 meters the island features dense, cool, and shady cloud forests. The highest mountain is 735-meter Gunung Satalibo. The south portion of the island, little frequented by visitors, offers wild mountain landscapes and empty seashores. One fishing village hugs the east coast on Teluk Slawi; two to three other temporary fishing encampments are maintained as long as the water supply lasts after the rains.

Prior to the wet season, the islanders burn off much of the island's grassland to improve the fresh growth of new grass for grazing. Komodo is a tropical savannah with dramatic landscapes of hills covered mostly in high, coarse, golden-green grass, scattered fire-resistant thickets, stunted scrub growth, thorny zizyphus trees, and tall, fan-leafed *lontar* palms that break the horizon like exploding artillery flak.

Volcanic in origin, the island is composed of pyroclastic-like ash which has solidified into arid tuffaceous hillsides. The whole east coast is an eroded cliff that plunges straight into the sea, with alluvial fans, occasional coastal mangroves, rocky streambeds, and great black ravines gouged out of cliffs. Perfect dragon country.

Climate
The wet season from November to April is heaviest during the monsoon months (Dec.-March), but the rain lasts just a few hours each day. Rain squalls during this period may prevent or delay sea travel. Between June and September, rainfall is very low. The dry season here can last 8-10 months, and standing water is rare even during the wet season. Komodo, in fact, receives the least rainfall of any of the surrounding islands. From April through the rest of the year, it's scorching hot, when searing winds from Australia desiccate the land. May is a good time to visit; water is more plentiful, grass is green, and temperatures are agreeable.

FLORA AND FAUNA

Only *lontar* palms and zizyphus trees (typical vegetation of the lesser Sundas) can survive during the dry spell. Riots of endemic orchids droop pellmell over the trails, and high grass covers the hills. Herds of deer and wild hogs, water buffalo, and cattle share the upland valleys of the island with the Komodo reserve, and serve as prey for the dragons. Cave bats (*kelelewar*) hover around black hollowed cliffs, and the island swarms with snakes. The strong yellow plastic-like webs of *Nephilia,* 15-centimeter-long spiders, stretch for as long as six meters across walking tracks.

Birds include the sulphur-crested cockatoo, which shrieks hysterically; equally noisy friar birds; stunning yellow-breasted sunbirds; black-naped orioles; masked cuckoo shrikes; spangled drongos; bee eaters; and a great number of sea and shore birds. Mound-building megapodes nest on southern Komodo and Rinca; dragons often raid their mounds for eggs. Dolphins, whales, and sea turtles are often seen in the straits.

GETTING THERE

Traveling to Komodo is getting easier all the time. If traveling overland from Bali, allow at least four days for the trip each way. The usual embarkation point, Labuhanbajo on Flores, has an airfield, hotels, and restaurants. The fastest possible land route involves taking an all-night bus from either Denpasar or Mataram to Sape (24 hours plus), which will get you there for the 0800 ferry to Komodo.

Regular Ferries

Running every day except Friday, the ferry from Sape in East Sumbawa departs at 0800 and arrives in Komodo at 1300, then continues on to Labuhanbajo. From Labuhanbajo, the ferry leaves at 0800, arrives at Komodo around 1100, and continues back to Sape.

Komodo is much closer to Labuhanbajo than Sape. The fares reflect this: from Sape to either Labuhanbajo or Komodo is Rp9000; from Labuhanbajo to Komodo, Rp2800. The ferry is

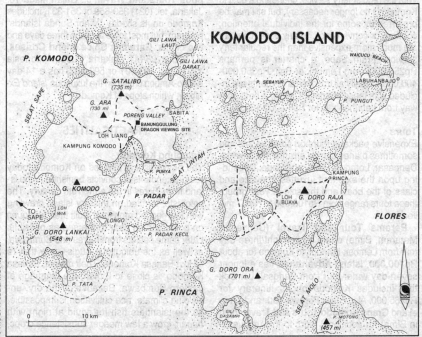

Komodo village

too big to come ashore at Komodo. Instead, you're shuttled to the national park pier on a small fishing *prahu* (Rp1500). Mind your luggage lest it end up on the seafloor.

Charters
With the regular ferry service, chartering a boat to Komodo is no longer necessary, but still may be preferred by some for the individual attention, comfort, or convenience. In any case, charters are much more expensive than the regular ferry service. From Sape, a charter is perhaps Rp250,000; from Lombok or Bali, Rp350,000-400,000. Usually all travel arrangements are included with these charters. Charter a boat one-way from Labuhanbajo for Rp60,000-100,000.

Tours
Expensive package tours on small yachts and sometimes planes can be arranged in Jakarta, Denpasar, Lombok, Bima, and Sape. Depending upon the extent of luxuries, the size and class of the boat, and the size of your group, these tours range from Rp105,000 to Rp1.7 million pp.
   Perama Tour and Travel (Denpasar, Mataram, Bima) offers a two-night/three-day tour from Lembar, Lombok to Komodo for about Rp100,000. **Island Adventures** has a longer seven-day water tour from Bangsal, Lombok that includes Komodo on its itinerary for Rp265,000. Also check **Parewa Tour and Travel** and **Grand Komodo Tours and Travel** (both in Bima) for additional tours to this unique is-

land. In Labuhanbajo, Perama offers a two-day/one-night trip to Komodo with other island destinations included for Rp30,000. Alternately, ask in Jakarta's or Denpasar's tourist office for the names of other travel companies or travel agencies specializing in Komodo tours. **Agaphos Tours and Travel,** Jl. Gajah Mada 16, Jakarta, tel. (021) 359-659 or 351-331, includes Komodo on its six-day "Minor Sunda Islands" program, but most tours average three days and two nights. **Garuda's Spice Island Cruises,** P.O. Box 98/MT, Jakarta Pusat, Indonesia 12910, tel. 593-401 or 593-402, has a 14-day Bali-to-Ambon cruise on the luxurious *Island Explorer,* which stops at Komodo.

PRACTICALITIES

Kampung Komodo
The native fishing families on Komodo today are descendants of convicts banished to the island from Flores in the early 16th century. The colonists, terrified on this dry island crawling with four-legged monsters, built their *kampung* on posts and as near to the sea as possible. Later came settlers from Flores and Sumbawa, as well as the ubiquitous Bugis—now they're all just Bangsa Komodo. Their dialect, Bahasa Komodo, is close to Biman, the language of eastern Sumbawa. Because of the dry, unyielding climate, rice cultivation is impossible, so the islanders fish for squid at night with *bagan,* grow a few meager subsistence crops,

and transport copra between Sumbawa and Flores.

This Islamic village is the island's only settlement. With a strictly controlled population of around 500, Kampung Komodo consists of a few rows of bamboo houses on stilts. There is no place to stay in this village; all tourists are required to use the visitors' accommodations at the PHPA park headquarters in Loh Liang. You can hire a boat (Rp10,000) out to Pulau Lasa in the middle of the bay to snorkel and swim. Komodo villagers earn cash as guides. Other charter boats run about Rp30,000 a day for points around the islands.

Permits

As Komodo is a national park, you need a permit (Rp2000) to visit. The permit, your room charge (Rp5500 a night), and an insurance fee (Rp50) are taken at the front office when you disembark the ferry at Loh Liang. Your visitor permit is good as long as you want to stay, but you must rent a room for every night you remain on the island.

From June to August about 15,000 people visit Komodo Island. The rest of the year sees about 9,000 people. Most come on cruise ships and sleep on board, but there are 52 beds for rent in several bungalows at the park headquarters.

Preparations

You'll need insect spray, suntan lotion, a hat, and long pants. Also take a telephoto lens—80 mm will do, 200 mm is better.

It's no longer acceptable to secure a goat or other animal as dragon bait. The PHPA has suspended artificial feedings of the dragons; the creatures are now required to fend for themselves. In previous years the extremely shy lizards were baited with dead goats, dead dogs, stinky fish heads, chicken feet, entrails, and other foul matter pungent enough to capture their olfactory attention.

EXPLORING KOMODO

DRAGON WATCHING

Best time to see these creatures is May-September. Early in the morning and/or late in the afternoon a PHPA guide takes a group from the camp to the dragon-watching site at **Banunggulung.** One or more guides (Rp2500 each) are required per group. This cost is split among the members of the group. Try being nice to the guides; they seem to get more than their fair share of abuse from tourists. The dry riverbed site is about a 30-minute walk (2.5 km) from Loh Liang. There you can safely view the dragons from above, from the edge of the ravine. Some of the area is protected by a fence. Red clothes and menstruating women are forbidden on this excursion.

Even without the bait the *ora* that feed at this site are quite active, not lethargic as they are in zoos. Since the lizards seldom move far from their feeding grounds, you're almost sure to find them there even without bait. The whole outing takes about an hour and a half.

Currently, more than 2,000 lizards on the island hunt for their sustenance. Follow the spoor trails left by dragons searching for carrion; these are visible imprints of the Komodo's claws and the scrape of its tail. Have the guide take you to the well-worn dragon trail in **Loh Kalo.** Extending from the bottom of the slope to a burrow complex at a point two-thirds of the way to the top, this 300-meter-long path is devoid of all brush and is used only by the giant lizards.

Safety

Never go looking for lizards without a guide. Loh Liang is the safest area, and *ora* here are not abused and killed. In most cases they show no interest in humans and you can often approach quite close to a large feeding dragon without it taking any notice of you. If they do approach, the guides keep them off you with long forked sticks. The younger dragons are the most curious—entering the camp, flicking their tongues at your feet. Often just a slight movement will send them scurrying.

An *ora* about to attack holds its head low, hisses, raises its back, inflates its neck, and arches its tail, ready for striking or lashing. If a dragon exhibits this type of threatening behavior, just hit the beast in the snout with a stick or tripod, or throw a handful of pebbles. Very few

(CONTINUED ON PAGE 895)

THE KOMODO DRAGON

The Komodo dragon (*Varanus komodoensis*) belongs to the group known as monitor lizards, from the ancient belief the creatures "monitor," or warn, of the presence of crocodiles. The Komodo is the largest species of monitor lizard, which are found throughout Asia, Africa, and Australia. The natives call the dragon *ora,* or *buaya darat* (land crocodile). Fossils strikingly similar to the Komodo dragon date back 130 million years. The creature has been extinct everywhere but here since the Jurassic period.

The area's isolation and strong ocean currents ensured the lizard's survival. Although Chinese traders had visited Komodo and taken dragon skins as early as the 12th century, the skins on the whole were considered too scarred for commercial use. The decorative granular skin was, however, much prized for native drums. *Ora* were also procured for their medicinal value, the tail fat boiled down and applied to burns. Because the animals are such remarkable swimmers, body fluids also provided the Chinese with "swimming medicine."

Named by a Dutch scientist, P.A. Ouwens, the dragons have lured visitors since their "discovery" in 1912. The *ora* came under the legislative protection of the sultan of Bima in 1915, a mere three years later. Yet hunting continued until 1937, when the Dutch finally put a stop to it. About 600 *ora* have been trapped, shot, or embalmed for museums in the past 60 years. Now the Wildlife Management Office in Bogor has set a limit of but five per year, *ora* killed strictly for scientific purposes.

The fiercest lizard known, *ora* can down deer, goat, or wild pig, ripping them apart with saw-like teeth. These highly specialized slicing teeth, as well as the lizard's predatory habits, are unique among reptiles.

Ora can lift up their heavy tails and bellies to sprint at up to 18 km per hour, but only for short distances. Dragons also enter the sea and swim, sometimes against strong tidal currents, up to 1,000 meters to offshore islets. They can plunge to depths of four meters, easily swimming 100 meters while submerged.

The *ora* has uncanny senses of smell and touch, and is one of the world's most intelligent reptiles. In captivity, they have the ability to recognize and obey only certain zookeepers. Barely a dozen specimens of this rare species are found in the world's zoos outside Indonesia, and if kept in captivity for long periods *ora* grow fat and phlegmatic, and usually die within a few years of amoebic parasites. In In-

donesia, specimens are kept in Jakarta, Yogyakarta, and Surabaya.

For the most thorough, definitive study of the Komodo dragon yet published, see *The Behavioral Ecology of the Komodo Monitor* by Walter Auffenberg, available from University Presses of Florida, 15 Northwest 15th St., Gainesville, FL 32603. With grateful acknowledgments, the following notes are drawn from that outstanding book.

Habitat

The Komodo dragon has the smallest permanent habitat range of any of the world's great carnivores. Confined to Komodo, Padar, Rinca, Uwada Sami, Gili Motong, and western Flores, their total area comprises just under 1,000 square km. Pulau Komodo is the largest single undisturbed *ora* habitat. The total number of lizards is estimated at 5,000-7,000. Population density averages 17 lizards per square km on Komodo, and six to seven per square km on Padar, Rinca, and western Flores.

Komodo monitors prefer naturally made burrows along the banks of dry riverbeds, or on the steep slopes of open hills, usually behind overhanging vegetation, big rocks, or tree roots. Komodo villagers know the best sites. The dragons seek refuge in these holes during really hot days; they're seldom used during the wet season. Burrows serve as a heat sink at high temperatures, conserving the panting lizard's body water. Burrows act as well as insulated chambers when night temperatures drop. Cold-blooded, the dragons don't usually emerge from their holes until after 0800-0900 when the air starts to get hot. Diurnal, they retire to their burrows by 1930 and are very deep sleepers.

Burrows are commandeered from rodents or porcupines, in length averaging only 1.5 meters. The reptile's head and shoulders therefore often protrude from the entrance; inside the burrow their tails are bent like hairpins. Sometimes several dragons use the same burrow, and there can be as many as 18 burrows to a burrow cluster.

Body Form

The longest specimen ever recorded was a male in the St. Louis Zoo that measured 3.13 meters from tail to snout. Villagers in the Lenteng area of Flores swear that 3.5-meter-long *ora* live in the vicinity, and through the years there have been absurd, unsubstantiated reports of dragons up to 14.5 meters long. Adults can weigh 150 kg, but most full-grown specimens are 1.7-1.8 meters long and average 35-55 kg in weight. Females attain only two-thirds the size of the average male.

The tail is the adult's best defense and most dangerous weapon. An adult runs through the grass with its tail lifted off the ground, lashing it about, or winds it like a snake and delivers mighty blows. Its thick, strong front legs and huge claws enable the lizard to climb hilly terrain and hold down carrion while ripping and tearing. The dragons are superlative diggers, able to excavate a meter-deep hole in less than an hour. When trapped in stockades, they can easily dig under the walls to escape. Starting in February the dragons shed their skins; the sloughing is completed by the end of the month.

Young dragons are the most unpredictable, the speediest, and the most skillful tree climbers. Sometimes you see them perched in trees preying on monkeys; some even live in hollow trees.

Coloration changes from speckled, multihued, greenish-yellow subadults to the standard dappled gray adults; larger male specimens have yellowish-green spots on their snouts. The clay color camouflages the mature *ora* as it waits in ambush, while the coloration of the young protects them as they scamper through leafy trees.

Senses

Komodo dragons are in large part scent-oriented, but they can also see well up to five to six meters. In spite of the popular belief that they're stone deaf, dragons hear moderately well—they just choose not to pay attention to noise, unless it pertains to food or danger. Much information is passed from lizard to lizard through scent: highly odoriferous fecal pellets of the larger dragons are often "read" by the smaller ones, who stop along the way and carry out exhaustive olfactory examinations. A ripe, putrifying carcass can draw a dragon from 11 km away, and *ora* can track the spoor of a deer in the wild as well as any hunting dog. The reptile's long tongue, forked and protrusible like a snake's, is both an organ of smell and taste, flicking out and taking scent "samples" before eating. These carnivores also use their all-important sense of smell to recognize territorial boundaries.

Diet

Newly hatched *ora* feed on small lizards and insects. Subadults prey on shellfish, rodents, eels, geckos, sea turtle eggs, bird eggs, and birds (swallowed live). Adults feed on roe deer, crab-eating macaques, feral dogs, and boars. Large dragons can kill water buffalo 10-15 times their weight. Drag-

ons will eat virtually anything they can catch or kill—including other dragons.

The carnivores show a marked preference for pregnant hoofed animals, and are able to distinguish these females by scent. On Flores and Pulau Rinca, a dragon will wait beneath a foaling mare so it can eat the newborn; the straining mare can only try to kick the lizard as she gives birth. Not only are the dragons fond of fetuses and afterbirth, but their harassment of the female so distresses and worries her it often causes a miscarriage, which then leaves her virtually incapacitated and more open to attack herself.

Hunting

Komodo dragons ambush deer and wild boar along the victims' accustomed trails by hiding to the side and waiting, or cunningly creep up to within striking distance while the victim sleeps in tangled thickets. Because of lack of cover, *ora* seldom hunt on open slopes. Dragons have also been known to come into a village in broad daylight to steal goats. Although almost exclusively active only during the day, occasionally *ora* raid the village at night for goats or fish kept under houses.

Dragons assume the attack posture when they hold their heads low, slightly cocked to one side, crouching low to the ground. Large ones often strike their prey with the tail, then grasp the prey by the throat and head, jerking it violently from side to side. It's a popular myth that dragons inflict poisonous bites; in fact, a great number of bitten deer who escape eventually die of massive infections.

Dragons forage up to 10 km per day from sea level to 500 meters, to offshore islets, mangrove swamps, grass thickets, even over reefs and bars, following their prey—the largest foraging area of any lizard. They feed erratically—it's feast or famine.

Feeding

With the exception of large snakes, varanids consume prey faster than any other large predator, including lions and crocodiles. They're equipped with lateral rows of jagged teeth, serrated and curved with sharp tips and wide bases—like curved scalpel blades—superlatively designed for cutting through flesh. If driven by hunger, dragons will swallow horns, hooves, antlers, hair, bones—everything.

They plunge their heads first into the bellies of carcasses to rip out the intestines and stomach. The only reptiles that cut their prey into sections before swallowing, varanids rock back and forth as they bite, bolting down each chunk after it's sawed off the body. A 40-kg *ora* can eat a 30-kg wild boar,

(CONTINUED ON NEXT PAGE)

THE KOMODO DRAGON
(CONTINUED)

swallowing the hindquarters whole. It takes several lizards three to five days to devour a 1,200-kg water buffalo. Articulate jaws like a snake's enable it to maneuver such odd shapes as horned heads and pelvic sections into their stomachs.

The dragon's powerful front legs, sharp claws, and thick back legs are vital for holding down carrion, tearing off rotted hide, ripping open underbellies, and digging out megapode nests and rodent burrows. In comparison with the world's other large carnivores, Komodos have the fewest competitors for carrion. Only with flies, wild dogs, beetles, crows, and kites is this magnificent scavenger-predator willing to share its carcass. But even the largest dragons can be driven from a kill on a hot day by a belligerent and persistent boar.

Varanids can go up to 1.5 months without water; when drinking they plunge their heads in up to their eyes, gulp water, then raise their heads like chickens to allow the water to run down their throats.

Hierarchy And Reproduction
A group of three to four *ora* feeding together on carrion is common; there could be as many as 20 at the banquet, ranging from juveniles to the largest adults. This is the only time when smaller varanids are tolerated. Behavior during feeding is very antagonistic, with a definite pecking order. The larger, dominant male takes his pick of the carcass, the best position around it, and most of the food. He determines when and where the carcass is moved. The younger *ora* help snap off ligaments and tendons which prevent the dominant male from swallowing really large chunks of the body.

Courting males exhibit themselves to the females by dancing, calling, posturing, and other conspicuous and curious visual behavior. Females behave likewise, with pushups, back-arching, and head-bobbing. Courtship takes place through nearly the entire year. Actual copulation often occurs near carrion and is usually preceded by tongue flicks over the female's back or by the male grasping the female's neck skin with his jaws. Females are very aggressive during courtship, biting the male trying to mount her, sometimes severely injuring or even killing him. A male must completely overpower the female in order to copulate successfully.

Approximately two weeks later the female digs out a half-meter-deep hole in the sand under a living shrub or on a hillside, then lays the soft, smooth, leathery, golfball-size eggs. The incubation period is about eight months, the young usually hatching in April or May. Occasionally, the male and female will eat some or all of a brood of eggs. The Komodo is perhaps the only lizard to use this method of controlling overpopulation.

Fighting
When fighting, Komodo lizards attack and parry with their open jaws. Zoologists call this "jaw fencing," a habit common among lizards. They also bite, tear, paw, and shake opponents, sometimes causing death.

feeding dragons

When high-ranking *ora* approach carrion, younger generation low-ranking individuals often scatter headlong into the underbrush. Smaller Komodos also go through elaborate appeasement displays in front of larger dragons to keep from being attacked. And for good reason: few vertebrates show such a disparity in size between young and adult. The larger the *ora*, the more likely s/he is to attack and kill others.

Mortality
The lifespan of *ora* in the wild is about 50 years maximum; in captivity it's half that. Size is directly related to the age of the reptile. Rats, dogs, cats, sea eagles, brahminy kites, osprey, and snakes prey on *ora* under one meter in length, while *kerbau*, desert vipers, and wild boar can kill larger specimens. Others die from burrow collapse, becoming trapped in land depressions, lack of water, starvation, and poaching.

Humans and dogs are the lizard's major competitors; dogs hunt deer and piglets in packs, and even compete for carrion, while people living in the dragons' habitat illegally poach about 150 deer yearly.

lizards will attack humans unprovoked, and most attacks occur in self-defense. Like people, some *ora* are meaner than others, and all should be watched carefully. The infection caused by a bite can be very dangerous. Only one recent death has been attributed to a Komodo Island *ora*. In 1974 an elderly Swiss gentleman from a cruise ship disappeared—only a few of his personal items were ever found. On Rinca, a local child was eaten while playing at home.

WATER SPORTS

Komodo is also a marine reserve with fine mangroves and coral reefs rich in diverse marine fauna (such as the *caranx* species) and shellfish. **Teluk Slawi** even has a resident population of baleen whales. After you're through viewing dragons, spend the rest of the afternoon snorkeling on the reef. The park office rents fins and asks Rp3000 per day. PHPA can advise you on the best spots, and can arrange boats and canoes. Snorkeling is particularly good off the north coast of the island, teeming with more than 180 species of fish. An outrigger costs Rp5000-10,000 per day. Local fishermen say the sharks are harmless; still, only snorkel in calm water close to the beach. More treacherous than sharks are the four- to five-knot currents in the straits between the islands. Komodo's numerous sheltered coves offer more safety.

LOH LIANG

Located at the north part of Teluk Slawi, Loh Liang is an area of open grasslands, riverbeds, old *ladang*, savannahs, and a small mangrove swamp on the bay's west end near the coast. It's also the location of the well-kept PHPA camp, two km north of Kampung Komodo. Tourists may only stay in the PHPA camp's visitor accommodations—several large bungalows costing Rp5500 per night. Generator-produced electricity operates until about 2200.

There is a cafeteria at the park headquarters which has an extensive menu, though it's somewhat expensive. This is the only place on the island to buy food. The place regularly runs out of items, including bottled water (but not beer) and occasionally rice. Folks there will, however, be able to fix something for you and it's usually prepared quite well. To be on the safe side, bring a few emergency food items and bottled water.

Loh Liang Bay
Explore this small, semicircular bay, a pristine area of white sulphur-crested cockatoos, megapode birds, *wili wili* birds, bellowing Timor deer, and snorting boars crashing through the grass. Walking from Loh Liang to Kampung Komodo (45-60 minutes), there are many rocks, so go at low tide. There is not much at Kampung Komodo except a few small shops, the boats, and children splashing about in the water. Villagers are not particularly welcoming and you won't actually succeed at buying much there. Above the coastal hills are green-forested highlands.

Follow only the marked trails to the Poreng Valley. Every time you leave the PHPA camp, a guide (Rp25,000 per day) must accompany you. When walking, always wear long pants and shoes to protect against snakes and poisonous insects. Other isolated bays in the northern part of the island are **Loh Boko** and **Loh Sorao,** with thick woods, rocky lava cliffs, and unspoiled coral gardens. *Ora* are larger here than on the village side of the island.

GUNUNG ARA

A beautiful dormant volcano surging right out of the sea, this mountain is covered in bamboo woods, monkeys, and wild buffalo. Many natives won't climb it for fear it's possessed by evil spirits and their reptile companions, the *naga*. The legend goes that a handful of Arabs once tried to settle Komodo, and relics of their settlement remain on this mountain; the wild buffalo found on Komodo are descended from their cattle.

Climb to the top through the well-trampled tracks made by wild pigs and deer; a path starts from behind Kampung Komodo. Count on it taking all day: three hours up, two hours' rest at the top (it's hot!), and two hours down. You'll need strong shoes. Thick, head-high *alang-alang* grass hides rubble and blocks of lava, so watch out. Marvelous savannah landscapes can be seen from the summit, with chains of valleys and bays in the distance; bring binoculars. **Gunung Satalibo** is a taller peak to the northeast, not as easy to get to, but at the top are dense, cool, cloud forests.

OTHER ISLANDS

Pulau Rinca

This 195-square-km island southeast of Komodo is also home to the *ora*. Flores is only two km away across a strait which, although very narrow, is not as treacherous as Selat Lintah and Selat Sape. Several villages lie on Rinca; tracks leading into the interior start at Kampung Rinca.

Northern Rinca is open, undulating country; the only high hills lie just west and south of Kampung Rinca. The grassy plains support many buffalo and horses gone wild from domestic stock: though small, they're fine, sturdy animals.

The horses and wild pigs are preyed upon by the Rincan lizards. The favorite destination for expeditions is Loh Buaya off the north coast of Rinca, where there's a small guesthouse, shelters, and viewing tower. Dense forests climb the slopes of Doro Ora ("Dragon Mountain"), while island-sheltered Teluk Dasampi provides good anchorage for exploring the southern part of the island, home to brush turkeys and megapode birds. There are few paths; watch out for wasps.

The best way to appreciate the attractions of the island is to stay overnight and get an early start each day. Accommodations are now available at the ranger guard post (*pos jaga*) in Loh Buaya; two double rooms (Rp15,000 each) and three single rooms (Rp10,000 each), plus five new rooms with *kamar mandi* (Rp25,000 each). Generator, electricity; fridge sometimes doesn't work. This ranger station is now nearly as large as the ranger complex at Komodo.

Pulau Padar

Separated from Komodo by the powerful Selat Lintah, 20-square-km Padar is drier than Komodo except in the rainy season. The currents and whirlpools that swirl around this tiny island can be extremely dangerous. Padar has some of the most spectacular scenery in the archipelago: pink beaches contrast with orange coral and a vividly ultramarine sea. There's only one source of water, on the northwest coast, so bring your own. You can find numerous campsites along attractive beaches.

There's little wildlife: competing with *ora* for food, packs of wild dogs bring down roe deer. For dragon viewing, the west side of the island is the most accessible observation locale, but lizards range all over the island, from its coastal mangrove swamps to its highest elevations. On small islands off southern Padar, edible bird nests are harvested from cliffs.

FLORES

A mostly Christian island becoming more popular with travelers, mountainous Flores could very well be the highlight of your visit to Nusatenggara. Considered by many one of Indonesia's most beautiful islands, Flores has grandiose volcanos, high mountain lakes, stretches of savannah, and tropical deciduous forests.

One of Indonesia's most fascinating ethnological regions, the island is home to intact tribes practicing their own brand of animism, as well as cultural and artistic traditions little known outside obscure missionary journals. Flores is particularly interesting as a foil for Bali, where human culture has created a symbiosis with nature. Flores offers similar natural conditions to Bali—a constant source of water from the mountains, sufficient rain for two and even three yearly rice crops—but the land remains undeveloped and resources are little used.

THE LAND

The island of Flores is about 360 km long as the crow flies, but because of its mountainous terrain, the road from one end to the other is 667 km long; the island averages 60 km wide (72 km at its widest). Frequently shaken by earthquakes and volcanic eruptions, Flores is riven with deep ravines and rugged valleys, which accounts for the difficulty of travel and the island's distinctive cultures.

Only Java and Sumatra have more active volcanos than Flores. One spectacular ridge of weathered mountains runs down the middle of the island, with 15 lazily smoking volcanos descending smoothly into the sea on both sides. The peaks of this range are all over 2,100 meters, and the highest, in the island's western end, is 2,400 meters. Flores's interior and eastern parts are covered in heavy tropical forests. The southern coast, known as the "male sea," has rougher seas than the northern coast, the "female" sea.

The wet season is Nov.-April. Rainfall can be irregular, leading to occasionally serious water shortages. Then when it does rain, roads frequently wash out and there are fuel shortages. Temperatures in the rainy season are slightly lower than in the mid-dry season, when they reach 30° C, and seem higher due to lack of water. The dry season is May-Oct.; eastern Flores is generally drier than western Flores. Near Ruteng, it can be decidedly cool at elevations over 2,000 meters.

Flora And Fauna

Above 500-700 meters, quasi-cloud forests harbor many endemic species of flora: rattan, bamboo groves, mosses, and species of high-elevation trees. Near sea level, monsoon forests dominated by thorny bamboo are widespread. Except for coconut plantations, *ladang* areas are generally used in rotation every 5-15 years. When these gardens are abandoned, they become covered with shrubs, low trees, and grasses. One spectacular species of grass, *Rottoehia escalbata,* reaches 3.5 meters in height during the course of one wet season.

An unbroken fringe of tangled, buttress-like roots has formed an almost impenetrable barrier along some of the island's coasts. Behind this tidal zone are thickets inhabited by wild boar. Flores is also well known for its large numbers of domestic horses. These animals are small but sturdy, standing only 1.2 meters high at the shoulder, and weighing an average of 250 kg. Although difficult to find, Komodo dragons also inhabit isolated spots on the remote western and northwestern coasts of Flores.

HISTORY

Giant bats, reptiles, stegosaurs, and one species of elephant once roamed this island. Over thousands of years, waves of migrants have passed through Flores, including early Veddoids, and later Hindus from India. Melanesian artifacts are also found. With its rich stores of sandalwood, textiles, and slaves, the island in the 14th century fell under the economic and political aegis of the Majapahit Empire, which established coastal states. A Portuguese explorer christened the island Cabo de Flores or "Cape of Flowers" in the 16th century. Ironically, Flores has few flowers and was known to Javanese sailors as "Stone Island." There is speculation that the "flowers" referred to were not terrestrial flowers, but colorful marine corals seen through the clear waters.

The Portuguese included Flores as a stop on their way to the Spice Islands, establishing several trading bases. In 1566 they built a fort on Pulau Solor to the east of Flores to guard their trading interests on Timor. Dominican priests were subsequently sent to the eastern part of Flores, where they began converting the island's inhabitants to Catholicism. Today the people of these areas have Portuguese names, practice old Portuguese customs and dances, and even look Portuguese.

In the coastal towns, Florinese began converting to Islam in the 15th and 16th centuries. In the 1660s Gowanese Muslims from South Celebes invaded Ende; their influence in that area remains evident to this day.

In 1859, the Dutch took over Flores from the Portuguese. Under their administration Dutch Jesuit and Franciscan priests were brought in, and entry to all other Christian denominations refused. The Dutch crushed a native rebellion in 1907-08, but it was not until 1936 that they considered the island safe enough for transfer from military to civil control.

THE PEOPLE

With 1,350,000 people, Flores is Nusatenggara's most populous island. The island features an amazing racial mix: Bimanese, Sumbawanese, Makassarese, Bugis, Solorese, Sumbanese. Flores is in fact a sort of transition point for the Papuan and Malay races; you find both types here in abundance. Many of its inhabitants, particularly in the east and the interior, look more Papuan than Malay, with dark brown to almost black skin, heavy brows, wide flat noses, stocky builds, and black, often curly hair. Along coastal areas and in the west live ethnic Malays.

Many people describe themselves as campur (mixed), naming different island ethnicities—Sikka, Lio—as well as Bugis, Makassarese, and Malay in their paternities. Life in the interior is simple; most Florinese live by fishing, hunting, and simple agriculture revolving around palm and taro cultivation. The indigenous peoples of the deep island areas can still be defensively hostile.

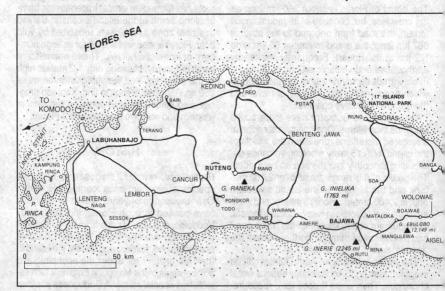

Agriculture

The daily routine is devoted to planting, harvesting, and protecting crops from rodents, while domesticated animals are allowed to forage for themselves. Rice is raised in the lowlands, maize and coffee are grown in the hilly districts, and coconut trees thrive along the coasts. Rice has been grown on this island only since the 1920s, from strains introduced by the Dutch from Vietnam. Before this, the Florinese were strictly hunters of small game and swidden farmers growing bananas and cassava. Even today these protein-deficient crops are still widely grown and account for many health problems among the Florinese.

The main farming method, slash-and-burn, exacerbates the island's erosion problem. Though the terrain is quite fertile, the markets in western Flores are impoverished because of ineffective use of resources, unreliable rainfall, and crop-destructive pests. Water can be as scarce here as on Timor; each year the people are near to famine because the food from last year's harvest is almost gone and the new crop isn't ready.

Religion

At least 85% of the population is Catholic, 11% or so Muslim, and the remainder animist. Christianity was brought to Flores by the Portuguese, who first established bases in Maumere and Sikka, which remain church administrative centers to this day. Today, Florinese traditions still closely adhere to the Portuguese Catholic heritage. Catholicism has flourished—Flores has the largest Catholic community in Indonesia, and the church has improved daily living conditions, initiated agricultural projects, and established health clinics. From the central towns to the most remote villages you find large, beautifully appointed concrete churches with lofty spires. One of the best shows in town is Sunday church service, when people arrive by boat, minibus, bicycle, and *bemo,* all dressed in their best.

But don't be deceived: not all Florinese wholeheartedly accept Western religion. Totemism and animism are widespread, and the island is steeped in witchcraft. Meet the *roh,* local shaman and healer, often an old woman. Megalithic cultures, animist belief systems, and ancestor spirit cults still persist in remote areas. Next to Nias Island off northwest Sumatra, Flores has the greatest collection of contemporary megaliths in Indonesia.

In round grass areas surrounded by stones, villagers dance for weddings, burials, and to celebrate planting and harvesting. Peculiar organic

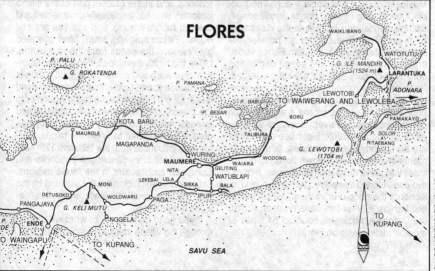

arrangements like scarecrows of dried branches and leaves are placed at certain sites to keep away evil spirits. Outside the village, stone pillars are set up to receive offerings to the gods and perpetuate the power of those who erected them; in eastern Flores an altar or totem pole is found in the village's largest traditional-style wooden hut (*kada*), in which idols and spirits are worshipped. You can still find Stonehenge-like tombs throughout Flores, and many people have modern tiled graves in their front yards.

The Missionaries

The missionaries are remarkable and unusual people who have to deal with bureaucrats, speak several dialects, meet payrolls, and accommodate local conditions. How you're treated by locals in a given area depends a lot on how the local pastor is regarded. The missions are quite strong and rich on Flores (everybody seems to work for them); in some areas you may have to depend on them for transportation and accommodations. The missionaries are an excellent source of information as well, and can be turned to for health problems. At nearly every mission there's at least a makeshift clinic, and in many cases the priest doubles as a medic.

Music

Musically, Flores is especially rich. The people love to sing hymns, dirges, work songs, satirical songs, and *pantun*. In the districts of Ende and Reo harvest songs are popular, the people of Manggaral in western Flores yodel, and in eastern Flores folk songs originating from 17th-century Portugal are still preserved. Percussion instruments are dominant—bamboo slit drums, small gongs, and simple xylophones. Hand-played drums are made from parchment stretched over the end of a hollow piece of coconut trunk. Florinese orchestras are particularly strong on flutes; other instruments include an end-blown bamboo instrument that plays deep thumping notes, a primitive one-stringed lute played with a bow, and idiochords (bamboo drum zithers), which sound like banjos. Earlier this century, Jaap Kunst, the Dutch musicologist, counted 54 types of musical instruments on Flores.

Dances

War-like dances are still practiced, and women perform graceful "round dances." In these, a solo dancer, man or woman, holds out a long scarf and dances with shuffling steps around a stone-edged grass area, hands fluttering and body gyrating while advancing, retreating, and encircling other dancers. Large groups also dance in a circle with arms linked, revolving counterclockwise.

In the *caci* whip duel, two dancers enter an open area, each with leather shields and painted wooden helmets tufted with horsehair, which protect the face like an uplifted welder's mask. They tie *sarung* over their pants, attach bells to their ankles, and wind towels around their arms to protect the skin from the blows. To the accompaniment of whistling, gongs, and drum beats, the dancers circle each other like cats, their snapping rawhide whips hissing through the air. Although they seldom show any sign of pain, each whips the other mercilessly. At intervals the men trade off weapons. *Caci* is now performed only at festivals in western Flores.

Crafts And Antiques

Exquisite cloths are handmade on Flores, but machine-spun imported cotton and synthetic dyes have made deep inroads. Locally grown cotton and organic dyes are still used in the hinterlands, and in the eastern part of the island intricately worked, fantastically ornamented and colored fabric, *sarung*, and scarves are still woven. Before spinning, small, hand-operated gins remove the seeds from the raw cotton. Using the highly developed, demanding, labor-intensive warp *ikat* method, the spun cotton is then bundled, tied tightly, and the pattern dyed into the warp threads before being wound onto the breastloom. Monochromatic, unpatterned threads, mostly store-bought and brightly colored, are then used to finish the textile. Portuguese influences from the 16th and 17th centuries are still in evidence: see peacocks and European architecture in the fabric designs. One can tell which clan did the weaving by the way the blue, reddish-brown, and yellow designs are arranged.

If you go to Sikka to shop, word will spread through the village that you're looking for cloth.

You'll be seated in front of a house and the women will show you *ikat* after *ikat*. A better place to buy cloth, with a greater selection and cheaper prices, is in the market of almost any village—women in the markets are more amenable to bargaining. In many places, such as in the Jopu and Sikka areas, cloth is sold open-ended so you can finish the piece yourself. In most other places, *ikat* cloth is made into *sarung*. Blankets show up occasionally, such as in Maumere's *pasar*. Don't wash organically dyed *ikat*: the indigo dye will turn your washbasin purple.

Antiques include old Venetian beads, probably brought by Arab traders, and greatly coveted by the people. Elephant tusks are still traded in eastern Flores. Orange or serrated red and blue Indian beads, from Hindu migrations centuries ago, are very rare and valuable. The Florinese believe they were given as gifts by mountaintop spirits (*nitu*).

GETTING THERE

By Air
Denpasar is the usual jumping-off point for flights to Ende (Rp196,000), Maumere (Rp181,000), Ruteng (Rp184,000), Labuhanbajo (Rp177,000), and Bajawa (Rp210,000). Scheduled Merpati flights also depart Sumbawa, Timor, Sumba, and Sulawesi to the six airstrips on the island. Now with the Darwin-Kupang connection established, flights from Kupang to Larantuka (Rp80,000), Maumere (Rp65,000), Ruteng (Rp121,000), and Ende (Rp85,000) have become especially popular.

To avoid the ferry crossing from Sumbawa to Labuhanbajo, take a Merpati flight from Bima to Labuhanbajo (Rp52,000), Ruteng, (Rp85,000), Bajawa (Rp85,000), Ende (Rp85,000), or Maumere (Rp104,000). Bouraq, serving only Maumere, flies from Denpasar (Rp181,000) and from Mataram via Denpasar (Rp224,000). There is no public transportation service to and from the Labuhanbajo, Ruteng, or Bajawa airports. Hire a *bemo,* or use your hotel's vehicle. Some make it part of the room price—these hotels send representatives to the airport to pick up prospective guests. Merpati and

Bouraq maintain offices in all the towns they service.

By Boat
From Sape, on Sumbawa, ferries depart daily except Friday for Labuhanbajo (Rp9000), and stop at Komodo en route. Also, regular Pelni and Perintis cargo ships call at Labuhanbajo, Reo, Ende, Maumere, and Larantuka. Ende is the island's largest port.

GETTING AROUND

By Air
Labuhanbajo, Ruteng, Bajawa, Ende, Maumere, and Larantuka have airstrips. Air travel might be your most convenient option during the wet season. Reservations are difficult to confirm; most locals seem to buy their air tickets on the morning of travel. Merpati handles most of the intraisland flights; Bouraq flies only into Maumere.

By Boat
Taking a boat between the coastal towns, from Labuhanbajo to Reo for example, is an attractive alternative, particularly in the wet season. Boats sail from Ende to Waingapu (Sumba) twice a week, and there's a daily boat from Ende to Nggela, sailing from Pelabuhan Ipi at around 0600. From Larantuka ferries and boats set sail for the Solor and Alor archipelagos and to Kupang.

By Road
The 667-km Trans-Flores Highway between Labuhanbajo and Waiklibang in the extreme northeast is paved almost all the way. The asphalt on some sections deteriorates rapidly due to harsh weather or less than adequate construction. In other areas, the road is under near continual repair due to landslides and washouts. It can still be hard going during the rainy season (Nov.-April). Buses seldom run through the night. There's regular transport from one end of the island to the other, with ample accommodations and restaurants in the major towns along the way. It takes about five days to cross Flores overland. No matter what the vehicle, all the rides in Flores are gorgeous.

WESTERN FLORES

LABUHANBAJO AND VICINITY

This tranquil fishing village, principal port of western Flores, is the favored departure point for Komodo and Sumbawa. It lies nestled into the hillside on a beautiful bay and offers great sunsets over the island-studded sea between Flores and Komodo. Quiet now, it's gearing up for growth—a new pier has recently been built to accommodate larger boats (a Pelni ship now makes a regular stop here); an extension to the airport runway is under construction, which will mean larger airplanes and more group travel; and new hotels, *losmen,* and eateries are appearing in eager anticipation. Most visitors come from June through August, when you'll find Labuhanbajo quite busy; the rest of the year is more relaxed.

Change your traveler's checks at **Bank Rakyat Indonesia,** the only bank in town. It changes only major currencies and four major traveler's checks; rates are low. Hours are Mon.-Fri. 0700-1230 and Saturday 0700-1100. The centrally located post office maintains regular hours, and the *wartel* (on the way to the airport) is open 24 hours a day. The old market in the center of town is still active on a daily basis, with a new market out past the police station open twice weekly.

Electricity is still not consistently available 24 hours a day; expect to spend some evenings by candlelight. There is still no local telephone service in town, but you can call long distance from the new *wartel.* Because of a new P.D.A.M. reservoir there is no longer a lack of fresh water during the dry season. A new irrigation system is under construction, and when completed will allow for rice growing in this area.

The airport is on a plateau, about two km from the center of town. The Merpati office is on the way, one half km before the airport. No public transport runs to the airport yet, but some accommodations will shuttle you into town for free. *Bemo* charge about Rp5000 from the airport to town. Anywhere in town, however, pay only Rp250 a ride.

Official information on Komodo Island is still difficult to come by. The Komodo National Park Office has but one brochure in English and the visitor's center near the harbor is only helpful in a general way. Try to find information at your hotel instead, or check the Perama travel office.

Visit the small harbor filled with native and Bugis *prahu.* Stilted Bajo fishermen's houses are built out over the water, with dugout canoes tied underneath. Forget about doing any snorkeling around the village as sewage and trash have killed the coral reefs, but there is good snorkeling and some nice shells in the sea gardens out in the bay. Charter a small catamaran for Rp15,000 and up for a half day to Pulau Badadari, although cheaper rates can be found by approaching individual fishermen at the harbor. Rent snorkeling equipment in Labuhanbajo from two dive shops. **Varanus Dive Shop** is located 100 meters up from the harbor; it runs dives to various locations including Sebolan, Sebayur, Rinca, and Komodo islands, where the skin diving and snorkeling are excellent. A two-tank dive with all equipment, transportation, guide, and lunch runs Rp135,000 (two-person minimum). Dives range up to Rp325,500 depending on location and type of boat. Similar dives are offered by the **Komodo Diving Resort** at the New Bajo Beach Hotel. The best beach around Labuhanbajo is Waecicu, but the snorkeling is second-rate due to reef destruction.

From Labuhanbajo, walk up the hill behind town for the sunset over the village and harbor, or visit **Batu Cermin** ("Mirror Cave"), in a hill about three km from town, on the far side of the runway from the air terminal. The road there leads around the end of the runway, through one village, and ends at a parking lot; from there a walk goes to the cave entrance. About 0900-1000 the sun shines through a crack in the cave roof, illuminating stones with shiny particles which cast sunbeams around the room. The cave is full of stalactites and stalagmites, and it's cool inside year-round. Bring a flashlight. From the rock outcrops above dangle long tree roots, some of which have wound their way into intricate patterns on the rock face. A petrified prehistoric forest, **Batu Fosil,** is 15 km south of town. Stone tree trunks lie in tangled broken heaps. People use the fossilized chunks of wood for stepping stones and walls. Go by hired *bemo* or motorcycle.

Accommodations And Food

A 10-minute walk from the harbor will bring you to the old standby **Bajo Beach Hotel.** Chinese-run, this tidy place has its own transportation, laundry service, tourist information, and a good restaurant. Rooms are Rp15,000 standard, Rp17,500 with fan and *mandi*; breakfast included. The same people now run a second establishment, two km south along the beach. This is the **New Bajo Beach Hotel and Cottages,** which promises to be the premier place in Labuhanbajo. Beyond the landscaped gardens are 16 rooms (four with a/c) and ten bungalows; the spacious rooms have showers and sit-down toilets. Rooms are Rp50,000 a/c and Rp30,000 with fan; bungalows run Rp20,000. All transportation around town is provided. The restaurant has a great sunset view, and a huge fish tank—choose your supper.

Across the street from the Bajo Beach Hotel is the **Mutiara Beach Hotel.** Set partly over the water, it's basic but adequate at Rp3500 s with shared *mandi* and Rp6000 d with fan and *mandi*. The restaurant has a good menu. Captained by Leonardo Kati, a reputed weasel, the hotel harbors one of Indonesia's most wonderful collection of *losmen* scalawags. Leo rents vehicles but will try to squeeze out every *rupiah*. Just a few steps toward the harbor, set on the hillside, is the new **Hotel Gardena.** Built in a simple beach-bungalow style, it has a pleasant setting. Good sunsets from the small restaurant. Rooms cost Rp8000 with shared *mandi* and Rp10,000 with private *mandi*; breakfast included. Another new place, 20 minutes on foot from the harbor, is **Hotel Wisata.** White tile, clean, somewhat sterile. It's not central and has no special location, but is good value for the money. Small restaurant attached. Rooms in the back are Rp7500 s and Rp10,000 d, while up front are rooms for Rp10,000 s and Rp15,000 d. Rates include fan, *mandi,* and breakfast.

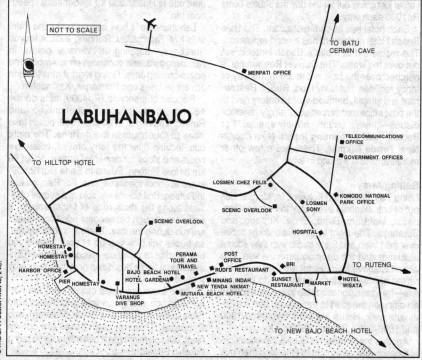

On the hill above town are two *losmen*. **Losmen Sony** is tattered but friendly and offers good food. Rates are Rp3500 s and Rp7000 d. Just up the hill toward the sunset lookout is **Losmen Chez Felix**. Rooms cost Rp4000-6000 s, Rp8000-10,000 d. A few other possibilities right near the harbor are the inexpensive **Homestay Gembira**, **Homestay Bahagia**, and **Losmen Pelangi**. The **Hilltop Hotel** overlooks the bay.

For those who want peace, quiet, and seclusion, the best place to stay is a short boat ride away. Good beach, great sunsets, no crowds, and no noise. A 20-minute shuttle-boat ride gets you to **Waecicu Beach Bungalows**; rooms for Rp6500 include three simple meals. Farther up the beach is the newer **Batu Gosok Cottages** where the rate is Rp12,500 with three meals. Each place has its own boat and will pick you up and drop you off at the Labuhanbajo pier; they meet the ferry from Sape/Komodo and buses from Ruteng. These shuttle boats are the only transportation to Waecicu and Batu Gosok. If you're just going out for the day the shuttle costs Rp1000 each way.

Each hotel has its own restaurant. The Bajo Beach Hotel restaurant has a good reputation. The restaurant at Mutiara Beach Hotel is set out over the water. The **Sunset Restaurant** is perched over the bay; not much in the way of fancy facilities, but tasty food. **Rudi's Restaurant** is a simple, bamboo-walled eatery next to the post office that serves surprisingly delicious dishes—there's usually a daily special. For Padang food try **Minang Indah**. Next door is **New Tenda Nikmat**. There are a few other restaurants and *warung* in town.

Getting Away

Using Twin Otters and Fokker 27s, Merpati flies out of Labuhanbajo every day to Ruteng, Denpasar, Mataram, Bima, Ende, Kupang, and Surabaya. The flight to Bima is unforgettable, over the Lintah and Sape straits with their scores of islands and the deep aquamarine sea. The airport is above town. Hotel reps will meet you on the runway and try to entice you to their hotels—free transportation into town. Merpati has an office on the road to the airport, about a 30-minute walk. Hours are Mon.-Sat. 0800-1300 and 1600-1700, Sunday 0800-1300.

Another travel option is to take the occasional local coaster overnight to Reo, and then bus to Ruteng. These *kapal motor* are more suitable for ponds than the open sea; if they lose their way in the dark, the journey could take as long as 16 hours—pray for calm weather and a safe arrival. From Labuhanbajo also are occasional boats to Ende, Maumere, and even Waingapu, Sumba. For small-boat departures and arrivals, ask at *kantor syahbandar* near the pier, where boat tickets are sold.

Ferries depart for Sape and stop at Komodo every day except Friday at 0800 (Rp9000 to Sape, Rp2800 to Komodo); bikes and motorbikes cost extra—no vehicles to Komodo. On this passage are very strong currents, especially between Padar and Rinca. You pass a hundred beautiful islands and may even see migrating whales. Approaching Komodo, see the Satalibo volcano rising out of the sea.

Boats to Komodo can be chartered from Labuhanbajo harbor. Ask your hotel manager to help find a reliable pilot. Prices range from Rp60,000 to Rp100,000 for a four-hour motorboat ride to Rp367,500 for a 45-minute speedboat trip.

Labuhanbajo is now connected by the Pelni ship KM *Tatamailau*. Running east, it leaves Surabaya, stopping at various points in Nusatenggara, and continues on to Ambon and points on Irian Jaya. Going west, it runs to north Javanese cities and Pontianak, Kalimantan.

Regular bus service (Rp4000) runs on the 137-km road between Labuhanbajo and Ruteng. Leaving at 0700 and 1500, buses take three to four hours in the daytime. The night bus, leaving after the ferry arrives, takes five hours and stops for dinner in Lembar, about 60 km before Ruteng. Buses to Ende (Rp12,500) leave at about the same time. For Reo, go first to Ruteng. Bus tickets are sold at a couple of offices along the main road of Labuhanbajo. If there are enough passengers additional buses will run during the day. There's no bus station, so buses will pick you up at your hotel if you buy a ticket in advance—recommended. Otherwise just flag a bus down as it makes its way around town.

There are a few ticket offices near the harbor entrance selling bus tickets for buses from Sape to Bima, Sumbawa Besar, Mataram, and Denpasar. These through buses are convenient, but you might get a better fare if you buy a ticket in Sape or Bima.

Perama Tour and Travel offers several excursions to Komodo, one from Labuhanbajo (Rp15,000) daily, and two that continue on from Komodo to Mataram (Rp75,000 and Rp80,000). Perhaps the most popular is a two-day trip that leaves Labuhanbajo twice a week and goes to Bidadori, Rinca, and on to Komodo before returning to Labuhanbajo for Rp30,000. The cost is Rp25,000 if you go only as far as Komodo and then transfer to one of the Perama boats going to Mataram, or if you take the public ferry from there.

Reo

Located two km from a rivermouth on the northwest coast, the port and pier are at Kedindi; pay Rp250 for a *bemo* from Reo. This little town has grown around a large Catholic mission. Not much to do here (the main attraction is you), but the people are friendly and there's a lovely beach five km from town. Local fishermen catch a certain small fish here that they sell to Taiwan for Rp40 per fish. The fish are transparent, have black eyes, and are very high in protein.

There's a post office in town. Stay at **Losmen Teluk Bayur,** Jl. Mesjit, tel. (0383) 17; Rp6000 s, Rp9000 d; the rooms on the second floor are more secluded. Or try **Nisang Nai**; Rp8000 s, breakfast and coffee included, located on the road to Kedindi outside of town. Eat at **Selera Anda** near the Gereja Katolik, or try the local *warung.* If you're arriving by boat from Labuhanbajo, a bus might be waiting at the docks to take you to Ruteng (Rp3500), a four-hour trip if weather permits. The road twists and climbs through the refreshing, cooler highlands, over the clouded mountains, past giant ferns, creepers, and huge bamboo thrusting up in thick growths.

On The Road To Ruteng

The road from Labuhanbajo to Ruteng is now sealed. Immediately upon leaving Labuhanbajo the road climbs over the shoulder of a thickly forested mountain. On the far side at **Rekas,** just south of the road, is the oldest church in the Manggarai district. The road drops down to the broad river plain at **Lembar,** an area of farming fields, few trees, and barren hillsides. Lembar, the usual rest stop for buses between Labuhanbajo and Ruteng, has a couple of Padang restaurants, shops, a post office, and

bank. The road once again goes up and over the side of a mountain and down to the broad agricultural plains of **Cancur.** Cancur has a post office, mission hospital, market, and shops. Near here are the **Tengku Lese Waterfall** and **Liang Bua Caves.** Once again up and over a mountain shoulder you enter the high and very pleasant area of Ruteng.

RUTENG

A cool, neat town set amidst the scenic hills of the Manggarai district, with broad streets, photogenic churches, and an airstrip that will put the fear of God in you. Ruteng is reachable by flights from Kupang (Rp121,000) and Denpasar (Rp184,000), with intermediate stops on the Denpasar route at Bima (Rp85,000) and Labuhanbajo (Rp42,000). This village is high (1,100 meters); you might need to don warm clothing by the late afternoon. Embroidered *sarung* are available in the *pasar.* The **post office** is on Jl. Baruk 6; poste restante letters are so scarce here they're tacked up in a display case. Just down the street in a traffic roundabout is a newly reconstructed former king's palace. Cash traveler's checks at **Bank Rakyat Indonesia**; open Mon.-Fri. 0700-1300, and Saturday until 1130; low rates. The town itself can be traversed in 20 minutes, so everything you need is within walking distance. *Bemo* around town charge a flat fee of Rp250.

Walk around Ruteng—excellent views of lush paddy fields, hills, mountains, and valleys. On a height overlooking the town sits the headquarters of the **Society of the Divine Word,** a German mission where Florinese are taught math, history, home economics, health care, and vocational skills like carpentry, blacksmithing, and masonry. The society, which started missionary activity on Flores in 1913, is also responsible for elementary and secondary schools throughout the island, as well as St. Rafael, the hospital and leper station (the best place to go if you're sick or injured in Ruteng). The society also tries to teach the people more efficient agricultural methods. This is a large market area; all around Ruteng are the productive mission farms that supply dairy products and meat. The missionaries are also a great source of local history and culture. The present Indonesian regime, however, considers missionaries a remnant of colonialism and is trying to force them out of the country.

Perhaps the best place to see the town, mountains, and surrounding agricultural fields, preferably in the early morning or late afternoon, is at **Golo Curu.** Walk north out of town past Losmen Agung I. Keep going straight over a vehicular bridge, where the road to Reo veers off to the left. About 200 meters farther on, past a church, a path leads off to the left through a residential area and zigzags up the hill, past stations of the cross, to the observation area at the top. Alternately, continue on from the church, past Chinese and Catholic cemeteries, and follow the path near the end of the road to the switchback path up the hill. From the top you can see the whole of Ruteng, its airstrip, terraced fields, and Gunung Raneka off to the southeast.

Traditional *caci* (whip fighting) dances can be arranged for about Rp75,000. They are usually performed only for a group. If a dance is being presented in town, try to latch onto a tour group for the show. Ask your hotel manager for information about performances and for help arranging to see a show.

Accommodations And Food

Well-run **Wisma Sindha,** Jl. Yos Sudarso 26, tel. (0383) 21197, has clean rooms for Rp7000-10,000 s and Rp13,000-18,000 d. Larger rooms cost Rp15,000 and Rp20,000, all with adjoining bathrooms. Excellent location—the bank is right across the street—with an expensive restaurant attached. **Losmen Agung II,** down an alley opposite the theater, is clean but not as well kept. Rooms with shared *mandi* run Rp6500 s and Rp8250, Rp13,000 d with *mandi* in room. On Jl.

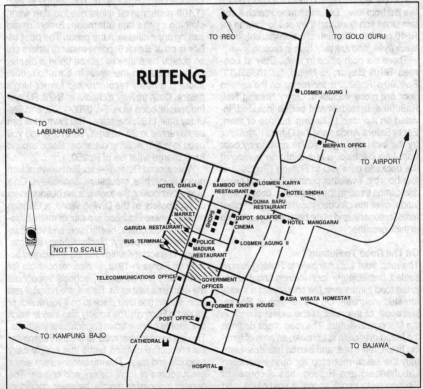

RUTENG

TO REO
TO GOLO CURU
TO LABUHANBAJO
LOSMEN AGUNG I
MERPATI OFFICE
TO AIRPORT
HOTEL DAHLIA
BAMBOO DEN RESTAURANT
LOSMEN KARYA
HOTEL SINDHA
DUNIA BARU RESTAURANT
MARKET
SHOPS
DEPOT SOLAFIDE
HOTEL MANGGARAI
CINEMA
GARUDA RESTAURANT
BUS TERMINAL
POLICE
MADURA RESTAURANT
LOSMEN AGUNG II
NOT TO SCALE
TELECOMMUNICATIONS OFFICE
GOVERNMENT OFFICES
ASIA WISATA HOMESTAY
FORMER KING'S HOUSE
TO KAMPUNG BAJO
POST OFFICE
CATHEDRAL
TO BAJAWA
HOSPITAL

© MOON PUBLICATIONS, INC.

Adi Sucepto 6 is the newer **Hotel Manggarai,** tel. 21008, with clean, open commons area, and large rooms for Rp7500 s and Rp15,000 d. Cheaper rooms in the back with shared *mandi.*

Hotel Dahlia, tel. 21377, on Jl. Kartini is the town's best. Breezy and clean, it has a restaurant with decent prices. Rooms: Rp30,000 VIP, Rp15,000 s and Rp20,000 d standard, and Rp7500 s and Rp20,000 d economy. Muslim-run **Losmen Karya,** Jl. Motangrua 34, charges Rp4000 s and Rp8000 d—down the street from three restaurants. A 20-minute walk north of center town gets you to **Losmen Agung I,** a pleasant place with large sitting room adjacent to rice paddies. Rooms cost Rp5000-8000 s and Rp7000-10,000 d; the VIP room is Rp25,000. Also 20 minutes from the city center, on the road to Ende, is the friendly, family-style **Asia Wisata Homestay,** which provides good tourist information. You eat with the family. Rooms run Rp3500 s and Rp7000 d.

Aside from the *losmen* restaurants, there are several good eateries in town. One of the best is the **Dunia Baru,** Jl. Motangrua 3, near the cinema, for Chinese and Indonesian. Two others next door are **Bamboo Den** and **Sari Bundo** for Padang-style food. Try **Depot Solafide** for delicious *gulai kambing* and *nasi campur ayam,* as well as cold beer. Pushcarts sell pastries on the street, and a number of other *rumah makan* and small *warung* occupy the bus terminal, including the **Garuda** and **Madura** restaurants. In the nearby market, buy all sorts of wonderful seasonal vegetables.

Getting Away

Merpati, tel. (0383) 21147, flies to Bima (Rp85,000), Denpasar (Rp184,000), Kupang (Rp121,000), Labuhanbajo (Rp42,000), and Surabaya (Rp262,000). Arrange a ride to the airport through your hotel—no public transportation exists yet. The flight to Labuhanbajo takes only 15 minutes. For the Merpati agent, only five minutes away, take a right coming out of Wisma Sindha, walk up two streets, take another right, then go down the little alley. The office is open 0730-1300 daily.

Most buses leave around 0700 for Labuhanbajo, Bajawa, and Ende; a few afternoon buses depart as well. Check times and make reservations through your hotel. The morning buses will pick you up at your door, except for buses to

Ende, which you must get at the bus station. Daily buses travel to Wairana (Rp2500) and on to Bajawa (Rp4200, six hours), as well as to Ende (Rp8500, 10 hours). Other destinations include Borong (Rp2000), Cancur (Rp600), Labuhanbajo (Rp4000), Bateng Jawa (Rp1600), Todo (Rp1250), and Reo (Rp3400). To points off the main highway, you might find trucks more numerous than buses.

VICINITY OF RUTENG

The Manggarai

A Malayan-Indonesian people, the Manggarai live in the western third of Flores, a mountainous land cut by deep valleys where rivers wend their way down to the north and south coasts. The Bimanese kingdom of East Sumbawa dominated the Manggarai region during the 17th century, establishing a principality in Cibal in the center of western Flores. But the catastrophic eruption of Sumbawa's Gunung Tambora so debilitated the kingdom that the Manggarai revolted in 1815. Backed by the Dutch, the Bimanese regained control over the Manggarai in 1851, only to be superseded by the Dutch in 1907. Catholic missionaries entered the area in 1913. Today the region is self-sufficient in rice and maize, and exports high-quality coffee, sturdy horses, and beef cattle. The Manggarai speak a language unintelligible to the Florinese.

Only in Todo and Pongkor, the former seats of two *rajas,* can you find many of the celebrated cone-like traditional houses of the Manggarai, built on piles one meter off the ground with no walls; a thatched roof and a central pillar rise six meters. At one time all the villages of the Manggarai had round houses but the Dutch discouraged their construction in favor of smaller, rectangular houses. Like the traditional houses, villages are also circular, with a central square and a large ceremonial *mbaru gendang* (drum house) occupied by a patrilineal clan and presided over by the *tuan tanah* (lord of the land).

In an open arena in the middle of the village stands a sacred tree surrounded by flat rocks (*kota*), where buffalo sacrifices used to take place. The Manggarai also cultivated round fields in which each clan received a pie-shaped section. Now most of the round houses, round villages, and round fields have disappeared.

You can now travel to **Todo,** 45 km southwest of Ruteng, and **Pangkor** by *bemo* (Rp1250) from Ruteng. Make this a day-trip. Ask to see some samples of local weaving, and the heirlooms of the former rulers.

One small vestige of round architecture survives near Ruteng in the village of **Kampung Ruteng,** three km from the center of Ruteng city. Take a *bemo* (Rp350) from in front of the market. In Kampung Ruteng, a round stone wall encircles the central tree and altar stones. To the side is a conical *rumah adat*; Rp1000 donation.

The volcano **Gunung Raneka** and the nearby peak Namparmos lie just southeast of Ruteng. The volcano erupted in late 1989 and continued to smoke into 1990. Walk the eight km up the zigzag road from Rabo or hire a sturdy four-wheel drive jeep to take you most of the way up. On top of Namparmos stands a tall telecommunications tower. Make this a day journey.

North of Ruteng, on a secondary road east of the road to Reo, is **Benteng Jawa** village. *Songket* weaving, considered the best of the Manggarai tradition, is produced here and in the nearby village of **Lambaleda.** These two villages are a rough and dusty 45 km (at least four hours one-way) from Ruteng.

Borong
Located on the south coast, Borong is three hours by bus from Ruteng. Tuesday is market day. There is only one *losmen* in town: **Losmen Sri Beach Inn,** not the cleanest and overpriced at Rp5000 per night. Eat across the street at **Minang Jaya.** Nice beach and small fishing boats in the tiny rivermouth harbor. Beautiful views all along the south coast.

Wairana
Fifty km southeast of Ruteng by road, Wairana is a little paradise in a small valley with streams running through it. Houses are built in Swiss-chalet style. The priest, Rene Dam, arrived in 1960 and built his house in a swamp where a man had been murdered. They say Rene's house shook for years. Market day is Saturday. No official accommodations are available as yet, but the local townspeople put up travelers. Superb hikes in this area; use Wairana as a base. The Dutch have established an irrigation project in the area. A bus regularly leaves Wairana around noon for Bajawa (Rp2500), or wait and see what else blows through. Buses to Ende are about Rp3500.

BAJAWA

The grueling ride from Ruteng to Bajawa is spectacular, although there is some grim evidence of slash-and-burn practices. Like Ruteng, this hill town is scenic and refreshingly cool. **Bank Rakyat Indonesia** changes major currencies and traveler's checks; all listed, poor rates. A few steps away are the post office and new *wartel.*

Don't miss Bajawa's **ancestral poles;** there are a few on Jl. Kartini and a whole group on the edge of town on the road to Ende. Called locally *ngadhu* for men and *bhaga* for women, these totems protect the town and fields against bad spirits (*polo*) and are said to be the resting place of the spirits of clan members.

Boxing matches are popular at area festivals; just the middle knuckle of a semi-clenched fist is used, with partners steering their fighter from behind like puppeteers. Another important event is the Catholic Maha Kudus Mass, in which a boisterous band of villagers leads a procession around town carrying the holy cross.

Bajawa makes a good base for excursions into surrounding villages such as Soa, Wago, Langa, and Bena. Gunung Inielika (1,763 meters) may or may not be climbable as it's still considered active, but Gunung Inerie (2,245 meters) can be climbed in three or four hours from the village of Bena.

Accommodations
Accommodations in Bajawa are grouped roughly in two areas—those below the town center, and those above the market. Many offer a hand-painted map of the area showing major sites. In the lower area on Jl. Ahmet Yani is **Hotel Korina,** tel. (0383) 21167, quiet, clean, and helpful in arranging transportation. Rooms, breakfast included, are Rp4000-10,000; evening meals also served. Down the street at the Y-intersection is **Losmen Dagalos.** Friendly family, but the traffic makes it a bit noisy. Rooms from Rp4000 include breakfast. Up the steps behind the Dagalos on Jl. Hayam Wuruk is the popular **Losmen Sunflower,** tel. 21236. Rooms here are Rp5000 s

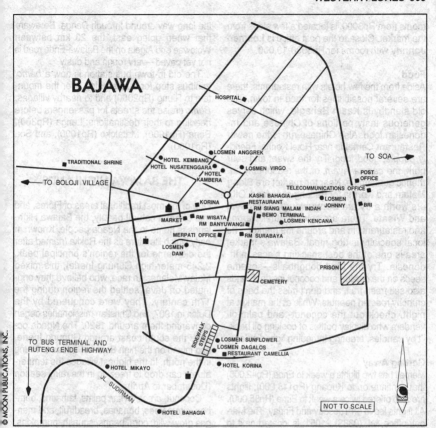

BAJAWA

HOSPITAL

LOSMEN ANGGREK

HOTEL KEMBANG
HOTEL NUSATENGGARA
LOSMEN VIRGO
HOTEL
KAMBERA

TRADITIONAL SHRINE

TO SOA

POST
OFFICE

TO BOLOJI VILLAGE

TELECOMMUNICATIONS OFFICE

KASHI BAHAGIA
RESTAURANT
KORINA
LOSMEN
JOHNNY
BRI
RM SIANG MALAM INDAH
MARKET
RM WISATA
BEMO TERMINAL
RM BANYUWANGI
LOSMEN KENCANA

MERPATI OFFICE
RM SURABAYA

LOSMEN
DAM

PRISON

CEMETERY

TO BUS TERMINAL AND
RUTENG / ENDE HIGHWAY

SIDEWALK
STEPS

LOSMEN SUNFLOWER
LOSMEN DAGALOS
RESTAURANT CAMELLIA

HOTEL MIKAYO

HOTEL KORINA

JL. SUDIRMAN

HOTEL BAHAGIA

NOT TO SCALE

© MOON PUBLICATIONS, INC.

and Rp8000 d with *mandi,* and Rp4000 s and Rp7000 d with shared *mandi.* Laundry service available. Although not large, the rooms in front offer a great view of Gunung Inerie. Down the hill along Jl. Sudirman are **Hotel Bahagia** and **Hotel Mikayo.**

Above the market are the somewhat fancier places. With its pretty flower garden, **Losmen Virgo,** tel. 21061, on Jl. Dwantoro seems the homiest. All rooms have *mandi;* Rp6500 s and Rp8000 d, including breakfast. Around the corner is **Hotel Kambera,** with a restaurant on the second floor. Rooms, including breakfast, are Rp3000-6000 s, and Rp6000-8000 d. Some *mandi* have Western toilets. The larger rooms in the front are okay, but the singles in back are cramped. Next door is **Hotel Nusatenggara,** a

pleasant place. Rooms are Rp3500-5000 s and Rp7500-9000 d, breakfast included. Kitty-corner is the more upscale **Hotel Anggrek,** with restaurant attached. All rooms except one have *mandi.* Rooms in front are Rp10,000 s and Rp15,000 d; in back Rp7500 s and Rp10,000 d. Room prices include breakfast. Down the street at Jl. El Tari 9 is **Hotel Kembara,** with perhaps the nicest rooms in town and a fine rose garden. Rooms are all Rp15,000, but the price may drop to Rp12,000 for single travelers. Hotels Virgo, Anggrek, and Kembara sometimes book tour groups, so it may not always be possible to find rooms at certain times.

Losmen Dam is on a dead-end alley behind the town's main church. The somewhat run-down and inexpensive **Hotel Kencana,** with rooms from Rp3000, is located a few steps from the market. Close to the post office is **Losmen Johnny** with rooms for Rp5000-10,000.

Food
Aside from the few hotels with restaurants, there are several possibilities for food in town. The old standby is **Kasih Bahagia**, which serves generous tasty portions of Chinese and Indonesian food. Also Chinese-run is the newer **Restaurant Camellia** near Hotel Korina. Friendly people, good food. Try the sweet and sour pork, the *cap cai ayam,* or the reasonably authentic guacamole. Near the market are **Siang Malam** and **Korina** for Padang-style food. Others worth a try are **Banyuwangi, Surabaya,** and **Wisata.** There are several other *warung* and restaurants in and around the market. The local specialty is dog meat. Bajawa's market area is one of the best snacking places in Indonesia. Try the fried doughballs—sesame seeds on the outside and coconut inside. Stands also sell fresh fruit, and don't miss the bags of crunchy roasted peanuts. While at the market at night, check out the coconut- and palm-oil venders who display bottles of cooking oil backlit by candles, creating intriguing light displays.

Getting Away
Merpati has two flights a week to Ende (Rp42,000) that continue on to Kupang (Rp118,000); flights are also offered twice a week to Bima (Rp85,000). All flights leave on Tuesday and Friday. The Merpati office, tel. (0383) 21051, is located next to the main market; office hours are 0800-1400 most days. The airport is inconveniently located 26 km north of Bajawa, three km outside the village of Soa. Merpati offers a shuttle service to the airport for Rp5000 pp; a charter vehicle costs about Rp20,000. Alternately, take a *bemo* (Rp1000) to Soa and walk the three km to the airport.

A new bus station at Watujaji is located two km outside of town (Rp300 by *bemo*) on the Ende-Ruteng highway. Frequent buses depart for Ende (Rp4000, four to five hours) throughout the day. Those to Ruteng (Rp4500, four to five hours) and Labuhanbajo (Rp8000, 8-10 hours) leave mostly in the morning beginning around 0700. There may also be an early morning bus (0400) to Labuhanbajo. Check the evening before in the market area where buses park for the night. There is also a daily bus to Riung (Rp4500), going

the long way around through Danga. Be aware that when going east, the 20 km between Wolowae and Aigela on the Bajawa-Ende road is not yet paved—very rough and dusty.

The old in-town bus station is now a *bemo/* minibus stop for trucks going over the mountain to Riung (Rp2000) and to nearby villages. *Bemo* cruise the streets for passengers before heading to their destinations: Langa (Rp300), Bena (Rp1000), Mataloko (Rp1000), and Soa (Rp1000).

THE BAJAWA HIGHLANDS

One of the most traditional areas of Flores, and one of great natural beauty, the Bajawa Highlands is home to the Ngada people. Known in early Dutch literature as the Rokka (named after the old name for the region's principal peak, 2,245-meter-high Gunung Inerie), this mixed Malay/Melanesian race, who believe they originated on Java, settled the region during the 17th century. They were conquered by the Dutch in 1907, and Christian missionaries began converting them around 1920. The Ngada occupy the south coast around Gunung Inerie, and inland on the high Bajawa Plateau to Riung in the north. In the highest villages the temperatures can drop to freezing in the rainy season (December to April).

Coconut, *areca, lontar,* palms, tamarind, bamboo, citrus trees, bananas, breadfruit, and mangos grow wild; corn, beans, squash, pumpkins, and other dry-land crops are raised. There is no irrigation system here so only small plots of rice are cultivated in a few riverine areas. The Ngada have domesticated the buffalo and horse, and keep pigs, chickens, and goats. They hunt from horses using bamboo spears and iron-tipped war lances. The Ngada practice ironsmithing and pottery, and dye cloth to make traditional *sarung* with yellow embroidery. This hand-woven cloth often has a black or dark blue background with simple animal designs in patterns. Some designs are tie-dyed.

Ngada villages consist of two rows of up to 50 closely spaced houses facing a central open square. Some of the villages have stone walls, pillars, megaliths, and ritual poles where buffalo sacrifices once took place. Their traditional raised wooden houses consist of living quarters

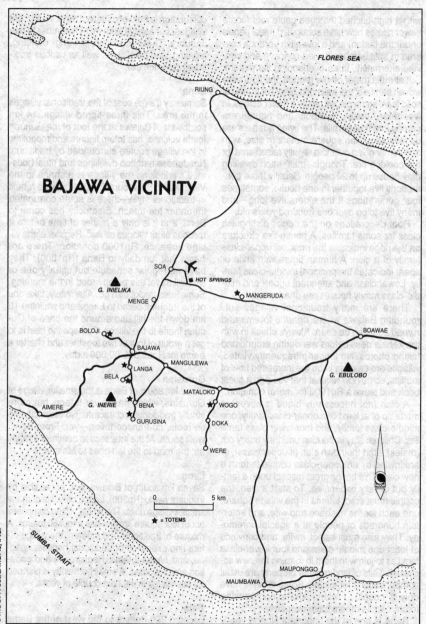

BAJAWA VICINITY

FLORES SEA

RIUNG

G. INIELIKA

SOA

HOT SPRINGS

MANGERUDA

MENGE

BOLOJI

BAJAWA

BOAWAE

LANGA

MANGULEWA

BELA

G. INERIE

MATALOKO

G. EBULOBO

BENA

WOGO

GURUSINA

DOKA

AIMERE

WERE

SUMBA STRAIT

0   5 km

★ = TOTEMS

MAUPONGGO

MAUMBAWA

© MOON PUBLICATIONS, INC.

with a high-pitched thatched gable roof (some newer homes now have corrugated metal panels under the thatch) and a low-pitch veranda covered in split bamboo turned concave and convex, alternately, in an overlapping tile pattern. Set about a meter off the ground, the floors are woven bamboo; the walls consist of flat panels of solid teak, some pieces nearly a meter across. In wealthier houses, symbols and figures are carved into these walls. The living quarters are usually about ten square meters in size, with one corner given over to a slightly raised area for the cooking fire. Though small, each dwelling may house up to 20 people. Usually three generations live together in one house, sometimes four generations if the elders live long—and many live to be over one hundred years old.

Roof decorations on the ridges distinguish class for some families. A house-like structure on the ridge indicates the principal upper-class family of a clan. A human figure with knife or spear indicates the principal middle-class family. Lower class and attendant upper- and middle-class family houses are unadorned.

There are many traditional villages surrounding Bajawa where *ngadhu* totems and *rumah adat* can be seen. Always check in with the *kepala desa* before wandering around and taking photos. No longer infrequently visited, villages are cashing in on the increased flow of tourists; some now request that you sign a guest book and leave a Rp1000 (or more) donation.

A clan (not necessarily blood relatives) is made up of at least one upper-class family, one middle-class family, and four lower class families. Children stay in the clan until they marry out (males), start their own clan (if upper class), or are invited by an upper-class couple to form a new clan. This brings great respect upon a family but is very expensive. To start a clan, the couple must erect totems in the village square, one each for the husband and wife, and entertain hundreds of people at a special ceremony. They also must select, invite, and convince at least one middle-class and four lower-class families to join with them in forming the new social unit. Gifts of land or other property are usual compensations for joining. Some villages have only a couple o clans and accompanying totems, while others have over sixty.

Reba is one of the important Ngada yearly celebrations. A new-year festivity, this multiday celebration is held on different days in different villages, but always from mid-December to late January. There is always singing, dancing, feasting, and frivolity, as well as various traditional ceremonies.

Bena

Some say it's the best of the traditional villages in the area. This three-tiered village, 14 km southeast of Bajawa at the foot of the Gunung Inerie volcano, has totem figures and megaliths in the village square surrounded by traditional Ngadanese bamboo dwellings and ritual houses. Overlooking the village is a shrine to the Virgin Mary. Bena burnt in 1961 but was rebuilt in traditional style—there is some corrugated tin under the thatch. Electricity has come to Bena, and it is only a matter of time before it reaches other villages as well. Register at the village entrance; Rp1000 donation. There are *bemo* that run daily to Bena (Rp1000). They have no regular schedule but usually one or two will travel this bumpy road in the morning. Sometimes trucks also go. Alternately, take one of the frequent *bemo* to Langa and walk the 10 km down the hill and around the base of Gunung Inerie to the village. Perhaps the best is to get a group of four or five together and charter a *bemo* for Rp60,000-80,000 a day.

Gurusina

Three km south of Bena is the smaller village of Gurusina, which has fewer totems but more strictly traditional architecture. No electricity, no tin roofs, no transportation—yet. From Bena, walk south. At the intersection continue straight on; the road to the left goes to Malanage.

Langa

Seven km south of Bajawa, and accessible by frequent *bemo* (Rp300), Langa consists of many smaller village units. The whole village comprises about four square km and has about 60 totems. A mixture of traditional and modern, the village offers fine examples of traditional houses, *ngadhu,* and *bhaga* totems. Registration and donation are requested. A small homestay is planned for this village in the next couple of years.

Bela

Located 300 meters to the west of the Bema road, about two km south of Langa, Bela is a

adat *house*
under construction

small, very traditional village that seems little affected by modernization. See women weaving on the verandas of the village houses. Behind Bela is a high promontory from where you can get a good view of this area and the sea. Be careful, though, as it's steep and has no well-worn paths.

Wogo

From Bajawa, take a *bemo* (Rp500) to Mataloko; from there it's a 10-15 minute walk south to Wogo (Wogo Baru). Here, too, are very good examples of *ngadhu* and *bhaga*. Wogo was moved some decades ago, and the megalith totems are still found abandoned at the old Wogo (Wogo Lama) site. To see them in their disarray, walk about one km farther down the road and then a couple of hundred meters off the road to the east. There's a market in Wogo on Saturday.

Boloji And Mangeruda

Other Ngadanese villages also have sites worth seeing. About an hour's walk west of Bajawa in Boloji are more fine *ngadhu* and *bhaga*. The village of Mangeruda also has totems and altars.

Soa

A subdistrict where the society of the Soa live, numbering about 6,000. From Soa you have wonderful views of the volcanic peaks in the entire Ngada region. In the not so distant past, yearly ritual deer hunts took place in this district, at which time the teeth of pubescent girls were filed

and blackened and boys were circumcised. After the deer was slain, the young girls would smear themselves with blood to increase their fertility. Even today, men hunt deer with spears. Many *bemo* and trucks travel down from Bajawa (Rp1000, 23 km, 45 minutes) to Soa's big market on Wednesday. Soa village is built around a huge amphitheater with tiers of great megaliths forming walls at different levels. Needle-like stones, with flatter stones on top serving as altars, are placed around the amphitheater. In the center stands a *peo* totem pole shaped like a doll. Soa has a fine *rumah adat*.

Guides And Tours

In Bajawa, many people will offer to guide you to the traditional villages in the Ngada region. Some are opportunists, while others are real lovers of the area, grew up here, and genuinely want to show you around. Ask around, and ask questions about the person and his tie to the area before hiring him. Two reputable guides are Lucas and Damianus. Lucas leads groups mainly to Langa, his home, for a full day (Rp7000-10,000 pp for a group of four to eight). Fluent in English, he has some command of German and Japanese. Contact him at Losmen Sunflower in the morning. Damianus takes small groups to Gurusina, his home town, as well as Bena, Wogo, and the hot springs near Soa (Rp80,000 for a group of eight). Contact him at Losmen Virgo. Both make all travel arrangements, provide some food, are founts of knowledge, and will tailor a tour to your needs.

Hot Spring

From the intersection in Soa, some two km from the Bajawa-Riung highway, walk about one hour (four km), gradually downhill to the east, to a left-hand turnoff (you pass the airport on the way). Two hundred meters down this road is the hot spring entrance (Rp100). As big as a backyard swimming pool and deep enough to sit in, the spring bubbles up through fissures in the earth and is comfortably hot. The water flows out and into the river about 30 meters away so you have your choice of hot or cold bath. The spring itself is clear and clean and shaded by large overhanging trees. A good spot for a soak and a picnic. There is regular transportation to Soa, mostly in the morning with return *bemo* and trucks into the late afternoon. Some *bemo* even run past the hot springs on the way to Mangeruda, but the schedule is flexible and untrustworthy. If you can gather a few friends and charter a *bemo*, go in the late afternoon when the weather is cooler and the bath more invigorating.

Gunung Inerie

An extinct volcano, Gunung Inerie can be climbed in about three hours. The trail starts just outside the village of Bena and goes up quite steeply to the top—spectacular views. Attempt this climb only in the dry season. Start early in the morning, as the mountain usually clouds over about midday. Stay the night in Bena and head up by daybreak. For guides, ask for Hermanus or others in the village

(Rp8000-10,000). Some guides from Bajawa will take you to the top and arrange transportation early from Bajawa (Rp22,500). Ask at Hotel Nusatenggara. Start at 0400.

Gunung Inielike is not climbable as it is very steep and still semi-active. Deeply etched Gunung Ebulobo, near Boawae, can be climbed, however, from a number of villages at the base of its northern slope.

Riung

Buses leave Bajawa's station every day to Riung (Rp4500, 125 km), going the long way around through Danga. Some days, buses and/or trucks run over the mountains to Riung (Rp2000), but this route is problematic as there is ongoing road construction. The many islands off the north coast near Riung make up **17 Island National Park,** home to several dozen varieties of coral (some of Nusatenggara's best), countless species of fish (great snorkeling), thousands of flying fox bats, and illusive, multicolored monitor lizards that might be seen on the clifftops from out at sea. Unlike the usual gray color that you see on Komodo, the dragons here are black, with shades of yellow, red, brown, blue—some with faint stripes. They're said to be the largest dragons found anywhere. Charter a boat to these islands for Rp35,000-40,000 a day. Coastal boats occasionally run from Riung to Maumere and Reo. Ask around in town for a reputable captain. A couple of accommodations have opened in the last few years. Try **Hotel Florida** or **Hotel Tamri.**

EASTERN FLORES

ENDE

Once an important port, administrative seat of the eastern archipelago, and the domain of a *raja*, Ende is now the capital of Flores, and many government offices are found here. Local aristocratic families trace their ancestry back to the Majapahit Empire. Ende was once a favorite city of the Dutch; old villas still stand on the hills around the cathedral. Ende makes a good base for exploring the *ikat* weaving villages of Jopu and Nggela, or a stopover on the road to Keli Mutu volcano. Also, a lot of *sarung* weaving

and dyeing goes on close to the market, and a new administrative district is located up from the airport.

Surrounded by steep volcanic peaks, Ende has a beautiful setting. To the west, across wide and gorgeous Ende Bay, rises Gunung Ebulobo. Wonderful sunsets appear over Pulau Ende, which sits in the middle of the bay. Gunung Ipi, still somewhat active, forms the short peninsula to the south of city center. Black-sand beaches stretch both east and west.

There is still evidence of the 1992 earthquake that struck eastern Flores. Piles of rubble lie where buildings once stood, many structures

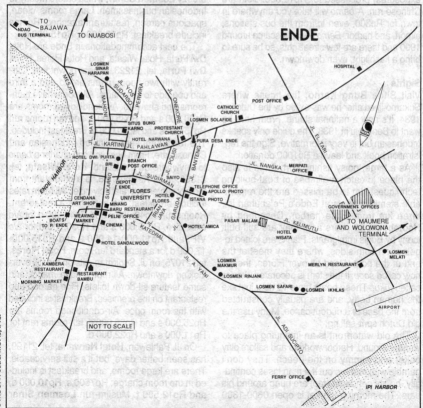

have big cracks in their walls, and parts of walls and roofs are missing. Limited reconstruction has taken place. Several hundred people were killed here during the quake.

Bank Rakyat Indonesia, temporarily located at the Dwi Putra Hotel, changes about a dozen major currencies, offering better rates than anywhere else on Flores. The new post office on Jl. Basuki Rahmat is open during regular business hours and offers stamps, international parcel service, and poste restante. Take a *bemo,* as it's inconveniently located up the hill on the edge of town. The old post office, now a branch office, is just around the corner from Flores University. The telephone office, still damaged, is open 24 hours a day. Get photo supplies at either Istana or Apollo photo shops, only a few steps away. Near complete photo service, with Fuji color slides (36 exposures) processed for Rp12,000. Both are Chinese run. A *bemo* will take you anywhere in town for Rp300, even to/from the bus stations, airport, and harbor. *Bemo* become scarce around 1900 and there are few streetlights, so be sure to bring a flashlight, even downtown.

Sights

Visit **Situs Bung Karno,** the house where Sukarno lived after he was exiled by the Dutch in 1934; it's now a national shrine. From here he went to Bengkulu in 1938. The guide only speaks Indonesian but is very informative. Sign the registration book and leave a Rp1000 donation.

As a large, noisy fishing port, Ende is also the place to catch a glimpse of boat-building techniques. Not to be missed are the remarkable stemless boats at Ende's Pelabuhan Ipi, three km from Ende harbor. Described by Nooteboom 50 years ago, they are still built today by Bugis immigrants. Planks are joined together on both sides, where they meet at the end of the boat. Used all over Flores, they're now called *sope;* if the stem is decorated, they're called *jukut.* These boats have 12 ribs, just like the human body, and are usually constructed from the base of a dugout canoe. Many use the old Dutch sprit-sail rig.

The old waterfront is an intriguing place to wander around. Harbor workers and sailors play poker and rummy on the beach. They don't gamble with money, but if a man loses continually, heavy pendants (*teo*) are hung around his ears. The morning market is open 0600-1300 (lots of fish), the night market 1600-2100 (food and clothing). Go after dark to the night market. Candlelight glows everywhere—very romantic. Incredible vegetables and fruits.

Accommodations

There are many *losmen* in Ende. **Losmen Ikhlas,** tel. (0383) 21695, on Jl. A. Yani is convenient and perhaps the best place for travelers. The walls are covered with maps, and the place offers information on sights and bus, ferry, and air schedules. It's conveniently located near the airport and Ipi harbor, and on a major *bemo* route for connections to both bus stations. Rooms cost Rp4500-10,000 s, Rp6000-15,000 d, Rp10,000-18,000 t. Rates do not include breakfast, but there's a decent kitchen. Laundry service available. Two doors away is open and breezy **Losmen Safari,** which caters mostly to Indonesian businessmen. Large rooms, clean, spacious garden, restaurant attached. Rooms include breakfast: Rp10,000 s, Rp15,000 d.

The best accommodations in Ende are Hotel Dwi Purta, Hotel Wisata, and Hotel Flores. **Hotel Dwi Purta,** tel. 21223, is near downtown. Currently with two floors, plans are to add a third and upgrade to star status. All rooms have bathrooms and showers. Air-conditioned rooms are Rp30,000 s and Rp35,000 d, and fan rooms run Rp15,000 s and Rp20,000 d. Breakfast included. The restaurant serves limited Indonesian and Chinese fare. From here you can charter a *bemo* to anywhere on the island. **Hotel Wisata,** tel. 21368, at Jl. Kelimutu 68, is a bit distant from the city center, but relatively quiet. All room rates include breakfast; the hotel has a restaurant. Rooms run Rp40,000 s and Rp45,000 d for a/c executive, Rp25,000 s and Rp30,000 d for a/c VIP, and Rp11,000-14,000 s and Rp15,000-17,000 d for a standard fan room. **Hotel Flores,** tel. 21075, on Jl. Sudirman, sits on the hill overlooking downtown. All rooms have *mandi,* and some feature sit-down toilets. Fine garden and restaurant on the premises. Breakfast is included with the room price. Air-conditioned rooms are Rp25,000 s and Rp35,000 d, fan rooms rent for Rp11,000 s and Rp22,000 d.

On Jl. Pahlawan, **Hotel Narwana,** tel. 21199, has seen better days, but it's still serviceable. There are large rooms, and breakfast is included in the room charge: Rp7500 s, Rp10,000 d, and Rp12,500 t. Muslim-run **Losmen Sinar**

Harapan, tel. 21436, on Jl. Mahoni is the closest to the Ndao bus terminal. Rooms run Rp5000 s and Rp10,000 d. Near the morning market on Jl. Kemakmuran, and the place with the best old-town setting, is the Chinese-run **Hotel Sandalwood,** tel. 21015. It's near a mosque and noisy in the early morning. Rooms run Rp5000 s and Rp10,000 d. At the entrance of the road to the airport is the somewhat ramshackle **Losmen Melati;** no restaurant, all rooms with *mandi,* Rp6600 s and Rp12,100 d. Somewhat dark, and with small rooms, is **Hotel Amica** on Jl. Garuda. Rooms Rp7000 s and Rp12,000 d include breakfast. If you're in a bind or simply want the cheapest place in town, try **Losmen Makmur** or **Losmen Rinjani,** next door to each other on Jl. A. Yani and near a mosque. Rooms in the Rp3500-8000 range.

Food

The better accommodations all have in-house restaurants. Aside from these, **Depot Ende** has a good reputation but slow service. In addition to the ordinary but tasty Indonesian fare, you'll find unusual items such as quail, passion fruit juice, *lassi* yogurt, and ice cream. **Depot Flores** at Hotel Flores serves both Indonesian and Chinese food. Both **Bambu,** near the morning market, and **Merlyn,** near Losmen Ikhlas, have Indonesian, Chinese, and seafood, as well as cold beer. For spicy Padang-style try **Saiyo** near Hotel Flores, **Minang Baru** near Ende harbor, or **Kambera,** also near the morning market.

Crafts

Check *pasar pagi* (morning market) near the waterfront for *sarung* and *ikat* from the Lio (northeast) and Jopu (east) areas of Ende: thin, stark black and yellow, with triangular motifs made up of continuous lines, like a maze. In Manokwari, Irian Jaya, where they're used as a bride price, Lio cloths fetch up to Rp250,000. Prices are lower and quality higher for *ikat* in the villages of Jopu, Nduria, Wolonjita, and Nggela. Yet in nearly every village in the area, even on the back streets of Ende, you can find weaving.

Getting Away

Landings terrify at Ende's paved, well-equipped, but windy airstrip. Wind whips across the bottleneck of a promontory formed by a small outlying volcano; you can see the palm heads toss as you come down. Merpati flies to Denpasar (Rp196,000) every day, stopping at Bajawa (Rp42,000), Bima (Rp85,000), Labuhanbajo (Rp97,000), and/or Mataram on different days of the week. This flight to Bali takes just two hours compared to two weeks on an overland journey. There's also a daily flight to Kupang (Rp85,000). The Merpati office is on Jl. Nangka, open Monday, Tuesday, Thursday, and Friday 0800-1300 and 1600-1700, Sunday and holidays 1000-1200, closed on Wednesday and Saturday. Get a *bemo* (Rp300) to the airport entrance; from there it's only a three-minute walk to the terminal. *Bemo* that wait at the terminal ask Rp1000-2000 for a ride to anywhere in town. That's convenient, but if you want to pay the usual fare, walk the 100 meters out to the roundabout and flag down any *bemo* going in your direction.

Ende has two harbors. The older is **Ende harbor,** the newer **Ipi harbor.** Most boat traffic now goes from Ipi harbor, with its long pier and deep anchorage. The KM *Kelimutu* connects Ende with Waingapu, Kupang, Dili, Kalabahi, Maumere, Makassar, Bima, Lembar, and Surabaya, departing once every two weeks in either direction. The Pelni office is located on the corner of Jl. Katedral up from the Ende harbor and opens at 0700.

The ASDP's regular passenger/cargo ferry KMP *Ile Mandiri* makes a circuit connecting Ende with Waingapu, Seba on Savu, and Kupang. Its route is as follows: Monday at 1400, Kupang to Ende, 16 hours; Tuesday at 1900, Ende to Waingapu, 12 hours; Wednesday at 1600, Waingapu to Seba, 13 hours; Thursday at 1600, Seba to Waingapu, 13 hours; Friday at 1900, Waingapu to Ende, 12 hours; and Saturday at 1300, Ende to Kupang, 16 hours. No departures on Sunday. Fares are: Ende to Kupang first class Rp21,300, economy Rp16,700; Ende to Waingapu first class Rp15,800, economy Rp11,200; and Waingapu to Seba Rp12,300. The ferry office is at the Ipi harbor and is open 0700-1400.

From the beach at Ipi harbor, a small motorboat makes a run every morning at about 0600-0700 for Nggela (Rp3000). It may pick up more passengers farther down the beach. Other boats may leave Ipi and Ende harbors for points on Flores, but there is no regular schedule. Check with the harbormaster's office for information.

Most *bemo* in town run past city-center Ende harbor. *Bemo* to Ipi harbor charge Rp300 and run down the dead-end road to the pier. Ipi Harbor is about three km from Ende harbor and less than one km from Losmen Ikhlas.

Ende has two bus terminals. **Ndao bus terminal** is located on the extreme west end of town for buses going to the west; **Wolowana bus terminal** is on the east end of town for buses to the east. From Ndao, buses leave at around 0700 for Labuhanbajo (Rp12,500, 14 hours), Ruteng (Rp8500, 10 hours), and Bajawa (Rp4000, four hours); a second bus to Bajawa leaves around 1200. Also from this station are buses to Aimere, Riung, and M'bai. From Wolowana many daily buses run until 1400 to Moni (Rp2000, two hours); the last bus to Maumere (Rp5000, six hours) leaves at 1900. The 148-km trip to Maumere is spectacular: Gunung Keli Mutu is almost halfway between Ende and Maumere. Buses also leave from Wolowana Terminal for Larantuka (Rp7500, 10 hours), Wolowaru (Rp2000), Jopu, (Rp2200), Wolojita (Rp2200), and once a day in the early morning for Nggela (Rp2500).

Vicinity Of Ende

Walk out around **Gunung Ipi,** the squat peak that creates the peninsula bulging out from Ende city. Start from either Ipi or Ende harbor. It's possible to climb Gunung Meja, which is the lower peak on this peninsula, from the southern side.

Ndano is a weaving village about four km (and Rp300 *bemo* ride) east of Ende on the coastal lowlands. The traditional village of **Wolotopo** is also a weaving village located about five km outside the city on a different road. No *bemo* run this bad track, so you must walk. From any spot on this littoral lowland are good views of Gunung Meja, Gunung Ipi, and the east side of Ende with its sheer mountain backdrop.

Three or four times a day *bemo* (Rp500) make their way to **Nuabosi,** from where you can enjoy your best views of Ende. Nuabosi is situated at the top of a mountain, in what appears to be an old caldera. Villagers harvest corn, tapioca, coffee, cloves, coconuts, vegetables, avocado, banana, papaya, beans, and vanilla, all in small quantities. On the highest point of the mountain ridge over the village is a *rumah adat,* occupied until the earthquake of 1992 when the family moved down the hill. The old house has a tin roof but is otherwise of traditional design: tall, steep-pitch roof, woven bamboo walls, bamboo and wood plank floors. To the front of the *rumah adat* is an altar and two graves. There are simple post carvings inside representing items of importance to the family: a man on a horse, a gong, grandmother figure, water buffalo, chicken, coconut tree, palm tree, ear of corn, a scorpion. There's also a stylized male figure carved into the threshold of the building's main doorway. About 200 meters down the ridge are the foundation remains of a colonial Dutch house, from where you get a great eagle-eye view of Ende. Soon there will be a tall telecommunications tower half a kilometer farther down the ridge that will partially mar this view. There are good panoramas of all of Ende Bay from the road up to Nuabosi.

About three km up this road from Ende at **Woloare** you'll find a natural spring that gushes from the ground around the roots of a huge tree. It's a five-minute walk from the main road. **Pura Puseh,** a Balinese temple, has been built here. To the west of Woloware, perched on a promontory with good views over Ende Bay, is **Kalibari.**

Thirteen km west toward Bajawa is **Nanganesa,** a good picnic place. Twelve km farther on is **Pangajawa Beach,** full of light green rocks sorted according to size and coloration and exported to Europe and Japan.

Halfway to Moni is **Detusoko,** a Catholic religious retreat. Go by *bemo* or bus (Rp1000). This village suffered a good deal of damage in the '92 quake but is rebuilding. It's a peaceful rest stop; walk in the fields, look around town, meditate. Across the valley on the distant ridge are three crosses representing Calvary. Stay at **Wisma St. Fransiskus.** Rooms are Rp25,000 pp; this includes a simple but neat room, mosquito net, three meals a day, and morning and afternoon tea and snacks.

The road east of Ende to Moni is spectacular. Sections are cut into precipitously steep and twisting valleys with sheer drops to the river below. This section suffered much damage from the earthquake and is being repaired. Though still quite bad in places, it's passable. Several new villages have been set up along this road to house people whose villages were destroyed. Roadside markets along the way.

KELI MUTU

Keli Mutu volcano is one of the more other-worldly sights in all of Indonesia. There are three lakes atop this extinct volcano, two separated by a low ridge and the third several hundred meters distant, all with different colored waters. The colors are in constant flux as the lakes leach minerals from the earth, which dissolve and color the water. Two of the lakes are now different shades of green, one dark and the other milky white; the third is nearly black. From the viewpoint, you can see the complex's highest peak (1,613 meters) and the even higher Keli Bara (1,731 meters) to the south. Rather dangerous trails run along the crater rims, from where the sides drop precipitously into the water. Be careful. Keli Mutu gets quite a few foreign tourists per year, but it's worth it even if there's a crowd. Dry season is April-October.

From Ende or Maumere, take the bus to Moni, from where you start climbing the volcano. It's best to stay the night in Moni and go to the top for sunrise, but it's possible to do Keli Mutu and get back to Ende the same day. On Sunday, busloads of local tourists assault the mountain, most of them directly from Ende. You might get a ride, but they often don't get to the top until around 1100, by which time the mountain has clouded over and there isn't much to see. Or follow Pak Harto's example and go by helicopter; a landing pad was cleared near the top for a visit he made in 1985.

The Climb

It's important to climb the volcano early in the morning, before clouds roll in, though some say the light is better for photography in the late afternoon if the weather is clear. To view the colored lakes by morning light, get up at 0200 and walk the whole 13 km to the top. Start about one km (15-minute walk) out of Moni toward Ende, just past Sao Ria Wisata, where an entrance arch has been set up over the road. The climb will take three to four hours, so carry water, snacks, and especially a flashlight. Gorgeous stars if there's no moon; follow the Southern Cross up to the crater. People in this region keep lamps burning in their houses at night to frighten the spirits (and calm themselves).

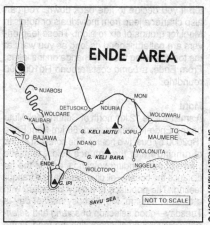

The mountain is steep, but the ascent isn't. Walking along the asphalted road is not difficult, even in the dark. About halfway up the mountain, at km six, is the PHPA checkpoint; the entrance fee is Rp400. From the checkpoint it's about six km to the top. You should reach the top around 0600 for sunrise.

There's a shortcut (*jalan potong*) from Moni that starts about one half km out of town toward the park road entrance. At the bottom of this trail is a waterfall; the top end is at the park checkpoint. Go in daylight to check out the shortcut, and keep an eye out for the wonderful green parrots in the trees. This way is steep and slippery and involves walking through one small gorge past a waterfall, crossing a narrow river, and passing through three small *kampung* where kids will hassle you for pens or candy. When it's raining, the shortcut should be avoided. If starting before sunrise, you might feel more comfortable sticking to the main road (*jalan raya*) on the way up and coming down by way of the shortcut (two hours from the top).

Alternatively, a truck to the top (Rp3000 pp one-way) leaves Moni around 0400, getting you there in time for sunrise. The truck leaves the top at 0700 for the return trip to Moni; either pay again to ride down, or walk. The guys on the truck sell coffee, tea, donuts, and pancakes at the top, and there may be some small vendors along the road on the way down during the day. Buy your ticket for the truck ride from your homestay; pay the driver for a return ticket at the top if you decide to ride back down. You can also charter a jeep from individuals or hotels in Moni for groups of six to eight. These jeep drivers are patient; spend as long as you want at the top, watching the light change on the lakes. From Ende, a *bemo* costs around Rp100,000 roundtrip.

Moni

A small village 12 km north of Gunung Keli Mutu on the Ende-Maumere road, 66 km from Ende (Rp2000 by bus, two hours). The constant sound of running water through rice fields, fantastic views of surrounding volcanos, and in the far distance the ocean—all give this village a tranquil feeling. The populace is mostly Christian, with a dash of Muslim. Moni's busy market day is Tuesday—good selection of *sarung* and *selendang*. Several small shops line the road, some selling *ikat*. A traditional dance is performed every evening at 2000 at the *rumah adat* (Rp2500 pp).

There are some bungalows made of native materials and a restaurant near the entrance to the road to Keli Mutu, with a nice view of the valley in which Moni is nestled. It's called **Sao Ria Wisata,** and rooms are Rp16,000 including breakfast—a good place for groups to stay. **Homestay Amina Moe** is Rp5000 pp including breakfast; great dinner. **Homestay Daniel** is a good place to stay and has a detailed map of the Keli Mutu climb, including landmarks for the shortcut. **Losmen Friendly,** Rp3000 pp with no breakfast, is not the cleanest place but the people are friendly. Other homestays include **Regal Jaya, Nusa Bunga,** and **John,** all in the Rp5000-8000 range. Behind Losmen Friendly is **Maria Homestay** (no sign). Here the four rooms are very basic (mosquito nets) but all right for a night; rates of Rp5000 s and Rp8000 d include a simple breakfast. The real draw here is Maria's cooking. She does full-blown Indonesian buffet meals only for her guests, Rp2500 for dinner. You always get delicious food and lots of it. If you choose not to eat at your homestay, try the restaurants at Sao Ria Wisata, **Moni Indah** or **Restaurant Ankermi.** The latter usually has a special every night.

Rumor has it there's a government plan to construct a star-rated hotel in Moni within five years to attract more affluent visitors. Nothing has been done about it yet, but if it happens the character of the village will change markedly.

Before the hotel the road system in this part of the island would have to be improved dramatically. If that happens, prepare for major changes.

THE WOLOWARU AREA

Wolowaru

Twelve km east of Moni on the road to Maumere. As you're coming into town, notice the cluster of old-style *rumah adat* with their high, steeply pitched roofs. **Losmen Keli Mutu** has some decent rooms starting at about Rp6000. Next door, **Jawa Timur** serves plain but filling Indonesian food. Also try **Andala** for Padang-style food. Buy blankets at Wolowaru's market on Saturday.

Daily buses depart in the mornings from Wolowaru to Ende (Rp2500) and Maumere (Rp3000); wait at Jawa Timur, where all the bus and *bemo* drivers stop to eat. Or flag down a bus or truck going east or west out front on the main road. Wolowaru is the start of the road south to Jopu, Wolonjita, and Nggela. Jopu is an easy five km walk south. Buses and trucks run direct to Jopu, Wolonjita, and once a day to Nggela from Ende. Wolonjita is four km beyond Jopu, Nggela another five km south of Wolonjita. Try the entire 20-km-round-trip walking tour (Wolowaru-Wolonjita) or bus to Nggela and walk up from there. Yet another alternative is to take the daily 0600-0700 boat from Ende's Pelabuhan Ipi to Nggela (Rp3000, two hours), then walk up through Wolonjita and Jopu to Wolowaru.

Jopu

An old-style Florinese village with steep-roofed *adat* houses and a distinctive Flemish-looking church, Jopu lies secluded in a valley with magnificent volcanos on all sides. There's also a small hospital here. Some of the best weaving in central Flores comes from Jopu and the surrounding six coastal villages. Beautiful, tapestry-like *sarung ikat* and other richly dyed fabrics; all you have to do is unthread the seam and you have a wall hanging. *Selendang* shawls for carrying *barang,* for warmth, and at one time for wrapping the dead are also for sale. The going rate for a reasonable-quality shawl is Rp20,000-25,000, but for the *ikat* the price can go as high as Rp130,000. Jopu has one *rumah makan,* but no official accommodations.

Other Villages

Ikat cloth, with unique motifs, is also fashioned in the neighboring villages of Nduria, Wolonjita, and Nggela, an interesting hilly part of Flores. **Nggela,** with traditional dwellings and weaving styles different from Jopu's, sits on a high cliff with stupendous views over the Savu Sea. The best *lio* cloths come from **Lio.** Reasonable prices for high-quality *sarung* are Rp17,000-20,000, but you can pay as high as Rp25,000-30,000 for an excellent one. First asking prices range from Rp35,000 to Rp50,000. You can climb Keli Mutu from Nggela (or from Jopu), but it's a much longer and steeper climb than from Moni.

MAUMERE

A port town 148 km east of Ende on the narrow eastern stretch of the island. A pretty place, and easy-going, Maumere is nicely situated on the bay with islands offshore to the north. It's a good base from which to explore this part of the island. In 1992 Maumere met with disaster in the form of a strong earthquake and tsunami. Although the epicenter was out in the bay, the city suffered great destruction. Many buildings were destroyed; some are still in rubble. Cement slabs of others show grim evidence of the damage; buildings stand with large cracks in the walls. Much new construction. Though some large concrete buildings have been erected,

smaller bamboo and wood structures are more numerous—they're not only easier, faster, and less costly to build but seem to be more flexible and take violent movement with less damage.

Built like a Spanish town with a main square and market occupying its center, Maumere's principal attraction is its large Catholic church. Inside are paintings of the Twelve Stations of the Cross executed by a local artist with Indonesian characters. The church was badly damaged during the quake of 1992, and there has been no major repair since then. Visit also the old musty cemetery in the rear.

A center of Catholic enterprise, the local mission finances and manages copra and coffee export businesses. The Catholic hospital, St. Elizabeth's (Western-trained staff), in the town of Lela, is the place to go if you get sick on Flores. The old central market was also badly damaged during the earthquake; a new market has been set up on the western edge of town. Buy thick, distinctive Maumere blankets (many times more expensive than on Bali); also see Sumatran ivory jewelry carved by local craftsmen. For Maumere-style *ikat* weaving, go to **Harapan Jaya** across from the old market in the city center.

You can change traveler's checks and currency at **Bank Rakyat Indonesia** though the exchange rate is very poor. The bank is open Mon.-Fri. 0800-1200 and Saturday until 1100. The *wartel* is kitty-corner from the bank and is open 24 hours. The **post office** is open Mon.-

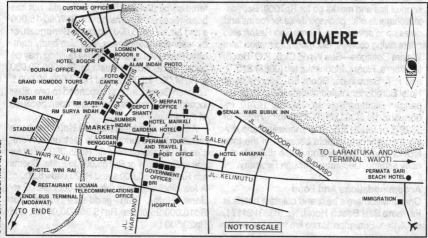

MAUMERE

CUSTOMS OFFICE
JL. SLAMET RIYADI
PELNI OFFICE
LOSMEN BOGOR II
HOTEL BOGOR
ALAM INDAH PHOTO
BOURAQ OFFICE
FOTO CANTIK
GRAND KOMODO TOURS
PASAR BARU
JL. RAJA CENTIS
JL. A. YANI
RM SARINA
MERPATI OFFICE
RM SURYA INDAH
DEPOT SHANTY
RM SUMBER INDAH
SENJA WAIR BUBUK INN
STADIUM
MARKET
HOTEL MAIWALI
GARDENA HOTEL
LOSMEN BENGGOAN
PERAMA TOUR AND TRAVEL
JL. SALEH
JL. KOMODOOR YOS. SUDARSO
JL. WAIR KLAU
POLICE
POST OFFICE
HOTEL HARAPAN
TO LARANTUKA AND TERMINAL WAIOTI
HOTEL WINI RAI
GOVERNMENT OFFICES
BRI
JL. KELIMUTU
PERMATA SARI BEACH HOTEL
RESTAURANT LUCIANA
ENDE BUS TERMINAL (MODAWAT)
TO ENDE
TELECOMMUNICATIONS OFFICE
JL. HARYONO
HOSPITAL
IMMIGRATION
NOT TO SCALE
© MOON PUBLICATIONS, INC.

Thurs. 0800-1400, Friday until 1100, and Saturday until 1230. For photo supplies try Alan Indah or Foto Cantik. Both have rolls of Fuji color slide film, 36 exposures for Rp12,500.

Once you've seen the church, visit Flores University or Maumere's copra-exporting harbor to observe the unusual stemless *sope* boats, a remnant of 17th-century Portuguese shipbuilding techniques.

Diving

Reputed to contain some of the finest diving sites in the world, the whole marine area within one hour by boat of Maumere comprises numerous detached coral reefs forming strings near the shore and several islands. Unfortunately, the earthquake of 1992 destroyed an estimated 40% of this coral. All the coral around Pulau Babi was destroyed, while the islands of Pulau Besar and Pulau Pemana were less affected. Dive sites range 200-2,000 meters deep and feature a great diversity of marinelife, shallow areas of seagrass (off Pulau Besar), spectacular world-class drop-offs with ultimate visibility of 50 meters or more, and an average water temperature of 30° Celsius.

In Waiara, 12 km east of Maumere, are two first-class dive resorts: **Sea World Club,** open since 1975, and **Flores Sao Resort,** one km farther. Both resorts are accessible by *bemo* (Rp500) from Maumere. Daily rates for dives, including all equipment, transportation, and snacks, are Rp110,000-145,000 pp per day; snorkel fins and masks go for Rp7000. Both establishments offer package deals for rooms and dives up to seven days. Flores Sao Resort also offers diving courses. Get more information from Waiara Cottages—Sea World Club, P.O. Box 3, Maumere, Flores, Indonesia, tel. (0383) 21570; and P.T. Saowisata, Room 6B, Second floor, Hotel Borobudur Intercontinental Offices, Jl. Lapangan Banteng Selatan, Jakarta, 10710, Indonesia, tel. (021) 370-333, ext. 78222 or 78227, or tel. 21555. The snorkeling and diving are very comfortable because of the total lack of swells and currents. Little diving in the rainy season, December through February.

Accommodations And Food

One of Maumere's best and quietest hotels is **Permata Sari Beach Hotel,** tel. (0383) 21171, on Jl. Jen. Sudirman 1, two km from the center of the city and one-half km from the airport. A friendly, relaxing place located right on the beach, the hotel also features a fine restaurant on the premises. Standard rooms are Rp17,500 s and Rp22,500 d; a/c rooms with hot and cold water and TV are Rp60,000 s and Rp75,000 d; breakfast included. The best deal here is the bungalows near the beach for Rp30,000 s and Rp40,000 d. Another very clean and well-managed place with large rooms is **Hotel Wini Rai,** tel. 21388, on Jl. Gajah Mada 50 near the west bus terminal. No restaurant but a simple breakfast is included with the room charge. Laundry service is available, as well as an expensive airport taxi service and local transportation charters. Single rooms from economy fan to a/c with TV run Rp7500-42,500, doubles Rp12,500-47,500.

Senja Wair Bubuk Inn can arrange for tours, traditional dance and musical exhibitions, and local transportation. A little dark and partially damaged by the quake, it has a wide variety of rooms for Rp6600-25,850 s and Rp11,000-35,700 d. Not far away, on Jl. Kutilang 18, is **Hotel Harapan,** tel. 21223, a small quiet place with 8-10 rooms for Rp6000 s, Rp12,000 d, Rp15,000 t.

Next to the Pelni office near the harbor on Jl. Salamet Riyadi is **Losmen Bogor II.** A Padang-style restaurant is located here. Breakfast is included in the room charge; rooms cost Rp5500-7500 s and Rp7000-12,000 d. Across the street is the fancier **Hotel Bogor I,** tel. 21191. It suffered some damage during the quake but has been repaired. Rooms go for Rp7000-15,000 s and a/c for Rp35,000. **Losmen Benggoan,** of questionable cleanliness, was also badly damaged during the quake; the new building may be better. Prices include breakfast: Rp8000-20,000 s, Rp14,000-25,000 d, and Rp17,500-30,000 t. Losmen Benggoan had expanded to two other locations, but both are no longer open because of the quake.

Although damaged, **Maiwali Hotel** has been repaired but no longer has a restaurant. Vehicles can be rented here for Rp65,000 a day for use in the vicinity or Rp185,000 to Ende. Rooms run Rp10,000-55,600 s and Rp20,000-78,900 d. A few blocks away is the small but clean **Gardena Hotel,** with good-size rooms for Rp10,000-25,000 s, Rp15,000-30,000 d, and Rp22,500 t.

Twelve km east of Maumere, in Waiara, are two resorts. Each is an upper-end place with nice bungalows on the beach, its own restaurant, abundant services, and a variety of diving options and packages. **Waiara Cottages—Sea World Club,** tel. 21570, has rooms for Rp21,000-52,500 s and Rp31,500-65,000 d, breakfast included. It offers dive and accommodation packages, dive equipment rental, and land excursions. **Flores Sao Resort,** tel. 21555, is a bit more luxurious and pricier at Rp73,500 s, 136,500 d, all meals extra. It too offers dive and accommodation packages, rentals, and operates its own tour and travel company.

Flores Froggies is an inexpensive *losmen* right on the beach, 28 km east of Maumere. Rates range from Rp4000 for a room, Rp12,000 for a beachside bungalow, to Rp18,000 for a bungalow with attached *mandi* and western toilet. Breakfast is included in the rates; laundry service available. There's a good restaurant on the premises, and snorkeling and sailing in the bay. Recommended.

The best place to eat in town is the Chinese restaurant **Sarina,** near the center of town. Maumere has several other *rumah makan* on Jl. Pasar Baru Barat. The Padang restaurant **Surya Indah** near the market is the best of the bunch, and now there's **Surya Indah II**—your only chance in Indonesia to eat tasty Padang-style food that isn't hot. Others on this street are **Sumber Indah** for Javanese-style food and seafood, and **Surabaya. Depot Shandy** is another option near the market. Other restaurants near the market are strong on Muslim-style goat *sate* and *gulai*. Delicious avocados, *zirzak,* and papaya are sold in the market. Next to Hotel Wini Rai is a nameless little place that serves up tasty dishes, and toward the west bus terminal is **Luciana** with an extensive menu of delicious Chinese food—a little expensive.

Getting Away

Maumere has good air connections to neighboring islands but none to other cities on Flores. Merpati flies three times a week to Ujung Pandang (Rp125,000), Palu (Rp250,000), Balikpapan (Rp276,000), and Tarakan (Rp409,000). Six times a week (every day except Sunday) there are flights to Kupang (Rp65,000). A daily flight goes to Bima (Rp104,000) and on to Denpasar (Rp181,000); from there you can make connec-

tions to Jakarta and other Javanese cities. Bouraq flies on Monday, Wednesday, and Friday to Kupang (65,000) and Denpasar (Rp181,000) direct. To Surabaya (Rp231,000), the flight goes via Denpasar. To Waingapu, you must go via Kupang and lay over one day. The Merpati office, Jl. Don Thomas 18, tel. (0383) 21342, is open Mon.-Sat. 0700-1400, Sunday 0900-1200. The Bouraq office on Jl. Nong Meak, tel. 21467, is open similar hours. Book in advance; these flights are popular and sometimes full.

Boats often call at this north coast port. Check the Pelni office on Jl. Slamet Riyadi near Losmen Bogor. Office hours are 0830-1200 and 1300-1500 daily. The KM *Kelimutu* calls at Maumere on its route from Banjarmasin and Surabaya to Ujungpandang. Sample economy class fares are: Ujung Pandang (Rp21,000), Dili (Rp19,000), Kalabahi (Rp11,000), Kupang (Rp31,000), Bima (Rp64,000), and Surabaya (Rp96,000). Ask the *syahbandar* about *kapal motor* heading for Reo, Labuhanbajo, Bima, and Ujung Pandang. There are no regularly scheduled passenger ships to these ports.

Maumere has two bus stations. The west bus station, **Terminal Modawat,** is about two km southwest of the city center. From here buses run to Ende (Rp4500). Several leave between 0700-0800 and four depart around 1600—but the night buses miss most of the beautiful scenery. Buses also go to Detusoko (Rp3750), Moni (Rp3500), Wolowaru (Rp3000), Paga (Rp1500), and Lekebai (Rp1250). *Bemo* use this station and head to Sikka (Rp800), Lela (Rp750), Nita (Rp350), Magapanda (Rp1000), and Kota Baru (Rp1400), among other destinations. The east bus station, three km east of the city center, is **Terminal Waioti.** From here buses run to Talibura (Rp1000), Nebe (Rp1500), and Larantuka (Rp4500, five hours). To Larantuka, several buses leave when full between 0900-1100 and several night buses leave around 1600-1700. *Bemo* from here run to Watublapi (Rp500), Geliting (Rp500), and Waiara (Rp500). Buses from Maumere still have the annoying habit of leaving the bus station to make a circuit of the market and city center before returning to the bus station, where they then leave for their destination.

Bemo around town charge a flat Rp300 fare, though drivers may ask extra to go up the road to the airport terminal. Charter *bemo* to the airport cost Rp5000.

Vicinity Of Maumere

Maumere is surrounded by coconut plantations; racks drying copra are everywhere. There's a beach close to town. Charter a *prahu* (one day, one night) out to Gunung Rokatenda, a volcano on Pulau Palu northwest of Maumere. Climb Rokatenda's peak in three hours from the *kampung* of **Uwa** on the southeast coast. Although this volcano erupts regularly, the people of Uwa always come back to reclaim their town.

The large Catholic seminary in **Ladelero**, 24 km southwest of Maumere, houses the **Blikon Blewut** museum, which exhibits weapons, Chinese porcelain, anthropological artifacts, rare *ikat* textiles from Sikka and Jopu, and other weavings from pre-Dutch times reflecting Flores's rich mosaic of ethnic groups. The museum is presided over by Father Peter, a Florinese priest. Leave a donation. The seminary has a wonderful view of the northern bay area. Some of the 300 students speak a little English and are very helpful in showing you around. Another Catholic seminary is in **Ritapiret**, a few km up the road. A mission is located in **Watublapi**, known for weaving and traditional dance. From this village, walk to the *kampung* of **Ohe** from where you can see both the northern and southern coasts of Flores. Magnificent.

Not far from Ladelero is **Nita**, a weaving center and regency of the former king of Nita. In the palace here are aristocratic heirlooms including clothing, jewelry, weapons, and elephant tusks.

Another important weaving center, Rp800 by minibus south of Maumere, is **Sikka**. The women greet arrivals, showing you their *sarung* and hoping you'll buy one. Watch the older women weave heavy *ikat*, spinning homegrown cotton thread using a device operated with their feet. Practically every house owns a primitive loom consisting of threads stretched between stakes stuck in the ground. Warp threads are tied tightly with grass fibers and then dyed with native indigo, red, and a yellow dye made from cudrania wood. *Sarung* in this district are often accented with narrow warp stripes of leaf-green. (Unfortunately, the brighter synthetic dyes are now making inroads.) Motifs include plants and animals such as lizards—a fertility symbol on Flores. Sikkanese dress and songs still show strong Portuguese influences dating back to the 16th century. A seat of Catholic power on Flores, the church dates from the 16th century and is one of the island's oldest. After Christmas Mass on 26 or 27 December, a play is performed in the courtyard before the local *raja*. Neither native Portuguese nor the people of Sikka understand the words, as the original Portuguese language has been so corrupted. Lela, Nita, and Koting are other villages in the area that faithfully preserve old Portuguese traditions.

Lela, a town on the south coast not far from Sikka, has an old church with a shrine to the Virgin Mary that's visited twice a year by pilgrims. A lovely palm-lined beach stretches between here and Sikka. Farther down the coast beyond **Paga** is Koka Beach, a very fine strand of white sand—one of the best on Flores—and a good place for swimming and picnicking. Down the coast to the east are the fishing villages of **Bola** and **Ipir**. The last *bemo* back to Maumere from here leaves in mid-afternoon.

For a different experience, visit the Bugis village of **Wuring** on the north coast, five km west of Maumere, where the houses are built over the water and wooden boats are constructed in a traditional style using traditional techniques.

LARANTUKA

A picturesque port on the island's far eastern tip, 667 km from Labuhanbajo. Towered over by Gunung Ile Mandiri (1,524 meters), Larantuka hugs the coast. This city has a long-established Eurasian colony and since Portuguese times has been the administrative center for the eastern neck of Flores and the island to the east. Travelers embark for the Solor and Alor archipelagos from Larantuka by crossing the narrow Selat Lewotobi.

Larantuka's main street, Jl. Niaga (also called Jl. Yos Sudarso, Jl. Fernandez, and Jl. Diponegoro along different sections), runs along the waterfront. It contains most of the government offices, the town's two churches, and many of the businesses. The **post office** is two km out of town past the *pasar* and Losmen Fortuna (take a *bemo,* Rp300); open Mon.-Thurs. 0800-1400, Friday until 1100, Saturday until 1230. The *wartel* is across the street. Change money at **Bank Rakyat Indonesia** near the harbor; poor exchange rates. Its business hours are 0800-1200 Mon.-Saturday. Across the street is a clinic and about five km east of town, on the way to

Weri Beach, is the public hospital. The tourist office is in *kantor bupati* next to the telephone and telegraph office. The *bemo* and bus station is opposite the main pier on Jl. Niaga; Rp300 flat rate for *bemo* all over town. Bus and *bemo* north to Waiklibang and to nearby villages depart throughout the day when full. Buses to Maumere (Rp4500, five hours) and Ende (Rp8500, 10 hours) leave from here in the morning. Have your *losmen* owner reserve a seat on the bus the evening before.

For centuries a Portuguese trading center, Larantuka still harbors traces of the Portuguese era in the old stone and stucco houses; in the large-boned, Latin-featured inhabitants; in family names such as Monteiros and da Silva; and even in the place-names in town such as *posto* (the town's center). With its prayers, ceremonies, Christmas and Good Friday processions, and Iberian church architecture, the Catholic religious life of Larantuka follows Portuguese traditions. Many of the prayers are recited in broken Portuguese, and during religious processions men carry a bier which symbolically contains the body of Jesus. They wear long white cloaks with high pointed hoods, costumes resembling those donned in Portugal during the Middle Ages. Every Easter, cruise ship passengers and numerous tourists visit Larantuka for its parades.

Old relics from the 1500s and 1600s are still preserved in bamboo chapels as village *pusaka*—vestments, devotional clothes, ivory crucifixes, silver chalices. A statue of a black Virgin Mary, claimed to have been washed ashore in a man's dream, is venerated. An old Portuguese bell hangs outside the **Church of Kapala Maria**. In the corner of the Peca da Penha is the Portuguese font where hundreds of Larantukans where baptized. The 1992 earthquake left its effect in Larantuka, mostly in the destruction of old colonial buildings, but the damage was not nearly as widespread as in Maumere. More destructive is the periodic flooding from waters draining off the steep mountainside at Larantuka's back. In 1979, for example, several villages were swept into the sea and scores of people perished.

Nearby Sights
There are several points of interest worth exploring in the vicinity of Larantuka. Just seven km north of the city, on the way to the airport, is **Weri Beach.** Take a *bemo* (Rp300). The sand beach is narrow but the water is all right for a swim. On the way you pass a spot where Pulau

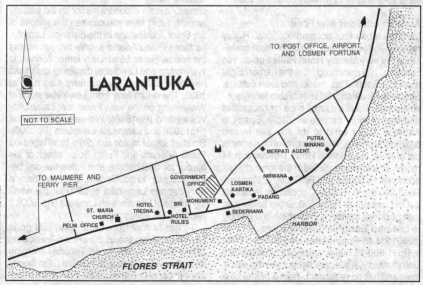

Adonara is only a few hundred meters across the channel. **Oka Hot Springs** is six km west of the city, on the road to Maumere. There's a beach nearby; take a dip in the sea and wash off in fresh water. One km west out of town at San Domingo Seminary is a **museum** that houses religious artifacts and cultural items relating to the history of Larantuka and its Portuguese influence. Going a bit farther afield, you can find many weaving villages on the slope of Gunung Ile Mandiri. Twenty minutes north of Larantuka is **Badug,** one such village; take a *bemo* (Rp600). There's a traditional *rumah adat* at **Desa Mokantarak.** Among other villages, **Riangkemie, Wailolong, Mukakeputu,** and **Lewoloba** also have *rumah adat* and practice some traditional ceremonies and dance. These villages and others are on the slope of Gunung Ile Mandiri. Small **Asmara Lake** is a one-hour walk out of Waiklibang. Bus (Rp1000) from Larantuka; bring food and water. **Botung Village** on Pulau Adonara is across the strait from Larantuka. Boats depart daily except Sunday and holidays. Leave Larantuka at 1130; the return boat is at 0730. There is no *losmen,* but ask for Nely—he puts people up. In this village you may see traditional dance and *arak*-making, or visit Batu Payung Beach. Good views of Larantuka and Ile Lewotobi across the strait.

Accommodations And Food

Larantuka has four accommodations. Highly recommended and the choice of most travelers is the very friendly **Hotel Rulies** on Jl. Yos Sudarso, 100 meters up from the harbor. Eight rooms at Rp6000 pp, *mandi* and toilet outside. Simple Indonesian food is available for reasonable prices. There's a small shop for necessities and *ikat*; laundry service available. Speak to Andreus about what to do and see in and around Larantuka, and for travel arrangements out of town. Next door is **Hotel Tresna,** with 14 rooms. Breakfast is included in the room charge: economy, Rp6000 s and Rp12,000 d; standard, Rp11,000 s and Rp22,000 d; and a/c (spacious but overpriced) at Rp38,500. Often booked up with business travelers. Also clean and friendly is **Losmen Fortuna,** Jl Diponegoro 171, tel. (0383) 21140. Rooms rates are Rp7500-11,000 s, Rp11,000-16,500 d, and Rp12,500-21,500 t. Unfortunately, it's located about two km out of town and has no restaurant. Take a *bemo*. **Losmen Kartika,** Rp4500 s and Rp9000 d and too expensive for what you get at those prices, is in the center of town near the *bemo* stop. None too quiet, none too clean.

All eateries in town are along the main street, but there's nothing too exciting about the food in Larantuka. Perhaps the best place to eat, and the town's only Chinese restaurant, is **Nirwana.** Try **Padang,** a restaurant that also sells Timorese honey for Rp3000 per bottle; **Minang** and **Sederhana I** also serve Padang-style food. Just around the corner, **RM Sederhana II** serves Javanese food. Vendors line the streets, selling fruit and crushed corn (Indonesian popcorn) for Rp500 per bag—have your *losmen* or a restaurant fry it up for you.

Getting There

Leaving Maumere for the 137-km trip (Rp4500, five hours) to Larantuka, you plunge from a region of tall, broad-leafed trees and magnificent scenery to coastal vegetation. Distinguished by identical box-type construction, several new communities for quake victims have sprung up along the Larantuka-Maumere highway. If you're arriving by boat from the east, buses wait near the wharf to take you to Maumere and points west.

Getting Away

Larantuka is an important harbor for the easterly islands. From here you can see the shapes of the Solor Archipelago in the distance. Larantuka faces Pulau Adonara, only two km across the narrow Flores Strait. Daily ferries connect to Waiwerang and Lewoleba, departing Larantuka harbor at 0830. A second ferry also runs at 1330. The return ferry from Lewoleba stops at Waiwerang on the way. Fares are: Larantuka-Waiwerang (Rp1500); Waiwerang-Lewoleba (Rp1500); and Larantuka-Lewoleba (Rp3000). Smaller *kapal motor* run daily to villages on Pulau Adonara and Pulau Solor; check at the harbor for destinations and times the day before you plan to go. Once a week on Friday a ferry departs Larantuka at 0900 for the whaling village of Lamalera on Lembata (Rp6000); it returns on Wednesday.

To get to Alor from Larantuka, first go to Lewoleba. From there, the once-a-week boat *Diana Express* departs on Tuesday morning and goes via Balauring to Kalabahi. On the return, it departs Kalabahi on Friday morning.

This trip takes two days and costs Rp12,500 one-way.

Pelni's KM *Tatamailau* connects Larantuka twice a month to Surabaya and other points west, and to Dili to the east. The Perintis ships KM *Elang* and KM *Nyala Perintis* run from Larantuka to ports on Solor and Alor, Kupang, and many ports on Flores, Sulawesi, and the Maluku. Contact the Pelni office for schedules and fares. The office, about 200 meters west of the harbor, on Jl. Yos Sudarso, is open from 0800.

From its new pier at Waibalun, five km west of downtown Larantuka, ASDP ferries KMP *Kerapu II* and KMP *Rokotenda* connect Larantuka with Kupang twice a week. Starting in Kupang, these ferries arrive at Larantuka on Tuesday and Saturday morning, and carry on to Waiwerang and Lewoleba; they return to Larantuka and depart for Kupang about 1500. For the time being, only these vehicular ferries leave from this new pier. The fare to Kupang is Rp12,500 (15 hours).

Taxis costs Rp5000 pp for the 10-km ride to the airport. Take a *bemo* for less than Rp1000. The Merpati agent, tel. 121, is opposite the big church, second house from the corner, no. 64; no sign. On Monday and Thursday there is a Merpati flight from Larantuka to Kupang via Lewoleba for Rp80,000. Notoriously unpredictable, this flight is often cancelled, or it may not fly to either Larantuka or Lewoleba if there are no reserved passengers. Don't count on it.

THE SOLOR AND ALOR ARCHIPELAGOS

Separated by swift, narrow straits, this small string of islands lies off the east coast of Flores. The people of the extreme eastern end of Flores, as well as the islands of Solor, Adonara, and Lembata, are referred to as Solorese. A mixture of Malay and Melanesian, they share strong cultural traits, speak the same language, and have experienced the same history.

These small islands are green but not thickly vegetated except at the higher elevations. Fishermen before farmers, the Solorese live in numerous communities that hug the shore, with scattered small villages on the interior slopes. Each island has something of historical and cultural interest: *adat* villages, *rumah adat*, caves, *moko* drums, elephant *tusk pusak,* traditional dances and ceremonies, as well as a few beaches.

With a sword in one hand and a Bible in the other, the Portuguese Dominican missionaries controlled the area during the 16th-19th cen-

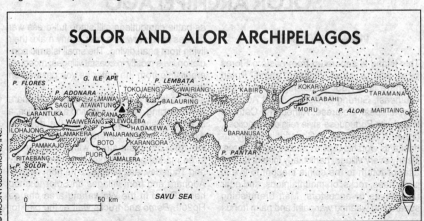

SOLOR AND ALOR ARCHIPELAGOS

turies. Dutch Jesuits and Franciscans arrived between 1860 and 1880. As a result of all this proselytizing, the majority of the population is Christian, although in the ports there are sizable Islamic communities.

For hundreds of years, the islands east of Flores were known as the "Isles of Murderers." Two clans, the Demons and the Padzis (like the American Hatfields and McCoys), carried on a deadly feud believed by anthropologists to have started between two brothers back in the 1500s. Today, however, the parties have been pacified.

Getting There

Larantuka is the starting point for scheduled ferries across the Flores Strait to Adonara and Lembata. Departing Larantuka daily at 0830 and 1330, they stop at Waiwerang (Adonara) before reaching Lewoleba on Lembata. Fares are Rp1500 Larantuka to Waiwerang, Rp1500 Waiwerang to Lewoleba, and Rp3000 from Larantuka to Lewoleba; one and a half hours from Larantuka to Waiwerang, four hours Larantuka to Lewoleba. Daily *kapal motor* connect Larantuka to towns on Solor; check with the *syahbandar* at the pier in Larantuka. Lamalera is serviced by scheduled *kapal motor* from Larantuka, Waiwerang, and Lewoleba. From Lembata, boats continue on to Pantar and Alor. The ASDP boats KMP *Kerapu II* and KMP *Rokotenda* leave Kupang, arriving in Larantuka early on Tuesday and Saturday mornings. From there, they carry on to Waiwerang and Lewoleba before turning around and heading back to Larantuka the same day. Leaving Larantuka at 1500, they return to Kupang. Also try the Perintis ship KM *Elang* for its many stops in these islands.

Merpati flies once a week from Kupang to Lewoleba and on to Larantuka. This flight is often cancelled to one or the other of these destinations for lack of booked passengers, so be sure to have a reservation in advance to ensure the flight will go. Five times a week Merpati flies to Kalabahi from Kupang. Tickets to these destinations cost Rp80,000.

Getting Around

All these small islands have limited and rather unrefined road systems. Roads improve slowly, perhaps more slowly than on the larger main islands of Nusatenggara due to the archipelago's relative economic backwater status. There is, however, some *bemo* and truck transportation on all the islands, although not necessarily regular or daily. To get to many villages you must walk or take *kapal motor* that shuttle from one coastal village to another. These boats usually don't run on any set schedule, so ask around in the village or at the pier for boats leaving for your preferred destination. Some scheduled *kapal motor* that run between the islands have designated routes and times; see individual island info below for more details.

SOLOR ARCHIPELAGO

PULAU ADONARA

This island is separated from eastern Flores by a narrow strait. Soaring above Pulau Adonara is a 1,650 meter-high peak to the southeast, Gurung Ile Boleng. Most Adonara people speak Solorese. Although a Catholic island with Portuguese-style religious practices, beneath the veneer of Christianity many inhabitants worship reptiles and other creatures. Nearly every village, particularly inland, has an altar or totem to the spirits thought to live in large trees, rocks, on mountaintops, and near the graves of ancestors. Men brandishing spears and wearing war paint and palm fronds as battle camouflage still stage full-dress war dances once or twice a year. Many make their living from pearl diving. The small Islamic population lives mostly in coastal villages; mosques are visible from the water as you pass by on the ferry.

The primary port and main town on Adonara is **Waiwerang.** Here you will find a post office, a branch of Bank Rakyat Indonesia that does not exchange foreign currency, a large church, mosque, one main street with shops, and a large market area. Market days are Monday and Thursday, and people come from all over Adonara and from villages on Solor to shop here. *Bemo* in the Waiwerang area charge Rp200. *Bemo* and trucks wait at the pier for each ferry and provide transportation to nearly every point on the island's limited road network.

Aside from the twice-daily ferries connecting Waiwerang to Larantuka and Lewoleba, and the ASDP ferry via Larantuka to Kupang, there are other boat connections from Waiwerang. On Monday and Thursday (market days) boats leave at 1000 for Pamakajo on Solor. To Lamakera, Solor's only whaling village, there is a daily boat; ask at the harbor for the current departure time. A boat to Lamalera, Pulau Lembata's whaling village, leaves every Friday at 1100.

About 50 meters up from the pier is **Losmen Taufik.** Rooms are dark and basic. The proprietor asks Rp6000 but will take Rp4000. **Losmen Asri** is also up from the pier. Opened in November 1993, **Ile Boleng Homestay** is located about 200 meters east of the pier. Follow the road around the side of Christus Raja church or cut in front of the beachside shops. This clean and friendly place has seven rooms, two of which look out over the channel to Solor and Lembata. Good views, breezy. Rooms are Rp5500 pp including tea and snacks. Also filling dinners for a reasonable price. Waiwerang has two hole-in-the-wall *rumah makan,* **Mayar Sari** and **Mampur.** Both are on the main road up from Losmen Taufik.

Sights

Although small, the island offers a few noteworthy sights. **Ene Burak Beach** (white sand) and **Wera Mata Beach** (red sand) are both to the east of Waiwerang and can be seen from the ferry to Lewoleba. **Lake Kota Kaya** is in the middle of the island. **Pukaona Village** has a *rumah adat,* while **Lamenele** and **Lamelaka** are traditional villages. **Sagu** is a port town on the north coast of Adonara, 20 minutes by truck from Waiwerang. An old Dutch cemetery is located here. Occasional boats run from Sagu to Larantuka. West of Sagu in the village of **Adonara** are remnants of a defensive town wall from the Dutch days. A few rusty cannon still point to sea in a decrepit show of former strength. **Wureh** village on the southwest coast has similar religious structure and practices to those in Larantuka. In fact, the church bell, inscribed with the date 10 December 1714, originally came from the Catholic church in Larantuka. Wander through the bamboo chapels with sand floors; many Portuguese and *adat* arti-

facts, some from Melaka and Goa (South Sulawesi). Prayers are uttered in almost indecipherable Portuguese.

PULAU SOLOR

For many years the rendezvous point for Portuguese sandalwood traders, 2,100 square-km Solor nestles between Flores, Adonara, and Lembata. In 1566, Dominican monks built the stone fortress of Henrique on the north coast, near the present-day village of **Lohajong,** a well-chosen spot that provided good anchorage. Although the fortress itself lies in ruins, its massive walls—two meters wide by four meters high—still stand, and some rusty cannons remain in the courtyard.

The small village of **Lamakera** on the east side is one of only two whaling villages in Indonesia. Since Solor is a volcanic island where only a few scanty crops are raised on the stony coastal soil, Lamakeran women must tramp up to the mountain villages to barter whale meat and oil for maize, rice, and cassava. To reach Solor, boats depart Larantuka each morning for Lohajong, as well as Pamakajo on the north coast. From Pamakajo, boats hop across to Waiwerang. Aside from Pamakajo, Ritaebang on the southwest coast is Solor's other administrative center and market town. Only a few *bemo* ply the island's roads.

PULAU LEMBATA

Also known as Lomblem, this is a dry island, due to hot, parching winds blowing up from Australia, creating expanses of scrub grasslands, inland stands of eucalyptus trees, and open savannahs. Wildlife is plentiful. Every district has its own dialect, customs, and brand of animism. A famous village in the south still practices a primitive form of whaling. The quality of Lembata's fine homespun *ikat* weaving and other fabrics is commensurate with Sumba's.

Two northern districts worth visiting, Ile Ape and Kedang, include scattered villages along the coast under the shadow of the volcanic peak Gunung Ile Ape. The best *sarung* are made in Ile Ape district, but you won't find them easily as they're mainly for ceremonial use and cost upward of Rp300,000. In Kedang district is a lot of porcelain, even in the inland villages, plus ivory (including whole tusks) from Sumatra. Expect to do a lot of walking, as there is only sporadic truck and boat transportation to the island's villages. *Bemo* run only in and around Lewoleba, Lembata's main town and administrative center.

The People

Most inhabitants practice slash-and-burn agriculture and are Melanesian-looking; some have Portuguese features, while others are unmistakably Papuan. A superstitious people with spooky beliefs and practices, some interior villagers still display the skulls of their ancestors in full view; in other villages no one goes out at night. The people are difficult to get to know beyond the initial meeting, though the men are fond of drinking *tuak* and often ask travelers to stop and drink with them along the trails. It's believed that if a stranger shares *tuak,* then he is not an enemy.

Islanders often call you "father" because most of the Westerners they meet are priests. The missionaries maintain a strong presence on the island, but tribalism and mysticism are still pervasive. Ask about the community houses (*kokay*), where you can observe rituals taking place right under the missionaries' noses.

Lembata Ikat

Lembata *ikat* is considered on a par with *ikat* from Sumba. Like Sumba *ikat,* pieces here may take up to a year to complete. *Ikat* is made all over the island of Lembata but the best is done around Gunung Ile Ape and are used in oft-practiced traditional ceremonies and as part of bridal dowries; most pieces cannot be bought. Adjacent **Mawa** and **Atawatun** villages, on the western slope of Ile Ape, produce the best *ikat.* Pieces for sale start at around Rp300,000. One exceptional heirloom with an elephant design reputedly sold for an incredible Rp10 million. Each village produces a different design, although production techniques are pretty much the same throughout the island. Cloth woven near Lewoleba sells for Rp75,000-250,000. Mostly natural dyes are used on locally spun cotton, although store-bought cotton and chemical dyes are now used as well. Beware. Know your stuff if you plan to buy.

To reach Mawa and Atawatun, go by truck from Lewoleba (one only on Saturday) or rent a mo-

torbike. It takes six to eight hours to walk to the area. There's no accommodation or restaurant there; ask to stay with the *kepala desa,* or take a guide with you to arrange a place to stay and eat.

Getting There And Around

Merpati flies to the landing strip near Lewoleba once a week for Rp80,000.

Catch the twice-daily ferry (0830 and 1330) from Larantuka to Waiwerang, which continues on to Lewoleba on the west coast of Lembata. The complete journey takes about four hours and costs Rp3000 from Larantuka to Lewoleba. Alternately, catch the ASDP ferries KMP *Kerapu II* or KMP *Rokotenda* on their way from Kupang, via Larantuka, to Waiwerang and Lewoleba. On their return, they leave Lewoleba on Tuesday and Saturday mornings for Kupang (Rp12,500). Traveling to Kalabahi (Alor) from Lembata is possible on a regular once-a-week basis. The *Diana Express* takes about two days to make this journey and costs Rp12,500 one-way. It leaves Lewoleba at 0700 on Tuesday and goes via Balauring and Wairiang on the way to Kalabahi. Stay in Balauring at the fine **Losmen Telaga Jan**; rooms are Rp6500 pp including three meals. There is no *losmen* in Wairiang. From Kalabahi, the *Diana Express* leaves on Friday morning for its return to Lewoleba. On occasion, the ferry KM *Inerie* also runs from Larantuka to Waiwerang, Lewoleba, Balauring, Baranusa, and Kalabahi, returning on the same route. Check its schedule with the ferry office in Lewoleba.

Infrequent boats ply the coastline between Lamalera, Lewoleba, and Balauring. Bad roads encircle Gunung Ile Ape. One runs north to Balauring and on to Wairiang, and another goes south toward Lamalera.

Land transport on Lembata is by foot, motorbike, or trucks that carry goods between the coastal towns. At the missions scattered around the island you can find food and accommodations, but only in Balauring and Lamalera are there *losmen* and homestays.

Lewoleba

The island's main town—a small, lazy village where boats from Larantuka dock. A *bemo* from the pier to town, and anywhere around town, is a flat Rp300; several bicycle pedicabs also ply the streets and charge Rp500 a ride. Lewoleba has a big market on Monday, and people come from far and wide, and even from neighboring islands, to shop. To the side of the market is the post office; they'll hold mail for you. Lewoleba now has its own *wartel,* open 24 hours a day for domestic and international phone calls. A branch of Bank Rakyat Indonesia is next door to the post office, but it can't cash foreign currency—the nearest exchange bank is in Larantuka. The manager of Losmen Rejeki will provide exchange service for you if necessary.

Merpati flies on Thursday at 0900 from Lewoleba to Kupang but only if there are reserved passengers, so flights are often cancelled. The airstrip is three km north of town; go by *bemo* or motorbike. This airstrip was newly expanded and paved in 1992 and a small terminal built. The manager of Losmen Rejeki is the Merpati agent. The office at the pier has current information on ferries and other boats to/from Lewoleba.

Stay at **Losmen Rejeki** in the *pasar* (15-minute walk from the pier), run by a nice Chinese family. Rooms with shared *mandi* are Rp5000; those with *mandi* in the room are Rp10,000. You'll be fed royally for Rp2500-3000. In the sitting room is a small shop with necessities, *ikat,* and craft items. Rejeki's manager can arrange a guide for island walks. Losmen Rejeki also runs a second place with eight rooms. Located about a 20-minute walk above town, it's quieter and a bit cooler. Rooms are the same price and meals are brought from the *losmen* in town. A new place, **Hotel Lewoleba,** is located a half a block up from the market. New, bright, and white, it's a bit sterile. All rooms have *mandi* and cost Rp10,000 s, Rp15,000 d, and Rp22,500 t; meals are Rp2000 for lunch and Rp3000 for dinner. There are some *warung* around the fringe of the market, but nothing beats the food at Losmen Rejeki.

There's not much to do in Lewoleba itself, but you can spend a day on the beach. Try the beach at the airstrip—not the best, but the water is shallow. Walk back along the beach and look for shells. People at the pearl-harvesting operation just past the airstrip might be willing to show you around. The oysters are actually raised out in the bay below buildings set on stilts. A better beach is at the village of **Waijarang,** several km west of Lewoleba—white sand, good snorkeling. To get there, arrange a

ride on a fishing boat from Lewoleba—some usually leave around 0500—and ask to be picked up on its way back to town. Negotiate the fare with the captain. Losmen Rejeki may be able to locate someone going that direction who is willing to take and retrieve you. Also, there's a Japanese-run pearl farm off the coast here as well. If it's operating at the time, workers might give you a ride and perhaps show you the operation. A road runs to the village of Waijarang, probably transversable via motorbike.

Climbing Gunung Ile Ape

Not for the weak of heart. Count on two to three days. First go to **Tokojaeng** on the northeast slope of Gunung Ile Ape. There you can stay the night and hire a guide from the village. Ask Losmen Rejeki to write a letter of introduction for hiring a guide, staying, and eating. One guide that often goes up with foreigners—he used to work at Losmen Rejeki—is Gabriel. Negotiate a price. Walk to Tokojaeng in five to six hours. Start before dawn as it gets very hot by midday. Alternately, catch the truck that goes out on Sunday, or return with the truck on Monday. Other trucks run to nearby villages on other days of the week; check with Losmen Rejeki. The climb starts in Tokojaeng and takes three to five hours. Bring food and plenty of water. The trail starts out on an easy incline. About halfway up it becomes much steeper, and as you approach the top your footing becomes treacherous as you scramble over loose rock. Begin the climb early, as clouds roll in by mid-morning. From the top, you can see all of Lembata, its surrounding coral reef, Lewoleba, and the neighboring islands. Near the top, the still-active volcano puffs smoke, so it's dangerous to hike to the actual crater rim. The climb down is faster but just as difficult. An alternate route, but much steeper most of the way, is from Kimokana on the southeast slope. It's closer to Lewoleba.

Balauring

Reach this village via boat from Lewoleba on Tuesday (Rp3000, five hours), by truck perhaps once weekly, or walk the 80 km in three days through fabulous country of tall grass, big green hills, swampy lowlands, and volcanos. In Balauring, stay at **Losmen Telaga Jan,** Rp6500 pp including three meals. A good place. Walk out of town to a back trail up through cornfields and high above the cliffs, then drop down to the villages along the shore. Eastern Lembata is rocky and beautiful. From Balauring, continue on to Pantar or Alor by the *Diana Express,* the KM *Elang,* or *prahu.*

Lamalera

A whaling village (pop. 3,000) on the south coast, one of only two in all Indonesia (the other is Lamakera on Solor). Few other villages on Lembata are so dependent on fishing and so poor agriculturally. Lamalera is comprised of settlers from the Kai Islands, Central Maluku, Ceram, and Flores, and each clan has its own boat and boathouse. Their boats (*pledang*)— painted, named, and decorated on the bow and sides with slogans in Bahasa Indonesia or Latin—are built without nails; only wooden pegs and rattan are used. Planks are cut with the necessary curve instead of being artificially bent. To maintain the flow of life force, plank ends from the base of the tree always lie toward the bow of the boat. A feast takes place when all the largest planks of a new boat have been fitted, and pig blood is smeared on the tools. When a manta ray is caught, they "feed" its brain to the boat. Though the population is Catholic, animist temples are placed around the village.

The whaling season runs from about May, when the rains end and the seas are calmer, until November when the rains return; perhaps the best months are May, June, and July. Villagers also hunt sea cows, manta rays, turtles, sharks, and porpoises, but always prefer to go after a whale. Boats are manned by 7-14 helmsmen, oarsmen, and harpooners. After spotting a whale and before they go in for the kill, the whole crew urinates, pulls down the sails, and says a communal *pater noster.*

From a platform extending forward from the bow, the harpooner leaps with his three meter-long harpoon to give it extra thrust, sometimes landing on the back of the whale like Captain Ahab. If the whale spouts bright crimson, it's a fatal wound. Sometimes a boat is pulled all the way to Timor by a maddened, runaway whale. The villagers take about 20 whales a year, mostly sperm whales, and place their skulls at the village gate.

Set on the hill overlooking town and the bay is **Guru Ben Homestay.** Rates are Rp7000 pp including three meals. Ben can arrange a ride on a whale boat for Rp15,000 if it's the right season. Two others are **Yosef Keraf Homestay** and **Abel Beding Homestay,** both Rp6500 including meals. Both can also put you up on a boat for Rp15,000. Guru Ben's is quiet and has nice scenery. The other two are down in the village. When a whale is caught the whole village gets excited, and when it's butchered the whole village stinks. At those times it would perhaps be better to stay on the hill above the village.

Once a week a regularly scheduled boat sails for Lamalera from Lewoleba. The *Sina Mutiara II* leaves at midnight (2400) on Monday (Rp3000, four to five hours) and returns on Tuesday. From Waiwerang, a boat departs each Friday for Lamalera. It's possible to go overland as well. Trucks from Lewoleba pass in front of Losmen Rejeki daily except Wednesday at about 0800 en route for either Boto or Puor (Rp2000, two to three hours), from where you must walk the remaining three to four hours over a bad road to Lamalera. To return, start your walk about 0600 to catch the truck, as it returns to Lewoleba from Boto or Puor at about 1100. Yet another way is to hike from Lewoleba down to Lamalera via Namaweke in 10-12 hours; ask the manager at Losmen Rejeki to assist you in finding a suitable guide. Take water. Villagers along the way are friendly. You can also hitch the occasional trucks that drive along the coastal road, or ride on the back of a motorcycle, which you can charter in Lewoleba.

ALOR ARCHIPELAGO

PULAU ALOR

Cut off for centuries from the cultural and historical changes taking place around it, the island of Alor (80 km by 50 km) lies approximately 60 km north of Timor. In 1908, *rajas* were installed by the Dutch in the principal coastal communities. Starting in the 1940s, Protestants opened missions and schools in the interior and began the systematic abolition of spirit-worship. The population today is sharply divided between Islamic peoples—for the most part immigrants from Flores, Timor, and Kisar—living in the relatively narrow lowlands, and an extraordinary number of indigenous ethnolinguistic groups living in the extremely mountainous interior.

These Christian/animist mountain dwellers speak some 70 dialects, most of them unintelligible to anyone living more than 20 km away. A number of Papuan languages linger as well. The isolated villages, which sit like fortresses on hilltops, have little contact with each other. Maize is the staple crop, grown on swiddens; secondary crops are rice (ceremonial), millet, beans, and tubers. The diet is supplemented by wild pig, hunted with bow and arrow during the dry season. In spite of the heavy Catholic presence, the *naga* cult persists, with sacrifices of meat and rice made to this protective deity. In the villages, carved wooden *naga* on posts, often surrounded by piles of stones, are endowed with magic properties. Women spend much of their time making baskets and weaving fine *ikat*-style cloth. Small islands off the coast of Alor still don't use Indonesian currency but rely on the barter system, trading fish for maize and tapioca.

With a population of 120,000, **Kalabahi** is the main town. It sits at the end of a 16-km-long bay which is more like an estuary because the current reverses violently as the tide turns. Stay at **Adhi Dharma,** with 10 rooms (five with private bath) for about Rp6500 pp; also try the **Marlina** or **Melati** *losmen.*

Alor is said to have some very good and little-explored coral beds, good for the diver or snorkeler who wants really out of the way locations.

Moko Drums

Among the most fascinating enigmas in Nusa-tenggara, these small cast-bronze kettle drums (*moko*) are found nowhere else in Indonesia in such incredible numbers. The drums are usually about one-half meter high and one-third to one-half meter in diameter, tapered in the middle like an hourglass with four ear-shaped grips around their circumferences, open at one end and closed at the other. All are decorated with Hindu motifs and have a rich, dark patina.

Imported originally by Indians, Makassarese, and Chinese traders on their way to Timor for sandalwood, the drums probably originated in North Vietnam, seat of the Dongson culture, whose bronze-casting skills reached Indonesia around 500 B.C. and spread as far as New Guinea. The Alorese have never had any expertise in working bronze and there is no copper for making bronze on the island.

A symbol of status and wealth, drums are used as currency to buy land (and, in the past, human heads). The exchange of *moko* and gongs still unofficially serves as a means of population control. When a man wants to marry, he is required by custom to give a *moko* to his in-laws. But since there's a limited number of the drums left, and new ones aren't made or imported, there aren't enough to go around and often the unlucky couple must leave the island to wed. Valued as high as Rp7.3 million, outsiders can't buy *moko* for any amount of money. Hundreds are said to be buried under the earth.

Transportation

Merpati flies to Kalabahi from Kupang five times weekly (Rp80,000). Also get to Kalabahi by ASDP ferry from Kupang (Rp15,000) on Thursday and Saturday at 1300, and from Atapupu (Rp7500) on Monday at 1030. Return to Atapupu on Sunday, and to Kupang on Tuesday and Friday. Land-and-sea travel entails first boarding a boat from Larantuka to Lewoleba. There catch the *Diana Express,* which leaves Lewoleba every Tuesday 0700 for Kalabahi. Alternately, truck from Lewoleba to Balauring, where you can also board the *Diana Express* about midday. A couple of times monthly the

Perintis ship KM *Elang* connects Larantuka and Kalabahi, calling at Waiwerang, Lewoleba, Balauring, and Baranusa (Pulau Pantar) en route. Twice a month the Pelni ship KM *Kelimutu* calls at Kalabahi on its way to/from Kupang, Dili, Maumere, and other ports.

Travel in Alor's interior is greatly affected by torrential rains during the winter months, when many of the tracks are impassable even on foot. The wet season (Nov.-March) is followed by a hot dry season that lasts through September. In the interior the mountains are so steep that even horses are useless. A number of inland villages have never been visited by white people. Luckily, most of the people have learned Bahasa Indonesia in the mission schools.

TIMOR

The easternmost islands of Nusatenggara, the Timor Archipelago—including the Outer Arc islands of Roti, Ndao, and Savu—is the largest of the Lesser Sunda island groups. The population of Timor, the main island (480 km long by 80 km wide), is 1.5 million. Because they experienced different histories, there are important cultural differences between Timor's eastern and western halves.

Timor was formerly divided between the Dutch in the west and the Portuguese in the east. When Indonesia gained its independence in 1950, the western portion of the island went to the Republic while the east remained with the Portuguese. After a military coup toppled the dictatorship in Portugal in April 1974, the Portuguese sought to rid themselves of all their colonial possessions. In 1975, the Portuguese-controlled half was thus granted complete independence by Lisbon. Fearing that separatism would inspire revolt in parts of Indonesia and that the new government would fall under the influence of communists, and perhaps also with an eye on the east's oil and gas reserves, the Indonesian military in 1975 brutally invaded and in 1976 annexed that territory. Now the whole island of Timor, divided into Timor Barat (West Timor) and Timor Timur (or "Tim Tim," East Timor) belongs to Indonesia.

Prior to annexation, Timor's eastern half was a popular stop between Australia and Singapore, but after Indonesia's occupation its borders were closed. East Timor was reopened in January 1989, yet today isolated fighting in Tim Tim continues and it's still a sensitive area politically. A steady stream of mostly Australian travelers enters Timor Barat via Kupang from Darwin; a 60-day entry stamp is issued at Kupang's airport upon arrival. They usually spend a short, enjoyable holiday snorkeling and sightseeing around Kupang, then island-hop westward, or fly directly to Bali.

THE LAND

Timor's landforms are markedly different from the rest of Indonesia. The island rose out of the sea relatively recently—only 15 million years ago—and you can still find seashells embedded in Timor's highest peaks. Today it's the fastest-rising island in the world, each year surging three millimeters out of the sea. A central mountain range marches across Timor, from western tip to east. The highest peak at 2,963 meters is Gunung Tata Mai Lau, with several other peaks exceeding 2,000 meters. The island's western half consists of rugged, rocky hills, high plateaus cut by deep valleys, and loose-soiled, grassy terrain. The eastern half is similar but more rugged, with higher peaks, narrower coastal plains, and numerous mountain-slashing rivers.

Climate

Timor is a transition point between humid, tropical Indonesia and more temperate Australia. The island's main climatic problem is rain—too little or too much. It is a land of harsh topography and capricious weather that has suffered drought and famine for centuries. Heavy rains fall Nov.-March, while during the rest of the year the island is one of the driest in Indonesia. More rain falls in the north than in the south and west.

The first rains in November turn the savannah into a vast garden: dust disappears, skies clear—Timor at its best. With monotonous regularity the rains come at the same time every day, with thunder, lightning, and rainbows on top of peaks. The countryside explodes when it rains, but much devastation occurs when trickling streams turn into crashing rivers, destroying much of the work done in the dry season. At the beginning of the wet season the rural people move out to the *ladang* and live in shelters; villages are practically deserted except for old people and children. When the rains really set in, the island becomes impassable anywhere off the main highway. Timor is the only island in the Lesser Sundas to get rain and wind of cyclonic force.

The end of the rainy season marks the high season in western Timor, when the maize is harvested, and all the *pasar* are alive with news and gossip. People travel and get married, visitors pass through, kids go to school, new hous-

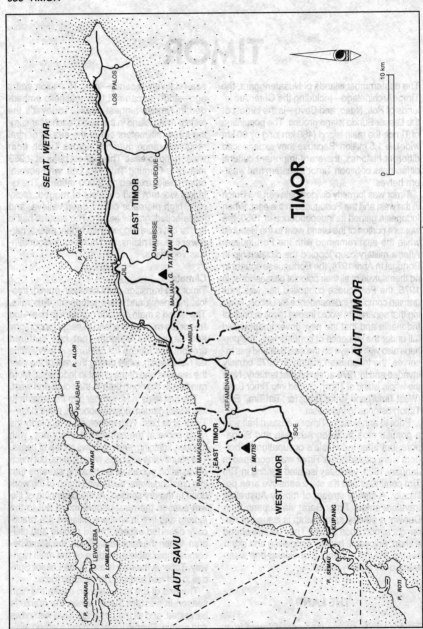

es are started. During the dry season (May-Sept.), the Timorese make salt, fell trees, collect beeswax, build houses, relax, feast, and dance. Landscapes during the dry are similar to the parched and brown Australian bush—leaves fall, rivers and wells dry up, drought sets in, the hot winds blow all day long. Later in the season dust and smoke from grass fires fill the air. When the rains are late the corn crop can fail. During this two- to three-month period each year, when food supplies are depleted and before the new harvest, the Timorese lay out strips of taro in rows in their yards; taro roots are processed into flour to be made into sago bread. This period is called *musim lapar,* "season of hunger."

FLORA AND FAUNA

Aromatic sandalwood has been Timor's "tree of destiny." By the 16th century Hindu-Javanese traders had discovered it, and by the end of the 19th century nearly all the sandalwood stands had been cut down, leaving behind large areas of open savannah grasslands. Acacia trees are a characteristic feature of the island's landscape, with their solitary flat-topped crowns and wide branches. Lantana palms cover 25-50% of West Timor. Only deep in the mountains of this highly eroded island are there traces of primary forests, especially in Tim Tim. Higher up are patches of original evergreen and eucalyptus forest. A mixture of both Australian- and Southeast Asian-type flora and fauna is found on the island.

HISTORY

Early History

Little is known of Timorese history prior to 1500 except that the island was split into dozens of independent, warring kingdoms. There is considerable evidence of early Hindu influence, and native princedoms were mentioned in ancient Chinese accounts. The sandalwood and beeswax of Timor attracted traders from Java and Malaya long before European contact. Starting in the 14th century, the aboriginal inhabitants, the Atoni, were displaced from their lands by invaders from southern Sulawesi and eastern Flores. These newcomers, known as the Tetum, or Belu, peoples, brought rice and maize, and

the federation they established in the eastern regions of West Timor lasted for hundreds of years.

Colonialism

Sandalwood first attracted the Portuguese to Timor in the early 1500s. After the traders came the priests. Dominican friars arrived in Flores and Timor in 1561 from Melaka to convert the natives to Christianity. The Dutch captured Melaka in 1641 and, after a prolonged struggle, eventually gained control of Kupang and western Timor. An expedition sent out by the Dutch in 1821 in search of the legendary Noil Noni ("River of Gold") failed; eight years later, with an escort of 1,200 men, the Dutch penetrated the interior, finally opening western Timor to the outside world.

For hundreds of years there was constant skirmishing with the Dutch over trade interests but the Portuguese were difficult to expel from eastern Timor because they had intermixed considerably with the natives and had created a group of Indo-Europeans called the "black Portuguese." For much of its history, the eastern half of Timor was ruled from Macao, the Portuguese colony south of Hong Kong. The neighboring islands of Solor and Adonara, as well as Larantuka in eastern Flores, also once belonged to the Portuguese, but they sold these districts to the Dutch (still not paid for!). Portuguese Timor was the earliest European enclave in Asia, predating much more powerful colonial holdouts like Macao and Goa that were established in the 17th century.

By 1655 the Portuguese had been ousted from all their most important settlements in Indonesia except for East Timor. The heated and longstanding territorial dispute between the Dutch and Portuguese over the sandalwood trade continued until 1904 when the two European powers finally carved up the island. The Portuguese were assigned the eastern half and the small enclave of Ocussi in the west, and the Dutch the remainder. But with few resources left to exploit, Timor was consigned to the backwaters of colonialism. The Portuguese thwarted East Timorese art and culture during hundreds of years of occupation, and failed to build roads, universities, or ports. Governing indirectly through local chiefs (*liurai*) elected from a federation of three to 10 *povoacaos* (villages), the

Portuguese kept the people ignorant and thus easier to control.

A series of popular revolts from 1894 to 1912 were mercilessly crushed. In 1958, after an unsuccessful coup by a group of army officers assisted by villagers in the eastern end of the island, more troops were sent. In 1974 there were 7,000 Portuguese soldiers in East Timor, which the government claimed were needed to keep another country from attacking. But they were really there to curb internal dissent. In the west, the impoverished Dutch territory was administered at an economic loss right up until Indonesia's independence.

World War II

During WW II, fighting by Australian, Dutch, and Japanese troops dragged Timor headlong into the war, and the island was eventually occupied by the Japanese. Australian commandos resisted for over a year, crediting their success—and many of their lives—to the wholehearted support they received from the Timorese. During the war the island's few towns and many villages were destroyed or badly damaged by Allied bombing, and over 50,000 Timorese civilians were killed outright or died in famines caused by food shortages.

It is cruelly ironic that after WW II, the victorious Allies favored independence for Indonesia under Sukarno and others who had collaborated with the Japanese, yet remained unopposed to the recolonization of East Timor by Portugal. In the 1950s, after the Indonesian revolution, Indonesia took control of the Dutch possessions but refrained from meddling in the Portuguese half. However, on 25 April 1974 military officers overthrew the Salazar dictatorship in Portugal, and the new socialist regime resolutely began dismantling the Portuguese colonial empire, including East Timor. For more on the history of East Timor, see "History" under "East Timor."

PRACTICALITIES

Getting There

Kupang is accessible from many points in the archipelago via Merpati, Sempati, and Bouraq airlines. Merpati charges, for example, Rp199,000 from Denpasar (three flights most days) or Rp393,000 from Jakarta. Bouraq charges Rp65,000 from Maumere (Flores) and Rp117,000 from Waingapu (Sumba). Both flights continue on to Denpasar. Sempati flies to Kupang from Denpasar, and like Merpati, also flies from Kupang to Dili for Rp82,000. From Kupang's El Tari Airport taxis cost Rp7500 for the 12-km ride into town. Pay the driver, not the taxi desk.

Merpati Fokker 28 aircraft also depart Darwin for Kupang, continuing on to Denpasar and Surabaya each Wednesday and Saturday at 1530; A$198 one-way (two hours) or A$330 roundtrip. At least three travel agencies in Darwin—San Michele, All Points Travel, and Natrabu—sell these tickets. No visa is required, as Kupang is now an official entry point.

Kupang's Tenau Harbor, eight km from the bemo terminal (Rp500), is home base for the Pelni ship KM Kelimutu, which follows a regular schedule to ports in East and West Nusatenggara and beyond. Since October 1993, the new KM Dobonsolo has also stopped at Kupang, sailing from Tanjung Priok, and continuing on to Dili and towns on the north coast of Irian Jaya. Also check out the KM Elang for a route that connects Kisar, and the Solor and Alor archipelagos, to Kupang. For schedules and fares from Kupang, check with the Pelni office, Jl. Pahlawan 5, Kupang, tel. (0391) 21977. Sample economy-class fares from Kupang on the KM Kelimutu are Dili (Rp17,000), Kalabahi (Rp21,700), Ende (Rp16,000), and Surabaya (Rp56,000). On the KM Dobonsolo fares include Ambon (Rp41,000), Jayapura (Rp117,000), and Tanjung Priok (Rp85,000).

From Kupang's Bolok Harbor, 12 km west of the bemo station, there are regular ASDP ferries to Roti, Savu, Sumba, the Solor and Alor groups, and Flores. There is a Rp100 harbor tax. The ASDP office is located near Kupang's main post office, about two km above the waterfront.

Getting Around

Timor's roads are quite good in the dry season; a government-built, well-surfaced trunk road runs all the way from Kupang through Dili to Los Palos. Back roads and trails are strewn with stones, and riverbeds are used for traffic. To reach really remote areas, like the Insana region, the only way is to walk. Travel to towns in West Timor like Soe (110 km), Kefamenanu (197 km), and Atambua

(283 km) on long-distance buses from Kupang's terminal. Bus and *bemo* connections to outlying areas from these towns are frequent and good. Be ready for long waits in the rainy season, especially off the main road, when landslides are common, mountain paths turn slippery, and roads and plains turn to mud—a time when it's difficult to travel even by four-wheel drive.

Since the start of the Darwin-Kupang flight in 1986, a tiny, budding travel industry has developed in Kupang. Representatives from a number of the city's hotels meet tourists at the airport and take them free of charge back to the hotel. Several hotels conduct relaxed and enjoyable snorkeling, picnicking, sunbathing, and sightseeing tours to outlying beaches and islands at an average cost of around Rp35,000 pp per day.

While roaming around the countryside, you'll notice how friendly the Timorese are. They wave from their fields, some bow, others will give you a sharp military salute—a holdover from the Japanese occupation. Hunters on horseback with bows and arrows may gallop alongside your vehicle, or you may wake up from a nap with 100 people staring down at you.

WEST TIMOR

ECONOMY

The West Timorese make a living from farming or the sea. The rapid spread of a cash economy in the postwar period has not greatly affected the subsistence patterns of the majority of the indigenous population. Soil is generally poor and thin; where rainfall and soil conditions permit, wet-rice agriculture and gardening are practiced. The villagers rely most of the year on crops of corn, sweet potatoes, cassava, and some millet, all grown in swidden gardens, as well as the cultivation of coconuts. Different locales grow different crops: the lowland villages of the central plain center their economy on corn, while the upland people of the north grow rice. West Timorese have never accepted the plow, and fields are still tilled by driving herds of water buffalo over the wet ground until it turns into a smooth sea of mud. In the upland areas, some use metal poles instead of spades or hoes to turn the soil.

Life on the parched inland is hard and the population exerts great pressure on available resources. Severe famine and drought are facts of life here. The open rainy grasslands of the island's western half make natural grazing regions, and the local economy is heavily tied to cattle raising. Bali cattle were introduced in Timor Barat by the Dutch on a large scale in the 1930s and distributed among the *rajas*. Raised for the export market, cattle are now twice as numerous as humans. Rain leaching the soil during the wet, together with the herds that run in the thousands, have resulted in serious overgrazing and erosion. The whole island is now experiencing progressive and irreversible ecological deterioration.

THE PEOPLE

West Timor is racially divided into two main groups: the Atoni, the indigenous Melanesian people, and the Belunese and Rotinese, who arrived at a later date and pushed the Atoni into the eroded mountains of the interior.

The patrilineal Atoni are short, with dark brown skin and frizzy hair like Papuans; Negrito types are also seen in the west. The native Atoni belong to 10 traditional princedoms (*swapraja*), now administrative districts, and speak a number of different Malayo-Polynesian languages. Their hamlets, containing a church and school, are usually found along ridges or slopes. Traditional Atoni dwellings (*lopo*), with dirt floors and bamboo frames, are characteristically beehive-shaped with high conical thatched roofs which extend downward almost to the ground. The different parts of the house are arranged according to cosmological beliefs, and are topped with animals, birds, or little people. Although the Indonesian government has depoliticized the native headmen (*rajas*), some are still quite powerful and control the allotment of village agricultural lands.

The people from Atambua share the same customs as the Belunese people of East Timor. The Helong are remnants of a group that once inhabited all of southwest Timor. By the 17th century, expanding native Atoni states had confined the Helong to a small coastal strip in far western Timor; still later they migrated to the offshore island of Semau. The dwindling Helong today live in one village near the port of Tenau in West Timor, and in several villages on Semau, where they grow dry-field rice and maize. The people of Roti and Savu on the islands of the Outer Arc trace their lineages back to the Majapahit Empire and practice traditional cultures quite distinct from mainland Timor's.

Lontar-palm tapping, to obtain the main ingredient in the alcoholic beverage sopo, is widespread. All ethnic groups in the Timor Archipelago chew sirih after meals and especially on ceremonial occasions. An adult chews 15 betelnut seeds a day; children start chewing at age seven or eight. Some natives of the deep interior still hunt with blowpipes; clubs (gada) with stone heads like tomahawks are used in places, and boomerangs are still employed in the southeast coastal regions.

Religion
Some 25% of the Timorese are Protestants, 20% are Catholic, and the rest are devotees of Islam. Nearly everyone you meet has a Christian name like Martinus, Augustus, or Daniatus. Christiani-

ty arrived in 1624, but wholesale conversions didn't take place until 1920, when the Dutch scholar-missionary Middelkoop began proselytizing, translating the Bible into Timorese.

In spite of the professed religion of most Timorese, traditional beliefs and rituals are still widely practiced. The Timorese believe that the afterlife contains all the same occupations, worries, and necessities of this earthly life. Reptiles play a vital role in the religion of the native West Timorese, particularly in the central and eastern districts. The most sacred reptile of all is the crocodile, revered as a fertility god. The Atoni prohibit hunting crocodiles; if one is killed in self-defense, it must be accorded all the privileges of a human burial. As late as the early 19th century virgins were reportedly sacrificed to hungry crocodiles. Crocodiles are still used frequently in Timorese weaving motifs.

Music
The Timorese enjoy music in their everyday lives, but to hear it you must seek it out. There's no gamelan, but one of the most unusual instruments in the Indonesian archipelago is the sasando, a plucked bamboo tube zither found on Roti, Timor, and surrounding islands. The sasando has up to 22 strings made from a civet's gut, stretched over pyramidal bridges

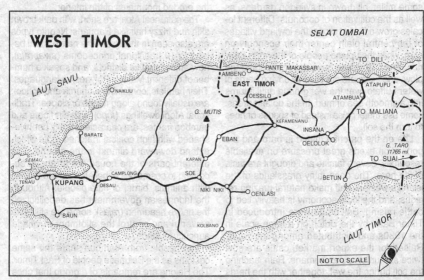

between two ends of a deep, boat-shaped body fashioned from dried *lontar* leaf. It makes a very high-pitched twangy sound.

Take a *bemo* (Rp400) to Oebelo, 15 km southwest of Kupang, where there's a *sasando* cottage industry. Ask for Pak Edupa, a masterful musician on the Timorese *sasando*. Hear him in his home at Lasiana Beach, 12 km from Kupang. He sits cross-legged and holds the head of the bamboo zither in his left hand while plucking the strings with his right fingernails. Eli Koamesakh plays traditional *sasando* at Kuanino Kampung in town.

High in the mountains people call each other with the *hoholo,* an instrument with a deep and penetrating voice made from buffalo horn. The *farafara,* which makes a harsh, vulgar sound, is used to frighten wild pigs from the crops. The *queuqueuquepere,* both a string and percussion instrument, is played by witch doctors to diagnose influences causing illness or misfortune. "Songs of Death," Timor's *Iliad,* tells of prehistoric migrations woven around the lives of ancestors. Some fetching melodies are Western in origin, but the rhythmical structure is Timorese—much wilder than Western renditions.

Crafts

Traditional weaving, plaiting, and basketry are still widely practiced inland. Atoni women decorate betelnut baskets (*oko*) with elaborate, vivid patterns. The weaving arts, such as tapestry weaving (*kelim*) and the embroidered warp technique (*songket*), are highly developed, among the most intricate in Indonesia. Both men and women wear traditional *kain, sarung,* and ornamental *selendang,* all symbols of wealth and often given as gifts.

All these cotton fabrics have naturalistic, ceremonial designs: bright geometric patterns, crocodiles, lizards, geckos, elongated ghost figures, sometimes mounted riders. Patterns indicate a person's princedom, and a strict etiquette governs wearing them. Using natural dyes, colors include solid black (Amfoan and Insana areas), shades of brown and black (Roti), and red, black, and white (Soba District).

Very expensive in the shops of Kupang, the women's *lau* garment can take six weeks of continuous work; cloth is sometimes buried to deepen the colors. In the central highlands, beautiful homemade *sarung* have narrow warpwise stripes of orange, yellow, red, or other bright colors, and incorporate designs that can be traced back to the Dongson period of over 2,000 years ago.

Timor has one of the largest reserves of antique ivory in the world. Originally brought by the sandalwood merchants from Flores, and before that from Sumatra, ivory is still used as part of the dowry price. A whole antique tusk costs Rp500,000, an old bracelet around Rp50,000. Note, however, that it's illegal to take ivory out of Indonesia, and illegal to import it to many countries. Aged ivory is like a dark, polished wood, taking years to turn brown from the oil in human skin. There's no stone or metal work, but the gold and silver ornaments produced by the roving Ndaonese (from a small island west of Roti) are highly prized.

KUPANG

This 300-year-old trading center is the largest urban area in Nusatenggara and the capital of Nusatenggara Timur. Lying only 483 km from the coast of northeast Australia, Kupang is closer to Darwin than to Jakarta. Having emigrated from surrounding islands and beyond, the friendly population comprises a rainbow of races: Atoni, Rotinese, Savunese, Chinese, Florinese, Kisarese, Alorese, Solorese, Ambonese, Javanese, Arabs, Eurasians. The vernacular Malay spoken here reflects the wide variety of peoples who settled this area.

Christianity is the predominant religion (90%), but there is also a small minority of Muslims (descendants of Arab traders), some 3,000 Balinese, a couple dozen Caucasian expats, and the Chinese, who own about 85% of the businesses. There's definitely a Melanesian flavor to the city. Due to Australia's close proximity and good flight connections, Kupang has an underlying yet distinctly Australian orientation and tourist focus.

Although there are now buildings several stories high, sidewalks, an excellent local phone system, and busy intersections full of *bemo* and government jeeps, the mood and pace are easy in this commercial and administrative center, which didn't get streetlights until 1971.

Kupang has a Catholic university, **Widya Mandira,** and a public university, **Nusa Cen-**

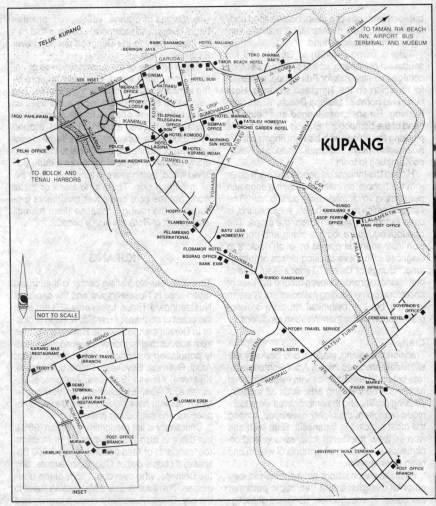

KUPANG

TELUK KUPANG

SEE INSET

TO BOLOK AND TENAU HARBORS

PELNI OFFICE

TAGU PAHLAWAN

BANK DANAMON

BERINGIN JAYA

JL. GARUDA

CINEMA

NATRABU

MERPATI
OFFICE

PITOBY
LODGE

IKANPAUS

TELEPHONE /
TELEGRAPH
OFFICE

BDN

POLICE

BANK INDONESIA

JL. SILIWANGI

JL. KOSASIH

JL. GUNUNG MEJA

JL. LAKAAN

HOTEL SUSI

JL. URIP
SUMOHARJO

HOTEL KOMODO

HOTEL
LAGUNA

MORNING
SUN HOTEL

HOTEL
KUPANG INDAH

TOMPELLO

JL. SOEKARNO

BANK DANAMON

HOTEL MALIANO

TIMOR BEACH HOTEL

BNI

TOKO DHARMA
BAKTI

JL. ALOR

JL. SUMBA

JL. A. TANI

JL. FLORES

HOTEL MARINA

FATULEU HOMESTAY

ORCHID GARDEN HOTEL

SEMPATI
OFFICE

JL. FATULEU

JL. NANGKA

JL. CAK
DOKO

BUNDO
KANDUANG II

ASOP FERRY
OFFICE

JL. LALAMENTIK

MAIN POST OFFICE

JL. PALAPA

GOVERNOR'S
OFFICE

CENDANA HOTEL

HOSPITAL

FLAMBOYAN

PELAMBANG
INTERNATIONAL

FLOBAMOR HOTEL

BOURAQ OFFICE

BANK EXIM

JL. PROF. YOHANES

BATU LESA
HOMESTAY

JL.
SUDIRMAN

BUNDO KANDUANG

PITOBY TRAVEL SERVICE

HOTEL ASTITI

JL. BENTENG

JL. SATSUI TUBUN

JL. JEN. SUHARTO

JL. HARIMAU

JL. EL TARI

MARKET
(PASAR INPRES)

UNIVERSITY NUSA CENDANA

POST OFFICE
BRANCH

NOT TO SCALE

TO TAMAN RIA BEACH
INN, AIRPORT, BUS
TERMINAL, AND MUSEUM

JL. TIM-TIM

INSET

KARANG MAS
RESTAURANT

TEDDY'S

JL. SILIWANGI

PITOBY TRAVEL
(BRANCH)

BEMO
TERMINAL

JL. IKANPAUS

JAYA RAYA
RESTAURANT

JL. SOEKARNO

MURAH

HEMILIKI RESTAURANT

BRI

POST OFFICE
BRANCH

LOSMEN EDEN

dana. Yet the city has almost no industry, only a local ice factory, an electrical generation plant, cement factory, sandalwood oil factory, and small fishing enterprises, so everybody wants to work for the civil service, army, police, hospitals, or the budding tourist industry. There's a tourism committee, but tourism seems slow to get started. A new tourist office and museum are out beyond the bus station in the new section of town. The museum is a grand place with a small collection, mostly *ikat* (nice samples),

some pottery and currency, and ethnographic articles of daily life. Worth a quick look.

History

Early in the 17th century, the Dutch established a trading post here. In 1653 they took possession of the town and then for more than a century struggled against the Portuguese for control of the island. The Dutch were almost repulsed from Timor in 1749 when a "black Portuguese" *raja* from the northern Portuguese enclave of

Ocussi threatened Kupang with a band of 200 angry men, but they were thrown back and the town saved. Finally, in 1859, the boundary between the Dutch and the Portuguese portions was formally drawn. In 1791, the irascible Captain Bligh ended his epic open-boat 6,500-km journey in Kupang.

In the first half of the 19th century, Kupang was a port of call for English and American whalers. Somerset Maugham's stories of Timor were set here. The Dutch established many schools and the city's first hospital in the early part of this century.

During the 1920s, Kupang's contact with the outside world increased when Dutch KPM steamers began to call at the small port. The old Dutch pier stood at the mouth of the Air Mata stream below what was Fort Concordia; only pilings remain today. After independence in 1949, Kupang's bureaucracy and population expanded exponentially. All the principal government offices are now located north of the city on a plateau called the Walikota. This highland area, which contains the governor's office, residence, regional senate (DPR), supreme court, and other provincial government offices, is cleaner, cooler, breezier and less congested than the city proper. Kupang is a major communications and transport hub for the region, with buses heading out to points in West Timor and Dili, as well as air and sea connections to all over Indonesia.

Sights

About 75 meters south of the bridge on the road heading to the harbor is a small road to the right leading to a promontory overlooking Kupang harbor. Some of Kupang's oldest buildings are here. The rather large graveyard has many old Dutch gravestones. On a Saturday night in Kupang it seems the whole town turns out on the main street to visit and hang out, with the usual assortment of *dukun* selling elixirs.

Have a Timorese friend take you to one of Kupang's many churches. Masses at the Catholic churches start at 0830 and 1030. On Sunday evenings, the streets are full of Bible-toting Timorese going to and from church.

Accommodations

Overnighting in any of Kupang's more than three dozen hostelries is no bargain—most charge in the Rp10,000-25,000 range. Private and very quiet **Fatuleu Homestay,** Jl. G. Fatuleu 1, tel. (0391) 31374, is recommended. Clean, beautiful garden, laundry service. Rooms without *mandi* are Rp7500 s and Rp10,000 d including breakfast (tea/coffee, bread, banana, even *nasi goreng* on request). Very friendly staff. Owner Jack Sine is also a tour operator and speaks English well.

At Jl. G. Fatuleu 2, across the street from Fatuleu Homestay, is the **Orchid Garden Hotel,** tel. 33707, the city's best. Full service: swimming pool, gourmet restaurant, in-house doctor, tennis courts, room service, free transfer to the airport, tour operator and ticketing agent on premises. All 60 rooms, with TV, radio, and video equipment, breakfast included, face the courtyard—standard Rp117,600, standard double Rp134,400, superior Rp155,400, and orchid suite Rp262,500.

A short distance back toward town at Jl A. Yani 79 is **Hotel Marina,** tel. 22566. A nice place, but it has no restaurant. Sempati Airlines maintains an office here. Fan rooms cost Rp10,000-15,000, a/c rooms Rp20,000-30,000; breakfast and tea included.

Hotel Laguna, Jl. Kelimutu 36, tel. 21348, is a sprawling complex of 23 rooms run as efficiently as a Singapore budget hotel. Rooms cost Rp7000 without *mandi* or fan and Rp12,000-18,000 with fan and *mandi*; a/c rooms run up to Rp60,000. Popular with businesspeople, the Laguna isn't a bad deal for Kupang. Coffee and sweetcakes are served at 0530. The restaurant here features Javanese food.

Next door at Jl. Kelimutu 35 is **Hotel Komodo,** tel. 31179. Recently renovated, this clean, efficiently run, multistoried hotel has laundry service but no restaurant. Standard rooms run Rp15,000-20,000, a/c rooms Rp25,000-27,000.

Around the curve along Jl. Kelimutu is **Hotel Kupang Indah,** tel. 22648. An older establishment, but clean and neat, it offers a simple breakfast but has no restaurant on site. Rooms are Rp10,000 s, Rp12,500 d, and Rp17,500 t; a/c rooms Rp20,000-25,000.

Down the street at Jl. Kelimutu 11a is the newest Kupang hotel, **Morning Sun Hotel,** tel. 32268. Owned and operated by Ruth Bowes, an Australian, it has an assortment of rooms: standard fan Rp10,000-12,500, or Rp17,500-22,000 for a larger room. Air-conditioned rooms from

Rp27,500 to Rp30,000. Discount on long-term stays and for Aussie government workers. Room charge includes afternoon tea and transfer to and from the airport or harbor. Beds in a bunk room for Rp4000 pp may be available; inquire. There are plans to open a Morning Glory Restaurant and Bar next door.

On Jl. Kosasi, just up from the Merpati office, is the centrally located, budget accommodation **Pitoby Lodge,** tel. 32910, with rooms from Rp5500. Some rooms have bunk beds, all have fans; some have *mandi,* others share facilities. YHA, VIP, or STA cardholders receive a 50% discount. In conjunction with the Pitoby Lodge is **Dive Kupang,** the only organized scuba diving operation on Timor. Across the street is the **Wisma Andhika.** Rooms downstairs are dark and go for Rp5000—ask for a larger, breezier room upstairs.

Hotel Susi, Jl. Sumatera 48, tel. 22172, charges from Rp10,000-19,000 for a room with a fan and Rp21,000-26,000 with a/c, breakfast included. Second- and third-floor rooms overlook the ocean. Beautiful rooftop for cool nights, and nice patio for cold beer. Clean enough but somewhat sterile.

Next door at no. 35 is **Hotel Maliano,** tel. 21879. Fourteen rooms on one level—homey, lived-in. Rooms are Rp19,000-23,000 s and Rp24,000-28,000 d, including breakfast. A bit expensive but you pay for the view. Just down the road, the **Maya Hotel** is undergoing a complete rebuilding.

Right on the waterfront, where Jl. Sumatera makes a jog away from the bay, is **Timor Beach Hotel,** tel. 31651. Economy rooms are Rp12,350 s and Rp16,800 d; a/c rooms Rp24,650 s and Rp30,800 d; rooms with a/c and TV Rp30,250 s and Rp36,400 d; with a "family room" for Rp49,300. This restaurant has a well regarded restaurant that serves seafood, Chinese, and Indonesian food.

Hotel Flobamor, tel. 21346, Jl. Jen. Sudirman 21, is basically a business hotel. Depending upon the floor and class of room, rates are Rp30,000-80,000, with one VIP room for Rp150,000. All rooms have a/c, hot water, satellite TV, telephone, and video. Very clean, spacious, and well kept with a nice lobby and breezy outdoor restaurant. Service is excellent except for exorbitant laundry costs. Many Australians stay here, as well as foreign project

workers and long-term businesspeople. A handy tour and travel agent's office is inside, as well as a gift shop and a bar/disco. The Merpati agent is next door. Also ask about the bungalows on Pulau Semau—Rp73,500 s, Rp126,000 d including transportation and three meals daily.

Fifty meters down an alley around the corner from the Hotel Flobamor is **Batu Lesa Homestay,** tel. 32863—Homey, cozy, inexpensive, and on a major *bemo* route. With 10 rooms, five in a new building, rates are Rp4000 with a shared *mandi* and Rp5000 with a *mandi* and fan.

Hotel Astiti, Jl. Jen. Sudirman 146, tel. 21810 or 21786, has economy rooms at Rp25,000 s and Rp30,000 d; other, nicer rooms from Rp37,500 to Rp65,000, including breakfast. Each room offers a/c and a TV. There is a restaurant on premises plus several in the immediate area. Astria Travel Service is located here. Although it isn't that strategically located (three km from the *bemo* terminal and no view), it's on the main *bemo* route into the city and on a good route to the bus terminal.

Air Nona is a quiet area to stay in, four km up the hill from the *bemo* terminal (Rp300 by *bemo*). There's a great 200-year-old spring-fed pool of cool water (the "lagoon") and many shady trees, so it's not so hot as downtown. Here at **Losmen Eden,** tel. 21921, run by ex-parliamentarian Papa Minggus, you pay Rp3000 pp. There are also bungalows and "family" rooms, but only tea and coffee for breakfast. His sons are guides. They also have a swimming pool and a bar, and tasty food is served at all hours (the best *gado-gado!*). Small fruit and vegetable market nearby, and a *warung* on the main road sells Rp800-1200 meals. From Air Nona, charter a *bemo* to the airport for Rp7500.

At **Cendana Hotel,** Jl. Raya El Tari 23, tel. 21541 or 21127, there are 44 rooms in all classes. The 12 economy rooms (Rp14,200 s and Rp19,700 d) in front with breakfast are a good deal because you can still take advantage of all the facilities. Or pay Rp24,500-46,200 for a/c rooms or suites with TV. All rooms have inside *mandi,* and the prices of all rooms include breakfast; three meals a day possible with an increase in the room charge of about Rp5000 pp. The food is mediocre but the atmosphere is definitely Indonesian. You could run into 73 nursing students or a government veterinarian convention. Although it's a bit far from downtown, *bemo* stop nearby and return as late as 2000. Room service, laundry, souvenir and art shops. The hotel *bemo* is available for hire. Travel agency attached.

Taman Ria Beach Inn, Jl. Tim Tim 69, tel. 31320, is a small amusement park converted to a hotel and restaurant, two km east of the city toward the airport. The old rides are still there rusting away, so it looks a bit surreal. A bit run-down, these are budget seaside accommodations—cool, tropical, calm surroundings—right on the beach so the breeze keeps the mosquitos away. Prices: Rp12,000 s and 15,000 d with *mandi* and fan. Ask the director about boat charters to Kupang's offshore islands.

Hotel Sasando, Jl. Kartini, tel. 22224, is a luxury hotel on a parched, windy, flat plateau six km east of town. Rates: Rp84,000-126,000, plus 21% service and government tax. All rooms face the ocean and the sunset. Facilities include telex, tennis courts, swimming pool, restaurant, and tour agency. One wonders how the Sasando ever got its two-star rating—a hotel is pretty hard up when the manager himself calls guests in their rooms to ask if they desire female companionship. The Sasando's fortunes may take an upswing as the city continues to build its administrative district, called Walikota, just behind the hotel. Take a taxi to and from Kupang for Rp6000 each way.

For a more unique stay try the **Uiasa Beach Cottage** on Semau Island, directly to the west of Kupang. Bamboo cottages, shower, Western toilets. Empty beaches, no crowds. Make reservations through Teddy's Bar in Kupang. Rates are Rp35,000 s, Rp50,000 d, and Rp60,000 t, which includes three meals a day and boat transportation to and from the island.

Food

Around the *bemo* station at night buy a carefully measured ounce of sweet potato chips (*kripik*), *tuak, es stroop,* ice cream, slices of fresh fruit, and honey from Amfoan. If loading up on snacks to take to Australia, don't buy unroasted peanuts, as Aussie customs will confiscate them. Beef is plentiful in Kupang, the animal protein of choice over chicken; sample some *daging se'i* (smoked beef).

The good **Hemiliki Restaurant** on Jl. Sukarno specializes in Chinese-style seafood dishes. Expensive but delicious. Serves one of the best *nasi goreng* in Indonesia. Friendly, relaxing setting; open 0800-1500 and 1800-2230. Directly to its front is a much more basic and inexpensive Indonesian place, appropriately called **Murah.**

Restaurant/bar **Teddy's,** on the waterfront and a hangout for expats, is owned by an Australian woman and her husband, a curly-haired Chinese who drove a taxi in Australia for eight years. Teddy's serves good seafood and steak dishes (Rp3000-7000).

Where Jl. Garuda meets Jl. Sumatera, at the Timor Beach Hotel, is the restaurant **Pantai Timor,** which specializes in seafood. Another outstanding restaurant is the **Istana Garden** on Jl. Tim Tim, out of town on the left just before the turnoff to the airport; it also has a bar, disco, and live music. One of the best restaurants is the 5 **Jaya Raya,** Jl. Sukarno 15, tel. (0391) 22254, by the *bemo* station. Decent value, dishes run Rp2000-10,000. The extensive menu, with shrimp and squid always available, is the real draw. The specialty is whole fish. Peek in at the disco upstairs for a look at people doing the foxtrot.

Bundo Kanduang, only a five-minute walk from Hotel Flobamor, is a big *nasi padang* restaurant. A good choice. The newer **Bundo Kanduang II** is located near the post office. The steak restaurant **Rotterdam,** near the mayor's office (*balai kota*), caters to *pegawai* and hotel guests from the Sasando in the new administrative district six km north of the city. The menu includes Indonesian, Chinese, and Western food, including beefsteak and chicken steak. Some patrons, however, say that everything that comes from the kitchen tastes the same.

At the **Karang Mas,** Jl. Siliwangi 84/88, the food's lousy, although it's a superlative place for a beer in the evening because of the brilliant sunsets. This place hasn't changed in the last 20 years—not even the stains on the wall. Like many of Kupang's restaurants, the Karang employs women from Roti. As you sit on the balcony jutting over the sea, look out over the very spot where Captain Bligh pulled into Kupang harbor in 1789. So valuable is this property along Kupang's waterfront that a Balinese once offered the Chinese family who owns the Karang Mas US$1 million for the restaurant; they refused to sell. For Padang-style, also try **Beringin Jaya** near the waterfront. Part way up the hill are the **Flamboyan** and **Pelambang International.**

Also try some of Kupang's hotel restaurants. The Flobamor, Astiti, and Orchid Garden offer a wide variety of Indonesian, Chinese, and Western food.

Shopping

Visit the large daily market, lively Pasar Inpres, where you can see all the peoples of eastern Nusatenggara in microcosm: work-hardened rustics from the mountain districts, natives from Roti, Savu, and Flores wearing resplendent woven garments. **Toko Dharma Bakti,** Jl. Sumba 32 A near Rumah Bupati, is Kupang's largest souvenir/crafts shop, selling sandalwood items, old statues, *lontar*-leaf weavings, flamboyant Rotinese hats, and *sarung, kain,* and *ikat* from all over Nusatenggara (up to Rp200,000 apiece).

The variety of *ikat* available on Timor is beyond belief. **Dharma Bakti** runs an *ikat* factory by the cement plant out toward the harbor, surrounded by elaborate murals, where you can watch the actual weaving. **Wisma Cendana,** with its piles of textiles, is another major crafts outlet. Also try **Toko Padang Sari,** Jl. Suharto 57, tel. (0391) 21538, and **Toko Sinar Baru,** Jl. Siliwangi 22, tel. 22056. **Loka Binkra,** located several km east of town, is a government-sponsored craft center.

Yayasan le Rai is the Savu Ikat Weavers Cooperative on Jl. Hati Mulia, tel. 22692, established to preserve *ikat* weaving on remote Savu; wares include small purses, blankets, and bedspreads. Farther afield, the inhabitants of the traditional village of **Kotabes** (40 km from Kupang) practice the Amarasi-style of *ikat* weaving. Another weaving village is **Sonraen,** Rp3000 by *bemo* from Kupang. **Oelolok** is a traditional weaving center in the Insana area, 20 km from Kefamenanu.

Kupang now has a few supermarkets, like the **Istana Supermarket** near the Flobamor Hotel. Others are located in the old part of town. There are several bookstores in each of these areas as well.

Services

The new tourist office near the museum is of dubious value; get tourist information from your hotel or a travel agency.

For photographic supplies, film processing and printing, try **Toko Sinar Jaya** on Jl. Sudirman next to Hotel Flobamor. Also try **Prima Photo** on Jl. Siliwangi; **Tari Photo,** Jl. Sudirman 51; **Sinar Baru,** Jl. Siliwangi 22; or **Roda Baru Photo,** on Jl. A Yani, near the Orchid Garden Hotel. Slide film must be sent out for processing—takes 10 days.

Bank Dagang Negara offers an outstanding rate for U.S. dollars (one of the best in Nusatenggara), not as good for Australian. Change money also at the main office of **BNI** next to Hotel Susi. **Bank Danamon** has good rates. Other exchange banks are **BRI** and **Bank Exim.**

A branch **post office** is near the waterfront, but have your poste restante mail addressed to the main post office, *kantor pos besar* on Jl. Palapa, open 0700-1400 daily. You may have to sift through the laundry basket of unsorted letters to find your own. Another branch post office is on Jl. Suharto near University Nusa Cendana.

The **telephone and telegraph** office is on Jl. Urip Sumoharjo (open 24 hours); the city prefix is 0391. The city hospital, **Umum,** is on Jl. Moh. Hatta. For medicines, go to **Apotik Kota,** Jl. Garuda 31, tel. (0391) 21303; **Apotik Sonbai,** Jl. Sudirman 93, tel. 21073; **Apotik Kupang Farma,** on Jl. Sudirman; or **Apotik Ani,** on Jl. A Yani.

Getting Around

Kupang is too spread out to explore on foot, so take a Philippine jeepney-like *bemo.* Painted and bedecked with lights and elaborate facades, pulsing loud American rhythms, they cruise all the main streets. *Bemo* can be found at the main *bemo* terminal or anywhere along the main thoroughfares. There is a dizzying number of *bemo* routes—too many to sort out easily—so ask at your hotel for the correct *bemo* to take to your destination. All *bemo* display numbers on their roof signs. *Bemo* charge Rp300 anywhere in town, Rp750 to/from the harbor, and Rp400 to/from the airport entrance road. Often used routes include no. 2, downtown to Jl. Sudirman and up the hill; no. 3, downtown to Bakunase and Air Nona; no. 5, downtown to Pasar Inpres and the post office; no. 7, from the Hotel Flobamor area to the bus station; no. 10, downtown to the bus station, museum, and tourist office; no. 15, to Pantai Lasiana; and no. 17, to the airport entrance road (then walk one km to the airport terminal).

El Tari Airport is 12 km from the city center. Take a taxi from town (Rp7500, or Rp8500 with a/c) to the terminal building. There are actually two small terminal buildings, separated by a restaurant, one for domestic and one for international flights. Each has a small snack shop and craft counter. Both foreign exchange and tourist information are available at the international terminal building, but only when flights from Darwin arrive. Upon leaving for Darwin, there is a Rp11,000 tax.

Getting Away

By Air: Merpati now has an extensive flight schedule from Kupang. Light aircraft fly five times per week to Alor, and twice a week to Roti, Savu, and Larantuka. Daily flights to points within Nusatenggara connect Kupang to Dili, Bima, Ende, Labuhanbajo, Maumere, and Ruteng; three times weekly to Waingapu and Mataram; and twice weekly to Bajawa. Farther afield, daily flights to the hubs of Denpasar, Surabaya, and Ujung Pandang connect Kupang

hanging out, bemo-*style*

to virtually all major cities in Indonesia. If you're flying west, sit on the right side to see Flores, Komodo, Sumba, and Sumbawa—a stupendous sight. The **Merpati** office is at Jl. Kosasi 2 (tel. 22088); there are also Merpati agents all over town. Good service here. The main office seems to be the only Merpati office in all of Nusatenggara with a computer link to Jakarta; reservations and flight information sent and received quickly and accurately.

The **Bouraq** office is at Jl. Sudirman 20A, tel. (0391) 21421, only five minutes from Hotel Flobamor, toward downtown. Flights leave three times weekly to Maumere, going on to Denpasar and Surabaya. Four times a week, there's a connection to Waingapu, which also continues on to Denpasar and Surabaya.

Sempati also flies out of Kupang to Dili and Denpasar three times a week. Its office is at Hotel Marina, at Jl. A. Yani 79, tel. 33044.

From Kupang to Darwin, Merpati charges A$198 one-way (two hours), A$330 return. Pay in *rupiah* or by credit card—no traveler's checks. This flight leaves Kupang every Wednesday and Saturday at 1130 and returns from Darwin the same day at 1530. Airport tax is Rp11,000. Get to the airport by taxi (Rp7500) or take *bemo* no. 15 or 16, or the one marked "Penfui." Be sure to get an Australian visa in Jakarta first.

By Sea: Inquire at **Pelni,** Jl. Pahlawan 5 (near Asrama Benteng Tentara), for ships to many of the principal ports of Nusatenggara and beyond. Pelni operates the KM *Kelimutu* between Surabaya, Banjarmasin, Benoa, Lembar, Ujung Pandang, Bima, Waingapu, Ende, Maumere, Kalabahi, Makassar, Kupang, and Dili—a full loop taking 14 days. Also on a two-week schedule is the KM *Dobonsolo,* which operates between Kupang, Dili, and ports in Maluku and the north coast of Irian Jaya. Refer to "Getting There" in the Timor Introduction for information about interisland ASDP ferries from Kupang.

Inquire about Pelni service from Kupang to Darwin, Australia; this trip should take about 26 hours and cost around Rp50,000 one-way.

By Land: A whole string of towns—Soe, Kefamenanu, Atambua, Atapupu—are connected by a trunk road that winds its way east into the interior to Dili, former capital of Portuguese Timor and now the provincial capital of Timor Timur. You head inland on a beautiful, wide, smooth road. Buses now leave from the **Oebo-**

lo bus terminal in Walikota, about six km from downtown Kupang; take *bemo* no. 10 (Rp300). All fares are posted. Sturdy buses run this main highway to major towns and to intermediate points off the highway on secondary roads. Buses start leaving for points east around 0600 and go when they fill up. There are many departures throughout the day, more to the nearer destinations. Sample destinations and fares: Camplong (Rp1000), Soe (Rp3500, two hours, 110 km), Niki Niki (Rp4300), Kefamenanu (Rp6200, five hours, 197 km), and Atambua (Rp8700, seven to eight hours, 274 km). Buses also run to Dili—Rp13,500 for the morning bus (0700 departure) and Rp15,000 for the night bus (1900 departure).

Periodically, the overland trip from West Timor to Dili is closed to foreign visitors without a *surat jalan*; however, there's almost never a problem going in the reverse direction. At these times it may be possible to get permission to cross from the military command in Atambua, but you may just as likely be told you need to apply to the military authorities in Kupang. Persist, because in Kupang you could be told papers are issued only in Denpasar or Jakarta. It seems nearly impossible to obtain accurate information and proper authorization, yet some do manage. If you run into a problem you can always fly.

Tours

Kupang has a number of private tour operators in addition to those connected to hotels. **Hotel Flobamor** offers a tour out to Pulau Semau, 12 km from Kupang, where there's a nice sandy beach, no roads, no cars, waving palm trees, crystal-clear cold natural bathing pools, small villages, and walks in the hills. The price (Rp63,000-126,000) includes accommodations, transportation, and meals. **Teddy's** owns a set of bamboo bungalows on Pulau Semau right on Uiasa Beach. They have showers, flush toilets, and cost Rp35,000-60,000 with three meals daily. Free transportation if you stay there.

All travel agents offer tours. The biggest and best organized is **Pitoby Travel Service,** Jl. Jen. Sudirman 118, tel. (0391) 32700. Pitoby offers a variety of half-day, full-day, and evening city tours, tours to Lasiana Beach and Pulau Semau, plus tours to West Timor inland destinations, Sumba, Flores, and Komodo. It also rents vehicles and makes international flight reservations. A branch office at Jl. Siliwangi 75, tel. 21222 or 21333, is only for ticketing. Inquire also at **Prahasti Citra Cendana,** Jl. Raya El Tari 23, tel. 21541, connected with Hotel Cendana; **Natrabu,** Jl. Gunung Mutis 18, tel. 21095, is also a full-service travel agency with tours of Kupang city and environs, as well as all the islands of Nusatenggara. Check also **Ultra Tour and Travel,** next to the *bemo* station, and **Teddy's** for various Timor and interisland tours.

Pitoby Water Sports/Dive Kupang, tel. 32910, the only dive company on Timor, is run out of the Pitoby Lodge, near the Merpati office. Dive/land/cultural tours around Kupang and to Roti—options range from a four-day/three-night program for Rp514,500 pp to an 11-day/10-night tour for Rp1.9 million pp; day and night dives. These include dive equipment, transportation, accommodations, meals, tour of Kupang, and an optional cultural show. Minimum of four people. Fully certified staff.

VICINITY OF KUPANG

Kupang Bay looks like Greece. The diving within a half-hour's drive of Kupang is as good as anywhere in Australia, though the reefs are shallow. **Pantai Lasiana** is a nice white-sand beach with grass huts, 12 km northeast of Kupang (Rp500 by *bemo*). The beach is one km from the main road. At **Kelapa Lima** on the road to the airport is a demolished WW II shore battery, a remnant of the war in the Pacific. At **Bakunase,** just beyond Air Nona, is a sandalwood oil processing factory.

Baun (Rp1500 by bus from Pasar Inpres) has a big Saturday market, Dutch colonial architecture, and traditional Timorese houses. The regent's wife still lives here, still makes (and sells) good-quality thick cotton *ikat* out of her home, and is delighted if you speak a few words of Indonesian. Baun was the summer residence of the Dutch governor and opposite the regent's wife's house are the ruins of the old governor's house. At 600 meters, Baun affords panoramic views of the rolling landscapes all the way to the sea. From the old Dutch *pasanggrahan,* see the beach where Japanese troops landed in 1942.

Oesau, 32 km east of Kupang (Rp700 by *bemo*), across the Noilbaki River, is where a battle between the Australians and Japanese occurred on 20 February 1942. Every day there's a colorful market at Oesau, but the biggest is on Friday. Fierce hand-to-hand combat also took place at **Tanah Merah** ("Red Earth") near Noilbaki, and at **Baubau** (25 km from Kupang), where there's a graveyard for Japanese war dead.

Heading inland from Kupang, the road passes dry bush and rugged fields of coral rock, climbing gradually to **Camplong,** a quiet, cool market town in the mountains 42 km east of Kupang (Rp1000 by bus), with an artificial lake and small forest. Eat at **Sederhana** opposite the town's *alun-alun.* Visit the Christian preschools. From Camplong, the road climbs to **Takari** (22 km east), passing wide, low, grass-thatched huts. From Takari, it's 39 km to Soe, the road running by wide, stony river basins, jagged cliffs, and patches of wet rice fields.

SOE AND VICINITY

This big mountain town sprawls across rolling hills 110 km east of Kupang in the Protestant half of West Timor. The fossilized coral all over the landscape looks like lava. Because of its many nearby tourist attractions and cool weather, Soe is the richest area for travelers in West Timor. It's also the capital, as well as the main cultural center, for Timor Tengah Selatan District. At night you'll need a blanket, but all the town's accommodations provide them; in June and July it can drop to 15° C. The Beatrix Tree, 500 meters from Losmen Anda, was planted in 1980 to commemorate the reign of Queen Beatrix of Holland.

Every day is market day in Soe, when tribal people come in from outlying villages to sell fresh fruit and vegetables, many wearing the brightly colored traditional garments for which the area is famous. A new tourist office is scheduled to open on Jl. Diponegoro, 200 meters down from Hotel Bahagia. The post office is next to the bus station; up the hill to the north is the *wartel.* One block away is Bank Rakyat Indonesia.

Bemo ply the streets until about 1930. They charge Rp250 and will drop you at your door. At night carry a flashlight, as there are few streetlights. Buses depart Kupang for Soe from 0700 to 1700 (Rp2000, two to three hours). Buses run east and west along the main highway to the larger West Timor cities, and north and south along secondary roads (often unpaved) to outlying towns.

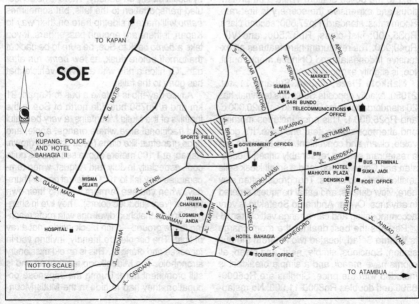

Accommodations

For **Losmen Anda,** the only family-style accommodations and the cheapest place to stay in town (Rp4000 pp, Rp3500 without morning and afternoon tea), take a *bemo* from the bus terminal and get dropped off at your door. Andrew, the proprietor, speaks English, Dutch, and French, is well informed and articulate, and can teach you traditional folk songs on the guitar. It's a rather bizarre place, with rooms set here and there, bright decor, and sculptures set into the plastered walls. Friendly and homey, this *losmen* is of dubious cleanliness. Simple meals are served, drinks and snacks are available, and the laundry service is cheap. Next door is **Wisma Chahaya,** which also charges Rp5000 pp.

Clean and well-organized **Hotel Bahagia,** Jl. Diponogoro 32, tel. (0391) 21015, has standard rooms for Rp12,500 s and Rp15,000 d, first-class rooms for Rp15,000 s and Rp17,500 d, and VIP rooms for Rp25,000, all with *mandi.* Rates include coffee and tea. One of the town's few restaurants is attached, and a gift shop is next door. The owners have expanded into a second, classier place, the town's best. **Hotel Bahagia II,** tel. 21095, Jl. Gajah Mada 95, is located about three km up the hill from town, next to the police station. While a bit pretentious and expensive the scenery is first-rate. Room rates: standard, Rp27,500; second class, Rp35,000; first class, Rp37,500; and VIP, Rp40,000. The restaurant here features an extensive Indonesian and Chinese menu, but it, too, is slightly expensive.

Mahkota Plaza, Jl. Jen. Suharto 11, tel. 21050, exactly opposite Soe's bus terminal, has 20 standard rooms for Rp12,500 s, Rp20,000 d, and Rp25,000 t. This price includes morning and afternoon coffee, tea, and cake. It's good value, clean, and convenient. The Mahkota has a restaurant serving reasonably priced Indonesian and Chinese food, and a small kiosk sells textiles and cold drinks. Tour groups often stay here, view dances, and eat at banquets ordered in advance. Owner Andrianto Soetektjo is very accommodating and can arrange vehicle rental.

Perhaps the best deal for the room charge is **Wisma Sejati,** located two km from the bus station. Spacious, simple, neat, and clean, all rooms have *mandi,* and a simple breakfast is included with the price. Singles are Rp6000-8500 and doubles Rp8000-11,000. No restau-rant here, but a simple neighborhood *warung* is across the street.

Food

Oddly, there are few restaurants in Soe. Pasar Baru (or Pasar Inpres) has the restaurants **Sari Bundo** and **Sumba Jaya;** additional *warung* here as well. At the Soe bus terminal there's the **Suka Jadi,** with a cheap, limited menu; **Densiko,** for Padang-style; and the more expensive but good restaurant at the Mahkota Plaza Hotel. Hotel Bahagia and Hotel Bahagia II both have places to eat, and a few hole-in-the-wall *warung* are scattered around town.

North Of Soe

Eleven km north of Soe, on the way to Kapan, is **Oehala Waterfall.** Take a *bemo* (Rp300) to the turnoff, then walk the three km down to the parking lot, which is the end of the road. The eight tiered waterfalls are about 100 meters down a ravine. They're referred to as the "Peace Waterfalls," as peace between two rival kingdoms was once made there. These spring-fed falls are surrounded by thick clumps of tall bamboo and a towering canopy of banyan trees. Fine for a lazy afternoon dip in the one pool. Visited by locals mostly on Sunday. There is no scheduled transportation to the falls, but sometimes *bemo* will make a sidetrip here on their way to Kapan, if there are enough passengers. If you take a *bemo* back to Soe, be sure to be back at the turnoff before dusk, as few *bemo* run after dark. Or hitch a ride with a private vehicle that has gone to the falls.

A nice day-trip is to take a bus to **Kapan,** 21 km and a Rp750 bus ride north of Soe in the foothills of the Mutis Mountains, a very beautiful and traditional area where orange, apple, and huge grapefruit-like citrus (*jeruk Bali*) are grown. Kapan, at 1,100 meters above sea level, is quite cool, especially in July and August, when temperatures may fall to 10° C. Market day is Thursday, when you see farmers wearing their own textiles (very subdued colors). They live in shaggy, elliptical thatched dwellings with roofs reaching to the ground—pitch black inside, not a ray of light. The people are friendly, inviting you in for coffee and oranges. This is an old missionary stronghold. The Middelkoop family was and is still prominent here. During the Japanese occupation, they had to hide in the Mutis Mountains to the north. Northwest of here is a prominent and craggy outcrop called **Nuasusu**, a holy spot of the local king. Walk to Nuasusu along a dirt track, starting a couple of km north of town, past several villages. From Kapan, a road runs northeast to Eban and on to Kefamenanu.

The road continues 20 km past Kapan to the village of **Fatamnasi** (Rp1000 by bus from Kapan). Fatamnasi is a semi-traditional village of farmers who raise *cor*, potatoes, sweet potatoes, beans, onions, garlic, melons, avocados, and oranges. At over 1,200 meters, it's cool and has an alpine feel—grassy knolls, stands of pines, eucalyptus forests. This village backs up against the dramatic outcrop Fatamnasi ("Old Rock").

Twelve km beyond Fatamnasi, at the foot of Mt. Mutis, is **Nenas Village** (1,500 meters). Sometimes a truck runs here from Soe or Kapan; otherwise walk from Fatamnasi. It's a 14 km walk to the top of Gunung Mutis from Nenas. Hire a guide to help find the way and to arrange food and accommodations, either in Nenas or Fatamnasi. At 2,427 meters, **Gunung Mutis** is the highest mountain in West Timor. At the top grow wild apples. Enjoy a panoramic view of the better part of West Timor.

Niki Niki

Bemo leave Soe every half-hour until 1800 (Rp750, 26 km) for Niki Niki, the center of one of the oldest Timorese kingdoms. Buses from Kupang usually stop in Niki Niki in search of more passengers for Kefamenanu. No accommodations. Market day is Wednesday—large and colorful. Visit the house of the old *raja*, Raja Nope, who used to skewer wrongdoers and display them on the hill above town. The Dutch conquered Nope's kingdom in 1912, employing Rotinese and Savunese mercenaries. Five hundred meters behind Raja Nope's house is the cave where the *raja* hid from the Dutch. They posted soldiers at both ends and finally smoked him to death. The *raja*'s descendants still live in his house. Also visit the family graves to the side of the house, and the meeting house to the front. The *raja* supported several wives and numerous children, and his descendants now number into the hundreds; there's quite a crowd every time a family ceremony or holiday gathering takes place. For a knowledgeable guide to Niki Niki and the entire region surrounding Soe, contact Pae Nope (a descen-

dent of Raja Nope) through the tourism office in Soe or your hotel. Rp10,000 guide fee for a full day is about right.

About 40 km east of Niki Niki gigantic rock formations rise suddenly above the surrounding countryside, looking like enormous ant heaps or the ruins of ancient castles. The largest is one km long and rises over 300 meters. Timorese mountain folk call these *fatukopa*, and have woven myths around them, believing the souls of the dead gather there and that the rocks are where the first marriages took place.

Boti, 30 km south of Soe, is a very traditional, very old village. With their woven garments and long hair tied in buns, these villagers are living reminders of what the Timorese looked like 50-60 years ago. Take a bus (Rp1100) to Oenlasi, then walk the remaining nine km. In the nearby village of Snok, the inhabitants still war with the neighboring Belunese. Police here say it's better to be sent to East Timor to fight than to be stationed in **Snok;** because it's such a dangerous area, they still carry rifles and machetes. Four people were killed in November 1989 the traditional way—disemboweled, heads chopped off.

Kolbano

A beautiful village near the sea on the south coast. Market day is Friday. No electricity but plenty of light from gas lamps. This wealthy village cultivates bananas, coconuts, and cassavas, and makes *tuak*. An abundance of fish is traditionally caught by spear fishermen using bamboo darts. The *kepala desa* is young and friendly, and the villagers are welcoming and look fit. Take a bus from Soe to Kolbano (Rp3000) on a really rough road. See the Old Man's Rock at Kolbano; if it's the dry season (April-Nov.), sleep on the beach and swim. **Sie** is up in the mountains; from there, on a clear night, you can see the lights of Darwin.

KEFAMENANU

Kefamenanu, often referred to simply as Kefa, is a rest-stop town on the highway about halfway between Kupang and Dili. Kefamenanu is the region's administrative center; it has a post office and *wartel*, but no place to exchange foreign currency. The bus station is about three km from the town center—take a *bemo*. *Bemo* charge Rp300 to anywhere in town. Sample bus fares: Kupang (Rp6000, 197 km, five hours), Soe (Rp2500, 87 km), Niki Niki (Rp1800, 60 km), Ambeno (Rp2000, 52 km), Atambua (Rp2500, 87 km, two hours). From Kefamenanu, buses to Kupang or Atambua leave around 0630, having circled the town for half an hour before departure.

The excellent road to Atambua passes by endless stony pastures and cattle corrals made of sticks or stones. Also along this road are many thatched conical structures, set up on posts and open underneath, in front of the traditional houses. Women sit and weave, and everyone congregates here for a midday rest; the area under the roof is used for storage. **Santa Maria Cave,** 27 km from Kefamenanu on the road to Atambua, was dug out by the Japanese in WW II but is now used as a pilgrimage site for Catholics.

From Kefamenanu, take a side trip along the north coast to the East Timorese enclave of Ambeno (formerly Oecussi). The town of Ambeno is an old port town, with remains of a Portuguese fort and other buildings. The principal town is now Pante Makassar; one *losmen*. Life is slow-paced here, with little or no tension from annexation by Indonesia, or the ensuing guerrilla movement that has gripped the rest of East Timor since 1975. On the way pass **Tano,** a traditional village with a great market.

Accommodations

Only five minutes' walk from Pasar Kefa is plain but adequate **Losmen Soko Windu,** tel. (0391) 21122, Jl. Kartini, which has eight rooms for Rp6500 s and Rp13,000 d, including coffee, tea, and a drink. The *mandi* is separate. Nice family, central to shops and market, clean sheets, and *bantal guling*. Street noise dies down after 2100. Up the street a bit is **Stella Maris.** Out of town on Jl. Patimura is **Losmen Sederhana,** tel. 21069; rooms cost Rp8000 s, Rp10,000 d, all with *kamar mandi*.

The best hotel in Kefamenanu is **Losmen Ariesta,** Jl. Basuki Rachmat, tel. 21007. It has different classes of rooms running from Rp8250 with outside *mandi* to Rp27,500 with a/c and *mandi*. Clean, good service, parking lot, nice garden with an oddly out-of-place cement dragon sculpture, and the town's best restaurant featuring the usual Indonesian dishes for good prices. The Ariesta hosts government officials and private contract workers; when the governor passes through Kefamenanu, he stays here.

ATAMBUA AND VICINITY

The administrative center of the Belu Plain bordering East Timor, Atambua is located on the old border crossing between Timor Barat and Portuguese Timor, seven hours and Rp8500 by bus from Kupang, and three to four hours and Rp5000 from Dili. Travelers no longer need to overnight in Atambua on their way to Dili; from Kupang the journey now takes 10-11 hours.

Atambua has a post office, and a *wartel* for domestic and international calls. Many government offices operate here, and there are lots of dry goods shops. Check Alam Subur Photo for film, developing, and cold drinks. None of the banks in town will change traveler's checks, but larger shops and the Catholic mission will change paper money in good condition. Atambua is the seat of one of the Timor bishops. His residence and the cathedral are about 200 meters north of the sports field at the center of town. The police station is on the east side of this sports field, and down the road is the military headquarters. Atambua has an airstrip, with Merpati and Pelni agents. In 1976, Atambua, then with a population of about 15,000, was besieged by 60,000 East Timorese refugees fleeing the fighting in East Timor. The influx was a heavy burden on the town's central government, from which it only slowly recovered. There is not much to do or see in town, although it's a pleasant enough place to spend the night. Several traditional villages are nestled in the mountains about an hour away, but they will not be easily accessible until bridges on the new mountain road are completed in a few years.

Handwoven Belu cloths from Kema and other areas of eastern West Timor are sold by old women in the market. Put out the word during the biggest market day—Sunday, starting at around 0700—that you want to buy cloth and you'll be mobbed. People will even offer clothes right off their bodies. This is a real *asli* market where you'll see country folk with betel-stained mouths wearing rich textiles and turbans. For old textiles, carvings, and jewelry, call at **Jems M. Lopez,** but barter his first price in half.

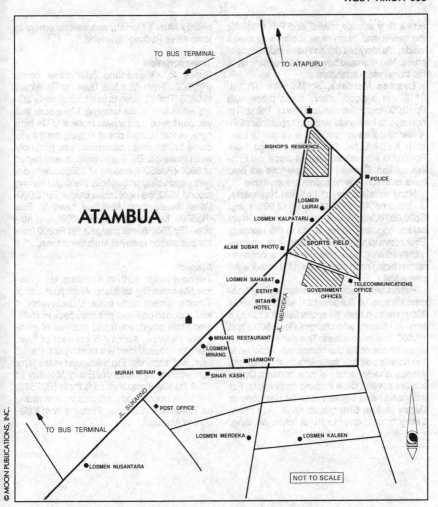

ATAMBUA

TO BUS TERMINAL

TO ATAPUPU

BISHOP'S RESIDENCE

POLICE

LOSMEN LIURAI

LOSMEN KALPATARU

SPORTS FIELD

ALAM SUBAR PHOTO

LOSMEN SAHABAT

ESTHY

INTAN HOTEL

TELECOMMUNICATIONS OFFICE

GOVERNMENT OFFICES

JL. MERDEKA

MINANG RESTAURANT

LOSMEN MINANG

HARMONY

MURAH MERIAH

SINAR KASIH

JL. SUKARNO

POST OFFICE

TO BUS TERMINAL

LOSMEN MERDEKA

LOSMEN KALBEN

LOSMEN NUSANTARA

NOT TO SCALE

© MOON PUBLICATIONS, INC.

Accommodations And Food

Homestay-style **Losmen Sahabat,** Jl. Merdeka 7, rents very plain rooms for Rp5500 pp; close to the sports field. Down the street at Jl. Merdeka 12A is **Hotel Intan,** tel. (0391) 21343, the newest and fanciest place in town. A multistoried structure frequented by government officials, it has a variety of clean Western-style rooms. Rates: economy Rp12,100 s and Rp19,800 d, economy fan Rp19,800 s and Rp26,400 d, a/c Rp26,400 s and Rp36,300 d,

a/c TV Rp36,300 s and Rp45,100 d. Prices include two daily snacks.

Quiet, clean, family-run **Losmen Kalpataru,** tel. 21351, is opposite the sports field. Rooms are Rp7500 pp with outside *mandi,* including a simple breakfast. Family-like, friendly, real down-to-earth. Run by Mr. Manek, a retired government official, who speaks English well, it's perhaps the most amicable place in town; highly recommended. Next to Losmen Kalpataru is **Losmen Liurai,** tel. 21187. Rooms are Rp5500 with a dirty outside *mandi,* and Rp11,000 for the newer and much nicer rooms with *mandi* inside. It's okay but doesn't have much atmosphere. Males should beware of the attentions of the transvestite attendant.

Losmen Merdeka, Jl. Merdeka 37, tel. 21197, is a good, clean, basic place with Rp10,000 rooms with fan and *mandi.* The staff is not used to foreigners and can't speak English. A few steps away around the corner is **Losmen Kalben,** tel. 21179. Rooms go from Rp10,000 with *mandi.* Decent place, no English spoken. Sometimes conferences are held here, at which time no rooms are available.

Many travelers stay at **Losmen Nusantara,** Jl. Sukarno 42, tel. 21117; Rp12,000 s and Rp20,000 d, with fan, *mandi,* and complimentary cakes, egg, and coffee or tea in the morning. Four restaurants and a few shops are conveniently nearby. Very clean, with nice open verandas facing each other. Around the corner is the post office.

Patronized mostly by businesspeople is **Losmen Minang,** Jl. Sukarno 12A, tel. 21153, about 200 meters up from the sports field. It's run by a shrewd Minang, who charges Rp15,500 s and 17,500 d; outside *mandi.* The owner is also an agent for one of the bus companies. Attached to this hotel is perhaps the town's best restaurant, serving a wide variety of *nasi padang.* Opposite are several more Padang restaurants. For Indonesian and Chinese food try **Harmony** or **Depot Makan Sinar,** both on Jl. Sudirman. **Esthy** is next door to Hotel Intan. **Minang,** nearby **Murah Meriah,** and several others in town serve Padang-style food.

Transportation

Buses to Kefamenanu take three hours (Rp2500). From Atambua, buses to Dili depart at 0800 (Rp500, three to four hours), while others leave later in the morning. Make sure that you don't need a *surat jalan* to travel to Dili from here, or that you get one in Kupang before you come to Atambua; otherwise, you probably won't make it to Dili. For Kupang, buses depart at 0800 (Rp8500), arriving at 1500; others depart periodically throughout the day. Leaving around 1600, the night buses charge Rp10,000. Other buses from Atambua head to Soe (Rp5000, two hours), Suai (Rp4000), and Atapupu (Rp750). *Bemo* charge a flat Rp300 from the bus station to anywhere around town.

Atapupu

Twenty-five km north of Atambua, on a narrow bay extending far inland, Atapupu is one of Timor's busiest cattle ports. Unbelievably, it was included on Riberiro's map back in 1529. Along this coast, you'll find patches of mangrove swamps. About 4.5 km east of town along the coastal road is a beach park, Pantai Laut, with cabanas. From Atapupu make ferry connections to Kalabahi. Every Monday at 1030 the KM *Kampaniru* sails there (Rp7500, five to six hours) and continues on to Kupang on Tuesday. On Sunday it returns from Kalabahi to Atapupu.

EAST TIMOR

For centuries the western half of the island of Timor was governed by Holland (and since 1950 by Indonesia), while the eastern half was an anachronistic, backwater Portuguese territory which slept on into the 20th century. This all ended in late 1975 when Indonesian troops brutally invaded East Timor. Today, life is slowly returning to normal. The capital of Dili still has the feel of a lazy Mediterranean port of the 1950s, with abandoned fishing trawlers washed up on shore, a long ocean promenade, good food, and very few tourists. Remnants of the Portuguese era are still evident in the architecture of the buildings and in the street names, and the territory's scenery can match anything in West Timor and Sumba.

Too many travelers speed through Kupang in West Timor in their rush to get to Bali, never considering East Timor worth a sidetrip. Official numbers show that since 1989 only about 7,000 travelers have entered East Timor, with most of these never venturing out of Dili to the outlying towns. Nearly one half of the visitors are from Australia and New Zealand. The greatest volume of visitors is in August. Some travelers don't even realize that the eastern half of the island has been open since January 1989; others think the former colony is still a war zone—not true, although sporadic guerrilla activity still occurs in the remote eastern mountain areas.

THE LAND

East Timor's land area is 14,609 square km, consisting of spectacularly rugged mountains extending right down to clear coastal waters. The highest point on the island of Timor is Gunung Tata Mai Lau (2,963 meters), directly south of Dili. The territory's rivers dry up in the dry season and become torrents in the wet. There are few lakes but many waterfalls and coastal lagoons, and highly variable vegetation, from dry grasslands and savannah forests to deep lush gullies and patches of dense rainforests. The longest river is the 80-km-long Laclo in the north to the east of Manatuto. East Timor's indigenous fauna resembles both Asia's and Australia's. Pigs run wild. Deer were introduced by Portuguese settlers. This dry rocky land is perfect for goats, and herds are found everywhere.

HISTORY

For East Timor's history prior to WW II, see "History" in the Timor Introduction.

When the Japanese surrendered in 1945, Portuguese troops quickly reoccupied East Timor while West Timor and the rest of the Dutch East Indies eventually gained their independence and became the nation of Indonesia. This is why, historically, East Timor has had little to do with Indonesia; it was never within the boundaries of colonial or postcolonial Indonesia, and the native peoples of the region always sought freedom. Thus, when Portugal announced it would grant East Timor independence in April 1974, the East Timorese zealously formed three main political parties.

The most popular was Fretilin, with its programs of social development and literacy campaigns appealing to more than 60% of the population. The party had strong links with the common people in the Timorese hinterlands. Fretilin could be described as a moderate, reformist, nationalist front advocating gradual steps toward complete independence, agrarian and educational reform, controlled foreign aid and investment, and a foreign policy of nonalignment.

Fretilin, an acronym which translates as "Revolutionary Front for the Independence of East Timor," was an unfortunate choice of name—it signalled a communist orientation to the Indonesians. Despite its progressive stance, Fretilin members were labeled as "Marxist terrorists" bent on totalitarianism. Several months of civil war ensued, during which political parties of the right and left bid for power in the political vacuum created by Portugal's withdrawal. Finally, Fretilin declared East Timor's full independence and assumed control of the territory.

Indonesia Invades
Under the pretext of restoring order, Indonesian attacks along the border escalated. On 7

December 1975, only hours after a visit by U.S. Secretary of State Henry Kissinger, Indonesia launched a full-scale land-sea-air invasion. In the weeks that followed, napalm was used by Indonesian troops, tank and mortar battles raged in Dili, Timorese were massacred, relief and aid supplies confiscated, and media "events" staged by Indonesian officials.

At first the ambushes, raids, and sniping by Fretilin irregulars severely tested the Indonesian armed forces; over 1,800 Indonesian troops were killed and Jakarta's hospitals filled with 7,000 wounded in the first four years of fighting. Against overpowering odds, small bands of Fretilin nationalists eventually faded into the arid hills that cover two-thirds of East Timor to wage protracted and bloody guerrilla warfare.

In July 1976, Indonesia formally annexed the territory as the country's 27th province, a move many view as a clear instance of Javanese imperialism to realize an Indonesian manifest destiny.

In 1977, due to a split in the party and a lack of outside support, Fretilin's fortunes declined. Well armed with U.S.-supplied attack helicopters and other Vietnam-surplus weapons, Indonesian troops during the next two years conducted ruthless "pacification" campaigns. Starvation and disease, in the wake of large-scale military operations, have been devastating. Since the start of the civil war in August 1975, the Timorese will tell you that 200,000 people out of a prewar population of 650,000 have died—probably an exaggeration. Informed estimates run around 100,000—a full one-sixth of East Timor's population. This is a clear, brutal case of genocide, yet the international press and world community have remained inexplicably silent.

In 1978 Australia, New Zealand, the U.S., and most Islamic countries formally recognized the Indonesian integration of East Timor, but in December 1978 the UN passed a resolution calling for the withdrawal of Indonesian troops from the territory. With East Timor alongside a deep-sea trench vital to the U.S. as a route for its nuclear-powered submarines, it appears that U.S. strategic interests have won out over the rights of the East Timorese. To date, the U.S. has not pressured Indonesia to withdraw its troops.

Since the passage of the resolution, Indonesia has doggedly tried to enlist international support for its territorial claim. One important success was Australia's Timor Gap Treaty. Signed by both Indonesia and Australia in 1989, this treaty detailed a management scheme for the joint exploration and development of undersea oil and gas reserves in the vast area between the coasts of Australia and East Timor. The treaty formalizes the seabed boundaries between the two countries.

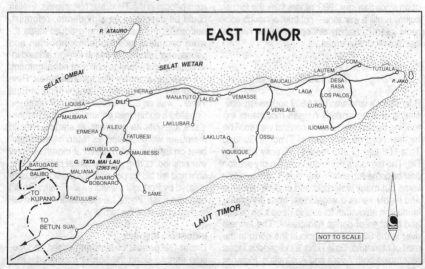

EAST TIMOR

NOT TO SCALE

© MOON PUBLICATIONS, INC.

Current Political Situation

East Timor today remains broken, dominated, and virtually forgotten, under the yoke of yet another colonial power. International pressure on Indonesia to withdraw is abating. So eager are the Indonesians to show the world that the situation has stabilized and a new era of freedom has begun for East Timor that, in January 1989, after some 15 years of tight control over access, they declared the territory officially "opened."

If you look deeper, though, it's obvious the Timorese have not dropped their efforts toward independence and self-determination. Fretilin guerrillas continue to fight. In September 1990 an Australian journalist, Robert Domm, made a hazardous trek into the mountains for the Australian Broadcasting Commission to conduct the first-ever interview with Xanana Gusmao, the East Timor guerrilla commander. According to Fretilin supporters—about 90% of the East Timorese—some 1,500 East Timorese guerrillas are pitted against 15,000 heavily armed Indonesian troops. In addition, there is an almost equal number of police and an unknown but large number of "cats" (spies). Vigilante activity by Indonesian soldiers in civilian dress continues, as does a high level of militarization. Refugees still report ongoing massacres of and atrocities against East Timorese by Indonesian troops. Most people you meet have lost a number of relatives in the war. Amnesty International has documented widespread use of torture, extra-judicial executions, and systematic intimidation of civilians. International human-rights groups and UN people on fact-finding missions are harassed by Indonesian troops. The military is a law unto itself. Farmers found in their fields after curfew have been shot and their bodies left to rot because they were suspected of contacting Fretilin guerrillas. The island of Atauro off the north coast functions as a detention center for about 130 political detainees suspected of guerrilla ties. Military posts are found on every strategic hilltop, and you see truckloads of soldiers everywhere, supposedly building bridges and roads. The Timorese feel almost totally repressed. An atmosphere of benign terror permeates the land.

At the end of 1993, Xanana Gusmao was captured by the Indonesian government; he allegedly made a public statement urging his comrades-in-arms to put down their weapons and cooperate with the Indonesian government. Whether the statement was coerced or not is debatable, but the fact that Fretilin's principal theoretician and leader is no longer in circulation is undoubtedly a blow to this flagging guerrilla organization.

Consequences Of Indonesian Rule

It can't be denied that integration has accelerated East Timor's development. Community health clinics (*puskesmas*) have been built in almost every subdistrict. There are now primary and secondary schools in every subdistrict and the literacy rate has nearly doubled. A university was established in 1986; it now has 87 lecturers and 800 students, 60% of whom are native Timorese. Polytechnic Institute opened in October 1990, its curriculum modeled after Bandung's ITB.

Almost the entire road network in the province has been asphalted, with Dili and regency capitals now linked. Outside Dili village life is still primitive, and most of the population lives in huts with thatched roofs and palm-frond walls. New government offices have sprouted up in all the main district centers. The Indonesian regime has also built the biggest cathedral in Southeast Asia, as well as a sports stadium. The government has upgraded bridges and installed electricity in dozens of villages; at the time of the invasion, only Dili had electricity. Shops and markets are full of everyday necessities. Even television programs have reached East Timor via satellite. But the Timorese still feel they've not received their fair share of the national budget. There's been a decided shift from military rebellion to civil discontent. The people feel colonized in a new way.

The New Immigrants

The biggest enemy of the Timorese is the fast and highly efficient Indonesianization of the region. The East Timorese culture has been gradually buried under a steady stream of immigrants over the past five years. Taking advantage of the "open door" policy, 25,000 heads of families have migrated voluntarily to East Timor from Java, Sumatra, Sulawesi, and the islands surrounding Timor.

There is an unmistakable and alarming gap between the newcomers, both civilian and military, and the local population. The Portuguese forbade the locals from establishing businesses, and they're still extremely naive in business matters. They don't even bargain—they weren't allowed to under the Portuguese, expected simply to hand over their produce to the Chinese at fixed prices.

With this cultural background the native community can't hope to compete with professional traders from other islands and those holding well-paid government jobs; you often see Timorese employed as *pembantu* (servants) and lowly *pegawai*. Newcomers drive up prices and the numerous Javanese civil servants exploit economic conditions in Dili. The capital already looks like any other Indonesian city, except for the Portuguese street names and the military presence. It's almost impossible to find any real Timorese food; all the *rumah makan* and *warung* are either Javanese, Sumatran, or Makassarese. The remaining 400,000 East Timorese feel they're already outnumbered by the immigrants. Even if East Timor gained independence next week, Fretilin would no longer receive a majority vote. And that's exactly what the Indonesian government intended.

Land is another big issue. From 1974 to 1980, many middle- and upper-class Timorese, frightened or unwilling to live under Indonesian rule, departed abroad, leaving their land behind. Today, newcomers can quickly secure land titles while the indigenous people cannot. Many are forced to eke out an existence on small pieces of nearly uncultivatable land. Prostitutes were nonexistent during the Portuguese colonial period, but after integration they started to arrive in numbers. Venereal disease is now a problem in the province.

ECONOMY

In the mid-1970s, the economy and agriculture of East Timor were totally disrupted because of the war. Gradually the economy has improved under Indonesian administration, with positive developments in health and education. Jobs outside the government sector, however, are few.

A war economy still prevails, with regulations and monopolies everywhere. For example, the army enjoys near monopolies on coffee and timber exports; coffee is sold strictly through the government cooperative, with its shadowy military connections, at the fixed official price. Farmers don't even see the scales where the beans are weighed. The province was once known as a producer of sandalwood and teak, but presently these are rare species in the territory's 45,211 hectares of production forest.

Agricultural production now is many times what it was during the Portuguese period. Annual rice production catapulted from 26,000 to 38,000 tons, corn from 16,000 to 58,000 tons. In 1989, about 24,000 families cultivated *ladang* in the province, using just a digging stick and rough hoe. If you see bright banners of bamboo with brown leaves waving in the breeze, this means grain or rice has been newly planted.

Making the dizzying leap from Neolithic farming to modern agriculture, East Timor now uses tractors introduced by the government. There's great potential for wet-rice cultivation in the fertile southern soils, but this region is less populated due to endemic malaria. Buffalo hooves are the preferred means of plowing, but war and famine wiped out nearly all the once numerous buffalo and horses. Buffalo are still an important mark of prestige and power, consumed as food, and in the mountain areas serve as currency in bartering for a bride.

Investors are reluctant to put capital into East Timor because of the political risk and the fact that the economy is largely managed and monopolized by the Indonesian army. Fisheries yield only about 700 tons of a potential 70,000 tons of fish a year. Along the coast around Dili you see men fishing with spears and boys catching crabs and shellfish in the rocks, but the people are not really sea-oriented. There are few words in their language describing products of the sea, compared with the complex terminology that describes horses and their equipment in the finest detail.

Tourism could enjoy a bright future in East Timor and provide jobs and income, as well as help preserve Timorese culture and raise valuable foreign exchange. Everyone realizes that, with its colorful Portuguese heritage, Dili has more potential for tourism than Kupang—it's only a matter of time before the province catches on and really opens up.

THE PEOPLE

The total population is approaching 700,000, with 29 ethnic groups. The people are very mixed, though the basic racial elements are

Papuan and Portuguese. Most faces bear unmistakable signs of Portuguese blood—dark bushy eyebrows, facial and arm hair, dark brown eyes.

East Timorese were never physically involved in Indonesia's achievement of independence from Dutch colonial rule. Mentally and ideologically, they feel little kinship with the Indonesian nation. Decolonization came through a bloody civil war that claimed many lives. Students now have to learn about the Pancasila in school and memorize facts about Indonesian historical figures uninvolved in their own history. Their culture, such as exhilarating traditional dances, is prohibited, put down as "activities of jungle people." This indoctrination in an alien culture has led to culture shock in all strata of East Timorese society.

Each ethnic group speaks a separate language, but the main dialect is Tetum. Like the Motu language of Papua New Guinea, Tetum contains many words also found in Polynesian languages. Most East Timorese speak three languages fluently: their own language, and those of their former and present colonizers. Speaking either Portuguese or Tetum in public is prohibited (when it's safe, boys will sing a song in Tetum for you). Children call Indonesian "the fucking language"; it's replaced Portuguese in all but some church schools. During the pope's visit in October 1989, the mass was celebrated in Indonesian rather than Tetum, but in the countryside the mass and catechism continue to be heard in Tetum. Since few people speak English, anyone going to Tim Tim should know at least some Indonesian or Portuguese.

Religion

In East Timor, Catholics comprise 91% of the population; the remainder are Muslims, Protestants, Hindus, Buddhists, and those adhering to local beliefs. Islam entered East Timor almost 300 years ago during Portuguese times. The number of Catholics has grown rapidly in recent years; many adopted it to quash all doubts about connections with Fretilin. The church was also very accommodating to the converts, allowing them to mix traditional Timorese religion with Catholic ritual. The farmer still spills blood before he tills the fields, and even the *lopo* (communal meetinghouse for men and boys) is tolerated. You see *lopo* throughout north-central

East Timor—a Catholic region—but you won't see it in the south-central area, which is controlled by the Dutch Reformed Church.

The people are ardent Catholics. Most towns, even remote villages, are dominated by a distinctive Portuguese-style Catholic church. Catholicism provides the people with both temporal and spiritual support and gives them their identity as East Timorese. War orphans are the wards of the Church, and people hunted by the military often take refuge in one of East Timor's 444 churches or chapels. Officials are always surprised to see East Timorese enthusiastically building churches but reluctant to build water canals.

The military realizes the position and power of the Church, a formidable challenge to the Indonesian government. Indonesian soldiers tell villagers the instability of East Timor is due solely to support given to the guerrillas by the all-powerful clergy. They maintain that a number of priests preach a violent Central American-style liberation theology.

Carlos Belo was consecrated bishop of East Timor by the pope in 1989, and the diocese of Dili falls directly under the head of the Holy See and not under the Indonesian Conference of Catholic Bishops (KWI). Pope John Paul II's visit to East Timor in October 1989 was an important political victory which, in the eyes of Indonesians, constituted a formal act of recognition by the Vatican of the integration of East Timor. The church today is torn between declaring itself on the side of the people or a government-appointed motivator for popular support of government programs.

GETTING THERE

Merpati flies a Fokker 28 daily from Kupang to Dili (Rp82,000), one leg of the following route: Yogyakarta, Surabaya, Denpasar, Kupang, Dili, return. If flying from Darwin to Dili, you must lay over a night in Kupang. There has been talk of reestablishing the former Darwin to Dili direct flight—popular with Australians when East Timor was still a Portuguese colony—but nothing has transpired yet. Merpati in the past has operated a flight from Kupang via Oeccusi and Atambua to Dili. The flight is no longer scheduled, but Merpati may revive it; the route is an interesting alternative into East Timor. Officials may or may not inspect your passport and luggage at Dili's Komoro Airport upon arrival or departure, but you should prepare for it.

The Pelni ship *Kelimutu* calls at Dili every second week of the month. The KM *Tatamailau* also stops at Dili twice a month, either en route to Java or to Maluku and Irian Jaya. The new KM *Dobonsolo*, based in Dili, arrives twice monthly to and from different ports on Java and Irian Jaya. Sample fares from Dili are: Ambon (Rp34,000), Tanjung Priok (Rp99,000), and Biak (Rp82,000). Periodically sailing from Dili are the Perintis ships KM *Dhuto Nusantara* and KM *Daya Nunst,* which both stop at many small port towns in Maluku. The KM *Dhuto Nusantara* route is Kupang, Dili, Kalabahi, Kisar, Romar, Damar, Saumlaki, Tual, Ambon, return. For the KM *Daya Nunst,* it's Dili, Ilwaki, Kisar, Lelang, Tepa, Marsela, Saumlaki, Tual, Ambon, return. Check with the Pelni office for current fare and schedule information; open Mon.-Fri. 0800-1600, Saturday 0800-1300.

From Hera, a small port seven km east of the Becora bus terminal, you can rent small motorboats (Rp100,000 for two days and one night) to Pulau Atauro. Occasionally, boats make the run from here to Alor. In Kalabahi, look for a *prahu motor* that calls at tiny ports on Alor and Pantar and occasionally takes people and cattle back to Dili. Bring food and books to read on this long, hot trip. Prepare for rough seas and waterproof your gear.

From Kupang daily buses leave for Dili at 0700 (Rp13,000) and 1900 (Rp15,000); Dili is three to four hours from Atambua (Rp5000) via the new coastal road. At the border is a checkpoint. Before boarding the bus, make sure you don't need a *surat jalan* to cross the provincial border. As East Timor is now open to tourism, none is usually required, but occasionally, due to political, social, and/or military concerns, the crossing may be closed to foreigners either one or both ways. Completely paved but for a short stretch near the provincial border, this road is scenic, sometimes running 50 meters above the sea, at other times two meters beside it. An even older, gravel road leads through Tim Tim's interior through such Portuguese towns as Maliano and Ermera to Dili. Consider taking the coastal road from Atambua to Dili, then the old Portuguese-built inland road back to Atambua. This inland road is often cut during Tim Tim's Nov.-March rainy season.

GETTING AROUND

Buses to all the main towns of Tim Tim emanate from Dili. Buses also start in Baucau for Viqueque and Los Palos, as well as back to Dili. Booking ahead is not usually necessary but could be useful during holidays. Bemo run regularly in all regional centers and also run to nearby villages and towns. Outside of Dili, buses will pick you up at your hotel and drop you off at your destination.

The northern coastal road is sealed and in good condition all the way to Los Palos. From Dili, the road mostly hugs the sea, passing the uninspiring town of **Manatuto,** which has a colonial-era church and is known for wood- and buffalo-horn carving. In **Lalela,** dramatically perched on a bluff, is another old church and the remains of a fortress. Farther on in **Vamasse** is yet another, newer, Portuguese church, circa 1936. From here, the road climbs to the Baucau Plateau and the town of **Baucau.** From Baucau, the road cuts down the cliffside and once again runs through the coastal plain to **Laga,** crossing two rivers, with the deep mauve Mata Bia Range in the distance. After Laga, where there's an old Portuguese fort, the road parallels the coastline facing the Wetar Strait. Here you must often drive right along the beach, with the waves washing the roadway; to one side are tall palms, on the other side buffalo graze. The road climbs again at Lautem to the plateau on which Los Palos sits. From here, it's about 30 km to Tutuala on the far eastern tip of the island.

Currently, three roads cross the province north to south. The first runs from Dili through Maubessi and Ainaro to Suai, passing below Gunung Tata Mai Lau, Timor's highest peak. The second heads south from Baucau to Viqueque. The third cuts off the north coast road before Lautem and goes to Iliomar. Work is currently in progress on a south coast road which will connect Los Palos to Viqueque, Same, and Suai—and on into West Timor.

DILI

The former capital of Portuguese Timor and now the capital of Timor Timur. Twenty years after the violent integration process, Dili today is

Map of Dili showing streets and landmarks including LIGHTHOUSE, DEKRANAS CRAFT SHOP, MATAEL CHURCH, MONUMENT TO INTEGRATION, HARBOR, and various other locations. "© MOON PUBLICATIONS, INC." "DILI" "NOT TO SCALE"

a delightful town with a distinct Mediterranean air. Its easy pace, shady squares, clean wide streets with light and fairly orderly motor traffic, and a sleepy seaside promenade are quite a distinct and refreshing change after busy, hot, noisy Kupang. The town bears few scars of war: old Portuguese buildings with terra-cotta-tiled roofs and white stucco walls overlook Dili Bay, miniplazas and office blocks have replaced the old Chinese shops, and the Indonesians have rebuilt the stadium, put in a new telecommunications station, new roads, schools, a library, a university, and a cathedral.

The *merah dan putih* (Indonesian flag) flaps on a pole in front of the governor's office, near the monument to East Timor's integration with Indonesia. The Indonesians have retained all the street names from Portuguese times—former Portuguese governors, war heroes, explorers. The Chinese, as they did in Portuguese times, run the important, high-profile

businesses. Just as in Portugal, the whole town takes a siesta 1200-1600. Goods and services cost a bit more in Dili but transport is cheap. Few travelers visit this small city, a situation that may change once the memory of violent annexation fades and the sociopolitical situation stabilizes.

Sights

The waterfront is picturesque, a long promenade with rusty cannon pointing skyward, broken sidewalks, cracked benches, giant *waringin* trees, grass lawns, barefoot boys selling textiles, dozens of food carts, children playing in the water, beached fishing boats, and goats grazing in front of rusty WW II landing barges run aground on the beach. Soldiers, once commonly encountered marching by with AR-16s in a show of strength, have now pretty much receded to their compounds and are largely unseen.

Start the day off with rich Ermera coffee and a warm *pao* (Portuguese bread), then take a stroll along the waterfront to the red-tiled **Matael** church, Timor's oldest, to hear the early-morning liturgy in archaic Portuguese. Just around the curve from the church is the old lighthouse. A second fine example of a newer Portuguese-style church is the **Paroqui de Balide**, located to the rear of town away from the water. Walk to the east, past Dili's harbor, the governor's office, a marble statue of the Virgin Mary, and long, quiet, residential streets. From here a seaside road continues about one km east to **Pasir Putih**, a beautiful white sand beach where a hotel is planned. The beach is usually deserted except on Sunday. Four km east is **Areia Branca,** another fine stretch of white sand. Offshore are coral gardens for snorkeling, with a neat drop-off. Firm powder sand. Walk or charter a taxi here for Rp5000. Notice the craggy peaks of Atauro Island offshore.

On the west side of town in Comoro is the very traditional **Mercado Comoro Market** selling fruit, vegetables, meat, fish, and hardware. Patronized almost exclusively by East Timorese people, it's a good place to meet them.

The white, sterile, and characterless **Katedral Immaculate,** the largest Catholic cathedral in Southeast Asia, was blessed by Pope John Paul II in October 1989 following an earlier opening ceremony by President Suharto. This ugly church has nothing ethnic or regional about it and could be found anywhere. During the pope's visit, Timorese walked into Dili without food from villages scores of miles away. Fretilin claimed the pope's open-air mass was held in a spot where the Indonesian military tortured and massacred thousands of Timorese.

There are a number of memorials to heroes of WW II. One in Taibesi commemorates Portuguese victims of the Japanese occupation. **Fatunaba Monument,** seven km up in the hills, is dedicated to Australians who served and died in Timor during the war. Another monument is dedicated to Artur Canto de Resende, who died in a Japanese POW camp on Alor in 1942. Manuel Pires, a hero of the battle at Bau Bau, is commemorated with another statue.

Visit the former Portuguese governor's residence in the hills above Dili, now serving as a government house (Gedung Negara) where Suharto and other dignitaries stay when they visit Tim Tim.

Accommodations

Villa Harmonia, tel. (0390) 22065, is inconveniently located several km east of downtown Dili on Jl. Bekora, up the street from the New Tropical Restaurant. A family-run place, its six rooms go for Rp7500 s, Rp12,500 d—the cheapest place to stay in Dili. On the premises is the **Mona Lisa II,** serving central Javanese food. The owner, Pedro S.C. Lebre, who speaks good English, fluent Portuguese, and a little Spanish, works in the tourist office and is also a guide.

Losmen Basmery Indah, Jl. Villa Verde, is a Portuguese-style building with a real grass back lawn, centrally located opposite the University of Tim Tim. Very basic, clean, and friendly, but with thin mattresses. Ask for a room on the exterior of the building, not a windowless inner room. Bring your own mosquito coils. Rooms are Rp8250 with shared facilities and Rp13,500 with *mandi* and fan.

Most centrally located, but on the noisy, busy, smelly, main intersection, is **Losmen Taufik,** tel. 22152. Second-floor rooms run from Rp10,000 s to Rp16,500 d. The lack of hospitality is not inviting.

A few steps back down the road toward the airport is capacious **Wisma Cendana,** tel. 21141, Jl. Americo Thomas. While on a main thoroughfare, it's set back and is quiet enough—ask for a room in the back. Nice garden, wide porch; some crafts and cloth are displayed in the lobby. All rooms have a/c and toilets, and go for Rp35,000. Order in advance either Western food or *makanan Porto* (the place has an old Portuguese cook). Nearby is **Beringin Jaya** for *nasi padang*. Behind Wisma Cendana on the quiet residential street Jl. Serparosa is **Wisma Flamboyan,** tel. 21658. It's pleasant enough and often full with long-staying guests, but if you can get a room they go for Rp13,500 s and Rp15,000 d.

Hotel Mahkota Timor, Jl. Av. Gov. Alves Aldeia, tel. 21664, is the new luxury hotel in town, and the fanciest in the province. Located across from the harbor, this multistoried hotel has full services, including car rental for Rp7500 an hour (two-hour minimum) or Rp90,000 a day. The comfy, quiet, low-lit restaurant serves Indonesian, Chinese, and Western food. Economy rooms are Rp22,000 s and Rp27,500 d, a/c standard are Rp45,000 s and Rp50,000 d, a/c deluxe are Rp55,000 s and Rp60,000 d, and the suites go for Rp75,000-110,000.

Directly to the side of the governor's office on Jl. Av. Bispo Madeiros is full-service **Hotel New Resende Inn,** tel. 22094 or 21768, which charges Rp35,000-44,000 s for standard a/c rooms, and Rp40,000-49,000 d for deluxe; 22 rooms. Prices don't include tax but do cover breakfast of bread, coffee, or tea. At the hotel is the very good **Diak Liu Restaurant** and a travel office for information about Dili and East Timor. Very near government offices, banks, cinema, post office, and police station; a Merpati office is next door. The affable owner, Adi Kresna Wijaja, will take care of your needs. Many government officials and tourists stay here.

To the east down the promenade along Jl. Av. Marchal Carmona is **Hotel Dili** (tel. 21871), which has four rooms in front for Rp17,000 and seven cooler, quieter, rear rooms for Rp15,000. A breakfast of bread and tea or coffee delivered by barefoot Melanesians is included in the price. A garden bar may serve cold beer if anyone is around to take your order. Located right on the waterfront, this is Tim Tim's oldest hotel. A bit faded and unkempt, it looks a little like something out of the '50s.

Turismo Beach Hotel, farther down the promenade on Jl. Av. Marchal Carmona, tel. 22651 or 22029, is a 49-room luxury hotel from the Portuguese period that has undergone something of a facelift. Beautifully located on the waterfront, far enough out to be quiet, but still just a 10-minute walk into town, with a beautiful garden that emulates the Raffles's Palm Court in Singapore. Cheapest rooms are Rp20,000 s and Rp24,000 d. Better sea-view rooms with balconies cost Rp36,000-85,000 s and Rp41,000-90,000 d. Breakfast is included in the room charge. Besides the good Indonesian food, the restaurant serves a few Portuguese and even Timorese dishes for Rp5000-10,000. In the morning, ask for the more substantial Portuguese bread *pao,* not white bread. Laundry service available; taxi service out front. Sempati Airlines maintains its office here. Swim off the beach when the cabanas are set up.

Food

Food is more expensive here than on Java. Even *gado-gado* costs Rp1000-2500; some restaurants charge Rp1000 for *nasi putih*. **Pasar Sengol** in Kampung Bidan is where you can enjoy such cheap and nutritious Javanese and Sulawesi dishes as *gado-gado, nasi pecel, coto makassar, ayam soto,* and *ikan bakar*. Some stalls are open until 2400. Many other *rumah makan* and *warung* around town. Fruit is expensive.

The large hotels like the Turismo, New Resende, and Mahkota each have fine restaurants serving a wide variety of Indonesian, European, and Chinese foods. Prices are characteristically high, but portions are large and tasty.

Although restaurants and foodstalls are overwhelmingly in the hands of non-Timorese, it's possible to find such local foods as *caldeirada* (vegetable meat stew) and *tukir* (veggies and meat cooked in green bamboo sections). The Arsenio family, behind the Turismo Beach Hotel, also prepare delicious Portuguese-style dinners if you give them one day's notice. The **New Tropical Restaurant,** Jl. Bekora 10 (*bemo* no. 1 or Rp2000 by taxi), features such Portuguese delicacies as *caldeirada* (Rp6000) and fish dishes (up to Rp15,000). Perhaps the best choice for Portuguese food is the Turismo Beach Hotel, as it has a wide. selection of fish, lamb, and other meat dishes, most in the Rp5000-12,000 range. Where Portuguese food is served you can also get a chilled carafe of Portuguese wine at Rp12,000-13,000 for a 750 ml bottle or a bottle of Mateuse Rose for Rp25,000. Tim Tim still enjoys duty-free status, so Tiger beer from Singapore can cost less than Bintang.

For Padang style, try **Beringin** near Wisma Cendana, **Padang Bobonaru** up the street from the post office, or **Bundo Kandung. Djakarta, 5 Jaya,** and **Pantai Laut** offer extensive selections and tasty portions of Indonesian and Chinese food, although they're a bit pricey.

People who were around during Portuguese times remember the bread. Well, the *pao timor* is still there and it's just as good as ever. If you're going inland, take some with you. The **Golden Bakery,** Jl. Jose Maria Marques 24, features a wide selection of delicious cakes and pastries behind glass. Go early. The **Aru Bakery,** Jl. Kolmera, has a plethora of cakes, sweet rolls, and snacks. **Pabrik Roti Bintang,** on Jl. Santa Cruz, is a large old Portuguese bakery with wonderful huge wood-fired brick ovens. Be there early to sample hand-baked biscuits and *pao*. Opened in 1968, another Chinese-run bakery, **YAP,** is on Jl. Belarmino Lobo with big mound-like brick ovens.

Shopping

There's a government art cooperative downtown on Av. Americo Thomas, called **Dekranasada,** with a great variety of handwoven textiles, belts, pottery, marble items, and woodcarvings. Next door is a replica of a typical *rumah adat* from the Rasa region. Also good is **Toko Dili Souvenir and Bookshop,** Jl. Av. Bispo Madeiros 11, tel. (0390) 21093, opposite the stadium. Buy weavings and crafts here from all of Tim Tim's districts. This is also the biggest bookshop in Tim Tim. Up the street on Jl. Juacinto Candido is **Karya Seni Timor Souvenir Shop** for more crafts from all over the province. Both these souvenir shops distribute simple but useful city maps.

The old Portuguese market, **Mercado Lama,** is no longer used but is of some architectural interest. The city's two major markets are on opposite sides of town, one in Bekora, the other in Comoro. Both lie several km from the city center.

Chinese-run dry goods shops and supermarkets are concentrated on Jl. Jose Maria Marques in the old downtown area, Jl. Infante de Henrique behind the Dili Hotel, and along Jl. 15 Oktober. For photographic needs, try **Jewita Photo** or **Multi Perona Photo,** both on Jl. Jose Maria Marques. For medicines, go to **Kamia Farma** or **Apotik Zedia Farma.** Remember that most shops close their doors for a siesta from 1200-1600, when the most reasonable thing to do is nap.

Services

Change money at **Bank Dagang Negara, Bank Rakyat Indonesian, Bank Negara Indonesia,** or **Bank Danamon,** all with convenient downtown locations; BRI and BD have the best rates in all of Nusatenggara. The **Multi Perona Maya** travel agency also can change money.

The **post office** is located on the waterfront to the side of the governor's office—staff claims there is no poste restante service. Across from both the stadium and the Mercado Lama is the new and efficient *wartel,* open 24 hours. Good satellite connections to all of Indonesia and the world. Kitty-corner from the New Resende Inn, behind the governor's office, is the *kantor polisi.* East of downtown, out beyond Pasar Sengol is the **public hospital.** On Jl. Kolmera, near the cathedral, are the **immigration offices.** The **East Timor Tourism Office,** tel. (0390) 21350, has some useful brochures, maps, and other information. Located on Jl. Kaikoli, behind the University of Tim Tim.

Getting Around

Old, broken down, mostly blue Nissan and Datsun station wagons are used for taxi (*taksi*) transportation around Dili, Rp750 for short distances and up to Rp2000 for long distances. For the 10-minute ride to the airport the charge is Rp5000-7500. Just flag one down on the street. Rattletrap public buses and new minivan *bemo* charge only Rp200, even all the way east to the Bekora bus terminal or west to the airport entrance road and the Tasitolu bus terminal.

There are several bus/*bemo* routes through town. Some of the more useful are: bus D or *bemo* no. 1 to the Becora bus terminal, New Tropical Restaurant, and Villa Harmonia; *bemo* no. 2 to Balide bus terminal from Becora or the east end of town; and bus A or B to Tasitolu bus terminal. All *bemo* and buses go past Mercado Lama (old Municipal Market) and the stadium on their way to/from their respective destinations.

Getting Away

Merpati has two offices in Dili. The head office is next door to the New Resende Inn. Sempati is located at the Turismo Beach Hotel. Or book tickets for both airlines through **Multi Perona Maya** travel agency.

Dili's Komoro Airport is five km west of downtown. A taxi to/from the airport costs Rp5000-7500 depending on your hotel location. Buses "A" and "B" run out along the highway past the airport entrance road; from there you can walk the 400 meters to the terminal building. The airport has a restaurant but no tourist information. You'll probably have to go through a security and baggage check when you fly out.

Dili now has three bus stations. For points east, buses leave from **Becora bus terminal** to Viqueque (Rp7000) and Los Palos (Rp7000) direct once a day at about 0700; there are others throughout the morning from Baucau. Buses to Baucau leave 0500-1200 (Rp4000, three hours). From the **Balide bus terminal** buses run to Maubessi (Rp3000), Same, Suai (Rp10,000, nine hours), Ainaro (Rp4000, four hours), and other points south. As there are fewer buses running these routes, it's best to book a ticket at the terminal office the day before your intended departure. For points west, use **Tasitolu bus terminal:** Liquisa (Rp1000), Maubara (Rp1500), Ermera, Bobonaru, Maliana, Atambua (Rp5000), and Kupang (Rp13,000 at 0700 and Rp15,000 at 1900).

Timor Indah, Jl. Komoro (on the way to the airport), sells tickets to Atambua and Kupang. Also try **PT Antar Nusa Arta Cipta** or **PT Bakau Inda,** both on Jl. Kaikoli, down from Mercado Lama.

For private vehicle rental and personalized travel arrangements, consult Johan Winarto Salim at **Natrabu,** Jl. 15 Oktober 10, tel. (0390) 21080. Also check the tour desk at the New Resende Inn and Hotel Mahkota for car rentals. **Multi Perona Maya,** tel. 21444, Jl. Dr. Carvalho, and **Indra Kelau,** tel. 21833, Jl. Kolmera, are two full-service travel agents specializing in tours to East Timor.

TRAVEL WITHIN EAST TIMOR

From 1976 to 1989, Tim Tim was effectively closed. Visitors had to obtain special permission to travel around, usually granted only to church officials, aid workers, and diplomats. The Indonesians thought the eastern part of the island secure enough in 1989 to declare it officially open. Domestic and foreign tourists may now visit all districts, even though there's only minimal tourist infrastructure in some of the outlying areas. There is still periodic guerrilla activity in the far eastern region.

Bahasa Indonesia is now the lingua franca. Taught in the schools, it's spoken by all young people and many elders. Some English is spoken in Dili's higher-priced hotels, but Portuguese is more useful throughout the province. *Losmen,* restaurants, and *warung* outside Dili are few in number and relatively expensive for the quality, but sufficient for the traveler. If you are caught somewhere and are unable to find food, accommodation, or transportation, or simply need help, contact the local police, *kepala desa,* or Catholic Pastora. Many of the police are from Bali and have had experience dealing with foreigners. In some areas the populous is not allowed to move around at night, and traffic is forbidden. It used to be that as you walked through the mountains, your presence was heralded by a system of whistles. Some people reported that the police and

army stopped and questioned travelers at checkpoints and asked to see their passports. This may still be the case in certain remote spots, but is not typical of travel through the province. You may be told to check in with the police in every town in which you stay the night, but it seems that registering at your hotel is sufficient. Most travelers now report no hassles and that everyone, including the police and army, are friendly and helpful. Travel to remote and little-frequented towns and into the mountains may still arouse some special interest on the part of the authorities (and locals), however, so be prepared for some questions by police and more reserve on the part of the Timorese.

There is now a private *losmen* or two, and at least one government-run hostelry (Mess), in each district. These outlying accommodations are not cheap—usually in the Rp15,000 range—but available.

Although the territory might be open to you, the East Timorese may not be. Usually people greet you with a smile or a wave, particularly schoolchildren in their neat uniforms. Full bows from the waist derive from the subservient gesture paid to Japanese invaders. Though it's fairly easy to meet people, the East Timorese hesitate to make contact. You can still see the fear and intimidation in their faces. Be extremely careful. Let them take the initiative. Wary of outsiders, they may be circumspect in conversation, particularly in the areas of government, politics, economy, social conditions, and the integration of East Timor into Indonesia. However, locals may open up if you make an effort to communicate in one of their languages about topics important to them. Tim Tim is full of spies, even among the native population. People are afraid they will be asked by the military what they said to tourists. Even now people can get killed because of "subversive activities," like talking politics to a foreigner. In fact, you may be specifically told by government or tourist officials not to talk with locals about politics. It's also an excellent idea not to take photos of police or military installations.

OUTLYING TOWNS

Liquisa And Maubara

West out of Dili, six km before Liquisa, the old Portuguese prison **Aipelu Jail** is undergoing a partial renovation of its walls and buildings. In town are other examples of Portuguese architecture, buildings now occupied by the Indonesian authorities, such as Kantor Kecamatan. At least one of these fine old structures is under renovation as well. Stay at **Wisma Tokodeke.** Take a *bemo* from Dili (Rp1000, 40 minutes). Forty km west of Dili (Rp1500 by *bemo*), and farther west than Liquisa, is **Maubara,** site of the old Dutch fort **Benteng Maubara.** Built in the 1600s, its walls are still in fine shape. The coastal scenery between Dili and Maubara is quite pleasing.

Balibo

About an hour from both Atambua (West Timor) and Maliana (East Timor), Balibo is where five Australian journalists were shot to death by Indonesian soldiers during the 1975 invasion; the Indonesians claim it was an accident, but many Australians believe the journalists were murdered. In Balibo is an old red-roofed fort on the top of a hill and an old Catholic church. There are also remains of a Portuguese fort at **Batugade,** on the coast near the provincial border.

concerned cockfighter

Not far away are the hot springs of **Marobo,** once frequented by the Portuguese. Spend some time at the **Balibo Cultural and Arts Festival,** held yearly on 30 November, for an introduction to the music, dance, and arts of the province.

Maliana

The government administrative and market center for Bobonaro District (pop. 68,000), Maliana has a *losmen* with three rooms in the market; each room has two beds and each bed costs Rp10,000. Communal bathroom. Electricity comes on from 1800 till morning. A government-run Mess is here as well. Eat food at the Padang-style restaurants. To get to Maliana, board a bus from Atambua or from Dili's Tasitolu bus terminal. The flooded Maliana Plain is a fertile rice-growing area known as Tim Tim's food barn. Prior to the Indonesian invasion, this district was also a stronghold for pro-Indonesia integrationist forces.

Bobonaro

A short drive up the hill is Bobonaro. During Easter of 1990, three Indonesian soldiers were reportedly killed southeast of here. In retaliation, an infantry battalion from Manado apparently killed more than 100 men, women, and children in Lour just north of Zumalai.

The Portuguese employed Africans as mercenaries in their military campaigns against the Dutch, their descendants eventually settling in the area around Bobonaro. In villages near Bobonaro you see people with African features—quite a stark difference between them and the indigenous peoples. They live in steep-walled huts with grass roofs just like in Africa. Also in Bobonaro is an old, very large cavalry stockade that has been converted into an agricultural high school.

From Bobonaro take the road to Ermera, passing by old Portuguese coffee plantations and also the army's newly rehabilitated plantations. Some interesting communities nestle in the mountains off this road, with old Catholic churches, town squares, and former Portuguese administration buildings.

Ermera

Tim Tim has four different kinds of coffee, but the best is mocha (or "Timor coffee") grown in Ermera District, the region of the largest coffee plantations. There is a coffee processing plant in **Fatubesi.** Several buses a day run to Ermera.

There are actually two Ermeras, a new town and an old town. Old Ermera is in a beautiful location and has a great old Portuguese church with decorative tiles, quite spectacular and well-preserved. See the former district head's house and the old cavalry fort (near the church), which has been turned into a police station. The new town is down in the valley where wet-rice is grown, a showcase project to prove to the locals that *sawah* cultivation will work in the region.

Suai

A port town on the south coast, Suai is the center of a relative backwater with many traditional houses, and some distinctive music and dance, particularly the Cobra Dance. Stay at either of the two private *losmen* or the government-run **Wisma Tatoli.** Bus from Dili (Rp10,000, nine hours) or from Atambua via Betun (West Timor).

Same

Seventy-five km south of Dili, Same is the center for a Catholic Relief Services project that is trying to introduce the plow for rice farming. The method presently in use is to first clear and irrigate a plot of land, then let 30-40 water buffalo into the *sawah* to plow it with their feet. Some weaving and woodcarving are done here. On the way from Dili (daily morning bus), you pass through the coffee-growing areas of Aileu and Maubessi. See Mt. Cobalaki in the distance. Stay at the new government hostel, **Losmen Same.**

Maubessi And Ainaro

Maubessi and Ainaro sit in a coffee growing area, one of the most attractive for travelers. Cool high valleys, fine scenery, several waterfalls. A traditional area with hilltop villages and houses of distinctively regional design. The nice people in this area still celebrate some harvest festivals. In the village of Hatubuilico, on the slope of Gunung Tata Mai Lau, is the **Tata Mai Lau Pension,** a solid old building with rooms for Rp15,000. No electricity. Rent a horse here and hire a guide for a climb up East Timor's highest mountain. Speak to the *Jamat* (head of the subregency) beforehand, to facilitate the arrangements. Horse rental is about Rp5000 a day; negotiate for the guide. Restaurants are available in Maubessi and Ainaro. Bus from Dili to Maubessi (Rp3000) and Ainaro (Rp4000).

Baucau

The second-largest town in Tim Tim, reachable from Dili by bus (Rp4000, three hours). Beautifully situated high above the water, Baucau is nestled under the edge of the Baucau Plateau. In the pre-invasion days Baucau was considered the loveliest town in Portuguese Timor, with its whitewashed houses roofed with coconut fiber. Thick with greenery and lots of flowering trees, the town has tight winding streets and splendid ocean vistas. Also here are fine examples of old Portuguese buildings, although the church is of newer vintage. See the old Portuguese radio station. The main market has been shifted, but the old **Mercado Municipal** is still used by the older people—a grand Portuguese-style building constructed in an open semicircular shape. Crumbling now, with makeshift stalls to its front, this was once the real vibrant center of the city. Since the town is almost 400 meters above the sea, it has a cool climate. It's quite a walk downhill to a superb beach five km away; locals may offer you a coconut along the way. Or charter a *bemo* to the beach for around Rp7500. Unfortunately the old town is going to seed, and an ugly new "Indonesian" town is under construction on the plateau above, with new houses, shopping areas, and government buildings, including the post office and *wartel.*

The bus station is still located in the center of town, however, across from the Mercado Municipal. From here buses run to Dili, Viqueque, Los Palos, and to nearby villages. Half a dozen small restaurants are located at the market. Perhaps the

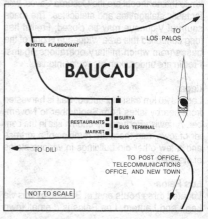

best is **Surya** (Padang-style) at the bus station—you can also buy tickets for the bus to Dili here.

The only hotel, the **Hotel Flamboyant** (formerly Hotel Baucau) charges Rp15,000 per room. Once used as a detention center by the Indonesians, and then by the Indonesian military, the hotel has a good location. The 20-plus rooms are clean and the staff is friendly. Each room has a private *mandi* and fan; some have a balcony. The hotel restaurant offers a limited menu of Indonesian and Portuguese dishes and provides music every night—a place for local boys and girls to meet under supervision.

Baucau has a good airport—strictly for the military—which you pass on your way from Dili. Baucau's Indonesian military cemetery has 175 Muslim soldier's graves and 40 Christian ones. Most are marked *gugur* (standard Indonesian military term for "fallen in battle"). Local farmers will tell you the *gugur* were Timorese militiamen, impressed by the army for guard duty and killed in Fretilin guerrilla attacks.

Viqueque

En route to Viqueque you come upon **Venilale**, where Japanese bunkers and caves were dug into the hills in 1943. Thousands of native slave laborers were shot to prevent them from telling Australian guerrillas of the location of the caves. See more recent war relics on the high plateaus, with sky-blue graves in cemeteries in the middle of nowhere. In Viqueque stay with the padre, who knows what's going on in the area (leave a donation), or try the new **Losmen Viqueque**. Nine km to the northeast are the Ossuroa Caves, with fantastic stalagmites and stalactites. The roads south of Viqueque may be closed; Fretilin has long controlled this area. Viqueque is one of the bases from which military operations against Fretilin are undertaken at regular intervals.

Laga

Laga is 20 km east of Baucau. Salt is harvested from nearby lakes from September to November. A newish Portuguese church sits in the center of town, and there are remains of a fortress and a few other old buildings in various states of disrepair.

Los Palos

Located three hours east of Baucau by bus via Laga and Lautem, Los Palos is a small town set on a 500 meter-high rangeland plateau (horses, cattle, goats, water buffalo). Some rice is cultivated here, as well as corn. An infantry battalion is stationed here. The streets of Los Palos are lined with small-town Portuguese buildings, shops, homes, offices, and a church, but the post office is new and the market is run down. In 1990, a Rasa-style *rumah adat* was constructed next to the market, also another fine building used for ceremonies and celebrations of all kinds. These are nice structures but the real thing can be seen in Desa Rasa. Los Palos has two mediocre restaurants. **Segar Baru** (Padang-style) is nothing to brag about but it's cheap; **Anda** is a few steps away, tucked into the side of the market building.

Los Palos receives on the average about one foreign visitor a day. Stay at **Losmen Paraja Agung** (no sign), right behind the hospital and next to the market. Rates are Rp6000 per room for the two rooms; tiny cubicles. There is no breakfast included in the room charge, only tea. Separate *mandi* and toilet. A newer, more comfortable place, though somewhat sterile, is the government-run *losmen,* located between the local government office and the police station. As yet without an official name, it's known as "Losmen Los Palos" or "Losmen Pariwisata" ("Tourist Losmen"). The eight rooms, all with *mandi,* toilet, and storage cabinets, go for Rp15,000-20,000.

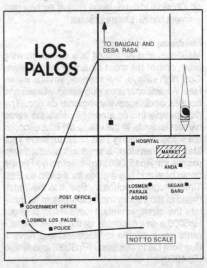

LOS PALOS

TO BAUCAU AND DESA RASA

HOSPITAL
MARKET
ANDA

LOSMEN PARAJA AGUNG
SEGAR BARU

POST OFFICE
GOVERNMENT OFFICE
LOSMEN LOS PALOS
POLICE

NOT TO SCALE

© MOON PUBLICATIONS, INC.

A bus from Baucau to Los Palos is Rp3000 (three hours), and the early-morning (0500-0600) bus from Dili is Rp7000 (six hours). Return buses to Baucau and Dili leave at about 0630, 1200, and 1300, with a 1500 bus only to Baucau. There is no bus station in Los Palos. You must wait at the bus company office at the town's main intersection or arrange with the driver the night before to pick you up at the *losmen*.

Desa Rasa

Twelve km before Los Palos (Rp500 by *bemo* from Los Palos), on the way up from Lautem, is the village of Desa Rasa. Here you'll find one fine, and still inhabited, example of a traditional East Timorese *rumah adat*. Standing next to it is a similar, unoccupied structure that tips like the leaning tower of Pisa. Both are only a few meters from the road, and virtually the only surviving houses of their kind; the vast majority were destroyed by guerrilla activity over the last two decades. These traditional houses, set on four stout posts, feature living areas raised a few meters above the ground. The roof, made of grass thatch, is as much as nine meters above the ground at its highest point. Other newer houses and granaries, in the traditional style but

smaller, closer to the ground, and without ladders, are found about 200 meters down the road in another part of the village. Desa Rasa sees few visitors, so be polite. Introduce yourself to the elders of the village—some only speak the local Fataluku language—before you wander around and take pictures. People are still quite genuine here. They seem happy to talk with you, so do your best with Bahasa Indonesia.

Tutuala

An out-of-the-way place on the far eastern tip of Timor, Tutuala is located about 30 km northeast of Los Palos over an unsealed road (Rp1500 and 1.5 hours from Los Palos). To Tutuala, there's one *bemo* a day at 0500; it returns around midmorning. At the intersection of the turnoff to Tutuala are the skeletal remains of a Portuguese fort. Overlooking the scenic confluence of the Wetar Strait and Timor Laut, the new **Pousada Tutuala** charges in the Rp15,000-25,000 range. Fantastic views over the ocean from here, with nine islands of Maluku visible in the distance. Dwellings in this eastern area are smaller, squarer in shape, and built on stilts. From Tutuala, rent a boat to **Jako island,** only a few hundred meters off Timor. Walk to the beach on the far side of the island.

THE OUTER ARC

Three rarely visited islands southwest of Timor—Roti, Ndao, and Savu—are known as the Outer Arc islands. Actually island kingdoms, the three are still ruled by royal lineages which trace their origins back to the Majapahit dynasty. Because of their isolation, these islands still practice a rich traditional culture with distinctive textile arts, dances, and music. The outside world intrudes only in the form of cruise ships that visit Savu for an afternoon three times a year to watch traditional welcoming dances.

It's thought that these dry, hot isles, more vulnerable to erosion than Sumba and Timor, became infertile hundreds of years ago. Gradually, the inhabitants learned to use the tens of thousands of palms that colonized their soil-depleted environment. Today the people depend to an extraordinary degree on the cultivation of *lontar*, "harvested" twice yearly. Providing all the necessities of life, the near-total exploitation of this

palm blesses the islands with a complex, successful, and diverse economy. After the trees are tapped, the menfolk of Roti, Ndao, and Savu have ample leisure time to engage in such pursuits as semipermanent gardening, offshore fishing, pig-, goat- and sheep-rearing, seaweed- and honey-gathering, and trading. Rotinese men, in fact, have so much time on their hands to devote to nonagricultural, nonsubsistence activities that they have a reputation as the most vigorous entrepreneurs of eastern Nusatenggara.

THE *LONTAR* CULTURE

On these islands grow a drought-resistant, solitary-stemmed, separately sexed species (*Borassus*) of the *lontar* palm. Attaining a height of up to 30 meters and a width of nearly .75 meter, this magnificent palm is the tree of life for the peoples of the Outer Arc. At the beginning and end of the dry season (April-Nov.), when the palm blossoms, a sweet juice is extracted from its huge leaves, which droop fanlike from the palm's crown. The islanders are highly skilled palm tappers, taking only 15-20 minutes to climb and tap a tree, servicing up to 15 trees per day. The tapper climbs the palm using a rope made of *lontar*-leaf stalks; on his belt are the *arit* tool to cut the spadix, and a *lontar*-leaf basket to collect the juice. Fatality awaits the inexperienced; you often hear of someone's death caused by "a fall from a tree."

Food Source

The *lontar* is one of the earth's most efficient sugar-producing plants and the islanders' guarantee against famine. During the tapping season the Rotinese and Savunese sustain themselves solely on the fresh juice of these trees. What juice is not drunk is cooked over clay earth ovens, producing a brown syrup that can be stored in vats for long periods. Diluted with water, the syrup provides nutrition during the off season.

The syrup can be crystallized to form thick, dark sugar squares, or fermented to make alcoholic toddy. The Rotinese distill a fine sweet gin from the mash, and even newborn babies are fed *lontar* sugar mixed with water. The froth from the boiling juice and the sago-mash from the soaked wood are fed to the pigs, thereby directly converting the palm to protein. Because of the year-round availability of *lontar* food products, Roti and Savu are the only islands in eastern Nusatenggara that do not experience the annual period of hunger (*lapar biasa*). Their population densities outstrip those on neighboring Timor and Sumba, and in some areas are comparable to the spectacular densities of the wet-rice cultivation regions of Java and Bali.

Lontar yields are very high: a single full-grown palm can produce over 100 liters of juice per month (which can be boiled down to about 15 liters of syrup), and a whole family can support itself from several palms' yields through an entire season. Tens of thousands of palms, all oozing sugary sap from their crowns, encourage huge populations of bees, and since the time of the Dutch East Indies honey has been a valuable export of Roti and Savu.

Crafts And Implements

Life is surrounded by this tree's products: *lontar* leaves and stalks can be bent, shaped, sliced, whittled, and tied to make furniture, rope, umbrellas, hats, sandals, belts, toys, cigarette papers, clothing, sailcloth, musical instruments, containers, saddlebags, and a mindboggling number of other household articles. The fan-shaped leaves provide thatch for house roofs and walls, and the fibrous leaf stalks are twined to fashion durable harnesses, bridles, and straps, or interlocked to build fences. The wood is converted into planks, while the hollow trunks are made into feeding troughs. A blanket of *lontar* leaves is spread over gardens and then burned to create excellent fertilizer. At the end of their lives the Rotinese are wrapped in *lontar*-mat shrouds and buried in a *lontar* coffins.

ROTI

Off the southwest tip of Timor, Roti is the southernmost island of the Indonesian archipelago. Geologically and climatically similar to Timor, Roti is a dry island with flat areas under cultivation, bare rolling hills, palm and acacia savannahs, patches of secondary forests, and almost no remaining primary forests. There are two distinct seasons: the east monsoon (April-Oct.) brings dry, gusty, hot winds, while the west monsoon (Nov.-March) brings sporadic rain. Rice, irrigated by laboriously built channels and diverted

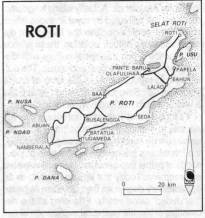

ROTI

© MOON PUBLICATIONS, INC.

rivers, is cultivated in the north and east areas of the island, while the *lontar* palm is harvested most intensively in the west, which has a proportionally higher population. The Rotinese, along with the Savunese, also keep large herds of sheep and goats, and water buffalo are prized as bride-wealth and as a means of plowing wet-rice fields. Driven in circles through fields, turning the ground into a muddy mire, the animals themselves function as plows.

The small, arid town of **Baa** serves as the island's government and trading center. There are several *losmen* in Baa, but for accommodations elsewhere, go directly to the *kepala desa* in each village. Be sure to try the famous sweet *tuak,* as well as *sopi, gula air, gula lempeng,* and *laru*—all drinks concocted from *lontar* palm juice. Some Rotinese men drink an average of 10 bottles of *tuak* daily.

There is rather good snorkeling and diving at Kakae and Papela on the east coast.

History
Myths of the present inhabitants of Roti claim their ancestors migrated via Timor from "the north." Portuguese Dominicans founded a mission on the island in the late 16th century, but by 1662 most of the autonomous states of Roti had signed treaties with the VOC. The Rotinese were close allies of the Dutch; they accepted Christianity as early as the 18th century and were active in the Dutch colonial service. The Rotinese, like the Ambonese, even fought some battles for the Dutch against rebellious natives on other islands.

As early as 1679 an extensive system of native schools, assisted first by the Dutch Missionary Society and later by the Dutch colonial government, was established for teaching Malay. By 1871, 34 local schools had been established on the island. Thus the Rotinese very early had a distinct educational advantage in eastern Indonesia, and upon independence their transition to Bahasa Indonesia was almost effortless.

Working as merchants, rice growers, *lontar* tappers, and civil servants, large numbers of Rotinese have migrated to northeast Timor, Kupang (where Rotinese form one-third of the population), and the islands of Semau, Sumba, and Flores. They participate in all levels of the Indonesian economy and national life.

The People
Roti is divided into 18 autonomous domains, each under its own "lord" (*manek*), and each adhering to its own dress, *adat,* and dialect. Malay in appearance, the Rotinese are characterized by their broad, sombrero-like *lontar*-leaf hats. These short, light-skinned, slightly built people have had longer contact with western Indonesia and are, in general, agriculturally, educationally, and politically more sophisticated than the Timorese. Christian Rotinese claim to be the oldest Protestants in the Timor area, but their Dutch Reformed Protestantism is interwoven with strong customs centering on ancestral spirts. Major ceremonies are held at marriage and death; minor rituals are held at the seventh month of pregnancy, at first hair-cutting, baptism, naming, and at specific times during the agricultural and palm-tapping cycles. The Rotinese have a long written and oral literary tradition and place great emphasis on storytelling and speaking well.

Most villages are located in and around stands of *lontar* palms, wherever there is enough fresh water for drinking and gardening. Wells and springs are usually owned by specific clans and managed by a "lord of the earth" (*dae langak*). Swidden agriculture has nearly disappeared; nowadays the Rotinese cultivate semi-permanent, fertilized household gardens, with some limited wet-rice cultivation. Their traditional houses, which resemble great furry hunched animals, are rectangular with gabled ends covered by immense stacks of *lontar* leaves reaching nearly to the ground.

Arts And Crafts
Roti cloth is usually red, black, and yellow with designs of flower rosettes formed by small squares of color, often with elongated triangles on the borders, which give their cloths a mosaic-like effect. Textiles play an integral role in burial ceremonies, and certain heirloom weavings are used to pass on oral legends and stories through the generations. Each of Roti's 18 kingdoms once had its own textile motifs so it was immediately apparent to which kingdom the wearer belonged; nowadays, with districts borrowing motifs from each other, these distinctions are blurred. Today, men dress up in a store-bought white shirt and plaid cotton *sarung,* with a homespun *selimut* draped over one shoulder. The Rotinese musical instrument, the *sasando,* is

like a bamboo zither with 22 civet catgut or copper strings and a hemispheric resonator made from a full, boat-shaped leaf of the *lontar* palm. Decorated antique axes with cast handles and blades are products of the Bronze Age, though the date of their origin on Roti is unknown.

The Rotinese make at least eight styles of hats from *lontar* leaves. Patterned after 16th- and 17th-century Portuguese helmets, the bright hats feature a jaunty cock feather or single woven "horn" curling up in front. Each hat has its own use in everyday life: to store tobacco in, work in, dance in, and so forth—see specimens in Kupang's tourist office. Also check out *lontar*-leaf baskets, plaited protective spirit figures (*maik* or *ola*), and heavy burlap-like clothing made from *lontar* leaf and still worn by laborers.

Getting There
Roti is separated from Timor by the 10-km-wide Roti Strait, which because of monsoonal turbulence July-Aug. has been called "the Grave of the Rotinese." Ferries leave Kupang's Bolok Harbor every day except Sunday at 0900 (Rp4500) for Terminal Pantai Baru near Baa on Roti. Selat Roti is also navigable by *prahu layar* from Kupang in two to three hours. On Tuesday and Saturday Merpati flies to Baa from Kupang (Rp35,000) at 1000, landing at Lekunik Airport 30 minutes later. This flight continues on to Savu (Rp55,000) at 1100, from where it returns to Roti and leaves again at 1300 for Kupang.

NDAO

A lonely, rocky, eroded island 12 km off Roti's northwest coast. Since the signing of a treaty with the Dutch in 1756, Ndao has been considered an autonomous domain of Roti which has traditionally absorbed Ndao's excess population. Like the Rotinese and Savunese, the Ndaonese are *lontar*-tappers; they speak a dialect of Savunese, drink palm-juice *tuak,* and wear distinctive *ikat*-dyed cloths and Rotinese-style *lontar* hats.

Nearly all the island's men supplement their *lontar*-based incomes by fashioning traditional silver and gold articles and selling *ikat* cloths and pandanus mats. Having had long contacts with Javanese artisans, the Ndaonese create

jewelry less elaborate and adorned than Yogyanese or Kendari work. At the beginning of each dry season, smiths wander throughout the Timor area making anklets, bracelets, and other finished jewelry; they also take advance orders and deliver the finished pieces the following dry season. In most cases the customer supplies the precious metal in the form of old coins or jewelry, and the jewelers are paid in food or small livestock. Most of the itinerant craftsmen return to Ndao by November, in time to tap their palms during the peak harvest season.

Because of the intensive cultivation of Ndao's overabundance of *lontar* palms, this tiny speck of an island (nine square km) has a population density of around 235 per square km, even higher than Roti and Savu. Between Roti and Ndao is yet another smaller island, Pulau Nusa, which supports a small Ndaonese settlement. To get there, take a local *prahu motor* from Baa.

SAVU

An isolated island group 100 km west of Roti and about midway between Sumba and Timor. The largest island of the group, with a population of about 30,000, is Pulau Savu. The main town, Seba, consists of one street, a dozen *toko,* a daily market, and a dozen motor vehicles.

In Seba, there are three **homestays:** the home of Ongko Kido Dena, a Chinese married to a Savunese, only 15 meters from the harbor; the home of Madu Buky, close by; and the home of Octo Djonaga, a member of the regional DPR

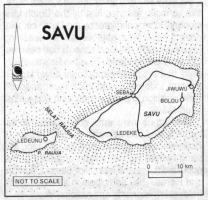

and director of the high school (SMA), about a km from harbor. Travelers must rely on village heads (*temugu*) to make sleeping arrangements.

This bare, stony island, uplifted on an ancient bed of coral limestone, endures parching heat and scorching wind each dry season (April-Oct.), while the west monsoon (Nov.-March) is a period of scant, spotty rain. The island's north and east portions are wetter than the southwest, but water is scarce all over Savu. No forests remain, and the island's highest elevation is 240 meters.

Despite this seemingly inhospitable environment, the Savunese are among the most cultured people of the Outer Arc islands, and their *ikat* weavings are among Indonesia's finest. Villages (*rae*) are often surrounded by stone walls, and each village is composed of members of one clan (*udu*). The island kingdom is ruled by a full-figured queen (*mone weto*), whom you can see attending important ceremonies.

Take the main track inland from Seba, crossing rice paddies and palm plantations, to **Namata,** an animistic site on a hill where you'll find a circle of huge lens-shaped boulders. Known to the local people as the "Oracle Stones," each weighs six tons and all are thought to be over 3,000 years old. On the summit of the hill is a small stone depicting on one side an early four-masted schooner under full sail and on the other side an inscription in English: "Stranded 1418." Tradition has it a ship ran aground here; the crew stayed on, entranced by the local women.

History

Savu has strong historical ties with Hindu Java and the people believe they are descended from a nobleman of the 15th-century Majapahit Empire. The Portuguese were the first Europeans to land on Savu, establishing several missions in the 16th century. The Dutch signed a treaty with the island's rulers in 1756, and united the separate kingdoms under a single *raja* (*douae*) in 1918. Savu is today divided into six native states (counting the tiny offshore island of Raijua), all recognized as administrative units by the Republic, each with its own complex priesthood, ritual events based on the lunar calendar, and established agricultural and *lontar* palm boundaries. Sizable Savunese colonies are also found on Sumba, Timor, and Flores.

Economy

As on Roti, the basis of the Savunese economy is the cultivation and harvesting of the island's tens of thousands of *lontar* palms. Individual palm enclosures are owned and harvested by households; the best-kept, family-worked *lontar* enclosures are found in **Liae** on the south coast and **Mesara** in the west. Some irrigated *sawah* are found in coastal areas, the fields worked to mud by water buffalo, and some pepper is grown. A seagrub (*nyale*), which appears in huge quantities off the south coast at about the same time each year, is harvested and then pickled in *lontar* vinegar. *Nyale* are considered a great delicacy. The Savunese also live by fishing, selling copra, and raising water buffalo, sheep, and fine, spirited, sturdy horses, one of the islanders' most prized exports.

Events

In spite of missionary efforts, Savu remains an animist stronghold where important collective rituals are still regularly staged. In the 18th and 19th centuries, fierce warfare between the native island domains was endemic, and feuding continues to this day. This warlike tradition can best be seen in Savunese dances. Like the nearby Sumbanese, the Savunese breed of horse plays a central role in their ceremonies; the *perhere jara* dance depicts the story of how horses saved the island from grasshopper plagues.

In the *pedoa* harvest dance, staged under the full moon between March and May, baskets of unhusked rice or dried peas are tied to the dancers' ankles; when shaken, they provide the dance's rhythmic accompaniment. In a blessing ritual (*dabba*), a sort of Savunese bar mitzvah, parents anoint a child's head with flowers and betelnut in the hopes of a good life. Savunese mortuary ceremonies are unbelievably complex. Cockfights between rival villages are popular, as well as being ritually important. The Savunese are also proud of their musical traditions.

Crafts

The Savunese weave exquisite *ikat* out of native cotton, typically with narrow design strips in somber blue, black, and white, with touches of beige, rust, brown, and red. Weaving designs, their significance long since forgotten, are unaltered from the time when the clans came into existence over 20 generations ago. Delicate floral and geometric motifs still serve as a system of clan identification. Some motifs have obviously been inspired by Portuguese and Dutch patterns: crocheted roses, grapevines, Western-style birds, lions from old Dutch coins, cherubs. Other traditional technology practiced is the plaiting of basketry, ropes, and harnesses.

Transportation

Fly with Merpati twice weekly from Kupang (Rp55,000) via Roti. An ASDP ferry departs Kupang every Monday and Friday at 1400 for the overnight trip to Savu (Rp12,000), and returns to Kupang on Tuesday and Saturday. There's also a connection between Savu and Waingapu on the Kupang, Ende, Waingapu, Savu, return route. This ferry leaves Waingapu on Wednesday at 1500 for the 13-hour crossing to Savu and returns to Waingapu Thursday at 1500. The fare between Waingapu and Savu is Rp12,300. Big cruise ships like the *Island Explorer* visit Savu many times a year. Take one of the island's four *bemo* from Seba to Savu Timor (the eastern district). No buses, but a few trucks run on the island. It takes just two days to walk completely around Savu on the coastal path.

SUMBA

Outlying, dry, mostly barren Sumba is one of the most fascinating islands of Nusatenggara. A principal island of the East Nusatenggara group, situated south of Flores and midway between Sumbawa and Timor, Sumba is the source of some of the most handsome *ikat* fabrics in Indonesia, and the breeding ground for the country's strongest horses. The island is also known for its ritual tribal life; flawlessly built, high-peaked, thatch-roofed structures; mammoth sculpted stone tombs; and excellent *tuak*. Here you find an authentic ancient culture with none of the layers of Hinduism, Islam, or Christianity found elsewhere in Indonesia.

About 300 km long by 80 km wide, Sumba's 11,100-square-km area is divided into east and west regencies, with significant topographic, climatic, cultural, linguistic, and historical differences between the two halves. The island's chief air- and seaport is Waingapu on the north coast, which is also the capital of the eastern *kabupaten*; Waikabubak is the principal town for the western half.

THE LAND

Lying outside the volcanic belt running through the length of the archipelago, much of interior Sumba consists of extensive plateaus with scattered, irregular hills. The climate is hot and dry, particularly in the east where widespread eucalyptus savannahs and large tracts of flat grasslands and steppe-like landscapes provide good grazing for cattle and support small-scale agriculture. The rainy season is Nov.-March. West Sumba receives a higher rainfall of 180 cm, while East Sumba gets 67 cm. East Sumba's soil is generally thin and nonvolcanic; the small unnavigable rivers which supply the island's only irrigation tend to be dry up to eight months of the year. At the approach of the rainy season the rivers are thick with spawning sea fish.

The 280,000 people of more verdant West Sumba (Sumba Barat) are mainly farmers, while the 150,000 or so East Sumbanese (Sumba Timur) raise horses, cattle, buffalo, and other livestock. Sumbans practice mostly subsistence agriculture: rice, tobacco, and maize are the main crops; coffee and coconuts are secondary. An archaic method of plowing is still used here, in which 20-30 buffalo are driven across flooded fields, trampling them to a muddy consistency.

Sumba's famous breed of sturdy "sandalwood" horses, symbols of wealth and status on the island, are some of Indonesia's finest, exported to Java and other islands for drawing carts. The island's forests yield cinnamon and sandalwood. Greed over the centuries has forced the government to forbid cutting down those few stands of sandalwood that remain; now you need a special license to export the fragrant wood from Indonesia. There are over 150 species of butterflies on the island, nine unique to Sumba.

SUMBA

HISTORY

Documented history begins with a reference to Sumba in 14th-century East Javanese chronicles as a dependency of the Majapahit Empire. During the 17th century Sumba fell under the dominance of the Bima rajadom of East Sumbawa, and later the entire island was subordinated to the powerful Goanese kingdom of southern Sulawesi. Right up until the 19th century, Bugis *prahu* regularly raided Sumba for slaves, transporting 20-30 boatloads each year for sale in Sulawesi, Lombok, and Bali.

In 1756, a contract was signed between the Dutch VOC and a coalition of Sumbanese *rajas*. Although Dutch civil officers were later assigned to Sumba as "political observers," it wasn't until around 1900 that the Netherlands began to actively intervene in Sumbanese internal affairs. As elsewhere in Indonesia, the Dutch governed the Sumbanese under a policy of indirect rule. Native rulers were appointed to administer the two regencies, East and West Sumba, an administrative division maintained by the Republic of Indonesia to this day.

In WW II, Waingapu was bombed by the Japanese and 3,000 Sumbanese were killed. When independence was declared by Sukarno on 17 August 1945, it took six months for the news to reach Waingapu.

THE PEOPLE

A harsh climate and difficult natural surroundings have forged a hardy people predominantly proto-Malay in appearance, with some Melanesian features. The men are farmers with weather-beaten faces who ride horses bareback, drape color-rich handwoven fabrics around their shoulders, and carry long knives with buffalo-horn hilts stuck in their waistbands. The eastern part of the island constitutes a relatively homogeneous ethnolinguistic entity, while the western half is more mixed. Minorities include immigrants from Savu, Timor, and Flores, plus Chinese merchants in the coastal towns.

Formerly, there were three castes in native Sumbanese society: *maramba* were nobility, the *kabisu* free commoners, while *ata* were ex-slaves and their descendants (the slave trade was abolished here in 1901). Although upon independence the new Indonesian Republic refused to recognize the authority of the native princedoms, some elements of this caste system are still in evidence; members of the nobility continue to hold the highest positions in the native civil service and exert strong influence. No kinship is felt or perceived with any other island; the local word for "foreigner" refers to anyone from any other island.

The Sumbanese variety of Bahasa Indonesia is spoken with an almost Italian-sounding accent. There are nine dialects on the island, each as different as Dutch from German. Missionaries introduced a common language, *kambera*, which is understood by everyone.

A transparent film of modern life is superimposed here on a wild society. Sumbanese men are turbaned, well-muscled, swashbuckling, mustachioed, with a dash of Arabian blood. Men and women alike—all the people of Sumba are handsome. Exceptions are the *sirih* addicts—not only does betelnut stain the teeth, lips, and gums a raw and bloody crimson, but some older people have filed their teeth almost to the gums, giving them the appearance of victims of some appalling disease.

Religion

Because it was sparsely populated and poor in resources, Sumba escaped the proselytizing zeal of Muslims and Christians. Though the majority of Sumbanese today are nominally Protestant, with colonies of Catholics and Muslims, the Sumbanese largely practice animism. The greatest concentration of those who worship ancestral and land spirits is found in Sumba Barat, where some two-thirds of the population hold on to the traditional religion.

The Sumbanese system of religious beliefs is known as *merapu*. The people believe this life is temporary; that, following death, eternal life is achieved in the world of spirits, *prai merapu*. All spirits consist of two elements, *ndewa* and *hamangu*, representing the balance of universal life through which happiness may be achieved. The Sumbanese associate the Great Mother (Ina Kalada) and Great Father (Ama Kalada) with the moon and the sun, the parents of the Sumbanese people. To honor *merapu* the people place statues on stone altars. These are most often made of wood, and depict human

faces; the altars receive offerings of *sirih pinang*, a dish containing betel leaves, nuts, and lime.

Traditional ceremonies, complex burial rites, and gift-exchange rituals are widespread. Forgiveness is asked of ancestral spirits if the harvest fails or someone falls from a tree or is thrown by a horse. Even megalithic cultures are still extant in the outlying areas, particularly in Sumba Barat, where you find large numbers of huge stone tombs and dolmens along roads, amid lush hilltop vegetation, around villages, and even in the front yards of houses. Anthropologists study these isolated Sumbanese societies to learn about similar cultures now dead or dying.

Village Life

The bulk of the population lives on the interior plateaus in fortified hilltop villages (*paraing*), where large clan houses face a central square containing the stone slab tombs of semidivine ancestors. Traditional Sumbanese houses, which resemble gigantic straw hats, consist of a big platform raised on piles, with low walls and thatched roofs sloping gently upward from all four sides, then rising sharply toward the center to characteristically high gables. As in Tanatoraja, some are also adorned with sacrificed buffalo horns and pig jawbones. Inside, massive center posts hold up the roof, and high in the rafters are stored precious ceremonial textiles and sacred objects of deified ancestors.

Sumbanese women as well as men chew betelnut, and the people are quite fond of coconut toddy and gin. Puberty for boys is marked by a token circumcision, while girls who come of age are tattooed and their teeth filed. Cross-cousin marriages were once strictly adhered to. Though traditional customs are now dying out, you still see older married women with blue horses and monkeys tattooed on their arms.

Every Sumbanese village has a *wunang* (spokesman) who is a master of the ceremonial language of *loluk*. The *wunang* is chosen for his melodious voice and fast, clear rhythms of speech. Arranged in couplets of parallel meanings, *loluk* is used in traditional ritual songs, love ballads, and animal stories, often containing moralistic or amusing comments on human nature.

Events

Family heads make great efforts to accumulate wealth (buffalo, horses, textiles, and jewelry), which is sacrificed or displayed at religious and funeral rites. In the *pasola,* the traditional battle of West Sumba, hundreds of horsemen fling spears at each other. Dances, along with bloody sacrifices and traditional boxing matches (*pajura*), are frequently staged during harvest festivals July to October. Prior to a boxing match, the fists of the combatants are wrapped in wild grass leaf; the barbed edges can produce vicious wounds. Swipes across the eyes are highly prized—blood flowing from such wounds blinds the opponent, usually bringing about his defeat.

While carrying shields and swords and letting out blood-tingling war cries, performers in tribal war dances perform energetic and rhythmic leaps. These expressive dances are not that far from reality, as clans still fight over land rights. The dancing of the girls of East Sumba, derived from weaving and spinning thread, feature many hand and shoulder movements but limited movements of the feet. Other women watching the lively dances let out a sort of excited, shrill warble called the *karakul.* These "vibrated shriek" songs of the women of Sumba were once ritually used to welcome husbands back from headhunting expeditions. The dances of West Sumba are, in contrast, slow and sedate.

Sumbanese horseracing begins annually on Independence Day and continues for about 10 days. This is a very masculine environment— young boys in numbered jerseys race horses four at a time. Trainers try to start the unruly mounts all at the same time, a process which can sometimes take up to ten minutes. The races are very exciting; the crowds go wild.

Visit the Kepala Seksi Kebudayaan in Waik-abubak for information on current cultural events; these genial officials can also help with hiring guides (see Mr. Mude).

Death And Funerals

The Sumbanese believe death is the last stage of human life, and the death ceremony must therefore be conducted properly so the spirit of the dead may proceed to *merapu* heaven undisturbed. From the time of sickness until death the soul must be treated carefully and with respect. Relatives, for instance, are not allowed to weep. Only after a prominent member of the family—a *rato*—calls the name of the dead four times and receives no answer may mourning begin. A gong is struck, and the family gathers and commences to weep. The body is bathed, and, in some places, smeared with coconut cream, milk, and oil. Afterwards it is dressed and carried to a large hall escorted by four corpse guards called *papanggang.*

Burial proceeds in two stages; the duration between the two is not fixed. In the primary stage the corpse is bound in a scarf wound from left to right and covered with *sarung;* the number of *sarung* is dependent upon the social status of the deceased. The body is then put into a wooden box or wrapped in buffalo skin, the knees and elbows broken so the corpse may return to the fetal position. The completed package is then temporarily interred in a tent.

stonedragging, Sumba

During the primary stage, the spirit of the departed is still present in the house and village. Relatives of highborn corpses must pay homage with buffalo, pigs, or horses, as well as expensive *sarung.* The day before the termination of the primary stage a *pahadang* ceremony is held to pray for the dead. The spirit is told it is time to proceed to the tomb, that it should no longer wander about the house.

For the second burial the tombstone must be prepared. The size of the stone depends on the importance of the dead. The stone should be dragged from a site outside the village with appropriate ceremony; often the entire village is involved. The Sumbanese use a hundred meters of long rope, made of plant or tree fiber, to drag stones. Drag time is dependent on the distance to the village, the weight of the stone, and the number of people participating. The relatives of the dead are expected to prepare food for all who transport the stone.

When the stone reaches the village the secondary stage of burial may begin. The corpse is removed from its tent and carried to the final burial place. The *papanggang* carry the corpse, others walk next to the bier or ride decorated horses. Occasionally people faint or are possessed by spirits. In former times slaves were buried alive with the deceased.

If you have a chance to attend a funeral for a deceased member of the nobility, don't miss it. As well as occasions for gaining immense social prestige, royal funerals are a major focus of Sumbanese culture and thus prime opportunities to witness the lavish display and destruction of family wealth. Multitudes of buffalo, pigs, dogs, and horses (and formerly slaves and captives) are slaughtered. Dutch officials at the turn of the century reported attending funerals where dazzling textile wealth and other valuables, after propitiary sacrifices, were interred with dead chiefs. Although not as widespread, this practice continues, with textiles, gold, porcelain, and antiques interred to feed, transport, and make life in the afterworld comfortable for the deceased. Your heart aches as magnificent *ikat* specimens are lowered into mother earth, tens of thousands of dollars' worth left to molder and decay.

Tombs are not built in a remote graveyard outside the village where thieves can work quietly, but right in front of the house. The people *live* with their dead. First a hole is dug in the ground and cement poured into it, with a room formed to hold the bones and the valuables. Then on each corner are rolled big, heavy stones, then another giant slab—with perhaps images of a man and a woman—is placed on top. These gigantic stone slabs and troughs, some weighing up to 40 tons, may require 40 men two years to cut and 1,000 men to drag, using ropes and rollers, from quarry to hilltop village. Great prestige attaches to the enormity of the stone and the distance covered. In October 1993 a 40-ton slab was dragged 10 km over numerous hills from the quarry at Wairasa to the village of Kapunduk.

IKAT SUMBA

Ikat is a very ancient tie-dye method of decorating rugs, shawls, and blankets. Each completed fabric represents a colossal amount of human labor and only isolated, feudal, agricultural societies like Sumba's still produce these handwoven textiles. Although *ikat* fabrics are also woven on nearby islands such as Flores and Roti, the craft here has reached an unusually high level. Woven from locally grown cotton, the cloths figure prominently in the ceremonial and social life of the island.

Each region has its own distinctive designs and shades. Some heirloom pieces are considered so priceless and magically powerful they cannot be viewed in safety but must be kept in sealed baskets high up among the roofbeams. The really fine blankets, family *pusaka,* you cannot buy. Families already have 1,000 buffalo, so why should they sell a blanket? It's easy to find more cattle, but difficult to make more blankets.

Types Of *Ikat*
Worn only by men, large rectangular cloths called *hinggi*—with horizontal rows of involved human and animal motifs—are usually made and sold in pairs. One is used as a shoulder cloth, the other to wrap around the hips; they also do duty as attractive wall decorations or door curtains. In addition, there are four classes of single-piece blankets (*selimut sumba*) which are traditionally used only in festivities or as burial shrouds. East Sumbanese *sarung,* called *lau,* feature light figures on dark backgrounds.

West Sumbanese *ikat* are more abstract, with blue the dominant color.

The Process

Under nearly every stilted house in East Sumba is a primitive loom. While sway-backed pigs grunt nearby and babies crawl across their laps to nurse, women weave these elaborate and beautiful works of art that can sell for upwards of US$2000 in Chicago or Sydney. Most of the steps in the weaving process can be seen in the well-known weaving villages around the island.

Locally grown cotton is used in the better pieces, store-bought cotton thread for the less expensive cloth. The cotton is picked, carded, and handspun into thread. This plain thread is wrapped around a bamboo frame about two meters in length. A design is then drawn on the stretched threads. According to the design, the threads are tightly tied and then dipped into the same color dye at least twice, allowed to dry in between. The parts of the thread that have been tied remain untreated, while the untied areas take up the dye. The binding is then removed and other areas are tied. When the next color is applied, the already dyed portions are bound up—the parts left blank receive the required coloring. Sometimes an already-dyed portion is dipped into another color to make a third color or shade of color. This process is repeated as often as required by the design and the number of colors. When all the dying is complete, the threads are stretched on a frame and each section of thread separated by hand so the design is correct. Sumba fabrics are often woven together unevenly and inexactly by moving the threads up or down a little in relation to the surrounding threads, which gives the cloth a strange, shimmering, three-dimensional effect. The threads are then stretched taut and the weaving process begins. Usually thread dyed to match one of the colors of the warp is used for the woof, and occasionally woven designs are added. Small simple pieces may take two to three months, most blankets four to six months, and very complicated and larger pieces up to a couple years. For piecework women are paid about Rp15,000-20,000 a piece. Finished blankets may sell for Rp150,000-500,000; some exceedingly fine pieces go for more than Rp3 million. Prices depend upon the size, intricacy of design, use or non-use of natural fiber and dyes, and who has created the design.

Looms seen in most villages are very simple. Many consist solely of two bamboo sections, one affixed to something solid, like the post of a house, and the second, at the other end of the threads, attached by rope to a wooden slat behind the weaver's waist to maintain tension. The weaver, usually seated on a mat on the ground or on a wooden floor, separates the warp threads by raising various wooden crosspieces; the shuttle is pushed back and forth by hand.

Colors

The age-old colors for *hinggi* are blue and white, or red and white and black. Dyes are usually made of natural ingredients, though artificial dyes are increasingly common. In East Sumba the rust color comes from the root of the *kombu* tree, dug up, chopped, and pounded into a pulp. Indigo is made from the tiny leaves of a low-growing indigo bush, always collected during the rainy season. In West Sumba the color from the blue indigo plant (*wora*) is preferred. Red is obtained by crushing and soaking the root and bark of certain trees. The weaver must sometimes wait for one particular week in the year when a certain berry appears to make a particular natural dye.

Many different shades can be derived from just two colors, depending upon how often the fabric is dipped into the dye bath. For example, dark brown or black is the result of consecutive immersions in red and blue dyes.

Motifs

Designs differ greatly, but all reflect the life, culture, and history of the island. The most frequent motifs are of tiny men on foot or armed on horseback, horses, Dutch lions, stags, chickens, dogs, monkeys, birds, snakes, crocodiles, turtles, lizards, Chinese dragons, crayfish, crabs, and octopuses. The blurred outline of the tree of life is a recurring pattern. The common skull tree motif dates from headhunting days, when captured heads were hung in celebration on the bare, blood-soaked limbs of a tree in the village center. Mana, or life-essence, was imbued in the heads, thus the skull tree ensured fertility and was the main religious object in the village.

Buying

Since *ikat* textiles are now mass-produced for export, a great deal of substandard junk is around. The price is not always indicative of quality; merchants could charge up to Rp150,000 for a worthless piece. Sellers use many, many tricks: if the colors are too faded, the cloth is sometimes painted to make it more vibrant. The fabric could also be starched to make it feel newer. Some traders also boil the fabric in a solution of water, tobacco juice, and *kayu kuning* to give it the look of great age. Caveat emptor.

Don't buy immediately; be patient and learn all you can first. On the genuine pieces look for smooth, sharp lines, clean colors (dyes must not run into each other), and intricate, tight designs. Smoothly curving lines is another sign of good work. Bargain relentlessly, for each and every piece.

In Waingapu, merchants want as much as Rp400,000 a piece (natural dyes); they can be purchased a little cheaper (Rp100,000 and up) in villages southeast of Waingapu such as Melolo, Rende, Kaliuda, and Pau. The weaving centers of Kawangu and Prailiu are located just outside Waingapu. You won't have to look far; armies of vendors approach you on foot or bicycles, *hinggi* wrapped around their arms, shoulders, and handlebars.

Other Crafts

Sumba boxes, made from *lontar* palm, come in all sizes. Much of Indonesia's precious Chinese porcelain originates in Sumba, dug up from old graves. Since the most valuable possessions of the deceased (gold, ivory, china, fabrics, and coins) were buried with the corpse, there are vast hoards of porcelain still under the earth. They could search you at the airport but some people manage (illegally) to get away with a few plates stuck down their pants or under their skirts.

TRANSPORTATION

Getting There

Sumba has two airports; the larger one is Mauhau Airport, six km outside Waingapu. Tambolaka Airport is 42 km and 1.5 hours from Waikabubak in West Sumba. Merpati flies three times a week (Monday, Thursday, Saturday) from Waingapu to Bima and Denpasar, with connections to Bandung, Yogyakarta, Semarang, Solo, and Surabaya. The same three days a week, a different plane flies to Bima, stopping in Tambaloka on the way. These flights leave about 0915 and 0920. There are flights to Kupang everyday except Tuesday. From Waingapu the fares are as follows: Kupang (Rp117,000), Tambaloka (Rp48,000), Bima (Rp77,000), and Denpasar (Rp160,000). Bouraq schedules flights on Tuesday, Thursday, Saturday, and Sunday at 0845 to Denpasar (Rp160,000), continuing on to Surabaya (Rp190,000) and Kupang (Rp117,000). The Merpati office is at the Elim Hotel at Jl. A. Yani

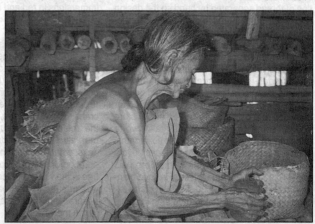

Sumbanese artist at work

73, while the Bouraq office is located at Jl. Yos Sudarso 57. Merpati's hours are Monday to Friday 0700-1700, Saturday until 1430, and Sunday 0900-1300. There are occasional *bemo* from Mauhau Airport to Waingapu. Some hotels also send vehicles to meet and deposit passengers. Otherwise, ask either Merpati or Bouraq for a lift in one of their vans.

The island's principal harbor is at Waingapu; there's another small harbor at Waikelo, 50 km northwest of Waikabubak. All ferries to Sumba stop at Waingapu. The KM *Kelimutu* stops every week in Waingapu either going east to Kupang and Dili (leaves 2400 on Wednesday) or west to Ende and Bima and beyond (leaves 0800 on Thursady). To Ende, fares are Rp15,900 economy, Rp30,000 second class, and Rp37,000 first class; to Kupang they're Rp22,650 economy, Rp50,450 second class, and Rp73,450 first class; to Ujung Pandang Rp75,450 economy, Rp200,450 second class, and Rp283,450 first class. Check the posted schedule for exact departure times and dates, and purchase tickets at the Pelni office 100 meters from the entrance to the pier. The KMP *Ile Mandiri* also calls at Waingapu twice a week on its Kupang-Ende-Waingapu-Seba return run. On Wednesday at 1600 it leaves Waingapu for Seba on Savu (Rp 12,300, 13 hours), and on Friday at 1900 it journeys to Ende (Rp15,800 first class, Rp11,200 economy, 12 hours).

Small boats heading to and from Flores also call at Waingapu. Check along the waterfront for who's going where and bargain with the captain for a ride.

Getting Around

Three times weekly, flights connect Sumba's main towns, Waingapu and Waikabubak, arriving at Tambolaka, 42 km from Waikabubak in West Sumba. Buses run back and forth down the 137-km paved road connecting Waingapu and Waikabubak; Rp4250 one-way, four hours. They fill up quickly, so get to the station early. Buses can take you to the remotest corners of the island, but some of Sumba's limited outlying road network is in bad shape. You can charter minibuses and four-wheel drive vehicles for Rp60,000-75,000 a day. Rent motorbikes from Permata Guest House in Waingapu for Rp15,000 a day. *Bemo* operate regularly in and around the two major towns and to most traditional villages, weaving centers, megalithic sites, and other tourist attractions.

In the east, herds of wild horses are exploited as mounts and for export; you see horses everywhere—on their own, with riders, in small groups, and on *ikat*. These sandalwood horses can be hired out; riding experience is essential as they can be quite temperamental. The hilly, rocky terrain—especially in the west—can be trying.

EAST SUMBA

East Sumba is characterized by flat, barren plateaus and canyons, and dramatic, world-class *ikat* weavings. A common language and elements of shared culture are found throughout this region of Sumba, which has received the lion's share of attention from anthropologists. Many of East Sumba's most traditional villages are located near Melolo and along the southeast coastline from Melolo to Baing. All are accessible by *bemo* from Melolo, but be sure to get an early start each day.

WAINGAPU

The district capital of East Sumba, the island's main town and seaport, and from 1906-49 a Dutch administrative and trading center. Change cash and traveler's checks at **Bank Rakyat Indonesia.** Both the post office and *wartel* are in the port area. *Bemo* (Rp300) run up and down the main streets of Waingapu, and on four established routes into the town's outskirts. In the hotel areas, you can walk to most anywhere. A small market is located in the harbor area, and a larger one is next to the bus station. **Istana Karang Photo** stocks most photo supplies. **Kuta Beach** is 12 km northwest of town. Waingapu is a good base from which to explore traditional villages to the southeast (Rende, Kaliuda, Umabara) and the north (Prainatang).

Accommodations And Food

Close to the port at Jl. Kartini 8 is **Permata Guest**

House, tel. 21516, also known as "Ali's Place," run by Ali Fadaq. Five clean, good-size budget rooms, all with *mandi*. No fans, but it's cool at night. Breakfast not included, but simple meals are available. Great dinners for Rp2000. Ali arranges local transportation and charter vehicles (four-wheel drive and motorbikes). **Ali's Place II,** a five-minute walk from the Permata, offers eight rooms for Rp2500-Rp5500, but it's in an unfortunate location under a mosque loudspeaker.

A short distance beyond the post office at Jl. Wanggameti 2 is **Hotel Lima Saudara,** tel. 21083. All rooms have a *mandi*; some offer bunkbeds. Rooms are Rp5500 s, Rp7500 d, which includes an afternoon snack.

Located between the port and the bus terminal, at Jl. A. Yani 73, is the quiet, Chinese-run **Elim Hotel,** tel. 21232. Somewhat tattered around the edges, there are a multitude of rooms, some with a/c, some with fans, some with *mandi*, some with

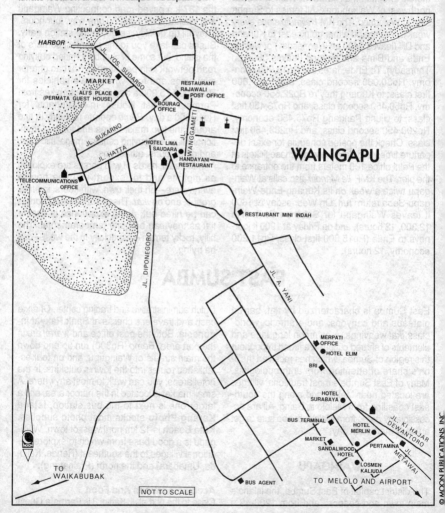

up to six beds. Rates run Rp5500-49,500. Midrange is a room with fan and *mandi* for Rp8250 s and Rp13,759 d, including breakfast and an afternoon snack. Local transportation can be arranged—Ali will get you a ten-person-capacity van for Rp80,000 per day, some Rp35,000 cheaper than the other hotels. Rp50,000 per day for a jeep. The **Eben Haezer Tour and Travel** agency, perhaps the best on the island, is located here, as is the Merpati office. In the restaurant is a fine map of Sumba, highlighting the tourist sites. Displayed on the walls are photographs of many of these sites.

Vying for the best place in town are the older Hotel Sandalwood and the Hotel Merlin. Clean, friendly, and well-kept, the more homey is **Hotel Sandalwood,** Jl. Panjaitan 23, tel. 21887. Standard rooms start at Rp10,000 s and Rp15,000 d, and run up to Rp35,000 s and Rp40,000 d for a/c suites; all include breakfast and afternoon snack. Serves Chinese and Indonesian food in a lobby restaurant, but the tablecloths tend to be dirty. Arrange local transportation and charter tours from Rp60,000 a day. Run by a Chinese family—all are characters. Next door is the newer, pseudo-palatial, and somewhat sterile **Hotel Merlin,** Jl. Panjaitan 25, tel. 21300. Offering all that its neighbor does, rooms run from Rp15,000 s and Rp20,000 d for a standard to Rp40,000 s and Rp50,000 d for suites. The restaurant features an extensive menu and a fine view over the town, but unfortunately it's on the fourth and top floor. The steep, high-tread stairs are a killer.

A clean and quiet alternative near here is the **Losmen Kaliuda,** Jl. Lalamentik 3, tel. 21264. Small and peaceful, comfortable, plenty of light, rooms from Rp10,000. Rooms are also available at the noisier **Hotel Surabaya**; restaurant attached.

Most of the hotels include restaurants; there are also three other restaurants in town. The restaurant at Hotel Sandalwood has a good reputaion; the food at Hotel Elim is nothing special; at Ali's Place the dishes are very simple. The **Mini Indah** serves very good Javanese and Sumbanese food and lots of it—not much to look at but the food is special. The **Rajawali** serves plentiful, tasty meals. Up from the pier is the small **Handayani** restaurant, and a few Padang-style restaurants are located in and around the large market next to the bus station.

The **Toko Kupang** bakery opens at 0600; good bread, cakes, biscuits. Good meals in the various *warung* around town.

Ikat

Amin Art Shop, Jl. Panjaitan 45, tel. 21638, is the only official art shop in town, specializing in statuary, basketry, and ready-made clothes. It's also the cheapest place on the island to purchase *ikat*. A cloth that would go for Rp500,000 elsewhere sells here for Rp250,000. The really special pieces Amin keeps in his bedroom, safely hidden. With enough persuasion, he'll bring them out for you. Most hotels don't tell travelers about Amin's because they're jealous—they don't want him to succeed. Only a two-minute walk from the Merlin.

The hotels **Elim, Sandalwood,** and **Merlin** all feature art and cloth shops. **Prai Liu,** near the center of town, is a weaving center; pieces go for Rp100,000-125,000. Also check **Louis Art Shop** for crafts, tapes, and *ikat.*

Getting Away

At least four buses per day leave for Waikabubak via Anakalang (Rp4250, four hours); book in advance. The Bumi Indah leaves at 0730; book at Hotel Surabaya. The Tambora Indah leaves at 0800 and 1300 and reserve-seat tickets are sold at the office west of the *pasar*. Buses run to all parts of eastern Sumba from Waingapu. About every half hour 0700-1700, buses travel to Melolo (Rp2000). Several during the day run beyond Melolo to the traditional village of Rende (Rp2250) and as far south as Baing (Rp3850). From Melolo, catch a bus to, among other places, Umabara and Nggongi (Rp3000). To the north, you can ride several times a day to Kodahang and Mondu (Rp1100). Running until the early evening, *bemo* charge a flat Rp300 around town, a bit more to the outlying areas. Route no. 1 will take you to the weaving centers of Prailiu and Kawangu, and route no. 4 goes to the weaving village of Lambanapu.

VICINITY OF WAINGAPU

Maru District

On the coast about 60 km northwest of Waingapu, this district and village sits at the foot of a former hilltop priestly capital. Different clans, including a warrior clan, once clustered around the king's residence. Now this royal walled village is deserted, the populace having moved down to the Maru River valley. In Maru are several traditional high-peaked houses. Major ceremonies take place in and around these houses; inside, treasures sacred to the deities are stored. During the Ratu Festival, prayers, sacrifices, and myth narration open the planting season.

Along this coast live the Kapunduk people, subsistence farmers whose divisions by class are still hereditary. The Kapunduk divide themselves into patrilineal clans, each claiming descent from a single founder (*marapu*). Brideprices are exceptionally high, a method of maintaining loyalty and class rigidity. Get to the main village of Kapunduk by bus from Waingapu, or rent a motorbike—however, the road for long stretches is not in very good condition.

Prainatang

On the way to Maru is a wonderful hilltop village called Prainatang, consisting of about a dozen high-peaked thatch roof houses set on a hilltop overlooking their riverside fields below. It's surrounded by remains of a rock wall, for protection against slavers—you can look out and see the ocean beyond the dry barren hills. There are many graves, mostly small and uncarved, packed into the courtyard of this picturesque community. It seems to be a perfect, and as yet non-Westernized, example of a traditional East Sumban village. There is one major drawback, however. An exorbitant fee is required just to walk around and take a few pictures. The Rp5000-10,000 per person charge is way high by any standard.

Take a bus to Mondu (Rp1100). Several leave every day starting as early as 0500. Get off at the Mondu market (market day is Friday) on the east side of town, and walk two km up a track to the village. The buses to Mondu go on to Kodahang. About 10 km outside of Waingapu on this road is the nonexciting **Kuta Beach**, located just past the shell of an old DC-3 airplane.

The Melolo Area

Melolo is a small town 60 km southeast of Waingapu at the end of a savannah-like plain pitted with deep craters and muddy pools. Take a bus (Rp2000, two hours). Buses run everyday throughout the day as far as Melolo. All is barren and brown, with the only color seeming to come from flowering trees and the rice fields that pop into view as you near town. On the way you'll pass scattered small villages, grazing Brahma cows, and goats. Recent road construction has made this trip faster and much more comfortable.

Stay at the new four-room **Losmen Hermindo** right on the main street—the only place in town. Rooms are neat and clean, and feature *mandi* and fan; Rp5000 pp includes a simple breakfast and snack. Ask Hermindo to direct you to other meals in town.

Melolo has its own diesel generator. At 2200 the electricity is abruptly shut off, followed by the deafening cackle of cocks. The whole area around Melolo is quite traditional and untouched, and the people are hospitable to visitors. Melolo is a good base for exploring the area. There's a big market in Melolo on Friday.

It's possible to continue farther down the coast from here: the *ikat*-weaving centers of **Mangili** and **Kaliuda** (a traditional-style village) can be reached by local *bemo* from Melolo, or by early bus leaving Waingapu and returning that afternoon. Farther down the coast is **Baing**, famous for its *hinggi kombu* scarves and superb waterskiing. Five km from Baing, at **Kalaia**, is a great surfing spot and one of the best beaches on Sumba; waves are best Dec.-May. A pricey sports fishing resort, owned and operated by an Australian, is also located here. Southwest of Melolo, in the village of **Nggongi**, are several large carved tombs.

Pau And Umabara

A nice four-km walk from Melolo is the kingdom of Pau. On the way, a short three km *bemo* ride from Melolo, is the village of Umabara, which contains three medium-size stone tombs (two with carvings) and four large and very high-peaked *adat* houses. Weaving can be seen at each house. In Pau, sign the visitor's book (Rp1000 donation) and ask the local *raja* if you can view his outstanding collection of exceptionally beautiful *ikat* blankets and *sarung*, many embroidered with shells and red and gold coral. Other pieces are offered for sale. The king, an impressive figure with long, white beard and white headscarf, is very knowledgeable about *ikat* styles.

Up another secondary road north of Melolo is the village of **Lailuru,** known for its fine weaving.

Rende

Seven km south of Melolo, Rende contains traditional clan houses and a row of huge 375-year-old carved megalithic stone tombs; Rp1000 donation. Take the 0700 bus from Waingapu direct (Rp2250), or a *bemo* from Melolo. On the way pass women in front of their houses dyeing yarn and weaving *ikat.* Rende overlooks a green river valley of coconut trees and rice fields, and

several small clusters of traditional houses. While some houses in Rende feature metal roofs, all are of traditional design. The largest house, that of the local *raja's* family, is in the slow process of being rebuilt after having been completely torn apart. This family is also preparing to ceremonially rebury the last head of the family. The former chief already has over 120 blankets wrapped around him, in which he will be reinterred. The large house will be reoccupied eight days prior to the burial. Lots of *ikat* are for sale here; Rp80,000-3,000,000.

WEST SUMBA

An area of gently sloping hills and savannahs and green forests, agriculturally based West Sumba is known for its giant megalithic stone memorial tablets; traditional villages; conical-shaped, thatch-roofed, high-peaked clan houses; and the *pasola,* a tribal war-game ritual held during Feb.-April. Events in Sumba Barat include *pajura* (traditional boxing), festivals of the Lunar New Year (October and November), Independence Day (17 August), horse races, and the building of *adat* houses and burials (July-Oct.). The isolated Bukambero in the Kodi subdistrict in the extreme west, numbering about 6,000, still practice their ancient ways and are considered a culture apart.

Less dry, cooler, more fertile, hillier, and greener than Sumba Timur, vegetables grow well in Sumba Barat. Many villages are located on a hilltop, a circle of tall houses around the ancestral graves; some villages are still walled and fortified. Houses typically have an open ground floor with chickens and pigs, where the weaving loom might be set up, sheltered from the hot sun. About a meter above is a bamboo floor, the actual living quarters. A veranda is often built on at least one side of the house. Large table-like slabs in the center of each *kampung* serve as a drying rack for roots, rice, buffalo dung, and chalk for *sirih.* Sometimes newly woven baskets are placed here; it's also where children play and old men sun themselves. Pegs-and-pebble gameboards are sometimes carved into the stone.

THE *PASOLA*

A ritual tribal war that takes place in different villages Feb.-April of each year, beginning several days after the full moon and coinciding with the ritual harvesting of a strange, multihued seaworm. Essentially a jousting match between horsemen carrying long wooden spears and shields, riders are frequently injured and, just as in American football or boxing matches, occasionally killed. The government allows the ritual to take place, but spears must now be blunted.

Famed as rugged, skilled horsemen, hundreds of Sumbanese combatants charge along circular runways tangent to each other. When their courses intersect they fling spears at each other or try to club opponents from their mounts with the butt end of their spears. Women are the chief observers and supporters of these mock combats, each cheering loudly for her favorites. Big thatch houses, grass-floor shelters, and foodstalls are set up in the spectator area for people streaming in from all over the island. The governor of Sumba and officials from Jakarta might even show up.

Shortly after the *pasola,* villagers will journey down to the sea to consult the *nyale,* a form of sea worm, on the people's fortunes for the coming year. The *ratu,* or senior priest, wades into the water, selects the appropriate worm, listens briefly, then returns to land to inform the village of its destiny.

Before setting out, find out in Waingapu exactly when the *pasola* takes place. During February, the ceremony occurs in **Kodi** and **Lamboya.** Lamboya is 20 km southwest of Waikabubak, Rp35,000-40,000 roundtrip by chartered *bemo* or truck. In March, the mock battle is staged in **Gaura** and **Wanokaka** (18 km from Waikabubak). In any of these villages, you may stay overnight with the local *raja*.

WAIKABUBAK

The laid-back capital of West Sumba, reached by bus (Rp3000, 127 km) in five hours from Waingapu—good road all the way. This cool, easygoing town, 500 meters above sea level, has the feel of a frontier settlement slowly lumbering into the 20th century. There's a Third World market full of betel-chewing tribal peoples, water buffalo wander the town, nearby fields are studded with table-shaped tombs, and in the afternoons literally thousands of schoolchildren fill the streets.

Waikabubak makes a great base—good restaurants, cheap prices, friendly people, lots of crafts, a multitude of day excursions. For a reliable guide, head for **Hotel Manandang,** the town's tourist nerve center and main gathering spot for guides, *ikat* sellers, and tour groups.

Inquire immediately upon arrival if there are any events or festivals scheduled in the area. Competent guides include H. B. Mude, Jl. E. Tari 10, tel. 21376, who served 15 years as the head of the Department of Culture; and Man Bamualim, Jl. A. Yani 29, tel. 21063, who charges around Rp125,000 for two energetic days touring via jeep. Motorcycles rent for Rp15,000 per day; inquire at the Hotel Manandang.

The **Merpati** agent is on Jl. A. Yani, less than a 10-minute walk from Hotel Manandang. The nearest airstrip is at sleepy Tambolaka, 42 km north and Rp3000 pp by taxi (one hour if there's no traffic). The flight from Bima to Tambolaka is only thirty minutes (Rp75,000, three times weekly).

Sights
In the center of Waikabubak are several traditional hilltop villages lined with megalithic tombs and high-peaked clan houses. In **Tarung,** sign the village guestbook and fork over Rp500. This village is sprawled across three small hills with old tumbled-down graves at odd angles and altitudes in the spaces between. Tarung feels like it's lost its identity, its coherence, absorbed and overwhelmed by the town that has grown around it.

Visit the handsome elderly woman at **Desa Elu,** only 500 meters from Hotel Manadang. She owns a magnificent 400-year-old, 3.5-meters-high totemic stone; this proud woman turned down an offer by Hamid's art shop to buy the stone for Rp50 million. To do so, she said, would have dishonored her ancestors.

Accommodations
One of the cheapest places around is Javanese-style **Aloha Hotel,** Jl. Gajah Mada, tel. 21024, with eight rooms at Rp10,000 s, Rp12,000 d. Located on a side street, five minutes from downtown, the Aloha caters mostly to Indonesian businesspeople. The **Rakuta** has large rooms for Rp12,000 s, but the meals are only so-so.

Hotel and Restoran Pelita, Jl. A Yani 2, tel. 21104 or 21392, charges Rp6000 s,

WAIKABUBAK

Rp8000 d for rooms in front. Includes a simple, stupid Western breakfast (egg, white bread, margarine, coffee). Order the *nasi goreng* instead. The six rooms in back are much better—clean, tile floors, good ventilation, showers, nice bathrooms, big verandas. Rp15,000 s, Rp25,000 d.

The **Monalisa,** Jl. Adyaksa, tel. 21020 or 21042, lies two km out of town on the side of a hill near the racetrack. Twenty-two big luxurious bungalows cost Rp42,000 s, Rp60,000 d; always under capacity because it's so isolated. Nicely furnished rooms with a suburban aesthetic, huge bathrooms, nice breezes. The restaurant serves Chinese/Indonesian food; see photos from the late '40s revealing traditional Sumbanese customs and architecture.

Waikabubak's best accommodation is the **Hotel Manandang,** Jl. Pemuda 4, tel. 197-292, with four classes of rooms ranging Rp8000-20,000. Nicely landscaped gardens. This hotel gets all the groups.

Food

The cheapest places to eat sit along the main street of Jl. A Yani, and include **Warung Surabaya** and a series of food tents near the Tambora Indah Bus Agency. The food in Hotel Manandang's big restaurant is the tastiest in town, though expensive, served in small portions, with an annoying 10% tax. **Gloria Restaurant,** Jl. Bhayangkara, tel. 21147, a little out of town on the way to the Monalisa Hotel, has very good prices and very cold drinks. Excellent food, though the *ayam gloria* (chicken) tends to be really tough. The small portions of *mie goreng* are good.

Shopping

In the back garden of **Hamid's Art Shop,** Jl. A Yani 99, tel. 21170, is a marvelous collection of wooden and stone statuary, menhirs, and plinths. Rich in symbolism, some pieces cost Rp3-5 million, plus another Rp420,000 to ship. It's worth visiting this large shop if only to see these precious, amazing museum-quality objects. Hamid will provide you with an official letter of certification that will allow you to leave the island with any item you purchase. He's a bit reluctant to bargain, as he has a corner on the art/antique market and is probably the largest art shop in Nusatenggara. Shop for *ikat* at **Pasar Inpres**; prices start at Rp35,000-50,000 but are fairly easy to bargain down to Rp15,000-20,000. Stacks and stacks of very attractive, very tribal pieces from Kodi, Lamoya, and Tossi.

VICINITY OF WAIKABUBAK

Most traditional villages surrounding Waikabubak are accessible by *bemo*, best visited during their colorful weekly open-air markets. Some are as close as one-half km; others, like **Pandedewatu** to the south, are a four-hour walk. Ask villagers along the way for the locations of the big stones, elaborate megaliths, and nice carvings. Different villages bury their dead in different ways, each with unusual carvings and arrangements of stones. The Christian cross is found on more recent graves, alongside such traditional ornaments as buffalo heads (symbolizing power and strength), the horse (a safe trip to heaven), and the dog (faithfulness).

The closest village is **Tarung,** a small hilltop *desa* and ceremonial center (*paraing*) with several tombs one-half km west of Waikabubak. The front of the *adat* houses here are embellished with sets of water buffalo horns, trophies of past sacrifices. If you're waiting for some ritual to take place or just want to relax, swim off the white-sand beach at **Pantai Rua,** 21 km south of town (Rp550, 30 minutes). Or try the natural freshwater pools at **Waikelo Sawah,** 10 km west of the city. *Bemo* will take you to both places.

Eighteen km south of Waikabubak in the district of Wanokaka is the traditional village of **Prai Goli,** believed to contain the oldest megalith—Watu Kajiwa—on Sumba. A few kilometers from Lamboya is **Sodan,** another traditional village, where an important Lunar New Year ceremony occurs in October. The village has a sacred drum, its playing surface covered in human skin from an enemy flayed long ago. The drum is used to call ancestor spirits.

Anakalang

Twenty-two km and Rp500 by *bemo* east of Waikabubak on the main road to Waingapu, the focal point of this village is its massive graveyard. Sumbanese believe the present world is just an antechamber to the palace of the next world and that death is the most important event in life. Note the beautifully built thatched, conical homes here, plus a concentration of old burial stones with strong carvings. Every two years a mass marriage ceremony, Purung Takadonga, is held in Anakalang in the early summer.

Check out the nearby village of **Pasunga,** where 50 years ago the last great ruler of the Anakalang Kingdom, Umbu Dongga, was buried in a unique tomb called Resi Moni. Resembling a giant's footstool, the huge 30-ton stone slab (now broken) sat on six short columns. It took two years to carve from a quarry, then thousands of men spent two months dragging the stone to its present site in the village square. The funeral feast lasted a week and 250 water buffalo and scores of horses, pigs, and chickens were slaughtered to honor the departed chief. Another vertical tomb, carved in 1926, features the figures of a man and a woman. Houses in Pasunga stand in two rows like gigantic brown straw hats. The traditional village of **Lai Tarung,** nearby, has numerous old graves.

Prai Bokul

In this village an hour's walk north of Anakalang (the path starts opposite the *tempat makam*), the heaviest single megalith on Sumba sits like a fallen meteor. This 70-ton sepulchre, known as **Umbu Sawola,** was erected by one of the richest *rajas* on the island, who hired 2,000 workers to chisel and haul it out of a remote mountain. The slab measures five meters long and four meters wide and rests on short columns. It took three years and three lives to transport it. When the rope broke and killed men it was not considered an accident; the men were but sacrifices to provide the necessary spiritual guardianship for the grave. Ten tons of rice were consumed and 250 buffalo sacrificed in the ritual accompanying the dragging, with priests egging the men on with invocations and chants, all in the belief the stone would ensure the owner's entrance into heaven. The whole project cost Rp105 million to complete, a sum present-day relatives are trying implacably to recoup by charging tourists Rp5000 per photo.

KALIMANTAN

Kalimantan comprises roughly the southern three-quarters of Borneo, the third largest island in the world. The Malaysian states of Sarawak and Sabah and the sultanate of Brunei lie to the north, occupying the island's top quarter. Despite exploration and development, many areas of Kalimantan are almost untouched by the Western world. The territory—with vast uncharted jungles laced with mighty rivers—makes a unique travel experience for the rough and ready traveler.

INTRODUCTION

Kalimantan is divided into four provinces, 24 regencies, and 346 subdistricts. The territory totals 539,500 square km, roughly 28% of Indonesia's land area, but has only 4.5% of its population (seven million), or about 12 people per square km. Tourist facilities are relatively developed but visitors are few. Most Westerners are solo backpackers or leftovers from the oil and wood booms of the 1970s, their jobs gradually being taken over by Indonesians.

Good roads run between Banjarmasin and Samarinda and around Pontianak, but rivers are the main transportation arteries. There are airports in major cities, and airstrips throughout the interior serviced by Pelita, DAS, and missionary aircraft.

THE LAND

No volcanic activity here, unlike most of Indonesia, though major eruptions wracked Kalimantan's interior over 50,000 years ago. Half of the territory's land area is under 150 meters in elevation, especially near the coasts. The island's

heavily eroded central mountain ranges appear like the spokes of a wheel, separated by broad river valleys. Kalimantan's highest peak is Gunung Murut, in the Iran Range, near the Sabah/Sarawak border. Kalimantan is crisscrossed by giant rivers, including the Mahakam, Barito, Sampit, and Kapuas. River deltas and much of the southern coastal areas are swampy.

Eighty percent of the territory is jungle, though the lush vegetation doesn't mean fertile soil. The rainforest's soil minerals and life energy never accumulate as humus. Nutrients are perpetually stored in the diverse plantlife, with the help of an extremely efficient recycling system: bacteria, fungi, insects, and animals. Soil avalanches are common on jungle slopes after heavy rains, even in areas undisturbed by human toil. Rain accumulates in the deep subsoil beneath the tangle of roots, then entire hillsides break away and slide in one mass into the valley below, leaving behind scars of raw, exposed earth.

A naturalist recently traveled through the deep interior for 26 days without seeing open sunlight or any sign of cultivation. Resource development makes a lasting impression, however, at

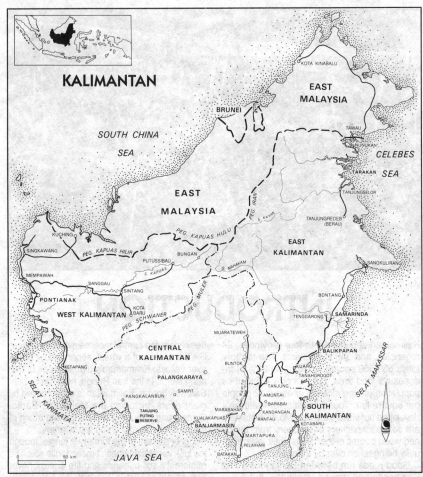

KALIMANTAN

SOUTH CHINA SEA

BRUNEI

EAST MALAYSIA

KOTA KINABALU

EAST MALAYSIA

TAWAU

NUNUKAN

CELEBES SEA

TARAKAN

TANJUNGSELOR

TANJUNGREDEB (BERAU)

KUCHING

PEG. KAPUAS HULU

S. KAYAN

SINGKAWANG

PEG. KAPUAS HILIR

BUNGAN

EAST KALIMANTAN

SANGKULIRANG

MEMPAWAH

PUTUSSIBAU

S. KAPUAS

S. MAHAKAM

SANGGAU

SINTANG

BONTANG

PONTIANAK

KOTA BARU

PEG. MULER

TENGGARONG

SAMARINDA

WEST KALIMANTAN

PEG. SCHWANER

BALIKPAPAN

MUARATEWEH

SELAT MAKASSAR

KETAPANG

CENTRAL KALIMANTAN

BUNTOK

KUARO

TANAHGROGOT

PALANGKARAYA

SAMPIT

TANJUNG

AMUNTAI

PANGKALANBUN

MARABAHAN

BARABAI

KANDANGAN

SOUTH KALIMANTAN

SELAT KARIMATA

TANJUNG PUTING RESERVE

KUALAKAPUAS

RANTAU

KOTABARU

BANJARMASIN

MARTAPURA

PELAIHARI

BATAKAN

JAVA SEA

0   50 km

© MOON PUBLICATIONS, INC.

major cost to the environment. Many areas have been devastated by logging, mining, and oil and natural gas drilling—activities which destroy the jungle's delicate balance. Conserving rainforests—necessarily a long-term effort—unfortunately collides with the nation's immediate political and economic goals.

Climate

Hot and humid. The temperature never falls below 21° C, and can go much higher. Rainfall averages 381 cm per year. Monsoons herald the arrival of the rainy season, Oct.-March; the most violent storms occur Nov.-March. July and August are drier. Rainstorms in the jungle can be torrential, a gentle rustling in the forest canopy quickly becoming a dark, gloomy curtain of rain in a primeval cathedral.

Upriver travel is often difficult because rivers are too low during the dry season (April-Sept.) and too high in the late wet season (Jan.-March). For these reasons, the best time to visit is in the wet season, either at the very beginning (October and November) or the very end (February to March). The worst time to attempt river journeys is during the dry season, when rivers run low and boat transport is limited to the lower reaches of the major arteries.

However, don't fear the rainy season. Rainstorms during the monsoons are surprisingly tolerable, often just late afternoon showers lasting less than an hour. And there's not a tourist in sight.

FLORA AND FAUNA

Flora

Kalimantan has a wide variety of montane and lowland forests, each an important genetic resource and wildlife habitat. None are adequately protected by Indonesia's reserves, which too often exist in name only. It's estimated that fewer than half the island's endemic species of rainforest plants and animals are known to science. These lowland forests are also rich in wild fruit and nut trees, a significant food source for people, primates, and other animals. Coastal swamp forests host nipa palms and a variety of valuable timber trees. Ironwood—immune to insect attacks and used for railway ties and roofing shingles—fringes the island's swampland. Pines are broadleafs here, since they don't need to conserve water.

Climbing rattan palms, vines, orchids, ferns, and insectivorous pitcher plants are also common. Kalimantan's veiled lady is a toxic fungus that shoots up out of the spongy earth in only 24 hours; its disgusting odor attracts scavenger flies and bees which spread its spores. Epiphytes and mosses are found in sandy heath forests. Kalimantan has 800 known types of orchids—the most beautiful hidden away in the high treetops—and 1,100 identified species of ferns. In heavily logged, cultivated, or soil-avalanche areas, giant sharp-stemmed ferns up to 2.5 meters high quickly form stable but unnatural plant communities which the jungle cannot reclaim for centuries.

Fauna

The region's wildlife is unusually diverse. With luck, you may see monkeys, gibbons, bearded wild pigs, deer, wild ox, civets, wildcats, flying lemurs, martins, weasels, badgers, otters, porcupines, mongeese, anteaters, 32 species of squirrels, and 41 types of bats.

Freshwater dolphins, found elsewhere only in the rivers and inland lakes of South America and Asia, thrive in the Mahakam River, playfully following river traffic. The elusive and endangered orangutan lives here and in northern Sumatra. The rare Sumatran rhinoceros is found only near Banamuda, in East Kalimantan. Wild elephants are occasionally spotted near the Malaysian border. Borneo's sun bear (*beruang*, meaning "has money") has a large white circle on its chest. The handsome silver and red *bakantan* or proboscis monkey can still be observed in the wild; males have very long pendulous noses, while females and young have prominent upturned noses. The clouded leopard is a jungle-camouflaged predator; indistinct splotches of black, brown, and yellowish gray blend ingeniously with the forest canopy.

Symbolically, the forest's most important creature is the black hornbill, the Dayak soul carrier. The hornbill's barking call disturbs the peace as it glides slowly and rhythmically, intercon-

---

PRIMATES OF BORNEO

Twenty-one species of primates live on Borneo. All have adapted to tree life and, like people, have developed large forward-facing eyes with binocular vision, useful in judging distances when leaping through trees. The spectacular tarsier comes from the Tertiary period of 70 million years ago, standing at a crossroads on the evolutionary chart where human and ape branch off from one another. The tarsier is scarcely larger than a rat, with ghostly globular eyes; the native Dayaks believe the souls of dead ancestors are reincarnated in its tiny body. As you walk along a river, macaque monkeys will often appear to follow and abuse you along the other bank. Gibbons stay together in families and live in the trees. Skilled gymnasts, they make terrifying piercing sounds which carry long distances through the jungle. A gibbon's pouch and throat swell up like a balloon, giving the call its booming quality. You can hear them moving through the trees; rarely will you see them.

The proboscis monkey (*bekantan*) is the yeti of Borneo. The creature bears an uncanny resemblance to human beings; Dayak tribes believe the *bekantan* is not an animal but a hairy human who lives in the jungle and eats fruit. The skunk monkey, no bigger than an alley cat, has a horrible stench.

nected air pouches beneath the skin acting as resonators. Prized by hunters for its feathers and beak and once nearly extinct, its numbers are now increasing. Hundreds of other exotic birds include parrots, parakeets, argus and crested fireback pheasants, bul-buls, flycatchers, quail, black partridges, and pigeons. Herons, egrets, and storks are common in Kalimantan's watery southern areas.

Also inhabiting the island are 134 kinds of snakes, including one which can flatten out and "fly." A venomous rear-fanged colubrid (*ular cincin mas*) or gold-ringed snake—prized by reptile fanciers for its glittering coloration and reasonable disposition—is found along the coast. The *koele* (panther snake), *apoei* (fire snake), and *ata-bla* (red water snake) are all as bad as they sound, but at least you can usually see them coming. Pythons and monitor lizards frequent riverbanks. Crocodiles inhabit swamp areas and river tributaries.

Borneo has 89 species of frogs: one species has webs of skin between its toes, enabling it to glide from branch to branch; another species never touches the ground, laying eggs in rain pools which collect on leaves. A flying lizard swoops between trees on leathery membranes stretched between its limbs and trunk.

Kalimantan is host to beautiful metallic green and blue butterflies, as well as hundreds of species of beetles. There are queer insects—poisonous polypods, brightly colored millipedes, giant walking sticks, and walking leaves. The island's version of a praying mantis looks like a miniature bright green banana leaf. Mosquitos and leeches abound, but bees, which often live in *tabang* trees, can be more dangerous. If disturbed, hundreds may swarm and sting intruders.

HISTORY

Borneo was a cultural crossroads in ancient times, a trade center on the route between Java's Majapahit Kingdom, the Philippines, and China. Migrants brought technology from the Sino-Vietnamese Dongson culture and China during the Neolithic period; Chou dynasty-style porcelain and bronze objects have been found in Kalimantan. In the 2nd century, the Greco-Roman geographer Ptolemy published an atlas containing an uncannily accurate description of Borneo; Indian traders traveling in merchant fleets of large, seagoing junks no doubt passed on the information. Roman and Marco Polo-vintage Chinese beads have been found here, as well as Hindu-Javanese relics from around A.D. 400. The Chinese may have traded with coastal Borneo, especially in the northwest, as early as the 7th century. On the Mahakam River, the oldest historic artifacts yet found in Indonesia have been uncovered: three rough plinths dating from the beginning of the 5th century recording in South Indian Palawa script "a gift to a Brahman priest."

Early History
Human immigration has always centered on the coasts and along major waterways. By A.D. 1000, Chinese trading posts flourished where Pontianak is today. Chinese mining communities, extracting gold and diamonds, also appeared on the island's south and west coasts. These areas gradually became Islamized during the 15th and 16th centuries, developing into small independent sultanates at Sambas, Kutai, and Banjarmasin; each had strong mercantile ties to the Islamic northern ports of Java.

Borneo's history also centers on the Brunei sultanate to the north; the sultan and his powerful maritime kingdom spread their influence over most of the island. Royal descendants still live in the East Kalimantan river ports of Tenggarong and Berau—small kingdoms deprived of political power when the Indonesian Republic gained real independence in 1949.

European Arrival
The first documented European arrival occurred in 1521, when one of Magellan's ships pulled into the harbor of Brunei. The word "Borneo" is the anglicized word for Brunei, an ancient kingdom named after the *berunai* fruit. Because of the island's interminable and inhospitable interior and its few natural harbors, the Europeans experienced difficulty in establishing control. Finally, in 1839, the British gained a foothold in the north, establishing the legendary dynasty of the White Rajas who ruled over Sarawak for more than 100 years. The British eventually took control of the northern part of the island, and during the second half of the 19th century the Dutch concluded treaties with the east coast sultans and assumed autocratic administration of the southern three-

quarters, bringing Borneo into the economic orbit of the Dutch East Indies empire. Except for minor disruptions such as the Banjarmasin War (1859-64), Kalimantan remained in Dutch hands until the Japanese invaded in 1942.

World War II

The Japanese occupied the island from 1942 to 1945; ruthless repression resulted in the deaths of as many as 20,000 intellectuals, missionaries, businessmen, and aristocrats. During its occupation, the island supplied Japan with almost half its wartime fuel oil. The U.S. invasion of the Philippines suddenly separated Borneo, its oil, and 30,000 defenders from Japan. Though both Australia and Britain thought that taking the island was of dubious value, early in 1945 General Douglas MacArthur decided to liberate Borneo and establish an Allied airbase and Pacific port for the British navy. There were subsequently three separate Allied landings on Borneo, all preceded by intense bombardments.

With Indonesian independence, the Javanese gave the territory its new name, Kalimantan, meaning "Rivers of Precious Stones"—an apt term to describe the many regions of the island known for rich deposits of gold, diamonds, amethysts, agates, sapphires, and emeralds.

ECONOMY

Kalimantan was for many years an economic burden on both the Dutch East Indies Company and the new Indonesian Republic. Then, in the 1950s, the island's oil, gas, and timber resources were finally tapped. Kalimantan is still not very developed, even less so than Sumatra. Most of the territory's wealth comes from East Kalimantan, which in 1978 produced nearly 25% of Indonesia's total export earnings.

Mineral resources are rich. Coal, petroleum, and natural gas production are big business here. So is the forest products industry: timber, rubber, copra, resin, gum, and camphor. Kalimantan also represents Indonesia's richest area for gems. Diamond mining and processing are vital; agate, amethyst, citrine, tiger eye, and topaz are plentiful. Gold and iron are also mined.

The Timber Industry

Between 1968 and 1978, East Kalimantan exported around 50% of Indonesia's timber, mostly from the Mahakam River and its tributaries. Huge, rugged tracts of primary rainforest are wantonly plundered by more than 100 overseas and domestic timber companies, with little concern for ecological and social consequences. Over 30 million hectares of tropical jungle have been earmarked for clearcutting, while unregulated transmigration settlements have turned marginal agricultural areas into a wasteland of *alang-alang*. As an indirect result of overlogging, one of the largest forest fires in recorded history took place in East Kalimantan in 1982-83. Reforestation efforts are meager and minimal.

THE PEOPLE

Most of Kalimantan's population lives near coastal areas, with Chinese and Malays predominating. Javanese, Buginese, and other Indonesians come here to find work, competing for skilled jobs. Under Indonesia's massive *transmigrasi* program, tens of thousands of Javanese and Balinese families were brought in to settle the island's hinterlands. Many resettlement projects have failed because of unsuitable land, lack of marketing opportunities, cultural and social conflicts, an ill-prepared resettlement infrastructure, or poor farming skills.

Most of the native Dayak peoples, almost half the territory's population, still live deep inland along the banks of major rivers and tributaries. Recent exposure to modernization is changing traditional life. The Indonesian government is abolishing multiple-family longhouses and replacing them with modern, single-family dwellings—a drastic change in village life. Tattooing, mastery of traditional crafts, and the custom of wearing huge bunches of metal earrings to elongate earlobes are all disappearing. Few Dayaks hunt with blowguns and poison darts or spears these days, preferring instead homemade Daniel Boone-style flintlocks. Though there are occasional unexplained decapitations in remote regions, the traditional practice of headhunting has official-ly ended.

Increasingly, young Dayaks leave their vil-lages to hire on with timber and oil companies or take menial jobs in Kalimantan boomtowns. Children of wealthy Dayaks study engineering, forestry, and other subjects in Indonesian and European universities.

The Penan

The Penan tribespeople are Borneo's original in-habitants, preceding even the Dayaks. With successive waves of migration over the cen-turies, the Penan gradually moved inland from the coast to continue their way of life; about 10,000 are left in isolated, scattered pockets in the upper Mahakam and the Apo Kayan.

Wizards in jungle craft and masters of the terrain, the Penan live off fruit, wild berries, and game. They hunt with blowpipes, using packs of hunting dogs to track wild pigs. The Penan may live in a village for a few weeks or months, then abandon it to become nomadic hunter-gatherers once again. You might see them in villages bar-tering their boar-tusk necklaces, panther teeth and skins, bear claws, and orangutan skulls for salt and tobacco. They smoke like locomotives.

THE DAYAK CULTURE

"Dayak" is a collective name for over 200 dif-ferent tribes living throughout Borneo's interi-or. Each *sukuh* (tribe) has a unique tribal name and dialect. Contrary to myth, the Dayak race is light-skinned, resembling the Chinese, with rounded, well-featured faces and slightly slant-ed eyes. Mountain Dayak tribespeople are phys-ically imposing, taller than most Asians, and heavily muscled, weighing 75 kg or more.

Numbering in the millions, Dayaks have tra-ditionally lived upriver in hill areas, thriving as hunters, gatherers, and, more recently, as slash-and-burn hill rice growers. Since the 1970s, the government has encouraged the Dayak to take up wet-rice cultivation and produce such cash crops as rubber, pepper, and cloves.

Other Indonesians call the Dayak villagers *orang bodoh* (stupid men), considering them backward because of their headhunting and other animist customs. The truth is, the Dayaks practice responsible local government with elect-ed members, maintain political boundaries, and even have a capital city, Palangkaraya. Dayak people are scrupulously honest by nature, though exposure to Christianity and modern values has muted this trait. Traditional villages have few modern problems, but the people suf-fer from curable diseases: malaria, dysentery, infections. Don't take advantage of Dayak village hospitality; returning generosity by giving useful gifts is a traditional gesture.

History

Since at least 5000 B.C., Dayak tribes have lived in splendid isolation throughout Kaliman-tan. Though flights now touch down on jungle airstrips hundreds of kilometers inland, Dayak territory is still some of the most inaccessible on earth. Historians and ethnologists have char-acterized Dayak culture as primitive, but by the late Neolithic period (1800 to 500 B.C.), when Europeans were wearing deerskins and throw-ing spears, Borneo's people already had a high-ly advanced culture, fashioning polished stone tools, earthenware pottery, bone ornaments, and cotton textiles. They buried their dead with great ceremony, believed in a cult of "death ships" which carried their loved ones to the af-terworld, and practiced elaborate spirit rituals. When Malays began to settle the island's coastal areas, the Dayaks retreated farther in-land, unwilling to become part of a religion and culture which prohibited their favorite food, pork. In the 1800s, when the Dutch began to settle and trade in the interior, the magnificent Dayak culture began to decline.

Dayak Society

A man seeks a wife outside his own village; the new couple may set up housekeeping in either the wife's or husband's village. Women and men share the work equally, including child care, though women don't hunt, and men usu-ally cook only when women aren't present. A child traces both its mother's and father's lin-eage; dependence on each is evident during the ear-piercing ritual—one ear is pierced by a relative of the mother, the other by paternal kin. Parents and children make up the basic family unit, with adopted children usually sharing equal rights and privileges.

The spirit of cooperation among relatives and between longhouse members is very strong.

DAYAK GLOSSARY

asa—old

ba'—baby carrier backpack, covered in colorful beadwork

baru—new, as in Kota Baru ("New Town"). It's common for villages to move to a new site when the surrounding land is exhausted by *ladang* agriculture.

buduk—mountain; *bukit* is the Malaysian and Indonesian word

burung enggang—rhinoceros hornbill bird

darat—land far from the river

hilir (or *ilir*)—downstream

hulu (or *ulu*)—upstream

konfrontasi—Indonesia's war of aggression against Malaysia in the early 1960s

ladang—hill rice fields (no irrigation), the traditional Dayak cultivation method

lama—old. Tering Lama, for example, is the oldest of three Tering villages.

lamin—longhouse

liang—a burial house

long—confluence of two rivers. Long Nawang village, for example, is the site where the Nawang joins the larger Krayan River.

mandau—a large bush knife often made in village forges from scrap steel; a smaller knife, or *pue*, is kept behind the large sheath

metik—tattoo

muara—estuary

payau—large deer of the elk family

pue—small knife usually tied to the *mandau* sheath

sampe'—large, flat lute, often with three strings

saop—large bush knife; same as a *mandau*

sumpit—blowpipe made from *ulin* wood

sungal—river, large or small

tel'o—barking deer

temator—rhinoceros

Tuhan—"Lord," in reference to Jesus

ubi kayu—cassava root

uma—rice field

wadian—medicine woman; shaman

Old women look after the children and do domestic chores, while old men sit, gossip, smoke, and repair implements. Children play on the covered longhouse veranda or in the nearby river. The longhouse leader, responsible for handling village affairs, usually lives in the center of the longhouse. Even in Christianized villages, shamans are responsible for the mental, physical, and spiritual health of the people.

Village social organization varies. The Kenyah and Kayan tribes of East Kalimantan practiced slavery until recent times; these villages are ruled by an indigenous aristocracy. The Iban of West Kalimantan are cheerful, cooperative, liberal, and highly democratic, with elected longhouse representatives serving at the pleasure of village elders.

Lamin

A special feature of Dayak life is the longhouse (*lamin* or *betang*). Built along riverbanks, these ridge-roofed structures can be up to 180 meters long and 9-18 meters wide. Several longhouses, each with 50 or more families and as many as 200 doors, may make up a Dayak village. Villagers, working cooperatively, can erect a new one in less than a week. Due to rapid tropical decomposition, longhouses usually don't last longer than 15 years.

Considerable variation exists in longhouse size, method of construction, and interior arrangement. Most are raised one to three meters off the ground on wooden piles—easier to replace than rotting floorboards. Pigs and chickens are kept underneath. The current of air below reduces vermin and prevents dry rot. Stilt construction also provides protection against snakes, floods, and enemies; longhouses evolved in a time of constant intertribal warfare. One or two logs with notched steps, or rough, flexible ladders, are pulled up at night.

In some areas, Dayak architecture and craftsmanship are magnificent, with many parts of the longhouse—door frames, galleries, posts—decoratively carved. Teakwood railings are carved into dragons, snakes, demons, or birds, with detail down to scales and feathers. There are even carved lessons in sex education. A covered veranda, the communal living area, runs the full length of the building, usually facing the river. The veranda is used for loafing, child care, visiting, repairing implements, and hanging

bearing a
ship of the dead

fish traps, boat paddles, weapons, and other articles of daily use. Clothes—and, in past times, heads—are hung out to dry here. One narrow longhouse door faces east, in honor of the sunrise and its association with life. Interior partitions separate family groups; distant relatives may live at the other end of the building. A loft upstairs is used for storing rice, baskets, stacks of woven mats, fishing nets, and firewood.

If invited to visit a *lamin* (always ask permission or wait for an invitation), remove your shoes and socks as a courtesy. Gratefully accept the food or drink offered you with both hands; one outstretched hand can be construed as a threat or challenge. Take useful items into the interior as gifts for your hosts; immediately reciprocate any kindness offered. Show respect for village animals—dogs, chickens, pigs—since the people believe mistreating them will cause various natural disasters.

Don't wait too long to visit a *lamin*—they're disappearing. The government thinks the longhouse concept is too communistic. With help from the government and Christian missionaries, the extended family structure is breaking down.

Life Events

Death is the major event of Dayak life, while birth and marriage are comparatively inconsequential. When a child is born, the celebration consists of offering a sacrifice of rice and chicken or pig blood to the river in which the midwife first bathes the child.

No fertility rites exist among the Dayak; marriage becomes official at the birth of the first child. Modern marriages may be simple, Christian affairs, with both bride and groom dressed in Western clothes. To see traditional animist ceremonies, the best time to visit is July and August, after the harvest.

Religion

All Dayak groups recognize a principal deity who is responsible for creating the world; other powerful deities include those in charge of weather cycles and agricultural yields. Belare, the thunder ghost, goes by the same name all

---

SHIP OF THE DEAD

The Dayak believe the dead will live on in the Land of the Dead, but they need a *prahu* to get there. At ceremonial funerals the people launch lavishly carved and decorated burial canoes containing the deceased; the craft drift downriver to the sea. These boat-shaped coffins are modeled after the water snake for men, the hornbill for women. The Dayak believe it takes three days to get to heaven, and even helpfully provide the dead with maps.

On the eve of the final sailing, men wear animal masks and grass cloaks and dance around the coffin. The dead are provided with painted hats for their trip to the afterworld. Funeral rites have now been modified in most tribes: decorative, canoe-like coffins may still be used, but the dead set sail from village graveyards. Elaborate funerals are now held only for tribal leaders, and Christian burials are the rule.

over Borneo. Every time he opens his mouth, thunder roars; lightning flashes whenever he winks an eye. *Siram,* a water-dripping ceremony, takes place during rice harvest: the rain ghosts pour water from the sky so river ghosts can float home. Legendary spirit heroes and supernatural beings usually include both male and female aspects, and traditionally there is very little anguish about death.

Animals and birds often have religious significance. The hornbill, for example, is associated with the world's creation and is sacred to the Dayak. Hearing or spotting certain birds and mammals can signify good or evil omens. Ritual sacrifices of animals (and at one time, people) appease the spirits and create magic. Before slaughtering village creatures, Dayaks explain their need and beg forgiveness. Beginning about 400 years ago, Chinese traders sold Dayak tribes huge porcelain jars decorated with dragons; the people believed the dragons' spirits lived inside. Many Dayak ideas of good and evil are based on the noises of the jungle. Before a cloudburst, the jungle becomes deathly silent, but when the rains stop, sounds begin again—cicadas, frogs, birds, monkeys, people, gods.

Placed outside villages, elaborately decorated *belawang* poles are hung with rotten eggs and other smelly matter to signify *katang,* an annual casting out of spirits accompanied by ritual dancing. Roads and paths leading to the village are blocked off for two or three days. Leaving the village is fine, since you'll take the spirits with you, but no one is allowed to enter until all the various rites are completed, for fear the spirits will sneak back into town.

Medicine Women

Shamans (*wadian* or *dajung*), in most cases older women, are a strong tradition here. These priestesses are the *dalang* of Dayak society. People will travel for days to see a famous *wadian.* The village *wadian,* with uncoiled hair and huge jangling bracelets, is a hypnotic entertainer capable of performing ritual dances for days on end. Many skills are required of her. She is a magician-healer who must seek out the cause of sickness or evildoing, a mistress of the ceremonial chanting which accompanies many ceremonies, and the local social historian.

In order to communicate directly with the spirits, a *wadian* must drop into a trance state, be-

lieved to be the door to the spirit world. These witch doctors have been known to yank out toenails without anesthesia. If someone comes down with fever or is possessed by demons, a *wadian* hired by the family may go into the jungle with a basket, imploring the devilish spirit to drop the wayward soul into the basket so she can return it.

Headhunting

Officially, headhunting doesn't exist in Kalimantan, though isolated jungle beheadings are still reported. In former times, men would awaken the spirit of courage, Bali Akang, to assist them during headhunting expeditions. After decapitating the enemy, great homecoming celebrations awaited returning warriors. The brains were carefully extracted through the nostrils, then fresh *ulu* (heads) were placed in plaited rattan nets and smoke-cured over fires.

Dried skulls provided the most powerful magic in the world, vital transfusions of energy. A good head could save a village from plague, produce rain, ward off evil spirits, or triple rice yields. Dayak people believed a man's spirit continued to inhabit his head after death. Surrounded by palm leaves, heads were offered food and cigarettes—already lit for smoking—so their spirits would forgive, forget, and feel welcome in their new home. New heads increased the prestige of the owner and impressed sweethearts; they were an initiation into manhood.

In some tribes, a head's powers increased over time; cherished skulls were handed down from generation to generation. In other tribes, a head's magic faded with age, so fresh heads were always needed. Villages without *ulu* were spiritually weak—easy prey for enemies and pestilence. In remote villages of Kalimantan, travelers still come across skulls—usually not fresh ones.

Sumpit

Dayak tribes once commonly used blowguns both in hunting pigs and hunting humans. *Sumpit,* two- to three-meter-long narrow tubes made of hardwood or bamboo fitted with iron sights, shot darts with deadly accuracy for distances of 100 meters or more. The small arrows are made of leaf ribs or the bark of palm trees, the sharp tips dipped in toxic tree sap, then dried until hard and brittle. The arrow shaft falls away on impact, the deadly tip firmly embedded in the victim's flesh. Paralysis occurs instantly, with death following in three minutes or less. Though most Dayak tribes have forsaken both the blowgun and the spear for homemade rifles, the aboriginal Penan still use *sumpit* for hunting.

Christianity

White Rheinische evangelists began work in south Borneo in 1835, first converting the village medicine women, who in turn converted the people, either actively or by example. Throughout the 1800s, Christian birth and marriage rituals began to take hold, undermining native death rites and other ceremonies. Longhouses were gradually abandoned in favor of Malay-type dwellings, and Malay dress was adopted. Villagers embraced Christianity because it tolerated their ideas about reincarnation; they also got to eat pork and keep their dogs. The Christian faith additionally freed families from the financial burden of *kaharingan*, the expensive traditional funeral rites. Christian missionaries spoke and translated the Bible into the Dayak language.

The Christians also set up schools, which changed the Dayaks' value system and attitudes. A common sight in Kalimantan now is young children holding satchels of books wending their way along muddy jungle trails to missionary schools. Still, elaborate Dayak mythology, ritual order, and ancient animist spirit cults persist in a number of places, such as the Barong Tongkok area and the Apo Kayan.

DAYAK ARTS AND CRAFTS

Each tribe specializes in its own handicrafts. Most craft products are utilitarian—for agriculture, daily village life, hunting, or fishing. Agriculturalists construct traps and snares to catch pigs, deer, and monkeys. Borneo people are also accomplished at devising cast nets, flat nets, and scoop nets; the Ngaju of the Upper Kahayan build a remarkable 50-meter-long bamboo and rattan fish trap (*mihing*) shaped like a slide.

The Dayaks fashion beautiful, high-quality bamboo receptacles of all shapes and sizes. Thin bamboo containers hold firemaking gear, jewelry, tobacco, sewing implements, and yarn;

thicker ones store darts for blowguns. Bamboo containers are often completely covered with intricate designs—yellowish red-floral decorations, spiral or triangular motifs, S-lines curving in opposite directions, battle scenes.

Men generally do the woodcarving and metallurgy; women do the tattooing, weaving, basketry, beadwork, embroidery, and sewing. Tangled, effusive S-patterns and curlicues are typical Dayak motifs, a mirror of their jungle environment.

China's highly sophisticated Late Chou style penetrated this island as nowhere else in Indonesia. Characterized by more typically Chinese motifs than the Dongson culture common throughout the remainder of the archipelago, Chou influence is apparent in the complex animal motifs, decorative designs, and mythological afterlife themes used in Dayak art, especially among the Iban people in the northwest. Hindu-Javanese inspiration includes exuberant arabesques and snake and tiger motifs, though tigers aren't found on Borneo.

Traditional Dances

Social dancing is more typical in the Malay coastal areas, while Dayak tribal and ritualistic dance is common up the rivers of the interior. The Indonesian national social dance, *joged*, is performed in the Ma'anjan area when a Banjar orchestra visits the area. Ritual dances, very popular in the interior, mark the transitional stages of life and important village events: coming of age, marriage, death, banishing illness, fighting wars, planting and harvesting rice.

Usually held at night, Dayak dances are exciting spectacles of screaming, tom-tomming dancers in animal skins and plumes of feathers. In mock battle dances, attackers noisily invade the village, then dance to the jugband equivalent of *gamelan*. The Dayaks are also renowned for their solo sword dances: the *ngejiak* shows the skill of a young man using a sharp *mandau*. The *kancet papatai* is a mock fight between two men, also wielding *mandau*. Animal-like demon masks with fangs, big noses, and bulging eyes are worn by some tribes.

Music

Some Dayak tribes still play a curious musical instrument, the *kledi*, a mouth organ akin to a bagpipe, with six or eight narrow strips of bamboo cane protruding from a hollow oval gourd.

Found on 9th century Borobudur bas reliefs, the *kledi,* known in Indoensia since the Bronze Age, survives only in the interior of Kalimantan. Another unusual instrument found among some tribes is the *sampe,* a large flat lute with rattan strings which resonate over a painted wooden box. Also played are goblet-shaped drums made from heavy, hollowed-out tree trunks. Natives of the northern regions play magnificent dragon gongs.

Tattooing

The Dayak's outstanding aesthetic sense is apparent in incredible tattoo designs combining snake, bird, and plant motifs. Woodcuts are usually made first, then colored with charcoal. The woodcut design is then stamped on the skin, which is punctured with brass needles dipped in dye. The most intricate tattooing may require months of hard work—and torture. Tattoos are not just decorative; they denote tribe, family, and social standing, or recognize acts of bravery. Now prohibited by Christian and government leaders, tattooing has become a lost art, though you can still see fine examples on older tribespeople in remote villages. The Kenyah and Kayan tribes of the northeast have the most attractive and complicated tattoo patterns.

Male tattoos are meant to beautify a man for heaven. Boys get their first tattoos at the age of 12. As they grow to manhood, all journeys, skirmishes, and spiritual events are recorded. At death, a historical and biological map of a man's life is tattooed on his shoulders, chest, and legs. Tattoos on certain parts of the female anatomy are related to rank; in some tribes, only wives and daughters of chiefs may have their thighs tattooed.

Plaiting

Traditional Dayak plaited mats are almost indistinguishable from some ancient Croatian weaving, suggesting links between the peoples of the Balkans and Borneo—probably during the "Pontianak Migration," which spread east across Europe to Asia and into the Tonkin area, giving rise to the Dongson culture.

Baskets for carrying rice and large objects, called *bambok* in West Kalimantan, are made of natural rattan, sometimes dyed or decorated in black and red. The Kantu make high-quality split bamboo mats, sought after by other Upper

Kapuas people; the Kapuas Penan and Ot Danum are also known for their excellent mats and basketmaking. Woven mats may feature the Ship of the Dead design. Food containers are also plaited, usually made from strips of pandanus leaves.

Among any family's most prized possessions are *ba',* baby carriers made of wood or rattan. Passed down from generation to generation and believed to magically protect infant spirits, *ba'* are elaborately beaded, carved, painted, or hung with ribbons, pieces of ivory, and coins.

Weaving

Many Dayak tribes are known for their colorful fabrics. Iban Dayak women weave exquisite multicolored *ikat* cloth. Large pieces of *ikat* are still used to mark sacred spots, but seldom worn; they were once used to carry fresh heads. At festivals and other special occasions you may see traditional woven costumes: kerchiefs, loincloths, decorated poncho-like coats (*jawat*), and a girdle of bark cloth wrapped around the waist, then passed through the legs. *Belet* are hundreds of fiber garters clipped around the legs at knee level. Women still wear *sholang* (shell skirts) or bright applique cloth skirts, an ancient technique in which black human figures and dogs are sewn onto light-colored fabrics. These traditional costumes are fast disappearing, worn now only in remote parts of East Kalimantan.

Sculpture
Dayak carving technique is unique. A small knife with a long handle is clamped tightly under the armpit: the object being carved is moved, not the knife. Such everyday objects as plates, bowls, spoons, seats, and footstools are carved and decorated; most carvings are of guardian figures and spirits. Carving is sometimes a religious function. Each Dayak has a personal spirit, about 12 cm tall; most are standing, but ancestral figures or *balian* (hereditary priest) figures may sit or crouch. Lifesize village guardians are made of ironwood and placed at the community entrance, or at the sites of accidents to prevent future misfortune. Figures with monkeys on their heads or hips are forest guardians. Tall, skinny, male wooden statues can be seen at burial grounds, with open arms, tusks, swords, and erect penises—devils hate to see sexual excitement.

Hampatong figures represent the live slaves who once accompanied and protected the soul of the dead on its journey to the afterworld; they have deformed faces and protruding tongues, and tigers sit atop their heads. *Hudog* (masks) are carved from single pieces of wood, are often bearded, and have two eyeteeth. Some tribes fashion one-meter-high to lifesize sacrificial hardwood columns (*temadu*), with male and female figures representing the dead.

Surreal, dynamic sculpture in the round is seen most frequently among the Ot Danum, Ngaju, and Dasan groups of southeastern Borneo. Central poles in meeting houses of East Kalimantan may be quite intricate, with carvings of flowing water, mandau, hornbills, and other creatures.

Metallurgy
The Dayak surpassed even the Javanese and Malays in the creation of iron products. Dayaks once forged axes, knives, and adzes out of their own iron, but this art has virtually been forgotten—the mines, ancient forges, and smelters reclaimed by the jungle. Only a few specimens of this traditional art exist. The brasswork of the braziers of Negara in southeast Kalimantan still reflects Hindu-Javanese influence. The Maloh of West Kalimantan are particularly skilled in the manufacture of brass and silver earrings, belts, bracelets, armlets, leg-rings, and anklets.

The most important Dayak weapon is the *mandau*, or sword, once worn in battle but now used mostly for decoration or magic. Known for their pliancy and strength, battle swords feature superb inlay work. Those made from rust-free Mantikai iron with carved staghorn hilts are masterpieces.

TRANSPORTATION

GETTING THERE

Kalimantan is often a stopover between Java and Sulawesi, although it's also possible to fly from Bali, Singapore, and Kuching. The most popular route is to fly or take Pelni from Java to Banjarmasin to see the floating market and trek the Loksado region, then bus or fly to Balikpapan and proceed to Samarinda, from where extended journeys can be made up the Mahakam River. From Samarinda, you can fly or take Pelni to Sulawesi, or fly to Pontianak, where buses depart daily for Kuching in East Malaysia. Allow a minimum of two weeks, or four weeks for interior boat explorations.

By Air
Flying to Kalimantan is easy but expensive. Bouraq, Merpati, and Garuda all fly into the territory's major cities and feature regular connecting flights. Bouraq and Merpati are generally less expensive than Garuda. All three carriers connect Balikpapan with Ujung Pandang, Surabaya, Jakarta, and Manado.

Balikpapan is the main destination for Garuda flights originating in Jakarta (Rp378,000, four or five times daily) and Surabaya (Rp242,000, twice daily). From Jakarta, Merpati also flies to Pontianak. Bouraq flies from Jakarta to Banjarmasin (Rp231,000, twice daily) and Balikpapan (Rp357,000, three times daily).

Bouraq even flies three times weekly from Denpasar to Banjarmasin (Rp284,000).

Overland treks between East Malaysia and Kalimantan are now legal, but crossing borders without a visa can get you jailed or deported. You can also fly. Tawau, in Sabah, is a busy Chinese commercial city. A little-known connection between Malaysia and Indonesia is the Tawau-Tarakan flight (M$100, four times weekly). It's sometimes cancelled or full, so allow a few extra days before your visa expires. You'll need an Indonesian visa, as Tarakan is not among Indonesia's official entry points.

The local agent is Merdata Travel Service, 41 Dunlop St., Tawau, tel. 72531. On the other side of the island, Merpati has flights from Kuching, Sarawak, to Pontianak for Rp208,000 roundtrip. Or take the daily 0700 bus from Kuching to Pontianak for Rp20,000. The land crossing is now legally open to tourists who are granted a two-month visitors permit—a convenient and inexpensive connection between the two countries.

By Boat
Pelni and other companies connect the east coast of Kalimantan to Java and Sulawesi. From Jakarta you can take a Pelni to Balikpapan via Surabaya and Ujung Pandang. Other passenger ships depart Surabaya for Banjarmasin twice weekly for Rp46,000. From Pare Pare or Ujung Pandang, take a frequent *kapal motor* to the East Kalimantan coast.

Going by ship or boat from the southern Philippines is more trouble than it's worth; you encounter all the usual official hassles plus the risk of piracy. It's easier to fly from Zamboanga to Tawau, then on to Tarakan; get an Indonesian visa in Manila, Singapore, or Kota Kinabalu.

Boats sail from Tawau, Sabah, to Nunukan, East Kalimantan, daily; M$35, two hours. From Nunukan each day at 0500, a somewhat larger boat leaves for Tarakan; Rp8000 (8.5 hours). From Tarakan, the big Pelni ship MV *Kerinci* sails to Balikpapan in three days.

Visas
Travelers reaching Pontianak from Kuching by bus or plane are automatically granted a two-month entry permit. Otherwise, get an Indonesian visa first; other than the Kuching-Pontianak land crossing, Kalimantan entry points don't issue 60-day tourist entry stamps on arrival. There are *imigrasi* offices only at Tarakan, Samarinda, Balikpapan, Banjarmasin, and Pontianak.

In East Malaysia, you'll find Indonesian consulates at Kuching and Kota Kinabalu in Sarawak, and at Tawau in Sabah. Unless you have a letter from Kota Kinabalu's main consular offices, Tawau's Wisma Indonesia won't issue visas to non-Malaysians. If you run out of time while traveling in the interior, ask the local police to write you a cover letter.

GETTING AROUND

No railways. The territory's four limited road systems—in Pontianak, Balikpapan/Samarinda, Banjarmasin, and from Banjarmasin to Samarinda—are fairly reliable, questionable only during the wet season.

Kalimantan's rivers are the island's main thoroughfares, traveled by sampan and motorized canoes (*ketingting*), canopied rivercraft (*klotok*), speedboats or longboats (*longbots*), and ferries. Seagoing ships travel up the large rivers, daily ferries connect Banjarmasin and Palangkaraya, and longboats run from Tarakan to both Berau and Nunukan.

Several small airlines fly regularly into the interior. MAF (Missionary Aviation Fellowship) has bases throughout Kalimantan; if space is available you can fly MAF into the most remote interior areas, and then from airstrip to airstrip. Pelita (owned by Pertamina) and DAS (Dirgantara Air Service) schedule many interior flights. Asahi Air, once the most important service to the interior, went bankrupt in early 1994.

Tours
If you require the services of a professional tour company, **Bolder Adventures** in Boulder, Colorado offers an Rp6.5-8 million monthlong "Indonesian Wildlife Safari," which includes river trips in Kalimantan, plus Torajaland, Sumatra, and the dragons of Komodo. Or try one of the most experienced domestic tour companies in East Kalimantan, **PT Tomaco,** Jakarta Theatre Bldg., Jl. Thamrin 9, Jakarta, tel. (021) 347-453, 354-551, or 320-087. Tomaco tours include the three-day "Banuaq Package" to Tenggarong and Tanjung Isui; the six-day "Enggang Package" to Muara Ancalong; plus helicoptor tours

and customized special-interest and/or adventure tours. The company uses local 20-meter-long boats and provides basic facilities. PT Tomaco has a branch office at Hotel Benakutai, Jl. Antasari, Balikpapan, tel. (0524) 21747 or 22747. Prices are Rp1 million per person for four to seven people, Rp983,000 per person for eight to 12 people, or Rp 949,000 per person for 13-16 people. Other travel agencies are listed under Samarinda and Banjarmasin.

THE INTERIOR

Everyone going to Kalimantan is well advised to learn at least some rudimentary Indonesian. Also, antimalarial pills should always be consumed everywhere in Kalimantan. Be sure to take all the *rupiah* you'll need; there are no banks or moneychangers in the interior. In Dayak country, the people's kindness and hospitality may be overwhelming. The head of the longhouse would love things like sunglasses or your clothes; pencils and paper go over big with children.

Jungle Officialdom
Make contact through passing on addresses ("I know somebody in a department . . ."). You might arrange to go upriver with a government party or on a police boat. Officials in Kalimantan, especially in remote areas, are unusually helpful—even willing to help you find accommodations and food.

River Travel
Some stretches of Kalimantan's rivers are so long and wide that amphibious aircraft can land on them. Traveling the interior is cheapest by boat on major rivers like the Kapuas, Barito, Mahakam, and their large tributaries. For traveling beyond cities and trading villages you'll need specially designed rivercraft. Many boats are decorated with painted bloodshot eyes to guide them safely through treacherous waters. Skippers steer by using mangrove trees, mudbanks, stumps, and other natural features as markers. Upriver areas are closed to larger craft because currents and courses are unpredictable. Seasonal flooding can be lethal; during heavy rains, rivers may double in size within hours. The farther inland you travel, the more it costs to live.

By Air
Pelita Air and DAS offer the most extensive interior flight network. Also check with Derayu. If there's room, MAF and other missionary air services will gladly take paying passengers; if you make advance arrangements, MAF (Box 82, Samarinda, Box 18, Tarakan) will even pick you up at remote interior villages. Due to uneven demand, MAF flights out of the interior are half the price of the same journey in, so plan your trip accordingly. If you're into skyhitching, try to get rides on aircraft leaving Balikpapan's airport.

It's popular now to fly with Pelita Air from Samarinda to Datah Dawai on the Upper Mahakam River; Rp50,000, leaving Monday and Thursday at 1000 or 1100. Then take a river bus upstream to Long Apari.

Trekking
Trekking in Borneo offers limitless possibilities. All the great Borneo routes interconnect to form

---

TREKKING ACROSS KALIMANTAN

Four California adventurers, loaded down with the latest in high-tech wilderness gear and sponsored by the R.J. Reynolds Tobacco Company, set out in July 1983 to cross Kalimantan from west to east, Pontianak to Tarakan. The team leader contracted typhoid and was airlifted out, but the remaining three finished the trip in 43 days—after wisely declining to run the formidable Embun rapids on East Kalimantan's Kayan River.

Another Californian, Eric Hansen, completed an unpublicized roundtrip trans-Borneo trek the year before. He brought no sleeping bag, camping equipment, water, food, or medicine except antimalarials, traveling alone—without government permission—from Malaysia south into Kalimantan. "If you travel like the native people, you don't have to bring anything," Hansen said later. "And you don't destroy the culture." He got along well with the remote Dayak tribes he encountered. "The key to getting along with these people is making a complete fool of yourself," he says. In his case, this included dancing dressed only in a loincloth, feather headdress, and bearskin vest. "If you can do that, they trust you." Read his book, *Stranger in the Forest: On Foot Across Borneo*, for more information on this amazing trek.

a vast network that's wide open for the adventurous. Routes between Malaysia and Kalimantan are now open to foreigners. Trans-Borneo treks are possible from Pontianak to Samarinda or vice versa; allow at least three or four weeks. The first coast-to-coast trek across Borneo's vast interior was accomplished in 1897 by a Dutch group with 110 porters and bodyguards. In 1858 Robert Burns (the poet's grandson) tried; he lost his head while exploring the island's northern reaches. Currently, several dozen travelers complete the trans-Kalimantan each month; tour companies now lead groups of travelers—a veritable highway. See the Putussibau and Long Apari sections for trekking details.

A good trek is from Putussibau in West Kalimantan to the Mahakam River. You can charter a *longbot* from Putussibau to Tanjung Lokan for Rp630,000; if you're lucky and find a boat already going, the charge is only Rp150,000. Guides can be hired in Tanjung Lokan for Rp10,000 per day—you'll need two. Although it's an easy four-day walk, guides want 10 days' pay, a total of about Rp200,000. You'll have to carry plenty of food, and a plastic sheet for makeshift camping is recommended. Along the way you'll see hornbills, macaques, lemurs, and plenty of leeches. When you reach the Mahakam you can buy passage on boats to Tiong Ohang (Rp50,000), then to Long Bagun, (Rp30,000), then take a water taxi to Samarinda for Rp15,000.

EAST KALIMANTAN

It was on the Mahakam River that Hindu culture first arrived in Indonesia, around A.D. 400. Traditional animist culture persists in isolated areas, but many tribes are thoroughly Christianized. Joseph Conrad visited Berau and Tanjungredeb four times, using "that Settlement hidden in the heart of the forest-land, up that sombre stream" as the setting for *Almayer's Folly* and *An Outcast of the Islands,* as well as the second part of *Lord Jim.*

Most rain falls between November and May in this land laced by rivers, swamps, and rainforests. Hundreds of different orchid varieties, including the rare black orchid, grow here; exotic animals include orangutans, proboscis monkeys, barking deer, bearded wild pigs, river dolphins, and pythons.

Most travelers visit East Kalimantan to explore the lower and middle stretches of the Mahakam River. Allow a minimum of one week—two or three are preferable. Inexpensive boats and homestays are plentiful in almost every village in the lower and middle sections of the Mahakam. Getting to the upper reaches of the Mahakam is time-consuming and expensive because of the shortage of ordinary transport. Aside from travelers crossing to West Kalimantan, the upper reaches are rarely visited.

Another area of interest is the more remote Apo Kayan region near the Sarawak border—a relatively untouched Dayak enclave easily reached with twice-weekly Pelita Air services from Samarinda. This is an area for determined explorers.

The Great Fire

Through late 1982 and the first quarter of 1983, the forests of East Kalimantan suffered a grievous loss of 3.5 million hectares. Ranking as one of the worst human-caused ecological catastrophes in history, the "Great Fire" destroyed more than 20% of the province's rainforests and eradicated dozens of plant and animal species. For months, ships off Balikpapan had to drop anchor because of poor visibility, and the gray-brown haze caused the cancellation of flights at Singapore's airport, 1,400 km to the west.

Experts attributed the fire to a pattern of unrestrained commercial logging activities. Logging debris on the forest floor kindled the flames, and because of widespread forest destruction, the remaining forests could no longer supply the moisture necessary to subdue the effects of the fire. As evidence of this, the primeval Kutai National Park escaped destruction even though the logged area surrounding it was completely engulfed in flames.

Getting There

Most visitors arrive by air in Balikpapan, one of Indonesia's busiest airports, eight km west of

EAST KALIMANTAN

EAST MALAYSIA

CELEBES SEA

TO KOTA KINABALU

LUMBIS

NUNUKAN

TAWAU

LONG BAWAN

ATAP

BINUANG

MALINAU

TIDANG PALE

TARAKAN

S. BAHAU

TANJUNGPALAS

TANJUNGSELOR

LONG PESO

LONG BIA

LONG PUJUNGAN

LONG JELET

LONG LAAI

GUNUNG TABUR

TANJUNGBATU

SAMBALIUNG

S. BERAU

TANJUNGREDEB (BERAU)

SEE "APO KAYAN" MAP

LONG NAWANG

LONG AMPUNG

S. KAT

S. KAYAN

LONG LE'ES

TANJUNGREDEB (BERAU)

MUARA WAHAU

LONG TEBUAN

MAHAK BARU

LONG LEBUSAN

LONG BENTUO

MUARALESAN

LONG MORAN

TALISAYAN

TRAIL

S. OGA

S. BOH

BATU AMPAR

LONG APARI

TIONG OHANG

LONG PAHANGAI

LONG BAGUN

RUKUN DAMAI

UJOH BILANG

MUARA BENGKAL

MUARA MAHAU

SANGKULIRANG

SEE "MAHAKAM RIVER" MAP

S. BELAYAN

S. TELEN

KEDANG KELAPA

TABANG

MUARA ANGGLONG

MUARA BENGKAL

KEMBANGJANGGUT

BONTANG

LONG IRAM

KARAHAN

MUARA KAMAN

BARONG TONGKOK

MELAK

MUARA PAHU

KOTA BANGUN

MUARA BADAK

MUARA TAWAI

SEBULU

DAMAI

MUARA MUNTAI

TENGGARONG

SAMARINDA

TANJUNG ISUI

PANTUNG

LOA KULU

ANGGANA

SANGASANGA

SEE "MID-MAHAKAM RIVER" MAP

LOA PALARAN

HANDIL

CENTRAL KALIMANTAN

MUARA JAWA

SAMBOJA

SELAT MAKASSAR

PENAJAM

WARU

BALIKPAPAN

LONG KALI

MUARA KOMAN

LONG IKIS

BATUSOPANG

TANAHGROGOT

KUARO

PASIR BELENGKONG

SOUTH KALIMANTAN

TANJUNGARU

0   50 km

TO BANJARMASIN

© MOON PUBLICATIONS, INC.

town at Sepinggan. Walk to the main road and take a local *kijang* (Rp500); taxis cost about Rp10,000. The airport has a bank (good rates), snack bar, post office counter, and offices for Garuda, Merpati, Bouraq, and Pelita Air.

Other travelers first arrive in Banjarmasin. From there, buses make the 12-hour (Rp20,000) trip to Balikpapan, then head to Samarinda. You can also enter from the state of Sabah in East Malaysia. Boats leave for Nunukan from Tawau on Monday, Wednesday, and Friday, costing M\$25 (two hours). Since Nunukan is not an official entry point you'll need an Indonesian visa. From Nunukan to Tarakan costs Rp10,000 (eight to nine hours). From Tarakan, take the plane to Balikpapan.

Boats, mostly wood-hulled *kapal motor*, also cross every two to three days from Pare Pare (South Sulawesi) to Balikpapan. Pelni (*Kambuna* and the *Kerinci*) and other shipping companies provide less frequent service from Surabaya and other Indonesian ports.

BALIKPAPAN

The discovery of coastal oil and gas here in the late 1960s quickly transformed traditional village life in the area, making Balikpapan the major economic transport center of East Kalimantan. Many American, European, and Australian oil and timber company employees ("oilies" and "chippies") once worked here or in nearby Badak. However, the completion of the oil refineries has meant the departure of most foreign oil workers. Today, only a handful work in Balikpapan.

The people of Balikpapan are friendly and helpful. Stay a couple days to see the combined effects of the oil boom and Indonesian cultural mixing: once-feared Dayaks serve cocktails to expatriates in air-conditioned bars and nightclubs on hills overlooking fishing *kampung*.

The city's central district at the waterfront sprawls up the hills to the northwest. New, expensive buildings are surrounded by trash piles and sewage ditches. All the main public buildings are on Jl. Jen. A. Yani. Americans, Australians, Europeans, and high-placed Indonesians live on hills overlooking the town. Walk up Pasir Ridge to the Union Oil Complex to see this "other world" of manicured lawns and trees, swimming pools, and modern suburban homes. Below are crowded *kampung* and Pertamina's oil refinery complex—a landscape of gas flares, pipes, tanks, and girders.

SIGHTS

Not much here. You get the best view of Balikpapan from **Tanki I,** Gunung Dubbs. North of the refinery is a whole neighborhood of houses on stilts connected by wooden walkways over a muddy estuary. There's an enormous, highly organized brothel called Lembah Harapan ("Valley of Hope") in an army camp: a long row of whitewashed huts, with rather worn-out Surabayan prostitutes. Relax with a drink in bars such as the Blue Sky Hotel, which has pool tables, pinball, and massage.

ACCOMMODATIONS AND FOOD

Accommodations

As in all boomtowns, expect to pay more for accommodations. **Hotel Sederhana** is the frequent choice of travelers on a budget. Located at Jl. A. Yani 290 (next to Bioskop Gelora on the waterfront), it has a/c rooms; cheaper rooms are in the *penginapan* of the same name in the same building. Rooms here cost Rp15,000-40,000 depending on facilities. Other cheapies around town such as the Penginapan Royal won't take foreigners—too much paperwork.

The best budget to midpriced hotel is the waterfront **Gajah Mada,** Jl. Sudirman 14, tel. (0542) 34634, fax 34636, with economy rooms from Rp25,000 to Rp30,000 and a/c standards from Rp50,000 to Rp60,000. Popular with travelers and tour groups watching their *rupiah*; a decent Padang restaurant is attached. Recommended.

A few kilometers from city center (take bus no. 5) is **Wisma Aida,** Jl. D.I. Penjaitan 50, tel. 21006. Fancy front but unprepossessing interior; inexpensive rooms are small but clean, with fan. The **Tirta Plaza,** Jl. D.I. Panjaitan 51-52, tel. 22324 or 22132, is an American-style hotel with

BALIKPAPAN

BUS STATION TO SAMARINDA
(BATU AMPAR BUS TERMINAL)

KAMPUNG BARU

NURLINA SHIPPING
BOATS TO BANJARMASIN
'BUS TERMINAL

JL. W. MONGINSIDI

JL. SUPRAPTO

POST OFFICE

JL. GUNUNG POLISI

JL. PIPA GUNUNG

JL. GUNUNG

JL. INPRES

STRAAT TIGA

STRAAT DUA

STRAAT SATU

BYPASS HWY.

BANK

BLUE SKY HOTEL

NIGHT WARUNG

JL. KARANG ANYAR

JL. GUNUNG SAMARINDA

RAPAK BUS TERMINAL

TO AIRPORT

PERTAMINA OIL FIELDS

JL. MINYAK

JL. PANORAMA

JL. KARANG REJO

WISMA AIDA

JL. D.I. PANJAITAN

JL. GUNUNG KAWI

TELUK BALIKPAPAN

GUNUNG PANCUR

TIRTA PLAZA HOTEL

JL. R.E. MARTADINATA

PARMAN

PUBLIC HOSPITAL

JL. SUTOYO

JL. INDUSTRY

OIL FIELDS

JL. YOS. SUDARSO

PASIR RIDGE

JL. ATAKA BESAR

NEW SHANGRILA RESTAURANT

JL. ANTASARI (JL. YANI)

JL. BLORA

BALIKPAPAN HARBOR

GUNUNG DUBBS

PELNI

JL. LOMBOK

JL. PRAPATAN

JL. SUDIRMAN

JL. TENDEAN

POST OFFICE

HOTEL SEDERHANA

ATOMIC CAFE
POLICE

GARUDA OFFICE

BONDY RESTAURANT

BOURAQ

HOTEL BUDIMAN

HOTEL ALTEA BENAKUTAI

TO SEPINGGAN AIRPORT (8 km)

IMMIGRATION

GAJAH MADA

HOTEL

BALIKPAPAN CENTER

JL. K.S. TUBIN

JL. YOS. SUDARSO

SELAT MAKASSAR

0   1 km

© MOON PUBLICATIONS, INC.

swimming pool; it also has bungalows for Rp45,000. Cheaper rates on the weekends.

Friendly, with excellent food and entertainment, is the completely reconstructed **Blue Sky Hotel,** Jl. Jen. Suprapto 1, tel. 35845, fax 24094. Rooms run from Rp80,000 (standard room, weekend) to Rp150,000 (deluxe, weekday). Facilities include a pool, fitness center, and comfortable rooms with views of the oil fields.

The **Mirama Hotel,** Jl. May. Jen. Sutoyo, tel. 22960, has a nice a/c lobby; breakfast included. On Jl. Antasari (opposite the Garuda office) is the spacious **Hotel Budiman;** Rp50,000-60,000 for a/c rooms—good downtown location.

Visitors with more to spend can stay at Balikpapan's original international-class hotel, the five-star 216-room **Altea Benakutai Hotel,** Jl. Yani, tel. 31896, fax 31823, which caters to oil workers and group tourists; rooms cost Rp294,000-756,000. Newer and much more luxurious is the five-star **Dusit Hotel** on the road to the airport, with all possible amenities plus a much more efficient management than the rather disorganized Altea. The Dusit opened in early 1994.

Food

The city's diverse population is reflected in the selection. *Warung* are scattered throughout the town, busiest at night. For fancier eating, Jl. Antasari is an excellent place to look for restaurants. The restaurant in the Hotel Altea Benakutai is too expensive, plus the food and service are second-rate. You'll do better at the **Atomic Cafe,** a Chinese restaurant popular with foreigners and known for its delicious chili crayfish.

Balikpapan's finest Chinese seafood is served in the immensely popular **New Shangrila**; extensive menu and reasonable prices. Arrive early. Also on Jl. Sutoyo is the open-air **Bondy Restaurant,** with seafood specialties in the rear courtyard, and the **Holland Bakery** for baked goods, hot dogs, ice cream, and steaks.

The **Blue Sky Restaurant** in the hotel of the same name is popular with expatriates and serves decent seafood, especially abalone. If you're hungry for very reasonably priced sirloin, try the **Barunawati** near the harbor. For Padang-style food, try **Minang Saiyo,** Jl. Gajah Mada 45, and similar places nearby. For Indonesian, Chinese, and European fare, head for the **Mirama,** in the Mirama Hotel.

SERVICES AND SHOPPING

Services And Information

The **post office** will hold poste restante mail for travelers. Balikpapan's telephone code is 0542. **Banks** and **moneychangers** are located on Jl. Antasari near Jl. Gajah Mada. Be sure to get all the *rupiah* you need before heading into the interior, where there are no banks. The banks in Balikpapan give the best rates in East Kalimantan, but rates vary so shop around. Exchange rates in Samarinda and Tarakan are only slightly lower. Scuba divers can contact **Derawa Dive Shop,** tel. (0542) 31896, in the Altea Benakutai Hotel. Dives to Derawan Island in Berau Regency (northeast Kalimantan) cost Rp315,000 per day, including transportation, meals, and equipment.

Crafts

Susila Art Shop, Jl. Suprapto, is a marvelous shop specializing in Dayak handicrafts and Chinese porcelain. Another, more touristy souvenir

shop is the **Syahda Mestika**, Jl. S. Parman. A really good buy in Balikpapan is 200- to 400-year-old Ming and Ching dynasty ceramics originally from the kingdom of Kutai to the north; small plates are Rp12,000-15,000. Also try the **Martapura Art Shop** adjacent to the Susila, and the **Kalimantan Art Shop** on Jl. Sutoyo near the New Shangrila Restaurant.

GETTING THERE AND AROUND

Getting There

Taxis from Sepinggan Airport to your hotel in Balikpapan cost Rp10,000, or you can walk out to the highway (300 meters), then catch a blue-and-white *kijang* into town for only Rp500. You can also charter a taxi direct to Samarinda (Rp35,000), Tenggarong (Rp40,000), or Pasar Baru (Rp25,000), where you board minibuses for Penajam and then down to Banjarmasin.

The latest wrinkle is motorcycle taxis that wait just outside the airport entrance near the highway. Strap on your backpack, pay about Rp6000, and hang on during the 15-minute backcountry ride direct to the bus terminal. This is the cheapest and fastest way to leave Balikpapan. Taxis from the airport to the bus terminal cost about Rp15,000.

Getting Around

Balikpapan is too spread out to walk everywhere, and the city's hundreds of *kijang* are the best transport option. The vehicles look like armored personnel carriers, and run frequently along the main streets; Rp200-500. Let the driver know when you want to get out by simply yelling "Stop!"—no Indonesian required. Local *kijang* transport helps in finding addresses, which can be difficult, as names for the same street change every few blocks.

Major *kijang* terminals are **Pasar Baru, Terminal Penajam** across Teluk Balikpapan, and **Rapak,** the central terminal in north Balikpapan. Three *kijang* are particularly useful. Orange *kijang* no. 5 goes from city center (downtown) to Rapak terminal, Blue Sky Hotel, and the boat pier for connections to Samarinda. As noted above, blue-and-white *kijang* connect the airport with city center. Red *kijang* no. 1 goes from Rapak terminal to the pier, Blue Sky Hotel, and Batu Ampar Bus Terminal for buses to Samarinda.

Tours

See **PT Tomaco,** tel. (0542) 21747 or 22747, in the Hotel Altea Benakutai on Jl. Antasari for river tours. Mahakam River trips are offered to such places as Tanjung Isui, Data Bilang, Rukun Damai, and Tering; cost is about Rp315,000 per day, depending on group size. If time is short and money long, this agency can also arrange a helicopter day-trip to Tanjung Isui. Much cheaper trips can be arranged in Samarinda.

GETTING AWAY

By Air

Balikpapan is served by Garuda/Merpati, Bouraq, and several small charters owned by oil companies and missionary groups. Sample fares: Banjarmasin (Rp63,000), Samarinda (Rp42,000), Palangkaraya (Rp84,000), Tarakan (Rp95,000), Surabaya (Rp150,000), Ujung Pandang (Rp150,000), Yogyakarta (Rp150,000), and Jakarta (Rp270,000). International departures include Singapore (Rp420,000), Brunei (Rp380,000), and Darwin via Bali. Most flights to small interior villages leave from Samarinda rather than Balikpapan. Check with Pelita Air Service, tel. (0542) 20500, in the Balikpapan Airport and in Samarinda.

Other Departures

To Samarinda: To get cheaply (not quickly) from the airport to Samarinda, take the blue-and-white *kijang* to downtown, then orange *kijang* no. 5 to Rapak terminal, then red *kijang* no. 1 to the Batu Ampur bus terminal. From the bus terminal, it's 2.5 hours and 113 km (Rp2500) by bus to Samarinda on the new paved road. Another way to Samarinda is to take a *kijang* to Pasar Baru (Rp450), then board a *spetbot* along the coast and then upriver to Samarinda (60 km). This trip takes five hours, and the price has come down due to competition from the new road.

To reach Banjarmasin, from Rapak terminal take a *kijang* to the pier on Jl. Monginsidi, then a *spetbot* (Rp1200) over to Penajam. Chartered taxis and buses depart Penajam to Banjarmasin and other points south. For Pare Pare and other Sulawesi destinations, check the boat offices of Nurlina Shipping near the Kampung Baru piers. Daily departures.

Three Pelni ships depart several times monthly to destinations within Indonesia. KM *Kambuna* sails to Sulawesi, Surabaya, and Jakarta. KM *Tidar* serves Tarakan, Ujung Pandang, and Surabaya. KM *Awu* reaches Tarakan, several ports in Sulawesi, and Surabaya. Departure dates can be confirmed and tickets purchased from the Pelni office, tel. 24171, on Jl. Pelabuhan near the Balikpapan harbor. Travel agents in town also make reservations and sell Pelni tickets.

VICINITY OF BALIKPAPAN

Get on the Union Oil boat just past Banana Town and take it out to very pretty Lawi Lawi Beach. Twenty km south of Balikpapan is **Panggar,** a quiet black-sand beach crowded on Sundays. Visit the oil rigs if you can go as a guest of one of the oil companies; after flying over miles of jungle and landing on helicopter pads, you'll discover the rigs are manned by men who could be sheriffs in Texas. Many of the helicopter pilots are Vietnam veterans. Look for experimental reforestation stations, where Caribbean pine, Indonesian albizzia, and Australian eucalyptus are planted.

Nearby small towns include Penajam and Tanahgrogot, the capital of the Pasir Regency. Both can be reached by bus and offer several accommodation and *warung* choices.

Pasir Belengkong Kingdom

This place is long forgotten by the outside world, but the people of Belengkong village carefully maintain the former sultan's palace, small museum, and mosque. The kingdom, founded in 1565, was known as Sadurangas. The Dutch purchased Pasir Kingdom in 1906 from Sultan Ibrahim. The "sale" didn't go over well with the local aristocracy, but the Dutch quickly put down their rebellion and exiled the sultan, ending the kingdom.

The old palace is architecturally unusual, with beautiful floral woodcarvings, Koranic inscriptions, and baroque figures. Now a museum, the building houses a small collection of Chinese dragon jars, locally made pottery, old Dayak carvings, gongs, and small cannons. These old relics are still considered magical and sacred by the local people; the cannons are wrapped in cloth and draped with strands of flowers. Small offerings may burn nearby. The sultan's mosque, still used by the village, is next door.

Pasir Belengkong is 45 minutes by boat downriver from Tanahgrogot. Look for riverside platforms where sago palm workers tread the pulp and wash out the flour. Easiest and least expensive is to take the trip on Pasir Belengkong's market days (Sunday and Wednesday); boats leave Tanahgrogot around sunrise and return midday. Fare is Rp750 each way.

SAMARINDA AND VICINITY

Sixty km upstream from the mouth of the Mahakam River, Samarinda is the capital of East Kalimantan, half the size of Balikpapan. You can see the giant silver-domed Mesjid Raya gleaming in the sun as you approach.

A trading town established in 1730, Samarinda is cheaper and more easygoing than Balikpapan. Its location on the northern bank of the Mahakam, with low hills in the background as you come upriver, is lovely. At this point, the Mahakam is up to two km wide at high water and deep enough to accommodate seagoing ships. Logs tied into rafts float everywhere and modern sawmills line the river's banks. All manner of watercraft chug back and forth on the river. Taxi boats depart frequently for upstream destinations, making Samarinda the natural starting point for trips to Dayak villages.

SIGHTS

Samarinda boasts one of the largest and most impressive **mosques** in Indonesia . . . if they ever finish those concrete minarets. A few Makassar schooners are moored at the south end of the pier. **Mulawarman University** has several campuses scattered around town. Samarinda's redlight district, **Air Biru,** commands an admission fee and is closed Thursday. Lumber mills line both sides of the river; climb the hills northeast of Samarinda to get a look at countryside ravaged by the timber concessions.

SAMARINDA

TO SEGIRI BUS TERMINAL
(BONTONG) AND MAF

MESRA HOTEL

PERTAMINA

CINEMA

TOURIST OFFICE

PHPA

JL. PAHLAWAN

SCHOOL

JL. KESUMA BANGSA

JL. SALIM

JL. THALIB

HOTEL ANDHIKA

MAHARANI HOTEL

MIRASA CAFE

JL. DAHLIA

JL. DAHLAN

JL. RAHMAT

ANGKASA TRAVEL

JL. HAKIM

JL. RAHMAT

JL. HASAN

JL. BHAYANGKARA

HOTEL RAHAYU

JL. BONJOL

TELEPHONE

HAYANI HOTEL

LOSMEN HIDAYAH 2

HOTEL SENYIUR PLAZA

WISMA PIRUS

GAJAH MADA DEPARTMENT STORE

JL. DIPONEGORO

0   100 m

JL. SUDIRMAN

SEWARGA INDAH HOTEL

MESIR HOTEL

BAKERY

JL. HIDAYA TULLAH

JL. BATUR

ART SHOPS

BANK DUTA MIRAMAR TRAVEL

POST OFFICE

JL. GAJAH MADA

PASAR PAGI

HIDAYAH 1 HOTEL

AIDA HOTEL

ART SHOPS

TAXIS

SUKARNI HOTEL

CITRA NIAGA SHOPPING COMPLEX

WARTEL

BOURAQ

JL. MULAWARAM

TO BRIDGE,
LONGBOAT PIER,
MAIN BUS TERMINAL
AND BALIKPAPAN

FERRY

JL. SUDARSO

HOLIDAY INDAH HOTEL

OLD SHIPS

HARBOR

MAHAKAM RIVER

BUS TERMINAL

SEBARANG

TO BALIKPAPAN

© MOON PUBLICATIONS, INC.

ACCOMMODATIONS

Budget

Losmen Hidayah 2, Jl. Abdul Hasan, wants Rp8000-12,000 for double beds, up to Rp20,000 for inside *mandi*. Very popular—for the money, these rooms are the nicest in town. Be sure to ask for a fan.

Hotel Rahayu, Jl. Abdul Hasan no. 17, asks Rp8000-12,000. No a/c but fans; spacious, clean (though dark), and central; eat at Depot Mirasa across the street. At Jl. Agus Salim 33 is the acceptable **Hotel Maharani,** tel. (0541) 31013, with budget rooms Rp6000-12,000 and rooms with private bath Rp13,000-20,000.

Hotel Andhika, Jl. A. Salim 37, tel. 42538, is much cleaner with economy rooms for Rp15,000-22,000 and standard rooms at Rp25,000-32,000. Across the river in Sebarang, stay in quieter **Losmen Loupathy** down Gang 8 off Jl. Antasari.

Moderate

Downtown, medium-priced hotels include the **Hidayah 1,** tel. (0541) 31408, on Jl. Temenggung, where standard rooms cost Rp20,000-24,000 and a/c rooms are Rp33,000-42,000, and the popular **Hotel Aida,** tel. 42572, with fancooled rooms for Rp17,000-20,000 and clean a/c rooms from Rp32,000. Avoid **Sukarni Hotel** and **Holiday Indah Hotel,** brothels filled with drunken sailors and traveling businessmen.

Two excellent hotels, with both new and old wings, are tucked away on a quiet side street. **Hotel Pirus** (tel. 41873) on Jl. Pirus 30 has economy rooms for Rp11,000-17,000 and deluxe a/c rooms from Rp50,000-66,000. Clean, friendly, comfortable. Across the street at no. 31 is **Hotel Hayani,** tel. 42653, with rooms running Rp22,000-31,000.

Luxury

Higher-priced hotels include the **Hotel Sewarga Indah,** Jl. Sudirman 11, tel. (0541) 42066, fax 43662, with room service, bar, coffee shop, travel service, and central a/c for Rp50,000-75,000. Downtown **Hotel Senyiur Plaza** is a first-class hotel owned by the daughter of the richest man in Kalimantan; opened in mid-1995.

Hotel Mesra on a hilltop at Jl. Pahlawan 1, tel. 32775, fax 35453, has a tennis court, golf course, a/c, restaurants, and nice location; Rp98,500-210,000. For a small fee, visitors may use a swimming pool.

OTHER PRACTICALITIES

Food

Jalan Abdul Hasan is busy at night with stalls selling *sate, martabak,* and various *soto*. Fruit can be found in stalls around **Terminal Kaltim** and along Jl. Adbul Hasan. There's an abundance of fish and seafood in Samarinda; a specialty is *udang galah* (giant river shrimp). The best Kalimantan-style river fish is found at **Restoran Haur Gading,** Rp5000 for an average meal. More expensive restaurants include the **Sari Bundo,** Jl. Batur; **Lezat Baru,** Jl. Mulawarman 34, featuring Chinese food; and **Lamin Indah,** Jl. Bayangkara 57. Expensive hotels such as Mesra also offer Western food.

Eat excellent Indonesian food at **Restaurant Gumarang** on Jl. Jen. Sudirman, with branches on Jl. Sulawesi and Jl. Veteran. Just around the corner is a great *soto ayam* (Rp1400) place, **Depot Pusaka Indah.**

Shopping

Samarinda's largest collection of Dayak art shops is on Jl. Martidinata, about three km west of town. Plenty of schlock in the Citra Niaga Shopping Complex, but the complex has won important awards for its architectural integrity and unique methods of owner financing; read the plaque that explains the history. Sellers of gold and gemstones are found in the market along Jl. Batur (try Toko Intan Jaya); several shops selling Dayak handicrafts are also here.

Sebarang, just across the Mahakam, is known for its finely woven *sarung*; buy beautiful pieces for Rp35,000-85,000 and watch the weavers work. Bugis women use a simple loom called the *gedokan*; *sutera* (silk) thread is used for *sarung samarinda,* woven in many designs and colors and made to last 100 years. Many shops sell these fabrics, but there are also many imitation *sarung* selling for the same price.

Pasar Pagi is Samarinda's biggest market; other markets include **Pasar Sungai Dama** over the bridge south of town, and **Pasar Segiri** in the north.

Services And Information

Visit the East Kalimantan **tourist office,** off Jl. Kesuma Bangsa; not much printed information but an enthusiastic crew. Ask for Dr. Rosihan Anwar.

The **post office** is on the corner of Jl. Awang-long and Jl. Gajah Mada. Samarinda's telephone code is 0541. *Imigrasi* is at Jl. A. Yamin, near RRI. Change money at **Bank Expor Impor Indonesia** or **Bank Negara Indonesia** Mon.-Thurs. 0800-1230, until 1130 on Friday and Saturday. Take plenty of *rupiah* if heading upriver.

Travel Agents And Tour Operators

PT Duta Miramar, Jl. Jen. Sudirman 20, tel. (0541) 43385, fax 35291, sells Garuda, Bouraq, and Merpati tickets, and offers tours up the Mahakam River. This agency is also the sole outlet for Pelita and Deraya Air.

Organized tours can be arranged at **Angkasa Travel,** tel. 38805, fax 433114, at Jl. Hasan 59, or through **Agus Wisata Travel,** tel. 32080, at Jl. Arga Mulia. Upriver tours cost Rp210,000-315,000 per day. Also, ask for Jailani at the Hotel Rahayu; he's extremely knowledgeable and a fluent English speaker, and can arrange river trips.

TRANSPORTATION

Getting There

Bouraq flies to Samarinda from Balikpapan, Banjarmasin, and Ujung Pandang. At the airport desk, hire a taxi into town (Rp5000) or walk five minutes down Jl. Pipit to Jl. Serindit and hop a minibus (Rp400).

By road from Balikpapan to Samarinda is 2.5 hours (Rp3000) by bus. This bus crosses the bridge, turns left, and drops you at the Samarinda bus terminal, four km west of city center. Minibuses into town cost Rp500; look for the Dayak art shops on your left.

Pelni sails to Samarinda from Surabaya in East Java, or Pare Pare, Palu, Pantoloan, or Donggala in Sulawesi.

Getting Around

Minibus taxis (Rp200) cruise major streets but not on fixed routes. To get around Samarinda, stop one and give your destination/street name to see if it's going there, but make it clear you don't want to charter. The main minibus taxi terminal is at the mosque; another terminal is at Pasar Kaltim. Or hire a sedan taxi from in front of Hotel Sewarga Indah, Rp4000 per hour.

Getting Away

Timindung Airport, on the north side of town, is used only by small aircraft. For long-distance flights, you must fly to Balikpapan on Bouraq and transfer to larger planes. **Pelita Air** flies from Samarinda to Datah Dawai on the Mahakam River every Friday (Rp44,000) and to Long Ampung in Apo Kayan on Wednesday and Saturday (Rp44,000). Buy tickets at **PT Duta Miramar,** Jl. Jen. Sudirman 20, tel. (0541) 43385, fax 35291.

The only alternatives to Pelita are **Deraya Air** and **Mission Aviation Fellowship (MAF),** missionary airlines that accept passengers on a space-available basis. Arrange trips directly with the pilot, who lives in a brown residence (Jl. Rubiu Rahaya II) on a hill near the main campus of the Mulawarman University in northern Samarinda. Call 43628 or write MAF, Box 82, Samarinda.

MAF flies to the following Mahakam River tributaries: Miau Baru (Wahau River), 185 km; Long Segar (Kedang Kepala River), 145 km; Long Lees (Kelinjau River), 161 km; Sentosa (Kelinjau River), 161 km; Makar Baru (Kelinjau River), 169 km. MAF also flies to the Apo Kayan villages of Mahak Baru, 300 km; Long Sule, 300 km; Long Nawang, 360 km; Data Dian, 360 km; Sungai Barang, 340 km; and Long Ampung, 355 km.

The taxiboat from Samarinda to Tenggarong takes two to three hours, and is more enjoyable than taking the road. Ordinary boats depart from a pier just beyond the bridge; board the green minibus from Jl. Gajah Mada to Pelabuhan Kapal Tanah Hulu (Rp500).

Destinations and distances for river buses up the Mahakam from Samarinda: Tenggarong, 44 km; Muara Kaman, 133 km; Kota Bangun, 161 km; Muara Muntai, 201 km; Muara Pahu, 269 km; Muara Angalong, 313 km; Muara Bengkai, 323 km; Melak, 325 km; Long Iram, 404 km.

For long-distance ships from Samarinda, check Pelni and other shipping offices in the port area. Ships depart for Tanjungredeb (Rp15,000, 48 hours); from there boats sail farther up to Tarakan and Tawau. For Pare

MAJOR DAYAK GROUPS OF EAST KALIMANTAN

Kenyah

Their homeland is the remote Apo Kayan of the upper Kayan River. Many have migrated during this century, some founding villages to the south on the Boh, Tabang, Kelinjau, and Kedang Kepala—all tributaries of the Mahakam. Kenyah have also migrated north to Sarawak in East Malaysia and east to the lower Kayan. Almost 100% is Protestant. In the upper Kayan and Boh rivers nearly all live in longhouses. Known for their handicrafts. Intermarriage is common among the Kenyah and Kayan.

Kayan

The Kayan homeland is the Apo Kayan, but most have now moved down onto the lower Kayan and its tributaries. Outwardly, the Kayan are similar to the Kenyah and sometimes both live together in the same village, but their language and customs are different. Like the Kenyah, the Kayan possess a hierarchical social order of aristocrats and commoners.

Bahau

The mostly Catholic Bahau live in the upper Mahakam in Long Iram, Long Bagun, Long Pahangai, and Long Apari. Not to be confused with the Bahau tributary of the Kayan River.

Modang

An offshoot of the Kenyah-Kayan complex, the Modang have moved from the heartland to the upper Mahakam basin in the Long Iram, Long Bagun, and Long Pahangai areas, as well as the upper parts of the Kelinjau and Kedang Kepala valleys. Most are Catholic.

Tanjung

Found near the middle Mahakam inland in the Melak and Barong Tongkok areas. Tanjung are a mixture of Catholics, Protestants, and animists.

Benuaq

The Benuaq live near the middle Mahakam in Muara Pahu, Damai, Muara Lawa, and Tanjung Isui. Most are Catholic. They weave *ikat* dresses and vests in a snake-scale pattern.

Bentian

The Catholic Bentians live in the Bentian Besar area on the upper Kedang River.

Penihing

The Long Apari area and Long Bagun are the domains of the Penihing.

Murut

Murut occupy the Bulungan District, including the Long Bawan and Malinau areas. Nearly 100% Protestant, they've largely abandoned their old ways; only a few longhouses remain.

Penan

Scattered in small groups throughout the interior, the Penan are nomadic hunter-gatherers who use *sumpit* (blowpipes), spears, and dogs in pursuit of wild pigs and other game. Most have not learned to grow rice. Penan build only simple shelters; villages move frequently. Some have settled and taken up rice growing, longhouse construction, even the languages of neighboring tribes. In the Apo Kayan, settlements are found at Long Ikang, Long Pipa, Long Sule, and Long Top. Other Penan live in the Bulungan and Berau districts.

Pare, inquire at **PT Harapanku Mekar,** Jl. Abdullah Marisi 7 (across from the Mesjid Raya), tel. 22689.

The new road from Samarinda to Tenggarong runs across the bridge and then along the south bank of the Mahakam; midway between Samarinda and Loa Kulu it branches off south to Balikpapan. Quickest way to Tenggarong is the minibus for Rp2000 (one hour). You can also charter a minibus; Rp6000-8000 (up to four people). The last minibuses go back to Balikpapan around 1900; after that they'll want Rp15,000 for charter.

TENGGARONG

Capital of the Kutai Regency and site of the former Kutai Kingdom, 39 km up the Mahakam from Samarinda. Though the new road has banished much of the town's charm, the people here are still friendly and there's no officialdom to contend with. Visit the **tourist office,** Jl. Diponegoro 2, for information and advice on traveling in the Mahakam River basin. A souvenir shop below sells Dayak Kenyah crafts. Near the Sporting and Cultural Complex is an

unusual mosque built during the reign of Haji Aji Pangeran Sosro Negoro (1926-35). Inside you'll find what is surely the only Indonesian public library housed in a minaret. **Doctor Achmad Thantawi,** Jl. Cut Nyak Dihn, practices acupuncture and is open Mon.-Sat. 1800-2000.

History
The Kutai Kingdom has its roots in the old Hindu kingdom of Martapura (Mulawarman), founded upriver at Muara Kaman around A.D. 400. In the 14th century a Muslim kingdom, Kartanegara, was founded downstream nearer the coast at Pamarangan. The two kingdoms waged war until the Muslims won; Kartanegara was then plagued by Philippine pirates. In 1782 the sultanate moved to a safer spot upstream, the site of present-day Tenggarong. The Chinese, impressed with the kingdom, which once included the Samarinda and Balikpapan areas as well as part of the Dayak territory, called it Ku-Tai ("Big Kingdom"). The original sultan's palace was reached by a long flight of steps from the river. The Buginese people gave it the name Tenggarong ("Palace Steps"). Aji Sultan Muhammad Parikesit, the 18th and final sultan, lost power when the Indonesian government abolished his kingdom in 1960. He donated his palace to the people as a museum, and the government presented him with a new house in exchange. The sultan died in 1982.

Mulawarman Museum Complex
This imposing white palace is the town's top attraction. An earlier wooden palace was torn down and this one built in its place in 1936. Designed by a Dutch architect, the large, solid structure was built in classical 1930s futurist style—what a Dutch man considered suitable for an Indonesian sultan.

All the gifts Dayak tribes presented to the sultan in recognition of his sovereignty are on display here. China's long contact with the Kutai and Dayak people can be seen in the ceramic collection, which includes Ming china. The bedroom is fantastic: the bridal bed decorated with elaborate beadwork, chairs made from deer antlers. See the startling representation of a *lembu suana,* a mythological animal with an elephant's trunk, tusks, and cow's legs, which originated in Burma in the 1800s. Museum labeling is hit-or-miss, but many items are described in English. Good luck understanding the "English-speaking" guide.

Accommodations
Penginapan Zaranah (Rp3500-6000 d) and **Penginapan Anda I** (Rp4000-8000) are right over the water and very conveniently located.

The **Anda II** is in two parts, a front building with Rp4000-8000 rooms, and larger, more expensive rooms in the rear for Rp11,000 s or d. This clean and friendly family-style hotel on stilts juts out on a pier. Or try quiet **Payung Asri,** Jl. A. Yani, tel. 61289, for Rp12,000-20,000; faces a garden. Both afternoon and evening meals cost Rp6000, extra bed Rp4000. Owner Jimmy Darongke can advise about river travel.

Best in town is the **Hotel Timbau Indah,** tel. 61367, fax 61369, at Jl. Mukhsin 15; a/c rooms cost Rp42,000-95,000.

Food
Cafeteria 17 on the boat landing is not really a cafeteria but offers some of the fanciest eating in town: Indonesian, Chinese, and Western dishes, plus ice drinks. For Padang food try **Padang,** Jl. Jen. Sudirman. **Tepian Pandan,** behind the Karya Indah Art Shop, offers *sate rusa* (venison *sate*) and very good *sate ayam* and curries. At night foodstalls are set up around Pasar Pagi. Wild *durian* are sold in Pasar Pagi. During the *durian* season, try *tempuyak,* a dish made of preserved *durian.* Or eat *gangan terong,* cassava soup with sour eggplant, hot chilies, and fish paste.

Shopping
Pasar Pagi is Tenggarong's main market. Dayak crafts are available here, but a better selection is at **Karya Indah Art Shop**: baskets, old stone necklaces, masks, *mandau,* and woodcarvings. A souvenir shop below the tourist office also sells Dayak Kenyah crafts (mostly new). Crafts can be purchased more cheaply in the villages, but you won't see the variety available in Tenggarong.

Events
Every year during the last week in September Tenggarong celebrates the anniversary of its founding. This cultural festival at the Taman Puskora (Cultural and Sports Center) includes traditional sports, rattan-lashing and blowpipe competitions, and a motorcycle race from Loa Janan to Tenggarong. Don't miss performances of traditional dances, such as the *belian* and *timbak,* with dancers chanting and accompanied by gongs; the male and female *nguwai,* with drums and gongs; the *ngibau,* a boy and girl wearing hornbill feathers dancing to *sampe'* accompaniment. You may even see the mass *gantar* dance, homage to the rice-planting time. This party can last as long as five days.

Transportation
Tenggarong is so small you can walk everywhere. At the *dermaga,* negotiate rides with one of the many *becak* (Rp2000 per hour) drivers or motorcyclists. Minibuses for Samarinda (Rp2000) and Balikpapan (Rp3750) stop at the *dermaga,* but most leave from Terminal Tepian Pandan, the last ones heading back to Samarinda Sebarang around 2000 or earlier. The travel agency **PT Mahakam Kutai Permai,** Jl. Diponegoro (right opposite Terminal Tepian Pandan), sells Merpati tickets.

THE MAHAKAM RIVER

This giant muddy river is the highway to the interior. Oceangoing ships travel as far as Samarinda, 60 km upstream from its mouth, to load huge logs floated down to the port. The lower half of the river valley is populated by Muslim Malay groups, including the native Kutai. Dayak tribes which originally moved upriver to avoid Islam have, since WW II, begun to move back into downstream river towns to avail themselves of education, jobs, and opportunity.

Don't expect to see longhouses lining the banks as you chug up the Mahakam; Western-style dwellings are steadily replacing them. Neither will your journey take you through impenetrable tropical forests—much of the jungle is secondary growth or has been clearcut by Weyerhauser. To see Dayak life, head up the river's tributaries, walk inland, or travel far upriver (*ulo*) to the Apo Kayan/Krayan regions. You'll see the unusual freshwater dolphin; crocodiles live in swamps and small tributaries of the lower Mahakam but not in the river itself.

Geographical Divisions
The Mahakam divides itself into three geographical sections. The **lower Mahakam** stretches from Samarinda to Muara Pahu just

beyond Lake Jembang, an easy tour for visitors short on time.

The **middle Mahakam** includes a series of villages between Melak and Long Iram, plus Data Bilang and Long Bagun—just before the treacherous rapids which often end all river traffic. Less touristy but still accustomed to foreign visitors.

The **upper Mahakam** from Batu Kelau to Long Apari at the headwaters is an isolated region generally reached by plane at the Datah Dawai airfield at Long Lunuk. The upper Mahakam and Apo Kayan district are the best places in East Kalimantan to see relatively undisturbed Dayak culture.

River Travel

The Mahakam up to Long Bagun is navigable year-round. It's best to travel up the smaller tributaries during the rainy season; but if they're too shallow, paddle canoes are the only option. When the water is high, you may have to portage your canoe. In a hard rain, you might have to wait two to three days for the waters to recede; about all you can do is try to stay dry and sleep. Water levels in the upper reaches of the Mahakam can change dramatically in a short time, so don't camp by riverbanks.

Though it now attracts only about 1,000 tourists per year, tourism in the region is growing. Most visitors see only the lower and middle Mahakam, seldom venturing north of Long Bagun. The key to doing the whole river cheaply is to take regular boats (not charters) all the way to Long Bagun; they run year-round. Venturing beyond Long Bagun takes luck, patience, or deep pockets.

Plenty of water is available, but you should bring along packaged vittles, as food in the Mahakam region is expensive and unimpressive. Also bring insect repellent, malaria pills, extra batteries, suntan lotion, toilet paper, flashlight, long pants and shirts, extra film, and waterproof plastic bags to keep everything dry. Supplies are readily available in the lower Mahakam, but prices skyrocket on the middle and upper stretches of the river. Useful gifts for your hosts include sugar, *kretek,* pens, salt, batteries, and liquor.

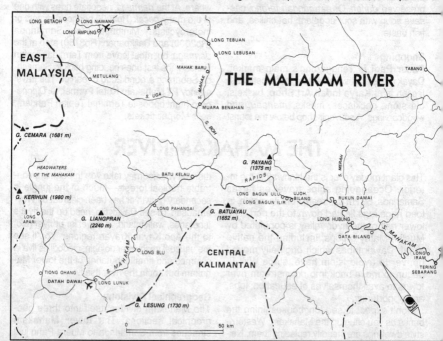

Transportation

Samarinda is the usual starting point for trips up the Mahakam. Taxi boats provide frequent, leisurely, 24-hour service at low cost. Except in the more remote regions, paddle canoes are used only for transport over short distances.

All boats from Samarinda stop at Tenggarong for a police check. Ordinary riverboats run year-round up to Long Iram, but are limited by a tough series of rapids just beyond Long Bagun. Several drownings occur here each year, and expensive charters may be necessary to reach the upper Mahakam towns of Long Pahangi, Long Lunuk, and Long Apari. For this reason, most travelers who intend to explore the upper Mahakam or trek to West Kalimantan usually take Pelita Air's twice weekly flight to Long Lunuk.

To reach Long Iram, about halfway up the Mahakam, takes two days. Long Bagun is three days farther. Beyond Long Bagun, rivercraft are infrequent and can be very expensive. Upriver from Long Bagun is a major fork where the Boh River comes in from the east. Longboats and *ketingting* travel up the Boh to the Benahan River. A two-day walk gets you to Mahak Baru in the Apo Kayan.

LOWER MAHAKAM

The best maps of the lower Mahakam are those from TAD, the big German development program headquartered in Kota Bagun; even the smaller walking paths are included. The lower river no longer has any jungle; all the land is cleared. The first longhouse up the Mahakam is at Tanjung Isui. Longhouses are also found at Tanjung Disur, past Muara Muntai. Tering is the first completely ethnic Dayak village you come to. A church here has an American pastor and a *losmen*. Look for orangutans about 10 km away in the Binulung Daerah area, Kecamatan Muara Kaman; ask the *kepala desa* where they are.

Losmen, homestays, and longhouses are located in almost every village and town along the

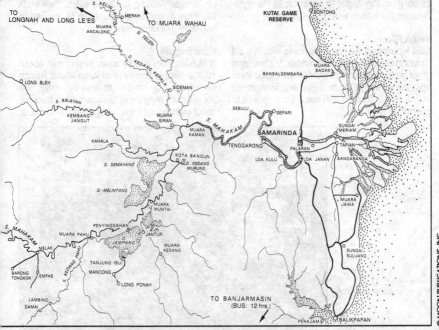

Mahakam. Standard charge is about Rp5000 per night; this often includes simple meals of rice, vegetables, and river fish. Bring extra food or endure an extremely monotonous diet.

Muara Kaman

Formerly the site of the Hindu Mulawarman Kingdom, Muara Kaman is now a Muslim town. You can still see a few ruins of the old kingdom: entrenchments, stone rice mortars, pig head monuments. By boat to Muara Kaman is five to six hours from Tenggarong, or two hours downstream from Kota Bangun. Get off here to take boats up the Kedang Kepala River to Gua Kombeng and Dayak villages.

Kedang Kepala River

Muara Ancalong is a Muslim Kutai and Kenyah Dayak town up the Kedang Kepala River from Muara Kaman. Taxiboats take 11 hours from Muara Kaman. If the water is high, river taxis can carry you as far as Muara Wahau; otherwise, travel by *longbot* or *ketingting*. MAF sometimes flies to airstrips at Makar Baru (downstream from Long Puh), Sentosa, and Long Le'es. Kenyah villages lie upstream to the northwest on the tributary Sungai Kelinjau.

Telen River

Gua Kombeng is a mountain cave with five old Hindu statues. Images of Brahma, Vishnu, and other gods were brought here to safeguard them from the spread of Islam in Borneo. Stalagmites are closing in fast, so visit soon. Be prepared to spend the night.

There are two ways to reach the cave: walk east eight hours from Jakluay, downstream from Muara Wahau; or, starting from Slahbing, a lumber camp one-half hour upstream from Muara Wahau, take a company vehicle east, then walk for a half hour. There's a longhouse in Muara Kenyak, a 30-minute walk from Muara Marah, downstream from Muara Wahau. There are other Kenyah villages between Muara Ancalong and Muara Wahau. MAF airstrips are located between these towns at Merah and Long Segar; Miau Baru, north of Muara Wahau, also has an MAF strip.

Belayan River

You can reach Tabang, a Kenyah village on Mahakam tributary Sungai Belayan, in two days by *longbot* if water levels are high enough. In shallow water, *ketinting* take three to five days and cost Rp35,000 per day chartered. Tabang also has an MAF airstrip across the river. Guides are essential for the trails through mountain jungles to the Apo Kayan, since the trek involves river travel and rugged hiking. From Tabang, walk two days around the rapids, paddle up Sungai Tabang for three days, then walk two days through the mountains to the Penan settlement of Long Suleh.

Kota Bagun

A Muslim town in a swampy region with about 10,000 people and several large lakes. Reach Kota Bagun by an 84-km-long dirt road, two hours from Tenggarong by motorbike or truck, or about eight hours from Tenggarong by taxi boat

along the river

MAHAKAM RIVERBOAT TRAVEL

Sample distances, times, and fares from Samarinda:

DESTINATION	DISTANCE	REGULAR BOAT	SPEEDBOAT
Kota Bangun	160 km	Rp3000; 10 hours	—
Muara Muntai	200 km	Rp4000; 14 hours	—
Tanjung Isui	240 km	Rp5000; 16 hours	Rp525,000; 5 hours
Muara Pahu	270 km	Rp6000; 18 hours	Rp525,000; 5 hours
Melak	325 km	Rp10,000; 24 hours	Rp630,000; 8 hours
Long Iram	410 km	Rp12,000; 30 hours	Rp893,000; 11 hours
Data Bilang	470 km	Rp13,000; 36 hours	Rp1.1 million; 14 hours
Long Hubung	480 km	Rp15,000; 38 hours	—
Long Bagun	525 km	Rp18,000; 40 hours	Rp1.3 million; 16 hours

(Rp3000). Stay at upscale **Sri Bangun Lodge**; Rp52,500 for a/c rooms.

Danau Kedang Murung is 30 minutes away by *ketinting*; it can be reached on foot if the water is low. From town, go upstream along the Mahakam a short distance, then turn left along a small river leading to the lake. **Danau Semayang** is on the other side of the Mahakam, one hour by *ketinting*. **Pela village** is on the shore near the outlet. There's a longhouse at Lamin Pulut on Sungai Berambi, which flows into the lake, five hours by *ketinting*. You'll find longhouses on a tributary north of Danau Melintang at Enggelam, five hours by *ketinting* from Kota Bangun.

Muara Muntai

This town—flat as a pancake and surrounded by lake country—is occupied mostly by Kutai and other Muslim people. Buildings are connected by gangplanks. To get to Muara Muntai, take a 10-hour taxi boat ride from Tenggarong, or travel three hours from Kota Bagun. For Tanjung Isui and Danau Jempang, take a taxiboat or *ketinting*; three hours (Rp3000). The boat returns from Tanjung Isui daily at 1500. An entire boat can be chartered for Rp15,000 one-way. The small motorized canoes are somewhat expensive at Rp15,000-25,000, but it's a lovely journey through thick jungle inhabited by colorful kingfishers, herons, and wild monkeys.

Stay at either **Penginapan Nitawardana** or **Sri Muntai Indah**. Both charge standard rates of about Rp5000, including a few simple meals.

Tanjung Isui

Muara Muntai is a good jumping-off point for Tanjung Isui, a beautiful Benuaq Dayak village on the south shore of the giant Danau Jempang, 184 km upstream from Tenggarong. Tanjung Isui is a popular place to view longhouses and traditional Dayak life. See *air tawar* (freshwater dolphins), birds feeding on fish, soft sunsets. There are two longhouses; the one in the center isn't very remarkable. The old longhouse is nicer—some handicrafts inside, and lots of *patong* around the courtyard. One *losmen,* but for the same price you can sleep in the old longhouse.

Tanjung Isui is the most popular Dayak village on the tourist trail. You might be able to watch a scheduled dance performance here—touristy, but great for photographers, since authentic rituals and dance are almost impossible to find in these regions.

From Tanjung Isui, reach Mancong and an unimpressive longhouse via a three-hour walk or canoe ride, or a half-hour ride in a car or motorcycle (Rp25,000 return). Four km from Mancong by chartered boat are three villages with better longhouses.

Muara Pahu

To reach Muara Pahu from Muara Muntai involves an exciting trip through some very narrow canals. You can cross to Central Kalimantan from Muara Pahu. First travel up Sungai Kedang Pahu to Lambing on semi-regular boats, then take a *ketinting* up the Lawa River to Dilang Puti. From here walk three to four days via

Swakong, Jelmusibak, Sembulan, Sambung, Randampas, and Tokuk to Payeng on the Teweh River, a tributary of the Barito. Take the Barito all the way down to Banjarmasin.

MIDDLE MAHAKAM

Animism

Animism has faded in most parts of Indonesia, but not in the Barong Tongkok area. Many villages here are predominantly animist, with longhouses occupied by traditional believers. Look for animist sites in villages and along trails: carved posts and statues, offerings of rice in small plaited baskets, rough-hewn offering tables, streamers hanging from poles, strangely shaped structures, bird carvings. Visit the *kuburan* outside the villages. Animist graves have unusual markers: painted wood boxes, carved posts, statues. Carved figures commonly show the sex of the deceased. Christian crosses are either clustered in a separate area nearby or scattered among animist gravestones. Ask around to find out if any animist ceremonies are planned. Visitors are usually welcome, and you might be able to take pictures. Ask first.

Transportation

Only a small part of Kecamatan Barong Tongkok borders the Mahakam River; taxi boats will stop at Bohok, 14 km east of Barong Tongkok town. Or get to Barong Tongkok by road from Melak, 18 km east, or from Tering Sebarang, 25 km north. A motorcyclist might ask Rp4000 to give you a lift; sometimes trucks travel these roads and cost less. Walking is cheaper still, and more enjoyable.

Melak

This picturesque Muslim riverside town is noted for its nearby orchid forest, **Kersik Luway,** where famous black orchids bloom at the end of the rainy season. Melak has six *losmen*; **Rachmat Abadi,** close to the dock, is the best place to stay. The owner, Bapak Effendi, can help with trekking details and transport needs. His prices for the latter are high, however, and you're better off with ordinary boats.

The area around Melak is still strongly animist. Stay in villages by asking the *kepala kampung,* and be sure to pay for food and accommodation. There are many easy trails to nearby villages, all commonly used by bicycles and motorbikes. A good gravel road goes to Barong Tongkok (18 km); another road south travels to the orchid reserve at Kersik Luway on the Tanjung Plateau (16 km). The road northwest to Tering Sebarang (cross the Mahakam there) is 43 km; to Long Iram, 51 km. If you get tired of walking, get a lift on a motorbike (Rp4000 from Melak-Barong Tongkok) or truck.

Barong Tongkok

An administrative center in an area of villages, rolling hills, small streams, waterfalls, and gardens—a lovely *kampung* to dwell in for a while.

Wisma Tamu Anggrek, a small house with a mattress on the floor, is maintained for visitors. **Barong Tongkok Losmen** is acceptable. Ask the local *camat* (headman) about upcoming Kaharigan rituals and nearby handicraft villages. You may stay in the villages; ask the *kepala kampung.* Camping is also a possibility, but ask first. There's usually a swimming hole or *mandi* spot near each village.

There are many hiking possibilities in Kecamatan Barong Tongkok. The terrain is flat or gently rolling; trails pass through groves of bamboo or small trees, gardens and rice fields, areas of overgrown clearings and scattered houses. *Babi hutan* (wild pig) and deer are abundant in the woods west of Barong Tongkok. Walk from Barong Tongkok to Tering on a very pleasant trail in six hours. Blacksmith sites are often found in villages, working a fire pit surrounded by hand-powered bamboo-tube blowers, a trough of water, and simple hand tools.

Eheng And Mencimai

Some of the best longhouses you'll see are in **Pepas/Eheng,** a mostly animist village noted for its *kuburan* (cemetery). Hire a motorcycle driver to get you to the big, dark longhouse in **Eheng;** see the *patong* out front, used to catch ghosts.

On the way to Eheng, be sure to stop in **Mencimai,** seven km south on the road from Barong Tongkok to Engkuni, with a small longhouse and several *patong*. Between Engkuni and Eheng is another small longhouse with some primitive totems. You can walk most of the way from Barong Tongkok to Damai; for the last portion you need to charter a *ketingting,* Rp8000.

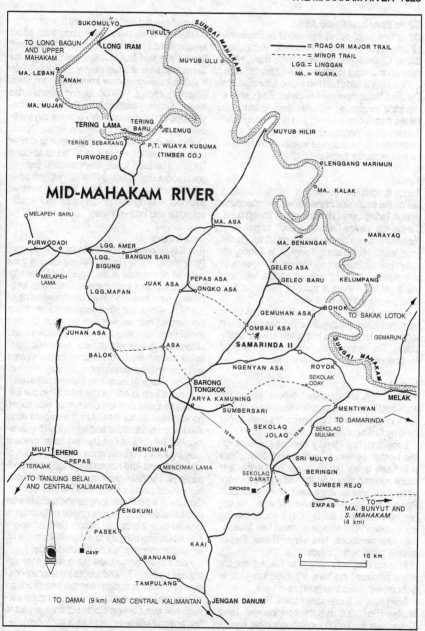

MID-MAHAKAM RIVER

Geleo Baru And Geleo Asa

Other fine longhouses are found at **Engkuni**, 12 km south of Barong Tongkok; and **Geleo Baru**, 13 km northeast. For Geleo Baru, head east on the road to Melak, then turn left after 2.5 km onto a wide trail (no sign). After nine km the road forks: bear right to Geleo Baru, where there's a longhouse with five animist families. **Geleo Asa** is one km west and features ruins of a much larger longhouse. In front of Geleo Asa's community hall is a carved wooden post used to tie up *kerbau* for sacrifice.

Tering

Tering is actually three villages. Tering Sebarang lies on the south side of the Mahakam; across the river is Tering Lama, downstream is Tering Baru. Tering has a large Catholic church, *rumah sakit* (hospital), and a timber company. A rough dirt road leads from Barong Tongkok to Tering, an easy six-hour, 25-km walk (or Rp6000 on back of a motorcycle). Don't believe people who say you'll get lost—there are only a few turns, and local people will point the way.

Tering Lama, a 1.5 hour walk from Long Iram, has a few posts (some with carvings) from long-gone longhouses but is still almost totally Dayak. The Tering Lama longhouse is only used for special occasions; worth a visit.

Long Iram

From Tering, it's an easy 1.5-hour, seven km walk past a lake and over a level terrain of gardens and jungles to Long Iram. It's easy to get here by taxi boat as well.

Long Iram is a friendly town on the equator, the border between upriver and down. You won't see many Dayak here. This is the last place you can count on for finding ice for your beer, *nasi goreng,* large *toko,* or a *kantor pos.* People arriving from downriver won't be impressed, but this is the Big City if you're coming from upriver. The village is about half Muslim, with four mosques. The native Bahau Dayak people are mostly Catholic.

Five km east is the village of Tukul; there are many lakes around here. It's three km north to Sukomulyo (the *camat's* office is here).

Long Iram is a one-street town. **Penginapan Wahyu** (Rp10,000 d) is the best *losmen.* **Jawa Timor,** near the ferry dock path, is a clean restaurant serving Javanese-style *mie, nasi goreng,* and curries—the best place to eat in town.

Boats of all varieties leave Long Iram often; keep in mind that boats run on *jam karet.* From Long Iram taxi boats head downstream for Samarinda several times weekly (Rp6000-8000). If you're traveling upriver from Long Iram, Data Bilang is six hours, Rp3000, leaving several times weekly. Ordinary boats to Long Bagun are cheap (Rp6000-8000), but take two or three days with overnight stops in Data Bilang and Rukun Damai. During the dry season, you might need to charter a longboat, which takes just 10 hours to Long Bagun. The four- to six-day roundtrip journey costs about Rp630,000-840,000; try to get other passengers to split the fare. There's another riverboat to Long Bagun, but it's on an irregular schedule and isn't very fast.

Data Bilang

Apo Kayan people recently founded this large, Protestant, 100% Dayak village, leaving their isolated homelands in the upper Mahakam for new opportunities and new lives. Traditional longhouses have been forsaken for modern single-family dwellings, but other facets of life are much the same. Older women with bunches of large metal rings dangling from their earlobes sport elaborate leg and arm tattoos. Authentic traditional dances are held in the intricately carved and painted longhouses every Sunday evening.

In this village there are no *losmen,* not even a *warung.* Sleep in one of the *toko,* or in the Elf-Aquitaine camp one km downriver: nice room, good meals, all for free. Ask the *kepala dasa* about accommodations and any upcoming ceremonies. Be sure to see the two large modern meeting halls overlooking the river; they're full of wild, curlicued Apo Kayan paintings and wood-carvings. The halls are supported by one-meter-high wood posts carved into human figures. Outside is a 30-meter-long canoe painted with traditional designs. Another piece of local art is located near the school soccer field: an angry carved dragon clinging to a massive post, with worried human figures on the other side.

Apo Kayan people are famous for their attractive baskets. Their impeccable sense of design and color is apparent in the beadwork on containers, ceremonial clothing, and baby carriers. Ask about buying crafts, but don't expect to find anyone willing to part with a baby carrier—they're family heirlooms.

Long Hubung

Located 30 minutes upriver from Data Bilang. The Catholic priest, Father Ding, promotes traditional culture and can arrange dance performances. Stay in the longhouse or check with the *kepala desa*—gifts of cigarettes, sugar, salt, batteries, and pens are appreciated.

Rukun Damai

Four hours upstream from Data Bilang, this village was established about 12 years ago by the Kenyahs from the mountains in the backland. Today it's a thriving community with two longhouses. A handsome people, they often hold dances in the longhouse on Sunday evenings. One hour by *ketingting* downstream and up a side river from Data Bilang is Matalibag, a Bahau Dayak village with a 200-year-old *lamin*. It's rarely visited, and the longhouse is in disuse. Most villagers are shy, but the headman can tell you some stories about old *patong,* the carved doors, and the skulls of former opponents.

Ujoh Bilang

Administrative center for the large Kecamatan Long Bagun, Ujoh Bilang contains a *kantor camat,* police station, small clinic, school, several small *toko,* and even streetlights. Nearly all 600 inhabitants are Catholic; only a few older people remain solidly animist.

Long Bagun

A series of three Ulu villages stretched out in a line, linked by a good trail. Uma Waj and other groups live here; total population is 400. See the 1.5-meter-tall carved animist post erected for a sick person. The large house of the *kepala adat* has carved posts, roof beams, and trim; a two-meter-long drum is suspended from the ceiling. The villages are predominantly Catholic, though some elders are still animist. Except for an odd pole, the longhouses have long since disappeared. A half-finished mosque sits sadly abandoned in an overgrown field.

Getting To The Apo Kayan

The easiest overland trip north to the Apo Kayan is from Long Bagun. A *longbot* can go up the Mahakam and Boh rivers to Muara Benahan in two days. A charter costs Rp450,000 and the boat can carry about eight passengers. You can stay free in temporary shelters used by workers who harvest rattan along the Boh River; there are no villages. Rapids make it impossible to take the Boh all the way. Instead, take a boat up the Benahan River to Muara Tanit, then walk two days to Mahak Baru. Or turn up the Uga River from the Boh and continue to Long Metulang, an Apo Kayan village. Trails lead from here to Long Ampung and Long Nawang on the Kayan River.

Between Long Bagun and Long Pahangai are about 13 rapids, seven major. Only *longbot* can make it up, taking two days (the return takes only a day). Ordinary longboats up the rapids to Long Pahangai ask about Rp63,000 per person. Charters cost Rp630,000. Long Bagun is the end of the line for most passengers, due to the rapids and sporadic, expensive boat services.

UPPER MAHAKAM

Long Pahangai

Travelers fortunate enough to reach Long Pahangai by longboat can stay in the rudimentary longhouse or contact the pastor at the Catholic mission for village homestays. You can hire canoes to explore the narrow and very quiet Pahangai River.

Long Lunuk

Because it's difficult to find river transport beyond Long Bagun, most travelers to the upper Mahakam arrive on the twice weekly Pelita Air flight from Samarinda (1.5 hours, Rp74,000). The plane lands at Datah Dawai, a small airstrip near Long Lunuk. On arrival, you should walk immediately to the river and check on boats heading upriver to Long Apari. Stay in Long Lunuk with the local schoolteacher (Rp5000), who can also arrange the six-hour longboat ride up to Long Apari. The ride costs Rp105,000-420,000, depending on the price of petrol and your bargaining skills; split the costs with other passengers.

Long Apari And Tiong Ohang

The final towns at the headwaters of the Mahakam. You can hire guides and porters in both towns for the seven-day trek to West Kalimantan for about Rp15,000-20,000 each per day. Agree on all prices and conditions in writing before you start your trek; misunderstandings are common. It's two tough days to the pass, then another five days down to the Bungan River, which flows into the Kapuas River.

THE APO KAYAN

The Apo Kayan area includes the headwaters of the Kayan River and tributaries above the great rapids (brem-brem), as well as the upper Boh River and its tributaries. On the north are the Iran Mountains, the natural and political border between East Kalimantan and Sarawak.

The Apo Kayan is divided into Kecamatan Kayan Hilir and Kecamatan Kayan Hulu. Most of the population lives in Kecamatan Kayan Hulu, the uppermost Kayan River area. Kayan people once controlled nearly the entire region but have now moved downstream. Several groups of Penan, formerly nomadic hunter-gatherers, have settled in the Apo Kayan, taking up long-house construction, rice growing, and the language of their Kenyah neighbors. People speak Kenyah or Kayan, not Indonesian.

The Apo Kayan jungles are among the most fascinating places on earth. Guides may be neccessary for longer treks since mountain ranges are irregular, some river sections are impassable, and animal trails may lead no-where. Also, the belief in spirits persists, and if you hike with local people you won't be mistaken for one.

The climate in the Apo Kayan is nearly ideal. There are pronounced wet and dry seasons. During August and September, the dry months, felled jungle is burned to make new ladang fields. Even then some rain falls. South toward Samarinda, the dry season is more pronounced, and there may be weeks with no rain at all. After a rain river travel is faster and easier, but in the jungles the leeches are friskier. The jungle of the Apo Kayan has fairly even temperatures—cool to warm during the day, and cooling off a bit at night. The jungle is perpetually humid, though, and while hiking the sweat pours off your skin. The jungle doesn't steam—you do.

Flora And Fauna

The jungle has hundreds of kinds of fruits. Some are edible and some not; local people can tell you the difference. Durian fanciers will enjoy the wild durian merah, which is bright orange inside and out. A minor hazard of hiking through the bush is the "wait a minute" vine; its hooks snag your clothing and skin. Look for insect-eating pitcher plants on rotting logs. Homesick Westerners will be happy to see familiar trees resembling oak and eucalyptus. Pine trees have the usual cones and sticky sap, but broad leaves.

Leeches, gnats, and mosquitos are plentiful. Most leeches are brown, bustling around on the ground and grabbing onto the first warm body to pass by. Another variety is green and drops down out of trees. Insect repellent applied to the tops of shoes, shoe eyelets, and other clothing openings will hold them back, but river trekking and rain will wash the repellent away. Expect at least a few leeches to get through. A firmly attached leech will come off with a drop of insect repellent, salt, or a hot match.

Termites are the hungriest and most industrious creatures in the jungle. Fallen timber doesn't last long, nor do buildings. Ants can grow as long as three cm, but rarely bite. Beetles come in an infinite variety of colors, shapes, and sizes. Butterflies are seen in a great variety of colors and patterns, often perched on stream banks, glittering in the sun.

Birds are very hard to see, though you can hear the vibrating wingbeats of the slowly cruising hornbill overhead. The best birdwatching takes place from a canoe. Some birds are quite musical, singing bits of familiar tunes.

History

One of the first Europeans to visit this region was Nieuwenhuis, a Dutchman who headed into the Apo Kayan in May 1900 with a photographer, two other Europeans, three Javanese collectors of flora and fauna, and a group of "Bahaus." Nieuwenhuis worked to settle the long-standing feud between the Kenyah and the Sarawak Ibans, who'd lost a number of heads to Apo Kayan raiding parties. To promote stability, the Dutch named the Lepo Tau leader as chief of all Apo Kayan.

The Dutch days were generally peaceful; intertribal warfare and most headhunting ceased. The Dutch built a post at Long Nawang in 1907, and established a school there in 1927. Trails to other villages were constructed. At the large rapids, which made travel to the coast difficult,

THE APO KAYAN

EAST MALAYSIA (SARAWAK)

EAST KALIMANTAN

TO BATU KELAU, LONG BANGUN, AND MAHAKAM RIVER

G. BATUBROK (1546 m)

© MOON PUBLICATIONS, INC.

0   25 km

⬭ = MAF AIRSTRIP
--- = TRAIL
L. = LONG

the Dutch carved out a portage route with warehouses at each end. Supplies for the Dutch garrison and Chinese shopkeepers at Long Nawang were transported by canoe from the coast to the lower warehouse, portaged to the upper one, then canoed to Long Nawang—a three-month trip in the days before motorboats. The Kenyah were often hired for this work; some even assisted in the exploration of New Guinea. This ended with the arrival of Japanese troops at Long Nawang during WW II. The garrison, taken by surprise, quickly surrendered; the Japanese executed 109 men, women, and children, including missionaries and British refugees from Sarawak. Missionaries returned after the war, but the Dutch never reestablished a garrison.

In 1929 George Fiske, an American with the Christian Missionary Alliance (CMA), started working at Tarakan, later moving to Tanjungselor on the lower Kayan River. By 1938 one village, Nahakramo, was over half Christian. In 1940, Fiske attempted the first flight into the Apo Kayan, making a daring landing at Data Dian in a floatplane. At first, Christianity and the *adat lama* (old religion) coexisted peacefully, with Christian and *adat lama* longhouses in the same village. But in the early 1950s villages started breaking apart. At Long Nawang, the *adat lama* people moved across the river and founded Nawang Baru. The Kenyah believe spirits cannot cross water and so lived peacefully.

Indonesian troops were stationed here from 1963 to 1965 during Sukarno's war against

Malaysia. Their presence affected many aspects of Kenyah life. Pagan beliefs were actively discouraged. With the troops came Lt. Herman, a Roman Catholic from Ambon. Holding up a Bible and a bullet, Herman went around to animist villages reminding people Indonesia is based on the five Pancasila beliefs, including the belief in God. Herman's message: adopt a "true religion," not animism, or be considered communist sympathizers. The army also removed Chinese traders and foreign missionaries from the interior, and village and regional leadership changed. The leader of all Apo Kayan, the Paran Bio, was deposed by Indonesian authorities; his replacement was elected under Indonesian military "guidance." In 1972 the first Apo Kayan airstrips were completed at Long Nawang and Data Dian, dramatically ending the area's extreme isolation.

The best recent book on the region is *Shooting the Boh* by Tracy Johnson—a very funny, harrowing, and memorable description of her ill-fated adventure in the Apo Kayan.

Economy

Kenyah life is centered on rice. Land is cleared of jungle and used for rice growing for up to three years. No irrigation is normally needed. Soil is poor; only one crop is harvested each year. Fields are commonly located an hour's walk from the village, so field houses are built for eating, sleeping, and rice storage. Planting usually begins in October, after the village chief has determined the proper date, and takes one to two weeks. Weeding takes place a month later, carried out with small hoes. The harvest, in February and March, is a happy time—the people can eat fresh rice again. Feasts, weddings, and a few animist rites follow the harvest. In the old days men celebrated with *mamat* ceremonies, venturing out to collect fresh heads.

Other crops include cassava, sugarcane, squash, corn, beans, small tomatoes, hot peppers, and green leafy vegetables. Pineapple, papaya, coconut, banana, tangerines, *durian*, and coffee are also grown. Sago palms are harvested by some Kenyah; others won't touch them. Wild *paku* ferns are harvested along riverbanks, immature wild grapes are used to spice up greens, and *petai* seedpods are collected in the jungle.

Workers also gather rattan from the forest, tie it into giant bundles, and drift it downstream.

Cane poles, nets, traps, and spears are used for fishing; spearfishing underwater or from canoes is common. Sometimes the *tuba* root is used for mass fish kills. Hunting is a favorite sport of the men; dogs are usually used in pursuit of wild pigs, deer, and small animals. Guns are the favored weapons, but both ammunition and firearms are scarce and expensive. More often the people use spears.

The People

Before the Dutch arrived, the Kenyah lived near the headwaters of the Kayan River, north across the divide and near the headwaters of the Rejang and Baram rivers. Since 1900, thousands have migrated, many moving to Sarawak along the Balui and upper Baram rivers. In all of East Kalimantan there are about 30,000 Kenyah, with 8,000 in Sarawak.

Superficially, the Kenyah are similar to their neighbors, the Kayan, but customs and languages are very different. Nomadic hunter-gatherers who originally learned rice cultivation in the Iwan headwaters, the Kenyah experienced a post-agriculture population increase that led to overcropping, resulting in migrations during the past 8-10 generations across to Sarawak and downstream on the Iwan to the Kayan. Large areas of *alang-alang* grass, indicating overcropping, remain in the Iwan River area to this day. Once populous, the area is now nearly deserted.

All Kenyah groups can trace their migration back to the Iwan River headwaters. Names of the 40 Kenyah subgroups are based on original longhouse locations; the Lepo Tau rose to prominence as the oldest and most culturally pure. The Lepo Tau village, Long Nawang, is the main administrative center for the Apo Kayan.

Traditional Customs

In the old days men wore a simple loincloth of cotton or bark cloth, while women wore rectangular cotton or bark cloth. Both men and women pierced their ears to hold heavy rings of silver or brass. Men also punched a one-cm hole in their upper ears. The men's earlobes were lengthened only a few cm, but women stretched theirs to their chests. Body hair was considered distasteful: beards, mustaches, and even eyebrows and eyelashes were plucked.

The Kenyah had three social classes: *panyin lamin* (slaves, war captives, and their offspring), *panyin* (commoners), and *paran* (aristocrats). *Metik* (tattooing) was common for both men and women, as decoration and as a sign of social status. Usually women did the tattooing, which could take months or even years to complete. Men had small tattoos on their arms, chest, legs, back, and sometimes the front of the neck. Associated with the taking of heads, tattooing on males all but disappeared with the end of head-hunting. Women of the *paran* class had exclusive designs tattooed on their arms and legs. The geometric designs and animal motifs were so finely detailed that from a distance they looked like solid colors. Women who endured the intense, prolonged pain of tattooing were considered strong and respected. The government has banned tattooing for health reasons, and the art is now found only on older women.

Marriage is mostly a Christian ceremony now, complete with pastor, best man, and maid of honor. The bride usually wears traditional clothing and decorations, the man a suit and tie. Traditionally, the bride and groom aren't allowed to become "lonely" on their wedding night, but are kept company by several of the bride's friends and siblings. It may be days or weeks before a husband can talk his wife into sending home the guests.

A burial house (*liang*) was once used for all Kenyah, but is now reserved only for chiefs and others of high social standing. The *liang* is a small, roofed structure one meter off the ground, supported by posts and decorated with paintings and ornate carvings. Ordinary graves may have a roof and carved, painted decorations. Gravesites are not maintained; grass and weeds grow quickly and the carvings slowly disintegrate.

Arts And Crafts

Villages often include a roofed shelter with anvil, air blowers, and a water trough where blacksmiths work. Chainsaw blades are a popular source of steel and are cut and shaped into knife blades. A Kenyah *mandau* (bushknife) makes a good souvenir.

Large baskets are used both for carrying rice from the fields and storing it. Smaller, more flexible shoulder bags are for personal use, and feature attractive designs of black on natural cane. The dye is added after weaving; only the outward, rough side of the cane strips absorbs the dye. A baby carrier (*ba'*) is prepared for

every child in Kenyah society. The symbols on the *ba'* show family status and have traditional religious significance. This carrier also protects the child's spirit, as loss of the soul is believed to be the prime reason for infant mortality.

Trekking

Long pants are best for hiking; some plants and vines are mildly poisonous and tough ferns will cut your legs. Boots should be sturdy, lightweight, and nonskid; old or untreated leather shoes may fall apart in the humid jungle. Bring foot powder, antiseptic for scratches and bites, and skin cream to relieve rashes from poison plants. Iodine purification tablets are a good idea; the Kenyah boil their water but it tastes like last night's fish stew. A tent is useful for extended trips: choose one that's lightweight, well ventilated, and insect-proof. Leeches and gnats will undoubtedly be looking for you. Don't forget antimalarial pills and insect repellent.

Large villages have small general stores (*toko*) which carry just a few shelves of the basics: soap, salt, men's underwear, sugar, pots and pans, thread. The only foods are usually biscuits, noodles, and tinned sardines. Prices are three times those on the coast, so bring in all your necessities.

APO KAYAN VILLAGES AND HIKES

All villages in the Apo Kayan make fascinating visits. For exploring the jungle and viewing *ladang* cultivation, day hikes are possible from any of them.

Long Ampung

Most visitors begin their Apo Kayan experience at Long Ampung, a large village of Ma'Jalan Kenyah upstream on the Kayan from Long Nawang. There's a small clinic; across the river is an airstrip.

Long Ampung can be reached by *ketingting* or canoe from Long Nawang, or walk it in five hours. Take the trail upstream along the bank. Soon after fording shallow Tepayan River, take the trail's right fork. Continue through forest and *ladang* fields to the Anye River, later crossing the suspension bridge over the Kayan to Long Ampung. A guide is recommended but not essential on the Long Nawang-Long Sungai Barang trails, which lead to Long Ampung.

Long Nawang

A six-hour hike on a jeep trail from Long Ampung, Long Nawang is home of the Lepo Tau Kenyah, the oldest aristocracy in the Apo Kayan. Today Long Nawang is the government administrative center, with an airstrip, clinic, police station, military post, *kantor camat,* school, two tiny *toko,* and several longhouses. This is one of the largest and richest *kampung* in the Apo Kayan, with a large number of *paran bui* (noblemen) thought to be direct descendants of Borneo's first people.

See the Kenyah paintings on rice barns. Three-dimensional wood sculptures decorate graves near the airstrip and on the trail to Nawang Baru. Outside the village are some *sawah,* a rarity in the Apo Kayan. Watch for women working a sugarcane crusher: they rock a giant log back and forth over stalks of sugarcane. Longhouses are located in the south part of the village, government offices in the north. Across from the village are single-family homes used by civil servants and the military.

Nawang Baru

A large village in a pretty setting along the Nawang River. *Adat lama* people split off from Long Nawang in the 1950s and formed this village to escape the onrushing Christians. Today, however, you'll see churches in the hills above town. From Long Nawang, it's only a half-hour walk to reach here. Cross the suspension bridge, then take either of the two trails to the left. The first follows the riverbanks, going upstream on the Kayan and Nawang rivers. The other goes straight up the hill and offers good views. After the trails rejoin there's a *kuburan* (gravesite) on the right with decorative paintings and woodcarvings.

Long Uro

A Lepo Tau village 2.5 hours by foot from Long Ampung. The small trail is easy to follow through the forest and *ladang.* Take the trail going upstream from Long Ampung, but don't cross the suspension bridge. Another suspension bridge is at Long Uro.

Lidung Payau is a Lepo Tau village a half hour down a good trail upstream from Long Uro. Ask about the rare stone Dayak image.

Long Sungai Barang

Sungai Barang means "River Things." The *kepala kampung*'s section of the longhouse has a higher roof, bigger veranda, and massive support timbers, with Kenyah artwork. From Lidung Payau, the trail to Long Sungai Barang climbs into the hills, passing many mountain streams. There are two trails; the higher one (left fork coming from Lidung Payau) is better. *Ladang* fields are near the villages, with forest in between.

Past Long Sungai Barang

The jungle forests in the area have attracted graduate students working on forestry and agricultural projects, and there may be an *orang putih* here. A suspension bridge across the Kayan connects the two parts of the village. The airstrip is a half-hour walk away.

From Sungai Barang, two trails lead south across the divide to Mahak Baru and Long Lebusan. Both routes involve hiking and river travel. The preferred way is to hike to the pass, then down to the Dumu Iran River in one day, then canoe to the Boh and on to Long Lissi (abandoned) or Long Lebusan, 1.5 days farther away. Mahak Baru is then 2.5-3 hours by trail. The other route from Sungai Barang is a 2.5-day hike over mountains, then one-half day by canoe down the Mahak River to Mahak Baru. Guides and canoes are needed for either journey. These trips are unbelievable: jungles of giant trees, clear streams full of fish, monkeys climbing overhead, birds flying across the river. The real Borneo.

Metulang

By continuing past Nawang Baru up the Nawang and following a trail over the mountain pass three to four days south you can reach this Uma Bakung Kenyah village. From Metulang it's possible to head downstream by boat to the Uga and Boh rivers, then journey on to the Mahakam.

Long Betaoh

A Badang Kenyah village on the Pengian River northwest of Long Nawang, four hours by canoe. The Malaysian border is just one day's travel farther up the Pengian. From the border north to the coast is a hazardous one-week boat trip via the Iran, Sahe, Aput, and Rajang rivers.

Long Payau

A small village—just one longhouse—of Uma Bakung Kenyah on the Tepayan River. A breathtaking two- to three-hour walk takes you up the Kayan River, then into the hills above the Tepayan River valley. The trail is fairly easy to follow without a guide; take the main trail southeast upriver about one hour to a small river, the Tepayan. Cross and follow the trail up the river valley, keeping left at the fork. The trail climbs high above the river, descends to cross it, then winds along to the village.

Sai Anai And Vicinity

Located northeast of Long Payau in Kecamatan Kayan Hilir, five-plus hours through rolling forested hills and rice fields. Some leeches; a guide is definitely needed. A route to Malaysia begins here: walk to Marong (northwest) in a half day, canoe up the Marong for about another half day, then walk one day to Long Musam in Sarawak. **Long Metun** is an Uma Bakung Kenyah village downstream (north) from Sai Anai, about one km before it meets the Kayan. If the water is high, this short trip can be made by canoe; or walk a very easy trail offering good views in two hours. No guide needed.

GETTING THERE

By Air

The easiest way to reach the area is to fly; it takes just an hour or two. **Pelita Air** flies twice weekly from Samarinda to a small airstrip near Long Ampung; roundtrip passage is about Rp210,000. At least a week is necessary to ex-plore the region, but a few days can suffice for visitors with limited time.

Check with the MAF pilot in Samarinda about alternative flights on a space-available basis. Keep a loose schedule: planes break down, pilots get sick or go on vacation, bad weather or emergencies can mean delays. Still, waiting beats slogging through leech-infested jungles and running dangerous river rapids for two months . . . for most people.

Overland

This is the hard way. There are at least five overland trips to the Apo Kayan—all involve extensive boat travel as well as jungle hiking, and all require a guide. There are several routes across from Sarawak; check the new border-crossing regulations. The easiest Indonesian route is from Long Bagun: a two-day trip by longboat or *ketingting* to Muara Benahan on the Boh River, then a two-day hike to Mahak Baru. Or head up the Uga River to the northwest from the Boh to Metulang, then north several days to Long Nawang by foot and canoe.

Guides

Necessary for any long hike. No topographic maps are available; maps in this book are about the best you'll find for hiking, and they're not good enough for navigation. The jungle offers many trails, some leading only to favorite pig wallows. There are no trail signs, no tourist offices, no park rangers. Local people are usually happy to guide you for Rp10,500-21,000 per day.

BERAU REGENCY

The capital of Berau Regency is Tanjungredeb, a secondary harbor since WW II. With a population of 32,000 this waterfront town of two-story buildings is 59 km from the mouth of the Berau River. Eight boats monthly arrive here from Samarinda or Balikpapan. The only road (10 km long) is between Tanjungredeb and Teluk Bayur. The autonomous kingdom of Berau, dating back to the 14th century, was divided in 1883, with the Berau River a natural boundary between new capitals established at Sambaliung and Gunung Tabur. In 1960 both kingdoms were abolished by Indonesian parliamentary decree. The two palaces still have small private museums. Take a canoe (Rp300) from Tanjungredeb across the river to see Istana Sambaliung. Stay at **Losmen Sempurna** or **Losmen Sederhana.** Food is expensive.

From Tanjungredeb, it's Rp9500 by fast, custom-built *longbot* to Tarakan, 55 km and nine hours north. Boats leave at least every other day. Up the unfrequented Kelai and Segan rivers, find the Dayak, Basap, Kenyah Tumbit, and Lebu tribes. Upriver by boat is two hours and 40 liters of fuel—and that's just the first stage of the trip.

The Land

The regency's upper Bahau area is one of few remaining areas of undisturbed lowland forest in Kalimantan. These forests are of immense ecological importance. The area is quite beautiful, with crystal waters—very rare, now that modern mechanical logging has penetrated so far inland. The ridges between the three rivers are very steep and well forested, having been affected little by the shifting cultivation of local tribes. The forest here is rich in edible fruit trees, tropical oaks, and ironwoods. Local paths cross the watershed into the upper tributaries of the Tubu and upper Bahau at Long Berini. The Tubu has many more rapids than the gentle Malinau, but the river is generally navigable downstream from Long Tete. Above Long Tua, the Bahau is not navigable; local trails continue to Long Berang and on to Sarawak.

The Krayan

The Krayan is tucked into the north corner of East Kalimantan, bordering Sabah and Sarawak. This region is very difficult to reach overland from Tarakan but an easy hour by plane. The first Dutch missionaries arrived here in 1927. Now the Krayan's Dayak are quite modern, dropping most old customs. Nearly all are members of the Kemah Injil Gereja Masehi Protestant church. Bahasa Indonesian is spoken by all but the oldest villagers; in some families the native Krayan language is secondary. The government encourages people to stay in their homeland by establishing clinics, schools, social programs, and regular Merpati flights to Long Bawan.

Krayan people, also known as Muruts, live on both sides of the border. There is much foot traffic across the border between the villages. Tourists, however, are not allowed to cross without advance permission from both countries. This is one of the easiest overland crossings between the countries: on foot it takes only half a day from Long Bawan, the main town of the Krayan, to Bakalalan in Sarawak. People walk there and back in the same day. Indonesians often work in Malaysia and bring goods and money back home.

Village Life

Old men and women with traditional tattoos and elongated earlobes are still here, but the heavy earrings are now gone. Longhouses still exist in some villages. Kurid has longhouses with up to five families; they're like tunnels with no interior walls. Five kitchens are lined up on one side; the other side is for working, eating, and sleeping. There is no outside veranda as in other Dayak villages. To see traditional longhouse life, dances, and crafts, it's best to visit the Apo Kayan, Penjungan, or upper Mahakam areas.

Recently church prohibitions against alcohol and tobacco have eased and many men are hooked on cigarettes and spend large sums of money on beer. Sodium cyclamate is being pushed by Indonesian chemical companies, sometimes under the brand name Tiga Tebu ("Three Sugar Canes"). Local people think this is a new, improved sugar, and leave their own natural sugarcane in the fields to consume doses of this highly potent synthetic, banned in the U.S. as a carcinogen.

Tall poles with firewood stacked around them are a common sight in Krayan villages. If the wood is stacked to the top and a banner waves from a pole, a wedding or other ceremony is about to take place.

LONG BAWAN

This main town of Kecamatan Krayan is the easiest place to reach in interior East Kalimantan; several flights in and out are available every week. Long Bawan is also the starting point of a wide array of hiking trips, from very easy to most difficult. No *losmen* here, but people are friendly and will help you find a place to stay. Be sure to leave a contribution.

Guinness Stout drinkers will be pleased to find their favorite brew here, as well as many other Western comforts, though no ice or refrigeration. The town's *toko* are reasonably well stocked with basic groceries. Rice is the most important food for the Krayan people; it's often served wrapped in leaves, *nasi bungkus*. Join in soccer, volleyball, or rattan ball games, or view videos and movies in the evenings, Rp400.

There are two Merpati flights a week (Rp60,000) and several MAF flights. The latter also flies frequently from Long Bawan to Malinau to the Apo Kayan. MAF is more expensive than Merpati flying into the Krayan, but cheaper flying out. There's a radio and MAF operator in Long Bawan, so it's possible to know when planes are expected. The Krayan area can be reached overland from the Apo Kayan by first traveling north to the headwaters of the Bahau, then walking across the divide to Pa' Ibang, Pa' Upan, and Long Bawan; allow two weeks. Overland travel to and from Tarakan is almost unknown these days, but is possible for the determined.

Hikes From Long Bawan

Many walks are possible from Long Bawan, ranging from very easy to extremely difficult. Rarely used trails lead south to the Long Pujungan area and east toward Malinau. The mountain trails can be difficult to follow; a guide is a wise investment. A trip north to Nukit Harun takes three days; wind and rain often force climbers to turn back. Between Long Paid and Long Rian it's possible to canoe seven hours upstream, five hours downstream.

Don't expect dense tropical jungle on these hikes. Soil is poor, and where land has been cleared, only shrubs and scrub trees have regrown. Up in the mountains are 30-meter-tall trees, flowers, waterfalls, spiraling vines, sparkling streams, and butterflies. And leeches. Get oriented by climbing Buduk Yuvai Samarin, a 45-minute walk east of Long Bawan; from the top you can see surrounding villages, *padi,* and mountains. Good forests on trails from Long Bawan to Pa' Padi, Pa' Padi to Kurid, Kurid to Lembudud.

Head southeast on the trail to Tenang Baru. After crossing the small stream Pa' Lutut, note the graves on the right covered by sheet metal roofs. Pass through a *kerbau* gate, then angle off to the left on a small track. Cross a small streambed, follow the Pa' Lutut a short way, then take the trail straight up the slope on the right—360 degree views. A small waterfall, Luyan, is one-half hour south. A small cave, Iluk, is west then north, a one-hour walk. You'll need someone to show you the way.

Easiest of the several trails to East Malaysia is the four-hour walk west on a good trail to Bakalalan in Sarawak. A much harder trip is north to Long Pesiat in Sabah; three days. From Lembudud, it's an easy four-hour walk south of Long Bawan. Trails go to Bakalalan and Bario in Sarawak; both villages have airstrips with small planes flying to the coast two or three times a week. Overland to the Malaysian or Brunei coast by canoe and trail takes about a week.

Kampung Baru

True to its name ("New Village"), this large settlement was hacked out of the jungle in 1982. The cleared land has a rough, naked look; few trees or grasses grow. Long rows of little whitewashed houses line the large open square. A four-year Bible school trains church workers for service over a large area of East Kalimantan. When walking north to Kampung Baru from Long Bawan, look for a well-trod trail to the left. If you reach the airstrip, you've gone too far.

The Kurid Loop

Loop walks of several days to more than a week are possible within the Krayan. You can see a good cross-section of Krayan villages and terrain in three to four easy days. Hike along nearly flat trails from Long Bawan past the airstrip and through Kuala Belawit, Brian Baru, Pa' Pirit, and Tanjung Karya to Lembudud; four hours. From Lembudud walk east straight up the mountain slope to the top (good views), then wind down through a forest and along a mountain stream to Kurid in another three to four hours. From Kurid (see the longhouses here) walk west through rice fields, then northeast over a mountain to Pa' Padi; two hours. From Pa' Padi head north into the mountain forests. Descend to rice fields at Pa' Matung a bit southwest of Terang Baru. Follow the river and turn left on the wide trail to Long Bawan, five to six hours from Pa' Padi.

Malinau

A town southeast of Kurid, 50 km as the hornbill flies. There are three routes; hardly anyone uses them anymore, but the trip is still possible in stages. All trails involve long rugged walks over narrow, rough trails, then a river trip by canoe or *ketingting.* Boats are infrequent; waits of up to a week are commonplace. Though the government encourages them to settle in permanent villages, some Penan remain upstream from Malinau, living in temporary huts and hunting with blowpipes.

The following hiking times are for local people, who walk *fast* over rough trails. The northern route requires eight days moving downstream, 11 upstream. Hike four hours to Long Umung, then six hours to Wayagung. It's another 1.5 days to Long Sepayang, then a one-day hike to Pa' Kelipal. Hike one day to Bang Niau, another to Long Nerang. Malinau is another two days by boat. The middle route takes seven days downstream, nine upstream. Hike 1.5 days to Long Rian, then continue on to Binuang, Lep Pupung, Long Semamu, and Long Seberang (one day each). From Long Seberang, Malinau is another two days by boat. The southern route consumes 7.5 days downstream, nine upstream. Hike to Pa' Padi, then on to Long Rungan, Pa' Sebangar, Bang Lan, and Long Sibiling (one day each). From there it's 1.5 days by boat to Malinau.

Long Punjungan

A Kenyah area on the Punjungan River where it joins the Bahau, about two weeks south via Lembudud, Pa' Upan, Pa' Ibang, and the Bahau River. There are airstrips along the river at Apau Ping and Long Aran, one half-hour by *ketingting* and one hour by canoe. Other airstrips are located at Long Bena and Apau Ping. A longboat departs Long Punjungan about once weekly to

Long Bia on the Kayan; two days. A boat from Long Bia to Tanjungselor takes six to eight hours, and continues to the coastal island of Tarakan.

People of the Long Punjungan area live in large longhouses and are nearly all Christian. A series of tombs here are built like miniature houses, supported by dwarfed pilings. The roofs are adorned with *lukir*, carved and painted wooden dragons. If you're lucky you'll see some Krayan dancing; there are dance platforms in many villages. See masked Krayan men and women in rice-sowing ceremonies.

Long Bia And Beyond

Beyond Long Bia is the notorious Giram Raya ("Grand Rapids") on the Kayan River, a 275-meter-long, 55-meter-wide gorge studded with rocky whirlpools and treacherous chunks of granite. A boat must head straight up through the central channel or capsize on the foaming cliffs. Passengers are often told to take the path along the banks.

TARAKAN AND VICINITY

Tarakan is the trading and supply town for northeast Kalimantan, located on an island off the coast near the border of Sabah. A short-lived though major battle took place here between the Japanese and Australians during WW II, and a number of Japanese bunkers and blockhouses still stand. The taking of Tarakan Island in May 1945 cost the Australian 26th Brigade 225 men. The objective of the assault, the island's airfield, was so heavily pockmarked by American bombing it was later of no use to the Allies.

Though Tarakan has an oil field, production is declining. The low hills overlooking the port are capped by oil tanks. Sixty percent of the population is Chinese; the rest are Bugis, Banjar, Javanese, and Dayaks. No special sights here but the markets offer a wealth of produce and seafood. The best is Pasar Lingkas; the fish section is on a pier out over the water. Find other markets near the traffic circle and on a side street in Kampung Bugis.

Accommodations

Kampung Bugis has the best selection of cheap and medium hotels, all on Jl. Jen. Sudirman. Good choices include the **Barito Hotel**, tel. (0551)

21212, with ordinary rooms from Rp10,000 and a/c rooms from Rp25,000, and the **Wisata Hotel**, tel. 21245, in the same price range.

Near Pasar Lingkas on Jl. Yos Sudarso are **Penginapan Taufig, Penginapan Alam Indah,** and top-of-the-line **Hotel Tarakan Plaza,** tel. 21870, with a/c, private bath, bar, and restaurant, Rp73,500-116,000. These nice people do your laundry in one day; good meals, great service—a wonderful place.

Food And Entertainment

Cahaya on Jl. Jen. Sudirman features delicious Chinese and seafood dishes for Rp3000-5000. On Jl. Jen. Sudirman near the traffic circle are several restaurants specializing in grilled fish for Rp2500-3500. Many small, inexpensive *warung* are scattered around town; try those at the intersection of Jl. Jen. Sudirman and Jl. Sudarso. Citrus fruits and apples are imported and cost over Rp3000 per kilogram. The **Nirwana Dance Hall Coffee House** has music, dancing, drinks, and food in the evenings. Three movie theaters, south of the traffic circle, offer the usual sex and violence. Two billiard halls lie across from Mesjid Kampung Bugis.

Services

Four banks, which will change U.S., Singapore, and Malaysian cash as well as U.S. traveler's checks, are scattered along Jl. Yos Sudarso; rates vary, but try **Bank Rakyat Indonesia** and **Bank Dagang Negara**. A **moneychanger** is located 200 meters south of Pasar Lingkas and open seven days a week, but is good only for cash—rates for traveler's checks are terrible.

Getting There And Around

Merpati, Bouraq, Sempati, and Pelita fly to Tarakan from Balikpapan, Samarinda, and Tanjungredeb in Berau Regency. The airport is only 2.5 km north of town. Taxis cost Rp6000, or walk a half-km to the main road and take a minibus taxi into the city (10 minutes) for Rp400, or just walk all the way in.

Tarakan is a cluster of *kampung* grown into a town; it has no real center. Minibus taxis run frequently on the two main roads, charging Rp200-500. Small boats are available for charter at the pier. Pelni's office, tel. (0551) 202, is in the port.

Getting Away

Pelita Air flies small planes south to Berau and on to Samarinda every day. Most travelers visit Tarakan simply to continue north to Tawau in Malaysia. Bouraq and Malaysian Air (MAS) fly several times weekly to Tawau, but as of this writing, visitors with a two-month Indonesian entry stamp cannot legally exit the country via this route. Before heading to Kalimantan, be sure to obtain the necessary exit permit from the Indonesian immigration office.

There's a MAF flight to the Long Bawan area almost daily, less frequently to the Punjungan

and Apo Kayan strips. The pilot's residence is at Jl. Sudirman, tel. 21181, a brown house on the hill between the airport and the town. MAF flies to Malinau (Rp42,000), Long Bawan (Rp84,000), Long Nawang in Apo Kayan (Rp147,000), and Data Dian (Rp147,000). Missionaries have priority and there's no guarantee of return flights from the interior.

Another way to reach Tawau in Malaysia is the 0900 longboat from the Tarakan harbor to the island of Nunukan, right on the border. The boat ride takes about 12 hours and costs Rp15,000. You can overnight in Nunukan and straighten out your paperwork with the Indonesian immigration office. Speedboats to Tawau depart Nunukan daily (four hours, Rp25,000). A final option is the daily speedboat from Tarakan to Tawau (six hours, Rp40,000), but make sure your paperwork is in proper order.

NUNUKAN

A timber town on a small island, Nunukan is the last town north before you reach the busy Chinese commercial city of Tawau. You'll never see so many moneychangers in your life.

Dayak tribes can be reached in the area around Pembelingan, 64 km up the Sebuku River. See the timber company PT Jamaker and get written permission to stay at the East Malaysia Camp or the Mukah Sawmill Camp, both in Indonesian territory. The office is in Tanjungselor in the "old town," one km from Nunukan. You might even get a free lift to the camp.

Hotel Sebar Menanti is a reasonable place to stay, or share a bed at **Losmen Arena. Losmen Nunukan** asks Rp6000 for acceptable rooms.

SOUTH KALIMANTAN

Straddling the equator, this southern province of predominantly flat swampland covers 37,600 square kilometers. Temperatures range 18-36° C in the lowlands; it's cooler in the mountains to the east. Mangrove forests and orchids are abundant and proboscis monkeys live on the Barito River.

Modern roads link some cities and villages, but rivers are still the primary transportation network. The Trans-Kalimantan Highway extends from Batakan to Sangkulirang in East Kalimantan. When completed, it will stretch all the way to Tarakan. The plywood industry is the number one money-earner in South Kalimantan, followed by rattan products. Another economic staple is diamond mining.

With its distinctive and colorful Banjarese culture, South Kalimantan deserves more tourists than it gets. Banjarmasin, the capital, is famous for its floating houses and markets. The Banjarese are friendly and the bureaucrats non-threatening. Yet tourism development is really an uphill battle in this province. Most visitors spend a few days exploring Banjarmasin—the "Venice" of Kalimantan—and then trek for a week or so in the nearby Losako Dayak region.

History

The Javanese Majapahit Kingdom took control of this region during the second half of the 14th century; today you can still see Java's influence in men's clothing styles, in some aspects of the region's *wayang kulit* forms, and in Banjarese dance-dramas. The sultan of Banjarmasin ruled the area until the mid-1800s; he traded the right to choose his successor to the Dutch in exchange for their protection. When the Dutch colonialists tried to enthrone the sultan's unpopular son in 1857, a Banjarese uprising challenged their choice. The rebellion was crushed, but with heavy Dutch losses, and it took more than 50 years to completely pacify the province. Once strictly the domain of the Orang Banjar, South Kalimantan's mangrove-sheltered coastline was unsafe due to piracy until the 1950s.

BANJARMASIN AND VICINITY

More than 450 years old, the city is renowned for its floating houses and network of criss-crossing rivers, streams, and canals. Banjarmasin is below sea level, and the water level rises and falls with the tides. Situated on the banks of the Martapura River, 22 km upriver from the sea, Banjarmasin is a convenient base for both Central and East Kalimantan.

The largest city in Kalimantan, Banjarmasin was once populated by pirates; today it's populated by Islamic conservatives, home to over 350,000 people. The Banjarese practice a decidedly more orthodox form of Islam than other Muslim groups on Indonesia's western islands. Thousands make the pilgrimage to Mecca each year; during Ramadan, piercing sirens announce the beginning and end of each day's fast. Modernity is fast approaching, and with it traffic jams, a thriving precious stones market, craft shops, and fine ethnic restaurants. If you want to hang out for a time in South Kalimantan, your cheapest bets are Martapura, Barabai, and Palangkaraya, though these cities lack the charms and idiosyncrasies of Banjarmasin, the "Venice of the East."

History

Banjarmasin has a long history of intrigue and murder. The Dutch came first for the pepper; in 1603 they began to trade with the sultan of Banjarmasin. Four years later, a Dutch East Indies vessel was attacked and its crew massacred, provoking a punitive assault that included razing the entire town. The sultan fled to Martapura. The Dutch were granted a pepper monopoly in 1635, but disgruntled growers murdered all 64 residents of the Dutch trading post; another 40 Dutch were slaughtered at

Kotawaringin. After further reprisals, the Dutch and the sultan drew up another monopoly agreement in 1658. When the English undermined the world market in 1669, the Dutch withdrew. They returned in 1733, building settlements at Banjarmasin and Fort Tatas at Tabanio, where they stayed until the 1800s. Many Portuguese merchants also set up shop here following the discovery of the southern route to Maluku.

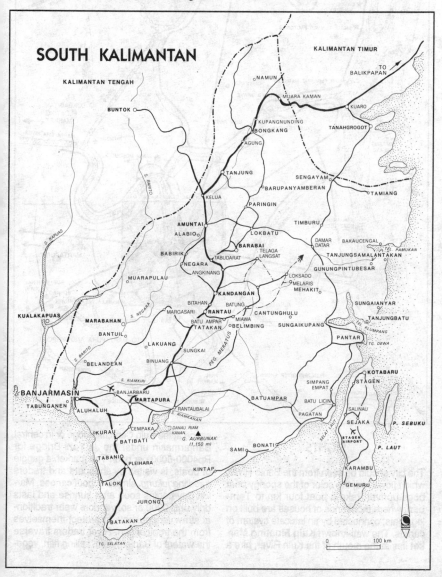

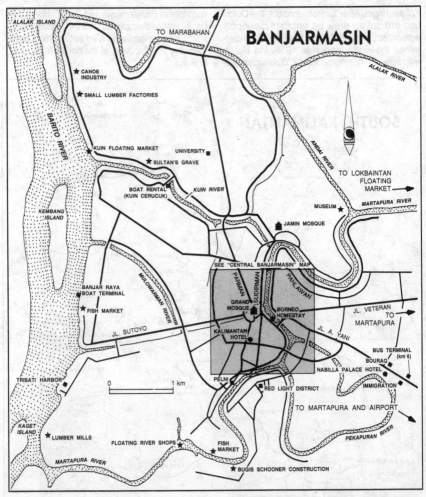

BANJARMASIN

ALALAK ISLAND
TO MARABAHAN
ALALAK RIVER
BARITO RIVER
★ CANOE INDUSTRY
★ SMALL LUMBER FACTORIES
ANDAI RIVER
★ KUIN FLOATING MARKET
UNIVERSITY ■
★ SULTAN'S GRAVE
TO LOKBAINTAN FLOATING MARKET
BOAT RENTAL (KUIN CERUCUK)
KUIN RIVER
KEMBANG ISLAND
MARTAPURA RIVER
MUSEUM ★
■ JAMIN MOSQUE
SEE "CENTRAL BANJARMASIN" MAP
BANJAR RAYA BOAT TERMINAL
MULOWARMAN RIVER
GRAND MOSQUE
BORNEO HOMESTAY
★ FISH MARKET
PAHLAWAN
PANGERAN
SUDIRMAN
JL. VETERAN TO MARTAPURA
JL. SUTOYO
KALIMANTAN HOTEL
JL. A. YANI
BUS TERMINAL (km 6)
BOURAQ
TRISATI HARBOR
0   1 km
PELNI
NABILLA PALACE HOTEL
IMMIGRATION
RED LIGHT DISTRICT
TO MARTAPURA AND AIRPORT
KAGET ISLAND
★ LUMBER MILLS
FLOATING RIVER SHOPS ★
★ FISH MARKET
PEKAPURAN RIVER
MARTAPURA RIVER
★ BUGIS SCHOONER CONSTRUCTION

© MOON PUBLICATIONS, INC.

SIGHTS

The city should be seen from the Barito River, which flows red, the color of the spongy peat bogs upriver; take a boat four km to **Tamban,** where thousands of houses are built on log floats, connected by an intricate system of canals. The well-known **Kuin Floating Market** lies at the mouth of the Kuin River; hire a canoe at the Kuin Cerucuk Bridge or in central Banjarmasin under the Jl. Yani Bridge for Rp4000-6000 per hour. The market, a gaggle of boats, is visited by shoppers and traders paddling *jukung,* simple dugout canoes. Market day begins soon after sunrise and lasts only until 0900 or so; vendors wear traditional straw *tanggui* hats to protect themselves from the tropical sun. River traders traverse the waters of Banjarmasin, selling fish, vegetables, fruits, and household necessities door-to-door.

A complete boat tour would include a visit to Kuin Floating Market at daybreak, then perhaps the small lumber factories and canoe builders near Alalak Island; then head downriver to Kembang and Kaget islands, passing the fish market, Trisakti Harbor, and the modern lumber mills at the mouth of the Martapura River. Ask the boatman to head up the Martapura, past the riverine shops to the Bugis schooners near the bend in the river. You can also visit the schooners on foot from central Banjarmasin.

Near the center of the city on Jl. Lambung Mangkurat, across from the Islamic University, is the massive **Mesjid Raya Sabilal Muhtadin** ("The Road Unto God's Blessings"), built on the site of the old Dutch fort. The main minaret is 45 meters high; the four smaller ones stand up to 21 meters. This modern-art mosque has a copper-colored dome shaped like an alien space vehicle.

If you're here on Independence Day, be sure to take in the canoe (*prahu dayung*) races. The **Ramadan Cake Fair** starts 30 days before Hari Raya, when super-sweet cakes are sold in the afternoons. These cakes, eaten to break the fast (*buka puasa*) each day, are prepared by rich people doing good deeds (*bikin amal*) and sold for Rp1000-2000. March is the traditional month for marriage; arrive then to see a Banjar wedding.

Visitors with extra time might also visit the **Jamin Mosque** and the **Banjarmasin Museum**, situated in a traditional *banjar* house near the Andai River.

Alalak, Kembang And Kaget Islands

On **Pulau Alalak**, see an old-style native Banjar timbermill. The delta island of **Pulau Kembang** features half-tame monkeys inclined to snatch peanuts from your pocket without warning. Be careful with your glasses. The Orang Banjar believe a person surrounded by monkeys will recieve good luck. An old Chinese temple is also located on the island. Charter a *klotok* (Rp10,000 roundtrip) from Banjarmasin's pier.

Pulau Kaget is just 12 km south of Banjarmasin by chartered riverboat (Rp40,000 roundtrip). The south end of this tiny Barito River island preserve is an ideal environment for the

proboscis monkey

leaf-eating proboscis monkey, found only on Borneo. These oddly attractive red and silver-gray primates have unusually long, vulnerable noses. You sometimes have to wait two days to see them, and then only with binoculars from your chartered *klotok* 100 meters away.

PRACTICALITIES

Accommodations

Most budget travelers head straight for the **Borneo Homestay**, Jl. Pos 87, tel. (0511) 66545, owned and operated by Johansyah and Nurlina Yasin, a pair of young, helpful attorneys. Both are experts in travel and will help with ticketing, local tours, and trekking in the Loksado district. Rooms are extremely basic, but there's a pleasant veranda overlooking the river. Also acceptable is the nearby **Diamond Homestay** (Rp10,000), operated by the managers of Adi Angkasa Travel on Jl. Hasanuddin 27. Not as well situated as the Borneo Homestay but conveniently located near the boat docks. The remainder of the *losmen* in Banjarmasin are either seedy dives, brothels, or refuse to accept Western visitors.

Hotel Beauty, Jl. Haryono M.T. 176, tel. 4493, is one of the best moderately priced hotels. Rooms feature fans, shared bathrooms, and *warung* close by. The very best bet for mid-level travelers is probably the centrally located and reasonably clean **Hotel Sabrina,** at Jl. Bank Rakyat 21, tel. 54442, where rooms cost Rp18,000-25,000 with fan and Rp32,000-38,000

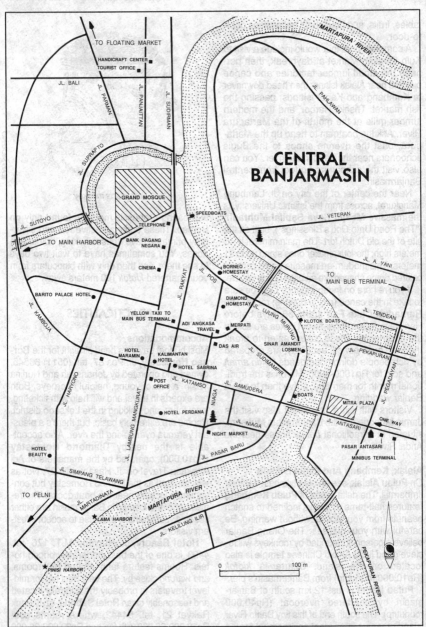

CENTRAL
BANJARMASIN

TO FLOATING MARKET

HANDICRAFT CENTER
TOURIST OFFICE

JL. BALI

JL. PARMAN

JL. PANJAITAN

JL. SUDIRMAN

JL. PAHLAWAN

MARTAPURA RIVER

JL. SUPRAPTO

GRAND MOSQUE

TELEPHONE

SPEEDBOATS

JL. VETERAN

JL. SUTOYO

TO MAIN HARBOR

BANK DAGANG
NEGARA

CINEMA

BORNEO
HOMESTAY

JL. A. YANI

JL. POS

JL. RAKYAT

TO
MAIN BUS TERMINAL

JL. TENDEAN

BARITO PALACE HOTEL

DIAMOND
HOMESTAY

JL. LUJUNG MURUNG

KLOTOK BOATS

JL. KAMBOJA

YELLOW TAXI TO
MAIN BUS TERMINAL

ADI ANGKASA
TRAVEL

MERPATI

SINAR AMANDIT
LOSMEN

JL. PEKAPURAN

HOTEL
MARAMIN

KALIMANTAN
HOTEL

DAS AIR

JL. SUDIMAMPIR

JL. HARYONO

HOTEL SABRINA

POST
OFFICE

JL. KATAMSO

JL. SAMUDERA

BOATS

MITRA PLAZA

JL. PEGADAYAN

JL. LAMBUNG MANGKURAT

NIAGA

HOTEL PERDANA

JL. NIAGA

JL. ANTASARI

ONE WAY

NIGHT MARKET

JL. PASAR BARU

PASAR ANTASARI

HOTEL
BEAUTY

JL. SIMPANG TELAWANG

MINIBUS TERMINAL

TO PELNI

JL. MARTADINATA

MARTAPURA RIVER

LAMA HARBOR

JL. KELILING ILIR

PINISI HARBOR

PEKAPURAN RIVER

0   100 m

cutting cane

a/c. Another choice in this price range is the old but friendly **Hotel Perdana,** tel. 68029.

The luxurious **Barito Palace Hotel,** Jl. Haryono 16, tel. 67300, fax 52240, offers an attractive pool, several restaurants, and rooms for Rp158,000-210,000. Best in town is the towering **Kalimantan Hotel,** Jl. Lambung Mangkurat, tel. 66818, fax 67345. Facilities include pool, fitness center, adjacent shopping center, and 180 classy rooms for Rp158,000-315,000. A surprisingly luxurious hotel in such a funky little town. The **Maramin Hotel,** Jl. Lambung Mangkurat 32, near Jl. Samudera intersection, tel. 68944, fax 53350, poses as a five-star hotel, but should be avoided; truly awful rooms for Rp65,000-100,000.

Food

The food is similar to Java's, with noodle soups, *sate,* and such. Local specialties such as spicy *soto banjar* are best tried at the night markets or street *warung*—great chicken in a tasty sauce is available at the *warung* outside the Hotel Racmat. There are many fascinating stalls along Jl. Pasar Baru and Jl. Niaga, south off Jl. Samudera, as well as at **Kelenteng Market** in the fabric bazaar.

Also find some good stalls at the market across the "new" bridge—the chicken is so fresh you might see the fowl meet its maker. Lots of cheap *warung* lie along Jl. Veteran. On the same street are the **Simpang Tiga** and **International** restaurants, with decent food fairly cheap. *Apam* is sold in front of Bioskop Cempaka each night. In fact, the whole street from

the Perdana Hotel to the cinema turns into a *pasar malam.*

Restaurants include the **Kobana Padang Restaurant,** Jl. Hasanuddin 19 (another one on Jl. Samudera), with reasonable *nasi padang* and quick service. On Jl. Haryono is **Prambanan,** with a Javanese menu offering Rp750-3500 meals including *udang bakar* and *ayam panggang*; big color TV and nice atmosphere. The **Blue Ocean,** Jl. Brig. Jen Katamso 44, has delicious Chinese food for Rp3500-5000, or go to the **Phoenix,** Jl. A. Yani, near the state hospital. The **Shinta,** Jl. Lambung Mangkurat, is the city's elite Chinese restaurant, with dishes running as high as Rp8000. European and Indonesian food is also available at the **Miramin Hotel** and the pricey **Banjar Permai Inn.**

For Banjarese food such as *sop banjar* (Rp1000) and *sayur asem,* go to **Simpang Ampat,** Jl. Simpang Ampat. But the real culinary delights of Banjarmasin are the twin restaurants **Depot Makan Kaganangan** and **Cendrawasih,** both on Jl. Samudera and both serving wonderful Banjarese specialties in a genuine atmosphere. Try *ikan saluangan* (small crispy fish), *es dewet* (a drink made from rice and coconut milk), baked river fish, huge *udang* with a musky sauce, fresh greens, and a delicate vegetable soup—pig out for under Rp10,000. These two restaurants are the best in town.

Shopping

This is the place to shop for diamonds and other precious and semiprecious gems: amethyst, agates, sapphires, light and dark emeralds. Diamonds that sell for US$5000 in Chicago can be purchased here for three million *rupiah* per karat; light-colored emeralds go for Rp300,000. Be prepared to bargain, and know your gems. Beware of pickpockets on this street. On Gang Malabar, a lane off Jl. Sudimampir, is a row of shops selling gems and Dayak stone beads (*manik-manik kalung*) from Rp5000-500,000. It seems every Banjarese of note wears a chunky semiprecious stone set in a gold-plated ring. Reliable gold shops are the **Toko Mas Sriwijaya** and **Toko Mas Gunung Kawi,** both on Jl. Sudimampir.

On Jl. Sudimampir II are several craft shops. **Ida** offers fine gems as well as some exquisite Ming-period pieces, *mandau,* swords, blowpipes, Dayak rattan mats and purses from Pandalaman, old Delft porcelain and silver coins, and ornamental Banjar brassware. Fascinating stuff, including miniature Dayak warriors crewing ships carved from rubber-like wood. Better prices in Pasar Baru or Martapura's market. Try **Toko Batik,** Jl. Sudimampir 108, for all manner of *sarung*—Bugis, Javanese, even Saudi Arabian. There's a bird market on Jl. Ujung Murung.

Services And Information

Visit the **South Kalimantan Tourist Office,** Dinas Pariwisata Kalimantan Selatan, Jl. Panjaitan 31, tel. (0511) 2982. You can call or send a telex to most major cities in Indonesia and overseas at the **telephone office,** Jl. Sudirman 92. Banjamasin's telephone code is 0511.

Check out the **university** and its library at Jl. Lambung Mangkurat 3. Banks, such as **Bank Expor Impor Indonesia** on Jl. Lambung Mangkurat, only accept U.S. traveler's checks or cash. If banks are closed, or if you have non-U.S. traveler's checks, **Adi Angkasa Travel** will help travelers change almost any kind of foreign currency. Best exchange rates are at **Bank Dagang Negara.** If you get sick, **Suaka Insan,** Jl. Pembanguan, is a hospital under Philippine management, and the doctors speak English well.

Of the 12 travel agents in Banjarmasin, only six do business with tourists. About half of that business goes through the very efficient **Adi Angkasa Travel,** Jl. Hasanuddin HM27, tel. 53131, fax 66200, open daily 0700-2200. Friendly staff will change traveler's checks, book hotels, sell airline tickets, supply chartered vehicles. All credit cards accepted.

Another excellent source of information on tours and trekking near Loksado is **Borneo Homestay,** tel 62511, fax 66545, at Jl. Pos 87. Best prices for both budget backpackers and group tours from Europe and the Americas.

TRANSPORTATION

Getting There

Merpati and Bouraq schedule two flights daily to Banjarmasin from Surabaya (Rp158,000), Balikpapan (Rp105,000), Jakarta (Rp252,000), and many other cities in Indonesia.

Syamsudin Noor Airport is situated 26 km from Banjarmasin, about halfway to Martapura. From the terminal, walk to the Banjarmasin-Martapura highway and flag down a *bemo* to the main bus terminal, six km east of city center. Yellow minibuses continue into town. Taxis from the airport taxi counter are a non-negotiable Rp12,000.

Passenger ships from Surabaya arrive twice weekly (14 hours, Rp30,000 economy); ships also arrive from numerous other ports. Or take the 12-hour bus ride from Panajam near Balikpapan for Rp15,000-25,000.

Getting Around

Though the local dialect is Banjarese, Bahasa Indonesia is spoken everywhere. Lots of *becak,* but the drivers ask high prices and are difficult to bargain with. Take a yellow minicab (*taxi kuning*) anywhere around town for a flat rate of Rp300. All local transport starts and ends at Terminal Antasari, the central city terminal.

Hire a *klotok* rivercraft to see the city from the water; boatmen charge about Rp6000 per hour. Inquire near the junction of Jl. Lambung Mangkurat and Jl. Pasar Baru.

Getting Away

The fastest way to get away is on one of many flights from Banjarmasin's Syamsudin Airport. Merpati, Bouraq, and Sempati fly all the standard routes. Smaller towns are served by small DAS aircraft. Ask your airline if it offers pick-up service to the airport. If you're traveling light, take a motorbike, or a *taxi kuning* to the terminal across the river, then a minibus in the direction of Martapura; get off at the airport road, then walk to the terminal. Taxis cost Rp12,000.

The delta canal connections near Banjarmasin also make it possible to travel inland by *taxi air* (riverboat). *Taxi air* leave when full for Marabahan and take about two hours, Rp2000. Chartered speedboats are faster but cost Rp50,000. From Trisakti Harbor, 1.5 km away, large ships cruise up the South Barito River as far as Muara Teweh. Also, regular ships to Surabaya cost Rp30,000-75,000; buy your tickets across from the harbormaster's office. **Pelni,** Jl. Martadinata 192, offers trips every two weeks to Surabaya and Semarang.

If leaving by land, you'll find there are many roads in the area in varying states of repair. The mountainous road via Rantau, Kandangan, Barabai, Amuntai, and Tanjung is in good condition. The long-distance terminal is Terminal Km 6, where buses leave frequently for Martapura, Banjarbaru, and other interior towns. The cheapest way to Balikpapan is by bus, Rp15,000-25,000. You can also go by road from Banjarmasin to Buntok in Central Kalimantan, but it's easier to take a riverboat or fly first to either Palangkaraya or Pangkalanbun.

VICINITY OF BANJARMASIN

Banjarbaru
About one-half hour southeast of Banjarmasin by minibus (Rp1000) from Terminal Km 6 on the road from Banjarmasin to Martapura, this new administrative center features numerous modern Indonesian buildings. Banjarbaru is usually cooler and less humid than Banjarmasin. Here you'll see lots of rattan processing, with raw fiber strips expertly peeled, split, twisted, and woven into fine carpets and mats.

Museum Lambung Mangkurat is housed in a building that follows the unique Banjarese architectural style. The present-day collection is paltry, dating only from 1967. The Japanese looted the museum during WW II, and the Dutch got most of what was left. The rest went to the National Museum in Jakarta. The museum covers much of South Kalimantan's history and culture, even Hindu antiquities dating back to the 14th century. The museum's library of coconut shells (Banjar was without paper for centuries) is fascinating; the hollowed-out interiors contain Malay inscriptions. Adjacent is a gallery featuring portraits and landscapes by the Banjar

painter Gusti Sholihin, who died on Bali in 1970; his artwork is reminiscent of the French Fauvist tradition. If you can't make it during regular hours, Tues.-Fri. 0830-1400, someone may be willing to give you an impromptu tour. Be sure to tip. On Sundays and holidays, the museum sometimes features traditional dancing, music, and games.

Cempaka
Extensive diamond-mining takes place along the shores of Riam Kanan, a reservoir near Cempaka, 10 km from Banjarbaru or 43 km from Banjarmasin. Get a public *bemo* to Cempaka from Martapura's bus station or charter one for Rp5000; there are also minibuses from Banjarmasin's Terminal Km 6.

Using traditional tools, miners try their luck in the diamond pits. Men dig holes up to 10 meters deep in the sour-smelling clay under a roof of loose thatch. They dig out gravel, sand, and heavy clay soil, handing it up from the pit in small baskets. Young girls carry the heavy load to sluicing areas along canals or the lakeshore, where women wash the raw sludge through sluice boxes, looking for the elusive *galuh* ("the lady"—raw diamonds).

Martapura
Behind the Martapura bus terminal is an enormous market on Tuesday and Friday, crowded with colorfully adorned Banjar women and children, with good prices on almost everything. High-quality diamonds are also sold in Martapura. South Kalimantan province is one of the major diamond-producing areas of Indonesia. Take the minibus from Terminal Km 6 outside Banjarmasin to Martapura (Rp1000, 45 minutes), or travel the short distance north from Banjarbaru or Cempaka.

Near Martapura's bus station and just across the playing field is a diamond-polishing factory—a good place to buy gems. This is a traditional workshop where over 150 people, using 200-year-old methods, work in each shed. Giant wheels, belts, and sluices are used to polish the cut stones—a process requiring two to three days for small gems, 30 days for large ones.

Don't buy diamonds unless you know about diamonds. Note that the mines are closed on Friday, and for the 10 days before Idul Fitri. Local people believe diamonds from Cempaka and

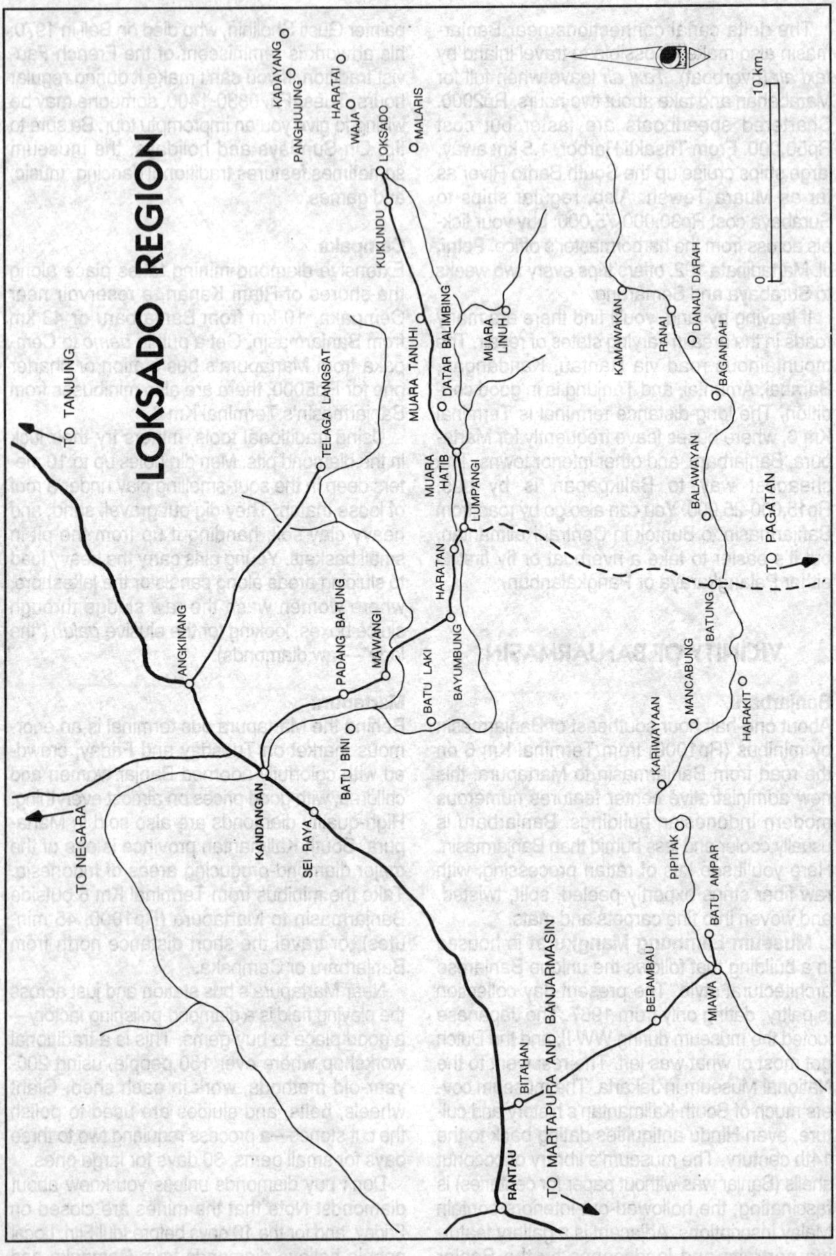

LOKSADO REGION

TO TANJUNG

TO NEGARA

KADAYANG
PANGHUUUNG
HARATAI
WAJA
MALARIS
LOKSADO
KUKUNDU

TELAGA LANGSAT

MUARA TANUHI
DATAR BALIMBING
MUARA DARAH
DANAU DARAH
MUARA HATIB
MUARA LINUH
RANAI

ANGKINANG
PADANG BATUNG
MAWANGI
LUMPANGI
KAMAWAKAN
BAGANDAH

BATU LAKI
HARATAN
BALAWAYAN
BAYUMBUNG

KANDANGAN
BATU BINI
BATUNG

TO PAGATAN

SEI RAYA
KARIWAYAN
MANCABUNG
HARAKIT

TO NEGARA
PIPITAK
BATU AMPAR

BERAMBAU

RANTAU
BITAHAN
MIAWA

TO MARTAPURA AND BANJARMASIN

© MOON PUBLICATIONS, INC.

0   10 km

other nearby places are magical, so local *dukun* do a very brisk trade. Buy loose stones and have them mounted here, or bargain for gold or silver rings with birthstones or other gems. Near Pasar Martapura are souvenir and gem shops. Martapura also has an impressive mosque.

The Loksado Area

To see Dayak tribes, most tourists head off to Mandomai and Palangkaraya. For the real thing, go to the Loksado or Batu Benawa areas.

Adi Angkasa Travel, Jl. Hasanuddin HM27, conducts six-day tours to Loksado. Independent travelers should take a minibus 138 km from Terminal Km 6 to Kandangan, 30 km south of Barabai; Rp2500. **Borneo Homestay** also organizes tours and offers advice to independent trekkers. Rock bottom prices and customized service; highly recommended.

Kandangan has several simple *losmen* on the main street. **Losmen Santosa** can arrange motorcycles and drivers to Loksado, but travel light—all gear is carried on your back or strapped to the gas tanks. Some *losmen* may be "full" because they don't want to serve Westerners. The police are helpful here, and might even offer to put you up. Market days are Tuesday and Friday.

From Kandangan, go east to visit the mountain Dayak people of the Loksado area. Loksado villagers arrive for Kandangan's market twice a week; ask a Dayak to guide you to his longhouse. Buses leave every two hours or so for Mawangi (Rp3000), 20 km east on a newly paved road which now reaches the town of Loksado. You can also follow the trail below the river (eight hours).

You'll need to register with the police in **Padang Batung,** a small town between Kandangan and Mawangi. Continue by jeep or hike from Padang Batung to Mawangi, then Bayumbung, Haratan, and Lumpangi, where the road continues up to Loksado or from Lumpangi it's a full-day hike to Loksado via the Westernized villages of Muara Hatib, Datar Balimbing, Niih, Muara Tanuhi, and Kukundu.

Loksado, a good base for exploring the region, features several inexpensive homestays and *losmen*; all cost Rp3000-5000. Better yet, walk three km to Melaris and stay with villagers. There are 29 *rumah adat* in the Loksado area, each two to three hours' walk apart. You can purchase souvenir-quality *mandau* knives, spears, and *sumpit* fairly cheaply.

Return to the main highway by rafting down the rapids of the Amandit River from Loksado to Muara Hariang, or make a three-day trek to Miawa via a dozen villages still quite traditional by Kalimantan standards. All feature communal *bale* longhouses that serve as homestays for Western trekkers. Donate Rp4000 for lodging and meals.

CENTRAL KALIMANTAN

The province of Central Kalimantan is large (156,610 square km), with vast areas of swampland and lowland terrain in the south. The Muller Mountains border the province in the far north, with the Schwaner Mountains to the west and northwest. Many rivers flow here, draining the highlands.

Central Kalimantan receives few visitors, primarily a handful of organized tours that visit the orangutan rehabilitation center at Tanjung Puting. For the visitor willing to travel in local rivercraft and make a few short flights, the rewards are plentiful: undisturbed rainforest, abundant wildlife, and some of the most traditional Dayak villages in all of Kalimantan. Best river trips are up the Barito from Banjarmasin and up the Kahayan from Palangkaraya.

The Barito River

Travel by land is difficult here; because stone must be imported, roads are expensive to build and maintain. Besides, river highways are already abundant. Navigable up to 750 km upriver, the Barito is the most expedient and economical way to enter the province. From Banjarmasin you can take the Barito River all the way to Muara Teweh and beyond. The boat is always stopping to pick up and deliver people and goods. Many Banjar settlements and agricultural areas are located in the rich marshy country along the river.

CENTRAL KALIMANTAN

Towns here are Islamic, with the ornate domes and spires of mosques nestled away in the trees. Villagers live by fishing, rice growing, and hand-sawing logs into planks. Traditionally, the people of Kalimantan decorate their homes with flow-ers. Along the Barito River grows the *pasak bumi*, the roots used in Strong Pa medicinal capsules for increasing men's sexual potency. Continuing north, you enter Dayak country and start to notice Christian churches.

PALANGKARAYA

A provincial capital not frequently visited by tourists, Palangkaraya was once intended as the capital of the entire territory. In the 1950s, when President Sukarno visited this town on the Kahayan River (then called Pahandut), he learned it was the mythical birthplace of the Dayak people, where the first human being descended to earth from the upper world. With his usual political astuteness, he ordered that

the governor's residence feature eight doors and 17 windows, symbolizing 17 August—the day Indonesia's Proclamation of Independence was signed in 1945. Concrete administrative buildings and asphalt roads suddenly appeared, and a military statue was erected in the center of a great traffic rotary—all totally incongruous and inappropriate in such a remote, undeveloped area.

Since Palangkaraya is strategically located on the Kahayan River, the best reason to visit is to make a river journey up to Tewah and Tumbang Mirih.

Sights

A surprising find in this small, backwater town is the striking local **Museum Balanga**, complete with classical white fluted pillars. Inside are Chinese ceramics, Kahayan Dayak *kayu besi* guardian figurines, ferocious weaponry, farming and forestry implements, and all types of original Dayak handicrafts. Behind the museum is a small zoo. Take a walk in the gardens; the museum is on five hectares of grounds and another five hectares are reserved as a Taman Budaya ("Cultural Garden").

Accommodations And Food

There's a concentration of cheap *losmen* by the docks. **Hotel Kalampangan**, Jl. Nias 17, tel. (0541) 21746, charges Rp5000 s, Rp8000 d. Across the street is **Losmen Mahkota**, and down the road at no. 2 is **Losmen Putir Sinta**, with cheaper rooms.

Higher priced is **Hotel Dandang Tingang** on Jl. Sudarso, tel. 21805, with a/c rooms for Rp46,200-94,500. The **Adidas** offers Rp36,000 rooms. **Hotel Virgo**, Jl. A. Yani, is in the middle range at Rp20,500 for a/c rooms, Rp15,500 non-a/c.

A few expensive *nasi padang* restaurants are within walking distance of Hotel Virgo. There are *warung* and foodstalls down at the docks and in the night markets, but you pay two to three times what you'd pay on Java. Even speaking Indonesian doesn't help.

Shopping And Services

Buy some of the museum's featured crafts in the market near the *dermaga*: rush baskets, the "Borneo bags" of Kuta Beach used for carrying food or babies on your back, gold and other precious metals, and weird green-rubber Dayak figures.

The **public library** is at Jl. Ade Irma Suryani Nasution 3; also visit the **University of Palangkaraya.** Be sure to bring all the *rupiah* you'll need before arriving in Central Kalimantan. Except at **Bank Dagang Negara,** Jl. A. Yani 11 in Palangkaraya, you can't change traveler's checks anywhere in the province.

Transportation

Palangkaraya is served by Merpati from Jakarta (Rp168,000) and Balikpapan (Rp94,500), by Bouraq from Banjarmasin (Rp73,500) and Pangkalabun (Rp84,000), and by DAS from Banjarmasin (Rp73,500).

The best way to reach Palangkaraya is by riverboat from Banjarmasin up the Barito River, then following connecting canals up to the Kayahan. From Banjarmasin, ordinary boats take 12 hours (Rp12,000), while speedboats consume five (Rp22,000). You won't spot any crocodiles—they nap in the afternoons—but you'll see honeycombs hanging from trees. Hope the boat's pilot avoids the angry bees. The *longbot* may stop at Kualakapuas, where there are two *losmen* and crumb-rubber factories, or at Pulangpisau, a river town of wooden platforms, swaying plank bridges, and buildings on stilts. At Palangkaraya, walk from the docks to the center of town in 20 minutes, or take one of the *bemo* around town for Rp200. You can also ride in one of the ubiquitous, hustling *becak*.

DAS, Jl. Milono, flies daily to the remote towns of Sampit (Rp52,500), Muara Teweh (Rp63,000), Buntok (Rp52,500), and Tumbang Samba (Rp63,000). **Merpati** has an office on Jl. A. Yani; the **Bouraq** office is at Jl. A. Yani 84, tel. (0541) 21622.

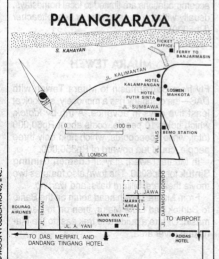

PALANGKARAYA

The Kahayan River begins in the Muller Mountains, emptying into the sea at Tanjung Tawas: you can travel upriver on the Kahayan past Palangkaraya to dozens of villages, then trek to more distant destinations. A *spetbot* to Banjarmasin costs Rp22,000 (five hours); buy your ticket an hour before departure at the little office on the pier.

NORTH OF PALANGKARAYA

TANGKILING

Only Rp1500 and 30 minutes from the *bemo* terminal on the western edge of Palangkaraya, this town is at the end of the province's only highway. Russians built 31 km of road, but suddenly found themselves unwelcome in Indonesia after 1965; Indonesians completed the last three km to nowhere. The road was supposed to reach Kasongan, but that plan was abandoned. It's a beautiful, well-built highway in the middle of the Kalimantan swamps, and nobody really knows why it was ever constructed. Few vehicles use the road, and because of the acidic soil no crops grow alongside it. Tangkiling's hill is known as Bukit Batu ("Stony Hill"), since there's a quarry and a few bungalows there. From Tangkiling's landing stage, it's three hours by *longbot* back to Palangkaraya, or about Rp1500 per person by shared taxi.

KAHAYAN RIVER

Ordinary longboats reach Tewah in 12 hours; speedboats take seven (Rp30,000). Possible stops include Bukitrawi, Bawan, or Kualakurun, but the scenery and authenticity of the *sandung* (small, elevated mausoleums) and *sepundung* dramatically improve beyond Tewah.

Transport beyond Tewah is tricky, due to the lack of ordinary river taxis. Speedboat charters are available to Tumbang Mirih (two hours, Rp168,000 roundtrip); from there you can get charters to Tumbang Hamptung (two hours, Rp63,000) and Tumbang Kurik (three hours, Rp84,000).

Bukitrawi
Take the air taxi upriver 1.5 hours (Rp4000) to this river town of about 1,000 people. Boats leave three or four times a day when there are enough passengers, or you could hitch a motorcycle ride along the tracks by the river, then head inland. Bukitrawi is a Protestant village with two primary schools and a secondary school. Walk down the sandy lanes with children shrieking behind you. Pressed natural rubber sheets drape fences; two crumb-rubber factories lie downstream.

Tewah
Tewah, a gold mining center on the upper Kahayan River, serves as the region's principal transportation and communications center. Home to both Ngaju and Ot Danum Dayaks, Tewah is the final stop for most visitors due to the scarcity of upriver transport and the expense of private charters.

Three simple *losmen* are located here, including the **Batu Mas,** which can arrange longboats to upriver towns such as Tumbang Hamputung and Tumbang Kurik. Beyond Tewah, accommodations are limited to local homestays, usually with the *kepala dasa* or schoolteacher (Rp5000).

MUARA TEWEH

Fly from Banjarmasin to Muara Teweh with DAS—the company has a monopoly, so book at least five days in advance. A trip by *klotok,* which holds 10 people, costs about Rp60,000 total, while speedboats, which hold only three people, could run upward of Rp350,000.

In Muara Teweh, stay at **Losmen Gunung Sintuk** for Rp6000. The town also features two movie theaters, billiard halls, and *warung.*

From Muara Teweh head south on the Barito to Buntok and Lake Matur, then on to Banjarmasin. Or hire a guide and trek east to the Mahakam River area.

TANJUNG PUTING RESERVE

The Land

Established in 1936, this is one of the largest lowland reserves in Kalimantan, with 305,000 hectares. Tanjung Puting consists mostly of a freshwater swamp forest featuring extensive peat bogs, with nipa palm swamps nearer the coast. Dry forest lands are to the north; some *ladang* lie to the east. The reserve covers most of Kotawaringin Sampit, the cape of Tanjung Puting on the south coast of Central Kalimantan between the Seruyan and Kumai rivers. The reserve's Camp Leakey Station specializes in orangutan research and rehabilitation.

There's a network of trails in the 3,500-hectare study area, where orangutans are accustomed to people and fairly easy to observe. Swamp trekking involves clambering over tree roots and wading—sometimes up to your chest—in the reddish waters (the color comes from tannins leached from trees and soil). You can also tour the reserve by boat along the Sekunyer River. You must have permission (requires two passport photos) from the PHPA in Kumai to visit the reserve.

Powerful economic interests in Jakarta have designs on Tanjung Puting's resources—within the park lies the last stand of ironwood in the region.

Flora And Fauna

You'll spot otters, false gavials, crocodiles, pythons, and monitor lizards in the wetter areas. The false gavial, which looks like a cross between a lizard and an alligator, has specialized jaws and teeth designed for catching and eating fish. The park is also home to dozens of species of frogs, colorful butterflies and moths, and the famous bony-tongued "dragon fish" (*arwan*).

Where it's drier, look for gibbons, macaques, sun bears, sambar deer, *muncak,* wild pigs, and squirrels. Along the river you can see macaques, Asian gray monkeys, and proboscis monkeys. In the bay, **Teluk Kumai,** a few *dugong* have been reported.

Birds are abundant—there are over 220 bird species here, including many deep forest birds and wetland species. The reserve is known for its "bird lakes," seasonal rookeries for endangered waterbirds. You'll probably see herons, storks, egrets, hornbills, pigeons, kingfishers, flycatchers, bulbuls, and *pitta.* The spectacular argus and fireback pheasants are rare, but sometimes seen. The reserve is also the only known nesting ground for Borneo's white egret.

Touring The Reserve

Each day's tour starts at the Rimba Hotel, across the river from the reserve, where you take *klotok* upriver to visit the research and rehabilitation centers. The beginning of the Sekunyer River is saltwater and tidal. The fresh water begins where you see the vegetation along the river change from nipa to pandanus palm.

As you move upriver, watch for monkeys moving in the branches of trees. When returning from Camp Leakey or Natai Lingkuas late in the afternoon, it seems every other tree bears proboscis monkeys—hundreds of them.

When hiking, wear socks and boots for protection against leeches and pit vipers. The minute it starts raining the leeches come out; snakes hide in the leaf litter.

A Guidebook to Tanjung Puting National Park, authored by Dr. Birute M.F. Galdikas, is the best guide available. Get a copy at the park for Rp20,000, or order it from Orangutan Foundation International, 822 Wellesley Ave., Los Angeles, CA 90049, U.S.A., tel. (310) 207-1655.

Camp Leakey

This center specializes in orangutan rehabilitation and research. Since 1971 more than 100 orangutans have been rehabilitated and returned to the wild by Dr. Birute Galdikas, assisted by students and volunteers. Of late Galdikas has concentrated on long-term research into orangutan social behavior, mother-infant relationships, and feeding ecology. Galdikas is friendly and hospitable, but remember this is a working research center—don't overstay your welcome.

Orangutan "camp followers" are accustomed to people and fairly easy to observe; all bear names like Friend, Boy, Rambo, or Princess. It's more challenging to try and find the wild ones deep in the forest. Feeding time is 1500.

Sometimes only a mother and child arrive for feeding, at other times 18 or 20 orangutans come in search of grub.

A few rules: don't look orangutans in the eye, as this is interpreted as a threatening gesture. Lock your shoulder bag—orangutans will unzip the thing and rummage around for goodies. Don't leave anything—especially food—loose or dangling from your clothing or body. Don't get too close, particularly to large males or nursing mothers; these creatures will actually bite off flesh. Don't hold baby orangutans without first donning a mask and washing your hands. Finally, don't stay too long, as an orangutan habituated to humans defeats the whole purpose of rehabilitation.

Pondok Tanggui

A rehabilitation center for semi-wild baby and infant orangutans, located 1.5 km upriver from the Rimba Hotel. The orangutans are fed as little as possible to encourage them to go wild again. See Pondok Tanggui as a happy ending to your visit to Tanjung Puting—a success in the making.

Natai Lengkuas Proboscis Research Station

The remarkable proboscis monkey is only found on Borneo. Of an estimated total world population of 3,000, some 2,000 live in this park. The proboscis has a forestomach that breaks down the food it consumes—like a small arboreal cow. Their diet is 52% leaves, 48% fruits and seeds. The nose is a species selection device—the female chooses only those males with long noses, a sign of sexual maturity. Proboscis monkeys are very difficult to keep in captivity; they often become depressed and succumb to respiratory fungal diseases. The proboscis is the only monkey with webbed feet, used to swim across rivers.

There has been a drastic decline in the proboscis population. Speedboat propellers kill many monkeys, and false gavial (also an endangered species) occasionally pick off a few. But the biggest toll is taken by the loss of timber forest and the degradations wrought by the Aspai gold mine upriver.

There are presently 11 groups of proboscis at the station. The guides are first class, the station has good trails and signs, and it's generally more remote and quieter here than at Camp Leakey. Don't be disappointed if you don't see any monkeys; you're almost certain to spot them in great numbers along the river. Climb the tower for a great view.

The Aspai Goldfields

The mines lie behind a terribly hot village consisting of two rows of bedraggled shacks and a few stores. Over 500 Javanese work here, using pumps driven by gas-powered motors and primitive sluices. Individuals, partners, or family enterprises produce three to four grams of gold per day, which they sell to government assayers for Rp21,000 per gram. Those who strike it rich move to Kumai.

Accommodations

The only official place to stay—and the most convenient—is the **Rimba Hotel,** on the opposite side of the river from the reserve. This wonderful Dayak-style jungle lodge consists of 35 double rooms (Rp52,000 s, Rp117,000 d) raised on wooden stilts above the swamp. Walkways connect the rooms, the beds are comfortable, and the electricity runs 24 hours a day. All rooms come equipped with mosquito nets, bath, fans, and mosquito coils. There are surprisingly few mosquitos, at least in the dry season.

You can use dugout canoes to paddle up and down the river to see the monkeys and birds. The food served in the lodge restaurant is good quality and priced at a premium (small cans of Bintang Rp5000), though meals often arrive cold.

Backpackers can stay with families at **Tanjung Harapan** for Rp2000 pp, then rent the village boat to Camp Leakey for Rp30,000. This village is only a 20-minute walk from the Rimba Hotel. There's a sister hotel to the Rimba in Pangkalanbun called the **Blue Kecabung.**

Officially tourists are not supposed to sleep on the *klotok* they use to visit the reserve, but you can probably get away with it.

Getting There

Plan on four days to a week for your trip. Pangkalanbun on the Arut River is the area's principal town; get there by flying from Banjarmasin on DAS or Bouraq (Rp75,000). Merpati also offers flights from Jakarta, and there's a daily morning flight from Semarang (1.5 hours). Book in advance. Pelni calls at Kumai's port.

It's 12 km by road (taxi Rp10,000) from the Pangkalanbun airport to the forestry headquarters and dock.

To reach the reserve, hire a *klotok* near the PHPA for the 2.5-hour trip to Pondok Tanggui on the Sekunyer River. From there it's an eight-minute boat ride to the Rimba Hotel. From the Rimba it's another 80 minutes to the Camp Leakey fork, then another hour to the camp. This tributary is narrow and sometimes the boat has to push aside clumps of swamp, felled trees, and floating islands of vegetation. From the dock, walk 300 meters to the ranger's office to register; you'll then be assigned a ranger to take you on a walk.

You can also get a public boat to the Rimba for only Rp1000, leaving at 1800 and returning at 1100. From the hotel to Camp Leakey is Rp70,000 by ordinary boat, Rp100,000 by speedboat. From the Kumai dock to the `Rimba Hotel by speedboat is Rp45,000. Count on paying about Rp70,000 per day for use of a 15-meter, canopied, one-lung *klotok* and crew. The ship moves at roughly 14-16 kph. Mats and pillows provided. Bring food and water; the crew will cook meals on board.

WEST KALIMANTAN

West Kalimantan is an immense, rugged, sparsely populated province where travel is slow and expensive. The 1,100-km-long "mother river" of the province, the Kapuas, connects areas near Pontianak with Sanggau, Sintang, Putussibau, and points near the Malaysian border. Life and work here are typical of riverine peoples: catching fish and selling them at market, transporting jungle products from the interior, delivering goods from the city to upriver villages.

Pontianak is the point of arrival and departure for the province: hop a ferry across the massive Kapuas to Terminal Siantan on the other side, then take a series of minibuses north to Kartiasa (west of Sambas), south to `Supadio, or east to Sintang.

The Land
The equator bisects Pontianak. The land is low and level near the coast, with extensive swamp-

MAJOR DAYAK GROUPS OF WEST KALIMANTAN

Kantu', Deberuang, Bugau, Sesa, Mualang
These groups inhabit the area around the great Kentungau River, a tributary of the Kapuas, as well as the Sintang District. Though they're culturally, historically, and linguistically related to the Iban of Sarawak, they do not call themselves Iban; the Iban had a fearsome reputation as aggressive headhunters.

Kayan
Found for the most part in East Kalimantan, a small pocket of Kayans inhabit the Mendalam River in the Upper Kapuas. As in East Kalimantan, they possess a stratified social order.

Maloh
Comprising three subgroups—Taman, Embaloh, and Kalis—the Maloh live deep in the interior of West Kalimantan. Skilled in metalwork, beadwork, woodworking, and painting.

Land Dayak
Living upstream on the Sanggau and Sekayam rivers in the lower basin of the Kapuas River, they form a diverse number of linguistically related subgroups. In former times the Land Dayak constructed a "head house," a separate building in the village for the storage of the heads of slain enemies.

Selaka, Kendayan
These groups live in the Sambas region north to the Lundu District of Sarawak and east of Pontianak in the lower reaches of the Kapuas. Their language is closely related to Malay. Most of the members of these two groups are Christian.

Ponoh Dayak, Desa, Lembang
Occupying the lower and middle sections of the Melawai River, these groups speak a language closely related to Malay, but their exact ethnic and cultural affiliations are unclear.

land. The Kapuas River dominates West Kalimantan. Indonesia's longest river, it's also wide and deep—seagoing ships can sail upriver as far as Putussibau. There are also many natural lakes, most good for fishing. Higher and hillier areas surround the Kapuas River basin.

Soil in West Kalimantan is generally poor and acidic; *ladang* cultivation is widespread. Wet-rice fields are found north of Pamangkat. The province has a hot and humid tropical climate. The annual rainfall averages 300 cm, with about 170 rainy days annually.

Flora And Fauna

Vegetation zones include a variety of swamp and lowland forests, jungle areas still pristine with abundant orchids and liana, and montane vegetation at higher elevations. You'll find here numerous snakes, including pythons, as well as such primates as leaf monkeys, the white-handed gibbon, the red-furred *kelasi,* and the *simpai.* In certain areas monkeys are heavily hunted, blamed for damaging the coconut crop. Other wild mammals include sun bears, sambar and mouse deer, *muncak,* bearded pigs, porcupines, and fruit bats. Bird species include chattering parrots, rare long-tailed parakeets, pheasant, rhinoceros and helmeted hornbills, and *pitta.*

History

During the 17th century, West Kalimantan's most important states were Sukadana, south of Pontianak, and Sambas, to the north. When the British attempted to colonize Sukadana, the

WEST KALIMANTAN

Dutch stepped in to support the Banjarese pirates who held the area. In 1778, the Dutch installed an Arab as sultan of Pontianak, but pulled out three years later due to a lack of men, guns, and money. Until the Japanese occupation in WW II, there were only two Dutch Residents—the total government of Borneo—stationed in Banjarmasin and Pontianak, with an Assistant Resident at Sambas.

West Kalimantan felt the full brunt of the Japanese occupation. Between October 1943 and July 1944, thousands of Indonesian intellectuals, members of the Islamic aristocracy, and prominent Chinese were rounded up and executed. After the war, mass graves were uncovered, the largest at Mandor (1,000 victims). Estimates of the total number of victims range from 3,000 to 20,000. The guerrilla group Majang Desa, comprised of Dayaks, Malays, and Chinese, emerged in 1945. Dayak warriors often attacked during forest-clearing operations, taking Japanese heads and hanging them on poles for all to see.

The People
West Kalimantan's population is about 2.2 million, averaging 19 people per square km. The most densely populated areas are near Singkawang and Pontianak. Orang Melayu, many brought in on *transmigrasi* schemes, make up 39% of the total population. Dayaks compose 41% of the population, Chinese 15%; the remaining 5% are Bugis, Madurese, and Minangkabau.

Initially brought in to mine gold ore by the sultan of Sambas in the 18th century, most Chinese today live in towns and the cities of Pontianak and Singkawang. Though they've gradually moved closer to the coasts to find jobs and education, the Dayak people have traditionally lived along the rivers. Most Iban Dayaks live north of the Kapuas, many in Sarawak where their culture is generally more intact than in Kalimantan.

Getting There
Supadio Airport, 20 km from Pontianak, is the main gateway into West Kalimantan, with three Garuda flights from Jakarta each day, taking 55 minutes by F-28 or 1.5 hours on an F-27. Merpati and Sempati fly from Jakarta as well. Merpati also flies to Pontianak from Kuching in Sarawak. Garuda schedules a flight from Balikpapan.

Pontianak is only 200 km south of Sarawak; it's now possible to cross by land from Pontianak to Kuching. No visa required; just show up at the border and receive your two-month entry permit.

Getting Around
From Pontianak, DAS and Deraya fly to Sintang, Nanga Pinoh, Putussibau, and other remote airstrips. MAF also takes passengers to the interior if space is available. Riverboats can reach Sintang, Putussibau, and other towns along the Kapuas River.

PONTIANAK

This overgrown village's name literally means "Vampire Ghosts of Women Dead in Childbirth," and refers to a baleful Indonesian spirit that lures young men into cemeteries. A bustling, sprawling town on the equator, Pontianak is also known as Kota Khatulistiwa ("Equator City") or the Floating Town. Founded in 1771 by Syarif Abdur, Pontianak is West Kalimantan's center of government, trade, banking, and culture. Hot and humid, its annual rainfall averages 320 cm.

Strategically located where the river Kapuas Kecil meets the Landak, Pontianak is Borneo's largest city and the province's rubber and plywood capital. Few tourists arrive here and the only foreigners present are Japanese and Koreans working in the plywood industry. Just 25 km

north of the Kapuas River, Pontianak is a good starting place for trips to interior Dayak villages.

Islam is the city's predominant religion. Chinese, who once mined gold but are now primarily traders, restaurateurs, and shopkeepers, comprise more than 60% of the population. Chinese residents even work as common laborers here—an unusual sight in the rest of Indonesia.

SIGHTS

The city has two large girder bridges spanning the river, a massive sports stadium, and numerous canals. Automobile, motorcycle, bicycle,

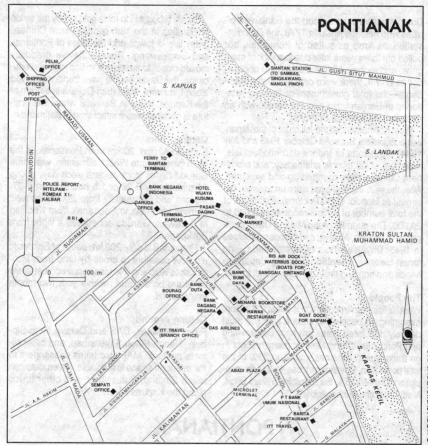

PONTIANAK

becak, bemo, and pedestrian traffic fills the streets day and night.

To get a feel for this bustling city, walk along Jl. Tanjungpura, visit the half dozen **Pinisi schooners** near the fruit market, then continue south along the rickety boardwalk that hugs the banks of the Kapuas. The riverside walk is much more colorful than the drab, congested boulevards. Walk over the **Pontianak Bridge** and continue west along another wooden boardwalk to the old **Sultan's Palace** and adjacent **Sultan's Mosque.** Finally, walk through the **floating village** of Kampung Dalam Bugis—the single most memorable sight in all of Pontianak.

The *kraton* of Sultan Muhammad Hamid, the only remnant of an ancient West Kalimantan kingdom, lies between the two bridges in East Pontianak. The massive 250-year-old **Sultan Jami Mosque,** in all its white-walled splendor, is in Kampung Dalam Bugis, as is **Istana Kadariyah,** the sultan's palace. Take a small boat from the west bank (Rp200).

In the main part of the city, the **Nusa Indah Plaza** is the new shopping area; take a stroll there in the evening. The **Pontianak Theater** nearby is a hive of activity in the evenings. Also south of the river is **Mesjid Mujahidin** on Jl. Jen. A. Yani.

The sports arena, **Gedung Arena Remaja,** lies south of the city on Jl. Sultan Abdur Rachman, within walking distance of the governor's mansion. See **Sekolah Santo Paulus** and **St. Joseph's Cathedral** for Dutch-style architecture. Traditional handicrafts, paintings, ceramics, and carvings are sold in the markets and in a half dozen shops along Jl. Tanjungpura; try the **Fazalally**, no. 59, and **H. Ahmadali**, no. 49.

Pontianak harbor, the center for both foreign and domestic trade, exports such products as rubber and timber. In the evening after it rains, thousands of sparrows swarm along the waterfront. A Chinese temple, **Yayasan Klenteng DW Darma Bakti,** is on Jl. Tanjungpura.

The regional museum, **Museum Negeri Propinsi,** is housed in a splendid building designed by a leading sculptor of Sanggau, Abdulazis Yusnian. Murals depicting scenes from the lives of the Dayak and Malay populations decorate the exterior. Inside is a collection from West Kalimantan's interior and coastal cultures: traditional implements, longhouse replicas, tattooing tools, wood statuary, *ikat* looms, fish-traps, and old ceramics. Open Tues.-Thurs. 0900-1300, Friday to 1100, Saturday 0900-1300. Free admission.

PRACTICALITIES

Accommodations

Everything but lodging is fairly reasonable in Pontianak. Even the dumpiest place in town asks Rp8000 and the cheapest livable room is about Rp12,000.

Probably the most popular budget spot is the **Hotel Khatulistiwa,** tel. (0561) 39856, fax 34930, on Jl. Diponegoro, with a variety of rooms for Rp12,000-20,000 and a/c rooms for Rp25,000-30,000, plus a handy location near the night *warung* and cafes.

Hotel Wijaya Kusuma, Jl. Kapt. Marsan 51, tel. 2547, has *sederhana* (ordinary) rooms for Rp12,000 and economy-class rooms at Rp20,000. Get the corner room with balconies right over the Kapuas terminal and the river. The central **Orient Hotel,** Jl. Tanjungpura 45, tel. 2650, has very plain rooms from Rp16,000.

In the moderate-priced category, the best deal by far is the homestay-style **Wisma Patria,** Jl. H.O.S. Cokroaminoto 497, with 18 large, comfortable, well-furnished rooms for Rp16,000-18,000 s or d. This *wisma* is quiet, clean, and run

well by a gracious family. The **Pontianak City Hotel,** Jl. Pak Kasih 44, tel. 438, very near the harbor area, offers rooms for Rp19,500-21,500.

If you're willing to spend still more for a room, try **Kapuas Palace Hotel,** Jl. Gajah Mada, tel. 4374, with Olympic-size swimming pool, disco, and in-house videos for Rp63,000-116,000. The best place in town is the **Hotel Mahkota,** tel. 36022, fax 36200, in a central location with English-speaking staff, restaurant, and 100 a/c rooms priced at Rp126,000-210,000.

Best location award goes to the clean and quiet **Kartika Hotel,** tel. 34401, fax 38457, with rooms overlooking the river for Rp84,000-137,000. Kartika also offers the most panoramic restaurant in town.

Food

There are many excellent Cantonese-style Chinese open-air restaurants, most without a menu, that serve up very good seafood dishes. Starting at around 1800, Jl. Tanjungkarang and Jl. Gajah Mada explode with foodstalls and carts as people emerge to walk and snack in the cool of the evening. Stalls are concentrated around the Kapuas terminal and Pontianak Theatre. *Nasi padang* places are found every 100 meters or so on Jl. Tanjungkarang, as are natural fruit drinks and cake shops.

The **Hawaii Restoran** on Jl. Tanjungpura in the middle of town offers *sop kepitang* (crab soup) and *udang angsio* (sweet and sour shrimp); sit upstairs and watch the street life below. This is a popular place with *pegawai* and expats. **Restoran Corina,** Jl. Tanjungkarang 124, serves excellent *mie baso.* In the seafood restaurants **Segar** and **Bamboo Kuning** opposite Dharma Hotel you won't get out for less than Rp5000 pp.

Italian Ice Cream and Steak House, Jl. Jen. Sudirman opposite Nusa Indah Plaza, features sundaes and imported steaks.

Services And Information

Most of the city lies on the south side of the river. In the vicinity of the Kapuas *bemo* terminal are the **Pelni** office, airline offices, banks, many hotels, several markets, and *warung.* Pontianak's telephone code is 0561. **Bank Bumi Daya** has the best exchange rate. Also try **Bank Negara Indonesia** and **Bank Dagang Negara.**

There are four hospitals, three run by the government; the best is **Sui Jawi.** Report to the **kantor polisi** at Jl. Zainuddin 8-10 for your *surat jalan* if you're going upriver. The **Menara Bookstore,** Jl. Asahan 4, tel. 493, stocks maps and some books in English.

Transportation

Garuda, Merpati, Bouraq, and Sempati all have regular flights from Jakarta (be sure to set your watch ahead an hour). Malaysian Airlines (MAS) flies twice weekly from Kuching (Rp158,000). Merpati flies daily from Balikpapan.

The laid-back airport, **Pelabuhan Udara Supadio,** is 20 km from Pontianak. Taxis ask Rp15,000 for a 30-minute journey, but it's fairly easy to find someone to share a ride. Or walk down to the main highway to Pontianak and catch an *oplet.*

Pontianak is an easy city to get around in; you can walk nearly the whole length of Jl. Tanjungpura under a covered walkway. There's reliable taxi service with a stand at the Dharma Hotel (Rp7000 for two hours). *Becak* abound; bargain with drivers for a fair rate. For a flat Rp300, *oplet* run on established "lines"; *bis kota* run up and down Jl. Tanjungpura. The main terminals are on Jl. Sisingamangaraja and just off Jl. Tanjungpura. From the ferry terminal off Jl. Ramadi Usman, a 24-hour ferry (Rp200) crosses the river to Terminal Siantan.

From Terminal Sisingamangaraja, take a minibus to the airport (you have to walk a bit). Most airlines fly regularly to Jakarta, some to Singapore. Garuda/Merpati has three flights daily to Jakarta (Rp168,000), Balikpapan (Rp179,000), Batam (Rp137,000), Medan (Rp273,000), and Singapore (Rp284,000). For internal flights, DAS and Derayu fly to Sintang (Rp63,000), Putussibau (Rp94,500), Ketapang (Rp63,000), Nanga Pinoh (Rp105,000). Flight schedules change frequently and are subject to cancellation when unfilled. MAF flies to about 50 remote interior airstrips. MAF's primary business is transporting church personnel and government officials, but the company will take paying passengers if space is available.

Riverboats (*bis air*) head into the interior to Sintang and even farther to Putussibau. The boat *Bandung* leaves once weekly and costs around Rp26,000 to Putussibau; see the Chinese Johnny in Paret Pekong (near bridge at end of Jl. Serayu). Boats also head for many destinations near Pontianak: Tayan (160 km), Sanggau (256 km), Sekadau (331 km), Sungai Ayak (357 km), Nanga Sepuak (380 km), Sintang (458 km), Putussibau (870 km), and Teluk Melano (takes 24 hours). From Pontianak, the riverbus to Nanga Pinoh turns up the Melawai River at Sintang, 578 km.

Pelni sails twice monthly to Jakarta (Rp40,000 economy, Rp100,000 second class). The Pelni office is on Jl. Pak Kasih at Pelabuhan Laut Dwikora. The MV *Lawit* also sails twice monthly to Semarang.

The long distance bus terminal **Batu Layan** is six km northwest of city center on the other side of the river. Take a minibus from Terminal Siantan to Batu Layan, a few km past the Equator Monument.

Many areas are accessible by road from the Batu Layang bus terminal, six km from city center and across the river. Buses head north for Sungai Duri, Singkawang, Pemangkat, Tebas, Sambas, and Kartiasa. Take the 0700 a/c bus to Sintang (10 hours) rather than the slow, ordinary buses.

To reach Malaysia, you can fly or take the bus. Malaysian Air flies twice weekly to Kuching for Rp158,000 (one hour); its office is in the Mahkota Hotel. Direct buses to Kuching (Rp30,000) depart at 0500 daily, arriving at 1600. Tickets can be purchased from SJS or Kirata bus companies; also try local travel agents. Your bus first reaches the Indonesian border town of Entikong, where you take care of paperwork. The bus then crosses the border and stops in the Malaysian town of Serian, where you'll automatically receive a Malaysian

---

AIRLINE OFFICES IN PONTIANAK

Merpati; Jl. Ir. H. Juanda 50A; tel. 2332

Bouraq; Jl. Gajah Mada, near the Orient Hotel; tel. 2683

DAS; Jl. Gajah Mada 67; tel. 4383

Deraya; Jl. Sisingamangaraja; tel. 4840

MAF; Jl. Jen. Urip; tel. 2757

Garuda; Jl. Ramadi Usman 8A; tel. 4986

Sempati; Jl. Gajah Mada; tel. 4350

entry permit. Be sure to request a full 30-day permit, which can be extended at the immigration office in Kuching.

Travel Agencies

Instead of running all over town to various airline offices, it's easier to go through a travel agency such as the highly efficient and central **Insan Tours** (also called ITT Travel), Jl. Tanjungpura 149 AB, tel. (0561) 36661, fax 36652. You can buy air tickets here; Visa accepted.

Another useful contact is Maria Tjung at **Jawa Holiday Tours,** tel. 34595, fax 39769, at Jl. Nusa Indah, Blok B 62. Maria speaks excellent English, works with foreign tour operators, and arranges eight- and 16-day (Rp1.7 million) adventure tours down the Kapuas River, flying first to Putussibau, then returning to Pontianak on the *Bandung* riverboat.

NORTH OF PONTIANAK

Equator Monument

Across the river in Pontianak Utara is the large **Siantan bus station.** Reach it by ferry from just off Jl. Ramadi Usman. About four km from the station on Jl. Khatulistiwa is a small, oft-photographed monument marking the precise location of the equator.

Traveling north on the road to Sambas, you'll pass many coconut and a few rubber plantations. Visit the fish market at **Jungkat.**

Mandor

About 40 km north of Pontianak. Take the bus or *bemo* north from Pontianak on the coast road toward Singkawang, then turn right at Sungai Pinyuh—an easy day-trip. Mandor's **War Memorial,** completed in 1977 and partly funded by the UN, commemorates a mass grave for victims of Japanese executions.

Near town, the beautiful 2,000-hectare **Mandor Nature Reserve** attracts locals and tends to be crowded on Sundays and holidays. You'll find scores of orchid varieties, peat and heath forests, the red *pinang* palm, some birds, and plenty of food and soft drink stands.

Singkawang

A clean, pleasant, well-built town 145 km northwest of Pontianak, accessible by minibus (Rp2510, three hours) on a picturesque drive from Batu Layang bus terminal. On the way up, stop at **Pulau Kijang,** a coastal rest stop just before Sungai Duri.

Singkawang's climate is cool, much like Bandung. This friendly, very Chinese place has a beautiful lake and pavilion in the center of town; Chinese temples. Unique traditional pottery is made at Saliung, seven km south of Singkawang.

Though less pricey than Pontianak, Singkawang's hotels still aren't cheap. Small *penginapan* offer rooms for Rp5000-8000. Opposite the bus station in the south end of town is **Hotel Sahuri.** Better values lie in the center of town, two km north of the bus terminal.

Losmen Bandung, Jl. Pasar Tengah, is an eight-minute walk from the bus station. Splurge at the **Palapa Hotel,** Jl. Ismail Tahir 152, Rp20,000-30,000. Top end choice is the impressive **Hotel Mahkota Singkawang,** tel. (0562) 31308, fax 31491, with pool, restaurant, and a/c rooms from Rp84,000-179,000. No shortage of inexpensive *rumah makan,* with fantastic fruits and delicious orange drinks.

The town's major attractions are its nearby beaches. **Batu Payung** is a lovely half-deserted beach where bungalows rent for Rp6000; very popular with the locals. A *losmen* and outdoor restaurants are also available. Hire a sampan from the fishermen.

Fifteen km away back toward Pontianak is the more remote **Pasir Panjang,** a five-km-long beach with golden sand. The *camat* in Singkawang rents out his big concrete beachhouse here at quite reasonable rates. Or you can bring camping gear and food.

Also visit **Gunung Puting** ("Nipple Mountain"), a curiously shaped limestone karst which once served as a Dutch hill resort. Stay at the neocolonial **Wisma Gunung Poteng.** Nipple Mountain is 12 km east of Singkawang; take any bus heading toward Benkayang.

Sambas

Many of the houses here are built on stilts along the river and above the water where the air is cool and fresh. The friendly people of the town go about their lives in the same quiet rhythm as the Sambas River, which flows nearby. Sambas is an old city, part of an ancient kingdom established over 400 years ago. Walk among the ruins of an old diamond mine.

Outside the *camat*'s office and on the palace grounds are old cannons.

The sultan's palace was built in 1812. Today, most of the servants have left the sultan to work in Pontianak mills. Next door is the oldest mosque in Sambas, built in the 1890s. The regency capital was moved from Sambas to Singkawang in 1954, turning this town into a secondary cultural center.

Stay in **Losmen Ujung Pandang** and sample the renowned Siamese citrus *jeruk manis Siam*. From Sambas, try to arrange cheap boat passage to Tanjung Pinang in Riau.

Some of Indonesia's most beautiful cloth is produced in villages near Sambas; ask about the superb *kain sambas*. This expensive cloth is

hand-stitched with gold thread in unique native motifs; it can take months to weave. Iban Dayak people in the area make the finest *ikat* fabrics, fashioned into reddish-brown skirts, jackets, kerchiefs, and blankets decorated with human figures. Ask around nearby *kampung* to find clothmakers.

Hutan Sambas Reserve is a proposed forest reserve adjacent to Sarawak's Samunsan Reserve along the coast north of Paloh. These joint "transfrontier" reserves are meant to protect mutual water-catchment areas, provide large genetic reservoirs of rainforest plant species, and protect arboreal animal habitat. Wildlife is abundant here; the turtle-nesting beaches are well worth a visit, if authorities allow it.

THE INTERIOR

The Kapuas, Indonesia's longest river, is the main highway deep into the interior; along the way you'll see rubber plantations, logging operations, and mostly Javanese settlements until you reach Putussibau. Isolated tribes of Dayak Iban, Sungkung, Bukat, and Kantuk live near

the border between West Kalimantan and Malaysia.

Traveling The Kapuas

Trips into the interior by plane or boat usually start in Pontianak. In many river towns you'll

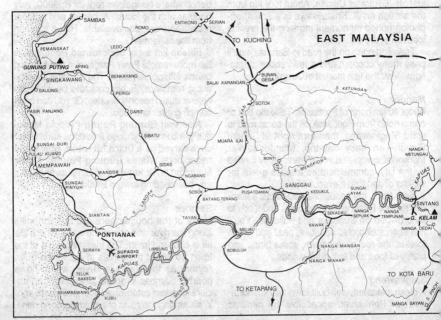

notice a traditional feature of the inland economy, the *toko terapung,* or floating shops. Deep in the interior you can see how high the rivers rise during the rainy season by the heights of docking platforms. During the drier season, people not working in modern industry catch and sell lake fish; all economic activity except logging stops when it's wet.

You can travel by boat or plane all the way to the Dayak fishing village of Putussibau in Kapuas Hulu ("Upper Kapuas"), nearly 900 km upriver. From here, some travelers boat and hike east across the whole island—extremely expensive, but possible. Beyond Putussibau, the Kapuas is navigable for almost another 300 km. The rest of the adventure involves overland treks, leeches, visits to isolated traditional Dayak villages, and weeks of canoeing and rafting down uncharted rivers.

The journey first reaches the headwaters of the Kapuas, then crosses the mountains to where the Mahakam begins its descent south through East Kalimantan. On the Mahakam, you can reach the coast near Samarinda; or continue on to Tarakan via the Boh and Kayan rivers. A popular option is to fly to Sintang, boat upriver

to Putussibau, and fly back to Pontianak—the Borneo experience with minimal hassles.

If the Kapuas challenge is too much, head south to the Kayan, Melawai, Pinoh, and Sayan river areas, then southwest toward the coast. The Bukit Baka area, adjacent to Central Kalimantan's Bukit Raya Reserve, is south of the Melawai River in the Schwaner Mountains.

Sanggau

There's a big pineapple and *durian* plantation at **Tayan** on the way to Sanggau with all the free *rambutan* you can eat. Reach Sanggau from Pontianak by river bus (16-18 hours), cheaper than the regular land bus. The trip upriver is tiring, mostly night travel, so rest for a while in Tayan. There are two small hotels in Sanggau; the **Narita** at Jl. Yani 31 and the **Carano** at Jl. Sudirman 7. Eat in the restaurant across from the Kitono, in the few *nasi padang* places, or at **Melati's,** which offers good Chinese food.

Sintang

Sintang is the entry point for the upper Kapuas River and the first place you might find Dayaks dressed in traditional clothing. Across the river

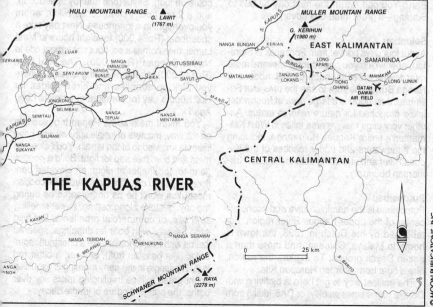

THE KAPUAS RIVER

HULU MOUNTAIN RANGE   G. LAWIT (1767 m)

MULLER MOUNTAIN RANGE   G. KERIHUN (1980 m)

EAST KALIMANTAN

TO SAMARINDA

S. MAHAKAM

LONG LUNUK

DATAH DAWAI AIR FIELD

LONG APARI

TIONG OHANG

TANJUNG LOKANG

NANGA BUNGAN   KERIAN

S. BUNGAN

MATALUMAI

PUTUSSIBAU

SAYUT

S. MANDAI

NANGA EMBALUH

NANGA BUNUT

BIKA

D. LUAR

SERIANG

D. SENTARUM

JONGKONG

SEMITAU

SELIMBAU

NANGA TEPUAI

NANGA MENTABAH

SELIRAM

S. KAPUAS

NANGA SUKAYAT

CENTRAL KALIMANTAN

S. KAYAN

NANGA TEBIDAH

MENUKUNG

NANGA SERAWAI

S. MELAWAI

ANGA PINOH

SCHWANER MOUNTAIN RANGE

G. RAYA (2278 m)

S. BARITO

0   25 km

© MOON PUBLICATIONS, INC.

lies the remains of the **Sultan's Palace** and small **Dara Juanti Museum.** The bus terminal and boat dock are on the south bank near the market, cinema, restaurants, and airline offices.

Take the a/c bus at 0700 from Pontianak's Batu Layang bus terminal. The bus arrives around nightfall; boats from Pontianak take two full days to travel up the very broad and muddy river.

Losmen choices include the rock-bottom **Ekaria,** the **Flamboyana** opposite the bus terminal, and the **Sasean** overlooking the river.

Melawi And Pinoh Rivers

The three-day roundtrip boat ride from Sintang south to the town of Kota Baru is an excellent alternative to the Kapuas. The trip resembles something from a Joseph Conrad novel, as the Melawi and Pinoh rivers are narrow and less disturbed than the main artery of the Kapuas.

Speedboats depart Sintang daily in the early morning and take six hours up the Melawi to reach Nanga Pinoh (Rp10,000), where two simple *losmen* face the river. The next day, take a speedboat (Rp10,000) six hours up to Kota Baru—a wonderful ride through thick jungle and isolated regions rarely visited by Westerners. Two inexpensive *losmen* are found in Kota Baru. You can return the next day by bus to Sintang—a great three-day adventure.

Selimbau

About four days upriver from Pontianak is **Semitau,** after which you pass through several more river towns on stilts, such as Selimbau and **Nanga Bunut.** Be sure to see the *mesjid* at Selimbau. Just north is a large area of freshwater lakes proposed for nature reserve status. Another very large reserve area takes in West Kalimantan's entire Kapuas Hulu range, including the headwaters and upper reaches of the Kapuas River and stretching east to the East Kalimantan boundary.

Putussibau

Putussibau is the administrative and economic center of the upper Kapuas River region. Established by the Dutch in 1895, the town is home to Malays, Chinese, and more than a dozen Dayak groups. To explore the region, hire a boat from Losmen Harapan Kita.

The easiest way to get here is by flying with Deraya (three times weekly) or DAS (daily) from Pontianak. River travel is another option. From Pontianak, the *Bandung* sails all the way up; other boat connections are possible. Lodging options include **Wisma Terapung** floating on the river, the small **Losmen Marisa** above a cafe, and **Harapan Kita,** with a very helpful owner who will arrange boat tours and extended excursions toward East Kalimantan.

To The East

The Kapuas and Mahakam rivers form an inverted "V"; the tip is near Putussibau in the interior's watershed highlands. From Putussibau, the cheapest way to Bungan is on ordinary boats during the wet season. Otherwise, the owner of Losmen Harapan Kita can help arrange expensive charter boats to Nanga Bungan (Rp525,000) and Tanung Lokang (Rp735,000), the starting point for treks across the Muller Mountains to the Mahakam River in East Kalimantan.

Upriver are raging rapids and whirlpools; the river might be swollen by rains, and is particularly dangerous where tributaries converge. Eventually the river becomes quieter and calmer, with giant trees hugging the banks.

The route from Putussibau is to Melapi (two hours on foot), Sayut (one hour by speedboat), and a three-hour trek to Lunsa Hiliar, where you overnight in a longhouse. Next day take a speedboat (Rp84,000) for eight hours to Mata Lumai; then comes a six-hour speedboat ride to Nanga Bungan (Rp84,000). The final boat (Rp147,000) reaches Tanjung Lokang, where you pick up supplies and hired guides for Rp21,000 a day for the eight-day trek to Long Apari.

You might meet some Penan tribespeople on the way, masters of jungle survival who have intimate knowledge of the terrain. You'll sleep on mats and burn tree sap for light. Build a *pondok* (lean-to) for shelter at night; an elevated bark floor keeps you dry. The nights are quite cool, so mosquitos won't be as bothersome as during the day, but take along netting, sweet-smelling *sirih olie,* or commercial repellents. Eat wild sago flavored with bear fat drippings, speared lizards with rice, *to kawat* (like a chestnut), *somboloc* (like passion fruit), or *soar,* a bitter red fruit. The jungle in the early morning is exquisite: bright green foliage in clinging mists, icy river baths, the pungent odors of jungle decay.

About four days from Tanjung Lokang, you reach the East Kalimantan border, a tangled jungle plateau 780 meters high. This is the halfway mark on the way to the Mahakam River. If your guides are willing to continue, have them build a raft you can take down the small tributaries toward the big river. You'll encounter many difficult rapids—poling could be more laborious than walking. After days of trudging and poling, you'll come to **Long Apari,** one of East Kalimantan's most isolated major settlements, at the headwaters of the Mahakam. From Long Apari, travel downriver to Samarinda. If you're trekking to the vicinity of Tarakan, try to reach the Boh River, then head overland to the Kayan.

SULAWESI

The world's most peculiarly shaped island, Sulawesi resembles anything from an open-jawed crocodile to a spastic letter "K." Lying between Kalimantan and Maluku, Sulawesi is Indonesia's third-largest island, with an area of 172,000 square km, about the size of Kansas. The population of this multiracial island is almost 11 million. An amazing diversity of societies exists here, with a distinct separation of old and new, traditional and modern within the many cultures themselves. There are the fiercely Islamic Bugis and Makassarese of the south, the animist Christian Torajans in the south central region, and the prosperous Christian Minahasans of the north. This variety, along with some spectacular mountains, coastline, lakes, and plains, makes Sulawesi a popular island with travelers, especially in the southern leg and Tanatoraja. Sulawesi also contains some of Indonesia's most remote jungle areas, with unusual flora and fauna and nearly unknown tribes; it's a unique place to explore. Transportation has improved greatly, and a road now connects Ujung Pandang in the south and Manado in the far north.

AIR NEW ZEALAND, PHOTO BY WALTER IMBER

INTRODUCTION

THE LAND

Four long, narrow peninsulas separated by three great gulfs are joined in the mountainous heart of Sulawesi. The main landmass is 1,300 km long, though in places only 56-200 km wide. Except for some narrow plains, almost all of Sulawesi consists of mountains—it's the most mountainous of any of Indonesia's large islands. Covered mostly in rainforests and high, uninhabited wasteland, volcanos stretch from north to south and range 1,800-3,000 meters in height, offering unspoiled, pollution-free, spectacular tropical scenery everywhere you turn.

Sulawesi is surrounded by very deep seas. Monsoons heave big surf onto beaches along beautiful but treacherous coasts. Few areas are more than 40 km from the sea. Lakes are widespread in the interiors. Sulawesi enjoys a constant temperature of around 22-30° C year-round. Rainfall is much heavier in the south around Ujung Pandang than in Palu (Central Sulawesi) or Manado (North Sulawesi).

Flora And Fauna

Separated from any land connection to either Asia or Australia since before the last great Ice Age, Sulawesi harbors unique flora and fauna. The four distinct peninsulas led to a mammalian evolution in isolation—nearly 40% of the birds and a remarkable 90% of Sulawesi's 59 species of mammals are endemic. The island is home to such extraordinary beasts as the *babirusa*, a pig-like creature with upward-curving tusks, and three species of *anoa*, a rare, fierce pygmy buffalo resembling an antelope. Also dwelling here are four primitive forms of black macaques, a genus of heavily built monkeys, as well as saucer-eyed tarsiers and cuscus. Over 220 known species of birds are found on Sulawesi; in the nature reserves of North Sulawesi, *maleo* (bush turkeys) dig nesting holes in ground heated by volcanic steam.

SULAWESI

LAUT CELEBES

KEP. SANGIHE

SULAWESI UTARA

MANADO
LIKUPANG
BITUNG
TONDANO

SANTIGI
TOLI-TOLI
LANU
BIAU
PIMPI
LOMBAGIN
KOTAMOBAGU

BORNEO

SIBOA
TOMINI
TINOMBO
KUANDANG
GORONTALO
TILAMUTA
MARISA
TALUDAA
DUMOGA

SULAWESI
TENGAH

MAPAGA
TORIBULU

TEL. TOMINI
KEP. TOGIAN

LAUT MALUKU

TG. KARANG
DONGGALA
PARIGI

PALU

SELAT WALEA
MALIK
TEKU
BOALANG
LUWUK

AMPANA

PASANGKAYU

LORE LINDU
RESERVE
TOJO

BATUI

PALAM
P. PELENG

KEP. SULA

KAROSA
GIMPU

POSO
MOROWALI
RESERVE

P. TALIABU

TENTENA
KEMBANI

P. BANGKULU

SULAWESI
SELATAN

D. POSO
PENDOLO

KOLONDALE
TEL. TOLO
KEP. BANGGAI

MESAMBA
SAROAKO
D. MATANA
SOKITA

MAMUJU
BONEBONE
D. TOWUTI

TALAPANG
RANTEPAO
MAULI
LABOTA

MAMASA
PALOPO
TOLALA

CENRANA
MAKALE
G. RANTEKOMBOLA
(3455 m)

POLEWALI

MAJENE
ENREKANG
MONDEODO

SULAWESI TENGGARA

PINRANG
SIWA

PANGKAJENE
SENGKANG SOPPENG
KOLAKA
KENDARI
MONSE

PARE PARE
D. TEMPE
BAULA
BENUA

SUMPANGBINANGAE
WATANGSOPPENG
TOWARI
SAMAK
RAHA

BARU
WATAMPONE (BONE)

PANGKAJENE
P. MUNA
BONE
P. BUTON

UJUNG
PANDANG
MAROS
BALANGNIPA
PISING
P. KABENA

MALINO
SINJAI
MAWASANGKA
PASARWAJO
KEP.
TUKANGBESI

TAKALAR
TANETTE
BULUKUMBA

BANTAENG
BIRA

JENEPONTO

BENTENG
P. SELAYAR
P. BATUATA

0   200 km

P. TANAHJAMPA
LAUT BANDA

P. KALAOTOA

© MOON PUBLICATIONS, INC.

PECULIAR PAIR

A unique animal found on Sulawesi and nearby islands is the babirusa (Babyrousa babyrussa, or literally "pig deer"), a very rare 100-kg boar with ornately curved tusks like the horns of a stag. Good swimmers in both salt and fresh water, the babirusa is found only in swampy forests. The upper canines of the male grow through the skin and bone of the upper jaw.

Another rarity is the anoa, or Anoa depressicornis. The smallest of the wild oxen and one of the oldest forms of all living oxen, the anoa is also known as the dwarf buffalo. This shy, hoofed animal, which has developed similar to an antelope, is confined to remote mountainous forests and is very seldom seen. The anoa stands only about one meter high at the shoulder and weighs around 200 kg.

A true paradise for lepidopterists, 86 species of butterfly and over 200 species of beetles inhabit Sulawesi, and its spiders can measure 15 cm long. The reptilian family is represented by 60 species of snakes and 40 different lizards; a Dutch doctor recorded in 1985 one of the few documented cases of a man-eating snake, a six-meter-long python in northern Central Sulawesi. The Togian Islands in Teluk Tomini are nesting grounds for giant sea turtles.

The island's flora consists of sago palms, wine palms, and a palm with a stem that grows corkscrew fashion, shooting out green spouts at each half circle. Ferns here grow in geometric shapes. The best places for observing natural phenomena are in the island's reserves: Morowali, Tanjung Api, and Lore Lindu in Central Sulawesi; Bone-Dumoga, Gunung Dua Saudara, and Panua in North Sulawesi.

HISTORY

On the west coast at Maros, 35 km northeast of Ujung Pandang, a Neolithic settlement and prehistoric remains have been discovered; small 4,000-year-old hollow-based stone arrowheads, known as Maros points, have also been found in other South Sulawesi locales. South Sulawesi ports were an important stop on international spice-trading routes for more than 1,000 years.

Buddhist images found at Sampaga on the southwest coast belong to the Indian Amarawati school of art that flourished in the second century. The famous bronze "Sulawesi Buddha," now in Jakarta's National Museum, reveals many stylistic similarities with Indian sculpture.

Mysterious megaliths, sarcophagi, and other prehistoric artifacts can be seen in the remote Besoa and Bada valleys of Central Sulawesi, and in North Sulawesi carved stone sarcophagi are scattered over a wide area of Minahasa—remnants of a vanished culture.

For centuries, Sulawesi was a refuge for pirates who hid out in its deserted coastal mangrove swamps. As new waves migrated to the coasts, the island's indigenous peoples fled into the mountainous interior. When the missionaries penetrated the mountains in the 19th century, they found ancient peoples like the Toala and Torajans living in almost total isolation.

The peoples of Sulawesi were among the very last to be converted to Islam; the Makassarese came under the sway of emerging Muslim kingdoms on Java's north coast only in 1605. They in turn forced Islam on the Bugis of South Sulawesi.

The Portuguese arrived soon after their conquest of Melaka in 1511. These seafarers believed the four tentacle-like arms of Sulawesi to be separate islands. They called the island Ponto dos Celebres ("Cape of the Infamous Ones"), their name for the cape north of Minahasa which had caused them so many shipwrecks; from this name was derived the English word for the island, Celebes. Also in the 16th century, Spanish missionaries began colonizing northern Sulawesi from their base in the Philippines. After the departure of the Spanish in the late 16th century, the spice sultanates of Ternate in northern Maluku exerted their authority over northern and eastern Sulawesi.

The Dutch gained complete control over the docile Minahasans in the north in the 17th century, but it was a long, bloody struggle to control the independent Muslim tribes of the south. The rebellious Bugis and Makassarese were finally conquered—but not completely subjugated—by a Dutch fleet in 1666-67. Although the Dutch imposed a maritime monopoly on spice trading in the southern part of the island, wars between the Dutch and the Islamic states of Gowa and Bone continued through the 19th century. It was

ruins of Kraton Bolyol, constructed by the Dutch, 1631

not until 1905-06 that the Dutch finally achieved political control over the Toraja highlands.

The Japanese occupied the island for 3.5 years starting in 1942; their overriding concern was the maintenance of law and order, the establishment of land defenses, and the efficient extraction of resources needed for the war effort.

Although Indonesian independence was declared in August 1945, there followed five years of chaotic guerrilla warfare against the Dutch in which thousands of suspected anti-Dutch rebels were killed.

In March 1957 the commander of the East Indonesia military region based in Ujung Pandang issued the Permesta Charter, demanding greater regional autonomy from the central government and a larger share of national revenues for local development. With the declaration of an autonomous state in North Sulawesi in June of that year, the dissension soon developed into a full-fledged separatist movement. The bombing of Manado and the landing of central government troops on Minahasa in 1958 neutralized the Permesta revolt, though it was not completely suppressed until 1961.

THE PEOPLE

Most of the population is concentrated in the island's southern and northern peninsulas, where relatively flat plains allow for large settlements. The people of the interior are still isolated, retaining their ethnic customs and traditions.

There are four major ethnic groups. The Islamic Makassarese and Buginese, inhabiting the southwestern peninsula, are well known as traders and seafarers; large numbers have migrated all over eastern Indonesia. The Torajans, once feared as headhunters, live in the highlands of south-central Sulawesi. A self-sufficient people, the Torajans practice dry-rice and shifting cultivation. Although nominally a Christian people, the cult of death is all-pervasive: the Torajans carry out bloody animal sacrifices and place their dead in trees and tombs cut into rock walls. The Christian Minahasans of the northern peninsula were more influenced by Dutch culture than any other group in Indonesia.

TRANSPORTATION

Getting There

Ujung Pandang (formerly Makassar) on the tip of the southwest peninsula is the major port of call and gateway to Sulawesi. Take a Pelni ship from Surabaya (30 hours), or fly there from just about anywhere in Indonesia. Garuda, Merpati, Bouraq, and Mandala all offer flights to Ujung Pandang. Manado/Bitung on the northern tip is another entry point.

From Java, most travelers fly out of Surabaya (the cheapest, flights twice daily), but some fly from Denpasar straight to Ujung Pandang. Garuda flies daily from Denpasar or Jakarta to Manado. Yet another approach is from Kalimantan; Bouraq hops across the Makassar Strait from

Balikpapan to Ujung Pandang, Banjarmasin to Palu, and Tarakan to Manado. Popular with travelers is the air loop from Surabaya to Ujung Pandang, traveling overland across lakes and bays from Ujung Pandang through Central Sulawesi to Manado, flying to Ternate and Ambon, then back to Surabaya by ship or plane.

The Pelni ships KM *Kambuna* and KM *Kerinci* stop at Ujung Pandang regularly en route from Java, Sumatra, and Kalimantan. From Ujung Pandang, the *Kambuna* sails to Bitung (Manado's port) with stops at Balikpapan and Pantoloan. Pelni's KM *Rinjani* sails Tanjung Priok-Surabaya-Ujung Pandang-Bau Bau-Ambon-Sorong-Ambon-Bau Bau-Ujung Pandang-Surabaya-Tanjung Priok-Belawan-Tanjung Priok. Inquire at a Pelni office for the latest schedules and prices. There's also the possibility of catching a ride on a Makassarese *pinisi* out of Surabaya to Ujung Pandang for around Rp20,000. It's fairly easy to get to such Sulawesi ports as Pare Pare, Donggala, and Palu from Balikpapan and Tarakan in Kalimantan, and regular *kapal motor* link Ternate and Bitung, North Sulawesi.

Getting Around

Flying is the easiest—and most expensive—option; Bouraq and Merpati are the principal carriers. Bouraq offers such tremendously time-saving flights as Ujung Pandang to Manado or Gorontalo, and Palu to Gorontalo or Manado. Merpati flies from Ujung Pandang to Kendari, and to such outlying areas as Pulau Buton and Pulau Salayar.

Also check out **Mandala Airlines,** Jl. Irian 2F, tel. (0411) 21289, 4288, or 3326, Ujung Pandang, and Jl. Sarapung 17, tel. (0431) 51743, 1324, 1824 or 2086, Manado, for such interesting flights as Ujung Pandang to Ambon.

Pelni ships embark from Ujung Pandang and sail up the west coast of Sulawesi to Pantoloan, Toli Toli, Kwandang, and Bitung; inquire at Ujung Pandang's Pelni office. In Central Sulawesi, fleets are clustered in Palu and Poso. From Palu, boats work the western coast of the northern peninsula, stopping at such small ports as Toli Toli and Kwandang. From Poso, ships cross Teluk Tomini to Gorontalo, calling at the Togian Islands on the way. Using these boats spares you the arduous road journey from central to northern Sulawesi.

The southwest peninsula and northern peninsula offer the best road systems on the island. Typical of the Outer Islands, the remainder is crisscrossed by poorly surfaced roads, which turn into quagmires during the monsoons. One can now, however, travel from Ujung Pandang to Manado by road.

SOUTH SULAWESI PROVINCE

This remarkable province offers spectacular limestone mountains, huge shallow lakes, hot springs, caves, waterfalls, fertile lowland rice lands, wide arid plains, exotic flora and fauna, an almost endless coastline with large harbors and picturesque fishing ports, megalithic remains, ancient and distinctive Islamic mosques and graves, Dutch fortress ruins, *prahu* building, and diverse and fascinating cultures with unequaled ceremonies and festivals.

The province comprises 82,768 square km, with a population of just over 6.5 million. Ujung Pandang is the capital, main port, and gateway to all of South Sulawesi, and the largest city in eastern Indonesia.

There are hotels, restaurants, and *warung* in all the big towns. Getting around the province is a snap with *bemo* and minibuses rolling on well-paved roads to every corner of South Sulawesi. You can arrange chauffeur-driven cars through your hotel in Ujung Pandang for around Rp73,500 per day plus fuel and driver's accommodation.

The four major cultures of the region are Bugis, Mandarese, Makassarese, and the Torajan, each of whom speaks a distinct and mutually unintelligible language. The Muslim Bugis and Makassarese, who live in the south and along the coasts, are renowned for their hand-built wooden schooners and seamanship. The

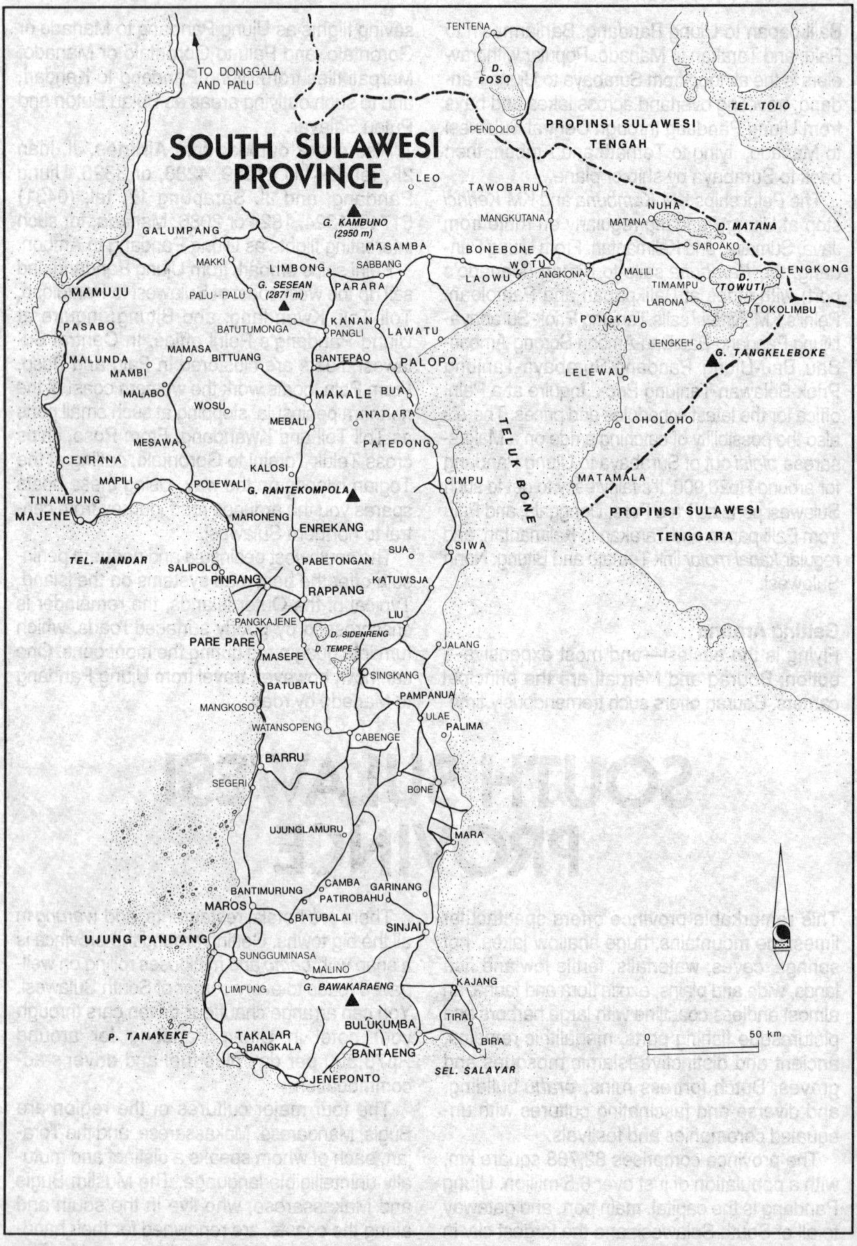

SOUTH SULAWESI PROVINCE

TO DONGGALA AND PALU

TENTENA

D. POSO

PENDOLO

PROPINSI SULAWESI TENGAH

TEL. TOLO

LEO

TAWOBARU

MANGKUTANA

MATANA

NUHA

D. MATANA

SAROAKO

GALUMPANG

G. KAMBUNO
(2950 m)

MASAMBA

BONEBONE

WOTU

MALILI

LENGKONG

MAKKI

LIMBONG

SABBANG

LAOWU

ANGKONA

TIMAMPU

D. TOWUTI

TOKOLIMBU

MAMUJU

PALU-PALU

G. SESEAN
(2871 m)

PARARA

LARONA

PASABO

BATUTUMONGA

KANAN
PANGLI

LAWATU

PONGKAU

LENGKEH

G. TANGKELEBOKE

MALUNDA

MAMASA

RANTEPAO

PALOPO

LELEWAU

MALABO

BITTUANG

MAKALE

BUA

MAMBI

WOSU

MEBALI

ANADARA

LOHOLOHO

MESAWA

PATEDONG

CENRANA

KALOSI

MATAMALA

MAPILI

POLEWALI

G. RANTEKOMPOLA

CIMPU

TINAMBUNG

MARONENG

PROPINSI SULAWESI TENGGARA

MAJENE

ENREKANG

TEL. MANDAR

SALIPOLO

PABETONGAN

SUA

SIWA

PINRANG

RAPPANG

KATUWSJA

TELUK BONE

PANGKAJENE

LIU

PARE PARE

D. SIDENRENG

JALANG

MASEPE

D. TEMPE

SINGKANG

BATUBATU

PAMPANUA

MANGKOSO

WATANSOPENG

ULAE

PALIMA

CABENGE

BARRU

BONE

SEGERI

UJUNGLAMURU

MARA

BANTIMURUNG

CAMBA

GARINANG

MAROS

PATIROBAHU

BATUBALAI

SINJAI

UJUNG PANDANG

SUNGGUMINASA

MALINO

KAJANG

LIMPUNG

G. BAWAKARAENG

TIRA

P. TANAKEKE

TAKALAR

BULUKUMBA

BIRA

BANGKALA

BANTAENG

SEL. SALAYAR

JENEPONTO

0   50 km

© MOON PUBLICATIONS, INC.

Christian Torajas of the north retain their old customs; their ceremonies and architecture are the primary reasons this province is the third most popular Indonesian tourist destination after Jakarta and Bali.

The people of the south have a stereotyped reputation, particularly among other Indonesians, for *kasar* (coarse) behavior, but in fact the manners of the Bugis and Makassarese differ little from the Javanese. Locals are generally curious and friendly to Western visitors. But travelers in South Sulawesi, especially women, should avoid extremes of behavior and dress. No, for instance, provocative shorts.

THE LAND

A mountain range runs down the spine of this Florida-like peninsula, which is cut in half by a narrow, Z-shaped plain. Through the mountains, ranging in altitude from 500-1,000 meters, flows the mighty Sa'dan River. The region has but one volcano, Gunung Lompobatang (2,871 meters), which is now dormant. Many caves of stalagmites and stalactites are found in South Sulawesi—the most famous is the ancient Leang-Leang Cave of the vanished Toala people near Maros. See also Mampu Cave near Watampone, as well as those at Sinjai.

The biggest of the region's many lakes lie in the central valley—Danau Sidenreng and Danau Tempe. These lakes, part of the sea itself in prehistoric times, are very shallow (only one to two meters deep), and are fished commercially. Waterfalls in this mountainous province are numerous. Beaches, found along the peninsula's south and west shores, are white because they lie near great coral reefs. Black-sand Barombang Beach south of Ujung Pandang is an exception.

Climate

South Sulawesi's mountain range creates two different rainy seasons. The *musim timor* blows April-September. The *musim barat* blows Sept.-April. It rains heaviest in December and January, when the whole countryside is verdant. As a result, South Sulawesi sees harvests twice a year and seldom experiences famine. The average temperature in Ujung Pandang is 25-29° C, but with a humidity of 72-89%. During June,

July, and August, the "high" tourist season, it is very hot. In the mountains the temperature is pleasant, but above 1,000 meters it can grow unexpectedly cold.

Flora And Fauna

South Sulawesi is home to species of animals and birds found nowhere else. There is, for example, the *anoa*, a small hoofed animal like an antelope, which lives wild in the forest. The *babirusa* (literally, "pig-deer") appears to be a cross between a pig and a deer; its legs are long like a deer's while the snout is short and flat. There are also unique species of monkeys, such as the almost tailless "black ape" which is actually a macaque.

Rice and corn are cultivated on Sulawesi, along with rubber, coffee, sugarcane, coconut, tobacco, and cloves. *Alang-alang, durian, duku,* pandanus, *kayu hitam* (ebony), rattan, mangrove swamps, nipa palms, and a great variety of beautiful forest orchids grow here.

HISTORY

Pleistocene vertebrate fossils have been discovered here, resembling similar fossils in the Philippines. The stone implements found in the region are similar to those unearthed in Central Java and provide a picture of life 400,000-500,000 years ago. Later the Toalas (their name means "Forest People") arrived, possibly from India, and there is some trace of Philippine Negritos, from about 10,000 B.C. The Negritos lived in lime mountain caves in Maros, Sinjai, Bone, and Soppeng; wall paintings of *babirusa* and hands have been found there, as well as stone tools.

Western influence began during the era of the European spice trade with Maluku. At this time, South Sulawesi consisted of many small kingdoms dominated by three larger ones: Luwu, Gowa (Makassar), and Bone. During this period of intensive trade there was much rivalry between the English, Portuguese, and Dutch. The Portuguese worked very closely with the regent of Makassar in the 16th century, but were defeated by the Dutch VOC company in the early 1600s. There was constant war between the *raja* of Makassar and the Dutch, who aggressively sought a monopoly over the Malukan spice trade. The Dutch enlisted the assistance of Aru Palakka, a Bugis prince, and together defeated the Makassarese in 1667. After this victory, the Dutch and Gowans went on to defeat the Mataram and Bantanese armies, which brought about the opening of Java itself for Dutch colonialism.

Although an increasing amount of South Sulawesi lands came under the control of the Dutch, the Bugis and Makassar did not submit passively. Rebellions continued for over 200 years, and it wasn't until 1905 that the Dutch finally achieved relative "peace" in the southern part of the island. Even then, sporadic armed struggle continued in the northern mountains of the province, ending in 1916 in Luwu and Torajaland and 1932 in Mamasa.

After WW II, the Dutch were determined to reoccupy the province but met fierce resistance from Republican youths trained by the Japanese on Java. To establish an East Indonesia State (NIT) here during the years 1945 to 1949, the Dutch committed many atrocities, including an infamous pacification campaign commanded by Captain "Turk" Westerling. Although it was claimed that over 40,000 local people were killed, 3,000 seems closer to the truth.

As elsewhere in Indonesia, there are many remnants of Dutch colonialism: Fort Rotterdam in Ujung Pandang, Dutch homes in Soppeng, Rantepao, and Mamasa. Numerous monuments commemorating the struggle against the Dutch are visible on a "Freedom Struggle" tour offered by Ujung Pandang tour companies. After the Dutch, the Indonesian military ruled with an iron fist from 1950 to 1965, until most rebellious groups were suppressed.

Economy

Irrigated *sawah* is the predominant agriculture; other crops include cotton, cassava, bananas, maize, cacao, pepper, nutmeg, sesame, cashews, and tea, all providing important revenues for South Sulawesi. There are also about 500,000 hectares of plantations producing coconuts, coffee, and rubber for export. The wide and fertile Jeneponto district offers salt, cotton, tobacco, and citrus. Sugarcane is cultivated in Bone; Luwu produces cloves and palm oil. The province also exports about 4,000 tons of seaweed to Japan, the U.S., and Europe each year.

With its extensive grass plains, South Sulawesi is able to support herds of cattle, and is Indonesia's second-largest exporter of the beasts.

THE PEOPLE

Seventy percent of the people make their living from agriculture; others work in fishing, industry and mining, government service, commerce, and tourism. The Buginese are distributed all over the province; the Makassarese are mostly clustered around Ujung Pandang. The Mandarese, the premier seafarers of the archipelago, live along the northeast coast of the peninsula around Polewali and Majene. Most of the Torajans live in the remote and mountainous highlands; others occupy the urban centers of South Sulawesi.

Religion

Islam first entered South Sulawesi at Gowa, the most powerful early Makassarese state, in the early 17th century. Today, southern Sulawesi is a fervent Muslim stronghold. Christianity was introduced by the Portuguese and the Dutch, but the religion was stymied until the Dutch took complete control of Tanatoraja in 1905. The Torajas of the interior practice a form of Christianity in which numerous animist rites and ceremonies survive. It is not contradictory for Torajans to attend church in the morning and in the afternoon slaughter scores of buffalo to accompany the deceased into the afterworld.

Events

Crowded, noisy, colorful religious and social festivals—such as circumcisions, weddings, and childbirth—are a great opportunity to see the South Sulawesi people in their native dress, practicing age-old customs and ceremonies. You can also hear traditional music and watch dancing and other dramatic performances, quite often for free. Monthly performances of traditional dance may occur at the Taman Budaya in Fort Rotterdam and regularly at such upmarket hotels as the Makassar Golden in Ujung Pandang. Most festivals take place after rice-harvesting times; others are the work of fishermen. Ritual events in highland Torajaland often revolve around death or the erection of a house.

PRAHU

The Bugis and Makassarese are the most skilled boatbuilders and sailors in Indonesia. They eschew the compass and sextant, and claim they can smell coral reefs or a coming tsunami. On board there is little distinction between captain and crew. Bunks below are useless; native sailors sleep and eat on deck in all weather.

Prahu are usually forward-tilting and square-bowed, with great oar-like rudders and seven sails ballooning from very high masts. In really strong winds *prahu* must drop their gigantic sails or capsize. Some *prahu* can sail as fast as 30 km an hour. A fully loaded oceangoing two-master with seven sails can cruise from Ujung Pandang to Jakarta in only five days. Bugis *prahu* were used extensively in the war for independence, and flotillas are still employed as a part of the Indonesian naval force.

Types Of *Prahu*

Some designs (*palari*), with their giant rectangular sails, still reflect Portuguese influence. There are numerous other types: *pinisi* weigh 50-200 tons and have two masts; the *lambo* is 25-50 tons with one mast; the *sande* is a fast and agile *prahu* of only two to three tons. Racing *prahu* have one or two outriggers; these very fast one-half-meter-wide boats can turn in just a few seconds, their outriggers clear out of the water. Under sail they have the grace of a bird. See a good variety of *prahu* at Ujung Pandang's Paotare harbor.

Prahu Building

Whole communities of shipwrights, sailors, and carpenters are involved in *prahu* construction. Expert *prahu* builders don't use plans, but build from knowledge and experience. The work takes place on a palm-shaded beach and the shipwrights have about eight tools between them—age-old equipment including iron scrapers, giant wooden mallets, and wooden planes. The only modern tools used are metal augers and steel blades. Hundreds of these highly seaworthy vessels are built each year, adding to an existing fleet of thousands.

The Bugis And Makassarese

Known in history as the sea gypsies, the Bugis and Makassarese peoples have always been extraordinary shipbuilders, sailors, merchants, settlers, slave runners, adventurers, and warriors. The most feared pirates of the Java Sea—the inspiration for the word "Boogeyman"—the Bugis hunted their prey in packs, their ships armed with cast-bronze bow rammers shaped like the gullets of dragons. South Sulawesi was already a formidable naval power in the 14th century; during the 17th and 18th centuries, the kingdom of Makassar became a political power on Borneo and Sumatra, and even maintained colonies as far away as Singapore. They traded with New Guinea, the Philippines, Burma, Cambodia, China, and India—there are even traces of Bugis words among the aboriginal tribes of Arnhem Land in northeastern Australia. Bugis wealth and influence persisted until the consolidation of Dutch control, whereupon the Dutch treated the Makassar kings as vassals.

In the precolonial days of petty states and kingdoms, the Bugis and Makassarese were preoccupied with social rank and status. Even today, among the nobility class structure is formalized and strictly adhered to. How one dresses, one's speech level when addressing people, where one sits, how and with whom one eats—all indicate position in society. Girls have their ears pierced and suffer clitoridectomies between ages three and seven, while boys are circumcised between 10 and 15. Brothers are intensely competitive; it falls to the brother to protect the honor and safety of sisters. Marriages, usually between second and third cousins, are often arranged by the parents.

The majority of Bugis and Makassarese work as rice farmers and fishermen. From Java and Kalimantan the Bugis *pinisi* carry general cargo—rice, beer, whatever the captain can find. Shipyards are always on a low stretch of riverbank so boats can be launched as the river swells during the monsoon flood. On land, the people live in solid wood houses on stilts, to catch the breeze. These are built entirely of wood and bamboo, and are similar to those in Malaysia. Both peoples are famous for their chanted heroic epic poems, recited by a storyteller who accompanies himself on a two-stringed lute played with a bow. The epic poems *I Caligo* and *I La Padoma* are mythical accounts of the tragic past.

UJUNG PANDANG

With a population of over 900,000, Ujung Pandang is the sixth-largest city in Indonesia. Formerly known as Makassar, this bustling commercial, shipping, and government center constitutes a major air-sea crossroads between western and eastern Indonesia—the largest and busiest mercantile and communications center in all of eastern Indonesia for over 500 years. It's also the capital of South Sulawesi, with scores of government buildings crowding downtown.

The area surrounding the city was once known as Jumpandang, or Pandan Point, named for its abundant *pandan* (screw pine) trees. A fort was built here by an early sultan of Gowa, to protect the strategic harbor from pirates; today it lies more or less in the center of town. The old fort was subsequently reconstructed by the Portuguese and then the Dutch; the latter renamed it Fort Rotterdam. They also rechristened the town Makassar, after the local people. In 1971, the name was changed to Ujung Pandang, closer to the original Jumpandang.

Today, Ujung Pandang is one of the most colorful cities in Indonesia, a unique and enjoyable place to wander. The metropolitan area consists of hundreds of separate ethnic *kampung* of Ambonese, Sangirese, Bandanese, Madurese, Batak, and Javanese. Ujung Pandang is also home to many Chinese, who run most of the businesses and restaurants. People are friendly, and many are eager to practice their English. The city features a number of large, relaxing, grassy areas, while Makassar Bay teems with sailing *prahu* and offers spectacularly beautiful sunsets.

SIGHTS

Clara L. Bundt's Orchid Garden And Shells
Downtown, a few blocks south of Fort Rotterdam at Jl. Mokthar Lufthi 15A, tel. (0411) 22572, visit Clara L. Bundt's collection of over 200 varieties of seashells (including giant clams), along with her father's 50-year-old orchid nursery. Peak orchid-blooming times are March and September. This is the largest orchid garden in Indonesia open to the public and is definitely worth a visit for a free tour by the friendly staff. Some shells and orchids may be purchased for Rp1000-35,000. Another, larger orchid garden owned by the Bundts is situated about seven km from the city and just over a half km off the main road north; obtain permission before entering.

Temples And Colonial Architecture
Ibu Agung Bahari, Jl. Sulawesi 41, is the most ornate of several Chinese temples found on or near Jl. Sulawesi. This 350-year-old Buddhist temple contains paintings and stone- and wood-

UJUNG PANDANG LEGEND

1. Hotel Nusantara
2. Malabar Restaurant
3. Parmato Bundo Restaurant
4. *kantor syahbandar*
5. Empang Restaurant
6. PT Sutras Raya
7. Bank Dagang Negara
8. King Barber Bath and Massage
9. Modern Photo
10. PT Bhakti Toko Buku
11. Bank Pembangunan Indonesia
12. BPK Gunung Mulia

13. Bank Indonesia
14. Ramayana Satrya Hotel
15. Hotel Benteng
16. Losari Beach Inn
17. Kanebo Art Shop
18. Hotel Purnama
19. Makassar Golden Hotel
20. Losari Beach Guesthouse
21. Marannu City Hotel
22. Rai Asia Baru
23. Clara L. Bundt's Orchid Garden

carvings—a riot of color. Farther south, on the corner of Jl. Sulawesi and Jl. Bali, is **Long Xian Gong Temple,** built in 1868. The early-18th-century **Tian Hou Gong Temple,** dedicated to a patroness of sailors, is on the corner of Jl. Sulawesi and Jl. Serui.

You'll find the highest concentration of surviving **18th-century architecture** in the oldest part of the city—a European, Chinese, and Christian enclave known as Vlaardingen in Dutch times. The old Dutch **governor's mansion,** now the Indonesian governor's residence, is on Jl. Jen. Sudirman.

Taman Mini Sulsel on Jl. Dangko is like a miniature version of Taman Mini in Jakarta; the emphasis is on South Sulawesi architecture, crafts, and culture. Close to the beach with *prahu*; entrance fee Rp1000. Swamps were reclaimed in

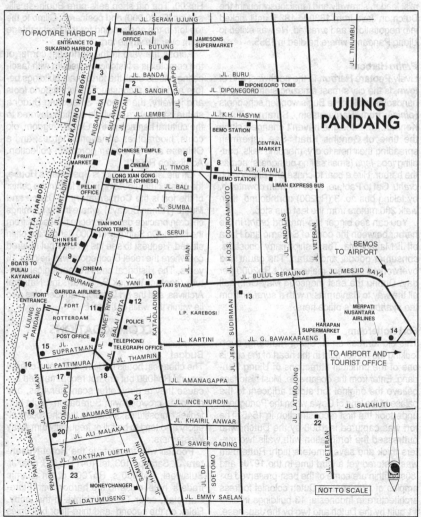

UJUNG PANDANG

the city's northeast to provide land for **Hasanud-din University,** established in 1956 and now the largest university in eastern Indonesia.

Diponegoro Monument
In a small cemetery on Jl. Diponegoro is Dipone-goro's Javanese-style grave and genealogy chart. Indonesians still pay homage at this tomb. Diponegoro, considered Indonesia's first nation-alist leader, shrewdly and tenaciously fought the Dutch on Java from 1830 to 1835, until tricked into negotiations and arrested. He was exiled to Ujung Pandang, where he died in 1855.

Prahu Harbors
Lively **Paotare Harbor,** in the northwest end of town, is the city's most amazing sight: rows of handsome, still-active Bugis wooden schooners (*pinisi*) from Banjarmasin, Surabaya, and Kendari. The designs haven't changed since the time of Genghis Khan. See fishermen spreading their nets to dry, mending sails, pad-dling *lepa-lepa* (small sailing outriggers) across the harbor. Hire a boat to chase and photograph *prahu.* Get to Paotare, three km from downtown, by taking bus no. 3 (Rp200) northbound, then walk 200 meters from the last bus stop.

You can see bigger two-masted *prahu* in the harbor between the ports of Sukarno and Hatta off Jl. Martadinata. These ships carry foodstuffs, consumer goods, and rattan. The gaunt and overworked laborers make about Rp2000 per day. During the east monsoon May-Oct., sail all the way to Banjarmasin with a *surat ijin* from the *syahbandar's* office here.

Fort Rotterdam
This old fortress on Jl. Ujung Pandang, over-looking the harbor right in the heart of the city, is one of the principal attractions of Ujung Pan-dang. Enter from the ocean side. Most historians believe the original fort stood adjacent to the palace of the king of Gowa when the Portuguese undertook the first reconstruction in 1545. The fort was captured in 1608 by the Dutch, who buttressed the fortification with walls two me-ters thick and seven meters high. Rotterdam was restored yet a third time in the 1970s and '80s. Within are some of the best-preserved ex-amples of 17th-century Dutch colonial fortress architecture in Indonesia, 13 buildings in all—11 built by the Dutch and two by the Japanese.

The fort's big **La Galigo Museum,** formerly warehouses, consists of two buildings, one cov-ering ethnology and the other history. The eth-nology museum contains ceramics, musical in-struments, miniature houses, traditional tools, handicrafts, and weapons. Local guides are available. Open Tues.-Thurs. 0800-1330, Fri-day 0800-1100, Saturday and Sunday 0800-1230, closed Monday and holidays. Entrance Rp200. The gift shop sells pure Buginese silk *sarung* (Rp20,000) and postcards. Climb to the top loft in the eastern end for the best vantage point over the whole fort.

Across the yard in the northeast corner of the complex is a historical museum with fasci-nating photos of all the fort's main buildings be-fore and after reconstruction, prehistoric tools and jewelry, the famous Sikendang Buddha statue, stoneware, a whole section devoted to the cultural heritage of the Gowa Kingdom, old coins, biographies of national heroes, and a Chinese and European porcelain collection. Admission Rp200.

On the left as you enter is **Speelman's House,** the oldest (1686) building in the fort. In the center of the fort is the **Conservatory of Dance and Music** (Taman Budaya), where in the mornings children practice dance or recite passages from the Koran. On Saturday at 2000 dances are often staged. Request to see the gloomy but revered cell where the rebel Diponegoro was held for 26 years. The Historical and Archaeological Insti-tute (contact Wiwiek P. Yusuf), the National Archives, and the Art Development Services also lie within the walls of the fort.

ACCOMMODATIONS

Budget
The cheapest hotels in Ujung Pandang charge around Rp4000 but are not recommended be-cause they're dirty, offer scant services, and are often crowded with Surabayan "night but-terflies" (prostitutes). Hotels in the cheapest cat-egory also tend to be full or frequently turn away Westerners.

Popular with travelers is the **Hotel Nusan-tara,** Jl. Sarappo 103, tel. (0411) 3163, near Jl. Sulawesi, Rp5000 s, Rp7000 d. An Islamic traders' hotel close to the harbor, with Flore-sian staff, color TV, and drinks in the lobby. Relax on the second- and third-floor balconies and look out over the busy market street below. The rooms are tiny but usually clean; windows don't close—lots of mosquitos for company; rats in the hallways. An automatic alarm system will have you up for predawn prayers at the mosque next door.

A more agreeable budget accommodation is **Dolly's Homestay,** Jl. Gunung Lompobatang 121, tel. 318-936, right in the middle of town, a 1.5-km Rp1000 *becak* ride from the main harbor. Rooms, including a good breakfast, are Rp5000 s, Rp7000 d. The proprietor, Mr. Rein, speaks fluent Dutch and English. He keeps a book of traveler's testimonials that is a very good source of information about Sulawesi, Kalimantan, and other islands. Clean.

One of the best places to stay for independent travelers is the **Mandar Inn,** Jl. Anuang 11, Box 245, tel. 82349. It has a very helpful staff, and offers information leaflets in five languages as well as a film of the tourist resorts of South Sulawesi. Very clean and located in a quiet neighborhood, about one km from the beach. Food is available in the hotel at the same prices as the local *warung.* Out of favor with travelers is the awful **Hotel Oriental,** Jl. Monginsidi (south of Jl. Saddang)—mosquito-ridden and dirty, unfriendly staff, no longer cheap.

Moderate

Most mid-range hotels cost Rp10,000-Rp20,000. **Hotel Wisata,** Jl. Hasanuddin 36-38, tel. (0411) 24344 or 22186, is much less expensive than the big hotels but it's clean and well-located. Shared bathroom, good breakfast, good service (porter). Avoid the least expensive rooms in the older part of the hotel in back—they're stultifyingly hot and lack ventilation. Ask for the newer and quite nice rooms in the front. Eat in the hotel restaurant (Rp2000), or try one of several good restaurants nearby.

Midtown accommodations include **Hotel Purnama,** Jl. Pattimura 3, tel. 3830; Rp11,000-17,000 with breakfast. Though centrally located just to the south of Fort Rotterdam, it's expensive for the drab rooms offered.

On the west side is the rather run-down, dank, and dismal **Hotel Benteng,** Jl. Ujung Pandang 8; Rp10,000 with *mandi.* It doubles as a bordello. Right on the waterfront, the **Losari Beach Guesthouse,** Jl. Penghibur 3, tel. 23609, asks Rp50,000 for rather overpriced a/c rooms with

hot water and breakfast included. Don't confuse it with the **Losari Beach Inn** on the same street to the north, which has a bar, restaurant, and karaoke parlor for the rich and boring. **Pasanggrahan Makassar Hotel,** Jl. Somba Opu 297, tel. 85421, Rp36,000 d, has next to no atmosphere, but the front rooms offer a beautiful view of the harbor, and the staff is very attentive.

To the east, just down the street from the Merpati office, is the **Ramayana Satrya Hotel,** Jl. Gunung Bawakaraeng, tel. 22165 or 24153. Take a *bemo* from downtown for Rp200 or alight from the *bemo* passing in front of the hotel from the airport. Rooms start at Rp14,000 s or d but because of the immense number of mosquitos an a/c room is recommended. Can be pretty dingy and mildewy. Many of the hotel policies—such as a 10% "tax" added to the already rip-off breakfast—seem designed to wheedle as much money out of people as possible. Staff is exceedingly lazy and the food is terrible. A foreign male who tries to stay here with an Indonesian woman will be thrown out. Still, the Ramayana is undeniably handy for early morning bus departures to Tator—they leave from right across the street.

Also recommended is **Hotel Widhana,** Jl. Botolempangan 53, tel. 22499, Rp30,000-55,000 for large, quiet, clean and comfortable a/c doubles. It's located in the center of town close to prime tourist attractions and shopping areas. **Pondok Delta,** Jl. Hasanuddin 25, tel. 22553, is a family hotel charging Rp35,000-45,000 (breakfast included) for good a/c rooms. Great food, cheap laundry rates, refrigerator in front—the kind of place you leave your key in the door. U.S. aid workers stay here months at a time, and it's a great place for kids. Far from the town center but close to the *bemo* route. **Hilda Tourist Hotel,** Jl. Amirullah 2, asks Rp12,000 s, Rp17,000 d (includes 10% tax).

Luxury

The city's top hotel is the **Marannu City Hotel,** Jl. Sultan Hasanuddin 3-5, tel. (0411) 21470 or 21806, near the post office, Garuda office, and shopping area. Rp110,000 (plus 21% tax and service) for big, well-lit rooms with fridge, TV, video, and all the amenities, including coffee shop, bar, billiard room, large swimming pool, and occasional buffets. Worth the price. Avoid the restaurant—Rp21,000 for overpriced, ordinary meals.

The three-star **Makassar Golden Hotel**, Jl. Pasar Ikan 52, tel. 22208, fax 71290, is terrific—the best view of any large city hotel. Commodious rooms, super magazine kiosk, disco, pool. Don't miss the sunset. Standard rooms Rp115,000 s; Toraja-style cottages at Rp155,400 s, Rp172,200 d right on the sea. Add to all prices tax and service charges. The restaurant is the pits and the food takes forever to arrive.

For something a little cheaper and more authentic, check out the old Dutch-style **Pondok Suada Indah**, Jl. Sultan Hasanuddin 14, tel. 7179, right across from the Marannu. With 14 enormous and slightly overpriced rooms at Rp35,000 s, Rp40,000 d (plus 10% tax), it feels like a guesthouse with a colonial air. The **Hotel Victoria Panghegar**, Jl. Jen. Sudirman 24, tel. 21292 or 21228, fax 21292, is a large, modern and expensive luxury hotel with outstanding service—the city's most "Westernized" international-standard hotel.

FOOD

Ujung Pandang is many travelers' favorite city because it's home to some of the best food anywhere. The city's *warung* and restaurants are renowned for their delicacies from the sea; barbecued fish and seafood (*ikan bakar*)—sea bass, red snapper, succulent crabs, huge prawns grilled over charcoal firepits—are a Makassarese specialty. Seafood meals prepared in this way, costing around Rp5000, are truly excellent. Another (in)famous regional specialty is *soto makassar,* a savory, nutritious soup made from buffalo guts offered in *warung* all over town.

Numerous stalls set up between 1600 and 2400 all along Makassar Bay south of the Makassar Golden Hotel on Jl. Penghubur. Enjoy enormous grilled king prawns, cuttlefish, rice, soup, fresh ketchups, and beer—all for Rp7500. The seafood is fresh and tasty, bursting with wholesome juiciness and served piping hot from the grill. Night markets open from 1800 to 2300 near the THR amusement park and Jl. Sungai Poso.

The **Central Market** (Pasar Sentral) is on Jl. Andalas near the Diponegoro monument. On Jl. Sulawesi are a couple of shops with a wide range of imported fruits—apples for Rp10,000 per kg, *longans* from California.

Cheap *warung* are found above this market, offering really good *es campur*. Lots of *warung* are along Jl. Sulawesi. Some of the best *martabak* in Indonesia is sold on Jl. Diponegoro at night; Rp500-2000 for both the sweet and savory varieties.

Just down the street from the Ramayana Satrya Hotel is the **Harapan Supermarket,** featuring a wide range of high-priced Western groceries; open 0900-2200.

Restaurants

Really good Padang restaurants are found along Jl. Sulawesi Nusantara. The **Asia Baru,** Jl. Salahutu 2, serves excellent grilled fish, shellfish, and *sate* in a tacky but unforgettable atmosphere. Here you get real *king* prawns. The price of a whole fish depends on the size, but expect to pay around Rp10,000-12,000. Try the delicious *pulu mara,* boiled fish in spiced sauce. **Empang,** Jl. Siau 7 in the harbor area, is a slightly better value for traditional Makassarese food.

For *martabak,* Indian curry, and *roti* (Rp2000), visit **Malabar,** Jl. Sulawesi 290 near the Nusantara Hotel. Four doors down, on the same side of the street as the Ramayana Satrya Hotel, is a place that serves outstanding *mie goreng* with crispy noodles, fresh vegetables, and seafood (Rp1750 half portion, Rp2500 mountainous portion).

The city's large Chinese population ensures good Chinese restaurants. Two very good spots are the Ujung Pandang at Jl. Irian 42, tel. (0411) 7193 or 7688, and the Oriental within a very short walk of the former. *Becak* drivers know both restaurants. The **Ujung Pandang** (open 0900-2300) specializes in barbecued/grilled fish, crabs, and prawns. The **Oriental** has perhaps the best Chinese food in the city. **Surya Supercrab,** Jl. Nusakambangan 16, is one of the finest crab, fish, and prawn restaurants in South Sulawesi. Very clean, no a/c.

A smaller and much cheaper place for Chinese food is **Hong Kong,** Jl. Timor 69, tel. 315-246. Sample the huge plate of big, perfectly prepared prawns in butter and garlic (Rp4000). Also available are scrumptious, very large fish (Rp5000) in ginger sauce with chilies. Top notch food.

Bakeries/Drinks/Desserts

Golden Ice Cream opposite the Golden Makassar Hotel sells a selection of pastries and ice cream flavors, including *durian,* litchi, and *salak* for Rp1000 per cone. **Modern Bakery,** at the end of Jl. Sutomo on Jl. Karunrun, is a good place for a continental breakfast with fine tea and coffee. On the corner of Jl. Gunung Latimojong and Jl. Bawakaraeng, another **Modern Bakery** sells sweet rolls, breads, and other baked goods. Don't leave Ujung Pandang without experiencing the superb Arabica coffee from Tanatoraja—you've never tasted anything quite like it.

ENTERTAINMENT

For a nice view of the harbor at sunset, try **Eva Ria** and **Kios Semarang,** both on Jl. Penghibur. Both have open-air third-floor decks and are popular with expats. They serve snacks, chilled bottled drinks, coffee, and fruit-and-ice combinations. Play billiards with the locals at the **Blue Ocean** and the **Marannu City Hotel.** The best of Ujung Pandang's discos is **Marannu's.** Witness the Japanese business community crooning in the **Irani** (fifth floor), the city's best karaoke lounge. Live music performances on the terrace at the **Makassar Golden Hotel** could feature the "Sweet Sisters" from Thailand, or Filipino duets. See Western and Hong Kong kung fu films at the **Studio 21** cinema complex on Jl. Ratulangi; take a sweater because of the lethal a/c.

But the best show in town happens nightly, has unlimited seating capacity, only takes an hour, and is free: the magnificent sunsets over Makassar Bay where scores of brightly painted craft with their wide sails look like butterflies on the wing. Claim some grass on the beachside boulevard; you won't be disappointed. The beach along Jl. Penghibur, however, is filthy.

SHOPPING

Ujung Pandang is a busy metalcrafts center where exquisite Kendari-style filigree-like silver jewelry is made and sold. The pieces are about 80% pure white silver. The Gowanese are known for their brilliant brasswork; brass bells and candleholders from Kuningan look almost Tibetan. The Bugis also produce some of the most attractive pottery in Indonesia.

Other regional crafts include unusual baskets and boxes made of orchid fibers from Bone on the east coast of South Sulawesi. Beautiful carved bamboo and wooden artifacts made by the Torajans are easy to find. Street hawkers and shops also sell mounted butterflies—including protected species—from the Bantimurung Waterfall area.

Jalan Somba Opu
The whole length of this street, south of Fort Rotterdam and east of the waterfront, is lined with shops selling jewelry, Gowa brasswork, Torajan trays and *tuak* containers, woven cloth, Bugis flutes, bonecarvings, seashells, antique Chinese ceramics, *celadon* stoneware, *ikat* weavings from Rongkong, and colorful silk cloth from Soppeng. Of the many gold shops on Jl. Somba Opu, **Tokos Jawa** and **Paris** have the highest quality craftsmanship and the fairest prices. The going rate for 22-carat gold is around Rp20,000 per ounce. Bugis and Makassarese women bedeck themselves in jewelry and much of a family's worth is invested in women's adornments.

Kanebo Art Shop, on the corner of Jl. Pattimura and Jl. Somba Opu, is a good introduction to the many fine crafts of South Sulawesi: mother-of-pearl brooches, intricate silver bracelets, clove artifacts, shells, Bone *lontar*-plaited articles, Torajan and Bugis *sarung.* Also peep in at the souvenir shops along Jl. Pasar Ikan.

Antiques
Genuine antique Chinese porcelain is still available in Ujung Pandang. **Asia Baru** on Jl. Somba Opu sells very fine but pricey museum-quality porcelain. Another recommended shop is **Maryam Art Shop,** Jl. Pattimura Pasar Baru 6 (second floor). Chinese porcelain is also sold at **Asdar Art Shop** and **Asia Art and Curio** at Jl. Somba Opu 207 and 2A respectively. Both shops are rather overpriced compared to Kalimantan. Know your porcelain.

Hawkers come around to the hotels and approach tour bus passengers with "antique" Chinese porcelain and highly suspect humongous "old" VOC two-and-a-half guilder coins. The counterfeit coins cost Rp2000; some may even be cast in real silver. Let the buyer beware— the street vendors of Indonesia sell amazingly realistic reproductions. If you do buy porcelain, you must obtain a permit from the office in the fort to remove it from Ujung Pandang.

Silk Factory

It's a wonderful experience to visit **Tenunan Sutera Alam** at Jl. Ontah 408. Here you can see the dyeing, spinning, and weaving processes, all under one roof. Mulberry leaves are grown out back; patterned silk *sarung* and other brilliantly dyed silk garments come out the front. Place special orders or buy your silk by the meter or *sarung*—lengths at fixed but reasonable prices. The silk factory lies in the southern part of the city between Jl. Dr. Ratulangi and Jl. Veteran, in the middle of the Chinese quarter.

SERVICES AND INFORMATION

Stella Maris Hospital, on Jl. Penghibur, and **Akademis** are the city's best hospitals. The city's biggest pharmacy is **Kimia Firma** on Jl. A. Yani; open 24 hours.

If you're starved for reading material, visit the lobby of the Makassar Golden Hotel for current magazines like *Garbage, USA Today,* and the *Asian Wall Street Journal,* as well as Indonesian newspapers.

Imigrasi is at Jl. Seram Ujung 8-12, near the harbor. The *kantor pos besar* is on the corner of Jl. Slamet Riyadi and Jl. Supratman (walking distance and southeast of the fort). The **telephone and telegraph office** on Jl. Sudirman is open Mon.-Thurs. 0730-2300, Friday 0730-1100 and 1400-2000, Saturday 0730-2000, Sunday 0900-1200. Ujung Pandang's telephone code is 0411.

Check different banks for the best rate of exchange—there could be a big difference. Start out with **Bank Rakyat Indonesia** on Jl. A. Yani; open Mon.-Thurs. 0800-1130 and 1330-1430, Friday 0800-1130, and 1330-1430, Saturday 0800-1130. Also try **Bank Indonesia** on Jl. Sudirman and **Bank Bumi Daya** on Jl. Nusantara, or any of the **moneychangers** in town such as Haji La Tunrung at Jl. Monginsidi 42 (north of the fort).

Information

A tourist information booth might be open at the airport; get the latest brochures. The people at the **tourist office** for South Sulawesi are friendly, offering maps, pamphlets, and excellent information. They also double as a sort of travel agency, arranging for guides, tickets, and car rentals. Open Mon.-Thurs. and Saturday 0700-1400, Friday 0700-1100. Unfortunately, it's inconveniently located four km southeast of the city center on Jl. A. Pangerang Pettarani, tel. (0411) 21142, heading east off the airport road. Take a *bemo* (Rp300) from the central *bemo* station, or a *bis kota* (Rp200) from the Central Market. After office hours, you can find good detailed information at **Mandar Inn Tourist Information,** Jl. Anuang 11, or **Mattappa Tourist Information,** Jl. Pattimura 34.

TRANSPORTATION

Getting There

The easiest, shortest, and fastest way to get to Ujung Pandang is to fly from Surabaya for around Rp175,000, although it's cheaper to fly from Denpasar for about Rp135,000. Garuda also flies to Ujung Pandang from Jakarta, Solo, Manado, and Medan. Merpati flies here from Maumere and Bima. Mandala Airlines, the cheapest of all, schedules flights to Ujung Pandang from Jakarta and Surabaya.

Hasanuddin Airport is in Mandai, 23 km northeast of the city. The tourist info booth is open 0800-1700, and a tout or two from hotel or tour companies will be near at hand. High-priced hotels like the Marannu City and the Makassar Golden offer free airport transfers. An a/c taxi into the city costs Rp13,000, or Rp11,000 for non-a/c. These yellow taxis can cause a lot of problems for tourists—the drivers always recommend only those hotels where they receive a commission of at least Rp5000. Other accommodations, they'll claim, are *tutup* (closed) or *tidak baik* (bad). To avoid the taxis, head to the small square just in front of the terminal, where you can hail "private" taxis or minibuses to haul three to six people into town for Rp6000.

Alternatively, simply walk (or take a *becak*) from the airport terminal 100 meters to an area in front of the Airport Police Station where every 10 minutes or so *bemo* arrive from Maros on their way into Ujung Pandang. Or catch a *bemo* or *becak* from the terminal one-half km to the main road, where you can flag down a local bus or *bemo* heading for Ujung Pandang's Central Market; these pass by every five minutes. The normal *bemo* rate into the city is Rp500 per person. If you have luggage, Rp1000 is a reasonable price.

If you're heading up to Tanatoraja, consider boarding a taxi direct for Rp90,000, or get out to the highway and flag down a passing bus (Rp10,000 on an a/c bus with reclining seats, eight hours). Your chances of finding an empty seat to Tanatoraja are best in the mornings.

The Pelni ship from Jakarta, the *Kambuna*, costs Rp42,000 in *klas ekonomi*. Pelni docks at Pelabuhan Hatta, close to the city center. From Surabaya, a Pelni ship leaves every 7-10 days, takes 40-plus hours, and charges Rp25,000-50,000 to Ujung Pandang. Some sail on to Kalimantan, some to Irian Jaya. From Jakarta to Ujung Pandang the tariff is Rp40,000-60,000.

Getting Around

The surly *becak* drivers of Ujung Pandang, the majority from the poor Jeneponto District to the south, seem brain damaged, and rarely know where anything is. Often they'll just take you to the post office, regardless of where you say you want to go. They can also be very pushy, and sometimes downright aggressive—travelers should avoid provoking them, especially late at night. Moreover, the going rates for *becak* are about twice those of Java. For Westerners, the average fare is Rp800-1000 to anywhere in the city.

A boat builder plies his craft.

Amal Taxis (white) and **Rosuwa Taxis** (baby blue) are metered (Rp800 flagfall, Rp400 each additional km). Late at night these are a good, if more expensive alternative to *pete-pete* (minibus, Rp200 average fare) and *becak*. Per-day hire for taxis is around Rp84,000. Taxis to Hasanuddin Airport cost less (Rp6000) than taxis from the airport (Rp11,000). Order your taxi in advance from one of the taxi stands in the city, or have your hotel arrange it. If you pay extra for the toll road, you can get to the airport in 15 minutes as opposed to 30 minutes.

There are two main transport hubs, the central *bemo* station at the northern end of Jl. Cokroaminoto, and the Panaikan bus terminal, four km east of the city. From the terminal along the north side of Central Market, *bemo* travel to all corners of the city: north to Paotare Harbor, southeast to the tourist office, south to Sungguminasa Palace and Pabaeng Baeng market. Too bad the destinations are not labeled. Fares in town range Rp200-300.

Double-decker buses (Rp200 flat fare) pass in front of the main *bemo* station and travel down Jl. Cokroaminoto, which changes farther south into Jl. Sudirman. All buses pass through the heart of the city, then head in only three directions: out Jl. Bawakaraeng to the airport, to the tourist office down Jl. A. Pangerang Pettarani, and to Sultan Hasanuddin's tomb. A very useful service. In the city, stand at the bus stops; outside downtown just flag the buses down.

Getting Away

A major transport hub and gateway to the "spice islands" to the east, you can fly to most major Indonesian cities from Ujung Pandang. The period around the *haj* is a difficult time to get in and out of Ujung Pandang, as Garuda's aircraft are diverted to ferrying pilgrims into Jakarta. Tour agencies could prove unreliable for airline reservations. It's best to go directly to **Garuda** at Jl. Slamet Riyadi 6, tel. (0411) 317-704 or 315-405, fax 23426, open Mon.-Fri. 0700-1600, Saturday 0700-1300, Sunday 0900-1200; **Merpati**, Jl. G. Bawakaraeng 109, tel. 4114 or 4118, near the Ramayana Satrya Hotel; **Mandala**, Jl. Cokroaminoto 7C, tel. 314-451, airport office tel. 3326; or **Bouraq**, Jl. Veteran Selatan 1, tel. 83039.

The orange **Pelni** office on the waterfront, at Jl. Martadinata 38, tel. 317-967 or 316-865, sells tickets for vessels to Sulawesi, Java, and Kalimantan. For Surabaya, Pelni has a new ship, the *Tatamazula*, with very good service and cabins.

The city's main bus station is a long way out of town—Rp200 by *bemo*. Hitching out of Ujung Pandang is fairly easy on the main roads, either as a paying passenger or for free. Minibus and bus companies provide frequent and inexpensive service to the other cities and towns in South Sulawesi. From the city's central *bemo* station at the end of Jl. Cokroaminoto, catch frequently departing *bemo* to Malino, Bantimurung, Barombang, or the airport.

For Torajaland, a beautiful journey into the hills on a smooth new road, take the Liman Express from Jl. Timor, tel. 5851. The journey consumes nine hours by day (Rp10,000) and seven hours by night, including snack and meal stops along the way. Be ready at 0600 at the depot opposite Ramayana Satrya Hotel, where you can also buy tickets. Purchase a day in advance and try to get a seat in the front, or risk bouncing around like iron filings in the back. If you're in a hurry, head to Tanatoraja on the same day you arrive in Ujung Pandang by taking the night coach at 2100. The route travels through Pare Pare, then turns inland. From Ujung Pandang, Merpati also serves the airstrip outside of Rantepao three times weekly.

From Ujung Pandang to Mamasa (eastern Tanatoraja), buses leave Wednesday, Thursday, Friday, and Sunday at 0800 and 1700 from the bus terminal (Rp10,000, nine hours). Or you can do it in stages: Ujung Pandang to Pare Pare for Rp3000, four hours, leaves when full; Pare Pare to Polewali by *bemo* or bus (Rp2000, two hours); Polewali to Mamasa three buses daily (0800, 1100, 1400), Rp3500, four hours.

Liman Express also offers direct services to Enrekang (five hours), Pare Pare (four hours), and Mamuju (seven hours), passing en route Majene on the coastal road. Another Liman bus leaves for Siwa (six hours), Palopo (eight hours), and Soroako (16 hours, passing Malili en route). Work out your own itinerary so you see as much of South Sulawesi as possible on your way to Tanatoraja. For example, hop your way up by way of the easterly route via Malino, Sinjai, Bone, Singkang, Siwa, Cimpu, and Palopo. From Rantepao, for variety's sake, return to Ujung Pandang via the westerly route through Makale, Enrekang, and Pare Pare.

On the way north you'll pass endless *sawah,* and, in the distance, steep limestone outcrops that were originally Tertiary-period coral reefs. In **Pangkajene,** 53 km north, visit the *kantor kebudayaan* to see ancient weapons, Chinese ceramics, models of *prahu,* musical instruments, and a famous 15th-century gold funerary mask. In **Segeri,** 74 km north, is a school for transvestite priests guarding the sacred regalia of a 17th-century Bugis kingdom. They officiate at the *mapilili* ceremony which opens the planting season each November. The last stretch of road before **Pare Pare** is a beautiful drive along the seashore through villages of *prahu* builders and white-sand beaches.

VICINITY OF UJUNG PANDANG

ISLANDS OF MAKASSAR BAY

Visit some fine beaches and peaceful fishing villages on islands way out in Makassar Bay—great places for swimming, snorkeling, and lazing about for a few days. The coral reefs around the nearer islands, just 15-20 minutes by motorboat from the pier opposite Fort Rotterdam, are half dead, so you need to go out at least 10 km to find underwater life. Bargain before accepting any offer. Buy snorkeling gear from sporting goods shops along Ujung Pandang's Jl. Somba Opu.

Lae Lae is the closest island, quite crowded, and too close to Ujung Pandang for safe swimming. Take a motorboat from Jl. Pasar Ikan, near the Losari Beach Inn. Touts roam the street nearby, ready to pounce on any Westerner. They'll ask Rp10,000 roundtrip; pay no more than Rp4000-5000.

Kayangan, crowded and run-down, with restaurants and an old "chalet," is also quite close to Ujung Pandang. Although many do, swimming is not advisable. Boats leave from the jetty near Jl. Pasar Ikan. A normal roundtrip price is Rp7000-8000 (15 minutes), although boat owners ask more from Westerners.

Samalona is the best island to visit, very small and much farther out than Lae Lae or Kayangan. Surrounded by reefs with clean, clear water, this floating bar offers safe and enjoyable swimming, nice white-sand beaches, and sufficient shade. Snorkeling is quite good just off the beach, and excellent about 100 meters offshore on the coral fringe. Hire little bamboo huts to laze around in all day. Quite good accommodations cost Rp30,000 per night, or stay with one of the island's eight fishing families. Eat fresh *cumi cumi* and play chess by the light of old kerosene lamps.

The night can be cool with a fresh sea breeze blowing so take a *sarung*. Travel to and from Samalona before 1400; at that time a rather sizable swell builds up, making the 45-minute trip in the dodgy old canoes rather harrowing. The touts on Jl. Pasar Ikan will ask Rp30,000 roundtrip; don't pay more than Rp20,000. Or

get one of the fishing boats to drop you for much less.

For superb swimming and snorkeling, try the half-deserted islands even farther out in the bay. **Kudingarang Keke** is a miniscule coral island one hour by motorized *prahu*, available by charter for Rp28,000 for the day. The only hut on the island is remarkably equipped with radio transmitter, television, and diesel generator. Fishermen will share their rice and freshly grilled fish with you. The coral reefs are glorious, but in serious danger from the sewage problem, which just gets worse and worse.

NORTH AND EAST OF UJUNG PANDUNG

Tallo

The walled compound of the 16th-century Tallo dynasty, which formed an alliance with the powerful Gowa Kingdom, lies three km north of Ujung Pandang on the other side of the Tallo River. Visit the coronation stone and sacred graves of Tallo's kings. Their greatest sultan, Karaeng Matoaya (1593-1636), credited with introducing Islam to southern Sulawesi, is buried in Old Gowa. Along the shore is a thick, 500-meter-long seawall built by the Portuguese in the 17th century.

The Maros Caves

The site of some of the oldest art in Indonesia, dating from the Mesolithic period. Handprints and paintings of *babirusa* and deer, believed to be 5,000-10,000 years old, have been found in 55 caves in southern Sulawesi. Small fee to enter. Located in steep limestone cliffs 38 km northeast of Ujung Pandang on the road to Bone, the well-signposted series of caves has been turned into a beautiful archaeological park with shrubbery, forests, clear cool mountain streams, and delightful walkways. Two Neolithic cave paintings of pig-deer are reminiscent of those at Lascaux in France. From Ujung Pandang's central station, take a *bemo* 30 km to Maros (Rp500, one hour), then another *bemo* eight km to the entrance of the park.

Bantimurung Waterfall

Located 41 km northeast of the city in a steep limestone valley with lush tropical vegetation. Cool off at the bottom of 12-meter-high falls, then follow the trail 15 minutes upstream from the first falls to a smaller upper waterfall with fewer people and deep enough for swimming. Also visit the high, one-km-long cave Gua Mimpi (Rp1000 entrance fee), with lights and a walkway. Frequent power cuts, which seem to be deliberate, darken the path, so bring a flashlight. At the end of the cave crawl out to the surface and look down on the valley. Great place to relax.

This valley was once famous for its swarms of colorful butterflies; the great naturalist Alfred Russell Wallace (1823-1913) collected specimens here in 1856. Sadly, few are left these days, as too many Indonesians catch them for souvenirs. The one place to stay is a beautifully landscaped *wisma*; Rp9000, park entrance included. *Warung* serve simple meals near the parking area. To get to Bantimurung, take a *bemo* direct from Ujung Pandang's central *bemo* station to Maros (one hour), then another *bemo* from Maros to Bantimurung (Rp250, 30 minutes). The park is extremely crowded on Saturday and Sunday. Entrance fee Rp500.

Malino

A cool, quiet hill resort 71 km east of Ujung Pandang, about Rp1000 (two hours) by minibus; these depart frequently in the mornings from Ujung Pandang's central *bemo* station. From Ujung Pandang, the road passes through Sungguminasa (11 km), site of the former sultan of Gowa's palace. Fifteen km from Ujung Pandang is a huge paper factory, **Pambrik Kertas Gowa**; 29 km away is a natural silk factory. A hill station since colonial times, Malino is 1,050 meters above sea level on the side of Gunung Bawakaraeng. Time your visit for the big market on Sunday mornings. Eat at **Riung Gunung Malino.** Numerous delightful walks among the imposing firs and pines of the Malino area. Hike four km to see spectacular **Takapala Falls.**

OLD GOWA

Sombaopu

Seven km south of Ujung Pandang, at the mouth of the Jeneberang River, are the remains of a massive 17th-century three-meter-wide brick-walled fortress, at one time the nerve center of a huge trading port. The fort also served as the residence of powerful Makassarese rulers. Overrun and then razed by Dutch and Bugis troops in 1669, the fort lay in ruins for 320 years before Indonesian archaeologists began excavating it. A palace, warehouses, inscribed bricks, bullets, and cannon balls have been uncovered. Visit the historical museum and the four living cultural villages representing the four main ethnic groups of South Sulawesi.

Take a *bemo* from Ujung Pandang's central station to Tanggul Patompo, hire a *sampan* to cross the river, then walk about a half-km to the excavations.

Hasanuddin's Tomb

The tomb of Sultan Hasanuddin, as well as the tombs of other Gowa kings, lie nine km south and a bit off the main road. Take the no. 2 double-decker *bis kota* (Rp500) from the central bus station. Ask the driver to let you off on the street to the tomb (note large sign); from there you can take a *becak* or walk the remaining 500 meters. Hasanuddin (1629-70) was the 12th and most famous of the Gowa kings, earning his place as a national hero by waging a long and vigorous war against the Dutch. He was finally defeated when a Dutch war fleet forced his surrender in 1660.

Next to the cemetery is the coronation stone of the Kingdom of Gowa, called the *tomanurunga*. The sultans of Gowa claimed to rule by divine right through their common ancestor, a heavenly female ruler called Tomanurunga, who descended from heaven onto this stone to marry the mortal Karaeng Bayo and beget the Gowa dynasty. Elaborate coronations were held here. About a 15-minute walk from the stone is Ujung Pandang's oldest mosque, the **Katangka Mosque,** supposedly built in 1605. Check out the massive royal crypts in the nearby graveyard.

Sungguminasa

Eleven km south of Ujung Pandang (Rp500 by *bemo*, 30 minutes), this was the site of the old Gowa Kingdom. The traditional wooden palace, mounted on stilts and dating from 1936, is now a historical museum called Ballalompoa. Ask in the *bupati*'s office for permission to see the room where the treasure (jewelry, 15.4-kg gold crown, gold bracelets), royal costumes, ceremonial regalia, and 7.5 kilos of gold weapons are on display. Open Mon.-Thurs. 0800-1300, Friday 0800-1030, Saturday 0800-1200, closed on Sunday and holidays.

THE SOUTHERN REGION

Bulukumba

A small town, 146 km by minibus from Ujung Pandang, of little two-story shops with balconies. You can also reach Bulukumba from Bone by bus, though you might have to change buses in Sinjai. Visit Bugis and Makassarese villages near Bulukumba to see houses on stilts, boatbuilding and repair. Outside Bulukumbu are scenic beaches.

Stay near the waterfront at **Penginapan Sinar Fajar,** Jl. Sawerigading 4, or near the market at **Penginapan Bawakaraeng,** Jl. Pahlawan, both Rp5000-8000. Though there's another *losmen,* staff always tell Westerners the place is full because they don't want to deal with the police. Bulukumba's market offers a wide selection of fish, local vegetables, and fruits. The ferry for Pulau Salayar (Rp5000, five hours) leaves from a spot two km east of town. Ride in a *becak* (Rp1000), or take a nice walk along the beach for free.

Bira

The shortest sea voyage to Pulau Salayar is from Bira, a small, quiet Bugis town east (Rp1500 by *bemo*) of Bulukumba. Bira is 197 km from Ujung Pandang; direct buses leave from Ujung Pandang's main terminal at 0700, arriving in time to catch the ferry at 1400 for Pamatata Harbor on the north end of Pulau Salayar. Bira is one of those places you go to for a day and stay a week. **Riswan Guesthouse,** at the ferry end of the village, offers very basic accommodations for Rp10,000 per person, including three varied, delicious, plentiful meals. Riswan and his "helpers" (especially Arif) are very attentive to your needs, providing maps and information.

From the guesthouse it's only 500 meters to a wonderful beach, **Pasir Putih,** with blinding white sand, crystal clear water, and good snor-

keling—a tropical paradise. Another *losmen* nearby and a hotel on the beach have opened; these are likely to bring many changes, beginning with electricity. Climb the mountain to see land's end. About seven km from Bira is **Maru Masa,** a big and very active shipyard where traditional *pinisi* are built.

The Kajang Area

A *kecamatan* in the Bulukumba region, about 60 km from Ujung Pandang by minibus, home of the Tana Toa people, who practice an animistic blend of Islam and Hinduism. Comprised of only about 100 families, this tribe wears only three colors: black for daily dress, white for the death ceremony, and red for other activities. The Tana Toa don't accept help in the form of clinics or schools, and are so poor they don't wear shoes. They subsist mainly on the tuberous plant *ubi keladi.* Visit the hermetically sealed traditional village of **Balobalo;** the leader of the village is Amma Toa. Stay at **Penginapan Sisihorong,** owned by a noblewoman; Rp55,000 d includes all meals, a local performance, and a loan of black clothing so you may enter the *tana toa* area.

Sinjai

A small Bugis town accessible from Bulukumba (Rp1500, 1.5 hours, 66 km), Bone (Rp1800 by *bemo*), or Ujung Pandang (Rp4300, six to seven hours, 220 km) on a good road via Sungguminasa, Jeneponto, and Bulukumba. Sooner or later you'll run into Aleks, who'll lead you to several caves north of town. Visit the hot springs at **Uwae,** about two km out of Sinjai. The port of Balanipa, two km (Rp200 by *bemo*) from Sinjai's bus station, features a Dutch fort built in the 1860s; it's now occupied by the police. From the wharf, take *kapal motor* three hours (Rp1000) out to the many fishing villages, pristine calm coral gardens, and white-sand beaches of **Pulau Sembilan.**

The best place to stay is **Wisma Tanka** (Rp6000 s or d) on Jl. Andi Pomogering Petta Rami. Clean, tidy, with few mosquitos. Every guest is served a free drink; guide service available. Near the central *bemo*/bus station is **Penginapan Linggar Jati,** Jl. Pramuka 45; Rp3500 s, Rp7000 d. **Hotel Rosyida** at Jl. Gunung Lompobattang 1, the older **Wisma Sanrego** on Jl. Sultan Hasanuddin, and **Penginapan Mutiara** on Jl. Dr. Sutomo all charge about the same as the Linggar Jati. Eat at **Nikmat Jawa Timur** on Jl. Persatuan Raya beside the Rachmat Restaurant, only 70 meters from the central *bemo* station. Seafood dishes cost around Rp1500. Surrounding the central market are many *warung* serving *ikan bakar.*

SALAYAR ISLAND

A long, narrow, rocky island in the Flores Sea 17 km off the southwest tip of Sulawesi. Salayar people live at a slower pace than those on the mainland. The five dialects spoken here are similar to Makassarese. Most of the population is Muslim, but one Christian church is found in the main town of **Benteng** in the central part of the west coast. Chief crops are copra, hemp, tobacco, and cotton. Though the island has much to offer, it's quite undeveloped for visitors, quiet (except for the market), and good for taking walks, observing village life, and watching men fashion wood-hulled ships with traditional tools.

In Benteng, **Hotel Berlian** is newer, nicer, and cleaner than the older **Hotel Harmita.** The Berlian charges Rp7500 s or d; the Harmita Rp3000 s. On the main street are several *warung.*

Sights
On the town's *alun-alun* check out the former Dutch *controleur's* residence and the old Dutch jail, both dating from the 1890s. Benteng's big *pasar,* the social and commercial center of the island, is busiest in the mornings, when a cornucopia of produce and fish is sold.

Big, wooden *prahu layar* and *kapal motor* are usually under construction along the beach several km south of Benteng. It may take two years for the small group of workmen to build a large boat. From the microwave station, walk up to **Gantarang** to see a pre-Islamic fortress with nine-meter-high walls, a 16th century mosque, and the rock footprint of a local Bugis hero.

A magnificent Dongson-era bronze drum, the **Nekara**, is kept in a well-guarded building near the *raja*'s palace in **Bontobangun,** three km south of Benteng. Measuring 95 by 115 cm, it's reputed to date from before the time of Christ. The drum is believed to have magic powers, and is still used on important occasions. In the same building are remnants of a royal *prahu.*

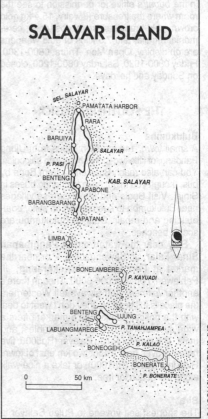

SALAYAR ISLAND

© MOON PUBLICATIONS, INC.

Getting There And Around
Boats leave most afternoons or evenings from two km east of Bulukumba for the five-hour Rp5000 crossing to Benteng. If you're prone to seasickness, try the ferry at 1400 from Bira, east of Bulukumba; just over two hours (17 km) to Pamatata Harbor in northern Pulau Salayar. Cabin space is Rp3000 extra and well worth it. You can also take the 0700 direct bus, which connects with the ferry, from Ujung Pandang's Panaikan station. The ferry from Pamatata Harbor back to Bira leaves at 1000. From the Benteng market, minibuses provide irregular transportation to inland villages. Ask drivers at the market about your destination.

ONWARD TO TANATORAJA

BONE

A quiet Bugis town, also known as Watampone, on the east coast Rp2000 and five hours (180 km) by bus or minibus from Ujung Pandang, Bone was the site of a powerful 17th-century kingdom led by the redoubtable and fearsome Aru Palakka. Continually rebellious against the Dutch, the city was conquered in 1824, 1859, and again in 1905. See old Dutch wooden houses from colonial times, and the large palace built in 1931 to house the son of the last Gowa sultan. Former royal possessions and relics—swords, sacred *kris,* ceremonial attire—are housed in **Museum Lapawawoi** on the *alun-alun.* Dutch-speaking guide. The royal grave complex is at **Bukaka** on the road to Singkang. You can buy locally produced basketry and silk-weaving at the **Usaha Rakyat Bone** handicrafts shop at Jl. Makmur 37.

Stay in charming **Wisma Bola Ridie,** Jl. Merdeka 6, tel. 412, only a short walk from the *alun-alun*; this large airy Dutch-style building includes six rooms for Rp10,000-15,000 s or d with breakfast and bathroom. **Wisma Merdeka** is next door. The town's most modern hotel is **Hotel Wisata Watampone,** Jl. Biru 14, tel. 362, with a/c, coffee shop, and swimming pool; Rp40,000-80,000 plus 21% tax and service. **Hotel Mario Pulana,** Jl. Kawerang 16, is another good hotel. Eat cheaply at the *martabak* stalls and *rumah makan* along Jl. Mesjid, or in the town's best restaurant, the Chinese-run **Pondok Selera** at Jl. Biru 28.

Vicinity Of Bone

Minibuses connect Bone with Bulukumba, 139 km south, Rp2000; and Sengkang, 69 km northwest. From Bone you can take a boat to Kolaka, capital of the island's southwestern peninsula. First take a *bemo* to the port of **Bajoe** (4 km, Rp500), then buy a ticket on the ferry which sails at 2300 and arrives at 0600. The fare is Rp10,000 first class with a/c and airline seats, or Rp4000 second class. The name Bajoe comes from a nomadic, boat-building shore people who once inhabited the waterways of Sulawesi.

Most of these former "sea nomads" now lead a sedentary lifestyle and occupy stilted houses over the water at the port.

For the largest and most spectacular cave system in South Sulawesi, travel first from Bone to **Ulae,** 34 km to the northwest. From Ulae, take a minibus to **Gua Mampu.** Many boys eager to guide you will be waiting with flashlights. Resembling human and animal forms, the rock formations in a series of upper and lower caves are the focus of many legends.

WATANSOPPENG

This district capital is a center for rice and silk production 240 km northeast of Ujung Pandang via Maros, or 75 km west of Bone. Silkworms are bred and raw silk produced for the weavers of Singkang, Rappang, and Enrekang in *pabrik sutera* (silkworm factories) north of town on the road to Pangkajene. Ten- to 15-meter pieces of silk cloth usually take about a week to produce on the big looms, though the finest is hand-loomed by village women who need an entire month to produce two meters. See women spin silk in the small cottage industries in Watansoppeng.

The remarkable residence of the Dutch *controleur,* built in 1911, is now a government *pasanggrahan.* Watansoppeng also boasts pretty gardens, flurries of bats in its tall tamarind trees, and an attractive hilly backdrop. On Jl. Kemakmuran, stay in either **Wisma Munasko** (no. 12), Rp10,000 with *mandi*; or the more comfortable **Hotel Makmur** (no. 104), for Rp15,000-20,000. Enjoy seafood dishes in the two Chinese-style *rumah makan* on Jl. Attang Benteng. Don't miss the tobacco market in **Cabenge,** nine km to the east, where villagers arrive in brightly decorated pony carts. Tobacco, palm sugar, cocoa, peanuts, and *kemiri* nuts are the principal crops of the region.

SINGKANG

Break your journey with a stop in this midsized Bugis town, offering good accommodations, restaurants, and shopping. The impressive white **Mesjid Raya** in the center of town bellows out calls to prayer starting at 0430; be ready to rise. Visit the silk factory on Jl. Sentosa Baru. Plentiful *bemo* and *becak* stand ready to take you anywhere in town. There's a fine view over Singkang, the town of Tempe on the lake, and the surrounding area from the government-run **Pasanggrahan Hirawati** on top of a hill. You need permission from the *kantor daerah* to stay there.

Brightly colored *prahu* cruise up and down the river through town. **Danau Tempe** and nearby **Danau Sidenreng** lie nine meters above sea level and are just two meters deep; both are slowly drying up due to erosion and resultant heavy silting. The remnant of a vast inland sea, Danau Tempe varies in size and depth with the seasons. Your hotel can arrange for a traditional boat with outboard motor for a visit to the lake; two hours, Rp3000. Or hitch a lift on a fisherman's *prahu* (Rp1000) to the wonderful Bugis fishing village of **Tempe** with its hundreds of stilt houses standing in the mud. Bare feet are best, as shoes get waterlogged. Time your visit to catch beautiful views of the sunrise or sunset from the lake. Walk on paths over wobbly bamboo suspension bridges (the old men aren't begging, but collecting the toll). Fields of sugarcane and peanuts surround the lake.

Accommodations And Food
Steep yourself in the old Bugis civilization at the **Hotel Apada** on Jl. Durian. Clean, well run; the noblewoman (Andi Bau Muddaria) who owns it charges Rp15,000-20,000 for quite comfortable rooms. Heading east toward Jl. Mesjid Raya is **Wisma Ayuni** at Jl. Puangrimaggalatung 18 in an old Dutch house; Rp5000 pp with *mandi*. **Hotel Al'Salam,** Jl. Sentosa 27, tel. 53, is Singkang's top hotel; Rp25,000 s or d. Very clean and few mosquitos, but the food is terrible (about Rp6000 for dinner) and there's no beer, as it's strictly Islamic.

Ikan bakar (grilled fish), *ayam kampung* (free-range chicken), and *lawa* (small shrimp) are local favorites served at Singkang's numerous high-quality *warung*. Stalls selling *martabak* and other Indonesian foods are scattered along the main street. The Bugis dishes on **Al'Salam II Hotel's** menu are good value (two dishes and rice feeds four) and very tasty. The best restaurant is the Chinese-owned **Rumah Makan Romantis**, Jl.

Petta Rani 2. Also good is **Jimmy:** Rp2500 dinner includes *ikan mas,* rice, veggies, sauce and chilies, salad, and iced tea. For chicken, go to **Warung Singkang** on Jl. Mesjid Raya.

Shopping
You can watch weaving on handlooms, using traditional Buginese designs and a wide variety of colors, in private homes in and near town; ask to see *tenun sutera* (silk weaving). Check out **Griya Sutera,** Jl. Hasanuddin 5; **Toko Akbar,** Jl. Kartini 16B; and **Mustaquiem,** Jl. A. Panggaru 1. Handspun two-meter-long silk *sarung* and *selendang* sets cost around Rp60,000. Lengths of patterned *kain* sell for Rp25,000-35,000; plain lengths are Rp4000-8000 cheaper.

Getting There And Away
Singkang is a convenient day-trip from Pare Pare (90 km, two hours, Rp2500). From Bone, it's 69 km and Rp2000 to Singkang; from Palopo, 177 km, six hours, Rp3500. From Ujung Pandang, it's Rp4500 one-way by bus. Singkang sits right in the middle of the southern peninsula, and buses, *bemo,* and minibuses head out in all directions from the town's central terminal—northeast to Palopo, north to Lake Tempe, west to Pare Pare, southeast to Bone, southwest to Ujung Pandang.

PARE PARE

The second-largest seaport of South Sulawesi, 155 km north of Ujung Pandang, Pare Pare is smaller and slower-paced than Ujung Pandang. A nice, clean city with friendly people, but nothing special except that it's the center of an area known for its delicious rice. Tourists often stop here for refreshment on their way to Mamasa or Rantepao in Tanatoraja. Pare Pare is located near areas that produce large quantities of export commodities, and the town's port is a major embarkation point for cargo and passenger boats to central and northern Sulawesi and over to East Kalimantan.

The city is divided into northern and southern commercial districts, with a quiet tree-lined government section in the center, and the waterfront is never far away. The harbor is the place to see the Bugis *bago,* with its long bowsprit and triangular mainsail. **Mesjid Raya,** with its white cupola surmounted by a silver spire, is a local landmark. Numerous *toko mas* (gold shops) are located on Jl. Lasinrang. In Cappa Galung village, two km before town, is the **Bangenge Museum of Ethnology,** featuring ceramics, gold ornaments, brassware, traditional implements and clothing dating from the Bacu Kiki kingdom. The curator, Haji Hamzah, is a descendant of its last ruler.

Accommodations And Food
Hotel Gandaria, Jl. Bau Masepe 171, charges Rp12,000 and up for an acceptable double, but if you don't mind the climbing ask for a room on the top (fifth) floor for Rp8000 d—very airy and good views all around. The owner, Haji Zainuddin, might let you see his priceless *pusaka,* dating from the kingdom of Suppa. In the south part of town, **Hotel Gemini** offers very nice, clean, big double rooms with fan, *mandi,* and real chairs; Rp9000 including breakfast and free tea. Small terrace. Cheeky boys try to peep in.

A *pasar malam* opens in the evenings along the waterfront. **Warung Sederhana** on the main street is excellent: delicious fish (Rp1000), rice, and tasty soup (Rp800). Extremely friendly; the beer is warm, but you can cool it with ice in a large bowl. Pare Pare also has a superb Chinese restaurant, **Restaurant Asia,** Jl. Baso Dg. Patompo 25, tel. 21415. Cold drinks. Don't miss the succulent *ikan goreng* and sautéed shrimp. The **Bukit Indah Hotel and Restaurant,** on the top of the hill in back of town, has a splendid view but rather ordinary food.

Getting There And Away
From Ujung Pandang frequent minibuses make the trip to Pare Pare in four hours, Rp2500. Alternatively, you can take a shared taxi for Rp3000; they start next door to the Hotel Nusantara on Jl. Sarappo in Ujung Pandang. The road passes through scenic rural villages and rice-paddy countryside with mountains rising in the east. From Balikpapan and Samarinda in East Kalimantan, small boats leave frequently for Pare Pare. From Pare Pare, buses and minibuses head out regularly in all directions from the bus station in the southeast part of town.

Prahu depart from docks in both northern and southern Pare Pare for the island's northern ports: Mamuju, Toli Toli, Donggala. Now that the road has been dramatically improved, you see more if you go overland through Central Sulawesi to the northern peninsula. *Kapal motor* also depart regularly for the east coast of Kalimantan: Tarakan, Nunukan, Samarinda, Balikpapan, and Sabah in East Malaysia. Numerous shipping companies and agents line Pare Pare's waterfront along Jl. Usahawan.

ENREKANG

This is a good place to stop if you find the heat and noise of Pare Pare too much. Stay at the very clean and pleasant **Hotel Rachmat,** Jl. Dr. Sam Ratulangi, the cleanest in town for Rp15,000 for two beds with *mandi,* Rp25,000 four beds with *mandi.* Price includes breakfast. Balcony, good food, warm beer available from **Toko Utama** on the same street (no. 41). While the proprietor and family of the hotel are strict Muslims, they'll allow you to bring demon drink inside.

POLEWALI

A small Bugis port town on Teluk Mandar, 92 km, 2.5 hours, and Rp2500 by *bemo* or minibus from Pare Pare. Polewali is divided into a southern section with market, port, and guesthouse, and a northern section comprising the administrative buildings of the Polewali Mamasa Regency. The town's best lodging is **Wisma Melati** on the main street close to the bus station; very good value at Rp10,000-12,000 with *mandi* and breakfast. If there've been no guests for awhile, the price will drop instantly to Rp7000-10,000. Slightly cheaper is **Losmen Mery** (sign on main road); Rp5000 s, Rp7500 d with breakfast. Eat at the good, cheap Chinese *warung* in front of the bus station.

For those headed for Mamasa, minibuses and jeeps negotiate the 92 km north over a twisting, scenic mountain road of ruts, sagging bridges, and landslides. Transport usually departs in the morning or early afternoon from the minibus station one km east of the port. The *bemo* fare is Rp3500.

MAMASA

Mamasa is a clean, cool mountain town in a large valley. Churches stand like sentinels on

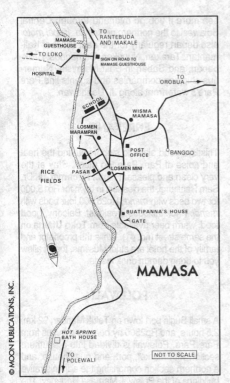

surrounding hills. Muslims, Protestants, Catholics, and followers of the old Aluk Todolo religion live here. Tourism has increased since the road to Mamasa was paved in 1987, and tour companies from Ujung Pandang now bring in groups. Appealing to those seeking interesting places less popular than Tanatoraja, this quiet, delightful little town has the nicest high street in Indonesia. Very few "Hallo Meesters!"

The Mamasa region is sometimes called "West Toraja" because the culture and language are similar to those of the better-known Torajans of Rantepao and Makale. However, the West Torajan culture is much less exploited. The Mamasa area has far fewer *kerbau* (water buffalo), and the funeral ceremonies lack the spectacle and bloody *kerbau* slaughter of the better known Torajans. But the wonderful scenery, architecture, and people are reason enough to spend time here. Mamasa has no banks, so bring plenty of cash.

Accommodations And Food

Losmen Mini is clean, with a nice location (balcony overlooking the street), and asks Rp4000-7500 with *mandi* for bed and breakfast of egg/onion soup and rice. Beer, soda, snacks, and excellent dinners are available for Rp3000. The restaurant is frequented by local police and government forestry officials, often very talkative. The manager, Daniel Sarrin, dispenses helpful information on walks to villages. **Losmen Marampan,** opposite the market, offers economy rooms for Rp4000 s, Rp6000 d without *mandi*. Standard rooms are Rp7000 s, Rp10,000 d with *mandi*. This comfortable Torajan-style house has its own resident interpreter, and lots of locals drop in for a chat and a look at the TV. Can be very noisy.

Mamase Guesthouse features a quiet, peaceful location across a bridge on the road to Loko. Four double rooms for Rp8000 d with *mandi* and Western toilets. Prices include coffee/tea plus towel and soap. Tour companies often book this guesthouse. The *pondok* next door is used as a dining room. **Wisma Mamasa** is reserved for government officials and does not accept tourists.

Meals at Losmen Mini's restaurant are quite good, but Losmen Marampan's restaurant has a more extensive menu, including tasty coconut chicken. Eat in the town *rumah makan,* on the corner opposite the market between Losmen Mini and Losmen Marampan—very cheap, all you can eat for Rp1500. The cook will create special vegetarian meals; her husband is an electronics whiz who built his own radio station, and now runs it from behind a curtain a few feet from your table. He may nonchalantly broadcast news of your arrival to the surrounding villages. The market is open every day; Monday and Thursday are busiest. Simple, cheap, good meals, snacks, and drinks at the *warung* in town.

Crafts

Mamasa *selimut* (striped sheets) cost around Rp35,000—just the thing for Mamasa's cold nights. The cost of a local *sambu* blanket depends on quality; count on around Rp50,000-100,000. Some of these eight-meter-long cloths take seven years to complete, on a loom consisting of nothing but stakes stuck in the ground.

Getting There

There's only one road to Mamasa, a 92-km stretch heading north from Polewali; the five-hour *bemo* journey costs Rp3500. Although the road is in good condition, passengers are jammed in like sardines, the *bemo* slipping and sliding around hairpin mountain turns. Passengers may be asked to walk across a few of the worst bridges. The journey could take as long as seven hours if the fanbelt snaps, or a bald tire blows out, or the driver chats interminably. Consider instead chartering a *bemo*, hiring a bike, or walking out of town and hitching a ride from one of the many road construction trucks. The ride starts out terribly hot, but by the end it's evening,

and decidedly cold. Nice views, though it can cloud up in the afternoons. You can also take a bus from Pare Pare (Rp7500), or from Ujung Pandang to Mamasa on Wednesday, Thursday, Friday, and Sunday at 0800 and 1700 (Rp10,000, 9-10 hours). From Mamasa to Ujung Pandang, a bus leaves Monday, Tuesday, Thursday, and Saturday at 0900 (Rp10,000).

Short Walks

The area offers many day-hike possibilities over rolling hills, rice terraces, and villages in the Mamasa Valley. Walking is best, as there are only 16 km of usable roads, though experienced motorcyclists and mountain bikers can reach

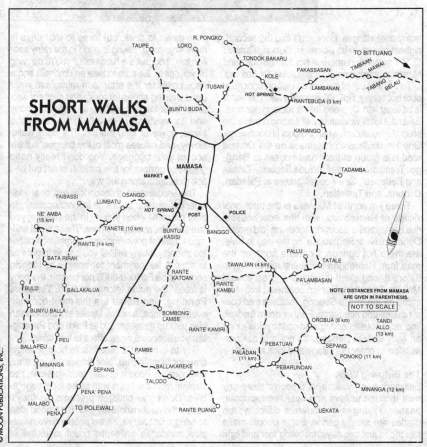

SHORT WALKS FROM MAMASA

NOTE: DISTANCES FROM MAMASA ARE GIVEN IN PARENTHESIS.

NOT TO SCALE

© MOON PUBLICATIONS, INC.

tempat mati *in*
Rantebuda village,
near Mamasa

BILL WEIR

many area villages. Here you'll find the second-highest mountain on Sulawesi, Gunung Quarles (3,107 meters); numerous hot springs surround Mamasa, though not all are suitable for bathing.

Two km south of town is an indoor, concrete-pool hot spring; Rp2000 entrance fee. The water is at least 40° C, piped into a rectangular pool. Beautiful local women in wet *sarung* provide the soap. Arrive at dusk when the pool is uncrowded. One km southeast of Mamasa on the Orobua road is a group of traditional houses at **Banggo.** Traditional villages include **Sepang, Tatale,** and **Ballapeu'.** See wooden graves at **Paladan, Orobua,** and **Tawalian.**

Three km north of Mamasa is the traditional village of **Rantebuda,** with fine *adat* houses, rice barns, and a decaying *kubur tua* (old grave). Donation. Near Rantebuda, on the way to Kole, are more hot springs. Continue north on the road from Rantebuda to several more villages before a long climb through the forest toward Makale. **Tawalian,** four km southeast from Mamasa on the trail to Sepang, features tradition-al houses and rice barns. Farther down the trail, find *adat* houses and scenic countryside along an easy walk to **Sepang.** It's polite to ask per-mission to enter the village and look around.

The Bittuang Walk

Bittuang, near Makale, is a scenic three-day hike through valleys and over two mountain passes. Hiking is of moderate difficulty; the grades are mostly gentle. Some people make this trip in just two days, traveling fast and light from dawn to dusk, but three to four days is more enjoyable. Hiking is good in the rainy sea-son too, though it's a hard walk if you're carrying all your gear. Be sure to take an umbrella and a pack cover for the afternoon rains, and wear good walking shoes for rocky and slippery sec-tions. Your *losmen* will help arrange for a pony and its master for Rp40,000; the fee is the same, however long the trip. The pony walks slowly, and refuses most of the bridges, but will accept your baggage. You don't really need guides or porters for this walk. Just set out and ask directions along the way.

The *kepala desa,* a schoolteacher, or any vil-lager can put you up. It's no longer necessary to offer presents when staying in the villages; you can stay just about anywhere. These small self-made "hotels" prefer money—sometimes rather too strongly. Many will tell you any lie to get you to stay. A fair payment for board and lodging seems to be Rp7000-8000 per person; the pony is free if the guide fetches its food. **Timbaan, Ponding,** and **Belau** are the most common overnight stops. A coffee farmer at **Pakassasan** also puts up travelers, and at **Paku** and **Pasang-tau** you'll receive more offers to bed down.

Try to arrive at a reasonable hour to allow time for washing up, sleeping arrangements, and cooking. Food is usually reddish-brown rice straight from the fields with some local vegeta-bles. Don't give children presents, as they'll pester the next visitors for gifts. It's a good idea to bring a first aid kit, as the people have no as-pirin, bandages, antiseptic, cough medicine, or insect bite balm. An antifungal cream is useful for you and them. Giving out penicillin isn't wise, though jungle ulcers are common.

From Mamasa, follow the road north along the river past **Rantebuda** (four km), **Lambanan** (eight km), and **Pakassasan** (12 km). From here the trail climbs high to a pass through a beautiful forest of big trees and ferns. There's no place to stay on this 14-km mountain section so get an early start or bring a tent. From the pass, the trail winds down to **Timbaan** (26 km), where there are three guesthouses in a row; Rp5000 for bed, breakfast, and dinner. These accommodations also feature kiosks where you can buy bananas, biscuits, *gula gula,* and cigarettes. From Timbaan, the trail drops gradually to **Mawai** (30 km) on the Mawai River where there are more places to stay. This is the halfway point to Bittuang.

From Mawai, the trail follows the river to the Masuppu River, then winds through the Masuppu Valley to a covered bridge (35 km). Cross the bridge and climb the steep trail to **Ponding** (39 km). Wash in the river just before Ponding. Saturday is market day in Ponding, with lots of crimson-mouthed, betel-chewing women, men selling bamboo tubes foaming with *tuak,* and young men hawking piles of dried fish. Very crowded and lively. From Ponding, continue

climbing through rice terraces to **Belau** (a *rumah adat* here), 42 km; **Paku,** 46 km; **Pasangtau,** 51 km (a house here sells food, tea, and coffee). From Pasangtau, walk through a forest to the pass, 54 km; you can camp here. From the summit, descend three km on an easy trail to the rice terraces of **Patongloan Desa,** 57 km; it's three more easy km into Bittuang, passing a hilltop church, a reservoir, and a school.

Bittuang is a delightful, cool market town— Monday is market day—with no electricity or asphalt roads. It's connected to Makale by a scenic but very rough 41-km road. In Bittuang stay in **Losmen Papongian** across from the *pasar;* Rp3000 per person for a charming, old-fashioned room, with *mandi* down in the yard. The food is simple but good and the place clean with few mosquitos. Hurricane lamps and smoky paraffin wick-lights, some converted from old beer cans. The old woman is gray-haired (a rarity) and quite beautiful, with a lovely smile. *Bemo* leave for Makale (Rp2500, three hours) in the morning and afternoon. For good views, walk the very bumpy first half of the road. **Se'seng,** about halfway, has a nice natural swimming hole. **Rembon,** 12 km before Makale, hosts a big market every six days. From Bittuang is a trail north (36 km, two days) to **Pangala.** From Pangala, trucks travel 58 km to Rantepao.

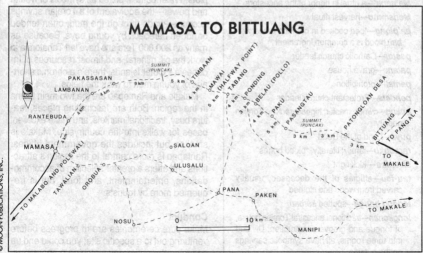

MAMASA TO BITTUANG

TANATORAJA

The name Toraja was given originally by the Buginese and means "People of the High Country," referring to those who occupy the core of central Celebes, from where the four peninsular legs radiate. These ancient peoples are believed to have originated from Cambodia; Toraja legends claim their ancestors arrived in a storm from the northern seas, pulled their splintered boats ashore, and used them as shelters. Today, the principal attractions of Tanatoraja include its houses: shaped like ships, they all face north, the direction of the people's origin. Other tourist draws are traditional villages, graves, scenery, farming, and the frequent and highly ritualistic religious ceremonies, including rites of birth, marriage, fertility, and death. Buffalo are sacrificed on a number of different occasions—a vivid, savage sight.

Tanatoraja, or Torajaland, is one of the country's most ruggedly magnificent regions—a high, mountain-bound, 3,600-square-km, fertile plateau. These mountains have protected patterns of life and custom which have evolved and changed little over centuries. Rice is grown in irrigated terraces, either carved by hand into the sides of hills or stretching into the farthest corners of the small valleys. The rice diet is supplemented with maize, cassava, and vegetables grown in small family plots. Water buffalo, prized as symbols of wealth and power—the equivalent of a Torajan savings account—wade through the mud, often tended or ridden bareback by young boys. Because as many as 200,000 Torajans have left Tanatoraja to work the oil, mineral, and timber resources of Indonesia's Outer Islands, there's a chronic shortage of young men to work the fields.

Makale and Rantepao are the two main towns in the region. Both are fascinating places, feature busy, traditional markets, and make excellent bases for walks into the countryside. Makale is smaller, but includes the government offices. Rantepao is more central to the region's attractions and offers a greater selection of accommodations, entertainment, and food, but is frequented more by tourists.

Conduct
Make sure ceremonies are in progress before venturing out to a specific site; you could end up spending the entire day watching preparations, with nothing really happening. Go with a local

TANATORAJA GLOSSARY

alang—rice barn

aluk—animist religion or symbolic ritual

Aluk Todolo—traditional religion of Torajaland

banua—house

bombo—ghost

erong—grave for a coffin, supported by wood beams driven into a cliff face

katik—mythical animal resembling a snake; symbolizes nobility. *Katik* are carved on the fronts of some *tongkonan*.

kaunan—slave, dependent

kerusu mengat—thank you

la'bo'—large knife

lo'ko—cave

liang—grave

Ma'bua'—an important smoke-rising ritual

Ma'nene'—a ritual in honor of the ancestors

Menammu—harvest ritual

pa'piong—food cooked in bamboo tubes; *kerbau* blood is a common ingredient

pastor—Catholic church leader

patane—grave house

pemali—prohibition

pendeta—Protestant church leader

puang—owner, master; highest-ranking Torajan nobility

puya—Land of the Dead

rarabuku—family; literally, "blood bones"

sisemba'—kick fight

tau-tau—effigies of the deceased, usually carved from wood and clothed

tedong bonga—spotted *kerbau*

tongkonan—traditional ancestral Torajan house, of tongue-and-groove construction. Divided into three rooms, all have symbolic carvings on the outside.

guide for a reasonable fee of around Rp5000; he'll keep you informed about what's going on during a ceremony. Or ask around in the hotels and restaurants, or at Rantepao's tourist office, before setting out. When attending a funeral, find out who the host and village dignitaries are, then approach and shake their hands. If you give cigarettes, perfume, soap, and the like, it means you share in their grief. At ceremonies, don't sit in any prepared or roped-off areas unless invited. Be discreet with your camera and dress. Men should wear shirts and pants, women full tops with sleeves, longish dresses, or *sarung.* Avoid bringing a nonlocal guide, as the Torajans interact easily and are happy to provide explanations. Also, they're more at ease if you're alone; guides tend to tell too many tall tales.

When To Visit

June, July, and August are very hot. Torajaland's best weather occurs April through October—the dry season. However, even in the dry season afternoon showers are not unusual, so start your sightseeing early, especially for photo-taking. In July and August Torajaland is flooded with European tourists toting video cameras. During this time it may be difficult to rent a room in Rantepao or Makale; prices tend to inflate. As many as 1,000 Europeans may rain down upon Rantepao; for a handout, groups of children will sing "Alouette" in perfect unison. The period with the fewest tourists is May-June. After the harvest, between September and December, is probably the best time to visit; the people have sufficient funds and free time to spend on such ritual occasions as funerals. To attract more tourists, the government now encourages the Torajans to space their death festivals throughout the year.

THE PEOPLE

Before the Dutch arrived in 1905, the Torajans were one of the fiercest and most remote people in Indonesia. Headhunters, they displayed the skulls of their enemies in a lodge (*lobo*) in the center of the village. Their skill with blowpipes and spears was uncanny; they could pin small animals and birds at 15 meters, and impale a man at 30 meters. The Torajans once lived in small walled fortress villages on top of hills, resembling European medieval fortifications. In the late 19th century, Torajaland was known for its coffee, which the Bugis and Makassarese traded for guns and cotton cloth. During this period Toraja's population was depleted by frequent raids from the lowlands for slaves. The Dutch invaded the highlands in 1905, and, after bitter resistence, vanquished and captured the last Torajan warlord, Pong Tiku, at his fortress in Pangala in 1906.

Precolonial Torajans lived in a highly stratified, nearly impervious feudal society in which villagers suspected of witchcraft or sorcery were tried by cultic ordeal. Their fingers were forced into burning pitch; if the hand burned, they were guilty, handed over to other villagers for sacrificial beheading. When the Dutch moved them down into the highland valleys and introduced agriculture, fixed boundaries, taxes, schools, Christianity, and disease, the old family structure and religion began to break down.

Although buffalo have now replaced human heads at sacrifices and the elaborate old religion has been diluted, this is still a society with very strong *adat.* An extensive oral literature, including animal stories, chants, rhymed poetry, and lullabies, exists among the Torajans. And there still exist three classes of Torajans. *Tokapua* are the noblemen; they generally have longer hair, wear special turbans and loincloths, and employ servants. Although only about five percent of Toraja's total population of 340,000, the *tokapua* own most of the land. The *tomokaka* are the middle-class tradespeople, one-quarter of the total. The *tobuda* are the common people, farmers and sharecroppers, about seven of every 10 Torajans.

Religion

The old religion is called Aluk Todolo ("Worship of the Spirits of Ancestors"). Today it's estimated only 25% of the people continue to practice it, mostly in remote areas, while around 65% claim allegiance to Christianity and 10% to Islam. Aluk Todolo divides the universe and the world of ritual in half: life and death. It's probable that, originally, equal attention was paid to both halves of the ritual world. But because the "life" side emphasized fertility, it was damned and forbidden by Christianity as "pagan"; funerals, on the other hand, have always been acceptable to the Church. Thus today the Torajans emphasize death over life.

Ironically, since Christianity has had such a democratizing effect, people can now hold as elaborate a funeral as they wish, and funerals have assumed a much greater importance in Torajan ritual life. Besides funerals, many of the old ceremonies and animist rites have been carried over into the Christian domain—indeed, there's a fantastic mixing of the two religions. For example, buffalo are still sacrificed at the Feast of the Dead; however, participants make sure they attend church that morning, too. The Aluk Todolo Torajans worshipped the buffalo as a fertility cult figure, and you still see people wear headdresses of buffalo horns in their dances.

The hereafter, called *puya,* is where everyone will live under the same conditions as he or she did on earth. This is why every Torajan tries to attain as much wealth as possible. Souls of animals follow their masters into heaven; thus the animal sacrifices. In a very real way, Torajans *live* for death.

Funerals

The Torajans believe that when a person dies, the soul leaves the body but not the general vicinity. It remains restless and dissatisfied until the burial ritual is complete. The corpse itself, partially embalmed, lies in the back of the house, or in a temporary grave, for the weeks or months necessary to complete the expensive funeral arrangements and assemble far-flung relatives. Much of a family's wealth, accumulated over an entire lifetime, is spent on staging the finest, most elaborate funeral possible, a strange blending of solemnity and celebration. The multiphased ceremony used to be held in special fields (*rante*) where tall spires that serve as monuments to ancestors stand. Temporary buildings were constructed, then burned afterwards. In olden times, freshly severed human heads were the required offerings at the final burial. After the funeral, the heads were hung in the *rumah adat* and in the houses of the closest kin. You can still find old heads in some houses.

Today, buffalo and pigs are slaughtered, a gruesome sight. Meat is distributed according to the rank and status of the funeral participants; the largest, choicest cuts go to the highest station. Often up to a thousand guests must be fed; 100 fat buffalo could be slaughtered at a very wealthy family's funeral, which can easily

last a week or two. Finally a gong is sounded, and a cock tied to a branch released, signifying the departure of the soul. This is the beginning of the "Festival of the Dead," a happy, almost orgiastic occasion. The corpse, embalmed and wrapped in many shrouds and looking like a big striped pillow, is kept company by professional mourners so it won't become lonely during the celebratory feasting. Villagers sing, dance, and drink palm wine; watch choreographed kick bouts and cock and buffalo fights.

The corpse is carried down from the house and placed inside a granary-shaped structure on a stretcher for transportation to its final resting place, *liang*. These sunken family graves in cliffs came into fashion after thieves from outside Tanatoraja began stealing the gold and jewels interred with the dead. Those Toraja who could afford the most extravagant funerals are buried the farthest up the cliff.

Athletic pallbearers carry the tightly wrapped body bundle up 4-30 meters on a notched, nearly vertical bamboo ladder. Every face looks up, then the corpse is placed into the hole. Although the opening is small, the interiors of these cave-graves stretch sometimes for kilometers, and are able to contain entire families. The Batutu-monga area is probably the best place to view Torajan burial sites. Open-air tourist museums like Lemo and Londa seem like abandoned ghost-villages.

Tau-Tau

For each *liang,* wooden effigies (*tau-tau*) stand eerily on balconies set into the limestone cliff. Since the Torajans engage in active ancestor worship, these outside galleries, in a sense, are their church. In the puppets dwell the ghosts of the deceased buried inside. Torajan sculptors have visited Bali, and today you see more naturalistic effigy faces on the *tau-tau,* complete with the deceased's wrinkles and moles. Standing like spectators, these realistic puppets are protected by thick paint. The head and arms are hinged so they can swivel; their clothing, worn by sun, wind, and rain, is changed at least once a year by relatives. Some of the figures have traveling sacks for their trip to the Land of Souls. Art collectors pay Muslim graverobbers handsomely, and you can find *tau-tau* today in antique shops from Los Angeles and Tokyo.

Torajan tau-tau

Children's Grave Tree

Children are buried in special trees called *terra* trees. Each village has one. The tree is very tall and very old. Little doors about 15-by-15 cm are cut in at various heights, made of matting from a nearby palm. When a baby dies, a grave is cut into the tree; the baby's body is placed inside, and the door closed. In a few years the tree heals and covers the baby's body and door.

Animists believe the soul of a baby who has not touched the earth will go directly to heaven. This is a comforting thought for grieving parents. An infant is defined as anyone from a stillborn child to a baby beginning to crawl. Great care is taken that the baby not touch the earth; infants sleep in hammocks and are held in their parents' hands when bathed.

There is a high infant mortality rate in Tanatoraja, and hundreds of children have been buried in some trees, like those in **Sangalla** and near **Tampong Allo**. Dim scars show where the bark has grown over old graves.

Other Ceremonies

Some fertility rites are still practiced by the older Torajans on the occasion of the birth of a baby or buffalo. Rice is the most important crop and has more than 10 ceremonies related to it. Blessing houses requires a series of important ceremonies. A small one marks the beginning of construction, followed by others during various stages of work. After completion, a major celebration is held which may include *pagellu* dancing. During the dance, relatives in the audience may dart among the dancers, stuffing Rp10,000 notes into their headbands. In ceremonies relating to death, wooden graves (*tedong-tedong*) are cleansed by relatives of the deceased each year and the clothing of the corpse is changed at least three times to ensure the soul rests in peace.

Another ritual is the *tuka,* performed for housewarming and harvest ceremonies. The *maro* ritual, associated with the fertility of the *sawah,* is staged to exorcise evil spells. In the *rambu tuka* ceremony offerings are made to Puang Matua (the Creator) to ward off epidemics and calamities. The *mabua* is a major event staged at 12-year intervals, a dance spiritually invaluable to the Torajans. Months of work are involved in getting ready for this nightlong ritual—preparing a ceremonial field, costumes, and miniature implements of everyday life. There are stately female singers, festival poles, war yells, and bonfires of exploding bamboo stalks. Priests wearing water buffalo headdresses rush about a sacred tree. Mabua concludes with a mock copulation with a buffalo.

ARTS AND CRAFTS

Architecture

Torajans are known for their remarkable dwellings (*tongkonan*), which also serve as reference points when tracing family ties. The placenta of each child born in the house is buried under the east side of the house, the direction of the rising sun, associated with life. Similar to the Batak buildings of North Sumatra, *tongkonan* are raised on wooden poles and look as if they could make a sea journey—their sweeping roofs resemble huge slope-prowed vessels navigating through an ocean of tropical foliage and verdant rice paddies. In villages where the houses and granaries stand in rows, it feels like you're in the middle of a fleet of ships floating on the wind. Set astride thick pillars and built solely by the tongue-and-groove method, using no nails, a traditional house has a layered bamboo roof; its sides a maze-like profusion of rich geometric ornamentation in black, red, and white, representing aspects of the festivals of Aluk Todolo.

People are allowed to place only those designs on their houses which are appropriate to their class. Horns of the buffalo, symbol of fertility, strength, prosperity, and protection from evil, decorate the gables of Torajan houses, each set representing a death feast. Villages are very simply designed: a row of residences with square columns faces another row of matching grain sheds with round columns. These rice barns can be moved intact on runners from one place to another. The number of barns indicates the family's wealth. All houses point north, while their entrances faces east. Though origin-houses in each village are still the focus of religious activity, modern technology is replacing much of the traditional saddle-roofed construction—zinc roofs instead of cooler bamboo, and metal nails. New buildings are now interspersed among the old. Government subsidy programs, however, encourage the use of the old techniques.

Dance

Torajan dances are slow-moving, rhythmical, even majestic, usually accompanied by taped music or the beat of a large drum. Dancers are dressed in long, colorful silk skirts and woven fabrics, adorning themselves in beaded corsets and capes, with gold jewelry draped from their necks and encircling their arms. Men wear spectacular kris in silver or gold scabbards. This regal pageantry can be seen even in tiny villages deep in the mountains of Torajaland. Dances are mostly ceremonial, though sometimes tourists are asked to join in circle dances.

The magellu dance is performed at a thanksgiving ceremony, after the harvest or the completion of a house. In this serene dance, three to five teenage girls wearing beaded costumes stretch out slender arms and flutter their fingers while advancing toward and retreating from the audience to the rhythm of a drum. In the manganda performance, a group of men wearing gigantic headdresses of silver coins, bulls' horns, and black velvet are accompanied by a bell and a leader's voice. These headdresses are so heavy the dance lasts only a few minutes. The maro dance rite is held when a sick person must be purified. The manimbong and ma'bugi are harvest dance ceremonies. The pa'daobulan is performed by a group of young people wearing long white dresses.

Music

The bamboo flute is the favorite Torajan instrument, played at funerals and harvests; schoolchildren play lively flute music out of sheer joy. There are both long and short transverse flutes, all decorated in the old style with poker work, beautifully engraved and colored. Other instruments are fashioned from palm leaves. Though their singing is monotonous and restricted to just a few notes, songs include chants, poetic love epics, and dirges. Singers are frequently accompanied by one-stringed lutes played with a bow.

Games

Sisemba (kick fights) are staged from late June to early August. This is a terrifying recreational sport where men fly through the air, sometimes knocking each other unconscious. The hands may not be used in this mock combat, in which individuals and sometimes whole villages take part. Takro is a ball game using a rattan ball kicked and bounced with the head and legs over a bamboo stick about one meter high, fixed parallel to the ground. Played something like volleyball, but with only two to three players.

Crafts

Torajan crafts are very similar to the Dayak art of Borneo, mostly two-dimensional and not very dynamic, yet some make striking wall ornaments and hangings. Torajans produce attractive carved wooden panels with stylized buffalo and betelnut leaves, embellished in subtle shades of blacks, whites, reds, and mustards. These panels are copied from those decorating houses and granaries. Craftsmen have since adapted these decorative panels to other uses, such as trays and plates.

Torajaland is very much a bamboo culture: roofs, water carriers, cooking vessels, winnowing trays, and engraved and decorated cases are all made from bamboo. The places to look for traditional implements are the markets. A big market occurs every six days, rotating between

Makale, Rembon, Rantepao, Bittuang, and Sangalla. Lime cases and bamboo flutes are covered with intricate black designs burnt in with a hot iron. If you go out to the villages themselves, flutes sell for Rp2000, bamboo necklaces Rp1500, small statuary Rp45,000, and carved murals Rp5000-20,000. In the interior you'll find fine expert pottery.

Textiles

Sa'dan is the Torajan weaving center, where local women have formed a cooperative. All designs seen in Torajan houses are also worked into their fabrics. Human figures are so cleverly interwoven into strict geometric patterns that it takes a sharp eye to pick out the figures from the lines. Much Torajan weaving is similar to Guatemalan weaving in texture, design, and even color—red, white, yellow, black. You can buy some beautiful *sarung* for Rp6000-8000 in the Rantepao market. Expensive, organically dyed *ikat* blankets take up to three months to make; the best come from Makki, Rongkong, and Seko, and cost Rp75,000-250,000. Reddish *ikat* weavings with black and blue patterns are artificially dyed and cost Rp55,000-160,000. Torajan *ikat* is most often handspun cotton funeral blankets with large geometric motifs in the traditional colors: rust, red, white, and black. Villages outside Rantepao are swamped with busloads of tourists, so prices are variable and unpredictable and bargaining is difficult.

Bark clothing (tapa or *fuyus*) reached a level of sophistication unknown anywhere else in the world and was widespread in the hinterlands until the 1930s. With the shortage of fabrics engendered by the Japanese occupation of WW II, there was a revival of the art, where fibrous inner tree bark is soaked in water for weeks, then beaten until soft and flexible. Small pieces are felted into large ones, eliminating the need for seams. You can find old examples in the interior; bark cloth is still produced in Kageroa and Bada. You can view some very rare Sulawesian tapa specimens in Jakarta's Textile Museum.

FOOD AND DRINK

Pa'piong is anything cooked in bamboo sections. Examples include rice in coconut milk, and meat and vegetables in buffalo or pig blood.

Pa'piong is available cheap and in large portions all over Rantepao; order it with the words *"Kami suka sekali makanan pedas"* ("We like hot food"). Traditional condiments—*sambal asli*—are included.

A typical Torajan breakfast is *songkolo,* made of sticky rice; *lombok* (chili); and coconut; it usually sells for Rp500. You can enjoy local specialties of fish and pork in the market; many local *warung* serve fiery hot *kerbau* dishes with all the trimmings. Also try *bale* and *lada* (fish and chilies), and the sweet snack *baje'* (fried coconut with brown sugar, four small packets for only Rp300)—completely natural and delicious.

World-class coffee is grown here, especially in the colder regions around Pangala and Nanggala. In Tokyo, Torajan coffee is highly prized and sells for around Rp42,000 per kilo. Buy it in the Rantepao market for Rp8000 per kilo. *Balok* (palm wine) is often consumed at Torajan ceremonies. Transported in long, foaming bamboo sections, *balok* is available in every village and is drunk all day long out in the *padi*. A mild, mellow booze; you feel more stoned than drunk. There are three varieties: sweet, medium sweet, and sour. Sweet *balok* (Rp500 for a tall bamboofull) turns sour in about two hours; it has the color of lemonade. Try mixing the sweet and sour together. The sour variety is redder; more coconut skin is added.

TRANSPORTATION

Getting There

From Ujung Pandang, Merpati serves the airstrip outside of Rantepao three times weekly (Rp48,000, leaving at 0900), but most travelers take the bus—they don't want to miss the magnificent mountain scenery on the way up the east coast from Ujung Pandang. The **Rantetayo Airport** lies 24 km southwest of Rantepao off the road between Makale and Rembon. A rather undependable service; flights are frequently cancelled because of the weather or lack of passengers. Flights return to Ujung Pandang at 1015.

Liman Express (Jl. Timor, tel. 5851) buses take nine hours and cost Rp10,000. They depart at 0600 from the depot opposite Ramayana Satrya Hotel (the night coach leaves at 2100) or from Panaikan bus station, 20 minutes by *bemo*

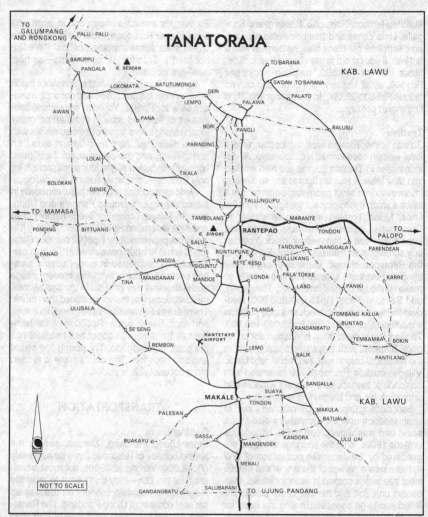

TANATORAJA

NOT TO SCALE

© MOON PUBLICATIONS, INC.

from town. Buy tickets a day ahead and get a seat in the front. Another way to reach the area is from South Sulawesi's east coast. From Palopo, a road corkscrews high into the mountains, then drops down to Rantepao; a two-hour trip by minibus (Rp3500).

The most scenic route to Tanatoraja passes through lush agricultural land on the western coastal plain to Pare Pare, then climbs through spectacular limestone mountains and rich val-

leys. The southern Torajans, who grow high-altitude crops like corn and *ubi gayo*, wear *sarung*, ride horses, worship Allah, and are ethnically the same as the Torajans. Friendly roadside restaurants have great views over deep ravines. When you see your first church and when the cattle start to give way to buffalo, you're in Torajaland. The actual entry point is 1,000-meter-high **Salu Barani**, with its elaborate gateway covered in Torajan motifs.

Getting Around

Torajan guides make trailfinding easier; ask at the hotels. Most speak good English and can organize everything. Guides usually specialize in certain areas and styles of travel. You can rent horses to carry gear for long-distance trips, but it's more pleasant to walk. For an eight-day trip, such as the **Simbuang Loop** passing through or near many traditional Torajan villages, expect to spend about Rp210,000-315,000. Using the map, create your own walks.

If you're in a hurry, you can hire minibuses (*kijang*) with drivers for Rp30,000 per day, plus all entrance fees and the lunch/drink costs of the driver and helper. For car, driver, guide, and entrance fees, the rate can go as high as Rp65,000 per day. Ask for *kijang* at Restaurant Rachmat in Rantepao. Or hire a vehicle and driver at the Ramayana Satrya Hotel in Ujung Pandang for Rp50,000 per day. You can try to hitch on workman's lorries; it's possible to reach many sites on one- to two-hour walks from Rantepao.

With your own vehicle you can easily see Londa, Lemo, and Kete Kesu in a single day. If you intend to design your own route off the main roads, rent a sturdy four-wheel-drive vehicle. Except for the roads to Makale, Palopo, and Kete Kesu, routes can be very rough, full of bone-jarring potholes and boulders.

Signs placed at the start of side roads announce the location of sites. Class one, such as Lemo, Londa, and Kete'Kesu, cost Rp1500 pp; class two, like Suaya, Rp1000; and class three destinations like Tampong Allo run Rp500. Admission to remote villages like Batutumonga is free. Cars cost Rp100 extra. Some keepers may be amenable to negotiations.

Some of the longer walks require communicating with villagers in Bahasa Indonesia. Buy a phrasebook and learn to use it; get tight with locals who don't speak English. They may take you around to remote locales where you could stumble Indiana Jones-style upon *tau-tau* in the midst of thick undergrowth.

RANTEPAO

Rantepao is a cool, busy, midsized mountain town with potholed roads, a huge market, and wide streets full of honking, bouncing *bemo* and whining motorcycles. A good place to base yourself, especially if walking, since most roads fan out from Rantepao. And despite all the tourists, the city is actually a manageable size, with lots of atmosphere. People are helpful and friendly; except for souvenirs, you're charged the same prices as the locals. It only takes a couple of days to learn your way around. *Becak* cruise up and down Jl. Mappanyuki looking for fares, but you can easily walk almost anywhere.

SIGHTS

Rantepao's fascinating market, on Jl. Abdul Gani 1.5 km northeast of town, is the region's largest. It offers an enormous variety of produce, merchandise, and handicrafts, and is open every day. See Torajan traditional life firsthand, without ever leaving town. An exotic place to explore—a cornucopia of fruits, vegetables, coffee, *tuak*, poultry, eels, dried fish, bamboo flutes, decorated containers, model houses, hand-forged swords, basketry, and giant conical hats. All is available cheaply—after bargaining, of course. Don't miss the squealing pig market. At **Pasar Hewan**, in a big open field in Bolu, dozens of tethered *kerbau* are surrounded by their owners and prospective buyers. The spotted buffalo have great ceremonial value and a correspondingly high price—up to Rp7 million. These beasts are rarely found outside Tanatoraja.

ACCOMMODATIONS

Rantepao offers a wide selection of reasonably priced places to stay. During late July, August, and September, however, hordes of Italian, French, Japanese, Dutch, and German tourists pour into town on tour buses, sometimes doubling the prices. Then you'll be lucky to secure a bed, and may have to settle for a *losmen* in Batutumonga or Pangala, an expensive hotel, or a place in Makale. The rest of the year hotels are dying for customers. If staying for several days or more, ask for a discount. The hotels on the main street are easily found, but quieter and more pleasant accommodations, often with their own private gardens alongside brilliant green rice fields, are available down the side roads.

Budget

Hotel Marlin is at Jl. Mappanyuki 75, tel. (0423) 21215, right next to the Liman Express office; guests receive a 10% discount on bus fare to Ujung Pandang. The balcony hangs over a noisy street. At first the place asks Rp15,000, but the price will plunge dramatically if there are no other guests—or no hot water, which is frequently the case. American breakfast Rp2500, continental breakfast Rp1500. **Wisma Rosa** has dark, dingy, mosquito-infested rooms for Rp6000 s. A better value is **Wisma Indo Grace**, Jl. Mappanyuki 72; Rp5000 s, Rp6000 d for bright, airy rooms. Helpful manager.

Moderate

Most midrange places start out at around Rp12,500 d, but in the off season many will go for Rp10,000 d. Always ask beforehand if there's any additional tax or service charge. **Wisma Maria I**, Jl. Ratulangi, tel. (0423) 21165, is living off its reputation and has become somewhat complacent. Rooms cost Rp7500 s, Rp12,500 d with cold *mandi*; Rp12,500 s, Rp18,000 d, Rp30,000 t with hot *mandi*. Breakfast with homemade bread is Rp2500. Attractive facilities. The cheaper rooms fill up fast. The more modern, upscale **Wisma Maria II** lies two km south of Rantepao on the road to Makale; Rp15,000-30,000 s and d.

Wisma Monika, Jl. Ratulangi 38, has a nice garden, courtyard, and sitting area, but bugs and ants infest the beds and some travelers complain they're charged more than the price originally quoted. Still, you get a huge and wonderful breakfast for Rp2000 and a free pot of tea three times a day. Non-tourist season prices are (allegedly) Rp8000 s, Rp12,500 d.

Wisma Irama, Jl. Abdul Gani, tel. 21371, charges Rp8000 s for bed and breakfast with

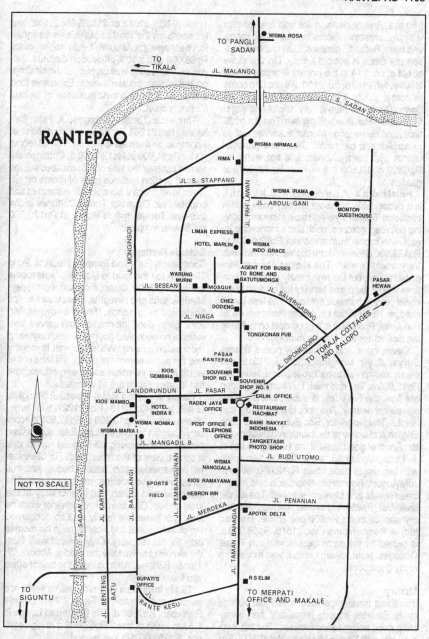

RANTEPAO

TO PANGLI SADAN

• WISMA ROSA

TO TIKALA

JL. MALANGO

S. SADAN

• WISMA NIRMALA

RIMA I

JL. S. STAPPANG

• WISMA IRAMA

JL. ABDUL GANI

MONTON GUESTHOUSE •

JL. PA'H' LAWAN

LIMAN EXPRESS •
HOTEL MARLIN •
• WISMA INDO GRACE

WARUNG MURNI ■
JL. SESEAN ■ MOSQUE

AGENT FOR BUSES TO BONE AND BATUTUMONGA

JL. SAUERIGADING

PASAR HEWAN ■

CHEZ DODENG ■

JL. NIAGA

TONGKONAN PUB ■

TO TORAJA COTTAGES AND PALOPO

PASAR RANTEPAO ■
SOUVENIR SHOP NO. 1 ■

KIOS GEMBIRA ■

SOUVENIR SHOP NO. 9 ■
ERLIN OFFICE

JL. LANDORUNDUN   JL. PASAR

KIOS MAMBO ■
RADEN JAYA OFFICE
RESTAURANT RACHMAT ■

HOTEL INDRA II ■
BANK RAKYAT INDONESIA ■

• WISMA MONIKA
POST OFFICE & TELEPHONE OFFICE ■

WISMA MARIA I •
TANGKETASIK PHOTO SHOP ■

JL. MANGADIL B.

JL. BUDI UTOMO

WISMA NANGGALA ■

KIOS RAMAYANA ■

SPORTS FIELD

HEBRON INN •

JL. PENANIAN

JL. MERDEKA

APOTIK DELTA ■

NOT TO SCALE

JL. KARTIKA

R S ELIM ■

BUPATI'S OFFICE ■

TO SIGUNTU

JL. RANTE KESU

TO MERPATI OFFICE AND MAKALE

JL. SADAN
JL. BENTENG BATU
JL. RATULANGI
JL. PEMBANGUNAN
JL. TAMAN BAHAGIA
JL. MONGINSIDI
JL. DIPONEGORO

free tea. A very clean, quiet and airy *losmen* with big, attractive rooms and spotless *mandi* and toilet. Beautiful gardens. During the off season the place is almost empty. On the same street at no. 14A is the homey **Monton Guest House,** tel. 21675, fax 2100. It's great to come in from a trek to a place with the beds turned down. The family here is very helpful and eager to please—Parubak will explain Torajan traditions, and can arrange Merpati tickets as well as motorbike and car rental. Clean and peaceful rooms with bath, shower, and hot water for Rp9500 d, 12,500 t; breakfast Rp3000. Nice garden.

Hotel Indra II, Jl. Landorundun 63, tel. 21163, is a dependable, pleasant, friendly hotel built in traditional Torajan style with a big restaurant serving *pa'piong,* gardens, pool, and a moneychanger. Clean rooms from a modest Rp63,000 d to Rp126,000 d for riverfront rooms. Add 16% tax. Very attentive staff. The kitchen seems overpriced at first, but the high quality and large portions render the prices fair. Try the chicken in coconut curry in bamboo sections. The less fancy, cheaper **Hotel Indra I** is across the street on Jl. Ratulangi; Rp11,500 s, a good deal considering the nice rooms and friendly management.

Clean, quiet, and reasonably priced **Wisma Surya,** Jl. Wr. Monginsidi 36, tel. 21312, has clean rooms with bathroom and toilet for Rp12,000 d. Tea and fresh fruit from the garden are free, the breakfast is super, and there's a restaurant nearby. The people are friendly and helpful. The proprietor, Ros Boby, speaks good English and works at the tourist information center. Another good hotel is the **Rantepao Inn** at Jl. Landorundun 35, tel. 21397. A twin room with two single beds costs Rp12,000, even in July/August. Rooms are clean, with cold *mandi*; clean sheets and blankets supplied. Tea is free; breakfast (Rp2500) is served downstairs. Laundry service costs Rp500 per article. **Hebron Inn,** Jl. Pembangunan, tel. 21519, Rp58,000 s, is owned by the same people who run Toraja Cottages. Neat, clean, central, well run, with a really good cook.

Luxury

You'll find three expensive hotels just outside town. Facilities include restaurant, bar, swimming pool, and meeting facilities. The big, two-star, two-part **Toraja Misiliana Hotel,** P.O. Box 1, tel. (0423) 21212 or 21537, fax 21512, two km south on the road to Makale, is designed for package tourists. A basic room costs Rp96,000 with a 10% off-season discount. Balconies, TV, wall-to-wall carpets, souvenir shop, courteous staff, transfer service. Expensive food and drink. If there are no busloads of tourists it's pretty quiet.

Three-star **Toraja Cottages,** Jl. Paku Balasara, tel. 21268, is three km northeast of Rantepao on the road to Palopo. The 63 rooms go for Rp84,000 s, Rp126,000 d. Cottages are spread out over the side of a landscaped hill; the second section features rows of rooms on different levels, with a big open-air restaurant and popular bar. Opposite Toraja Cottages is the four-star **Toraja Prince Hotel,** at Rp130,000 pp. Swimming pool.

Outside Rantepao

Comfortable **Pia's and Poppies Hotel,** Jl. Pong Tiku 27A (on the road to Makale), rents rooms for Rp5000-7000. Clean, nice bathrooms, psychedelic tubs and skylights, great views of rice fields and carp ponds. The chef-owner, Mr. Paul, gives good information and serves sensational homecooked gourmet French-style and Indonesian cuisine. While the wait is lengthy and the prices somewhat steep, the food is well worth it. The pumpkin soup, egg frittata, and fish in spicy sauce are all wonderful.

Near Pia's is the **Hotel Pison,** Jl. Pongtiku G II/8, tel. (0423) 21344 or 21221, with large, clean rooms for Rp10,000 s, Rp12,500 d economy. Bargain for longer stays. Each room has a private terrace looking out on quiet *sawah,* and a superb view of the mountains. For breakfast eat homemade bread, butter, cheese, jam, fruit salad, very good coffee, *marquisa* juice. The owner speaks Dutch and is secretary of the local church. One traveler reports that when he took sick the whole family was so concerned the church council and vicar came to his room to pray for his recovery. Only a short walk from the center of town; take the road to Makale, Jl. Taman Bahagia. After passing the tourist office you'll see the sign.

Tikala Indah is a very nice *wisma* set in rice fields in the direction of Tikala 2.7 km outside Rantepao, Rp7500 d. The **Rantepao Lodge** is 1.5 km south of town; Rp53,000 d in high season, Rp25,000 d in low season.

FOOD AND ENTERTAINMENT

Rantepao's *warung* offer standard Indonesian foods—*martabak, sate, nasi goreng,* fish and vegetables. In the market you'll find a wide variety of fruits, especially bananas. Nice, smooth *balok* is sold in the center of the square behind the main market buildings. The town's restaurants are generally expensive. You'll find Rantepao's *tuak* market in the northern part of town just before the bridge.

Warung Murni, on Jl. Sesean near the mosque, is a local travelers' hangout that serves good *nasi campur* (Rp2000). Another popular and reasonable eatery is **Rima I,** Jl. Mappanyuki, north of town center, with complete menu from breakfast (great pancakes) to full-course dinners (really nice salad with tomatoes and garlic).

Eat excellent *pa'piong* at many of the hotel restaurants; place your order in advance. Order *tuak* to accompany your meal. Near the Toraja Misiliana Hotel is **Pondok Ikan,** a new restaurant on stilts in the middle of a lake filled with croaking frogs. Splendid location. The only local restaurant where you can consume Padang dishes is **Saputo Padang Food**— excellent quality and low-priced meals prepared by cooks who learned their trade in Bukittinggi. Avoid the **Chez Dodeng;** poor value. **Dodeng II** is better. Dinner excellent and very reasonable at **Alios Mambo;** fat sandwiches wrapped for traveling.

Entertainment

Tongkonan Pub, on the main street, is where you'll find the nightlife: Indonesian hard rock bands, great mimics, sometimes a guest singer from Europe. No pressure to buy drinks; you can just go and dance. Tables full of Italians, French, and Germans.

The sons of the owner of Hotel Pison, particularly Luther, like to play chess with Westerners. Batak singers will entertain you at Toraja Cottage's pavilion restaurants; performances of the *paranding* dance are staged at the Misiliana and other top-drawer hotels.

SHOPPING AND SERVICES

Souvenir shops on Jl. Pahlawan offer the best selection of Torajan handicrafts and antiques.

Prices are higher than in the market or villages. Look for old woodcarvings, knives, bead necklaces, and *ikat*-dyed cloth. Bargain for engraved and painted boxes, miniature replicas of *tongkanan,* statues made of wood and *kerbau* bone, glass beads. Both **Art Shop Marura** (Jl. Mappanyuki 21) and **Gemini Mulia** (Jl. Mappanyuki 9) feature a complete range of items at reasonable prices. For both new and antique weavings, try **Sa'dan Tobarana** and **Sa'dan Sangkombong** (Rp63,000-294,000).

Those 200-year-old European and American coins selling for Rp4000 are ingenious copies of the real thing. In the *pasar,* look for bamboo basketware, flat sifting trays woven in attractive colors, work and dress hats, old *ikat,* and *pisau labok'* (machetes) with buffalo horn handles. A good buy from street vendors is vanilla pods, about eight to a plastic pouch for Rp1500. You can easily find unroasted Robusta for Rp1000 per liter in the downtown market, but roasted coffee costs Rp11,000 per liter. Or buy coffee in 250-gram plastic bags for only Rp2000—delicious. Arabica is very expensive and hard to find. Check out the drinks, snacks, and sweets in Hotel Indra's small store.

Near the big intersection is the town's largest hardware/general store, **Toko Abadi** (Jl. A. Yani 102), which cashes traveler's checks and also gives cash for Visa and MasterCard. **Bank Rakyat Indonesia,** Jl. Mappanyuki, also changes money. Film and processing at **Toko Foto Duta Wisata** on the corner of Jl. Landorundun and Jl. A. Yani. Try **Apotik Delta,** Jl. A. Yani 48, for medicine. The **post office** (Jl. A. Yani 111) is open Mon.-Thurs. 0800-1400, Friday 0800-1100; poste restante service. The **telephone office** next door is open round the clock. Rantepao telephone code is 0423. Make overseas telephone calls via satellite. The **tourist information center,** Jl. A. Yani 63, tel. (0423) 21277, is long on cheerfulness but chronically short of literature. Check out the bulletin board heralding upcoming events. Medan K., who works here, lives in a house behind the center and will work as a guide.

TRANSPORTATION

Getting There

Although it's not that reliable and flights are heavily booked July-Aug., the alternative to a long eight-hour-plus bus ride is the scenic 45-minute flight (Rp60,000) with **Merpati,** leaving at 0900 from Ujung Pandang's airport. The return flight to Ujung Pandang takes off from Rantetayo Airport at 1015. Find Rantepao's Merpati agent in Hotel Pison. Staff will make reservations and sell tickets, but allow a day or two for them to radio Ujung Pandang and wait for a reply. If arriving from Makale or Palopo, *bemo* stop at the station behind the small downtown market. **Liman Express,** Jl. Laiya, leaves Rantepao for Ujung Pandang three times daily. Another company to try is **Litha.**

Getting Away

If tired of walking out to nearby villages, take local minibuses or *bemo*—find them on Rantepao's main street near the traffic circle. Or hop on a *bemo* heading down to Makale (17 km south, Rp400) and jump out when you see the Londa and Lemo signs—a good enough place to begin. All vehicles leave only when full. You can easily reach the northern towns of Palawa, Pangli, and Sa'dan on Rantepao's big market day, when *kijang* and *bemo* leave constantly for these northern villages, returning each hour until nightfall. Charter *kijang* and minibuses for Rp60,000 per day. You can hire *bemo* for Rp5000 per hour, or about Rp30,000 per day. Hire bicycles from some of the hotels; rent motorcycles for Rp12,000 per day from **Studio Foto Hibar.**

The **Liman, Erlin,** and **Fa. Lithah Express** offices are on Jl. Mappanyuki, a short walk from the traffic island. Buses depart at 0700, 1300, and 1800 for Ujung Pandang (Rp10,000) with a rest/meal stop in Pare Pare. **Liman Express** will pick up passengers at various hotels around Rantepao. Starting at around 0900 buses leave from near the traffic circle to head over the mountain to the harbor town of Palopo (Rp2500, two to three hours). This amazingly scenic road is routinely washed out during the monsoons. Halfway down is an excellent coffee shop with a view down the valley toward Palopo.

From Rantepao all the way to Palu is a grueling three-day trip (Rp45,000). If heading for Poso via Mangkutana (Rp33,000, 24 hours), it's better to travel to Palopo first, then buy a ticket to Mangkutana and travel onward to Poso; when you change your "direct" Rantepao-Mangkutana bus in Palopo, confusion might arise as to whether you've paid or not. It's easier on your body to take your time and stop along the way anyway.

Tour Guides

You'll be approached by a lot of self-appointed local tour guides demanding Rp10,000-20,000 per day. English-speaking youth will want to show you around, but for most sites they're unnecessary. People are friendly and helpful and seem pleasantly surprised to see unguided tourists. The eight to 10 guides working out of the **Indra Hotel** are all licensed—Rantepao's best. In an attempt to crack down on unofficial "guides," the **Himpunan Pramuwisata Indonesia** at Jl. Landorundun 7 now trains and certifies guides. Travel agents in Kuta on Bali offer five-day tours to Torajaland for around Rp630,000. A reliable local tour company is **Toraja Highlands Tour and Travel** at Toraja Cottages; see manager Herman Nari.

Trekking

Though Rantepao can be afflicted with tourists even in the off season, just move a kilometer out of town and you're in a tropical Xanadu. People invite you to attend their ceremonies or spend the night with them. Since the roads in Torajaland are so bone-jarring, walking can be a great relief. The trekking season is March-Nov., but is best in the late dry season when clouds protect you from the intense sun. In the rainy season (Dec.-Feb.) trails are muddy and slippery, and the leeches plentiful.

You'll need sturdy footwear, an umbrella, hat, sleeping bag and mat, long shorts, sweater, flashlight, and *sarung* for bathing. It's always a good idea to take a water bottle, as drinking spots are few and day-walking is very hot. If you're headed into the mountains, take salt, dried fish, and sugar, as well as cigarettes as friendly offerings. Don't give out candy or money; dispense ballpoint pens or pencils instead. When hiking to distant villages, take a good first aid kit with sunblock and medicine for skin infections, and a cheap (Rp700) bottle of baby powder for rashes.

There are always people around to provide directions, provided you speak Indonesian—you'll be handicapped without it. There are some amazing *losmen* deep in the countryside. Virtually anywhere in Torajaland you can spend the night in *tongkonan* houses, or ask the *kepala kampung* for help with accommodations. Always give the lady of the house Rp6000-8000 per day for food. Although some *kampung* will slaughter a chicken for you, don't expect much more than rice straight from the *padi*; vegetables like *jagung* (corn), *sayur labuk* (pumpkin), or cucumber; and sometimes *daging babi* and *daging kerbau.* There are coffee and tea stands in most villages. If you're in one of the small *kampung* when swarms of European tourists overrun the place, don't despair. They'll be gone in 20 minutes or so, after buying up everything in sight, including all the beer.

VICINITY OF RANTEPAO

The walks around Rantepao are gorgeous. A wonderful all-day walk, for example, is from Rantepao to Tikala-Pana-Lokomata-Batutumonga-Lempo-Deri-Bori-Parinding, then back to Rantepao by *bemo.* There are few travelers along the way and you'll enjoy lots of meaningful contact with the villagers. The views from Batutumonga and Lokomata of the *sawah* and Rantepao below are spectacular, especially toward sunset. Set out for more distant villages in the early morning when it's cool; visit villages closer to Rantepao later in the day. Most are quite close to one another and you can easily visit a number of villages in an afternoon. Take lunch with you.

SOUTH OF RANTEPAO

Karasik is just one km south of Rantepao on the road to Makale, then a 400-meter-walk up a rocky trail. Constructed in 1983 for a funeral, this horseshoe-shaped row of *rumah adat* is arranged around a group of menhir, some carved in decorative patterns.

Londa lies six km south of Rantepao on the road to Makale, then 1.5 km east. Entrance fee of Rp1000. See two natural burial caves under a cliff face, with interconnecting passages. Inside are stacks of old wooden coffins arranged in family groups, with skulls and bones strategically placed for show. The impressive entrance is guarded by a balcony full of replacement *tau-tau.* Guides with gas lamps take tourists through both caves for an exorbitant Rp2000; just bring your own flashlight. Children hold onto your hands until you give them something.

There's an incredible vantage point on the other side of the rice fields, affording a view of the towering limestone cliff above the caves. Get a glimpse of the graves of two noblemen interred high up the cliff; see the glint of gold from their coffins. At this viewpoint is a carver who turns out better and cheaper tourist-grade *tau-tau* than the craftsman in Lemo. A trail to the east leads to an infant grave tree.

Tilanga is nine km south of Rantepao on the main road, then east for two km on a really beautiful, bumpy, sometimes muddy cross-country trail. Find here a crowded natural swimming hole; entrance fee Rp600. The swimming pool and changing rooms are in a decrepit state. On Sunday, food and drinks are sold. A path through *sawah* leads from Tilanga to Londa, but be sure to ask directions along the way.

Twelve km south on the main road, then east for two km is **Lemo.** Entrance fee Rp1500. Rows of *tau-tau* peer down from balconies jutting out from 30 funerary niches carved from the cliffs—one of the largest *tau-tau* groupings in all of Torajaland. The effigies are new, replacing stolen originals. Photographers should arrive early, before the figures are obscured by shadows. See the three traditional houses and two rice barns near the souvenir stalls.

SOUTHEAST OF RANTEPAO

On the road to Kete Kesu stop in **Buntupune** to see several *tongkonan* and six rice barns. The *tongkonan* to the west belonged to Pong Maramba, a nobleman who rebelled against the Dutch and was exiled to Ambon for the rest of his life. Buntupune is a half km from the junction.

Walk two km south on the road to Makale, then turn east at the sign and continue another two km to reach **Kete Kesu.** At the base of a cliff, 100 meters behind the *tongkonan,* are scattered bones, skulls, and rotted wood coffins with dragon motifs. On the cliff face are *erong* (hanging graves) on wood posts and platforms. Kete Kesu is one of the more commercial, touristy villages in the region. As is **Sullukang,** an old, secluded village about two km past Kete Kesu. This *kampung* has some tall *rante* as well as statues seated in a run-down shack near the village. Look for a sign on the road to Kantor Desa La'bo; the statues are 100 meters beyond.

Nine km from Rantepao is **Pala'tokke.** While human bones crunch underfoot, see two 800-year-old *erong* on the limestone cliff. As at Lemo, these very scenic cliffs are also used for stone graves. Local legend claims the people of Pala'tokke can climb the cliff face like geckos. Entrance fee Rp2000.

Buntao, a village with a *patane* (grave house), is 16 km from Rantepao, Rp500 by *bemo*. Another approach is from Nanggala off the Palopo road; it's a full day's walk via Paniki over a mountainous area. No signs, so keep asking the way. Time your visit for market day. **Tembamba** is a mountain pass village only three km from Buntao—old graves and an awesome panorama.

SOUTHWEST OF RANTEPAO

One km from Rantepao is **Singki Hill.** From the southern edge of town, walk on the road beside the river, cross the bridge, then look on the right for the trail going up the hill—a short but precipitous climb. Good views of Rantepao and surroundings.

Five km from town is **Siguntu',** a traditional village with views of the valley below. Continue walking past the Singki Hill turnoff to Singki village and beyond, then look for a road to the right up the hill. See the remarkable carving on the nobleman's house, filled with trichromatic symbolic forms. Impressive rice barns; seldom visited. Continue past the Siguntu' turnoff, then turn right on the next road to **Mandoe,** a typical Torajan village six km from Rantepao and just off the Siguntu'-Alang Alang road.

Salu lies 15 km from Rantepao, close to good places to swim near a bamboo bridge over the river.

EAST OF RANTEPAO

Marante is six km from Rantepao, located on the left just off the road to Palopo. Marante offers

a mixture of traditional Torajan dwellings and wooden houses, with some coffins and *tau-tau*. There's a huge step suspension bridge here that daring tourists like to cross. Quite scary.

Nine km farther is **Tandung,** a spectacular area with pine forests, 18-meter-high bamboo, and a gorgeous lake. One-half km off the road to Palopo, 15 km from Rantepao (Rp500 by *bemo*), is **Nanggala,** a traditional Torajan village known for its large *tongkonan* and 14 rice barns with superb carvings—the best around. Entrance fee Rp1500. Packages of beans and ground coffee for sale. Huge fruit bats hang from trees.

From Nanggala, walk south on a dirt trail over mountains 10 km (three hours) to Paniki, then on to the Buntao area (two more hours), a full day's walk. **PT Toraco Jaya** is a Japanese-Indonesian coffee-growing and exporting company between Nanggala and Paniki. The field workers earn Rp2000 a day while roasted coffee beans sell for around Rp8000 per kilo. If you pass through the plantation, you must register at the office. From Buntao, return to Rantepao (15 km) by *bemo*.

NORTH OF RANTEPAO

Only a 20-minute walk from Rantepao is **Tallunglipu.** Stay in the Chez Dodeng Resthouse in this hamlet of about 15 houses in the middle of paddy fields; Rp8000 for a double with *mandi* and breakfast.

Walk north from Rantepao and cross the river, turn left at the intersection, then keep right at the Tikala road intersection to reach **Parinding.** Easy, pleasant, mostly level walking through rice fields. Infrequent vehicles on this route. Parinding is in two parts, both with handsome *tongkonan* and rice barns.

One km beyond Parinding is **Bori,** with one of the best *rante* in the region. Many other villages have *rante,* but here the stones are huge, some towering four meters high. Bori is getting quite touristy—you have to pay to enter now. A small trail near Bori climbs to **Deri,** passing many *tongkonan* on the way.

In **Pangli,** eight km from Rantepao, see the house grave 200 meters above the church; the stone statue features the realistic likeness of a dead man, one Pong Massangka. House graves are built when there are no cliff faces for carving out deep burial pockets; graves are dug into the earth and a small statue or miniature *tongkonan* is built over the top. Each house grave contains members of an entire family, wrapped in shrouds and interred without coffins. Pangli is also the source of a famous *tuak*.

About one km north of Pangli, then one km west on a side road, is **Palawa.** This traditional village has numerous *tongkonan* and rice barns, fine examples of Torajan domestic architecture turned into souvenir kiosks. Large numbers of *kerbau* horns are attached to the fronts of some *tongkonan.* Palawa is built on terraces; the highest features seven big houses facing seven big storehouses. Also visit Palawa's Stonehenge-like circle of stones.

Sa'dan To'barana is 13 km from Rantepao. Hyped as the weaving center of Tanatoraja, the cultural significance of the place is greatly exaggerated. Most products, sold at fixed prices, are made to suit the tastes and pocketbooks of package tourists. Women demonstrate traditional weaving at a center near Sa'dan, where you can bargain for old and new cloth. Sa'dan has the best distilleries of the strong palm toddy drink, *tuak sissing biang.*

Twenty-five km from Rantepao, at the end of a Rp1500, 70-minute rough *bemo* ride, is **Lempo.** This traditional village has a *tongkonan* with 100 sets of *kerbau* horns. The walk from here to Pana and Tikala is outstanding.

Batutumonga

A nice place to hang out in the countryside, Batutumonga sits on the slopes of Gunung Sesean, with some of the best trekking in the region and superb views of the valleys below all the way to Rantepao. Batutumonga is the main town in one of the most traditional and remote areas on the island. It's about 23 km by road from Rantepao, but only 11 km by trail via Tikala and Pana. The climb is steep and should be attempted before the afternoon rains turn the trail into slippery mud. *Bemo* also travel to Lempo direct from Rantepao (Rp1500), then you walk one hour to Batutumonga. Or you can take a *bemo* to either Tikala, Bori, or Deri and walk to Batutumonga in a couple of hours.

There are a number of places to stay—bungalow hotels for around Rp10,000-12,000 d, homestay/*losmen* for Rp8000-9000 per person full board in rather basic rooms, and some tra-

ditional-style structures, a few as cheap as Rp5000 per person with meals. One of the most isolated is **Mama Siska.** The food is good (try the coconut cookies); strong homegrown coffee served. It's quiet, mosquito nets are provided, and the family is unctuously friendly. Mama Siska, an interesting personality, can advise about one, two, and three-day hikes in the vicinity of Gunung Sesean.

Other accommodations lie along the main road. **Marthen Tonapa Guest House,** modern and psuedo-Western in atmosphere, offers stupendous views of rice terraces, large double rooms, and *mandi.* Price includes an excellent dinner and breakfast. Look for the big Coffee Shop sign. Even if you don't stay here, don't miss a meal or drink in the restaurant. **Betania Homestay,** in a Torajan house a half km past Mama Siska's toward Batutumonga, is very comfortable. Rooms are small but nice with mosquito nets, clean sheets, and lots of windows. Food is plain but good. The terrace has incredibly beautiful 360-degree views. **Hasker Homestay** is old and dumpy. Although the manager, Anton, is friendly, and the place has a genuine, spontaneous Indonesian atmosphere, it also features vicious barking dogs, no view, and is located right next to a school. Anton's 11 children give you ample opportunity to practice your Indonesian.

From Batutumonga walk uphill to the turnoff south to Pana. On this wonderful walk are great panoramas and *rante* stones. From Pana it's 1.5 hours down to Tikala; from there you can take a *bemo* to Rantepao (Rp1500). The complete 670 meter descent from Batutumonga, with beautiful views at almost every turn, takes three to four hours.

Pana To Pangala

From Rantepao you can take a *bemo* direct to **Pana** for Rp2000. Near Pana is a very old, hidden set of cliff graves in a wild setting—some of the best *rante* and *liang* in Toraja. After Pana look for a small trail up the bank to the left. If you pass a large school you've gone about 300 meters too far. Coming from Tikala, look for the small trail to the graves on your right, some 300 meters after the school. The *tau-tau* near **Tikala** are rarely visited. It takes a local with a machete to hack a path through the jungle to get to them. You can actually climb up and stand next to them; unusual.

Thirty-five km from Rantepao is **Lokomata.**
Take a *bemo* to Tikala (Rp1000), then walk
three hours up a steep clay track to Lokomata.
Or from Lempo walk 1.5 hours west to Lokomata. A huge, round, three-story-tall boulder
beside the road is studded with about 60 board-
ed-up funereal niches carved into three sides.
Many other boulders with graves in this area.
Some of the burials are recent, and you might
even see a guy chipping away at a boulder.
The walk from Batutumonga to Lokomata is
level, with nearly continuous panoramas of rice
terraces, mountains, and the valley below.
Northeast of Lokomata is **Gunung Sesean,** the
highest mountain in Tanatoraja. Climb it early in
the morning; guide recommended. From Lokomata, walk 45 minutes to the junction to Pana,
which you'll reach in a 30-minute walk.

Kijang and trucks drive to **Pangala,** 58 km
from Rantepao, a coffee-growing area also
known for its dancers. The amazing **Wisma
Sandro** here, owned by a rich man from Jakarta, has rooms for Rp12,000 s or d. Nice and
clean, hardly used. Mindblowing to find such
extravagance out here in the hills. Food okay
but overpriced. Nice walking around here—
scenic, friendly people, and the children don't
beg. Small trails lead south to Bittuang (36 km,
two-day walk) and north to Galumpang (six-
day walk). A jeep leaves for Rantepao (Rp4000
per person) from Pangala's market around
1000.

The Rantepao To Galumpang Trek

The trail to Galumpang, in the northern reaches
of South Sulawesi, offers long forest sections,
lots of mud and mountains, big rivers, snakes,
lizards, and wild orchids. From Rantepao you
can make it to Galumpang in a minimum of
seven days. But unless you really want to suffer,
plan 9-10 days of walking, not counting time
spent resting up. Start early each day, or expect to get wet—in any season.

There are no *kampung,* so come prepared.
Bring food, particularly on the Palu-Palu to Makki
section, where there are *no* people. Also bring
warm clothing—it's freezing at night. Nothing
to eat but rice and rats on a stick; the guide will
set traps. Or you might meet a hunter and buy a
slab of *anoa* off him. The people of this region
are very poor—barefoot, hand-woven packs,
diet of rice and rats.

First walk from Rantepao to Batutumonga
(10 km, three hours). It's worth it to stay here for
the day before moving on. From Batutumonga
to Palu-Palu is a seven-hour walk; the trail to
Palu-Palu actually starts in Nanggala, 4.5 km
west of Batutumonga. Two-thirds of the way to
Palu-Palu you pass through **Sapen,** which has
a big, interesting market every Sunday. This
walk up and down hills and valleys offers beautiful views and is not difficult. In Palu-Palu stay
with the *kepala dusan* in his *rumah adat.* Children are assigned to take care of you and they
do a great job. Nothing like coming in from the
cold rain to hot Torajan coffee.

You can move from Palu-Palu to Makki in
three days and two nights—if you walk your ass
off. Otherwise, plan more time. A guide is a
must on this segment. Don't hire a guide in
Rantepao; hire in Palu-Palu instead. This region is about as wild and remote as you can
get. Pass through dense moss-covered forests
during 80% of the walk—overgrown trails, wild
anoa, caribou, giant squirrels. Fantastic vegetation. The trail is very difficult and painful—slippery log bridges, river crossings, fallen trees,
mud, leeches. Pure hell until you've finished,
and begin to remember the beauty of it all. The
only accommodations along the way are grass
and stick shelters only high enough to sit under.

Makki lies in the middle of nowhere. No nothing. Gets about one foreigner a year; usually a
missionary. So you don't feel like a zoo freak,
stay in one of the *kampung* around Makki instead of Makki itself. A good choice is **Rattele-
mo,** situated between a river and a steep hill. Although a foreigner here is even rarer than in
Makki, the people are completely different—
laid-back, friendly, curious but respectful. Other
kampung, all within an hour's walk, are similar—beautiful, peace and quiet, horses, caribou, pigs, lots of singing and guitar-playing.

From Makki to Galumpang is 12.5 hours—
the locals do it in about eight hours. A fantastic
walk; the path follows a river the whole way on
an easy trail level almost the entire way. Lovely
scenery. People from as far away as Mamuju
come here to live in temporary shacks while
planting and harvesting rice.

The small river town of **Galumpang** isn't that
interesting. No food stores, but you'll probably
be invited in to buy a meal. You'll think of little
else but food after the walk getting here. From

Galumpang a truck costs Rp5000 to Tarilu, a boat Rp10,000. From Tarilu catch a *bemo* to Mamuju; the ordinary price is Rp5000 but they ask double of *orang asing*.

From **Mamuju** are boats every morning and night to Donggala and other points along the coast. A boat to Donggala is Rp17,000; it's supposed to take 12 hours but may require over 40 due to breakdowns. Mostly old cars make the short drive from Donggala to **Palu**; Rp1250 to the edge of Palu, another Rp250 for a *bemo* into town.

MAKALE

Makale, an administrative center built by the Dutch in 1925, is the district capital. Located 17 km south of Rantepao, Makale's hilltop churches and Torajan-style government buildings overlook an artificial lotus-filled lake. The town is steadily expanding northward along the road to Rantepao, with new hotels appearing each year. The region's only tertiary level school, run by a Protestant church, is in Makale, offering a three-year degree program. Although it's cleaner than Rantepao, few tourists stay in Makale. A tourist office is located in the Bupati Daerah building, two km north of town, but the staff does little but drink tea all day. Makale's large market is worth a visit to see local produce and the people from surrounding villages. The hospital, **Fatimah**, is at Jl. Pongtiku 103. Some fine walks in the area.

Accommodations And Food

Right in the center of town is **Losmen Litha**, Jl. Nusantara; Rp4000 s, Rp6000 d for small rooms with thin walls. However, the place is clean, and offers great laundry facilities, two sitting areas with comfortable couches and chairs, a balcony overlooking the street, friendly manager, unlimited drinking water, free breakfast and coffee.

Up the street toward Rantepao, on Jl. Pahlawan near the center of town, is the popular **Losmen Merry**. Disguised as a stationery shop, it's basic but has a large balcony (Rp7500 s).

North one-half km on the road to Rantepao is pleasant, family-run **Wisma Martha**, Jl. Pongtiku 75. **Losmen Indra**, Jl. Jen. Sudirman 7, tel. 43, is just south of the *mesjid*; the best rooms are upstairs (Rp7500 s or d). The one-star **Batupapan Hotel**, Jl. Pongtiku, tel. 22259, costs Rp12,500 s or d for economy-class rooms and Rp17,500 s or d for first-class rooms. Restaurant, bar, telephone, hot and cold water in a quiet location on a hill near the river. About 20 meters from the hotel is a hanging bridge and a small mosque. The best hotel in the Makale area is the **Marannu City Hotel**, four km north; its 40 rooms go for Rp88,000 d. Complete facilities. The small market near town has some good, cheap *warung*. *Martabak* is sold at night near the town square.

Getting There And Away

Minibuses arrive frequently from Rantepao (Rp500, half hour), Pare Pare, and Ujung Pandang. When there are enough passengers, Merpati flies from Ujung Pandang to the airstrip at Rantetayo, 12 km northwest of Makale. From Makale, local trucks and minibuses travel west into the mountains to Bittuang (Rp1500, three hours); northeast to Sangalla (Rp500, half hour); and southeast to Kandora (Rp300, 15 minutes). Most minibuses leave from around Jl. Nusantara. Buy long-distance bus tickets from agents at both **Losmen Litha** and **Losmen Merry**. The **Liman Express** and other bus agency offices are scattered along Jl. Ihwan Rombe.

WALKS FROM MAKALE

One-half km from Makale is **Tondon**. Walk from the Makale market east on a small road. A row of *tau-tau* in the cliff overlooks cliff graves. Old caskets, bones, and skulls are found in small caves around the cliffs. An easy six-km excursion from Makale is **Suaya**, which has a lovely church. Walk by spectacular, small limestone mountains, then along rice fields. Turn left 250 meters to the village at the base of a limestone hill. In the cliff is a row of 40 amazing *tau-tau* and scattered cliff graves. Suaya is one of the best places to see *tau-tau*. On the ground is a row of old coffins full of bones; some have elaborate geometric designs and several are carved in the shape of *kerbau*.

One km before Suaya is **Tampong Allo,** with seldom-visited hanging graves in a cave. Note the effigy of a mother holding an infant. Because she died in childbirth, she was given a "child" to accompany her in the afterlife. About one km before Tampong Allo is a tree grave. Here only babies nine months or younger are buried in trees, covered in *atap* to protect them from birds and animals.

Eight km from Makale is **Buntukalando.** On the right is a king's *tongkonan,* housing a small museum (Rp300) of royal possessions and Torajan household artifacts. One of the rice barns is unusually large, with 10 supporting pillars instead of the usual six. A *rante* consisting of huge, strangely shaped stones is on the other side of the road.

Sangalla lies six km east of Makale. A palace has been built here on a leveled-off hill with picturesque surroundings. Bear in mind that a Torajan "palace" means "grand bamboo house." Sangala is also the residence of a *tari pageullu* dance troupe, **Group Husik Bambu.** See the children's grave tree, easily accessible. There are three graves, at heights of two meters, 2.5 meters, and 3.5 meters, on one side of the tree; two fairly recent graves are carved into the other side.

Bemo run direct from Makale to Sangalla (Rp500). On the way is Kalembang Homestay, a row of traditionally built houses on top of a small hill. From Sangalla, make the excellent two-hour walk to Buntao, where you can find a minibus back to Rantepao. From the north side of town, a road traversed by minibuses leads west for seven km to the main Makale-Rantepao highway; it comes out at a point four km north of Makale. From the south side of Sangalla a small road heads west to Suaya. A good trail continues from Suaya to Tondon and Makale.

Twenty km east of Makale, after a fairly level hike, is **Makula.** The old government *pasanggrahan* here has bathtubs inside the rooms, fed by a steaming hot spring. There's also a spring-fed swimming pool outside. You'll find a good natural swimming hole in nearby **Se'seng.** The road then winds for 21 km into the mountains to **Bittuang,** a market town (Monday is the big day). *Bemo* carry passengers and goods to Makale (Rp2000, three hours). From Bittuang a trail heads north to **Pangala** (36 km, two days). The 60-km trail to Mamasa in western Toraja can be walked in three days, with gorgeous scenery of valleys, mountains, villages, and rice terraces. From Mamasa you can readily travel south by minibus to Ujung Pandang via Polewali and Pare Pare.

LAWU REGENCY

PALOPO

A small Muslim port, Palopo is the administrative capital of the Lawu Regency. This district curves around the northwest and western stretch of Teluk Bone. Before the arrival of the Dutch, the Lawu Kingdom was a major power in the region, exacting tribute from both Torajaland and Kolaka. Palopo was the port from which chained Torajan slaves were sold and shipped to Java and Siam. In the late 1930s Lawu became a center for Dutch-sponsored transmigration settlements, gradually shifting the land use from sago to wet-rice cultivation. The *durian* grown in this region is famous for its flavor—the whole of Lawu smells overripe during the Nov.-March *durian* season. The climate in Palopo is hot and humid. *Becak* are plentiful and cheap.

The giant **Kris Memorial** in town, with its lethal bamboo-spear fencing, commemorates the fight for independence. Nearby, across from the post office at Jl. A. Jemma 1, is **Barara Guru,** a small museum in the old Dutch-style Lawu palace opposite the *mesjid kuno.* Inside you'll find a miserable collection of broken plates, dusty relics, and moth-eaten rags. On the way out somebody will make you sign your name in the register and try to get you to pay the ridiculous tourist price of Rp1750—just laugh and pay the local price of Rp250. The **Mesjid Kuno,** built in 1603, is the oldest in South Sulawesi; royal graves are to the right of the mosque. From the mosque, head toward Rantepao for three km, then take a right (northwest) up the high grassy ridge for a spectacular view over the town, bay, rice paddies, and mountains.

If you have no sense of smell or are bored, walk to the end of Palopo's two-km-long pier for views of native outriggers and the mountains behind Palopo. For a swim, take a *bemo* from Pasar Sentral three km southwest to Lattuppa, where there's a swimming pool still known by its Dutch name, Zwembat. There are no beaches in Palopo, just mudflats, but there's snorkeling and scuba diving on reefs four to five km offshore. From the *pelabuhan,* charter a *ketingting* for the day to the coral reefs; ask for

Basso. Another good spot for snorkeling is reached from Bassean. Go by road 37 km south, then travel seven km east to the end of the road. Charter a *ketingting* (Rp25,000) for excellent snorkeling reefs with many fish.

Accommodations And Food

Choose from lots of inexpensive (Rp3000-8000) places to stay, but you sacrifice in cleanliness what you save in *rupiah.* **Losmen Marlia,** Jl. Diponegoro 25, offers rather grotty doubles with common *mandi* for Rp5000. Loud music emanates from the next door cinema in the afternoons.

The **Buana Hotel,** Jl. K. H. A. Dahlan 89, tel. 664, is acceptable at Rp15,000 d. It offers a kiosk, *warung,* taxi and laundry service, and a souvenir shop. Slightly pretentious **Hotel Bumi Sawerigading,** a Rp500 *becak* ride from the bus station, is dirty, run-down, and friendly. Doubles with bathrooms, bathtub, telephone, and private veranda cost Rp15,000. **Hotel Adifati,** near the military complex, is cleaner and costs Rp16,000 with a/c. Another Hotel Adifati, near the Victoria Restaurant, is superior. **Hotel al Salaam** has two houses on different streets; one is budget, the other is better (Rp10,000). The best hotel in town is **Wisma Kumda Indah,** Jl. Opu Tosapaille across from the police station; Rp12,000-18,000 for non-a/c rooms, Rp18,000-22,000 for a/c rooms.

Seafood is Palopo's savior. The foodstalls alongside the market serve good rice, *ikan bakar,* and vegetables. Beef and curry soup for Rp1500. Most restaurants are on Jl. Diponegoro. Enjoy Indonesian or Chinese meals at the town's official "tourist restaurant," the **Restaurant Victoria,** Jl. Diponegoro 1, tel. 147, near the Apollo Cinema. The crab-corn soup (Rp6000) is very good. Just down the street is **Kios Mimi Indah** for excellent Javanese-style *nasi campur.* **Restaurant Segar** on Jl. Sawerigading serves food almost as good as the Victoria's.

Getting There

Minibuses depart frequently from Rantepao down the mountain road to Palopo (Rp3000, three hours). On the way there's a *pasanggrahan* in Desa Battang in a mountain valley overlooking a deep gorge, located 25 km west of Palopo at Puncak. Good meals at the *warung*. Sample brown sugar candy; exotic butterflies sell for Rp600-4000. Connect to Palopo by bus from Singkang, six hours; Bone, six hours; Pare Pare, seven hours; Ujung Pandang, eight hours.

Getting Away

The nearest airport to Palopo is at Masamba, 63 km north, offering only several flights weekly to Ujung Pandang. Since there are no boats directly to Kolaka from Palopo, go by road to Bone, then by boat to Kolaka and overland to Kendari. Minibuses to Bone cost Rp6000; departure 0900, six hours, 247 km. Except for the nightly ferry to Malili across Teluk Bone, boats are rarely used for transportation.

From the main terminal, numerous minibuses and buses depart for Ujung Pandang (Rp10,000, eight hours) either via Rantepao or along the coast via Singkang (Rp5000, six hours). Buses also travel to Pare Pare. The Rantepao and Makale (Rp5000) buses leave from out of town, mostly in the morning; you can easily hike or take a *bemo* to the depot. The 62-km (Rp4000) trip to Rantepao is on a scenic road through a mountain pine forest. During the rains, there could be landslides. Minibuses and buses leave from Pasar Sentral heading north to Wotu (139 km, three hours), Malili (188 km, six hours, Rp5000), and Saroako (228 km, five hours).

Some buses try to make it all the way to Poso, but they're likely to encounter some problems along the way. Taking a jeep to Poso from Palopo's bus station (Rp20,000) is a better bet, although you'll probably have to endure all the expected and unexpected trouble. Huge a/c Mercedes buses leave several times daily for Mangkutana (Rp5000, four hours). There, minibuses meet buses for the 12-hour trip over a rough mountain road to Pendolo on the south shore of Lake Poso.

TELUK BONE

Wotu

A small, nondescript crossroads town 139 km northeast of Palopo, Rp3000 and three hours by minibus. Traveling north from Palopo, it's best to take the bus through Wotu to Mangkutana,

WOTU TO POSO

where you connect by bus or jeep through Central Sulawesi via Pendolo on the south shore of Lake Poso. Eastbound, a minibus runs from Palopo through Wotu another 50 km to Malili. If you have to stay in Wotu's drab hotel (Rp5000), beware of kids peering through peepholes. **Pantai Lemo Beach** features good snorkeling; take the road to the *pelabuhan* (three km), then charter a *ketingting* (Rp15,000). For a white sand beach and pristine coral in inner and outer reefs, travel from Wotu downriver to the coast, then turn right and go two to three km.

Malili

On the northeast shore of Teluk Bone, the mining company **PT Inco** built the port of Malili—complete with administrative buildings, schools, a clinic, and Indonesian government customs station. This serves as its Sulawesi headquarters. For accommodations, **Setia II** is better than **Setia I.** Other cheap *losmen* lie along the waterfront close to the harbor.

Saroako And Vicinity

Soroako is a mining community 52 km north-east of Malili at the end of a good road. This town produces an extraordinary eight percent of the world's supply of nickel. Saroako was a tiny impoverished village of several hundred *ladang* cultivators when Inco moved in and constructed a smelting works in 1972, one of the biggest non-oil high-tech investments in Indonesia. Hundreds of a/c prefab houses, two airstrips, golf course, modern canteen. Only one *losmen.*

In this region are two magnificent, cool, and very deep lakes, Towuti and Matana. Inco maintains elegant lakeside villas; there are recreational speedboats for Inco staff on **Danau Matana,** Indonesia's deepest nonvolcanic lake. Excellent for swimming, water-skiing, or sailing. Boats are available to **Matana village** at the head of the lake and to **Nuha** village directly across the lake from Saroako. This is an area of caves, and a repository of spearheads and helmets.

Danau Towuti is the largest lake in Sulawesi. Other than the bus from Malili to **Larona** and **Timampu** on the shore of Towuti, Inco has the only vehicles to the lakes and maintains the only launch.

CENTRAL AND SOUTHEAST SULAWESI PROVINCES

CENTRAL SULAWESI PROVINCE

The province of mountainous Sulawesi Tengah offers beautiful forest scenery, vast stretches of coastline, fantastic diving on coral reefs, unusual natural phenomena, arid plains with cacti, remote tribes, ancient megaliths, and sleepy port towns. Its population of 1.5 million is for the most part Muslims living in the coastal towns. Christians and animists, about 20% of the population, live in the remote villages of the interior, linked only by bridle trails. While the human geography is not as colorful as Sumatra's or Nusatenggara's, it does offer unspoiled natural beauty and friendly people. Forests cover about 60% of the land; timber products are Central Sulawesi's principal source of revenue.

Until recently, this rugged province was isolated, but now, with the new Trans-Sulawesi Highway, there is access from the far northern and southern tips of the island. Even so, hillsides occasionally collapse on the roads and you might roam for days without meeting other travelers. Palu, the province capital, has a tourist office, good hotels, and a cultural museum, but few tourists. Adventurous treks are possible from here easier and cheaper than in Irian Jaya or Kalimantan.

In Central Sulawesi ample food is set on the table and you pay a set price (Rp2000-3000) no matter how much you eat. Eel season at Lake Poso is Jan.-June, and all year round tasty *ikan mas* are on the menu.

© MOON PUBLICATIONS, INC.

You can reach Central Sulawesi by flying into Mutiara Airport near Palu; Bouraq has flights four days a week from Ujung Pandang (Rp113,000). The majority of visitors head east by minibus from Rantepao to Palopo, then northeast to Wotu, Mangkutana, and into Central Sulawesi. The section of road from Wotu to Pendolo is nightmarish, with ditches in the middle of the road and long muddy stretches; if traveling north along the coast, it's faster to take boats. The road was originally built by slave laborers (*romusha*) during WW II at a terrible cost

in lives. There's a monument to the *romusha* at **Perbatasan,** the highest point on the road from Wotu to Pendolo.

Mangkutana is a tiny, pleasant town with a market three times weekly. This is the jumping-off point for jeep rides over the tortuous mountain road to Lake Poso. The two *losmen* in Mangkutana are right across from each other on the highway. **Wisma Sikumbang** charges Rp5000-7500 s or d; good Padang food for Rp3500. You'll probably be dropped off at the **PT Jawah Indah** terminal for four-wheel drive vehicles to Pendolo;

Rp15,000 per person for five to six passengers. The first part of the road is fine, but soon you hit the mud. Some road construction is underway, but in the meantime expect to get stuck at least once, plus one breakdown and one flat tire. Learn such useful expressions as *licin* (slippery), *lumpur* (mud), and *setengah mati* (half-dead). The journey can take as little as four or as long as 24 hours, depending on road conditions and the technical reliability of the jeep. Two *warung* on this stretch of road do a roaring trade in noodle soup and coffee.

PENDOLO

A highland village on the south shore of Danau Poso. This huge lake is still remarkably clean, clear, and beautiful. For swimming, go down to the pier and turn right. Accommodations are all on the lakeshore. A wonderful homestay with nice people called **Victory** lies on the beach close to the dock for the boat from Tentena. It has a small terrace above the lake where you can eat your breakfast. Clean rooms include *mandi* and free tea; cheap at Rp2500 per person. The Christian service is sung next door. **Wisma Masamba** charges Rp2500 s or d; good, cheap food. Eat at the inexpensive *warung* along Jl. Pelabuhan.

The ferry **KM Wisata** leaves for Tentena at 0600 or 0700 (Rp6000 per person, four hours); after that, boats could leave anytime they're full, depending on the weather. You can also charter

a boat to Tentena for Rp40,000. A road through the mountains along the eastern shore of the lake connects Pendolo with Tentena by minibus (four to five hours, Rp7000), though the boat is a smoother and more scenic experience. South to Mangkutana, jeeps leave all hours of the day and night—a spectacular but terrible and frightening trip, especially at night. There's a fantastic waterfall 15 km before Mangkutana.

TENTENA

Tentena is a small Christian town on the north shore of Danau Poso, a stunning 440-meter-deep lake ringed by high forested mountains. Coffee, vegetables, and *cengkih* grow in neat plantations on the surrounding hills; irrigated rice is the staple. The best way to reach Tentena is from Pendolo by boat over the lake (Rp1500, 15 hours). Tentena makes for a restful pitstop on the trans-Sulawesi journey, and is a good point from which to visit some white-sand beaches, waterfalls, and the Bada Valley. The town has a small grass airstrip served by the missionary airline MAF, but because of rising local demand don't count on a place on a flight. It helps if you telegram at least a week ahead (MAF Pilot, Tentena, Kab. Poso, Sulawesi Tengah, Sulawesi).

Accommodations And Food

Accommodations are clustered along Jl. Yos Sudarso—a strip of shops, *losmen,* and *warung* across from the wharf. **Penginapan Wisata**

playing in the band

Remaja is near the boat landing, very convenient for the boat south across the lake; Rp7500 s or d for large, clean rooms with *mandi*. No eating facilites. This *penginapan* is great for people-watching though it can be noisy in the mornings with buses revving up their engines. **Wisma Rio,** down the street, is Rp5000 s or d; small rooms with big beds.

Hotel/Restaurant Pamona Indah occupies a quieter location looking down the lake from the end of the commercial strip. Nice, clean bungalows of wood and bamboo sit next to the lake; Rp12,500 d with *mandi* and porch, or Rp2500 per person in bunk rooms with five to six beds. Spacious indoor lounge area, restaurant, and paddleboat rental. Clean and comfortable **Hotel Wasantara** charges Rp10,000-20,000 d (no single rate); nice view of the lake.

A one-km walk on the road to Poso is church-run **Wisma Tiberias,** Rp2500 per person with *mandi.* Quiet **Hotel Panorama** lies two km north of the wharf on Jl. Setiabudi past the big white Protestant church on the left—quite a hike up the hillside from the valley floor. *Bemo* will take you to the access road for Rp1000. Although far from everything, rooms are huge and clean (Rp15,000 including tax) with private *mandi.* Fantastic view over the lake from the front porch, but the best part is the plentiful, fresh, and delicious food.

Good value, basic *ruman makan* are found along Jl. Yos. Sudarso. **Cahaya Bone** is narrow and dark but serves delicious local fish for Rp2000, and the hottest food outside of Bukittinggi. **Moro Seneng,** Jl. Yos Sudarso 30, offers East Javanese cuisine at near-Javanese prices. Basic menu of rice and noodle dishes, Rp1000-2000. Open from early morning to late night. Friendly folks. **Warung Makan** has simple, filling dishes (Rp750-Rp1500); no surprises but good food. Turn right after the post office, just before crossing the bridge. **Harmonis** is located four km north of the covered bridge at the Tentena/Poso-Kolonodale intersection, where Jl. Panorama comes down from the hotel. Serves local fish and some chicken dishes. Good place to eat while waiting to catch buses to Kolonodale. Buy water and snacks for the trip in the store next door.

Getting Away
The MAF pilot is from Iowa and his six-seater Cessna flies on Tuesday and Thursday to Gintu

in the Bada Valley (Rp25,000)—only 20 minutes as compared to a three-day walk. Reasonably priced flights to Masamba, Rantepao, Palu, Betelema, and Soroako are also available. On Wednesday, Saturday, and Sunday no flights are scheduled, so it might be possible to charter the plane. The luggage fee varies with the distance—for Bada, Rp240 per kg; Rantepao, Rp710 per kg.

Buy bus tickets at Hotel Wasantara. In contrast to the Mangkutana-Pendolo road, the road from Tentena north to Poso is well-surfaced with fairly frequent minibuses (Rp3000, 57 km, two to three hours). There are also buses to Palu (Rp8000, 10 hours). The small wooden passenger ferry to Pendolo, on the southern shore of the lake, departs every afternoon between 1500 and 1600 (Rp1500, three hours). Board at the rickety wooden pier at the end of Jl. Yos. Sudarso by Hotel Pamona Indah.

Tentena is a good starting point to Kolonodale and the **Morowali Nature Reserve** on Tolo Bay. From Tentena, buses travel the 178-km road to Kolonodale in six to eight hours. Local boats depart Kolonodale for Baturubi and the reserve. Manuel Lapasila (Jl. Yos. Sudarso 22) was the guide for the original 1979 scientific expedition that resulted in the creation of the park. He really knows the area and the people there. Manual's guide fee is Rp105,000 for four days, plus Rp50,000 for boat charter in Tomori Bay.

VICINITY OF TENTENA

Caves are found in the limestone hills north of town. **Gua Latea** is an authentic burial site under a cliff ledge. Nice walks in the area.

Two Balinese transmigration villages, Tonusu and Toinasa, are located on the northwest shore of Lake Poso, both accessible from Tentena by *bemo.* Nice walks around **Tonusu.** There's a palm beach two km west, and 1.5 km from Tonusu is one of the most exciting waterfalls in Indonesia. Like a giant cascading cauliflower; climb 30 meters to the top on non-slippery stones. No one knows where the falls actually end, as they continue horizontally into the forest. North of Tentena are the impressive and rough Sulewana rapids (Rp1000 admission).

Lake Poso

Lakefront **Hotel Wasantara** has huge, brightly-colored plastic duck paddle boats for Rp2500 per hour. They're a great laugh, and a quiet way to see the lake. Or you can charter an outrigger or motorized craft and tour the entire 37-km-long-by-13-km-wide lake; about five hours. The owner of the Pamona Hotel, Pak Satigi, hires his speedboat for about Rp20,000 per hour. From Tentena you can pay for a ride on the back of a motorcycle to **Peura** village. From **Taripa** on the west shore, hike three km to a high promontory with spectacular views over the lake, or walk the incredible lakeside trail all the way from Taripa to Pendolo. South of Taripa is seven-hectare **Bancea Orchid Reserve,** boasting over 50 species of orchids that bloom in January, May, and August. Roundtrip boat charters start at around Rp40,000.

To The Bada Valley

To see 4.5-meter stone statues and other huge, mysterious, freestanding stone megaliths, head southwest to the Bada Valley. First take a frequent *bemo* 12 km west to Tonusu (Rp1000), then connect with people walking to Bada. There's a rough road 60 km to Gintu, a beautiful two-day walk through magnificent jungle with one river to ford. Convoys of jeeps travel this road in the dry season, Rp20,000 pp. Bomba, 53 km from Tentena, is the first village you come to in the Bada Valley.

On this walk, watch out for poisonous snakes, giant centipedes, and *anoa*—they attack when encountered. There are no *losmen* or *warung,* so bring a tent and food. No English speakers, and except for occasional groups of Germans with a guide from Palu, no tourists. From Bada, follow the same trail 42 km to Gimpu, where transportation is available to Palu. Inquire at Tentena hotels about guides.

POSO

The main port town on the southern shore of Teluk Tomini, Rp2000 by minibus from Tentena, Poso serves as a transit point for travelers heading west to Palu or sailing north across the bay to Gorontalo on the south shore of the northern peninsula. Although fairly spread out, *bemo* cruise the streets of this small, tidy city (Rp200). Most hotels and restaurants are within walking distance of the Poso River, which is on the town's west side; small outriggers cross the river to Pasar Sentral.

Change money at **Bank Negara Indonesia** on Jl. Yos Sudarso. The **telegraph and telephone office** and **post office** are on Jl. Sumoharjo. Poso's beach is filthy and not fit for swimming. The **tourist office** is at Jl. P. Kalimantan 15. Sooner or later you'll be found by Pak Amir Kiat, the local government tourist information officer. He's friendly, kind-hearted, speaks good

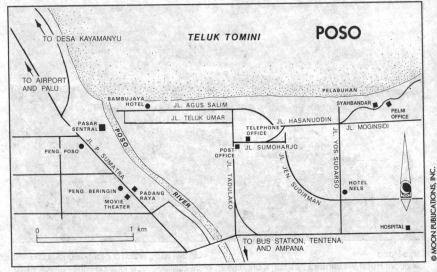

English, and is so full of misinformation you'll readily understand why his boss lets him spend all his time outside playing with tourists rather than reporting to the office.

Accommodations And Food

The cheapest places to stay (Rp6000-8000) are near the central market: **Penginapan Beringin** and **Penginapan Poso,** both on Jl. P. Sumatra. Also check out **Penginapan Sulawesi** on the corner of Jl. Agus Salim and Jl. Imam Bonjol. Many *warung* nearby.

The town's best hotel is **Bambujaya,** Jl. Agus Salim 105, tel. 21570 or 21886, right on the bay. Amenities include a TV, karaoke lounge, hair salon, and a rather expensive restaurant with high quality food and big portions. Non-a/c rooms are Rp15,000 d, a/c rooms Rp22,000 d, suites Rp45,000. All rooms have *mandi* and the price includes a continental breakfast. Quite comfortable for the money is **Hotel Nels,** Jl. Yos Sudarso 9; Rp10,000-15,000 includes *mandi* and meals. Avoid **Hotel Wisata,** Jl. Pattimura 19, with its dimly lit, grungy rooms and high prices.

Not to be missed is *cap tikus campur madu*, or *arak* mixed with honey—a wonderful combination. Sold from big cooling boxes next to the bus station for Rp1000 per liter. Careful—the alcohol percentage can vary from 35% to 70%

or more. For Padang food, head for **Padang Raya** across from **Penginapan Beringin.** Other places to eat include **Mekar** on Jl. Imam Bonjol and **Warung Lamayan** on Jl. Teluk Umar on the left, north of the traffic circle. Poso's best Chinese food is available at **RM Jawa Timur** on Jl. P. Sumatra.

Getting Away

Only **Merpati** (Jl. P. Sumatra 69A, tel. 94619) serves Poso, with flights to many points on Sulawesi as well as Surabaya and Jakarta. Flights to Palu leave Monday, Friday, and Sunday. The airport is 13 km west at **Kasiguncu**; the airline will fetch you at your hotel for Rp2000.

Gorontalo and Bitung in North Sulawesi can be reached by government cargo ships for Rp15,000—Poso-Gorontalo, 20 hours. The regular passenger ship is Rp25,000, two days. Watch the harbor. En route the Gorontalo-bound boats often stop at the Togian Islands. Poso is also the gateway to the isolated east end of Central Sulawesi. Bus companies at the station sell tickets to Ampana (six hours, Rp8000) along the coast road. Luwuk is 18 hours farther, another Rp22,000.

The major shipping offices and harbor are located in the northern part of town, about a 15-minute walk from Penginapan Sulawesi. A **Pelni** (Jl. Pattimura) vessel calls at Poso about every two weeks. For this and other boats, check several times a day at the pier and at the *syah-bandar's* office, Jl. Pattimura 3 near the Pelni office. One plan involves taking the boat to Parigi, then traveling by road to Palu. Boats to Gorontalo in North Sulawesi depart every two to three days. Tariffs start at Rp22,000 and the passage requires two days, stopping at Dolong in the Togian Islands (superlative diving).

It's a six-to-seven-hour minibus ride (Rp6000 non-a/c, Rp8000 a/c) on a good road to Besusu station, Palu. Buses depart at 1300, 1400, and 2200; buy tickets at the *stasiun bis,* agency offices around Pasar Sentral, or at the Bina Wisata Bus Company in the Merpati office (Jl. P. Sumatra 69A). Several companies run medium-sized buses along the mountainous route south to Tentena: **Sinar Sulawesi,** Jl. P. Sumatra 19, tel. 21819; **Pa'antobu,** Terminal Kasintuwu, tel. 21872; **Awa Indah; Omega;** and **Pamona Indah.** Tell *bemo* drivers to take you to Terminal Tentena. Buses leave when full (frequently) from 0900 to 1600. If requested ahead of time, they'll pick you up at your hotel. Including delays, the trip takes two to three hours, but feels a lot longer.

Vicinity Of Poso
Beaches in Poso town are badly trashed; head instead for the fishing village of **Kayamanyu,** northwest of the market. Good snorkeling on the reefs off **Polande,** a two-hour drive west. Charter a *ketinting* for the half-hour trip offshore. **Togolu,** seven km to the south, is a center for ebony woodcarvings in the form of imaginative trays, tables, and miniature people and animals.

THE EASTERN PENINSULA

This is Sulawesi's most untouristed region. The main town is **Ampana,** located about 150 km northeast of Poso or six hours (Rp8000) by minibus—*if* no bridges are out. Or take a passenger ferry from Poso to Ampana twice weekly for Rp10,000 per person (eight hours).

Stay at **Hotel Mekar** for Rp4000 per person. The **Irama,** also on Jl. Kartini, is another option. Take *bendi* (Rp300) from near the market to anywhere in town. South of Ampana in the mountains live the isolated Ta people; this province is home to thousands of unassimilated, isolated tribespeople. Other major groups include the Bugis and Bajau "sea gypsies."

At **Tanjung Api** ("Fire Cape"), three km east of Ampana on the coast, a flame is fed by underground natural gas—a magical spot to the locals. Reach the flame by motorized *prahu* (Rp25,000 roundtrip, 30-45 minutes each way) from Ampana's docks. Most dramatic at night. Snorkeling is good, there are nice walking paths in the vicinity, and the reserve offers Sulawesi macaques, deer, pigs, pythons, and *babirusa.* A beautiful six-hour drive by regular minibus from Ampana along the coast to Luwuk.

Ampana and Poso are embarkation points for Gorontalo across the Gulf of Tomini in North Sulawesi. On the way the 60- to 100-ton boats often stop at Wakai or Dolong in the **Togian Islands.** The Togian islanders practice Islam and make their living from the sea. Besides their ethnic diversity, these islands offer superb beaches, some of Indonesia's best coral reefs, seabird rookeries, sea turtles, and numerous forest *babirusa.* Rent scuba diving gear from Edi Jusuf in Wakai on Pulau Batudaka. Small Pulau Unauna has an active volcano. On the coast between Uwekuli and Ampana live colonies of amazing megapode birds.

Luwuk
A small port and district capital on the Peleng Strait on the east end of Central Sulawesi. The **Safari Beach Hotel** charges Rp15,000 including meals. **Eicke's Bavarian Homestay** offers simple but friendly accommodations for Rp2500 per person. Wolfgang, the German owner, also arranges jungle treks and boat trips to island beaches. He and his English-speaking wife are a mine of local information. The **Safari Restaurant** is a great place to eat. From Luwuk to Gorontalo by boat takes 16 hours; it's better to take the minibus to Pagimana and proceed from there.

Good diving and swimming at **Kilo Lima,** five km from Luwuk. A road to the southwest along the coast passes 75-meter-high **Hanga-Hanga Waterfall,** three km from Luwuk. At **Batui** wildlife, including megapode birds, can be observed. The road leads south all the way to **Baturubi,** gateway to the Morowali Nature Reserve. At **Bangkiriang,** 96 km east of Luwuk, is a *maleo* hatchery protected by the PHPA. Just three hours by boat from Luwuk are the Banggai Islands, with wonderful beaches, snorkeling, fishing, wild sea cows, and nature walks.

Morowali Nature Reserve

A large, isolated wilderness area on the south shore of Tomori Bay, with varied topography ranging from open grassland to sparse pine forest, from thick lowland forest to 2,600-meter-high peaks. The flora and fauna is as varied as the topography. Morowali also contains the famous Danau Ranu ("Moon Lakes"), known for their eerie silence, as the emission of marsh gases keeps birds and animals away. Sir Francis Drake's ship, the *Golden Hind,* ran aground

off Morowali in 1580. Five rivers flow through the reserve, three into long, narrow Tomori Bay. There are no roads, hotels, or other facilities. Buy all the film you'll need before leaving Poso or Rantepao. Get there by road from Kolonodale, which sits on the south shore of Tomori Bay, or from Baturubi. MAF maintains landing strips at Kolonodale and Baturubi.

Another approach is from Tentena. Ask for Manuel Lapasila, Jl. Yos. Sudarso 22. Manuel was the guide of the original 1979 scientific expedition that resulted in the creation of the park. He knows the area best, and is well-known and liked by the local Wana people. He still acts as their unofficial representative with the authorities, their only contact with the outside world, and a supplier of small goods such as salt, tobacco, and kitchenware. Though you'll see hundreds of species of unusual butterflies, you can forget about the zoological wonders. The *anoa* is a sad captive little cow with a leg missing, and the *maleo* bird turns out to be a *maleo* egg. Stay with the friendly and unsuspicious Wana people who fish with spearguns and hunt with blowpipes, eat wild pig and lizard and drink rice wine, swim in the Morowali River, and go for a superb sightseeing tour of Tomori Bay on the trip back. Cost: Rp105,000 for a four-day guide fee, Rp50,000 for boat charter.

Yet another way to reach Kolonodale and the reserve is north by road from Soroako. More of a trail than a road, motorbikes make the trip regularly. Negotiate for a bike and driver in Soroako, cross Lake Matana to Nuha, then ride the 42 km to Beteleme in about three hours (around Rp2000). From Beteleme regular *bemo* run to Kolonodale (Rp1000, 33 km).

Kolonodale

A small, quiet Bugis town about 180 km east of Tentena or 235 km southeast of Poso, at the south end of Tomori Bay. Worth a stop on the Soroako/Beteleme/Poso road. There are daily buses from Poso at 0900 or 1000, arriving in Tentena at 1200 or 1300. They then proceed on to Kolonodale, arriving at 1900 or 2000 (Rp7500 non-a/c, eight or nine hours in all). Or motorbike up from Soroako. Kolonodale consists mostly of traditional fishermen's houses on stilts with only one real street. Besides fishing, the town also serves as a collection point for rattan and *damar* resin from the nearby forests.

MOROWALI RESERVE

TANJUNG API RESERVE

AMPANA

TEL TOMINI

S. BONGKA

BONE

S. SAMBU

UWEKULI

TO POSO

R. SAMARA

S. SOLATO

G. TAMBUSISI (2,422 m)

G. TOKALA (2,630 m)

G. MOROWALI (2,280 m)

BATURUBI

TAMBIOLI

KAYU POLI

TOKALA ATAS

TANDIONDO

D. RANU

MOROWALI RESERVE

MOROWALI

TEL TOMORI

KOLONODALE

BETELEME

0   20 km

© MOON PUBLICATIONS, INC.

People are curious and friendly; very few people speak more than a few words of English. In lieu of reporting your arrival to the local police, pay a visit to the effusive and knowledgeable *pembantu bupati,* Pak Theo Tumakaka: be prepared to speak Bahasa Indonesia. For evening entertainment, try the billiard hall on Jl. Yos Sudarso, Rp250 per game and open until midnight. The nearest bank is one hour away in Beteleme.

Penginapan Sederhana, close to the market on the main street of Jl. Yos Sudarso, has clean wooden rooms with iron beds and short mosquito nets, common *mandi*; Rp2500 per person. One of the nicest and friendliest places to stay in Indonesia. Big meals, Rp1200 per person. Nice balcony overlooking the water. **Penginapan Lestari,** on Jl. Yos Sudarso, has clean average-sized doubles with *mandi*, clean sheets, and funny old furniture; Rp3500 per person. Run by an authoritarian matron. Bountiful meals cost Rp2000 per person per meal. Front rooms tend to be noisy. The large garden in back juts out into the calm bay, with beautiful views of the sunrise. **Penginapan Rejeki Jaya,** on the Beteleme road a 10-minute walk from Kolonodale's "center," offers large, cool doubles and common *mandi*; Rp2500 per person. Meals are Rp2000 per person, tea Rp250. **Kios Jumpandang** serves six different dishes, most chronically unavailable, in the Rp1000-2000 bracket. Better to eat in your *losmen.*

Beaches in Kolonodale are unswimmable; the nearest swimming beach is 1.5-2 hours by boat. Tomori Bay is absolutely superb on a sunny day, a labyrinth of valleys and jungle-covered islands, with pristine green waters, coral for snorkeling (wait for low tide), fishermen's villages (stop for tea with the *kepala desa* and 67 children staring at you), and lots of tiny beaches where you can scavenge a couple of coconuts. Charter a motorized canoe for Rp25,000 per day; with luck you'll see dolphins.

Two boats a week sail from Kolonodale to Luwuk (Rp7500), and one boat a week from Kolonodale to Kendari (Rp15,000). At least two buses a day depart Kolonodale for Tentena (Rp5500) or Poso (Rp6000). The main interest of this route is avoiding the 24-hour jeep ride from Kolonodale to Pendolo. If the journey is interrupted, stay in **Beteleme** in either Penginapan Jawa Timor (Rp3000 per person) or Pengina-

pan Vibros. You'll find a cluster of *rumah makan* along the main road. Beteleme is a clean, green, and oversized village in a nice valley, with an airstrip served by MAF. There's also a hot spring, but not much else to do except wait for a bus.

PALU

A major port and the administrative capital of Central Sulawesi, this small, predominantly Bugis city occupies an attractive location at the south end of spacious Palu Bay. This is a real *kantor* town; everyone seems to work in some government office. The commercial neighborhood is on the west side of the river; the east bank hosts most of the government buildings and the airport. The old *pasar* is located in the southwest part of town on the river's west bank, while the big new market is on Jl. Sapiri past the provincial museum. You can buy *kain donggala ikat* textiles at **Fauzia Hassan's,** Jl. Jambu 11, tel. (0451) 22940, for Rp100,000-180,000 per piece. *Bemo* (here called *taksi*) travel to anywhere in town for Rp250. There are also *ojek* and *dokar.*

Sights

The large **Museum of Central Sulawesi** on Jl. Sapiri has some fine exhibits and also houses an impressive library of books in Dutch, English, and Indonesian on the anthropology and archaeology of Central Sulawesi. The building was inspired by a Kaili *lobo,* or ceremonial meeting house. In front are reproductions of the Bada megaliths and a stone burial vat. See Kaili costumes and jewelry, basketry, valuable heirloom *ikat* textiles, photos of Easter Island-like stone sculptures and dolmens, and prehistoric artifacts. Open Tues.-Fri. 0800-1700, Saturday and Sunday 0900-1400, Monday closed. Central Sulawesi's oldest mosque, on Jl. Kyai Haji Agust Salim, was founded by Islam proselytizer Dato Karama in the 17th century.

Accommodations

Losmen Pasifik, Jl. Gajah Mada 42, offers Rp7000 d rooms with lots of mosquitos near the noisy street, or Rp10,000 rooms out back with *mandi* and fan. Try to get a room upstairs. Though some readers describe the Pasifik as horrible, everyone seems to stay there. **Penginapan**

Arafah is just off the main street on Jl. S. Wuno, close to Losmen Pasifik. The rooms (Rp5000-7000) are tiny, the walls are thin, and it looks out over a dusty street. No *mandi* in any of the rooms.

Hotel Pattimura, Jl. Pattimura, asks Rp10,000 for no a/c or Rp20,000 for a/c. Expensive for what you get; the rooms are kind of drab. Could be noisy. **Hotel Taurus,** Jl. Hasanuddin, tel. (0451) 21567, has small but clean rooms.

Wisata Hotel, Jl. Letjen. S. Parman 39, tel. 21175 or 21162, fax 22427, rents first-class rooms for Rp50,000 d with a/c, TV, *mandi,* breakfast, and afternoon tea/coffee. Economy rooms cost Rp25,000 d; a/c, radio, common *mandi,* breakfast, tea/coffee. Expensive laundry service, expensive and empty restaurant, bar, TV lounge. Rooms are quiet and well-spaced. Photocopy service, telephones in the rooms, room service. Service is quick but not yet up to Western standards. More guests stay here than at the **Palu Beach Hotel,** which is on the shore along Jl. S. Parman, a 10-minute walk from the main post office, tel. 21326 or 21426. You can bargain the price down to Rp30,000. Pool, hot water, a/c, restaurant with nice view, no shortage of mosquitos, erratic TV. Few guests, and the beach is too dirty for swimming.

Food

No problem locating good food. Many stalls set up nightly on Jl. Gajah Mada. *Gado-gado* goes for Rp500, *es campur* is Rp250, small sesame-seed-covered balls with bean paste filling are good value at Rp100 each. Other *warung* and *rumah makan* are located all over town, especially on the street behind Jamesons Supermarket on Jl. Hasanuddin. **Warung Pangkep,** on Jl. Gajah Mada, a two-minute walk from Losmen Pasifik, has fantastic *ikan bakar* up to a foot long with rice, soup, and vegetables for Rp2000—great deal. *Martabak* sellers roll in at night near the central bridge along Jl. Hasanuddin. The best Chinese food and seafood dishes are served at **Restaurant Meranu Setia Budi** on Jl. Setia Budi 44. For *nasi padang,* go to **Padang Raya** at Jl. Imam Bonjol 55.

For some unknown reason, Palu has excellent ice cream. **Milanos,** in the new shopping area in back of Jl. Hasanuddin, is run by a German with an Italian last name who speaks broken English with an Australian accent. He and his Sulawesian wife provide info on day-trips around Palu and arrange trekking tours in the nearby mountains. Milanos also serves a poor imitation of Western food and small and attractively presented Indonesian dishes. Try the snack bar attached to **Golden Photo** on Jl. Hasanuddin.

Entertainment

Cool off during the day in the pool at the Palu Beach Hotel, Rp1000 if it has water. Cool off in the evening in either of the two Istana Theaters at opposite ends of Jl. Gajah Mada. The **Gedung Olah Seni** building, on Jl. Muhammed Yamin SH near *kantor imigrasi,* features exhibits of local arts, and stages dances and musical recitals. Inquire if any performances are planned.

Services

Change money at **Bank Negara Indonesia** or **Bank Bumi Daya** (Jl. Gajah Mada). *Kantor imigrasi* is on Jl. Kartini; the efficient **post office** is located on Jl. Prof. Dr. Mohyamin. Don't go to the *kantor pos* on Jl. Gajah Mada; using a 19th-century scale, these people have no idea what they're doing. You'll find another post office at Jl. Jen. Sudirman 15-17. The central post office is on Jl. Prof. Mohd. Yamin in the southeastern corner of the city.

Permits are necessary for touring most parts of Morowali, Tanjung Api, or Lore Lindu reserves. Get your *surat ijin,* maps, and information at **Kantor PHPA,** Jl. Prof. Mohd. Yamin, one km past the central post office on the right. Meet engaging Pak Yonas Marunduh for permits and a mine of information in Indonesian. He'll also give you a letter of introduction to the *pembantu bupati* in Kolonodale—married to his younger sister—to help smooth the trip to Morowali. He can additionally recommend guides for the reserve. Ask to see the four-inch Tarsier monkey, smallest in the world.

Obtain local maps and information at the very friendly and helpful **tourist office,** Jl. Cik Ditiro 22. Good English-language brochures and free postcards. Find out what roads are currently undergoing construction, an important topic of conversation in Central Sulawesi.

Getting There

Bouraq flies to Palu from Manado, Rp144,000; Ujung Pandang, Rp113,000. Merpati flies daily from Ujung Pandang. To Palu by a/c bus is

Rp8500 (12 hours) from Tentena; real luxury if the a/c works. The road is bad from Tentena to Poso, but all right from Poso to Palu. Lots of leg room, complimentary mineral water, bread, candy, and two videos—one kung fu, one barbarian warrior. The bus drops you off in Palu wherever you want. Taxis are Rp5000 from the airport seven km into town. Or hitch a ride—the highway is visible.

Getting Away

From Palu to Manado, Rp144,000 with Garuda; same with Bouraq (three times weekly). Bouraq also schedules flights to Balikpapan, Rp88,000; Gorontalo, Rp84,000; Jakarta, Rp380,000; Surabaya, Rp246,000; Ternate, Rp219,000; and Ujung Pandang, Rp113,000. Merpati flies daily to Toli Toli and Luwuk, and three times weekly to Poso, Manado, and Kendari. Airline offices: **Bouraq,** Jl. Mawar 5, tel. 21195; **Garuda,** Jl. S. Aldjufrie, tel. 21095; **Merpati,** Jl. Hasanuddin 33, tel. 21295. **MAF** flies to its base in Tentena at least once weekly. Palu's Mutiara Airport is seven km southeast of Palu, Rp5000 by *bemo*. Airport tax is Rp5000.

From the ports of Donggala, Wani, or Pantaloan board *kapal motor* to such places as Toli Toli, Pare Pare, and even Balikpapan or Tawau in East Kalimantan. Pantaloan is 25 km, Rp500 (30 minutes) by minibus from Jl. Gajah Mada. From Pantaloan to Toli Toli, first class Rp38,500, economy Rp13,500; Balikpapan, first class Rp42,000, economy Rp16,500; Ujung Pandang, first class Rp72,000, economy Rp24,500; Surabaya, first class Rp113,500, economy Rp39,000; Tarakan, first class Rp62,000, economy Rp20,500.

The small boat harbor of Wani lies two km beyond Pantaloan. Donggala is 34 km north of Palu on a nice road; catch minibuses (Rp1000) on Jl. Imam Bonjol near the Istana Theater. Also check the Pelni office upstairs at Jl. Gajah Mada 86 in Palu. The Pelni ship *Kerinci* leaves Pantaloan on Saturday, and every second week two days later on Monday; Pelni's *Kambuna* leaves on Sunday and on alternate weeks two days later on Tuesday. This means there's a boat to Balikpapan every week either on Monday or Tuesday.

Palu is a major transport hub for Central Sulawesi. For Poso, buses depart every day at approximately 1000 (Rp10,000), arriving even

more approximately six to seven hours later. Road surfaced all the way. The bus stops between Parigi and Sausu for lunch. The stretch after Sausu is lined with Balinese transmigrant settlements complete with temples—a surreal sight. Buy tickets at **Sinar Sulawesi,** Jl. Sultan Hasanuddin 47, tel. 21868; **Jawa Indah,** just down from Sinar Sulawesi on Jl. Hasanuddin, and also on Jl. S. Parman; or **Bina Wisata Sulteng,** Jl. Sis Aljufri next to the Garuda office. All use medium-sized buses; no a/c buses yet. Westerners with long legs should reserve front seats one to two days in advance; they'll pick you up at your hotel. From Poso, head for such points south as Tentena (eight to nine hours, Rp8000), Pendolo, Wotu, and Rantepao (two days, Rp30,000).

Buses to Gorontalo leave from the **Masomba terminal** from 1700 to 1900; Rp20,000 (29-30 hours). Buy tickets at **Rajawali Motors,** which has agents clustered around the terminal. For Rp30,000 go all the way to Manado; because of competition, you can probably bargain the fare down to Rp25,000 on a cheaper bus. The bus ride from Palu terminates in Gorontalo; from there you switch buses. Gorontalo to Manado is a major route, with buses leaving all the time.

From Palu to **Toboli,** on the Trans-Sulawesi Highway, is Rp2000. Daytime buses heading north from Poso to Gorontalo are rare, so just hop one to **Kotaraya;** Rp5000, 12-13 hours. From Kotaraya to Gorontalo the fare is Rp15,000. You'll find *losmen* in **Tinombo** and **Tomini** on the way up. After leaving Mautong, you'll arrive in Gorontalo at around midnight. Buses make meal stops at **Marisa** where there's a *penginapan* in the *rumah makan* next to the bridge.

In places, the "highway" bears a remarkable resemblance to a walking track, and can be quite useless in the wet season. The Central Sulawesi section is very flat and stays right on the coast most of the way, although before reaching **Mautong** it climbs sharply. The North Sulawesi section is more uneven. The road is extremely rough and sleeping on the bus is virtually impossible. Expect breakdowns, flat tires, fallen trees, mud and bog problems, and the driver stopping every 20 minutes to eat or piss. Most of the bridges are out, replaced by temporary structures, or the bus fords creeks directly.

VICINITY OF PALU

Palu's surrounding green hills create an unusual climate; the Palu Valley is one of the driest places in Indonesia, receiving less than 50 cm yearly rainfall despite the rainforests nearby. Visit the hot springs at Pasaku 25 km south of Palu.

The road up the west coast of Sulawesi's northern peninsula to Toli Toli is intermittently paved; it's easier to travel by boat from Donggala or Wani Harbor. Toli Toli is also accessible by Merpati flight from Palu. The coast is lined with copra and clove plantations worked by *transmigrasi* settlers. You'll find a ruined Dutch fort at Salumpaga village, 70 km north of Toli Toli.

Traveling by road from Palu over to the east coast of the northern peninsula of Central Sulawesi, the bus makes a refreshing stop at Kebun Kopi, a former Dutch coffee plantation between Palu and Parigi. Check out the clove-blanketed mountainsides and breathe the cool, fresh air. Beautiful vegetables sold along the road.

Donggala

This sleepy old port, situated at the tip of a hilly peninsula, was once the largest and most important settlement in Central Sulawesi, a focal point of trade between South Sulawesi and the east coast of Borneo. A *kraton* and Dutch residency house here were destroyed by Japanese bombers in WW II. In the 1950s, the surrounding hills were used by guerrillas fighting Indonesian government forces. Over the years, Donggala's harbor silted up; today only small boats can use the port. With its quiet rhythms, red-tiled roofs, breezy weather, and friendly people, Donggala is a nice place for a night. The beach outside of town is also worth some time.

For Tanjung Karang Beach, walk north two km (30 minutes) along a rocky road. At the Y intersection, bear right and walk for 30 minutes down to a long beach with beautiful white sand, waving *pohon kelapa,* and excellent snorkeling—a friendly place and not much traveled. There's a fishing village here, very relaxed and friendly; stay with a family right on the beach. On weekdays, you can have the beach all to yourself.

Climb Bale Hill for a good view of Donggala harbor, full of sleek sailing vessels; there's a village on top. At Boneage village, seven km

from Donggala, is another nice beach; walk north of town and at the intersection bear left. Next to Wisma Rame take a *bemo* 12 km (Rp500) from Donggala and visit the village of Tawale on the west coast to see *kain donggala* made from silk thread imported from China. While here, climb down seven meters to the Pusenasi salt-water swimming hole.

Only two places in town to stay: Wisma Rame has large dirty rooms with slimy *mandi* and squashed cockroaches on the floor. The place wants Rp5000 pp (!) but you can bargain down to Rp3000 pp. During the night rats may visit your room. Losmen Mukmar offers basic but clean rooms with *mandi,* Rp3000 per person. Friendly people, cool sea breeze.

The food in the village isn't that good, but there's cold beer. Maduratna offers large servings of *sate,* rice, and chicken soup (Rp1500). Depot Duna Baru has an extensive and expensive menu. The best deal is the excellent *nasi campur* for Rp2000; also try the delicious ice cream. At Gembira, nothing is under Rp2000 for Chinese food. For its size, the fruit and vegetable market is incredibly well stocked; open every day. Fill up on papaya, jackfruit, and bananas.

Minibuses for Donggala leave Palu frequently from the Manonda terminal, near Palu's Pasar Inpres. It's a 39-km ride (Rp1000) over a winding all-weather coastal road. Shared taxis cost Rp1500 per person (35 minutes). From Donggala, a road north along the west coast leads to Sabang (155 km). Gorontalo, North Sulawesi, is two days by road.

There are boats to Wani Harbor daily at 1130 (Rp1000). Small *kapal motor* also embark north to Toli Toli, 24 hours; south to Pare Pare, 48 hours; and west to East Kalimantan. Ask at the *syahbandar* office on the waterfront. It's also possible to board Bugis schooners carrying copra for Surabaya, or charter *prahu sunde* (outrigger canoe) for inexpensive sightseeing, fishing, and diving on the ship sunk in Donggala harbor, or for crossing over to Pantoloan.

Lore Lindu

This rugged park 50 km southeast of Palu consists of a large, beautiful highland lake (Danau Lindu), heavily forested mountains, boggy valley bottoms, and open grasslands ranging in altitude from 200 to 2700 meters. Ninety percent of the park is covered in montane forests. Get information from Pak Yonas Marunduh or Pak Rolex at **Kantor PHPA** out towards the airport on Jl. Prof. Mohd. Yamin in Palu. Although you can enter the park without a permit, you need one if you want to stay in the huts at the ranger station. A permit is issued in exchange for a donation, usually Rp5000.

The ranger station is at **Kamarora** on the northeast border of the park; huts cost Rp5000 per person per night. You'll probably be the only one there. It can get chilly, so bring a sleeping bag. The ranger and his family are very friendly and you might be lucky enough to recieve some of the corn they grow in the field next to the huts. Birdwatching is excellent: hornbills, parrots, bee-eaters, kingfishers, egrets. Sulawesi's endemic species, such as black macaques, *anoa*, and *babirusa*, are much more difficult to spot.

Gunung Nokilalaki (elevation 2,355 meters) is near the lake; climbing permit required. A trail up the mountain starts a few km down the road from the ranger station. Buy provisions at Kamarora, about one km from the huts, or at the market in Palu. The climb consumes 12 hours up and five down; no trail to the summit. The usual method is to climb up one day and camp. Next morning make the summit—eerie moss forests near the top—then return to the road.

You can approach the park from a number of directions. From the east (Poso) by road it's three hours by *bemo* to **Wuasa,** 100 km southeast of Palu on the eastern boundary of the park. The bus to **Kamarora** (and ultimately to Wuasa) leaves Palu from the Masomba bus terminal next to the market. The cost to Kamarora is Rp2000, two to three hours; look for buses to Palolo.

From Palu's Masomba station take a minibus three hours south to **Toro,** 80 km south of Palu and right in the middle of the park. The PHPA office here can help you find a guide. From Toro walk all the way to Wuasa, or four hours east on a good trail to the lake. You can join groups of highlanders walking, or fall in with one of the horse caravans that crisscross the park. Good campsites along the rivers, but don't go swimming, walk barefoot, or drink untreated water from Lake Lindu—this is one of the only places in Southeast Asia with the blood-fluke disease schistosomiasis.

You can cross the park from **Sidaunta** to Wuasa via Danau Lindu in about three days. Or walk to the lake from Sidaunta in about seven hours (20 km). At the southern end of the park, and accessible from Toro or Sidaunta, are the Besoa and Bada valleys, with ancient water cisterns and cryptic megaliths.

The Besoa Wells
The main attraction of this region are giant stone statues and other huge freestanding stone megaliths. No one knows who constructed them, or why; they were there when the local people arrived. A Dutch missionary, Dr. A. C. Kruyt, first reported the stone statues in 1908. To reach the Besoa Wells you can travel five hours by minibus 99 km south of Palu to **Gimpu** (Rp6000), the end of the road. Gimpu's *kepala desa* will arrange accommodations for the night. The next day, negotiate for a guide and perhaps a packhorse, the local mode of transport within the park.

From Gimpu, the **Besoa Valley** is one day's walk to the east. This valley is famed for its 10 strange monuments; they look like wells but aren't deep enough to have held water. Though they're made of gray stone, there's no trace of such rock here. The largest of the stone cisterns is over one meter high and 1.5 meters deep; a few include covers nearly two meters wide. Archaeologists speculate the "wells" of Besoa were either treasuries, baths, or aristocratic tombs.

The Bada Valley
Another route, which takes three days, starts from Gimpu and leads south to Moa and on to **Gintu** in the Bada Valley, 15 km south of Lore Lindu National Park. This two-day walk is a more interesting and easier (flatter) walk than the trek from Tentena to Gintu and Gimpu. Another approach is to drive from Palu to Wuasa via Kamaroa, then walk two days south to Gintu.

In the morning, the trail from Gimpu leads through a magic land of forests, stately trees, and giant tropical ferns. In the afternoon, the trail narrows and climbs up the side of a mountain, following the course of the mighty Karanganan River below. By evening you arrive in **Moa,** with its thatched houses, bright poinsettias, coffee and fruit gardens, and steepled church. Villagers will put you up; bathe in the

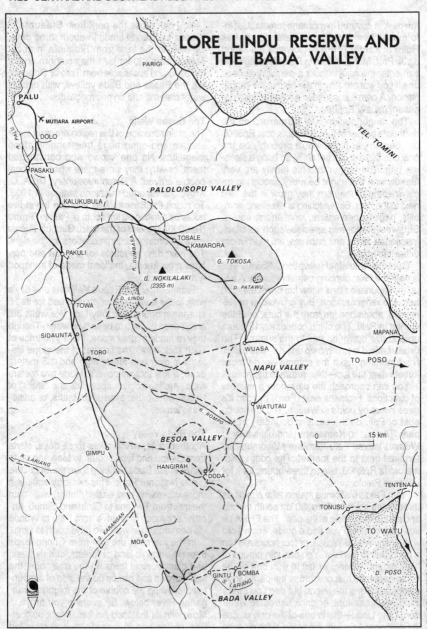

LORE LINDU RESERVE AND
THE BADA VALLEY

PARIGI

PALU

MUTIARA AIRPORT

DOLO

R. PALU

PASAKU

TEL. TOMINI

PALOLO/SOPU VALLEY

KALUKUBULA

TOSALE

KAMARORA

G. TOKOSA

PAKULI

G. NOKILALAKI
(2355 m)

D. PATAWU

D. LINDU

R. GUMBASA

TOWA

SIDAUNTA

MAPANA

TORO

WUASA

TO POSO

NAPU VALLEY

WATUTAU

R. ROMPO

BESOA VALLEY

0   15 km

GIMPU

R. LARIANG

HANGIRAH

DODA

TENTENA

S. KABANGAN

TONUSU

MOA

TO WATU

GINTU   BOMBA

S. LARIANG

D. POSO

BADA VALLEY

© MOON PUBLICATIONS, INC.

river. In this area men still hunt wild pigs with spears, women pound rice in hollow tree trunk mortars, and both sexes wear bark clothing.

Early the next morning, walk hard another day over a forested mountain to the Bada Valley, with its sleepy villages, irrigation canals, neat rice terraces, grazing water buffalo, and wobbly suspension bridges. This is the home of some 7,000-odd Bada people inhabiting 14 villages in the valley. After crossing a grassy, unpopulated plateau, you'll reach the village of **Gintu**. A small hotel here charges Rp12,000 pp room and board. A youth will accompany you to the local police station to register. Bring your passport.

The Bada Man is near Sepe, about 1.5 km north of Bewa. Children will lead you across the Lariang River near Bewa on a bamboo raft; on the other side you'll see the outline of the giant stone sculpture in a meadow surrounded by hills. The impact of the legless megalith is derived from its simplicity, size, and symbols—upright penis, faint slit mouth, flared nose, round stone eyes, high forehead, topknot.

Besides the Bada Man, which goes by the local name of Palindo, the Bada Valley also contains 13 other statues ranging in size from one to four meters, plus numerous large stone vats. All the oval-shaped humanoid statues share the same flat, minimalist characteristics, with large round faces carved in high relief. You can reach most of the megaliths by following rough jeep roads or trails wet and slippery from September to May. A statue sits just outside the village of Gintu; others are found in Badangkai, Bakekau, and Bulili. To see the megaliths, you'll definitely need a guide from one of the villages; Rp6000-Rp10,000 per day. Stay along the way with *kepala desa* for Rp10,000 with meals.

SOUTHEAST SULAWESI PROVINCE

The lower right leg of spider-shaped Sulawesi, much of the 38,000 square km of Sulawesi Tenggara consists of rugged mountains. The highest point, Gunung Menkongga in the west, is 2,790 meters, while in the south lie vast plains and forests. With the eastern peninsula of Central Sulawesi, Southeast Sulawesi is the island's most isolated, least developed, and least traveled area. A basic knowledge of Indonesian is required, as well as a sufficient amount of *rupiah*—banks here don't cash traveler's checks.

This is a heavily Islamized province, its 1.2 million people comprised of a number of ethnic groups speaking distinct languages. Bugis and Makassarese live along the coasts, while Javanese, Balinese, and Sasak transmigrants as well as native Tolaki, Munanese, and Tomoronene occupy the interiors. The province grows rice, maize, cacao, cashews, coffee, and *kapok* for cash, and exports marine and forest products (teak, ebony, rattan). It's famous for its finely wrought filigree-style silver crafts, and boasts a Japanese ferro-nickel project 25 km south of Kolaka.

The province is accessible only by boat or air. From Bajowe Harbor boats cruise across Teluk Bone to Kolaka, a small port on the west coast of the southeast peninsula. The ferry leaves at 2000 and arrives around 0800 the next morning; Rp6000-9000, depending on class. A well-surfaced, 140-km-long road links Kolaka with Kendari, the provincial capital on the peninsula's east coast. Or fly straight to Kendari from Ujung Pandang or Palu with Merpati or Garuda.

Kolaka
A transit town where the ferry docks. Most travelers shoot through to Kendari if they decide not to visit Kolaka's principle attraction, the *air panas* 15 km north. In the center of town is **Wisma Mustika**, Rp3500 per person. Two quite reasonable *losmen* are the **Alkaosar** on Jl. Jen. Sudirman 20 (rooms Rp6000-10,000), and the **Rahmat** at Jl. Kadue 6 (Rp8000 per room). Other places to check out are **Losmen Aloha**, Jl. Kewanangan 19 (Rp7000 pp) and **Losmen Family**, Jl. Jen. Sudirman 6 (Rp6000 per room). Eat at **Santana**, Jl. Kadue 17, or **Cita Rasa**, Jl. Repelita.

Take *bemo* around town, Rp300 to anywhere. From Kolaka take a minibus (140 km, Rp4500, four hours) from the main terminal to Kendari, leaving frequently. Kendari's **Wawotobi terminal** is eight km before town; take another *bemo* into town. The ferry from Kolaka to Watampone's harbor at **Bajowe** leaves at 2100.

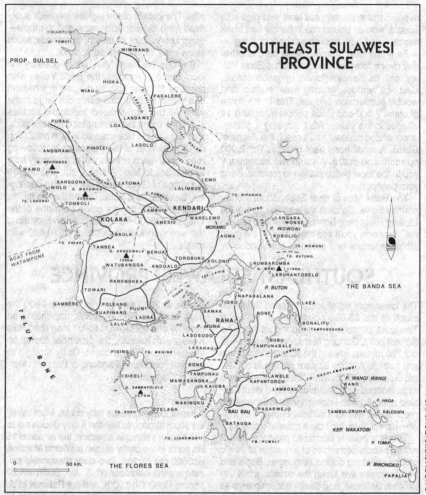

SOUTHEAST SULAWESI PROVINCE

© MOON PUBLICATIONS, INC.

KENDARI

This provincial capital of 120,000 inhabitants is spread out along the east coast in a fertile plain at the base of two legs of the central mountain range. During WW II, the Japanese built an airfield that stopped dead at the foot of the mountains to prevent American strafing. Today, Kendari has an 18-hole golf course patronized mostly by mining people.

Kendari is the chief entry point for tourists, most of whom fly in from Palu (daily flights) or Ujung Pandang (four flights weekly). Take minibuses all over town, Rp200 fixed fare. Boats, vehicles, and minibuses can be rented from the **Badan Pekerjaan Umum** (BPU), Jl. Konggoasa 48, tel. (0401) 21019. Ask about the glass-bottomed boat. For guided tours by English-speaking guides, see **PT Alam Jaya**, Jl. Kongoasa 50, tel. 21729, telex 71447.

Southeast Sulawesi's largest city, Kendari offers all the amenities, most on the eight-km-long main street running along the north shore of the bay. There are moderately priced to expensive hotels, good *warung* and restaurants, scores of shops, banks, a tourist office, *pasar sentral,* and bus station. A slew of government offices are also located here. The tourist office, Kantor Pariwisata, tel. 21764, sits on a hill behind the harbor.

Kendari-style ware—brooches, necklaces, lizards with emerald eyes, large ships, and fruit bowls—display some of the most intricate patterns imaginable, spun from cobweb-like silver threads, a technique learned centuries ago from the Chinese. Check out relatively inexpensive, good quality goldwork. At **Pusat Kerajinan** on Jl. A. Yani observe the jewelry-making process as well as *ikat*-dyeing; the shop sells silver and ironwood and teak crafts. Open 0800-1330, closed Sunday. Across from the BPU, on Jl. Abdullah Silonda, is the **Handicraft Exhibition Center,** which sells jewelry and other crafts.

Accommodations And Food

The best in the budget class is **Wisma Cendrawasih** on Jl. Diponegoro. Also check out **Wisma Dua** on Jl. Drs. Abdullah Silondae and **Wisma Nirmala,** Jl. Ir. Sukarno 115 near the Merpati office. **Armins Hotel,** Jl. Diponegoro 55, is hot and small but reasonable—Rp16,000-24,000 s, Rp20,000-30,000 d. Kendari's best hotel is hilltop **Kendari Beach Hotel,** Jl. Sultan Hasanuddin 44, tel. (0401) 21988—incredible view, beautiful gardens, tennis court, a/c rooms for Rp60,000 s Rp70,000 d.

Along the waterfront, one km from the harbor, night *warung* serve *nasi campur* and *soto daging;* even cheaper foodstalls around the cinema. The town's best food, particularly Chinese-style seafood dishes, is served at the **Kendari Beach Hotel.** Restaurants include the **Royal** on Jl. Diponegoro, opposite the Armins Hotel, and the Javanese-style **Pekalongan** on Jl. Sultan Hasanuddin.

Getting Away

As capital of Southeast Sulawesi, Kendari serves as an air hub for the region. **Merpati,** Jl. Sudirman 29, tel. (0401) 360 or 109, offers flights to Luwuk, Namlea, Raha, Surabaya, and Ujung Pandang. Also check the fares and flight schedules at the **Garuda** office, Jl. Diponegoro

59, tel. 21729. The airport is 35 km from town, Rp5000 by regular minibus.

In Kendari harbor, a ferry departs each day at 1400, arriving in Raha at 2100; the same ferry departs Raha at 2200 and arrives in Bau Bau at 0500. From Bau Bau the next day the ferry departs at 1300 and arrives in Raha at 1700. Occasionally boats leave for the Tukangbesi Group.

Vicinity Of Kendari

Huge Kendari Bay is enclosed, making it an excellent place for water sports. There's a recreation park a few kilometers from Kendari toward the bay; beyond lie coastal villages of stilt houses. Visit the fine beach at **Desa Mata,** five km from town, and pristine **Pulau Hari,** 30 minutes by boat from Kendari harbor. There are sago palm marshes in the vicinity—the people prefer sago to rice. Seventy-five km south (Rp2000 by minibus, two hours) is the impressive, seven-level **Air Terjun Moramo.** From the falls climb seven km to two high mountain lakes. Nearby **Moramo Bay** features white-sand beaches and excellent snorkeling.

PULAU BUTON AND VICINITY

This mountainous island off the southwest coast of Southeast Sulawesi was formerly a center of piracy and the slave trade. Buton was ruled by an unbroken dynasty from the 14th to the mid-20th centuries, its level of commerce at one time rivaling that of Makassar and Melaka. The irrepressible Butonese stubbornly retained their independence, even successfully repelling an invasion by Dutch warships in 1740 with the help of Portuguese-made cannons fired from a European-style fortress overlooking the harbor of Bau Bau. The region came under Dutch control only in 1906.

Famous for their seamanship and boatbuilding, the Islamic Butonese have migrated all over Eastern Indonesia, particularly to Maluku, where 600,000 now live. Of the *kabupaten*'s 500,000 population, a large number are Buginese. Maize, millet, and *ubi* are staples in the hinterlands. Basket- and mat-weaving are the only crafts.

Bau Bau

The old seat of the Wolio sultanate, Bau Bau (pop. 54,000) is the island's major town—a charming little port nestled at the foot of hills far from the tyranny of the clock. The ferry departs Kendari at 1400 and arrives in Bau Bau at 0500. Everywhere in town worth visiting lies within walking distance. At **Pasar Sentral,** you can rent *microlet* for Rp4000 per hour.

From the Bau Bau pier take a right past old wooden Dutch officers' and civil servants' quarters. The white *kantor bupati,* once the home of the assistant Dutch resident, was built in 1903. Large, tasty cashew nuts (season Oct.-Jan.) sell for Rp8000 per unroasted kilo and Rp1000 per toasted and salted ounce. Buy them at **Toko Sinar Alam** on Jl. Kartini near the downtown mosque.

The best place to stay is **Losmen Debora,** Jl. Kartini 15; Rp50,000 for a/c rooms, Rp20,000 without a/c. Fifty meters from the hotel is a view of the harbor. Meals (fried crab), picnic lunch, Indonesian or continental breakfast. The hotel also contains the **Iramasuka** tour agency. **Losmen Mutiara,** Jl. Moh. Thamrin, charges Rp5000 s or d, all rooms with private bath. **Losmen Pelangi,** on the waterfront, is cheaper than the Mutiara. The best places to eat are **Warung Sukabumi** and **Warung Kenangan**—good *mie pangsit* and *nasi campur.*

Two km in back of town, Rp300 by *bemo,* a white coral fortification, dating from 1613, encircles the Wolio sultanate's traditional hilltop *kraton.* From the parapets enjoy a magnificent view over the strait. Ask to see the weathered VOC cannon. Also on the grounds is the oldest mosque in eastern Indonesia (16th century), the grave of the first Sultan of Buton (15th century), and perhaps the oldest flag mast in Indonesia (300 years old, made of teak). The last sultan died in 1960; his descendants still reside in the palace. The structure contains some fascinating historical objects, such as helmets and Butonese cloth money.

Marine tourism is increasing in this unpolluted area. White-sand **Nirwana Beach,** 11 km southeast of Bau Bau, is very popular with the locals. Catch a *bemo* to Sulaa, leaving when full; on Sunday, no problem. Fish market every Sunday and Thursday; go early. Pelni's KM *Rinjani* sails to Ujung Pandang (first class ticket Rp65,000) once monthly. A hotel boy will take you to the office. The ship departs in the late afternoon and arrives in Ujung Pandang at 0700. Or you can take the ferry up to Kendari

and then the Merpati flight to Ujung Pandang; Rp95,000.

Pulau Muna

A predominantly Islamic island with one of Indonesia's most stunning lagoons; it also offers horsefighting and prehistoric cave paintings. The principle staples are swidden-grown cassava and maize, with cashews grown for export. Muna is laced with well-maintained roads. In Raha, the district capital, *becak* cost Rp300 to anywhere in town.

The island is accessible by ferry from Kendari or Bau Bau. A bus-ferry combination all the way from Kendari to Raha costs only Rp8000. First take a bus two hours from Kendari to the small port of Torobuku on the Tiworo Strait, then board a ferry two hours to Tampo on the northern coast of Pulau Muna. From Tampo it's an hour by bus to Raha. From Pulau Buton, the daily ferry leaves Bau Bau's *dermaga* at 1300, arriving at 1800 in Raha; Rp6000 for a berth or Rp3500 for deck.

In Raha, stay at one of seven *losmen.* The best hotel is the **Andalas** (Rp20,000 s, Rp30,000 d), with a restaurant serving Western meals. For Chinese and Indonesian food head for the **Hawaii** or **Pacific** restaurants. The *kantor bupati* serves as the district's tourist office and can arrange for a guide. Or seek out English-speaking Siddo Thamrin of the Iramasuka tour company, Jl. Pelita 5, tel. 283. Charter a minibus with driver from Hotel Andalas for around Rp60,000 per day.

The cave paintings are in **Bolo** village, nine km from Raha on a good road. Start the day early—it's hot, and takes about an hour to walk the four km to **Liang Toko** cave, home to most of the paintings. There are at least ten other caves in the area worth visiting. Sixteen km south of Raha is the magnificent **Napabale Lagoon,** where the swimming is superb and you can rent *prahu* to dive on the coral. Horsefighting, which once had ritualistic significance, is staged for around Rp300,000 at **Latungo,** 24 km from Raha. Blood is drawn but the horses are separated before grave injuries occur.

The Tukangbesi Group

There's world-class snorkeling in sea gardens near **Ambeua** off Pulau Kaledupa south of Pulau Wangi Wangi. This clean, clear dive site offers underwater vegetation and very colorful coral. Take a public bus from Bau Bau to Pasarwejo (Rp2000, 1.5 hours, 48 km), then board a local "johnson" (speedboat) for Pulau Kaledupa (departures depending on weather) for around Rp5000, 10 hours. Or board the regular boat from Bau Bau (Rp10,000, 14 hours). Take your own snorkel and flippers and stay with the fishermen.

Wangi Wangi is a small island in the Tukangbesi Group off the west coast of Pulau Butong. You sail into a beautiful lagoon with a narrow, shallow entrance which surrounds the *kampung* of **Wanci**. The only *penginapan* in the Tukangbesi Group is here. Just outside town, enter a hole in the ground to an underground cavern with a cool freshwater spring. Ships from Ujung Pandang often stop at Wangi Wangi on their way to Ambon.

NORTH SULAWESI PROVINCE

A pretty land of vast coconut and clove plantations, high active volcanos, mountain lakes, picturesque villages, hot springs and fumaroles, ancient burial sites, white-sand coral islands, abundant marine life, and outstanding snorkeling and diving. Sulawesi Utara, with an area of 27,515 square km, makes up the narrow northern peninsula of the island, over 602 km long with an average width of 50 km. One of the wonders of North Sulawesi is that it combines both terrestrial and marine parks; if you feel a bit waterlogged, you can don sturdy boots and hike deep into the forest. Along this peninsula are six dormant volcanos, each towering 1,800-2,400 meters. The dry season is May to October, rainy season November to April. So near the equator is the Minahasan peninsula that telephone poles cast no shadows at noon.

Heavy, regular rainfall and rich volcanic ash have blessed North Sulawesi with extremely fertile land. The narrow lowlands and valleys of the province have been particularly successful agriculturally, producing rice, vanilla, nutmeg, corn, coconut palms, and cloves. Forest products include rattan, ebony, resins, and gums. Valuable *cingke* (cloves) are grown everywhere in Minahasa, and during harvest their fragrance is everywhere. Land not cultivated with this Christmas tree-like spice are planted with coconut palms for copra. With an estimated 25 million trees, this is the largest copra production area of Indonesia— 18,000 tons exported per month. Everyone— including teachers, bankers, and army colonels—tends their coconut palms after hours. Other important sources of income are fishing

(especially tuna), freshwater fish raised in ponds, and mining of copper in Gorontalo and gold in Bolaang Mongondow.

North Sulawesi's population of nearly 2.6 million is comprised of an ethnic mix of peoples from mainland Southeast Asia, Indonesia, the Philippines, and the ex-colonial countries of Spain, Portugal, and the Netherlands. A major food and fish processing province, Sulawesi Utara has a higher standard of living and better health care and education systems than most other regions of Indonesia. In fact, this very wealthy province sometimes feels like a separate republic. Its geographic isolation from the rest of Indonesia, and its rebellious history, accentuate this impression.

Most travelers use Manado as a base. Coming from the south, it's possible to travel by bus from Palu (leaving 1700 or 1900) in Central Sulawesi to the North Sulawesi peninsula, then up to Manado via Gorontalo. This approach is still quite challenging (29-30 hours, Rp20,000). For Rp25,000-Rp30,000 you can ride all the way from Palu to Manado. It's easier to fly from Palu to Gorontalo (Rp84,000, three times weekly with Bouraq) and travel the remaining 520 km overland to Manado. Bouraq also schedules flights from Gorontalo to Manado (Rp71,000, four times a week) and Palu to Manado (Rp144,000, three times weekly).

Yet another way to get to Sulawesi Utara is to cross Teluk Tomini via the Togian Islands by boat from Poso, Ampana, or other small ports along the eastern peninsula of Central Sulawesi to Gorontalo. One can also take *kapal motor*

NORTH SULAWESI PROVINCE

from Palu's Wani or Pantoloan harbors to such northern peninsular ports as Toli Toli, Kwandang, and Manado.

HISTORY

Legends say the original Minahasan tribe was divided by the god Muntu Untu at a huge boulder called Batu Pinabetengan. At Manado intersections you'll notice statues of the ferocious, legendary warriors who once guarded the city. For hundreds of years this northern arm of Sulawesi was under the suzerainty of the Ternate sultanate to the east. Portuguese trader-adventurers were the first Westerners to arrive, as early as 1563. At **Amurang** are the remains of the fort the Portuguese built; they also used

Manado Tua off the coast as a base. Emanating from the Philippines to the north, the Spaniards were next on the scene, arriving in the late 1500s to convert the population to Catholicism and introduce horses, maize, and chili peppers.

In the words of A.R. Wallace, in the early part of the 19th century this area was "a wilderness, the people naked savages, garnishing their rude houses with human heads." The region first attracted Dutch attention as a source of provisions for the factories they'd established on the spice-rich but soil-poor Maluku islands to the east. In the mid-17th century, the Minahasans called on the Dutch VOC to help them expel the Spaniards. The Dutch built a wooden fort in Manado in 1657, and drove out the Spanish within three years. From 1679 until Indonesian

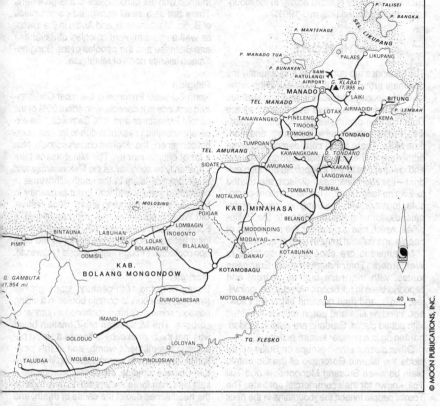

independence 270 years later, the Dutch monopolized the Sulawesi spice trade.

In the early 1800s Dutch planters began cultivating coffee in the interior, and the Minahasans converted wholesale to Protestantism and started making spectacular progress as agriculturalists. Because of its close religious, military, and economic ties with the colonial power, Minahasa soon became known as the "12th Province of Holland." The people's literacy rate was rivaled only by the Minangkabaus, and disproportionate numbers held important posts in the civil service. The Minahasans even supplied mercenary troops for the colonial army, helping the Dutch quell indigenous anticolonial revolts on other islands. This earned the Minahasans the contempt of other Indonesians, who called them *anjing belanda* (Dutch dogs).

The Japanese occupation from January 1942 to August 1945 was followed by the politically turbulent and unstable '50s, when tensions between Jakarta and the Outer Islands reached the breaking point. Vice President Hatta's resignation in December 1956 worsened the situation. Finally, in early 1958, regionalist forces in North Sulawesi seceded from the republic and established their own government. Finding common cause with the revolutionary government of West Sumatra, the so-called Permesta insurgents of North Sulawesi demanded greater regional autonomy and a more just distribution of national wealth. Sukarno charged that the rebels received American aid, which soured relations with the U.S. and encouraged Sukarno to develop closer relations with China and the Soviet Union. By the end of July the brief rebellion was crushed, except for guerrilla activity in the mountains that continued until mid-1961.

THE PEOPLE

The Minahasa are numerically and culturally the dominant group in North Sulawesi, living in the relatively densely populated valleys and plateaus of the interior. They were appreciated by the Dutch for their administrative and teaching abilities, Protestant work ethic, soldiering, and maritime skills. There is still considerable Eurasian admixture in the population. Strong historical and cultural ties to the Philippines are also evident—the two Minahasan dialects are related to Filipino languages. This far northern peninsula, together with the Sangihe-Talaud archipelagos, forms a natural bridge to the Philippines, which has allowed for the movement of people and cultural traits in both directions.

Minahasans are especially hospitable to Westerners. Their houses reflect European tastes, with trim rose bushes in front and sapodilla trees in full bloom; hibiscus, bougainvillea, citrus, and neat gardens bright with flowers. Window sills and porch railings are lined with potted plants. Gardens are lavishly tended; gardening is a popular leisure activity.

Other distinct ethnic groups on Sulawesi include the Islamic Gorontalo of the Gorontalo plain between Bolaang Mongondow and Toli Toli, known for their commercial aptitude. The Tomini people inhabit the mountains in the neck of the peninsula. Urban Chinese have inter-

married with the Minahasans to a large extent. There are also small immigrant communities of Bugis, Makassarese, and Arabs in the towns, as well as transmigrant colonies of Javanese and Balinese and the peoples of the Sangihe-Talaud islands north of Minahasa.

Religion

North Sulawesi Province is the most Christianized province in Indonesia, with about 90% of the people Protestants and 10% Catholics. The excellent education system is due to intense competition among the different church schools, plus a lot of church money. The Minahasans take Christianity as seriously as the Makassarese and Bugis practice Islam in the south. Christmas is celebrated joyfully and with great pageantry in Manado and surrounding areas. Such festive, Old World practices as mumming (masking), a Spanish legacy, still survive. Also surviving are animist beliefs in supernatural spirits called *opo-opo* contacted through native priests (*mawasal*).

Waruga

Dating from the 10th century, stone graves (*waruga*) were built to contain bodies in a sitting position; some may have contained a number of corpses. The Minahasan pre-Christian belief was that the human baby is born in a sitting position in the mother's womb, and in this position must pass on to eternity. Looking like miniature Chinese temples, the largest *waruga* are a little less than three meters tall. Engravings on the headstones depict the cause of death, and the deceased's hobby, character, and occupa-

Minahasan Christians

tion. Today, coconut shells offered at the base of *waruga* have replaced human skulls.

Originally, each family had its own burial ground, but because of hygiene and grave robbers the local government has since 1817 ensured that all *waruga* are gathered in one communal burial ground. See *waruga* at Airmadidi and Sawangan.

Music, Dance, And Crafts

In May, at the end of the harvest (*panen*), is the festive season, when celebrations are held all over Minahasa, featuring pre-Christian dancing such as the fierce warlike *cakalele,* conch-shell jug bands, and performances of the mesmerizing wooden xylophonic *kolintang* orchestra—as exciting a sound as the wildest Jamaican beat. *Kolintang* are found in almost every village; performances usually taking place on Sundays. In Manado, *kolintang* sometimes perform at popular Chinese restaurants; you can purchase tapes of traditional *kolintang* music at shops in that city. The *marambak* and *maengket* are typical Minahasan group dances once performed during harvest, at the inauguration of a newly built house, or at a party when a man introduced his fiancee. You can charter traditional dances in Tara Tara for around Rp100,000.

Few traditional handicrafts survive. "Maybe because the Lord gave us cloves" is one explanation offered. Basketry is an active craft, and the Sangihe-Talaud Group is known for its woodcarving. From the Bolaang Mongondow district comes *karawang* cross-stitch fabrics and garments. *Karawang* sheets, pillowcases, and tablecloths can be purchased in Gorontalo.

Events

On 23 September, the anniversary of the official establishment of North Sulawesi Province (1964) is celebrated throughout the province. In Manado, there are costume shows and cultural performances, as well as horse and bull racing. Don't miss the Chinese Taoist festival of Tai Pei Kong in Manado, held two weeks after the Lunar New Year. Although this celebration has been greatly reduced in size and splendor due to government restrictions, it remains the largest of its kind in Southeast Asia. The festival dates back over 200 years, when a small band of Chinese settlers, braving rough seas, arrived in Manado harbor.

Food

Minahasans enjoy their own rather spicy cuisine. Enormous goldfish (*ikan mas*) are served at special roadside restaurants built out over fishponds. A kitchen hand catches the live fish, which is then served spiced and glowing a rich golden-brown. Eat *ikan mas* slowly, as there are many sharp bones. Another regional delicacy is papaya leaves; the fruit itself is fed to pigs, but the leaves are served up as cooked greens. Other dishes include *kawaok* (fried field rats), *rintek wuuk* (spiced dog), and *kelalawar pangang* (bat stew). Out in the small towns, restaurants specializing in Minahasan cooking are the best and cheapest places to sample these flavorful delicacies.

MANADO

The predominantly Christian capital of North Sulawesi Province, this busy city of 420,000 people is built on gentle hills sloping down to a beautiful bay. Two volcanos overlook the city—an inspired setting. Yet for any tourist who is not a water sport enthusiast, Manado holds little of interest; there are few historical sights, no cultural centers or museums of note, and sparse nightlife.

The city has become a collection of the best and the worst in terms of buildings, sanitation, and government services. The most impressive buildings in town, aside from the governor's offices/residence on the hill, are the banks. Surrounding these massive, ugly structures are corrugated tin hovels dominating the entire waterfront boulevard area—very grim even by Jakarta standards. The beach is filthy—human excrement, miscellaneous animal parts, flotsam of all descriptions.

But with the gross exception of the waterfront, the city is clean and tidy, and there's a good selection of accommodations, restaurants, and modern shops quite Western style-conscious and trendy. Almost all the women prefer skirts and blouses to traditional dress. Most locals are happy to make friends and do favors for any Westerner, and they're not bashful about

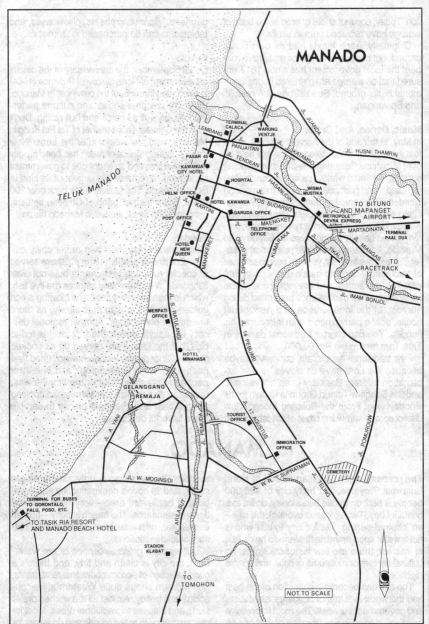

MANADO

TELUK MANADO

JL. LEMBANG
TERMINAL CALACA
WARUNG VENTJE
JL. JUANDA
JL. PANJAITAN
JL. KATAMSO
JL. HUSNI THAMRIN
PASAR 45
JL. TENDEAN
KAWANUA CITY HOTEL
HOSPITAL
JL. HASANUDIN
WISMA MUSTIKA
PELNI OFFICE
JL. KARTINI
HOTEL KAWANUA
JL. YOS SUDARSO
GARUDA OFFICE
METROPOLE DEVRA EXPRESS
TO BITUNG AND MAPANGET AIRPORT
POST OFFICE
JL. MAHAKERET
JL. MAENGKET TELEPHONE OFFICE
JL. DIPONEGORO
JL. KUMARAKA
JL. MARTADINATA
JL. MIANGAS
HOTEL NEW QUEEN
TIKALA
TO RACETRACK
JL. S. RATULANGI
JL. 14 PEBUARI
JL. IMAM BONJOL
MERPATI OFFICE
HOTEL MINAHASA
GELANGGANG REMAJA
TOURIST OFFICE
JL. 17 AGUSTUS
JL. PEMUDA
IMMIGRATION OFFICE
JL. POMUROUW
JL. A. YANI
JL. W. R. T. SUPRATMAN
JL. TELING
CEMETERY
JL. W. MOGINSIDI
TERMINAL FOR BUSES TO GORONTALO, PALU, POSO, ETC.
TO TASIK RIA RESORT AND MANADO BEACH HOTEL
JL. ARILASIT
STADION KLABAT
TO TOMOHON
NOT TO SCALE

© MOON PUBLICATIONS, INC.

asking for material things or money in return. If you refuse, you'll never see them again. This is true for all social classes, top to bottom.

SIGHTS

Manado has a large Chinese population. **Ban Hian Kiong** is a small, colorful 19th-century Confucian-Buddhist temple in the center of town (Jl. Panjaitan 7A). The oldest in East Indonesia, this temple is the center of international attention during the Toa Pe Kong festival each February. Climb up to the balcony at the top for a view of the downtown. Near here are several smaller Confucian temples and a **Kuan Yin** temple just before Megawati Bridge. **Kwan Im Tong,** Jl. Sisingamangaraja, is one of the oldest temples in Manado. The city's numerous Christian churches bear such familiar names as Zion, Bethesda, and Advent.

The **Provincial Museum of North Sulawesi,** on Jl. W.R. Supratman, contains cultural artifacts of Minahasa as well as historical remains from Dutch and Portuguese times. Near the waterfront is the large market, **Pasar 45,** a motley sprawl of semi-permanent shops selling just about everything. This is also where all the city's *oplet* seem to converge. **Pasar Bersehati,** near Jumbo Supermarket north of the harbor, is the largest and busiest food market in Manado.

Few Westerners take advantage of bicycle tours around town, particularly along the waterfront boulevard in the late afternoon or all day Sunday. There are several good reasons why you shouldn't. One, it can be rather dangerous at times to pedal amidst the *oplet,* trucks, and Toyota carryalls. Two, the population of Manado has not yet become accustomed to the presence of *orang asing* and they stare unmercifully for long periods of time. Nonetheless, bicycle touring is recommended for the adventurous (and careful).

ACCOMMODATIONS

Budget
Of the city's 52 accommodations, **Penginapan Jakarta Jaya** and **Penginapan Keluarga,** both on Jl. Hasanuddin near the Megawati Bridge, are the most popular with travelers. Both are almost always full, except when they periodically decide not to receive foreigners. Reach these *penginapan* by *oplet* traveling to Tuminting (Rp200).

The most likely place to accept your presence—especially if you have some foreign coins to give the owner—is the **Flamboyan,** across the street from Penginapan Jakarta Jaya. Quite basic (Rp4000 per person) but adequate rooms. Friendly people, very good eats downstairs, and a balcony over the rather noisy street. Ask to see Pak Asrul's coin collection; he has some rare VOC coins a relative unearthed in an Ujung Pandang cemetery. Check out the travelers' testimonials; some can be useful.

The **Hotel Kawanua,** Jl. Sudirman 40, tel. (0431) 63842, lies opposite the hospital in Kampung Kodok. The nice lobby does not accurately represent the condition of the rooms. For Rp24,000 (not bargainable), you get a/c that probably worked alright last year, two twin beds with no linens, no mirrors in room or bath, no sink or toilet seat, no towels, no desk or rack to hang clothes or stack anything, no screens on windows with panes missing.

Alternatively, stay at one of the diving/snorkeling clubs outside of the city. For example, negotiate a quiet a/c bungalow with hot water, tub and shower, and enclosed patio at the **Nusantara Diving Center** in Molas for around Rp15,000 per day. Even better is to stay out on Bunaken Island in Manado Bay where there are at least 14 inexpensive *losmen* and *penginapan* for Rp10,000 per person with all meals.

Moderate
The best values are **Guesthouse Maria** (Rp25,000-30,000) and **Hotel Minahasa,** both on Jl. Sam Ratulangi. Both are very clean, with good food, and easy to locate. Hotel Minahasa, no. 199, tel. (0431) 62559, in an old Dutch mansion, rents fan rooms for Rp30,000 and a/c rooms for Rp38,000. Sheets and towels are changed every day; incredible meals, plus tea, snacks, and *zirzak.* Excellent people, good service. From the hotel, catch any *oplet* along Jl. Sam Ratulangi into town. Returning, catch one to either Sario or Waneo.

At Jl. Sam Ratulangi 37, tel. 4049, is **Hotel Jeprinda;** Rp20,000 s for rooms with fan, Rp25,000 for a/c, conveniently located opposite a travel agent, near downtown and the main

main square,
Manado

post office. No restaurant. Not a bad deal, but nowhere as good as the Minahasa. **Wisma Charlotte**, Jl. Yos Sudarso 56, tel. 62265, fax 65100, is a small guesthouse charging Rp25,000 s or d. Coffee and tea free, free airport service, rates include all taxes and service. Located between the city and the airport, with souvenir shop, travel bureau, drugstore, laundry service, taxi, doctor on call, sports facilites, and games. Dine at the **Pondok Bambu** restaurant nearby—specialties are fried chicken and *ikan mas*.

Luxury
The city's only three-star hotel is the **Kawanua City Hotel**, Jl. Sam Ratulangi 1, tel. (0431) 52222, fax 65220, in the center of town near the business district. With central a/c, elevators, two restaurants, lounge, travel agent, shops, large swimming pool, American breakfast, and sanitized toilet seats, this place tries very hard to be a Holiday Inn—but it's absolute robbery. The service is appalling and the pool green and slimy. A better deal is two-star **Manado Sahid Hotel**, Jl. Babe Palar 1, tel. 52688; Rp35,000 s Rp40,000 d, deluxe Rp90,000 s, Rp106,000 d.

Two-star **New Queen Hotel**, Jl. Wakeke 12-14, tel. 64440, fax 52748, is a small "big" hotel, very service-oriented and efficient; Rp30,400-68,400 s, Rp38,000-Rp79,000 d, plus 21% service and government tax. Credit cards accepted. If booked by the tourist office at the airport, the price is Rp25,000—free airport pickup for guests. Good restaurant with bad coffee; over-priced laundry service. From the roof is a sweeping view over the whole neighborhood and the waterfront.

The city's first international hotel is the four-star **Manado Beach Hotel**, P.O. Box 1030, Manado, tel. 67001, fax 67007, on Tasik Ria Beach about 32 km from the city. It has 250 a/c rooms decorated in traditional style, TV and video rooms, minibars, private balconies overlooking the ocean, coffee shops, restaurants, two swimming pools, fitness center, tennis courts, squash courts, jogging track, disco, shops, banks, travel agencies, free transfer to airport, fax, massage, and taxis. Tranquil, peaceful, expensive. Rp126,000 s, Rp140,000 d and up, with all rates subject to 15.5% service and government tax.

FOOD
It's not advisable to eat any local food served from street vendors or the small *warung* scattered around town. The rate of infection from all manner of disease—pinworms, hepatitis, cholera—is rising rapidly. Besides, there are plenty of decent *rumah makan* that serve great inexpensive food from *nasi padang* to Sundanese. **Penginapan Jakarta Jaya**, on Jl. Hasanuddin, is the place to try really delicious *ikan mas*. Food and service are also quite good at **Hotel Minahasa**—the Rp5000 per person meal can actually feed two people. Order ahead of time.

Across the street from Pasar 45 on Jl. Ratulangi is the new, huge **Pasar Swalayan**, a gigantic modern a/c grocery store that sells just about everything. The second floor has an Indonesian restaurant and the expensive **California Spicy Chicken**—other than the fantastic lemon ice tea, not worth the money. On the third floor is the **Jumbo Restaurant,** serving Western and Indonesian dishes.

For shopping, try either **Jumbo Supermarket,** diagonally across the street from the Kawanua City Hotel, or **Fiesta Ria** supermarket on Jl. Ratulangi in the Ranotano area. Both are well-supplied with a great many Western foods and other amenities. Local beer, Anker and Bintang, costs Rp1600 per can; combat bottles go for around Rp2450 per. The cans are a better deal.

Restaurants

Minahasan food tends to be hot and spicy. Try the local dishes—fruitbats, field mice, dog—at **Selera Minahasa** on Jl. Dotulolang Lasut, or the **Tinoor Jaya** on Jl. Sam Ratulangi. Both are very reasonable. Dog meat is also available in a section of **Pasar Bersehati** near Jumbo Supermarket.

Try fresh seafood in the city's Chinese restaurants. A fresh seafood specialty restaurant, the open-air **Manado Seaside Cottages and Restaurant,** is in Malalayang south of the city. Go for the sunset; you can stay here in one of seven nice cottages. **Bunaken Indah** serves impeccable Chinese and European food; it's on top of the Jumbo Supermarket on Jl. Suprapto. The **Klabat Indah,** Jl. Sam Ratulangi 211, is another reliable choice for seafood; the *cumi-cumi* dishes are outstanding. The **Fiesta Ria Restaurant** on Jl. Sam Ratulangi, next door to the supermarket by the same name, is another fine Chinese restaurant.

For Javanese-style food, head for **Surabaya** on Jl. Sam Ratulangi, tel. (0431) 52317, or the **Kalasan,** Jl. Sudirman 9, tel. 3253, the latter known for its "special chicken." Enjoy *nasi padang* at the **Singgalang Sago,** Jl. Sam Ratulangi 164, tel. 52573.

Desserts And Beverages

Try the Italian ice cream at **Turin Restaurant and Bakery,** Jl. Sam Ratulangi 50 near the Hotel Jepindra. An **American Donut** in the eastern part of Pasar 45 is no different from any other cheap bakery. The best bakery around is located on the same floor as the *bioskop* on Jl.

Tendean near Pasar 45. In the **Pasar 45** market try the local sago wine, *tuak saguer.*

Manado has very good sweets—coconut cookies (*kue kelapa*), sago cookies (*bagea*), and nutmeg candies (*pala manis*)—as well as high-quality *arak.* **Warung Ventje,** Jl. Panjaitan 67, tel. (0431) 65105, is a small cake shop passed down through three generations (started in 1936). A larger shop, **Warung Ventje II,** is at Jl. Sam Ratulangi 184. Both sell every possible traditional Minahasan cookie, made from coconut, rice, nutmeg, peanuts, *kenari* nuts—all in small packets (Rp400-2000) for snacking.

PRACTICALITIES

Shopping

The **Bunaken Souvenir Shop,** Jl. Sam Ratulangi 178, tel. (0431) 62303, is the best such shop in Manado, featuring arts and crafts made of wood, rattan, bamboo, seashell, and traditional *krawang* embroidery from Gorontalo. Buy a beautiful sailing ship carved from black ebony for only Rp21,000. Sample nutmeg, coconut, and *kenari* cookies. Open 0800-2000, closed Sunday. **U.D. Kawanua,** Jl. Balai Kota 1/30 (near Lapangan Tikala), and **Krawang** on Jl. Walanda Maramis, sell only *krawang.*

A small sales counter in the **Kawanua City Hotel** sells souvenirs but the management there must really like the products, because the prices are 50% higher than at the Bunaken Souvenir Shop. For inexpensive clothing, cruise the **Makmur** and **Ramayana** department stores on Jl. Walanda Maramis.

Entertainment

There are three discos, two located at or near the Plaza Hotel complex, and the other over by the University. All charge a Rp5000 cover, and sometimes even serve cold beer. Occasionally, you have to troop downstairs and beg for ice (Rp2000). The only other place for Westerners (after 2100) is the **Tarsius Pub** in Malalayang—not recommended for more than one visit. Beer and food are expensive: Rp3250 for a draft Anker, Rp8000-plus for generally drab and ill-prepared Indonesian and Western food.

For the sports-minded who enjoy walking or jogging, Manado is home to a small branch of Hash House Harriers. This small organization, sponsored by mostly Canadian expats, conducts a run/walk somewhere in Manado or the surrounding countryside every two weeks. Bulletins are usually posted at the **Fiesta Ria Supermarket** and the **Tarsius Pub** in Malalayang. Usually the fee is Rp5000, which includes an HHH T-shirt, any food offered afterwards, and transportation. Nice tennis courts in the **Sario Sports Complex** on Jl. A. Yani in the southern part of the city.

Events
Bull-cart, horse, and *bendi* races are held twice yearly at Manado's large **Ranomuut Racetrack** on Jl. Ranomuut in eastern Manado.

Toa Pe Kong, a traditional Chinese parade with origins in the 14th century, takes place in Manado—the largest ceremony of its kind in all of Southeast Asia. This Taoist festival occurs two weeks after the Chinese New Year, usually sometime in February. People come from Jakarta and even as far as Tokyo to see this dynamic and inscrutably ritualistic festival.

Another good day to visit Manado is 23 September: it's the anniversary of the official establishment of the province of North Sulawesi. Parades, performances, costume shows, races.

Information And Services
The **North Sulawesi Tourist Office** is now located at Jl. Diponegoro 111, Manado 95112, tel. (0431) 51723 or 51835. Go there for pamphlets and other useful publications; the director is F. H. Warokka. Hours 0700-1400, Friday until 1100, Saturday till 1230. There's also a very helpful tourist information booth at Sam Ratulangi Airport (open 0830-1600) which provides discounts on hotels.

The only beauty shop in town with English-speaking attendants and fairly modern methods and procedures is **Ginza** on the south side of the Kawanua City Hotel; men's haircuts cost Rp5000. Buy film and order 24-hour film processing from **Angkasa Color Photo Service,** Jl. Yos Sudarso 20, tel. 62467, and **PT Modern Photo Film Co.** on Jl. M.T. Haryono between the *alun-alun* and the Jumbo Supermarket.

Manado's best hospital, **Rumah Sakit Umum,** is on Jl. Yos. Sudarso. An even better hospital, run by Seventh-Day Adventists, is the **Bethesda,** upcountry in Tomohon. Manado has become too poor to support the platoons of doc-

tors and dentists in town. While many speak English, Dr. Polliton is recommended. His practice is in the same building as Apotik Setia on Jl. Sam Ratulangi. Open daily except Sunday, 1700-2000. Arrive by 1645 and sign up on the waiting list to avoid a long wait. An office call is Rp15,000, plus drugs.

The helpful **PHPA** office is at Jl. Babe Palar, P.O. Box 80, Manado, tel. 62680; get your permit (Rp1000) for the Tangkoko-Batuangus National Park here. See the *kepala,* Susanto. *Kantor imigrasi* is on Jl. 17 Agustus, tel. 63491. The poste restante is at the rear of the main post office, Jl. Sam Ratulangi 23, a short walk from the Kawanua City Hotel. Open Mon.-Fri. 0800-2000, Saturday and Sunday 0800-1800. For domestic telephone calls, **Perumtel** on Jl. Sam Ratulangi (between the post office and Kawanua City Hotel) is open 24 hours. Place international calls only at upmarket hotels at exorbitant rates. Manado's telephone code is 0431.

You've never seen so many banks in one town as in Manado. Most are in the city center and are open 0700-1230. **Bank Dagang Negara,** Jl. Dotulolong Lasut, tel. 63278, has a branch office in Los Angeles which you may use to wire money; it costs $25 per wire on the L.A. end. Very professional, with English-speaking clerks, and the exchange rates are usually the best in town. **Bank Bumi Daya** is the only bank open later than 1400. A night teller is on duty until 1900; walk around the right side of the building towards the back. **Bank Central Asia** is on Jl. Dotoholong Lasut, tel. 52778. The **moneychanger** opposite the Minahasa Hotel gives decent rates.

TRANSPORTATION

Getting There
Garuda flies from Jakarta to Manado for Rp515,000; Merpati flies from Jakarta early in the morning via Ujung Pandang for around Rp492,000, arriving before noon. Bouraq's flight from Jakarta is also Rp492,000, but stops at a number of places in East Kalimantan. Arriving, helpful tourist office staff are on hand at Manado's airport (open 0800-1630) to hand out free pamphlets and provide information. Take a taxi seven km into the city for Rp6000; only 20 minutes to the Kawanua City Hotel).

If you arrive by ship at Bitung, 46 km east of Manado, take a *bis umum* to Manado for Rp1000 or a taxi for around Rp25,000. Two Pelni ships, the KM *Umsini* and the KM *Kambuna* sail from Jakarta to Bitung (five days); check Pelni schedules.

It's still a long hard trip to travel by road from Palu to Manado. By bus from Palu, it's around Rp30,000 and two days to Manado. Take this journey in the dry season. From Gorontalo, the bus is Rp10,000 (18 hours).

Getting Around

No *becak* in Manado. *Bendi* are little horse-drawn carts that carry passengers and goods, but many areas are off-limits to them. Hire one from outside a market for Rp200-300 for short rides or Rp1000-2000 for longer ones. What are called *bemo* elsewhere are known as *oplet* here; use these to get around town. Amazing swarms of them—like Jakarta—run frequently to and from Pasar 45, Manado's main *oplet* station. There's also a massing of blue *oplet* under the pedestrian bridge near Jumbo Supermarket on Jl. Sam Ratulangi. The current price is Rp250 to anywhere on set routes. If asked, they'll detour out of their way to drop you off within their general area, and you can even charter an *oplet* for around Rp3000 per hour, cheaper than a taxi.

Taxi meters drop at Rp700 for the first kilometer; Manado taxis always use the meter. There are two taxi stands, one in front of the Plaza Hotel complex, the other next to the Pelni ticket office at Jl. Sam Ratulangi 3. Taxis are also available at the Kawanua City and other city hotels, or call **Dian Taksi,** tel. 62421. The fare from the Plaza Hotel complex to the Nusantara Diving Center is Rp3200. It has become somewhat expensive to charter taxis as touring vehicles, generally Rp7000-10,000 per hour with a five-hour minimum. Charter one for Rp70,000 per day to Lake Tandano. To Airmadidi, Bitung, Lake Tondano, Tomohon, Tinoor, and back to Manado takes five to six hours.

Getting Away

To attract more tourists, the government has opened Manado's Sam Ratulangi Airport as an international airport, allowing foreign airlines to fly direct to Manado. A Singapore-based airline, **Silkair,** now schedules direct flights between Manado and Singapore; Rp1 million roundtrip. **Sempati,** with an agent in the Kawanua City Hotel, flies from Manado to Jakarta and Surabaya.

The **Merpati** office is at Jl. Sam Ratulangi 138, tel. (0431) 64027; take a Sario- or Wanea-bound *bemo* from Pasar 45 down Jl. Sam Ratulangi. Open Mon.-Sat. 0800-1500, Sunday 0900-1200. Merpati schedules flights to Ambon (Rp212,000), Gorontalo (Rp83,000), Poso (Rp194,000), Palu (Rp163,000), and Ternate (Rp87,000). **Garuda,** Jl. Diponegoro 15, tel. 62242, is open Mon.-Sat. 0700-1600, Sunday 1000-1600. Garuda flies daily to Ujung Pandang, Surabaya, Jakarta, and Denpasar. International flights connect Manado directly with Melbourne, Sydney, Singapore, Amsterdam, and Frankfurt.

Bouraq, Jl. Sarapung 27, tel. 62757, flies at least once daily to Gorontalo (Rp75,000), Palu (Rp154,000), Balikpapan (Rp224,000), Surabaya (Rp358,000), and Jakarta (Rp472,000), and to Ternate (Rp82,000) four times weekly. Bouraq also offers the new Manado-Davao (Philippines) 628-km-flight, used by many travelers to obtain a new entry permit. Flights depart on Wednesday and Saturday, returning Thursday and Sunday; Rp550,800 roundtrip, Rp315,000 one-way. The **Philippines consulate** is at Jl. Sam Ratulangi 186, tel. 64447.

Pola Pelita Express Tours and Travel, Jl. Sam Ratulangi 113, charges an administrative fee of 10% on all credit card purchases, the only agency in town charging this ridiculous fee.

Sam Ratulangi Airport is 15 km from Manado in Mapanget. Take an *oplet* bound for Terminal Paal Dua (Rp200), then transfer to another *oplet* for Lapangan (Rp300)—the Lapangan-bound *oplet* goes straight to the airport. The whole ride from Pasar 45 to the airport consumes about half an hour. Or take a taxi for Rp5500-6000; 20 minutes. Airport tax is Rp1800.

The city's harbor terminal and shipping offices are north of Pasar 45. Since Manado's harbor is so silted up, it can only handle smaller boats. The main deep-water port for northern Sulawesi is Bitung on the eastern coast of the peninsula, 48 km east. To sail anywhere east of Sulawesi you often have to go to Ternate in North Maluku first (Rp20,000).

The **Pelni** offices are located on Jl. Sam Ratulangi 3, tel. 62844, a five-minute walk south of the Kawanua City Hotel. Its ships call at

Bitung every two weeks. Pelni has another office in Bitung on Jl. Jakarta, tel. 226 or 152, where it might be easier to get a place on board. The KM *Kambuna* sails the Medan-Padang-Jakarta-Surabaya-Ujung Pandang-Balikpapan-Pantoloan-Bitung-Medan loop. Another Pelni ship, the KM *Umsini,* calls only at Jakarta-Surabaya-Ujung Pandang-Bitung-Ternate-Ambon-Jayapura. From Manado to Jayapura, *ekonomi* class costs Rp56,570 and takes three nights.

Terminal Paal Dua, at the end of Jl. Martadinata near the corner of Jl. Sudirman, has buses to all easterly directions, such as the airport, Airmadidi, Bitung, Likupang, and Kemo. This busy station is accessible by *oplet* from Pasar 45. There are different ways Paal Dua is denoted on the signboards of *bemo*; you may see it written Paal Dua, Paal Paal, Pal 2, or Paal II.

From **Terminal Bahu** on Jl. Mongonsidi, take *oplet* to Gorontalo (Rp10,000, 12 hours) or Palu (Rp25,000, 2.5 days). To reach Terminal Bahu, take a Sario-bound *oplet* from Pasar 45. From **Terminal Wanea** get buses to points south like Tomohon, Tandano, and Kawangkoan. Finally, for northern directions like Wari and Molosgo go to **Stasiun Tuminting.**

VICINITY OF MANADO

An 18-hole golf course at **Kayubatu** (means "Stone Wood," and refers to the ancient Minahasans' first golf clubs), five km from Manado, has well-tended fairways set amidst towering coconut palms.

There are as many as 15 "inns" here, featuring hot springs with both public and private facilities, located no more than 20 km from Manado toward Tondano and Gunung Mahawu. Some of these places are very nice, with spring water piped to every guest room.

On the way to Tomohon, sample delicious spicy food at such roadside restaurants as **Inspirasi, Tindoor Indah,** and the **Tinoor Jaya** in Tinoor. All feature breath-catching views.

Lotak
Seven km south of Manado at Lotak is the tomb of Imam Bonjol, one of Indonesia's most famous freedom fighters. Bonjol led the Padri War in West Sumatra against Dutch tyranny. The Dutch captured and exiled him in 1841; he died in Lotak in 1864. The people of the village of **Pineleng** are descended from Imam Bonjol's family. There's a Catholic seminary in the middle of this village. Enjoy the specialty of the house—*ikan mas*—at the **Kelapa Gading** restaurant. Visit copra plantations in the area; thick coconut plantations cover all the coastal areas, while cloves are grown in the highlands. For Lotak, take an *oplet* from Pasar 45 in the direction of Pineleng.

Beaches
It's not advisable to swim anywhere in Manado Bay due to the raw sewage and other filth discharged from the city in at least 20 spots. Some people travel nearly 32 km to the Manado Beach Hotel in **Tasik Ria** to use the artificial beach—access fee charged for nonguests. The 10-room **Tasik Ria Beach Cottages** is a very relaxing place to stay. The reef and cove offer good snorkeling, safe swimming, and a variety of water sports. To call the beach at **Molas,** north of Manado, a beach is really a misnomer: it should actually be called the Molas Mangrove Swamp.

Malalayang Beach, west of the city, consists of fist-sized rocks from shore to water. In Malalayang, stay at the **Kolongan Beach Hotel** on Jl. Raya Manado-Tanahwangko, tel. 51001; Rp23,000 s and Rp27,000 d for fan rooms, Rp29,000 s and Rp33,000 d for a/c. Restaurant, catamaran, speedboat, scuba, and snorkeling. **Happy Beach Hotel,** Jl. Kayu Wulan, tel. 65444, fax 66487, not far from the Piere Tendean and Monginsidi monuments, offers a/c rooms for Rp50,000 d and full facilities and services. The majority of the rooms enjoy seaside views.

BUNAKEN NATIONAL MARINE PARK

The magnificent reefs of Manado Bay were declared a marine park in 1989. Curtains of millions of brilliantly hued small fish, snakes, and seahorses, as well as dense colonies of black-spined sea urchins, inhabit the coral flats. Bunaken Island has a wide coral platform and a complex marine ecology in caves, crevices, walls, and hanging corals. Its reef is host to a rich panoply of fish, invertebrates, sponges, tu-

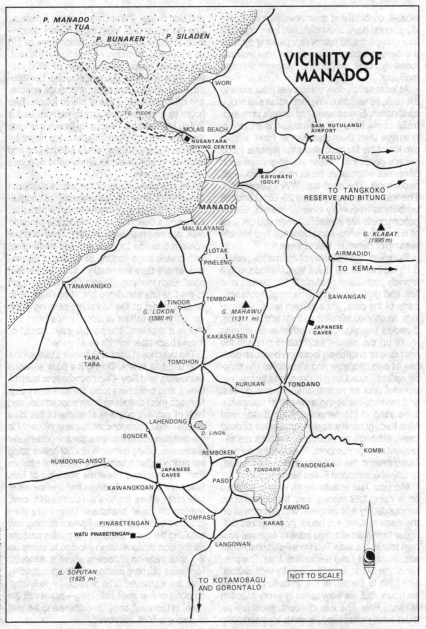

VICINITY OF MANADO

P. MANADO TUA

P. BUNAKEN

P. SILADEN

FERRY

TG. PISOK

WORI

MOLAS BEACH

NUSANTARA DIVING CENTER

SAM RUTULANGI AIRPORT

TAKELU

KAYUBATU (GOLF)

MANADO

TO TANGKOKO RESERVE AND BITUNG

MALALAYANG

LOTAK

PINELENG

G. KLABAT (1995 m)

AIRMADIDI

TO KEMA

TANAWANGKO

TEMBOAN

SAWANGAN

TINOOR

G. LOKON (1580 m)

G. MAHAWU (1311 m)

JAPANESE CAVES

KAKASKASEN II

TARA TARA

TOMOHON

RURUKAN

TONDANO

LAHENDONG

D. LINON

SONDER

REMBOKEN

KOMBI

RUMOONGLANSOT

D. TONDANO

TANDENGAN

JAPANESE CAVES

PASO

KAWANGKOAN

KAWENG

PINABETENGAN

TOMPASO

KAKAS

WATU PINABETENGAN

LANGOWAN

G. SOPUTAN (1825 m)

NOT TO SCALE

TO KOTAMOBAGU AND GORONTALO

© MOON PUBLICATIONS, INC.

nicates, crinoids, and anemones. Some 58 genera of coral have been identified here. You can see groupers and parrot fish plowing through the deeper waters, while on the reef wall are found hydroids, gorgonians, feather stars, and mollusks.

At least seven dive companies offer tours to the park, as well as diving instruction and scuba certification. Even marine enthusiasts from Australia come here—the Bunaken is more impressive than their own Barrier Reef. Within two km of the Manado shore the water is 1,200 meters deep; this means you might see such deep-sea animals as manta rays, sharks, eels, and whales. There are also WW II shipwrecks. The water averages a balmy 25-28° C and the visibility is frequently over 30 meters. Glass-bottom boats are available. When you get tired of diving, the white-sand beaches and friendly *warung* of Bunaken Island await.

Bunaken, the mainstay of the marine park, is a 15-km-long island 15 km from Manado, with a friendly population of about 3,000 people who fish and grow coconuts. The most accessible parts of the park, the southern reefs of Bunaken, lie only 40 minutes by boat from Manado. Besides Bunaken, three other main islands make up the park. It's difficult to pinpoint the best dive or snorkeling locations because each has its own character and attractions. The dropoff wall at Teluk Liang is described by international divers as sensational—caves, gullies, and caverns harboring a wealth of marinelife. Dive sites at Montehagen, Nain Besar, and Nain Kecil generally display large areas of dead coral, although barracuda and sharks are still present in large numbers. The cleanest diving is found around the backside of Bunaken Island, or anywhere around Pulau Manado Tua.

Manado Tua is actually an extinct volcanic cone rising 822 meters from the ocean floor, surrounded by a fringing reef with mangroves on the eastern side; 1.5 hours by motorized outrigger from Manado. You have to organize your own tour to Manado Tua from Pelabuhan Manado; inquire at Toko Samudera Jaya. The people of the island are still quite shy with visitors. The path to the top of the volcano consumes six hours, but the view takes in every island in Manado Bay. The island's coral reefs are almost totally unspoiled, superb for snorkeling

and skin diving. The volcano rests on a plateau, and the water is at most three meters deep—ideal for coral and sponges, which grow as big as a meter in diameter. At the edge of the reef, the plateau drops off to a depth of 2000 meters—a whole new underwater world. Barracuda, tuna, *kakap,* and other enormous species are often sighted. Take a picnic lunch. Two hours by motorized outrigger to the northeast is **Pulau Montehage,** famous for its sea gardens. Another island, **Pulau Siladen,** 1.5 hours by boat from Manado, also offers good diving and snorkeling and beautiful white-sand beaches with many shells.

Unfortunately, many of the area's sheltered reefs, which once offered unparalleled snorkeling and scuba diving, are no longer a paradise. Bunaken's beaches, at least on the Manado side, are also fast degenerating. Trash has become a scourge for beaches and reefs alike, with plastic bags floating at depths of 20 meters where they eventually catch on the reef coral. Each morning villagers carry all their trash to the tide line and dump it in. If you happen to be on the reef as the tide starts carrying it out, you can't see fish for plastic. If you explain that this is a problem, the people say "*nanti,*" or "come back later and it'll be all gone."

The beaches in front of Bunaken's villages are also used as toilets. During the busy seasons (June-Aug. and Nov.-Dec.) hundreds of tourists, divers, and snorkelers roam the area every day. Perhaps most disturbing is the poor attitude and lack of professionalism of some of the dive guides—their behavior contributes significantly to the deterioration of this once pristine underwater wilderness. Some consume alcohol before going out on the water; others pull snakes and lobsters from the sea, and allow the spearing of fish. Boats are occasionally driven into shallow water over reefs, where anchors are carelessly thrown, tearing off coral branches. Divers are then dropped overboard, their flippers kicking and breaking the coral. Because the guides possess no flotation devices, they're forced to stamp on the coral instead of floating above it. Although Manado's offshore islands and the surrounding seas are supposed to be protected—no fishing, no coral or live shell collecting—this is not the case. In fact everybody fishes here and the reef in places is 50% destroyed.

Dive Tours

Most operators charge a daily rate of about Rp147,000 per person plus 20% service tax (minimum two people), including full board, two dives, boat, tanks, weights, mask, snorkel, fins, and wetsuit. Your regulator may not work when you tilt your head, but the crew can usually fix it. To offset these high rates, some clubs routinely provide a 10% discount off the listed price. Also, the different dive clubs compete for customers by offering extras. Most will fetch you at the airport or your hotel (just call them), and drive you into town whenever you want—free. For snorkeling only, expect to pay around Rp63,000 per day. Most operators accept credit cards.

Make sure you agree on a schedule. Don't let the boat crew yank you out of the water after only 25 minutes. It's no fun living life as a clock-watcher, but for this kind of money you want to make sure you get a full day. Book reservations any time of year except the monsoon season from December to February. On Sunday groups of people come out from Manado, and in the European summer the tourists flock in, but in midweek in late April you'll have the whole reef to yourself. The best windsurfing month is windy December.

Of the seven tour operators in the Manado area, the **Nusantara Diving Center**, tel. (0437) 3988, P.O. Box 75, Manado 95007, is the class act—the oldest of Manado's dive outfits. It's located on seven hectares of land on the mainland near the town of **Molas**, northeast of Manado, about 15 minutes by taxi. The owner, Loki Herlambang, is a likable man. The facility is comfortable, quiet, and well-maintained by his large staff—more than 70 at last count. Dive rates are generally Rp63,000 per tank, regardless of destination, unless you're able to negotiate something lower (not likely). Meals cost Rp5200 (breakfast), Rp7300 (lunch), and Rp8400 (dinner). All meals served buffet style. For short stays the food is excellent, but after a while it gets repetitive. The rooms—fan, private *mandi*, hot water—are very nice. There's another scuba/snorkeling center nearby, the **Barracuda**, which is a lot smaller but also good.

Manado Underwater Explorations, or Murex, Jl. Sudirman 28, tel. (0341) 66280, fax 062 431 52116, is a small resort and dive shop in Kalasay, a *kampung* between Manado and Tasik Ria. Murex offers a nice dining room and

10 clean and roomy fan-cooled bungalows facing Manado Bay. With diving and snorkeling equipment available, guests may enjoy day tours to Bunaken and surroundings. Run by professionals Dr. and Mrs. Batuna, an intelligent, conscientious couple who took Jacques Cousteau to Halmahera. They and their guides are particularly conscious about protecting the reefs. Murex doesn't have the party atmosphere of Nusantara Diving Center; it's more laid-back, peaceful, and very romantic. The food is delicious.

Manado Land and Sea was set up to lure noisy Australians from their traditional lair in Bali. This is the only group with an expressed aim to assist tavelers in experiencing the beauty of Sulawesi. The business has established links with the head of the *kehutanan* in the Dumoga Bone Park, so it gets preferential treatment in accommodations and assistance from forest guides. Land and Sea has also impressed upon its instructors the importance of caring for the environment. The dive masters have been tested according to both NAUI and PADI standards by a FAUI-trained Australian instructor/diver and have passed with flying colors. Instructors have even been sent to Australia for maintenance courses on specialized equipment. As a perfect adjunct to the diving/snorkeling package, consider the 16-hour national park tour—Rp94,000 per person, with reduced rates for groups or longer periods of time.

Accommodations

Boats pull into the village of Bunaken, where visitors can eat, sleep, rent equipment, hire a boat to the reefs, and take lessons from the various dive centers. Stay on this island for a whole week for the same amount the dive clubs on the mainland want for one day. Bunaken now has approximately 14 small *penginapan* and *losmen* on the beach with a total of at least 30 rooms costing Rp10,000-15,000 per day, including three meals and sometimes even snorkeling equipment thrown in. Other bungalows run Rp20,000-25,000 per person per day, including meals. All fresh water shipped in from Manado daily; electricity sporadically available from privately owned generators.

A comfortable, relaxing place to stay is **Rusli Kampong**; the boatman will drop you at the place. Rusli will take you to the most interesting spots on the reef; spend four to five hours each day snorkeling and see something new each time. Another terrific *losmen* is **Papa Boa's,** run by very nice people. Mama cooks great meals: fresh lobster, fish, *cumi cumi*. At **Taman Laut,** right on the reef, is quiet **Mr. Jan's.** Or stay at **Losmen Daniel** with Daniel, his wife Grace, who feeds you to the bursting point, and their three kids. This homestay is right on the beach, a five-minute swim out to the reef. Snorkels and masks rent for Rp2500 per day.

Getting There
Inquire at **Toko Samudra,** Kali Jengki 20, or any of the shops backing the river behind Pasar Bersehati. The public boat is Rp1000 and normally leaves between 1200 and 1500, taking more or less two hours. Let the boatman know where you want to get off. A one-way charter on an outboard-powered outrigger runs about Rp5000. You can get an early start, spend a few hours on the reef, and return to Manado that same afternoon.

AIRMADIDI

In this mountain village, 19 km southeast of Manado, are the best examples of *waruga,* pre-Christian tombs of the ancestral Minahasans. Hewn from single blocks of limestone, *waruga* are shaped like small Chinese temples with enormous roof-shaped covers. Often they're lavishly decorated with intricate animal and anthropomorphic carvings, Portuguese gentlemen in 18th-century attire, or features of important Minahasans. Once common over a large area of Minahasa, as Christianity spread *waruga* were either forgotten or destroyed. Because they contained valuables, many have been plundered. Now they've been collected and assembled in places like Airmadidi.

The name "Airmadidi" means "boiling water"—there are two natural hot springs near the *waruga,* with amazingly clear water.

Airmadidi is Rp400 by *oplet* from Manado's Terminal Paal Dua; the *waruga* are just down the road from the Airmadidi *oplet* terminal. A small museum is open 0800-1700. Just before town in Suwaan is **Pongkor,** offering such Minahasan delicacies as baked or fried *ikan mas*; *kolintang* bands play in the restaurant on Saturday nights.

Vicinity Of Airmadidi
At **Taman Waruga Sawangan,** 144 ancient *waruga* have been collected within the confines of a tranquil terraced garden. Because they've been so beautifully restored, the *waruga* at Sawangan are more interesting, varied, and detailed than those at Airmadidi. Take an *oplet* from Airmadidi to Sawangan (Rp100, six km). There are other *waruga* sites at **Kema** on the coast south of Bitung, and at **Likupang** on the northern tip of the peninsula.

From Airmadidi, you're within range of some of Indonesia's most beautiful landscapes. It's only a 45-minute *oplet* ride (Rp1000) farther to Bitung or 50 minutes (Rp1000) down to Tondano on Lake Tondano. **Gunung Klabat** is a stiff five- to six-hour climb from the path near the Airmadidi police station. Tackle it during a full-moon night; shiver while waiting for the sunrise at the top. Register with the police before climbing—there may be wild *anoa* on the trail.

BITUNG

Though sleepy looking, this is the major Minahasan port on the east coast, Rp300 from Girian or one hour (Rp1000, 48 km) by *oplet* on a good road from Manado's Terminal Paal Dua. From Manado, you're dropped off at Terminal Mapalus, 10 minutes and Rp250 by *oplet* from Bitung. The city's natural harbor, from which timber, coffee, cloves, and copra are exported, is protected by **Pulau Lembeh,** a large island just offshore. *Oplet* around town cost Rp200.

The best place for travelers is **Hotel Victoria** on the far side of town in Pateten opposite Gareja Nazeret, a Rp300 *bendi* ride from town. **Hotel Yordan** is a long way out of town on the Manado side, Jl. H.V. Worang Kadoodan, tel. 283; six rooms, fan, Rp30,000 d. **Penginapan Samudera Jaya,** Jl. Sam Ratulangi 2, tel. 114, opposite Minang Jaya Restaurant, charges outrageous prices of Rp7500-15,000 for smelly, windowless tombs. The town's number one accommodation is the **Dynasty Hotel,** Jl. Yos Sudarso 10, tel. 22111, with rooms starting at Rp50,000 d.

Many *rumah makan* on Jl. Sudarso sell *nasi goreng, cap cai, fu yung hae,* and lots of *es.* Prices range Rp1500-2000; *es* is Rp750. Dog lovers should beware of the menu item listed as R.W.—dog meat. For outstanding seafood, try the Chinese restaurants **Virgo** on Jl. Yos Sudarso and the **Hawaii** on Jl. Pertamina.

Within the harbor complex on Jl. Jakarta is the **Pelni** office, tel. 21167, which sells tickets for the ships *Kambuna* and *Umsini*. Pelni now has competition on this route from a private company. The ship KM *Arthirah* runs every 10 days, stopping at Ternate, Bitung, Balikpapan, Ujung Pandang, Surabaya, and Tanjung Priok. The fare from Bitung to Tanjung Priok is Rp865,500, but the facilities are good. For tickets, see the **Kalla Line** agent, with offices all over Manado and Bitung. There are also boats sailing from Bitung each week to Poso in Central Sulawesi via Gorontalo, Pagimana, and Ampana.

Attractive beaches lie out of town, with excellent skindiving and snorkeling from islands off Bitung. **Aertembuga,** a few km from Bitung, is the commercial fishing center of North Sulawesi. South of Bitung, on the southern side of the northern peninsula, is **Kema,** an important seaport in Portuguese times and the site of a Portuguese fort, as well as *waruga.* Take an *oplet* from Bitung (Rp200).

Gunung Saudara National Park

This 3,000-hectare nature reserve, 30 km north of Bitung, was established around the peaks of **Gunung Dua Saudara, Gunung Tangkoko,** and **Gunung Batuangus,** and includes coastline and coral gardens offshore. A real cross-section of Sulawesi's endemic animal life inhabits this geologically fascinating area of hot springs and volcanic craters. There are tarsiers, Indonesia's highest density of crested macaques, monkeys, the bear cuscus, the aggressive *anoa,* flying lizards, the curious *maleo,* hornbills, cockatoos, and in the coastal fringes such marine birds as frigates and sea eagles.

First, obtain a permit (Rp1000 per person) from the helpful PHPA office on Jl. Babe Palar in Manado. It's possible to get a permit on arrival at the park, but you can also be ripped off—people have paid Rp5000-7500 per person. From Airmadidi, it's a Rp500-600 ride on a Bitung-bound *microlet* to **Girian,** where you switch to a jeep for the track up to **Batuputih** (Rp1000, one hour on a very rough road) at the northern entrance of the reserve. Or you can take a jeep all the way from Manado (Rp100,000, four to five hours), walk three hours through the jungle, eat lunch, and return. Inquire at Pola Pelita Tours and Travel in Manado.

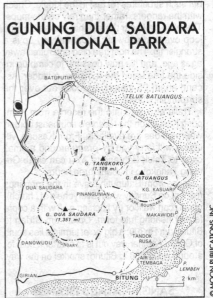

GUNUNG DUA SAUDARA NATIONAL PARK

BATUPUTIH

TELUK BATUANGUS

G. TANGKOKO (1.109 m)

G. BATUANGUS

DUA SAUDARA

PINANGUNIAN

KG. KASUARI

PARK BOUNDARY

G. DUA SAUDARA (1.351 m)

MAKAWIDEI

TANDOK RUSA

PARK BOUNDARY

DANOWUDU

AIR TEMBAGA

P LEMBEH

GIRIAN

BITUNG

0   2 km

© MOON PUBLICATIONS, INC.

The park office lies just on the other side of the bridge. Accommodations are available in the village near the bridge, but you're better off staying in the government *pasanggrahan* about one km farther down the coast. Bring your own food or let the rangers cook for you; Rp1500 breakfast, Rp2500 lunch and tea. The hut, set right on the volcanic black sand beach and right next to the forest, features three rooms for two people each. Few people stay here, and you'll probably be by yourself. You can also try the basic but nice **Tangkoko Beach Cottage** in Batuputih for Rp2000 per person; lunch and dinner Rp3000 per person.

Hand in all your permits at the front office. Don't let them talk you into dropping off the copies at **Donowudu**—that's their job, not yours. The guides are friendly and available for Rp10,000 per day. Even if you explore without one, you may still see quite a lot, including numerous hornbills, troops of black macaques, groups of cuscus. Go early (0600-0900) to the *maleo* nesting area.

The huts and blinds shown on the PHPA map don't exist. There's a tower next to a *maleo* nest site built by a Japanese camera crew in 1991, but such structures rot fast in the jungle. Check with the rangers, rather than rely on the maps. There's a trail near the hut that makes a circuit loop over a nearby hill; about halfway up is a strangler fig. The host tree died and rotted away ages ago, and it's now possible to climb up inside the tree using the roots like a ladder. Ascend about 25 meters and look out over the surrounding forest.

Trails also lead into the reserve from Kampung Kasuari on the reserve's southeast border, where guides are available. From Kasuari, villagers will ferry you by *prahu* around a small cape to Teluk Batuangus. You can climb Gunung Tangkoko in about three hours.

Jeeps from Batuputih leave in the mornings (except on Sunday when everyone's at church), or you can walk or try hitching a lift with a copra farmer headng into town. *Oplet* from **Girian** to Bitung run Rp300; a big *oplet* terminal lies south of Girian. Another way out is to charter a boat for around Rp35,000 to Bitung; snorkel on the way.

SANGIR-TALAUD ISLANDS

An archipelago that stretches from the northern tip of North Sulawesi nearly all the way to Mindanao Island in the Philippines. Not only physical features but also the languages spoken in Sangir-Talaud are closely related to those in the Philippines. Before the arrival of the Portuguese, the Islamic sultanate of Ternate ruled over Sangir-Talaud. The Dutch occupied the islands in the late 17th century, eventually converting most of the population to Christianity. The principal industries today are copra and clove production. The total population of the islands is around 300,000. The light-complexioned natives, famous for their delicate carving of black mahogany, are believed to have originated from somewhere in northern Polynesia. Though the northernmost islands of the Talaud group are only 120 km from Mindanao—the closest point to the Philippines in Indonesia— you can't get to the Philippines from here.

With their sandy beaches, coral reefs, and small fishing *kampung*, these islands present silence and beauty all their own. Like the islands of Maluku, this is a highly volcanic chain. Gunung Awu on Pulau Sangir has a long record of explosions, with the most recent eruption in 1966. The ground on the island is very shaky. Gunung Ruang, Gunung Karanggetang, and Gunung Banua are also very volatile. Many rare and distinctive palms, notably the *kavesu* and the *sago barok,* grow in the region.

The *Agape* sails three times weekly from Manado; the faster, better express *Pan Marine* also leaves Manado harbor thrice weekly— Rp20,000-25,000 roundtrip, two days and two nights. Even in the first-class cabin 17 people will stare at you the entire voyage; for more privacy, fork over an additional Rp20,000 for the captain's cabin. Inquire about latest prices and schedules at **PT Putra Utara** or **PT Holpers,** both on Jl. Pelabuhan in Manado.

Tahuna
The capital of the group is the town of Tahuna, situated on the main island of Sangir. Here is the best TV reception in North Sulawesi, where Filipino and even Malaysian stations are pulled out of the sky. The best accommodations in town are at the **New Victory Veronica,** Jl. Raramenusa 16, tel. 79 or 111; good food, no a/c, nice rooms. Also check out **Tagaroa,** Jl. Malahasa 1; rooms with private bath go for Rp20,000-70,000. Cheaper is **Wisma Anugah** at Rp15,000 pp; meals served. Eat at restaurants **Yenny, Al Fajar,** and **Madorosa.** There's no beach where you won't be bothered by village children, and the whole coast is dotted with villages.

Pulau Siau
The largest of the southern islands in the Sangir group, Pulau Siau has historically fallen under the administrative control of the Manado district of North Sulawesi. Its large, active volcano, Gunung Awu, has the same name as Pulau Sangir's. It erupted in 1974, forcing the evacuation of the island's entire population of 42,000 to Minahasa. For information on climbing Gunung Awu, inquire at the volcanologist office in Tahuna.

Getting There
Merpati flies directly from Manado to Naha Airport, 21 km from Tahuna on Pulau Sangir; Rp60,000. Or fly with Merpati from Manado to Melanguane Airport on Pulau Karakelang; twice weekly, Rp70,000. It's cheaper to catch cargo boats departing at least four times weekly from Manado harbor. Boats also depart from

Bitung about five times weekly, stopping at ports such as Beo and Lirung for 12-36 hours, depending upon the time required to load and unload supplies.

TOMOHON AND VICINITY

Tomohon is a pretty, windy, sunny town with still-active **Gunung Lokon** (1,580 meters) towering in the background and the sea visible beyond. The smell of sulphur can be very strong. One of the highest villages of the district, the town has a pleasantly cool climate, not unlike a European summer. Known as Kota Kembang ("Flower City"), every wooden house seems to be draped with orchid plants, while household gardens burst with enormous zinnias, dahlias, marigolds, and glorious perennial gladiolas. Tomohon is the location of a Christian theology school at nearby **Bukit Inspirasi** ("Hill of Inspiration").

People are very friendly. The town is renowned for its wheelwrights, who supply most of the wheels for the *bendi* of Manado; Tomohon's streets echo with the sound of horses' hooves. Take the road by the Christian University leading to Bukit Inspirasi, from where you can see Gunung Lokon and Manado; descend the steps back down. A fine market on Tuesday, Thursday, and Saturday features roasted dogs, giant roasted rats, snakes, and bats. One of the best hospitals in Sulawesi is Tomohon's **Bethesda,** operated by Seventh-Day Adventists. From Tomohon, take an *oplet* to Tondano (Rp500, 30 minutes) and Kawangkoan (Rp550, 45 minutes).

From Manado's Pasar Karombasan, take a public bus or minibus direct to Tomohon (Rp600). Enjoy wonderful views of the city; at night see strings of lights below. Cafes, restaurants, and hot spring spas perch on the side of the road all the way to Tomohon. This pine-forest region offers one of Indonesia's highest concentrations of hot springs. Buy *durian, langsat,* mangos, and other monsoon fruits at **Pineleng,** a village just above Tomohon. The bus continues to climb through the plantations between the volcanos of Lokon and Mahawu.

At **Temboan,** halfway up the mountain to Tomohon, experience real ethnic Minahasan cooking: mice, dog (very peppery hot), wild pig (*babi* *hutan*), and a gin called *cap tikus,* plus sago wines (*tuak saguer*) of varying potency. The food is heavily spiced, and visitors who don't like hot food should ask for food *"tidak pedas."* Superb views of Manado and the bay. Approaching Tomohon, see the *ikan mas* raised in the ponds on the left.

Vicinity Of Tomohon

This is a lovely area, comparable to the mountain towns of Java. An oft-expressed greeting in upcountry Minahasa is: *"Pakatua'an wo paka-lawiren!"* ("Wishing you long life and health!"). Because of the rich *cingke* cash crops, the people in surrounding villages are comparatively well off. Many horsecarts, so plenty of transportation; Rp500-1000 per ride.

Two km out of Tomohon, on the road to **Tara Tara,** are WW II Japanese ammunition caves. In **Kinilow,** five km before Tomohon, is **Indraloka,** with a large modern swimming pool, natural hot springs, and public baths; hostesses offer rubdowns. Cottages for Rp20,000 s or d.

At **Kakaskasen I,** three km before Tomohon, dances are sometimes held on Saturday night; Rp250 admission. **Kakaskasen II** sits in the shadows of two volcanos, **Gunung Lokon** and **Gunung Mahawu.** Both have crater lakes of considerable beauty, duck-egg blue and smoking, within 1.5 hours walk of the village. Lokon is usually considered the more beautiful of the two, and the casual climb should be no problem for anyone in reasonable condition. Guides for around Rp5000 may be found with the help of the *kepala desa.* The walk takes you through fields of corn and *enau* (palm oil trees). The final 30 minutes follows a frozen lava flow that has formed a rock river holding rainwater pools for refreshment. The steaming crater lies 600 meters below the peak of the mountain; it threatens to erupt every 10 years. The lake is about 60 meters deep, crusted with yellow sulphur. Start from Kakaskasen II no later than 0700, arriving at the Lokon crater while the morning is still cool and the sun fills the crater.

Tara Tara

Thirty km southwest of Manado. In Tomohon, turn right at the ticket office and either walk eight km or take an *oplet.* In Tara Tara, a traditional mill is located toward the end of the road to the right. Powered by a fast-running stream at the bottom of a small ravine, the immense water wheel drives an intricate maze of belts, pulleys, and wooden gears—the final achievement is the vertical operation of a group of heavy log pounders that pulverize the grain. It's possible to travel along this road to **Tanawangko,** then circle back to Manado.

Contact the *hukum tua* in Tara Tara to charter extraordinary dances for around Rp100,000: *maengket, kebesaran,* old Portuguese, harvest, and Christian dances. Music is provided by a group of *kolintang* players, using homemade bamboo and brass instruments. Very lively and characteristically Minahasan—more pleasing to the Western ear than most Asian orchestras. Please give a donation to the village. Stay at the **Tamaska.**

Lahendong

A few km south of Tomohon on the main road to Langowan, Rp250 by *oplet.* There's a hot springs on the right before Lahendong village, but it's a real commercial operation. Better to get off just after the bridge on the edge of the village, where there's a huge lava flow with small, bubbling, steaming craters, and a hot springs alongside the river. Interesting walk around the area. Danau Linon, a small, highly sulphurous lake with steam jets, bubbles at the edges. The lake's colors change depending upon the light and viewing perspective: shades of light blue, green, turquoise. Hundreds of large white birds and beautiful small songbirds in residence—a fairy-tale environment. In the water sticks with strings attract dragonflies, which the local youths capture at night, then fry and eat. Bathe in the hot spring by the side of the lake near the power project. Take an *oplet* to Lahendong, get off at the Kantor Vulkanolog sign, and walk 700 meters to the lake.

Sonder

This clove village, 20 km southwest of Tomohon, consists of one main street with three churches (Minahasa, Seventh-Day Adventist, Catholic). During the harvest (July-Oct.), one can hardly drive through the streets because of the *cingke* which people have put out to dry on mats—their yards are already overflowing. Even stilted traditional-style wooden homes sport color TV sets, kitchen gadgetry, and expensive furniture. With a per capita income of US$5500, this is one of the richest towns in Asia.

Rurukan

A colorful 900-meter-high mountain village perched halfway between Tomohon and Tandano, five km up a twisting, rough, mountain road. From the center of the village, take the road to Kumelebuag. Turn right after 400 meters, follow a dirt path for 100 meters, then turn left and go straight along a jungle path to reach some fine hot springs. Backtracking to the village, follow the main road down to Tondano, another six km; this is a beautiful walk with a panoramic view of Lake Tondano.

TONDANO AREA

Tondano is a large market town located in the middle of a fertile rice-growing plateau. Catch a minibus or *oplet* from Tomohon, or from Manado's Terminal Karombasan. Stay at the excellent, clean, and cool **Asri;** Rp18,000 per room includes breakfast, tea, and coffee. Eat at the **Pemandangan** or **Fireball** restaurants on the main road, Jl. Raya Tomohon. From Tondano, continue to other resort towns surrounding **Danau Tondano,** a large, scenic lake beautifully situated between paddies and the Lembean Mountains. This 50-square-km lake, about 30 km southeast of Manado, is the region's largest. Its abundant fish provide a livelihood for the native population. The tiny island in the middle is known as Likri. The waterfall of Tondano is famous.

Vicinity Of Tondano

From Tondano take the road north to Airmadidi, which carves its way through thick plantations of endless coconut, following the Tondano River, with dramatic views of the Klabat volcano and evening mists filling the valley. See extensive Japanese-made caves about one-hour's walk on this road.

From Tondano, pay Rp500 to travel around the west or east side of the lake. Eastbound, stop in at **Tandengan** and **Eris,** both with nice views of the lake. Westbound, **Remboken** has a better selection of pottery than Manado; also try the hot springs at the **Taman Wisata.** At **Paso,** bathe in large steaming concrete tanks; ask for *air panas umum* (Rp500). Stay at **Tempat Pemandian Florida,** Rp10,000. From Paso there are lovely views of Lake Tondano across

Minahasan waruga

steaming fields of hot springs bubbling amongst the rice.

Heading south from Tondano, you wind up in **Kakas.** No *losmen* here, but contact the *kepala desa* who'll turn you on to some accommodations if you're willing to teach English. From Kakas, take a small *prahu* across the lake to Kaweng. Five km southwest of Kakas is **Langowan,** a mountain village with hot springs, *sawah,* and virgin pine forests.

Kawangkoan

Located between Langowan and Amurang, Kawangkoan is a crossroads village reached by *oplet* from Manado's Pasar Karombasan (two hours). Eat at **Restaurant Harmoni.** Enjoy local coffee and hot *biapong,* soft pastry cakes with a meat and vegetable filling, at **Kopi Gembira,** open 0500-2100. This village is known for

bull-cart racing, celebrated *kolintang* performances, and an underground Japanese fortress and storage caves. Eat in the restaurant opposite the caves. You can charter the *maengket* dance in **Tompaso,** between Kawangkoan and Langowan. Don't miss the flaming red and yellow gladioli (*bunga mas*) of **Pinabetengan** village, five km to the south.

Watu Pinabetengan

A megalithic ancestor stone near Kawangkoan, its surface covered in crude, mysterious line drawings and scripts that have never been deciphered. According to Minahasan history, this is the place where their ancestors first divided the land between the people; Watu Pinabetengan means "The Stone of Discussion about the Division." This memorial boulder, two meters high and four meters long, shaped like the top of a *waruga,* has served as a political gathering place for Minahasan elders since time immemorial. There have been at least six major discussions at the stone: the first division of the tribes, a reconciliation of the differences between the tribes, a resolution in the 17th century to drive out the Spanish, a meeting to organize a defense against attackers from Bolaang Mongondow to the south, a 1939 demand for Indonesian independence, and a blessing of the new Indonesian Republic in 1945. Though each of the six Minahasan tribes speaks its own dialect, they are today united as one people; Mina Esa means "Become One" or "United."

From Kawangkoan, take a *bendi* three km (Rp300, 30 minutes) to Desa Pinabetengan. Then walk two km along a road to the site, in a beautiful forest on the slopes of a mountain with a majestic view over Minahasa. Unfortunately, the government has buried the sacred stone in an ugly concrete crypt, like a white-tiled grave. It should have been situated on a lovely grass hillock for everyone to see and enjoy. To make it worse, the concrete roof makes the place even darker, and birds who live under the roof shit on the revered object. A pity, as the site could be an important tourist attraction. Don't visit during the first part of the year: thousands of people converge on the memorial stone during the month of January. Bathe in the hot springs nearby.

BOLAANG MONGONDOW DISTRICT

This beautiful rural district of undulating *sawah,* mountains, and magnificent sea coast is primarily an agricultural region growing rice, sago, maize, yams, and cassava; coconuts and coffee are cash crops. It's inhabited by the coastal Bolaang, who merged with the inland Mongondow. Village heads are called *sangadi.* Villages, formerly consisting of longhouses, are strung out along the roads. Islam, which replaced an indigenous ancestor cult, first arrived around 1830; Protestant missionaries have also made inroads.

KOTAMOBAGU

Kotamobagu is the cultural center and capital of the Bolaang Mongondow District, situated in the upland plateau between the Minahasa and Gorontalo districts and surrounded by mountains. An attractive, clean, friendly and quite modern Muslim town, it has many new buildings and three new supermarkets; an Rp5000, four-hour, 218-km bus journey from Manado's Terminal Karombasan. If coming from the south, the road up from Bintauna (six hours) on the coast is excellent and a real delight after the Trans-Sulawesi Highway.

Accommodations
Losmen Lely is one of the cheapest at Rp6000 d. If you demur, the owner will send you off to his sister's, **Hotel Ade Irama** on Jl. Ade Irama near the *rumah sakit;* Rp12,000-20,000 d. The beds look like they come from the *rumah sakit* and the rooms are as hot as Lely's. **Losmen Widura** wants Rp10,000 d, Rp12,500 with double bed; **Hotel Tentram** on Jl. Adampe Dolot charges Rp8000-10,000 plus 10% tax.

Better than all of the above is **Hotel Ramayana** on Jl. Adampe Dolot, just down the road from Lely and Tentram. Bargaining begins at Rp10,000 d but management will drop to Rp8000—*mandi,* breakfast, big airy rooms with fan, friendly staff, quite modern. For more upscale accommodations, check out the **New Plaza,** Jl. Mayjen Suoyo, for Rp17,500 s, Rp20,000 d, Rp25,000 VIP. The **Kabela,** on the same street, rents rooms for Rp10,000 s or d.

Food
Supermarket Paris near the roundabout is a local landmark and hangout; check out the bakery. The **Putra Minang** next door is a good Padang-style restaurant; the *nangka* curry is an excellent value for vegetarians. Good *gado-gado* stalls are open around town at night; the **Nasional** sells very good, very reasonably priced Chinese food and drink. The dirty and grotty market area is a big contrast to the rest of town; it's here that *martabak* and *es* sellers congregate. Unlike elsewhere in Indonesia, the *martabak* stalls seem to operate in the day only. Only sweet *martabak* is available here, and it's quite inferior. The *es* is also quite plain. One interesting item available in the market is *kedelei,* roasted soybean powder which serves as a very good coffee substitute.

Getting Away
Take buses to Manado from Terminal Gelora in Kotamobagu. Walk about one km north along the main street; then, when almost at the top of the hill, turn right at the Sekolah Dasar Katolik (Rp4000, 3.5 hours). From Terminal Bahu in Manado, take a *bemo* into town for Rp200.

NORTH OF KOTAMOBAGU

From Kotamobagu, catch a local bus north to **Amurang.** A nice day-trip is to picturesque **Bilalang** village, three km north of town. Ten km northeast of Kotamobagu is **Modayag,** a cool, high goldmine village. Stay at the *pasanggrahan.*

Every Sunday a 1,000-meter horserace—with betting on the side—takes place at Togop, three km north of Kotamobagu; free entry.

Gunung Ambang National Park
A good day-trip from Kotamobagu, only about a half-hour drive (27 km), this reserve offers crater lakes, montane forests, sulphur fumaroles, and hot mudpools. The park, at 1,100-1,800 meters above sea level, is filled with *pigafetta* palms, tree ferns, and flowering shrubs. The locals use the good trails to hunt rats, bats, and snakes.

From the Kotamobagu bus terminal, take a *bemo* headed north to Modayag and disembark at **Bong Kudai Baru.** This is a beautiful drive on a good road through coffee plantations. The fare is Rp500, more if you change *bemo.*

Report at the **Taman Nasional Dumoga-Bone** office back down the road three km, just opposite the entrance to the lake. The ranger is likely to insist you hire a guide; you get the impression he really wants only to assert his authority, and may grant you permission to enter unescorted provided you report back to his office. When you return later that afternoon, the place could well be deserted.

If you try to find your own way, you may find yourself on top of an adjoining mountain. To avoid this, walk up the cobblestone path in Bong Kudai Baru for about 200 meters and follow it as it veers sharply to the left. This is basically the end of the road, though a faint path continues past it. If you take the other route near the PHPA hut, it's easy to get lost, as the paths are transitory and change with the vegetable plantings. The suggested path is a bullsled track—a novel form of transport used to carry goods in this muddy area. If you stick to the left, this path continues almost all the way to the fumaroles. The last section is a footpath through the *alang-alang* grass. The walk takes an hour and fifteen minutes.

SOUTH OF KOTAMOBAGU

Imandi
Buses leave for Doloduo every morning before 0900; Rp600. The route passes through 50 km of splendid river and mountain country over a good, sealed road. Stop in at Imandi, a small quiet village, and an ideal place to relax. Stay at **Penginapan Ingat Budi,** Rp8000 per bed. **Penginapan Sweetheart,** right in the village itself, charges Rp8000, or Rp10,000 full board; better food than at Ingat Budi. From Imandi, walk or take a *bendi* seven km to **Desa Werdhi Agung** (pop. 600), a Balinese *transmigrasi* colony, where you'll find heart-shaped Balinese faces, one *pura,* a *gamelan* orchestra, Balinese *bubur* rice cakes, and *legong* dances. Crafts also made here. Another, smaller Balinese *kampung,* **Desa Merta,** is only three km from Imandi.

Doloduo
There are irrigation systems just like Bali's seven km beyond Imandi in Doloduo. Stay at **Losmen Sabar Menanti,** which also provides meals. From Doloduo to **Molibagu** is a 20-km walk over a small mountain range through a beautiful forest with lots of butterflies. Plan on about four hours; you can make the roundtrip in a day. From Molibagu, boats embark for Gorontalo or Bitung at least three times weekly; try to find out in Doloduo when the next boat leaves, as there's no *losmen* in Molibagu, only an eight-room *pasanggrahan.* One of the local policemen usually puts up Westerners, but his hospitality is embarrassing—three huge meals a day while the whole family watches. Best to arrive the day before the boat sails. Boats are either *prahu* with outboards and outriggers or big, fast 15- to 20-meter-long jobs with large outriggers and diesel engines. To Gorontalo it's Rp8000-10,000, 12 hours, an overnight trip. Might not operate July-Sept. due to big seas and easterly winds.

Dumoga-Bone National Park
The remote and fascinating 300,000-hectare Dumoga-Bone National Park offers a superior walking environment, greater variety of wildlife, and better accommodations and food than the Tangkoko-Batuangus Reserve. Since its establishment in 1984, farms have steadily—and recently, very rapidly—encroached upon the boundaries of the park. The *maleo* birds, found at the Tumokang and Tambun nesting grounds in the park, are still endangered by egg poachers who sell the eggs in Jakarta. The pig deer (*babirusa*) is also threatened by poachers.

Joining ecological tours will help prolong the lives of these beasties, and great efforts are made to conserve the park because of its incredible biodiversity. If traveling with your own vehicle from, say, Manado, your travel costs will make up the large part of your expenses. Since it costs the same to transport one or ten people to this park, it's in your best interest to find others interested in the journey. Or you can take a public bus from Kotamobagu to **Doloduo.** Ask the driver to drop you off at the eastern entrance to the park, four km beyond Doloduo.

At the park office ask permission to stay in the guesthouse (Rp2000 per person). If your purpose is "rekreasi," not "scientific research," Mr. Palete will grant permission. The accommodation is good quality and the food wonderful. Plead with the head ranger to give you a map of the park with walking trails marked. Eat in the *warung* by the dam (Rp1500); there are also a few small restaurants near the entrance. If you're going to spend the night in the forest, you'll need a hammock and basher—Dumoga-Bone is extremely rich in insect life.

You've got a good chance of seeing the famous Celebes ape (*Macaque nigra*), which is not really an ape but a tailless monkey. They often feed at the edge of the forest, behind the guesthouse. Dumoga Bone is also a birdwatcher's paradise. Orinthologists have spotted 100 species of birds within a one km radius of the park headquarters. The great hornbill, many species of kingfishers, birds of prey, parrots, pigeons, and a number of species endemic to Sulawesi are denizens of the park. Bats also abound, with at least two species endemic to the park. Those with spider fear should beware—there are 103 species of *laba laba* found just along the forest edge.

THE NORTH COAST

Inobonto

A small Muslim port town along the highway from Manado to Gorontalo, accessible by road from Kotamobagu. A pleasant place to hang out; quiet and relaxing. **Hotel Kotabuan,** 500 meters from the harbor, is the best place to stay. **Losmen Tepi Laut** ("Edge of the Sea") is so close to the harbor you can hear the waves. **Losmen Haji Idrus** right around the corner is cheaper and has better food, but the lighting leaves you a little in the dark. Eat local food at one of the food stations in **Air Anjing,** 12 km to the northeast.

Boats out of Inobonto have become quite rare since the completion of the Trans-Sulawesi Highway. Have tea with the harbormaster on his porch on the beach and find out what boats he's expecting. You might have to wait three to four days, but he'll send a boy to your *losmen* when your ship comes in. It won't leave for hours anyway. Boats west to Kwandang stop in small Muslim coastal towns like Bintauna, Baroko, and Buko; pay no more than Rp8000-9000 through to Kwandang. If you speak Arabic along this western section of Bolaang Mongon-

dow, you're in. Boats also carry copra between Inobonto and Bitung; ride along for Rp8500.

To experience Sulawesi scenery at its finest, take the Rp2000 bus trip from Inobonto over the mountain northeast to **Poigar** village. Visit Poigar's Minahasan village on the far bank of the river for fresh fish or spiced dog—black dogs are supposedly the tastiest.

Lolak

Northwest of Kotamobagu. A nice-looking cottage-style hotel here, the **Molosing Beach Motel and Cottages,** lies close to the beach, a perfect opportunity to engage in some fishing, canoeing, and boating. There are also facilities for tennis, volleyball, and badminton. The powdery white-sand beach is ideal for sunbathing. For reservations, call the Manado office, tel. 62162. The motel overlooks **Pulau Molosing,** where several families tend coconut plantations. The motel maintains three bungalows on the island.

Labuhan Uki

The tiny isolated village of Labuhan Uki, west of Inobonto, offers clear water and a white sand beach. Go first southwest to Lolak, then walk eight km along the beach or travel nine km by road. There are no vehicles to Labuhan Uki. You can see the bare patches on the mountain slope across the bay where timber has been felled for boatbuilding.

Bintauna

Ruins of a Portuguese fort, 60 km west of Inobonto. If coming from Gorontalo, you'll probably be let off at **Safari Gorontalo,** with small rooms for Rp2000 per person. Staff is prepared to cook a meal as late as 2000, but the food is poor, usually Padang-style with fish or chicken; sometimes they dig up some cucumber and eggs. If heading for Kotamobagu, buses leave Bintauna each morning at around 0700 or 0800. Don't wait in the restaurant, as the bus may not even stop there; flag it down. The road is very nice along this section, moving through coconut plantations with many fine sea views. Just before **Maelang** stop for lunch in a *warung* on a sea cliff, one of many in the area. The vegetables are very good. The Maelang District is quite prosperous and the residents house-proud with colorful, well-tended gardens. From Bintauna to Kotamobagu consumes six hours.

GORONTALO DISTRICT

Most travelers who visit North Sulawesi usually fly out without seeing Gorontalo, though this fertile, rice growing area is fascinating for its isolated and conservative Islamic culture. The half million people of the Gorontalo plain consist of a number of different groups—the Buol, Limboto, Kwandang, Soewawa, and Attingola.

The district is 95% Muslim. Four dialects are spoken here; those in the west are closer to Torajan, while those in the east are distinctly Filipino. Governed from the Ternate sultanate, who probably introduced Islam; a federation of all the different principalities formed in 1673. The Gorontalo District came under Dutch control in the 1890s. Swidden rice, maize, and sago are the staples of the region, while on Lake Limboto nets, traps, and harpoons are used to catch fish.

GORONTALO

The port of Gorontalo, on the south-central coast of the northern peninsula, is the main town of the Gorontalo District and the second largest urban center in North Sulawesi. Only recently has Gorontalo been connected to the rest of North Sulawesi by road; it's a pleasant enough place to recover from the punishing overland journey by bus from Palu. This city of one-story buildings has a rich local culture, history, and handicrafts.

Dutch provincial architecture is still in evidence; fine specimens include the **Mini Saronde Hotel**, the art-deco **Mitra Cinema** on Jl. S. Parman 45, and the **RS Umum** on Jl. Jend. A. Yani. Although spread out, all the important offices, hotels, and eateries lie within a small central business district.

Accommodations
Dutch-built and aging **Penginapan Teluk Kau,** Jl. Jen. S. Parman 42, tel. 21785, Rp8000-12,000, is roomy, with gigantic canopied double beds and high ceilings. Though not a tremendous value, don't be surprised if it's full. **Hotel Asia,** down the road from the Teluk Kau at no. 10, is basically in the same shape at the same price, though the tariff includes a boiled egg and tea/coffee. Very friendly.

A nice place to stay is **Hotel Melati,** on the road to the harbor next to the Ideal Theater and across the road from the playing field. A beautiful big colonial house, restaurant, great veranda, large rooms with old paintings and artifacts, Rp10,000 d. **Hotel Wisata,** Jl. 23 Januari 19, tel. 21736, is good value at Rp10,000 s, Rp12,000 d, Rp15,000-20,000 standard, and Rp25,000-30,000 deluxe with a/c; good food. The Merpati office is here.

The city's top hotel is the **Mini Saronde Hotel** in a converted Dutch-built villa, Jl. Walanda Maramis 17, tel. 2677 or 21735. Rooms, set around a courtyard, run Rp45,000-50,000 for a/c, hot water, balcony, and fridge. Breakfast included. The delightful owner speaks good English. **Hotel Indah Ria,** Jl. Jen. A. Yani 20, tel. 21296, is another of the city's best. Rp20,000 for fan-cooled rooms, Rp30,000 for a/c rooms; central, clean, basic, friendly, private. Tariff includes all meals.

Food
Eat *nasi campur* or *nasi kuning* in the *warung* down the narrow alleyways in and around Pasar Sentral for as little as Rp1000. Around the *bioskop* in the city center is another collection of inexpensive *warung.* Inexpensive, good foodstalls on Jl. Pertiwi at night; try the local delicacy *milu siram* (fish broth with corn, *santan,* and lemon juice). Across the street from the *bemo* station, a 15-minute walk from Penginapan Teluk Kau, is a good fruit and vegetable market.

Dirgahayu on Jl. Pertiwi downtown specializes in tasty goat dishes like *sate,* curry, and soup. Also very central is **Olympic,** which offers primarily seafood. For Padang-style food, try the **Padang** on Jl. Sam Ratulangi; excellent meals for the price. The best Chinese food in town is at the **Milado** in the town's center. **Brantas,** Jl. Hasanuddin 5, has great baked goods and delicious Indonesian cuisine.

Shopping And Services
For local basketry, try **Pasar Sentral;** for *krawang* embroidery, peep in at the shops along Jl. Jen. Suprapto. The **main post office** is at Jl. Jen. A. Yani 14. **Perumtel,** the telephone/telegraph office, is at Jl. 23 Januari 35. Change money at

Bank Rakyat Indonesia and **Bank Negara Indonesia,** both on Jl. Jen. A. Yani near the intersection of Jl. M. T. Haryono.

Getting There

From Manado's Terminal Malalayang, take a public bus to Amurang (Rp1700); from there, the north coast road leads via Lolak to Kwandang. From Kwandang, take a minibus one hour south to Gorontalo. Another possibility is to take a bus Manado-Inobonto-Kotamobagu, then a minibus to Dumogabesar, Imandi, and Molibagu on the coast. From there it's Rp7000-9000 by motorized *prahu* to Gorontalo. You can also reach the city by bus from Palu in 36 hours.

Getting Around

If arriving by air, minibuses wait to take passengers into town (Rp3500); on the way you pass through the lovely lakeside village of Limboto. It's an easy walk from the downtown to the Pasar Sentral at the intersection of Jl. Dr. Sam Ratulangi and Jl. Pattimura. From the market, the main bus terminal is across (north) Jl. Dr. Sam Ratulangi. *Oplet* run from the terminal to all over town, Rp250 flat fee. Catch *oplet* which run often from Pasar Sentral to the long-distance bus station, **Terminal Andalas,** on the outskirts of town. There are also hundreds of *bendi* (Rp200-250). Hire a *bendi* (Rp2000 per hour) or a *microlet* (Rp4000 per hour) for a complete tour around Gorontalo. The harbor is in the eastern part of town, Rp200 by *oplet* (15 minutes).

Getting Away

The **Merpati** office is in Hotel Wisata, Jl. 23 January 19, tel. 21736, with service to Manado, Palu, Poso, and Toli Toli. From Manado, connect to Surabaya, Ujung Pandang, Jakarta, and Ternate. Next to the BNI bank, at Jl. Jen. A. Yani 34, tel. 70870, is **Bouraq,** which schedules flights at least three times weekly to Manado (Rp78,000) and Palu (Rp92,000). Flights to Samarinda are Rp198,000 via Palu; Surabaya Rp333,000 via Palu and Balikpapan; Tarakan Rp279,000 via Palu and Balikpapan; Ternate Rp146,000 via Manado, and Ujung Pandang Rp197,000 via Palu. The Merpati/Bouraq people will pick you up at your hotel and take you to Gorontalo's **Jalaluddin Airport** 32 km to the north; Rp4000, 45 minutes. Line it up at their respective offices.

Ships headed for ports along the northern arm of Sulawesi embark from the port of Kwandang, two hours by bus from Gorontalo. **Pelni** has an office in Kwandang; the KM *Umsini* sails to Ujung Pandang for Rp152,000 first class, Rp110,000 second class, Rp38,000 economy. Pelni in Gorontalo, Jl. 23 January 31, tel. 20419, runs a fairly regular boat to Poso, Kendari, then Ujung Pandang. Another shipping line is **PT Gapsu** on Jl. Pertiwi 55, tel. 88173, in Gorontalo, with another office in the harbor at Jl. Mayor Dullah, tel. 198. From Gorontalo harbor leave many ships of all sizes to Bitung, Rp12,000-15,000, 20 hours; Poso, Rp23,000 deck class, 48 hours, with stops in the Togian Islands en route; and sometimes to Kendari.

From Gorontalo harbor embark at least two small *kapal motor* weekly to the southern side of Teluk Tomini. The easy way is to take a boat to Parigi, then travel by *oplet* or minibus to Palu or Donggala. Alternatively, take a boat from Gorontalo harbor, two to three days, to either Bunta, Pagimana, or Ampana. From any of these villages there are boats or minibuses leaving for Poso on the south shore of Tomini Bay. Be prepared for a wait, as departure times are irregular, particularly during the rain.

There are bus offices and ticket agencies at the long-distance **Andalas bus station.** Approximately 10 companies offer service to Manado, but all leave at 1700. This 12-14 hour (Rp12,500) trip is sheer overnight hell. For Kotamobagu, first get an *oplet* to Pasar Sentral (Rp200), then another to Terminal Andalas in Telaga (Rp200). Buses leave at 1700 for Kotamobagu (Rp8500) and Manado. If you're not willing to wait until 1700, you can connect with a bus to Bintauna about two-thirds of the way.

Whatever you do, don't pay up front "for petrol" at the station as it's not uncommon to be ripped off and asked for Rp7500. The actual fare to Bintauna is Rp5000, which you should pay to the driver. The road to Bintauna is fairly flat, although it veers inland and climbs quite a bit just before Boroko. It's also in very bad condition. Until just before the turnoff to Kotamobagu the road is a goat track, and although tarred in some sections it's extremely potholed. Ten hours to Bintauna.

There are also direct buses leaving Terminal Andalas to Palu (Rp20,000, 24 hours) and Poso.

VICINITY OF GORONTALO

Good beaches lie along the coastal road to the east of Gorontalo. Inland, **Dahawalolo,** in the Lake Limboto area 13 km from Gorontalo (Rp750 by *bemo*), offers a hot springs in a concrete complex. Not too clean, not too hot (thermally), obnoxious kids, but a great view of Lake Limboto. **Lake Limboto,** only three meters deep, lies in a fertile rice-growing area only five km northwest of Gorontalo. Hire a *prahu* to visit small lakeside fishing villages.

Other places to visit in this upland plain are **Utapato,** a bathing place with a view over the lake; and **Batudia,** where you can bathe in steaming water.

Check out the travel agencies in Gorontalo to arrange budget travel to hot springs around Kwandang, Limboto Lake, and the north coast, as well as pigeon-hunting, swimming, and jungle jaunts. **Lombongo,** a hot springs and bathing spot, is located in the jungle 40 km from Gorontalo. Dive in the cold nearby river after.

Near the school in Dembe is a recently renovated Portuguese fortress, **Benteng Otanaha.**

Three crumbling towers on a hill are all that remain, with a superb view of Lake Limboto. Take a *bendi* or *oplet* from Gorontalo to the start of the path up the hill; look for the sign. **Panua Reserve,** on the coast near Marisa, about 100 km west of Gorontalo, is a sanctuary for the extraordinary *maleo* bird. Take a bus from Gorontalo's Terminal Andalas.

Kwandang

A port since the time of the Portuguese, Kwandang lies north of Gorontalo on the northern shore of the northern arm of Sulawesi, Rp2000 and two hours by bus from Gorontalo's Terminal Andalas. This small coastal town consists of a police station, school, Pelni office, one hotel, and several foodstalls. To the harbor is Rp200 by *bemo.*

Just before the beginning of town is an old Portuguese fortress, **Benteng Ota Mas Udangan,** with a tower and wall segments still standing. This fort was once on the sea, which has now receded. Another Portuguese ruin, partially restored **Benteng Oranje,** is a short walk from the main Kwandang-Gorontalo road. The path begins on the left just after the bridge.

MALUKU

The first discovered and most famous of all the Indonesian islands, today the islands of Maluku are still the most unexplored and least developed. These were the original "Spice Islands" of Dutch colonial history that spurred Columbus to cross the Atlantic and discover America. Fought over by Spanish, Portuguese, British, and Dutch merchant fleets for their nutmeg and cloves, used to preserve meat, the fabulous wealth of these islands changed the world's balance of power. This 25th province of Indonesia stretches over an area 50% greater than Kalimantan, yet its thousand islands make up less than four percent of Indonesia's total land area.

INTRODUCTION

Maluku is divided into three administrative districts: North Maluku, Central Maluku, and Southeast Maluku. Militarily, it is of great strategic importance, guarding the shortest sea and air lanes north from Australia to the Philippines and Japan. The Dutch navy established its second-largest base in the Indies in Amboina harbor, which the Japanese neutralized early in WW II. Maluku is also a transition zone for Asian and Australian flora and fauna, as well as for the human cultures of Melanesia and Southeast Asia. Only about 1.5 million people live here, many of them skilled agriculturalists and seafarers. Animists—Papuan, proto-Malayan, and Negrito—occupy the interiors. Those islands most visited are Ambon, Ternate, Tidore, and the Bandas. The only real urban center in Maluku is Ambon City, or Amboina, on Pulau Ambon.

THE LAND

The total land area of these thousand or so islands is 87,100 square km, about two-thirds the size of Java; territorial waters comprise 294,946 square km. To the east Maluku is bordered by Irian Jaya, to the south by Nusatenggara, to the west by Sulawesi, to the north by the Philippines. The 5,000-meter-deep Maluku Sea adds to their geographical remoteness. The islands vary in size from tiny uninhabited atolls, the tops of submerged volcanos, to Halmahera, Buru, and Ceram, each over 4,000 square km. Most of the northern and central islands feature dense tropical jungles, active volcanos, deserted beaches, colorful coral gardens, and wild, rugged mountainous interiors. Some island groups, such as the Arus, lie at such low elevations they consist mainly of great stretches of mangrove swamps, tidal salt marshes, and sea grass. Other islands, particularly in North Maluku, are volcanic in origin; mountains on Halmahera and Ceram reach heights of over 3,000 meters. Lying right in the middle of the great chain of volcanos known as the "Ring of Fire," Maluku is a volatile territory, with 70 eruptions recorded in the last 400 years; earth-

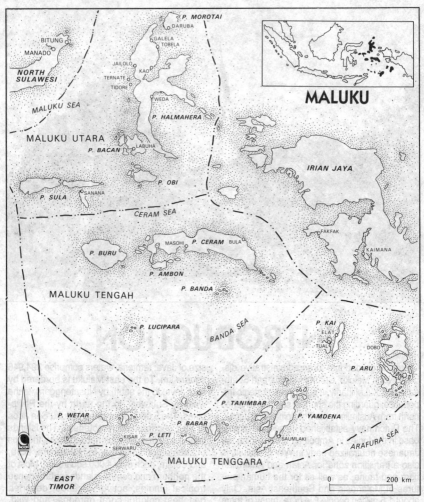

MALUKU

© MOON PUBLICATIONS, INC.

quakes are not uncommon on Ternate, Ambon, and the Bandas.

Climate

Maluku is wet, humid, and tropical, though tempered by fresh sea breezes. Temperatures vary from 24-29° C during the dry season (Sept.-March) to 19-22° C in the rainy season of April to August. The sea is too rough during this time for small boats. Rainfall is heavy throughout the year, the volume dependent upon the height and ori-

entation of the mountain chains. The best season for sea travel, or *musim teduh,* is Sept.-March, when the seas are calm and interisland shipping most frequent. This is also the fishing season, which means abundant seafood.

FLORA AND FAUNA

Despite unrelenting pressure from timber concessions and human settlements, Maluku still offers the naturalist a striking example of the luxuriance and beauty of tropical animal life. It was here in the 19th century that Alfred R. Wallace developed his theory of evolution, which greatly influenced Darwin's work. A transition zone between the Asian and Australasian/Papuan plant and animal kingdoms, many unique species are found on the islands of Maluku. The Aru and Kai islands feature marsupials, including a dwarf species of tree kangaroo only 30 cm tall and the tree-living cuscus, a small opposum-like animal.

About 90 species of butterflies are found in Maluku, 25 of which are endemic, including gaily colored birdwing species as large as small birds. There's a rich variety of other rare insects, and an indigenous species of frilled lizards. Yet, in spite of the unbroken chain of islands which seems to link Maluku with the Asian continent, there is a conspicuous absence of land mammals. Wild deer, wild pigs, and the tiny shrew have reached certain parts of Maluku. There are monkeys on Pulau Bacan, and the Sulawesi black baboon and *babirusa* are found as far as the Sula Islands. Ornamental fish, shellfish, and other marine forms abound in extraordinary variety.

Before traveling extensively in Maluku, read A.R. Wallace's *The Malay Archipelago,* still the most complete book in English on the area's natural history. In Karangpanjang, a suburb of Ambon, is a lush garden where you'll find a great variety of Malukan flora, including endemic orchids. The Siliwama Museum there offers natural history exhibits.

Birds

The region's profuse birdlife, particularly plumage birds, shows great affinity to New Guinea species. There are many kinds of honeyeaters, 22 species of parrots, the famous racket-tailed kingfisher, the giant red-crested Malukan cockatoo, four species of nutmeg-eating pigeons, and even, on Aru, two species of bird of paradise. The region is well known for its parakeets and the vividly colored black-capped, purple, and green lories. Ceram is home to dazzling white fruit pigeons. As Australians are proud of their black swans, Malukans are equally proud of their black cockatoos. Yet there's a widespread absence of such common Asian species as woodpeckers, thrushes, jays, tits,

and pheasants. In these eastern islands, people keep lorikeets and king parrots as pets. The large, mound-building megapode bird lays its eggs in mounds of rotting vegetation—the heat hatches the eggs. This curious bird, sometimes called the jungle fowl or *maleo,* is found on Ceram, Buru, and Haruku. On Ceram and the southern islands lives the huge, nearly wingless cassowary. The brown booby is also common in Maluku.

Flora

The vegetation of Maluku is extravagant, with many Australian forms intermingled with the Asiatic. Cloves are found all over Central Maluku, particularly on Ceram and the Liassers. Nutmeg is also cultivated throughout Central Maluku. Other products include copra, *damar* resin, and hardwood timber such as the red-and-white *meranti. Kayuputih* (cajeput) oil is derived from the region's eucalyptus trees, while the all-important sago tree provides the main staple in the Malukan diet, as well as bark to make walls for houses and leaves to make roof thatch. An indigenous orange prune-like fruit, the *gandaria,* grows in Poka and Rumahtiga on Ambon. A curious species of banana, the red-brown *pisang tongka langit,* does not hang down but grows up. Wild forest orchids are found on the Tanimbars and Kais.

HISTORY

Early History

Nutmeg and cloves have brought trade to these islands since at least 300 B.C. They were known by Chinese, Javanese, Indians, and Arabs long before the Portuguese "discovered" Maluku in 1498. Chinese Tang literature of the 7th century mentions Mi Lu Ku. In A.D. 846, Ibn Khordadhbih wrote about the "Spice Islands" located some 15 sailing days off Java. Maluku was always treated as a satellite by various Javanese kingdoms; the 13th century Singosari dynasty prospered hugely on the spice trade with Maluku. From the 14th century the spice trade in the islands was dominated by powerful Muslim sultans on Ternate, Tidore, and Djailolo (Halmahera). When the Portuguese captured Melaka in the early 16th century, Maluku was known as Jazirat-al-Muluk, the "Land of Many Kings."

The Search

In 15th-century Europe, nutmeg and cloves were the preferred way to preserve and flavor meat. These spices were also used in incense, lotions, perfumes, and medications to relieve gout, colic, and rheumatism. Aristocratic ladies wore nutmeg in gold and silver lockets, sweetening their breath with these spices. Gentlemen added zest to their grogs and soups with grated nutmeg, which they carried in fancy cases equipped with tiny graters. At that time Maluku was the only place in the world where these precious aromatic spices were grown. For centuries, Europeans could obtain the spices only through Arab traders; European monarchs dreamed of one day controlling the source.

In the second half of the 15th century, various European nations launched expeditions in search of these legendary islands, the "Indies." Christopher Columbus was searching for a shorter, westerly route to the Indies when he stumbled upon the Americas in 1492. Spices were the main incentive behind Magellan's voyage of discovery; he too was looking for a shortcut to the Indies when he discovered the Strait of Magellan and crossed the Pacific to the Philippines. It is a testament to European greed and perseverance that ruins of 400-year-old European fortresses litter scores of Malukan islands today.

The Portuguese Era

Portuguese rule (1512-1605) was cruel and brutal. The Portuguese navigator Albuquerque captured Goa (India) in 1510 and Melaka (Peninsular Malaysia) in 1511. Soon after, he also located an outstanding map of the smaller islands north of Java, from which the Portuguese were able to trace the origin of nutmeg and mace to the Banda Islands, and cloves to Tidore, Ternate, Halmahera, Bacan, Makian, and Moti. By 1512 the Portuguese were in Central Maluku in force, busily converting the inhabitants to Catholicism. Magellan's crews arrived in Ternate mad with joy in 1521, after a journey of 27 months.

Antonio Galvao established economic control over Maluku in 1529, monopolizing the spice trade in Ambon and the Bandas. By 1550 it was claimed that nine missionaries had converted 20,000 souls on Halmahera and Ternate, and another 20,000 on Ambon. In 1570, when a nephew of Captain Sancho de Vasconcelos

murdered Sultan Hairun, the people of Ternate attacked and routed the Portuguese. The Portuguese later returned to neighboring Tidore, but their fortunes had taken a bad turn. They were forced out of Hitu in 1601, and driven entirely out of Tidore and Ambon by 1605.

The Spanish Era

By virtue of Magellan's passage around Cape Horn, the Spanish laid claim to Maluku under the Treaty of Tordesillas. Early Spanish influence was eclipsed by the Portuguese, but the Spanish and their Filipino lackeys sent expeditions from Manila and finally subdued Ternate in 1606 after a hard fight, also grabbing some islands off Tidore and parts of Halmahera. In 1616 another expedition was mounted to drive out the Dutch, but its commander died en route and the journey was called off. The Spanish finally evacuated northern Maluku in 1663.

The Dutch Era

The Dutch period lasted from around 1605 to 1942. The Dutch tried to create a world monopoly of the valuable nutmeg, cinnamon, and clove trade. In 1607 they gained power by signing a treaty with the sultans of Tidore and Ternate, mandating that the price of cloves was to be fixed, the Dutch would "defend" Ternate against the Spaniards, and the sultan would pay the Dutch for the cost of all battles fought on his behalf. At the time Malukans were grateful to the Dutch for driving out the Portuguese and Spanish, and for the fact they offered such high prices for their spices.

But the Dutch soon revealed their true motives, imposing a ruthless system of forced cultivation which remained in place for hundreds of years. Plantations were laid waste and production reduced to keep profits high. Anyone caught buying or selling even the smallest parcel of spices was executed. On the basis of the spice trade, the Netherlands East India Company was established, prospering until rampant corruption and intense competition drove it into bankruptcy in 1799. The Dutch government took over the company's affairs at the beginning of the 19th century. During the 19th- and 20th-century colonial wars, eastern Indonesia was a traditional supplier of military manpower on the side of the Dutch against popular uprisings in Java and Sumatra.

The Decline

At the end of the 18th century, world demand for cloves and nutmeg fell drastically. Coffee, tea, and cacao were the big-money crops and the value of spices gradually declined. At about the same time the British and French smuggled out seedlings and succeeded in planting clove and nutmeg trees in their colonies in India and Africa, breaking the back of the monopoly. Maluku soon became an economic backwater. Ambon, Ternate, and the Bandas were opened to foreign shipping in 1854, but it wasn't until 1863, when a liberal constitution was adopted in Holland, that forced cultivation at last ceased and all monopolies were terminated.

Modern History

Maluku was taken by the Japanese in the first two months of 1942, and recaptured by the Allies in 1945. After Indonesia declared its independence in 1945, civilians and former military members (KNIL) of the Dutch colonial army created—with Dutch backing—the Republik Maluku Selatan in 1947; the republic broke off ties with Indonesia in 1949. When the Dutch refused the next year to continue backing the new nation, secession was abandoned and some 40,000 sympathetic Malukans were evacuated to the Netherlands.

Today a sizable number of Malukans make up the Indonesian population of Holland; many have never seen their homeland. Malukans disappointed with life in Holland returned to Indonesia in the 1970s to face problems of readjustment and cultural conflicts with Ambonese who never left. Some Malukans in Holland still harbor the futile dream of returning and liberating their country; the dream exploded in violence in 1977 when a band of youthful Malukan malcontents seized the Indonesian consulate and hijacked a commuter train in Holland, killing one passenger and holding the rest hostage.

ECONOMY

In the golden days of the spice trade, Maluku was the richest commercial region in the Dutch East Indies. Today, foreign investors and government joint ventures are extracting tin, asbestos, and oil. Timber is the big growth industry, with mills on Buru, Ceram, Halmahera, Taliabu, and Mongole. Plywood, for export to Japan, Singapore, and Hong Kong, is processed at plants in Batu Gong near Passo on Ambon, and at Waisarisa on Ceram. Besides timber, agriculture, and fishing, the mainstays of the local economy are raising sheep and goats, and, in Christian villages, pigs.

Agriculture

Copra, cacao, coffee, rice, sago, maize, sugarcane, and fruit are important agricultural products. Copra is one of the chief money crops. Rice is grown on Ceram, eucalyptus oil is produced on Pulau Buru. The islands' most important products are no longer exotic spices, though cloves, nutmeg, and resins are still cultivated on some islands. Cloves (buah cengkeh) are sun-dried buds of the clove tree. The trees require very little maintenance and each carries 30,000-50,000 buds which, when dry, yield three kg of cloves selling for around Rp8000-9000 per kg. The spicy smoke of Indonesian cigarettes (kretek) wafting through the kampung or pasar and now popular around the world, bears the distinctive odor of cloves. Cloves are also used in pharmaceuticals.

Nutmeg (pala), produced only in Ambon and the Banda Islands, comes from the inner seed of the nut from the nutmeg tree. The lacy scarlet flesh surrounding the shiny chestnut-colored seed is used in the making of mace.

Fishing

In Maluku are some of the richest fishing grounds in Indonesia, especially for shrimp, crab, trepang (sea cucumber), and tuna. The surrounding oceans are at present being criminally raped by the Japanese. The government has established a frozen fish packing plant in Galela (Halmahera); near Kate Kate and Rumahtiga on Ambon are frozen-shrimp-processing plants, a joint Japanese/Indonesian venture. Fish mills have also opened up in the Arus in Southeast Maluku. Pearls are cultivated in Kao Bay (Halmahera) and on Kai and Aru islands. If you get the chance, it's great fun to make the rounds at night on the mudflats with a Malukan crabber. Carrying a torch, he plunges a cylinder of split bamboo over the scuttling kepiting, placing them in a sack slung around his shoulders.

Tourism

In Dutch times these islands were so remote they were called Groote Oost ("The Great East"), a term that applied to all the small archipelagos between Sulawesi and New Guinea. Because of lack of transportation, no one but a few Dutch officials ever visited the region. Now more travelers and tourists are turning up in Ambon and even in the more far-flung island groups. Marine tourism holds almost unlimited promise: skin diving in the gin-clear waters from Ambon to Ternate is unbelievable. The local *adat* protects Maluku's ecological resources. The province's sandy beaches are beautiful and often empty, and the maritime climate splendid. Although the people are friendly and helpful, funds are lacking to develop tourism facilities.

THE PEOPLE

Maluku is a fascinating ethnographic, linguistic, and anthropological environment. With a total population of 1.5 million, the average population density of these many scattered islands is around 13 per square km. The islands are inhabited by a number of distinct, relatively isolated ethnic groups: the Alfuros, dark-skinned frizzy-haired proto-Malays, the original inhabitants of Maluku; lighter-skinned straight-haired deutero-Malays, who arrived many centuries later; minority groups like Chinese, Arabs, Javanese, and Malukans of European descent who trace their lineage from colonists. One of the major ethnic groups is the Ambonese, living along the coastal areas of the islands of Ambon, Saparua, Nusa Laut, and western Ceram. Roving colonies of "sea gypsies" (Orang Laut) moor their boats in the many ports of the archipelago.

The Alfuros

Alfuros is the collective name for all of the indigenous peoples living in the interior mountainous areas of Maluku. Foreign traders—whether European, Javanese, or Chinese—have always settled the coastal areas of Maluku, forcing inland the dark-complexioned aborigines, called by the Portuguese Alifuro, meaning "uncouth, savage, pagan." The Spanish were not able to subjugate them on the is-

lands of Buru and Ceram, and even as late as 1890 they were still described as head-hunting savages, dressed only in a *cidako*, which covered the genitals. With government encouragement and support, many of these isolated inland tribes have been relocated to the coasts, where they continue their forest-oriented gathering of coconuts rather than taking up the Malay-style livelihood of fishing. The term Alfuro still bears an unfavorable stigma. The Alfuros do not inhabit Ambon, Haruku, Saparua, or Nusa Laut.

Religion

European Catholic and Protestant missionaries started proselytizing in this region over 100 years ago. In Central Maluku, Christians and Muslims are equally divided. Generally, Muslims outnumber Christians in North Maluku, while Christians predominate in the south. But like so many of Indonesia's ethnic groups, the locals also govern themselves by local *adat*. Many tribes, particularly in the southeast islands, also believe strongly in supernatural and ancestor spirits, both benevolent and malevolent. All over eastern Indonesia there is a widespread belief in witches (*swangi*).

ARTS AND CRAFTS

Music And Dance

Maluku has a rich traditional music; many popular Indonesian folk songs originated here, particularly from Ambon. The special type of *gamelan* played here is called *totabuang*. Bamboo flutes are played unceasingly by schoolchildren. There are a number of original dances, many containing elements imported from abroad: in the *bambu gila* dance, bamboo poles about 2-2.5 meters long are placed crosswise and clicked rhythmically together. As the tempo gradually speeds up, dancers step between and around the poles. A *dukun* puts a spell on the bamboo and can order it to go anywhere he commands; seven men are powerless to hold it back. The *badapus* dance is similar to the Balinese *kris* dance; though men stab themselves with sharp weapons, their flesh isn't pierced. Even the spectators who take part cannot harm themselves. Also performed is the slow, hypnotic handkerchief dance.

Crafts

On Ambon and Ternate, model ships and houses are built completely of cloves; clove artifacts have been tourist souvenirs since at least the 19th century. For handwoven fabrics, each Malukan island has retained its own artistic styles, motifs, and dyeing methods. The tribes of Ceram make the finest woven crafts. On the Kai Islands, the people produce unique earthenware with arabesque and curlicue designs. Freed from hard labor thanks to the widely available and easily harvested sago palm, Malukans are excellent boatbuilders and seamen who have traditionally embarked on long trading expeditions. Notice the wide use of outrigger canoes, indicating your location on the periphery of Melanesia.

ACCOMMODATIONS AND FOOD

Ambon and Ternate offer a number of *losmen,* as well as modern, comfortable hotels with a/c and *wisma.* Prices often include two meals per day. Although prices tend to be at least twice those on Java and Bali, in Maluku you can sometimes stay with a family for much less. This is a quality experience; ask at the tourist office which family in town offers guest rooms. In Southeast Maluku, it's possible to stay with missionaries and at the residences of priests (*pastoran*) for as little as Rp4000 per person per day, including meals. If your host doesn't ask for any money, be sure to give a donation. Take lots of cash in a moneybelt. Your Visa or MasterCard is absolutely useless in Maluku; the people either ignore it, laugh, or just say "no." Traveler's checks can be difficult to cash.

Minang-style restaurants are found in Ambon, but otherwise the regional food is quite basic. Fish is the main source of protein; there's an abundance of crab, shrimp, and tuna. In the villages, meat and fowl are generally eaten only at feasts or celebrations. One of the main sources of carbohydrates is a meal extracted from the heart of the sago palm, a tree that grows wild. Sago fronds are also used to thatch huts, while the leaf midrib is utilized to build walls and ceilings. Sago bread comes in the form of a giant waffle. A unique dish of this region is *papeda,* prepared by pulverizing and straining the sago pulp. This "flour" is then boiled to form a taste-less, jelly-like mass eaten hot or cold. *Papeda* has the consistency of, and even looks like, wallpaper paste. If you don't swallow it straightaway, you think you're drowning. Thankfully, *papeda* is often served with a flavorful fish-curry soup which makes it almost palatable. This sago diet is supplemented by cassava and sweet potatoes. Other popular regional dishes include boiled sweet potatoes, roast fish (*ikan bakar*), and sour sauce, all served, of course, with sago cakes.

In North Maluku you'll find a delicious yellow saffron-flavored rice (*nasi kunyit*) accompanying *sate* and curry. Instead of peanut sauce on *gado-gado,* the Malukans use *kanari* nut, a cousin to the almond. Chinese and Arabian families have a more imaginative cuisine with more animal protein served, and Malukans of European descent follow European-style eating habits, serving such dishes as red bean soup and pig's feet. There's the full range of fruits found everywhere in Indonesia. One regional fruit is the *gandaria,* an orange-colored prune. Over 22 varieties of bananas of matchless flavor grow throughout these islands, including one tiny species, *pisang tuju,* which reaches maturity in only seven months. There's also the gargantuan one-half-meter-long *pisang raja,* which Ambonese women aren't permitted to eat because it's thought the fruit will wreck a marriage.

GETTING THERE

Ambon, the provincial capital, is the gateway to Maluku from Java and Ujung Pandang; Ternate is the gateway from Manado in North Sulawesi. Garuda flies to Ambon from Jakarta and Surabaya. Merpati flies from Ujung Pandang to Ambon or from Manado daily to Ternate. Bouraq and Mandala airlines also schedule regular flights to Ambon from Ujung Pandang, and Bouraq flies thrice weekly from Jakarta to Ternate, stopping at Balikpapan (Kalimantan), Palu, Gorontalo, and Manado en route.

One "outer island" loop is to fly from Surabaya to Ujung Pandang, then head overland up through Sulawesi (visiting Torajaland on the way) to Poso, take a boat across Teluk Poso to Gorontalo, travel overland to Manado, fly or take a boat to Ternate, then fly or take a boat to Ambon and back to Ujung Pandang or Java.

Some travelers, on the Los Angeles to Jakarta flight, get off at Biak on Irian Jaya and fly down to Ambon (one hour, three flights weekly). You can even fly from Guam to Manado, then hop over to Ternate and work your way down through Maluku from there. Ambon is also accessible from Jakarta on Pelni's luxurious KM *Rinjani.*

GETTING AROUND

Air travel is the most expedient but costliest way to see Maluku. Merpati schedules a very useful flight from Ternate to the small airstrips of Bacan and Halmahera. Merpati also serves Ternate, Galela (Halmahera), Labuha (Bacan), Ambon, Namlea (Buru), Sanana and Amahai (Ceram), Bandaneira (Banda), Langgur (near Tual, Kais), Saumlaki (Tanimbars), and Mangole (Sula). Ambon has the only jet-length runway in the province.

Between the main ports of call, the only regular sea links are provided by Pelni and Perintis ships which sail from one island group to another at two- to three-week intervals. This means you must either explore the island of your choice while the ship is in harbor, or wait for the next ship. The deep-water harbor of Ambon is Maluku's principal port. Pelni's ship KM *Baruna Bhakti* departs for Ternate and north-ern Malukan ports, returning to Ambon every three weeks; the KM *Niaga X* does the three-week southern loop (Banda, Tual, Saumlaki, and back to Ambon). Regular ships also connect Ternate to Bitung, the main port on Sulawesi's northern peninsula. Fares are cheap, and it's possible to rent a space in a cramped crewmember's cabin with a small fan.

It's fairly easy to hitch a ride on a local boat working the coasts—from *kapal motor* to small dugouts with 15-hp motors. Regional craft are called *prahu, jungku, arombai,* or simply *bot.* Interisland ferries are also widely available, especially during the dry season (Sept.-March). For example, a regular ferry leaves Langgur (Kai Kecil) to Elat (Kai Besar) in the morning and returns that same afternoon, costing only Rp2000. Local, inexpensive ferries connect Ambon to its neighboring islands of Saparua and Nusa Laut. At least four vessels depart twice weekly from Ambon to coastal villages on Ceram and to Buru. Ideally, though, this is a region that should be explored in your own self-contained, seaworthy craft, with plenty of time. Be prepared for adventure.

Of about 1,800 km of roads, less than 500 km are paved. Minibuses and *bemo* travel the main roads; terminals are usually in the center of town near the *pasar* or *stanplats.* Roads are virtually nonexistent in the interiors of the Outer Islands; expect to walk practically everywhere.

NORTH MALUKU

The fabulous spice islands of North Maluku, or Maluku Utara, have been lauded in literature and fable since 1667, when Ternate and Tidore appeared in Milton's *Paradise Lost*. The district's land area is 32,000 square km, while its sea territory covers 207,381 square km. Most of the islands are volcanic in origin; immense areas of the district's larger islands are covered with dense rainforests. Commercial crops include cloves and nutmeg; sago and a great variety of forest orchids grow all over the district.

The forests of Halmahera, Obi, Bacan, and Sula provide the best opportunities for wildlife observation. Birdlife, particularly on Halmahera, is profuse—*anggang, kasumba, maleo,* parrots, giant crestless and orange-crested cockatoos, gong bird. Wild animals include deer, cuscus, the Bacan monkey of Pulau Bacan, lizards on Pulau Obi and Halmahera, and a wide variety of butterflies. The seas teem with ornamental fish, colorful coral, seashells, and the *kenari* crab. The rainy season on Maluku Utara is about the same as in the rest of Indonesia. The administrative seat and capital of the province is Ternate.

History

Islam came to North Maluku with Javanese traders, probably during the 15th century. Before the arrival of Europeans in the early 16th century, the rival kingdoms of Tidore and Ternate had long warred with one another over control of the lucrative spice trade. Their domains once stretched as far as Flores, Sulawesi, and Cebi in the Philippines. For hundreds of years these and other nearby sultanates traded with Chinese, Arab, and Javanese merchants. The first European account of the islands comes from the Portuguese Barbosa in a manuscript dated 1516. North Maluku became well known in Europe during the 16th and 17th centuries as the sole supplier of cloves; in the hopes of wresting this monopoly away from the four sultanates of the region, the Portuguese established themselves on Ternate in 1521. However, eventual conflict with the sultans led to their expulsion from Ternate in 1574 and Tidore in 1581.

The Dutch, arriving in North Maluku at the beginning of the 17th century, were first welcomed by the sultan of Ternate, anxious to keep the Spaniards and Portuguese in check. In granting the Dutch a spice monopoly, it was the sultan's intention to extend his power, with Dutch help, over not only Maluku but to Makassar in southern Sulawesi. The Dutch, however, bolstered the power of the sultanates only as long as it suited their purposes. When the Dutch

musician and dancers of the court of the sultan of Ternate, 1890

decided to confine clove cultivation to Ambon, they destroyed the clove gardens of northern Maluku and brought all smuggling to a halt. Although these harsh measures caused widespread revolt throughout the islands, the Dutch prevailed, shearing the sultan of his power. Ruins of colonial forts—Portuguese, Spanish, English, and Dutch—can be found today on every major spice-producing island in the area.

Economy
The economy of North Maluku centers on timber, fishing, copra, and spices. The islands of the Sula and Obi archipelagos are important timber-producing areas, while top quality cacao is produced on Pulau Bacan. Ternate, Tidore, Makian, and Moti are still major clove-producing islands, enjoying resurgent prosperity due to the worldwide popularity of clove cigarettes. The district today cultivates nearly 500,000 *cengkeh* (clove) trees on over 3,000 hectares.

Getting There And Around
Ternate is the focus of air and sea transportation in the region. Merpati provides service from

Ambon 11 times weekly and from Manado in North Sulawesi twice daily. Bouraq flies from Balikpapan, Tarakan, Manado, Jakarta, and Surabaya. Within Maluku Utara, Merpati flies from Ternate to Galela and Kao on neighboring Halmahera three times weekly, as well as to remote islands like Mongole and Morotai once weekly, and Sanana on Pulau Sulabesi twice weekly.

Sea transport is well developed. Public motorized *prahu* and motorboats travel between all the main administrative and market centers. Pelni and Perintis coasters connect the main ports of North Maluku to North Sulawesi, as well as to Ambon and elsewhere in Maluku. For only around Rp15,000 per person, Pelni's KM *Baruna Bakti* makes a loop every two weeks from Ambon to Ternate.

If traveling by road within North Maluku, take *bendi* (Rp300-400 per person within Ternate), public *bemo* (Rp200 in urban areas), and island buses. Roads circle the islands of Ternate and Tidore, and there are small road systems around Jailolo and Galela on Halmahera, Sanana on Pulau Sulabesi, and Labuha on Pulau Bacan.

TERNATE ISLAND

The northernmost of a series of seven islands off the west coast of Halmahera, Ternate's small area—only 65 square km with a width of but 9.7 km—is all out of proportion to its tempestuous 500-year history. Scores of overgrown and ill-maintained Portuguese and Dutch fortifications litter the island, which consists almost entirely of the active volcanic cone of Gunung Gamalama (1,721 meters). This lofty mountain boasts three peaks—Madina, Arfat, and Kekan—a grotesque shape brought about by numerous deadly eruptions. Within the last four centuries most have affected the northern half of the island. The worst was in 1763, devastating the prosperous seaport of Fort Takome and so obliterating one slope it has since been known as Batu Angus ("Burnt Corner"). An eruption in 1840 destroyed every house in Ternate City. The island is still very geophysically unstable, with frequent earth tremors. All this volcanic history ensures that most of the towns are coastal, connected by a

road around the island. A loop around the island costs only Rp500 and takes two hours.

History
At one time Ternate, Tidore, Moti, Mare, and Makian were the world's only suppliers of cloves. A traditional power center for all of northern Maluku, the Portuguese entrenched themselves here in 1521 with the aim of turning Ternate into one of their chief spice-producing centers. In a clumsy attempt to monopolize the spice trade, they assassinated Sultan Hairun in 1570. The hatred this engendered led to their expulsion, and eventually cost them the East Indies. The Spaniards, after founding Manila in 1570, moved south and captured the weakened Portuguese garrison in Ternate in 1574. Sir Francis Drake called at Ternate in 1579, taking on five tons of cloves. The English buccaneer was much impressed by the thriving port and the sultan's fabulous wealth. Although he was warmly re-

ceived, Drake's visit was never followed by further English trade.

The island's history took a turn in 1599 with the arrival of the opportunistic Dutch. Relying on Dutch assistance against the Portuguese and Spanish, and bent on expanding his control over adjacent islands, the sultan granted the newcomers a spice monopoly. For more than 80 years Ternate rose in power, until the Dutch decided to confine clove production to Ambon. The Dutch voided all contracts with Ternate in 1683; in a single stroke the Ternate sultanate lost control of the northern Malukan islands, vast territories henceforth administered by the Dutch. The sultan and his descendants were reduced to titular rule, in effect pensioned off by the Dutch. Before WW II, Ternate was a regular port of call for Dutch packet steamers, a service entirely disrupted by the Japanese invasion of 1942.

Economy
Much of the island is still densely wooded, and the timber trade is an important source of revenue. The volcanic, fertile land produces the staples of sago, bananas, and cassava, supplemented by a little rice, maize, vegetables, and sugarcane. Copra, cacao, and coffee are important cash crops. The scent of cloves and nutmeg hangs heavy in the air. Coral is found everywhere along the coast and there are some outstanding dive sites for pearls.

The People
The native population is of very mixed blood, with the Malay physical type predominant. Because of extensive trade contacts with Arab merchants and other Islamic groups, the population today is 90% Muslim. These northern islands feature a very strong orthodox Islamic presence; groups of young schoolgirls in white veils and sky-blue blouses are frequently seen in the streets of Ternate. There's also a tiny Christian community, the Orang Seracci, descendants of natives converted in the 17th century by the Portuguese. The bell in Ternate's only church is believed to have been presented by St. Francis Xavier himself. Witchcraft (*keswange*) is widespread; mediums are capable of communication with spirits called *manganitu* and may function as healers who perform many important rituals.

TERNATE CITY

This town, now the administrative center of North Maluku, has clung to the side of a smoking volcano since the 1500s. Lying on a flat strip of land on the southeast side of the island, Ternate is today a picturesque seaport and major shipping center, Gunung Gamalama rising majestically above a main street filled with *bemo* and *bendi*. Though Ambon is more cosmopolitan, Ternate is quieter and more relaxing, except for the nightly earth tremors. Ternate's fervent Muslims are in general generous, warm, and friendly. You'll also encounter few "hello Misters!" here. Wander down to the harbor in the southern end of town; from there you can easily make out the island of Halmahera. South of the harbor area is **Bastion,** where you catch

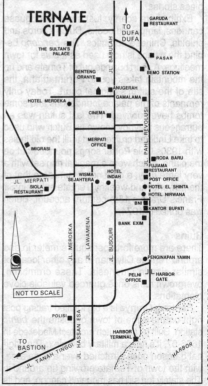

boats to motor over to the neighboring island of Tidore.

The Sultan's Palace

Located above the town on Jl. Babulah past Benteng Oranye on the road to the airport. Also known as the *kedaton,* the palace has been converted to a museum and is open to the public. The original structure dates from 1234. Designed by an English architect, the palace resembles a European country villa. Take a *bemo* from the Jl. Pahlawan Revolusi station (Rp100), then walk up the majestic flight of steps to the veranda. If the gate to the museum is locked, try to locate the curator. Amidst the royal regalia and heavy atmosphere of decay, you can still see by special request the extraordinary "jeweled" crown Drake described in his 1579 visit, though all the priceless jewels and ornaments have been replaced by cheap glass stones.

Exhibits are scanty; just some Portuguese cannons, lamps, old books, Dutch swords and shields, Chinese ceramics. The *pendopo* behind the palace is now used as a *bale* for town meetings. A short bus ride out of Ternate and up the mountain takes you to **Foramadiaha,** the site of the sultan's original court. Today only remnants of the palace foundations and some tombs have survived. The last sultan was an outrageous playboy known as Butch who used to take Lindblad cruises and thrill the old ladies with 1930s Cole Porter songs pounded out on the piano. Butch wore a magical ring set with a very large ruby, a gem not dissimilar to that of the powerful and wealthy Ternate sultan in Sir Francis Drake's 15th-century account. Butch was buried in 1974.

Ruins

There are more forts per square meter in and around Ternate City than in any other locale of similar size in Indonesia. These crumbling, overgrown ruins once guarded valuable clove plantations.

Benteng Oranye is a big fortified trading post right on the edge of town opposite the *bemo* station. Built by the Dutch architect Madeliede in 1606-07, it's now a military complex. The original garrison once stretched over a huge area, with the town of Ternate growing up around it. The stately fort still has mounted cannon, and its VOC seal is intact. Informal tours are conducted by the soldiers.

From Benteng Oranye, it's a pleasant two-km walk north of town on the road to the airport, or a Rp300 *bemo* ride, to **Benteng Toloko,** just past Desa Dufa Dufa on the right. This small, well-maintained Portuguese fort was erected on a hill by Albuquerque in 1512. Inside you can enjoy a sweeping panorama of Ternate City. The structure is in such splendid condition the 16th-century official seal is still quite visible. The inscription and coat of arms at the entrance are Dutch, placed there by one of the first Dutch governors of Ternate, Peter Boit; here he falsely claims to have built the fort. Benteng Toloko is shaped so much like a male sexual organ this must have been the architect's intention.

The shape of **Benteng Kayu Merah** represents the complementary female sexual organ, but here the similarity is not so obvious. It's Rp300 by *bemo* along the road in front of Penginapan Yamin to this serene, unfinished fort in the south of town. Complete with a moat, the edge of the sea laps at the walls of this structure begun in 1510. North of Kayu Merah is Pelabuhan Bastion, where you catch *kapal motor* to Tidore. Another two km south of Kayu Merah, a heap of old stones is all that's left of **Kota Janji,** the fortress where the Portuguese murdered Sultan Hairun in 1570.

A 15-minute, 11-km *bemo* ride from town down a lovely road to Kastela (or Rp200 past Kota Janji) is **Benteng Kastela,** erected by the Portuguese captain Antonio de Brito in 1522. Named after the Portuguese castle nearby, this wrecked fortification's gateways still stand. Kastela was also the center of a town called Ave. The remains of the hospital can be seen in thick undergrowth and an old Portuguese well nearby is still used by the locals. The ramparts at the circumference of the town are clearly visible. Fort Kastela, believed at the time impregnable, was abandoned only 50 years after it was built; it now protects a papaya patch.

Accommodations

Most places to stay in town are on the expensive side. Many hotels might be booked up, or may decline to accept foreigners. Usually there are separate rates for rooms with meals; be sure to establish rates, and any hidden taxes, in advance. A good deal is **Wisma Alhilal,** Jl. Monunutu 2/32, tel. (0921) 21404; rooms cost Rp10,000-20,000. Outstanding meals, very helpful staff. Although family-style **Wisma Sejahtera,** Jl. Lawamena 21, has small rooms, it's quite comfortable and homey, with prices similar to the Alhilal. **Penginapan Yamin,** just outside the harbor gates, is one of the cheapest lodgings in town. Other hotels include **Anda,** Jl. Ketilang 49; **Massa,** Jl. Busouri 27; **Merdeka,** Jl. Merdeka 19; **Thamrin,** Jl. Merdeka 28; and **Nusantara,** Jl. Lawamena 18A. All charge around Rp7000 s, Rp10,000-15,000 d with meals.

Down near the harbor is **Hotel Nirwana,** Jl. Pahlawan Revolusi 58, tel. 21787; Rp20,000 with meals. The **El Shinta,** next to Hotel Nirwana, charges up to Rp40,000 d without attached bathrooms. **Hotel Merdeka,** Jl. Monunutu, runs Rp15,000 for big rooms; tariff includes meals. Also check out **Hotel Chrysan,** Jl. A. Yani, tel. 377 or 210, Rp15,000-25,000; and **Hotel Anda Baru,** Jl. Ketilang 49, tel. 155, Rp10,000 s. **Hotel Indah,** Jl. Bosouri 3, tel. 21334, in the middle of Ternate, has no private bathrooms but is quite good value at Rp20,000. The a/c rooms are almost twice the price. The **Angin Mamiri,** Jl. Babulah 17, tel. 21245, offers Rp10,000-15,000 rooms; and higher-priced a/c rooms. Meals cost extra, Rp5000 per person lunch or dinner.

Food

Experience such traditional North Malukan dishes as *kenari* crab, *mamuya* (lobster eggs), yellow rice, *bagea, dabu-dabu,* and cassava cakes. Also try *ikan bakar* (roasted fish) with *cohoh-coloh* sauce, an area specialty. Enjoy local food in the town's *warung.* Several good *es jus* street stalls operate along Jl. Pahlawan Revolusi. During January and February the streets and markets are flooded with *durian* at Rp1500-2000 apiece.

Anugerah, on Jl. Busouri across from the *bemo* station, serves meals for about Rp1000; **Gamalama,** Jl. Pahlawan Revolusi, offers inexpensive meals and specializes in *coto ternate.* For Padang-style food, try the **Jaya,** Jl. Busouri, and the **Roda Baru,** Jl. Pahlawan Revolusi. For Chinese food, the **Garuda Restaurant** on Jl. Babulah opposite the *bioskop* is the place. The **Fujiama,** Jl. Pahlawan Revolusi (next to the post office), is the swankiest and priciest restaurant in town.

Crafts

During the golden age of the spice trade, Ternate's markets overflowed with fantastic merchandise. Today, a few shops sell tortoiseshell bracelets, *kulit mutiara* (mother of pearl) articles, and jewelry. Perhaps a woman might try to sell you *batu bacan* and other semiprecious stones at inflated prices. In the markets find green, red, or dazzling white *kakatua raja* (king parrot) and big blue pigeons for sale. Beware of vendors of old coins—there's a lot of fake casting going on. Test if it's silver by dropping it against concrete and listening to the ring. Douglas Capp, at Calvari Mission in Ternate City, is an avid shell collector.

Events

See the *soya soya,* performed by 13 men. For information on the esoteric Muslim rite of self-mortification with knives (*badubus*), as well as local magic acts such as the *gambu gila,* contact friendly Haji Ulmar, a part-time tourist guide. You'll find him at the mosque in Kampung Falajawa just before the harbor.

Services

Three banks on the main street change money; **Bank Dagang Negara** on Jl. Nukula presents the fewest hassles. **Bank Negara Indonesia** and **Bank Expor Impor Indonesia** on Jl. Pahlawan Revolusi (adjacent to the harbor) also change U.S. dollar traveler's checks; open Mon.-Fri. 0800-1100, Saturday 0800-1000. The **post office** is on Jl. Pahlawan Revolusi next to the Fujiama Restaurant and near Bank Negara Indonesia. The tourist office, *Kantor pariwisata,* provides little information. With luck you might score a map of Maluku. *Kantor imigrasi* is on Jl. Merpati, a road up above the town. Here you must apply for a *surat jalan* to visit any of the out-islands.

Getting There And Around

Flying into Ternate is spectacular. From **Ba Ullah Airport** at Tarau, walk out to the main road and flag down a *bemo* into town, Rp300. Or take a taxi, Rp3000. Pelni's KM *Umsini* sails from Jakarta to Ternate for Rp70,000 economy, Rp180,000 first class. There are no *becak* on Ternate; *bemo* cost Rp150 to anywhere in town. A ring road runs entirely around the island, passing through all the coastal villages;

without stops the complete circuit can be accomplished in about two hours. Suggested itinerary for a round-the-island circuit: Dufa Dufa, for 16th-century Fort Toloko; "Burnt Corner," the lava flow Batu Angus; Sulamandaha, a small village, the northernmost point on the island, with a black-sand beach opposite Pulau Hiri; the villages of Loto and Taduma; Kastela village, the site of another historical ruin; Akerica, a sacred spring; Aftador, the scene of a Japanese WW II atrocity; Kulumata, another ruined fortification; and Kayu Merah, yet another ruin; and finally to Bastion and back to Ternate City.

From Ternate, Merpati flies to Ambon daily, Galela three times weekly, Gebe, Kao, Labuha, Manado, and Sanana. Bouraq flies thrice weekly to Balikpapan, Jakarta, Manado, Surabaya, and Ujung Pandang. The Merpati office is located on Jl. Busouri, tel. 21605 or 21651; you'll find Bouraq at Jl. Pahlawan Revolusi 58, tel. (0921) 22365.

PT Premut's ships Semangap, Pulau Mas, and Gunung Mas sail north to Doruba, and Galela and Tobelo on Halmahera, for Rp10,000. Futuru Jaya's ships Morotai Star and Kasratu Indah also make this trip for about the same price. Pelni, with an office near the harbor at Jl. A. Yani 1, offers irregular economy-class service to Kendari, Luwuk, Poso, Gorontalo, Ujung Pandang, Surabaya, Tanjung Priok, and Bitung. Perintis Lines sails to Bitung, Jailolo, Tobelo, Sorong, Sausapor, Manokwari, Biak, Jayapura, and other locations. Sri Wijaya (swing right just before the harbor gates and follow the road south) sends ships to Ujung Pandang, Surabaya, and Jakarta once a month.

From Ternate's harbor, or from the port of Bastion, kapal motor and motorized prahu leave regularly for ports on the surrounding islands of Makian, Tidore, Bacan, and Halmahera, as well as such destinations as Pulau Morotai north of Halmahera. The syahbandar office, Jl. A. Yani 1, tel. 21214 or 21206, down on the waterfront, will tell you which boats go where and for how much. To charter a boat to see the volcano on Pulau Maitara costs as much as Rp50,000; try to negotiate with a fisherman to take you for less.

Perintis Maluku's Baruna Bakti takes 10 days to reach Ambon via Lubuha, Lawui, Falabisahaya, Dofa, Bobong, and Sawana. If you take this boat, you can count on wall-to-wall passengers, tropical songbirds, minimal sanitary facilities, and beautiful scenery. A test of endurance. Meals are sold on the boat for Rp750 each. It's possible to rent a space in a cramped cabin with a small fan for Rp18,000-25,000; a whole cabin goes for Rp65,000. This boat also sails north to Doruba, Bere-Bere, Galela, and Tobelo before returning to Ternate and Ambon. The Perintis ship Bendulu also sails to Ambon, but is smaller, makes more stops, and takes longer; the company's office is opposite Pelni's in the harbor.

AROUND THE ISLAND

Dufa Dufa is a fishing village three km from town, the site of Fort Toloko. Nice white-sand beaches around this village. Cengkeh Afu, four km from town in Kampung Maliaro and 650 meters above sea level, is the world's oldest clove tree—382 years old. Over 36 meters high, almost two meters wide, 4.26 meters in diameter—three people can't join their arms around it. This tree yields up to 600 kilos of cloves each year. See others nearly as huge in the clove plantations nearby, and on the road between Ternate and Kayu Merah.

Gunung Gamalama

An active volcano with three craters on the island's northern side. The central crater has collapsed, forming a lake with vertical sides 80 meters high. It's extremely unstable geophysically; an eruption in September 1980 forced two-thirds of Ternate's inhabitants to evacuate to neighboring Tidore. Gunung Gamalama erupted again in 1983. You can climb the volcano on foot from Ternate town, but before setting out consult Udin at Wisma Sejahtera. Take a bemo or hike up a steep road three km to Desa Marikrubu. From there, it's another three km to the Cengkeh Afu tree. Take particular care crossing the bamboo bridge; one of the poles may be rotten. From the clove tree it's two to three hours up to the top and back. It can be quite dangerous on the rim; there's a sheer drop into the cavernous crater. If you throw a rock into it, there's no sound. At the top you must walk on hot marble-sized stones, the residue of a 1737 eruption.

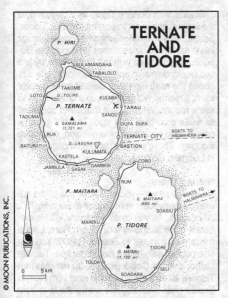

Batu Angus

"Burnt Corner." To the north between Tarau and Kulaba (catch a *bemo* from Tarau), this is where a river of lava from Gunung Gamalama plowed its way down to the sea in the 18th century. A

Japanese war memorial stands nearby. The ravaged north coast has always borne the brunt of Ternate's devastating volcanic activity, standing out in contrast to the luxurious forests and vegetation in the eastern and southern coasts of the island.

Lakes, Beaches, Reefs

Inland are two volcanic lakes covered in lotus flowers. Beautiful, inviting, spring-fed **Lake Laguna** lies seven km southwest of Ternate City. Past Laguna, the road leads up the mountain to Foramadiaha. **Lake Tolire** is just a 10-minute walk off the main road, about 24 km from Ternate City; catch a *bemo* to Takome, then walk. The locals are afraid to swim in this deep, green-shaded lake; they claim its waters are home to crocodiles and demons.

    Bastion Beach is three km from Ternate town. **Ngade** is a white-sand beach seven km from town. **Sulamandaha Beach** is a good swimming spot 16 km away. The whole stretch of coast on the northeast between Tabalolo and Dufa Dufa offers white-sand beaches and splendid reefs; no sharks, but watch the very strong currents. Averaging only about two meters deep, direct sunlight goes straight to the bottom; there you can see black lava piled upon black sand, with white coral on top.

TIDORE

With an area of about 78 square km, slightly larger than its sister island, Tidore lies just 1.5 km southwest of Ternate. Both islands are but volcanic cones emerged from the sea. The southern portion of Pulau Tidore is occupied almost entirely by an extinct volcanic peak, **Gunung Matabu** (1,730 meters). The soaring peaks of Tidore and Ternate are only two of 10 conical volcanos which form a line off the west coast of Halmahera. Below the 300-meter level, coffee, fruit, and tobacco are cultivated in very fertile soil. The northern half of Tidore consists mostly of hills, with a few level strips along the coast.

    With its relaxed people, many skilled smithies, and craftsmen, Tidore feels completely different than Ternate. The natives, originally of Alfuro stock, have intermixed considerably with outsiders. Even though Islam arrived here rela-

tively late (around A.D. 1430), the Tidorese are now Muslims all. The only accommodation on the island is in the main town of Soasiu, but you could probably make arrangements to board in a private home. The best days to visit Tidore are the market days, Tuesday and Saturday, when the island's towns are a spectacle of color, and transportation is plentiful.

History

Like Ternate, Tidore was the seat of an ancient and once-powerful sultanate that ruled over immense areas of eastern Indonesia as far as New Guinea. European contact began in the 16th century. After Magellan was killed in the Philippines, his crew reached Ternate in 1521. The Portuguese fought the sultans of both Tidore and Ternate, destroying their palaces and alienating the people. Later, the Spaniards took over the island and helped the Tidorese maintain their independence from the sultan of Ternate and the Dutch. In 1654, the Dutch finally conquered the island, but subsidized the sultan and allowed him to rule his subjects and retain his rank and title. During the period of Dutch rule in the 18th century, a young French adventurer—Pierre Poivre, the "Viper"—stole, from right under the noses of the Dutch, young clove tree seedlings which he successfully transplanted on the tiny French island of Mauritius in the Indian Ocean. The Japanese occupied Tidore in 1942.

Sights

Rum is the island's main port, where the boats arrive from Ternate. A short *prahu* ride from Rum is **Pulau Maitara**; about a 25-minute walk from the Rum *pasar* are the ruins of a Portuguese fortress. Shop and eat in Rum's many bamboo market stalls; Sunday is market day, when clove ships are sold. The south coast village of **Seli** consists of a row of houses along the sea, made of bamboo and volcanic rock. From Seli, **Pulau Moti,** famed for its cloves, and **Pulau Mare** are visible. The road from Rum all the way to Seli is well maintained.

Soasiu, with Gunung Tidore as a backdrop, is the largest and most important town on Tidore. Soasiu was the Indonesian headquarters for the West New Guinea campaign during the Republic's 1965 clash with the Dutch. Nearby are two overgrown ruins of Spanish forts: one sits above the road high over the sea as you enter town. Children will lead you up a difficult trail to see a mountain fortress, a maze-like complex, its walls crumbled long ago. The old sultan's palace, also reclaimed by vegetation, sits above the town. There's also a restored mosque. Stay in **Losmen Gebura.**

Getting There

No airstrip as yet—you must take one of the numerous motorboats from Bastion to Rum, Rp750, 30 minutes. As you cross see to the left Halmahera's huge shadowy form. From Rum, take a minibus 45 minutes to Soasiu, Rp800. You can also occasionally take a motorboat from Ternate harbor over to **Cobo** (Rp750, 30 minutes) on Tidore's far northern tip. On the road from Rum to Soasiu near Soadara, see where the lava from Gunung Matubu slid over the road in a 1968 eruption that killed 11 people. Since then, an entirely new town has been built on the ash and rubble.

HALMAHERA

This grotesquely shaped island, largest and northernmost in Maluku, is about 322 km long, with an area, including smaller satellite islands, of a staggering 16,835 square km. In shape and geography a smaller version of Sulawesi, the island's four tentacles are high, densely forested mountain chains tumbling together into the center. These peninsulas enclose three great bays—Kao, Buli, and Weda—all of which open toward the east. The isthmus connecting the northern peninsula is only eight km wide. The northern peninsula is volcanic, with three active and two semiquiescent peaks; the other sections are nonvolcanic. Tsunami caused by volcanic eruptions wiped out whole coastal villages as late as 1969.

Halmahera is a well-kept travelers' secret. It remains economically and agriculturally undeveloped. Mother-of-pearl and *trepang* are harvested from the sea. Many pearl divers live on Kao Bay, in particular in the Magaliho Islands,

accessible by motorboat from Tobelo. Rice is grown on the plain south of Galela; sago is also an important subsistence crop. Cash crops include *damar,* copra, wild nutmeg, and forest hardwoods. Halmahera's heavy tropical forests contain a great variety of trees, including the ironwood *Nania vera,* as well as such botanical wonders as the trumpet-shaped, pure white, 7.5-cm-wide *fagraea* flower.

History

Halmahera was settled first by Malayan sea gypsies, Orang Laut. In the Middle Ages, a native state evolved on the Bay of Jailolo. This sultanate prospered until it was supplanted by Ternate in 1380, but even those powerful usurpers were only able to control the coastal regions of the island. The Portuguese and Spanish were better acquainted with Halmahera (called "Moro" at the time) than with many other parts of the archipelago. The Dutch first secured a footing on Halmahera with the sultan of Ternate's aid, but since Halmahera grew only negligible quantities of lesser-grade spices and possessed few other marketable commodities, it was neglected by the colonial administration. In WW II, the Japanese occupied Halmahera, using their big base on Kao Bay as their command headquarters for the whole southwest Pacific. In Kao Bay you can still find many downed Japanese planes in the jungle and at the bottom of the sea; wrecked landing craft and amphibious tanks rust on the beach.

The People

The population of over 100,000 is made up of immigrants and merchants from other islands, Malayan fishermen, and hybrid Melanesian Alfuro in the interior. The vast majority of Halmahera's inhabitants are Islamic, though missionary efforts in the north have converted as many as 10,000 to Christianity. The approximately 30 distinct tribes of inland Halmahera have remained untouched by the more sophisticated sultanate islands. Thus, much of their traditional culture remains intact.

These mixed Papuan-Malay types, called Orang Primitif by other Halmaherans, have crisp, wavy hair, light skin, and strong builds—a true forest people. Several groups live in the Galela and Tobelo areas. These people have tall, muscular Polynesian physiques with oval faces, high open brows, aquiline noses, cinnamon skin, and thick beards. Formerly, this tribe hunted with barbed ironwood spears and bows and arrows, built and maintained temples (*sabuas*), and believed in an afterlife. One theory holds they're remnants of Caucasian groups who migrated across the Pacific in prehistoric times.

Ask one of these natives to make you a palm-leaf cup, a unique souvenir. The Tobelo, Galela, and Tabau tribes in the northern part of this island produce amazingly intricate plaited mats and decorated bark fabrics given as marriage gifts or used in mortuary festivities. Sleeping mats two meters long are made of pandanus leaves. Some pieces take years to complete, especially the ornamental display mats.

Getting There And Around

There were once more hassles and formalities on Pulau Halmahera than on most other islands of Maluku Utara, but of late the bureaucrats are easing up. Still, take along extra passport photos.

Merpati flies from Ternate to Galela for about Rp35,000. Or board a *kapal motor* at Bastion harbor, south of Ternate City, to Dodinga on Pulau Halmahera (Rp2500, 45 minutes). From Dodinga, take a minibus for Babaneigo on Teluk Kao (Rp3500), then a coaster north to the town of Kao (Rp4000), then proceed by daily motorboat to Tobelo. From Tobelo buses leave for Galela, Rp3500. Pelni vessels stop at Jailolo, Galela, Tobelo, and Weda. There are two daily ferrys from Ternate to Halmahera, leaving 0800 and 1300; Rp1800. Return on the same craft at 1100 and 1530 daily.

With no good navigable rivers, and roads only around the principal towns, travel in the rugged interior is arduous. It's fairly easy to travel from Dodinga to Galela; anywhere else you must often walk or take boats along the coasts. From Sidangoli to Molijut runs a very bad gravel road, full of holes. The bus companies Horino and Nikmah Tidore sell tickets for jaunts from Sidangoli to Tobelo (Rp12,500, six hours) and Galela (Rp13,500). The missionaries, mostly based on the northern peninsula, are a valuable source of information.

AROUND THE ISLAND

Northwest of Dodinga is **Sidangoli**, with white sandy beaches, beautiful coral marine gardens, and breathless panoramas. To reach the coral rent a *prahu* from Rp2500; you'll be there in 15 minutes. Ten minutes by bus from Sidangoli is **Batu Pituh**, a nature reserve where it's possible to see birds of paradise. *Losmen* here cost Rp8000 per person; three daily meals Rp5000 extra. The manager will guide you into the reserve for Rp10,000 per day. From Dodinga east to Buli on Teluk Buli is a two-day walk. **Maba**, south of Buli, is the reputed black magic area of the island.

Jailolo

Boats from Ternate make the two-hour trip to Jailolo at least once daily for Rp1000; buy your ticket on the boat at Bastion. Visit the unusual regional *adat* houses in this town. Take a motorboat out to the 13th-century ruins of the sultan's palace. From Jailolo, it's Rp200 by *bemo* to

P. MOROTAI

BUSOBUSO

SUPU

PUTI   SANGOWO

SELAT MORATAI

ASIMIRO

TEL. GALELA
GALELA
LUAR
LOLODA   TOBELO
UPA
TEL. LOLODA   1335 m

IBU   TOGIUS

PADIWANG

TATAM   AKELAMO
TEL. AKELAMO

GOROGORO   GAMLAHA
DORO

SAHU   MOMODA   KAO
TEL.
WASILE
1070 m

JAILOLO   GURUA

TEL. JAILOLO   AKESELAKA   1442 m

P. TERNATE   SIDANGOLI   WAJAMALI
BABANEIGO
TERNATE   DODINGA   WAJOL   BULI
P. TIDORE   OBA
SOASUI   MABA   H A L M A H E R A
TATOMUTU   1170 m   1042 m   S E A
P. MOTI   GUMI   GOTOWASI
NGOTAKIAHA   KOBE   SEPO   BITJOLI
P. MAKIAN   MESA
TELUK
PAJAHI   WEDA   TELUK
WEDA   PATANI   390 m
725 m
P. KAYOA   MAIDI

MAFA
SEMO   WOSI

0   90 km

SAKETA

GOROGORO   425 m   BESUI
P. BACAN   1155 m
BABANG.
TEL.
LABUHA   LAPAN   MUILIJK
2111 m
TEL.
WAJANA   GANI.   HALMAHERA

TG. LIHOBO

© MOON PUBLICATIONS, INC.

Babaneigo. The aboriginal areas of the Tobelo and Ibu tribes are 70 km inland.

Tobelo

Accommodations include **Toko Megaria**; the recently enlarged **Hotel Pantai Indah,** with 21 rooms, 15 with a/c, for Rp20,000-40,000; **Wisma Sibua Lamo**; and **Hotel President,** with fan and a/c rooms for Rp15,000-50,000. A large hospital run by a church group operates a coconut plantation on the side. The New Tribes Mission is based here.

About once a week ships travel from Bastion to Tobelo, Rp6000. From Tobelo, take a bus to Galela, Rp1500; Upa, Rp200. It's about a 30-km walk to the villages of **Desa Pickwang** and **Kusuri,** home to aborigines. Or take a minibus, Rp1000 to Kusuri.

Galela

This town is famous for the five lakes in its vicinity. **Lake Duma,** with its lovely surroundings, is especially worth visiting. Climb 930-meter **Gunung Mamuja,** an active volcano that emits rivers of lava. Travel 16 km from town by road, then hike three km to the top. There's a hot spring at **Kalimede.** Fly from Galela on Merpati to Ternate. From the airport into town is Rp500 by *bemo.* Or take a coaster to Ternate for around Rp8000.

Loloda

A magnesium mine here is run by a joint local government/Japanese venture. One of Halmahera's longest and most interesting rivers is the Loloda, coming down the mountain and emptying into the Bay of Loloda. Hire a motorized *prahu* to the three islands in the southern part of Loloda Bay. These amazing islands rise straight up from narrow beaches, forming pinnacles of rock up to 90 meters high, clothed with dense vegetation clear to their tops. Caves and tunnels dug out by the waves, and the exposed rocks of the cliffs themselves, sculpted by tropical rains, combine to create some of the strangest scenery on the island.

Pulau Morotai

To the northeast of the northern peninsula of Halmahera lies this 1,600-square-km island, more than 80 km long and 20-42 km wide. Some mountains, such as the Sabotai Range, reach 1,130 meters high. The strait separating Morotai from Halmahera is only 16 km wide; Wallace concluded the two must have been connected in some remote epoch. Pulau Morotai today is a big copper-producing island with tens of thousands of coconut palms waving in the wind. Other main crops include chocolate, *damar* gum, and rattan.

The island is populated by a mixture of races, with Papuans predominating—Morotai is only 320 km west of Irian Jaya. Morotai was a big Japanese airbase during WW II. From here Japanese bombers raided Darwin, Australia. During the Pacific campaign, **Doruba** served as a temporary headquarters for MacArthur. The island experienced heavy fighting during the war; Doruba's harbor is full of old wrecks. The town boasts a good market. A Pelni ship stops here from Ternate.

THE OUTER ISLANDS

THE BACAN ISLANDS

The 80 Bacan Islands, off the southwest tip of Halmahera, are green, hilly, volcanic in origin, and covered in forests. The sultanate of Bacan formerly traveled in a gorgeous cabined barge with gilded roof, fluttering flags, and bravely clad rowers. Although the island contains gold, copper, and coal, its mineral wealth has never been exploited. On the main island cacao and copra are produced; there's a Japanese-run pearl farm as well.

The Bacanese Malay natives are mostly Islamic with only a few hundred Christians on the islands, descendants of the Portuguese. There are also small groups of people from Galela, as well as descendents of Tomore colonists, brought from Sulawesi at their own request to escape intertribal warfare. To reach Labuha, the main town, fly with Merpati from Ternate, or take a daily *kapal motor* for Rp15,000 from Ternate harbor. Two Pelni boats, coming and going on the Ternate-Ambon run, stop here for two hours.

Dutch **Fort Barneveld** (1615) is only a half-hour's walk from Labuha harbor. It's said the

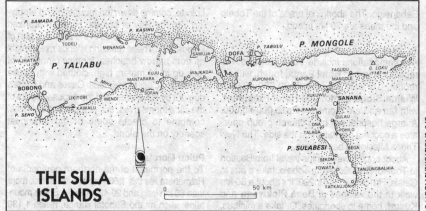

© MOON PUBLICATIONS, INC.

fort is haunted by the souls of soldiers formerly stationed there; during the full moon you can hear cadence being called and the shuffling footsteps of drilling men. The sultan's palace, 30% of which is still intact, dates back to the 13th century. **Air Belanda,** a former Dutch bathing place, lies three km from Labuha. Climb Gunung Sibela for a marvelous panorama over the surrounding islands.

In Labuha, stay at **Wisma Eka Endar,** Jl. Usman Sjah, which has four double rooms with private bathroom for Rp9500 full board (a very good price). Also check out **Wisma Harmonis,** rooms without bathrooms, Rp9000 per person. **Penginapan Borero** offers 13 rooms for Rp12,500-16,500. The *warung* near the pier is clean and friendly. A limited number of Bacan's famed *batu bacan* (semiprecious stones) can be purchased at unmarked **Toko Sibela** near Labuha harbor. Or look for stones in nearby *perusahaan* (workshops)—they come in translucent red and white, as well as other striking color combinations.

THE SULA ISLANDS

An island group in the southwest region of Maluku Utara, between Pulau Buru and Sulawesi. Combined, the three large islands and innumerable smaller isles have an area of near-

ly 13,000 square km. For the most part, the Sulas are nonvolcanic, with hilly interiors and low-lying swampy coasts. The people are primarily proto-Malay. Some primitive seminomadic groups still live along the coasts; animists inhabit the interior of Pulau Taliabu only. Rice is grown on these islands, while the forests are worked by Japanese and Filipino timber companies. From Bobong (Pulau Taliabu) it's about a day's walk to **Gunung Godo,** home to the Mangai and Sibojo people. The villages of Kadai and Mange have wonderful *adat* houses with *atap* roofs. The Mangai and Kadai people also live on Pulau Mongole. By Sanana harbor is an old fort, dating from Portuguese times, ruined but in good condition. Cannon lie in the entrance and you'll find a wildflower garden inside.

The Sulas are difficult to reach by sea, but Pelni's KM *Baruna Bakti* stops in Sanana (Pulau Sulabesi) on its Ambon-Ternate voyage. Other ships often stop in Sanana to unload cargo. For Pulau Mongole take a ship from Ternate for Rp15,000 to Sanana, then hire a small motorboat to Dofa for Rp5000. From Sanana to Bobong it's one day by *kapal motor* (Rp7500); departures daily. From Bobong, ships sail to Banggai, then to Kendari or Luwuk in southeast Sulawesi. Merpati flies from Sanana to Ambon twice weekly, Labuha, Morotai, and Ternate.

CENTRAL MALUKU

The land area of Central Maluku (Maluku Tengah) is 37,701 square km; its territorial waters total 265,316 square km. The population of over 450,000 lives in about 480 villages. Maluku Tengah consists of hundreds of islands, including the immense and partially unexplored islands of Ceram and Buru. The province also contains fabled Ambon, an island on the crossroads of the colonial struggle for control of the Spice Islands, and the district capital since Dutch times. Masohi on Ceram is the province's busiest urban and principal economic center. To the south are the Bandas, the nutmeg islands. On these islands during the 16th and 17th century, money literally grew on trees. Today the Bandas are more renowned for their historical remnants and pristine diving sites.

A number of natural reserves are found in Central Maluku: the dazzling 1,000-hectare marine gardens of Pulau Pombo east of Ambon; the spectacular *meranti* forests of Wai Mual and Wai Nua in central Ceram; the *maleo* (jungle fowl) preserves of Pulau Kasa north of Ambon; and the seabird refuges of the Lucipara-Penju groups southwest of the Bandas. For permits, inquire at Ambon's tourist office, first floor, Kantor Gubernor, Jl. Pattimura.

Getting There And Around

Garuda flies to Ambon from Surabaya via Ujung Pandang daily. Merpati schedules the same flight at least three times weekly. In July '92 a Mandala craft crashed into the mountains near Ambon Airport, killing 71 environmental scientists. Other air approaches are from Denpasar, Jakarta, and Manado. From Brisbane flights to Ambon via Denpasar and Ujung Pandang run A$1172.

Consider a ship from Jakarta, Surabaya, Ujung Pandang, or Manado via Ternate. There's also the option of taking Pelni and Perintis coasters, *kapal motor,* motorized outriggers, and even *kapal layar* from island to island. Other modes of transport often used by travelers include dugout canoes for around Rp6000 per hour and motorboats at about Rp20,000 per hour.

For road transport within Central Maluku, use buses, minibuses, and *becak.* Merpati provides interisland service out of Central Maluku to a number of distant island groups; Mandala and Pelita airlines also service the area.

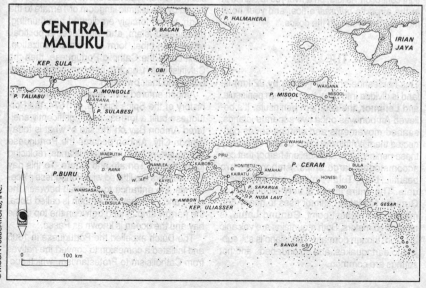

AMBON ISLAND

The Uliasser Islands—commercial, communication, administrative, and geographic center of Maluku—consist of four mountainous islands southwest of Ceram: from west to east Ambon, Haruku, Saparua, and Nusa Laut. Their total area is 1,295 square km, of which Ambon takes 777 square km. *Embun* means "dew" in Indonesian; this island is almost always enclosed by fog or mist. Another theory has it the name derives from *apon,* which means "plantation." In Ambon's long history of exploitation, commerce has always been handled by outsiders, beginning with the Chinese and Arabs, then Europeans, and now Indonesians from other islands.

Predominantly Christian, Ambon is today a sort of "mini-Maluku," offering beautiful tropical landscapes, historic buildings, churches and ruins, picturesque country walks, and fascinating *kampung* with traditions intact. On this island you can photograph some of the most spectacular vistas in the whole archipelago. Officially, the island's main city is called Amboina, although nobody much uses the name anymore—both the island and city are called Ambon. There is tight control on visitors; on arrival you're signed in at the airport's *imigrasi* office, and your hotel must register you with the police.

THE LAND

This horseshoe-shaped (48 km by 22 km) island is divided into **Hitu,** the northern peninsula, and **Leitimor,** the southern peninsula. It's believed Ambon was once two separate islands; seabed movements and shifting sands connected them. Within the loops of land created by these peninsulas is an excellent harbor that can accommodate large ships. Ambon has two beautiful bays, **Teluk Ambon** and **Teluk Baguala.** The entire island is very mountainous; **Gunung Horiel** in Leitimor rises to nearly 580 meters; the highest point, **Gunung Latua,** is nearly 915 meters. Both mountains are volcanic in origin, though dormant. The island is still subject to earthquakes, and sulphur beds and hot springs are common.

Ambon's rich soil gives rise to nutmeg, clove, cinnamon, betelnut, and palm plantations; a variety of orchids grows wild on shrubs and trees. Although a profusion of tropical blossoms sprout outside windows, plastic flowers are prized, and are found in every home, hotel lobby, and hotel room. The main staples are sago, tubers, vegetables, and cassava, which grows wild in swampy areas. Fish provide most of the protein. Cloves and nutmeg are still among the primary cash crops, though not nearly on the scale of the past. Swidden crops such as squash and other gourds, plus spinach, are also cultivated; the Ambonese preference for root crops betrays their Melanesian origins.

HISTORY

Early History
The ancestors of the present inhabitants of Central Malukan villages migrated from West Ceram or Makian Island no later than the 15th century; this is evident in their *adat.* Divided into small kinship groups, the Ambonese were originally slash-and-burn cultivators. They were first dominated by the Islamic kingdom of Ternate to the north, which forcibly eradicated headhunting, propagated Islam, and introduced a political, rather than tribal, form of social organization. Next came the Catholic Portuguese, then the Calvinist Dutch, each in turn converting the Ambonese to their own faith.

Ambon entered quite late into the tumultuous history of the Spice Islands. In 1574, the Portuguese built a fortress on magnificently sheltered Ambon Bay on the site of what is today Ambon City. Ambon became the Portuguese headquarters for the eastern islands, replacing fortresses on Ternate and Tidore. To this day the Uliassers are littered with Portuguese placenames: the entrance to the strait between the outer and inner bays of Ambon is called Boca, the narrow strip of land between the top of the bay and the ocean is known as Passo.

The Dutch expelled the Portuguese in 1605 and initiated a campaign to convert the natives from Catholicism to Protestantism, which suc-

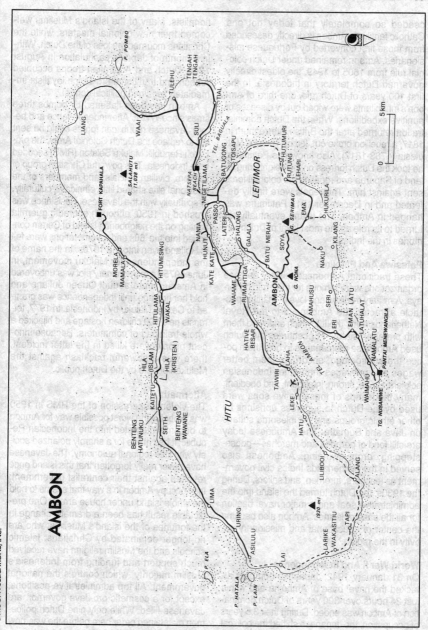

AMBON

0 5 km

P. POMBO

TENGAH
TENGAH

TULEHU

LIANG
WAAI
SULI   TIAL

MORELA
MAMALA
HITUMESING   NATSEPA
BEACH
NEGERILAMA
BATUGONG
TOISAPU
TEL BAGUALA
CHUTUMURI
RUTUNG
LEHARI   LEITIMOR
HUKURILA
EMA
G. SERIMAU
KILANG
NAKU
SERI   G. NONA
EMAN LATU
LATUHALAT
NAMALATU
PANTAI MENEWANGLA
TG. NUSANIWE

G. SALAHUTU
(1,038 m)

FORT KAPAHALA

HITULAMA
WAKAL
KATE KATE
HUNUT
NANIA
LATERI
PASSO
HALONG   BATU MERAH
GALALA
AMBON
AMAHUSU
ERI
WAIAME
RUMAHTIGA
HATIVE
BESAR
AHA
TAWIRI
LEKE   HATU

HILA
(ISLAM)

HILA
(KRISTEN)

KAITETU

HATUNUKU
BENTENG
SEITH
BENTENG
WAWANE

HITU

LIMA

URING
ASILULU
LAI
LARIKE
WAKASITIU
LILIBOOI
ALANG
TAPI
(930 m)

P. ELA
P. HATALA
P. LAIN

TEL AMBON

WAIMAHU

SOYA

KATE

© MOON PUBLICATIONS, INC.

ceeded so completely that today not one Catholic family on Ambon is directly descended from those first converted by Portuguese missionaries. Ambon remained under Dutch colonial rule from 1605 to 1949, the oldest directly governed Dutch territory in Indonesia. In the first 100 years of Dutch rule, one-third of Ambon's inhabitants were wiped out by diseases or punitive expeditions. When the Dutch administration returned after the British interregnum in 1817, a rebellion broke out, led by Thomas Matulesia (1783-1817). Also known as Pattimura, he took the Dutch fortress on the neighboring island of Saparua and repelled the colonial force sent against him. The rebels were finally defeated and in December 1817 Pattimura was hanged in Ambon. The island eventually returned to its role as the most loyal of Dutch territories in the Indies.

Patasiwa And Patalima
These traditional Ambonese military defense organizations were famous for their raiding forays. A military tradition and love of martial spectacle attracted the Ambonese to the Royal Netherlands Army (KNIL), which endowed them with preferred status. For centuries the Dutch used Ambonese mercenaries to help them police the archipelago, according them better wages and privileges than other Indonesian soldiers. Brave, strong, intelligent, and obedient, many thousands of these native sons were used by the Dutch to suppress uprisings by other ethnic groups and troublesome sultans on Java and Sumatra. The Ambonese today are still fond of parades and marches—goose-stepping, arms swinging. Ambonese also served in the Netherlands Indies civil government as teachers, foremen, and sailors. During the 1930s, the Dutch turned the island into the administrative seat and a major naval bastion for all the eastern islands. Ambon also became the center of educational and missionary activity in the region.

World War II And Independence
On 31 January 1942, Japanese bombers attacked the naval base of Amboina and within just 24 hours over 300 years of Dutch domination of Ambon was ended. During their 3.5 years of occupation, the Japanese shifted the political balance from the *adat* elite to Ambonese nationalists. Many of the island's Muslims welcomed their new colonial masters, while the Christians mourned the loss of the Dutch. Within a month of Japan's capitulation in August 1945, Dutch and Australian troops occupied Ambon and traditional pro-Dutch loyalists immediately regained political control.

Ambon has been flattened by bombs three times since WW II. After independence and before Javanese republican forces could be sent out to replace the Dutch Colonial Army, the pro-Dutch Republik Maluku Selatan (RMS) seceded from Indonesia. This powerful Christian group of soldiers, civilian officials, and members of the traditional elite shared little ethnically, culturally, or spiritually with the Javanese. Resistance was crushed in 1950, although sporadic guerrilla fighting on the neighboring island of Ceram continued into the '60s and reverberations were felt in Holland even into the 1970s. In the name of the Independence for Maluku movement, in June 1975 an extraordinary plot was uncovered in Amsterdam to abduct Queen Juliana and hold her hostage until independence was granted to Central Maluku by Indonesia. In 1977, terrorists held 100 children hostage and hijacked a whole trainload of commuters. Because innocent people were killed in the latter incident, there was a powerful backlash against the Malukan people by the Dutch public.

Aftermath
The violent suppression of the RMS in 1950 was probably the worst possible way for Ambon to become integrated into the Indonesian Republic; it has made for a sharply polarized society with little regional autonomy. The Javanese have never really forgotten that this island once revolted against their centralist government; they occupy Ambon in a way that seems to hold the whole island under house arrest. One predictable result has been a dramatic change in the fortunes of the island's Muslims, who are no longer dominated by Christians. Islamic schools and the Muslim religion have received much support and funding from Indonesia's Muslim majority, which controls the national government. All top administrative positions, except for a cosmetic pro-Java governor, are Javanese-filled. While only nine Dutch policemen maintained order here before the war, now it takes thousands of Javanese soldiers to con-

trol the island. The less you say about politics in public on Ambon, the better.

THE PEOPLE

A very striking people, the Ambonese have mixed racially with Portuguese, Alfuros, Malays, Javanese, and the Dutch, creating a sort of creole Malukan culture. This amalgam is most obvious in the lighter-skinned coastal villagers; interior peoples have darker complexions with more pronounced Melanesian features. A strong Melanesian element is also evident in the urban population, as people from surrounding islands arrive in Ambon to seek work. The Ambonese tongue is classified as belonging to the Ambon-Timor group of Malayo-Polynesian languages. European languages have made a deep impression. Portuguese lives on in Ambonese: *mui* from *muito* for "very much"; religious terms such as *perdeos* and *komunyan*; and *nyora* for "Mrs." In some families and among the elderly, Dutch is still spoken as a second language. More Ambonese—largely political refugees—live in Holland than on Ambon.

Village Organization
The majority of Ambonese live in coastal villages. Each Ambonese village is either *patasiwa* or *patalima,* "nine divisions" or "five divisions"—territorial quasipolitical patrilineal federations (*uli*) dating from the 15th century. These federations protected the Ambonese against war and colonial repression. The Dutch later abolished the federations and made each village politically independent, governed by a ruling council. From this native elite a village headman—the *raja*—is chosen or inherits the title. Other traditional officers who help govern the village are the head of the *soa* (administrative subdistrict), the Lord of the Land (*tuan tanah*), the *adat*-chief, the war leader (*kapitan,* now a purely ceremonial office), the chief of the forest police (*kepala kewang*), the village messenger (*marinyo*), and the village priest (*mauwang*). Each of the important lineages on the island has an honorific title, belongs to a sacred spring, and maintains its own cultivated plots (*dati*). Many villages also maintain an ancestral memorial stone in an "original settlement" (*negeri lama*) in the hills.

Adat
Although Ambonese villages are either Christian or Muslim, they're all nearly identical in their social and cultural fabric. Scratch the skin of a Muslim or a Christian and you find *adat.* Socially approved *adat* behavior is equated with the will of the ancestors, and violation of *adat* can incur the wrath of ancestral spirits. Village councils enforce *adat* and carry out temporal punishment of offenders if necessary.

One classic example of living *adat* is the *pela* system. This ritual form of truce between warring villages dates back to the 15th and 16th centuries, when Christianity and Islam were introduced into Maluku. Over 50 *pela* confederations were formed to avoid the harmful mistrust which could develop between villages adhering to different religions. When several or more villages have adopted a *pela* alliance, this common law is even stronger than blood relationships. To avoid conflict, the youngsters of *pela* villages are strictly forbidden to marry, a union which is looked upon as a form of incest. Sometimes Christians help their Muslim neighbors build a mosque or Muslims help their Christian neighbors build a church; *pela* villages also help each other plant and harvest crops, share the financial burden of funerals and weddings, and together celebrate national and religious holidays. Despite the experience of the rebellious RMS movement in the 1950s—in which Christian soldiers victimized Muslims, deeply dividing the two communities—the alliances are still strong. Even the sizable Malukan exile communities living in the Netherlands practice *pela.*

Religion
Ambon's Christian community is a product of European contact, while the island's Islamic community came into being as a result of early trading with Ternate, Makassar, and Java. Saint Francis Xavier established a mission on Ambon as early as 1547; by the 17th century there were as many as 50,000 Catholics in Central Maluku. Today, Christianity and Islam are equally represented on Ambon, to the extent that sometimes you see a mosque and a church in the same *kampung.* These modern religions have largely replaced indigenous animism. The church and mosque congregations exert a powerful social and moral force in village life.

SHOPPING

Although more expensive than Java or Bali, you can find about anything you want if you're willing to wander around. Ambon City has hundreds of mostly Chinese-owned shops. The city market is fascinating, but the crowds are heavy. Buy black coral bracelets (*akar bahar*) or turtle shell bracelets for Rp1500; *gigi duyung* (sea cow teeth) cost Rp5000 or more. Great Ming platters run Rp150,000-300,000; the Naulu people of Ceram have loads of 16th-century Ming cheaper, but you have to really hike for it. Pulau Buru is the origin of *kayuputih* oil, which is processed and sold quite cheaply on Ambon. *Runut* is the local name for the tissue that covers the young leaves of a coconut tree. In the past it was used as a sieve for sago washing, but its contemporary use is as a basic material for fans, bags, and wall decorations.

Clove Artifacts

Ambon's oldest craft, sold to Dutch tourists for generations. The first designs were of the *kora kora*, the Malukan gondola, built entirely of cloves. The art was invented by the Mustamu family of Mardika, the skill passed down from father to son. Nowadays, clove artifacts are also produced in Latuhalat but sometimes their stock is depleted because they sell mostly to retailers. Designs include baskets, flowers, birds, cigarette and cigar boxes, and whole ships mounted in glass cases and built completely out of cloves with tiny seamen, oars, and lanterns on deck: Rp15,000-20,000 depending on size and the workmanship invloved. Also try the shops along Jl. A.Y. Patty.

Shops

You'll find craft shops along Jl. J. Latu Harhary and A.Y. Patty in Ambon City. In Rumahtiga village, visit Frans C. Tita's **Salawaku Art Shop,** a shell-crafts cottage industry. Board a ferry or outrigger from near Galala, northeast of Ambon, to Rumahtiga across Ambon Bay, Rp300. **Batumerah,** a section of Ambon, is the center of production for attractive pearl and tortoiseshell articles.

Garments

Malukan shirts and jackets are either painted or embroidered with beautiful designs of traditional Malukan decorative patterns. Ambonese Christians have been known, since Dutch times, for their black clothing, worn to church. Women wear a black jacket and shawl (*kain pikul*) and sometimes go barefoot, especially in the village; men wear a black coat with white shirt and shell buttons. Young women's festive dress comes in all shades of red, while older women wear more subdued blue and violet colors. These Malukanstyle garments are available at hotel gift shops; also ask the tourist office which tailors in town produce traditional jackets and blouses.

EVENTS

Most Ambonese *adat* ceremonies have fizzled out, but a few are still practiced. When a new *baileo* (communal meetinghouse) is constructed, there's a purification ceremony by village headmen and elders called *cuci baileo*. This cleansing festival is also used on old consecrated *baileo* such as the one in Soya, southeast of Ambon City, on the second Friday of December. Newly elected *raja* enjoy inauguration ceremonies. Try to get in on an infant baptism and a Christian confirmation ceremony, both of which retain a number of pre-Christian indigenous features. **Kunci Tahun Baru,** meaning "locking in the New Year," is celebrated by feasting on sago, sweet potatoes, and wild game. Ambonese funerals are conducted by the village priest or elder. At the gravesite service flutes are played and sometimes graveside vigils are held on the third and 40th days after interment.

At Ambonese weddings, spiritual, civil, and *adat* practices come into full play. The marriage first is performed before the village *raja*, at his home or office, then at the church, then come the *adat* rituals. The groom's relatives carry the bride's dowry—textiles, brandy, Chinese porcelain, money, motorscooter—to the bride's family. Formerly, heads were offered in payment for the bride. Sudden elopements and mock wife-stealings, to avoid paying the bride-price, are frequent, and are actually encouraged by parents to save costs.

Music And Dance

An extraordinarily musical people, the Ambonese are known for their many songs of lament, farewell, and fishing; they're also very adept at choir singing. The women of the island sing like angels; go to the New Garden Restaurant to hear the customers sing. There are 20-30 flute bands in Ambon City, usually connected with a church. Other Ambonese musical instruments are made from seashells. Shell orchestras (*orkes kulibia*) are composed of individual players each with a large triton shell. Like a European bell or Sundanese *angklung* orchestra, each player plays individual notes. Dances include the rowing dance, the fishtrapping dance, and various village folk dances such as the clove harvest dance, the sago-beating dance, and the thatch-knitting dance. Perhaps the most famous is the traditional war dance, the *cakalele*.

Folk dances are sometimes held on the weekends or by arrangement in the Fine Arts Building beside the sports arena in Karangpanjang, a suburb of Ambon. The *sasapu*, performed in Mamala 40 km from Ambon, lauds the magical properties of Mamala oil, a medicinal rubbing oil. After the dancers hit each other with the hard stems of palm leaves, wounds are instantly cured with application of the oil. Such dances as the *horlapep, katreji,* and the *cakaiba* originate from Portuguese and Dutch times. Another remnant of Portuguese (actually Moorish) times are the melancholy *keroncong* ballads sung to a small five-stringed guitar-like instrument.

Sports

The famous Darwin-Ambon International Yacht Classic Race began in 1976 with only six yachts; by 1986 there were 26. Yachts from Australia, New Zealand, Germany, and the U.S. take part, and even Ambon's tourist office has its own yacht. Local sailing competitions and *arumbai manggurebe,* or gondola-rowing contests, are also popular. *Pencak silat* (martial arts) is widely practiced. The north coast town of Mamala practices a sport called *sapulidi* (or "broom fighting") using palm fibers tied to a stick. *Sapulidi* usually takes place in August.

GETTING AROUND

The airport is at Laha, 46 km from Ambon on the southern shore of the island's northern peninsula. This little airport takes its job seriously—there's a dispensary, post office, police and immigration checks, restaurant, and airline desks. The pun-

ishing taxi fare is anywhere from Rp15,000 to Rp25,000 (one hour). Or you can choose a hotel (look for signs) that pays your fare in if you stay there. People at the information desk push hotels from which they receive commissions. Alternatively, take a minibus (Rp5000 between seven to eight people), leaving when full, or wait out on the highway for a public bus for Rp1000. The road from the airport runs around Ambon Bay and affords wonderful views. On the way you pass Universitas Pattimura in Poka, with fisheries and shipbuilding facilities. If you want to get off at Poka, there's a speedboat over to Ambon for only Rp150. Hitching is also possible.

Minibuses travel the whole island from the terminal at Mardika Pantai in Ambon City. Ambon is a small island and no bus or minibus trip anywhere is more than about Rp2000. Taxis run Rp4000 per hour. Public *bemo* are available, but it's difficult to take pictures; views and stops en route are possible. Local ferries or motorized *prahu,* called here *pok-pok,* are very reasonable.

Visiting Villages And Ruins

Ask questions at Ambon's bus station about the places you wish to visit; often the drivers come from the village where the bus is headed. Although the Ambonese speak their own dialect of Indonesian, you shouldn't have any trouble communicating out in the villages. It's essential that you first pay a call to the *raja,* if he's there. A *raja* often lives in Ambon City and visits his village only when his presence is absolutely required. Some villages won't give you food or put you up without his permission, but this is rare; most will accommodate you. In Christian areas don't wear a *kain* or *sarung*; in Muslim areas they'll love you if you do.

There are at least 40 ruins of old fortresses (*benteng*) on Pulau Ambon. If you're going to do a lot of walking around ruins, first get a letter from the police or the tourist office; this may enable you to stay for free in places that receive very few Western visitors. Since a fort could be hallowed ground, people may deny the forts actually exist. Always ask before wandering around out areas; you don't want to disturb ancestors in their shrines. While crawling over old forts be careful of treacherous land coral. There's a ban on photographing some old forts, such as Fort Victoria, which is also a military installation.

AMBON CITY

The administrative capital of Maluku Tengah, Ambon City is a disparate collection of government offices and closely knit *kampung*, the most important Indonesian city between Ujung Pandang and Jayapura. Set on a high, rocky coastline on Leitimor, the southern peninsula, the city occupies a lovely setting divided by steep ravines. Walk around town in the afternoon when families relax on their front verandas sipping tea. Join in a Christian service on Sunday in one of the town's numerous churches, a real window into Ambonese culture. The Islamic community lives in the southwest of town.

Food, accommodations, and transportation in this fair-sized city are as expensive as in Bandung, but the pace is slower. You see few foreigners here except missionaries and occasional Dutch, Australian, or New Zealand tourists. The Ambonese seem to like the Dutch enough to hate them, absolutely despise the Japanese, consider most Americans too loud, and positively love Australians. As a foreigner you'll be the object of constant attention, but there are usually enough friendly Ambonese around to make your stay worthwhile. Music is everywhere; all the latest Western tapes pulsate from shopfronts, transistors, and taxi buses, guitars are played on porches and street corners, and everyone owns and exchanges cassettes. Ambon is one of the few places in Indonesia where you see drunks on the street, especially on Sunday afternoons and in the evenings.

History

This city has had a hard history since the Portuguese first established a fort here 400 years ago. Because of the worldwide popularity of its spices, Ambon has been caught in crossfires and destroyed many times. Before the arrival of Europeans, the land now occupied by the town was called Honipopu, and consisted of four villages. Ambon was for centuries an important way-station for the spice traffic between Ternate and the Banda Islands.

The great blind Dutch naturalist, Rumphius (1628-1702), was buried in the garden of his former home in Ambon but his grave has long since disappeared. Rumphius worked for over 50 years in and around Ambon collecting hundreds of new tropical species. His uncanny illustrations of the region's biota still stand today as some of the finest and most beautiful ever drawn.

Known all over the Indies as "Beautiful Amboina," prewar Ambon had spacious squares with tall trees, shady cobblestone streets, promenades and gardens, and a charming tree-lined waterfront, with the white houses of the Dutch interspersed among native palm houses. The town was all but demolished by Allied bombs in 1945. A new administrative center, with many government buildings and official residences, was built in the 1970s in the suburb of Karangpanjang—the "Brasilia" of Ambon.

SIGHTS

Historic

The statue with the upraised sword in the town park is of **Kapitan Pattimura,** who fought against Dutch oppression. The statue is located on the spot where the guerrilla leader was hanged by the Dutch. His last words to his captives were "have a pleasant day." Pattimura's most famous action was leading an assault on Fort Duurstede on Pulau Saparua, east of Ambon, on 5 March 1817. The memorial to freedom-fighter **Martha Christina Tiahahu,** in the suburb of Karangpanjang, overlooks the whole of Ambon City and Ambon Bay. Both day and twilight views are superb. Tiahahu and her father served in Pattimura's guerrilla forces; she died on a POW ship to Java. Near the statue is the Provincial House of Assembly where elected members meet periodically. Other colonial-era remnants, all on Jl. Pahlawan Revolusi, include the mausoleum of **Sunan Pakubuwono VI,** a Solonese ruler who died here in exile in 1849; the former Dutch governor's mansion; and the former home of the Javanese **Prince Diponegoro,** exiled here for several years. See the huge mural in the church on Jl. A. Rhebok depicting the holy cross as a stairway to heaven.

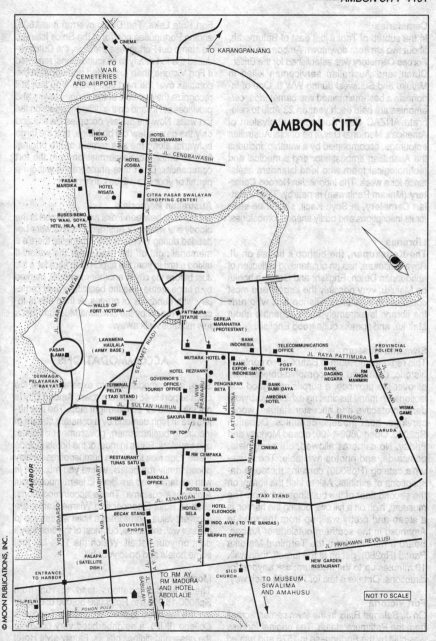

AMBON CITY

TO KARANGPANJANG

CINEMA

TO WAR CEMETERIES AND AIRPORT

NEW DISCO

HOTEL CENDRAWASIH

JL. MUTIARA

JL. CENDRAWASIH

HOTEL JOSIBA

JL. TULUKABESSY

PASAR MARDIKA

HOTEL WISATA

CITRA PASAR SWALAYAN (SHOPPING CENTER)

KALI MARDIKA

BUSES/BEMO TO WAAI, SOYA, HITU, HILA, ETC.

JL. MARDIKA PANTAI

WALLS OF FORT VICTORIA

PATTIMURA STATUE

GEREJA MARANATHA (PROTESTANT)

BANK INDONESIA

TELECOMMUNICATIONS OFFICE

JL. RAYA PATTIMURA

PROVINCIAL POLICE HQ.

LAWAMENA HAULALA (ARMY BASE)

JL. SELAMET RIADI

MUTIARA HOTEL

HOTEL REZFANNY

BANK EXPOR-IMPOR INDONESIA

POST OFFICE

BANK DAGANG NEGARA

RM ANGIN MAMMIRI

JL. JEND A. YANI

PASAR LAMA

GOVERNOR'S OFFICE/ TOURIST OFFICE

PENGINAPAN BETA

BANK BUMI DAYA

DERMAGA PELAYARAN RAKYAT

TERMINAL PELITA (TAXI STAND)

JL. WIM REAWARU

AMBOINA HOTEL

WISMA GAME

JL. SULTAN HAIRUN

JL. BERINGIN

GARUDA

CINEMA

SAKURA

HALIM

TIP TOP

P. LATUMAHINA

HARBOR

RESTAURANT TUNAS SATU

RM CEMPAKA

CINEMA

MANDALA OFFICE

HOTEL SILALOU

JL. SAID PERINTAH

JL. MR J. LATU HARHARY

JL. SULTAN BABULLAH

JL. A.Y. PATTY

BECAK STAND

JL. KENANGAN

HOTEL SELA

HOTEL ELEONOOR

TAXI STAND

SOUVENIR SHOPS

INDO AVIA (TO THE BANDAS)

JL. A. RHEBOK

MERPATI OFFICE

JL. PAHLAWAN REVOLUSI

PALAPA (SATELLITE DISH)

ENTRANCE TO HARBOR

S. POHON PULE

TO RM AY, RM MADURA AND HOTEL ABDULALIE

SILO CHURCH

TO MUSEUM, SIWALIMA AND AMAHUSU

NEW GARDEN RESTAURANT

PELNI

JL. YOS SUDARSO

NOT TO SCALE

© MOON PUBLICATIONS, INC.

Cemeteries

In the suburb of Tantui just east of Batumerah, about two km from downtown Ambon, an **Allied Forces Cemetery** was established for the British, Dutch, and Australian servicemen killed in Maluku and Sulawesi during WW II. One of Indonesia's best-maintained war cemeteries, ceremonies are held each year on 23 April to celebrate ANZAC Day, Australia's equivalent of America's Memorial Day. The official Australian entourage, accompanied by a warship, includes the Australian ambassador and a medical and technological team who lend islanders assistance for a week. The Indonesian **Heroes Cemetery** (Makam Pahlawan) is nearby. The **Christian Cemetery,** in Soya Kecil, should be seen for its inscriptions and oddly shaped tombstones.

Libraries

The **Keuskupan,** the bishop's house on Jl. Raya Pattimura, has an outstanding collection of antiquarian Dutch, English, and German books on Maluku, very possibly the largest and most complete in existence. Bishop Sol, who runs the library, is extremely knowledgeable about Maluku, and speaks quite good English.

Siwalima Museum

This regional museum in Batu Capeo contains historic, craft, and ethnographic objects from all over the province, a surprisingly good collection with many fascinating exhibits: *ikat,* wonderful protective and ancestor statues, woodcarvings, boat models, ceramics. Donation Rp2000. Open 0800-1400; closed Monday and Friday. No cameras allowed, but pamphlets, postcards, and photos available. The museum's catalog (Rp5000) contains thorough descriptions of exhibits. Ask to visit the library on the second floor of the building next door. The museum, high on a hill overlooking the harbor, is a steep and pretty walk up from the road to Amahusu in the southern outskirts of Ambon. Board a minibus from the Terminal Mardika Pantai (Rp250), get off at the turnoff, then walk 10 minutes up to the museum; ask anyone for directions. Or take a taxi for Rp4000 each way.

Fort Victoria

On Jl. Selamat Riadi in the town center, across from the Pattimura statue. The original fortress was built by the Portuguese in 1575 and named Fort Kota Laka. The Dutch overran it in 1605, ending Portuguese control of the Spice Islands. To stamp out Portuguese prestige, the Dutch reduced the fort nearly to its foundations, renamed it Fort Victoria, then expanded and updated the complex over the next 350 years. You can still recognize the symbols of the various towns and provinces of Holland on the different crests on the fort walls. Now the military occupies the site and only the gate, a few old buildings, and the large bulwarks along the sea remain of the original fort. To enter, obtain permission from the fort commander. Don't take photographs without a permit or your film will be confiscated.

Australian Memorials

On the road between Poka and the airport is the bloody site where 72 Australian POWs were beheaded during WW II by the Japanese; there's a memorial right off the road, near the water. If taking a taxi in from the airport stop here for a bit. Just before the city is another memorial, marked by a huge statue; see the beautifully kept cemetery with hundreds of graves. A third site is located on the hill by the Siwalima Museum, just a few minutes walk away.

ACCOMMODATIONS

Since accommodations are expensive and the city's airport is 46 km from town, Ambon City is not the place for an overnight stop. The few hotels are in high demand by a constant stream of incoming businessmen, government officials, and travelers. Rates in most of the hotels include meals. One nice touch is a number of reasonably priced family-run hotels, where you mix right in with the family and are likely to learn much about Ambonese customs. These accommodations, such as Hotel Eleonoor and Wisma Game, are excellent value. Sometimes a hotel will ask you to register with the police, but most of the time they'll do it on your behalf. Watch the 10% tax that some hotels add on to your bill.

Moderate

These accommodations tend to run from Rp8000-15,000 s to Rp25,000-35,000 d. Cheapest are the basic *losmen* around the Teacher's College (IKIP), a neighborhood very handy to the *pasar* and airlines offices. Family-style **Hotel**

Sela, Jl. A. Rhebok, has rooms with *kamar mandi*—a clean, comfortable hotel on a quiet street. Hotel Silalou, run by a very helpful old man, is behind the Teacher's College, Jl. Sedap Malam 41, tel. (0911) 3197. Meals also served.

Hotel Rezfanny, Jl. Wim Reawaru 115, tel. 42300, has drab upstairs rooms, but better, slicker rooms downstairs with *mandi* inside, a/c, and sitting area. Barely drinkable coffee. Be sure to light your mosquito coil. Very near the governor's office and Dinas Pariwisata. Next door, Penginapan Beta, Jl. Wim Reawaru 114, tel. 3463, is the best value in town. Run by a Protestant family, the top floor rooms have a cool balcony and easy access to the breezy roof. Even the cheapest rooms have *mandi* inside. Next door is the Hotel Hero, with rates from Rp30,000; no tax or service charge.

Wisma Game, Jl. Jen. A. Yani, tel. 3525, is a good deal, located near the Garuda office; a small, very clean, family-run hotel, the price includes breakfast (toast), free tea, sandals and towel. The proprietor, Mr. Kasturian, speaks Dutch. Hotel Eleonoor, Jl. A. Rhebok 30, tel. 2834, next door to the Chinese Protestant church and across the street from Hotel Sela, is also clean and comfortable. A family-style place on a semi-busy street; comfortable, nice breakfast. A *penginapan* opposite the airport charges a scandalous Rp40,000; dirty and decrepit.

On the beach 14 km from the city is Lelisa Beach Resort, Jl. Raya Namalatu, tel. 51990 or 51989. Rp45,000 for rooms with a/c, hot water; Rp65,000 for rooms with a/c, hot water, TV, refrigerator. Prices do not include meals; restaurant on site. Ibu Wanda Latumahina is very friendly and speaks both English and Dutch. If you don't wish to spend the night you're free to vist the resort to swim, relax, and spend the day.

Luxury

There's still no international-class hotel in all of Maluku. In the town's higher-priced hotels the a/c and TVs could be dead most of the time. Be prepared for a 5-10% tax and 5-10% service charge added onto your bill. The Mutiara, Jl. Pattimura 90, tel. (0911) 3075 or 3076, comes closest to international standards—its 12 a/c rooms cost Rp25,500 s, Rp35,000 d with inside *mandi*, video, and minibar. Some rooms have private terraces. Anggrek, Jl. A. Yani, tel. 2139, is an old colonial hotel in a residential district

with pleasant porches and a central location. It has some new a/c rooms, but the rest are shabby. Good meals included in the price. Hotel Amboina, Jl. Kapt. Ulupaha 5, tel. 41725 or 3354, is a one-star hotel, supposedly the best in Ambon. It's probably the best base for a businessperson; reasonably good restaurant, right in the town center. Telex, room service, restaurant, erratic TV, all credit cards accepted. Prices range from Rp60,000 per night for very basic a/c singles to Rp120,000 for clean double rooms with large bathrooms. Travelers arriving at the airport are sometimes offered a 15% discount to stay here; 20% discount for stays of more than one night.

The Wisata, Jl. Mutiara SK 3-15, tel. 3293 or 3567, is a close, tight, cozy place right on the waterfront. Rooms with private bath, TV, hot water, a/c, and fridge cost Rp27,500 s, Rp30,000 d. Run by Mr. Yunan, who was born in Dobo; this character speaks a number of languages and is quite sharp and informative. Very good food in the clean dining room. No credit cards accepted. Not a great value despite the automatic 10% discount. Josiba Hotel, Jl. Tulukabessy 27, tel. 41280, is nothing special; Hotel Amboina is a better deal.

A little farther up the same side of the street is Hotel Cendrawasih, tel. 2487. Although you can get a 20% discount without much bargaining, standards are poor. Located in one of the busiest parts of Ambon. The Abdulalie, Jl. Sultan Babulah, tel. 2796, consists of a new expensive modern building and an older building with cheaper rates. Located in the Muslim quarter near outstanding restaurants.

FOOD

Most of the town's many *warung* serve tasty *nasi ikan* with vegetables or *mie goreng* for Rp2000. Try the stands around the corner from the Garuda office. *Bakmie* wagons peddle soup, Rp1000. Other *warung* dishes served in town tend to be more expensive; for example, in front of Mesjid Raya at night massive portions of baked fish and baked potatoes cost Rp5000.

Local Dishes

Try the Ambonese sweet-sour sauce *colo-colo*, made with a citrus base and red chilies; it's especially piquant with baked fish. Out in the villages the place to eat is the *pasar,* where women sell snacks of rice and vegetables heated on the spot and wrapped in banana leaf. Other regional dishes include the *kohu-kohu,* a Malukan fish salad; and *laor,* a marine seaworm harvested during the full moon at the end of March. Also sample the famous *papeda,* a kind of sago porridge. Cold, it's rolled into a lump on a banana leaf or dried in small cakes; warm, it's eaten with chopsticks (*gata-gata*), served with a fish sauce (*kuah ikan*), or cooked with Spanish peppers (*cili*) or shellfish.

Restaurants

Dining out is not a big tradition with the Ambonese, who prefer family-style homecooking, but because of the influx of immigrant workers a number of *warung* and restaurants have appeared. Head for the *rumah makan* along Jl. A.Y. Patty and around the harbor, as well as those on Jl. Said Perintah. There are three good ones in a row on Jl. Sultan Hairun—**Halim Restaurant,** Jl. Sultan Hairun SK 3/37, tel. (0911) 97126, beside *kantor gubernor,* has a full menu: crab soup, Rp5500; the best *mie goreng,* Rp2000; also known for its ice cream. Nice open-air sitting area. Also try the **Tip Top** next door—good food, popular with Australians. The **Tifa Club** serves quality Indonesian food; staff is very obliging, and may give you cash on your Visa. For *asli* Java-style food such as *ayam goreng kalasan,* Yogyakarta-style, eat at **Restaurant Sakura** next to the Tip Top. There are several good *nasi padang* restaurants, such as the **Minang Jaya** on Jl. Kemakmuran. The hotel restaurants serve simple but good food; don't expect gourmet dishes. Because of lack of pasture land, most meats are imported.

Several wonderful Madurese eateries, including **RM Ai** and **RM Madura,** face each other in the Muslim quarter on Jl. Sultan Babulah close to Hotel Abdulalie. Feast on a full range of genuine Islamic-Indonesian dishes such as *gado-gado* with super fresh veggies (Rp1000), perfect *soto ay madura* (Rp1100), and a selection of ice juices. *Sate* smoke wafts through crowded, noisy rooms. Both are open 0700-0100. Nearby, the **Adbulalie Coffee Shop and Restaurant** has sirloin steak, spaghetti, all kinds of soup, and ice cream—a popular place with the city's affluent. Buy *kayuputih* oil here. **Restoran Kakatoe,** Jl. Perintah, offers a wide variety of what it describes as European food:

salad with fried chicken in garlic butter Rp4500, pizza topped with minced beef and chili peppers Rp7500, Indian-style prawns Rp10,000. The **New Garden Restaurant** on Jl. Pahlawan Revolusi is the best Chinese restaurant in town—crowded even on Monday nights. Consume classical Mandarin fare, with dishes in the Rp5000 range, while an organ and vocalist perform for your dining pleasure. A fun place.

Fruits, Desserts, And Drinks

Pineapple (Rp1250, but much less in season in December) and *durian* (Rp1500, cheaper in May) are unbelievably expensive, so stick with the cheaper indigenous fruits like *pala gula,* sweet-and-sour raw nutmeg; Rp250 for a one-ounce bag. Exquisite fruits such as *rambutan* and mangosteen are available in season. The island's bananas—all 22 varieties—are famous throughout the archipelago for their size and flavor. *Nasi goreng* here is made with plantains cut into very small cubes to resemble rice and prepared in the same way as fried rice. Used for baby food, the largest *pisang tongka langit* grow 50-75 cm in length and grow upward instead of down. *Gandaria,* 10 for Rp700, is a sweet orange plum found only on Ambon. *Ucapi* are yellow, peach-like fruits with translucent pulp—similar to *duku* in taste—10 for Rp400. *Tomi-tomi* are small, sour cherries. *Kutu katak* are branches of bitter berries.

This island's alcoholic *sopi* is a potent palm wine served in back rooms. The best is made in Latere. *Sopi rusa* has a two-month-old deer fetus in the bottle; supposedly possesses curative and strengthening powers. It takes about four glasses, at Rp750 per glass (Rp3000 per bottle), to get a good buzz going. Cold Bintang beer, Rp2000 per bottle.

Spices

The price of nutmeg is not stable, ranging from Rp3000 to Rp8000 per kilo, generally dependent on quality. Buy *minyak cengkeh,* bottles of powerful, burning hot oil made from clove leaves. A small 10 cc bottle runs around Rp650.

OTHER PRACTICALITIES

Entertainment

A number of small movie houses are scattered around town; the one opposite the *stanplats* offers Saturday midnight shows. There are at least four nightclubs in town; the **Santai Bar and Restaurant** has a restaurant, cafeteria, live band, and hostesses. A disco called **Number One** is located on the other side of the bus terminal; Rp5000 cover, large cold beer for Rp2750. Totally dark except for the dance floor; staff circulate constantly, forever refilling your glass. No one seems to drink at the **Top Ten** but Westerners; if you ask for a whiskey it comes from a bottle that's collected dust for a month. Rp7500 cover; large beer Rp4000. High-tech, great audiovisual, beautifully set up. Ambon also offers some karaoke bars; bloody terrible, but popular with the Japanese. Music and other performances are occasionally held at the **Gedung Kesenian** beside the sports hall in Karangpanjang.

Events

Pattimura Anniversary is celebrated on 15 May each year: runners arrive from Saparua carrying lighted torches used to ignite a huge bonfire in front of the Pattimura Monument. Each July the **Darwin-Ambon sailing race** finishes at Amahusu. Celebrations commemorating **the founding of Ambon City** take place each 17 September; festivities include *arumbai mangurebe* (boat racing).

Shopping

Crafts and souvenirs are generally expensive. The only reasonable items are pretty tortoise-shell rings, fans, bracelets, and hair clasps. Ships and *prahu* are dominant themes: inside bottles, with sails made of shells, small ships of tortoiseshell (Rp45,000), or boats made entirely of cloves. In all shapes and sizes, Rp8500-30,000. Flowers and baskets are made of cloves. You'll also find bracelets, necklaces, pendants, wall hangings, flower arrangements, and hairpins made from *kulit mutiara* (mother-of-pearl).

For local crafts, it's best to locate the source and buy directly, though the island's craft villages are becoming hip to the prices in the stores. Compare before you buy. Try **Rumahtiga** for shell and other indigenous crafts.

Peddlers will come around the hotels selling pearls for Rp200,000; if the things are harder than your teeth, they're real pearls. Peddlers also push statues from "Tenggara" for Rp10,000;

don't believe their claims of antiquity. You'll also be confronted with opportunities to buy Ming china, Rp50,000 per plate; *ikat* clothing, Rp30,000 after bargaining; and precious stones from Biak and Java.

The city has several souvenir shops. Up to 50% of the crafts come from Tanatoraja, Bali, or other islands, so ask before you buy. Shops specialize in shellwork, clove crafts, *sarung*, *kayuputih* and *lawang* oil. Visit the Chinese antique shop **Toko Lima,** Jl. J. Latu Harhary A/III/5, for exquisite blue-and-white ceramics. Also check out the souvenir shops along Jl. Pattimura and Jl. A.Y. Patty; **Toko Sulawesi** on Jl. A.Y. Patty has a very complete selection of souvenirs. **Murni,** also on Jl. A.Y. Patty, offers jewelry and handicrafts; good service. Just down the street is **Umum,** with gold and mother-of-pearl.

Tempat Masyarakat Maluku Tenggara is a cottage industry where Tanimbar-style weaving is produced. **Kantor Perindustrian,** in Karangpanjang, also sells crafts. *Kayuputih* oil is processed and bottled on Ambon, used as a surface balm for itching and may be swallowed for a stomach ache. Most attractively packaged by **Abdulalie** on Jl. Sultan Abdulalie; Rp500-900. The place also sells Minyak Kulit Lawang, which is twice as expensive; this is a hot oil for itching, rheumatism, and the healing of cuts. Also buy pure, green clove oil here for only Rp1000 per bottle—if the place hasn't lost the key to the showcase.

Services

The **tourist office,** Dinas Pariwisata Dati I Maluku, is on the ground floor of *kantor gubernor* on Jl. Pattimura. Open Mon.-Thurs. 0800-1400, Friday until 1130, Saturday until 1300. The officer for tourism, Mr. Oratmangun, can answer your questions and make it easier for you to visit places that present bureaucratic difficulties. Dinas Pariwisata also rents snorkeling equipment and masks: full tanks (Rp17,500 per day), fins, and masks (Rp2500).

The best doctors work in **Umum Hospital** where there are specialists (one internist has been trained in Italy); **Tentara,** the military hospital, has good doctors and service. One-hour photo service for Kodak, Agfa, and Fuji at **Union Color Photo Service,** Jl. A.Y. Patty 3, tel. 3349 or 3569; Rp250 per print.

Change U.S., U.K., or Australian currency at **Bank Dagang Negara,** Jl. Raya Pattimura. Compare the rates with those of **Bank Expor Impor Indonesia** just down from the post office, also on Jl. Raya Pattimura; open Monday to Friday 0800-1300, Saturday 0800-1100. Probably the best place to change money is the **Bank Of Central Asia,** open 0800-1400 Mon.-Fri., Saturday 0800-1200. If using your Visa, staff will probably have to ring Jakarta; remember the two-hour time difference between here and there. The **post office** is on Jl. Raya Pattimura; the *wartel* lies opposite. Ambon's telephone code is 0911. *Kantor imigrasi* is on Jl. Dr. Kaijadu, a new building opposite a small church; get there by *bemo* from the *stanplats*, Rp200. Another small immigration office at the airport stamps your passport upon arrival. Your hotel usually registers you with the police. Some travelers don't even bother registering and get clean away with it.

TRANSPORTATION

Getting There

Garuda flies to Ambon from Surabaya via Ujung Pandang every day; Merpati makes the same flight three times a week. From Manado, Merpati schedules flights six times a week. Take a minibus, *bemo*, or taxi over the narrow road from the airport via Passo, or the vehicle ferry from Rumahtiga to Ambon City (Rp150). The Merpati bus might take you into the city office for free.

The Pelni boat KM *Rinjani* sails about every two weeks from Jakarta via Surabaya, Ujung Pandang, Bau Bau, Ambon, and Sorong. In front of Terminal Luar Kota (or Terminal Mardika Pantai) on Jl. Mardika Pantai is the small boat harbor of Dermaga Pelayaran Rakyat, where small *kapal* from other Malukan islands call.

Getting Around

Since the city consists of only a half-dozen main streets, stretching out along the waterfront for three km, you can easily walk to just about anywhere. The harbor is located at the northern end of Jl. Pahlawan Revolusi. Thousands of *becak* are color-coded red, yellow, and white and are only permitted to carry passengers on the days designated for each color. Many of these people will quote rates akin to robbery; bargain hard. From Terminal Pasar Mardika, *bemo* travel out to the suburbs—Air Salobar, four km; Karangpanjang, 4.5 km; Ahuru, six km; Batumerah, two km; Tantui, 3.5 km; Dermaga (ferry to Rumahtiga), 4.5 km. The bus fare is Rp200 to anywhere in town. Taxis are available at the taxi stand down from the Amboina Hotel; Rp4000 per hour.

Getting Away

Merpati, the most active carrier in the region, flies to Ternate, Amahai, Bandaneira, Manado, Tual, Saumlaki, and Galela via Ternate. During the wet season (April-Aug.), many of the small unsurfaced landing strips on Maluku's outer islands are unfit for aircraft. Garuda is the only airline that flies to Jayapura, Biak, and Sorong. Two Garuda flights per week head to Timika on the south coast of Irian Jaya, then continue to Jayapura. Mandala and Merpati fly to Ujung Pandang, Surabaya, and Jakarta.

If you miss your plane, camp on the pretty beach of Air Manis in Laha village, only two km from the airport. Airline offices: Garuda, Jl. Jen. A. Yani, tel. (0911) 2481; Merpati, Jl. A. Rhebok, tel. 42480 or 3480; Mandala, Jl. A.Y. Patty SH 4/18, tel. 2444. Domestic airport tax is Rp1400.

Ambon is a center for interisland sea transport on either small *kapal motor* or bigger ships to Central, North, and Southeast Maluku. For the latest fares and ships, visit the **Dermaga Pelayaran Rakyat** at the northern end of Jl. Sultan Hairun and ask the friendly *syahbandar*. Also inquire at the Pelni office, Jl. Pelabuhan 1, tel. 34. Timetables change constantly. During the monsoon season sea travel is restricted in South Maluku, though the weather doesn't hinder larger seagoing vessels. Larger boats have more reliable departure times and more comfortable passages. For the smaller boats, March-April is the best time to travel around Banda, Kai, and the Tanimbars. Clove boats to East Ceram and other Central and North Malukan ports mostly travel during the clove season September to December when seas are calm.

From Dermaga Pelayaran Rakyat, catch boats to **Taniwel** (Rp10,000, eight hours) and other Ceramese ports. From Tulehu on Ambon's east coast, boats depart to many locations on Ceram. For example, board *spetbot* to

Kairatu (1.5 hours), diesel-powered boats to **Amahai** (three hours). Boats from Tulehu to **Tehoru** leave irregularly except during clove season. Charging around Rp15,000, the vessels sail right through the night (eight hours), an uncomfortable but exciting voyage. Between Tulehu and Waai there's a harbor called **Hurnala** for the big fast boats to Pararua and points on Ceram. From Hitu, catch *prahu* and the more expensive motorized *prahu* to **Waiputih, Whu, Waijase,** and **Piru.**

The Kai, Tanimbar, and Banda islands can be reached by small boat from Ambon; allow at least 10 days roundtrip. Perintis may have ships sailing from Ambon to Banda, Tual, Elat, Dobo, or Larat depending on demand for cargo. Pelni has two ships running regularly. KM *Niaga XII* runs the long route: Ambon-Banda-Tual-Elat-Dobo-Larat-Saumlaki-Tual-Banda-Ambon; *Niagas* takes the "shorter" route: Ambon-Banda-Tual-Elat-Dobo-Larat-Saumlaki-Tual-Banda-Ambon. Be aware that on these boats people are packed like beetles under miserable hygienic conditions, though there's some relief in crew cabin space rented at steep prices.

For **Namlea** on Pulau Buru, take *kapal motor* from Ambon's Dermaga Pelayaran Rakyat (Rp7500), leaving every night. To Ternate there are twice-monthly Perintis ships: *Baruna Bakti* and the smaller, long-routed *Pendulu.* Rustbuckets, such as the KM *Tolsuti*, are rare. To Ujung Pandang and Surabaya, Pelni's KM *Rinjani* runs twice a month between Ambon, Bau Bau, Ujung Pandang, Surabaya, and Jakarta.

Takes 10 days. Pelni's KM *Rinjani* sails every other week to Sorong and Jayapura in Irian Jaya.

Bemo and buses leave often from Terminal Pasar Mardika. For destinations outside the city minibuses depart from the new terminal at Mardika Pantai. This 48- by 22-km island has only around 200 km of asphalted roads. To get to Soya, take a bus (line 1) from Terminal Pasar Mardika.

Tours

Ambon travel agencies offer local and intraisland nature/cultural tours. For groups of three to five, **Sumber Budi Tour and Travel,** Jl. Mardika 2/16, tel. (0911) 3205, offers a three-day, two-night sightseeing tour of Ambon City and nearby nutmeg and clove plantations (Rp420,000 pp); a three-day, two-night snorkeling, skin diving, and safari fishing tour (Rp840,000 pp); and a six-day historical tour of the Banda Islands (Rp1 million pp). Its most creative tour is the all-day lobster-catching excursion off Saparua (Rp1.1 million pp); you get to eat your catch afterwards. See Mr. J.G.B. Nanlohy.

Natrabu Tour and Travel, Jl. Rijali 53, tel. 3537, offers such exotic group tours as "Babi Island Diving" (Rp1.2 million pp); "Amboina City Tour" (Rp46,200 per person for a two-person group); tours to Waai (Rp63,000 per person) and Soya, Sirimau, Ema (Rp132,000). Most prices include transfer service from airport, guide, a choice of accommodations, breakfast and lunch, airfare from Ambon, and all transport costs. For tickets, see **PT Daya Patal,** Jl. Said Perintah SK 11/27A, tel. 3529 or 41136.

AROUND AMBON ISLAND

LEITIMOR PENINSULA

Take a *bemo* to Benteng, then turn right and climb two hours to the top of **Gunung Nona** for relief from the noise and heat of the city.

Air Salobar offers a sometimes quiet beach, always rocky shoreline, and old fishing village. Close by, near the sea and five km from Ambon, is **Batu Capeo,** a gigantic hat-shaped coral rock along a small beach. Legend has it a man lost his top hat in the sea; it returned to land as this

rock. Three km from Air Salobar is Amahusu, where there are *rumah makan.*

Kusu Kusu is the largest cave on Ambon, well known and a fairly easy walk from the city. Take a minibus out to the *rumah sakit* (hospital), then turn down Jl. Mangga Dua. It's an hour's walk from the hospital to the cave. From the main entrance down into the cave is a steep descent, but once inside it's mostly level. A few bats inside; expect a muddy floor.

Batu Merah is a suburb northeast of Ambon City on the road to Passo, Rp150 by *bemo.* Tortoiseshell and other crafts are made nearby.

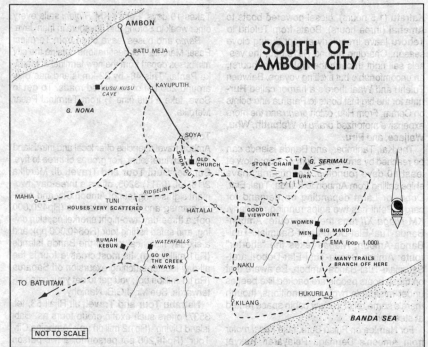

SOUTH OF
AMBON CITY

AMBON
BATU MEJA
KUSU KUSU CAVE
KAYUPUTIH
G. NONA
SOYA
SHORTCUT
OLD CHURCH
STONE CHAIR
G. SERIMAU
URN
MAHIA
RIDGELINE
TUNI
HOUSES VERY SCATTERED
HATALAI
GOOD VIEWPOINT
WOMEN
MEN
BIG MANDI
EMA (pop. 1,000)
RUMAH KEBUN
WATERFALLS
GO UP THE CREEK A WAYS
NAKU
MANY TRAILS BRANCH OFF HERE
TO BATUITAM
KILANG
HUKURILA
BANDA SEA
NOT TO SCALE

© MOON PUBLICATIONS, INC.

See the old mosque in this Muslim village.
Check out the scores of tuna boats moored at
Galala, Rp125 (six km) from Ambon by *bemo.*
From Galala, take the relaxing Rp125 ferry ride
across Ambon Bay to Rumahtiga. A car and
passenger ferry also makes the crossing from
Galala to Poka (Rp100), the location of Pattimura University. An oceanographic research
station was established here by the Russians.
Try the local specialty, smoked tuna, sold at
warung (Rp1500). A Chinese family produces
crafts here. **Waiame** is a white-sand, clear-water
beach west of Rumahtiga. Nice view of the city,
particularly at dusk.

You can reach **Halong** from Ambon for
Rp200 (seven km) by minibus. At this point it's
only 1.5 km across the bay as the fish swim;
over 30 km if you follow the shore road. **Passo
and Baguala** are Rp250 by *bemo* from Ambon,
on both sides of the narrow isthmus joining Ambon's two peninsulas. **Natsepa Beach,** just east
of Passo and 14 km from Ambon (Rp500, 45
minutes by minibus) is a large, beautiful, white-

sand beach with a view over Leitimor. It seems
all of Ambon empties out to bathe and picnic
here on Sundays. **Toisapu** is a more secluded beach 18 km from Ambon.

In the village of **Amahusu,** Rp150 and eight
km southwest of Ambon City, are radiant marine
gardens only a short distance from the beach.
Hire an outrigger. Good swimming here, and a
panoramic view of Hitu Peninsula. This village
has an *angkutan laut,* the finishing point for the
five-day Darwin-Ambon sailing race held annually in July. Farther to the southeast, 26 km from
Ambon, is **Namalatu,** with clear, calm water
surrounded by a white sandy beach and coral
reefs. Good bathing and fishing. Coconut trees
along the beach provide shade and refreshment. There's a guesthouse here as well.

Latuhalat is a Rp325, 45-minute (17 km)
minibus or *bemo* ride from Ambon along a
bumpy, snake-like road. Between Amahusu and
Eri notice the numerous Japanese WW II pillboxes. Latuhalat, on the south coast of Leitimor Peninsula, features a beautiful secluded

beach, coral reefs, and good scuba diving and snorkeling (wear thongs because of razor-sharp coral). Best time to visit is September to December, when the seas are calm. Farther up the coast from Latuhalat is **Nama Latu,** where you can see up to 15 meters below the water. You don't need a mask, only a snorkel. Or just stick your head under the water; it's like swimming inside an aquarium.

Soya

There's an air of mysticism about this place. It's said that the last 32 Portuguese families in Maluku were driven to this mountain village in the early 17th century; they held onto their Catholic faith until finally converted to Protestantism. The old church in Soya was built by the Portuguese in 1817. Nearby are huge boulders surrounding a square, once a *baileo.* From the church, turn left and follow a small, twisting footpath, keeping to the right for 15 minutes to the top of Gunung Serimau. If you find the right vantage point, the view from here takes in the long inlet that separates the two peninsulas. On Gunung Serimau there's a foot-high sacred stone chair surrounded by a hedge, believed to be where the first *raja* sat. The trench surrounding the throne area was dug by the Dutch. A WW II concrete pillbox, overlooking Ambon Bay, stands 10 meters away. In a slope in back of the throne is the *tampayang keramat,* a clay water urn which never goes dry. It's visited by locals seeking good fortune, a cure for illness, or a perfect marriage partner. Locals planning to leave the area will take water from the urn to give themselves protection wherever they go. The original urn was stolen in 1980, replaced by the present one.

To reach Soya, take a *bemo* from Ambon. If you want to walk, a red clay path leads southeast of Ambon up to this village (two hours) through a countryside full of steep-sided valleys and rainy hills covered in buffalo grass, palm groves, and Amboina conifers.

Vicinity Of Soya

Naku lies about 15 minutes farther along the path from Soya. Descendants of the Portuguese still live here. The name of the neighboring village, **Hatalai,** is very close in spelling to the town of Atalaia in Ribatejo, Portugal. The men's shirts are the same style as those once worn in Ribatejo, and the *kapitan* of Hatalai, Antonio

Parera, will perform an old dance uncannily similar to the 17th-century fandango of the Ribatejo district. Another way to reach Hatalai is to take a *bemo* from Ambon to Kayuputih (Rp300), then walk up the hill. A fantastic waterfall lies along the path from Naku to **Batuitam.** Take the path to Batuitam and cross the river; the next river has the waterfall. You can also reach Batuitam from Kusu Kusu via Mahia, then return to the city via Hatalai. It's also possible to walk on a jungle path from Soya to Ema; on the way you pass a point on Gunung Serimau where you can see the whole south coast. **Ema** is a friendly village on top of the mountain. From Ema walk down to the coastal villages of **Hukurila** or **Lehari.**

Rutung

Located on the south coast of Leitimor, this village is a 24-km motorcycle ride from Ambon right across the center of the peninsula. Pass through avenues of eucalyptus trees, over rolling rhododendron-blanketed hills, past dense forests with beautiful mauve orchids growing out of giant tree trunks, and clear streams at the bottom of ravines. At last there's a chain of hills before the coast and an incredible panorama of the Banda Sea and long sweeping stretches of yellow beaches. Then descend down to the village. **Hutumuri,** a bit northeast of Rutung, has a complete shell orchestra. Hire an outrigger, *kapal layar,* or motorboat to take you from Rutung to Passo, passing limestone cliffs and caves, tiny bays, sea gardens of pink coral, amber seaweed, and multicolored tropical fish along the way.

HITU PENINSULA

By *bemo* Rp450 (24 km) from Ambon, the small harbor of **Tulehu** is the departure point for *spetbot* to Ceram, Saparua, and the Haruku Islands. Coming into town, the first structure you see is the silver-domed mosque. From Tulehu you can view Pulau Haruku in the distance. Curative hot springs are located along the beach just south of Tulehu; a hotel is nearby.

Waai

This friendly, prosperous Christian village, Rp550 by minibus (31 km) from Ambon, is home to people originally from Hawaii—hence the curious name. People here even look Dutch Polynesian. At the bottom of nearby Gunung Salahutu is a sacred pool beneath a 60-meter-high waterfall; holy fish appear here from under the sea. Watch a 10-year-old girl call a giant eel by thumping on the water, then feed it eggs. If the eel shows up, it means a bright future for all who see it. You can get in and swim among the eels, which are very large, sometimes four inches thick. Keep your fingers and legs together if you don't wish to be bitten and nipped.

From Waai it's a five- to six-hour climb to the summit of 1,038-meter **Gunung Salahutu.** Hire your guide from the family of Marcus Watatula. Fee? Free. Hard, hands-and-knees climbing, but worth it for the stunning views from the top. Before you reach the summit you'll pass through a sacred forest where it is forbidden to speak or otherwise generate noise. In this place thrive trees similar to the Brazilian cherry, trunks covered in long club moss, dripping with great droplets of dew. Fine, rare, magical rainforest, sunlight streaming in through breaks in the billowing, wispy clouds.

Liang

The journey to Liang, Rp750 (41 km) by minibus from Ambon, takes you along the coast via Galala, Passo, and Tulehu; at low tide you can see rusting shipwrecks transformed into sea gardens. Liang is known for its friendly people, good beach, and swimming.

Hitulama And Vicinity

Thirty km north of Ambon is the oldest Islamic *kampung* on the island; some believe it was founded by Arab or Javanese traders as early as the 11th century. The Portuguese landed at Hitu in the 16th century; you can still see the ruins of their first trading post. The *kapal motor* for northern Ceram leaves from Hitulama. The section of coastline from Hitu to Liang is very rugged; a fairly good road leads east to **Mamala,** where an unusual traditional event takes place each year at the end of Ramadan. Now a form of ritualized warfare, in *sapulidi* (broom-fighting) combatants whip each other with coconut-fiber brooms. A *dukun* treats the open wounds with Mamala oil, which is said to have almost magical curative qualities.

From Mamala, proceed northeast to **Morela.** Though there doesn't even seem to be a trail along parts of this coast, persevere. East of Morela is the old stone fortress of **Kapahala,** captured by the Dutch in 1646. Follow the track into a hilly area past weirdly shaped caves and bizarre rock formations, finally ascending stone stairs to the fortress, protected on three sides by a precipitous drop. Inside are graves of Kapahala's suicidal defenders.

Hila

A village of great tradition 12 km west of Hitulama on a bumpy road, or a Rp1000 (45-km, 1.5-hour) minibus ride from Ambon. The air is heavy with the scent of mace, nutmeg, and cloves, laid out on *tikar* in the streets to dry. The people of Hila venerate several Portuguese helmets, looking upon them as protective mascots and sources of strength. The entire village and its 300 screaming children adopt you. A Christian church here, built in 1772, features a Dutch-inscribed plaque.

Kaitetu

In neighboring Kaitetu, visit the blockhouse, **Benteng Amsterdam** (1659), which has an unfortunate location (next to a kindergarten) along the bay; schoolchildren throng around you. It's not certain how much of this trading post was of Portuguese and how much of Dutch construction. Nothing is left but the walls. Near the blockhouse is the oldest church on Ambon, still in use, dating from 1780 with a Dutch-inscribed plaque. Children will paddle you down the coast to view more ruins, or just start walking. From Kaitetu, walk along a dreamy pebble beach; the giant island of Ceram looms in the distance. Reach the clove plantations by climbing high up into the hills behind Hila; follow the road along the beach. To prevent another devastating Hitu War, in the 16th century the Dutch built Fort Rotterdam in Lima, 16 km southwest of Hila. It's presently dilapidated.

Alang

A Christian coastal village on the southwest tip of the island, reachable mornings by ferry from Ambon pier (Rp750). Only larger boats can make the passage during the "east season" (April-July), when high winds and waves make the sea hazardous. For over 400 years Alang has guarded the entrance to Ambon Bay. The village sits unsteadily on the rocky terraced slopes rising steeply from the bright green sea. Because of the lack of level space, its houses are built very close together on very few streets. Nutmeg and cloves are the main crops; Alang is also known for its *kanari* nuts. People in this village love to sing, especially folk songs. Listen to the choirs and flute orchestras in the large church.

OFFSHORE ISLANDS

Pulau Pombo And Pulau Kasa

Pombo and Kasa are two small undeveloped, unprotected island marine reserves near Ambon. Both contain nesting sites for seabirds, megapodes, and an endemic species of lizard, *Hydrosaurus amboinensis*. Pulau Kasa has the larger and better reefs, but both have suffered from fishing with explosives, said to have been learned from the Japanese during the war. Whatever you take onto the islands, please take it out again. Information and a visitor's pass should first be obtained from the Oceanographic Institute at Pattimura University in Poka. A small run-down shelter exists on Pulau Pombo, but there's no fresh water on either island. Camping is easy and pleasant, with no mosquitos.

Kasa (60 hectares) is the larger of the two islands, still well forested despite continued disturbance by local fishermen and wood collectors. Found here are the megapode bird and numerous pigeons. The megapode builds a mound of leaves and other bits of vegetation which, in the process of rotting, provides sufficient heat to incubate its eggs. To dig themselves out, the chicks hatch fully clawed.

The small, uninhabited coral atoll of Pulau Pombo ("Pigeon Island"), off Ambon's east coast, is covered with shrubs and nesting trees for birds. There's a sandy white reef-sheltered beach, sweeping panoramas, untouched snorkeling sites, and stunning sunsets.

Pulau Pombo is 30 minutes by *kapal motor* from Tulehu or Waai on the east coast of Ambon. You can reach Pulau Kasa in three hours by *kapal motor*. Tulehu and Waai are easily accessible from Ambon's terminal on a paved road; the minibus takes you straight to the wharf.

SAPARUA

A small coral isle of 202 square km, 74 east of Ambon. There's a big clove plantation in the center and many other plantations dot the coast. Saparua is very hilly, rising steeply from the sea. The island's main city and capital, Saparua, has a big market Wednesday and Saturday. There are two ruins and an old church on the island. A 15-minute *bemo* ride from the ferry landing is a nice hotel; here swim tame *dugong*.

History

As a center of nutmeg and clove cultivation, Saparua has a torrid history. Spice has been traded from coastal villages on this and adjacent islands for over 500 years. Old Dutch fortifications litter the coasts, most obliterated. Saparua was the site of a revolt under the leadership of Thomas Matulessy, alias Kapitan Pattimura; the island still celebrates Pattimura Day in honor of this national hero. A flaming torch is carried by relay runners from each village until it arrives for the official ceremony in Ambon, where it's used to ignite a huge bonfire.

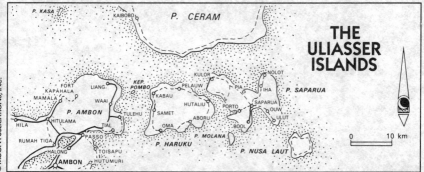

Sights

Visit the well-restored Dutch fort of **Duurstede,** its battlements and cannon still in place, pointing over the rocky shore. The fort was attacked in 1817 by Pattimura and his forces. Opposite the fort is a **museum** with miniature three-dimensional displays depicting the history of the fort and the life of Pattimura. **Saniri Hill** is a historic spot where *kapitan* (warlords) from all over the Uliassers gathered to choose a commander; Pattimura was selected and sworn in as their leader. At **Nolot,** about 13 from Saparua town, there's an old *baileo,* the traditional Malukan meetinghouse.

Waisisilia, a white coral beach, was the site of a decisive battle between Pattimura and the Dutch. In **Haria** village, Pattimura's battle dress is in the custody of a village elder, Manuhutu, and may be viewed upon request. **Ouw** is a big traditional pottery center which turns out most of the island's distinctive earthenware. This is not art pottery, but pots, water urns, and sago molds intended for everyday use.

Accommodations

In Kota Saparua stay at **Penginapan Ibu Sien Pietersz,** located on the road to the fort. Rooms cost Rp12,500 with breakfast and afternoon tea. Also try **Penginapan Lisa Beli,** on Jl. Rumnah Sakit Umum. **Siri Serini** is a *losmen* in a new two-story building off the main road, a 10-minute walk from the beach. Rooms with *mandi*

and breakfast cost Rp22,000 s, Rp24,000 d. The **Mahu Village Resort** offers bungalows with meals; Rp50,000 d. Visit the sago plantation nearby. The owners will arrange excursions to other villages, snorkeling, and diving. Very beautiful setting in a coconut grove. It's also possible to arrange accommodations with local families.

Getting There And Around

Take ferries from Tulehu on Ambon (Rp3000), leaving at least twice each morning, docking in Haria. Speedboats for the same price. Boats to Saparua also leave from Waai, but less often. This comfortable passage takes you past numerous islands, with Ceram looming in the background. From Haria you can grab a *bemo* to Ouw and the other side of the island. Minibuses travel from Haria to Kota Separua; from there you can take buses to destinations all over the island.

Lovely beaches and curative hot springs are found on **Nusa Laut,** an island southeast of Saparua and the most westerly of the Uliassers. On market days, Wednesday and Saturday, it's possible to ride a motorboat from Saparua to Nusa Laut; otherwise arrange a charter. The isle of **Haruku** lies seven km east of Ambon, between Saparua and Ambon. Once an important clove-growing island, there are ruins of Portuguese fortifications here, as well as nice views and hot sulphur springs esteemed for curing skin diseases.

CERAM

THE LAND

This primitively beautiful island stretches 340 km from east to west, with an area of 17,354 square km—about half the size of Holland. It's the second largest and one of the least known islands of the region. Ceram is very wooded, watered, and mountainous. The island's mountains rise over 2,000 meters; the highest peak in the center, Gunung Murkele Besar, reaches 3,027 meters in height. Some of its impenetrable central forests have never been explored. Ceram's northern coasts are covered in long stretches of swamplands, while the southern coasts are steep and rocky. The island's rivers are almost useless for navigation and there are few natural harbors. Luckily, Ceram's difficult terrain has prevented extensive exploitation of its resources. A rough and wild place, Ceram was of little value to Dutch colonists.

The island's coasts were settled early by Malays; the Alfuros, primitive and indomitable headhunters, lived in the interior. The Dutch maintained four trading posts; at Wahai were European coffee and cacao plantations. European fortresses are today in ruins, smothered in vegetation. The first man to go around the world was an Alfuro slave from Ceram named Henry, a member of Magellan's crew whom the navigator had taken to Europe on his first voyage.

From a traveler's standpoint, there are two reasons to visit Ceram: the clean white beaches on the south coast, many accessible from Masohi, and the unforgettable walk through the center of the island from Hatumetan to Wahai. But you don't need to tackle the trans-Ceram walk to see native life; just get away from the coasts and you'll start to find indigenous people.

Climate

This island has different weather entirely from Ambon's; if it's clear on Ceram, it's probably raining on Ambon. Most of Maluku has—for Indonesia—a unique rainy season but in the central part of Ceram rainfall is fairly even throughout the year, averaging 200 cm. The best season for visiting the inner valleys is June to Oc-

tober; if traveling to Ceram by sea, avoid the south coast during July and August. The north coast is exposed to strong winds Jan.-March.

Flora And Fauna

Ceram's steep hills, sharp ridges, and deep river valleys have protected most of its endemic flora and fauna from excessive hunting, export, or loss of habitat. As in neighboring Irian Jaya, there are few native mammals—no monkeys, cats, or squirrels—and only several marsupial species, mainly cuscus and bandicoots. There are 13 species of fruit bats, 11 insectivorous bats, three phalangers, and two species of mongoose. Some mammals have been introduced by humans; in eastern Ceram wild pigs come down to the beach to hunt for crabs. Numerous deer roam the forests around Sawai; beaters and dogs force them to jump from granite cliffs into the sea, where they're retrieved by hunters in rowboats.

The island's birdlife is probably the most colorful in all of Maluku: bright-colored lories, parrots, cockatoos, kingfishers, and pigeons, as well as cassowaries, megapodes, hornbills, friar birds, honeyeaters, and white eyes. The pigeons are particularly eye-catching, especially the golden Nicobar pigeon which lives deep in the forest; it has bright green feathers contrasting with a snow-white tail. Another remarkable species is the racket-tailed kingfisher; its head, nape, and shoulders are light blue, the beak a brilliant coral, its back and wings a rich purple, with two long tailfeathers fanning out like a spoon at the tip.

There are tree-climbing fish along the shores of Ceram, rare purplish pythons in jungle shadows, crocodiles and lizards splashing in estuaries. Ceram is famous for its bright butterflies; be on the lookout for the striking *Papilio ulysses* (the Blue Mountain butterfly), which ranges from Ceram to the Solomon Islands.

Economy

Ceram's principal source of income is petroleum products. With its virgin forests and hundreds of kilometers of wilderness coasts, the island's biggest potential growth industry is tourism.

Except for limited employment at the Bula oil center on the northeast coast, not many opportunities exist for earning a living. The island's principal products are resin, coral, fish, rice, maize, sugarcane, spices, coconuts, and fruits. The native peoples of the interior still depend upon forest products such as roots and wild sago, cultivate coconuts, and sell copra and Agathis resin (*damar*), cockatoos, and lories. Some natives earn a secondary cash income cultivating spices and vegetables.

THE PEOPLE

An ethnologically rich island, Ceram's local name is Nusa Ina ("Mother Island"), possibly alluding to the fact that the founding aristocratic families of Ambon and other central Malukan islands originated here. In the east live the tribal peoples; the west is home to more Malays. The bulk of the island's population lives in the coastal areas; successive waves of alien ethnic groups pushed the original Ceramese inland, yet a considerable admixture is evident among the coastal peoples. Among the most notorious headhunters in the old Dutch East Indies, the native Ceramese proved very difficult to govern. In the 19th century, the Dutch administration resettled many villages from the inaccessible interior to the coast to better control the indigenous people. Today comparatively few people live in the interior.

The inland villagers, courteous and friendly to travelers, are completely different from the coastal people. In the west and along the southern coasts live the largest concentration of these deutero-Malay groups; on the far west coasts

are located completely ethnic Javanese villages. At 90-140 people per square km, Ceram's southern coast is one of the most densely populated areas of Maluku.

When traveling this island be sure to ask permission before photographing women. Expensive hotels and a few less expensive *losmen* are found in Amahai and Masohi. Inland, you may stay with missionaries; if you're in a real bind the police will always put you up or turn you on to a place. Out in the villages fruits are as cheap as you'll find in Indonesia. Rice cultivation, except by the *transmigrasi* settlers, is unknown. As rice is imported you'll generally find the village people eating *papeta* and other sago products, tapioca roots or potatoes, and vegetables.

Tribal Peoples

When the Portuguese arrived in the region in the late 16th century, they found the natives living only in the mountain regions. Today, all interior tribes, such as the Borera and Nuaulu peoples, live in fairly permanent settlements and practice shifting cultivation which provides for more than half of their subsistence needs. These indigenous people have a tripartite mode of production in which hunting and gathering still plays a surprisingly large role. Some of the best stick and staff fighters in Indonesia, bows and arrows are still commonly used by the mountain people of western Ceram—a tall, excitable, dark-complexioned people.

Until relatively recently, the taking of heads was an essential part of the ceremonial life of some tribes. The number of heads determined a man's status in the community and was indicated by black rings on the belt of his *tjidako*. Heads were given to the Lord of the Heavens, portrayed in the form of concentric circles symbolizing the sun. The Alfuro reputation for savagery persists, undeservedly, to this day. Every so often a rumor spreads that they're seeking a head to be used, for example, in a bridge-dedication ceremony. Resident Westerners then post guards in their living rooms, and people stay in at night. Even the Ambonese will tell you they feel more secure when the rainy season cuts Ceram off from Ambon. The central districts of Ceram are sparsely inhabited by mixed Alfuro tribes, with less warlike traditions. The marshes and hills of eastern Ceram shelter a Veddoid people, the Bonfia, who are shy, peaceful, and almost untouched by any cultural influence from the outside world.

Religion

In the past, the people's religion was a form of animism, a belief that stones, trees, forests, and mountains are populated by spirits, often the souls of the dead (*nitu nitu*). Their religion was similar to the old religion of the Bataks of North Sumatra. Ceram was famous for its village *kakihan* societies made up exclusively of adult males. These groups practiced periodic initiation of pubescent boys by means of ritually "devouring" the initiates by a crocodile figure, sacrificing pigs on stone altars, and issuing frightening noises from spirit houses—strikingly similar to certain New Guinea rites.

Later Islamization, combined with the inexorable Indonesianization of the territory, has made deep inroads into these native religious systems. Though Ceram does retain its socioreligious institutions to a higher degree than anywhere else in Central Maluku, out of a total native population of around 60,000 today 16,000 are Islamic and 12,000 Christian; the remainder are animists.

TRANSPORTATION

Getting There

Fly once weekly from Ambon to Amahai with Merpati for about Rp18,000. Merpati also flies between Amahai and Langgur. From Waai (Pulau Ambon), get boats to Kamal, Nurue, Waisamu, Hatusua, and Kairatu. From Tulehu on Ambon there are boats to Masohi, Tehoru (south coast), Kairatu, Seruawan, Tihulale, Ka-

marian, Rumahkai, Latu, Liang, Waraka, Makariki, Sepa, Rutah, and Tamilu.

Getting Around

Plan on walking; motorized transport is scarce. You need three months to really get around the island, as Ceram's traditional culture is only found deep in the interior. Roads are restricted to the immediate area around the principal towns of Amahai, Masohi, and Wahai. The east is quite remote and inaccessible. A trans-Ceram highway to the north coast is under construction; in other places, land travel in the interior is entirely over tracks. To get to nearby coastal villages from Amahai you can also take *prahu,* though not all boats run daily. If you want to head for the eastern part of the island, allow four or five days. If there's no intraisland boat transport, return to Tulehu on Pulau Ambon, then depart again for another point on Ceram.

SIGHTS

Masohi-Amahai Area

The *kampung* where the boat docks is **Soahuku,** and it costs Rp300 to get up to Masohi, the government headquarters. Between Soahuku and Masohi is Amahai, consisting of only a school, post office, a few houses, and a stretch of fields and woods. Stay in the town's *penginapan.* Amahai can be very bureaucratic; you might register at one police station, then a cop will come around and complain you didn't register at his station too. People might even ap-

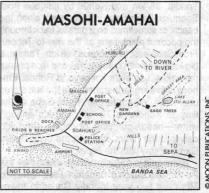

MASOHI-AMAHAI

NOT TO SCALE

© MOON PUBLICATIONS, INC.

proach you on the street to ask to see your passport, pretending to be police. *Kantor pos* are found in Amahai and Masohi; there are no more for a long way east.

Nice walks in this area: a short one out around **Tanjung Kwako** (wear shorts and thongs or you'll never get the vicious grass seeds out of your clothes), and a longer jaunt up to **Lake Itu Allah**—not for the novice trailfinder. Here there's a sago swamp; the lake itself is at the end of a long, swampy meadow. **Kawa Pool** is located roughly between Amahai and Masohi, easily reached from either town. The pool, which runs down to the sea via a small stream, contains sacred fish and eels.

With its thousand-kilometer coastline, many Ceram beaches are scenic and suitable for swimming and fishing. Among the more accessible are **Tanjung Kwako, Rutah, Uneputi, Piru, Elpaputih,** and **Soleman,** all in southern Ceram and reached by minibus from Amahai or Masohi. **Marsegu** is a coral atoll in the western part of the island, 60 km from Ambon, where 33 species of sea lilies are found.

You can also take a minibus from Amahai to Sepa (24 km) and beyond. On this road east you pass through the villages of **Rutah** and **Rohoa** where some Nuaulu tribesmen live, descendants of aborigines. Regular motorboats make the run from Masohi to Tehora.

The Walk East

Popular with travelers is the walk east along the fascinating coastal track from Sepa to Haya, Tehoru, Saunulu, Yaputih, and Hatumetan; allow at least a week. The road goes as far as Tamilu, 36 km and Rp800 by minibus from Soahuku. From Sepa you can walk along the beach, or sometimes on a parallel track through the coconut plantations all the way to Tehoru. From Sepa east to **Rohoa** is five km; **Tamilu,** a big *kampung* with many stores and nice peanut pancakes, lies eight km beyond Rohoa. **Empera** is five km farther; here are the last stores until Haya, 40 km farther. From Sepa all the way to Tehoru is 70 km. There's enough water—needs purifying, of course—and you can ford the rivers easily in the dry season. Camp or stay with the *bapak raja*.

Namasula is a Muslim village where they ask Rp400 for a bunch of bananas. **Salamaha** and **Misa** are two very friendly Christian towns

where the people might treat you to *kelapa muda* if you're thirsty. **Haya** is a big, mostly Muslim town. Twelve km later, the trail ends at **Tehoru,** which is the *camat's* headquarters but has no post office. Luxury items such as blocks or ice or a box of matches are expensive (Rp400 each). From Tehoru, take a *prahu* across the bay to Mosso; if you try to walk, you'll have to cross an estuary.

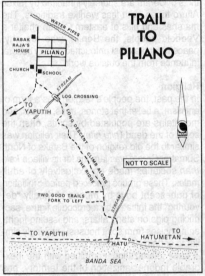

TRAIL TO PILIANO

NOT TO SCALE

BANDA SEA

Piliano

Isolated tribal villages are located 30 km north of Yaputih, but the trail from Yaputih is too difficult; instead take trails north from Hatumetan or Hatu. Piliano is a half-day walk uphill from just west of Hatu. From Hatumetan, two trails lead to Piliano; to avoid a big ford, walk west from Hatu and turn inland just before the first large stream. Cross the river a bit beyond on a log. Farther along are two main forks—go right, because the left heads for Yaputih. After this, take the best-used trail inland. Go down to the big river and cross a stick bridge (*titian*), then climb up through clove groves to Piliano.

Manusela Reserve

There are two approaches to this 100,000-hectare forest reserve. From the south, take a

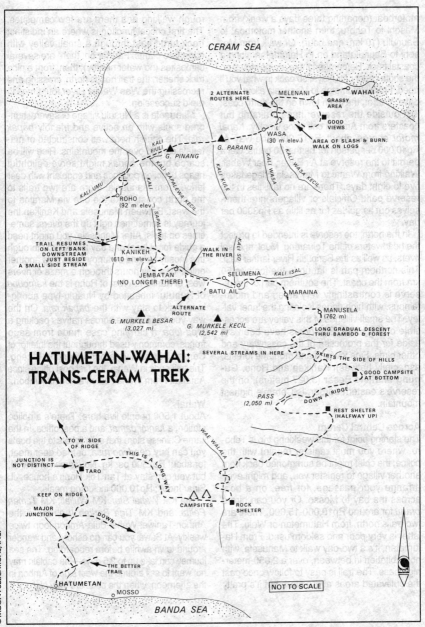

CERAM SEA

2 ALTERNATE
ROUTES HERE

MELENANI ■ WAHAI
GRASSY
AREA

WASA ○ GOOD
(30 m elev.) VIEWS

KALI FIULI AREA OF SLASH & BURN;
WALK ON LOGS

G. PINANG ▲ ▲ G. PARANG

KALI WASA KECIL
KALI WASA

KALI SAPALEWA KECIL
KALI KULE

KALI FIULI

KALI UMU

ROHO
(92 m elev.) ● KALI SAPALEWA

KALI SO

TRAIL RESUMES WALK IN
ON LEFT BANK KANIKEH THE RIVER
DOWNSTREAM (610 m elev.) KALI ISAL
JUST BESIDE SELUMENA
A SMALL SIDE STREAM JEMBATAN
(NO LONGER THERE) BATU AIL
MARAINA

ALTERNATE MANUSELA
ROUTE (762 m)
G. MURKELE BESAR
(3,027 m) G. MURKELE KECIL LONG GRADUAL DESCENT
(2,542 m) THRU BAMBOO & FOREST

SKIRTS THE SIDE OF HILLS

HATUMETAN-WAHAI:
TRANS-CERAM TREK

SEVERAL STREAMS IN HERE

GOOD CAMPSITE
AT BOTTOM

PASS DOWN A RIDGE
(2,050 m)

REST SHELTER
(HALFWAY UP)

TO W. SIDE WAE WALAIA
OF RIDGE
THIS IS A LONG WAY

JUNCTION IS
NOT DISTINCT ● TARO

KEEP ON RIDGE

MAJOR △ △
JUNCTION ● DOWN CAMPSITES

ROCK
SHELTER
THE BETTER
TRAIL

HATUMETAN ○ MOSSO

BANDA SEA

NOT TO SCALE

motorboat (departing three days a week) from Masohi to Tehoru, then another motorboat to Saunulu (10 km, one hour). Or walk from Masohi to Saunulu and on to Hatumetan along a coastal track. Remember, there are no stores on the south coast until Haya, so pack in what you'll need. From Hatumetan to Manusela allow three days. **Wahai,** the main town on the north coast just outside the reserve, has no airstrip but coasters from Ambon call twice weekly. *Kapal motor* charge about Rp15,000 one-way or Rp40,000 per person for berths; 30 hours. Get a permit to the reserve at Air Besar, near Wahai. Walking from Wahai to Manusela village takes five to eight days. There are no facilities in the reserve park. Officials or villagers hire themselves out as guides for as little as Rp3000 per day.

In the north, the reserve is intended to protect the headwaters of the Toluarang, Mual, and Isal rivers, as well as the Sariputih River farther east. This northern part is flat up to the foothills 50 km from the coast. The southern part of the reserve is contrastingly very steep and mountainous, with high ridges isolating the inner valley. The small villages of this valley are accessible only by foot. Preserves have been set aside for the protection of the cassowary and other birds. Fine lowland and montane forests, especially between Kanikeh and Roho. **Gunung Murkele Besar** (3,027 meters), on the reserve's eastern border, is Ceram's highest mountain.

Across Central Ceram

The starting point for this weeklong trip is Tehoru, where you must register (again) with the police; the chief might be summoned back from another village to register you, and might even arrange your passage, for free, on a boat across the bay to Mosso. Or you can hire a *prahu* for around Rp10,000-15,000. There are two trails north, from Hatumetan or Wolu. The latter is very poor and seldom used. From Hatumetan, it's a two-day walk to Manusela, with no habitation in between, over a 2,050-meter-high pass. The trail is easy to follow once past the cultivated areas at the start, but it's pretty

rough walking and there are few campsites. The first critical junction is where an indistinct track turns east through a small valley with huge taro plants. Farther on, there are several campsites (no water nearby); then, from a nice rock shelter, the trail heads north, crossing and recrossing the Wae Walala River four times in rapid succession.

Manusela is a Nuaulu village of several hundred souls with an active and friendly *bapak raja.* The church here was constructed of materials carried over the mountains. Rice will be scarce but the *bapak* might serve delightful heaps of boiled potatoes and eggplant with deer jerky. From Manusela, there are two trails to the north coast. Take the one via Maraina to the west. Between Manusela and Kanikeh the journey is sometimes right up the rivers, sometimes on trails. After Manusela, you might need a guide for at least one day to take you through this mostly flat and swampy area, plus another guide for a few hours through a maze of rivers west of Kanikeh. West of Roho is the *kampung* of **Huaulu,** inhabited by Nuaulu-type aborigines. Ask to stay with the *bapak raja.* On the way you might come across natives packing a *lopa-lopa,* a carrying case made from sago fronds, commonly used throughout the interior of Ceram. Parrots live around Gunung Pinang. The trail ends in Wahai, the first post office since Amahai. From Wahai, catch a boat to Ambon.

Wahai

About 1,500 people live here. There's a police station, a *kantor camat,* and a post office. In the same Chinese store that sells tickets to the boats you can buy *dendeng rusa,* or fried deer meat, for about Rp2500 per kg. No *losmen* in Wahai, but you can stay at Tan Tok Hong's house, Jl. Sinar Indok; Rp10,000 including meals.

The KM *Wahai Star,* KM *Wuliati,* KM *Taman Pelita,* and KM *Tiga Berlian II* all make the Ambon-Taniwel-Wahai-Bula-Ambon loop twice weekly. At Sawai you can go ashore and wander around town awhile before reboarding. The sea journey can take up to 2.5 days—the captain may not want to sail around the west side of Ambon in the afternoon, when the seas are very high.

BURU ISLAND

Buru is a large, magnificently wild island west of Ceram. One of Maluku's three largest islands, it has an area of 8,806 square km, slightly larger than Bali. The island is surrounded by coral barriers and covered in impenetrable eucalyptus forests, elephant grass, and vine-shrouded mountains. The soil is poor, with some savannahs. Coastal areas are flat and marshy, dotted with impoverished fishing villages. There are very few roads; only one river is navigable by small boats. In the western part of Buru is 670-meter-high **Lake Wakolo,** with a 60-km circumference. In the northwest corner is the Kaku Palatmada mountain range, with a volcanic peak rising over 2,100 meters. Dense forests crowd right down to the sea.

Although the VOC built a fort on Buru as early as 1657, most of the island has only recently been explored. A third the size of Holland, Buru was ruled by a single Dutch Resident during the later colonial era. In 1861, the indefatigable A.R. Wallace spent May and June here wading barefoot through the island's muddy swamps, where he "discovered" no fewer than 17 new species of birds. Since independence, the island's main claim to fame is that it was the penal colony for Javanese prisoners suspected of involvement in the 1965 coup.

Buru produces timber, its principal industry, as well as *kayuputih* oil derived from a species of eucalyptus tree. The oil has been exported since Portuguese times. The main town is **Namlea,** a dusty village on the northeast coast composed of Chinese shopkeepers, natives, Arabs, and Javanese. Some *transmigrasi* settlements have been established here, especially since the island's political prisoners were sent home. Now that the prisoners are gone, no special military clearance is required to visit the island.

The People
Buru's population of around 63,000 is divided between the animist and proto-Malayan Gebmelia of the interior and mixed racial groups along the coasts known as Gebmasin, of both Christian and Muslim faiths. Until 1969 cannibalism was still practiced deep in the island's rugged interior. Isolated aboriginal tribes around the Lake Wakolo region—the Rana, Waeloa, Waetenum, and Waejapo—number about 3,000. These first-wave inhabitants continue to hold on to their hunting and foraging culture.

The Prisoners
From 1969 to 1979, Buru was the "rehabilitation center" for political detainees (*tapol*) suspected of complicity in or sympathy with the nearly successful coup of 1965. During this period Pulau Buru was a forbidden island, sealed off from the rest of Indonesia and the world by the Kopkamtib, or Indonesian State Security Agency. The giant center, located inland from Namlea on the Wai Apu River, held as many as 13,000 prisoners by the end of 1975.

Prisoners attended compulsory indoctrination lectures, the aim being to replace communist ideology with the government Pancasila philosophy. Detainees were forced to faithfully attend a mosque or church—imagine hundreds of communist voices singing "Jesus is my Shepherd," resounding eerily through the Buru jungles. The wet-rice cultivation introduced by the government failed miserably. There were no newspapers, movies, radios, or TV. Prisoners lived under harsh conditions, and were sometimes tortured, deprived of water, and fed salted food.

The many writers, artists, and other intellectuals confined to the camps as "prisoners of conscience" read like a cultural "Who's Who" of Indonesia: Subronto Admojo, one of Indonesia's leading composer-conductors; Basuki Effendi, Indonesia's foremost film director (he was the camp violinist and instrument-maker); and probably Indonesia's greatest prose writer, Pramoedya Ananta Toer, who'd spent two years in prison for fighting the Dutch—all imprisoned without trial after the abortive coup.

There were no watchtowers or barbed wire, and camp guards weren't armed. They didn't need to be. Buru was an ideal isle of exile, from which no prisoner ever escaped alive. Thirty-eight people escaped the camp in 1974, only to perish of exposure in the jungle within days.

The Release
Finally, under pressure from foreign govern-

ments and such humanist organizations as Amnesty International, plans were made in 1975 to begin releasing the prisoners. With the collapse of the anticommunist regimes in South Vietnam, Cambodia, and Laos, and the financial bankruptcy of its state oil company Pertamina, Indonesia felt more conciliatory toward its Japanese, American, and European allies. With the election of President Jimmy Carter and his human rights policies in 1976, conditions began to improve, and the pace of the release process quickened. By 1979, all prisoners had gone home, replaced for the most part by *transmigrasi* settlers exploiting the millions of dollars the government spent on Buru and the work started by the *tapol*, who hacked their settlement literally right out of the jungle.

Getting There And Around

Merpati flies from Ambon to Namlea for Rp35,000 (30 minutes). The plane lands close to Namlea on a coral airstrip still pockmarked with bomb craters from the 1950 Indonesian attack on the Republic of South Maluku.

The KM *Bedalu* and KM *Baruna Bakti* stop at Buru in their passages to and from Ambon and Ternate. More regular are the ships KM *Wahai Star, Suliati, Tiga Berlian II,* and *Dewi Jaya,* which all sail from Ambon to Namlea (Rp10,000) and Airbuaya (Rp15,000) twice weekly. The KM *Usaha Baru III* also sails from Ambon to Leksula on Buru.

There are a few roads around Namlea, but on the rest of the island are only muddy jungle tracks.

THE BANDA ISLANDS

Nine small volcanic islands 160 km southeast of Ambon on the northeast fringe of the Banda Sea, the Banda Group became world famous in the 17th-19th centuries as the original Spice Islands of the Dutch East Indies. These islands played a gigantic role in Indonesia's early history. To acquire control of the nutmeg trade, in 1619 the ruthless 31-year-old Dutch Governor-General Jan Pieterszoon Coen exterminated Banda's indigenous population—one of the blackest days in Dutch colonial history.

Now comprising the southernmost islands of the Central Maluku District and governed from Ambon, the two main islands are close together and you can get around them easily by *prahu*. There is magnificent scenery, beautiful sandy beaches, puffing volcanos, easygoing accommodations, crumbling Dutch forts and ruined mansions, one of the finest harbors in the archipelago, and peerless coral gardens and reefs.

The Bandas receive a trickle of travelers and odd adventurers. Wealthy tourists, retracing "the footsteps of Magellan," arrive on the luxury cruise ship *Lindblad Explorer.* As yet uncorrupted by tourism, there are few vehicles on the islands; one will meet you at the airport. Theft is practically unknown. Electricity is very sporadic; the generator is turned on at 1800 or 2100 (you never know) and is always shut off by 0600.

THE LAND

The early romantic vision of the Bandas was a jewel-like cluster of forgotten tropical islands surrounded by crystal waters and brilliant coral reefs, containing hills lined with aromatic spice trees on which perched flocks of green and red parrots, all presided over by a still-active volcano resembling Mt. Fuji in miniature. This vision is also the reality. Considered the most beautiful cluster of islands in Maluku, the forests are remarkably green and the surrounding waters so clear that coral and even minute objects can be seen to depths of up to eight fathoms.

The group consists of four main islands—Lontar (Banda Besar or "Great Banda," the largest at 32 square km), Neira (which contains the principal town, Bandaneira), Run, and Ai, plus five smaller islands, all volcanic in origin. Since 1586, eruptions have been reported on an average of once every 21 years.

Flora And Fauna

Banda is home to the best-known commercial species of nutmeg, *Myristica fragrans.* The tree, which can grow eight to 12 meters in height, is always in bloom, and the fruit ripens year-round. When mature and yellow the five-cm-wide fruit splits open, revealing a dark red aril surrounding a crimson seed. The aril is carefully stripped off and dried, forming mace. The seed is a thin, hard shell around a wrinkled kernel. When dried, this kernel is the nutmeg. The islands remain the most important world producer of nutmeg, exporting about 500 tons per year. Ironically, while the rest of the world considers nutmeg a delicacy, the inhabitants of these islands reputedly have never used it as a condiment.

Deer and pigs have been introduced to the islands; also inhabiting the isles are big nutmeg pigeons, *Ducula concinna,* a species distinct to the Kai, Banda, and Watabela islands. The Bandas are also fortunate to have their own 2,500-hectare marine reserve based on the coral gardens on the lee side of Pulau Lontar. The actual reserve area no longer contains the best coral; **Pulau Suanggi,** Bandas' farthest outlier, has the most extensive coral reefs and the finest sand beaches, and is a nesting site for boobies and other seabirds. Some 167 fish species are found in these sheltered waters, including the magnificent flashlight fish (*Photoblepharon bandanensis*) and 24 species of butterfly fish. Watch for lurking sharks. Tiny fluorescent algae also live in the waves, turning the water sparkling white. This "milk sea" is at its weakest in June and July, but is very pronounced in August. The **Penju Islands,** 200 km southwest of the Bandas, are nesting grounds for giant sea turtles.

HISTORY

To really appreciate Banda it helps to have a keenly developed sense of history. Before going, borrow a copy of Willard A. Hanna's *Indonesian Banda* from a well-stocked Asian Studies library; copies are also available at Bandaneira's museum and Hotel Laguna. The only detailed study of the islands' culture and history over the past 400 years, this is an engrossing and provocative study of the colonial system in microcosm, as well as the whole evolution of modern Indonesia.

Spice

These islands derive their name from the Javanese word *bandau,* meaning "united"; another interpretation traces the origin to Nusa Banda, "Islands of Wealth." Spices are bound up inextricably in the history of these islands. For centuries the Bandanese sold their spices to such traditional regional trading partners as the Bugis, Chinese, and Arabs, receiving in exchange medicine, ceramics, and *batik* and other textiles. Scholars believe Hindu-Javanese merchants were the first to introduce nutmeg and mace in the international emporia, the commodities reaching Europe around A.D. 500.

The demand for spices as preservatives accelerated in Europe to such an extent that by the 16th century expeditions were dispatched in search of the source. The Portuguese captain Antonio d'Abreu discovered the Bandas in 1511, inaugurating a profitable Bandanese-Portuguese trade which lasted nearly 100 years. Atypically, the Portuguese did not leave a trail of intrigue and exploitation in the Bandas, as they did in the other Malukan spice islands. The Portuguese kept a tenuous hold on the islands until the arrival of the Dutch in the early 17th century.

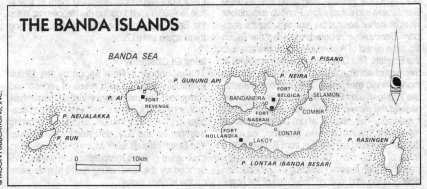

Early Dutch Expeditions

The Dutch first attempted to lure the Bandanese away from the politically and economically bankrupt Portuguese. In 1599 the Dutch Vice Admiral van Heemskerk arrived with two ships and 200 men to barter iron goods, heavy woolens and velvets, gunpowder, mirrors, and trinkets. For these inappropriate and unwanted goods, the Dutch demanded the island's entire crop of nutmeg and mace. Under tremendous pressure, village elders signed a written treaty, not realizing the Dutch considered the document to carry the full force of law. After signing, the Bandanese ignored the treaty and went back to freely selling spices to their traditional buyers, which included the English on the island of Run. When the Dutch found out, they were outraged, threatened reprisals, and demanded even more stringent agreements.

Finally, under the auspices of the Dutch East Indies Co., in 1609 Admiral Pieter Verhoeffe brought a war fleet of 13 ships and a thousand men into Bandaneira's harbor to impose an airtight monopoly on all spices leaving the Bandas. After cursory negotiations, the admiral began constructing a massive fort upon the foundations of a former Portuguese fort—a premature and provocative act. Under pretense of further negotiations, the Bandanese lured the unarmed Dutch into an ambush in which the admiral and 45 of his entourage were killed.

Dutch Conquest

After the ambush, the chiefs and much of the population deserted the spice gardens around the fort and fled into the hills. Dutch survivors blockaded the islands, attempting to starve the Bandanese into submission. Punitive expeditions were launched against the islanders, but the stubborn Bandanese resisted, expelled the Dutch from the island of Ai, and continued to trade with the English. The Dutch were getting nowhere in this war of attrition, and at last decided to take more drastic measures. The new commander, the ruthless Jan Pieterszoon Coen, had witnessed the murder of Verhoeffe during the 1609 expedition. This man, of whom Dutch historians have said "his name reeks of blood," gave no quarter. Invading the Bandas from Batavia with a force of 2,000 men, Coen's mercenaries rampaged through the islands razing villages, burning boats, raping, and looting. Two-thirds of the population was wiped out, the remainder sold into slavery or driven into the hills to die of exposure. Only 1,000 Bandanese survived in the archipelago out of an original population of 15,000.

Monopoly

In Coen's attempt to impose a monopoly, British factories and forts first had to be destroyed, stocks of spices confiscated, and merchants and seamen beaten and thrown into chains. Coen began setting up a closed horticultural preserve to control the growing and sale of spices. To keep supply down and prices up, nutmeg groves on all but the two main islands were destroyed. Coen carved up the remaining gardens into 68 concessions, or *perken,* which were offered free to Dutch planters called *perkeniers—* mostly rogues and drifters. To work the nutmeg trees on these now unpopulated islands, the holder of each land grant was provided with 1,500 imported slaves. The Dutch East Indies Co. controlled demand and fixed prices, ensuring a guaranteed income for the *perkeniers* and astronomical profits for the company.

In And Out With The English

Continued English interference in the region led to the "Amboina Massacre" in 1623, in which merchants and their Javanese guards were beheaded. This convinced the English of the futility of maintaining a presence in Maluku; in the 1667 Treaty of Breda, the English relinquished all claims to the Bandas in exchange for the small and insignificant Dutch island of Manhattan in the Americas. The British returned in 1795 and by a mere show of force took the islands to protect them from Napoleon, restoring them to Dutch rule in 1803. In 1811 during the Napoleonic Wars the English again seized the Bandas, returning them again in 1817.

Isles Of Obscurity

The monopoly system begun by the Dutch eventually declined as a result of widespread corruption. The *perkeniers* enriched themselves further by smuggling and selling subsidized supplies on the black market, eventually growing degenerate and lazy, detested by their slaves and Dutch officials alike. Many of these planters took slave girls as mistresses and wives, evidenced by the fascinating racial blends seen on the islands today.

During the Napoleonic Wars the English, with great foresight, transplanted prime nutmeg seedlings to their colonies in Sumatra, Penang, Colombo, and Calcutta, which eventually broke the back of the Dutch monopoly. The price nutmeg and mace could command on the world market was drastically reduced, and the Bandas became an economic backwater. Rampant graft and larceny finally drove the Dutch East Indies Co. into bankruptcy in the 1790s with a staggering debt of 12 million guilders.

When the new Dutch colonial administration took over the affairs of the shattered company in the early 1800s, it began to institute long overdue reforms. Slavery was abolished in 1862, the plantation workers replaced with imported convicts and gangs of Javanese coolies. The *perkeniers* gained title to their landholdings in the 1870s, but managed their finances so poorly their *perken* were purchased at rock-bottom prices by Chinese and Arab competitors, and by an official government agency created for that purpose. The late 19th and early 20th centuries saw Dutch colonialists sponsoring churches, schools, and public works. In contrast to its stormy beginnings, these tiny islands, under the paternalistic rule of the Dutch, returned to a state of relative peace and prosperity which lasted into the mid-20th century. The tiny and once-famous Bandas became a remote and nearly forgotten outpost of the empire.

Isles Of Exile

With nationalist demands for self-determination gaining momentum through the 1920s and '30s, all was not peaceful elsewhere in the archipelago. In the 1930s Banda was chosen as the isle of exile for several of Indonesia's most popular revolutionary leaders, including Sutan Sjahrir and Mohammed Hatta. Transferred from the infamous Boven Digul detention camp in West New Guinea, these famous visitors arrived on 11 February 1936. Their presence immediately made a subtle impact on the Bandanese, who felt they were once again put on the map.

The fervent revolutionaries rented excolonialist quarters, mingled with and endeared themselves to the townsfolk, ordered books from Batavia and the Netherlands, and started tutoring the local children—all under the watchful eye of the Dutch warden who occupied the jail next to their dwellings. The nationalists swam, fished, and hiked in what amounted to a delightful exile in an idyllic tropical setting, which ended abruptly in 1942 with the Japanese invasion. Fearful they could fall into Japanese hands and be used for propaganda purposes, the Dutch flew Hatta and Sjahrir from Bandaneira on 31 January 1942 to Java, just before the Japanese attacked. When the Republic of Indonesia was proclaimed in 1945, Hatta became vice-president; Sjahrir later became prime minister.

The Japanese Occupation

During WW II the Japanese military had little interest in developing spice commodities and thus nutmeg production virtually ceased. Forced to fend for themselves, the Bandanese reverted to a subsistence economy, planting cassava and sweet potatoes and trading fish for sago from Ambon. Later the Japanese used Bandaneira as a rendezvous point for their warships when other ports in the Banda Sea were strafed by Allied bombers. Just before the return of the Dutch in early 1945, American bombers flying out of New Guinea occasionally bombed and strafed Bandaneira. On one occasion, a stray bomb landed in the middle of a wedding party, killing 100 people and injuring hundreds more. The old prewar Bandaneira pier, where stately KPM ships once tied up to unload cargo and passengers, is now a twisted mass of iron, a grotesque memorial to this tragedy.

The Postwar Years

By the end of the Japanese occupation, the once beautiful and high-yield nutmeg estates had fallen into sad disrepair. The *perkenier* were demoralized; no new planting had taken place for years. The increasing use of refrigeration to keep meat fresh further eroded clove and nutmeg markets. The Dutch at last gave up their Indonesian possessions in 1949, and the Banda Islands lost their importance in the international trade arena forever. During the Sukarno era, the Bandas were associated with the Central Malukan rebellion instigated by the Ambonese, and the nutmeg gardens were nationalized. The whole spice enterprise, rife with corruption, fell into further neglect. The industry has been only partially rehabilitated.

ECONOMY

Bandaneira has always been an entrepôt for the Tanimbar and Aru islands, as well as for the coastal towns of southern Irian Jaya. But this historical trade has always been small scale: its production of *trepang*, tortoiseshell, and shark fins is modest, and what fruit and vegetables are grown can only supply the local market. Employment opportunities are dismal. As soon as the youth of Banda are able, they migrate to Ambon. Finding jobs there almost as nonexistent as in Banda, they move on to Ujung Pandang, and, inevitably, wind up in the streets of Jakarta, adding to the already swollen mass of that city's jobless. Seldom do they ever return.

The Nutmeg Industry

Ever since VOC times, Banda has been run like one big nutmeg plantation, with little economic development in any other sector. On the decline for decades, the depression of the 1930s brought even more deterioration to the nutmeg industry, and WW II and the political and social turbulence of the '40s and '50s nearly killed it for good. Yet Bandanese spices, still considered peerless in quality, might yet stage a comeback. It is with this in mind that the government has begun to allocate funds to revitalize the nutmeg industry. The principal trading partner for the spice is, ironically, Holland, where Dutchmen still like to sprinkle the spice over their vegetables. And all over the world, prime nutmeg and mace are still considered essential in gourmet cooking. In Indonesia itself, Sulawesi and Java have outstripped Banda in production, while Grenada in the West Indies is also a major producer. One of the largest enterprises in the islands is PT Perkebunan Pala Banda, the walled-in headquarters for the state-run nutmeg cooperative. Here the nutmeg is processed, then shipped, usually to Ambon, from where it is exported.

Fishing

Besides tourism, the only other sector of the island economy which shows any promise is fishing. These seas are a rich reservoir of high-quality swordfish, tuna, and grouper. Although Bandanese fishermen put out to sea in over 60 *arumbai* (traditional Bandanese fishing vessels), so far only the Japanese have exploited these waters to any commercial extent. Their wanton robbery of the waters of the Banda Sea, to absolutely no enrichment of the region's inhabitants, has raised vehement protests, but to little effect. Fishing remains a small, indigenous industry that barely supplies the local market. When there's a surplus, it's dried, salted, and exported to Ambon. Plans by the government to modernize fishing fleets and canning facilities have never gotten off the ground, and the chance of this ever happening in such an economic backwater is unlikely.

THE PEOPLE

The Banda Islands have lost their aboriginal population. Two-thirds of the original Bandanese people were wiped out by the Dutch, who then imported Makassarese convicts, Javanese coolies, and Papuan and Timorese slaves to work the nutmeg plantations. These were later joined by an influx of Europeans, Eurasians, Chinese, Buginese, Arab merchants, and other immigrants. The contract laborers in time earned their freedom, and many of the present-day inhabitants of the Bandas are descended from them. All these variegated races, languages, and religions eventually produced today's homogenous, highly distinct, and complex Bandanese people. In some of these islands an archaic dialect is spoken which is not used anywhere else in Indonesia.

Although utterly devoid of any productive employment opportunities for the young, Banda does offer its inhabitants a good number of blessings, even dignity. Banda islanders do not share the grinding poverty of Java's urban poor, housing quality is above average, and the people can feed themselves adequately with the help of government subsidies. The seven schools of the group have an enrollment of over 1,000 students at the primary and secondary levels, though they are ludicrously underequipped and understaffed.

Events

The Portuguese occupied the Bandas for over 100 years; the local dances still retain a distinctive Portuguese flavor. The *cakelele* dance is staged whenever the *orang besar,* Des Alwi, asks for it. Des is the owner of the islands' premier hotel. In this war dance, village men dance around a large bronze drum decorated with leaf offerings. In other Portuguese-derived dances, celebrants don and display old costumes, blunderbusses, helmets, and shields. Another dance sometimes held in Bandaneira resembles the Chinese dragon dance, in which children dress up in sackcloth costumes with papier-mâché masks. The *mako-mako* and *maru-maru* dances are still seen on occasion in the Bandas.

BANDANEIRA

The principal town on Pulau Neira, Bandaneira is perched on the edge of a gigantic crater. This quiet, peaceful town, today just a few short streets filled with Mediterranean-style homes and shops, was once the Dutch administrative center for the whole region, famous all over the Dutch East Indies for its beauty. Bandaneira's dilapidated buildings, though reflecting the turbulent history they have seen, have a mysterious air of decay about them. The town features an old Dutch church (Jl. Gereja) and ancient Fort Nassau (built in 1621); along Jl. Pelabuhan are the grand mansions of the *perkeniers.* Around town are other examples of gracious Dutch colonial architecture, most crumbling into ruin. On a plateau above Bandaneira, backed by a 240-meter-high rock, is massive Fort Belgica, commenced in 1611, which has survived numerous earthquakes. You may tour all the historical sites, and since there aren't many tourists you really get top treatment.

Two resident cassowaries prance down the middle of the main street—no traffic, so why not? A few years ago Holland dug 35 wells; the holes are all there, but only five pumps have survived. The show at Bandaneira's single cinema is the town's nightlife. Bandaneira's landlocked harbor, with no visible outlet, was once one of the finest in the Indies. The wharf faces the narrow strait; in the middle sits the imposing Gunung Api volcano. Between Pulau Neira and Pulau Lontar are colorful sea gardens.

Churches
In the center of town, the **Dutch Reform Church** (1852) overlooks the neglected park surrounding Fort Nassau. The lovely church is a severe structure that replaced an earlier building destroyed in an earthquake. The church has a clock that doesn't work; apparently it clicked its last the very moment of the Japanese invasion 47 years ago. Near the church are a Christian and a Chinese cemetery with lichen-covered inscriptions; probably one of the most fascinating collections of old tombstones in all of Indonesia. The Dutch governor of Banda is buried here.

Bandaneira's old **Catholic church** has a clockface with only eight numbers on it, and no hands—a haunting touch even for the Bandas. Services are held here only once a week, but the church is well cared for; see caretaker Julius, who'll show you around. Ask to view the church service, a whole set of 17th-century pewter that would probably fetch £100,000 at auction in London.

Governor's Palace
The magnificent palace was once the Dutch *controlleur*'s mansion, built in the 1820s with giant granite paving slabs, bright floor tiles, shiny marble, heavily carved beams, huge wooden doors, and shuttered windows. Although the building is still used as Banda's administrative headquarters, the top *kabupaten* administrator nowadays uses Ambon as his base; Indonesian *pegawai* consider a posting to Banda the bureaucratic equivalent of exile. Behind the building, in the garden, is a statue of the Dutch King Willem III. Ask to see the inscription by a 19th-century French prisoner who scratched a lament on the wall. A stern, heavy, colonial air still pervades this building.

Middenstraat
This residential street that runs along the waterfront is now called Jl. Pelabuhan. Here are the giant *perkeniers*' stone mansions, the majority in serious disrepair. These buildings are occupied now by the military or police. One of the grandest of these waterfront buildings is the former **Harmonie Club,** the center of Dutch social life, where the *perkenier* set would socialize with their wives in the cool of the evening, smoking cigars, drinking Bols gin, playing cards. There were often balls and banquets as well as musical or theatrical performances by traveling troupes. Today the Harmonie Club is in ruins. Another big Dutch villa is being converted into a bank.

Museums

The **Mohammed Hatta Museum** is housed in a building once occupied by the freedom-fighter Dr. Mohammed Hatta. It contains exile memorabilia, as well as the desk and pens he used. The **Rumah Badya** museum, formerly a *perkenier* mansion converted into a mosque, is now the home of the Baadillah family, who claim descent from Arab sea captains. The head of the family, Des Alwi, runs two hotels in Bandaneira and also rents out snorkeling and diving equip-

ment. This historical museum, which also rents rooms in the back, contains artifacts tracing the whole nutmeg culture, plus paintings, big ceramic vases, and old coins.

Forts

Fort Belgica is a pentagonal-shaped Dutch fort built in 1611 on the ruins of a 16th-century Portuguese fort, above Bandaneira about 500 meters from the harbor. Although overgrown, the structure is still standing and in fairly good con-

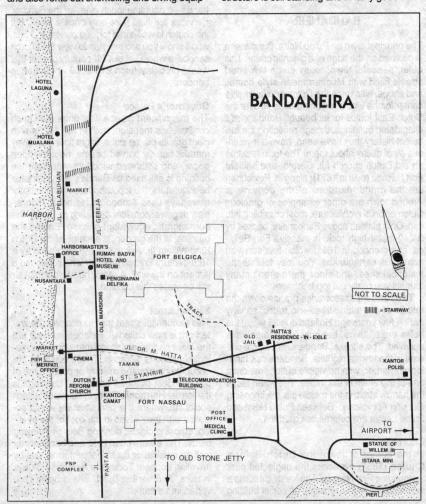

BANDANEIRA

NOT TO SCALE

||||||| = STAIRWAY

HOTEL LAGUNA

HOTEL MUALANA

MARKET

HARBOR

JL. PELABUHAN

JL. GEREJA

HARBORMASTER'S OFFICE

RUMAH BADYA HOTEL AND MUSEUM

PENGINAPAN DELFIKA

NUSANTARA

OLD MANSIONS

FORT BELGICA

TRACK

MARKET

PIER MERPATI OFFICE

CINEMA

DUTCH REFORM CHURCH

KANTOR CAMAT

TAMAN

JL. DR. M. HATTA

JL. ST. SYAHIR

FORT NASSAU

OLD JAIL

HATTA'S RESIDENCE - IN - EXILE

TELECOMMUNICATIONS BUILDING

POST OFFICE

MEDICAL CLINIC

KANTOR POLISI

TO AIRPORT →

PNP COMPLEX

JL. PANTAI

TO OLD STONE JETTY

STATUE OF WILLEM III

ISTANA MINI

PIER

© MOON PUBLICATIONS, INC.

*old Dutch fort,
Bandaneira*

dition considering it was last restored in 1935. Cannons point out over Bandaneira's sleepy harbor. Climb up to one of the towers for a sweeping view over the town, volcano, and nutmeg groves. Remains of a moat are still visible. Also visit the overgrown, crumbling walls of **Fort Nassau,** below Fort Belgica near the church. Just a gateway, a rusting cannon, and three walls remain of this fort built in 1609 by the Dutch. In the repressive atmosphere of Banda's plantation system in the 17th and 18th centuries, the major reason for building these fortifications was to protect the white population against slave uprisings.

Skin Diving

Some dazzling coral gardens are found in the straits between Pulau Neira, Gunung Api, and Pulau Lontar, a body of water which constitutes a large, broken-up crater lake. The configuration of these three main islands has created one of the most beautiful natural harbors in Indonesia. The Banda Sea is a very deep blue, and the colors of the sand, rocks, and sky vivid and bright, while objects at the bottom of the transparent sea are visible for many meters. You could find yourself swimming in the middle of a school of 100 dolphins frolicking in the water. Hire diving equipment from Des Alwi at Hotel Complex: snorkel, mask, and fins, Rp2000 per day, tank for Rp12,000 per day. Motorboats, going for around Rp15,000 per hour, are prefer-able. Smaller canoes, although quite maneuverable and able to travel great distances, usually capsize when you attempt to climb in. While snorkeling, be careful of stonefish and angelfish. The most beautiful coral reefs surround **Pulau Karaka,** which lies off Gunung Api. The paddle canoe from Bandaneira's harbor costs Rp3000-4000 per hour. There's only one, very friendly old man living on the island.

Volcanos

The main harbor of the Bandas is dominated by the **Gunung Api** volcano rising 676 meters out of the sea. Though its main crater is thought to be dormant, the volcano is constantly puffing away and has a treacherous history. On 2 April 1778, a violent eruption was accompanied by an earthquake, hurricane, and tsunami. Fires flared up all over Pulau Neira, destroying 500,000 nutmeg trees and nearly obliterating the town of Bandaneira. In 1820 another eruption occurred. Today you can reach the rim of the crater by first taking a motorboat or canoe from Neira harbor, then climbing up a 500-meter-long footpath; two hours roundtrip. From the top is a splendid view over the town and the whole Banda chain.

Also climb Pulau Neira's 250-meter-high mountain, **Gunung Papenberg,** on a poorly maintained trail, some sections of which have stone steps. The trail begins beyond town and anyone can show you the way. On the side of

Gunung Papenberg are the ruined mansions and sheds of the rich Lans family, as well as the dilapidated estates of two other *perkenier* families. Ask the locals about the springs on Gunung Kele, known locally as **Airmata Cilubintang.**

Accommodations
The cheapest places to stay in Bandaneira, both run by friendly people, are **Penginapan Delfika,** in an old *perkenier* mansion, Rp15,000 with meals; and **Penginapan Selecta,** for the same price. More expensive is the **Hotel Laguna,** the principal tourist hotel, which everyone tries to steer you toward. Rates are Rp35,000 s or Rp60,000 with full board plus 10% tax; use the CB radio to haggle with the Arab owner in Jakarta to get the price down. Staff expects you to take all your meals there, and they'll pack a lunch if you go out for the day. The Laguna rents canoes, motorboats, and snorkeling equipment, and arranges tours and marine excursions.

Also try the pricey **Hotel Mualana** on Jl. Pelabuhan on the waterfront; **Hotel Complex** (rent diving gear here); the peaceful **Rumah Badya Hotel** (Rp10,000 pp, in back of the museum); and the **Naira Hotel** (Jl. Pantai), each about the same price as Hotel Laguna. Best is to ask around and try to stay with a Bandanese family; they'll not only put you up, but act as guides and counselors. Inquire at the police station for families that take travelers; expect to give a donation of around Rp7500 per day. Elsewhere on the islands, stay with the *kepala kampung.*

Food
Except at Hotel Laguna, there are no refrigerators in town. Bandaneira is chronically short on vegetables and eggs; even rice is expensive here. At the *pasar,* near the government nutmeg cooperative, buy fruits, vegetables, and fish; only open when a ship comes in. **Nusantara** serves good *nasi campur* and *ikan bakar.* The price of fish depends upon the size of the day's catch. Dog is still eaten on Banda; even a skinny one fetches Rp10,000. The locals will tell you that for some illnesses, you must consume *sate anjing.*

Services
There are no banks. Avoid any dealings with the local *imigrasi* office; real sonsabitches, absolutely

the worst in all of Indonesia. Bandaneira's *rumah sakit umum,* with its Indonesian doctor, can handle minor ailments and injuries but for anything serious you need to go to Ambon.

Getting There
The Merpati flight from Ambon to Banda costs about Rp60,000, departing twice weekly (if enough passengers). You're only allowed to take 10 kilos pp, but you can leave your stuff with your hotel proprietor in Ambon. This flight continues on to Tual and Langgur in the Kais. Buy only a one-way ticket, as you might be able to return on a boat to Ambon. Buy return tickets at the Merpati office on Jl. Pelabuhan in Bandaneira. Arriving in Banda, a car meets you at the airport to drive you into town for Rp2000. Or walk into town in about 20 minutes if you take the shortcut that comes out beside Rumah Badya.

Frequent coasters leave from Ambon to Banda, a 200-km trip taking 14-16 hours and costing around Rp7000. The Pelni ship, KM *Niaga X,* sails every three weeks for a swing around the entire Banda Sea, stopping at Banda on both ends. Other ships of the line, such as the *Nusantara Daya,* are of dubious seaworthiness. Crews rent out their cabins for around Rp15,000. Also check Perintis Lines, which has vessels to Banda from Ambon about every three weeks. Best, of course, is to visit by private yacht.

Getting Around
There are only a few vehicles on Neira, and the island's principal road leads from town to the airport. Move like the natives: walk or ride bicycles. Some very picturesque tracks lead from Bandaneira around the island. Use boats to see the other islands in the group. The seas are calm Sept.-Dec., although in March and April it's also possible to travel. The charter rate for motorboats (find them near the market) runs Rp30,000-75,000 per day; figure on about Rp150,000 to Pulau Ai and back. It's cheaper to hire or borrow from the locals canoes and other types of rowing vessels at Rp3000-4000 per hour. For other islands in the province, about every three weeks either Pelni or Perintis ships call at Bandaneira, providing transport to Tual, Rp7000; Elat, Rp7500; Dobo, Rp12,250; Larat, Rp17,300; and Saumlaki, Rp22,250.

OUTER ISLANDS

Pulau Lontar And Vicinity

Pulau Lontar, also known as Banda Besar, is located directly south of Pulau Neira. The largest of the Banda Group, this long, thin island is covered in nutmeg orchards; during the days of forced cultivation it supported half a million nutmeg trees. Plantations still thrive under the island's remaining *kanari* trees. You can reach Lontar by chartered motorboat from near Bandaneira's *pasar*. Boatmen want Rp15,000 roundtrip, but the school boat goes over at around 0900 for Rp2000 pp and returns at around noon, ample time for you to get up to see **Fort Hollandia**, the island's main attraction. Located on the island's central spine near the village of **Lontar**, a steep flight of steps leads up to the overgrown hilltop fortress. This once huge fort, devastated by an earthquake in 1743, was built by the Dutch in 1621 during a punitive visit by the redoubtable Jan Pieterszoon Coen. Nice view of the volcano from the top. Near Tanjung Burang is an underwater holy urn, **Tempayang Keramat,** said to be watched over by a white tortoise and holy fish. Accessible by canoe or motorboat from Bandaneira. **Laci** is a well on Pulau Lontar renowned for its purification ceremonies which take place every 13 years; the next is scheduled for 2002.

To reach any of the outer islands of the Banda Group, charter a motorboat from Bandaneira. **Pulau Ai** is a small island to the west of Gu-nung Api, 21 km from Bandaneira (two hours by motorboat); its name means "water" in Bandanese. Pulau Ai was conquered by the Dutch in 1616; they built a fort and a blockhouse here called "Revenge." Made of coral-lime, the structure rises straight up from the sea. During the Napoleonic era, the island was occupied by the English, who grew cloves here. To the southwest, **Pulau Neijalakka** was a British stronghold until the Ambon Massacre of 1623. **Pulau Suanggi,** a favorite habitat for seabirds 125 km northwest of Bandaneira, has gorgeous natural panoramas and pristine white sandy beaches. **Pulau Manuk,** a volcanic island 80 km south of the Banda Group, is an untouched nesting ground for seabirds, with beautiful marine gardens for skin diving and snorkeling.

Lucipara-Penju Groups

An isolated, uninhabited group of reefs, sandy beaches, and coral cays 200-230 km southwest of the Bandas, about a 14-hour sea voyage from Bandaneira. Pulau Mai is nestled among the Lucipara Group, surrounded by a huge platform reef holding a veritable treasury of sealife. This island is one of few on the planet still in its primeval state. With the exception of a few coconut palms, Pulau Mai supports a natural flora undisturbed by humans. Also inhabiting the island is a distinct species of mound-building megapodes. Pulau Mai's reef edge is one of the most spectacular drop-offs anywhere, plunging to a depth of over 900 meters. These islands are breeding grounds for a huge colony of sea turtles.

SOUTHEAST MALUKU

This remote district extends from Wetar, off the eastern tip of Timor, to the Aru Group, only 240 km from the underbelly of Irian Jaya. The territorial waters of the region are immense, totaling 320,470 square km, while its land area is only 28,000 square km. In all there are 287 islands and islets, 199 inhabited, stretching in a long chain on the edge of the Arafura Sea between Australia and Irian Jaya. Most of the islands are hilly to mountainous, some are volcanic in origin, others feature extensive marshlands and lowland swamps. The economy of the region centers on fishing, logging (*kayu besi*), forest products, and pearls. Isolated from the main currents of Indonesian culture and economy, Maluku Tenggara is a forgotten place: difficult to get to, difficult to travel. Tourism is nil. Accommodations, food, and transportation are expensive or nonexistent. Yet travel here is rewarding, because, as a direct result of their inaccessibility, native customs, crafts, dress, and traditions are still very much alive.

FLORA AND FAUNA

The fauna and flora of the region show marked affinity to species found in Australia and New Guinea, including a profuse variety of butterflies, marsupials such as cuscus and miniature kangaroos on Aru and Kai, wild buffalo on Moa and Luang, the wild goats of Wetar, several species of cockatoo, green parrots, and several species of the bird of paradise. Marinelife includes sea turtles nesting on the island of Enu, a dazzling array of ornamental fish off the islands of Luang and Sermatang, shrimp west of Yamdena, pearls in the Arus, sea cucumbers around the islands of Selaru, Sera, Tayando, and the Arus, octopus everywhere, and a huge variety of shellfish. The sea is also home to *akar bahar* (black coral), sea *kasuari, agar agar,* and seaweeds. Wild orchids (*lelemuku*) bloom on Tanimbar at least four months of the year; other varieties of orchids, such as *macan tutul* and *macan kumbang,* are found on Kai and in the far southern islands. Exotic woods like *meranti* and *salamoni* (black ironwood) grow in scattered locations. Ordinary ironwood is found on the Kais; there are a few sago forests on Aru and Tanimbar.

Ecological Devastation

Wild animal life in Maluku Tenggara, on both land and sea, is in danger of extinction. This region is no different from any other area of Indonesia—the rape just started a bit later than most. Officially, a number of nature reserves have been established on the Tanimbars, Arus, and other islands, but these are a joke.

SOUTHEAST MALUKU

BANDA SEA

KEP. KAI

KEP. ARU

KEP. TANIMBAR

KEP. BABAR

EAST TIMOR

0   200 km

© MOON PUBLICATIONS, INC.

As everywhere else in Indonesia, these islands are rapidly being stripped of fish, shrimp, turtles, sharks, trees, and birds. On Kai Kecil there are almost 30 villages where people are chopping down trees as fast as they can, planting whatever they think will grow, killing whatever they can eat, and just generally raising hell with the environment. It's almost impossible to get away from coconut palms, tapioca, bananas, and sago fields. People in Ambon are willing to pay Rp100,000 for a white cockatoo, so there are any number of people eager to supply the market—even if their share of the loot is only Rp2000.

The Japanese and Taiwanese have brought their fishing factories to the islands, so in Dobo it's nearly impossible to find fresh shrimp or any variety of the many fish supposedly plentiful everywhere in Aru waters. Since shark fins are worth as much as Rp50,000 per kilo, everything that floats is out reaping the harvest, nets extending as much as one kilometer from the boat.

HISTORY

Until recently, Southeast Maluku has been little influenced by the outside world. Even the Portuguese and Dutch could divine little of economic interest in this remote group, and thus paid it scant attention. Still, there are ruined Dutch forts in the Tanimbars and the Arus. Late in the 19th century Christian missionaries began proselytizing here with great success, and today the majority of Southeast Maluku's inhabitants are at least nominally Protestant or Catholic. Christianity has made the deepest inroads on Leti, Kisar, and Tanimbar, though animism still pervades the lives of the people, particularly the interior tribes. In coastal areas, Islamic communities predominate.

THE PEOPLE

Southeast Maluku has a population of around 280,000, living in some 550 villages. Of mixed proto-Malayan and Papuan races, Melanesian features become more noticeable in the eastern islands of Aru and Tanimbar, and are less pronounced in the west. The region has long been known for the ferocity of its tribes, with frequent accounts of headhunting and cannibalism. Up until the early 1960s, most communities in the islands between Alor and Kai were divided into three fixed hereditary castes—nobility, commoners, and slaves. The nobility were often of mixed Malay-indigenous origin, the commoners of indigenous races, while the slaves were curly-haired natives imported or indentured from New Guinea. A hereditary land-owning class still holds much of the power. Life is centered on the sea; some villages are laid out in the form of a boat. No systematic ethnographic study has ever been made of the cultures of this isolated region, and anthropological literature is scarce.

The main diet on the islands of Kisar and Babar is maize; on the volcanic islands of Damar, Teun, Nila, and Serua it's bananas; on Tanimbar the root products ubi and cassava are the staples; on the Kais cassava; in Aru sago. On Tanimbar and Babar you find some dry-rice cultivation. Cassava is beginning to inundate the entire area.

Arts And Crafts

Although the southwest and southeast Malukan islands are racially and culturally mixed, their arts are rather homogeneous. A good many of their traditions—woodcarving, weaving, and pearl-diving—are largely intact. Primitive woodcarving is a living art, especially in the Tanimbars, and is seen in statuary, on doorposts, and on the prows of local prahu. The art of the peoples of Alor Kai can be traced back as far as the ornamental Dongson-style of Annam. This style incorporates numerous Oriental motifs, as seen in their small carved wooden ancestor statues. At present nearly all the old ancestor statues, sculptures, carvings, and figurines have either been burned by fervid Ambonese ministers or sold to foreign "collectors." You'll find a great number of beautiful specimens in the Siwalima Museum in Batu Capeo; a visit here is an excellent introduction to the art of the area. New figurines, resembling the old sculptures, are made by a few Tanimbarese and Babarese living in Ambon. The best islands for traditional architecture, in homes and public meeting halls, are Tanimbar, Babar, Kisar, and Serwaru. Antiques found in the region are chinaware, swords, shields, and ancestral carvings.

Except for the Kais, ikat backstrap handloom weaving is found on every island. The motifs and colors have much in common with those used on Savu, but are quite different from those produced on Sumba and Timor. Factory-made cotton and artificial dyes are increasingly common. Prices vary from Rp25,000 to Rp75,000, depending on size, age, and patterns.

Local musical instruments include shellhorns, *totobuang, tifa,* gongs, bamboo flutes, and violin. See many work dances; Kai *sul sawat* and Tanimbar *angkosi* and *badendang* social dances; *tnabar ilaa* and *cakalele* war dances; and *rubai dab* and *tiwa nam* traditional dances.

TRANSPORTATION

Getting There
If you don't have the time to journey by sea, fly Merpati from Ambon to Saumlaki, twice weekly (Rp75,700), or to Langgur, once daily (Rp84,600); both destinations are in the Tanimbars. From Saumlaki or Langgur, take a Pelni ship or some other watercraft to the outlying islands. The regular routes are run by overcrowded, filthy, cheap Pelni-Perintis ships from Ambon or Kupang, sailing about once every three weeks. Some 250-300 passengers pile on at a time; the ships are almost complete disasters. The sanitary conditions are disgusting, but people patiently endure the whole thing—it's the only way to travel.

The KM *Dukuh* travels the short route from Ambon twice monthly, while the KM *Niaga XIV* takes care of the extended one twice a month. Sample ticket prices: Ambon-Tual, Rp20,000; Ambon-Tepa, Rp30,000; pay extra for cabins, beds, food.

Getting Around And Away
Since few minibuses or buses exist, most of the villagers walk; hire rowing, sailing, or motorized vessels along the coasts, or take one of the local ferries. You can get a ship to almost anyplace in Southeast Maluku if you hang around long enough—just realize this could mean a week or so. Boats are more frequent to Ambon and Banda than to Babar, Kisar, and Wetar; some outliers are approachable only by chartered boat. In the wet season (April-Aug.) there are very few boats to anywhere.

Accommodations are limited, and proper hotels are found only in such administrative/commercial centers as Tual, Saumlaki, and Dobo. Everywhere else, ask the missionaries or police to put you up for suitable remuneration, or stay on the boat.

THE KAI ISLANDS

Two fairly large and many tiny islands covering a total area of about 900 square km. With heavy forests and rugged mountains, these nonvolcanic islands are singularly picturesque. Their coasts rise hundreds of meters above the sea, forming an arc of uplifted coral reefs. With bays of dazzling white sand, magnificent butterflies and beetles, many species of pigeon and exotic birds, the Kais were once a real discovery for the naturalist and traveler alike. Today they're on the brink of an ecological catastrophe.

Tual, on Pulau Dullah, is the principal town and administrative center of Southeastern Maluku. **Elat** on Kai Besar is the capital of the Kai Islands, seat of the Dutch *controlleur* during colonial times.

The Kai islanders cultivate taro, yams, maize, and rice. Sago is collected from the swamps. Regional dishes include *embal,* or cassava cakes. Mango stones (seeds) are soaked in brine for three to seven days to soften and pickle them, then they're boiled or made into cakes to supplement the diet during the dry season. Much of the people's cash income is derived from timber, boatbuilding, copra production, and *trepang* collection. All but two villages are coastal.

THE PEOPLE

The inhabitants of the Kais are Papuan in origin. Although the original population has become more mixed with later immigrant groups, the Melanesian strain observed by A.R. Wallace in the 19th century is still very much in evidence.

Three classes or status-groups make up this society: the aristocrats, or ruling lineage (*melmel*); the common people (*ven-ven*); and the recently freed ex-slaves (*hiri-hiri*), who still live with the stigma of slavery. Descent is patrilineal.

Bride-prices are often paid, though the groom has the option of substituting bride-price service (*nafdu*). The bride-price could be reciprocated by a gift from the girl's parents.

Today the population of the Kais is actually declining because of the very high incidence of malaria and cholera, which kill hundreds each year. This is a place where you don't want to drink the water, and do want to down your malaria medication.

Religion

About one-third of the people are animist. The remainder of the population is equally divided between Islam and Christianity. To counter the spread of Islam introduced by Buginese missionaries, the Dutch brought in Protestant and Catholic missionaries and by the turn of the century large numbers had converted. Some state their religion is Agama Hindu; on Kai Besar a few villages are said to be Hindu.

Arts And Crafts

Besides Ambon, Kai is the most musical area of Maluku. The islanders also carve wood. On **Pulau Tayandu,** a small island west of Kai Kecil, pottery-making is a thriving cottage industry. The Kai islanders were once noted boatbuilders, but since the forests of the islands have been so plundered that art is declining. Wallace observed magnificent long canoes, with the bow and stern rising up in a peak several meters high, decorated with shells and waving plumes or cassowary hair. These *prahu,* made without a nail or piece of iron, could hold 60 men and 20-30 tons of cargo, and were able to sail on any sea to Singapore. To this day the harbors are always full of *prahu* weighing 5-200 tons, and islanders still fish at night from elaborate and skillfully built dugout canoes and plank outriggers.

TRANSPORTATION

Getting There

Merpati flies daily from Ambon to Langgur in the Kais for about Rp130,000. Extra baggage is expensive, so travel light. You'll touch down at Banda on the way to Langgur; landings are pretty rough. Flights also depart from Saumlaki to Langgur for Rp50,000. You'll land at Dumaatuban Airport just outside of Langgur and must cross a bridge to reach Tual, five km distant on Pulau Dullah.

Another approach is by sea. From Kaimana on the southern coast of Irian Jaya take a *kapal motor* or sailing *prahu* to Tual, Rp15,000. There's a brisk trade between Kaimana and the Kais, so boats are frequent. On the way they sometimes stop in the Mengawitu Islands. These small boats seldom venture out over open seas during the rainy season, though this doesn't stop the Pelni and Perintis ships, the KM *Dukuh* and the KM *Niaga XIV,* which stop in Kai Kecil about once every three weeks year-round. Be prepared for the ship showing up a week or so late.

Getting Around

Transport on Kai Kecil is surprisingly developed, with new Japanese minibuses. The roads may not be perfectly smooth, but they're definitely passable at all times and traffic is steady in all directions. Fares are cheap. Road systems are less developed on Kai Besar; you must walk to the more distant villages. Motorized *prahu* are available for charter at expensive prices. You can get a ship to almost any place in Southeast Maluku if you hang around long enough.

KAI BESAR

Known as "Great Kai," this is the largest island in the Kais, about 80 km long and very narrow. Part of the spectacular limestone arc system of eastern Indonesia, scenic Kai Besar's topography is quite mountainous; the highest peak is Gunung Dab (688 meters). There are very few roads on Kai Besar; expect to walk. **Elat,** on Pulau Kai Besar, is the capital of the subdistrict. In Banda-Elat and Eli on Kai Besar live the Muslim descendants of the survivors of the Dutch genocide on the Banda Islands in the 17th century. They produce fine boats, woodcarvings, and silver- and goldwork.

Most villages on the east coast are animistic. **Onoilim,** located on a small hill, is a primitive *kampung gunung* that shows signs of influence from the Aru Islands. **Ohoiwait,** also on the east coast, is a sacred village; a footpath connects it with the west coast. **Haar** is a tiny village on the northeast tip divided into three *kampung*— Catholic, Protestant, and Muslim. Only about six meters separates each community, yet they have little to do with one another.

Accommodations And Food

Best place to stay is the **Catholic Mission** (Pastoran Katolik), 200 meters from the airport; Rp2000 with meals for a nice room, with access to the priestly sanitary arrangements. The food is quite acceptable and you'll eat with the father and brothers while listening to highly amusing accounts of the day's religious events. The **Linda Mas** in Tual, five km down the road, costs Rp18,000 per night including meals; small rooms, hard beds, weird toilets. There's also a *pasanggrahan* for government officials; you can stay if there's a vacancy.

Transportation

Tual is the center of trade and shipping for the Kai islands. From Ambon to Tual fly Merpati daily for Rp75,000. Minibuses travel often (Rp100, five km) between Langgur and Tual. From Tual there's a daily boat to Elat on the west coast of Pulau Kai Besar; Rp1000, three hours. About once every three weeks there's a Pelni ship to Dobo in the Arus; Rp3500 for deck class; rent a crew member's cabin for around Rp20,000. Buy tickets at the Pelni office on the dock or on the boat itself.

PULAU DULLAH AND KAI KECIL

Pulau Dullah and Kai Kecil are two islands west of Kai Besar. Generally flat, they consist mostly of swampland and coconut palm groves, with

some ironwood forests. **Tual,** on Pulau Dullah, is the main town and port. About a dozen Dutch missionaries and teachers live here. There's a good road system on both islands, with minibuses heading everywhere; you can also borrow bicycles from the mission. In some villages you'll find large squatting wooden statues representing hero ancestors; other villages feature thick defensive stone walls. Along sea cliffs are inscribed paintings of natives and their *prahu*; nothing is known of these paintings except that they're very old.

Sights

Just outside of Tual is an open-air museum of *belang* (*prahu*) right on the shore. **Pasir Panjang Beach** is three km long with deep blue water and nice coral. **Ohoider,** 12 km from Tual, is a white sandy beach ideal for swimming, rowing, and diving in marine gardens. At the far end of Ohoider Beach is sacred **Gua Luat,** containing strange, undeciphered inscriptions. **Difur,** about 13 km north of Tual, is a center for traditional pearl cultivation.

Wearblel Lake is a three-square-km lake with a depth of 21 meters; good fishing. At **Danau,** a pond surrounded by grass meadows and cemara trees, watch wild animals come down to drink. Clear, blue **Mas II** reservoir provides drinking water for the town of Tual. The traditional-minded people from the island of **Ur,** west of Pulau Kai Kecil, are quite different from other Kai people. They keep almost totally to themselves, though they have set up a sort of marriage-exchange system with the nearby island of Kai Tanimbar.

THE ARU ISLANDS

The unusual Aru Islands, located in the middle of the Banda Sea, consist of several large islands surrounded by many small closely packed isles. Consisting of low-lying limestone formations, the islands share a similar topography to the Kais. Most of the group's 21 islands are flat and swampy, their extensive marshes broken by low hills. Lying about 640 km southeast of Ambon and only 240 km from the coast of West New Guinea, the Arus probably once formed part of that giant island.

Between these islands are deep, narrow channels known locally as *tanah besar,* or "big land." The numerous islands and islets on the Great Aru Bank to the east are called *belakang tanah,* or "beyond the land." These saltwater straits give rise to numerous and beautiful waterfalls. Essentially an unknown region, forests here cover the interiors, growing directly out of limestone

rock with very little topsoil; there are endless white-sand beaches. The main town and principal trading and shipping center for the district is Dobo, on the small island of Wamar.

FAUNA

On the Arus the fauna of Asia and Australasia meet. There is small game, deer, cuscus, wallabies, kangaroos, crocodiles, monitor lizards, an amazing variety of insects, and wonderful birdlife: lories, rainbow lorikeets, parakeets, cassowaries, and the great black palm and yellow-crested cockatoos, living on the *kanari* nuts other birds are unable to crack. Two species of bird of paradise reach full plumage in the courting season, May through September. Under unremitting pressure from human settlement, birds are now scarce on Wamar, and soon will be in danger of extinction. Wildlife on the *belakang tanah* islands to the east is said to be the least disturbed.

It was here that Wallace wrote for the first time his thoughts on the faunal differences he'd observed during seven years of travel. He and Darwin jointly announced to the world their Theory of Evolution in London in 1858, but because Darwin had emphasized human evolution he received the lion's share of credit/blame. Once Wallace was able to collect all manner of fascinating and unusual wild things on a walk from Dobo to Wangil; today you're never out of sight or sound of village life.

HISTORY

For centuries Dobo has been a famous native trading station. Chinese traders came from as far away as Goram and Makassar; pirate Malay *prahu* from the Sulas would occasionally attack and burn villages. To guard their spice monopoly, the Dutch finally built a fortress on Pulau Wokam in 1659. Dutch trade declined in the second half of the 18th century, and the Makassarese and Buginese quickly filled the vacuum. In 1882, the Dutch reopened trade with the establishment of an administrative settlement in

THE ARU ISLANDS

P. WAMAR   P. WOKAM
DOBO
NAFAR
P. KOBROOR

P. TRANGAN
WORKAI

0   50 km

P. ENU

© MOON PUBLICATIONS, INC.

Dobo, and by 1904 had regained control over the islands. Today trade is mainly again in the hands of the Makassarese and Buginese. Dobo was one of the few places in the Indies where Japanese were numerous before 1941, engaged primarily in pearl production. In the 1960s the Arus played a strategic role in the war of liberation in Irian Jaya. In Dobo you can see a commemorative column to Yos Sudarso, who perished in the battle of Trikora.

ECONOMY

Vast quantities of marine wealth come from these isolated waters: *agar-agar,* turtle shell, *trepang,* and edible birds' nests. Although illegal, collection of bird of paradise skins thrives. The *trepang* which used to lie so thickly on the banks have now become hard to find, and shark fishing with imported nets has greatly increased the catches of *dugong,* one of the rarest of sea mammals. *Dugong* are chiefly valued for their ivory teeth. Made into cigarette holders, they're an important Indonesian status symbol. These islands were once famous for their pearls, of great purity and high value, but today the pearl and mother-of-pearl industries are languishing, to say the least.

THE PEOPLE

The ethnic groups of the Arus resemble those of the Kais and the Tanimbars; pure Papuan Alfuro communities now live only in the interior of Pulau Wokam—primitive, nomadic bands that seldom come in contact with outsiders. Inhabitants of the western coasts have mixed more with Malayan immigrants, are lighter skinned, and tend to look down upon those on the east coast. But unlike the neighboring Tanimbarese, the peaceful Arus rarely warred among themselves.

Because of their changeable terrain, these flat islands are among the most sparsely inhabited regions of Indonesia. At high tide many areas are underwater, even though the land, so densely forested by mangroves, *seems* to be terra firma. Since clearings for cultivation are often washed out, the scattered native Alfuros are often on the move. In the southern islands they gather sago and paddy melons, harvest wild mangosteens and honey, practice slash-and-burn agriculture, and in times of food shortages hunt pig, deer, cassowary, and tree kangaroo. Although today the islanders are ostensibly a mix of Christian and Muslims, animism persists.

Crafts

The Arus share many historical and cultural affinities with New Guinea; their plastic arts reflect this association. In the Arus the finest mother-of-pearl in the world is found. The islands are a production center for shell artifacts, tortoiseshell, *akar bahar, dugong-* and crocodile-teeth pipes, and cassowary eggshell crafts. The Catholics are trying to revive the creation of native pottery, which once resulted in strikingly painted and engraved clay dishes and pots. Large squatting ancestor statues watch over the centers and entrances to villages; they also occupy mountaintops.

PRACTICALITIES

Getting There

There's only one airstrip on the Arus, in a small village south of Dobo called Bendjina, where a navy patrol plane drops in whenever the pilot feels like it. You could conceivably hitch a ride on that plane, but don't bank on it. For the moment the nearest civilian airport is at Langgur on Kai Kecil.

The only reliable way to reach the Arus is by Pelni ship on the "long route" out of Ambon. The regular port of call for ships in the Arus is Dobo on Pulau Wamar. From Tual to Dobo it's about 24 hours by Pelni boat; you usually leave in the afternoon and arrive in Dobo early the next morning. The ship has a canteen on it, so you can buy sandwiches, candy, and drinks. Still, carry boiled water and snacks. The basic fare is Rp3500; buy your ticket either on the boat or at the Pelni office on the dock in Tual. Coasting vessels also call at Dobo from Kaimana in Irian Jaya.

Getting Around

There's a road under construction from Dobo to a Pertamina installation at a small village called **Wamar** southeast of Dobo, but they've been working on it since 1984 and are only a few kilometers along. Since waterways so cut up the islands, land travel is difficult. Hollowed-out canoes with small 15-hp outboards are available for local transport. Occasionally, motorboats are available, but expect to pay a minimum of Rp30,000 for a half-day trip—you probably won't get farther than **Nafar,** a small village on the southwest corner of Pulau Wokam. The calm season for interisland sea travel is September through December; at other times the seas can be rough. **Pulau Enu** to the south and other nearby islets are only accessible those four months of the year. The dry season is May through August, when whole villages often move to streamside locations.

Accommodations And Food
For accommodations and guides, avail yourself of the *camat,* village head, traditional lineage

heads, or *orang kaya.* There's no hotel in Dobo; most travelers stay at the **Pastoran,** Rp2000 per day including meals. A woman comes in during the day to wash up and do the laundry and housekeeping. The food comes from a local restaurant and consists of several dishes of fish, vegetables, occasional meat (almost always venison), and soup. For the evening and morning meals you're provided with reheated leftovers. A young Indonesian seminarian, Father Segers, is an all-around assistant to the priest, a kind, elderly Dutchman responsible for about 20 village churches scattered throughout the Arus. Sometimes he makes seven- to eight-day trips to visit several of these churches, traveling as far as Pulau Workai; you could hitch a ride with him. This is probably your best opportunity to see the real Aru jungle.

THE TANIMBARS

The Tanimbar Islands, with a total land area of 5,568 square km, consist of about 66 nonvolcanic islands; only seven are inhabited. Located 675 km southeast of Ambon, this isolated group is the southernmost in Maluku, accessible by air and sea. The Tanimbars offer nu-

merous empty beaches, pristine coral reefs and sealife, a strong traditional culture, unique flora, and superb scenery. The islands are famous among botanists for the Larat orchids that grow only here—in fact, another name for the Tanimbars is Lelemuku, the local word for "orchid." Saumlaki is the largest town, located on the southern coast of Pulau Yamdena, the largest island of the group.

THE TANIMBARS

P. MOLU
LARAT
P. NUSWÓTAR
P. LARAT
P. YAMDENA
P. SERA
ARUIBAB
OLILIT
SAUMLAKI
ADAUT
P. SELARU

0   25 km

© MOON PUBLICATIONS, INC.

History
The Buginese and Makassarese traded with the Tanimbars as early as the 16th century. The Dutch established a fortified factory here in 1645 but abandoned it several years later. They returned in the late 19th century to attempt to settle the islands; they were not warmly received. Wearing magnificent battle costumes and headdresses, native Tanimbarese long engaged in savage internecine warfare, headhunting, and cannibalism. The Dutch weren't able to pacify the islands until 1907, after building a garrison and bolstering their police force.

The People
The Tanimbars are composed of a mix of peoples: Irianese, Negritos, Melanesians, and Orang Maluku. Papuan physical features predominate. A number of subgroups are scattered throughout the islands, each speaking its own

mutually unintelligible dialect. Slaves here could marry into a higher class and thus gain their freedom. Alfuro aborigines have for the most part retained their traditional culture and animist religion; on some islands shark cults flourish.

It's an ancient custom for village elders to occupy ancestral stone seats, indicating their origins and reinforcing their right to rule. The Alfuro are some of the best spearmen in Indonesia; they still use blowpipes, but only as a hunting weapon. Maize is the staple dish, supplemented by cassava, yams, and taro baked in Polynesian-style pit ovens. Fowl and pig are consumed on special occasions. *Tuak* is very popular; with tobacco and betelnut, it's an important component in rituals.

Crafts

In the Saumlaki (Pulau Yamdena) and Larat (Pulau Larat) areas you can find high-quality plaiting and *ikat* weaving decorated with symbolic traditional patterns. *Tikar* weaving, shell jewelry, coil pottery, and metallurgy are widespread; wood- and some stone carvings are also exported. You'll see carvings on *adat* houses as well as on the bows of the large *belang,* a gondola-like vessel used by the local *rajas.* Tanimbarese are skilled boatbuilders, fashioning their own plank boats and dugout canoes with outriggers; see them drawn up on the beach in Yamdena coastal villages. Traditional dwellings (*das*) feature steep, thatched gable roofs, with buffalo horn decorations placed at the ridge poles. Inside are small compartments that sleep an extended family of up to 20 people. Sometimes there's a separate men's and boys' building (*lingat*) where head-hunting raids were once planned and prepared; *lingat* now serve as eating and gathering places.

Economy

Except for several timber companies, a subsistence economy predominates on these islands. The soil is worked by the slash-and-burn method and food staples are typically Melanesian. During droughts or food shortages, the people hunt and collect sago. Fish supplements the diet; the Tanimbarese practice torchlight fishing using harpoons and lines.

Transportation

Merpati flies from Ambon to Saumlaki. There are also flights from Saumlaki in the Kais for Rp50,000. Perintis sends a ship out of Ambon for southeast Maluku about once every three weeks. On the islands themselves there are few vehicles, so count on walking. Rowing canoes, outriggers, and *kapal motor* are available between isles. Plenty of sharks in these waters.

YAMDENA ISLAND

The largest island of the Tanimbars. The Yamden language spoken along the east coast is related to Tetum in the Timor archipelago. The people are involved primarily in agriculture and fishing; the main crops are coconut, candlenut, and beans. From Saumlaki, walk through the villages up the east coast. See rare orchids and endemic birds such as the *kesturi,* cockatoos, and egrets. Take care: herds of wild bulls occasionally kill people on this island. **Lakateri Beach** offers white sand and coral gardens. **Bangruti, Bangdas,** and **Weritubun** caves feature stalactites and stalagmites. Natural salt mines are found between the villages of **Otimmer/Selwasa** and **Wowonda,** in the center of Pulau Yamdena.

Saumlaki

The largest town in the Tanimbars. There's a nice mission here where you can always secure a bed or bath. One good small hotel, the **Ratulel,** is run by kind people; Rp15,000 per person with food. Visit the delightful harbormaster and Odilon, the amicable Chinese merchant. The *ikat* weaving center is in **Olilit,** north of Saumlaki.

Transportation

About every three to four weeks a Pelni ship stops at Saumlaki and then departs for Babar, Sermatang, and Kisar to the southwest. Pelni's KM *Dukuh* docks at Saumlaki on the short route from Ambon. Sometimes *kapal motor* sail for Aru and Kai. From Saumlaki you can catch *prahu* to the southern end of Selaru and its main town of Adaut; pay Rp4000 or trade two packs of good tobacco. Pulau Selaru is a poor island, low and bushy. There's not a lot of food; meals of dried fish cost Rp400-600. Trade a bottle of beer for a black coral bracelet (*akhar bahar*). The surrounding islands are known for pearl diving and gorgeous coral reefs.

Deforestation And Obliteration

It's possible Pulau Yamdena may slip beneath the sea before you have a chance to visit. Although Yamdena was declared a protected forest and research area in 1971, twenty years later the government granted a logging concession to a company controlled by one of the most powerful men in Indonesia, Liem Sioe Liong. To date Liong has been authorized to fell fully half the island's trees.

Yamdena is a coral island where 80% of the topography is rolling, with slopes of 15-60 percent. The topsoil is but 50 to 60 cm deep; beneath is limestone. It is estimated that on islands like Yamdena 100 to 200 years are required to form one cm of soil. Logging will cause erosion at the rate of 10 tons per hectare per year. At such a pace the island itself cannot last; eventually it will simply blow and flow away.

Efforts by the people of Yamdena and international environmental interests to halt the logging have proved futile. In early 1993 the minister of forestry announced the completion of a government study on the effects of timber cutting on Yamdena. He refused to reveal the results of the report, but noted snidely that if the logging perpetrated by Liong was adjudged environmentally harmful, then all other timber cutting—including that by residents—should also come to a halt.

The sinking of Yamdena would not be unique. Pulau Tapak Kuda in North Sumatra was stripped of its mangrove forests and is now slowly disappearing beneath the waves. The government is appealing to the inhabitants to leave the island.

SOUTHWESTERN MALUKU

Southwest of Banda off the northeast coast of Timor, this group can be divided into two main archipelagos: the northern arc of islands, mostly volcanic and wooded; and the southern arc, generally less fertile with savannah-like landscapes. All these islands share cultural and historical similarities emanating from a common cultural capital, **Pulau Luang,** located in the geographic center of the region. The Dutch established themselves here in the 17th century; since the 1800s the islands have been administered from Ambon. All the southwest islands are noted for their plaiting and weaving; the Babar, Leti, and Damar groups are the haunt of anthropologists.

The People

Natives were notorious for their savagery and headhunting; today the inhabitants are a mixture of Papuan, Malay, Negrito, and Arab peoples. Most are Christian, although the old paganism persists. Ancestor spirits are depicted in wood and bone, and religious chiefs perform a renewal festival called Porka every seven years; at one time Porka rites involved public orgies and the taking of heads. Originally, a rigid caste system predominated; the Dutch, however, instituted administration by local *rajas,* ruling with the help of appointed headmen and hereditary *adat* chiefs.

Adat villages today often contain a communal council house; in front stands a wooden ancestor statue of the village founder. Single family structures are now replacing the traditional large raised extended family dwellings. As is typical throughout Maluku Tenggara, the people consume a heavy starch diet of maize, rice, sweet potatoes, cassava, and millet. Inhabitants of the islands of Kisar, Babar, Romang, and Damar subsist on sago. In the Romang-Damar group, breadfruit, bananas, and coconut are the rule; on Wetar wild honey is an important exchange commodity.

THE BABAR ISLANDS

An isolated group of six economically unimportant islands, with a combined area of about 650 square km, named after the largest central island of Babar. The islands of the group are nonvolcanic, high, and rugged. About one-third of the population lives in Tual, Ambon, Dobo, and Ceram, seeking jobs, education, medical help. Although Christianized, the inhabitants of these nearly inaccessible islands still maintain a phallic-animist religious structure. Be sure to see Babar's unique *bero*; islanders sail as far as Tanimbar in these canoes with one outrigger.

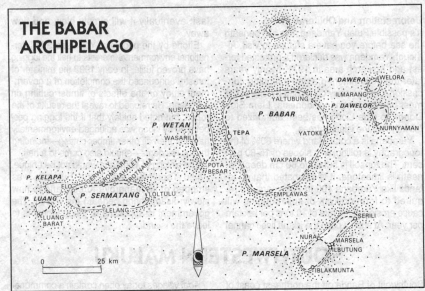

THE BABAR
ARCHIPELAGO

© MOON PUBLICATIONS INC.

During festivals, the traditional circle dance *seka* is performed; accompanied by *tifa* drums, these dances last all night. Arriving in Tepa on Pulau Babar you must report to the *camat*, police, and military office. In every village you may stay in the *kepala desa*'s house; give him Rp2000-3000 per day for food, and bring some cigarettes. A footpath around Babar connects the villages; it takes three to four days to complete the circuit. Be careful: an innocent chat with an unmarried girl may make the Babarese *toli belik* (beat a tin drum), which may mean you're obliged to marry her.

Sights
Near **Tepa** at Watrorona is a 150-meter-high stone staircase at the base of a steep mountain; climb to the top for the view. A natural geyser lies 10 km from Tepa. Near the villages of **Yatoke** and **Wakpapapi** are guarded sacred caves containing skulls and other ancestor artifacts. The islands of **Dawelor** and **Dawera** offer similar sacred caves. The sandy beaches on **Pulau Sermatang**, west of Pulau Babar, are a striking rust-iron and green-black.

Pulau Wetan, a few km west of Pulau Babar, offers sacred caves near the villages of **Lektu-**pang and **Nusiata,** ancestral burial places. The skull cave near **Pota Besar** is an old defensive stronghold, fenced in by human skulls. **Pulau Marsela,** southeast of Pulau Babar, is the weaving and plaiting center of the group. *Seka* dances in traditional costumes are performed in the villages of **Ilbutung** and **Marsela.** This island is well known for its mildly alcoholic *sopi*, distilled from the juice of the *lontar* (here called the *koli*) tree.

Pulau Luang
The Luang Islands—Luang, Sermatang, and Kelapa—have a combined area of 389 square km. Luang was once the cultural heart of the Leti and Babar islands. The languages of Leti and West Babar are similar, more or less dialects of Luangese. Half the proto-Malayan Luangese profess Christianity, the other half Islam, while animism is strongest among the Sermatangs. Luang's goldsmiths once traveled all over the region to make gold earrings; these are still part of the bride-price. Today Luang is well known for its marine products (*hasil laut*), ideal fishing grounds, and *ikat* weaving. The island is overgrown with olive trees, and some areas are inhabited by wild buffalo. Marine gardens extend out to sea; at

ebbtide you can walk from Pulau Luang to the uninhabited island of Pulau Kelapa.

THE OUTER ISLANDS

The Leti Group

Located east of Kisar and Timor, the Letis have an area of around 900 square km. They are nonvolcanic and comparatively infertile. The proto-Malay natives are half Christian, half Muslim. Porka festivals are held every few years with phallic rites. **Tutukei** village, the pottery, basketry, and weaving center, is the only link to Leti's past; it's on a hilltop near Serwaru, the administrative center. From Serwaru

it's not difficult to find a fishing boat to East Timor.

Pulau Kisar

East of Pulau Wetar, this 250-square-km island supports a population of around 9,000. The landscape is hilly, almost denuded of trees, and the soil infertile. Ninety percent of the Kisarese are Islamic, the remainder Christian. Proto-Malays live here except for one district inhabited by descendants of Dutch soldiers and Kisarese women; over 100 years ago the Dutch maintained a garrison on the island. Although they still have Dutch names and do not mix with the island's aborigines, the people no longer speak Dutch.

IRIAN JAYA

Politically a part of Indonesia since 1969, Irian Jaya is Indonesia's most spectacular region for tourism, and the greatest intact natural history museum in existence. The province comprises roughly the western half of the island of New Guinea, the world's second-largest island; Papua New Guinea (PNG) occupies the eastern half. Although the province makes up 22% of Indonesia's total land surface, only one percent of the nation's people live here; it's the least visited, least populated, most remote province in Indonesia. The provincial capital, Jayapura, is 3,520 km from Jakarta. Decades behind Java, it's also the country's least economically developed territory. With the exception of large coastal cities like Jayapura, Biak, Sorong, Manokwari, and Merauke, the vast landmass of Irian Jaya is punctuated by just a dozen or so frontier towns connected with one another only by air or sea. Between these posts stretch thousands of kilometers of mountains and jungle, most of it isolated and primitive.

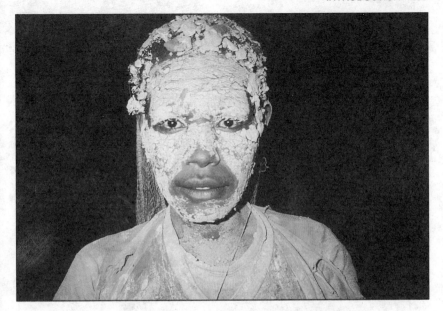

INTRODUCTION

Irian Jaya is one of the last places on the planet where whole great swaths of earth can still be accurately described as totally wild. There are people here who have resolutely refused to move into any sort of "civilization" as defined by white Europeans. Creatures once throught extinct elsewhere on the globe seem now to flourish here; the Irian mountains, swamps, and jungles are filled with animals and plants unknown and unclassified by Western science. Though tourism has increased markedly since the late 1980s, there are still plenty of places in Irian Jaya that seem to bear no human footprint at all.

THE LAND

Irian Jaya features wilder landscapes and more impenetrable, treacherous jungle than any other tropical region in the world, including the Amazon Basin. The territory contains white-sand beaches lined with coconut palms, wild forest streams plunging down sheer rock faces, glittering mountain snowfields, jewel-like turquoise-green lakes strewn with glacial debris, heaths and yellow marshes bursting with head-high grass, vast stands of pine trees, wild sugarcane meadows, groves of casuarina, and moss-carpeted forests with bright flowers growing riotously. Fifty types of pandanus grow naturally in Irian Jaya. Forests still cover 31.5 million hectares and occupy 75% of the land area.

The majority of the territory is mountainous, with a high central backbone extending for 650 km, dividing Irian into south and north. Some mountains are so high planes must fly between them to avoid turbulence. The highest, Puncak Jaya, is 5,039 meters. Although situated just four degrees below the equator, a number of mountaintops are permanently covered in snow and ice. High mountain regions are broken up by coarse grassy valleys and rainforests.

IRIAN JAYA

✈ = AIRFIELD

0   100 km

© MOON PUBLICATIONS, INC.

Climate

Hot and humid on the coastal fringes. Mountain areas above 1,800 meters are warm in the daytime but sometimes experience frosts at night. The climate varies through the highlands. One valley might suffer through a dry season as a second is drenched in the wet, a third receiving rainfall evenly distributed throughout the year. The Baliem and its sister valleys to the north are quite broad and receive more sunshine than the steep, narrow valleys to the south. There are no well-defined seasons, but December and January are generally warmer, while August and September are misty and cold. The southern lowlands have a very distinct dry season; in Merauke it sometimes doesn't rain for five straight months.

Because of its phenomenal rainfall—in some places up to 1,000 cm per annum—Irian Jaya possesses some of Indonesia's largest rivers. Originating in the mountains, these mighty watercourses flow like undulating snakes through evergreen forests. In the south and southwest, they've created mosaic river systems winding through a million square kilometers of mangrove swamps, casuarina groves, and tidal forests. The great Baliem, Mamberamo, Tariku, Taritatu, and Digul rivers writhe with many rapids and waterfalls.

Flora

The island is home to many species of liana, beech trees, tree ferns, tree orchids, and the so-called "anthouse plants," which are potato-shaped and honeycombed with tunnels inhabited by biting ants, tree frogs, and lizards. From the *lagenaria* come gourds used by the Irianese as bottles and dippers. *Libodedrus* is an incense tree found at high elevations. At night the mold of the rainforest floor glows and flickers with decomposing bacteria.

For centuries highland peoples burnt off forests to flush game and prepare the ground for agriculture. This created the great highland grass plains of the Baliem Valley and the Wissel Lakes Country. The native plant with the widest variety of uses is the coconut, which provides food, drink, oil, wood, leaves for thatching, fiber for matting, and shells for water vessels. Nipa and *arca* palm leaves are also used for thatching. Native plants consumed as food include sugarcane, banana, sweet potato, sago palm, taro, papaya, yam, and breadfruit.

Fauna

The whole territory holds immense fascination for the naturalist. Freshwater and terrestrial vertebrates are nearly all of the Australian type. Many species may appear in one locale of Irian Jaya but not in another, possibly due to the varying amounts of rainfall. Except for freshwater eels, fish are restricted to the coastal regions. Some highland tribes have never seen a fish, only eels, freshwater crayfish, and tadpoles with flattened heads attached to rocks in fast-flowing streams. The province is host to fabulously colored butterflies, some exceedingly rare. The coral islands east of the Bird's Head Peninsula in Cendrawasih Bay are famous as feeding grounds for sea turtles and *dugong*, and serve as important nesting sites for seabirds. On land there are cuscus, bandicoots, bats, rats, mice, snakes, tortoises, frilled lizards, and giant monitor lizards. Irian Jaya is home to the world's largest tree-climbing water rat. The spiny anteater is a nocturnal marsupial with a long beak-like snout, small black eyes, powerful set of claws, no tail or teeth, and a very long thin tongue used to consume ants, termites, and other insects. It has one exit for both solid and liquid excreta; the only other animal like it is the platypus, absent from Irian Jaya.

Tree kangaroos with gray-brown coats live in the higher regions. The phalanger has fox-like ears and a long bushy tail. The marsupial cat presumably chases marsupial mice. Other marsupials include the possum; these vary in size from the mouse-like flying possum to the furry cuscus, the largest member of the possum family. There are 11 crocodile ranches in Irian, each with 300-400 crocodiles; their skins are purchased by such high fashion houses as Gucci and Christian Dior and exported mostly to France.

Irian Jaya is renowned for its over 650 species of exquisite, colorful, and plentiful birds which, having developed in isolation, are unique and spectacular. These include at least 38 protected species of the exotic bird of paradise. For many years it was believed this bird needed no feet—they never landed on earth, but flew always in the sunlight. The Papuans call them "Birds of the Gods," and the bird of paradise is pictured on the national flag of Papua New Guinea. A spectacular example of overadaptation to species-specific evolution, the bird of paradise averages 43-46 cm from the tip of its beak to its tail, with

THE SEARCH FOR THE TASMANIAN TIGER

The world's largest carnivorous marsupial was once believed native only to Tasmania, Australia's island state, where it was known as the Tasmanian tiger (*Thylacinus cynocephalus*) and ruthlessly hunted to extinction by white sheepherders. Recent evidence, however, suggests the animal may also inhabit the island of Irian Jaya.

Until the 1830s Australians regarded the Tasmanian tiger as just another small curious antipodean animal. But with the introduction of sheep the creature was transformed in the public mind into a savage economic threat. Its reputation as a sheep killer grew to demonic proportions; the tiger was blamed for the victims of poor farming, dogs, theft, and aboriginal attacks. In 1887 the government began offering bounties for dead tigers; this officially sponsored program of annihilation continued for 25 years. The Tasmanian tiger was not granted full protection of the law until 1936, some months after the last known tiger died in the Hobart zoo.

Thylacinus cynocephalus means "pouched dog with a wolf head." An adult Tasmanian tiger averages 20 kilograms, 200 centimeters from tailtip to nose, standing about 60 centimeters at the shoulder. Like kangaroos, tigers have long stiff tails; they also possess a unique rearfacing pouch. Fifteen to 20 brown-black stripes streak its yellow-brown coat from the base of the tail almost to the shoulders. The animal is nocturnal, hunting from dusk to dawn. It isn't fast, but will most often stalk its prey to exhaustion. It can open its mouth to an extraordinary 120 degrees and possesses far more force in its jaws than most animals. The tiger is silent but for the occasional coughing bark.

In the late '80s missionaries working in the highlands of Irian Jaya began to report that tribespeople shown photographs of the Tasmanian tiger insisted the creature inhabited the surrounding high country. Locals rarely see the animal in full daylight; it's usually spotted hunting at dawn or dusk for small marsupials and birds. The people say they are afraid of it; they associate the animal with evil spirits, and use its feces to perform magic on enemies. Its dens, they say, are usually found in rocks or caves. They described a creature with a head and shoulders like a dog's, except for a huge, strong mouth; a long, stiff tail; and many stripes from the ribs to the hips. Tribespeople even have a name for the beast: *dobsegna*.

Ned Terry, an Australian grazier obsessed with discovering a living Tasmanian tiger, is convinced *dobsegna* and the tiger are one and the same. Fossil evidence proves conclusively the tiger once roamed the island, and the local Irianese consistently produce, spontaneously, detailed and accurate descriptions of the tiger-like *dobsegna*. "They know its living habits too well for it not to have been there very recently," Terry says. "They know where it slept, how it hunts, what it eats, and the difference between its paw print and that of a dog's." If the tiger has survived, he adds, it makes sense that the creature found refuge in the Baliem Valley, "the wildest place left on the face of the earth."

---

half-meter sprays of luxurious tail feathers and plumes beneath its wings. The yellow bird of paradise uses its long golden plumes as a display tree. Some species display in groups, though you only see this in the wild. Some decorate nests with castoff snake skins. These birds are difficult to glimpse through the thick vegetation; listen for the silken rustling of wings. Wondrous acrobats, they fly up suddenly, alarmed and frantic; when they settle down again it's with a dull, heavy sound. The great bird of paradise has a mythological appearance: rich coffee-brown body, fine straw-yellow feathered crown, metallic emerald-green throat, golden-orange feathers, black middle tail feathers, blue beak, red eyes. The female of each species, although very discerning in its choice of a mate, is usually drab brown and quite plain.

Other birds include parrots, lovely green pigeons, honeyeaters, and plumed herons. The blue-gray *mambruk* (crown pigeon), named for its crown of tufted down, inhabits the coastal marshes, as does the multihued kingfisher. The male bowerbird dances and parades before females on a display ground made of a layer of moss surrounded by a one-meter-high wall brightly decorated with flower petals, leaves, fruit, and berries.

In 1992 a University of Chicago doctoral candidate discovered on the island the world's only known poisonous fowl. The feathers, skin, and flesh of an orange-and-black jungle songbird known as the New Guinea pitohi contain one of nature's most powerful toxins, homobatrachotoxin, the same substance exuded by the South American poison dart frog. The Irianese have long avoided the creature, calling it "a rubbish bird." The pitohi probably developed the poison as a defense against snakes and hawks, in Irian Jaya highly effective predators of songbirds. The pitohi's weapon is so effective other jungle songbirds have copied its coloration scheme. Naturalists recently determined that pitohi in certain areas of the island do not contain the toxin; it is now theorized the bird requires some sort of food source—berries, insects—to produce it.

HISTORY

The First Settlers

Negritos settled New Guinea beginning perhaps 30,000 years ago. Some believe the original mountain Papuans came from the great plains to the south or even from as far away as Australia; their features and languages are similar to those of the Australian aboriginals. During Neolithic times the Melanesians arrived from the east, bringing with them the bow and arrow, the ax blade, pottery, crop plants, the calendar, cowrie shells for money, tattooing, betel-chewing, decorative woodcarving, outrigger canoes and seagoing vessels, the dog and the pig, men's and women's clubhouses, ritualized cannibalism, and warfare.

The subsequent discovery and coastal exploration of western New Guinea came about because of the Malukan spice trade. Arab, Chinese, and Malay traders were the first to arrive. The Portuguese stumbled upon the island in 1512, the Spanish in 1526, and in 1605 the first Dutch ship, captained by William Janz, reached the mainland, where nine of his crew were eaten by tribesmen. When early 17th-century European navigators circling the island saw snow-capped peaks, they thought they were clouds. In 1623, the Dutch captain Jan Carstensz first glimpsed the glacier later given his name: Carstensz Toppen. When he returned to Europe and reported snow so close to the equator, he was laughed at.

Colonization

The Spanish, British, and Germans all tried to establish colonies in the territory, but most ended in disaster. Western New Guinea was officially

Dutchmen examine a batch of seized heads, circa 1920.

COURTESY OF THE ROYAL TROPICAL INSTITUTE IN AMSTERDAM

annexed by the Dutch in 1848. They built their first capital at Manokwari in 1898, then garrisoned men at Fakfak on the west coast and Merauke to the southwest. A settlement at the present site of Jayapura was founded in 1910; this was a political move. The town, located 22 km from the New Guinea border, laid real claim to the western half of the island—keeping it from the Germans, who at the time controlled land east of the border. The highlands of western New Guinea were not penetrated until 1933, when Catholic, Lutheran, and Seventh-Day Adventist proselytizers began creeping into the interior. More than a few ended their missions in the stewpot. Well into this century maps of Netherlands New Guinea still included great blank patches in the center marking territory unknown to any white person. By 1938 Hollandia, as Jayapura was then called, had a population of only 800 Indonesians and 400 Dutch.

World War II

The war swirled furiously around this island. By the spring of 1944, General Douglas MacArthur's forces had captured most of the Bismarck archipelago and the Admiralty Islands and neutralized the advance Japanese base at Rabaul, successfully penetrating Japan's rear zone of defense in the southwest Pacific. MacArthur then moved westward on the island of New Guinea to prepare for his next campaign, the Philippines.

American forces stormed the beach near Jayapura one April morning in 1944, meeting only token resistance. Over the coming months, Hollandia became a gigantic staging area. Since MacArthur had obliterated most of the coastal towns during the war to uproot the Japanese, as a war reparation gesture he built a new town on the north coast in 1944.

In MacArthur's airy hilltop residence, which overlooked the whole magnificent harbor, he planned the liberation of the Philippines. By October, a huge armada of over 500 ships rendezvoused in Hollandia's harbor. Eyewitnesses reported that the fleet, interconnected by catwalks with thousands of glowing lamps, looked like a great city floating on the water. United States Army camps, where whole divisions once bivouacked, now lie smothered in jungle, and a few rusting landing barges on the beach at Hamadi are the only remnants left. Most of the hulks were long ago turned into spatulas and eggbeaters by Hong Kong merchants.

The Dutch Colony

After the surrender of Japan in 1945, the Allies handed West New Guinea back to the Dutch. While losing the rest of the archipelago piece by piece, the Dutch increasingly regarded West New Guinea as the last pearl in their former island empire. The Dutch openly encouraged Papuan nationalism and prepared the territory for self-government by training the Irianese in the necessary administrative and technical skills. The chances of the colony ever supporting itself were poor; Holland's purpose in continuing to hold on to the territory was more a matter of emotion and prestige. Holland also believed its settlements in New Guinea would prove politi-

cally invaluable if the unstable Indonesian Republic began breaking apart.

Ironically, the Dutch refusal to leave brought the young and chaotic Indonesian nation together. All through the 1950s and early 1960s, as the Indonesian Republic seemed to totter—its economy in shambles, regional rebellions flaring up on Sumatra, Sulawesi, and Maluku—the specter of the Dutch bogeyman continued to spook the Indonesian masses. Sukarno held the whole wobbly state together by vehemently accusing the Dutch of plotting to reconquer Indonesia from their base in West New Guinea. Dutch imperialism was godsent, probably the most powerful cohesive force in the new republic.

"Self-Determination"

The Indonesian Republic's claim to the territory was based on the historic half-truth that West New Guinea once lay under the suzerainty of the Malukan sultan of Tidore. The Indonesians also argued that *all* the former Netherlands East Indies were promised to the republic in truce agreements. After years of futile haggling, in the early 1960s Sukarno launched his *konfrontasi* campaign to oust the Dutch. To lead Irianese villagers in rebellion and sabotage against the Dutch, more than 2,000 Indonesian soldiers parachuted into wild jungle or put ashore in various parts of the Dutch-held territory. Sukarno boasted that the Irianese kept Indonesian flags hidden in their homes, ready for raising once the war of liberation began.

Actually, few informed Irianese wished to become part of Indonesia—or the Netherlands, for that matter. The majority wanted total independence from both. Most of Indonesia's military forays in the area ended in catastrophe—hundreds of Indonesian troops were captured and killed. World opinion, power politics, and a fateful meeting between Robert Kennedy and Sukarno—not military ferocity or prowess—did more to force the Dutch out.

A 1962 agreement between Holland and Indonesia provided the Irianese with an opportunity to vote; joining the Indonesian Republic, if it occurred, would be an "Act of Free Choice." But in 1969, the year of the vote, Suharto waived the referendum and selected 1,025 "representative" delegates instead. Curiously, the delegates in this carefully orchestrated referendum voted to join Indonesia 1,025 to 0. In August 1969,

Dutch West New Guinea officially became a part of Indonesia. The Indonesians renamed the territory Irian Jaya; Irian is an abbreviation of Ikut Repoublik Indonesia Anbti Nederland, while Jaya means "Victorious."

POLITICS

The OPM

Believing they are Melanesian and not Asian, Papuans have never had any feelings of strong cultural or historic affinity with Indonesia. Feelings of opposition have been compounded by the way Papuans have been treated by the Indonesians. The changeover from Dutch colony to Indonesian colony took place during a period of severe repression under Indonesian military occupation. Since the 1960s, West Papuans have suffered numerous violations of their rights: racial discrimination, arrest and detention, torture, disappearances, and extrajudicial killings. The result is a separatist liberation movement, the Operasi Papua Merdeka ("Free Papua Movement"). These roving bands of guerrillas, never invited to the ballot box, are intent on uniting Irian Jaya with its eastern half, Papua New Guinea, and erasing the incongruous straight line that politically bisects the island.

The OPM operates primarily in dense jungle lowlands near the northernmost boundary with Papua New Guinea. Although there are skirmishes between Indonesian troops and OPM guerrillas along the border, ambushes of Indonesian army patrols, and an occasional assassination, most incidents are successfully hushed up. Beginning in 1977, many thousands of Irianese have been killed in military sweeps bent on suppressing the OPM movement. Political troubles brought on by the elections of that year led to uprisings in the central highlands; Danis attacked police posts with spears and pounded stakes into airfields to prevent the landing of reinforcements.

There are protests each year on 14 December, the anniversary of the 1961 declaration of independence by Papuan nationalists. More a state of mind than a state of war, symbolic raisings of the West Papuan flag are usually the focus of these demonstrations, an act that can lead to harsh jail sentences. In 1989 in Jayapura there was a major protest—hundreds of police

stopped Papuans and checked IDs, and over 400 people were detained. Private homes were raided, and cooking knives and axes seized by police fearing attacks. The Australian-trained anthropologist Arnold Ap, killed by Indonesians while in custody in April 1984, is revered as a martyr by young Papuan intellectuals.

The OPM today is essentially contained and doesn't constitute a real threat to the government. OPM harassment is more economic than military. The Freeport mine in Tembagapura, one of Indonesia's largest mining enterprises, has been the target of low-level OPM sabotage for decades. To counteract OPM influence, the Indonesians have used a combination of military repression, tight political control, economic development, co-optation of Irianese radicals, and a nationalistic education policy, all aimed at instilling in the Irianese a sense of kinship with the Indonesian nation. Obliteration has become the fate of an entire people: cultural obliteration as well as the obliteration of their cause through neglect by the world community. Because the dominant minority is not white, Irian oppression is an issue that has hardly ever been raised in the UN. Papuan defiance attracts only slight attention in the international press, and virtually none in domestic Indonesian media coverage.

Indonesian Occupation

Indonesians generally display a paternalistic attitude toward the Irianese, whom they regard as inferior. But harsh early "civilizing" policies, such as attempts to coerce highland Irianese to wear clothes instead of their traditional penis gourds, have been replaced by a more realistic, humane approach utilizing education and wage labor to impose a more "Indonesian" lifestyle. Economically, it's a classic case of occupation by a colonial power. In the bigger towns like Jayapura, Biak, and Wamena, you never see a shop or *warung* run, managed, or owned by a black person, though you do see plenty of dark-skinned Papuans unloading trucks, sweeping *losmen*, and working as guards, petty clerks, gardeners, and houseboys. When a UN delegation recently visited Irian, one African delegate became visibly enraged at Indonesia's absurd and iniquitous Irian colonial policy.

The Indonesians place much emphasis on education and indoctrination, expending a full one-third of the region's development budget on schooling since the early 1980s. Nearly 40% of all civil service employees work for the Education Department. Vocational schools for high school students are everywhere under construction. Peek in schools in outlying villages and see hundreds of barefoot Papuan children and one very unhappy Javanese schoolteacher.

A trickle of Irianese are beginning to fill lower echelon positions in the civil service sector as teachers and police. It's difficult for them, because sometimes they must act against their own people. Most key government officials are still recruited from outside the province. An incredible gulf exists between the Javanese rulers and the native Irianese.

Transmigrasi

A great source of friction between Melanesians and Indonesians is the government's transmigration policy. Officials maintain the Irianese have no right to lay claim to land that is not being "used"—and the government does not consider collecting wild food and hunting game as valid and productive "use." The new immigrants are mostly ethnic Javanese, plus Bugis, Butonese, and Makassarese from Sulawesi. At present, Asian-Indonesians mostly occupy coastal settlements and the main urban centers. The government's ultimate aim seems to be an Irian Jaya where Asian-Indonesians outnumber the Papuans.

There is no doubt that immigrants have contributed to the growth of the local economy, establishing construction industries, cheap minibus transport in all the major towns, thriving market gardens, and makeshift consumer markets. To some extent the Irianese have copied the trading practices and farming, fishing, and other skills of the immigrants, but the latter have severely limited the level of Irianese employment. Not only political positions but most white collar jobs are filled by outsiders. The OPM finds the *transmigrasi* policy its most effective recruitment device.

THE ECONOMY

Natural Resources

Crucial to an understanding of Indonesia's determination to hold on to and develop Irian Jaya is the fact that it contains the world's richest copper deposits, some of Indonesia's largest oil fields, and important gold, uranium, and timber resources. Since 1969 the Javanese have ruthlessly exploited the territory's inland and offshore wealth. The Japanese are robbing its deep seas to the north by paying off influential Indonesian politicians. Although its soil is generally poor, this province produces rattan, copra, and the finest and widest variety of timber in Indonesia, including tough, weather- and borer-resistant ironwood. The province's total exports Jan.-Aug. 1990 were valued at US$374.7 million. Non-oil/gas exports—copper, nickel concentrate, crocodile hide, canned tuna, sawn timber, plywood—for the same period stood at US$292 million.

Irian's mineral, petroleum, ocean, and forest resources are exploited with little benefit to the Irianese, providing employment for only an infinitesimal fraction of the total workforce. Except as laborers, natives aren't employed by foreign companies; higher-echelon personnel are also recruited from the outside. It's difficult to believe the extent of the assault on Irian's environment. One Japanese firm alone, Marubeni, signed a contract in 1990 with an Indonesian firm which commits them to export—from one of the world's last virgin mangrove forests—300,000 tons of pulp annually over the next 19 years.

Copper deposits discovered at Tembagapura in south-central Irian Jaya are among the world's largest. Starting with nothing, and in the middle of a Stone Age culture, Freeport Minerals Co. in the '70s put in tramways and the world's longest slurry pipeline to carry ore through the mountains down to the sea. The company also constructed a huge processing mill, a modern loading port, and a 112-km road from the coast to the mountains. In 1989, Freeport announced plans to expand its copper-mining operations with a US$511 million investment, seeking to achieve a production of 300,000 tons of concentrate per year by 1993. In that year the company met its goal. Freeport is Indonesia's largest taxpayer; the government owns 20% of the company.

THE PEOPLE

Irian Jaya is Indonesia's most sparsely populated province. Only the areas around Manokwari on the east coast of the Vogelkop ("Bird's

rife but now have been all but stamped out by missionaries and the Indonesian government.

Irian Jaya offers more security than Papua New Guinea. In Papua New Guinea, because of all the rowdy drinking, you can't really go out at night—it's too dangerous, particularly for women. But in West Irian, even in the Jayapura area, it's entirely safe any time of night. The difference is that the Indonesians imposed a somewhat compatible Asian culture on the native peoples, whereas in Papau New Guinea a wild and uninhibited Australian way of life was thrust upon a totally unprepared Melanesian culture. If an Irianese says a spirit lives in a certain tree, a Javanese will thank him for the information—it's not a far-fetched idea. In Papua New Guinea, such a concept is so totally foreign to Australians they'll scoff at the notion.

Some tribes continue to resist any contact with the outside world. Negritos of the purest blood and a few little-known, extremely isolated pygmy tribes still live in the rough Sudirman Range, raising crops and pigs on land as high as 3,000 meters. The majority of the Papuans in the central mountain regions thrive in small clans isolated by terrain, dialect, and customs. These upland Irianese generally possess more complex social, spiritual, and family structures than the coastal peoples. Indonesian immigrants live in trading and fishing communities and in oil and timber centers along the coasts, and on satellite islands off western New Guinea.

Head"), the Schouten Islands in Geelvink Bay, the north coast near Jayapura, and several fertile highland valleys feature relatively high population densities. A few inland valleys are "crowded" with 10-15 people per square km, though most regions have fewer than six people per square km or are totally uninhabited. Of the total population, about 79% is Irian-born.

The native Papuans are divided into the Negroids of the high valleys and plateaus whose skins are brown and black, and the coastal and foothills Papuans, a blending of the Melanesian and Negroid races. Papuans have little ethnic, linguistic, historic, or spiritual relationship with other Indonesians. There's a giddy variety of tribes and over 300 distinct languages, with no one language intelligible to more than 150,000 people. Some languages are spoken by as few as 2,000 people.

While Irian Jaya's mountain people cultivate gardens, its coastal peoples are hunters and gatherers whose staple diet is sago. Coastal dwellers, like the Asmat, traditionally paddle their canoes in the standing position and are masterful woodcarvers. Headhunting and cannibalism were once

Central highlanders still live a largely Stone Age existence. In high, fertile valleys like the Baliem, the people have for centuries constructed complicated irrigation systems. Fields are generally cleared by men, though planting and harvesting are the province of women. Each wife has her own garden plot. In the higher regions, tribesmen slash and burn forests to grow vegetables. They terrace and cultivate mountain slopes that sometimes lie at 50 degree angles, far above the frost line. Dani women wear a traditional grass skirt with a net-bag; the men wear only penis sheaths (horim) made from dried gourds. The illiteracy rate among the Dani is low, but in areas outside the central Baliem Valley "literacy" is nonexistent. The Grand Valley of the Baliem is one of the longest settled areas of the interior upland region, and the Dani therein have over the years become quite skilled at playing rival missionaries and civil authorities against one another.

Highland Irianese accept you as you are. There is no eye avoidance here. Known for their wide grins, they let out little yelps of delight, walk with you through the valley, take you back to their villages, maybe play a bamboo mouth organ for your entertainment. In really remote interior areas, blonde hair fills the natives with wonder. They'll want to stroke it because it's so soft and smooth, and may lift your trouser leg to make sure you're white and hairy all over. When you shave or brush your teeth they may run off, thinking you've gone mad, foaming as you are at the mouth.

Arts And Crafts

Irianese crafts are less affected by commercialism than in Papau New Guinea. The Asmat of the Casuarina Coast in the south carve striking wooden shields, ancestral and serpent totem poles, dugout canoes, prows, paddles, masks, soul ships, ironwood shields and spears, sago pounders, and grub trays. Traditional colors are red, black, and white. Formerly the Asmat carved using only animal teeth and shells, and stone axes obtained through trade with the mountain people, but since WW II they've begun employing metal tools. Irianese make ingenious wheeled toys out of figs and banana leaves which they race at great speeds along winding paths.

In the highlands natives may begin offering you items for sale the moment you step off the plane. Usually these wares are examples of their own clothing. The women's bark-string bag (*noken*) is made from rolled bark fibers, often dyed in red and purple stripes. The *noken* hangs down the back, supported by a strap around the forehead. In it women carry heavy loads of sweet potatoes, babies, piglets, and tools—sometimes all at once. When empty, it's worn over the shoulders and down the back to keep the woman warm in the cold mornings and evenings. The yellow penis gourd, *horim,* is common all the way from Telefomin on the Sepik River in Papau New Guinea to Teluk Bintuni south of the Bird's Head. Measuring 7.5 cm to .5 meters long, the *horim* is made from the outer rind of an elongated pumpkin-like gourd. Men wear no clothing except for this penis sheath, which seems to actually accentuate their nakedness. Each man has a wardrobe of several sizes and shapes of *horim,* which he selects according to mood. A very short *horim* is

worn when a man goes boar-hunting; an elongated one is donned for festive occasions. The *horim* may be decorated with a tassle of fur on top, strips of colorful fabric, or a spiky cocoon. In some mountain tribes the penis sheath is also used as a betelnut container or a place to keep money. Uplanders also make stone axes by cracking a cliff-face with fire high on a scaffold or by hammering on cold rock, methods at least 30,000 years old.

PAPERWORK

There's no land entry into Irian Jaya. A route popular with travelers is to depart from Cairns in Australia for Port Moresby or Vanimo in Papua New Guinea, where one can apply for an Indonesian tourist visa. From Port Moresby, fly or make your way overland to Vanimo, then hop another flight over to Jayapura. Ujung Pandang is a favorite departure point for Biak and Jayapura. The best months to travel in Irian Jaya are June and July; the weather is drier and it's easier then to find guides.

Visas

Jayapura, the provincial capital of Irian Jaya, is not an official tourist gateway into Indonesia, so a 30-day Indonesian visa is required upon arrival from another country. However, foreign tourists may enter the territory via Biak, an island off the northwest coast, and receive the usual automatic 60-day tourist pass.

If you intend to enter Jayapura from Papua New Guinea, a visa is fairly easy to obtain from the Indonesian consulate in either Port Moresby or Vanimo. You'll need an onward ticket out of Jayapura and two passport photos; the visa takes two days. From Jayapura to Vanimo, get a Papua New Guinea visa in the consulate in Jayapura or Jakarta. Remember that relations between Indonesia and Papau New Guinea run hot and cold; you can never be sure of the consulate's policy until you actually arrive in either Irian or Papau New Guinea or hear from another traveler who's visited either spot. Don't believe what any consulate official abroad says. Even if you have a Papua New Guinea visa, it's not possible to cross the border into that country from Merauke. Very tight security in the border areas.

Surat Jalan

When in Irian Jaya itself, you need a *surat jalan* from the police in Biak or Jayapura to visit such places as the Baliem Valley, Agats, Nabire, Oksibil, Merauke, and anywhere near the border with Papau New Guinea. Without proper documentation, travelers may be shoved right back on the plane. You can receive a *surat jalan* quickly and cheaply in Jayapura or Biak. Or obtain a *surat jalan* for Irian Jaya in Jakarta at MABAK, Turun Walikota, Jl. Truno Joyo, Blok M. You may be able to grab it the same day you apply if you arrive early. Travel agents like Tunas and Pacto in Jakarta can secure you a permit in two to four days, but will charge you for it.

Some travelers report that since the publication of George Monbiot's controversial book *Poisoned Arrows,* the Jakarta MABAK office requires you to be a member of a tour group (minimum five people) sponsored by a legitimate travel agency. Sometimes staff require two photos and a form letter from the Directorate of Tourism to Army Headquarters, then a visit to the police station to fill out more forms and submit two more passport photos for final approval; takes a minimum of three days. You must also have your *surat jalan* stamped in the Jayapura police station, even if you've already obtained it in Jakarta. Expect to pay an "administrative fee" of approximately Rp4000. Watch as the police captain's English skills totally deteriorate when you ask for a receipt.

All areas you might visit should be written on the *surat jalan.* Check in with the police within 24 hours of arrival in each town or village. It's wise to make a few photocopies of your *surat jalan,* which usually considerably reduces your wait in local police stations. The police in Jayapura can tell you which areas are off-limits.

Generally, travel restrictions have been eased considerably since Visit Indonesia Year in 1991. As of this writing the only areas closed to tourists are the entire Panai Lakes area, the Tembagapura and Puncak Jaya region, and some locales along the border with Papua New Guinea. Officials who say otherwise are simply on a power trip. It's now possible to get Oksibil on your *surat jalan,* but the military may not let you out of town. Even if you wrangle a *surat jalan* to Enarotali, the local police will probably make you report to the station every day, and you won't be able to leave town overnight.

The police in Wamena are said to be more lenient about allowing visits to remote central highland areas, so wait until you arrive there for *surat jalan* to such places as Ninia and Soba. As a rule, *surat jalan* are issued only for district capitals; if you want to travel deeper into the interior, you need to reapply in the appropriate district capital.

GETTING THERE

By Air

Garuda flies four times weekly from Los Angeles, stopping in Honolulu, Biak, and Denpasar. Once a week, Air Niugini flies between Vanimo and Jayapura one-way; reserve tickets through Merpati in Jayapura. Garuda also connects Irian with Java, Sulawesi, and Bali on a daily basis. Special routings are Manado-Sorong-Biak twice weekly, and Ambon-Biak-Timika-Jayapura-Merauke five times a week. Take the Garuda flight to Biak from Jakarta, then hop another plane to Jayapura. Biak is also accessible on Garuda from Ujung Pandang and Denpasar. Merpati flies to Jayapura from Ambon, Biak, Jakarta, Surabaya, and Ujung Pandang. Once in Jayapura, you can reach just about any other worthwhile destination in Irian Jaya via Merpati and/or missionary aircraft.

Air Niugini flies from Honolulu to Port Moresby each Sunday evening at 1830. The Garuda flight from Honolulu to Bali passes through Biak. Since the airline has switched from DC10s to Boeing 747s the quality of this flight has deteriorated noticeably; it's now so bad the airline warns you the plane will certainly be 12 to 24 hours late. Sometimes those hours can stretch into weeks. Hopefully service will improve, but be prepared for the worst. Factors worth considering are the 64 kg luggage limit and the very lax Biak authorities. They barely glance at your luggage and for a few greenbacks will let just about anything out of the country. This is especially important for those who are barking mad for Asmat carvings.

Qantas flies from Cairns to Port Moresby; Air Niugini flies to Irian Jaya from Brisbane and Sydney. Once in Port Moresby, travel up through Papua New Guinea, then take the Air Niugini flight from Vanimo to Jayapura.

If flying from Papua New Guinea into Irian Jaya, stock up on about US$20 in Indonesian *rupiah* at the Wespac Bank in Wewak, then change the rest of your money in the Sentani or Jayapura banks that offer better rates. You can also fly direct to Jayapura from Port Moresby or Wewak. Using this back door approach into Indonesia, hop down to Bali via Ujung Pandang. The Darwin-Kupang-Mataram-Denpasar route is cheapest.

Arriving

At Sentani Airport, go right up to the counter and buy your taxi ticket at the government-controlled price—you need to be careful of shady characters here, both drivers and corrupt police. A board advertises all the correct prices: Rp17,500 to Jayapura, Rp12,000 to Abepura, Rp5000 to Sentani. After buying your ticket hunt up the taxi chief, who loads people into cabs. Also available are shared rides into Jayapura on small buses. If you walk one-half km down the road in front of the airport to catch a minibus the charge is only Rp2000 into Jayapura, with one changeover in Abepura.

Instead of spending the night in noisy and unglamorous Jayapura, you can stay in more agreeable Sentani village. You do have to go into Jayapura to obtain your *surat jalan*, but this you can do in one morning by minibus. On the way back, hit the museum in Abepura. Returning from Wamena, you'll fly out of Sentani anyway. You can even get the *pas foto* required for your *surat jalan* in Sentani in the photo shop next to the Virgo restaurant. Or, even better, some hotel proprietors will obtain your *surat jalan* for you.

By Sea

Irian Jaya's smaller coastal towns lack regular shipping services, but Pelni sails to such major towns as Biak, Sorong, and Jayapura, providing a reliable and cheap way to cover great distances. Departing Jakarta, Pelni's KM *Umsini* sails every fortnight to Surabaya, Ujung Pandang, Bitung, Ternate, Manokwari, Jayapura, Sorong, Ternate, Ujung Pandang, then back to Jakarta for Rp93,900 economy and Rp226,500 first class. Don't count on Pelni schedules to be exact. The KM *Serimau* also travels to Irian, with stops in Biak, Manokwari, Serui, Nabire and Jayapura. Another ship sails the south

coast—Fakfak, Kaimana, Agats, and Merauke. These are good, new ships, quite comfortable, even in fourth class. Other shipping lines also have vessels embarking for Maluku and Irian Jaya from Java. Inquire in the harbormasters' offices in Surabaya and Jakarta. Locally, the KM *Perintis Nagura* plies Irian's north coast once a month; another Perintis ship covers the south coast. Be aware you might grow a long beard waiting for these vessels.

GETTING AROUND

Road networks only exist around urban centers. None of the district capitals are yet linked by road, nor are the highlands connected by road to the coast. Irian Jaya's most important ports include Jayapura, Sorong, Manokwari, Biak, Fakfak, Merauke, and Amampare. Sorong and Jayapura are served by the *Umsini* and *Rinjani*. Local watercraft can be used to navigate the province's rivers and lakes.

Until the trans-Irian highway from Jayapura to Merauke is completed, planes are about the only reasonable means of travel in the interior. Merpati has the cheapest and widest selection of flights within the province. From Wamena you can fly to Jayapura daily, Karubaga on Saturday, and Kelila and Bokondini on Friday.

Merpati is infamous for its nonservice. Don't trust the printed schedules, and check all flights at local offices. Remain flexible, and always carry a map to check alternate routes. Planes will often not fly to certain destinations for months on end, for a variety of reasons. Often Merpati blames poor weather. The airline tries to assess a Rp1200 per kg fee for overweight luggage, though sometimes you can talk your way out of it. Reporting time is around 0600, although the plane may not leave until 1000. Bring a book and a good dose of patience.

Missionary Aircraft

With light fixed-wing aircraft, missionary organizations fly to tiny, remote missionary stations, but charge more than Merpati. Missionary Aviation Fellowship (MAF), the largest air transport organization, serves Protestant missions and lands at over a hundred airstrips. Associated Missions Aviation (AMA), next door to MAF's offices at Sentani Airport, is smaller, serving Roman Catholic missions. Both carry cargo, accept charter business, and accommodate passengers—if there's room.

MAF flies regularly from Wamena to Pyramid, Tiom, Karubaga, Angguruk, Kanggine, and Senggo. For the Sentani-Wamena flight, MAF prefers you use Merpati. If heading for Agats, contact AMA directly. AMA also schedules now and then a Wamena-Enarotali flight. MAF flies out of Nabire on Monday to Beoga, then journeys back to Nabire, but your chance of securing a seat on this flight is remote. MAF has a fleet of Cessnas that charter for around Rp300,000 per hour. A chartered Wamena-to-Senggo flight costs over a million *rupiah*.

Most missionary groups maintain offices at Sentani Airport. Be sure to record your destination in your *surat jalan* prior to flying into the interior. It's best to reserve scheduled flights at least a week in advance. Scheduled flights are more reliable, but even these are subject to weather or

maintenance problems. If one plane is down, it could torpedo the whole MAF schedule for weeks. Travel light—you're charged for any baggage over 20 kilos on MAF or 15 kilos on AMA. Request additional baggage space in advance; priority is given to missionaries and/or supplies.

Another option is to join a tour group. For the really remote areas, this is what the government, missionaries, and police prefer. A recommended trekking specialist in Irian is **Dani Sangrila Tours,** Jl. Pembangunan 19, Jayapura, tel. (0967) 21610, offering tours to the Baliem Valley, the Angguruk Jaly tribes, and the Senggo and Asmat regions. Dani Sangrila agents include **PT Astura Tours and Travel,** tel. (021) 548-1879 or 530-0064 in Jakarta, and **Astura-Geckotours P/L,** tel. (0022) 311-522 or 235-629 in Australia. Also contact **Balindo Star Tours and Travel,** P.O. Box 455, Denpasar 80001, Bali, tel. (0361) 25372 or 28669, or after hours, tel. 22497.

THE NORTHERN PROVINCES

JAYAPURA AND VICINITY

Known as Hollandia during the reign of the Dutch, this city was the capital of Netherlands New Guinea. At the time it was a small, attractive town in an amphitheater-like setting, with red-tiled roofs sheltering Dutch civil servants. The Dutch put in permanent hardtop roads, expensive dock facilities, and sturdy public buildings. When Irian Jaya fell into the hands of the Indonesian Republic it became Sukarnopurna, then Kota Baru; in the late 1960s it was renamed Jayapura, or "City of Victory," to commemorate its "liberation" from the Dutch.

Located on the northeast coast of Irian Jaya, this thriving, noisy, sweltering provincial capital is wedged into a flat strip of land between steep coastal hills and the sea. The picture-postcard harbor is surrounded by perpetually green hills. Most houses are built on slopes, while the administrative portion occupies the level region beneath. This area contains all the

worst features of a modern Indonesian city— dirty streets, polluting traffic, garish blaring cassette shops.

Peopled by an extraordinary mix of gentle Melanesians, immigrant merchants and laborers, and Javanese bureaucrats, in this city Southeast Asia and the Pacific meet. On the streets you'll see tribesmen, vendors with Javanese-style *pikulan,* Minang shopowners, expat oil and timber men, Bugis fishermen, sailors from Makassar, and a trickle of travelers. The town is dead from 1200 to 1600, when most shops and offices close, but in the evenings Japapura's four main streets pulsate with life. Prices are relatively high and it's difficult to bargain. For magnificent views over Jayapura and its harbor, share the charter of a minibus up to **Pemancar Stasiun TVRI,** a steep two-km climb from the highway to the top of a mountain between Jayapura and Hamadi. For nightlife, Jaya-

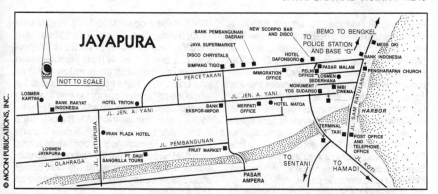

© MOON PUBLICATIONS, INC.

pura has three discos: the New Scorpio, Tropical, and Chrystals.

Jayapura is still a fairly unpleasant necessity for getting to the Baliem Valley. The police will tell you the *surat jalan* permit office is open 24 hours a day, but don't believe it. Once in, however, it's quite a painless process—you can be in and out within half an hour. Make sure you bring all the relevant *juju*. The *surat jalan* is now free, but you could always make a donation towards a new office typewriter.

ACCOMMODATIONS AND FOOD

Accommodations

All the following rates may include meals; try to bargain for a room without meals and eat in one of Jayapura's *pasar malam*.

One of the cheapest places to stay is **Losmen Jayapura,** Jl. Olah Raga 4, tel. (0967) 21216; Rp12,000-14,000 d, all rooms with fans. Avoid staying here on weekends unless you want to hear bedsprings creaking all night long; it's here that Jayapuran lads entertain their ladies of the evening. A better, newer *losmen* is clean **Losmen Kartini,** Jl. Kurabesi 2; Rp8000 s, Rp12,000 d. The owner lives there and keeps the place well managed; good security (next to the military police). Many *warung* in front.

A good deal is **Losmen Ayu,** Jl. Tugu II 101, tel. 22263—very friendly, clean, good water, close to town and the *bemo* stop, free telephone, laundry service, Rp10,000 s with a different breakfast each day. Or pay Rp15,000 d for a room with three beds and huge *mandi*. **Losmen Sederhana,** Jl. Halmahera 2, tel.

22157, charges Rp20,000 for a basic single. Located in a lively area opposite the night market. **Hotel Nombai,** Jl. Trikora, Dok V, rents rooms for Rp25,000-30,000 with a/c and hot water on request. Clean, with the best views in town. Close to the main road, where you can hop a *bemo umum* into town for Rp250. Good, cheap restaurants nearby.

The **Dafonsoro,** Jl. Percetakan 20-24, tel. 31695, 31696, or 31697, fax 22055, charges Rp24,000-48,000. All rooms are a/c, carpeted, clean, some with balcony; prices include breakfast but not the 21% government tax and service. This well-run hotel lies in the middle of the city near the harbor and taxi terminal. **Hotel Triton,** Jl. Jen. A. Yani 52, P.O. Box 33, tel. 21218 or 21171, offers spare and smelly economy rooms for Rp17,500 plus 20% tax, which includes a breakfast of egg, bread, and coffee. The more expensive rooms are a better deal at Rp36,000, but make sure they come with both a/c and hot water. The "free" pickup service to the airport is iffy.

Jayapura's best hotel, where all the *orang barat* stay, is the **Matoa** on the main street near the banks, a comfortable European-style hotel costing Rp40,000-50,000—expensive even for Jayapura. Upmarket types might also consider the new **Irian Plaza Hotel** on Jl. Setiapura—apparently the best in town, with a/c rooms for Rp26,000-60,000. Alternately, many travelers choose to stay near the airport in Sentani.

Food

Jayapuran food, because of the Indonesian influence, is cheaper and tastier than in Papua New Guinea. Try the delectable *nasi campur* in *warung* all over town for around Rp800. A cheap *warung* serving delicious Javanese food is situated right beside *kantor perdaganan* on Jl. Nindya 17. Good *gado-gado* for only Rp600. Probably the best place to eat is the *pasar malam* close to the waterfront: order the *ikan kakap* with rice, sauce, and jackfruit for Rp2000—more delicious than *gurami*. The fish grills offer up delectable *cumi-cumi*; tuna dishes are only Rp2000. For *ikan bakar* and other seafood, try **Kebon Siri,** right in front of the Irian Plaza Hotel. Directly next to the Irian Plaza is **Satya House**; clean and jaunty, with reasonable food at reasonable prices.

A number of restaurants along Jl. Percetakan serve European, Indonesian, and Chinese food. **Hawaii Restaurant,** near the waterfront and the IMBI cinema, serves *soto ayam* for Rp15,000, fish and shrimp for Rp17,000, and Rp5000-6000 *nasi* dishes. Less expensive is **Mandala Restaurant,** on the city side of *kantor gubernor* on the waterfront, with a/c and a good view over the harbor. The **Jaya Grill,** also with a scenic view of the harbor, is known for its popular Chinese and European food. Probably Jayapura's best Padang-style restaurant is the big, well-ventilated, and central **Simpang Tigo.**

Beer here is ridiculously expensive in restaurants, Rp2500 for a small bottle. Buy beer instead from the extremely well-stocked supermarkets, Rp1500 for a cold one.

SHOPPING AND SERVICES

Shopping
There are three markets in Jayapura. At **Jaya Supermarket** buy cold New Zealand apples and American ice cream. Most craft shops are concentrated in Jayapura's Pasar Ampera, on Jl. Polimak, and at the museum in Abepura. Some of the town's travel agencies and hotels also feature small shops. Irianese *batik* is sold in **Toko Batik Khas Irian** near Disco Chrystals on Jl. Percetakan. Items in the souvenir shop at the airport are far too expensive. The travel agent **Agent MNA** carries carvings, statuary, paintings, and woven goods.

Services
The **tourist office** is located in the building to the left of Gedung Gubernor on Jl. Sua Sio, tel.

(0967) 21381, open 0730-1500, Friday until 1100, Sunday closed. Take a *bemo* from town (Rp250). Change money at the **Bank Ekspor-Impor,** Jl. Jen. A. Yani. At **Bank Pembangunan Daerah** you can get up to two million *rupiah* on your credit card. Make international calls at the telephone office; don't pay for the time it takes to connect Jayapura with Jakarta. The telephone code for all of Irian Jaya is 0967. The only place in town that carries the English daily *Jakarta Post* is Bank Ekspor-Impor. A **bookstore** across from the Pelni office near the harbor resells subscriber copies of magazines. The best barber shop/beauty salon in town is **Salon Ronald** on Jl. Percetakan.

You can obtain visas for Papua New Guinea at the PNG consulate, Jl. Serui 81, Perbukitan Dok VIII. *Imigrasi* is centrally located on Jl. Jen. A. Yani; open Mon.-Thurs. 0730-1430, Friday 0730-1100, Saturday 0730-1300. If you have a social visa you need to get your *surat jalan* from Polda police headquarters, Jl. Sam Ratulangi next to GKI Mess (open 0730-1200). This is also where you obtain your permit to visit such points in the interior as Ilaga, Oksibil, Enarotali, and Wamena. Open 0800-2400: you'll need to fill out forms and hand over four passport photos and Rp1000. Get photos at **Happy Photo Studio,** Jl. Jen. A. Yani near Hotel Matoa, or at **Variant Photo Studio** near the Triton. About Rp5000 for four, with a 45-minute wait.

TRANSPORTATION

Getting There
You can only officially enter Irian Jaya from Papua New Guinea if you have a 60-day Indonesian tourist pass. Check with the Indonesian embassy in Port Moresby or the Indonesian consulate in Vanimo for the latest regulations. Fly with Garuda to Sentani Airport from Biak, Jakarta, Manado, and Surabaya. Merpati flies to Jayapura from Biak, Sorong, Merauke, Timika, and other points in Irian. Or take the Pelni ship KM *Umsini* from Tanjung Priok, stopping at ports in Sulawesi and Maluku en route. There's no customs check at Sentani Airport.

Getting Around
Jayapura's central business district is small enough so you can walk anywhere. Take mini-

buses or *bemo* (Rp200-750) from the terminal near the Ekspor-Impor Bank on Jl. Jen. A. Yani; minibuses also run up and down Jl. Jen. A. Yani looking for fares. Taxis operate all over Jayapura and Abepura. Sample fares: to Abepura Rp500, to Angkasa Rp550, from Abepura to Sentani Rp800. Expect to be ripped off from time to time.

Getting Away
Garuda and Merpati share the same office at Jl. Jen. A. Yani 15, tel. (0967) 21327, 21810, 21913, or 21111, open Mon.-Thurs. 0800-1200 and 1300-1600. Garuda flies from Jayapura to Ambon, Ujung Pandang, Jakarta, Denpasar, and Manado; book in advance at the Garuda office and get to the airport 1.5 hours before departure time as flights are heavily booked. When flying from Jayapura to Wamena or vice versa, make sure your ticket gets in the hands of the airline representative. Don't wait in line. Having confirmed reservations is less insurance than showing up early.

Merpati flies to Wamena and Biak at least 10 times weekly; Merauke, Serui, and Nabire three times weekly; Tanah Merah on Monday; Oksibil on Wednesday; Timika on Thursday; Sorong on Friday; and Karubaga on Saturday. Change

JAYAPURA AND VICINITY

your big *rupiah* bills into Rp100s if heading into the interior.

Air Niugini flies every Wednesday to Vanimo, then on to Wewak and Port Moresby. You need a valid cholera vaccination—not older than six months, not within the past week—before flying to Papua New Guinea. Suffer through the shots, two within eight days, in Jayapura at the *immunasi* next to the police station.

Pelni sails to Ujung Pandang, Jakarta, or Surabaya every seven to 10 days. It takes a slow-moving four to five days to reach Ujung Pandang and another one or two days to make Surabaya. There are calls en route at Sorong, Ternate, and Bitung. You usually spend a couple days at sea, then have a few days to walk around the port. Hang out close to the ship, as departure times often change. Inquire at the Pelni office in downtown Jayapura, Jl. Halmahera 1, tel. 21270, or at the *syahbandar* office on Jl. Koti, tel. 21923.

VICINITY OF JAYAPURA

Bestiji
From the terminal at the harbor end of Jl. Percetakan, take a minibus (Rp300) to Bestiji, an Indonesianization of the name of the wartime American military "Base G." After a successful amphibious assault in April 1944, General Douglas MacArthur established his Pacific Headquarters here on a hill overlooking the beautiful harbor. You can still see his old command post, the huts now used for fish farming. The site can be visited with permission from the military. From Bestiji, walk 10 minutes (400 meters) down to a deserted beach; nice swimming but beware of theft.

Hamadi
A town over the hills about five km east of Jayapura. A war memorial in Hamadi marks the spot where Allied forces landed on 22 April 1944. See rusting wartime amphibious landing craft and a Sherman tank down a nearby beach. Visit the fish market. This is the place to buy mass-produced Asmat carvings, most actually crafted in Sentani. Female figures, once known for their sexual symbology, now feature bikinis, and heavy wood is painted with shoe polish—do a chip test before buying. Carved panels aver-

age around Rp35,000-50,000 for 1.5 meters and Rp50,000-80,000 for two to 2.5 meters. About 10 souvenir shops line the main street, selling statuary, beads, Dani artifacts, woven baskets, and postcards.

Dirty but cheap **Wisma Asia**, Jl. Perikanan 18, tel. (0967) 22277, costs Rp8500 s, Rp13,000 d. The Chinese-owned love hotel **Losmen Agung** is located in the middle of a noisy *kampung*; Rp25,000; see the sign on the left when heading into Hamadi from Jayapura. **Losmen Argapura** charges but Rp7500 for a single.

Museum Negeri

Next to the Ekspo in Waena, on Jl. Raya Sentani, about 18 km from Jayapura. Open Mon.-Thurs. 0800-1400, Friday 0800-1100, Saturday 0800-1300, Sunday 1000-1500. The museum features traditional weapons, baskets, historical and archaeological relics, shell money, old china, reconstructed *honnay* and miniature traditional dwellings, fishing and hunting implements, bark clothing looms, sago-making tools, and stuffed birds of paradise. The museum also sells such crafts as penis gourds (Rp2500), bark string bags (Rp15,000), and stone axes (Rp7000-20,000).

Abepura

In this village is a smaller version of the Museum Negeri. Here you can see some of the finest pieces of Irianese art extant, on the grounds of Cendrawasih University. Visit on the way into Jayapura from Sentani Airport, or from Jayapura take a minibus (Rp500). The museum, **Loka Budaya,** Jl. Senanit, tel. (0967) 81224, exhibits such artifacts as an alligator skin drum from Fakfak, Lake Sentani sculpture and pottery, beautiful long war spears, carved prow decorations, fish traps, a very strong collection of Asmat statuary, wooden coffins, and an old collection of Korwar statues from Biak. Captions and the museum's catalogue are in Indonesian. Open Mon.-Thurs. 0730-1430, Friday until 1100 and Saturday to 1330. Admission charge Rp500; fees of Rp3500 for photographs and Rp5000 for video cameras. If you want the place opened up during holidays call the director: he'll "charter" you a visit for Rp15,000. Also at the university is a 45,000-volume library.

An extremely clean and efficient *nasi padang* restaurant lies 800 meters down the road on the left towards Jayapura. At **Mahligai Jaya** meals run Rp400-3000; above-average ice juices. Also in Abepura is the **Cemetery of National Heroes,** the final resting place of Indonesian casualties of the militarily disastrous but politically successful Irian campaign of the early 1960s. South of Abepura is **Proyek Batik Khas Irian Jaya,** two km from the main road, where Irianese-style *batik* is produced. Three-meter-long *sarung* cost Rp18,000; shirts are Rp20,000-28,000.

SENTANI AND VICINITY

SENTANI

With the feel of a small village, Sentani is a more agreeable place than Jayapura. The Sentani Airport is located between Lake Sentani and the Cyclops Mountains, a small but steep coastal range that begins on the outskirts of Jayapura. Sentani has a serious malaria problem, so don't forget your mosquito net.

The post office is about a three-minute walk from the Minang Jaya, just down the lane and across the street. You can even have your passport photo taken in Sentani, in a shop next to the Virgo restaurant.

Accommodations

Every accommodation in Sentani offers free transport to and from the airport, and a set of houseboys whose social life revolves around their Western guests. They drive you to dinner, guide you around town, take an extreme personal interest in you.

One of the cheapest places to stay is **Losmen Ratna,** tel. (0967) 91435, a beauty parlor that rents out rooms. Rp16,500 s, Rp28,000 d for rooms with fan; Rp36,000 d for a/c. Drab, but cheap for Sentani. The Mickey Mouse restaurant is across the street. Good place to stay despite the noise from the roadway. From the airport, turn left after reaching the Sentani-Jayapura highway, then walk about 100 meters.

Perhaps the best place to stay in Sentani is **Losmen Minang Jaya,** Jl. Raya Sentani, P.O. Box 231, tel. 27143. Clean and well-run, it costs Rp11,000 s and Rp18,000 d for rooms with fans, toilets, and fresh towels; Rp18,000 s, Rp23,000 d for a/c rooms with toilets. Price includes breakfast of coffee, tea, and bread. On a side street off the main boulevard through town, the Minang Jaya offers attentive and good-natured houseboys, cold beer, good eating places nearby, and lively travelers' gatherings in the evenings. **Losmen Mansapur Rani,** Jl. Yabaso 113, tel. 99, charges Rp10,000 s and Rp12,000 d including breakfast of bread, fried bananas, and coffee. Ten rooms with *mandi,* cool water always available, closest *losmen* to the airport. The propri-

etor, Mr. Bernard, is very proud of his former position as chairman of the Irian Jaya Hotel and Restaurant Association, which allowed him to meet Suharto in 1989. Two giant portraits in his living room commemorate the momentous occasion. Mr. Bernard will take you to or from the airport for free, or arrange Rp15,000 charters into Jayapura. He also claims he can secure a *surat jalan* even at night.

Sentani Inn, Jl. Raya Sentani, tel. 21207, has 12 a/c rooms for Rp20,000 s, Rp25,000 d. The very plain, smallish rooms have inside *mandi* but no washbowl; small terraces. Friendly service, small TV room, coffee dispenser. Since you can't get warm meals here, the place provides free transportation to and from the Mickey Mouse.

Food

The **Mickey Mouse,** 125 meters from Losmen Minang Jaya, tel. (0967) 119, caters to the many Aussie and American missionary families in the area. Good hamburgers for Rp2500, as well as a passable approximation of a taco. Also Indonesian food; *bihun goreng* Rp1500. There's a well-stocked grocery store next to the Mickey Mouse. In Sentani's *pasar sengol* are baked goodies. A good *nasi padang* restaurant is in the town shopping complex. **Virgo,** on the Sentani-Jayapura highway, offers a full menu with ice juices. The **Lili** and **Sari,** opposite Virgo, are probably the cheapest places around for good quality meals. The Sari serves up a huge but quite peppery *gado-gado* for only Rp750. On the same side as Virgo, up the street 100 meters, is **Pojok,** featuring Indonesian food. Fifteen km from Sentani toward Jayapura on the lakeshore is **Yougwa,** home to a garrulous cockatoo. Chicken, noodle, and vegetable dishes run Rp2500-7000; freshwater fish cost Rp6000-7500; goldfish are served for Rp6000-15,000.

Getting Around And Away

The hotel vehicle at Mansapur Rani can be chartered into Jayapura for Rp15,000. Taxis run from 0500-2200 and cost Rp17,500 into Jayapura. Merpati flies from Sentani to Wamena, Nabire, Fakfak, Sorong, Manokwari, and

Biak. On the Catholic AMA airline or the larger Protestant MAF you need to book at least seven to 14 days in advance. The MAF office is open 0800-1600, and will also change money and traveler's checks. Before leaving home you can write Merpati about its flights from here to outlying airstrips.

VICINITY OF SENTANI

There's an *air terjun* four km behind the Losmen Minang Raya. Two routes to reach it; ask the way. The first three km are flat; for the final kilometer, you have to climb. Very cold water. Hire a guide for Rp5000 (two people) for a whole day; he'll do the toting. Two other waterfalls in the area require a two-hour journey from Sentani.

Seven km out of Sentani on the right is a small crocodile farm. Nine km out is a monument to four men killed in a helicopter crash in the late '80s; just beyond is a magnificent viewpoint over Lake Sentani. In 1946 an American B-24 bomber crashed into the Cyclops Mountains; completely shrouded in the thick forests, it wasn't discovered until 1992. The skeletons of the pilot and copilot still manned the cockpit. Twenty-seven km from Sentani, on the right, is a beautiful Buddhist temple; on the left is a Balinese *pura*. Both are situated on hills.

Visit the strange group of stones at **Doyo Lama,** Jl. Genyem, five km west of Sentani. Here are 76 mysterious dolmen and menhir standing atop a hill. The largest stone is only one-half meter high. Check out the engravings—figures with jutting chins and small noses. Other big rocks in the area feature cloud and spiral motifs. No one knows who erected these stones; local legend has it that if they fall down they stand themselves up again.

Gunung Ifar is six km from Sentani, with superb views over the lake and town of Sentani; Rp10,000 by airport taxi there and back. **MacArthur Lookout** is located opposite the Asmer Jaya airstrip. Travel five km up Jl. MacArthur to this military training area, featuring signs like Prepare Your Physical And Mental State and If You Hesitate, Go Back. Take a picnic lunch. Or you can buy fried chicken at the KFC opposite the road to Ifarguni. The place is not really a KFC, the woman who runs it just calls herself KFC. In **Abar,** see village craftsmen carve tree bark and make clay pottery. The houses of tribal chiefs bear human, crocodile, fish, bird, and snake carvings.

Depapre

In this village, but a day-trip from Jayapura, you can commission a beautiful carved miniature *prahu* for an average cost of Rp21,000-

In some areas of Irian Jaya, young women once had "coming out frocks" tattooed upon their skins, the patterns worked with thorns dipped in dye and hammered into the flesh.

FIELD MUSEUM OF NATURAL HISTORY, CHICAGO

42,000. Whole *prahu* sides are available; these are not antiques, but are carved to this day. One of the area's most spectacular coral reefs is located at **Tanah Merah Depapre,** a completely native Irianese fishing village on the north coast east of Depapre. Take a bus from Sentani west to Depapre for Rp1000, then charter a boat for Rp20,000 to Tanah Merah Depapre; arrange to be picked up the next day. Or take public boats (Rp2000-4000) to different villages along the coast. Go only in the dry season, March-October. There's a market in Depapre three times a week where you can buy all the food and supplies you'll need. Fresh water is available (boil it); get fish and coconuts from the villagers. Obtain a *surat jalan* before you go.

Lake Sentani

Lake Sentani is a former arm of the sea, now landlocked. It's home to a species of freshwater sawfish and a tribe of people who make their living from products of the lake. Located on the other side of the airstrip, the water's edge is only 1.5 km from Losmen Mansapur Rani. This lake is very picturesque, especially from the air. The lake sprawls in all directions, with sleepy rows of stilted houses lining the bottom of the hills. Fish-traps set below the water catch saltwater fish which enter the lake; it's the women's job to retrieve the catches. Lake Sentani natives carve intricate panels with raised surfaces painted black and white. They create pottery as well, a craft not found in abundance in Irian Jaya. At **Sarmi,** on the north shore, villagers make clothing of bark (*tenun tervo*). To tour the lake, contact a travel agency in Jayapura or Anton to charter a 15-meter-long *prahu matoa,* about Rp30,000 per hour—magnificent. Motorized *prahu* rent for Rp20,000-25,000 hourly; unmotorized canoes run Rp5000 hourly. The nearest village is **Netar,** 2.5 km from the airstrip.

BIAK

Hot and bright, like glittering sequins, Biak is also known as Kota Karang, "City of Coral." Located just one degree south of the equator on the island of the same name, Biak is a travelers' way station and the easternmost international gateway to Indonesia. An easy, lazy, friendly town, Biak would be all but comatose if it weren't for the screech of jets flying over six or seven times a day. The city serves as a big Indonesian naval base, a supply center for offshore oil rigs in the Sorenarwa Straits and Irian Bay, and a major port for Irian Jaya's tuna industry. Biak also played an important role in General MacArthur's WW II island-hopping campaign through the southwest Pacific.

Today Biak is a typical middle-sized Outer Island town, with restaurants, Chinese supermarkets, and three cinemas. Because of the midday heat, shops open at 0530 or 0600. Biak was well appreciated by the Dutch; even today, everyone seems to speak the language. It's a bird-smuggling center; you can see all manner of exotic birds at Pasar Panir, including "protected" bird-of-paradise skins from Serui. Also for sale are live lorikeets and ravens. Biak woodcarvings are sold at the airport terminal shop and at workshops in the village of **Swapodibo.**

On Biak you can buy all the usual Papuan artifacts available on the mainland—stone axes, bows, arrows. They're much cheaper here than in the Baliem Valley.

War Relics

Exploiting the successes of the Hollandia campaign, on 27 May 1944 the Hurricane Task Force of the U.S. Sixth Army landed at Bosnik on Biak Island. The Japanese defense was based on a brilliant use of unfriendly terrain. The Japanese purposely withheld their main forces until U.S. troops had advanced to the rugged limestone hills beyond the beaches. Then, from the cliffs and caves overlooking the advancing Allied columns, the Japanese launched a savage counterattack, succeeding in driving a block between the beachhead and the invading force. After a week of bitter, heavy fighting, the Japanese retreated to a network of enormous interlocking caves known in American military annals as The Sump. During the night the Japanese left their cave positions to launch harassing attacks; by day they fired mortars on the newly captured airdromes. The Americans finally poured aviation gas and TNT down the enemy's long command tunnel, then lit a match: thousands of Japanese soldiers were instantly incinerated.

The cave system, Gua Nippon, is now a tourist attraction. Once a year, Japanese come to pay homage to the 6,000 who died here. To see both Bosnik and The Sump, charter a taxi at the airport for Rp5000 per hour. Or you can reach the caves by walking up a path about 30 minutes from the far side of the airport. More remnants of the war lie all over the beaches and highlands of Biak. Rusted hulls of trucks, jeeps, tanks, and planes remain where they were once abandoned, covered now by flowering creepers. A line of tanks, covered with shells and coral, has been pressed into service as a pier; torpedos have been hollowed out and used as gongs. Bunkers on cliffs face the beaches of the Mokmer Airdrome, and a nearby Quonset hut houses a large family.

Accommodations

The best budget accommodation in Biak is **Losmen Solo** on Jl. Imam Bonjol, near the Garuda office and 50 meters from Bank Impor-Ekspor. Clean, though hot and noisy. Rp5500 s for cubicle rooms, with showers and bathrooms down the hall. Upstairs rooms, facing the sea, receive breezes. Other cheapies include **Losmen Rahayu,** in back of the mosque; **Losmen Sinar Kayu,** 500 meters from Pasar Inpres; and **Losmen Madju.**

Hotel Dahlia, Jl. Selat Madura 6, tel. (0967) 21851, rents rooms for Rp20,000-35,000 s or d; price depends on inside or outside *mandi.* Typical Javanese *losmen*; very plain. A *nasi padang* restaurant next door is open 1100-2000. The **Marisen Hotel,** Jl. Majapahit, tel. 33416, offers full a/c rooms for reasonable prices. The new **Airport Beach Hotel,** Jl. Prof. M. Yamin, tel. 21496, 22311, or 22345, is opposite the Pertamina depot only 250 meters from the airport. Three classes of rooms; the best are those facing the ocean, Rp54,000 without bath. Simple rooms go for Rp25,000.

Laid-back **Hotel Mapia,** Jl. Jen. A. Yani 23, tel. 21383, P.O. Box 68, is about a five-minute walk from Bank Impor-Ekspor, the Garuda office, police station, and market. Twenty a/c double rooms for Rp24,200 s, Rp30,250 d; with lunch and dinner Rp28,200 s, Rp38,250. Rooms with fans, toilet, and *mandi* are Rp15,215 s, Rp20,570 d with just breakfast, or Rp22,150 s,

Rp32,200 d with all meals. TV lounge in the back; all rooms nicely furnished.

One of Indonesia's handsomest hotels and the perfect setting for a grade B American movie is **Hotel Irian,** just opposite the airport, tel. 21839 or 21139, and only a 20-minute walk into town. Built of solid teakwood in 1952, this single-story hotel has a huge dining room, all original fittings and furnishings, a well-kept seaside garden, and 80 rooms, most with verandas, all within earshot of the thundering surf. Rooms with a/c, *mandi,* and breakfast go for Rp45,980 s, Rp72,600 d. Economy rooms run Rp27,830-48,400. Leaves and other decaying matter lie between you and the beach—as well as bugs, flies, and mosquitos—but you can't beat the front lawn.

The **Basan Inn** is located at Jl. A Yani 36, tel. 21398 or 21956. New rooms, clean, with a/c, TV, and hot and cold water. The tariff runs Rp45,000 for a single to Rp149,000 for a suite. The **Titawaka,** on Jl. Salat Mahassar, tel. 21835, with a nice ocean view, has carpeted a/c rooms with bath and Euro-toilet. Very clean, excellent service. The price of Rp36,000 s and Rp72,000 d includes all meals, ice water, tea and coffee all day, and transfer to and from the airport. The manager, Mr. Engels, speaks English and Dutch. Rp58,000 s, Rp88,000 d for big VIP big rooms with full a/c, TV, shower, and hot and cold water. Price includes breakfast, lunch, and dinner. Fax, phone, refrigerator, room service, pool, laundry service, bike rental. Very central and convenient. You eat in the hotel dining room; there's also a bland and greasy restaurant, and a snack and ice cream parlor on the premises. Get yer hot dogs and pizza here.

Food

Divemasters and oil industry people like to eat at air-conditioned **Restaurant 99,** Jl. Imam Bonjol 32. Whole large fried fish with fried mushrooms Rp12,000—delicious. Asparagus crab soup (large) Rp15,000, fried noodles Rp2500. Located right next to a beauty parlor where you can get a haircut for Rp5000 or perm for Rp10,000. **Jakarta** is up the street by the Hadi Supermarket. Good *cumi-cumi* with veggies Rp12,000, *cap cai* with tofu Rp8000, and the best *mie kuah* for the money (Rp3500) in all Indonesia.

Coffee House Nirwana, Jl Jen. Sudirman 22, serves all kinds of delicious cakes and snacks. Liter of ice cream Rp12,000, whole black forest cake Rp40,000, zebra cake Rp10,000, coffee and tea. Nice, breezy place to sit, take in the street life, and listen to syrupy Indonesian pop music.

Get delicious, cheap food at the *warung* which spring up at night in the *pasar malam* between the bank and Losmen Solo; don't miss the *ikan bakar* and the wonderfully fresh tuna steaks. Twenty meters past Restaurant 99 is the best *sate* place in Biak. Also try the **Anda, Himalaya,** and the **New Garden. Gloria Food Mart** is open 1000-1500 and 1800-2300. All the usual Indonesian dishes, and the best prices in town— *nasi agan panggang* Rp3500, *nasi campur ika* Rp1500, *nasi rawan* Rp3500. **Toko Setuju,** where you can buy the cheapest cold beer in Biak, is next door.

Shopping And Services

Buy your Asmat carvings here for Rp30,000-40,000, cheaper than in Asmat. Vendors hang around the lobbies of the Titawaka and Irian hotels. **Jaya Art Shop,** Jl. Sel Makassar 65, tel. (0967) 2213, offers some interesting items. **Pusaka Art Shop,** deeper inside the market, features a better selection, including Irian handicrafts, jewelry, coins, porcelain, ceramics, and stone statues. Be sure to visit the inner sanctum, where all the high-quality work is stored. Pray the electricity is on so you can actually see the stuff.

The unofficial **tourist office** is at Jl. Jen. A. Yani 36, opposite Hotel Mapia, in PT Sentosa Tosiga's main office. The **police station** is on Jl. Ratulangi. Get your *surat jalan* for Wamena here—Rp1000, one photo, 30 minutes—to avoid the trip to Jayapura. The **post office** is on the right on Jl. Prof. M. Yamin, coming in from the airport. *Kantor imigrasi* is located at the corner of Jl. Imam Bonjol and Jl. Jen. A. Yani. Also on the corner of Jl. Imam Bonjol and Jl. Jen. A. Yani is **Bank Impor-Ekspor** (open Mon.-Fri. 0800-1400, Saturday 0800-1000, Sunday closed), which cashes traveler's checks. **Sentosa Tosiga** is a tour agent and money-changer on Jl. Jen. A. Yani, tel. 21398 or 21956; change money here until 2000. **PT Biak Paradise Tours and Travel** offers birdwatching expeditions to Yapen, and snorkeling and diving tours to the islands off Biak.

The best **pharmacy** in town is Apotik Gandhawati on Jl. Yos Sudarso. At the *wartel* you can dial direct to your home; Rp5000 per minute

to the United States. It's cheaper to use the Indosat International Box in the airport transit corridor; just punch in your country code to connect with the home country operator.

Getting There And Around

Garuda schedules one flight daily (at 0500) from Jakarta via Ujung Pandang to Biak's Frans Kaisiepo Airport. After arriving, walk from the airport down Jl. Prof. M. Yamin into town, hitch, or take a minibus (Rp250) or public *bemo* (Rp350). From the airport five km to town by taxi is Rp9500. Biak is small enough so you can walk anywhere in five or 10 minutes. Catch minibuses from Jl. Prof. M. Yamin or Jl. Jen. A. Yani out to the airport.

Taxi rates run around Rp10,000 per hour. It costs Rp50,000 to reach eastern Biak, Rp60,000 to enter northern Biak, and Rp70,000 to tour western Biak.

Getting Away

Consider using Biak as a base, rather than Jayapura. Biak is an important air hub for coastal Irian Jaya, with Merpati flying to and from Sorong, Manokwari, Serui, and Nabire on the north coast, and Fakfak, Kaimana, and Merauke to the south. Garuda flies from Biak to Ambon on a one-hour flight that's an easy way to reach Maluku. The Garuda offices are located on Jl. Jen. A. Yani, tel. (0967) 21416 or 21331; open 0700-1200 and 1300-1600. You'll find Merpati, tel. 21213 or 21386, across the road from the airport. Both accept Visa or MasterCard. In town, PT Sentosa Tosiga also sells Merpati tickets.

Biak is an oil base and there's heavy sea traffic to and from the island. Monsoons begin in August and last up to two months; there are more ships when the seas are not so rough (Nov.-July). The Pelni office is located near the harbor entrance on Jl. Jen. A. Yani, opposite the taxi terminal. All vessels heading west sail via Ambon. Inquire at the *syahbandar* at the harbor about crowded coasters to Serui, Manokwari, Fakfak, and Sorong. *Prahu* with outboard motors also travel to such islands as Pulau Yapen.

Setia Tours and Travel, Jl. Jen. A. Yani 36, tel. 21398 or 21956, arranges trips for tourists, but if you're on your own it's cheaper to rent a minibus with driver for Rp5000 per hour. **Adventure Travel Expeditions** at Jl. Selat Makassar, tel. 22554, offers several local tours, including rental of your own private desert island for Rp210,000 per day. Traditional palm hut, bedding, pots and pans, food, double outriggers, snorkeling, and fishing. Houseboy optional. An entire island, they say, is yours.

AROUND THE ISLAND

Beaches

Biak is primarily agricultural, which has helped preserve the island's virgin beaches and unpolluted waters. From the town of Biak, take a minibus eight km to rocky Yendidori Beach. About 26 km from Biak (Rp600 by minibus) is **Bosnik,** the first Dutch capital of Biak. On the way, don't miss the incredible Telaga Biru ("Blue Lagoon"). Bosnik is a beautiful white-sand beach with palm trees; from here you can see the 17 islands of the Owi Group to the southeast. Near Bosnik is a bird park (*taman burung*) featuring birds from Irian Jaya, including the bird of paradise. Fifteen minutes by taxi past Bosnik the good road ends. Walk one km more and arrive in **Sabah,** a quiet, untouristed fishing village.

In Bosnik you can stay in the Merau Hotel, a huge accommodation owned by the Japanese. Down the road is a public beach with a pavilion. This is where the Americans first landed in 1944; see rusted old American landing craft. Children sell shells. If you start from here by roofed boat, it takes only one hour to reach Auki Island, where there are numerous good places to snorkel. Full-day rate is Rp150,000 for up to 15-20 people. Leave at 0800 and return at 1700. There's a nice pool for swimming in the middle of a reef, the coral like undulating mountains of red, green, blue, white, and brown.

Korim Beach

On the north coast, 40 km from Biak, the Bay of Korim is surrounded by rocks and jungle. Ride on a well-paved road through tropical landscapes of Melanesian hill villages, tunnels of butterflies, and tall dead trees with orchids perched on top. Sleep in a house on the beach,

or ask the *kepala kampung* for a bed in the very traditional *kampung*. From Biak it's Rp1500 by *bemo* to Korim (one hour); go early, before it rains, when *bemo umum* fill up fast. Near Korim visit the Japanese caves, where human skeletons are displayed. War freaks should seek out John Vandevijver, a half-Dutchman living halfway between Biak and Korim (ask for the *belanda*); he knows a couple of unusual places. Also on the north coast, accessible by dirt track, is the **Biak Nature Reserve,** which protects species of cockatoos and parrots. On **Pulau Sipiori,** two hours away by boat, is another sizable nature reserve.

Warso is a small village northeast of Korim, located at the mouth of a river. From there you can charter a canoe or motorboat to explore upriver. See two waterfalls and exotic birdlife, watch villagers forage from boats or along the banks, visit remote wildlife sanctuaries.

The 150 reefs around Biak offer some of the greatest dropoffs outside the Cayman Islands, some starting only a meter from shore. Together with the big islands of Supiori and Numfoor, there are 43 islands in the Biak-Numfoor District.

The Owi Islands

Directly out front and to the right of Bosnik is Pulau Owi; Auki is to the left. Owi is a very sleepy, idyllic island, with no cars or motorcycles and nice walking paths. It used to be an old U.S. Navy supply and communications base; see the remains of concrete foundations and wrecked planes inland. You can stay overnight with villagers. They love Americans here and the old men remember WW II vividly. As you approach the island you'll probably see the whole village gathered under a banyan tree, with one man playing a ukelele. Mr. Johannsan forges machetes by hand for Rp15,000-20,000; bring a bottle of *awak*. Boat prices vary significantly, from Rp150,000-250,000 for a half day to Rp250,000-500,000 for a full day. You can get anything from an open motorized outrigger to a roofed launch with seats. The crossing to Owi takes about thirty minutes.

CENDRAWASIH DISTRICT

The northwest peninsula of Irian Jaya was known as **Vogelkop** ("Bird's Head") in Dutch times. The inhabitants of this coastal district are a striking mixture of Irianese, Buginese, Filipino, and Chinese. There has also been much contact with the people of Maluku; the native languages here are reminiscent of those of Halmahera. Along the district's coasts are many picturesque small towns with fishing and sawmill operations. Though removed from the main sea lanes, this region offers many natural harbors. Historically, the small, wiry mountain men of the Arfak Mountains—the Moiray, Hattam, and Meach clans—were the most notorious headhunters of western New Guinea. Ancestors' skulls were often worn as charms or kept in an honored part of the house. During WW II, these tribes fought and ate the Japanese using rifles dropped from Allied planes. Some tribes living deep in the interior still shun all contact with outsiders, refusing to move down to the Warmare settlement south of Manokwari.

MANOKWARI

The English built a fort at Dore, near Manokwari, in 1790, but so many people died of beriberi and starvation the place was abandoned five years later. Caves excavated by the Japanese during WW II are scattered all over town. Though only covering a small area, the land in this district is agriculturally very rich and supports a population of nearly 130,000. Manokwari is known as the fruit capital of Irian Jaya; the Dutch introduced numerous types of fruits to the area. The town is situated around a big bay; the Arfak Mountains behind come right down to the sea. There are many *toko*, and a cinema. Traveler's checks and hard currency are accepted at Bank Ekspor-Impor. There's a post office on Jl. Merdaka across from the harbor. The *wartel* is also on Jl. Merdaka, offering international phone and fax service. Go to the World Wildlife Fund office in Manokwari to learn about flora, fauna, and hiking in the Arfak Mountains; consult the detailed maps. Taxi from the airport Rp10,000. If you walk 50 meters to the

road you can flag down a regular taxi for Rp300. Charter taxis for Rp10,000 an hour. Good roads lead out of town to Arfak, Amban, Pasir Putih, and Andai.

Accommodations And Food

The cheapest *losmen* in town is **Losmen Abose,** located near the Merpati office; rooms rent for Rp7500 pp. The old Dutch government hotel, **Hotel Arfak,** Jl. Brawijaya 18, tel. (0967) 21293 or 21195, runs Rp20,000 pp with breakfast and dinner plus coffee and tea all day. Situated on a hill with a nice view over the city; rooms have fans and *mandi.* Best value rooms are in the front of the hotel.

The deluxe **Mutiara Hotel,** Jl. Yos Sudarso, tel. 98311, opposite the daily market, offers a/c rooms with bath, showers, hot water, carpet, video, and restaurant. Rooms go for Rp30,000-65,000; all prices include breakfast plus tea or coffee with snacks and 21% government tax and service. **Losmen Mulia,** just down the road from the Mutiara, charges Rp16,000 for a clean room. **Hotel Mokwam,** on a noisy shopping street, has carpeted rooms with a/c for Rp40,000 d with bath and toilet. Free transport to and from the airport; breakfast included.

Enjoy good food at **Eka Ria**; the owner will show you his butterfly collection. The best *es campur* in town is at **Sori Bakery,** Jl. Merdeka. Try the *ikan bakar* stand in the *warung* across from the Mutiara. For a more formal meal dine at the **Hawaii,** on Jl. Sudirman. Good *ikan bakar* in the **Kebun Sirih,** a few doors down from the Hawaii.

Getting Away

Merpati flies to Biak every day; Sorong on Tuesday, Thursday, and Sunday; and Jakarta on Friday and Sunday. MAF schedules flights to Minyambau and Anggi almost every day, occasionally to Ransiki and other outposts. From Manokwari ferries run twice a week to Ransiki (Rp5000) and weekly to Wasior (Rp7000), leaving from the wharf near the market. From the large cacao plantation at Ransiki hike to the **Anggi Lakes** in three days. Stay with the schoolteacher, Sam Ahoren, in Suruei, the *kampung* near the airstrip. Bring appropriate footwear and waterproof your gear, as it often rains and the nights can be cold. Also bring tea, coffee, and canned fish or instant noodles. The locals stick to potatoes and beans. In both Anggi and Ransiki the police want to see your *surat jalan*.

Vicinity Of Manokwari

On **Gunung Ajamberi** between the beaches and town is a beautiful forest reserve inhabited by hornbills and other rare birds. Remains of the first mission (1855) in Irian Jaya and the ruins of an old church are found on **Pulau Manisam**, about 150 meters offshore. A monument and an old weathered grave mark the spot. Take a two-day hike into the **Arfak Mountains** from Maripi, south of Manokwari.

Universitas Cendrawasih, specializing in agriculture and forestry, is located at **Amban,** three km south of Manokwari harbor. Formerly the site of a Dutch agricultural research station, the spot offers a great view of the Pacific. From here walk four km along a trail through a forest reserve to see a Japanese war monument. The trail continues down the hill to town. The road to the university continues on to the Pacific coast, where you can walk along endless black-sand beaches. Watch the sandflies, and beware of the strong undertow. **Pasir Putih** a few km northeast of town offers good swimming and decent snorkeling. On weekends it's a popular spot, so it can get busy in the afternoons. The road past Pasir Putih continues on for nearly 20 km around the Manokwari peninsula, and ends up back at Universitas Cendrawasih. Charter a *prahu* for Rp35,000 to Pulau Manisnam, where you'll find good snorkeling. You can take a taxi to the *transmigrasi* area at **Warmare,** 60 km west of Manokwari. Aside from small holder farms there's a large oil palm plantation and processing plant.

The road south along the coast to **Oransbari** (70 km) and **Ransiki** (120 km) is quite good, except for the odd landslide in the wet season (Nov.-April). Taxis leave from the main terminal every morning on this very scenic trip. In the rainy season you may not be able to get through every day, as there are several rivers to cross. There are no official accommodations in either town. Inland from Ransiki is **Anggi,** on the shore of the Anggi lakes. This region supplies vegetables for the Manokwari district. Merpati flies here

twice weekly direct from Manokwari, but flights are often cancelled due to bad weather. You can get stuck here for several days, or walk out to Ransiki. Hike into the Arfak mountains from Warmare, Anggi, or Ransiki; the trails are slippery, wet, and steep. Not for the faint of heart; always take a guide. Locals on bare feet will put to shame even the most fit Westerners and their clumsy and all but useless shoes. Let the natives carry your goods; that's the only way you'll have a chance of keeping up with them.

SORONG AND VICINITY

A big Pertamina oil and timber base. The capital of the Sorong District, Sorong lies at the western tip of the Bird's Head. Lots of young, unemployed, non-Irian men hanging around in the market area playing billards and waiting to hassle you. There's a beautiful seaside in front of Sorong, but not much else to see or do.

Accommodations And Food

Stay at **Losmen Pondok Ngeri,** only Rp2500. An excellent deal for the price, hence it's almost always full. So try **Penginapan Sagawin,** Rp7500 including tea or coffee. Both places are located in the *pasar* area. **Losmen Murah** (Rp5000) is also near the *pasar*. Food prices in the market are incredibly cheap compared to the rest of Irian Jaya.

Nearby Islands

Head over to **Doom Island,** a nice place to visit for a few hours. There's a trail around it, an hour's walk through villages and a graveyard, with lots of children for company. For Europeans, Doom has a particularly bleak history: an early British colony was wiped out by malaria and beriberi, and a number of too-persistent Dutch missionaries were speared to death here. See the graves of these missionary "martyrs."

From Sorong, rent dugouts for Rp5000 per hour for island-exploring. **Pulau Salawati,** one of the closest, is home to the bird of paradise, an endemic myra, the orange lori, and white-crowned koel. You can charter a longboat without floats for Salawati; for islands farther out, larger motorized craft are recommended, especially during the rough seas of the northwest monsoons (Nov.-March). On this coast outboard motors are given as part of the dowry, so if you want to start a family, bring a Johnson. Sorong's Jefman Airport is situated on a small island 30 km offshore; the regular daily airport ferry is a ripoff Rp5000 one-way, but there's no other way to get into town.

CAPE ABBA

On the south shore of Teluk Bintuni, south of the Bird's Head. Here you'll find many caves and galleries with rock wall drawings executed by artists some 400 to 1,000 years ago. The drawings are rendered in high coastal cliffs accessible only by sea. The Abba cave features one whole wall covered with silhouettes of hands, red ochre splattered around them. See also a wild, chaotic, multicolored collection of stenciled footprints, figures of people, sea animals, lizard gods, fish, turtles, birds, boats, crescent moons, solar eclipses, and setting suns. One cave includes a drawing of a hornbill with x-rayed ribs. Some figures are hauntingly drawn, others little more than scribbles. These marvelous paintings reveal artists in a very close relationship with the sea and the cosmos. There are other cave paintings near Kokas and Kaimana.

FAKFAK

Pronounced "fuckfuck." A beautiful, scenic town nestled on a hill rolling down to the sea, one of the hidden gems of Irian Jaya. Surprisingly large considering its location, Fakfak offers three banks, a big market, a telecommunications office, frequent bemo service, and plenty of fruit trees. Everything about the place reminds you of Dutch colonization; most older people still speak fluent Dutch, and will frequently ask if you're from Holland and capable of speaking Bahasa Belanda—they're really disappointed if you can't. Many older men in civil service jobs went to high school in the Netherlands. Dutch tourists return here for, as the Indonesians put it, "nostalgia." Dutch architecture is everywhere and every house has a beautiful garden. In fact, the whole town gives the impression of a professional landscape artist's creation.

The town contains a curious mix of Irianese and people from nearby islands. There are more Muslims here than anywhere else in Irian; Fakfak has traded with other islands since the 17th century. The rainy season is reversed in this region, with the wettest months May-November. Fakfak is known as the nutmeg and durian capital of Irian Jaya. Good snorkeling nearby. The hills around town are karst, and thus the area is difficult to explore; from the air it looks like a giant egg carton. People are laid-back and friendly, though hordes of children freaked out by white aliens can prove a hassle.

Accommodations And Food

Try the **Hotel Tambagapura,** Jl. Izak Telussa 16, with rooms for Rp15,000-30,000. Prices include breakfast of roti and kopi. There's a restaurant attached, the **Kumawa,** with expensive but good food. The only other available food stations are a few cheap, strictly nasi ikan foodstalls.

Another recommended accommodation is **Losmen Harahna,** Rp20,000 d including breakfast; meals Rp3500. The Irianese manager, Pak Eduard, will arrange tours and guides; ask him about the jaunt to Kokas, 40 km north on Bintuni Bay. Take taxis part of the journey; proceed the rest of the way on foot along a good trail. **Losmen Sulinah,** Jl. Tambaruni 79, tel. (0967) 292, is Rp22,000 s or d, including three meals.

Practicalities

Change money at **Bank Impor-Ekspor,** Jl. Izak Telussa, with the best exchange rate for traveler's checks. Also try **Bank Pembangunun Daerah** on Jl. Tambaruni. **Pasar Tambaruni** on Jl. Tambaruni along the waterfront has great atmosphere. In **Toko Andalas,** tel. (0967) 2532, on Jl. Tambaruni buy recent editions of the English Jakarta Post and even Newsweek and Time. The airport lies four km out of town. Halfway there is a Bintang distributor, where you can drink ice-cold beer and soda in a serene garden with a blue lagoon.

Getting There

Be prepared for the airstrip at Fakfak. It's insanely short, with steep dropoffs on either end. Only Twin Otters can land here, and even they have to come in at a very steep angle. Strong crosswinds often throw the plane around upon descent. This hair-raising arrival experience, as well as its location among steep hills preventing urban expansion, ensures Fakfak will not soon lose its charms.

KAIMANA

A small, expensive town on the underside of the Bird's Head, capital of the Fakfak District. In 1828 the Dutch built a fort on Triton Bay, but nearly the whole contingent soon perished of malaria, beriberi, starvation, and native attacks. Utarom Airstrip covers the spot today.

Stay at the *pasanggrahan* or in the mission station. The mission offers maps good for a number of walks in the surrounding jungle, though there are few native villages left intact. You can trek from here to **Teluk Bintani** in about one week. In the dry season there's a small boat to **Kokonau** on the south coast, where there's a mission station. From Kokonau you can hop a plane to Timika. Merpati schedules flights from Kaimana to Biak, Enarotali, Fakfak, and Nabire.

THE CENTRAL HIGHLANDS

In the Central Highlands mountain rivers have cut magnificent valleys that are home to hundreds of thousands of people. Because the peaks are higher in the west, the Baliem Valley is more spectacular than its eastern counterpart, the Wahgi in Papua New Guinea. The remarkable quiltwork of sweet potato gardens gives the valley an incredibly ordered look. Natives in the area engage in a form of agriculture that is quite different from the slash-and-burn system practiced elsewhere on the island.

Although volcanos are found at the north end of the island there are none in the Central Highlands. Earthquakes are likewise very rare. The Baliem Valley offers an equatorial climate, without seasons, where the steady pressure of the tradewinds makes for rain and sunshine every day. There are no high winds, torrential downpours, or droughts. Because the Baliem climate is so equitable and mild, the natives cannot blame natural disasters on weather-identified supernatural powers, and thus are not a particularly superstititous people.

The pig is all-important in the highlanders' ceremonial and economic life—a crucial part of their social organization, and a major source of protein. Pork is essential for feasts, as payment of personal debts, and to make tribal reparations. A man's main interests are pigs and women—new wives are purchased with fat pigs and *rupiah*—and his social status is determined by how many of each he owns. Women here are usually seen bent beneath heavy loads carried in a multicolored *bilum*; the long braided handle of the bag is looped around the forehead, so the burden is borne by the head and neck. The pressure of all this weight is padded by a small, sweatsoaked, grimy towel positioned between the *bilum* handle and the forehead. A series of three or four bark net bags may hang down a woman's back, containing separate cargos of vegetables, pigs, and babies. Women walk along singing softly to their babies, who often lie asleep, unseen, in the deep dark folds at the bottom of the bags. Here they stay all day, except when at the breast. The mother's walking serves to rock the baby; you can hear the child murmur contentedly inside.

Although the Dani, the area's best known tribe, are not cannibals, the practice has been known to occur among tribes in the southern valleys. In the 1960s an Aso Lokopals raiding party was cut off and wiped out by a group of Hisaro. The twenty dead men were roasted in a big rock fire and ritually eaten. Their bones were placed in the forest on taboo ground, considered extremely dangerous because of its high concentration of angry, vengeful ghosts.

Flora And Fauna
Highland plantlife is remarkable both for its oddity and its relative paucity of species. Fewer species inhabit the upland areas; those that do are most often peculiar, rare. Confined to the high ranges, many are endemic to the region. Perched atop some eucalyptus trees you'll see large white rhododendron blossoms, the corolla spanning as wide as five inches from lip to lip. This species, *rhododendron levcogigas*, possesses the largest flower of any member of the

genus. The dark pandanus yields a large red fruit; the people squeeze its juice over their tubers. Pandanus are planted in village gardens; each tree is owned by a particular man, tended and eventually harvested by him. The *daluga* and *duge pandanus,* which produce nuts, grow wild in the forest.

Snakes are rare here because of the vast number of foraging pigs. Tree frogs, large tree lizards, and small bronze-colored skinks are plentiful; there are no toads, salamanders, or turtles. The Dani don't eat amphibians or reptiles but catch and consume many insects and almost any sort of mammal, marsupial, or bird, including bats and cormorants. Rats are considered a delicacy, given to young boys who open them with bone needles to remove their entrails. The gutted rodents are placed along the edge of a fire and singed, then roasted over the flames at the end of pointed sticks. Rats in religious ceremonies are wrapped neatly in leaves and grass, left as offerings in ghost-purging ceremonies. There are huge cicadas, tropical butterflies, and beautiful hesperid moths in the highlands. The mountain duck, a solitary, rare, small species, is black and white with a bright orange bill. Freshwater crayfish attain a length of four to five inches in the smaller streams everywhere in the Baliem Valley. Boys feel for them with their toes as they walk through the mud.

The Missionaries

Missionaries were the first outsiders to enter the interior, attempting settlement as early as the 1940s. Many have been and are sensitive, intelligent, and dedicated. Since 1977, missionaries have built over 800 schools, 130 hospitals, and 240 first-aid posts, and their private air services are the most extensive on the island. There are important Protestant and Catholic agricultural projects at Mulia, Angguruk, Soba, and Ninia, as well as an agricultural program at the Bible and Vocational Institute in Sentani. Due to their efforts and those of the Indonesian government, schools all over the central highlands now teach Bahasa Indonesia. Though the missionaries have been gradually training Indonesians to take over mission work and replace them, they remain extremely important agents of change between the Irianese and the Indonesian authorities.

Success in conversion has varied from tribe to tribe. In some cases, barely comprehensible Christian doctrines were force-fed to Papuans who already practiced their own proud, integrated spiritual beliefs. Sometimes spectacular shifts to Christianity occurred; other times the missionaries were pretty much ignored. Occasionally, they were eaten.

The greatest missionary successes came in discouraging war. Only after an area was rendered "safe" by missionaries would government officials and soldiers arrive. Yet the missionaries also brought disease and, to the horror of historians and anthropologists, encouraged the destruction of priceless works of art, fetishes, and handicrafts. A large portion of the money flowing into Irian Jaya from people overseas goes to support missionaries and not the Irianese people.

TREKKING

Irian Jaya's highlands are home to very sensitive, fossilized, wholly intact traditional cultures, so visitors must be on their very best behavior. Some European visitors think they're in the Garden of Eden, surrounded by noble savages, but these cultures are actually very complex. Just because the natives are half-naked, it doesn't mean visitors may bathe naked in the rivers. Though women wear just a G-string girdle, there are involved rules governing how it is worn, according to the woman's age and marital or societal status. Without this scant covering, highland Irianese women feel naked.

Practicalities

If heading into remote areas, take plenty of small bills. Minibuses from Wamena only venture 14 km, as far as Yiwika. Motorcycles are expensive, hard to arrange, and impractical. Your feet will take you to many more places. There are hundreds of kilometers of good hiking trails linking villages throughout the central highlands. Streams not easily forded will have bridges of some sort. Conditions vary widely, depending on terrain and weather. Hiking can be like a Sunday stroll through the park or it can mean clambering over steep slippery rock faces, sliding down muddy paths, and wobbling over dangerous bridges.

BALIEM VALLEY TREKS

EASY

Kurima to Tangma; three hours roundtrip

Kurima to Polimo; two hours roundtrip

MODERATE

Kurima to Tangma; five hours roundtrip

Pugima to Sekon to Suroba; two to three days roundtrip; jungle

Jiwika to Iluw; six hours roundtrip

STRENUOUS

Kurima to Pasema; three days one way; jungle

Prongoli to Anggruk; one day one way; hill, jungle

Manda to Wolo to Ilugwa; three days roundtrip; jungle, cave

Munak to Bokondini; three days one way

Bokondini to Karaubaga; three days one way

Ibele to Lake Habema; three days one way

DIFFICULT

Kurima to Soba; three days one way; jungle, steep climb

Kurima to Ninia; six days one way; jungle

Kurima to Prongolo; five days one way; jungle, climbs

Mbua to Lake Habema; eight days one way; jungle, caves, waterfall, cold nights

Kurima to Holowon; eight to nine days one way

Kosarek to Nipsan; two days

If considering a trek into the Baliem Valley it's a good idea to buy most of your provisions in Jayapura. Carry tins and packets of noodles on the plane as hand luggage; don't forget cigarettes and chocolate. The closer you get to Baliem the greater the price of imported food. You can't buy a beer in the valley; it's prohibited. Bring good footwear, a hat, sunglasses, wind- and rainproof gear, a medical kit that includes sterile pads and bandages, light clothing, and a warm sweater and windbreaker for the cool highland nights. If camping, bring a sleeping bag and mosquito-proof tent. Shorts are the most com-

fortable attire for trailwalking. Lay in a supply of sun-protection cream, lip balm, and insect repellent. Cheap costume jewelry, ballpoint pens, rice, and salt make good gifts. The best present is probably the common safety pin, or *pineti*, which is the Swiss Army Knife of the Dani culture. They have about 12 different uses for the thing—fishhook, decoration, surgical tool, wood gouger. They seem to like velcro, too.

Guides And Porters

Guides and porters are usually easy to find in any village, *losmen,* or airport. Costs can vary widely. Be prepared for heavy rip-offs if you hire a guide in Wamena, where you're expected to pay from Rp10,000 to Rp20,000 per day plus food for a guide and perhaps Rp5000 and up per porter. It's better to work on a day-by-day basis with village men who ask about Rp2000-3000 per day; a prearranged guide from Wamena will demand Rp60,000 for a five-day trek. Get advice on pay rates from local missionaries, teachers, police, and government officials. One man might carry for you without worrying about receiving any pay while another might expect an exorbitant sum. Still others you meet along the trail will accompany you to where you're going if it's more or less in the same direction they're headed. Bargain and establish the fee in advance. Be sure to ascertain who pays carriers, food, and lodging for all parties. Don't let them overbuy food; you may end up feeding whole families.

Many guide positions are being taken over by the Javanese. While they may be nice people, few speak the Dani dialects of the outlying villages, reducing their value considerably. The native people also greatly resent the Indonesians, an attitude that will affect their behavior toward visitors with Javanese guides. On the other hand, don't expect an Irianese guide or porter to accompany you much more than a day's travel from his village; he might be afraid of old enemies. It's often taboo for them to climb a mountain, believing it will fall down and crush them; it could also be the forbidden home of ancestors. Problems also pop up with guides arranged in Jayapura. Best to hire locally and hire Dani.

Never force porters to walk later than they think wise. Mountain Irianese know best where to find good shelter and plentiful firewood. They can build huts from tree trunks and branches within minutes or light fires without matches in complete darkness with soaking wet wood. Irianese are proud people, not servants. They won't wait on you hand and foot. A contract is made at the start for them to carry so much for so long to such and such a place for an agreed payment, and that's it. Small boys and young men will fetch water, light fires, cook breakfast, and erect tents; the older men won't. Be prepared to carry your own pack if prices escalate or your porter suddenly decides to return home. Young boys may be eager to carry your gear but often tire before reaching your destination. Bring stacks of small bills (Rp100-1000 notes) to cover expenses.

Certain areas are not open to travelers. Recently three Americans climbed Gunung Trikora without mishap, slogging through the mud, rain, wind, and cold. Occasionally they stayed in huts with native hunters; otherwise they were alone with the fleas. Soon after, two Germans tried to hang glide off the peak; they flew into a forest and broke their legs. The Indonesians subsequently closed the mountain.

ACCOMMODATIONS AND FOOD

Overnighting

Usually it's possible to stay in village huts, with the village schoolteacher or pastor, at the local police post, or in the homes of missionaries, but haul around an insect-proof tent in case you can't. In the Painan Lake country, for example, you must be entirely self-sufficient. Police will often let you sleep for free in their yard. Always check in at police stations to lessen the chance of suspicion. In the larger villages, you can sleep on the floor of the schoolhouse or church. Expect to donate Rp3000 to Rp5000 per night.

You can probably also stay in a traditional Dani *honnay*. Many travelers shun them because they're often infested with cockroaches, pig fleas (*kutu babi*), and rats, but bites will fade while memories grow—you can't beat the *honnay* for atmosphere. This ultra-macho men's hut is full of weapons, charms, and mummified body parts of enemies killed in battle. It can be very warm inside, but the smoke keeps the mosquitos away. Only brave men who've proven themselves in battle can sleep in a *honnay*; young, untested men are often afraid to, believing they'll suffer terrible nightmares.

The men sit naked on the grass floor around the fire, continually smoking a very strong tobacco rolled in dried leaves. Smoke with them and you're guaranteed a high. The stuff is so strong it acts like pot, and will really mellow you out if you inhale as deeply as the men do. Before staying in village huts, determine first if there's a charge. You could be presented in the morning with an itemized bill for Rp5000 for sleeping and sweet potatoes. Danis may be naked but they're not stupid.

Staying With Missionaries

The insensitivity of tourists has caused some strained relations with the missionaries. Many missionaries have spent lifetimes building their missions and are very possessive about what they've accomplished. Some tourists believe missionaries have no right to be in Irian at all, while missionaries feel tourists all too often impose themselves without any forewarning or compensation.

Travelers are often so ignorant of the harsh conditions and rugged terrain, and arrive so ill-prepared, that missionaries end up taking care of them. Some travelers have ruined the reception for those who follow by taking help for granted, disregarding private property, and helping themselves to missionary supplies. These factors mean many missionaries are not enthusiastic about the growth of tourism in Irian Jaya.

If you intend to stay in a mission, it's a matter of courtesy to contact the place before you arrive. If you know only the general region you wish to visit, write David Wunsch, MAF flight operations manager, at P.O. Box 239, Sentani, Irian Jaya 99352, tel. (0967) 179. If MAF doesn't visit the area, Wunsch will pass your letter on to the appropriate office.

Food And Health

Cooked sweet potatoes are almost always available, a fairly complete food nutritionally though some find them tiresome day after day after day. In many villages you can also secure potatoes, carrots, cabbage, corn, green beans, rice, pineapples, papayas, and citrus fruits. Everything seems to cost Rp100, no matter what or how big it is—except a chicken, which is Rp7000. Always ask for the price of everything beforehand; you might be charged as much as Rp6000 for *nasi putih*. To break up the monotony, bring tins of meat and snack foods from

Jayapura or Wamena. Canned food is sometimes available from a local *toko* or missionaries, but don't count on either source outside Wamena. Clean water is often difficult to obtain; it all comes from mountain streams, which run through villages dripping with pig shit. You definitely need water-purification tablets or a water filter here. Malaria and tuberculosis, imported by transmigrants and travelers, are the most serious health hazards for the Irianese.

THE BALIEM VALLEY

The Baliem Valley was "discovered" by a wealthy American explorer during a botanical and zoological expedition in 1938. He believed this 1,600-meter-high valley inhabited by a lost civilization. When the clouds cleared, the expedition members beheld a vast, beautifully tended garden of checkerboard squares with neat stone fences, clean-cut networks of canals, and meticulously terraced mountain slopes. The Grand Valley of the Baliem received worldwide publicity in 1945 when a sightseeing plane out of wartime Hollandia crashed and its survivors were subsequently rescued in a daring glider operation. An American nurse in the group called the valley a Shangri-La. The first outsiders to settle here were missionaries landed by floatplane in 1945 near Hetagima on the Baliem River. The Dutch established a settlement at Wamena in 1956, bringing in schoolteachers, new breeds of livestock, modern clothing, and metal tools. Wamena remained under Dutch control for just six short years, until Indonesia wrested West New Guinea from Holland in 1962. The year before, Harvard's Peabody Museum sponsored a major expedition to the Grand Baliem to document the area's stone age culture. This journey is documented in Peter Matthiessen's magnificent *Under the Mountain Wall*. Beyond the Baliem live other peoples, such as the Yali, Mek, and Kim Yal, some uncontacted until the 1960s and '70s. Villagers here occasionally use human skulls as pillows; the Kim Yal were eating missionaries as recently as 1969.

The government's "Indonesianization" campaign has yet to succeed. Even in the main town of Wamena people still wear traditional dress. The villages and gardening systems are still much as they were, although steel tools have all but replaced traditional polished wood, stone, bone, and sharpened bamboo implements. Children are not taught about their own history, culture, and environment, but are indoctrinated with pan-Indonesian nationalism. The valley offers magnificent scenery and unlimited tourist potential. Yet the increasing population is putting a strain on the surviving forests; most of the trees between Wamena and Karubaga have already been cut down for timber.

The Land

The Grand Valley is 72 km long by 16-32 km wide, inhabited by tribes of Neolithic warrior farmers, the Dani. The Baliem River pours down from Gunung Trikora, running like a snake through a valley of stony riverbeds, jungled ravines, *kampung* of round and long houses, plots of green cultivated fields, and stone walls. The valley lies one mile above the sea; 50 miles southeast of the head of the valley the river drops into an extensive and spectacular gorge system to run itself out in the vast marshes and mud of the southern coast. The river and its tributaries provide water for the Danis' elaborate chessboard-patterned drainage and irrigation systems, which look more like New England farmlands than the home of Stone Age people.

The Dani have practiced pig-raising and horticulture for 5,000 years, and are today some of the most meticulous gardeners in the world. They plant bushes to prevent erosion, use leaf mulch to heat the soil, and cultivate casuarina trees to siphon off some of the loam's excess moisture. Ditches are also used as compost heaps, so that each new crop can take root on fertilized soil. Droughts and pests are uncommon; there are no dangerous animals and disease is rare.

Sweet potato (*hiperi*), grown on raised plots and cultivated only with digging sticks, is the Dani's staple crop, accounting for 90% of their diet. Just as the Eskimo language contains numerous words for snow and various Arabic tongues feature numberless terms for camels, so do the Dani have 790 different words for the sweet potato. There are basically two kinds: some with grayish or cream-colored meat, others colored yellow to orange. The tuber is never eaten raw but roasted in coals or steamed in a pit. The leaf of the young vine is also consumed; it tastes a lot like spinach. Some varieties are thought to taste particularly good while others are fit only for pigs.

Climate

The temperature is mild and the rainfall moderate, though highly variable. If it's raining in the southern part of the valley, it might be sunny in the north, or vice versa. September through October is the season of high winds, usually rising in the afternoon. It's frequently cloudy except in the early morning when all the surrounding mountains are in clear view.

WAMENA

Wamena is a study in cultural incongruities. Streets are gridded like any small Australian town but flow with very little traffic. In Wamena you'll find Dani tribesmen, Indonesian schoolboys, international aid workers, backpackers, tourists, missionaries, and the police, all strolling beneath cloud-wreathed mountain peaks. There are statues of Dani warriors here, penis gourds pointing proudly upward. Wamena is a Dani handicrafts and marketing center; there are an increasing number of traditional Dani fences and thatched compound entrances erected around town.

Still, it's odd that in a city that's the center of a pig-loving tribal culture the largest and most opulent building is a mosque. Restaurants here are run exclusively by Javanese and Sumatrans. Tribespeople are mustered for the occasional pig feast or as carriers for short walks around the valley, but these activities generate a pittance compared with the economic returns for Indonesians.

Wamena is a small town with row upon row of mission offices, schools, and what seems like hundreds of government offices, all sprawling across the flat Baliem Valley floor. As everything is flown in, prices are some of the highest in Indonesia. You can cut down on your costs if you eat in the markets and stay in the nearby villages. Wamena's market, bustling with farmers selling produce, is the town's premier tourist attraction. This is also the place to view Wamena's extraordinary mixture of cultures and customs—craggy Dani tribesmen, tall stately Minangs, Western-attired Javanese, curly-haired Ambonese. For additional entertainment, the military shows movies every night (Rp2000) and there are regular TV broadcasts. Almost every night the electricity goes out, so be sure to bring a flashlight.

Accommodations

The cheapest and best *losmen* in town is the **Syahrial Jaya**, Jl. Gatot Subroto 51, tel. (0967)

THE BALIEM VALLEY

TO MULIA
TO MAMIT
KANGIME
(4,050 m)
KARUBAGA — WUNEN
TIOM
BOKONDINI
KELILA
PIT RIVER
JUGWA
MAGI
FLIGHT FROM JAYAPURA
PYRAMID
WOLO RIVER
WOLO
WOOGI
BUGI
ILUGWA
MUSAKFAK
WOSI
ELEGAIMA
JIWAKA
SINATMA
HOM HOM
AKIMA
WAMENA RIVER
WAMENA
PUGIMA
WORUBA
HETAGIMA
(4,240 m)
KURIMA
SEINMA
(3,690 m)
BALIEM RIVER
WET
SOBA
(3,960 m)
PASEMA
NINIA
(3,700 m)
HOLOWON
HELUK RIVER
0   10 km

151), Rp10,000 pp with fan and *mandi*; a/c rooms cost Rp18,000 s. Price includes breakfast. Easy to find, close to the airport runway; Sam will probably be out at the airport to greet you. The Indonesian manager, Hamzah Tanjung, is very responsible and helpful. You can even arrange to clean up there, stay half a day, and leave things in the locked storage room without checking in as a guest—a big help when trekking. Sit around in the evenings with the locals and sing Dani songs.

The **Nayak,** at Jl. Gatot Subroto 1, tel. 31067 or 31030, has 15 clean, basic rooms for Rp30,000 s, Rp40,000 d. Tariff includes breakfast, service tax, and attached *mandi*. Also check out nice, clean **Losmen Sri Lestari** across from the market with rooms for Rp15,000 s and Rp27,000 d. The place is sprayed every night for mosquitos. **Losmen Anggrek**, Jl. Ambon 1, tel. 31242, rents rooms for Rp30,000-40,000. Balcony overlooks the neighborhood. Clean, *mandi*-style bath, Western toilet.

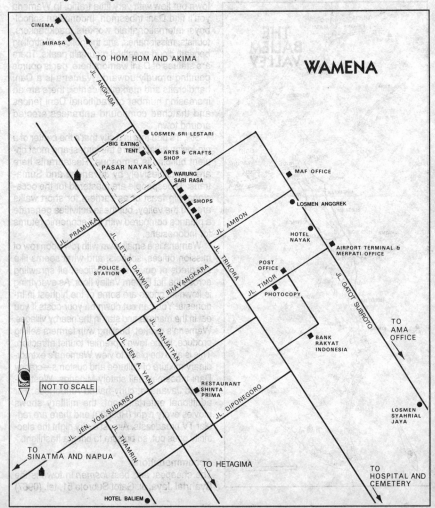

More comfortable and expensive is the **Hotel Baliem** on Jl. Thamrin, tel. 31370, the oldest luxury hotel in Wamena. Rooms run Rp35,500 s, Rp55,000 d; price includes all taxes, continental breakfast, and afternoon snack. Clean bungalows built in typical Dani style with sitting areas, Western-style bathrooms, but no hot water and weak electricity. Seventeen rooms in 11 *honnay*-shaped buildings; even the restaurant resembles a *honnay*. Very nice dining room with good breakfast and full-course meals (Rp5000). The superb map in the office shows most of the villages and rivers of the Baliem.

The small, central **Baliem Palace Hotel** charges Rp55,000 s, Rp65,000 d for clean, comfortable rooms, and sells good maps of the Baliem Valley for Rp7500. It's almost always full in the high season, even for meals. The **Wamena Hotel**, on Jl. Trikora, tel. 81292, about 1.5 km from the market on the road out of town to the north, is a typical Indonesian businessman's hotel with Western toilet and cold-water *mandi*. Beware of annoying abbreviated "short sheets." Sinks, but no water. Light breakfast of marmalade and hardboiled egg. Ishak, a good guide, works out of this hotel. Rates are Rp32,000 but you can probably bargain for less. The **Hotel Trendy**, right next to the Baliem Palace towards the market, tel. 31092, offers rooms for Rp22,000 s, Rp27,000 d. Ten rooms, all with bath. The air is closed and stuffy but the *ibu* is friendly. Breakfast, coffee, cold drinks, tea.

The **Wio Silimo Traditional Dani Hotel** is a *losmen* built in the traditional style of the Dani tribe. Dani tools hang on walls. Rp5,000 for a loft, Rp10,000 s, Rp15,000 d. Generator electricity. Julius Yikma here works here as a guide; he smokes like a chimney, and speaks three languages of the Baliem Valley as well as English.

Avoid the **Merrano Hotel.** The owners here are more interested in buying fancy new computers than serving a decent breakfast, and they don't seem to care that all the toilets are broken. Also in the broken toilet category is the **Merannu,** with single economy rooms for Rp36,000 and double rooms for Rp44,000. Not a working john in sight. Restaurant attached with drinks and simple meals.

Walk east across the bridge to Pugima or go north to Yiwika for cheap village accommodations. Dani tribesmen may even approach you in Wamena with offers to come and stay in their villages. Or just go to the market—in five minutes you'll find somebody to stay with for Rp5000. A lot more interesting than a *losmen.*

Food

At the **Shinta Prima** *rumah makan* ask for the local specialty, *udang asam manis saus*—fresh Baliem River crawfish the size of lobsters for Rp1700 apiece. The **Bougainiville Restaurant** is Chinese-run, with ordinary food and the decor of an Iowa barbecue joint. *Sate ayam* costs Rp7500, *nasi putih* Rp1000. The *pakpak* provides pickup and dropoff service to and from anywhere in town. At **Mas Budi's,** Jl. Trikora 116, tel. (0967) 31214, the *mie kuah* for Rp2500 is delicious, as is the Rp1000 *es jerish. Nasi goreng* Rp2500, *mie bakso* Rp25000, *cap cai* Rp3000, *udang goreng* Rp30,000, fried fish Rp8000. Great for Javanese food; best traveler's hangout in town.

The *warung* in the market dish up excellent filling *nasi campur* for Rp800; with *ikan,* Rp1000. The big tent by the market serves good, fresh, cheap food such as fried rice and noodles for around Rp2000. Right across the street is **Warung Sari Rasa**—excellent *mie goreng* dishes for Rp1500. **Flower's Coffee Shop** is the best place for breakfast, new and clean, with good coffee. Visit **Pasar Nayak** for snack foods, fresh vegetables, *durian,* oranges, fish, and canned goods. You can see tribespeople here walking around in full dress for the express purpose of having themselves photographed for Rp500.

Shopping

The local market, Pasar Nayak, is an unbelievable hodgepodge of foreign and domestic goods. Stone axes (*kapak*) sell for Rp5000-10,000, the cost depending on size, the type of stone used, and the labor involved. The cheaper variety is sold in the market stalls. Ax blades are mostly common black; green stone is the hardest and considered the finest. The Dani are now aware such things can bring a lot of money, and some specimens look filed or lathed on machines, obviously turned out for tourists. The oruder and larger the blade, the more likely it's the real thing. Buy from a guy who's just walked in from an outlying village.

At least 20 kiosks in the market sell Dani artificats—bibs, Asmat-style carvings, headdresses, bone and wood carvings, fossils, exchange stones. Also look for thin hand-woven rattan bracelets (*sekan*), Rp300 for nice ones, and women's grass skirts (*yokal*) made from *alang-alang*, found everywhere in the highlands. *Noken*, the cloak-like bark-string bags, come in a variety of sizes and make handy carriers—small ones are Rp3000, large ones Rp7000. The most popular souvenir for visiting Indonesians seems to be the giant-size men's penis-sheath, selling for around Rp200-300. There's a good selection of postcards (Rp1000), Memory Irian games (Rp25,000), and maps of the Baliem Valley (Rp8000) for sale at most of the hotels. Mailing Irianese crafts home from Jayapura's central post office can be a real bureaucratic hassle, so wait until you get to Ambon, Ujung Pandang, or Singapore.

Services

Wamena is the center for bureaucratic activity in the highlands. Arriving, the police at the airport will stamp and sign your *surat jalan* in five minutes. The **post office** on Jl. Timor is open Mon.-Thurs. 0800-1200, Friday 0800-1000, Saturday 0800-1100. Change money at **Bank Rakyat Indonesia** Mon.-Fri. 0800-1500, Saturday 0800-1200; fairly low rate. In Wamena, you can use Rp5000 and Rp10,000 bills, but when you get just a couple of hours' walk away they want only the red ones (Rp100). Danis expect Rp100 per photo or piece of fruit.

Getting There

From Jayapura take the Merpati flight out of Sentani Airport—a fantastic flight. Or fly with Airfast or another charter group. Missionary aircraft are more expensive but may be your only choice if flying to Wamena from a remote area. Never believe airline personnel or your guide regarding the availability of flights from outlying locales to Wamena. Some travelers have been told flights from Karubaga to Wamena would be "no problem" but ended up waiting three days at the airport. Because the clouds and mists come over in the afternoon, the morning flight could be crowded. Sometimes the only two passes into the Baliem accessible to non-pressurized aircraft are closed. Those flying into Wamena or any other remote region of Irian

Jaya should be prepared for the occasional disconcerting aviation experience, such as the copilot asking to borrow a screwdriver to tighten the screws that have rattled loose in the aircraft's dashboard.

A siren chases all people and animals off Wamena's runway when a plane is about to land. The best transport from the airport to town is your feet. No problem: one hotel is quite near the airstrip, while others are only a 15- or 20-minute walk away. Strapping Dani boys will stride off to your hotel with your luggage, with you trotting behind trying to keep up.

It is assumed the construction of a road from Jayapura to Wamena will eventually deliver more tourists to the highlands. The Indonesian government and swarms of local businesspeople have already developed a sort of cargo cult mentality about this uncompleted roadway, establishing and expanding businesses all over Wamena in great expectation of the arriving hordes. No one seems to have considered just how many tourists will want to spend days and days bouncing around an overpacked *bemo* for hundreds of kilometers over a poorly maintained road running through areas heavily infested with multiple strains of malaria.

Getting Away

The Merpati flight to Jayapura usually leaves at 0830 and arrives in time to connect with onward flights to Ujung Pandang and Surabaya. Buy tickets two hours before departure at the office adjacent to the airport terminal. Open Mon.-Fri. 0530-1700, closed Saturday and Sunday. The Airfast agent in the tower at the terminal sells tickets to Jayapura. Departure times depend on cargo, passengers, and weather, so you never really know when flights are leaving. Inquire at the missionary MAF and AMA offices at the airport for flights within the highlands.

Reliable Sam Chandra of **Chandra Nusantara Tours and Travel,** Jl. Trikora No. Tromel Post 41, tel. (0967) 143, will organize any kind of trek or difficult expedition, either in the highlands or the Asmat area. Another outfit that arranges package tours is **PT Insos Moon Wijaya Tours and Travel,** Jl. Sulawesi 57, Wamena.

The *terminal taksi* is located opposite the airport. Fares to Sinagara Rp500, Kimbim Rp3500, Ibele Rp2000, Wanima Rp1500, Munda Rp4000, Tanahmerah Rp1000, Kurulu

THE BALIEM VALLEY 1271

Rp2000, Osolimo Rp1500, Sogohmo Rp2500, Kurian Rp3000, Maki Rp12,5000, and Pirimie Rp17,500. To reach the Pugima caves you must charter a vehicle for Rp20,000.

SHORT WALKS FROM WAMENA

Hiking From Wamena

Walking on the numerous and generally well-maintained dirt footpaths and hard-gravel roads of the Baliem Valley is an invigorating and unforgettable experience. It's difficult to find vehicles—even motorbikes—to charter, and even if you do the cost is high. The climate is ideal for walking, though rains can turn the trails slippery. The people are friendly and welcoming, approaching you on the paths hands extended. Old men still ask you to take their photo for Rp100—it seems you can buy almost everything from the Dani for the worthless red Rp100 notes. Women are generally weighed down under loads of sweet potatoes, piglets, and ba-

trekking in the Baliem

bies and tend to walk past you with averted eyes. Greet men with *"Narak!"* followed by a handshake; to women, shout *"La'uk!"*

Any of the hotels can help you find guides and porters for the longer walks. Having someone along to translate between Indonesian and the local language makes for a more rewarding trip. Look for recommendations from other travelers. Guides frequent Losmen Syahrial Jaya, such as Benji (highly recommended), who speaks excellent English and is full of information. Sam Payokwa will charge three people Rp10,000 to take them to Yiwika. Sam's friend Selias Morip is an excellent cook, porter, and great companion as well. Good reports also on Benny Wehda, who hangs out at Losmen Sri Lestari.

Another school holds you don't really need a guide within the Baliem. Even if you speak only a little Indonesian, it's easy to get around. The valley is populated enough there's almost always someone around to ask directions from. If you reach a difficult stretch and find you need a guide, just go back to the nearest *kampung* and hire one there for as long as you need him. Guides from Wamena often have to ask directions too.

Sinatma

A Protestant mission one hour's walk west of Wamena. From Sinatma walk to the power station dam, then follow Wamena River to two suspension bridges made of vines and rough wood. Continue out to Napua and then over to Walesa.

Pugima

An easy walk from Wamena east across the Baliem River. Walk south on the road beside the airport for about three-fourths of the runway length, then turn left on a path over rocks polished by bare feet, cross the runway—stay alert for planes—and then continue east on the trail to the bridge over the river. The water here is deep and calm enough for swimming. Follow the trail a short distance further to Pugima village, where the chief sells ornately carved arrows at about the same prices as in Wamena.

Woruba

A nice eight- to 10-hour roundtrip walk to the east of Wamena via Pugima. There's a point here where you can look out over the entire valley. Not a flat walk, the scenery really changes along the way. In Woruba there's a big house with a friendly family from Timor who are happy to put people up for the night, though it's more interesting to stay in nearby *kampung*.

Akima

At the end of a two-hour walk north from Wamena is the infamous smoked mummy of Akima. Walk northwest on the compacted gravel road from Wamena, turning left at the intersection, past the jail to Hom Hom. Turn down to the river and cross the bridge. Continue on the dirt road to Akima. A tourist sight, it costs Rp10,000 per group to view the decorated mummy, so if you want to see it take others along with you. The mummy is not for sale; it's the chief's grandfather. These are the Soka people, so don't call them Dani. Akima is also accessible by taxi from Wamena.

Yiwika

An easy five- to six-hour (15 km) walk north from Wamena, Yiwika consists of two traditional longhouses, a thatch roof shelter, and a *honnay* surrounded by gardens and women working the fields. *Bemo* run 1100 to 1600 from in front of the Wamena market to Yiwika; a charter for three people costs around Rp10,000 each way. A short walk from Yiwika is the **Lauk Inn**; Rp7000 pp, Rp9000 with breakfast, or Rp12,000 for all meals. Keep a light burning at night to shoo the rats away. Nice restaurant—fresh bread in the mornings.

Alternately stay in traditional Dani village huts for Rp3000 s, Rp5000 d, including light breakfast, extra for other meals. Meet Kurulu Mabel,

---

OBAHOROK'S LAST STAND

One of the last acknowledged skirmishes to occur in the Baliem Valley was in 1971, when the American anthropologist Wyn Sargent married the Dani chief Obahorok to observe at close range the tribal habits of the Dani. It is said that Obahorok, egged on by his new wife, then staged a tribal war for his bride's benefit. When the Indonesians got wind of this they expelled the American and Obahorok became the object of worldwide attention. To this day the local authorities remain suspicious of anthropologists, journalists, and Americans in general.

---

chief of the Yiwika confederation of villages, paramount chief of the northeast side of the Baliem River, and proud owner of some 65 wives. His first wife and two sons were killed by a raiding party; Mabel started a war, captured the killers, and ate them. The startled mummy with the gaping mouth in Yiwika comes with a donation book.

Consider using Yiwika as a base from which to see the northeast end of the valley. It's an agreeable place to recover from the aches and bites received from sleeping in village *honnay* and trekking knee-deep in mud. From this village of modern-style houses walk to nearby *kampung* to see dome-shaped *honnay*. In several nearby villages you can also see some smoke-cured ancestors.

Steep paths lead into the hills to the villages of **Wosi, Bugi,** and **Wolo.** See splendid dances at **Woogi,** a six to seven hour walk north of Wamena. To photograph a funeral or dance, it's good manners to pay Rp3000-5000.

The Salt Pools

One hour's walk up a steep hillside path in a valley behind Yiwika you can see the centuries-old process of collecting salt. Banana leaves are first pounded to a pulp, then carried up the hill on shoulder poles. Next, the pulp is dipped into a pool of natural saline spring water, squeezed and prodded until saturated. It's then spread on rocks to dry. Women carry up to 70-kg stem sections back to the village for further drying and burning. The ashes are blown away; salt is what's left behind. Go early in the morning if you want to see the women collecting salt; by noon they've all gone home.

Bat Caves

Another walk, 2.5-3 hours north of Yiwika, takes you to a whole series of magnificent bat caves known simply as **Goa.** Children will light torches and take you down to see stalactites and stalagmites. Climb out through the back of the cave for some really impressive views of the valley. You'll find other caves at Pugima, Usilimo, and Minimo.

Pyramid

A seven- to nine-hour walk north on a vehicular road leads all the way from Sinatma via Elegaima to this mission station and airstrip with beautiful views. The site is named for a pyramid-shaped mountain here. If walking, take the track leading from Wamena to Hom Hom, Musatfak, Woogi, and Pyramid—a long, hot, baking, uninteresting walk not worth it in itself, unless returning or heading to Tiom. You can also catch a *bemo* all the way to Pyramid.

Hetagima

From Wamena, Hetagima is an easy three- to four-hour 15 km walk. After two hours walking, a track turns off toward a village you can see in the distance. Ask directions along the way. Or take a taxi past Hetagima to the end of the line. Stay as a guest in one of the village's beehive huts. Beware of the bridge downriver from Hetagima—it's in very poor shape; rotting, missing planks, badly swaying, loose cables.

Kurima

Beyond Hetagima and near the entrance of the Baliem Gorge is Kurima, a five- to six-hour walk south of Wamena (25 km). In the rainy season, be careful at the mudwash and when fording the small river. Stay with the Catholic nuns in Kurima. There's a great market three times weekly, with the best and biggest on Tuesday. Past the village soccer field and suspension bridge on the other side of a dip is the **Halok Inn,** an accommodation for travelers. You enter a compound to find a big *honnay*-style hut called Pondok Wisata divided into a sleeping room and dining room. Foam mattresses, pillows, sheets, and use of attached kitchen and toilet, Rp12,500 pp. If you haven't brought food, the inn will take care of that too. The Baliem River roars 100 meters below.

The Baliem Valley abruptly ends here, and a narrow canyon of soaring rock walls begins. On a clear day, it's worth it to walk three to four hours from Kurima in the direction of Soba up and above the Baliem River. Really beautiful walk, with fantastic views.

LONGER WALKS FROM WAMENA

Wolo Valley

A scenic side valley of the Baliem with friendly people and a good trail. From Wamena head north following the main trail through Yiwika and Wosi and on to the Wolo River. Follow this small river about two km upstream to Bugi, a 12-hour walk from Wamena. Bugi would be just a few hours from Pyramid if there were a way across the Baliem River. Hiking upstream along the Wolo River you pass impressive high cliffs, many gardens, several caves, and superb panoramas. The flight from Jayapura to Wamena often enters the Baliem by this side valley. About three hours beyond Bugi is the school and airstrip of Wolo. Another mission station, **Ilugwa,** is higher still, an additional three hours' walk.

Karubaga

If you really want to get off the beaten path, this five- to six-day hike via Bokondini actually leaves the Baliem Valley and crosses over a high mountain pass with an incredible 360-degree view. It requires at least 12 hours to get up and over. A guide is definitely a good idea here, as the path continually crosses and recrosses a stream. As you descend the mountain, there are two major trails. The right heads to Karubaga, the left to Tiom. You can also fly to Karubaga with Merpati once weekly and walk back to Wamena.

In Karubaga there's a hydro station, a mission complex with a guesthouse-cum-kitchen (Rp4000), and a *warung* where a jolly lady bakes bread or cake on demand. From Karubaga, fly back, walk back, or make the Karubaga-Tangome-Mamit-Karubaga trek (three days). Sleep in deserted mission houses. Karubaga to Tiom is three rough days. The walk from Tiom to Wamena takes two days, following the Baliem River through some beautiful valleys. An easy walk and highly recommended for its spectacular scenery.

THE BALIEM DANI

Dani is often used as a generic term to apply to all the tribes of the Baliem Valley, but actually there are a number of other tribes in the area. The exact origin of these people is unknown. All have Negroid features and dark brown skin, but each tribe's language, customs, and even physical appearance can be quite distinct. Indonesian is now widely known and many younger Danis can read and write.

The Dani have a high degree of social organization, an extraordinarily sophisticated form of agriculture, and demonstrate advanced en-

*bringing home the
bacon, Dani-style*

gineering skill in the construction of rattan bridges and dwellings. They have a complicated system of trading and bartering, importing bird-of-paradise feathers, *scere*-bird plumes, cowrie shells, and the finest spear-wood from distant villages. The Danis spend most of their lives working the fields—cleaning, draining, pruning vines, weeding beds, scooping up the rich, dark soil to enrich their gardens—so their strength is phenomenal. Watch one run through the forest barefoot or walk for kilometers with a man on his shoulders. Yet the Danis have the gentlest handshake you'll ever experience.

Dress
The loincloths of other tribes and the clothing of white people are repugnant to the rural Dani. Except for the rolled grass or reed skirts of the women and the tube-like yellow gourds over the genitals of the men, no clothing is worn. Apart from ringbeards and beehive-hairdos, Dani men find hair on the rest of the body repulsive and untidy, so they diligently remove it from the arms, legs, chest, back, and all other parts of the body with tweezers made of araucaria twigs. The village chief wears only a hat, necklace, and three-foot-long *horim* supported at the waist with twine. Body decorations worn every day are *nonken,* cowrie shell necklaces, and armbands of pig scrotums which the Dani believe ward off ghosts. Some Dani men wear ropes of dried black pig intestines around their necks. Dani men also put ballpoint pens, drinking straws, boar tusks, or pieces of tin cans

through their noses, and insert anything from cigarettes to diaper pins into their pierced earlobes. For festive occasions, and during battles, men are elaborately adorned with headdresses of cassowary whisks, white egret feathers, and anklets of parrot feathers, all of which make them appear ready to take flight.

Danis don't believe in washing but smear their bodies with a mixture of soot and earth, a thick layer of rancid pig fat, or red or white clay to keep themselves warm in the often cold climate. In the chilly mornings, Dani men stand with their arms wrapped around their necks to keep themselves warm. The upper lips of both children and adults are almost always encrusted with a layer of dried mucus, a symptom of respiratory infection. Strings of mucus, rising and falling as they breathe, are a chronic feature of the Dani face, as is spitting, blowing, and hawking. Otherwise, the Dani are a remarkably strong, healthy, clear-skinned people.

In the '70s the Indonesian government launched Operation Koteka, or Operation Penis Gourd, wherein the military sought to "civilize" the Dani. The army attempted to take away the Dani *horim* and force them down out of their treehouses and into cotton clothing. Skin disease and respiratory ailments became rife, and the campaign was abandoned. Now the Dani are seen as worth preserving, if only for their potential to generate tourist dollars. Recently a group of Dani generously offered to donate a supply of *horim* to a remote Irian tribe that goes completely naked.

Crafts

Tourism preserves and develops Dani crafts and also serves to introduce a cash economy to the people. Dani are enthusiastic craftsmen and great designers of tools and dwellings; they also use shells, feathers, and other organic articles for self-adornment. Powerful warriors who hunt wild boar with spears can sit for hours making delicate skirts or orchid-fiber necklaces for their wives. Spiderwebs are harvested in the forest and hung around the throat in unique, woven patterns. Men also produce the ancestor sculptures, musical instruments, and sacred ritual objects which are kept in the men's ceremonial house, often referred to as the center of the cosmos.

Dani spears are usually made of heavy reddish myrtle wood from the eucalyptus-like *yoli* tree. Some spears reach up to 18 feet, with an ornamental sleeve below the blade, and are tapered to a dull point at the butt so they can be stuck in the ground. Bows are small, only about four feet long, scarcely longer than the arrows. Most often bows are cut from laurel or a special woodland rhododendron tree. The bowstring is made of flat, hard strips of rattan, about one-quarter inch thick, too wide for use with notched arrows. The fact that Dani arrows are unfeathered and unnotched makes the accuracy of the men all the more uncanny. Thin shafts of hard cane, the arrows differ mostly in the heads, each meant for different uses. The bleeding arrow is used for hunting and killing pigs. Heads knobbed with two to five prongs are designed to down birds and small game. War arrows are often made of myrtle and are unbarbed, about a foot in length, the tip inserted in the cane and bound by fine strands of ground vine. Other war arrows are notched with files of jagged teeth. Sometimes the arrowhead has notches reversed close to the shaft so the arrow can't be drawn through an arm or a leg. All arrows are weakened at the base of the point so they'll snap off inside the wound.

Economy

Traditionally, most of the fieldwork was done by the women, leaving the men free to guard them and go off on periodic raiding parties. But since these activities have been in large part prohibited by the government, the men now work the fields. Men and women use different tools: there's a large oarlike stick for the males,

and a smaller, pointed stick for females. The sticks double as weapons in case of ambush. Though the women tend the gardens, the men do all the heavy work of creating and rebuilding fields and ditches.

A Dani man's status is reckoned by how many pigs and wives he owns. Pigs and shells are still media of exchange and circulate freely at weddings, funerals, and feasts; salt and pigs are traded for the forest products of other tribes. With their fertile and self-sufficient gardens and herds of fat pigs, the Dani are potentially a prosperous people.

Only sugar and bananas are native to the region; other vegetables were brought in by Papuans relatively recently, some 5,000 years ago. Since 1954, the missionaries and both the Dutch and Indonesian governments have introduced a variety of vegetables into the fertile valley. *Rambutans,* apples, mangos, mangosteens, and *durian* were introduced from East Java in the early 1970s. Although the Dani grow these products, they rarely eat them, preferring to sell the fruit in Wamena, Jayapura, or Tembagapura. This is the only way they're able to raise the cash to buy electronic, plastic, and metal goods.

Village Life

Designed originally as mini-fortresses, Dani villages feature U-shaped courtyards not unlike African *kraal,* guarded by a swing door easily defended. A typical settlement is also surrounded by a sturdy fence which keeps the *kampung* pigs in and the neighbors' pigs out. The fence is constructed of pilings, nestled in straw to protect the raw wood from rot. Straw-thatched, dome-roofed, windowless roundhouses, plus a longhouse for the women, are grouped around the open space. Nearby are taro, tobacco, and banana gardens. Gourd vines grow under the roof eaves. Dani buildings are held together with only rattan vines or elephant grass (*logob*). Roofs may be made of juniper tree bark or pandanus leaves interlocked like roof tiles, making the structures water- and windproof. Long tunnel-like passages sometimes connect the structures so the people do not have to move about outdoors on cold nights.

A village contains a ritual men's house (*iwool*) which only initiated males may enter. The round grass men's house (*honnay*) is used by males over age eight for sleeping at night. Divided into a lower level with a firepit and an upstairs sleeping section, coals from the first floor fireplace provide even heat throughout the whole structure. What smoke doesn't escape through the bamboo slats keeps down the mosquitos, which are horrendous. A small door, giving the only light, is barred at night with heavy wooden planks. The *honnay* is stocked with an arsenal of bows and arrows, spare bowstrings, new arrow points wrapped in neat packets and stored in rafters, fine shell bibs, gourds containing small fetish objects, net bags of tobacco, stone adzes, bird feather headdresses, extra *holim,* digging sticks, sets of boar tusk knives, cane mouth harps, dog fur amulets, bamboo tobacco containers, and wooden tongs for moving hot coals. Tobacco is wrapped and smoked in course leaf. Women, children, and pigs live in the long women's houses (*wew umah*). Heated rocks are placed around inside to sit on and the sweet, acrid smell of ashes permeates the air. The fire area is delimited by four wood uprights at its corners. The uprights help support the ceiling and also prevent people from rolling into the fire—a common accident among small children. New wooden houses with corrugated roofs are being built for the Dani, but the new houses aren't insulated and are thus freezing at night.

The *kaio* is a lookout tower built of tall young saplings bound into a column with liana thongs, rising to a stick platform some 25 feet above the ground. Once they stretched along the perimeter of villages and cultivated areas for as far as the eye could see. These watchtowers allowed Dani men to scan the no-man's-land between settlements and detect enemy raids before they occurred. Each tower was the responsiblity of those men who had gardens in the vicinity. While the women worked in the fields, the men took turns as sentries, messages and challenges called from one tower to another.

Family Life

Men and women lead altogether separate lives and the major divisions of labor follow the lines of age and sex. Though a man will sometimes work with his wives, the two sexes never mix in large groups. Women have a definite market value; previously they were purchased with pigs and cowrie shells, today with pigs and *rupiah.* After the day's work, the men gather to chat, joke, and work in the *kampung* yard or

communal *honnay,* while the women cultivate sweet potato gardens, tend children, or cook in the women's houses. Babies aren't weaned until they're four or five years old and during that time a man may not sleep with his wife. When asked why this is necessary, the Danis reply that the ghosts demand it. Polygamy, practiced only by the wealthier chiefs, witchdoctors, and teachers, is thought to have evolved as a result of this custom.

The sequence of wives dictates their dominance. The first wife is the highest ranking and can expect help from the others. Although the wives share a common kitchen, each woman has her own hearth, and prepares food for herself and her children. The women alternate feeding the husband. Until they marry, Dani girls wear grass skirts like those found on other Pacific islands. When a man buys a wife, the bridegroom's village drapes her with a married woman's skirt made of seeds strung together and worn just below the abdomen. Though her breasts are exposed, her buttocks are always scrupulously covered. She also wears a *noken.*

Diet And Feasts

A Dani woman preparing the evening meal will first heat rocks in a fire while gathering a pile of fresh, damp grass. The hot rocks are placed in the grass and covered with broad vegetable leaves. The whole thing is then bundled up in more grass and left for an hour or so. The leaves are cooked by the hot rocks, creating steam from the wet grass, which at the same time serves as insulation for the primitive oven.

Lacking cooking pots, the Dani cook meat in the same way. Although women cook the daily meals, the men take over at festivals. There are no regular eating times; the Danis eat when they're hungry. Sweet potatoes, of which there are 70 different varieties, comprise 90% of their diet. They're eaten skin and all, along with the protein-rich leaves, at least twice a day. Sweet potatoes are usually roasted directly on the embers of the fire, but are steamed at festivals. The Danis don't store or plant seeds but plant instead vegetative parts such as sprouts, tubers, rootstocks, and slips. Ginger, yams, cucumbers, spinach, beans, bananas, and tobacco are also grown. The Dani eat almost anything else they can lay their hands on: roots, dragonfly larvae, mice, raw tadpoles, frogs, caterpillars, spiny anteater and other marsupial entrails. No knives or forks or cooking vessels are used, just round water gourds.

The Pig

Pigs are the most highly valued animal in the Dani culture. Pigs were formerly used as a means of "living currency" and are still used today as part of the bride-price. The Dani believe pigs possess a soul similar to that of humans. Pigs are raised as family members, called by ancestors' names, fed in the kitchen, take their rightful place around the hearth, and are stroked and fondled by their masters. Piglets share the same net bag as babies, carried about together by the women; human infants must sometimes compete with hungry orphaned pig-

lets for mother's milk. Tame pigs walk alongside the Danis without a leash. Adult pigs consume daily the same quantity of sweet potatoes as a man, so they provide the women with an equal amount of work. Although raised by the women, pigs are owned by the men. Each family cuts holes or notches on their pigs' ears so they can be immediately recognized. The word for pig fat may not be pronounced in the presence of women; using it is a man's prerogative.

Pigs are put out to pasture, usually in a sweet potato field gone fallow, where they eat greens and unharvested vegetables, root for grubs, and seek frogs, mice, and small skinks living in the ditches. In the villages pigs are fed *hiperi* skins and other offal from the fires. Until the day it is slaughtered the Dani pig leads a pleasant and structured life, prized and honored on all sides.

Pig flesh is eaten only on festive occasions such as mass marriages or funerals. Whereas in former days a man reached the status of "Big Man" by his brave deeds as a warrior or hunter, today he acquires that prestigious title as a successful wild boar hunter and by the number of large pig feasts he sponsors in his lifetime. Try to get in on one of these big pig feasts, which usually coincide with the ripening of the taro roots the Dani serve with steamed pork.

For slaughter, a pig is held chest high, one man holding it by the ears, another by its haunches. The pig is shot with an arrow from a distance of only a few inches, driving the shaft into its lungs. The arrow tip is a half-shaft of bamboo, sharpened at both edges to the tip,

divvying up the pig

designed to open a wound of maximum size and bleed the pig as quickly as possible. Squealing and screaming the creature is dropped to the ground, where it runs about wildly spurting blood. Men sometimes work the pig's lungs with their feet like a bellows while it gasps upon the mud, weakening and finally dying.

The dead pig is laid on banana fronds on the ground, on its belly, legs stretched out front and back. The animal's ears and tails are lopped off for use as fetishes. A fire is built between two logs and the pig is singed blotchy black and white, then the bristles and mud are scraped off. A cooking pit is dug with long digging sticks—three feet deep, narrow at the bottom, with smooth mud sides. Lathes are then laid on the fire, along with hot stones and damp leaves to hold the heat. A dark, heavy smoke pours out of the pit. Fresh leaves and stones are tiered into the pit in between the hot stones, carried from the fire with tongs made of split staves. Sweet potatoes, leaves and ferns, vegetables, pig meat, and hot stones are laid in layers till the conical shaped mound rises three to four feet above the ground, bound by a long coil of rattan. Using bamboo and bone knives the pigs are dressed and cut up into small pieces. The Danis smash bones with rocks to get at the marrow, suck flesh from the jaws, nibble at vertebrae, gnaw at the kidneys—the whole pig vanishes. Often the women must content themselves with sweet potatoes as all the pig is taken by the men. Occasionally children get to play with the tripe. Spoons are later made from pig pelvic bones. On the spiritual level, consuming their beloved pets symbolizes the incorporation of the pigs' spirit into the spirit of the human host.

Death

Cremation is the customary method of disposing of a corpse. If the stature of the deceased warrants it, his body is sometimes dried and displayed; see mummified remains in Akima and one hanging on a building at Blai on the Kemabu River to the west of the Grand Valley. After a death, the whole village mourns and wails. Sometimes women try to throw themselves on the funeral pyre; women commonly smear their upper bodies and faces with yellow clay to show their grief. Once the mud dries, it turns the skin a bluish-white, which gives a mourning woman a ghostly pallor.

In former times, female relatives of the dead, starting at about 12 years old, had their fingers amputated up to the second joint. If a warrior had neither a pig nor a ritual stone to bring to a funeral, he might offer the fingers of his child. The girl's fingers were bound very tightly, to cut off circulation, then just prior to amputation the child's "funny bone" was struck to render the hand numb. The fingers were placed on a piece of wood and cut off with a blow of a stone adze by a man considered skilled in this sort of operation. The severed fingers were hung in the cooking shed to dry and then buried the next day in a special place behind the compound. The wound was dressed in banana leaves and husks, bound with a mixture of clay and ashes, and proudly displayed around the village. A girl or woman could refuse to make such a sacrifice without fear of persecution; her shame was considered punishment enough. Now prohibited, this practice of ritual mutilation continues only in remote areas. You'll still notice many fingerless women over 40 years old.

Dani Warfare

Broken up into a number of fierce clans, Danis practiced what anthropologists call ritual warfare; they regularly faced each other in formal battle. The Dani do not fight war (*weem*) for an ideology, or to annex land or dominate people, but to avenge ghosts of dead warriors or relatives. Battles are called out in the mornings, one alliance in the valley against another. If the battle is not cancelled because of rain, about 200 men enjoy the fight. If a Dani does not want to participate, he is not called a coward or made to suffer. Sallies are highly ritualistic, not intended to wreak carnage. Frontline fighting seldom lasts for more than 10-15 minutes. The main force relaxes on a hill nearby, watching, smoking, gossiping, meeting friends from other areas.

When darkness comes and the battle is almost over, warriors on both sides hurl abuse and taunts at each other, causing much laughter. Rarely does a man die unless he is clumsy or stupid. If a death does occur, the rectum and ventral base of the dead man's penis are plugged with grass to prevent bad magic from entering. When a Dani clan learns later that an enemy has died of wounds, they will congregate on hilltops to sing pitched, victorious choruses and yodels, sounding something like cheers from a football stadium.

MODERN DANI WARFARE

Although the official claim is that the Indonesian government has eliminated all warfare between Dani tribes, Freeport expats, missionaries, and locals say otherwise. A reader reports that, while trekking near Tiom in March 1991, he ran into about 30 men with spears, bows and arrows, and axes. Not knowing what was up, he started shaking hands all around. In the middle of this someone yelled and the Dani all charged up a hill, weapons at the ready. They stopped for a while, then ran off again. At first he figured they were hunting some animal, then he found they were going to war with another tribe. Why? One of their members had been killed in an argument with someone from the other tribe while both were in Wamena.

Later, this same reader tried to walk from Wamena to Soba but found it impossible to find the trail up a hill. When he returned to find a guide, he learned the reason the trail was so overgrown was because of an ongoing war between the two tribes on either side of the hill. He couldn't find anyone willing to guide him, and after two days on his own he gave up. Two Dani guards with spears on rotating day shifts were posted on the path to warn their people in case of attack. In Wamena the more you ask about warfare, the more stories you hear. It still goes on.

THE YALI

About 35 miles southeast of Wamena begins the valley of the Yali. A mountain trail climbs from the Baliem Valley floor to the northern Kurelu, continues past the Ilueraiuma salt pools, over a ridge, and into Rass Valley. From there a three-day journey will take you to Yali Valley, steep and forested and home to a people who are very skillful hunters. The Yali practice less sophisticated cultivation techniques than the Dani and keep fewer pigs. They provide the Dani with decorative bird feathers as well as tree kangaroo and cuscus pelts and fine rare woods, long disappeared from the Baliem Valley itself.

Yali men begin to wear penis sheaths around the time of puberty, fashioned from long, hollowed gourds. Some stretch as long as two feet, and serve as a mix of protection, modesty, and

style. Each man has several, one to fit any occasion. At the southern reaches of the valley warriors also wear extraordinary coiled corsets of hard vines around their stomachs and chests. These layers of thick hoops can measure more than 100 feet end to end and act as armor. The Yali are small in stature, the men just over five feet, the women standing a few inches shorter. The Yali have a reputation as fierce and dangerous fighters, and the Indonesian government allows them neither guns nor alcohol. Yali tools have not changed in thousands of years—stone axes of pointed shards wrapped tightly onto a wooden stick, net carrying bags supported from the forehead, thick bows five or six feet long, and arrowheads carved to a purpose—broad and flat for large game, a triple barb for birds, notched and tapered black for settling tribal disputes. In 1990 one such "dispute," over the ownership of a pig, resulted in 18 casualties. It is said that somebody kills somebody in this valley just about every week, but travelers are safe so long as they don't make any moves towards women or pigs, have previously murdered no Yali relatives, and refrain from the missionary mistake of trying a little too hard to make the Yali do something they don't want to.

The Yali came into contact with the outside world only in 1961. At that time American missionaries forged an agreement to split up the interior of Irian Jaya, with the Protestants winning the Yali district. Before first contact a low-flying reconnaissance aircaft completely spooked the Yali, causing suspension of all farming activities and the mass slaughter of the people's sacred pigs. Because each Yali village is usually operating under some form of undeclared war with another village, there were substantial communication problems and most of the Yali were not involved in the initial missionary encounter. But after a few years the busy biblebeaters got around to just about everybody, encouraging the Yali to visit their fellows in other villages. This only served to revive long dormant feuds, and culminated in the Jaxole Valley massacre, where many of the losers were eaten. It was then that the Yali got their first look at Indonesian rifles. They now understand that certain types of behavior are likely to attract the wrath of the "bum bow" people who carry dangerous weapons and do not speak their language. Still, this doesn't stop them from engaging in the occasional cannibal feast on the airstrip at Angguruk.

Planes that are late arriving in the Yali Valley are presumed to have crashed. To reach the area many fly through, not over, the mountains of the central highlands. In 1990 the Yali were encouraged to look for a missing plane with an offer of sharing in the downed craft's cargo. The "prizes" included a Johnson outboard motor.

THE SENGGO AREA

A big mission post here. Get your *surat jalan* for Senggo, 100 km east of Agats, in Jayapura. The river tours of this area are popular now. Write Dr. Werner Weiglein, Ikarus Expeditionen, GMBH, Fasanenweg 1, P.O. Box 1247, D-6240 Konigstein/TS, Germany. Or go on your own. Merpati and Merauke fly here once weekly; if you're obstinate you may be able to charter an MAF flight. From Senggo, go upriver to the Brazza or Dairam rivers. This isn't easy. To reach the Dairam Hitam or Dairam Kabur—where there are treehouses 20 meters above the ground—hire Mr. Duhari, who owns a *toko* and *losmen* in Senggo. If you want to try the

Brazza, Siretsj, Kolff, Steenboom, or Modera rivers, you have to make a deal with the police chief in Senggo, who'll want Rp160,000-200,000. The area has been declared unsafe so you have to be "protected." Don't worry, it's dangerous only for Indonesians. Everyone else is welcome, because they spread information about what's really going on.

You travel in a police dugout with armed cops and drivers. You won't go far upriver because your "guides" are reluctant to leave well-trodden paths, but you'll see enough. The most poignant sight is that of a totally lost humanity, sick, anxious, resettled in permanent villages, when for centuries they lived as nomads in the forests. No more shields. No more rituals. Nothing left of a brilliant past. The forced settlements are built with planks, without ventilation, on the ground and not on piles. The most terrifying example is Patipi, last village on the Brazza. The health situation is disastrous and you'll see lots of elephantiasis. On the Kolff River, it's been said people shoot Indonesians with arrows. But the trigger-happy chief of police in Senggo handles the situation with a firm hand, the money you gave him going directly into his pocket.

THE SOUTH COAST

FREEPORT COPPER MINE

The towns of Tembagapura and Timika are supply bases for the Freeport Copper Mine, located 10 km from the mine site and mill at Gunung Bijh ("Mineral Mountain"). Discovered in 1936 by Dutchman Jean Jacques Dozy, Freeport is one of the world's largest outcrops of base metal, literally a whole mountain of solid copper. In 1967, with the Suharto regime actively wooing foreign investment, an agreement was reached with Freeport Copper Co. to develop the gigantic project. Today Freeport is one of the largest mines in the world.

The mining town of Tembagapura is nicely laid out, with modern homes for the supervisory expats and dormitories for the 2,000 plus mineworkers from all over Indonesia and 22 other nations. The town sits on a mountain-

ous slope under the vertical face of Gunung Zaagham; after a hard rain, some 50 waterfalls pour from the tropical vegetation and bare rocks of its uppermost slopes. Facilities include schools, tennis courts, clubs, indoor sports complex, football field, video movies, commissaries, and bars. Towering over all is glacier-packed Puncak Jaya, at 5,039 meters the world's highest peak between the Himalayas and the Andes.

The Mine

Though the all-weather road from Tembagapura is only 10 km long, to reach the mine site you must climb 1,066 meters in elevation and pass through a 900-meter-long tunnel. At the processing mill you'll see the globe's highest refinery and the beginning of the world's longest slurry pipeline (120 km), as well as the world's longest (762 meters) aerial tramway, built over one of

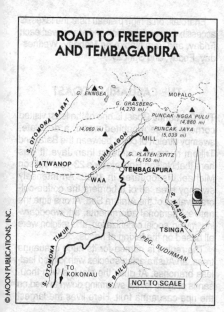

ROAD TO FREEPORT AND TEMBAGAPURA

NOT TO SCALE

© MOON PUBLICATIONS, INC.

the roughest and most inaccessible terrains outside Antarctica. Tramway cars carrying the rich ore pass through clouds and over ghostly 500-meter-high waterfalls, dumping their loads at the mill before returning to the mine in a neverending circular journey. At the mill the ore is crushed, the valuable minerals separated to produce concentrate that flows in the slurry pipeline to the port of Amamapare on the Arafura Sea, where it's dehydrated and shipped to Japan. The mine's average daily copper production is now around 60,000 tons of ore. Freeport is also Indonesia's largest gold producer, mining some three tons of the stuff per year.

The Damage
In September 1993 Freeport denied that recent outbreaks of diarrhea and skin disease among the local populace were caused by its copper mining activities. A company director suggested instead that such afflictions are common in the province due to poor hygiene and sanitation. A group called the Sympathizers For The Mimika-Amungme Community additionally charged the mine with contributing to an increased number of miscarriages; government health officials preferred to blame the epidemic of spontaneous

explusions on poor nutrition, extreme maternal youth, and venereal disease.

Freeport processes 60,000 tons of ore each day, and, after the separating process, more than 95% of this material is dumped into nearby rivers as tailings. Freeport and its government hirelings admit this dumping increases sedimentation in waterways, but argues the same thing occurs every day naturally.

PUNCAK JAYA

Puncak Jaya, or Carstensz Toppen, is, at 5,039 meters, the highest mountain in Southeast Asia, and one of the three remaining tropical icefields in the world. The European name was bestowed on the peak in honor of the Dutch sea captain Jan Carstensz, who in 1623 gazed upon the ice-covered mountain from his ship as it sailed off the south coast of Irian Jaya. Back home his reports of snowy peaks in the tropics were met by ridicule and derision; it was not until the 1930s that a Dutch expedition penetrated the region to confirm the Carstensz sighting. The Irianese call this region Dugundugu, which means "Reed Flower," so named for the white hanging flowers of the reed plants growing in the area's marshlands.

When last the mountain was legally open to trekkers, it required about a month to secure the necessary permissions. These included permits from the minister of sports and recreation, the director of army intelligence, and the head of the police. In Ilaga, the approved departure point for the climb, additional *surat jalan* had to be obtained from the police, sector police, and regional military command. The cost of permits in Jakarta alone was Rp500,000. Climbers were required to join an authorized American adventure tour outfit like Ecosummer, Wilderness Travel, or Mountain Travel. Officers of the Ilaga police were supposed to accompany all climbing parties, but usually grew weak-kneed and frightened of the cold, turning back to Ilaga in a day or two—after collecting their Rp15,000 food/drink tariff for the entire 21-day trek.

Tour operators usually arrive with 10 people, plus 25 porters, with all the usual mountaineering equipment required. The climb involves bare sloping limestone faces and alpine meadows, with Antarctic landscapes. The entire three weeks trekkers spend in weather frigidly cold. In the afternoons temperatures average 6-9° C; at night the mercury often falls to zero. Very soft snow and rain showers fill the afternoons. Near the summit icicles form on your tent. The mountain features five square kilometers of snowfields at the top; from there one can view Gunung Idenburg's snowcapped peak and gaze out to the Arafura Sea.

In the early '90s the World Wildlife Fund was asked to develop plans for a new national park in the region, to be called Lorentz. One of the park's most spectacular attractions would be the glaciated peaks known as the Carstensz Mountain Range, including Puncak Jaya. It seems freelance mountaineers were frequently approaching the mountain from the side of the sea, in the process crossing Freeport Copper property. The Freeport people were disturbed; the government asked WWF to develop alternate routes. As part of its overall Lorentz tourism plan, WWF teams explored, surveyed, and mapped likely Puncak Jaya trails. When the area is again opened to tourists it is hoped both the park and legal ascent of Puncak Jaya will follow.

PANIAI LAKES

Discovered by a Dutch flier in 1936 during an aerial survey for an oil company, these enchanted lakes are entirely surrounded by blue mountains. The most spectacular is **Lake Paniai**; there are also two smaller, olive-green lakes. None of the three contain fish, only freshwater shrimp. No mosquitos. Women seine the lakes at night from log boats, building fires aboard to keep warm. A heavy mist comes in low over the waters in early morning, and from 0900 clouds begin to obscure the mountain walls around the lakes. The surface is calm until 1100, when strong winds sweep across and breakers crash against the shores.

This area is home to the Moni and Ekagi peoples. The Ekagi are a healthy, muscular, black-skinned people less than 1.5 meters tall. One of the first Europeans to enter the area described them as "childlike, carefree, undependable, selfish, deceitful, transparent, credulous, superstitious, fairly industrious, timid, but not without racial pride."

Enarotali, on a high plateau near the lakes, is accessible by air from Biak and Manokwari each Friday, and from Nabire on Monday, Wednesday, Friday, and Sunday.

THE CASUARINA COAST

The Casuarina Coast is one of the least visited corners of the inhabited world, a desolate, swampy stretch of coast between the Barai and Trikom rivers in southeast Irian Jaya. It was here that Nelson Rockefeller's 23-year-old son Michael disappeared in 1962. An intensely swampy area, all of it borders the coffee-colored waters of the Arafura Sea. At one time the natives' personal adornments, art, woodcarving, music, social organization, and religion were all based on the taking of heads.

The region is named for its huge casuarina trees, an Australasian species with jointed leafless branches. At dusk the sky fills with thousands of flying foxes, swarming down to feed on the ripe casuarina fruit. Here lives the largest

Casuarina cannibal

of the New Guinea parrots, the *kakatua raja,* or king parrot. Vast mangrove, sago, and bamboo forests crowd the sloping swampland environment, formed of mud sediment over millennia. The natives depend on the surrounding 20,000 square km of forests as a hunting ground.

It is probable that headhunting and cannibalism are still practiced in these swamps, home to some of the most untouched tribes in the world. For centuries the people have prepared human meat like pig meat; the body cut into pieces by the women, then roasted over a fire. Human food has long been known here as "long pig," though it is said human flesh is juicier than the flesh of the swine.

The whole Casuarina Coast is now threatened by ecological disaster. The pristine area of the Asmat and other tribes has been allotted to concessionaires who employ the Irianese to fell trees and float them downriver for collection. There are no reforestation efforts, and overlogging is occurring farther and farther away from the rivers. Even more serious is the erosion caused by uncontrolled logging. Unless timber cutting is stopped, several large rivers could eventually completely submerge the region.

LAND OF THE ASMAT

The name most probably comes from the Asmat word *asakat,* which means "human being." The Asmat's neighbors to the west, the Mimika, however, claim the name is derived from their word for the tribe—*manue,* meaning "maneater."

The Land

Almost the entire Asmat region is covered in water during the rainy season, when high tide reaches up to two km inland and low tide flows up to two km out to sea. This is the largest alluvial swamp in the world, a low-lying stoneless territory of bog forests and meandering rivers emptying into the Arafura Sea. Several rivers are wide enough to allow boats to sail up to 50 km upriver; a widely used means of transport is *motor mappi,* the Asmat motorboat. The rivers swarm with shrimp, fish, lobster, crab, freshwater dolphin, sea snakes, and crocodiles. Living along the banks are lizards, known as cuscus, that grow longer than the Komodo dragon. The forests contain palms, ironwood, *merak* wood,

and mangroves, and are home to crown pigeons, hornbills, and cockatoos. There are grass meadows, and flowers like the Dedrobium orchid. The rainy season stretches from October to May, with an average of 40 cm of precipitation each year. The east monsoon season runs from April to June; west monsoons strike December to March, causing high waves and very hot afternoon temperatures. In the dry season it's often difficult to find water fit for human consumption. The low-lying land, often covered in water, makes roadbuilding and farming difficult. From Agats to sites 25 miles north is a very muddy area. Tides sometimes reach as high as Sawo and the Atay district.

The People

Natives of the region are divided into two main groups: those living along the coasts, and those in the interior. They differ in dialect, way of life, social structure, and ceremonies. The coastal people are further divided into two groups, the Bisman people between the Sinetsy and Nin Rivers, and the Simai people.

The 70,000 Asmat, the area's largest tribe, are scattered in 100 villages in a territory of roughly 27,000 square km, an area a little larger than the Netherlands. Asmat legend says a mythological hero once traveled the area building men's clubhouses, decorating the halls with carved wooden figurines. One day, by beating a lizard-skin drumhead, he brought all the statues to life, and thereby populated Asmat lands.

The tribe was untouched by civilization until recent times. Dutch outposts, missionary settlements, and foreign expeditions finally made inroads on this isolated culture during the 1950s and '60s. Formerly, the families of the entire tribe resided together in houses up to 28 meters long called *yeus.* Today, in such coastal villages as Basiem and Agats, families occupy separate dwellings built on pilings. Catwalks or log paths are necessary to cope with the spongy terrain and torrential rainfall. *Yeus* are still used, but now only by men, as clubhouses where bachelors sleep. Upriver Asmat still live in longhouses; some even construct houses in treetops. The Indonesian government encourages nomadic Asmat to settle in permanent villages and has built schools and clinics to lure them downriver.

The Asmat live on sago, their staple, as well as mussels, snails, and fat insect larvae collected from decaying stumps of sago palms. These last are eaten to the accompaniment of throbbing drums and ritual dances; larval feasts can sometimes last up to two weeks. The Asmat also gather forest products such as rattan, and catch fish and shrimp in large hoop nets. When traveling on the rivers, the Asmat stand to guide long narrow canoes, using three-meter-long paddles.

For the most part, these former cannibals and headhunters live in a constant nightmare of fear, fighting off powerful supernatural enemies by wearing bones of dead relatives around their necks. Constantly carried, fondled, and polished, the bones eventually aquire the patina and sheen of old ivory. Dead ancestor spirits are invited to attend festivities, but only for a night, after which they're driven away. Almost every household article is given a dead person's name. War implements were traditionally also named after dead relatives, to remind the owner of his obligation to take revenge. In the upper river reaches, tribes wrap their dead in bark and lay them out on scaffolding only a few meters away from the house. The bodies are left there to rot, until only the skeleton is left; then the bones are brought into the house. A man might wear the skull of his mother around his neck so she can protect him in death as she did in life. Ritual wife-swapping (*papisj*) is practiced by some tribes to increase bonds between men in times of stress, and some men have a male "exchange friend" (lover) in addition to a wife. Before heading for this coast, read *Where the Spirits Dwell: An Odyssey in the New Guinea Jungle* by Tobias Schneebaum, which provides a vivid picture of Asmat tribal life.

Asmat Art

The whole estuary region is famous for its carvers. Much of the highly original art of the Asmat is symbolic of warfare, headhunting, and warrior-ancestor veneration. For centuries the Asmat were preoccupied with the necessity of appeasing ancestor spirits, producing a wealth of superbly designed shields, canoes, sculpted figures, and drums.

Working in freshly cut wood, the Asmat paint with only three colors—red, white, and black—derived from mixing crushed shells, lime, earth, charcoal, and water. Until the end of WW II, the only tools utilized were shells, animal teeth, tusks, and precious stone axes obtained by

trade with mountain people. Today, flattened nails set into wooden handles and iron axes and chisels have replaced the old-style tools; shell and bone are still used for scraping and smoothing finished pieces. The general design is first traced with a single incised line, then the detail is carved in deep relief.

When tribal warfare was outlawed in the 1950s, and the warrior's way of life began to disappear, it threatened to curtail the people's artistic production. For example, their huge *bisj*, or phallic ancestor poles, were carved solely to commemorate forebears mighty in battle. In 1969, a UN-financed project revived local handicrafts, but by the late 1980s its purchasing depot had closed down. You can still purchase good-quality carvings from Agats carvers for cash or barter goods; a beautiful, intricate meter-high woodcarving that sells here for Rp10,000 goes for Rp200,000 on Bali. For authentic ancestor poles, paint-mixing vessels, grub trays, soulships, paddles, canoe prows, shields, spears, masks, drums, and personal ornaments you must travel inland or down the coast.

Agats

The starting point for visiting Asmat villages. The missionaries founded a timber mill here and raised wooden walkways all over town; these have since fallen into disrepair, and are now quite dangerous in places. Of the village's two *losmen,* the **New Asmat Inn** is the cheapest at Rp15,000 s, Rp20,000 d. Nothing special and definitely not worth the price. The other *losmen* has no name; it charges Rp17,000 s, Rp25,000 d, which is more or less a rip-off. The six rooms in the guesthouse of Father Suwada run Rp25,000; the dining room features a gigantic poster of the Rocky Mountains. Father Suwada imports fruits and mangos from the Aru Islands; he also manages the local museum. Another *penginapan,* located down by the river, is a trader's hotel; Rp10,000-12,000 tariff.

It's extremely easy to make arrangements to stay with an Asmat family in town for Rp5000 per night or less. People here welcome you with open arms; they're very affable. Just about anybody will be glad to put you up for a little cash. Staying with an Asmat family is cheaper; a non-Irian family will always want more *rupiah*.

Only three *warung* in town; all are expensive. Two serve *soto ayam* and nothing else, day after day. The third is run by the same Chinese family who runs the New Asmat Inn and offers more variety—usually dried fish, vegetables, and rice at Rp3000 a meal.

Agats's main attraction is its unique **museum** of primitive woodcarvings and weaponry, run by the aforementioned Father Suwada. Ironwood carvings produced here include hafts for stone axes, one- to two-meter-tall ceremonial shields, sago bowls, copulation figurines, solid wood human heads, arabesque panels, and canoe paddles. There are also knives and necklaces made from the thigh bones and vertebrae of the giant cassowary bird. *Prahu* are painted in bright colors, ornamented with superb carvings. Across from the museum is the **Catholic Mission,** featuring a fantastic library. If you really get bored, at night seek out the dark house in town where you can buy coconut wine for Rp2000 per bottle from a decrepit old man. A lot of backroom card gambling sessions in Agats, but your tablemates never cough up the dough when you win.

Getting There And Away
From Wamena, Merpati flies once weekly to Agats for Rp63,700. Flights are often delayed, postponed, or cancelled. The plane comes to earth on a grass airstrip in Ewer near Agats on the Per River; only small Islanders or Cessnas can safely make the landing. From here you have to catch a boat to Agats (Rp5000, 20 minutes). Sometimes flights leave from Timika, depending on the whims of Merpati, which dispatches the planes from Merauke. You can also rent your very own Merpati Twin Otter in these parts: the tariff is roughly Rp11 million, with an 850-kilogram maximum weight limit.

A *kapal Pelni perintis,* the KM *Nasuna,* sails all the way to Sorong in nine days for an incredibly cheap Rp21,300. Deck class only, though it's possible to rent crew cabin rooms. A worthwhile trip; the ship stops at such remote spots as Bade, Agats, Pomako, Dobo, Elat, Tual, and Kaimana. Food is not included in the fare, but is quite decent—a large plate of rice and vegetables with fish or egg for Rp1000. The usual crowded ship conditions, but not too bad. Members of the crew might let you use their bathroom. From Merauke to Sorong requires 12 days; the ship sits in Sorong for three days, then returns. Another ship runs this route as well, so there's a boat leaving every two weeks.

River Travel
Unless you're packing big money, don't come to Agats planning to visit Asmat villages upriver. Fuel and boat rental prices are high; it costs at least Rp200,000 per day to travel anywhere by boat. Because of the expense, the missionaries don't run a regular service to any villages upriver. You can charter a missionary boat with *atap* for Rp750,000 including crew. A motorized canoe runs Rp350,000; no roof, but it travels three times faster. These last are available for rent from Bugis timber people.

River travel can be quite hazardous—unbelievably strong river currents cut away at the ground, ripping out trees and great chunks of earth. Riverbanks are choked with bush, trees, ferns, gnarled roots, and flowers. Going upriver you'll spot freshwater turtles, crocodiles, white herons, Indian sea eagles, kingfishers, parrots, and slow-flapping hornbills. At night trees are brilliantly lit by fireflies. Pass by red flowering trees hidden in the jungle and little stilted villages hugging the banks. When inhabitants are unhappy in a location they pack up the whole town and move elsewhere, so never expect a village you've heard about to still be there when you float by.

TANAH MERAH

Means "Red Clay." Take a riverboat from the mouth of the Digul River near Mapi three days to this jungle outpost over 300 km upriver. Or fly with Merpati from Merauke on Monday, or from Jayapura or Biak on Friday. Called Boven Digul in Dutch times, this was originally a large internment camp built on a malarial swamp. In 1926, many of the communist leaders of the Madiun Rebellion were sent here by the Dutch. During revolutionary times, notable Indonesian political personalities were exiled here. There were never any successful escapes; all those who fled were invariably eaten by cannibals or died before they reached the coast. During the post-independence era, it was a sort of nationalist status symbol to have survived internment in this notorious penal colony.

MERAUKE AND VICINITY

A forlorn, singularly unattractive destination on the southeast coast, Merauke is the most easterly major town in Indonesia—the outer limits of the archipelago. With its serious dry spells, the climate here is different from the rest of Irian Jaya. Merauke is an arid windswept town of one-story concrete houses, shanties, and huge police barracks. Stay in the reasonably priced government *pasanggrahan* on Jl. Biak, in **Hotel Asmat,** or **Hotel Gedung Putih.** Eat at **Bahagia** near the Gedung Bina Ria movie theater. There are several *warung* near the Kores police station. Merauke is accessible from Sorong by ship, or you can fly from Jayapura or Biak.

Transmigration Sites

Roads to the north lead to barren, godforsaken transmigration sites. This is some of the poorest

tropical soil in the world, a region where only white-barked gum trees, scrub, and the residents of giant ant heaps can survive. The settlement of **Salor,** north of Merauke, was spotlighted in George Monbiot's *Poisoned Arrows,* a blistering indictment of Indonesia's *transmigrasi* program. **Erom,** another transmigrant site, is Rp7500 by *bemo.* The 40,000 or so transmigrants of this impoverished region live in abject, hopeless poverty. Merauke is filled with refugees from drought- and pest-ridden *transmigrasi* sites. Most of the women have turned to prostitution, servicing the police, while the men scrape by as taxi drivers, vendors, shop assistants, and clerks. Yet the government's goal is to continue to bring ever more transmigrants into Irian Jaya, year after year.

BAHASA INDONESIA

Any seasoned traveler will tell you the ability to speak the language of your host country will have a huge effect on the quality of your experience there. It's not necessary to commit to memory hundreds of complicated sentences. A basic grasp of such simple, everyday phrases as "Good morning," "Thank you," and variations of the theme "I want to eat/sleep" are enough to explain what you want, make friends, find your way, learn correct prices, and generally make your stay more enjoyable. You'll be amazed at how much you can say with only a 500-word vocabulary.

Don't worry about grammar and sentence construction at first. Just concentrate on memorizing the most important commonly used words and phrases in this appendix, all selected specifically for their value to travelers. Your emphasis should be on effective, speedy communication. The most important phrase in this section is *"Saya belum lancar di Bahasa Indonesia"* ("I'm not yet fluent in Indonesian"). Say this first, then ask your questions. If you don't first admit your ignorance, any inquiry is likely to produce an outpouring of verbiage impossible to comprehend.

At first, Indonesian might appear extremely simple. It's a nontonal language with no tense suffixes or prefixes, no case genders or definite articles, no declensions, no conjugations, not even a verb "to be." In actuality, however, the very lack of obvious rules makes it difficult to speak the language correctly or express yourself in a natural way. To speak enough Indonesian to get by is easy—easier than English. But to speak Indonesian well is another matter; it's as difficult and sophisticated as any of the world's great languages. But the surprised expressions and smiles of those you address will be your reward. *Selamat belajar!*

SPELLING

Bahasa Indonesia is written in Latin script and consists of 21 letters. Spelling is strictly phonetic; small children after a very few years of schooling can read adult literature aloud to their grandparents. In 1972 Indonesia simplified its spelling, making revisions in the language to conform to Malay, though pronunciation remains the same. Sometimes the old spelling is used on road signs and maps, and in publications and dictionaries.

In the "new" spelling, every "j" becomes "y" (as in "yarn"), every "dj" changes to "j" (as in "jam"), every "tj" to "c" (as in "chair"), "ch" to "kh," "nj" to "ny," and "sj" to "sy." To make matters even more confusing, there are spelling variations everywhere you go, depending on the island or even the district of the island. Words from other major languages of Indonesia have also influenced Bahasa Indonesian. Many Javanese words change "o" for "a" when translated into Indonesian; Diponegoro becomes Dipanegara and Solo becomes Sala. Some Indonesians spell *tolong* (please) as *tulang*.

Until about 1947, Indonesian words on signs, maps, and other materials were transcribed using Dutch sounds—e.g., Bandoeng (Bandung) and Boekoe (Buku). Occasionally you'll still come across these archaic spellings.

GREETINGS

Selamat may be used in conjunction with almost any action word. Together they form a phrase which translates as "May your (action) be prosperous, blessed!" Thus, *"Selamat tinggal"* means literally "May your remaining be prosperous"; *"Selamat tidur"* means "Sleep well"; *"Selamat bekerja"* means "Enjoy your work." By itself, *"Selamat"* means "Congratulations" or "Good luck" (literally, "Health"). *"Asalamu alaikum"* (literally, "Peace be unto you") is a greeting used before entering someone's house in Muslim areas; the reply is *"Walaikum salam"* ("And unto you, peace").

Good morning/Good afternoon/Good night
Selamat pagi/Selamat siang/Selamat malam

Where are you going? (a common greeting)
Mau kemana? or *Pergi ke mana?*

I'm taking a walk. (a common answer)
Jalan-jalan.

please/go right ahead
silahkan

Come in please. Please sit down.
Silahkan masuk. Silahkan duduk.

Hot today, isn't it? It will rain soon.
*Panas sekali, ya? Sebentar lagi (hari) mau
hujan.*

It's a beautiful day, isn't it? Nice day, isn't it?
Harinya indah, ya? Harinya enak, ya?

Nice view, isn't it?
Pemandangannya indah sekali, ya?

pleased/be happy
senang

Thank you/Excuse me (Pardon me)
Terima kasih/Ma'af

Bon appetit! This food is delicious.
Selamat makan! Makanan ini nikmat sekali.

Happy Hari Raya! Merry Christmas! Happy
New Year!
*Selamat Hari Raya! Selamat Hari Natal!
Selamat Tahun Baru!*

Thanks for the invitation.
Terima kasih atas undangan anda.

Have a good trip.
Selamat berjalan.

Welcome (literally, "Good fortune on arrival").
Selamat datang.

very interesting/very beautiful (of buildings,
monuments)
sangat menarik/bagus sekali

INTRODUCTIONS

How are you?/What's new?
Apa kabar?

Fine, thanks, and you?
Kabar baik, terima kasih, dan Tuan?

Don't be shy.
Jangan malu-malu.

Do you know Mr. Ali?
Apakah saudara kenal Tuan Ali?

I'm glad to meet you. (literally, "Good fortune
on meeting.")
Saya senang bertemu dengan anda.

I want you to meet my father/mother.
*Saya perkenalkan anda dengan ayah/ibu
saya.*

This is Mrs. Ahmad.
Ini Nyonya Ahmad.

Hello, what's your name? My name is
Mohammad.
*Halo, siapa namamu? Nama saya
Mohammad.*

Do you know Mr. Panggabean? I know him
well.
*Saudara kenal Tuan Panggabean? Saya
kenal baik dia.*

Are you Mr. Jones? Where are you from?
*Apa saudara bernama Jones? Dari mana
asal anda?*

I'm from New York. Here is my card.
Saya berasal dari New York. Ini kartu saya.

May I offer you something to drink or eat?
Anda ingin minuman atau makanan?

Perhaps no. Are you sure?
Mungkin tidak. Apakah anda pasti?

You are very hospitable. It's very kind of you.
Anda sangat ramah tamah. Anda baik sekali.

Excuse me. Come again.
*Permisi (asking for permission to leave).
Silahkan datang lagi.*

DO YOU SPEAK INDONESIAN?

Can you speak Indonesian?
Dapatkah anda berbahasa Bahasa Indonesia?

I don't speak Indonesian.
Saya tidak bicara Bahasa Indonesia.

Please speak slowly.
Tolong bicara pelan-pelan.

Yes, a little. Just enough to make myself
  understood.
Ya, sedikit. Hanya cukup untuk dimengerti.

Where did you learn it? I learned it by myself.
*Tuan belajarnya dimana? Saya belajar
  sendiri.*

Your Indonesian is fluent. Your pronunciation
  is good.
*Bahasa Indonesia anda lancar. Ucapan kata-
  kata anda baik.*

How long have you been studying
  Indonesian?
*Sudah berapa lama anda belajar Bahasa
  Indonesia?*

Do you speak English? May I practice my
  English with you?
*Apa saudara dapat bicara Bahasa Inggeris?
  Boleh saya praktek Bahasa Inggeris pada
  anda?*

I'm very sorry. Perhaps another time.
Ma'af sekali. Mungkin lain waktu.

What is the name for this? What does this
  word mean?
Apa namanya ini? Apa arti kata ini?

What do you call this? What is this (that)
  called in Indonesian?
*Ini namanya apa? Apa namanya ini (itu)
  dalam Bahasa Indonesia?*

How do you spell it? How do you pronounce
  it?
*Bagaimana mengejanya? Bagaimana
  mengucapannya?*

What did he (she) say? Please repeat. Say it
  again.
Apa katanya? Coba ulangi lagi. Sekali lagi.

I understand. I don't understand.
Saya mengerti. Saya kurang mengerti.

What is *pembangunan* in English?
*Apakah arti "pembangunan" dalam
  Bahasa Inggeris?*

How do you translate *jam karet* into English?
*Bagaimana terjemahan "jam karet" dalam
  Bahasa Inggeris?*

CONVERSATION

Where are you from? I'm from the U.S.A.
*Anda berasl dari negara mana? Saya berasal
  dari U.S.A.*

My nationality is Australian/American/Dutch.
*Saya berkebangsaan Australi/orang
  Amerika/orang Belanda.*

How old are you? I'm twenty years old.
*Umur berapa anda? Saya berumur duapuluh
  tahun.*

Are you a tourist? What's your address?
*Adakah anda seorang wisatawan? Dimana
  alamat anda?*

When did you arrive here? How long have
  you been here?
*Kapan anda tiba disini? Sudah berapa lama
  anda disini?*

I've just arrived in Indonesia.
Saya baru datang di Indonesia303

Have you ever been here before? Where are
  you going?
*Apakah anda sudah pernah kemari sebelum
  ini? Mau kemana?*

Will you stay long in Indonesia? No, just a
  couple of months.
*Anda akan tinggal lama di Indonesia? Tidak,
  hanya beberapa bulan.*

Have you already been to Bali? Yes, already.
Sudah pernah ke Bali? Ya, sudah.

No, I've never been to Torajaland.
Belum, saya belum pernah ke Tanatoraja.

How do you like the climate of Indonesia?
  The climate is wonderful!
*Bagaimana tentang iklim Indonesia? Iklimnya
  baik sekali!*

Do you smoke? May I have a light (for a cigarette)?
Anda suka merokok? Boleh saya minta korek api?

What's your ocupation?
Apakah pekerjaan anda?

I'm a businessman. I go to school.
Saya adalah seorang pengusaha. Saya seorang pelajar.

My occupation is artist/sailor/teacher/writer.
Pekerjaan saya seniman/pelaut/guru/penulis.

What's your religion? I'm a Christian/Jew/Muslim.
Agama apa anda? Saya orang Kristen/orang Jahudi/orang Islam.

Are you married? Yes, I am. Not yet. Do you have children?
Apa anda sudah kawin? Ya, sudah. Belum. Sudah punya anak?

Do you like Indonesian cooking?
Apakah anda suka makanan Indonesia.

Yes, but some dishes are too hot for me.
Ya, tetapi sebagian masakan pedas bagi saya.

Will you be free this evening?
Anda tidak akan sibuk malam nanti?

Would you like to come to my house?
Maukah anda datang ke rumah saya?

Where shall we meet? Let's meet in front of . . .
Dimana kita akan jumpa? Kita jumpa saja di depan . . .

Okay, no problem. I'm sorry, I can't.
Baiklah, tidak ada masalah. Ma'af, saya tak dapat.

USEFUL PHRASES

yes
ya (Dutch spelling and pronunciation)

no
tidak (with an adjective or verb) or *bukan* (with a noun)

this, that
ini, itu (after the noun)

I do not have . . .
Saya tidak punya . . .

There is . . . There is not . . .
Ada . . . Tidak ada . . .

Yes, you're right.
Ya, anda benar.

It seems wrong. It's not necessary.
Rupanya salah. Ini tidak penting.

In my opinion. That's right.
Saya rasa or *saya kira* or *menurut saya. Itu betul* or *Itu benar.*

As much as possible.
Sebanyak mungkin.

I'm tired/hungry/thirsty.
Saya lelah/lapar/haus.

I want . . . Do you want . . .? I'm looking for . . .
Say mau . . . Anda mau . . .? Saya mencari . . .

I'm interested (in) . . . to like . . .
Saya tertarik . . . suka . . .

I need . . . I like . . . I hope so.
Saya perlu . . . Saya suka . . . Saya harap begitu.

I want to borrow . . . Do you have . . .?
Saya mau pinjam . . . Anda punya . . .?

Don't . . . I don't like that . . . I don't want . . .
Jangan . . . Saya tidak suka itu . . . Saya tidak mau . . .

I like Indonesia. Fine, okay.
Saya suka Indonesia. Baik.

I know. I don't know.
Saya tahu. Saya tidak tahu.

I think so. I don't think so.
Saya kira begitu. Saya kira tidak begitu.

I have . . . Of course.
Saya punya . . . Tentu saja.

an expression of surprise or pain
Aduh!

in the future . . . in that manner . . . in this manner . . .
pada masa yang akan datang . . . begitu . . . begini . . .

Yes, you're right. You're wrong.
Ya, anda benar. Anda salah.

It's possible. It's not possible. To be able.
Mungkin. Tidak mungkin. Bisa or *dapat* (may) or *boleh*

I'm glad to hear it.
Saya senang mendengarnya.

Thanks for the gift. It's very kind of you.
Terima kasih atas hadiah anda. Anda baik hati sekali.

Excuse me for being late. Excuse me for interrupting.
Ma'afkan, saya terlambat. Ma'afkan, saya mengganggu.

Excuse me for a moment. May I be excused?
Ma'afkan saya sebentar. Bolehkah saya tidak ikutserta?

I beg your pardon.
Saya mohon ma'af. or *Ma'afkan saya.*

Excuse me, what did you say?
Ma'af, apa yang anda katakan?

I'm sorry, I can't help you.
Ma'af, saya tidak dapat menolong anda.

ACCOMMODATIONS

Where's a hotel? Where's a *losmen*?
Dimana ada hotel? Dimana ada losmen?

Which is the best hotel/*losmen*?
Hotel/losmen mana yang terbaik?

Please recommend a good first-class hotel.
Tunjukkan lah hotel kelas satu yang baik.

I want a quiet, small hotel.
Saya ingin hotel yang tenang dan kecil.

That hotel is near the town square, far from the airport.
Hotel itu terletak dekat alun-alun, jauh dari lapangan terbang.

Please take me to Wisma Borobudur.
Tolong antar saya ke Wisma Borobudur.

Do you have a room available? Sorry, there aren't any rooms.
Ada kamar kosong? Ma'af, tidak ada.

Can I have a room for one night?
Bisakah saya dapat kamar untuk semalam?

We have a reservation. We want to reserve a room.
Kami telah memesan kamar. Saya ingin memesan kamar.

How long are you staying?
Berapa lama anda akan tinggal disini?

I will stay two days. On Tuesday I travel to Malang.
Saya akan tinggal dua hari. Hari selasa saya terus ke Malang.

One or two people? I'm alone.
Untuk satu atau dua orang? Saya sendiri.

Single, please. Two (three) of us, one room.
Untuk satu orang. Dua (tiga) orang, satu kamar.

One room, two beds. Clean and tidy.
Kamar dengan dua tempat tidur. Bersih dan rapih.

Have you a room with a private bath?
Apa ada kamar yang pakai kamar mandi tersendiri?

hot and cold water
air panas dan dingin

How much for one night? One person?
Berapa harga satu malam? Satu orang?

What is the rate per day? Week? Month?
Berapa taripnya sehari? Minggu? Bulan?

Does the price include breakfast? It includes
three daily meals.
*Apakah sewanya termasuk makan pagi?
Termasuk tiga kali makan.*

What time do I have to check out?
Jam berapa harus saya keluar?

May I see the room first? What's my room
number?
*Bolehkah saya melihat kamarnya dulu?
Nomor berapa kamar saya?*

I'm leaving tomorrow midday.
Saya berangkat besok tengah hari.

Here is the key to your room. It's unlocked.
Ini kunci kamar anda. Tidak dikunci.

Is it safe here? First floor. Second floor.
*Amankah disini? Lantai pertama. Lantai
kedua.*

Is there a bathroom on this floor? Where's the
toilet?
*Apa ada kamar mandi di lantai ini? Dimana
WCnya?*

Please spray my room. It has mosquitos.
*Tolong semprot kamar saya. Ada nyamuk
didalam.*

The mattress is too hard. I want to change
rooms.
*Kasurnya terlalu keras. Saya mau ganti
kamar.*

I want a better room/cheaper room.
*Saya minta kamar yang lebih baik/kamar
yang lebih murah*

larger room/smaller room/quiet room
*kamar yang lebih besar/kamar yang lebih
kecil/kamar yang tenang*

Have you anything cheaper? Have you
anything better?
*Adakah yang lebih murah? Adakah yang
lebih baik?*

I'll take this one. It'll do.
Saya ambil yang ini. Boleh juga.

Please put out the light, I want to sleep.
Tolong padamkan lampunya, saya mau tidur.

Please turn down the radio, it's loud.
Pelankan radio itu, suaranya terlalu keras.

HOTEL SERVICES

Just ring for service. May I have . . . ?
*Telpon saja untuk pelayanan. Bolehkah saya
minta . . . ?*

I want another pillow. Another blanket.
Saya ingin bantal lagi. Satu selimut lagi.

Dutch wife/hot water/ice/ice water
bantal guling/air panas/es/es batu

Please clean my room.
Tolong bersihkan kamar saya.

to make a bed
membereskan tempat tidur

soap/toilet paper/towel
sabun/kertas toilet/handuk

I want to speak to the manager.
Saya mau bicara dengan pengurus.

May I deposit my passport/luggage with you?
*Boleh saya titip paspor/barang saya dengan
anda?*

May I use your telephone?
Bolehkah saya meminjam telpon?

Is there a message for me? I'm sorry, you
were out.
*Ada pesan untuk saya? Ma'af, anda sedang
tidak ada disini.*

I need a porter. Will you please fetch my
suitcases.
*Saya memerlukan seorang portir. Tolong
ambil kopor-kopor saya.*

Please call a taxi.
Tolong panggilkan taxi.

Can I have breakfast in my room?
Bisakah saya makan pagi di kamar?

Please send my breakfast up.
Tolong kirimkan makan pagi saya keatas.

Is there someone who washes clothes?
Please wash these clothes.
Ada orang yang mencuci pakaian? Tolong cucikan pakaian ini.

Can I have them back tomorrow? Yes, all these are mine.
Apakah bisa selesai besok? Ya, ini semua punya saya.

Please wake me up at 0600/before sunrise/very early.
Harap bangunkan saya pukul enam pagi/subuh/pagi-pagi.

Don't wake me up.
Jangan bangunkan saya.

I want to check out now. Give me my bill, please.
Saya mau keluar sekarang. Saya minta rekening saya.

I will return next week.
Saya akan kembali minggu yang akan datang.

Can you store my things for five days?
Bisakah anda menyimpan barang-barang saya untuk lima hari?

AT THE RESTAURANT/MARKET

I'm hungry. I'm going to go to a downtown restaurant.
Saya lapar. Saya akan pergi ke restoran di pusat kota.

Where's a good restuarant?
Restoran mana yang baik?

Can we stop for lunch/dinner?
Dapatkah kita berhenti untuk makan siang/makan malam.

Let's have lunch. Who'll join me?
Mari kita makan siang. Siapa ikut saya?

This is the best foodstall here.
Ini warung yang terbaik disini.

I'm a vegetarian, I don't eat any meat. Vegetables only.
Saya seorang vegetaris, saya tidak makan daging-dagingan. Sayur saja.

I want Indonesian food.
Saya mau makanan Indonesia.

What time is breakfast? It's served at seven o'clock.
Jam berapa waktu makan pagi? Makan pagi dihidangkan pada pukul tujuh.

Waiter! I want a table for five people.
Pelayan! Saya ingin meja untuk lima orang.

I'm sorry, this table is reserved.
Ma'af, meja ini sudah dipesan.

Give me tea instead of coffee.
Berilah saya teh untuk gantinya kopi.

Do you take sugar and milk?
Anda pakai gula dan susu?

Is this water drinkable? No, it's not drinkable.
Apa air ini bisa diminum? Tidak, itu tak bisa diminum.

I'm thirsty. Please get me a glass of ice water.
Saya haus. Tolong ambil segelas air es.

Please give me some hot water. I want boiled water (for drinking).
Tolong beri saya air panas. Saya minta air matang (untuk minum).

May I see the menu? What's the specialty in this restaurant?
Boleh saya lihat daftar makanan? Apa keistimewaan rumah makan ini?

We're in a hurry, please bring our orders quickly.
Kami terburu-buru, tolong cepatkan pesanan kami.

When will it be ready? What's the price?
Kapan siapnya? Berapa harganya?

That's too expensive. Have you got Indonesian dishes?
Itu terlalu mahal. Apakah anda menyajikan makanan Indonesia?

Let's have some *sate*. Don't make it too spicy!
Mari kita makan sate. Jangan terlalu pedas!

What is that/this? I'd like another helping. Is there more?
Apa itu/ini? Saya mau tambah lagi. Ada lagi?

Please bring us some hot chili sauce. Bring me coffee.
Bawakan lah kami sambal. Bawakan untuk saya kopi.

Bring me another glass. What do you have for dessert?
Ambilkan untuk saya gelas yang lain. Apa yang anda punyai untuk makanan perwei mulut?

I have had enough. I want a banana.
Saya sudah kenyang. Saya ingin pisang.

I want to wash my hands. Where's the toilet?
Saya mau cuci tangan. Dimana kamar kecil?

Good. Waiter, please bring me the bill.
Bagus. Bung, saya minta nota.

Can you change a 10,000-*rupiah* bill?
Bisakah anda menukar sepuluh ribu rupiah uang kertas?

at the same time/each person/if there is any/finished
pada waktu yang sama/setiap orang/kalau ada/habis

to like very much/really delicious/Enjoy your meal!
suka sekali/enak sekali/Selamat makan!

a little/too little/a little more
sedikit/terlalu sedikit/sedikit lagi

fresh/clean/dirty/to taste
segar/bersih/kotor/mencicipi, merasa

lukewarm/hot/underdone/well done
hangat/panas/mentah/matang

cold/hot (temperature)/hot (spicy)
dingin/panas/pedas

to cook/one serving/forbidden (for Muslims)
memasak/satu porsi/haram

to boil/to fry/to slice/to squeeze (fruit)
merebus/menggoreng/mengiris/memeras

salty/sour/vinegar/sweet/honey/bitter (or plain)
asin/asam/cuka/manis/madu/pahit

plastic bag/bottled drinking water
tas plastik/botol air minum

fork/spoon/knife/glass/plate/bowl/cup
garpu/sendok/pisau/gelas/piring/mangkok/cangkir

rice (after cooking)/rice noodles/sticky white rice
nasi/bakmi/ketan

beans/fermented white soybeans/soybean curd/shrimp paste
buncis/tempe/tahu/terasi

soup/noodle soup/curried chicken/fried rice/fried noodles
sup/mie kuah/ayam kari/nasi goreng/mie goreng

fish/prawns/squid/crab/carp/lobster/eel
ikan/udang/cumi/kepiting/ikan mas/udang karang/belut

meat/liver/heart/beefsteak/water buffalo/frog legs
daging/hati/jantung/bistik/daging kerbau/kaki kodok

beef/chicken/lamb/mutton/pork
daging sapi/daging ayam/daging domba/daging kambing/daging babi

vegetables/tomato/onion/cabbage/corn/potato/sweet potato/carrots/avocado
sayur/tomat/bawang/kol/jagung/kentang/ubi/wortel/apokat

salt/ginger/chili/cinnamon/pepper/cloves/
garlic/lemon
*garam/jahe/cabe/kayu\manis/merica/cengkeh/
bawang putih/jeruk*

beer/rice wine/water/cordial/ice/orange
juice/soda water
bir/tuak/air/strop/es/air jeruk/air soda

bread/toast/cake/cracker/spring rolls
roti/roti bakar/kue/biskuit/lumpia

butter/cheese/cream/milk/ice cream
mentega/keju/kepala susu/susu/es krim

egg/fried egg/omelette/boiled egg/soft-boiled
egg
*telur/telur mata sapi/telur dadar/telur
rebus/telur setengah matang*

snacks/peanuts/candy/shrimp chips
*makanan kecil/kacang tanah/gula-
gula/krupuk udang*

Where can I buy fruit? Where's the market?
*Dimana saya bisa beli buah-buahan? Pasar
dimana?*

apple/coconut/citrus fruit/papaya/pineapple/
banana fritters
*apel/kelapa/jeruk/papaya/nanas/pisang
goreng*

to pick out good ones/ripe/remove the skin
pilih yang baik/matang/kupas

How does one eat this? Peel it and then you
can eat it as is.
*Bagaimana cara makannya? Dikupas, lalu
bisa dimakan begitu saja.*

TRANSPORTATION

What are the tourist places I should visit?
*Apa nama tempat pariwisata yang harus saya
kunjungi?*

There are two caves near the hot springs.
Ada dua gua dekat sumber air panas.

Is it safe to swim here?
Aman berenang disini?

Where do you want to go?
Anda mau pergi ke mana?

I want to go to Yogyakarta.
Saya mau pergi ke Yogyakarta.

When are you leaving?
Kapan anda berangkat?

I depart tommorrow/today.
Saya berangkat besok/hari ini.

not sure/not certain
belum tentu/belum pasti

I'm worn out.
Saya agak capai.

How far is it from here? Is it near?
Berapa jauh dari sini. Dekat?

Far from here. This way/that way. Which
way?
Jauh dari sini. Kesini/kesana. Kemana?

Turn left at the corner.
Belok ke kiri di prapatan.

Go straight ahead and then turn to the
left/right.
*Jalan terus dan kemudian belok
kekiri/kekanan.*

Go back to the intersection, then follow the
sign.
*Kembali kepersimpangan jalan, lalu ikuti
tanda arah.*

My address is . . . /I live on Melati Street.
Alamat saya . . . /Saya tinggal di Jalan Melati.

Straight ahead. On the right. On the left.
Terus. Disebelah kanan. Disebelah kiri.

Cross here. Wait here. Stop here.
*Di sini menyeberang. Tunggulah disini.
Berhenti disini.*

to back up or go backwards/to go forward or
advance
mundur/maju

To search for. Where can I find a post office?
Mencari. Kantor pos dimana?

Please show me the way to the highway.
Tolong tunjukkan ke jalan raya.

I want to find this address. I am lost.
Saya mau mendapat alamat ini. Saya tersesat.

Please show me on this map.
Tolong tunjukkan dipeta ini.

What is the name of this street?
Apa nama jalan ini?

What town does this road lead to?
Jalan ini menuju kekota apa?

Where can I catch a . . . ? Where can I rent a . . . ?
Dimana saya akan naik . . . ? Dimana bisa menyewa . . . ?

How many kilometers is it to Rantepao?
Berapa kilometer ke Rantepao?

What's the best route to follow?
Jalan mana yang terbaik?

This road is under repair.
Jalan ini sedang diperbaiki.

This road is very slippery. Look out.
Jalan ini sangat licin. Hati-hati.

My car has broken down. Where can I find a mechanic?
Mobil saya mogok. Dimana saya bisa dapat seorang montir?

I have a flat tire. Will you please repair the tire?
Ban saya kempis. Harap perbaiki ponpa itu?

What's wrong with the engine? Switch off the engine.
Apa yang rusak pada mesin ini? Berhentikah mesin.

The engine won't start. Is there enough gasoline?
Mesin ini mogok. Apakah bensinnya cukup?

Fill it up please. Check the oil.
Tolong diisi penuh. Periksa olinya.

at the bus/train station.
di stasiun bis/stasiun kereta api.

Where is the ticket window?
Dimana ada loket?

How long does it take from here to Bogor?
Berapa lama perjalanan dari sini ke Bogor?

Where's the airport?
Dimana lapangan terbang?

How much does a taxi to the airport cost?
Berapa tarip taxi kepelabuhan udara?

Please help me with my luggage.
Bung, tolong bawakan barang-barang saya.

There are three pieces.
Semuanya ada tiga barang.

Where is the passport and customs checkpoint?
Dimana tempat pemeriksaan paspor dan barang?

Which gate do I go to for the plane for Singapore?
Saya harus pergi kepintu mana untuk naik pesawat ke Singapura?

When is the next flight?
Jam berapa ada penerbangan berikutnya?

When is the next flight to Jambi?
Kapan ada penerbangan lagi ke Jambi?

At what time does the plane for Ambon leave?
Jam berapa pesawat terbang ke Ambon berangkat?

Is there a nonstop flight between Jakarta and Samarinda?
Apakah ada pesawat langsung antara Jakarta dan Samarinda?

What's the fare to Solo?
Berapa ongkosnya ke Solo?

I want a single/return ticket.
Saya mau beli karcis sejalan/pulang pergi.

Stewardness, are we near Kupang?
Pramugari, apakah kita sudah dekat dengan Kupang?

Where is the railway station?
Dimana stasiun kereta api?

Where is the railway information desk?
Dimana tempat bertanya?

Where is the baggage room?
Dimana kamar bagasi?

I want a ticket to Bandung. What's the fare?
Saya mau beli karcis ke Bandung. Berapa ongkosnya?

Which class do you want? First class or second class?
Kelas berapa yang anda mau? Kelas satu atau kelas dua?

How much is a first class roundtrip ticket to Bogor?
Berapa harga karcis kelas satu pulang-pergi ke Bogor?

Is it half price for a child?
Apakah anak-anak setengah harga?

I want to reserve two seats to Bandung on Monday.
Saya mau pesan dua kursi untuk ke Bandung pada hari senin.

What time is the first train for Banyuwangi?
Jam berapa kereta-api pertama menuju Banyuwangi?

Is this seat taken? Sorry, already full.
Apakah kursi ini kosong? Ma'af, sudah ada orang.

There's room for one more. Take a seat, please.
Ada tempat untuk satu orang lagi. Silahkan duduk.

How long does the train stop here?
Berapa lama kereta-api berhenti disini?

What time does the train arrive?
Jam berapa kereta api datang?

Does this train go to . . . ?
Apakah kereta api ini ke . . . ?

We will arrive in Cilacap at around noon.
Kita akan sampai di Cilacap kira-kira tengah hari.

time of arrival
waktu kedatangan or *jam datang*

What time will the ship be sailing?
Jam berapa kapal ini akan berangkat?

Where do I get the boat to Balikpapan?
Darimanakah dapat saya naik kapal ke Balikpapan?

Perhaps on Monday.
Barangkali hari senin.

Which class are you traveling?
Perjalanan anda di kelas berapa?

First class (or cabin)/Economy class
Kelas satu/Kelas ekonomi

It's time to go on board.
Sekarang ini waktu untuk naik ke kapal.

to take a *becak*/call a *becak*
naik becak or *berbecak/panggil becak*

turn to the right/left
belok ke kanan/kiri

What is the *becak* fare there?
Berapa ongkos becak ke sana?

Don't pay more than 1500 *rupiah*.
Jangan bayar lebih dari seribu limaratus rupiah.

Driver, take me to Losmen Matahari.
Bung, bawa saya ke Losmen Matahari.

Two thousand! How is it possible nowadays, sir!
Duaribu! Mana bisa sekarang ini, Pak!

All right, make it one thousand.
Ayo, satu ribu!

What time will the bus leave? Let's get on the bus.
Jam berapa bis ini akan berangkat? Mari kita naik bis.

Are there buses that go there? How long from here to there?
Apa ada bis yang ke sana? Berapa lama dari sini kesana?

Which bus will take us downtown?
Bis yang mana yang akan ke kota?

Does this bus go directly to Bukittinggi?
Apakah bis ini pergi langsung ke Bukittinggi?

Are there any empty seats? No standing room!
Ada tempat duduk yang kosong? Tak ada tempat untuk berdiri!

Where shall we get off? Let's get off the bus here!
Dimana kita akan turun? Kita turun disini!

At the next stop, please let me off.
Saya akan berhenti dipemberhentian berikut.

Do we need to take a taxi? We have to take a taxi.
Perlu kita naik taksi? Kita harus naik taksi.

call a taxi/please get me a taxi
panggil taksi/tolong panggilkan saya taksi

Where is the taxi stand? Is this taxi taken?
Dimana tempat taksi? Apakah taksi ini ada yang pakai?

How much is this taxi per hour? That taxi has a meter.
Berapa sewa taksi ini per jam? Taksi itu pakai meter.

Taxi! To the airport!/Drive me to . . .
Taksi! Ke lapangan terbang!/Antar saya ke . . .

Take me to a cheap/expensive hotel.
Antarkan saya kehotel yang murah/mahal.

I want to see the city. Please drive me around for sightseeing.
Saya ingin melihat kota. Tolong antar saya berkeliling lihat-lihat kota.

Drive a bit faster. I'm in a hurry.
Cepat sedikit. Saya buru-buru.

Please slow down. Please drive more slowly.
Kurangi kecepatan. Jalan pelan-pelan saja.

Stop here. What's the fare, driver?
Berhenti disini. Berapa ongkosnya, Bung?

STREET SIGNS

Parking—*Parkir*
No parking—*Dilarang parkir*
Cross here—*Menyeberang di sini*
Women/Men—*Wanita/Laki-laki*
Keep Out—*Dilarang Masuk*
Entrance—*Pintu Masuk*
Exit—*Pintu Keluar*
Caution—*Awas/Hati-hati*
Open/Closed—*Buka/Tutup*
Danger—*Bahaya*
Waiting Room—*Ruang Tunggu*
Information—*Penerangan*
Up/Down—*Naik/Turun*
Push/Pull—*Dorong/Tarik*
Police—*Polisi*
Police Station—*Kantor Polisi*
Headquarters—*Kantor Pusat*
Branch—*Cabang*

RECREATION AND SIGHTSEEING

Where's the theater/moviehouse/music hall?
Dimana gedung sandiwara/gedung bioskop/gedung musik?

What kind of play (movie) would you like to see?
Sandiwara (film) apa yang anda suka?

What's on at the Jakarta Theatre tonight? What's showing?
Film apa di Jakarta Theatre malam ini? Film apa yang diputar?

Is there a matinee today? What's the admission?
Adakah matinee hari ini? Berapa harga karcisnya?

Please reserve two tickets for Friday.
Saya mau pesan dua karcis untuk hari Jumat.

What time does it start? It will start at 1800.
Jam berapa mulainya? Mulainya jam 6 sore.

Let's sit in the first row. This is a good seat.
Mari kita duduk dibaris depan. Disini baik juga.

Sorry, all tickets have been sold out. Sorry, the house is full.
Ma'af, karcis sudah habis terjual. Ma'af, kami sudah penuh.

Where can we go to dance? Is there a discotheque in this hotel?
Dimana kita bisa berdansa? Ada diskotik di hotel ini?

I'd like to dance to live music. Is there a nightclub here?
Saya suka berdansa dengen diiringi band. Ada kelab-malam disini?

Would you like to dance?
Maukah anda berdansa?

Is there a lot to interest tourists around here?
Apakah disini banyak pemandangan yang menarik untuk turis?

What is there to see around here?
Pemandangan apa yang bisa dilihat di daerah ini?

Is there a tourist office near here?
Apakah ada kantor pariwisata di sekitar ini?

What's the fare for a roundtrip to the Loksado area?
Berapa ongkos pulang-pergi ke daerah Loksado?

What will we see on that trip?
Apa saja yang akan dilihat di perjalanan itu?

What shall we bring on the trip?
Apa saja yang harus kita bawa?

How much do you charge per hour? What's included in the price?
Berapa taripnya sejam? Termasuk apa saja itu?

What time does the bus leave? What time do we get back?
Jam berapa bisnya berangkat? Jam berapa kita kembali?

I want a guide who speaks English.
Saya ingin seorang petunjuk-jalan yang bisa bicara Bahasa Inggeris.

Is it all right to take photographs?
Bolehkah memotret?

What's that building? Where can I see good paintings?
Gedung apa itu? Dimanakah saya bisa melihat lukisan-lukisan yang baik?

Is there a cave near here? Where's the waterfall?
Ada gua dekat sini? Dimana air terjun?

I want to climb to the peak of that volcano.
Saya mau naik kepuncak gunung itu.

From where can one start the climb? From a village to the north.
Dari mana bisa berangkat? Dari desa ke utara.

How long (time) to the top?
Berapa lama keatas?

Is it safe to swim here? Yes, it's shallow here.
Aman berenang disini? Ya, disini dangkal.

Don't swim too far. It's very calm. Rough. Deep. Dangerous.
Jangan berenang terlalu jauh. Tenang sekali. Berombak. Dalam. Bahaya.

There's a bathing spot on the river.
Di sungai itu ada tempat pemandian.

I only want to sunbathe. Is there a quieter beach?
Saya hanya mau berjemur. Ada pantai yang lebih sepi?

I'm a good swimmer. I like big waves and white sand.
Saya perenang yang baik. Saya suka ombak besar dan pasir putih.

I want to hire a mat/sailboat/tent.
Saya mau menyewa tikar/perahu layar/tenda.

May I go fishing? What time is high/low tide?
Bolehkah saya memancing? Jam berapa air pasang/surut?

Note: Banners on buildings, stretched out over streets, and hanging from fences and walls announce current and upcoming events, performances, dramas, and movies. Checking banners is one of the best ways to keep abreast of the events in a town or city.

concert/solo concert/recital
konser/konser tunggal/pertunjukan

theater/play/movie/art exhibition
teater/sandiwara, drama/bioskop/pameran lukisan

SHOPPING

I want to buy . . . Where can I buy . . . ?
Saya mau beli . . . Dimana saya bisa beli . . . ?

Where's the shopping center in this town? How do I get there?
Dimanakah pusat pertokoan di kota ini? Naik apa saya pergi kesana?

Do you sell arts and crafts here? May I see some *batik*?
Tuan ada menjual barang kesenian dan kerajinan tangan di sini? Boleh saya lihat batik?

I'd like to buy silver crafts.
Saya mau membeli barang-barang kerajinan perak.

I'm just looking around.
Saya hanya melihat-lihat.

I'd like to look at blouses. Which one (do you) want?
Saya ingin melihat-lihat blus. Mau yang mana?

Do you have many kinds? I only want this one.
Punya banyak macam? Saya hanya mau yang ini.

Do you have it in other colors?
Apakah ini ada warna yang lain?

I prefer something of better quality. These are better.
Saya lebih suka kwalitas yang lebih baik. Ini lebih baik.

I want one which is new. Can you show me something else?
Saya mau yang baru. Tolong tunjukkan yang lainnya?

May I try on this dress? Where is the fitting room?
Boleh saya mencoba rok? Dimana kamar pasnya?

Will it fade/shrink? Where are these goods made?
Ini bisa luntur/menyusut? Barang-barang ini dibuat dimana?

Those are bad. Same or different? Is there enough?
Itu jelek. Sama atau lain? Apakah cukup?

What is the price of this? May I bargain?
Ini berapa harganya? Boleh ditawar?

That's too expensive. Do you have a cheaper one?
Itu terlalu mahal. Ada yang lebih murah?

Can you come down in price? No, the price is fixed.
Bisa saudara kurangkan harganya? Tidak, ini harga pasti.

When will it be ready? Can you deliver it to my hotel?
Kapan selesainya? Bisa anda antarkan kehotel saya?

I'll take it with me.
Saya akan membawanya sendiri.

How much is it altogether? May I have a receipt, please?
Berapa jumlah semuanya? Boleh saya minta tanda terimanya?

Please wrap this with thick paper.
Tolong bungkuskan dengan kertas yang tebal.

Let's go to the market.
Mari, kita pergi ke pasar.

What is this? What are you making?
Apakah ini? Sedang bikin apa disini?

Do you sell mosquito nets? Yes (there is), sir.
Jual kelambu? Ada, Tuan.

How much is this mosquito net?
Berapa harga kelambu ini?

Six thousand-five hundred *rupiah*, sir.
Enamribu limaratus rupiah, Tuan.

Don't give me a crazy price! I've seen some that are cheaper.
Jangan beri harga gila! Saya pernah lihat ada yang lebih murah.

I'll come back later.
Saya akan kembali lagi.

I can only pay five and a half thousand.
Saya hanya bisa bayar lima ribu limaratus rupiah.

If you want it for five thousand *rupiah*, just take it.
Kalau Tuan mau lima ribu rupiah, ambil saja.

Last price. It's up to you.
Harga akhir. Terserah Tuan.

Here is four and a half thousand *rupiah*. Is it enough?
Ini empat ribu limaratus rupiah. Cukup?

Please wrap it up for me. Please make a very strong package.
Tolong bungkuskan. Tolong bungkuskan yang kuat sekali.

for sale/to pick out/to point out
untuk dijual/memilih/menunjukkan

cheap/expensive/to make a profit
murah/mahal/membuat untung

to pay/to pay cash
membayer/membayar kontan

there is/there is not/as much again
ada/tidak ada/sekali lagi

big and little/little (not much)/same
besar dan kecil/sedikit/sama

on top of/in front of
diatas/dimuka or *didepan*

maker or doer/merchant or shopkeeper/antique dealer
tukang/pedagang, penjual/pedagang antik

AT THE BANK

Where's a bank? Where's the nearest bank?
Dimana bank? Dimanakah bank yang terdekat?

What time does the bank open?
Jam berapa bank buka?

Where can I cash traveler's checks?
Dimana boleh saya menguangkan cek perjalanan turis?

Is there a wire transfer for me?
Ada kiriman uang untuk saya?

I'm sorry, it hasn't arrived yet.
Ma'af, belum datang.

Please contact the Jakarta branch for me.
Tolong hubungi cabang Jakarta untuk saya.

I want to change some American dollars.
Saya mau menukar dolar Amerika.

What's the exchange rate for the dollar?
Berapa kurs uang dolar?

Two thousand one hundred *rupiah* for one dollar.
Duaribu seratus rupiah untuk satu dollar.

Give me five thousand *rupiah* notes.
Beri saya uang lima ribuan.

I want to change this into small money.
Saya ingin tukar ini uang kecil.

AT THE POST OFFICE

I'm looking for the post office.
Saya sedang mencari kantor pos.

Where can I mail this? Do not fold!
Dimana saya dapat mengirimkan ini? Jangan dilipat!

Please post this letter/parcel for me.
Tolong poskan surat/bungkusan ini untuk saya.

I want to send this letter via regular mail/airmail.
Saya mau mengirim surat ini biasa/pos udara.

I want to register this letter.
Saya mau surat ini tercatat.

This is a special-delivery letter.
Ini adalah surat kilat.

Airmail to New York is Rp1800.
Pos udara untuk New York Rp1800.

Please weigh this letter/packet.
Tolong timbang surat/paket ini.

Please give me postage stamps/aerograms/postcards.
Saya mau beli perangko/warkatpos udara/kartu pos.

This package is overweight.
Paket ini terlalu berat.

Do you want a return receipt?
Tuan ingin surat tanda terima?

to tie with nylon string/to wrap with paper/scotch tape
mengikat dengan tali/bungkus dengan kertas/pita plastik

TELEPHONE

May I use the telephone?
Bolehkah meminjan telpon anda?

I want to make a long-distance call.
Saya ingin menelpon untuk interlokal.

How much is a long-distance call to . . .?
Berapa ongkos interlokal ke . . .?

Can I dial direct?
Dapatkah saya menelpon langsung?

What number are you calling?
Anda minta nomor berapa?

the line is busy/out of order
telponnya sedang bicara/telpon ini rusak

hold the line/there's no answer
tunggu sebentar/tidak ada jawaban

He's not in. Who's speaking?
Ia tak ada di tempat. Siapakah ini?

Is this telephone directory still new?
Buku telpon ini masih baru?

wrong number/the line was interrupted
salah sambung/hubungan telpon terganggu

May I speak with . . . ?/Wait a minute.
Boleh saya bicara dengan . . . ?/Tunggu sebentar.

I want to speak to Mr. Sujono.
Saya mau bicara dengan Tuan Sujono.

PHOTOGRAPHY

May I take photographs here?
Bolehkah saya mengambil foto disini?

I have a camera. Photography prohibited.
Saya punya tustel (fototustel). Dilarang memotret.

Where is the nearest photo studio?
Dimanakah foto studio yang terdekat?

Where can I get photographic materials?
Dimana saya bisa memperoleh bahan-bahan fotografi?

Can I buy a roll of film? Please develop this film.
Dapatkah saya membeli satu rol film? Tolonglah cuci film ini.

I want to have my photo taken.
Saya ingin difoto.

I want to have this film developed and printed.
Saya mau mencuci dan mencetak film ini.

Can you enlarge this photo? I want this size.
Dapatkah anda memperbesar foto ini? Saya mau ukuran ini.

Let me have a proof, please.
Coba lihat contohnya.

When will it be ready? Can you make it earlier?
Kapan selesainya? Bisa lebih cepat?

What type of paper do you use (to print film)?
Kertas produksi apa yang anda pakai (untuk mencetak film)?

NUMBERS AND AMOUNTS

0—*nol*
1—*satu*
2—*dua*
3—*tiga*
4—*empat*
5—*lima*
6—*enam*
7—*tujuh*
8—*delapan*
9—*sembilan*
10—*sepuluh*
11—*sebelas*
12—*duabelas*
15—*limabelas*
20—*duapuluh*
30—*tigapuluh*
40—*limapuluh*
100—*seratus*
200—*duaratus*

500—*limaratus*
1,000—*seribu*
3,000—*tigaribu*
10,000—*sepuluh ribu*
100,000—*seratus ribu*
268—*duaratus enampuluh delapan*
150—*seratus limapuluh*
307—*tigaratus tujuh*
537—*limaratus tigapuluh tujuh*
11,347—*sebelas ribu tiga ratus empatpuluh tujuh*
first—*pertama, kesatu*
second—*kedua*
third—*ketiga*
fourth—*keempat*
fifth—*kelima*
sixth—*keenam*
seventh—*ketujuh*
eighth—*kedelapan*
ninth—*kesembilan*
tenth—*kesepuluh*
eleventh—*kesebelas*
twelfth—*keduabelas*
one-half—*setengah*
one-quarter—*seperempat*
three-quarters—*tigaperempat*
1.5—*satu setengah*
2.5%—*dua setengah persen*
one-third—*sepertiga*
two-thirds—*dua pertiga*
one-fifth—*seperlima*
one-tenth—*sepersepuluh*
divide—*bagi*
multiply—*kali*
to slice—*iris, potong*
one slice—*satu iris, sepotong*
a dozen—*duabelas/satu lusin*
to cut—*potong*
number—*nomor*
total/quantity—*jumlah*
to add—*tambah*
to subtract—*kurang*
more (quantity)—*lagi*
approximately—*kira-kira*
how many/much—*berapa*
many/much—*banyak*
too—*terlalu*
too many—*terlalu banyak*
few—*sedikit*
enough—*cukup*
a handful—*segenggam*
a spoonful—*satu sendok penuh*

fix two slices (pieces) of meat—*bikin dua iris (potong) daging*
buy four fish—*beli empat ekor ikan*
I need five eggs.—*Saya perlu lima biji telur.*
I need five shirts.—*Saya perlu lima helai baju.*
sheets of/paper/cloth—*helai/kertas/kain*
three sheets of paper—*tiga lembar kertas*

TIME, SEASONS, MEASUREMENTS, COLORS

What time is it?
Jam berapa?

I was ten minutes late.
Saya terlambat sepuluh menit.

How long? It takes only ten minutes.
Berapa lama? Itu hanya sepuluh menit.

When? What time does it start?
Kapan? Jam berapa mulai?

earlier/already/ago/recently
tadi/sudah/yang lalu/baru-baru ini

now/once again/just now
sekarang/sekali lagi/baru saja

immediately/quick
segera/cepat

later/afterwards
nanti/kemudian or *sesudah*

to be late/already late (in the day)
terlambat/hari sudah siang

not yet/nearly finished
belum/hampir habis

a few hours/a few minutes ago
beberapa jam/beberapa menit yang lalu

just a moment longer
sebentar lagi or *segera*

it's not going to happen/it won't come about
tidak jadi/tidak akan terjadi

very flexible schedule; "rubber time"
jam karet

When did you leave Sydney?
Kapan anda meninggalkan Sydney?

I arrived here only yesterday.
Saya sampai disini kemarin.

many times/just this once
sering kali/baru sekali ini

for the first time
untuk pertama kali

I saw him a week ago.
Saya ketemu dia seminggu yang lalu.

I left San Francisco two months ago.
Saya pergi dari San Francisco dua bulan yang lalu.

0500-0700 (5-7 a.m.)
pagi pagi

0700-1200 (7 a.m.-noon)
pagi

1200-1500 (noon-3 p.m.)
siang

1500-1900 (3-7 p.m.)
sore

1900-0500 (7 p.m.-5 a.m.)
malam

today/yesterday/the day before yesterday
hari ini/kemarin/kemarin dulu

tomorrow/the day after tomorrow/tomorrow morning
besok/besok lusa/besok pagi

two more days/in the daytime
dua hari lagi/di siang hari

next month
bulan yang akan datang or *bulan depan*

day off/everyday/nowadays
hari libur/tiap hari/sekarang ini or *sahat ini*

midday/later in the afternoon
tengah hari/nanti sore

last night/tonight/the whole night/midnight
*tadi malam/malam ini/semalamsuntuk/
tengah malam*

thirty minutes
tigapuluh menit

second
detik

hour/o'clock
jam/pukul

past or after
lewat

quarter past five
jam lima lewat seperempat

six-thirty
setengah tujuh

just seven o'clock
tepat pukul tujuh

It's seven-ten.
Sekarang pukul tujuh lewat sepuluh menit.

quarter to eight
jam delapan kurang seperempat

twenty to nine
jam sembilan kurang duapuluh menit

It's eleven-thirty.
Jam setengah duabelas.

week/last week/next week
minggu/minggu yang lalu/minggu depan

once a week/in a week
seminggu sekali/seminggu lagi

Monday/Tuesday/Wednesday
Hari Senin/Hari Selasa/Hari Rabu

Thursday/Friday/Saturday/Sunday
Hari Kamis/Hari Jum'at/Hari Sabtu/Hari Minggu

What day is today? Monday morning.
Hari ini hari apa? Senin pagi.

Tomorrow is Tuesday.
Besok hari Selasa.

It's Friday, the twenty-second.
Ini hari Jum'at, tanggal duapuluh dua.

Yesterday was Sunday.
Kemarin hari Minggu.

January/February/March/April
Januari/Februari/Maret/April

May/June/July/August
Mei/Juni/Juli/Agustus

September/October/November/December
September/Oktober/Nopember/Desember

What date is today?
Tanggal berapa hari ini? or *Tanggal berapa
sekarang?*

It's the sixteenth of July.
Hari ini tanggal enambelas Juli.

What date was it yesterday?
Kemarin tanggal berapa?

Do you have a calendar?
Apa saudara punya tanggalan?

17 May 1941
*Tujuhbelas Mei, sembilanbelas empatpuluh
satu.*

this year/for years and years
tahun ini/bertahun-tahun

season/dry season/hot season/rainy season
*musim/musim kemarau/musim panas/musim
hujan*

wind/humid/nice day/beautiful weather
angin/lembab/hari bagus/cuaca bagus

clear/cloudy/cool/hot/foggy
terang/mendung/sejuk/panas/berkabut

measurement/distance
ukuran/jarak

to weigh/width/length
timbang/lebarnya/panjangnya

to measure (for size)/to measure (for volume)
mengukur/menakar

depth/height/bigger than that
dalamnya/tingginya/lebih besar dari itu

black/white/yellow/red/blue/green/brown/orange
hitam/putih/kuning/merah/biru/hijau/coklat/oranje

HEALTH

Where is the nearest drugstore? Hospital?
Dimanakah apotik (toko obat) yang terdekat? Rumah sakit?

What's your ailment? I need medicine for diarrhea.
Sakit apa? Saya perlu obat untuk berak-berak.

Do you have something for an upset stomach? Insect bites?
Apakah ada obat untuk gangguan perut? Gigitan serangga?

My throat is very sore. Can you make up this prescription?
Tenggorokan saya sakit sekali. Tolong buatkan resep ini?

"enter wind" (to catch a cold or flu)/dry cough/itching
masuk angin/batuk kering/gatal

I have a splitting headache/stomachache/sore eye/disease
Saya pusing sekali/sakit perut/sakit mata/penyakit

earache/toothache/backache/stomach cramp
sakit telinga/sakit gigi/sakit punggung/kejang perut mules

infection/malaria/cough (n.)/cough (v.)
infeksi/malaria/batuk-batuk/batuk

healthy/seriously sick
sehat/sakit keras

broken arm/broken leg
lengan patah/kaki patah

I don't sleep well. I have a cough/fever.
Tidur saya tidak nyenyak. Saya batuk/demam.

take medicine/take a pill
minum obat/minum pil

How many pills shall I take a day? Three times daily.
Berapa tablet harus saya makan sehari? Tiga kali sehari.

Take three teaspoons before/after meals.
Minumlah tiga sendok teh sebelum/sesudah makan.

on getting up/on going to bed/sleepy
waktu bangun tidur/jika mau tidur/ngantuk

I'm sick. I want to see a doctor.
Saya sakit. Saya mau pergi ke dokter.

Where is there a doctor who speaks English?
Dimana ada dokter yang bisa berbicara Bahasa Inggeris?

doctor's consulting hours/patient
jam bicara/pasien

Please call a doctor. That wound/cut needs dressing.
Tolong panggilkan dokter. Luka itu perlu dibalut.

How long have you had this cold? About a week.
Sudah berapa lama anda menderita masuk angin? Kurang lebih satu minggu.

You're very pale. Is your temperature still high?
Anda pucat. Apakah suhu badan anda masih tinggi?

Where's the pain? How's your appetite?
Dibagian mana yang anda rasakan sakit? Bagaimana nafsu makan anda?

I'll write you a prescription.
Saya akan menuliskan resep untuk anda.

Wash the cut in boiled water.
Basuh luka itu dengan air panas.

medicine/alcohol/antiseptic cream/aspirin
obat/alkohol/krem antiseptik/aspirin

bandage/plasters/cotton/injection
perban/plester/kapas/suntikan

cough medicine/laxative/ointment/powder
obat batuk/obat peluntur/salep/bedak

sedative/sleeping pill/talcum powder/
  tranquilizer
*obat untuk meredakan sakit/obat tidur/bedak
  talek/obat penenang*

urine specimen/stool specimen
contoh buang air kecil/contoh buang air besar

to rub (with salve)
menggosok

TROUBLES, DIFFICULTIES, HASSLES

Indonesia is not a violent environment and you
very seldom hear of muggings, rapes, or fights.
But due to its huge population base, there is an
element of the population who are illbred and
rude (*kasar*, in Indonesian). If anyone is ever
bothering you or touching you indecently, it's
usually enough to say *"Jangan begitu, itu tidak
baik"* ("Don't act like that, it's not nice"). This is
sufficiently firm, yet polite, and will cover most
unpleasant situations.

Please help me for a moment. I've missed the
  train.
*Tolonglah saya sebentar. Saya ketinggalan
  kereta api.*

I've been robbed. I've been held up. What a
  pity!
*Saya baru dirampok. Saya baru di todong.
  Kasihan!*

My money has been stolen. Our bags are
  missing.
*Uang saya dicuri orang. Barang-barang kami
  hilang.*

I've lost my passport. All my IDs are gone.
*Paspor saya hilang. Semua pengenalan saya
  hilang.*

Where's the police station? Please call the
  police.
Dimana kantor polisi? Tolong panggilkan polisi.

Can I speak with the manager? I am angry.
*Bisakah saya bicara dengan pengurus? Saya
  marah.*

Let's talk over the problem with . . .
*Marilah, kita bicarakan persoalan
  ini dengan . . .*

Is there anybody here who speaks English?
Ada yang bisa berbahasa Inggeris disini?

Is there a translator here?
Ada penterjemah disini?

Where's the information desk? Where's the
  moneychanger?
*Dimana "information desk?" Dimana tempat
  menukar uang?*

Don't be angry with me. Don't be ill-
  mannered.
*Janganlah marah kepada saya. Jangan
  kurang ajar.*

Don't do that. Absolutely not!
Jangan bikin itu. Sama sekali tidak!

Don't talk nonsense! Don't bother me!
Jangan omong kosong! Jangan ganggu saya!

Excuse me, I must be going now.
Ma'af, saya harus pergi sekarang.

I want to go away from here.
Saya ingin pergi dari sini.

Will you please leave me alone? Please go
  away. Go away!
*Sudikah anda membiarkan saya sendiri?
  Pergilah. Pergi!*

Be patient, please! Don't disturb me. Leave
  her alone.
*Sabarlah sebentar! Jangan ganggu saya.
  Jangan ganggu dia.*

What's the matter? Be careful of him.
Ada apa? Hati-hati sama dia.

His manners are very vulgar. He's ill-
  mannered (impolite/rude).
Dia tidak sopan. Dia kurang ajar.

Never mind. That's all right. Forget it!
Tidak apa-apa. Itu tak mengapa. Lupakan saja!

GLOSSARY

A

acar—cucumber pickle salad

adat—traditional law or custom; unwritten rules of behavior covering such matters as inheritance rights, land ownership, cooking, eating, courtship, ceremonies of birth, marriage, and death.

Airlangga—an East Javanese hermit-king whose rule (A.D. 1019-1049) saw the flowering of intense literary and artistic activity during Indonesia's Golden Age. Airlangga achieved the unification of nearly all Java.

air panas—literally means "hot springs," but could also be a medicinal spring or health spa

alun-alun—a town square or park where public meetings, festivals, and sports events take place

Amir Hamzah—tales of the prophet Mohammed's uncle, derived from 7th-century Persian history. Indonesianized in the 15th century, they tell of battles, wars, and love affairs of the warrior-missionaries of Java.

angklung—hollow bamboo tubes cut to graduated lengths, producing a strange xylophonic sound; used by the Sundanese to accompany folk dances

anoa—a timid animal resembling a miniature buffalo, indigenous to the forests of Sulawesi

apam—a thick doughy pancake, spread with sugar and crushed nuts or coconut, then folded over

arak—distilled rice brandy

Arjuna Wiwaha—a play composed by Mpu Kanwa in A.D. 1035, inspired by the Mahabharata

asarco—coed dormitory or hostel

ASEAN—Association of South East Asian Nations (Singapore, Thailand, Malaysia, Indonesia, Philippines); political/economic/military organization founded in 1968 to check the growth of communism

asli—native, original, authentic; can also mean high-born or noble

asram—student dormitory or student flats. Only in its broadest sense does it mean "retreat" or "school."

asuransi—insurance; usually included in the price of a ship ticket

atap—palm thatch

Atoni—the native peoples of West Timor, living mainly in the inland mountain areas

ayam—chicken

B

babirusa—an Indonesian mammal, the "hog deer" (*Babyrousa babyrussa*)

badak—Javan or Sumatran rhinoceros

bahasa—language, dialect

Bahasa Indonesia—the Indonesian national language

bajaj—a motorized three-wheel *becak* used in Jakarta

bajigur—a delicious drink made of coconut milk, thickened with rice and sweetened condensed milk. Sometimes boiled with ginger flour and stirred with coffee.

bale—platform. Also written *balai*.

Bali Aga—aboriginal pre-Hindu inhabitants of Bali

banci—female impersonators or transsexuals, found particularly in Jakarta. Also called "sister boys." The polite word is *waria*, a combination of *wanita* (female) and *pria* (male).

bandrek—a Sundanese drink made from ginger milk, coconut, and brown sugar

banteng—Indonesia's wild cattle. Looks like a cow but has longer limbs; the *banteng* symbolizes freedom and nationalism.

banyan—a fig tree with writhing arteries spreading out some 10-15 meters, a sturdy trunk, and an umbrella-shaped crown. This tree is believed to never die, replenishing itself from seedlings which drop from its branches. It may never be cut down, for powerful spirits may dwell within.

bapak—father, headman, leader, male teacher, department head, boss

Batak—a proto-Malayan people of northern Sumatra, one of the ancient peoples of Indonesia

batik—a traditional way of decorating cloth by the wax-resist, or "negative" painting method

becak—Indonesia's bicycle trishaw. Carries two or more passengers, plus goods.

bedaya—a sedate court dance of the Central Javanese *kraton* also seen in East Kalimantan

bemo—a small three- or four-wheeled covered vehicle, with seats for up to nine passengers. In Jakarta, a *bemo* is a motorized tricycle, like the *helicak* but larger.

bendi—a versatile horse-drawn two-wheeled cart used extensively in rural Java and West Sumatra

benteng—an old fortress, either Portuguese, Dutch, Indonesian, or English

bersih desa—an annual village cleansing festival staged after the harvest to rid a town of evil

betelnut—see *sirih*

Bharta-yuddha—a poem masterpiece begun by the court poet Mpu Sedah in A.D. 1157, describing an epic battle in Indian mythology between the five Pandava brothers and their evil cousins the Korawas. The most popular stories and figures of today's *wayang* plays are based directly on this involved story.

bhikku (female: *bhikksuni*)—the Pali form for "religious hermit." On Java it means a Hindu or Buddhist teacher.

Bhinneka Tunggal Ika—an old Sanskrit term attributed to a 13th-century poet and now Indonesia's official motto, meaning "We are many, but we are one," or "Unity in diversity"

Bima—a warrior-lover of the Ramayana. One of the five Pandava brothers, the biggest and baddest, the black-headed giant hero.

bioskop—a movie theater which usually shows violent films from the U.S. or Hong Kong

bis air—a river ferry used in Kalimantan and Sumatra

bis kota—city bus

bis malam—special, fast, more expensive buses that travel long distances at night on Java, Bali, Sulawesi, and Sumatra

blimbing (or "star fruit")—a crispy, watery, thirst-quenching sour fruit that looks like a starfish. Usually yellow, but there are white and green varieties too.

bonze—a Buddhist monk

Brahma—the four-headed Hindu god of creation who gave birth to the Hindu castes; head of the Hindu Trinity. Brahma appears in white robes and rides a goose. Seldom worshipped in Indonesia.

Brahman—the highest Hindu caste

breadfruit—related to figs, the breadfruit (*Artocarpus*) grows all over Indonesia and Polynesia. This massive globose fruit, sometimes weighing 20 kilos, must be cooked before eating. Breadfruit wood is easily worked and its inner bark was once used to make *tapa* cloth.

brem—fiery Balinese wine made from fermented black rice

bubur—Indonesian porridge, a soft semi-liquid food made from rice, coconut, or beans

bupati—a local native chief or government district officer appointed by the minister of internal affairs. *Bupati* is the embodiment of traditional elite culture. In larger towns his function can now be compared to the position of mayor.

C

calung—a xylophonic bamboo instrument of the Tengenan villagers of East Bali

camat—civilian assistant head of a district, second in command after the *bupati*

candi—a Hindu or Buddhist tomb-temple

canting—an implement used for drawing (waxing) *batik* designs

cap—a tin or copper stamp used in the hand-stamped *batik* process

cap cai—Indonesian vegetable and/or meat chop suey

casuarina—a tough, incredibly fire-resistant tree prevalent over Indonesia's drier eastern islands. Sometimes called the "Australian pine," the casuarina has dense, needle-like branches that serve as leaves. In Indonesian, it's called *cemara*.

cecak—small household lizards, formidable killers of mosquitos

cek jalanan turis—traveler's check

cella—a niche in an ancient stone temple containing a divinity, or his or her symbol, or a reincarnated king, nobleman, or noblewoman

cemara—see casuarina

ciku—a sweet, soft fruit, shaped like an egg, brown outside and in

colt—(pronounced "coal") a Japanese-made van. Used all over Indonesia to transport passengers quickly from town to town. More expensive than buses but faster, the closest vehicle extant to an "express" service.

copra—dried coconut meat, from which coconut oil is extracted

cuscus—a nocturnal, tree-dwelling marsupial with soft fur and sharp claws and teeth, found in Irian Jaya, its satellite islands, and Maluku

D

dagob—the highest pinnacle of a stupa

dalang—the *wayang* puppeteer who either manipulates the puppets and speaks the words, or narrates a plot for live actors

Damar Wulan—a Majapahit hero in East Javanese theater

Darul Islam—a murderous group of rebels active around Bandung from 1948 to 1962. Its goal was to set up an Islamic state.

datu—a Batak medicine man, priest, prophet, or physician

debus (or *dabus*)—an awl-like dagger that participants in mystical trance ceremonies use to inflict wounds upon themselves

delman—a large, horse-drawn wagon carrying up to six people

dermaga—pier

desa—a small agrarian village

Dewi Sri—the rice goddess of Java and Bali

dokar—a light, two-wheeled horse carriage for four to six passengers

duku—fruits the size of a ping-pong ball, sweet with a sour tinge

dukun—could be a folk doctor, witch doctor, black magic advocate, herbalist, druggist, village healer, chronicler, bard, diviner, or conjuror and spiritual leader of great prestige

durian—an odorous spiked fruit, with three or four compartments of cream-colored pulp surrounding large pods

E

empu—a *kris* maker

erong—graves hung from high cliffs in Torajaland, South Sulawesi

es—ice; could also mean sweet frozen fruit-flavored water on a stick

es buah (also called *sterup*)—a mixture of fruit with shaved ice and/or sweetened condensed milk, coconut, *bubur,* and chocolate syrup on top

es jus—a combination of fruit, crushed ice, and sweet syrup mixed in a blender. Some spike their *es jus* with liquor.

F

fahombe—a stone-jumping sport of the Nias islanders, once used to train warriors for battle and to prove a young man's fitness to take a wife. Now a tourist spectacle.

G

gado-gado—a rich dish of steamed green beans, soy beans, potatoes, cabbage, or bean sprouts covered in a tangy peanut sauce

Galungan—a Balinese festival when the gods come down to visit the island for a week

gamelan—a Javanese or Balinese percussion-type orchestra, consisting of bronze and wooden xylophones shaped like discs, cylinders, keys, or bulbous hollow bowls beaten with hammers

Ganesha—in Hindu mythology, the household god, god of learning, and god of prosperity. Worshipped before every undertaking to assure success.

gang—alleyway, small lane, path, or street

garuda—a legendary bird, the mount of Vishnu. A common motif in Indonesian art, the bird is the official emblem of the Indonesian Republic.

gayung—water dipper or scoop.

genggong—a Balinese mouth organ

gotong royong—village socialism. A traditional village practice of mutual cooperation in planting, irrigation, and harvesting.

gringsing—in East Bali, the "flaming cloth" weaving design

gudeg—a Yogyanese culinary specialty combining rice with boiled young jackfruit, chicken, egg, and a spicy coconut cream sauce. Sometimes served with boiled buffalo hide.

gunung—mountain. Gunung Merapi means "Mount Merapi."

gunungan—meaning "the story," this is the triangular symbol of the *wayang* theater, set in the middle of the stage when the shadow play begins and ends. It can also be the link that connects different portions of a play; by its motions or the angle in which it is set, it shows the mood of the next scene. The *gunungan* also represents the world cosmic order, harmony and peace with nature, and the Tree of Life.

guru—in the Indonesian sense, anyone who teaches

H

haj—the pilgrimage made by Muslims to Mecca, undertaken by some 40,000 Indonesians each year. A *haji* is a man who has made the pilgrimmage; he wears the white skullcap called a *peci*. *Hajah* is the feminine form. The honorific title "Haji" or "Hajah" may precede a person's name.

halus—describes all behavior or temperaments which are refined, noble, sophisticated

hansip—civil defense units often given neighborhood patrol tasks

Hari Raya—(or Idul Fitri) the Islamic New Year. Several days of festivities which end Ramadan.

helicak—a small motorized three-wheeled vehicle carrying five to eight passengers

hukum tua—in Minahasa, North Sulawesi, the head of a village

huta—Toba-Batak settlement, a small group of houses standing like an island in the midst of a rice field

I

ibu—mother. Also a deferential or affectionate title used to address any older woman.

Idul Fitri—see Hari Raya

ikan bakar—baked fish

ikat—a tie-dye technique which results in a highly unusual and colorful overall design

imigrasi—the immigration department or office

istana—a palace or castle

J

jambu-air—the rose apple (*Syzygium jambos*). A juicy pink, light green, or white bell-shaped fruit about the size of a large strawberry.

jambu-batu—a guava

jam karet—rubber time

jamu—herbal medicine made from a mixture of roots, barks, and grasses, usually steeped in hot water. Some *jamu* are applied directly on the skin, or simply eaten.

jeruk—a term applicable to all citrus fruits. In some parts of Indonesia it means orange or mandarin; in other parts, a grapefruit or a lemon.

jeruk Bali—pomelo (coconut-sized citrus)

jimmy (or *jimny*)—a small, powerful, fuel-efficient Suzuki vehicle

joget (or *joged*)—Indonesia's all-purpose social dance, a kind of contactless cha-cha

juru kunci—caretaker or "keeper of the shrine." You must go to this man for the keys to let you into the temple, monument, museum, or historical site.

K

kabupaten—a regency of a province

kain—a length of material (2.75 meters by 1.2 meters) worn by both men and women, fastened at the waist by a sash. *Kain kebaya* is the national dress of Indonesian women.

kakawin—a classical style of poetry of ancient Javanese courts

kala—a demon that haunts desolate places like the seashores, the deep forests, cemeteries, and crossroads. *Kala* can enter people's bodies and make them idiotic or insane. A *kala*-head is the carved stone head of a monster over temple gates and recesses to ward off demonic forces by magic means; looks like a stylized lion's head.

kamar mandi—bathroom, washroom

kambing—goat

kampung—a village, neighborhood, homestead family, or migrant living compound in the country or city *kanari*—a nut similar to an almond

kancil—also called the "mouse-deer," the *kancil* is not a true deer and has no antlers. Smallest of all hoofed, cud-chewing mammals, it stands no more than one-half meter at the shoulders.

kantor—office

kantor pariwisata—tourist office

kapal laut—a seagoing ship

kapal motor—a small motorboat used for traveling along coasts, up rivers, and across channels or straits

kapok—a silky, waxy fiber taken from the pods of the kapok tree, which grows on higher slopes. Kapok resists vermin and moisture and is good filler for life preservers. Oil from its seeds is used in munitions, food, and soap.

kasar—a term used to describe uncivilized, ungracious, impolite, coarse traits in objects, people, or skills; in poor taste; inappropriate

kauman—the orthodox Islamic quarter of a city, known for its strict adherence to Muslim customs and traditions

Kawi—Old Javanese; the classical literary language of early Javanese and Balinese poetry

kayu besi—ironwood

kayuputih oil—a panacea derived from the *kayuputih* tree (*Eucalyptus alba*). Drink diluted or rub on full strength for stomach aches, head colds, and rashes. Found only in the dry areas of eastern Indonesia.

kebaya—a Chinese long-sleeved blouse with shaped bodice worn by Indonesian women

kecak—a seated choral dance-drama by Balinese men, often called the "monkey dance" because of its characteristic staccato chorus ("*chaka, chaka, chaka*") and body contortions.

kecamatan—subdistrict, the administrative unit that comes under the *kabupaten*

kecap—ketchup or soy sauce

kecapi—a plucked stringed musical instrument used in South Sulawesi; similar instruments are found in the Batak and Gayo areas of northern Sumatra. *Kecapi suling* refers to the lute and flute music of the Sundanese of West Java.

kedai kopi—coffee shop, a local gathering place for men

Kediri—an East Javanese dynasty (A.D. 1049-1222) known mainly for its poetry. Such a large number of literary works were produced that this period is known as Indonesia's Golden Age of Literature.

keelong—a raised platform used by fishermen all over the archipelago to catch fish

kelapa—the coconut tree or its fruit

Ken Arok—a 13th-century Javanese king, subject of a classic of Kawi literature called *The Magic Kris*

kepala desa—village leader or headman. Other names include: *lurah, kepala kampung, kepala negeri,* and *pengulu kampung.*

kerbau—water buffalo.

keroncong—see *kroncong*

ketinting—a small motorized canoe designed for river travel in the interior of Kalimantan

ketoprak—a Javanese folk play

klotok—a specialized, canopied, motorized river craft of Kalimantan

kolintang—a wooden xylophonic orchestra used in Minahasa, North Sulawesi

Konfrontasi—the period (1962-65) when the Sukarno regime threatened Malaysia with military intervention because of Malaysia's alleged neocolonialist policies

korupsi—corruption, graft

kraton—a small walled and fortified palace city, the supreme center of worship in the Hindu-Javanese system of rule

kretek—clove cigarettes

kris—a Javanese or Balinese double-edged dagger, simultaneously a weapon, an ornament, a cultic object, and the finest example of Indonesian metalcraft

kris dance—the most violent and dramatic of Balinese dances; used often as an exorcism. Also called the *barong* dance.

Krishna—a Hindu god of human form, a magnificent warrior and a great lover, the eighth incarnation of Vishnu, worshipped in his own right

kroncong—the Indonesian ukulele; gentle melancholy music played in Nusatenggara and Jakarta

krupuk—fried prawn or fish crisps

kuda kepang—a flat hobby horse made of painted bamboo used in a folk-play trance dance of the same name

kulkul—a drum tower found in Javanese and Balinese villages which sounds the alarm or calls people to meetings

L

ladang—slash-and-burn cultivation

lahar—lava or mud emitted from active volcanos

lakon—the content or plot of a *wayang* play

lapangan—field, square, park, shopping plaza

laskar—paramilitary troops or guerrillas

legong—a classical Balinese dance performed by two young girls, considered by many the most beautiful and graceful of the Balinese dance ballets

leyak—on Bali, an evil spirit that haunts dark, lonely places, roads, and graveyards. The *leyak* can assume any shape, devours the entrails of babies and corpses, casts spells, and drinks blood from the necks of sleeping people.

liana—any of various high-climbing, usually woody vines common in the tropics

liang—graves hewn out of cliffs by the Torajas of South Sulawesi

linga—a Hindu religious symbol in the form of an upright stone column; the phallic emblem of Shiva and of male potency

loket—train or bus ticket window

longbot—a long, thin river craft capable of high speeds, propelled by as many as three outboard motors, used in Kalimantan

longsat—a small round fruit with a yellowish white skin and sweet white meat

lontar—a species of palm tree (*Corypha gebanga*) which provides food, shelter, utensils, and ornaments. Its fan-like leaves are used to plait sacks and as fishing nets, food covers, and baskets.

lontong—rice steamed in a banana leaf

losmen—rooms to let; cheaper than hotels but just as adequate. On Bali, a *losmen* is usually a native-style house, a family-run inn.

ludruk—a theater form, created this century, which is popular in the big cities of Indonesia

lurah—a village head on Java elected traditionally by secret ballot but now sometimes appointed by the government

lurik—a finely woven striped textile of Yogyakarta

M

Mahabharata—a Hindu epic containing 100,000 couplets, the longest epic poem in the world. The legend of a tremendous 18-day battle between two family groups during the Vedic Age in India (1500-500 B.C.). Translated into Kawi in the Middle Ages, this Indian masterpiece by Vyasa plays a gigantic part in Indonesian literature, art, and theater.

Majapahit—an ancient East Javanese empire that held power over much of Indonesia from A.D. 1294-1398. The mightiest indigenous kingdom in Indonesia's history, it was finally dissolved by Indonesian princes in A.D. 1527.

makara—a formalized mythical aquatic animal figure in old Javanese sculpture, combining the features of a dolphin with those of a crocodile. Also the Asian zodiac sign of Cancer.

maleo—a jungle-fowl (*Megapodiidae*). Some species lay their eggs in black volcanic beach sand.

mambruk—the crown pigeon; a large blue-gray bird with a purple-brown breast, wings marked by two transverse bars, and a tuft of finely ramified feathers on its head. Found only in Maluku and Irian Jaya; now a protected species.

mandau—the traditional sword of Kalimantan's Dayak tribes

mandi—a cement, palm, or bamboo bathroom with a large cement tub; you dip water from the tub and throw it over your body, elephant-fashion.

mangosteen—a round purple-black skinned fruit with a whorl of green sepals on top. Inside, white, sweet-sour juicy segments huddle into a ball. Comes into season Jan.-March.

martabak—a thin, fried Arabian pancake stuffed with meat, egg, and/or vegetables

Mataram—a Hindu empire which reached its apogee in the 16th and 17th centuries, represented today in the sultanates of Yogyakarta and Solo. Though it professed Islam, Mataram retained a Hindu-Buddhist state structure.

Menak Jonggo—a deadly enemy of the Majapahit hero Damar Wulan, a very evil literary character, used as a central theme in *wayang golek*

merdeka—freedom

meru—a Javanese mountain of heaven, named for the sacred mountain of India. *Meru* is also a pagoda-like thatch roof found on Bali.

mesin becak—a motorcycle with sidecar; motorized *becak*

mesjid—mosque

mie—noodles

mie goreng—fried noodles with meat and/or vegetables

muara—estuary, mouth of a river

muezzin—the men who call Muslims to prayer from high towers on the mosques

mufakat—discussion to reach a consensus agreement

muncak—a small, graceful variety of deer found on Timor and Java, sometimes called the "barking deer"

N

naga—a Hindu mythological serpent charged with magic powers

nangka—jackfruit; sweet, refreshing, fibrous, segmented fruit weighing up to 20 kilos

nasi—rice

nasi campur—a combination of eggs, vegetables, meat or fish, and sauce on top of a heap of steamed rice

nasi liwet—a Solonese specialty of rice cooked in *santen* with garnishes

nasi padang—rice with many side dishes, usually quite spicy-hot (*pedas*)

nasi pecal—a breakfast dish similar to *gado-gado* with boiled vegetables and fried soybean cake

negeri—district

Nyai Loro Kidul—the South Sea goddess, said to be the legendary wife of a 16th-century Mataram ruler, still venerated along the south coast of Java

nyale—sea worm believed to possess oracular powers

O

oplet—a small covered pickup truck with side benches in back, used to transport passengers in cities and between villages and towns for short distances cheaply. In Sumatra, an *oplet* is a small bus seating about 25 or more people.

OPM—Operasi Papua Merdeka. A guerrilla force in Irian Jaya which has resisted Indonesian occupation since 1969

orang—man, people

Orang Laut—aboriginal nomadic sea gypsies or fishermen

owa—a tailless gibbon easily recognizable by its face ringed by a hood of fine tufted white hair; found in Sumatra, Kalimantan, and West Java

P

Padri War—a violent Muslim reform movement in the Minangkabau region of West Sumatra (1804-37)

pala—a sweet-sour nutmeg fruit of the nutmeg tree of Maluku and North Sulawesi

pamong—in Solo, a "guide" for spiritual development. Could also mean caretaker, supporter, mentor, educator, teacher.

panakawan—grotesque figures offering comic relief in *wayang* performances, equivalent to medieval court jesters

Pancasila—a Sanskrit phrase meaning "The Five Principles," a political philosophy put forth in 1945 by Sukarno to provide a constitutional basis for the Republic. The five principles are belief in one of the four great universal religions, nationalism, Indonesian-style "guided" democracy, humanitarianism, and a just and prosperous society.

pandanus—leaves of a species of tree native to Indonesia. Used in building, making utensils, wrapping, or for clothing. *Pandan* in Indonesian.

pangeran—literally prince, lord; an honorific term for a saint, royal personage, or nobleman

pangolin—anteater; *trenggiling* in Indonesian

Panji Cycle—an extensive cycle of 15th-century Javanese stories, of many different written and oral versions. Staged often at wedding parties, this cycle serves as theme for mask plays (*topeng*) and some puppet plays.

parang—chopping knife, machete, cleaver

pasanggrahan—government lodge, resthouse, or forestry hut which may accept travelers for a modest price or free; sometimes a commercial venture or hotel

pasar—market

pas jalan—See *surat jalan*

pastoran—parish house

peci (or *kopiah*)—Indonesian felt or velvet cap, an Islamic religious symbol of tradition and power

pedanda—a high priest of the Bali-Hindu religion

pegawai—a white-collar worker, functionary, staff member, or employee. Most often a civil servant or government official.

pemangku—curators of the temple; temple priests

pemuda—young man; youth. During the 1945-50 independence struggle, the word was synonymous with "revolutionary bands."

pencak silat—the national Indonesian art of self-defense; both a lethal fighting skill and a graceful art form

pendeta—Protestant clergyman; Hindu or Buddhist priest

pendopo—a traditional, ornate, open-air pillared pavilion with a low pyramidal overhanging roof found usually in a *kraton* or in front of a Javanese nobleman's house

pengulu—a headman in a Batak or Sumbawan village

penginapan—a cheap hotel with plain facilities

penjaga—guard or watchman at a temple site, bank, residence, hotel

perkutut—a Javanese singing bird that looks like a dove with a pale blue head and rosy breast. Highly valued by the Javanese and Chinese; mythology claims selection and care of the right *perkutut* will result in good luck.

Pertamina—Indonesia's mammoth state-run oil company

pesarian—Islamic school

PHPA—Dinas Perlindungan dan Pengawetan Alam, the Indonesian Forestry Service

pikulan—a pole that looks like an archery bow and rests on the shoulders of a laborer or peddler on the move. Bricks, water, and other burdens are suspended from each end.

pisang—banana

PKI—Partai Komunis Indonesia. The Communist Party of Indonesia, dissolved on 12 March 1966 by order of President Suharto.

plangi—a tie-dye technique practiced in Lombok, Palembaŋ in South Sumatra, and the eastern districts of Java and Bali

polisi—police

pondok—cottage, hut, cabin, hotel, or Muslim boarding school

prahu—swift, strong, wooden sailing boat or outrigger of Malay origin

pria—man, male

pribumi—of native stock, not of immigrant blood

priyayi—the established aristocratic administrative class of Java. Roughly the successor of the old Hindu Satriya caste, today they're senior officials and professionals, generally the intelligentsia and new business group. Now the term is used more to describe a cultured person or cultured behavior.

puak—tribe, ethnic group, or clan

puasa—Islamic fasting month

puputan—Balinese ritual suicide

pura—a Balinese terrace temple consisting of three tiers enclosed by walls

puri—on Bali, a palace of a prince

pusaka—sacred heirlooms

R

rafflesia—a giant flower of Sumatra and Kalimantan

raja—a prince, lord, or king. On Bali it may still be used to refer to male Hindu royalty.

raksasa—a mythical giant from Hindu mythology; sculptures and reliefs of *raksasa* figures often guard entrances to temples

Ramadan (or Puasa)—the Muslim month of fasting which takes place on the ninth month of the Muslim calendar

Ramayana—an Indian epic poem containing 18 books and 24,000 verses divided into 500 songs, all about an Aryan king of the Indian Vedic Age. The hero Rama (Vishnu reincarnated) defeats the wicked King Rawana of Ceylon, who has stolen his consort and is generally troubling the world.

rambutan—litchi; a hairy red-skinned fruit with sweet white juicy meat; tastes like a very sweet grape

rante—a special field for funeral ceremonies in Torajaland

rawon—rice with spiced sauce. Some versions are a spicy-hot beef or buffalo meat soup with fried onions sprinkled on top and served with *lontong*.

rebab—a one-stringed violin of Arab-Persian origin

rempeyek—round peanut crisps fried in spiced batter

rendang—spiced beef in a thick rich sauce made from a Minangkabau recipe of West Sumatra; can last without refrigeration for as long as a month

reyog—form of *wayang topeng,* a masked dance with a small number of performers, including a ferocious tiger with a peacock atop it, a red warrior figure, and a giant

rijstaffel—means literally "rice table." A tropical smorgasbord, a banquet specialty. Boiled rice is the base, with 20-40 individual spicy side dishes: meat, fish, eggs, and vegetables in various curries and sauces, fruit, fish, dried coconuts and nuts, and on and on.

romusha—slave laborers used by the Japanese during WW II

ronde—a warm Javanese drink sold in *warung* and by street vendors, made from ginger syrup, peanuts, fruit slices, hot water, and yellow balls of glutinous rice

rotan—rattan, a tough pliable vine used to make handicrafts and furniture

rumah adat—a traditional native-style house, usually old

rumah makan—eating place, restaurant, cafe

rumah sakit—hospital or clinic

rupiah—the Indonesian monetary unit

rusa—deer (*Cervus timorensis*)

S

sago—a starchy, low protein food extracted from the sago palm, the staple diet of the rural populations of Indonesia's eastern islands

Sailendra—the builders of Borobudur, a feudal Buddhist dynasty that ruled around A.D. 700-856

salak—a pear-shaped, plum-sized soury fruit with a brown snake-like skin; comes from a palm tree

sambal—a hot spicy chili sauce consisting of fresh chilies, garlic, sugar, salt, vinegar, and onions

sambar—a deer (*Cervus unicolor*) with a set of three-pointed antlers, related to the European red deer and the American wapati. Used synonymously with *rusa.*

sampan—a small sailboat used over short distances in western Indonesia

sanghyang dedari—a famous Balinese trance dance performed by two untrained young girls who dance in unison on top of men's shoulders

santri—a Muslim who embraces the ethics and values of orthodox Islam and commerce

sarung—a *kain* with both ends sewn together, used by men, women, and children. Worn with a tight sheathlike effect, the slack of this long, loose tubular-shaped step-in skirt is folded and tucked in.

sasando—plucked bamboo tube zither of Roti, Timor, and surrounding islands

sate—a national dish, much like the *kebab* found throughout the Arab world. Chicken, beef, mutton, seafood, or entrails (the Chinese prepare it with pork) are threaded on thin bamboo skewers and grilled over a charcoal fire. Often served with a sharp peanut sauce.

sawah—flooded fields of rich, deep mud artificially constructed, often terraced, and continuously cultivated with a specialized crop, usually rice

sawo—a fruit, the sapodilla plum, shaped like a potato; has the texture and flavor of sweetbread

Sekaten—Mohammed's birthday. Celebrated with special week-long ceremonies and festivals in Yogyakarta and Solo.

sekotang—a spicy-hot herb-flavored tea

selamatan—ceremonial meal

selendang—a long narrow shawl or shoulder cloth; also may be worn around the breast. It can be used as a backsling for carrying babies and burderns, but is generally thrown over one shoulder or wrapped around the head for warmth or fashion. On Bali, called a *kamben cerik.*

selimut raja—the finest of the handwoven *ikat* burial blankets made on the island of Sumba, Nusatenggara

serimpi—any of the dances of the Central Javanese palace courts characterized by fluttering scarves and straight-backed dancers. Dating from Hindu times, this is the basic classical dance of Javanese women.

serow—the goat antelope of Sumatra, adapted to life in high mountain areas

Shiva—in the Hindu galaxy of gods Shiva is one of the mightiest, the destroyer of the world. Still the most venerated of the gods of India. In Indonesia he also takes the form of the supreme teacher, Maha Guru, or the supreme god, Maha Dewa.

siamang—a black gibbon or lesser ape found on Sumatra and in Western Malaysia

Simalungun—one of the five main Batak clans of eastern North Sumatra

Singosari—an ancient, ruthless Javanese dynasty (A.D. 1222-1293) with an official faith of Buddhist-Shivaite syncretism

sirih—betelnut; its scarlet seeds, chewed mostly by older people all over Indonesia, cause a mild euphoric state

sirsak—soursop, a rich, sweet-sour fruit with a creamy texture

songket—a gold-threaded fabric woven by the floating-weft technique. *Sarung songket* is the traditional wear for Indonesian bridegrooms.

sopi—an alcoholic drink; Indonesian gin

soto—a spicy soup found all over Indonesia; served with rice or *lontong,* soybean sprouts, chicken, mutton, or beef, and garnished with onions

soto ayam—Javanese chicken broth

soto madura—a rich coconut-milk soup full of noodles, bean sprouts and other vegetables, and chicken

spetbot—a long motorboat with an outboard motor used in western Indonesia

Sriwijaya—an empire which may have flourished in southern Sumatra near present-day Palembang during the 12th century

stanplats—a bus, *oplet, bemo,* colt, or taxi station; an assembly point for all these conveyances

stasiun kereta api—railroad station

stempel—a long narrow river craft of Kalimantan that travels at high speeds and rides so close to the water passengers often get wet

stupa—a bell-shaped burial place for the remains or relics of Buddha or one of his disciples, or of Buddhists

subak—the village water board in southern Balinese villages that controls irrigation, canal building, and maintainance

Subud—a religious, commercial, nondenominational association on Java. Embracing much Islamic philosophy, Subud has centers all over the world.

suling—flute

sunan—the titular and spiritual head of Solo's Kraton Hadiningrat. Also the title of a *wali* and the name of his burial place. See *wali.*

Sundanese—the main ethnic group of West Java

surat ijin—see *surat jalan*

surat jalan—a letter or travel permit that may be required in the Outer Islands

surau—a Minangkabau meeting house for men and boys; here they study cooking and the Koran

syahbandar—the harbormaster, found in every port in Indonesia

T

tanuk—tapir, a prehistoric pig-like animal still extant in the forests of Sumatra and Kalimantan

tau-tau—lifesize statues representing deceased people placed on balconies outside cliffside graves in Torajaland

tegalan—a permanent garden or field. Planted with rice during the wet season, and maize, cassava, sweet potatoes, ground nuts, chili peppers, and vegetables during the dry. This system is used in areas that can't be irrigated and rely on rainwater.

tempe—a protein-rich cake made from fermented soybeans

Tempo Doeloe—roughly translated "the Old Days," of or pertaining to the time of the Netherlands East Indies empire

THR—Taman Hiburan Rakyat or "People's Parks"; entertainment complexes found in towns and cities all over Indonesia

toko—shop, store

tongkonan—a special ceremonial house used for religious activities, burials, and marriages, and also for sleeping. Built by upper-class Torajas.

transmigrasi—a government program aimed at depopulating Java and Bali by resettling Javanese and Balinese individuals or communities in the Outer Islands

trapel cek—traveler's check; *cek jalanan turis* is perhaps a more widely understood term

trepang—smoked and dried sea cucumber; the Chinese put it in soups

tritik—a textile-decorating process in which designs are stitched on the fabric, then the thread is pulled tightly so only the exposed areas are dyed, leaving the areas underneath the threads and tucks colorless until re-dyed or restitched in a different pattern

tuak—rice, palm (*arin*), or sago beer

tugbot—a long, flat-bottomed, motorized, slow river craft with a shelter; used in Kalimantan

tukang—artisan, workman, skilled laborer; one who does something, i.e. *tukang portret* (photographer), *tukang listerik* (electrician)

U

udang—shrimp

ulos—an oblong fabric created by the *ikat* process, worn in the Bataklands of North Sumatra by both men and women. Dull deep colors are characteristic.

V

Vishnu—in the Hindu pantheon of gods, the guardian of the world. Vishnuism attached great value to the service and love of God, thereby achieving identity of existence with him.

VOC—Vereenigde Oost-Indische Compagnie, the United East India Company

W

wadian—female shaman in Kalimantan's Dayak regions

wakil—a government agent, representative, deputy; the civilian counterpart of a military jurisdictional commander

wali—one of the nine legendary holy men who introduced Islam into Java

wanita—woman

waringin—see banyan

waruga—a pre-Christian Minahasan sarcophagus, shaped like a prism

warung—a poor man's restaurant; a foodstall or portable kitchen. Many also sell coffee, soft drinks, cigarettes, canned foods, and *sirih*.

wayang—a dramatic puppet theater. In the strict sense it means flat, carved-leather puppets of the shadow play, but in a broad sense it could mean any dramatic performance.

wisma—guesthouse

Y

YHA—Youth Hostel Association

yoni—a stylized vagina usually carved out of stone; the Hindu symbol of female life-giving force

BOOKLIST

ANTHROPOLOGY

Barley, Nigel. *Not A Hazardous Sport*. London: Penguin, 1989. Accounts of Torajan responses to Western customs are a bright spot in an otherwise unmemorable book.

Dove, Michael R., ed. *The Real and Imagined Role of Culture in Development: Case Studies From Indonesia*. Honolulu: University of Hawaii Press, 1988. An examination of the interaction between government development policies and traditional cultures throughout Indonesia. Nine case studies from Western and Indonesian scholars.

Dumarcay, Jacques. *The House in South-East Asia*. Singapore: Oxford University Press, 1987. Covers domestic architectural forms from the earliest reconstructions of the Dongson culture through the different regional variants of the archipelago. Lavishly illustrated.

Hefner, Robert W. *Hindu Javanese: Tengger Tradition and Islam*. Princeton, NJ: Princeton University Press, 1989. A scholarly study of Tengger religion and culture, past and present.

Lebar, Frank M., ed. *Ethnic Groups of Insular Southeast Asia*. New Haven, CT: Human Relations Area Files Press, 1972. One of the very few systematic surveys of the people and cultures of insular Southeast Asia. Includes bibliographies and ethnolinguistic maps.

Wallace, Alfred Russell. *The Malay Archipelago*. Singapore: Graham Brash Pte. Ltd., 1983. A reprint of the 1869 classic. Represents seven years of research by this great British naturalist on the flora, fauna, and ethnology of numerous outer islands. Still a brilliant, exhaustive, and valid study of natural phenomena, as well as an exciting travelogue.

ARTS AND CRAFTS

Borneo and Beyond: Tribal Arts of Indonesia, East Malaysia and Madagascar. Singapore: Bareo Gallery, 1990. Stunning color photos of tribal artifacts fill this expertly printed large-format book. Includes tools, masks, and ancestor figures.

Draeger, Donn. *Weapons and Fighting Arts of the Indonesian Archipelago*. Rutland, VT: Charles E. Tuttle, 1972. The only book on the subject. Incorporates entertaining travel anecdotes.

Elliott, Inger McCabe. *Batik: Fabled Cloth of Java*. New York: Clarkson N. Potter, 1984. A sumptuous book of color photos examining 120 extraordinary *batik* pieces; extensive black and white photos and text.

Feldman, Jerome. *The Eloquent Dead*. Los Angeles: UCLA Museum of Cultural History, 1985. Covers the ancestral art of the Nias, Batak, Dayak, Torajan, Lesser Sundas, Maluku, and Biak areas, as well as other linguistically related areas of Southeast Asia.

Fraser-Lu, Sylvia. *Indonesian Batik: Processes, Patterns and Places*. Oxford: Oxford University Press, 1986. Describes the traditional *batik* of Central Java; as well as north coast art.

Frey, Edward. *The Kris: Mystic Weapon of the Malay World*. Oxford: Oxford University Press, 1986. This mysterious weapon examined by a leading expert in Malay weaponry.

Hering, B. *Candi and Pura: A Pictorial History*. Australia: Centre for Southeast Asian Studies, James Cooke University, 1985. Photos vividly depict the most striking examples of early medieval Indonesian monumental art.

Hitchcock, Michael. *Indonesian Textile Techniques*. Aylesbury, U.K.: Shire Publications, 1985. A concise volume on the complex and fascinating textile traditions of Indonesia.

Holt, Claire. *Art in Indonesia: Continuities and Change*. Ithaca, NY: Cornell University Press, 1967. The best on this very broad subject. Covers the ancient ruins of Java and Bali, as well as the performing and plastic arts.

Horridge, Adrian. *Sailing Craft of Indonesia*. Oxford: Oxford University Press, 1986. An introduction to the various types of sailing craft used in Indonesia.

Kartomi, Margaret J. *Musical Instruments of Indonesia*. Melbourne: Indonesian Arts Society, 1985. An illustrated survey of the full range of musical instruments used in Indonesia, from xylophones and gongs to bowed strings and mouth organs.

Kempers, Bernet. *Ancient Indonesian Art*. Amsterdam: D.P.J. van der Peet, 1959. The be-all, end-all book for this subject. Very scholarly, accurate information. Know your Hindu mythology before diving in.

Spee, Miep. *Traditional and Modern Batik*. Kenthurst, Australia: Kangaroo Press, 1982. Covers all aspects of *batik* from its ancient origins to modern forms. A useful handbook for beginners.

Wagner, Frits A. *The Art of an Island Group*. New York: Greystone Press, 1967. Useful general account covering art, literature, dance, and drama from prehistoric times to independence.

Willetts, William. *Ceramic Art of Southeast Asia*. Singapore: S.E. Asia Ceramics Society, 1971. Though difficult to find, this book is one of the best on the subject.

BALI

Bali. Singapore: Times Editions, 1986. Vivid full-color photos depict every facet of Balinese daily life and culture.

Baum, Vicki. *A Tale From Bali*. Singapore: Oxford University Press, 1984. First published in 1937, this historical novel portrays the famous *puputan* death charge of Balinese royalty in 1906. A remarkable study of Balinese character, customs, and way of life.

Black, Star, and Willard A. Hanna. *Insight Guides: Bali*. Singapore: APA Publications, 1989. This fascinating photographic overview of Bali has been a classic from the day it first left the presses in 1970.

Charlé, Suzanne. *An Illustrated Guide to Bali*. Hong Kong: The Guidebook Company, 1990. This colorful travel guide by a Bali resident includes profiles of individual islanders and focuses on Bali's changing culture.

Coast, John. *Dancers of Bali*. New York: G.P. Putnam's Sons, 1953. After joining with the Indonesian nationalists to help expel the Dutch, Coast was the first dance impresario to organize a tour of Balinese dancers and musicians to Europe and America.

Covarrubias, Miguel. *Island of Bali*. Oxford University Press, 1972. Written and illustrated by a Mexican painter who lived and worked in Bali for two years in the 1930s; Covarrubias was one of the first to call what the Balinese were living and creating "art."

Daniel, Ana. *Bali: Behind the Mask*. New York: Alfred A. Knopf, Inc., 1981. During several extended stays in Bali, the author/photographer documented her experiences studying under one of Bali's last great classical dancers, I Nyoman Kakul.

de Zoete, Beryl, and Walter Spies. *Dance and Drama in Bali*. New York: Harper and Brothers Publishers, 1939. Best introduction to the traditional dances and dance dramas of Bali. Out of print.

Djelantik, A.A.M. *Balinese Paintings*. Singapore: Oxford University Press, 1986. A concise study of Balinese painting styles. Extensively illustrated.

Eiseman, Fred, and Margaret Eiseman. *Woodcarvings of Bali*. Berkeley: Periplus, 1988. The history, styles, and practicalities of Balinese woodcarving are presented in detail in this colorful guide.

Eiseman, Fred B., Jr. *Bali: Sekala and Niskala*. Vol. 1. Berkeley: Periplus, 1989. A collection of essays examining Balinese religion, rituals, and art.

Gorer, Geoffrey. *Bali and Angkor*. Singapore: Oxford University Press, 1986. A 1930s travel writer analyzes the roles played by art and religion in the life of the Balinese.

Kemper, A.J. Bernet. *Monumental Bali*. Netherlands: Van Goor Zonen Den Haag, 1977. A good introduction to Balinese archaeology, concentrating on the mysterious early period but with many connections to later Balinese culture.

Koke, Louise G. *Our Hotel in Bali*. New Zealand: January Books, 1987. How two young Americans made their dream come true by opening one of the first Balinese tourist hotels on Kuta Beach in the 1930s.

Mabbett, Hugh. *The Balinese*. New Zealand, January Books, 1985. An excellent introduction to all elements of Balinese life.

McPhee, Colin. *A House in Bali*. Singapore: Oxford University Press, 1985. An amusing and sympathetic look at Balinese society and a rare look at the importance of music in Balinese life.

Mason, Victor, and Frank Jarvis. *Birds of Bali*. Berkeley: Periplus, 1989. Over 100 notable species are included, with color illustrations, descriptions, and scientific information.

Powell, Hickman. *The Last Paradise*. Singapore: Oxford University Press, 1986. A description of Bali's inhabitants, customs, and beliefs before the advent of modern tourism.

Ramseyer, Urs. *The Art and Culture of Bali*. Singapore: Oxford University Press, 1986. This large-format book explains the social,

religious, and philosophic concepts that rule the lives of the Balinese.

Vickers, Adrian. *Bali: A Paradise Created*. Ringwood, Victoria, Australia: Penguin Books Australia, 1989. An overview of Bali history, from its "savage" beginnings to modern tourism. Thoroughly researched and well-presented.

Winterton, Bradley. *The Insider's Guide to Bali*. Edison, NJ: Hunter Publishing, 1989. A thorough guide, packed with color photos, for travelers seeking an "earthly paradise."

GENERAL

Blair, Lawrence. *Ring of Fire: Exploring the Last Remote Places of the World*. New York: Bantam Books, 1988. The story of two brothers who, for 12 years starting in 1973, penetrated and filmed some of the most remote regions of Indonesia.

Dalton, Bill. *Introduction to Indonesia*. Hong Kong: Odyssey Guides, 1991. A detailed introductory guide for the traveler, packed with color photos and maps. Includes literary excerpts concerning Indonesia.

Dekker, N.A. Douwes. *Tanah Air Kita*. The Hague: W. Van Houve Ltd. A wonderful pictorial mosaic of 350 black and white and 16 color photos taken in the 1950s. This large-format book is a valuable record of postwar Indonesia.

Draine, Cathie, and Barbara Hall. *Culture Shock! Indonesia*. Singapore: Times Books International, 1986. An excellent guide to interacting with Indonesians at all social and business levels: the character of the people, their social etiquette, customs, world view, and expectations.

Indonesia: A Country Study. United States Government, 1983. A good broad introduction to the historical setting, society, environment, economy, government, and politics of Indonesia. Useful maps.

Indonesia: A Voyage Through the Archipelago. Paris: Millet Weldon Owen, 1990. Photographers from around the world capture the striking beauty of the archipelago in this luxurious coffee-table book.

Indonesia From the Air. Jakarta and Singapore: PT Humpuss and Times Editions, 1985. One of the few books to capture the breathtaking patterns and rhythms of the entire archipelago.

Jones, Howard Palfrey. *Indonesia: The Possible Dream.* New York: Harcourt Brace Jovanovich, Inc., 1971. A former U.S. Ambassador's relationships with Sukarno and other political and military leaders, as well as his account of the explosive aftermath of the 1965 coup.

Kipp, Rita Smith, and Susan Rodgers. *Indonesian Religions in Transition.* Tucson: University of Arizona Press, 1987. Examines mantric Islam among the Javanese, Sufism among the Highland Gayo, new syncretisms formed from *adat,* and the transformation of "primitive" religious rituals by the expanding tourist industry.

Krannich, Ronald L., and Caryl Rae Krannich. *Shopping and Traveling in Exotic Indonesia.* Woodbridge, VA: Impact Publications, 1991. A handy guide for the traveler looking for bargains.

Neill, Wilfred T. *Twentieth-Century Indonesia.* New York: Columbia University Press, 1973. A very thorough survey of Indonesia's physical environment, history, and culture.

Oey, Eric. *Indonesia.* Singapore: APA Productions, 1986. This thorough guide presents the Indonesian archipelago in all its compelling beauty and diversity.

Palmier, Leslie. *Understanding Indonesia.* Hampshire, England: Gower Publishing Co., 1985. Revised versions of a lecture series given at Oxford in 1983.

Stewart, Ian Charles. *Indonesians: Portraits from an Archipelago.* Singapore: Concept Media Pte Ltd., 1983. Some 280 full-color photos of all the main geographic and cultural regions of Indonesia.

Wilhelm, Donald. *Emerging Indonesia.* London: Quiller Press Ltd., 1985. Indonesia's dynamic pace of development examined against the critical political events of the past 40 years.

Winks, Robin W., and James R. Rush. *Asia In Western Fiction.* Honolulu: University of Hawaii Press, 1990. A scholarly guide to literary stereotyping of Asia and its peoples, with a chapter on Indonesia.

HISTORY

Adams, Cindy. *Sukarno: An Autobiography as Told by Cindy Adams.* New York: Bobbs-Merrill Co., Inc., 1965. Details conditions in Indonesia during Dutch rule. Sukarno's charisma jumps from every page.

Benda, Harry J. *The Crescent and the Rising Sun: Indonesian Islam Under the Japanese Occupation 1942-1945.* The Hague: W. van Hoeve, 1958. An excellent treatise on Islam in Indonesia. The war years are given the most detailed treatment.

Day, Clive. *The Dutch in Java.* New York: Oxford University Press, 1966. Though some of the material is historically inaccurate, this history is fascinating reading.

Hanifah, Abu. *Tales of a Revolution.* Australia: Angus and Robertson Pty Ltd., 1972. An Indonesian's personal experiences during the struggle for independence against the Dutch.

Hughes, John. *Indonesian Upheaval.* New York: David McKay Company, 1967. Describes the alleged communist coup of 1965 and ensuing events. Valuable despite its red-baiting; written in a suspenseful, tight style.

Kahin, Audrey. *Regional Dynamics of the Indonesian Revolution.* Honolulu: University of Hawaii Press, 1985. Essays on the postwar social revolution pitting Indonesian against Indonesian in a scramble for power.

Lovestrand, Harold. *Hostage in Djakarta.* Chicago: Moody Press, 1967. A missionary's experience of imprisonment and trial in Indonesia during the political turmoil of the 1960s.

Masselman, George. *The Cradle of Colonialism.* New Haven: Yale University Press, 1963. The author puts a new perspective on the early history of the Netherlands East Indies by utilizing long-neglected Dutch archives.

McCoy, Alfred. *Southeast Asia Under Japanese Occupation.* New Haven: Yale University Southeast Asia Studies, 1985. Nine essays which reassess the thesis that the "Japanese interregnum" formed a distinct and decisive epoch in Southeast Asian history.

Mossman, James. *Rebels in Paradise.* London: Jonathon Cape, 1961. A journalist's view of Indonesia's civil war (1958) in which North Sulawesi and West Sumatra declared themselves separate states.

Raffles, Thomas S. *The History of Java.* Vols. 1 and 2. London: Black, Parbury, and Allen, 1965. A monumental work written by the English governor-general in the early 19th century.

Reid, Anthony. *The Indonesian National Revolution.* Hawthorn, Victoria, Australia: Longman, 1974. Concise account of the Indonesian revolution and the formation of the Indonesian state.

Simatupang, T. *Report from Banaran: Experiences During the People's War.* New York: Cornell University Southeast Asia Program, 1972. The first full-length book in any language devoted to the climax of the 1948 revolution.

Tantri, K'Tut. *Revolt in Paradise.* London: Heinemann, 1960. A passionate book by an American woman who went to Bali in the 1930s, was adopted by a Balinese *raja,* thrown in prison and tortured by the Japanese, and fought for Indonesian independence after WW II.

Van Heekeren, H.R. *The Stone Age of Indonesia.* Amsterdam: M. Nijhoff, 1958. One of the best studies of Indonesia's prehistory. See also companion volume, *The Bronze Age of Indonesia.*

Wilson, Greta O. *Regents, Reformers, and Revolutionaries.* Honolulu: University Press of Hawaii, 1978. An anthology illustrating diverse aspects of early 20th century Indonesian social change.

IRIAN JAYA

Harrar, Heinrich. *I Come From the Stone Age.* London: R. Hart-Davis, 1964. A famous explorer's account of his mountain-climbing expedition to West New Guinea.

Merrifield, Gregerson, and Ajamiseba. *Gods, Heroes, Kinsmen.* Dallas: International Museum of Cultures, 1983. Ethnographic studies of the spirits and belief systems of seven different Irian Jaya tribes.

Mitton, Robert. *The Lost World of Irian Jaya.* Melbourne: Oxford University Press, 1985. A pictorial study of the cultures and environments of five distinct groups living along the Baliem River.

Monbiot, George. *Poisoned Arrows: An Investigative Journey Through Indonesia.* London: Abacus, 1989. An adventurous investigation of the effects of transmigration on the indigenous peoples of Irian Jaya's "forbidden territories."

Muller, Kal. *New Guinea: Journey Into the Stone Age.* Chicago: Passport Books, 1990. The first comprehensive travel guide to this undeveloped land, with maps and color photos.

Schneebaum, Tobias. *Asmat Images.* Minneapolis: Crosier Missions, 1985. A detailed guide, in English and Indonesian, to a selection of Asmat museum artifacts. (Order from Crosier Missions, 3204 E. 43rd St., Minneapolis, MN 55406.)

Temple, Philip. *Nawok*. London: J.M. Dent, 1962. A 1961 New Zealand expedition into Irian Jaya's highest mountain ranges.

JAVA

Abeyasekere, Susan. *Jakarta: A History*. Oxford: Oxford University Press, 1987. The first general history of Jakarta, with maps and photos excellently presented. In spite of its charitable treatment of the Suharto regime, this book is banned in Indonesia.

Banner, Hubert S. *Romantic Java*. Philadelphia: J.B. Lippincott, 1927. An early 20th-century description of Java's peoples, customs, arts, and natural beauty.

Carpenter, Frank G. *Java and the East Indies*. New York: Doubleday, Page and Co., 1923. Covers Java (mostly), Sumatra, Sulawesi, the Maluku, Borneo, and West New Guinea.

De Wit, Augusta. *Java: Facts and Fancies*. Oxford: Oxford University Press, 1987. Travels in Java at the outset of the new Dutch "Ethical Policy" during the first decade of this century. An important social document and a good read.

Dumarcay, Jacques. *Borobudur*. Oxford: Oxford University Press, 1985. A complete examination of one of the largest religious monuments in the world.

Dumarcay, Jacques. *The Temples of Java*. Oxford: Oxford University Press, 1986. A study of all the main Hindu and Buddhist monuments of Central and East Java constructed between the 7th and 15th centuries.

Geertz, Clifford. *The Religion of Java*. Chicago: University of Chicago Press, 1976. A reprint of a 1961 classic. Still a gold mine of highly readable details of Javanese religion, customs, and values.

Hatley, Ron, J. Schiller, A. Lucas, and B. Martin-Schiller. *Other Javas Away From the Kraton*. Australia: Monash University, 1984. Examines Java's relative place in Austronesia, the status of *priyayi* on Java's north coast, three revolutionary biographies, and life in a Javanese mountain village.

Heuken, Adolph. *Historical Sights of Jakarta*. Jakarta: Cipta Loka Caraka, 1982. Guides the reader into Jakarta's past—its ancient mansions, churches, temples, mosques, palaces.

Hutton, Peter. *Insight Guides: Java*. Hong Kong: APA Productions, 1990. Contains hundreds of photos, dozens of maps and charts, and a section of travel information.

Lindsay, Jennifer. *Javanese Gamelan: Traditional Orchestra of Indonesia*. Oxford: Oxford University Press, 1986. Provides a listening framework so the exotic sounds of the *gamelan* make musical and cultural sense. Includes a list of sites offering *gamelan* music.

Ponder, H.W. *Java Pageant: Impressions of the 1930s*. Singapore: Oxford University Press, 1989. An account, originally published in 1934, of the author's residence in Java during the 1920s and 1930s.

Scidmore, E.R. *Java: The Garden of the East*. Oxford: Oxford University Press, 1986. A late-19th-century travel book written by an American visitor offering unique glimpses of Javanese and Dutch-Javanese life in the heyday of colonial rule.

Smithies, Michael. *Yogyakarta: Cultural Heart of Indonesia*. Oxford: Oxford University Press, 1986. An erudite yet practical guide to Yogyakarta.

Van Ness, Edward C., and Shita Prawirohardjo. *Javanese Wayang Kulit*. Oxford: Oxford University Press, 1985. An excellent primer to *wayang kulit* traditions, characters, and plots, and the medium's importance in the everyday life of the Javanese.

KALIMANTAN

Ave, Jan B., and Victor T. King. *Borneo: The People of the Weeping Forest*. Leiden, Netherlands: National Museum of Ethnology, 1986. Outstanding treatment of the land

and people, Dayak tribal life, and the deep ecological and social changes on the island of Borneo.

Barclay, James. *A Stroll Through Borneo.* London: Hodder and Stoughton, 1980. A five-month trek across Borneo provides a sympathetic picture of such tribes as the Penans, Ibans, and Kayans.

Beeckman, Captain Daniel. *Voyage to Borneo.* New York: Harper and Row, 1973. A reprint of a travelogue first published in 1718 which records the 1713 voyage of the *Eagle Galley* to Banjarmasin. Beeckman's detailed eye-witness accounts of the Banjarese and Dayaks of the time continue to fascinate present-day anthropologists.

Hansen, Eric: *Stranger in the Forest: On Foot Across Borneo.* For seven months, Eric Hansen lived and hunted with the Penan, one of the last surviving rainforest dwellers in the world.

MacKinnon, John, et al. *Borneo.* Amsterdam: Time-Life International B.V., 1975. A magnificent book that explains the flora, fauna, geology, and history of this jungle island. More than just a beautiful coffee table book.

Miller, Charles C. *Black Borneo.* New York: Modern Age Books, 1942. Heart-thumping adventures from the "come back alive" school of explorer. Miller, born on Java, made many trips to Borneo in the company of his father, a captain in the Dutch East Indies Army.

O'Hanlon, Redmond. *Into the Heart of Borneo.* New York: Random House, 1984. An exuberant, hilarious narrative of a hazardous 1983 journey on foot and by boat into the center of Borneo.

LANGUAGE

Almatsier, A.M. *How to Master Bahasa Indonesia.* Jakarta: Penerbit Djambatan, 1974. A short-term course for English-speaking foreigners. Sold all over Indonesia.

Echols, John, and H. Shaddily. *An English-Indonesian Dictionary.* Ithaca, NY: Cornell University Press, 1975. With 25,000 headwords, the only truly comprehensive modern English-Indonesian dictionary. Includes modern idioms and slang, many abbreviations, technical terms, and cross references, especially to irregular noun forms and noun plurals.

Echols, John, and H. Shaddily. *An Indonesian-English Dictionary.* Ithaca, NY: Cornell University Press, 1989. A well-balanced register of the Indonesian vocabulary with clear, accurate definitions and sample sentences that illustrate usage. None better for the serious English-speaking student.

Johnson, Helen L., and Rossall J. Johnson. *Indonesian-English English-Indonesian Dictionary.* New York: Hippocrene Books, 1990. Includes prefixes in verb listings, rather than just the root verbs. Designed for the business traveler, with appendices for everyday vocabulary.

Kramer, A.L.N. *Van Goor's Indonesian Dictionary.* Rutland, VT: Charles E. Tuttle Co., 1986. This easy-to-use bilingual dictionary features colloquial usages, easy-to-read type, multiple definitions, and pronunciation aids. One of the best compact dictionaries available.

Kwee, John B. *Teach Yourself Indonesian.* Kent, England: Hodder and Stoughton, 1984. Carefully graded lessons take the student to the point where he or she will be able to take part in everyday conversation and read simple texts. Distributed in the U.S. by David McKay Co., 2 Park Ave., New York, NY 10016.

Sarumpaet, J.P. *Modern Usage in Bahasa Indonesia.* Carlton, Australia: Pitman Publishing Pty. Ltd., 1980. A guide to correct spelling, nuances of meaning, situations in which a word might be taboo, and regional varieties.

Wolff, John U. *Say it in Indonesian.* New York: Dover Publications, 1983. Some 2,100 up-to-date practical entries, easy pronunciation transcription, every entry numbered and indexed, quick word substitution for every need, handy bilingual glossary.

LITERATURE

Alberts, A. *The Islands*. Amherst: University of Massachusetts Press, 1983. Library of the Indies series. An original collection of stories by an outstanding Dutch writer on Indonesia.

Aman, Dra. S.D.B. *Folk Tales From Indonesia*. Djambatan, 1982. Popular myths and legends from all over Indonesia.

Aveling, Harry. *Contemporary Indonesian Poetry*. Brisbane, Australia: University of Queensland Press, 1975. Poems in Indonesian and English by such modern poets as Rendra, Rosidi, Heraty, Sastrowardjo, and Ismai.

Couperus, Louis. *The Hidden Force*. Amherst: University of Massachusetts Press, 1985. A masterpiece of psychological fiction by one of Holland's greatest novelists. Although written 45 years before Indonesian independence, it reveals many reasons why the Dutch colonial empire was destined to fail.

de Nijs, E. Briton. *Faded Portraits*. Amherst: University of Massachusetts Press, 1982. A fictionalized memoir of family life in the colonial Dutch East Indies. Reminiscent of the literature of the American South, this book wistfully records the passing of an era.

Dekker, Douwes. *Max Havelaar*. Amherst: University of Massachusetts Press, 1982. Library of the Indies series. First published in 1860. Describes the exploitation of the Javanese peasant under the control of rapacious Dutch colonial policy in the infamous Cultuur Stelsel period. This book did much to bring that period to an end.

Dermout, Maria. *The Ten Thousand Things*. Amherst: University of Massachusetts Press, 1983. Set in Maluku, this haunting, offbeat novel draws on the author's rich memories and knowledge of Indonesian customs and folklore.

du Perron, E. *Country of Origin*. Amherst: University of Massachusetts Press, 1984. Second only to *Max Havelaar* as an important Dutch work on Indonesia, this novel teems with the atmosphere of the tropics and evokes the colonial scene in great detail.

Forbes, Anna. *Unbeaten Tracks in the Islands of the Far East*. Oxford: Oxford University Press, 1987. The experiences of a Victorian woman who traveled from Batavia to Sulawesi, Maluku, and Timor. Anna was the wife of the distinguished naturalist Henry O. Forbes.

Hendon, Rufus S. *Six Indonesian Short Stories*. New Haven: Yale University Southeast Asian Studies, 1968. Samples of work produced by Indonesian short-story writers in the 1940s and early 1950s, a high point in the development of Indonesian fiction and the refinement of the Indonesian language as a literary vehicle.

Kartini, Raden Adjeng. *Letters of a Javanese Princess*. Lanham, MD: University Press of America, 1985. The first Indonesian nationalist, Kartini argued that all Indonesian women have a right to be educated.

Koch, C.J. *The Year of Living Dangerously*. New York: Penguin Books, 1978. A complex drama of loyalty and betrayal played out in the eye of the political storm of 1965.

Lubis, Mochtar. *A Road With No End*. Singapore: Graham Brash Pte. Ltd., 1982. A story set between the time of the reoccupation of Indonesia by the Dutch in 1946 and the First Police Action of 1947.

Lubis, Mochtar. *The Indonesian Dilemma*. Singapore: Graham Brash Pte. Ltd., 1983. A distillation of an electrifying three-hour critique Lubis delivered on 6 April 1977 at the TIM in Jakarta focusing on what he feels are weak character traits of the Javanese people.

Lubis, Mochtar. *The Outlaw and Other Stories*. Singapore: Oxford University Press, 1987. This selection of tragic stories is representative of Lubis at the peak of his literary career.

Lubis, Mochtar. *Twilight in Djakarta*. Oxford: Oxford University Press, 1986. One of the best documents of daily life in 1950s Jakarta, especially its underbelly: *becak* drivers, derelicts, prostitutes.

Moore, Cornelia Niekus. *Insulinde: Selected Translations from Dutch Writers of Three Centuries on the Indonesian Archipelago*. Honolulu: University Press of Hawaii, 1978. Mainly autobiographical short stories centering on the Dutch experience in Indonesia during colonization.

Nieuwenhuys, Rob. *Mirror of the Indies: A History of Dutch Colonial Literature*. Amherst: University of Massachusetts Press, 1982. The definitive literary history of the colonial Dutch East Indies.

Savage, Victor R. *Western Impressions of Nature and Landscape in Southeast Asia*. Singapore: Singapore University Press, 1984. Popular literature by Western sojourners and travelers who've written of their experiences in Indonesia over the centuries.

Toer, Pramoedya Ananta. *The Fugitive*. Hong Kong: Heinemann Educational Books (Asia) Ltd., 1975. Set in August 1945, immediately after the declaration of independence from the Dutch. Pramoedya himself was captured and tortured by the Dutch; *The Fugitive* was smuggled out of prison by sympathetic Dutch intellectuals.

Van Schendel, Arthur. *John Company*. Amherst: University of Massachusetts Press, 1983. A vivid, panoramic sea journey during the early years of the Dutch East Indies Company.

Vuyk, Beb, and H.J. Friedericy. *Two Tales of the East Indies*. Amherst: University of Massachusetts Press, 1983. An autobiographical novel set on the island of Buru in Maluku, and the story of the relationship between a young Dutch government official and an older and wiser administrator in southern Sulawesi in the 1920s.

Watson, Lyall. *Gifts of Unknown Things*. London: Hodder and Stoughton, 1983. A fascinating book that records the mystical happenings on a small volcanic island somewhere in Indonesia.

MALUKU

Deane, Shirley. *Ambon: Island of Spices*. London: John Murray. A description of *adat* customs in Ambonese society through the author's own experience living on Ambon in the early 1970s.

Hanna, Willard A. *Indonesian Banda: Colonialism and its Aftermath in the Nutmeg Islands*. Philadelphia: Institute for the Study of Human Issues, 1978. Demonstrates how the Dutch became their own worst enemies, creating a monopolistic system in the Bandas that eventually declined into economic chaos.

Muller, Kal. *Spice Islands: Exotic Eastern Indonesia*. Chicago: Passport Books, 1990. A comprehensive guide to Maluku, with over 100 color prints and photos, detailed maps.

NATURAL PHENOMENA

Beekman, E.M. *The Poison Tree*. Amherst: University of Massachusetts Press, 1981. Selected writings of the renowned Dutch naturalist Rumphius (1628-1702) on the tropical flora, shellfish, minerals, and precious stones of the Dutch East Indies. Also an intriguing and erudite sourcebook on the native use of plants, native customs, lore, religion, and historical information of the period.

Dharma, Dr. A.P. *Indonesian Medicinal Plants*. Jakarta: Balai Pustaka, 1987. Catalogs 145 plants, with illustrations, descriptions, and medicinal uses.

Elisofon, Eliot. *Java Diary*. Toronto: Macmillan Company, 1969. An adventure-packed diary of the author's experiences in the Ujung Kulon Nature Reserve of West Java, recording in 130 black and white and 17 color photos the fauna typical of the Greater Sunda Islands.

Farrelly, David. *The Book of Bamboo*. San Francisco: Sierra Club Books, 1984. A complete sourcebook of the bamboo culture, including its hundreds of uses, plus how to cultivate, maintain, and harvest this astonishing plant.

Gradwohl, Judith, and Russell Greenberg. *Saving the Tropical Forests*. Washington, D.C.: Island Press, 1988. Presents practical solutions for preserving tropical forests worldwide, including three promising reserves in Indonesia.

Kavanagh, Michael. *A Complete Guide to Monkeys, Apes and Other Primates*. New York: The Viking Press, 1983. A complete, up-to-date, fully illustrated guide to all the world's living primates. Includes distribution maps and full-color photos illustrating every genus.

Maple, Terry L. *Orangutan Behavior*. New York: Van Nostrand Reinhold Co., 1980. A discussion of the natural history, behavioral patterns, and conservation of the orangutan.

McNeely, Jeffrey A., and Paul Spencer Wachtel. *Soul of the Tiger: Searching for Nature's Answers in Exotic Southeast Asia*. New York: Doubleday, 1988. Two American conservationists and adventurers give fascinating, bizarre, and humorous accounts of the vital connections between Southeast Asians and their animals.

Merrill, E. *Plant Life of the Pacific World*. Rutland, VT: Charles E. Tuttle Co., 1981. A well-organized overview of the plantlife of the whole Pacific region. First published in 1945.

Veevers-Carter, W. *Land Mammals of Indonesia*. Jakarta: PT Intermasa, 1979. Contains drawings, field notes, distribution, and zoological data on all Indonesian mammals.

Veevers-Carter, W. *Nature Conservation in Indonesia*. Jakarta: PT Intermasa, 1978. Sponsored by the Indonesian Wildlife Fund. An island-by-island guide to the nature reserves of Indonesia.

NUSATENGGARA

Attenborough, D. *Zoo Quest for a Dragon*. Oxford: Oxford University Press, 1986. A vivid and entertaining account of travel to Bali, Java, the interior of Borneo, and Komodo, this last to acquire a Komodo dragon for the London Zoo.

Auffenberg, W. *The Behavioral Ecology of the Komodo Monitor*. Gainesville, FL: University Presses of Florida, 1981. Reporting the findings of the author's 13-month field study of the ecology and behavior of the spectacular Komodo dragon.

Budiardjo, Carmel, and Liem Soei Liong. *The War Against East Timor*. London: Zed Books Ltd., 1984. Analyzes Indonesia's military and political strategy to subjugate and integrate this former Portuguese colony.

Fox, J. *The Flow of Life*. Cambridge: Harvard University Press, 1980. Erudite essays by international scholars on the social anthropology of eastern Indonesia.

Kessler, C. *Lombok—Just Beyond Bali*. Jakarta: PT Indira, 1984. A picture essay on Lombok, with short sections on historical background, the people, and the land. One of the very few books in print on Lombok and for sale only on that island and in Jakarta.

Traube, E. *Cosmology and Social Life*. Chicago: University of Chicago Press, 1986. An ethnographic study of ritual life in an eastern Indonesian society, that of the Mambai of East Timor.

POLITICS AND ECONOMY

Geertz, C. *Agricultural Involution: The Processes of Ecological Change in Indonesia*. Los Angeles: University of California Press, 1963. An incisive account of Indonesian agricultural history, primarily covering the period of Dutch control from 1619 to 1942.

Jenkins, David. *Suharto and His Generals: Indonesian Military Politics 1975-1983*. Ithaca, NY: Cornell Modern Indonesia Project, 1984. An exhaustive examination of the army's involvement in Indonesian political life.

Legge, J.D. *Sukarno: A Political Biography*. Boston: Allen and Unwin, 1972. A standard biography and one of the best introductions to Sukarno.

Lubis, Mochtar. *The Indonesian Dilemma*. Singapore: Graham Brash Pte. Ltd., 1983. Defines the Indonesian character and encourages Indonesians to reassert their ethical values to achieve national security.

May, Brian. *The Indonesian Tragedy*. Singapore: Graham Brash Pte. Ltd., 1984. May concludes that Indonesia's "tragedy" is the ruling junta's attempt to force a Western economic model on a backward and superstitious people.

McDonald, Hamish. *Suharto's Indonesia*. Australia: Fontana Books, 1981. The best introduction to Indonesian politics of the 1970s.

Roeder, O.G. *The Smiling General: President Soeharto of Indonesia*. Jakarta: Gunung Agung, 1969. Follows Suharto's rise from obscurity to president.

SULAWESI

Reid, Helen, and Anthony Reid. *South Sulawesi*. Berkeley: Periplus, 1988. A detailed guide emphasising the region's cultures and traditions.

Volkman, Toby Alice, and Ian Caldwell, eds. *Sulawesi: Island Crossroads of Indonesia*. Chicago: Passport Books, 1990. Lots of maps and color photos in this comprehensive guide to Sulawesi.

SUMATRA

Errington, Frederick. *Manners and Meaning in West Sumatra*. New Haven: Yale University Press, 1984. An engrossing analysis of how the Minangkabau conduct and interpret their lives and an exploration of the contrasts between Minang consciousness and Western thought processes. A beautifully written and richly illustrated book.

Freidus, Alberta. *Sumatran Contributions to the Development of Indonesian Literature, 1920-1942*. Honolulu: University Press of Hawaii, 1977. A tribute to the genius of Minang poets

and writers in the development of a modern Indonesian literature.

Frey, Katherine. *Journey to the Land of the Earth Goddess*. Jakarta: Gramedia Publishing Division, 1986. A panoramic view of the Minangkabau culture: their myths, customs, practice and worship of Islam, archaeology, contemporary life, rituals, and ceremonies.

Leigh, Barbara. *Hands of Time: The Crafts of Aceh*. Jakarta: Penerbit Djambatan, 1989. Lots of photos and illustrations in this collection of Aceh artifacts. Text in English and Indonesian.

Marsden, William. *The History of Sumatra*. Oxford: Oxford University Press, 1986. A reprint of the esteemed 1811 edition, this "history" includes authenticated facts in the fields of geography, linguistics, botany, and zoology.

Salim, Leon. *Prisoners at Kota Cane*. Ithaca: Cornell Modern Indonesia Project, 1986. A memoir, from the Indonesian perspective, of the final days of Dutch colonial rule on Sumatra in 1942.

Schnitger, F.M. *Forgotten Kingdoms in Sumatra*. Singapore: Oxford University Press, 1989. First published in 1939; details Sumatran ruins, legends, and folk tales.

Stoler, Ann. *Capitalism and Confrontation in Sumatra's Plantation Belt*. New Haven: Yale University Press, 1985. Analyzes how popular resistance molded the form of colonial expansion and the experience of the Javanese laboring communities on Sumatra's 19th century plantations. Fascinating.

Szeleky, Ladislao. *Tropic Fever*. Oxford: Oxford University Press, 1979. A remarkable account of a planter's life in Sumatra during the first two decades of this century.

Whitten, A., D. Sengli, A. Jazanul, and H. Nazaruddin. *The Ecology of Sumatra*. Yogyakarta: Gadjah Mada University Press, 1984. A comprehensive overview of the impact of agricultural, social, and industrial developments on the ecosystems of Sumatra and its surrounding islands.

Whitten, Tony. *The Gibbons of Siberut.* London: J.M. Dent and Sons Ltd., 1982. The first full-length, popular account of gibbon life as well as a study of Siberut Island's botany, wildlife, and people.

TRAVELOGUE

Arndt, H.W. *Asian Diaries.* Singapore: Chopmen Publishers, 1987. An Australian economist's perceptive diaries spanning three decades of travel in Asia. Included are chapters on Indonesia, Bali, and Aceh.

Clune, Frank. *Isles of Spice.* New York: E.P. Dutton and Co., Inc., 1942. An extensive pre-WW II journey through the Dutch East Indies, Indochina, and North Australia.

de Leeuw, Hendrik. *Crossroads of the Java Sea.* New York: Garden City Publishing Co., 1931. A travel narrative by a Dutch-American describing the strange customs and other interesting data he came across on Java, Sumatra, Borneo, Sulawesi, and Bali.

Fairchild, D. *Garden Islands of the Great East.* New York: Charles Scribner's Sons, 1943. A botanist's hunt in a Chinese junk for exotic plants in the far-flung isles of the East Indies in the 1930s.

Gibson, A. *The Malay Peninsula and Archipelago.* London: J.M. Dent and Sons, Ltd., 1928. About one-third of this travelogue is devoted to "Insulinde," or the Dutch East Indies.

Hanbury-Tenison, R. *A Pattern of Peoples.* New York: Charles Scribner's Sons, 1975. Covers a wide cross-section of peoples from the highly cultured Torajans to the Stone-Age Dani.

Hilton, J. *The Story of Dr. Wassell.* Boston: Little, Brown and Co., 1943. A true story of an American Navy doctor who brought his wounded men out of Java through the turmoil of the Japanese invasion in WWII.

Mackellar, C.D. *Scented Isles and Coral Gardens.* London: John Murray, 1912. A collection of letters written in the 1890s describing the author's travels in the Indies. The extensive black and white photos are unique.

McDougall, W. *Six Bells Off Java.* New York: Charles Scribner's Sons, 1948. The fast-moving story of the author's wartime escape from Shanghai to Palembang and ultimate capture and imprisonment by the Japanese.

Pelzer, D. *Trek Across Indonesia.* Singapore: Graham Brash Pte. Ltd., 1982. A photographic record of traditional house forms.

Schreider, H., and J. Schreider. *The Drums of Tonkin.* New York: Coward-McCann, Inc., 1963. An account of a young couple's 13-month journey across the Indonesian archipelago in a seagoing jeep. A first-rate tale of adventure.

Stevenson, W. *Bird's Nest in Their Beards.* Boston: Houghton Mifflin Co., 1963. A journalist's coverage of the turbulent period beginning with the first Afro-Asian conference held in Bandung in 1955 and ending eight years later at the Moshi conference in Africa.

INDEX

Page numbers in **boldface** indicate the primary reference to a given topic. *Italicized* page
numbers indicate information in captions, illustrations, maps, or special topics.

ABOUT THE AUTHORS

BILL DALTON

*Bill Dalton was born in
Waltham, Massachusetts, in
1944. After four years as a
student at the University of
Copenhagen, he embarked
on a seven-year journey
through 81 countries, working as a letter-sorter in
Scandinavia, an apple pick-
er in Israel, and an English
teacher in war-torn Cambodia. Dalton founded Moon
Publications in a youth hos-*

Bill Dalton and friends

*tel in Queensland, Australia in 1973, and has worked writing and publishing travel books
ever since. Though his travels have taken him around the world, he has a special interest in
the Pacific Rim. During the past 25 years Dalton has explored every crack and crevice of
many of the archipelago's 13,000 islands, visiting Indonesia dozens of times, amassing a
total of more than six years on the islands.*

CARL PARKES

Carl Parkes

Carl Parkes was born into an American Air Force family and spent his childhood in California, Nebraska, Alabama, and Japan. It was while living in this last that his love affair with Asia first surfaced. Years later, a chance encounter with Bill Dalton in Singapore led to the release of Parkes' highly acclaimed Southeast Asia Handbook. *Parkes has since published* Thailand Handbook, *and is currently working on Moon Travel Handbooks to Malaysia and Singapore.*

ROBERT NILSEN

Born and raised in Minnesota, Robert Nilsen left the largely insular Midwest in 1973 to gain an appreciation for the wider world. He joined the Peace Corps and spent two years working at a public health center in rural South Korea. Two additional years of teaching in Korea and two more of traveling through Asia from Japan to Pakistan gave him a deeper and wider understanding of the people and cultures of Asia and the Pacific. Living now in Chico, California, Robert has returned to Asia and the Pacific six times to write about Korea, Hawaii, and Indonesia.

Robert Nilsen

HONG KONG HANDBOOK by Kerry Moran, 300 pages, $15.95
Hong Kong has been called "the most cosmopolitan city on earth,"
yet it's also one of the few places where visitors can witness
Chinese customs as they have been practiced for centuries.
Award-winning author Kerry Moran explores this unusual
juxtaposition of tradition and modern life in *Hong Kong Handbook*.
Moran traces the history and cultural development of the British
Colony, and anticipates the changes to come in 1997, when this
fascinating city reverts to Chinese rule.

INDONESIA HANDBOOK by Bill Dalton, 1,300 pages, $25.00
"Looking for a fax machine in Palembang, a steak dinner on
Ambon or the best place to photograph Bugis prahus in Sulawesi?
Then buy this brick of a book, which contains a full kilogram of
detailed directions and advice." —*Asia, Inc. Magazine*

"One of the world's great guides." —*All Asia Review of Books*

"The classic guidebook to the archipelago."
—*Condé Nast Traveler*

JAPAN HANDBOOK by J.D. Bisignani, 952 pages, $22.50
"The scope of this guide book is staggering, ranging from an
introduction to Japanese history and culture through to the best
spots for shopping for pottery in Mashie or silk pongee in
Kagoshima." —*Golden Wing*

"More travel information on Japan than any other guidebook."
—*The Japan Times*

NEPAL HANDBOOK by Kerry Moran, 378 pages, $12.95
"This is an excellent guidebook, exploring every aspect of the
country the visitor is likely to want to know about with both wit and
authority." —*South China Morning Post*

PHILIPPINES HANDBOOK by Peter Harper and Laurie
Fullerton, 638 pages, $17.95
"The most comprehensive travel guide done on the Philippines.
Excellent work." —*Pacific Stars & Stripes*

SOUTHEAST ASIA HANDBOOK by Carl Parkes, 1,100 pages,
$21.95
"Plenty of information on sights and entertainment, also provides
a political, environment and cultural context that will allow visitors
to begin to interpret what they see." —*London Sunday Times*

"Carl Parkes is the savviest of all tourists in Southeast Asia."
—Arthur Frommer

TRAVEL MATTERS

Travel Matters is Moon Publications' free quarterly newsletter, loaded with specially commissioned travel articles and essays that tell it like it is. Recent issues have been devoted to Asia, Mexico, and North America, and every issue includes:

Feature Stories: Travel writing unlike what you'll find in your local newspaper. Andrew Coe on Mexican professional wrestling, Michael Buckley on the craze for wartime souvenirs in Vietnam, Kim Weir on the Nixon Museum in Yorba Linda.

Transportation: Tips on how to get around. Rick Steves on a new type of Eurail pass, Victor Chan on hiking in Tibet, Joe Cummings on how to be a Baja road warrior.

Health Matters: Articles on the most recent findings by Dr. Dirk Schroeder, author of *Staying Healthy in Asia, Africa, and Latin America*. Japanese encephalitis, malaria, the southwest U.S. "mystery disease" . . . forewarned is forearmed.

Book Reviews: Informed assessments of the latest travel titles and series. The Rough Guide to *World Music,* Let's Go vs. Berkeley, Dorling Kindersley vs. Knopf.

The Internet: News from the cutting edge. The Great Burma Debate in rec.travel.asia, hotlists of the best WWW sites, updates on Moon's massive "Road Trip USA" exhibit.

TRAVEL MATTERS

ISSUE 12   FOCUS ON U.S.A.   SPRING 1995

BLACKJACK, BLUES, AND BALES OF COTTON
Travels and Tangents in the New Mississippi Delta
by Jeff Perk

At night, the first you see of Tunica, Mississippi are the searchlights. Coming down Highway 61 from Memphis, or west on Route 304 from the Interstate, you see the swirling circles of light against low clouds, long white beams cutting through the humid night air, clearly visible even through the spattering rain of bugs against your windshield. All around in the darkness is a rural landscape of farms, fields, and wood lots: the Mississippi Delta.

Technically speaking, the Delta begins around Cairo, Illinois, a full thousand river miles from the Gulf, but nobody pays attention to technicalities here. The Delta, as cotton historian David Cohn wrote, "begins in the lobby of the Peabody Hotel in Memphis and ends on Catfish Row in Vicksburg." The Delta is history and culture, as deep and fertile as the alluvial soil. The Delta is a century of King Cotton, from which a few reaped enormous wealth while everyone else was yoked with backbreaking labor. The Delta is field hands tilling and picking and praying and creating a musical tradition of hymns and hollers that begat blues, jazz, country, gospel and even, eventually, that hip-slinging white boy who rolled it all together, Elvis Aaron Presley. The Delta is the memory of slavery and secession and a chorus of ghosts as poignant and garrulous as they ever were alive, for here in the Delta, the dead aren't allowed to rest: Robert Johnson, Tennessee Williams, and old Sam Grant (General

Ulysses S. to you) still exist in the present tense, as if they just stepped out for a drink or piss and might yet return. Past and present are swirled together like the bourbon and water in a frosty mint julep you might be able to tell 'em apart to start, but after a few swigs, why try?

This, then, is the countryside through which you drive: old skeletons rattling around, fat brown moths staining your radiator, loose tufts of white cotton twirling beside the road in your wake, and, up ahead, dancing white beams of light. Lights that promise a dramatic change for the Delta, on par with Grant's armies, the Corps of Engineers, or the mechanized cotton harvester. Because behind those lights is money—lots of money, all just itching to build as much tackiness as traffic will bear.

Welcome to the new Delta: the land that gave us the blues now gives us blackjack, progressive slots, and lounge entertainers like the Gary Puckett and Suzanne Somers. The land that exhausted the mule of many a poor sharecropper, that filled the inkwell of Faulkner's pen, now clamors to the sound of quarters dropping in slot trays and cards slapping felt. The change is dizzying: two-lane farm roads being turned into four-lane highways, mini-marts and motels and an endless parade of casino billboards sprouting like kudzu. Stand still and you're likely to be paved over.

Tunica County in the northwest corner of Mississippi is the scene of greatest transformation, but it isn't the only game along Old Man River. There are riverboat casinos up and down the Mississippi, from

continued on page 3

There are also booklists, Letters to the Editor, and anything else we can find to interest our readers, as well as Moon's latest titles and ordering information for other travel products, including Periplus Travel Maps to Southeast Asia.

To receive a free subscription to *Travel Matters,* call (800) 345-5473, write to Moon Publications, P.O. Box 3040, Chico, CA 95927-3040, or e-mail travel@moon.com.

Please note: subscribers who live outside the United States will be charged $7.00 per year for shipping and handling.

MOON TRAVEL HANDBOOKS

ASIA AND THE PACIFIC

Bali Handbook (3379) $12.95
Bangkok Handbook (0595) $13.95
Fiji Islands Handbook (3921) $11.95
Hong Kong Handbook (0560) $15.95
Indonesia Handbook (0625) $25.00
Japan Handbook (3700) $22.50
Micronesia Handbook (3808) $11.95
Nepal Handbook (3646) $12.95
New Zealand Handbook (3883) $18.95
Outback Australia Handbook (3794) $15.95
Philippines Handbook (0048) $17.95
Southeast Asia Handbook (0021) $21.95
South Korea Handbook (3204) $14.95
South Pacific Handbook (3999) $19.95
Tahiti-Polynesia Handbook (3875) $11.95
Thailand Handbook (3824) $16.95
Tibet Handbook (3905) $30.00
*Vietnam, Cambodia & Laos Handbook (0293) $18.95

NORTH AMERICA AND HAWAII

Alaska-Yukon Handbook (0161) $14.95
Alberta and the Northwest Territories Handbook (0676) . . . $17.95
Arizona Traveler's Handbook (0536) $16.95
Atlantic Canada Handbook (0072) $17.95
Big Island of Hawaii Handbook (0064) $13.95
British Columbia Handbook (0145) $15.95
Catalina Island Handbook (3751) $10.95
Colorado Handbook (0137) $17.95
Georgia Handbook (0609) $16.95
Hawaii Handbook (0005) $19.95
Honolulu-Waikiki Handbook (0587) $14.95
Idaho Handbook (0617) $14.95
Kauai Handbook (0013) $13.95
Maui Handbook (0579) $14.95
Montana Handbook (0544) $15.95
Nevada Handbook (0641) $16.95
New Mexico Handbook (0153) $14.95

Northern California Handbook (3840) $19.95
Oregon Handbook (0102) $16.95
Texas Handbook (3867) $13.95
Utah Handbook (0684) $16.95
Washington Handbook (0552) $15.95
Wyoming Handbook (3980) $14.95

MEXICO
Baja Handbook (0528) $15.95
*Cabo Handbook (0285) $14.95
Cancún Handbook (0501) $13.95
Central Mexico Handbook (0234) $15.95
*Mexico Handbook (0315) $21.95
Northern Mexico Handbook (0226) $16.95
Pacific Mexico Handbook (0056) $15.95
*Puerto Vallarta Handbook (0250) $14.95
Yucatán Peninsula Handbook (0242) $15.95

CENTRAL AMERICA AND THE CARIBBEAN
Belize Handbook (3956) $13.95
*Caribbean Handbook (0277) $16.95
Costa Rica Handbook (0080) $17.95
Jamaica Handbook (0129) $14.95

INTERNATIONAL
Egypt Handbook (3891) $18.95
*Moon Handbook (0668) $10.00
Moscow-St. Petersburg Handbook (3913) $13.95
Staying Healthy in Asia, Africa, and Latin America (0269) . . $11.95

* New title, please call for availability

PERIPLUS TRAVEL MAPS
All maps $7.95 each

Bali	Hong Kong	Penang
Bandung/W. Java	Jakarta	Phuket/S. Thailand
Bangkok/C. Thailand	Java	Sarawak
Batam/Bintan	Ko Samui/S. Thailand	Singapore
Cambodia	Kuala Lumpur	Vietnam
Chiangmai/N. Thailand	Lombok	Yogyakarta/C. Java

WHERE TO BUY MOON TRAVEL HANDBOOKS

BOOKSTORES AND LIBRARIES: Moon Travel Handbooks are sold worldwide. Please write to our sales manager for a list of wholesalers and distributors in your area.

TRAVELERS: We would like to have Moon Travel Handbooks available throughout the world. Please ask your bookstore to write or call us for ordering information. If your bookstore will not order our guides for you, please contact us for a free title listing.

Moon Publications, Inc.
P.O. Box 3040
Chico, CA 95927-3040 U.S.A.
Tel: (800) 345-5473
Fax: (916) 345-6751
E-mail: travel@moon.com

IMPORTANT ORDERING INFORMATION

PRICES: All prices are subject to change. We always ship the most current edition. We will let you know if there is a price increase on the book you order.

SHIPPING AND HANDLING OPTIONS: Domestic UPS or USPS first class (allow 10 working days for delivery): $3.50 for the first item, 50 cents for each additional item.

EXCEPTIONS:

Tibet Handbook and *Indonesia Handbook* shipping $4.50; $1.00 for each additional *Tibet Handbook* or *Indonesia Handbook*.

Moonbelt shipping is $1.50 for one, 50 cents for each additional belt.

Add $2.00 for same-day handling.

UPS 2nd Day Air or Printed Airmail requires a special quote.

International Surface Bookrate 8-12 weeks delivery: $3.00 for the first item, $1.00 for each additional item. Note: Moon Publications cannot guarantee international surface bookrate shipping. Moon recommends sending international orders via air mail, which requires a special quote.

FOREIGN ORDERS: Orders that originate outside the U.S.A. must be paid for with either an international money order or a check in U.S. currency drawn on a major U.S. bank based in the U.S.A.

TELEPHONE ORDERS: We accept Visa or MasterCard payments. Minimum order is US$15.00. Call in your order: (800) 345-5473, 8 a.m.-5 p.m. Pacific Standard Time.

ORDER FORM

Be sure to call (800) 345-5473 for current prices and editions or for the name of the bookstore
nearest you that carries Moon Travel Handbooks • 8 a.m.–5 p.m. PST.
(See important ordering information on preceding page.)

Name: _____ Date: _____

Street: _____

City: _____ Daytime Phone: _____

State or Country: _____ Zip Code: _____

QUANTITY	TITLE	PRICE

Taxable Total _____

Sales Tax (7.25%) for California Residents _____

Shipping & Handling _____

TOTAL _____

Ship: ☐ UPS (no P.O. Boxes) ☐ 1st class ☐ International surface mail

Ship to: ☐ address above ☐ other _____

_____

_____

Make checks payable to: **MOON PUBLICATIONS, INC.** P.O. Box 3040, Chico, CA 95927-3040
U.S.A. We accept Visa and MasterCard. **To Order:** Call in your Visa or MasterCard number, or send
a written order with your Visa or MasterCard number and expiration date clearly written.

Card Number: ☐ **Visa** ☐ **MasterCard**

☐☐☐☐ ☐☐☐☐ ☐☐☐☐ ☐☐☐☐

Exact Name on Card: _____

Expiration date: _____

Signature: _____

S/95–A

THE METRIC SYSTEM

1 inch = 2.54 centimeters (cm)
1 foot = .304 meters (m)
1 mile = 1.6093 kilometers (km)
1 km = .6124 miles
1 fathom = 1.8288 m
1 chain = 20.1168 m
1 furlong = 201.168 m
1 acre = .4047 hectares
1 sq km = 100 hectares
1 sq mile = 2.59 square km
1 ounce = 28.35 grams
1 pound = .4536 kilograms
1 short ton = .90718 metric ton
1 short ton = 2000 pounds
1 long ton = 1.016 metric tons
1 long ton = 2240 pounds
1 metric ton = 1000 kilograms
1 quart = .94635 liters
1 US gallon = 3.7854 liters
1 Imperial gallon = 4.5459 liters
1 nautical mile = 1.852 km

To compute celsius temperatures, subtract 32 from Fahrenheit and divide by 1.8. To go the other way, multiply celsius by 1.8 and add 32.

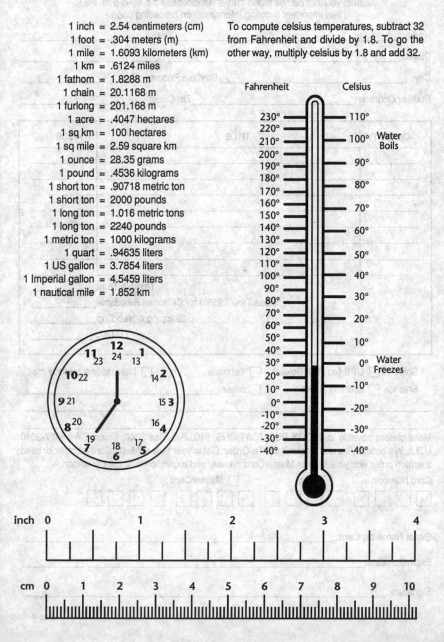